PS
3566
.L27
Z459
1986

Matovich, Richard
M., 1936-

A concordance to The
collected poems of
Sylvia Plath

DATE		

A CONCORDANCE TO
THE COLLECTED POEMS OF
SYLVIA PLATH

GARLAND REFERENCE LIBRARY
OF THE HUMANITIES
(Vol. 618)

A CONCORDANCE TO
THE COLLECTED POEMS OF
SYLVIA PLATH

Richard M. Matovich

GARLAND PUBLISHING, INC. • NEW YORK AND LONDON
1986

Ref

Library of Congress Cataloging-in-Publication Data

Matovich, Richard M., 1936–
  A concordance to The collected poems of Sylvia Plath.

  (Garland reference library of the humanities ; vol. 618)
  Includes index.
  1. Plath, Sylvia—Concordances. I. Plath, Sylvia.
Poems. II. Title. III. Series: Garland reference
library of the humanities ; v. 618.
PS3566.L27Z459 1986   811'.54   85-45126
ISBN 0-8240-8664-3 (alk. paper)

534 68087

Printed on acid-free, 250-year-life paper
Manufactured in the United States of America

CONTENTS

PREFACE

This concordance is intended to assist critics and scholars in the study of the poetry of Sylvia Plath (October 27, 1932–February 11, 1963), who in her brief but brilliant career reminds us of those other inheritors of, thankfully, fulfilled renown, John Keats, Hart Crane, and Dylan Thomas.

The present work uses the text of *The Collected Poems of Sylvia Plath*, edited by Ted Hughes (New York; Harper & Row, 1981). I am grateful to Harper & Row for permission to use this edition.

All of the poetry in the *Collected Poems* is analyzed in this concordance, except for the literal, prosaic translation of Rilke's "A Prophet" (p. 296). All epigraphs to the poems are included. In place of line numbers, the following abbreviations are used for the indicated special instances:

D	Dedication	SD	Stage direction
DR	Draft	ST	Subtitle
DP	*Dramatis personae*	T	Title
E	Epigraph		

The first part of the work is an alphabetical listing of all the words used in the *Collected Poems*. The frequency is given in parentheses. Under the entry word appear all the lines of the poetry in which the word is used. After each use is the title of the poem, the page number where this use occurs in the *Collected Poems*, and the line number of this particular use. The lines are numbered consecutively throughout the poem, as they appear on the page, except (a) where the lines are in dramatic blank verse, in which case a link of iambic pentameter, however divided among speakers, counts as a single line and (b) where a long poem is divided into individual poems by means of subtitles, in which case each section, each individual poem so subtitled, is treated as a separate poem and the numbering begins afresh with one. (Therefore, long poems with numbered sections are treated as single poems.) All numerals have been changed to the corresponding words according to

the A.L.A. cataloging rules. Hyphenated words are entered under only the first word. A word sometimes hyphenated and sometimes not is entered separately under each form. If a word is spelled in different ways, it is entered separately under each spelling.

Some words that are used a large number of times and whose inclusion the compiler felt would not add to the value of this concordance are only listed in the concordance. These words, which have only been counted, are as follows:

A 1675	CAN'T 14	I'M 23	NOR 40	THEY 354
AM 172	EITHER 6	IN 1138	NOT 233	THIS 294
AN 155	FOR 284	INTO 109	OF 1744	THOSE 65
AND 1710	FROM 279	IS 656	ON 440	THROUGH . . . 97
ARE 337	HAD 54	IT 600	OR 188	TO 1003
AT 262	HAS 62	ITS 201	OUR 158	US 100
BE 165	HAVE 162	IT'S 29	SHE 188	WAS 104
BEEN 29	HE 186	I'VE 14	THAT 391	WE 162
BUT 180	HER 272	ME 273	THE 3847	WERE 56
BY 237	HIM 78	MY 531	THEIR 284	WITH 445
CAN 98	HIS 274	NEITHER 13	THEM 107	YOU 393
CANNOT 25	I 988	NO 242	THESE 120	YOUR 229

When space was limited an (*) was used to clearly separate the line of poetry from the title. Wherever possible, the complete title is cited, but for reasons of space, the following abbreviations have been used:

APPEARANCE. . . . . AN APPEARANCE 189
THE ARRIVAL. . . . . THE ARRIVAL OF THE BEE BOX 212
BABY. . . . . THE BABYSITTERS 174
BARREN. . . . . BARREN WOMAN 157
BEE. . . . . THE BEE MEETING 211
BEEKEEPER'S. . . . . THE BEEKEEPER'S DAUGHTER 118
BERCK. . . . . BERCK-PLAGE 196
BIRTHDAY. . . . . A BIRTHDAY PRESENT 206
BLACK PINE TREE. . . . . BLACK PINE TREE
                                              IN AN ORANGE LIGHT 328
BLACK ROOK I. . . . . BLACK ROOK IN RAINY WEATHER 56
BLACKBER. . . . . BLACKBERRYING 168
BURNING. . . . . BURNING THE LETTERS 204
CHANNEL C. . . . . CHANNEL CROSSING 26
COMPANIONABLE. . . . . THE COMPANIONABLE ILLS 105
CONJURING. . . . . ON THE DIFFICULTY OF
                                              CONJURING UP A DRYAD 65
CONVERSATION. . . . . CONVERSATION AMONG THE RUINS 21
COURAGE. . . . . THE COURAGE OF SHUTTING-UP 209
CROSSING THE W. . . . . CROSSING THE WATER 190

DETECTIVE. . . . . THE DETECTIVE 208
DIALOGUE B. . . . . DIALOGUE BETWEEN GHOST
AND PRIEST 38
DIALOGUE O. . . . . DIALOGUE OVER A OUIJA BOARD 276
DREAM WITH C. . . . . DREAM WITH CLAM-DIGGERS 43
ELECTRA ON. . . . . ELECTRA ON AZALEA PATH 116
ELLA MASON A. . . . . . . ELLA MASON AND HER ELEVEN CATS 53
EPITAPH FOR F. . . . . EPITAPH FOR FIRE AND FLOWER 45
EPITAPH IN THREE. . . . . EPITAPH IN THREE PARTS 337
EVERLASTING MONDAY. . . . . . THE EVERLASTING MONDAY 62
FATHERLESS. . . . . FOR A FATHERLESS SON 205
FEMALE A. . . . . FEMALE AUTHOR 301
FEVER. . . . . FEVER 103° 231
GETTING. . . . . GETTING THERE 247
GHOST'S. . . . . THE GHOST'S LEAVETAKING 90
GO GET. GO GET THE GOODLY SQUAB 313
GORING. . . . . THE GORING 47
GREEN ROCK. . . . . GREEN ROCK, WINTHROP BAY 104
THE HANGING. . . . . THE HANGING MAN 141
HARDCASTLE C. . . . . HARDCASTLE CRAGS 62
INSOLENT STORM. . . . . INSOLENT STORM STRIKES
AT THE SKULL 325
LADY AND T. . . . . THE LADY AND THE
EARTHENWARE HEAD 69
LESSON. . . . . A LESSON IN VENGEANCE 80
LETTER IN NOV. . . . . LETTER IN NOVEMBER 253
LOVE IS A PAR. . . . . LOVE IS A PARALLAX 329
METAMORPHOSES. . . . . . METAMORPHOSES OF THE MOON 307
MISS DRAKE P. . . . . MISS DRAKE PROCEEDS TO SUPPER 41
MONOLOGUE AT 3. . . . . MONOLOGUE AT 3 A.M. 40
MOON. . . . . THE MOON AND THE YEW TREE 172
MORNING IN THE HOS. . . . . MORNING IN THE
HOSPITAL SOLARIUM 332
MUNICH. . . . . THE MUNICH MANNEQUINS 262
MUSSEL HUNTER. . . . . . MUSSEL HUNTER AT ROCK HARBOR 95
NARCISSI. . . . . AMONG THE NARCISSI 190
NET-. . . . . THE NET-MENDERS 121
NEVER TRY TO TRICK. . . . . NEVER TRY TO TRICK ME
WITH A KISS 319
NEW YEAR ON. . . . . NEW YEAR ON DARTMOOR 176
NOVEMBER G. . . . . NOVEMBER GRAVEYARD 56
ON LOOKING INTO THE EYES. . . . . ON LOOKING INTO THE
EYES OF A DEMON LOVER 325
OTHER TWO. . . . . THE OTHER TWO 68
OXBOW. . . . . ABOVE THE OXBOW 87

PARLIAMENT H. .... PARLIAMENT HILL FIELDS 152
PLASTER. .... IN PLASTER 158
PLETHORA OF DRYADS. .... ON THE PLETHORA OF DRYADS   67
POEM.1.WHO. .... POEM FOR A BIRTHDAY 1. WHO 131
POEM.2.DARK. .... POEM FOR A BIRTHDAY 2. DARK HOUSE 132
POEM.3.MAENAD. ...... POEM FOR A BIRTHDAY 3. MAENAD 133
POEM.4.BEAST. ...... POEM FOR A BIRTHDAY 4. THE BEAST 134
POEM.5.F. .... POEM FOR A BIRTHDAY 5.
                       FLUTE NOTES FROM A REEDY POND 134
POEM.6.W.. ..... POEM FOR A BIRTHDAY 6. WITCH BURNING 135
POEM.7.S.. .... POEM FOR A BIRTHDAY 7. THE STONES 136
POP.OCT. .... POPPIES IN OCTOBER 240
THE PRINCESS. .... THE PRINCESS AND THE GOBLINS 333
PRIVATE G. .... PRIVATE GROUND 130
QUEEN'S C. .... THE QUEEN'S COMPLAINT   28
THE RABBIT. .... THE RABBIT CATCHER 193
RHODODENDRON. .... FABLE OF THE
                        RHODODENDRON STEALERS 103
SLEEP. .... SLEEP IN THE MOJAVE DESERT 143
SNOWMAN O. .... THE SNOWMAN ON THE MOOR   58
SONG FOR A REVOLU. . SONG FOR A REVOLUTIONARY LOVE 322
SONNET: EVA. .... SONNET: TO EVA 304
A SORCERER B. .... A SORCERER BIDS FAREWELL TO SEEM 324
SPINACH-PICKER. .... MEMOIRS OF A SPINACH-PICKER   89
STARS. .... STARS OVER THE DORDOGNE 165
SUICIDE. .... SUICIDE OFF EGG ROCK 115
SURGEON. .... THE SURGEON AT 2 A.M. 170
SWARM. .... THE SWARM 215
THREE. .... THREE WOMEN 176
TO EVA DESCENDING. ..... TO EVA DESCENDING THE STAIR 303
TOUR. .... THE TOUR 237
TWO CAMP. .... TWO CAMPERS IN CLOUD COUNTRY 144
TWO LOVERS. .... TWO LOVERS AND A BEACHCOMBER
                         BY THE REAL SEA 327
TWO VIEWS. .... TWO VIEWS OF A CADAVER ROOM 114
VERTICAL. .... I AM VERTICAL 162
VIRGIN. .... VIRGIN IN A TREE   81
WAKING. .... WAKING IN WINTER 151
WATERCOLOR. .... WATERCOLOR OF
                        GRANTCHESTER MEADOWS 111
WINTER LANDSCAPE,. .. WINTER LANDSCAPE, WITH ROOKS   21
WORDS HEARD. .... WORDS HEARD BY ACCIDENT
                        OVER THE PHONE 202
WREATH F. .... WREATH FOR A BRIDAL   44
YADWIGHA. . YADWIGHA, ON A RED COUCH, AMONG LILIES   85
ZOO K. .... ZOO KEEPER'S WIFE 154

The second part is a list of the words in the concordance, in order of frequency. Character names were not counted.

I must express several debts of gratitude to those persons and institutions whose assistance helped me to complete this work. Again, I should like to thank Harper & Row for their permission to use *The Collected Poems of Sylvia Plath*. The faculty and administration of California University of Pennsylvania granted me a sabbatical leave for the academic year 1983–84, during which this project was begun and largely completed, and I am grateful to them for this opportunity to pursue a project that I might otherwise not have found the leisure to undertake. Professor Sumner Ferris of the English Department of my University assisted me with his knowledge of Sylvia Plath and other modern poets and recent concordances. Walter Trach of Belle Vernon, Pennylvania shared with me his knowledge of computers and programming that enabled me to list and count the words. But my family is owed great and warm thanks for smoothing my daily way while I worked on this concordance, even at the cost of sometimes seeming to ignore them during a whole year when I "wasn't working." It is not customary to dedicate reference works such as this to anybody, but if I were to do so, I should certainly dedicate it to my beloved wife Mary, my son Mark, and my daughter Melanie (who did actually help with some data input!).

THE CONCORDANCE

A (1675)
ABASES (1)
    THE MOON, TOO, ABASES HER SUBJECTS, ...THE RIVAL 166   11
ABATED (1)
    HIS TALKING WHIRLWIND, ABATED HIS EXCESSIVE TEMPER ....OUIJA   77   16
ABC (1)
    ABC, HER EYELIDS SAY. ....;.............AN APPEARANCE 189   18
ABDUCTING (1)
    OF SQUADRONS UNDERGROUND ABDUCTING HIM *THE PRINCESS AND THE GOBLINS 333   22
ABEYANCE (1)
    THIS IS THE SEA, THEN, THIS GREAT ABEYANCE. ....BERCK-PLAGE 196   1
ABLAZE (1)
    GERD WHIRLS THE BALL ABLAZE: "ROUGH STORM," SHE GRANTS,
        "MAY WREAK .... CRYSTAL GAZER   55   22
ABLE (1)
    SIX MONTHS IN THE WORLD, AND SHE IS ABLE ....MAGI 148   10
ABLUTION (1)
    THAN PHYSICAL ABLUTION, AND THE TOWEL ....TALE OF A TUB   24   12
ABORTED (1)
    IN THE BOWL THE HARE IS ABORTED, ...TOTEM 264   11
ABORTIONS (1)
    KNOWING NEITHER ABORTIONS NOR BITCHERY, ...WINTER TREES 258   6
ABORTS (1)
    FLEES AND ABORTS LIKE DROPPED MERCURY. ....THALIDOMIDE 252   26
ABOUT (50)
    SCARCELY VISIBLE. ABOUT AND ABOUT THE SLOPE ....SPIDER   48   14
    SCARCELY VISIBLE. ABOUT AND ABOUT THE SLOPE ....SPIDER   48   14
    ELLA FLOUNCED ABOUT, MINX-THIN AND HAUGHTY, ...ELLA MASON A.   53   14
    AND, SPRINGING ALL ABOUT, ...CRYSTAL GAZER   55   15
    ABOUT TO BE ....SOW   60   14
    ABOUT A QUINTESSENTIAL BEAUTY ....ON THE PLETHORA OF DRYADS   67   2
    LIKE BUBBLES ABOUT TO BREAK, YOU FED ....THE DISQUIETING MUSES   75   19
    ENTER THE CHILLY NO-MAN'S LAND OF ABOUT ....THE GHOST'S LEAVETAKING   90   1
    WENT ABOUT THEIR BUSINESS, WHICH ......MUSSEL HUNTER AT ROCK HARBOR   97   61
    ABOUT SAM: WHITENESS AND THE GREAT RUN ....WHITENESS I REMEMBER 102   2
    THE PIER PILINGS SEEM ABOUT TO COLLAPSE ....A WINTER SHIP 113   15
    IF I DON'T MOVE ABOUT, I'LL KNOCK NOTHING OVER. SO I SAID,*POEM.6.W. 135   14
    IF THEY MISSED OUT ON WALKING ABOUT LIKE PEOPLE ....STILLBORN 142   4
    DENSE AND EXPRESSIONLESS ROUND ABOUT. ....LOVE LETTER 147   23
    ABOUT A BALD, HOSPITAL SAUCER. ....A LIFE 150   22
    YOU'RE NO HAPPIER THAN I ABOUT IT. ....WHITSUN 154   17
    BUT WHAT DO YOU KNOW ABOUT THAT ....ZOO KEEPER'S WIFE 155   14
    THEY STAND LIKE SHADOWS ABOUT THE GREEN LANDSCAPE -- ....WIDOW 164   28
    WALKING ABOUT IN AFRICA MAYBE, BUT THINKING OF ME. ....THE RIVAL 167   17
    THEY STAND ABOUT IN GRANDMOTHERLY DISGUISE, ...WUTHERING HEIGHTS 167   25
    BLOOM ABOUT ME LIKE NIGHT FLOWERS, WITH A GOOD SMELL. ...LAST WORDS 172   22
    AND A COOK AND A MAID, AND KNEW ABOUT THE KEY TO THE BOURBON. *BABY. 175   21
    SETTING: A MATERNITY WARD AND ROUND ABOUT ....THREE WOMEN 176   SD
    I WATCHED THE MEN WALK ABOUT ME IN THE OFFICE. THEY WERE
        SO FLAT! ....THREE WOMEN 177   16
    THERE WAS SOMETHING ABOUT THEM LIKE CARDBOARD, AND NOW I HAD
        CAUGHT IT, ...THREE WOMEN 177   17
    I AM DUMB AND BROWN. I AM A SEED ABOUT TO BREAK. ....THREE WOMEN 179   99
    NOW I BREAK UP IN PIECES THAT FLY ABOUT LIKE CLUBS. ....ELM 192   19
    BUT HOW ABOUT THE EYES, THE EYES, THE EYES? ....COURAGE. 210   26
    DO NOT WORRY ABOUT THE EYES -- ....THE COURAGE OF SHUTTING-UP 210   30
    HOW ABOUT THIS SUIT --- ....THE APPLICANT 221   20
    AND YOU WANT TO BE SHOWN ABOUT! ....THE TOUR 237   7
    NOBODY'S ABOUT. IN THE HOTELS ....THE MUNICH MANNEQUINS 263   17
    KINDNESS GLIDES ABOUT MY HOUSE. ....KINDNESS 269   1
    THE MOON HAS NOTHING TO BE SAD ABOUT, ...EDGE 273   17
    ASKING ABOUT MONEY? I'M SICK OF THAT. ..DIALOGUE OVER A OUIJA BOARD 277   50
    REALLY WANT TO KNOW ABOUT? EVERYTHING. DIALOGUE OVER A OUIJA BOARD 278   54
    SIFT HIM ABOUT THE AFTER-LIFE THAN THIS:*DIALOGUE OVER A OUIJA BOARD 278   60
    DANGERS, BUT DON'T MIND HEARING ABOUT THE ONES ....DIALOGUE O. 278   64
    TEDIOUS. THAT'S WHAT WE'D SAY. ABOUT ROT*DIALOGUE OVER A OUIJA BOARD 279 101
    AS HE STOLE OUR PERPLEXITIES ABOUT THE POOLS ....DIALOGUE O. 279 103
    IN THIS DAY BEFORE THE DAY NOBODY IS ABOUT.*QUEEN MARY'S ROSE GARDEN 290   1
    IN WHICH THE MINUTES COULD ADMIRE THEIR REFLECTIONS AND
        FORGET ABOUT ME. ....THE RIVAL/DR 291   7
    THEY TALKED ABOUT THE RUSSIANS. ....BITTER STRAWBERRIES 299   2
    YOU SIT, SOLEMN-EYED, ABOUT TO VOMIT, ...THE TRIAL OF MAN 312   13
    WINGED RABBITS REVOLVING ABOUT HIS KNEES, ...CIRCUS IN THREE RINGS 322   16
    ABOUT EACH COSMIC PRO AND CON; ....LOVE IS A PARALLAX 329   15
    AS GREAT WEIGHTS DROP ALL ABOUT HER ....AERIALIST 331   17
    ABOUT A GOBLIN RAID ON MINER'S HUT ....THE PRINCESS AND THE GOBLINS 334   38
    LOOPING LIKE FAITH ABOUT HER BLEEDING FEET, ...THE PRINCESS. 334   48
    AND COO QUADRILLES ABOUT THE BLIGHTED CORE ....THE PRINCESS. 335   67
ABOVE (23)
    ABOVE THE APPALLING RUIN; IN BLEAK LIGHT .............CONVERSATION.   21   6
    THE AUSTERE SUN DESCENDS ABOVE THE FEN, ...WINTER LANDSCAPE.   21   6
    ABOVE: LEAF-WRAITHED WHITE AIR, WHITE CLOUD. ....BUCOLICS   24   12
    ABOVE PITCH OF PEDESTRIAN EAR, ...STREET SONG   36   23
    ABOVE THE SIMPLE VEIN, ...RECANTATION   42   15
    NEAR HIS SMALL STONEHENGE ABOVE THE ANTS' ROUTE, ...SPIDER   48   11

```
                                                    TITLE           PAGE  LINE
ABOVE (CONT.)
   AS IF, ABOVE LOVE'S RUINAGE, WE WERE  .................THE OTHER TWO    69   34
   ABOVE WHORLED, SPINDLING GORSE,  ..............TWO VIEWS OF WITHENS     71    1
   FLOATING ABOVE ME IN BLUEST AIR  ............THE DISQUIETING MUSES      75   42
   RAVEL ABOVE US, MISTILY DESCEND,  ...........................OUIJA      77   20
   ABOVE THE OXBOW  ......................................ABOVE THE OXBOW  87    T
   FOUR-WAY VERANDA, VIEW-KEEPING ABOVE  ...............ABOVE THE OXBOW    88   36
   INTACT, STRANGELY STRAYED ABOVE  .......MUSSEL HUNTER AT ROCK HARBOR    97   70
   THEN, TO SQUALL ABOVE THE LEVEL  .............................OWL      102   10
   ABOVE THE FIREPLACE;  ........................YADDO: THE GRAND MANOR    123   14
   ARCHES ABOVE US. O FATHER, ALL BY YOURSELF  .........THE COLOSSUS      129   17
   THE MOLTS ARE TONGUELESS THAT SANG FROM ABOVE THE WATER  ..POEM.5.F.   135   17
   THERE IS THIS WHITE WALL, ABOVE WHICH THE SKY CREATES ITSELF --  ...
                                                 ... APPREHENSIONS        195    1
   LIKE AN OLIVE-BEAKED DOVE ABOVE THE ENGULFING FACT:  ....DIALOGUE O.   279  112
   TO PROPEL HIS PLAYFULNESS, BUT ON YOU, ABOVE  ..........DIALOGUE O.    282  230
   PLOTS DOOM FROM ABOVE,  ..........................TRIO OF LOVE SONGS   314   14
   KNOWS NOT OF DEATH NOR CALCULUS ABOVE  ..........LOVE IS A PARALLAX    331   77
   IN THE AIR ABOVE MY ISLAND FLIES  ............EPITAPH IN THREE PARTS   337   12
ABRACADABRA (2)
   ABRACADABRA OF THE RAIN  ........INSOLENT STORM STRIKES AT THE SKULL   326   13
   WITH ABRACADABRA FROM THE ALPHABET.  ...THE PRINCESS AND THE GOBLINS   335   59
ABRADED (1)
   SAND ABRADED THE MILKLESS LIP.  .......................I WANT, I WANT  106    5
ABRADING (1)
   ABRADING MY LID, THE SMALL GRAIN BURNS:  ...............THE EYE-MOTE   109   16
ABSENCE (10)
   SO, PERHAPS I, KNELLED DUMB BY YOUR ABSENCE,  ...........STREET SONG    36   24
   HE IS GRATIFIED BY THE ABSENCE OF ICECAKES.  ...............ON DECK    143   27
   YOUR ABSENCE IS INCONSPICUOUS;  ...........PARLIAMENT HILL FIELDS      152    4
   A SENSE OF ABSENCE IN ITS OLD SHINING PLACE.*STARS OVER THE DORDOGNE   166   33
   THE ABSENCE OF SHRIEKS  .........................THE RABBIT CATCHER    194   17
   YOU WILL BE AWARE OF AN ABSENCE, PRESENTLY,  ...FOR A FATHERLESS SON   205    1
   THE MOUTH FIRST, ITS ABSENCE REPORTED  ...............THE DETECTIVE    209   27
   THERE WAS NO ABSENCE OF LIPS, THERE WERE TWO CHILDREN,*THE DETECTIVE   209   34
   ABSENCE, I  ........................................PURDAH            243   31
   PUNCHING OUT ABSENCE! LIKE CANNON.  ..................GETTING THERE    248    8
ABSENCES (1)
   BLOOD-CAUL OF ABSENCES.  ..................................THALIDOMIDE 252   16
ABSENT (1)
   METHINKS I SHALL ABSENT ME FOR A WHILE  ..............A SORCERER B.    324    3
ABSENTLY (1)
   TO BE SCRATCHED ABSENTLY,  ...........................EAVESDROPPER    260    5
ABSENT-MINDED (1)
   SHE LET IN THE DRAFTS AND BECAME MORE AND MORE ABSENT-MINDED.  ...
                                                 ... IN PLASTER          159   32
ABSINTHE (1)
   WITH ABSINTHE EYE  .........................................PROSPECT   28   10
ABSOLUTE (5)
   THE SHAPE THAT SHUTS US IN? ABSOLUTE FACT  ............TALE OF A TUB    25   29
   ABSOLUTE POWER  .......................SOLILOQUY OF THE SOLIPSIST      37   25
   LOOMED ABSOLUTE AS THE ANTIQUE WORLD WAS  .........HARDCASTLE CRAGS     63   38
   THE ABSOLUTE SACRIFICE.  .........................THE MUNICH MANNEQUINS 263   7
   SKY WON'T BE DRAWN CLOSER: ABSOLUTE,  .....METAMORPHOSES OF THE MOON   307    7
ABSOLUTELY (3)
   ABSOLUTELY ALIEN  ......................MUSSEL HUNTER AT ROCK HARBOR    96   54
   THIS NEW ABSOLUTELY WHITE PERSON AND THE OLD YELLOW ONE, *IN PLASTER   158    2
   YOUR CLEAR EYE IS THE ONE ABSOLUTELY BEAUTIFUL THING.  ........CHILD   265    1
ABSOLUTES (2)
   ALL ABSOLUTES THAT ANGELS GIVE   INSOLENT STORM STRIKES AT THE SKULL   326   23
   THE ALGEBRA OF ABSOLUTES  .......................LOVE IS A PARALLAX    330   51
ABSORB (2)
   (TOO QUICK FOR THE PAIR TO ABSORB IT),  ..........DIALOGUE EN ROUTE    309   41
   THE TENTS OF SUN ABSORB.  ......................TRIO OF LOVE SONGS     314   20
ABSORBENT (1)
   ABSORBENT AS A SPONGE;  ............................FAMILY REUNION     301   28
ABSTAIN (1)
   THE FALLING MAN WHO NEVER WILL ABSTAIN  ...METAMORPHOSES OF THE MOON   307   10
ABSTRACT (1)
   ELOPING FROM THEIR SLABS, ABSTRACT  ....................DANSE MACABRE  321   19
ABSTRACTIONS (1)
   ENDLESSLY PROCEED -- AND THE COLD ANGELS, THE ABSTRACTIONS.  THREE.   177   20
ABSTRACTS (1)
   THE ABSTRACTS HOVER LIKE DULL ANGELS:  ........................MAGI   148    1
ABSURD (3)
   WHERE, ABSURD AND OUT-OF-SEASON, A SINGLE SWAN  ...WINTER LANDSCAPE,    21    3
   A BEDRAGGLED SNAKE, HANGING LIMP AS THE ABSURD MOUTH  .......PERSEUS    83   38
   MUST HAVE BEEN WHOLLY SOMEONE ELSE. IT'S ABSURD,  .......DIALOGUE O.   285  309
ABUSES (2)
   NOT GUNS, NOT ABUSES,  ...........................THE THIN PEOPLE      64   16
   BUT BY SUCH ABUSES  .........................A LESSON IN VENGEANCE     80    6
ABYSS (3)
   THAT RIVET IN PLACE ABYSS AFTER ABYSS.  .................THREE WOMEN   182  203
   THAT RIVET IN PLACE ABYSS AFTER ABYSS.  .................THREE WOMEN   182  203
   THE SHADOW OF THIS LIP, AN ABYSS.  ........................GULLIVER    251   24
```

4

	TITLE	PAGE	LINE

ACADEMIES (1)
    HERE IN THIS VALLEY OF DISCREET ACADEMIES ....ABOVE THE OXBOW   87   1
ACANTHINE (1)
    YOUR FLUTED BONES AND ACANTHINE HAIR ARE LITTERED .....THE COLOSSUS   130   20
ACANTHUS (1)
    THESE CROWNS OF ACANTHUS, ...THE MANOR GARDEN   125   10
ACCEPT (3)
    SHOULD ACCEPT SO FELL A WOUND, ...BUCOLICS   24   18
    IT IS NOT MINE. DO NOT ACCEPT IT. ....THE COURIERS   247   2
    DO NOT ACCEPT IT. IT IS NOT GENUINE. ....THE COURIERS   247   4
ACCEPTABLE (1)
    BETTER, BETTER, AND MORE ACCEPTABLE ....THE RAVAGED FACE   116   12
ACCEPTING (1)
    OPENS AND SHUTS, ACCEPTING THEM AMONG ITS REFLECTIONS. ..PRIVATE G.   131   24
ACCIDENT (5)
    OR AN ACCIDENT ....BLACK ROOK IN RAINY WEATHER   56   5
    WORDS HEARD, BY ACCIDENT, OVER THE PHONE ....WORDS HEARD.   202   T
    AFTER ALL I AM ALIVE ONLY BY ACCIDENT. ....A BIRTHDAY PRESENT   206   14
    IT WAS AN ACCIDENT. ....LADY LAZARUS 245   36
    FROM THE COMIC ACCIDENT OF BIRTH ....DIRGE FOR A JOKER   303   9
ACCIDENTAL (1)
    WAITING FOR SOME ACCIDENTAL BREAK ....TALE OF A TUB   25   21
ACCOMMODATE (2)
    THE POLITE SKYS OVER BOSTON COULDN'T POSSIBLY ACCOMMODATE.*TWO CAMP.   145   11
    THEY ACCOMMODATE THEMSELVES TO MY MILKBOTTLE, FLATTENING THEIR
        SIDES. ....BLACKBERRYING 168   9
ACCOMMODATES (1)
    SAYING: "SOMETHING'S ADDLED IN A WOMAN WHO ACCOMMODATES ...
                              ... ELLA MASON AND HER ELEVEN CATS   53   5
ACCOMPANIED (1)
    ACCOMPANIED YOU. SO THEY NODDED AT THE COUCH WITH THE MOON*YADWIGHA.   86   32
ACCOMPLISH (1)
    I LAST. I LAST IT OUT. I ACCOMPLISH A WORK. ....THREE WOMEN   180 129
ACCOMPLISHED (1)
    WHOSE IS THAT LONG WHITE BOX IN THE GROVE, WHAT HAVE THEY
        ACCOMPLISHED, WHY AM I COLD. ....THE BEE MEETING   212   55
ACCOMPLISHMENT (1)
    BODY WEARS THE SMILE OF ACCOMPLISHMENT, ...EDGE   272   3
ACCORD (1)
    ROUND OF ITS OWN ACCORD. ....THE TIMES ARE TIDY 107   5
ACCORDING (2)
    STAYING PUT ACCORDING TO HABIT. ....LOVE LETTER 147   4
    AND STUNG ACCORDING TO THE WITCH'S PLAN, ...THE PRINCESS.   333   9
ACCOUNTING (1)
    IS ACCOUNTING FOR ITS COW. I SHUT MY EYES ..STARS OVER THE DORDOGNE 166   39
ACCOUNTS (1)
    LOADED, AS THEY ARE, WITH ACCOUNTS OF BASTARDIES. ....COURAGE.   210   6
ACCUMULATED (1)
    BUT ALL THE ACCUMULATED LAST GRUNTS, GROANS, ...PERSEUS   83   17
ACCURACY (1)
    SUCH STARKNESS; ACCURACY MUST NOT STALK AT LARGE: ....TALE OF A TUB   25   35
ACCURATE (1)
    AN ACCURATE ASSAULT UPON THE EYES ....EPITAPH IN THREE PARTS   337   14
ACCURST (1)
    ACCURST AS WILD-CATS. ....ELLA MASON AND HER ELEVEN CATS   54   42
ACCUSED (4)
    I AM ACCUSED. I DREAM OF MASSACRES. ....THREE WOMEN 180 148
    I SHALL NOT BE ACCUSED BY ISOLATE BUTTONS, ...THREE WOMEN   182 198
    I SHALL NOT BE ACCUSED, I SHALL NOT BE ACCUSED. ....THREE WOMEN   182 201
    I SHALL NOT BE ACCUSED, I SHALL NOT BE ACCUSED. ....THREE WOMEN   182 201
ACE (2)
    SIGHED EVE, THE ELEVATOR-GIRL ACE, ...DIALOGUE EN ROUTE   308   2
    EVE, THE ELEVATOR-GIRL ACE, ...DIALOGUE EN ROUTE   309   32
ACETIC (2)
    ACETIC ACID IN A SEALED TIN? ....THE COURIERS   247   3
    OF AN ACETIC STAR. ....JILTED 304   4
ACETYLENE (1)
    AM A PURE ACETYLENE ....FEVER. 232   46
ACH (1)
    ACH, DU. ....DADDY 222   15
ACHE (4)
    ASKEW, SHE'LL ACHE AND WAKE ....VIRGIN IN A TREE   82   40
    THE WOODS CREAK AND ACHE, AND THE DAY FORGETS ITSELF.*PRIVATE GROUND 131   19
    ATTENDING HER COT IS LESS THAN A BELLY ACHE, ...MAGI 148   13
    I WAIT AND ACHE. I THINK I HAVE BEEN HEALING. ....THREE WOMEN   187 358
ACHES (1)
    THE CITY WAITS AND ACHES. THE LITTLE GRASSES ....THREE WOMEN   187 370
ACHIEVE (1)
    MYSELF THE ROSE YOU ACHIEVE -- ....CHILDLESS WOMAN   259   7
ACHIEVED (1)
    IT IS HE WHO HAS ACHIEVED THESE SYLLABLES. ....WORDS HEARD.   202   5
ACHOO (1)
    BARELY DARING TO BREATHE OR ACHOO. ....DADDY   222   5
ACID (3)
    THE ACID BATHS, THE SKYFULS OFF OF YOU. ....LESBOS 228   47

	TITLE	PAGE	LINE

ACID (CONT.)
O VASE OF ACID, ...LESBOS 229 71
ACETIC ACID IN A SEALED TIN? ....THE COURIERS 247 3
ACIDS (1)
ITS SNAKY ACIDS KISS. ....ELM 193 40
ACORN-STOMACHED (1)
SAVED FOR THE ACORN-STOMACHED SAINT OR EYES ....DIALOGUE O. 280 129
ACQUIRE (1)
ACQUIRE THE AIR. ....MUSHROOMS 139 6
ACRE (1)
O THE KING'S TIDY ACRE IS UNDER THE SEA, ...THE BULL OF BENDYLAW 108 19
ACRES (3)
HER DAINTY ACRES HE RAMPED THROUGH ....THE QUEEN'S COMPLAINT 28 6
FOR HIS LEAST LOOK, SCANT ACRES YIELD: ....ODE FOR TED 29 13
OVER THE WEEDY ACRES OF YOUR BROW ....THE COLOSSUS 129 13
ACROBAT (1)
ACROBAT OF SPACE, ...TRIO OF LOVE SONGS 314 25
ACROBATICS (1)
IN TIGHTROPE ACROBATICS. ....AERIALIST 331 6
ACROPOLIS (1)
CHUCK THE BROKEN ACROPOLIS OUT, ...SONG FOR A REVOLUTIONARY LOVE 323 6
ACROSS (20)
ACROSS BARBED STILE, THROUGH FLOCKED BROWN COWS. ....BUCOLICS 23 4
ACROSS THE JUT OF OCHREOUS ROCK ....DEPARTURE 51 18
DAMNED, HOWLING IN THEIR SHROUDS ACROSS THE MOOR NOVEMBER GRAVEYARD 56 16
ACROSS MOOR SNOWS ....THE SNOWMAN ON THE MOOR 58 16
ACROSS ATLANTIC FURROWS, DARK, UNSURE -- ....MAYFLOWER 60 11
STRAIGHTFORWARDLY ACROSS THE SPRINGING GREEN. ......ABOVE THE OXBOW 89 52
AND YOU, ACROSS THOSE WHITE ....MAN IN BLACK 119 15
ACROSS THE INDIAN CARPET, THE COLD FLOOR, ...BY CANDLELIGHT 237 25
IT IS RUSSIA I HAVE TO GET ACROSS, IT IS SOME WAR OR OTHER.*GETTING. 248 9
THE GLASS CRACKS ACROSS, ...THALIDOMIDE 252 24
WHILE WE'RE SITTING, FACE TO FACE ACROSS THE COFFEE- ...DIALOGUE O. 276 3
AND YOU, SHACKLED ASHEN ACROSS THE RIFT, A SPECTER ....DIALOGUE O. 285 321
ACROSS THE RUTTED ROAD. ....BITTER STRAWBERRIES 299 17
ACROSS THEM ALL ....FAMILY REUNION 300 21
AND BLOOD REFLECTS ACROSS THE MANUSCRIPT; ....FEMALE AUTHOR 301 10
AND PROFANE WORDS SCRAWLED BLACK ACROSS THE SUN. ....DOOM OF EXILES 318 12
ACROSS THAT SULTRY AIR, ...AERIALIST 331 14
ACROSS THE FROSTED GRASS SHE MARKS THE SHEEN ....THE PRINCESS. 334 31
ROCKING ACROSS THE LAPIS LAZULI SEA ....EPITAPH IN THREE PARTS 337 1
CAPER ON LEAFSTALK LEGS ACROSS MY DOORSILL, EPITAPH IN THREE PARTS 337 24
ACT (11)
SHREWD CATCH SILTING OUR EACH BRIGHT ACT BACK ....FIRESONG 30 13
WHOSE STARK ACT ALL COMING DOUBLE LUCK JOINS. ..WREATH FOR A BRIDAL 44 6
HUSH A LUMPED MAN-SHAPE. THE WHOLE ACT FORMAL, FLUENT AS A DANCE. ...
... THE GORING 47 9
ACT, BUT -- HOW THOSE FEATHERS SHINE! ....RHYME 50 16
HEAD ALONE SHOWS YOU IN THE PRODIGIOUS ACT ....PERSEUS 82 1
EVERY LITTLE WORD HOOKED TO EVERY LITTLE WORD, AND ACT TO ACT. ...
... THREE WOMEN 178 55
EVERY LITTLE WORD HOOKED TO EVERY LITTLE WORD, AND ACT TO ACT. ...
... THREE WOMEN 178 55
AND ACT BEAR WITNESS, IN THE CRUX OF TIME, ...DIALOGUE O. 286 362
SHEER SILVER BLURS THEIR PHANTOM ACT. ....DANSE MACABRE 321 21
THE CULTIVATED ACT, A FIERCE BRIEF FUSION ....LOVE IS A PARALLAX 330 58
IN DEAD CENTER OF HER ACT ....AERIALIST 331 16
ACTED (3)
YOU ACTED, ACTED, ACTED FOR THE THRILL. ....LESBOS 228 43
YOU ACTED, ACTED, ACTED FOR THE THRILL. ....LESBOS 228 43
YOU ACTED, ACTED, ACTED FOR THE THRILL. ....LESBOS 228 43
ACTION (2)
TO LEAF-SIZE FROM LACK OF ACTION: ....THE TIMES ARE TIDY 107 9
LINK TO HIS LYRIC ACTION ....TRIO OF LOVE SONGS 314 35
ACTIONS (1)
HOW FAR HE IS NOW, HIS ACTIONS ....BERCK-PLAGE 199 82
ACTIVE (1)
IN THE MORTAL ACTIVE VERB, ...TOUCH-AND-GO 336 18
ACTORS (3)
THE STONY ACTORS POISE AND PAUSE FOR BREATH. *ELECTRA ON AZALEA PATH 117 37
WHILE ALL THE ACTORS HALT IN MORTAL SHOCK: ....DOOMSDAY 316 5
BRAZEN ACTORS MOCK AT HIM, ...LOVE IS A PARALLAX 330 45
ACTS (2)
BRAVE ACTS PLAYED OUT IN PEACE, IN WAR; ALL DANGERS*CHANNEL CROSSING 27 39
AND THE AIR DANGEROUS. NOONDAY ACTS QUEERLY ....SLEEP. 143 3
ACTUAL (2)
NAKED IN THE MERELY ACTUAL ROOM, ...TALE OF A TUB 24 5
WATER WILL RUN BY RULE; THE ACTUAL SUN ....TWO LOVERS. 327 21
A.D. (1)
...COFFIN OF THE FOURTH CENTURY A.D. CONTAINING THE
SKELETONS... ....ALL THE DEAD DEARS 70 E/2
ADAM (5)
SIDE OF GREEN ADAM, I ....PURDAH 242 4
TO ADAM THE ARROGANT MATADOR ....DIALOGUE EN ROUTE 308 3
SHAM ADAM THE MATADOR CRIED: ....DIALOGUE EN ROUTE 308 14

6

	TITLE	PAGE	LINE

ADAM (CONT.)
ADDED ADAM, THAT SIMIAN SWELL, ...DIALOGUE EN ROUTE 309 25
AND ADAM THE ARROGANT MATADOR ....DIALOGUE EN ROUTE 309 33
ADAM'S (2)
COULD BE THIS ADAM'S WOMAN ....ODE FOR TED   30 22
THICK, RED AND SLIPPING. IT IS ADAM'S SIDE, ...GETTING THERE 248 36
ADAZZLE (1)
ADAZZLE WITH BRIGHT SHARDS ....MISS DRAKE PROCEEDS TO SUPPER   41 19
ADDED (2)
SHE ADDED PETTISHLY, "I CAN'T SEE WHY ....BITTER STRAWBERRIES 300 25
ADDED ADAM, THAT SIMIAN SWELL, ...DIALOGUE EN ROUTE 309 25
ADDING (1)
YOU ARE SILVER-SUITED FOR THE OCCASION. O ADDING MACHINE --- ...
                                      ... A BIRTHDAY PRESENT 207 44
ADDLED (2)
SHE, ADDLED IN HER GOOSE-WIT, STRUTS ....RHYME   50   4
SAYING: "SOMETHING'S ADDLED IN A WOMAN WHO ACCOMMODATES ...
                            ... ELLA MASON AND HER ELEVEN CATS   53   5
ADDRESS (4)
STUBBORNLY HANGING ON TO MY NAME AND ADDRESS. ....TULIPS 161 23
YES, YES, THIS IS MY ADDRESS. ....THE TOUR 237   8
PLUMMET TO THEIR DARK ADDRESS, ...NICK AND THE CANDLESTICK 241 36
THE MAGIC SAWDUST WRITES: ADDRESS UNKNOWN. ....DENOUEMENT 327 17
ADDRESSED (2)
"HOW NOW," FATHER SHAWN CRISPLY ADDRESSED THE GHOST ....DIALOGUE B.   38 11
EACH WITH A TELEGRAM ADDRESSED TO ME. ....EPITAPH IN THREE PARTS 337   3
ADDRESSING (1)
ADDRESSING IT, WHILE THE HILLS ROLL THE NOTES OF THE DEAD BELL; ...
                                      ... BERCK-PLAGE 200 95
ADHERE (1)
WHO WOULD ADHERE TO ME: I UNDO HER FINGERS LIKE BANDAGES: I GO. ...
                                      ... THREE WOMEN 184 273
ADHERING (1)
ADHERING TO RULES, TO RULES, TO RULES. ....A BIRTHDAY PRESENT 206   8
ADIRONDACKS (1)
TO THE ADIRONDACKS, TO NORTHERN MONADNOCK, ...ABOVE THE OXBOW   87   3
ADJECTIVE (1)
THE DARING ADJECTIVE ....TRIO OF LOVE SONGS 314 26
ADJECTIVES (1)
WHERE ADJECTIVES PLAY CROQUET WITH FLAMINGO NOUNS; ...A SORCERER B. 324   2
ADMIRALS (1)
THE WHITE BUSTS OF MARSHALS, ADMIRALS, GENERALS ....THE SWARM 217 44
ADMIRE (4)
THE BLOOD IS A SUNSET. I ADMIRE IT. ....THE SURGEON AT 2 A.M. 171 21
HOW I ADMIRE THE ROMANS -- ....THE SURGEON AT 2 A.M. 171 27
I WOULD ADMIRE THE DEEP GRAVITY OF IT, ITS TIMELESS EYES. *BIRTHDAY 208 57
IN WHICH THE MINUTES COULD ADMIRE THEIR REFLECTIONS AND FORGET
        ABOUT ME. ....THE RIVAL/DR 291   7
ADMIRERS (1)
TOWARD THEIR ADMIRERS IN THE TABLETOP: ....LEAVING EARLY 146 12
ADMIRER'S (1)
THE FOND ADMIRER'S ....ON LOOKING INTO THE EYES OF A DEMON LOVER 325 11
ADMIRING (1)
LET US SIT DOWN TO IT, ONE ON EITHER SIDE, ADMIRING THE GLEAM, ...
                                      ... A BIRTHDAY PRESENT 207 24
ADMIT (3)
BLIND WITH STEAM, WILL NOT ADMIT THE DARK ....TALE OF A TUB   24 15
ALTHOUGH, I ADMIT, I DESIRE, ...BLACK ROOK IN RAINY WEATHER   57 11
ME. ASK, ANYHOW. I ADMIT IT: I'M AFRAID,*DIALOGUE OVER A OUIJA BOARD 278 67
ADMONITIONS (1)
ADMONITIONS ....ADMONITIONS 319   T
ADMONITORY (1)
ADMONITORY CLIFFS, AND THE SEA EXPLODING ....FINISTERRE 169   3
ADOLESCENCE (1)
OF CHILDHOOD AND ADOLESCENCE, STICKY WITH DREAMS, ...INSOMNIAC 163 10
ADORED (1)
I DIDN'T MIND HER WAITING ON ME, AND SHE ADORED IT. ......IN PLASTER 159 22
ADORES (1)
EVERY WOMAN ADORES A FASCIST, ...DADDY 223 48
ADRIFT (1)
ADRIFT IN THE GUISE OF SOME GREAT-TALONED BIRD ....DIALOGUE O. 285 311
ADROIT (3)
ADROIT LOBSTERS ....AQUATIC NOCTURNE 306 22
BUT ADROIT CONJUNCTION ....TRIO OF LOVE SONGS 314 33
EACH NIGHT, THIS ADROIT YOUNG LADY ....AERIALIST 331   1
ADULTERERS (1)
GREASING THE BODIES OF ADULTERERS ....FEVER. 231 25
ADULTERIES (1)
SULFUROUS ADULTERIES GRIEVE IN A DREAM. ....THE OTHER 202 25
ADVANCE (1)
NOW WITH STAKE AND PITCHFORK THEY ADVANCE, FLINT EYES FIXED
        ON MURDER. .... DREAM WITH CLAM-DIGGERS   44 28
ADVANCES (1)
OUR CREDITOR ADVANCES WITH A BOW ....THE DISPOSSESSED 318 10

	TITLE	PAGE	LINE

ADVANCING (2)
    ADVANCING ALWAYS AT MY BACK; ....PURSUIT   22   6
    SHOWS, RANK ON RANK, THE HUNGRY SEAS ADVANCING.   ...CHANNEL CROSSING   26   8
ADVANTAGES (1)
    SHE BEGAN TO WARM UP, AND I SAW HER ADVANTAGES.   ....IN PLASTER 159   14
ADVICE (1)
    THEY ARE ROUND AND FLAT AND FULL OF DARK ADVICE. *CROSSING THE WATER   190   6
AERIALIST (1)
    AERIALIST   ....AERIALIST   331   T
AFAR (1)
    HEARING A WEIRD CACKLE FROM AFAR, ...THE PRINCESS AND THE GOBLINS   334   41
AFFABLE (1)
    AND LOVERS AFFABLE, DOVELIKE.   ....IN MIDAS' COUNTRY   99   15
AFFAIR (2)
    THE SECOND CARCASS MAKES A DUEL OF THE AFFAIR: ....BLUE MOLES   126   8
    I SHOULD WEAR TIGER PANTS, I SHOULD HAVE AN AFFAIR.   ....LESBOS   228   30
AFFECTS (1)
    IS IT ANY WONDER HE AFFECTS A BLACK CASSOCK?   ....BERCK-PLAGE   196   13
AFFIRMING (1)
    EIGHT GREAT TONGUES AFFIRMING THE RESURRECTION.   ....MOON.   173   13
AFFLICTED (1)
    BY THIS TUMULT AFFLICTED, SHE   ....SPINSTER   49   7
AFFLUENCE (1)
    IN A GLASSED TABLEAU OF AFFLUENCE.   ....OWL   102   7
AFLAME (1)
    HIS GREED HAS SET THE WOODS AFLAME, ...PURSUIT   22   3
AFLOAT (1)
    HE, AFLOAT IN THE SEA OF HER BLUE SATIN *TWO VIEWS OF A CADAVER ROOM   114   14
AFRAID (2)
    DO NOT BE AFRAID, IT IS NOT SO.   ....A BIRTHDAY PRESENT 207   32
    ME. ASK, ANYHOW. I ADMIT IT: I'M AFRAID,*DIALOGUE OVER A OUIJA BOARD   278   67
AFRICA (2)
    WALKING ABOUT IN AFRICA MAYBE, BUT THINKING OF ME.   ......THE RIVAL   167   17
    ON INDIA, AFRICA, AMERICA, THESE MIRACULOUS ONES, ...THREE WOMEN   183 229
AFRICAN (4)
    THEY ARE OPENING LIKE THE MOUTH OF SOME GREAT AFRICAN CAT, ..TULIPS   162   59
    ON THE INFERNO OF AFRICAN ORANGES, THE HEEL-HUNG PIGS.   THREE WOMEN   184 283
    WITH THE SWARMY FEELING OF AFRICAN HANDS *THE ARRIVAL OF THE BEE BOX   213   13
    THROUGH THE AFRICAN GIRAFFE IN ITS EDENY GREENERY, ...A SECRET   219   12
AFTER (53)
    SUN HOISTS SOUL UP AFTER LIDS FALL SHUT;   ....VANITY FAIR   33   28
    AFTER A LEAN DAY'S WORK   ....STRUMPET SONG   33   3
    IN BLACK NOVEMBER. AFTER A SLIDING RAIN   ....DIALOGUE B.   38   3
    AFTER YOUR LIFE'S END, WHAT JUST EPILOGUE   ....DIALOGUE B.   39   24
    SHE LIFTS ONE WEBBED FOOT AFTER THE OTHER   ....MISS DRAKE P.   41   24
    CANNOT FOLLOW AFTER, BUT LIES   ....THE SHRIKE   42   8
    SCATHED, STAINED AFTER TEDIOUS PILGRIMAGES. DREAM WITH CLAM-DIGGERS   43   4
    THEY NAMED THEIR SHIP AFTER THE FLOWER OF MAY.   ....MAYFLOWER   60   14
    AFTER THE HORIZONS, STRETCHING THE NARROWED EYE   ....ABOVE THE OXBOW   88   25
    OF THE SPINACH PATCH. BUNCH AFTER BUNCH OF GREEN   ...SPINACH-PICKER.   89   7
    SCRIM AFTER SCRIM LIKE FISHNETS   ....LORELEI   94   5
    ALREADY THE FARMER'S AFTER HIS CROP, ...IN MIDAS' COUNTRY   100   23
    GLUT THESE HUNTERS AFTER AN OLD MEAT, ...AFTERMATH   113   7
    THEIR MUSK ENCROACHES, CIRCLE AFTER CIRCLE,*THE BEEKEEPER'S DAUGHTER   118   3
    AFTER THE FAT CHILDREN OF ROOT AND ROCK.   ....BLUE MOLES   126   25
    AFTER THE OTHER   ....DARK WOOD, DARK WATER   127   23
    NOW COLDNESS COMES SIFTING DOWN, LAYER AFTER LAYER, ...POEM.5.F.   134   1
    THEY ARE TURNING THE BURNERS UP, RING AFTER RING. POEM.6.W.   135   16
    MUSKY AS A LOVEBED THE MORNING AFTER.   ....LEAVING EARLY   146   19
    NOW SILENCE AFTER SILENCE OFFERS ITSELF.   ....PARLIAMENT HILL FIELDS   152   19
    SIMPLY BECAUSE SHE LOOKED AFTER ME SO BADLY.   ....IN PLASTER 159   34
    AFTER ALL, IT WAS A KIND OF MARRIAGE, BEING SO CLOSE.   ...IN PLASTER   160   51
    LETTING IN THE LIGHT, PEEPHOLE AFTER PEEPHOLE --   ....INSOMNIAC   163   3
    ARRIVE AT TWILIGHT, AND THEN AFTER SOME EFFORT.   ....STARS.   165   10
    IT DRAGS THE SEA AFTER IT LIKE A DARK CRIME; IT IS QUIET   .....MOON.   173   10
    THE EYES LIFT AFTER IT AND FIND THE MOON. *THE MOON AND THE YEW TREE   173   16
    RISES TOWARD HER DAY AFTER DAY, LIKE A TERRIBLE FISH.   ....MIRROR   174   18
    ON TRIAL, FROM IRELAND, SHE BURNED BATCH AFTER BATCH OF COOKIES   ...
                                                      THE BABYSITTERS   175   26
    I LOSE LIFE AFTER LIFE. THE DARK EARTH DRINKS THEM.   ....THREE WOMEN   181 154
    THE BLUE COLOR PALES. HE IS HUMAN AFTER ALL.   ....THREE WOMEN   181 166
    MONTH AFTER MONTH, WITH ITS VOICES OF FAILURE.   ....THREE WOMEN   182 187
    THAT RIVET IN PLACE ABYSS AFTER ABYSS.   ....THREE WOMEN   182 203
    IT STRIVES AFTER THEM WITH ITS LIGHTS.   ....THREE WOMEN   186 346
    AND SO WE ARE AT HOME TOGETHER, AFTER HOURS.   ....THREE WOMEN   187 362
    HOW YOU LIE AND CRY AFTER IT   ....ELM   192   8
    DIMINISHED AND FLAT, AS AFTER RADICAL SURGERY.   ....ELM   192   26
    THESE CHILDREN ARE AFTER SOMETHING, WITH HOOKS AND CRIES, ...BERCK.   198   44
    PASSES CLOUD AFTER CLOUD.   ....BERCK-PLAGE   200 105
    AFTER ALL I AM ALIVE ONLY BY ACCIDENT.   ....A BIRTHDAY PRESENT   206   14
    MASS AFTER MASS, SAYING SHH!   ....THE SWARM   216   10
    UNLOOSING THEIR MOONS, MONTH AFTER MONTH, TO NO PURPOSE.   ...MUNICH.   263   5
    AFTER WHOSE STROKE THE WOOD RINGS, ...WORDS   270   2
    A LIFE AFTER THIS LIFE? HE SHOOTS SO SWIFT   ....DIALOGUE O.   278   72
    FOR YES, DRAGGING OUR FINGERS AFTER. HOW*DIALOGUE OVER A OUIJA BOARD   278   75

AFTER (CONT.)
AND TRICKED US TO TRUST HIS VISION, WHILE NIGHT AFTER NIGHT HE ...
                           ... DIALOGUE OVER A OUIJA BOARD 279 104
YOUR HEAD AFTER ALL. IT SEEMS HIS LAUGH *DIALOGUE OVER A OUIJA BOARD 282 238
IN THE CENTER OF THE GARDEN NAMED AFTER QUEEN MARY. ..QUEEN MARY'S. 290   3
THE ROSES ARE NAMED AFTER QUEENS AND PEOPLE OF NOTE ..QUEEN MARY'S. 290 17
OR AFTER GAY DAYS, OR COLORS THE GROWER FOUND GOOD. ..QUEEN MARY'S. 290 18
AFTER, THEY STAGGER AND WEAVE, UNDER NO BANNER. ....STINGS/DR 293 11
AFTER, THEY CRAWL ....STINGS/DR 293 12
FLING THE SEVEN WONDERS AFTER THAT ...SONG FOR A REVOLUTIONARY LOVE 323   7
ANNOUNCING AFTER GLUTTED BIRDS HAVE FLOWN: ..EPITAPH IN THREE PARTS 337 21
AFTERBIRTH (1)
LET US EAT IT LIKE PLATO'S AFTERBIRTH, ...TOTEM 264 14
AFTER-HELL (1)
THIS IS THE AFTER-HELL: I SEE THE LIGHT. POEM.7.S. 136 22
AFTER-LIFE (2)
OUR WORK. LOVE. THE AFTER-LIFE . . . DO YOU ....DIALOGUE O. 278 55
SIFT HIM ABOUT THE AFTER-LIFE THAN THIS:*DIALOGUE OVER A OUIJA BOARD 278 60
AFTERMATH (1)
AFTERMATH ....AFTERMATH 113   T
AFTERNOON (2)
ALL AFTERNOON THESE LOVERS LAY ....BUCOLICS   24 13
THE AFTERNOON AT A BAD END UNDER THE CROWD'S TRUCULENCE, THE GORING   47   2
AFTERTHOUGHT (1)
AFTERTHOUGHT OFTEN WOULD HAVE THEM ALTER ....POEMS, POTATOES 106   7
AGAIN (29)
GROW GREEN AGAIN? WHO'D WALK IN THIS BLEAK PLACE? WINTER LANDSCAPE,   22 15
TRICKS OF RADIANCE MIRACLES. THE WAIT'S BEGUN AGAIN, BLACK ROOK I.   57 38
OUT THEIR STALKY LIMBS AGAIN THOUGH PEACE ....THE THIN PEOPLE   64   9
OF THAT UNCOUTH SHAPE TO SIMPLE SOD AGAIN ....LADY AND T.   70 27
TOWARD THE ROWDY BELLOW AND BACK AGAIN ....THE BULL OF BENDYLAW 108 11
IN THE EAR OF THE VETERAN, AND AGAIN ....BLUE MOLES 126 20
SKYWARD AGAIN, WITHOUT HOPE, OF COURSE, ...LOVE LETTER 147   7
A SECOND TIME, TO HAVE HIM NEAR AGAIN -- ....WIDOW 164 16
AGAIN, THIS IS A DEATH. IS IT THE AIR, ...THREE WOMEN 177 37
I AM MYSELF AGAIN. THERE ARE NO LOOSE ENDS. ....THREE WOMEN 184 274
NOTHING THAT CANNOT BE ERASED, RIPPED UP AND SCRAPPED,
   BEGUN AGAIN. ....THREE WOMEN 184 277
I AM SIMPLE AGAIN. I BELIEVE IN MIRACLES. ....THREE WOMEN 185 319
I FIND MYSELF AGAIN. I AM NO SHADOW ....THREE WOMEN 187 368
NOT TO BE SPREAD AGAIN. ....BERCK-PLAGE 200 103
THEM HUGE AGAIN, VIOLENT GIANTS ON THE WALL. ....BY CANDLELIGHT 236 14
I HAVE DONE IT AGAIN. ....LADY LAZARUS 244   1
PLUMAGE OF WHAT, PAN? P . . . HE STARTS AGAIN, ...DIALOGUE O. 279 85
BEFORE HE SPELLS AGAIN, SHOULD HIS NEXT WRIT ....DIALOGUE O. 281 193
TO THE END OF IT. HE STARTS AGAIN: I-N- *DIALOGUE OVER A OUIJA BOARD 282 217
I'VE DREAMED OF DOING IT AGAIN. AND NOW *DIALOGUE OVER A OUIJA BOARD 285 303
IS ITSELF AGAIN, AND OURS. THE DREAM ...DIALOGUE OVER A OUIJA BOARD 286 358
THE SAME AGAIN: ....TO A JILTED LOVER 310 20
AGAIN WE ARE DELUDED AND INFER ....APRIL AUBADE 312 13
MY EXTRAVAGANT HEART BLOWS UP AGAIN ....CIRCUS IN THREE RINGS 321   3
AND AGAIN TOGETHER BEGIN IT ALL. .....SONG FOR A REVOLUTIONARY LOVE 323 24
HELLO, AND THEN HELLO AGAIN IN DEAF ....LOVE IS A PARALLAX 330 40
NOW KISS AGAIN: TILL OUR STRICT FATHER LEANS ...LOVE IS A PARALLAX 330 43
O NEVER AGAIN WILL THE EXTRAVAGANT STRAW ....THE PRINCESS. 335 72
THERE AND THERE AND THERE AGAIN, AND THEN ...EPITAPH IN THREE PARTS 337 27
AGAINST (34)
THAN AGAINST THIS ONSLAUGHT, THESE CASUAL BLASTS OF ICE CHANNEL C.   27 17
AGAINST VIRGIN PRAYER ....VANITY FAIR   33 21
AGAINST THE FLOWER IN THE BLOOD: ....RECANTATION   42 13
HIGH AGAINST HEAVEN, GULLS WENT WHEELING SOUNDLESS ...DREAM WITH C.   44 13
RODE OUT AGAINST THE FIFTH BULL TO BRACE HIS PIKE AND SLOWLY BEAR ...
                                            ... THE GORING   47   6
AND, PLAINTIFF AGAINST EACH DAY, DECRY ....THE BEGGARS   47   4
AGAINST MUTINOUS WEATHER ....SPINSTER   50 27
AGAINST WHICH THE BRUNT OF OUTER SEA ....DEPARTURE   51 14
HE ALSO AGAINST BLACK FROST ....THE EVERLASTING MONDAY   62   7
FOR STRONGHOLD AGAINST THEIR STIFF ....THE THIN PEOPLE   65 42
AGAINST BARE, WHITEWASHED WALLS, THE FURNITURE ....THE OTHER TWO   68   8
STOOD STUBBORN IN ITS JUNGLE: RED AGAINST GREEN, ...YADWIGHA.   85 18
RED AGAINST FIFTY VARIANTS OF GREEN, ...YADWIGHA.   85 19
AGAINST OUR SKY: THEY ARE WHAT WE LOOK SOUTHWARD TO *ABOVE THE OXBOW   88 11
SHUT AGAINST ME. ALL HELD STILL. ......MUSSEL HUNTER AT ROCK HARBOR   95 20
AGAINST THE WEIGHTY IMAGE OF THEIR FALL. ....MOONRISE   98 24
AGAINST MY LEANING DOWN, WOULD NOT EXCHANGE .........INCOMMUNICADO 100   5
OF RIDING AGAINST THE LIZARD, ...THE TIMES ARE TIDY 107   7
HOVE UP AGAINST BENDYLAW. ....THE BULL OF BENDYLAW 108   3
TAILS STREAMING AGAINST THE GREEN ....THE EYE-MOTE 109   3
KEPT HOUSE AGAINST ....POINT SHIRLEY 110 11
AGAINST BOTH BAR AND TOWER THE BLACK SEA RUNS. ....POINT SHIRLEY 111 48
UNFISTS AGAINST THE DUN ....MAN IN BLACK 119   5
THEMSELVES UP AGAINST THE WALL ....OLD LADIES' HOME 120   6
AGAINST THE CRACKING CLIMATE. ....PRIVATE GROUND 130   6
A PAPER IMAGE TO LAY AGAINST HER HEART ....WIDOW 164 17
LIKE BLUE MARY'S ANGEL, DOVELIKE AGAINST A PANE ....WIDOW 165 38

9

AGAINST (CONT.)
    WHO WALL UP THEIR BACKS AGAINST HIM. ....BERCK-PLAGE 196 15
    MIND AGAINST ALL THAT WHITE. ....WINTERING 218 33
    AGAINST FIRE AND BOMBS THROUGH THE ROOF. ....THE APPLICANT 221 24
    THAN AGAINST GRAVITY'S GRIP, TABLES RISING; THE DRINK ..DIALOGUE O. 279 122
    WHAT GREENHORN VENTS HIS VENOM AGAINST GIANTS ....DIALOGUE O. 281 199
    AGAINST A SILENCE WEARING THIN. ....FAMILY REUNION 300   9
    BLACK AGAINST THE ORANGE LIGHT: BLACK PINE TREE IN AN ORANGE LIGHT 328   3
AGAWP (1)
    AGAWP AT THE IMPECCABLE MOON. ....LETTER TO A PURIST   37 16
AGE (10)
    STILL AS A SHELL: HEAR WHAT AN AGE OF GLASS ....EPITAPH FOR F.   45 16
    AGE MANHANDLES ME ....WORDS FOR A NURSERY   74 42
    AGE, AND AGES OF PROSE, HAVE UNCOILED ....OUIJA   77 15
    HERALDRY OF A STARKER AGE, ...ON THE DECLINE OF ORACLES   78 19
    PITYS FROM PAN'S ASSAULT! AND THOUGH AGE DROP .....VIRGIN IN A TREE   81 17
    AGE, ANOTHER PLANET SURELY. FLANKED ....CHILD'S PARK STONES 101   8
    HOW SHALL I AGE INTO THAT STATE OF MIND? ...ELECTRA ON AZALEA PATH 117 41
    AGE WEARS THE BEST BLACK FABRIC ....OLD LADIES' HOME 120 13
    AGE AND TERROR, LIKE NURSES, ATTEND HER, ...A LIFE 150 33
    UNDO THE DOINGS OF THE FATHERING AGE: *SONG FOR A REVOLUTIONARY LOVE 323   5
AGED (1)
    CHOKING THE AGED AND THE MEEK, ...FEVER. 231 17
AGENT (1)
    THE RECTOR, THE MIDWIFE, THE SEXTON, THE AGENT FOR BEES. ......BEE. 211   2
AGES (4)
    AGE, AND AGES OF PROSE, HAVE UNCOILED ....OUIJA   77 15
    IN THE DOUR AGES ....A LESSON IN VENGEANCE   80   1
    AGES BEAT LIKE RAINS ....FULL FATHOM FIVE   93 27
    ENOUGH AGES LAPSED TO WIN ....MUSSEL HUNTER AT ROCK HARBOR   95 22
AGILE (2)
    AGILE MINNOWS ....AQUATIC NOCTURNE 305 11
    AGILE AS A STAR ....TRIO OF LOVE SONGS 314 19
AGITATE (1)
    IS IT FOR SUCH I AGITATE MY HEART? ....ELM 193 36
AGITATES (1)
    A CURRENT AGITATES THE WIRES POEM.7.S. 137 29
AGITATION (1)
    SHE REWARDS ME WITH TEARS AND AN AGITATION OF HANDS. ....MIRROR 174 14
AGO (4)
    TWENTY YEARS AGO, THE FAMILIAR TUB ....TALE OF A TUB   25 17
    A DAY AGO, TWO DAYS, THREE DAYS AGO. IT WAS A FRIDAY. ..THREE WOMEN 183 248
    A DAY AGO, TWO DAYS, THREE DAYS AGO. IT WAS A FRIDAY. ..THREE WOMEN 183 248
    "WE OUGHT TO HAVE BOMBED THEM LONG AGO." ....BITTER STRAWBERRIES 299 21
AGOG (1)
    WE PEERED AGOG THROUGH THE COBWEBBED DOOR ....ELLA MASON A.   54 26
AGONIES (1)
    I AM A GARDEN OF BLACK AND RED AGONIES. I DRINK THEM, ..THREE WOMEN 180 149
AGONIZED (1)
    THE AGONIZED ....PURDAH 242   3
AGONY (4)
    UNDER THE STRICT MASK OF HIS AGONY. ....CHANNEL CROSSING   26 12
    OF HUMAN AGONY: A LOOK TO NUMB ....PERSEUS   83 15
    ITS CARGO OF AGONY TOWARD ME, INESCAPABLE, TIDAL. ......THREE WOMEN 179 110
    THIS EARTH I RISE FROM, AND I IN AGONY. ....GETTING THERE 248 37
AGREE (1)
    "WELL THEN, IF WE AGREE, IT IS NOT ODD ....LOVE IS A PARALLAX 329   7
AGUEY (1)
    THE AGUEY TENDON, THE SIN, THE SIN. ....FEVER. 231   7
AHAB (1)
    AHAB, FULFILL YOUR BOAST: ....BATTLE-SCENE   84 27
AHEAD (7)
    GRIP THE RAIL, SQUINT AHEAD, AND WONDER HOW MUCH LONGER   CHANNEL C.   26   6
    AHEAD, IT FATTENED ....HARDCASTLE CRAGS   62 15
    THAT GLIDE AHEAD OF THE VERY THIRSTY. ...SLEEP IN THE MOJAVE DESERT 144 13
    OR BRAG AHEAD OF TIME HOW I'D AVENGE MYSELF. ....IN PLASTER 160 47
    PUMPED AHEAD BY THESE PISTONS, THIS BLOOD ....GETTING THERE 248 30
    WHITE TOWERS OF SMITHFIELD AHEAD, ...TOTEM 264   7
    TO KNOW AT ALL. AND YET I GO AHEAD. ....DIALOGUE OVER A OUIJA BOARD 278 69
AHISS (1)
    NOW THE ROOM IS AHISS. THE INSTRUMENT ....WORDS HEARD. 203 11
AHS (1)
    ATTRACTING MY SHARE OF AHS AND SPECTACULARLY PAINTED, *I AM VERTICAL 162   6
AIM (2)
    SO BEGGAR GERD MIGHT AIM HER LOOK ....CRYSTAL GAZER   55 40
    MY WISH ONE WITH YOUR AIM. ONCE, IN A DREAM, ...DIALOGUE O. 284 301
AIMS (1)
    WITH A THUNDER LIKE LIONS; ALL AIMS ....AERIALIST 331 32
AIR (85)
    ABOVE: LEAF-WRAITHED WHITE AIR, WHITE CLOUD. ....BUCOLICS   24 12
    FAR FROM THE SWEET STENCH OF THAT PERILOUS AIR ....CHANNEL CROSSING   27 13
    THE AIR WAS BRIGHT FOR LOOKING: ....SONG FOR A SUMMER'S DAY   31   6
    LIKE POLLEN ON BRIGHT AIR. LULLED ....TWO SISTERS OF PERSEPHONE   32 15
    CLEAVING FURRED AIR ....VANITY FAIR   32 11
    NOW THROUGH HER AMBUSHED AIR, ...MISS DRAKE PROCEEDS TO SUPPER   41 18

AIR (CONT.)
   THE SINGULAR AIR, ...THE SHRIKE   42   6
   ITS CLEAR AIR WINNOWED BY ANGELS; SHE WAS COME ....DREAM WITH C. 43   2
   TO PREVENT FALL, OR ANCHOR THE FLUENT AIR ....EPITAPH FOR F. 45   3
   BLOOD FAULTLESSLY BROACHED REDEEMED THE SULLIED AIR,
      THE EARTH'S GROSSNESS. ....THE GORING   47   10
   OBSERVED HER LOVER'S GESTURES UNBALANCE THE AIR, ...SPINSTER 49   8
   WALK FORTH INTO SUN-MONEYED AIR, QUICKENED ....CRYSTAL GAZER   55   26
   WHICH PEOPLES THE BARE ROOM, THE BLANK, UNTENANTED AIR. *NOVEMBER G. 56   18
   STONE-BUILT TOWN, THAT SHE HEARD THE QUICK AIR IGNITE *HARDCASTLE C. 62   4
   AND THE OPULENT AIR GO STUDDED WITH SEED, ...CONJURING. 66   36
   NOT ONE LEAF WRINKLED IN THE CLEARING AIR. ....THE OTHER TWO 68   6
   THROUGH AIR STREAMING AND GREEN-LIT, ...THE GREAT CARBUNCLE   72   2
   FLOATING ABOVE ME IN BLUEST AIR ....THE DISQUIETING MUSES 75   42
   WHEN WORDS, LIKE LOCUSTS, DRUMMED THE DARKENING AIR ....OUIJA   77   17
   OF THE AIR EDDIES' LOOP AND ARCH THOUGH AIR'S AT REST ....OXBOW. 88   32
   THE WATER HAD AN IRON TASTE, AND THE AIR, ...SPINACH-PICKER. 89   15
   IMAGES OF LIGHT AND AIR ....SCULPTOR 91   7
   FATHER, THIS THICK AIR IS MURDEROUS. ....FULL FATHOM FIVE   93   44
   IN SUNLESS AIR, UNDER PINES ....CHILD'S PARK STONES 100   1
   FROM BLIND AIR, FROM COMPLETE ECLIPSE. ...............RHODODENDRON. 103   16
   IN AN EBONY AIR, ON WINGS OF WITCH CLOTH, ...GOATSUCKER 111   10
   THERE, SPRING LAMBS JAM THE SHEEPFOLD. IN AIR ....WATERCOLOR. 111   1
   HOW IN SUCH MILD AIR ....WATERCOLOR OF GRANTCHESTER MEADOWS 112   27
   TO FATHER DYNASTIES. THE AIR IS RICH. .....THE BEEKEEPER'S DAUGHTER 118   12
   TIP, RIVETING STONES, AIR, ...MAN IN BLACK 120   20
   HIS BRUSH IN THE STRINGENT AIR. ....MAGNOLIA SHOALS   122   20
   AIR, AND BLUR. ....YADDO: THE GRAND MANOR   123   3
   AIR. THE SILVER- ....POLLY'S TREE   128   15
   SHALL UNHUSK HIMSELF AND STEER INTO THE AIR. POEM.5.F. 135   20
   ACQUIRE THE AIR. ....MUSHROOMS 139   6
   THOUGH THEY HAVE A PIGGY AND A FISHY AIR -- ....STILLBORN 142   12
   AND THE AIR DANGEROUS. NOONDAY ACTS QUEERLY ....SLEEP. 143   3
   THE FIRST THING I SAW WAS SHEER AIR ....LOVE LETTER 147   20
   FLOATING THROUGH THE AIR IN MY SOUL-SHIFT ....LOVE LETTER 147   35
   WHILE THE CHILD SMILES INTO THIN AIR. ....MAGI 148   9
   IT WILL PING LIKE A CHINESE CHIME IN THE SLIGHTEST AIR STIR A LIFE 150   7
   AIR LIKE A MEDICINE. ....WHITSUN 153   6
   BEFORE THEY CAME THE AIR WAS CALM ENOUGH, ...TULIPS 161   50
   NOW THE AIR SNAGS AND EDDIES ROUND THEM THE WAY A RIVER .....TULIPS 161   53
   BEHIND WHICH THE SECRET PASSAGE LIES -- STALE AIR, ...WIDOW 164   8
   IN THIS CLEAR AIR AND NEVER NOTICE IT -- ....WIDOW   164   33
   UNWARMED BY THE SWEET AIR OF THIS PEACH ORCHARD. ....STARS.   166   36
   THE AIR TO ORANGE ....WUTHERING HEIGHTS   167   5
   OF PEOPLE THE AIR ONLY ....WUTHERING HEIGHTS   168   33
   AGAIN, THIS IS A DEATH. IS IT THE AIR, ...THREE WOMEN 177   37
   THE AIR IS THICK. IT IS THICK WITH THIS WORKING. ....THREE WOMEN 180 144
   THEIR FOOTSOLES ARE UNTOUCHED. THEY ARE WALKERS OF AIR. *THREE WOMEN 183 231
   THERE IS A KIND OF SMOKE IN THE SPRING AIR, ...THREE WOMEN 186 354
   BY PALE GIRLS, TRAVEL THE AIR IN SCORCHED HANDS. ....BERCK-PLAGE 196   4
   THE VOICE OF THE PRIEST, IN THIN AIR, ...BERCK-PLAGE 200   93
   IS IT FOR THIS THE AIR MOTES DEPART? ....THE OTHER   201   11
   THEY ARE NOT AIR MOTES, THEY ARE CORPUSCLES. ....THE OTHER   201   12
   DYEING THE AIR, ...BURNING THE LETTERS   205   54
   TO YOU THEY ARE ONLY TRANSPARENCIES, CLEAR AIR.   A BIRTHDAY PRESENT 207   38
   WE WALK ON AIR, WATSON. ....THE DETECTIVE 209   38
   AND THE NOISE IT FLAYS FROM THE AIR, ONCE IT GETS GOING! ..COURAGE. 210   20
   WE SHOULD MEET IN ANOTHER LIFE, WE SHOULD MEET IN AIR, ...LESBOS   228   31
   THERE'S ALWAYS A BLOODY BABY IN THE AIR. ....STOPPED DEAD 230   13
   AND LIVE IN GIBRALTAR ON AIR, ON AIR. ....STOPPED DEAD 230   25
   AND LIVE IN GIBRALTAR ON AIR, ON AIR. ....STOPPED DEAD 230   25
   HANGING ITS HANGING GARDEN IN THE AIR, ...FEVER. 231   21
   HAULS ME THROUGH AIR --- ....ARIEL 239   16
   OF AIR THAT ALL DAY FLIES ....PURDAH   243   45
   AND I EAT MEN LIKE AIR. ....LADY LAZARUS   247   84
   TURNING AND TURNING IN THE MIDDLE AIR, ...GETTING THERE 249   53
   THERE IS A GREEN IN THE AIR, ...LETTER IN NOVEMBER 253   8
   THE AIR IS A MILL OF HOOKS -- ....MYSTIC 268   1
   IN THE FETID WOMBS OF BLACK AIR UNDER PINES IN SUMMER. ......MYSTIC 268   5
   INVISIBLE AIR DRIFTS, ...BALLOONS 271   6
   GLOBES OF THIN AIR, RED, GREEN, ...BALLOONS 271   14
   AS IF THE AIR WERE LABORING TO PRODUCE   DIALOGUE OVER A OUIJA BOARD 279   89
   A SOLID SHAPE ON AIR. MAY THE DECORUM ..DIALOGUE OVER A OUIJA BOARD 286 360
   THE ASTEROIDS TURN TRAITOR IN THE AIR,   TO EVA DESCENDING THE STAIR 303   4
   THE MUTE AIR MERELY THINS AND THINS. .....METAMORPHOSES OF THE MOON 307   6
   HE CATAPULTS IN AIR; ....TRIO OF LOVE SONGS 314   30
   AIR ALTERS INTO GLASS AND THE WHOLE SKY ....PROLOGUE TO SPRING 322   4
   UPON THE POURING AIR UNTIL ....SONG FOR A REVOLUTIONARY LOVE 323   18
   ACROSS THAT SULTRY AIR, ...AERIALIST   331   14
   AND HONOR THE GREAT GODDESS OF THE AIR *THE PRINCESS AND THE GOBLINS 335   62
   IN THE AIR ABOVE MY ISLAND FLIES ....EPITAPH IN THREE PARTS   337   12
AIRBUBBLES (1)
   NO AIRBUBBLES START FROM MY HEART, I AM LUNGLESS   ZOO KEEPER'S WIFE 154   5
AIRING (1)
   I THINK OF THE LIZARDS AIRING THEIR TONGUES ....SLEEP. 144   14

```
                                            TITLE              PAGE  LINE
AIR-MOTES (1)
    TO CALL MY OWN EXCEPT THE AIR-MOTES, ....................LANDOWNERS   53    2
AIRPORT (1)
    FROM LOGAN AIRPORT OPPOSITE. ..............GREEN ROCK, WINTHROP BAY  105   16
AIRS (2)
    TILL, SICK OF THEIR RULER'S GODLING AIRS, ..........NATURAL HISTORY   71    7
    BLACK BAT AIRS ............................NICK AND THE CANDLESTICK  240    6
AIR'S (2)
    OF THE AIR EDDIES' LOOP AND ARC THOUGH AIR'S AT REST ........OXBOW.   88   32
    AND WHILE THE AIR'S CLEAR ..................DARK WOOD, DARK WATER   127   18
AIRY (2)
    HIGH ON THE AIRY THATCHING ...........MUSSEL HUNTER AT ROCK HARBOR   97   67
    BREATHING WAS EASY IN HIS AIRY HOLDING. ..............POEM.4.BEAST.  134    3
AISLES (1)
    TO PEOPLE THE TWIGGED AISLES; LEAD BABEL TONGUES*WREATH FOR A BRIDAL  45   14
AJAR (1)
    THE FRENCH WINDOW AJAR ................................THE SLEEPERS  122    6
ALACRITY (1)
    WITH BLACK ALACRITY BOUND ROUND HIS PRISONER. ...............SPIDER   49   28
ALARMCLOCK (1)
    AS THE LOUD ALARMCLOCK STOPS. ..........................AERIALIST   332   42
ALAS (1)
    "HOW SAD, ALAS, IT IS ......................THE QUEEN'S COMPLAINT    29   24
ALBATROSS (1)
    BEARDED AND BLOWN, AN ALBATROSS OF FROST, ............A WINTER SHIP  113   26
ALCHEMY (1)
    LET THEM START THE QUEER ALCHEMY .....................EAVESDROPPER   260   21
ALGEBRA (1)
    THE ALGEBRA OF ABSOLUTES .......................LOVE IS A PARALLAX  330   51
ALIAS (1)
    BY CLAW-CUTS OF THE GOATSUCKER, ALIAS DEVIL-BIRD, .......GOATSUCKER  111    7
ALICANTE (2)
    ALICANTE LULLABY ..............................ALICANTE LULLABY     43    T
    IN ALICANTE THEY BOWL THE BARRELS .................ALICANTE LULLABY   43    1
ALICE (1)
    SEND MY MUSE ALICE PACKING WITH GAUDY SCRAPS .........A SORCERER B.  324    7
ALIEN (2)
    ABSOLUTELY ALIEN ......................MUSSEL HUNTER AT ROCK HARBOR   96   54
    I FEEL IT ENTER ME, COLD, ALIEN, LIKE AN INSTRUMENT. ...THREE WOMEN  182  183
ALIGHTING (1)
    CHEEKS ALIGHTING EACH MOMENT TO MELT ...................LOVE LETTER  147   14
ALIVE (4)
    AS THOUGH ALIVE, SHRIVELING IN TORMENT THUS ............DIALOGUE B.   39   35
    IT WOULD BE BETTER IF THEY WERE ALIVE, AND THAT'S WHAT THEY WERE. ...
                                                     ... STILLBORN      142   13
    IF I'M ALIVE NOW, THEN I WAS DEAD, ....................LOVE LETTER   147    2
    AFTER ALL I AM ALIVE ONLY BY ACCIDENT. ..........A BIRTHDAY PRESENT  206   14
ALL (195)
    OF ALL DECORUM WHICH HOLDS THE WHIRLWIND BACK. .......CONVERSATION.   21    4
    LAST SUMMER'S REEDS ARE ALL ENGRAVED IN ICE ......WINTER LANDSCAPE,   22   11
    ALL AFTERNOON THESE LOVERS LAY ..............................BUCOLICS  24   13
    GILDS ALL OUR AVENUE, ...........................SOUTHERN SUNRISE    26   15
    LAYS ALL WALLS WASTE; PRIVATE ESTATES ARE TORN, ...CHANNEL CROSSING   27   31
    BRAVE ACTS PLAYED OUT IN PEACE, IN WAR; ALL DANGERS*CHANNEL CROSSING   27   39
    WHY, ALL THE WINDOWS BROKE WHEN HE STALKED IN.*THE QUEEN'S COMPLAINT   28    5
    TO SUMMON IN HER SLIGHT ALL DOUGHTY MEN ......THE QUEEN'S COMPLAINT   29   17
    WHEN ALL EARTH HIS WORDS DO SUMMON .......................ODE FOR TED   30   23
    WHICH HAULS DOWN BUCK, COCK, TROUT, TILL ALL MOST FAIR ....FIRESONG   30    6
    SO SHE WILLS ALL TO THE BLACK KING. .....................VANITY FAIR   33   29
    AND ALL GREEN DREAMS NOT WORTH MUCH, ................STRUMPET SONG    33    2
    UNTIL ALL OWLS IN THE TWIGGED FOREST .........................FAUN    35    3
    TO WARD OFF, AT ALL COST, SUSPICIONS ..................STREET SONG    36   16
    THESE DREAMING HOUSES ALL SNUFF OUT; ...SOLILOQUY OF THE SOLIPSIST   37    6
    ALL YOUR BEAUTY, ALL YOUR WIT, IS A GIFT, MY DEAR, ...
                           ... SOLILOQUY OF THE SOLIPSIST               38   35
    ALL YOUR BEAUTY, ALL YOUR WIT, IS A GIFT, MY DEAR, ...
                           ... SOLILOQUY OF THE SOLIPSIST               38   35
    THAT ALL MERIT'S IN BEING MEAT .........................THE GLUTTON   40    5
    AND ALL ELSE I'VE TAUGHT .............................RECANTATION    42   12
    CROWNS, PALACE, ALL ......................................THE SHRIKE   42   19
    NO CHANGE MET HER: GARDEN TERRACE, ALL SUMMER ........DREAM WITH C.   44    9
    WHOSE STARK ACT ALL COMING DOUBLE LUCK JOINS. ..WREATH FOR A BRIDAL   44    6
    CALL HERE WITH FLYING COLORS ALL WATCHFUL BIRDS *WREATH FOR A BRIDAL   45   13
    FROM THIS HOLY DAY ON, ALL POLLEN BLOWN ........WREATH FOR A BRIDAL   45   19
    ON ALL BUT CATS. ..................ELLA MASON AND HER ELEVEN CATS    54   18
    AND, SPRINGING ALL ABOUT, ..........................CRYSTAL GAZER    55   15
    FOCUSING ALL TIME'S DAY-SUNS IN ONE ...................CRYSTAL GAZER   55   39
    BULKS REAL, ALL SAINTS' TONGUES FALL QUIET: .....NOVEMBER GRAVEYARD   56   11
    ALL THE NIGHT GAVE HER, IN RETURN .................HARDCASTLE CRAGS   63   26
    NEIGHBORHOOD COCKCROW -- ALL NATURE'S PRODIGAL BACKTALK, CONJURING.   66    4
    HAD ALL MY LOVE. ......................ON THE PLETHORA OF DRYADS     67    6
    ALL SUMMER WE MOVED IN A VILLA BRIMFUL OF ECHOES, ....THE OTHER TWO   68    1
    FREE FROM ALL MOLESTING. ROUGH BOYS, ....................LADY AND T.   69    9
    ALL THE DEAD DEARS ...............................ALL THE DEAD DEARS   70    T
    ALL THE LONG GONE DARLINGS: THEY .................ALL THE DEAD DEARS   71   25
```

ALL (CONT.)
ONE WHITE HORSE DROWNED, AND ALL THE UNCONQUERED PINNACLES   LESSON.   80   9
ALL AMOROUS ARROWS. FOR TO SHEATHE THE VIRGIN SHAPE*VIRGIN IN A TREE   81   7
BEEN STRUCK TO KEEP ALL GLORY IN THE GRIP ....VIRGIN IA A TREE   82   32
UNTONGUED, ALL BEAUTY'S BRIGHT JUICE SOURS.   ....VIRGIN IN A TREE   82   43
BUT ALL THE ACCUMULATED LAST GRUNTS, GROANS, ...PERSEUS   83   17
ALL CREATION, WERE IT NOT FOR A BIGGER BELLY ....PERSEUS   83   33
AND SO ALL CHILDREN SING ....BATTLE-SCENE   85   32
IN THE MIDST OF ALL THAT GREEN AND THOSE GREAT LILIES! ...YADWIGHA.   86   39
AND ALL YOU SANTA'S DEER WHO BROWSE ....A WINTER'S TALE   87   21
OF THE DESULTORY CURRENTS -- ALL THAT UNIQUE ....ABOVE THE OXBOW   89   45
OF, NOT FATHOMED. ALL OBSCURITY ....FULL FATHOM FIVE   92   14
ALL STILLNESS. YET THESE SHAPES FLOAT ....LORELEI   94   9
SHUT AGAINST ME. ALL HELD STILL. ......MUSSEL HUNTER AT ROCK HARBOR   95   20
AND FROM THE TRENCH-DUG MUD, ALL .....MUSSEL HUNTER AT ROCK HARBOR   96   30
STOOD SHUT OUT, FOR ONCE, FOR ALL, ...MUSSEL HUNTER AT ROCK HARBOR   96   52
THROWN: FEAR, WISDOM, AT ONE: ALL COLORS ......WHITENESS I REMEMBER   103   32
ONE COURTING DOCTORS OF ALL SORTS, ...THE DEATH OF MYTH-MAKING   104   4
STEADILY ROOTED THOUGH THEY WERE ALL FLOWING ....THE EYE-MOTE   109   7
OLD GOATHERDS SWEAR HOW ALL NIGHT LONG THEY HEAR ....GOATSUCKER   111   1
IN THE DISTANCE. ALL AROUND US THE WATER SLIPS ....A WINTER SHIP   113   18
PAST KEEPING TO THE HOUSE, PAST ALL DISCRETION --   THE RAVAGED FACE   115   7
I FOUND YOUR NAME, I FOUND YOUR BONES AND ALL*ELECTRA ON AZALEA PATH   117   16
ALL OF IT, TOGETHER. ....MAN IN BLACK   120   21
ARCHES ABOVE US. O FATHER, ALL BY YOURSELF ....THE COLOSSUS   129   17
ALL MORNING, WITH SMOKING BREATH, THE HANDYMAN ......PRIVATE GROUND   130   7
I NEED HARDLY GO OUT AT ALL. ....PRIVATE GROUND   130   14
THEY GLITTER LIKE EYES, AND I COLLECT THEM ALL. .....PRIVATE GROUND   131   22
EATEN OR ROTTEN. I AM ALL MOUTH. POEM.1.WHO.   131   2
FOR WEEKS I CAN REMEMBER NOTHING AT ALL. POEM.1.WHO.   132   33
I MUST SWALLOW IT ALL. POEM.3.MAENAD.   133   21
THE LIQUOR OF INDOLENCE, AND ALL THINGS SINK POEM.5.F.   134   8
I AM LOST, I AM LOST, IN THE ROBES OF ALL THIS LIGHT. POEM.6.W.   136   24
OF JULY TO ALL FOOLS' DAY, ...YOU'RE   141   8
A CREEL OF EELS, ALL RIPPLES. ....YOU'RE   141   15
THE REAL THING, ALL RIGHT: THE GOOD, THE TRUE -- ....MAGI   148   6
TO ROCK ON ALL FOURS LIKE A PADDED HAMMOCK. ....MAGI   148   11
AND THE OWNER PAST THIRTY, NO BEAUTY AT ALL. ....CANDLES   148   9
HOW SHALL I TELL ANYTHING AT ALL ....CANDLES   149   32
ALL NIGHT I HAVE DREAMED OF DESTRUCTION, ANNIHILATIONS -- ..WAKING.   151   4
I SUPPOSE IT'S POINTLESS TO THINK OF YOU AT ALL. .....PARLIAMENT H.   152   24
I CAN SMELL THE SALT, ALL RIGHT. ....WHITSUN   154   13
I CAN STAY AWAKE ALL NIGHT, IF NEED BE -- ....ZOO KEEPER'S WIFE   154   1
MUMMY-CLOTHS, SMILING: I'M ALL RIGHT. ....FACE LIFT   155   3
THEY'VE CHANGED ALL THAT. TRAVELING ....FACE LIFT   156   9
ALL NIGHT YOUR MOTH-BREATH ....MORNING SONG   157   10
AFTER ALL, IT WAS A KIND OF MARRIAGE, BEING SO CLOSE. ...IN PLASTER   160   51
A BONEWHITE LIGHT, LIKE DEATH, BEHIND ALL THINGS. ....INSOMNIAC   163   4
STRETCHING ITS FINE, IRRITATING SAND IN ALL DIRECTIONS. ..INSOMNIAC   163   7
THAT OPENS AT THE TOP ONTO NOTHING AT ALL. . . ..WIDOW   164   10
BLINDED TO ALL BUT THE GRAY, SPIRITLESS ROOM ....WIDOW   165   39
THE SMALLER AND MORE TIMID NEVER ARRIVE AT ALL ....STARS.   165   12
ALL WIG CURLS AND YELLOW TEETH ....WUTHERING HEIGHTS   167   26
AMONG ALL HORIZONTALS. ....WUTHERING HEIGHTS   168   38
I DO NOT THINK THE SEA WILL APPEAR AT ALL. ...........BLACKBERRYING   168   13
A FEW MORE BREATHS, AND IT WILL REFLECT NOTHING AT ALL.   LAST WORDS   172   12
INSIDE THE CHURCH, THE SAINTS WILL BE ALL BLUE, ...MOON.   173   24
THE BOLD GULLS DOVE AS IF THEY OWNED IT ALL. ....THE BABYSITTERS   175   37
AND ALL I COULD SEE WAS DANGERS: DOVES AND WORDS, ...THREE WOMEN   178   47
SHE IS THE VAMPIRE OF US ALL. SO SHE SUPPORTS US, ...THREE WOMEN   18   155
THE BLUE COLOR PALES. HE IS HUMAN AFTER ALL. ....THREE WOMEN   181 166
LOOK, THEY ARE SO EXHAUSTED, THEY ARE ALL FLAT OUT .....THREE WOMEN   18: 219
THEY HAVE LIVED BEHIND GLASS ALL THEIR LIVES, THEY HAVE BEEN
     CARED FOR TENDERLY. ....THREE WOMEN 184 264
WHITE AS AN EYE ALL OVER! ....LITTLE FUGUE   187   7
OR JUST TO BE VISITED AT ALL. ....PHEASANT   191   6
ALL NIGHT I SHALL GALLOP THUS, IMPETUOUSLY, ...ELM   192   10
ALL DAY I FEEL ITS SOFT, FEATHERY TURNINGS, ITS MALIGNITY. .....ELM   193   33
AFTER ALL I AM ALIVE ONLY BY ACCIDENT. ....A BIRTHDAY PRESENT   206   14
THERE IS NO BODY IN THE HOUSE AT ALL. ....THE DETECTIVE   209   16
THE BODY DOES NOT COME INTO IT AT ALL. ....THE DETECTIVE   209   25
AND THEY ARE ALL GLOVED AND COVERED, WHY DID NOBODY TELL ME? ..BEE.   211   4
IT IS THE NOISE THAT APPALLS ME MOST OF ALL, ...THE ARRIVAL.   213   17
IS THERE ANY QUEEN AT ALL IN IT? ....STINGS   214   15
A FLYING HEDGEHOG, ALL PRICKLES. ....THE SWARM   216   32
THEY ARE NOT HANDS AT ALL ....THE SWARM   217   53
MIND AGAINST ALL THAT WHITE. ....WINTERING   218   33
THE BEES ARE ALL WOMEN, ...WINTERING   218   38
I DIDN'T CALL YOU AT ALL. ....MEDUSA   225   22
IS THAT ALL HE CAN COME UP WITH, ...THE JAILER   226   4
ALL DAY, GLUING MY CHURCH OF BURNT MATCHSTICKS, ...THE JAILER   227   26
IT IS ALL HOLLYWOOD, WINDOWLESS, ...LESBOS   227   3
DARLING, ALL NIGHT ....FEVER.   231   28
ALL BY MYSELF I AM A HUGE CAMELLIA ....FEVER.   232   41

ALL (CONT.)
     DOWN THE DRAIN WITH ALL OF IT! ....AMNESIAC   233   11
     AND MONEY THE SPERM FLUID OF IT ALL. ....AMNESIAC   233   20
     AT FIRST THE CANDLE WILL NOT BLOOM AT ALL -- ....BY CANDLELIGHT   236   16
     POOR HEIRLOOM, ALL YOU HAVE, ...BY CANDLELIGHT   237   32
     ALL COGS, WEIRD SPARKLE AND EVERY COG SOLID GOLD. ....THE TOUR   237   5
     OF AIR THAT ALL DAY FLIES ....PURDAH   243   45
     TO LAST IT OUT AND NOT COME BACK AT ALL. ....LADY LAZARUS   245   38
     ALL TO ITSELF ON THE TOP OF EACH ....THE COURIERS   247   9
     ALL THE GODS KNOW IS DESTINATIONS. ....GETTING THERE   248   17
     ALL COOL, ALL BLUE. UNLIKE YOU --- ....GULLIVER   251   9
     ALL COOL, ALL BLUE. UNLIKE YOU --- ....GULLIVER   251   9
     ALL NIGHT I CARPENTER ....THALIDOMIDE   252   17
     STARS STUCK ALL OVER, BRIGHT STUPID CONFETTI. ....YEARS   255   8
     ALL MORNING THE ....SHEEP IN FOG 262   8
     TALKERS: "YOU ALL RIGHT?" ....PARALYTIC   266   15
     I SMILE, A BUDDHA, ALL ....PARALYTIC   267   33
     ALL THE FALL OF WATER AN EYE ....GIGOLO   268   30
     THE REST OF THE BODY IS ALL WASHED OUT, ...CONTUSION   271   2
     IN ALL. PLUS YES. PLUS NO. AND THIS BARE BOARD. ....DIALOGUE O.   276   14
     TO KNOW AT ALL. AND YET I GO AHEAD. ....DIALOGUE OVER A OUIJA BOARD   278   69
     CASTLES UPON THE SMUG-SHAPED CHAIRS. ALL THIS I ....DIALOGUE O.   279 118
     LIKE ALL THE OTHERS AND SWEAR THAT HE'S A PUMA ....DIALOGUE O.   281 176
     ALL, IF YOU'LL HIDE HOPES OF HEAVEN IN A HAT ....DIALOGUE O.   282 231
     YOUR HEAD AFTER ALL. IT SEEMS HIS LAUGH *DIALOGUE OVER A OUIJA BOARD   282 238
     WORK AT ALL? HOW CAN WE HELP BUT BATTLE *DIALOGUE OVER A OUIJA BOARD   284 286
     SOME LIGHT. I GLIMPSE NO LIGHT AT ALL AS LONG ....DIALOGUE O.   284 290
     BEING NOT YOU, NOR I, NOR US AT ALL, ...DIALOGUE OVER A OUIJA BOARD   285 308
     ALL NIGHT LONG, EVEN SHOULD OUR EYES SHUT ....DIALOGUE O.   286 354
     RULE THEIR BEDS LIKE BEHEADED AND RESURRECTED AND ALL SILENT
          ROYALTY, ...QUEEN MARY'S ROSE GARDEN   290   5
     WHAT GOOD IS ALL THAT SPACE IF IT CAN'T DRAW YOU OFF? THE RIVAL/DR   291   13
     INTO A DARK WORLD I CANNOT SEE AT ALL. ....ELM/DR 292   10
     ALL NIGHT I HAVE HEARD ....FEVER./DR   294   1
     ALL THAT MORNING IN THE STRAWBERRY FIELD ....BITTER STRAWBERRIES   299   1
     AND WE ALL TURNED BACK TO PICKING. ....BITTER STRAWBERRIES   300   33
     ACROSS THEM ALL ....FAMILY REUNION 300   21
     ALL DAY SHE PLAYS AT CHESS WITH THE BONES OF THE WORLD: ..FEMALE A.   301   1
     THE SLIME OF ALL MY YESTERDAYS ....APRIL 18   301   1
     AND GILDED COUPLES ALL IN WHIRLING TRANCE ....CINDERELLA 304   9
     UNTIL NEAR TWELVE THE STRANGE GIRL ALL AT ONCE ....CINDERELLA 304   11
     ALL RIGHT, LET'S SAY YOU COULD TAKE A SKULL AND BREAK IT*SONNET:EVA.   304   1
     WITH THE PILOT WHO DARES ALL HEAVEN'S HARMS .........METAMORPHOSES.   307   2
     "O MAY G-MEN ALL DIE OF THE CHOLER, ...DIALOGUE EN ROUTE   308   15
     IN THE MORNING ALL SHALL BE ....TO A JILTED LOVER   310   19
     WHEN I ROSE AND OPENED ALL ....THE DREAM 310   4
     WOULD AVOID ALL PENALTY. ....THE DREAM 311   23
     RAISED TO TOAST A THOUSAND KINGS, FOR ALL GIVES ....SONNET: TO TIME   311   11
     DIRECTS ALL ZODIAC. ....TRIO OF LOVE SONGS 313   4
     YET ALL ANGELIC REASON ....TRIO OF LOVE SONGS 314   15
     WHILE ALL THE ACTORS HALT IN MORTAL SHOCK: ....DOOMSDAY   316   5
     GOD'S MONKEY WRENCH HAS BLASTED ALL MACHINES; ....DOOMSDAY   316   13
     ALL MOONSTRUCK MAGIC ....MOONSONG AT MORNING 317   19
     ALL WE FIND ARE ALTARS IN DECAY ....DOOM OF EXILES   318   11
     WE'VE SQUANDERED ALL THE BANKER WILL ALLOW ....THE DISPOSSESSED   319   16
     THE MAGIC GOLDEN APPLES ALL LOOK GOOD ....ADMONITIONS   319   4
     AND LUCKY STARS ALL EXIT ON THE RUN: ....ADMONITIONS   319   17
     THE OLD MAID IN THE GABLE CRIES ALL DAY: ....NEVER TRY TO TRICK.   320   11
     WHILE THE ANGELS ALL APPLAUD. ....CIRCUS IN THREE RINGS   321   6
     AND SUSPENDED ALL THAT MIGHT OCCUR? ....PROLOGUE TO SPRING   322   12
     GREEN-SINGING BIRDS EXPLODE FROM ALL THE ROCKS. PROLOGUE TO SPRING   322   15
     O THROW IT AWAY, THROW IT ALL AWAY ON THE WIND: SONG FOR A REVOLU.   322   1
     AND AGAIN TOGETHER BEGIN IT ALL. .....SONG FOR A REVOLUTIONARY LOVE   323   24
     YOU OVERCAST ALL ORDER'S NOONDAY RANK ....SONNET TO SATAN   323   7
     ALL WHO LOOK: ....ON LOOKING INTO THE EYES OF A DEMON LOVER   325   4
     ALL ABSOLUTES THAT ANGELS GIVE   INSOLENT STORM STRIKES AT THE SKULL   326   23
     THE COLORED TENTS ALL TOPPLE IN THE BAY; ....DENOUEMENT   327   16
     OUTLAWS ALL EXTRAPOLATION ....TWO LOVERS. 327   10
     A GRAIN OF SAND IS ALL WE HAVE. ....TWO LOVERS.   327   20
     BUT MORE PRAGMATIC THAN ALL OF THIS, ...BLACK PINE TREE.   328   16
     NOTHING CHANGES, FOR ALL THE BLAZING OF ....LOVE IS A PARALLAX   329   16
     GRAVES ALL CAROL IN REPLY. ....LOVE IS A PARALLAX   330   42
     AS GREAT WEIGHTS DROP ALL ABOUT HER ....AERIALIST   331   17
     WITH A THUNDER LIKE LIONS; ALL AIMS ....AERIALIST   331   32
     WHICH ALL THE ARTFUL WIZARDS CANNOT CRIMP ....THE PRINCESS.   333   17
     HOW ALL THEIR PLAY IS TOUCH-AND-GO: ....TOUCH-AND-GO   335   12
     AND ALL THE GOLD APPLES ....TEMPER OF TIME   336   3
     WHERE THE WATER BLOTS OUT ALL FOOTSTEPS." ...EPITAPH IN THREE PARTS   337   6
     THE THIRD CRIES OUT AS ALL THE SHIPS GO DOWN:*EPITAPH IN THREE PARTS   337   10
     AND HIDDEN ALL THE BRIGHT ANGELIC MEN. ......EPITAPH IN THREE PARTS   338   31
ALLAY (1)
     WHICH ALLAY THE MALICE ....MISS DRAKE PROCEEDS TO SUPPER   41   3
ALLEY (2)
     EACH GESTURE FLEES IMMEDIATELY DOWN AN ALLEY ....INSOMNIAC   163   23
     A BLACKBERRY ALLEY, GOING DOWN IN HOOKS, AND A SEA ...BLACKBERRYING   168   3

		TITLE	PAGE	LINE

ALLEYS (1)
      GREEN ALLEYS WHERE WE REVELED HAVE BECOME ....DOOM OF EXILES   318   5
ALL-MOUTH (1)
      ALL-MOUTH LICKS UP THE BUSHES POEM.2.DARK.   132   17
ALLOW (1)
      WE'VE SQUANDERED ALL THE BANKER WILL ALLOW ....THE DISPOSSESSED 319   16
ALL'S (3)
      FROM HIS CRABBED MIDDEN WHERE ALL'S WROUGHT SO AWRY ....FIRESONG   30   10
      ALL'S PEACE AND DISCIPLINE DOWN THERE. TILL LATELY WE ....OXBOW.   89   53
      ALL'S POLISHED TO A DULL LUSTER ....IN MIDAS' COUNTRY   99   5
ALMANAC (1)
      AND THE SNAKE-FIGURED ALMANAC ....MONOLOGUE AT 3 A.M.   40   5
ALMOND (2)
      WHITE HOUSE AND ALMOND GROVE. THE BEGGARS ....THE BEGGARS   48   18
      HALFWAY DOWN FROM GROVES WHERE THE THIN, BITTER ALMOND PIPS ..NET-.   121   2
ALMOST (11)
      LOUD ON EARTH'S BEDROCK, ALMOST THROWN, NOT ...WHITENESS I REMEMBER   103   31
      A WELL OF SCENTS ALMOST TOO DENSE TO BREATHE IN. ......BEEKEEPER'S.   118   4
      GROWN MILKY, ALMOST CLEAR, LIKE THE BODIES OF SAINTS. ......CANDLES   148   4
      YOU COULD TELL ALMOST AT ONCE SHE HAD A SLAVE MENTALITY. *IN PLASTER   159   21
      ALMOST TOO SMALL FOR THE MISTS TO BOTHER WITH. ....FINISTERRE   169   12
      WARMED BY MUCH HANDLING. THEY ALMOST PURR. ....LAST WORDS   172   18
      AND THE SNARES ALMOST EFFACED THEMSELVES -- .....THE RABBIT CATCHER   194   14
      SQUARE AS A CHAIR AND ALMOST TOO HEAVY TO LIFT. ....THE ARRIVAL.   212   2
      IT IS ALMOST OVER. ....STINGS   214   31
      TO ALMOST NOTHING, TO A DULL BLUE DUD. ....BY CANDLELIGHT   236   18
      TUGGING US THROUGH PLUMAGE. I ALMOST FEEL ....DIALOGUE O.   279   86
ALOFT (4)
      MOST FAR IN BLUE, ALOFT, ...SONG FOR A SUMMER'S DAY   31   7
      HAND ALOFT, GOODBYE, GOODBYE, NOT DOWN .....THE GHOST'S LEAVETAKING   90   23
      SUSPENDED ALOFT WITHIN HER PLANET-SHINE. ....THE PRINCESS.   335   63
      ALOFT, A LONE GULL HALTS UPON THE WIND, ...EPITAPH IN THREE PARTS   337   20
ALONE (10)
      ALONE CAN HEAR ....STREET SONG   36   25
      I WALK ALONE; ....SOLILOQUY OF THE SOLIPSIST   37   2
      BY WITS ALONE: TO FORESEE HER LOVER'S FAITH ....CRYSTAL GAZER   55   33
      "WITH MY FANTASY ALONE," BRAGS THE IMPORTUNATE HEAD, ...CONJURING.   66   9
      HEAD ALONE SHOWS YOU IN THE PRODIGIOUS ACT ....PERSEUS   82   1
      OF DIGESTING WHAT CENTURIES ALONE DIGEST: ....PERSEUS   82   2
      DOWN THERE ONE IS ALONE. ....BLUE MOLES   126   27
      IF ONLY THE WIND WOULD LEAVE MY LUNGS ALONE. POEM.1.WHO.   131   10
      LEAVE HER ALONE NOW. ....A LIFE   150   30
      ALONE TO THAT AUTHENTIC ISLAND WHERE ....A SORCERER B.   324   13
ALONG (5)
      ALONG RED NETWORK OF HIS VEINS ....PURSUIT   22   11
      LURCHING HOME ALONG RIVER BANK. ....FAUN   35   7
      ALONG BOX-LINED WALKS IN THE FLORID SUN ....THE BULL OF BENDYLAW   108   10
      ALONG THE VEIN, ...MOONSONG AT MORNING   316   4
      ALONG BRIGHT ASTERISKS BY MILKY WAY. ..THE PRINCESS AND THE GOBLINS   333   12
ALONGSIDE (1)
      ALONGSIDE THE SIBILANT HARBOR THE LOVERS ....ALICANTE LULLABY   43   11
ALOOF (2)
      ALOOF, SQUATTING MUMMY-WISE, GERD SCANS ....CRYSTAL GAZER   55   28
      IT HOLDS ALOOF, A SHROUDED PARACHUTE .....METAMORPHOSES OF THE MOON   307   8
ALOUD (2)
      ALOUD, CROSSLEGGED ON THE STERN SEAT, FROM THE GENERATION OF VIPERS.   ...
                                      ... THE BABYSITTERS   175   32
      LAUGHING ALOUD, THE DAZZLED BOY DEMANDS*THE PRINCESS AND THE GOBLINS   335   64
ALPENSTOCK (1)
      OLD JOSEPH HOLDS AN ALPENSTOCK. ....A WINTER'S TALE   86   5
ALPHABET (1)
      WITH ABRACADABRA FROM THE ALPHABET. ...THE PRINCESS AND THE GOBLINS   335   59
ALPHABETICAL (1)
      FROM MY ALPHABETICAL FINGERS, ORDERING PARTS, ...THREE WOMEN   177   28
ALPHABETS (1)
      AND PRISTINE ALPHABETS AND COWS THAT MOO ...THE GHOST'S LEAVETAKING   91   36
ALPS (1)
      OF NINE BLACK ALPS. ....THE COURIERS   247   10
ALREADY (10)
      ALREADY VEILING THE GRAY SPOOL OF STONE ....SPIDER   48   18
      ALREADY THE FARMER'S AFTER HIS CROP, ...IN MIDAS' COUNTRY   100   23
      ALREADY HALF UNSTRUNG. A VINEGARY FUME   TWO VIEWS OF A CADAVER ROOM   114   3
      ALREADY YELLOW THE HEAVENS. ....THE MANOR GARDEN   125   15
      BARE NO SINISTER SPACES. ALREADY ....BLUE MOLES   126   13
      ALREADY FROG-MOUTH AND FISH-MOUTH DRINK POEM.5.F.   134   7
      ALREADY YOUR DOLL GRIP LETS GO. ....PARLIAMENT HILL FIELDS   152   25
      ALREADY HE CAN FEEL DAYLIGHT, HIS WHITE DISEASE, ...INSOMNIAC   163   31
      I SEE THEM ALREADY -- THE PALE, STAR-DISTANCE FACES. ....LAST WORDS   172   6
      WHAT HOLES THIS PAPERY DAY IS ALREADY FULL OF! ....THE JAILER   226   17
ALSO (10)
      GREEN, ALSO, THE GRAPES ON THE GREEN VINE ....DEPARTURE   51   2
      HE ALSO AGAINST BLACK FROST ....THE EVERLASTING MONDAY   62   7
      ALSO OF HIGH WINDOWS. WORSE ....LORELEI   94   28
      SUPERIOR PAGE; THE BLUNT STONE ALSO. ....POEMS, POTATOES   106   13
      THE WALLS, ALSO, SEEM TO BE WARMING THEMSELVES. ....TULIPS   162   57

15

                                                        TITLE   PAGE LINE
ALSO (CONT.)
    THE MOON, ALSO, IS MERCILESS: SHE WOULD DRAG ME ....ELM   192   22
    THE CONSTRICTION KILLING ME ALSO. ....THE RABBIT CATCHER   194   30
    MY LIMBS, ALSO, HAVE LEFT ME. ....EVENT   195   20
    ANGELS SWIM IN IT, AND THE STARS, IN INDIFFERENCE ALSO. ...
                                             ... APPREHENSIONS   195   3
    THE SEA, ALSO, IS INEFFECTUAL. ....THE RIVAL/DR   291   15
ALTAR (2)
    ON THAT GREEN ALTAR ....TWO SISTERS OF PERSEPHONE   32   20
    THEN BRISKLY SCALED HIS ALTAR TIERED WITH TETHERED ANTS, ...SPIDER   49   22
ALTARS (1)
    ALL WE FIND ARE ALTARS IN DECAY ....DOOM OF EXILES   318   11
ALTER (2)
    AFTERTHOUGHT OFTEN WOULD HAVE THEM ALTER ....POEMS, POTATOES   106   7
    TO ALTER HER WILL OUR WAY. SHALL WE GO ON ....DIALOGUE O.   277   49
ALTERED (1)
    YOU NEVER ALTERED YOUR AMUSED BELIEF ....DIRGE FOR A JOKER   302   7
ALTERING (3)
    AND RECOIL IN THE ALTERING LIGHT: THE RADIANT LIMB ..EPITAPH FOR F.   46   33
    VALLEYS OF GRASS ALTERING ....THE GREAT CARBUNCLE   72   4
    HORSES WARPED ON THE ALTERING GREEN, ...THE EYE-MOTE   109   12
ALTERNATELY (1)
    PARENTAL FACES ON TALL STALKS, ALTERNATELY STERN AND TEARFUL, ...
                                             ... INSOMNIAC   163   11
ALTERS (2)
    ALTERS SHADOWS OF ROSE AND IRIS -- ....CHILD'S PARK STONES   101   13
    AIR ALTERS INTO GLASS AND THE WHOLE SKY ....PROLOGUE TO SPRING   322   4
ALTHOUGH (6)
    ALTHOUGH, I ADMIT, I DESIRE, ...BLACK ROOK IN RAINY WEATHER   57   11
    ALTHOUGH EACH TEACHER FOUND MY TOUCH ....THE DISQUIETING MUSES   75   35
    GIVEN AN INCH. NOT THAT THEY'RE GROSS (ALTHOUGH ...POEMS, POTATOES   106   6
    ALTHOUGH THE RAINS DISSOLVE A BLOODY DYE: ...ELECTRA ON AZALEA PATH   117   27
    MY FINGERS WOULD ENTER ALTHOUGH ....BURNING THE LETTERS   204   17
    ALTHOUGH THE WICKED WITCH HAS POISONED ONE. ....ADMONITIONS   319   5
ALTITUDE (2)
    DROPS ME FROM A TERRIBLE ALTITUDE. ....THE JAILER   226   13
    GULPS AND RECOVERS ITS SMALL ALTITUDE, ...NICK AND THE CANDLESTICK   241   21
ALTOGETHER (1)
    "DO AWAY WITH IT ALTOGETHER." ....A SECRET   220   33
ALUMINUM (1)
    TUBULAR STEEL WHEELCHAIRS, ALUMINUM CRUTCHES. ....BERCK-PLAGE   197   39
ALWAYS (23)
    ADVANCING ALWAYS AT MY BACK; ....PURSUIT   22   6
    YET ALWAYS THE RIDICULOUS NUDE FLANKS URGE ....TALE OF A TUB   25   33
    BUT ALWAYS EXPOSE ....DEPARTURE   51   12
    THEY ARE ALWAYS WITH US, THE THIN PEOPLE ....THE THIN PEOPLE   64   1
    MOTHER, WHOSE WITCHES ALWAYS, ALWAYS ....THE DISQUIETING MUSES   75   11
    MOTHER, WHOSE WITCHES ALWAYS, ALWAYS ....THE DISQUIETING MUSES   75   11
    DOWN HERE THE SKY IS ALWAYS FALLING. POEM.4.BEAST.   134   20
    TILTED AND DISPARATE, AND ALWAYS UNSTABLE. ......WUTHERING HEIGHTS   167   2
    WE WERE ALWAYS CRYING, IN OUR SPARE ROOMS, LITTLE PUT-UPON SISTERS, ...
                                             ... THE BABYSITTERS   174   4
    I HAVE ALWAYS BEEN SCARED OF YOU, ...DADDY   223   41
    THEY ALWAYS KNEW IT WAS YOU. ....DADDY   224   79
    IN ANY CASE, YOU ARE ALWAYS THERE, ...MEDUSA   225   16
    THERE'S ALWAYS A BLOODY BABY IN THE AIR. ....STOPPED DEAD   230   13
    THE LYONIANS HAD ALWAYS THOUGHT ....LYONNESSE   234   11
    THAT'S HOW YOU ALWAYS TALK BEFORE WE START. ....DIALOGUE O.   277   15
    ALWAYS, THE GLASS WILL BLURT WHAT I DON'T WANT ....DIALGGUE O.   278   68
    YOU'RE ALWAYS TALKING THIS WAY . . ." ....BITTER STRAWBERRIES   300   26
    FAT ALWAYS, AND OUT OF BREATH, ...FAMILY REUNION   300   13
    ALWAYS IN THE MIDDLE OF A KISS ....DIRGE FOR A JOKER   302   1
    ALWAYS FROM THE PULPIT DURING SERVICE ....DIRGE FOR A JOKER   302   3
    ALWAYS THE SAME DISTANCE FROM ..........METAMORPHOSES OF THE MOON   307   9
    IS ALWAYS TO BE MADE: INNOCENCE ........METAMORPHOSES OF THE MOON   308   40
    TRAIN TRACKS ALWAYS MEET, NOT HERE, BUT ONLY ....LOVE IS A PARALLAX   329   2
AM (172)
A.M. (2)
    MONOLOGUE AT 3 A.M. ....MONOLOGUE AT 3 A.M.   40   T
    THE SURGEON AT 2 A.M. ....THE SURGEON AT 2 A.M.   170   T
AMAZINGLY (1)
    FROM HER AMAZINGLY WHITE TORSO, AND I COULDN'T HELP BUT NOTICE ...
                                             ... IN PLASTER   159   24
AMBER (3)
    ON THIS AMBER BANK WHERE GRASSES BLEACH. ....IN MIDAS' COUNTRY   100   22
    A SECRET...AN EXTRA AMBER ....A SECRET   219   17
    BE PLUCKED FROM CAVES OF DAPPLED AMBER WHERE ....MIDSUMMER MOBILE   324   9
AMBIGUOUS (3)
    WHICH SHROUDS OUR PROSPECTS IN AMBIGUOUS SHADOW? .....TALE OF A TUB   24   16
    WITH VOICES OF THAT AMBIGUOUS SEA ....ON THE DECLINE OF ORACLES   78   4
    TO MAKE ORANGE AND BLACK AMBIGUOUS. ....BLACK PINE TREE.   328   18
AMBIVALENCE (1)
    ON THE QUICKSANDS OF AMBIVALENCE ....LOVE IS A PARALLAX   329   11
AMBLE (1)
    AMBLE DARKLY OLIVE ....AQUATIC NOCTURNE   306   23

	TITLE	PAGE	LINE

AMBROSIAL (1)
   OF AMBROSIAL REVELATION. AND SO DEPARTS. ...THE GHOST'S LEAVETAKING   90   15
AMBULANCE (1)
   NOR THE WOMAN IN THE AMBULANCE ....POPPIES IN OCTOBER   240   2
AMBUSH (2)
   LURKS THE LITHE ONE; IN DREAMS' AMBUSH ....PURSUIT   23   30
   LAUGHED AT THE AMBUSH OF ANGELS' TONGUES, ...LAMENT   315   14
AMBUSHED (3)
   NOW THROUGH HER AMBUSHED AIR, ...MISS DRAKE PROCEEDS TO DINNER   41   18
   AMBUSHED BIRDS BY ....THE SNOWMAN ON THE MOOR   59   34
   OR HER OWN WORD, AMBUSHED IN AN EQUIVOCAL ....DIALOGUE O.   286   351
AMERICA (2)
   IMAGINING HIMSELF A HEADWAITER IN AMERICA, ...CANDLES   149   21
   ON INDIA, AFRICA, AMERICA, THESE MIRACULOUS ONES, ...THREE WOMEN   183   229
AMERICANA (1)
   AMERICANA. MAGI NEAR ....A WINTER'S TALE   86   3
AMETHYST (1)
   ROSE AND AMETHYST. ....BATTLE-SCENE   84   26
AMID (3)
   IN WAIT AMID SNARLED WEED AND WRACK OF WAVE DREAM WITH CLAM-DIGGERS   44   26
   AS AMID THE HECTIC MUSIC AND COCKTAIL TALK ....CINDERELLA   304   13
   AMID THE TICKING JEWELED CLOCKS THAT MARK ....SONNET: TO TIME   311   2
AMISS (1)
   SOONER OR LATER SOMETHING GOES AMISS; ....NEVER TRY TO TRICK.   320   16
AMNESIA (1)
   HIS HIGH COLD MASKS OF AMNESIA. ....THE JAILER   227   31
AMNESIAC (1)
   AMNESIAC ....AMNESIAC   232   T
AMNESIAS (1)
   THROUGH THE BLACK AMNESIAS OF HEAVEN. ....THE NIGHT DANCES   250   21
AMOEBAS (1)
   PLANETS PULSE IN THE LAKE LIKE BRIGHT AMOEBAS; ....TWO CAMP.   145   23
AMONG (60)
   CONVERSATION AMONG THE RUINS ..........................CONVERSATION.   21   T
   AMONG SACRED ISLANDS OF THE MAD TILL DEATH ....TALE OF A TUB   25   47
   SPRAWLS, HUNCHED IN BLACK, AMONG BAGGAGE, WINCING CHANNEL CROSSING   26   11
   AMONG ORANGE-TILE ROOFTOPS ....PROSPECT   28   1
   AMONG THE COMMON ROUT ....STREET SONG   35   2
   AMONG HER SECRET COMBINATIONS OF EGGSHELLS ....MISS DRAKE P.   41   7
   ESCAPED AMONG MOON-PLUMAGED STRANGERS; ....THE SHRIKE   42   14
   THE RITUAL DEATH EACH TIME BOTCHED AMONG DROPPED CAPES,
       ILL-JUDGED STABS, ...THE GORING   47   3
   A BEGGAR STOPS AMONG EGGS AND LOAVES, ...THE BEGGARS   48   10
   HIS TEETH ARE CHATTERING AMONG THE LEPROUS ..THE EVERLASTING MONDAY   62   5
   ARROGANT AMONG ROOK-TONGUED SPACES, ...CONJURING.   66   10
   FLOATING, AMONG THE FLOATING ....THE GREAT CARBUNCLE   73   21
   IN TARNISHED MODES, MAUNDERING AMONG THE WASTES, ...OUIJA   77   13
   YADWIGHA, ON A RED COUCH, AMONG LILIES ....YADWIGHA.   85   T
   TO ROOT DEEP AMONG KNUCKLES, SHINBONES, ...FULL FATHOM FIVE   93   35
   GRUB-WHITE MULBERRIES REDDEN AMONG LEAVES. ....MOONRISE   98   1
   AMONG THE SOCKETED WHITE STARS, YOUR FACE ....MOONRISE   98   26
   AMONG THE PITHLESS REEDS. FLIES FAIL US. ....FROG AUTUMN   99   7
   YOU MOVE AMONG THE MANY-BREASTED HIVES, ...THE BEEKEEPER'S DAUGHTER   118   6
   KEEP HOUSE AMONG THE GRASSES. KNEELING DOWN*THE BEEKEEPER'S DAUGHTER   118   16
   OF OUR HUSBANDS AND SONS MOVE SURE AMONG THE LOW STARS. ......NET-.   121   19
   UP HERE AMONG THE GULL CRIES ....MAGNOLIA SHOALS   121   1
   AMONG PETALS PALE AS DEATH ....THE SLEEPERS   123   13
   FIRST FROST, AND I WALK AMONG THE ROSE-FRUIT, THE MARBLE TOES ...
       ... PRIVATE GROUND   130   1
   OPENS AND SHUTS, ACCEPTING THEM AMONG ITS REFLECTIONS. ..PRIVATE G.   131   24
   I AM AT HOME HERE AMONG THE DEAD HEADS. POEM.1.WHO.   131   6
   A RED TONGUE IS AMONG US. POEM.3.MAENAD.   133   13
   AMONG EMMETS AND MOLLUSKS, ...POEM.4.BEAST.   134   24
   ARCHAEOLOGIST AMONG ....THE BURNT-OUT SPA   138   15
   MASKED AMONG BLACK ROCKS AS A BLACK ROCK ....LOVE LETTER   147   10
   AMONG BIRD FEET AND THE STEMS OF PLANTS. ....LOVE LETTER   147   27
   AMONG ICE BUCKETS, FROSTY NAPKINS. ....CANDLES   149   23
   TOOK ITS PLACE AMONG THE ELEMENTS. ....MORNING SONG   156   3
   FLICKERS AMONG THE FLAT PINK ROSES. I WAKE TO LISTEN: MORNING SONG   157   11
   THEY STEP AMONG THE ARCHETYPES. ....HEAVY WOMEN   158   17
   I WALK AMONG THEM, BUT NONE OF THEM ARE NOTICING. ....I AM VERTICAL   162   13
   TO WHITEN MY BONES AMONG THEM. ....WUTHERING HEIGHTS   167   18
   AMONG ALL HORIZONTALS. ....WUTHERING HEIGHTS   168   38
   I WALK AMONG THEM, AND THEY STUFF MY MOUTH WITH COTTON. FINISTERRE   169   17
   I WALK AMONG SLEEPERS IN GAUZE SARCOPHAGI. ...THE SURGEON AT 2 A.M.   171   47
   PICKING AMONG THE DUMB MINERALS, THE ROOTS. ....LAST WORDS   172   5
   I AM A MOUNTAIN NOW, AMONG MOUNTAINY WOMEN. ....THREE WOMEN   179   113
   THE DOCTORS MOVE AMONG US AS IF OUR BIGNESS ....THREE WOMEN   179   114
   STARS OPEN AMONG THE LILIES. ....CROSSING THE WATER   190   10
   AMONG THE NARCISSI ....AMONG THE NARCISSI   190   T
   PERCY BOWS, IN HIS BLUE PEAJACKET, AMONG THE NARCISSI. ..NARCISSI.   190   2
   THERE IS NO TALK OF IMMORTALITY AMONG THESE! .........APPREHENSIONS   196   18
   HERE HE COMES NOW, AMONG THE MACKEREL GATHERERS ....BERCK-PLAGE   196   14
   NECESSARY AMONG THE FLOWERS, ...BERCK-PLAGE   200   101
   I PUT MY HANDS AMONG THE FLAMES. NOTHING BURNS. ....POPPIES IN JULY   203   4

17

	TITLE	PAGE	LINE

AMONG (CONT.)
INSOLVENT AMONG THE MOUNTAINS. ....THE COURAGE OF SHUTTING-UP 210 35
IN AMONG THESE SILK ....PURDAH 243 22
AMONG THESE PARAKEETS, MACAWS! ....PURDAH 243 35
AMONG THE BLANCHED, BOILED INSTRUMENTS, THE VIRGINAL
   CURTAINS. ....FEVER./DR 294 8
WE REACHED AMONG THE LEAVES ....BITTER STRAWBERRIES 300 35
EVEN THE DEAD LAUGH AMONG THE GOLDENROD. ....GOLD MOUTHS CRY 302 9
DOWN AMONG STRICT ROOTS AND ROCKS, ...DANSE MACABRE 320 1
A LONE BEACHCOMBER SQUATS AMONG THE WRACK ....TWO LOVERS. 327 13
LIES AMONG SHEETS ....AERIALIST 331 2
AMONG THE JAGGED MAZES OF THE ROCKS. ..THE PRINCESS AND THE GOBLINS 334 34
AMOROUS (3)
RICH IN STRAYINGS WITH EVERY AMOROUS OAF, ...VANITY FAIR 33 17
BUT FLORIDLY, HIS AMOROUS NOSTALGIAS. ....OUIJA 78 32
ALL AMOROUS ARROWS. FOR TO SHEATHE THE VIRGIN SHAPE*VIRGIN IN A TREE 81 7
AMPERSANDS (1)
FROM HER LIPS AMPERSANDS AND PERCENT SIGNS ....AN APPEARANCE 189 4
AMPLE (2)
BRED AN AMPLE BATCH OF OMENS; BUT NOW ....TALE OF A TUB 25 18
LULLED IN THE AMPLE WOMB OF THE FULL-TILT GLOBE. ....THE DEAD 320 4
AMPUTATIONS (1)
AMPUTATIONS CRAWL AND APPALL -- ....THALIDOMIDE 252 5
AMUSED (4)
AMUSED COURT HALLS: ....THE SNOWMAN ON THE MOOR 59 42
AMUSED SHOUT: ....LADY LAZARUS 246 54
YOU NEVER ALTERED YOUR AMUSED BELIEF ....DIRGE FOR A JOKER 302 7
WHILE WANTONLY AMUSED BY THIS, INSOLENT STORM STRIKES AT THE SKULL 325 5
AN (155)
ANACONDA (1)
ANACONDA. IMAGINE: THE WORLD ....PERSEUS 83 24
ANALYSE (1)
TO ANALYSE THE FIN, ...TRIO OF LOVE SONGS 315 46
ANANSI (1)
ANANSI, BLACK BUSYBODY OF THE FOLKTALES, ...SPIDER 48 1
ANARCHY (1)
IN THEIR OLD ANARCHY TO THE HORIZON-LINE. ....THE COLOSSUS 130 21
ANATOMY (1)
TREE-TWIST WILL APE THIS GROSS ANATOMY ....VIRGIN IN A TREE 82 44
ANCESTRAL (2)
CONDEMNED BY OUR ANCESTRAL FAULT, ...PURSUIT 22 14
NOW, DISCIPLINED IN THE STRICT ANCESTRAL CHAIR, ...THE TRIAL OF MAN 312 12
ANCESTRESS (1)
WITH MY GIPSY ANCESTRESS AND MY WEIRD LUCK ....DADDY 223 38
ANCHOR (4)
TO PREVENT FALL, OR ANCHOR THE FLUENT AIR ....EPITAPH FOR F. 45 3
AND RIDE THAT FLUX AT ANCHOR, UPSIDE DOWN. ....WATERCOLOR. 112 11
THE PEASANTS ANCHOR THEM WITH CONCHES. ONE IS TOLD: .....FINISTERRE 170 30
ONE SCARF WILL CATCH AND ANCHOR IN THE WHEEL. ....FEVER. 231 13
ANCHORED (5)
GOD'S WORK STOOD ANCHORED IN THAT GLARE ....CRYSTAL GAZER 55 38
ANCHORED ITSELF, GRIFFIN-LEGGED AND DARKLY GRAINED. ..THE OTHER TWO 68 9
THE WHOLE FLAT HARBOR ANCHORED IN ....A WINTER SHIP 113 9
BOOMERANG LIKE ANCHORED ELASTICS, HURTING THE OWNER. ...BERCK-PLAGE 196 11
FOR THOSE ANCHORED ATTITUDES ....TOUCH-AND-GO 335 2
ANCIENT (7)
DREAM-FILMED. WHAT A VISION OF ANCIENT HOGHOOD MUST ....SOW 61 27
WHO DRAG OUR ANCIENT FATHER AT THE HEEL, ...MOONRISE 98 28
THE MISTS ARE PART OF THE ANCIENT PARAPHERNALIA -- ......FINISTERRE 169 13
THEY ARE SMILING AND TAKING OUT VEILS TACKED TO ANCIENT HATS. BEE. 211 5
THAT LENGTHEN FROM ANCIENT CATHEDRALS ....MYSTIC 268 14
NO ANCIENT BLUEPRINT BUILDS AN ARK ....INSOLENT STORM. 326 17
WHERE ANCIENT, INFINITE, AND BEAUTIFUL,*THE PRINCESS AND THE GOBLINS 333 14
AND (1710)
ANEMIC (1)
AT NOON, ANEMIC HUSBANDS VISIT THEM. ....MORNING IN THE HOS. 333 27
ANEMONE (1)
OR AN ANEMONE, THAT SEA ....LESBOS 229 87
ANESTHETIST (2)
WHEN I WAS NINE, A LIME-GREEN ANESTHETIST ....FACE LIFT 155 4
AND MY HISTORY TO THE ANESTHETIST AND MY BODY TO SURGEONS. ..TULIPS 160 7
ANESTHETIZED (1)
MAY BE PINNED ANY MINUTE, ANESTHETIZED. ....KINDNESS 269 15
ANGEL (7)
OF WHATEVER ANGEL MAY CHOOSE TO FLARE ..BLACK ROOK IN RAINY WEATHER 57 26
THE LONG WAIT FOR THE ANGEL, ...BLACK ROOK IN RAINY WEATHER 57 39
A BALD ANGEL BLOCKS AND SHAPES ....SCULPTOR 91 10
LIKE BLUE MARY'S ANGEL, DOVELIKE AGAINST A PANE ....WIDOW 165 38
THAT WANES AND WANES, FACING THE COLD ANGEL? ....THREE WOMEN 177 39
AN ANGEL. PLUMAGE. O-F-R. HE'LL ....DIALOGUE OVER A OUIJA BOARD 279 90
ANGEL OF COLDNESS, ...THE RIVAL/DR 291 20
ANGELDOM (1)
YOU'LL ISSUE HIM HIS PASS TO ANGELDOM ..DIALOGUE OVER A OUIJA BOARD 281 192
ANGEL-FOOD (1)
FROM HERE THE MOON SEEMS SMOOTH AS ANGEL-FOOD, ...ADMONITIONS 319 7

```
                                                    TITLE              PAGE  LINE
ANGELIC (3)
   IMPALED UPON A STERN ANGELIC STARE  ................THE TRIAL OF MAN  312   9
   YET ALL ANGELIC REASON  ...........................TRIO OF LOVE SONGS 314  15
   AND HIDDEN ALL THE BRIGHT ANGELIC MEN.  ......EPITAPH IN THREE PARTS  338  31
ANGELS (21)
   THAT WRESTLE WITH US LIKE ANGELS; THE MERE CHANCE  CHANNEL CROSSING   27   18
   ITS CLEAR AIR WINNOWED BY ANGELS; SHE WAS COME  .......DREAM WITH C.  43    2
   WHERE, BEDDED LIKE ANGELS, TWO BURN ONE IN FEVER.  ........WREATH F.  45   18
   BUT NO HOCUS-POCUS OF GREEN ANGELS  .....................CONJURING.  66   17
   WITH STARS, WITH ANGELS, HE CONVERSED  .............NATURAL HISTORY   71    6
   ANGELS ARE RUMORED, CLEARLY  ....................THE GREAT CARBUNCLE  73   20
   ANGELS -- MORE FEMININE AND DOUCE  ...................A WINTER'S TALE  86    9
   ANGELS WEEPING OVER DULL NATURES,  ......................LOVE LETTER  147   16
   THE ABSTRACTS HOVER LIKE DULL ANGELS:  ........................MAGI  148    1
   MULTIPLIED TO INFINITY LIKE ANGELS ON A PINHEAD  ..ZOO KEEPER'S WIFE  155   22
   THE ANGELS OF MORPHIA HAVE BORNE HIM UP.  .....THE SURGEON AT 2 A.M.  171   44
   ENDLESSLY PROCEED -- AND THE COLD ANGELS, THE ABSTRACTIONS.   THREE.  177   20
   ANGELS SWIM IN IT, AND THE STARS, IN INDIFFERENCE ALSO.  ...
                                               ...  APPREHENSIONS  195    3
   THEY WOULD FLUTTER OFF, BLACK AND GLITTERING, THEY WOULD BE COAL
       ANGELS  ...................................BURNING THE LETTERS  204   33
   WHILE ANGELS WEAR A WAKEFUL ATTITUDE  ..................ADMONITIONS  319   13
   NOR CAN GOD'S STERN, SHOCKED ANGELS CRY THEM UP  ...........THE DEAD  320   13
   WHILE THE ANGELS ALL APPLAUD.  .................CIRCUS IN THREE RINGS  321    6
   SCATTER SMUG ANGELS WITH YOUR HAND.  ..SONG FOR A REVOLUTIONARY LOVE  322    4
   BRIGHT ANGELS BLACK OUT OVER LOGIC'S LAND .........SONNET TO SATAN   323    3
   ALL ABSOLUTES THAT ANGELS GIVE   INSOLENT STORM STRIKES AT THE SKULL  326   23
   COLONNADES OF ANGELS NOD HER IN  .......THE PRINCESS AND THE GOBLINS  333   13
ANGEL'S (2)
   ANGEL'S EYE IN THE AUDIENCE, THEN WHISK THEM OUT  ......DIALOGUE O.   282  233
   THE ANGEL'S FRAME  ...........................MOONSONG AT MORNING    317   34
ANGELS' (3)
   OF ANGELS' BAY  .....................................SOUTHERN SUNRISE  26   17
   THAT WILL KINDLE ANGELS' ENVY, SCORCH AND DROP  .....EPITAPH FOR F.   45    6
   LAUGHED AT THE AMBUSH OF ANGELS' TONGUES,  ..................LAMENT  315   14
ANGEL-SHAPE (1)
   SOME ANGEL-SHAPE WORTH WEARING  ...........................FIRESONG   30    9
ANGER (4)
   CLEAVES FORWARD INTO FURY; DARK AS ANGER,  ........CHANNEL CROSSING   26    3
   GRIEF AND ANGER, EXORCIZED,  ....................................A LIFE  150   29
   BUT NOW THAT ANGER COOLS, I'VE A SENSE OF SORROW  .......DIALOGUE O.  285  310
   AND AT THE JET-PLANE ANGER OF GOD'S ROAR  .........THE TRIAL OF MAN   312    7
ANGRILY (2)
   HE IS LOOKING SO ANGRILY!  .............................THREE WOMEN   181  164
   BLACK ON BLACK, ANGRILY CLAMBERING.  .....THE ARRIVAL OF THE BEE BOX  213   15
ANGRY (4)
   "THOR IS ANGRY: BOOM BOOM BOOM!  .............THE DISQUIETING MUSES   75   22
   THOR IS ANGRY: WE DON'T CARE!"  ..............THE DISQUIETING MUSES   75   23
   EITHER WAY WE CHOOSE, THE ANGRY WITCH  ....METAMORPHOSES OF THE MOON  308   43
   STARS PALE BEFORE THE ANGRY DAWN;  .................TO A JILTED LOVER  310   21
ANIMAL (7)
   WHICH NO GRUFF ANIMAL MISINTERPRETS.  ...................INCOMMUNICADO 100   11
   ANIMAL, COME FROM ANOTHER  ......................CHILD'S PARK STONES  101    7
   KING OF THE DISH, MY LUCKY ANIMAL.  ..................POEM.4.BEAST.   134    2
   NO ANIMAL SPOILS ON HER GREEN DOORSTEP.  ..........THE BURNT-OUT SPA  138   30
   AN IMAL  ...................................................LESBOS   229   55
   TURN, LIKE AN ANIMAL,  .....................................LYONNESSE  234   24
   AN ANIMAL  ...............................................GETTING THERE  249   56
ANIMALCULES (1)
   WHAT HONEY SUMMONS THESE ANIMALCULES?  ....................STINGS/DR  293    1
ANIMALS (4)
   OF ANIMALS TO CHOIR: "LOOK WHAT THRESH OF WINGS *WREATH FOR A BRIDAL  45   15
   WHERE TREES AND CLOUDS AND ANIMALS PAY NO NOTICE;  ........TWO CAMP.  144    8
   THE TULIPS SHOULD BE BEHIND BARS LIKE DANGEROUS ANIMALS;  ....TULIPS  162   58
   THEY ENTER AS ANIMALS FROM THE OUTER  .......................YEARS   255    1
ANIMOSITY (1)
   A GULLIBLE HEAD UNTOUCHED BY THEIR ANIMOSITY,  ......THE BEE MEETING  212   40
ANKLE (1)
   FIRELESS, SEVEN CHILL SEAS CHAINED TO HIS ANKLE. *EVERLASTING MONDAY  62   12
ANKLE-BONE (2)
   ...OF A WOMAN, A MOUSE AND A SHREW. THE ANKLE-BONE OF THE... ...
                                        ...  ALL THE DEAD DEARS  70  E/3
   THAT BATTENED FOR A DAY ON HER ANKLE-BONE.  ......ALL THE DEAD DEARS  70    6
ANKLES (4)
   CRUEL NETTLES STUNG HER ANKLES RAW.  ......................BUCOLICS   24   16
   THEY SAILED TILL TIDE FOAMED ROUND THEIR ANKLES  ......DREAM WITH C.  44   19
   MY ANKLES BRIGHTEN. BRIGHTNESS ASCENDS MY THIGHS.  ........POEM.6.W.  136   23
   PRICKLING MY ANKLES AND MURMURING OF THEIR HUMILITY.  .........MOON.  172    4
ANNIHILATE (1)
   TO ANNIHILATE EACH DECADE.  ...........................LADY LAZARUS   245   24
ANNIHILATES (1)
   THE SMILE OF ICEBOXES ANNIHILATES ME.  .................AN APPEARANCE  189    1
ANNIHILATING (1)
   OF SOMETHING BEAUTIFUL, BUT ANNIHILATING.  .................THE RIVAL  166    3
```

19

```
                                                      TITLE         PAGE  LINE
ANNIHILATION (1)
    BY THE DOVE'S ANNIHILATION,  ...............................BRASILIA  259   22
ANNIHILATIONS (1)
    ALL NIGHT I HAVE DREAMED OF DESTRUCTION, ANNIHILATIONS -- ..WAKING.  151    4
ANNOUNCER'S (1)
    TILL THE ANNOUNCER'S VOICE IS LOST  ...............INSOLENT STORM.  326   35
ANNOUNCES (1)
    ANNOUNCES A NEW SOUL. THE BED IS BLUE.  .......THE SURGEON AT 2 A.M.  171   42
ANNOUNCING (1)
    ANNOUNCING AFTER GLUTTED BIRDS HAVE FLOWN:  ..EPITAPH IN THREE PARTS  337   21
ANNUNCIATION (1)
    IS THIS THE ONE FOR THE ANNUNCIATION?  ...........A BIRTHDAY PRESENT  206    9
ANOINTS (1)
    WHOSE HOLY BLUE ANOINTS HER INJURED HAND.  ............THE PRINCESS.  333    6
ANONYMOUS (2)
    THE SOFT ANONYMOUS  ....................................PARALYTIC  266   14
    OF AN ANONYMOUS CLAM,  .........................NOTES TO A NEOPHYTE  306    3
ANOTHER (23)
    AS THE GODS BEGAN ONE WORLD, AND MAN ANOTHER,  ........SNAKECHARMER   79    1
    ANIMAL, COME FROM ANOTHER  .......................CHILD'S PARK STONES  101    7
    AGE, ANOTHER PLANET SURELY. FLANKED  ...........CHILD'S PARK STONES  101    8
    ANOTHER KIND OF REDNESS BOTHERS ME:  ........ELECTRA ON AZALEA PATH  117   29
    INTO ANOTHER TIME.  ...................................THE SLEEPERS  123   24
    I AM BECOMING ANOTHER.  ..............................POEM.3.MAENAD.  133   15
    THE BLUE SISTERS SENT ME TO ANOTHER SCHOOL.  .........POEM.4.BEAST.  134    7
    DOING THINGS WITH THEIR HANDS, ONE JUST THE SAME AS ANOTHER, *TULIPS  160   13
    A BODILESS SOUL COULD PASS ANOTHER SOUL  .....................WIDOW  164   32
    BUT FROM ANOTHER PLACE, TROPICAL AND BLUE,  ............FINISTERRE  170   34
    WITH SEVEN HOLES THUMBED IN. THE SOUL IS ANOTHER LIGHT. ...SURGEON.  170    8
    NOT LOOKING, THROUGH THE THICK DARK, FOR THE FACE OF ANOTHER.*THREE.  178   77
    GREAT SILENCE OF ANOTHER ORDER.  ....................LITTLE FUGUE  188   37
    SHE IS OLD, OLD, OLD, SHE MUST LIVE ANOTHER YEAR, AND SHE KNOWS IT. ...
                                              ... THE BEE MEETING  212   44
    HERE IS HIS SLIPPER, HERE IS ANOTHER,  .......................STINGS  215   42
    TO ENTER ANOTHER YEAR? ...................................WINTERING  219   48
    WE SHOULD MEET IN ANOTHER LIFE, WE SHOULD MEET IN AIR,  .....LESBOS  228   31
    AND OF ANOTHER COLOR. ....................................AMNESIAC  233   16
    TO GIVE ANOTHER INCH. IF YOU PREFER, ...DIALOGUE OVER A OUIJA BOARD  281  179
    ONE CAMOUFLAGING ITSELF BEHIND ANOTHER. ................THE RIVAL/DR  291    5
    O RANSACK THE FOUR WINDS AND FIND ANOTHER ...................LAMENT  316   16
    OR PLAY ANOTHER CARD GAME WHEN YOU'VE WON; ............ADMONITIONS  319    2
    MORNING: ANOTHER DAY, AND TALK  ....MORNING IN THE HOSPITAL SOLARIUM  332   10
ANOTHER'S (1)
    THAT ONE MAN'S DEVIL IS ANOTHER'S GOD  ..........LOVE IS A PARALLAX  329    8
ANSWER (5)
    THOUGH NOBODY IN THERE LOOKS UP OR BOTHERS TO ANSWER.  .......A LIFE  150    8
    I BLAMED HER FOR EVERYTHING, BUT SHE DIDN'T ANSWER.  .....IN PLASTER  159   10
    QUESTIONS WITHOUT ANSWER,  ...................................MYSTIC  268    2
    HE LIVES. HIS ANSWER WILL PUT AN END TO GIBES  ..........DIALOGUE O.  281  174
    AND CHANCE OF A TRUE ANSWER. YOU WASTE NO TIME  ........DIALOGUE O.  281  188
ANT (3)
    HE TRIPPED AN ANT WITH A ROPE  ...............................SPIDER   48   13
    EACH TIME ROUND WINDING THAT ANT  ...........................SPIDER   48   16
    I CRAWL LIKE AN ANT IN MOURNING  .......................THE COLOSSUS  129   12
ANTELOPE (3)
    HER ANTELOPE WHO MEANT HIM NAUGHT BUT GOOD.  ..THE QUEEN'S COMPLAINT   28   10
    BUT LET THE GALLOPING ANTELOPE RUN.  ........GO GET THE GOODLY SQUAB  313   12
    LET THE GALLOPING ANTELOPE RUN  .............GO GET THE GOODLY SQUAB  313   13
ANTENNA (1)
    TOUCHY ANTENNA,  ............................WORDS FOR A NURSERY   74   22
ANTEROOM (1)
    I ROLL TO AN ANTEROOM WHERE A KIND MAN  ...................FACE LIFT  156   12
ANTHERS (1)
    THE ANTHERS NOD THEIR HEADS, POTENT AS KINGS  ..........BEEKEEPER'S.  118   11
ANTICIPATES (1)
    ANTICIPATES THE WARNING SOUND  .......................DANSE MACABRE  321   23
ANTIGONE (1)
    THE CLASSIC LIMBS OF STUBBORN ANTIGONE?  ....................PERSEUS   83   40
ANTIMACASSARS (1)
    ON ANTIMACASSARS  ..................ELLA MASON AND HER ELEVEN CATS   54   21
ANTIQUE (9)
    LOOMED ABSOLUTE AS THE ANTIQUE WORLD WAS  .........HARDCASTLE CRAGS   63   38
    AN ANTIQUE HAG-HEAD, TOO TOUGH FOR KNIFE TO FINISH,  ....LADY AND T.   70   33
    THIS ANTIQUE MUSEUM-CASED LADY  ...............ALL THE DEAD DEARS   70    3
    FRAIL AS ANTIQUE EARTHENWARE  .......................OLD LADIES' HOME  120    2
    GARDENS IN AN ANTIQUE BOOK  .........................MAGNOLIA SHOALS  122    9
    BOSSED, BRAZEN, AN ANTIQUE SHIELD,  ...............A BIRTHDAY PRESENT  207   30
    THEN THERE IS THAT ANTIQUE BILLHOOK, THE TONGUE,  ........COURAGE.  210   17
    AREN'T VOUCHSAFED TO ANTIQUE VIRGINS ONLY:  ............DIALOGUE O.  282  220
    UNRAVEL ANTIQUE SAMPLERS, UNWIND THE CLOCKS,  ....SONG FOR A REVOLU.  323   13
ANTS (4)
    FROM WHICH COILS, CAUGHT ANTS WAVED LEGS IN  ................SPIDER   49   19
    THEN BRISKLY SCALED HIS ALTAR TIERED WITH TETHERED ANTS,  ....SPIDER   49   22
    THE ANTS -- A FILE OF COMERS, A FILE OF GOERS --  ...........SPIDER   49   29
    WHERE SMALL ANTS ROLL THEIR EGGS, WHERE GRUBS FATTEN.  .....MOONRISE   98   17
```

	TITLE	PAGE	LINE

ANTS' (1)
NEAR HIS SMALL STONEHEDGE ABOVE THE ANTS' ROUTE, ...SPIDER 48 11
ANT-SIZE (1)
ONE-THIRD ANT-SIZE, A LEGGY SPOT, ...SPIDER 48 12
ANVIL (2)
AN ANVIL, HOOVES FOUR HAMMERS TO JOLT ....WHITENESS I REMEMBER 102 21
I LIE ON A GREAT ANVIL. POEM.7.S. 136 2
ANXIOUSNESS (1)
OR ANY SIGNAL OF DISTRESS OR ANXIOUSNESS. ..STARS OVER THE DORDOGNE 165 7
ANY (45)
AND SALLOW AS ANY LEMON, ...TWO SISTERS OF PERSEPHONE 32 25
NO FIRE IS, NOR IN ANY BOOK PROOF ....VANITY FAIR 33 27
AND, MORE DAFT THAN ANY GOOSE, ...STREET SONG 36 29
TO BOYCOTT COLOR AND FORBID ANY FLOWER ..SOLILOQUY OF THE SOLIPSIST 38 26
THEIR FOND HEARTS CHARRED AS ANY MATCH. EPITAPH FOR FIRE AND FLOWER 45 7
ANY MORE IN THE DESULTORY WEATHER SOME DESIGN, ...BLACK ROOK I. 57 8
ONE MIGHT SAY LOVE. AT ANY RATE, I NOW WALK ....BLACK ROOK I. 57 22
NOR DID ANY WORD BODY WITH A NAME ....HARDCASTLE CRAGS 63 17
ANY MORE THAN THE OLD WOMAN IN HER MUD HUT COULD ...THE THIN PEOPLE 64 26
THAN FLESH OF ANY BODY ....ON THE PLETHORA OF DRYADS 67 17
ANY TOUCH, TASTE, TANG'S ....ALL THE DEAD DEARS 71 29
DRUMMING UP ANY FEVER ....NIGHT SHIFT 76 4
IRREPROACHABLE AS ANY LETTUCE HEAD, ...MEMOIRS OF A SPINACH-PICKER 89 10
SEEN BY ANY MAN WHO KEPT HIS HEAD, ...FULL FATHOM FIVE 93 38
NOR BY ANY LEARNED MAN. ....THE BULL OF BENDYLAW 108 18
YET IT NEVER MILKED ANY GOAT, NOR DEALT COW DEATH ....GOATSUCKER 111 12
SOME SCANDAL MIGHT ANY MINUTE OOZE ....AFTERMATH 113 4
MOVES HUMBLY AS ANY HOUSEWIFE THROUGH ....AFTERMATH 114 10
MY MOTHER SAID; YOU DIED LIKE ANY MAN. ......ELECTRA ON AZALEA PATH 117 40
LEAF UNLIKE ANY ....POLLY'S TREE 128 5
ANY SILK FAN ....POLLY'S TREE 128 12
WITHOUT DREAMS OF ANY SORT. POEM.1.WHO. 132 24
ANY DAY I MAY LITTER PUPPIES POEM.2.DARK. 132 12
CALL HIM ANY NAME, HE'LL COME TO IT. POEM.4.BEAST. 134 16
THE WINGY MYTHS WON'T TUG AT US ANY MORE: POEM.5.F. 135 16
HERE THEY CAN DOCTOR HEADS, OR ANY LIMB. POEM.7.S. 137 35
IT WASN'T FOR ANY LACK OF MOTHER-LOVE. ....STILLBORN 142 5
I WASN'T IN ANY POSITION TO GET RID OF HER. ....IN PLASTER 159 43
SO I WAS CAREFUL NOT TO UPSET HER IN ANY WAY ....IN PLASTER 160 46
I DIDN'T WANT ANY FLOWERS, I ONLY WANTED ....TULIPS 161 29
COMING AND GOING, BREATH BY BREATH, WITHOUT ANY FUSS. ....TULIPS 161 51
OR ANY SIGNAL OF DISTRESS OR ANXIOUSNESS. ..STARS OVER THE DORDOGNE 165 7
IS IT ANY WONDER HE PUTS ON DARK GLASSES? ....BERCK-PLAGE 196 12
IS IT ANY WONDER HE AFFECTS A BLACK CASSOCK? ....BERCK-PLAGE 196 13
I WOULD HAVE KILLED MYSELF GLADLY THAT TIME ANY POSSIBLE WAY. ...
                                       ... A BIRTHDAY PRESENT 206 15
IS THERE ANY QUEEN AT ALL IN IT? ....STINGS 214 15
ANY MORE, BLACK SHOE ....DADDY 222 2
ANY LESS THE BLACK MAN WHO ....DADDY 223 55
IN ANY CASE, YOU ARE ALWAYS THERE, ...MEDUSA 225 16
MAY BE PINNED ANY MINUTE, ANESTHETIZED. ....KINDNESS 269 15
ON HIM SOMETIMES. HE'S LAZY. LIKE ANY YOUNG ....DIALOGUE O. 281 182
THEM ANY MORE THAN YOU DID. OH, LET IT GO. ....DIALOGUE O. 283 265
THAN ANY ORCHID. YOU BROKE HIM THEN. I BROKE ....DIALOGUE O. 285 324
IT IS SIX IN THE MORNING AND FINER THAN ANY SUNDAY -- *QUEEN MARY'S. 290 8
SO IF YOU CAN DREAM UP ANY SAVING PLAN ....THE DISPOSSESSED 318 2
ANYBODY (3)
THIS BLACK BOOT HAS NO MERCY FOR ANYBODY. ....BERCK-PLAGE 197 19
ONLY THEY HAVE NOTHING TO SAY TO ANYBODY. ....BURNING THE LETTERS 204 34
IS ANYBODY THERE? IT GOES. IT GOES .....DIALOGUE OVER A OUIJA BOARD 277 26
ANYHOW (1)
ME. ASK, ANYHOW. I ADMIT IT: I'M AFRAID,*DIALOGUE OVER A OUIJA BOARD 278 67
ANYONE (2)
THUMB CAN MAKE ANYONE WINCE, BUT THE WHOLE GLOBE ....PERSEUS 83 28
I AM TOO PURE FOR YOU OR ANYONE. ....FEVER. 232 34
ANYTHING (8)
AND SHE COULD SCARCELY MAKE OUT ANYTHING*TWO VIEWS OF A CADAVER ROOM 114 7
I HAD NOTHING TO DO WITH GUILT OR ANYTHING ..ELECTRA ON AZALEA PATH 116 9
ANYTHING CAN HAPPEN WHERE THEY ARE GOING. ....ON DECK 143 18
HOW SHALL I TELL ANYTHING AT ALL ....CANDLES 149 32
WITH NO BOTTOM, OR ANYTHING ON THE OTHER SIDE OF IT, ...FINISTERRE 169 4
THEY ARE SO JEALOUS OF ANYTHING THAT IS NOT FLAT! THEY ARE
     JEALOUS GODS ....THREE WOMEN 179 86
I AM NOT READY FOR ANYTHING TO HAPPEN. ....THREE WOMEN 180 125
IF ANYTHING SHOULD HAPPEN . . ." ....BITTER STRAWBERRIES 299 12
ANYWAY (1)
I DO NOT WANT MUCH OF A PRESENT, ANYWAY, THIS YEAR. ......BIRTHDAY. 206 13
ANYWHERE (1)
NEVER, NEVER, FOUND ANYWHERE. ....THE DISQUIETING MUSES 76 45
APART (8)
AS LIFT HIM APART ....THE SHRIKE 42 3
DRAGGED EACH DAZZLED SENSE APART ....ON THE PLETHORA OF DRYADS 67 26
SHAPELESS AS FLUNG GLOVES, A FEW FEET APART -- ....BLUE MOLES 126 3
I TALK TO MYSELF, MYSELF ONLY, SET APART -- ....THREE WOMEN 179 106
I AM BREAKING APART LIKE THE WORLD. THERE IS THIS BLACKNESS, *THREE. 180 142

21

APART (CONT.)
  HARD AND APART AND WHITE. ....LESBOS   229 58
  SMIRK. SAINTS' DOOR APART, BACKDOOR'S A DOOR, ...DIALOGUE O.   280 131
  OUR PAINTED STAGES FALL APART BY SCENES ....DOOMSDAY   316   4
APARTMENTS (2)
  BETWEEN THE SNUFF AND RED TAR-PAPER APARTMENTS, ...ABOVE THE OXBOW   88 13
  HER RUINED APARTMENTS, TAKING STOCK ....AFTERMATH   114 11
APE (2)
  APE OF HER LOOK. BEST RID ....THE LADY AND THE EARTHENWARE HEAD   69   5
  TREE-TWIST WILL APE THIS GROSS ANATOMY ....VIRGIN IN A TREE   82 44
APES (2)
  NIGHTLY NOW I FLOG APES OWLS BEARS SHEEP ....ZOO KEEPER'S WIFE   155 39
  S. HE CALLS US APES. I'LL SETTLE HIM! ..DIALOGUE OVER A OUIJA BOARD   284 299
A-P-E-S (1)
  HIS MANNERS ARE ATROCIOUS. A-P-E-S. ..DIALOGUE OVER A OUIJA BOARD   284 298-9
APHRODISIAC (1)
  THE APHRODISIAC SQUID. ....GIGOLO   267 17
APHRODISIACS (2)
  WHO HAS SALTIER APHRODISIACS ....OUIJA   77 23
  "O FOR UBIQUITOUS FREE APHRODISIACS, ...DIALOGUE EN ROUTE   309 27
APOLLOS (1)
  MOTHER OF A WHITE NIKE AND SEVERAL BALD-EYED APOLLOS.   BARREN WOMAN   157   7
APOTHECARY (1)
  YOU HAD A ROSE GARDEN AND A GUEST COTTAGE AND A MODEL APOTHECARY
    SHOP ....THE BABYSITTERS   174 20
APPALL (4)
  OF THE WHEELS MOVE, THEY APPALL ME --- ....GETTING THERE   248   4
  AMPUTATIONS CRAWL AND APPALL -- ....THALIDOMIDE   252   5
  SHALL THE HOOD OF THE COBRA APPALL ME --- ....TOTEM   264 19
  AND GOD OR VOID APPALL US TILL WE DROWN ....LOVE IS A PARALLAX   330 74
APPALLED (1)
  APALLED BY SECRET WANT, I RUSH ....PURSUIT   23 43
APPALLING (3)
  ABOVE THE APPALLING RUIN; IN BLEAK LIGHT ..............CONVERSATION.   21   6
  APPALLING TO WITNESS, ...SPIDER   49 24
  CHINESE YELLOW ON APPALLING OBJECTS --- ....WINTERING   218 16
APPALLS (1)
  IT IS THE NOISE THAT APPALLS ME MOST OF ALL, ...THE ARRIVAL.   213 17
APPARENTLY (1)
  AND APPARENTLY INDESTRUCTIBLE. ....A WINTER SHIP   112   4
APPARITION (2)
  THIS IS THE KINGDOM OF THE FADING APPARITION, ...GHOST'S.   90   8
  THIS APPARITION IN A GREEN HELMET, ...THE BEE MEETING   211 28
APPEAR (6)
  END: GREEN SHORES APPEAR; WE ASSUME OUR NAMES, ...CHANNEL CROSSING   27 40
  KNOW YOU APPEAR ....SOLILOQUY OF THE SOLIPSIST   38 29
  I DO NOT THINK THE SEA WILL APPEAR AT ALL. ...........BLACKBERRYING   168 13
  "IS THIS THE ONE I AM TO APPEAR FOR, ...A BIRTHDAY PRESENT   206   5
  FAILS TO APPEAR, TURN, AND, TURNING, SHRINK ....DIALOGUE O.   279 120
  A RIGOR SEIZED ME: I SAW CRACKS APPEAR, *DIALOGUE OVER A OUIJA BOARD   285 319
APPEARANCE (1)
  AN APPEARANCE ....AN APPEARANCE   189   T
APPEARED (1)
  WHEN THE SWEETHEART FROM ENGLAND APPEARED, WITH HER CREAM SKIN
    AND YARDLEY COSMETICS, ...THE BABYSITTERS   174   6
APPEARS (1)
  AND APPEARS TO HAVE SUFFERED A SORT OF PRIVATE BLITZKRIEG. ..A LIFE   150 24
APPENDAGES (1)
  DELVING FOR THE APPENDAGES ....BLUE MOLES   126 30
APPETITE (2)
  DOOM CONSUMMATES THAT APPETITE. ....PURSUIT   22 20
  THE DREAMER REINS HIS WAKING APPETITE ....TERMINAL   328   2
APPLAUD (2)
  WHILE THE ANGELS ALL APPLAUD. ....CIRCUS IN THREE RINGS   321   6
  THE LEAVES APPLAUD, AND SANTA CLAUS FLIES IN ....LOVE IS A PARALLAX   329 34
APPLAUSE (1)
  SHE DRAWS APPLAUSE; BRIGHT HARNESS ....AERIALIST   331 23
APPLE (6)
  "I SEE TWO STALWART APPLE TREES ....CRYSTAL GAZER   55 13
  AND APPLE CAKES TO COOL. WHAT IS IT ....POINT SHIRLEY   110 28
  WHERE APPLE BLOOM ICES THE NIGHT ....EVENT   195 13
  STAB A FEW CLOVES IN AN APPLE, ...A SECRET   220 30
  OF SLOW DISASTER: THE BITTEN APPLE ENDS ..METAMORPHOSES OF THE MOON   307 14
  IN A BATCH OF RAVELED APPLE RINDS. ....THE PRINCESS AND THE GOBLINS   335 68
APPLES (6)
  PLENITUDE: APPLES GOLD ON THE BOUGH, ...IN MIDAS' COUNTRY   99 12
  I'VE EATEN A BAG OF GREEN APPLES, ...METAPHORS   116   8
  THE SNAILS BLEW KISSES LIKE BLACK APPLES. ....ZOO KEEPER'S WIFE   155 38
  THE APPLES ARE GOLDEN, ...LETTER IN NOVEMBER   253 24
  THE MAGIC GOLDEN APPLES ALL LOOK GOOD ....ADMONITIONS   319   4
  AND ALL THE GOLD APPLES ....TEMPER OF TIME   336   3
APPLE-TREE (1)
  I TRIED MY SIGHT ON AN APPLE-TREE ....ON THE PLETHORA OF DRYADS   67   4
APPLICANT (1)
  THE APPLICANT ....THE APPLICANT   221   T

	TITLE	PAGE	LINE

APPREHENDING (1)
OF APPREHENDING BLUENESS, OR STARS. ....LOVE LETTER 147 8
APPREHENSIONS (1)
APPREHENSIONS ....APPREHENSIONS 195 T
APPROACH (1)
COLD BLANKS APPROACH US: ...........................APPREHENSIONS 196 19
APPROACHED (1)
FROM THE LAUREL THICKET. NO ONE APPROACHED. .........RHODODENDRON. 103 19
APPROACHES (1)
INCENSE OF DEATH. YOUR DAY APPROACHES. ....THE MANOR GARDEN 125 2
APPROACHING (1)
APPROACHING HIS COTTAGE ....TEMPER OF TIME 336 17
APPROVE (2)
SEASONED HOW HE'D MOST APPROVE; ....THE GLUTTON 40 6
LOW MOOS OF APPROVE; LET SUN SURPLICED IN BRIGHTNESS .....WREATH F. 44 4
APPROVING (1)
APPROVING CHASED GIRLS WHO GET THEM TO A TREE .....VIRGIN IN A TREE 81 4
APPURTENANCES (1)
SCREENS, THESE RUSTLING APPURTENANCES. ....PURDAH 243 23
APRIL (4)
DURING A CEREMONIOUS APRIL WALK ....SPINSTER 49 2
APRIL SNOWDROP, INDIAN PIPE, ...CHILD 265 5
APRIL 18 ....APRIL 18 301 T
APRIL AUBADE ....APRIL AUBADE 312 T
APT (1)
IN APT IAMBICS, IF PRODDED TO RECITE ...DIALOGUE OVER A OUIJA BOARD 280 143
AQUARIUM (1)
OF AN UNDULANT AQUARIUM. ....MORNING IN THE HOSPITAL SOLARIUM 332 9
AQUATIC (1)
AQUATIC NOCTURNE ....AQUATIC NOCTURNE 305 T
AQUEDUCTS (1)
AQUEDUCTS, THE BATHS OF CARACALLA, THE EAGLE NOSE! ....SURGEON. 171 28
ARABESQUES (1)
AND PRAISED MY ARABESQUES AND TRILLS ....THE DISQUIETING MUSES 75 34
ARABIC (1)
THEY PAINT SUCH SECRETS IN ARABIC, CHINESE! ....THREE WOMEN 179 98
ARBOR (1)
THE QUEEN IN THE MULBERRY ARBOR STARED ....THE BULL OF BENDYLAW 108 4
ARC (3)
OF THE AIR EDDIES' LOOP AND ARC THOUGH AIR'S AT REST ....OXBOW. 88 32
ARC OF TEAR-PEARLED ....POLLY'S TREE 129 39
THE BROWN ARC ....ARIEL 239 8
ARCADIAN (1)
ARCADIAN GREEN ....WATERCOLOR OF GRANTCHESTER MEADOWS 112 20
ARCHAEOLOGICAL (1)
IN THE ARCHAEOLOGICAL MUSEUM IN CAMBRIDGE IS A STONE... ...
                                          ... ALL THE DEAD DEARS 70 E/1
ARCHAEOLOGIST (1)
ARCHAEOLOGIST AMONG ....THE BURNT-OUT SPA 138 15
ARCHAIC (2)
FOR THE ARCHAIC TRENCHED LINES ....FULL FATHOM FIVE 93 25
FROM THE ARCHAIC ....DARK WOOD, DARK WATER 127 4
ARCHED (1)
ON THE ARCHED GREEN ....RESOLVE 52 14
ARCHES (2)
ARCHES ABOVE US. O FATHER, ALL BY YOURSELF ....THE COLOSSUS 129 17
STUCCO ARCHES, THE BANKED ROCKS SUNNING IN ROWS, ...WHITSUN 153 2
ARCHETYPES (1)
THEY STEP AMONG THE ARCHETYPES. ....HEAVY WOMEN 158 17
ARCS (4)
WHERE TRAINS, FAITHFUL TO THEIR STEEL ARCS, ...THE SWARM 216 35
FIXED TO THEIR ARCS LIKE GODS, ...GETTING THERE 248 14
DESCRIBING ARCS OF LOVE. ....TRIO OF LOVE SONGS 314 28
ARCS UP TO THE TALL TREE TIP; ....TOUCH-AND-GO 335 14
ARCTIC (2)
RIDING MY ARCTIC ....BURNING THE LETTERS 204 27
IT IS THE ARCTIC, ...LETTER IN NOVEMBER 253 5
ARDENT (2)
INTO AN ARDENT BLAZING. ....SONG FOR A SUMMER'S DAY 31 15
BLOWS ASH IN EACH LOVER'S EYE; THE ARDENT LOOK ......EPITAPH FOR F. 46 34
ARDOR (1)
HIS ARDOR SNARES ME, LIGHTS THE TREES, ...PURSUIT 23 33
ARE (337)
ARENA (2)
AN ARENA OF YELLOW EYES ....FAUN 35 11
ARENA DUST RUSTED BY FOUR BULLS' BLOOD TO A DULL REDNESS,*THE GORING 47 1
AREN'T (2)
ONE DAY IT WON'T COME BACK. THINGS AREN'T LIKE THAT. ....LAST WORDS 172 16
AREN'T VOUCHSAFED TO ANTIQUE VIRGINS ONLY: ....DIALOGUE O. 282 220
ARGUE (2)
TO THIS CREST OF GRASS. INLAND, THEY ARGUE, PARLIAMENT HILL FIELDS 152 7
THE BEES ARGUE, IN THEIR BLACK BALL, ...THE SWARM 216 31
ARGUED (1)
ARGUED MY CONSCIENCE CLEAR WHICH ROBBED .............RHODODENDRON. 103 11

23

```
                                                TITLE              PAGE  LINE
ARGUMENT (1)
    ARGUMENT TO THE HOUSE NEXT DOOR. OR IF   DIALOGUE OVER A OUIJA BOARD  280  166
ARGUMENTS (3)
    WE DREAMED THEIR ARGUMENTS, THEIR STRICKEN VOICES.  ...THE OTHER TWO   69   29
    AND CASUIST ARGUMENTS RUN RIOT   INSOLENT STORM STRIKES AT THE SKULL  326   21
    WE RAISE OUR ARGUMENTS LIKE SITTING DUCKS  ......LOVE IS A PARALLAX   329   19
ARIEL (1)
    ARIEL ...........................................................ARIEL   239    T
ARISING (1)
    LARKS' NIP AND TUCK ARISING  ................SONG FOR A SUMMER'S DAY    31    9
ARK (2)
    I ENTERED YOUR BIBLE, I BOARDED YOUR ARK  .........ZOO KEEPER'S WIFE   155   28
    NO ANCIENT BLUEPRINT BUILDS AN ARK  ..................INSOLENT STORM.  326   17
ARM (7)
    HE LIFTS AN ARM TO BRING HER CLOSE, BUT SHE  ..........THE OTHER TWO    68   18
    AS ITSELF -- NO FIDDLER'S ARM  .........MUSSEL HUNTER AT ROCK HUNTER    96   34
    AN ARM AND A LEG, AN ARM, A LEG.  .......................LOVE LETTER   147   32
    AN ARM AND A LEG, AN ARM, A LEG.  .......................LOVE LETTER   147   32
    GLOVED MY ARM TO THE ELBOW.  ......................ZOO KEEPER'S WIFE   155   37
    I AM LEFT WITH AN ARM OR A LEG,  ..............THE SURGEON AT 2 A.M.   171   33
    I HOLD YOU ON MY ARM.  ...............................BY CANDLELIGHT   236    6
ARMADILLO (1)
    THE ARMADILLO DOZED IN HIS SANDBIN  ................ZOO KEEPER'S WIFE   155   20
ARMCHAIR (1)
    AND TO SANCTUARY: USURPING THE ARMCHAIR  .........ALL THE DEAD DEARS    71   31
ARMED (1)
    ARMED WITH FEATHERS TO TICKLE AS WELL AS FLY,  ..............PERSEUS    83   35
ARMIES (2)
    STALEMATED THEIR ARMIES STOOD, WITH TOTTERING BANNERS:  ..SNOWMAN O.    58    1
    ARMIES OF THEM. THEY ARE CARBON MONOXIDE.  .......A BIRTHDAY PRESENT   207   40
ARMING (1)
    ARMING MYSELF WITH THE MOST REASONABLE ITEMS  ...........STREET SONG    36   15
ARMOR (3)
    PINE-NEEDLE ARMOR PROTECTS  .........................VIRGIN IN A TREE    81   16
    IN HIS PINK PLUME AND ARMOR.  ...........................BATTLE-SCENE    84   10
    WITH HIS ARMOR OF FAKERY,  ................................THE JAILER   227   30
ARMORPLATE (2)
    HIS ARMORPLATE, HIS TOPPLED STONES  ...............THE BURNT-OUT SPA   138   12
    IN THEIR BLACK ARMORPLATE AND CRY.  ......SLEEP IN THE MOJAVE DESERT   144   23
ARMORY (1)
    WITH ITS YELLOW PURSES, ITS SPIKY ARMORY.  ..........THE BEE MEETING   211   32
ARMPIT (1)
    THE SUN SAT IN HIS ARMPIT.  .........................POEM.4.BEAST.    134    4
ARMPITS (2)
    FRIENDS, FRIENDS. THEY STINK OF ARMPITS  ............LEAVING EARLY    146   17
    BREASTPLATES OF CHEESECLOTH KNOTTED UNDER THE ARMPITS.  ........BEE.   211   14
ARMS (9)
    ON ARMS AND LEGS IN A FRINGE OF KELP; GREEN SOAP  .....TALE OF A TUB    25   43
    THE FLIMSY LIGHT; ARMS FOLDED  ............................SCULPTOR    91   11
    MY SWADDLED LEGS AND ARMS SMELL SWEET AS RUBBER.  .........POEM.7.S.   137   34
    THOSE LITTLE SICK ONES THAT ELUDE MY ARMS.  .............THREE WOMEN   178   67
    ITS END AND RUNS TOWARD IT, ARMS HELD OUT IN LOVE.  .....THREE WOMEN   181  151
    THE BODY OF A STARFISH CAN GROW BACK ITS ARMS  .........THREE WOMEN   184  257
    LEGS, ARMS PILED OUTSIDE  ............................GETTING THERE   248   26
    ARMS FOLDED, EAR COCKED,  ...........................EAVESDROPPER    261   38
    I AM MAD, CALLS THE SPIDER, WAVING ITS MANY ARMS.  ............TOTEM   265   28
ARMY (2)
    TWO PEOPLE ONLY ARE BLIND TO THE CARRION ARMY:  .........TWO VIEWS.   114   13
    SO MUCH FOR THE CHARIOTEERS, THE OUTRIDERS, THE GRAND ARMY!  SWARM.   217   39
AROUND (15)
    THIS DREAM BUDDED BRIGHT WITH LEAVES AROUND THE EDGES,*DREAM WITH C.    43    1
    AROUND OUR BED THE BARONIAL FURNITURE  .................THE OTHER TWO    68    4
    NODDING BY NIGHT AROUND MY BED,  .............THE DISQUIETING MUSES     75   15
    SHAPES ITS IMAGES AROUND HIS SONGS.  ...................SNAKECHARMER    79    7
    NODDED THEIR PETALED HEADS AROUND YOUR COUCH.  ............YADWIGHA.    86   30
    RED CINDER AROUND WHICH I MYSELF,  ....................THE EYE-MOTE    109   17
    IN THE DISTANCE. ALL AROUND US THE WATER SLIPS  .......A WINTER SHIP   113   18
    AROUND OUR TENT THE OLD SIMPLICITIES SOUGH  ................TWO CAMP.  145   25
    THESE BODIES MOUNDED AROUND ME NOW, THESE POLAR SLEEPERS --  THREE.   181  181
    IT IS SHE THAT DRAGS THE BLOOD-BLACK SEA AROUND  .......THREE WOMEN   182  186
    HOW LONG CAN I BE A WALL AROUND MY GREEN PROPERTY?  ....THREE WOMEN   185  295
    AROUND HIM LIKE LIVINGROOM FURNITURE, LIKE A DECOR.  ....BERCK-PLAGE   199   83
    AROUND THE RING. I THINK IT MUST BE MAKING SURE  .......DIALOGUE O.   277   22
    NOW BOUND AROUND HER WRIST TILL SHE REDEEM  ...........THE PRINCESS.  333   24
    DOZING AROUND THEIR SILVERED SENTRY BOX.  .............THE PRINCESS.  334   30
ARRANGED (1)
    ARRANGED IN SHEETS OF ICE, THE FOND  .................DANSE MACABRE   321    4
ARRANGING (4)
    ARRANGING AND REARRANGING ITS FEATHERS IN THE RAIN.  ..BLACK ROOK I.    56    3
    HE IS ARRANGING HIS BROWN FEATHERS.  ....................THREE WOMEN   176   12
    ARRANGING MY MORNING.  ...............................LITTLE FUGUE    189   50
    WAS SHE ARRANGING CUPS? IT IS IMPORTANT.  ............THE DETECTIVE   208    3
ARRIVAL (3)
    SURVIVES ARRIVAL; WE WALK THE PLANK WITH STRANGERS.*CHANNEL CROSSING    27   42
    OUR VOICES ECHO, MAGNIFYING YOUR ARRIVAL. NEW STATUE.   MORNING SONG   157    4
```

24

```
                                              TITLE            PAGE  LINE
ARRIVAL (CONT.)
    THE ARRIVAL OF THE BEE BOX  ..............THE ARRIVAL OF THE BEE BOX  212   T
ARRIVE (4)
    ARRIVE AT TWILIGHT, AND THEN AFTER SOME EFFORT.  ..............STARS.  165   10
    THE SMALLER AND MORE TIMID NEVER ARRIVE AT ALL  ..............STARS.   165   12
    ARRIVE THROUGH THE MAILSLOT WITH LOVING REGULARITY,  ......THE RIVAL   166   14
    LEAVE AND ARRIVE, AND THERE IS NO END TO THE COUNTRY.  ....THE SWARM   217   36
ARRIVES (2)
    AND NIGHT ARRIVES IN ONE GIGANTIC STEP.*TWO CAMPERS IN CLOUD COUNTRY  145   16
    AT THIS FACET THE BRIDEGROOM ARRIVES  ......................PURDAH    242   19
ARROGANT (3)
    ARROGANT AMONG ROOK-TONGUED SPACES,  .....................CONJURING.   66   10
    TO ADAM THE ARROGANT MATADOR  ...................DIALOGUE EN ROUTE    308    3
    AND ADAM THE ARROGANT MATADOR  ..................DIALOGUE EN ROUTE    309   33
ARROW (4)
    INDEX THE ARROW,  ................................WORDS FOR A NURSERY  73   14
    TONGUE A ROSE-COLORED ARROW.  ...........................MEDALLION    124    7
    DID IT COME LIKE AN ARROW, DID IT COME LIKE A KNIFE?  THE DETECTIVE   209   21
    AM THE ARROW,  ................................................ARIEL  239   27
ARROW-BACKS (1)
    FOLLOW THE BLACK ARROW-BACKS OF SWIFTS ON THEIR TRACK  .......OXBOW.   88   31
ARROWS (6)
    ALL AMOROUS ARROWS. FOR TO SHEATHE THE VIRGIN SHAPE*VIRGIN IN A TREE   81    7
    AND NO BODIES, SINGING LIKE ARROWS UP TO HEAVEN.  .............WIDOW   164   25
    SCRATCHING AT MY SLEEP LIKE ARROWS,  ....................THREE WOMEN   182  214
    SHRIEK FROM MY BELLY LIKE ARROWS, AND THESE I RIDE.  ......THE OTHER   202   19
    DYNASTY OF BROKEN ARROWS!  ...........................GETTING THERE   248   33
    ARROWS THAT LACERATE THE SKY, WHILE KNOWING  ....LOVE IS A PARALLAX   330   61
ARROWY (1)
    ON ARROWY STEMS,  ................................SOUTHERN SUNRISE     26    8
ARSENIC (1)
    AND THIS IS THE FRUIT OF IT: TIN-WHITE, LIKE ARSENIC.  .........ELM   192   15
ART (4)
    INSTINCT FOR ART BEGAN WITH THE BULL'S HORN LOFTING IN THE MOB'S  ...
                                                   ... THE GORING   47    8
    NOW, SNARED BY THIS MIRACULOUS ART,  ......ON THE PLETHORA OF DRYADS   67   28
    THE ART STUDENTS IN WEST BERLIN.  ..........................ON DECK   143   24
    IS AN ART, LIKE EVERYTHING ELSE.  .....................LADY LAZARUS   245   44
ARTFUL (3)
    SO THE ARTFUL GLASS WON'T CHANGE ITS CHILL FOR HEART'S   DIALOGUE O.   277   17
    WITH A LAST ARTFUL DODGE SHE LEAPS  .....................AERIALIST     332   39
    WHICH ALL THE ARTFUL WIZARDS CANNOT CRIMP  ............THE PRINCESS.   333   17
ARTICULATING (1)
    ARTICULATING SONG.  ............................TRIO OF LOVE SONGS    315   40
ARTIFICE (2)
    IN AN ARTIFICE OF ICE;  .........................NOTES TO A NEOPHYTE  306   15
    FOR MOST EXQUISITE TRUTHS ARE ARTIFICE  ...METAMORPHOSES OF THE MOON  307   25
ARTIFICIAL (2)
    THE ARTIFICIAL RED SAGE DOES NOT STIR  .......ELECTRA ON AZALEA PATH  117   24
    THE WHITE LIGHT IS ARTIFICIAL, AND HYGIENIC AS HEAVEN.  ....SURGEON.   170    1
ARTILLERY (1)
    THE COURAGE OF THE SHUT MOUTH, IN SPITE OF ARTILLERY!  .....COURAGE.  209    1
ART'S (1)
    ART'S SAKE THAN GOD'S. FAR FROM SEA -- *MUSSEL HUNTER AT ROCK HARBOR   97   82
ARTWORK (1)
    DOWN DEEP INTO THE BENT BULL-NECK. CUMBROUS ROUTINE, NOT ARTWORK.  ...
                                                   ... THE GORING   47    7
ARYAN (1)
    AND YOUR ARYAN EYE, BRIGHT BLUE.  ............................DADDY   223   44
AS (400)
    FLOATS CHASTE AS SNOW, TAUNTING THE CLOUDED MIND   WINTER LANDSCAPE,   21    4
    BROODING AS THE WINTER NIGHT COMES ON.  ..........WINTER LANDSCAPE,    21   10
    AS IS YOUR IMAGE IN MY EYE; DRY FROST  ...........WINTER LANDSCAPE,    22   12
    FINE AS HAND-  .......................................SOUTHERN SUNRISE  26    5
    CLEAVES FORWARD INTO FURY; DARK AS ANGER,  .........CHANNEL CROSSING   26    3
    OUR LUGGAGE, AS DOCKS HALT OUR BRIEF EPIC; NO DEBT  CHANNEL CROSSING   27   41
    GRAY AS RATS,  ...........................................PROSPECT     28    4
    LOOKS FIERCE AND BLACK AS ROOKS;  .............THE QUEEN'S COMPLAINT    28    4
    BUT IN SPECKLED THICKETS, WARTED AS A TOAD,  .............FIRESONG     30    3
    TOOK MY HEART AS IF  .......................SONG FOR A SUMMER'S DAY    31   12
    AS SHE CALCULATES EACH SUM.  ..............TWO SISTERS OF PERSEPHONE   31    9
    BRONZED AS EARTH, THE SECOND LIES,  .......TWO SISTERS OF PERSEPHONE   32   13
    AND SALLOW AS ANY LEMON,  ..................TWO SISTERS OF PERSEPHONE  32   25
    THIS WITCH SIDLES, FINGERS CROOKED, AS IF  ................VANITY FAIR  32    2
    RIGHT TO BLAZE AS SATAN'S WIFE;  ..........................VANITY FAIR  33   32
    AS CAN SPARE BREATH  ...................................STRUMPET SONG   34   15
    BRIGHT AS BLOOD.  ..............TINKER JACK AND THE TIDY WIVES         34    9
    AND BLOODIED AS A COW'S SPLIT FRAME  ...................STREET SONG     36    9
    AS A GREENLY ESCAPED IDIOT,  ...........................STREET SONG     36   12
    EVEN AS MY EACH MANGLED NERVE-END  .....................STREET SONG     36   21
    CAUGHT (AS IT WERE) IN THE MUCK-TRAP  ...........LETTER TO A PURIST     37   11
    AS THOUGH ALIVE, SHRIVELING IN TORMENT THUS  ..........DIALOGUE B.      39   35
    TO ATONE AS SHADE FOR SIN THAT LURED BLIND MAN."  .......DIALOGUE B.    39   36
    (WITH HEAT SUCH AS NO MAN COULD HAVE  ..................THE GLUTTON     40    3
    FOOTING SALLOW AS A MOUSE  ...........MISS DRAKE PROCEEDS TO SUPPER     41    9
```

	TITLE	PAGE	LINE

AS (CONT.)
AS LIFT HIM APART ....THE SHRIKE 42 3
KUMQUAT-COLORED TROLLEYS DING AS THEY TRUNDLE .....ALICANTE LULLABY 43 8
WITH SHINGLES BURNISHED AS GLASS, ...DREAM WITH CLAM-DIGGERS 43 7
GRIM AS GARGOYLES FROM YEARS SPENT SQUATTING AT SEA'S BORDER ...
... DREAM WITH CLAM-DIGGERS 44 25
SUCH PACT AS IS MADE ONCE ONLY; WHAT MATTER ....WREATH FOR A BRIDAL 44 2
YOU MIGHT AS WELL HAUL UP ....EPITAPH FOR FIRE AND FLOWER 45 1
IN QUARTZ, AS CRACK YOUR SKULL TO KEEP   EPITAPH FOR FIRE AND FLOWER 45 4
THEIR FOND HEARTS CHARRED AS ANY MATCH. EPITAPH FOR FIRE AND FLOWER 45 7
STILL AS A SHELL: HEAR WHAT AN AGE OF GLASS ....EPITAPH FOR F. 45 16
AS IF TO OUTFLAME A PHOENIX, THE MOMENT'S SPUR ......EPITAPH FOR F. 46 24
EVEN AS LOVE'S DEAR FOOLS CRY EVERGREEN,*EPITAPH FOR FIRE AND FLOWER 46 30
HUSH A LUMPED MAN-SHAPE. THE WHOLE ACT FORMAL, FLUENT AS A DANCE. ...
... THE GORING 47 9
AS A SLEDGE HAMMER, AS A MAN'S BUNCHED FIST, ...SPIDER 48 4
AS A SLEDGE HAMMER, AS A MAN'S BUNCHED FIST, ...SPIDER 48 4
EXACT AS A SNOWFLAKE. ....SPINSTER 50 18
AS NO MERE INSURGENT MAN COULD HOPE TO BREAK ....SPINSTER 50 28
NOW, AS I HONE MY KNIFE, SHE BEGS ....RHYME 50 11
AND SEE THAT FIRST HOUSE, AS IF BETWEEN ....LANDOWNERS 53 6
DEATH AS STRIKING ROOT ON ONE LAND-TRACT; ....LANDOWNERS 53 14
RUM AND RED-FACED AS A WATER-MELON, HER VOICE ....ELLA MASON A. 53 7
WE SNICKERED AS SHE SHAMBLED DOWN SOMERSET TERRACE ...ELLA MASON A. 54 32
ACCURST AS WILD-CATS. ....ELLA MASON AND HER ELEVEN CATS 54 42
PLAGUE-PITTED AS THE MOON: EACH BUD ....CRYSTAL GAZER 56 44
BUT LET SPOTTED LEAVES FALL AS THEY FALL, ...BLACK ROOK I. 57 9
AS IF A CELESTIAL BURNING TOOK ....BLACK ROOK IN RAINY WEATHER 57 17
AS TO SEIZE MY SENSES, HAUL ....BLACK ROOK IN RAINY WEATHER 57 29
SHE STALKED INTRACTABLE AS A DRIVEN GHOST ..THE SNOWMAN ON THE MOOR 58 15
AND, BRIGHT AS BLOOD-DROPS, PROVED NO BRAVE BRANCH DIES ..MAYFLOWER 60 3
NOW, AS GREEN SAP ASCENDS THE STEEPLED WOOD, ...MAYFLOWER 60 5
AS SPRANG FROM JOSEPH'S ROD, AND TESTIFIES ....MAYFLOWER 60 7
PRODIGIOUS IN GLUTTONIES AS THAT HOG WHOSE WANT ....SOW 61 41
BUT THE ECHOES DIED AT HER BACK AS THE WALLS ......HARDCASTLE CRAGS 62 8
TIRELESS, TIED, AS A MOON-BOUND SEA ....HARDCASTLE CRAGS 62 12
KNELT IN THE MEADOW MUTE AS BOULDERS; ....HARDCASTLE CRAGS 63 33
LOOMED ABSOLUTE AS THE ANTIQUE WORLD WAS ....HARDCASTLE CRAGS 63 38
MEAGER OF DIMENSION AS THE GRAY PEOPLE ....THE THIN PEOPLE 64 2
THEMSELVES AS THE DAWN ....THE THIN PEOPLE 65 33
MAKING THE WORLD GO THIN AS A WASP'S NEST ....THE THIN PEOPLE 65 46
SELF-SUFFICIENT AS THEY ARE." ....CONJURING. 66 16
AS NYMPHS; COLD VISION ....CONJURING. 66 30
COOL AS THE PEARLED INTERIOR OF A CONCH. ....THE OTHER TWO 68 2
HEAVY AS STATUARY, SHAPES NOT OURS ....THE OTHER TWO 68 15
THEY POISE AND GRIEVE AS IN SOME OLD TRAGEDY. ....THE OTHER TWO 68 21
AS IF, ABOVE LOVE'S RUINAGE, WE WERE ....THE OTHER TWO 69 34
SHE BLENCHED, AS ONE WHO DROWNS,   THE LADY AND THE EARTHENWARE HEAD 69 21
TO PROVE IT. AS I THINK NOW OF HER HEAD, ...ALL THE DEAD DEARS 70 18
DEADLOCKED WITH THEM, TAKING ROOT AS CRADLES ROCK. ...
... ALL THE DEAD DEARS 71 36
LUCENT AS PORCELAIN, THE EARTH'S ....THE GREAT CARBUNCLE 72 7
AS A FLATFISH, I ....WORDS FOR A NURSERY 74 32
LIKE A SOAP-BUBBLE AS YOU CALLED: COME HERE!   THE DISQUIETING MUSES 76 47
FACES BLANK AS THE DAY I WAS BORN, ...THE DISQUIETING MUSES 76 51
IMAGINE THEIR DEEP HUNGER, DEEP AS THE DARK ....OUIJA 77 8
AS PONDERABLE TOKENS OF HER LOVE. ....OUIJA 77 29
AND AS I LISTENED ITS COLD TEETH SEETHED   ON THE DECLINE OF ORACLES 78 3
AS THE GODS BEGAN ONE WORLD, AND MAN ANOTHER, ...SNAKECHARMER 79 1
AND AS HIS NOTES TWINE GREEN, THE GREEN RIVER .........SNAKECHARMER 79 6
AS OUT OF EDEN'S NAVEL TWIST THE LINES ................SNAKECHARMER 79 19
AS SMACK OF SPITE AND THE OVERSCRUPULOUS ....A LESSON IN VENGEANCE 80 7
NEVER GRIP, AS THEIR GRANDSIRES DID, THAT DEVIL WHO CHUCKLES*LESSON. 80 24
AS YOU ETCH ON THE INNER WINDOW OF YOUR EYE ....VIRGIN IN A TREE 82 34
STIFF AS TWIGS, HER BODY WOODENLY ....VIRGIN IA A TREE 82 39
ARMED WITH FEATHERS TO TICKLE AS WELL AS FLY, ...PERSEUS 83 35
ARMED WITH FEATHERS TO TICKLE AS WELL AS FLY, ...PERSEUS 83 35
A BEDRAGGLED SNAKE, HANGING LIMP AS THE ABSURD MOUTH ....PERSEUS 83 38
AND SINEWS BUNCHED, VICTORIOUS, AS THE COSMIC ....PERSEUS 83 44
HALOES LUSTROUS AS SIRIUS -- ....A WINTER'S TALE 87 11
INTO THE BLUE. TOPS DEFINE THEMSELVES AS PLACES ....ABOVE THE OXBOW 88 29
AS ROSES BROACH THEIR CARMINE IN A MIRROR. FLUX ....ABOVE THE OXBOW 89 44
IRREPROACHABLE AS ANY LETTUCE HEAD, ...MEMOIRS OF A SPINACH-PICKER 89 10
DUNGAREES, PROUD AS A LADY IN A SEA ....MEMOIRS OF A SPINACH-PICKER 90 18
UPRAISED, AS A HAND, EMBLEMATIC OF FAREWELL.*THE GHOST'S LEAVETAKING 90 11
AND MOO AS THEY JUMP OVER MOONS AS NEW .....THE GHOST'S LEAVETAKING 91 37
AND MOO AS THEY JUMP OVER MOONS AS NEW .....THE GHOST'S LEAVETAKING 91 37
AS THAT CRISP CUSP TOWARDS WHICH YOU VOYAGE NOW. ....GHOST'S. 91 38
PALPABLE AS HIS, AND WEIGHTY. ....SCULPTOR 91 4
A DRAGNET, RISING, FALLING, AS WAVES ....FULL FATHOM FIVE 92 5
AS KEELED ICE-MOUNTAINS ....FULL FATHOM FIVE 92 12
DISPLACED THEIR DOMES AS TINY ....MUSSEL HUNTER AT ROCK HARBOR 96 27
AS ITSELF -- NO FIDDLER'S ARM ....MUSSEL HUNTER AT ROCK HARBOR 96 34
AS I COULD BETWEEN BARE TOES? ....MUSSEL HUNTER AT ROCK HARBOR 96 50
ORDER AS I MIGHT PUZZLE ....MUSSEL HUNTER AT ROCK HARBOR 96 55

	TITLE	PAGE	LINE

AS (CONT.)

GRIMACED AS SKULLS GRIMACE: IT ....MUSSEL HUNTER AT ROCK HARBOR	97	78
BUILD UP FROM A ROCK ROOT, AS FOUNTAINS BUILD ....MOONRISE	98	23
AND GOLDENROD AS ON GOLD LEAF. ....IN MIDAS' COUNTRY	99	10
BLACK AS THE CHARRED KNUCKLE-BONES ....CHILD'S PARK STONES	100	5
QUICK AS THEY. TO FOLLOW THE LIGHT'S TINT ......CHILD'S PARK STONES	101	18
WARMING AT CORE ONLY AS ....CHILD'S PARK STONES	101	25
FIRST HORSE UNDER ME, HIGH AS THE ROOFS, ...WHITENESS I REMEMBER	102	13
WE GAVE GOOD USE AS SHIP AND HOUSE IS BLACK*GREEN ROCK, WINTHROP BAY	105	11
TOLERABLE NOW AS MOLES ON THE FACE ....THE COMPANIONABLE ILLS	105	2
DUG IN FIRST AS GOD'S SPURS ....THE COMPANIONABLE ILLS	105	5
CAN ONLY HAUNT. STURDY AS POTATOES, ...POEMS, POTATOES	106	4
STIFF AS A QUEEN ON A PLAYING CARD. ....THE BULL OF BENDYLAW	108	5
BLAMELESS AS DAYLIGHT I STOOD LOOKING ....THE EYE-MOTE	109	1
OUTLANDISH AS DOUBLE-HUMPED CAMELS OR UNICORNS, ...THE EYE-MOTE	109	13
STILLED, SILVERED AS WATER IN A GLASS ....WATERCOLOR.	111	2
AS WOOD AND FORMAL, IN A JACKET OF ASHES, ...A WINTER SHIP	113	8
THE PROSPECT IS DULL AS AN OLD ETCHING. ....A WINTER SHIP	113	13
THEY LOITER AND STARE AS IF THE HOUSE ....AFTERMATH	113	2
BURNT-OUT WERE THEIRS, OR AS IF THEY THOUGHT ....AFTERMATH	113	3
MOVES HUMBLY AS ANY HOUSEWIFE THROUGH ....AFTERMATH	114	10
THEY HAD FOUR MEN LAID OUT, BLACK AS BURNT TURKEY, ...TWO VIEWS.	114	2
HE SMOLDERED, AS IF STONE-DEAF, BLINDFOLD, ...SUICIDE OFF EGG ROCK	115	14
OUTLANDISH AS A CIRCUS, THE RAVAGED FACE ....THE RAVAGED FACE	115	1
AS IF YOU HAD NEVER EXISTED, AS IF I CAME ...ELECTRA ON AZALEA PATH	116	6
AS IF YOU HAD NEVER EXISTED, AS IF I CAME ...ELECTRA ON AZALEA PATH	116	6
SMALL AS A DOLL IN MY DRESS OF INNOCENCE ....ELECTRA ON AZALEA PATH	116	11
THE ANTHERS NOD THEIR HEADS, POTENT AS KINGS ....BEEKEEPER'S.	118	11
IN BURROWS NARROW AS A FINGER, SOLITARY BEES ....BEEKEEPER'S.	118	15
ROUND, GREEN, DISCONSOLATE AS A TEAR. .....THE BEEKEEPER'S DAUGHTER	118	18
BACKBONE UNBENDABLE AS ....THE HERMIT AT OUTERMOST HOUSE	119	11
FRAIL AS ANTIQUE EARTHENWARE ....OLD LADIES' HOME	120	2
DISTANT AND COLD AS PHOTOS, ...OLD LADIES' HOME	120	11
RUST-RED OR GREEN AS LICHENS, ...OLD LADIES' HOME	120	14
THE HOUSES ARE WHITE AS SEA-SALT GOATS LICK FROM THE ROCKS. ..NET-.	121	10
THEY TALK OF BRIDE-LACE, OF LOVERS SPUNKY AS GAMECOCKS. ......NET-.	121	14
AS IF IT WERE SUMMER STILL. ....MAGNOLIA SHOALS	121	4
THE LATE MONTH WITHERS, AS WELL. ....MAGNOLIA SHOALS	122	12
MUSSELS CLUSTER BLUE AS GRAPES: ....MAGNOLIA SHOALS	122	17
THEY LIE AS IF UNDER WATER ....THE SLEEPERS	122	4
AMONG PETALS PALE AS DEATH ....THE SLEEPERS	123	13
WOOD STOVES BURN WARM AS TOAST. ....YADDO: THE GRAND MANOR	124	17
INERT AS A SHOELACE; DEAD ....MEDALLION	124	4
AS I TURNED HIM IN THE LIGHT; ....MEDALLION	124	11
THIN AS PINS IN THE DARK BRUISE ....MEDALLION	125	22
WHERE HIS INNARDS BULGED AS IF ....MEDALLION	125	23
SHAPELESS AS FLUNG GLOVES, A FEW FEET APART -- ....BLUE MOLES	126	3
THE MOLES LOOK NEUTRAL AS THE STONES. ....BLUE MOLES	126	14
OF FINAL SURFEIT IS JUST AS FAR ....BLUE MOLES	127	33
FROM THE DOOR AS EVER. WHAT HAPPENS BETWEEN US ....BLUE MOLES	127	34
EASY AND OFTEN AS EACH BREATH. ....BLUE MOLES	127	36
FLAT AS PAPER AND ....POLLY'S TREE	128	8
VAPORISH AS FROST-BREATH, ...POLLY'S TREE	128	10
AS THE HALO ....POLLY'S TREE	128	18
WHOLE AS A COBWEB, ...POLLY'S TREE	129	35
YOU ARE PITHY AND HISTORICAL AS THE ROMAN FORUM. ......THE COLOSSUS	129	18
FLEX AS THE MUD FREEZES. ....PRIVATE GROUND	131	21
THIS SHED'S FUSTY AS A MUMMY'S STOMACH: ....POEM.1.WHO.	131	4
THEIR VEINS WHITE AS PORKFAT. ....POEM.1.WHO.	131	18
I AM ROUND AS AN OWL, ...POEM.2.DARK.	132	10
FOOTLINGS, BONELESS AS NOSES, ...POEM.2.DARK.	133	25
THE BEAN LEAVES ARE DUMB AS HANDS. ....POEM.3.MAENAD.	133	10
AND HOW A GOD FLIMSY AS A BABY'S FINGER ....POEM.5.F.	135	19
SITTING UNDER A POTLID, TINY AND INERT AS A RICE GRAIN. ..POEM.6.W.	135	15
DRUNK AS A FOETUS ....POEM.7.S.	136	17
MY SWADDLED LEGS AND ARMS SMELL SWEET AS RUBBER. ....POEM.7.S.	137	34
I SHALL BE GOOD AS NEW. ....POEM.7.S.	137	45
AS RESIN DROPS OOZED FROM PINE BARK. ....THE BURNT-OUT SPA	137	5
PROCEEDS CLEAR AS IT EVER DID ....THE BURNT-OUT SPA	138	20
TRAWLING YOUR DARK AS OWLS DO. ....YOU'RE	141	6
MUTE AS A TURNIP FROM THE FOURTH ....YOU'RE	141	7
VAGUE AS FOG AND LOOKED FOR LIKE MAIL. ....YOU'RE	141	10
SNUG AS A BUD AND AT HOME ....YOU'RE	141	13
JUMPY AS A MEXICAN BEAN. ....YOU'RE	141	16
WRAPPED UP IN THEMSELVES AS IN THICK VEILING ....ON DECK	142	2
AND MUTE AS MANNEQUINS IN A DRESS SHOP, ...ON DECK	142	3
ON HIM HAND AND FOOT, QUIET AS A DIAMOND. ....ON DECK	143	33
YET THEY RECEDE, UNTOUCHABLE AS TOMORROW,*SLEEP IN THE MOJAVE DESERT	144	11
THE DESERT IS WHITE AS A BLIND MAN'S EYE,*SLEEP IN THE MOJAVE DESERT	144	17
COMFORTLESS AS SALT. SNAKE AND BIRD .....SLEEP IN THE MOJAVE DESERT	144	18
THE HORIZONS ARE TOO FAR OFF TO BE CHUMMY AS UNCLES; .....TWO CAMP.	145	14
I LEAN TO YOU, NUMB AS A FOSSIL. TELL ME I'M HERE. ....TWO CAMP.	145	21
SLEEPILY AS LETHE, TRYING TO GET IN. ..TWO CAMPERS IN CLOUD COUNTRY	145	26
WE'LL WAKE BLANK-BRAINED AS WATER IN THE DAWN. ....TWO CAMP.	145	27
ME, SITTING HERE BORED AS A LEOPARD ....LEAVING EARLY	145	3

AS (CONT.)

MUSKY AS A LOVEBED THE MORNING AFTER. ....LEAVING EARLY   146   19
THEY TOE OLD WATER THICK AS FOG. ....LEAVING EARLY   146   22
MAGENTA AS THIS FUBSY SOFA. ....LEAVING EARLY   146   33
MASKED AMONG BLACK ROCKS AS A BLACK ROCK ....LOVE LETTER   147   10
LIMPID AS SPIRITS. MANY STONES LAY ....LOVE LETTER   147   22
MY FINGER-LENGTH GREW LUCENT AS GLASS. ....LOVE LETTER   147   30
PURE AS A PANE OF ICE. IT'S A GIFT. ....LOVE LETTER   147   36
NOTHING SO VULGAR AS A NOSE OR AN EYE ....MAGI   148   2
SALUTARY AND PURE AS BOILED WATER, ...MAGI   148   7
LOVELESS AS THE MULTIPLICATION TABLE. ....MAGI   148   8
AS A SCHOOL GIRL SHE GAVE ROSES TO FRANZ JOSEF. ....CANDLES   149   18
THESE LITTLE GLOBES OF LIGHT ARE SWEET AS PEARS. ....CANDLES   149   24
AS THESE DRAUGHTY EPHEMERIDS. ....CANDLES   149   30
THIS EGG-SHAPED BAILIWICK, CLEAR AS A TEAR. ....A LIFE   149   2
PALM-SPEAR AND LILY DISTINCT AS FLORA IN THE VAST ....A LIFE   149   4
THE INHABITANTS ARE LIGHT AS CORK, ...A LIFE   150   9
AS VICTORIAN CUSHIONS. THIS FAMILY ....A LIFE   150   16
FACELESS AND PALE AS CHINA ....PARLIAMENT HILL FIELDS   152   2
THIN AS THE SKIN SEAMING A SCAR. ....PARLIAMENT HILL FIELDS   153   39
AS IF IN HOSPITAL. ....WHITSUN   154   12
GREEN AS A POOL TABLE, WHERE CABBAGE BUTTERFLIES ....WHITSUN   154   19
PEEL OFF TO SEA AS GULLS DO, ...WHITSUN   154   20
COLD AS AN EEL, WITHOUT EYELIDS. ....ZOO KEEPER'S WIFE   154   2
OBSCENE AND BALD AS A PIG, THE WHITE MICE ....ZOO KEEPER'S WIFE   155   21
DIRTY AS A BOOTSOLE AND BIG AS A HOSPITAL SINK ...ZOO KEEPER'S WIFE   155   35
DIRTY AS A BOOTSOLE AND BIG AS A HOSPITAL SINK ...ZOO KEEPER'S WIFE   155   35
NUDE AS CLEOPATRA IN MY WELL-BOILED HOSPITAL SHIFT, ...FACE LIFT   156   10
SKIN DOESN'T HAVE ROOTS, IT PEELS AWAY EASY AS PAPER. ....FACE LIFT   156   20
PINK AND SMOOTH AS A BABY. ....FACE LIFT   156   32
SHADOWS OUR SAFETY. WE STAND ROUND BLANKLY AS WALLS. ..MORNING SONG   157   6
YOUR MOUTH OPENS CLEAN AS A CAT'S. THE WINDOW SQUARE ..MORNING SONG   157   15
BLANK-FACED AND MUM AS A NURSE. ....BARREN WOMAN   157   10
AS VENUS, PEDESTALED ON A HALF-SHELL ....HEAVY WOMEN   158   2
FLOATS CALM AS A MOON OR A CLOUD. ....HEAVY WOMEN   158   7
DEVOUTLY AS THE DUTCH BULB ....HEAVY WOMEN   158   9
I GAVE HER A SOUL, I BLOOMED OUT OF HER AS A ROSE ....IN PLASTER   159   16
NOT HER WHITENESS AND BEAUTY, AS I HAD AT FIRST SUPPOSED.*IN PLASTER   159   19
AS IF MY HABITS OFFENDED HER IN SOME WAY. ....IN PLASTER   159   31
AS THE LIGHT LIES ON THESE WHITE WALLS, THIS BED, THESE HANDS. ...
                                                      ... TULIPS   160   4
DOING THINGS WITH THEIR HANDS, ONE JUST THE SAME AS ANOTHER, *TULIPS   160   13
MY BODY IS A PEBBLE TO THEM, THEY TEND IT AS WATER ....TULIPS   160   15
AND COMES FROM A COUNTRY FAR AWAY AS HEALTH. ....TULIPS   162   63
HIS FOREHEAD IS BUMPY AS A SACK OF ROCKS. ....INSOMNIAC   163   13
ARE RIDING TO WORK IN ROWS, AS IF RECENTLY BRAINWASHED. ..INSOMNIAC   163   35
ONE SOUL PASS THROUGH THE OTHER, FRAIL AS SMOKE ....WIDOW   165   34
STARS ARE DROPPING THICK AS STONES INTO THE TWIGGY ....STARS.   165   1
THEY ARE SCRUBBED AND SELF-ASSURED AS THE GREAT PLANETS. ...STARS.   165   16
SPITEFUL AS A WOMAN, BUT NOT SO NERVOUS, ...THE RIVAL   166   9
WHITE AND BLANK, EXPANSIVE AS CARBON MONOXIDE. ....THE RIVAL   166   15
LIKE A SERIES OF PROMISES, AS I STEP FORWARD. ....WUTHERING HEIGHTS   167   9
GRAY AS THE WEATHER. ....WUTHERING HEIGHTS   167   21
LIMPID AS THE SOLITUDES ....WUTHERING HEIGHTS   167   29
AND BLACK AS PURSES, THE HOUSE LIGHTS ....WUTHERING HEIGHTS   168   44
BIG AS THE BALL OF MY THUMB, AND DUMB AS EYES ........BLACKBERRYING   168   5
BIG AS THE BALL OF MY THUMB, AND DUMB AS EYES ........BLACKBERRYING   168   5
THE HIGH, GREEN MEADOWS ARE GLOWING, AS IF LIT FROM WITHIN. ...
                                                 ... BLACKBERRYING   168   14
SUCH AS FINGERS MIGHT EMBROIDER, CLOSE TO DEATH, ...FINISTERRE   169   11
THE WHITE LIGHT IS ARTIFICIAL, AND HYGIENIC AS HEAVEN. ...SURGEON.   170   1
AS USUAL THERE IS NO FACE. A LUMP OF CHINESE WHITE ....SURGEON.   170   7
ROUND AS THE MOON, TO STARE UP. ....LAST WORDS   172   3
THE GRASSES UNLOAD THEIR GRIEFS ON MY FEET AS IF I WERE GOD, MOON.   172   3
WHITE AS A KNUCKLE AND TERRIBLY UPSET. ...THE MOON AND THE YEW TREE   173   9
JUST AS IT IS, UNMISTED BY LOVE OR DISLIKE. ....MIRROR   173   3
STOPPED AND AWFUL AS A PHOTOGRAPH OF SOMEBODY LAUGHING. .....BABY.   175   35
THE BOLD GULLS DOVE AS IF THEY OWNED IT ALL. ....THE BABYSITTERS   175   37
I AM SLOW AS THE WORLD. I AM VERY PATIENT, ...THREE WOMEN   176   1
SHE PASSES AND REPASSES, LUMINOUS AS A NURSE. ....THREE WOMEN   176   5
I AM DYING AS I SIT. I LOSE A DIMENSION. ....THREE WOMEN   177   30
AS A CHILD I LOVED A LICHEN-BITTEN NAME. ....THREE WOMEN   177   41
WENT ON SHAPING ITSELF WITH LOVE, AS IF I WAS READY. ...THREE WOMEN   178   63
THE DOCTORS MOVE AMONG US AS IF OUR BIGNESS ....THREE WOMEN   179 114
AND WHAT IF THEY FOUND THEMSELVES SURPRISED, AS I DID? THREE WOMEN   180 118
SHINY AND STRANGE, AS IF HE HAD HURTLED FROM A STAR? ...THREE WOMEN   181 163
THEY ARE STITCHING ME UP WITH SILK, AS IF I WERE A MATERIAL. *THREE.   181 168
AND SOFT AS A MOTH, HIS BREATH. ....THREE WOMEN   181 173
I AM HELPLESS AS THE SEA AT THE END OF HER STRING. ......THREE WOMEN   182 188
I SEE MYSELF AS A SHADOW, NEITHER MAN NOR WOMAN, ...THREE WOMEN   182 191
I AM BEAUTIFUL AS A STATISTIC. HERE IS MY LIPSTICK. ...THREE WOMEN   183 245
AS IF I HAD LOST AN EYE, A LEG, A TONGUE. ....THREE WOMEN   183 252
AWAY ON WHEELS, INSTEAD OF LEGS, THEY SERVE AS WELL. ...THREE WOMEN   184 254
AS PRODIGAL IN WHAT LACKS ME. ....THREE WOMEN   184 259
I AM BLED WHITE AS WAX, I HAVE NO ATTACHMENTS. ....THREE WOMEN   184 275

```
                                                        TITLE           PAGE  LINE
AS (CONT.)
  TO BE SO OPEN: IT IS AS IF MY HEART  ....................THREE WOMEN   185  300
  TO LOVE ME AS I LOVE HIM,  .......................THREE WOMEN         186  335
  THEY ARE BLACK AND FLAT AS SHADOWS.  .....................THREE WOMEN 186  340
  I AM SOLITARY AS GRASS. WHAT IS IT I MISS?  .............THREE WOMEN   186  342
  I AM YOUNG AS EVER, IT SAYS. WHAT IS IT I MISS?  ........THREE WOMEN   186  350
  WITH PINKNESS, AS IF A TENDERNESS AWOKE,  ...............THREE WOMEN   186  356
  SAFE ON THE MATTRESS, HANDS BRACED, AS FOR A FALL.  .....THREE WOMEN   187  367
  WHITE AS AN EYE ALL OVER!  ............................LITTLE FUGUE    187    7
  EMPTY AND SILLY AS PLATES,  ...........................LITTLE FUGUE    188   17
  BLACK AND LEAFY, AS IN MY CHILDHOOD,  .................LITTLE FUGUE    188   24
  IS IT NOT AS TORTURED?  ...............................LITTLE FUGUE    188   30
  SPRY, WRY, AND GRAY AS THESE MARCH STICKS,  ......AMONG THE NARCISSI   190    1
  THE FLOWERS VIVID AS BANDAGES, AND THE MAN MENDING.  ......NARCISSI.   190    8
  AS IF I THOUGHT IT HAD A SPIRIT.  .........................PHEASANT    191    8
  IT UNCLAPS, BROWN AS A LEAF, AND LOUD,  ...................PHEASANT    191   21
  DIMINISHED AND FLAT, AS AFTER RADICAL SURGERY.  ................ELM    192   26
  AND A WEED, HAIRY AS PRIVATES.  .......................BERCK-PLAGE     197   36
  AS THE PALLORS GATHER ---  ............................BERCK-PLAGE     199   84
  THICK AS FOREIGN COFFEE, AND WITH A SLUGGY PULSE.  .....WORDS HEARD.   202    2
  INVOLVED AS A FOETUS.  .........................BURNING THE LETTERS    205   41
  WHITE AS BABIES' BEDDING AND GLITTERING WITH DEAD BREATH. O IVORY!  ...
                                        ... A BIRTHDAY PRESENT          206   18
  IT STANDS AT MY WINDOW, BIG AS THE SKY.  ..........A BIRTHDAY PRESENT  207   49
  PURE AND CLEAN AS THE CRY OF A BABY,  .............A BIRTHDAY PRESENT  208   61
  THE MILK CAME YELLOW, THEN BLUE AND SWEET AS WATER.  ..THE DETECTIVE   209   33
  LOADED, AS THEY ARE, WITH ACCOUNTS OF BASTARDIES.  ........COURAGE.    210    6
  I AM NUDE AS A CHICKEN NECK, DOES NOBODY LOVE ME?  ..THE BEE MEETING   211    6
  THE WHITE HIVE IS SNUG AS A VIRGIN,  ...................THE BEE MEETING 212   34
  SQUARE AS A CHAIR AND ALMOST TOO HEAVY TO LIFT.  ........THE ARRIVAL.  212    2
  BROOD CELLS GRAY AS THE FOSSILS OF SHELLS  ...................STINGS   214   12
  AS THE MOON, FOR ITS IVORY POWDERS, SCOURS THE SEA.  .........STINGS   215   37
  STINGS BIG AS DRAWING PINS!  ..............................THE SWARM   217   56
  NAKED AS PAPER TO START  ...............................THE APPLICANT  221   30
  BIG AS A FRISCO SEAL  ........................................DADDY    222   10
  GREEN AS EUNUCHS, YOUR WISHES  ...........................MEDUSA       226   38
  IMPOTENT AS DISTANT THUNDER,  ..........................THE JAILER     227   37
  YOU ARE SUNK IN YOUR SEVEN CHINS, STILL AS A HAM.  .....STOPPED DEAD   230   16
  ARE DULL, DULL AS THE TRIPLE  ...............................FEVER.    231    3
  THE SHEETS GROW HEAVY AS A LECHER'S KISS.  ..................FEVER.    231   30
  HURTS ME AS THE WORLD HURTS GOD. I AM A LANTERN ---  .......FEVER.     232   36
  KNEELS, BACK BENT, AS BEST HE CAN  ...................BY CANDLELIGHT   237   27
  OFF AND ON, AS IF I JUST HAD TO RETCH.  ...................THE TOUR    238   25
  AND RETURNED THEM STEAMED AND PRESSED AND STIFF AS SHIRTS. *THE TOUR   238   34
  BRIGHT AS A NAZI LAMPSHADE,  ...........................LADY LAZARUS   244    5
  AS A SEASHELL.  .......................................LADY LAZARUS    245   40
  PURE AS A BABY.  ......................................GETTING THERE   249   68
  AND A LITTLE FLAT, AS IF THEY  ............................GULLIVER    251    3
  THEY ENTER AS ANIMALS FROM THE OUTER  ........................YEARS    255    1
  UNGODLY AS A CHILD'S SHRIEK.  ......................CHILDLESS WOMAN     259   10
  COLD AS SNOW BREATH, IT TAMPS THE WOMB  .....THE MUNICH MANNEQUINS     262    2
  AS FLAT AS SHE, WHO WHISPER "WE'RE YOUR DAUGHTERS."  ....PARALYTIC     266   26
  AS FLAT AS SHE, WHO WHISPER "WE'RE YOUR DAUGHTERS."  ......PARALYTIC   266   26
  GLITTERING AND DRUNK AS FLIES  .............................MYSTIC     268    3
  WHAT IS SO REAL AS THE CRY OF A CHILD?  ...................KINDNESS    269    6
  CONTEMPLATING A WORLD CLEAR AS WATER.  ...................BALLOONS     272   28
  THEM BACK INTO HER BODY AS PETALS  ...........................EDGE     273   13
  WITH WINTER AS YOU CLAIM IT DOES. THE COAL  ...........DIALOGUE O.     277   19
  AND BACK TO P, AS IF HE KNEW US WELL  ...DIALOGUE OVER A OUIJA BOARD   277   30
  AT FAME OR NOT? AS FOR LOVE, I FIGURE WHEN WE'RE  .......DIALOGUE O.   278   57
  THE GLASS YET AS HE GLIDES. P-L-U-  .....DIALOGUE OVER A OUIJA BOARD   278   77
  AS IF THE AIR WERE LABORING TO PRODUCE   DIALOGUE OVER A OUIJA BOARD   279   89
  AS HE STOLE OUR PERPLEXITIES ABOUT THE POOLS  ...........DIALOGUE O.   279  103
  PALMED OFF OUR OWN HUNCHES AS ORACLES.   DIALOGUE OVER A OUIJA BOARD   279  105
  SELVES POSING AS PROPHET AND SLYLY POACHING  ...........DIALOGUE O.    280  134
  PAN AS IF HE WERE OUR FIRST-BREACHED BRAT  .............DIALOGUE O.    280  138
  MINOR IMPS PIPE UP, SO LONG AS EACH  ...DIALOGUE OVER A OUIJA BOARD    280  152
  AS IF TEMPTING OUR GROSS GULLIBILITY  ...DIALOGUE OVER A OUIJA BOARD   281  178
  EATING YOUR WORDS: YOU'LL REVOKE HIS GODHOOD SOON AS  ...DIALOGUE O.   281  189
  MIGHT DO AS A GOD'S MOUTHPIECE IF A WHIRLWIND  .........DIALOGUE O.    281  202
  AND NOT EXTINCT, AS EVERYONE SUPPOSED.   DIALOGUE OVER A OUIJA BOARD   283  247
  PAN AS OUR EVENING GUEST IF HE'S SO FREE*DIALOGUE OVER A OUIJA BOARD   283  252
  WILL BE OUR BEAT, JUST AS THE GIFT IS OURS,  ...........DIALOGUE O.    283  257
  AND TONGUE, AND THOUGHT, AS WELL AS THE BLOOD-HEAT  ....DIALOGUE O.    283  258
  AND TONGUE, AND THOUGHT, AS WELL AS THE BLOOD-HEAT  ....DIALOGUE O.    283  258
  OTHER THAN YOUR OWN. AS HE BORES YOU  ...DIALOGUE OVER A OUIJA BOARD   283  261
  YOU INHABIT. PLAINLY AS YOU CAN,  ........DIALOGUE OVER A OUIJA BOARD  283  273
  AS IF BLOODHOUNDS BORE HIM DOWN. I-N-C-O . . .  ........DIALOGUE O.    283  275
  SOME LIGHT. I GLIMPSE NO LIGHT AT ALL AS LONG  .........DIALOGUE O.    284  290
  AS WE TWO GLOWER FROM OUR SEPARATE CAMPS,  .............DIALOGUE O.    284  291
  AS A BAD JOB. WAIT. HE STIRS. HE ROMPS  *DIALOGUE OVER A OUIJA BOARD   284  293
  AS IF I'D HALF-BELIEVED IN HIM, AND HE, *DIALOGUE OVER A OUIJA BOARD   285  307
  DEEPER WITHIN THE DARK, AND AS I PITCHED FURTHER  ......DIALOGUE O.    285  317
  AS THE GLASS FLEW TO ITS FRAGMENTS. LET US STAKE  ......DIALOGUE O.    285  328
  AS IS THE USE WITH VAMPIRES, AND RESIGN OUR STAND  .....DIALOGUE O.    285  330
```

29

AS (CONT.)
   WHY, YOUR HAND'S COLD AS ICE! THEN CHAFE THE COLD ......DIALOGUE O. 285 333
   BLUE AS LIZARD-SCALES. FROST SHEENS THE STREET. ....DIALOGUE O. 286 340
   THE TABLE LOOKS AS IF IT WOULD STAY A TABLE ....DIALOGUE O. 286 353
   AS SURE AS THOSE COALS BURN, THE LIVINGROOM ....DIALOGUE O. 286 357
   AS SURE AS THOSE COALS BURN, THE LIVINGROOM ....DIALOGUE O. 286 357
   COMPARED TO YOU, I AM CORRUPTIBLE AS A LOAF OF BREAD.   THE RIVAL/DR 291   1
   THEIR MAGNIFIED HEADS AND PLAN TO KILL ME AS SOON AS POSSIBLE. ...
                                              ... THE RIVAL/DR 291   3
   THEIR MAGNIFIED HEADS AND PLAN TO KILL ME AS SOON AS POSSIBLE. ...
                                              ... THE RIVAL/DR 291   3
   AS A DESK DRAWER HIDES A POISON PEN LETTER, ...THE RIVAL/DR 291   9
   AND LET THE DEAD SLEEP AS THEY DESERVE. ....THE RIVAL/DR 291   28
   OF COOL MOUTHS AND HANDS OPEN AND NATURAL AS ROSES. ......FEVER./DR 294   10
   WHILE ROUGH AS SPLINTERED WOOD ....FAMILY REUNION 300   20
   ABSORBENT AS A SPONGE; ....FAMILY REUNION 301   28
   SUCH AS PREGNANCY OR CONSTIPATION ....APRIL 18 301   5
   INFREQUENT AS A MOON OF GREENCHEESE ....APRIL 18 302   8
   NOURISHING AS VIOLET LEAVES ....APRIL 18 302   10
   AS EASILY AND IRRETRIEVABLY ....APRIL 18 302   15
   AS A TENNIS BALL AT TWILIGHT ....APRIL 18 302   16
   OF SILVER AS THE RONDO SLOWS; NOW REELS ....CINDERELLA 303   3
   AS AMID THE HECTIC MUSIC AND COCKTAIL TALK ....CINDERELLA 304   13
   BLUNT AS THE FACELESS GUT ....NOTES TO A NEOPHYTE 306   2
   VERNACULAR AS THE STRUT ....NOTES TO A NEOPHYTE 306   4
   AS THEY SHOT PAST THE FORTY-NINTH FLOOR ....DIALOGUE EN ROUTE 308   4
   FAST AS A FALLIBLE FALCON. ....DIALOGUE EN ROUTE 308   6
   AS THE WORLD SWIVELED ROUND IN ITS ORBIT ....DIALOGUE EN ROUTE 309   38
   INCANDESCENT AS A GOD; ....TO A JILTED LOVER 310   15
   AGILE AS A STAR ....TRIO OF LOVE SONGS 314   19
   NIMBLE AS A NOUN, ...TRIO OF LOVE SONGS 314   29
   AS THE DOOMSTRUCK CITY CRUMBLES BLOCK BY BLOCK: ....DOOMSDAY 316   8
   AS THEIR GOLDEN JAILER ....MOONSONG AT MORNING 317   27
   FROM HERE THE MOON SEEMS SMOOTH AS ANGEL-FOOD, ...ADMONITIONS 319   7
   COUCHED IN CAULS OF CLAY AS IN HOLY ROBES, ...THE DEAD 320   2
   DARING AS DEATH AND DEBONAIR ....CIRCUS IN THREE RINGS 321   7
   MOCKING AS MEPHISTOPHELES, ...CIRCUS IN THREE RINGS 322   13
   GROWS BRITTLE AS A TILTED CHINA BOWL; ....PROLOGUE TO SPRING 322   5
   YET AS WE WONDER WHAT CAN COME OF ICE ....PROLOGUE TO SPRING 322   14
   HORIZONS BEAT A RETREAT AS WE EMBARK ....LOVE IS A PARALLAX 329   4
   ONLY TO REOPEN AS FLESH CONGEALS: ....LOVE IS A PARALLAX 330   65
   SURRENDER: TO BUILD OUR BED AS HIGH AS JACK'S ...LOVE IS A PARALLAX 330   70
   SURRENDER: TO BUILD OUR BED AS HIGH AS JACK'S ...LOVE IS A PARALLAX 330   70
   SHREDDED FINE AS SNOWFLAKES ....AERIALIST 331   3
   AS GREAT WEIGHTS DROP ALL ABOUT HER ....AERIALIST 331   17
   AS THE LOUD ALARMCLOCK STRIKES. ....AERIALIST 332   42
   NOW AS PENALTY FOR HER SKILL, ...AERIALIST 332   43
   THE THIRD CRIES OUT AS ALL THE SHIPS GO DOWN:*EPITAPH IN THREE PARTS 337   10
ASBESTOS (1)
   BUT ASBESTOS RECEPTACLES. ....THE SWARM 217   54
ASCEND (1)
   TO LEAVE HER BED OF FEVER AND ASCEND ..THE PRINCESS AND THE GOBLINS 333   4
ASCENDED (1)
   FROM STONE TO CLOUD, SO I ASCENDED. ....LOVE LETTER 147   33
ASCENDS (3)
   NOW, AS GREEN SAP ASCENDS THE STEEPLED WOOD, ...MAYFLOWER   60   5
   MY ANKLES BRIGHTEN. BRIGHTNESS ASCENDS MY THIGHS. POEM.6.W. 136   23
   AND SAP ASCENDS THE STEEPLE OF THE VEIN. ....APRIL AUBADE 312   4
ASH (8)
   THE GUTTED FOREST FALLS TO ASH; ....PURSUIT   23   42
   BLOWS ASH IN EACH LOVER'S EYE; THE ARDENT LOOK ......EPITAPH FOR F.   46   34
   AND THE TONGUE, SAPPHIRE OF ASH. ....BERCH-PLAGE 198   54
   LIKE HIROSHIMA ASH AND EATING IN. ....FEVER. 231   26
   ASH, ASH -- ....LADY LAZARUS 246   73
   ASH, ASH -- ....LADY LAZARUS 246   73
   OUT OF THE ASH ....LADY LAZARUS 247   82
   MOUTH-ASH, ASH OF EYE. ....MARY'S SONG 257   14
ASHAMED (1)
   DO NOT BE ASHAMED -- I DO NOT MIND IF IT IS SMALL. ....BIRTHDAY. 206   22
ASHEN (2)
   SOUTHWARD, OVER KENTISH TOWN, AN ASHEN SMUDGE*PARLIAMENT HILL FIELDS 152   21
   AND YOU, SHACKLED ASHEN ACROSS THE RIFT, A SPECTER .....DIALOGUE O. 285 321
ASHES (1)
   AS WOOD AND FORMAL, IN A JACKET OF ASHES, ...A WINTER SHIP 113   8
ASH-HEAP (1)
   GLOWERING SULLEN AND POMPOUS FROM AN ASH-HEAP, ...LADY AND T.   69   11
ASIDE (8)
   BUT, HEAVY-FOOTED, STOOD ASIDE ....THE DISQUIETING MUSES   75   29
   PALMING THE EARTH ASIDE, GRUBBERS ....BLUE MOLES 126   24
   THEY ARE DEPARTING IN THEIR TRANSPARENT GARMENTS, TURNED ASIDE ...
                                       ... THE SURGEON AT 2 A.M. 170   3
   ASIDE WERE DRAGGING ME IN FOUR DIRECTIONS. ....THREE WOMEN 178   58
   I WILL ONLY TAKE IT AND GO ASIDE QUIETLY. ....A BIRTHDAY PRESENT 207   33
   POOLS ASIDE, WILLS ASIDE, DO WE ....DIALOGUE OVER A OUIJA BOARD 278   53

ASIDE (CONT.)
     POOLS ASIDE, WILLS ASIDE, DO WE ....DIALOGUE OVER A OUIJA BOARD 278   53
     CASTLES WHEN WE GLANCE ASIDE. THAT'S THAT.   ....DIALOGUE O. 286 356
ASININITY (1)
     BLACK ASININITY. DECAY.   ....WINTERING 218   17
ASK (8)
     "I DON'T ASK YOU TO SPIN SOME RIDICULOUS FABLE ....DIALOGUE B.   39   22
     THE DISKS REVOLVE, THEY ASK TO BE HEARD -- ....COURAGE. 209   5
     YOU TO ASK WHO'S HOME, OR I? I WILL.   ...DIALOGUE OVER A OUIJA BOARD 277   25
     ME. ASK, ANYHOW. I ADMIT IT: I'M AFRAID,*DIALOGUE OVER A OUIJA BOARD 278   67
     THE STINT OF SISYPHUS. ASK PAN, THEN, WHERE ....DIALOGUE O. 281 173
     I'LL ASK. DO. WE'VE KEPT HIM WAITING LONG ....DIALOGUE O. 281 180
     IS SMALL THESE DAYS. DON'T BE SO SMART. I'LL ASK, ...DIALOGUE O. 281 204
     TOO LATE TO ASK IF END WAS WORTH THE MEANS, ...DOOMSDAY 316   16
ASKED (3)
     "WHAT LOVE," ASKED FATHER SHAWN, "BUT TOO GREAT LOVE ...DIALOGUE B.   39   31
     I HAD NOT ASKED FOR SUCH A BLOOD SISTERHOOD; THEY MUST LOVE ME. ...
                                              ... BLACKBERRYING 168   8
     BUSINESSLIKE SHE ASKED US, "HOW MANY QUARTS?" ..BITTER STRAWBERRIES 300   31
ASKEW (4)
     ASKEW WITH BLOTCH, DINT, SCAR ....STRUMPET SONG   33   12
     WITH BIRD-QUICK EYE COCKED ASKEW .....MISS DRAKE PROCEEDS TO SUPPER   41   14
     ASKEW, SHE'LL ACHE AND WAKE ....VIRGIN IN A TREE   82   40
     YOUR SPECKLED STONE ASKEW BY AN IRON FENCE.   ELECTRA ON AZALEA PATH 117   18
ASKING (4)
     BLAND-MANNERED, ASKING ....MUSHROOMS 139   21
     ASKING ABOUT MONEY? I'M SICK OF THAT. ..DIALOGUE OVER A OUIJA BOARD 277   50
     FEED YOUR OWN WISHFUL THINKING. TRY ASKING HIM ....DIALOGUE O. 283 268
     FROM ASKING, BUT INVENTIVE, HOPES; IN VAIN*METAMORPHOSES OF THE MOON 307   11
ASKS (3)
     "NO HARDSHIP THEN?" HE ASKS. "WE'LL TAKE ....CRYSTAL GAZER   55   19
     AND IT ASKS NOTHING, A NAME TAG, A FEW TRINKETS. ....TULIPS 161   33
     ASKS NOTHING OF LIFE.   ....PARALYTIC 267   40
ASLANT (1)
     ASLANT: THEIR HILL OF STINGING NETTLE; ....BUCOLICS   24   10
ASLEEP (1)
     SHE IS A SMALL ISLAND, ASLEEP AND PEACEFUL, ...THREE WOMEN 184 260
ASP (1)
     AND EVERY PRIVATE TWINGE A HISSING ASP ....PERSEUS   83   20
ASPARAGUS (1)
     OF ASPARAGUS HEADS. CARS RUN THEIR SUAVE ....ABOVE THE OXBOW   89   50
ASPIC (1)
     BUT OUT OF THE WATERY ASPIC, LAURELED BY FINS, ...LADY AND T.   69   18
ASSAIL (1)
     STENCHES AND COLORS ASSAIL ME.   ....THE SURGEON AT 2 A.M. 170   14
ASSAILANT (2)
     FOR BEING SUCH A RUDE ASSAILANT ....THE DREAM 311   16
     FOR YOUR FATE INVOLVES A DARK ASSAILANT." ...EPITAPH IN THREE PARTS 337   9
ASSAILED (1)
     BUZZED AND ASSAILED THE VAULTED BRAINCHAMBER.   SUICIDE OFF EGG ROCK 115   18
ASSAILING (1)
     THEY ARE ASSAILING YOUR BRAIN LIKE NUMERALS, ...STINGS/DR 293   4
ASSASSINS (1)
     PARCELED OUT BY WHITE-JACKETED ASSASSINS.   ....STREET SONG   36   10
ASSAULT (7)
     FROM SUCH ASSAULT OF RADIANCE.   ....PURSUIT   23   44
     ASSAULT OF SNOW-FLAWED WINDS FROM THE DOUR SKIES ....MAYFLOWER   60   2
     PITYS FROM PAN'S ASSAULT! AND THOUGH AGE DROP .....VIRGIN IN A TREE   81   17
     IF YOU ASSAULT A FISH ....TRIO OF LOVE SONGS 315   45
     ASSAULT A SLEEPING VIRGIN'S SHROUD ....DANSE MACABRE 321   14
     TO ASSAULT THE SCENE AND MAKE SOME *MORNING IN THE HOSPITAL SOLARIUM 333   24
     AN ACCURATE ASSAULT UPON THE EYES ....EPITAPH IN THREE PARTS 337   14
ASSAULTING (2)
     WAVES WALLOP, ASSAULTING THE STUBBORN HULL.   ....CHANNEL CROSSING   26   4
     THEY LIE, CUT-GRASS ASSAULTING EACH SEPARATE SENSE ....WREATH F.   44   8
ASSAULTS (3)
     SUCH POVERTY ASSAULTS THE EGO; CAUGHT ....TALE OF A TUB   24   4
     THE ENVIOUS ASSAULTS OF SEA ....LETTER TO A PURIST   36   3
     ASSAULTS THE SLEEPING CITADEL,   INSOLENT STORM STRIKES AT THE SKULL 325   2
ASSEMBLE (1)
     ASSEMBLE WITH THE FRAIL PALENESS OF MOTHS, ...OUIJA   77   4
ASSEMBLY-LINE (1)
     AN ASSEMBLY-LINE OF CUT THROATS, AND YOU AND I ....WAKING IN WINTER 151   5
ASSERT (1)
     THE COLORS ASSERT THEMSELVES WITH A SORT OF VENGEANCE. ...TWO CAMP. 145   14
ASSIDUOUS (1)
     WERE BEWITCHED TO ASSIDUOUS LOVERS, ...DIALOGUE EN ROUTE 309   20
ASSISTANTS (1)
     A MAT OF ROOTS. MY ASSISTANTS HOOK THEM BACK. *THE SURGEON AT 2 A.M. 170   13
ASSOCIATIONS (1)
     THEY HAVE SWABBED ME CLEAR OF MY LOVING ASSOCIATIONS.   ....TULIPS 161   24
ASSORTED (1)
     SIPPING THEIR LIQUIDS FROM ASSORTED POTS, ...LEAVING EARLY 145   8
ASSUME (1)
     END: GREEN SHORES APPEAR; WE ASSUME OUR NAMES, ...CHANNEL CROSSING   27   40

	TITLE	PAGE	LINE

ASSUMES (2)
OF OUR MEAT-AND-POTATO THOUGHTS ASSUMES THE NIMBUS ....GHOST'S. 90 14
ASSUMES, LIKE A MEATHOOK, THE BURDEN OF HIS PARTS. ....THE OTHER 201 6
ASTERISKS (1)
ALONG BRIGHT ASTERISKS BY MILKY WAY. ..THE PRINCESS AND THE GOBLINS 333 12
ASTEROIDS (1)
THE ASTEROIDS TURN TRAITOR IN THE AIR, TO EVA DESCENDING THE STAIR 303 4
ASTONISHED (1)
SHE IS SIMPLY ASTONISHED AT FERTILITY. ....THREE WOMEN 176 7
ASTOUND (2)
LET THEM ASTOUND HIS HEART WITH THEIR MERIT. ....MAGI 148 17
DOES NOT MY HEAT ASTOUND YOU. AND MY LIGHT. ....FEVER. 232 40
ASTOUNDED (2)
OF ASTOUNDED GENERATIONS; THEY WRESTLE EPITAPH FOR FIRE AND FLOWER 45 19
THIS IS THE SILENCE OF ASTOUNDED SOULS. ....CROSSING THE WATER 190 12
ASTOUNDINGLY (1)
WHOSE RED HEART BLOOMS THROUGH HER COAT SO ASTOUNDINGLY ---*POP.OCT. 240 3
ASTOUNDS (1)
EACH HEDGE WITH SUCH WHITE BLOOM ASTOUNDS OUR EYES ....MAYFLOWER 60 6
ASTRAY (1)
THE MORBID COBRA'S WITS HAVE RUN ASTRAY; ....DENOUEMENT 327 13
ASTRIDE (1)
STOOD ASTRIDE ....LETTER TO A PURIST 36 2
ASTROLOGER (1)
THE ASTROLOGER AT HER ELBOW (A LEO) ....ON DECK 143 25
ASTRONOMIC (1)
YET ASTRONOMIC FOUNTAINS ....TRIO OF LOVE SONGS 314 7
AT (262)
ATE (4)
IT WAS THE GANGRENE ATE YOU TO THE BONE .....ELECTRA ON AZALEA PATH 117 39
THE SMALL DELL EATS WHAT ATE IT ONCE. ....THE BURNT-OUT SPA 138 18
IT ATE SEVEN MAIDS AND A PLUMBER ....THE TOUR 238 33
THE GRAVE CAVE ATE WILL BE ....LADY LAZARUS 244 17
ATHLETIC (1)
ATHLETIC THAN A VERB, ...TRIO OF LOVE SONGS 314 18
ATLANTIC (3)
ACROSS ATLANTIC FURROWS, DARK, UNSURE -- ....MAYFLOWER 60 11
AND A HEAD IN THE FREAKISH ATLANTIC ....DADDY 222 11
OLD BARNACLED UMBILICUS, ATLANTIC CABLE, ...MEDUSA 225 14
ATLAS (2)
BENT-BACKED ATLAS, OUR TRAVELED PRAWN. ....YOU'RE 141 12
HE IS YOURS, THE LITTLE BRASSY ATLAS -- ....BY CANDLELIGHT 237 31
ATMOSPHERE (4)
BUT TOWARD A REGION WHERE OUR THICK ATMOSPHERE ....GHOST'S. 90 25
THE CLEAR, GREEN, QUITE BREATHABLE ATMOSPHERE, ...LYONNESSE 234 16
CRYPTIC STARS WIND UP THE ATMOSPHERE, ..TO EVA DESCENDING THE STAIR 303 10
CRIMPED LIKE FERN IN THE QUARTZ ATMOSPHERE; .....PROLOGUE TO SPRING 322 8
ATOMS (2)
ATOMS THAT CRIPPLE DRIP ....NICK AND THE CANDLESTICK 242 38
AND SHATTER TO ATOMS ....AERIALIST 332 35
ATONE (1)
TO ATONE AS SHADE FOR SIN THAT LURED BLIND MAN." ....DIALOGUE B. 39 36
ATOP (2)
ATOP THE FLIGHT OF STAIRS I STAND. ....FAMILY REUNION 301 26
ATOP THE BROKEN UNIVERSAL CLOCK: ....DOOMSDAY 316 2
ATROCIOUS (1)
HIS MANNERS ARE ATROCIOUS. A-P-E- ......DIALOGUE OVER A OUIJA BOARD 284 298
ATROCITY (2)
I AM THE CENTER OF AN ATROCITY. ....THREE WOMEN 180 132
I HAVE SUFFERED THE ATROCITY OF SUNSETS. ....ELM 192 16
ATROCITIES (1)
FISH-GREASE, FISH-BONES, REFUSE OF ATROCITIES. ....FEVER./DR 294 6
AT'S (1)
WE START AT'S THE SAME POST WE FINISH BY, ...ABOVE THE OXBOW 88 19
ATTACH (1)
ATTACH HER TO HEAVEN. ....VANITY FAIR 32 5
ATTACHED (1)
WITH NO STRINGS ATTACHED. ....GULLIVER 251 8
ATTACHMENTS (3)
WITH NO ATTACHMENTS, LIKE A FOETUS IN A BOTTTLE, ...A LIFE 150 26
I AM BLED WHITE AS WAX, I HAVE NO ATTACHMENTS. ....THREE WOMEN 184 275
IT IS SO BEAUTIFUL TO HAVE NO ATTACHMENTS! ....THREE WOMEN 186 341
ATTACKED (1)
WHEN ATTACKED, THEN SCOOTING TO REST, BARELY TREMBLING. ...BALLOONS 271 8
ATTACKS (1)
THEY BOW AND STAND: THEY SUFFER SUCH ATTACKS! ...AMONG THE NARCISSI 190 9
ATTEND (3)
AGE AND TERROR, LIKE NURSES, ATTEND HER, ...A LIFE 150 33
PINK-BUTTOCKED INFANTS ATTEND THEM. ....HEAVY WOMEN 158 15
LEAVES AND PETALS ATTEND ME. I AM READY. ....THREE WOMEN 177 14
ATTENDANT (1)
I AM NOT A NURSE, WHITE AND ATTENDANT, ...BERCK-PLAGE 197 42
ATTENDANTS (4)
ATTENDANTS OF THE EYELASH! ....PURDAH 243 37
ATTENDANTS OF THE LIP! ....PURDAH 243 40

	TITLE	PAGE	LINE

ATTENDANTS (CONT.)
ATTENDANTS! ....PURDAH 243 48
ATTENDANTS! ....PURDAH 243 49
ATTENDED (1)
ATTENDED BY ROSES, ...FEVER. 232 48
ATTENDING (1)
ATTENDING HER COT IS LESS THAN A BELLY ACHE, ...MAGI 148 13
ATTENTION (7)
NO GESTURE OF YOURS OR MINE COULD CATCH THEIR ATTENTION, TWO CAMP. 144 4
AND IT WAS I WHO ATTRACTED EVERYBODY'S ATTENTION, ...IN PLASTER 159 18
THEY CONCENTRATE MY ATTENTION, THAT WAS HAPPY ....TULIPS 161 55
TOO CLOSE ATTENTION, THEY WILL INVITE ME ....WUTHERING HEIGHTS 167 17
REGARDING ME WITH ATTENTION. ....THREE WOMEN 176 3
WHAT HAPPENS IN ME WILL HAPPEN WITHOUT ATTENTION. ......THREE WOMEN 176 10
AND A SKY LIKE A PIG'S BACKSIDE, AN UTTER LACK OF ATTENTION. ...
... FOR A FATHERLESS SON 205 5
ATTENTIONS (1)
INSTEAD, THE DEAD INJURE ME WITH ATTENTIONS, AND NOTHING CAN
HAPPEN. ....BARREN WOMAN 157 8
ATTIC (5)
FROM MY RENTED ATTIC WITH NO EARTH ....LANDOWNERS 53 1
HOW DID WE MAKE IT UP TO YOUR ATTIC? ....LEAVING EARLY 146 40
AND AT LEAST IT WILL BE A GOOD PLACE NOW, THE ATTIC. ......BURNING. 204 22
INTO THE ATTIC OF THE SKULL. ....TWO LOVERS. 327 8
BEHIND THE ZODIAC ON ATTIC DOOR ....THE PRINCESS AND THE GOBLINS 335 58
ATTIRE (1)
OF RICH ATTIRE ....THE QUEEN'S COMPLAINT 28 13
ATTITUDE (1)
WHILE ANGELS WEAR A WAKEFUL ATTITUDE ....ADMONITIONS 319 13
ATTITUDES (2)
COT LEGS MELTED IN TERRIBLE ATTITUDES, AND THE NURSES -- ...WAKING. 151 12
FOR THOSE ANCHORED ATTITUDES ....TOUCH-AND-GO 335 2
ATTRACT (1)
A SANCTUM TO ATTRACT ....VIRGIN IN A TREE 82 26
ATTRACTED (1)
AND IT WAS I WHO ATTRACTED EVERYBODY'S ATTENTION, ...IN PLASTER 159 18
ATTRACTING (1)
ATTRACTING MY SHARE OF AHS AND SPECTACULARY PAINTED, I AM VERTICAL 162 6
AUBADE (1)
APRIL AUBADE ....APRIL AUBADE 312 T
AUCTION (1)
AND AUCTION OFF EACH RARE WHITE-RABBIT VERB; ....A SORCERER B. 324 6
AUDIENCE (1)
ANGEL'S EYE IN THE AUDIENCE, THEN WHISK THEM OUT ....DIALOGUE O. 282 233
AUGUST (2)
AUGUST GIVES OVER ITS MIDAS TOUCH, ...IN MIDAS' COUNTRY 100 24
AND SEVEN WINTER COATS LAST AUGUST) ....ON DECK 143 22
AUNT (3)
MOTHER, MOTHER, WHAT ILLBRED AUNT ....THE DISQUIETING MUSES 74 1
O MAIDEN AUNT, YOU HAVE COME TO CALL. ....THE TOUR 237 1
FROM AUNT ELIZABETH; ....FAMILY REUNION 300 13
AUNTIE (4)
AUNTIE, IT MIGHT BITE! ....THE TOUR 237 14
AND THAT'S WHY I HAVE NO HAIR, AUNTIE, THAT'S WHY I CHOKE THE TOUR 238 24
BUT AUNTIE, SHE'S AWFULLY NICE. ....THE TOUR 238 44
WELL I HOPE YOU'VE ENJOYED IT, AUNTIE! ....THE TOUR 238 48
AUNTS (1)
"I WISH MILLIONAIRE UNCLES AND AUNTS ....DIALOGUE EN ROUTE 308 7
AUREATE (1)
THE OLD GOD, TOO, WRITES AUREATE POETRY ....OUIJA 77 12
AUREOLED (1)
AT TWELVE, EACH SKULL IS AUREOLED ....DANSE MACABRE 321 10
AUSCHWITZ (1)
A JEW TO DACHAU, AUSCHWITZ, BELSEN. ....DADDY 223 33
AUSTERE (5)
THE AUSTERE SUN DESCENDS ABOVE THE FEN, ...WINTER LANDSCAPE, 21 6
SCRUPULOUSLY AUSTERE IN ITS ORDER ....SPINSTER 49 14
AUSTERE, CORPSE-WHITE ....THE SNOWMAN ON THE MOOR 59 30
BLOOD-SPOOR OF THE AUSTERE TRAGEDIES. ....AFTERMATH 113 8
O SHE IS GRACIOUS AND AUSTERE, ...THE BURNT-OUT SPA 138 27
AUSTRALIA (1)
FARTHER OFF THAN AUSTRALIA. ....YOU'RE 141 11
AUSTRALIAN (1)
A DEATH TREE, COLOR GONE, AN AUSTRALIAN GUM TREE -- ....FATHERLESS. 205 3
AUTHENTIC (2)
THE AUTHENTIC SEA DENIES THEM AND WILL PLUCK ....TALE OF A TUB 25 23
ALONE TO THAT AUTHENTIC ISLAND WHERE ....A SORCERER B. 324 13
AUTHOR (1)
FEMALE AUTHOR ....FEMALE AUTHOR 301 T
AUTOCRATIC (1)
WITH HEAVEN'S AUTOCRATIC STATION, ...INSOLENT STORM. 326 30
AUTUMN (2)
FROG AUTUMN ....FROG AUTUMN 99 T
AND THE INVOLVED MALADIES OF AUTUMN, ...LEAVING EARLY 146 18

33

	TITLE	PAGE	LINE

AUTUMNS (2)
    REMEMBERING A THOUSAND AUTUMNS ....GOLD MOUTHS CRY   302   3
    REMEMBERING A THOUSAND AUTUMNS, ...GOLD MOUTHS CRY   302   12
AVENGE (1)
    OR BRAG AHEAD OF TIME HOW I'D AVENGE MYSELF. ....IN PLASTER   160   47
AVENUE (1)
    GILDS ALL OUR AVENUE, ...SOUTHERN SUNRISE   26   15
AVERSE (1)
    I AM BITTER? I'M AVERSE? ....THE TOUR   238   35
AVOID (3)
    OR TO AVOID ME. THEY MOVED ....MUSSEL HUNTER AT ROCK HARBOR   96   45
    WOULD AVOID ALL PENALTY. ....THE DREAM   311   23
    "DESTROY YOUR MIRROR AND AVOID MISHAPS," ....EPITAPH IN THREE PARTS   337   4
AWAITED (1)
    HOW THEY AWAITED HIM, THOSE LITTLE DEATHS! ......THE RABBIT CATCHER   194   24
AWAITING (1)
    AWAITING MASSES ....BRASILIA   258   4
AWAKE (2)
    I CAN STAY AWAKE ALL NIGHT, IF NEED BE -- ....ZOO KEEPER'S WIFE   154   1
    TO SIT UP STARK AWAKE ....AERIALIST   332   41
AWARE (2)
    AND I AM AWARE OF MY HEART: IT OPENS AND CLOSES ....TULIPS   162   60
    YOU WILL BE AWARE OF AN ABSENCE, PRESENTLY, ...FOR A FATHERLESS SON   205   1
AWAY (38)
    WAVER, FAINTLY GREEN, SHUDDERING AWAY ....TALE OF A TUB   25   26
    SEEING HER FREEZE, HE TURNS HIS FACE AWAY. ....THE OTHER TWO   68   20
    BUT THE LITTLE PLANET BOBBED AWAY ....THE DISQUIETING MUSES   76   46
    HE WILLED HIS BOOKS AND SHELL AWAY. ......ON THE DECLINE OF ORACLES   78   10
    LAUGH DOES AWAY WITH THE UNSTITCHING, PLAGUEY WOUNDS ....PERSEUS   83   45
    DREAMED YOURSELF AWAY IN THE MOON'S EYE ....YADWIGHA.   86   28
    TO MAKE AWAY WITH THE GROUND- ....FULL FATHOM FIVE   93   31
    PROFITED MEMORY, BUT DID AWAY WITH THE OLD SCENERY .....GREEN ROCK.   105   5
    AWAY TO THE LEFT LIKE REEDS IN A SEA ....THE EYE-MOTE   109   8
    THE CROWD SUCKS HER LAST TEAR AND TURNS AWAY. ....AFTERMATH   114   14
    THE FOOD TUBES EMBRACE ME. SPONGES KISS MY LICHENS AWAY.   POEM.7.S.   136   19
    TO FIDDLE THE SHORT NIGHT AWAY. ....SLEEP IN THE MOJAVE DESERT   144   26
    AWAY FROM THE LABELED ELMS, THE TAME TEA-ROSES. ....TWO CAMP.   144   9
    SKIN DOESN'T HAVE ROOTS, IT PEELS AWAY EASY AS PAPER. ....FACE LIFT   156   20
    AND MY SKIN ITCHED AND FLAKED AWAY IN SOFT PIECES ....IN PLASTER   159   33
    AND COMES FROM A COUNTRY FAR AWAY AS HEALTH. ....TULIPS   162   63
    TO FUNNEL MY HEAT AWAY. ....WUTHERING HEIGHTS   167   15
    AWAY ON WHEELS, INSTEAD OF LEGS, THEY SERVE AS WELL. ...THREE WOMEN   184 254
    CREEPS AWAY, MANY-SNAKED, WITH A LONG HISS OF DISTRESS. *BERCK-PLAGE   196   18
    AND I CAN'T KEEP AWAY FROM IT. ....THE ARRIVAL OF THE BEE BOX   213   8
    DO AWAY WITH THE BASTARD. ....A SECRET   220   32
    "DO AWAY WITH IT ALTOGETHER." ....A SECRET   220   33
    TO BRING TEACUPS AND ROLL AWAY HEADACHES ....THE APPLICANT   221   12
    I WISH HIM DEAD OR AWAY. ....THE JAILER   227   39
    A LIGHT, AND RIGHT AWAY A RAVING ....THE DREAM   310   10
    THE STING OF BEES TOOK AWAY MY FATHER ....LAMENT   315   1
    THE STING OF BEES TOOK AWAY MY FATHER. ....LAMENT   315   6
    BUT THE STING OF BEES TOOK AWAY MY FATHER. ....LAMENT   315   12
    THE STING OF BEES TOOK AWAY MY FATHER ....LAMENT   316   18
    THE SINGING BIRDS PACK UP AND FLY AWAY; ....NEVER TRY TO TRICK.   320   17
    O THROW IT AWAY, THROW IT ALL AWAY ON THE WIND: SONG FOR A REVOLU.   322   1
    O THROW IT AWAY, THROW IT ALL AWAY ON THE WIND: SONG FOR A REVOLU.   322   1
    TO BURN AWAY THE HUMBUG RUST ....SONG FOR A REVOLUTIONARY LOVE   323   23
    THE TELEGRAM SAYS YOU HAVE GONE AWAY ....DENOUEMENT   326   1
    THE TELEGRAM SAYS YOU HAVE GONE AWAY. ....DENOUEMENT   326   6
    THE TELEGRAM SAYS YOU HAVE GONE AWAY. ....DENOUEMENT   327   12
    THE TELEGRAM SAYS YOU HAVE GONE AWAY; ....DENOUEMENT   327   18
    AWAY OUR RATIONED DAYS AND WEEKS. ....LOVE IS A PARALLAX   330   72
AWE (1)
    MOST MOCK-HEROIC, TO CLOAK OUR WAKING AWE ....CHANNEL CROSSING   27   28
AWFUL (6)
    LIGHTLY, THROUGH THEIR WHITE SWADDLINGS, LIKE AN AWFUL BABY. *TULIPS   161   38
    STOPPED AND AWFUL AS A PHOTOGRAPH OF SOMEBODY LAUGHING, ...BABY.   175   35
    THE BLIND, WHITE, AWFUL, INACCESSIBLE SLANT. ..NEW YEAR ON DARTMOOR   176   5
    AND THE MAN I WORK FOR LAUGHED: "HAVE YOU SEEN SOMETHING AWFUL? ...
                                                        ... THREE WOMEN   177   22
    I AM CALM. I AM CALM. IT IS THE CALM BEFORE SOMETHING AWFUL: *THREE.   179   92
    THE AWFUL ....YEARS   255   20
AWFULLY (1)
    BUT AUNTIE, SHE'S AWFULLY NICE. ....THE TOUR   238   44
AWKWARD (2)
    AND A NAKED MOUTH, RED AND AWKWARD. ....BERCK-PLAGE   201 124
    LEAPING AWKWARD AND LONG-LEGGED ....BITTER STRAWBERRIES   299   16
AWOKE (1)
    WITH PINKNESS, AS IF A TENDERNESS AWOKE, ...THREE WOMEN   186 356
AWRY (2)
    FROM HIS CRABBED MIDDEN WHERE ALL'S WROUGHT SO AWRY ....FIRESONG   30   10
    NO FORM'S GONE SO AWRY, ...TINKER JACK AND THE TIDY WIVES   34   15
A-W-W (1)
    A-W-W. HE'S GONE OFF: WHAT ENGLISH .....DIALOGUE OVER A OUIJA BOARD   279   93

```
                                    TITLE           PAGE  LINE
AXE (1)
    THAN AXE COULD CUT. ...................ON THE PLETHORA OF DRYADS   67   12
AXE-CRACK (1)
    FROM BRUNT OF AXE-CRACK ..................THE SNOWMAN ON THE MOOR   59   46
AXED (1)
    THE INDIAN'S AXED YOUR SCALP. ...................................CUT  235   10
AXES (1)
    AXES .........................................................WORDS  270    1
AXLE (1)
    WHILE FAR OFF, THE AXLE OF WINTER ....................HEAVY WOMEN  158   19
AZALEA (2)
    ELECTRA ON AZALEA PATH ....................ELECTRA ON AZALEA PATH  116    T
    BREAKS THE SOIL. THIS IS AZALEA PATH. .......ELECTRA ON AZALEA PATH  117   21
AZALEAS (2)
    OF AZALEAS, SACROSANCT .......................CHILD'S PARK STONES  101   10
    OF THE AZALEAS, YET BURNT OUT ................CHILD'S PARK STONES  101   17
BAAS (1)
    AND HARD, MARBLY BAAS. ..........................WUTHERING HEIGHTS  167   27
BABEL (4)
    TO PEOPLE THE TWIGGED AISLES; LEAD BABEL TONGUES*WREATH FOR A BRIDAL   45   14
    BY THE BIRDS' IRREGULAR BABEL ............................SPINSTER   49    5
    HER HEAD CUPPED THE BABEL. ....................HARDCASTLE CRAGS   63   25
    OF LEAVES' BICKER AND WHISK IN BABEL TONGUES, ..PLETHORA OF DRYADS.   67   21
BABIES (9)
    IN THEIR JARS THE SNAIL-NOSED BABIES MOON AND GLOW. .....TWO VIEWS.  114   10
    NOW THEY ARE NOTHING, THEY ARE NOT EVEN BABIES. .........LAST WORDS  172    7
    BUT I DIDN'T KNOW HOW TO COOK, AND BABIES DEPRESSED ME. ......BABY.  174   13
    THE SNAKES, THE BABIES, THE TITS ........THE COURAGE OF SHUTTING-UP  210   12
    I AM PACKING THE BABIES, ...............................LESBOS  229   69
    FOUR BABIES AND A COOKER! ........................................AMNESIAC  233    6
    THE BABIES LOOK IN THEIR HOSPITAL .....................DEATH & CO.  254   14
    OF TWO BABIES .....................................EAVESDROPPER  261   61
    THE MEANINGLESS CRY OF BABIES. SUCH A SEA ...............FEVER./DR  294    4
BABIES' (2)
    WHITE AS BABIES' BEDDING AND GLITTERING WITH DEAD BREATH. O IVORY! ...
                                    ... A BIRTHDAY PRESENT  206   18
    CIRCLE, WITH ITS TAWN SILK GRASSES -- BABIES' HAIR.   LETTER IN NOV.  253    7
BABOON (1)
    WITH THE SACRED BABOON IN HIS WIG AND WAX EARS ...ZOO KEEPER'S WIFE  155   29
BABUSHKA (1)
    BABUSHKA ........................................................CUT  236   31
BABY (27)
    OPEN-MOUTHED, THE BABY GOD .........................I WANT, I WANT  106    1
    PLATONIC TABLE WHERE IT LIVES. THE BABY CARP ........PRIVATE GROUND  130   11
    PINK AND SMOOTH AS A BABY. ..............................FACE LIFT  156   32
    LIGHTLY, THROUGH THEIR WHITE SWADDLINGS, LIKE AN AWFUL BABY. *TULIPS  161   38
    AND THE SWEET, DRUGGED WAKING OF A FORGETFUL BABY. .......INSOMNIAC  163   19
    I HAD TO SLEEP IN THE SAME ROOM WITH THE BABY ON A TOO-SHORT COT, ...
                                    ... THE BABYSITTERS  174    7
    THESE ARE MY FINGERS, THIS MY BABY. ..................LITTLE FUGUE  189   51
    PURE AND CLEAN AS THE CRY OF A BABY, ............A BIRTHDAY PRESENT  208   61
    OR A SQUARE BABY .......................THE ARRIVAL OF THE BEE BOX  212    4
    AN ILLEGITIMATE BABY -- ................................A SECRET  220   25
    DWARF BABY, .............................................A SECRET  220   45
    THE BABY SMILES, FAT SNAIL, ..............................LESBOS  228   23
    YOU HAVE ONE BABY, I HAVE TWO. ...........................LESBOS  228   28
    MEANWHILE THERE'S A STINK OF FAT AND BABY CRAP. .............LESBOS  228   33
    GEE BABY, YOU ARE RARE." ................................LESBOS  228   42
    CLOSE ON YOU LIKE THE FIST OF A BABY .....................LESBOS  229   86
    WITH A GODDAM BABY SCREAMING OFF SOMEWHERE. ..........STOPPED DEAD  230   12
    THERE'S ALWAYS A BLOODY BABY IN THE AIR. ..............STOPPED DEAD  230   13
    HOTHOUSE BABY IN ITS CRIB, ...............................FEVER.  231   19
    YOU ARE THE BABY IN THE BARN. ..............NICK AND THE CANDLESTICK  242   42
    THE PURE GOLD BABY ...................................LADY LAZARUS  246   69
    PURE AS A BABY. .....................................GETTING THERE  249   68
    THE THOUGHT OF A BABY -- .............................THE FEARFUL  256   11
    AND MY BABY A NAIL ......................................BRASILIA  258    7
    THE BABY LACE, THE GREEN-LEAVED CONFECTIONERY,*THE MUNICH MANNEQUINS  263   25
    ITS BABY HEAD OUT OF THE WAY, EMBALMED IN SPICE, ...........TOTEM  264   12
    MY BABY IS SLEEPING. .................................FEVER./DR  294   12
BABY-HEADED (1)
    IMMENSE, BALD, THOUGH BABY-HEADED, ..................I WANT, I WANT  106    2
BABYLON'S (1)
    OF GOD'S CITY AND BABYLON'S ..................A LESSON IN VENGEANCE   80   10
BABY'S (2)
    RINSING THOSE STABLES: A BABY'S TEARS WOULD DO IT. .........PERSEUS   82    7
    AND HOW A GOD FLIMSY AS A BABY'S FINGER ..................POEM.5.F.  135   19
BABYSITTERS (1)
    THE BABYSITTERS ......................................THE BABYSITTERS  174    T
BACHELOR
    EACH VIRILE BACHELOR DREADS PARALYSIS, .........NEVER TRY TO TRICK.  320   10
BACK (71)
    OF ALL DECORUM WHICH HOLDS THE WHIRLWIND BACK. .......CONVERSATION.   21    4
    ADVANCING ALWAYS AT MY BACK; ................................PURSUIT   22    6
    IS CLOSED; THE TUB EXISTS BEHIND OUR BACK: ...........TALE OF A TUB   25   31
```

35

BACK (CONT.)
SHREWD CATCH SILTING OUR EACH BRIGHT ACT BACK ....FIRESONG   30   13
SHOULD TRIM BACK TO SHAPE. ....TINKER JACK AND THE TIDY WIVES   34   4
BACK TO HER EARLY SEA-TOWN HOME ....DREAM WITH CLAM DIGGERS   43   3
PLUCKED BACK THUS SUDDEN TO THAT FAR INNOCENCE, ...DREAM WITH C.   44   21
BUT THE ECHOES DIED AT HER BACK AS THE WALLS ......HARDCASTLE CRAGS   62   8
SHE TURNED BACK. ....HARDCASTLE CRAGS   63   45
RIGGED POKER-STIFF ON HER BACK ....ALL THE DEAD DEARS   70   1
GET BACK, THOUGH, SOON, ...ALL THE DEAD DEARS   71   26
AND PIPES THE WORLD BACK TO THE SIMPLE FABRIC .........SNAKECHARMER   79   23
SHOWS ITS HEAD, AND THOSE GREEN WATERS BACK TO ........SNAKECHARMER   79   26
SWITCHED HER INCOMPARABLE BACK ....VIRGIN IN A TREE   81   10
BACK OF THE CONNECTICUT, THE RIVER-LEVEL ....ABOVE THE OXBOW   88   7
THEY CALLED THE PLACE LOOKOUT FARM. BACK THEN, THE SUN ...
                           ... MEMOIRS OF A SPINACH-PICKER   89   1
AND FACED ME, BACK TO A LEDGE OF DIRT, TO RATTLE .....INCOMMUNICADO   100   3
MORE THAN EIGHT DECADES BACK ....THE TIMES ARE TIDY   107   12
TOWARD THE ROWDY BELLOW AND BACK AGAIN ....THE BULL OF BENDYLAW   108   11
WHAT I WANT BACK IS WHAT I WAS ....THE EYE-MOTE   109   25
WHEN I WORMED BACK UNDER MY MOTHER'S HEART. ELECTRA ON AZALEA PATH   116   10
THE GREAT COROLLAS DILATE, PEELING BACK THEIR SILKS. ..BEEKEEPER'S.   118   2
THEY SET THEIR STOUT CHAIRS BACK TO THE ROAD AND FACE THE DARK*NET-.   121   5
THAT SEASON HAS TURNED ITS BACK. ....MAGNOLIA SHOALS   121   5
DUST DULLED HIS BACK TO OCHRE ....MEDALLION   124   14
THREADING BACK, FILAMENT BY FILAMENT, TO THE PURE ...PRIVATE GROUND   130   10
GIVE ME BACK MY SHAPE. I AM READY TO CONSTRUE THE DAYS ...POEM.6.W.   136   21
IN THE MIRROR THEIR DOUBLES BACK THEM UP. ....LEAVING EARLY   146   34
GULLS HAVE THREADED THE RIVER'S MUD BED BACK *PARLIAMENT HILL FIELDS   152   6
IN MY COURTYARD A FOUNTAIN LEAPS AND SINKS BACK INTO ITSELF,*BARREN.   157   3
AND WHERE I LIE NOW, BACK TO MY OWN DARK STAR. ....STARS.   166   34
HER MARBLE SKIRTS BLOWN BACK IN TWO PINK WINGS. ....FINISTERRE   169   20
A MAT OF ROOTS. MY ASSISTANTS HOOK THEM BACK. *THE SURGEON AT 2 A.M.   170   13
ONE DAY IT WON'T COME BACK. THINGS AREN'T LIKE THAT. ....LAST WORDS   172   16
I SEE HER BACK, AND REFLECT IT FAITHFULLY. ....MIRROR   174   13
VOICES STAND BACK AND FLATTEN. THEIR VISIBLE HIEROGLYPHS*THREE WOMEN   179   96
THE MIRROR GIVES BACK A WOMAN WITHOUT DEFORMITY. ....THREE WOMEN   183 240
THE NURSES GIVE BACK MY CLOTHES, AND AN IDENTITY. ......THREE WOMEN   183 241
THE BODY OF A STARFISH CAN GROW BACK ITS ARMS ....THREE WOMEN   184 257
LAP AT MY BACK INELUCTABLY. ....THREE WOMEN   185 293
THE SWIFTS ARE BACK. THEY ARE SHRIEKING LIKE PAPER ROCKETS.   THREE.   185 310
BACK TO BACK. I HEAR AN OWL CRY ....EVENT   194   4
BACK TO BACK. I HEAR AN OWL CRY ....EVENT   194   4
STEPS AT MY BACK SPIRAL INTO A WELL. .................APPREHENSIONS   195   8
YOU ARE TOO BIG. THEY MUST TAKE YOU BACK! ....WORDS HEARD.   203   15
THEY CAN BE SENT BACK. ....THE ARRIVAL OF THE BEE BOX   213   24
IF I JUST UNDID THE LOCKS AND STOOD BACK AND TURNED INTO A TREE. ...
                           ... THE ARRIVAL OF THE BEE BOX   213   28
THE HUMP OF ELBA ON YOUR SHORT BACK, ...THE SWARM   216   8
THE KNIFE IN YOUR BACK. ....A SECRET   220   46
AND GET BACK, BACK, BACK TO YOU. ....DADDY   224   59
AND GET BACK, BACK, BACK TO YOU. ....DADDY   224   59
AND GET BACK, BACK, BACK TO YOU. ....DADDY   224   59
DADDY, YOU CAN LIE BACK NOW. ....DADDY   224   75
THEN SPEWS IT BACK. ....LESBOS   229   76
I SAY I MAY BE BACK. ....LESBOS   230   90
KNEELS, BACK BENT, AS BEST HE CAN ....BY CANDLELIGHT   237   27
TO LAST IT OUT AND NOT COME BACK AT ALL. ....LADY LAZARUS   245   38
YOU, THERE ON YOUR BACK, ...GULLIVER   251   10
DEAD ON THE CHAIR BACK, ...EAVESDROPPER   261   59
ON MY BARE BACK ....PARALYTIC   266   32
THE SEA SLIDES BACK, ...CONTUSION   271   11
BACK, FAT JUG ....BALLOONS   272   27
THEM BACK INTO HER BODY AS PETALS ....EDGE   273   13
AND BACK TO P, AS IF HE KNEW US WELL ...DIALOGUE OVER A OUIJA BOARD   277   30
AND WE ALL TURNED BACK TO PICKING. ....BITTER STRAWBERRIES   300   33
I AM SENDING BACK THE KEY ....BLUEBEARD   305   1
I AM SENDING BACK THE KEY; ....BLUEBEARD   305   4
I AM SENDING BACK THE KEY ....BLUEBEARD   305   7
HANDS REACH BACK TO RELICS OF ....DANSE MACABRE   321   7
BACK INTO THE HOLOCAUST ....SONG FOR A REVOLUTIONARY LOVE   323   22
TURN BACK TO INJURE ......ON LOOKING INTO THE EYES OF A DEMON LOVER   325   13
BACK-ALLEY (1)
BELOW THE RAMSHACKLE BACK-ALLEY BALCONIES, ...ALICANTE LULLABY   43   4
BACKBONE (1)
BACKBONE UNBENDABLE AS ....THE HERMIT AT OUTERMOST HOUSE   119   11
BACKCLOTH (1)
I THINK THEY WOULD NOT WISH FOR THIS DRESSY BACKCLOTH ....STARS.   166   29
BACKDOOR'S (1)
SMIRK. SAINTS' DOOR APART, BACKDOOR'S A DOOR, ...DIALOGUE O.   280 131
BACKDROP (1)
BACKDROP OF SYCAMORES. SUN WAS STRIKING ....THE EYE-MOTE   109   4
BACKS (2)
WHO WALL UP THEIR BACKS AGAINST HIM. ....BERCK-PLAGE   196   15
AT THE UNREAL FRONTIER. LET OUR BACKS, NOW BOLD, ...DIALOGUE O.   285 331

```
                                               TITLE        PAGE  LINE
BACKSIDE (1)
  AND A SKY LIKE A PIG'S BACKSIDE, AN UTTER LACK OF ATTENTION.  ...
                             ... FOR A FATHERLESS SON  205    5
BACKTALK (2)
  OCCASIONALLY, SOME BACKTALK  ............BLACK ROOK IN RAINY WEATHER  57   12
  NEIGHBORHOOD COCKCROW -- ALL NATURE'S PRODIGAL BACKTALK, ...
                      ... ON THE DIFFICULTY OF CONJURING UP A DRYAD  66    4
BACKTALKS (1)
  BACKTALKS AT THE RAVEN  .................................VANITY FAIR  32   10
BACKTRACK (1)
  THAT CHUCKLES IN BACKTRACK OF THE WAVE;  .................TWO LOVERS.  327   18
BACKTRACKING (1)
  BACKTRACKING TAIL. I'D COME FOR  .......MUSSEL HUNTER AT ROCK HARBOR  95    8
BACKWARD (5)
  MY BACKWARD IMAGE.  ........................WORDS FOR A NURSERY  74   35
  WE TAKE A BACKWARD LOOK.  ...............................THE SLEEPERS  123   12
  O I AM TOO BIG TO GO BACKWARD:  .....................POEM.3.MAENAD.  133    8
  WHEN I GRIN, THE STITCHES TAUTEN. I GROW BACKWARD. I'M TWENTY,*FACE.  156   21
  BACKWARD WE TRAVELED TO RECLAIM THE DAY  .............DOOM OF EXILES  318    9
BAD (13)
  THE AFTERNOON AT A BAD END UNDER THE CROWD'S TRUCULENCE, *THE GORING  47    2
  INTO OUR BAD DREAMS, THEIR MENACE  ...............THE THIN PEOPLE  64   15
  GRAZING AT THE MARGINS OF A BAD MONOCHROME, ...........THE EYE-MOTE  109   14
  BLIND TWINS BITTEN BY BAD NATURE.  ........................BLUE MOLES  126    9
  NEVER TRESPASSING IN BAD TEMPER:  ............................A LIFE  150   12
  BOOMED WITH BAD DREAMS AND THE JOVIAN VOICES OF SURGEONS. *FACE LIFT  156    6
  HOW YOUR BAD DREAMS POSSESS AND ENDOW ME.  ......................ELM  192   27
  OPEN YOUR HANDBAG. WHAT IS THAT BAD SMELL?  ...............THE OTHER  201   13
  BLACK AND STIFF, BUT NOT A BAD FIT.  ...................THE APPLICANT  221   21
  YOU WHO HAVE BLOWN YOUR TUBES LIKE A BAD RADIO  ............LESBOS  228   17
  CURTSEYED TO YOURS. TOO BAD YOU CALLED PAN UP  .........DIALOGUE O.  284  280
  AS A BAD JOB. WAIT. HE STIRS. HE ROMPS   DIALOGUE OVER A OUIJA BOARD  284  293
  GO BAD TO THE CORE.  ...........................TEMPER OF TIME  336    4
BADGE (1)
  THE LAST BADGE OF VICTORY.  ............................THE SWARM  217   41
BADLY (3)
  SIMPLY BECAUSE SHE LOOKED AFTER ME SO BADLY.  ...........IN PLASTER  159   34
  HE TELLS ME HOW BADLY I PHOTOGRAPH.  ....................DEATH & CO.  254   12
  SURELY IT IS NOT I YOU WANT SO BADLY.  .................THE RIVAL/DR  291   21
BAFFLE (1)
  BAFFLE THE DARK, THE PITYING EYE.  ......................THE BEGGARS  48   21
BAFFLES (1)
  IN A SCABBARD OF WOOD BAFFLES PURSUERS,  ...........VIRGIN IN A TREE  81    8
BAG (5)
  I'VE EATEN A BAG OF GREEN APPLES,  .......................METAPHORS  116    8
  GUTS BAG WOULD CLACK LIKE A CHILD'S RATTLE,  .....ZOO KEEPER'S WIFE  154   12
  THAT SPLITS FROM ITS RIPPED BAG AND DOES NOT STOP ........BURNING.  205   51
  MARBLE-HEAVY, A BAG FULL OF GOD,  ............................DADDY  222    8
  DRAGGED ITS BLOOD BAG, SICK  ................................LESBOS  229   54
BAGGAGE (2)
  SPRAWLS, HUNCHED IN BLACK, AMONG BAGGAGE, WINCING   CHANNEL CROSSING  26   11
  NOW I HAVE LOST MYSELF I AM SICK OF BAGGAGE ---  .............TULIPS  160   18
BAGPIPES (1)
  CRACK-THROATED MISTRESS OF BAGPIPES AND CYMBALS,  ..ALICANTE LULLABY  43   16
BAGS (3)
  JANGLING THEIR GREAT MONEY BAGS.  ............................RHYME  50    8
  TWO GRAY, PAPERY BAGS --  ............................APPREHENSIONS  195   13
  DUST BAGS IN AND OUT,  .................................PARALYTIC  266    7
BAILIWICK (1)
  THIS EGG-SHAPED BAILIWICK, CLEAR AS A TEAR.  ...............A LIFE  149    2
BAIT (2)
  BECOME HIS STARVING BODY'S BAIT.  ............................PURSUIT  22   24
  AND BAIT THE DROWSING TROUT BY THE BROOK'S BRIM;  ...........GO GET.  313   18
BAKED (1)
  GOT BAKED INTO GINGERBREAD, I WONDER  .........THE DISQUIETING MUSES  75   12
BAKING (1)
  POODLES ARE BAKING COOKIES IN  .....................A WINTER'S TALE  87   18
BALANCE (3)
  AND REPOISE UNTIL TIME STOP, THE CELESTIAL BALANCE  .........PERSEUS  84   48
  IN THIS COUNTRY THERE IS NEITHER MEASURE NOR BALANCE  .....TWO CAMP.  144    1
  THE WINTER LANDSCAPE HANGS IN BALANCE NOW,  ......PROLOGUE TO SPRING  322    1
BALANCED (1)
  UNDER A BALANCED RULER.  ...............................LORELEI  94   20
BALANCES (1)
  NIGHTLY SHE BALANCES  ...............................AERIALIST  331    7
BALCONIES (4)
  SHUTTERS, THEIR BALCONIES  ......................SOUTHERN SUNRISE  26    4
  BELOW THE RAMSHACKLE BACK-ALLEY BALCONIES,  ........ALICANTE LULLABY  43    4
  HOW THE BALCONIES ECHOED! HOW THE SUN LIT UP  .......WAKING IN WINTER  151    9
  ON THE BALCONIES OF THE HOTEL, THINGS ARE GLITTERING.  ..BERCK-PLAGE  197   37
BALD (21)
  MOUTHLESS, EYELESS, WITH STITCHED BALD HEAD.   THE DISQUIETING MUSES  75   16
  A BALD ANGEL BLOCKS AND SHAPES  ........................SCULPTOR  91   10
  IMMENSE, BALD, THOUGH BABY-HEADED,  ....................I WANT, I WANT  106    2
  THE BALD, WHITE TUMULI OF YOUR EYES.  .................THE COLOSSUS  129   15
```

BALD (CONT.)
     LOVE IS THE UNIFORM OF MY BALD NURSE. POEM.7.S.   137   39
     A WORLD OF BALD WHITE DAYS IN A SHADELESS SOCKET. ..THE HANGING MAN   141   4
     NOR LEAVE ME TO SET MY SMALL BALD EYE ....LOVE LETTER   147   6
     THEY MOLLIFY THE BALD MOON. ....CANDLES   149   26
     ABOUT A BALD, HOSPITAL SAUCER. ....A LIFE   150   22
     ON THIS BALD HILL THE NEW YEAR HONES ITS EDGE. ....PARLIAMENT H.   152   1
     BALD EYES OR PETRIFIED EGGS, ...WHITSUN   153   3
     OBSCENE AND BALD AS A PIG, THE WHITE MICE ....ZOO KEEPER'S WIFE 155   21
     THE MIDWIFE SLAPPED YOUR FOOTSOLES, AND YOUR BALD CRY   MORNING SONG   156   2
     THE BALD SLOTS OF HIS EYES STIFFENED WIDE-OPEN ....INSOMNIAC   163   27
     THE MOON SEES NOTHING OF THIS. SHE IS BALD AND WILD. ....MOON.   173   27
     THEY ARE BALD AND IMPOSSIBLE, LIKE THE FACES OF MY CHILDREN, *THREE.   178   66
     THERE ARE SOME WITH THICK BLACK HAIR, THERE ARE SOME BALD. ..THREE.   183 222
     THE LINES OF THE EYE, SCALDED BY THESE BALD SURFACES, ..BERCK-PLAGE   196   10
     SHE MAY BE BALD, SHE MAY HAVE NO EYES, ...THE TOUR   238   43
     NAKED AND BALD IN THEIR FURS. ....THE MUNICH MANNEQUINS   263   13
     BALD AND SHINY, WITH POCKETS OF WISHES. ....TOTEM   264   26
BALDERDASH (1)
     INSTEAD OF BREWING US SUCH A BALDERDASH *DIALOGUE OVER A OUIJA BOARD   279   97
BALD-EYED (1)
     MOTHER OF A WHITE NIKE AND SEVERAL BALD-EYED APOLLOS.   BARREN WOMAN   157   7
BALD-FACED (1)
     FACE, TO FACE THE BALD-FACED SUN. .....MUSSEL HUNTER AT ROCK HARBOR   97   91
BALD-HEAD (1)
     AND DEATH, THAT BALD-HEAD BUZZARD, ...OLD LADIES' HOME   120   19
BALDING (1)
     BALDING, GELDED BY LIGHTNING -- AN ILLUSION. ..FOR A FATHERLESS SON   205   4
BALL (13)
     THIS MOON-POCKED CRYSTAL BALL ....RECANTATION   41   6
     THE BURNISHED BALL HANGS FIRE IN HER HANDS, A LENS ...CRYSTAL GAZER   54   5
     SLOWLY SHE SPINS THE BALL: ....CRYSTAL GAZER   55   12
     GERD WHIRLS THE BALL ABLAZE: "ROUGH STORM," SHE GRANTS. "MAY WREAK ...
                                                           CRYSTAL GAZER   55   22
     NOW WORKS HIS HELL OF MONDAYS IN THE MOON'S BALL,*EVERLASTING MONDAY   62   11
     THEIR EYES REVOLVE THE WHOLE TOWN LIKE A BLUE AND GREEN BALL. *NET-. 121   12
     BIG AS THE BALL OF MY THUMB, AND DUMB AS EYES ........BLACKBERRYING   168   5
     THE BEES ARGUE, IN THEIR BLACK BALL, ...THE SWARM   216   31
     NOW THEY BALL IN A MASS, ...WINTERING   218   31
     HE IS HUGGING HIS BALL AND CHAIN DOWN BY THE GATE ....LESBOS   229   73
     AS A TENNIS BALL AT TWILIGHT ....APRIL 18   302   16
     THEN HURL THE BARE WORLD LIKE A BLUEGREEN BALL ..SONG FOR A REVOLU. 323   21
     OF BLACK WEIGHT, BLACK BALL, BLACK TRUCK, ...AERIALIST   332   38
BALLED (3)
     THE BALLED ....CUT   236   33
     BALLED HEDGEHOG. ....BY CANDLELIGHT   236   20
     AND BALLED, LIKE BLAKE'S. ....DEATH & CO.   254   4
BALLOON (4)
     ON A GREEN BALLOON BRIGHT WITH A MILLION .....THE DISQUIETING MUSES   76   43
     THEY SHOULD HAVE GONE OUT WITH BALLOON FLIGHTS AND THE
            STEREOPTICON. ....CANDLES   149   12
     A SORT OF CELLOPHANE BALLOON. ....PARLIAMENT HILL FIELDS   153   47
     HIS BALLOON SQUEAK LIKE A CAT. ....BALLOONS   272   22
BALLOONS (3)
     MOONY BALLOONS TIED BY A STRING ....ON DECK   143   34
     THE CLEAR VOWELS RISE LIKE BALLOONS. ....MORNING SONG   157   18
     BALLOONS ....BALLOONS   271   T
BALLS (7)
     OVALS AND BALLS, ...FIESTA MELONS   46   4
     POLLARDED GREEN BALLS, THE TREES MARCH TO CHURCH. ......BERCK-PLAGE   199   92
     SO THE SWARM BALLS AND DESERTS ....THE SWARM   216   17
     FIVE BALLS! FIVE BRIGHT BRASS BALLS! ....BY CANDLELIGHT   237   35
     FIVE BALLS! FIVE BRIGHT BRASS BALLS! ....BY CANDLELIGHT   237   35
     HOLDING THEIR GOLD-RUDDY BALLS ....LETTER IN NOVEMBER   253   27
     SQUAT, BOWLING BLACK BALLS AT HER. ....AERIALIST   331   30
BALUSTRADE (1)
     BALUSTRADE OF A SAG-BACKED BRIDGE. ....THE BURNT-OUT SPA 138   23
BAMBOO (1)
     OF PINK AND BEIGE, IMPECCABLE BAMBOO, ...MORNING IN THE HOS.   332   4
BAN (1)
     TO CAST LOCK, STOCK AND BARREL UNDER BAN; ....THE DISPOSSESSED   318   11
BANANA (1)
     FED ME BANANA GAS THROUGH A FROG-MASK. THE NAUSEOUS VAULT *FACE LIFT 156   5
BANDAGE (3)
     THE WIND STOPS MY BREATH LIKE A BANDAGE. ....PARLIAMENT HILL FIELDS   152   20
     BE A BANDAGE TO HIS HURT, AND MY WORDS ....THREE WOMEN   185 297
     AND MY HEART TOO SMALL TO BANDAGE THEIR TERRIBLE FAULTS.*BERCK-PLAGE 198   45
BANDAGED (1)
     WITH FINGER BANDAGED WHERE THE WASPISH PIN ....THE PRINCESS.   333   7
BANDAGES (4)
     THEY WILL ROLL ME UP IN BANDAGES, THEY WILL STORE MY HEART ...
                                                       ... LAST WORDS   172   23
     WHO WOULD ADHERE TO ME: I UNDO HER FINGERS LIKE BANDAGES: I GO. ...
                                                       ... THREE WOMEN   184 273
     THE FLOWERS VIVID AS BANDAGES, AND THE MAN MENDING. ......NARCISSI.   190   8

	TITLE	PAGE	LINE

BANDAGES (CONT.)
   OF OLD BANDAGES, BOREDOMS, OLD FACES ....GETTING THERE 249 66
BANDED (1)
   THE DUMB, BANDED BODIES ....THE SWARM 217 47
BANDS (1)
   HE IS STILL SWADDLED IN WHITE BANDS. ....THREE WOMEN 186 326
BANDY-LEG (1)
   CROOK-BACK OR BANDY-LEG, ...TINKER JACK AND THE TIDY WIVES 34 16
BANK (4)
   LURCHING HOME ALONG RIVER BANK. ....FAUN 35 7
   ON THE BANK OF THE RIVER'S ....MUSSEL HUNTER AT ROCK HARBOR 95 7
   ON THIS AMBER BANK WHERE GRASSES BLEACH. ....IN MIDAS' COUNTRY 100 22
   BLOOD AND BANK WRIST, ELBOW, SHOULDER, LIP ....DIALOGUE O. 277 18
BANKED (1)
   STUCCO ARCHES, THE BANKED ROCKS SUNNING IN ROWS, ...WHITSUN 153 2
BANKER (1)
   WE'VE SQUANDERED ALL THE BANKER WILL ALLOW ....THE DISPOSSESSED 319 16
BANKING (1)
   SUCCEED IN BANKING THEIR FIRES ....WINTERING 219 47
BANKRUPT (2)
   WITH SUCH BLIGHT WROUGHT ON OUR BANKRUPT ESTATE, ...CONVERSATION. 21 13
   AND LEFT OUR BANKRUPT CIRCUS ON ITS OWN; ....DENOUEMENT 326 2
BANNER (1)
   AFTER, THEY STAGGER AND WEAVE, UNDER NO BANNER. ....STINGS/DR 293 11
BANNERS (1)
   STALEMATED THEIR ARMIES STOOD, WITH TOTTERING BANNERS: ..SNOWMAN O. 58 1
BANQUET (1)
   THE WALNUT BANQUET TABLE, THE TWELVE CHAIRS ....THE OTHER TWO 68 13
BAPTIZED (1)
   A LIFE BAPTIZED IN NO-LIFE FOR A WHILE, ...INSOMNIAC 163 18
BAR (1)
   AGAINST BOTH BAR AND TOWER THE BLACK SEA RUNS. ....POINT SHIRLEY 111 48
BARB (2)
   SUCH A BARRICADE OF BARB AND CHECK ....SPINSTER 50 26
   IT STUCK IN A BARB WIRE SNARE. ....DADDY 223 26
BARBAROUS (4)
   TO THE BARBAROUS OUTLOOK, FROM THERE CHOSE ....SPIDER 49 25
   OF THE BASE, BARBAROUS PRINCE OW. ....NATURAL HISTORY 71 12
   GOTHIC AND BARBAROUS, PURE GERMAN. ....LITTLE FUGUE 188 26
   THE BARBAROUS HOLLY WITH ITS VIRIDIAN ....LETTER IN NOVEMBER 253 19
BARBECUE (1)
   CHILDBIRTHS OR A FAMILY BARBECUE: ....ALL THE DEAD DEARS 71 28
BARBED (2)
   ACROSS BARBED STILE, THROUGH FLOCKED BROWN COWS. ....BUCOLICS 23 4
   WE HEFT GLOBED FLINT, RACKED IN VEINS' BARBED BINDINGS; ...FIRESONG 30 18
BARBS (1)
   BARBS ON THE CROWN OF GILDED WIRE, ...I WANT, I WANT 106 11
BARB-WIRED (1)
   BARB-WIRED HEADLAND OF ....MAN IN BLACK 119 6
BARE (20)
   RECORDS BARE PAINTED WALLS, WHILE AN ELECTRIC LIGHT ..TALE OF A TUB 24 2
   HE MADE HER SHOULDERS BARE ....THE QUEEN'S COMPLAINT 28 14
   PLUCKS BARE THAT COMET'S FLOWERING. ....EPITAPH FOR FIRE AND FLOWER 46 28
   WHICH PEOPLES THE BARE ROOM, THE BLANK, UNTENANTED AIR. NOVEMBER G. 56 18
   THROUGH BARE WHISTLING HEATHER, OVER STILES OF BLACK STONE, ...
                ... THE SNOWMAN ON THE MOOR 58 21
   AGAINST BARE, WHITEWASHED WALLS, THE FURNITURE ....THE OTHER TWO 68 8
   I FOUND BETWEEN BARE MOOR, ...TWO VIEWS OF WITHENS 72 12
   AS I COULD BETWEEN BARE TOES? ....MUSSEL HUNTER AT ROCK HARBOR 96 50
   OF HER BARE SHOULDER, WHILE SHE BENDS, TWO VIEWS OF A CADAVER ROOM 114 16
   THE HORIZON'S BARE OF SHIPS, ...MAGNOLIA SHOALS 122 21
   THE BEACH AND THE ROCKS ARE BARE. ....MAGNOLIA SHOALS 122 22
   BARE NO SINISTER SPACES. ALREADY -------------------------BLUE MOLES 126 13
   SCARED AND BARE ON THE GREEN PLASTIC-PILLOWED TROLLEY ....TULIPS 161 25
   I SAW DEATH IN THE BARE TREES, A DEPRIVATION. ....THREE WOMEN 177 24
   POOR AND BARE AND UNQUEENLY AND EVEN SHAMEFUL. ....STINGS 214 19
   ON MY BARE BACK ....PARALYTIC 266 32
   HER BARE ....EDGE 272 6
   IN ALL. PLUS YES. PLUS NO. AND THIS BARE BOARD. ....DIALOGUE O. 276 14
   THE ONLY FARE ON MY BARE BREAKFAST PLATE. QUEEN MARY'S ROSE GARDEN 290 6
   THEN HURL THE BARE WORLD LIKE A BLUEGREEN BALL ..SONG FOR A REVOLU. 323 21
BARED (2)
   BARED BY EACH FALLING TIDE, ...MAN IN BLACK 119 14
   THE SPIDERY JAWS, THE SPINE BONES BARED FOR A MOMENT ....ZOO K. 154 9
BAREFOOT (2)
   BAREFOOT, SHE STOOD, IN SHOCK OF THAT RETURNING, ...DREAM WITH C. 43 5
   SO WE SHALL WALK BAREFOOT ON WALNUT SHELLS ......LOVE IS A PARALLAX 330 67
BARE-HANDED (2)
   BARE-HANDED, I HAND THE COMBS. ....STINGS 214 1
   THE MAN IN WHITE SMILES, BARE-HANDED, ...STINGS 214 2
BARELY (2)
   BARELY DARING TO BREATHE OR ACHOO. ....DADDY 222 5
   WHEN ATTACKED, THEN SCOOTING TO REST, BARELY TREMBLING. ...BALLOONS 271 8
BARES (2)
   BARES ITS LOW LINTEL TO CORRODING WEATHERS: ....DEPARTURE 51 17

	TITLE	PAGE	LINE

BARES (CONT.)
WIND BARES A FLINTIER LANDSCAPE. ....IN MIDAS' COUNTRY 100 25
BARGES (1)
RED AND ORANGE BARGES LIST AND BLISTER ....A WINTER SHIP 112 2
BARGE-TAR (1)
BARGE-TAR CLOTTED AT THE TIDE-LINE, THE WRECKED PIER ...GREEN ROCK. 104 2
BARITONE (1)
RASPS THE JARRING BARITONE OF UNCLE PAUL; ....FAMILY REUNION 300 22
BARK (3)
"HOWEVER I WRENCH OBSTINATE BARK AND TRUNK ....CONJURING. 66 25
STREAK AND MOTTLE OF TAWN BARK, ...ON THE PLETHORA OF DRYADS 67 22
AS RESIN DROPS OOZED FROM PINE BARK. ....THE BURNT-OUT SPA 137 5
BARK'S (1)
AND PUT ON BARK'S NUN-BLACK ....VIRGIN IN A TREE 81 5
BARN (1)
YOU ARE THE BABY IN THE BARN. ....NICK AND THE CANDLESTICK 242 42
BARNACLE (2)
FOR THAT BRAG, WE BARNACLE THESE IRON THIGHS." ....SNOWMAN O. 59 43
THESE BARNACLE DEAD! ....ALL THE DEAD DEARS 70 14
BARNACLED (1)
OLD BARNACLED UMBILICUS, ATLANTIC CABLE, ...MEDUSA 225 14
BARNACLE-PATED (1)
A BARNACLE-PATED, MOSS-WIGGED, LOBSTER-LIMBED ....DIALOGUE O. 283 244
BARNACLES (1)
BEYOND THE BREAKWATER, SPOTTY WITH BARNACLES? ....BERCK-PLAGE 197 41
BARNS (2)
MAZE OF BARNS TO THE LINTEL OF THE SUNK STY DOOR ....SOW 60 9
ON BLACK STONE. BARNS ....HARDCASTLE CRAGS 63 30
BARNYARD (4)
THE BARNYARD LIKE THOSE TALONED HAGS ....RHYME 50 5
NOR EVEN ONE OF THE COMMON BARNYARD SOWS, ...SOW 61 17
IT'S WORSE THAN A BARNYARD. ....THE COLOSSUS 129 5
MOTHER, KEEP OUT OF MY BARNYARD, ...POEM.3.MAENAD. 133 14
BAROMETER (1)
THEY BOTH WATCHED THE BAROMETER SINK ....DIALOGUE EN ROUTE 309 37
BARON (1)
NOTABLE ROBBER BARON, ...SPIDER 48 9
BARONIAL (1)
AROUND OUR BED THE BARONIAL FURNITURE ....THE OTHER TWO 68 4
BAROQUE (1)
CAME TO BE LYING ON THIS BAROQUE COUCH ....YADWIGHA. 85 2
BARRED (1)
THEN, FROM THE BARRED YARD, THE CHILDREN ....BERCK-PLAGE 200 118
BARREL (2)
THEN WITH A JOCULAR FIST THWACKED THE BARREL NAPE, ...SOW 61 35
TO CAST LOCK, STOCK AND BARREL UNDER BAN; ....THE DISPOSSESSED 318 11
BARRELS (2)
IN ALICANTE THEY BOWL THE BARRELS ....ALICANTE LULLABY 43 1
THEY ARE UNLOADING THREE BARRELS OF LITTLE CRABS. ....A WINTER SHIP 113 14
BARREN (8)
AT THIS BARREN ENTERPRISE ....TWO SISTERS OF PERSEPHONE 31 10
OF UGLY SPINSTERS AND BARREN SIRS ....VIRGIN IN A TREE 82 33
BARREN WOMAN ....BARREN WOMAN 157 T
OLD WINTER-FACE, OLD BARREN ONE, OLD TIME BOMB. ....THREE WOMEN 181 158
CRUELLY, BEING BARREN. ....ELM 192 23
THE BARREN BODY OF HAWTHORN, ETHERIZING ITS CHILDREN. ....BEE. 211 25
BARREN, THE LOT ARE BARREN! ....AMNESIAC 233 15
BARREN, THE LOT ARE BARREN! ....AMNESIAC 233 15
BARRETTE (1)
ONE CHILD DROPS A BARRETTE OF PINK PLASTIC; PARLIAMENT HILL FIELDS 152 16
BARRICADE (1)
SUCH A BARRICADE OF BARB AND CHECK ....SPINSTER 50 26
BARS (3)
THE TULIPS SHOULD BE BEHIND BARS LIKE DANGEROUS ANIMALS; ....TULIPS 162 58
GROWS TALL. YOU CLUTCH YOUR BARS. ....BY CANDLELIGHT 237 22
TIME IS A GREAT MACHINE OF IRON BARS ....SONNET: TO TIME 311 13
BARTER (1)
COME TO BARTER ENDLESSLY ....SCULPTOR 91 2
BASALT (1)
MY CHEEK OF BASALT. THEY TURNED TO TEARS, ...LOVE LETTER 147 15
BASE (2)
OF THE BASE, BARBAROUS PRINCE OW. ....NATURAL HISTORY 71 12
ON THE ROUND BASE OF THE INVERTED WINE-GLASS HERE, ...DIALOGUE O. 276 5
BASEMENTS (1)
FROM DEEP-SUNK BASEMENTS ....OWL 102 8
BASILISK-BLINK (1)
LIMBS: NOT A BASILISK-BLINK, NOR A DOUBLE WHAMMY, ...PERSEUS 83 16
BASILISK-LOOK (1)
BY ONE JOT ITS BASILISK-LOOK OF LOVE. ....LADY AND T. 70 35
BASIN (3)
INTO THE STONE BASIN. I SNIPPED FABLE OF THE RHODODENDRON STEALERS 103 7
I BEND OVER THIS DRAINED BASIN WHERE THE SMALL FISH PRIVATE GROUND 131 20
THEN MOTHER SWAM UP, HOLDING A TIN BASIN. ....FACE LIFT 156 7
BASINS (1)
RETCHING IN BRIGHT ORANGE BASINS; A REFUGEE ....CHANNEL CROSSING 26 10

	TITLE	PAGE	LINE

BASKET (2)
```
    LAYER ON LAYER, AND YOU HAD A BASKET  ...MEMOIRS OF A SPINACH-PICKER    89    9
    IN THE BASKET OF PLASTIC EVERGREENS THEY PUT *ELECTRA ON AZALEA PATH   117   25
```
BASKETS (3)
```
    WITH A HUNDRED BUSHEL BASKETS ON THE EDGE  ..........SPINACH-PICKER.    89    6
    PURE LEAFAGE. A HUNDRED BASKETS BY DAY'S END.  ......SPINACH-PICKER.    89   11
    MY WORLD PYRAMIDED WITH LADEN BASKETS.  MEMOIRS OF A SPINACH-PICKER    90   20
```
BASKETWORK (1)
```
    FRAMED IN A BASKETWORK OF CAT-TAILS.  ..............THE BURNT-OUT SPA   138   26
```
BASKIN (1)
```
    FOR LEONARD BASKIN  .......................................SCULPTOR    91    D
```
BASKING (1)
```
    THE LINE PINK AND QUIET, A WORM, BASKING.*THE COURAGE OF SHUTTING-UP   209    2
```
BASTARD (4)
```
    DO AWAY WITH THE BASTARD.  .....................................A SECRET   220   32
    DADDY, DADDY, YOU BASTARD, I'M THROUGH.  .....................DADDY   224   80
    BASTARD  ................................................DEATH & CO.   254   23
    FUSING TWO TALENTS, A SORT OF PSYCHIC BASTARD  ..........DIALOGUE O.   280  139
```
BASTARDIES (2)
```
    LOADED, AS THEY ARE, WITH ACCOUNTS OF BASTARDIES.  .........COURAGE.   210    6
    BASTARDIES, USAGES, DESERTIONS AND DOUBLENESS,  ............COURAGE.   210    7
```
BASTARD'S (1)
```
    THE BASTARD'S A GIRL.  .........................................LESBOS   228   16
```
BAT (3)
```
    THE BLACK BUNCHED IN THERE LIKE A BAT,  .....................WINTERING   218   13
    FLAPPING AND SUCKING, BLOOD-LOVING BAT.  ......................LESBOS   229   80
    BLACK BAT AIRS  .............................NICK AND THE CANDLESTICK   240    6
```
BATCH (4)
```
    BRED AN AMPLE BATCH OF OMENS; BUT NOW  .................TALE OF A TUB    25   18
    ON TRIAL, FROM IRELAND, SHE BURNED BATCH AFTER BATCH OF COOKIES  ...
                                          ...  THE BABYSITTERS   175   26
    ON TRIAL, FROM IRELAND, SHE BURNED BATCH AFTER BATCH OF COOKIES  ...
                                          ...  THE BABYSITTERS   175   26
    IN A BATCH OF RAVELED APPLE RINDS.  ....THE PRINCESS AND THE GOBLINS   335   68
```
BATH (1)
```
    THE SHRIEK IN THE BATH,  .......................................PURDAH   244   56
```
BATHER (1)
```
    TROUNCING THE SEA LIKE A RAGING BATHER,  ....................LAMENT   315    7
```
BATHS (2)
```
    AQUEDUCTS, THE BATHS OF CARACALLA, THE EAGLE NOSE!  ........SURGEON.   171   28
    THE ACID BATHS, THE SKYFULS OFF OF YOU.  .....................LESBOS   228   47
```
BATHTUB (1)
```
    THEIR BATHTUB BATTLES DEEP,  ...........................BATTLE-SCENE    85   33
```
BATMAN (1)
```
    THE CAPTAIN'S BATMAN,  .........................WORDS FOR A NURSERY    74   37
```
BATS (3)
```
    YOU WOOED ME WITH THE WOLF-HEADED FRUIT BATS  .....ZOO KEEPER'S WIFE   155   17
    HER BLUE GARMENTS UNLOOSE SMALL BATS AND OWLS.  ..............MOON.   173   18
    NOW FOLD THEIR WINGS LIKE BATS AND DISAPPEAR  ..........TWO LOVERS.   327    7
```
BAT-SHAPES (1)
```
    NOVEMBER'S DONE WITH. THE BLOWN LEAVES MAKE BAT-SHAPES, *DIALOGUE O.   286  337
```
BATTALIONS (1)
```
    BATTALIONS. SEE, HOW THE TREE BOLES FLATTEN  ........THE THIN PEOPLE    65   43
```
BATTENED (1)
```
    THAT BATTENED FOR A DAY ON HER ANKLE-BONE.  .......ALL THE DEAD DEARS    70    6
```
BATTER (1)
```
    CRAVES MOST TO COOK BATTER  ............................VANITY FAIR    33   16
```
BATTERED (1)
```
    SO, OVER THIS BATTERED, OBSTINATE SPIT  ................POINT SHIRLEY   110   30
```
BATTLE (4)
```
    THIS PAIR SEEK SINGLE STATE FROM THAT DUAL BATTLE.  .......WREATH F.    44   10
    BATTLE HOWEVER I WOULD  ................ON THE PLETHORA OF DRYADS    67   19
    BEFORE IT MADE THE BULL'S-EYE. DO WE HAVE TO BATTLE  ...DIALOGUE O.   284  282
    WORK AT ALL? HOW CAN WE HELP BUT BATTLE *DIALOGUE OVER A OUIJA BOARD   284  286
```
BATTLEFIELD (1)
```
    THIS BOARD OUR BATTLEFIELD. LET'S GIVE PAN UP  ..........DIALOGUE O.   284  292
```
BATTLEMENT (1)
```
    BUT SAT ON, GUARDING HIS GRIM BATTLEMENT.  ..THE SNOWMAN ON THE MOOR    58    7
```
BATTLES (1)
```
    THEIR BATHTUB BATTLES DEEP,  ...........................BATTLE-SCENE    85   33
```
BATTLE-SCENE (1)
```
    BATTLE-SCENE  .............................................BATTLE-SCENE    84    T
```
BATTLESHIPS (1)
```
    COMES A FLOCK OF BOTTLE BATTLESHIPS  .........EPITAPH IN THREE PARTS   337    2
```
BATTLE-SHOUTS (1)
```
    NIGHTLY THE BATTLE-SHOUTS START UP  .....................BLUE MOLES   126   19
```
BAWDY (2)
```
    THAN VIRGINS' TEARS. THAT BAWDY QUEEN OF DEATH,  .............OUIJA    77   24
    MULE-BRAY, PIG-GRUNT AND BAWDY CACKLES  ...............THE COLOSSUS   129    3
```
BAY (8)
```
    OF ANGELS' BAY  ........................................SOUTHERN SUNRISE    26   17
    THE SCRAGGY ROCK SPIT SHIELDING THE TOWN'S BLUE BAY  ......DEPARTURE    51   13
    OF LOVE: CLAWS BRACED, AT BAY, MY CURRENCY NOT HERS.  INCOMMUNICADO   100    7
    GREEN ROCK, WINTHROP BAY  ...................GREEN ROCK, WINTHROP BAY   104    T
    FIFTEEN YEARS BETWEEN ME AND THE BAY  ......GREEN ROCK, WINTHROP BAY   105    4
```

41

BAY (CONT.)
     THEY DO NOT COME FROM THE BAY OF THE DEAD DOWN THERE, ...FINISTERRE   170   33
     THAT KEEPS THE SKY AT BAY, ...BY CANDLELIGHT   237   29
     THE COLORED TENTS ALL TOPPLE IN THE BAY; ....DENOUEMENT   327   16
BAY'S (1)
     THE BAY'S SHEER, EXTRAVAGANT BLUE, ...THE BEGGARS   48   17
BAY-TREE (1)
     FOR A BAY-TREE HIDE, RESPECT'S ....VIRGIN IN A TREE   81   11
BE (165)
BEACH (3)
     THE BEACH AND THE ROCKS ARE BARE. ....MAGNOLIA SHOALS   122   22
     THEN STEPPED DOWN THE STEEP BEACH SHELF AND INTO THE WATER. ..BABY.   175   39
     AND I, A SHELL, ECHOING ON THIS WHITE BEACH ....THREE WOMEN   179 111
BEACHCOMBER (2)
     TWO LOVERS AND A BEACHCOMBER BY THE REAL SEA ....TWO LOVERS.   327   T
     A LONE BEACHCOMBER SQUATS AMONG THE WRACK ....TWO LOVERS.   327   13
BEACHED (3)
     OF THE THREE FISHING SMACKS BEACHED ...MUSSEL HUNTER AT ROCK HARBOR   95   6
     HIS BODY BEACHED WITH THE SEA'S GARBAGE, ...SUICIDE OFF EGG ROCK   115   15
     BEACHED UNDER THE SPUMY BLOOMS, WE LIE ....WHITSUN   154   23
BEACHES (1)
     BREAKING ON LEGENDARY BEACHES; IN FAITH ....TALE OF A TUB   25   45
BEADED (1)
     WHEN THEY FREE ME, I AM BEADED WITH TEARS. ....FINISTERRE   169   18
BEADS (2)
     COLORED BEADS ON THE STRUNG ROADS, AND THE PEOPLE STROLL ....OXBOW.   89   51
     THE BEADS OF HOT METAL FLY, AND I, LOVE, I ....FEVER.   232   45
BEAK (7)
     AND WITH RED BEAK ....THE SHRIKE   42   21
     ENGINEERED THE GANNET'S BEAK. ....I WANT, I WANT   106   8
     HIS BEAK BRINGS THE HARVEST IN. ....MAGNOLIA SHOALS   122   18
     SMOKE WHEELS FROM THE BEAK OF THIS EMPTY JAR. POEM.6.W.   135   12
     UNDER THE GLUED SHEET FROM WHICH HIS POWDERY BEAK ......BERCK-PLAGE   198   63
     CONDONING THE BEAK, THE CLAW, THE GRIN OF THE DOG ....THE SWARM   216   22
     I AM RED MEAT. HIS BEAK ....DEATH & CO.   254   10
BEAKS (2)
     TRUMPET-THROATS OPEN TO THE BEAKS OF BIRDS.*THE BEEKEEPER'S DAUGHTER   118   8
     I SPREAD TO THE BEAKS OF BIRDS. ....THE JAILER   226   15
BEAN (7)
     THE RED TOMATO'S IN, THE GREEN BEAN; ....YADDO: THE GRAND MANOR   123   4
     SAT BY MY FATHER'S BEAN TREE POEM.3.MAENAD.   133   2
     THE BEAN LEAVES ARE DUMB AS HANDS. POEM.3.MAENAD.   133   10
     JUMPY AS A MEXICAN BEAN. ....YOU'RE   141   16
     FEATHER DUSTERS FANNING THEIR HANDS IN A SEA OF BEAN FLOWERS,   BEE.   211   17
     CREAMY BEAN FLOWERS WITH BLACK EYES AND LEAVES LIKE BORED HEARTS. ...
                                             ... THE BEE MEETING   211   18
     WHERE IT POURS BEAN GREEN OVER BLUE ....DADDY   222   12
BEANFIELD (1)
     THEIR SMILES AND THEIR VOICES ARE CHANGING. I AM LED THROUGH A
          BEANFIELD. ....THE BEE MEETING   211   15
BEANSTALK (1)
     BOLD BEANSTALK; LIE AND LOVE TILL SHARP SCYTHE HACKS *LOVE IS A PAR.   330   71
BEANSTALKS (1)
     GODS AND REAR THEM LIKE BEANSTALKS FROM OUT THESE RIBS   DIALOGUE O.   280 170
BEAR (7)
     RODE OUT AGAINST THE FIFTH BULL TO BRACE HIS PIKE AND SLOWLY BEAR ...
                                             ... THE GORING   47   6
     THESE THREE, UNMASKED NOW, BEAR ....ALL THE DEAD DEARS   70   7
     OF MIXIE BLACKSHORT THE HEROIC BEAR, ...THE DISQUIETING MUSES   75   10
     BEAR UP THE SEAFARER, ...BATTLE-SCENE   84   8
     I BROUGHT MY LOVE TO BEAR, AND THEN YOU DIED.*ELECTRA ON AZALEA PATH   117   38
     AND ACT BEAR WITNESS, IN THE CRUX OF TIME, ...DIALOGUE O.   286 362
     GO SNARE THE SLEEPING BEAR IN LEAF-LINED DEN*GO GET THE GOODLY SQUAB   313   9
BEARD (3)
     FLOURED HIS WHIRLING BEARD, AND AT HIS TREAD*THE SNOWMAN ON THE MOOR   59   33
     CAPPED: WHITE HAIR, WHITE BEARD, FAR-FLUNG, ...FULL FATHOM FIVE   92   4
     THE KING FINGERED HIS BEARD. ....THE BULL OF BENDYLAW   108   6
BEARDED (1)
     BEARDED AND BLOWN, AN ALBATROSS OF FROST, ...A WINTER SHIP   113   26
BEARDS (2)
     UPROOT THEM: THEIR BEARDS ARE EVER- ....CHILD'S PARK STONES   101   27
     IN ELBOW-SCARVES, BEARDS ....DARK WOOD, DARK WATER   127   3
BEARERS (1)
     THE CURIOUS BEARERS AND THE RAW DATE ....BERCK-PLAGE   199   71
BEAR-FURRED (1)
     AND THE BEAR-FURRED, BIRD-EATING SPIDER ....ZOO KEEPER'S WIFE   155   30
BEARING (1)
     GRINDS ROUND, BEARING DOWN WITH THE STRAW, ...HEAVY WOMEN   158   20
BEARS (5)
     SHE BEARS A KING. TURNED BITTER ....TWO SISTERS OF PERSEPHONE   32   24
     BEARS A BURDEN TOO WEIGHTY ....LORELEI   94   17
     THEIR WHITENESS BEARS NO RELATION TO LAUNDRY, ...MAGI   148   4
     NIGHTLY NOW I FLOG APES OWLS BEARS SHEEP ....ZOO KEEPER'S WIFE   155   39
     THEIR FLESH BEARS NO RELATION. ....THE NIGHT DANCES   250   11

BEAST (5)
    THE BEAST ....POEM.4.BEAST. 134 ST
    AN OLD BEAST ENDED IN THIS PLACE: ....THE BURNT-OUT SPA 137   1
    SILVER BEAST BETWEEN TWO DARK CANYONS, ..THE COURAGE OF SHUTTING-UP 210   9
    THE LABYRINTH AND IGNORE WHAT MANNER OF BEAST ....DIALOGUE O. 286 343
    IF YOU FLAY A BEAST ....TRIO OF LOVE SONGS 315 41
BEASTS (1)
    BEASTS OF OASIS, A BETTER TIME. ....THE EYE-MOTE 109 15
BEAT (9)
    FOR THE PALTRY GIFT OF HER BULK AND THE BEAT ......HARDCASTLE CRAGS   63 27
    AGES BEAT LIKE RAINS ....FULL FATHOM FIVE   93 27
    A MACHINE TO BREATHE AND BEAT FOREVER. ....SUICIDE OFF EGG ROCK 115 16
    HIS SOUL MAY BEAT AND BE BEATING AT HER DULL SENSE ....WIDOW 165 37
    WE PICKED UP STICKS OF DRIFTWOOD AND BEAT THEM OFF, *THE BABYSITTERS 175 38
    OF POETRY FROM THESE LETTERS, BUT THE BEAT ....DIALOGUE O. 283 256
    WILL BE OUR BEAT, JUST AS THE GIFT IS OURS, ...DIALOGUE O. 283 257
    THE DULL DRUMS OF MY PULSES BEAT ....FAMILY REUNION 300   8
    HORIZONS BEAT A RETREAT AS WE EMBARK ....LOVE IS A PARALLAX 329 14
BEATEN (3)
    HISTORY'S BEATEN THE HAZARD. ....THE TIMES ARE TIDY 107 10
    OF JAPANESE PAPER, MY GOLD BEATEN SKIN ....FEVER. 232 38
    BEATEN IN STARRY METALS. ....BALLOONS 272 19
BEATING (8)
    IT WAS NOT A HEART, BEATING, ...NIGHT SHIFT   76   1
    ME OFF INTO THEIR SPACE OF BEATING, ...WHITENESS I REMEMBER 102 22
    AND HIS BLOOD BEATING THE OLD TATTOO ....SUICIDE OFF EGG ROCK 115   8
    HIS SOUL MAY BEAT AND BE BEATING AT HER DULL SENSE ....WIDOW 165 37
    THE GRASS IS BEATING ITS HEAD DISTRACTEDLY. ......WUTHERING HEIGHTS 168 39
    BEATING AND BEATING AT AN INTRACTABLE METAL. .........BLACKBERRYING 169 27
    BEATING AND BEATING AT AN INTRACTABLE METAL. .........BLACKBERRYING 169 27
    BOY, HE NEEDS A BEATING NOW AND THEN ..DIALOGUE OVER A OUIJA BOARD 281 183
BEATINGS (1)
    TO COLLECT HIS BEATINGS. AND IF HE'S A GO-BETWEEN ......DIALOGUE O. 281 185
BEATS (1)
    BEATS, IS BRUTAL ENDLESSLY. ....DEPARTURE   51 15
BEAUTIES (3)
    OF THE GREEK BEAUTIES YOU BROUGHT ....PRIVATE GROUND 130   2
    SIT EMPTIED OF BEAUTIES, THE GIFT ....THE NIGHT DANCES 250   8
    WHERE BEAUTIES CHAR ......ON LOOKING INTO THE EYES OF A DEMON LOVER 325 22
BEAUTIFUL (21)
    EVERY POCK AND STAIN BULKED MORE BEAUTIFUL*ON THE PLETHORA OF DRYADS   67 16
    WITH THE ROOMS, OR THE SMILES, OR THE BEAUTIFUL RUBBER PLANTS, ...
                                             ... WAKING IN WINTER 151 15
    OF SOMETHING BEAUTIFUL, BUT ANNIHILATING. ....THE RIVAL 166   3
    SHE IS IN LOVE WITH THE BEAUTIFUL FORMLESSNESS OF THE SEA. ...
                                             ... FINISTERRE 170 37
    TONIGHT, FOR THIS PERSON, BLUE IS A BEAUTIFUL COLOR. ......SURGEON. 171 43
    THE FACE IN THE POOL WAS BEAUTIFUL, BUT NOT MINE -- ....THREE WOMEN 177 45
    I AM NOT UGLY. I AM EVEN BEAUTIFUL. ....THREE WOMEN 183 239
    I AM BEAUTIFUL AS A STATISTIC. HERE IS MY LIPSTICK. ....THREE WOMEN 183 245
    IT IS SO BEAUTIFUL TO HAVE NO ATTACHMENTS! ....THREE WOMEN 186 341
    THE NURSES IN THEIR WING-CAPS ARE NO LONGER SO BEAUTIFUL; ...BERCK. 198 58
    IT IS SO BEAUTIFUL UP HERE: IT IS A STOPPING PLACE. ....BERCK-PLAGE 199 90
    FOLLOWING THE COFFIN ON ITS FLOWERY CART LIKE A BEAUTIFUL WOMAN, ...
                                             ... BERCK-PLAGE 200 115
    THEY ARE MORE BEAUTIFUL THAN MY BODILESS OWL, ..BURNING THE LETTERS 204 30
    WHAT IS THIS, BEHIND THIS VEIL, IS IT UGLY, IS IT BEAUTIFUL? ...
                                             ... A BIRTHDAY PRESENT 206   1
    IN THE WATERS OFF BEAUTIFUL NAUSET. ....DADDY 222 13
    ONCE YOU WERE BEAUTIFUL. ....LESBOS 228 40
    THERE IS NOTHING TO DO WITH SUCH A BEAUTIFUL BLANK BUT
        SMOOTH IT. ....AMNESIAC 232   2
    SQUELCHING AND SQUELCHING THROUGH THE BEAUTIFUL RED. *LETTER IN NOV. 253 15
    YOUR CLEAR EYE IS THE ONE ABSOLUTELY BEAUTIFUL THING. ....CHILD 265   1
    BEAUTIFUL; ....MOONSONG AT MORNING 317 16
    WHERE ANCIENT, INFINITE, AND BEAUTIFUL,*THE PRINCESS AND THE GOBLINS 333 14
BEAUTIFULLY (2)
    IRREFUTABLE, BEAUTIFULLY SMUG ....HEAVY WOMEN 158   1
    HOW BEAUTIFULLY THE LIGHT INCLUDES THESE THINGS. ....THREE WOMEN 186 353
BEAUTY (15)
    BEAUTY FROM HAG. ....TINKER JACK AND THE TIDY WIVES   34 18
    ALL YOUR BEAUTY, ALL YOUR WIT, IS A GIFT, MY DEAR, ...
                                             ... SOLILOQUY OF THE SOLIPSIST   38 35
    A FASHIONABLE BEAUTY, ...ELLA MASON AND HER ELEVEN CATS   53 15
    ABOUT A QUINTESSENTIAL BEAUTY ....ON THE PLETHORA OF DRYADS   67   2
    THEY DESCANT ON THE SERENE AND SERAPHIC BEAUTY ....VIRGIN IN A TREE   82 29
    O THE BEAUTY OF USAGE! POEM.1.WHO. 131 19
    AND THE OWNER PAST THIRTY, NO BEAUTY AT ALL. ....CANDLES 148   9
    NOT HER WHITENESS AND BEAUTY, AS I HAD AT FIRST SUPPOSED.*IN PLASTER 159 19
    NOR AM I THE BEAUTY OF A GARDEN BED ....I AM VERTICAL 162   5
    THEY HAD AN EFFICIENCY, A GREAT BEAUTY, ...THE RABBIT CATCHER 193   9
    STEALER OF CELLS, STEALER OF BEAUTY -- ....THE FEARFUL 256 12
    AT NIGHTFALL THERE IS THE BEAUTY OF DROWNED FIELDS, ...TOTEM 264   4
    AND A TITLED LADY MAY FREQUENTLY BE A BEAUTY. ....QUEEN MARY'S. 290 22
    HERE IS A WHITE SKY. HERE IS THE BEAUTY ....FEVER./DR 294   9

BEAUTY (CONT.)
    INTOLERANT BEAUTY NEVER WILL BE LEARNING. ....TO EVA DESCENDING. 303   17
BEAUTY'S (3)
    TO DISTRACT BEAUTY'S THOUGHT; ....VANITY FAIR   33   23
    HOW BEST BEAUTY'S BORN OF HARDIHOOD. ....MAYFLOWER   60   8
    UNTONGUED, ALL BEAUTY'S BRIGHT JUICE SOURS. ....VIRGIN IN A TREE   82   43
BECAME (3)
    IT STABLED IN; LONG-USED, BECAME WELL-LOVED   THE COMPANIONABLE ILLS 105   7
    I BECAME A STILL PEBBLE. POEM.7.S.   136   8
    SHE LET IN THE DRAFTS AND BECAME MORE AN MORE ABSENT-MINDED. ...
                                                    ... IN PLASTER   159   32
BECAUSE (13)
    AND I WAS SCARED, BECAUSE SHE WAS SHAPED JUST THE WAY I WAS*PLASTER. 158   7
    SIMPLY BECAUSE SHE LOOKED AFTER ME SO BADLY. ....IN PLASTER 159   34
    THAN THE DARK OF THE SKY BECAUSE IT IS QUITE STARLESS. ......STARS. 165   3
    THAT WOULD HAVE THE WHOLE WORLD FLAT BECAUSE THEY ARE.   THREE WOMEN 179   87
    LESS DREAD OF THE WORLD BEYOND THAN OURS. THAT'S BECAUSE*DIALOGUE O. 278   62
    YOU'RE MELTING NOW, BECAUSE YOU THINK HE'S HIT ....DIALOGUE O. 278   80
    BECAUSE PAN BLUNTLY SPELT OUT GOD'S HEAD, NOT ....DIALOGUE O.   282 237
    BECAUSE OF SOME EXPLICABLE PHENOMENON ....APRIL 18 301   4
    OR THAT BECAUSE OF SLEEP ....APRIL 18 302   7
    THAT BECAUSE OF FOOD ....APRIL 18 302   9
    THAT BECAUSE OF THESE ....APRIL 18 302   11
    BECAUSE HE WOULD MAKE LOVE TO ME ....BLUEBEARD   305   3
    BECAUSE NEW EXCAVATIONS CAME TOO NEAR   THE PRINCESS AND THE GOBLINS 334   39
BECKON (1)
    SUCH ROYAL DREAMS BECKON THIS MAN ....THE SHRIKE   42   2
BECKONER (1)
    CHENILLE BECKONER, ...EAVESDROPPER 260   33
BECKONING (2)
    LEWDLY BECKONING, AND HER COURAGE WAVERED: ....LADY AND T.   69   20
    BECKONING MY WORDS IN -- ...............................EAVESDROPPER 260   34
BECOME (8)
    BECOME HIS STARVING BODY'S BAIT. ....PURSUIT   22   24
    FREELY BECOME SUN'S BRIDE, THE LATTER ....TWO SISTERS OF PERSEPHONE   32   21
    BECOME QUITE YELLOW ....RESOLVE   52   9
    IS VISIBLE. THE SNAKE-SCALES HAVE BECOME ...........SNAKECHARMER   79   13
    LEAF, BECOME EYELID; SNAKE-BODIES, BOUGH, BREAST ......SNAKECHARMER   79   14
    IN SLEEP. THE CHAIRS WON'T VANISH OR BECOME ....DIALOGUE O.   286 355
    GREEN ALLEYS WHERE WE REVELED HAVE BECOME ....DOOM OF EXILES   318   5
    REFECTORIES WHERE HE REVELED HAVE BECOME ....TERMINAL   328   5
BECOMING (2)
    THE ONCE-KNOWN WAY BECOMING ....THE GREAT CARBUNCLE   72   17
    I AM BECOMING ANOTHER. POEM.3.MAENAD.   133   15
BED (29)
    THEY PITCHED THEIR COATS, COME TO GREEN BED. ....BUCOLICS   23   8
    NEAR A BED OF POPPIES, ...TWO SISTERS OF PERSEPHONE   32   16
    AROUND OUR BED THE BARONIAL FURNITURE ....THE OTHER TWO   68   4
    NODDING BY NIGHT AROUND MY BED, ...THE DISQUIETING MUSES   75   15
    BED OF A REED. LOOK: ....VIRGIN IN A TREE   81   15
    YOUR SHELLED BED I REMEMBER. ....FULL FATHOM FIVE   93   43
    NO THIRST DISTURBS A STONE'S BED. ....CHILD'S PARK STONES   101   30
    BEFORE THE BED, BEFORE THE KNIFE, ...THE EYE-MOTE   109   26
    SHARK LITTERED IN THE GERANIUM BED -- ....POINT SHIRLEY 110   16
    HER WIDE BED WORE THE STAIN OF DIVINITY. ...ELECTRA ON AZALEA PATH   116   8
    OUSTED FROM THAT WARM BED ....THE SLEEPERS 123   19
    I BED IN A FISH PUDDLE. POEM.4.BEAST. 134   19
    WEAR MASKS OF HORN TO BED. POEM.5.F.   135   14
    IN THE MONTH OF RED LEAVES I CLIMB TO A BED OF FIRE. POEM.6.W.   135   6
    SPACE! SPACE! THE BED LINEN WAS GIVING OUT ENTIRELY. ....WAKING. 151   11
    GULLS HAVE THREADED THE RIVER'S MUD BED BACK *PARLIAMENT HILL FIELDS 152   6
    ONE CRY, AND I STUMBLE FROM BED, COW-HEAVY AND FLORAL   MORNING SONG 157   13
    SHE LAY IN BED WITH ME LIKE A DEAD BODY ....IN PLASTER 158   6
    AS THE LIGHT LIES ON THESE WHITE WALLS, THIS BED, THESE
        HANDS. ....TULIPS   160   4
    NOR AM I THE BEAUTY OF A GARDEN BED ....I AM VERTICAL 162   5
    OVER ONE BED IN THE WARD, A SMALL BLUE LIGHT   THE SURGEON AT 2 A.M. 171   41
    ANNOUNCES A NEW SOUL. THE BED IS BLUE. ....THE SURGEON AT 2 A.M. 171   42
    BLIND IN MY BED, WITH MY DEAR BLIND SWEET ONE, ...THREE WOMEN 178   76
    FROM THE LONG FALL, AND FIND MYSELF IN BED, ...THREE WOMEN   187 366
    THE BED IS ROLLED FROM THE WALL. ....BERCK-PLAGE   198   60
    AND WHEN AT LAST THEY BLUNDER INTO BED ....THE DEAD   320   7
    SURRENDER: TO BUILD OUR BED AS HIGH AS JACK'S ...LOVE IS A PARALLAX 330   70
    FROM BED TO STRICT TRYOUTS ....AERIALIST 331   5
    TO LEAVE HER BED OF FEVER AND ASCEND ..THE PRINCESS AND THE GOBLINS 333   4
BEDDED (3)
    SILENT AND SHINING ON A GREEN ROCK BEDDED IN MUD, ...DREAM WITH C.   44   15
    WHERE, BEDDED LIKE ANGELS, TWO BURN ONE IN FEVER. ....WREATH F.   45   18
    THOUGH HE BEDDED IN ERMINE, GORGED ON ROAST, ...NATURAL HISTORY   71   3
BEDDING (3)
    TO SQUANDER OWL-HOURS ON BRACKEN BEDDING, ...VANITY FAIR   33   19
    THE LEAFY BEDDING, ...MUSHROOMS   139   12
    WHITE AS BABIES' BEDDING AND GLITTERING WITH DEAD BREATH. O IVORY! ...
                                                    ... A BIRTHDAY PRESENT 206   18

BEDFELLOWS (1)
    BEDFELLOWS OF THE SPIRIT'S DEBAUCH, FOND MASTERS. ...COMPANIONABLE. 105   8
BEDLAM (1)
    REEL GIDDY IN BEDLAM SPRING: ....SPINSTER   50   23
BEDRAGGLED (1)
    A BEDRAGGLED SNAKE, HANGING LIMP AS THE ABSURD MOUTH ....PERSEUS   83   38
BEDROCK (1)
    LOUD ON EARTH'S BEDROCK. ALMOST THROWN, NOT ...WHITENESS I REMEMBER   103   31
BEDS (2)
    FROM BEDS BOXED-IN LIKE COFFINS ....OLD LADIES' HOME 120   17
    RULE THEIR BEDS LIKE BEHEADED AND RESURRECTED AND ALL SILENT
        ROYALTY, ... QUEEN MARY'S ROSE GARDEN   290   5
BEDSPREAD (1)
    UPON OUR BEDSPREAD. ....THE EVERLASTING MONDAY   62   4
BEE (3)
    THE QUEEN BEE MARRIES THE WINTER OF YOUR YEAR. ....BEEKEEPER'S.   118   21
    THE BEE MEETING ....THE BEE MEETING 211   T
    THE ARRIVAL OF THE BEE BOX ....THE ARRIVAL OF THE BEE BOX   212   T
BEEKEEPER'S (1)
    THE BEEKEEPER'S DAUGHTER ....THE BEEKEEPER'S DAUGHTER 118   T
BEELZEBUB (1)
    GABRIEL OR BEELZEBUB: I SEE, ...DIALOGUE OVER A OUIJA BOARD   280 150
BEEN (29)
BEER (1)
    THE SNOWS OF THE TYROL, THE CLEAR BEER OF VIENNA ....DADDY   223   36
BEES (18)
    WHERE BEES, STRIPED BLACK AND GOLD, SLEEP OUT THE BLIZZARD ...
                                     ... ELECTRA ON AZALEA PATH   116   3
    HIERATICAL IN YOUR FROCK COAT, MAESTRO OF THE BEES, ...BEEKEEPER'S.   118   5
    IN BURROWS NARROW AS A FINGER, SOLITARY BEES ....BEEKEEPER'S.   118   15
    THE RECTOR, THE MIDWIFE, THE SEXTON, THE AGENT FOR BEES. ......BEE.   211   2
    YES, HERE IS THE SECRETARY OF BEES WITH HER WHITE SHOP SMOCK, BEE.   211   7
    NOW I AM MILKWEED SILK, THE BEES WILL NOT NOTICE. ..THE BEE MEETING   211   9
    THE BEES FOUND HIM OUT, ...STINGS 215   48
    THE BEES HAVE GOT SO FAR. SEVENTY FEET HIGH! ....THE SWARM   216   26
    THE BEES ARGUE, IN THEIR BLACK BALL, ...THE SWARM   216   31
    IT SEEMS BEES HAVE A NOTION OF HONOR, ...THE SWARM   217   57
    THIS IS THE TIME OF HANGING ON FOR THE BEES -- THE BEES ..WINTERING   218   22
    THIS IS THE TIME OF HANGING ON FOR THE BEES -- THE BEES ..WINTERING   218   22
    THE BEES ARE ALL WOMEN, ...WINTERING   218   38
    THE BEES ARE FLYING. THEY TASTE THE SPRING. ....WINTERING   219   50
    THE STING OF BEES TOOK AWAY MY FATHER ....LAMENT   315   1
    THE STING OF BEES TOOK AWAY MY FATHER ....LAMENT   315   6
    BUT THE STING OF BEES TOOK AWAY MY FATHER ....LAMENT   315   12
    THE STING OF BEES TOOK AWAY MY FATHER ....LAMENT   316   18
BEE'S (1)
    YOU INHERIT WHITE HEATHER, A BEE'S WING, ...THE MANOR GARDEN   125   12
BEE-SELLER (1)
    HE HAS NOTHING TO DO WITH THE BEE-SELLER OR WITH ME. ....STINGS   215   39
BEETHOVEN (1)
    HE COULD HEAR BEETHOVEN: ....LITTLE FUGUE 187   13
BEETLES (3)
    SHARDED IN BLACK, LIKE BEETLES, ...OLD LADIES' HOME 120   1
    OF BEETLES, SWEETBREADS, SHARDS -- TO BE EATEN ....BLUE MOLES   126   31
    MOTHER OF BEETLES, ONLY UNCLENCH YOUR HAND: POEM.6.W.   135   19
BEETROOT (1)
    RED CLOVER OR GNAW BEETROOT .....WATERCOLOR OF GRANTCHESTER MEADOWS   112   17
BEFORE (41)
    BEFORE HE PART ....TINKER JACK AND THE TIDY WIVES   35   32
    REPENT, DEPART, BEFORE GOD'S TRUMP-CRACK SPLITS THE SKY." ...
                         ... DIALOGUE BETWEEN GHOST AND PRIEST   3   46
    WILL BREAK BEFORE IT HELP; ....RECANTATION   4   7
    BEFORE TIME ENDS ....RECANTATION 42   18
    STEEL ON MYSELF BEFORE PROFIT ....RHYME 50   14
    OF HER SMALL HEAT OUT, BUT BEFORE THE WEIGHT ......HARDCASTLE CRAGS   63   42
    BUT BEFORE I MIGHT BLIND SENSE ....ON THE PLETHORA OF DRYADS   67   13
    SO THESE POSED SHEETS, BEFORE THEY THIN TO NOTHING, ...GHOST'S.   90   18
    I CAME BEFORE THE WATER- ....MUSSEL HUNTER AT ROCK HARBOR   95   1
    THE BLACK BULL BELLOWED BEFORE THE SEA. ....THE BULL OF BENDYLAW   108   1
    BEFORE THE BED, BEFORE THE KNIFE, ...THE EYE-MOTE   109   26
    BEFORE THE BED, BEFORE THE KNIFE, ...THE EYE-MOTE   109   26
    BEFORE THE BROOCH-PIN AND THE SALVE ....THE EYE-MOTE   109   27
    THEY GO BEFORE: OPENING THE VEINS, ...BLUE MOLES 126   29
    IN THE BLUE HOUR BEFORE SUNUP. ....SLEEP IN THE MOJAVE DESERT   144   10
    YOU SHOULD HAVE JUNKED THEM BEFORE THEY DIED. ....LEAVING EARLY   146   28
    NOBODY WATCHED ME BEFORE, NOW I AM WATCHED. ....TULIPS   161   43
    BEFORE THEY CAME THE AIR WAS CALM ENOUGH, ...TULIPS   161   50
    BEFORE THE DISTANCES THEY PIN EVAPORATE, ...WUTHERING HEIGHTS   167   6
    THESE ARE OUR CREPES. EAT THEM BEFORE THEY BLOW COLD." ..FINISTERRE   170   36
    I AM CALM. I AM CALM. IT IS THE CALM BEFORE SOMETHING AWFUL: *THREE.   179   92
    THE YELLOW MINUTE BEFORE THE WIND WALKS, WHEN THE LEAVES*THREE WOMEN   179   93
    WHAT DID MY FINGERS DO BEFORE THEY HELD HIM? ....THREE WOMEN   181 169
    THE BENT PRINT BULGING BEFORE HIM LIKE SCENERY. ....BERCK-PLAGE   197   23
    YOU DIED BEFORE I HAD TIME --- ....DADDY   222   7
    TODDLE ON HOME, BEFORE THE WEATHER'S WORSE. ....THE TOUR   238   41

	TITLE	PAGE	LINE

BEFORE (CONT.)
MY SOUL DIES BEFORE IT. ....YEARS 255 13
THAT'S HOW YOU ALWAYS TALK BEFORE WE START. ....DIALOGUE O. 277 15
WE THOUGHT WE'D TRAINED HIM, BEFORE GOING HAYWIRE. TRUTH*DIALOGUE O. 277 41
BEFORE ONE HEAVED HIMSELF THROUGH HEAVEN'S TENT ....DIALOGUE O. 281 171
BEFORE HE SPELLS AGAIN, SHOULD HIS NEXT WRIT ....DIALOGUE O. 281 193
I KNEW HE'D GOT IT MIXED BEFORE: VISIONS*DIALOGUE OVER A OUIJA BOARD 282 219
BEFORE IT MADE THE BULL'S-EYE. DO WE HAVE TO BATTLE ....DIALOGUE O. 284 282
IN THIS DAY BEFORE THE DAY NOBODY IS ABOUT.*QUEEN MARY'S ROSE GARDEN 290 1
CUPPING THE BERRY PROTECTIVELY BEFORE ....BITTER STRAWBERRIES 300 37
STARS PALE BEFORE THE ANGRY DAWN; ....TO A JILTED LOVER 310 21
THAT CAME BEFORE THE CHANGE OF WEATHER ....THE DREAM 310 3
BEFORE THAT PAPAL PARAGON, THE SUN. ....APRIL AUBADE 312 8
BEFORE WE FELL, LIKE ICARUS, UNDONE; ....DOOM OF EXILES 318 10
WHY HE SHOULD KNEEL BEFORE A SILLY SCENE ....THE PRINCESS. 335 65
WHO WEEPS BEFORE THE DESOLATE TABLEAU   THE PRINCESS AND THE GOBLINS 335 74
BEGAN (10)
SHE, IN HER SHABBY TRAVEL GARB, BEGAN ......DREAM WITH CLAM-DIGGERS 44 22
INSTINCT FOR ART BEGAN WITH THE BULL'S HORN LOFTING IN THE MOB'S ...
... THE GORING 47 8
AS THE GODS BEGAN ONE WORLD, AND MAN ANOTHER, ...SNAKECHARMER 79 1
THE GREAT BRONZE GATE BEGAN TO CRACK, ...THE BULL OF BENDYLAW 108 13
SHE BEGAN TO WARM UP, AND I SAW HER ADVANTAGES. ....IN PLASTER 159 14
AND SECRETLY SHE BEGAN TO HOPE I'D DIE. ....IN PLASTER 159 39
I BEGAN TO TALK LIKE A JEW. ....DADDY 223 34
WOULD TRAFFIC IN. LET HIM FINISH WHAT HE BEGAN. ....DIALOGUE O. 278 84
FROM WHICH THE FUR BEGAN. ....TRIO OF LOVE SONGS 315 44
WE BROKE THE MINUTE THAT THE WORLD BEGAN ....THE DISPOSSESSED 318 14
BEGGAR (2)
A BEGGAR STOPS AMONG EGGS AND LOAVES, ...THE BEGGARS 48 10
SO BEGGAR GERD MIGHT AIM HER LOOK ....CRYSTAL GAZER 55 40
BEGGARED (2)
WHILE THIS BEGGARED BRAIN *ON THE DIFFICULTY OF CONJURING UP A DRYAD 66 37
WHICH, WITHOUT HIM, WERE BEGGARED ....SCULPTOR 92 18
BEGGARS (3)
THE BEGGARS ....THE BEGGARS 47 T
BY LACK AND LOSS THESE BEGGARS ENCROACH ....THE BEGGARS 48 13
WHITE HOUSE AND ALMOND GROVE. THE BEGGARS ....THE BEGGARS 48 18
BEGGING (1)
NO USE, NO USE, NOW, BEGGING RECOGNIZE! ....AMNESIAC 232 1
BEGIN (7)
AND SHE'LL PERISH WITH EMPTINESS THEN, AND BEGIN TO MISS ME. ...
... IN PLASTER 160 56
LIKE LIVE WHITE RABBITS, READY TO BEGIN *DIALOGUE OVER A OUIJA BOARD 282 234
FAVORED (WHILE SUDDENLY THE RAINS BEGIN ....FEMALE AUTHOR 301 2
BEGIN ON TILTED VIOLINS TO SPAN ....CINDERELLA 303 4
WHILE THE GNAWINGS OF LOVE BEGIN. ....CIRCUS IN THREE RINGS 322 12
AND AGAIN TOGETHER BEGIN IT ALL. .....SONG FOR A REVOLUTIONARY LOVE 323 24
BEGIN BY DIPPING YOUR BRUSH INTO CLEAR LIGHT. .....MIDSUMMER MOBILE 324 1
BEGINNING (2)
AT THE BEGINNING I HATED HER, SHE HAD NO PERSONALITY -- IN PLASTER 158 5
THEY ARE BEGINNING TO REMEMBER THEIR DIFFERENCES. ......THREE WOMEN 183 224
BEGINS (5)
SO THE SNAKECHARMER BEGINS A SNAKY SPHERE .............SNAKECHARMER 79 2
SICKNESS BEGINS HERE: I AM A DARTBOARD FOR WITCHES. POEM.6.W. 135 4
BEGINS. A JERK. AND NOW THE FIRST SLOW RAMBLE ....DIALOGUE O. 277 21
TO RAID THE ZONE WHERE FATE BEGINS, ...METAMORPHOSES OF THE MOON 307 3
TELL NOW, WE TAUNT, WHERE BLACK OR WHITE BEGINS   LOVE IS A PARALLAX 330 49
BEGONIA (1)
WITH BEGONIA AND BUILDING BLOCKS. ....SONG FOR A REVOLUTIONARY LOVE 323 16
BEGRUDGE (1)
OF WATER. WAIT. GODPIE I DON'T BEGRUDGE *DIALOGUE OVER A OUIJA BOARD 282 213
BEGS (1)
NOW, AS I HONE MY KNIFE, SHE BEGS ....RHYME 50 11
BEGUILE (1)
TO BEGUILE SIGHT: ....ON THE DIFFICULTY OF CONJURING UP A DRYAD 66 21
BEGUILES (2)
IT BEGUILES -- ....BATTLE-SCENE 84 1
DISGUISE BEGUILES AND MORTAL MISCHIEF'S DONE: ....ADMONITIONS 319 14
BEGUN (3)
TRICKS OF RADIANCE MIRACLES. THE WAIT'S BEGUN AGAIN,   BLACK ROOK I. 57 38
NOTHING THAT CANNOT BE ERASED, RIPPED UP AND SCRAPPED, BEGUN
AGAIN. ....THREE WOMEN 184 277
FOLLOW HOLIDAY REVEL BEGUN LONG SINCE, ...CINDERELLA 304 10
BEHAVIOR (2)
SMILING AT THIS BEHAVIOR, SUBJUGATING THEIR ENEMIES ....LESSON. 80 22
I COULDN'T UNDERSTAND HER STUPID BEHAVIOR! ....IN PLASTER 159 11
BEHEADED (2)
TO THE BEHEADED HEAD OF A SULLEN DOLL, ONE BRAID, ...PERSEUS 83 37
RULE THEIR BEDS LIKE BEHEADED AND RESURRECTED AND ALL SILENT
ROYALTY, ... QUEEN MARY'S ROSE GARDEN 290 5
BEHIND (31)
BEHIND SNARLED THICKETS OF MY EYES ....PURSUIT 23 29
IS CLOSED; THE TUB EXISTS BEHIND OUR BACK: ....TALE OF A TUB 25 31
STILL DREAM BEHIND ....SOUTHERN SUNRISE 26 3

BEHIND (CONT.)
    BEHIND A GOATHERD'S HUT: ....SPIDER   48   10
    BEHIND SHUT DOORS; THE DAIRY HERDS ....HARDCASTLE CRAGS   63   32
    LEAVES AND LILIES FLATTENED TO PAPER BEHIND YOU ....YADWIGHS.   85   16
    NOBODY WINTERING NOW BEHIND ....POINT SHIRLEY   110   25
    BEHIND HIM THE HOTDOGS SPLIT AND DRIZZLED .....SUICIDE OFF EGG ROCK   115   1
    LEAVES BEHIND US WARP AND LAPSE. ....MAGNOLIA SHOALS   122   11
    DOZE BEHIND THE OLD MASKS OF FURY. ......SLEEP IN THE MOJAVE DESERT   144   19
    BLUE SHRUB BEHIND THE GLASS ....PARLIAMENT HILL FIELDS   153   45
    THE TULIPS TURN TO ME, AND THE WINDOW BEHIND ME ....TULIPS   161   44
    THE TULIPS SHOULD BE BEHIND BARS LIKE DANGEROUS ANIMALS; ....TULIPS   162   58
    A BONEWHITE LIGHT, LIKE DEATH, BEHIND ALL THINGS. ....INSOMNIAC   163   4
    BEHIND WHICH THE SECRET PASSAGE LIES -- STALE AIR, ...WIDOW   164   8
    THEY HAVE LIVED BEHIND GLASS ALL THEIR LIVES, THEY HAVE BEEN
        CARED FOR TENDERLY. ....THREE WOMEN   184 264
    I LEAVE MY HEALTH BEHIND. I LEAVE SOMEONE ....THREE WOMEN   184 272
    LIMBS, IMAGES, SHRIEKS. BEHIND THE CONCRETE BUNKERS ....BERCK-PLAGE   197   29
    BEHIND THE GLASS OF THIS CAR ....BERCK-PLAGE   200 109
    GLIDING UP IN LOW GEAR BEHIND THE CART. ....BERCK-PLAGE   200 112
    WHAT IS THIS, BEHIND THIS VEIL, IS IT UGLY, IS IT BEAUTIFUL? ...
                                        ... A BIRTHDAY PRESENT   206   1
    THERE ARE BLACK DISKS BEHIND IT, THE DISKS OF OUTRAGE, ...COURAGE.   209   3
    BEHIND TWO EYES IN WHICH NOTHING IS REFLECTED BUT MONKEYS. *A SECRET   219   20
    AND CRAWLS BEHIND IT LIKE A WORM. ....THE FEARFUL   256   2
    ONE CAMOUFLAGING ITSELF BEHIND ANOTHER. ....THE RIVAL/DP. 291   5
    BEHIND MOCK-CEREMONY OF YOUR GRIEF ....DIRGE FOR A JOKER   302   5
    "BEHIND ME THEN I HEARD A VOICE ....THE DREAM   311   19
    AND THE SNOW BLOW UP BEHIND: ....GO GET THE GOODLY SQUAB   313   14
    FEVER FROM THE WORLD BEHIND. ....DANSE MACABRE   321   6
    BEHIND WHICH THE DECLINING MOON HAS SET, ...THE PRINCESS.   334   36
    BEHIND THE ZODIAC ON ATTIC DOOR ....THE PRINCESS AND THE GOBLINS   335   58
BEIGE (1)
    OF PINK AND BEIGE, IMPECCABLE BAMBOO, ...MORNING IN THE HOS.   332   4
BEING (18)
    THAT ALL MERIT'S IN BEING MEAT ....THE GLUTTON   40   5
    WHITENESS BEING WHAT I REMEMBER ....WHITENESS I REMEMBER   102   1
    I SAID: I MUST REMEMBER THIS, BEING SMALL. POEM.1.WHO.   132   28
    LIKE LOCAL TROLLS IN THE SPELL OF A SUPERIOR BEING. ......TWO CAMP.   144   6
    AFTER ALL, IT WAS A KIND OF MARRIAGE, BEING SO CLOSE. ...IN PLASTER   160   51
    IT IS LIKE BEING MAILED INTO SPACE, ...WUTHERING HEIGHTS   167   23
    CRUELLY, BEING BARREN. ....ELM 192   23
    OF BEING WHEELED OFF UNDER CROSSES AND A RAIN OF PIETAS. ...
                                        ... APPREHENSIONS   195   15
    I MADE A FIRE; BEING TIRED ....BURNING THE LETTERS   204   1
    THAT BEING FREE. WHAT WOULD THE DARK ....THE JAILER   227   41
    SHOVE INTO BEING, DRAGGING ....THALIDOMIDE   252   14
    MOVING, BEING MOVED. AND WE'LL IMAGINE   DIALOGUE OVER A OUIJA BOARD   276   8
    AND STILL I'M SKEPTIC. I KNOW. I'M BEING FOOLISH ....DIALOGUE O.   277   35
    SPRUNG TO BEING ON OUR WEDDING NIGHT ...DIALOGUE OVER A OUIJA BOARD   280 140
    BEING NOT YOU, NOR I, NOR US AT ALL, ...DIALOGUE OVER A OUIJA BOARD   285 308
    FOR BEING TOO WELL-BRED AND SMELLESS AND LIKING THE CITY. ...
                                        ... QUEEN MARY'S ROSE GARDEN   290   20
    BEING CRYSTALLIZED FROM CARBON ....NOTES TO A NEOPHYTE   307   23
    FOR BEING SUCH A RUDE ASSAILANT ....THE DREAM   311   16
BELCHED (1)
    BELCHED INTO BLAZE AND, THOUGH RED-HOT, KEPT WHOLE .....DIALOGUE O.   280 158
BELGE (1)
    BELGE TROLL, THE LOW ................................EAVESDROPPER   261   49
BELIEF (3)
    OF CAMBRIC OR WATERDROPS, WHO KNOWS WHAT BELIEF ....DIALOGUE O.   282 224
    MIGHT WORK ON THIS GLASS MEDIUM. BELIEF, YES, ...DIALOGUE O.   282 225
    YOU NEVER ALTERED YOUR AMUSED BELIEF ....DIRGE FOR A JOKER   302   7
BELIEVE (10)
    TO BELIEVE BEYOND HEART'S FLARE ....VANITY FAIR   33   26
    THE HONEY-FEAST OF THE BERRIES HAS STUNNED THEM; THEY BELIEVE IN
        HEAVEN. ....BLACKBERRYING   169   17
    HOW I WOULD LIKE TO BELIEVE IN TENDERNESS --- ....MOON.   173   19
    WHEN I FIRST SAW IT, THE SMALL RED SEEP, I DID NOT BELIEVE IT. ...
                                        ... THREE WOMEN   177   15
    I COULD NOT BELIEVE IT. IS IT SO DIFFICULT ....THREE WOMEN   177   25
    I AM SIMPLE AGAIN. I BELIEVE IN MIRACLES. ....THREE WOMEN   185 319
    I DO NOT BELIEVE IN THOSE TERRIBLE CHILDREN ....THREE WOMEN   185 320
    BELIEVE ME, THEY'LL BURY YOU IN IT. ....THE APPLICANT   221   25
    YOU DON'T QUITE BELIEVE IN IT. YOU'RE DEAF TO REAL .....DIALOGUE O.   278   63
    BELIEVE, IF THEY COULD MANAGE TO CONVINCE ....DIALOGUE O.   278   66
BELL (5)
    THE SKY'S GREAT BELL GLASS AND BRIEFLY ENGRAVE ...IN MIDAS' COUNTRY   99   8
    ON THIS HILL, WITH ITS VIEW OF LIT CASTLES, EACH SWUNG BELL STARS.   166   38
    ADDRESSING IT, WHILE THE HILLS ROLL THE NOTES OF THE DEAD BELL; ...
                                        ... BERCK-PLAGE   200   95
    THE DEAD BELL, ...DEATH & CO.   255   29
    THE DEAD BELL. ....DEATH & CO.   255   30
BELLED (1)
    CLOCKS BELLED TWELVE. MAIN STREET SHOWED OTHERWISE ....OWL   101   1

BELLIED (2)
      STUDY WINDOWS BELLIED IN ....THE DISQUIETING MUSES   75   18
      BELLIED ON A NIMBUS OF SUN-GLAZED BUTTERCUP. ....WATERCOLOR.   112   18
BELLIES (3)
      PLUMPED THE BELLIES OF THE MICE ....THE THIN PEOPLE   64   10
      BELLIES PALLID AND UPTURNED, ...MUSSEL HUNTER AT ROCK HARBOR   97   85
      HANGING THEIR BLUEGREEN BELLIES AND THEIR WING PANES IN A CHINESE
         SCREEN. ....BLACKBERRYING   168   16
BELLING (1)
      SETTLE IN THEIR BELLING DRESSES. ....HEAVY WOMEN   158   5
BELL-JAR (1)
      UNDER THE BELL-JAR OF A WONDERLAND. ....QUEEN MARY'S ROSE GARDEN   290   14
BELLOW (1)
      TOWARD THE ROWDY BELLOW AND BACK AGAIN ....THE BULL OF BENDYLAW   108   11
BELLOWED (1)
      THE BLACK BULL BELLOWED BEFORE THE SEA. ....THE BULL OF BENDYLAW   108   1
BELLRINGERS (1)
      OF BELLRINGERS AND SINGERS ROUSE ....A WINTER'S TALE   87   33
BELLS (8)
      OF BELLS CALLS HOLY ONES, HER TONGUE ....VANITY FAIR 32   9
      BELLS, HOOVES, OF THE HIGH-STEPPING BLACK GOATS WOKE US. OTHER TWO.   68   3
      THE CLIFFS ARE EDGED WITH TREFOILS, STARS AND BELLS .....FINISTERRE   169   10
      TWICE ON SUNDAY, THE BELLS STARTLE THE SKY --- ....MOON.   173   12
      SQUEEZING THE BREATH FROM THE BLOOD BELLS ....MEDUSA   225   28
      POPPING UPWARD FROM THE MOUTHS OF BELLS ....LYONNESSE   234   9
      THE DULL BELLS TONGUE THE HOUR. ....BY CANDLELIGHT   236   8
      HOOVES, DOLOROUS BELLS --- ....SHEEP IN FOG   262   7
BELL-TONGUED (1)
      LET BELL-TONGUED BIRDS DESCANT IN BLACKEST FEATHER .....LADY AND T.   69   25
BELLY (11)
      ALL CREATION, WERE IT NOT FOR A BIGGER BELLY ....PERSEUS   83   33
      OF THE FERRYING CURRENTS, BELLY ....OWL   102   13
      AND THE ROYAL ROSE IN THE BULL'S BELLY, ...THE BULL OF BENDYLAW   108   20
      GOD-FATHERED INTO THE WORLD FROM MY MOTHER'S BELLY: ...ELECTRA ON.   116   7
      YET HIS BELLY KEPT ITS FIRE ....MEDALLION   124   16
      OR MOTHER A HORSE, MY BELLY MOVES. POEM.2.DARK.   132   13
      THE CELLAR'S BELLY. THEY'VE BLOWN MY SPARKLER OUT. POEM.6.W.   135   8
      THE STONES OF THE BELLY WERE PEACEABLE, ...POEM.7.S.   136   9
      ATTENDING HER COT IS LESS THAN A BELLY ACHE, ...MAGI   148   13
      AND UGLY, MY BELLY A SILK STOCKING ....ZOO KEEPER'S WIFE   154   6
      SHRIEK FROM MY BELLY LIKE ARROWS, AND THESE I RIDE. ......THE OTHER   202   19
BELLYACHE (1)
      FINE FOR THE MIGRAINE OR THE BELLYACHE. AND THIS ....THE TOUR   238   19
BELLY-BEDDED (1)
      OF A SOW LOUNGED BELLY-BEDDED ON THAT BLACK COMPOST, ...SOW   61   25
BELLY-SCALE (1)
      IN EACH OPAQUE BELLY-SCALE: ....MEDALLION   124   19
BELONG (2)
      THEY ARE NOT MINE. THEY DO NOT BELONG TO ME. ....THREE WOMEN   185 322
      THE CHAIRS BELONG TO ITS DARKNESS. I SMELL DECAY ....DIALOGUE O.   285 314
BELOW (7)
      BELOW: A FEN WHERE WATER STOOD; ....BUCOLICS   24   9
      BELOW, ROCKED HAVOC-SICK, VOYAGERS LIE ....CHANNEL CROSSING   26   9
      BELOW THE RAMSHACKLE BACK-ALLEY BALCONIES, ...ALICANTE LULLABY   43   4
      BELOW SHOULDERS NOT ONCE ....FULL FATHOM FIVE   93   37
      WITH THE LANGUOR OF IDOLS BELOW ....IN MIDAS' COUNTRY   99   7
      BELOW US A WHITE GULL KEEPS ....MAGNOLIA SHOALS   122   13
      IT FLOWS OFF BELOW THE GREEN AND WHITE ....THE BURNT-OUT SPA   138   22
BELSEN (1)
      A JEW TO DACHAU, AUSCHWITZ, BELSEN. ....DADDY   223   33
BELT (1)
      WORSE -- SAW DANGLING FROM THAT SPIKE-STUDDED BELT ......SNOWMAN O.   59   37
BENCHES (1)
      THE EMPTY BENCHES OF MEMORY LOOK OVER STONES, ...BERCK-PLAGE   199   88
BEND (4)
      THE GESTURE, BEND AND HOLD THE PRONE MAN'S HEAD. ..CHANNEL CROSSING   27   36
      I BEND OVER THIS DRAINED BASIN WHERE THE SMALL FISH   PRIVATE GROUND   131   20
      WIDOW, THE COMPASSIONATE TREES BEND IN, ...WIDOW   164   26
      THE SPRY HOOKS THAT BEND AND CRINGE, AND THE SMILES, THE SMILES. ...
                                           ... BURNING THE LETTERS   204   21
BENDING (2)
      POURS BY LIKE DESTINY, BENDING ....WUTHERING HEIGHTS   167   12
      BENDING, ON ME IN PARTICULAR, ITS MILD EYES. ....MOON.   173   21
BENDS (2)
      OF HER BARE SHOULDER, WHILE SHE BENDS,   TWO VIEWS OF A CADAVER ROOM   114   16
      NOW I AM A LAKE. A WOMAN BENDS OVER ME, ...MIRROR   174   10
BENDYLAW (2)
      THE BULL OF BENDYLAW ....THE BULL OF BENDYLAW   108   T
      HOVE UP AGAINST BENDYLAW. ....THE BULL OF BENDYLAW   108   3
BENEATH (6)
      BLACK BENEATH BLAND MIRROR-SHEEN, ...LORELEI   94   3
      I SMELL THAT WHITENESS HERE, BENEATH THE STONES ....MOONRISE   98   16
      SEATED BENEATH THE TONELESS WATER! ....THE BURNT-OUT SPA   138   28
      BENEATH THE FLAT HANDKERCHIEF YOU WEAR INSTEAD OF A HAT. STINGS/DR   293   6
      BENEATH THE FRINGES OF FORBIDDEN ROBE, ...METAMORPHOSES OF THE MOON   308   32

BENEATH (CONT.)
    ECLIPSED BENEATH BLIND LID OF LAND ....DANSE MACABRE   320   2
BENEFACTRESS (1)
    OR YOUR WHITE-HAIRED BENEFACTRESS, WHO MAY SEE FIT .....DIALOGUE O. 277   48
BENIDORM (1)
    IN BENIDORM THERE ARE MELONS, ...FIESTA MELONS   46   1
BENIGN (1)
    HEDGING MEADOWS OF BENIGN ....WATERCOLOR OF GRANTCHESTER MEADOWS 112   19
BENT (9)
    DOWN DEEP INTO THE BENT BULL-NECK. CUMBROUS ROUTINE, NOT ARTWORK. ...
                                                     ... THE GORING   47   7
    O BENT BOW OF THORNS ....RESOLVE   52   16
    THE GIRL BENT HOMEWARD, BRIMFUL OF GENTLE TALK ....SNOWMAN O.   59   50
    BENT UNDER A BUNDLE ....THE EVERLASTING MONDAY 62   2
    I BENT OVER THE PLANTS IN MY LEATHER-KNEED ....SPINACH-PICKER.   89   17
    AT A FIELD OF HORSES, NECKS BENT, MANES BLOWN, ...THE EYE-MOTE 109   2
    AND I SLEPT ON LIKE A BENT FINGER. ....LOVE LETTER 147   19
    THE BENT PRINT BULGING BEFORE HIM LIKE SCENERY. ....BERCK-PLAGE 197   23
    KNEELS, BACK BENT, AS BEST HE CAN ....BY CANDLELIGHT 237   27
BENT-BACKED (1)
    BENT-BACKED ATLAS, OUR TRAVELED PRAWN. ....YOU'RE 141   12
BEQUEATHS (1)
    UNTIL HIS CHISEL BEQUEATHS ....SCULPTOR   92   22
BERCK-PLAGE (1)
    BERCK-PLAGE ....BERCK-PLAGE 196   T
BEREFT (1)
    BEREFT OF MOSES AND OF MORES; ..INSOLENT STORM STRIKES AT THE SKULL 326   16
BERG (1)
    TAKE A LOOK AT THE WHITE, HIGH BERG ON HIS FOREHEAD -- ...LYONNESSE 233   3
BERLIN (1)
    THE ART STUDENTS IN WEST BERLIN. ....ON DECK 143   24
BERRIES (9)
    BERRIES REDDEN. A BODY OF WHITENESS ....MOONRISE   98   13
    WHITE-BEARDED, WEARY. THE BERRIES PURPLE ....MOONRISE   98   29
    FEED ME THE BERRIES OF DARK. POEM.3.MAENAD.   133   17
    LIKE MONDAY DRUNKARDS. THE MILKY BERRIES ....LEAVING EARLY 145   10
    I COME TO ONE BUSH OF BERRIES SO RIPE IT IS A BUSH OF FLIES, ...
                                             ... BLACKBERRYING   168   15
    THE HONEY-FEAST OF THE BERRIES HAS STUNNED THEM; THEY BELIEVE IN
        HEAVEN. ....BLACKBERRYING 169   17
    ONE MORE HOOK, AND THE BERRIES AND BUSHES END. .......BLACKBERRYING 169   18
    BERRIES CAST DARK ....ARIEL   239   11
    THE BLOOD BERRIES ARE THEMSELVES, THEY ARE VERY STILL. ....YEARS 255   23
BERRY (1)
    CUPPING THE BERRY PROTECTIVELY BEFORE ....BITTER STRAWBERRIES 300   37
BERYL (1)
    TO A BERYL JUNGLE, AND DREAMED THAT BRIGHT MOON-LILIES ...YADWIGHA.   86   29
BESET (1)
    AND SHADOWS ONLY -- CAVE-MOUTH BRISTLE BESET -- ....GOATSUCKER 111   13
BESIDE (9)
    BESIDE A NEIGHBOR'S HOUSE ....DREAM WITH CLAM-DIGGERS   43   6
    SUSPENDS BESIDE IT THE FIRST POINT, THE STARTING ....GHOST'S.   91   30
    OBJECT BESIDE THE MAD, STRAIGHT ROAD ....SLEEP IN THE MOJAVE DESERT 143   6
    BESIDE THE POSTCARD STALLS. ....FINISTERRE   170   29
    GROWING BESIDE YOU, LIKE A TREE, ...FOR A FATHERLESS SON   205   2
    AND YOU OUT COLD BESIDE ME IN YOUR CHAIR. ....STOPPED DEAD 230   5
    THE WALKING BESIDE STILL WATER? MEMORY? ....MYSTIC   268   17
    IF THAT ELDERBERRY BUSH BESIDE THE GATE *DIALOGUE OVER A OUIJA BOARD 280 157
    BESIDE A SUNBLUE SEA, AND MOURN THE FLAGON ....SONNET: TO TIME   311   10
BEST (12)
    VIES WITH BEST QUEEN OVER ....VANITY FAIR 33   31
    LIKE A LAST STORM-CROSSED LEAF? BEST GET YOU GONE ......DIALOGUE B.   39   44
    HOW BEST BEAUTY'S BORN OF HARDIHOOD. ....MAYFLOWER 60   8
    APE OF HER LOOK. BEST RID ....THE LADY AND THE EARTHENWARE HEAD   69   5
    STILL, THEY'RE OUR BEST MUSTERING OF HEIGHT: BY ....ABOVE THE OXBOW   88   5
    AGE WEARS THE BEST BLACK FABRIC ....OLD LADIES' HOME 120   13
    EVEN MY BEST FRIEND THINKS I'M IN THE COUNTRY. ....FACE LIFT   156   19
    SHE HUMORED MY WEAKNESS LIKE THE BEST OF NURSES; ....IN PLASTER 159   26
    KNEELS, BACK BENT, AS BEST HE CAN ....BY CANDLELIGHT 237   27
    IT IS BEST TO MEET IN A CUL-DE-SAC, ...GIGOLO   267   4
    OUR WORLD AND THEIRS WE'D BEST PLAY SAFE AND GROOM .....DIALOGUE O. 281 186
    COUNTS. SUCH DUELS INFECT BEST FRIENDSHIPS. PAN ....DIALOGUE O. 283 271
BESTOWING (1)
    BY BESTOWING LARGESSE, HONOR, ...BLACK ROOK IN RAINY WEATHER   57   21
BET (1)
    DIRECT TO YES. I BET IT'S PAN. WHO'LL ..DIALOGUE OVER A OUIJA BOARD 277   27
BETRAY (1)
    WILL BETRAY THE COMPANY I KEEP. ....THE DISQUIETING MUSES   76   56
BETRAYED (2)
    IN WHICH OUR COMRADES ARE BETRAYED, WE FREEZE .....CHANNEL CROSSING   27   14
    BETRAYED IN MUTE GEOMETRY OF BROKEN ....SONNET: TO EVA 304   6
BETRAYS (2)
    STOPS US, BETRAYS US; ....MUSHROOMS 139   8
    "PERSPECTIVE BETRAYS WITH ITS DICHOTOMY: ....LOVE IS A PARALLAX 329   1

BETTER (12)
  OF NATURE: WHAT BETTER WAY TO TEST TAUT FIBER .....CHANNEL CROSSING   27   16
  BETTER THAT EVERY FIBER CRACK ....MONOLOGUE AT 3 A.M.   40   1
  I SHOULD HAVE KNOWN BETTER. ....GREEN ROCK, WINTHROP BAY   104   3
  BUT THE CHILDREN ARE BETTER FOR IT, ...THE TIMES ARE TIDY   107   14
  BEASTS OF OASIS, A BETTER TIME. ....THE EYE-MOTE   109   15
  BETTER THE FLAT LEER OF THE IDIOT, ...THE RAVAGED FACE   116   9
  BETTER, BETTER, AND MORE ACCEPTABLE ....THE RAVAGED FACE   116   12
  BETTER, BETTER, AND MORE ACCEPTABLE ....THE RAVAGED FACE   116   12
  IT WOULD BE BETTER IF THEY WERE ALIVE, AND THAT'S WHAT THEY
    WERE. ....STILLBORN   142   13
  IN YOUR HOUSE, THE MAIN HOUSE, YOU WERE BETTER OFF. *THE BABYSITTERS 174   19
  "IT SMELLS OF SALT COD, YOU HAD BETTER ....A SECRET 220   29
  THERE! THAT SHUTS HIM UP! SO. BETTER SO,*DIALOGUE OVER A OUIJA BOARD 284 300
BETWEEN (39)
  PLAYS BETWEEN THESE. ....TWO SISTERS OF PERSEPHONE   31   4
  DIALOGUE BETWEEN GHOST AND PRIEST *DIALOGUE BETWEEN GHOST AND PRIEST   38   T
  BETWEEN THE CABBAGE-ROSES ....MISS DRAKE PROCEEDS TO SUPPER   41   10
  AND SEE THAT FIRST HOUSE, AS IF BETWEEN ....LANDOWNERS   53   6
  FLOWER FORGET-ME-NOTS BETWEEN THE STONES ....NOVEMBER GRAVEYARD   56   7
  BETWEEN TICK ....ALL THE DEAD DEARS   71   32
  TO CHOOSE BETWEEN YOUR WORLD OF JUNGLE GREEN ....YADWIGHA.   85   9
  BETWEEN THE SNUFF AND RED TAR-PAPER APARTMENTS, ...ABOVE THE OXBOW   88   13
  AT THIS JOINT BETWEEN TWO WORLDS AND TWO ENTIRELY ....GHOST'S.   90   12
  AS I COULD BETWEEN BARE TOES? ....MUSSEL HUNTER AT ROCK HARBOR   96   50
  FIFTEEN YEARS BETWEEN ME AND THE BAY ......GREEN ROCK, WINTHROP BAY 105   4
  BETWEEN THE ROAD AND THE LAKE WATER, ...BLUE MOLES   126   12
  FROM THE DOOR AS EVER. WHAT HAPPENS BETWEEN US ....BLUE MOLES   127   34
  SOFT SUEDE TONGUES BETWEEN HIS BONES. ....THE BURNT-OUT SPA 138   11
  THEY HAVE PROPPED MY HEAD BETWEEN THE PILLOW AND THE SHEET-CUFF ...
                                                          ... TULIPS   160   8
  LIKE AN EYE BETWEEN TWO WHITE LIDS THAT WILL NOT SHUT. ......TULIPS   160   9
  BETWEEN THE EYE OF THE SUN AND THE EYES OF THE TULIPS, ...TULIPS   161   47
  OF IMMORTAL BLANKNESS BETWEEN STARS ....WIDOW   164   24
  HAND FOLDING HAND, AND NOTHING IN BETWEEN. ....WIDOW.   164   31
  FROM BETWEEN TWO HILLS A SUDDEN WIND FUNNELS AT ME, ..BLACKBERRYING 169   20
  I FOLLOW THE SHEEP PATH BETWEEN THEM. A LAST HOOK BRINGS ME
                                                  ... BLACKBERRYING   169   23
  AND WHAT IF TWO LIVES LEAKED BETWEEN MY THIGHS? ....THREE WOMEN   180 120
  TASTING THE BITTERNESS BETWEEN MY TEETH. ....THREE WOMEN   184 286
  TIGHT WIRES BETWEEN US, ...THE RABBIT CATCHER   194   27
  STREAMING BETWEEN MY WALLS? ....THE OTHER   201   4
  BETWEEN MYSELF AND MYSELF. ....THE OTHER   202   27
  BETWEEN THIS WISH AND THAT WISH. ....BURNING THE LETTERS   204   28
  BETWEEN THE YELLOW LETTUCES AND THE GERMAN CABBAGE ....BURNING.   205   39
  SILVER BEAST BETWEEN TWO DARK CANYONS, ..THE COURAGE OF SHUTTING-UP   210   9
  HAVE A THOUSAND CLEAN CELLS BETWEEN US, ...STINGS   214   6
  A DIFFERENCE BETWEEN US? ....A SECRET   219   5
  THERE IS NOTHING BETWEEN US. ....MEDUSA   226   41
  THE FIRE'S BETWEEN US. ....GETTING THERE   249   51
  IN MUNICH, MORGUE BETWEEN PARIS AND ROME, ...THE MUNICH MANNEQUINS   263   12
  SQUATTED DOWN BETWEEN THE ROWS ....BITTER STRAWBERRIES   299   3
  BETWEEN THUMB AND FOREFINGER. ....BITTER STRAWBERRIES   300   39
  BETWEEN STEEL PALMS OF INCLINATION, TAKE IT, ...SONNET: TO EVA   304   3
  THE CHOICE BETWEEN THE MICA MYSTERY ......METAMORPHOSES OF THE MOON   308   37
  A CROSS OF CONTRADICTION, RACKED BETWEEN METAMORPHOSES OF THE MOON   308   47
BEWARE (4)
  BEWARE, BEWARE ....BATTLE-SCENE 84   19
  BEWARE, BEWARE ....BATTLE-SCENE 84   19
  BEWARE ....LADY LAZARUS 246 80
  BEWARE. ....LADY LAZARUS 246 81
BEWITCHED (1)
  WERE BEWITCHED TO ASSIDUOUS LOVERS, ...DIALOGUE EN ROUTE   309   20
BEYOND (13)
  AND OCTOPUS -- SCRABBLING JUST BEYOND THE VIEW, ...TALE OF A TUB   25   20
  SUCH FORCE CAN LAST; BUT BEYOND, THE NEUTRAL VIEW CHANNEL CROSSING   26   7
  TO BELIEVE BEYOND HEART'S FLARE ....VANITY FAIR   33   26
  SUFFERING-TOUGHENED BEYOND THE FETCH ....THE BEGGARS   48   15
  HORIZONS BEYOND VISION, SPILL VISION ....ABOVE THE OXBOW   88   24
  BEYOND THE MUNDANE ORDER, ...LORELEI   94   22
  BORNE, FOR A USE BEYOND MY ....MUSSEL HUNTER AT ROCK HARBOR   96   37
  BEYOND THE BREAKWATER, SPOTTY WITH BARNACLES? ....BERCK-PLAGE   197   41
  LESS DREAD OF THE WORLD BEYOND THAN OURS. THAT'S BECAUSE*DIALOGUE O. 278   62
  BEYOND THE WINDOW-FRAME TONIGHT. WIND WARNS ....DIALOGUE O.   286 336
  BEYOND THE WINDOW) SHE LIES ON CUSHIONS CURLED ....FEMALE AUTHOR 301   3
  BEYOND THE INTERVAL OF NOW AND HERE: ....TWO LOVERS. 327   11
  BEYOND THE INCONSTANT GREEN ....TOUCH-AND-GO   335   6
BIBLE (1)
  I ENTERED YOUR BIBLE, I BOARDED YOUR ARK ....ZOO KEEPER'S WIFE 155   28
BICKER (1)
  OF LEAVES' BICKER AND WHISK IN BABEL TONGUES, ..PLETHORA OF DRYADS.   67   21
BICKERING (2)
  AND BICKERING SHOPS; ....STREET SONG 35   4
  THE SHINGLE BOOMS, BICKERING UNDER ....POINT SHIRLEY 110   2

                                             TITLE   PAGE LINE
BIDS (1)
   A SORCERER BIDS FAREWELL TO SEEM ..A SORCERER BIDS FAREWELL TO SEEM 324   T
BIER (1)
   THE SEAWALL AND DROPS ONTO A BIER ....POINT SHIRLEY 110   6
BIG (26)
   MILK-SPOUT, BIG FINGER ....WORDS FOR A NURSERY   73   7
   A BIG HANDKERCHIEF WITH BLUE ....MUSSEL HUNTER AT ROCK HARBOR   97 63
   NOTHING IS BIG OR FAR. ....WATERCOLOR OF GRANTCHESTER MEADOWS 111   3
   THIS LOAF'S BIG WITH ITS YEASTY RISING. ....METAPHORS 116   5
   THIS IS A DARK HOUSE, VERY BIG. POEM.2.DARK. 132   1
   O I AM TOO BIG TO GO BACKWARD: POEM.3.MAENAD. 133   8
   HERE ON THE LAST FRONTIER OF THE BIG, BRASH SPIRIT ....TWO CAMP. 145 12
   DIRTY AS A BOOTSOLE AND BIG AS A HOSPITAL SINK ...ZOO KEEPER'S WIFE 155 35
   THE PEACEFULNESS IS SO BIG IT DAZES YOU, ...TULIPS 161 32
   THE BIG DIPPER IS MY ONLY FAMILIAR. ....STARS OVER THE DORDOGNE 165 17
   BIG AS THE BALL OF MY THUMB, AND DUMB AS EYES .......BLACKBERRYING 168   5
   ON THE GAMEROOM PIANO, WHEN THE "BIG PEOPLE" WERE OUT, ...BABY. 175 23
   LIKE A BIG SEA. FAR OFF, FAR OFF, I FEEL THE FIRST WAVE TUG THREE. 179 109
   I HAVE PAPERED HIS ROOM WITH BIG ROSES, ...THREE WOMEN 186 328
   I ENVY THE BIG NOISES, ...LITTLE FUGUE 188 19
   THE NARCISSI, TOO, ARE BOWING TO SOME BIG THING: *AMONG THE NARCISSI 190   4
   THE PRINT OF ITS BIG FOOT LAST WINTER, ...PHEASANT 191 11
   THIS IS RAIN NOW, THIS BIG HUSH. ....ELM 192 14
   YOU ARE TOO BIG. THEY MUST TAKE YOU BACK! ....WORDS HEARD. 203 15
   IT STANDS AT MY WINDOW, BIG AS THE SKY. ....A BIRTHDAY PRESENT 207 49
   STINGS BIG AS DRAWING PINS! ....THE SWARM 217 56
   THAT BIG BLUE HEAD -- ....A SECRET 220 26
   BIG AS A FRISCO SEAL ....DADDY 222 10
   THAT THE BIG GOD ....LYONNESSE 234 20
   THE BIG STRIP TEASE. ....LADY LAZARUS 245 29
   TO THE ELECTRIC MILKER, THE WIFEY, THE BIG BLUE EYE ...EAVESDROPPER 261 43
BIGGER (2)
   ALL CREATION, WERE IT NOT FOR A BIGGER BELLY ....PERSEUS   83 33
   ON A SQUARE NO BIGGER THAN A CARPET ....ON DECK 142 12
BIGNESS (1)
   THE DOCTORS MOVE AMONG US AS IF OUR BIGNESS ....THREE WOMEN 179 114
BIKINIS (1)
   OBSCENE BIKINIS HIDE IN THE DUNES, ...BERCK-PLAGE 197 24
BILLHOOK (1)
   THEN THERE IS THAT ANTIQUE BILLHOOK, THE TONGUE, ...COURAGE. 210 17
BILLS (1)
   BREED INNUMERABLE BILLS, BONA FIDE: ....DIALOGUE EN ROUTE 308 17
BINDINGS (1)
   WE HEFT GLOBED FLINT, RACKED IN VEINS' BARBED BINDINGS; ...FIRESONG   30 18
BINGE (1)
   A BINGE OF JEERS. LOOK. HE'S RUNNING THROUGH ....DIALOGUE O. 284 296
BINGO (1)
   THE BINGO PLAYERS, THE PLAYERS AT LOVE ....ON DECK 142 11
BIRD (13)
   THE WARNING WHIRR AND BURRING OF THE BIRD ....GOATSUCKER 111   2
   EACH THUMB-SIZE BIRD ....WATERCOLOR OF GRANTCHESTER MEADOWS 112   6
   COMFORTLESS AS SALT. SNAKE AND BIRD ....SLEEP IN THE MOJAVE DESERT 144 18
   AMONG BIRD FEET AND THE STEMS OF PLANTS. ....LOVE LETTER 147 27
   GHOST OF A LEAF, GHOST OF A BIRD. ....PARLIAMENT HILL FIELDS 153 28
   WHAT IS THAT BIRD THAT CRIES ....THREE WOMEN 186 348
   ADRIFT IN THE GUISE OF SOME GREAT-TALONED BIRD ....DIALOGUE O. 285 311
   THE IDIOT BIRD LEAPS UP AND DRUNKEN LEANS ....SONNET: TO EVA 305 13
   IF YOU DISSECT A BIRD ....TRIO OF LOVE SONGS 315 37
   THE IDIOT BIRD LEAPS OUT AND DRUNKEN LEANS ....DOOMSDAY 316   1
   THE IDIOT BIRD LEAPS OUT AND DRUNKEN LEANS. ....DOOMSDAY 316   6
   THE IDIOT BIRD LEAPS OUT AND DRUNKEN LEANS. ....DOOMSDAY 316 12
   THE IDIOT BIRD LEAPS OUT AND DRUNKEN LEANS, ...DOOMSDAY 316 18
BIRD-BEAKED (1)
   NEEDLES KNIT IN A BIRD-BEAKED ....OLD LADIES' HOME 120   8
BIRD-EATING (1)
   AND THE BEAR-FURRED, BIRD-EATING SPIDER ....ZOO KEEPER'S WIFE 155 30
BIRD-FEET (1)
   MUFFLES THEIR BIRD-FEET: THEY WHISTLE FOR JOY. ....LEAVING EARLY 146 37
BIRD-FOOT (1)
   THROUGH LICHEN-LID AND PASSING BIRD-FOOT ....TOUCH-AND-GO 335   4
BIRDMILK (1)
   BIRDMILK IS FEATHERS, ...POEM.3.MAENAD. 133   9
BIRD-QUICK (1)
   WITH BIRD-QUICK EYE COCKED ASKEW .....MISS DRAKE PROCEEDS TO SUPPER   41 14
BIRD-RACKETING (1)
   UNTIL BIRD-RACKETING DAWN ....THE SHRIKE   42 16
BIRDS (24)
   AT HIS HAND'S STAUNCH HEST, BIRDS BUILD. ....ODE FOR TED   29 18
   CALL HERE WITH FLYING COLORS ALL WATCHFUL BIRDS *WREATH FOR A BRIDAL   45 13
   AMBUSHED BIRDS BY ....THE SNOWMAN ON THE MOOR   59 34
   SHEEP DROWSED STONEWARD IN THEIR TUSSOCKS OF WOOL, AND BIRDS, ...
                                          ... HARDCASTLE CRAGS   63 34
   LET BELL-TONGUED BIRDS DESCANT IN BLACKEST FEATHER .....LADY AND T.   69 25
   AND BIRDS OF PARADISE, AND THE ROUND MOON, ...YADWIGHA   86 24
   TRUMPET-THROATS OPEN TO THE BEAKS OF BIRDS.*THE BEEKEEPER'S DAUGHTER 118   8

	TITLE	PAGE	LINE

BIRDS (CONT.)
THE SMALL BIRDS CONVERGE, CONVERGE ....THE MANOR GARDEN 125 19
THESE HALLS ARE FULL OF WOMEN WHO THINK THEY ARE BIRDS. *POEM.1.WHO. 131 21
THE BIRDS MADE MILK. POEM.3.MAENAD. 133   4
BRIGHT BIRDS IN THE SKY, CONSOLING, CONSOLING? ....THREE WOMEN 185 298
THERE ARE NO TREES OR BIRDS IN THIS WORLD, ...APPREHENSIONS 195   9
ON A BLACK WALL, UNIDENTIFIABLE BIRDS ...............APPREHENSIONS 195 16
SO I POKE AT THE CARBON BIRDS IN MY HOUSEDRESS. ....BURNING. 204 29
I SPREAD TO THE BEAKS OF BIRDS. ....THE JAILER 226 15
GRAY BIRDS OBSESS MY HEART, ...MARY'S SONG 257 13
TO PEOPLE THE BOUGHS WITH TALKING BIRDS. I'D PLANT .....DIALOGUE O. 280 169
PRETENDING THAT THE BIRDS ARE HERE TO STAY; ....NEVER TRY TO TRICK. 319   2
THE SINGING BIRDS PACK UP AND FLY AWAY; ....NEVER TRY TO TRICK. 320 17
GREEN-SINGING BIRDS EXPLODE FROM ALL THE ROCKS. PROLOGUE TO SPRING 322 15
THE MAESTRO GIVES THE SINGING BIRDS THEIR PAY ....DENOUEMENT 326   4
AN INSIGHT LIKE THE FLIGHT OF BIRDS: ....LOVE IS A PARALLAX 330 60
BLACK BIRDS OF OMEN ....TEMPER OF TIME 336   5
ANNOUNCING AFTER GLUTTED BIRDS HAVE FLOWN: ..EPITAPH IN THREE PARTS 337 21
BIRDS' (1)
BY THE BIRDS' IRREGULAR BABEL ....SPINSTER   49   5
BIRTH (3)
SET CLOSE, LIKE BIRTH PANGS. ....THE RABBIT CATCHER 194 16
OR IS IT A BIRTH CRY? ....STOPPED DEAD 230   2
FROM THE COMIC ACCIDENT OF BIRTH ....DIRGE FOR A JOKER 303   9
BIRTH-CRY (1)
THE TRUTH IS, ONE LATE OCTOBER, AT MY BIRTH-CRY ....ELECTRA ON. 117 34
BIRTHDAY (4)
POEM FOR A BIRTHDAY ....POEM FOR A BIRTHDAY 131   T
IN YOUR SISTER'S BIRTHDAY PICTURE START TO GLOW. .....PARLIAMENT H. 153 42
A BIRTHDAY PRESENT ....A BIRTHDAY PRESENT 206   T
THERE WOULD BE A NOBILITY THEN, THERE WOULD BE A BIRTHDAY.*BIRTHDAY. 208 59
BIRTH-DROWSE (1)
TO THIS INFANT STILL IN A BIRTH-DROWSE? ....CANDLES 149 33
BIRTHMARKS (1)
THE BIRTHMARKS THAT ARE HIS TRADEMARK --- ....DEATH & CO. 254   6
BIRTHSPOT (1)
TO PRINT YOUR FLAMING IMAGE IN BIRTHSPOT ....SONNET TO SATAN 323 11
BISCUITS (1)
LEMON TEA AND EARWIG BISCUITS -- CREEPY-CREEPY. ....THE TOUR 238 39
BIT (9)
BIT BY BIT TO THEIR FRIENDLY ....MUSSEL HUNTER AT ROCK HARBOR   97 89
BIT BY BIT TO THEIR FRIENDLY ....MUSSEL HUNTER AT ROCK HARBOR   97 89
BUT SHE'LL SOON FIND OUT THAT THAT DOESN'T MATTER A BIT. *IN PLASTER 160 54
I MAY BE A BIT OF A JEW. ....DADDY 223 40
BIT MY PRETTY RED HEART IN TWO. ....DADDY 224 56
IT'S A BIT BURNT-OUT, ...THE TOUR 237 11
A BIT OF A WILD MACHINE, A BIT OF A MESS! ....THE TOUR 237 12
A BIT OF A WILD MACHINE, A BIT OF A MESS! ....THE TOUR 237 12
OR A BIT OF BLOOD ....LADY LAZARUS 246 63
BITCHERY (1)
KNOWING NEITHER ABORTIONS NOR BITCHERY, ...WINTER TREES 258   6
BITCHES (1)
BITCHES TO RIPPLES OF SILVER ....GIGOLO 268 23
BITE (3)
I SHALL TAKE NO BITE OF YOUR BODY, ...MEDUSA 225 34
THE WHEELS, TWO RUBBER GRUBS, BITE THEIR SWEET TAILS. STOPPED DEAD 230   6
AUNTIE, IT MIGHT BITE! ....THE TOUR 237 14
BITES (2)
HE BITES, ...BALLOONS 272 25
BITES KEEN INTO EACH BRAVE LIMB ....AERIALIST 331 24
BITS (6)
ONE BREATH MIGHT SHIVER TO BITS, ...OLD LADIES' HOME 120   3
THE GARNET BITS BURNED LIKE THAT. ....MEDALLION 124 13
BITS OF BURNT PAPER WHEELING IN A BLOWN SKY. .........BLACKBERRYING 168 11
PARTS, BITS, COGS, THE SHINING MULTIPLES. ....THREE WOMEN 177 29
SPLITTING LIKE QUARTZ INTO A MILLION BITS. ....LESBOS 228 51
THOSE GLASS BITS IN THE GRATE STRIKE ME CHILL: ....DIALOGUE O. 285 306
BITTEN (3)
AND LEFT THE COBS TO RATTLE, BITTEN CLEAN. ....OUIJA   77 18
BLIND TWINS BITTEN BY BAD NATURE. ....BLUE MOLES 126   9
OF SLOW DISASTER: THE BITTEN APPLE ENDS ..METAMORPHOSES OF THE MOON 307 14
BITTER (7)
SHE BEARS A KING. TURNED BITTER ....TWO SISTERS OF PERSEPHONE   32 24
HALFWAY DOWN FROM GROVES WHERE THE THIN, BITTER ALMOND PIPS ..NET-. 121   2
WIDOW. THE BITTER SPIDER SITS ....WIDOW 164 11
A GROOVE OF OLD FAULTS, DEEP AND BITTER. ....EVENT 195 15
I AM BITTER? I'M AVERSE? ....THE TOUR 238 35
BITTER STRAWBERRIES ....BITTER STRAWBERRIES 299   T
OR THE BITTER BLINKING YELLOW ....JILTED 304   3
BITTERNESS (1)
TASTING THE BITTERNESS BETWEEN MY TEETH. ....THREE WOMEN 184 286
BITTERS (1)
HOW NATURE, SENSING THIS, COMPOUNDS HER BITTERS. ....DEPARTURE   51   5
BLACK (158)
ROOTED TO YOUR BLACK LOOK, THE PLAY TURNED TRAGIC: ...CONVERSATION.   21 12

52

BLACK (CONT.)
PLUNGES HEADLONG INTO THAT BLACK POND ....WINTER LANDSCAPE,   21   2
THE BLACK MARAUDER, HAULED BY LOVE ....PURSUIT   22   27
SPRAWLS, HUNCHED IN BLACK, AMONG BAGGAGE, WINCING   CHANNEL CROSSING   26   11
TWO BLACK ROOKS HUNCH ....PROSPECT   28   7
LOOKS FIERCE AND BLACK AS ROOKS; ....THE QUEEN'S COMPLAINT   28   4
SO SHE WILLS ALL TO THE BLACK KING. ....VANITY FAIR   33   29
WHICH OUT FROM BLACK TARN, DITCH AND CUP ....STRUMPET SONG   34   17
GONE BLACK OF POLISH ....TINKER JACK AND THE TIDY WIVES   34   2
FLAPPED BLACK TO LOOK AND BROOD ....FAUN   35   4
IN BLACK NOVEMBER. AFTER A SLIDING RAIN ....DIALOGUE B.   38   3
SO FITTED IS FOR MY BLACK LUCK ....THE GLUTTON   40   2
ON MY BLACK PILGRIMAGE ....RECANTATION   41   5
WHEN NIGHT COMES BLACK ....THE SHRIKE   42   1
IN BLACK AND WHITE, OR PUT ON ICE ......EPITAPH FOR FIRE AND FLOWER   45   10
OF BLANCHED SEEDS OR BLACK SEEDS,....................FIESTA MELONS   47   16
ANANSI, BLACK BUSYBODY OF THE FOLKTALES, ...SPIDER   48   1
WITH BLACK ALACRITY BOUND ROUND HIS PRISONER. ....SPIDER   49   28
UP BY A SPRY BLACK DEUS ....SPIDER   49   34
OF WHITE AND BLACK ....SPINSTER   49   15
A FLASH LIKE DOOMCRACK RENT NIGHT'S BLACK: ....CRYSTAL GAZER   55   37
BLACK ROOK IN RAINY WEATHER ....BLACK ROOK IN RAINY WEATHER   56   T
HUNCHES A WET BLACK ROOK ....BLACK ROOK IN RAINY WEATHER   56   2
ORDERING ITS BLACK FEATHERS CAN SO SHINE*BLACK ROOK IN RAINY WEATHER   57   28
THROUGH BARE WHISTLING HEATHER, OVER STILES OF BLACK STONE, ...
     ... THE SNOWMAN ON THE MOOR   58   21
THROUGHOUT BLACK WINTER THE RED HAWS WITHSTOOD ....MAYFLOWER   60   1
OF A SOW LOUNGED BELLY-BEDDED ON THAT BLACK COMPOST, ...SOW   61   25
HE ALSO AGAINST BLACK FROST ....THE EVERLASTING MONDAY   62   7
TACKING IN MOON-BLUED CROOKS FROM THE BLACK ....HARDCASTLE CRAGS   62   3
OF ITS HILLS, AND ITS PASTURES BORDERED BY BLACK STONE SET ...
     ... HARDCASTLE CRAGS   63   29
ON BLACK STONE. BARNS ....HARDCASTLE CRAGS   63   30
TO STUN SKY BLACK OUT, DRIVE GIBBERING MAD ....CONJURING.   66   12
BELLS, HOOVES, OF THE HIGH-STEPPING BLACK GOATS WOKE US. *OTHER TWO.   68   3
RISES TO THE GLASS FROM HIS BLACK FATHOMS. ....OUIJA   77   2
A BLACK SHEEP LEADS THE SHEPHERDS' FLOCK. ....A WINTER'S TALE   86   7
FOLLOW THE BLACK ARROW-BACKS OF SWIFTS ON THEIR TRACK ....OXBOW.   88   31
BLACK BENEATH BLAND MIRROR-SHEEN, ...LORELEI   94   3
BLACK AS THE CHARRED KNUCKLE-BONES ....CHILD'S PARK STONES   100   5
WE GAVE GOOD USE AS SHIP AND HOUSE IS BLACK ....GREEN ROCK.   105   11
THE BLACK BULL BELLOWED BEFORE THE SEA. ....THE BULL OF BENDYLAW   108   1
THE BLACK DUCKS DIVE. ....POINT SHIRLEY   111   43
AGAINST BOTH BAR AND TOWER THE BLACK SEA RUNS. ....POINT SHIRLEY   111   48
THEY HAD FOUR MEN LAID OUT, BLACK AS BURNT TURKEY, ...TWO VIEWS.   114   2
WHERE BEES, STRIPED BLACK AND GOLD, SLEEP OUT THE BLIZZARD ...
     ... ELECTRA ON AZALEA PATH   116   3
A GARDEN OF MOUTHINGS. PURPLE, SCARLET-SPECKLED, BLACK *BEEKEEPER'S.   118   1
MAN IN BLACK ....MAN IN BLACK   119   T
BLACK COAT, BLACK SHOES, AND YOUR ....MAN IN BLACK   120   17
BLACK COAT, BLACK SHOES, AND YOUR ....MAN IN BLACK   120   17
BLACK HAIR TILL THERE YOU STOOD, ...MAN IN BLACK   120   18
SHARDED IN BLACK, LIKE BEETLES, ...OLD LADIES' HOME   120   1
AGE WEARS THE BEST BLACK FABRIC ....OLD LADIES' HOME   120   13
DRESSED IN BLACK, EVERYBODY IN MOURNING FOR SOMEONE.*THE NET-MENDERS   121   4
I OPEN MY LUNCH ON A HILL OF BLACK CYPRESS. ....THE COLOSSUS   130   19
IN THIS LIGHT THE BLOOD IS BLACK. POEM.3.MAENAD.   133   24
IN THEIR BLACK ARMORPLATE AND CRY. ......SLEEP IN THE MOJAVE DESERT   144   23
MASKED AMONG BLACK ROCKS AS A BLACK ROCK ....LOVE LETTER   147   10
MASKED AMONG BLACK ROCKS AS A BLACK ROCK ....LOVE LETTER   147   10
THE TUMULUS, EVEN AT NOON, GUARDS ITS BLACK SHADOW: ..PARLIAMENT H.   153   26
THE SNAILS BLEW KISSES LIKE BLACK APPLES. ....ZOO KEEPER'S WIFE   155   38
MY PATENT LEATHER OVERNIGHT CASE LIKE A BLACK PILLBOX, ...TULIPS   160   19
OR EVEN LIKE BLACK HOLES CUT OUT OF IT. ....WIDOW   164   29
THE BLACK SLOTS OF THEIR PUPILS TAKE ME IN. ......WUTHERING HEIGHTS   167   22
BLACK STONE, BLACK STONE. ....WUTHERING HEIGHTS   168   36
BLACK STONE, BLACK STONE. ....WUTHERING HEIGHTS   168   36
AND BLACK AS PURSES, THE HOUSE LIGHTS ....WUTHERING HEIGHTS   168   44
OVERHEAD GO THE CHOUGHS IN BLACK, CACOPHONOUS FLOCKS -- ..BLACKBER.   168   10
CRAMPED ON NOTHING. BLACK ....FINISTERRE   169   2
A PEASANT WOMAN IN BLACK ....FINISTERRE   170   22
THE TREES OF THE MIND ARE BLACK. THE LIGHT IS BLUE. ....MOON.   172   2
THAT SUMMER WE WORE BLACK GLASSES TO HIDE OUR EYES. *THE BABYSITTERS   174   3
THE LETTERS PROCEED FROM THESE BLACK KEYS, AND THESE BLACK KEYS
     PROCEED ....THREE WOMEN   177   27
THE LETTERS PROCEED FROM THESE BLACK KEYS, AND THESE BLACK KEYS
     PROCEED ....THREE WOMEN   177   27
HE GLIDED BY; HIS EYE HAD A BLACK MEANING. ....THREE WOMEN   178   53
I SAW THE WORLD IN IT -- SMALL, MEAN AND BLACK, ...THREE WOMEN   178   54
I AM A GARDEN OF BLACK AND RED AGONIES. I DRINK THEM, ..THREE WOMEN   180   149
THERE ARE SOME WITH THICK BLACK HAIR, THERE ARE SOME BALD. ..THREE.   183   222
THESE LITTLE BLACK TWIGS DO NOT THINK TO BUD, ...THREE WOMEN   184   278
MY BLACK GOWN IS A LITTLE FUNERAL: ....THREE WOMEN   185   303
THEY ARE BLACK AND FLAT AS SHADOWS. ....THREE WOMEN   186   340
THE YEW'S BLACK FINGERS WAG; ....LITTLE FUGUE   187   1

BLACK (CONT.)
  I LIKE BLACK STATEMENTS. ....LITTLE FUGUE   187   5
  BLACK YEW, WHITE CLOUD, ...LITTLE FUGUE   187 14
  BLACK AND LEAFY, AS IN MY CHILDHOOD, ...LITTLE FUGUE   188 24
  DEATH OPENED, LIKE A BLACK TREE, BLACKLY. ....LITTLE FUGUE   188 48
  BLACK LAKE, BLACK BOAT, TWO BLACK, CUT-PAPER PEOPLE.*CROSSING THE W. 190   1
  BLACK LAKE, BLACK BOAT, TWO BLACK, CUT-PAPER PEOPLE.*CROSSING THE W. 190   1
  BLACK LAKE, BLACK BOAT, TWO BLACK, CUT-PAPER PEOPLE.*CROSSING THE W. 190   1
  WHERE DO THE BLACK TREES GO THAT DRINK HERE? ....CROSSING THE WATER   190   2
  ITS BLACK SPIKES, ...THE RABBIT CATCHER 193   7
  A BLACK GAP DISCLOSES ITSELF. ....EVENT   195 17
  ON A BLACK WALL, UNIDENTIFIABLE BIRDS .................APPREHENSIONS   195 16
  IS IT ANY WONDER HE AFFECTS A BLACK CASSOCK? ....BERCK-PLAGE   196 13
  THEY ARE HANDLING THE BLACK AND GREEN LOZENGES LIKE THE
                        PARTS OF A BODY. ....BERCK-PLAGE   196 16
  THIS BLACK BOOT HAS NO MERCY FOR ANYBODY. ....*BERCK-PLAGE 197 19
  THE WIDOW WITH HER BLACK POCKETBOOK AND THREE DAUGHTERS.*BERCK-PLAGE 200 100
  SIX ROUND BLACK HATS IN THE GRASS AND A LOZENGE OF WOOD,*BERCK-PLAGE 201 123
  THEY WOULD FLUTTER OFF, BLACK AND GLITTERING, THEY WOULD BE
                        COAL ANGELS ....BURNING THE LETTERS 204 33
  AND A NAME WITH BLACK EDGES ....BURNING THE LETTERS   205 42
  IS THIS THE ELECT ONE, THE ONE WITH BLACK EYE-PITS AND A SCAR? ...
                                    ... A BIRTHDAY PRESENT   206   6
  THERE ARE BLACK DISKS BEHIND IT, THE DISKS OF OUTRAGE, ...COURAGE.   209   3
  WHICH IS THE RECTOR NOW, IS IT THAT MAN IN BLACK? ..THE BEE MEETING   211 11
  EVERYBODY IS NODDING A SQUARE BLACK HEAD, THEY ARE KNIGHTS
                        IN VISORS, ...THE BEE MEETING 211 13
  CREAMY BEAN FLOWERS WITH BLACK EYES AND LEAVES LIKE BORED
                        HEARTS. ....THE BEE MEETING 211 18
  AND A BLACK VEIL THAT MOLDS TO MY FACE, THEY ARE MAKING ME ONE
                        OF THEM. ....THE BEE MEETING 211 22
  BLACK ON BLACK, ANGRILY CLAMBERING. .....THE ARRIVAL OF THE BEE BOX   213 15
  BLACK ON BLACK, ANGRILY CLAMBERING. .....THE ARRIVAL OF THE BEE BOX   213 15
  IT CAN MAKE BLACK ROSES. ....THE SWARM 216   4
  SEVENTY FEET UP, IN A BLACK PINE TREE. ....THE SWARM 216 18
  THE BEES ARGUE, IN THEIR BLACK BALL, ...THE SWARM 216 31
  A BLACK INTRACTABLE MIND. ....THE SWARM 217 58
  THE BLACK BUNCHED IN THERE LIKE A BAT, ...WINTERING   218 13
  BLACK ASININITY. DECAY. ....WINTERING   218 17
  BLACK ....WINTERING   218 32
  WILL IT SHOW IN THE BLACK DETECTOR? ....A SECRET   219   9
  BLACK AND STIFF, BUT NOT A BAD FIT. ....THE APPLICANT   221 21
  ANY MORE, BLACK SHOE ....DADDY   222   2
  SO BLACK NO SKY COULD SQUEAK THROUGH. ....DADDY   223 47
  ANY LESS THE BLACK MAN WHO ....DADDY   223 55
  A MAN IN BLACK WITH A MEINKAMPF LOOK ....DADDY   224 65
  THE BLACK TELEPHONE'S OFF AT THE ROOT, ...DADDY   224 69
  THERE'S A STAKE IN YOUR FAT BLACK HEART ....DADDY   224 76
  INTO A BLACK SACK ....THE JAILER   226   8
  WHERE IT DRIVES IN, WHITE AND BLACK, ...LESBOS   229 75
  A SORT OF BLACK HORSEHAIR, ...BY CANDLELIGHT   236   2
  THE SACK OF BLACK! IT IS EVERYWHERE, TIGHT, TIGHT! ..BY CANDLELIGHT   237 30
  BLACK SWEET BLOOD MOUTHFULS, ...ARIEL   239 13
  BLACK BAT AIRS ....NICK AND THE CANDLESTICK   240   6
  OF NINE BLACK ALPS. ....THE COURIERS   247 10
  OF KRUPP, BLACK MUZZLES ....GETTING THERE   248   6
  STEP TO YOU FROM THE BLACK CAR OF LETHE, ...GETTING THERE   249 67
  THROUGH THE BLACK AMNESIAS OF HEAVEN. ....THE NIGHT DANCES   250 21
  THIS LITTLE BLACK ....LETTER IN NOVEMBER   253   6
  IN YOUR VACUOUS BLACK, ...YEARS   255   7
  AND THE BLACK PHONES ON HOOKS ....THE MUNICH MANNEQUINS 263 24
  IN THE FETID WOMBS OF BLACK AIR UNDER PINES IN SUMMER. ....MYSTIC 268   5
  WHILE I SLEEP, THE BLACK SPORES NOD ....THE RIVAL/DR   291   2
  BLUE SKY OR BLACK ....THE RIVAL/DR   291 11
  THE BLACK VEIL MOLDS TO YOUR LIPS: ....STINGS/DR   293   9
  THROUGH MY WINDOW-SQUARE OF BLACK: ....TO A JILTED LOVER   309   3
  DOWN THE DARK IN A BLACK HEARSE ....THE DREAM 310   8
  WHERE THE BLACK WAVE TOPPLES DOWN; ....GO GET THE GOODLY SQUAB   313 22
  AND PROFANE WORDS SCRAWLED BLACK ACROSS THE SUN. ....DOOM OF EXILES   318 12
  BRIGHT ANGELS BLACK OUT OVER LOGIC'S LAND ....SONNET TO SATAN   323   3
  WHOSE MOONS OF BLACK .....ON LOOKING INTO THE EYES OF A DEMON LOVER   325   2
  BLACK PINE TREE IN AN ORANGE LIGHT ....BLACK PINE TREE. 328   T
  BLACK AGAINST THE ORANGE LIGHT: BLACK PINE TREE IN AN ORANGE LIGHT   328   3
  NINE BLACK MICE WITH EBON COACH, *BLACK PINE TREE IN AN ORANGE LIGHT 328   6
  A DEVIL'S CATARACT OF BLACK .....BLACK PINE TREE IN AN ORANGE LIGHT   328   8
  TATTOOS BLACK LEAVES ON TANGERINE. ....BLACK PINE TREE. 328 12
  READ BLACK MAGIC OR HOLY BOOK ...BLACK PINE TREE IN AN ORANGE LIGHT   328 13
  OR LYRIC OF LOVE IN THE ORANGE AND BLACK ....BLACK PINE TREE. 328 14
  TO MAKE ORANGE AND BLACK AMBIGUOUS. ....BLACK PINE TREE. 328 18
  TELL NOW, WE TAUNT, WHERE BLACK OR WHITE BEGINS   LOVE IS A PARALLAX 330 49
  SQUAT, BOWLING BLACK BALLS AT HER. ....AERIALIST   331 30
  OF BLACK WEIGHT, BLACK BALL, BLACK TRUCK, ...AERIALIST   332 38
  OF BLACK WEIGHT, BLACK BALL, BLACK TRUCK, ...AERIALIST   332 38
  OF BLACK WEIGHT, BLACK BALL, BLACK TRUCK, ...AERIALIST   332 38
  BLACK BIRDS OF OMEN ....TEMPER OF TIME   336   5

BLACKBERRIES (3)
NOBODY IN THE LANE, AND NOTHING, NOTHING BUT BLACKBERRIES,*BLACKBER.   168   1
BLACKBERRIES ON EITHER SIDE, THOUGH ON THE RIGHT MAINLY,   BLACKBER.   168   2
SOMEWHERE AT THE END OF IT, HEAVING. BLACKBERRIES ....BLACKBERRYING   168   4
BLACKBERRY (2)
THE HOOPS OF BLACKBERRY STEMS MADE ME CRY. POEM.1.WHO.   132   31
A BLACKBERRY ALLEY, GOING DOWN IN HOOKS, AND A SEA ...BLACKBERRYING   168   3
BLACKBERRYING (1)
BLACKBERRYING ....BLACKBERRYING   168   T
BLACKBIRDS (1)
WITH BLACKBIRDS -- TWENTY-FOUR, AND EVERY ONE ....DIALOGUE O.   282 215
BLACKBOARD (2)
DARKNESS WIPES ME OUT LIKE CHALK ON A BLACKBOARD. . . ...FACE LIFT   156   15
YOU STAND AT THE BLACKBOARD, DADDY, ...DADDY   223   51
BLACKEN (1)
SETTLES IN THE ROOM NOW. ITS WINGS BLACKEN THE TABLE. ..DIALOGUE O.   285 313
BLACKENING (2)
BLACKENING THE TIME ....MONOLOGUE AT 3 A.M.   40   11
MORNING HAS BEEN BLACKENING, ...SHEEP IN FOG   262   9
BLACKENS (1)
BLACKENS FLESH TO BONE AND DEVOURS THEM.*EPITAPH FOR FIRE AND FLOWER   46   35
BLACKEST (1)
LET BELL-TONGUED BIRDS DESCANT IN BLACKEST FEATHER .....LADY AND T.   69   25
BLACK-GOWNED (2)
DISENCHANT MY TWELVE BLACK-GOWNED EXAMINERS ....RESOLVE   52   21
BLACK-GOWNED, BUT UNAWARE ....WATERCOLOR OF GRANTCHESTER MEADOWS   112   26
BLACK-LEAVED (1)
THE RUBBISH OF SUMMERS, THE BLACK-LEAVED FALLS. ..THE BURNT-OUT SPA   138   9
BLACKLY (1)
DEATH OPENED, LIKE A BLACK TREE, BLACKLY. ....LITTLE FUGUE   188   48
BLACKNESS (8)
GREEN TO THE POINT OF BLACKNESS, SOME ....CHILD'S PARK STONES   100   2
AND THE MESSAGE OF THE YEW TREE IS BLACKNESS -- BLACKNESS AND
     SILENCE. ....THE MOON AND THE YEW TREE   173   28
AND THE MESSAGE OF THE YEW TREE IS BLACKNESS -- BLACKNESS AND
     SILENCE. ....THE MOON AND THE YEW TREE   173   28
I AM BREAKING APART LIKE THE WORLD. THERE IS THIS BLACKNESS, *THREE.   180 142
THIS RAM OF BLACKNESS. I FOLD MY HANDS ON A MOUNTAIN. ..THREE WOMEN   180 143
MY EYES ARE SQUEEZED BY THIS BLACKNESS. ....THREE WOMEN   180 146
I SHALL MOVE NORTH. I SHALL MOVE INTO A LONG BLACKNESS. *THREE WOMEN   182 190
THE SPIRIT OF BLACKNESS IS IN US, IT IS IN THE FISHES. ...
                      ... CROSSING THE WATER   190   8
BLACKOUT (1)
PILLAR OF WHITE IN A BLACKOUT OF KNIVES. ....THE BEE MEETING   212   52
BLACKS (2)
AND I, IN MY SNAZZY BLACKS, ...GIGOLO   267   12
HER BLACKS CRACKLE AND DRAG. ....EDGE   273   20
BLACK-SHARDED (1)
A BLACK-SHARDED LADY KEEPS ME IN A PARROT CAGE. POEM.6.W.   135   9
BLACKSHORT (1)
OF MIXIE BLACKSHORT THE HEROIC BEAR, ...THE DISQUIETING MUSES   75   10
BLACKTHORN (1)
BY BLACKTHORN THICKET, FLOWER SPRAY ....BUCOLICS   23   7
BLADE (1)
BURNS OPEN TO SUN'S BLADE. ....TWO SISTERS OF PERSEPHONE   32   19
BLADES (2)
THERE IS THE SUNLIGHT, PLAYING ITS BLADES, ...THE DETECTIVE   209   18
THE HOSTELRY OF WORMS, RAPACIOUS BLADES ....TERMINAL   328   6
BLAKE'S (1)
AND BALLED, LIKE BLAKE'S, ...DEATH & CO.   254   4
BLAME (4)
OR MUST TAKE LOOPHOLE AND BLAME TIME ......GREEN ROCK, WINTHROP BAY   105   22
A STONY HOLE. HE'S TO BLAME. POEM.2.DARK.   132   20
IT IS EASY TO BLAME THE DARK: THE MOUTH OF A DOOR, ...POEM.6.W.   135   7
THEY ARE TO BLAME FOR WHAT I AM, AND THEY KNOW IT. .....THREE WOMEN   180 116
BLAMED (1)
I BLAMED HER FOR EVERYTHING, BUT SHE DIDN'T ANSWER. .....IN PLASTER   159   10
BLAMELESS (1)
BLAMELESS AS DAYLIGHT I STOOD LOOKING ....THE EYE-MOTE   109   1
BLANCHED (3)
CURDED OVER WITH CLOUDS AND CHALK CLIFFS BLANCHED   CHANNEL CROSSING   27   24
OF BLANCHED SEEDS OR BLACK SEEDS ....FIESTA MELONS   47   16
AMONG THE BLANCHED, BOILED INSTRUMENTS, THE VIRGINAL
     CURTAINS. ....FEVER./DR   294   8
BLANCHING (1)
THE SOURCE OF BLANCHING LIGHT THAT CONJURED HER ....THE PRINCESS.   333   3
BLAND (4)
BLACK BENEATH BLAND MIRROR-SHEEN, ...LORELEI   94   3
AND MEANDER IN BLAND PLEATINGS UNDER ....IN MIDAS' COUNTRY   99   3
THE BLAND GRANTA DOUBLE THEIR WHITE AND GREEN ....WATERCOLOR.   112   9
AND I, ON THE SKY-MIRRORING, BLAND SANDS ....THE RIVAL/DR   291   17
BLAND-MANNERED (1)
BLAND-MANNERED, ASKING ....MUSHROOMS   139   21
BLANK (14)
ITS GLITTERING SURFACES ARE BLANK AND TRUE. ....TALE OF A TUB   25   32

BLANK (CONT.)
  WITH HER BLANK BROWN EYES STARVED WIDE, ...THE SHRIKE   42   9
  WHICH PEOPLES THE BARE ROOM, THE BLANK, UNTENANTED AIR. *NOVEMBER G. 56 18
  THE BLANK MOOD SHE WALKED IN. ONCE PAST ....HARDCASTLE CRAGS   63 18
  FACES BLANK AS THE DAY I WAS BORN, ...THE DISQUIETING MUSES 76 51
  EVERYTHING GLITTERED LIKE BLANK PAPER. ....SUICIDE OFF EGG ROCK 115 20
  TABLETS OF BLANK BLUE, COULDN'T ......THE HERMIT AT OUTERMOST HOUSE 118   2
  ON THE BLANK STONES OF THE LANDING. ....THE COLOSSUS 130 30
  HOURLY THE EYE OF THE SKY ENLARGES ITS BLANK POEM.5.F. 134   5
  IT RESEMBLES THE MOON, OR A SHEET OF BLANK PAPER ....A LIFE 150 23
  AND EVERYWHERE PEOPLE, EYES MICA-SILVER AND BLANK, ...INSOMNIAC 163 34
  WHITE AND BLANK, EXPANSIVE AS CARBON MONOXIDE. ....THE RIVAL 166 15
  THERE IS NOTHING TO DO WITH SUCH A BEAUTIFUL BLANK BUT SMOOTH IT. ...
                          ... AMNESIAC 232   2
  YOUR SHERLOCK HOLMESING STEERED TO A BLANK WALL ....DIALOGUE O. 280 167
BLANK-BRAINED (1)
  WE'LL WAKE BLANK-BRAINED AS WATER IN THE DAWN. ....TWO CAMP. 145 27
BLANK-FACED (1)
  BLANK-FACED AND MUM AS A NURSE. ....BARREN WOMAN 157 10
BLANKLY (1)
  SHADOWS OUR SAFETY. WE STAND ROUND BLANKLY AS WALLS. ..MORNING SONG 157   6
BLANKNESS (2)
  HOURS OF BLANKNESS. SOME HARD STARS ....THE MANOR GARDEN 125 14
  OF IMMORTAL BLANKNESS BETWEEN STARS ....WIDOW 164 24
BLANKS (2)
  BOSSING THE ETHEREAL BLANKS OF THEIR FACE-OVALS. ....MAGI 148   3
  COLD BLANKS APPROACH US: .............................APPREHENSIONS 196 19
BLASTED (2)
  GOD'S MONKEY WRENCH HAS BLASTED ALL MACHINES; ....DOOMSDAY 316 13
  FACTS HAVE BLASTED ....MOONSONG AT MORNING 317 33
BLASTS (1)
  THAN AGAINST THIS ONSLAUGHT, THESE CASUAL BLASTS OF ICE   CHANNEL C. 27 17
BLAZE (3)
  RIGHT TO BLAZE AS SATAN'S WIFE; ....VANITY FAIR 33 32
  AND KINDLES A DAY'S-END BLAZE ....CHILD'S PARK STONES 101 15
  BELCHED INTO BLAZE AND, THOUGH RED-HOT, KEPT WHOLE .....DIALOGUE O. 280 158
BLAZING (6)
  INTO AN ARDENT BLAZING. ....SONG FOR A SUMMER'S DAY 31 15
  IN THEIR HEARTBEATS' BLAZING WAKE UNTIL RED COCK ....EPITAPH FOR F. 46 27
  EACH LOVE BLAZING BLIND TO ITS GUTTED END -- ....CRYSTAL GAZER 56 46
  THE DAY IS BLAZING. IT IS VERY MOURNFUL. ....THREE WOMEN 184 262
  BLAZING IN MY GOLDEN HELL. ....TO A JILTED LOVER 310 27
  NOTHING CHANGES, FOR ALL THE BLAZING OF ....LOVE IS A PARALLAX 329 16
BLAZON (1)
  BLAZON SKY BLUE, AND ENDOW THE SUN ......SOLILOQUY OF THE SOLIPSIST 37 22
BLAZONED (1)
  THE GREAT GRANDAM! -- OUR MARVEL BLAZONED A KNIGHT, ...SOW 61 29
BLEACH (1)
  ON THIS AMBER BANK WHERE GRASSES BLEACH. ....IN MIDAS' COUNTRY 100 22
BLEACHED (2)
  AND INNARDS BLEACHED AND BLOWN OFF ....MUSSEL HUNTER AT ROCK HARBOR 97 72
  BLEACHED AND FINISHED, I SURFACE ....FEVER./DR 294   7
BLEAK (3)
  ABOVE THE APPALLING RUIN; IN BLEAK LIGHT .............CONVERSATION. 21   6
  GROW GREEN AGAIN? WHO'D WALK IN THIS BLEAK PLACE? WINTER LANDSCAPE, 22 15
  WITH RADIANCE, PEACOCK-COLORED; INSTEAD, BLEAK ROCKS ....CHANNEL C. 27 22
BLEARED (1)
  TIME'S SOOT IN BLEARED EYE ....TINKER JACK AND THE TIDY WIVES 34 12
BLEB (1)
  ELBA, ELBA, BLEB ON THE SEA! ....THE SWARM 217 43
BLED (3)
  I AM BLED WHITE AS WAX, I HAVE NO ATTACHMENTS. ....THREE WOMEN 184 275
  BLED WHITE WITH BRIARS BY A BUSY CONSCIENCE ....DIALOGUE O. 281 197
  DEATH'S TWO DREAMS DOWN WITH THE BODY THAT BLED THE VEIN,
                 ... DIALOGUE OVER A OUIJA BOARD 285 329
BLEED (6)
  OF A WHALE WITH HOLES AND HOLES, AND BLEED HIM WHITE ....PERSEUS 82   5
  AND BLEED. THE WHITE STOMACH MAY RIPEN YET. ....MOONRISE 98 30
  IF I COULD BLEED, OR SLEEP! --- ....POPPIES IN JULY 203 11
  GOLDS BLEED AND DEEPEN, THE MOUTHS OF THERMOPYLAE. ..LETTER IN NOV. 254 35
  TO BLEED, IF IT COMES TO THAT. .........................EAVESDROPPER 260   6
  STIFFENS AND ODORS BLEED ....EDGE 273 15
BLEEDING (4)
  BLEEDING HEARTS ON ITS SLEEVE ....POLLY'S TREE 129 40
  THE SUN DISSOLVES ON THIS WALL, BLEEDING ITS LIGHTS. APPREHENSIONS 195   5
  BLEEDING AND PEELING ....THE NIGHT DANCES 250 20
  LOOPING LIKE FAITH ABOUT HER BLEEDING FEET, ...THE PRINCESS. 334 48
BLENCHED (1)
  SHE BLENCHED, AS ONE WHO DROWNS,   THE LADY AND THE EARTHENWARE HEAD 69 21
BLESS (1)
  LET NIGHT BLESS THAT LUCK-ROOTED MEAD OF CLOVER *WREATH FOR A BRIDAL 45 17
BLESSED (1)
  EATS AT POINT SHIRLEY. SHE DIED BLESSED, ...POINT SHIRLEY 111 36
BLESSING (3)
  IT IS A BLESSING, IT IS A BLESSING: ....BERCK-PLAGE 199 69

	TITLE	PAGE	LINE

BLESSING (CONT.)
```
IT IS A BLESSING, IT IS A BLESSING:  ....................BERCK-PLAGE   199   69
PEACOCKS BLESSING  .............................................BALLOONS   272   17
```
BLESSINGS (2)
```
FALLING LIKE BLESSINGS, LIKE FLAKES  ...............THE NIGHT DANCES   250   24
BLESSINGS RIGHT AND LEFT AND CRY  ...............LOVE IS A PARALLAX   330   39
```
BLEW (4)
```
UNTIL SWEET WIND CHANGED TUNE, BLEW HARM:  ..................BUCOLICS    24   15
TO A PINCH OF FLAME, BLEW ITS BURDENED WHISTLE  ....HARDCASTLE CRAGS    63   23
THE SNAILS BLEW KISSES LIKE BLACK APPLES.  .........ZOO KEEPER'S WIFE   155   38
WHAT WAS SHE DOING WHEN IT BLEW IN  ...................THE DETECTIVE   208    1
```
BLIGHT (1)
```
WITH SUCH BLIGHT WROUGHT ON OUR BANKRUPT ESTATE,  .....CONVERSATION.    21   13
```
BLIGHTED (1)
```
AND COO QUADRILLES ABOUT THE BLIGHTED CORE  ...........THE PRINCESS.   335   67
```
BLIMP (1)
```
A BLIMP SWIMS UP LIKE A DAY-MOON OR TIN  ..............A WINTER SHIP   113   11
```
BLIND (23)
```
BLIND WITH STEAM, WILL NOT ADMIT THE DARK  .............TALE OF A TUB    24   15
TO ATONE AS SHADE FOR SIN THAT LURED BLIND MAN."  .......DIALOGUE B.    39   36
EACH LOVE BLAZING BLIND TO ITS GUTTED END --  .........CRYSTAL GAZER    56   46
BUT BEFORE I MIGHT BLIND SENSE  ............ON THE PLETHORA OF DRYADS    67   13
FROM BLIND AIR, FROM COMPLETE ECLIPSE.  ................RHODODENDRON.   103   16
BLIND TO WHAT WILL BE AND WHAT WAS.  .....................THE EYE-MOTE   109   23
TWO PEOPLE ONLY ARE BLIND TO THE CARRION ARMY:  ..........TWO VIEWS.   114   13
BLIND TWINS BITTEN BY BAD NATURE.  .......................BLUE MOLES   126    9
THE DESERT IS WHITE AS A BLIND MAN'S EYE,*SLEEP IN THE MOJAVE DESERT   144   17
I LOSE SIGHT OF YOU ON YOUR BLIND JOURNEY,  ..PARLIAMENT HILL FIELDS   153   33
NUN-HEARTED AND BLIND TO THE WORLD. MARBLE LILIES  .....BARREN WOMAN   157    4
THE BLIND, WHITE, AWFUL, INACCESSIBLE SLANT.  ..NEW YEAR ON DARTMOOR   176    5
I HAVE TRIED TO BE BLIND IN LOVE, LIKE OTHER WOMEN,  ....THREE WOMEN   178   75
BLIND IN MY BED, WITH MY DEAR BLIND SWEET ONE,  .........THREE WOMEN   178   76
BLIND IN MY BED, WITH MY DEAR BLIND SWEET ONE,  .........THREE WOMEN   178   76
HE IS TURNING TO ME LIKE A LITTLE, BLIND, BRIGHT PLANT. *THREE WOMEN   183  235
SIGNAL THE BLIND, AND ARE IGNORED.  .....................LITTLE FUGUE   187    4
THE EYE OF THE BLIND PIANIST  ...........................LITTLE FUGUE   187    8
SO THE BLIND SMILE.  ....................................LITTLE FUGUE   188   18
THE BLIND MIRROR OF IT. I LOOK IN  .............FOR A FATHERLESS SON   205    8
AND HIS EYES GONE BLIND WITH LEAVES.  ...............GOLD MOUTHS CRY   302   14
LEST THE BLIZZARD DRIVE YOU BLIND.  .........GO GET THE GOODLY SQUAB   313   16
ECLIPSED BENEATH BLIND LID OF LAND  ...................DANSE MACABRE   320    2
```
BLINDED (3)
```
BLINDED TO ALL BUT THE GRAY, SPIRITLESS ROOM  ...............WIDOW   165   39
ARE YOU NOT BLINDED BY SUCH EXPRESSIONLESS SIRENS?   CROSSING THE W.   190   11
RISING AND FLYING, BUT BLINDED.  ...............BURNING THE LETTERS   204   32
```
BLINDERED (1)
```
BLINDERED BY GREEN, UNDER A GREEN-GRAINED SKY  ......ABOVE THE OXBOW    88   28
```
BLINDFOLD (1)
```
HE SMOLDERED, AS IF STONE-DEAF, BLINDFOLD,  ....SUICIDE OFF EGG ROCK   115   14
```
BLINDING (1)
```
BLINDING ME WITH ITS LIGHTS, THE LIVES OF THE DEAD  .....THE RABBIT.   193    4
```
BLINDINGLY (2)
```
THE LIGHT FALLS WITHOUT LETUP, BLINDINGLY.  ...................A LIFE   150   20
ISSUING FROM THE STEEL NEEDLE THAT FLIES SO BLINDINGLY? *APPEARANCE.   189   11
```
BLINDS (1)
```
BLINDS LOWERED ON THAT HOT MORNING.  ........DREAM WITH CLAM-DIGGERS    43    8
```
BLINK (1)
```
NOR GUESS THAT IF I CHOOSE TO BLINK  .....SOLILOQUY OF THE SOLIPSIST    37   17
```
BLINKING (3)
```
BLINKING GREEN-EYED AND SOLITARY  ....ELLA MASON AND HER ELEVEN CATS    54   38
BLINKING FLASHLIGHTS LIKE FIREFLIES  ..........THE DISQUIETING MUSES    75   26
OR THE BITTER BLINKING YELLOW  ..................................JILTED   304    3
```
BLINKS (1)
```
NOBODY BLINKS A LID, GAPES,  ...........................STREET SONG    35    5
```
BLISS (1)
```
THE SUAVE ETERNAL SERPENTS PROMISE BLISS  .......NEVER TRY TO TRICK.   320   13
```
BLISTER (1)
```
RED AND ORANGE BARGES LIST AND BLISTER  ...............A WINTER SHIP   112    2
```
BLITHE (1)
```
YOUNG WIVES STILL BLITHE,  ..........TINKER JACK AND THE TIDY WIVES    35   27
```
BLITZEN (1)
```
DONNER, BLITZEN,  .......................................A WINTER'S TALE    87   20
```
BLITZKRIEG (1)
```
AND APPEARS TO HAVE SUFFERED A SORT OF PRIVATE BLITZKRIEG.  ..A LIFE   150   24
```
BLIZZARD (4)
```
OF A BLIZZARD, THE GIANT ROARED UP WITH HIS CHITTERING TROPHIES.  ...
                        ...  THE SNOWMAN ON THE MOOR    59   45
WHERE BEES, STRIPED BLACK AND GOLD, SLEEP OUT THE BLIZZARD  ...
                        ...  ELECTRA ON AZALEA PATH   116    3
HE PAINTS A BLIZZARD OF GULLS,  .....................MAGNOLIA SHOALS   122   23
LEST THE BLIZZARD DRIVE YOU BLIND.  .........GO GET THE GOODLY SQUAB   313   16
```
BLOAT (1)
```
BLOAT TUN OF MILK  ...............................................SOW    61   20
```
BLOATS (1)
```
BLOATS LIKE A SPINNAKER. HAT-BRIMS  .......................WHITSUN   154   10
```

	TITLE	PAGE	LINE

BLOCK (2)
    AS THE DOOMSTRUCK CITY CRUMBLES BLOCK BY BLOCK: ....DOOMSDAY 316 8
    AS THE DOOMSTRUCK CITY CRUMBLES BLOCK BY BLOCK: ....DOOMSDAY 316 8
BLOCKS (2)
    A BALD ANGEL BLOCKS AND SHAPES ....SCULPTOR 91 10
    WITH BEGONIA AND BUILDING BLOCKS. ....SONG FOR A REVOLUTIONARY LOVE 323 16
BLOND (3)
    SHAWLED IN BLOND HAIR AND THE SALT ....HEAVY WOMEN 158 3
    THERE IS THE LABURNUM, ITS BLOND COLONNADES, ...THE ARRIVAL. 213 29
    WITH BLOND BRAIDS. ....BITTER STRAWBERRIES 299 23
BLOOD (57)
    CRYING: BLOOD, LET BLOOD BE SPILT; ....PURSUIT 22 15
    CRYING: BLOOD, LET BLOOD BE SPILT; ....PURSUIT 22 15
    TO QUENCH HIS THIRST I SQUANDER BLOOD; ....PURSUIT 23 38
    BLOOD QUICKENS, GONGING IN MY EARS: ....PURSUIT 23 48
    OUR LONE LUCK NOW, COMPELLED BY BOND, BY BLOOD, ...CHANNEL CROSSING 27 33
    WHEREBY SHE TREKS IN BLOOD THROUGH SUN AND SQUALL ....QUEEN'S C. 29 22
    LEAPS TO LAUD SUCH MAN'S BLOOD! ....ODE FOR TED 30 24
    IS TRICKED TO FALTER IN SPILT BLOOD. ....FIRESONG 30 7
    OF PETALED BLOOD ....TWO SISTERS OF PERSEPHONE 32 18
    BRIGHT AS BLOOD. ....TINKER JACK AND THE TIDY WIVES 34 9
    BLOOD DRENCHING VIVID ....MONOLOGUE AT 3 A.M. 40 3
    AGAINST THE FLOWER IN THE BLOOD: ....RECANTATION 42 13
    DRIVES NIMBLE BLOOD TOO QUICK ....EPITAPH FOR FIRE AND FLOWER 46 25
    ARENA DUST RUSTED BY FOUR BULLS' BLOOD TO A DULL REDNESS,*THE GORING 47 1
    BLOOD FAULTLESSLY BROACHED REDEEMED THE SULLIED AIR, THE EARTH'S
                   GROSSNESS. .....THE GORING 47 10
    IN A CLENCH OF BLOOD, THE SLEEP-TALKING VIRGIN ....MAUDLIN 51 2
    OURSELVES THE HAUNTERS, AND THEY, FLESH AND BLOOD; ...THE OTHER TWO 69 33
    BLOOD AND WHISTLE MY MARROW CLEAN ....ALL THE DEAD DEARS 70 17
    FAR OFF, NOT BLOOD IN THE EARS ....NIGHT SHIFT 76 3
    CRIED THEN FOR THE FATHER'S BLOOD ....I WANT, I WANT 106 6
    AND HIS BLOOD BEATING THE OLD TATTOO ....SUICIDE OFF EGG ROCK 115 8
    IN THIS LIGHT THE BLOOD IS BLACK. POEM.3.MAENAD. 133 24
    VELVET PILLOWS THE COLOUR OF BLOOD PUDDING ....LEAVING EARLY 145 5
    I HAD NOT ASKED FOR SUCH A BLOOD SISTERHOOD; THEY MUST LOVE ME. ...
                   ... BLACKBERRYING 168 8
    THE BLOOD IS A SUNSET. I ADMIRE IT. ....THE SURGEON AT 2 A.M. 171 21
    THE RED NIGHT LIGHTS ARE FLAT MOONS. THEY ARE DULL WITH BLOOD. ...
                   ... THE SURGEON AT 2 A.M. 171 48
    THE NIGHT LIGHTS ARE FLAT RED MOONS. THEY ARE DULL WITH BLOOD. ...
                   ... THREE WOMEN 180 124
    A RED LOTUS OPENS IN ITS BOWL OF BLOOD; ....THREE WOMEN 181 167
    OLD BLOOD OF CAKED WALLS THE SUN HEALS, ...BERCK-PLAGE 200 98
    OLD BLOOD OF LIMB STUMPS, BURNT HEARTS. ....BERCK-PLAGE 200 99
    THE BLOOD THAT RUNS IS DARK FRUIT -- ....THE OTHER 202 29
    IS IT BLOOD CLOTS THE TENDRILS ARE DRAGGING UP THAT STRING? ...BEE. 211 19
    JEALOUSY CAN OPEN THE BLOOD, ...THE SWARM 215 3
    AND DRANK MY BLOOD FOR A YEAR, ...DADDY 224 73
    SQUEEZING THE BREATH FROM THE BLOOD BELLS ....MEDUSA 225 28
    DRAGGED ITS BLOOD BAG, SICK ....LESBOS 229 54
    BLACK SWEET BLOOD MOUTHFULS, ...ARIEL 239 13
    THE BLOOD BLOOMS CLEAN ....NICK AND THE CANDLESTICK 241 27
    OR A BIT OF BLOOD ....LADY LAZARUS 246 63
    THE MEN THE BLOOD STILL PUMPS FORWARD, ...GETTING THERE 248 25
    PUMPED AHEAD BY THESE PISTONS, THIS BLOOD ....GETTING THERE 248 30
    THE BLOOD BERRIES ARE THEMSELVES, THEY ARE VERY STILL. ....YEARS 255 23
    RED EARTH, MOTHERLY BLOOD. ....BRASILIA 258 17
    UTTERING NOTHING BUT BLOOD -- ....CHILDLESS WOMAN 259 13
    THE BLOOD FLOOD IS THE FLOOD OF LOVE, ...THE MUNICH MANNEQUINS 263 6
    FAT HAUNCHES AND BLOOD ON THEIR MINDS. ....TOTEM 264 8
    THE BLOOD JET IS POETRY, ...KINDNESS 270 18
    BLOOD AND BANK WRIST, ELBOW, SHOULDER, LIP ....DIALOGUE O. 277 18
    FAITH FAST: A MIRACLE AND THE SMELL OF BLOOD ....DIALOGUE O. 280 161
    TO QUICKEN HIS SLUGGARD'S BLOOD. BUT HE NEEDN'T COME ...DIALOGUE O. 281 184
    AND BLOOD REFLECTS ACROSS THE MANUSCRIPT; ....FEMALE AUTHOR 301 10
    BLOOD SPRINGS ETERNAL IF THE HEART BE BURNING. ....TO EVA DESCENDING. 303 8
    WHERE DIAMONDS JANGLE HYMNS WITHIN THE BLOOD ....APRIL AUBADE 312 3
    METRONOMES THE BLOOD, ...TRIO OF LOVE SONGS 314 10
    LURED BY BRIGANDS IN THE BLOOD, ...DANSE MACABRE 321 16
    OF CLOCKWORK THAT MAKES THE ROYAL BLOOD RUN COLD. ....THE PRINCESS. 335 75
    BLOOD RUNS IN A GLISSANDO FROM THE HAND .....EPITAPH IN THREE PARTS 337 18
BLOOD-BERRIED (1)
    THE BLOOD-BERRIED HAWTHORN HIDES ITS SPINES WITH WHITE. *WATERCOLOR. 112 21
BLOOD-BLACK (1)
    IT IS SHE THAT DRAGS THE BLOOD-BLACK SEA AROUND ....THREE WOMEN 182 186
BLOOD-CAUL (1)
    BLOOD-CAUL OF ABSENCES. ....THALIDOMIDE 252 16
BLOOD-DROP (1)
    LAST BLOOD-DROP OF THAT TRUANT HEART. ....THE SHRIKE 42 23
BLOOD-DROPS (1)
    AND, BRIGHT AS BLOOD-DROPS, PROVED NO BRAVE BRANCH DIES ..MAYFLOWER 60 3
BLOOD-FLUSH (1)
    DAWN SAYS, WITH ITS BLOOD-FLUSH. ....TOTEM 264 23

                                                          TITLE   PAGE LINE
BLOOD-HEAT (3)
   FOR THE BLOOD-HEAT THAT WOULD RUDDLE OR RECLAIM. ....OUIJA   77   9
   THE GLASS MOUTH SUCKS BLOOD-HEAT FROM MY FOREFINGER. ....OUIJA   77   10
   AND TONGUE, AND THOUGHT, AS WELL AS THE BLOOD-HEAT .....DIALOGUE O.   283 258
BLOOD-HOT (1)
   THE WORLD IS BLOOD-HOT AND PERSONAL ....TOTEM   264   22
BLOODHOUNDS (1)
   AS IF BLOODHOUNDS BORE HIM DOWN. I-N-C-O*DIALOGUE OVER A OUIJA BOARD   283 275
BLOODIED (3)
   AND BLOODIED AS A COW'S SPLIT FRAME ....STREET SONG   36   9
   I REMEMBER THE BLOODIED CHICKS AND THE QUARTERED RABBITS. ...ZOO K.   155   24
   A MOUTH JUST BLOODIED. ....POPPIES IN JULY   203   7
BLOOD-LOVING (1)
   FLAPPING AND SUCKING, BLOOD-LOVING BAT. ....LESBOS   229   80
BLOOD'S (1)
   BLOOD'S BROTH, ...THE GLUTTON   40   7
BLOOD-SOAKED (1)
   ENACTED TRAGEDIES ON THESE BLOOD-SOAKED BOARDS, ...PERSEUS   83   19
BLOOD-SPOOR (1)
   BLOOD-SPOOR OF THE AUSTERE TRAGEDIES. ....AFTERMATH   113   8
BLOODSPOT (1)
   THE BLOODSPOT, ...GETTING THERE   249   58
BLOODY (6)
   THORNS ON THE BLOODY ROSE-STEM. ....I WANT, I WANT 106   12
   THE SUN SINKS UNDER BOSTON, BLOODY RED. ....POINT SHIRLEY   111   40
   ALTHOUGH THE RAINS DISSOLVE A BLOODY DYE: ...ELECTRA ON AZALEA PATH   117   27
   A GRAY WALL NOW, CLAWED AND BLOODY. .................APPREHENSIONS   195   6
   LITTLE BLOODY SKIRTS! ....POPPIES IN JULY   203   8
   THERE'S ALWAYS A BLOODY BABY IN THE AIR. ....STOPPED DEAD   230   13
BLOOM (6)
   EACH HEDGE WITH SUCH WHITE BLOOM ASTOUNDS OUR EYES ....MAYFLOWER   60   6
   DOGBODY NOSES THE PETALS. THEY BLOOM UPSIDE DOWN. POEM.1.WHO.   131   11
   BLOOM ABOUT ME LIKE NIGHT FLOWERS, WITH A GOOD SMELL. ...LAST WORDS   172   22
   WHERE APPLE BLOOM ICES THE NIGHT ....EVENT   195   13
   AT FIRST THE CANDLE WILL NOT BLOOM AT ALL -- ....BY CANDLELIGHT   236   16
   OF ONE I LOVED. I SAW DIVISION BLOOM ...DIALOGUE OVER A OUIJA BOARD   285 322
BLOOMED (1)
   I GAVE HER A SOUL, I BLOOMED OUT OF HER AS A ROSE ....IN PLASTER   159   16
BLOOMS (7)
   BEACHED UNDER THE SPUMY BLOOMS, WE LIE ....WHITSUN   154   23
   BLOOMS OUT OF A VASE OF NOT VERY VALUABLE PORCELAIN, ...IN PLASTER   159   17
   ITS BOWL OF RED BLOOMS OUT OF SHEER LOVE OF ME. ....TULIPS   162   61
   WHOSE RED HEART BLOOMS THROUGH HER COAT SO ASTOUNDINGLY--- *POP.OCT.   240   3
   THE BLOOD BLOOMS CLEAN ....NICK AND THE CANDLESTICK   241   27
   THE SUN BLOOMS, IT IS A GERANIUM. ....MYSTIC   269   30
   AND HOTHOUSE ROSES SHED IMMORAL BLOOMS. ....FEMALE AUTHOR   301   8
BLOT (1)
   THE PINES BLOT OUR VOICES UP IN THEIR LIGHTEST SIGHS. ....TWO CAMP.   145   24
BLOTCH (2)
   ASKEW WITH BLOTCH, DINT, SCAR ....STRUMPET SONG   33   12
   UNTIL NO CHASTE TREE BUT SUFFERS BLOTCH ..ON THE PLETHORA OF DRYADS   68   34
BLOTS (1)
   WHERE THE WATER BLOTS OUT ALL FOOTSTEPS." ...EPITAPH IN THREE PARTS   337   6
BLOTTER (1)
   ON THEIR BLOTTER OF FOG THE TREES ....WINTER TREES   257   2
BLOW (6)
   THESE ARE OUR CREPES. EAT THEM BEFORE THEY BLOW COLD." ..FINISTERRE   170   36
   ONLY TO BLOW ....BY CANDLELIGHT   236   13
   WHERE THE YEW TREES BLOW LIKE HYDRAS, ...THE MUNICH MANNEQUINS   262   3
   AND THE SNOW BLOW UP BEHIND; ....GO GET THE GOODLY SQUAB 313   14
   AND PAGE BY PRIDE THE GOOD BOOKS BLOW;*SONG FOR A REVOLUTIONARY LOVE   322   3
   SIBYL'S LEAVES BLOW. ....TEMPER OF TIME   336   8
BLOWING (1)
   HE KEPT BLOWING ME KISSES. POEM.4.BEAST.   134   9
BLOWN (12)
   HEARING TICKS BLOWN GOLD ....TWO SISTERS OF PERSEPHONE   32   14
   FROM THIS HOLY DAY ON, ALL POLLEN BLOWN ....WREATH FOR A BRIDAL   45   19
   AND INNARDS BLEACHED AND BLOWN OFF ....MUSSEL HUNTER AT ROCK HARBOR   97   72
   AT A FIELD OF HORSES, NECKS BENT, MANES BLOWN, ...THE EYE-MOTE   109   2
   BEARDED AND BLOWN, AN ALBATROSS OF FROST, ...A WINTER SHIP   113   26
   THE CELLAR'S BELLY. THEY'VE BLOWN MY SPARKLER OUT. POEM.6.W.   135   8
   SETTLING AND STIRRING LIKE BLOWN PAPER .....PARLIAMENT HILL FIELDS   152   8
   BITS OF BURNT PAPER WHEELING IN A BLOWN SKY. ........BLACKBERRYING   168   11
   HER MARBLE SKIRTS BLOWN BACK IN TWO PINK WINGS. ....FINISTERRE   169   20
   THE WIND GAGGING MY MOUTH WITH MY OWN BLOWN HAIR,*THE RABBIT CATCHER   193   2
   YOU WHO HAVE BLOWN YOUR TUBES LIKE A BAD RADIO ....LESBOS   228   17
   NOVEMBER'S DONE WITH. THE BLOWN LEAVES MAKE BAT-SHAPES, *DIALOGUE O.   286 337
BLOWS (2)
   BLOWS ASH IN EACH LOVER'S EYE; THE ARDENT LOOK ......EPITAPH FOR F.   46   34
   MY EXTRAVAGANT HEART BLOWS UP AGAIN ....CIRCUS IN THREE RINGS   321   3
BLOWSY (1)
   MORE MAMMOTH AND BLOWSY WITH EVERY SEASON; ....ELLA MASON A.   54   34
BLOWZE (1)
   RETROGRESSED TO BLOWZE, I NEXT CHOSE RED; ............RHODODENDRON.   103   10

                                                    TITLE   PAGE   LINE
BLOWZY (1)
  MIRE-SMIRCHED, BLOWZY, ...SOW   61   18
BLUBBERY (1)
  A COMMUNION WAFER? BLUBBERY MARY? ....MEDUSA 225   33
BLUE (108)
  AND OUT OF THE BLUE DRENCH ....SOUTHERN SUNRISE   26   16
  TAUNTS US TO VALOR. BLUE SAILORS SANG THAT OUR JOURNEY ..CHANNEL C.   27   20
  BLUE FUR, MOLES HAVE; HEFTING CHALK-HULLED FLINT ....ODE FOR TED   29   9
  MOST FAR IN BLUE, ALOFT, ...SONG FOR A SUMMER'S DAY   31   7
  BLAZON SKY BLUE, AND ENDOW THE SUN .....SOLILOQUY OF THE SOLIPSIST   37   22
  EACH THORN; SPIRING FROM WET EARTH, A BLUE HAZE ....DIALOGUE B.   38   5
  FROM YOUR BLUE PALLOR, I'D SAY YOU INHABITED THE FROZEN WASTE ...
                      ... DIALOGUE BETWEEN GHOST AND PRIEST   38   14
  SLOPED SEAWARD TO PLUNGE IN BLUE; FED BY WHITE FIRE, DREAM WITH C.   44   11
  THE BAY'S SHEER, EXTRAVAGANT BLUE, ...THE BEGGARS   48   17
  THE SCRAGGY ROCK SPIT SHIELDING THE TOWN'S BLUE BAY ......DEPARTURE   51   13
  REPORT WHITE PILLARS, A BLUE SKY, ...TWO VIEWS OF WITHENS   72   17
  SKIES ONCE WEARING A BLUE, DIVINE HAUTEUR ....OUIJA   77   19
  THE SIGHT OF THOSE BLUE, UNSEEN WAVES ....ON THE DECLINE OF ORACLES   78   14
  INTO THE BLUE. TOPS DEFINE THEMSELVES AS PLACES ....ABOVE THE OXBOW   88   29
  THE BLUE WATER-MISTS DROPPING ....LORELEI   94   4
  FREE FISH-BAIT: THE BLUE MUSSELS ......MUSSEL HUNTER AT ROCK HARBOR   95   9
  THE MUSSELS HUNG DULL BLUE AND ....MUSSEL HUNTER AT ROCK HARBOR   95   17
  A BIG HANDKERCHIEF WITH BLUE ....MUSSEL HUNTER AT ROCK HARBOR   97   63
  A BLUE SEA, FOUR HORNY BULL-FEET, ...THE BULL OF BENDYLAW 108   7
  EVEN OUR SHADOWS ARE BLUE WITH COLD. ....A WINTER SHIP 113   23
  HE, AFLOAT IN THE SEA OF HER BLUE SATIN *TWO VIEWS OF A CADAVER ROOM 114   14
  RAY BUT EGG ROCK ON THE BLUE WASTAGE. ....SUICIDE OFF EGG ROCK 115   22
  MY OWN BLUE RAZOR RUSTING IN MY THROAT. .....ELECTRA ON AZALEA PATH 117   43
  TABLETS OF BLANK BLUE, COULDN'T ......THE HERMIT AT OUTERMOST HOUSE 118   2
  THEIR EYES REVOLVE THE WHOLE TOWN LIKE A BLUE AND GREEN BALL. *NET-. 121   12
  MUSSELS CLUSTER BLUE AS GRAPES: ....MAGNOLIA SHOALS 122   17
  IN A BLUE, UNCHANGING LIGHT, ...THE SLEEPERS 122   5
  A BLUE MIST IS DRAGGING THE LAKE. ....THE MANOR GARDEN 125   4
  BLUE MOLES ....BLUE MOLES 126   T
  BLUE SEUDE A DOG OR FOX HAS CHEWED. ....BLUE MOLES 126   4
  BLUE MISTS MOVE OVER ....DARK WOOD, DARK WATER 127   6
  BLUE LARKSPUR STAR. ....POLLY'S TREE 129   42
  A BLUE SKY OUT OF THE ORESTEIA ....THE COLOSSUS 129   16
  THE BLUE SISTERS SENT ME TO ANOTHER SCHOOL. POEM.4.BEAST. 134   7
  THE FLAT BLUE SKY-CIRCLE POEM.7.S. 136   3
  OF PALE BLUE VITREOUS STUFF, OPAQUE ....THE BURNT-OUT SPA 137   4
  BLUE AND IMPROBABLE PERSON ....THE BURNT-OUT SPA 138   25
  I SIZZLED IN HIS BLUE VOLTS LIKE A DESERT PROPHET. THE HANGING MAN 141   2
  IN THE BLUE HOUR BEFORE SUNUP. ....SLEEP IN THE MOJAVE DESERT 144   10
  KNOTTING AND STOPPING, ILL-ASSORTED, IN BLUE UNIFORMS,*PARLIAMENT H. 152   14
  THE BLUE NIGHT PLANTS, THE LITTLE PALE BLUE HILL ....PARLIAMENT H. 153   41
  THE BLUE NIGHT PLANTS, THE LITTLE PALE BLUE HILL ....PARLIAMENT H. 153   41
  BLUE SHRUB BEHIND THE GLASS ....PARLIAMENT HILL FIELDS 153   45
  HE IS IMMUNE TO PILLS: RED, PURPLE, BLUE -- ....INSOMNIAC 163   15
  LIKE BLUE MARY'S ANGEL, DOVELIKE AGAINST A PANE ....WIDOW 165   38
  BUT FROM ANOTHER PLACE, TROPICAL AND BLUE, ...FINISTERRE 170   34
  THE INTRICATE, BLUE PIPING UNDER THIS PALE MARBLE. ......SURGEON. 171   26
  OVER ONE BED IN THE WARD, A SMALL BLUE LIGHT   THE SURGEON AT 2 A.M. 171   41
  ANNOUNCES A NEW SOUL. THE BED IS BLUE. ......THE SURGEON AT 2 A.M. 171   42
  TONIGHT, FOR THIS PERSON, BLUE IS A BEAUTIFUL COLOR. ......SURGEON. 171   43
  THE BLUE EYE OF MY TURQUOISE WILL COMFORT ME. ....LAST WORDS 172   20
  THE TREES OF THE MIND ARE BLACK. THE LIGHT IS BLUE. ....MOON. 172   2
  HER BLUE GARMENTS UNLOOSE SMALL BATS AND OWLS. ....MOON. 173   18
  BLUE AND MYSTICAL OVER THE FACE OF THE STARS. ....MOON. 173   23
  INSIDE THE CHURCH, THE SAINTS WILL BE ALL BLUE, ...MOON. 173   24
  A HOT BLUE DAY HAD BUDDED INTO SOMETHING. ....THREE WOMEN 178   56
  DUSK HOODS ME IN BLUE NOW, LIKE A MARY. ....THREE WOMEN 179 102
  WHO IS HE, THIS BLUE, FURIOUS BOY, ...THREE WOMEN 181 162
  THE BLUE COLOR PALES. HE IS HUMAN AFTER ALL. ....THREE WOMEN 181 166
  WHAT BLUE, MOONY RAY ICES THEIR DREAMS? ....THREE WOMEN 181 182
  HIS WIDE EYE IS THAT GENERAL, FLAT BLUE. ....THREE WOMEN 183 234
  INTERCEPTING THE BLUE BOLTS OF A COLD MOON? ....THREE WOMEN 185 291
  I REMEMBER A BLUE EYE, ...LITTLE FUGUE 188   45
  SUCH BLUE CURRENTS IN THE VEINS OF MY LOVED ONE! .....AN APPEARANCE 189   2
  PERCY BOWS, IN HIS BLUE PEAJACKET, AMONG THE NARCISSI. ...NARCISSI. 190   2
  HE IS QUITE BLUE; THE TERRIBLE WIND TRIES HIS BREATHING. NARCISSI. 190   11
  MARBLE FACADES WITH BLUE VEINS, AND JELLY-GLASSFULS OF DAFFFODILS. ...
                      ... BERCK-PLAGE 199   89
  SMILINGLY, BLUE LIGHTNING ....THE OTHER 201   5
  INVOLVED IN ITS WEIRD BLUE DREAMS, ...BURNING THE LETTERS 205   40
  THE SMALL SKULLS, THE SMASHED BLUE HILLS, THE GODAWFUL HUSH. ...
                      ... FOR A FATHERLESS SON 206   13
  OVER THE SEVEN HILLS, THE RED FURROW, THE BLUE MOUNTAIN? *DETECTIVE. 208   2
  THE MILK CAME YELLOW, THEN BLUE AND SWEET AS WATER. ..THE DETECTIVE 209   33
  TATTOOING OVER AND OVER THE SAME BLUE GRIEVANCES, ...COURAGE. 210   11
  WHICH IS THE MIDWIFE, IS THAT HER BLUE COAT? ....THE BEE MEETING 211   12
  BLUE DEW FROM DANGEROUS SKIN. ....STINGS 214   27
  YOU ARE BLUE AND HUGE, A TRAFFIC POLICEMAN, ...A SECRET 219   3

                                                    TITLE   PAGE LINE
BLUE (CONT.)
    THAT BIG BLUE HEAD -- ....A SECRET 220 26
    WHERE IT POURS BEAN GREEN OVER BLUE ....DADDY 222 12
    AND YOUR ARYAN EYE, BRIGHT BLUE. ....DADDY 223 44
    THE SAME PLACARD OF BLUE FOG IS WHEELED INTO POSITION ...THE JAILER 226   2
    MY SLEEPING CAPSULE, MY RED AND BLUE ZEPPELIN ....THE JAILER 226 12
    FLOGGED TROLLEY. THE SPARKS ARE BLUE. ....LESBOS 228 49
    THE BLUE SPARKS SPILL, ...LESBOS 228 50
    A GREEN DRINK, ONE A BLUE. ....AMNESIAC 233 22
    THE BLUE, GREEN, ...LYONNESSE 234   5
    TO ALMOST NOTHING, TO A DULL BLUE DUD. ....BY CANDLELIGHT 236 18
    THEN THE SUBSTANCELESS BLUE ....ARIEL 239   2
    I AM A MINER. THE LIGHT BURNS BLUE. ......NICK AND THE CANDLESTICK 240   1
    ALL COOL, ALL BLUE. UNLIKE YOU --- ....GULLIVER 251   9
    IN BLUE DISTANCE THE PISTONS HISS. ....YEARS 256 25
    THE WET DAWN INKS ARE DOING THEIR BLUE DISSOLVE. ......WINTER TREES 257   1
    TO THE ELECTRIC MILKER, THE WIFEY, THE BIG BLUE EYE ...EAVESDROPPER 261 43
    THEY BUZZ LIKE BLUE CHILDREN ....TOTEM 265 31
    THE BLUE AND RED JEWELS OF HER RINGS SMOKE ....KINDNESS 269   3
    YELLOW CATHEAD, BLUE FISH --- ....BALLOONS 271   9
    CAN ONCE IN A BLUE MOON CATCH THE SHADOWS OF ....DIALOGUE O. 282 222
    BLUE AS LIZARD-SCALES. FROST SHEENS THE STREET. ....DIALOGUE O. 286 340
    BLUE SKY OR BLACK ....THE RIVAL/DR 291 11
    THE NIGHT IS A BLUE POOL; SHE IS VERY STILL. ....ELM/DR 292   6
    THE SKY WAS HIGH AND BLUE. ....BITTER STRAWBERRIES 299 13
    HER BLUE EYES SWAM WITH VAGUE TERROR. ....BITTER STRAWBERRIES 300 24
    GOT UP TO LET THE SUAVE BLUE POLICEMAN IN. ......THE TRIAL OF MAN 312   8
    REAP THE ROUND BLUE PIGEON FROM ROOF RIDGE, *GO GET THE GOODLY SQUAB 313   3
    TRANSFIXED BY GLARE OF BLUE FROM GORGON'S EYE; ..PROLOGUE TO SPRING 322   2
    BLUE VIEWS ARE BOARDED UP; OUR SWEET VACATION ....TWO LOVERS. 327   3
    RIDING HOME FROM CREDULOUS BLUE DOMES, ...TERMINAL 328   1
    THEN LET THE BLUE TENT TOPPLE, STARS RAIN DOWN, LOVE IS A PARALLAX 330 73
    WHOSE HOLY BLUE ANOINTS HER INJURED HAND. ....THE PRINCESS. 333   6
BLUEBEARD (1)
    BLUEBEARD ....BLUEBEARD 305   T
BLUEBEARD'S (2)
    THAT LET ME INTO BLUEBEARD'S STUDY; ....BLUEBEARD 305   2
    THAT LET ME INTO BLUEBEARD'S STUDY. ....BLUEBEARD 305   8
BLUEBIRDS (1)
    FLOWERS AND BLUEBIRDS THAT NEVER WERE ....THE DISQUIETING MUSES 76 44
BLUEBLACK (3)
    PELLMELL, BLUEBLACK. ....THE BULL OF BENDYLAW 108 15
    BLUEBLACK, A SPECTACULAR PLUM FRUIT. ....ZOO KEEPER'S WIFE 154   4
    BLUEBLACK, WITH THE MUCH-POKED PERIODS OF STARS ....INSOMNIAC 163   2
BLUE-BLOODED (1)
    BLUE-BLOODED IN COARSE COUNTRY REIGNED; ....NATURAL HISTORY 71   2
BLUE-CAPED (1)
    THE RED-NOSED, BLUE-CAPED WOMEN RING ....A WINTER'S TALE 87 14
BLUEGREEN (2)
    HANGING THEIR BLUEGREEN BELLIES AND THEIR WING PANES IN A CHINESE
        SCREEN. ....BLACKBERRYING 168 16
    THEN HURL THE BARE WORLD LIKE A BLUEGREEN BALL ..SONG FOR A REVOLU. 323 21
BLUE-GREEN (1)
    OF THIS BLUE-GREEN TOY. ....WORDS FOR A NURSERY 73 20
BLUENESS (1)
    OF APPREHENDING BLUENESS, OR STARS. ....LOVE LETTER 147   8
BLUEPRINT (2)
    LIKE THE WHITE LINES ON A BLUEPRINT. ....ZOO KEEPER'S WIFE 154 10
    NO ANCIENT BLUEPRINT BUILDS AN ARK ....INSOLENT STORM. 326 17
BLUE-RED (2)
    WITH BLUE-RED JUICES. THESE THEY SQUANDER ON MY FINGERS. BLACKBER. 168   7
    NAVEL CORDS, BLUE-RED AND LUCENT, ...THE OTHER 202 18
BLUES (2)
    GRAYNESS BLUES, REDDENS, AND THE OUTLINE ....THE THIN PEOPLE 65 34
    REDS, GREENS, BLUES. ....ON THE PLETHORA OF DRYADS 68 36
BLUE'S (2)
    MY PROMISE OF AN IDYLL. THE BLUE'S WORN OUT: ....GREEN ROCK. 105   8
    THE BLUE'S A JEWEL. ....THE TOUR 238 29
BLUEST (1)
    FLOATING ABOVE ME IN BLUEST AIR ....THE DISQUIETING MUSES 75 42
BLUNDER (1)
    AND WHEN AT LAST THEY BLUNDER INTO BED ....THE DEAD 320   7
BLUNT (13)
    WITH EACH TILT, SHOCK AND SHUDDER, OUR BLUNT SHIP CHANNEL CROSSING 26   2
    BLUNT IN SELF-INTEREST ....SPIDER 48   3
    OF BLUNT PENCILS, ROSE-SPRIGGED COFFEE CUP, ...CONJURING. 65   2
    THUMBHEAD, BLUNT HELPER, ...WORDS FOR A NURSERY 73 15
    TENDING, WITHOUT STOP, THE BLUNT ....NIGHT SHIFT 77 23
    AND BUFFS AND SLEEKS THE BLUNT HULLS ..MUSSEL HUNTER AT ROCK HARBOR 95   5
    SUPERIOR PAGE; THE BLUNT STONE ALSO. ....POEMS, POTATOES 106 13
    BLUNT AND FLAT ENOUGH TO FEEL NO LACK. I FEEL A LACK. ..THREE WOMEN 182 193
    I FELT HANDS ROUND A TEA MUG, DULL, BLUNT, ...THE RABBIT CATCHER 194 22
    BLUNT, PRACTICAL BOATS ....BERCK-PLAGE 199 76
    THE BLUNT, CLUMSY STUMBLERS, THE BOORS. ....WINTERING 219 41
    COMES BLUNT AND WAN ....AQUATIC NOCTURNE 306 26

BLUNT (CONT.)
    BLUNT AS THE FACELESS GUT ....NOTES TO A NEOPHYTE 306   2
BLUNTED (1)
    THEIR WHETSTONE TO THE BLUNTED EDGE ....THE DEATH OF MYTH-MAKING 104   9
BLUNTLY (1)
    BECAUSE PAN BLUNTLY SPELT OUT GOD'S HEAD, NOT ....DIALOGUE O. 282 237
BLUR (3)
    EVER BLUR THE INTRANSIGENT LINES WHICH DRAW ....TALE OF A TUB   25   28
    AIR, AND BLUR. ....YADDO: THE GRAND MANOR 123   3
    WHO WILL LOVE ME THROUGH THE BLUR OF MY DEFORMITY ......THREE WOMEN 183 251
BLURS (3)
    A MILK-FILM BLURS ....RESOLVE   52   10
    PROW-LIKE THROUGH BLURS ....TWO VIEWS OF WITHENS   72   4
    SHEER SILVER BLURS THEIR PHANTOM ACT. ....DANSE MACABRE 321   21
BLURT (1)
    ALWAYS, THE GLASS WILL BLURT WHAT I DON'T WANT ....DIALOGUE O. 278   68
BOA (1)
    WITH THE BOA CONSTRICTOR IN THE FELLOWS' GARDEN.   ZOO KEEPER'S WIFE 155   26
BOAR (1)
    BOAR, FABULOUS ENOUGH TO STRADDLE THAT SOW'S HEAT. ....SOW   61   33
BOARD (4)
    WE SHALL BOARD OUR IMAGINED SHIP AND WILDLY SAIL .....TALE OF A TUB   25   46
    DIALOGUE OVER A OUIJA BOARD ....DIALOGUE OVER A OUIJA BOARD 276   T
    IN ALL. PLUS YES. PLUS NO. AND THIS BARE BOARD. ....DIALOGUE O. 276   14
    THIS BOARD OUR BATTLEFIELD. LET'S GIVE PAN UP ....DIALOGUE O. 284 292
BOARDED (4)
    BOARDED THE TRAIN THERE'S NO GETTING OFF. ....METAPHORS 116   9
    SOON EACH WHITE LADY WILL BE BOARDED UP ....PRIVATE GROUND 130   5
    I ENTERED YOUR BIBLE. I BOARDED YOUR ARK ....ZOO KEEPER'S WIFE 155   28
    BLUE VIEWS ARE BOARDED UP; OUR SWEET VACATION ....TWO LOVERS. 327   3
BOARDS (1)
    ENACTED TRAGEDIES ON THESE BLOOD-SOAKED BOARDS, ...PERSEUS   83   19
BOAST (1)
    AHAB, FULFILL YOUR BOAST: ....BATTLE-SCENE   84   27
BOAT (4)
    I HAVE LET THINGS SLIP, A THIRTY-YEAR-OLD CARGO BOAT ....TULIPS 161   22
    AND RENTED AN OLD GREEN BOAT. I ROWED. YOU READ ....THE BABYSITTERS 175   31
    BLACK LAKE, BLACK BOAT, TWO BLACK, CUT-PAPER PEOPLE.*CROSSING THE W. 190   1
    I ROCK YOU LIKE A BOAT ....BY CANDLELIGHT 237   24
BOATS (2)
    HALFWAY UP FROM THE LITTLE HARBOR OF SARDINE BOATS, *THE NET-MENDERS 121   1
    BLUNT, PRACTICAL BOATS ....BERCK-PLAGE 199   76
BOBBED (2)
    BUT THE LITTLE PLANET BOBBED AWAY ....THE DISQUIETING MUSES   76   46
    SO WE BOBBED OUT TO THE ISLAND. IT WAS DESERTED --   THE BABYSITTERS 175   33
BOCKLIN (2)
    OLD BOCKLIN MISSED, WHO HELD A SHELL .....ON THE DECLINE OF ORACLES   78   5
    FOR WHICH THE GHOST OF BOCKLIN GRIEVES. ..ON THE DECLINE OF ORACLES   78   15
BODIES (9)
    WHITE BODIES IN A WOODEN GIRDLE, ROOT TO TOP ......VIRGIN IN A TREE   81   22
    VISION, WISDOM, FOR BODIES ....SCULPTOR   91   3
    DWARFING US. OUR BODIES FLICKER ....SCULPTOR   92   16
    OF PLACE, TIME, AND THEIR BODIES. ....SCULPTOR   92   19
    GROWN MILKY, ALMOST CLEAR, LIKE THE BODIES OF SAINTS. ......CANDLES 148   4
    AND NO BODIES, SINGING LIKE ARROWS UP TO HEAVEN. ....WIDOW 164   25
    THESE BODIES MOUNDED AROUND ME NOW, THESE POLAR SLEEPERS -- THREE. 181 181
    THE DUMB, BANDED BODIES ....THE SWARM 217   47
    GREASING THE BODIES OF ADULTERERS ....FEVER. 231   25
BODILESS (3)
    TO HIS HOUSE THE BODILESS ....SCULPTOR   91   1
    A BODILESS SOUL COULD PASS ANOTHER SOUL ....WIDOW 164   32
    THEY ARE MORE BEAUTIFUL THAN MY BODILESS OWL, ..BURNING THE LETTERS 204   30
BODY (49)
    NOR DID ANY WORD BODY WITH A NAME ....HARDCASTLE CRAGS   63   17
    THAN FLESH OF ANY BODY ....ON THE PLETHORA OF DRYADS   67   17
    IN ONE BODY THOSE EARTHBORN COMMONERS ....NATURAL HISTORY   71   8
    DOWN: THE BODY WEIGHS LIKE STONE. ....THE GREAT CARBUNCLE   73   30
    AND HIS LOVE'S BODY. ....WORDS FOR A NURSERY   74   40
    STIFF AS TWIGS, HER BODY WOODENLY ....VIRGIN IN A TREE   82   39
    AND BODY WHITER THAN ITS FRILL OF LILIES: ....YADWIGHA.   85   14
    BERRIES REDDEN. A BODY OF WHITENESS ....MOONRISE   98   13
    THOUGH THE BODY WALK OUT IN CLEAN LINEN. ....MOONRISE   98   15
    HIS BODY BEACHED WITH THE SEA'S GARBAGE, ...SUICIDE OFF EGG ROCK 115   15
    THE WAX IMAGE OF MYSELF, A DOLL'S BODY. POEM.6.W. 135   3
    THE RAFTERS AND STRUTS OF HIS BODY WEAR ....THE BURNT-OUT SPA 138   6
    SHE LAY IN BED WITH ME LIKE A DEAD BODY ....IN PLASTER 158   6
    AND MY HISTORY TO THE ANESTHETIST AND MY BODY TO SURGEONS. ..TULIPS 160   7
    MY BODY IS A PEBBLE TO THEM, THEY TEND IT AS WATER ....TULIPS 160   15
    BODY, A SHEET OF NEWSPRINT ON THE FIRE ....WIDOW 164   2
    THE BODY UNDER IT IS IN MY HANDS. ....THE SURGEON AT 2 A.M. 170   6
    THE BODY IS A ROMAN THING. ....THE SURGEON AT 2 A.M. 171   29
    THE BODY IS RESOURCEFUL. ....THREE WOMEN 184 256
    THE BODY OF A STARFISH CAN GROW BACK ITS ARMS ....THREE WOMEN 184 257
    HOW HER BODY OPENS AND SHUTS -- ....AN APPEARANCE 189   14

                                             TITLE   PAGE LINE
BODY (CONT.)
  THEY ARE HANDLING THE BLACK AND GREEN LOZENGES LIKE THE PARTS
    OF A BODY. ....BERCK-PLAGE   196   16
  A BODY INTO A PIPE, AND THE SMOKE RISING. ....THE DETECTIVE 208   11
  THERE IS NO BODY IN THE HOUSE AT ALL. ....THE DETECTIVE 209   16
  THIS IS A CASE WITHOUT A BODY. ....THE DETECTIVE 209   24
  THE BODY DOES NOT COME INTO IT AT ALL. ....THE DETECTIVE 209   25
  THE BARREN BODY OF HAWTHORN, ETHERIZING ITS CHILDREN. ....BEE. 211   25
  HER WINGS TORN SHAWLS, HER LONG BODY ....STINGS 214   17
  WITH HER LION-RED BODY, HER WINGS OF GLASS? ....STINGS 215   55
  IT SPREADS ITSELF OUT, A MILE-LONG BODY OF MEISSEN, ...WINTERING 218   35
  HER BODY A BULB IN THE COLD AND TOO DUMB TO THINK. ....WINTERING 219   45
  I SHALL TAKE NO BITE OF YOUR BODY, ...MEDUSA   225   34
  WORKING IT LIKE DOUGH, A MULATTO BODY, ...LESBOS   229   61
  YOUR BODY ....FEVER. 232   35
  I AM DRAGGING MY BODY ....GETTING THERE 248   10
  THE BODY OF THIS WOMAN, ...GETTING THERE 249   46
  OVER YOUR BODY THE CLOUDS GO ....GULLIVER 251   1
  THIS BODY, ...CHILDLESS WOMAN 259   8
  YOUR BODY ONE ....EAVESDROPPER 260   13
  FLEA BODY! ....EAVESDROPPER 261   53
  THE REST OF THE BODY IS ALL WASHED OUT, ...CONTUSION 271   2
  BODY WEARS THE SMILE OF ACCOMPLISHMENT, ...EDGE 272   3
  THEM BACK INTO HER BODY AS PETALS ....EDGE 273   13
  DEATH'S TWO DREAMS DOWN WITH THE BODY THAT BLED THE VEIN, ...
                              ... DIALOGUE OVER A OUIJA BOARD 285 329
  MY X-RAYED HEART, DISSECTED BODY: ....BLUEBEARD   305   6
  EACH SACRED BODY ....MOONSONG AT MORNING 317   29
  TILL HER STUBBORN BODY BURNS. ....DANSE MACABRE   321   15
  TAKES ON THE BODY ....ON LOOKING INTO THE EYES OF A DEMON LOVER 325   7
  UNTIL DREAM TAKES HER BODY ....AERIALIST 331   4
BODYGUARD (1)
  THIS MINER'S BOY FROM GOBLIN BODYGUARD.*THE PRINCESS AND THE GOBLINS 333   25
BODY'S (1)
  BECOME HIS STARVING BODY'S BAIT. ....PURSUIT   22   24
BODY-TREE (1)
  A SOUL GROWN FEVERISH, CLUTCHING ITS DEAD BODY-TREE ....DIALOGUE B.   39   43
BOG (1)
  FOR MY CUBE OF SUGAR: ITS BOG BREATH ....ZOO KEEPER'S WIFE 155   36
BOGGLING (1)
  A WEATHER FIGURE, BOGGLING, ...EAVESDROPPER   261   48
BOILED (2)
  SALUTARY AND PURE AS BOILED WATER, ...MAGI   148   7
  AMONG THE BLANCHED, BOILED INSTRUMENTS, THE VIRGINAL
    CURTAINS. ....FEVER./DR   294   8
BOILS (1)
  IT BOILS FOR FORTY HOURS AT A STRETCH. ....THE TOUR   238   30
BOLD (5)
  THE BOLD GULLS DOVE AS IF THEY OWNED IT ALL. ....THE BABYSITTERS 175   37
  WITH YOUR BOLD ....THE TOUR 237   3
  AT THE UNREAL FRONTIER. LET OUR BACKS, NOW BOLD, ...DIALOGUE O. 285 331
  BOLD BEANSTALK; LIE AND LOVE TILL SHARP SCYTHE HACKS *LOVE IS A PAR. 330   71
  OF THE BOLD SAILOR FALLING UNDER DRENCH .....EPITAPH IN THREE PARTS 337   15
BOLES (2)
  BATTALIONS. SEE, HOW THE TREE BOLES FLATTEN ....THE THIN PEOPLE   65   43
  DOWN BOLES OF THE FIR. ....DARK WOOD, DARK WATER   127   24
BOLT (3)
  I BOLT THE DOOR, EACH DOOR I BOLT. ....PURSUIT   23   47
  I BOLT THE DOOR, EACH DOOR I BOLT. ....PURSUIT   23   47
  AND BOLT IT UP BY TAKING OATH NO GUESS   DIALOGUE OVER A OUIJA BOARD 286 345
BOLTS (1)
  INTERCEPTING THE BLUE BOLTS OF A COLD MOON? ....THREE WOMEN 185 291
BOMB (2)
  OLD WINTER-FACE, OLD BARREN ONE, OLD TIME BOMB. ....THREE WOMEN 181 158
  "BOMB THEM OFF THE MAP." ....BITTER STRAWBERRIES   299   6
BOMBED (1)
  "WE OUGHT TO HAVE BOMBED THEM LONG AGO." ....BITTER STRAWBERRIES 299   21
BOMBS (1)
  AGAINST FIRE AND BOMBS THROUGH THE ROOF. ....THE APPLICANT 221   24
BONA (1)
  BREED INNUMERABLE BILLS, BONA FIDE: ....DIALOGUE EN ROUTE   308   17
BONBON (1)
  AND NIBBLES AN OCCASIONAL BONBON OF SIN. ....FEMALE AUTHOR 301   4
BOND (1)
  OUR LONE LUCK NOW, COMPELLED BY BOND, BY BLOOD, ...CHANNEL CROSSING   27   33
BONE (25)
  FANTASTIC FLESH DOWN TO THE HONEST BONE. ....TALE OF A TUB   25   24
  OF SKIN AND BONE, ...LETTER TO A PURIST   37   12
  TO THIS WHITE BONE; ....DIALOGUE BETWEEN GHOST AND PRIEST   39   28
  BLACKENS FLESH TO BONE AND DEVOURS THEM.*EPITAPH FOR FIRE AND FLOWER   46   35
  TO UNPICK THE HEART, PARE BONE ....NOVEMBER GRAVEYARD   56   9
  OF CANDOR PARES WHITE FLESH TO THE WHITE BONE, ...MOONRISE   98   27
  RAISED HIS MEN OF SKIN AND BONE, ...I WANT, I WANT 106   10
  IT WAS THE GANGRENE ATE YOU TO THE BONE .....ELECTRA ON AZALEA PATH 117   39
  THE DARK'S HIS BONE. POEM.4.BEAST.   134   15

BONE (CONT.)
    LOVE IS THE BONE AND SINEW OF MY CURSE. POEM.7.S.   137   40
    GRINNING OVER ITS BONE OF IVORY ....THE SWARM   216   24
    I MAY BE SKIN AND BONE, ...LADY LAZARUS   245   33
    FLESH, BONE, THERE IS NOTHING THERE --- ....LADY LAZARUS   246   75
    GRAY TALLOW, FROM BONE AND BONE. ......................EAVESDROPPER   260   23
    GRAY TALLOW, FROM BONE AND BONE. ......................EAVESDROPPER   260   23
    STARING FROM HER HOOD OF BONE. ....EDGE   273   18
    IT KEEPS WASHING YOU UP LIKE AN OLD BONE. ....THE RIVAL/DR   291   16
    THE WAY YOU'D CRACK A CLOCK; YOU'D CRUSH THE BONE ...SONNET: TO EVA   304   2
    TO THE GRANITE GRIN OF BONE. ....NOTES TO A NEOPHYTE   306   12
    THE GENERATING BONE. ....TRIO OF LOVE SONGS   315   48
    THESE BONE SHANKS WILL NOT WAKE IMMACULATE ....THE DEAD   320   10
    SHANKS OF BONE NOW RESURRECT. ....DANSE MACABRE   321   17
    SKEPTIC CYCLONES TRY THE BONE ..INSOLENT STORM STRIKES AT THE SKULL   325   7
    THEY SHOOT THE DICE FOR ONE REMAINING BONE; ....DENOUEMENT   326   8
    NO SEA-CHANGE DECKS THE SUNKEN SHANK OF BONE ....TWO LOVERS.   327   17
BONE-BARE (1)
    SACKED LARDER'S GONE BONE-BARE. ....THE GLUTTON   40   14
BONELESS (1)
    FOOTLINGS, BONELESS AS NOSES, ...POEM.2.DARK.   133   25
BONES (19)
    AND GRAYER; NOT EVEN MOVING THEIR BONES. ....THE THIN PEOPLE   65   47
    HER WORMY COURIERS ARE AT HIS BONES. ....OUIJA   77   25
    BONES, BONES ONLY, PAWED AND TOSSED, ...POINT SHIRLEY   111   38
    BONES, BONES ONLY, PAWED AND TOSSED, ...POINT SHIRLEY   111   38
    I FOUND YOUR NAME, I FOUND YOUR BONES AND ALL*ELECTRA ON AZALEA PATH   117   16
    BONES OF THE GREAT TREES. ....DARK WOOD, DARK WATER   127   5
    YOUR FLUTED BONES AND ACANTHINE HAIR ARE LITTERED .....THE COLOSSUS   130   20
    SOFT SUEDE TONGUES BETWEEN HIS BONES. ....THE BURNT-OUT SPA   138   11
    THE SKULLS, THE UNBUCKLED BONES FACING THE VIEW! ..WAKING IN WINTER   151   10
    THE SPIDERY JAWS, THE SPINE BONES BARED FOR A MOMENT ....ZOO K.   154   9
    HOLDING MY BONES IN PLACE SO THEY WOULD MEND PROPERLY. ..IN PLASTER   159   27
    TO WHITEN MY BONES AMONG THEM. ....WUTHERING HEIGHTS   167   18
    I WOULD NOT MIND IF IT WAS BONES, OR A PEARL BUTTON. .....BIRTHDAY.   206   12
    BUT THEIR BONES SHOWED, AND THE MOON SMILED. ....THE DETECTIVE   209   35
    I THOUGHT EVEN THE BONES WOULD DO. ....DADDY   224   60
    OUR BONES, OUR HAIR. ....LESBOS   228   37
    BONES NOSING FOR DISTANCES. ....BRASILIA   258   10
    MY BONES HOLD A STILLNESS, THE FAR ....SHEEP IN FOG   262   11
    ALL DAY SHE PLAYS AT CHESS WITH THE BONES OF THE WORLD: ..FEMALE A.   301   1
BONEWHITE (1)
    A BONEWHITE LIGHT, LIKE DEATH, BEHIND ALL THINGS. ....INSOMNIAC   163   4
BONFIRE (1)
    BY THE ORANGE AND FUCHSIA BONFIRE ....CHILD'S PARK STONES   101   9
BONG (1)
    AT THE END, THEY SOBERLY BONG OUT THEIR NAMES. ....MOON.   173   14
BONNETED (1)
    THE BONNETED LADIES GRIN. ....OLD LADIES' HOME   120   18
BONWIT'S (1)
    THAN MODELS FROM BONWIT'S OR JAY'S, ...A WINTER'S TALE   86   10
BONY (2)
    OUR OWN GRIST DOWN TO ITS BONY FACE. ....ALL THE DEAD DEARS   70   12
    LUCINA, BONY MOTHER, LABORING ....MOONRISE   98   25
BOOK (8)
    NO FIRE IS, NOR IN ANY BOOK PROOF ....VANITY FAIR   33   27
    THE WORDS IN HIS BOOK WORMED OFF THE PAGES. ...SUICIDE OFF EGG ROCK   115   19
    GARDENS IN AN ANTIQUE BOOK ....MAGNOLIA SHOALS   122   9
    CAN TURN AND TURN THE PAGES OF A BOOK. ....THREE WOMEN   187 361
    WHO PLUMBS THE WELL OF HIS BOOK, ...BERCK-PLAGE   197   22
    THEY PROPPED HIS JAW WITH A BOOK UNTIL IT STIFFENED ....BERCK-PLAGE   198   65
    HIS BOOK OF INSULTS. NERVE OR NOUMENON. *DIALOGUE OVER A OUIJA BOARD   284 297
    READ BLACK MAGIC OR HOLY BOOK ..BLACK PINE TREE IN AN ORANGE LIGHT   328   13
BOOKENDS (1)
    BY TWO BRONZE BOOKENDS OF SHIPS IN SAIL,   ON THE DECLINE OF ORACLES   78   2
BOOKS (5)
    HE WILLED HIS BOOKS AND SHELL AWAY. ......ON THE DECLINE OF ORACLES   78   10
    THE BOOKS BURNED UP, SEA TOOK THE SHELL,   ON THE DECLINE OF ORACLES   78   11
    I WATCHED MY TEASET, MY BUREAUS OF LINEN, MY BOOKS ....TULIPS   161   26
    THE BOOKS I CARRY WEDGE INTO MY SIDE. ....THREE WOMEN   185 305
    AND PAGE BY PRIDE THE GOOD BOOKS BLOW;*SONG FOR A REVOLUTIONARY LOVE   322   3
BOOKS' (1)
    POSTAGE STAMPS, STACKED BOOKS' CLAMOR AND YAWP, ...CONJURING.   65   3
BOOKSHELF (1)
    ON THE LONG BOOKSHELF IT STOOD ...THE LADY AND THE EARTHENWARE HEAD   69   3
BOOM (5)
    HEAR LOUDSPEAKERS BOOM ....ALICANTE LULLABY   43   12
    "THOR IS ANGRY: BOOM BOOM BOOM! ....THE DISQUIETING MUSES   75   22
    "THOR IS ANGRY: BOOM BOOM BOOM! ....THE DISQUIETING MUSES   75   22
    "THOR IS ANGRY: BOOM BOOM BOOM! ....THE DISQUIETING MUSES   75   22
    THAT MUTED BOOM, THAT CLANGOR ....NIGHT SHIFT   76   2
BOOMED (1)
    BOOMED WITH BAD DREAMS AND THE JOVIAN VOICES OF SURGEONS. *FACE LIFT   156   6
BOOMERANG (1)
    BOOMERANG LIKE ANCHORED ELASTICS, HURTING THE OWNER. ...BERCK-PLAGE   196   11

```
                                                       TITLE          PAGE  LINE
BOOMS (1)
  THE SHINGLE BOOMS, BICKERING UNDER  ...................POINT SHIRLEY  110    2
BOORS (1)
  THE BLUNT, CLUMSY STUMBLERS, THE BOORS.  ................WINTERING    219   41
BOOT (4)
  FROM UNDER CRUNCH OF MY MAN'S BOOT  .....................ODE FOR TED   29    1
  WHERE SECOND WIND, HIP BOOT  ...................TWO VIEWS OF WITHENS    72    9
  THIS BLACK BOOT HAS NO MERCY FOR ANYBODY.  ..............BERCK-PLAGE  197   19
  THE BOOT IN THE FACE, THE BRUTE  ...............................DADDY  223   49
BOOTSOLE (1)
  DIRTY AS A BOOTSOLE AND BIG AS A HOSPITAL SINK  ...ZOO KEEPER'S WIFE  155   35
BOOTSOLES (1)
  STEPPING STONES FOR FRENCH BOOTSOLES.  ....................THE SWARM  216   14
BORDER (4)
  GRIM AS GARGOYLES FROM YEARS SPENT SQUATTING AT SEA'S BORDER  ...
                                     ... DREAM WITH CLAM-DIGGERS         44   25
  ICE AND ROCK, EACH SENTIMENT WITHIN BORDER,  ..............SPINSTER    49   16
  I WALK DRY ON YOUR KINGDOM'S BORDER  .............FULL FATHOM FIVE     93   41
  SNAILS SCROLL THE BORDER  ...................DARK WOOD, DARK WATER    127    8
BORDERED (1)
  OF ITS HILLS, AND ITS PASTURES BORDERED BY BLACK STONE SET  ...
                                     ... HARDCASTLE CRAGS                63   29
BORDERS (1)
  BY DAY, DESCANT FROM BORDERS  .............................LORELEI     94   26
BORE (2)
  AND THIS IS THE KINGDOM YOU BORE ME TO,  ......THE DISQUIETING MUSES   76   54
  AS IF BLOODHOUNDS BORE HIM DOWN. I-N-C-O ...  ........DIALOGUE O.     283  275
BORED (4)
  ME, SITTING HERE BORED AS A LEOPARD  ..................LEAVING EARLY  145    3
  BORED HOODLUM IN A RED ROOM  .........................THE DETECTIVE   209   19
  CREAMY BEAN FLOWERS WITH BLACK EYES AND LEAVES LIKE BORED HEARTS. ...
                                     ... THE BEE MEETING                211   18
  BORED HIM. HE'S MORE PHILOSOPHER, IT SEEMS,  ...........DIALOGUE O.   277   43
BOREDOM (4)
  A VULTUROUS BOREDOM PINNED ME IN THIS TREE.  .........THE HANGING MAN  142    5
  OUT OF SHEER BOREDOM. TANGLED IN THE SWEAT-WET SHEETS  .......ZOO K.  155   23
  IN A NEST OF ROOT-HAIRS AND BOREDOM --  .........BURNING THE LETTERS  205   45
  EXUDES FROM ITS DEAD BOREDOM.  ............NICK AND THE CANDLESTICK   240    5
BOREDOMS (1)
  OF OLD BANDAGES, BOREDOMS, OLD FACES  ..................GETTING THERE  249   66
BORES (3)
  ETERNITY BORES ME,  ............................................YEARS  255    9
  HE LEECHES BY OUR LENIENCE. HE STILL BORES  ............DIALOGUE O.   283  259
  OTHER THAN YOUR OWN. AS HE BORES YOU  ...DIALOGUE OVER A OUIJA BOARD  283  261
BORN (7)
  BORN GREEN WE WERE  ..........................................FIRESONG   30    1
  HOW BEST BEAUTY'S BORN OF HARDIHOOD.  ......................MAYFLOWER   60    8
  FACES BLANK AS THE DAY I WAS BORN,  ..........THE DISQUIETING MUSES    76   51
  UNLUCKY THE HERO BORN  ...........................THE TIMES ARE TIDY  107    1
  NOBODY DIES OR IS BORN WITHOUT THEIR KNOWING IT.  ...THE NET-MENDERS  121   13
  SHE'S PINK, SHE'S A BORN MIDWIFE --  .......................THE TOUR  238   45
  AND THOUSANDS WERE BORN AND DROPPED DEAD,  .......DIALOBUE EN ROUTE   309   39
BORNE (3)
  A TREASON NOT TO BE BORNE. LET IDIOTS  .....................SPINSTER   50   22
  BORNE, FOR A USE BEYOND MY  ...........MUSSEL HUNTER AT ROCK HARBOR    96   37
  THE ANGELS OF MORPHIA HAVE BORNE HIM UP.  ...THE SURGEON AT 2 A.M.   171   44
BORNING (1)
  WITH THEIR GIFTS TO A DIFFICULT BORNING.  ..........THE MANOR GARDEN  125   20
BORROW (1)
  I BORROW THE STILTS OF AN OLD TRAGEDY.  ......ELECTRA ON AZALEA PATH  117   33
BORROWED (3)
  WHO BORROWED FEATHERS FOR YOUR FEET, NOT LEAD,  .............PERSEUS   83   12
  THEY LEFT ME A BORROWED MAID NAMED ELLEN, "FOR PROTECTION",  ..BABY.  174   17
  IF A BUSH BORROWED TONGUES AND SPOKE TO YOU. YOU'D KNEEL*DIALOGUE O.  280  163
BORROWERS (1)
  BOTH OF YOU ARE GREAT LIGHT BORROWERS.  ...................THE RIVAL  166    4
BOSSED (1)
  BOSSED, BRAZEN, AN ANTIQUE SHIELD,  ..............A BIRTHDAY PRESENT  207   30
BOSSING (1)
  BOSSING THE ETHEREAL BLANKS OF THEIR FACE-OVALS.  ............MAGI    148    3
BOSTON (4)
  ON BOSTON COMMON A RED STAR  ........................A WINTER'S TALE   86    1
  ON GRASS THAT ONCE FED BOSTON COWS.  ................A WINTER'S TALE   87   23
  THE SUN SINKS UNDER BOSTON, BLOODY RED.  .........POINT SHIRLEY      111   40
  THE POLITE SKIES OVER BOSTON COULDN'T POSSIBLY ACCOMMODATE.  ...
                                     ... TWO CAMPERS IN CLOUD COUNTRY  145   11
BOTANICAL (1)
  SEEM A BOTANICAL DRAWING --  .........................WINTER TREES   257    3
BOTCHED (1)
  THE RITUAL DEATH EACH TIME BOTCHED AMONG DROPPED CAPES,
                                ILL-JUDGED STABS, ....THE GORING        47    3
BOTH (7)
  MEEK AND PROUD BOTH FALL; STARK VIOLENCE  .........CHANNEL CROSSING    27   30
  AGAINST BOTH BAR AND TOWER THE BLACK SEA RUNS.  .......POINT SHIRLEY  111   48
  BOTH OF THEM DEAF TO THE FIDDLE IN THE HANDS  ...........TWO VIEWS.  114   18
```

	TITLE	PAGE	LINE
BOTH (CONT.)

IT WAS MY LOVE THAT DID US BOTH TO DEATH.   ...ELECTRA ON AZALEA PATH   117   46
BOTH OF YOU ARE GREAT LIGHT BORROWERS.   ....THE RIVAL   166   4
THEY BOTH WATCHED THE BAROMETER SINK   ....DIALOGUE EN ROUTE   309   37
BOTH SERAPH SONG AND VIOLINS ARE DUMB;   ....DOOM OF EXILES   318   7

BOTHER (2)

ALMOST TOO SMALL FOR THE MISTS TO BOTHER WITH.   ....FINISTERRE   169   12
HE COUNTED THE GUNS OF GOD A BOTHER, ...LAMENT   315   13

BOTHERS (2)

ANOTHER KIND OF REDNESS BOTHERS ME: ...ELECTRA ON AZALEA PATH   117   29
THOUGH NOBODY IN THERE LOOKS UP OR BOTHERS TO ANSWER.   ....A LIFE   150   8

BOTTLE (6)

WITH NO ATTACHMENTS, LIKE A FOETUS IN A BOTTLE, ...A LIFE   150   26
TO RATTLE IN A BOTTLE AND TAKE HOME, ...THE SURGEON AT 2 A.M.   171   35
AN EXPLODED BOTTLE OF STOUT, ...A SECRET   220   42
BOTTLE IN WHICH I LIVE, ...MEDUSA   225   35
CLUTCHING MY BOTTLE   ....CUT   235   15
COMES A FLOCK OF BOTTLE BATTLESHIPS   ....EPITAPH IN THREE PARTS   337   2

BOTTLES (3)

THE EMPTY BOTTLES ON THE WINDOWSILL   ....RESOLVE   52   11
AND THE BOTTLES OF EMPTY GLITTERS ---   ....WINTERING   218   9
IN SQUARE HERMETIC BOTTLES, WHILE THE SUN   ......THE TRIAL OF MAN   312   3

BOTTOM (6)

OF SWAYS AND COILINGS, FROM THE SNAKE-ROOTED BOTTOM   ...SNAKECHARMER   79   11
TO PEOPLE WHO LIVE IN THE BOTTOM OF VALLEYS   ....ABOVE THE OXBOW   88   15
WITH NO BOTTOM, OR ANYTHING ON THE OTHER SIDE OF IT,   ...FINISTERRE   169   4
I KNOW THE BOTTOM, SHE SAYS. I KNOW IT WITH MY GREAT TAP ROOT: ELM   192   1
FROM THE BOTTOM OF THE POOL, FIXED STARS   ....WORDS   270   19
BOTTOM OF YOUR BRAIN. BY SOME MISHAP,   ..DIALOGUE OVER A OUIJA BOARD   282   241

BOTTOMLESS (1)

THE THICK GERMANS SLUMBERING IN THEIR BOTTOMLESS STOLZ.   ....MUNICH.   263   23

BOUDOIR (1)

TESSELLATED BOUDOIR. HEARING FLUTES, YOU   ....YADWIGHA.   86   27

BOUDOIRS (1)

IN THESE LITTLE BOUDOIRS STREAKED WITH ORANGE AND RED   BEEKEEPER'S.   118   10

BOUGH (4)

LEAF, BECOME EYELID; SNAKE-BODIES, BOUGH, BREAST   ......SNAKECHARMER   79   14
TILL IRONY'S BOUGH BREAK.   ....VIRGIN IN A TREE   82   45
PLENITUDE: APPLES GOLD ON THE BOUGH, ...IN MIDAS' COUNTRY   99   12
NOW PROWL ON THE BOUGH;   ....TEMPER OF TIME   336   6

BOUGHS (4)

BOUGHS WHERE THOSE OWLS SAT.   ....FAUN   35   10
ON HAWTHORN BOUGHS, WITH GOODWILL TO ENDURE   ....MAYFLOWER   60   13
LAIN SPLAYED TOO LONG IN THE TORTUOUS BOUGHS: OVERRIPE   .....VIRGIN.   82   37
TO PEOPLE THE BOUGHS WITH TALKING BIRDS. I'D PLANT   ....DIALOGUE O.   280   169

BOULDERS (1)

KNELT IN THE MEADOW MUTE AS BOULDERS;   ....HARDCASTLE CRAGS   63   33

BOUND (3)

WITH BLACK ALACRITY BOUND ROUND HIS PRISONER.   ....SPIDER   49   28
TRADING THEIR POISONS, THE NORTH AND SOUTH BOUND CARS*PRIVATE GROUND   130   16
NOW BOUND AROUND HER WRIST TILL SHE REDEEM   ....THE PRINCESS.   333   24

BOUNDS (1)

IN EIGHT GREAT BOUNDS, A GREAT SCAPEGOAT.   ....STINGS   215   41

BOURBON (1)

AND A COOK AND A MAID, AND KNEW ABOUT THE KEY TO THE BOURBON. *BABY.   175   21

BOW (9)

O BENT BOW OF THORNS   ....RESOLVE   52   16
BOW, AND RECOVER THEIR LOOK   ....MAGNOLIA SHOALS   122   7
BOW DOWN, A LOCAL CONSTELLATION, ...LEAVING EARLY   145   11
AT THEIR FEET, THE SEA WAVES BOW IN SINGLE FILE, ...A LIFE   150   11
I WEAR WHITE CUFFS, I BOW.   ....AN APPEARANCE   189   9
THEY BOW AND STAND: THEY SUFFER SUCH ATTACKS!   ...AMONG THE NARCISSI   190   9
WHILE TULIPS BOW LIKE A COLLEGE OF CARDINALS   ....APRIL AUBADE   312   7
OUR CREDITOR ADVANCES WITH A BOW   ....THE DISPOSSESSED   318   10
SHE TELLS THE GREENHORN MINER TO BOW DOWN   ....THE PRINCESS.   335   61

BOWEL (1)

IN THE BOWEL OF THE ROOT. POEM.2.DARK.   133   27

BOWEL-PULSE (1)

IT IS THE BOWEL-PULSE, LOVER OF DIGESTIBLES.   ....WORDS HEARD.   202   4

BOWELS (1)

OF IMPERFECTIONS HIS BOWELS WERE PART OF --   ...SUICIDE OFF EGG ROCK   115   4

BOWEL'S (1)

FIDO LITTLESOUL, THE BOWEL'S FAMILIAR. POEM.4.BEAST.   134   13

BOWER (1)

TO OUR BOWER AT THE LILY ROOT. POEM.5.F.   134   2

BOWING (2)

BOWING AND TRUCKLING LIKE AN OLD-SCHOOL ORIENTAL.   ....WHITSUN   154   16
THE NARCISSI, TOO, ARE BOWING TO SOME BIG THING: *AMONG THE NARCISSI   190   4

BOWL (7)

IN ALICANTE THEY BOWL THE BARRELS   ....ALICANTE LULLABY   43   1
BOWL ONE HOMEWARD TO TASTE   ....FIESTA MELONS   46   9
TEN FINGERS SHAPE A BOWL FOR SHADOWS. POEM.7.S.   137   43
ITS BOWL OF RED BLOOMS OUT OF SHEER LOVE OF ME.   ....TULIPS   162   61
A RED LOTUS OPENS IN ITS BOWL OF BLOOD;   ....THREE WOMEN   181   167
IN THE BOWL THE HARE IS ABORTED, ...TOTEM   264   11

BOWL (CONT.)
    GROWS BRITTLE AS A TILTED CHINA BOWL; ....PROLOGUE TO SPRING   322   5
BOWLERS (1)
    DULLED TO A HALT UNDER BOWLERS. ....POPPIES IN OCTOBER   240   9
BOWLING (1)
    SQUAT, BOWLING BLACK BALLS AT HER. ....AERIALIST   331   30
BOWLS (1)
    IRON ENTRAILS, ENAMEL BOWLS, ...THE BURNT-OUT SPA   138   16
BOWS (1)
    PERCY BOWS, IN HIS BLUE PEAJACKET, AMONG THE NARCISSI. ...NARCISSI.   190   2
BOX (14)
    FIVE WORMS IN A BOX ....WORDS FOR A NURSERY   74   49
    CLAMBERING ROUND ITS GLASS BOX LIKE AN EIGHT-FINGERED HAND.   ZOO K.   155   31
    I DO NOT WANT A PLAIN BOX, I WANT A SARCOPHAGUS ....LAST WORDS   172   1
    WHOSE IS THAT LONG WHITE BOX IN THE GROVE, WHAT HAVE THEY
        ACCOMPLISHED, ...THE BEE MEETING   212   55
    THE ARRIVAL OF THE BEE BOX ....THE ARRIVAL OF THE BEE BOX   212   T
    I ORDERED THIS, THIS CLEAN WOOD BOX .....THE ARRIVAL OF THE BEE BOX   212   1
    THE BOX IS LOCKED, IT IS DANGEROUS. .....THE ARRIVAL OF THE BEE BOX   213   6
    I HAVE SIMPLY ORDERED A BOX OF MANIACS.   THE ARRIVAL OF THE BEE BOX   213   23
    THE BOX IS ONLY TEMPORARY. ....THE ARRIVAL OF THE BEE BOX   213   36
    THAT'S MY FROST BOX, NO CAT, ...THE TOUR 237   15
    GOES THE GRASS-EMBROIDERED BOX. ....DANSE MACABRE   320   3
    DOZING AROUND THEIR SILVERED SENTRY BOX. ....THE PRINCESS.   334   30
    MY ROOM IS A TWITTERING GRAY BOX WITH A WALL *EPITAPH IN THREE PARTS   337   26
    ENORMOUS BOX OF GRAY WHERE GOD HAS GONE .....EPITAPH IN THREE PARTS   338   30
BOXCARS (1)
    QUIETLY THROUGH THE STRAW OF THE BOXCARS. ....GETTING THERE   248   11
BOXED-IN (1)
    FROM BEDS BOXED-IN LIKE COFFINS ....OLD LADIES' HOME   120   17
BOXES (1)
    NOW EMPTY BOXES OF THE HOODWINKED DEAD*SONG FOR A REVOLUTIONARY LOVE   323   17
BOX-LINED (1)
    ALONG BOX-LINED WALKS IN THE FLORID SUN ....THE BULL OF BENDYLAW   108   10
BOY (13)
    AND A CABIN BOY WHO COULD DECORATE CAKES IN SIX-COLORED
        FROSTING. ....THE BABYSITTERS   174   12
    WHO IS HE, THIS BLUE, FURIOUS BOY, ...THREE WOMEN 181 162
    MY BOY, IT'S YOUR LAST RESORT. ....THE APPLICANT 222   39
    YOU COULD EAT HIM. HE'S A BOY. ....LESBOS   228   25
    BOY, PRONE TO COMPOSE QUEER POETRY .....DIALOGUE OVER A OUIJA BOARD   280 142
    BOY, HE NEEDS A BEATING NOW AND THEN ...DIALOGUE OVER A OUIJA BOARD   281 183
    LIKE A GOOD BOY. BE CAREFUL. I'M NOT SURE THAT HE ......DIALOGUE O.   282 207
    CERTAINTY OF THE BRONZE BOY ....GOLD MOUTHS CRY   302   2
    THE BRONZE BOY STANDS KNEEDEEP IN CENTURIES, ...GOLD MOUTHS CRY   302   10
    THIS MINER'S BOY FROM GOBLIN BODYGUARD.*THE PRINCESS AND THE GOBLINS   333   25
    FROM THE PRAGMATIC BOY CONFINED WITHIN,*THE PRINCESS AND THE GOBLINS   334   45
    THE PRINCESS COAXES THE INCREDULOUS BOY*THE PRINCESS AND THE GOBLINS   334   51
    LAUGHING ALOUD, THE DAZZLED BOY DEMANDS*THE PRINCESS AND THE GOBLINS   335   64
BOYCOTT (1)
    TO BOYCOTT COLOR AND FORBID ANY FLOWER ..SOLILOQUY OF THE SOLIPSIST   38   26
BOYS (3)
    FREE FROM ALL MOLESTING. ROUGH BOYS, ...LADY AND T.   69   9
    THE WHITE-SMOCKED BOYS STARTED WORKING. *TWO VIEWS OF A CADAVER ROOM   114   5
    PREDICTING THREE BOYS AN HOUR HENCE WILL PLAY ....DIALOGUE O.   279 124
BRACE (2)
    RODE OUT AGAINST THE FIFTH BULL TO BRACE HIS PIKE AND
        SLOWLY BEAR ....THE GORING   47   6
    A BRACE OR A HOOK, ...THE APPLICANT 221   4
BRACED (2)
    OF LOVE: CLAWS BRACED, AT BAY, MY CURRENCY NOT HERS.   INCOMMUNICADO   100   7
    SAFE ON THE MATTRESS, HANDS BRACED, AS FOR A FALL. .....THREE WOMEN   187 367
BRACKEN (1)
    TO SQUANDER OWL-HOURS ON BRACKEN BEDDING, ...VANITY FAIR   33   19
BRACING (1)
    BRACING THEIR KNEES. ON UNSEEN TOWLINES ....IN MIDAS' COUNTRY   99   17
BRAG (2)
    FOR THAT BRAG, WE BARNACLE THESE IRON THIGHS." ....SNOWMAN O.   59   43
    OR BRAG AHEAD OF TIME HOW I'D AVENGE MYSELF. ....IN PLASTER   160   47
BRAGS (1)
    "WITH MY FANTASY ALONE," BRAGS THE IMPORTUNATE HEAD, ...CONJURING.   66   9
BRAID (2)
    FACED IN HIS RICH YELLOWS, TASSELS, POMPONS, BRAID, THE PICADOR ...
        ...   THE GORING   47   5
    TO THE BEHEADED HEAD OF A SULLEN DOLL, ONE BRAID, ...PERSEUS   83   37
BRAIDS (1)
    WITH BLOND BRAIDS. ....BITTER STRAWBERRIES   299   23
BRAIN (5)
    WHILE THIS BEGGARED BRAIN *ON THE DIFFICULTY OF CONJURING UP A DRYAD   66   37
    AND THE OUTRAGE OF A SKY, THE LINED BRAIN OF IT. ....COURAGE.   209   4
    SO THE DISKS OF THE BRAIN REVOLVE, LIKE THE MUZZLES OF CANNON. ...
        ...   THE COURAGE OF SHUTTING-UP   210   16
    BOTTOM OF YOUR BRAIN. BY SOME MISHAP, ..DIALOGUE OVER A OUIJA BOARD   282 241
    THEY ARE ASSAILING YOUR BRAIN LIKE NUMERALS, ...DIALOGUE O.   293   4

                                         TITLE   PAGE   LINE
BRAINCHAMBER (1)
   BUZZED AND ASSAILED THE VAULTED BRAINCHAMBER. SUICIDE OFF EGG ROCK   115   18
BRAINS (1)
   THE TERRIBLE BRAINS ....GETTING THERE   248   5
BRAINWASHED (1)
   ARE RIDING TO WORK IN ROWS, AS IF RECENTLY BRAINWASHED. ..INSOMNIAC   163   35
BRAKES (1)
   A SQUEAL OF BRAKES. ....STOPPED DEAD   230   1
BRAMBLE (1)
   TO SPRIGGED HEDGE OF BRAMBLE, ...ODE FOR TED   29   5
BRAMBLED (1)
   AND OUTWIT THEIR BRAMBLED PLAN; ......MISS DRAKE PROCEEDS TO SUPPER   41   17
BRANCH (2)
   WHILE ON SPOTTED BRANCH ....PROSPECT   28   5
   AND, BRIGHT AS BLOOD-DROPS, PROVED NO BRAVE BRANCH DIES ..MAYFLOWER   60   3
BRANCHES (3)
   HUNG CAUGHT IN DARK-WEBBED BRANCHES LIKE A FABULOUS HERON. ...
                             ... DIALOGUE BETWEEN GHOST AND PRIEST   38   6
   COUPLED BY BRANCHES INTERTWINED ....CRYSTAL GAZER   55   14
   SO MURDEROUS IN ITS STRANGLE OF BRANCHES? --- ....ELM   193   39
BRANCHING (1)
   FIVE-ANTLERED, BRANCHING ....WORDS FOR A NURSERY   74   21
BRAND (1)
   TO PATCH WITH BRAND OF LOVE THIS RANK GRIMACE ....STRUMPET SONG   34   16
BRANDS (1)
   WHEN BURNS AND BRANDS THAT YELLOW GAZE? ....PURSUIT   23   36
BRANDY (2)
   BRANDY FINGER ....A SECRET   219   18
   BUT I'VE BROUGHT BRANDY AND BUILT THE FIRE UP ....DIALOGUE O.   277   16
BRASH (1)
   HERE ON THE LAST FRONTIER OF THE BIG, BRASH SPIRIT ....TWO CAMP.   145   12
BRASILIA (1)
   BRASILIA ....BRASILIA   258   T
BRASS (4)
   SUN'S BRASS, THE MOON'S STEELY PATINAS, ...DEPARTURE   51   10
   WHILE THE BRASS MAN ....BY CANDLELIGHT   237   26
   AT HIS HEELS A PILE OF FIVE BRASS CANNONBALLS, ...BY CANDLELIGHT   237   33
   FIVE BALLS! FIVE BRIGHT BRASS BALLS! ....BY CANDLELIGHT   237   35
BRASSILY (1)
   THEY BRASSILY PICKED, SLOWED BY NO CHAGRIN, ...RHODODENDRON.   104   24
BRASSY (1)
   HE IS YOURS, THE LITTLE BRASSY ATLAS -- ....BY CANDLELIGHT   237   31
BRAT (1)
   PAN AS IF HE WERE OUR FIRST-BREACHED BRAT ....DIALOGUE O.   280 138
BRAVE (6)
   BRAVE ACTS PLAYED OUT IN PEACE, IN WAR; ALL DANGERS*CHANNEL CROSSING   27   39
   BRAVE LOVE, DREAM ....FIRESONG   30   19
   AND, BRIGHT AS BLOOD-DROPS, PROVED NO BRAVE BRANCH DIES ..MAYFLOWER   60   3
   THE THROATS OF OUR WRISTS BRAVE LILIES. ....STINGS   214   4
   LOVED ME AND A BRAVE EMBRACE ....THE DREAM   311   22
   BITES KEEN INTO EACH BRAVE LIMB ....AERIALIST   331   24
BRAVED (1)
   AND THEIR FUTURE LOT, SHE BRAVED ....CRYSTAL GAZER   55   34
BRAWN (1)
   SQUANDERS A SUMMER AND THE BRAWN OF HIS HEROES*A LESSON IN VENGEANCE   80   17
BRAY (1)
   TAIL ON EACH TOY DONKEY THAT WILL BRAY   DIALOGUE OVER A OUIJA BOARD   283 250
BRAZEN (6)
   TABLE-TOP, CUPBOARD SHELF, CATS LOUNGED BRAZEN, ...ELLA MASON A.   54   22
   NEITHER BRAZEN SWAN NOR BURNING STAR, ...ON THE DECLINE OF ORACLES   78   18
   BOSSED, BRAZEN, AN ANTIQUE SHIELD, ...A BIRTHDAY PRESENT   207   30
   THE BRAZEN JACKANAPES ....TRIO OF LOVE SONGS   314   23
   BRAZEN ACTORS MOCK AT HIM, ...LOVE IS A PARALLAX   330   45
   SUDDENLY A BRAZEN SONG IS HEARD ....THE PRINCESS AND THE GOBLINS   334   44
BREAD (4)
   BUYING WINE, BREAD, ...STREET SONG   36   13
   WILL THERE BE FIRE, WILL THERE BE BREAD? ....GETTING THERE   248   20
   COMPARED TO YOU, I AM CORRUPTIBLE AS A LOAF OF BREAD.   THE RIVAL/DR   291   1
   OF DAY-OLD BREAD AND EGG-STAINED PLATES; PERHAPS ....METAMORPHOSES.   307   29
BREAK (15)
   LIKE A DAUNTED WITCH, QUITTING CASTLE WHEN REAL DAYS BREAK. ...
                             ... CONVERSATION AMONG THE RUINS   21   8
   WAITING FOR SOME ACCIDENTAL BREAK ....TALE OF A TUB   25   21
   WILL BREAK BEFORE IT HELP; ....RECANTATION   41   7
   NO MATTER HOW FIERCELY LIT; STAUNCH CONTRACTS BREAK   EPITAPH FOR F.   46   32
   AS NO MERE INSURGENT MAN COULD HOPE TO BREAK ....SPINSTER   50   28
   OF STONES AND HILLS OF STONES COULD BREAK ....HARDCASTLE CRAGS   63   43
   TO BREAK THROUGH THAT PATCHWORK ....ON THE PLETHORA OF DRYADS   67   20
   LIKE BUBBLES ABOUT TO BREAK, YOU FED ....THE DISQUIETING MUSES   75   19
   SAW EVIL BREAK OUT OF THE NORTH. ....ON THE DECLINE OF ORACLES   78   32
   TILL IRONY'S BOUGH BREAK. ....VIRGIN IN A TREE   82   45
   SNOWCAKES BREAK AND WELTER. THIS YEAR ....POINT SHIRLEY   110   4
   I AM DUMB AND BROWN. I AM A SEED ABOUT TO BREAK. ....THREE WOMEN   179   99
   NOW I BREAK UP IN PIECES THAT FLY ABOUT LIKE CLUBS. ....ELM   192   19
   ALL RIGHT, LET'S SAY YOU COULD TAKE A SKULL AND BREAK IT*SONNET:EVA.   304   1

                                                    TITLE   PAGE LINE
BREAK (CONT.)
    LET MY TRANSIENT EYE BREAK A TEAR ....TOUCH-AND-GO   336   19
BREAKABLE (1)
    AND BREAKABLE HUMMINGBIRDS, ...MISS DRAKE PROCEEDS TO SUPPER   41   8
BREAKFAST (2)
    MY NIGHT SWEATS GREASE HIS BREAKFAST PLATE. ....THE JAILER 226   1
    THE ONLY FARE ON MY BARE BREAKFAST PLATE.   QUEEN MARY'S ROSE GARDEN 290   6
BREAKING (4)
    BREAKING ON LEGENDARY BEACHES; IN FAITH ....TALE OF A TUB   25   45
    I AM BREAKING APART LIKE THE WORLD. THERE IS THIS BLACKNESS, *THREE. 180 142
    (BREAKING GLASS) ....DIALOGUE OVER A OUIJA BOARD   284   SD
    BREAKING THROUGH GRAVITY'S GARRISON, ...DIALOGUE EN ROUTE 309   31
BREAKS (3)
    BREAKS THE SOIL. THIS IS AZALEA PATH. ....ELECTRA ON AZALEA PATH 117   21
    WHEN WILL IT BE, THE SECOND WHEN TIME BREAKS ....THREE WOMEN 179 104
    UNDERSTANDING BREAKS THROUGH THE SKULL'S SHELL ......METAMORPHOSES. 307   16
BREAKWATER (1)
    BEYOND THE BREAKWATER, SPOTTY WITH BARNACLES? ....BERCK-PLAGE 197   41
BREAKWATERS (1)
    BREAKWATERS TAKE THE SHOVE ....MAN IN BLACK 119   2
BREAST (2)
    LEAF, BECOME EYELID; SNAKE-BODIES, BOUGH, BREAST ......SNAKECHARMER   79   14
    THE STARCHED, INACCESSIBLE BREAST. ....PARALYTIC 266   16
BREASTPLATES (1)
    BREASTPLATES OF CHEESECLOTH KNOTTED UNDER THE ARMPITS. ....BEE. 211   14
BREASTS (6)
    BREASTS AND HIPS A CONFECTIONER'S SUGAR ....BERCK-PLAGE 197   25
    A CREST OF BREASTS, EYELIDS AND LIPS ....BERCK-PLABE 200 116
    IT IS SHIMMERING, HAS IT BREASTS, HAS IT EDGES?   A BIRTHDAY PRESENT 206   2
    THE BREASTS NEXT. ....THE DETECTIVE 209   31
    RUBBER BREASTS OR A RUBBER CROTCH, ...THE APPLICANT 221   5
    MILL A LITTER OF BREASTS LIKE JELLYFISH. ....GIGOLO 267   13
BREATH (28)
    AS CAN SPARE BREATH ....STRUMPET SONG   34   15
    SHE EDGES WITH WARY BREATH, ...MISS DRAKE PROCEEDS TO SUPPER   41   21
    THAT EVERY BREATH, THUS TEEMING, SET THE LAND ..WREATH FOR A BRIDAL   45   21
    THE DAY YOUR SLACK SAIL DRANK MY SISTER'S BREATH ....ELECTRA ON. 117   30
    THE STONY ACTORS POISE AND PAUSE FOR BREATH. *ELECTRA ON AZALEA PATH 117   37
    ONE BREATH MIGHT SHIVER TO BITS, ...OLD LADIES' HOME 120   3
    SHORTENS WITH EACH BREATH DRAWN. ....OLD LADIES' HOME 120   21
    EASY AND OFTEN AS EACH BREATH. ....BLUE MOLES 127   36
    ALL MORNING, WITH SMOKING BREATH, THE HANDYMAN ......PRIVATE GROUND 130   7
    PRAYS UNDER HER BREATH THAT SHE MAY SAVE ....ON DECK   143   23
    THE WIND STOPS MY BREATH LIKE A BANDAGE. ....PARLIAMENT HILL FIELDS 152   20
    FOR MY CUBE OF SUGAR: ITS BOG BREATH ....ZOO KEEPER'S WIFE 155   36
    COMING AND GOING, BREATH BY BREATH, WITHOUT ANY FUSS. ....TULIPS 161   51
    COMING AND GOING, BREATH BY BREATH, WITHOUT ANY FUSS. ....TULIPS 161   51
    AND SOFT AS A MOTH, HIS BREATH. ....THREE WOMEN 181 173
    THAT YOU SUCK BREATH LIKE MILEAGE? ....THE OTHER   202   24
    WHITE AS BABIES' BEDDING AND GLITTERING WITH DEAD BREATH. O
        IVORY! ....A BIRTHDAY PRESENT 206   18
    TREMULOUS BREATH AT THE END OF MY LINE, ...MEDUSA   225   17
    SQUEEZING THE BREATH FROM THE BLOOD CELLS ....MEDUSA   225   28
    OF THE FUCHSIA. I COULD DRAW NO BREATH, ...MEDUSA   225   29
    I HOLD MY BREATH UNTIL YOU CREAK TO LIFE, ...BY CANDLELIGHT 236   19
    THE SOUR BREATH ....LADY LAZARUS   244   14
    OF YOUR SMALL BREATH, THE DRENCHED GRASS ....THE NIGHT DANCES 250   9
    THE TRAIN LEAVES A LINE OF BREATH. ....SHEEP IN FOG 262   4
    COLD AS SNOW BREATH, IT TAMPS THE WOMB ....THE MUNICH MANNEQUINS 262   2
    FAT ALWAYS, AND OUT OF BREATH, ...FAMILY REUNION 300   13
    SPREAD GAY CONTAGION WITH EACH CLEVER BREATH. ....DIRGE FOR A JOKER 303   12
    TO PAY THE PIPER WITH EACH BREATH, YET LOVE .....LOVE IS A PARALLAX 331   76
BREATHABLE (1)
    THE CLEAR, GREEN, QUITE BREATHABLE ATMOSPHERE, ...LYONNESSE 234   16
BREATHE (13)
    I WOULD BREATHE WATER. ....FULL FATHOM FIVE   93   45
    A MACHINE TO BREATHE AND BEAT FOREVER. ....SUICIDE OFF EGG ROCK 115   16
    A WELL OF SCENTS ALMOST TOO DENSE TO BREATHE IN. ......BEEKEEPER'S. 118   4
    THE SMALL GREEN NOSTRILS BREATHE, ...THE SLEEPERS 123   17
    EVEN THROUGH THE GIFT PAPER I COULD HEAR THEM BREATHE ....TULIPS 161   37
    I FLAKE UP PAPERS THAT BREATHE LIKE PEOPLE, ...BURNING THE LETTERS 204   37
    SWEETLY, SWEETLY I BREATHE IN, ...A BIRTHDAY PRESENT 207   41
    THIS IS THE ROOM I COULD NEVER BREATHE IN. ....WINTERING 218   12
    BARELY DARING TO BREATHE OR ACHOO. ....DADDY   222   5
    THIS HALOEY RADIANCE THAT SEEMS TO BREATHE ....BY CANDLELIGHT 236   11
    I BREATHE, AND THE MOUTH ....PURDAH   243   24
    THE CHIMNEYS OF THE CITY BREATHE, THE WINDOW SWEATS, ...MYSTIC 269   28
    MAY TWO REAL PEOPLE BREATHE IN A REAL ROOM. ....DIALOGUE O. 286 364
BREATHES (2)
    IT BREATHES FROM MY SHEETS, THE COLD DEAD CENTER *A BIRTHDAY PRESENT 207   50
    HOW IT BREATHES IN THE BUREAU DRAWER! ....A SECRET 220   27
BREATHING (6)
    OF DRAGONS BREATHING WITHOUT THE FRAME OF FABLES, ...LESSON.   80   3
    SMALL NOSTRILS ARE BREATHING. POEM.2.DARK.   133   23
    BREATHING WAS EASY IN HIS AIRY HOLDING. POEM.4.BEAST. 134   3

TITLE   PAGE LINE

BREATHING (CONT.)
    HE IS QUITE BLUE; THE TERRIBLE WIND TRIES HIS BREATHING.   NARCISSI.   190   11
    STEAMING AND BREATHING, ITS TEETH ....GETTING THERE   248   39
    BREATHING THE GOD'S WORD, OR THE DEVIL'S WORD, ...DIALOGUE O.   286 350
BREATHLESS (1)
    GOLD LEAVES METAL AND BREATHLESS. ....LETTER IN NOVEMBER   253   30
BREATHS (1)
    A FEW MORE BREATHS, AND IT WILL REFLECT NOTHING AT ALL.   LAST WORDS   172   12
BRED (1)
    BRED AN AMPLE BATCH OF OMENS; BUT NOW ....TALE OF A TUB   25   18
BREED (2)
    GOD KNOWS HOW OUR NEIGHBOR MANAGED TO BREED ....SOW   60   1
    BREED INNUMERABLE BILLS, BONA FIDE: ....DIALOGUE EN ROUTE   308   17
BREEZE (2)
    STARES THROUGH US; HIS HOOVES CHEW THE BREEZE. ....WHITSUN   154   8
    SCRIM OF A SEA BREEZE, THE WOMEN ....HEAVY WOMEN   158   4
BREWING (1)
    INSTEAD OF BREWING US SUCH A BALDERDASH *DIALOGUE OVER A OUIJA BOARD   279   97
BRIAR (1)
    HIS KISSES PARCH, EACH PAW'S A BRIAR, ...PURSUIT   22   19
BRIARS (1)
    BLED WHITE WITH BRIARS BY A BUSY CONSCIENCE ....DIALOGUE O.   281 197
BRIBERY (1)
    NOW IS THE TIME FOR BRIBERY. ....GETTING THERE   248   12
BRIBES (1)
    THEIR BRIBES --- ....THE NIGHT DANCES   251   14
BRIC-A-BRAC (2)
    RAVENING THROUGH THE PERSISTENT BRIC-A-BRAC ....CONJURING.   65   1
    WITH ITS PRIM BRIC-A-BRAC, WITHOUT A MOON ....YADWIGHA.   85   11
BRICK (3)
    OF IDENTICAL GRAY BRICK HOUSES, ...LANDOWNERS   53   4
    FROM WATER-TOWER HILL TO THE BRICK PRISON ....POINT SHIRLEY   110   1
    FLUNG BRICK PERFECTED HIS LAUGH. ....MEDALLION   125   27
BRICKDUST-COMPLECTED (1)
    FIT NOWHERE: BRICKDUST-COMPLECTED, EYE UNDER A DENSE LID, ...
                    ... THE LADY AND THE EARTHENWARE HEAD   69   2
BRICKRED (1)
    SHADING THE BRICKRED PORCH TILES. ....DEPARTURE   51   3
BRIDAL (2)
    WREATH FOR A BRIDAL ....WREATH FOR A BRIDAL   44   T
    THAT VAIN JADES SULK SINGLE DOWN BRIDAL NIGHTS, ...ELLA MASON A.   54   41
BRIDE (8)
    FREELY BECOME SUN'S BRIDE, THE LATTER ....TWO SISTERS OF PERSEPHONE   32   21
    WHILE SHE, ENVIOUS BRIDE, ...THE SHRIKE   42   7
    HIS BRIDE ECHOES HIS WORD. AT THAT, ...CRYSTAL GAZER   55   21
    HAIRTUSK'S BRIDE. POEM.4.BEAST.   134   26
    AND THE BRIDE FLOWERS EXPEND A FRESHNESS, ...BERCK-PLAGE   200 106
    AND THE SOUL IS A BRIDE ....BERCK-PLAGE   200 107
    A CURTAIN OF WAX DIVIDING THEM FROM THE BRIDE FLIGHT, ...BEE.   212   47
    HIS OWN PALE BRIDE UPON A FLAMING TRAY: ....TERMINAL   328   12
BRIDEGROOM (2)
    FATHER, BRIDEGROOM, IN THIS EASTER EGG ....THE BEEKEEPER'S DAUGHTER   118   19
    AT THIS FACET THE BRIDEGROOM ARRIVES ....PURDAH   242   19
BRIDE-LACE (1)
    THEY TALK OF BRIDE-LACE, OF LOVERS SPUNKY AS GAMECOCKS. ......NET-.   121   14
BRIDES (1)
    HOUSED IN EARTH, THOSE MILLION BRIDES SHRIEK OUT. ......VANITY FAIR   33   33
BRIDGE (2)
    BALUSTRADE OF A SAG-BACKED BRIDGE. ....THE BURNT-OUT SPA   138   23
    WHO ARE THESE PEOPLE AT THE BRIDGE TO MEET ME? THEY ARE THE
            VILLAGERS --- ....THE BEE MEETING   211   1
BRIDGES (2)
    NEATLY, NICELY, BY DISBELIEF OR BRIDGES, ...A LESSON IN VENGEANCE   80   23
    OF WAREHOUSES, DERRICKS, SMOKESTACKS AND BRIDGES .....A WINTER SHIP   113   17
BRIEF (3)
    OUR LUGGAGE, AS DOCKS HALT OUR BRIEF EPIC; NO DEBT *CHANNEL CROSSING   27   41
    A BRIEF RESPITE FROM FEAR ....BLACK ROOK IN RAINY WEATHER   57   31
    THE CULTIVATED ACT, A FIERCE BRIEF FUSION ....LOVE IS A PARALLAX   330   58
BRIEFCASE (1)
    A BRIEFCASE OF TANGERINES. ....LITTLE FUGUE   188   46
BRIEFLY (1)
    THE SKY'S GREAT BELL GLASS AND BRIEFLY ENGRAVE ...IN MIDAS' COUNTRY   99   8
BRIGANDS (1)
    LURED BY BRIGANDS IN THE BLOOD, ...DANSE MACABRE   321   16
BRIGHT (39)
    BRIGHT THOSE CLAWS THAT MAR THE FLESH ....PURSUIT   23   31
    INCH BY BRIGHT INCH ....SOUTHERN SUNRISE   26   14
    RETCHING IN BRIGHT ORANGE BASINS; A REFUGEE ....CHANNEL CROSSING   26   10
    NONE OF THAT GREENHORN LOT MATCHED HER BRIGHT CROWN. ....QUEEN'S C.   29   20
    BRIGHT GRAIN SPRUNG SO RARELY ....ODE FOR TED   29   16
    SHREWD CATCH SILTING OUR EACH BRIGHT ACT BACK ....FIRESONG   30   13
    THE AIR WAS BRIGHT FOR LOOKING: ....SONG FOR A SUMMER'S DAY   31   6
    LIKE POLLEN ON BRIGHT AIR. LULLED ....TWO SISTERS OF PERSEPHONE   32   15
    BRIGHT AS BLOOD. ....TINKER JACK AND THE TIDY WIVES   34   9
    ADAZZLE WITH BRIGHT SHARDS ....MISS DRAKE PROCEEDS TO SUPPER   41   19

                              70

BRIGHT (CONT.)
    THIS DREAM BUDDED BRIGHT WITH LEAVES AROUND THE EDGES,*DREAM WITH C.   43   1
    BRIGHT GREEN AND THUMPABLE ....FIESTA MELONS   46   5
    AND, BRIGHT AS BLOOD-DROPS, PROVED NO BRAVE BRANCH DIES ..MAYFLOWER   60   3
    ON A GREEN BALLOON BRIGHT WITH A MILLION .....THE DISQUIETING MUSES   76   43
    UNTONGUED, ALL BEAUTY'S BRIGHT JUICE SOURS. ....VIRGIN IN A TREE   82   43
    TO A BERYL JUNGLE, AND DREAMED THAT BRIGHT MOON-LILIES ...YADWIGHA.   86   29
    BRIGHT WATERLIGHTS ARE ....DARK WOOD, DARK WATER   127   21
    PLANETS PULSE IN THE LAKE LIKE BRIGHT AMOEBAS; ....TWO CAMP.   145   23
    THEY BRING ME NUMBNESS IN THEIR BRIGHT NEEDLES, THEY BRING
        ME SLEEP. ....TULIPS 160   17
    OR ELSE THEY ARE PRESENT, AND THEIR DISGUISE SO BRIGHT ......STARS.   165   22
    HE IS TURNING TO ME LIKE A LITTLE, BLIND, BRIGHT PLANT   THREE WOMEN 183 235
    BRIGHT BIRDS IN THE SKY, CONSOLING, CONSOLING? ....THREE WOMEN 185 298
    THESE ARE THE CLEAR BRIGHT COLORS OF THE NURSERY, ...THREE WOMEN 185 317
    BRIGHT HAIR, SHOE-BLACK, OLD PLASTIC, ...THE OTHER   201   8
    AND YOUR ARYAN EYE, BRIGHT BLUE. ....DADDY   223   44
    FIVE BALLS! FIVE BRIGHT BRASS BALLS! ....BY CANDLELIGHT   237   35
    BRIGHT AS A NAZI LAMPSHADE, ...LADY LAZARUS   244   5
    STARS STUCK ALL OVER, BRIGHT STUPID CONFETTI. ....YEARS 255   8
    BRIGHT FISH HOOKS, THE SMILES OF WOMEN ....GIGOLO   267   10
    OR PICKING UP THE BRIGHT PIECES ....MYSTIC   269   18
    NINE MONTHS TOO SOON FOR COMFORT, BUT A BRIGHT ....DIALOGUE O. 280 141
    AND WE ARE GLAD IN THIS BRIGHT METAL SEASON. ....GOLD MOUTHS CRY 302   8
    OF BRIGHT TINFOIL ....AQUATIC NOCTURNE   305   5
    AND TOOK THE WOMAN'S BRIGHT SUBPOENA ....THE DREAM 311   26
    BRIGHT ANGELS BLACK OUT OVER LOGIC'S LAND ....SONNET TO SATAN   323   3
    SHE DRAWS APPLAUSE; BRIGHT HARNESS ....AERIALIST   331   23
    BRIGHT WINDOW-SQUARES UNTIL THE WOMEN SEEM .....MORNING IN THE HOS. 332   7
    ALONG BRIGHT ASTERISKS BY MILKY WAY. ..THE PRINCESS AND THE GOBLINS 333   12
    AND HIDDEN ALL THE BRIGHT ANGELIC MEN. ......EPITAPH IN THREE PARTS 338   31
BRIGHTEN (1)
    MY ANKLES BRIGHTEN. BRIGHTNESS ASCENDS MY THIGHS. POEM.6.W. 136   23
BRIGHTENS (2)
    THAT NEVER BRIGHTENS OR GOES DOWN. ....THE DISQUIETING MUSES   76   53
    THE SUN BRIGHTENS TARDILY ....FROG AUTUMN   99   6
BRIGHTNESS (3)
    LOW MOOS OF APPROVE; LET SUN SURPLICED IN BRIGHTNESS .....WREATH F.   44   4
    MY ANKLES BRIGHTEN. BRIGHTNESS ASCENDS MY THIGHS. POEM.6.W. 136   23
    SUCH A WASTE OF BRIGHTNESS I CAN'T UNDERSTAND. ....QUEEN MARY'S. 290   7
BRILLIANT (2)
    FROM MY WORLDLING LOOK ITS BRILLIANT VEIN *ON THE PLETHORA OF DRYADS   67   10
    AND THE SNOW, MARSHALING ITS BRILLIANT CUTLERY ....THE SWARM 216   9
BRIM (3)
    AND BRIM; THE CITY MELTS LIKE SUGAR. ....PARLIAMENT HILL FIELDS 152   12
    YOU: A PRIEST-BAKED PASTY STUFFED TO THE BRIM ....DIALOGUE O. 282 214
    AND BAIT THE DROWSING TROUT BY THE BROOK'S BRIM; ....GO GET. 313   18
BRIMFUL (2)
    THE GIRL BENT HOMEWARD, BRIMFUL OF GENTLE TALK ....SNOWMAN O.   59   50
    ALL SUMMER WE MOVED IN A VILLA BRIMFUL OF ECHOES, ...THE OTHER TWO   68   1
BRING (12)
    "COME LADY, BRING THAT POT ....TINKER JACK AND THE TIDY WIVES   34   1
    "COME LADY, BRING THAT FACE ....TINKER JACK AND THE TIDY WIVES   34   10
    WILL BRING CROP'S INCREASE, AND HARVEST FRUIT ....CRYSTAL GAZER   55   17
    LET HIM SEND POLICE AND HOUNDS TO BRING HER IN. ....SNOWMAN O.   58   19
    HE LIFTS AN ARM TO BRING HER CLOSE, BUT SHE ....THE OTHER TWO   68   18
    BRING HOME EACH STORIED HEAD. ....BATTLE-SCENE   84   28
    YOU BRING ME GOOD NEWS FROM THE CLINIC, ...FACE LIFT 155   1
    THEY BRING ME NUMBNESS IN THEIR BRIGHT NEEDLES, THEY BRING
        ME SLEEP. ....TULIPS 160   17
    THEY BRING ME NUMBNESS IN THEIR BRIGHT NEEDLES, THEY BRING
        ME SLEEP. ....TULIPS 160   17
    OR SHALL I BRING YOU THE SOUND OF POISONS? ....ELM   192   13
    TO BRING TEACUPS AND ROLL AWAY HEADACHES ....THE APPLICANT 221   12
    SHE CAN BRING THE DEAD TO LIFE ....THE TOUR   238   46
BRINGS (4)
    HIS BEAK BRINGS THE HARVEST IN. ....MAGNOLIA SHOALS   122   18
    I FOLLOW THE SHEEP PATH BETWEEN THEM. A LAST HOOK BRINGS ME ...
                                         ... BLACKBERRYING   169   23
    ONE NURSE BRINGS IN ....AMNESIAC   233   21
    THE NIGHT BRINGS VIOLETS, ...PARALYTIC 266   11
BRIOS (1)
    LET BE YOUR CON BRIOS, YOU CAPRICCIOSOS, ...ALICANTE LULLABY   43   17
BRISK (2)
    PACED BRISK FATHER SHAWN. A COLD DAY, A SODDEN ONE IT WAS ...
               ... DIALOGUE BETWEEN GHOST AND PRIEST   38   2
    WHERE DO YOU LIVE? HE MOVES. HE'S MOVING BRISK ....DIALOGUE O. 281 206
BRISKLY (1)
    THEN BRISKLY SCALED HIS ALTAR TIERED WITH TETHERED ANTS, ...SPIDER   49   22
BRISTLE (1)
    AND SHADOWS ONLY -- CAVE-MOUTH BRISTLE BESET -- ....GOATSUCKER 111   13
BRITTLE (1)
    GROWS BRITTLE AS A TILTED CHINA BOWL; ....PROLOGUE TO SPRING 322   5
BROACH (1)
    AS ROSES BROACH THEIR CARMINE IN A MIRROR. FLUX ....ABOVE THE OXBOW   89   44

BROACHED (1)
     BLOOD FAULTLESSLY BROACHED REDEEMED THE SULLIED AIR, THE EARTH'S
                              GROSSNESS. ....THE GORING   47   10
BROAD (2)
     COMEBACK IN BROAD DAY ....LADY LAZARUS   246   52
     INTO WHICH BROAD TOES WILL GO TOMORROW. ......THE MUNICH MANNEQUINS 263   20
BROADCAST (1)
     SHALL STREW BROADCAST SO RARE A SEED ON WIND ...WREATH FOR A BRIDAL   45   20
BROBDINGNAG (1)
     BROBDINGNAG BULK ....SOW   61   24
BROCADES (1)
     A CAVIARE DECAY OF RICH BROCADES. ....TERMINAL 328   8
BROKE (7)
     WHY, ALL THE WINDOWS BROKE WHEN HE STALKED IN.*THE QUEEN'S COMPLAINT   28   5
     BUT THOSE LADIES BROKE THE PANES. ....THE DISQUIETING MUSES   75   24
     THE SEA BROKE IN AT EVERY CRACK, ...THE BULL OF BENDYLAW 108   14
     WERE SQUEALING WHERE COMBERS BROKE AND THE SPINDRIFT ......SUICIDE.   115   10
     THAN ANY ORCHID. YOU BROKE HIM THEN. I BROKE ....DIALOGUE O.   285 324
     THAN ANY ORCHID. YOU BROKE HIM THEN. I BROKE ....DIALOGUE O.   285 324
     WE BROKE THE MINUTE THAT THE WORLD BEGAN ....THE DISPOSSESSED   318   14
BROKEN (7)
     OF BROKEN GLASS, ...MISS DRAKE PROCEEDS TO SUPPER   41   20
     NOURISHES THESE BROKEN FLUTINGS, ...THE MANOR GARDEN 125   9
     FROM THE BROKEN THROAT, THE MARSHY LIP. ....THE BURNT-OUT SPA 138   21
     DYNASTY OF BROKEN ARROWS! ....GETTING THERE 248   33
     BETRAYED IN MUTE GEOMETRY OF BROKEN ....SONNET: TO EVA 304   6
     ATOP THE BROKEN UNIVERSAL CLOCK: ....DOOMSDAY 316   2
     CHUCK THE BROKEN ACROPOLIS OUT, ...SONG FOR A REVOLUTIONARY LOVE 323   6
BRONZE (9)
     BY TWO BRONZE BOOKENDS OF SHIPS IN SAIL,   ON THE DECLINE OF ORACLES   78   2
     BUT SURE STATIONS IN BRONZE, WOOD, STONE. ....SCULPTOR   91   8
     BRONZE DEAD DOMINATE THE FLOOR, ...SCULPTOR   91   14
     THE GREAT BRONZE GATE BEGAN TO CRACK, ...THE BULL OF BENDYLAW 108   13
     THE BRONZE SNAKE LAY IN THE SUN ....MEDALLION 124   3
     CERTAINTY OF THE BRONZE BOY ....GOLD MOUTHS CRY 302   2
     PERSUADED BY HIS BRONZE HEROIC REASON. ....GOLD MOUTHS CRY 302   6
     THE BRONZE BOY STANDS KNEEDEEP IN CENTURIES, ...GOLD MOUTHS CRY 302   10
     LIKE THE BRONZE TONE ....AQUATIC NOCTURNE 306   27
BRONZED (2)
     BRONZED AS EARTH, THE SECOND LIES, ...TWO SISTERS OF PERSEPHONE   32   13
     THE FIELDS WERE FULL OF BRONZED YOUNG MEN ......BITTER STRAWBERRIES 299   18
BRONZES (1)
     VERMILIONS, BRONZES, COLORS OF THE SUN ....OUIJA   77   6
BROOCH-PIN (1)
     BEFORE THE BROOCH-PIN AND THE SALVE ....THE EYE-MOTE 109   27
BROOD (4)
     FLAPPED BLACK TO LOOK AND BROOD ....FAUN   35   4
     BROOD, ROOTED IN THEIR HEAPED LOSSES. ....PARLIAMENT HILL FIELDS 153   31
     SEALING OVER HER BROOD CELLS, HER HONEY, AND QUIETLY HUMMING. ..BEE. 212   35
     BROOD CELLS GRAY AS THE FOSSILS OF SHELLS ....STINGS 214   12
BROODING (1)
     BROODING AS THE WINTER NIGHT COMES ON. ....WINTER LANDSCAPE,   21   10
BROODS (2)
     GUARDED BROODS AND LITTERS ....HARDCASTLE CRAGS   63   31
     BROODS IN THE NEWSPRINT! ....FEVER./DR 294   5
BROODY (1)
     BROODY AND IN LONG SKIRTS ON MY FIRST HUSBAND'S SOFA, MY
                         FINGERS ....FACE LIFT 156   22
BROOK'S (1)
     AND BAIT THE DROWSING TROUT BY THE BROOK'S BRIM; ....GO GET.   313   18
BROOM (1)
     SHE WORE HER BROOM STRAWS TO THE NUB. ....POINT SHIRLEY 110   18
BROTH (1)
     BLOOD'S BROTH, ...THE GLUTTON   40   7
BROTHER (3)
     MY BROTHER AND ME COOKIES AND OVALTINE ....THE DISQUIETING MUSES   75   20
     YOUR BROTHER WILL TRIM MY HEDGES! .......................EAVESDROPPER 260   1
     BROTHER IS MAKING ....BALLOONS 272   21
BROTHERS (1)
     KNOCKING OUR BROTHERS DOWN, WE STRIKE A STANCE ....CHANNEL CROSSING   27   27
BROTHER-SISTER (1)
     SPARKING OFF THEIR BROTHER-SISTER REARS ....AMNESIAC 233   18
BROUGHT (4)
     I BROUGHT MY LOVE TO BEAR, AND THEN YOU DIED.*ELECTRA ON AZALEA PATH 117   38
     OF THE GREEK BEAUTIES YOU BROUGHT ....PRIVATE GROUND 130   2
     BUT I'VE BROUGHT BRANDY AND BUILT THE FIRE UP ....DIALOGUE O.   277   16
     THE ORDINARY MILKMAN BROUGHT THAT DAWN ....THE TRIAL OF MAN 312   1
BROW (2)
     HIS CROWN USURPED BY THE LOW BROW ....NATURAL HISTORY   71   11
     OVER THE WEEDY ACRES OF YOUR BROW ....THE COLOSSUS 129   13
BROWN (11)
     ACROSS BARBED STILE, THROUGH FLOCKED BROWN COWS. ....BUCOLICS   23   4
     LIKE ICEBERGS, WHILE MINUTE BROWN HAIRS RISE ....TALE OF A TUB   25   42
     RICH, BROWN, SUDDEN IN SUNGLINT. ....ODE FOR TED   29   12
     WITH HER BLANK BROWN EYES STARVED WIDE, ...THE SHRIKE   42   9

                                   72

BROWN (CONT.)
     HE IS ARRANGING HIS BROWN FEATHERS. ....THREE WOMEN 176   12
     I AM DUMB AND BROWN. I AM A SEED ABOUT TO BREAK. ....THREE WOMEN 179   99
     THEIR SKIN TINTS ARE PINK OR SALLOW, BROWN OR RED; .....THREE WOMEN 183 223
     IT UNCLAPS, BROWN AS A LEAF, AND LOUD, ...PHEASANT 191   21
     AND IN PUNISHMENT WAS HUNG OUT LIKE BROWN FRUIT ......THE DETECTIVE 209   29
     THE BROWN MOTHERLY FURROWS, THE WHOLE ESTATE. ....THE DETECTIVE 209   37
     THE BROWN ARC ....ARIEL 239   8
BROWN-BACKED (1)
     BROWN-BACKED, WHITE-BELLIED ....WORDS FOR A NURSERY   74   31
BROWNING (1)
     THEY ARE BROWNING, LIKE TOUCHED GARDENIAS. ....BERCK-PLAGE 198   59
BROWNNESS (1)
     THE BROWNNESS IS MY DEAD SELF, AND IT IS SULLEN: ....THREE WOMEN 179 100
BROWNS (3)
     AND LOSE THEIR GOOD BROWNS ....THE THIN PEOPLE   65   44
     OF BROWNS AND GREENS. EACH WORE ONE ...MUSSEL HUNTER AT ROCK HARBOR   96   32
     BUNCHES ITS KNOBBY BROWNS ON A VASTLY ....POEMS, POTATOES 106   12
BROWSE (1)
     AND ALL YOU SANTA'S DEER WHO BROWSE ....A WINTER'S TALE   87   21
BROWSING (1)
     BROWSING IN THEIR DIRTY WOOL-CLOUDS, ...WUTHERING HEIGHTS 167   20
BRUEGHEL'S (1)
     IN BRUEGHEL'S PANORAMA OF SMOKE AND SLAUGHTER ....TWO VIEWS. 114   12
BRUISE (2)
     THIN AS PINS IN THE DARK BRUISE ....MEDALLION 125   22
     THEY BRUISE THE ROCKS OUT OF EXISTENCE, THEN RESURRECT THEM. ...
                                                        ... FINISTERRE 169   15
BRUISES (1)
     WHITE BRUISES TOWARD COLOR, ELSE COLLAPSES. ....MOONRISE   98   12
BRUISING (1)
     OUT OF THE SUN'S BRUISING) ....SONG FOR A SUMMER'S DAY   31   19
BRUIT (3)
     COLD SQUINT STEALS SKY'S COLOR; WHILE BRUIT ....VANITY FAIR   32   8
     MERE BRUIT OF HER TAKES OUR STREET ....STRUMPET SONG   33   5
     STILL RINGING WITH BRUIT OF INSULTS AND DISHONORS ....SNOWMAN O.   58   3
BRUNT (3)
     AGAINST WHICH THE BRUNT OF OUTER SEA ....DEPARTURE   51   14
     FROM BRUNT OF AXE-CRACK ....THE SNOWMAN ON THE MOOR   59   46
     BY NOON AND THROUGHOUT THE BRUNT ....CHILD'S PARK STONES 101   20
BRUSH (3)
     HIS BRUSH IN THE STRINGENT AIR. ....MAGNOLIA SHOALS 122   20
     THERE IS MY COMB AND BRUSH. THERE IS AN EMPTINESS. .....THREE WOMEN 184 268
     BEGIN BY DIPPING YOUR BRUSH INTO CLEAR LIGHT. .....MIDSUMMER MOBILE 324   1
BRUTAL (1)
     BEATS, IS BRUTAL ENDLESSLY. ....DEPARTURE   51   15
BRUTE (4)
     THE BOOT IN THE FACE, THE BRUTE ....DADDY 223   49
     BRUTE HEART OF A BRUTE LIKE YOU. ....DADDY 223   50
     BRUTE HEART OF A BRUTE LIKE YOU. ....DADDY 223   50
     TO THE SAME PLACE, THE SAME FACE, THE SAME BRUTE ......LADY LAZARUS 246   53
BUBBLE (1)
     AND A ROUND BUBBLE ....LYONNESSE 234   8
BUBBLES (1)
     LIKE BUBBLES ABOUT TO BREAK, YOU FED ....THE DISQUIETING MUSES   75   19
BUCK (1)
     WHICH HAULS DOWN BUCK, COCK, TROUT, TILL ALL MOST FAIR ....FIRESONG   30   6
BUCKED (1)
     BUCKED AT THE GARDEN GATE. ....THE BULL OF BENDYLAW 108   9
BUCKETS (1)
     AMONG ICE BUCKETS, FROSTY NAPKINS. ....CANDLES 149   23
BUCOLIC (1)
     THE EDEN OF BUCOLIC EVE: ...............METAMORPHOSES OF THE MOON 307   15
BUCOLICS (1)
     BUCOLICS ....BUCOLICS   23   T
BUD (9)
     PLAGUE-PITTED AS THE MOON: EACH BUD ....CRYSTAL GAZER   56   44
     THOUGH DOOMSDAY BUD. NEGLECT'S ....VIRGIN IN A TREE   82   41
     AN ORANGE BUD, POCKETED IT. WHEN *FABLE OF THE RHODODENDRON STEALERS 103   8
     YET TODAY, A YELLOW BUD IN MY HAND, ...RHODODENDRON. 103   17
     SNUG AS A BUD AND AT HOME ....YOU'RE 141   13
     YOU HANDED ME GIN IN A GLASS BUD VASE. ....LEAVING EARLY 146   41
     I STARTED TO BUD LIKE A MARCH TWIG: ....LOVE LETTER 147   31
     THESE LITTLE BLACK TWIGS DO NOT THINK TO BUD, ...THREE WOMEN 184 278
     IT SNUFFS ITS BUD ....BY CANDLELIGHT 236   17
BUDDED (2)
     THIS DREAM BUDDED BRIGHT WITH LEAVES AROUND THE EDGES,*DREAM WITH C.   43   1
     A HOT BLUE DAY HAD BUDDED INTO SOMETHING. ....THREE WOMEN 178   56
BUDDHA (1)
     I SMILE, A BUDDHA, ALL ....PARALYTIC 267   33
BUDDHAS (1)
     THE PEARS FATTEN LIKE LITTLE BUDDHAS. ....THE MANOR GARDEN 125   3
BUDGE (1)
     THE SEA CANNONS INTO THEIR EAR, BUT THEY DON'T BUDGE. ...FINISTERRE 169   8

```
                                                    TITLE            PAGE  LINE
BUDS (1)
    THE INDELIBLE BUDS, ....................................THALIDOMIDE  252   11
BUFFS (1)
    AND BUFFS AND SLEEKS THE BLUNT HULLS  ..MUSSEL HUNTER AT ROCK HARBOR   95    5
BUGGY (1)
    A GARDEN OF BUGGY ROSES THAT MADE HIM CRY. ...............INSOMNIAC  163   12
BUGS (1)
    THE STAR BUGS WON'T SAVE ME THIS MONTH. ..............POEM.4.BEAST.  134   22
BUILD (5)
    AT HIS HAND'S STAUNCH HEST, BIRDS BUILD. .................ODE FOR TED   29   18
    BUILD UP FROM A ROCK ROOT, AS FOUNTAINS BUILD ............MOONRISE   98   23
    BUILD UP FROM A ROCK ROOT, AS FOUNTAINS BUILD ............MOONRISE   98   23
    TO BUILD HIS CANTING TOWERS. WHILE YOU, YOU LONG .......DIALOGUE O.  280  136
    SURRENDER: TO BUILD OUR BED AS HIGH AS JACK'S ...LOVE IS A PARALLAX  330   70
BUILDING (1)
    WITH BEGONIA AND BUILDING BLOCKS.  ....SONG FOR A REVOLUTIONARY LOVE  323   16
BUILDS (1)
    NO ANCIENT BLUEPRINT BUILDS AN ARK .................INSOLENT STORM.  326   17
BUILT (1)
    BUT I'VE BROUGHT BRANDY AND BUILT THE FIRE UP ..........DIALOGUE O.  277   16
BULB (3)
    NOW THEY LIGHT ME UP LIKE AN ELECTRIC BULB. ............POEM.1.WHO.  132   32
    DEVOUTLY AS THE DUTCH BULB .............................HEAVY WOMEN  158    9
    HER BODY A BULB IN THE COLD AND TOO DUMB TO THINK. .......WINTERING  219   45
BULBOUS (1)
    OF BULBOUS JELLYFISH ............................AQUATIC NOCTURNE  306   17
BULBS (1)
    CLUMPED LIKE BULBS AT THE GRASS-ROOT ..MUSSEL HUNTER AT ROCK HARBOR   95   10
BULGED (2)
    WHERE HIS INNARDS BULGED AS IF ...........................MEDALLION  125   23
    THEIR LITTLE FOREHEADS BULGED WITH CONCENTRATION. ........STILLBORN  142    3
BULGING (1)
    THE BENT PRINT BULGING BEFORE HIM LIKE SCENERY. ........BERCK-PLAGE  197   23
BULK (4)
    BROBDINGNAG BULK ...............................................SOW   61   24
    FOR THE PALTRY GIFT OF HER BULK AND THE BEAT ......HARDCASTLE CRAGS   63   27
    THAT BULK SO CALM ........................................CONJURING   66   14
    GULP AT MY BULK .............................................GIGOLO  267   11
BULKED (1)
    EVERY POCK AND STAIN BULKED MORE BEAUTIFUL*ON THE PLETHORA OF DRYADS   67   16
BULKING (1)
    BULKING MORE REAL THAN WE THINK WE ARE: WE FACE ........DIALOGUE O.  279  115
BULKS (1)
    BULKS REAL, ALL SAINTS' TONGUES FALL QUIET ......NOVEMBER GRAVEYARD   56   11
BULL (6)
    RODE OUT AGAINST THE FIFTH BULL TO BRACE HIS PIKE AND SLOWLY BEAR ...
                                               ... THE GORING   47    6
    THE BULL OF BENDYLAW .........................THE BULL OF BENDYLAW  108    T
    THE BLACK BULL BELLOWED BEFORE THE SEA. .......THE BULL OF BENDYLAW  108    1
    THE BULL SURGED UP, THE BULL SURGED DOWN, .....THE BULL OF BENDYLAW  108   16
    THE BULL SURGED UP, THE BULL SURGED DOWN, .....THE BULL OF BENDYLAW  108   16
    AND THE BULL ON THE KING'S HIGHWAY. ...........THE BULL OF BENDYLAW  108   21
BULLDOZERS (1)
    BULLDOZERS, GUILLOTINES, WHITE CHAMBERS OF SHRIEKS PROCEED,   THREE.  177   19
BULLETS (1)
    SO DUMB IT THINKS BULLETS ARE THUNDER. ....................THE SWARM  216   20
BULL-FEET (1)
    A BLUE SEA, FOUR HORNY BULL-FEET, .............THE BULL OF BENDYLAW  108    7
BULLMAN (1)
    HE WAS BULLMAN EARLIER, ..............................POEM.4.BEAST.  134    1
BULL-NECK (1)
    DOWN DEEP INTO THE BENT BULL-NECK. CUMBROUS ROUTINE, NOT ARTWORK. ...
                                               ... THE GORING   47    7
BULLS' (3)
    ARENA DUST RUSTED BY FOUR BULLS' BLOOD TO A DULL REDNESS,*THE GORING   47    1
    INSTINCT FOR ART BEGAN WITH THE BULL'S HORN LOFTING IN THE MOB'S ...
                                               ... THE GORING   47    8
    AND THE ROYAL ROSE IN THE BULL'S BELLY, .......THE BULL OF BENDYLAW  108   20
BULL'S-EYE (1)
    BEFORE IT MADE THE BULL'S-EYE. DO WE HAVE TO BATTLE ....DIALOGUE O.  284  282
BULL-SNOUTED (1)
    A BULL-SNOUTED SEA THAT WOULDN'T STAY PUT, ....THE BULL OF BENDYLAW  108    8
BUMBLINGLY (1)
    BUMBLINGLY OVER THE NUBS OF THE COBBLES ...........ALICANTE LULLABY   43    2
BUMP-RINDED (1)
    BUMP-RINDED CANTALOUPES .............................FIESTA MELONS   46   13
BUMPY (1)
    HIS FOREHEAD IS BUMPY AS A SACK OF ROCKS. .................INSOMNIAC  163   13
BUNCH (4)
    OR BUNCH MY FIST ..........................................RESOLVE   52   22
    OF THE SPINACH PATCH. BUNCH AFTER BUNCH OF GREEN ...SPINACH-PICKER.   89    7
    OF THE SPINACH PATCH. BUNCH AFTER BUNCH OF GREEN ...SPINACH-PICKER.   89    7
    TO A KNOT OF LAUNDRY, WITH A CLASSIC BUNCH OF SHEETS ......GHOST'S.   90   10
BUNCHED (4)
    AS A SLEDGE HAMMER, AS A MAN'S BUNCHED FIST, ................SPIDER   48    4
```

	TITLE	PAGE	LINE

BUNCHED (CONT.)
AND SINEWS BUNCHED, VICTORIOUS, AS THE COSMIC ....PERSEUS 83 44
THE BLACK BUNCHED IN THERE LIKE A BAT, ...WINTERING 218 13
THE ROADS BUNCHED TO A KNOT, ...CHILDLESS WOMAN 259 5
BUNCHES (1)
BUNCHES ITS KNOBBY BROWNS ON A VASTLY ....POEMS, POTATOES 106 12
BUNDLE (1)
BENT UNDER A BUNDLE ....THE EVERLASTING MONDAY 62 2
BUNKERS (1)
LIMBS, IMAGES, SHRIEKS. BEHIND THE CONCRETE BUNKERS ....BERCK-PLAGE 197 29
BURDEN (2)
BEARS A BURDEN TOO WEIGHTY ....LORELEI 94 17
ASSUMES, LIKE A MEATHOOK, THE BURDEN OF HIS PARTS. ....THE OTHER 201 6
BURDENED (2)
TO A PINCH OF FLAME, BLEW ITS BURDENED WHISTLE ....HARDCASTLE CRAGS 63 23
BURDENED IN SUCH A WAY WE SEEMED THE LIGHTER -- ......THE OTHER TWO 69 32
BURDOCK (1)
A FIELD OF BURDOCK OPENS TO THE SOUTH. ......ELECTRA ON AZALEA PATH 117 22
BUREAU (3)
CHAIR AND BUREAU ARE THE HIEROGLYPHS ....THE GHOST'S LEAVETAKING 90 16
DAYBREAK DISCOVERED THE BUREAU LID ....LEAVING EARLY 146 29
HOW IT BREATHES IN THE BUREAU DRAWER! ....A SECRET 220 27
BUREAUS (2)
OF CHAIRS AND BUREAUS AND SLEEP-TWISTED SHEETS. ....GHOST'S. 90 7
I WATCHED MY TEASET, MY BUREAUS OF LINEN, MY BOOKS ....TULIPS 161 26
BURGEONING (1)
BUT HERE -- A BURGEONING ....SPINSTER 50 19
BURGERS (1)
THE BURGHERS SWEATED AND WEPT. THE CHILDREN WORE WHITE. ....CANDLES 149 19
BURGLAR (1)
AND LIKE A BURGLAR STEAL THEIR FANCY: ....MORNING IN THE HOS. 333 26
BURIAL (1)
OF YOUR BURIAL MOVE ME ....FULL FATHOM FIVE 93 22
BURIED (2)
BURIED IN THE LAMBSWOOL OF THE DEAD POODLE; ....FACE LIFT 156 23
I WAS TEN WHEN THEY BURIED YOU. ....DADDY 224 57
BURLESQUE (1)
LURKED THE BURLESQUE INSTINCT OF THE HAM; ....DIRGE FOR A JOKER 302 6
BURN (14)
LEAN TO MY WOUND; BURN ON, BURN ON. ....FIRESONG 30 21
LEAN TO MY WOUND; BURN ON, BURN ON. ....FIRESONG 30 21
SOME BURN SHORT, SOME LONG, ...VANITY FAIR 33 34
WHERE, BEDDED LIKE ANGELS, TWO BURN ONE IN FEVER. ....WREATH F. 45 18
WOOD STOVES BURN WARM AS TOAST. ....YADDO: THE GRAND MANOR 124 17
NUN-SOULED, THEY BURN HEAVENWARD AND NEVER MARRY. ....CANDLES 149 27
MY RED FILAMENTS BURN AND STAND, A HAND OF WIRES. ....ELM 192 18
I TURN AND BURN. ....LADY LAZARUS 246 71
BURN, FOR YOUR INHALATION, ...EAVESDROPPER 260 17
WITH THE COLD BURN DRY ICE HAS. YET THE CLOCK ....DIALOGUE O. 276 11
AS SURE AS THOSE COALS BURN, THE LIVINGROOM ....DIALOGUE O. 286 357
I NEVER THOUGHT HIS FLESH WOULD BURN ....TO A JILTED LOVER 310 12
AND BURN TO DEATH WITHIN YOUR NEON HELL. ....THE TRIAL OF MAN 312 11
TO BURN AWAY THE HUMBUG RUST ....SONG FOR A REVOLUTIONARY LOVE 323 23
BURNED (4)
THE BOOKS BURNED UP, SEA TOOK THE SHELL, ON THE DECLINE OF ORACLES 78 11
THE GARNET BITS BURNED LIKE THAT. ....MEDALLION 124 13
ON TRIAL, FROM IRELAND, SHE BURNED BATCH AFTER BATCH OF COOKIES ...
... THE BABYSITTERS 175 26
HUNG, STARVED, BURNED, HOOKED. ....THE JAILER 227 35
BURNERS (1)
THEY ARE TURNING THE BURNERS UP, RING AFTER RING. POEM.6.W. 135 16
BURNING (11)
WHILE SHE STANDS BURNING, VENOM-GIRT, ...BUCOLICS 24 23
AS IF A CELESTIAL BURNING TOOK ....BLACK ROOK IN RAINY WEATHER 57 17
I RIDE EARTH'S BURNING CARROUSEL ....ON THE PLETHORA OF DRYADS 67 29
NEITHER BRAZEN SWAN NOR BURNING STAR, ...ON THE DECLINE OF ORACLES 78 18
WITCH BURNING ....POEM.6.W. 135 ST
BURNING THE LETTERS ....BURNING THE LETTERS 204 T
THIS IS THE SMELL OF YEARS BURNING, HERE IN THE KITCHEN, *DETECTIVE. 208 12
HE HAS BEEN BURNING ME WITH CIGARETTES, ...THE JAILER 226 18
BURNING LIKE KNOTHOLES FROM A NUN'S SHROUD-CIRCLED .....DIALOGUE O. 280 130
BLOOD SPRINGS ETERNAL IF THE HEART BE BURNING. ..TO EVA DESCENDING. 303 8
BURNING DARTS ....ON LOOKING INTO THE EYES OF A DEMON LOVER 325 12
BURNISHED (3)
CLOUDS STEERED A BURNISHED DRIFT; ....SONG FOR A SUMMER'S DAY 31 8
WITH SHINGLES BURNISHED AS GLASS, ...DREAM WITH CLAM-DIGGERS 43 7
THE BURNISHED BALL HANGS FIRE IN HER HANDS, A LENS ...CRYSTAL GAZER 54 5
BURNS (10)
WHEN BURNS AND BRANDS THAT YELLOW GAZE? ....PURSUIT 23 36
BURNS OPEN TO SUN'S BLADE. ....TWO SISTERS OF PERSEPHONE 32 19
AND THE COAL FIRE BURNS ....RESOLVE 52 7
ABRADING MY LID, THE SMALL GRAIN BURNS: ....THE EYE-MOTE 109 16
THIS WOOD BURNS A DARK ....DARK WOOD, DARK WATER 127 1
ONE TOUCH: IT BURNS AND SICKENS. ....EVENT 194 11
I PUT MY HANDS AMONG THE FLAMES. NOTHING BURNS. ....POPPIES IN JULY 203 4

BURNS (CONT.)
     I AM A MINER. THE LIGHT BURNS BLUE. ....NICK AND THE CANDLESTICK   240   1
     TILL HER STUBBORN BODY BURNS. ....DANSE MACABRE   321   15
     THERE BURNS THROUGHOUT THE LINE OF WORDS, ...LOVE IS A PARALLAX   330   57
BURNT (7)
     OF THE AZALEAS, YET BURNT OUT ....CHILD'S PARK STONES   101   17
     THE LAST CRONE GOT BURNT UP ....THE TIMES ARE TIDY   107   11
     THEY HAD FOUR MEN LAID OUT, BLACK AS BURNT TURKEY, ...TWO VIEWS.   114   2
     THE TREES STIFFEN INTO PLACE LIKE BURNT NERVES. ...WAKING IN WINTER   151   3
     BITS OF BURNT PAPER WHEELING IN A BLOWN SKY. .........BLACKBERRYING   168   11
     OLD BLOOD OF LIMB STUMPS, BURNT HEARTS. ....BERCK-PLAGE   200   99
     ALL DAY, GLUING MY CHURCH OF BURNT MATCHSTICKS, ...THE JAILER   227   26
BURNT-OUT (5)
     BURNT-OUT WERE THEIRS, OR AS IF THEY THOUGHT ....AFTERMATH   113   3
     THE BURNT-OUT SPA ....THE BURNT-OUT SPA   137   T
     IT'S A BIT BURNT-OUT, ...THE TOUR   237   11
     OVER THE CICATRIX OF POLAND, BURNT-OUT ....MARY'S SONG   257   10
     OVER SCOURED POLAND, BURNT-OUT ....MARY'S SONG/DR   294   1
BURRING (1)
     THE WARNING WHIRR AND BURRING OF THE BIRD ....GOATSUCKER   111   2
BURROWS (2)
     INCHED FROM THEIR PIGMY BURROWS ....MUSSEL HUNTER AT ROCK HARBOR   96   29
     IN BURROWS NARROW AS A FINGER, SOLITARY BEES ....BEEKEEPER'S.   118   15
BURST (1)
     A RED BURST AND A CRY ....BURNING THE LETTERS   205   50
BURSTING (1)
     THE NERVES BURSTING LIKE TREES, AND THIS IS THE SURGEON:*BERCK-PLAGE   198   47
BURY (3)
     BELIEVE ME, THEY'LL BURY YOU IN IT. ....THE APPLICANT   221   25
     I SHALL BURY THE WOUNDED LIKE PUPAS, ...GETTING THERE   249   60
     I SHALL COUNT AND BURY THE DEAD. ....GETTING THERE   249   61
BUSH (5)
     STEM OF MY NEIGHBOR'S ROSE BUSH ....RESOLVE   52   15
     I COME TO ONE BUSH OF BERRIES SO RIPE IT IS A BUSH OF FLIES, ...
                                                 ... BLACKBERRYING   168   15
     I COME TO ONE BUSH OF BERRIES SO RIPE IT IS A BUSH OF FLIES, ...
                                                 ... BLACKBERRYING   168   15
     IF THAT ELDERBERRY BUSH BESIDE THE GATE *DIALOGUE OVER A OUIJA BOARD   280 157
     IF A BUSH BORROWED TONGUES AND SPOKE TO YOU. YOU'D KNEEL*DIALOGUE O.   280 163
BUSHEL (1)
     WITH A HUNDRED BUSHEL BASKETS ON THE EDGE ....SPINACH-PICKER   89   6
BUSHES (4)
     A SPASM TOOK THE RHODODENDRON BUSHES: ..............RHODODENDRON.   103   20
     THEY RATTLE LIKE HYDRANGEA BUSHES. POEM.1.WHO.   131   12
     ALL-MOUTH LICKS UP THE BUSHES POEM.2.DARK.   132   17
     ONE MORE HOOK, AND THE BERRIES AND BUSHES END. .......BLACKBERRYING   169   18
BUSH-STINK (1)
     A KIND OF BUSH-STINK. .............................EAVESDROPPER   260   9
BUSHY (1)
     LITTLE BUSHY POLYPS, ...PURDAH   242   15
BUSILY (1)
     IT IS YOUR KNITTING, BUSILY ....THE OTHER   201   14
BUSINESS (4)
     "WHAT MANNER OF BUSINESS ARE YOU ON? ....DIALOGUE B.   38   13
     WENT ABOUT THEIR BUSINESS, WHICH ......MUSSEL HUNTER AT ROCK HARBOR   97   61
     THE ROUND SKY GOES ON MINDING ITS BUSINESS.   PARLIAMENT HILL FIELDS   152   3
     THE SMILE OF A MAN OF BUSINESS, INTENSELY PRACTICAL. .....THE SWARM   217   52
BUSINESSLIKE (1)
     BUSINESSLIKE SHE ASKED US, "HOW MANY QUARTS?" ..BITTER STRAWBERRIES   300   31
BUSTS (1)
     THE WHITE BUSTS OF MARSHALS, ADMIRALS, GENERALS ....THE SWARM   217   44
BUSY (2)
     EVERY ONE OF THEM PERMANENTLY BUSY. ....A LIFE   150   10
     BLED WHITE WITH BRIARS BY A BUSY CONSCIENCE ....DIALOGUE O.   281 197
BUSYBODY (1)
     ANANSI, BLACK BUSYBODY OF THE FOLKTALES, ...SPIDER   48   1
BUSYNESS (1)
     I FELT A STILL BUSYNESS, AN INTENT. ....THE RABBIT CATCHER   194   21
BUT (180)
BUTCHER (2)
     IS IT THE BUTCHER, THE GROCER, THE POSTMAN, SOMEONE I KNOW? ...BEE.   211   30
     IF YOU MUST BUTCHER MOTHER GOOSE TO DO IT. ....DIALOGUE O.   280 149
BUTCHER'S (2)
     REEKS OF THE BUTCHER'S CLEAVER. ....STREET SONG   36   7
     THE BUTCHER'S GUILLOTINE THAT WHISPERS: "HOW'S THIS, HOW'S THIS?" ...
                                                 ... TOTEM   264   10
BUTLER (1)
     THE FIENDISH BUTLER SAUNTERS IN AND SERVES ....TERMINAL   328   10
BUTT (1)
     WITH THE BUTT OF A RAKE ....BURNING THE LETTERS   204   36
BUTTER (1)
     SPREADING ITSELF, LIKE BUTTER. ......................EAVESDROPPER   261   51
BUTTERCUP (1)
     BELLIED ON A NIMBUS OF SUN-GLAZED BUTTERCUP. ....WATERCOLOR.   112   18

	TITLE	PAGE	LINE
BUTTERCUPS (1)			
HOT NOON IN THE MEADOWS. THE BUTTERCUPS ....THREE WOMEN		186	337
BUTTERFLIES (3)			
GREEN AS A POOL TABLE, WHERE CABBAGE BUTTERFLIES ....WHITSUN		154	19
MY JAPANESE SILKS, DESPERATE BUTTERFLIES, ...KINDNESS		269	14
AND HANDS LIKE NERVOUS BUTTERFLIES; ....FAMILY REUNION		300	19
BUTTON (2)			
COIN, BUTTON, TRIGGER ....WORDS FOR A NURSERY		74	39
I WOULD NOT MIND IF IT WAS BONES, OR A PEARL BUTTON. .....BIRTHDAY.		206	12
BUTTONING (1)			
BUTTONING THE CUFFS AT MY WRISTS AND THE SLIT FROM MY NECK			
TO MY KNEES. .... THE BEE MEETING		211	8
BUTTONS (1)			
I SHALL NOT BE ACCUSED BY ISOLATE BUTTONS, ...THREE WOMEN		182	198
BUY (1)			
AND THEY BUY TICKETS FOR THE TROPIC ZONE; ....DENOUEMENT		326	5
BUYING (2)			
BUYING WINE, BREAD, ...STREET SONG		36	13
WHAT AM I BUYING, WORMY MAHOGANY? ....STINGS		214	14
BUZZ (1)			
THEY BUZZ LIKE BLUE CHILDREN ....TOTEM		265	31
BUZZARD (1)			
AND DEATH, THAT BALD-HEAD BUZZARD, ...OLD LADIES' HOME		120	19
BUZZED (2)			
BUZZED AND ASSAILED THE VAULTED BRAINCHAMBER. SUICIDE OFF EGG ROCK		115	18
HORSEFLIES BUZZED, PAUSED AND STUNG. ....BITTER STRAWBERRIES		299	7
BY (237)			
BYRON'S (1)			
IN BYRON'S POOL ....WATERCOLOR OF GRANTCHESTER MEADOWS		112	13
BYSTANDING (1)			
WILL TOLERATE NO BYSTANDING: I MUST SHRIEK. ....ELM		192	21
C (1)			
DOES HE WRITE C FOR G? NO. HE DARTS ....DIALOGUE OVER A OUIJA BOARD		284	276
CABBAGE (3)			
OWN THEIR CABBAGE ROOTS, A SPACE OF STARS, ...LANDOWNERS		53	10
GREEN AS A POOL TABLE, WHERE CABBAGE BUTTERFLIES ....WHITSUN		154	19
BETWEEN THE YELLOW LETTUCES AND THE GERMAN CABBAGE ....BURNING.		205	39
CABBAGEHEADS (1)			
CABBAGEHEADS: WORMY PURPLE, SILVER-GLAZE, ...POEM.1.WHO.		131	16
CABBAGE-ROSES (2)			
BETWEEN THE CABBAGE-ROSES ....MISS DRAKE PROCEEDS TO SUPPER		41	10
FRIEZE OF CABBAGE-ROSES AND CORNFLOWERS PALES ......THE THIN PEOPLE		65	37
CABBAGES (2)			
CABBAGES ARE CABBAGES; KINGS: KINGS. ....A SORCERER B.		324	14
CABBAGES ARE CABBAGES; KINGS: KINGS. ....A SORCERER B.		324	14
CABIN (1)			
AND A CABIN BOY WHO COULD DECORATE CAKES IN SIX-COLORED			
FROSTING. ....THE BABYSITTERS		174	12
CABINET (1)			
THAT CABINET WITHOUT WINDOWS OR DOORS: ....THE OTHER TWO		68	17
CABINETS (1)			
THEY WOULD HAVE YOU SLEEP IN THEIR CABINETS, ...GULLIVER		251	18
CABINS (1)			
THE DEAD SMELL OF SUN ON WOOD CABINS, ...MYSTIC		268	7
CABLE (1)			
OLD BARNACLED UMBILICUS, ATLANTIC CABLE, ...MEDUSA		225	14
CACKLE (1)			
HEARING A WEIRD CACKLE FROM AFAR, ...THE PRINCESS AND THE GOBLINS		334	41
CACKLES (2)			
SCUTTLE REPOSE WITH CROWNS AND CACKLES. ....ALICANTE LULLABY		43	7
MULE-BRAY, PIG-GRUNT AND BAWDY CACKLES ....THE COLOSSUS		129	3
CACOPHONOUS (1)			
OVERHEAD GO THE CHOUGHS IN BLACK, CACOPHONOUS FLOCKS -- ..BLACKBER.		168	10
CACOPHONY (1)			
O CACOPHONY, GODDESS OF JAZZ AND OF QUARRELS, ...ALICANTE LULLABY		43	15
CADAVER (2)			
TWO VIEWS OF A CADAVER ROOM ....TWO VIEWS OF A CADAVER ROOM		114	T
THE HEAD OF HIS CADAVER HAD CAVED IN, ..TWO VIEWS OF A CADAVER ROOM		114	6
CADENZAS (1)			
CRESCENDOS, CADENZAS, PRESTOS AND PRESTISSIMOS, ...ALICANTE LULLABY		43	18
CADDIS (1)			
CADDIS WORMS DROWSE IN THEIR SILK CASES, ...POEM.5.F.		135	11
CADILLACS (1)			
AND FOR PUMPKINS TO PURR INTO CADILLACS ....DIALOGUE EN ROUTE		309	28
CAESAR (1)			
I AM NOT A CAESAR. ....THE ARRIVAL OF THE BEE BOX		213	22
CAESARS (1)			
NO SPIRITUAL CAESARS ARE THESE DEAD; ....THE DEAD		320	5
CAGE (4)			
SHAKING IN HER SKULL'S CAGE ....THE SHRIKE		42	12
A BLACK-SHARDED LADY KEEPS ME IN A PARROT CAGE. ....POEM.6.W.		135	9
IN HIS CAGE OF ETHER, HIS CAGE OF STARS. ....LYONNESSE		234	25
IN HIS CAGE OF ETHER, HIS CAGE OF STARS. ....LYONNESSE		234	25
CAGES (2)			
HOW OUR COURTSHIP LIT THE TINDERY CAGES -- ....ZOO KEEPER'S WIFE		155	33

```
                                              TITLE              PAGE  LINE
CAGES (CONT.)
    LIKE PETULANT PARAKEETS CORKED UP IN CAGES  .....MORNING IN THE HOS.  332  19
CAHOOTS (1)
    "MISS ELLA'S GOT LOONY FROM KEEPING IN CAHOOTS  .......ELLA MASON A.   54  35
CAIRN (1)
    AND CONFRONTS A CAIRN OF IRON ORE.  ....THE PRINCESS AND THE GOBLINS  334  43
CAKE (2)
    LIT LIKE A TWO-TIERED WEDDING CAKE  .........................ON DECK  142   7
    A CAKE OF SOAP,  ......................................LADY LAZARUS  246  76
CAKED (1)
    OLD BLOOD OF CAKED WALLS THE SUN HEALS,  ...............BERCK-PLAGE  200  98
CAKES (3)
    AND APPLE CAKES TO COOL. WHAT IS IT  ...............POINT SHIRLEY  110  28
    AND A CABIN BOY WHO COULD DECORATE CAKES IN SIX-COLORED
        FROSTING.  ...........................................THE BABYSITTERS  174  12
    MILLIONS OF NEEDLY GLASS CAKES!  .........................THE TOUR  238  18
CALAMITY'S (1)
    COMPELLED BY CALAMITY'S MAGNET  .........................AFTERMATH  113   1
CALCIUM (1)
    OLD CAVE OF CALCIUM  .....................NICK AND THE CANDLESTICK  241  10
CALCULATE (1)
    TOO LATE TO CALCULATE THE TOPPLING STOCK:  ...............DOOMSDAY  316  17
CALCULATES (1)
    AS SHE CALCULATES EACH SUM.  .............TWO SISTERS OF PERSEPHONE   31   9
CALCULUS (1)
    KNOWS NOT OF DEATH NOR CALCULUS ABOVE  ..........LOVE IS A PARALLAX  331  77
CALDER (1)
    LIKE A RARE CALDER MOBILE IN YOUR MIND.  ..........MIDSUMMER MOBILE  324  14
CALENDARS (1)
    DISRUPT THE CALENDARS NEXT; SEND THE DUTEOUS  ....SONG FOR A REVOLU.  323   9
CALF (1)
    I'M A MEANS, A STAGE, A COW IN CALF.  .....................METAPHORS  116   7
CALIFORNIA (1)
    IN THE CALIFORNIA DELICATESSEN  ........................LITTLE FUGUE  188  32
CALL (19)
    ON THE CALL THIS MAN MADE.  ..........................................FAUN   35   5
    CALL HERE WITH FLYING COLORS ALL WATCHFUL BIRDS *WREATH FOR A BRIDAL   45  13
    TO CALL MY OWN EXCEPT THE AIR-MOTES,  .................LANDOWNERS   53   2
    IF YOU CARE TO CALL THOSE SPASMODIC  ....BLACK ROOK IN RAINY WEATHER   57  37
    CALL HIM ANY NAME, HE'LL COME TO IT.  ...............POEM.4.BEAST.  134  16
    AND FROM OUR OPPOSITE CONTINENTS WE WAVE AND CALL.  THE BABYSITTERS  175  44
    I DIDN'T CALL YOU.  ................................................MEDUSA  225  21
    I DIDN'T CALL YOU AT ALL.  .......................................MEDUSA  225  22
    I CALL YOU ORPHAN, ORPHAN. YOU ARE ILL.  ....................LESBOS  228  38
    I'D CALL IT A SUNSET, BUT  ...............................STOPPED DEAD  230  14
    O MAIDEN AUNT, YOU HAVE COME TO CALL.  ....................THE TOUR  237   1
    THEY HAD TO CALL AND CALL  ...........................LADY LAZARUS  245  41
    THEY HAD TO CALL AND CALL  ...........................LADY LAZARUS  245  41
    I GUESS YOU COULD SAY I'VE A CALL.  ..................LADY LARARUS  245  48
    COME ON CALL LIKE THAT BUT PAN? HE'S  ...DIALOGUE OVER A OUIJA BOARD  277  28
    YOU SAY HE'S TOLD TWO LIES . . . CALL THEM TWO PLUCKED  DIALOGUE O.  283 266
    CHILD TO SEE WHICH ONE OF US CAN CALL  ..DIALOGUE OVER A OUIJA BOARD  284 284
    TO CALL FOR CURTAIN ON OUR THOUSAND SCENES;  .....LOVE IS A PARALLAX  330  44
    WHICH DREAMERS CALL REAL, AND REALISTS, ILLUSION:*LOVE IS A PARALLAX  330  59
CALLA (1)
    COLD FOLDS OF EGO, THE CALLA,  .....................THE NIGHT DANCES  250  12
CALLED (6)
    SHE CAME, AND CALLED HELL TO SUBDUE AN UNRULY MAN  .......SNOWMAN O.   59  23
    LIKE A SOAP-BUBBLE AS YOU CALLED: COME HERE!  THE DISQUIETING MUSES   76  47
    ELEVATIONS TO BE CALLED SOMETHING MORE THAN HILLS.  ABOVE THE OXBOW   88   9
    THEY CALLED THE PLACE LOOKOUT FARM. BACK THEN, THE SUN  ...
                       ... MEMOIRS OF A SPINACH-PICKER   89   1
    I CALLED.  ..................................................EAVESDROPPER  261  46
    CURTSEYED TO YOURS. TOO BAD YOU CALLED PAN UP  ..........DIALOGUE O.  284 280
CALLING (2)
    MAINTAINS IT HAS NO MORE HOLY CALLING  .................TALE OF A TUB   24  11
    OF YOUR ICE-HEARTED CALLING --  .............................LORELEI   95  31
CALLS (3)
    OF BELLS CALLS HOLY ONES, HER TONGUE  .....................VANITY FAIR   32   9
    I AM MAD, CALLS THE SPIDER, WAVING ITS MANY ARMS.  .............TOTEM  265  28
    S. HE CALLS US APES. I'LL SETTLE HIM!  ..DIALOGUE OVER A OUIJA BOARD  284 299
CALM (7)
    THAT BULK SO CALM  ........ON THE DIFFICULTY OF CONJURING UP A DRYAD   66  14
    FLOATS CALM AS A MOON OR A CLOUD.  ....................HEAVY WOMEN  158   7
    BEFORE THEY CAME THE AIR WAS CALM ENOUGH,  ...................TULIPS  161  50
    I AM CLAM. I AM CALM. IT IS THE CALM BEFORE SOMETHING AWFUL: *THREE.  179  92
    I AM CLAM. I AM CALM. IT IS THE CALM BEFORE SOMETHING AWFUL: *THREE.  179  92
    I AM CLAM. I AM CALM. IT IS THE CALM BEFORE SOMETHING AWFUL: *THREE.  179  92
    ENGRAVING ITSELF IN SILVER WITH MARVELOUS CALM.  ........BERCK-PLAGE  199  72
CALMNESS (1)
    HER TIDINESS AND HER CALMNESS AND HER PATIENCE:  .........IN PLASTER  159  25
CAMBRIC (1)
    OF CAMBRIC OR WATERDROPS, WHO KNOWS WHAT BELIEF  ........DIALOGUE O.  282 224
CAMBRIDGE (1)
    IN THE ARCHAEOLOGICAL MUSEUM IN CAMBRIDE IS A STONE ... *DIALOGUE O.   70 E/1
```

CAME (21)
   MAYDAY: TWO CAME TO FIELD IN SUCH WISE: ....BUCOLICS   23   1
   CAME IN FOR MY LOVE'S PRAISING. ....SONG FOR A SUMMER'S DAY   31   10
   TILL THE NIGHT MISTS CAME RISING. ....SONG FOR A SUMMER'S DAY   31   20
   LAST SUMMER I CAME UPON YOUR SPANISH COUSIN, ...SPIDER   48   8
   SHE CAME, AND CALLED HELL TO SUBDUE AN UNRULY MAN ....SNOWMAN O.   59   23
   WE CAME OVER THE MOOR-TOP ....THE GREAT CARBUNCLE   72   1
   THE NOISE CAME FROM OUTSIDE: ....NIGHT SHIFT   76   6
   CAME TO BE LYING ON THIS BAROQUE COUCH ....YADWIGHA.   85   2
   I CAME BEFORE THE WATER- ....MUSSEL HUNTER AT ROCK HARBOR   95   1
   COLORISTS CAME TO GET THE ....MUSSEL HUNTER AT ROCK HARBOR   95   2
   AS IF YOU HAD NEVER EXISTED, AS IF I CAME ...ELECTRA ON AZALEA PATH   116   6
   BEFORE THEY CAME THE AIR WAS CALM ENOUGH, ...TULIPS   161   50
   WHEN I CAME TOO CLOSE TO THE WASTEBASKET. ......BURNING THE LETTERS   204   4
   THE MILK CAME YELLOW, THEN BLUE AND SWEET AS WATER. ..THE DETECTIVE   209   33
   WHERE THOSE WORMS CAME FROM. I SWEAR I DIDN'T EXPECT ...DIALOGUE O.   283 264
   CAME SLIDING DOWN HIS SHOULDERBLADES ....GOLD MOUTHS CRY   302   5
   CAME THE PROFANE STIMULUS TO COUGH; ....DIRGE FOR A JOKER   302   2
   CAME A GARGANTUAN GALACTIC WINK. ....DIALOGUE EN ROUTE   309   42
   THAT CAME BEFORE THE CHANGE OF WEATHER ....THE DREAM   310   3
   "CRYING, SHE CAME TO THE ISLAND ....THE DREAM   311   13
   BECAUSE NEW EXCAVATIONS CAME TOO NEAR   THE PRINCESS AND THE GOBLINS   334   39
CAMELLIA (1)
   ALL BY MYSELF I AM A HUGE CAMELLIA ....FEVER.   232   41
CAMELS (1)
   OUTLANDISH AS DOUBLE-HUMPED CAMELS OR UNICORNS, ...THE EYE-MOTE   109   13
CAMERA-EYE (1)
   SEEK NO STONY CAMERA-EYE TO FIX ....EPITAPH FOR FIRE AND FLOWER   45   8
CAMOUFLAGED (1)
   CAMOUFLAGED IN MOTTLED MAIL ....MUSSEL HUNTER AT ROCK HARBOR   96   31
CAMOUFLAGING (1)
   ONE CAMOUFLAGING ITSELF BEHIND ANOTHER. ....THE RIVAL/DR   291   5
CAMPERS (1)
   TWO CAMPERS IN CLOUD COUNTRY ....TWO CAMPERS IN CLOUD COUNTRY   144   T
CAMPS (1)
   AS WE TWO GLOWER FROM OUR SEPARATE CAMPS, ...DIALOGUE O.   284 291
CAN (98)
CANACEE (1)
   TO CANACEE CRIES GIBBERISH TO COARSENED EARS. ........INCOMMUNICADO   100   14
CANADA (2)
   (ROCK LAKE, CANADA) ....TWO CAMPERS IN CLOUD COUNTRY   144   ST
   THEIR SHADOWS MUST COVER CANADA. ....CROSSING THE WATER   190   3
CANCELS (1)
   LOSS CANCELS PROFIT. ....GREEN ROCK, WINTHROP BAY   105   18
CANCEROUS (1)
   RISE, WITH HER CANCEROUS PALLORS, ...PURDAH   242   13
CANDELABRUM (1)
   QUEER CANDELABRUM. ....POLLY'S TREE   128   23
CANDID (2)
   DRUNK, AND TEA-LEAVES CANDID; THE CLAIRVOYANT SEIZURE ..DIALOGUE O.   279 123
   THROUGH CANDID KITCHENS IN THE RISING SUN ....THE PRINCESS.   334   52
CANDIES (1)
   IT IS YOUR STICKY CANDIES. ....THE OTHER   201   16
CANDLE (6)
   RAYED ROUND A CANDLE FLAME, ...POLLY'S TREE   128   19
   FLICKERING AND POURING, A PITIFUL CANDLE. ....BERCK-PLAGE   199   80
   OF A SNUFFED CANDLE! ....FEVER.   231   10
   THE MIRROR FLOATS US AT ONE CANDLE POWER. ....BY CANDLELIGHT   236   9
   AT FIRST THE CANDLE WILL NOT BLOOM AT ALL -- ......BY CANDLELIGHT   236   16
   THE CANDLE ....NICK AND THE CANDLESTICK   241   20
CANDLE-FLOWERS (1)
   THE EXTREME UNCTION OF ITS YELLOW CANDLE-FLOWERS.*THE RABBIT CATCHER   193   8
CANDLELIGHT (1)
   BY CANDLELIGHT ....BY CANDLELIGHT   236   T
CANDLES (8)
   FIVE WICKLESS CANDLES ....WORDS FOR A NURSERY   74   45
   CARRIES ITS CANDLES SLOWLY OFF. ....ON DECK   142   8
   CANDLES ....CANDLES   148   T
   THEY ARE THE LAST ROMANTICS, THESE CANDLES: ....CANDLES   148   1
   THE FACE OF EFFIGY, GENTLED BY CANDLES, ..THE MOON AND THE YEW TREE   173   20
   THEN SHE TURNS TO THOSE LIARS, THE CANDLES OR THE MOON. .....MIRROR   174   12
   ROSE CANDLES FLICKER ON THE LILAC WALL ....CINDERELLA   304   7
   CAPER WITH CANDLES IN THEIR HEADS; ....LOVE IS A PARALLAX   329   33
CANDLE'S (1)
   I'LL FLY THROUGH THE CANDLE'S MOUTH LIKE A SINGELESS MOTH.*POEM.6.W.   135   20
CANDLESTICK (1)
   NICK AND THE CANDLESTICK ....NICK AND THE CANDLESTICK   240   T
CANDOR (2)
   OF CANDOR PARES WHITE FLESH TO THE WHITE BONE, ...MOONRISE   98   27
   WHOSE CANDOR EXPOSES ....MOONSONG AT MORNING   317   23
CANDY (1)
   SCATTERING CANDY FROM A ZEPPELIN, ...LOVE IS A PARALLAX   329   35
CANNON (2)
   SO THE DISKS OF THE BRAIN REVOLVE, LIKE THE MUZZLES OF CANNON. ...
                                    ... THE COURAGE OF SHUTTING-UP   210   16

	TITLE	PAGE	LINE

CANNON (CONT.)
PUNCHING OUT ABSENCE! LIKE CANNON. ....GETTING THERE 248 8
CANNONBALLS (1)
AT HIS HEELS A PILE OF FIVE BRASS CANNONBALLS, ...BY CANDLELIGHT 237 33
CANNONS (1)
THE SEA CANNONS INTO THEIR EAR, BUT THEY DON'T BUDGE. ...FINISTERRE 169 8
CANNOT (25)
CANT (1)
E.G., BY CANT OF LIGHT ...ON THE DIFFICULTY OF CONJURING UP A DRYAD 66 22
CAN'T (14)
CANTALOUPES (1)
BUMP-RINDED CANTALOUPES ....FIESTA MELONS 46 13
CANTING (1)
TO BUILD HIS CANTING TOWERS. WHILE YOU, YOU LONG ....DIALOGUE O. 280 136
CANVAS-SIDED (1)
IN THEIR CANVAS-SIDED COTS, NAMES TIED TO THEIR WRISTS, *THREE WOMEN 183 220
CANYONS (1)
SILVER BEAST BETWEEN TWO DARK CANYONS, ..THE COURAGE OF SHUTTING-UP 210 9
CAP (1)
MONKEY LIVED UNDER THE DUNCE CAP. POEM.4.BEAST. 134 8
CAPACITY (1)
TO FULL CAPACITY. WE CLIMB IN HOPES ....ABOVE THE OXBOW 88 26
CAPE (1)
GOOD OF THE CAPE LIGHT THAT SCOURS ....MUSSEL HUNTER AT ROCK HARBOR 95 3
CAPER (2)
CAPER WITH CANDLES IN THEIR HEADS; ....LOVE IS A PARALLAX 329 33
CAPER ON LEAFSTALK LEGS ACROSS MY DOORSILL, EPITAPH IN THREE PARTS 337 24
CAPES (1)
THE RITUAL DEATH EACH TIME BOTCHED AMONG DROPPED CAPES,
                         ILL-JUDGED STABS, ...THE GORING 47 3
CAPRICCIOSOS (1)
LET BE YOUR CON BRIOS, YOUR CAPRICCIOSOS, ...ALICANTE LULLABY 43 17
CAPRICE (1)
OF CAPRICE. ....MOONSONG AT MORNING 317 12
CAPS (1)
THEY PASS THE WAY GULLS PASS INLAND IN THEIR WHITE CAPS, ...TULIPS 160 12
CAPSULE (2)
OR YOUR LIQUORS SEEP TO ME, IN THIS GLASS CAPSULE, POPPIES IN JULY 203 13
MY SLEEPING CAPSULE, MY RED AND BLUE ZEPPELIN ....THE JAILER 226 12
CAPSULES (1)
WHERE ARE YOUR OPIATES, YOUR NAUSEOUS CAPSULES? ....POPPIES IN JULY 203 10
CAPTAIN'S (1)
THE CAPTAIN'S BATMAN, ...WORDS FOR A NURSERY 74 37
CAR (8)
BEHIND THE GLASS OF THIS CAR ....BERCK-PLAGE 200 109
GRINNED LIKE A GETAWAY CAR. ....BURNING THE LETTERS 204 8
SIMPLY OPEN THE DOOR AND STEP OUT OF THE CAR ....STOPPED DEAD 230 24
NAME, HOUSE, CAR KEYS, ...AMNESIAC 232 3
STEP TO YOU FROM THE BLACK CAR OF LETHE, ...GETTING THERE 249 67
A CAR DOOR SLAM; VOICES COMING NEAR; ....FAMILY REUNION 300 2
TO HALT OUR CAR IN HEADLONG COURSE. ....THE DREAM 310 12
OUR YEARS. DEATH COMES IN A CASUAL STEEL CAR, YET ..SONNET: TO TIME 311 3
CARACALLA (1)
AQUEDUCTS, THE BATHS OF CARACALLA, THE EAGLE NOSE! ....SURGEON. 171 28
CARAPACE (1)
CARAPACE SMASHED, ...THE JAILER 226 14
CARAVAN (1)
OF WEEVIL TRIBE AND LOCUST CARAVAN ....THE DISPOSSESSED 318 8
CARBON (7)
THE NIGHT SKY IS ONLY A SORT OF CARBON PAPER, ...INSOMNIAC 163 1
WHITE AND BLANK, EXPANSIVE AS CARBON MONOXIDE. ....THE RIVAL 166 15
SO I POKE AT THE CARBON BIRDS IN MY HOUSEDRESS. *BURNING THE LETTERS 204 29
ARMIES OF THEM. THEY ARE CARBON MONOXIDE. ....A BIRTHDAY PRESENT 207 40
IGNITING ITS CARBON MONOXIDES, BY EYES ....POPPIES IN OCTOBER 240 8
DOWN SHOES FOR A POLISH OF CARBON ....THE MUNICH MANNEQUINS 263 19
BEING CRYSTALLIZED FROM CARBON ....NOTES TO A NEOPHYTE 307 23
CARBUNCLE (1)
THE GREAT CARBUNCLE ....THE GREAT CARBUNCLE 72 T
CARCASS (2)
THE SECOND CARCASS MAKES A DUEL OF THE AFFAIR: ....BLUE MOLES 126 8
HOW LONG HIS CARCASS HAS FOUNDERED UNDER ....THE BURNT-OUT SPA 138 8
CARD (2)
STIFF AS A QUEEN ON A PLAYING CARD. ....THE BULL OF BENDYLAW 108 5
OR PLAY ANOTHER CARD GAME WHEN YOU'VE WON; ....ADMONITIONS 319 2
CARDBOARD (2)
THERE WAS SOMETHING ABOUT THEM LIKE CARDBOARD, AND NOW I HAD
        CAUGHT IT, ...THREE WOMEN 177 17
OF CARDBOARD CARTONS THE COLOR OF CEMENT OR A DOG PACK ....BURNING. 204 11
CARDINALS (1)
WHILE TULIPS BOW LIKE A COLLEGE OF CARDINALS ....APRIL AUBADE 312 7
CARE (3)
IF YOU CARE TO CALL THOSE SPASMODIC ....BLACK ROOK IN RAINY WEATHER 57 37
THOR IS ANGRY: WE DON'T CARE!" ....THE DISQUIETING MUSES 75 23
NOW, YOU REALLY DON'T MUCH CARE WHICH, OR WHAT ....DIALOGUE O. 280 151

CARED (1)
    THEY HAVE LIVED BEHIND GLASS ALL THEIR LIVES, THEY HAVE BEEN
         CARED FOR TENDERLY. ....THREE WOMEN 184 264
CAREER (2)
    THERE'S NO CAREER IN THE VENTURE ....THE TIMES ARE TIDY 107   6
    COULD CLIMAX HIS CAREER, ...TRIO OF LOVE SONGS 314   32
CAREFUL (2)
    SO I WAS CAREFUL NOT TO UPSET HER IN ANY WAY ....IN PLASTER 160   46
    LIKE A GOOD BOY. BE CAREFUL. I'M NOT SURE THAT HE ......DIALOGUE O. 282 207
CAREFULLY (2)
    WEARS PURPLE, STEPS CAREFULLY ....MISS DRAKE PROCEEDS TO SUPPER   41   6
    AND WALKED CAREFULLY, PRECARIOUSLY, LIKE SOMETHING RARE.*THREE WOMEN 178   73
CARGO (2)
    I HAVE LET THINGS SLIP, A THIRTY-YEAR-OLD CARGO BOAT ....TULIPS 161   22
    ITS CARGO OF AGONY TOWARD ME,INESCAPABLE, TIDAL. ....THREE WOMEN 179 110
CARICATURES (1)
    CARICATURES ITSELF AND THRIVES ....THE BEGGARS   47   8
CARMINE (1)
    AS ROSES BROACH THEIR CARMINE IN A MIRROR. FLUX ....ABOVE THE OXBOW   89   44
CAROL (1)
    GRAVES ALL CAROL IN REPLY. ....LOVE IS A PARALLAX 330   42
CAROLING (1)
    THERE'S CAROLING ....A WINTER'S TALE   87   16
CAROUSALS (1)
    TO GET YOUR CAROUSALS TOLD: ....SPIDER   48   6
CARP (2)
    GOLD CARP LOOM IN THE POOLS. ....YADDO: THE GRAND MANOR 123   8
    PLATONIC TABLE WHERE IT LIVES. THE BABY CARP ....PRIVATE GROUND 130   11
CARPENTER (1)
    ALL NIGHT I CARPENTER ....THALIDOMIDE 252   17
CARPET (5)
    COUCH, CARPET, FLOOR ....MONOLOGUE AT 3 A.M.   40   4
    ON A SQUARE NO BIGGER THAN A CARPET ....ON DECK 142   12
    CARPET ROLLS ....CUT 235   12
    ACROSS THE INDIAN CARPET, THE COLD FLOOR, ...BY CANDLELIGHT 237   25
    ROLLS OUT A CARPET, A HUSH. ....GIGOLO 268   24
CARPETS (1)
    THERE IS THE SMELL OF POLISH, THERE ARE PLUSH CARPETS.*THE DETECTIVE 209   17
CARPET'S (1)
    INTO THE CARPET'S DESIGN. ....MISS DRAKE PROCEEDS TO SUPPER   41   13
CARRIAGES (1)
    THE CARRIAGES ROCK, THEY ARE CRADLES. ....GETTING THERE 249   64
CARRIES (1)
    CARRIES ITS CANDLES SLOWLY OFF. ....ON DECK 142   8
CARRION (1)
    TWO PEOPLE ONLY ARE BLIND TO THE CARRION ARMY: ....TWO VIEWS. 114   13
CARROT (1)
    IN RINGING ORANGE LIKE A STELLAR CARROT. ...THE GHOST'S LEAVETAKING   91   28
CARROUSEL (1)
    I RIDE EARTH'S BURNING CARROUSEL ....ON THE PLETHORA OF DRYADS   67   29
CARRY (6)
    NO WORD MAKE THEM CARRY WATER OR FIRE THE KINDLING ....TWO CAMP. 144   5
    THIS IS A DISEASE I CARRY HOME, THIS IS A DEATH. ....THREE WOMEN 177   36
    QUIET, LIKE THE LITTLE EMPTINESSES I CARRY. ....THREE WOMEN 178   70
    THE BOOKS I CARRY WEDGE INTO MY SIDE. ....THREE WOMEN 185 305
    THEY CAN ONLY CARRY THEIR DEAD. ....WINTERING 218   37
    I'LL CARRY IT OFF LIKE A RICH PRETTY GIRL, ...STOPPED DEAD 230   23
CARRYING (1)
    A WORKMAN WALKS BY CARRYING A PINK TORSO. POEM.7.S. 137   31
CARS (3)
    OF ASPARAGUS HEADS. CARS RUN THEIR SUAVE ....ABOVE THE OXBOW   89   50
    TRADING THEIR POISONS, THE NORTH AND SOUTH BOUND CARS*PRIVATE GROUND 130   16
    THE CARS IN THE PLACE DE LA CONCORDE -- ....A SECRET 220   38
CART (2)
    GLIDING UP IN LOW GEAR BEHIND THE CART. ....BERCK-PLAGE 200 112
    FOLLOWING THE COFFIN ON ITS FLOWERY CART LIKE A BEAUTIFUL WOMAN, ...
                                                  ... BERCK-PLAGE 200 115
CARTONS (1)
    OF CARDBOARD CARTONS THE COLOR OF CEMENT OR A DOG PACK ....BURNING. 204   11
CARVE (1)
    AND THE KNIFE NOT CARVE, BUT ENTER ....A BIRTHDAY PRESENT 208   60
CARVED (3)
    TWO CARVED SLEIGHS ....YADDO: THE GRAND MANOR 123   15
    I THINK HER LITTLE HEAD IS CARVED IN WOOD, ...THREE WOMEN 182 211
    HIS LITTLE FACE IS CARVED IN PAINED, RED WOOD. ....EVENT 194   9
CARVING (1)
    AND THE WHITE-HAIRED JEWELER FROM DENMARK IS CARVING ....ON DECK 143   31
CASE (6)
    MY PATENT LEATHER OVERNIGHT CASE LIKE A BLACK PILLBOX, ...TULIPS 160   19
    OF UNANSWERED LETTERS, COFFINED IN A LETTER CASE. ......THREE WOMEN 182 200
    A GLASS CASE ....BURNING THE LETTERS 204   16
    THIS IS A CASE WITHOUT A BODY. ....THE DETECTIVE 209   24
    IT IS A CASE OF VAPORIZATION. ....THE DETECTIVE 209   26
    IN ANY CASE, YOU ARE ALWAYS THERE, ...MEDUSA 225   16

TITLE   PAGE LINE

CASES (2)
CADDIS WORMS DROWSE IN THEIR SILK CASES, ...POEM.5.F. 135 11
THE PILLOW CASES ARE SWEETENING. ....BERCK-PLAGE 198 68
CASK (1)
TAPPED LIKE A CASK, THE YEARS DRAINING INTO MY PILLOW. ...FACE LIFT 156 18
CASKETS (1)
LOCKED IN CRYSTAL CASKETS ARE THE LAKES, ...PROLOGUE TO SPRING 322 13
CASQUES (1)
KNIGHTS MIGHT DOFF THEIR CASQUES. THE CRABS ....MUSSEL HUNTER.   96 28
CASSIOPEIA'S (1)
I MISS ORION AND CASSIOPEIA'S CHAIR. MAYBE THEY ARE ....STARS. 165 18
CASSOCK (1)
IS IT ANY WONDER HE AFFECTS A BLACK CASSOCK? ....BERCK-PLAGE 196 13
CAST (6)
IN THE SHADOW CAST BY MY DISMAL-HEADED ....THE DISQUIETING MUSES   75 30
CAST A ROUND WHITE SHADOW IN THEIR DYING. ....MOONRISE   98   6
WE CAST OUR SKINS AND SLIDE ....THE SLEEPERS 123 23
BERRIES CAST DARK ....ARIEL 239 11
I CAST OFF MY IDENTITY ....FAMILY REUNION 301 29
TO CAST LOCK, STOCK AND BARREL UNDER BAN; ....THE DISPOSSESSED 318 11
CASTANETS (1)
HER SALLOW RODENT TEETH LIKE CASTANETS ...............INCOMMUNICADO 100   4
CASTING (1)
OVER MY MIND, CASTING A SHADOW. SORROW   DIALOGUE OVER A OUIJA BOARD 285 312
CASTLE (3)
LIKE A DAUNTED WITCH, QUITTING CASTLE WHEN REAL DAYS BREAK. ...
... CONVERSATION AMONG THE RUINS   21   8
THE MASSIVE CASTLE TURRETS ....LORELEI   94   7
COMING AT ME, LIKE A CASTLE, FROM THE TOP OF THE RIVER. *THREE WOMEN 178 51
CASTLED (1)
AND CASTLED IN IT LIKE A KING. ....ON DECK 143 15
CASTLES (4)
OF DRAFTY CELLS AND DRAFTIER CASTLES, ...A LESSON IN VENGEANCE   80   2
ON THIS HILL, WITH ITS VIEW OF LIT CASTLES, EACH SWUNG BELL   STARS. 166 38
CASTLES UPON THE SMUG-SHAPED CHAIRS. ALL THIS I ....DIALOGUE O. 279 118
CASTLES WHEN WE GLANCE ASIDE. THAT'S THAT. ....DIALOGUE O. 286 356
CASUAL (3)
THAN AGAINST THIS ONSLAUGHT, THESE CASUAL BLASTS OF ICE   CHANNEL C.   27 17
OUR YEARS. DEATH COMES IN A CASUAL STEEL CAR, YET ..SONNET: TO TIME 311   3
TICKS TEMPO TO THE CASUAL CLIMB ...MORNING IN THE HOSPITAL SOLARIUM 332 16
CASUIST (1)
AND CASUIST ARGUMENTS RUN RIOT   INSOLENT STORM STRIKES AT THE SKULL 326 21
CAT (14)
IN THE WAKE OF THIS FIERCE CAT, ...PURSUIT   22 21
THE ONE-EARED CAT ....RESOLVE   52   5
THE CAT UNSHEATHES ITS CLAWS ....RESOLVE   52 17
GOLDFINCH, GOLDFISH, GOLDEN TIGER CAT STOCK- .....IN MIDAS' COUNTRY   99 13
WITH THE LOVE-HOT HERB, THE TALKING CAT, ...THE TIMES ARE TIDY 107 13
I HADN'T A CAT YET. ....FACE LIFT 156 24
THEY ARE OPENING LIKE THE MOUTH OF SOME GREAT AFRICAN CAT, ..TULIPS 162 59
I SCRATCH LIKE A CAT. ....THE OTHER 202 28
WHERE I RELAX, FOETUS OR CAT, ...THE JAILER 226   9
THAT'S MY FROST BOX, NO CAT, ...THE TOUR 237 15
THOUGH IT LOOKS LIKE A CAT, WITH ITS FLUFFY STUFF, PURE WHITE.*TOUR. 237 16
AND LIKE THE CAT I HAVE NINE TIMES TO DIE. ....LADY LAZARUS 244 21
HIS BALLOON SQUEAK LIKE A CAT. ....BALLOONS 272 22
IT'S TIME TO VANISH LIKE THE CHESHIRE CAT ....A SORCERER B. 324 12
CATACOMBS (2)
A TALL METROPOLIS OF CATACOMBS ....DOOM OF EXILES 318   3
IN PANIC AT THE CROP OF CATACOMBS ....TERMINAL 328   3
CATALPA (2)
HEART-SHAPED LEAVES, LIKE CATALPA LEAVES, AND LILIES .....YADWIGHA.   85   6
WHITE CATALPA FLOWERS TOWER, TOPPLE, ...MOONRISE   98   5
CATAPULTS (1)
HE CATAPULTS IN AIR; ....TRIO OF LOVE SONGS 314 30
CATARACT (1)
A DEVIL'S CATARACT OF BLACK .....BLACK PINE TREE IN AN ORANGE LIGHT 328   8
CATASTROPHE (1)
CATASTROPHE A WRITHING LENGTH OF COBRA, ...PERSEUS   83 22
CATCH (9)
SHREWD CATCH SILTING OUR EACH BRIGHT ACT BACK ....FIRESONG   30 13
LET JACK CATCH FIRE." ....TINKER JACK AND THE TIDY WIVES   35 33
NO GESTURE OF YOURS OR MINE COULD CATCH THEIR ATTENTION, TWO CAMP. 144   4
THEIR SMILES CATCH ONTO MY SKIN, LITTLE SMILING HOOKS. ......TULIPS 160 21
HER CRIES ARE HOOKS THAT CATCH AND GRATE LIKE CATS. ....THREE WOMEN 182 207
ONE SCARF WILL CATCH AND ANCHOR IN THE WHEEL. ....FEVER. 231 13
OF THE NECK I CANNOT CATCH, ...ARIEL 239   9
MIRROR TALK YOU LOVE TO CATCH ME AT. ..................EAVESDROPPER 260 36
CAN ONCE IN A BLUE MOON CATCH THE SHADOWS OF ....DIALOGUE O. 282 222
CATCHER (1)
THE RABBIT CATCHER ....THE RABBIT CATCHER 193   T
CAT-CLEVER (1)
CAT-CLEVER ON PERILOUS WIRE ....AERIALIST 331   8
CATERWAUL (1)
ON STORM-STRUCK DECK, WIND SIRENS CATERWAUL; ......CHANNEL CROSSING   26   1

CATGUT (1)
   VOLT UPON VOLT. CATGUT STITCHES MY FISSURES. POEM.7.S.   137   30
CAT-HAUNT (1)
   ON SEEING OUR NEIGHBOR'S CAT-HAUNT,   ELLA MASON AND HER ELEVEN CATS   53   4
CATHEAD (1)
   YELLOW CATHEAD, BLUE FISH --- ....BALLOONS   271   9
CATHEDRALS (1)
   THAT LENGTHEN FROM ANCIENT CATHEDRALS ....MYSTIC   268   14
CAT-LADY (1)
   "LOOK! THERE SHE GOES, CAT-LADY MASON!" ....ELLA MASON A.   54   31
CATS (14)
   CATS PLAY IN THE STALKS. ....DEPARTURE   51   8
   ELLA MASON AND HER ELEVEN CATS ......ELLA MASON AND HER ELEVEN CATS   53   T
   OLD ELLA MASON KEEPS CATS, ELEVEN AT LAST COUNT, ...ELLA MASON A.   53   1
   THAT MANY CATS." ....ELLA MASON AND HER ELEVEN CATS   53   6
   OF FINICAL CATS. ....ELLA MASON AND HER ELEVEN CATS   53   12
   ON ALL BUT CATS. ....ELLA MASON AND HER ELEVEN CATS   54   18
   TABLE-TOP, CUPBOARD SHELF, CATS LOUNGED BRAZEN, ...ELLA MASON A.   54   22
   SUCH STENTORIAN CATS! ....ELLA MASON AND HER ELEVEN CATS   54   24
   OF GUARDIAN CATS CROUCHED ROUND THEIR IDOL, ...ELLA MASON A.   54   28
   SPHINX-QUEEN OF CATS. ....ELLA MASON AND HER ELEVEN CATS   54   30
   WITH ELEVEN CATS." ....ELLA MASON AND HER ELEVEN CATS   54   36
   NIGHTLONG, IN THE GRANITE YARD, INVISIBLE CATS ....INSOMNIAC   163   29
   HER CRIES ARE HOOKS THAT CATCH AND GRATE LIKE CATS. ....THREE WOMEN   182   207
   I AM PACKING THE SICK CATS. ....LESBOS   229   70
CAT'S (4)
   YOUR MOUTH OPENS CLEAN AS A CAT'S. THE WINDOW SQUARE ..MORNING SONG   157   15
   SIX CAT'S EYES IN THE WINE CELLAR, ...WINTERING   217   5
   THEY ARE MAKING A CAT'S CRADLE, THEY ARE SUICIDAL. ....STINGS/DR   293   7
   THE STARCHED WHITE COAT, THE CAT'S PAW WALK, ...MORNING IN THE HOS.   332   12
CAT-TAILS (2)
   CAT-TAILS PART WHERE THE TAME CYGNETS STEER. ....WATERCOLOR.   112   14
   FRAMED IN A BASKETWORK OF CAT-TAILS. ....THE BURNT-OUT SPA   138   26
CATTLE (3)
   THEN, HONOR-BOUND, MUTE GRAZING CATTLE; ....BUCOLICS   24   11
   DREAMS THAT HIS FATTEST CATTLE DWINDLE, FEVERED ....GOATSUCKER   111   6
   HEN HUTS AND CATTLE GREEN ....MAN IN BLACK   119   9
CAT-VOICE (1)
   TATTLING IN ITS CAT-VOICE OF DEPARTURE, DEPARTURE. ....A LIFE   150   32
CAUGHT (11)
   SUCH POVERTY ASSAULTS THE EGO; CAUGHT ....TALE OF A TUB   24   4
   CAUGHT IN A HAZARDOUS MEDIUM THAT MIGHT ....VANITY FAIR   32   3
   CAUGHT (AS IT WERE) IN THE MUCK-TRAP ....LETTER TO A PURIST   37   11
   HUNG CAUGHT IN DARK-WEBBED BRANCHES LIKE A FABULOUS HERON. ...
          ... DIALOGUE BETWEEN GHOST AND PRIEST   38   6
   FROM WHICH COILS, CAUGHT ANTS WAVED LEGS IN ....SPIDER   49   19
   KNOTTED, CAUGHT, SURVIVES ....FULL FATHOM FIVE   92   9
   THERE WAS SOMETHING ABOUT THEM LIKE CARDBOARD, AND NOW I HAD
          CAUGHT IT, ...THREE WOMEN   177   17
   HER RADIANCE SCATHES ME. OR PERHAPS I HAVE CAUGHT HER. ....ELM   192   24
   THE SPIDER-MEN HAVE CAUGHT YOU, ...GULLIVER   251   12
   IT IS LIKE SOMETHING SHE HAS CAUGHT FOR ME. ....ELM/DR   292   5
   AND I, LIKE THE CHILDREN, CAUGHT ....TOUCH-AND-GO   336   17
CAUL (1)
   INTO A SOFT CAUL OF FORGETFULNESS. POEM.5.F.   135   9
CAULDRON (2)
   EYE, THE CAULDRON OF MORNING. ....ARIEL   240   31
   CAULDRON, TALKING AND CRACKLING ....THE COURIERS   247   8
CAULS (1)
   COUCHED IN CAULS OF CLAY AS IN HOLY ROBES, ...THE DEAD   320   2
CAUSE (2)
   OF FLAWED EARTH-FLESH COULD CAUSE THIS SORRY PASS? .....DIALOGUE B.   39   32
   HIS NEXT MARTYR TO THE GROSS CAUSE ....SPIDER   49   26
CAUSED (1)
   WHICH HAD CAUSED HIS DEAR GIRL PAIN. ....BUCOLICS   24   20
CAUSEWAYS (1)
   CROSSED BY THREE CAUSEWAYS, ...WORDS FOR A NURSERY   74   28
CAUSTIC (2)
   SHE HEARS THE CAUSTIC TICKING OF THE CLOCK. ....CINDERELLA   304   14
   TONIGHT THE CAUSTIC WIND, LOVE, ...JILTED   304   5
CAVE (5)
   OLD CAVE OF CALCIUM ....NICK AND THE CANDLESTICK   241   10
   I HAVE HUNG OUR CAVE WITH ROSES, ...NICK AND THE CANDLESTICK   241   32
   THE GRAVE CAVE ATE WILL BE ....LADY LAZARUS   244   17
   OUTSIDE THE CAVE WHOSE CONTOURS MOST REMIND ....DIALOGUE O.   281   200
   HIDE, HIDE, IN THE SAFE CAVE ....GO GET THE GOODLY SQUAB   313   15
CAVED (1)
   THE HEAD OF HIS CADAVER HAD CAVED IN, ..TWO VIEWS OF A CADAVER ROOM   114   6
CAVE-MOUTH (1)
   AND SHADOWS ONLY -- CAVE-MOUTH BRISTLE BESET -- ....GOATSUCKER   111   13
CAVES (2)
   LEAVES, UNDOING THEIR YELLOW CAVES ....BLUE MOLES   126   11
   BE PLUCKED FROM CAVES OF DAPPLED AMBER WHERE ......MIDSUMMER MOBILE   324   9
CAVIARE (1)
   A CAVIARE DECAY OF RICH BROCADES. ....TERMINAL   328   8

	TITLE	PAGE	LINE

CEASE (2)
CEASE, AND I NEARED THE SILENCED ......MUSSEL HUNTER AT ROCK HARBOR 95 15
TODAY WE MOVE IN JADE AND CEASE WITH GARNET ....SONNET: TO TIME 311 1
CEILING (4)
JUST HOW GUILTY ARE WE WHEN THE CEILING ....TALE OF A TUB 24 9
OF THE OLD STAR-MAP ON THE CEILING. ....ON DECK 142 5
HE FLOATS AN INCH FROM THE CEILING, ...THE SURGEON AT 2 A.M. 171 45
CEILING WITHOUT A STAR. ....CHILD 265 12
CELEBRATE (2)
OF OTHER MEN, WHERE STATUES CELEBRATE ....CHANNEL CROSSING 27 38
CRIES: "CELEBRATE SYRINX WHOSE DEMURS ....VIRGIN IN A TREE 81 13
CELEBRATION (1)
A CELEBRATION, THIS IS. ....CUT 235 17
CELERY (1)
HOEING LETTUCE, WEEDING CELERY. ....BITTER STRAWBERRIES 299 19
CELESTIAL (5)
OVER GABLES THE MOON'S CELESTIAL ONION ..SOLILOQUY OF THE SOLIPSIST 37 8
AS IF A CELESTIAL BURNING TOOK ....BLACK ROOK IN RAINY WEATHER 57 17
AND REPOISE UNTIL TIME STOP, THE CELESTIAL BALANCE ....PERSEUS 84 48
AT ITS CRYPTIC CELESTIAL ORIGIN. ....DIALOGUE EN ROUTE 309 36
AND VIOLATES CELESTIAL CUSTOM ..INSOLENT STORM STRIKES AT THE SKULL 326 31
CELIBATE (1)
O LOVE, O CELIBATE. ....LETTER IN NOVEMBER 254 31
CELL (3)
CELL BY CELL FROM A QUIET CORNER, ...POEM.2.DARK. 132 3
CELL BY CELL FROM A QUIET CORNER, ...POEM.2.DARK. 132 3
IT'S EASY ENOUGH TO DO IT IN A CELL. ....LADY LAZARUS 245 49
CELLAR (2)
SHIP TIMBERS IN THROUGH THE CELLAR WINDOW; ....POINT SHIRLEY 110 14
SIX CAT'S EYES IN THE WINE CELLAR, ...WINTERING 217 5
CELLARS (1)
IT HAS SO MANY CELLARS, ...POEM.2.DARK. 132 8
CELLAR'S (1)
THE CELLAR'S BELLY. THEY'VE BLOWN MY SPARKLER OUT. POEM.6.W. 135 8
CELLOPHANE (3)
LAY OVER THE LEAVES LIKE A CLEAR CELLOPHANE, ...SPINACH-PICKER. 89 4
A SORT OF CELLOPHANE BALLOON. ....PARLIAMENT HILL FIELDS 153 47
CELLOPHANE I CANNOT CRACK. ....PARALYTIC 266 31
CELLOS (1)
THE CELLOS OF MOANS I EAT EGGS -- ....GIGOLO 267 15
CELLS (8)
OF DRAFTY CELLS AND DRAFTIER CASTLES, ...A LESSON IN VENGEANCE 80 2
SEALING OFF HER BROOD CELLS, HER HONEY, AND QUIETLY HUMMING. ..BEE. 212 35
WHILE IN THEIR FINGERJOINT CELLS THE NEW VIRGINS ...THE BEE MEETING 212 45
HAVE A THOUSAND CLEAN CELLS BETWEEN US, ...STINGS 214 6
BROOD CELLS GRAY AS THE FOSSILS OF SHELLS ....STINGS 214 12
PLYING THEIR WILD CELLS IN MY KEEL'S SHADOW, ...STINGS 225 7
STEALER OF CELLS, STEALER OF BEAUTY -- ....THE FEARFUL 256 12
DRIVING THE DULL CELLS WILD. .........................EAVESDROPPER 260 18
CEMENT (2)
OF CARDBOARD CARTONS THE COLOR OF CEMENT OR A DOG PACK ....BURNING. 204 11
IN A SORT OF CEMENT WELL ....LESBOS 227 13
CENTER (11)
YOU SPUN THE COSMIC WEB: YOU SQUINT FROM CENTER FIELD. ......SPIDER 48 7
AND, FIXED IN THE CRYSTAL CENTER, GRINNING FIERCE: ...CRYSTAL GAZER 56 47
AND SITS IN THE CENTER OF HER LOVELESS SPOKES. ....WIDOW 164 12
I AM THE CENTER OF AN ATROCITY. ....THREE WOMEN 180 132
IT BREATHES FROM MY SHEETS, THE COLD DEAD CENTER *A BIRTHDAY PRESENT 207 50
RED STIGMATA AT THE VERY CENTER, ...MEDUSA 225 9
OFF FROM THE CENTER LIKE HORSES. ....WORDS 270 5
IN THE CENTER OF THE GARDEN NAMED AFTER QUEEN MARY. ..QUEEN MARY'S. 290 3
AT THE CENTER SHE IS STILL, VERY STILL WITH WISDOM. ....ELM/DR 292 7
ON ENVIOUS STRINGS, AND YOU ARE THE CENTER. ....STINGS/DR 293 3
IN DEAD CENTER OF HER ACT ....AERIALIST 331 16
CENTRE (1)
TOAD-STONE! I SEE I MUST WEAR YOU IN THE CENTRE OF MY FOREHEAD ...
... THE RIVAL/DR 291 27
CENTURIES (3)
OF DIGESTING WHAT CENTURIES ALONE DIGEST: ....PERSEUS 82 2
THE SMUG CENTURIES OF THE PIG -- ....THE MANOR GARDEN 125 6
THE BRONZE BOY STANDS KNEEDEEP IN CENTURIES, ...GOLD MOUTHS CRY 302 10
CENTURY (1)
..COFFIN OF THE FOURTH CENTURY A.D. CONTAINING THE
SKELETON... ....ALL THE DEAD DEARS 70 E/2
CERBERUS (1)
TONGUES OF DULL, FAT CERBERUS ....FEVER. 231 4
CEREMONIOUS (1)
DURING A CEREMONIOUS APRIL WALK ....SPINSTER 49 2
CEREMONIOUSLY (1)
AND RESOLVED MORE CEREMONIOUSLY TO LODGE ....LADY AND T. 69 22
CEREMONY (3)
WHAT CEREMONY OF WORDS CAN PATCH THE HAVOC? .........CONVERSATION. 21 14
THE STRONGEST WILL SEEMED A WILL TOWARD CEREMONY. OBESE, DARK- ...
... THE GORING 47 4

CEREMONY (CONT.)
    WITHOUT CEREMONY, OR PORTENT. ....BLACK ROOK IN RAINY WEATHER   57   10
CERISE (1)
    OF CERISE AND PINK FROM THE RHODODENDRON, ...RHODODENDRON.   104   22
CERTAIN (3)
    A CERTAIN MINOR LIGHT MAY STILL ....BLACK ROOK IN RAINY WEATHER   57   14
    BE CERTAIN SOME SUCH PACT'S ....VIRGIN IN A TREE   82   31
    BUT A CERTAIN MEANING GREEN. ....THE HERMIT AT OUTERMOST HOUSE   119   16
CERTAINLY (2)
    AND THE WHITE PERSON IS CERTAINLY THE SUPERIOR ONE. ......IN PLASTER   158   3
    SEA-COLD, SEA-COLD IT CERTAINLY IS. ....LYONNESSE   233   2
CERTAINTY (1)
    CERTAINTY OF THE BRONZE BOY ....GOLD MOUTHS CRY   302   2
CESSATION (2)
    THERE IS THIS CESSATION. THIS TERRIBLE CESSATION OF EVERYTHING. ...
                                                ... THREE WOMEN   181   180
    THERE IS THIS CESSATION. THIS TERRIBLE CESSATION OF EVERYTHING. ...
                                                ... THREE WOMEN   181   180
CHAFE (1)
    WHY, YOUR HAND'S COLD AS ICE! THEN CHAFE THE COLD ......DIALOGUE O.   285   333
CHAGRIN (4)
    LONGER ON THIS LANDSCAPE OF CHAGRIN; .................CONVERSATION.   21   8
    THEY BRASSILY PICKED, SLOWED BY NO CHAGRIN, ...RHODODENDRON.   104   24
    PUT UP WITH UNTIL CHAGRIN GIVES PLACE ....THE COMPANIONABLE ILLS   105   3
    BY SOME UNUTTERABLE CHAGRIN, ...THE RAVAGED FACE   115   3
CHAIN (2)
    NOT TO BE STAYED BY A DAISY CHAIN ....THE BULL OF BENDYLAW   108   17
    HE IS HUGGING HIS BALL AND CHAIN DOWN BY THE GATE ....LESBOS   229   73
CHAINED (1)
    FIRELESS, SEVEN CHILL SEAS CHAINED TO HIS ANKLE. *EVERLASTING MONDAY   62   12
CHAINMAIL (1)
    GOING UNDER THE CHAINMAIL, ...MEDALLION   124   17
CHAIR (9)
    OF KNOTTED TABLE AND CROOKED CHAIR, ..MISS DRAKE PROCEEDS TO SUPPER   41   4
    OUT OF KITCHEN TABLE OR CHAIR ....BLACK ROOK IN RAINY WEATHER   57   16
    CHAIR AND BUREAU ARE THE HIEROGLYPHS ....THE GHOST'S LEAVETAKING   90   16
    I MISS ORION AND CASSIOPEIA'S CHAIR. MAYBE THEY ARE ....STARS.   165   18
    SQUARE AS A CHAIR AND ALMOST TOO HEAVY TO LIFT. ....THE ARRIVAL.   212   2
    AND YOU OUT COLD BESIDE ME IN YOUR CHAIR. ....STOPPED DEAD   230   5
    DEAD ON THE CHAIR BACK, ...EAVESDROPPER 261   59
    NOW, DISCIPLINED IN THE STRICT ANCESTRAL CHAIR, ...THE TRIAL OF MAN   312   12
    DEFENDING MY PERILOUS WOUNDS WITH A CHAIR ....CIRCUS IN THREE RINGS   322   11
CHAIRARMS (1)
    CHAIRARMS AND TABLES, ...WORDS FOR A NURSERY   74   44
CHAIRS (9)
    THE WALNUT BANQUET TABLE, THE TWELVE CHAIRS ....THE OTHER TWO   68   13
    TABLES AND CHAIRS. GRAVITY'S ....THE GREAT CARBUNCLE   73   22
    LIGHT WITHDRAWS. CHAIRS, TABLES DROP ....THE GREAT CARBUNCLE   73   29
    OF CHAIRS AND BUREAUS AND SLEEP-TWISTED SHEETS. ....GHOST'S.   90   7
    THEY SET THEIR STOUT CHAIRS BACK TO THE ROAD AND FACE THE DARK*NET-.   121   5
    TABLES AND CHAIRS CAN ELBOW US WITH EASE*DIALOGUE OVER A OUIJA BOARD   279   113
    CASTLES UPON THE SMUG-SHAPED CHAIRS. ALL THIS I ....DIALOGUE O.   279   118
    THE CHAIRS BELONG TO ITS DARKNESS. I SMELL DECAY ......DIALOGUE O.   285   314
    IN SLEEP. THE CHAIRS WON'T VANISH OR BECOME ....DIALOGUE O.   286   355
CHALK (6)
    CURDED OVER WITH CLOUDS AND CHALK CLIFFS BLANCHED   CHANNEL CROSSING   27   24
    OF STICKS. THE LIGHT FALLS CHALK AND COLD ...THE EVERLASTING MONDAY   62   3
    SNOW, CHALK OR SUCHLIKE. THEY'RE ....MAGI   148   5
    DARKNESS WIPES ME OUT LIKE CHALK ON A BLACKBOARD... ....FACE LIFT   156   15
    HOW WINTER FILLS MY SOUL! AND THAT CHALK LIGHT ....THREE WOMEN   181   177
    THE MOONLIGHT, THAT CHALK CLIFF ....EVENT   194   2
CHALK-HULLED (1)
    BLUE FUR, MOLES HAVE; HEFTING CHALK-HULLED FLINT ....ODE FOR TED   29   9
CHALLENGE (1)
    FLAYED BY SPRAY, WE TAKE THE CHALLENGE UP, ...CHANNEL CROSSING   26   5
CHALLENGES (1)
    CHALLENGES THE SILENT DOME. ..............METAMORPHOSES OF THE MOON   307   12
CHAMBER (3)
    THE PHOTOGRAPHIC CHAMBER OF THE EYE ....TALE OF A TUB   24   1
    A WIND UNSTOPPERS THE CHAMBER POEM.6.W. 136   23
    I HAVE SEEN THE WHITE CLEAN CHAMBER WITH ITS INSTRUMENTS. ...THREE.   180   121
CHAMBERS (5)
    OUR FOOTSTEPS MULTIPLIED IN THE SHADOWY CHAMBERS, ...THE OTHER TWO   68   11
    PEBBLE SMELLS, TURNIPY CHAMBERS. POEM.2.DARK.   133   22
    BULLDOZERS, GUILLOTINES, WHITE CHAMBERS OF SHRIEKS PROCEED, THREE.   177   19
    THE VILLAGERS OPEN THE CHAMBERS, THEY ARE HUNTING THE QUEEN. ..BEE.   212   42
    THE CHAMBERS WHERE THEIR FIENDISH QUEEN WOULD SIT. ...THE PRINCESS.   334   40
CHAMPAGNE-COLORED (1)
    IN A RAMPAGE OF CHAMPAGNE-COLORED RAIN ....CIRCUS IN THREE RINGS   321   4
CHANCE (2)
    THAT WRESTLE WITH US LIKE ANGELS; THE MERE CHANCE   CHANNEL CROSSING   27   18
    AND CHANCE OF A TRUE ANSWER. YOU WASTE NO TIME ....DIALOGUE O.   281   188
CHANCES (2)
    I HAVE HAD MY CHANCES. I HAVE TRIED AND TRIED. ....THREE WOMEN   178   71
    CHANCES TO MASTER MINE. THEY SAY THE THIRD TIME ....DIALOGUE O.   283   270

	TITLE	PAGE	LINE

CHANDELIER (1)
THE CHANDELIER ....PURDAH 243 44
CHANEL (1)
IN A SHOWER OF CHANEL, DIOR GOWNS, ...DIALOGUE EN ROUTE 308 9
CHANGE (6)
NO CHANGE MET HER: GARDEN TERRACE, ALL SUMMER ....DREAM WITH C. 44 9
IT IS COMFORTABLE, FOR A CHANGE, TO MEAN SO LITTLE. ......TWO CAMP. 145 17
NOT EASY TO STATE THE CHANGE YOU MADE. ....LOVE LETTER 147 1
GLEAM LIKE SMALL CHANGE. ....WUTHERING HEIGHTS 168 45
SO THE ARTFUL GLASS WON'T CHANGE ITS CHILL FOR HEART'S   DIALOGUE O. 277 17
THAT CAME BEFORE THE CHANGE OF WEATHER ....THE DREAM 310 3
CHANGED (3)
UNTIL SWEET WIND CHANGED TUNE, BLEW HARM: ....BUCOLICS 24 15
ESTRANGED, CHANGED, SUSPENDED WHERE ....THE GREAT CARBUNCLE 73 19
THEY'VE CHANGED ALL THAT. TRAVELING ....FACE LIFT 156 9
CHANGES (1)
NOTHING CHANGES, FOR ALL THE BLAZING OF ....LOVE IS A PARALLAX 329 16
CHANGING (2)
WATCHED THE CHANGING SHAPE HE CUT, ...FAUN 35 12
THEIR SMILES AND THEIR VOICES ARE CHANGING. I AM LED THROUGH A
BEANFIELD. ....THE BEE MEETING 211 15
CHANNEL (1)
CHANNEL CROSSING ....CHANNEL CROSSING 26 T
CHANNELS (1)
ON THE UNBEATEN CHANNELS ....FULL FATHOM FIVE 93 28
CHANTING (1)
THE SHADOWS OF RINGDOVES CHANTING, BUT EASING NOTHING. *WINTER TREES 258 15
CHAPEL (2)
FOR WEDLOCK WROUGHT WITHIN LOVE'S PROPER CHAPEL.*WREATH FOR A BRIDAL 44 12
WHILE CHAPEL PINNACLES OVER THE ROOFS, ...THE EYE-MOTE 109 5
CHAPELS (1)
FESTERING ON THE DIM WALLS OF EUROPE'S CHAPELS, ...PERSEUS 82 10
CHAR (2)
THEIR CHAR OF KARAKUL STILL. I CAN'T TELL ....THE BURNT-OUT SPA 138 7
WHERE BEAUTIES CHAR ......ON LOOKING INTO THE EYES OF A DEMON LOVER 325 22
CHARACTERS (1)
WITH CHARACTERS NO COCKCROW CAN DEFACE. ....SONNET TO SATAN 323 12
CHARADES (1)
PLAYING HIS PRODIGAL CHARADES. ....LOVE IS A PARALLAX 329 36
CHARGE (6)
FOR SMALL CHARGE ....TINKER JACK AND THE TIDY WIVES 34 14
BUT GAVE ME PAUSE, MY ROSE A CHARGE, ...RHODODENDRON. 104 26
THERE IS A CHARGE ....LADY LAZARUS 246 57
FOR THE EYEING OF MY SCARS, THERE IS A CHARGE ....LADY LAZARUS 246 58
AND THERE IS A CHARGE, A VERY LARGE CHARGE ....LADY LAZARUS 246 61
AND THERE IS A CHARGE, A VERY LARGE CHARGE ....LADY LAZARUS 246 61
CHARIOTEERS (1)
SO MUCH FOR THE CHARIOTEERS, THE OUTRIDERS, THE GRAND ARMY! SWARM. 217 39
CHARITY (1)
IN THIS CHARITY WARD, THIS POORHOUSE, WHERE THE DEAD ...ELECTRA ON. 117 19
CHARLES (1)
FROM CHARLES STREET TO THE CUSTOM HOUSE, ...A WINTER'S TALE 87 35
CHARRED (5)
CHARRED AND RAVENED WOMEN LIE, ...PURSUIT 22 23
THEIR FOND HEARTS CHARRED AS ANY MATCH. *EPITAPH FOR FIRE AND FLOWER 45 7
BLACK AS THE CHARRED KNUCKLE-BONES ....CHILD'S PARK STONES 100 5
OF CHARRED SHOES, THE SODDEN UPHOLSTERY: ....AFTERMATH 114 12
CHARRED SKIRTS AND DEATHMASK ....GETTING THERE 249 47
CHART (2)
GRAPHS A FEVER CHART, ...TRIO OF LOVE SONGS 313 6
TO CHART THE MEASURE OF FORTUNE'S WHEEL; ....SONG FOR A REVOLU. 323 11
CHARTS (1)
YOU CHECKED THE DIET CHARTS AND TOOK ME TO PLAY ..ZOO KEEPER'S WIFE 155 25
CHARY (1)
MOON FULL, MOON DARK, THE CHARY DAIRY FARMER ....GOATSUCKER 111 5
CHASED (1)
APPROVING CHASED GIRLS WHO GET THEM TO A TREE .....VIRGIN IN A TREE 81 4
CHASTE (4)
FLOATS CHASTE AS SNOW, TAUNTING THE CLOUDED MIND   WINTER LANDSCAPE, 21 4
INTO MY MOST CHASTE OWN EYES ....STRUMPET SONG 34 18
UNTIL NO CHASTE TREE BUT SUFFERS BLOTCH ..ON THE PLETHORA OF DRYADS 68 34
KNIFELIKE, HE WAS CHASTE ENOUGH, ...MEDALLION 125 25
CHASTITY'S (1)
TO CHASTITY'S SERVICE: LIKE PROPHETS, LIKE PREACHERS, ...VIRGIN. 82 28
CHATTERERS (1)
O CHATTERERS ....PURDAH 243 36
CHATTERING (1)
HIS TEETH ARE CHATTERING AMONG THE LEPROUS ..THE EVERLASTING MONDAY 62 5
CHEATED (1)
CHEATED OF THE PYRE AND THE RACK, ...AFTERMATH 114 13
CHECK (1)
SUCH A BARRICADE OF BARB AND CHECK ....SPINSTER 50 26
CHECKED (1)
YOU CHECKED THE DIET CHARTS AND TOOK ME TO PLAY ..ZOO KEEPER'S WIFE 155 25

86

                                                         TITLE   PAGE LINE
CHEEK (2)
   MY CHEEK OF BASALT. THEY TURNED TO TEARS, ...LOVE LETTER   147   15
   A GREASY SMACK ON EVERY CHEEK ....FAMILY REUNION   300   14
CHEEKS (1)
   CHEEKS ALIGHTING EACH MOMENT TO MELT ....LOVE LETTER   147   14
CHEERFUL (2)
   THE GRAFTERS ARE CHEERFUL, ...POEM.7.S.   137   27
   THE CITY IS A MAP OF CHEERFUL TWITTERS NOW, ...INSOMNIAC   163   33
CHEESECLOTH (2)
   BREASTPLATES OF CHEESECLOTH KNOTTED UNDER THE ARMPITS. ....BEE.   211   14
   OUR CHEESECLOTH GAUNTLETS NEAT AND SWEET, ...STINGS   214   3
CHEESEPARING (1)
   STARS, NOT OUR CHEESEPARING PSYCHES. IT *DIALOGUE OVER A OUIJA BOARD   281 195
CHEF (1)
   FOR FEAST THE SWEETEST MEAT OF HELL'S CHEF D'OEUVRES: .....TERMINAL   328   11
CHENILLE (1)
   CHENILLE BECKONER, ...EAVESDROPPER   260   33
CHEQUERED (1)
   WITH CHEQUERED WAVES AND GAILY ....BATTLE-SCENE   84   7
CHERRY (2)
   AND THE PETTICOATS OF THE CHERRY. ....THE ARRIVAL OF THE BEE BOX   213   30
   WHOSE NEWS IS THE OPEN CHERRY, THE OPEN CLOVER? ....STINGS   214   30
CHERUBIM (1)
   BY KISSES, BY CHERUBIM, ...FEVER.   232   49
CHESHIRE (1)
   IT'S TIME TO VANISH LIKE THE CHESHIRE CAT ....A SORCERER B.   324   12
CHESS (2)
   SHH! THESE ARE CHESS PEOPLE YOU PLAY WITH, ...THE SWARM   216   11
   ALL DAY SHE PLAYS AT CHESS WITH THE BONES OF THE WORLD: ..FEMALE A.   301   1
CHESTNUT (1)
   ON PINCKNEY, MOUNT VERNON, CHESTNUT, ...A WINTER'S TALE   87   25
CHEVROLET (1)
   INCHING OFF IN THE GRAY CHEVROLET, DRINKING THE GREEN ......WAKING.   151   6
CHEW (1)
   STARES THROUGH US; HIS HOOVES CHEW THE BREEZE. ....WHITSUN   154   8
CHEWED (1)
   BLUE SUEDE A DOG OR FOX HAS CHEWED. ....BLUE MOLES   126   4
CHEWING (1)
   CHEWING AT THE GRAY PAPER, ...POEM.2.DARK.   132   4
CHICKEN (2)
   I AM NUDE AS A CHICKEN NECK, DOES NOBODY LOVE ME? ..THE BEE MEETING   211   6
   LEMON WATER, CHICKEN ....FEVER.   232   32
CHICKEN-GUT (1)
   WITH CREAM AND CHICKEN-GUT FEASTING THE PALATES ......ELLA MASON A.   53   11
CHICKENS (2)
   HAWK MISFORTUNE LIKE FIGS AND CHICKENS ....THE BEGGARS   47   3
   WINKS LIKE MONEY UNDER THE RINGED TOES OF THE CHICKENS. ......NET-.   121   9
CHICKS (1)
   I REMEMBER THE BLOODIED CHICKS AND THE QUARTERED RABBITS. ...ZOO K.   155   24
CHIDING (1)
   SHE SPOKE MOST CHIDING IN HIS EAR ....THE QUEEN'S COMPLAINT   28   11
CHILD (18)
   TWO WAXEN OXEN FLANK THE CHILD. ....A WINTER'S TALE   86   6
   WHILE THE CHILD SMILES INTO THIN AIR. ....MAGI   148   9
   THE EYES OF THE CHILD I NURSE ARE SCARCELY OPEN. ....CANDLES   149   28
   ONE CHILD DROPS A BARRETTE OF PINK PLASTIC;   PARLIAMENT HILL FIELDS   152   16
   MY HUSBAND AND CHILD SMILING OUT OF THE FAMILY PHOTO; ....TULIPS   160   20
   AS A CHILD I LOVED A LICHEN-BITTEN NAME. ....THREE WOMEN   177   41
   THE CHILD IN THE WHITE CRIB REVOLVES AND SIGHS, ...EVENT   194   7
   AND MY CHILD -- LOOK AT HER, FACE DOWN ON THE FLOOR, ...LESBOS   227   8
   NO CHILD, NO WIFE. ....BY CANDLELIGHT   237   34
   WHERE THE CHILD CAN NEVER SWIM, ...THE FEARFUL   256   17
   O GOLDEN CHILD THE WORLD WILL KILL AND EAT. ....MARY'S SONG   257   21
   CHILD ....CHILD   265   T
   WHAT IS SO REAL AS THE CRY OF A CHILD? ....KINDNESS   269   6
   EACH DEAD CHILD COILED, A WHITE SERPENT, ...EDGE   272   9
   CHILD TO SEE WHICH ONE OF US CAN CALL ..DIALOGUE OVER A OUIJA BOARD   284 284
   FROM GRAY CHILD FACES CRYING IN THE STREETS. ....FEMALE AUTHOR   301   14
   KNIT UP A GILDED FABLE FOR THE CHILD ..THE PRINCESS AND THE GOBLINS   335   73
   OF CHILD, LEAF AND CLOUD, ...TOUCH-AND-GO   336   21
CHILDBIRTHS (1)
   CHILDBIRTHS OR A FAMILY BARBECUE: ....ALL THE DEAD DEARS   71   28
CHILDHOOD (2)
   OF CHILDHOOD AND ADOLESCENCE, STICKY WITH DREAMS, ...INSOMNIAC   163   10
   BLACK AND LEAFY, AS IN MY CHILDHOOD, ...LITTLE FUGUE   188   24
CHILDLESS (1)
   CHILDLESS WOMAN ....CHILDLESS WOMAN   259   T
CHILDREN (31)
   OVER TIDAL-FLATS WHERE THREE CHILDREN PLAYED*DREAM WITH CLAM-DIGGERS   44   14
   SPROUTING FRUIT, FLOWERS, CHILDREN MOST FAIR IN LEGION ...WREATH F.   45   22
   ONCE WE CHILDREN SNEAKED OVER TO SPY MISS MASON ......ELLA MASON A.   54   19
   FOR THRIFTY CHILDREN, NOR DOLT PIG RIPE FOR HECKLING, ...SOW   60   13
   AND SO ALL CHILDREN SING ....BATTLE-SCENE   85   32
   AND GHOST OF OUR DREAMS' CHILDREN, IN THOSE SHEETS ....GHOST'S.   91   33

CHILDREN (CONT.)
    BUT THE CHILDREN ARE BETTER FOR IT, ...THE TIMES ARE TIDY 107   14
    I AM, I AM, I AM. CHILDREN ....SUICIDE OFF EGG ROCK 115   9
    TO TIMOROUS CHILDREN, TO THE LADY ON THE STREET. ..THE RAVAGED FACE   116   13
    AFTER THE FAT CHILDREN OF ROOT AND ROCK. ....BLUE MOLES 126   25
    ON FRIDAYS THE LITTLE CHILDREN COME POEM.7.S.   137   36
    THE BURGHERS SWEATED AND WEPT. THE CHILDREN WORE WHITE. ...CANDLES   149   19
    THEY ARE BALD AND IMPOSSIBLE, LIKE THE FACES OF MY CHILDREN, *THREE. 178   66
    OTHER CHILDREN DO NOT TOUCH ME: THEY ARE TERRIBLE. .....THREE WOMEN   178   68
    I DO NOT BELIEVE IN THOSE TERRIBLE CHILDREN ....THREE WOMEN   185 320
    THE NARCISSI LOOK UP LIKE CHILDREN, QUICKLY AND WHITELY.   NARCISSI.   190   12
    THESE CHILDREN ARE AFTER SOMETHING, WITH HOOKS AND CRIES, ...BERCK.   198   44
    THEN, FROM THE BARRED YARD, THE CHILDREN ....*BERCK-PLAGE   200 118
    THERE WAS NO ABSENCE OF LIPS, THERE WERE TWO CHILDREN,*THE DETECTIVE 209   34
    THE BARREN BODY OF HAWTHORN, ETHERIZING ITS CHILDREN. ....BEE.   211   25
    MOURNED BY RELIGIOUS FIGURES, BY GARLANDED CHILDREN. GETTING THERE   249   48
    PERFECTION IS TERRIBLE, IT CANNOT HAVE CHILDREN. ....MUNICH.   262   1
    THEY BUZZ LIKE BLUE CHILDREN ....TOTEM 265   31
    THE CHILDREN LEAP IN THEIR COTS. ....MYSTIC   269   29
    YOU HAND ME TWO CHILDREN, TWO ROSES. ....KINDNESS   270   20
    TWO CHILDREN LAUGHED AT TAG ....BITTER STRAWBERRIES 299   14
    TO MORTAL CHILDREN LONGING TO BE GAY; ....NEVER TRY TO TRICK.   320   14
    TILL UNRULY CHILDREN STREAM DOWN THE SKY ....SONG FOR A REVOLU.   323   14
    WHERE VIVID CHILDREN TWIRL ....TOUCH-AND-GO   335   9
    AND I, LIKE THE CHILDREN, CAUGHT ....TOUCH-AND-GO   336   17
    HIS WIFE AND HIS CHILDREN ....TOUCH-AND-GO   336   21
CHILDREN'S (1)
    IT IS TEN YEARS, NOW, SINCE WE ROWED TO CHILDREN'S ISLAND. ...BABY. 174   1
CHILD'S (5)
    CHILD'S PARK STONES ....CHILD'S PARK STONES   100   T
    GUTS BAG WOULD CLACK LIKE A CHILD'S RATTLE, ...ZOO KEEPER'S WIFE 154   12
    LIKE A CHILD'S TOO-SIMPLE MATHEMATICAL PROBLEM. ....STARS.   165   20
    THE CHILD'S CRY ....ARIEL   239   24
    UNGODLY AS A CHILD'S SHRIEK. ....CHILDLESS WOMAN   259   10
CHILL (6)
    DEW STOOD IN CHILL SWEAT ON EACH STALK, ...DIALOGUE B.   38   4
    FIRELESS, SEVEN CHILL SEAS CHAINED TO HIS ANKLE. EVERLASTING MONDAY   62   12
    GULLS STIFFEN TO THEIR CHILL VIGIL IN THE DRAFTY HALF-LIGHT; ...
                                    ... PARLIAMENT HILL FIELDS   153   49
    AND DRINK THE SMALL NIGHT CHILL LIKE NEWS OF HOME. ....STARS.   166   40
    SO THE ARTFUL GLASS WON'T CHANGE ITS CHILL FOR HEART'S   DIALOGUE O. 277   17
    THOSE GLASS BITS IN THE GRATE STRIKE ME CHILL: ....DIALOGUE O. 285 306
CHILLING (1)
    THE WILLOWS WERE CHILLING, ...THREE WOMEN   177   44
CHILLS (1)
    CHILLS ME TO DEATH ....TO A JILTED LOVER 309   8
CHILLY (2)
    IT IS A CHILLY GOD, A GOD OF SHADES, ...OUIJA   77   1
    ENTER THE CHILLY NO-MAN'S LAND OF ABOUT ....THE GHOST'S LEAVETAKING   90   1
CHIME (1)
    IT WILL PING LIKE A CHINESE CHIME IN THE SLIGHTEST AIR STIR   A LIFE 150   7
CHIMERA (1)
    CHIMERA ON THE HOOK, WHO CLAIMS HE'S LATE ....DIALOGUE O. 283 245
CHIMERICAL (1)
    AND MY EVERY CHIMERICAL DOLLAR ....DIALOGUE EN ROUTE   308   16
CHIMNEY (2)
    AND CHIMNEY POTS ....PROSPECT   28   2
    ORANGE ROOF-TILES, ORANGE CHIMNEY POTS, ...LANDOWNERS   53   5
CHIMNEYS (1)
    THE CHIMNEYS OF THE CITY BREATHE, THE WINDOW SWEATS, ...MYSTIC 269   28
CHIN (1)
    A CLEFT IN YOUR CHIN INSTEAD OF YOUR FOOT ....DADDY   223   53
CHINA (8)
    THIS WAS NO ROSE-AND-LARKSPURRED CHINA SUCKLING ....SOW 60   11
    AND THE WHITE CHINA FLYING FISH FROM ITALY. ....LEAVING EARLY   145   6
    THEY RING TRUE, LIKE GOOD CHINA. ....A LIFE   150   18
    FACELESS AND PALE AS CHINA ....PARLIAMENT HILL FIELDS   152   2
    RINGING THE WHITE CHINA. ....THE RABBIT CATCHER   194   23
    FULL OF DRESSES AND HATS AND CHINA AND MARRIED DAUGHTERS. ...BERCK. 199   77
    WHICH OCCURRED TO ME IN CHINA." ....THE DREAM   311   30
    GROWS BRITTLE AS A TILTED CHINA BOWL; ....PROLOGUE TO SPRING 322   5
CHINESE (7)
    THE CHINESE LADIES USE ....POLLY'S TREE   128   13
    LITTERED WITH CHINESE HANDS. NOW I'M STARED AT ....LEAVING EARLY 146   30
    IT WILL PING·LIKE A CHINESE CHIME IN THE SLIGHTEST AIR STIR A LIFE 150   7
    HANGING THEIR BLUEGREEN BELLIES AND THEIR WING PANES IN A CHINESE
         SCREEN. ....BLACKBERRYING   168   16
    AS USUAL THERE IS NO FACE. A LUMP OF CHINESE WHITE ....SURGEON. 170   7
    THEY PAINT SUCH SECRETS IN ARABIC, CHINESE! ....THREE WOMEN   179   98
    CHINESE YELLOW ON APPALLING OBJECTS --- ....WINTERING   218   16
CHINS (1)
    YOU ARE SUNK IN YOUR SEVEN CHINS, STILL AS A HAM. .....STOPPED DEAD 230   16
CHIP (1)
    ITS EYE, FLASHLIT, A CHIP OF RUBY FIRE. ....GOATSUCKER 111   8

	TITLE	PAGE	LINE
CHIPS (1)			
OF QUAHOG CHIPS, ...POINT SHIRLEY	110	7
CHIRP (1)			
TO CHIRP THE HOUR IN LUNATIC THIRTEENS. ....SONNET: TO EVA	305	14
CHIRPS (1)			
CHIRPS THE FIRST: "LIVE ON A SILENT ISLAND ..EPITAPH IN THREE PARTS	337	5
CHISEL (2)			
UNTIL HIS CHISEL BEQUEATHS ....SCULPTOR	92	22
THE JEWELMASTER DRIVES HIS CHISEL TO PRY ....POEM.7.S.	136	20
CHITTERING (2)			
OF A BLIZZARD, THE GIANT ROARED UP WITH HIS CHITTERING TROPHIES. ...			
... THE SNOWMAN ON THE MOOR	59	45
THE CHITTERING CRACKPOTS THAT HE MADE.*SONG FOR A REVOLUTIONARY LOVE	323	20
CHITTERS (1)			
THE SMALL SHREW CHITTERS FROM ITS WILDERNESS ....WATERCOLOR.	112	4
CHOCOLATE (1)			
CHOCOLATE FANCIES IN ROSE-PAPERED ROOMS ....FEMALE AUTHOR	301	6
CHOICE (2)			
CHOICE WASSAIL MAKES, COOKED HOT, ...THE GLUTTON	40	9
THE CHOICE BETWEEN THE MICA MYSTERY ......METAMORPHOSES OF THE MOON	308	37
CHOIR (2)			
OF ANIMALS TO CHOIR: "LOOK WHAT THRESH OF WINGS ....WREATH F.	45	15
AND HELPED THE TWO OF US TO CHOIR: ....THE DISQUIETING MUSES	75	21
CHOKE (1)			
AND THAT'S WHY I HAVE NO HAIR, AUNTIE, THAT'S WHY I CHOKE THE TOUR	238	24
CHOKING (1)			
CHOKING THE AGED AND THE MEEK, ...FEVER.	231	17
CHOLER (1)			
"O MAY G-MEN ALL DIE OF THE CHOLER, ...DIALOGUE EN ROUTE	308	15
CHOOSE (5)			
NOR GUESS THAT IF I CHOOSE TO BLINK .....SOLILOQUY OF THE SOLIPSIST	37	17
CHOOSE AN EGG-SHAPE, A WORLD-SHAPE, ...FIESTA MELONS	46	8
OF WHATEVER ANGEL MAY CHOOSE TO FLARE ..BLACK ROOK IN RAINY WEATHER	57	26
TO CHOOSE BETWEEN YOUR WORLD OF JUNGLE GREEN ....YADWIGHA.	85	9
EITHER WAY WE CHOOSE, THE ANGRY WITCH ....METAMORPHOSES OF THE MOON	308	43
CHORD (1)			
YOU'LL CUT THE CHORD ....TRIO OF LOVE SONGS	315	39
CHORUS (1)			
THE FAITH-MAKER, FISTED IN HIS CLOUD, OR THE CHORUS ....DIALOGUE O.	279	109
CHOSE (3)			
TO THE BARBAROUS OUTLOOK, FROM THERE CHOSE ....SPIDER	49	25
SO WHEN STAUNCH ISLAND STOCK CHOSE FORFEITURE ....MAYFLOWER	60	9
RETROGRESSED TO BLOWZE, I NEXT CHOSE RED; ............RHODODENDRON.	103	10
CHOSEN (1)			
AND LEADS HIM HOME TO BE HER CHOSEN KNIGHT. ....THE PRINCESS.	334	50
CHOUGHS (1)			
OVERHEAD GO THE CHOUGHS IN BLACK, CACOPHONOUS FLOCKS -- ..BLACKBER.	168	10
CHRIST (6)			
O OEDIPUS. O CHRIST. YOU USE ME ILL. ....THE RAVAGED FACE	116	14
THE YEW MY CHRIST, THEN. ....LITTLE FUGUE	188	29
CHRIST! THEY ARE PANES OF ICE, ...NICK AND THE CANDLESTICK	241	15
LET US EAT IT LIKE CHRIST. ....TOTUM	264	15
THE MOUTH OF CHRIST ....GIGOLO	267	19
OF CHRIST IN THE FACES OF RODENTS, ...MYSTIC	269	19
CHRISTENED (1)			
CHRISTENED IN A SPINDRIFT OF SNOWDROP STARS, ...APRIL AUBADE	312	9
CHRISTENING (2)			
UNASKED TO MY CHRISTENING, THAT SHE ....THE DISQUIETING MUSES	74	4
THE SHADOWS STOOP OVER LIKE GUESTS AT A CHRISTENING. ....CANDLES	149	35
CHRISTMAS (2)			
WHAT WILL THEY TASTE OF, THE CHRISTMAS ROSES? ....WINTERING	219	49
SINCE CHRISTMAS THEY HAVE LIVED WITH US, ...BALLOONS	271	1
CHRISTUS (1)			
IS IT A CHRISTUS, ...YEARS	255	19
CHROMIUM (2)			
FLAYS THE CHROMIUM NERVES OF PLUMBING RAW; ....TALE OF A TUB	24	3
THE STOPPED HORSE ON HIS CHROMIUM POLE ....WHITSUN	154	7
CHRONICLER (1)			
FAIR CHRONICLER OF EVERY FOUL DECLENSION. ....OUIJA	77	14
CHRYSANTHEMUMS (2)			
YELLOW-CASQUED CHRYSANTHEMUMS -- ....STREET SONG	36	14
BY CHRYSANTHEMUMS THE SIZE ....LEAVING EARLY	146	31
CHUCK (2)			
CHUCK THE BROKEN ACROPOLIS OUT, ...SONG FOR A REVOLUTIONARY LOVE	323	6
ITEM: CHUCK OUT ROYAL RIGMAROLE OF PROPS ....A SORCERER B.	324	5
CHUCKLES (2)			
NEVER GRIP, AS THEIR GRANDSIRES DID, THAT DEVIL WHO CHUCKLES*LESSON.	80	24
THAT CHUCKLES IN BACKTRACK OF THE WAVE; ....TWO LOVERS.	327	18
CHUFFING (1)			
CHUFFING ME OFF LIKE A JEW. ....DADDY	223	32
CHUMMY (1)			
THE HORIZONS ARE TOO FAR OFF TO BE CHUMMY AS UNCLES; .....TWO CAMP.	145	13
CHURCH (5)			
CHURCH CURSE TO KEN THAT CROOKED OATH ....CRYSTAL GAZER	55	35
INSIDE THE CHURCH, THE SAINTS WILL BE ALL BLUE, ...MOON.	173	24

89

```
                                                        TITLE            PAGE  LINE
CHURCH (CONT.)
   POLLARDED GREEN BALLS, THE TREES MARCH TO CHURCH.  ......BERCK-PLAGE  199  92
   ALL DAY, GLUING MY CHURCH OF BURNT MATCHSTICKS,  .........THE JAILER  227  26
   CHURCH SMILE  ...........................................EAVESDROPPER  261  50
CHURCHES (1)
   EMPTY SCHOOLROOMS, EMPTY CHURCHES. O SO MUCH EMPTINESS! *THREE WOMEN  181 179
CHURCH-GOING (1)
   WAYLAYS SIMPLE GIRLS, CHURCH-GOING,  ...................VANITY FAIR    32  14
CHURCHYARD (2)
   THE DAY I WOKE, I WOKE ON CHURCHYARD HILL.  ..ELECTRA ON AZALEA PATH  117  15
   CHURCHYARD EARS UNTIL THE STARLIT STIFF  .........LOVE IS A PARALLAX  330  41
CHURLISH (1)
   FOR A CHURLISH WELCOME.  ...................GREEN ROCK, WINTHROP BAY  105  24
CHURN (1)
   THEIR MERCILESS CHURN.  .........................................YEARS  255  15
CICATRIX (1)
   OVER THE CICATRIX OF POLAND, BURNT-OUT  .................MARY'S SONG  257  10
CIDER-JUICE (1)
   OVER WINDFALLS TO SIP CIDER-JUICE.  .........YADDO: THE GRAND MANOR  123  10
CIGAR (1)
   CIGAR OVER HIS RINK OF FISHES.  .......................A WINTER SHIP  113  12
CIGARETTE (1)
   WHITE CIGARETTE,  ......................................EAVESDROPPER  260  16
CIGARETTES (2)
   TICKING YOUR FINGERS ON THE MARBLE TABLE, LOOKING FOR
       CIGARETTES,  ..............................................THE RIVAL  166   8
   HE HAS BEEN BURNING ME WITH CIGARETTES,  .................THE JAILER  226  18
CINDER (4)
   RED CINDER AROUND WHICH I MYSELF,  .....................THE EYE-MOTE  109  17
   THE SUN PUTS ITS CINDER OUT. WHERE WE LIE*SLEEP IN THE MOJAVE DESERT  144  21
   TO A CINDER, THAN MEET A POOR UPSTART OF OUR NETHER  ....DIALOGUE O.  280 133
   LEST THE LIGHTNING STRIKE YOU TO CINDER.  ...GO GET THE GOODLY SQUAB  313   8
CINDERELLA (1)
   CINDERELLA  .............................................CINDERELLA  303   T
CINDERS (2)
   SHRIVELING TO CINDERS AT ITS SOURCE,  .................CRYSTAL GAZER   56  45
   WITH KISS OF CINDERS, GHOSTS DESCEND,  ................DANSE MACABRE  321  25
CINDER'S (1)
   TO CONQUER CINDER'S KINGDOM IN THE STROKE OF AN HOUR *EPITAPH FOR F.   45  20
CIPHERS (1)
   THE CIPHERS THAT WATCH IT.  ..........................EAVESDROPPER  261  45
CIRCLE (11)
   UPSTANDING SPINACH-TIPS WEDGED IN A CIRCLE --  ......SPINACH-PICKER.   89   8
   GULLS CIRCLE GRAY UNDER SHADOW OF A STEELIER FLIGHT.  ...GREEN ROCK.  105  17
   THEIR MUSK ENCROACHES, CIRCLE AFTER CIRCLE,*THE BEEKEEPER'S DAUGHTER  118   3
   THEIR MUSK ENCROACHES, CIRCLE AFTER CIRCLE,*THE BEEKEEPER'S DAUGHTER  118   3
   A WOMAN IS DRAGGING HER SHADOW IN A CIRCLE  ..................A LIFE  150  21
   I CIRCLE THE WRITHEN TREES. I AM TOO HAPPY.  PARLIAMENT HILL FIELDS  153  29
   CIRCLE A WOMB OF MARBLE.  ...................................THE OTHER  202  22
   THEY ARE LEADING ME TO THE SHORN GROVE, THE CIRCLE OF HIVES.  ..BEE.  211  23
   CIRCLE, WITH ITS TAWN SILK GRASSES -- BABIES' HAIR.  LETTER IN NOV.  253   7
   DOWN TO A CIRCLE OF LETTERS: TWENTY-SIX *DIALOGUE OVER A OUIJA BOARD  276  13
   INVIOLATE IN THE CIRCLE OF THAT SKEIN, *THE PRINCESS AND THE GOBLINS  334  47
CIRCLED (1)
   UNDERSHIRTS CIRCLED, TENDING  ...........................NIGHT SHIFT   77  21
CIRCLES (1)
   CIRCLES HER LIKE A PREY SHE'D LOVE TO KILL  ...................WIDOW  164  15
CIRCLING (1)
   CIRCLING ZODIAC COMPELS THE YEAR.  ......TO EVA DESCENDING THE STAIR  303  16
CIRCUITS (1)
   NOTIONS AND TICKETS, SHORT CIRCUITS AND FOLDING MIRRORS.  .....TOTEM  265  27
CIRCUMFLUENT (1)
   AND PAINTS THE RIVER'S PALE CIRCUMFLUENT STILLNESS   ABOVE THE OXBOW   89  43
CIRCUS (7)
   I LEARN, GOOD CIRCUS  ...........................WORDS FOR A NURSERY   73  11
   THEY STUNT LIKE CLOWNS IN THE CIRCUS.  .............IN MIDAS' COUNTRY  100  20
   OUTLANDISH AS A CIRCUS, THE RAVAGED FACE  ..........THE RAVAGED FACE  115   1
   TREADING CIRCUS TIGHTROPES  .......................TRIO OF LOVE SONGS  314  21
   CIRCUS IN THREE RINGS  .......................CIRCUS IN THREE RINGS  321   T
   IN THE CIRCUS TENT OF A HURRICANE  .........CIRCUS IN THREE RINGS  321   1
   AND LEFT OUR BANKRUPT CIRCUS ON ITS OWN;  ...............DENOUEMENT  326   2
CITADEL (1)
   ASSAULTS THE SLEEPING CITADEL,   INSOLENT STORM STRIKES AT THE SKULL  325   2
CITIES (1)
   AND SO WE SAIL TOWARD CITIES, STREETS AND HOMES  ...CHANNEL CROSSING   27  37
CITY (14)
   OF GOD'S CITY AND BABYLON'S  ...................A LESSON IN VENGEANCE   80  10
   O LITTLE CITY ON A HILL!  ...................A WINTER'S TALE   87  31
   LOOK UPON? RATS' TEETH GUT THE CITY  .............................OWL  102  15
   THIS IS THE CITY WHERE MEN ARE MENDED.  .....................POEM.7.S.  136   1
   THE PEOPLE OF THE CITY HEARD IT.  ...........................POEM.7.S.  136  14
   THIS IS THE CITY OF SPARE PARTS.  ...........................POEM.7.S.  137  33
   AND BRIM; THE CITY MELTS LIKE SUGAR.  ........PARLIAMENT HILL FIELDS  152  12
   THE CITY IS A MAP OF CHEERFUL TWITTERS NOW,  .............INSOMNIAC  163  33
```

CITY (CONT.)
    THE CITY WAITS AND ACHES. THE LITTLE GRASSES ....THREE WOMEN 187 370
    THE CHIMNEYS OF THE CITY BREATHE, THE WINDOW SWEATS, ...MYSTIC 269   28
    THE SKY OF THE CITY IS WHITE; THE LIGHT FROM THE COUNTRY. ...
                        ... QUEEN MARY'S ROSE GARDEN 290   10
    FOR BEING TOO WELL-BRED AND SMELLESS AND LIKING THE CITY. ...
                        ... QUEEN MARY'S ROSE GARDEN 290   20
    MOST PLASTIC-WINDOWED CITY, I CAN HEAR ....SONNET: TO TIME 311   6
    AS THE DOOMSTRUCK CITY CRUMBLES BLOCK BY BLOCK: ....DOOMSDAY 316   8
CIVIL (1)
    SINCE THOSE TWO CIVIL SERVANTS SET ....THE DEATH OF MYTH-MAKING 104   8
CLACK (1)
    GUTS BAG WOULD CLACK LIKE A CHILD'S RATTLE, ...ZOO KEEPER'S WIFE 154   12
CLACKED (1)
    MOURNFULLY THE DRY TONGUES CLACKED THEIR GUILT: ....SNOWMAN O.   59   39
CLAIM (2)
    CLAIM AND WEIGHT GONE OUT OF THEM. ....THE GREAT CARBUNCLE   72   8
    WITH WINTER AS YOU CLAIM IT DOES. THE COAL ....DIALOGUE O. 277   19
CLAIMING (1)
    CLAIMING YOU FEEL ....SOLILOQUY OF THE SOLIPSIST   38   32
CLAIMS (2)
    CHIMERA ON THE HOOK, WHO CLAIMS HE'S LATE ....DIALOGUE O. 283 245
    OUR NOBLE DOCTOR CLAIMS THE PAIN IS HIS, ...NEVER TRY TO TRICK. 320   7
CLAIRVOYANT (2)
    THAT CLAIRVOYANT QUARTZ WHICH ONCE, AT HER OWN WISHING, ...
                        ... CRYSTAL GAZER   55   29
    DRUNK, AND TEA-LEAVES CANDID; THE CLAIRVOYANT SEIZURE ..DIALOGUE O. 279 123
CLAM (1)
    OF AN ANONYMOUS CLAM, ...NOTES TO A NEOPHYTE 306   3
CLAMBERING (3)
    CLAMBERING ROUND ITS GLASS BOX LIKE AN EIGHT-FINGERED HAND.   ZOO K. 155   31
    BLACK ON BLACK, ANGRILY CLAMBERING. .....THE ARRIVAL OF THE BEE BOX 213   15
    CLAMBERING UP THE CREAKING HEIGHTS OF HEAT ....THE PRINCESS. 334   55
CLAM-DIGGERS (2)
    DREAM WITH CLAM-DIGGERS ....DREAM WITH CLAM-DIGGERS   43   T
    CLAM-DIGGERS ROSE UP OUT OF DARK SLIME AT HER OFFENSE.*DREAM WITH C.   44   24
CLAMOR (1)
    POSTAGE STAMPS, STACKED BOOKS' CLAMOR AND YAWP, ...CONJURING.   65   3
CLANGOR (1)
    THAT MUTED BOOM, THAT CLANGOR ....NIGHT SHIFT   76   2
CLAPBOARD (1)
    POISON OF STILLED LAWNS, THE LITTLE CLAPBOARD GRAVESTONES,   WAKING. 151   7
CLAPPED (1)
    CLAPPED SHUT, FLATTEN THIS MAN OUT. ..THE HERMIT AT OUTERMOST HOUSE 118   3
CLAPS (1)
    CLAPS SIDEWISE: I AM NOT HIS YET. ....DEATH & CO. 254   11
CLARET (1)
    HATCHED WITH A CLARET HOGSHEAD TO SWIG ....MAUDLIN   51   5
CLARITIES (1)
    SHIFTING MY CLARITIES. ....PURDAH 242   7
CLASH (1)
    OH, HEAR THE CLASH OF PEOPLE MEETING -- ....FAMILY REUNION 300   11
CLASSIC (2)
    THE CLASSIC LIMBS OF STUBBORN ANTIGONE? ....PERSEUS   83   40
    TO A KNOT OF LAUNDRY, WITH A CLASSIC BUNCH OF SHEETS ......GHOST'S.   90   10
CLASSICAL (2)
    NOW THE PILLS ARE WORN-OUT AND SILLY, LIKE CLASSICAL GODS.*INSOMNIAC 163   20
    SHOULD BE GRAND AND CLASSICAL ....CHILD 265   9
CLATTER (1)
    FOR THAT WARY CLATTER SOUND OR GESTURE .............INCOMMUNICADO 100   6
CLAUS (1)
    THE LEAVES APPLAUD, AND SANTA CLAUS FLIES IN ....LOVE IS A PARALLAX 329   34
CLAW (3)
    CLAW SWOLLEN TO A SHIELD LARGE ....MUSSEL HUNTER AT ROCK HARBOR   96   33
    CONDONING THE BEAK, THE CLAW, THE GRIN OF THE DOG ....THE SWARM 216   22
    THE CLAW ....PARALYTIC 267   37
CLAW-CUTS (1)
    BY CLAW-CUTS OF THE GOATSUCKER, ALIAS DEVIL-BIRD, ...GOATSUCKER 111   7
CLAWED (1)
    A GRAY WALL NOW, CLAWED AND BLOODY. ..................APPREHENSIONS 195   6
CLAW-FOOT (1)
    THE GREAT GODS, STONE-HEAD, CLAW-FOOT,*THE HERMIT AT OUTERMOST HOUSE 118   4
CLAWS (9)
    BRIGHT THOSE CLAWS THAT MAR THE FLESH ....PURSUIT   23   31
    THE CAT UNSHEATHES ITS CLAWS ....RESOLVE   52   17
    EYEING ME. GRASS PUT FORTH CLAWS; .....MUSSEL HUNTER AT ROCK HARBOR   96   25
    PLEASURABLE UNDER CLAWS ....MUSSEL HUNTER AT ROCK HARBOR   96   49
    WHERE RED-FRECKLED CRAB-BACKS, CLAWS ..MUSSEL HUNTER AT ROCK HARBOR   97   83
    OF LOVE: CLAWS BRACED, AT BAY, MY CURRENCY NOT HERS.   INCOMMUNICADO 100   7
    RED-MOTTLED RELICS, SHELLS, CLAWS ....MAGNOLIA SHOALS 121   3
    WITH COPPER CLAWS; ....FAMILY REUNION 300   6
    ON SHREWD CLAWS: ....AQUATIC NOCTURNE 306   24
CLAW-THREAT (1)
    AND CLAW-THREAT, REALIZED THAT. ......THE HERMIT AT OUTERMOST HOUSE 118   6

CLAY (4)
    FIRED IN SANGUINE CLAY, THE MODEL HEAD   ....LADY AND T.   69   1
    THEMSELVES ON THE CLAY TOES AND SHORT CLUBFOOT   ......METAMORPHOSES.   308   35
    COUCHED IN CAULS OF CLAY AS IN HOLY ROBES, ...THE DEAD   320   2
    THE LION AND THE TIGERS TURN TO CLAY   ....DENOUEMENT   327   10
CLEAN (13)
    BLOOD AND WHISTLE MY MARROW CLEAN   ....ALL THE DEAD DEARS   70   17
    AND LEFT THE COBS TO RATTLE, BITTEN CLEAN.   ....OUIJA   77   18
    THOUGH THE BODY WALK OUT IN CLEAN LINEN.   ....MOONRISE 98   15
    A CLEAN SLATE, WITH YOU OWN FACE ON.   ....YOU'RE   141   18
    YOUR MOUTH OPENS CLEAN AS A CAT'S. THE WINDOW SQUARE ..MORNING SONG   157   15
    TOMORROW THE PATIENT WILL HAVE A CLEAN, PINK PLASTIC LIMB. *SURGEON.   171   40
    I HAVE SEEN THE WHITE CLEAN CHAMBER WITH ITS INSTRUMENTS.   ...THREE. 180 121
    O GOD, HOW SHALL I EVER CLEAN THE PHONE TABLE?   ....WORDS HEARD. 202   8
    PURE AND CLEAN AS THE CRY OF A BABY, ...A BIRTHDAY PRESENT 208   61
    I ORDERED THIS, THIS CLEAN WOOD BOX   .....THE ARRIVAL OF THE BEE BOX 212   1
    HAVE A THOUSAND CLEAN CELLS BETWEEN US, ...STINGS 214   6
    OF LICKING CLEAN   ....FEVER. 231   6
    THE BLOOD BLOOMS CLEAN   ....NICK AND THE CANDLESTICK   241   27
CLEAR (36)
    THOUGH IT'S QUITE CLEAR   ....SOLILOQUY OF THE SOLIPSIST   38   34
    ITS CLEAR AIR WINNOWED BY ANGELS; SHE WAS COME   ....DREAM WITH C. 43   2
    OF THE WORLD COMES CLEAR AND FILLS WITH COLOR.   .....THE THIN PEOPLE 65   35
    BUT IT'S THE CLEAR CONVERSION AT THE TOP CAN HOLD ..ABOVE THE OXBOW   88   20
    LAY OVER THE LEAVES LIKE A CLEAR CELLOPHANE, ...SPINACH-PICKER. 89   4
    OF THE NORTH, TO BE STEERED CLEAR   ....FULL FATHOM FIVE 92   13
    OF A WORLD MORE FULL AND CLEAR   ....LORELEI 94   15
    AT THE CLEAR TAIL OF HALLEY'S   ....MUSSEL HUNTER AT ROCK HARBOR 96   56
    SIGNS SAY NOTHING. THE FALCON WHO SPOKE CLEAR   ........INCOMMUNICADO 100   13
    ARGUED MY CONSCIENCE CLEAR WHICH ROBBED   .............RHODODENDRON.   103   11
    FILTER INTO THIS CLEAR   ....YADDO: THE GRAND MANOR   123   2
    COME CLEAR OF THE SHADOW. HISTORY   ....THE MANOR GARDEN 125   8
    THE SKY'S FAR DOME IS SANE AND CLEAR.   ....BLUE MOLES 126   10
    AND WHILE THE AIR'S CLEAR   ....DARK WOOD, DARK WATER   127   18
    TO MEND THE IMMENSE SKULL-PLATES AND CLEAR   ....THE COLOSSUS   129   14
    PROCEEDS CLEAR AS IT EVER DID   ....THE BURNT-OUT SPA 138   20
    GROWN MILKY, ALMOST CLEAR, LIKE THE BODIES OF SAINTS.   ......CANDLES 148   4
    THIS EGG-SHAPED BAILIWICK, CLEAR AS A TEAR.   ....A LIFE 149   2
    THE CLEAR VOWELS RISE LIKE BALLOONS.   ....MORNING SONG   157   18
    THEY HAVE SWABBED ME CLEAR OF MY LOVING ASSOCIATIONS.   ....TULIPS 161   24
    IN THIS CLEAR AIR AND NEVER NOTICE IT --   ....WIDOW 164   33
    I HAVE NEVER SEEN A THING SO CLEAR.   ....THREE WOMEN   181 171
    THESE ARE THE CLEAR BRIGHT COLORS OF THE NURSERY, ...THREE WOMEN   185 317
    THE GLASSY LIGHT WAS A CLEAR WALL, ...THE RABBIT CATCHER   194   19
    FLICKERING LIKE THAT, WRINKLY AND CLEAR RED, LIKE THE SKIN
        OF A MOUTH.   ....POPPIES IN JULY   203   6
    SANDS WHERE A DREAM OF CLEAR WATER   ....BURNING THE LETTERS 204   7
    TO YOU THEY ARE ONLY TRANSPARENCIES, CLEAR AIR. A BIRTHDAY PRESENT   207   38
    THE SNOWS OF THE TYROL, THE CLEAR BEER OF VIENNA   ....DADDY   223   36
    CLEAR OF VOICES AND HISTORY, THE STATICKY   ....LESBOS 228   18
    THE CLEAR, GREEN, QUITE BREATHABLE ATMOSPHERE, ...LYONNESSE   234   16
    YOUR CLEAR EYE IS THE ONE ABSOLUTELY BEAUTIFUL THING.   ....CHILD 265   1
    A CLEAR   ....PARALYTIC   266   30
    GUILELESS AND CLEAR, ...BALLOONS 271   2
    CONTEMPLATING A WORLD CLEAR AS WATER.   ....BALLOONS   272   28
    AND GET US CLEAR OF THIS. OH, HE'LL GO CLEVER   ....DIALOGUE O. 281 175
    BEGIN BY DIPPING YOUR BRUSH INTO CLEAR LIGHT.   .....MIDSUMMER MOBILE 324   1
CLEARING (1)
    NOT ONE LEAF WRINKLED IN THE CLEARING AIR.   ....THE OTHER TWO 68   6
CLEARLY (2)
    ANGELS ARE RUMORED, CLEARLY   ....THE GREAT CARBUNCLE 73   20
    FROST DROPS EVEN THE SPIDER. CLEARLY   ....FROG AUTUMN 99   9
CLEARNESS (1)
    RAVEL TO CLEARNESS ON THE DAWN SEA.   ....FULL FATHOM FIVE 93   20
CLEAVE (1)
    THEY CLEAVE THE RIVER'S GREENING PATINAS;   ....IN MIDAS' COUNTRY 100   18
CLEAVER (1)
    REEKS OF THE BUTCHER'S CLEAVER, ...STREET SONG 36   7
CLEAVERS (1)
    THERE IS NO MERCY IN THE GLITTER OF CLEAVERS, ...TOTEM 264   9
CLEAVES (2)
    CLEAVES FORWARD INTO FURY; DARK AS ANGER, ...CHANNEL CROSSING 26   3
    HOW FLESH CLEAVES FAST TO FROZEN JOINT, ...INSOLENT STORM.   326   10
CLEAVING (1)
    CLEAVING FURRED AIR   ....VANITY FAIR 32   11
CLEFT (2)
    THOSE ROCKS, CLEFT AND WORN, THEMSELVES THEN GROW   ....PERSEUS 83   30
    A CLEFT IN YOUR CHIN INSTEAD OF YOUR FOOT   ....DADDY 223   53
CLEMATIS (1)
    UNDER THE SPOKES OF THE CLEMATIS.   ....MYSTIC   269   23
CLENCH (1)
    IN A CLENCH OF BLOOD, THE SLEEP-TALKING VIRGIN   ....MAUDLIN   51   2
CLEO (1)
    ECLIPSING EVA, CLEO AND HELEN OF TROY: ....VIRGIN IN A TREE   81   19

CLEOPATRA (2)
   NUDE AS CLEOPATRA IN MY WELL-BOILED HOSPITAL SHIFT, ...FACE LIFT 156 10
   CLEOPATRA FROM A SLUT. ..................METAMORPHOSES OF THE MOON 307 24
CLEVER (5)
   OH NO, FOR I STRUT IT CLEVER ....STREET SONG 36 11
   IS SHE HIDING, IS SHE EATING HONEY? SHE IS VERY CLEVER. ....BEE. 212 43
   AND GET US CLEAR OF THIS. OH, HE'LL GO CLEVER ....DIALOGUE O. 281 175
   SPREAD GAY CONTAGION WITH EACH CLEVER BREATH. ....DIRGE FOR A JOKER 303 12
   THE CLEVER WOOLLY DOGS HAVE HAD THEIR DAY ....DENOUEMENT 326   7
CLEVEREST (1)
   YET OF DEVILS THE CLEVEREST ....SPIDER 48   5
CLICKER (1)
   SPEWED RELICS CLICKER MASSES IN THE WIND, ...POINT SHIRLEY 110 32
CLICKING (1)
   AND HIGH HEELS CLICKING UP THE WALK; ....FAMILY REUNION 300   4
CLICKS (1)
   ON A STICK THAT RATTLES AND CLICKS, A COUNTERFEIT SNAKE. .....TOTEM 264 18
CLIFF (4)
   WISH FOR EVEN GROUND, AND IT'S THE LAST CLIFF ......ABOVE THE OXBOW 88 22
   A POLICEMAN POINTS OUT A VACANT CLIFF ....WHITSUN 154 18
   THE MOONLIGHT, THAT CHALK CLIFF ....EVENT 194   2
   OVER THE ENGLISH CLIFF AND UNDER SO MUCH HISTORY! ....LYONNESSE 234 22
CLIFFS (4)
   CURDED OVER WITH CLOUDS AND CHALK CLIFFS BLANCHED CHANNEL CROSSING 27 24
   SNUFF-COLORED SAND CLIFFS RISE ....MAN IN BLACK 119 12
   ADMONITORY CLIFFS, AND THE SEA EXPLODING ....FINISTERRE 169   3
   THE CLIFFS ARE EDGED WITH TREFOILS, STARS AND BELLS ....FINISTERRE 169 10
CLIMATE (1)
   AGAINST THE CRACKING CLIMATE. ....PRIVATE GROUND 130   6
CLIMAX (1)
   COULD CLIMAX HIS CAREER, ...TRIO OF LOVE SONGS 314 32
CLIMB (3)
   TO FULL CAPACITY. WE CLIMB IN HOPES ....ABOVE THE OXBOW 88 26
   IN THE MONTH OF RED LEAVES I CLIMB TO A BED OF FIRE. POEM.6.W. 135   6
   TICKS TEMPO TO THE CASUAL CLIMB ...MORNING IN THE HOSPITAL SOLARIUM 332 16
CLIMBING (1)
   TO BE MEANT FOR CLIMBING. A PECULIAR LOGIC ....ABOVE THE OXBOW 88 17
CLIMBS (3)
   IT IS BY THESE HOOKS SHE CLIMBS TO MY NOTICE. ....THREE WOMEN 182 208
   IT IS THE EXCEPTION THAT CLIMBS THE SORROWFUL HILL .....THREE WOMEN 186 332
   UP WHICH THE WAKEFUL PRINCESS CLIMBS TO FIND ....THE PRINCESS. 333   2
CLINGS (1)
   GUILT-STRICKEN HALTS, PALES, CLINGS TO THE PRINCE ....CINDERELLA 304 12
CLINIC (1)
   YOU BRING ME GOOD NEWS FROM THE CLINIC, ...FACE LIFT 155   1
CLINKING (1)
   GLINTING AND CLINKING IN A SAINT'S FALSETTO. ONLY YOU NEW YEAR ON. 176   3
CLOAK (3)
   MOST MOCK-HEROIC, TO CLOAK OUR WAKING AWE ....CHANNEL CROSSING 27 28
   THE CLOAK OF HOLES. ....PURDAH 244 57
   ERECT IN HIS FOLDEROL CLOAK ....DIALOGUE EN ROUTE 308 13
CLOAKED (1)
   TO UNMADE MUD CLOAKED BY SOUR SKY. ....FIRESONG 30 14
CLOAKS (1)
   MIDNIGHT CLOAKS THE SULTRY GROVE; ....PURSUIT 22 26
CLOCK (10)
   AND TACK OF THE CLOCK, UNTIL WE GO, ...ALL THE DEAD DEARS 71 33
   THE SHADOWS OF THE GRASSES INCHED ROUND LIKE HANDS OF A CLOCK,*BABY. 175 43
   THE CLOCK SHALL NOT FIND ME WANTING, NOR THESE STARS ...THREE WOMEN 182 202
   WITH THE COLD BURN DRY ICE HAS. YET THE CLOCK ....DIALOGUE O. 276 11
   SHE HEARS THE CAUSTIC TICKING OF THE CLOCK. ....CINDERELLA 304 14
   THE WAY YOU'D CRACK A CLOCK; YOU'D CRUSH THE BONE ...SONNET: TO EVA 304   2
   YOU'LL HALT THE CLOCK ....TRIO OF LOVE SONGS 315 51
   ATOP THE BROKEN UNIVERSAL CLOCK: ....DOOMSDAY 316   2
   EACH CLOCK TICK CONSECRATES THE DEATH OF STRANGERS. DOOM OF EXILES 318   8
   OUR DRASTIC JARGON, BUT CLOCK HANDS THAT MOVE ...LOVE IS A PARALLAX 329 17
CLOCKCASE (1)
   IN A ROCKETING VERTICAL CLOCKCASE, ...DIALOGUE EN ROUTE 308   5
CLOCKED (1)
   THE MORNING PAPER CLOCKED THE HEADLINE HOUR ....THE TRIAL OF MAN 312   5
CLOCKS (9)
   CLOCKS BELLED TWELVE. MAIN STREET SHOWED OTHERWISE ....OWL 101   1
   THE SHEETS, THE FACES, ARE WHITE AND STOPPED, LIKE CLOCKS. ..THREE. 179 95
   CLOCKS CRY: STILLNESS IS A LIE, MY DEAR;*TO EVA DESCENDING THE STAIR 303   1
   CLOCKS CRY: STILLNESS IS A LIE, MY DEAR.*TO EVA DESCENDING THE STAIR 303   6
   CLOCKS CRY: STILLNESS IS A LIE, MY DEAR.*TO EVA DESCENDING THE STAIR 303 12
   CLOCKS CRY: STILLNESS IS A LIE, MY DEAR.*TO EVA DESCENDING THE STAIR 303 18
   AMID THE TICKING JEWELED CLOCKS THAT MARK ....SONNET: TO TIME 311   2
   UNRAVEL ANTIQUE SAMPLERS, UNWIND THE CLOCKS, ...SONG FOR A REVOLU. 323 13
   OBSCURE THE SCALDING SUN TILL NO CLOCKS MOVE. .....SONNET TO SATAN 323 14
CLOCKWORK (1)
   OF CLOCKWORK THAT MAKES THE ROYAL BLOOD RUN COLD. ....THE PRINCESS. 335 75
CLOISTERS (1)
   COUCHED DAYLONG IN CLOISTERS OF STINGING NETTLE *WREATH FOR A BRIDAL 44   7

```
                                                  TITLE          PAGE  LINE
CLOISTRAL (1)
     INVADE THE CLOISTRAL EYE LIKE PAGES  ......ON THE DECLINE OF ORACLES   78   23
CLOSE (10)
     HE LIFTS AN ARM TO BRING HER CLOSE, BUT SHE  ..........THE OTHER TWO   68   18
     AFTER ALL, IT WAS A KIND OF MARRIAGE, BEING SO CLOSE.  ...IN PLASTER  160   51
     IT IS WHAT THE DEAD CLOSE ON, FINALLY; I IMAGINE THEM  .......TULIPS  161   34
     TOO CLOSE ATTENTION, THEY WILL INVITE ME  .........WUTHERING HEIGHTS  167   17
     SUCH AS FINGERS MIGHT EMBROIDER, CLOSE TO DEATH,  ........FINISTERRE  169   11
     SET CLOSE, LIKE BIRTH PANGS.  ....................THE RABBIT CATCHER  194   16
     WHEN I CAME TOO CLOSE TO THE WASTEBASKET.  ......BURNING THE LETTERS  204    4
     CLOSE ON YOU LIKE THE FIST OF A BABY  .........................LESBOS  229   86
     OF A ROSE CLOSE WHEN THE GARDEN  .................................EDGE  273   14
     TO NORMAL. LET'S CLOSE THE CURTAINS. IT LOOKS WILD  .....DIALOGUE O.  286  335
CLOSED (2)
     IS CLOSED; THE TUB EXISTS BEHIND OUR BACK:  ..........TALE OF A TUB   25   31
     HAD LAZILY CLOSED ONE EYE AND LET THEM SLIP  ...............LYONNESSE  234   21
CLOSELY (1)
     SHE STOPPED FITTING ME SO CLOSELY AND SEEMED OFFISH.  ....IN PLASTER  159   29
CLOSER (1)
     SKY WON'T BE DRAWN CLOSER: ABSOLUTE,  .....METAMORPHOSES OF THE MOON  307    7
CLOSES (1)
     AND I AM AWARE OF MY HEART: IT OPENS AND CLOSES  .............TULIPS  162   60
CLOSET (2)
     FROM A SMOKE-CHOKED CLOSET INTO LIGHT;  ...................AFTERMATH  113    5
     COME HERE, SWEETIE, OUT OF THE CLOSET.  ...............THE APPLICANT  221   28
CLOSETS (1)
     THROUGH CLOSETS OF COPSES  ..........................TEMPER OF TIME  336    9
CLOSING (1)
     A RED FIST, OPENING AND CLOSING,  ....................APPREHENSIONS  195   12
CLOTH (6)
     THE FABRICATION OF SOME CLOTH TO COVER  ...............TALE OF A TUB   25   34
     OF SNAKE-WARP, SHAKE-WEFT. PIPES THE CLOTH OF SNAKES  ..SNAKECHARMER   79   24
     IN AN EBONY AIR, ON WINGS OF WITCH CLOTH,  ...............GOATSUCKER  111   10
     THE FLAT SEA PURPLED LIKE THAT EVIL CLOTH  ...ELECTRA ON AZALEA PATH  117   31
     HENNA HAGS: CLOTH OF YOUR CLOTH.  ....................LEAVING EARLY  146   21
     HENNA HAGS: CLOTH OF YOUR CLOTH.  ....................LEAVING EARLY  146   21
CLOTHES (4)
     THE NURSES GIVE BACK MY CLOTHES, AND AN IDENTITY.  ......THREE WOMEN  183  241
     THERE ARE THE CLOTHES OF A FAT WOMAN I DO NOT KNOW.  ....THREE WOMEN  184  267
     I AM PACKING THE HARD POTATOES LIKE GOOD CLOTHES,  ...........LESBOS  229   68
     OR A PIECE OF MY HAIR OR MY CLOTHES.  ..................LADY LAZARUS  246   64
CLOTS (1)
     IS IT BLOOD CLOTS THE TENDRILS ARE DRAGGING UP THAT STRING?  ...BEE.  211   19
CLOTTED (1)
     BARGE-TAR CLOTTED AT THE TIDE-LINE, THE WRECKED PIER  ...GREEN ROCK.  104    2
CLOUD (16)
     ABOVE: LEAF-WRAITHED WHITE AIR, WHITE CLOUD.  .............BUCOLICS   24   12
     INANE WORLDS OF WIND AND CLOUD.  .........................SCULPTOR   91   13
     TWO CAMPERS IN CLOUD COUNTRY  ..........TWO CAMPERS IN CLOUD COUNTRY  144    T
     IT TOOK THREE DAYS DRIVING NORTH TO FIND A CLOUD  .........TWO CAMP.  145   10
     FROM STONE TO CLOUD, SO I ASCENDED.  ...................LOVE LETTER  147   33
     I WATCH THEIR SPILT TEARS CLOUD AND DULL TO PEARLS.  ........CANDLES  149   31
     THAN THE CLOUD THAT DISTILLS A MIRROR TO REFLECT ITS OWN SLOW  ...
                                                    ... MORNING SONG  157    8
     FLOATS CALM AS A MOON OR A CLOUD.  ....................HEAVY WOMEN  158    7
     IT FINDS THEIR SHAPES IN A CLOUD.  ....................THREE WOMEN  186  347
     THE FEATURELESSNESS OF THAT CLOUD, NOW!  .............LITTLE FUGUE  187    6
     BLACK YEW, WHITE CLOUD,  .............................LITTLE FUGUE  187   14
     PASSES CLOUD AFTER CLOUD.  ............................BERCK-PLAGE  200  105
     PASSES CLOUD AFTER CLOUD.  ............................BERCK-PLAGE  200  105
     OF CLOUD TO GIVE THEM EXPRESSION,  .......................BRASILIA  258    5
     THE FAITH-MAKER, FISTED IN HIS CLOUD, OR THE CHORUS  ....DIALOGUE O.  279  109
     OF CHILD, LEAF AND CLOUD,  ...........................TOUCH-AND-GO  336   21
CLOUDBANK (1)
     IT COULD BE A SNOWFIELD OR A CLOUDBANK.  .....PARLIAMENT HILL FIELDS  152   23
CLOUD-CUCKOO (2)
     CLOUD-CUCKOO,  ...................................LETTER TO A PURIST   37   15
     TO THE CLOUD-CUCKOO LAND OF COLOR WHEELS  ...THE GHOST'S LEAVETAKING   91   35
CLOUDED (1)
     FLOATS CHASTE AS SNOW, TAUNTING THE CLOUDED MIND  WINTER LANDSCAPE,   21    4
CLOUDING (1)
     MY MIRROR IS CLOUDING OVER --  ..........................LAST WORDS  172   11
CLOUDS (17)
     CURDED OVER WITH CLOUDS AND CHALK CLIFFS BLANCHED   CHANNEL CROSSING   27   24
     CLOUDS STEERED A BURNISHED DRIFT;  .........SONG FOR A SUMMER'S DAY   31    8
     HOLDING THE HORSES, THE CLOUDS, THE LEAVES  ..........THE EYE-MOTE  109    6
     THE PASSAGE, SAY, OF THESE MAN-SHAMING CLOUDS.  ...........TWO CAMP.  144    3
     WHERE TREES AND CLOUDS AND ANIMALS PAY NO NOTICE;  ........TWO CAMP.  144    8
     OVERHEAD, THE CLOUDS SIT TASSELED AND FANCY  .................A LIFE  150   15
     I HAVE FALLEN A LONG WAY. CLOUDS ARE FLOWERING  ..............MOON.  173   22
     I WASN'T READY. THE WHITE CLOUDS REARING  ...............THREE WOMEN  178   57
     COLD CLOUDS GO OVER.  ................................LITTLE FUGUE  187    2
     NOW SIMILAR CLOUDS  ..................................LITTLE FUGUE  188   41
     THE CLOUDS ARE A MARRIAGE DRESS, OF THAT PALLOR.  ......LITTLE FUGUE  189   52
     CLOUDS PASS AND DISPERSE.  .........................................ELM  193   34
```

CLOUDS (CONT.)
　　TELLING THE PARTICLES OF THE CLOUDS, THE LEAVES, THE WATER *BURNING.　205　55
　　BUT MY GOD, THE CLOUDS ARE LIKE COTTON.　.........A BIRTHDAY PRESENT　207　39
　　IN THE FURNACE OF GREED. CLOUDS, CLOUDS.　.................THE SWARM　216　16
　　IN THE FURNACE OF GREED. CLOUDS, CLOUDS.　.................THE SWARM　216　16
　　OVER YOUR BODY THE CLOUDS GO　...........................GULLIVER　251　1
CLOUD-STUFF (1)
　　OF CLOUD-STUFF, TIPPING HER　...........................POLLY'S TREE　128　22
CLOUDWRACK (1)
　　CLOUDWRACK AND OWL-HOLLOWED WILLOWS SLANTING OVER　......WATERCOLOR.　112　8
CLOVER (3)
　　LET NIGHT BLESS THAT LUCK-ROOTED MEAD OF CLOVER *WREATH FOR A BRIDAL　45　17
　　RED CLOVER OR GNAW BEETROOT　.....WATERCOLOR OF GRANTCHESTER MEADOWS　112　17
　　WHOSE NEWS IS THE OPEN CHERRY, THE OPEN CLOVER?　............STINGS　214　30
CLOVES (1)
　　STAB A FEW CLOVES IN AN APPLE,　..........................A SECRET　220　30
CLOWN (1)
　　TIGER-TAMER AND GRINNING CLOWN　.........................AERIALIST　331　29
CLOWNLIKE (1)
　　CLOWNLIKE, HAPPIEST ON YOUR HANDS,　.........................YOU'RE　141　1
CLOWNS (1)
　　THEY STUNT LIKE CLOWNS IN THE CIRCUS.　............IN MIDAS' COUNTRY　100　20
CLUBFOOT (1)
　　THEMSELVES ON THE CLAY TOES AND SHORT CLUBFOOT　......METAMORPHOSES.　308　35
CLUBS (1)
　　NOW I BREAK UP IN PIECES THAT FLY ABOUT LIKE CLUBS.　............ELM　192　19
CLUMPED (1)
　　CLUMPED LIKE BULBS AT THE GRASS-ROOT　..MUSSEL HUNTER AT ROCK HARBOR　95　10
CLUMSY (1)
　　THE BLUNT,CLUMSY STUMBLERS, THE BOORS.　...................WINTERING　219　41
CLUNG (1)
　　OF THE DEATH VATS CLUNG TO THEM;　.......TWO VIEWS OF A CADAVER ROOM　114　4
CLUSTER (1)
　　MUSSELS CLUSTER BLUE AS GRAPES:　...................MAGNOLIA SHOALS　122　17
CLUSTERS (1)
　　THREE GIRLS, ENGROSSED, WERE WRENCHING FULL CLUSTERS　RHODODENDRON.　104　21
CLUTCH (1)
　　GROWS TALL. YOU CLUTCH YOUR BARS.　...................BY CANDLELIGHT　237　22
CLUTCHES (1)
　　SHE CLUTCHES AT THE TALISMANIC CORD　...THE PRINCESS AND THE GOBLINS　334　42
CLUTCHING (2)
　　A SOUL GROWN FEVERISH, CLUTCHING ITS DEAD BODY-TREE　....DIALOGUE B.　39　43
　　CLUTCHING MY BOTTLE　..CUT　235　15
CO. (1)
　　DEATH & CO.　...DEATH & CO.　254　T
COACH (1)
　　NINE BLACK MICE WITH EBON COACH, *BLACK PINE TREE IN AN ORANGE LIGHT　328　6
COAL (6)
　　AND THE COAL FIRE BURNS　..RESOLVE　52　7
　　IN THE COAL FIRE WILL NOT WHOLLY CONSOLE THEM.　.................OUIJA　77　7
　　THEY WOULD FLUTTER OFF, BLACK AND GLITTERING, THEY WOULD BE COAL
　　　　ANGELS　...BURNING THE LETTERS　204　33
　　EACH COAL A HOT CROSS-STITCH -- A LOVELY LIGHT!　............THE TOUR　238　21
　　COAL GAS IS GHASTLY STUFF.　................................THE TOUR　238　26
　　WITH WINTER AS YOU CLAIM IT DOES. THE COAL　.............DIALOGUE O.　277　19
COAL-FIRE (1)
　　GLOWERING AT THE COAL-FIRE: "COME FIND ME" -- HER LAST TAUNT.　...
　　　　...　THE SNOWMAN ON THE MOOR　58　5
COALS (1)
　　AS SURE AS THOSE COALS BURN, THE LIVINGROOM　............DIALOGUE O.　286　357
COARSE (3)
　　BLUE-BLOODED IN COARSE COUNTRY REIGNED;　............NATURAL HISTORY　71　2
　　THAT KNITS TO EACH ORIGINAL ITS COARSE COPY. A DARK TARN*LADY AND T.　69　15
　　WHILE THEIR FINGERS WORK WITH THE COARSE MESH AND THE FINE　...NET-.　121　11
COARSENED (1)
　　TO CANACEE CRIES GIBBERISH TO COARSENED EARS.　........INCOMMUNICADO　100　14
COAT (9)
　　WHILE YOU STAND HEROIC IN COAT AND TIE, I SIT　........CONVERSATION.　21　10
　　DISGUISING THE CONSTANT HORROR IN A COAT　.............TALE OF A TUB　25　37
　　HIERATICAL IN YOUR FROCK COAT, MAESTRO OF THE BEES,　...BEEKEEPER'S.　118　5
　　BLACK COAT, BLACK SHOES, AND YOUR　.....................MAN IN BLACK　120　17
　　A THICKET OF SHADOWS IS A POOR COAT. I INHABIT　...........POEM.6.W.　135　2
　　I AM THE SUN, IN MY WHITE COAT,　.............THE SURGEON AT 2 A.M.　171　49
　　WHICH IS THE MIDWIFE, IS THAT HER BLUE COAT?　.......THE BEE MEETING　211　12
　　WHOSE RED HEART BLOOMS THROUGH HER COAT SO ASTOUNDINGLY ---*POP.OCT.　240　3
　　THE STARCHED WHITE COAT, THE CAT'S PAW WALK,　...MORNING IN THE HOS.　332　12
COATS (5)
　　THEY PITCHED THEIR COATS, COME TO GREEN BED.　..............BUCOLICS　23　8
　　SMALL DROPS SPOT THEIR COATS, THEIR GLOVES:　.................ON DECK　143　16
　　AND SEVEN WINTER COATS LAST AUGUST)　.........................ON DECK　143　22
　　IT WILL MAKE LITTLE DRESSES AND COATS,　.................AN APPEARANCE　189　12
　　THE WAITRESS HOLDS OUR COATS AND WE PUT ON　......LOVE IS A PARALLAX　329　22
COAXES (1)
　　THE PRINCESS COAXES THE INCREDULOUS BOY*THE PRINCESS AND THE GOBLINS　334　51

	TITLE	PAGE	LINE

COBALT (1)
   WAKENS, MORNINGS, TO A COBALT SKY, ...YADDO: THE GRAND MANOR 124 19
COBBLED (1)
   HE LUMPS IT DOWN THE PLASTIC COBBLED HILL, ...LESBOS 228 48
COBBLES (1)
   BUMBLINGLY OVER THE NUBS OF THE COBBLES ....ALICANTE LULLABY 43 2
COBRA (4)
   CATASTROPHE A WRITHING LENGTH OF COBRA, ...PERSEUS 83 22
   COBRA LIGHT ....MEDUSA 225 27
   SHALL THE HOOD OF THE COBRA APPALL ME --- ....TOTEM 264 19
   THE SUAVE DISSEMBLING COBRA WEARS A HOOD ....ADMONITIONS 319 10
COBRA'S (1)
   THE MORBID COBRA'S WITS HAVE RUN ASTRAY; ....DENOUEMENT 327 13
COBS (1)
   AND LEFT THE COBS TO RATTLE, BITTEN CLEAN. ....OUIJA 77 18
COBWEB (1)
   WHOLE AS A COBWEB, ...POLLY'S TREE 129 35
COBWEBBED (1)
   WE PEERED AGOG THROUGH THE COBWEBBED DOOR ....ELLA MASON A. 54 26
COCK (6)
   WHICH HAULS DOWN BUCK, COCK, TROUT, TILL ALL MOST FAIR ....FIRESONG 30 6
   IN THEIR HEARTBEATS' BLAZING WAKE UNTIL RED COCK ....EPITAPH FOR F. 46 27
   TROUT, COCK, RAM, ...ON THE DIFFICULTY OF CONJURING UP A DRYAD 66 13
   THE GILDED COCK WILL TURN FOR ME ....TO A JILTED LOVER 310 22
   WE NEVER THOUGHT TO HEAR THE HOLY COCK: ....DOOMSDAY 316 14
   TILL DARK IS CONQUERED BY ORANGE COCK, ...BLACK PINE TREE. 328 15
COCKCHAFERS (1)
   COCKCHAFERS AND THE WAN, GREEN LUNA MOTH. ....GOATSUCKER 111 14
COCKCROW (4)
   "MAY COCKCROW GUARD US SAFE," SAID HE; ....BUCOLICS 23 6
   NEIGHBORHOOD COCKCROW -- ALL NATURE'S PRODIGAL BACKTALK, CONJURING. 66 4
   OF COCKCROW CRYING UP THE DAWN. ....DANSE MACABRE 321 24
   WITH CHARACTERS NO COCKCROW CAN DEFACE. ....SONNET TO SATAN 323 12
COCKED (4)
   COCKED ON THE LONE, LATE, ...PROSPECT 28 11
   WITH BIRD-QUICK EYE COCKED ASKEW .....MISS DRAKE PROCEEDS TO SUPPER 41 14
   THE SWARM IS KNOCKED INTO A COCKED STRAW HAT. ....THE SWARM 217 42
   ARMS FOLDED, EAR COCKED, ...EAVESDROPPER 261 38
COCKLE-SHELL (1)
   WALTZING UP TO ME OUT OF HER COCKLE-SHELL." ......DIALOGUE EN ROUTE 309 30
COCKLE-SHELLS (1)
   DECKED FORTH IN COCKLE-SHELLS, ...DREAM WITH CLAM-DIGGERS 44 18
COCKS (2)
   WHILE THE COCKS AND HENS ....ALICANTE LULLABY 43 5
   COCKS CROW UP A RIVAL ....MOONSONG AT MORNING 316 5
COCK'S (1)
   AND SOLACED HER, BUT QUIT HER AT COCK'S CROWING. QUEEN'S COMPLAINT 28 15
COCKTAIL (1)
   AS AMID THE HECTIC MUSIC AND COCKTAIL TALK ....CINDERELLA 304 13
COCOON (1)
   TIGHTER TO THE COCOON ....SPIDER 48 17
COD (2)
   FERRYING THE SMELLS OF DEAD COD AND TAR. ....A WINTER SHIP 113 20
   "IT SMELLS OF SALT COD, YOU HAD BETTER ....A SECRET 220 29
COFFEE (4)
   OF BLUNT PENCILS, ROSE-SPRIGGED COFFEE CUP, ...CONJURING. 65 2
   THICK AS FOREIGN COFFEE, AND WITH A SLUGGY PULSE. .....WORDS HEARD. 202 2
   THE IMPOTENT HUSBAND SLUMPS OUT FOR A COFFEE. ....LESBOS 228 44
   YOU DRANK YOUR COFFEE LIKE ORIGINAL SIN, ...THE TRIAL OF MAN 312 6
COFFEE-TABLE (1)
   WHILE WE'RE SITTING, FACE TO FACE ACROSS THE COFFEE-TABLE, ...
            ... DIALOGUE OVER A OUIJA BOARD 276 3-4
COFFIN (5)
   ...COFFIN OF THE FOURTH CENTURY A.D. CONTAINING THE
        SKELETON... ....ALL THE DEAD DEARS 70 E/2
   LIVING WITH HER WAS LIKE LIVING WITH MY OWN COFFIN: .....IN PLASTER 160 48
   THE LONG COFFIN OF SOAP-COLORED OAK, ...BERCK-PLAGE 199 70
   FOLLOWING THE COFFIN ON ITS FLOWERY CART LIKE A BEAUTIFUL WOMAN, ...
            ... BERCK-PLAGE 200 115
   I WOULD SAY IT WAS THE COFFIN OF A MIDGET*THE ARRIVAL OF THE BEE BOX 212 3
COFFINED (2)
   GROWNUPS COFFINED IN STOCKINGS AND JACKETS, ...WHITSUN 153 4
   OF UNANSWERED LETTERS, COFFINED IN A LETTER CASE. ......THREE WOMEN 182 200
COFFINS (1)
   FROM BEDS BOXED-IN LIKE COFFINS ....OLD LADIES' HOME 120 17
COG (1)
   ALL COGS, WEIRD SPARKLE AND EVERY COG SOLID GOLD. ....THE TOUR 237 5
COGS (3)
   PARTS, BITS, COGS, THE SHINING MULTIPLES. ....THREE WOMEN 177 29
   ALL COGS, WEIRD SPARKLE AND EVERY COG SOLID GOLD. ....THE TOUR 237 5
   COGS AND DISKS, INANE MECHANIC WHIMS, ...SONNET: TO EVA 304 7
COIL (3)
   AND THE DECLINE OF EMPIRES THE THICK COIL OF A VAST ....PERSEUS 83 23
   AND I SAW WHITE MAGGOTS COIL ....MEDALLION 124 21
   THESE ORCHIDS ARE SPLENDID. THEY SPOT AND COIL LIKE SNAKES.*SURGEON. 170 16

| | | TITLE | PAGE | LINE |

COILED (1)
EACH DEAD CHILD COILED, A WHITE SERPENT, ...EDGE 272 9
COILED-SPRING (1)
FUSTY REMEMBRANCES, THE COILED-SPRING STAIR ....WIDOW 164 9
COILINGS (1)
OF SWAYS AND COILINGS, FROM THE SNAKE-ROOTED BOTTOM ...SNAKECHARMER 79 11
COILS (4)
FROM WHICH COILS, CAUGHT ANTS WAVED LEGS IN ....SPIDER 49 19
WITH COILS OF RAM'S-HORN. ....DARK WOOD, DARK WATER 127 10
THE COILS AND PIPES THAT MADE HIM RUN. ....THE BURNT-OUT SPA 138 17
AND IDLE COILS OF JARGON YET UNSPOKEN. ....SONNET: TO EVA 304 8
COIN (2)
MY JILTING LADY SQUANDER COIN, GOLD LEAF STOCK DITCHES, CONJURING. 66 35
COIN, BUTTON, TRIGGER ....WORDS FOR A NURSERY 74 39
COINS (2)
ON THE COINS OF PITY. AT RANDOM ....THE BEGGARS 47 9
LOOK, THEY ARE MELTING LIKE COINS IN THE POWERFUL JUICES -- ZOO K. 154 8
COLD (50)
COLD SQUINT STEALS SKY'S COLOR; WHILE BRUIT ....VANITY FAIR 32 8
PACED BRISK FATHER SHAWN. A COLD DAY, A SODDEN ONE IT WAS ...
... DIALOGUE BETWEEN GHOST AND PRIEST 38 2
NIGHTFALL, COLD EYE -- NEITHER DISHEARTENS ....THE BEGGARS 47 1
OF STICKS. THE LIGHT FALLS CHALK AND COLD ...THE EVERLASTING MONDAY 62 3
AS NYMPHS; COLD VISION ...ON THE DIFFICULTY OF CONJURING UP A DRYAD 66 30
COLD POLE AND HOT PLATE. ....WORDS FOR A NURSERY 74 25
AND AS I LISTENED ITS COLD TEETH SEETHED ON THE DECLINE OF ORACLES 78 3
WHEN SEAS WASH COLD, FOAM- ....FULL FATHOM FIVE 92 3
THEIR DREAM OF THE WINTER'S COLD; STONES ....CHILD'S PARK STONES 101 24
THE SEA IN ITS COLD GIZZARD GROUND THOSE ROUNDS. .....POINT SHIRLEY 110 24
EVEN OUR SHADOWS ARE BLUE WITH COLD. ....A WINTER SHIP 113 23
DISTANT AND COLD AS PHOTOS, ...OLD LADIES' HOME 120 11
THEY ARE CONCEIVING A DYNASTY OF PERFECT COLD. ....TWO CAMP. 145 19
KNEE-DEEP IN THE COLD AND SWAMPED BY FLOWERS? ....LEAVING EARLY 146 44
AND A DROWNED MAN, COMPLAINING OF THE GREAT COLD, ...A LIFE 150 34
COLD AS AN EEL, WITHOUT EYELIDS. ....ZOO KEEPER'S WIFE 154 2
I COULDN'T SLEEP FOR A WEEK, SHE WAS SO COLD. ....IN PLASTER 158 9
THESE ARE OUR CREPES. EAT THEM BEFORE THEY BLOW COLD." ..FINISTERRE 170 36
WHEN THE SOLES OF MY FEET GROW COLD, ...LAST WORDS 172 19
THIS IS THE LIGHT OF THE MIND, COLD AND PLANETARY. ....MOON. 172 1
FLOATING ON THEIR DELICATE FEET OVER THE COLD PEWS, ...MOON. 173 25
ENDLESSLY PROCEED -- AND THE COLD ANGELS, THE ABSTRACTIONS. THREE. 177 20
THAT WANES AND WANES, FACING THE COLD ANGEL? ....THREE WOMEN 177 39
I REMEMBER A WHITE, COLD WING ....THREE WOMEN 178 49
I FEEL IT ENTER ME, COLD, ALIEN, LIKE AN INSTRUMENT. ...THREE WOMEN 182 183
INTERCEPTING THE BLUE BOLTS OF A COLD MOON? ....THREE WOMEN 185 291
COLD CLOUDS GO OVER. ....LITTLE FUGUE 187 2
COLD WORLDS SHAKE FROM THE OAR. ....CROSSING THE WATER 190 7
FROM ITS COLD INDIGO. ....EVENT 194 5
COLD BLANKS APPROACH US: ............................APPREHENSIONS 196 19
COLD GLASS, HOW YOU INSERT YOURSELF ....THE OTHER 202 26
IT BREATHES FROM MY SHEETS, THE COLD DEAD CENTER *A BIRTHDAY PRESENT 207 50
WHOSE IS THAT LONG WHITE BOX IN THE GROVE, WHAT HAVE THEY
ACCOMPLISHED, WHY AN I COLD. ....THE BEE MEETING 212 55
THEY TAKE IT. THE COLD SETS IN. ....WINTERING 218 30
HER BODY A BULB IN THE COLD AND TOO DUMB TO THINK. ....WINTERING 219 45
HIS HIGH COLD MASKS OF AMNESIA. ....THE JAILER 227 31
AND YOU OUT COLD BESIDE ME IN YOUR CHAIR. ....STOPPED DEAD 230 5
COLD GRITS UNDERFOOT, ...LYONNESSE 234 17
ACROSS THE INDIAN CARPET, THE COLD FLOOR, ...BY CANDLELIGHT 237 25
COLD HOMICIDES. ....NICK AND THE CANDLESTICK 241 8
COLD FOLDS OF EGO, THE CALLA, ...THE NIGHT DANCES 250 12
COLD AS SNOW BREATH, IT TAMPS THE WOMB ....THE MUNICH MANNEQUINS 262 2
WITH THE COLD BURN DRY ICE HAS. YET THE CLOCK ....DIALOGUE O. 276 11
WHY, YOUR HAND'S COLD AS ICE! THEN CHAFE THE COLD ......DIALOGUE O. 285 333
WHY, YOUR HAND'S COLD AS ICE! THEN CHAFE THE COLD ......DIALOGUE O. 285 333
COLD MOONS WITHDRAW, REFUSING TO COME TO TERMS ......METAMORPHOSES. 307 1
COLD ON MY NARROW COT I LIE ....TO A JILTED LOVER 309 1
NIPPLED MOONS, EXTINCT AND COLD, ...DANSE MACABRE 321 8
COLD AND FINAL, THE IMAGINATION ....TWO LOVERS. 327 1
OF CLOCKWORK THAT MAKES THE ROYAL BLOOD RUN COLD. ....THE PRINCESS. 335 75
COLD-BLOODED (1)
SUMMER GROWS OLD, COLD-BLOODED MOTHER. ....FROG AUTUMN 99 1
COLDNESS (3)
NOW COLDNESS COMES SIFTING DOWN, LAYER AFTER LAYER, ...POEM.5.F. 134 1
SUCH COLDNESS, FORGETFULNESS. ....THE NIGHT DANCES 250 17
ANGEL OF COLDNESS, ...THE RIVAL/DR 291 20
COLDS (1)
DOURLY THE LONG HOTS AND COLDS, ...THE HERMIT AT OUTERMOST HOUSE 119 8
COLLAPSE (3)
THE SEA'S COLLAPSE. ....POINT SHIRLEY 110 3
THE PIER PILINGS SEEM ABOUT TO COLLAPSE ....A WINTER SHIP 113 15
THEY COLLAPSE LIKE LUNGS, THE ESCAPED WATER ....PRIVATE GROUND 130 9
COLLAPSES (1)
WHITE BRUISES TOWARD COLOR, ELSE COLLAPSES. ....MOONRISE 98 12

97

COLLAR (1)
   DEATH IS THE DRESS SHE WEARS, HER HAT AND COLLAR. ....WIDOW 164   13
COLLECT (3)
    THEY GLITTER LIKE EYES, AND I COLLECT THEM ALL. .....PRIVATE GROUND 131   22
    AND A DEW COLLECT ON THEM, DEARER THAN MONEY, ...SLEEP. 144   9
    TO COLLECT HIS BEATINGS. AND IF HE'S A GO-BETWEEN ......DIALOGUE O. 281 185
COLLECTING (1)
   I'M COLLECTING MY STRENGTH; ONE DAY I SHALL MANAGE WITHOUT HER, ...
             ... IN PLASTER 160   55
COLLECTOR (1)
   OF VALENTINE-FACES MIGHT PLEASE A COLLECTOR: ....A LIFE 150   17
COLLECTS (1)
   KEEPER COLLECTS HALF-DOLLARS FOR THE SLOPES ....ABOVE THE OXBOW   88   40
COLLEGE (1)
   WHILE TULIPS BOW LIKE A COLLEGE OF CARDINALS ....APRIL AUBADE 312   7
COLLEGES (1)
   TODAY THE COLLEGES ARE DRUNK WITH SPRING. ....THREE WOMEN 185 302
COLLUSION (1)
   SUCH COLLUSION OF MULISH ELEMENTS ....POINT SHIRLEY 110   17
COLONNADES (2)
   THERE IS THE LABURNUM, ITS BLOND COLONNADES, ...THE ARRIVAL. 213   29
   COLONNADES OF ANGELS NOD HER IN ....THE PRINCESS AND THE GOBLINS 333   13
COLOR (28)
   FROM THE GENUINE COLOR OF SKIN; CAN OUR DREAMS ....TALE OF A TUB   25   27
   COLOR OF LEMON, MANGO, PEACH, ...SOUTHERN SUNRISE   26   1
   COLD SQUINT STEALS SKY'S COLOR; WHILE BRUIT ....VANITY FAIR   32   8
   TO BOYCOTT COLOR AND FORBID ANY FLOWER ..SOLILOQUY OF THE SOLIPSIST   38   26
   OF THE WORLD COMES CLEAR AND FILLS WITH COLOR. .....THE THIN PEOPLE   65   35
   TO THE CLOUD-CUCKOO LAND OF COLOR WHEELS ...THE GHOST'S LEAVETAKING   91   35
   HIS WORLD OF MUD -- GREEN COLOR ....MUSSEL HUNTER AT ROCK HARBOR   97   71
   WHITE BRUISES TOWARD COLOR, ELSE COLLAPSES. ....MOONRISE   98   12
   I CAN SEE NO COLOR FOR THIS WHITENESS. ....MOONRISE   98   20
   FLITS NIMBLE-WINGED IN THICKETS, AND OF GOOD COLOR. ....WATERCOLOR. 112   7
   OF A COLOR ....POLLY'S TREE 128   9
   WINTER DAWN IS THE COLOR OF METAL, ...WAKING IN WINTER 151   2
   UPSETTING ME WITH THEIR SUDDEN TONGUES AND THEIR COLOR, ...TULIPS 161   41
   WEIGHTING THE PALE SKY WITH A SOLIDER COLOR. .....WUTHERING HEIGHTS 167   7
   TONIGHT, FOR THIS PERSON, BLUE IS A BEAUTIFUL COLOR. ......SURGEON. 171   43
   O COLOR OF DISTANCE AND FORGETFULNESS! -- ....THREE WOMEN 179 103
   THE BLUE COLOR PALES. HE IS HUMAN AFTER ALL. ....THREE WOMEN 181 166
   THEY COLOR MY SLEEP, ...LITTLE FUGUE 188   34
   WHAT IS THE NAME OF THAT COLOR? --- ....BERCK-PLAGE 200   97
   OF CARDBOARD CARTONS THE COLOR OF CEMENT OR A DOG PACK ....BURNING. 204   11
   A DEATH TREE, COLOR GONE, AN AUSTRALIAN GUM TREE -- ....FATHERLESS. 205   3
   SURELY THE SKY IS NOT THAT COLOR, ...THE JAILER 226   24
   AND OF ANOTHER COLOR. ....AMNESIAC 233   16
   SUDDENLY TURNS, TURNS COLOR. THE STREETLIGHT ....LETTER IN NOVEMBER 253   2
   HORSE THE COLOR OF RUST, ...SHEEP IN FOG 262   6
   I WANT TO FILL IT WITH COLOR AND DUCKS, ...CHILD 265   2
   COLOR FLOODS TO THE SPOT, DULL PURPLE. ....CONTUSION 271   1
   THE COLOR OF PEARL. ....CONTUSION 271   3
COLORED (4)
   COLORED BEADS ON THE STRUNG ROADS, AND THE PEOPLE STROLL ....OXBOW.   89   51
   COLORED TO DULL THE PIGMENT ....CHILD'S PARK STONES 101   16
   THE COLORED TENTS ALL TOPPLE IN THE BAY; ....DENOUEMENT 327   16
   LIKE COLORED TOPS THROUGH TIME ....TOUCH-AND-GO 335   10
COLORLESS (3)
   A COLORLESS WEATHER, ...TWO VIEWS OF WITHENS   72   13
   BUT COLORLESS. COLORLESS. ....POPPIES IN JULY 203   15
   BUT COLORLESS. COLORLESS. ....POPPIES IN JULY 203   15
COLORS (12)
   KNOBBED QUARTZ; FLAYED COLORS RIPEN ....ODE FOR TED   29   11
   CALL HERE WITH FLYING COLORS ALL WATCHFUL BIRDS *WREATH FOR A BRIDAL   45   13
   VERMILIONS, BRONZES, COLORS OF THE SUN ....OUIJA   77   6
   THROWN: FEAR, WISDOM, AT ONE: ALL COLORS ......WHITENESS I REMEMBER 103   32
   THE FUGITIVE COLORS DIE. POEM.5.F. 135   10
   THE COLORS ASSERT THEMSELVES WITH A SORT OF VENGEANCE. ...TWO CAMP. 145   14
   THEIR POPPY-SLEEPY COLORS DO HIM NO GOOD. ....INSOMNIAC 163   21
   STENCHES AND COLORS ASSAIL ME. ....THE SURGEON AT 2 A.M. 170   14
   THEY HAVE TOO MANY COLORS, TOO MUCH LIFE. THEY ARE NOT QUIET,*THREE. 178   69
   THE COLORS REPLENISH THEMSELVES, AND THE WET ....THREE WOMEN 185 313
   THESE ARE THE CLEAR BRIGHT COLORS OF THE NURSERY, ...THREE WOMEN 185 317
   OR AFTER GAY DAYS, OR COLORS THE GROWER FOUND GOOD. ..QUEEN MARY'S. 290   18
COLOSSAL (2)
   OF OUR COLOSSAL SLEEP, COME HOME TO FIND ....DOOM OF EXILES 318   2
   THEY LOLL FOREVER IN COLOSSAL SLEEP; ....THE DEAD. 320   12
COLOSSUS (2)
   THAT GRANDIOSE COLOSSUS WHO ....LETTER TO A PURIST   36   1
   THE COLOSSUS ....THE COLOSSUS 129   T
COLOUR (1)
   VELVET PILLOWS THE COLOUR OF BLOOD PUDDING ....LEAVING EARLY 145   5
COLUMBUS (1)
   OR HEADSTRONG COLUMBUS CRAB. ....MUSSEL HUNTER AT ROCK HARBOR   97   76
COLUMN (2)
   I STAND IN A COLUMN ....STINGS 214   20

COLUMN (CONT.)
    COLUMN OF DAZZLE DRAWS MY EYES TO THE WALL ....DIALOGUE O. 279   88
COMB (2)
    THERE IS MY COMB AND BRUSH. THERE IS AN EMPTINESS. .....THREE WOMEN 184 268
    I SHOULD SIT ON A ROCK OFF CORNWALL AND COMB MY HAIR. ....LESBOS 228   29
COMBAT (1)
    UNHORSED AND SHREDDED IN THE GROVE OF COMBAT ....SOW   61   31
COMBERS (1)
    WERE SQUEALING WHERE COMBERS BROKE AND THE SPINDRIFT ......SUICIDE. 115   10
COMBINATIONS (1)
    AMONG HER SECRET COMBINATIONS OF EGGSHELLS ....MISS DRAKE P.   41   7
COMBS (2)
    BARE-HANDED, I HAND THE COMBS. ....STINGS 214   1
    EIGHT COMBS OF YELLOW CUPS, ...STINGS 214   7
COME (65)
    THEY PITCHED THEIR COATS, COME TO GREEN BED. ....BUCOLICS   23   8
    SO SHE IS COME TO THIS RARE PASS ....THE QUEEN'S COMPLAINT   29   21
    NOT OF STAUNCHING SUCH STRICT FLAME, BUT COME, ...FIRESONG   30   20
    "COME LADY, BRING THAT POT ....TINKER JACK AND THE TIDY WIVES   34   1
    "COME LADY, BRING THAT FACE ....TINKER JACK AND THE TIDY WIVES   34   10
    "COME, COME," FATHER SHAWN GAVE AN IMPATIENT SHRUG, ...DIALOGUE B.   39   21
    "COME, COME," FATHER SHAWN GAVE AN IMPATIENT SHRUG, ...DIALOGUE B.   39   21
    IS NOT YET COME. ....DIALOGUE BETWEEN GHOST AND PRIEST   39   38
    WHAT'S TO COME, ...RECANTATION   42   9
    ITS CLEAR AIR WINNOWED BY ANGELS; SHE WAS COME ....DREAM WITH C.   43   2
    FRESH LEAVED OUT IN VOWS: "COME TELL ....CRYSTAL GAZER   55   8
    WHATEVER TRIAL'S TO COME, SO SAY TRUE." ....CRYSTAL GAZER   55   20
    GLOWERING AT THE COAL-FIRE: "COME FIND ME" -- HER LAST TAUNT. ...
                                  ... THE SNOWMAN ON THE MOOR   58   5
    HE DID NOT COME ....THE SNOWMAN ON THE MOOR   58   6
    IN THINNESS, TO COME, LATER, ...THE THIN PEOPLE   64   14
    COME, SO UNLIKE US, TO A STIFF IMPASSE, ...THE OTHER TWO   69   31
    LIKE A SOAP-BUBBLE AS YOU CALLED: COME HERE! THE DISQUIETING MUSES   76   47
    DARK FACE. SO MIGHT RIGOR MORTIS COME TO STIFFEN ....PERSEUS   83   32
    COME TO BARTER ENDLESSLY ....SCULPTOR   91   2
    THEN YOU COME IN WITH THE TIDE'S COMING ....FULL FATHOM FIVE   92   2
    BACKTRACKING TAIL. I'D COME FOR ....MUSSEL HUNTER AT ROCK HARBOR   95   8
    ANIMAL, COME FROM ANOTHER ....CHILD'S PARK STONES 101   7
    AND I COME BY ....POINT SHIRLEY 111   37
    WE WANTED TO SEE THE SUN COME UP ....A WINTER SHIP 113   24
    NO HARM CAN COME TO THEM. ....THE SLEEPERS 123   22
    COME CLEAR OF THE SHADOW. HISTORY ....THE MANOR GARDEN 125   8
    CALL HIM ANY NAME, HE'LL COME TO IT. POEM.4.BEAST. 134   16
    ON FRIDAYS THE LITTLE CHILDREN COME POEM.7.S. 137   36
    AND THE CRICKETS COME CREEPING INTO OUR HAIR ....SLEEP. 144   25
    I COME TO WHEEL RUTS, AND WATER ....WUTHERING HEIGHTS 167   28
    I COME TO ONE BUSH OF BERRIES SO RIPE IT IS A BUSH OF FLIES, ...
                                  ... BLACKBERRYING 168   15
    THE ONLY THING TO COME NOW IS THE SEA. ...............BLACKBERRYING 169   19
    THEY DO NOT COME FROM THE BAY OF THE DEAD DOWN THERE, ...FINISTERRE 170   33
    I WANT TO BE LOOKING AT THEM WHEN THEY COME ....LAST WORDS 172   4
    ONE DAY IT WON'T COME BACK. THINGS AREN'T LIKE THAT. ....LAST WORDS 172   16
    O WHAT HAS COME OVER US, MY SISTER! ....THE BABYSITTERS 175   28
    WE HAVE ONLY COME TO LOOK. YOU ARE TOO NEW ....NEW YEAR ON DARTMOOR 176   8
    "THIS IS WHERE YOU WILL COME WHEN YOU ARE READY." ......THREE WOMEN 180 123
    THE LITTLE SILVER TROPHIES THEY'VE COME SO FAR FOR. ....THREE WOMEN 183 221
    LOVE CANNOT COME HERE. ....EVENT 195   16
    YOU COME IN LATE, WIPING YOUR LIPS. ....THE OTHER 201   1
    LET IT NOT COME BY THE MAIL, FINGER BY FINGER. ..A BIRTHDAY PRESENT 208   52
    LET IT NOT COME BY WORD OF MOUTH, I SHOULD BE SIXTY ......BIRTHDAY. 208   53
    DID IT COME LIKE AN ARROW, DID IT COME LIKE A KNIFE? THE DETECTIVE 209   21
    DID IT COME LIKE AN ARROW, DID IT COME LIKE A KNIFE? THE DETECTIVE 209   21
    THE BODY DOES NOT COME INTO IT AT ALL. ....THE DETECTIVE 209   25
    HERE THEY COME, THE OUTRIDERS, ON THEIR HYSTERICAL ELASTICS. ..BEE. 212   38
    WILL IT COME OUT ....A SECRET 219   10
    COME HERE, SWEETIE, OUT OF THE CLOSET. ....THE APPLICANT 221   28
    IS THAT ALL HE CAN COME UP WITH, ...THE JAILER 226   4
    O MAIDEN AUNT, YOU HAVE COME TO CALL. ....THE TOUR 237   1
    TO LAST IT OUT AND NOT COME BACK AT ALL. ....LADY LAZARUS 245   38
    AND HERE YOU COME, WITH A CUP OF TEA ....KINDNESS 270   16
    WE HAVE COME SO FAR, IT IS OVER. ....EDGE 272   8
    COME ON CALL LIKE THAT BUT PAN? HE'S ...DIALOGUE OVER A OUIJA BOARD 277   28
    TO QUICKEN HIS SLUGGARD'S BLOOD. BUT HE NEEDN'T COME ...DIALOGUE O. 281 184
    A DEVIL. WAIT: HE SHIFTS. HE HASN'T COME*DIALOGUE OVER A OUIJA BOARD 282 216
    COLD MOONS WITHDRAW, REFUSING TO COME TO TERMS ......METAMORPHOSES. 307   1
    AND VOLUPTUOUS VENUS TO COME ....DIALOGUE EN ROUTE 309   29
    UNTIL THE PEAK OF NOON HAS COME ....TO A JILTED LOVER 310   24
    AND COME TO THIS ....MOONSONG AT MORNING 317   10
    OF OUR COLOSSAL SLEEP, COME HOME TO FIND ....DOOM OF EXILES 318   2
    THEY WANT NO PROUD PATERNAL KINGDOM COME; ....THE DEAD 320   6
    YET AS WE WONDER WHAT CAN COME OF ICE ....PROLOGUE TO SPRING 322   14
    GAUDY MIRACLE OCCUR,TO COME ....MORNING IN THE HOSPITAL SOLARIUM 333   25
COMEBACK (1)
    COMEBACK IN BROAD DAY ....LADY LAZARUS 246   52

COMERS (1)
   THE ANTS -- A FILE OF COMERS, A FILE OF GOERS -- ....SPIDER   49   29
COMES (15)
   BROODING AS THE WINTER NIGHT COMES ON. ....WINTER LANDSCAPE,   21   10
   TIME COMES ROUND FOR THAT FOUL SLUT: ....STRUMPET SONG   33   4
   WHEN NIGHT COMES BLACK ....THE SHIRIKE   42   1
   OF THE WORLD COMES CLEAR AND FILLS WITH COLOR. .....THE THIN PEOPLE   65   35
   COMES TO ROOST THERE, FRAIL ....POLLY'S TREE   128   17
   NOW COLDNESS COMES SIFTING DOWN, LAYER AFTER LAYER, ...POEM.5.F.   134   1
   AND COMES FROM A COUNTRY FAR AWAY AS HEALTH. ....TULIPS   162   63
   I AM IMPORTANT TO HER. SHE COMES AND GOES. ....MIRROR   174   15
   HERE HE COMES NOW, AMONG THE MACKEREL GATHERERS ....BERCK-PLAGE   196   14
   TO BLEED, IF IT COMES TO THAT. ........................EAVESDROPPER   260   6
   FOR FORTUNE-TELLING? AND WHERE IS IT FORTUNE COMES ....DIALOGUE O.   277   45
   IF NOTHING COMES OF IT. ON THE OTHER HAND, ...DIALOGUE O.   281 198
   COMES BLUNT AND WAN ....AQUATIC NOCTURNE   306   26
   OUR YEARS. DEATH COMES IN A CASUAL STEEL CAR, YET ..SONNET: TO TIME   311   3
   COMES A FLOCK OF BOTTLE BATTLESHIPS ....EPITAPH IN THREE PARTS   337   2
COMET (5)
   COMET COOLLY GIVING MY ....MUSSEL HUNTER AT ROCK HARBOR   96   57
   SCAR IN THE SKY, RED COMET ....STINGS 215   58
   A COMET TAIL! ....AMNESIAC   233   19
   COMMANDING THAT CORKSCREW COMET JET FORTH INK ......SONNET TO SATAN   323   5
   OF COMET HARA-KIRI THROUGH THE DARK ....LOVE IS A PARALLAX   329   29
COMETS (1)
   THE COMETS ....THE NIGHT DANCES   250   15
COMET'S (1)
   PLUCKS BARE THAT COMET'S FLOWERING. ....EPITAPH FOR FIRE AND FLOWER   46   28
COMFORT (2)
   THE BLUE EYE OF MY TURQUOISE WILL COMFORT ME. ....LAST WORDS   172   20
   NINE MONTHS TOO SOON FOR COMFORT, BUT A BRIGHT ....DIALOGUE O.   280 141
COMFORTABLE (2)
   IT IS COMFORTABLE, FOR A CHANGE, TO MEAN SO LITTLE. ......TWO CAMP.   145   17
   WHOSE HOPES ARE SO LOW THEY ARE COMFORTABLE -- ....MYSTIC   269   21
COMFORTLESS (1)
   COMFORTLESS AS SALT. SNAKE AND BIRD .....SLEEP IN THE MOJAVE DESERT   144   18
COMIC (3)
   FROM A GROSS COMIC STRIP, AND TOWARD .....ON THE DECLINE OF ORACLES   78   24
   FROM THE COMIC OPERATIC FANTASY THE SEAFARER ....BATTLE-SCENE   84   ST
   FROM THE COMIC ACCIDENT OF BIRTH ....DIRGE FOR A JOKER   303   9
COMING (14)
   COMING UP AND UP THE STAIRS. ....PURSUIT   23   50
   WHOSE STARK ACT ALL COMING DOUBLE LUCK JOINS. ..WREATH FOR A BRIDAL   44   6
   IT TOOK ROOT AT MY COMING ....NIGHT SHIFT   76   12
   AND THOSE MEN COMING UP THE STAIR. ....ON THE DECLINE OF ORACLES   78   21
   COMING UP, THOSE THREE. WORTH ....ON THE DECLINE OF ORACLES   78   28
   IN GOING UP FOR THE COMING DOWN IF THE POST ....ABOVE THE OXBOW   88   18
   THEN YOU COME IN WITH THE TIDE'S COMING ....FULL FATHOM FIVE   92   2
   COMING AND GOING, BREATH BY BREATH, WITHOUT ANY FUSS. ....TULIPS   161   51
   COMING AT ME, LIKE A CASTLE, FROM THE TOP OF THE RIVER. *THREE WOMEN   178   51
   GLOWING AND COMING AND GOING, FLUSH ON FLUSH. ....FEVER.   232   42
   I AM NEVER, NEVER, NEVER COMING HOME! ....AMNESIAC   233   27
   A CAR DOOR SLAM; VOICES COMING NEAR; ....FAMILY REUNION   300   2
   WE IGNORE THE COMING DOOM OF GOLD ....GOLD MOUTHS CRY   302   7
   GILDED, COMING CORRECT ....AERIALIST   331   13
COMMANDING (2)
   SHE STOOD UP, A THIN COMMANDING FIGURE ....BITTER STRAWBERRIES   300   29
   COMMANDING THAT CORKSCREW COMET JET FORTH INK ......SONNET TO SATAN   323   5
COMMENCE (1)
   AND COMMENCE TO SWING. ....AERIALIST 331   18
COMMENDED (1)
   BUT ONE DUSK OUR QUESTIONS COMMENDED US TO A TOUR ....SOW   60   7
COMMISSION (1)
   BY LEAVE OF THE PARK COMMISSION ....A WINTER'S TALE   87   22
COMMITTING (1)
   PLAYING AND RESTING WITHOUT COMMITTING ITSELF. ....TULIPS   161   56
COMMON (10)
   NOW, FREE, BY HAZARD'S QUIRK, FROM THE COMMON ILL   CHANNEL CROSSING   27   26
   AMONG THE COMMON ROUT ....STREET SONG 35   2
   NOR EVEN ONE OF THE COMMON BARNYARD SOWS, ...SOW   61   17
   AT THE COMMON HOMECOMING ....THE GREAT CARBUNCLE   73   28
   ON BOSTON COMMON A RED STAR ....A WINTER'S TALE   86   1
   LANTERN-JAWED REASON, SQUAT COMMON SENSE,   THE DEATH OF MYTH-MAKING   104   3
   AND PERIWINKLES, SHRUNK TO COMMON ....GREEN ROCK, WINTHROP BAY   105   13
   I WILL HIM TO BE COMMON, ...THREE WOMEN   186 334
   BUT THE NAME OF THE TOWN IS COMMON. ....DADDY   222   19
   WILL PROVE TO BE SOME COMMON PARLOR FAKE: ..........METAMORPHOSES.   307   22
COMMONERS (1)
   IN ONE BODY THOSE EARTHBORN COMMONERS ....NATURAL HISTORY   71   8
COMMON-SENSE (1)
   GILLED LIKE A FISH. A COMMON-SENSE ....YOU'RE   141   3
COMMUNICATE (1)
   I CAN'T COMMUNICATE." ....LESBOS   229   84
COMMUNICATION (1)
   NOW EARTH REJECTS COMMUNICATION *INSOLENT STORM STRIKES AT THE SKULL   326   29

COMMUNION (4)
   SHUTTING THEIR MOUTHS ON IT, LIKE A COMMUNION TABLET. ....TULIPS   161   35
   A COMMUNION WAFER? BLUBBERY MARY? ....MEDUSA   225   33
   ITS FIRST COMMUNION OUT OF MY LIVE TOES. ..NICK AND THE CANDLESTICK   241   19
   THE PILL OF THE COMMUNION TABLET, ...MYSTIC   268   16
COMPANIONABLE (1)
   THE COMPANIONABLE ILLS ....THE COMPANIONABLE ILLS   105   T
COMPANIONED (1)
   LIES, COMPANIONED BY THE GIMCRACK ....ALL THE DEAD DEARS   70   4
COMPANIONS (1)
   AND I FACED MY TRAVELING COMPANIONS. ....THE DISQUIETING MUSES   76   48
COMPANY (4)
   WILL BETRAY THE COMPANY I KEEP. ....THE DISQUIETING MUSES   76   56
   WHAT GIRL EVER FLOURISHED IN SUCH COMPANY? ....MAGI   148   18
   OR MUCH COMPANY, OR THE MILDNESS OF THE SOUTH. ....STARS.   166   30
   FOR A LIFE IN SUCH COMPANY; ....WUTHERING HEIGHTS   168   41
COMPARED (2)
   COMPARED WITH ME, A TREE IS IMMORTAL ....I AM VERTICAL   162   8
   COMPARED TO YOU, I AM CORRUPTIBLE AS A LOAF OF BREAD.   THE RIVAL/DR   291   1
COMPARISON (2)
   COMPARISON WITH THE SUNKEN SILVER-GRIZZLED ....ABOVE THE OXBOW   88   6
   IN COMPARISON TO THESE ORGANS! ....THE SURGEON AT 2 A.M.   171   19
COMPASS (1)
   PACKING WITHOUT A COMPASS OR SCALE ...SONG FOR A REVOLUTIONARY LOVE   323   10
COMPASSIONATE (1)
   WIDOW, THE COMPASSIONATE TREES BEND IN, ...WIDOW   164   26
COMPELLED (3)
   OUR LONE LUCK NOW, COMPELLED BY BOND, BY BLOOD, ...CHANNEL CROSSING   27   33
   COMPELLED BY CALAMITY'S MAGNET ....AFTERMATH   113   1
   COMPELLED TO DEADLOCK UNDERGROUND. ....DANSE MACABRE   321   26
COMPELS (2)
   COMPELS A TOTAL SACRIFICE. ....PURSUIT   23   40
   CIRCLING ZODIAC COMPELS THE YEAR. ......TO EVA DESCENDING THE STAIR   303   16
COMPLAIN (1)
   FROM THE MUTE SKY, I CAN'T HONESTLY COMPLAIN: ....BLACK ROOK I.   57   13
COMPLAINING (1)
   AND A DROWNED MAN, COMPLAINING OF THE GREAT COLD, ...A LIFE   150   34
COMPLAINT (2)
   THE QUEEN'S COMPLAINT ....THE QUEEN'S COMPLAINT   28   T
   EMPTY OF COMPLAINT, FOREVER ....THE THIN PEOPLE   64   19
COMPLAINTS (1)
   ONLY MUCH WHITER AND UNBREAKABLE AND WITH NO COMPLAINTS. *IN PLASTER   158   8
COMPLAISANCE (1)
   TO A WRY COMPLAISANCE -- ....THE COMPANIONABLE ILLS   105   4
COMPLETE (3)
   FROM BLIND AIR, FROM COMPLETE ECLIPSE. .............RHODODENDRON.   103   16
   WITH THE O-GAPE OF COMPLETE DESPAIR. I LIVE HERE. ....MOON.   173   11
   THIS IS WHAT IT IS TO BE COMPLETE. IT IS HORRIBLE. .....BERCK-PLAGE   198   61
COMPLEXION (2)
   WHITE: IT IS A COMPLEXION OF THE MIND. ....MOONRISE   98   21
   I SHOULD HAVE A STEEL COMPLEXION LIKE YOURS ....THE RIVAL/DR   291   6
COMPLICATING (1)
   COMPLICATING HIS FEATURES. ....STINGS   215   50
COMPLICATIONS (1)
   THE HORRIFIC COMPLICATIONS. ....LITTLE FUGUE   187   15
COMPOSE (3)
   SHEEP GREENS, FINNED FALLS, "I SHALL COMPOSE A CRISIS ...CONJURING.   66   11
   MUSE, COMPOSE. ....YADDO: THE GRAND MANOR   123   12
   BOY, PRONE TO COMPOSE QUEER POETRY ....DIALOGUE OVER A OUIJA BOARD   280 142
COMPOSED (1)
   COMPOSED IN GRECIAN TUNIC AND PSYCHE-KNOT, ...CONVERSATION.   21   11
COMPOST (1)
   OF A SOW LOUNGED BELLY-BEDDED ON THAT BLACK COMPOST, ...SOW   61   25
COMPOUNDS (1)
   HOW NATURE, SENSING THIS, COMPOUNDS HER BITTERS. ....DEPARTURE   51   5
COMRADES (1)
   IN WHICH OUR COMRADES ARE BETRAYED, WE FREEZE .....CHANNEL CROSSING   27   14
CON (2)
   LET BE YOUR CON BRIOS, YOUR CAPRICCIOSOS, ...ALICANTE LULLABY   43   17
   ABOUT EACH COSMIC PRO AND CON; ....LOVE IS A PARALLAX   329   15
CONCATENATION (1)
   A CONCATENATION OF RAINBOWS. ....PURDAH   243   28
CONCEAL (2)
   WHICH CONCEAL INCONGRUOUS ...............METAMORPHOSES OF THE MOON   307   27
   THAT HAPPENS TO CONCEAL THE LID OF ONE ......EPITAPH IN THREE PARTS   338   29
CONCEALING (1)
   RUN FOLD UPON FOLD FAR OFF, CONCEALING THEIR HOLLOWS, ..BERCK-PLAGE   199   74
CONCEDE (1)
   SLOWLY CONCEDE TO SUN AND SERUM. ..MORNING IN THE HOSPITAL SOLARIUM   332   18
CONCEIT (1)
   RIVALS HER WHETTED LOOK, DIVINING WHAT CONCEIT ....VANITY FAIR   32   13
CONCEIVE (1)
   FOR THE SPIRIT TO CONCEIVE A FACE, A MOUTH? ....THREE WOMEN   177   26
CONCEIVES (1)
   HATING MYSELF, HATING AND FEARING. AND NOW THE WORLD CONCEIVES ...
                                              ... THREE WOMEN   181 150

	TITLE	PAGE	LINE

CONCEIVING (1)
THEY ARE CONCEIVING A DYNASTY OF PERFECT COLD. ....TWO CAMP. 145 19
CONCENTRATE (1)
THEY CONCENTRATE MY ATTENTION, THAT WAS HAPPY ....TULIPS 161 55
CONCENTRATION (1)
THEIR LITTLE FOREHEADS BULGED WITH CONCENTRATION. ....STILLBORN 142   3
CONCEPT (1)
LEDGE WILL DISLODGE OUR CRAMPED CONCEPT OF SPACE, UNWALL ....OXBOW. 88 23
CONCEPTION (1)
WITH SUFFERING FROM CONCEPTION UPWARDS, AND THERE ....PERSEUS 83 26
CONCEPTIONS (2)
STARS AND SHOWERS OF GOLD -- CONCEPTIONS, CONCEPTIONS! THREE WOMEN 178 48
STARS AND SHOWERS OF GOLD -- CONCEPTIONS, CONCEPTIONS! THREE WOMEN 178 48
CONCERN (4)
TO KEEP SOME UNSAID PACT; PERHAPS CONCERN ....CHANNEL CROSSING 27 34
IS NO MORE MY CONCERN. ....RECANTATION 41   4
THE MOON'S CONCERN IS MORE PERSONAL: ....THREE WOMEN 176   4
DO NOT THINK I UNDERESTIMATE YOUR GREAT CONCERN. ......LADY LAZARUS 246 72
CONCERNING (1)
OF NOTCHED TIN PLATITUDES CONCERNING WEATHER, ...SONNET: TO EVA 305 11
CONCH (2)
COOL AS THE PEARLED INTERIOR OF A CONCH. ....THE OTHER TWO 68   2
MY FATHER KEPT A VAULTED CONCH ....ON THE DECLINE OF ORACLES 78   1
CONCHES (1)
THE PEASANTS ANCHOR THEM WITH CONCHES. ONE IS TOLD: .....FINISTERRE 170 30
CONCLUDES (1)
EACH DAY CONCLUDES IN A HUGE SPLURGE OF VERMILIONS ....TWO CAMP. 145 15
CONCLUDING (1)
CRIES AND HEROIC COUPLETS CONCLUDING THE MILLION ....PERSEUS 83 18
CONCOCT (1)
CONCOCT A DAPHNE; ....ON THE DIFFICULTY OF CONJURING UP A DRYAD 66 23
CONCORDE (1)
THE CARS IN THE PLACE DE LA CONCORDE -- ....A SECRET 220 38
CONCRETE (1)
LIMBS, IMAGES, SHRIEKS. BEHIND THE CONCRETE BUNKERS ....BERCK-PLAGE 197 29
CONCUPISCENCE (1)
OF CONCUPISCENCE. ONCE MORE ....SPIDER 49 27
CONDEMNED (2)
CONDEMNED BY OUR ANCESTRAL FAULT, ...PURSUIT 22 14
YOU WERE CONDEMNED TO SERVE THE LEGAL LIMIT ....THE TRIAL OF MAN 312 10
CONDITION (1)
SOME DAMNED CONDITION YOU ARE IN: *DIALOGUE BETWEEN GHOST AND PRIEST 39 33
CONDONING (1)
CONDONING THE BEAK, THE CLAW, THE GRIN OF THE DOG ....THE SWARM 216 22
CONDOR (1)
VERDIGRIS OF THE CONDOR. ....DEATH & CO. 254   9
CONDUCTING (1)
OF THREAD CONDUCTING HER TO THE WORN TRACKS ....THE PRINCESS. 334 32
CONFECTIONER'S (1)
BREASTS AND HIPS A CONFECTIONER'S SUGAR ....BERCK-PLAGE 197 25
CONFECTIONERY (1)
THE BABY LACE, THE GREEN-LEAVED CONFECTIONERY,*THE MUNICH MANNEQUINS 263 22
CONFESS (1)
THE POLICE LOVE YOU, YOU CONFESS EVERYTHING. ....THE OTHER 201   7
CONFESSED (1)
BUT TO A FRIEND, IN PRIVATE, ROUSSEAU CONFESSED HIS EYE ..YADWIGHA. 86 35
CONFETTI (2)
TO STREW LIKE CONFETTI ....FIESTA MELONS 47 17
STARS STUCK ALL OVER, BRIGHT STUPID CONFETTI. ....YEARS 255   8
CONFIDENCE (1)
CONFIDENCE OF SAFE-CONDUCT ....MUSSEL HUNTER AT ROCK HARBOR 95 23
CONFINED (1)
FROM THE PRAGMATIC BOY CONFINED WITHIN,*THE PRINCESS AND THE GOBLINS 334 45
CONFLAGRATIONS (1)
USED UTTERLY, IN THE SUN'S CONFLAGRATIONS, THE STAINS ....MYSTIC 268 13
CONFOUNDED (2)
CONFOUNDED INEPT GUESSWORK: ....NIGHT SHIFT 76 14
WHETHER NICETY STOOD CONFOUNDED BY LOVE, ...RHODODENDRON. 104 27
CONFRONTS (2)
CONFRONTS ITS SMALL ....CUT 236 35
AND CONFRONTS A CAIRN OF IRON ORE. ....THE PRINCESS AND THE GOBLINS 334 43
CONGEAL (1)
WHERE SPILT LIVES CONGEAL AND STIFFEN TO HISTORY.*A BIRTHDAY PRESENT 208 51
CONGEALS (2)
AND A LANGUOR OF WAX CONGEALS THE VEIN EPITAPH FOR FIRE AND FLOWER 46 31
ONLY TO REOPEN AS FLESH CONGEALS: ....LOVE IS A PARALLAX 330 65
CONGREGATE (1)
THE HEAT-CRACKED CRICKETS CONGREGATE ....SLEEP IN THE MOJAVE DESERT 144 22
CONJUNCTION (1)
BUT ADROIT CONJUNCTION ....TRIO OF LOVE SONGS 314 33
CONJURED (2)
WHICH CONJURED US ....MOONSONG AT MORNING 317   8
THE SOURCE OF BLANCHING LIGHT THAT CONJURED HER ......THE PRINCESS. 333   3
CONJURES (1)
LIGHTNING CONJURES GOD'S GLOBE OFF ITS ....INSOLENT STORM. 326 25

CONJURING (1)
    ON THE DIFFICULTY OF CONJURING UP A DRYAD ....CONJURING.   65   T
CONNECTICUT (2)
    BACK OF THE CONNECTICUT, THE RIVER-LEVEL ....ABOVE THE OXBOW   88   7
    CURRENTS OF THE CONNECTICUT FAN ....IN MIDAS' COUNTRY 99   2
CONQUER (1)
    TO CONQUER CINDER'S KINGDOM IN THE STROKE OF AN HOUR *EPITAPH FOR F. 45 20
CONQUERED (1)
    TILL DARK IS CONQUERED BY ORANGE COCK, ...BLACK PINE TREE. 328 15
CONSCIENCE (4)
    OF FINEST CONSCIENCE. NIGHTFALL OBSCURES ....THE BEGGARS   48 16
    ARGUED MY CONSCIENCE CLEAR WHICH ROBBED ..............RHODODENDRON. 103 11
    STONES, WITHOUT CONSCIENCE, WORD AND LINE ENDURE, ..POEMS, POTATOES 106   5
    BLED WHITE WITH BRIARS BY A BUSY CONSCIENCE ....DIALOGUE O. 281 197
CONSECRATE (2)
    WAITING FOR HIS GRACE TO CONSECRATE. ....TERMINAL 328 14
    THAT LIFTS TO CONSECRATE THE SUNKEN MAN. ....EPITAPH IN THREE PARTS 337 19
CONSECRATES (1)
    EACH CLOCK TICK CONSECRATES THE DEATH OF STRANGERS.   DOOM OF EXILES 318   8
CONSECRATING (1)
    GREEN VIRGINS, CONSECRATING LIMB AND LIP ....VIRGIN IN A TREE   82 27
CONSEQUENCE (1)
    I THOUGHT I COULD DENY THE CONSEQUENCE -- ....THREE WOMEN 178 61
CONSEQUENTIAL (1)
    IT HAD A CONSEQUENTIAL LOOK, LIKE EVERYTHING ELSE, ...THREE WOMEN 177 46
CONSIDER (1)
    PERHAPS YOU CONSIDER YOURSELF AN ORACLE, ...THE COLOSSUS 129   6
CONSIDERED (1)
    I CONSIDERED THE POETRY I RESCUED*FABLE OF THE RHODODENDRON STEALERS 103 15
CONSISTENT (1)
    IT SEEMS THE CONSISTENT CRITICS WANTED YOU ....YADWIGHA.   85   8
CONSOLE (3)
    IN THE COAL FIRE WILL NOT WHOLLY CONSOLE THEM. ....OUIJA   77   7
    MOLDERING HEADS CONSOLE ME, ...POEM.1.WHO. 131 13
    THEY CONSOLE ME -- ....BURNING THE LETTERS 204 31
CONSOLING (2)
    BRIGHT BIRDS IN THE SKY, CONSOLING, CONSOLING? ....THREE WOMEN 185 298
    BRIGHT BIRDS IN THE SKY, CONSOLING, CONSOLING? ....THREE WOMEN 185 298
CONSPICUOUS (1)
    CONSPICUOUS, YET IT SEEMED ....MUSSEL HUNTER AT ROCK HARBOR   95 18
CONSTANCE (1)
    WITH SAVOR; COUPLED SO, PURE PARAGONS OF CONSTANCE, ...WREATH F.   44   9
CONSTANT (2)
    DISGUISING THE CONSTANT HORROR IN A COAT ....TALE OF A TUB   25 37
    YOU KNOW ME LESS CONSTANT, ...PARLIAMENT HILL FIELDS 153 27
CONSTELLATION (1)
    BOW DOWN, A LOCAL CONSTELLATION, ...LEAVING EARLY 145 11
CONSTELLATIONS (1)
    I SEE THOSE CONSTELLATIONS IN MY HEAD, ...STARS OVER THE DORDOGNE 166 35
CONSTIPATION (1)
    SUCH AS PREGNANCY OR CONSTIPATION ....APRIL 18 301   5
CONSTRAINT (1)
    OF KITCHEN SLOPS AND STOMACHING NO CONSTRAINT, ...SOW   61 43
CONTRARY (1)
    STEEPLING SNAKE IN THAT CONTRARY LIGHT ....SONNET TO SATAN 323   9
CONSTRICTION (1)
    THE CONSTRICTION KILLING ME ALSO. ....THE RABBIT CATCHER 194 30
CONSTRICTOR (1)
    WITH THE BOA CONSTRICTOR IN THE FELLOWS' GARDEN.   ZOO KEEPER'S WIFE 155 26
CONSTRICTS (1)
    FOR A FASHION THAT CONSTRICTS ....VIRGIN IN A TREE   81 21
CONSTRUE (2)
    I SEE HIM, HORNY-SKINNED AND TOUGH, CONSTRUE ....OUIJA   77 27
    GIVE ME BACK MY SHAPE. I AM READY TO CONSTRUE THE DAYS ...POEM.6.W. 136 21
CONSUME (1)
    CONSUME THIS PIPER AND HE TIRES OF MUSIC ..............SNAKECHARMER   79 22
CONSUMES (1)
    WIDOW. THE WORD CONSUMES ITSELF -- ....WIDOW 164   1
CONSUMMATES (1)
    DOOM CONSUMMATES THAT APPETITE. ....PURSUIT   22 20
CONTAGION (1)
    SPREAD GAY CONTAGION WITH EACH CLEVER BREATH. ....DIRGE FOR A JOKER 303 12
CONTAIN (2)
    I CANNOT CONTAIN IT. I CANNOT CONTAIN MY LIFE. ....THREE WOMEN 182 196
    I CANNOT CONTAIN IT. I CANNOT CONTAIN MY LIFE. ....THREE WOMEN 182 196
CONTAINING (1)
    ...COFFIN OF THE FOURTH CENTURY A.D. CONTAINING THE
        SKELETON... ....ALL THE DEAD DEARS   70 E/2
CONTEMPLATING (1)
    CONTEMPLATING A WORLD CLEAR AS WATER. ....BALLOONS 272 28
CONTENDING (1)
    OF CONTENDING WORDS. SOME PYTHONESS ....DIALOGUE OVER A OUIJA BOARD 286 347
CONTENT (2)
    PATCH TOGETHER A CONTENT ....BLACK ROOK IN RAINY WEATHER   57 35
    BUT I AM CONTENT WITH THIS MORE POMPOUS LOT. ....QUEEN MARY'S. 290 25

		TITLE	PAGE	LINE

CONTEST (1)
    HERE IS A QUEENSHIP NO MOTHER CAN CONTEST -- ....BEEKEEPER'S. 118 13
CONTINENT (1)
    THE SEVEN TROUGHED SEAS AND EVERY EARTHQUAKING CONTINENT. ......SOW 61 45
CONTINENTS (1)
    AND FROM OUR OPPOSITE CONTINENTS WE WAVE AND CALL.   THE BABYSITTERS 175 44
CONTINUALLY (1)
    THIS RED WALL WINCES CONTINUALLY: ....................APPREHENSIONS 195 11
CONTINUING (1)
    MERELY BY ITS CONTINUING ....VANITY FAIR 32 4
CONTINUOUSLY (1)
    SHORTCHANGE ME CONTINUOUSLY: WHETHER ....POEMS, POTATOES 106 9
CONTORT (1)
    THEY CONTORT YOUR HAIR ....STINGS/DR 293 5
CONTOURS (1)
    OUTSIDE THE CAVE WHOSE CONTOURS MOST REMIND ....DIALOGUE O. 281 200
CONTRACT (1)
    AND IF MY STOMACH WOULD CONTRACT ....APRIL 18 301 3
CONTRACTED (1)
    IN THE CONTRACTED COUNTRY OF THE HEAD ....THE THIN PEOPLE 64 25
CONTRACTS (1)
    NO MATTER HOW FIERCELY LIT; STAUNCH CONTRACTS BREAK   EPITAPH FOR F. 46 32
CONTRADICT (2)
    TO CONTRADICT ME. YOUR SHOULDERING WORDS OUTSTRIP ......DIALOGUE O. 281 172
    AND CONTRADICT OURSELVES FOR FUN; ....LOVE IS A PARALLAX 329 21
CONTRADICTION (1)
    A CROSS OF CONTRADICTION, RACKED BETWEEN   METAMORPHOSES OF THE MOON 308 47
CONTRADICTIONS (1)
    WHAT AM I TO MAKE OF THESE CONTRADICTIONS? ....AN APPEARANCE 189 8
CONTRIVE (1)
    AND I CONTRIVE, ...POINT SHIRLEY 111 45
CONTROL (3)
    AT THIS RARE RUMPUS WHICH NO MAN CAN CONTROL: .....CHANNEL CROSSING 27 29
    WINGSPREAD IN CONTROL ....OWL 102 12
    I AM IN CONTROL. ....STINGS 214 32
CONTUSION (1)
    CONTUSION ....CONTUSION 271 T
CONUNDRUM (1)
    TO CORRAL THE CONUNDRUM OF SPACE ....DIALOGUE EN ROUTE 309 35
CONUNDRUMS (1)
    OF SULFUROUS DREAMSCAPES AND OBSCURE LUNAR CONUNDRUMS .....GHOST'S. 90 4
CONVALESCENT (1)
    PATRONIZED BY CONVALESCENT WIVES;   MORNING IN THE HOSPITAL SOLARIUM 332 5
CONVERGE (2)
    THE SMALL BIRDS CONVERGE, CONVERGE ....THE MANOR GARDEN 125 19
    THE SMALL BIRDS CONVERGE, CONVERGE ....THE MANOR GARDEN 125 19
CONVERGING (1)
    OUT IN A CONVERGING STREAM ....MUSSEL HUNTER AT ROCK HARBOR 96 40
CONVERSATION (2)
    CONVERSATION AMONG THE RUINS ........CONVERSATION AMONG THE RUINS 21 T
    THEN THE SKY AND I ARE IN OPEN CONVERSATION, ...I AM VERTICAL 162 18
CONVERSE (1)
    THEY CONVERSE IN THE VALLEY OF YOUR FINGERS, THEY ARE INCHWORMS. ...
                                                    ... GULLIVER 251 17
CONVERSED (1)
    WITH STARS, WITH ANGELS, HE CONVERSED ....NATURAL HISTORY 71 6
CONVERSING (1)
    I SEE THE FATHER CONVERSING WITH THE SON. ....THREE WOMEN 179 88
CONVERSION (1)
    BUT IT'S THE CLEAR CONVERSION AT THE TOP CAN HOLD ..ABOVE THE OXBOW 88 20
CONVICTION (1)
    INTO MYSELF AND INTO MY CONVICTION .....DIALOGUE OVER A OUIJA BOARD 285 318
CONVINCE (2)
    BUT DIDN'T CONVINCE ME. THOSE TEARS FROZE. ....LOVE LETTER 147 17
    BELIEVE, IF THEY COULD MANAGE TO CONVINCE ....DIALOGUE O. 278 66
CONVULSION (1)
    IN THE DEEP CONVULSION GRIPPING YOUR FACE, MUSCLES ....PERSEUS 83 43
CONVULSORS (1)
    WHICH OF THE NERVE-CURLERS, THE CONVULSORS? DID IT ELECTRIFY? ...
                                                ... THE DETECTIVE 209 23
COO (1)
    AND COO QUADRILLES ABOUT THE BLIGHTED CORE ....THE PRINCESS. 335 67
COOING (1)
    ROOSTING AND COOING "YOU, YOU" ....A SECRET 219 19
COOK (6)
    CRAVES MOST TO COOK BATTER ....VANITY FAIR 33 16
    THE COOK LUGS A PUMPKIN ....YADDO: THE GRAND MANOR 123 5
    BUT I DIDN'T KNOW HOW TO COOK, AND BABIES DEPRESSED ME. ......BABY. 174 13
    AND A COOK AND A MAID, AND KNEW ABOUT THE KEY TO THE BOURBON. *BABY. 175 21
    THE COOK HAD ONE WALL EYE AND COULDN'T SLEEP, SHE WAS SO NERVOUS. ...
                                                ... THE BABYSITTERS 175 25
    IT CAN SEW, IT CAN COOK, ...THE APPLICANT 222 34
COOKED (1)
    CHOICE WASSAIL MAKES, COOKED HOT, ...THE GLUTTON 40 9

```
                                            TITLE               PAGE   LINE
COOKER (1)
    FOUR BABIES AND A COOKER!  ...................................AMNESIAC  233   6
COOKIES (3)
    MY BROTHER AND ME COOKIES AND OVALTINE  .......THE DISQUIETING MUSES   75  20
    POODLES ARE BAKING COOKIES IN  .......................A WINTER'S TALE   87  18
    ON TRIAL, FROM IRELAND, SHE BURNED BATCH AFTER BATCH OF COOKIES  ...
                                               ... THE BABYSITTERS  175  26
COOKING (3)
    LET ME HAVE MY COPPER COOKING POTS, LET MY ROUGE POTS  ...LAST WORDS  172  21
    WHEN I AM QUIET AT MY COOKING I FEEL IT LOOKING, I FEEL IT THINKING  ...
                                               ... A BIRTHDAY PRESENT  206   4
    THE SMOG OF COOKING, THE SMOG OF HELL  .......................LESBOS  228  35
COOKS (1)
    WHERE THE MOST WATCHFUL COOKS GO JOBLESS  ........THE TIMES ARE TIDY  107   3
COOL (9)
    WHAT LULL, WHAT COOL CAN LAP ME IN  .........................PURSUIT   23  35
    COOL AS THE PEARLED INTERIOR OF A CONCH.  .............THE OTHER TWO   68   2
    WHO KEEP COOL AND HOLY MAKE  .......................VIRGIN IN A TREE   81  25
    WELL-WATER KEPT COOL AT THE START OF THE ROWS.  .....SPINACH-PICKER.   89  14
    AND APPLE CAKES TO COOL. WHAT IS IT  ...................POINT SHIRLEY  110  28
    A COOL WIND SHOULD INHABIT THOSE LEAVES    SLEEP IN THE MOJAVE DESERT  144   8
    THE TREES AND FLOWERS HAVE BEEN STREWING THEIR COOL ODORS.  ..TULIPS  162  12
    ALL COOL, ALL BLUE. UNLIKE YOU ---  .......................GULLIVER  251   9
    OF COOL MOUTHS AND HANDS OPEN AND NATURAL AS ROSES.  ......FEVER./DR  294  10
COOLLY (2)
    AND NEVER SAW HOW COOLLY WE MIGHT MOVE. FOR ONCE  ...ABOVE THE OXBOW   89  55
    COMET COOLLY GIVING MY  ................MUSSEL HUNTER AT ROCK HARBOR   96  57
COOLNESS (1)
    THEY MOUND A SUMMER COOLNESS IN OUR VIEW.  ..........ABOVE THE OXBOW   88  14
COOLS (1)
    BUT NOW THAT ANGER COOLS, I'VE A SENSE OF SORROW  .......DIALOGUE O.  285 310
COOT (1)
    NO SOUND BUT A DRUNKEN COOT  .....................................FAUN   35   6
COPPER (3)
    AND SHINE THAT KETTLE OF COPPER  .....TINKER JACK AND THE TIDY WIVES   34   7
    LET ME HAVE MY COPPER COOKING POTS, LET MY ROUGE POTS  ...LAST WORDS  172  21
    WITH COPPER CLAWS;  ...................................FAMILY REUNION  300   6
COPSES (1)
    THROUGH CLOSETS OF COPSES  ...........................TEMPER OF TIME  336   9
COPY (2)
    CROW'S-FEET COPY VEINING ON STAINED LEAF;  ..............VANITY FAIR   32   7
    THAT KNITS TO EACH ORIGINAL ITS COARSE COPY. A DARK TARN*LADY AND T.   69  15
CORD (2)
    WHO IS THE DESTINATION OF THE CORD  ....THE PRINCESS AND THE GOBLINS  333  23
    SHE CLUTCHES AT THE TALISMANIC CORD  ...THE PRINCESS AND THE GOBLINS  334  42
CORDIAL (1)
    THE CORDIAL STRAINS  ...................................A WINTER'S TALE   87  32
CORDS (1)
    NAVEL CORDS, BLUE-RED AND LUCENT,  ......................THE OTHER  202  18
CORE (6)
    HEARTS OF THOSE WHO PIERCED TIME'S CORE.  .............CRYSTAL GAZER   55  42
    WARMING AT CORE ONLY AS  .......................CHILD'S PARK STONES  101  25
    TO R NOW. E. IN CORE . . . O-F-N-E-  ....DIALOGUE OVER A OUIJA BOARD  284 277
    R-V-E. IN CORE OF NERVE! I HOPE  ........DIALOGUE OVER A OUIJA BOARD  284 278
    AND COO QUADRILLES ABOUT THE BLIGHTED CORE  ...........THE PRINCESS.  335  67
    GO BAD TO THE CORE.  ...................................TEMPER OF TIME  336   4
CORES (1)
    WITH ORANGE CORES.  ...................................FIESTA MELONS   46  14
CORK (2)
    THE INHABITANTS ARE LIGHT AS CORK,  .........................A LIFE  150   9
    I SEE US FLOATING THERE YET, INSEPARABLE -- TWO CORK DOLLS.  ..BABY.  175  41
CORKED (1)
    LIKE PETULANT PARAKEETS CORKED UP IN CAGES  .....MORNING IN THE HOS.  332  19
CORKSCREW (3)
    THEIR CORKSCREW NOSES, THEIR WHITE HANDS  ...............BLUE MOLES  126  15
    COMMANDING THAT CORKSCREW COMET JET FORTH INK  ......SONNET TO SATAN  323   5
    OBSCURE GOD'S EYE WITH CORKSCREW FLECK;  ...........BLACK PINE TREE.  328   9
CORN (2)
    THE SUN SHINES ON UNRIPE CORN.  .........................DEPARTURE   51   7
    GO GET THE GOODLY SQUAB IN GOLD-LOBED CORN   GO GET THE GOODLY SQUAB  313   1
CORNER (3)
    AT EYE'S ENVIOUS CORNER  .......................................VANITY FAIR   32   6
    FOOLISH, DELICATE, IN THE LOWER RIGHT HAND CORNER.  ......TWO VIEWS.  114  22
    CELL BY CELL FROM A QUIET CORNER,  ....................POEM.2.DARK.  132   3
CORNFLOWERS (2)
    FRIEZE OF CABBAGE-ROSES AND CORNFLOWERS PALES  .......THE THIN PEOPLE   65  37
    IN A FOREST OF FROST, IN A DAWN OF CORNFLOWERS.  POPPIES IN OCTOBER  240  12
CORNUCOPIA (2)
    NIGHTS, I SQUAT IN THE CORNUCOPIA  ....................THE COLOSSUS  130  24
    IT'S A LITTLE CORNUCOPIA.  ...........................PHEASANT  191  20
CORNWALL (1)
    I SHOULD SIT ON A ROCK OFF CORNWALL AND COMB MY HAIR.  .......LESBOS  228  29
COROLLAS (1)
    THE GREAT COROLLAS DILATE, PEELING BACK THEIR SILKS.  ..BEEKEEPER'S.  118   2
```

	TITLE	PAGE	LINE

CORONAL (1)
    UNDER THE CORONAL OF SUGAR ROSES ....THE BEEKEEPER'S DAUGHTER 118 20
CORONATION (1)
    PITCHERS AND CORONATION GOBLETS ....LEAVING EARLY 145 9
CORPSE (1)
    MEETS THE CORPSE AT THE GATE, ...BERCK-PLAGE 200 94
CORPSES (3)
    I AM RESTLESS. RESTLESS AND USELESS. I, TOO, CREATE CORPSES. *THREE. 182 189
    AND THE WALL OF OLD CORPSES. ....LETTER IN NOVEMBER 253 21
    GLEAMING WITH THE MOUTHS OF CORPSES. ....CHILDLESS WOMAN 259 18
CORPSE-WHITE (1)
    AUSTERE, CORPSE-WHITE ....THE SNOWMAN ON THE MOOR 59 30
CORPUSCLES (1)
    THEY ARE NOT AIR MOTES, THEY ARE CORPUSCLES. ....THE OTHER 201 12
CORRAL (1)
    TO CORRAL THE CONUNDRUM OF SPACE ....DIALOGUE EN ROUTE 309 35
CORRECT (3)
    I'LL CORRECT EACH MAR ....TINKER JACK AND THE TIDY WIVES 34 5
    BY CORRECT GREEN LINES AND NO SEEDY FREE-FOR-ALL ...ABOVE THE OXBOW 89 49
    GILDED, COMING CORRECT ....AERIALIST 331 13
CORRESPONDS (1)
    THEIR REDNESS TALKS TO MY WOUND, IT CORRESPONDS. ....TULIPS 161 39
CORRIDOR (1)
    CORRIDOR OF INANE REPLICAS, ...LANDOWNERS 53 8
CORRODING (1)
    BARES ITS LOW LINTEL TO CORRODING WEATHERS: ....DEPARTURE 51 17
CORROSIVE (2)
    EVERYTHING SHRANK IN THE SUN'S CORROSIVE ......SUICIDE OFF EGG ROCK 115 21
    THE TREES WITHER IN THE STREET. THE RAIN IS CORROSIVE. THREE WOMEN 180 135
CORRUPTIBLE (1)
    COMPARED TO YOU, I AM CORRUPTIBLE AS A LOAF OF BREAD. THE RIVAL/DR 291 1
CORRUPTS (1)
    AND SUCH GRIT CORRUPTS MY EYES ....ON THE PLETHORA OF DRYADS 67 31
CORSETS (1)
    THEIR YELLOW CORSETS WERE READY TO SPLIT. ....LEAVING EARLY 146 25
COSMETIC (1)
    AN EFFECT, A COSMETIC. ....THE OTHER 202 30
COSMETICS (1)
    WHEN THE SWEETHEART FROM ENGLAND APPEARED, WITH HER CREAM SKIN AND
        YARDLEY COSMETICS, ...THE BABYSITTERS 174 6
COSMIC (3)
    YOU SPUN THE COSMIC WEB: YOU SQUINT FROM CENTER FIELD. ......SPIDER 48 7
    AND SINEWS BUNCHED, VICTORIOUS, AS THE COSMIC ....PERSEUS 83 44
    ABOUT EACH COSMIC PRO AND CON; ....LOVE IS A PARALLAX 329 15
COST (1)
    TO WARD OFF, AT ALL COST, SUSPICIONS ....STREET SONG 36 16
COT (4)
    ATTENDING HER COT IS LESS THAN A BELLY ACHE, ...MAGI 148 13
    COT LEGS MELTED IN TERRIBLE ATTITUDES, AND THE NURSES -- ...WAKING. 151 12
    I HAD TO SLEEP IN THE SAME ROOM WITH THE BABY ON A TOO-SHORT
        COT, ...THE BABYSITTERS 174 7
    COLD ON MY NARROW COT I LIE ....TO A JILTED LOVER 309 1
COTS (2)
    IN THEIR CANVAS-SIDED COTS, NAMES TIED TO THEIR WRISTS, *THREE WOMEN 183 220
    THE CHILDREN LEAP IN THEIR COTS. ....MYSTIC 269 29
COTTAGE (3)
    YOU HAD A ROSE GARDEN AND A GUEST COTTAGE AND A MODEL
        APOTHECARY SHOP .... THE BABYSITTERS 174 20
    THE HUMPBACK IN HIS SMALL, WASHED COTTAGE ....MYSTIC 269 22
    APPROACHING HIS COTTAGE ....TEMPER OF TIME 336 17
COTTAGES (1)
    TO WALL OF THE DARK, DWARFED COTTAGES. ....HARDCASTLE CRAGS 62 7
COTTON (2)
    I WALK AMONG THEM, AND THEY STUFF MY MOUTH WITH COTTON. FINISTERRE 169 17
    BUT MY GOD, THE CLOUDS ARE LIKE COTTON. ....A BIRTHDAY PRESENT 207 39
COUCH (15)
    SO WERE THEY ONE; SO SOUGHT THEY COUCH, ...BUCOLICS 23 3
    COUCH, CARPET, FLOOR ....MONOLOGUE AT 3 A.M. 40 4
    YADWIGHA, ON A RED COUCH, AMONG LILIES ....YADWIGHA. 85 T
    CAME TO BE LYING ON THIS BAROQUE COUCH ....YADWIGHA. 85 2
    AND THE FASHIONABLE MONDE OF THE RED COUCH ....YADWIGHA. 85 10
    OR, AT MOST, TO A MILLE-FLEURS TAPESTRY. BUT THE COUCH ...YADWIGHA. 85 17
    THE COUCH GLARED OUT AT THE PROSAIC EYE. ....YADWIGHA. 85 20
    SO ROUSSEAU, TO EXPLAIN WHY THE RED COUCH ....YADWIGHA. 86 21
    ON A RED VELVET COUCH WITHIN YOUR GREEN- ....YADWIGHA. 86 26
    NODDED THEIR PETALED HEADS AROUND YOUR COUCH. ....YADWIGHA. 86 30
    AND THAT, ROUSSEAU TOLD THE CRITICS, WAS WHY THE COUCH ...YADWIGHA. 86 31
    ACCOMPANIED YOU. SO THEY NODDED AT THE COUCH WITH THE MOON*YADWIGHA. 86 32
    SO POSSESSED BY THE GLOWING RED OF THE COUCH WHICH YOU, ..YADWIGHA. 86 36
    YADWIGHA, POSE ON, THAT HE PUT YOU ON THE COUCH ....YADWIGHA. 86 37
    DRUM OF MY SLEEPING COUCH ....PARALYTIC 266 21
COUCHED (2)
    COUCHED DAYLONG IN CLOISTERS OF STINGING NETTLE *WREATH FOR A BRIDAL 44 7
    COUCHED IN CAULS OF CLAY AS IN HOLY ROBES, ...THE DEAD 320 2

	TITLE	PAGE	LINE

COUGH (1)
  CAME THE PROFANE STIMULUS TO COUGH; ....DIRGE FOR A JOKER 302   2
COULD (55)
  COULD BE THIS ADAM'S WOMAN ....ODE FOR TED   30 22
  COULD UNLOCK ....FIRESONG   30 12
  OF FLAWED EARTH-FLESH COULD CAUSE THIS SORRY PASS? .....DIALOGUE B.   39 32
  (WITH HEAT SUCH AS NO MAN COULD HAVE ....THE GLUTTON   40   3
  NO SCRUPLE COULD DISRUPT, ...SPIDER   49 31
  AS NO MERE INSURGENT MAN COULD HOPE TO BREAK ....SPINSTER   50 28
  WARY (FOR IT COULD HAPPEN ....BLACK ROOK IN RAINY WEATHER   57 23
  OF STONES AND HILLS OF STONES COULD BREAK ....HARDCASTLE CRAGS   63 43
  SO WEEDY A RACE COULD NOT REMAIN IN DREAMS, ...THE THIN PEOPLE   64 23
  COULD NOT REMAIN OUTLANDISH VICTIMS ....THE THIN PEOPLE   64 24
  ANY MORE THAN THE OLD WOMAN IN HER MUD HUT COULD ...THE THIN PEOPLE   64 26
  THAN AXE COULD CUT. ....ON THE PLETHORA OF DRYADS   67 12
  AND SINGING THE GLOWWORM SONG, I COULD ....THE DISQUIETING MUSES   75 27
  TO HEAR THE SEA HE COULD NOT HEAR. ....ON THE DECLINE OF ORACLES   78   6
  A GIRL COULD WADE WITHOUT WETTING HER SHINS.   A LESSON IN VENGEANCE   80 20
  IN SAFE PERSPECTIVE, COULD OUTFACE THE GORGON-GRIMACE ......PERSEUS   83 14
  AND TRICKLE. COULD THEY FEEL MUD ......MUSSEL HUNTER AT ROCK HARBOR   96 48
  AS I COULD BETWEEN BARE TOES? ....MUSSEL HUNTER AT ROCK HARBOR   96 50
  IF THEY COULD SEE, I WAS ONE ....MUSSEL HUNTER AT ROCK HARBOR   97 65
  FROST FORMS. NO MAN'S CROWBAR COULD ....CHILD'S PARK STONES 101 26
  WHAT THE SLUTTISH, RUTTED SEA COULD DO. ....POINT SHIRLEY 110 12
  AND SHE COULD SCARCELY MAKE OUT ANYTHING*TWO VIEWS OF A CADAVER ROOM 114   7
  NO GESTURE OF YOURS OR MINE COULD CATCH THEIR ATTENTION,   TWO CAMP. 144   4
  IT COULD BE A SNOWFIELD OR A CLOUDBANK. ....PARLIAMENT HILL FIELDS 152 23
  YOU COULD TELL ALMOST AT ONCE SHE HAD A SLAVE MENTALITY. *IN PLASTER 159 21
  THEN SHE COULD COVER MY MOUTH AND EYES, COVER ME ENTIRELY, *PLASTER. 159 40
  EVEN THROUGH THE GIFT PAPER I COULD HEAR THEM BREATHE ....TULIPS 161 37
  A BODILESS SOUL COULD PASS ANOTHER SOUL ....WIDOW 164 32
  AND A CABIN BOY WHO COULD DECORATE CAKES IN SIX-COLORED FROSTING. ...
                                          ... THE BABYSITTERS 174 12
  I COULD NOT BELIEVE IT. IS IT SO DIFFICULT ....THREE WOMEN 177 25
  AND ALL I COULD SEE WAS DANGERS: DOVES AND WORDS, ...THREE WOMEN 178 47
  I THOUGHT I COULD DENY THE CONSEQUENCE -- ....THREE WOMEN 178 61
  THE FACE OF THE DEAD ONE THAT COULD ONLY BE PERFECT ....THREE WOMEN 178 80
  IN ITS EASY PEACE, COULD ONLY KEEP HOLY SO. ....THREE WOMEN 178 81
  HE COULD HEAR BEETHOVEN: ....LITTLE FUGUE 187 13
  IF I COULD BLEED, OR SLEEP! --- ....POPPIES IN JULY 203 11
  IF MY MOUTH COULD MARRY A HURT LIKE THAT! ....POPPIES IN JULY 203 12
  I COULD NOT RUN WITHOUT HAVING TO RUN FOREVER. .....THE BEE MEETING 212 33
  THIS IS THE ROOM I COULD NEVER BREATHE IN. ....WINTERING 218 12
  SO I NEVER COULD TELL WHERE YOU ....DADDY 223 22
  I NEVER COULD TALK TO YOU. ....DADDY 223 24
  I COULD HARDLY SPEAK. ....DADDY 223 28
  SO BLACK NO SKY COULD SQUEAK THROUGH. ....DADDY 223 47
  OF THE FUCHSIA. I COULD DRAW NO BREATH, ...MEDUSA 225 29
  YOU COULD EAT HIM. HE'S A BOY. ....LESBOS 228 25
  I GUESS YOU COULD SAY I'VE A CALL. ....LADY LAZARUS 245 48
  BELIEVE, IF THEY COULD MANAGE TO CONVINCE ....DIALOGUE O. 278 66
  I AM RESOLVED. NO REASON COULD UNTWIST   DIALOGUE OVER A OUIJA BOARD 286 341
  COULD GROPE ITS WAY TO GOSPEL THROUGH THAT WELTER ......DIALOGUE O. 286 346
  IN WHICH THE MINUTES COULD ADMIRE THEIR REFLECTIONS AND
               FORGET ABOUT ME. ....THE RIVAL/DR 291   7
  ALL RIGHT, LET'S SAY YOU COULD TAKE A SKULL AND BREAK IT*SONNET:EVA. 304   1
  NOT MAN NOR DEMIGOD COULD PUT TOGETHER ....SONNET: TO EVA 305   9
  COULD CLIMAX HIS CAREER, ...TRIO OF LOVE SONGS 314 32
  FOR WHAT FIRE COULD DAMAGE*ON LOOKING INTO THE EYES OF A DEMON LOVER 325 19
  SO WE COULD RAVE ON, DARLING, YOU AND I, ...LOVE IS A PARALLAX 329 13
COULDN'T (7)
  TABLETS OF BLANK BLUE, COULDN'T, ...THE HERMIT AT OUTERMOST HOUSE 118   2
  THE POLITE SKIES OVER BOSTON COULDN'T POSSIBLY ACCOMMODATE. ...
                                   ... TWO CAMPERS IN CLOUD COUNTRY 145 11
  I COULDN'T SLEEP FOR A WEEK, SHE WAS SO COLD. ....IN PLASTER 158   9
  I COULDN'T UNDERSTAND HER STUPID BEHAVIOR! ....IN PLASTER 159 11
  FROM HER AMAZINGLY WHITE TORSO, AND I COULDN'T HELP BUT NOTICE ...
                                          ... IN PLASTER 159 24
  THE COOK HAD ONE WALL EYE AND COULDN'T SLEEP, SHE WAS SO NERVOUS. ...
                                   ... THE BABYSITTERS 175 25
  I COULDN'T STOP LOOKING. ....LITTLE FUGUE 187 12
COUNT (3)
  OLD ELLA MASON KEEPS CATS, ELEVEN AT LAST COUNT, ...ELLA MASON A.   53   1
  IS LEAKING FROM THE FINGER-VENTS. AT THE COUNT OF TWO ....FACE LIFE 156 14
  I SHALL COUNT AND BURY THE DEAD. ....GETTING THERE 249 61
COUNTED (2)
  THOUGH I COUNTED SCANT SECONDS, ...MUSSEL HUNTER AT ROCK HARBOR   95 21
  HE COUNTED THE GUNS OF GOD A BOTHER, ...LAMENT 315 13
COUNTENANCE (1)
  OUT OF OUR VERY COUNTENANCE BY SIMPLY ..DIALOGUE OVER A OUIJA BOARD 279 114
COUNTERFEIT (3)
  WILL HAVE NO COUNTERFEIT   ON THE DIFFICULTY OF CONJURING UP A DRYAD   66 31
  ON A STICK THAT RATTLES AND CLICKS, A COUNTERFEIT SNAKE. .....TOTEM 264 18
  SOMERSAULTS TO COUNTERFEIT ECLIPSE: ....SONNET TO SATAN 323   2

COUNTERMAGIC (1)
    WHAT COUNTERMAGIC CAN UNDO THE SNARE ....PROLOGUE TO SPRING   322   10
COUNTERPOINT (1)
    COUNTERPOINT TO THEIR VOICES: ....OLD LADIES' HOME   120   9
COUNTIES (1)
    A MILLION GREEN COUNTIES FROM HERE, ...MONOLOGUE AT 3 A.M.   40   7
COUNTING (1)
    COUNTING THE RED STARS AND THOSE OF PLUM-COLOR. ....THE COLOSSUS 130   26
COUNTRIES (1)
    "NEITHER OF THOSE COUNTRIES DO I FREQUENT: ....DIALOGUE B.   38   19
COUNTRY (17)
    WITH MY OWN COUNTRY LOVE ....SONG FOR A SUMMER'S DAY   30   2
    IN THE CONTRACTED COUNTRY OF THE HEAD ....THE THIN PEOPLE   64   25
    BLUE-BLOODED IN COARSE COUNTRY REIGNED; ....NATURAL HISTORY   71   2
    HERE, IN A WELL-STEERED COUNTRY, ...LORELEI   94   19
    IN MIDAS' COUNTRY ....IN MIDAS' COUNTRY   99   T
    OF COUNTRY HEDGEROWS AND COW PASTURES ....WHITENESS I REMEMBER 102   16
    IT IS A COUNTRY ON A NURSERY PLATE. ....WATERCOLOR.   112   15
    YET DESOLATION, STALLED IN PAINT, SPARES THE LITTLE COUNTRY ...
                              ... TWO VIEWS OF A CADAVER ROOM 114   21
    TWO CAMPERS IN CLOUD COUNTRY ....TWO CAMPERS IN CLOUD COUNTRY 144   T
    IN THIS COUNTRY THERE IS NEITHER MEASURE NOR BALANCE .....TWO CAMP. 144   1
    EVEN MY BEST FRIEND THINKS I'M IN THE COUNTRY. ....FACE LIFT   156   19
    AND COMES FROM A COUNTRY FAR AWAY AS HEALTH. ....TULIPS 162   63
    OF A COUNTRY NO LONGER HEARD OF, ...THE COURAGE OF SHUTTING-UP 210   33
    LEAVE AND ARRIVE, AND THERE IS NO END TO THE COUNTRY. ...THE SWARM   217   36
    A ROUGH, DUMB COUNTRY STUFF ....BY CANDLELIGHT   236   3
    THE SKY OF THE CITY IS WHITE; THE LIGHT FROM THE COUNTRY. ...
                              ... QUEEN MARY'S ROSE GARDEN 290   10
    REPOSE OF SCULPTURE HOLDS THE COUNTRY STILL. ....PROLOGUE TO SPRING 322   9
COUNTS (1)
    COUNTS. SUCH DUELS INFECT BEST FRIENDSHIPS. PAN ....DIALOGUE O. 283 271
COUPLED (3)
    WITH SAVOR; COUPLED SO, PURE PARAGONS OF CONSTANCE, ...WREATH F.   44   9
    COUPLED BY BRANCHES INTERTWINED ....CRYSTAL GAZER   55   14
    I COUPLED WITH DUST IN THE SHADOW OF A STONE. POEM.6.W.   136   22
COUPLES (2)
    AND GILDED COUPLES ALL IN WHIRLING TRANCE ....CINDERELLA 304   9
    COUPLES COURT BY MILK OF MOON: ....DANSE MACABRE   321   20
COUPLETS (1)
    CRIES AND HEROIC COUPLETS CONCLUDING THE MILLION ....PERSEUS   83   18
COURAGE (3)
    LEWDLY BECKONING, AND HER COURAGE WAVERED: ....LADY AND T.   69   20
    THE COURAGE OF SHUTTING-UP ....THE COURAGE OF SHUTTING-UP 209   T
    THE COURAGE OF THE SHUT MOUTH, IN SPITE OF ARTILLERY! .....COURAGE. 209   1
COURIERS (2)
    HER WORMY COURIERS ARE AT HIS BONES. ....OUIJA   77   25
    THE COURIERS ....THE COURIERS 247   T
COURSE (5)
    PERSEVERED ON A SET COURSE ....SPIDER   49   30
    SKYWARD AGAIN, WITHOUT HOPE, OF COURSE, ...LOVE LETTER   147   7
    WITHOUT ME, SHE WOULDN'T EXIST SO OF COURSE SHE WAS GRATEFUL. ...
                              ... IN PLASTER 159   15
    TWO, OF COURSE THERE ARE TWO. ....DEATH & CO.   254   1
    TO HALT OUR CAR IN HEADLONG COURSE. ....THE DREAM   310   12
COURT (7)
    TO JUDGMENT IN A HIGHER COURT OF GRACE. ....DIALOGUE B.   39   45
    "THERE SITS NO HIGHER COURT .....DIALOGUE BETWEEN GHOST AND PRIEST   39   49
    AMUSED COURT HALLS: ....THE SNOWMAN ON THE MOOR   59   42
    THE TAIL-TRACK, ON THE SNOW IN OUR COURT -- ....PHEASANT   191   12
    TO COURT REMORSE. OR SOMEONE ELSE. I'D RATHER ....DIALOGUE O.   278   59
    I ENJOY PETTICOATS AND VELVETS AND GOSSIP OF COURT, ..QUEEN MARY'S. 290   21
    COUPLES COURT BY MILK OF MOON: ....DANSE MACABRE   321   20
COURTFOLK (1)
    IN RUCK AND QUIBBLE OF COURTFOLK ....THE QUEEN'S COMPLAINT   28   1
COURTING (1)
    ONE COURTING DOCTORS OF ALL SORTS, ...THE DEATH OF MYTH-MAKING 104   4
COURTSHIP (1)
    HOW OUR COURTSHIP LIT THE TINDERY CAGES -- ....ZOO KEEPER'S WIFE 155   33
COURTYARD (1)
    IN MY COURTYARD A FOUNTAIN LEAPS AND SINKS BACK INTO ITSELF,*BARREN. 157   3
COUSIN (4)
    LAST SUMMER I CAME UPON YOUR SPANISH COUSIN, ...SPIDER   48   8
    COUSIN DID YOU SO UNWISELY KEEP ....THE DISQUIETING MUSES   74   3
    INDEFATIGABLE COUSIN ....PURDAH 242   12
    OF COUSIN JANE, OUR SPINSTER WITH ....FAMILY REUNION   300   17
COVEN (1)
    STAKED IN PRIDE'S COVEN. ....VANITY FAIR   33   35
COVER (6)
    THE FABRICATION OF SOME CLOTH TO COVER ....TALE OF A TUB   25   34
    SIX FEET OF YELLOW GRAVEL COVER YOU. ....ELECTRA ON AZALEA PATH 117   23
    THEN SHE COULD COVER MY MOUTH AND EYES, COVER ME ENTIRELY, *PLASTER. 159   40
    THEN SHE COULD COVER MY MOUTH AND EYES, COVER ME ENTIRELY, *PLASTER. 159   40
    IT WILL COVER A DYNASTY. ....AN APPEARANCE   189   13
    THEIR SHADOWS MUST COVER CANADA. ....CROSSING THE WATER 190   3

COVERED (1)
AND THEY ARE ALL GLOVED AND COVERED, WHY DID NOBODY TELL ME? ..BEE. 211 4
COVERS (1)
FOR RECREATION DOWN UNDER THE COVERS: ....DIALOGUE EN ROUTE 309 23
COW (7)
OF COUNTRY HEDGEROWS AND COW PASTURES ....WHITENESS I REMEMBER 102 16
THE COW MILKS CREAM AN INCH THICK. ....THE TIMES ARE TIDY 107 15
YET IT NEVER MILKED ANY GOAT, NOR DEALT COW DEATH ....GOATSUCKER 111 12
I'M A MEANS, A STAGE, A COW IN CALF. ....METAPHORS 116 7
IS ACCOUNTING FOR ITS COW. I SHUT MY EYES ..STARS OVER THE DORDOGNE 166 39
IN A DESERT OF COW PEOPLE ............................EAVESDROPPER 261 41
AN ODD DISEASE HAS HIT OUR HOLY COW, ...THE DISPOSSESSED 318 4
COW-HEAVY (1)
ONE CRY, AND I STUMBLE FROM BED, COW-HEAVY AND FLORAL   MORNING SONG 157 13
COW-PARSLEY (1)
IF I STAND VERY STILL, THEY WILL THINK I AM COW-PARSLEY, ...BEE. 212 39
COWS (9)
ACROSS BARBED STILE, THROUGH FLOCKED BROWN COWS. ....BUCOLICS 23 4
I SAW SLOW FLOCKED COWS MOVE ....SONG FOR A SUMMER'S DAY 30 3
THAT OWL VOICE SOLE "YES", WHILE COWS UTTER ....WREATH FOR A BRIDAL 44 3
ON GRASS THAT ONCE FED BOSTON COWS. ....A WINTER'S TALE 87 23
AND PRISTINE ALPHABETS AND COWS THAT MOO ...THE GHOST'S LEAVETAKING 91 36
SPOTTED COWS REVOLVE THEIR JAWS AND CROP ....WATERCOLOR. 112 16
WIDEN AND DIE IN THE HEDGEROWS. I HEAR THE MOO OF COWS. *THREE WOMEN 185 312
THAT IS THE VALLEY OF DEATH, THOUGH THE COWS THRIVE.   THE DETECTIVE 208 6
PEOPLE AND COWS. ....LYONNESSE 234 10
COW'S (1)
AND BLOODIED AS A COW'S SPLIT FRAME ....STREET SONG 36 9
COY (1)
COY PAPER STRIPS FOR DOORS -- ....LESBOS 227 5
CRAB (3)
WATER FAUCETS SPAWN NO DANGER; EACH CRAB ....TALE OF A TUB 25 19
(A CRAB TO NAP ON ....WORDS FOR A NURSERY 74 43
OR HEADSTRONG COLUMBUS CRAB. ....MUSSEL HUNTER AT ROCK HARBOR 97 76
CRAB-BACKS (1)
WHERE RED-FRECKLED CRAB-BACKS, CLAWS ..MUSSEL HUNTER AT ROCK HARBOR 97 83
CRABBED (2)
FROM HIS CRABBED MIDDEN WHERE ALL'S WROUGHT SO AWRY ....FIRESONG 30 10
MY THOUGHTS ARE CRABBED AND SALLOW, ...JILTED 304 1
CRAB-CLAW (1)
ROCK-FACE, CRAB-CLAW VERGED ON GREEN. *THE HERMIT AT OUTERMOST HOUSE 119 18
CRAB-FACE (1)
THE CRAB-FACE, ETCHED AND SET THERE, ..MUSSEL HUNTER AT ROCK HARBOR 97 77
CRABS (6)
KNIGHTS MIGHT DOFF THEIR CASQUES. THE CRABS ....MUSSEL HUNTER. 96 28
KNEW NOTHING OF. SO THE CRABS ....MUSSEL HUNTER AT ROCK HARBOR 97 60
MUSSELS. FROM WHAT THE CRABS SAW, ...MUSSEL HUNTER AT ROCK HARBOR 97 64
AND WHOLE CRABS, DEAD, THEIR SOGGY ....MUSSEL HUNTER AT ROCK HARBOR 97 84
THEY ARE UNLOADING THREE BARRELS OF LITTLE CRABS. ....A WINTER SHIP 113 14
HUSTLES OTHER GULLS OFF. CRABS ....MAGNOLIA SHOALS 122 15
CRACK (13)
BETTER THAT EVERY FIBER CRACK ....MONOLOGUE AT 3 A.M. 40 1
IN QUARTZ, AS CRACK YOUR SKULL TO KEEP   EPITAPH FOR FIRE AND FLOWER 45 4
KING EGG-HEAD SAW HIS DOMAIN CRACK, ...NATURAL HISTORY 71 10
THE GREAT BRONZE GATE BEGAN TO CRACK, ...THE BULL OF BENDYLAW 108 13
THE SEA BROKE IN AT EVERY CRACK, ...THE BULL OF BENDYLAW 108 14
THROUGH THE NARROW CRACK ....THE SLEEPERS 122 8
CRACK THROUGH STONE, AND THEY ARE GREEN WITH LIFE. .....THREE WOMEN 187 371
CELLOPHANE I CANNOT CRACK. ....PARALYTIC 266 31
THE WAY YOU'D CRACK A CLOCK; YOU'D CRUSH THE BONE ...SONNET: TO EVA 304 2
WITH VALENTINO'S CRACK TECHNICAL TALENT ....DIALOGUE EN ROUTE 309 22
AND THE SKIES CRACK THROUGH WITH THUNDER; ..GO GET THE GOODLY SQUAB 313 6
STREETS CRACK THROUGH IN HAVOC-SPLIT RAVINES ....DOOMSDAY 316 7
STILL, STUBBORNLY WE TRY TO CRACK THE NUT ....DOOM OF EXILES 318 13
CRACKED (5)
HE STAMPED AND CRACKED STALKS TO THE GROUND ....BUCOLICS 24 19
INTO CRACKED HEART ....TINKER JACK AND THE TIDY WIVES 34 24
THIS CRACKED WORLD'S INCESSANT GABBLE AND HISS. ....STREET SONG 36 30
THE DRY VOLCANOES CRACKED AND SPIT, ...I WANT, I WANT 106 4
HE HANDS HER THE CUT-OUT HEART LIKE A CRACKED HEIRLOOM.   TWO VIEWS. 114 11
CRACKER (1)
ARE RATTLING THE CRACKER PACKETS. FINE FLOUR ....LEAVING EARLY 146 36
CRACKING (1)
AGAINST THE CRACKING CLIMATE. ....PRIVATE GROUND 130 6
CRACKLE (2)
YOU WILL NOT EVEN HEAR ME OPENING IT, NO PAPER CRACKLE, ..BIRTHDAY. 207 34
HER BLACKS CRACKLE AND DRAG. ....EDGE 273 20
CRACKLESS (1)
FAGGOT-BEARING JACK IN HIS CRACKLESS EGG: ....MAUDLIN 51 4
CRACKLING (2)
GLORIFIED FOR PRIME FLESH AND GOLDEN CRACKLING ....SOW 60 15
CAULDRON, TALKING AND CRACKLING ....THE COURIERS 247 8
CRACKPOTS (1)
THE CHITTERING CRACKPOTS THAT HE MADE.*SONG FOR A REVOLUTIONARY LOVE 323 20

CRACKS (7)
    REVEALS NO CRACKS THAT CAN BE DECODED? WHEN WASHBOWL   TALE OF A TUB   24 10
    SEE, THE DARKNESS IS LEAKING FROM THE CRACKS. ....THREE WOMEN   182 195
    THE GLASS CRACKS ACROSS, ...THALIDOMIDE   252 24
    THE SUNDAY LAMB CRACKS IN ITS FAT. ....MARY'S SONG   257   1
    CRACKS RED. NOTHING HAPPENS. WAIT. ITS TRIP ....DIALOGUE O.   277 20
    SUCH SKEPTIC CRACKS. WITH SENSE SEALED WATERTIGHT ......DIALOGUE O.   280 155
    A RIGOR SEIZED ME: I SAW CRACKS APPEAR, *DIALOGUE OVER A OUIJA BOARD   285 319
CRACK-THROATED (1)
    CRACK-THROATED MISTRESS OF BAGPIPES AND CYMBALS, ..ALICANTE LULLABY   43 16
CRADLE (3)
    AT THE CRADLE OF SPANISH WALNUT, ...WINTERING   219 44
    THEY ARE MAKING A CAT'S CRADLE, THEY ARE SUICIDAL. ....STINGS/DR   293   7
    THERE'S A HEX ON THE CRADLE ....TEMPER OF TIME   336 23
CRADLED (1)
    ROLLED ROUND WITH GOODLY LOAM AND CRADLED DEEP, ...THE DEAD 320   9
CRADLES (2)
    DEADLOCKED WITH THEM, TAKING ROOT AS CRADLES ROCK. ...
                                    ... ALL THE DEAD DEARS   71 36
    THE CARRIAGES ROCK, THEY ARE CRADLES. ....GETTING THERE 249 64
CRAFT (1)
    A CRAFT WITH PAINT AND POWDER THAT CAN MAKE .........METAMORPHOSES. 307 23
CRAFTY (1)
    SAY HOW CRAFTY THE PAINTER WAS ..BLACK PINE TREE IN AN ORANGE LIGHT 328 17
CRAGS (1)
    HARDCASTLE CRAGS ....HARDCASTLE CRAGS 62   T
CRAM (1)
    THOUGH PRIME PARTS CRAM EACH RICH MEAL, ...THE GLUTTON   40 11
CRAMPED (3)
    LEDGE WILL DISLODGE OUR CRAMPED CONCEPT OF SPACE, UNWALL ....OXBOW.   88 23
    ENLISTED IN A CRAMPED NECROPOLIS, ...ELECTRA ON AZALEA PATH 117 17
    CRAMPED ON NOTHING. BLACK ....FINISTERRE 169   2
CRANNIES (1)
    WIDEN THE CRANNIES, ...MUSHROOMS   139 17
CRAP (2)
    WHERE THEY CRAP AND PUKE AND CRY AND SHE CAN'T HEAR. ....LESBOS 228 14
    MEANWHILE THERE'S A STINK OF FAT AND BABY CRAP. ....LESBOS 228 33
CRASH (1)
    EVERY DOWNFALL AND CRASH ....STREET SONG   36 27
CRASHED (1)
    WITH MANY MEN UNTIL I CRASHED ....THE DREAM   310   9
CRASHES (1)
    I STALLED AT SUDDEN NOISY CRASHES*FABLE OF THE RHODODENDRON STEALERS 103 18
CRATERED (1)
    EDGE OF A CRATERED POOL-BED ....MUSSEL HUNTER AT ROCK HARBOR   95 16
CRATERS (2)
    PEAKS AND CRATERS OF THOSE EXTINCT VOLCANOES.*THE EVERLASTING MONDAY   62   6
    DILATING TO CRATERS IN THIS LIVINGROOM, *DIALOGUE OVER A OUIJA BOARD 285 320
CRAVED (1)
    THEN, A FREE-GADDING HOYDEN, GERD HAD CRAVED ....CRYSTAL GAZER   55 31
CRAVES (2)
    CRAVES MOST TO COOK BATTER ....VANITY FAIR   33 16
    SKELETON STILL CRAVES TO HAVE ....DANSE MACABRE   321   5
CRAVING (1)
    WHAT FIRES RUN, WHAT CRAVING WAKES? ....PURSUIT   22 12
CRAWL (5)
    NO PIT OF SHADOW TO CRAWL INTO, ...SUICIDE OFF EGG ROCK 115   7
    I CRAWL LIKE AN ANT IN MOURNING ....THE COLOSSUS   129 12
    LOOK, LOOK! IT IS WANTING TO CRAWL." ....A SECRET   220 36
    AMPUTATIONS CRAWL AND APPALL -- ....THALIDOMIDE   252   5
    AFTER, THEY CRAWL ....STINGS/DR   293 12
CRAWLED (1)
    YOU CRAWLED OUT, ...EAVESDROPPER 261 47
CRAWLS (4)
    A WASP CRAWLS ....YADDO: THE GRAND MANOR   123   9
    CRAWLS UP OUT OF THE SEA. ....A LIFE   150 35
    AND CRAWLS BEHIND IT LIKE A WORM. ....THE FEARFUL 256   2
    CRAWLS DOWN THE WALL. ....CONTUSION   271   9
CREAK (2)
    THE WOODS CREAK AND ACHE, AND THE DAY FORGETS ITSELF.*PRIVATE GROUND 131 19
    I HOLD MY BREATH UNTIL YOU CREAK TO LIFE, ...BY CANDLELIGHT   236 19
CREAKING (3)
    A GALLERY OF CREAKING PORCHES AND STILL INTERIORS,   THE BABYSITTERS 175 34
    WHERE POLISHED HIGHBOYS WHISPER CREAKING CURSES ......FEMALE AUTHOR 301   7
    CLAMBERING UP THE CREAKING HEIGHTS OF HEAT ....THE PRINCESS.   334 55
CREAM (3)
    WITH CREAM AND CHICKEN-GUT FEASTING THE PALATES ......ELLA MASON A.   53 11
    THE COW MILKS CREAM AN INCH THICK. ....THE TIMES ARE TIDY 107 15
    WHEN THE SWEETHEART FROM ENGLAND APPEARED, WITH HER CREAM SKIN
                AND YARDLEY COSMETICS, ...THE BABYSITTERS 174   6
CREAMING (2)
    THE FORGETFUL SURF CREAMING ON THOSE LEDGES. ..SUICIDE OFF EGG ROCK 115 24
    TO SCOUR THE CREAMING CRESTS ....STINGS 215 36
CREAM-SMOOTH (1)
    CREAM-SMOOTH HONEYDEWS, ...FIESTA MELONS   46 11

CREAMY (1)
CREAMY BEAN FLOWERS WITH BLACK EYES AND LEAVES LIKE BORED HEARTS. ...
... THE BEE MEETING   211   18
CREATE (3)
EACH DAY DEMANDS WE CREATE OUR WHOLE WORLD OVER, ...TALE OF A TUB   25   36
TO CREATE SUCH A RUIN. ....THE COLOSSUS   130   23
I AM RESTLESS. RESTLESS AND USELESS. I, TOO, CREATE CORPSES. *THREE.   182 189
CREATES (1)
THERE IS THIS WHITE WALL, ABOVE WHICH THE SKY CREATES ITSELF -- ...
... APPREHENSIONS   195   1
CREATION (3)
ALL CREATION, WERE IT NOT FOR A BIGGER BELLY ....PERSEUS   83   33
GETS READY TO FACE THE READY-MADE CREATION   THE GHOST'S LEAVETAKING   90   6
PAN'S PROWESS OUR OWN CREATION, AND NOT THE OTHER'S ....DIALOGUE O.   284 285
CREATURE (1)
LITTLE VICTIM UNEARTHED BY SOME LARGE CREATURE ....BLUE MOLES   126   6
CREDIT (1)
I DO NOT THINK YOU CREDIT ME WITH THIS DISCRETION. ....BIRTHDAY.   207   36
CREDITOR (1)
OUR CREDITOR ADVANCES WITH A BOW ....THE DISPOSSESSED   318   10
CREDULITY (1)
I NEVER KNEW SUCH CREDULITY TO PITCH ...DIALOGUE OVER A OUIJA BOARD   280 154
CREDULOUS (1)
RIDING HOME FROM CREDULOUS BLUE DOMES, ...TERMINAL   328   1
CREEL (1)
A CREEL OF EELS, ALL RIPPLES. ....YOU'RE   141   15
CREEP (2)
THE OLD WOMEN CREEP OUT HERE ....OLD LADIES' HOME   120   4
THE WRINKLES CREEP UP LIKE WAVES, ...THE RIVAL/DR   291   4
CREEPING (2)
AND THE CRICKETS COME CREEPING INTO OUR HAIR ....SLEEP.   144   25
CREEPING UP WITH HER HATFUL OF TRIVIAL REPETITIONS. ......INSOMNIAC   163   32
CREEPS (1)
CREEPS AWAY, MANY-SNAKED, WITH A LONG HISS OF DISTRESS. *BERCK-PLAGE   196   18
CREEPY-CREEPY (1)
LEMON TEA AND EARWIG BISCUITS -- CREEPY-CREEPY. ....THE TOUR   238   39
CREPES (1)
THESE ARE OUR CREPES. EAT THEM BEFORE THEY BLOW COLD." ..FINISTERRE   170   36
CRESCENDOS (1)
CRESCENDOS, CADENZAS, PRESTOS AND PRESTISSIMOS, ...ALICANTE LULLABY   43   18
CRESCENT (1)
A GREEN CRESCENT OF PALMS ....SOUTHERN SUNRISE   26   10
CRESCENTS (1)
FIVE MOONY CRESCENTS ....WORDS FOR A NURSERY   73   4
CREST (4)
CREST AND TROUGH. MILES LONG ....FULL FATHOM FIVE   92   6
RAVELED WIND-RIPPED FROM THE CREST OF THE WAVE.*SUICIDE OFF EGG ROCK   115   11
TO THIS CREST OF GRASS. INLAND, THEY ARGUE,   PARLIAMENT HILL FIELDS   152   7
A CREST OF BREASTS, EYELIDS AND LIPS ....BERCK-PLAGE   200 116
CRESTS (2)
ARE HUSTLED OVER THE CRESTS AND TROUGHS, ...ON DECK   143   13
TO SCOUR THE CREAMING CRESTS ....STINGS   215   36
CREVICE (2)
IN THE CREVICE OF AN EXTREMELY SMALL SHADOW ....SLEEP.   144   15
STUCK TO HER TRIPOD, OVER THE FUMING CREVICE, ...DIALOGUE O.   286 349
CREVICES (1)
THE STREETS ARE LIZARDY CREVICES ....GIGOLO   267   2
CREW (1)
AND THE FAIR SHIP SANK, ITS CREW KNELLED HOME FOR DINNER. ...
... DREAM WITH CLAM-DIGGERS   44   20
CRIB (4)
AND AT THE LEFT SIDE OF MY CRIB? ....THE DISQUIETING MUSES   75   8
THEY WANT THE CRIB OF SOME LAMP-HEADED PLATO. ....MAGI   148   16
THE CHILD IN THE WHITE CRIB REVOLVES AND SIGHS, ...EVENT   194   7
HOTHOUSE BABY IN ITS CRIB, ...FEVER.   231   19
CRICKET (1)
IMPORTUNATE CRICKET POEM.7.S.   136   12
CRICKETS (3)
ARE AN ESPLANADE FOR CRICKETS. ....THE BURNT-OUT SPA   138   13
THE HEAT-CRACKED CRICKETS CONGREGATE ....SLEEP IN THE MOJAVE DESERT   144   22
AND THE CRICKETS COME CREEPING INTO OUR HAIR ....SLEEP.   144   25
CRICKETS' (1)
A HIGH HUSH QUIETENS THE CRICKETS' CRY. ....ABOVE THE OXBOW   89   56
CRIED (7)
"FOND PHANTOM," CRIED SHOCKED FATHER SHAWN, ...DIALOGUE B.   39   41
GODMOTHERS, AND YOU CRIED AND CRIED: ....THE DISQUIETING MUSES   75   31
GODMOTHERS, AND YOU CRIED AND CRIED: ....THE DISQUIETING MUSES   75   31
CRIED OUT FOR THE MOTHER'S DUG. ....I WANT, I WANT   106   3
CRIED THEN FOR THE FATHER'S BLOOD ....I WANT, I WANT   106   6
ON THAT DAY-OFF THE TWO OF US CRIED SO HARD TO GET   THE BABYSITTERS   175   29
SHAM ADAM THE MATADOR CRIED: ....DIALOGUE EN ROUTE   308   14
CRIES (17)
OR CRIES THAT THIS RAW FLESH ....STREET SONG   35   6
SUCH POVERTY. NO DEAD MEN'S CRIES ....NOVEMBER GRAVEYARD   56   6

                                                   TITLE   PAGE LINE
CRIES (CONT.)
   CRIES: "CELEBRATE SYRINX WHOSE DEMURS ....VIRGIN IN A TREE   81   13
   CRIES AND HEROIC COUPLETS CONCLUDING THE MILLION ....PERSEUS   83   18
   TO CANACEE CRIES GIBBERISH TO COARSENED EARS. ........INCOMMUNICADO   100   14
   SIZE. THE CRIES OF SCAVENGING GULLS SOUND THIN ....GREEN ROCK.   105   14
   UP HERE AMONG THE GULL CRIES ....MAGNOLIA SHOALS   121   1
   HER CRIES ARE HOOKS THAT CATCH AND GRATE LIKE CATS. ....THREE WOMEN   182 207
   AND FROM THE OPEN MOUTH ISSUE SHARP CRIES ....THREE WOMEN   182 213
   I HAD A DREAM OF AN ISLAND, RED WITH CRIES. ....THREE WOMEN   185 307
   WHAT IS THAT BIRD THAT CRIES ....THREE WOMEN   186 348
   THESE CHILDREN ARE AFTER SOMETHING, WITH HOOKS AND CRIES, ...BERCK.   198   44
   THE TINDER CRIES. ....FEVER.   231   8
   THE TENT OF UNENDING CRIES --- ....GETTING THERE   248   27
   NO RINGS THROUGH THE NOSE, NO CRIES. ....GIGOLO   267   9
   THE OLD MAID IN THE GABLE CRIES ALL DAY: ....NEVER TRY TO TRICK.   320   11
   THE THIRD CRIES OUT AS ALL THE SHIPS GO DOWN:*EPITAPH IN THREE PARTS   337   10
CRIME (1)
   IT DRAGS THE SEA AFTER IT LIKE A DARK CRIME; IT IS QUIET .....MOON.   173   10
CRIMINAL (1)
   INDETERMINATE CRIMINAL, ...THE JAILER   227   33
CRIMP (2)
   AND CRIMP THEIR WRINKLES IN A GRIN, ...RHYME   50   7
   WHICH ALL THE ARTFUL WIZARDS CANNOT CRIMP ....THE PRINCESS.   333   17
CRIMPED (1)
   CRIMPED LIKE FERN IN THE QUARTZ ATMOSPHERE; .....PROLOGUE TO SPRING   322   8
CRINGE (2)
   DROVE THE DOGS TO CRINGE AND WHINE, ...THE DEATH OF MYTH-MAKING   104   13
   THE SPRY HOOKS THAT BEND AND CRINGE, AND THE SMILES, THE SMILES. ...
                                            ... BURNING THE LETTERS   204   21
CRIPPLE (1)
   ATOMS THAT CRIPPLE DRIP ....NICK AND THE CANDLESTICK   242   38
CRIPPLES (2)
   THE DARK IS MELTING. WE TOUCH LIKE CRIPPLES. ....EVENT   195   22
   TRANSFORM TO CRIPPLES ....ON LOOKING INTO THE EYES OF A DEMON LOVER   325   3
CRISIS (1)
   SHEEP GREENS, FINNED FALLS, "I SHALL COMPOSE A CRISIS ...CONJURING.   66   11
CRISP (2)
   AS THAT CRISP CUSP TOWARDS WHICH YOU VOYAGE NOW. ....GHOST'S.   91   38
   YOUR SHIRT OF CRISP LINEN ....WHITSUN   154   9
CRISPLY (1)
   "HOW NOW," FATHER SHAWN CRISPLY ADDRESSED THE GHOST ....DIALOGUE B.   38   11
CRITIC (1)
   THOUGH PRIMA DONNA POUTS AND CRITIC STINGS, ...LOVE IS A PARALLAX   330   56
CRITICIZING (1)
   I FELT HER CRITICIZING ME IN SPITE OF HERSELF, ...IN PLASTER   159   30
CRITICS (2)
   IT SEEMS THE CONSISTENT CRITICS WANTED YOU ....YADWIGHA.   85   8
   AND THAT, ROUSSEAU TOLD THE CRITICS, WAS WHY THE COUCH ...YADWIGHA.   86   31
CRIVELLI (1)
   THAT REVOLVE IN CRIVELLI, UNTOUCHABLE. ....GULLIVER   251   22
CROAK (4)
   NOW, RICH ORDER OF WALLS IS FALLEN; ROOKS CROAK ......CONVERSATION.   21   5
   FROM GAUNT HEMLOCK, ROOKS CROAK HAVOC: ....WINTER LANDSCAPE,   22   7
   RATHER THAN CROAK OUT ....RECANTATION   42   8
   CROAK AND WITHER. ....FROG AUTUMN 99   4
CROCK (1)
   A CROCK OF DUST IS MY DEAR HOME." DIALOGUE BETWEEN GHOST AND PRIEST   39   40
CROCODILE (1)
   A CROCODILE OF SMALL GIRLS ....PARLIAMENT HILL FIELDS   152   13
CRONE (1)
   THE LAST CRONE GOT BURNT UP ....THE TIMES ARE TIDY   107   11
CROOK (1)
   LIKE A CUP OR A ROOM. THE MOON'S CROOK WHITENS, ...PARLIAMENT H.   153   38
CROOK-BACK (1)
   CROOK-BACK OR BANDY-LEG, ...TINKER JACK AND THE TIDY WIVES   34   16
CROOKED (6)
   THIS WITCH SIDLES, FINGERS CROOKED, AS IF ....VANITY FAIR   32   2
   OF KNOTTED TABLE AND CROOKED CHAIR, ..MISS DRAKE PROCEEDS TO SUPPER   41   4
   AND THAT CROOKED LINE ....RECANTATION   41   2
   CHURCH CURSE TO KEN THAT CROOKED OATH ....CRYSTAL GAZER   55   35
   UNHINGED AND HIS GRIN CROOKED, ...MEDALLION   124   6
   BY CROOKED DETOUR, ...TEMPER OF TIME   336   18
CROOKS (1)
   TACKING IN MOON-BLUED CROOKS FROM THE BLACK ....HARDCASTLE CRAGS   62   3
CROP (3)
   ALREADY THE FARMER'S AFTER HIS CROP, ...IN MIDAS' COUNTRY   100   23
   SPOTTED COWS REVOLVE THEIR JAWS AND CROP ....WATERCOLOR.   112   16
   IN PANIC AT THE CROP OF CATACOMBS ....TERMINAL   328   3
CROP'S (1)
   WILL BRING CROP'S INCREASE, AND HARVEST FRUIT ....CRYSTAL GAZER   55   17
CROQUET (1)
   WHERE ADJECTIVES PLAY CROQUET WITH FLAMINGO NOUNS; ...A SORCERER B.   324   2
CROSS (3)
   SMALL AND CROSS. THE YELLOW KNIFE ....BY CANDLELIGHT   237   21
   HAVE SUCH A SPACE TO CROSS, ...THE NIGHT DANCES   250   16

	TITLE	PAGE	LINE

CROSS (CONT.)
A CROSS OF CONTRADICTION, RACKED BETWEEN   METAMORPHOSES OF THE MOON   308   47
CROSSED (3)
    CROSSED BY THREE CAUSEWAYS, ...WORDS FOR A NURSERY   74   28
    SPUN INTO A RIVER, THE RIVER CROSSED. ....THE SWARM   216   30
    YOUR CROSSED POSITION. ....NICK AND THE CANDLESTICK   241   26
CROSSES (2)
    CROSSES THE LAKE. THE WORMS ....THE MANOR GARDEN 125   17
    OF BEING WHEELED OFF UNDER CROSSES AND A RAIN OF PIETAS. ...
                                                ... APPREHENSIONS 195   15
CROSSHATCH (1)
    THROUGH CROSSHATCH OF SPARROW AND STARLING. ....PHEASANT   191   14
CROSSING (3)
    CHANNEL CROSSING ....CHANNEL CROSSING 26   T
    CROSSING THE WATER ....CROSSING THE WATER   190   T
    CROSSING AND RECROSSING: A FINE THING! ....PHEASANT   191   18
CROSSLEGGED (1)
    ALOUD, CROSSLEGGED ON THE STERN SEAT, FROM THE GENERATION OF
        VIPERS. ....THE BABYSITTERS   175   32
CROSS-LEGGED (1)
    SMILE, CROSS-LEGGED, ...PURDAH 242   5
CROSS-PURPOSES (1)
    TO SUCH CROSS-PURPOSES? AT LAST YOU GLIMPSE ....DIALOGUE O.   284 289
CROSSROAD (1)
    OR SHOUTS OF WALKERS: CROSSROAD TRAFFIC ....WHITENESS I REMEMBER   103   25
CROSS-STITCH (1)
    EACH COAL A HOT CROSS-STITCH -- A LOVELY LIGHT! ....THE TOUR   238   21
CROTCH (2)
    AN IVORY PALACE, A CROTCH PINE. ....THE SWARM   217   50
    RUBBER BREASTS OR A RUBBER CROTCH, ...THE APPLICANT   221   5
CROTCHED (1)
    THE MIMIC HEAD -- IN A CROTCHED WILLOW, GREEN- ....LADY AND T.   69   23
CROUCHED (1)
    OF GUARDIAN CATS CROUCHED ROUND THEIR IDOL, ...ELLA MASON A.   54   28
CROW (3)
    AND THE CROW SETTLES HER GARMENTS. ....THE MANOR GARDEN   125   11
    THERE IS ONLY A CROW IN A TREE. MAKE NOTES. ....THE DETECTIVE   209   40
    COCKS CROW UP A RIVAL ....MOONSONG AT MORNING   316   5
CROWBAR (1)
    FROST FORMS. NO MAN'S CROWBAR COULD ....CHILD'S PARK STONES   101   26
CROW-COLORS (1)
    DOMINOES OF THEIR DOORWAYS. SUN GRAINS THEIR CROW-COLORS, ...NET-.   121   6
CROWD (5)
    THE WREATHED DOORS OPEN TO THE CROWD. ....A WINTER'S TALE   87   26
    THE CROWD SUCKS HER LAST TEAR AND TURNS AWAY. ....AFTERMATH   114   14
    CROWD FOOT TO FOOT, HEAD TO HEAD, NO FLOWER   ELECTRA ON AZALEA PATH   117   20
    THE PEANUT-CRUNCHING CROWD ....LADY LAZARUS   245   26
    A CROWD OF SHINING GULLS THAT PLUNGE TO LAUNCH ...EPITAPH IN THREE.   337   13
CROWED (4)
    THE HOUR IS CROWED IN LUNATIC THIRTEENS. ....DOOMSDAY   316   3
    THE HOUR IS CROWED IN LUNATIC THIRTEENS. ....DOOMSDAY   316   9
    THE HOUR IS CROWED IN LUNATIC THIRTEENS. ....DOOMSDAY   316   15
    THE HOUR IS CROWED IN LUNATIC THIRTEENS. ....DOOMSDAY   316   19
CROWDS (1)
    FOR MONEY. LORD, THE CROWDS ARE FIERCE! ....A WINTER'S TALE   87   15
CROWD'S (1)
    THE AFTERNOON AT A BAD END UNDER THE CROWD'S TRUCULENCE, *THE GORING   47   2
CROWING (1)
    AND SOLACED HER, BUT QUIT HER AT COCK'S CROWING.   QUEEN'S COMPLAINT   28   15
CROWN (4)
    NONE OF THAT GREENHORN LOT MATCHED HER BRIGHT CROWN. ...
                                    ... THE QUEEN'S COMPLAINT   29   20
    IN THE WHORL OF HER EAR, AND LIKE A SCOOPED-OUT PUMPKIN CROWN ...
                                    ... HARDCASTLE CRAGS   63   24
    HIS CROWN USURPED BY THE LOW BROW ....NATURAL HISTORY   71   11
    BARBS ON THE CROWN OF GILDED WIRE, ...I WANT, I WANT   106   11
CROWNING (2)
    AND, CROWNING IT, ONE ....POLLY'S TREE   129   41
    TO KEEP THE YOUNG GIRL FROM HER CROWNING GOAL. ....THE PRINCESS.   333   18
CROWNS (4)
    CROWNS, PALACE, ALL ....THE SHRIKE   42   19
    SCUTTLE REPOSE WITH CROWNS AND CACKLES. ....ALICANTE LULLABY   43   7
    THEIR LEAFY CROWNS, THEIR FAME SOARS, ...VIRGIN IN A TREE   81   18
    THESE CROWNS OF ACANTHUS, ...THE MANOR GARDEN   125   10
CROWS (1)
    TO FEED THE THIN CROWS. ....WORDS FOR A NURSERY   74   50
CROW'S-FEET (1)
    CROW'S-FEET COPY VEINING ON STAINED LEAF; ....VANITY FAIR   32   7
CRUDE (1)
    A GLITTER OF WHEAT AND CRUDE EARTH. ....BERCK-PLAGE   200   96
CRUEL (4)
    CRUEL NETTLES STUNG HER ANKLES RAW. ....BUCOLICS   24   16
    I AM NOT CRUEL, ONLY TRUTHFUL -- ....MIRROR   173   4
    THERE IS NO MIRACLE MORE CRUEL THAN THIS. ....THREE WOMEN   180 127
    NEITHER CRUEL NOR INDIFFERENT, ...WINTERING   218   20

```
                                                TITLE              PAGE  LINE
CRUELLY (1)
  CRUELLY, BEING BARREN.  ..........................................ELM  192   23
CRUISE (1)
  I SEE THEM START TO CRUISE AND DIP FOR FOOD*QUEEN MARY'S ROSE GARDEN   290   13
CRUISES (1)
  WHEN THE SPORTY WIFE AND HER DOCTOR HUSBAND WENT ON ONE OF
    THEIR CRUISES  .....................................THE BABYSITTERS  174   16
CRUISING (1)
  WHITE HULKS ON THEIR DAY'S CRUISING;  .......SONG FOR A SUMMER'S DAY    31    4
CRUMB (2)
  STARS GRINDING, CRUMB BY CRUMB,  ..................ALL THE DEAD DEARS   70   11
  STARS GRINDING, CRUMB BY CRUMB,  ..................ALL THE DEAD DEARS   70   11
CRUMBLED (1)
  CRUMBLED TO SMOKE.  .......................THE SNOWMAN ON THE MOOR      59   48
CRUMBLES (1)
  AS THE DOOMSTRUCK CITY CRUMBLES BLOCK BY BLOCK:  ...........DOOMSDAY   316    8
CRUMBS (1)
  ON CRUMBS OF SHADOW,  .......................................MUSHROOMS  139   20
CRUNCH (1)
  FROM UNDER CRUNCH OF MY MAN'S BOOT  ......................ODE FOR TED   29    1
CRUSH (2)
  THE WAY YOU'D CRACK A CLOCK; YOU'D CRUSH THE BONE  ...SONNET: TO EVA   304    2
  YOUR HANDS WILL CRUSH  ...........................TRIO OF LOVE SONGS   315   47
CRUSTY (1)
  HEARD A QUEER CRUSTY SCRABBLE  .........MUSSEL HUNTER AT ROCK HARBOR    95   14
CRUTCH (2)
  PROPS A LEG-STUMP UPON A CRUTCH,  ........................THE BEGGARS   48   11
  A GLASS EYE, FALSE TEETH OR A CRUTCH,  .................THE APPLICANT  221    3
CRUTCHES (1)
  TUBULAR STEEL WHEELCHAIRS, ALUMINUM CRUTCHES.  ..........BERCK-PLAGE   197   39
CRUTCHLESS (1)
  WAVING AND CRUTCHLESS, HALF THEIR OLD SIZE.  ............BERCK-PLAGE   196    9
CRUX (2)
  NOW IN THE CRUX OF THEIR VOWS HANG YOUR EAR,  ........EPITAPH FOR F.    45   15
  AND ACT BEAR WITNESS, IN THE CRUX OF TIME,  .............DIALOGUE O.   286  362
CRY (37)
  MARK, I CRY, THAT MOUTH  .................................STRUMPET SONG  33    9
  EVEN AS LOVE'S DEAR FOOLS CRY EVERGREEN,*EPITAPH FOR FIRE AND FLOWER   46   30
  A HIGH HUSH QUIETENS THE CRICKETS' CRY.  .............ABOVE THE OXBOW   89   56
  SHAKEN BY OWL CRY.  .....................................................OWL  102   16
  THE OWL SHALL STOOP FROM HIS TURRET, THE RAT CRY OUT.  ..WATERCOLOR.   112   28
  THE HOOPS OF BLACKBERRY STEMS MADE ME CRY.  ............POEM.1.WHO.    132   31
  IN THEIR BLACK ARMORPLATE AND CRY.  ......SLEEP IN THE MOJAVE DESERT   144   23
  YOUR CRY FADES LIKE THE CRY OF A GNAT.  ......PARLIAMENT HILL FIELDS   153   32
  YOUR CRY FADES LIKE THE CRY OF A GNAT.  ......PARLIAMENT HILL FIELDS   153   32
  THE MIDWIFE SLAPPED YOUR FOOTSOLES, AND YOUR BALD CRY   MORNING SONG   156    2
  ONE CRY, AND I STUMBLE FROM BED, COW-HEAVY AND FLORAL   MORNING SONG   157   13
  A GARDEN OF BUGGY ROSES THAT MADE HIM CRY.  ................INSOMNIAC   163   12
  ONE CRY. IT IS THE HOOK I HANG ON.  .....................THREE WOMEN   183  236
  DEAD MEN CRY FROM IT.  ................................LITTLE FUGUE    188   27
  HOW YOU LIE AND CRY AFTER IT  ..................................ELM    192    8
  I AM INHABITED BY A CRY.  ......................................ELM    193   28
  BACK TO BACK. I HEAR AN OWL CRY  .............................EVENT    194    4
  SWIVEL THEIR HEADS AND CRY.  ...........................APPREHENSIONS  195   17
  A RED BURST AND A CRY  ..........................BURNING THE LETTERS   205   50
  PURE AND CLEAN AS THE CRY OF A BABY,  ...........A BIRTHDAY PRESENT    208   61
  WHERE THEY CRAP AND PUKE AND CRY AND SHE CAN'T HEAR.  .......LESBOS    228   14
  OR IS IT A BIRTH CRY?  ................................STOPPED DEAD    230    2
  THE CHILD'S CRY  ...............................................ARIEL  239   24
  THAT THESE LATE MOUTHS SHOULD CRY OPEN  .........POPPIES IN OCTOBER    240   11
  WHAT IS SO REAL AS THE CRY OF A CHILD?  ...................KINDNESS    269    6
  A RABBIT'S CRY MAY BE WILDER  ............................KINDNESS     269    7
  THE MEANINGLESS CRY OF BABIES. SUCH A SEA  ................FEVER./DR   294    4
  GOLD MOUTHS CRY  .................................GOLD MOUTHS CRY      302    1
  GOLD MOUTHS CRY WITH THE GREEN YOUNG  ............GOLD MOUTHS CRY      302    1
  CLOCKS CRY: STILLNESS IS A LIE, MY DEAR.*TO EVA DESCENDING THE STAIR   303    1
  CLOCKS CRY: STILLNESS IS A LIE, MY DEAR.*TO EVA DESCENDING THE STAIR   303    6
  CLOCKS CRY: STILLNESS IS A LIE, MY DEAR.*TO EVA DESCENDING THE STAIR   303   12
  CLOCKS CRY: STILLNESS IS A LIE, MY DEAR.*TO EVA DESCENDING THE STAIR   303   18
  SO CRY FOR THE PAGAN GIRL LEFT PICKING OLIVES  ......SONNET: TO TIME   311    9
  NOR CAN GOD'S STERN, SHOCKED ANGELS CRY THEM UP  ...........THE DEAD   320   13
  BLESSINGS RIGHT AND LEFT AND CRY  .................LOVE IS A PARALLAX  330   39
  BUT, GO! THEY CRY, AND THE SWING  ....................TOUCH-AND-GO     335   13
CRYING (13)
  CRYING: BLOOD, LET BLOOD BE SPILT;  ........................PURSUIT    22   15
  TILL HE SOME PITY TOOK UPON HER CRYING;  ......THE QUEEN'S COMPLAINT    28   12
  HUMBLED THEN, AND CRYING,  ...................THE SNOWMAN ON THE MOOR   59   49
  THE MOUTH-HOLE CRYING THEIR LOCATIONS.  ...................POEM.7.S.  136   16
  WE WERE ALWAYS CRYING, IN OUR SPARE ROOMS, LITTLE PUT-UPON
    SISTERS,  ........................................THE BABYSITTERS   174    4
  SHE IS CRYING THROUGH THE GLASS THAT SEPARATES US.  .....THREE WOMEN  182  205
  SHE IS CRYING, AND SHE IS FURIOUS.  .....................THREE WOMEN  182  206
  SHE IS CRYING AT THE DARK, OR AT THE STARS  .............THREE WOMEN  182  209
  STOP CRYING.  ..........................................THE APPLICANT 221    8
  FROM GRAY CHILD FACES CRYING IN THE STREETS.  .........FEMALE AUTHOR  301   14
```

		TITLE	PAGE	LINE

CRYING (CONT.)
"CRYING, SHE CAME TO THE ISLAND ....THE DREAM 311 13
VOICE CRYING EXCLUSION IN MY EAR. ....SONNET: TO TIME 311   8
OF COCKCROW CRYING UP THE DAWN. ....DANSE MACABRE 321 24
CRYPT (1)
OF FESTERING GARDENIAS IN A CRYPT, ...FEMALE AUTHOR 301 12
CRYPTIC (3)
CRYPTIC STARS WIND UP THE ATMOSPHERE, ..TO EVA DESCENDING THE STAIR 303 10
AT ITS CRYPTIC CELESTIAL ORIGIN. ....DIALOGUE EN ROUTE 309 36
POINTING TOWARD THE SPINDLE'S CRYPTIC WHIR, ...THE PRINCESS. 335 60
CRYSTAL (5)
THIS MOON-POCKED CRYSTAL BALL ....RECANTATION   41   6
CRYSTAL GAZER ....CRYSTAL GAZER   54   T
AND, FIXED IN THE CRYSTAL CENTER, GRINNING FIERCE: ...CRYSTAL GAZER   56 47
SAND GRIT TO SIDED CRYSTAL ....MUSSEL HUNTER AT ROCK HARBOR   95   4
LOCKED IN CRYSTAL CASKETS ARE THE LAKES, ...PROLOGUE TO SPRING 322 13
CRYSTALLIZED (2)
THE SEA, THAT CRYSTALLIZED THESE, ...BERCK-PLAGE 196 17
BEING CRYSTALLIZED FROM CARBON ....NOTES TO A NEOPHYTE 307 23
CRYSTALS (3)
OF LITTLE CRYSTALS, TITILLATING THE LIGHT, ...BERCK-PLAGE 197 26
ITS CRYSTALS ....PURDAH 243 46
ITS CRYSTALS A LITTLE POULTICE. ....KINDNESS 269 11
CUBE (1)
FOR MY CUBE OF SUGAR: ITS BOG BREATH ....ZOO KEEPER'S WIFE 155 36
CUCKOO (1)
AND LIKE A CUCKOO IN THE NEST MAKES HELL   METAMORPHOSES OF THE MOON 307 17
CUDDLY (1)
HERE'S A CUDDLY MOTHER. POEM.2.DARK. 133 28
CUFFS (2)
I WEAR WHITE CUFFS, I BOW. ....AN APPEARANCE 189   9
BUTTONING THE CUFFS AT MY WRISTS AND THE SLIT FROM MY NECK TO MY
KNEES. ....THE BEE MEETING 211   8
CUIRASS (1)
HELMED, IN CUIRASS, ...SOW   61 30
CUL-DE-SAC (1)
IT IS BEST TO MEET IN A CUL-DE-SAC, ...GIGOLO 267   4
CULL (1)
GO CULL THE PURPLE SNAILS FROM SLOTHFUL SHELLS ....GO GET. 313 17
CULLING (1)
OF PRIZE ROSES, CULLING THE FULLEST FLORETS; ....SPINACH-PICKER.   90 19
CULTIVATED (1)
THE CULTIVATED ACT, A FIERCE BRIEF FUSION ....LOVE IS A PARALLAX 330 58
CUMBROUS (2)
DOWN DEEP INTO THE BENT BULL-NECK. CUMBROUS ROUTINE, NOT ARTWORK. ...
... THE GORING   47   7
WATCHES HIS CUMBROUS WORLD ECLIPSE ....SCULPTOR   91 12
CUNNING (1)
AND PLANETS PLOT WITH OLD ELLIPTIC CUNNING; .....TO EVA DESCENDING. 303   5
CUP (6)
WHICH OUT FROM BLACK TARN, DITCH AND CUP ....STRUMPET SONG   34 17
JIGGLES HIS TIN CUP AT THE GOODWIVES. ....THE BEGGARS   48 12
OF BLUNT PENCILS, ROSE-SPRIGGED COFFEE CUP, ...CONJURING.   65   2
LIKE A CUP OR A ROOM. THE MOON'S CROOK WHITENS, ...PARLIAMENT H. 153 38
THE WHITE SKY EMPTIES OF ITS PROMISE, LIKE A CUP. ......THREE WOMEN 177 33
AND HERE YOU COME, WITH A CUP OF TEA ....KINDNESS 270 16
CUPBOARD (3)
TABLE-TOP, CUPBOARD SHELF, CATS LOUNGED BRAZEN, ...ELLA MASON A.   54 22
I'VE MARRIED A CUPBOARD OF RUBBISH. POEM.4.BEAST. 134 18
THE STOMACH OF INDIFFERENCE, THE WORDLESS CUPBOARD. POEM.7.S. 136   6
CUPBOARDS (1)
PEBBLES WE PRESERVE IN OUR OWN CUPBOARDS*DIALOGUE OVER A OUIJA BOARD 280 135
CUPPED (3)
CUPPED QUICK TO MOUTH; ....THE GLUTTON   40 10
HER HEAD CUPPED THE BABEL. ....HARDCASTLE CRAGS   63 25
WHAT CUPPED SIGHS, WHAT SALT IN THE THROAT.... ......BERCK-PLAGE 197 32
CUPPING (2)
EARS CUPPING THE SEA'S INCOHERENCES, ...MEDUSA 224   3
CUPPING THE BERRY PROTECTIVELY BEFORE ....BITTER STRAWBERRIES 300 37
CUPS (3)
DRINKING VINEGAR FROM TIN CUPS: THEY WORE ....THE THIN PEOPLE   64 20
WAS SHE ARRANGING CUPS? IT IS IMPORTANT. ....THE DETECTIVE 208   3
EIGHT COMBS OF YELLOW CUPS, ...STINGS 214   7
CURB (1)
SO KISS: THE DRUNKS UPON THE CURB AND DAMES .....LOVE IS A PARALLAX 329 31
CURBSIDE (1)
STALLING CURBSIDE AT HIS ONCOMING, ...WHITENESS I REMEMBER 103 26
CURDED (1)
CURDED OVER WITH CLOUDS AND CHALK CLIFFS BLANCHED   CHANNEL CROSSING   27 24
CURE (1)
SUGAR CAN CURE EVERYTHING, SO KINDNESS SAYS. ....KINDNESS 269   9
CURIOSITY (1)
SEDUCED BY CURIOSITY, ...METAMORPHOSES OF THE MOON 308 33
CURIOUS (2)
TO SATISFY THE QUESTIONS OF A CURIOUS OLD FOOL?" ....DIALOGUE B.   39 26

	TITLE	PAGE	LINE

CURIOUS (CONT.)
THE CURIOUS BEARERS AND THE RAW DATE ....BERCK-PLAGE 199 71
CURLED (2)
AND I'D SOONER BE STAKED FOR A WITCH, KINDLED, AND CURLED ...
... DIALOGUE OVER A OUIJA BOARD 280 132
BEYOND THE WINDOW) SHE LIES ON CUSHIONS CURLED ....FEMALE AUTHOR 301 3
CURLS (1)
ALL WIG CURLS AND YELLOW TEETH ....WUTHERING HEIGHTS 167 26
CURRENCY (1)
OF LOVE: CLAWS BRACED, AT BAY, MY CURRENCY NOT HERS. INCOMMUNICADO 100 7
CURRENT (1)
A CURRENT AGITATES THE WIRES POEM.7.S. 137 29
CURRENTS (4)
OF THE DESULTORY CURRENTS -- ALL THAT UNIQUE ....ABOVE THE OXBOW 89 45
CURRENTS OF THE CONNECTICUT FAN ....IN MIDAS' COUNTRY 99 2
OF THE FERRYING CURRENTS, BELLY ....OWL 102 13
SUCH BLUE CURRENTS IN THE VEINS OF MY LOVED ONE! .....AN APPEARANCE 189 2
CURSE (6)
WITH STARE, WITH CURSE ....MONOLOGUE AT 3 A.M. 40 10
WITH CURSE, FIST, THREAT ....SPINSTER 50 29
GIBBETS WITH HER CURSE THE MOON'S MAN, ...MAUDLIN 51 3
CHURCH CURSE TO KEN THAT CROOKED OATH ....CRYSTAL GAZER 55 35
LOVE IS THE BONE AND SINEW OF MY CURSE. POEM.7.S. 137 40
WHERE WE STOPPED, AND WITH A CURSE ....THE DREAM 311 14
CURSES (2)
TWISTING CURSES IN THE TANGLED SHEET ....THE SHRIKE 42 10
WHERE POLISHED HIGHBOYS WHISPER CREAKING CURSES ......FEMALE AUTHOR 301 7
CURSING (1)
GAILY CURSING THE WHOLE GOBLIN HORDE. THE PRINCESS AND THE GOBLINS 334 46
CURTAIN (5)
ONE CURTAIN IS FLICKERING FROM THE OPEN WINDOW, ...BERCK-PLAGE 199 79
A CURTAIN OF WAX DIVIDING THEM FROM THE BRIDE FLIGHT, ...BEE. 212 47
VEIL STIRS ITS CURTAIN ....PURDAH 243 25
DO NOT THINK I DON'T NOTICE YOUR CURTAIN -- ..........EAVESDROPPER 260 28
TO CALL FOR CURTAIN ON OUR THOUSAND SCENES; .....LOVE IS A PARALLAX 330 44
CURTAINED (1)
CURTAINED WITH YELLOW LACE. ....THE SLEEPERS 122 7
CURTAINS (4)
NOW THERE ARE THESE VEILS, SHIMMERING LIKE CURTAINS, ...BIRTHDAY. 206 16
STAGE CURTAINS, A WIDOW'S FRIZZ. ....LESBOS 227 6
TO NORMAL. LET'S CLOSE THE CURTAINS. IT LOOKS WILD .....DIALOGUE O. 286 335
AMONG THE BLANCHED, BOILED INSTRUMENTS, THE VIRGINAL
CURTAINS. ....FEVER./DR 294 8
CURTAIN'S (1)
THICKET OF WORDS. THE CURTAIN'S DRAWN ON THAT. ....DIALOGUE O. 286 352
CURTSEYED (1)
CURTSEYED TO YOURS. TOO BAD YOU CALLED PAN UP ....DIALOGUE O. 284 280
CURTSIES (1)
THEN, THIS TOUGH STINT DONE, SHE CURTSIES ....AERIALIST 331 25
CURVE (2)
POINT OF EDEN, NEXT THE NEW MOON'S CURVE. ..THE GHOST'S LEAVETAKING 91 31
CURVE OF WATER UPLEAPING ....MEDUSA 225 18
CUSHIONS (3)
AS VICTORIAN CUSHIONS. THIS FAMILY ....A LIFE 150 16
IT CUSHIONS ME LOVINGLY. ....LETTER IN NOVEMBER 253 10
BEYOND THE WINDOW) SHE LIES ON CUSHIONS CURLED ....FEMALE AUTHOR 301 3
CUSP (1)
AS THAT CRISP CUSP TOWARDS WHICH YOU VOYAGE NOW. ....GHOST'S. 91 38
CUSTOM (2)
FROM CHARLES STREET TO THE CUSTOM HOUSE, ...A WINTER'S TALE 87 35
AND VIOLATES CELESTIAL CUSTOM ..INSOLENT STORM STRIKES AT THE SKULL 326 31
CUT (11)
WATCHED THE CHANGING SHAPE HE CUT, ...FAUN 35 12
THAN AXE COULD CUT. ....ON THE PLETHORA OF DRYADS 67 12
I FORGET YOU, HEARING THE CUT FLOWERS ....LEAVING EARLY 145 7
AN ASSEMBLY-LINE OF CUT THROATS, AND YOU AND I ....WAKING IN WINTER 151 5
OR EVEN LIKE BLACK HOLES CUT OUT OF IT. ....WIDOW 164 29
RED, MOTTLED, LIKE CUT NECKS. ....LITTLE FUGUE 188 35
INDEFATIGABLE, PURPLE. MUST IT BE CUT OUT? ....COURAGE. 210 18
SHE'LL CUT HER THROAT AT TEN IF SHE'S MAD AT TWO. ....LESBOS 228 22
CUT ....CUT 235 T
OF DREAMERS IS DISPELLED. ONCE MORE WE CUT ....DIALOGUE O. 286 359
YOU'LL CUT THE CHORD ....TRIO OF LOVE SONGS 315 39
CUTE (1)
I SEE YOUR CUTE DECOR ....LESBOS 229 85
CUT-GRASS (1)
THEY LIE, CUT-GRASS ASSAULTING EACH SEPARATE SENSE ....WREATH F. 44 8
CUTLERY (1)
AND THE SNOW, MARSHALING ITS BRILLIANT CUTLERY ....THE SWARM 216 9
CUT-OUT (1)
HE HANDS HER THE CUT-OUT HEART LIKE A CRACKED HEIRLOOM. TWO VIEWS. 114 11
CUT-PAPER (2)
AND I SEE MYSELF, FLAT, RIDICULOUS, A CUT-PAPER SHADOW ......TULIPS 161 46
BLACK LAKE, BLACK BOAT, TWO BLACK, CUT-PAPER PEOPLE.*CROSSING THE W. 190 1

CUTTING (3)
   KEEP FROM CUTTING FAT MEAT ....THE THIN PEOPLE   65   27
   MEASURING THE FLOUR, CUTTING OFF THE SURPLUS, ...A BIRTHDAY PRESENT 206   7
   HIS THREE TEETH CUTTING ....BRASILIA 258   12
CYCLING (1) -
   CYCLING PHOENIX NEVER STOPS. ....LOVE IS A PARALLAX 330   66
CYCLONES (1)
   SKEPTIC CYCLONES TRY THE BONE ..INSOLENT STORM STRIKES AT THE SKULL 325   7
CYCLOPS-EYE (1)
   AN ORANGE CYCLOPS-EYE, SCORNING TO LOOK ....WINTER LANDSCAPE,   21   7
CYGNETS (1)
   CAT-TAILS PART WHERE THE TAME CYGNETS STEER. ....WATERCOLOR. 112   14
CYMBALS (1)
   CRACK-THROATED MISTRESS OF BAGPIPES AND CYMBALS, ..ALICANTE LULLABY   43   16
CYPRESS (1)
   I OPEN MY LUNCH ON A HILL OF BLACK CYPRESS. ....THE COLOSSUS 130   19
CYPRESSES (1)
   THESE FAITHFUL DARK-BOUGHED CYPRESSES ....PARLIAMENT HILL FIELDS 153   30
CYRUS (1)
   WHILE THERE IRATE CYRUS ....A LESSON IN VENGEANCE   80   16
DA (1)
   I REMEMBER YOU PLAYING "JA DA" IN A PINK PIQUE DRESS*THE BABYSITTERS 175   22
DACHAU (1)
   A JEW TO DACHAU, AUSCHWITZ, BELSEN. ....DADDY 223   33
DADDY (7)
   DADDY ....DADDY 222   T
   DADDY, I HAVE HAD TO KILL YOU. ....DADDY 222   6
   YOU STAND AT THE BLACKBOARD, DADDY, ...DADDY 223   51
   SO DADDY, I'M FINALLY THROUGH. ....DADDY 224   68
   DADDY, YOU CAN LIE BACK NOW. ....DADDY 224   75
   DADDY, DADDY, YOU BASTARD, I'M THROUGH. ....DADDY 224   80
   DADDY, DADDY, YOU BASTARD, I'M THROUGH. ....DADDY 224   80
DAFFODILS (1)
   MARBLE FACADES WITH BLUE VEINS, AND JELLY-GLASSFULS OF DAFFODILS. ...
                                                    ... BERCK-PLAGE 199   89
DAFT (2)
   AND, MORE DAFT THAN ANY GOOSE, ...STREET SONG   36   29
   WHERE THE DAFT FATHER WENT DOWN ....ALL THE DEAD DEARS   71   23
DAINTY (1)
   HER DAINTY ACRES HE RAMPED THROUGH ....THE QUEEN'S COMPLAINT   28   6
DAIRY (2)
   BEHIND SHUT DOORS; THE DAIRY HERDS ....HARDCASTLE CRAGS   63   32
   MOON FULL, MOON DARK, THE CHARY DAIRY FARMER ....GOATSUCKER 111   5
DAISIED (1)
   "A DAISIED MEAD," EACH SAID TO EACH, ...BUCOLICS   23   2
DAISIES (1)
   HER WINTER-BEHEADED DAISIES, MARROWLESS, GAUNT, ...SNOWMAN O.   58   9
DAISY (2)
   NOT TO BE STAYED BY A DAISY CHAIN ....THE BULL OF BENDYLAW 108   17
   WHITE DAISY WHEELS AND ....POLLY'S TREE 128   26
DALLY (1)
   WHO SEEKS TO DALLY IN THE PORT TILL DAWN, ...EPITAPH IN THREE PARTS 337   8
DALMATIAN (1)
   AND A SMALL DALMATIAN. ....THE BABYSITTERS 174   18
DAMAGE (1)
   FOR WHAT FIRE COULD DAMAGE*ON LOOKING INTO THE EYES OF A DEMON LOVER 325   19
DAMAGED (1)
   HAVE BEEN HOWLING LIKE WOMEN, OR DAMAGED INSTRUMENTS. ....INSOMNIAC 163   30
DAMAGING (1)
   AND DAMAGING THE WHOLE UNSEEN ....THE DREAM 311   17
DAMASKS (1)
   DAMASKS WITH DAZZLE THE THREADBARE EYE; ....CONJURING.   66   18
DAME (1)
   DAME KINDNESS, SHE IS SO NICE! ....KINDNESS 269   2
DAMES (1)
   SO KISS: THE DRUNKS UPON THE CURB AND DAMES .....LOVE IS A PARALLAX 329   31
DAMN (1)
   AND THAT DAMN SCRUPULOUS TREE WON'T PRACTICE WILES ......CONJURING.   66   20
DAMNATION (1)
   SUN STRUCK THE WATER LIKE A DAMNATION. ....SUICIDE OFF EGG ROCK 115   6
DAMNED (2)
   SOME DAMNED CONDITION YOU ARE IN: *DIALOGUE BETWEEN GHOST AND PRIEST   39   33
   DAMNED, HOWLING IN THEIR SHROUDS ACROSS THE MOOR *NOVEMBER GRAVEYARD   56   16
DAMPER (1)
   A SANDY DAMPER KILLS THE VIBRATIONS; ....BERCK-PLAGE 196   7
DANCE (1)
   HUSH A LUMPED MAN-SHAPE. THE WHOLE ACT FORMAL, FLUENT AS A DANCE. ...
                                                    ... THE GORING   47   9
DANCED (2)
   WHEN ON TIPTOE THE SCHOOLGIRLS DANCED, ...THE DISQUIETING MUSES   75   25
   SQUALL WAVES ONCE DANCED ....POINT SHIRLEY 110   13
DANCES (3)
   THE NIGHT DANCES ....THE NIGHT DANCES 249   T
   AND HOW WILL YOUR NIGHT DANCES ....THE NIGHT DANCES 249   3
   FOOTING HER DELICATE DANCES ....AERIALIST 331   10

	TITLE	PAGE	LINE

DANCING (1)
    THEY ARE DANCING AND STAMPING ON YOU. ....DADDY 224 78
DANDELIONS (1)
    SNUFF-RUFFED DANDELIONS, ...POLLY'S TREE 128 25
DANDIES (1)
    SLAYING THE DANDIES WITH HER EMERALD EYES; ....ELLA MASON A. 54 16
DANGER (3)
    WATER FAUCETS SPAWN NO DANGER; EACH CRAB ....TALE OF A TUB 25 19
    STARTS WITH A DANGER: ....FULL FATHOM FIVE 92 15
    AND INFLAME TO DANGER ....ON LOOKING INTO THE EYES OF A DEMON LOVER 325 15
DANGEROUS (5)
    AND THE AIR DANGEROUS. NOONDAY ACTS QUEERLY ....SLEEP. 143 3
    THE TULIPS SHOULD BE BEHIND BARS LIKE DANGEROUS ANIMALS; ....TULIPS 162 58
    IT HAS NINE TAILS, IT IS DANGEROUS. .....THE COURAGE OF SHUTTING-UP 210 19
    THE BOX IS LOCKED, IT IS DANGEROUS. .....THE ARRIVAL OF THE BEE BOX 213 6
    BLUE DEW FROM DANGEROUS SKIN. ....STINGS 214 27
DANGERS (5)
    BRAVE ACTS PLAYED OUT IN PEACE, IN WAR; ALL DANGERS*CHANNEL CROSSING 27 39
    YOUR DANGERS ARE MANY. I ....FULL FATHOM FIVE 92 16
    AND ALL I COULD SEE WAS DANGERS: DOVES AND WORDS, ...THREE WOMEN 178 47
    DANGERS, BUT DON'T MIND HEARING ABOUT THE ONES ....DIALOGUE O. 278 64
    THE INFERNAL HAUNT OF DEMON DANGERS; ....DOOM OF EXILES 318 6
DANGLES (1)
    DANGLES THE PUPPET-PEOPLE ....SOLILOQUY OF THE SOLIPSIST 37 14
DANGLING (1)
    WORSE -- SAW DANGLING FROM THAT SPIKE-STUDDED BELT ......SNOWMAN O. 59 37
DANS (1)
    DANS LE FOND DES FORETS VOTRE IMAGE ME SUIT. ....PURSUIT 22 E
DANSE (1)
    DANSE MACABRE ....DANSE MACABRE 320 T
DAPHNE (2)
    CONCOCT A DAPHNE; ....ON THE DIFFICULTY OF CONJURING UP A DRYAD 66 23
    WHETHER GOAT-THIGHED OR GOD-HALOED. EVER SINCE THAT FIRST DAPHNE ...
            ... VIRGIN IN A TREE 81 9
DAPPLE (1)
    YET THE DAPPLE TONING HIS WHITE DOWN ....WHITENESS I REMEMBER 102 10
DAPPLED (1)
    BE PLUCKED FROM CAVES OF DAPPLED AMBER WHERE ......MIDSUMMER MOBILE 324 9
DARED (1)
    LIKE THE RED-HEADED SISTER HE NEVER DARED TO TOUCH, ...AMNESIAC 233 13
DARES (1)
    WITH THE PILOT WHO DARES ALL HEAVEN'S HARMS .........METAMORPHOSES. 307 2
DARING (4)
    AND I WANT THE ONE'S LONGEVITY AND THE OTHER'S DARING.*I AM VERTICAL 162 10
    BARELY DARING TO BREATHE OR ACHOO. ....DADDY 222 5
    THE DARING ADJECTIVE ....TRIO OF LOVE SONGS 314 26
    DARING AS DEATH AND DEBONAIR ....CIRCUS IN THREE RINGS 321 7
DARK (72)
    FEATHERED DARK IN THOUGHT, I STALK LIKE A ROOK, ..WINTER LANDSCAPE, 21 9
    I SHUT MY DOORS ON THAT DARK GUILT, ...PURSUIT 23 46
    BLIND WITH STEAM, WILL NOT ADMIT THE DARK ....TALE OF A TUB 24 15
    CLEAVES FORWARD INTO FURY; DARK AS ANGER, ...CHANNEL CROSSING 26 3
    IN HER DARK WAINSCOTED ROOM ....TWO SISTERS OF PERSEPHONE 31 5
    RED, PALE OR DARK. ....STRUMPET SONG 33 7
    CLAM-DIGGERS ROSE UP OUT OF DARK SLIME AT HER OFFENSE.*DREAM WITH C. 44 24
    BAFFLE THE DARK, THE PITYING EYE. ....THE BEGGARS 48 21
    GERD SITS SPINDLE-SHANKED IN HER DARK TENT, ...CRYSTAL GAZER 54 1
    ACROSS ATLANTIC FURROWS, DARK, UNSURE -- ....MAYFLOWER 60 11
    TO WALL OF THE DARK, DWARFED COTTAGES. ....HARDCASTLE CRAGS 62 7
    THAT KNITS TO EACH ORIGINAL ITS COARSE COPY. A DARK TARN*LADY AND T. 69 15
    TO WAG AT THE DARK) ....WORDS FOR A NURSERY 74 46
    IMAGINE THEIR DEEP HUNGER, DEEP AS THE DARK ....OUIJA 77 8
    DARK FACE. SO MIGHT RIGOR MORTIS COME TO STIFFEN ....PERSEUS 83 32
    OF TIGERS TO BE STILLED BY YOUR DARK EYE ....YADWIGHA. 85 13
    THESE STONES GUARD A DARK REPOSE ....CHILD'S PARK STONES 101 11
    NEEDLING IT DARK. THEN I WAS SEEING ....THE EYE-MOTE 109 10
    MOON FULL, MOON DARK, THE CHARY DAIRY FARMER ....GOATSUCKER 111 5
    A FRUIT THAT'S DEATH TO TASTE: DARK FLESH, DARK PARINGS.
         ... THE BEEKEEPER'S DAUGHTER 118 14
    A FRUIT THAT'S DEATH TO TASTE: DARK FLESH, DARK PARINGS. ...
         ... THE BEEKEEPER'S DAUGHTER 118 14
    THEY SET THEIR STOUT CHAIRS BACK TO THE ROAD AND FACE THE DARK*NET-. 121 5
    DARK THICKETS HEDGE THE HOUSE. ....THE SLEEPERS 123 11
    THIN AS PINS IN THE DARK BRUISE ....MEDALLION 125 22
    DARK WOOD, DARK WATER ....DARK WOOD, DARK WATER 127 T
    DARK WOOD, DARK WATER ....DARK WOOD, DARK WATER 127 T
    THIS WOOD BURNS A DARK ....DARK WOOD, DARK WATER 127 1
    DARK HOUSE ....POEM.2.DARK. 132 ST
    THIS IS A DARK HOUSE, VERY BIG. POEM.2.DARK. 132 1
    FEED ME THE BERRIES OF DARK. POEM.3.MAENAD. 133 17
    IT IS EASY TO BLAME THE DARK: THE MOUTH OF A DOOR, ...POEM.6.W. 135 7
    TRAWLING YOUR DARK AS OWLS DO. ....YOU'RE 141 6
    LIKE A DEAD LAKE THE DARK ENVELOPS ME, ...ZOO KEEPER'S WIFE 154 3
    THE DARK STILL NURSES ITS SECRET. ....HEAVY WOMEN 158 11

DARK (CONT.)
    AND I'D BEEN KEEPING HER IN THE DARK, AND SHE WAS RESENTFUL -- ...
                                        ... IN PLASTER   159   37
    THAN THE DARK OF THE SKY BECAUSE IT IS QUITE STARLESS. ......STARS.   165   3
    AND WHERE I LIE NOW, BACK TO MY OWN DARK STAR, ...STARS.   166   34
    I SHALL HARDLY KNOW MYSELF. IT WILL BE DARK, ...LAST WORDS   172   25
    IT DRAGS THE SEA AFTER IT LIKE A DARK CRIME; IT IS QUIET .....MOON.   173   10
    NOT LOOKING, THROUGH THE THICK DARK, FOR THE FACE OF ANOTHER.*THREE.   178   77
    DARK TUNNEL, THROUGH WHICH HURTLE THE VISITATIONS. ....THREE WOMEN   180 130
    I LOSE LIFE AFTER LIFE. THE DARK EARTH DRINKS THEM. ....THREE WOMEN   181 154
    SHE IS CRYING AT THE DARK, OR AT THE STARS ....THREE WOMEN   182 209
    IT UTTERS SUCH DARK SOUNDS IT CANNOT BE GOOD. ....THREE WOMEN   182 217
    SUCH A DARK FUNNEL, MY FATHER! ....LITTLE FUGUE   188   22
    THEY ARE ROUND AND FLAT AND FULL OF DARK ADVICE. *CROSSING THE WATER   190   6
    THE JUT OF THAT ODD, DARK HEAD, PACING ....PHEASANT   191   3
    I AM TERRIFIED BY THIS DARK THING ....ELM   193   31
    THE DARK IS MELTING. WE TOUCH LIKE CRIPPLES. ....EVENT   195   22
    IS IT ANY WONDER HE PUTS ON DARK GLASSES? ....BERCK-PLAGE   196   12
    THE BLOOD THAT RUNS IS DARK FRUIT -- ....THE OTHER   202   29
    SILVER BEAST BETWEEN TWO DARK CANYONS, ..THE COURAGE OF SHUTTING-UP   210   9
    IT IS DARK, DARK, ...THE ARRIVAL OF THE BEE BOX   213   12
    IT IS DARK, DARK, ...THE ARRIVAL OF THE BEE BOX   213   12
    WINTERING IN A DARK WITHOUT WINDOW ....WINTERING   218   6
    THAT BEING FREE. WHAT WOULD THE DARK ....THE JAILER   227   41
    BERRIES CAST DARK ....ARIEL   239   11
    PLUMMET TO THEIR DARK ADDRESS, ...NICK AND THE CANDLESTICK   241   36
    YOUR DARK ....THALIDOMIDE   252   4
    THE DARK FRUITS REVOLVE AND FALL. ....THALIDOMIDE   252   23
    TASTE IT, DARK RED! ....CHILDLESS WOMAN   259   14
    STARLESS AND FATHERLESS, A DARK WATER. ....SHEEP IN FOG   262   15
    WRINGING OF HANDS, THIS DARK ....CHILD   265   11
    DEEPER WITHIN THE DARK, AND AS I PITCHED FURTHER ....DIALOGUE O.   285 317
    INTO A DARK WORLD I CANNOT SEE AT ALL. ....ELM/DR   292   10
    DOWN THE DARK IN A BLACK HEARSE ....THE DREAM   310   8
    WE VAUNT OUR DAYS IN NEON AND SCORN THE DARK. ....SONNET: TO TIME   311   4
    TO NAVIGATE THIS FINAL DARK. ...INSOLENT STORM STRIKES AT THE SKULL   326   18
    TILL DARK IS CONQUERED BY ORANGE COCK, ...BLACK PINE TREE.   328   15
    OF COMET HARA-KIRI THROUGH THE DARK ....LOVE IS A PARALLAX   329   29
    HOPING FOR SOME INCREDIBLE DARK MAN*MORNING IN THE HOSPITAL SOLARIUM   333   23
    FOR YOUR FATE INVOLVES A DARK ASSAILANT." ...EPITAPH IN THREE PARTS   337   9
DARK-BOUGHED (1)
    THESE FAITHFUL DARK-BOUGHED CYPRESSES ....PARLIAMENT HILL FIELDS   153   30
DARKEN (1)
    THEY DARKEN YOUR HOUSE, ...EAVESDROPPER   260   2
DARKENING (3)
    WHEN WORDS, LIKE LOCUSTS, DRUMMED THE DARKENING AIR ....OUIJA   77   17
    NOW SHE HERSELF IS DARKENING ....ELM/DR   292   9
    THE DARKENING STAIR, UNDOES THE PALACE LATCH ....THE PRINCESS.   334   28
DARKENS (1)
    DARKENS AND TARNISHES AND WHEN ....CUT   236   32
DARKER (1)
    PICKFT OF TREES WHOSE SILHOUETTE IS DARKER   STARS OVER THE DORDOGNE   165   2
DARK-FACED (1)
    THE STRONGEST WILL SEEMED A WILL TOWARD CEREMONY. OBESE, DARK-FACED ...
                                        ... THE GORING   47 4-5
DARKLY (3)
    AND DARKLY GLARE, ...PROSPECT   28   8
    ANCHORED ITSELF, GRIFFIN-LEGGED AND DARKLY GRAINED. ..THE OTHER TWO   68   9
    AMBLE DARKLY OLIVE ....AQUATIC NOCTURNE   306   23
DARKNESS (15)
    LIKE A PLANET, A STONE, SWALLOWED IN A GREAT DARKNESS,*THE OTHER TWO   68   25
    SHROUDED TO SUCKLE DARKNESS? ONLY THEY ....VIRGIN IN A TREE   81   24
    WHO WAKES WITH DARKNESS AND TILL DAWN WORKS HARD ....GOATSUCKER   111   3
    HAPPENS IN DARKNESS, VANISHES ....BLUE MOLES   127   35
    I SUCK AT THE PAPS OF DARKNESS. POEM.7.S.   136   18
    DARKNESS WIPES ME OUT LIKE CHALK ON A BLACKBOARD... ....FACE LIFT   156   15
    DARKNESS TERRIFIES IT. ....WUTHERING HEIGHTS   168   42
    FACES AND DARKNESS SEPARATE US OVER AND OVER. ....MIRROR   173   9
    EACH MORNING IT IS HER FACE THAT REPLACES THE DARKNESS. .....MIRROR   174   16
    SEE, THE DARKNESS IS LEAKING FROM THE CRACKS. ....THREE WOMEN   182 195
    STASIS IN DARKNESS. ....ARIEL   239   1
    BUT GREENNESS, DARKNESS SO PURE ....YEARS   255   4
    THE SNOW DROPS ITS PIECES OF DARKNESS, ...THE MUNICH MANNEQUINS   263   16
    THE CHAIRS BELONG TO ITS DARKNESS. I SMELL DECAY ......DIALOGUE O.   285 314
    ON DARKNESS, MORE VIVID AND UNNATURAL ..DIALOGUE OVER A OUIJA BOARD   285 323
DARKROOM (2)
    IN HIS EYE'S DARKROOM I CAN SEE ....BLUEBEARD   305   5
    IN DARKROOM OF YOUR EYE THE MOONLY MIND ....SONNET TO SATAN   323   1
DARK'S (2)
    THEY'RE OUT OF THE DARK'S RAGBAG, THESE TWO ....BLUE MOLES   126   1
    THE DARK'S HIS BONE. POEM.4.BEAST.   134   15
DARK-SUITED (1)
    AND I AM DARK-SUITED AND STILL, A MEMBER OF THE PARTY,   BERCK-PLAGE   200 111
DARK-WEBBED (1)
    HUNG CAUGHT IN DARK-WEBBED BRANCHES LIKE A FABULOUS HERON. ...

		TITLE	PAGE	LINE

DARK-WEBBED (CONT.)
... DIALOGUE BETWEEN GHOST AND PRIEST 38 6
DARLING (8)
MY DARLING RAVENS ARE FLOWN. ....RECANTATION 42 10
HOWEVER YOU MAY SWEAT TO HOLD SUCH DARLING WRECKS ...EPITAPH FOR F. 45 13
DARLING, ALL NIGHT ....FEVER. 231 28
TELL ME QUICK, DARLING, TELL ME NOW. ....THE DISPOSSESSED 318 3
TELL ME QUICK, DARLING, TELL ME NOW. ....THE DISPOSSESSED 318 9
TELL ME QUICK, DARLING, TELL ME NOW. ....THE DISPOSSESSED 318 15
TELL ME QUICK, DARLING, TELL ME NOW! ....THE DISPOSSESSED 319 19
SO WE COULD RAVE ON, DARLING, YOU AND I, ...LOVE IS A PARALLAX 329 13
DARLINGS (1)
ALL THE LONG GONE DARLINGS: THEY ....ALL THE DEAD DEARS 71 25
DARNING (1)
OLD SOCK-FACE, SAGGED ON A DARNING EGG. ....FACE LIFT 156 27
DARNING-EGGS (1)
WITH HEADS LIKE DARNING-EGGS TO NOD ....THE DISQUIETING MUSES 75 6
DARTBOARD (1)
SICKNESS BEGINS HERE: I AM A DARTBOARD FOR WITCHES. POEM.6.W. 135 4
DARTMOOR (1)
NEW YEAR ON DARTMOOR ....NEW YEAR ON DARTMOOR 176 T
DARTS (2)
DOES HE WRITE C FOR G? NO. HE DARTS ....DIALOGUE OVER A OUIJA BOARD 284 276
BURNING DARTS ....ON LOOKING INTO THE EYES OF A DEMON LOVER 325 12
DATE (1)
THE CURIOUS BEARERS AND THE RAW DATE ....BERCK-PLAGE 199 71
DAUGHTER (3)
YOUR GATE, FATHER -- YOUR HOUND-BITCH, DAUGHTER, FRIEND.*ELECTRA ON. 117 45
THE BEEKEEPER'S DAUGHTER ....THE BEEKEEPER'S DAUGHTER 118 T
MY DAUGHTER HAS NO TEETH. HER MOUTH IS WIDE. ....THREE WOMEN 182 216
DAUGHTERS (5)
SONS, DAUGHTERS, DAUGHTERS AND SONS, ...OLD LADIES' HOME 120 10
SONS, DAUGHTERS, DAUGHTERS AND SONS, ...OLD LADIES' HOME 120 10
FULL OF DRESSES AMD HATS AND CHINA AND MARRIED DAUGHTERS. ...BERCK. 199 77
THE WIDOW WITH HER BLACK POCKETBOOK AND THREE DAUGHTERS,*BERCK-PLAGE 200 100
AS FLAT AS SHE, WHO WHISPER "WE'RE YOUR DAUGHTERS." ......PARALYTIC 266 26
DAUNTED (1)
LIKE A DAUNTED WITCH, QUITTING CASTLE WHEN REAL DAYS BREAK. ...
... CONVERSATION AMONG THE RUINS 21 8
DAVY'S (1)
OF DAVY' LOCKER, AND THE LORD'S TO HOME,*DIALOGUE OVER A OUIJA BOARD 283 246
DAWN (23)
A QUARTZ-CLEAR DAWN ....SOUTHERN SUNRISE 26 13
UNTIL BIRD-RACKETING DAWN ....THE SHRIKE 42 16
DAWN SNUFFS OUT STAR'S SPENT WICK, ...EPITAPH FOR FIRE AND FLOWER 46 29
THEMSELVES AS THE DAWN ....THE THIN PEOPLE 65 33
IN A LIGHT NEITHER OF DAWN ....THE GREAT CARBUNCLE 72 5
RAVEL TO CLEARNESS ON THE DAWN SEA. ....FULL FATHOM FIVE 93 20
DAWN TIDE STOOD DEAD LOW. I SMELT .....MUSSEL HUNTER AT ROCK HARBOR 95 12
WHO WAKES WITH DARKNESS AND TILL DAWN WORKS HARD ....GOATSUCKER 111 3
WE'LL WAKE BLANK-BRAINED AS WATER IN THE DAWN. ....TWO CAMP. 145 27
WINTER DAWN IS THE COLOR OF METAL, ...WAKING IN WINTER 151 2
SMELLING THE DAWN DRAFTS. ....THE SURGEON AT 2 A.M. 171 46
DAWN FLOWERS IN THE GREAT ELM OUTSIDE THE HOUSE. ......THREE WOMEN 185 309
IN A FOREST OF FROST, IN A DAWN OF CORNFLOWERS. POPPIES IN OCTOBER 240 12
THE WET DAWN INKS ARE DOING THEIR BLUE DISSOLVE. ......WINTER TREES 257 1
DAWN GLIDS THE FARMERS LIKE PIGS, ...TOTEM 264 5
DAWN SAYS, WITH ITS BLOOD-FLUSH. ....TOTEM 264 23
STARS PALE BEFORE THE ANGRY DAWN; ....TO A JILTED LOVER 310 21
THE ORDINARY MILKMAN BROUGHT THAT DAWN ....THE TRIAL OF MAN 312 1
TO WAKEN DREAMERS IN THE MILKY DAWN, ...APRIL AUBADE 312 6
DAWN SHALL DISSEVER ....MOONSONG AT MORNING 317 13
TO TRUMPET-TOPPLING DAWN OF DOOMSTRUCK DAY: ....THE DEAD 320 11
OF COCKCROW CRYING UP THE DAWN. ....DANSE MACABRE 321 24
WHO SEEKS TO DALLY IN THE PORT TILL DAWN, ...EPITAPH IN THREE PARTS 337 8
DAY (64)
ONE DAY I'LL HAVE MY DEATH OF HIM; ....PURSUIT 22 2
EACH DAY DEMANDS WE CREATE OUR WHOLE WORLD OVER, ...TALE OF A TUB 25 36
IN SULLEN LIGHT OF THE INAUSPICIOUS DAY. ....CHANNEL CROSSING 27 25
SONG FOR A SUMMER'S DAY ....SONG FOR A SUMMER'S DAY 30 T
PACED BRISK FATHER SHAWN. A COLD DAY, A SODDEN ONE IT WAS ...
... DIALOGUE BETWEEN GHOST AND PRIEST 38 2
"THE DAY OF DOOM ....DIALOGUE BETWEEN GHOST AND PRIEST 39 37
FROM THIS HOLY DAY ON, ALL POLLEN BLOWN ....WREATH FOR A BRIDAL 45 19
AND, PLAINTIFF AGAINST EACH DAY, DECRY ....THE BEGGARS 47 4
DAY OF MIST: DAY OF TARNISH ....RESOLVE 52 1
DAY OF MIST: DAY OF TARNISH ....RESOLVE 52 1
DAY IN, DAY OUT, ...ON THE PLETHORA OF DRYADS 67 30
DAY IN, DAY OUT, ...ON THE PLETHORA OF DRYADS 67 30
THAT BATTENED FOR A DAY ON HER ANKLE-BONE. ......ALL THE DEAD DEARS 70 6
I WOKE ONE DAY TO SEE YOU, MOTHER, ...THE DISQUIETING MUSES 75 41
DAY NOW, NIGHT NOW, AT HEAD, SIDE, FEET, ...THE DISQUIETING MUSES 76 49
FACES BLANK AS THE DAY I WAS BORN, ...THE DISQUIETING MUSES 76 51
EVEN, A TANG OF METAL. DAY IN, DAY OUT, *MEMOIRS OF A SPINACH-PICKER 89 16

DAY (CONT.)
    EVEN, A TANG OF METAL. DAY IN, DAY OUT, *MEMOIRS OF A SPINACH-PICKER   89   16
    BY DAY, DESCANT FROM BORDERS ....LORELEI   94   26
    THE SEA, TILL THAT DAY ORDERLY, ...THE BULL OF BENDYLAW   108   2
    THE DAY SHE VISITED THE DISSECTING ROOM *TWO VIEWS OF A CADAVER ROOM   114   1
    THE DAY YOU DIED I WENT INTO THE DIRT, ...ELECTRA ON AZALEA PATH   116   1
    THE DAY I WOKE, I WOKE ON CHURCHYARD HILL. ..ELECTRA ON AZALEA PATH   117   15
    THE DAY YOUR SLACK SAIL DRANK MY SISTER'S BREATH ....ELECTRA ON.   117   30
    INCENSE OF DEATH. YOUR DAY APPROACHES. ....THE MANOR GARDEN   125   2
    BY DAY, ONLY THE TOPSOIL HEAVES. ....BLUE MOLES   126   26
    THE WOODS CREAK AND ACHE, AND THE DAY FORGETS ITSELF.*PRIVATE GROUND   131   19
    ANY DAY I MAY LITTER PUPPIES POEM.2.DARK.   132   12
    OF JULY TO ALL FOOLS' DAY, ...YOU'RE   141   8
    EACH DAY CONCLUDES IN A HUGE SPLURGE OF VERMILIONS ....TWO CAMP.   145   15
    THE DAY EMPTIES ITS IMAGES ....PARLIAMENT HILL FIELDS   153   37
    I'M COLLECTING MY STRENGTH; ONE DAY I SHALL MANAGE WITHOUT HER, ...
                                                        ... IN PLASTER   160   55
    WHERE ONCE A DAY THE LIGHT SLOWLY WIDENS AND SLOWLY THINS, ..TULIPS   161   45
    NO DAY IS SAFE FROM NEWS OF YOU, ...THE RIVAL   167   16
    ONE DAY IT WON'T COME BACK. THINGS AREN'T LIKE THAT. ....LAST WORDS   172   16
    RISES TOWARD HER DAY AFTER DAY, LIKE A TERRIBLE FISH. ......MIRROR   174   18
    RISES TOWARD HER DAY AFTER DAY, LIKE A TERRIBLE FISH. ....MIRROR   174   18
    A HOT BLUE DAY HAD BUDDED INTO SOMETHING. ....THREE WOMEN   178   56
    A DAY AGO, TWO DAYS, THREE DAYS AGO. IT WAS A FRIDAY. ..THREE WOMEN   183   248
    THE DAY IS BLAZING. IT IS VERY MOURNFUL. ....THREE WOMEN   184   262
    ALL DAY I FEEL ITS SOFT, FEATHERY TURNINGS, ITS MALIGNITY. ....ELM   193   33
    MADE A HOLE IN THE HOT DAY, A VACANCY. ....THE RABBIT CATCHER 194   18
    ONE DAY YOU MAY TOUCH WHAT'S WRONG ....FOR A FATHERLESS SON   205   12
    NO, NO, IT IS SCARLET FLOWERS THAT WILL ONE DAY BE EDIBLE. ....BEE.   211   20
    WHAT HOLES THIS PAPERY DAY IS ALREADY FULL OF! ....THE JAILER   226   17
    ALL DAY, GLUING MY CHURCH OF BURNT MATCHSTICKS, ...THE JAILER   227   26
    EVERY DAY YOU FILL HIM WITH SOUL-STUFF, LIKE A PITCHER. .....LESBOS   229   77
    OF AIR THAT ALL DAY FLIES ....PURDAH   243   45
    WILL VANISH IN A DAY. ....LADY LAZARUS   244   15
    COMEBACK IN BROAD DAY ....LADY LAZARUS   246   52
    TWO TIMES A DAY ....LETTER IN NOVEMBER   253   17
    WHILE THE DAY OUTSIDE GLIDES BY LIKE TICKER TAPE. ....PARALYTIC   266   10
    IN THIS DAY BEFORE THE DAY NOBODY IS ABOUT.*QUEEN MARY'S ROSE GARDEN   290   1
    IN THIS DAY BEFORE THE DAY NOBODY IS ABOUT.*QUEEN MARY'S ROSE GARDEN   290   1
    ALL DAY SHE PLAYS AT CHESS WITH THE BONES OF THE WORLD: ..FEMALE A.   301   1
    BACKWARD WE TRAVELED TO RECLAIM THE DAY ....DOOM OF EXILES   318   9
    THE OLD MAID IN THE GABLE CRIES ALL DAY: ....NEVER TRY TO TRICK.   320   11
    TO TRUMPET-TOPPLING DAWN OF DOOMSTRUCK DAY: ....THE DEAD   320   11
    SUSPEND THIS DAY, SO SINGULARLY DESIGNED, ...MIDSUMMER MOBILE   324   13
    THE CLEVER WOOLLY DOGS HAVE HAD THEIR DAY ....DENOUEMENT   326   7
    SOME DAY, MOVING, ONE WILL DROP. ....LOVE IS A PARALLAX 330   63
    BY DAY SHE MUST WALK IN DREAD ....AERIALIST   332   44
    MORNING: ANOTHER DAY, AND TALK ...MORNING IN THE HOSPITAL SOLARIUM   332   10
    TO SEEK THE STAIRCASE BY THE GLARE OF DAY. ....THE PRINCESS.   334   53
DAYBREAK (1)
    DAYBREAK DISCOVERED THE BUREAU LID ....LEAVING EARLY   146   29
DAY-CLOTHES (1)
    I HAVE GIVEN MY NAME AND MY DAY-CLOTHES UP TO THE NURSES ....TULIPS   160   6
DAYLIGHT (4)
    BLAMELESS AS DAYLIGHT I STOOD LOOKING ....THE EYE-MOTE   109   1
    AND DAYLIGHT LAYS ITS SAMENESS ON THE WALL. POEM.7.S.   137   26
    DAYLIGHT WOULD BE MORE JUDICIOUS, ...CANDLES   148   10
    ALREADY HE CAN FEEL DAYLIGHT, HIS WHITE DISEASE, ...INSOMNIAC   163   31
DAYLONG (2)
    DAYLONG A DUET OF SHADE AND LIGHT ....TWO SISTERS OF PERSEPHONE   31   3
    COUCHED DAYLONG IN CLOISTERS OF STINGING NETTLE *WREATH FOR A BRIDAL   44   7
DAY-MOON (2)
    A BLIMP SWIMS UP LIKE A DAY-MOON OR TIN ....A WINTER SHIP   113   11
    THE DAY-MOON LIGHTS UP LIKE A SORRY MOTHER, ...SLEEP.   144   24
DAY-OFF (1)
    ON THAT DAY-OFF THE TWO OF US CRIED SO HARD TO GET   THE BABYSITTERS   175   29
DAY-OLD (1)
    OF DAY-OLD BREAD AND EGG-STAINED PLATES; PERHAPS ....METAMORPHOSES.   307   29
DAYS (21)
    LIKE A DAUNTED WITCH, QUITTING CASTLE WHEN REAL DAYS BREAK. ...
                                            ... CONVERSATION AMONG THE RUINS 21   8
    GOD ORDAINED TO FOLLOW UP YOUR DAYS. IS IT SUCH TROUBLE *DIALOGUE B.   39   25
    VILLAGE STORIES GO THAT IN OLDEN DAYS ....ELLA MASON A. 53   13
    STAUNCH SAPLINGS; TO THIS HOUSE, THRIVING DAYS ....CRYSTAL GAZER   55   16
    GIVE ME BACK MY SHAPE. I AM READY TO CONSTRUE THE DAYS ...POEM.6.W.   136   21
    A WORLD OF BALD WHITE DAYS IN A SHADELESS SOCKET. ..THE HANGING MAN   141   4
    IT TOOK THREE DAYS DRIVING NORTH TO FIND A CLOUD ....TWO CAMP.   145   10
    FOR FIVE DAYS I LIE IN SECRET, ...FACE LIFT   156   17
    WASTING HER DAYS WAITING ON A HALF-CORPSE! ....IN PLASTER   159   38
    EXPOSES EMBARRASSMENTS -- THE MIZZLING DAYS ....INSOMNIAC   163   9
    I SHOULD SUGAR AND PRESERVE MY DAYS LIKE FRUIT! ....LAST WORDS   172   10
    A DAY AGO, TWO DAYS, THREE DAYS AGO. IT WAS A FRIDAY. ..THREE WOMEN   183   248
    A DAY AGO, TWO DAYS, THREE DAYS AGO. IT WAS A FRIDAY. ..THREE WOMEN   183   248
    IF YOU ONLY KNEW HOW THE VEILS WERE KILLING MY DAYS. .....BIRTHDAY.   207   37
    INTO WHICH, ON WARM DAYS, ...WINTERING   218   36

DAYS (CONT.)
  THREE DAYS. THREE NIGHTS. ....FEVER. 232 31
  IS SMALL THESE DAYS. DON'T BE SO SMART. I'LL ASK, ...DIALOGUE O. 281 204
  OF OUR DAYS SUSTAIN US. MAY EACH THOUGHT*DIALOGUE OVER A OUIJA BOARD 286 361
  OR AFTER GAY DAYS, OR COLORS THE GROWER FOUND GOOD. ..QUEEN MARY'S. 290 18
  WE VAUNT OUR DAYS IN NEON AND SCORN THE DARK. ......SONNET: TO TIME 311 4
  AWAY OUR RATIONED DAYS AND WEEKS. ....LOVE IS A PARALLAX 330 72
DAY'S (3)
  WHITE HULKS ON THEIR DAY'S CRUISING; ....SONG FOR A SUMMER'S DAY 31 4
  AFTER A LEAN DAY'S WORK ....STRUMPET SONG 33 3
  PURE LEAFAGE. A HUNDRED BASKETS BY DAY'S END. ......SPINACH-PICKER. 89 11
DAY'S-END (1)
  AND KINDLES A DAY'S-END BLAZE ....CHILD'S PARK STONES 101 15
DAY-SUNS (1)
  FOCUSING ALL TIME'S DAY-SUNS IN ONE ....CRYSTAL GAZER 55 39
DAYTIME (1)
  BUT IN THE DAYTIME SHE IS RIDICULOUS. ....THE RIVAL 166 12
DAZES (1)
  THE PEACEFULNESS IS SO BIG IT DAZES YOU, ...TULIPS 161 32
DAZZLE (4)
  THE PASSING DAZZLE OF EACH FACE ....EPITAPH FOR FIRE AND FLOWER 45 9
  DAMASKS WITH DAZZLE THE THREADBARE EYE; ....CONJURING. 66 18
  DEFLECT THE WATERY DAZZLE; THE PEOPLE IDLE ....WHITSUN 154 11
  COLUMN OF DAZZLE DRAWS MY EYES TO THE WALL ....DIALOGUE O. 279 88
DAZZLED (3)
  OF HELL, AND NOT THE FIERY PART. YET TO JUDGE BY THAT DAZZLED LOOK, ...
                      ... DIALOGUE BETWEEN GHOST AND PRIEST 38 15
  DRAGGED EACH DAZZLED SENSE APART ....ON THE PLETHORA OF DRYADS 67 26
  LAUGHING ALOUD, THE DAZZLED BOY DEMANDS*THE PRINCESS AND THE GOBLINS 335 64
DAZZLING (2)
  TILL YOUR EYES FOIST A VISION DAZZLING ON THE WIND: ....NOVEMBER G. 56 14
  TO MY WATER ROD, DAZZLING AND GRATEFUL, ...MEDUSA 225 19
DE (1)
  THE CARS IN THE PLACE DE LA CONCORDE -- ....A SECRET 220 38
DEAD (82)
  A SOUL GROWN FEVERISH, CLUTCHING ITS DEAD BODY-TREE ....DIALOGUE B. 39 43
  SUCH POVERTY. NO DEAD MEN'S CRIES ....NOVEMBER GRAVEYARD 56 6
  DOZENS DROPPED DEAD IN THE HEDGES: O SHE FELT ....SNOWMAN O. 59 35
  ALL THE DEAD DEARS ....ALL THE DEAD DEARS 70 T
  THESE BARNACLE DEAD! ....ALL THE DEAD DEARS 70 14
  BRONZE DEAD DOMINATE THE FLOOR, ...SCULPTOR 91 14
  DAWN TIDE STOOD DEAD LOW. I SMELT .....MUSSEL HUNTER AT ROCK HARBOR 95 12
  AND WHOLE CRABS, DEAD, THEIR SOGGY ....MUSSEL HUNTER AT ROCK HARBOR 97 84
  IN MY GRANDMOTHER'S SAND YARD. SHE IS DEAD, ...POINT SHIRLEY 110 9
  FERRYING THE SMELLS OF DEAD COD AND TAR. ....A WINTER SHIP 113 20
  FLIES FILING IN THROUGH A DEAD SKATE'S EYEHOLE *SUICIDE OFF EGG ROCK 115 17
  IN THIS CHARITY WARD, THIS POORHOUSE, WHERE THE DEAD ...ELECTRA ON. 117 19
  STONES, STRODE OUT IN YOUR DEAD ....MAN IN BLACK 120 16
  INERT AS A SHOELACE; DEAD ....MEDALLION 124 4
  MOLES DEAD IN THE PEBBLED RUT, ...BLUE MOLES 126 2
  MOUTHPIECE OF THE DEAD, OR OF SOME GOD OR OTHER. ......THE COLOSSUS 129 7
  I AM AT HOME HERE AMONG THE DEAD HEADS. POEM.1.WHO. 131 6
  THE DEAD RIPEN IN THE GRAPELEAVES. POEM.3.MAENAD. 133 12
  WHAT LARGE EYES THE DEAD HAVE! POEM.6.W. 135 10
  DEAD MEN LEAVE EYES FOR OTHERS. POEM.7.S. 137 38
  BUT THEY ARE DEAD, AND THEIR MOTHER NEAR DEAD WITH DISTRACTION, ...
                              ... STILLBORN 142 14
  BUT THEY ARE DEAD, AND THEIR MOTHER NEAR DEAD WITH DISTRACTION, ...
                              ... STILLBORN 142 14
  IF I'M ALIVE NOW, THEN I WAS DEAD, ...LOVE LETTER 147 2
  EACH DEAD HEAD HAD A VISOR OF ICE. ....LOVE LETTER 147 18
  LIKE A DEAD LAKE THE DARK ENVELOPS ME, ...ZOO KEEPER'S WIFE 154 3
  BURIED IN THE LAMBSWOOL OF THE DEAD POODLE; ....FACE LIFT 156 23
  INSTEAD, THE DEAD INJURE ME WITH ATTENTIONS, AND NOTHING CAN HAPPEN. ...
                              ... BARREN WOMAN 157 8
  SHE LAY IN BED WITH ME LIKE A DEAD BODY ....IN PLASTER 158 6
  IT IS WHAT THE DEAD CLOSE ON, FINALLY; I IMAGINE THEM ....TULIPS 161 34
  WIDOW. THE DEAD SYLLABLE, WITH ITS SHADOW ....WIDOW 164 6
  THEY DO NOT COME FROM THE BAY OF THE DEAD DOWN THERE, ...FINISTERRE 170 33
  BUT TEN YEARS DEAD. ....THE BABYSITTERS 175 36
  IS THIS THE ONE SIN THEN, THIS OLD DEAD LOVE OF DEATH? THREE WOMEN 177 42
  THE FACE OF THE DEAD ONE THAT COULD ONLY BE PERFECT ....THREE WOMEN 178 80
  THE BROWNNESS IS MY DEAD SELF, AND IT IS SULLEN: ....THREE WOMEN 179 100
  A DEAD SUN STAINS THE NEWSPRINT. IT IS RED. ....THREE WOMEN 181 153
  DEAD MEN CRY FROM IT. ....LITTLE FUGUE 188 27
  BLINDING ME WITH ITS LIGHTS, THE LIVES OF THE DEAD .....THE RABBIT. 193 4
  WHY SHOULD IT, IT IS THE HEARSE OF A DEAD FOOT, ...BERCK-PLAGE 197 20
  THE HIGH, DEAD, TOELESS FOOT OF THIS PRIEST ....BERCK-PLAGE 197 21
  THIS IS THE TONGUE OF THE DEAD MAN: REMEMBER, REMEMBER. *BERCK-PLAGE 199 81
  ADDRESSING IT, WHILE THE HILLS ROLL THE NOTES OF THE DEAD BELL; ...
                              ... BERCK-PLAGE 200 95
  WITH THE DEAD EYE ....BURNING THE LETTERS 205 52
  WHITE AS BABIES' BEDDING AND GLITTERING WITH DEAD BREATH. O IVORY! ...
                              ... A BIRTHDAY PRESENT 206 18

DEAD (CONT.)
    IT BREATHES FROM MY SHEETS, THE COLD DEAD CENTER *A BIRTHDAY PRESENT   207   50
    THE DEATH WEAPON? NO ONE IS DEAD. ....THE DETECTIVE   208   15
    AND THE FOX HEADS, THE OTTER HEADS, THE HEADS OF DEAD RABBITS. ...
                                ... THE COURAGE OF SHUTTING-UP   210   23
    THE FACE THAT LIVED IN THIS MIRROR IS THE FACE OF A DEAD MAN. ...
                                ... THE COURAGE OF SHUTTING-UP   210   29
    IS SHE DEAD, IS SHE SLEEPING? ....STINGS   215   53
    THEY CAN ONLY CARRY THEIR DEAD. ....WINTERING   218   37
    DEAD AND MONEYLESS, ...MEDUSA   225   30
    I WISH HIM DEAD OR AWAY. ....THE JAILER   227   39
    STOPPED DEAD ....STOPPED DEAD   230   T
    AND HERE WE ARE, HUNG OUT OVER THE DEAD DROP ....STOPPED DEAD   230   3
    DEAD WHITE. ....CUT   235   7
    SHE CAN BRING THE DEAD TO LIFE ....THE TOUR   238   46
    DEAD HANDS, DEAD STRINGENCIES. ....ARIEL   239   21
    DEAD HANDS, DEAD STRINGENCIES. ....ARIEL   239   21
    EXUDES FROM ITS DEAD BOREDOM. ....NICK AND THE CANDLESTICK   240   5
    I SHALL COUNT AND BURY THE DEAD. ....GETTING THERE   249   61
    THE DEAD BELL, ...DEATH & CO.   255   29
    THE DEAD BELL. ....DEATH & CO.   255   30
    MORE AND MORE LIKE A DEAD ONE, ...THE FEARFUL   256   8
    SHE WOULD RATHER BE DEAD THAN FAT, ...THE FEARFUL   256   13
    DEAD AND PERFECT, LIKE NEFERTIT, ...THE FEARFUL   256   14
    DEAD ON THE CHAIR BACK, ...EAVESDROPPER   261   59
    DEAD EGG, I LIE ....PARALYTIC   266   17
    MY WIFE, DEAD AND FLAT, IN 1920 FURS, ...PARALYTIC   266   23
    THE DEAD SMELL OF SUN ON WOOD CABINS, ...MYSTIC   268   7
    INSTEAD OF DEAD FURNITURE! ....BALLOONS   271   11
    HER DEAD ....EDGE   272   2
    EACH DEAD CHILD COILED, A WHITE SERPENT, ...EDGE   272   9
    DEAD, YOU'D SWEAR HIM A VICTIM OF OUR OWN VAIN ....DIALOGUE O.   278   82
    AND LET THE DEAD SLEEP AS THEY DESERVE. ....THE RIVAL/DR   291   28
    THE MOON IS LET GO, LIKE A DEAD THING. ....ELM/DR   292   8
    EVEN THE DEAD LAUGH AMONG THE GOLDENROD. ....GOLD MOUTHS CRY   302   9
    AND THOUSANDS WERE BORN AND DROPPED DEAD, ...DIALOGUE EN ROUTE   309   39
    THE DEAD ....THE DEAD   320   T
    DEAD MEN RENDER LOVE AND WAR NO HEED, ...THE DEAD   320   3
    NO SPIRITUAL CAESARS ARE THESE DEAD; ....THE DEAD   320   5
    NOW EMPTY BOXES OF THE HOODWINKED DEAD*SONG FOR A REVOLUTIONARY LOVE   323   17
    IN DEAD CENTER OF HER ACT ....AERIALIST   331   16
DEADLOCK (1)
    COMPELLED TO DEADLOCK UNDERGROUND. ....DANSE MACABRE   321   26
DEADLOCKED (1)
    DEADLOCKED WITH THEM, TAKING ROOT AS CRADLES ROCK. ...
                                ... ALL THE DEAD DEARS   71   36
DEADLY (1)
    FOR DEADLY SECRETS STRIKE WHEN UNDERSTOOD ....ADMONITIONS   319   16
DEAF (4)
    BOTH OF THEM DEAF TO THE FIDDLE IN THE HANDS ....TWO VIEWS.   114   18
    SO THE DEAF AND DUMB ....LITTLE FUGUE   187   3
    YOU DON'T QUITE BELIEVE IN IT. YOU'RE DEAF TO REAL .....DIALOGUE O.   278   63
    HELLO, AND THEN HELLO AGAIN IN DEAF ....LOVE IS A PARALLAX   330   40
DEAFNESS (1)
    DEAFNESS IS SOMETHING ELSE. ....LITTLE FUGUE   188   21
DEAL (1)
    THERE IS A GREAT DEAL ELSE TO DO. MY HANDS ....THREE WOMEN   187 359
DEALT (1)
    YET IT NEVER MILKED ANY GOAT, NOR DEALT COW DEATH ....GOATSUCKER   111   12
DEAR (12)
    WHICH HAD CAUSED HIS DEAR GIRL PAIN. ....BUCOLICS   24   20
    ALL YOUR BEAUTY, ALL YOUR WIT, IS A GIFT, MY DEAR, ...
                                ... SOLILOQUY OF THE SOLIPSIST   38   35
    A CROCK OF DUST IS MY DEAR HOME." DIALOGUE BETWEEN GHOST AND PRIEST   39   40
    EVEN AS LOVE'S DEAR FOOLS CRY EVERGREEN,*EPITAPH FOR FIRE AND FLOWER   46   30
    WELL OR ILL." GERD SLANTS A LOOK AT EACH: MOST DEAR,   CRYSTAL GAZER   55   10
    FROM MUSES UNHIRED BY YOU, DEAR MOTHER. ......THE DISQUIETING MUSES   75   40
    BLIND IN MY BED, WITH MY DEAR BLIND SWEET ONE. ....THREE WOMEN   178   76
    HERE'S YOUR SPECS, DEAR, HERE'S YOUR PURSE. ....THE TOUR   238   36
    CLOCKS CRY: STILLNESS IS A LIE, MY DEAR;*TO EVA DESCENDING THE STAIR   303   1
    CLOCKS CRY: STILLNESS IS A LIE, MY DEAR.*TO EVA DESCENDING THE STAIR   303   6
    CLOCKS CRY: STILLNESS IS A LIE, MY DEAR.*TO EVA DESCENDING THE STAIR   303   12
    CLOCKS CRY: STILLNESS IS A LIE, MY DEAR.*TO EVA DESCENDING THE STAIR   303   18
DEARER (1)
    AND A DEW COLLECT ON THEM, DEARER THAN MONEY, ...SLEEP.   144   9
DEARIES (1)
    TO MARKET FOR HER DEARIES, ...ELLA MASON AND HER ELEVEN CATS   54   33
DEARS (1)
    ALL THE DEAD DEARS ....ALL THE DEAD DEARS   70   T
DEATH (51)
    ONE DAY I'LL HAVE MY DEATH OF HIM; ....PURSUIT   22   2
    AMONG SACRED ISLANDS OF THE MAD TILL DEATH ....TALE OF A TUB   25   47
    THE RITUAL DEATH EACH TIME BOTCHED AMONG DROPPED CAPES,
                                ILL-JUDGED STABS, ...THE GORING   47   3

                                                           TITLE   PAGE LINE
DEATH (CONT.)
    DEATH AS STRIKING ROOT ON ONE LAND-TRACT; ....LANDOWNERS   53   14
    AND WORSE-SERVED WHEN DEATH ....WORDS FOR A NURSERY   74   47
    THAN VIRGINS' TEARS. THAT BAWDY QUEEN OF DEATH, ...OUIJA   77   24
    A SAMURAI DEATH MASK DONE ....MUSSEL HUNTER AT ROCK HARBOR   97   80
    DEATH MAY WHITEN IN SUN OR OUT OF IT. ....MOONRISE   98   18
    DEATH WHITENS IN THE EGG AND OUT OF IT. ....MOONRISE   98   19
    THE DEATH OF MYTH-MAKING ....THE DEATH OF MYTH-MAKING   104   T
    YET IT NEVER MILKED ANY GOAT, NOR DEALT COW DEATH ......GOATSUCKER   111   12
    OF THE DEATH VATS CLUNG TO THEM; ....TWO VIEWS OF A CADAVER ROOM   114   4
    IT WAS MY LOVE THAT DID US BOTH TO DEATH. ...ELECTRA ON AZALEA PATH   117   46
    A FRUIT THAT'S DEATH TO TASTE: DARK FLESH, DARK PARINGS. ...
                                      ... THE BEEKEEPER'S DAUGHTER   118   14
    AND DEATH, THAT BALD-HEAD BUZZARD, ...OLD LADIES' HOME 120   19
    AMONG PETALS PALE AS DEATH ....THE SLEEPERS   123   13
    INCENSE OF DEATH. YOUR DAY APPROACHES. ....THE MANOR GARDEN   125   2
    LIGHT'S DEATH TO THEM: THEY SHRIVEL IN IT. ....BLUE MOLES   126   22
    THIS IS NOT DEATH, IT IS SOMETHING SAFER. POEM.5.F.   135   15
    A BONEWHITE LIGHT, LIKE DEATH, BEHIND ALL THINGS. .....INSOMNIAC   163   4
    DEATH IS THE DRESS SHE WEARS, HER HAT AND COLLAR. ....WIDOW   164   13
    SUCH AS FINGERS MIGHT EMBROIDER, CLOSE TO DEATH, ...FINISTERRE   169   11
    I SAW DEATH IN THE BARE TREES, A DEPRIVATION. ....THREE WOMEN   177   24
    THIS IS A DISEASE I CARRY HOME, THIS IS A DEATH. ......THREE WOMEN   177   36
    AGAIN, THIS IS A DEATH. IS IT THE AIR, ...THREE WOMEN   177   37
    IS THIS MY LOVER THEN? THIS DEATH, THIS DEATH? ....THREE WOMEN   177   40
    IS THIS MY LOVER THEN? THIS DEATH, THIS DEATH? ....THREE WOMEN   177   40
    IS THIS THE ONE SIN THEN, THIS OLD DEAD LOVE OF DEATH? THREE WOMEN   177   42
    IT IS A LOVE OF DEATH THAT SICKENS EVERYTHING. ....THREE WOMEN   181 152
    THE SUN IS DOWN. I DIE. I MAKE A DEATH. ....THREE WOMEN   181 161
    DEATH OPENED, LIKE A BLACK TREE, BLACKLY. ....LITTLE FUGUE   188   48
    LETTERS AND THEIR DEATH RATTLE ....BURNING THE LETTERS   204   3
    A DEATH TREE, COLOR GONE, AN AUSTRALIAN GUM TREE -- ....FATHERLESS.   205   3
    IF IT WERE DEATH ....A BIRTHDAY PRESENT   208   56
    THAT IS THE VALLEY OF DEATH, THOUGH THE COWS THRIVE.   THE DETECTIVE   208   6
    THE DEATH WEAPON? NO ONE IS DEAD. ....THE DETECTIVE 208   15
    HE HAS SEEN TOO MUCH DEATH, HIS HANDS ARE FULL OF IT. .....COURAGE.   210   15
    THEIR DEATH RAYS FOLDED LIKE FLAGS ......THE COURAGE OF SHUTTING-UP   210   32
    THEY THOUGHT DEATH WAS WORTH IT, BUT I ....STINGS   215   51
    I AM SICK TO DEATH OF HOT SALT. ....MEDUSA   225   37
    THE SCALE-SHEEN ON THE SAND SCARED ME TO DEATH. ....LESBOS   229   59
    DEATH & CO. ....DEATH & CO.   254   T
    DEATH WITH ITS MANY STICKS. ....TOTEM   265   34
    TO THE FINAL GROTESQUE JOKE OF DEATH ....DIRGE FOR A JOKER   303   10
    CHILLS ME TO DEATH ....TO A JILTED LOVER   309   8
    OUR YEARS. DEATH COMES IN A CASUAL STEEL CAR, YET ..SONNET: TO TIME   311   3
    AND BURN TO DEATH WITHIN YOUR NEON HELL. ....THE TRIAL OF MAN   312   11
    EACH CLOCK TICK CONSECRATES THE DEATH OF STRANGERS. DOOM OF EXILES   318   8
    DARING AS DEATH AND DEBONAIR ....CIRCUS IN THREE RINGS   321   7
    KNOWS NOT OF DEATH NOR CALCULUS ABOVE ....LOVE IS A PARALLAX   331   77
    AND DEATH IN THE POT. ....TEMPER OF TIME   336   24
DEATH-GOWNS (1)
    DEATH-GOWNS, ...DEATH & CO.   254   18
DEATHLY (1)
    THE DEATHLY GUESTS HAD NOT BEEN SATISFIED ....WAKING IN WINTER   151   14
DEATHMASK (1)
    CHARRED SKIRTS AND DEATHMASK ....GETTING THERE 249   47
DEATH-PEGS (1)
    THEIR DEATH-PEGS STUD YOUR GLOVES, IT IS NO USE RUNNING. STINGS/DR   293   8
DEATHS (3)
    NO DEATHS, NO PRODIGIOUS INJURIES ....AFTERMATH   113   6
    HOW THEY AWAITED HIM, THOSE LITTLE DEATHS! ......THE RABBIT CATCHER   194   24
    UNDER A STONE. THOSE TWO DREAMED DEATHS TOOK ....DIALOGUE O.   285 326
DEATH'S (3)
    EARTH'S EVER-GREEN DEATH'S HEAD. ....CRYSTAL GAZER   56   48
    A SOLIDER REPOSE THAN DEATH'S. ....SCULPTOR   92   24
    DEATH'S TWO DREAMS DOWN WITH THE BODY THAT BLED THE VEIN, ...
                                 ... DIALOGUE OVER A OUIJA BOARD   285 329
DEATH'S-HEAD (1)
    OF THE DEATH'S-HEAD SHADOWING THEIR SONG. ....TWO VIEWS. 114   19
DEATH'S-METAL (1)
    PURE DEATH'S-METAL. THE YARDMAN'S ....MEDALLION   125   26
DEATH-SOUP (1)
    IN A THICK GRAY DEATH-SOUP, ...LETTER IN NOVEMBER 253   28
DEATH-STENCH (1)
    AND WE PICNIC IN THE DEATH-STENCH OF A HAWTHORN. ....WHITSUN   154   21
DEBASED (1)
    GRIEF'S HONEST GRIMACE, DEBASED BY TIME, ...THE BEGGARS 47   7
DEBAUCH (1)
    BEDFELLOWS OF THE SPIRIT'S DEBAUCH, FOND MASTERS. ...COMPANIONABLE.   105   8
DEBONAIR (1)
    DARING AS DEATH AND DEBONAIR ....CIRCUS IN THREE RINGS   321   7
DEBT (1)
    OUR LUGGAGE, AS DOCKS HALT OUR BRIEF EPIC; NO DEBT *CHANNEL CROSSING   27   41
DECADE (1)
    TO ANNIHILATE EACH DECADE. ....LADY LAZARUS   245   24

DECADES (1)
    MORE THAN EIGHT DECADES BACK   ....THE TIMES ARE TIDY   107   12
DECAY (5)
    BLACK ASININITY. DECAY.   ....WINTERING   218   17
    THE CHAIRS BELONG TO ITS DARKNESS. I SMELL DECAY   ....DIALOGUE O.   285 314
    ALL WE FIND ARE ALTARS IN DECAY   ....DOOM OF EXILES   318   11
    FROM THEIR FOND, FINAL, INFAMOUS DECAY.   ....THE DEAD   320   14
    A CAVIARE DECAY OF RICH BROCADES.   ....TERMINAL   328   8
DECEITS (1)
    THESE ARE THE DECEITS, TACKED UP LIKE FAMILY PHOTOGRAPHS,*DETECTIVE.   208   13
DECK (3)
    ON STORM-STRUCK DECK, WIND SIRENS CATERWAUL;   ......CHANNEL CROSSING   26   1
    ON DECK   ....ON DECK   142   T
    MIDNIGHT IN THE MID-ATLANTIC. ON DECK.   ....ON DECK   142   1
DECKED (1)
    DECKED FORTH IN COCKLE-SHELLS, ...DREAM WITH CLAM-DIGGERS   44   18
DECKS (1)
    NO SEA-CHANGE DECKS THE SUNKEN SHANK OF BONE   ....TWO LOVERS.   327   17
DECLARE (1)
    LOUD THE IMMORTAL NIGHTINGALES DECLARE: *TO EVA DESCENDING THE STAIR   303   13
DECLENSION (1)
    FAIR CHRONICLER OF EVERY FOUL DECLENSION.   ....OUIJA   77   14
DECLINE (2)
    ON THE DECLINE OF ORACLES   ....ON THE DECLINE OF ORACLES   78   T
    AND THE DECLINE OF EMPIRES THE THICK COIL OF A VAST   ....PERSEUS   83   23
DECLINING (1)
    BEHIND WHICH THE DECLINING MOON HAS SET, ...THE PRINCESS.   334   36
DECODED (1)
    REVEALS NO CRACKS THAT CAN BE DECODED? WHEN WASHBOWL ..TALE OF A TUB   24   10
DECOMPOSE (1)
    WHERE THE HEADS AND TAILS OF MY SISTERS DECOMPOSE.*ZOO KEEPER'S WIFE   154   7
DECOR (2)
    AROUND HIM LIKE LIVINGROOM FURNITURE, LIKE A DECOR.   ....BERCK-PLAGE   199   83
    I SEE YOUR CUTE DECOR   ....LESBOS   229   85
DECORATE (1)
    AND A CABIN BOY WHO COULD DECORATE CAKES IN SIX-COLORED
        FROSTING.   ....THE BABYSITTERS   174   12
DECORUM (3)
    OF ALL DECORUM WHICH HOLDS THE WHIRLWIND BACK.   .......CONVERSATION.   21   4
    STIRRUPS UNDONE, AND DECORUM. AND   ....WHITENESS I REMEMBER   103   23
    A SOLID SHAPE ON AIR. MAY THE DECORUM ..DIALOGUE OVER A OUIJA BOARD   286 360
DECREE (1)
    RULED DECREE OF DOOMSDAY ON THE FLOOR.   ....THE TRIAL OF MAN   312   4
DECRY (1)
    AND, PLAINTIFF AGAINST EACH DAY, DECRY   ....THE BEGGARS   47   4
DEEP (15)
    DOWN DEEP INTO THE BENT BULL-NECK. CUMBROUS ROUTINE, NOT ARTWORK. ...
                                                   ... THE GORING   47   7
    WE OWN NO WILDERNESSES RICH AND DEEP ENOUGH   ....THE THIN PEOPLE   65   41
    IMAGINE THEIR DEEP HUNGER, DEEP AS THE DARK   ....OUIJA   77   8
    IMAGINE THEIR DEEP HUNGER, DEEP AS THE DARK   ....OUIJA   77   8
    IN THE DEEP CONVULSION GRIPPING YOUR FACE, MUSCLES   ....PERSEUS   83   43
    THEIR BATHTUB BATTLES DEEP, ...BATTLE-SCENE   85   33
    TO ROOT DEEP AMONG KNUCKLES, SHINBONES, ...FULL FATHOM FIVE   93   35
    DEEP IN YOUR FLUX OF SILVER   ....LORELEI   95   34
    PEGS TOO DEEP TO UPROOT, AND A MIND LIKE A RING   THE RABBIT CATCHER   194   28
    A GROOVE OF OLD FAULTS, DEEP AND BITTER.   ....EVENT   195   15
    I WOULD ADMIRE THE DEEP GRAVITY OF IT, ITS TIMELESS EYES. *BIRTHDAY.   208   57
    FROM THE SWEET, DEEP THROATS OF THE NIGHT FLOWER.   ....EDGE   273   16
    DEEP IN LIQUID INDIGO   ....AQUATIC NOCTURNE   305   1
    HIDE, HIDE, IN THE DEEP NEST   ....GO GET THE GOODLY SQUAB   313   7
    ROLLED ROUND WITH GOODLY LOAM AND CRADLED DEEP, ...THE DEAD   320   9
DEEPEN (1)
    GOLDS BLEED AND DEEPEN, THE MOUTHS OF THERMOPYLAE. ..LETTER IN NOV.   254   35
DEEPER (3)
    FAR DEEPER IN GROSS WOOD   ....ON THE PLETHORA OF DRYADS   67   11
    DEEPER THAN YOUR OWN OCEAN FLOOR, AND GOT   ....DIALOGUE O.   283 243
    DEEPER WITHIN THE DARK, AND AS I PITCHED FURTHER   ....DIALOGUE O.   285 317
DEEPS (1)
    SIMPLY TO PLUMB THE DEEPS OF AN EYE   ....CANDLES   148   7
DEEP-SUNK (1)
    FROM DEEP-SUNK BASEMENTS   ....OWL   102   8
DEER (2)
    AND ALL YOU SANTA'S DEER WHO BROWSE   ....A WINTER'S TALE   87   21
    THE DEER ISLAND PRISON   ....MAN IN BLACK   119   7
DEFACE (1)
    WITH CHARACTERS NO COCKCROW CAN DEFACE.   ....SONG FOR A REVOLU.   323   12
DEFENDING (1)
    DEFENDING MY PERILOUS WOUNDS WITH A CHAIR   ....CIRCUS IN THREE RINGS   322   11
DEFERRING (1)
    SHE IS DEFERRING TO REALITY.   ....THREE WOMEN   184 284
DEFINE (2)
    EYEFUL, WHICH, ENVIOUS, WOULD DEFINE   ....LANDOWNERS   53   13
    INTO THE BLUE. TOPS DEFINE THEMSELVES AS PLACES   ....ABOVE THE OXBOW   88   29

                                     125

DEFINING (1)
   THE WORD, DEFINING, MUZZLES; THE DRAWN LINE ....POEMS, POTATOES 106 1
DEFINITELY (1)
   IN RITUAL, TO STRIKE -- IS DEFINITELY GONE; ....TALE OF A TUB 25 22
DEFLECT (1)
   DEFLECT THE WATERY DAZZLE; THE PEOPLE IDLE ....WHITSUN 154 11
DEFLECTS (1)
   HABIT WHICH DEFLECTS ....VIRGIN IN A TREE 81 6
DEFORMITY (2)
   THE MIRROR GIVES BACK A WOMAN WITHOUT DEFORMITY. ....THREE WOMEN 183 240
   WHO WILL LOVE ME THROUGH THE BLUR OF MY DEFORMITY ......THREE WOMEN 183 251
DEFT (1)
   BY DEFT DUCK AND TWIRL ....AERIALIST 331 22
DEFY (2)
   YOU DEFY QUESTIONS; ....FULL FATHOM FIVE 93 39
   YOU DEFY OTHER GODHOOD. ....FULL FATHOM FIVE 93 40
DEGREES (1)
   FEVER [ONE HUNDRED THREE DEGREES] ....FEVER. 231 T
DEIGN (1)
   GOD-PIE. WHY, THEN, DID YOU DEIGN TO INTRODUCE ....DIALOGUE O. 283 251
DELECTABLE (1)
   SOFT, DELECTABLE. ....LETTER IN NOVEMBER 253 9
DELICACY (1)
   TO DELICACY, TO POISE) BUT THAT THEY ....POEMS, POTATOES 106 8
DELICATE (7)
   WITH GREEN ROCK GLIDING, A DELICATE SCHOONER*DREAM WITH CLAM-DIGGERS 44 17
   FOOLISH, DELICATE, IN THE LOWER RIGHT HAND CORNER. ......TWO VIEWS. 114 22
   HEATING THE PINCERS, HOISTING THE DELICATE HAMMERS. POEM.7.S. 137 28
   IT IS TOO DELICATE ....WUTHERING HEIGHTS 168 40
   FLOATING ON THEIR DELICATE FEET OVER THE COLD PEWS, ...MOON. 173 25
   INFINITELY DELICATE AND INFINITELY EXPENSIVE. ....FEVER. 232 39
   FOOTING HER DELICATE DANCES ....AERIALIST 331 10
DELICATESSEN (1)
   IN THE CALIFORNIA DELICATESSEN ....LITTLE FUGUE 188 32
DELIGHTING (1)
   DELIGHTING ....BALLOONS 271 15
DELIVERED (2)
   BY THE TIME THE WHOLE OF IT WAS DELIVERED, AND TOO NUMB TO USE IT. ...
               ... A BIRTHDAY PRESENT 208 54
   OF DESTINY, DELIVERED TO THE DOOR ....THE TRIAL OF MAN 312 2
DELL (1)
   THE SMALL DELL EATS WHAT ATE IT ONCE. ....THE BURNT-OUT SPA 138 18
DELUDED (1)
   AGAIN WE ARE DELUDED AND INFER ....APRIL AUBADE 312 13
DELVED (1)
   UP FROM DELVED WORM-HAUNT; ....ODE FOR TED 29 8
DELVING (1)
   DELVING FOR THE APPENDAGES ....BLUE MOLES 126 30
DELVINGS (1)
   SUCH EELISH DELVINGS! POEM.2.DARK. 132 9
DEMAND (1)
   THE SIZE OF MY DEMAND TO MAGIC: NO MORE *DIALOGUE OVER A OUIJA BOARD 279 121
DEMANDED (1)
   DEMANDED THAT I PAY A FINE ....THE DREAM 311 15
DEMANDING (2)
   OPENS ITS MOUTH NOW, DEMANDING. ....EVENT 194 8
   DEMANDING SATISFACTION; NO DUEL TAKES PLACE: ........METAMORPHOSES. 307 5
DEMANDS (2)
   EACH DAY DEMANDS WE CREATE OUR WHOLE WORLD OVER, ...TALE OF A TUB 25 36
   LAUGHING ALOUD, THE DAZZLED BOY DEMANDS*THE PRINCESS AND THE GOBLINS 335 64
DEMARCATING (1)
   DEMARCATING GOOD FROM EVIL, ...INSOLENT STORM STRIKES AT THE SKULL 326 20
DEMIGOD (1)
   NOT MAN NOR DEMIGOD COULD PUT TOGETHER ....SONNET: TO EVA 305 9
DEMON (5)
   WHEREBY ONE HIRES A DEMON. ....CRYSTAL GAZER 55 36
   IT WAS NO FIRE-BLURTING FORK-TAILED DEMON ..THE SNOWMAN ON THE MOOR 59 25
   THE INFERNAL HAUNT OF DEMON DANGERS; ....DOOM OF EXILES 318 6
   MY DEMON OF DOOM TILTS ON A TRAPEZE, ...CIRCUS IN THREE RINGS 322 15
   ON LOOKING INTO THE EYES OF A DEMON LOVER *ON LOOKING INTO THE EYES. 325 T
DEMURE (1)
   DEMURE ONES, LITHE ONES, NEEDING NO LESSON ....ELLA MASON A. 54 40
DEMURS (1)
   CRIES: "CELEBRATE SYRINX WHOSE DEMURS ....VIRGIN IN A TREE 81 13
DEN (2)
   GO SNARE THE SLEEPING BEAR IN LEAF-LINED DEN*GO GET THE GOODLY SQUAB 313 9
   I INVADE MY LION'S DEN; ....CIRCUS IN THREE RINGS 321 8
DENIES (1)
   THE AUTHENTIC SEA DENIES THEM AND WILL PLUCK ....TALE OF A TUB 25 23
DENMARK (1)
   AND THE WHITE-HAIRED JEWELER FROM DENMARK IS CARVING ....ON DECK 143 31
DENOUEMENT (1)
   DENOUEMENT ....DENOUEMENT 326 T
DENSE (6)
   PIERCED MY DENSE LID. ....ON THE PLETHORA OF DRYADS 67 24

DENSE (CONT.)
   FIT NOWHERE: BRICKDUST-COMPLECTED, EYE UNDER A DENSE LID, ...
                        ... THE LADY AND THE EARTHENWARE HEAD   69   2
   OF THE DENSE GRASSES I FOUND ....MUSSEL HUNTER AT ROCK HARBOR   97   68
   A WELL OF SCENTS ALMOST TOO DENSE TO BREATHE IN. ......BEEKEEPER'S.   118   4
   DENSE AND EXPRESSIONLESS ROUND ABOUT. ....LOVE LETTER   147   23
   AND DRIED PLATES WITH MY DENSE HAIR. ....STINGS   214   25
DENSE-FEATHERED (1)
   DENSE-FEATHERED, FEARFULLY SOFT TO ....OWL   102   14
DENSE-GRAINED (1)
   OBDURATE, IN DENSE-GRAINED WOOD, ...SCULPTOR   91   9
DENY (1)
   I THOUGHT I COULD DENY THE CONSEQUENCE -- ....THREE WOMEN   178   61
DENYING (1)
   DENYING YOU SPRANG OUT OF MY HEAD, ...SOLILOQUY OF THE SOLIPSIST   38   31
DEPART (3)
   AND, UNDER HONOR, WILL DEPART; ....BUCOLICS   24   22
   REPENT, DEPART, BEFORE GOD'S TRUMP-CRACK SPLITS THE SKY." ...
                        ... DIALOGUE BETWEEN GHOST AND PRIEST   39   46
   IS IT FOR THIS THE AIR MOTES DEPART? ....THE OTHER   201   11
DEPARTING (1)
   THEY ARE DEPARTING IN THEIR TRANSPARENT GARMENTS, TURNED ASIDE ...
                        ... THE SURGEON AT 2 A.M.   170   3
DEPARTS (1)
   OF AMBROSIAL REVELATION. AND SO DEPARTS. ...THE GHOST'S LEAVETAKING   90   15
DEPARTURE (4)
   DEPARTURE ....DEPARTURE   51   T
   TATTLING IN ITS CAT-VOICE OF DEPARTURE, DEPARTURE. ....A LIFE   150   32
   TATTLING IN ITS CAT-VOICE OF DEPARTURE, DEPARTURE. ....A LIFE   150   32
   RIDING THE RIP TIDE TO THE NEAREST POINT OF DEPARTURE, ...MEDUSA   225   10
DEPARTURES (2)
   TRAINS ROAR IN MY EARS, DEPARTURES, DEPARTURES! ....THREE WOMEN   177   31
   TRAINS ROAR IN MY EARS, DEPARTURES, DEPARTURES! ....THREE WOMEN   177   31
DEPENDED (1)
   YET I STILL DEPENDED ON HER, THOUGH I DID IT REGRETFULLY.*IN PLASTER   160   49
DEPRESSED (1)
   BUT I DIDN'T KNOW HOW TO COOK, AND BABIES DEPRESSED ME. ......BABY.   174   13
DEPRIVATION (1)
   I SAW DEATH IN THE BARE TREES, A DEPRIVATION. ....THREE WOMEN   177   24
DEPTHS (1)
   DRUNKENNESS OF THE GREAT DEPTHS. ....LORELEI   95   32
DERANGING (1)
   DERANGING BY HARMONY ....LORELEI   94   21
DERRICKS (2)
   WITH HANDS LIKE DERRICKS, ...THE QUEEN'S COMPLAINT   28   3
   OF WAREHOUSES, DERRICKS, SMOKESTACKS AND BRIDGES .....A WINTER SHIP   113   17
DES (1)
   DANS LE FOND DES FORETS VOTRE IMAGE ME SUIT. ....PURSUIT   22   E
DESCANT (3)
   LET BELL-TONGUED BIRDS DESCANT IN BLACKEST FEATHER .....LADY AND T.   69   25
   THEY DESCANT ON THE SERENE AND SERAPHIC BEAUTY ....VIRGIN IN A TREE   82   29
   BY DAY, DESCANT FROM BORDERS ....LORELEI   94   26
DESCEND (2)
   RAVEL ABOVE US, MISTILY DESCEND, ...OUIJA   77   20
   WITH KISS OF CINDERS, GHOSTS DESCEND, ...DANSE MACABRE   321   25
DESCENDED (1)
   DESCENDED ON YOUR FAVORITES, AND YET ...DIALOGUE OVER A OUIJA BOARD   281   191
DESCENDING (1)
   TO EVA DESCENDING THE STAIR ....TO EVA DESCENDING THE STAIR   303   T
DESCENDS (2)
   THE AUSTERE SUN DESCENDS ABOVE THE FEN, ...WINTER LANDSCAPE,   21   6
   NO GLORY DESCENDS ....RESOLVE   52   12
DESCENT (1)
   FOR THAT RARE, RANDOM DESCENT. ....BLACK ROOK IN RAINY WEATHER   57   40
DESCRIBED (1)
   DESCRIBED HOW YOU FELL DREAMING AT FULL OF MOON, ...YADWIGHA.   86   25
DESCRIBING (1)
   DESCRIBING ARCS OF LOVE. ....TRIO OF LOVE SONGS   314   28
DESCRIED (1)
   THAT ONCE DESCRIED TROY'S TOWERS FALL, ...ON THE DECLINE OF ORACLES   78   31
DESERT (9)
   NIGHTLY WE LEFT THEM IN THEIR DESERT PLACE. ....THE OTHER TWO   68   27
   MY PAGE THIS DESERT ....WORDS FOR A NURSERY   74   27
   I SIZZLED IN HIS BLUE VOLTS LIKE A DESERT PROPHET. THE HANGING MAN   141   2
   SLEEP IN THE MOJAVE DESERT ....SLEEP IN THE MOJAVE DESERT   143   T
   THE DESERT IS WHITE AS A BLIND MAN'S EYE,*SLEEP IN THE MOJAVE DESERT   144   17
   HE SUFFERS HIS DESERT PILLOW, SLEEPLESSNESS ....INSOMNIAC   163   6
   OR SITS IN THE DESERT AND HURTS HIS MOTHER'S HEART. ....THREE WOMEN   186   333
   IN A DESERT OF COW PEOPLE ............................EAVESDROPPER   261   41
   WHICH PROPS YOU THROUGH THIS DESERT LIKE A DREAM ....DIALOGUE O.   282   212
DESERTED (1)
   SO WE BOBBED OUT TO THE ISLAND. IT WAS DESERTED --   THE BABYSITTERS   175   33
DESERTIONS (1)
   BASTARDIES, USAGES, DESERTIONS AND DOUBLENESS, ...COURAGE.   210   7

	TITLE	PAGE	LINE

DESERTS (1)
  SO THE SWARM BALLS AND DESERTS ....THE SWARM 216 17
DESERVE (1)
  AND LET THE DEAD SLEEP AS THEY DESERVE. ....THE RIVAL/DR 291 28
DESIGN (2)
  INTO THE CARPET'S DESIGN. ....MISS DRAKE PROCEEDS TO SUPPER 41 13
  ANY MORE IN THE DESULTORY WEATHER SOME DESIGN, ...BLACK ROOK I. 57 8
DESIGNED (2)
  DESIGNED BY A DRUNKEN GOD ....CIRCUS IN THREE RINGS 321 2
  SUSPEND THIS DAY, SO SINGULARLY DESIGNED, ...MIDSUMMER MOBILE 324 13
DESIGNS (1)
  FROZEN IN DESIGNS OF LOVE. ....DANSE MACABRE 321 9
DESIRE (2)
  ALTHOUGH, I ADMIT, I DESIRE, ...BLACK ROOK IN RAINY WEATHER 57 11
  WANTS, DESIRE ....PARALYTIC 267 34
DESK (2)
  I SAT AT MY DESK IN MY STOCKINGS, MY HIGH HEELS, ...THREE WOMEN 177 21
  AS A DESK DRAWER HIDES A POISON PEN LETTER, ...THE RIVAL/DR 291 9
DESOLATE (1)
  WHO WEEPS BEFORE THE DESOLATE TABLEAU   THE PRINCESS AND THE GOBLINS 335 74
DESOLATION (1)
  YET DESOLATION, STALLED IN PAINT, SPARES THE LITTLE COUNTRY ...
                                     ... TWO VIEWS OF A CADAVER ROOM 114 21
DESPAIR (3)
  THE HEAVEN THOSE TWO DREAMED OF, IN DESPAIR. ....THE OTHER TWO 69 35
  PONDEROUS AND EXTEND DESPAIR ON EARTH'S ....PERSEUS 83 31
  WITH THE O-GAPE OF COMPLETE DESPAIR. I LIVE HERE. ....MOON. 173 11
DESPERATE (1)
  MY JAPANESE SILKS, DESPERATE BUTTERFLIES, ...KINDNESS 269 14
DESPITE (1)
  DESPITE HER WRUNG HANDS, HER TEARS, HER PRAYING: VANISH!*LADY AND T. 70 30
DESPOTS (1)
  THOSE OLD DESPOTS, IF HE SAT ....THE HERMIT AT OUTERMOST HOUSE 119 9
DESTINATION (2)
  INSANE FOR THE DESTINATION, ...GETTING THERE 249 57
  WHO IS THE DESTINATION OF THE CORD ....THE PRINCESS AND THE GOBLINS 333 23
DESTINATIONS (1)
  ALL THE GODS KNOW IS DESTINATIONS. ....GETTING THERE 248 17
DESTINY (2)
  POURS BY LIKE DESTINY, BENDING ....WUTHERING HEIGHTS 167 12
  OF DESTINY, DELIVERED TO THE DOOR ....THE TRIAL OF MAN 312 2
DESTROY (1)
  "DESTROY YOUR MIRROR AND AVOID MISHAPS," ....EPITAPH IN THREE PARTS 337 4
DESTRUCTION (2)
  ALL NIGHT I HAVE DREAMED OF DESTRUCTION, ANNIHILATIONS -- ..WAKING. 151 4
  THE PARTICLES OF DESTRUCTION I SUCK UP? AM I A PULSE ...THREE WOMEN 177 38
DESTRUCTIONS (1)
  THAT FLAT, FLAT, FLATNESS FROM WHICH IDEAS, DESTRUCTIONS, ...THREE. 177 18
DESULTORY (3)
  ANY MORE IN THE DESULTORY WEATHER SOME DESIGN, ...BLACK ROOK I. 57 8
  OF THE DESULTORY CURRENTS -- ALL THAT UNIQUE ....ABOVE THE OXBOW 89 45
  THE HOUSEWIFE'S, DESULTORY. ....THE DEATH OF MYTH-MAKING 104 15
DETECTIVE (1)
  THE DETECTIVE ....THE DETECTIVE 208 T
DETECTOR (1)
  WILL IT SHOW IN THE BLACK DETECTOR? ....A SECRET 219 9
DETERRED (1)
  EX MACHINA, NOR DID THEY SEEM DETERRED BY THIS. ....SPIDER 49 35
DETONATING (1)
  A METAL DETONATING ....NIGHT SHIFT 76 7
DETONATIONS (1)
  AND NOW DETONATIONS --- ....GETTING THERE 249 49
DETOUR (1)
  BY CROOKED DETOUR, ...TEMPER OF TIME 336 18
DEUS (1)
  UP BY A SPRY BLACK DEUS ....SPIDER 49 34
DEVIATION (1)
  GOING'S BEEN TAME DEVIATION. WHITE, ...WHITENESS I REMEMBER 102 4
DEVIL (9)
  NEVER GRIP, AS THEIR GRANDSIRES DID, THAT DEVIL WHO CHUCKLES*LESSON. 80 24
  AND MINCED THE MUDDLING DEVIL ....THE DEATH OF MYTH-MAKING 104 10
  ONLY THE DEVIL CAN EAT THE DEVIL OUT. POEM.6.W. 135 5
  ONLY THE DEVIL CAN EAT THE DEVIL OUT. POEM.6.W. 135 5
  IT IS THE EXCEPTION THAT INTERESTS THE DEVIL. ....THREE WOMEN 186 331
  BUT NO LESS A DEVIL FOR THAT, NO NOT ....DADDY 223 54
  A DEVIL. WAIT: HE SHIFTS. HE HASN'T COME*DIALOGUE OVER A OUIJA BOARD 282 216
  LEANED THE DEVIL PROMPTING YOU TO LAUGH. ....DIRGE FOR A JOKER 302 4
  THAT ONE MAN'S DEVIL IS ANOTHER'S GOD ....LOVE IS A PARALLAX 329 8
DEVIL-BIRD (1)
  BY CLAW-CUTS OF THE GOATSUCKER, ALIAS DEVIL-BIRD, ...GOATSUCKER 111 7
DEVILISH (2)
  DEVILISH LEOPARD! ....FEVER. 231 22
  ONLY TO VANISH WITH DEVILISH EASE ....CIRCUS IN THREE RINGS 322 17
DEVILS (1)
  YET OF DEVILS THE CLEVEREST ....SPIDER 48 5

DEVIL'S (3)
   READY TO ROLL, LIKE A DEVIL'S. ....GETTING THERE   248   40
   BREATHING THE GOD'S WORD, OR THE DEVIL'S WORD, ...DIALOGUE O.   286 350
   A DEVIL'S CATARACT OF BLACK .....BLACK PINE TREE IN AN ORANGE LIGHT   328   8
DEVON (1)
   A DEVON MEADOW MIGHT OFFER A SIMPLER SORT   QUEEN MARY'S ROSE GARDEN   290   23
DEVOUR (1)
   TO DEVOUR AND DRAG HER DOWN ....MISS DRAKE PROCEEDS TO SUPPER   41   12
DEVOURER (1)
   DOG-HEAD, DEVOURER: POEM.3.MAENAD.   133   16
DEVOURING (1)
   DEVOURING GREEN GARDENS INCH BY INCH. ....EPITAPH IN THREE PARTS   337   17
DEVOURS (1)
   BLACKENS FLESH TO BONE AND DEVOURS THEM.*EPITAPH FOR FIRE AND FLOWER   46   35
DEVOUT (1)
   RUNNING NECK AND NECK WITH THE MOST DEVOUT ....DIALOGUE O.   282 235
DEVOUTLY (1)
   DEVOUTLY AS THE DUTCH BULB ....HEAVY WOMEN   158   9
DEW (7)
   DEW STOOD IN CHILL SWEAT ON EACH STALK, ...DIALOGUE B.   38   4
   AND A DEW COLLECT ON THEM, DEARER THAN MONEY, ...SLEEP.   144   9
   AND THE LOCKED DROPS RISING IN A DEW ....LOVE LETTER   147   21
   BLUE DEW FROM DANGEROUS SKIN. ....STINGS   214   27
   THE DEW THAT FLIES ....ARIEL   240   28
   LET THEIR SOULS WRITHE IN A DEW, ...GETTING THERE   249   62
   THE DEW MAKES A STAR, ...DEATH & CO.   255   28
DEWDROP (1)
   A MINUTE, A DEWDROP. ....GETTING THERE   248   42
DEWLAPPED (1)
   NOW SHE'S DONE FOR, THE DEWLAPPED LADY ....FACE LIFT   156   25
DIABOLIC (1)
   BUT OUTSIDE THE DIABOLIC STEEL OF THIS ....SONNET: TO TIME   311   5
DIAGNOSIS (1)
   THESE POEMS DO NOT LIVE: IT'S A SAD DIAGNOSIS. ....STILLBORN   142   1
DIAGRAM (2)
   DIAGRAM OF MOUNTAINS ....TRIO OF LOVE SONGS   313   5
   TO DIAGRAM THE TONGUE, ...TRIO OF LOVE SONGS   315   38
DIAGRAMS (1)
   DIAGRAMS THE FALLING YEARS, ...TO A JILTED LOVER   309   6
DIALOGUE (4)
   DIALOGUE BETWEEN GHOST AND PRIEST *DIALOGUE BETWEEN GHOST AND PRIEST   38   T
   DIALOGUE OVER A OUIJA BOARD ....DIALOGUE OVER A OUIJA BOARD   276   T
   A VERSE DIALOGUE ....DIALOGUE OVER A OUIJA BOARD   276   ST
   DIALOGUE EN ROUTE ....DIALOGUE EN ROUTE   308   T
DIAMOND (5)
   SECURE IN MUSEUM DIAMOND FOR THE STARE   EPITAPH FOR FIRE AND FLOWER   45   18
   DIAMOND RINGS, POTTED ROSES, FOX-SKINS ....OWL   101   5
   ON HIM HAND AND FOOT, QUIET AS A DIAMOND. ....ON DECK   143   33
   BUT EVEN HER TONNAGE DOESN'T IMPRESS A DIAMOND. ....THE RIVAL/DR   291   24
   AND IT TOOK THE DIAMOND STONE ....NOTES TO A NEOPHYTE   307   21
DIAMOND-PANED (1)
   A DIAMOND-PANED WINDOW, ...YADDO: THE GRAND MANOR   124   20
DIAMONDS (1)
   WHERE DIAMONDS JANGLE HYMNS WITHIN THE BLOOD ....APRIL AUBADE   312   3
DIAPHANOUS (1)
   THE DIAPHANOUS SATINS OF A JANUARY WINDOW ....A BIRTHDAY PRESENT   206   17
DIARY (1)
   NIGHTS, I WROTE IN MY DIARY SPITEFULLY, MY FINGERS RED ....BABY.   174   14
DICE (1)
   THEY SHOOT THE DICE FOR ONE REMAINING BONE; ....DENOUEMENT   326   8
DICHOTOMY (1)
   "PERSPECTIVE BETRAYS WITH ITS DICHOTOMY: ....LOVE IS A PARALLAX   329   1
DID (35)
   WHAT LOVE DID THEN, LOVE DOES NOW:*DIALOGUE BETWEEN GHOST AND PRIEST   39   29
   EX MACHINA; NOR DID THEY SEEM DETERRED BY THIS. ....SPIDER   49   35
   HE DID NOT COME ....THE SNOWMAN ON THE MOOR   58   6
   NOR DID ANY WORD BODY WITH A NAME ....HARDCASTLE CRAGS   63   17
   WE MIGHT EMBRACE, BUT THOSE TWO NEVER DID, ...THE OTHER TWO   69   30
   COUSIN DID YOU SO UNWISELY KEEP ....THE DISQUIETING MUSES   74   3
   NEVER GRIP, AS THEIR GRANDSIRES DID, THAT DEVIL WHO CHUCKLES*LESSON.   80   24
   THE GROUNDHOG ON THE MOUNTAIN DID NOT RUN ...........INCOMMUNICADO   100   1
   THE PARK OF LESS RED THAN WITHERING DID. .............RHODODENDRON.   103   12
   PROFITED MEMORY, BUT DID AWAY WITH THE OLD SCENERY .....GREEN ROCK.   105   5
   IT WAS MY LOVE THAT DID US BOTH TO DEATH. ...ELECTRA ON AZALEA PATH   117   46
   PROCEEDS CLEAR AS IT EVER DID ....THE BURNT-OUT SPA   138   20
   IF HE WERE I, HE WOULD DO WHAT I DID. ....THE HANGING MAN   142   6
   HOW DID WE MAKE IT UP TO YOUR ATTIC? ....LEAVING EARLY   146   40
   YET I STILL DEPENDED ON HER, THOUGH I DID IT REGRETFULLY.*IN PLASTER   160   49
   WHEN I FIRST SAW IT, THE SMALL RED SEEP, I DID NOT BELIEVE IT. ...
                                          ... THREE WOMEN   177   15
   I DID NOT LOOK. BUT STILL THE FACE WAS THERE, ...THREE WOMEN   178   77
   AND WHAT IF THEY FOUND THEMSELVES SURPRISED, AS I DID? THREE WOMEN   180 118
   WHAT DID MY FINGERS DO BEFORE THEY HELD HIM? ....THREE WOMEN   181 169
   WHAT DID MY HEART DO, WITH ITS LOVE? ....THREE WOMEN   181 170
   IT WAS A DREAM, AND DID NOT MEAN A THING. ....THREE WOMEN   185 308

DID (CONT.)
    A TENDERNESS THAT DID NOT TIRE, SOMETHING HEALING. .....THREE WOMEN   186 357
    WHAT DID I LEAVE UNTOUCHED ON THE DOORSTEP -- ....THE OTHER   201   2
    WHAT DID THEY KNOW THAT I DIDN'T? ....BURNING THE LETTERS   204   5
    DID IT COME LIKE AN ARROW, DID IT COME LIKE A KNIFE?   THE DETECTIVE   209   21
    DID IT COME LIKE AN ARROW, DID IT COME LIKE A KNIFE?   THE DETECTIVE   209   21
    WHICH OF THE NERVE-CURLERS, THE CONVULSORS? DID IT ELECTRIFY? ...
                                              ... THE DETECTIVE   209   23
    AND THEY ARE ALL GLOVED AND COVERED, WHY DID NOBODY TELL ME? ..BEE.   211   4
    DID I ESCAPE, I WONDER? ....MEDUSA   225   12
    HOW DID I GET HERE? ....THE JAILER   227   32
    THEY DID NOT SEE HIM SMILE, ...LYONNESSE   234   23
    O LOVE, HOW DID YOU GET HERE? ....NICK AND THE CANDLESTICK   241   23
    DID. IT'S SMALL, BUT THE VOLUME OF THE VOICE ....DIALOGUE O.   281 203
    GOD-PIE. WHY, THEN, DID YOU DEIGN TO INTRODUCE ....DIALOGUE O.   283 251
    THEM ANY MORE THAN YOU DID. OH, LET IT GO. ....DIALOGUE O.   283 265
DIDN'T (15)
    WE'D WINK AT IF WE DID'T HEAR ....ALL THE DEAD DEARS   70   10
    DIDN'T GO DOWN IN SUCH A HURRY. HOW IT MEMOIRS OF A SPINACH-PICKER   89   2
    THE MOTHER OF MOUTHS DIDN'T LOVE ME. POEM.3.MAENAD.   133   6
    YOU DIDN'T JUST TOE ME AN INCH, NO -- ....LOVE LETTER   147   5
    BUT DIDN'T CONVINCE ME. THOSE TEARS FROZE. ....LOVE LETTER   147   17
    I DIDN'T KNOW WHAT TO MAKE OF IT. ....LOVE LETTER   147   24
    I BLAMED HER FOR EVERYTHING, BUT SHE DIDN'T ANSWER. .....IN PLASTER   159   10
    I DIDN'T MIND HER WAITING ON ME, AND SHE ADORED IT. .....IN PLASTER   159   22
    I DIDN'T WANT ANY FLOWERS, I ONLY WANTED ....TULIPS   161   29
    BUT I DIDN'T KNOW HOW TO COOK, AND BABIES DEPRESSED ME. ......BABY.   174   13
    WHAT DID THEY KNOW THAT I DIDN'T? ....BURNING THE LETTERS   204   5
    I DIDN'T CALL YOU. ....MEDUSA   225   21
    I DIDN'T CALL YOU AT ALL. ....MEDUSA   225   22
    I SUPPOSE. IF I DIDN'T TRUST YOU AT THIS*DIALOGUE OVER A OUIJA BOARD   277   36
    WHERE THOSE WORMS CAME FROM. I SWEAR I DIDN'T EXPECT ...DIALOGUE O.   283 264
DIE (14)
    THEY DIE. ....SOLILOQUY OF THE SOLIPSIST   37   18
    AND SEEMS TO DIE: SO VAPORS ....FULL FATHOM FIVE   93   19
    THE FUGITIVE COLORS DIE. POEM.5.F.   135   10
    LET HER DIE THERE, OR WITHER INCESSANTLY FOR THE NEXT FIFTY
                       YEARS, ...FACE LIFT   156   29
    AND SECRETLY SHE BEGAN TO HOPE I'D DIE. ....IN PLASTER   159   39
    THE SUN IS DOWN. I DIE. I MAKE A DEATH. ....THREE WOMEN   181 161
    WIDEN AND DIE IN THE HEDGEROWS. I HEAR THE MOO OF COWS. *THREE WOMEN   185 312
    THEY CAN DIE, I NEED FEED THEM NOTHING, I AM THE OWNER.*THE ARRIVAL.   213   25
    AT TWENTY I TRIED TO DIE ....DADDY   224   58
    I DIE WITH VARIETY -- ....MEDUSA   227   34
    AND LIKE THE CAT I HAVE NINE TIMES TO DIE. ....LADY LAZARUS   244   21
    THEY DO NOT DIE. ....MARY'S SONG   257   12
    "O MAY G-MEN ALL DIE OF THE CHOLER, ...DIALOGUE EN ROUTE   308   15
    AND, DROPPING, DIE, TO TRACE A WOUND THAT HEALS LOVE IS A PARALLAX   330   64
DIED (11)
    BUT THE ECHOES DIED AT HER BACK AS THE WALLS ......HARDCASTLE CRAGS   62   8
    MY FATHER DIED, AND WHEN HE DIED ....ON THE DECLINE OF ORACLES   78   9
    MY FATHER DIED, AND WHEN HE DIED ....ON THE DECLINE OF ORACLES   78   9
    DIED RECLUSE OR SUICIDE ....MUSSEL HUNTER AT ROCK HARBOR   97   75
    EATS AT POINT SHIRLEY. SHE DIED BLESSED, ...POINT SHIRLEY   111   36
    THE DAY YOU DIED I WENT INTO THE DIRT, ...ELECTRA ON AZALEA PATH   116   1
    NOBODY DIED OR WITHERED ON THAT STAGE. ......ELECTRA ON AZALEA PATH   116   13
    I BROUGHT MY LOVE TO BEAR, AND THEN YOU DIED.*ELECTRA ON AZALEA PATH   117   38
    MY MOTHER SAID; YOU DIED LIKE ANY MAN. ....ELECTRA ON AZALEA PATH   117   40
    YOU SHOULD HAVE JUNKED THEM BEFORE THEY DIED. ....LEAVING EARLY   146   28
    YOU DIED BEFORE I HAD TIME --- ....DADDY   222   7
DIES (3)
    AND, BRIGHT AS BLOOD-DROPS, PROVED NO BRAVE BRANCH DIES ..MAYFLOWER   60   3
    NOBODY DIES OR IS BORN WITHOUT THEIR KNOWING IT. ...THE NET-MENDERS   121   13
    MY SOUL DIES BEFORE IT. ....YEARS   255   13
DIET (2)
    DIET ON WATER, ...MUSHROOMS   139   19
    YOU CHECKED THE DIET CHARTS AND TOOK ME TO PLAY ..ZOO KEEPER'S WIFE   155   25
DIFFERENCE (1)
    A DIFFERENCE BETWEEN US? ....A SECRET   219   5
DIFFERENCES (1)
    THEY ARE BEGINNING TO REMEMBER THEIR DIFFERENCES. ......THREE WOMEN   183 224
DIFFERENT (2)
    AND WHAT IF THE SKY HERE IS NO DIFFERENT, ..STARS OVER THE DORDOGNE   166   25
    IT DOES NOT WISH TO BE MORE, OR DIFFERENT. ....THREE WOMEN   179 101
DIFFICULT (3)
    WITH THEIR GIFTS TO A DIFFICULT BORNING. ....THE MANOR GARDEN   125   20
    DIFFICULT TO IMAGINE HOW FURY STRUCK -- ....BLUE MOLES   126   17
    I COULD NOT BELIEVE IT. IS IT SO DIFFICULT ....THREE WOMEN   177   25
DIFFICULTIES (1)
    THE OLD DREGS, THE OLD DIFFICULTIES TAKE ME TO WIFE.   PARLIAMENT H.   153   48
DIFFICULTY (1)
    ON THE DIFFICULTY OF CONJURING UP A DRYAD ....CONJURING.   65   T
DIGEST (1)
    OF DIGESTING WHAT CENTURIES ALONE DIGEST: ....PERSEUS   82   2

	TITLE	PAGE	LINE

DIGESTIBLES (1)
   IT IS THE BOWEL-PULSE, LOVER OF DIGESTIBLES. ....WORDS HEARD. 202 4
DIGESTING (3)
   OF DIGESTING WHAT CENTURIES ALONE DIGEST: ....PERSEUS 82 2
   HE WERE DIGESTING A MOUSE. ....MEDALLION 125 24
   GLITTERING AND DIGESTING ....THE MUNICH MANNEQUINS 263 26
DIGNITY (1)
   THERE IS A DIGNITY TO THIS; THERE IS A FORMALITY -- ......NARCISSI. 190 7
DILATE (3)
   THE GREAT COROLLAS DILATE, PEELING BACK THEIR SILKS. ..BEEKEEPER'S. 118 2
   DILATE LITHE AND ....AQUATIC NOCTURNE 305 14
   INVADES THE DILATE LENS OF GENESIS ....SONNET TO SATAN 323 10
DILATING (1)
   DILATING TO CRATERS IN THIS LIVINGROOM, *DIALOGUE OVER A OUIJA BOARD 285 320
DILUTE (1)
   OF DILUTE LIGHT ....AQUATIC NOCTURNE 305 3
DIM (3)
   FESTERING ON THE DIM WALLS OF EUROPE'S CHAPELS, ...PERSEUS 82 10
   THOUGHTS GONE DIM. ....I AM VERTICAL 162 16
   WHILE FOOTLIGHTS FLARE AND HOUSELIGHTS DIM. .....LOVE IS A PARALLAX 330 48
DIMENSION (2)
   MEAGER OF DIMENSION AS THE GRAY PEOPLE ....THE THIN PEOPLE 64 2
   I AM DYING AS I SIT. I LOSE A DIMENSION. ....THREE WOMEN 177 30
DIMENSIONS (1)
   SHE HAS ONE TOO MANY DIMENSIONS TO ENTER. ....A LIFE 150 28
DIMINISH (3)
   AND TREES DIMINISH ....SOLILOQUY OF THE SOLIPSIST 37 12
   REFUSING TO DIMINISH ....THE LADY AND THE EARTHENWARE HEAD 70 34
   THE SUN WILL DIMINISH IT SOON ENOUGH: ....A WINTER SHIP 113 29
DIMINISHED (2)
   THE MOTHER OF PESTLES DIMINISHED ME. POEM.7.S. 136 7
   DIMINISHED AND FLAT, AS AFTER RADICAL SURGERY. ....ELM 192 26
DIMINISHES (1)
   DIMINISHES, AND GOD KNOWS WHAT IS THERE. ...THE GHOST'S LEAVETAKING 91 26
DIMINISHING (1)
   OF DIMINISHING PERSPECTIVES, AND ITS SIGNIFICANCE ....INSOMNIAC 163 24
DIN (2)
   OF WHITE AND PEWTER LIGHTS, AND A DIN LIKE SILVERSMITHS ..BLACKBER. 169 26
   WERE THERE NOT SUCH A DIN IN IT. ....THE ARRIVAL OF THE BEE BOX 212 5
DING (1)
   KUMQUAT-COLORED TROLLEYS DING AS THEY TRUNDLE .....ALICANTE LULLABY 43 8
DINING (1)
   OF THE PATIENTS' DINING ROOM. ....MISS DRAKE PROCEEDS TO SUPPER 41 26
DINNER (1)
   AND THE FAIR SHIP SANK, ITS CREW KNELLED HOME FOR DINNER. ...
         ... DREAM WITH CLAM-DIGGERS 44 20
DINT (1)
   ASKEW WITH BLOTCH, DINT, SCAR ....STRUMPET SONG 33 12
DIOR (1)
   IN A SHOWER OF CHANEL, DIOR GOWNS, ...DIALOGUE EN ROUTE 308 9
DIP (2)
   O I SHOULDN'T DIP MY HANKIE IN, IT HURTS! ....THE TOUR 238 31
   I SEE THEM START TO CRUISE AND DIP FOR FOOD*QUEEN MARY'S ROSE GARDEN 290 13
DIPPED (1)
   OF HOLOFERNES' HEAD, DIPPED IN THE SAME ....LEAVING EARLY 146 32
DIPPER (1)
   THE BIG DIPPER IS MY ONLY FAMILIAR. ....STARS OVER THE DORDOGNE 165 17
DIPPING (1)
   BEGIN BY DIPPING YOUR BRUSH INTO CLEAR LIGHT. .....MIDSUMMER MOBILE 324 1
DIRECT (1)
   DIRECT TO YES. I BET IT'S PAN. WHO'LL ..DIALOGUE OVER A OUIJA BOARD 277 27
DIRECTION (2)
   SKIRTS, SINGS IN THE DIRECTION ....TWO VIEWS OF A CADAVER ROOM 114 15
   EVERYTHING IN ONE DIRECTION. ....WUTHERING HEIGHTS 167 13
DIRECTIONS (2)
   STRETCHING ITS FINE, IRRITATING SAND IN ALL DIRECTIONS. ..INSOMNIAC 163 7
   ASIDE WERE DRAGGING ME IN FOUR DIRECTIONS. ....THREE WOMEN 178 58
DIRECTS (1)
   DIRECTS ALL ZODIAC. ....TRIO OF LOVE SONGS 313 4
DIRGE (1)
   DIRGE FOR A JOKER ....DIRGE FOR A JOKER 302 T
DIRT (3)
   AND FACED ME, BACK TO A LEDGE OF DIRT, TO RATTLE .....INCOMMUNICADO 100 3
   THE DAY YOU DIED I WENT INTO THE DIRT, ...ELECTRA ON AZALEA PATH 116 1
   TO LEVER THE DIRT. ....A SECRET 220 23
DIRTY (4)
   DIRTY AS A BOOTSOLE AND BIG AS A HOSPITAL SINK ...ZOO KEEPER'S WIFE 155 35
   BROWSING IN THEIR DIRTY WOOL-CLOUDS, ...WUTHERING HEIGHTS 167 20
   DIRTY GIRL, ...CUT 236 39
   ELEMENTS LIKE DIRTY SOCKS AND SCRAPS .....METAMORPHOSES OF THE MOON 307 28
DISAPPEAR (2)
   LITTLE UNSTRUNG PUPPET, KICKING TO DISAPPEAR -- ....LESBOS 227 9
   NOW FOLD THEIR WINGS LIKE BATS AND DISAPPEAR ....TWO LOVERS. 327 7
DISAPPEARED (1)
   EACH NURSE PATCHED HER SOUL TO A WOUND AND DISAPPEARED. ....WAKING. 151 13

131

	TITLE	PAGE	LINE

DISAPPOINT (1)
  REGARD ME SADLY, I DISAPPOINT THEM. ....SHEEP IN FOG 262 3
DISARRAY (1)
  SHE JUDGED PETALS IN DISARRAY, ...SPINSTER 49 11
DISASTER (2)
  OF SLOW DISASTER: THE BITTEN APPLE ENDS ..METAMORPHOSES OF THE MOON 307 14
  WITH A HISS OF DISASTER ....TEMPER OF TIME 336 7
DISBELIEF (1)
  NEATLY, NICELY, BY DISBELIEF OR BRIDGES, ...A LESSON IN VENGEANCE 80 23
DISCHARGES (1)
  DISCHARGES ITSELF FROM THE TREE WITH NOWHERE TO GO. *CHILDLESS WOMAN 259 3
DISCIPLINE (3)
  AND HEART'S FROSTY DISCIPLINE ....SPINSTER 50 17
  ALL'S PEACE AND DISCIPLINE DOWN THERE. TILL LATELY WE ....OXBOW. 89 53
  WITH STRUCTURAL DISCIPLINE: ....NOTES TO A NEOPHYTE 306 9
DISCIPLINED (1)
  NOW, DISCIPLINED IN THE STRICT ANCESTRAL CHAIR, ...THE TRIAL OF MAN 312 12
DISCIPLINES (1)
  FRAMED IN DISCIPLINES OF FIRE AND ICE ....METAMORPHOSES OF THE MOON 307 26
DISCLAIMS (1)
  DRYLY DISCLAIMS THAT FIERCE TROLL FACES LURK ....TALE OF A TUB 24 13
DISCLOSES (1)
  A BLACK GAP DISCLOSES ITSELF. ....EVENT 195 17
DISCONSOLATE (1)
  ROUND, GREEN, DISCONSOLATE AS A TEAR. .....THE BEEKEEPER'S DAUGHTER 118 18
DISCORD (1)
  EMULOUS SPIRITS MAKE DISCORD, ...SCULPTOR 92 20
DISCOVER (1)
  TO DISCOVER THAT METAPHYSICAL TREE WHICH HID ...PLETHORA OF DRYADS. 67 9
DISCOVERED (2)
  DAYBREAK DISCOVERED THE BUREAU LID ....LEAVING EARLY 146 29
  BUT TONIGHT THEY HAVE DISCOVERED THIS RIVER WITH NO TROUBLE, *STARS. 165 15
DISCREET (1)
  HERE IN THIS VALLEY OF DISCREET ACADEMIES ....ABOVE THE OXBOW 87 1
DISCREETLY (1)
  WHITELY, DISCREETLY, ...MUSHROOMS 139 2
DISCRETION (2)
  PAST KEEPING TO THE HOUSE, PAST ALL DISCRETION -- THE RAVAGED FACE 115 7
  I DO NOT THINK YOU CREDIT ME WITH THIS DISCRETION. ....BIRTHDAY. 207 36
DISEASE (3)
  ALREADY HE CAN FEEL DAYLIGHT, HIS WHITE DISEASE, ...INSOMNIAC 163 31
  THIS IS A DISEASE I CARRY HOME, THIS IS A DEATH. ....THREE WOMEN 177 36
  AN ODD DISEASE HAS HIT OUR HOLY COW, ...THE DISPOSSESSED 318 4
DISENCHANT (1)
  DISENCHANT MY TWELVE BLACK-GOWNED EXAMINERS ....RESOLVE 52 21
DISENCHANTMENT (1)
  UNTIL IN DISENCHANTMENT OUR EYES GLUT ....METAMORPHOSES OF THE MOON 308 34
DISFIGURED (1)
  OR WHAT DISFIGURED AND UNSIGHTLY ....THE DISQUIETING MUSES 74 2
DISGUISE (4)
  OR ELSE THEY ARE PRESENT, AND THEIR DISGUISE SO BRIGHT STARS OVER. 165 22
  THEY STAND ABOUT IN GRANDMOTHERLY DISGUISE, ...WUTHERING HEIGHTS 167 25
  DISGUISE BEGUILES AND MORTAL MISCHIEF'S DONE: ....ADMONITIONS 319 14
  ECLIPSED BY MAGICIAN'S DISGUISE, ...CIRCUS IN THREE RINGS 322 14
DISGUISES (2)
  THE VILLAGERS ARE UNTYING THEIR DISGUISES, THEY ARE SHAKING HANDS. ...
                      ... THE BEE MEETING 212 54
  NO SWEET DISGUISES ....MOONSONG AT MORNING 317 21
DISGUISING (1)
  DISGUISING THE CONSTANT HORROR IN A COAT ....TALE OF A TUB 25 37
DISH (2)
  ON SILVER DISH, ...TINKER JACK AND THE TIDY WIVES 34 6
  KING OF THE DISH, MY LUCKY ANIMAL. POEM.4.BEAST. 134 2
DISHEARTENS (1)
  NIGHTFALL, COLD EYE -- NEITHER DISHEARTENS ....THE BEGGARS 47 1
DISHONORS (1)
  STILL RINGING WITH BRUIT OF INSULTS AND DISHONORS ....SNOWMAN O. 58 3
DISINFECTANTS (1)
  SWABBED AND LURID WITH DISINFECTANTS, SACRIFICIAL. .....THREE WOMEN 179 107
DISKS (5)
  THERE ARE BLACK DISKS BEHIND IT, THE DISKS OF OUTRAGE, ...COURAGE. 209 3
  THERE ARE BLACK DISKS BEHIND IT, THE DISKS OF OUTRAGE, ...COURAGE. 209 3
  THE DISKS REVOLVE, THEY ASK TO BE HEARD -- ....COURAGE. 209 5
  SO THE DISKS OF THE BRAIN REVOLVE, LIKE THE MUZZLES OF CANNON. ...
                ... THE COURAGE OF SHUTTING-UP 210 16
  COGS AND DISKS, INANE MECHANIC WHIMS, ...SONNET: TO EVA 304 7
DISLIKE (1)
  JUST AS IT IS, UNMISTED BY LOVE OR DISLIKE. ....MIRROR 173 3
DISLODGE (1)
  LEDGE WILL DISLODGE OUR CRAMPED CONCEPT OF SPACE, UNWALL ....OXBOW. 88 23
DISMAL-HEADED (1)
  IN THE SHADOW CAST BY MY DISMAL-HEADED ....THE DISQUIETING MUSES 75 30
DISMEMBERED (2)
  WHO HAS DISMEMBERED US? ....EVENT 195 21
  DISMEMBERED, TO A TOD OF IVY. ....THE SWARM 217 38

132

	TITLE	PAGE	LINE

DISORGANIZATION (1)
   O HEART, SUCH DISORGANIZATION! ....AN APPEARANCE   189   16
DISPARAGING (1)
   AND I HAVE NO INTENTION OF DISPARAGING THEM*QUEEN MARY'S ROSE GARDEN   290   19
DISPARATE (1)
   TILTED AND DISPARATE, AND ALWAYS UNSTABLE. ....WUTHERING HEIGHTS   167   2
DISPATCHED (1)
   DISPATCHED, INTO TRENCHES OF GRASS. ....STINGS/DR   293   13
DISPELLED (1)
   OF DREAMERS IS DISPELLED. ONCE MORE WE CUT ....DIALOGUE O.   286   359
DISPERSE (1)
   CLOUDS PASS AND DISPERSE. ....ELM   193   34
DISPLACED (2)
   ITS ROUND PERIOD, DISPLACED AND GREEN, ...THE GHOST'S LEAVETAKING   91   29
   DISPLACED THEIR DOMES AS TINY ....MUSSEL HUNTER AT ROCK HARBOR   96   27
DISPOSSESSED (1)
   THE DISPOSSESSED ....THE DISPOSSESSED   318   T
DISQUIETING (1)
   THE DISQUIETING MUSES ....THE DISQUIETING MUSES   74   T
DISRUPT (2)
   NO SCRUPLE COULD DISRUPT, ...SPIDER   49   31
   DISRUPT THE CALENDARS NEXT; SEND THE DUTEOUS ....SONG FOR A REVOLU.   323   9
DISSATISFACTIONS (2)
   YOUR DISSATISFACTIONS, ON THE OTHER HAND, ...THE RIVAL   166   13
   ITS DISSATISFACTIONS? ....ELM   192   5
DISSATISFY (1)
   MORE OR OTHER, THEY STILL DISSATISFY. ....POEMS, POTATOES   106   10
DISSECT (1)
   IF YOU DISSECT A BIRD ....TRIO OF LOVE SONGS   315   37
DISSECTED (1)
   MY X-RAYED HEART, DISSECTED BODY: ....BLUEBEARD   305   6
DISSECTING (1)
   THE DAY SHE VISITED THE DISSECTING ROOM *TWO VIEWS OF A CADAVER ROOM   114   1
DISSEMBLING (1)
   THE SUAVE DISSEMBLING COBRA WEARS A HOOD ....ADMONITIONS   319   10
DISSEVER (1)
   DAWN SHALL DISSEVER ....MOONSONG AT MORNING   317   13
DISSIPATE (1)
   MORNINGS DISSIPATE IN SOMNOLENCE. ....FROG AUTUMN   99   5
DISSOLUTE (1)
   IS DISSOLUTE: ....MOONSONG AT MORNING   317   20
DISSOLVE (5)
   ALTHOUGH THE RAINS DISSOLVE A BLOODY DYE: ...ELECTRA ON AZALEA PATH   117   27
   BUT THEY ONLY DISSOLVE AND DISSOLVE ....WUTHERING HEIGHTS   167   8
   BUT THEY ONLY DISSOLVE AND DISSOLVE ....WUTHERING HEIGHTS   167   8
   AND DISSOLVE OF SORROW. ....THE APPLICANT   221   17
   THE WET DAWN INKS ARE DOING THEIR BLUE DISSOLVE. ......WINTER TREES   257   1
DISSOLVED (1)
   DISSOLVED NOW, SMOKE OF AN OLD WAR. ....BLUE MOLES   126   18
DISSOLVES (1)
   THE SUN DISSOLVES ON THIS WALL, BLEEDING ITS LIGHTS.   APPREHENSIONS   195   5
DISSOLVING (2)
   ON THE WAVES' DISSOLVING TURN ....MUSSEL HUNTER AT ROCK HARBOR   97   87
   (MY SELVES DISSOLVING, OLD WHORE PETTICOATS) --- ....FEVER.   232   53
DISTAIN (1)
   DROWNS NOAH'S PRAYERS WITH DISTAIN, ...INSOLENT STORM.   326   14
DISTANCE (9)
   GIANT HEAVED INTO THE DISTANCE, STONE-HATCHETED, ...SNOWMAN O.   59   31
   IN THE DISTANCE. ALL AROUND US THE WATER SLIPS ....A WINTER SHIP   113   18
   OF POPLARS IN THE MIDDLE DISTANCE, THE ONLY ....SLEEP.   143   5
   THE SILVER TRACK OF TIME EMPTIES INTO THE DISTANCE, ...THREE WOMEN   177   32
   O COLOR OF DISTANCE AND FORGETFULNESS! -- ....THREE WOMEN   179   103
   THAT AT SUCH A DISTANCE FROM US SHINE AND WHIRL. ....THREE WOMEN   182   210
   IN BLUE DISTANCE THE PISTONS HISS. ....YEARS   256   25
   IT STRETCHES INTO THE DISTANCE. IT WILL BE EATEN NEVERTHELESS.*TOTEM   264   2
   ALWAYS THE SAME DISTANCE FROM ............METAMORPHOSES OF THE MOON   307   9
DISTANCES (4)
   BEFORE THE DISTANCES THEY PIN EVAPORATE, ...WUTHERING HEIGHTS   167   6
   POUR OF TOR AND DISTANCES. ....ARIEL   239   3
   STEP OFF SEVEN LEAGUES, LIKE THOSE DISTANCES ....GULLIVER   251   21
   BONES NOSING FOR DISTANCES. ....BRASILIA   258   10
DISTANCING (1)
   BUT NEARING MEANS DISTANCING: ....THE GREAT CARBUNCLE   73   27
DISTANT (3)
   DISTANT AND COLD AS PHOTOS, ...OLD LADIES' HOME   120   11
   WOODSMOKE AND A DISTANT LOUDSPEAKER ....YADDO: THE GRAND MANOR   123   1
   IMPOTENT AS DISTANT THUNDER, ...THE JAILER   227   37
DISTILLS (1)
   THAN THE CLOUD THAT DISTILLS A MIRROR TO REFLECT ITS OWN SLOW ...
                                                ... MORNING SONG   157   8
DISTINCT (1)
   PALM-SPEAR AND LILY DISTINCT AS FLORA IN THE VAST ....A LIFE   149   4
DISTRACT (1)
   TO DISTRACT BEAUTY'S THOUGHT; ....VANITY FAIR   33   23

                                                           TITLE   PAGE LINE
DISTRACTEDLY (2)
    THE GRASS IS BEATING ITS HEAD DISTRACTEDLY. ......WUTHERING HEIGHTS 168   39
    A MARBLE SAILOR KNEELS AT HER FOOT DISTRACTEDLY, AND AT HIS FOOT ...
                                                   ... FINISTERRE 170   21
DISTRACTION (2)
    BUT THEY ARE DEAD, AND THEIR MOTHER NEAR DEAD WITH DISTRACTION, ...
                                                   ... STILLBORN 142   14
    HERALD DISTRACTION: A FLOCK OF PASTEL PILLS, ...MORNING IN THE HOS. 332   13
DISTRACTIONS (1)
    MY DISTRACTIONS, MY PALLORS. .........................EAVESDROPPER 260   20
DISTRESS (3)
    OR ANY SIGNAL OF DISTRESS OR ANXIOUSNESS. ..STARS OVER THE DORDOGNE 165   7
    THE HEART IS A RED-BELL-BLOOM, IN DISTRESS. ..THE SURGEON AT 2 A.M. 171   17
    CREEPS AWAY, MANY-SNAKED, WITH A LONG HISS OF DISTRESS. *BERCK-PLAGE 196   18
DISTURBANCE (1)
    A DISTURBANCE IN MIRRORS, ...THE COURIERS 247   11
DISTURBING (1)
    WITH YOUR WILD FURIES, DISTURBING GARLANDS OF FRUIT ..CONVERSATION.   21   2
DISTURBS (1)
    NO THIRST DISTURBS A STONE'S BED. ....CHILD'S PARK STONES 101   30
DITCH (1)
    WHICH OUT FROM BLACK TARN, DITCH AND CUP ....STRUMPET SONG   34   17
DITCHES (1)
    MY JILTING LADY SQUANDER COIN, GOLD LEAF STOCK DITCHES, CONJURING.   66   35
DITHERS (1)
    DITHERS WITH THE OTHER WAY OUT ....LETTER TO A PURIST   37   13
DIVE (2)
    THE BLACK DUCKS DIVE. ....POINT SHIRLEY 111   43
    DIVE AT YOUR MIRROR ....MOONSONG AT MORNING 317   39
DIVER (1)
    LIKE A DIVER ON A LOFTY SPAR OF LAND ....FAMILY REUNION 301   25
DIVIDENDS (1)
    NO VIOLATION BUT GIVES DIVIDENDS .........METAMORPHOSES OF THE MOON 307   13
DIVIDING (1)
    A CURTAIN OF WAX DIVIDING THEM FROM THE BRIDE FLIGHT, ...BEE. 212   47
DIVINE (1)
    SKIES ONCE WEARING A BLUE, DIVINE HAUTEUR ....OUIJA   77   19
DIVINING (1)
    RIVALS HER WHETTED LOOK, DIVINING WHAT CONCEIT ....VANITY FAIR   32   13
DIVINITY (2)
    HER WIDE BED WORE THE STAIN OF DIVINITY. ....ELECTRA ON AZALEA PATH 116   8
    HER LIPS SWEET WITH DIVINITY. ....FINISTERRE 170   25
DIVISION (1)
    OF ONE I LOVED. I SAW DIVISION BLOOM ...DIALOGUE OVER A OUIJA BOARD 285 322
DO (111)
    I DO NOT KNOW ....THE QUEEN'S COMPLAINT   28   8
    WHEN ALL EARTH HIS WORDS DO SUMMON ....ODE FOR TED   30   23
    MADE TO DO VIOLENCE ON, ...STRUMPET SONG   33   10
    "NEITHER OF THOSE COUNTRIES DO I FREQUENT: ....DIALOGUE B.   38   19
    AND DO GOOD ....RECANTATION   42   19
    HOW WE SHALL DO TOGETHER, ...CRYSTAL GAZER   55   9
    I DO NOT EXPECT A MIRACLE ....BLACK ROOK IN RAINY WEATHER   56   4
    NOW THE THIN PEOPLE DO NOT OBLITERATE ....THE THIN PEOPLE   65   32
    SO FINE WE CANNOT DO IT. ....THE GREAT CARBUNCLE   73   26
    SWIM THE SEA OF DO, ...WORDS FOR A NURSERY   74   33
    RINSING THOSE STABLES: A BABY'S TEARS WOULD DO IT. ....PERSEUS   82   7
    I'LL GO OUT AND SIT IN WHITE LIKE THEY DO, ...MOONRISE   98   2
    GREEN. NOR DO THEY, ONCE IN A HUNDRED ....CHILD'S PARK STONES 101   28
    UNLESS YOU DO THIS TAWDRY HARBOR ....GREEN ROCK, WINTHROP BAY 105   19
    WHAT THE SLUTTISH, RUTTED SEA COULD DO. ....POINT SHIRLEY 110   12
    I HAD NOTHING TO DO WITH GUILT OR ANYTHING ..ELECTRA ON AZALEA PATH 116   9
    NO LONGER DO I LISTEN FOR THE SCRAPE OF A KEEL ....THE COLOSSUS 130   29
    IF I AM A LITTLE ONE, I CAN DO NO HARM. POEM.6.W. 135   13
    MY MENDINGS ITCH. THERE IS NOTHING TO DO. POEM.7.S. 137   44
    TRAWLING YOUR DARK AS OWLS DO. ....YOU'RE 141   6
    IF HE WERE I, HE WOULD DO WHAT I DID. ....THE HANGING MAN 142   6
    THESE POEMS DO NOT LIVE: IT'S A SAD DIAGNOSIS. ....STILLBORN 142   1
    AND THEY STUPIDLY STARE, AND DO NOT SPEAK OF HER. ....STILLBORN 142   15
    PEEL OFF TO SEA AS GULLS DO, ...WHITSUN 154   20
    BUT WHAT DO YOU KNOW ABOUT THAT ....ZOO KEEPER'S WIFE 155   14
    I AM NOBODY; I HAVE NOTHING TO DO WITH EXPLOSIONS. ....TULIPS 160   5
    THEIR POPPY-SLEEPY COLORS DO HIM NO GOOD. ....INSOMNIAC 163   21
    NOR DO THEY SEND UP FIRES WHERE THEY FALL ..STARS OVER THE DORDOGNE 165   6
    I DO NOT THINK THE SEA WILL APPEAR AT ALL. ...........BLACKBERRYING 168   13
    THEY DO NOT COME FROM THE BAY OF THE DEAD DOWN THERE, ...FINISTERRE 170   33
    IT IS A GARDEN I HAVE TO DO WITH -- TUBERS AND FRUITS .....SURGEON. 170   11
    I DO NOT WANT A PLAIN BOX, I WANT A SARCOPHAGUS ....LAST WORDS 172   1
    I DO NOT TRUST THE SPIRIT. IT ESCAPES LIKE STEAM ....LAST WORDS 172   14
    IS SHE SORRY FOR WHAT WILL HAPPEN? I DO NOT THINK SO. ..THREE WOMEN 176   6
    I DO NOT HAVE TO THINK, OR EVEN REHEARSE. ....THREE WOMEN 176   9
    OTHER CHILDREN DO NOT TOUCH ME: THEY ARE TERRIBLE. .....THREE WOMEN 178   68
    WHAT DID MY FINGERS DO BEFORE THEY HELD HIM? ....THREE WOMEN 181 169
    WHAT DID MY HEART DO, WITH ITS LOVE? ....THREE WOMEN 181 170
    I DO NOT EVEN NEED A HOLIDAY; I CAN GO TO WORK TODAY. ..THREE WOMEN 183 249

DO (CONT.)
  THERE ARE THE CLOTHES OF A FAT WOMAN I DO NOT KNOW. ....THREE WOMEN   184 267
  THESE LITTLE BLACK TWIGS DO NOT THINK TO BUD, ...THREE WOMEN   184 278
  NOR DO THESE DRY, DRY GUTTERS DREAM OF RAIN. ....THREE WOMEN   184 279
  I DO NOT BELIEVE IN THOSE TERRIBLE CHILDREN ....THREE WOMEN   185 320
  THEY ARE NOT MINE. THEY DO NOT BELONG TO ME. ....THREE WOMEN   185 322
  I DO NOT WILL HIM TO BE EXCEPTIONAL. ....THREE WOMEN   186 330
  THERE IS A GREAT DEAL ELSE TO DO. MY HANDS ....THREE WOMEN   187 359
  DO YOU SAY NOTHING? ....LITTLE FUGUE 188   43
  WHERE DO THE BLACK TREES GO THAT DRINK HERE? ....CROSSING THE WATER 190   2
  THEIR LEAVES DO NOT WISH US TO HURRY: ....CROSSING THE WATER 190   5
  DO NOT KILL IT. IT STARTLES ME STILL, ...PHEASANT 191   2
  I DO NOT FEAR IT: I HAVE BEEN THERE. ....ELM 192   3
  DO YOU DO NO HARM? ....POPPIES IN JULY   203   2
  DO YOU DO NO HARM? ....POPPIES IN JULY   203   2
  DO NOT TOUCH. ....BURNING THE LETTERS   204   19
  I DO NOT WANT MUCH OF A PRESENT, ANYWAY, THIS YEAR. ......BIRTHDAY. 206   13
  CAN YOU NOT SEE I DO NOT MIND WHAT IT IS. ......A BIRTHDAY PRESENT   206   20
  DO NOT BE ASHAMED -- I DO NOT MIND IF IT IS SMALL. ......BIRTHDAY.   206   22
  DO NOT BE ASHAMED -- I DO NOT MIND IF IT IS SMALL. ......BIRTHDAY.   206   22
  DO NOT BE MEAN, I AM READY FOR ENORMITY. ....A BIRTHDAY PRESENT   207   23
  DO NOT BE AFRAID,IT IS NOT SO. ....A BIRTHDAY PRESENT   207   32
  I DO NOT THINK YOU CREDIT ME WITH THIS DISCRETION. ......BIRTHDAY.   207   36
  DO NOT WORRY ABOUT THE EYES -- ....THE COURAGE OF SHUTTING-UP   210   30
  HE HAS NOTHING TO DO WITH THE BEE-SELLER OR WITH ME. ......STINGS   215   39
  DO AWAY WITH THE BASTARD. ....A SECRET   220   32
  "DO AWAY WITH IT ALTOGETHER." ....A SECRET   220   33
  DO YOU WEAR ....THE APPLICANT 221   2
  AND DO WHATEVER YOU TELL IT. ....THE APPLICANT 221   13
  WELL, WHAT DO YOU THINK OF THAT? ....THE APPLICANT 221   29
  YOU DO NOT DO, YOU DO NOT DO ....DADDY 222   1
  YOU DO NOT DO, YOU DO NOT DO ....DADDY 222   1
  YOU DO NOT DO, YOU DO NOT DO ....DADDY 222   1
  YOU DO NOT DO, YOU DO NOT DO ....DADDY 222   1
  I THOUGHT EVEN THE BONES WOULD DO. ....DADDY 224   60
  AND THEN I KNEW WHAT TO DO. ....DADDY 224   63
  AND I SAID I DO, I DO. ....DADDY 224   67
  AND I SAID I DO, I DO. ....DADDY 224   67
  WHO DO YOU THINK YOU ARE? ....MEDUSA 225   32
  DO WITHOUT FEVERS TO EAT? ....THE JAILER 227   42
  DO WITHOUT EYES TO KNIFE, WHAT WOULD HE ....THE JAILER 227   44
  DO, DO, DO WITHOUT ME? ....THE JAILER 227   45
  DO, DO, DO WITHOUT ME? ....THE JAILER 227   45
  DO, DO, DO WITHOUT ME? ....THE JAILER 227   45
  I DO NOT SPEAK. ....LESBOS 229   67
  WHO DO YOU THINK I AM, ...STOPPED DEAD 230   17
  WHERE DO YOU STASH YOUR LIFE? ....STOPPED DEAD 230   20
  THERE IS NOTHING TO DO WITH SUCH A BEAUTIFUL BLANK BUT SMOOTH IT. ...
                                                   ... AMNESIAC   232   2
  DO STEP INTO THE HALL! ....THE TOUR 237   2
  DO I TERRIFY? --- ....LADY LAZARUS 244   12
  I DO IT EXCEPTIONALLY WELL. ....LADY LAZARUS 245   45
  I DO IT SO IT FEELS LIKE HELL. ....LADY LAZARUS 245   46
  I DO IT SO IT FEELS REAL. ....LADY LAZARUS 245   47
  IT'S EASY ENOUGH TO DO IT IN A CELL. ....LADY LAZARUS 245   49
  IT'S EASY ENOUGH TO DO IT AND STAY PUT. ....LADY LAZARUS 245   50
  DO NOT THINK I UNDERESTIMATE YOUR GREAT CONCERN. ......LADY LAZARUS 246   72
  IT IS NOT MINE. DO NOT ACCEPT IT. ....THE COURIERS 247   2
  DO NOT ACCEPT IT. IT IS NOT GENUINE. ....THE COURIERS 247   4
  WHAT DO WHEELS EAT, THESE WHEELS ....GETTING THERE 248   13
  I DO NOT STIR. ....DEATH & CO. 255 26
  THEY DO NOT DIE. ....MARY'S SONG 257   12
  DO NOT THINK I DON'T NOTICE YOUR CURTAIN -- ...........EAVESDROPPER 260   28
  POOLS ASIDE, WILLS ASIDE, DO WE ....DIALOGUE OVER A OUIJA BOARD   278   53
  OUR WORK. LOVE. THE AFTER-LIFE . . . DO YOU ....DIALOGUE O.   278   55
  DO YOU KNOW HOW MY FATHER IS? HE'S LEFT *DIALOGUE OVER A OUIJA BOARD 278   74
  IF YOU MUST BUTCHER MOTHER GOOSE TO DO IT. ....DIALOGUE O.   280 149
  I'LL ASK. DO. WE'VE KEPT HIM WAITING LONG ....DIALOGUE O.   281 180
  MIGHT DO AS A GOD'S MOUTHPIECE IF A WHIRLWIND ....DIALOGUE O.   281 202
  WHERE DO YOU LIVE? HE MOVES. HE'S MOVING BRISK ....DIALOGUE O.   281 206
  TELL US THE TRUTH. WHERE DO YOU LIVE? HE STARTS ....DIALOGUE O.   283 274
  BEFORE IT MADE THE BULL'S-EYE. DO WE HAVE TO BATTLE ...DIALOGUE O.   284 282
  LIKE THE UNDERSIDE OF MUSHROOMS. DO YOU FEEL ....DIALOGUE O.   285 315
  I DO NOT TELL YOU THE NIGHTMARE ....THE DREAM   311   29
DOCK (1)
  SHACKLED TO THE DOCK, OUTMODED, GAUDY, ...A WINTER SHIP 112   3
DOCKS (1)
  OUR LUGGAGE, AS DOCKS HALT OUR BRIEF EPIC; NO DEBT CHANNEL CROSSING 27   41
DOCTOR (6)
  "MY TROUBLE, DOCTOR, IS: I SEE A TREE, ...CONJURING. 66   19
  HERE THEY CAN DOCTOR HEADS, OR ANY LIMB. POEM.7.S. 137   35
  I PICK AND PRY LIKE A DOCTOR OR ....THE BURNT-OUT SPA 138   14
  WHEN THE SPORTY WIFE AND HER DOCTOR HUSBAND WENT ON ONE OF
     THEIR CRUISES ....THE BABYSITTERS 174   16
  NURSES THE SIZE OF WORMS AND A MINUTE DOCTOR ....AMNESIAC   233   7

                                                        TITLE   PAGE LINE
DOCTOR (CONT.)
    OUR NOBLE DOCTOR CLAIMS THE PAIN IS HIS, ...NEVER TRY TO TRICK.   320   7
DOCTORS (2)
    ONE COURTING DOCTORS OF ALL SORTS, ...THE DEATH OF MYTH-MAKING   104   4
    THE DOCTORS MOVE AMONG US AS IF OUR BIGNESS ....THREE WOMEN   179 114
DODDERING (1)
    HE, GODLY, DODDERING, SPELLS ....OUIJA   78   30
DODGE (1)
    WITH A LAST ARTFUL DODGE SHE LEAPS ....AERIALIST   332   39
DODGES (1)
    THE VELVET DODGES OF THE HYPOCRITE: ....THE RAVAGED FACE   116   11
DODO'S (1)
    THUMBS-DOWN ON THE DODO'S MODE. ....YOU'RE   141   4
DOES (23)
    WHAT LOVE DID THEN, LOVE DOES NOW: ....DIALOGUE B.   39   29
    LAUGH DOES AWAY WITH THE UNSTITCHING, PLAGUEY WOUNDS ....PERSEUS   83   45
    THE ARTIFICIAL RED SAGE DOES NOT STIR ....ELECTRA ON AZALEA PATH   117   24
    AT THE HEADSTONE NEXT TO YOURS, NOR DOES IT ROT, ...ELECTRA ON.   117   26
    SHE DOES NOT HEAR WHAT THE SAILOR OR THE PEASANT IS SAYING -- ...
                                                    ... FINISTERRE   170   26
    I HAVE NOT SEEN IT; IT DOES NOT FLY UP. ....THE SURGEON AT 2 A.M.   170   9
    IT DOES NOT WISH TO BE MORE, OR DIFFERENT. ....THREE WOMEN   179 101
    HE DOES NOT WALK. HE DOES NOT SPEAK A WORD. ....THREE WOMEN   186 325
    HE DOES NOT WALK. HE DOES NOT SPEAK A WORD. ....THREE WOMEN   186 325
    THAT SPLITS FROM ITS RIPPED BAG AND DOES NOT STOP ....BURNING.   205   51
    BUT IT SHIMMERS, IT DOES NOT STOP, AND I THINK IT WANTS ME. ...
                                                    ... A BIRTHDAY PRESENT   206   11
    THE BODY DOES NOT COME INTO IT AT ALL. ....THE DETECTIVE   209   25
    THE SURGEON IS QUIET, HE DOES NOT SPEAK. *THE COURAGE OF SHUTTING-UP   210   14
    I AM NUDE AS A CHICKEN NECK, DOES NOBODY LOVE ME? ..THE BEE MEETING   211   6
    THE OLD QUEEN DOES NOT SHOW HERSELF, IS SHE SO UNGRATEFUL? ....BEE.   212   50
    I AM THE MAGICIAN'S GIRL WHO DOES NOT FLINCH. ......THE BEE MEETING   212   53
    PURE? WHAT DOES IT MEAN? ....FEVER.   231   1
    DOES NOT MY HEAT ASTOUND YOU. AND MY LIGHT. ....FEVER.   232   40
    HE DOES NOT SMILE OR SMOKE. ....DEATH & CO.   254   20
    THE OTHER DOES THAT, ...DEATH & CO.   254   21
    DOES THE SEA ....MYSTIC   269   25
    WITH WINTER AS YOU CLAIM IT DOES. THE COAL ....DIALOGUE O.   277   19
    DOES HE WRITE C FOR G? NO. HE DARTS ...DIALOGUE OVER A OUIJA BOARD   284 276
DOESN'T (5)
    THE STONE FACE OF THE MAN WHO DOESN'T FEEL, ...THE RAVAGED FACE   116   10
    SKIN DOESN'T HAVE ROOTS, IT PEELS AWAY EASY AS PAPER. ....FACE LIFT   156   20
    SHE DOESN'T NEED FOOD, SHE IS ONE OF THE REAL SAINTS. ...IN PLASTER   158   4
    BUT SHE'LL SOON FIND OUT THAT THAT DOESN'T MATTER A BIT. *IN PLASTER   160   54
    BUT EVEN HER TONNAGE DOESN'T IMPRESS A DIAMOND. ....THE RIVAL/DR   291   24
D'OEUVRES (1)
    FOR FEAST THE SWEETEST MEAT OF HELL'S CHEF D'OEUVRES: .....TERMINAL   328   11
DOFF (1)
    KNIGHTS MIGHT DOFF THEIR CASQUES. THE CRABS ....MUSSEL HUNTER.   96   28
DOG (5)
    DOG THAT I AM, HOW ....WORDS FOR A NURSERY   73   12
    BLUE SUEDE A DOG OR FOX HAS CHEWED. ....BLUE MOLES   126   4
    OF CARDBOARD CARTONS THE COLOR OF CEMENT OR A DOG PACK ...BURNING.   204   11
    CONDONING THE BEAK, THE CLAW, THE GRIN OF THE DOG ....THE SWARM   216   22
    A DOG PICKED UP YOUR DOGGY HUSBAND. HE WENT ON. ....LESBOS   229   63
DOGBODY (1)
    DOGBODY NOSES THE PETALS. THEY BLOOM UNSIDE DOWN. POEM.1.WHO.   131   11
DOG-FACED (1)
    A DOG-FACED SEA. ....POINT SHIRLEY   111   39
DOGGED (1)
    LIGHTS OUT, THEY DOGGED US, SLEEPLESS AND ENVIOUS: ...THE OTHER TWO   68   28
DOGGY (1)
    A DOG PICKED UP YOUR DOGGY HUSBAND. HE WENT ON. ....LESBOS   229   63
DOG-HEAD (1)
    DOG-HEAD, DEVOURER: POEM.3.MAENAD.   133   16
DOGS (3)
    DROVE THE DOGS TO CRINGE AND WHINE, ...THE DEATH OF MYTH-MAKING   104   13
    THE DOGS ARE TEARING A FOX. THIS IS WHAT IT IS LIKE -- ....BURNING.   205   49
    THE CLEVER WOOLLY DOGS HAVE HAD THEIR DAY ....DENOUEMENT   326   7
DOING (8)
    DOING NOTHING. JULY'S JUICE ROUNDS THEIR NUBS. ....MOONRISE   98   3
    WE SLEPT LIKE STONES. LADY, WHAT AM I DOING ....LEAVING EARLY   146   42
    LOOPING WOOL, DOING NOTHING IN PARTICULAR, ...HEAVY WOMEN   158   16
    DOING THINGS WITH THEIR HANDS, ONE JUST THE SAME AS ANOTHER, *TULIPS   160   13
    WHAT WAS SHE DOING WHEN IT BLEW IN ....THE DETECTIVE   208   1
    THIS IS THE EASY TIME, THERE IS NOTHING DOING. ....WINTERING   217   1
    THE WET DAWN INKS ARE DOING THEIR BLUE DISSOLVE. ......WINTER TREES   257   1
    I'VE DREAMED OF DOING IT AGAIN. AND NOW *DIALOGUE OVER A OUIJA BOARD   285 303
DOINGS (1)
    UNDO THE DOINGS OF THE FATHERING AGE: *SONG FOR A REVOLUTIONARY LOVE   323   5
DOKTOR (1)
    SO, SO, HERR DOKTOR. ....LADY LAZARUS   246   65
DOLL (7)
    TO THE BEHEADED HEAD OF A SULLEN DOLL, ONE BRAID, ...PERSEUS   83   37
    SMALL AS A DOLL IN MY DRESS OF INNOCENCE ....ELECTRA ON AZALEA PATH   116   11

	TITLE	PAGE	LINE

DOLL (CONT.)
```
    THE OLD MAN SHRANK TO A DOLL. ....................POEM.3.MAENAD.    133    7
    FLEW OFF LIKE THE HAT OF A DOLL  ........................POEM.7.S.   136    4
    ALREADY YOUR DOLL GRIP LETS GO.  ............PARLIAMENT HILL FIELDS  152   25
    A LIVING DOLL, EVERYWHERE YOU LOOK.  ...............THE APPLICANT    221   33
    DOLL HE GUARDS LIKE A HEART --  ..............................PURDAH  244   54
DOLLAR (1)
    AND MY EVERY CHIMERICAL DOLLAR  ...................DIALOGUE EN ROUTE  308   16
DOLLS (2)
    I SEE US FLOATING THERE YET, INSEPARABLE -- TWO CORK DOLLS.  ..BABY.  175   41
    A HOSPITAL OF DOLLS.  .................................GETTING THERE  248   28
DOLL'S (1)
    THE WAX IMAGE OF MYSELF, A DOLL'S BODY.  ...............POEM.6.W.     135    3
DOLOROUS (1)
    HOOVES, DOLOROUS BELLS ---  ...........................SHEEP IN FOG   262    7
DOLT (1)
    FOR THRIFTY CHILDREN, NOR DOLT PIG RIPE FOR HECKLING,  ..........SOW   60   13
DOMAIN (1)
    KING EGG-HEAD SAW HIS DOMAIN CRACK,  ...............NATURAL HISTORY   71   10
DOME (2)
    THE SKY'S FAR DOME IS SANE AND CLEAR.  ...................BLUE MOLES  126   10
    CHALLENGES THE SILENT DOME.  .............METAMORPHOSES OF THE MOON  307   12
DOMED (1)
    THE DOMED STATE HOUSE.  ...........................A WINTER'S TALE    86    4
DOMES (4)
    DISPLACED THEIR DOMES AS TINY  .........MUSSEL HUNTER AT ROCK HARBOR   96   27
    THE GILT AND PINK DOMES OF RUSSIA MELT AND FLOAT OFF  .....THE SWARM  216   15
    NOW WE, RETURNING FROM THE VAULTED DOMES  ...........DOOM OF EXILES  318    1
    RIDING HOME FROM CREDULOUS BLUE DOMES,  ...................TERMINAL  328    1
DOMESTICITY (1)
    O THE DOMESTICITY OF THESE WINDOWS,  ..........THE MUNICH MANNEQUINS  263   21
DOMINANCE (1)
    TO REDRESS THE DOMINANCE OF ROCKS AND WOODS,  .............TWO CAMP.  144    2
DOMINATE (1)
    BRONZE DEAD DOMINATE THE FLOOR,  ...........................SCULPTOR   91   14
DOMINION (1)
    DOMINION. THE STARS ARE NO NEARER.  .....................POEM.5.F.    134    6
DOMINOES (1)
    DOMINOES OF THEIR DOORWAYS. SUN GRAINS THEIR CROW-COLORS,  ....NET-.  121    6
DONE (11)
    SO HUMBLY DONE, I'D TURN THIS KEEN  ...........................RHYME   50   13
    A SAMURAI DEATH MASK DONE  ............MUSSEL HUNTER AT ROCK HARBOR   97   80
    NOW SHE'S DONE FOR, THE DEWLAPPED LADY  ...................FACE LIFT  156   25
    I HAVE DONE IT AGAIN.  .....................................LADY LAZARUS  244    1
    SOMEBODY'S DONE FOR.  ....................................DEATH & CO.  255   31
    DYING TO FLY AND BE DONE WITH IT?  ...........................YEARS   255   11
    IT'S DONE. IT'S DONE, AND THERE'S NO MENDING HIM.  ......DIALOGUE O.  285  304
    IT'S DONE. IT'S DONE, AND THERE'S NO MENDING HIM.  ......DIALOGUE O.  285  304
    NOVEMBER'S DONE WITH. THE BLOWN LEAVES MAKE BAT-SHAPES, *DIALOGUE O.  286  337
    DISGUISE BEGUILES AND MORTAL MISCHIEF'S DONE:  .........ADMONITIONS  319   14
    THEN, THIS TOUGH STINT DONE, SHE CURTSIES  ...............AERIALIST   331   25
DONKEY (2)
    WRAPPED IN FLEA-RIDDEN DONKEY SKINS,  ...............THE THIN PEOPLE   64   18
    TAIL ON EACH TOY DONKEY THAT WILL BRAY   DIALOGUE OVER A OUIJA BOARD  283  250
DONKEY-CARTS (1)
    WHOLE DONKEY-CARTS FULL  .............................FIESTA MELONS   46    2
DONNA (1)
    THOUGH PRIMA DONNA POUTS AND CRITIC STINGS,  .....LOVE IS A PARALLAX  330   56
DONNER (1)
    DONNER, BLITZEN,  .....................................A WINTER'S TALE   87   20
DON'T (21)
    "I DON'T ASK YOU TO SPIN SOME RIDICULOUS FABLE  .........DIALOGUE B.   39   22
    THOR IS ANGRY: WE DON'T CARE!"  ...............THE DISQUIETING MUSES   75   23
    INMATES WHO DON'T HIBERNATE.  ..........................POEM.1.WHO.   131   15
    IF I DON'T MOVE ABOUT, I'LL KNOCK NOTHING OVER. SO I SAID,*POEM.6.W.   135   14
    OVER THEIR IRON STILE. AND STILL DON'T SLEEP.  ....ZOO KEEPER'S WIFE  155   40
    I DON'T KNOW A THING.  ....................................FACE LIFT  156   16
    THE SEA CANNONS INTO THEIR EAR, BUT THEY DON'T BUDGE.  ...FINISTERRE  169    8
    DON'T KNOW WHAT TO MAKE OF THE SUDDEN SLIPPINESS,  .....NEW YEAR ON.  176    4
    TODDLE ON HOME, AND DON'T TRIP ON THE NURSE! --  ...........THE TOUR  238   42
    DO NOT THINK I DON'T NOTICE YOUR CURTAIN --  .........EAVESDROPPER    260   28
    UNDER YOUR FINGER? I MEAN, YOU DON'T PUSH  .............DIALOGUE O.   277   33
    EVEN A LITTLE? YOU KNOW I DON'T, AND STILL ...  ......DIALOGUE O.     277   34
    YOU DON'T QUITE BELIEVE IN IT. YOU'RE DEAF TO REAL  .....DIALOGUE O.  278   63
    DANGERS, BUT DON'T MIND HEARING ABOUT THE ONES  .........DIALOGUE O.  278   64
    ALWAYS, THE GLASS WILL BLURT WHAT I DON'T WANT  .........DIALOGUE O.  278   68
    NOW, YOU REALLY DON'T MUCH CARE WHICH, OR WHAT  .........DIALOGUE O.  280  151
    IS SMALL THESE DAYS. DON'T BE SO SMART. *DIALOGUE OVER A OUIJA BOARD  281  204
    OF WATER. WAIT. GODPIE I DON'T BEGRUDGE *DIALOGUE OVER A OUIJA BOARD  282  213
    FOR ROT. DON'T THINK YOU HAD ME FOOLED. I KNEW  .........DIALOGUE O.  283  263
    A THIRD TIME. DON'T GLOAT. YOUR WILL MISFIRED TWICE  ....DIALOGUE O.  284  281
    "DON'T," PLEADED THE LITTLE GIRL  ...............BITTER STRAWBERRIES  299   22
DOOM (8)
    DOOM CONSUMMATES THAT APPETITE.  ............................PURSUIT   22   20
    "THE DAY OF DOOM  ................DIALOGUE BETWEEN GHOST AND PRIEST   39   37
```

	TITLE	PAGE	LINE

DOOM (CONT.)
THE DOOM MARK ....CONTUSION 271 8
HIS DRIFT ENDORSES YOUR INKLINGS OF A DOOM ....DIALOGUE O. 281 190
WE IGNORE THE COMING DOOM OF GOLD ....GOLD MOUTHS CRY 302 7
PLOTS DOOM FROM ABOVE, ...TRIO OF LOVE SONGS 314 14
DOOM OF EXILES ....DOOM OF EXILES 318 T
MY DEMON OF DOOM TILTS ON A TRAPEZE, ...CIRCUS IN THREE RINGS 322 15
DOOMCRACK (1)
A FLASH LIKE DOOMCRACK RENT NIGHT'S BLACK: ....CRYSTAL GAZER 55 37
DOOM-NOISE (1)
SOULS, ROLLED IN THE DOOM-NOISE OF THE SEA. ....FINISTERRE 169 14
DOOMSDAY (3)
THOUGH DOOMSDAY BUD. NEGLECT'S ....VIRGIN IN A TREE 82 41
RULED DECREE OF DOOMSDAY ON THE FLOOR. ....THE TRIAL OF MAN 312 4
DOOMSDAY ....DOOMSDAY 316 T
DOOMSTRUCK (2)
AS THE DOOMSTRUCK CITY CRUMBLES BLOCK BY BLOCK: ....DOOMSDAY 316 8
TO TRUMPET-TOPPLING DAWN OF DOOMSTRUCK DAY: ....THE DEAD 320 11
DOOR (22)
I BOLT THE DOOR, EACH DOOR I BOLT. ....PURSUIT 23 47
I BOLT THE DOOR, EACH DOOR I BOLT. ....PURSUIT 23 47
NOW, RUN TO FAT, SHE'S A SPINSTER WHOSE DOOR SHUTS ...ELLA MASON A. 54 17
WE PEERED AGOG THROUGH THE COBWEBBED DOOR ....ELLA MASON A. 54 26
MAZE OF BARNS TO THE LINTEL OF THE SUNK STY DOOR ....SOW 60 9
FROM THE DOOR AS EVER. WHAT HAPPENS BETWEEN US ....BLUE MOLES 127 34
IT IS EASY TO BLAME THE DARK: THE MOUTH OF A DOOR, ...POEM.6.W. 135 7
OUR FOOT'S IN THE DOOR. ....MUSHROOMS 140 33
THE MOON IS NO DOOR. IT IS A FACE IN ITS OWN RIGHT, ...MOON. 173 8
WHAT KEYHOLE HAVE WE SLIPPED THROUGH, WHAT DOOR HAS SHUT? ....BABY. 175 42
YOU PEER FROM THE DOOR, ...LESBOS 229 82
SIMPLY OPEN THE DOOR AND STEP OUT OF THE CAR ....STOPPED DEAD 230 24
IS IT A TIGER THIS YEAR, THIS ROAR AT THE DOOR? ....YEARS 255 18
SMIRK. SAINTS' DOOR APART, BACKDOOR'S A DOOR, ...DIALOGUE O. 280 131
SMIRK. SAINTS' DOOR APART, BACKDOOR'S A DOOR, ...DIALOGUE O. 280 131
ARGUMENT TO THE HOUSE NEXT DOOR. OR IF DIALOGUE OVER A OUIJA BOARD 280 166
MIGHT RANGE IN IT. I ONLY SHUT THE DOOR *DIALOGUE OVER A OUIJA BOARD 286 344
A CAR DOOR SLAM; VOICES COMING NEAR; ....FAMILY REUNION 300 2
THE DOOR NOW OPENS FROM WITHIN. ....FAMILY REUNION 300 10
OF DESTINY, DELIVERED TO THE DOOR ....THE TRIAL OF MAN 312 2
BEHIND THE ZODIAC ON ATTIC DOOR ....THE PRINCESS AND THE GOBLINS 335 58
OF THE WOLF AT THE DOOR. ....TEMPER OF TIME 336 20
DOORBELL (1)
THE DOORBELL RENDS THE NOONDAY HEAT ....FAMILY REUNION 300 5
DOORMAN (1)
GODS GROW TOO PROUD TO PRACTICE DOORMAN DUTIES ....DIALOGUE O. 280 127
DOORS (6)
I SHUT MY DOORS ON THAT DARK GUILT, ...PURSUIT 23 46
BEHIND SHUT DOORS; THE DAIRY HERDS ....HARDCASTLE CRAGS 63 32
THAT CABINET WITHOUT WINDOWS OR DOORS: ....THE OTHER TWO 68 17
THE WREATHED DOORS OPEN TO THE CROWD. ....A WINTER'S TALE 87 26
COY PAPER STRIPS FOR DOORS -- ....LESBOS 227 5
HANDS WILL BE OPENING DOORS AND SETTING ......THE MUNICH MANNEQUINS 263 18
DOORSILL (2)
LAUGH-SHAKEN ON HIS DOORSILL, ...THE HERMIT AT OUTERMOST HOUSE 119 10
CAPER ON LEAFSTALK LEGS ACROSS MY DOORSILL, EPITAPH IN THREE PARTS 337 24
DOORSTEP (3)
BY THE DOORSTEP ....THE SNOWMAN ON THE MOOR 58 8
NO ANIMAL SPOILS ON HER GREEN DOORSTEP. ....THE BURNT-OUT SPA 138 30
WHAT DID I LEAVE UNTOUCHED ON THE DOORSTEP -- ....THE OTHER 201 2
DOORSTEPS (1)
HOLLOW DOORSTEPS GO FROM GRASS TO GRASS; ....WUTHERING HEIGHTS 168 31
DOORWAY (1)
EAT ME. WASTEBASKET GAPER, SHADOW OF DOORWAY. POEM.1.WHO. 132 27
DOORWAYS (3)
DOMINOES OF THEIR DOORWAYS. SUN GRAINS THEIR CROW-COLORS, ...NET-. 121 6
DRIVES PRIEST AND PROSTITUTE IN DOORWAYS, ...INSOLENT STORM. 326 15
IN DUBIOUS DOORWAYS FORGET THEIR MONDAY NAMES, ..LOVE IS A PARALLAX 329 32
DOPED (2)
FLATTEN THE DOPED SNAKES TO RIBBON. IN HERE, THE GRASSES *PRIVATE G. 130 17
I'M DOPED AND THICK FROM MY LAST SLEEPING PILL. ....LESBOS 228 34
DORDOGNE (1)
STARS OVER THE DORDOGNE ....STARS OVER THE DORDOGNE 165 T
DOUANIER (1)
A SESTINA FOR THE DOUANIER ..YADWIGHA, ON A RED COUCH, AMONG LILIES 85 ST
DOUBLE (4)
OF DOUBLE STAR-EYES LIT ....FAUN 35 9
WHOSE STARK ACT ALL COMING DOUBLE LUCK JOINS. ..WREATH FOR A BRIDAL 44 6
LIMBS: NOT A BASILISK-BLINK, NOR A DOUBLE WHAMMY, ...PERSEUS 83 16
THE BLAND GRANTA DOUBLE THEIR WHITE AND GREEN ....WATERCOLOR. 112 9
DOUBLECROSS (1)
TO DOUBLECROSS THE FIRMAMENT. ..INSOLENT STORM STRIKES AT THE SKULL 326 28
DOUBLE-HUMPED (1)
OUTLANDISH AS DOUBLE-HUMPED CAMELS OR UNICORNS, ...THE EYE-MOTE 109 13
DOUBLENESS (1)
BASTARDIES, USAGES, DESERTIONS AND DOUBLENESS, ...COURAGE. 210 7

138

	TITLE	PAGE	LINE

DOUBLES (1)
IN THE MIRROR THEIR DOUBLES BACK THEM UP. ....LEAVING EARLY 146 34
DOUBLING (1)
DOUBLING THEMSELVES IN A GLASS ....LORELEI 94 8
DOUBT (2)
"NO DOUBT NOW IN DREAM-PROPERTIED FALL SOME MOON-EYED, ..CONJURING. 66 33
THE FACT OF DOUBT, THE FAITH OF DREAM. ...METAMORPHOSES OF THE MOON 308 48
DOUBTING (1)
MAY TESTIFY TO DRIVE YOUR DOUBTING OUT. *DIALOGUE OVER A OUIJA BOARD 280 153
DOUCE (1)
ANGELS -- MORE FEMININE AND DOUCE ....A WINTER'S TALE 86 9
DOUGH (1)
WORKING IT LIKE DOUGH, A MULATTO BODY, ...LESBOS 229 61
DOUGHTY (1)
TO SUMMON IN HER SLIGHT ALL DOUGHTY MEN ....THE QUEEN'S COMPLAINT 29 17
DOUR (4)
STRUCK BY EACH DOUR YEAR. ....STRUMPET SONG 34 13
TO ELEGIAC DRYADS, AND DOUR GRASS ....NOVEMBER GRAVEYARD 56 3
ASSAULT OF SNOW-FLAWED WINDS FROM THE DOUR SKIES ....MAYFLOWER 60 2
IN THE DOUR AGES ....A LESSON IN VENGEANCE 80 1
DOUR-FACED (1)
NOW, DOUR-FACED, HER FINGERS ....VIRGIN IN A TREE 82 38
DOURLY (1)
DOURLY THE LONG HOTS AND COLDS, ...THE HERMIT AT OUTERMOST HOUSE 119 8
DOUSING (1)
FOR THE RELISH OF HEAVEN, RELENTLESS, DOUSING WITH PRICKLES *LESSON. 80 14
DOVE (4)
OF TENDERNESS DOVE THROUGH THEIR PURGATORY ....THE OTHER TWO 68 24
TO THAT SPUMIEST DOVE. ....POINT SHIRLEY 111 47
THE BOLD GULLS DOVE AS IF THEY OWNED IT ALL. ....THE BABYSITTERS 175 37
LIKE AN OLIVE-BEAKED DOVE ABOVE THE ENGULFING FACT: ....DIALOGUE O. 279 112
DOVELIKE (2)
AND LOVERS AFFABLE, DOVELIKE. ....IN MIDAS' COUNTRY 99 15
LIKE BLUE MARY'S ANGEL, DOVELIKE AGAINST A PANE ....WIDOW 165 38
DOVES (2)
AND USED HER GENTLE DOVES WITH MANNERS RUDE; THE QUEEN'S COMPLAINT 28 7
AND ALL I COULD SEE WAS DANGERS: DOVES AND WORDS, ...THREE WOMEN 178 47
DOVE'S (1)
BY THE DOVE'S ANNIHILATION, ...BRASILIA 259 22
DOWN (91)
WHICH HUNGERS TO HAUL THE WHITE REFLECTION DOWN. WINTER LANDSCAPE, 21 5
THERE IS A PANTHER STALKS ME DOWN: ....PURSUIT 22 1
FANTASTIC FLESH DOWN TO THE HONEST BONE. ....TALE OF A TUB 25 24
KNOCKING OUR BROTHERS DOWN, WE STRIKE A STANCE ....CHANNEL CROSSING 27 27
WHICH HAULS DOWN BUCK, COCK, TROUT, TILL ALL MOST FAIR ....FIRESONG 30 6
TO DEVOUR AND DRAG HER DOWN ....MISS DRAKE PROCEEDS TO SUPPER 41 12
NEEDLING SPUMILY DOWN FROM THE WIRES: ....ALICANTE LULLABY 43 10
DOWN DEEP INTO THE BENT BULL-NECK. CUMBROUS ROUTINE, NOT ARTWORK. ...
... THE GORING 47 7
WE SNICKERED AS SHE SHAMBLED DOWN SOMERSET TERRACE ...ELLA MASON A. 54 32
THAT VAIN JADES SULK SINGLE DOWN BRIDAL NIGHTS, ...ELLA MASON A. 54 41
SKIN WORN DOWN TO THE KNUCKLEBONES ....CRYSTAL GAZER 54 3
DOWN FROM PRIDE'S SIZE: INSTEAD, A GRISLY-THEWED, ...SNOWMAN O. 59 29
THE LONG WIND, PARING HER PERSON DOWN ....HARDCASTLE CRAGS 63 22
HER DOWN TO MERE QUARTZ GRIT IN THAT STONY LIGHT ..HARDCASTLE CRAGS 63 44
STARVING MY FANTASY DOWN ....ON THE PLETHORA OF DRYADS 67 8
OUR OWN GRIST DOWN TO ITS BONY FACE. ....ALL THE DEAD DEARS 70 12
WHERE THE DAFT FATHER WENT DOWN ....ALL THE DEAD DEARS 71 23
DOWN: THE BODY WEIGHS LIKE STONE. ....THE GREAT CARBUNCLE 73 30
THAT NEVER BRIGHTENS OR GOES DOWN. ....THE DISQUIETING MUSES 76 53
I SHALL GO DOWN THE SHABBY STAIR AND MEET,*ON THE DECLINE OF ORACLES 78 27
IN GOING UP FOR THE COMING DOWN IF THE POST ....ABOVE THE OXBOW 88 18
ALL'S PEACE AND DISCIPLINE DOWN THERE. TILL LATELY WE ....OXBOW 89 53
DIDN'T GO DOWN IN SUCH A HURRY. HOW IT MEMOIRS OF A SPINACH-PICKER 89 2
HAND ALOFT, GOODBYE, GOODBYE, NOT DOWN .....THE GHOST'S LEAVETAKING 90 23
WAIST DOWN, YOU MAY WIND ....FULL FATHOM FIVE 93 33
STONE, STONE, FERRY ME DOWN THERE. ....LORELEI 95 36
A PIGEON RUDDERS DOWN. ITS FAN-TAIL'S WHITE. ....MOONRISE 98 7
AGAINST MY LEANING DOWN, WOULD NOT EXCHANGE ..........INCOMMUNICADO 100 5
YEARS, GO DOWN TO DRINK THE RIVER: ....CHILD'S PARK STONES 101 29
YET THE DAPPLE TONING HIS WHITE DOWN ....WHITENESS I REMEMBER 102 10
THE BULL SURGED UP, THE BULL SURGED DOWN, ...THE BULL OF BENDYLAW 108 16
AND RIDE THAT FLUX AT ANCHOR, UPSIDE DOWN. ....WATERCOLOR. 112 11
SAWS DOWN A REED AND SWIMS FROM HIS LIMBER GROVE, ...WATERCOLOR. 112 23
MY MOTHER DREAMED YOU FACE DOWN IN THE SEA. ELECTRA ON AZALEA PATH 117 36
THE GOLDEN RAIN TREE DRIPS ITS POWDERS DOWN. ....BEEKEEPER'S. 118 9
KEEP HOUSE AMONG THE GRASSES. KNEELING DOWN*THE BEEKEEPER'S DAUGHTER 118 16
HALFWAY DOWN FROM GROVES WHERE THE THIN, BITTER ALMOND PIPS ..NET-. 121 2
DOWN THERE ONE IS ALONE. ....BLUE MOLES 126 27
DOWN THERE THE LATE YEAR ....DARK WOOD, DARK WATER 127 12
DOWN BOLES OF THE FIR. ....DARK WOOD, DARK WATER 127 24
DOGBODY NOSES THE PETALS. THEY BLOOM UNSIDE DOWN. POEM.1.WHO. 131 11
DOWN HERE THE SKY IS ALWAYS FALLING. POEM.4.BEAST. 134 20
NOW COLDNESS COMES SIFTING DOWN, LAYER AFTER LAYER, ...POEM.5.F. 134 1
BOW DOWN, A LOCAL CONSTELLATION, ...LEAVING EARLY 145 11

DOWN (CONT.)
   UPSIDE DOWN HEARTS OF LIGHT TIPPING WAX FINGERS, ...CANDLES 148   2
   GRINDS ROUND, BEARING DOWN WITH THE STRAW, ...HEAVY WOMEN 158 20
   THEY ARE SUBTLE: THEY SEEM TO FLOAT, THOUGH THEY WEIGH ME DOWN, ...
                                                     TULIPS 161 40
   IT IS MORE NATURAL TO ME, LYING DOWN. ....I AM VERTICAL 162 17
   AND I SHALL BE USEFUL WHEN I LIE DOWN FINALLY: ....I AM VERTICAL 162 19
   EACH GESTURE FLEES IMMEDIATELY DOWN AN ALLEY ....INSOMNIAC 163 23
   A BLACKBERRY ALLEY, GOING DOWN IN HOOKS, AND A SEA ...BLACKBERRYING 168   3
   THEY DO NOT COME FROM THE BAY OF THE DEAD DOWN THERE, ...FINISTERRE 170 33
   THE SUN FLAMED STRAIGHT DOWN THAT NOON ON THE WATER OFF
      MARBLEHEAD. ....THE BABYSITTERS 174   2
   THEN STEPPED DOWN THE STEEP BEACH SHELF AND INTO THE WATER. ..BABY. 175 39
   THE SUN IS DOWN. I DIE. I MAKE A DEATH. ....THREE WOMEN 181 161
   LET US SIT DOWN TO IT, ONE ON EITHER SIDE, ADMIRING THE GLEAM, ...
                         ... A BIRTHDAY PRESENT 207 24
   ONLY LET DOWN THE VEIL, THE VEIL, THE VEIL. .....A BIRTHDAY PRESENT 208 55
   IT MUST BE SHOT DOWN. POM! POM! ....THE SWARM 216 19
   AND MY CHILD -- LOOK AT HER, FACE DOWN ON THE FLOOR, ...LESBOS 227   8
   HE LUMPS IT DOWN THE PLASTIC COBBLED HILL, ...LESBOS 228 48
   HE IS HUGGING HIS BALL AND CHAIN DOWN BY THE GATE ....LESBOS 229 73
   IS THAT SPAIN DOWN THERE? ....STOPPED DEAD 230   7
   DOWN THE DRAIN WITH ALL OF IT! ....AMNESIAC 233 11
   DOWN SHOES FOR A POLISH OF CARBON ....THE MUNICH MANNEQUINS 263 19
   CRAWLS DOWN THE WALL. ....CONTUSION 271   9
   DOWN TO A CIRCLE OF LETTERS: TWENTY-SIX *DIALOGUE OVER A OUIJA BOARD 276 13
   AS IF BLOODHOUNDS BORE HIM DOWN. I-N-C-O ....DIALOGUE O. 283 275
   DEATH'S TWO DREAMS DOWN WITH THE BODY THAT BLED THE VEIN, ...
                     ... DIALOGUE OVER A OUIJA BOARD 285 329
   SOME DUCKS STEP DOWN OFF THEIR GREEN-REEDED SHELF ....QUEEN MARY'S. 290 11
   SQUATTED DOWN BETWEEN THE ROWS ....BITTER STRAWBERRIES 299   3
   CAME SLIDING DOWN HIS SHOULDERBLADES ....GOLD MOUTHS CRY 302   5
   DOWN WHERE SOUND ....AQUATIC NOCTURNE 306 25
   FOR RECREATION DOWN UNDER THE COVERS: ....DIALOGUE EN ROUTE 309 23
   DOWN THE DARK IN A BLACK HEARSE ....THE DREAM 310   8
   WHERE THE BLACK WAVE TOPPLES DOWN; ....GO GET THE GOODLY SQUAB 313 22
   A SCOWL OF SUN STRUCK DOWN MY MOTHER, ...LAMENT 315 10
   FRACTURED GLASS FLIES DOWN IN SMITHEREENS; ....DOOMSDAY 316 10
   ERECTED DOWN THE GANGWAYS OF OUR MIND. ....DOOM OF EXILES 318   4
   DOWN AMONG STRICT ROOTS AND ROCKS, ...DANSE MACABRE 320   1
   TILL UNRULY CHILDREN STREAM DOWN THE SKY ......SONG FOR A REVOLU. 323 14
   TO PITCH THE WHITE WORLD DOWN IN SWIVELING FLOOD, ..SONNET TO SATAN 323   6
   SHUTS DOWN ITS FABLED SUMMER HOUSE; ....TWO LOVERS. 327   2
   TO KNOCK THEM DOWN WITH LOGIC OR WITH LUCK ......LOVE IS A PARALLAX 329 20
   LIKE AN ENORMOUS OYSTER, DOWN ....LOVE IS A PARALLAX 329 27
   THE MOON LEANS DOWN TO LOOK; THE TILTING FISH ...LOVE IS A PARALLAX 330 37
   THEN LET THE BLUE TENT TOPPLE, STARS RAIN DOWN, LOVE IS A PARALLAX 330 73
   AND SERENELY PLUMMETS DOWN ....AERIALIST 331 26
   HER LEGENDARY GODMOTHER LEANS DOWN, ...THE PRINCESS AND THE GOBLINS 333 15
   OF THAT MERCURIAL STRAND, THE GIRL GOES DOWN ....THE PRINCESS. 334 27
   SHE TELLS THE GREENHORN MINER TO BOW DOWN ....THE PRINCESS. 335 61
   THE THIRD CRIES OUT AS ALL THE SHIPS GO DOWN:*EPITAPH IN THREE PARTS 337 10
DOWNFALL (1)
   EVERY DOWNFALL AND CRASH ....STREET SONG   36 27
DOWNWARD (1)
   WHERE NOTHING HIGHER'S TO BE LOOKED TO. DOWNWARD LOOKS ......OXBOW.   88 30
DOZE (2)
   DOZE BEHIND THE OLD MASKS OF FURY. ......SLEEP IN THE MOJAVE DESERT 144 19
   AND YOU DOZE ON, NOSE TO THE WALL. ....LEAVING EARLY 146 38
DOZED (1)
   THE ARMADILLO DOZED IN HIS SANDBIN ....ZOO KEEPER'S WIFE 155 20
DOZEN (3)
   A DOZEN RED LEAD SINKERS ROUND MY NECK. ....TULIPS 161 42
   BUT A DOZEN WOULD BE WORTH HAVING, ...PHEASANT 191 16
   SAYS THERE ARE A DOZEN OR TWO. ....DADDY 223 21
DOZENS (1)
   DOZENS DROPPED DEAD IN THE HEDGES: O SHE FELT ....SNOWMAN O.   59 35
DOZER (1)
   NO POCKET DOZER, ...WORDS FOR A NURSERY   73 18
DOZING (1)
   DOZING AROUND THEIR SILVERED SENTRY BOX*THE PRINCESS AND THE GOBLINS 334 30
DRAB (1)
   OF HER HAND, THE HOUSE STILL HUGS IN EACH DRAB ....POINT SHIRLEY 110 20
DRABBLED (1)
   FOR THE ROCK'S DWARFED LUMP, FOR THE DRABBLED SCUM, ...GREEN ROCK. 105 23
DRAFT (1)
   "THE DRAFT IS PASSED," THE WOMAN SAID. ....BITTER STRAWBERRIES 299 20
DRAFTIER (1)
   OF DRAFTY CELLS AND DRAFTIER CASTLES, ...A LESSON IN VENGEANCE   80   2
DRAFTINESS (1)
   THE VOICE OF GOD IS FULL OF DRAFTINESS, ...WIDOW 164 22
DRAFTS (4)
   SHE LET IN THE DRAFTS AND BECAME MORE AND MORE ABSENT-MINDED. ...
                                   ... IN PLASTER 159 32
   GULL-COLORED LACES FLAP IN THE SEA DRAFTS ....FINISTERRE 170 28

	TITLE	PAGE	LINE

DRAFTS (CONT.)
    SMELLING THE DAWN DRAFTS. ....THE SURGEON AT 2 A.M. 171 46
    TARTING WITH THE DRAFTS THAT PASS, ...EAVESDROPPER 260 31
DRAFTY (3)
    OF DRAFTY CELLS AND DRAFTIER CASTLES, ...A LESSON IN VENGEANCE 80 2
    GULLS STIFFEN TO THEIR CHILL VIGIL IN THE DRAFTY HALF-LIGHT; ...
        ... PARLIAMENT HILL FIELDS 153 49
    IN A DRAFTY MUSEUM, YOUR NAKEDNESS ....MORNING SONG 157 5
DRAG (6)
    TO DEVOUR AND DRAG HER DOWN ....MISS DRAKE PROCEEDS TO SUPPER 41 12
    WHO DRAG OUR ANCIENT FATHER AT THE HEEL, ...MOONRISE 98 28
    DRAG UP FALSE, EDWARDIAN SENTIMENTS, ...CANDLES 149 16
    THE MOON, ALSO, IS MERCILESS: SHE WOULD DRAG ME ....ELM 192 22
    HER BLACKS CRACKLE AND DRAG. ....EDGE 273 20
    LEST THE WATER DRAG YOU TO DROWN. ....GO GET THE GOODLY SQUAB 313 24
DRAGGED (3)
    DRAGGED EACH DAZZLED SENSE APART ....ON THE PLETHORA OF DRYADS 67 26
    I AM DRAGGED BY THE HORSES, THE IRON HOOVES. ....THREE WOMEN 180 128
    DRAGGED ITS BLOOD BAG, SICK ....LESBOS 229 54
DRAGGING (10)
    A BLUE MIST IS DRAGGING THE LAKE. ....THE MANOR GARDEN 125 4
    A WOMAN IS DRAGGING HER SHADOW IN A CIRCLE ....A LIFE 150 21
    ASIDE WERE DRAGGING ME IN FOUR DIRECTIONS. ....THREE WOMEN 178 58
    IS IT BLOOD CLOTS THE TENDRILS ARE DRAGGING UP THAT STRING? ...BEE. 211 19
    DRAGGING THEIR JESUS HAIR ....MEDUSA 225 11
    DRAGGING TREES -- ....PURDAH 242 14
    I AM DRAGGING MY BODY ....GETTING THERE 248 10
    THE TRAIN IS DRAGGING ITSELF, IT IS SCREAMING --- ....GETTING THERE 249 55
    SHOVE INTO BEING, DRAGGING ....THALIDOMIDE 252 14
    FOR YES, DRAGGING OUR FINGERS AFTER. HOW*DIALOGUE OVER A OUIJA BOARD 278 75
DRAGGLED (1)
    WHERE THE WAKING HEAD RUBBISHES OUT THE DRAGGLED LOT ......GHOST'S. 90 3
DRAGNET (1)
    A DRAGNET, RISING, FALLING, AS WAVES ....FULL FATHOM FIVE 92 5
DRAGON (1)
    SORROW; WEEP FOR THE LEGENDARY DRAGON. ....SONNET: TO TIME 311 12
DRAGONFLY (1)
    A PANE OF DRAGONFLY WING, WHEN THEY LEFT ME ....SPINACH-PICKER. 89 5
DRAGONS (1)
    OF DRAGONS BREATHING WITHOUT THE FRAME OF FABLES, ...LESSON. 80 3
DRAGON'S (1)
    TO SLAY SPAWN OF DRAGON'S TEETH: SPEAKING THIS PROMISE, ..WREATH F. 45 23
DRAGS (2)
    IT DRAGS THE SEA AFTER IT LIKE A DARK CRIME; IT IS QUIET .....MOON. 173 10
    IT IS SHE THAT DRAGS THE BLOOD-BLACK SEA AROUND ....THREE WOMEN 182 186
DRAIN (1)
    DOWN THE DRAIN WITH ALL OF IT! ....AMNESIAC 233 11
DRAINED (1)
    I BEND OVER THIS DRAINED BASIN WHERE THE SMALL FISH PRIVATE GROUND 131 20
DRAINING (2)
    HAS BEEN DRAINING THE GOLDFISH PONDS. ....PRIVATE GROUND 130 8
    TAPPED LIKE A CASK, THE YEARS DRAINING INTO MY PILLOW. ...FACE LIFT 156 18
DRAINS (2)
    DRAINS LIKE WATER OUT THE HOLE AT THE FAR END. ....INSOMNIAC 163 25
    THAT DRAINS ETERNALLY THE MILK OF STARS. ....SONNET: TO TIME 311 14
DRAKE (1)
    MISS DRAKE PROCEEDS TO SUPPER ....MISS DRAKE PROCEEDS TO SUPPER 41 T
DRAMA (1)
    DRAMA OF EACH SEASON ....TRIO OF LOVE SONGS 314 13
DRANK (3)
    THE DAY YOUR SLACK SAIL DRANK MY SISTER'S BREATH ....ELECTRA ON. 117 30
    AND DRANK MY BLOOD FOR A YEAR, ...DADDY 224 73
    YOU DRANK YOUR COFFEE LIKE ORIGINAL SIN, ...THE TRIAL OF MAN 312 6
DRAPED (1)
    WALKING THE PLANK DRAPED WITH MOTHER FRANCE'S UPHOLSTERY THE SWARM 217 48
DRASTIC (1)
    OUR DRASTIC JARGON, BUT CLOCK HANDS THAT MOVE ...LOVE IS A PARALLAX 329 17
DRAUGHTY (1)
    AS THESE DRAUGHTY EPHEMERIDS. ....CANDLES 149 30
DRAW (4)
    EVER BLUR THE INTRANSIGENT LINES WHICH DRAW ....TALE OF A TUB 25 28
    I DRAW ON THE OLD MOUTH. ....THREE WOMEN 183 246
    OF THE FUCHSIA. I COULD DRAW NO BREATH, ...MEDUSA 225 29
    WHAT GOOD IS ALL THAT SPACE IF IT CAN'T DRAW YOU OFF? THE RIVAL/DR 291 13
DRAWER (3)
    HOW IT BREATHES IN THE BUREAU DRAWER! ....A SECRET 220 27
    AS A DESK DRAWER HIDES A POISON PEN LETTER, ...THE RIVAL/DR 291 9
    BUT THERE IS NO DRAWER TO HOLD YOU. ....THE RIVAL/DR 291 10
DRAWING (2)
    STINGS BIG AS DRAWING PINS! ....THE SWARM 217 56
    SEEM A BOTANICAL DRAWING -- ....WINTER TREES 257 3
DRAWN (6)
    THE WORD, DEFINING, MUZZLES; THE DRAWN LINE ....POEMS, POTATOES 106 1
    SHORTENS WITH EACH BREATH DRAWN. ....OLD LADIES' HOME 120 21
    DRAWN LIKE A LONG MATERIAL ....BERCK-PLAGE 197 34

DRAWN (CONT.)
    WISER FOR TONIGHT'S WISE WORDS. I FELT DRAWN ....DIALOGUE O.   285 316
    THICKET OF WORDS. THE CURTAIN'S DRAWN ON THAT. ....DIALOGUE O.   286 352
    SKY WON'T BE DRAWN CLOSER: ABSOLUTE, ...METAMORPHOSES OF THE MOON 307   7
DRAWS (3)
    HOW THE SUN'S POULTICE DRAWS ON MY INFLAMMATION. ....BERCK-PLAGE   196   2
    COLUMN OF DAZZLE DRAWS MY EYES TO THE WALL ....DIALOGUE O.   279   88
    SHE DRAWS APPLAUSE; BRIGHT HARNESS ....AERIALIST   331   23
DREAD (2)
    LESS DREAD OF THE WORLD BEYOND THAN OURS. THAT'S BECAUSE*DIALOGUE O.   278   62
    BY DAY SHE MUST WALK IN DREAD ....AERIALIST   332   44
DREADFUL (1)
    WITH FANGED AND DREADFUL HEAD. ....BATTLE-SCENE   84   18
DREADS (1)
    EACH VIRILE BACHELOR DREADS PARALYSIS, ...NEVER TRY TO TRICK.   320   10
DREAM (30)
    STILL DREAM BEHIND ....SOUTHERN SUNRISE   26   3
    BRAVE LOVE, DREAM ....FIRESONG   30   19
    DREAM WITH CLAM-DIGGERS ....DREAM WITH CLAM-DIGGERS   43   T
    THIS DREAM BUDDED BRIGHT WITH LEAVES AROUND THE EDGES,*DREAM WITH C.   43   1
    THE DREAM-PEOPLED VILLAGE, HER EYES ENTERTAINED NO DREAM, ...
                                          ... HARDCASTLE CRAGS   63   19
    THEIR DREAM OF THE WINTER'S COLD; STONES ....CHILD'S PARK STONES   101   24
    I DREAM THAT I AM OEDIPUS. ....THE EYE-MOTE   109   24
    WE ARE A DREAM THEY DREAM. ....THE SLEEPERS   123   20
    WE ARE A DREAM THEY DREAM. ....THE SLEEPERS   123   20
    A DREAM TREE, POLLY'S TREE: ....POLLY'S TREE   128   1
    A DREAM TREE. POLLY'S TREE ....POLLY'S TREE   129   37
    I AM ACCUSED. I DREAM OF MASSACRES. ....THREE WOMEN   180 148
    NOR DO THESE DRY, DRY GUTTERS DREAM OF RAIN. ....THREE WOMEN   184 279
    I HAD A DREAM OF AN ISLAND, RED WITH CRIES. ....THREE WOMEN   185 307
    IT WAS A DREAM, AND DID NOT MEAN A THING. ....THREE WOMEN   185 308
    SULFUROUS ADULTERIES GRIEVE IN A DREAM. ....THE OTHER   202   25
    SANDS WHERE A DREAM OF CLEAR WATER ....BURNING THE LETTERS   204   7
    DREAM OF A DUEL THEY WILL WIN INEVITABLY, ...THE BEE MEETING   212   46
    OF THEIR DREAM, THE HIVED STATION ....THE SWARM   216   34
    I DREAM OF SOMEONE ELSE ENTIRELY. ....THE JAILER   227   27
    WHICH PROPS YOU THROUGH THIS DESERT LIKE A DREAM ....DIALOGUE O.   282 212
    MY WISH ONE WITH YOUR AIM. ONCE, IN A DREAM, ...DIALOGUE O.   284 301
    I SMASHED A GLASS, AND EVER SINCE THAT DREAM ....DIALOGUE O.   285 302
    IS ITSELF AGAIN, AND OURS. THE DREAM ...DIALOGUE OVER A OUIJA BOARD   286 358
    THE FACT OF DOUBT, THE FAITH OF DREAM. ...METAMORPHOSES OF THE MOON   308   48
    THE DREAM ....THE DREAM   310   T
    "IN THE FIRST DREAM I WAS DRIVING ....THE DREAM   310   7
    SO IF YOU CAN DREAM UP ANY SAVING PLAN ....THE DISPOSSESSED   318   2
    UNTIL DREAM TAKES HER BODY ....AERIALIST   331   4
    THROUGH HOOP OF THAT HAZARDOUS DREAM ....AERIALIST   332   40
DREAMED (10)
    WE DREAMED HOW WE WERE PERFECT, AND WE WERE. ....THE OTHER TWO   68   7
    WE DREAMED THEIR ARGUMENTS, THEIR STRICKEN VOICES. ...THE OTHER TWO   69   29
    THE HEAVEN THOSE TWO DREAMED OF, IN DESPAIR. ....THE OTHER TWO   69   35
    DREAMED YOURSELF AWAY IN THE MOON'S EYE ....YADWIGHA.   86   28
    TO A BERYL JUNGLE, AND DREAMED THAT BRIGHT MOON-LILIES ...YADWIGHA.   86   29
    WHICH SEEMED, WHEN DREAMED, TO MEAN SO PROFOUNDLY MUCH, ...GHOST'S.   90   5
    MY MOTHER DREAMED YOU FACE DOWN IN THE SEA.   ELECTRA ON AZALEA PATH 117   36
    ALL NIGHT I HAVE DREAMED OF DESTRUCTION, ANNIHILATIONS -- ..WAKING.   151   4
    I'VE DREAMED OF DOING IT AGAIN. AND NOW *DIALOGUE OVER A OUIJA BOARD   285 303
    UNDER A STONE. THOSE TWO DREAMED DEATHS TOOK ....DIALOGUE O.   285 326
DREAMER (1)
    THE DREAMER REINS HIS WAKING APPETITE ....TERMINAL   328   2
DREAMERS (3)
    OF DREAMERS IS DISPELLED. ONCE MORE WE CUT ....DIALOGUE O.   286 359
    TO WAKEN DREAMERS IN THE MILKY DAWN, ...APRIL AUBADE   312   6
    WHICH DREAMERS CALL REAL, AND REALISTS, ILLUSION:*LOVE IS A PARALLAX   330   59
DREAM-FILMED (1)
    DREAM-FILMED. WHAT A VISION OF ANCIENT HOGHOOD MUST ....SOW   61   27
DREAM-FISH (1)
    TO FLOAT LIKE DREAM-FISH IN THE LANGUID LIMBO ..MORNING IN THE HOS.   332   8
DREAMGIRLS (1)
    ON MERMAIDS AND TWO-LEGGED DREAMGIRLS. ..THE COURAGE OF SHUTTING-UP   210   13
DREAMING (4)
    THESE DREAMING HOUSES ALL SNUFF OUT; ....SOLILOQUY OF THE SOLIPSIST   37   6
    DESCRIBED HOW YOU FELL DREAMING AT FULL OF MOON ....YADWIGHA.   86   25
    OF THE PROFANE GRAIL, THE DREAMING SKULL. ..THE GHOST'S LEAVETAKING   91   40
    I LAY DREAMING YOUR EPIC, IMAGE BY IMAGE. ...ELECTRA ON AZALEA PATH   116   12
DREAM-PEOPLED (1)
    THE DREAM-PEOPLED VILLAGE, HER EYES ENTERTAINED NO DREAM, ...
                                          ... HARDCASTLE CRAGS   63   19
DREAM-PROPERTIED (1)
    "NO DOUBT NOW IN DREAM-PROPERTIED FALL SOME MOON-EYED, ..CONJURING.   66   33
DREAMS (19)
    FROM THE GENUINE COLOR OF SKIN; CAN OUR DREAMS ....TALE OF A TUB   25   27
    AND ALL GREEN DREAMS NOT WORTH MUCH, ...STRUMPET SONG   33   2
    SUCH ROYAL DREAMS BECKON THIS MAN ....THE SHRIKE   42   2
    INTO OUR BAD DREAMS, THEIR MENACE ....THE THIN PEOPLE   64   15

DREAMS (CONT.)
   SO WEEDY A RACE COULD NOT REMAIN IN DREAMS, ...THE THIN PEOPLE   64   23
   DREAMS THAT HIS FATTEST CATTLE DWINDLE, FEVERED ....GOATSUCKER   111   6
   WITHOUT DREAMS OF ANY SORT. POEM.1.WHO.   132   24
   TO THEIR OWNERS' WRISTS, THE LIGHT DREAMS FLOAT ....ON DECK   143   35
   BOOMED WITH BAD DREAMS AND THE JOVIAN VOICES OF SURGEONS. *FACE LIFT   156   6
   OF CHILDHOOD AND ADOLESCENCE, STICKY WITH DREAMS, ...INSOMNIAC   163   10
   IN DREAMS, THROUGH MOUTH-HOLE OR EYE-HOLE. I CAN'T STOP IT. *LAST W.   172   15
   WHAT BLUE, MOONY RAY ICES THEIR DREAMS? ....THREE WOMEN   181 182
   HOW YOUR BAD DREAMS POSSESS AND ENDOW ME. ....ELM 192   27
   INVOLVED IN ITS WEIRD BLUE DREAMS, ...BURNING THE LETTERS   205   40
   LEVER OF HIS WET DREAMS. ....THE JAILER   226   10
   HE DREAMS OF A NEW ONE -- ....AMNESIAC   233   14
   DEATH'S TWO DREAMS DOWN WITH THE BODY THAT BLED THE VEIN, ...
                                ... DIALOGUE OVER A OUIJA BOARD   285 329
   A SEA OF DREAMS WASHES THE EDGE OF MY GREEN ISLAND ...QUEEN MARY'S.   290   2
   EXCEPT FOR TWO UNCANNY DREAMS ....THE DREAM   310   2
DREAMS' (2)
   LURKS THE LITHE ONE; IN DREAMS' AMBUSH ....PURSUIT   23   30
   AND GHOST OF OUR DREAMS' CHILDREN, IN THOSE SHEETS ....GHOST'S.   91   33
DREAMSCAPES (1)
   OF SULFUROUS DREAMSCAPES AND OBSCURE LUNAR CONUNDRUMS .....GHOST'S.   90   4
DREAR (1)
   THROUGH DREAR AND DULCET WEATHER. *THE LADY AND THE EARTHENWARE HEAD   70   28
DREDGE (2)
   TO DREDGE THE SILT FROM YOUR THROAT. ....THE COLOSSUS 129   9
   IS ON YOU NOW, FOR PLANNING TO DREDGE UP*DIALOGUE OVER A OUIJA BOARD   282 239
DREGS (2)
   HER RUBY DREGS. ....RHYME   50   18
   THE OLD DREGS, THE OLD DIFFICULTIES TAKE ME TO WIFE.   PARLIAMENT H.   153   48
DRENCH (3)
   AND OUT OF THE BLUE DRENCH ....SOUTHERN SUNRISE   26   16
   WHERE WAVE PRETENDS TO DRENCH REAL SKY." ....LOVE IS A PARALLAX   329   6
   OF THE BOLD SAILOR FALLING UNDER DRENCH ....EPITAPH IN THREE PARTS   337   15
DRENCHED (2)
   WOULD BE FULL OF SUN, WHITE GULLS, AND WATER DRENCHED ...CHANNEL C.   27   21
   OF YOUR SMALL BREATH, THE DRENCHED GRASS ....THE NIGHT DANCES   250   9
DRENCHING (1)
   BLOOD DRENCHING VIVID ....MONOLOGUE AT 3 A.M.   40   3
DRESS (6)
   SMALL AS A DOLL IN MY DRESS OF INNOCENCE ....ELECTRA ON AZALEA PATH   116   11
   AND MUTE AS MANNEQUINS IN A DRESS SHOP, ...ON DECK   142   3
   DEATH IS THE DRESS SHE WEARS, HER HAT AND COLLAR. ....WIDOW   164   13
   I REMEMBER YOU PLAYING "JA DA" IN A PINK PIQUE DRESS*THE BABYSITTERS   175   22
   THE CLOUDS ARE A MARRIAGE DRESS, OF THAT PALLOR. ......LITTLE FUGUE   189   52
   IN MY SLEEVELESS SUMMERY DRESS I HAVE NO PROTECTION,*THE BEE MEETING   211   3
DRESSED (1)
   DRESSED IN BLACK, EVERYBODY IN MOURNING FOR SOMEONE.*THE NET-MENDERS   121   4
DRESSES (3)
   SETTLE IN THEIR BELLING DRESSES. ....HEAVY WOMEN   158   5
   IT WILL MAKE LITTLE DRESSES AND COATS, ...AN APPEARANCE   189   12
   FULL OF DRESSES AND HATS AND CHINA AND MARRIED DAUGHTERS. ...BERCK.   199   77
DRESSING (1)
   A DRESSING OF MULE EARS, MOTHY PELTS, BUT GREEN-HEARTED,*POEM.1.WHO.   131   17
DRESSY (1)
   I THINK THEY WOULD NOT WISH FOR THIS DRESSY BACKCLOTH ....STARS.   166   29
DRIBBLES (1)
   THE OLD GOD DRIBBLES, IN RETURN, HIS WORDS. ....OUIJA   77   11
DRIED (2)
   PIG HOVE, LETTING LEGEND LIKE DRIED MUD DROP, ...SOW   61   37
   AND DRIED PLATES WITH MY DENSE HAIR. ....STINGS   214   25
DRIFT (4)
   CLOUDS STEERED A BURNISHED DRIFT; ....SONG FOR A SUMMER'S DAY   31   8
   LOST IN THE LIFT AND DRIFT OF ....THE GREAT CARBUNCLE   73   23
   DRIFT OF GOLDPIECES ....DARK WOOD, DARK WATER   127   20
   HIS DRIFT ENDORSES YOUR INKLINGS OF A DOOM ....DIALOGUE O.   281 190
DRIFTING (1)
   O RIVER, I SEE DRIFTING ....LORELEI   95   33
DRIFTS (1)
   INVISIBLE AIR DRIFTS, ...BALLOONS 271   6
DRIFTWOOD (1)
   WE PICKED UP STICKS OF DRIFTWOOD AND BEAT THEM OFF, *THE BABYSITTERS   175   38
DRINK (8)
   WITHOUT MEAT OR DRINK I SAT ....ON THE PLETHORA OF DRYADS 67   7
   YEARS, GO DOWN TO DRINK THE RIVER: ....CHILD'S PARK STONES   101   29
   ALREADY FROG-MOUTH AND FISH-MOUTH DRINK POEM.5.F.   134   7
   AND DRINK THE SMALL NIGHT CHILL LIKE NEWS OF HOME. ....STARS.   166   40
   I AM A GARDEN OF BLACK AND RED AGONIES. I DRINK THEM, ..THREE WOMEN   180 149
   WHERE DO THE BLACK TREES GO THAT DRINK HERE? ....CROSSING THE WATER   190   2
   A GREEN DRINK, ONE A BLUE. ....AMNESIAC   233   22
   THAN AGAINST GRAVITY'S GRIP, TABLES RISING; THE DRINK .DIALOGUE O.   279 122
DRINKING (3)
   DRINKING VINEGAR FROM TIN CUPS: THEY WORE ....THE THIN PEOPLE   64   20
   INCHING OFF IN THE GRAY CHEVROLET, DRINKING THE GREEN ......WAKING.   151   6
   RELIGION, DRINKING ....NICK AND THE CANDLESTICK   241   18

```
                                                TITLE          PAGE  LINE
DRINKS (2)
    I LOSE LIFE AFTER LIFE. THE DARK EARTH DRINKS THEM.  ....THREE WOMEN  181  154
    THE TWO DRINKS FLAME AND FOAM.  .........................AMNESIAC  233   24
DRIP (4)
    THE ERSATZ PETALS DRIP, AND THEY DRIP RED.  ..ELECTRA ON AZALEA PATH  117   28
    THE ERSATZ PETALS DRIP, AND THEY DRIP RED.  ..ELECTRA ON AZALEA PATH  117   28
    DRIP AND THICKEN, TEARS  ...................NICK AND THE CANDLESTICK  240    3
    ATOMS THAT CRIPPLE DRIP  ...................NICK AND THE CANDLESTICK  242   38
DRIPS (2)
    THE GOLDEN RAIN TREE DRIPS ITS POWDERS DOWN.  ..........BEEKEEPER'S.  118    9
    INCENSE. PALE MOSS DRIPS  .....................DARK WOOD, DARK WATER  127    2
DRIVE (4)
    TO STUN SKY BLACK OUT, DRIVE GIBBERING MAD  .............CONJURING.   66   12
    SUICIDAL, AT ONE WITH THE DRIVE  ...........................ARIEL  240   29
    MAY TESTIFY TO DRIVE YOUR DOUBTING OUT. *DIALOGUE OVER A OUIJA BOARD  280  153
    LEST THE BLIZZARD DRIVE YOU BLIND.  .........GO GET THE GOODLY SQUAB  313   16
DRIVEN (4)
    EACH VAIN GIRL'S DRIVEN  ...................................VANITY FAIR   33   25
    SHE STALKED INTRACTABLE AS A DRIVEN GHOST  ..THE SNOWMAN ON THE MOOR   58   15
    DRIVEN, DRIVEN IN.  .......................................BRASILIA  258    8
    DRIVEN, DRIVEN IN.  .......................................BRASILIA  258    8
DRIVES (4)
    DRIVES NIMBLE BLOOD TOO QUICK  .........EPITAPH FOR FIRE AND FLOWER   46   25
    THE JEWELMASTER DRIVES HIS CHISEL TO PRY  .................POEM.7.S.  136   20
    WHERE IT DRIVES IN, WHITE AND BLACK,  .......................LESBOS  229   75
    DRIVES PRIEST AND PROSTITUTE IN DOORWAYS,  ..........INSOLENT STORM.  326   15
DRIVING (3)
    IT TOOK THREE DAYS DRIVING NORTH TO FIND A CLOUD  .........TWO CAMP.  145   10
    DRIVING THE DULL CELLS WILD.  .........................EAVESDROPPER  260   18
    "IN THE FIRST DREAM I WAS DRIVING  ......................THE DREAM  310    7
DRIZZLED (1)
    BEHIND HIM THE HOTDOGS SPLIT AND DRIZZLED  .....SUICIDE OFF EGG ROCK  115    1
DROLL (1)
    DROLL, VEGETARIAN, THE WATER RAT *WATERCOLOR OF GRANTCHESTER MEADOWS  112   22
DROLL-FLECKED (1)
    AND PLUCK THE DROLL-FLECKED QUAIL WHERE THICK THEY LIE;  ...GO GET.  313    2
DROOLS (1)
    AND DROOLS AT THE RECEPTION LINE.  ....................FAMILY REUNION  301   24
DROOP (1)
    GIVEN HER LIPS THAT LEMON-TASTING DROOP:  .........VIRGIN IN A TREE   82   42
DROOPS (1)
    DROOPS UPON ITS WIZENED STEM  ................................JILTED  304   11
DROP (13)
    THAT WILL KINDLE ANGELS' ENVY, SCORCH AND DROP  ......EPITAPH FOR F.   45    6
    PIG HOVE, LETTING LEGEND LIKE DRIED MUD DROP,  ...................SOW   61   37
    LIGHT WITHDRAWS. CHAIRS, TABLES DROP  ..........THE GREAT CARBUNCLE   73   29
    PITYS FROM PAN'S ASSAULT! AND THOUGH AGE DROP  .....VIRGIN IN A TREE   81   17
    LET DROP ITS SPITTLE OF SLUGGISH GREEN  .............RHODODENDRON.  103    6
    THE WOODS ARE A WELL. THE STARS DROP SILENTLY.  ............STARS.  165    4
    THEY SEEM LARGE, YET THEY DROP, AND NO GAP IS VISIBLE.  ......STARS.  165    5
    AND HERE WE ARE, HUNG OUT OVER THE DEAD DROP  .........STOPPED DEAD  230    3
    TOAD-YELLOW UNDER THE DROP  .........................EAVESDROPPER  261   39
    THAT WOULD NOT, WOULD NOT DROP  ......................EAVESDROPPER  261   40
    SO, YOU'LL SCOFF, AND YET YOU'D DROP TO KNEEL  ..........DIALOGUE O.  280  156
    SOME DAY, MOVING, ONE WILL DROP,  ..............LOVE IS A PARALLAX  330   63
    AS GREAT WEIGHTS DROP ALL ABOUT HER  ......................AERIALIST  331   17
DROPLET (1)
    AND THE TOAD GUARDING HIS HEART'S DROPLET.  ..................SLEEP.  144   16
DROPPED (4)
    THE RITUAL DEATH EACH TIME BOTCHED AMONG DROPPED CAPES,
                        ILL-JUDGED STABS,  ....THE GORING   47    3
    DOZENS DROPPED DEAD IN THE HEDGES: O SHE FELT  ..........SNOWMAN O.   59   35
    FLEES AND ABORTS LIKE DROPPED MERCURY.  .................THALIDOMIDE  252   26
    AND THOUSANDS WERE BORN AND DROPPED DEAD,  ........DIALOGUE EN ROUTE  309   39
DROPPING (3)
    THE BLUE WATER-MISTS DROPPING  ...............................LORELEI   94    4
    STARS ARE DROPPING THICK AS STONES INTO THE TWIGGY  .........STARS.  165    1
    AND DROPPING, DIE, TO TRACE A WOUND THAT HEALS  ..LOVE IS A PARALLAX  330   64
DROPS (11)
    TWO WATER DROPS POISE  ....................................RESOLVE   52   13
    FROST DROPS EVEN THE SPIDER. CLEARLY  ....................FROG AUTUMN   99    9
    THE SEAWALL AND DROPS ONTO A BIER  ....................POINT SHIRLEY  110    6
    OOZING THE GLUE DROPS,  ............................POEM.2.DARK.  132    5
    AS RESIN DROPS OOZED FROM PINE BARK.  .............THE BURNT-OUT SPA  137    5
    SMALL DROPS SPOT THEIR COATS, THEIR GLOVES:  .............ON DECK  143   16
    AND THE LOCKED DROPS RISING IN A DEW  ....................LOVE LETTER  147   21
    ONE CHILD DROPS A BARRETTE OF PINK PLASTIC;   PARLIAMENT HILL FIELDS  152   16
    DROPS ME FROM A TERRIBLE ALTITUDE.  .....................THE JAILER  226   13
    THE SNOW DROPS ITS PIECES OF DARKNESS,  .......THE MUNICH MANNEQUINS  263   16
    THAT DROPS AND TURNS,  ....................................WORDS  270   11
DROVE (2)
    DROVE THE DOGS TO CRINGE AND WHINE,  .......THE DEATH OF MYTH-MAKING  104   13
    THEN DROVE TO YOU UPON THE WIND. . . .  .............THE DREAM  311   28
DROWN (10)
    IT IS NO NIGHT TO DROWN IN:  .................................LORELEI   94    1
```

```
                                                          TITLE          PAGE  LINE
DROWN (CONT.)
  AND ETERNITY ENGULFS IT, AND I DROWN UTTERLY?  ..........THREE WOMEN    179  105
  YOU SAY I SHOULD DROWN THE KITTENS. THEIR SMELL!  ............LESBOS    228   20
  YOU SAY I SHOULD DROWN MY GIRL. .............................LESBOS    228   21
  LEST THE WATER DRAG YOU TO DROWN.  ..........GO GET THE GOODLY SQUAB    313   24
  AND DROWN WITHIN. ...............................MOONSONG AT MORNING    317   40
  AND GOD OR VOID APPALL US TILL WE DROWN  .........LOVE IS A PARALLAX    330   74
  "THERE IS MORE THAN ONE GOOD WAY TO DROWN."  EPITAPH IN THREE PARTS    337   11
  "THERE IS MORE THAN ONE GOOD WAY TO DROWN."  EPITAPH IN THREE PARTS    337   22
  "THERE IS MORE THAN ONE GOOD WAY TO DROWN."  EPITAPH IN THREE PARTS    338   33
DROWNED (5)
  ONE WHITE HORSE DROWNED, AND ALL THE UNCONQUERED PINNACLES  LESSON.     80    9
  AND A DROWNED MAN, COMPLAINING OF THE GREAT COLD,  ..........A LIFE    150   34
  WHITENED BY THE FACES OF THE DROWNED. ...................FINISTERRE    169    5
  IN ME SHE HAS DROWNED A YOUNG GIRL, AND IN ME AN OLD WOMAN  ..MIRROR    174   17
  AT NIGHTFALL THERE IS THE BEAUTY OF DROWNED FIELDS,  .........TOTEM    264    4
DROWNS (2)
  SHE BLENCHED, AS ONE WHO DROWNS,   THE LADY AND THE EARTHENWARE HEAD    69   21
  DROWNS NOAH'S PRAYERS WITH DISTAIN,  ................INSOLENT STORM.    326   14
DROWSE (1)
  CADDIS WORMS DROWSE IN THEIR SILK CASES,  .................POEM.5.F.    135   11
DROWSED (2)
  WHILE ELLA DROWSED WHISKERED WITH SLEEK FACE, SLY WITS:  ...
                           ... ELLA MASON AND HER ELEVEN CATS            54   29
  SHEEP DROWSED STONEWARD IN THEIR TUSSOCKS OF WOOL, AND BIRDS,  ...
                                       ... HARDCASTLE CRAGS             63   34
DROWSING (1)
  AND BAIT THE DROWSING TROUT BY THE BROOK'S BRIM;  ...........GO GET.    313   18
DRUDGE (1)
  I AM NO DRUDGE  ...............................................STINGS    214   23
DRUGGED (2)
  AND THE SWEET, DRUGGED WAKING OF A FORGETFUL BABY.  .......INSOMNIAC    163   19
  I HAVE BEEN DRUGGED AND RAPED. ..........................THE JAILER    226    6
DRUGS (1)
  GRAY FACES, SHUTTERED BY DRUGS, FOLLOW ME LIKE FLOWERS.  ...SURGEON.    171   50
DRUM (1)
  DRUM OF MY SLEEPING COUCH  .............................PARALYTIC    266   21
DRUMMED (2)
  WHEN WORDS, LIKE LOCUSTS, DRUMMED THE DARKENING AIR  ..........OUIJA    77   17
  I AM USED. I AM DRUMMED INTO USE. .....................THREE WOMEN    180  145
DRUMMING (2)
  DRUMMING UP ANY FEVER  ...................................NIGHT SHIFT    76    4
  WINGS DRUMMING IN THE WINTER. .......................MAGNOLIA SHOALS    122   24
DRUMS (1)
  THE DULL DRUMS OF MY PULSES BEAT  ...................FAMILY REUNION    300    8
DRUNK (6)
  LAUGH, KISS, GET DRUNK,  .................SOLILOQUY OF THE SOLIPSIST    37   16
  DRUNK AS A FOETUS .....................................POEM.7.S.    136   17
  TODAY THE COLLEGES ARE DRUNK WITH SPRING. ...............THREE WOMEN    185  302
  DRUNK ON ITS OWN SCENTS, ..................................PARALYTIC    267   39
  GLITTERING AND DRUNK AS FLIES ................................MYSTIC    268    5
  DRUNK, AND TEA-LEAVES CANDID; THE CLAIRVOYANT SEIZURE  ..DIALOGUE O.    279  123
DRUNKARDS (1)
  LIKE MONDAY DRUNKARDS. THE MILKY BERRIES  .............LEAVING EARLY    145   10
DRUNKEN (7)
  NO SOUND BUT A DRUNKEN COOT  .................................FAUN    35    6
  THE IDIOT BIRD LEAPS UP AND DRUNKEN LEANS  ..........SONNET: TO EVA    305   13
  THE IDIOT BIRD LEAPS OUT AND DRUNKEN LEANS  ...............DOOMSDAY    316    1
  THE IDIOT BIRD LEAPS OUT AND DRUNKEN LEANS.  ..............DOOMSDAY    316    6
  THE IDIOT BIRD LEAPS OUT AND DRUNKEN LEANS.  ..............DOOMSDAY    316   12
  THE IDIOT BIRD LEAPS OUT AND DRUNKEN LEANS,  ..............DOOMSDAY    316   18
  DESIGNED BY A DRUNKEN GOD  ..................CIRCUS IN THREE RINGS    321    2
DRUNKENNESS (1)
  DRUNKENNESS OF THE GREAT DEPTHS. ...........................LORELEI    95   32
DRUNKS (1)
  SO KISS: THE DRUNKS UPON THE CURB AND DAMES  .....LOVE IS A PARALLAX    329   31
DRY (17)
  AS IS YOUR IMAGE IN MY EYE; DRY FROST  ...........WINTER LANDSCAPE,    22   12
  DRY TICKS MARK TIME  ...................TWO SISTERS OF PERSEPHONE    31    8
  MOURNFULLY THE DRY TONGUES CLACKED THEIR GUILT:  .......SNOWMAN O.    59   39
  DRY WITNESS  ......................................ALL THE DEAD DEARS    70    8
  I WALK DRY ON YOUR KINGDOM'S BORDER  ..............FULL FATHOM FIVE    93   41
  THE DRY VOLCANOES CRACKED AND SPIT,  ..................I WANT, I WANT    106    4
  VAMPIRING DRY OF MILK EACH GREAT GOAT UDDER.  ............GOATSUCKER    111    4
  THE FOUNTAINS ARE DRY AND THE ROSES OVER. ...........THE MANOR GARDEN    125    1
  IN THE MARKETPLACE THEY ARE PILING THE DRY STICKS.  .......POEM.6.W.    135    1
  HOT GRAINS, SIMPLY. IT IS DRY, DRY.  .....SLEEP IN THE MOJAVE DESERT    143    2
  HOT GRAINS, SIMPLY. IT IS DRY, DRY.  .....SLEEP IN THE MOJAVE DESERT    143    2
  NOR DO THESE DRY, DRY GUTTERS DREAM OF RAIN.  ...........THREE WOMEN    184  279
  NOR DO THESE DRY, DRY GUTTERS DREAM OF RAIN.  ...........THREE WOMEN    184  279
  TO WRINKLE AND DRY. .................................THE DETECTIVE    209   30
  THEN THE DRY WOOD, THE GATES, ........................THE DETECTIVE    209   36
  WORDS DRY AND RIDERLESS, ......................................WORDS    270   16
  WITH THE COLD BURN DRY ICE HAS. YET THE CLOCK  ..........DIALOGUE O.    276   11
```

```
                                           TITLE              PAGE  LINE
DRYAD (1)
   ON THE DIFFICULTY OF CONJURING UP A DRYAD  ..............CONJURING.    65    T
DRYADS (3)
   TO ELEGIAC DRYADS, AND DOUR GRASS  ..............NOVEMBER GRAVEYARD    56    3
   ON THE PLETHORA OF DRYADS  .................ON THE PLETHORA OF DRYADS  67    T
   I MUST WATCH SLUTTISH DRYADS TWITCH  ......ON THE PLETHORA OF DRYADS   67   32
DRY-EYED (1)
   DRY-EYED, THE INVETERATE PATRIARCH  ...................I WANT, I WANT  106   9
DRYLY (1)
   DRYLY DISCLAIMS THAT FIERCE TROLL FACES LURK  .........TALE OF A TUB   24   13
DRY-PAPPED (1)
   I WOULD GET FROM THESE DRY-PAPPED STONES  ..............POINT SHIRLEY  111   41
DRY-WET (1)
   OBLIQUELY WITH A DRY-WET  .............MUSSEL HUNTER AT ROCK HARBOR     96   46
DU (1)
   ACH, DU.  .........................................................DADDY  222   15
DUAL (1)
   THIS PAIR SEEK SINGLE STATE FROM THAT DUAL BATTLE.  .......WREATH F.    44   10
DUBIOUS (1)
   IN DUBIOUS DOORWAYS FORGET THEIR MONDAY NAMES,  ..LOVE IS A PARALLAX   329   32
DUCHESS (2)
   SORROWS OF MALFI'S GENTLE DUCHESS? GONE  .....................PERSEUS    83   42
   DUCHESS OF NOTHING,  .....................................POEM.4.BEAST.  134   25
DUCK (1)
   BY DEFT DUCK AND TWIRL  ...................................AERIALIST    331   22
DUCK-FEET (1)
   WITH ORANGE DUCK-FEET WINNOWING HIS HAIR --  .....ALL THE DEAD DEARS    71   24
DUCKS (5)
   THE BLACK DUCKS DIVE.  ....................................POINT SHIRLEY  111   43
   THE TALKING DUCKS, THE HAPPY LAMBS.  .....................THREE WOMEN   185  318
   I WANT TO FILL IT WITH COLOR AND DUCKS,  .......................CHILD   265    2
   SOME DUCKS STEP DOWN OFF THEIR GREEN-REEDED SHELF  ...QUEEN MARY'S.    290   11
   WE RAISE OUR ARGUMENTS LIKE SITTING DUCKS  .......LOVE IS A PARALLAX   329   19
DUD (1)
   TO ALMOST NOTHING, TO A DULL BLUE DUD.  .............BY CANDLELIGHT    236   18
DUEL (3)
   THE SECOND CARCASS MAKES A DUEL OF THE AFFAIR:  .........BLUE MOLES    126    8
   DREAM OF A DUEL THEY WILL WIN INEVITABLY,  .........THE BEE MEETING    212   46
   DEMANDING SATISFACTION; NO DUEL TAKES PLACE:  ........METAMORPHOSES.   307    5
DUELS (1)
   COUNTS. SUCH DUELS INFECT BEST FRIENDSHIPS. PAN  ........DIALOGUE O.   283  271
DUET (1)
   DAYLONG A DUET OF SHADE AND LIGHT  ........TWO SISTERS OF PERSEPHONE    31    3
DUFY-BLUE (1)
   THEN SYNCOPATE A SKY OF DUFY-BLUE  .................MIDSUMMER MOBILE   324    2
DUG (2)
   DUG IN FIRST AS GOD'S SPURS  .................THE COMPANIONABLE ILLS    105    5
   CRIED OUT FOR THE MOTHER'S DUG.  ......................I WANT, I WANT   106    3
DULCET (1)
   THROUGH DREAR AND DULCET WEATHER. *THE LADY AND THE EARTHENWARE HEAD    70   28
DULL (28)
   ARENA DUST RUSTED BY FOUR BULLS' BLOOD TO A DULL REDNESS,*THE GORING    47    1
   EVEN IN THIS DULL, RUINOUS LANDSCAPE); SKEPTICAL,  ....BLACK ROOK I.    57   24
   WORTHLESS SUCH VISION TO EYES GONE DULL  ..ON THE DECLINE OF ORACLES    78   30
   THE MUSSELS HUNG DULL BLUE AND  .......MUSSEL HUNTER AT ROCK HARBOR     95   17
   ALL'S POLISHED TO A DULL LUSTER  ....................IN MIDAS' COUNTRY   99    5
   COLORED TO DULL THE PIGMENT  ....................CHILD'S PARK STONES   101   16
   THE PROSPECT IS DULL AS AN OLD ETCHING.  ...............A WINTER SHIP  113   13
   THIS IS A DULL SCHOOL.  ..........................................POEM.1.WHO.  132   22
   ANGELS WEEPING OVER DULL NATURES,  ......................LOVE LETTER   147   16
   THE ABSTRACTS HOVER LIKE DULL ANGELS:  ...........................MAGI   148    1
   I WATCH THEIR SPILT TEARS CLOUD AND DULL TO PEARLS.  .......CANDLES    149   31
   WHITENS AND SWALLOWS ITS DULL STARS. AND NOW YOU TRY  ..MORNING SONG   157   16
   HIS SOUL MAY BEAT AND BE BEATING AT HER DULL SENSE  ..........WIDOW    165   37
   THE RED NIGHT LIGHTS ARE FLAT MOONS. THEY ARE DULL WITH BLOOD.  ...
                                              ... THE SURGEON AT 2 A.M.   171   48
   THE NIGHT LIGHTS ARE FLAT RED MOONS. THEY ARE DULL WITH BLOOD.  ...
                                              ... THREE WOMEN            180  124
   I FELT HANDS ROUND A TEA MUG, DULL, BLUNT,  ......THE RABBIT CATCHER   194   22
   A TARRED FABRIC, SORRY AND DULL,  .........................BERCK-PLAGE  200  114
   A DULL POM, POM IN THE SUNDAY STREET.  ......................THE SWARM  215    2
   ARE DULL, DULL AS THE TRIPLE  .................................FEVER.   231    3
   ARE DULL, DULL AS THE TRIPLE  .................................FEVER.   231    3
   TONGUES OF DULL, FAT CERBERUS  ................................FEVER.   231    4
   THE DULL BELLS TONGUE THE HOUR.  ...................BY CANDLELIGHT     236    8
   TO ALMOST NOTHING, TO A DULL BLUE DUD.  .............BY CANDLELIGHT    236   18
   DRIVING THE DULL CELLS WILD.  ........................EAVESDROPPER     260   18
   COLOR FLOODS TO THE SPOT, DULL PURPLE.  ...................CONTUSION   271    1
   THE DULL DRUMS OF MY PULSES BEAT  ...................FAMILY REUNION    300    8
   DULL LUNAR GLOBES  ..................................AQUATIC NOCTURNE   306   16
   DUPE THE DULL SOW LOUNGING SNOUT IN MUD,  ...GO GET THE GOODLY SQUAB   313   11
DULLED (3)
   DUST DULLED HIS BACK TO OCHRE  ..............................MEDALLION  124   14
   AND THEY ARE WAN, DULLED BY MUCH TRAVELLING.*STARS OVER THE DORDOGNE   165   11
   DULLED TO A HALT UNDER BOWLERS.  .................POPPIES IN OCTOBER   240    9
```

DULLING (1)
    DULLING AND STILLING. ....POPPIES IN JULY 203   14
DULLY (1)
    DULLY, UNDER A PACK OF MEN IN RED JACKETS, ...BURNING THE LETTERS 204   13
DUMB (13)
    SO, PERHAPS I, KNELLED DUMB BY YOUR ABSENCE, ...STREET SONG   36   24
    THE BEAN LEAVES ARE DUMB AS HANDS. POEM.3.MAENAD. 133   10
    BIG AS THE BALL OF MY THUMB, AND DUMB AS EYES ........BLACKBERRYING 168   5
    PICKING AMONG THE DUMB MINERALS, THE ROOTS. ....LAST WORDS 172   5
    I AM DUMB AND BROWN. I AM A SEED ABOUT TO BREAK. ....THREE WOMEN 179   99
    SO THE DEAF AND DUMB ....LITTLE FUGUE 187   3
    DUMB FISH ....BURNING THE LETTERS 204   24
    BUT RIGHT NOW YOU ARE DUMB. ....FOR A FATHERLESS SON 205   6
    SO DUMB IT THINKS BULLETS ARE THUNDER. ....THE SWARM 216   20
    THE DUMB, BANDED BODIES ....THE SWARM 217   47
    HER BODY A BULB IN THE COLD AND TOO DUMB TO THINK. ....WINTERING 219   45
    A ROUGH, DUMB COUNTRY STUFF ....BY CANDLELIGHT" 236   3
    BOTH SERAPH SONG AND VIOLINS ARE DUMB; ....DOOM OF EXILES 318   7
DUMBSHOW (1)
    PERFORMED A DUMBSHOW IN THE POLISHED WOOD, ...THE OTHER TWO   68   16
DUMP (1)
    NOW IT IS ONLY GLOOMY, A DUMP OF ROCKS -- ....FINISTERRE 169   6
DUN (1)
    UNFISTS AGAINST THE DUN ....MAN IN BLACK 119   5
DUNCE (1)
    MONKEY LIVED UNDER THE DUNCE CAP. POEM.4.BEAST. 134   8
DUNES (1)
    OBSCENE BIKINIS HIDE IN THE DUNES, ...BERCK-PLAGE 197   24
DUNGAREES (2)
    DUNGAREES, PROUD AS A LADY IN A SEA ....MEMOIRS OF A SPINACH-PICKER   90   18
    IN FADED DUNGAREES. ....BITTER STRAWBERRIES 300   30
DUPE (1)
    DUPE THE DULL SOW LOUNGING SNOUT IN MUD, ...GO GET THE GOODLY SQUAB 313   11
DURABLE (3)
    EVERYTHING TOOK PLACE IN A DURABLE WHITENESS.*ELECTRA ON AZALEA PATH 117   14
    WHERE THE DURABLE ONES KEEP HOUSE. ....THE BURNT-OUT SPA 138   32
    THE FEW I AM USED TO ARE PLAIN AND DURABLE; *STARS OVER THE DORDOGNE 166   28
DURANCE (1)
    DURANCE ARE WHIRLPOOLS ....FULL FATHOM FIVE   93   30
DURING (4)
    DURING A CEREMONIOUS APRIL WALK ....SPINSTER   49   2
    IT WAS DURING THE LONG HUNGER-BATTLE ....THE THIN PEOPLE   64   12
    AND YOU, DURING THE GREAT WAR ....LITTLE FUGUE 188   31
    ALWAYS FROM THE PULPIT DURING SERVICE ....DIRGE FOR A JOKER 302   3
DUSK (3)
    BUT ONE DUSK OUR QUESTIONS COMMENDED US TO A TOUR ....SOW   60   7
    DUSK HOODS THEM IN MARY-BLUE ....HEAVY WOMEN 158   18
    DUSK HOODS ME IN BLUE NOW, LIKE A MARY. ....THREE WOMEN 179 102
DUST (11)
    A CROCK OF DUST IS MY DEAR HOME." DIALOGUE BETWEEN GHOST AND PRIEST   39   40
    ARENA DUST RUSTED BY FOUR BULLS' BLOOD TO A DULL REDNESS,*THE GORING   47   1
    AND THE SANDMAN'S DUST ....HARDCASTLE CRAGS   63   20
    MEADOWS OF GOLD DUST. THE SILVER ....IN MIDAS' COUNTRY   99   1
    PURPLES THE FIG IN THE LEAF'S SHADOW, TURNS THE DUST PINK. ...NET-. 121   7
    DUST DULLED HIS BACK TO OCHRE ....MEDALLION 124   14
    I COUPLED WITH DUST IN THE SHADOW OF A STONE. POEM.6.W. 136   22
    WITH A LUNG FULL OF DUST AND A TONGUE OF WOOD, ...LEAVING EARLY 146   43
    BUT STAY, SITTING FAR OUT, IN THEIR OWN DUST. ....STARS. 165   13
    THOUGH FOR YEARS I HAVE EATEN DUST ....STINGS 214   24
    DUST BAGS IN AND OUT, ...PARALYTIC 266   7
DUSTBINS (1)
    A DUSTBIN'S ENOUGH FOR HIM. POEM.4.BEAST. 134   14
DUSTERS (1)
    FEATHER DUSTERS FANNING THEIR HANDS IN A SEA OF BEAN FLOWERS, BEE. 211   17
DUTCH (1)
    DEVOUTLY AS THE DUTCH BULB ....HEAVY WOMEN 158   9
DUTEOUS (1)
    DISRUPT THE CALENDARS NEXT; SEND THE DUTEOUS ....SONG FOR A REVOLU. 323   9
DUTIES (1)
    GODS GROW TOO PROUD TO PRACTICE DOORMAN DUTIES ....DIALOGUE O. 280 127
DWARF (1)
    DWARF BABY, ...A SECRET 220   45
DWARFED (2)
    TO WALL OF THE DARK, DWARFED COTTAGES. ....HARDCASTLE CRAGS   62   7
    FOR THE ROCK'S DWARFED LUMP, FOR THE DRABBLED SCUM, ...GREEN ROCK. 105   23
DWARFING (1)
    DWARFING US. OUR BODIES FLICKER ....SCULPTOR   92   16
DWINDLE (2)
    WHO, UNAWARE HOW THEY DWINDLE, ...SOLILOQUY OF THE SOLIPSIST   37   15
    DREAMS THAT HIS FATTEST CATTLE DWINDLE, FEVERED ....GOATSUCKER 111   6
DWINDLES (2)
    THE ORACULAR GHOST WHO DWINDLES ON PIN-LEGS *THE GHOST'S LEAVETAKING   90   9
    DWINDLES IN THE HOUR-GLASS. ....TWO LOVERS. 327   4
DYE (1)
    ALTHOUGH THE RAINS DISSOLVE A BLOODY DYE: ...ELECTRA ON AZALEA PATH 117   27

```
                                           TITLE              PAGE  LINE
DYEING (1)
  DYEING THE AIR,  ................................BURNING THE LETTERS  205   54
DYING (10)
  THE DYING GAUL AND THOSE INNUMERABLE PIETAS  ................PERSEUS   82    9
  CAST A ROUND WHITE SHADOW IN THEIR DYING.  .................MOONRISE   98    6
  AND DYING TO SAY SOMETHING UNANSWERABLE.  .................THE RIVAL  166   10
  I AM DYING AS I SIT. I LOSE A DIMENSION.  ...............THREE WOMEN  177   30
  DYING  ................................................LADY LAZARUS  245   43
  DYING TO FLY AND BE DONE WITH IT?  ..........................YEARS  255   22
  THE DYING MAN WILL SCOFF IN SCORN AT THIS.  .....NEVER TRY TO TRICK.  319    3
  THE DYING MAN WILL SCOFF IN SCORN AT THIS.  .....NEVER TRY TO TRICK.  320    9
  THE DYING MAN WILL SCOFF IN SCORN AT THIS.  .....NEVER TRY TO TRICK.  320   15
  THE DYING MAN WILL SCOFF IN SCORN AT THIS.  .....NEVER TRY TO TRICK.  320   19
DYNASTIES (1)
  TO FATHER DYNASTIES. THE AIR IS RICH.  .....THE BEEKEEPER'S DAUGHTER  118   12
DYNASTY (3)
  THEY ARE CONCEIVING A DYNASTY OF PERFECT COLD.  ..........TWO CAMP.  145   19
  IT WILL COVER A DYNASTY.  .............................AN APPEARANCE  189   13
  DYNASTY OF BROKEN ARROWS!  .............................GETTING THERE  248   33
E (1)
  TO R NOW. E. IN CORE . . . O-F-N-E  .....DIALOGUE OVER A OUIJA BOARD  284  277
EACH (97)
  HIS KISSES PARCH, EACH PAW'S A BRIAR,  ......................PURSUIT   22   19
  I BOLT THE DOOR, EACH DOOR I BOLT.  .........................PURSUIT   23   47
  "A DAISIED MEAD," EACH SAID TO EACH,  ......................BUCOLICS   23    2
  "A DAISIED MEAD," EACH SAID TO EACH,  ......................BUCOLICS   23    2
  WATER FAUCETS SPAWN NO DANGER; EACH CRAB  .............TALE OF A TUB   25   19
  EACH DAY DEMANDS WE CREATE OUR WHOLE WORLD OVER,  .....TALE OF A TUB   25   36
  WITH EACH TILT, SHOCK AND SHUDDER, OUR BLUNT SHIP  CHANNEL CROSSING   26    2
  EACH FINGER-FURROWED FIELD  .............................ODE FOR TED   29   14
  SHREWD CATCH SILTING OUR EACH BRIGHT ACT BACK  ............FIRESONG   30   13
  AS SHE CALCULATES EACH SUM.  ...............TWO SISTERS OF PERSEPHONE   31    9
  EACH VAIN GIRL'S DRIVEN  ...................................VANITY FAIR   33   25
  STRUCK BY EACH DOUR YEAR.  ............................STRUMPET SONG   34   13
  I'LL CORRECT EACH MAR  ...........TINKER JACK AND THE TIDY WIVES   34    5
  EVEN AS MY EACH MANGLED NERVE-END  ....................STREET SONG   36   21
  DEW STOOD IN CHILL SWEAT ON EACH STALK,  .................DIALOGUE B.   38    4
  EACH THORN; SPIRING FROM WET EARTH, A BLUE HAZE  ........DIALOGUE B.   38    5
  THOUGH PRIME PARTS CRAM EACH RICH MEAL,  .................THE GLUTTON   40   11
  FROM EACH NEON-LIT PALM  ............................ALICANTE LULLABY   43   13
  THEY LIE, CUT-GRASS ASSAULTING EACH SEPARATE SENSE  .....WREATH F.   44    8
  LET FLESH BE KNIT, AND EACH STEP HENCE GO FAMOUS.  .......WREATH F.   45   24
  THE PASSING DAZZLE OF EACH FACE  .......EPITAPH FOR FIRE AND FLOWER   45    9
  BLOWS ASH IN EACH LOVER'S EYE; THE ARDENT LOOK  ......EPITAPH FOR F.   46   34
  EACH WEDGE WEARS A STUDDING  ..........................FIESTA MELONS   47   15
  THE RITUAL DEATH EACH TIME BOTCHED AMONG DROPPED CAPES,
                                   ILL-JUDGED STABS,  ....THE GORING   47    3
  AND, PLAINTIFF AGAINST EACH DAY, DECRY  .................THE BEGGARS   47    4
  EACH TIME ROUND WINDING THAT ANT  ...........................SPIDER   48   16
  ICE AND ROCK, EACH SENTIMENT WITHIN BORDER,  ...............SPINSTER   49   16
  FISH-TAILED GIRLS PURCHASE EACH WHITE LEG.  .................MAUDLIN   51    8
  WELL OR ILL." GERD SLANTS A LOOK AT EACH: MOST DEAR,  CRYSTAL GAZER   55   10
  EACH TO THE OTHER; FIT FIBER FOR STERN WEATHER.  ...CRYSTAL GAZER   55   11
  PLAGUE-PITTED AS THE MOON: EACH BUD  ...............CRYSTAL GAZER   56   44
  EACH LOVE BLAZING BLIND TO ITS GUTTED END --  ......CRYSTAL GAZER   56   46
  EACH HEDGE WITH SUCH WHITE BLOOM ASTOUNDS OUR EYES  ....MAYFLOWER   60    6
  HOW THEY PROP EACH OTHER UP!  .......................THE THIN PEOPLE   65   40
  EACH PARTICULAR QUIRK SO RAVISHED ME  .....ON THE PLETHORA OF DRYADS   67   15
  DRAGGED EACH DAZZLED SENSE APART  .........ON THE PLETHORA OF DRYADS   67   26
  WOULD NOT BE EASED, RELEASED. OUR EACH EXAMPLE  .......THE OTHER TWO   68   23
  THAT KNITS TO EACH ORIGINAL ITS COARSE COPY. A DARK TARN*LADY AND T.   69   15
  EACH SKULLED-AND-CROSSBONED GULLIVER  .............ALL THE DEAD DEARS   71   34
  ALTHOUGH EACH TEACHER FOUND MY TOUCH  .........THE DISQUIETING MUSES   75   35
  OF EACH SCROLLED SEA-BEAST  .............................BATTLE-SCENE   84   22
  BRING HOME EACH STORIED HEAD.  .........................BATTLE-SCENE   84   28
  OF BROWNS AND GREENS. EACH WORE ONE  ...MUSSEL HUNTER AT ROCK HARBOR   96   32
  OF HER HAND, THE HOUSE STILL HUGS IN EACH DRAB  .......POINT SHIRLEY  110   20
  VAMPIRING DRY OF MILK EACH HAN GREAT GOAT UDDER.  .........GOATSUCKER  111    4
  EACH THUMB-SIZE BIRD  ............WATERCOLOR OF GRANTCHESTER MEADOWS  112    6
  EACH WAVE-TIP GLITTERS LIKE A KNIFE.  ...................A WINTER SHIP  113   30
  BARED BY EACH FALLING TIDE,  ............................MAN IN BLACK  119   14
  SHORTENS WITH EACH BREATH DRAWN.  .................OLD LADIES' HOME  120   21
  IN EACH OPAQUE BELLY-SCALE:  ...............................MEDALLION  124   19
  EASY AND OFTEN AS EACH BREATH.  ............................BLUE MOLES  127   36
  EACH SPECKLED TWIG  .....................................POLLY'S TREE  128    3
  SOON EACH WHITE LADY WILL BE BOARDED UP  .............PRIVATE GROUND  130    5
  EACH STALLED IN HIS PARTICULAR MINUTE  ....................ON DECK  143   14
  EACH DAY CONCLUDES IN A HUGE SPLURGE OF VERMILIONS  .......TWO CAMP.  145   15
  CHEEKS ALIGHTING EACH MOMENT TO MELT  ...................LOVE LETTER  147   14
  EACH DEAD HEAD HAD A VISOR OF ICE.  .....................LOVE LETTER  147   18
  EACH NURSE PATCHED HER SOUL TO A WOUND AND DISAPPEARED.  ...WAKING.  151   13
  LIGHT UP. EACH RABBIT-EARED  ...............PARLIAMENT HILL FIELDS  153   44
  OLD GRIEVANCES JOSTLING EACH OTHER, SO MANY LOOSE TEETH.  ...ZOO K.  154   13
  OVER EACH WEIGHTY STOMACH A FACE  .......................HEAVY WOMEN  158    6
  SO THAT EACH MARCH I MAY GLEAM INTO LEAF,  ............I AM VERTICAL  162    4
```

EACH (CONT.)
MEMORIES JOSTLE EACH OTHER FOR FACE-ROOM LIKE OBSOLETE FILM
STARS. ....INSOMNIAC 163 14
EACH GESTURE FLEES IMMEDIATELY DOWN AN ALLEY ....INSOMNIAC 163 23
ON THIS HILL, WITH ITS VIEW OF LIT CASTLES, EACH SWUNG BELL STARS. 166 38
EACH MORNING IT IS HER FACE THAT REPLACES THE DARKNESS. .....MIRROR 174 16
MUST YOU STAMP EACH PIECE IN PURPLE, ...A BIRTHDAY PRESENT 207 46
THIS IS THE FLUID IN WHICH WE MEET EACH OTHER, ...BY CANDLELIGHT 236 10
EACH COAL A HOT CROSS-STITCH -- A LOVELY LIGHT! ....THE TOUR 238 21
TO ANNIHILATE EACH DECADE. ....LADY LAZARUS 245 24
ALL TO ITSELF ON THE TOP OF EACH ....THE COURIERS 247   9
THE SILVER LIMBO OF EACH EYE ....THE FEARFUL 256 16
EACH DEAD CHILD COILED, A WHITE SERPENT, ...EDGE 272   9
ONE AT EACH LITTLE ....EDGE 272 10
EACH TIME MUST LEARN THE LETTERS NEW. ARE ....DIALOGUE O. 277 24
MINOR IMPS PIPE UP, SO LONG AS EACH ....DIALOGUE OVER A OUIJA BOARD 280 152
TAIL ON EACH TOY DONKEY THAT WILL BRAY DIALOGUE OVER A OUIJA BOARD 283 250
OF OUR DAYS SUSTAIN US. MAY EACH THOUGHT*DIALOGUE OVER A OUIJA BOARD 286 361
SPREAD GAY CONTAGION WITH EACH CLEVER BREATH. ....DIRGE FOR A JOKER 303 12
IT'S LIKELY THAT EACH SECRET SOUGHT ......METAMORPHOSES OF THE MOON 307 21
EACH ONE AN INVETERATE GALLANT ....DIALOGUE EN ROUTE 309 21
DRAMA OF EACH SEASON ....TRIO OF LOVE SONGS 314 13
OF EACH SYLLABLE, ...TRIO OF LOVE SONGS 314 22
EACH SACRED BODY ....MOONSONG AT MORNING 317 29
EACH CLOCK TICK CONSECRATES THE DEATH OF STRANGERS. DOOM OF EXILES 318   8
EACH VIRILE BACHELOR DREADS PARALYSIS, ...NEVER TRY TO TRICK. 320 10
AT TWELVE, EACH SKULL IS AUREOLED ....DANSE MACABRE 321 10
EACH FALLEN LEAF IS TRAPPED BY SPELL OF STEEL, ..PROLOGUE TO SPRING 322   7
AND AUCTION OFF EACH RARE WHITE-RABBIT VERB; ....A SORCERER B. 324   6
EACH LOVELY LADY ....ON LOOKING INTO THE EYES OF A DEMON LOVER 325   5
ABOUT EACH COSMIC PRO AND CON; ....LOVE IS A PARALLAX 329 15
THAT JAR, WHILE EACH POLEMIC JACKANAPES ....LOVE IS A PARALLAX 330 53
TO PAY THE PIPER WITH EACH BREATH, YET LOVE ....LOVE IS A PARALLAX 331 76
EACH NIGHT, THIS ADROIT YOUNG LADY ....AERIALIST 331   1
BITES KEEN INTO EACH BRAVE LIMB ....AERIALIST 331 24
FOR EACH QUICK, FLARING GAME ....TOUCH-AND-GO 336 20
EACH WITH A TELEGRAM ADDRESSED TO ME. ......EPITAPH IN THREE PARTS 337   3
EAGER (1)
WALKING EAGER TOWARD WATER, WHEN THERE, ONE BY ONE, ..DREAM WITH C. 44 23
EAGLE (4)
AQUEDUCTS, THE BATHS OF CARACALLA, THE EAGLE NOSE! ....SURGEON. 171 28
LET THIS EYE BE AN EAGLE, ...GULLIVER 251 23
BUT LET THE FAST-FEATHERED EAGLE FLY. ......GO GET THE GOODLY SQUAB 313   4
LET THE FAST-FEATHERED EAGLE FLY ....GO GET THE GOODLY SQUAB 313   5
EAR (17)
SHE SPOKE MOST CHIDING IN HIS EAR ....THE QUEEN'S COMPLAINT 28 11
ABOVE PITCH OF PEDESTRIAN EAR, ...STREET SONG 36 23
NOW IN THE CRUX OF THEIR VOWS HANG YOUR EAR, ...EPITAPH FOR F. 45 15
IN THE WHORL OF HER EAR, AND LIKE A SCOOPED-OUT PUMPKIN CROWN ...
... HARDCASTLE CRAGS 63 24
SURFEITING EYE, EAR, TASTE, TOUCH, SMELL; ON THE PLETHORA OF DRYADS 67 27
AND THE HOURS OF PRACTICING, MY EAR ....THE DISQUIETING MUSES 75 37
WHAT THE SEASHELL SPOKE TO HIS INNER EAR ON THE DECLINE OF ORACLES 78   7
SET IN MY EAR, AND IN MY EYE ......ON THE DECLINE OF ORACLES 78 13
IN THE EAR OF THE VETERAN, AND AGAIN ....BLUE MOLES 126 20
OF YOUR LEFT EAR, OUT OF THE WIND, ...THE COLOSSUS 130 25
OF THE EAR, OLD WORRIER. POEM.7.S. 136 24
A FAR SEA MOVES IN MY EAR. ....MORNING SONG 157 12
THE SEA CANNONS INTO THEIR EAR, BUT THEY DON'T BUDGE. ...FINISTERRE 169   8
I LAY MY EAR TO FURIOUS LATIN. ....THE ARRIVAL OF THE BEE BOX 213 21
ARMS FOLDED, EAR COCKED, ...EAVESDROPPER 261 38
ONE OF A GIANT'S EAR? I GUESS THIS GLASS*DIALOGUE OVER A OUIJA BOARD 281 201
VOICE CRYING EXCLUSION IN MY EAR. ....SONNET: TO TIME 311   8
EAR-FLAPS (1)
RUMBAS AND SAMBAS NO EAR-FLAPS CAN MUFFLE. ......ALICANTE LULLABY 43 14
EARLESS (1)
EARLESS AND EYELESS, ...MUSHROOMS 139 15
EARLIER (2)
HE WAS BULLMAN EARLIER, ...POEM.4.BEAST. 134   1
OPPOSE WHAT WE FACED EARLIER. FEEL MY HAND. ....DIALOGUE O. 285 332
EARLIEST (1)
ONCE, IN ITS EARLIEST SWAY OF LYMPH AND SAP, ...HARDCASTLE CRAGS 63 39
EARLY (6)
JUTTED EARLY TO MARK OUR GOING, WHILE SKY ....CHANNEL CROSSING 27 23
HE HAULS TO HIS WILL EARLY; ....ODE FOR TED 29 17
BACK TO HER EARLY SEA-TOWN HOME ....DREAM WITH CLAM-DIGGERS 43   3
LEAVING EARLY ....LEAVING EARLY 145   T
IN THE MORNING SHE WOKE ME EARLY, REFLECTING THE SUN ....IN PLASTER 159 23
WHILE LIKE AN EARLY SUMMER PLUM, ...JILTED 304   9
EARN (1)
ROUND TO EARN HIS PAY: HE'LL HAVE US KEEP ....DIALOGUE O. 284 294
EARPIECE (1)
THEY ARE PRESSING OUT OF THE MANY-HOLED EARPIECE, THEY ARE LOOKING
FOR A LISTENER. ......WORDS HEARD, BY ACCIDENT, OVER THE PHONE 203   9

	TITLE	PAGE	LINE

EAR-RING (1)
    YOUR VOICE MY EAR-RING, ...LESBOS   229   79
EARS (11)
    BLOOD QUICKENS, GONGING IN MY EARS: ....PURSUIT   23   48
    FAR OFF, NOT BLOOD IN THE EARS ....NIGHT SHIFT   76   3
    TO CANACEE CRIES GIBBERISH TO COARSENED EARS. ........INCOMMUNICADO   100   14
    A DRESSING OF MULE EARS, MOTHY PELTS, BUT GREEN-HEARTED,*POEM.1.WHO.   131   17
    WHISTLING, WIGGLING MY EARS, ...POEM.2.DARK.   132   6
    WITH THE SACRED BABOON IN HIS WIG AND WAX EARS ...ZOO KEEPER'S WIFE   155   29
    TRAINS ROAR IN MY EARS, DEPARTURES, DEPARTURES! ....THREE WOMEN   177   31
    EARS CUPPING THE SEA'S INCOHERENCES, ...MEDUSA   224   3
    EYES, NOSE AND EARS, ...PARALYTIC   266   29
    CHURCHYARD EARS UNTIL THE STARLIT STIFF ....LOVE IS A PARALLAX   330   41
    GRASSHOPPER GOBLINS WITH GREEN POINTED EARS   EPITAPH IN THREE PARTS   337   23
EAR'S (1)
    FOR THE WHORLED EAR'S LISTENING ....LORELEI   94   18
EARTH (21)
    WHEN ALL EARTH HIS WORDS DO SUMMON ....ODE FOR TED   30   23
    BRONZED AS EARTH, THE SECOND LIES, ...TWO SISTERS OF PERSEPHONE   32   13
    HOUSED IN EARTH, THOSE MILLION BRIDES SHRIEK OUT. ......VANITY FAIR   33   33
    EACH THORN; SPIRING FROM WET EARTH, A BLUE HAZE ....DIALOGUE B.   38   5
    EARTH IS MY HAUNT." ....DIALOGUE BETWEEN GHOST AND PRIEST   38   20
    FROM MY RENTED ATTIC WITH NO EARTH ....LANDOWNERS   53   1
    TO HOODWINK THE HONEST EARTH WHICH POINTBLANK ....CONJURING.   66   28
    THAN EARTH, AND THERE IS NOTHING ....THE GREAT CARBUNCLE   73   25
    THE EARTH TURNS NOW. IN HALF AN HOUR .....ON THE DECLINE OF ORACLES   78   26
    INTO THE ROCKY GIZZARD OF THE EARTH, ...THE GHOST'S LEAVETAKING   90   24
    WORK OF THE EARTH AND THE SKY'S RIDGEPOLE. ....FULL FATHOM FIVE   93   32
    ODORS OF WET EARTH RISE. ....THE SLEEPERS   122   9
    PALMING THE EARTH ASIDE, GRUBBERS ....BLUE MOLES   126   24
    INHERIT THE EARTH. ....MUSHROOMS   140   32
    I LOSE LIFE AFTER LIFE. THE DARK EARTH DRINKS THEM. ....THREE WOMEN   181 154
    A GLITTER OF WHEAT AND CRUDE EARTH. ....BERCK-PLAGE   200   96
    THIS EARTH I RISE FROM, AND I IN AGONY. ....GETTING THERE   248   37
    RED EARTH, MOTHERLY BLOOD. ....BRASILIA   258   17
    I THOUGHT EARTH MIGHT USE YOU. ....THE RIVAL/DR   291   22
    GAVE MOLTEN EARTH A FRAME, ...NOTES TO A NEOPHYTE   306   20
    NOW EARTH REJECTS COMMUNICATION *INSOLENT STORM STRIKES AT THE SKULL   326   29
EARTHBORN (1)
    IN ONE BODY THOSE EARTHBORN COMMONERS ....NATURAL HISTORY   71   8
EARTHEN (2)
    AND THE IRON HILLS THAT ENCLOSE THEM. EARTHEN FINGERS ....NET-.   121   16
    THE EARTHEN WOMB ....NICK AND THE CANDLESTICK   240   4
EARTHENWARE (2)
    THE LADY AND THE EARTHENWARE HEAD   THE LADY AND THE EARTHENWARE HEAD   69   T
    FRAIL AS ANTIQUE EARTHENWARE ....OLD LADIES' HOME   120   2
EARTH-FLESH (1)
    OF FLAWED EARTH-FLESH COULD CAUSE THIS SORRY PASS? .....DIALOGUE B.   39   32
EARTHQUAKING (1)
    THE SEVEN TROUGHED SEAS AND EVERY EARTHQUAKING CONTINENT. ......SOW   61   45
EARTH'S (6)
    BLOOD FAULTLESSLY BROACHED REDEEMED THE SULLIED AIR, THE EARTH'S
                                  GROSSNESS. ....THE GORING   47   10
    EARTH'S EVER-GREEN DEATH'S HEAD. ....CRYSTAL GAZER   56   48
    I RIDE EARTH'S BURNING CARROUSEL ....ON THE PLETHORA OF DRYADS   67   29
    LUCENT AS PORCELAIN, THE EARTH'S ....THE GREAT CARBUNCLE   72   7
    PONDEROUS AND EXTEND DESPAIR ON EARTH'S ....PERSEUS   83   31
    LOUD ON EARTH'S BEDROCK. ALMOST THROWN, NOT ...WHITENESS I REMEMBER   103   31
EARTH-WIFE'S (1)
    FROM HIS EARTH-WIFE'S SIDE ....THE SHRIKE   42   4
EARWIG (1)
    LEMON TEA AND EARWIG BISCUITS -- CREEPY-CREEPY. ....THE TOUR   238   39
EASE (4)
    THERE IS TOO MUCH EASE HERE; THESE STARS TREAT ME TOO WELL.   STARS.   166   37
    TABLES AND CHAIRS CAN ELBOW US WITH EASE*DIALOGUE OVER A OUIJA BOARD   279 113
    ONLY TO VANISH WITH DEVILISH EASE ....CIRCUS IN THREE RINGS   322   17
    A MERMAID ODALISQUE LOLLS AT HER EASE ....MIDSUMMER MOBILE   324   10
EASED (1)
    WOULD NOT BE EASED, RELEASED. OUR EACH EXAMPLE ....THE OTHER TWO   68   23
EASIER (1)
    AN EASIER ELEMENT ....THE GREAT CARBUNCLE   73   24
EASILY (1)
    AS EASILY AND IRRETRIEVABLY ....APRIL 18   302   15
EASING (2)
    NEITHER TEARS NOR THE EASING FLUSH ....THE EYE-MOTE   109   19
    THE SHADOWS OF RINGDOVES CHANTING, BUT EASING NOTHING. *WINTER TREES   258   15
EASTER (2)
    THEY GLEAM LIKE EASTER EGGSHELLS, ...BATTLE-SCENE   84   25
    FATHER, BRIDEGROOM, IN THIS EASTER EGG ....THE BEEKEEPER'S DAUGHTER   118   19
EASY (11)
    EASY AND OFTEN AS EACH BREATH. ....BLUE MOLES   127   36
    BREATHING WAS EASY IN HIS AIRY HOLDING. POEM.4.BEAST.   134   3
    IT IS EASY TO BLAME THE DARK: THE MOUTH OF A DOOR, ...POEM.6.W.   135   7
    NOT EASY TO STATE THE CHANGE YOU MADE. ....LOVE LETTER   147   1

EASY (CONT.)
  SKIN DOESN'T HAVE ROOTS, IT PEELS AWAY EASY AS PAPER. ....FACE LIFT 156   20
  IN ITS EASY PEACE, COULD ONLY KEEP HOLY SO. ....THREE WOMEN 178   81
  SETTLES IN THE ELM, AND IS EASY. ....PHEASANT 191   22
  THIS IS THE EASY TIME, THERE IS NOTHING DOING. ....WINTERING 217   1
  IT'S EASY ENOUGH TO DO IT IN A CELL. ....LADY LAZARUS 245   49
  IT'S EASY ENOUGH TO DO IT AND STAY PUT. ....LADY LAZARUS 245   50
  SHE IS NOT EASY, SHE IS NOT PEACEFUL; ....ELM/DR 292   1
EAT (22)
  LEANS TO PECK OPEN THOSE LOCKED LIDS, TO EAT ....THE SHRIKE   42   18
  WHILE I EAT GRITS ....RHYME   50   9
  EAT ME. WASTEBASKET GAPER, SHADOW OF DOORWAY. POEM.1.WHO. 132   27
  MOLEY-HANDED, I EAT MY WAY. POEM.2.DARK. 132   16
  ONLY THE DEVIL CAN EAT THE DEVIL OUT. POEM.6.W. 135   5
  THE VIVID TULIPS EAT MY OXYGEN. ....TULIPS 161   49
  THESE ARE OUR CREPES. EAT THEM BEFORE THEY BLOW COLD." ..FINISTERRE 170   36
  MEN HAVE USED HER MEANLY. SHE WILL EAT THEM. ....THREE WOMEN 181 159
  EAT THEM, EAT THEM, EAT THEM IN THE END. ....THREE WOMEN 181 160
  EAT THEM, EAT THEM, EAT THEM IN THE END. ....THREE WOMEN 181 160
  EAT THEM, EAT THEM, EAT THEM IN THE END. ....THREE WOMEN 181 160
  LET US EAT OUR LAST SUPPER AT IT, LIKE A HOSPITAL PLATE. BIRTHDAY. 207   26
  DO WITHOUT FEVERS TO EAT? ....THE JAILER 227   42
  YOU COULD EAT HIM. HE'S A BOY. ....LESBOS 228   25
  AND I EAT MEN LIKE AIR. ....LADY LAZARUS 247   84
  WHAT DO WHEELS EAT, THESE WHEELS ....GETTING THERE 248   13
  O GOLDEN CHILD THE WORLD WILL KILL AND EAT. ....MARY'S SONG 257   21
  O YOU WHO EAT ....BRASILIA 258   18
  LET US EAT IT LIKE PLATO'S AFTERBIRTH, ...TOTEM 264   14
  LET US EAT IT LIKE CHRIST. ....TOTEM 264   15
  THE CELLOS OF MOANS I EAT EGGS -- ....GIGOLO 267   15
  A FUNNY PINK WORLD HE MIGHT EAT ON THE OTHER SIDE OF IT, ..BALLOONS 272   24
EATEN (9)
  I'VE EATEN A BAG OF GREEN APPLES, ...METAPHORS 116   8
  OF BEETLES, SWEETBREADS, SHARDS -- TO BE EATEN ....BLUE MOLES 126   31
  EATEN OR ROTTEN. I AM ALL MOUTH. POEM.6.WHO. 131   2
  THEY ARE EATEN IMMEDIATELY BY THE PINES. ...STARS OVER THE DORDOGNE 165   8
  THOUGH FOR YEARS I HAVE EATEN DUST ....STINGS 214   24
  MY RIBS SHOW. WHAT HAVE I EATEN? ....THE JAILER 226   22
  IN WHOSE SHADOW I HAVE EATEN MY GHOST RATION. ....THE JAILER 227   38
  IT STRETCHES INTO THE DISTANCE. IT WILL BE EATEN NEVERTHELESS.*TOTEM 264   2
  EATEN BY WEEDY GREENS. ....WORDS 270   13
EATERIES (1)
  PAST THE YELLOW-PAELLA EATERIES, ...ALICANTE LULLABY   43   3
EATING (5)
  TO THE GROSS EATING GAME ....ALL THE DEAD DEARS   70   9
  EATING THE FINGERS OF WISDOM. POEM.3.MAENAD. 133   3
  IS SHE HIDING, IS SHE EATING HONEY? SHE IS VERY CLEVER. ....BEE. 212   43
  LIKE HIROSHIMA ASH AND EATING IN. ....FEVER. 231   26
  EATING YOUR WORDS: YOU'LL REVOKE HIS GODHOOD SOON AS ...DIALOGUE O. 281 189
EATS (4)
  HE EATS, AND STILL HIS NEED SEEKS FOOD, ...PURSUIT   23   39
  EATS AT POINT SHIRLEY. SHE DIED BLESSED, ...POINT SHIRLEY 111   36
  THE SMALL DELL EATS WHAT ATE IT ONCE. ....THE BURNT-OUT SPA 138   18
  THE MASK INCREASES, EATS THE WORM, ...THE FEARFUL 256   5
EAVESDROPPER (1)
  EAVESDROPPER ....EAVESDROPPER 260   T
EBBING (1)
  IN PAN: IT'S BEEN EBBING EVER SINCE THE MESS ....DIALOGUE O. 277   38
EBON (2)
  EBON IN THE HEDGES, FAT .............................BLACKBERRYING 168   6
  NINE BLACK MICE WITH EBON COACH, *BLACK PINE TREE IN AN ORANGE LIGHT 328   6
EBONY (1)
  IN AN EBONY AIR, ON WINGS OF WITCH CLOTH, ...GOATSUCKER 111   10
ECCENTRIC (1)
  THAT FOR ECCENTRIC KNOB AND WART ....ON THE PLETHORA OF DRYADS   67   5
ECHO (4)
  OUR VOICES ECHO, MAGNIFYING YOUR ARRIVAL. NEW STATUE.   MORNING SONG 157   4
  EMPTY, I ECHO TO THE LEAST FOOTFALL, ...BARREN WOMAN 157   1
  OF AN ECHO, EXPOSES THE PANEL IN THE WALL ....WIDOW 164   7
  IN THAT VALLEY THE TRAIN SHRIEKS ECHO LIKE SOULS ON HOOKS. ...
                                         ... THE DETECTIVE 208   5
ECHOED (1)
  HOW THE BALCONIES ECHOED! HOW THE SUN LIT UP ......WAKING IN WINTER 151   9
ECHOER (1)
  ICICLES, OLD ECHOER. ....NICK AND THE CANDLESTICK 241   11
ECHOES (8)
  HIS BRIDE ECHOES HIS WORD. AT THAT, ...CRYSTAL GAZER   55   21
  SUCH A RACKET OF ECHOES FROM THE STEELY STREET, ...HARDCASTLE CRAGS   62   2
  A FIREWORK OF ECHOES FROM WALL ....HARDCASTLE CRAGS   62   6
  BUT THE ECHOES DIED AT HER BACK AS THE WALLS ......HARDCASTLE CRAGS   62   8
  ALL SUMMER WE MOVED IN A VILLA BRIMFUL OF ECHOES, ...THE OTHER TWO   68   1
  THESE ARE MY FEET, THESE MECHANICAL ECHOES. ....THREE WOMEN 177   34
  AND THE ECHOES! ....WORDS 270   3
  ECHOES TRAVELING ....WORDS 270   4

	TITLE	PAGE	LINE

ECHOING (3)
    AND I, A SHELL, ECHOING ON THIS WHITE BEACH ....THREE WOMEN 179 111
    ECHOING, ECHOING. ....ELM 192 12
    ECHOING, ECHOING. ....ELM 192 12
ECLIPSE (4)
    WATCHES HIS CUMBROUS WORLD ECLIPSE ....SCULPTOR   91 12
    FROM BLIND AIR, FROM COMPLETE ECLIPSE. ...............RHODODENDRON. 103 16
    AND ECLIPSE THAT OVAL ....MOONSONG AT MORNING 317   7
    SOMERSAULTS TO COUNTERFEIT ECLIPSE: ....SONNET TO SATAN 323   2
ECLIPSED (2)
    ECLIPSED BENEATH BLIND LID OF LAND ....DANSE MACABRE 320   2
    ECLIPSED BY MAGICIAN'S DISGUISE, ...CIRCUS IN THREE RINGS 322 14
ECLIPSING (2)
    ECLIPSING THE SPITTED OX I SEE ....ON THE DECLINE OF ORACLES   78 17
    ECLIPSING EVA, CLEO AND HELEN OF TROY: ....VIRGIN IN A TREE   81 19
ECSTASY'S (1)
    THE SECRET OF THEIR ECSTASY'S IN GOING; ....LOVE IS A PARALLAX 330 62
EDDIES (2)
    NOW THE AIR SNAGS AND EDDIES ROUND THEM THE WAY A RIVER .....TULIPS 161 53
    SNAGS AND EDDIES ROUND A SUNKEN RUST-RED ENGINE. ....TULIPS 161 54
EDDIES' (1)
    OF THE AIR EDDIES' LOOP AND ARC THOUGH AIR'S AT REST*ABOVE THE OXBOW   88 32
EDDY (1)
    FROST-BITTEN PIGEONS, EDDY FORTH ....A WINTER'S TALE   87 34
EDEN (3)
    IN THE GREEN OF EDEN, PRETEND FUTURE'S SHINING FRUIT   TALE OF A TUB   25 39
    POINT OF EDEN, NEXT THE NEW MOON'S CURVE. ..THE GHOST'S LEAVETAKING   91 31
    THE EDEN OF BUCOLIC EVE: ................METAMORPHOSES OF THE MOON 307 15
EDEN'S (2)
    AS OUT OF EDEN'S NAVEL TWIST THE LINES ................SNAKECHARMER   79 19
    INUNDATING EDEN'S QUIET: ....INSOLENT STORM STRIKES AT THE SKULL 326 22
EDENY (1)
    THROUGH THE AFRICAN GIRAFFE IN ITS EDENY GREENERY, ...A SECRET 219 12
EDGE (8)
    TO THE WORLD'S WHITE EDGE ....THE SNOWMAN ON THE MOOR   59 22
    TO US, SINCE WE SEE NO LEAF EDGE STIR HIGH ....ABOVE THE OXBOW   88 33
    WITH A HUNDRED BUSHEL BASKETS ON THE EDGE ....SPINACH-PICKER.   89   6
    EDGE OF A CRATERED POOL-BED ....MUSSEL HUNTER AT ROCK HARBOR   95 16
    THEIR WHETSTONE TO THE BLUNTED EDGE ....THE DEATH OF MYTH-MAKING 104   9
    ON THIS BALD HILL THE NEW YEAR HONES ITS EDGE. ....PARLIAMENT H. 152   1
    EDGE ....EDGE 272   T
    A SEA OF DREAMS WASHES THE EDGE OF MY GREEN ISLAND ...QUEEN MARY'S. 290   2
EDGED (1)
    THE CLIFFS ARE EDGED WITH TREFOILS, STARS AND BELLS .....FINISTERRE 169 10
EDGES (4)
    SHE EDGES WITH WARY BREATH, ...MISS DRAKE PROCEEDS TO SUPPER   41 21
    THIS DREAM BUDDED BRIGHT WITH LEAVES AROUND THE EDGES,*DREAM WITH C.   43   1
    AND A NAME WITH BLACK EDGES ....BURNING THE LETTERS 205 42
    IT IS SHIMMERING, HAS IT BREASTS, HAS IT EDGES?   A BIRTHDAY PRESENT 206   2
EDIBLE (2)
    WE ARE EDIBLE, ...MUSHROOMS 139 27
    NO, NO, IT IS SCARLET FLOWERS THAT WILL ONE DAY BE EDIBLE. ....BEE. 211 20
EDIFICE (1)
    AND WITH THEM THAT RICKETY EDIFICE ....A WINTER SHIP 113 16
EDWARDIAN (1)
    DRAG UP FALSE, EDWARDIAN SENTIMENTS, ...CANDLES 149 16
EEL (1)
    COLD AS AN EEL, WITHOUT EYELIDS. ....ZOO KEEPER'S WIFE 154   2
EELISH (1)
    SUCH EELISH DELVINGS! POEM.2.DARK. 132   9
EELS (2)
    A CREEL OF EELS, ALL RIPPLES. ....YOU'RE 141 15
    EELS TWIRL ....AQUATIC NOCTURNE 306 19
EELY (1)
    OFF, OFF, EELY TENTACLE! ....MEDUSA 226 40
EFFACE (1)
    AND I HAVE NO FACE, I HAVE WANTED TO EFFACE MYSELF. ....TULIPS 161 48
EFFACED (1)
    AND THE SNARES ALMOST EFFACED THEMSELVES -- .....THE RABBIT CATCHER 194 14
EFFACEMENT (1)
    EFFACEMENT AT THE WIND'S HAND. ....MORNING SONG 157   9
EFFECT (1)
    AN EFFECT, A COSMETIC. ....THE OTHER 202 30
EFFICIENCY (1)
    THEY HAD AN EFFICIENCY, A GREAT BEAUTY, ...THE RABBIT CATCHER 193   9
EFFIGY (2)
    NO PLACE, IT SEEMED, FOR THE EFFIGY TO FARE ....LADY AND T.   69   8
    THE FACE OF THE EFFIGY, GENTLED BY CANDLES, ...MOON. 173 20
EFFORT (1)
    ARRIVE AT TWILIGHT, AND THEN AFTER SOME EFFORT. ....STARS. 165 10
EFFORTLESSLY (1)
    THEY SEED SO EFFORTLESSLY! ....WINTER TREES 258   8
EFFORTS (1)
    THE SWEAT OF HIS EFFORTS A RAIN ....STINGS 215 46

```
                                                            TITLE          PAGE  LINE
E.G. (1)
    E.G., BY CANT OF LIGHT  ...ON THE DIFFICULTY OF CONJURING UP A DRYAD    66   22
EGG (8)
    FAGGOT-BEARING JACK IN HIS CRACKLESS EGG:  ..................MAUDLIN     51    4
    DEATH WHITENS IN THE EGG AND OUT OF IT.  ....................MOONRISE    98   19
    SUICIDE OFF EGG ROCK  .........................SUICIDE OFF EGG ROCK    115    T
    RAY BUT EGG ROCK ON THE BLUE WASTAGE.  .........SUICIDE OFF EGG ROCK   115   22
    FATHER, BRIDEGROOM, IN THIS EASTER EGG  ....THE BEEKEEPER'S DAUGHTER   118   19
    TO STIR ROBIN'S EGG  ...............................POLLY'S TREE       128   14
    OLD SOCK-FACE, SAGGED ON A DARNING EGG.  ...................FACE LIFT  156   27
    DEAD EGG, I LIE  ..........................................PARALYTIC   266   17
EGG-HEAD (1)
    KING EGG-HEAD SAW HIS DOMAIN CRACK,  .................NATURAL HISTORY   71   10
EGGS (6)
    A BEGGAR STOPS AMONG EGGS AND LOAVES,  ....................THE BEGGARS  48   10
    HONEYCOMBED WITH GOLDEN EGGS,  ..................................RHYME  50    2
    WHERE SMALL ANTS ROLL THEIR EGGS, WHERE GRUBS FATTEN.  .....MOONRISE    98   17
    BALD EYES OR PETRIFIED EGGS,  ..............................WHITSUN    153    3
    THE CELLOS OF MOANS I EAT EGGS --  ..........................GIGOLO    267   15
    EGGS AND FISH, THE ESSENTIALS,  ............................GIGOLO     267   16
EGG-SHAPE (1)
    CHOOSE AN EGG-SHAPE, A WORLD-SHAPE,  ..................FIESTA MELONS    46    8
EGG-SHAPED (1)
    THIS EGG-SHAPED BAILIWICK, CLEAR AS A TEAR.  .................A LIFE   149    2
EGGSHELLS (2)
    AMONG HER SECRET COMBINATIONS OF EGGSHELLS  ...........MISS DRAKE P.    41    7
    THEY GLEAM LIKE EASTER EGGSHELLS,  .....................BATTLE-SCENE    84   25
EGG-STAINED (1)
    OF DAY-OLD BREAD AND EGG-STAINED PLATES; PERHAPS  ....METAMORPHOSES.   307   29
EGGSTONES (1)
    THE PURPLE EGG-STONES: FROM GREAT HEAD'S KNOB  ........POINT SHIRLEY   110   22
EGO (2)
    SUCH POVERTY ASSAULTS THE EGO; CAUGHT  ................TALE OF A TUB    24    4
    COLD FOLDS OF EGO, THE CALLA,  ....................THE NIGHT DANCES    250   12
EGOTISTS (1)
    UNABLE TO FACE THE FINGERS, THOSE EGOTISTS.  ......A BIRTHDAY PRESENT  208    9
EGYPTIAN (2)
    THE ORANGE POMPONS, THE EGYPTIAN PAPYRUS  ....PARLIAMENT HILL FIELDS   153   43
    A GREAT FRIEZE, EGYPTIAN, PERHAPS, OR GREEK,  ..........DIALOGUE O.    276    9
EIDERS (1)
    GREY WAVES THE STUB-NECKED EIDERS RIDE.  .............POINT SHIRLEY    110   33
EIGHT (5)
    THE EIGHT PILGRIMS TOWARDS ITS SOURCE --  .......THE GREAT CARBUNCLE    72   10
    MORE THAN EIGHT DECADES BACK  .....................THE TIMES ARE TIDY  107   12
    EIGHT GREAT TONGUES AFFIRMING THE RESURRECTION.  ..............MOON.   173   13
    EIGHT COMBS OF YELLOW CUPS,  ................................STINGS    214    7
    IN EIGHT GREAT BOUNDS, A GREAT SCAPEGOAT.  ..................STINGS    215   41
EIGHTEENTH (1)
    APRIL [EIGHTEENTH]  .........................................APRIL 18  301    T
EIGHT-FINGERED (1)
    CLAMBERING ROUND ITS GLASS BOX LIKE AN EIGHT-FINGERED HAND.  ZOO K.   155   31
EITHER (6)
ELABORATE (2)
    IN THOSE ELABORATE RITUALS  ..........MISS DRAKE PROCEEDS TO SUPPER     41    2
    ELABORATE SCAFFOLD OF SKY OVERHEAD  .......................AERIALIST   332   47
ELASTICS (2)
    BOOMERANG LIKE ANCHORED ELASTICS, HURTING THE OWNER.  ...BERCK-PLAGE   196   11
    HERE THEY COME, THE OUTRIDERS, ON THEIR HYSTERICAL ELASTICS.  ..BEE.   212   38
ELATE (1)
    THE ELATE PALLORS OF FLYING IRIS.  ......................BERCK-PLAGE   199   86
ELEVATOR-GIRL (2)
    SIGHED EVE, THE ELEVATOR-GIRL ACE,  ...............DIALOGUE EN ROUTE   308    2
    EVE, THE ELEVATOR-GIRL ACE,  ......................DIALOGUE EN ROUTE   309   32
ELBA (3)
    THE HUMP OF ELBA ON YOUR SHORT BACK,  .....................THE SWARM   216    8
    ELBA, ELBA, BLEB ON THE SEA!  .............................THE SWARM   217   43
    ELBA, ELBA, BLEB ON THE SEA!  .............................THE SWARM   217   43
ELBOW (5)
    SUDDENLY AT MY ELBOW. I ONLY KNOW THAT A ROOK  ........BLACK ROOK I.    57   27
    THE ASTROLOGER AT HER ELBOW (A LEO)  .........................ON DECK  143   25
    GLOVED MY ARM TO THE ELBOW.  ....................ZOO KEEPER'S WIFE     155   37
    BLOOD AND BANK WRIST, ELBOW, SHOULDER, LIP  .............DIALOGUE O.   277   18
    TABLES AND CHAIRS CAN ELBOW US WITH EASE*DIALOGUE OVER A OUIJA BOARD   279  113
ELBOWS (2)
    I AM UP TO MY ELBOWS IN IT, RED AND SQUEAKING.*THE SURGEON AT 2 A.M.   171   22
    WINGED ELBOWS AND EYEHOLES  ................................BRASILIA    258    3
ELBOW-SCARVES (1)
    IN ELBOW-SCARVES, BEARDS  ....................DARD WOOD, DARK WATER     127    3
ELDERBERRY (1)
    IF THAT ELDERBERRY BUSH BESIDE THE GATE *DIALOGUE OVER A OUIJA BOARD   280  157
ELDERLY (1)
    WHERE THE WIRELESS TALKS TO ITSELF LIKE AN ELDERLY RELATIVE.  ...
                                                    ... THE DETECTIVE     209   20
ELECT (1)
    IS THIS THE ELECT ONE, THE ONE WITH BLACK EYE-PITS AND A SCAR?  ...
                                                    ... A BIRTHDAY PRESENT 206   6
```

	TITLE	PAGE	LINE

ELECTRA (1)
    ELECTRA ON AZALEA PATH ....ELECTRA ON AZALEA PATH   116   T
ELECTRIC (3)
    RECORDS BARE PAINTED WALLS, WHILE AN ELECTRIC LIGHT ..TALE OF A TUB   24   2
    NOW THEY LIGHT ME UP LIKE AN ELECTRIC BULB. POEM.1.WHO.   132   32
    TO THE ELECTRIC MILKER, THE WIFEY, THE BIG BLUE EYE ...EAVESDROPPER   261   43
ELECTRIFY (1)
    WHICH OF THE NERVE-CURLERS, THE CONVULSORS? DID IT ELECTRIFY? ...
        ... THE DETECTIVE   209   23
ELECTRIFYINGLY-COLORED (1)
    ELECTRIFYINGLY-COLORED SHERBETS, SCOOPED FROM THE FREEZE*BERCK-PLAGE   196   3
ELECTRODE (1)
    THE FUTURE AN ELECTRODE IN YOUR SKULL. ....THE TRIAL OF MAN   312   14
ELEGANT (3)
    THROUGH PORTICO OF MY ELEGANT HOUSE YOU STALK ........CONVERSATION.   21   1
    EROTIC AND ELEGANT EPISODES." ....DIALOGUE EN ROUTE   309   24
    OF MAGAZINES IN ELEGANT ENNUI, ...MORNING IN THE HOSPITAL SOLARIUM   332   22
ELEGIAC (1)
    TO ELEGIAC DRYADS, AND DOUR GRASS ....NOVEMBER GRAVEYARD   56   3
ELEGIES (1)
    PARSLEYED WITH ELEGIES, SHE LIES IN STATE ....TERMINAL   328   13
ELEMENT (6)
    AN EASIER ELEMENT ....THE GREAT CARBUNCLE   73   24
    ELEMENT -- THIS RELIC SAVED ....MUSSEL HUNTER AT ROCK HARBOR   97   90
    FACE THE VOICES THAT OVERWHELM, THE TERRIBLE ELEMENT. ..THREE WOMEN   179 112
    IT IS SIMPLY IN ITS ELEMENT. ....PHEASANT   191   9
    MAKE THEIR OWN ELEMENT. THEY WILL NOT RISE, ...FEVER.   231   15
    AND INTO THE SILVER ELEMENT OF THE POND. ..QUEEN MARY'S ROSE GARDEN   290   12
ELEMENTS (4)
    SUCH COLLUSION OF MULISH ELEMENTS ....POINT SHIRLEY   110   17
    TOOK ITS PLACE AMONG THE ELEMENTS. ....MORNING SONG   156   3
    HOW THE ELEMENTS SOLIDIFY!-- ....EVENT   194   1
    ELEMENTS LIKE DIRTY SOCKS AND SCRAPS .....METAMORPHOSES OF THE MOON   307   28
ELEPHANT (2)
    AN ELEPHANT, A PONDEROUS HOUSE, ...METAPHORS   116   2
    NO GETTING UP BY ELEPHANT OR WHEEL OR SHOE. ...NEW YEAR ON DARTMOOR   176   7
ELEVATIONS (1)
    ELEVATIONS TO BE CALLED SOMETHING MORE THAN HILLS.   ABOVE THE OXBOW   88   9
ELEVEN (5)
    ELLA MASON AND HER ELEVEN CATS ......ELLA MASON AND HER ELEVEN CATS   53   T
    OLD ELLA MASON KEEPS CATS, ELEVEN AT LAST COUNT, ...ELLA MASON A.   53   1
    WITH ELEVEN CATS." ....ELLA MASON AND HER ELEVEN CATS   54   36
    ELEVEN WEEKS, AND I KNOW YOUR ESTATE SO WELL ....PRIVATE GROUND   130   13
    O IT WAS RICHNESS! -- ELEVEN ROOMS AND A YACHT .....THE BABYSITTERS   174   10
ELIZABETH (1)
    FROM AUNT ELIZABETH; ....FAMILY REUNION   300   15
ELLA (5)
    ELLA MASON AND HER ELEVEN CATS ......ELLA MASON AND HER ELEVEN CATS   53   T
    OLD ELLA MASON KEEPS CATS, ELEVEN AT LAST COUNT, ...ELLA MASON A.   53   1
    LONG GONE TO WHEEZE AND SEED, ELLA MASON ....ELLA MASON A.   53   8
    ELLA FLOUNCED ABOUT, MINX-THIN AND HAUGHTY, ...ELLA MASON A.   53   14
    WHILE ELLA DROWSED WHISKERED WITH SLEEK FACE, SLY WITS: ...
        ... ELLA MASON AND HER ELEVEN CATS   54   29
ELLA'S (1)
    "MISS ELLA'S GOT LOONY FROM KEEPING IN CAHOOTS ....ELLA MASON A.   54   35
ELLEN (1)
    THEY LEFT ME A BORROWED MAID NAMED ELLEN, "FOR PROTECTION", ..BABY.   174   17
ELLIPTIC (1)
    AND PLANETS PLOT WITH OLD ELLIPTIC CUNNING; .....TO EVA DESCENDING.   303   5
ELM (4)
    FROM HIS ORBIT UNDER THE ELM ROOT. ....BLUE MOLES   126   7
    DAWN FLOWERS IN THE GREAT ELM OUTSIDE THE HOUSE. ....THREE WOMEN   185 309
    SETTLES IN THE ELM, AND IS EASY. ....PHEASANT   191   22
    ELM ....ELM   192   T
ELMS (1)
    AWAY FROM THE LABELED ELMS, THE TAME TEA-ROSES. ....TWO CAMP.   144   9
ELM'S (1)
    THROUGH THE UNCUT GRASS ON THE ELM'S HILL. ....PHEASANT   191   4
ELOPING (1)
    ELOPING FROM THEIR SLABS, ABSTRACT ....DANSE MACABRE   321   19
ELOQUENTLY (1)
    ELOQUENTLY SHALL ....TRIO OF LOVE SONGS   314   34
ELSE (16)
    AND ALL ELSE I'VE TAUGHT ....RECANTATION   42   12
    WHITE BRUISES TOWARD COLOR, ELSE COLLAPSES. ....MOONRISE   98   12
    HARD GODS WERE THERE, NOTHING ELSE. ..THE HERMIT AT OUTERMOST HOUSE   119   13
    STILL HE THUMBED OUT SOMETHING ELSE.   THE HERMIT AT OUTERMOST HOUSE   119   14
    THINKING OF SOMETHING ELSE. POEM.2.DARK.   132   7
    OR ELSE THEY ARE PRESENT, AND THEIR DISGUISE SO BRIGHT ......STARS.   165   22
    IT HAD A CONSEQUENTIAL LOOK, LIKE EVERYTHING ELSE, ...THREE WOMEN   177   46
    THERE IS A GREAT DEAL ELSE TO DO. MY HANDS ....THREE WOMEN   187 359
    DEAFNESS IS SOMETHING ELSE. ....LITTLE FUGUE   188   21
    I DREAM OF SOMEONE ELSE ENTIRELY. ....THE JAILER   227   27
    HEAVEN WOULD BE SOMETHING ELSE, ...LYONNESSE   234   12
    SOMETHING ELSE ....ARIEL   239   15

ELSE (CONT.)
    IS AN ART, LIKE EVERYTHING ELSE. ....LADY LAZARUS   245   44
    THE LETTERS LIVE IN THE SAME PLACE. OR ELSE ....DIALOGUE O.   277   23
    TO COURT REMORSE. OR SOMEONE ELSE. I'D RATHER ....DIALOGUE O.   278   59
    MUST HAVE BEEN WHOLLY SOMEONE ELSE. IT'S ABSURD, ...DIALOGUE O.   285 309
ELSEWHERE (3)
    I LEARNED, I LEARNED, I LEARNED ELSEWHERE, ...THE DISQUIETING MUSES   75   39
    HOUSES HIMSELF ELSEWHERE. OUR FOLK THIN ....FROG AUTUMN   99   11
    ELSEWHERE THE LANDSCAPE IS MORE FRANK. ....A LIFE   150   19
ELUDE (1)
    THOSE LITTLE SICK ONES THAT ELUDE MY ARMS. ....THREE WOMEN   178   67
ELUSIVE (2)
    THE ELUSIVE ROSE. POEM.7.S. 137   42
    ON ELUSIVE TAILS: ....AQUATIC NOCTURNE   306   21
EMBALMED (2)
    THERE IS ONLY THE MOON, EMBALMED IN PHOSPHORUS. ......THE DETECTIVE   209   39
    ITS BABY HEAD OUT OF THE WAY, EMBALMED IN SPICE, ...TOTEM   264   12
EMBARK (1)
    HORIZONS BEAT A RETREAT AS WE EMBARK ....LOVE IS A PARALLAX   329   4
EMBARRASS (1)
    SUCH A LUXURY OF STARS WOULD EMBARRASS ME.   STARS OVER THE DORDOGNE   166   27
EMBARRASSMENTS (1)
    EXPOSES EMBARRASSMENTS -- THE MIZZLING DAYS ....INSOMNIAC   163   9
EMBELLISHING (1)
    AND THE TIGER, EMBELLISHING ITSELF --- ....THE NIGHT DANCES   250   13
EMBLEMATIC (1)
    UPRAISED, AS A HAND, EMBLEMATIC OF FAREWELL.*THE GHOST'S LEAVETAKING   90   11
EMBRACE (4)
    THESE LOVERS PROPHESY TO LOCK EMBRACE ..EPITAPH FOR FIRE AND FLOWER   45   17
    WE MIGHT EMBRACE, BUT THOSE TWO NEVER DID, ...THE OTHER TWO   69   30
    THE FOOD TUBES EMBRACE ME. SPONGES KISS MY LICHENS AWAY. POEM.7.S.   136   19
    LOVED ME AND A BRAVE EMBRACE ....THE DREAM   311   22
EMBROIDER (1)
    SUCH AS FINGERS MIGHT EMBROIDER, CLOSE TO DEATH, ...FINISTERRE   169   11
EMBROIDERY (1)
    FLEW FROM THE INTRICATE EMBROIDERY ....THE PRINCESS AND THE GOBLINS   333   8
EMBRYO (1)
    O EMBRYO ....NICK AND THE CANDLESTICK   241   24
EMERALD (3)
    HEAVES FORTH STALK, LEAF, FRUIT-NUBBED EMERALD; ....ODE FOR TED   29   15
    SLAYING THE DANDIES WITH HER EMERALD EYES; ....ELLA MASON A.   54   16
    GUARDS THE HARD-HEARTED EMERALD OF ITS GRASSINESS*NOVEMBER GRAVEYARD   56   4
EMMETS (1)
    AMONG EMMETS AND MOLLUSKS, ...POEM.4.BEAST.   134   24
EMPIRES (1)
    AND THE DECLINE OF EMPIRES THE THICK COIL OF A VAST ....PERSEUS   83   23
EMPTIED (2)
    SIT EMPTIED OF BEAUTIES, THE GIFT ....THE NIGHT DANCES   250   8
    THAT EMPTIED ONE MAN INTO SPACE ....MARY'S SONG   257   17
EMPTIES (3)
    THE DAY EMPTIES ITS IMAGES ....PARLIAMENT HILL FIELDS   153   37
    THE SILVER TRACK OF TIME EMPTIES INTO THE DISTANCE, ...THREE WOMEN   177   32
    THE WHITE SKY EMPTIES OF ITS PROMISE, LIKE A CUP. ......THREE WOMEN   177   33
EMPTINESS (3)
    AND SHE'LL PERISH WITH EMPTINESS THEN, AND BEGIN TO MISS ME. ...
                                                ... IN PLASTER   160   56
    EMPTY SCHOOLROOMS, EMPTY CHURCHES. O SO MUCH EMPTINESS! *THREE WOMEN   181 179
    THERE IS MY COMB AND BRUSH. THERE IS AN EMPTINESS. .....THREE WOMEN   184 268
EMPTINESSES (1)
    QUIET, LIKE THE LITTLE EMPTINESSES I CARRY. ....THREE WOMEN   178   70
EMPTY (17)
    THE EMPTY BOTTLES ON THE WINDOWSILL ....RESOLVE   52   11
    EMPTY OF COMPLAINT, FOREVER ....THE THIN PEOPLE   64   19
    SMOKE WHEELS FROM THE BEAK OF THIS EMPTY JAR. POEM.6.W.   135   12
    EMPTY, I ECHO TO THE LEAST FOOTFALL, ...BARREN WOMAN   157   1
    TO LIE WITH MY HANDS TURNED UP AND BE UTTERLY EMPTY. ....TULIPS   161   30
    LAYING ITS SCALES ON THE WINDOWS, THE WINDOWS OF EMPTY OFFICES, ...
                                                ... THREE WOMEN   181 178
    EMPTY SCHOOLROOMS, EMPTY CHURCHES. O SO MUCH EMPTINESS! *THREE WOMEN   181 179
    EMPTY SCHOOLROOMS, EMPTY CHURCHES. O SO MUCH EMPTINESS! *THREE WOMEN   181 179
    EMPTY AND SILLY AS PLATES, ...LITTLE FUGUE   188   17
    THE EMPTY BENCHES OF MEMORY LOOK OVER STONES, ...BERCK-PLAGE   199   88
    AND THE BOTTLES OF EMPTY GLITTERS --- ....WINTERING   218   9
    EMPTY? EMPTY. HERE IS A HAND ....THE APPLICANT   221   10
    EMPTY? EMPTY. HERE IS A HAND ....THE APPLICANT   221   10
    NOW YOUR HEAD, EXCUSE ME, IS EMPTY. ....THE APPLICANT   221   26
    PITCHER OF MILK, NOW EMPTY. ....EDGE   272   11
    NO MILK OR HONEY FILLS THE EMPTY CAN; ....THE DISPOSSESSED   318   5
    NOW EMPTY BOXES OF THE HOODWINKED DEAD*SONG FOR A REVOLUTIONARY LOVE   323   17
EMPTY-PURSED (1)
    WHILE SUBJECTS HUNGERED, EMPTY-PURSED, ...NATURAL HISTORY   71   5
EMULOUS (1)
    EMULOUS SPIRITS MAKE DISCORD. ....SCULPTOR   92   20
EN (1)
    DIALOGUE EN ROUTE ....DIALOGUE EN ROUTE   308   T

```
                                                    TITLE           PAGE   LINE
ENACTED (1)
   ENACTED TRAGEDIES ON THESE BLOOD-SOAKED BOARDS, ...........PERSEUS    83   19
ENAMEL (1)
   IRON ENTRAILS, ENAMEL BOWLS,  .....................THE BURNT-OUT SPA  138   16
ENAMELED (1)
   WITH EXCESSIVE LOVE I ENAMELED IT  ..........................STINGS  214   10
ENCASED (1)
   ENCASED IN A GLASSY PELLICLE.  .......................A WINTER SHIP  113   28
ENCHANTING (1)
   ENCHANTING MEN  ...............................MOONSONG AT MORNING   316    2
ENCLOSE (1)
   AND THE IRON HILLS THAT ENCLOSE THEM. EARTHEN FINGERS  ........NET-.  121   16
ENCOUNTER (2)
   LEANING OVER, I ENCOUNTER ONE  ....................THE BURNT-OUT SPA  138   24
   ENCOUNTER THEM ON THE ROAD ---  .............................WORDS   270   15
ENCROACH (1)
   BY LACK AND LOSS THESE BEGGARS ENCROACH  ...............THE BEGGARS   48   13
ENCROACHES (1)
   THEIR MUSK ENCROACHES, CIRCLE AFTER CIRCLE,*THE BEEKEEPER'S DAUGHTER 118    3
END (30)
   END: GREEN SHORES APPEAR; WE ASSUME OUR NAMES,  ....CHANNEL CROSSING  27   40
   AFTER YOUR LIFE'S END, WHAT JUST EPILOGUE  .............DIALOGUE B.   39   24
   THE AFTERNOON AT A BAD END UNDER THE CROWD'S TRUCULENCE, *THE GORING  47    2
   EACH LOVE BLAZING BLIND TO ITS GUTTED END --  .........CRYSTAL GAZER  56   46
   PURE LEAFAGE. A HUNDRED BASKETS BY DAY'S END.  ......SPINACH-PICKER.  89   11
   WHICH SIGNIFY OUR ORIGIN AND END,  ..........THE GHOST'S LEAVETAKING  91   34
   DRAINS LIKE WATER OUT THE HOLE AT THE FAR END.  ...........INSOMNIAC  163   25
   SOMEWHERE AT THE END OF IT, HEAVING. BLACKBERRIES  ...BLACKBERRYING  168    4
   ONE MORE HOOK, AND THE BERRIES AND BUSHES END.  .......BLACKBERRYING  169   18
   THIS WAS THE LAND'S END: THE LAST FINGERS, KNUCKLED AND
      RHEUMATIC,  ....................................FINISTERRE        169    1
   AT THE END, THEY SOBERLY BONG OUT THEIR NAMES.  ...............MOON.  173   14
   ITS END AND RUNS TOWARD IT, ARMS HELD OUT IN LOVE.  .....THREE WOMEN  181  151
   EAT THEM, EAT THEM, EAT THEM IN THE END.  ...............THREE WOMEN  181  160
   AND THAT MAD, HARD FACE AT THE END OF IT, THAT O-MOUTH   THREE WOMEN  182  184
   I AM HELPLESS AS THE SEA AT THE END OF HER STRING.  ....THREE WOMEN  182  188
   AND HERE IS AN END TO THE WRITING,  ............BURNING THE LETTERS  204   20
   NO FALLING RIBBONS, NO SCREAM AT THE END.  .......A BIRTHDAY PRESENT  207   35
   THE MIND OF THE HIVE THINKS THIS IS THE END OF EVERYTHING.  ....BEE.  212   37
   LEAVE AND ARRIVE, AND THERE IS NO END TO THE COUNTRY.  ...THE SWARM  217   36
   TO THUMB SHUT YOUR EYES AT THE END  ..................THE APPLICANT  221   16
   TREMULOUS BREATH AT THE END OF MY LINE,  ...................MEDUSA   225   17
   THERE IS A MINUTE AT THE END OF IT  ...................GETTING THERE  248   41
   THE FACE AT THE END OF THE FLARE.  ...................GETTING THERE  249   59
   ROPED IN AT THE END BY THE ONE  .............................TOTEM   265   33
   WHEN MY ENGINE REACHES THE END OF IT.  ......................GIGOLO  267   20
   AND THERE IS NO END, NO END OF IT.  .........................GIGOLO  268   25
   AND THERE IS NO END, NO END OF IT.  .........................GIGOLO  268   25
   HE LIVES. HIS ANSWER WILL PUT AN END TO GIBES  .........DIALOGUE O.  281  174
   TO THE END OF IT. HE STARTS AGAIN: I-N- *DIALOGUE OVER A OUIJA BOARD  282  217
   TOO LATE TO ASK IF END WAS WORTH THE MEANS,  ..............DOOMSDAY  316   16
ENDED (2)
   THAT QUESTION ENDED IT -- I  ..........MUSSEL HUNTER AT ROCK HARBOR   96   51
   AN OLD BEAST ENDED IN THIS PLACE:  ................THE BURNT-OUT SPA  137    1
ENDING (2)
   OF WEEDS WE TACKLE TOWARDS WAY'S RANK ENDING;  .............FIRESONG   30   16
   ENDING IN A THIN-PANED  ................................POLLY'S TREE  128    4
ENDLESS (2)
   THEIR FABULOUS HEYDAY ENDLESS.  ............DREAM WITH CLAM-DIGGERS   44   16
   ITS ENDLESS GLITTER.  ................................POEM.3.MAENAD.  133   20
ENDLESSLY (3)
   BEATS, IS BRUTAL ENDLESSLY.  .............................DEPARTURE   51   15
   COME TO BARTER ENDLESSLY  ................................SCULPTOR    91    2
   ENDLESSLY PROCEED -- AND THE COLD ANGELS, THE ABSTRACTIONS.   THREE.  177   20
ENDORSES (1)
   HIS DRIFT ENDORSES YOUR INKLINGS OF A DOOM  ............DIALOGUE O.  281  190
ENDOW (2)
   BLAZON SKY BLUE, AND ENDOW THE SUN  ......SOLILOQUY OF THE SOLIPSIST   37   22
   HOW YOUR BAD DREAMS POSSESS AND ENDOW ME.  ....................ELM   192   27
ENDS (3)
   BEFORE TIME ENDS  .......................................RECANTATION   42   18
   I AM MYSELF AGAIN. THERE ARE NO LOOSE ENDS.  ...........THREE WOMEN  184  274
   OF SLOW DISASTER: THE BITTEN APPLE ENDS  ..METAMORPHOSES OF THE MOON  307   14
ENDURE (2)
   ON HAWTHORN BOUGHS, WITH GOODWILL TO ENDURE  ..............MAYFLOWER   60   13
   STONES, WITHOUT CONSCIENCE, WORD AND LINE ENDURE,  ..POEMS, POTATOES  106    5
ENDURED (2)
   YET, SHRINED ON HER SHELF, THE GRISLY VISAGE ENDURED,  ..LADY AND T.   70   29
   FOR WHAT, THEN, HAD THEY ENDURED  .....THE HERMIT AT OUTERMOST HOUSE  119    7
ENEMIES (1)
   SMILING AT THIS BEHAVIOR, SUBJUGATING THEIR ENEMIES  ........LESSON.   80   22
ENEMIES' (1)
   JOINS HIS ENEMIES' RECRUITS.  ...................LOVE IS A PARALLAX  330   54
ENEMY (2)
   O MY ENEMY.  ...........................................LADY LAZARUS  244   11
```

ENEMY (CONT.)
    SO, HERR ENEMY. ....LADY LAZARUS   246   66
ENFOLDS (2)
    TONIGHT, LIKE A SHAWL, THE MILD LIGHT ENFOLDS HER, ...CANDLES   149   34
    ENFOLDS HER FACE LIKE FINE LINEN, ...BERCK-PLAGE   200 102
ENGENDERING (1)
    MIRRORS, ENGENDERING A SPECTRAL ....LANDOWNERS   53   7
ENGINE (6)
    SNAGS AND EDDIES ROUND A SUNKEN RUST-RED ENGINE. ....TULIPS   161   54
    OVER THE ENGINE THAT KILLED HER --- ....STINGS   215   59
    AN ENGINE, AN ENGINE ....DADDY   223   31
    AN ENGINE, AN ENGINE ....DADDY   223   31
    THE ENGINE IS KILLING THE TRACK, THE TRACK IS SILVER, ...TOTEM   264   1
    WHEN MY ENGINE REACHES THE END OF IT. ....GIGOLO   267   20
ENGINEERED (1)
    ENGINEERED THE GANNET'S BEAK. ....I WANT, I WANT   106   8
ENGLAND (2)
    WHEN THE SWEETHEART FROM ENGLAND APPEARED, WITH HER CREAM SKIN AND
        YARDLEY COSMETICS, ...THE BABYSITTERS   174   6
    IT ISN'T ENGLAND, IT ISN'T FRANCE,IT ISN'T IRELAND. ...STOPPED DEAD   230   10
ENGLISH (3)
    SELLING THE WELSH AND ENGLISH MOTHERS ....ON DECK   143   29
    OVER THE ENGLISH CLIFF AND UNDER SO MUCH HISTORY! ....LYONNESSE   234   22
    A-W-W. HE'S GONE OFF: WHAT ENGLISH .....DIALOGUE OVER A OUIJA BOARD   279   93
ENGRAVE (1)
    THE SKY'S GREAT BELL GLASS AND BRIEFLY ENGRAVE ...IN MIDAS' COUNTRY   99   8
ENGRAVED (2)
    LAST SUMMER'S REEDS ARE ALL ENGRAVED IN ICE ......WINTER LANDSCAPE,   22   11
    WHAT GERD SAW THEN ENGRAVED HER MIND ....CRYSTAL GAZER   56   43
ENGRAVES (1)
    A WAVE OF GRASS ENGRAVES UPON THE STONE: ....EPITAPH IN THREE PARTS   338   32
ENGRAVING (1)
    ENGRAVING ITSELF IN SILVER WITH MARVELOUS CALM. ....BERCK-PLAGE   199   72
ENGRAVINGS (1)
    HUNG UP IN THE LIBRARY WITH THE ENGRAVINGS OF RANGOON .....COURAGE.   210   22
ENGROSS (1)
    THUS WHOLLY ENGROSS ....SOW   61   28
ENGROSSED (2)
    PURE PHILOSOPHY HIS LOVE ENGROSSED: ....NATURAL HISTORY   71   4
    THREE GIRLS, ENGROSSED, WERE WRENCHING FULL CLUSTERS   RHODODENDRON.   104   21
ENGULFING (1)
    LIKE AN OLIVE-BEAKED DOVE ABOVE THE ENGULFING FACT: ...DIALOGUE O.   279 112
ENGULFS (1)
    AND ETERNITY ENGULFS IT, AND I DROWN UTTERLY? ....THREE WOMEN   179 105
ENIGMATICAL (1)
    ENIGMATICAL, ...PURDAH   242   6
ENJOY (1)
    I ENJOY PETTICOATS AND VELVETS AND GOSSIP OF COURT, ..QUEEN MARY'S.   290   21
ENJOYED (1)
    WELL I HOPE YOU'VE ENJOYED IT, AUNTIE! ....THE TOUR   238   48
ENLARGES (1)
    HOURLY THE EYE OF THE SKY ENLARGES ITS BLANK POEM.5.F.   134   5
ENLISTED (1)
    ENLISTED IN A CRAMPED NECROPOLIS, ...ELECTRA ON AZALEA PATH   117   17
ENNUI (1)
    OF MAGAZINES IN ELEGANT ENNUI, ...MORNING IN THE HOSPITAL SOLARIUM   332   22
ENORMITY (1)
    DO NOT BE MEAN, I AM READY FOR ENORMITY. ....A BIRTHDAY PRESENT   207   23
ENORMOUS (8)
    THERE WERE SUCH ENORMOUS FLOWERS, ...POEM.1.WHO.   132   29
    I THINK I MAY BE ENORMOUS, ...LETTER IN NOVEMBER   253   12
    THE ENORMOUS MORTGAGE MUST BE PAID SOMEHOW, ...THE DISPOSSESSED   318   1
    THE ENORMOUS MORTGAGE MUST BE PAID SOMEHOW. ....THE DISPOSSESSED   318   6
    THE ENORMOUS MORTGAGE MUST BE PAID SOMEHOW. ....THE DISPOSSESSED   318   12
    THE ENORMOUS MORTGAGE MUST BE PAID SOMEHOW: ....THE DISPOSSESSED   319   18
    LIKE AN ENORMOUS OYSTER, DOWN ....LOVE IS A PARALLAX   329   27
    ENORMOUS BOX OF GRAY WHERE GOD HAS GONE .....EPITAPH IN THREE PARTS   338   30
ENOUGH (25)
    THIS SORCERESS SETS MIRRORS ENOUGH ....VANITY FAIR   33   22
    LOVE FIERY ENOUGH TO PROVE FLESH REAL, ..SOLILOGUY OF THE SOLIPSIST   38   33
    UNRULY ENOUGH TO PITCH HER FIVE QUEENLY WITS ....SPINSTER   50   20
    BOAR, FABULOUS ENOUGH TO STRADDLE THAT SOW'S HEAT. ....SOW   61   33
    ENOUGH TO SNUFF THE QUICK ....HARDCASTLE CRAGS   63   41
    WE OWN NO WILDERNESSES RICH AND DEEP ENOUGH ....THE THIN PEOPLE   65   41
    INDISSOLUBLE ENOUGH TO RIDDLE THE GUTS ....PERSEUS   82   4
    FLATS OF HADLEY FARMS, THEY'RE LOFTY ENOUGH ....ABOVE THE OXBOW   88   8
    ENOUGH AGES LAPSED TO WIN ....MUSSEL HUNTER AT ROCK HARBOR   95   22
    VOCATION ENOUGH: OPENING, SHUTTING ....MOONRISE   98   8
    ENOUGH FOR FINGERNAILS TO MAKE HALF-MOONS ....MOONRISE   98   10
    THE SUN WILL DIMINISH IT SOON ENOUGH: ....A WINTER SHIP   113   29
    KNIFELIKE, HE WAS CHASTE ENOUGH, ...MEDALLION   125   25
    ONE, BY HIMSELF, SEEMED PITIABLE ENOUGH, ...BLUE MOLES   126   5
    A DUSTBIN'S ENOUGH FOR HIM. POEM.4.BEAST.   134   14
    THEY GREW THEIR TOES AND FINGERS WELL ENOUGH, ...STILLBORN   142   2
    BEFORE THEY CAME THE AIR WAS CALM ENOUGH, ...TULIPS   161   50

ENOUGH (CONT.)

BLUNT AND FLAT ENOUGH TO FEEL NO LACK. I FEEL A LACK. ..THREE WOMEN 182 193
I AM MYSELF. THAT IS NOT ENOUGH. ....THE JAILER 226 20
IT'S EASY ENOUGH TO DO IT IN A CELL. ....LADY LAZARUS 245 49
IT'S EASY ENOUGH TO DO IT AND STAY PUT. ....LADY LAZARUS 245 50
ENOUGH FOR NICKNAMES. HOW ARE YOU, PAN? F- ....DIALOGUE O. 277 31
YOU'D PRESUME YOUR INNER VOICE GOD-PLUMED ENOUGH ......DIALOGUE O. 280 168
ENOUGH. BUT BE POLITE. YOU'RE TOO SEVERE*DIALOGUE OVER A OUIJA BOARD 281 181
OLD ENOUGH TO GO. ....BITTER STRAWBERRIES 299 11

ENTER (14)

TWO ENTER TO TAP HER SIGHT, A GREEN PAIR ....CRYSTAL GAZER 55 7
STILL THAN SWALLOWS JOY. YOU ENTER NOW, ...PERSEUS 83 34
ENTER THE CHILLY NO-MAN'S LAND OF ABOUT ....THE GHOST'S LEAVETAKING 90 1
TRY ENTRY, ENTER NIGHTMARES ....SCULPTOR 92 21
I ENTER THE SOFT PELT OF THE MOLE. ....BLUE MOLES 126 21
AND WE SHALL NEVER ENTER THERE ....THE BURNT-OUT SPA 138 31
SHE HAS ONE TOO MANY DIMENSIONS TO ENTER. ....A LIFE 150 28
I ENTER THE LIT HOUSE. ....PARLIAMENT HILL FIELDS 153 50
I FEEL IT ENTER ME, COLD, ALIEN, LIKE AN INSTRUMENT. ...THREE WOMEN 182 183
INTOLERABLE VOWELS ENTER MY HEART. ....EVENT 194 6
MY FINGERS WOULD ENTER ALTHOUGH ....BURNING THE LETTERS 204 17
AND THE KNIFE NOT CARVE, BUT ENTER ....A BIRTHDAY PRESENT 208 60
TO ENTER ANOTHER YEAR? ....WINTERING 219 48
THEY ENTER AS ANIMALS FROM THE OUTER ....YEARS 255 1

ENTERED (2)

WHEN I FELL OUT OF THE LIGHT. I ENTERED POEM.7.S. 136 5
I ENTERED YOUR BIBLE, I BOARDED YOUR ARK ....ZOO KEEPER'S WIFE 155 28

ENTERING (3)

ENTERING THE TOWER OF MY FEARS, ...PURSUIT 23 45
BUT THREE MEN ENTERING THE YARD, ...ON THE DECLINE OF ORACLES 78 20
SCRATCHING AT MY SLEEP, AND ENTERING MY SIDE. ....THREE WOMEN 182 215

ENTERPRISE (1)

AT THIS BARREN ENTERPRISE ....TWO SISTERS OF PERSEPHONE 31 10

ENTERTAINED (1)

THE DREAM-PEOPLED VILLAGE, HER EYES ENTERTAINED NO DREAM, ...
... HARDCASTLE CRAGS 63 19

ENTIRE (1)

WOULD HAVE ME SWALLOW THE ENTIRE SUN ....LOVE IS A PARALLAX 329 26

ENTIRELY (6)

AT THIS JOINT BETWEEN TWO WORLDS AND TWO ENTIRELY ....GHOST'S. 90 12
I SHALL NEVER GET YOU PUT TOGETHER ENTIRELY, ...THE COLOSSUS 129 1
SPACE! SPACE! THE BED LINEN WAS GIVING OUT ENTIRELY. ......WAKING. 151 11
THEN SHE COULD COVER MY MOUTH AND EYES, COVER ME ENTIRELY, *PLASTER. 159 40
I DREAM OF SOMEONE ELSE ENTIRELY. ....THE JAILER 227 27
THE WORLD FOREVER, I SHALL NOT ENTIRELY ....THE NIGHT DANCES 250 7

ENTOMBED (1)

TONIGHT THE PARTS ARE ENTOMBED IN AN ICEBOX. THE SURGEON AT 2 A.M. 171 37

ENTRAILS (1)

IRON ENTRAILS, ENAMEL BOWLS, ...THE BURNT-OUT SPA 138 16

ENTRY (1)

TRY ENTRY, ENTER NIGHTMARES ....SCULPTOR 92 21

ENVELOPS (1)

LIKE A DEAD LAKE THE DARK ENVELOPS ME, ...ZOO KEEPER'S WIFE 154 3

ENVIOUS (8)

AT EYE'S ENVIOUS CORNER ....VANITY FAIR 32 6
THE ENVIOUS ASSAULTS OF SEA ....LETTER TO A PURIST 36 3
WHILE SHE, ENVIOUS BRIDE, ...THE SHRIKE 42 7
EYEFUL, WHICH, ENVIOUS, WOULD DEFINE ....LANDOWNERS 53 13
LIGHTS OUT, THEY DOGGED US, SLEEPLESS AND ENVIOUS: ...THE OTHER TWO 68 28
AN ENVIOUS PHOSPHORESCENCE IN THEIR WINGS. ....OUIJA 77 5
SOLID THE SPACES LEAN ON, ENVIOUS. ....NICK AND THE CANDLESTICK 242 41
ON ENVIOUS STRINGS, AND YOU ARE THE CENTER. ....STINGS/DR 293 3

ENVY (2)

THAT WILL KINDLE ANGELS' ENVY, SCORCH AND DROP ......EPITAPH FOR F. 45 6
I ENVY THE BIG NOISES, ...LITTLE FUGUE 188 19

EPHEMERIDS (1)

AS THESE DRAUGHTY EPHEMERIDS. ....CANDLES 149 30

EPIC (2)

OUR LUGGAGE, AS DOCKS HALT OUR BRIEF EPIC; NO DEBT *CHANNEL CROSSING 27 41
I LAY DREAMING YOUR EPIC, IMAGE BY IMAGE. ...ELECTRA ON AZALEA PATH 116 12

EPILOGUE (1)

AFTER YOUR LIFE'S END, WHAT JUST EPILOGUE ....DIALOGUE B. 39 24

EPISODES (1)

EROTIC AND ELEGANT EPISODES." ....DIALOGUE EN ROUTE 309 24

EPITAPH (2)

EPITAPH FOR FIRE AND FLOWER ....EPITAPH FOR FIRE AND FLOWER 45 T
EPITAPH IN THREE PARTS ....EPITAPH IN THREE PARTS 337 T

EQUILIBRIUM (1)

IN FATAL EQUILIBRIUM ...................METAMORPHOSES OF THE MOON 308 45

EQUIVOCAL (1)

OR HER OWN WORD, AMBUSHED IN AN EQUIVOCAL ....DIALOGUE O. 286 351

ERA (1)

YOU MOVE THROUGH THE ERA OF FISHES, ...THE MANOR GARDEN 125 5

ERASED (2)

NOTHING THAT CANNOT BE ERASED, RIPPED UP AND SCRAPPED,

	TITLE	PAGE	LINE

ERASED (CONT.)
      BEGUN AGAIN. ....THREE WOMEN 184 277
ERASED, SIGH, SIGH. ....AMNESIAC 233 5
ERECT (1)
    ERECT IN HIS FOLDEROL CLOAK ....DIALOGUE EN ROUTE 308 13
ERECTED (1)
    ERECTED DOWN THE GANGWAYS OF OUR MIND. ....DOOM OF EXILES 318 4
ERECTING (1)
    ON THE MIND'S EYE, ERECTING A LINE ......SLEEP IN THE MOJAVE DESERT 143 4
ERMINE (1)
    THOUGH HE BEDDED IN ERMINE, GORGED ON ROAST, ...NATURAL HISTORY 71 3
EROS (1)
    AND THE HOUSE OF EROS ....TWO VIEWS OF WITHENS 72 14
EROTIC (1)
    EROTIC AND ELEGANT EPISODES." ....DIALOGUE EN ROUTE 309 24
ERSATZ (1)
    THE ERSATZ PETALS DRIP, AND THEY DRIP RED. ..ELECTRA ON AZALEA PATH 117 28
ESCAPE (1)
    DID I ESCAPE, I WONDER? ....MEDUSA 225 12
ESCAPED (3)
    AS A GREENLY ESCAPED IDIOT, ...STREET SONG 36 12
    ESCAPED AMONG MOON-PLUMAGED STRANGERS; ....THE SHRIKE 42 14
    THEY COLLAPSE LIKE LUNGS, THE ESCAPED WATER ....PRIVATE GROUND 130 9
ESCAPES (1)
    I DO NOT TRUST THE SPIRIT. IT ESCAPES LIKE STEAM ....LAST WORDS 172 14
ESCARPMENTS (1)
    OF SUCH SEEING UP THE LEAF-SHUTTERED ESCARPMENTS, ..ABOVE THE OXBOW 88 27
ESPLANADE (1)
    ARE AN ESPLANADE FOR CRICKETS. ....THE BURNT-OUT SPA 138 13
ESSAYING (1)
    (ESSAYING, WAVE BY WAVE, ...LETTER TO A PURIST 36 4
ESSENTIAL (1)
    AT THE ESSENTIAL LANDSCAPE STARE, STARE ....NOVEMBER GRAVEYARD 56 13
ESSENTIALS (1)
    EGGS AND FISH, THE ESSENTIALS, ...GIGOLO 267 16
ESTABLISHMENTS (1)
    IN ESTABLISHMENTS WHICH IMAGINED LINES ....POEMS, POTATOES 106 3
ESTATE (5)
    WITH SUCH BLIGHT WROUGHT ON OUR BANKRUPT ESTATE, ...CONVERSATION. 21 13
    IT'S A NIGGARD ESTATE, ...GREEN ROCK, WINTHROP BAY 105 9
    ELEVEN WEEKS, AND I KNOW YOUR ESTATE SO WELL ....PRIVATE GROUND 130 13
    WIDOW: THAT GREAT, VACANT ESTATE! ....WIDOW 164 21
    THE BROWN MOTHERLY FURROWS, THE WHOLE ESTATE. ....THE DETECTIVE 209 37
ESTATES (1)
    LAYS ALL WALLS WASTE; PRIVATE ESTATES ARE TORN, ...CHANNEL CROSSING 27 31
ESTRANGED (1)
    ESTRANGED, CHANGED, SUSPENDED WHERE ....THE GREAT CARBUNCLE 73 19
ETCH (1)
    AS YOU ETCH ON THE INNER WINDOW OF YOUR EYE ....VIRGIN IN A TREE 82 34
ETCHED (1)
    THE CRAB-FACE, ETCHED AND SET THERE, ..MUSSEL HUNTER AT ROCK HARBOR 97 77
ETCHING (1)
    THE PROSPECT IS DULL AS AN OLD ETCHING. ....A WINTER SHIP 113 13
ETERNAL (3)
    OF AN ETERNAL SUFFERER. TO YOU ....PERSEUS 83 46
    BLOOD SPRINGS ETERNAL IF THE HEART BE BURNING. ..TO EVA DESCENDING. 303 8
    THE SUAVE ETERNAL SERPENTS PROMISE BLISS ....NEVER TRY TO TRICK. 320 13
ETERNALLY (2)
    THROUGH WHICH THE SKY ETERNALLY THREADS ITSELF? ....TOTEM 264 21
    THAT DRAINS ETERNALLY THE MILK OF STARS. ....SONNET: TO TIME 311 14
ETERNITY (2)
    AND ETERNITY ENGULFS IT, AND I DROWN UTTERLY? ....THREE WOMEN 179 105
    ETERNITY BORES ME, ...YEARS 255 9
ETHER (1)
    IN HIS CAGE OF ETHER, HIS CAGE OF STARS. ....LYONNESSE 234 25
ETHEREAL (1)
    BOSSING THE ETHEREAL BLANKS OF THEIR FACE-OVALS. ....MAGI 148 3
ETHERIZING (1)
    THE BARREN BODY OF HAWTHORN, ETHERIZING ITS CHILDREN. ....BEE. 211 25
EUNUCHS (1)
    GREEN AS EUNUCHS, YOUR WISHES ....MEDUSA 226 38
EUROPE (1)
    O EUROPE! O TON OF HONEY! ....THE SWARM 217 60
EUROPE'S (2)
    FESTERING ON THE DIM WALLS OF EUROPE'S CHAPELS, ...PERSEUS 82 10
    OFF EUROPE'S RELIC HEAP ....PRIVATE GROUND 130 3
EVA (3)
    ECLIPSING EVA, CLEO AND HELEN OF TROY: ....VIRGIN IN A TREE 81 19
    TO EVA DESCENDING THE STAIR ....TO EVA DESCENDING THE STAIR 303 T
    SONNET: TO EVA ....SONNET: TO EVA 304 T
EVAPORATE (2)
    BEFORE THE DISTANCES THEY PIN EVAPORATE, ...WUTHERING HEIGHTS 167 6
    AND SEEN MY STRANGENESS EVAPORATE, ...STINGS 214 26
EVE (4)
    THE EDEN OF BUCOLIC EVE: .................METAMORPHOSES OF THE MOON 307 15

	TITLE	PAGE	LINE

EVE (CONT.)
SIGHED EVE, THE ELEVATOR-GIRL ACE, ...DIALOGUE EN ROUTE 308 2
SAID EVE: "I WISH VENOMOUS NEMATODES ....DIALOGUE EN ROUTE 309 19
EVE, THE ELEVATOR-GIRL ACE, ...DIALOGUE EN ROUTE 309 32
EVEN (38)
INTRUDES EVEN WHEN THE REVOLTED EYE ....TALE OF A TUB 25 30
EVEN AS MY EACH MANGLED NERVE-END ....STREET SONG 36 21
EVEN AS LOVE'S DEAR FOOLS CRY EVERGREEN,*EPITAPH FOR FIRE AND FLOWER 46 30
EVEN IN THIS DULL, RUINOUS LANDSCAPE); SKEPTICAL, ...BLACK ROOK I. 57 24
NOR EVEN ONE OF THE COMMON BARNYARD SOWS, ...SOW 61 17
AND GRAYER; NOT EVEN MOVING THEIR BONES. ....THE THIN PEOPLE 65 47
WISH FOR EVEN GROUND, AND IT'S THE LAST CLIFF ......ABOVE THE OXBOW 88 22
EVEN, A TANG OF METAL. DAY IN, DAY OUT, *MEMOIRS OF A SPINACH-PICKER 89 16
EVEN THAN YOUR MADDENING ....LORELEI 94 29
FROST DROPS EVEN THE SPIDER. CLEARLY ....FROG AUTUMN 99 9
EVEN OUR SHADOWS ARE BLUE WITH COLD. ....A WINTER SHIP 113 23
EVEN THE PAVING. ....MUSHROOMS 139 13
THEY ARE NOT PIGS, THEY ARE NOT EVEN FISH, ...STILLBORN 142 11
THE TUMULUS, EVEN AT NOON, GUARDS ITS BLACK SHADOW: ..PARLIAMENT H. 153 26
EVEN MY BEST FRIEND THINKS I'M IN THE COUNTRY. ....FACE LIFT 156 19
I HAD EVEN FORGOTTEN HOW TO WALK OR SIT, ...IN PLASTER 159 45
EVEN THROUGH THE GIFT PAPER I COULD HEAR THEM BREATHE ....TULIPS 161 37
OR EVEN LIKE BLACK HOLES CUT OUT OF IT. ....WIDOW 164 29
NOW THEY ARE NOTHING, THEY ARE NOT EVEN BABIES. ....LAST WORDS 172 7
I DO NOT HAVE TO THINK, OR EVEN REHEARSE. ....THREE WOMEN 176 9
I AM NOT UGLY. I AM EVEN BEAUTIFUL. ....THREE WOMEN 183 239
I DO NOT EVEN NEED A HOLIDAY; I CAN GO TO WORK TODAY. ..THREE WOMEN 183 249
YOU WILL NOT EVEN HEAR ME OPENING IT, NO PAPER CRACKLE, ..BIRTHDAY. 207 34
NOT EVEN NODDING, A PERSONAGE IN A HEDGEROW. ....THE BEE MEETING 212 41
POOR AND BARE AND UNQUEENLY AND EVEN SHAMEFUL. ....STINGS 214 19
I THOUGHT EVEN THE BONES WOULD DO. ....DADDY 224 60
EVEN IN YOUR ZEN HEAVEN WE SHAN'T MEET. ....LESBOS 230 92
EVEN THE SUN-CLOUDS THIS MORNING CANNOT MANAGE SUCH SKIRTS.*POP.OCT. 240 1
EVEN THE NEWTS ARE WHITE, ...NICK AND THE CANDLESTICK 241 12
REMEMBERING, EVEN IN SLEEP, ...NICK AND THE CANDLESTICK 241 25
EVEN IN HIS ....PURDAH 243 30
AND HE WAS NOT EVEN MALICIOUS. ........................EAVESDROPPER 260 27
EVEN A LITTLE? YOU KNOW I DON'T, AND STILL . . . .DIALOGUE O. 277 34
THAT'S SOMETHING TO STUDY EVEN IF IT'S NOT ....DIALOGUE O. 279 108
EVEN IF YOU SEEM PACIFIED, PREFER ......DIALOGUE OVER A OUIJA BOARD 280 145
ALL NIGHT LONG, EVEN SHOULD OUR EYES SHUT ....DIALOGUE O. 286 354
BUT EVEN HER TONNAGE DOESN'T IMPRESS A DIAMOND. ....THE RIVAL/DR 291 24
EVEN THE DEAD LAUGH AMONG THE GOLDENROD. ....GOLD MOUTHS CRY 302 9
EVENING (5)
IN THE RECTORY GARDEN ON HIS EVENING WALK ....DIALOGUE B. 38 1
TO IMPOSE ON THE EVENING. ....NIGHT SHIFT 76 5
HOW THEY LIT THE TEDIUM OF THE PROTRACTED EVENING! ....INSOMNIAC 163 16
IS HE WEARING PAJAMAS OR AN EVENING SUIT ....BERCK-PLAGE 198 62
PAN AS OUR EVENING GUEST IF HE'S SO FREE*DIALOGUE OVER A OUIJA BOARD 283 252
EVENINGS (1)
I AM AT HOME IN THE LAMPLIGHT. THE EVENINGS ARE LENGTHENING. *THREE. 186 351
EVENT (2)
WHEN I WALK OUT, I AM A GREAT EVENT. ....THREE WOMEN 176 8
EVENT ....EVENT 194 T
EVER (12)
EVER BLUR THE INTRANSIGENT LINES WHICH DRAW ....TALE OF A TUB 25 28
WHETHER GOAT-THIGHED OR GOD-HALOED. EVER SINCE THAT FIRST DAPHNE ...
 ... VIRGIN IN A TREE 81 9
FROM THE DOOR AS EVER. WHAT HAPPENS BETWEEN US ....BLUE MOLES 127 34
PROCEEDS CLEAR AS IT EVER DID ....THE BURNT-OUT SPA 138 20
WHAT GIRL EVER FLOURISHED IN SUCH COMPANY? ....MAGI 148 18
SHALL I EVER FIND IT, WHATEVER IT IS? ....THREE WOMEN 186 343
I AM YOUNG AS EVER, IT SAYS. WHAT IS IT I MISS? ....THREE WOMEN 186 350
O GOD, HOW SHALL I EVER CLEAN THE PHONE TABLE? ....WORDS HEARD. 202 8
MORE TERRIBLE THAN SHE EVER WAS, RED ....STINGS 215 57
IN PAN: IT'S BEEN EBBING EVER SINCE THE MESS ....DIALOGUE O. 277 38
I SMASHED A GLASS, AND EVER SINCE THAT DREAM ....DIALOGUE O. 285 302
WHAT PRINCE HAS EVER SEIZED THE SHINING GRAIL .......METAMORPHOSES. 307 19
EVEREST (1)
THEMSELVES MERE ROCKY HILLOCKS TO AN EVEREST. ......ABOVE THE OXBOW 87 4
EVERGREEN (1)
EVEN AS LOVE'S DEAR FOOLS CRY EVERGREEN,*EPITAPH FOR FIRE AND FLOWER 46 30
EVER-GREEN (2)
EARTH'S EVER-GREEN DEATH'S HEAD. ....CRYSTAL GAZER 56 48
UPROOT THEM: THEIR BEARDS ARE EVER-GREEN. ......CHILD'S PARK STONES 101 27-8
EVERGREENS (1)
IN THE BASKET OF PLASTIC EVERGREENS THEY PUT *ELECTRA ON AZALEA PATH 117 25
EVERLASTING (2)
THE EVERLASTING MONDAY ....THE EVERLASTING MONDAY 62 T
THOU SHALT HAVE AN EVERLASTING... ....THE EVERLASTING MONDAY 62 E/1
EVERY (33)
RICH IN STRAYINGS WITH EVERY AMOROUS OAF, ...VANITY FAIR 33 17
UNTIL EVERY MAN, ...STRUMPET SONG 33 6
EVERY DOWNFALL AND CRASH ....STREET SONG 36 27
BETTER THAT EVERY FIBER CRACK ....MONOLOGUE AT 3 A.M. 40 1

EVERY (CONT.)
    THAT EVERY BREATH, THUS TEEMING, SET THE LAND ....WREATH F.   45   21
    AND HAVE EVERY WEATHER COCK KISS HANG FIRE ....EPITAPH FOR F.   46   23
    MORE MAMMOTH AND BLOWSY WITH EVERY SEASON; ....ELLA MASON A.   54   34
    THE SEVEN TROUGHED SEAS AND EVERY EARTHQUAKING CONTINENT. ......SOW   61   45
    EVERY POCK AND STAIN BULKED MORE BEAUTIFUL*ON THE PLETHORA OF DRYADS   67   16
    FAIR CHRONICLER OF EVERY FOUL DECLENSION. ....OUIJA   77   14
    AND EVERY PRIVATE TWINGE A HISSING ASP ....PERSEUS   83   20
    TO PETRIFY YOUR EYES, AND EVERY VILLAGE ....PERSEUS   83   21
    THE SEA BROKE IN AT EVERY CRACK, ...THE BULL OF BENDYLAW   108   14
    RELIC OF TOUGH WEATHER, EVERY WINCH AND STAY ....A WINTER SHIP   113   27
    THEY ARE PROPER IN SHAPE AND NUMBER AND EVERY PART. *THE HANGING MAN   142   7
    EVERY ONE OF THEM PERMANENTLY BUSY. ....A LIFE   150   10
    THIS IS NEWNESS: EVERY LITTLE TAWDRY ....NEW YEAR ON DARTMOOR   176   1
    EVERY LITTLE WORD HOOKED TO EVERY LITTLE WORD, AND ACT TO ACT. ...
                                            ... THREE WOMEN   178   55
    EVERY LITTLE WORD HOOKED TO EVERY LITTLE WORD, AND ACT TO ACT. ...
                                            ... THREE WOMEN   178   55
    I THOUGHT EVERY GERMAN WAS YOU. ....DADDY   223   29
    EVERY WOMAN ADORES A FASCIST, ...DADDY   223   48
    EVERY DAY YOU FILL HIM WITH SOUL-STUFF, LIKE A PITCHER. .....LESBOS   229   77
    SAD HAG. "EVERY WOMAN'S A WHORE. ....LESBOS   229   83
    REDCOATS, EVERY ONE. ....CUT   235   20
    ALL COGS, WEIRD SPARKLE AND EVERY COG SOLID GOLD. ....THE TOUR   237   5
    ONE YEAR IN EVERY TEN ....LADY LAZARUS   244   2
    IN EVERY RESPECT LIKE EVERY OTHER NIGHT:*DIALOGUE OVER A OUIJA BOARD   276   2
    IN EVERY RESPECT LIKE EVERY OTHER NIGHT:*DIALOGUE OVER A OUIJA BOARD   276   2
    WITH BLACKBIRDS -- TWENTY-FOUR, AND EVERY ONE ....DIALOGUE O.   282   215
    A GREASY SMACK ON EVERY CHEEK ....FAMILY REUNION   300   14
    AND MY EVERY CHIMERICAL DOLLAR ....DIALOGUE EN ROUTE   308   16
    AND MISLAID EVERY VITAL TALISMAN; ....THE DISPOSSESSED   319   17
    OF EVERY PENDULUM; ....AERIALIST   331   21
EVERYBODY (4)
    DRESSED IN BLACK, EVERYBODY IN MOURNING FOR SOMEONE.*THE NET-MENDERS   121   4
    GIVING EVERYBODY A FAIR HEARING. ....CANDLES   149   11
    EVERYBODY IS NODDING A SQUARE BLACK HEAD, THEY ARE KNIGHTS IN
        VISORS, ...THE BEE MEETING   211   13
    LIKE THE PACK, THE PACK, LIKE EVERYBODY. ....THE SWARM   216   25
EVERYBODY'S (1)
    AND IT WAS I WHO ATTRACTED EVERYBODY'S ATTENTION, ...IN PLASTER   159   18
EVERYDAY (1)
    THE INCALCULABLE MALICE OF THE EVERYDAY. ....THREE WOMEN   184   287
EVERYONE (1)
    AND NOT EXTINCT, AS EVERYONE SUPPOSED.   DIALOGUE OVER A OUIJA BOARD   283   247
EVERYTHING (19)
    EVERYTHING GLITTERED LIKE BLANK PAPER. ....SUICIDE OFF EGG ROCK   115   20
    EVERYTHING SHRANK IN THE SUN'S CORROSIVE ......SUICIDE OFF EGG ROCK   115   21
    EVERYTHING TOOK PLACE IN A DURABLE WHITENESS.*ELECTRA ON AZALEA PATH   117   14
    I BLAMED HER FOR EVERYTHING, BUT SHE DIDN'T ANSWER. .....IN PLASTER   159   10
    LOOK HOW WHITE EVERYTHING IS, HOW QUIET, HOW SNOWED-IN. .....TULIPS   160   2
    STUPID PUPIL, IT HAS TO TAKE EVERYTHING IN. ....TULIPS   160   10
    AND YOUR FIRST GIFT IS MAKING STONE OUT OF EVERYTHING. ...THE RIVAL   166   6
    EVERYTHING IN ONE DIRECTION. ....WUTHERING HEIGHTS   167   13
    EVERYTHING HAS HAPPENED. ....THE BABYSITTERS   175   45
    IT HAD A CONSEQUENTIAL LOOK, LIKE EVERYTHING ELSE, ...THREE WOMEN   177   46
    IT IS A LOVE OF DEATH THAT SICKENS EVERYTHING. ....THREE WOMEN   181   152
    THERE IS THIS CESSATION. THIS TERRIBLE CESSATION OF EVERYTHING. ...
                                            ... THREE WOMEN   181   180
    I HAVE PAINTED LITTLE HEARTS ON EVERYTHING. ....THREE WOMEN   186   329
    THE POLICE LOVE YOU, YOU CONFESS EVERYTHING. ....THE OTHER   201   7
    THE MIND OF THE HIVE THINKS THIS IS THE END OF EVERYTHING. ....BEE.   212   37
    NAPOLEON IS PLEASED, HE IS PLEASED WITH EVERYTHING. ......THE SWARM   217   59
    IS AN ART, LIKE EVERYTHING ELSE. ....LADY LAZARUS   245   44
    SUGAR CAN CURE EVERYTHING, SO KINDNESS SAYS. ....KINDNESS   269   9
    REALLY WANT TO KNOW ABOUT? EVERYTHING.   DIALOGUE OVER A OUIJA BOARD   278   54
EVERYWHERE (3)
    AND EVERYWHERE PEOPLE, EYES MICA-SILVER AND BLANK, ...INSOMNIAC   163   34
    A LIVING DOLL, EVERYWHERE YOU LOOK. ....THE APPLICANT   221   33
    THE SACK OF BLACK! IT IS EVERYWHERE, TIGHT, TIGHT! ..BY CANDLELIGHT   237   30
EVIDENTLY (3)
    NATIVE, EVIDENTLY, TO ....NIGHT SHIFT   76   8
    YOU'RE SATISFIED. MY WILL HAS EVIDENTLY *DIALOGUE OVER A OUIJA BOARD   284   279
    HEDGED IN AND EVIDENTLY INVIOLATE ....QUEEN MARY'S ROSE GARDEN   290   15
EVIL (6)
    IN A WAR MAKING EVIL HEADLINES WHEN WE ....THE THIN PEOPLE   64   6
    SAW EVIL BREAK OUT OF THE NORTH. ....ON THE DECLINE OF ORACLES   78   32
    THE FLAT SEA PURPLED LIKE THAT EVIL CLOTH ...ELECTRA ON AZALEA PATH   117   31
    FOR HER, THE HEAVY NOTION OF EVIL ....MAGI   148   12
    DEMARCATING GOOD FROM EVIL, ...INSOLENT STORM STRIKES AT THE SKULL   326   20
    WHILE EVIL STARS WHIR ....TEMPER OF TIME   336   2
EVILEST (1)
    OUTLAST THEIR EVILEST STAR, WRYLY ....THE BEGGARS   48   19
EVIL-STARRED (1)
    STEADFAST AND EVIL-STARRED, ...THE LADY AND THE EARTHENWARE HEAD   70   31

TITLE   PAGE LINE

EX (1)
 EX MACHINA. NOR DID THEY SEEM DETERRED BY THIS. ....SPIDER 49 35
EXACT (2)
 EXACT AS A SNOWFLAKE. ....SPINSTER 50 18
 I AM SILVER AND EXACT. I HAVE NO PRECONCEPTIONS. ....MIRROR 173 1
EXACTED (1)
 EXACTED HER FIRST SIMPLE SIGHT FOR THIS STRICT SECOND.*CRYSTAL GAZER 55 30
EXACTING (2)
 TO SERVE HER EXACTING TURN: ......THE LADY AND THE EARTHENWARE HEAD 69 17
 NO LITTLE MAN LIVES IN THE EXACTING MOON ....TWO LOVERS. 327 23
EXAMINERS (1)
 DISENCHANT MY TWELVE BLACK-GOWNED EXAMINERS ....RESOLVE 52 21
EXAMPLE (1)
 WOULD NOT BE EASED, RELEASED. OUR EACH EXAMPLE ....THE OTHER TWO 68 23
EXCAVATIONS (1)
 BECAUSE NEW EXCAVATIONS CAME TOO NEAR THE PRINCESS AND THE GOBLINS 334 39
EXCEPT (3)
 TO CALL MY OWN EXCEPT THE AIR-MOTES, ...LANDOWNERS 53 2
 EXCEPT FOR A SORT OF A HINGE ....CUT 235 4
 EXCEPT FOR TWO UNCANNY DREAMS ....THE DREAM 310 2
EXCEPTION (2)
 IT IS THE EXCEPTION THAT INTERESTS THE DEVIL. ....THREE WOMEN 186 331
 IT IS THE EXCEPTION THAT CLIMBS THE SORROWFUL HILL .....THREE WOMEN 186 332
EXCEPTIONAL (1)
 I DO NOT WILL HIM TO BE EXCEPTIONAL. ....THREE WOMEN 186 330
EXCEPTIONALLY (1)
 I DO IT EXCEPTIONALLY WELL. ....LADY LAZARUS 245 45
EXCESSIVE (2)
 HIS TALKING WHIRLWIND, ABATED HIS EXCESSIVE TEMPER ....OUIJA 77 16
 WITH EXCESSIVE LOVE I ENAMELED IT ....STINGS 214 10
EXCHANGE (1)
 AGAINST MY LEANING DOWN, WOULD NOT EXCHANGE .........INCOMMUNICADO 100 5
EXCITABLE (1)
 THE TULIPS ARE TOO EXCITABLE, IT IS WINTER HERE. ....TULIPS 160 1
EXCITED (2)
 THEY WAITED LIKE SWEETHEARTS. THEY EXCITED HIM. THE RABBIT CATCHER 194 25
 I AM EXCITED, SEEING IT THERE. ....ELM/DR 292 4
EXCLAMATION (1)
 A POINT OF EXCLAMATION MARKS THAT SKY ......THE GHOST'S LEAVETAKING 91 27
EXCLUSION (1)
 VOICE CRYING EXCLUSION IN MY EAR. ....SONNET: TO TIME 311 8
EXCUSE (1)
 NOW YOUR HEAD, EXCUSE ME, IS EMPTY. ....THE APPLICANT 221 26
EXCUSES (1)
 NO LAME EXCUSES CAN GLOSS OVER ....GREEN ROCK, WINTHROP BAY 104 1
EXHALE (1)
 EXHALE THEIR PALLOR LIKE SCENT. ....BARREN WOMAN 157 5
EXHALES (1)
 EXHALES AN INDIGO NIMBUS, ...PARLIAMENT HILL FIELDS 153 46
EXHAUSTED (5)
 STILL IT SEEPS UP, IT IS NOT EXHAUSTED. ....THE SURGEON AT 2 A.M. 171 23
 LOOK, THEY ARE SO EXHAUSTED, THEY ARE ALL FLAT OUT .....THREE WOMEN 183 219
 I AM EXHAUSTED, I AM EXHAUSTED --- ....THE BEE MEETING 212 51
 I AM EXHAUSTED, I AM EXHAUSTED --- ....THE BEE MEETING 212 51
 YOU ARE SO EXHAUSTED. ....LESBOS 229 78
EXHAUSTS (1)
 AND IT EXHAUSTS ME TO WATCH YOU ....POPPIES IN JULY 203 5
EXHIBITING (1)
 WHIPPING OFF YOUR SILK SCARF, EXHIBITING THE TIGHT WHITE FACE LIFT 155 2
EXHIBITS (2)
 EXHIBITS ITS GLAUCOUS SILKS, ...WHITSUN 154 15
 WHO EXHIBITS ....DEATH & CO. 254 5
EXILED (1)
 EXILED TO NO GOOD. ....FULL FATHOM FIVE 93 42
EXILES (1)
 DOOM OF EXILES ....DOOM OF EXILES 318 T
EXIST (1)
 WITHOUT ME, SHE WOULDN'T EXIST, SO OF COURSE SHE WAS GRATEFUL. ...
              ... IN PLASTER 159 15
EXISTANCE (1)
 THEY BRUISE THE ROCKS OUT OF EXISTENCE, THEN RESURRECT THEM. ...
              ... FINISTERRE 169 15
EXISTED (1)
 AS IF YOU HAD NEVER EXISTED, AS IF I CAME ...ELECTRA ON AZALEA PATH 116 6
EXISTS (1)
 IS CLOSED; THE TUB EXISTS BEHIND OUR BACK: ....TALE OF A TUB 25 31
EXIT (5)
 EXIT FROM A SMOKING SLIT ....RHYME 50 17
 EXIT LIKE KISSES. ....AN APPEARANCE 189 5
 THERE IS ONLY A LITTLE GRID, NO EXIT. ...THE ARRIVAL OF THE BEE BOX 213 10
 EXIT FROM THE HEART. ....TRIO OF LOVE SONGS 314 8
 AND LUCKY STARS ALL EXIT ON THE RUN: ....ADMONITIONS 319 17
EXORCIZED (1)
 GRIEF AND ANGER, EXORCIZED, ...A LIFE 150 29

EXPANSIVE (1)
    WHITE AND BLANK, EXPANSIVE AS CARBON MONOXIDE. ....THE RIVAL 166   15
EXPECT (3)
    I DO NOT EXPECT A MIRACLE ....BLACK ROOK IN RAINY WEATHER   56   4
    OF MANDATORY VOICES YOU HALF EXPECT ....DIALOGUE OVER A OUIJA BOARD 279 110
    WHERE THOSE WORMS CAME FROM. I SWEAR I DIDN'T EXPECT ...DIALOGUE O. 283 264
EXPEND (1)
    AND THE BRIDE FLOWERS EXPEND A FRESHNESS, ...BERCK-PLAGE 200 106
EXPENSIVE (1)
    INFINITELY DELICATE AND INFINITELY EXPENSIVE. ....FEVER. 232   39
EXPLAIN (1)
    SO ROUSSEAU, TO EXPLAIN WHY THE RED COUCH ....YADWIGHA.   86   21
EXPLICABLE (1)
    BECAUSE OF SOME EXPLICABLE PHENOMENON ....APRIL 18 301   4
EXPLICIT (1)
    IN ITS EXPLICIT FOLDS? OR WHEN THE WINDOW, ...TALE OF A TUB   24   14
EXPLODE (1)
    GREEN-SINGING BIRDS EXPLODE FROM ALL THE ROCKS. PROLOGUE TO SPRING 322   15
EXPLODED (2)
    AN EXPLODED BOTTLE OF STOUT, ...A SECRET 220   42
    IT SIMPLY EXPLODED ONE NIGHT, ...THE TOUR 238   22
EXPLODES (1)
    EXPLODES IN A KALEIDOSCOPE OF SHAPES ....LOVE IS A PARALLAX 330   52
EXPLODING (1)
    ADMONITORY CLIFFS, AND THE SEA EXPLODING ....FINISTERRE 169   3
EXPLOSIONS (1)
    I AM NOBODY; I HAVE NOTHING TO DO WITH EXPLOSIONS. ....TULIPS 160   5
EXPORT (2)
    MINUTE AND SHRUNK FOR EXPORT, ...THE ARRIVAL OF THE BEE BOX 213   14
    THEY ARE FOR EXPORT, ...A SECRET 219   15
EXPOSE (1)
    BUT ALWAYS EXPOSE ....DEPARTURE   51   12
EXPOSED (1)
    TILL THE THUDDING SOURCE, EXPOSED, ...NIGHT SHIFT   76   13
EXPOSES (3)
    EXPOSES EMBARRASSMENTS -- THE MIZZLING DAYS ....INSOMNIAC 163   9
    OF AN ECHO, EXPOSES THE PANEL IN THE WALL ....WIDOW 164   7
    WHOSE CANDOR EXPOSES ....MOONSONG AT MORNING 317   23
EXPRESSION (3)
    I THINK THEY ARE MADE OF WATER; THEY HAVE NO EXPRESSION.*THREE WOMEN 183 225
    AND THE STUFFED EXPRESSION, BUT GOES ON ....BURNING THE LETTERS 205   53
    OF CLOUD TO GIVE THEM EXPRESSION, ...BRASILIA 258   5
EXPRESSIONLESS (2)
    DENSE AND EXPRESSIONLESS ROUND ABOUT. ....LOVE LETTER 147   23
    ARE YOU NOT BLINDED BY SUCH EXPRESSIONLESS SIRENS? CROSSING THE W. 190   11
EXPRESSIVE (1)
    EXPRESSIVE OF GRIEF TURNS GODS, LIKE KINGS, TO ROCKS. ......PERSEUS   83   29
EXQUISITE (1)
    FOR MOST EXQUISITE TRUTHS ARE ARTIFICE ...METAMORPHOSES OF THE MOON 307   25
EXTEND (2)
    PONDEROUS AND EXTEND DESPAIR ON EARTH'S ....PERSEUS   83   31
    EXTEND THE RADIAL SHEAVES ....FULL FATHOM FIVE   92   7
EXTINCT (5)
    PEAKS AND CRATERS OF THOSE EXTINCT VOLCANOES.*THE EVERLASTING MONDAY   62   6
    OF A GIANT OR EXTINCT ....CHILD'S PARK STONES 101   6
    AND I, NEARLY EXTINCT, ...BRASILIA 258   11
    AND NOT EXTINCT, AS EVERYONE SUPPOSED. DIALOGUE OVER A OUIJA BOARD 283 247
    NIPPLED MOONS, EXTINCT AND COLD, ...DANSE MACABRE 321   8
EXTINCTION (1)
    TOWARD EXTINCTION IN THOSE EYES ....SCULPTOR   92   17
EXTINGUISHES (1)
    WARM RAIN GREASES MY HAIR, EXTINGUISHES NOTHING.*BURNING THE LETTERS 205   47
EXTRA (2)
    IS HELPLESS HERE, QUITE EXTRA, YET WE MUST MAKE ...CHANNEL CROSSING   27   35
    A SECRET...AN EXTRA AMBER ....A SECRET 219   17
EXTRACTOR (1)
    I HAVE WHIRLED THE MIDWIFE'S EXTRACTOR, ...WINTERING 217   2
EXTRAPOLATION (1)
    OUTLAWS ALL EXTRAPOLATION ....TWO LOVERS. 327   10
EXTRAVAGANT (5)
    THE BAY'S SHEER, EXTRAVAGANT BLUE, ...THE BEGGARS   48   17
    AND WERE EXTRAVAGANT, LIKE TORTURE. ....THE RABBIT CATCHER 193   10
    TO INDULGE MY EXTRAVAGANT WANTS." ....DIALOGUE EN ROUTE 308   12
    MY EXTRAVAGANT HEART BLOWS UP AGAIN ....CIRCUS IN THREE PARTS 321   3
    O NEVER AGAIN WILL THE EXTRAVAGANT STRAW ....THE PRINCESS. 335   72
EXTREME (1)
    THE EXTREME UNCTION OF ITS YELLOW CANDLE-FLOWERS.*THE RABBIT CATCHER 193   8
EXTREMELY (1)
    IN THE CREVICE OF AN EXTREMELY SMALL SHADOW ....SLEEP. 144   15
EXUDES (1)
    EXUDES FROM ITS DEAD BOREDOM. ....NICK AND THE CANDLESTICK 240   5
EYE (88)
    OF YOUR STORMY EYE, MAGIC TAKES FLIGHT ...............CONVERSATION.   21   7
    AS IS YOUR IMAGE IN MY EYE; DRY FROST ....WINTER LANDSCAPE,   22   12

EYE (CONT.)
    THE PHOTOGRAPHIC CHAMBER OF THE EYE ....TALE OF A TUB   24   1
    INTRUDES EVEN WHEN THE REVOLTED EYE ....TALE OF A TUB   25   30
    RANSACKED IN THE PUBLIC EYE. WE FORSAKE ....CHANNEL CROSSING   27   32
    WITH ABSINTHE EYE ....PROSPECT   28   10
    TIME'S SOOT IN BLEARED EYE ....TINKER JACK AND THE TIDY WIVES   34   12
    WITH BIRD-QUICK EYE COCKED ASKEW .....MISS DRAKE PROCEEDS TO SUPPER   41   14
    BLOWS ASH IN EACH LOVER'S EYE; THE ARDENT LOOK ......EPITAPH FOR F.   46   34
    NIGHTFALL, COLD EYE -- NEITHER DISHEARTENS ....THE BEGGARS   47   1
    BAFFLE THE DARK, THE PITYING EYE. ....THE BEGGARS   48   21
    IN MY EYE, NOR SEEK ....BLACK ROOK IN RAINY WEATHER   57   7
    NO LOVE IN HIS EYE, ...THE SNOWMAN ON THE MOOR   59   36
    DAMASKS WITH DAZZLE THE THREADBARE EYE; ....CONJURING.   66   18
    STEPS OUT RADIANT IN LIMB, EYE, LIP, ...CONJURING.   66   27
    SURFEITING EYE, EAR, TASTE, TOUCH, SMELL; *ON THE PLETHORA OF DRYADS   67   27
    FIT NOWHERE: BRICKDUST-COMPLECTED, EYE UNDER A DENSE LID, ...
                  ... THE LADY AND THE EARTHENWARE HEAD   69   2
    SET IN MY EAR, AND IN MY EYE ....ON THE DECLINE OF ORACLES   78   13
    INVADE THE CLOISTRAL EYE LIKE PAGES ......ON THE DECLINE OF ORACLES   78   23
    PUTS UP HIS PIPE, AND LIDS HIS MOONY EYE. .............SNAKECHARMER   79   28
    AS YOU ETCH ON THE INNER WINDOW OF YOUR EYE ....VIRGIN IN A TREE   82   34
    YOU HAVE IT IN HAND. GRIT IN THE EYE OR A SORE ....PERSEUS   83   27
    UPHOLSTERED IN RED VELVET, UNDER THE EYE ....YADWIGHA.   85   3
    TO TURN YOU LUMINOUS, WITHOUT THE EYE ....YADWIGHA.   85   12
    OF TIGERS TO BE STILLED BY YOUR DARK EYE ....YADWIGHA.   85   13
    THE COUCH GLARED OUT AT THE PROSAIC EYE. ....YADWIGHA.   85   20
    DREAMED YOURSELF AWAY IN THE MOON'S EYE ....YADWIGHA.   86   28
    BUT TO A FRIEND, IN PRIVATE, ROUSSEAU CONFESSED HIS EYE ..YADWIGHA.   86   35
    TO FEED HIS EYE WITH RED: SUCH RED! UNDER THE MOON, ...YADWIGHA.   86   38
    AFTER THE HORIZONS, STRETCHING THE NARROWED EYE ....ABOVE THE OXBOW   88   25
    MUSK SATISFIED MY NOSE, RED MY EYE, ...RHODODENDRON.   103   13
    WHEN THE SPLINTER FLEW IN AND STUCK MY EYE, ...THE EYE-MOTE   109   9
    ITS EYE, FLASHLIT, A CHIP OF RUBY FIRE. ....GOATSUCKER   111   8
    MAUDLIN FROM LEAKY EYE TO SWOLLEN NOSE. ....THE RAVAGED FACE   115   4
    I SET MY EYE TO A HOLE-MOUTH AND MEET AN EYE ....BEEKEEPER'S.   118   17
    I SET MY EYE TO A HOLE-MOUTH AND MEET AN EYE ....BEEKEEPER'S.   118   17
    HIS LITTLE VERMILION EYE ....MEDALLION   124   9
    HOURLY THE EYE OF THE SKY ENLARGES ITS BLANK POEM.5.F.   134   5
    OPEN ONE STONE EYE. POEM.7.S.   136   21
    ON THE MIND'S EYE, ERECTING A LINE ......SLEEP IN THE MOJAVE DESERT   143   4
    THE DESERT IS WHITE AS A BLIND MAN'S EYE,*SLEEP IN THE MOJAVE DESERT   144   17
    NOR LEAVE ME TO SET MY SMALL BALD EYE ....LOVE LETTER   147   6
    NOTHING SO VULGAR AS A NOSE OR AN EYE ....MAGI   148   2
    SIMPLY TO PLUMB THE DEEPS OF AN EYE ....CANDLES   148   7
    LIKE AN EYE BETWEEN TWO WHITE LIDS THAT WILL NOT SHUT. ......TULIPS   160   9
    BETWEEN THE EYE OF THE SUN AND THE EYES OF THE TULIPS, ...TULIPS   161   47
    THAT WILL PUT HER HEART OUT LIKE AN ONLY EYE. ....WIDOW   164   5
    THE BLUE EYE OF MY TURQUOISE WILL COMFORT ME. ....LAST WORDS   172   20
    THE EYE OF A LITTLE GOD, FOUR-CORNERED. ....MIRROR   173   5
    THE COOK HAD ONE WALL EYE AND COULDN'T SLEEP, SHE WAS SO NERVOUS. ...
                  ... THE BABYSITTERS   175   25
    HE GLIDED BY; HIS EYE HAD A BLACK MEANING. ....THREE WOMEN   178   53
    HIS WIDE EYE IS THAT GENERAL, FLAT BLUE. ....THREE WOMEN   183 234
    AS IF I HAD LOST AN EYE, A LEG, A TONGUE. ....THREE WOMEN   183 252
    WHITE AS AN EYE ALL OVER! ....LITTLE FUGUE   187   7
    THE EYE OF THE BLIND PIANIST ....LITTLE FUGUE   187   8
    I REMEMBER A BLUE EYE, ...LITTLE FUGUE   188   45
    THE LINES OF THE EYE, SCALDED BY THESE BALD SURFACES, ..BERCK-PLAGE   196   10
    WHILE A GREEN POOL OPENS ITS EYE, ...BERCK-PLAGE   197   27
    ONE MIRRORY EYE --- ....BERCK-PLAGE   198   48
    WITH ONE TIN EYE, ...BURNING THE LETTERS   204   25
    WITH THE DEAD EYE ....BURNING THE LETTERS   205   52
    I PUT MY EYE TO THE GRID. ....THE ARRIVAL OF THE BEE BOX   213   11
    I HAVE ONE EYE, YOU HAVE TWO. ....A SECRET   219   6
    A GLASS EYE, FALSE TEETH OR A CRUTCH, ...THE APPLICANT   221   3
    YOU HAVE AN EYE, IT'S AN IMAGE. ....THE APPLICANT   222   38
    AND YOUR ARYAN EYE, BRIGHT BLUE. ....DADDY   223   44
    HAD LAZILY CLOSED ONE EYE AND LET THEM SLIP ....LYONNESSE   234   21
    EYE, THE CAULDRON OF MORNING. ....ARIEL   240   31
    MY EYE ....PURDAH   243   26
    THE NOSE, THE EYE PITS, THE FULL SET OF TEETH? ....LADY LAZARUS   244   13
    LET THIS EYE BE AN EAGLE, ...GULLIVER   251   23
    THE SILVER LIMBO OF EACH EYE ....THE FEARFUL   256   16
    MOUTH-ASH, ASH OF EYE. ....MARY'S SONG   257   14
    TO THE ELECTRIC MILKER, THE WIFEY, THE BIG BLUE EYE ..EAVESDROPPER   261   43
    THE LONELINESS OF ITS EYE, THE EYE OF THE MOUNTAINS ....TOTEM   264   20
    THE LONELINESS OF ITS EYE, THE EYE OF THE MOUNTAINS ....TOTEM   264   20
    YOUR CLEAR EYE IS THE ONE ABSOLUTELY BEAUTIFUL THING. ....CHILD   265   1
    ALL THE FALL OF WATER AN EYE ....GIGOLO   268   30
    OBLITERATION HOURLY UNLESS OUR EYE .....DIALOGUE OVER A OUIJA BOARD   279 116
    ANGEL'S EYE IN THE AUDIENCE, THEN WHISK THEM OUT ....DIALOGUE O.   282 233
    YOU ARE THE ONE EYE OUT THERE. ....THE RIVAL/DR   291   14
    WHILE FROM THE MOON, MY LOVER'S EYE ....TO A JILTED LOVER   309   7
    TRANSFIXED BY GLARE OF BLUE FROM GORGON'S EYE; ..PROLOGUE TO SPRING   322   2
    IN DARKROOM OF YOUR EYE THE MOONLY MIND ....SONNET TO SATAN   323   1

EYE (CONT.)
    OBSCURE GOD'S EYE WITH CORKSCREW FLECK; ....BLACK PINE TREE.   328   9
    IN THE IMPOSSIBLE MIND'S EYE; ....LOVE IS A PARALLAX   329   3
    SHE MOUNTS THROUGH MALICE OF THE NEEDLE'S EYE, ...THE PRINCESS.   333   10
    LET MY TRANSIENT EYE BREAK A TEAR ....TOUCH-AND-GO   336   19
EYEBALL (1)
    TOUCH IT: IT WON'T SHRINK LIKE AN EYEBALL, ...A LIFE   149   1
EYEBALLS (1)
    MOBS OF EYEBALLS LOOKING UP. ....LEAVING EARLY   146   13
EYEBATHS (1)
    OF EYEBATHS CAN UNSEAT THE SPECK: ....THE EYE-MOTE   109   20
EYE-BUTTON (1)
    THE ROUND OF HIS YELLOW EYE-BUTTON. ....A WINTER SHIP   113   10
EYEFUL (2)
    MY EYEFUL OF REFLECTIONS A GHOST'S ....LANDOWNERS   53   12
    EYEFUL, WHICH, ENVIOUS, WOULD DEFINE ....LANDOWNERS   53   13
EYEHOLE (2)
    FLIES FILING IN THROUGH A DEAD SKATE'S EYEHOLE *SUICIDE OFF EGG ROCK 115   17
    IN DREAMS, THROUGH MOUTH-HOLE OR EYE-HOLE. I CAN'T STOP IT. *LAST W.   172   15
EYEHOLES (1)
    WINGED ELBOWS AND EYEHOLES ....BRASILIA   258   3
EYEING (2)
    EYEING ME. GRASS PUT FORTH CLAWS; .....MUSSEL HUNTER AT ROCK HARBOR   96   25
    FOR THE EYEING OF MY SCARS, THERE IS A CHARGE ....LADY LAZARUS   246   58
EYELASH (1)
    ATTENDANTS OF THE EYELASH! ....PURDAH   243   37
EYELESS (2)
    MOUTHLESS, EYELESS, WITH STITCHED BALD HEAD. THE DISQUIETING MUSED   75   16
    EARLESS AND EYELESS, ...MUSHROOMS   139   15
EYELID (2)
    LEAF, BECOME EYELID; SNAKE-BODIES, BOUGH, BREAST ......SNAKECHARMER   79   14
    THE NIGHTS SNAPPED OUT OF SIGHT LIKE A LIZARD'S EYELID:*THE HANGING.   141   3
EYELIDS (5)
    MY EYELIDS UP, AND GRANT ....BLACK ROOK IN RAINY WEATHER   57   30
    THEIR EYELIDS KEEP THE SHADE. ....THE SLEEPERS   123   21
    COLD AS AN EEL, WITHOUT EYELIDS. ....ZOO KEEPER'S WIFE   154   2
    ABC, HER EYELIDS SAY. ....AN APPEARANCE 189   18
    A CREST OF BREASTS, EYELIDS AND LIPS ....BERCK-PLAGE   200 116
EYE-MOTE (1)
    THE EYE-MOTE ....THE EYE-MOTE   109   T
EYE-PITS (1)
    IS THIS THE ELECT ONE, THE ONE WITH BLACK EYE-PITS AND A SCAR? ...
                                      ... A BIRTHDAY PRESENT   206   6
EYE-RINGS (1)
    IS IT FOR THIS YOU WIDEN YOUR EYE-RINGS? ....THE OTHER   201   10
EYES (88)
    BEHIND SNARLED THICKETS OF MY EYES ....PURSUIT   23   29
    RAT-SHREWD GO HER SQUINT EYES, ...TWO SISTERS OF PERSEPHONE   31   11
    INTO MY MOST CHASTE OWN EYES ....STRUMPET SONG   34   18
    AN ARENA OF YELLOW EYES ....FAUN   35   11
    WHEN MY EYES SHUT ....SOLILOQUY OF THE SOLIPSIST   37   5
    WITH HER BLANK BROWN EYES STARVED WIDE, ...THE SHRIKE   42   9
    NOW WITH STAKE AND PITCHFORK THEY ADVANCE, FLINT EYES FIXED
        ON MURDER. .... DREAM WITH CLAM-DIGGERS   44   28
    SLAYING THE DANDIES WITH HER EMERALD EYES; ....ELLA MASON A.   54   16
    TILL YOUR EYES FOIST A VISION DAZZLING ON THE WIND: .....NOVEMBER G. 56   14
    EACH HEDGE WITH SUCH WHITE BLOOM ASTOUNDS OUR EYES ....MAYFLOWER   60   6
    FAT-RUTTED EYES ....SOW   61   26
    THE DREAM-PEOPLED VILLAGE, HER EYES ENTERTAINED NO DREAM, ...
                                      ... HARDCASTLE CRAGS   63   19
    UNALTERED BY EYES, ...HARDCASTLE CRAGS   63   40
    AND SUCH GRIT CORRUPTS MY EYES ....ON THE PLETHORA OF DRYADS   67   31
    FOR EYES TO LIGHT ME ....WORDS FOR A NURSERY 73   5
    WORTHLESS SUCH VISION TO EYES GONE DULL ..ON THE DECLINE OF ORACLES   78   30
    TO PETRIFY YOUR EYES, AND EVERY VILLAGE ....PERSEUS 83   21
    TOWARD EXTINCTION IN THOSE EYES ....SCULPTOR   92   17
    THEIR EYES REVOLVE THE WHOLE TOWN LIKE A BLUE AND GREEN BALL. *NET-. 121   12
    THE BALD, WHITE TUMULI OF YOUR EYES. ....THE COLOSSUS   129   15
    THEY GLITTER LIKE EYES, AND I COLLECT THEM ALL. .....PRIVATE GROUND 131   22
    THE ORANGE PUMPKINS HAVE NO EYES. POEM.1.WHO.   131   20
    WHAT LARGE EYES THE DEAD HAVE! POEM.6.W.   135   10
    DEAD MEN LEAVE EYES FOR OTHERS. POEM.7.S.   137   38
    FIRE SMELTED HIS EYES TO LUMPS ....THE BURNT-OUT SPA   137   3
    THE EYES OF THE CHILD I NURSE ARE SCARCELY OPEN. ....CANDLES   149   28
    FROM THE LINKED PONDS THAT MY EYES WINCE ...PARLIAMENT HILL FIELDS   152   11
    BALD EYES OR PETRIFIED EGGS, ...WHITSUN   153   3
    THEN SHE COULD COVER MY MOUTH AND EYES, COVER ME ENTIRELY, *PLASTER.   159   40
    BETWEEN THE EYE OF THE SUN AND THE EYES OF THE TULIPS, ...TULIPS   161   47
    UNDER THE EYES OF THE STARS AND THE MOON'S RICTUS ....INSOMNIAC   163   5
    THE BALD SLOTS OF HIS EYES STIFFENED WIDE-OPEN ....INSOMNIAC   163   27
    AND EVERYWHERE PEOPLE, EYES MICA-SILVER AND BLANK, ...INSOMNIAC   163   34
    AND IT IS MY EYES THAT HAVE BEEN SHARPENING THEMSELVES? .....STARS.   166   26
    IS ACCOUNTING FOR ITS COW. I SHUT MY EYES ..STARS OVER THE DORDOGNE   166   39
    BIG AS THE BALL OF MY THUMB, AND DUMB AS EYES ........BLACKBERRYING   168   5
    THE EYES LIFT AFTER IT AND FIND THE MOON. *THE MOON AND THE YEW TREE   173   16

EYES (CONT.)
    BENDING, ON ME IN PARTICULAR, ITS MILD EYES. ....MOON.   173   21
    THAT SUMMER WE WORE BLACK GLASSES TO HIDE OUR EYES. *THE BABYSITTERS   174   3
    MY EYES ARE SQUEEZED BY THIS BLACKNESS. ....THREE WOMEN   180 146
    A RED, HARD WOOD, EYES SHUT AND MOUTH WIDE OPEN. ....THREE WOMEN   182 212
    WHO INJURE MY SLEEP WITH THEIR WHITE EYES, THEIR FINGERLESS
        HANDS. ....THREE WOMEN 185 321
    I CANNOT SEE YOUR EYES. ....EVENT 194   12
    THEIR EYES OPENING ....BERCK-PLAGE 201 121
    AND THE EYES AND TIMES OF THE POSTMARKS. ....BURNING THE LETTERS   204   14
    PALE EYES, PATENT-LEATHER GUTTURALS! ....BURNING THE LETTERS   205   46
    I WOULD ADMIRE THE DEEP GRAVITY OF IT, ITS TIMELESS EYES. *BIRTHDAY.   208   57
    AND THE EYES OF THE KILLER MOVING SLUGLIKE AND SIDELONG, *DETECTIVE.   208   8
    BUT HOW ABOUT THE EYES, THE EYES, THE EYES? ....COURAGE.   210   26
    BUT HOW ABOUT THE EYES, THE EYES, THE EYES? ....COURAGE.   210   26
    BUT HOW ABOUT THE EYES, THE EYES, THE EYES? ....COURAGE.   210   26
    DO NOT WORRY ABOUT THE EYES -- ....THE COURAGE OF SHUTTING-UP   210   30
    CREAMY BEAN FLOWERS WITH BLACK EYES AND LEAVES LIKE BORED HEARTS. ...
        ... THE BEE MEETING 211   18
    SIX CAT'S EYES IN THE WINE CELLAR, ...WINTERING   217   5
    BEHIND TWO EYES IN WHICH NOTHING IS REFLECTED BUT MONKEYS. *A SECRET   219   20
    TO THUMB SHUT YOUR EYES AT THE END ....THE APPLICANT   221   16
    EYES ROLLED BY WHITE STICKS, ...MEDUSA   224   2
    DO WITHOUT EYES TO KNIFE, WHAT WOULD HE ....THE JAILER   227   44
    SEA OF HIS EYES WASHING OVER IT ....LYONNESSE   234   7
    SHE MAY BE BALD, SHE MAY HAVE NO EYES, ...THE TOUR   238   43
    IGNITING ITS CARBON MONOXIDES, BY EYES ....POPPIES IN OCTOBER   240   8
    I FLY TO A NAME, TWO EYES. ....GETTING THERE   248   19
    ON MY EYES, MY LIPS, MY HAIR ....THE NIGHT DANCES   250   26
    EYES TO THE SKY. ....GULLIVER   251   11
    OF TWO WET EYES AND A SCREECH. ....THALIDOMIDE   252   20
    THE ONE WHO NEVER LOOKS UP, WHOSE EYES ARE LIDDED ......DEATH & CO.   254   3
    STRIPES FOR MOUTH AND EYES AND NOSE, ...THE FEARFUL   256   6
    EYES LIKE MICE ....EAVESDROPPER   261   54
    OPENING THE FAT SMILES, THE EYES .....................EAVESDROPPER   261   60
    THEIR ROUND EYES, THEIR TEETH, THEIR GRIMACES ....TOTEM   264   17
    MULTIPLIED IN THE EYES OF THE FLIES. ....TOTEM   265   30
    TAPESTRIES OF EYES, ...PARALYTIC   266   12
    EYES, NOSE AND EARS, ...PARALYTIC   266   29
    AND THEIR EYES LOOKING OUT OF IT: KEEN, *DIALOGUE OVER A OUIJA BOARD   276   10
    COLUMN OF DAZZLE DRAWS MY EYES TO THE WALL ....DIALOGUE O.   279   88
    SAVED FOR THE ACORN-STOMACHED SAINT OR EYES ....DIALOGUE O.   280 129
    ALL NIGHT LONG, EVEN SHOULD OUR EYES SHUT ....DIALOGUE O.   286 354
    HER BLUE EYES SWAM WITH VAGUE TERROR. ....BITTER STRAWBERRIES   300   24
    THE FADED EYES ....FAMILY REUNION   300   18
    AND HIS EYES GONE BLIND WITH LEAVES. ....GOLD MOUTHS CRY   302   14
    HER GREEN EYES SLANT, HAIR FLARING IN A FAN ....CINDERELLA   303   2
    UNTIL IN DISENCHANTMENT OUR EYES GLUT ....METAMORPHOSES OF THE MOON   308   34
    IN A SMOKE THAT SEARS MY EYES. ....CIRCUS IN THREE RINGS   322   18
    ON LOOKING INTO THE EYES OF A DEMON LOVER *ON LOOKING INTO THE EYES.   325   T
    AND GET SAFE HOME; BUT, TURNING WITH TRAINED EYES, ...AERIALIST   331   28
    AND STAUNCH STONE EYES THAT STARE ....TOUCH-AND-GO   335   3
    THOSE STONIER EYES LOOK, ...TOUCH-AND-GO   336   23
    AN ACCURATE ASSAULT UPON THE EYES ....EPITAPH IN THREE PARTS   337   14
EYE'S (2)
    AT EYE'S ENVIOUS CORNER ....VANITY FAIR   32   6
    IN HIS EYE'S DARKROOM I CAN SEE ....BLUEBEARD   305   5
EYESORE (1)
    GILDING WHAT'S EYESORE, ...GREEN ROCK, WINTHROP BAY   105   21
EYE-STONES (1)
    WHERE ARE THE EYE-STONES, YELLOW AND VALUABLE, ...BERCK-PLAGE   198   53
FABLE (4)
    "I DON'T ASK YOU TO SPIN SOME RIDICULOUS FABLE ....DIALOGUE B.   39   22
    HOW THIS TART FABLE INSTRUCTS ....VIRGIN IN A TREE   81   1
    FABLE OF THE RHODODENDRON STEALERS ................RHODODENDRON.   103   T
    KNIT UP A GILDED FABLE FOR THE CHILD ..THE PRINCESS AND THE GOBLINS   335   73
FABLED (2)
    FABLED HORIZON ....MOONSONG AT MORNING 317   11
    SHUTS DOWN ITS FABLED SUMMER HOUSE; ....TWO LOVERS.   327   2
FABLES (3)
    OF DRAGONS BREATHING WITHOUT THE FRAME OF FABLES, ...LESSON.   80   3
    SO FABLES GO. ....BATTLE-SCENE   85   31
    SO FABLES SAY THE GOATSUCKER MOVES, MASKED FROM MEN'S SIGHT ...
        ... GOATSUCKER 111   9
FABLING (1)
    HAS NEVER FAILED TO SEE OUR FABLING SHEARED ....DIALOGUE O.   276   12
FABRIC (4)
    AND PIPES THE WORLD BACK TO THE SIMPLE FABRIC .........SNAKECHARMER   79   23
    AGE WEARS THE BEST BLACK FABRIC ....OLD LADIES' HOME   120   13
    A TARRED FABRIC, SORRY AND DULL, ...BERCK-PLAGE   200 114
    WHICH QUAINTLY WOVE THE FABRIC OF HER FATE ....THE PRINCESS.   335   57
FABRICATION (2)
    THE FABRICATION OF SOME CLOTH TO COVER ....TALE OF A TUB   25   34
    FROM FABRICATION SPRINGS THE SPIRAL STAIR ....THE PRINCESS.   333   1

                                                    TITLE   PAGE LINE
FABULOUS (5)
    AND THE FABULOUS LUTES AND PEACOCKS, RENDING THE NET   CONVERSATION.   21   3
    SHATTERS THE FABULOUS STARS AND MAKES US REAL. ....TALE OF A TUB   25   48
    HUNG CAUGHT IN DARK-WEBBED BRANCHES LIKE A FABULOUS HERON. ...
                        ... DIALOGUE BETWEEN GHOST AND PRIEST   38   6
    THEIR FABULOUS HEYDAY ENDLESS. ....DREAM WITH CLAM-DIGGERS   44   16
    BOAR, FABULOUS ENOUGH TO STRADDLE THAT SOW'S HEAT. ....SOW   61   33
FACADES (1)
    MARBLE FACADES WITH BLUE VEINS, AND JELLY-GLASSFULS OF DAFFODILS. ...
                        ... BERCK-PLAGE   199   89
FACE (70)
    THAT SEAMED FACE ....STRUMPET SONG   33   11
    "COME LADY, BRING THAT FACE ....TINKER JACK AND THE TIDY WIVES   34   10
    THE PASSING DAZZLE OF EACH FACE ....EPITAPH FOR FIRE AND FLOWER   45   9
    WHILE ELLA DROWSED WHISKERED WITH SLEEK FACE, SLY WITS: ...
                        ... ELLA MASON AND HER ELEVEN CATS   54   29
    LEAN FACE GONE TAWN WITH SEASONS, ...CRYSTAL GAZER   54   2
    SEEING HER FREEZE, HE TURNS HIS FACE AWAY. ....THE OTHER TWO   68   20
    OUR OWN GRIST DOWN TO ITS BONY FACE. ....ALL THE DEAD DEARS   70   12
    DARK FACE. SO MIGHT RIGOR MORTIS COME TO STIFFEN ....PERSEUS   83   32
    IN THE DEEP CONVULSION GRIPPING YOUR FACE, MUSCLES ....PERSEUS   83   43
    GETS READY TO FACE THE READY-MADE CREATION   THE GHOST'S LEAVETAKING   90   6
    OF YOUR GRAINED FACE SHED TIME IN RUNNELS: ....FULL FATHOM FIVE   93   26
    UP TOWARD ME, TROUBLING THE FACE ....LORELEI   94   10
    FACE, TO FACE THE BALD-FACED SUN. .....MUSSEL HUNTER AT ROCK HARBOR   97   91
    FACE, TO FACE THE BALD-FACED SUN. .....MUSSEL HUNTER AT ROCK HARBOR   97   91
    AMONG THE SOCKETED WHITE STARS, YOUR FACE ....MOONRISE   98   26
    TOLERABLE NOW AS MOLES ON THE FACE ....THE COMPANIONABLE ILLS   105   2
    THE RAVAGED FACE ....THE RAVAGED FACE   115   T
    OUTLANDISH AS A CIRCUS, THE RAVAGED FACE ....THE RAVAGED FACE   115   1
    THE STONE FACE OF THE MAN WHO DOESN'T FEEL, ...THE RAVAGED FACE   116   10
    MY MOTHER DREAMED YOU FACE DOWN IN THE SEA.   ELECTRA ON AZALEA PATH   117   36
    THEY SET THEIR STOUT CHAIRS BACK TO THE ROAD AND FACE THE DARK*NET-.   121   5
    A CLEAN SLATE, WITH YOUR OWN FACE ON. ....YOU'RE   141   18
    FACE LIFT ....FACE LIFT   155   T
    OVER EACH WEIGHTY STOMACH A FACE ....HEAVY WOMEN   158   6
    AND WEAR MY PAINTED FACE THE WAY A MUMMY-CASE ....IN PLASTER   159   41
    WEARS THE FACE OF A PHARAOH, THOUGH IT'S MADE OF MUD AND WATER. ...
                        ... IN PLASTER   159   42
    AND I HAVE NO FACE, I HAVE WANTED TO EFFACE MYSELF. ....TULIPS   161   48
    SLAPPING ITS PHANTOM LAUNDRY IN MY FACE. .............BLACKBERRYING   169   21
    TO THE HILLS' NORTHERN FACE, AND THE FACE IS ORANGE ROCK   BLACKBER.   169   24
    TO THE HILLS' NORTHERN FACE, AND THE FACE IS ORANGE ROCK   BLACKBER.   169   24
    AS USUAL THERE IS NO FACE. A LUMP OF CHINESE WHITE ....SURGEON.   170   7
    WITH TIGERY STRIPES, AND A FACE ON IT ....LAST WORDS   172   2
    AND THE SHINE OF THESE SMALL THINGS SWEETER THAN THE FACE OF
        ISHTAR. ....LAST WORDS   172   26
    THE MOON IS NO DOOR. IT IS A FACE IN ITS OWN RIGHT, ...MOON.   173   8
    THE FACE OF THE EFFIGY, GENTLED BY CANDLES, ...MOON.   173   20
    BLUE AND MYSTICAL OVER THE FACE OF THE STARS. ....MOON.   173   23
    EACH MORNING IT IS HER FACE THAT REPLACES THE DARKNESS. .....MIRROR   174   16
    FOR THE SPIRIT TO CONCEIVE A FACE, A MOUTH? ....THREE WOMEN   177   26
    THE FACE IN THE POOL WAS BEAUTIFUL, BUT NOT MINE -- ...THREE WOMEN   177   45
    BUT IT WAS TOO LATE FOR THAT. IT WAS TOO LATE, AND THE FACE   THREE.   178   62
    NOT LOOKING, THROUGH THE THICK DARK, FOR THE FACE OF ANOTHER *THREE.   178   77
    I DID NOT LOOK. BUT STILL THE FACE WAS THERE, ...THREE WOMEN   178   78
    THE FACE OF THE UNBORN ONE THAT LOVED ITS PERFECTIONS,   THREE WOMEN   178   79
    THE FACE OF THE DEAD ONE THAT COULD ONLY BE PERFECT ...THREE WOMEN   178   80
    FACE THE VOICES THAT OVERWHELM, THE TERRIBLE ELEMENT. ..THREE WOMEN   179 112
    AND THAT MAD, HARD FACE AT THE END OF IT, THAT O-MOUTH ...THREE WOMEN   182 184
    NOW THEY FACE A WINTER OF WHITE SHEETS, WHITE FACES. ...THREE WOMEN   184 265
    PUT ON A FACE AND WALKED INTO THE WORLD. ....THREE WOMEN   185 301
    WHAT IS THIS, THIS FACE ....ELM   193   38
    HIS LITTLE FACE IS CARVED IN PAINED, RED WOOD. ....EVENT   194   9
    A WEDDING-CAKE FACE IN A PAPER FRILL. ....BERCK-PLAGE   198   55
    ENFOLDS HER FACE LIKE FINE LINEN, ...BERCK-PLAGE   200 102
    AND FIND NO FACE BUT MY OWN, AND YOU THINK THAT'S FUNNY.*FATHERLESS.   205   9
    UNABLE TO FACE THE FINGERS, THOSE EGOTISTS. ....THE DETECTIVE   208   9
    THE FACE THAT LIVED IN THIS MIRROR IS THE FACE OF A DEAD MAN. ...
                        ... THE COURAGE OF SHUTTING-UP   210   29
    THE FACE THAT LIVED IN THIS MIRROR IS THE FACE OF A DEAD MAN. ...
                        ... THE COURAGE OF SHUTTING-UP   210   29
    AND A BLACK VEIL THAT MOLDS TO MY FACE, THEY ARE MAKING ME ONE OF
        THEM. ....THE BEE MEETING   211   22
    THE BOOT IN THE FACE, THE BRUTE ....DADDY   223   49
    AND MY CHILD -- LOOK AT HER, FACE DOWN ON THE FLOOR, ...LESBOS   227   8
    HER FACE RED AND WHITE, A PANIC, ...LESBOS   227   11
    MY FACE A FEATURELESS, FINE ....LADY LAZARUS   244   8
    TO THE SAME PLACE, THE SAME FACE, THE SAME BRUTE ......LADY LAZARUS   246   53
    THE FACE AT THE END OF THE FLARE. ....GETTING THERE   249   59
    WHILE WE'RE SITTING, FACE TO FACE ACROSS THE COFFEE- ...DIALOGUE O.   276   3
    WHILE WE'RE SITTING, FACE TO FACE ACROSS THE COFFEE- ...DIALOGUE O.   276   3
    BULKING MORE REAL THAN WE THINK WE ARE: WE FACE ....DIALOGUE O.   279 115
    YOU TO TAUNTS THOUGH, WHEN HE REFLECTS A FACE ....DIALOGUE O.   283 260
    OF MOONLIGHT OR THE POCKMARKED FACE WE SEE*METAMORPHOSES OF THE MOON   308   38

FACE (CONT.)
    TO MOCK YOUR FACE ....MOONSONG AT MORNING   316   6
    A WITCH'S FACE? ....ON LOOKING INTO THE EYES OF A DEMON LOVER   325   20
FACED (3)
    AND I FACED MY TRAVELING COMPANIONS. ....THE DISQUIETING MUSES   76   48
    AND FACED ME, BACK TO A LEDGE OF DIRT, TO RATTLE .....INCOMMUNICADO 100   3
    OPPOSE WHAT WE FACED EARLIER. FEEL MY HAND. ....DIALOGUE O. 285 332
FACELESS (3)
    FACELESS AND PALE AS CHINA ....PARLIAMENT HILL FIELDS 152   2
    THE FACELESS FACES OF IMPORTANT MEN. ....THREE WOMEN 179   84
    BLUNT AS THE FACELESS GUT ....NOTES TO A NEOPHYTE 306   2
FACE-OVALS (1)
    BOSSING THE ETHEREAL BLANKS OF THEIR FACE-OVALS. ....MAGI 148   3
FACE-ROOM (1)
    MEMORIES JOSTLE EACH OTHER FOR FACE-ROOM LIKE OBSOLETE FILM
        STARS. ....INSOMNIAC 163   14
FACES (28)
    DRYLY DISCLAIMS THAT FIERCE TROLL FACES LURK ....TALE OF A TUB   24   13
    NOR NIGHTFALL, OUR HANDS, FACES ....THE GREAT CARBUNCLE   72   6
    FACES BLANK AS THE DAY I WAS BORN, ...THE DISQUIETING MUSES   76   51
    PARENTAL FACES ON TALL STALKS, ALTERNATELY STERN AND TEARFUL, ...
                                                   ... INSOMNIAC 163   11
    WHITENED BY THE FACES OF THE DROWNED. ....FINISTERRE 169   5
    GRAY FACES, SHUTTERED BY DRUGS, FOLLOW ME LIKE FLOWERS. ...SURGEON. 171   50
    I SEE THEM ALREADY -- THE PALE, STAR-DISTANCE FACES. ....LAST WORDS 172   6
    THE FLOWERS AND THE FACES WHITEN TO A SHEET. ....LAST WORDS 172   13
    THEIR HANDS AND FACES STIFF WITH HOLINESS.*THE MOON AND THE YEW TREE 173   26
    FACES AND DARKNESS SEPARATE US OVER AND OVER. ....MIRROR 173   9
    HOW WHITE THESE SHEETS ARE. THE FACES HAVE NO FEATURES. *THREE WOMEN 178   65
    THEY ARE BALD AND IMPOSSIBLE, LIKE THE FACES OF MY CHILDREN, *THREE. 178   66
    AND THEN THERE WERE OTHER FACES. THE FACES OF NATIONS,   THREE WOMEN 179   82
    AND THEN THERE WERE OTHER FACES. THE FACES OF NATIONS,   THREE WOMEN 179   82
    THE FACELESS FACES OF IMPORTANT MEN. ....THREE WOMEN 179   84
    THE SHEETS, THE FACES, ARE WHITE AND STOPPED; LIKE CLOCKS. ..THREE. 179   95
    THE VISITATIONS, THE MANIFESTATIONS, THE STARTLED FACES.*THREE WOMEN 180 131
    HOLES IN THE HEELS OF SOCKS, THE WHITE MUTE FACES ......THREE WOMEN 182 199
    NOW THEY FACE A WINTER OF WHITE SHEETS, WHITE FACES. ...THREE WOMEN 184 265
    THE NARCISSI OPEN WHITE FACES IN THE ORCHARD. ....THREE WOMEN 185 315
    ARE THOSE THE FACES OF LOVE, THOSE PALE IRRETRIEVABLES? ....ELM 193   35
    THE PALLORS OF HANDS AND NEIGHBORLY FACES, ...BERCK-PLAGE 199   85
    THEIR FACES TURNING, WORDLESS AND SLOW, ...BERCK-PLAGE 201 120
    BUT WITH THE SAME FACES, ...LYONNESSE 234   13
    OF OLD BANDAGES, BOREDOMS, OLD FACES ....GETTING THERE 249   66
    FACES THAT ....THALIDOMIDE 252   13
    OF CHRIST IN THE FACES OF RODENTS, ...MYSTIC 269   19
    FROM GRAY CHILD FACES CRYING IN THE STREETS. ....FEMALE AUTHOR 301   14
FACET (2)
    A FACET OF KNOWLEDGE. ....BERCK-PLAGE 198   49
    AT THIS FACET THE BRIDEGROOM ARRIVES ....PURDAH 242   19
FACETED (1)
    A PERFECTLY FACETED WIFE TO WAIT ....ON DECK 143   32
FACETS (1)
    YOUR FACETS ARE INDESTRUCTIBLE; ....THE RIVAL/DR 291   25
FACE-TO-THE-WALL (1)
    MY FAT PORK, MY MARROWY SWEETHEART, FACE-TO-THE-WALL? ....ZOO K. 155   15
FACING (2)
    THE SKULLS, THE UNBUCKLED BONES FACING THE VIEW! ..WAKING IN WINTER 151   10
    THAT WANES AND WANES, FACING THE COLD ANGEL? ....THREE WOMEN 177   39
FACT (4)
    THE SHAPE THAT SHUTS US IN? ABSOLUTE FACT ....TALE OF A TUB   25   29
    INDEFATIGABLE FACT. ....NIGHT SHIFT   77   24
    LIKE AN OLIVE-BEAKED DOVE ABOVE THE ENGULFING FACT: ....DIALOGUE O. 279 112
    THE FACT OF DOUBT, THE FAITH OF DREAM. ...METAMORPHOSES OF THE MOON 308   48
FACTORY (3)
    SILVER FACTORY, IMMENSE ....NIGHT SHIFT   76   16
    GAS TANKS, FACTORY STACKS -- THAT LANDSCAPE ...SUICIDE OFF EGG ROCK 115   3
    UNCLE, PANTS FACTORY FATSO, MILLIONAIRE. ....STOPPED DEAD 230   4
FACTS (1)
    FACTS HAVE BLASTED ....MOONSONG AT MORNING 317   33
FADE (1)
    IN WAIT FOR SHARPER SMART TO FADE. ....BUCOLICS   24   24
FADED (2)
    IN FADED DUNGAREES. ....BITTER STRAWBERRIES 300   30
    THE FADED EYES ....FAMILY REUNION 300   18
FADES (1)
    YOUR CRY FADES LIKE THE CRY OF A GNAT. ......PARLIAMENT HILL FIELDS 153   32
FADING (1)
    THIS IS THE KINGDOM OF THE FADING APPARITION, ...GHOST'S.   90   8
FAGGOT-BEARING (1)
    FAGGOT-BEARING JACK IN HIS CRACKLESS EGG: ....MAUDLIN   51   4
FAGGOTS (1)
    THE HORIZONS RING ME LIKE FAGGOTS, ...WUTHERING HEIGHTS 167   1
FAIL (1)
    AMONG THE PITHLESS REEDS. FLIES FAIL US. ....FROG AUTUMN   99   7

	TITLE	PAGE	LINE

FAILED (1)
HAS NEVER FAILED TO SEE OUR FABLING SHEARED ....DIALOGUE O. 276 12
FAILS (1)
FAILS TO APPEAR, TURN, AND, TURNING, SHRINK ....DIALOGUE O. 279 120
FAILURE (1)
MONTH AFTER MONTH, WITH ITS VOICES OF FAILURE. ....THREE WOMEN 182 187
FAINLIGHT (1)
FOR RUTH FAINLIGHT ....ELM 192 D
FAINT (2)
BUT THE TORCH AND ITS FAINT ....WINTERING 218 15
FAINT, UNDULANT WATERMARK. ....A SECRET 219 8
FAINTLY (1)
WAVER, FAINTLY GREEN, SHUDDERING AWAY ....TALE OF A TUB 25 26
FAIR (7)
WHICH HAULS DOWN BUCK, COCK, TROUT, TILL ALL MOST FAIR ....FIRESONG 30 6
VANITY FAIR ....VANITY FAIR 32 T
STILL FAIR, ...TINKER JACK AND THE TIDY WIVES 35 28
AND THE FAIR SHIP SANK, ITS CREW KNELLED HOME FOR DINNER. ...
... DREAM WITH CLAM-DIGGERS 44 20
SPROUTING FRUIT, FLOWERS, CHILDREN MOST FAIR IN LEGION ...WREATH F. 45 22
FAIR CHRONICLER OF EVERY FOUL DECLENSION. ....OUIJA 77 14
GIVING EVERYBODY A FAIR HEARING. ....CANDLES 149 11
FAIRYTALE (1)
IN HELL, SINCE HELL'S A FAIRYTALE. I WOULD ....DIALOGUE O. 278 65
FAIRY-TALE (1)
IS A FAIRY-TALE; INTELLIGENCE ...........METAMORPHOSES OF THE MOON 308 41
FAITH (9)
BREAKING ON LEGENDARY BEACHES; IN FAITH ....TALE OF A TUB 25 45
AND HOARD FAITH SAFE IN A FOSSIL. ......EPITAPH FOR FIRE AND FLOWER 45 21
BY WITS ALONE: TO FORESEE HER LOVER'S FAITH ....CRYSTAL GAZER 55 33
I WOULDN'T TRUST MYSELF. THE FAULT'S MY FAITH ....DIALOGUE O. 277 37
TO FRACTURE THESE FOUR WALLS. YOUR FAITH FLIES ....DIALOGUE O. 279 111
FAITH FAST: A MIRACLE AND THE SMELL OF BLOOD ....DIALOGUE O. 280 161
THE FACT OF DOUBT, THE FAITH OF DREAM. ...METAMORPHOSES OF THE MOON 308 44
WITH RADIANCE OF HIS FROZEN FAITH. ....TO A JILTED LOVER 309 9
LOOPING LIKE FAITH ABOUT HER BLEEDING FEET, ...THE PRINCESS. 334 48
FAITHFUL (2)
THESE FAITHFUL DARK-BOUGHED CYPRESSES ....PARLIAMENT HILL FIELDS 153 30
WHERE TRAINS, FAITHFUL TO THEIR STEEL ARCS, ...THE SWARM 216 35
FAITHFULLY (1)
I SEE HER BACK, AND REFLECT IT FAITHFULLY. ....MIRROR 174 13
FAITH-MAKER (1)
THE FAITH-MAKER, FISTED IN HIS CLOUD, OR THE CHORUS ...DIALOGUE O. 279 109
FAKE (1)
WILL PROVE TO BE SOME COMMON PARLOR FAKE: *METAMORPHOSES OF THE MOON 307 22
FAKERY (1)
WITH HIS ARMOR OF FAKERY, ...THE JAILER 227 30
FALCON (2)
SIGNS SAY NOTHING. THE FALCON WHO SPOKE CLEAR ........INCOMMUNICADO 100 13
FAST AS A FALLIBLE FALCON. ....DIALOGUE EN ROUTE 308 6
FALL (19)
MEEK AND PROUD BOTH FALL; STARK VIOLENCE ....CHANNEL CROSSING 27 30
SUN HOISTS SOUL UP AFTER LIDS FALL SHUT; ....VANITY FAIR 33 28
TO PREVENT FALL, OR ANCHOR THE FLUENT AIR ....EPITAPH FOR F. 45 3
BULKS REAL, ALL SAINTS' TONGUES FALL QUIET: .....NOVEMBER GRAVEYARD 56 11
BUT LET SPOTTED LEAVES FALL AS THEY FALL, ...BLACK ROOK I. 57 9
BUT LET SPOTTED LEAVES FALL AS THEY FALL, ...BLACK ROOK I. 57 9
"NO DOUBT NOW IN DREAM-PROPERTIED FALL SOME MOON-EYED, ..CONJURING. 66 33
STALLED, LET FALL THEIR VERTICAL ....NIGHT SHIFT 76 18
THAT ONCE DESCRIED TROY'S TOWERS FALL, ...ON THE DECLINE OF ORACLES 78 31
AGAINST THE WEIGHTY IMAGE OF THEIR FALL. ....MOONRISE 98 24
NOR DO THEY SEND UP FIRES WHERE THEY FALL ..STARS OVER THE DORDOGNE 165 6
FROM THE LONG FALL, AND FIND MYSELF IN BED, ...THREE WOMEN 187 366
SAFE ON THE MATTRESS, HANDS BRACED, AS FOR A FALL. .....THREE WOMEN 187 367
POM! POM! THEY FALL ....THE SWARM 217 37
THE DARK FRUITS REVOLVE AND FALL. ....THALIDOMIDE 252 23
ALL THE FALL OF WATER AN EYE ....GIGOLO 268 30
OUR PAINTED STAGES FALL APART BY SCENES ....DOOMSDAY 316 4
TANGLING IN THE TIDE'S GREEN FALL ....TWO LOVERS. 327 6
FALL RACKETING FINALE ON HER LUCK. ....AERIALIST 332 48
FALLEN (6)
NOW, RICH ORDER OF WALLS IS FALLEN; ROOKS CROAK........CONVERSATION. 21 5
FALLEN FROM LUSTER. ....TINKER JACK AND THE TIDY WIVES 34 11
THE FALLEN TIMBERS OF ITS ONCE REMARKABLE ....ABOVE THE OXBOW 88 37
FROM WHAT GRACE AM I FALLEN. TONGUES ARE STRANGE, ...INCOMMUNICADO 100 12
I HAVE FALLEN A LONG WAY. CLOUDS ARE FLOWERING ....MOON. 173 22
EACH FALLEN LEAF IS TRAPPED BY SPELL OF STEEL, ..PROLOGUE TO SPRING 322 7
FALLIBLE (1)
FAST AS A FALLIBLE FALCON. ....DIALOGUE EN ROUTE 308 6
FALLING (13)
A DRAGNET, RISING, FALLING, AS WAVES ....FULL FATHOM FIVE 92 5
BARED BY EACH FALLING TIDE, ...MAN IN BLACK 119 14
DOWN HERE THE SKY IS ALWAYS FALLING. POEM.4.BEAST. 134 20
NO FALLING RIBBONS, NO SCREAM AT THE END. ....A BIRTHDAY PRESENT 207 35
FALLING LIKE BLESSINGS, LIKE FLAKES ....THE NIGHT DANCES 250 24

FALLING (CONT.)
    FALLING FROM ME LIKE RINGS ....PARALYTIC 267 35
    THE FALLING MAN WHO NEVER WILL ABSTAIN ...METAMORPHOSES OF THE MOON 307 10
    DIAGRAMS THE FALLING YEARS, ...TO A JILTED LOVER 309 6
    AND SCORNED THE TICK OF THE FALLING WEATHER. ....LAMENT 315 3
    AND SCORNED THE TICK OF THE FALLING WEATHER. ....LAMENT 315 9
    AND SCORNED THE TICK OF THE FALLING WEATHER. ....LAMENT 315 15
    WHO SCORNED THE TICK OF THE FALLING WEATHER. ....LAMENT 316 19
    OF THE BOLD SAILOR FALLING UNDER DRENCH .....EPITAPH IN THREE PARTS 337 15
FALLS (7)
    THE GUTTED FOREST FALLS TO ASH; ....PURSUIT 23 42
    OF STICKS. THE LIGHT FALLS CHALK AND COLD ...THE EVERLASTING MONDAY 62 3
    SHEEP GREENS, FINNED FALLS, "I SHALL COMPOSE A CRISIS ...CONJURING. 66 11
    THE RUBBISH OF SUMMERS, THE BLACK-LEAVED FALLS. ..THE BURNT-OUT SPA 138 9
    THE LIGHT FALLS WITHOUT LETUP, BLINDINGLY. ....A LIFE 150 20
    WHEN ONE OF THEM FALLS IT LEAVES A SPACE, ..STARS OVER THE DORDOGNE 166 32
    TO JUGGLE WITH, MY LOVE, WHEN THE SKY FALLS. ....BY CANDLELIGHT 237 36
FALSE (2)
    DRAG UP FALSE, EDWARDIAN SENTIMENTS, ...CANDLES 149 16
    A GLASS EYE, FALSE TEETH OR A CRUTCH, ...THE APPLICANT 221 3
FALSETTO (1)
    GLINTING AND CLINKING IN A SAINT'S FALSETTO. ONLY YOU NEW YEAR ON. 176 3
FALTER (1)
    IS TRICKED TO FALTER IN SPILT BLOOD. ....FIRESONG 30 7
FAME (2)
    THEIR LEAFY CROWNS, THEIR FAME SOARS, ...VIRGIN IN A TREE 81 18
    AT FAME OR NOT? AS FOR LOVE, I FIGURE WHEN WE'RE ....DIALOGUE O. 278 57
FAMILIAR (3)
    TWENTY YEARS AGO, THE FAMILIAR TUB ....TALE OF A TUB 25 17
    FIDO LITTLESOUL, THE BOWEL'S FAMILIAR. POEM.4.BEAST. 134 13
    THE BIG DIPPER IS MY ONLY FAMILIAR. ....STARS OVER THE DORDOGNE 165 17
FAMILY (11)
    CHILDBIRTHS OR A FAMILY BARBECUE: ....ALL THE DEAD DEARS 71 28
    BY A FAMILY NAME IT ....MUSSEL HUNTER AT ROCK HARBOR 96 59
    TWO SUICIDES, THE FAMILY WOLVES, ...THE MANOR GARDEN 125 13
    UPLIFTED, STIFFEN IN A FAMILY POSE. ....BLUE MOLES 126 16
    NO FAMILY TREE, ...POLLY'S TREE 128 29
    A WHOLE FAMILY OF PROMINENT OBJECTS ....CANDLES 148 6
    AS VICTORIAN CUSHIONS. THIS FAMILY ....A LIFE 150 16
    MY HUSBAND AND CHILD SMILING OUT OF THE FAMILY PHOTO; ....TULIPS 160 20
    THESE ARE THE DECEITS, TACKED UP LIKE FAMILY PHOTOGRAPHS,*DETECTIVE. 208 13
    THERE ARE NO FAMILY PHOTOGRAPHS, ...GIGOLO 267 8
    FAMILY REUNION ....FAMILY REUNION 300 T
FAMILY-FEATURED (1)
    TO NO FAMILY-FEATURED GHOST, ...HARDCASTLE CRAGS 63 16
FAMISHED (1)
    WERE SMALL THAT THEY FAMISHED AND ....THE THIN PEOPLE 64 7
FAMOUS (1)
    LET FLESH BE KNIT, AND EACH STEP HENCE GO FAMOUS. ....WREATH F. 45 24
FAN (4)
    CURRENTS OF THE CONNECTICUT FAN ....IN MIDAS' COUNTRY 99 2
    ANY SILK FAN ....POLLY'S TREE 128 12
    I FAN THEM OUT ....BURNING THE LETTERS 205 38
    HER GREEN EYES SLANT, HAIR FLARING IN A FAN ....CINDERELLA 303 2
FANCIES (1)
    CHOCOLATE FANCIES IN ROSE-PAPERED ROOMS ....FEMALE AUTHOR 301 6
FANCY (2)
    OVERHEAD, THE CLOUDS SIT TASSELED AND FANCY ....A LIFE 150 15
    AND LIKE A BURGLAR STEAL THEIR FANCY: ....MORNING IN THE HOS. 333 26
FANG (1)
    SEA-DRAGON FOR SOFA, FANG ....BATTLE-SCENE 85 36
FANGED (1)
    WITH FANGED AND DREADFUL HEAD. ....BATTLE-SCENE 84 18
FANGS (1)
    BUT MISSED THE MARK WITH SNAKING FANGS: ....LAMENT 315 5
FANNING (1)
    FEATHER DUSTERS FANNING THEIR HANDS IN A SEA OF BEAN FLOWERS, BEE. 211 17
FAN-TAILS (1)
    WHITE PETALS, WHITE FAN-TAILS, TEN WHITE FINGERS. ....MOONRISE 98 9
FAN-TAIL'S (1)
    A PIGEON RUDDERS DOWN. ITS FAN-TAIL'S WHITE. ....MOONRISE 98 7
FANTASTIC (1)
    FANTASTIC FLESH DOWN TO THE HONEST BONE. ....TALE OF A TUB 25 24
FANTASY (3)
    "WITH MY FANTASY ALONE," BRAGS THE IMPORTUNATE HEAD, ...CONJURING. 66 9
    STARVING MY FANTASY DOWN ....ON THE PLETHORA OF DRYADS 67 8
    FROM THE COMIC OPERATIC FANTASY THE SEAFARER ....BATTLE-SCENE 84 ST
FAR (31)
    FAR FROM THE SWEET STENCH OF THAT PERILOUS AIR ....CHANNEL CROSSING 27 13
    MOST FAR IN BLUE, ALOFT, ...SONG FOR A SUMMER'S DAY 31 7
    BY GOING FAR; MY LOOK'S LEASH ....SOLILOQUY OF THE SOLIPSIST 37 13
    PLUCKED BACK THUS SUDDEN TO THAT FAR INNOCENCE, ...DREAM WITH C. 44 21
    FAR DEEPER IN GROSS WOOD ....ON THE PLETHORA OF DRYADS 67 11
    FAR OFF, NOT BLOOD IN THE EARS ....NIGHT SHIFT 76 3
    LORDED PERSPECTIVES. MAPLIKE, THE FAR FIELDS ARE RULED ......OXBOW. 89 48

FAR (CONT.)
    ART'S SAKE THAN GOD'S. FAR FROM SEA -- *MUSSEL HUNTER AT ROCK HARBOR   97   82
    NOTHING IS BIG OR FAR. ....WATERCOLOR OF GRANTCHESTER MEADOWS   111   3
    FIXED VORTEX ON THE FAR ....MAN IN BLACK   120   19
    THE SKY'S FAR DOME IS SANE AND CLEAR. ....BLUE MOLES   126   10
    OF FINAL SURFEIT IS JUST AS FAR ....BLUE MOLES   127   33
    TINY AND FAR, A SINGLE SHIP ....ON DECK   142   6
    THE HORIZONS ARE TOO FAR OFF TO BE CHUMMY AS UNCLES; .....TWO CAMP.   145   13
    A FAR SEA MOVES IN MY EAR. ....MORNING SONG   157   12
    WHILE FAR OFF, THE AXLE OF WINTER ....HEAVY WOMEN   158   19
    AND COMES FROM A COUNTRY FAR AWAY AS HEALTH. ....TULIPS   162   63
    DRAINS LIKE WATER OUT THE HOLE AT THE FAR END. ....INSOMNIAC   163   25
    BUT STAY, SITTING FAR OUT, IN THEIR OWN DUST. ....STARS.   165   13
    LIKE A BIG SEA. FAR OFF, FAR OFF, I FEEL THE FIRST WAVE TUG   THREE.   179 109
    LIKE A BIG SEA. FAR OFF, FAR OFF, I FEEL THE FIRST WAVE TUG   THREE.   179 109
    THE LITTLE SILVER TROPHIES THEY'VE COME SO FAR FOR. ...THREE WOMEN   183 221
    RUN FOLD UPON FOLD FAR OFF, CONCEALING THEIR HOLLOWS, ..BERCK-PLAGE   199   74
    HOW FAR HE IS NOW, HIS ACTIONS ....BERCK-PLAGE   199   82
    THE BEES HAVE GOT SO FAR. SEVENTY FEET HIGH! ....THE SWARM   216   26
    HOW FAR IS IT? ....GETTING THERE   247   1
    HOW FAR IS IT NOW? ....GETTING THERE   247   2
    HOW FAR IS IT? ....GETTING THERE   248   34
    HOW FAR IS IT? ....GETTING THERE   248   43
    MY BONES HOLD A STILLNESS, THE FAR ....SHEEP IN FOG   262   11
    WE HAVE COME SO FAR, IT IS OVER. ....EDGE   272   8
FARE (2)
    NO PLACE, IT SEEMED, FOR THE EFFIGY TO FARE ....LADY AND T.   69   8
    THE ONLY FARE ON MY BARE BREAKFAST PLATE. QUEEN MARY'S ROSE GARDEN   290   6
FAREWELL (3)
    UPRAISED, AS A HAND, EMBLEMATIC OF FAREWELL.*THE GHOST'S LEAVETAKING   90   11
    HAIL AND FAREWELL. HELLO, GOODBYE. O KEEPER *THE GHOST'S LEAVETAKING   91   39
    A SORCERER BIDS FAREWELL TO SEEM ..A SORCERER BIDS FAREWELL TO SEEM   324   T
FAR-FLUNG (1)
    CAPPED: WHITE HAIR, WHITE BEARD, FAR-FLUNG, ...FULL FATHOM FIVE   92   4
FARM (1)
    THEY CALLED THE PLACE LOOKOUT FARM. BACK THEN, THE SUN ...
                              ... MEMOIRS OF A SPINACH-PICKER   89   1
FARMBOY'S (1)
    AND TURNED THE FARMBOY'S TEMPER WOLFISH, ..THE DEATH OF MYTH-MAKING   104   14
FARMER (3)
    "NO PITCHFORKED FARMER, PLEASE," SHE SAID; ....BUCOLICS   23   5
    BUT OUR FARMER WHISTLED, ...SOW   61   34
    MOON FULL, MOON DARK, THE CHARY DAIRY FARMER ....GOATSUCKER   111   5
FARMERS (1)
    DAWN GILDS THE FARMERS LIKE PIGS, ...TOTEM   264   5
FARMER'S (1)
    ALREADY THE FARMER'S AFTER HIS CROP, ...IN MIDAS' COUNTRY   100   23
FARMLAND (1)
    THROUGH FEN AND FARMLAND WALKING ....SONG FOR A SUMMER'S DAY   30   1
FARMS (3)
    STONE FARMS FOUNDERING IN IT, ...THE GREAT CARBUNCLE   72   3
    FLATS OF HADLEY FARMS, THEY'RE LOFTY ENOUGH ....ABOVE THE OXBOW   88   8
    RIVER-VERGE FARMS WHERE RYE-HEADS WHITEN. ....IN MIDAS' COUNTRY   99   4
FARTHER (2)
    FARTHER OUT, THE WAVES WILL BE MOUTHING ICECAKES -- ..A WINTER SHIP   113   21
    FARTHER OFF THAN AUSTRALIA. ....YOU'RE   141   11
FASCIST (1)
    EVERY WOMAN ADORES A FASCIST, ...DADDY   223   48
FASHION (1)
    FOR A FASHION THAT CONSTRICTS ....VIRGIN IN A TREE   81   21
FASHIONABLE (3)
    A FASHIONABLE BEAUTY, ...ELLA MASON AND HER ELEVEN CATS   53   15
    AND THE FASHIONABLE MONDE OF THE RED COUCH ....YADWIGHA.   85   10
    NOW THEY ARE GIVING ME A FASHIONABLE WHITE STRAW ITALIAN HAT ..BEE.   211   21
FAST (4)
    THEY FLY TOO FAST TO FEEL THE WET. ....ON DECK   143   17
    FAITH FAST: A MIRACLE AND THE SMELL OF BLOOD ....DIALOGUE O.   280 161
    FAST AS A FALLIBLE FALCON. ....DIALOGUE EN ROUTE   308   6
    HOW FLESH CLEAVES FAST TO FROZEN JOINT, ...INSOLENT STORM.   326   10
FAST-FEATHERED (2)
    BUT LET THE FAST-FEATHERED EAGLE FLY. ......GO GET THE GOODLY SQUAB   313   4
    LET THE FAST-FEATHERED EAGLE FLY ....GO GET THE GOODLY SQUAB   313   5
FAT (22)
    NOW, RUN TO FAT, SHE'S A SPINSTER WHOSE DOOR SHUTS ...ELLA MASON A.   54   17
    KEEP FROM CUTTING FAT MEAT ....THE THIN PEOPLE   65   27
    MONEY'S NEW-MINTED IN THIS FAT PURSE. ....METAPHORS   116   6
    AFTER THE FAT CHILDREN OF ROOT AND ROCK. ....BLUE MOLES   126   25
    HE'S A FAT SORT. POEM.2.DARK. 132   21
    MY FAT PORK, MY MARROWY SWEETHEART, FACE-TO-THE-WALL? ....ZOO K.   155   15
    LOVE SET YOU GOING LIKE A FAT GOLD WATCH. ....MORNING SONG   156   1
    EBON IN THE HEDGES, FAT ...............................BLACKBERRYING   168   6
    THERE ARE THE CLOTHES OF A FAT WOMAN I DO NOT KNOW. ....THREE WOMEN   184 267
    THERE'S A STAKE IN YOUR FAT BLACK HEART ....DADDY   224   76
    FAT AND RED, A PLACENTA ....MEDUSA   225   25
    THE BABY SMILES, FAT SNAIL, ...LESBOS   228   23

	TITLE	PAGE	LINE

FAT (CONT.)
MEANWHILE THERE'S A STINK OF FAT AND BABY CRAP. ....LESBOS 228 33
TONGUES OF DULL, FAT CERBERUS ....FEVER. 231 4
SHE WOULD RATHER BE DEAD THAN FAT, ...THE FEARFUL 256 13
THE SUNDAY LAMB CRACKS IN ITS FAT. ....MARY'S SONG 257 1
THE FAT ....MARY'S SONG 257 2
OPENING THE FAT SMILES, THE EYES ......................EAVESDROPPER 261 60
FAT HAUNCHES AND BLOOD ON THEIR MINDS. ....TOTEM 264 8
BACK, FAT JUG ....BALLOONS 272 27
INSTEAD OF FAT FISH ON THE LINE, YOU'VE PLUMBED ....DIALOGUE O. 282 242
FAT ALWAYS, AND OUT OF BREATH, ...FAMILY REUNION 300 13
FATAL (5)
NO, IT IS NOT FATAL. ....THE OTHER 202 32
AND MAKE THE FATAL PLUNGE. ....FAMILY REUNION 301 30
AND IN A FEW FATAL YARDS OF GRASS ....APRIL 18 302 12
IN FATAL EQUILIBRIUM ...................METAMORPHOSES OF THE MOON 308 45
YET I FLOURISH MY WHIP WITH A FATAL FLAIR ....CIRCUS IN THREE RINGS 322 10
FATE (3)
TO RAID THE ZONE WHERE FATE BEGINS, ...METAMORPHOSES OF THE MOON 307 3
WHICH QUAINTLY WOVE THE FABRIC OF HER FATE ....THE PRINCESS. 335 57
FOR YOUR FATE INVOLVES A DARK ASSAILANT." ...EPITAPH IN THREE PARTS 337 9
FATHER (25)
PACED BRISK FATHER SHAWN. A COLD DAY, A SODDEN ONE IT WAS ...
   ... DIALOGUE BETWEEN GHOST AND PRIEST 38 2
FATHER SHAWN PERCEIVED A GHOST ...DIALOGUE BETWEEN GHOST AND PRIEST 38 9
"HOW NOW," FATHER SHAWN CRISPLY ADDRESSED THE GHOST ....DIALOGUE B. 38 11
"COME, COME," FATHER SHAWN GAVE AN IMPATIENT SHRUG .....DIALOGUE B. 39 21
"WHAT LOVE," ASKED FATHER SHAWN, "BUT TOO GREAT LOVE ...DIALOGUE B. 39 31
"FOND PHANTOM," CRIED SHOCKED FATHER SHAWN, ...DIALOGUE B. 39 41
WHERE THE DAFT FATHER WENT DOWN ....ALL THE DEAD DEARS 71 23
MY FATHER KEPT A VAULTED CONCH ....ON THE DECLINE OF ORACLES 78 1
MY FATHER DIED, AND WHEN HE DIED ....ON THE DECLINE OF ORACLES 78 9
GO, GHOST OF OUR MOTHER AND FATHER, GHOST OF US, ...GHOST'S. 91 32
FATHER, THIS THICK AIR IS MURDEROUS. ....FULL FATHOM FIVE 93 44
WHO DRAG OUR ANCIENT FATHER AT THE HEEL, ...MOONRISE 98 28
FOUNDING FATHER SET THESE LOBED, WARPED STONES CHILD'S PARK STONES 100 3
YOUR GATE, FATHER -- YOUR HOUND-BITCH, DAUGHTER, FRIEND.*ELECTRA ON. 117 45
TO FATHER DYNASTIES. THE AIR IS RICH. ....THE BEEKEEPER'S DAUGHTER 118 12
FATHER, BRIDEGROOM, IN THIS EASTER EGG ....THE BEEKEEPER'S DAUGHTER 118 19
ARCHES ABOVE US. O FATHER, ALL BY YOURSELF ....THE COLOSSUS 129 17
I SEE THE FATHER CONVERSING WITH THE SON. ....THREE WOMEN 179 88
SUCH A DARK FUNNEL, MY FATHER! ....LITTLE FUGUE 188 22
DO YOU KNOW HOW MY FATHER IS? HE'S LEFT *DIALOGUE OVER A OUIJA BOARD 278 74
THE STING OF BEES TOOK AWAY MY FATHER ....LAMENT 315 1
THE STING OF BEES TOOK AWAY MY FATHER. ....LAMENT 315 6
BUT THE STING OF BEES TOOK AWAY MY FATHER. ....LAMENT 315 12
THE STING OF BEES TOOK AWAY MY FATHER ....LAMENT 316 18
NOW KISS AGAIN: TILL OUR STRICT FATHER LEANS ....LOVE IS A PARALLAX 330 43
FATHERING (1)
UNDO THE DOINGS OF THE FATHERING AGE: *SONG FOR A REVOLUTIONARY LOVE 323 5
FATHERLESS (2)
FOR A FATHERLESS SON ....FOR A FATHERLESS SON 205 T
STARLESS AND FATHERLESS, A DARK WATER. ....SHEEP IN FOG 262 15
FATHERS (1)
I IMAGINE THEM WITHOUT FATHERS OR MOTHERS, LIKE THE FIRST GODS. ...
   ... LAST WORDS 172 8
FATHER'S (3)
IN THE HURRICANE, WHEN FATHER'S TWELVE ....THE DISQUIETING MUSES 75 17
CRIED THEN FOR THE FATHER'S BLOOD ....I WANT, I WANT 106 6
SAT BY MY FATHER'S BEAN TREE POEM.3.MAENAD. 133 2
FATHOM (1)
FULL FATHOM FIVE ....FULL FATHOM FIVE 92 T
FATHOMED (2)
OUR VOICES FATHOMED A PROFOUNDER SOUND: ....THE OTHER TWO 68 12
OF, NOT FATHOMED. ALL OBSCURITY ....FULL FATHOM FIVE 92 14
FATHOMS (1)
RISES TO THE GLASS FROM HIS BLACK FATHOMS. ....OUIJA 77 2
FATIGUE (1)
OF FATIGUE, I SHALL ....BLACK ROOK IN RAINY WEATHER 57 34
FATLY (1)
BUT FATLY SCUTTLED INTO THE SPLAYED FERN .............INCOMMUNICADO 100 2
FATNESS (1)
THE NATURAL FATNESS OF THESE LIME LEAVES! --- ....BERCK-PLAGE 199 91
FAT-RUTTED (1)
FAT-RUTTED EYES ....SOW 61 26
FATSO (1)
UNCLE, PANTS FACTORY FATSO, MILLIONAIRE. ....STOPPED DEAD 230 4
FATTEN (3)
WHERE SMALL ANTS ROLL THEIR EGGS, WHERE GRUBS FATTEN. .....MOONRISE 98 17
FATTEN IN GREEN-POCKED PODS, THE THREE NET-MENDERS SIT OUT, ..NET-. 121 3
THE PEARS FATTEN LIKE LITTLE BUDDHAS. ....THE MANOR GARDEN 125 3
FATTENED (1)
AHEAD, IT FATTENED ....HARDCASTLE CRAGS 62 15
FATTENS (2)
SHE FATTENS ON THE FINEST GRAIN. ....RHYME 50 10

172

```
                                             TITLE        PAGE  LINE
FATTENS (CONT.)
   FATTENS US, IS KIND. HER MOUTH IS RED.  .................THREE WOMEN  181 156
FATTEST (1)
   DREAMS THAT HIS FATTEST CATTLE DWINDLE, FEVERED  .........GOATSUCKER  111   6
FAUCET (1)
   UNDERGOING THE FAUCET WATER, ITS VEILS, VEILS IN A NUNNERY,*GETTING.  248  23
FAUCETS (1)
   WATER FAUCETS SPAWN NO DANGER; EACH CRAB  ..............TALE OF A TUB   25  19
FAULT (1)
   CONDEMNED BY OUR ANCESTRAL FAULT,  ..........................PURSUIT   22  14
FAULTLESSLY (1)
   BLOOD FAULTLESSLY BROACHED REDEEMED THE SULLIED AIR, THE EARTH'S
          GROSSNESS.  ......................................THE GORING   47  10
FAULTS (4)
   IT PETRIFIES THE WILL. THESE ARE THE ISOLATE, SLOW FAULTS  ......ELM  193  41
   A GROOVE OF OLD FAULTS, DEEP AND BITTER.  ....................EVENT  195  15
   AND MY HEART TOO SMALL TO BANDAGE THEIR TERRIBLE FAULTS.*BERCK-PLAGE  198  45
   MAJOR FAULTS IN GRANITE  ........................TRIO OF LOVE SONGS  313   1
FAULT'S (1)
   I WOULDN'T TRUST MYSELF. THE FAULT'S MY FAITH  ..........DIALOGUE O.  277  37
FAUN (3)
   FAUN  ......................................................FAUN   35   T
   HAUNCHED LIKE A FAUN, HE HOOED  .................................FAUN   35   1
   THE RAW WIND LIKE A SCARF; LOVE IS A FAUN  .......LOVE IS A PARALLAX  329  23
FAVORED (1)
   FAVORED (WHILE SUDDENLY THE RAINS BEGIN  .............FEMALE AUTHOR  301   2
FAVORITES (1)
   DESCENDED ON YOUR FAVORITES, AND YET  ...DIALOGUE OVER A OUIJA BOARD  281 191
FAWN (1)
   THIS FIRE MAY LICK AND FAWN, BUT IT IS MERCILESS:  .........BURNING.  204  15
FEAR (10)
   A BRIEF RESPITE FROM FEAR  .............BLACK ROOK IN RAINY WEATHER   57  31
   THROWN: FEAR, WISDOM, AT ONE: ALL COLORS  ......WHITENESS I REMEMBER  103  32
   THAT IS THE FEAR SHE HAS -- THE FEAR  ..........................WIDOW  165  36
   THAT IS THE FEAR SHE HAS -- THE FEAR  ..........................WIDOW  165  36
   IT IS WHAT YOU FEAR.  ...........................................ELM  192   2
   I DO NOT FEAR IT: I HAVE BEEN THERE.  ...........................ELM  192   3
   THEY WILL NOT SMELL MY FEAR, MY FEAR, MY FEAR.  .....THE BEE MEETING  211  10
   THEY WILL NOT SMELL MY FEAR, MY FEAR, MY FEAR.  .....THE BEE MEETING  211  10
   THEY WILL NOT SMELL MY FEAR, MY FEAR, MY FEAR.  .....THE BEE MEETING  211  10
   WHAT FEAR? IT HAS SET THEM ZINGING  ......................STINGS/DR  293   2
FEARFUL (1)
   THE FEARFUL  ...........................................THE FEARFUL  256   T
FEARFULLY (1)
   DENSE-FEATHERED, FEARFULLY SOFT TO  ...........................OWL  102  14
FEARING (1)
   HATING MYSELF, HATING AND FEARING. AND NOW THE WORLD CONCEIVES  ...
                                                  ... THREE WOMEN  181 150
FEARS (1)
   ENTERING THE TOWER OF MY FEARS,  ...........................PURSUII   23  45
FEAST (2)
   THE PEASANTS FEAST AND MULTIPLY.  .........ON THE DECLINE OF ORACLES   78  16
   FOR FEAST THE SWEETEST MEAT OF HELL'S CHEF D'OEUVRES:  .....TERMINAL  328  11
FEASTING (1)
   WITH CREAM AND CHICKEN-GUT FEASTING THE PALATES  ......ELLA MASON A.   53  11
FEAT-FOOT (1)
   ON THE MOVE, HEDGED BY A LITTER OF FEAT-FOOT NINNIES  ..........SOW   61  21
FEATHER (6)
   LET BELL-TONGUED BIRDS DESCANT IN BLACKEST FEATHER  .....LADY AND T.   69  25
   FEATHER AND ROSE.  ...................................POLLY'S TREE  129  33
   FEATHER DUSTERS FANNING THEIR HANDS IN A SEA OF BEAN FLOWERS,  BEE.  211  17
   ONE FEATHER, LIKE THE PEACOCK.  ..............................PURDAH  243  39
   OLD GROUND WITH A FEATHER  ................................BALLOONS  272  18
   THE SHUTTERS TO LET WARM WIND FEATHER  ....................THE DREAM  310   5
FEATHERED (2)
   FEATHERED DARK IN THOUGHT, I STALK LIKE A ROOK,  ..WINTER LANDSCAPE,   21   9
   GULLS IN A FEATHERED FUGUE OF WINGS. OUTDO  ........MIDSUMMER MOBILE  324   4
FEATHERS (8)
   ACT, BUT -- HOW THOSE FEATHERS SHINE!  .....................RHYME   50  16
   ARRANGING AND REARRANGING ITS FEATHERS IN THE RAIN.  ..BLACK ROOK I.   56   3
   ORDERING ITS BLACK FEATHERS CAN SO SHINE  ............BLACK ROOK I.   57  28
   WHO BORROWED FEATHERS FOR YOUR FEET, NOT LEAD,  .............PERSEUS   83  12
   ARMED WITH FEATHERS TO TICKLE AS WELL AS FLY,  .............PERSEUS   83  35
   BIRDMILK IS FEATHERS,  ...............................POEM.3.MAENAD.  133   9
   HE IS ARRANGING HIS BROWN FEATHERS.  ...................THREE WOMEN  176  12
   FEATHERS WINNOWING THE ROOM. A THIN  ...DIALOGUE OVER A OUIJA BOARD  279  87
FEATHERY (1)
   ALL DAY I FEEL ITS SOFT, FEATHERY TURNINGS, ITS MALIGNITY.  .....ELM  193  33
FEATURELESS (2)
   IN A STILL PLACE, AND THE GROOM IS RED AND FORGETFUL,
          HE IS FEATURELESS.  .............................. BERCK-PLAGE  200 108
   MY FACE A FEATURELESS, FINE  .........................LADY LAZARUS  244   8
FEATURELESSNESS (1)
   THE FEATURELESSNESS OF THAT CLOUD, NOW!  ..............LITTLE FUGUE  187   6
```

```
                                                          TITLE          PAGE  LINE
FEATURES (3)
    HOW WHITE THESE SHEETS ARE. THE FACES HAVE NO FEATURES. *THREE WOMEN   178   65
    THEIR FEATURES ARE SLEEPING, LIKE LIGHT ON QUIET WATER. *THREE WOMEN   183  226
    COMPLICATING HIS FEATURES. ...................................STINGS   215   50
FED (4)
    SLOPED SEAWARD TO PLUNGE IN BLUE; FED BY WHITE FIRE,   DREAM WITH C.    44   11
    LIKE BUBBLES ABOUT TO BREAK, YOU FED .........THE DISQUIETING MUSES     75   19
    ON GRASS THAT ONCE FED BOSTON COWS. ................A WINTER'S TALE     87   23
    FED ME BANANA GAS THROUGH A FROG-MASK. THE NAUSEOUS VAULT *FACE LIFT   156    5
FEE (1)
    WITH HER WIGGLY FINGERS AND FOR A VERY SMALL FEE. .........THE TOUR    238   47
FEED (5)
    TO FEED THE THIN CROWS. ....................WORDS FOR A NURSERY         74   50
    TO FEED HIS EYE WITH RED: SUCH RED! UNDER THE MOON, ......YADWIGHA.     86   38
    FEED ME THE BERRIES OF DARK. ........................POEM.3.MAENAD.    133   17
    THEY CAN DIE, I NEED FEED THEM NOTHING, I AM THE OWNER.*THE ARRIVAL.   213   25
    FEED YOUR OWN WISHFUL THINKING. TRY ASKING HIM .........DIALOGUE O.    283  268
FEEDING (1)
    FEEDING AT THE ROOT OF THINGS. HE STOLE THAT, TOO, .....DIALOGUE O.    279  102
FEEL (20)
    CLAIMING YOU FEEL ......................SOLILOQUY OF THE SOLIPSIST       38   32
    AND TRICKLE. COULD THEY FEEL MUD ......MUSSEL HUNTER AT ROCK HARBOR     96   48
    THE STONE FACE OF THE MAN WHO DOESN'T FEEL, .......THE RAVAGED FACE    116   10
    THEY FLY TOO FAST TO FEEL THE WET. ...........................ON DECK  143   17
    FISTS MY FINGERS FOR ME. HE MAKES ME FEEL SOMETHING PRECIOUS  FACE.    156   13
    ALREADY HE CAN FEEL DAYLIGHT, HIS WHITE DISEASE, .........INSOMNIAC    163   31
    I CAN FEEL IT TRYING ............................WUTHERING HEIGHTS     167   14
    LIKE A BIG SEA. FAR OFF, FAR OFF, I FEEL THE FIRST WAVE TUG   THREE.   179  109
    I FEEL IT ENTER ME, COLD, ALIEN, LIKE AN INSTRUMENT. ...THREE WOMEN    182  183
    BLUNT AND FLAT ENOUGH TO FEEL NO LACK. I FEEL A LACK. ..THREE WOMEN    182  193
    BLUNT AND FLAT ENOUGH TO FEEL NO LACK. I FEEL A LACK. ..THREE WOMEN    182  193
    ALL DAY I FEEL ITS SOFT, FEATHERY TURNINGS, ITS MALIGNITY. .....ELM    193   33
    WHEN  I AM QUIET AT MY COOKING I FEEL IT LOOKING, I FEEL IT
        THINKING .....................................A BIRTHDAY PRESENT  206    4
    WHEN I AM QUIET AT MY COOKING I FEEL IT LOOKING, I FEEL IT
        THINKING .....................................A BIRTHDAY PRESENT  206    4
    "I FEEL WEAK." ......................................................A SECRET  220   47
    I-N-E, HE SAYS. YOU FEEL HIM PULL .....DIALOGUE OVER A OUIJA BOARD     277  312
    IT'S NOT SO IMMINENT. AT LEAST I FEEL ..DIALOGUE OVER A OUIJA BOARD    278   61
    TUGGING US THROUGH PLUMAGE. I ALMOST FEEL .............DIALOGUE O.     279   86
    LIKE THE UNDERSIDE OF MUSHROOMS. DO YOU FEEL ..........DIALOGUE O.     285  315
    OPPOSE WHAT WE FACED EARLIER. FEEL MY HAND. ..........DIALOGUE O.      285  332
FEELING (2)
    WITH THE SWARMY FEELING OF AFRICAN HANDS *THE ARRIVAL OF THE BEE BOX   213   13
    PAPERY FEELING. ......................................................CUT  235   26
FEELS (2)
    I DO IT SO IT FEELS LIKE HELL. .........................LADY LAZARUS   245   46
    I DO IT SO IT FEELS REAL. ..............................LADY LAZARUS   245   47
FEET (25)
    ROUSED BY THORNED HANDS, FEET, HEAD, ....................STREET SONG    36   17
    SPINS ITSELF FROM UNDER MY FEET; ........SOLILOQUY OF THE SOLIPSIST     37    4
    UNDER THE FEET OF ........................................FIESTA MELONS  47   18
    FLINTLIKE, HER FEET STRUCK ........................HARDCASTLE CRAGS     62    1
    DAY NOW, NIGHT NOW, AT HEAD, SIDE, FEET, .....THE DISQUIETING MUSES     76   49
    WHO BORROWED FEATHERS FOR YOUR FEET, NOT LEAD, ............PERSEUS      83   12
    SIX FEET OF YELLOW GRAVEL COVER YOU. ........ELECTRA ON AZALEA PATH    117   23
    SHAPELESS AS FLUNG GLOVES, A FEW FEET APART -- ..........BLUE MOLES    126    3
    FEET TO THE STARS, AND MOON-SKULLED, ......................YOU'RE      141    2
    AMONG BIRD FEET AND THE STEMS OF PLANTS. ..............LOVE LETTER     147   27
    AT THEIR FEET, THE SEA WAVES BOW IN SINGLE FILE, ............A LIFE     150   11
    AT OUR FEET, THE WEED-MUSTACHIOED SEA ....................WHITSUN      154   14
    WHEN THE SOLES OF MY FEET GROW COLD, ....................LAST WORDS    172   19
    UNDER MY FEET IN A NEAT PARCEL. .........................LAST WORDS    172   24
    THE GRASSES UNLOAD THEIR GRIEFS ON MY FEET AS IF I WERE GOD,  MOON.    172    3
    FLOATING ON THEIR DELICATE FEET OVER THE COLD PEWS, .........MOON.     173   25
    THESE ARE MY FEET, THESE MECHANICAL ECHOES. ..........THREE WOMEN      177   34
    THOUGH THERE IS A SHADOW STARTING FROM MY FEET. I AM A WIFE. *THREE.   187  369
    SEVENTY FEET UP, IN A BLACK PINE TREE. ....................THE SWARM   216   18
    THE BEES HAVE GOT SO FAR. SEVENTY FEET HIGH! ...............THE SWARM  216   26
    THERE IS MUD ON MY FEET, ............................GETTING THERE     248   35
    THEN TWO LITTLE FEET. ...................................DEATH & CO.   254   19
    FEET SEEM TO BE SAYING: .................................................EDGE  272    7
    WHERE ON PINK-FLUTTED FEET THE PIGEONS PASS ..........APRIL AUBADE     312   10
    LOOPING LIKE FAITH ABOUT HER BLEEDING FEET, ..........THE PRINCESS.    334   48
FELL (6)
    SHOULD ACCEPT SO FELL A WOUND, .........................BUCOLICS        24   18
    DESCRIBED HOW YOU FELL DREAMING AT FULL OF MOON ..........YADWIGHA.     86   25
    WHEN I FELL OUT OF THE LIGHT. I ENTERED .................POEM.7.S.     136    5
    A SMILE FELL IN THE GRASS. .........................THE NIGHT DANCES   249    1
    WOULD FRACTURE IF HE FELL. .......................TRIO OF LOVE SONGS   314   24
    BEFORE WE FELL, LIKE ICARUS, UNDONE; ................DOOM OF EXILES    318   10
FELLA (1)
    MARY SAID SLOWLY, "I'VE GOT A FELLA ...........BITTER STRAWBERRIES     299   10
FELLOWS (2)
    AND SUFFERED THEIR LIVELIER FELLOWS TO STRUGGLE. ............SPIDER     49   21
```

174

	TITLE	PAGE	LINE

FELLOWS (CONT.)
WE ARE FULL OF STARCH, MY SMALL WHITE FELLOWS. WE GROW. ..POEM.6.W.   135   17
FELLOWS' (1)
WITH THE BOA CONSTRICTOR IN THE FELLOWS' GARDEN.   ZOO KEEPER'S WIFE   155   26
FELT (8)
DOZENS DROPPED DEAD IN THE HEDGES: O SHE FELT ....SNOWMAN O.   59   35
STILL, SHE FELT LOATH TO JUNK IT. THE LADY AND THE EARTHENWARE HEAD   69   7
IN THE PUBLIC PARK; AT HOME FELT THE WANT ............RHODODENDRON.   103   2
I FELT HER CRITICIZING ME IN SPITE OF HERSELF, ...IN PLASTER   159   30
HE FELT FOR HIS FOOD. ....LITTLE FUGUE 187   10
I FELT A STILL BUSYNESS, AN INTENT. ....THE RABBIT CATCHER 194   21
I FELT HANDS ROUND A TEA MUG, DULL, BLUNT, ...THE RABBIT CATCHER   194   22
WISER FOR TONIGHT'S WISE WORDS? I FELT DRAWN ....DIALOGUE O.   285 316
FEMALE (1)
FEMALE AUTHOR ....FEMALE AUTHOR   301   T
FEMININE (2)
ANGELS -- MORE FEMININE AND DOUCE ....A WINTER'S TALE   86   9
PRIM, PINK-BREASTED, FEMININE, SHE NURSES ....FEMALE AUTHOR   301   5
FEN (5)
THE AUSTERE SUN DESCENDS ABOVE THE FEN, ...WINTER LANDSCAPE,   21   6
BELOW: A FEN WHERE WATER STOOD; ....BUCOLICS   24   9
THE FEN FOG SLIPS, ...PROSPECT   28   3
THROUGH FEN AND FARMLAND WALKING ....SONG FOR A SUMMER'S DAY   30   1
THE FEN SICKENS. ....FROG AUTUMN   99   8
FENCE (1)
YOUR SPECKLED STONE ASKEW BY AN IRON FENCE.   ELECTRA ON AZALEA PATH 117   18
FENDING (1)
FENDING OFF JAG AND TOOTH, ...MISS DRAKE PROCEEDS TO SUPPER   41   22
FEN-FROST (1)
FROM GROVE OF MOON-GLINT AND FEN-FROST ....FAUN   35   2
FERN (3)
THROUGH A RANK WILDERNESS OF FERN AND FLOWER. ....SPINSTER   49   10
BUT FATLY SCUTTLED INTO THE SPLAYED FERN ............INCOMMUNICADO   100   2
CRIMPED LIKE FERN IN THE QUARTZ ATMOSPHERE; .....PROLOGUE TO SPRING 322   8
FERRIES (1)
FERRIES THE FISHPOND SINBAD ....BATTLE-SCENE   84   13
FERRY (1)
STONE, STONE, FERRY ME DOWN THERE. ....LORELEI   95   36
FERRYING (2)
OF THE FERRYING CURRENTS, BELLY ....OWL 102   13
FERRYING THE SMELLS OF DEAD COD AND TAR. ....A WINTER SHIP   113   20
FERTILE (1)
BUT THE SPAWN PERCOLATE IN MY HEART. THEY ARE FERTILE. *WORDS HEARD. 203   13
FERTILITY (1)
SHE IS SIMPLY ASTONISHED AT FERTILITY. ....THREE WOMEN   176   7
FESTERING (2)
FESTERING ON THE DIM WALLS OF EUROPE'S CHAPELS, ...PERSEUS   82   10
OF FESTERING GARDENIAS IN A CRYPT, ...FEMALE AUTHOR   301   12
FETCH (1)
SUFFERING-TOUGHENED BEYOND THE FETCH ....THE BEGGARS   48   15
FETCHER (1)
MY MASTER'S FETCHER, ...WORDS FOR A NURSERY   73   16
FETID (1)
IN THE FETID WOMBS OF BLACK AIR UNDER PINES IN SUMMER. ......MYSTIC 268   5
FETTERS (1)
WINDING AND TWINING THEIR PETTY FETTERS, ...GULLIVER   251   13
FEVER (9)
WHERE, BEDDED LIKE ANGELS, TWO BURN ONE IN FEVER. ....WREATH F.   45   18
DRUMMING UP ANY FEVER ....NIGHT SHIFT   76   4
FOR FEVER IN A SLEEP. ....BATTLE-SCENE   85   38
THE FEVER TRICKLES AND STIFFENS IN MY HAIR. ....THE JAILER 226   21
FEVER 103 [DEGREES] ....FEVER. 231   T
FOUR O'CLOCK, AND THE FEVER SOAKS FROM ME LIKE HONEY. ....FEVER./DR 294   1
GRAPHS A FEVER CHART, ...TRIO OF LOVE SONGS 313   6
FEVER FROM THE WORLD BEHIND. ....DANSE MACABRE 321   6
TO LEAVE HER BED OF FEVER AND ASCEND ..THE PRINCESS AND THE GOBLINS 333   4
FEVER-DRY (1)
SEASICK AND FEVER-DRY. ....WHITSUN   154   24
FEVERED (1)
DREAMS THAT HIS FATTEST CATTLE DWINDLE, FEVERED ....GOATSUCKER 111   6
FEVERISH (1)
A SOUL GROWN FEVERISH, CLUTCHING ITS DEAD BODY-TREE ....DIALOGUE B.   39   43
FEVERS (1)
DO WITHOUT FEVERS TO EAT? ....THE JAILER 227   42
FEW (10)
OF FOG IN THAT HINTERLAND FEW ....TWO VIEWS OF WITHENS   72   5
SHAPELESS AS FLUNG GLOVES, A FEW FEET APART -- ....BLUE MOLES 126   3
SOME FEW PASSENGERS KEEP TRACK ....ON DECK 142   4
AND IT ASKS NOTHING, A NAME TAG, A FEW TRINKETS. ....TULIPS 161   33
THE FEW I AM USED TO ARE PLAIN AND DURABLE; *STARS OVER THE DORDOGNE 166   28
REMEMBERS A FEW ODD SYLLABLES. ....WUTHERING HEIGHTS 168   34
A FEW MORE BREATHS, AND IT WILL REFLECT NOTHING AT ALL. LAST WORDS 172   12
STAB A FEW CLOVES IN AN APPLE, ...A SECRET 220   30
AND IN A FEW FATAL YARDS OF GRASS ....APRIL 18 302   12
IN A FEW SPACES OF SKY AND TREETOPS ....APRIL 18 302   13

```
                                                 TITLE           PAGE  LINE
FIBER (3)
   OF NATURE: WHAT BETTER WAY TO TEST TAUT FIBER  .....CHANNEL CROSSING   27   16
   BETTER THAT EVERY FIBER CRACK  .................MONOLOGUE AT 3 A.M.    40    1
   EACH TO THE OTHER; FIT FIBER FOR STERN WEATHER.  ......CRYSTAL GAZER   55   11
FIBS (2)
   WITH FIBS? THE FIBS ARE OURS, NOT HIS, PAN'S FINE  ......DIALOGUE O.  283  253
   WITH FIBS? THE FIBS ARE OURS, NOT HIS, PAN'S FINE  ......DIALOGUE O.  283  253
FICTION (1)
   SPURNS SUCH FICTION  ......ON THE DIFFICULTY OF CONJURING UP A DRYAD   66   29
FICTIONS (2)
   OF MANY-COLORED FICTIONS; WE MASK OUR PAST  ...........TALE OF A TUB   25   38
   OR THOSE GLITTERY FICTIONS OF SPILT WATER*SLEEP IN THE MOJAVE DESERT  144   12
FICTIVE (1)
   FREE OF THE FICTIVE VEIN. WHEN ONE STARK SKELETON*NOVEMBER GRAVEYARD   56   10
FIDDLE (2)
   BOTH OF THEM DEAF TO THE FIDDLE IN THE HANDS  .............TWO VIEWS.  114   18
   TO FIDDLE THE SHORT NIGHT AWAY.  .........SLEEP IN THE MOJAVE DESERT  144   26
FIDDLER-CRAB (1)
   THE HUSK OF A FIDDLER-CRAB,  ...........MUSSEL HUNTER AT ROCK HARBOR   97   69
FIDDLER'S (1)
   AS ITSELF -- NO FIDDLER'S ARM  ........MUSSEL HUNTER AT ROCK HARBOR   96   34
FIDDLING (1)
   WASN'T FIDDLING, AND I FILLED  .........MUSSEL HUNTER AT ROCK HARBOR   97   62
FIDE (1)
   BREED INNUMERABLE BILLS, BONA FIDE:  ..............DIALOGUE EN ROUTE  308   17
FIDO (1)
   FIDO LITTLESOUL, THE BOWEL'S FAMILIAR.  ................POEM.4.BEAST.  134   13
FIELD (9)
   MAYDAY: TWO CAME TO FIELD IN SUCH WISE:  ...................BUCOLICS   23    1
   EACH FINGER-FURROWED FIELD  .............................ODE FOR TED   29   14
   YOU SPUN THE COSMIC WEB: YOU SQUINT FROM CENTER FIELD.  ......SPIDER   48    7
   OUR LIMBS' IMAGE ON A FIELD OF STRAW  ............IN MIDAS' COUNTRY   99    9
   AT A FIELD OF HORSES, NECKS BENT, MANES BLOWN,  .........THE EYE-MOTE  109    2
   A FIELD OF BURDOCK OPENS TO THE SOUTH.  .....ELECTRA ON AZALEA PATH  117   22
   ROVE OVER HIS FIELD OF STONE;  .....................MAGNOLIA SHOALS  122   16
   AND THE SPIDERY WATER-DAZZLE ON FIELD AND STREET.  ........LYONNESSE  234   18
   ALL THAT MORNING IN THE STRAWBERRY FIELD  .......BITTER STRAWBERRIES  299    1
FIELDS (7)
   GAVE WAY TO FIELDS AND THE INCESSANT SEETHE OF GRASSES*HARDCASTLE C.   62    9
   LORDED PERSPECTIVES. MAPLIKE, THE FAR FIELDS ARE RULED  ......OXBOW.   89   48
   PARLIAMENT HILL FIELDS  ......................PARLIAMENT HILL FIELDS  152    T
   FIELDS SHRUNK TO A PENNY  ................................THE SWARM  216   29
   FIELDS MELT MY HEART.  ..................................SHEEP IN FOG  262   12
   AT NIGHTFALL THERE IS THE BEAUTY OF DROWNED FIELDS,  .........TOTEM  264    4
   THE FIELDS WERE FULL OF BRONZED YOUNG MEN  ......BITTER STRAWBERRIES  299   18
FIENDISH (2)
   THE FIENDISH BUTLER SAUNTERS IN AND SERVES  .................TERMINAL  328   10
   THE CHAMBERS WHERE THEIR FIENDISH QUEEN WOULD SIT.  ...THE PRINCESS.  334   40
FIERCE (8)
   IN THE WAKE OF THIS FIERCE CAT,  .........................PURSUIT   22   21
   DRYLY DISCLAIMS THAT FIERCE TROLL FACES LURK  .........TALE OF A TUB   24   13
   LOOKS FIERCE AND BLACK AS ROOKS;  .............THE QUEEN'S COMPLAINT   28    4
   FIERCE FIRE'S WROUGHT  ................TINKER JACK AND THE TIDY WIVES   34   20
   AND, FIXED IN THE CRYSTAL CENTER, GRINNING FIERCE:  ..CRYSTAL GAZER   56   47
   FOR MONEY. LORD, THE CROWDS ARE FIERCE!  ...........A WINTER'S TALE   87   15
   HEARING THE FIERCE MASK MAGNIFY  ....................THE FEARFUL  256   15
   THE CULTIVATED ACT, A FIERCE BRIEF FUSION  .......LOVE IS A PARALLAX  330   58
FIERCELY (1)
   NO MATTER HOW FIERCELY LIT; STAUNCH CONTRACTS BREAK   EPITAPH FOR F.   46   32
FIERY (2)
   LOVE FIERY ENOUGH TO PROVE FLESH REAL,  ..SOLILOQUY OF THE SOLIPSIST   38   33
   OF HELL, AND NOT THE FIERY PART. YET TO JUDGE BY THAT DAZZLED LOOK, ...
                         ... DIALOGUE BETWEEN GHOST AND PRIEST   38   15
FIESTA (1)
   FIESTA MELONS  ..........................................FIESTA MELONS   46    T
FIESTA-GOERS (1)
   FIESTA-GOERS.  ..........................................FIESTA MELONS   47   20
FIFTEEN (1)
   FIFTEEN YEARS BETWEEN ME AND THE BAY  ......GREEN ROCK, WINTHROP BAY  105    4
FIFTH (1)
   RODE OUT AGAINST THE FIFTH BULL TO BRACE HIS PIKE AND SLOWLY BEAR ...
                         ... THE GORING   47    6
FIFTY (3)
   RED AGAINST FIFTY VARIANTS OF GREEN,  .....................YADWIGHA.   85   19
   LET HER DIE THERE, OR WITHER INCESSANTLY FOR THE NEXT FIFTY
                         YEARS,  .........................FACE LIFT  156   29
   IN FIFTY, GOLD.  ......................................THE APPLICANT  221   32
FIG (2)
   THE FIGS ON THE FIG TREE IN THE YARD ARE GREEN;  ..........DEPARTURE   51    1
   PURPLES THE FIG IN THE LEAF'S SHADOW, TURNS THE DUST PINK.  ...NET-.  121    7
FIGS (2)
   HAWK MISFORTUNE LIKE FIGS AND CHICKENS  ..................THE BEGGARS   47    3
   THE FIGS ON THE FIG TREE IN THE YARD ARE GREEN;  ..........DEPARTURE   51    1
FIGURE (3)
   A WEATHER FIGURE, BOGGLING,  ..........................EAVESDROPPER  261   48
```

FIGURE (CONT.)
    AT FAME OR NOT? AS FOR LOVE, I FIGURE WHEN WE'RE ....DIALOGUE O.   278   57
    SHE STOOD UP, A THIN COMMANDING FIGURE ....BITTER STRAWBERRIES   300   29
FIGURED (1)
    FIGURED IN THE MIDNIGHT SKY, ...TO A JILTED LOVER   309   4
FIGURES (2)
    STILL FIGURES OF IVORY. ....THE SWARM   216   12
    MOURNED BY RELIGIOUS FIGURES, BY GARLANDED CHILDREN.   GETTING THERE   249   48
FILAMENT (3)
    OF HIS REDOUBT HE RAN HIS NIMBLE FILAMENT, ...SPIDER   48   15
    THREADING BACK, FILAMENT BY FILAMENT, TO THE PURE ...PRIVATE GROUND   130   10
    THREADING BACK, FILAMENT BY FILAMENT, TO THE PURE ...PRIVATE GROUND   130   10
FILAMENTS (2)
    MY RED FILAMENTS BURN AND STAND, A HAND OF WIRES. ....ELM   192   18
    WHAT A MILLION FILAMENTS. ....LADY LAZARUS   245   25
FILCHED (1)
    FILCHED BY HIS HAND, ...THE GLUTTON   40   8
FILE (3)
    THE ANTS -- A FILE OF COMERS, A FILE OF GOERS -- ....SPIDER   49   29
    THE ANTS -- A FILE OF COMERS, A FILE OF GOERS -- ....SPIDER   49   29
    AT THEIR FEET, THE SEA WAVES BOW IN SINGLE FILE, ...A LIFE   150   11
FILENE'S (1)
    FILENE'S SHOW WINDOWS. GRANT US GRACE, ...A WINTER'S TALE   87   19
FILET (1)
    FILET MIGNON AND WALLOPING WINES, ...DIALOGUE EN ROUTE   308   10
FILING (2)
    FLIES FILING IN THROUGH A DEAD SKATE'S EYEHOLE *SUICIDE OFF EGG ROCK   115   17
    FILING LIKE SOLDIERS ....WINTERING   218   24
FILL (5)
    AND STILL THE LUNGS WON'T FILL AND THE HEART WON'T START. *STILLBORN   142   10
    I MUST SEAL OFF AND LET FILL ....THE SURGEON AT 2 A.M.   171   25
    TO FILL IT AND WILLING ....THE APPLICANT   221   11
    EVERY DAY YOU FILL HIM WITH SOUL-STUFF, LIKE A PITCHER. .....LESBOS   229   77
    I WANT TO FILL IT WITH COLOR AND DUCKS, ...CHILD   265   2
FILLED (2)
    WASN'T FIDDLING, AND I FILLED ....MUSSEL HUNTER AT ROCK HARBOR   97   62
    THEN THE TULIPS FILLED IT UP LIKE A LOUD NOISE. ....TULIPS   161   52
FILLED-IN (1)
    TO THE FILLED-IN GUT ....POINT SHIRLEY   110   23
FILLING (3)
    FILLING MY VEINS WITH INVISIBLES, WITH THE MILLION ....BIRTHDAY.   207   42
    A GOLD FILLING. ....LADY LAZARUS   246   78
    ARE FILLING WITH SMILES. ....KINDNESS   269   5
FILLS (3)
    OF THE WORLD COMES CLEAR AND FILLS WITH COLOR. .....THE THIN PEOPLE   65   35
    HOW WINTER FILLS MY SOUL! AND THAT CHALK LIGHT ....THREE WOMEN   181 177
    NO MILK OR HONEY FILLS THE EMPTY CAN; ....THE DISPOSSESSED   318   5
FILM (1)
    MEMORIES JOSTLE EACH OTHER FOR FACE-ROOM LIKE OBSOLETE FILM
        STARS. ....INSOMNIAC   163   14
FILTER (1)
    FILTER INTO THIS CLEAR ....YADDO: THE GRAND MANOR   123   2
FILTERING (1)
    A LITTLE LIGHT IS FILTERING FROM THE WATER FLOWERS. *CROSSING THE W.   190   4
FIN (2)
    TO ANALYSE THE FIN, ...TRIO OF LOVE SONGS   315   46
    A TINSEL PIZZICATO ON FISH FIN ....MIDSUMMER MOBILE   324   8
FINAL (5)
    OF FINAL SURFEIT IS JUST AS FAR ....BLUE MOLES   127   33
    TO THE FINAL GROTESQUE JOKE OF DEATH ....DIRGE FOR A JOKER   303   10
    FROM THEIR FOND, FINAL, INFAMOUS DECAY. ....THE DEAD   320   14
    TO NAVIGATE THIS FINAL DARK.   ...INSOLENT STORM STRIKES AT THE SKULL   326   18
    COLD AND FINAL, THE IMAGINATION ....TWO LOVERS.   327   1
FINALE (1)
    FALL RACKETING FINALE ON HER LUCK. ....AERIALIST   332   48
FINALLY (3)
    IT IS WHAT THE DEAD CLOSE ON, FINALLY; I IMAGINE THEM ....TULIPS   161   34
    AND I SHALL BE USEFUL WHEN I LIE DOWN FINALLY: ....I AM VERTICAL   162   19
    SO DADDY, I'M FINALLY THROUGH. ....DADDY   224   68
FINANCIER (1)
    THAN FINANCIER. WHAT GOOD IS HE, IF NOT *DIALOGUE OVER A OUIJA BOARD   277   44
FIND (16)
    GLOWERING AT THE COAL-FIRE: "COME FIND ME" -- HER LAST TAUNT. ...
                                ... THE SNOWMAN ON THE MOOR   58   5
    IT TOOK THREE DAYS DRIVING NORTH TO FIND A CLOUD ....TWO CAMP.   145   10
    BUT SHE'LL SOON FIND OUT THAT THAT DOESN'T MATTER A BIT. *IN PLASTER   160   54
    THE EYES LIFT AFTER IT AND FIND THE MOON. *THE MOON AND THE YEW TREE   173   16
    THE CLOCK SHALL NOT FIND ME WANTING, NOR THESE STARS ...THREE WOMEN   182 202
    SHALL I EVER FIND IT, WHATEVER IT IS? ....THREE WOMEN   186 343
    FROM THE LONG FALL, AND FIND MYSELF IN BED, ...THREE WOMEN   187 366
    I FIND MYSELF AGAIN. I AM NO SHADOW ....THREE WOMEN   187 368
    AND FIND NO FACE BUT MY OWN, AND YOU THINK THAT'S FUNNY.*FATHERLESS.   205   9
    HONESTLY WANT TO FIND IF YOU'LL HAVE A FLING ....DIALOGUE O.   278   56
    FIND YOU OVER AND OVER, LIPPED LIKE A SKATE AND SMILING, ...
                                ... THE RIVAL/DR   291   18

FIND (CONT.)
    TO FIND WHAT MAKES IT MOVE, ...TRIO OF LOVE SONGS   315   50
    O RANSACK THE FOUR WINDS AND FIND ANOTHER ....LAMENT   316   16
    OF OUR COLOSSAL SLEEP, COME HOME TO FIND ....DOOM OF EXILES 318   2
    ALL WE FIND ARE ALTARS IN DECAY ....DOOM OF EXILES   318   11
    UP WHICH THE WAKEFUL PRINCESS CLIMBS TO FIND ....THE PRINCESS. 333   2
FINDS (1)
    IT FINDS THEIR SHAPES IN A CLOUD. ....THREE WOMEN   186 347
FINE (15)
    FINE AS HAND- ....SOUTHERN SUNRISE   26   5
    THEIR FINE SKIN SERE, ...TINKER JACK AND THE TIDY WIVES 35   30
    SO FINE WE CANNOT DO IT. ....THE GREAT CARBUNCLE 73   26
    O RED FRUIT, IVORY, FINE TIMBERS! ....METAPHORS 116   4
    WHILE THEIR FINGERS WORK WITH THE COARSE MESH AND THE FINE ...NET-. 121 11
    ARE RATTLING THE CRACKER PACKETS. FINE FLOUR ....LEAVING EARLY 146   36
    STRETCHING ITS FINE, IRRITATING SAND IN ALL DIRECTIONS. ..INSOMNIAC 163   7
    AND THEIR FINE LINES SINGE ....WUTHERING HEIGHTS   167   4
    CROSSING AND RECROSSING: A FINE THING! ....PHEASANT   191   18
    ENFOLDS HER FACE LIKE FINE LINEN, ...BERCK-PLAGE   200 102
    FINE FOR THE MIGRAINE OR THE BELLYACHE. AND THIS ....THE TOUR 238   19
    MY FACE A FEATURELESS, FINE ....LADY LAZARUS   244   8
    WITH FIBS? THE FIBS ARE OURS, NOT HIS, PAN'S FINE .....DIALOGUE O. 283 253
    DEMANDED THAT I PAY A FINE ....THE DREAM   311   15
    SHREDDED FINE AS SNOWFLAKES ....AERIALIST   331   3
F-I-N-E (1)
    ENOUGH FOR NICKNAMES. HOW ARE YOU, PAN? F-I-N-E, ...DIALOGUE O. 277 31-2
FINED (1)
    "BUT YET I WAITED TO BE FINED ....THE DREAM   311   25
FINER (1)
    IT IS SIX IN THE MORNING AND FINER THAN ANY SUNDAY -- *QUEEN MARY'S. 290 8
FINEST (2)
    OF FINEST CONSCIENCE. NIGHTFALL OBSCURES ....THE BEGGARS   48   16
    SHE FATTENS ON THE FINEST GRAIN. ....RHYME   50   10
FINGER (12)
    MILK-SPOUT, BIG FINGER ....WORDS FOR A NURSERY   73   7
    IN BURROWS NARROW AS A FINGER, SOLITARY BEES ....BEEKEEPER'S. 118   15
    HEAD, TOE AND FINGER ....THE MANOR GARDEN   125   7
    AND HOW A GOD FLIMSY AS A BABY'S FINGER POEM.5.F. 135   19
    AND I SLEPT ON LIKE A BENT FINGER. ....LOVE LETTER 147   19
    LET IT NOT COME BY THE MAIL, FINGER BY FINGER. ..A BIRTHDAY PRESENT 208 52
    LET IT NOT COME BY THE MAIL, FINGER BY FINGER. ..A BIRTHDAY PRESENT 208 52
    BRANDY FINGER ....A SECRET   219   18
    O I SHOULDN'T PUT MY FINGER IN THAT ....THE TOUR 237   13
    NOT A TOE, NOT A FINGER, AND USED, ...MYSTIC   268   12
    UNDER YOUR FINGER? I MEAN, YOU DON'T PUSH ....DIALOGUE O.   277   33
    WITH FINGER BANDAGED WHERE THE WASPISH PIN ....THE PRINCESS. 333   7
FINGERED (1)
    THE KING FINGERED HIS BEARD. ....THE BULL OF BENDYLAW 108   6
FINGER-FURROWED (1)
    EACH FINGER-FURROWED FIELD ....ODE FOR TED 29   14
FINGERING (2)
    FINGERING A LEAFLET OF MUSIC, OVER HIM, *TWO VIEWS OF A CADAVER ROOM 114 17
    NODDING AND ROCKING AND FINGERING HER THIN HAIR. ....FACE LIFT 156 30
FINGERJOINT (1)
    WHILE IN THEIR FINGERJOINT CELLS THE NEW VIRGINS ...THE BEE MEETING 212 45
FINGER-LENGTH (1)
    MY FINGER-LENGTH GREW LUCENT AS GLASS. ....LOVE LETTER 147   30
FINGERLESS (1)
    WHO INJURE MY SLEEP WITH THEIR WHITE EYES, THEIR FINGERLESS
        HANDS. ....THREE WOMEN 185 321
FINGERNAIL (1)
    FLICK THE GLASS WITH YOUR FINGERNAIL: ....A LIFE 150   6
FINGERNAILS (1)
    ENOUGH FOR FINGERNAILS TO MAKE HALF-MOONS ....MOONRISE   98   10
FINGERS (37)
    THIS WITCH SIDLES, FINGERS CROOKED, AS IF ....VANITY FAIR   32   2
    WITH TALONED FINGERS, ...THE SHRIKE   42   11
    NOW, DOUR-FACED, HER FINGERS ....VIRGIN IN A TREE   82   38
    WHITE PETALS, WHITE FAN-TAILS, TEN WHITE FINGERS. ......MOONRISE   98   9
    WHILE THEIR FINGERS WORK WITH THE COARSE MESH AND THE FINE ...NET-. 121 11
    AND THE IRON HILLS THAT ENCLOSE THEM. EARTHEN FINGERS ....NET-. 121 16
    EATING THE FINGERS OF WISDOM. POEM.3.MAENAD. 133   3
    TEN FINGERS SHAPE A BOWL FOR SHADOWS. POEM.7.S.   137   43
    THEY GREW THEIR TOES AND FINGERS WELL ENOUGH, ...STILLBORN 142   2
    TAPPING AND TICKING LIKE NERVOUS FINGERS. ....LEAVING EARLY 146   27
    UPSIDE DOWN HEARTS OF LIGHT TIPPING WAX FINGERS, ...CANDLES 148   2
    AND THE FINGERS, TAKEN IN BY THEIR OWN HALOES, ...CANDLES   148   3
    FISTS MY FINGERS FOR ME. HE MAKES ME FEEL SOMETHING PRECIOUS FACE. 156 13
    BROODY AND IN LONG SKIRTS ON MY FIRST HUSBAND'S SOFA, MY
        FINGERS ....FACE LIFT   156   22
    TICKING YOUR FINGERS ON THE MARBLE TABLE, LOOKING FOR CIGARETTES, ...
        ... THE RIVAL   166   8
    THAT FLEE THROUGH MY FINGERS. ....WUTHERING HEIGHTS 168   30
    WITH BLUE-RED JUICES. THESE THEY SQUANDER ON MY FINGERS. BLACKBER. 168   7

FINGERS (CONT.)
  THIS WAS THE LAND'S END: THE LAST FINGERS, KNUCKLED AND RHEUMATIC, ...
                                        ... FINISTERRE   169   1
  SUCH AS FINGERS MIGHT EMBROIDER, CLOSE TO DEATH, ...FINISTERRE   169   11
  NIGHTS, I WROTE IN MY DIARY SPITEFULLY, MY FINGERS RED ....BABY. 174   14
  FROM MY ALPHABETICAL FINGERS, ORDERING PARTS, ...THREE WOMEN 177   28
  WHAT DID MY FINGERS DO BEFORE THEY HELD HIM? ....THREE WOMEN 181 169
  I HOLD MY FINGERS UP, TEN WHITE PICKETS. ....THREE WOMEN 182 194
  AND LEARN TO SPEAK WITH FINGERS, NOT A TONGUE. ....THREE WOMEN 184 255
  WHO WOULD ADHERE TO ME: I UNDO HER FINGERS LIKE BANDAGES: I GO. ...
                                        ... THREE WOMEN   184 273
  THE YEW'S BLACK FINGERS WAG; ....LITTLE FUGUE 187   1
  HIS FINGERS HAD THE NOSES OF WEASELS. ....LITTLE FUGUE 187   11
  THESE ARE MY FINGERS, THIS MY BABY. ....LITTLE FUGUE 189   51
  MY FINGERS WOULD ENTER ALTHOUGH ....BURNING THE LETTERS 204   17
  UNABLE TO FACE THE FINGERS, THOSE EGOTISTS. ....THE DETECTIVE 208   9
  THE FINGERS WERE TAMPING A WOMAN INTO A WALL, ...THE DETECTIVE 208   10
  WITH HER WIGGLY FINGERS AND FOR A VERY SMALL FEE. ....THE TOUR 238   47
  THEY CONVERSE IN THE VALLEY OF YOUR FINGERS, THEY ARE INCHWORMS. ...
                                        ... GULLIVER   251   17
  NO FINGERS TO GRIP, NO TONGUE, ...PARALYTIC 266   3
  TABLE, TRYING OUR LUCK, INDEX FINGERS SET ....DIALOGUE O. 276   4
  FOR YES, DRAGGING OUR FINGERS AFTER. HOW*DIALOGUE OVER A OUIJA BOARD 278   75
  THE GARNETS ON HER FINGERS TWINKLE QUICK ....FEMALE AUTHOR 301   9
FINGERTIPS (2)
  THE PETALS' NAP MY FINGERTIPS: ..FABLE OF THE RHODODENDRON STEALERS 103   14
  CAN SPELL SARCASM THROUGH OUR FINGERTIPS. ....DIALOGUE O. 282 208
FINGER-TRAPS (1)
  FINGER-TRAPS -- A TUMULT OF KEYS. ....LITTLE FUGUE 187   16
FINGER-VENTS (1)
  IS LEAKING FROM THE FINGER-VENTS. AT THE COUNT OF TWO ....FACE LIFT 156   14
FINICAL (2)
  OF FINICAL CATS. ....ELLA MASON AND HER ELEVEN CATS   53   12
  MORE FINICAL THAN ....POLLY'S TREE 128   11
FINISH (3)
  AN ANTIQUE HAG-HEAD, TO TOUGH FOR KNIFE TO FINISH, ...LADY AND T.   70   33
  WE START AT'S THE SAME POST WE FINISH BY, ...ABOVE THE OXBOW   88   19
  WOULD TRAFFIC IN. LET HIM FINISH WHAT HE BEGAN. ....DIALOGUE O. 278   84
FINISHED (3)
  THE MONTH OF FLOWERING'S FINISHED. THE FRUIT'S IN, ...POEM.1.WHO. 131   1
  UNTIL IT FINISHED, AND THEN LOOK FURTIVELY ....DIALOGUE O. 280 164
  BLEACHED AND FINISHED, I SURFACE ....FEVER./DR 294   7
FINISTERRE (1)
  FINISTERRE ....FINISTERRE 169   T
FINNED (1)
  SHEEP GREENS, FINNED FALLS, "I SHALL COMPOSE A CRISIS ...CONJURING.   66   11
FINS (2)
  BUT OUT OF THE WATERY ASPIC, LAURELED BY FINS, ...LADY AND T.   69   18
  BUT FINS AND SCALES ....BATTLE-SCENE   84   21
FIR (2)
  FOR PIES. THE FIR TREE'S THICK WITH GRACKLES.*YADDO: THE GRAND MANOR 123   7
  DOWN BOLES OF THE FIR. ....DARK WOOD, DARK WATER 127   24
FIRE (25)
  NO FIRE IS, NOR IN ANY BOOK PROOF ....VANITY FAIR   33   27
  LET JACK CATCH FIRE." ....TINKER JACK AND THE TIDY WIVES   35   33
  OF GILDED HARPS OR GNAWING FIRE: SIMPLY TELL ....DIALOGUE B.   39   23
  SLOPED SEAWARD TO PLUNGE IN BLUE; FED BY WHITE FIRE, DREAM WITH C.   44   11
  EPITAPH FOR FIRE AND FLOWER ....EPITAPH FOR FIRE AND FLOWER   45   T
  AND HAVE EVERY WEATHERCOCK KISS HANG FIRE ....EPITAPH FOR F.   46   23
  AND THE COAL FIRE BURNS ....RESOLVE   52   7
  THE BURNISHED BALL HANGS FIRE IN HER HANDS, A LENS ...CRYSTAL GAZER   54   5
  TO SET THE SIGHT ON FIRE ....BLACK ROOK IN RAINY WEATHER   57   6
  IN THE COAL FIRE WILL NOT WHOLLY CONSOLE THEM. ....OUIJA   77   7
  ITS EYE, FLASHLIT, A CHIP OF RUBY FIRE. ....GOATSUCKER 111   8
  YET HIS BELLY KEPT ITS FIRE ....MEDALLION 124   16
  IN THE MONTH OF RED LEAVES I CLIMB TO A BED OF FIRE. POEM.6.W. 135   6
  FIRE SMELTED HIS EYES TO LUMPS ....THE BURNT-OUT SPA 137   3
  NO WORD MAKE THEM CARRY WATER OR FIRE THE KINDLING ....TWO CAMP. 144   5
  BODY, A SHEET OF NEWSPRINT ON THE FIRE ....WIDOW 164   2
  I MADE A FIRE; BEING TIRED ....BURNING THE LETTERS 204   1
  THIS FIRE MAY LICK AND FAWN, BUT IT IS MERCILESS: ....BURNING. 204   15
  AGAINST FIRE AND BOMBS THROUGH THE ROOF. ....THE APPLICANT 221   24
  WILL THERE BE FIRE, WILL THERE BE BREAD? ....GETTING THERE 248   20
  THE FIRE MAKES IT PRECIOUS, ...MARY'S SONG 257   5
  THE SAME FIRE ....MARY'S SONG 257   6
  BUT I'VE BROUGHT BRANDY AND BUILT THE FIRE UP ....DIALOGUE O. 277   16
  FRAMED IN DISCIPLINES OF FIRE AND ICE ....METAMORPHOSES OF THE MOON 307   26
  FOR WHAT FIRE COULD DAMAGE*ON LOOKING INTO THE EYES OF A DEMON LOVER 325   19
FIRE-BLURTING (1)
  IT WAS NO FIRE-BLURTING FORK-TAILED DEMON ..THE SNOWMAN ON THE MOOR   59   25
FIRED (2)
  FIRED IN SANGUINE CLAY, THE MODEL HEAD ....LADY AND T.   69   1
  TILL SHE WAS FIRED. ....THE BABYSITTERS 175   27
FIREDOGS (1)
  WE SWELTER LIKE FIREDOGS IN THE WIND. ...SLEEP IN THE MOJAVE DESERT 144   20

                                                          TITLE   PAGE   LINE
FIREFLIES (1)
     BLINKING FLASHLIGHTS LIKE FIREFLIES ....THE DISQUIETING MUSES   75   26
FIRELESS (1)
     FIRELESS, SEVEN CHILL SEAS CHAINED TO HIS ANKLE. *EVERLASTING MONDAY   62   12
FIREPLACE (1)
     ABOVE THE FIREPLACE; ....YADDO: THE GRAND MANOR   123   14
FIRES (4)
     WHAT FIRES RUN, WHAT CRAVING WAKES? ....PURSUIT   22   12
     NOR DO THEY SEND UP FIRES WHERE THEY FALL ..STARS OVER THE DORDOGNE   165   6
     SUCCEED IN BANKING THEIR FIRES ....WINTERING   219   47
     INDEPENDENT REBEL FIRES ....INSOLENT STORM STRIKES AT THE SKULL   326   34
FIRE'S (2)
     FIERCE FIRE'S WROUGHT ....TINKER JACK AND THE TIDY WIVES   34   20
     THE FIRE'S BETWEEN US. ....GETTING THERE   249   51
FIRESIDE (1)
     AT YOUR FIRESIDE ....TINKER JACK AND THE TIDY WIVES   34   8
FIRESONG (1)
     FIRESONG ....FIRESONG   30   T
FIREWORK (2)
     FIREWORK OF FRONDS. ....SOUTHERN SUNRISE   26   12
     A FIREWORK OF ECHOES FROM WALL ....HARDCASTLE CRAGS   62   6
FIRMAMENT (1)
     TO DOUBLECROSS THE FIRMAMENT. ..INSOLENT STORM STRIKES AT THE SKULL   326   28
FIRM-FIXED (1)
     IF ROOT'S FIRM-FIXED AND RESOLUTION GOOD. ....MAYFLOWER   60   4
FIRST (30)
     THE FIRST WORKS PROBLEMS ON ....TWO SISTERS OF PERSEPHONE   31   6
     LOVESICK AT FIRST FOND SONG, ...VANITY FAIR   33   24
     TO TRAP THIS WAYWARD GIRL AT HER FIRST MOVE OF LOVE,   DREAM WITH C.   44   27
     AND SEE THAT FIRST HOUSE, AS IF BETWEEN ....LANDOWNERS   53   6
     EXACTED HER FIRST SIMPLE SIGHT FOR THIS STRICT SECOND.*CRYSTAL GAZER   55   30
     HEIR OF THE FIRST FIVE ....WORDS FOR A NURSERY   73   2
     WHETHER GOAT-THIGHED OR GOD-HALOED. EVER SINCE THAT FIRST DAPHNE ...
                                       ... VIRGIN IN A TREE   81   9
     SUSPENDS BESIDE IT THE FIRST POINT, THE STARTING ....GHOST'S.   91   30
     FIRST HORSE UNDER ME, HIGH AS THE ROOFS, ...WHITENESS I REMEMBER   102   13
     DUG IN FIRST AS GOD'S SPURS ....THE COMPANIONABLE ILLS   105   5
     FIRST FROST, AND I WALK AMONG THE ROSE-FRUIT, THE MARBLE TOES ...
                                           ... PRIVATE GROUND   130   1
     IT HURTS AT FIRST. THE RED TONGUES WILL TEACH THE TRUTH.   POEM.6.W.   135   18
     THE FIRST THING I SAW WAS SHEER AIR ....LOVE LETTER   147   20
     BROODY AND IN LONG SKIRTS ON MY FIRST HUSBAND'S SOFA, MY
         FINGERS ....FACE LIFT   156   22
     NOT HER WHITENESS AND BEAUTY, AS I HAD AT FIRST SUPPOSED.*IN PLASTER   159   19
     THE TULIPS ARE TOO RED IN THE FIRST PLACE, THEY HURT ME. ....TULIPS   161   36
     AND YOUR FIRST GIFT IS MAKING STONE OUT OF EVERYTHING. ...THE RIVAL   166   6
     I IMAGINE THEM WITHOUT FATHERS OR MOTHERS, LIKE THE FIRST GODS. ...
                                           ... LAST WORDS   172   8
     WHEN I FIRST SAW IT, THE SMALL RED SEEP, I DID NOT BELIEVE IT. ...
                                           ... THREE WOMEN   177   15
     LIKE A BIG SEA. FAR OFF, FAR OFF, I FEEL THE FIRST WAVE TUG   THREE.   179 109
     THE MOUTH FIRST, ITS ABSENCE REPORTED ....THE DETECTIVE   209   27
     FIRST, ARE YOU OUR SORT OF A PERSON? ....THE APPLICANT   221   1
     AT FIRST THE CANDLE WILL NOT BLOOM AT ALL -- ....BY CANDLELIGHT   236   16
     ITS FIRST COMMUNION OUT OF MY LIVE TOES. ...NICK AND THE CANDLESTICK   241   19
     THE FIRST TIME IT HAPPENED I WAS TEN. ....LADY LAZARUS   245   35
     BEGINS. A JERK. AND NOW THE FIRST SLOW RAMBLE ....DIALOGUE O.   277   21
     OF FORMAL SCORN, UNTIL THE FIRST SIGN OF AN ....DIALOGUE O.   282 232
     "IN THE FIRST DREAM I WAS DRIVING ....THE DREAM   310   7
     FIRST LET THE HEAVENLY FOLIAGE GO, ...SONG FOR A REVOLUTIONARY LOVE   322   2
     CHIRPS THE FIRST; "LIVE ON A SILENT ISLAND ..EPITAPH IN THREE PARTS   337   5
FIRST-BREACHED (1)
     PAN AS IF HE WERE OUR FIRST-BREACHED BRAT ....DIALOGUE O.   280 138
FISH (18)
     TWIST OLD WORDS INTO THE WEB-THREADS: TONIGHT MAY THE FISH ...NET-.   121   17
     A LAKE THICK WITH FISH. ....DARK WOOD, DARK WATER   127   7
     I BEND OVER THIS DRAINED BASIN WHERE THE SMALL FISH   PRIVATE GROUND   131   20
     I BED IN A FISH PUDDLE. POEM.4.BEAST.   134   19
     GILLED LIKE A FISH. A COMMON-SENSE ....YOU'RE   141   3
     THEY ARE NOT PIGS, THEY ARE NOT EVEN FISH, ...STILLBORN   142   11
     AND THE WHITE CHINA FLYING FISH FROM ITALY. ....LEAVING EARLY   145   6
     RISES TOWARD HER DAY AFTER DAY, LIKE A TERRIBLE FISH. ....MIRROR   174   18
     DUMB FISH ....BURNING THE LETTERS   204   24
     AND THE FISH, THE FISH --- ....NICK AND THE CANDLESTICK   241   14
     AND THE FISH, THE FISH --- ....NICK AND THE CANDLESTICK   241   14
     BRIGHT FISH HOOKS, THE SMILES OF WOMEN ....GIGOLO   267   10
     EGGS AND FISH, THE ESSENTIALS, ...GIGOLO   267   16
     YELLOW CATHEAD, BLUE FISH --- ....BALLOONS   271   9
     INSTEAD OF FAT FISH ON THE LINE, YOU'VE PLUMBED ....DIALOGUE O.   282 242
     IF YOU ASSAULT A FISH ....TRIO OF LOVE SONGS   315   45
     A TINSEL PIZZICATO ON FISH FIN ....MIDSUMMER MOBILE   324   8
     THE MOON LEANS DOWN TO LOOK; THE TILTING FISH ...LOVE IS A PARALLAX   330   37
FISH-BAIT (1)
     FREE FISH-BAIT: THE BLUE MUSSELS ......MUSSEL HUNTER AT ROCK HARBOR   95   9

```
                                                    TITLE           PAGE  LINE
FISH-BONES (1)
  FISH-GREASE, FISH-BONES, REFUSE OF ATROCITIES.  ...........FEVER./DR   294    6
FISHERMEN (1)
  THOUGH FISHERMEN ARE SLEEPING,  ...........................LORELEI     94    6
FISHES (3)
  CIGAR OVER HIS RINK OF FISHES.  .....................A WINTER SHIP    113   12
  YOU MOVE THROUGH THE ERA OF FISHES,  ...............THE MANOR GARDEN  125    5
  THE SPIRIT OF BLACKNESS IS IN US, IT IS IN THE FISHES.  ...
                                          ... CROSSING THE WATER        190    8
FISH-GREASE (1)
  FISH-GREASE, FISH-BONES, REFUSE OF ATROCITIES.  ...........FEVER./DR   294    6
FISHING (1)
  OF THE THREE FISHING SMACKS BEACHED  ...MUSSEL HUNTER AT ROCK HARBOR   95    6
FISH-MOUTH (1)
  ALREADY FROG-MOUTH AND FISH-MOUTH DRINK  ..................POEM.5.F.  134    7
FISHNETS (1)
  SCRIM AFTER SCRIM LIKE FISHNETS  ..........................LORELEI     94    5
FISHPOND (2)
  AND AN IMAGE LOOMS UNDER THE FISHPOND SURFACE  ...ALL THE DEAD DEARS   71   22
  FERRIES THE FISHPOND SINBAD  .........................BATTLE-SCENE     84   13
FISH-TAILED (1)
  FISH-TAILED GIRLS PURCHASE EACH WHITE LEG.  ................MAUDLIN    51    8
FISHY (1)
  THOUGH THEY HAVE A PIGGY AND A FISHY AIR --  ..............STILLBORN  142   12
FISSURED (1)
  UP FROM THE FISSURED VALLEY AND HUNG SHOULDER-HIGH  HARDCASTLE CRAGS   62   14
FISSURES (1)
  VOLT UPON VOLT. CATGUT STITCHES MY FISSURES.  .............POEM.7.S.  137   30
FIST (8)
  AS A SLEDGE HAMMER, AS A MAN'S BUNCHED FIST,  .................SPIDER   48    4
  WITH CURSE, FIST, THREAT  ....................................SPINSTER  50   29
  OR BUNCH MY FIST  ............................................RESOLVE   52   22
  THEN, WITH A JOCULAR FIST THWACKED THE BARREL NAPE,  ............SOW    61   35
  A RED FIST, OPENING AND CLOSING,  ....................APPREHENSIONS   195   12
  CLOSE ON YOU LIKE THE FIST OF A BABY  .......................LESBOS   229   86
  SHRED IN HIS LITTLE FIST.  .................................BALLOONS   272   30
  KNOW: WHICH IS WHY I, WHEN THE WONDROUS FIST  ...........DIALOGUE O.  279  119
FISTED (3)
  IT OGLED THROUGH ROCK-FAULT, WIND-FLAW AND FISTED WAVE--*LADY AND.    70   32
  FISTED TO A FOETUS HEAD, RAVINED, SEAMED  ..................PERSEUS    83   25
  THE FAITH-MAKER, FISTED IN HIS CLOUD, OR THE CHORUS  ....DIALOGUE O.  279  109
FISTS (3)
  SOFT FISTS INSIST ON  ....................................MUSHROOMS   139   10
  FISTS MY FINGERS FOR ME. HE MAKES ME FEEL SOMETHING PRECIOUS  FACE.  156   13
  OF THE WHITE FISTS OF OLD  ....................BURNING THE LETTERS    204    2
FIT (10)
  WHOSE FORCE MIGHT FIT  ......................THE QUEEN'S COMPLAINT     29   18
  AND FIT FOR USE.  ....................TINKER JACK AND THE TIDY WIVES   34   22
  EACH TO THE OTHER; FIT FIBER FOR STERN WEATHER.  ......CRYSTAL GAZER   55   11
  INSTEAD, A WANTON FIT  ...................ON THE PLETHORA OF DRYADS    67   25
  FIT NOWHERE: BRICKDUST-COMPLECTED, EYE UNDER A DENSE LID,  ...
                        ... THE LADY AND THE EARTHENWARE HEAD           69    2
  FIT FOR THOSE OUTLAWS TO RIDE HOME ON,  ..........ALL THE DEAD DEARS   71   30
  THIS MONTH IS FIT FOR LITTLE.  ........................POEM.3.MAENAD  133   11
  BLACK AND STIFF, BUT NOT A BAD FIT.  ..................THE APPLICANT  221   21
  OR YOUR WHITE-HAIRED BENEFACTRESS, WHO MAY SEE FIT  .....DIALOGUE O.  277   48
  IN HER PROPHETIC FIT HEARD WHAT WE HEARD,  .............DIALOGUE O.   286  348
FITFUL (1)
  US TO THE OBLIQUE ROAD, IN SPITE OF A FITFUL  .......ABOVE THE OXBOW   88   21
FITS (1)
  THIS MIZZLE FITS ME LIKE A SAD JACKET.  ...............LEAVING EARLY  146   39
FITTED (1)
  SO FITTED IS FOR MY BLACK LUCK  .........................THE GLUTTON   40    2
FITTING (1)
  SHE STOPPED FITTING ME SO CLOSELY AND SEEMED OFFISH.  ....IN PLASTER  159   29
FIVE (13)
  UNRULY ENOUGH TO PITCH HER FIVE QUEENLY WITS  ..............SPINSTER   50   20
  HEIR OF THE FIRST FIVE  ..........................WORDS FOR A NURSERY  73    2
  FIVE MOONY CRESCENTS  ............................WORDS FOR A NURSERY  73    4
  WITH FIVE WHORLED LANDSPITS.  ....................WORDS FOR A NURSERY  74   30
  FIVE WICKLESS CANDLES  ...........................WORDS FOR A NURSERY  74   45
  FIVE WORMS IN A BOX  .............................WORDS FOR A NURSERY  74   49
  FIVE O'CLOCK IN THE MORNING, THE NO-COLOR VOID  ...........GHOST'S.   90    2
  FULL FATHOM FIVE  ...................................FULL FATHOM FIVE  92    T
  FOR FIVE DAYS I LIE IN SECRET,  .........................FACE LIFT   156   17
  I AM ONE IN FIVE, SOMETHING LIKE THAT. I AM NOT HOPELESS.  ...THREE.  183  244
  AT HIS HEELS A PILE OF FIVE BRASS CANNONBALLS,  ......BY CANDLELIGHT  237   33
  FIVE BALLS! FIVE BRIGHT BRASS BALLS!  ................BY CANDLELIGHT  237   35
  FIVE BALLS! FIVE BRIGHT BRASS BALLS!  ................BY CANDLELIGHT  237   35
FIVE-ANTLERED (1)
  FIVE-ANTLERED, BRANCHING  ........................WORDS FOR A NURSERY  74   21
FIX (1)
  SEEK NO STONY CAMERA-EYE TO FIX  ........EPITAPH FOR FIRE AND FLOWER   45    8
FIXED (7)
  NOW WITH STAKE AND PITCHFORK THEY ADVANCE, FLINT EYES FIXED
```

```
                                                   TITLE              PAGE  LINE
FIXED (CONT.)
        ON MURDER. ..........................  DREAM WITH CLAM-DIGGERS   44   28
    AND, FIXED IN THE CRYSTAL CENTER, GRINNING FIERCE: ...CRYSTAL GAZER  56   47
    FIXED ME IN THIS PARENTHESIS; ....................THE EYE-MOTE      109   28
    FIXED VORTEX ON THE FAR .........................MAN IN BLACK       120   19
    FIXED TO THEIR ARCS LIKE GODS, .......................GETTING THERE 248   14
    FROM THE BOTTOM OF THE POOL, FIXED STARS ...................WORDS   270   19
    PERFUME, POLITICS, AND FIXED IDEALS. ...........SONNET: TO EVA      305   12
FIXING (1)
    FIXING HIS SNARE ...........................................FIRESONG  30   5
FIZZ (2)
    SHE SHIED SIDEWAYS: A WHITE FIZZ! AND THE GIANT, PURSUING, ...
                                  ... THE SNOWMAN ON THE MOOR            59   47
    OF PINK FIZZ. ......................................................CUT  235  16
FIZZLE (1)
    PASSENGERS UNDER AN INDIGO FIZZLE .................ALICANTE LULLABY   43   9
FIZZY (1)
    FIZZY WITH SEDATIVES AND UNUSUALLY HUMOROUS, .............FACE LIFT  156   11
FLAGON (1)
    BESIDE A SUNBLUE SEA, AND MOURN THE FLAGON .........SONNET: TO TIME  311   10
FLAGONS' (1)
    REFLECTING IN A MILLION FLAGONS' SHINE, ..................CINDERELLA  304   8
FLAGS (1)
    THEIR DEATH RAYS FOLDED LIKE FLAGS ......THE COURAGE OF SHUTTING-UP  210   32
FLAIR (1)
    YET I FLOURISH MY WHIP WITH A FATAL FLAIR ....CIRCUS IN THREE RINGS  322   10
FLAKE (2)
    I FLAKE UP PAPERS THAT BREATHE LIKE PEOPLE, ....BURNING THE LETTERS  204   37
    SO YOUR GESTURES FLAKE OFF --- ....................THE NIGHT DANCES  250   18
FLAKED (1)
    AND MY SKIN ITCHED AND FLAKED AWAY IN SOFT PIECES ........IN PLASTER 159   33
FLAKES (2)
    FLAKES FROM MY HEELS. .........................................ARIEL  239   18
    FALLING LIKE BLESSINGS, LIKE FLAKES ...............THE NIGHT DANCES  250   24
FLAME (7)
    NOT OF STAUNCHING SUCH STRICT FLAME, BUT COME, ............FIRESONG   30   20
    TO A PINCH OF FLAME, BLEW ITS BURDENED WHISTLE ....HARDCASTLE CRAGS   63   23
    IGNITED WITH A GLASSED FLAME ............................MEDALLION   124   10
    RAYED ROUND A CANDLE FLAME, ..........................POLLY'S TREE   128   19
    THE TWO DRINKS FLAME AND FOAM. .........................AMNESIAC     233   24
    MOON AND SUN REFLECT HIS FLAME. ...................TO A JILTED LOVER  310   18
    KINDLING HER WITHIN A STEEPLED FLAME, THE PRINCESS AND THE GOBLINS   333   20
FLAMED (1)
    THE SUN FLAMED STRAIGHT DOWN THAT NOON ON THE WATER OFF MARBLEHEAD. ...
                                  ... THE BABYSITTERS                    174   2
FLAMES (4)
    LITTLE POPPIES, LITTLE HELL FLAMES, .................POPPIES IN JULY  203   1
    I PUT MY HANDS AMONG THE FLAMES. NOTHING BURNS. ....POPPIES IN JULY  203   4
    LOVE FLAMES FOREVER IF THE FLESH BE YEARNING. ...TO EVA DESCENDING.  303   14
    A ROSE OF JEOPARDY FLAMES IN MY HAIR .........CIRCUS IN THREE RINGS  321   9
FLAMILY (1)
    PALELY AND FLAMILY ...........................POPPIES IN OCTOBER      240   7
FLAMING (2)
    TO PRINT YOUR FLAMING IMAGE IN BIRTHSPOT .........SONNET TO SATAN    323   11
    HIS OWN PALE BRIDE UPON A FLAMING TRAY: ...................TERMINAL   328   12
FLAMINGO (1)
    WHERE ADJECTIVES PLAY CROQUET WITH FLAMINGO NOUNS; ...A SORCERER B.  324   2
FLANK (1)
    TWO WAXEN OXEN FLANK THE CHILD. .....................A WINTER'S TALE   86   6
FLANKED (1)
    AGE, ANOTHER PLANET SURELY. FLANKED ............CHILD'S PARK STONES  101   8
FLANKS (2)
    YET ALWAYS THE RIDICULOUS NUDE FLANKS URGE ..........TALE OF A TUB    25   33
    SEURAT: FLECK SCHOONER FLANKS WITH SUN AND SET ....MIDSUMMER MOBILE  324   5
FLAP (3)
    HUSTLED A GULL FLOCK TO FLAP OFF THE SANDSPIT. *SUICIDE OFF EGG ROCK 115   13
    GULL-COLORED LACES FLAP IN THE SEA DRAFTS ...............FINISTERRE  170   28
    A FLAP LIKE A HAT, ................................................CUT  235   6
FLAPPED (1)
    FLAPPED BLACK TO LOOK AND BROOD ...............................FAUN   35   4
FLAPPING (1)
    FLAPPING AND SUCKING, BLOOD-LOVING BAT. ......................LESBOS  229   80
FLAPS (2)
    NIGHTLY IT FLAPS OUT ...........................................ELM   193   29
    LEVERING LETTER FLAPS, ...............................EAVESDROPPER   261   56
FLARE (7)
    SHE SEES HOW THEIR RED SILK FLARE ........TWO SISTERS OF PERSEPHONE   32   17
    TO BELIEVE BEYOND HEART'S FLARE .........................VANITY FAIR   33   26
    MOUTH'S INSTANT FLARE FOR FUTURE LOOKS; *EPITAPH FOR FIRE AND FLOWER  45   11
    WHATEVER LOST GHOSTS FLARE, ...................NOVEMBER GRAVEYARD     56   15
    OF WHATEVER ANGEL MAY CHOOSE TO FLARE ..BLACK ROOK IN RAINY WEATHER   57   26
    THE FACE AT THE END OF THE FLARE. ....................GETTING THERE  249   59
    WHILE FOOTLIGHTS FLARE AND HOUSELIGHTS DIM. .....LOVE IS A PARALLAX  330   48
FLARED (1)
    THE WHOLE SCENE FLARED WELCOME TO THIS ROAMER. .......DREAM WITH C.   44   12
```

FLARING (4)
    AND I RUN FLARING IN MY SKIN; ....PURSUIT   23   34
    HER GREEN EYES SLANT, HAIR FLARING IN A FAN ....CINDERELLA   303   2
    FLARING GREEN THROUGH PHILODENDRON LEAVES ......MORNING IN THE HOS.   332   2
    FOR EACH QUICK, FLARING GAME ....TOUCH-AND-GO   336   20
FLASH (1)
    A FLASH LIKE DOOMCRACK RENT NIGHT'S BLACK: ....CRYSTAL GAZER   55   37
FLASHING (1)
    THE STARS ARE FLASHING LIKE TERRIBLE NUMERALS. ....AN APPEARANCE   189   17
FLASHLIGHTS (1)
    BLINKING FLASHLIGHTS LIKE FIREFLIES ....THE DISQUIETING MUSES   75   26
FLASHLIT (1)
    ITS EYE, FLASHLIT, A CHIP OF RUBY FIRE. ....GOATSUCKER   111   8
FLAT (28)
    THE WHOLE FLAT HARBOR ANCHORED IN ....A WINTER SHIP   113   9
    BETTER THE FLAT LEER OF THE IDIOT, ...THE RAVAGED FACE   116   9
    THE FLAT SEA PURPLED LIKE THAT EVIL CLOTH ...ELECTRA ON AZALEA PATH   117   31
    FLAT AS PAPER AND ....POLLY'S TREE   128   8
    WHEN IT THUNDERED I HID UNDER A FLAT STONE. POEM.3.MAENAD.   133   5
    THE FLAT BLUE SKY-CIRCLE POEM.7.S.   136   3
    FLICKERS AMONG THE FLAT PINK ROSES. I WAKE TO LISTEN: MORNING SONG   157   11
    AND I SEE MYSELF, FLAT, RIDICULOUS, A CUT-PAPER SHADOW ......TULIPS   161   46
    THE RED NIGHT LIGHTS ARE FLAT MOONS. THEY ARE DULL WITH BLOOD. ...
                                        ... THE SURGEON AT 2 A.M.   171   48
    I WATCHED THE MEN WALK ABOUT ME IN THE OFFICE. THEY WERE SO
        FLAT! ....THREE WOMEN   177   16
    THAT FLAT, FLAT, FLATNESS FROM WHICH IDEAS, DESTRUCTIONS, ...THREE.   177   18
    THAT FLAT, FLAT, FLATNESS FROM WHICH IDEAS, DESTRUCTIONS, ...THREE.   177   18
    THEY ARE SO JEALOUS OF ANYTHING THAT IS NOT FLAT! THEY ARE
        JEALOUS GODS ....THREE WOMEN   179   86
    THAT WOULD HAVE THE WHOLE WORLD FLAT BECAUSE THEY ARE.   THREE WOMEN   179   87
    THE NIGHT LIGHTS ARE FLAT RED MOONS. THEY ARE DULL WITH BLOOD. ...
                                        ... THREE WOMEN   180 124
    BLUNT AND FLAT ENOUGH TO FEEL NO LACK. I FEEL A LACK. ..THREE WOMEN   182 193
    LOOK, THEY ARE SO EXHAUSTED, THEY ARE ALL FLAT OUT .....THREE WOMEN   183 219
    HIS WIDE EYE IS THAT GENERAL, FLAT BLUE. ....THREE WOMEN   183 234
    I AM FLAT AND VIRGINAL, WHICH MEANS NOTHING HAS HAPPENED, ...THREE.   184 276
    THEY ARE BLACK AND FLAT AS SHADOWS. ....THREE WOMEN   186 340
    THEY ARE ROUND AND FLAT AND FULL OF DARK ADVICE. *CROSSING THE WATER 190   6
    DIMINISHED AND FLAT, AS AFTER RADICAL SURGERY. ....ELM   192   26
    SCRAPED FLAT BY THE ROLLER ....DADDY   222   17
    TODDLE ON HOME TO TEA NOW IN YOUR FLAT HAT. ....THE TOUR   238   37
    AND A LITTLE FLAT, AS IF THEY ....GULLIVER   251   3
    MY WIFE, DEAD AND FLAT, IN 1920 FURS, ...PARALYTIC   266   23
    AS FLAT AS SHE, WHO WHISPER "WE'RE YOUR DAUGHTERS." ......PARALYTIC   266   26
    BENEATH THE FLAT HANDKERCHIEF YOU WEAR INSTEAD OF A HAT. STINGS/DR   293   6
FLATFISH (1)
    AS A FLATFISH, I ....WORDS FOR A NURSERY   74   32
FLATNESS (3)
    THAT FLAT, FLAT, FLATNESS FROM WHICH IDEAS, DESTRUCTIONS, ...THREE.   177   18
    SUCH FLATNESS CANNOT BUT BE HOLY. ....THREE WOMEN   179   89
    THEY HUG THEIR FLATNESS LIKE A KIND OF HEALTH. ....THREE WOMEN   180 117
FLATS (2)
    FLATS OF HADLEY FARMS, THEY'RE LOFTY ENOUGH ....ABOVE THE OXBOW   88   8
    ON THE PUBLIC GRILLS, AND THE OCHREOUS SALT FLATS, ...SUICIDE.   115   2
FLATTEN (6)
    BATTALIONS. SEE, HOW THE TREE BOLES FLATTEN ....THE THIN PEOPLE   65   43
    CLAPPED SHUT, FLATTEN THIS MAN OUT. ..THE HERMIT AT OUTERMOST HOUSE   118   3
    FLATTEN THE DOPED SNAKES TO RIBBON. IN HERE, THE GRASSES *PRIVATE G.   130   17
    "LET US FLATTEN AND LAUNDER THE GROSSNESS FROM THESE SOULS." *THREE.   179   91
    VOICES STAND BACK AND FLATTEN. THEIR VISIBLE HIEROGLYPHS*THREE WOMEN   179   96
    FLATTEN TO PARCHMENT SCREENS TO KEEP THE WIND OFF. ....THREE WOMEN   179   97
FLATTENED (2)
    LEAVES AND LILIES FLATTENED TO PAPER BEHIND YOU ....YADWIGHA.   85   16
    THE OBSOLETE HOUSE, THE SEA, FLATTENED TO A PICTURE ....A LIFE   150   27
FLATTENING (1)
    THEY ACCOMMODATE THEMSELVES TO MY MILKBOTTLE, FLATTENING THEIR
        SIDES. ....BLACKBERRYING   168   9
FLAWED (3)
    TO THIS FLAWED GARDEN, ...FIRESONG   30   2
    OF FLAWED EARTH-FLESH COULD CAUSE THIS SORRY PASS? .....DIALOGUE B.   39   32
    FLAWED BY LOVE'S PRINTS. ....ON THE PLETHORA OF DRYADS   67   18
FLAY (1)
    IF YOU FLAY A BEAST ....TRIO OF LOVE SONGS   315   41
FLAYED (5)
    FLAYED BY THORNS I TREK THE ROCKS, ...PURSUIT   22   9
    FLAYED BY SPRAY, WE TAKE THE CHALLENGE UP, ...CHANNEL CROSSING   26   5
    KNOBBED QUARTZ; FLAYED COLORS RIPEN ....ODE FOR TED   29   11
    FROM THE FLAYED SIDE. ....STREET SONG   36   20
    FLAYED OF FUR AND HUMANITY. ....TOTEM   264   13
FLAYS (2)
    FLAYS THE CHROMIUM NERVES OF PLUMBING RAW; ....TALE OF A TUB   24   3
    AND THE NOISE IT FLAYS FROM THE AIR, ONCE IT GETS GOING! ..COURAGE.   210   20
FLEA (1)
    FLEA BODY! ....EAVESDROPPER   261   53

```
                                             TITLE            PAGE  LINE
FLEA-RIDDEN (1)
  WRAPPED IN FLEA-RIDDEN DONKEY SKINS,  ...............THE THIN PEOPLE   64  18
FLECK (2)
  SEURAT: FLECK SCHOONER FLANKS WITH SUN AND SET  ....MIDSUMMER MOBILE  324   5
  OBSCURE GOD'S EYE WITH CORKSCREW FLECK;  ...........BLACK PINE TREE.  328   9
FLEE (1)
  THAT FLEE THROUGH MY FINGERS.  ...................WUTHERING HEIGHTS  168  30
FLEES (2)
  EACH GESTURE FLEES IMMEDIATELY DOWN AN ALLEY  ..............INSOMNIAC  163  23
  FLEES AND ABORTS LIKE DROPPED MERCURY.  .................THALIDOMIDE  252  26
FLEMISH (1)
  THESE FLEMISH LOVERS FLOURISH; NOT FOR LONG.  ............TWO VIEWS.  114  20
FLESH (21)
  BRIGHT THOSE CLAWS THAT MAR THE FLESH  .....................PURSUIT   23  31
  FANTASTIC FLESH DOWN TO THE HONEST BONE.  .............TALE OF A TUB   25  24
  FLESH UNSHRIVEN.  .........................................VANITY FAIR   33  20
  GOES GRAVEWARD WITH FLESH LAID WASTE,  ....TWO SISTERS OF PERSEPHONE   32  27
  OR CRIES THAT THIS RAW FLESH  ...........................STREET SONG   35   6
  LOVE FIERY ENOUGH TO PROVE FLESH REAL,  ..SOLILOQUY OF THE SOLIPSIST   38  33
  LET FLESH BE KNIT, AND EACH STEP HENCE GO FAMOUS.  ........WREATH F.   45  24
  BLACKENS FLESH TO BONE AND DEVOURS THEM.*EPITAPH FOR FIRE AND FLOWER   46  35
  GLORIFIED FOR PRIME FLESH AND GOLDEN CRACKLING  ................SOW   60  15
  THAN FLESH OF ANY BODY  ....................ON THE PLETHORA OF DRYADS   67  17
  OURSELVES THE HAUNTERS, AND THEY, FLESH AND BLOOD;  ...THE OTHER TWO   69  33
  OF CANDOR PARES WHITE FLESH TO THE WHITE BONE,  ...........MOONRISE   98  27
  I WEAR THE PRESENT ITCH FOR FLESH,  ...................THE EYE-MOTE  109  22
  A FRUIT THAT'S DEATH TO TASTE: DARK FLESH, DARK PARINGS.  ...
                                    ...  THE BEEKEEPER'S DAUGHTER  118  14
  SOON, SOON THE FLESH  .....................................LADY LAZARUS  244  16
  FLESH, BONE, THERE IS NOTHING THERE ---  ..............LADY LAZARUS  246  75
  THEIR FLESH BEARS NO RELATION.  .....................THE NIGHT DANCES  250  11
  LOVE FLAMES FOREVER IF THE FLESH BE YEARNING.  ...TO EVA DESCENDING.  303  14
  I NEVER THOUGHT HIS FLESH WOULD BURN  ..............TO A JILTED LOVER  310  12
  HOW FLESH CLEAVES FAST TO FROZEN JOINT,  ...........INSOLENT STORM.  326  10
  ONLY TO REOPEN AS FLESH CONGEALS:  .............LOVE IS A PARALLAX  330  65
FLESHED (1)
  THIS PARK IS FLESHED WITH IDIOT PETALS.  ...................MOONRISE   98   4
FLEW (5)
  WHEN THE SPLINTER FLEW IN AND STUCK MY EYE,  ...........THE EYE-MOTE  109   9
  FLEW OFF LIKE THE HAT OF A DOLL  .........................POEM.7.S.  136   4
  HE FLEW INTO THE ROOM, A SHRIEK AT HIS HEEL.  ..........THREE WOMEN  181 165
  AS THE GLASS FLEW TO ITS FRAGMENTS. LET US STAKE  .......DIALOGUE O.  285 328
  FLEW FROM THE INTRICATE EMBROIDERY  ....THE PRINCESS AND THE GOBLINS  333   8
FLEX (1)
  FLEX AS THE MUD FREEZES.  .............................PRIVATE GROUND  131  21
FLICK (3)
  FLICK THE GLASS WITH YOUR FINGERNAIL:  .........................A LIFE  150   6
  GECKO, THE LITTLE FLICK!  ...................................THE TOUR  237   4
  GALLOP AND FLICK OF LIGHT  .............................TOUCH-AND-GO  335   7
FLICKER (5)
  DWARFING US. OUR BODIES FLICKER  ..........................SCULPTOR   92  16
  ON THE INCESSANT HEAT-LIGHTNING FLICKER OF SITUATIONS.  ...INSOMNIAC  163  28
  YOU FLICKER. I CANNOT TOUCH YOU.  ...................POPPIES IN JULY  203   3
  ROSE CANDLES FLICKER ON THE LILAC WALL  ..................CINDERELLA  304   7
  FLICKER GILT:  ......................................AQUATIC NOCTURNE  305  12
FLICKERING (6)
  ON GRUNT, UP IN THE FLICKERING LIGHT TO SHAPE  ................SOW   61  39
  NO FLOOR: A WAVE OF FLICKERING GRASS TONGUES  .........SNAKECHARMER   79   9
  ONE CURTAIN IS FLICKERING FROM THE OPEN WINDOW,  ........BERCK-PLAGE  199  79
  FLICKERING AND POURING, A PITIFUL CANDLE.  .............BERCK-PLAGE  199  80
  FLICKERING LIKE THAT, WRINKLY AND CLEAR RED, LIKE THE SKIN
     OF A MOUTH.  .....................................POPPIES IN JULY  203   6
  I HAVE BEEN FLICKERING, OFF, ON, OFF, ON.  ..................FEVER.  231  29
FLICKERS (2)
  FLICKERS AMONG THE FLAT PINK ROSES. I WAKE TO LISTEN:  MORNING SONG  157  11
  I THINK IT IS A PART OF MY HEART. BUT IT FLICKERS.  .........MIRROR  173   8
FLICKING (1)
  FLICKING OVER MY PROPERTY,  ..........................EAVESDROPPER  261  55
FLIES (13)
  FLIES WATCH NO RESURRECTIONS IN THE SUN.  ........NOVEMBER GRAVEYARD   56  12
  AMONG THE PITHLESS REEDS. FLIES FAIL US.  ..............FROG AUTUMN   99   7
  FLIES FILING IN THROUGH A DEAD SKATE'S EYEHOLE *SUICIDE OFF EGG ROCK  115  17
  I COME TO ONE BUSH OF BERRIES SO RIPE IT IS A BUSH OF FLIES,  ...
                                    ...  BLACKBERRYING  168  15
  ISSUING FROM THE STEEL NEEDLE THAT FLIES SO BLINDINGLY? *APPEARANCE.  189  11
  THE DEW THAT FLIES  ..........................................ARIEL  240  28
  OF AIR THAT ALL DAY FLIES  ................................PURDAH  243  45
  MULTIPLIED IN THE EYES OF THE FLIES.  .......................TOTEM  265  30
  GLITTERING AND DRUNK AS FLIES  .............................MYSTIC  268   3
  TO FRACTURE THESE FOUR WALLS. YOUR FAITH FLIES  .........DIALOGUE O.  279 111
  FRACTURED GLASS FLIES DOWN IN SMITHEREENS;  ..............DOOMSDAY  316  10
  THE LEAVES APPLAUD, AND SANTA CLAUS FLIES IN  ....LOVE IS A PARALLAX  329  34
  IN THE AIR ABOVE MY ISLAND FLIES  ...........EPITAPH IN THREE PARTS  337  12
FLIGHT (5)
  OF YOUR STORMY EYE, MAGIC TAKES FLIGHT  ...............CONVERSATION.   21   7
```

	TITLE	PAGE	LINE

FLIGHT (CONT.)
GULLS CIRCLE GRAY UNDER SHADOW OF A STEELIER FLIGHT. ...GREEN ROCK. 105 17
A CURTAIN OF WAX DIVIDING THEM FROM THE BRIDE FLIGHT, ...BEE. 212 47
ATOP THE FLIGHT OF STAIRS I STAND. ....FAMILY REUNION 301 26
AN INSIGHT LIKE THE FLIGHT OF BIRDS: ....LOVE IS A PARALLAX 330 60
FLIGHTS (1)
THEY SHOULD HAVE GONE OUT WITH BALLOON FLIGHTS AND THE STEREOPTICON. ...
... CANDLES 149 12
FLIMSILY (1)
FLIMSILY PEOPLED. BUT LANDOWNERS ....LANDOWNERS 53 9
FLIMSY (2)
THE FLIMSY LIGHT; ARMS FOLDED ....SCULPTOR 91 11
AND HOW A GOD FLIMSY AS A BABY'S FINGER POEM.5.F. 135 19
FLINCH (1)
I AM THE MAGICIAN'S GIRL WHO DOES NOT FLINCH. ......THE BEE MEETING 212 53
FLING (2)
HONESTLY WANT TO FIND IF YOU'LL HAVE A FLING ....DIALOGUE O. 278 56
FLING THE SEVEN WONDERS AFTER THAT ..SONG FOR A REVOLUTIONARY LOVE 323 7
FLINGS (2)
WHAT IS IT THAT FLINGS THESE INNOCENT SOULS AT US? .....THREE WOMEN 183 218
FLINGS SILVER GAUNTLET OF HIS PLANE AT SPACE, ...METAMORPHOSES. 307 4
FLINT (4)
BLUE FUR, MOLES HAVE; HEFTING CHALK-HULLED FLINT ....ODE FOR TED 29 9
WE HEFT GLOBED FLINT, RACKED IN VEINS' BARBED BINDINGS; ...FIRESONG 30 18
NOW WITH STAKE AND PITCHFORK THEY ADVANCE, FLINT EYES FIXED
ON MURDER. .... DREAM WITH CLAM-DIGGERS 44 28
WATER MOLLIFIES THE FLINT LIP, ...POEM.7.S. 137 25
FLINTIER (1)
WIND BARES A FLINTIER LANDSCAPE. ....IN MIDAS' COUNTRY 100 25
FLINTLIKE (1)
FLINTLIKE, HER FEET STRUCK ....HARDCASTLE CRAGS 62 1
FLINTY (1)
WHAT FLINTY PEBBLES THE PLOUGHBLADE UPTURNS ....OUIJA 77 28
FLITS (1)
FLITS NIMBLE-WINGED IN THICKETS, AND OF GOOD COLOR. ....WATERCOLOR. 112 7
FLOAT (8)
UNIMAGINABLE. YOU FLOAT NEAR ....FULL FATHOM FIVE 92 11
ALL STILLNESS. YET THESE SHAPES FLOAT ....LORELEI 94 9
TO THEIR OWNERS' WRISTS, THE LIGHT DREAMS FLOAT ....ON DECK 143 35
THEY ARE SUBTLE: THEY SEEM TO FLOAT, THOUGH THEY WEIGH ME DOWN, ...
... TULIPS 161 40
THE GILT AND PINK DOMES OF RUSSIA MELT AND FLOAT OFF .....THE SWARM 216 15
THEIR THICK PALLS FLOAT ....MARY'S SONG 257 9
TO FLOAT LIKE DREAM-FISH IN THE LANGUID LIMBO ..MORNING IN THE HOS. 332 8
FLOATED (1)
FLOATED ON A GLASS THAT WAS INVISIBLE. ....GULLIVER 251 4
FLOATING (7)
FLOATING, AMONG THE FLOATING ....THE GREAT CARBUNCLE 73 21
FLOATING, AMONG THE FLOATING ....THE GREAT CARBUNCLE 73 21
FLOATING ABOVE ME IN BLUEST AIR ....THE DISQUIETING MUSES 75 42
FLOATING THROUGH THE AIR IN MY SOUL-SHIFT ....LOVE LETTER 147 35
FLOATING IN A HIGH-CHURCH HUSH ....CANDLES 149 22
FLOATING ON THEIR DELICATE FEET OVER THE COLD PEWS, ...MOON. 173 25
I SEE US FLOATING THERE YET, INSEPARABLE -- TWO CORK DOLLS. ..BABY. 175 41
FLOATS (5)
FLOATS CHASTE AS SNOW, TAUNTING THE CLOUDED MIND WINTER LANDSCAPE. 21 4
FLOATS CALM AS A MOON OR A CLOUD. ....HEAVY WOMEN 158 7
HE FLOATS AN INCH FROM THE CEILING, ...THE SURGEON AT 2 A.M. 171 45
FLOATS OUR HEADS, TWO VENOMOUS OPPOSITES, ...LESBOS 228 36
THE MIRROR FLOATS US AT ONE CANDLE POWER. ....BY CANDLELIGHT 236 9
FLOCK (5)
A BLACK SHEEP LEADS THE SHEPHERDS' FLOCK. ....A WINTER'S TALE 86 7
HUSTLED A GULL FLOCK TO FLAP OFF THE SANDSPIT. *SUICIDE OFF EGG ROCK 115 13
AT OWL-CALL THE OLD GHOSTS FLOCK ....OLD LADIES' HOME 120 15
HERALD DISTRACTION: A FLOCK OF PASTEL PILLS, ...MORNING IN THE HOS. 332 13
COMES A FLOCK OF BOTTLE BATTLESHIPS ....EPITAPH IN THREE PARTS 337 2
FLOCKED (2)
ACROSS BARBED STILE, THROUGH FLOCKED BROWN COWS. ....BUCOLICS 23 4
I SAW SLOW FLOCKED COWS MOVE ....SONG FOR A SUMMER'S DAY 30 3
FLOCKS (2)
OVERHEAD GO THE CHOUGHS IN BLACK, CACOPHONOUS FLOCKS -- ..BLACKBER. 168 10
AND THE OCTOGENARIAN LOVES THE LITTLE FLOCKS. ...AMONG THE NARCISSI 190 10
FLOG (1)
NIGHTLY NOW I FLOG APES OWLS BEARS SHEEP ....ZOO KEEPER'S WIFE 155 39
FLOGGED (1)
FLOGGED TROLLEY. THE SPARKS ARE BLUE. ....LESBOS 228 49
FLOOD (5)
THE BLOOD FLOOD IS THE FLOOD OF LOVE, ...THE MUNICH MANNEQUINS 263 6
THE BLOOD FLOOD IS THE FLOOD OF LOVE, ...THE MUNICH MANNEQUINS 263 6
PROCEEDS FROM PRIVATE FLOOD. ....TRIO OF LOVE SONGS 314 12
HE RODE THE FLOOD IN A PRIDE OF PRONGS ....LAMENT 315 8
TO PITCH THE WHITE WORLD DOWN IN SWIVELING FLOOD, ..SONNET TO SATAN 323 6
FLOODS (2)
COLOR FLOODS TO THE SPOT, DULL PURPLE. ....CONTUSION 271 1
RIVER FLOODS TRANSCEND THE LEVEL*INSOLENT STORM STRIKES AT THE SKULL 326 19

```
                                              TITLE          PAGE  LINE
FLOOR (11)
   COUCH, CARPET, FLOOR  ...........................MONOLOGUE AT 3 A.M.   40    4
   NO FLOOR: A WAVE OF FLICKERING GRASS TONGUES  ..........SNAKECHARMER   79    9
   BRONZE DEAD DOMINATE THE FLOOR,  ...........................SCULPTOR   91   14
   AND MY CHILD -- LOOK AT HER, FACE DOWN ON THE FLOOR,  ........LESBOS  227    8
   ACROSS THE INDIAN CARPET, THE COLD FLOOR,  ...........BY CANDLELIGHT  237   25
   DEEPER THAN YOUR OWN OCEAN FLOOR, AND GOT  .............DIALOGUE O.  283  243
   AS THEY SHOT PAST THE FORTY-NINTH FLOOR  .........DIALOGUE EN ROUTE  308    4
   SHOT PAST THE NINETY-FOURTH FLOOR  ................DIALOGUE EN ROUTE  309   34
   RULED DECREE OF DOOMSDAY ON THE FLOOR.  ............THE TRIAL OF MAN  312    4
   TO TRAVERSE GLASS FLOOR  .................................AERIALIST   331   27
   WHILE SUNLIGHT WINDS ITS YARN UPON THE FLOOR.  ........THE PRINCESS.  335   71
FLOORBOARDS (1)
   HOW PERILOUS NEEDLES GRAIN THE FLOORBOARDS  ...........MISS DRAKE P.   41   16
FLORA (1)
   PALM-SPEAR AND LILY DISTINCT AS FLORA IN THE VAST  ...........A LIFE  149    4
FLORAL (1)
   ONE CRY, AND I STUMBLE FROM BED, COW-HEAVY AND FLORAL   MORNING SONG  157   13
FLORETS (1)
   OF PRIZE ROSES, CULLING THE FULLEST FLORETS;  .......SPINACH-PICKER.   90   19
FLORID (1)
   ALONG BOX-LINED WALKS IN THE FLORID SUN  .......THE BULL OF BENDYLAW  108   10
FLORIDLY (1)
   BUT FLORIDLY, HIS AMOROUS NOSTALGIAS.  ........................OUIJA   78   32
FLOUNCED (1)
   ELLA FLOUNCED ABOUT, MINX-THIN AND HAUGHTY,  ..........ELLA MASON A.   53   14
FLOUNDER (2)
   PALE FLOUNDER  ....................................AQUATIC NOCTURNE  305    7
   FLOUNDER IN THE RELATIVE.  ......INSOLENT STORM STRIKES AT THE SKULL  326   24
FLOUR (2)
   ARE RATTLING THE CRACKER PACKETS. FINE FLOUR  ........LEAVING EARLY  146   36
   MEASURING THE FLOUR, CUTTING OFF THE SURPLUS,  ...A BIRTHDAY PRESENT  206    7
FLOURED (1)
   FLOURED HIS WHIRLING BEARD, AND AT HIS TREAD*THE SNOWMAN ON THE MOOR   59   33
FLOURISH (2)
   THESE FLEMISH LOVERS FLOURISH; NOT FOR LONG.  ............TWO VIEWS.  114   20
   YET I FLOURISH MY WHIP WITH A FATAL FLAIR  ....CIRCUS IN THREE RINGS  322   10
FLOURISHED (1)
   WHAT GIRL EVER FLOURISHED IN SUCH COMPANY?  .....................MAGI  148   18
FLOURISHING (1)
   TO SAVOR THEIR SPAN OF FLOURISHING.  .................CRYSTAL GAZER   55   27
FLOW (1)
   IF YOU'VE A PLOT TO HALT THE LETHAL FLOW  ..........THE DISPOSSESSED  318    7
FLOWER (12)
   BY BLACKTHORN THICKET, FLOWER SPRAY  .....................BUCOLICS    23    7
   TO BOYCOTT COLOR AND FORBID ANY FLOWER  ..SOLILOQUY OF THE SOLIPSIST   38   26
   AGAINST THE FLOWER IN THE BLOOD:  .........................RECANTATION   42   13
   EPITAPH FOR FIRE AND FLOWER  ..........EPITAPH FOR FIRE AND FLOWER    45    T
   THROUGH A RANK WILDERNESS OF FERN AND FLOWER.  ..............SPINSTER   49   10
   FLOWER FORGET-ME-NOTS BETWEEN THE STONES  .......NOVEMBER GRAVEYARD   56    7
   THEY NAMED THEIR SHIP AFTER THE FLOWER OF MAY.  ..........MAYFLOWER   60   14
   CROWD FOOT TO FOOT, HEAD TO HEAD, NO FLOWER   ELECTRA ON AZALEA PATH  117   20
   OR IN A GHOST FLOWER  .................................POLLY'S TREE   128    7
   THE FROST MAKES A FLOWER,  ...............................DEATH & CO.  255   27
   A FLOWER LEFT OUT.  .................................SHEEP IN FOG     262   10
   FROM THE SWEET, DEEP THROATS OF THE NIGHT FLOWER.  ............EDGE   273   16
FLOWER-HEAD (1)
   AND A FLOWER-HEAD NOT TALL, BUT MORE STARTLING,  ......I AM VERTICAL  162    9
FLOWERING (2)
   PLUCKS BARE THAT COMET'S FLOWERING.  ....EPITAPH FOR FIRE AND FLOWER   46   28
   I HAVE FALLEN A LONG WAY. CLOUDS ARE FLOWERING  ..............MOON.  173   22
FLOWERING'S (1)
   THE MONTH OF FLOWERING'S FINISHED. THE FRUIT'S IN,  .....POEM.1.WHO.  131    1
FLOWER-NIBBLERS (1)
   THE TAME FLOWER-NIBBLERS, THE ONES  ..........................MYSTIC  269   20
FLOWERPOT (1)
   LET ME SIT IN A FLOWERPOT,  ..............................POEM.1.WHO.  131    7
FLOWERS (24)
   SPROUTING FRUIT, FLOWERS, CHILDREN MOST FAIR IN LEGION  ...WREATH F.   45   22
   FLOWERS AND BLUEBIRDS THAT NEVER WERE  ........THE DISQUIETING MUSES   76   44
   WHITE CATALPA FLOWERS TOWER, TOPPLE,  .....................MOONRISE    98    5
   THERE WERE SUCH ENORMOUS FLOWERS,  ....................POEM.1.WHO.   132   29
   LADY, YOUR ROOM IS LOUSY WITH FLOWERS.  ............LEAVING EARLY    145    1
   I FORGET YOU, HEARING THE CUT FLOWERS  .................LEAVING EARLY  145    7
   KNEE-DEEP IN THE COLD AND SWAMPED BY FLOWERS?  .......LEAVING EARLY  146   44
   I DIDN'T WANT ANY FLOWERS, I ONLY WANTED  .................TULIPS    161   29
   THE TREES AND FLOWERS HAVE BEEN STREWING THEIR COOL ODORS.*VERTICAL.  162   12
   THEN THE TREES MAY TOUCH ME FOR ONCE, AND THE FLOWERS HAVE TIME
        FOR ME.  .............................................I AM VERTICAL  162   20
   GRAY FACES, SHUTTERED BY DRUGS, FOLLOW ME LIKE FLOWERS.  ...SURGEON.  171   50
   THE FLOWERS AND THE FACES WHITEN TO A SHEET.  .........LAST WORDS    172   13
   BLOOM ABOUT ME LIKE NIGHT FLOWERS, WITH A GOOD SMELL.  ...LAST WORDS  172   22
   THE FLOWERS IN THIS ROOM ARE RED AND TROPICAL.  .........THREE WOMEN  184  263
   DAWN FLOWERS IN THE GREAT ELM OUTSIDE THE HOUSE.  .......THREE WOMEN  185  309
   A LITTLE LIGHT IS FILTERING FROM THE WATER FLOWERS. *CROSSING THE W.  190    4
```

TITLE   PAGE LINE
FLOWERS (CONT.)
   THE FLOWERS VIVID AS BANDAGES, AND THE MAN MENDING. ......NARCISSI.   190   8
   NECESSARY AMONG THE FLOWERS, ...BERCK-PLAGE   200 101
   AND THE BRIDE FLOWERS EXPEND A FRESHNESS, ...BERCK-PLAGE   200 106
   FEATHER DUSTERS FANNING THEIR HANDS IN A SEA OF BEAN FLOWERS,   BEE.   211   17
   CREAMY BEAN FLOWERS WITH BLACK EYES AND LEAVES LIKE BORED HEARTS. ...
                                         ... THE BEE MEETING   211   18
   NO, NO, IT IS SCARLET FLOWERS THAT WILL ONE DAY BE EDIBLE. ....BEE.   211   20
   WHITE WITH PINK FLOWERS ON IT, ...STINGS   214   9
   IT IS TATE AND LYLE THEY LIVE ON, INSTEAD OF FLOWERS. ....WINTERING   218   29
FLOWERY (1)
   FOLLOWING THE COFFIN ON ITS FLOWERY CART LIKE A BEAUTIFUL WOMAN, ...
                                         ... BERCK-PLAGE   200 115
FLOWING (1)
   STEADILY ROOTED THOUGH THEY WERE ALL FLOWING ....THE EYE-MOTE   109   7
FLOWN (3)
   MY DARLING RAVENS ARE FLOWN. ....RECANTATION   42   10
   THE STUFFED SHAPE OF HER FLOWN MATE ....THE SHRIKE   42   13
   ANNOUNCING AFTER GLUTTED BIRDS HAVE FLOWN: ..EPITAPH IN THREE PARTS   337   21
FLOWS (2)
   IT FLOWS OFF BELOW THE GREEN AND WHITE ....THE BURNT-OUT SPA   138   22
   FLOWS IN THE SCROLLS OF HER TOGA, ...EDGE   272   5
FLUENT (4)
   ON FLUENT HAUNCHES, KEEPS MY SPEED. ....PURSUIT   23   28
   TO PREVENT FALL, OR ANCHOR THE FLUENT AIR ....EPITAPH FOR F.   45   3
   HUSH A LUMPED MAN-SHAPE. THE WHOLE ACT FORMAL, FLUENT AS A DANCE. ...
                                         ... THE GORING   47   9
   HORSES FLUENT IN THE WIND, ...THE EYE-MOTE   109   29
FLUFFY (1)
   THOUGH IT LOOKS LIKE A CAT, WITH ITS FLUFFY STUFF, PURE WHITE.*TOUR.   237   16
FLUID (6)
   THEY SIT SO NICELY IN THE PICKLING FLUID! ....STILLBORN   142   8
   TO POUR MYSELF OUT LIKE A FLUID ....LOVE LETTER   147   26
   O MUD, MUD, HOW FLUID! --   WORDS HEARD, BY ACCIDENT, OVER THE PHONE   202   1
   AND MONEY THE SPERM FLUID OF IT ALL. ....AMNESIAC   233   20
   THIS IS THE FLUID IN WHICH WE MEET EACH OTHER, ...BY CANDLELIGHT   236   10
   SUGAR IS A NECESSARY FLUID, ...KINDNESS   269   10
FLUNG (3)
   SHE FLUNG FROM A ROOM ....THE SNOWMAN ON THE MOOR   58   2
   FLUNG BRICK PERFECTED HIS LAUGH. ....MEDALLION   125   27
   SHAPELESS AS FLUNG GLOVES, A FEW FEET APART -- ....BLUE MOLES   126   3
FLUORESCENT (1)
   THE FLUORESCENT LIGHT WINCING ON AND OFF LIKE A TERRIBLE MIGRAINE, ...
                                         ... LESBOS   227   4
FLUSH (3)
   NEITHER TEARS NOR THE EASING FLUSH ....THE EYE-MOTE   109   19
   GLOWING AND COMING AND GOING, FLUSH ON FLUSH. ....FEVER.   232   42
   GLOWING AND COMING AND GOING, FLUSH ON FLUSH. ....FEVER.   232   42
FLUSHED (1)
   I AM FLUSHED AND WARM. ....LETTER IN NOVEMBER   253   11
FLUTE (1)
   FLUTE NOTES FROM A REEDY POND ....POEM.5.F.   134   ST
FLUTED (1)
   YOUR FLUTED BONES AND ACANTHINE HAIR ARE LITTERED .....THE COLOSSUS   130   20
FLUTES (2)
   TESSELLATED BOUDOIR. HEARING FLUTES, YOU ....YADWIGHA.   86   27
   AND SEPARATE THE FLUTES FROM VIOLINS: ....LOVE IS A PARALLAX   330   50
FLUTINGS (2)
   NOURISHES THESE BROKEN FLUTINGS, ...THE MANOR GARDEN   125   9
   THEN THE FLUTINGS OF THEIR IONIAN ....DEATH & CO.   254   17
FLUTTER (1)
   THEY WOULD FLUTTER OFF, BLACK AND GLITTERING, THEY WOULD BE COAL
       ANGELS ....BURNING THE LETTERS   204   33
FLUTTERING (1)
   THE WOMEN WAIT, FLUTTERING, TURNING PAGES ......MORNING IN THE HOS.   332   21
FLUX (5)
   OF MAKING HARBOR THROUGH THIS RACKETING FLUX ......CHANNEL CROSSING   27   19
   UNDER FLUX OF THOSE SEDUCTIVE ....ON THE PLETHORA OF DRYADS   68   35
   AS ROSES BROACH THEIR CARMINE IN A MIRROR. FLUX ....ABOVE THE OXBOW   89   44
   DEEP IN YOUR FLUX OF SILVER ....LORELEI   95   34
   AND RIDE THAT FLUX AT ANCHOR, UPSIDE DOWN. ....WATERCOLOR.   112   11
FLY (15)
   ARMED WITH FEATHERS TO TICKLE AS WELL AS FLY, ...PERSEUS   83   35
   I'LL FLY THROUGH THE CANDLE'S MOUTH LIKE A SINGELESS MOTH.*POEM.6.W.   135   20
   THEY FLY TOO FAST TO FEEL THE WET. ....ON DECK   143   17
   I HAVE NOT SEEN IT; IT DOES NOT FLY UP. ......THE SURGEON AT 2 A.M.   170   9
   NOW I BREAK UP IN PIECES THAT FLY ABOUT LIKE CLUBS. ....ELM   192   19
   NOW THE WASHED SHEETS FLY IN THE SUN, ...BERCK-PLAGE   198   67
   THE BEADS OF HOT METAL FLY, AND I, LOVE, I ....FEVER.   232   45
   I FLY TO A NAME, TWO EYES. ....GETTING THERE   248   19
   DYING TO FLY AND BE DONE WITH IT? ....YEARS   255   22
   SCRUTINIZING THE FLY .................................EAVESDROPPER   261   57
   THE SIZE OF A FLY, ...CONTUSION   271   7
   BUT LET THE FAST-FEATHERED EAGLE FLY. ......GO GET THE GOODLY SQUAB   313   4
   LET THE FAST-FEATHERED EAGLE FLY ....GO GET THE GOODLY SQUAB   313   5

	TITLE	PAGE	LINE

FLY (CONT.)
  THE SINGING BIRDS PACK UP AND FLY AWAY; ....NEVER TRY TO TRICK.   320   17
  AND OLD MAIDS ON IMPROMPTU PETTICOATS FLY ....SONG FOR A REVOLU.   323   15
FLY-BY-NIGHT (1)
  WELL-NAMED, ILL-FAMED A KNAVISH FLY-BY-NIGHT, ...GOATSUCKER   111   11
FLYING (8)
  CALL HERE WITH FLYING COLORS ALL WATCHFUL BIRDS *WREATH FOR A BRIDAL   45   13
  AND THE WHITE CHINA FLYING FISH FROM ITALY. ....LEAVING EARLY   145   6
  THE ELATE PALLORS OF FLYING IRIS. ....BERCK-PLAGE   199   86
  THEY ARE FLYING OFF INTO NOTHING: REMEMBER US. ....BERCK-PLAGE   199   87
  RISING AND FLYING, BUT BLINDED. ....BURNING THE LETTERS   204   32
  NOW SHE IS FLYING ....STINGS   215   56
  A FLYING HEDGEHOG, ALL PRICKLES. ....THE SWARM   216   32
  THE BEES ARE FLYING. THEY TASTE THE SPRING. ....WINTERING   219   50
FOAM (3)
  SLACK FOAM IN THE LAP. ....A SECRET   220   43
  THE TWO DRINKS FLAME AND FOAM. ....AMNESIAC   233   24
  FOAM TO WHEAT, A GLITTER OF SEAS. ....ARIEL   239   23
FOAM-CAPPED (1)
  WHEN SEAS WASH COLD, FOAM-CAPPED: ....FULL FATHOM FIVE   92 3-4
FOAMED (1)
  THEY SAILED TILL TIDE FOAMED ROUND THEIR ANKLES ......DREAM WITH C.   44   19
FOCUSING (1)
  FOCUSING ALL TIME'S DAY-SUNS IN ONE ....CRYSTAL GAZER   55   39
FOETUS (5)
  FISTED TO A FOETUS HEAD, RAVINED, SEAMED ....PERSEUS   83   25
  DRUNK AS A FOETUS POEM.7.S.   136   17
  WITH NO ATTACHMENTS, LIKE A FOETUS IN A BOTTLE, ...A LIFE   150   26
  INVOLVED AS A FOETUS. ....BURNING THE LETTERS   205   41
  WHERE I RELAX, FOETUS OR CAT, ...THE JAILER   226   9
FOG (7)
  THE FEN FOG SLIPS, ...PROSPECT   28   3
  OF FOG IN THAT HINTERLAND FEW ....TWO VIEWS OF WITHENS   72   5
  VAGUE AS FOG AND LOOKED FOR LIKE MAIL. ....YOU'RE   141   10
  THEY TOE OLD WATER THICK AS FOG. ....LEAVING EARLY   146   22
  THE SAME PLACARD OF BLUE FOG IS WHEELED INTO POSITION ...THE JAILER   226   2
  ON THEIR BLOTTER OF FOG THE TREES ....WINTER TREES   257   2
  SHEEP IN FOG ....SHEEP IN FOG   262   T
FOIST (2)
  TILL YOUR EYES FOIST A VISION DAZZLING ON THE WIND: ....NOVEMBER G.   56   14
  CAN WHIPCRACK THE TABLES INTO TIGERS AND FOIST ....DIALOGUE O.   279 117
FOLD (4)
  THIS RAM OF BLACKNESS. I FOLD MY HANDS ON A MOUNTAIN. ..THREE WOMEN   180 143
  RUN FOLD UPON FOLD FAR OFF, CONCEALING THEIR HOLLOWS, ..BERCK-PLAGE   199   74
  RUN FOLD UPON FOLD FAR OFF, CONCEALING THEIR HOLLOWS, ..BERCK-PLAGE   199   74
  NOW FOLD THEIR WINGS LIKE BATS AND DISAPPEAR ....TWO LOVERS.   327   7
FOLDED (5)
  THE FLIMSY LIGHT; ARMS FOLDED ....SCULPTOR   91   11
  AND FOLDED HIS HANDS, THAT WERE SHAKING: GOODBYE, GOODBYE. ..BERCK.   198   66
  THEIR DEATH RAYS FOLDED LIKE FLAGS ......THE COURAGE OF SHUTTING-UP   210   32
  ARMS FOLDED, EAR COCKED, ...EAVESDROPPER   261   38
  SHE HAS FOLDED ....EDGE   272   12
FOLDEROL (1)
  ERECT IN HIS FOLDEROL CLOAK ....DIALOGUE EN ROUTE   308   13
FOLDING (2)
  HAND FOLDING HAND, AND NOTHING IN BETWEEN. ....WIDOW   164   31
  NOTIONS AND TICKETS, SHORT CIRCUITS AND FOLDING MIRRORS. .....TOTEM   265   27
FOLDS (2)
  IN ITS EXPLICIT FOLDS? OR WHEN THE WINDOW, ...TALE OF A TUB   24   14
  COLD FOLDS OF EGO, THE CALLA, ...THE NIGHT DANCES   250   12
FOLIAGE (2)
  VAULTED BY FOLIAGE: ....THE LADY AND THE EARTHENWARE HEAD   69   24
  FIRST LET THE HEAVENLY FOLIAGE GO, ...SONG FOR A REVOLUTIONARY LOVE   322   2
FOLK (1)
  HOUSES HIMSELF ELSEWHERE. OUR FOLK THIN ....FROG AUTUMN   99   11
FOLKTALES (1)
  ANANSI, BLACK BUSYBODY OF THE FOLKTALES, ...SPIDER   48   1
FOLLOW (8)
  GOD ORDAINED TO FOLLOW UP YOUR DAYS. IS IT SUCH TROUBLE *DIALOGUE B.   39   25
  CANNOT FOLLOW AFTER, BUT LIES ....THE SHRIKE   42   8
  FOLLOW ON KIND WIND." ....CRYSTAL GAZER   55   18
  FOLLOW THE BLACK ARROW-BACKS OF SWIFTS ON THEIR TRACK ....OXBOW.   88   31
  QUICK AS THEY. TO FOLLOW THE LIGHT'S TINT ......CHILD'S PARK STONES   101   18
  I FOLLOW THE SHEEP PATH BETWEEN THEM. A LAST HOOK BRINGS ME ...
                                                    ... BLACKBERRYING   169   23
  GRAY FACES, SHUTTERED BY DRUGS, FOLLOW ME LIKE FLOWERS. ...SURGEON.   171   50
  FOLLOW HOLIDAY REVEL BEGUN LONG SINCE, ...CINDERELLA   304   10
FOLLOWED (1)
  WOMAN FOLLOWED US AND RUSHED ....THE DREAM   310   11
FOLLOWING (1)
  FOLLOWING THE COFFIN ON ITS FLOWERY CART LIKE A BEAUTIFUL WOMAN, ...
                                                    ... BERCK-PLAGE   200 115
FOND (8)
  DANS LE FOND DES FORETS VOTRE IMAGE ME SUIT: ....PURSUIT   22   E

	TITLE	PAGE	LINE

FOND (CONT.)
LOVESICK AT FIRST FOND SONG, ...VANITY FAIR 33 24
"FOND PHANTOM," CRIED SHOCKED FATHER SHAWN, ...DIALOGUE B. 39 41
THEIR FOND HEARTS CHARRED AS ANY MATCH. *EPITAPH FOR FIRE AND FLOWER 45 7
BEDFELLOWS OF THE SPIRIT'S DEBAUCH, FOND MASTERS. ...COMPANIONABLE. 105 8
FROM THEIR FOND, FINAL, INFAMOUS DECAY. ....THE DEAD 320 14
ARRANGED IN SHEETS OF ICE, THE FOND ....DANSE MACABRE 321 4
THE FOND ADMIRER'S ....ON LOOKING INTO THE EYES OF A DEMON LOVER 325 11
FONTAINEBLEAU (1)
GLITTER LIKE FONTAINEBLEAU ....GIGOLO 268 28
FOOD (7)
HE EATS, AND STILL HIS NEED SEEKS FOOD, ...PURSUIT 23 39
TO MOVE, SERVE, STEER FOOD, ...WORDS FOR A NURSERY 73 13
THE FOOD TUBES EMBRACE ME. SPONGES KISS MY LICHENS AWAY. POEM.7.S. 136 19
SHE DOESN'T NEED FOOD, SHE IS ONE OF THE REAL SAINTS. ...IN PLASTER 158 4
HE FELT FOR HIS FOOD. ....LITTLE FUGUE 187 10
I SEE THEM START TO CRUISE AND DIP FOR FOOD*QUEEN MARY'S ROSE GARDEN 290 13
THAT BECAUSE OF FOOD ....APRIL 18 302 9
FOOL (4)
TO SATISFY THE QUESTIONS OF A CURIOUS OLD FOOL?" ....DIALOGUE B. 39 26
AND I, GREAT MAGNANIMOUS FOOL, THUS WRENCHED FROM ..MONOLOGUE AT 3. 40 13
ONE A FOOL, THE OTHER A FOOL. ....A SECRET 219 16
ONE A FOOL, THE OTHER A FOOL. ....A SECRET 219 16
FOOLED (2)
I WASN'T FOOLED. I KNEW YOU AT ONCE. ....LOVE LETTER 147 28
FOR ROT. DON'T THINK YOU HAD ME FOOLED. I KNEW ....DIALOGUE O. 283 263
FOOLISH (2)
FOOLISH, DELICATE, IN THE LOWER RIGHT HAND CORNER. ......TWO VIEWS. 114 22
AND STILL I'M SKEPTIC. I KNOW. I'M BEING FOOLISH ....DIALOGUE O. 277 35
FOOLS (5)
EVEN AS LOVE'S DEAR FOOLS CRY EVERGREEN,*EPITAPH FOR FIRE AND FLOWER 46 30
"OUR WIT MADE FOOLS ....THE SNOWMAN ON THE MOOR 59 40
FRIGHTENED THE MIND. THEY SMILE LIKE FOOLS. ....THREE WOMEN 179 115
THEY ARE FOOLS. ....STINGS/DR 293 10
A PACK OF PHILANTHROPICAL FOOLS ....DIALOGUE EN ROUTE 308 11
FOOLS' (1)
OF JULY TO ALL FOOLS' DAY, ...YOU'RE 141 8
FOOT (25)
SAW HOOF HARDEN FROM FOOT, SAW SPROUT ....FAUN 35 13
WITH ONE FOOT ....LETTER TO A PURIST 37 10
SHE LIFTS ONE WEBBED FOOT AFTER THE OTHER ....MISS DRAKE P. 41 24
SET FOOT NIGHTLY IN HER YARD ....THE THIN PEOPLE 65 29
AND NOD AND NOD AT FOOT AND HEAD ....THE DISQUIETING MUSES 75 7
NOT LIFT A FOOT IN THE TWINKLE-DRESS ....THE DISQUIETING MUSES 75 28
SUPPORTS HIS FOOT. HE PIPES A WORLD OF SNAKES, ...SNAKECHARMER 79 10
I'D ONLY TO SET ONE FOOT IN WILDERNESS--*MEMOIRS OF A SPINACH-PICKER 90 21
CROWD FOOT TO FOOT, HEAD TO HEAD, NO FLOWER   ELECTRA ON AZALEA PATH 117 20
CROWD FOOT TO FOOT, HEAD TO HEAD, NO FLOWER   ELECTRA ON AZALEA PATH 117 20
MY HEART UNDER YOUR FOOT, SISTER OF A STONE. ....BEEKEEPER'S. 118 7
WAITED ON HIM HAND AND FOOT. POEM.4.BEAST. 134 6
ON HIM HAND AND FOOT, QUIET AS A DIAMOND. ....ON DECK 143 33
A MARBLE SAILOR KNEELS AT HER FOOT DISTRACTEDLY, AND AT
    HIS FOOT ....FINISTERRE 170 21
A MARBLE SAILOR KNEELS AT HER FOOT DISTRACTEDLY, AND AT
    HIS FOOT ....FINISTERRE 170 21
THE PRINT OF ITS BIG FOOT LAST WINTER, ...PHEASANT 191 11
WHY SHOULD IT, IT IS THE HEARSE OF A DEAD FOOT, ...BERCK-PLAGE 197 20
THE HIGH, DEAD, TOELESS FOOT OF THIS PRIEST ....BERCK-PLAGE 197 21
WILTS AT MY FOOT, ...BURNING THE LETTERS 205 43
IN WHICH I HAVE LIVED LIKE A FOOT ....DADDY 222 3
PUT YOUR FOOT, YOUR ROOT, ...DADDY 223 23
A CLEFT IN YOUR CHIN INSTEAD OF YOUR FOOT ....DADDY 223 53
MY RIGHT FOOT ....LADY LAZARUS 244 6
THEM UNWRAP ME HAND AND FOOT --- ....LADY LAZARUS 245 28
A SIX AND A HALF FOOT WEDDING-CAKE. ...................EAVESDROPPER 260 26
FOOTBALL (1)
HE MADE OF THE FOOTBALL POOLS -- TEASING US WITH ....DIALOGUE O. 277 39
FOOTFALL (1)
EMPTY, I ECHO TO THE LEAST FOOTFALL, ...BARREN WOMAN 157 1
FOOTING (2)
FOOTING SALLOW AS A MOUSE ....MISS DRAKE PROCEEDS TO SUPPER 41 9
FOOTING HER DELICATE DANCES ....AERIALIST 331 10
FOOTLESS (1)
TASTING THE WINDS, THAT ARE FOOTLESS, ...WINTER TREES 258 9
FOOTLIGHTS (1)
WHILE FOOTLIGHTS FLARE AND HOUSELIGHTS DIM. .....LOVE IS A PARALLAX 330 48
FOOTLINGS (1)
FOOTLINGS, BONELESS AS NOSES, ...POEM.2.DARK. 133 25
FOOT'S (1)
OUR FOOT'S IN THE DOOR. ....MUSHROOMS 140 33
FOOTSOLES (3)
LOST LUSTRE UNDER HER FOOTSOLES. ....HARDCASTLE CRAGS 63 21
THE MIDWIFE SLAPPED YOUR FOOTSOLES, AND YOUR BALD CRY   MORNING SONG 156 2
THEIR FOOTSOLES ARE UNTOUCHED. THEY ARE WALKERS OF AIR. *THREE WOMEN 183 231

	TITLE	PAGE	LINE
FOOTSTEPS (2)			
OUR FOOTSTEPS MULTIPLIED IN THE SHADOWY CHAMBERS, ...THE OTHER TWO		68	11
WHERE THE WATER BLOTS OUT ALL FOOTSTEPS." ...EPITAPH IN THREE PARTS		337	6
FOR (284)			
FORBID (1)			
TO BOYCOTT COLOR AND FORBID ANY FLOWER ..SOLILOQUY OF THE SOLIPSIST		38	26
FORBIDDEN (1)			
BENEATH THE FRINGES OF FORBIDDEN ROBE, ...METAMORPHOSES OF THE MOON		308	32
FORCE (3)			
SUCH FORCE CAN LAST; BUT BEYOND, THE NEUTRAL VIEW CHANNEL CROSSING		26	7
WHOSE FORCE MIGHT FIT ....THE QUEEN'S COMPLAINT		29	18
IT WAS A PLACE OF FORCE -- ....THE RABBIT CATCHER		193	1
FOREFINGER (2)			
THE GLASS MOUTH SUCKS BLOOD-HEAT FROM MY FOREFINGER. ....OUIJA		77	10
BETWEEN THUMB AND FOREFINGER. ....BITTER STRAWBERRIES		300	39
FOREHEAD (4)			
THE MOON LAYS A HAND ON MY FOREHEAD, ...BARREN WOMAN		157	9
HIS FOREHEAD IS BUMPY AS A SACK OF ROCKS. ....INSOMNIAC		163	13
TAKE A LOOK AT THE WHITE, HIGH BERG ON HIS FOREHEAD -- ...LYONNESSE		233	3
TOAD-STONE! I SEE I MUST WEAR YOU IN THE CENTRE OF MY FOREHEAD ...			
... THE RIVAL/DR		291	27
FOREHEADS (1)			
THEIR LITTLE FOREHEADS BULGED WITH CONCENTRATION. ....STILLBORN		142	3
FOREIGN (1)			
THICK AS FOREIGN COFFEE, AND WITH A SLUGGY PULSE. .....WORDS HEARD.		202	2
FORESEE (1)			
BY WITS ALONE: TO FORESEE HER LOVER'S FAITH ....CRYSTAL GAZER		55	33
FOREST (5)			
THE GUTTED FOREST FALLS TO ASH; ....PURSUIT		23	42
UNTIL ALL OWLS IN THE TWIGGED FOREST ....FAUN		35	3
IF THE THIN PEOPLE SIMPLY STAND IN THE FOREST, ...THE THIN PEOPLE		65	45
IN A FOREST OF FROST, IN A DAWN OF CORNFLOWERS. POPPIES IN OCTOBER		240	12
AND MY FOREST ....CHILDLESS WOMAN		259	15
FORETS (1)			
DANS LE FOND DES FORETS VOTRE IMAGE ME SUIT: ....PURSUIT		22	E
FOREVER (6)			
EMPTY OF COMPLAINT, FOREVER ....THE THIN PEOPLE		64	19
A MACHINE TO BREATHE AND BEAT FOREVER. ....SUICIDE OFF EGG ROCK		115	16
I COULD NOT RUN WITHOUT HAVING TO RUN FOREVER. .....THE BEE MEETING		212	33
THE WORLD FOREVER, I SHALL NOT ENTIRELY ....THE NIGHT DANCES		250	7
LOVE FLAMES FOREVER IF THE FLESH BE YEARNING. ...TO EVA DESCENDING.		303	14
THEY LOLL FOREVER IN COLOSSAL SLEEP; ....THE DEAD		320	12
FORFEITURE (1)			
SO WHEN STAUNCH ISLAND STOCK CHOSE FORFEITURE ....MAYFLOWER		60	9
FORGE (1)			
BUT TINKER JACK CAN FORGE ....TINKER JACK AND THE TIDY WIVES		34	17
FORGET (5)			
I FORGET YOU, HEARING THE CUT FLOWERS ....LEAVING EARLY		145	7
I WONDER IF THEY WOULD FORGET ME ....THE ARRIVAL OF THE BEE BOX		213	27
THAT SKEIN OF VOICES. WE PROMISED TO FORGET ....DIALOGUE O.		286	342
IN WHICH THE MINUTES COULD ADMIRE THEIR REFLECTIONS AND			
FORGET ABOUT ME. ....THE RIVAL/DR		291	7
IN DUBIOUS DOORWAYS FORGET THEIR MONDAY NAMES, ..LOVE IS A PARALLAX		329	32
FORGETFUL (3)			
THE FORGETFUL SURF CREAMING ON THOSE LEDGES. ..SUICIDE OFF EGG ROCK		115	24
AND THE SWEET, DRUGGED WAKING OF A FORGETFUL BABY. ....INSOMNIAC		163	19
IN A STILL PLACE, AND THE GROOM IS RED AND FORGETFUL, HE IS			
FEATURELESS. ....BERCK-PLAGE		200	108
FORGETFULNESS (3)			
INTO A SOFT CAUL OF FORGETFULNESS. ....POEM.5.F.		135	9
O COLOR OF DISTANCE AND FORGETFULNESS! -- ....THREE WOMEN		179	103
SUCH COLDNESS, FORGETFULNESS. ....THE NIGHT DANCES		250	17
FORGET-ME-NOTS (1)			
FLOWER FORGET-ME-NOTS BETWEEN THE STONES ....NOVEMBER GRAVEYARD		56	7
FORGETS (1)			
THE WOODS CREAK AND ACHE, AND THE DAY FORGETS ITSELF.*PRIVATE GROUND		131	19
FORGOT (1)			
IT NEVER OCCURRED THAT THEY HAD BEEN FORGOT, ...LYONNESSE		234	19
FORGOTTEN (1)			
I HAD EVEN FORGOTTEN HOW TO WALK OR SIT, ...IN PLASTER		159	45
FORKED (1)			
SENDS UP ITS FORKED ....SOUTHERN SUNRISE		26	11
FORKS (1)			
IN A MONTH WE'LL WONDER WHAT PLATES AND FORKS ARE FOR. ...TWO CAMP.		145	20
FORK-TAILED (1)			
IT WAS NO FIRE-BLURTING FORK-TAILED DEMON ..THE SNOWMAN ON THE MOOR		59	25
FORM (1)			
CANNOT LOOK MUCH BUT YOUR FORM SUFFERS ....FULL FATHOM FIVE		92	17
FORMAL (3)			
HUSH A LUMPED MAN-SHAPE. THE WHOLE ACT FORMAL, FLUENT AS A DANCE. ...			
... THE GORING		47	9
AS WOOD AND FORMAL, IN A JACKET OF ASHES, ...A WINTER SHIP		113	8
OF FORMAL SCORN, UNTIL THE FIRST SIGN OF AN ....DIALOGUE O.		282	232
FORMALITY (1)			
THERE IS A DIGNITY TO THIS; THERE IS A FORMALITY -- ......NARCISSI.		190	7

FORMING (1)
    FORMING ITS TWENTY PETALS. ....HEAVY WOMEN   158   10
FORMLESSNESS (1)
    SHE IS IN LOVE WITH THE BEAUTIFUL FORMLESSNESS OF THE SEA. ...
                                        ... FINISTERRE   170   27
FORMS (1)
    FROST FORMS. NO MAN'S CROWBAR COULD ....CHILD'S PARK STONES   101   26
FORM'S (1)
    NO FORM'S GONE SO AWRY, ...TINKER JACK AND THE TIDY WIVES   34   15
FORNICATIONS (1)
    THE STOLEN HORSES, THE FORNICATIONS ....THE OTHER   202   21
FORSAKE (2)
    RANSACKED IN THE PUBLIC EYE. WE FORSAKE ....CHANNEL CROSSING   27   32
    INVEIGLED TO FORSAKE THE SOD. ....DANSE MACABRE   321   18
FORSWEAR (1)
    "FORSWEAR THOSE FREEZING TRICKS OF SIGHT ....RECANTATION   42   11
FORTH (6)
    HEAVES FORTH STALK, LEAF, FRUIT-NUBBED EMERALD; ....ODE FOR TED   29   15
    DECKED FORTH IN COCKLE-SHELLS, ...DREAM WITH CLAM-DIGGERS   44   18
    WALK FORTH INTO SUN-MONEYED AIR, QUICKENED ....CRYSTAL GAZER   55   26
    FROST-BITTEN PIGEONS, EDDY FORTH ....A WINTER'S TALE   87   34
    EYEING ME. GRASS PUT FORTH CLAWS; .....MUSSEL HUNTER AT ROCK HARBOR   96   25
    COMMANDING THAT CORKSCREW COMET JET FORTH INK .....SONNET TO SATAN   323   5
FORTUNE (2)
    HATCHES NO FORTUNE, ...ON THE DIFFICULTY OF CONJURING UP A DRYAD   66   38
    FOR FORTUNE-TELLING? AND WHERE IS IT FORTUNE COMES .....DIALOGUE O.   277   45
FORTUNE'S (1)
    TO CHART THE MEASURE OF FORTUNE'S WHEEL; ....SONG FOR A REVOLU.   323   11
FORTUNE-TELLING (1)
    FOR FORTUNE-TELLING? AND WHERE IS IT FORTUNE COMES .....DIALOGUE O.   277   45
FORTY (1)
    IT BOILS FOR FORTY HOURS AT A STRETCH. ....THE TOUR   238   30
FORTY-NINTH (1)
    AS THEY SHOT PAST THE FORTY-NINTH FLOOR ....DIALOGUE EN ROUTE   308   4
FORUM (1)
    YOU ARE PITHY AND HISTORICAL AS THE ROMAN FORUM. ......THE COLOSSUS   129   18
FORWARD (3)
    CLEAVES FORWARD INTO FURY; DARK AS ANGER, ...CHANNEL CROSSING   26   3
    LIKE A SERIES OF PROMISES, AS I STEP FORWARD. ....WUTHERING HEIGHTS   167   9
    THE MEN THE BLOOD STILL PUMPS FORWARD, ...GETTING THERE   248   25
FOSSIL (2)
    AND HOARD FAITH SAFE IN A FOSSIL. ......EPITAPH FOR FIRE AND FLOWER   45   21
    I LEAN TO YOU, NUMB AS A FOSSIL. TELL ME I'M HERE. ....TWO CAMP.   145   21
FOSSILS (1)
    BROOD CELLS GRAY AS THE FOSSILS OF SHELLS ....STINGS   214   12
FOUL (2)
    TIME COMES ROUND FOR THAT FOUL SLUT: ....STRUMPET SONG   33   4
    FAIR CHRONICLER OF EVERY FOUL DECLENSION. ....OUIJA   77   14
FOUND (15)
    FOUND HERSELF, OF A SUDDEN, INTOLERABLY STRUCK ....SPINSTER   49   4
    THEY FOUND THEIR TALENT TO PERSEVERE ....THE THIN PEOPLE   64   13
    I FOUND BARE MOOR, ...TWO VIEWS OF WITHENS   72   12
    ALTHOUGH EACH TEACHER FOUND MY TOUCH ....THE DISQUIETING MUSES   75   35
    NEVER, NEVER, FOUND ANYWHERE. ....THE DISQUIETING MUSES   76   45
    OF THE DENSE GRASSES I FOUND ....MUSSEL HUNTER AT ROCK HARBOR   97   68
    I FOUND YOUR NAME, I FOUND YOUR BONES AND ALL*ELECTRA ON AZALEA PATH   117   16
    I FOUND YOUR NAME, I FOUND YOUR BONES AND ALL*ELECTRA ON AZALEA PATH   117   16
    TAP, TAP, TAP, STEEL PEGS. I AM FOUND WANTING. ....THREE WOMEN   177   35
    AND WHAT IF THEY FOUND THEMSELVES SURPRISED, AS I DID?   THREE WOMEN   180   118
    TILL THEN YOUR SMILES ARE FOUND MONEY. ....FOR A FATHERLESS SON   206   14
    THE BEES FOUND HIM OUT, ...STINGS   215   48
    OR AFTER GAY DAYS, OR COLORS THE GROWER FOUND GOOD. ..QUEEN MARY'S.   290   18
    BUT FOUND RADIANT VENUS ..ON LOOKING INTO THE EYES OF A DEMON LOVER   325   23
    THOUGHTS THAT FOUND A MAZE OF MERMAID HAIR ....TWO LOVERS.   327   5
FOUNDERED (2)
    FOUNDERED THROUGH LEVELS OF LIGHT SEAGREEN AND STRANGE.   OTHER TWO.   68   5
    HOW LONG HIS CARCASS HAS FOUNDERED UNDER ....THE BURNT-OUT SPA   138   8
FOUNDERING (1)
    STONE FARMS FOUNDERING IN IT, ...THE GREAT CARBUNCLE   72   3
FOUNDING (1)
    FOUNDING FATHER SET THESE LOBED, WARPED STONES   CHILD'S PARK STONES   100   3
FOUNTAIN (1)
    IN MY COURTYARD A FOUNTAIN LEAPS AND SINKS BACK INTO ITSELF,*BARREN.   157   3
FOUNTAINS (4)
    BUILD UP FROM A ROCK ROOT, AS FOUNTAINS BUILD ....MOONRISE   98   23
    THE FOUNTAINS ARE DRY AND THE ROSES OVER. ....THE MANOR GARDEN   125   1
    IT TAKES PATIENCE. IF VERONICAS AND FOUNTAINS ....DIALOGUE O.   282   221
    YET ASTRONOMIC FOUNTAINS ....TRIO OF LOVE SONGS   314   7
FOUR (10)
    ARENA DUST RUSTED BY FOUR BULLS' BLOOD TO A DULL REDNESS,*THE GORING   47   1
    AN ANVIL, HOOVES FOUR HAMMERS TO JOLT ....WHITENESS I REMEMBER   102   21
    A BLUE SEA, FOUR HORNY BULL-FEET, ...THE BULL OF BENDYLAW   108   7
    THEY HAD FOUR MEN LAID OUT, BLACK AS BURNT TURKEY, ...TWO VIEWS.   114   2
    ASIDE WERE DRAGGING ME IN FOUR DIRECTIONS. ....THREE WOMEN   178   58
    FOUR BABIES AND A COOKER! ....AMNESIAC   233   6

	TITLE	PAGE	LINE

FOUR (CONT.)
   MIDNIGHT, FOUR O'CLOCK, ...EAVESDROPPER 260 29
   TO FRACTURE THESE FOUR WALLS. YOUR FAITH FLIES ....DIALOGUE O. 279 111
   FOUR O'CLOCK, AND THE FEVER SOAKS FROM ME LIKE HONEY. ....FEVER./DR 294 1
   O RANSACK THE FOUR WINDS AND FIND ANOTHER ....LAMENT 316 16
FOUR-CORNERED (1)
   THE EYE OF A LITTLE GOD, FOUR-CORNERED. ....MIRROR 173 5
FOURS (1)
   TO ROCK ON ALL FOURS LIKE A PADDED HAMMOCK. ....MAGI 148 11
FOURTH (2)
   ...COFFIN OF THE FOURTH CENTURY A.D. CONTAINING THE SKELETONS...
   ... ALL THE DEAD DEARS 70 E/2
   MUTE AS A TURNIP FORM THE FOURTH ....YOU'RE 141 7
FOUR-WAY (1)
   FOUR-WAY VERANDA, VIEW-KEEPING ABOVE ....ABOVE THE OXBOW 88 36
FOX (4)
   STALKS RED FOX, SHREWD STOAT. ....ODE FOR TED 29 6
   BLUE SUEDE A DOG OR FOX HAS CHEWED. ....BLUE MOLES 126 4
   THE DOGS ARE TEARING A FOX. THIS IS WHAT IT IS LIKE -- ....BURNING. 205 49
   AND THE FOX HEADS, THE OTTER HEADS, THE HEADS OF DEAD RABBITS. ...
   ... THE COURAGE OF SHUTTING-UP 210 23
FOX-SKINS (1)
   DIAMOND RINGS, POTTED ROSES, FOX-SKINS ....OWL 101 5
FRACTURE (2)
   TO FRACTURE THESE FOUR WALLS. YOUR FAITH FLIES ....DIALOGUE O. 279 111
   WOULD FRACTURE IF HE FELL ....TRIO OF LOVE SONGS 314 24
FRACTURED (3)
   FRACTURED PILLARS FRAME PROSPECTS OF ROCK; ...........CONVERSATION. 21 9
   FRACTURED GLASS FLIES DOWN IN SMITHEREENS; ....DOOMSDAY 316 10
   PROBING FRACTURED VENUS WITH A STICK ....TWO LOVERS. 327 15
FRAGMENTS (2)
   AS THE GLASS FLEW TO ITS FRAGMENTS. LET US STAKE ....DIALOGUE O. 285 328
   AND THE FRAGMENTS WHIR LIKE A WEATHER VANE ...CIRCUS IN THREE RINGS 321 5
FRAIL (4)
   ASSEMBLE WITH THE FRAIL PALENESS OF MOTHS, ...OUIJA 77 4
   FRAIL AS ANTIQUE EARTHENWARE ....OLD LADIES' HOME 120 2
   COMES TO ROOST THERE, FRAIL ....POLLY'S TREE 128 17
   ONE SOUL PASS THROUGH THE OTHER, FRAIL AS SMOKE ....WIDOW 165 34
FRAME (6)
   FRACTURED PILLARS FRAME PROSPECTS OF ROCK; ...........CONVERSATION. 21 9
   ROOT-PALE HER MEAGER FRAME. ....TWO SISTERS OF PERSEPHONE 31 12
   AND BLOODIED AS A COW'S SPLIT FRAME ....STREET SONG 36 9
   OF DRAGONS BREATHING WITHOUT THE FRAME OF FABLES, ...LESSON. 80 3
   GAVE MOLTEN EARTH A FRAME, ...NOTES TO A NEOPHYTE 306 20
   THE ANGEL'S FRAME ....MOONSONG AT MORNING 317 34
FRAMED (3)
   FRAMED IN WINDOWS OF MAIN STREET'S ....NIGHT SHIFT 76 15
   FRAMED IN A BASKETWORK OF CAT-TAILS. ....THE BURNT-OUT SPA 138 26
   FRAMED IN DISCIPLINES OF FIRE AND ICE ....METAMORPHOSES OF THE MOON 307 26
FRANCE (1)
   IT ISN'T ENGLAND, IT ISN'T FRANCE, IT ISN'T IRELAND. ..STOPPED DEAD 230 10
FRANCE'S (1)
   WALKING THE PLANK DRAPED WITH MOTHER FRANCE'S UPHOLSTERY THE SWARM 217 48
FRANK (1)
   ELSEWHERE THE LANDSCAPE IS MORE FRANK. ....A LIFE 150 19
FRANZ (1)
   AS A SCHOOLGIRL SHE GAVE ROSES TO FRANZ JOSEF. ....CANDLES 149 18
FREAKISH (1)
   AND A HEAD IN THE FREAKISH ATLANTIC ....DADDY 222 11
FREE (12)
   NOW, FREE, BY HAZARD'S QUIRK, FROM THE COMMON ILL CHANNEL CROSSING 27 26
   FREE OF THE FICTIVE VEIN. WHEN ONE STARK SKELETON*NOVEMBER GRAVEYARD 56 10
   FREE FROM ALL MOLESTING. ROUGH BOYS, ...LADY AND T. 69 9
   FREE FISH-BAIT: THE BLUE MUSSELS ......MUSSEL HUNTER AT ROCK HARBOR 95 9
   HOW FREE IT IS, YOU HAVE NO IDEA HOW FREE --- ....TULIPS 161 31
   HOW FREE IT IS, YOU HAVE NO IDEA HOW FREE --- ....TULIPS 161 31
   WHEN THEY FREE ME, I AM BEADED WITH TEARS. ....FINISTERRE 169 18
   TOMORROW I WILL BE SWEET GOD, I WILL SET THEM FREE. ...THE ARRIVAL. 213 35
   THAT BEING FREE. WHAT WOULD THE DARK ....THE JAILER 227 41
   THE HEART LIKE WISHES OR FREE ....BALLOONS 272 16
   PAN AS OUR EVENING GUEST IF HE'S SO FREE*DIALOGUE OVER A OUIJA BOARD 283 252
   "O FOR UBIQUITOUS FREE APHRODISIACS, ...DIALOGUE EN ROUTE 309 27
FREE-FOR-ALL (1)
   BY CORRECT GREEN LINES AND NO SEEDY FREE-FOR-ALL ...ABOVE THE OXBOW 89 49
FREE-GADDING (1)
   THEN, A FREE-GADDING HOYDEN, GERD HAD CRAVED ....CRYSTAL GAZER 55 31
FREELY (1)
   FREELY BECOME SUN'S BRIDE, THE LATTER ....TWO SISTERS OF PERSEPHONE 32 21
FREES (1)
   THE PRINCESS FREES THE MINER, STONE BY STONE, ...THE PRINCESS. 334 49
FREEZE (6)
   IN WHICH OUR COMRADES ARE BETRAYED, WE FREEZE .....CHANNEL CROSSING 27 14
   SEEING HER FREEZE, HE TURNS HIS FACE AWAY. ....THE OTHER TWO 68 20
   ELECTRIFYINGLY-COLORED SHERBETS, SCOOPED FROM THE FREEZE*BERCK-PLAGE 196 3
   THEY FREEZE AND ARE. ....YEARS 255 5

```
                                                    TITLE              PAGE  LINE
FREEZE (CONT.)
   WE POISE ON PERILOUS POLES THAT FREEZE US IN  ........METAMORPHOSES.  308   46
   THE SKATERS FREEZE WITHIN A STONE TABLEAU.  ......PROLOGUE TO SPRING  322    3
FREEZES (1)
   FLEX AS THE MUD FREEZES.  ...........................PRIVATE GROUND   131   21
FREEZING (1)
   "FORSWEAR THOSE FREEZING TRICKS OF SIGHT  ...............RECANTATION   42   11
FRENCH (2)
   THE FRENCH WINDOW AJAR  ...............................THE SLEEPERS   122    6
   STEPPING STONES FOR FRENCH BOOTSOLES.  ....................THE SWARM  216   14
FREQUENT (1)
   "NEITHER OF THOSE COUNTRIES DO I FREQUENT:  .............DIALOGUE B.   38   19
FREQUENTLY (2)
   BUT HE IS PINK AND PERFECT. HE SMILES SO FREQUENTLY.  ...THREE WOMEN  186  327
   AND A TITLED LADY MAY FREQUENTLY BE A BEAUTY.  ........QUEEN MARY'S.  290   22
FRESH (2)
   FRESH LEAVED OUT IN VOWS: "COME TELL  ..............CRYSTAL GAZER      55    8
   FRESH FROM THE MELLOW PALETTE OF MATISSE:  .........MIDSUMMER MOBILE  324   12
FRESHNESS (1)
   AND THE BRIDE FLOWERS EXPEND A FRESHNESS,  .............BERCK-PLAGE   200  106
FRETFUL (1)
   THE YOUNGEST NEPHEW GIVES A FRETFUL WHINE  ...........FAMILY REUNION  301   23
FRIDAY (1)
   A DAY AGO, TWO DAYS, THREE DAYS AGO. IT WAS A FRIDAY.  ..THREE WOMEN  183  248
FRIDAYS (1)
   ON FRIDAYS THE LITTLE CHILDREN COME  ......................POEM.7.S.  137   36
FRIEND (5)
   BUT TO A FRIEND, IN PRIVATE, ROUSSEAU CONFESSED HIS EYE ..YADWIGHA.   86   35
   YOUR GATE, FATHER -- YOUR HOUND-BITCH, DAUGHTER, FRIEND.*ELECTRA ON. 117   45
   EVEN MY BEST FRIEND THINKS I'M IN THE COUNTRY.  ..........FACE LIFT  156   19
   MY POLACK FRIEND  ...............................................DADDY 222   20
   "I KNOW, I KNOW," I TOLD MY FRIEND.  ....................THE DREAM   311   24
FRIENDLY (1)
   BIT BY BIT TO THEIR FRIENDLY  .........MUSSEL HUNTER AT ROCK HARBOR   97   89
FRIENDS (2)
   FRIENDS, FRIENDS. THEY STINK OF ARMPITS  .............LEAVING EARLY  146   17
   FRIENDS, FRIENDS. THEY STINK OF ARMPITS  .............LEAVING EARLY  146   17
FRIENDSHIPS (1)
   COUNTS. SUCH DUELS INFECT BEST FRIENDSHIPS. PAN  ......DIALOGUE O.   283  271
FRIEZE (2)
   FRIEZE OF CABBAGE-ROSES AND CORNFLOWERS PALES  .......THE THIN PEOPLE  65   37
   A GREAT FRIEZE, EGYPTIAN, PERHAPS, OR GREEK,  .........DIALOGUE O.   276    9
FRIGHT (1)
   FROM ME LIKE ISADORA'S SCARVES, I'M IN A FRIGHT  ............FEVER.   231   12
FRIGHTENED (1)
   FRIGHTENED THE MIND. THEY SMILE LIKE FOOLS.  ...........THREE WOMEN  179  115
FRILL (4)
   AND BODY WHITER THAN ITS FRILL OF LILIES:  ...............YADWIGHA.   85   14
   A WEDDING-CAKE FACE IN A PAPER FRILL.  ..................BERCK-PLAGE  198   55
   THEY STARE FROM A SQUARE, STIFF FRILL.  ....................A SECRET  219   14
   FRILL AT THE NECK,  .......................................DEATH & CO.  254   16
FRINGE (3)
   ON ARMS AND LEGS IN A FRINGE OF KELP; GREEN SOAP  .....TALE OF A TUB   25   43
   FRINGE OF MUNDANE VISION, THIS GHOST GOES  ..THE GHOST'S LEAVETAKING   90   22
   IN ITS HOLLOW OF SHADOWS, ITS FRINGE OF REEDS,  ............CANDLES  148    8
FRINGES (1)
   BENEATH THE FRINGES OF FORBIDDEN ROBE,  ...METAMORPHOSES OF THE MOON  308   32
FRISCO (1)
   BIG AS A FRISCO SEAL  .........................................DADDY  222   10
FRIZZ (1)
   STAGE CURTAINS, A WIDOW'S FRIZZ.  ............................LESBOS  227    6
FROCK (1)
   HIERATICAL IN YOUR FROCK COAT, MAESTRO OF THE BEES,  ...BEEKEEPER'S.  118    5
FROG (1)
   FROG AUTUMN  ............................................FROG AUTUMN   99    T
FROG-COLORED (1)
   WON HER THE FROG-COLORED SKIN, PALE PITH AND WATERY  ......VIRGIN.    81   14
FROG-MASK (1)
   FED ME BANANA GAS THROUGH A FROG-MASK. THE NAUSEOUS VAULT *FACE LIFT 156    5
FROG-MOUTH (1)
   ALREADY FROG-MOUTH AND FISH-MOUTH DRINK  ...................POEM.5.F.  134    7
FROM (279)
FRONDS (1)
   FIREWORK OF FRONDS.  ..............................SOUTHERN SUNRISE    26   12
FRONTIER (2)
   HERE ON THE LAST FRONTIER OF THE BIG, BRASH SPIRIT  .......TWO CAMP.  145   12
   AT THE UNREAL FRONTIER. LET OUR BACKS, NOW BOLD,  .......DIALOGUE O.  285  331
FRONTS (1)
   OF PALE FRONTS, STRAW THATCHINGS, THE HARD ROAD*WHITENESS I REMEMBER  102   20
FROST (13)
   AS IS YOUR IMAGE IN MY EYE; DRY FROST  ............WINTER LANDSCAPE,   22   12
   WITH WHITE FROST GONE  ................................STRUMPET SONG   33    1
   IN VOICE FURRED WITH FROST,  ......DIALOGUE BETWEEN GHOST AND PRIEST   38   17
   HE ALSO AGAINST BLACK FROST  ................THE EVERLASTING MONDAY    62    7
   FROST DROPS EVEN THE SPIDER. CLEARLY  ..................FROG AUTUMN    99    9
```

193

```
                                                     TITLE              PAGE  LINE
FROST (CONT.)
    FROST FORMS. NO MAN'S CROWBAR COULD  ............CHILD'S PARK STONES  101   26
    BEARDED AND BLOWN, AN ALBATROSS OF FROST,  ............A WINTER SHIP  113   26
    FIRST FROST, AND I WALK AMONG THE ROSE-FRUIT, THE MARBLE TOES  ...
                                          ...  PRIVATE GROUND            130    1
    THAT'S MY FROST BOX, NO CAT,  ............................THE TOUR   237   15
    IN A FOREST OF FROST, IN A DAWN OF CORNFLOWERS.  POPPIES IN OCTOBER  240   12
    FROST ON A LEAF, THE IMMACULATE  .....................THE COURIERS   247    7
    THE FROST MAKES A FLOWER,  ............................DEATH & CO.    255   27
    BLUE AS LIZARD-SCALES. FROST SHEENS THE STREET.  ........DIALOGUE O. 286  340
FROST-BITTEN (1)
    FROST-BITTEN PIGEONS, EDDY FORTH  ...................A WINTER'S TALE   87   34
FROST-BREATH (1)
    VAPORISH AS FROST-BREATH,  ...........................POLLY'S TREE   128   10
FROSTED (1)
    ACROSS THE FROSTED GRASS SHE MARKS THE SHEEN  .........THE PRINCESS.  334   31
FROSTING (1)
    AND A CABIN BOY WHO COULD DECORATE CAKES IN SIX-COLORED
        FROSTING.  .....................................THE BABYSITTERS  174   12
FROST-THICK (1)
    THROUGH FROST-THICK WEATHER  ...........................VANITY FAIR   32    1
FROSTY (2)
    AND HEART'S FROSTY DISCIPLINE  ...........................SPINSTER    50   17
    AMONG ICE BUCKETS, FROSTY NAPKINS.  ......................CANDLES    149   23
FROWN (1)
    MOTHER, MOTHER. BUT NO FROWN OF MINE  .........THE DISQUIETING MUSES   76   55
FROZE (2)
    WHOSE LAUNDRY SNAPPED AND FROZE HERE, WHO  ............POINT SHIRLEY  110   10
    BUT DIDN'T CONVINCE ME. THOSE TEARS FROZE.  .............LOVE LETTER  147   17
FROZEN (5)
    FROM YOUR BLUE PALLOR, I'D SAY YOU INHABITED THE FROZEN WASTE  ...
                          ...  DIALOGUE BETWEEN GHOST AND PRIEST          38   14
    THE SCALDED SHEET IS A SNOWFIELD, FROZEN AND PEACEFUL.  ....SURGEON.  170    5
    WITH RADIANCE OF HIS FROZEN FAITH.  .................TO A JILTED LOVER 309    9
    FROZEN IN DESIGNS OF LOVE.  ..........................DANSE MACABRE   321    9
    HOW FLESH CLEAVES FAST TO FROZEN JOINT,  ............INSOLENT STORM.  326   10
FRUIT (13)
    WITH YOUR WILD FURIES, DISTURBING GARLANDS OF FRUIT  ..CONVERSATION.   21    2
    IN THE GREEN OF EDEN, PRETEND FUTURE'S SHINING FRUIT  TALE OF A TUB    25   39
    SPROUTING FRUIT, FLOWERS, CHILDREN MOST FAIR IN LEGION  ...WREATH F.   45   22
    WILL BRING CROP'S INCREASE, AND HARVEST FRUIT  ........CRYSTAL GAZER   55   17
    O RED FRUIT, IVORY, FINE TIMBERS!  .......................METAPHORS   116    4
    A FRUIT THAT'S DEATH TO TASTE: DARK FLESH, DARK PARINGS.  ...
                                  ...  THE BEEKEEPER'S DAUGHTER           118   14
    BLUEBLACK, A SPECTACULAR PLUM FRUIT.  .............ZOO KEEPER'S WIFE  154    4
    YOU WOOED ME WITH THE WOLF-HEADED FRUIT BATS  .....ZOO KEEPER'S WIFE  155   17
    I SHOULD SUGAR AND PRESERVE MY DAYS LIKE FRUIT!  .........LAST WORDS  172   10
    AND THIS IS THE FRUIT OF IT: TIN-WHITE, LIKE ARSENIC.  .........ELM   192   15
    THE BLOOD THAT RUNS IS DARK FRUIT --  .................THE OTHER      202   29
    AND IN PUNISHMENT WAS HUNG OUT LIKE BROWN FRUIT  ......THE DETECTIVE  209   29
    TUGGING THE WORLD TO FRUIT.  ..............................STINGS     215   47
FRUIT-NUBBED (1)
    HEAVES FORTH STALK, LEAF, FRUIT-NUBBED EMERALD;  ........ODE FOR TED   29   15
FRUITS (3)
    IT IS A GARDEN I HAVE TO DO WITH -- TUBERS AND FRUITS  .....SURGEON.  170   11
    THE DARK FRUITS REVOLVE AND FALL.  ......................THALIDOMIDE  252   23
    FRUITS OF YOUR WILLFUL TREE: GOD-HEAD, GOD-PIE  .........DIALOGUE O.  283  267
FRUIT'S (1)
    THE MONTH OF FLOWERING'S FINISHED. THE FRUIT'S IN,  .....POEM.1.WHO.  131    1
FUBSY (1)
    MAGENTA AS THIS FUBSY SOFA.  .........................LEAVING EARLY   146   33
FUCHSIA (2)
    BY THE ORANGE AND FUCHSIA BONFIRE  .............CHILD'S PARK STONES   101    9
    OF THE FUCHSIA. I COULD DRAW NO BREATH,  ....................MEDUSA   225   29
FUG (1)
    FUG OF THE SMALL MAMMAL HOUSE.  ...................ZOO KEEPER'S WIFE  155   19
FUGE (1)
    THE YEW HEDGE OF THE GROSSE FUGE.  ....................LITTLE FUGUE   188   20
FUGITIVE (1)
    THE FUGITIVE COLORS DIE.  ................................POEM.5.F.   135   10
FUGUE (3)
    LITTLE FUGUE  .........................................LITTLE FUGUE   187    T
    GULLS IN A FEATHERED FUGUE OF WINGS. OUTDO  ........MIDSUMMER MOBILE  324    4
    WHILE ON THIS SAME FUGUE, UNMOVED,  ....................TOUCH-AND-GO  336   22
FULFILL (1)
    AHAB, FULFILL YOUR BOAST:  .............................BATTLE-SCENE   84   27
FULL (27)
    WOULD BE FULL OF SUN, WHITE GULLS, AND WATER DRENCHED  ...CHANNEL C.   27   21
    WHOLE DONKEY-CARTS FULL  ..............................FIESTA MELONS   46    2
    RIDING IN THE FULL  ...............................HARDCASTLE CRAGS    62   10
    DESCRIBED HOW YOU FELL DREAMING AT FULL OF MOON  .........YADWIGHA.    86   25
    TO FULL CAPACITY. WE CLIMB IN HOPES  .................ABOVE THE OXBOW  88   26
    FULL FATHOM FIVE  .....................................FULL FATHOM FIVE 92    T
    A FULL MOON, RIVER LAPSING  ...............................LORELEI     94    2
    OF A WORLD MORE FULL AND CLEAR  ..........................LORELEI      94   15
```

194

	TITLE	PAGE	LINE

FULL (CONT.)
```
    THE GARDEN'S REMAINDER IN FULL PAINT. .................RHODODENDRON.   103    4
    THREE GIRLS, ENGROSSED, WERE WRENCHING FULL CLUSTERS   RHODODENDRON.   104   21
    MOON FULL, MOON DARK, THE CHARY DAIRY FARMER ...........GOATSUCKER.   111    5
    THESE HALLS ARE FULL OF WOMEN WHO THINK THEY ARE BIRDS. *POEM.1.WHO.   131   21
    WE ARE FULL OF STARCH, MY SMALL WHITE FELLOWS. WE GROW. ..POEM.6.W.   135   17
    THE STOREROOMS ARE FULL OF HEARTS. ......................POEM.7.S.   137   32
    WITH A LUNG FULL OF DUST AND A TONGUE OF WOOD, .......LEAVING EARLY   146   43
    THE VOICE OF GOD IS FULL OF DRAFTINESS, ......................WIDOW   164   22
    THEY ARE ROUND AND FLAT AND FULL OF DARK ADVICE. *CROSSING THE WATER   190    6
    FULL OF DRESSES AND HATS AND CHINA AND MARRIED DAUGHTERS. ...BERCK.   199   77
    HE HAS SEEN TOO MUCH DEATH, HIS HANDS ARE FULL OF IT. .....COURAGE.   210   15
    MARBLE-HEAVY, A BAG FULL OF GOD, .............................DADDY   222    8
    WHAT HOLES THIS PAPERY DAY IS ALREADY FULL OF! ..........THE JAILER   226   17
    IT IS LOVE YOU ARE FULL OF. YOU KNOW WHO YOU HATE. ..........LESBOS   229   72
    THE NOSE, THE EYE PITS, THE FULL SET OF TEETH? ........LADY LAZARUS   244   13
    FULL OF WINGS, OTHERWORLDLINESS. .......................WINTER TREES   258   11
    MOUTH FULL OF PEARLS, ...................................PARALYTIC   266   24
    WEB-WINGED AND FURIOUS. THE FULL MOONLIGHT ..............DIALOGUE O.   286  338
    THE FIELDS WERE FULL OF BRONZED YOUNG MEN ......BITTER STRAWBERRIES   299   18
FULLEST (1)
    OF PRIZE ROSES, CULLING THE FULLEST FLORETS; .......SPINACH-PICKER.    90   19
FULL-TILT (1)
    LULLED IN THE AMPLE WOMB OF THE FULL-TILT GLOBE. ..........THE DEAD   320    4
FUMBLING (1)
    POOLING IN HEEL-PRINTS, FUMBLING PEBBLE AND STEM. ....PARLIAMENT H.   153   36
FUME (1)
    ALREADY HALF UNSTRUNG. A VINEGARY FUME   TWO VIEWS OF A CADAVER ROOM   114    3
FUMES (1)
    THERE ARE FUMES THAT I CANNOT TOUCH. ...............POPPIES IN JULY   203    9
FUMING (1)
    STUCK TO HER TRIPOD, OVER THE FUMING CREVICE, .........DIALOGUE O.   286  349
FUMY (1)
    FUMY, SPIRITOUS MISTS INHABIT THIS PLACE   THE MOON AND THE YEW TREE   172    5
FUN (1)
    AND CONTRADICT OURSELVES FOR FUN; ..............LOVE IS A PARALLAX   329   21
FUNERAL (3)
    MY BLACK GOWN IS A LITTLE FUNERAL: ......................THREE WOMEN   185  303
    IN MY MOON SUIT AND FUNERAL VEIL. ........THE ARRIVAL OF THE BEE BOX   213   32
    MY FUNERAL, ...........................................CHILDLESS WOMAN   259   16
FUN-HOUSE (1)
    AND A FUN-HOUSE MIRROR THAT TURNS THE TRAGIC MUSE ..........PERSEUS    83   36
FUNICULAR (1)
    FUNICULAR RAILWAY, WITNESS TO GONE .................ABOVE THE OXBOW    88   38
FUNNEL (4)
    TO FUNNEL MY HEAT AWAY. .........................WUTHERING HEIGHTS   167   15
    SUCH A DARK FUNNEL, MY FATHER! .........................LITTLE FUGUE   188   22
    MUCK FUNNEL, MUCK FUNNEL --*WORDS HEARD, BY ACCIDENT, OVER THE PHONE   203   14
    MUCK FUNNEL, MUCK FUNNEL --*WORDS HEARD, BY ACCIDENT, OVER THE PHONE   203   14
FUNNELED (1)
    THEIR SHRILL, GRAVELLY GOSSIP'S FUNNELED OFF.*PARLIAMENT HILL FIELDS   152   18
FUNNELS (1)
    FROM BETWEEN TWO HILLS A SUDDEN WIND FUNNELS AT ME, ..BLACKBERRYING   169   20
FUNNY (2)
    AND FIND NO FACE BUT MY OWN, AND YOU THINK THAT'S FUNNY.*FATHERLESS.   205    9
    A FUNNY PINK WORLD HE MIGHT EAT ON THE OTHER SIDE OF IT, ..BALLOONS   272   24
FUR (4)
    THE SINGEING FURY OF HIS FUR; .............................PURSUIT    22   18
    BLUE FUR, MOLES HAVE; HEFTING CHALK-HULLED FLINT .......ODE FOR TED    29    9
    FLAYED OF FUR AND HUMANITY. ...................................TOTEM   264   13
    FROM WHICH THE FUR BEGAN. ......................TRIO OF LOVE SONGS   315   44
FURIES (1)
    WITH YOUR WILD FURIES, DISTURBING GARLANDS OF FRUIT ..CONVERSATION.    21    2
FURIOUS (4)
    WHO IS HE, THIS BLUE, FURIOUS BOY, .....................THREE WOMEN   181  162
    SHE IS CRYING, AND SHE IS FURIOUS. .....................THREE WOMEN   182  206
    I LAY MY EAR TO FURIOUS LATIN. ..........THE ARRIVAL OF THE BEE BOX   213   21
    WEB-WINGED AND FURIOUS. THE FULL MOONLIGHT ..............DIALOGUE O.   286  338
FURNACE (4)
    IN THE FURNACE OF GREED. CLOUDS, CLOUDS. ...................THE SWARM   216   16
    IS WHERE I KEPT THE FURNACE, ..............................THE TOUR   238   20
    HEAT FURNACE OF PARADOX .........................NOTES TO A NEOPHYTE   306   14
    SO I STARED IN THAT FURNACE ...............ON LOOKING INTO THE EYES.   325   21
FURNITURE (5)
    AROUND OUR BED THE BARONIAL FURNITURE .................THE OTHER TWO    68    4
    AGAINST BARE, WHITEWASHED WALLS, THE FURNITURE .......THE OTHER TWO    68    8
    AROUND HIM LIKE LIVINGROOM FURNITURE, LIKE A DECOR. ....BERCK-PLAGE   199   83
    INSTEAD OF DEAD FURNITURE! ..................................BALLOONS   271   11
    IN THE WINGS SOMEWHERE, OR LIKE HEIRLOOM FURNITURE .....DIALOGUE O.   276    7
FURRED (4)
    CLEAVING FURRED AIR .......................................VANITY FAIR    32   11
    IN VOICE FURRED WITH FROST, ......DIALOGUE BETWEEN GHOST AND PRIEST    38   17
    WHICH ARE SLOWLY OPENING THEIR FURRED PETALS ........MISS DRAKE P.    41   11
    ONE GRUFF-TIMBRED PURR ROLLING FROM FURRED THROATS: ..ELLA MASON A.    54   23
```

	TITLE	PAGE	LINE

FURROW (2)
OVER THE SEVEN HILLS, THE RED FURROW, THE BLUE MOUNTAIN? *DETECTIVE. 208 2
PIVOT OF HEELS AND KNEES! -- THE FURROW ....ARIEL 239 6
FURROWS (2)
ACROSS ATLANTIC FURROWS, DARK UNSURE -- ....MAYFLOWER 60 11
THE BROWN MOTHERLY FURROWS, THE WHOLE ESTATE. ....THE DETECTIVE 209 37
FURS (2)
NAKED AND BALD IN THEIR FURS, ...THE MUNICH MANNEQUINS 263 13
MY WIFE, DEAD AND FLAT, IN 1920 FURS, ...PARALYTIC 266 23
FURTHER (1)
DEEPER WITHIN THE DARK, AND AS I PITCHED FURTHER ....DIALOGUE O. 285 317
FURTIVELY (1)
UNTIL IT FINISHED, AND THEN LOOK FURTIVELY ....DIALOGUE O. 280 164
FURY (7)
THE SINGEING FURY OF HIS FUR; ....PURSUIT 22 18
CLEAVES FORWARD INTO FURY; DARK AS ANGER, ...CHANNEL CROSSING 26 3
WHAT FURY URGED HIM SLAY ....THE QUEEN'S COMPLAINT 28 9
AND FURY MAKE HEAD, ...MONOLOGUE AT 3 A.M. 40 2
AND IN FURY LEFT HIM ....THE SNOWMAN ON THE MOOR 58 4
DIFFICULT TO IMAGINE HOW FURY STRUCK -- ....BLUE MOLES 126 17
DOZE BEHIND THE OLD MASKS OF FURY. ......SLEEP IN THE MOJAVE DESERT 144 19
FUSING (2)
FUSING TIME'S THREE HORIZONS. ....CRYSTAL GAZER 54 6
FUSING TWO TALENTS, A SORT OF PSYCHIC BASTARD ....DIALOGUE O. 280 139
FUSION (1)
THE CULTIVATED ACT, A FIERCE BRIEF FUSION ....LOVE IS A PARALLAX 330 58
FUSS (1)
COMING AND GOING, BREATH BY BREATH, WITHOUT ANY FUSS. ....TULIPS 161 51
FUSTY (2)
THIS SHED'S FUSTY AS A MUMMY'S STOMACH: POEM.1.WHO. 131 4
FUSTY REMEMBRANCES, THE COILED-SPRING STAIR ....WIDOW 164 9
FUTURE (7)
MOUTH'S INSTANT FLARE FOR FUTURE LOOKS; *EPITAPH FOR FIRE AND FLOWER 45 11
AND THEIR FUTURE LOT, SHE BRAVED ....CRYSTAL GAZER 55 34
LESS THAN PRESENT, PAST -- THIS FUTURE. ..ON THE DECLINE OF ORACLES 78 29
THE FUTURE IS A GRAY SEAGULL ....A LIFE 150 31
REALLY CAN SEE INTO THE FUTURE. WHAT, ..DIALOGUE OVER A OUIJA BOARD 278 52
A FUTURE WAS LOST YESTERDAY ....APRIL 18 302 14
THE FUTURE AN ELECTRODE IN YOUR SKULL. ....THE TRIAL OF MAN 312 14
FUTURE'S (3)
IN THE GREEN OF EDEN, PRETEND FUTURE'S SHINING FRUIT TALE OF A TUB 25 39
WHAT FURY URGED HIM SLAY ....THE QUEEN'S COMPLAINT 28 9
AND FURY MAKE HEAD, ...MONOLOGUE AT 3 A.M. 40 2
G (1)
DOES HE WRITE C FOR G? NO. HE DARTS ....DIALOGUE OVER A OUIJA BOARD 284 276
GABBLE (1)
THIS CRACKED WORLD'S INCESSANT GABBLE AND HISS. ....STREET SONG 36 30
GABLE (1)
THE OLD MAID IN THE GABLE CRIES ALL DAY: ....NEVER TRY TO TRICK. 320 11
GABLE-ENDS (1)
WHERE PIGEONS PROMENADE THE GABLE-ENDS *THE PRINCESS AND THE GOBLINS 335 66
GABLES (1)
OVER GABLES THE MOON'S CELESTIAL ONION ..SOLILOQUY OF THE SOLIPSIST 37 8
GABLE-TOPS (1)
STRIKES THE TILES OF THE NEIGHBORS' GABLE-TOPS ....DIALOGUE O. 286 339
GABRIEL (2)
NO SUCCINCT GABRIEL FROM THE LETTERS HERE ....OUIJA 78 31
GABRIEL OR BEELZEBUB: I SEE, ...DIALOGUE OVER A OUIJA BOARD 280 150
GABRIEL'S (1)
GOING TO GET GABRIEL'S THUMB INTO THE PIE ....DIALOGUE O. 280 148
GAGGING (1)
THE WIND GAGGING MY MOUTH WITH MY OWN BLOWN HAIR,*THE RABBIT CATCHER 193 2
GAILY (4)
WITH CHEQUERED WAVES AND GAILY ....BATTLE-SCENE 84 7
GAILY, GAILY, ...BATTLE-SCENE 84 9
GAILY, GAILY, ...BATTLE-SCENE 84 9
GAILY CURSING THE WHOLE GOBLIN HORDE. THE PRINCESS AND THE GOBLINS 334 46
GAIN (1)
OUR QUESTIONS IN HUMBLE HABIT TO GAIN GRACE ....DIALOGUE O. 281 187
GAIT (1)
HIS GAIT STRAY UNEVEN ....SPINSTER 49 9
GALACTIC (1)
CAME A GARGANTUAN GALACTIC WINK. ....DIALOGUE EN ROUTE 309 42
GALES (1)
POLEMIC GALES PROVE POINT BY POINT ....INSOLENT STORM. 325 9
GALLANT (2)
EACH ONE AN INVETERATE GALLANT ....DIALOGUE EN ROUTE 309 21
THE SECOND SINGS: "RECEIVE NO ROVING GALLANT *EPITAPH IN THREE PARTS 337 7
GALLERY (1)
A GALLERY OF CREAKING PORCHES AND STILL INTERIORS, THE BABYSITTERS 175 34
GALLOP (3)
A MONGREL WORKING HIS LEGS TO A GALLOP ....SUICIDE OFF EGG ROCK 115 12
ALL NIGHT I SHALL GALLOP THUS, IMPETUOUSLY, ...ELM 192 10
GALLOP AND FLICK OF LIGHT ....TOUCH-AND-GO 335 7

196

GALLOPED (1)
  AND GALLOPED WOODWARD IN THAT GUISE. ....FAUN   35   15
GALLOPING (2)
  BUT LET THE GALLOPING ANTELOPE RUN. ....GO GET THE GOODLY SQUAB 313   12
  LET THE GALLOPING ANTELOPE RUN ....GO GET THE GOODLY SQUAB 313   13
GAMBLING-GAME (1)
  HEARTED GAMBLING-GAME YOU WARILY PRACTICE ....DIALOGUE O. 282 227
GAME (3)
  TO THE GROSS EATING GAME ....ALL THE DEAD DEARS 70   9
  OR PLAY ANOTHER CARD GAME WHEN YOU'VE WON; ....ADMONITIONS 319   2
  FOR EACH QUICK, FLARING GAME ....TOUCH-AND-GO 336   20
GAMECOCKS (1)
  THEY TALK OF BRIDE-LACE, OF LOVERS SPUNKY AS GAMECOCKS. ......NET-. 121   14
GAMEROOM (1)
  ON THE GAMEROOM PIANO, WHEN THE "BIG PEOPLE" WERE OUT, ...BABY. 175   23
GANGRENE (1)
  IT WAS THE GANGRENE ATE YOU TO THE BONE .....ELECTRA ON AZALEA PATH 117   39
GANGWAYS (1)
  ERECTED DOWN THE GANGWAYS OF OUR MIND. ....DOOM OF EXILES 318   4
GANNET'S (1)
  ENGINEERED THE GANNET'S BEAK. ....I WANT, I WANT 106   8
GAP (3)
  THEY SEEM LARGE, YET THEY DROP, AND NO GAP IS VISIBLE. ......STARS. 165   5
  A BLACK GAP DISCLOSES ITSELF. ....EVENT 195   17
  OUT OF A GAP ....CUT 235   18
GAPE (3)
  TO GAPE AT IT: ....SOW   60   10
  OPEN IN ITS GAPE OF PERPETUAL GRIEVING. ....THREE WOMEN 182 185
  THE WHITE GAPE OF HIS MIND WAS THE REAL TABULA RASA. .....LYONNESSE 234   27
GAPER (1)
  EAT ME. WASTEBASKET GAPER, SHADOW OF DOORWAY. POEM.1.WHO. 132   27
GAPES (1)
  NOBODY BLINKS A LID, GAPES, ...STREET SONG   35   5
GARB (2)
  SHE, IN HER SHABBY TRAVEL GARB, BEGAN ......DREAM WITH CLAM-DIGGERS   44   22
  OF MUSHROOM SIMILE AND GRYPHON GARB. ....A SORCERER B. 324   8
GARBAGE (1)
  HIS BODY BEACHED WITH THE SEA'S GARBAGE, ...SUICIDE OFF EGG ROCK 115   15
GARDEN (19)
  TO THIS FLAWED GARDEN, ...FIRESONG   30   2
  IN THE RECTORY GARDEN ON HIS EVENING WALK ....DIALOGUE B.   38   1
  NO CHANGE MET HER: GARDEN TERRACE, ALL SUMMER ....DREAM WITH C.   44   9
  LONG, SHORT, LONG -- IN THE LIT GARDEN ....CHILD'S PARK STONES 101   14
  I WALKED THE UNWALKED GARDEN OF ROSE-BEDS ............RHODODENDRON. 103   1
  BUCKED AT THE GARDEN GATE. ....THE BULL OF BENDYLAW 108   9
  A GARDEN OF MOUTHINGS. PURPLE, SCARLET-SPECKLED, BLACK *BEEKEEPER'S. 118   1
  THE MANOR GARDEN ....THE MANOR GARDEN 125   T
  WITH THE BOA CONSTRICTOR IN THE FELLOWS' GARDEN. ZOO KEEPER'S WIFE 155   26
  NOR AM I THE BEAUTY OF A GARDEN BED ....I AM VERTICAL 162   5
  A GARDEN OF BUGGY ROSES THAT MADE HIM CRY. ....INSOMNIAC 163   12
  IT IS A GARDEN I HAVE TO DO WITH -- TUBERS AND FRUITS .....SURGEON. 170   11
  YOU HAD A ROSE GARDEN AND A GUEST COTTAGE AND A MODEL APOTHECARY
      SHOP ....THE BABYSITTERS 174   20
  I AM A GARDEN OF BLACK AND RED AGONIES. I DRINK THEM, ..THREE WOMEN 180 149
  IN HER GARDEN THE LIES WERE SHAKING OUT THEIR MOIST SILKS*DETECTIVE. 208   7
  HANGING ITS HANGING GARDEN IN THE AIR, ...FEVER. 231   21
  OF A ROSE CLOSE WHEN THE GARDEN ....EDGE 273   14
  QUEEN MARY'S ROSE GARDEN ....QUEEN MARY'S ROSE GARDEN 290   T
  IN THE CENTER OF THE GARDEN NAMED AFTER QUEEN MARY. ..QUEEN MARY'S. 290   3
GARDENIAS (2)
  THEY ARE BROWNING, LIKE TOUCHED GARDENIAS. ....BERCK-PLAGE 198   59
  OF FESTERING GARDENIAS IN A CRYPT, ...FEMALE AUTHOR 301   12
GARDENS (5)
  THOUGH THE GREEN SEA GARDENS STALL, ...MAGNOLIA SHOALS 121   6
  GARDENS IN AN ANTIQUE BOOK ....MAGNOLIA SHOALS 122   9
  WELL, ONE WEARIES OF THE PUBLIC GARDENS: ONE WANTS A VACATION ...
              ... TWO CAMPERS IN CLOUD COUNTRY 144   7
  IN GARDENS OF SQUALOR ....MOONSONG AT MORNING 317   25
  DEVOURING GREEN GARDENS INCH BY INCH. ....EPITAPH IN THREE PARTS 337   17
GARDEN'S (1)
  THE GARDEN'S REMAINDER IN FULL PAINT. .................RHODODENDRON. 103   4
GARGANTUAN (2)
  GROWN GARGANTUAN BY TRADE, ...MUSSEL HUNTER AT ROCK HARBOR   96   35
  CAME A GARGANTUAN GALACTIC WINK. ....DIALOGUE EN ROUTE 309   42
GARGOYLES (1)
  GRIM AS GARGOYLES FROM YEARS SPENT SQUATTING AT SEA'S BORDER ...
              ... DREAM WITH CLAM-DIGGERS   44   25
GARLANDED (2)
  MOURNED BY RELIGIOUS FIGURES, BY GARLANDED CHILDREN. GETTING THERE 249   48
  MY LOVE AND I GO GARLANDED WITH GRASS. ....APRIL AUBADE 312   12
GARLANDS (1)
  WITH YOUR WILD FURIES, DISTURBING GARLANDS OF FRUIT ..CONVERSATION.   21   2
GARMENTS (4)
  AND THE CROW SETTLES HER GARMENTS. ....THE MANOR GARDEN 125   11

GARMENTS (CONT.)
    THEY ARE DEPARTING IN THEIR TRANSPARENT GARMENTS, TURNED ASIDE ...
                                ... THE SURGEON AT 2 A.M.   170   3
    HER BLUE GARMENTS UNLOOSE SMALL BATS AND OWLS. ....MOON.   173   18
    THEY ARE THE REAL MONKS AND NUNS IN THEIR IDENTICAL GARMENTS.*THREE.   183 227
GARNET (2)
    THE GARNET BITS BURNED LIKE THAT. ....MEDALLION   124   13
    TODAY WE MOVE IN JADE AND CEASE WITH GARNET ....SONNET: TO TIME   311   1
GARNETS (1)
    THE GARNETS ON HER FINGERS TWINKLE QUICK ....FEMALE AUTHOR   301   9
GARRISON (1)
    BREAKING THROUGH GRAVITY'S GARRISON, ...DIALOGUE EN ROUTE   309   31
GAS (3)
    GAS TANKS, FACTORY STACKS -- THAT LANDSCAPE ...SUICIDE OFF EGG ROCK   115   3
    FED ME BANANA GAS THROUGH A FROG-MASK. THE NAUSEOUS VAULT *FACE LIFT   156   5
    COAL GAS IS GHASTLY STUFF. ....THE TOUR   238   26
GATE (9)
    BUCKED AT THE GARDEN GATE. ....THE BULL OF BENDYLAW   108   9
    THE GREAT BRONZE GATE BEGAN TO CRACK, ...THE BULL OF BENDYLAW   108   13
    YOUR GATE, FATHER -- YOUR HOUND-BITCH, DAUGHTER, FRIEND.*ELECTRA ON.   117   45
    BY THE GATE WITH STAR AND MOON ....MEDALLION   124   1
    MEETS THE CORPSE AT THE GATE, ...BERCK-PLAGE   200   94
    HE IS HUGGING HIS BALL AND CHAIN DOWN BY THE GATE ....LESBOS   229   73
    WHO WHEEZES AT THE GATE. INCAPABLE ....FEVER.   231   5
    OF WHAT GREEN STARS CAN MAKE IT TO OUR GATE. ....BY CANDLELIGHT   236   5
    IF THAT ELDERBERRY BUSH BESIDE THE GATE *DIALOGUE OVER A OUIJA BOARD   280 157
GATES (1)
    THEN THE DRY WOOD, THE GATES, ...THE DETECTIVE   209   36
GATHER (2)
    AS THE PALLORS GATHER --- ....BERCK-PLAGE   199   84
    GATHER IDLE OYSTERS FROM GREEN SHOALS, ...GO GET THE GOODLY SQUAB   313   19
GATHERERS (1)
    HERE HE COMES NOW, AMONG THE MACKEREL GATHERERS ....BERCK-PLAGE   196   14
GAUDY (3)
    SHACKLED TO THE DOCK, OUTMODED, GAUDY, ...A WINTER SHIP   112   3
    SEND MY MUSE ALICE PACKING WITH GAUDY SCRAPS ....A SORCERER B.   324   7
    GAUDY MIRACLE OCCUR, TO COME ......MORNING IN THE HOSPITAL SOLARIUM   333   25
GAUL (1)
    THE DYING GAUL AND THOSE INNUMERABLE PIETAS ....PERSEUS   82   9
GAUNT (2)
    FROM GAUNT HEMLOCK, ROOKS CROAK HAVOC: ....PURSUIT   22   7
    HER WINTER-BEHEADED DAISIES, MARROWLESS, GAUNT, ...SNOWMAN O.   58   9
GAUNTLET (1)
    FLINGS SILVER GAUNTLET OF HIS PLANE AT SPACE, ...METAMORPHOSES.   307   4
GAUNTLETS (2)
    OUR CHEESECLOTH GAUNTLETS NEAT AND SWEET, ...STINGS   214   3
    STEEL GAUNLETS OF TRAFFIC, TERROR-STRUCK ....AERIALIST   332   45
GAUZE (3)
    MOTHER TO MYSELF, I WAKE SWADDLED IN GAUZE, ...FACE LIFT   156   31
    I WALK AMONG SLEEPERS IN GAUZE SARCOPHAGI. ...THE SURGEON AT 2 A.M.   171   47
    GAUZE KU KLUX KLAN ....CUT   235   30
GAUZE-EDGED (1)
    WAVERING THERE, GAUZE-EDGED, SMELLING OF WOODSMOKE, ...DIALOGUE B.   38   12
GAVE (11)
    "COME, COME," FATHER SHAWN GAVE AN IMPATIENT SHRUG .....DIALOGUE B.   39   21
    GAVE WAY TO FIELDS AND THE INCESSANT SEETHE OF GRASSES*HARDCASTLE C.   62   9
    ALL THE NIGHT GAVE HER, IN RETURN ....HARDCASTLE CRAGS   63   26
    HE GAVE ME. I'VE GONE NOWHERE SINCE BUT ....WHITENESS I REMEMBER   102   3
    BUT GAVE ME PAUSE, MY ROSE A CHARGE, ...RHODODENDRON.   104   26
    WE GAVE GOOD USE AS SHIP AND HOUSE IS BLACK*GREEN ROCK, WINTHROP BAY   105   11
    FOR WHOM THE GOOD LORD PROVIDES (HE GAVE ....ON DECK   143   20
    GAVE UP THE GHOST LAST NIGHT. HIGH TIME. ....LEAVING EARLY   146   24
    AS A SCHOOLGIRL SHE GAVE ROSES TO FRANZ JOSEF. ....CANDLES   149   18
    I GAVE HER A SOUL, I BLOOMED OUT OF HER AS A ROSE ....IN PLASTER   159   16
    GAVE MOLTEN EARTH A FRAME, ...NOTES TO A NEOPHYTE   306   20
GAY (4)
    OR AFTER GAY DAYS, OR COLORS THE GROWER FOUND GOOD. ..QUEEN MARY'S.   290   18
    SPREAD GAY CONTAGION WITH EACH CLEVER BREATH. ....DIRGE FOR A JOKER   303   12
    TO MORTAL CHILDREN LONGING TO BE GAY; ....NEVER TRY TO TRICK.   320   14
    IN GAY VENTRILOQUY FROM WING TO WING ....LOVE IS A PARALLAX   330   47
GAZE (1)
    WHEN BURNS AND BRANDS THAT YELLOW GAZE? ....PURSUIT   23   36
GAZER (1)
    CRYSTAL GAZER ....CRYSTAL GAZER   54   T
GEAR (1)
    GLIDING UP IN LOW GEAR BEHIND THE CART. ....BERCK-PLAGE   200 112
GECKO (1)
    GECKO, THE LITTLE FLICK! ....THE TOUR   237   4
GEE (1)
    GEE BABY, YOU ARE RARE." ....LESBOS   228   42
GEESE (1)
    GEESE AND THE MONKEY TREES. ....THE TOUR   237   10
GELDED (2)
    BALDING, GELDED BY LIGHTNING -- AN ILLUSION, ..FOR A FATHERLESS SON   205   4
    GELDED AND WINGLESS. NOT HEROES. NOT HEROES. ....STINGS/DR   293   15

GEM (1)
   OF PERSONAGE -- SINGLE-SKIRTED, PERFUMED, A GEM -- ...QUEEN MARY'S. 290 24
GENERAL (2)
   HIS WIDE EYE IS THAT GENERAL, FLAT BLUE. ....THREE WOMEN 183 234
   TAKE THE GENERAL MUMBLE, ...NOTES TO A NEOPHYTE 306   1
GENERALS (1)
   THE WHITE BUSTS OF MARSHALS, ADMIRALS, GENERALS ....THE SWARM 217 44
GENERATING (1)
   THE GENERATING BONE. ....TRIO OF LOVE SONGS 315 48
GENERATION (1)
   ALOUD, CROSSLEGGED ON THE STERN SEAT, FROM THE GENERATION OF
      VIPERS. ....THE BABYSITTERS 175 32
GENERATIONS (2)
   OF ASTOUNDED GENERATIONS; THEY WRESTLE EPITAPH FOR FIRE AND FLOWER   45 19
   OF SNAKY GENERATIONS: LET THERE BE SNAKES! ...........SNAKECHARMER   79 20
GENEROUS (1)
   OUT OF THE SIDE OF THE GENEROUS MOON WHEN IT ....THE THIN PEOPLE   65 28
GENESIS (1)
   INVADES THE DILATE LENS OF GENESIS ....SONNET TO SATAN 323 10
GENIUS (1)
   THE GENIUS OF PLENITUDE ....FROG AUTUMN   99 10
GENTLE (4)
   AND USED HER GENTLE DOVES WITH MANNERS RUDE; THE QUEEN'S COMPLAINT   28   7
   THE GIRL BENT HOMEWARD, BRIMFUL OF GENTLE TALK ....SNOWMAN O.   59 50
   SORROWS OF MALFI'S GENTLE DUCHESS? GONE ....PERSEUS   83 42
   THE WORLD PURRS, SHUT-OFF AND GENTLE. ....BERCK-PLAGE 200 110
GENTLED (1)
   THE FACE OF THE EFFIGY, GENTLED BY CANDLES, ...MOON. 173 20
GENTLEMAN (1)
   AND SWAGGERS LIKE A PROPER GENTLEMAN; ....ADMONITIONS 319 11
GENTLEMEN (1)
   GENTLEMEN, LADIES ....LADY LAZARUS 245 30
GENTLING (1)
   GENTLING THE SUN WITH THE SHADE OF MY HAND, ...THREE WOMEN 185 290
GENTLY (1)
   TENDS TO THE PEBBLES IT MUST RUN OVER, SMOOTHING THEM GENTLY.*TULIPS 160 16
GENTLY-GRADED (1)
   OVER A SURFACE OF GENTLY-GRADED ....BATTLE-SCENE   84 4-5
GENUINE (3)
   FROM THE GENUINE COLOR OF SKIN; CAN OUR DREAMS ....TALE OF A TUB   25 27
   DO NOT ACCEPT IT. IT IS NOT GENUINE. ....THE COURIERS 247   4
   TO PROVE IT GENUINE. YOU'D KNEEL, TOO, DIALOGUE OVER A OUIJA BOARD 280 162
GEOMETRY (1)
   BETRAYED IN MUTE GEOMETRY OF BROKEN ....SONNET: TO EVA 304   6
GERANIUM (3)
   SHARK LITTERED IN THE GERANIUM BED -- ....POINT SHIRLEY 110 16
   MY HEART IS A STOPPED GERANIUM. POEM.1.WHO. 131   9
   THE SUN BLOOMS, IT IS A GERANIUM. ....MYSTIC 269 30
GERANIUMS (1)
   THE RED GERANIUMS I KNOW. ....LEAVING EARLY 146 16
GERD (7)
   GERD SITS SPINDLE-SHANKED IN HER DARK TENT, ...CRYSTAL GAZER   54   1
   WELL OR ILL." GERD SLANTS A LOOK AT EACH: MOST DEAR, CRYSTAL GAZER   55 10
   GERD WHIRLS THE BALL ABLAZE: "ROUGH STORM," SHE GRANTS, "MAY WREAK ...
                               ... CRYSTAL GAZER   55 22
   ALOOF, SQUATTING MUMMY-WISE, GERD SCANS ....CRYSTAL GAZER   55 28
   THEN, A FREE-GADDING HOYDEN, GERD HAD CRAVED ....CRYSTAL GAZER   55 31
   SO BEGGAR GERD MIGHT AIM HER LOOK ....CRYSTAL GAZER   55 40
   WHAT GERD SAW THEN ENGRAVED HER MIND ....CRYSTAL GAZER   56 43
GERMAN (4)
   GOTHIC AND BARBAROUS, PURE GERMAN. ....LITTLE FUGUE 188 26
   BETWEEN THE YELLOW LETTUCES AND THE GERMAN CABBAGE ....BURNING. 205 39
   IN THE GERMAN TONGUE, IN THE POLISH TOWN ....DADDY 222 16
   I THOUGHT EVERY GERMAN WAS YOU. ....DADDY 223 29
GERMANS (1)
   THE THICK GERMANS SLUMBERING IN THEIR BOTTOMLESS STOLZ. ....MUNICH. 263 23
GERMANY (3)
   RUSSIA, POLAND AND GERMANY! ....THE SWARM 216 27
   GERMANY. ....MARY'S SONG 257 11
   GERMANY. ....MARY'S SONG/DR 294   2
GESTURE (4)
   THE GESTURE, BEND AND HOLD THE PRONE MAN'S HEAD. ..CHANNEL CROSSING   27 36
   FOR THAT WARY CLATTER SOUND OR GESTURE ..............INCOMMUNICADO 100   6
   NO GESTURE OF YOURS OR MINE COULD CATCH THEIR ATTENTION, TWO CAMP. 144   4
   EACH GESTURE FLEES IMMEDIATELY DOWN AN ALLEY ....INSOMNIAC 163 23
GESTURES (3)
   OBSERVED HER LOVER'S GESTURES UNBALANCE THE AIR, ...SPINSTER   49   8
   MIRRORED THE INTRICATE GESTURES OF TWO OTHERS. ....THE OTHER TWO   68 14
   SO YOUR GESTURES FLAKE OFF --- ....THE NIGHT DANCES 250 18
GET (27)
   LAUGH, KISS, GET DRUNK, ...SOLILOQUY OF THE SOLIPSIST   37 16
   LIKE A LAST STORM-CROSSED LEAF? BEST GET YOU GONE ......DIALOGUE B.   39 44
   TO GET YOUR CAROUSALS TOLD: ....SPIDER   48   6
   GET BACK, THOUGH, SOON, ...ALL THE DEAD DEARS   71 26
   HIKERS GET TO: ....TWO VIEWS OF WITHENS   72   6

GET (CONT.)
    APPROVING CHASED GIRLS WHO GET THEM TO A TREE .....VIRGIN IN A TREE   81   4
    COLORISTS CAME TO GET THE ....MUSSEL HUNTER AT ROCK HARBOR   95   2
    I WOULD GET FROM THESE DRY-PAPPED STONES ....POINT SHIRLEY   111   41
    I SHALL NEVER GET YOU PUT TOGETHER ENTIRELY, ...THE COLOSSUS   129   1
    SLEEPILY AS LETHE, TRYING TO GET IN. ..TWO CAMPERS IN CLOUD COUNTRY   145   26
    I CAN'T GET IT OUT OF MY MIND ....ZOO KEEPER'S WIFE   155   32
    I SHALL NEVER GET OUT OF THIS! THERE ARE TWO OF ME NOW: IN PLASTER   158   1
    I WASN'T IN ANY POSITION TO GET RID OF HER. ....IN PLASTER   159   43
    I SIMPLY CANNOT SEE WHERE THERE IS TO GET TO. ....MOON.   173   7
    ON THAT DAY-OFF THE TWO OF US CRIED SO HARD TO GET   THE BABYSITTERS   175   29
    THERE WAS ONLY ONE PLACE TO GET TO. ....THE RABBIT CATCHER   193   11
    "BUT IT WANTS TO GET OUT! ....A SECRET   220   35
    AND GET BACK, BACK, BACK TO YOU. ....DADDY   224   59
    HOW DID I GET HERE? ....THE JAILER   227   32
    O LOVE, HOW DID YOU GET HERE? ....NICK AND THE CANDLESTICK   241   23
    IT IS RUSSIA I HAVE TO GET ACROSS, IT IS SOME WAR OR OTHER.*GETTING.   248   9
    GO GET THE GLASS, THEN. BUT I KNOW TONIGHT WILL BE .....DIALOGUE O.   276   1
    GOING TO GET GABRIEL'S THUMB INTO THE PIE ....DIALOGUE O.   280 148
    AND GET US CLEAR OF THIS. OH, HE'LL GO CLEVER ....DIALOGUE O.   281 175
    GO GET THE GOODLY SQUAB ....GO GET THE GOODLY SQUAB   313   T
    GO GET THE GOODLY SQUAB IN GOLD-LOBED CORN   GO GET THE GOODLY SQUAB   313   1
    AND GET SAFE HOME; BUT, TURNING WITH TRAINED EYES, ...AERIALIST   331   28
GETAWAY (1)
    GRINNED LIKE A GETAWAY CAR. ....BURNING THE LETTERS   204   8
GETS (2)
    GETS READY TO FACE THE READY-MADE CREATION   THE GHOST'S LEAVETAKING   90   6
    AND THE NOISE IT FLAYS FROM THE AIR, ONCE IT GETS GOING! ..COURAGE.   210   20
GETTING (5)
    BOARDED THE TRAIN THERE'S NO GETTING OFF. ....METAPHORS   116   9
    THERE'S NO GETTING UP BY THE WORDS YOU KNOW.*NEW YEAR ON DARTMOOR   176   6
    NO GETTING UP BY ELEPHANT OR WHEEL OR SHOE. ...NEW YEAR ON DARTMOOR   176   7
    GETTING THERE ....GETTING THERE   247   T
    THE PLACE I AM GETTING TO, WHY ARE THERE THESE OBSTACLES --- ...
                                            ... GETTING THERE   249   45
GHASTLY (4)
    GHASTLY STATUE WITH ONE GRAY TOE ....DADDY   222   9
    GHASTLY VATICAN. ....MEDUSA   225   36
    THE GHASTLY ORCHID ....FEVER.   231   20
    COAL GAS IS GHASTLY STUFF. ....THE TOUR   238   26
GHOST (20)
    DIALOGUE BETWEEN GHOST AND PRIEST *DIALOGUE BETWEEN GHOST AND PRIEST   38   T
    FATHER SHAWN PERCEIVED A GHOST ...DIALOGUE BETWEEN GHOST AND PRIEST   38   9
    "HOW NOW," FATHER SHAWN CRISPLY ADDRESSED THE GHOST ....DIALOGUE B.   38   11
    GHOST SAID TO PRIEST: ....DIALOGUE BETWEEN GHOST AND PRIEST   38   18
    GHOST SWORE TO PRIEST: ....DIALOGUE BETWEEN GHOST AND PRIEST   39   48
    SHE STALKED INTRACTABLE AS A DRIVEN GHOST ..THE SNOWMAN ON THE MOOR   58   15
    SUNDAY'S GHOST OF SUN; ....THE EVERLASTING MONDAY   62   10
    TO NO FAMILY-FEATURED GHOST, ...HARDCASTLE CRAGS   63   16
    FOR WHICH THE GHOST OF BOCKLIN GRIEVES. ..ON THE DECLINE OF ORACLES   78   15
    THE ORACULAR GHOST WHO DWINDLES ON PIN-LEGS *THE GHOST'S LEAVETAKING   90   9
    FRINGE OF MUNDANE VISION, THIS GHOST GOES ..THE GHOST'S LEAVETAKING   90   22
    GO, GHOST OF OUR MOTHER AND FATHER, GHOST OF US, ...GHOST'S.   91   32
    GO, GHOST OF OUR MOTHER AND FATHER, GHOST OF US, ...GHOST'S.   91   32
    AND GHOST OF OUR DREAMS' CHILDREN, IN THOSE SHEETS .....GHOST'S.   91   33
    I AM THE GHOST OF AN INFAMOUS SUICIDE, ...ELECTRA ON AZALEA PATH   117   42
    OR IN A GHOST FLOWER ....POLLY'S TREE   128   7
    GAVE UP THE GHOST LAST NIGHT. HIGH TIME. ....LEAVING EARLY   146   24
    GHOST OF A LEAF, GHOST OF A BIRD. ....PARLIAMENT HILL FIELDS   153   28
    GHOST OF A LEAF, GHOST OF A BIRD. ....PARLIAMENT HILL FIELDS   153   28
    IN WHOSE SHADOW I HAVE EATEN MY GHOST RATION. ....THE JAILER   227   38
GHOST-COLUMN (1)
    IT MUST BE A TUSK THERE, A GHOST-COLUMN. ....A BIRTHDAY PRESENT   206   19
GHOSTS (5)
    WHATEVER LOST GHOSTS FLARE, ...NOVEMBER GRAVEYARD   56   15
    RIDDLED WITH GHOSTS, TO LIE ....ALL THE DEAD DEARS   71   35
    THE GHOSTS, KINDLY. ....TWO VIEWS OF WITHENS   72   18
    AT OWL-CALL THE OLD GHOSTS FLOCK ....OLD LADIES' HOME   120   15
    WITH KISS OF CINDERS, GHOSTS DESCEND, ...DANSE MACABRE   321   25
GHOST'S (2)
    MY EYEFUL OF REFLECTIONS A GHOST'S ....LANDOWNERS   53   12
    THE GHOST'S LEAVETAKING ....THE GHOST'S LEAVETAKING   90   T
GIANT (5)
    THIS GIANT HULKED, I TELL YOU, ON HER SCENE ..THE QUEEN'S COMPLAINT   28   2
    GIANT HEAVED INTO THE DISTANCE, STONE-HATCHETED, ...SNOWMAN O.   59   31
    OF A BLIZZARD, THE GIANT ROARED UP WITH HIS CHITTERING TROPHIES. ...
                                      ... THE SNOWMAN ON THE MOOR   59   45
    SHE SHIED SIDEWAYS: A WHITE FIZZ! AND THE GIANT, PURSUING, ...
                                      ... THE SNOWMAN ON THE MOOR   59   47
    OF A GIANT OR EXTINCT ....CHILD'S PARK STONES   101   6
GIANTS (2)
    THEM HUGE AGAIN, VIOLENT GIANTS ON THE WALL. ....BY CANDLELIGHT   236   14
    WHAT GREENHORN VENTS HIS VENOM AGAINST GIANTS ....DIALOGUE O.   281 199
GIANT'S (1)
    ONE OF A GIANT'S EAR? I GUESS THIS GLASS*DIALOGUE OVER A OUIJA BOARD   281 201

                                                        TITLE   PAGE LINE
GIBBERING (1)
    TO STUN SKY BLACK OUT, DRIVE GIBBERING MAD ....CONJURING.   66   12
GIBBERISH (1)
    TO CANACEE CRIES GIBBERISH TO COARSENED EARS. ........INCOMMUNICADO   100   14
GIBBETS (1)
    GIBBETS WITH HER CURSE THE MOON'S MAN, ...MAUDLIN   51   3
GIBES (1)
    HE LIVES. HIS ANSWER WILL PUT AN END TO GIBES ....DIALOGUE O.   281 174
GIBRALTER (1)
    AND LIVE IN GIBRALTAR ON AIR, ON AIR. ....STOPPED DEAD   230   25
GIDDY (2)
    REEL GIDDY IN BEDLAM SPRING: ....SPINSTER   50   23
    TO A GIDDY JOG. THEN FOR ILL WILL ....WHITENESS I REMEMBER   102   17
GIFT (9)
    ALL YOUR BEAUTY, ALL YOUR WIT, IS A GIFT, MY DEAR, ...
                            ... SOLILOQUY OF THE SOLIPSIST   38   35
    FOR THE PALTRY GIFT OF HER BULK AND THE BEAT ......HARDCASTLE CRAGS   63   27
    PURE AS A PANE OF ICE. IT'S A GIFT. ....LOVE LETTER 147   36
    EVEN THROUGH THE GIFT PAPER I COULD HEAR THEM BREATHE ....TULIPS 161   37
    AND YOUR FIRST GIFT IS MAKING STONE OUT OF EVERYTHING. ...THE RIVAL 166   6
    A GIFT, A LOVE GIFT ....POPPIES IN OCTOBER   240   4
    A GIFT, A LOVE GIFT ....POPPIES IN OCTOBER   240   4
    SIT EMPTIED OF BEAUTIES, THE GIFT ....THE NIGHT DANCES 250   8
    WILL BE OUR BEAT, JUST AS THE GIFT IS OURS, ...DIALOGUE O. 283 257
GIFTS (2)
    WITH THEIR GIFTS TO A DIFFICULT BORNING. ....THE MANOR GARDEN 125   20
    THESE GIFTS ARE GIVEN. AND WHEN WITHHELD, YOU'LL SAY ...DIALOGUE O. 279 126
GIGANTIC (5)
    AND THE SNAKECHARMER'S SONG AND THE GIGANTIC LILIES, ...YADWIGHA.   86   33
    STILL IN ONE GIGANTIC TAPESTRY -- ....IN MIDAS' COUNTRY 99   14
    AND NIGHT ARRIVES IN ONE GIGANTIC STEP. ....TWO CAMP. 145   16
    THE GIGANTIC GORILLA INTERIOR ....GETTING THERE 247   3
    IN A GIGANTIC HALL, ...AERIALIST 331   9
GIGGLE (1)
    WITH POKE AND GIGGLE, READY TO SKEDADDLE, ...ELLA MASON A.   54   25
GIGOLO (1)
    GIGOLO ....GIGOLO   267   T
GILDED (6)
    OF GILDED HARPS OR GNAWING FIRE: SIMPLY TELL ....DIALOGUE B.   39   23
    BARBS ON THE CROWN OF GILDED WIRE, ...I WANT, I WANT 106   11
    AND GILDED COUPLES ALL IN WHIRLING TRANCE ....CINDERELLA 304   9
    THE GILDED COCK WILL TURN FOR ME ....TO A JILTED LOVER 310   22
    GILDED, COMING CORRECT ....AERIALIST 331   13
    KNIT UP A GILDED FABLE FOR THE CHILD ..THE PRINCESS AND THE GOBLINS 335   73
GILDING (1)
    GILDING WHAT'S EYESORE, ...GREEN ROCK, WINTHROP BAY 105   21
GILDS (2)
    GILDS ALL OUR AVENUE, ...SOUTHERN SUNRISE   26   15
    DAWN GILDS THE FARMERS LIKE PIGS, ...TOTEM   264   5
GILLED (1)
    GILLED LIKE A FISH. A COMMON-SENSE ....YOU'RE 141   3
GILT (4)
    GILT TRUMPETS RAISE. ....A WINTER'S TALE   87   12
    THE GILT AND PINK DOMES OF RUSSIA MELT AND FLOAT OFF .....THE SWARM 216   15
    GRAY, INDETERMINATE GILT ....LYONNESSE   234   6
    FLICKER GILT: ....AQUATIC NOCTURNE 305   12
GIMCRACK (1)
    LIES, COMPANIONED BY THE GIMCRACK ....ALL THE DEAD DEARS   70   4
GIMLETS (1)
    O LITTLE GIMLETS -- ....THE JAILER 226   16
GIN (2)
    YOU HANDED ME GIN IN A GLASS BUD VASE. ....LEAVING EARLY 146   41
    SIR SO-AND-SO'S GIN. ....WINTERING 218   10
GINGERBREAD (1)
    GOT BAKED INTO GINGERBREAD, I WONDER ....THE DISQUIETING MUSES   75   12
GIPSY (1)
    WITH MY GIPSY ANCESTRESS AND MY WEIRD LUCK ....DADDY 223   38
GIRAFFE (1)
    THROUGH THE AFRICAN GIRAFFE IN ITS EDENY GREENERY, ...A SECRET 219   12
GIRDLE (1)
    WHITE BODIES IN A WOODEN GIRDLE, ROOT TO TOP ......VIRGIN IN A TREE   81   22
GIRL (20)
    WHICH HAD CAUSED HIS DEAR GIRL PAIN. ....BUCOLICS 24   20
    TO TRAP THIS WAYWARD GIRL AT HER FIRST MOVE OF LOVE,   DREAM WITH C.   44   27
    NOW THIS PARTICULAR GIRL ....SPINSTER 49   1
    THE GIRL BENT HOMEWARD, BRIMFUL OF GENTLE TALK ....SNOWMAN O.   59   50
    A GIRL COULD WADE WITHOUT WETTING HER SHINS.   A LESSON IN VENGEANCE   80   20
    WHAT GIRL EVER FLOURISHED IN SUCH COMPANY? ....MAGI   148   18
    IN ME SHE HAS DROWNED A YOUNG GIRL, AND IN ME AN OLD WOMAN ..MIRROR 174   17
    I SEE HER IN MY SLEEP, MY RED, TERRIBLE GIRL. ....THREE WOMEN   182 204
    I AM THE MAGICIAN'S GIRL WHO DOES NOT FLINCH. ......THE BEE MEETING 212   53
    THE BASTARD'S A GIRL. ....LESBOS 228   16
    YOU SAY I SHOULD DROWN MY GIRL. ....LESBOS 228   21
    I'LL CARRY IT OFF LIKE A RICH PRETTY GIRL, ...STOPPED DEAD 230   23
    DIRTY GIRL, ...CUT 236   39

		TITLE	PAGE	LINE

GIRL (CONT.)
"DON'T," PLEADED THE LITTLE GIRL ....BITTER STRAWBERRIES 299 22
THE PRINCE LEANS TO THE GIRL IN SCARLET HEELS, ...CINDERELLA 303 1
UNTIL NEAR TWELVE THE STRANGE GIRL ALL AT ONCE ....CINDERELLA 304 11
SO CRY FOR THE PAGAN GIRL LEFT PICKING OLIVES ......SONNET: TO TIME 311 9
LESSONED THUS, THE GIRL ....AERIALIST 331 19
TO KEEP THE YOUNG GIRL FROM HER CROWNING GOAL. ....THE PRINCESS. 333 18
OF THAT MERCURIAL STRAND, THE GIRL GOES DOWN ....THE PRINCESS. 334 27
GIRLS (9)
TWO GIRLS THERE ARE: WITHIN THE HOUSE ....TWO SISTERS OF PERSEPHONE 31 1
WAYLAYS SIMPLE GIRLS, CHURCH-GOING, ...VANITY FAIR 32 14
FISH-TAILED GIRLS PURCHASE EACH WHITE LEG. ....MAUDLIN 51 8
AT GIRLS WHO MARRY -- ....ELLA MASON AND HER ELEVEN CATS 54 39
APPROVING CHASED GIRLS WHO GET THEM TO A TREE .....VIRGIN IN A TREE 81 4
THREE GIRLS, ENGROSSED, WERE WRENCHING FULL CLUSTERS RHODODENDRON. 104 15
A CROCODILE OF SMALL GIRLS ....PARLIAMENT HILL FIELDS 152 13
BY PALE GIRLS, TRAVEL THE AIR IN SCORCHED HANDS. ....BERCK-PLAGE 196 4
TWO GIRLS ....PARALYTIC 266 25
GIRL'S (1)
EACH VAIN GIRL'S DRIVEN ....VANITY FAIR 33 25
GIVE (14)
GIVE GRASS ITS GREEN ....SOLILOQUY OF THE SOLIPSIST 37 21
GIVE ME BACK MY SHAPE. I AM READY TO CONSTRUE THE DAYS ...POEM.6.W. 136 21
AND SEEMED TO GIVE HER WARMTH, LIKE A LIVE SKIN. ....WIDOW 164 19
THE NURSES GIVE BACK MY CLOTHES, AND AN IDENTITY. ...THREE WOMEN 183 241
CAN YOU NOT GIVE IT TO ME? ....A BIRTHDAY PRESENT 206 21
I KNOW WHY YOU WILL NOT GIVE IT TO ME, ...A BIRTHDAY PRESENT 207 27
THERE IS THIS ONE THING I WANT TODAY, AND ONLY YOU CAN GIVE
IT TO ME. ....A BIRTHDAY PRESENT 207 48
HOW CAN WE GIVE YOU A THING? ....THE APPLICANT 221 7
OF CLOUD TO GIVE THEM EXPRESSION, ...BRASILIA 258 5
TO GIVE ANOTHER INCH. IF YOU PREFER, ...DIALOGUE OVER A OUIJA BOARD 281 179
TO NAME HIS HOME A THIRD TIME. GIVE YOUR WILL THREE ....DIALOGUE O. 283 269
THIS BOARD OUR BATTLEFIELD. LET'S GIVE PAN UP ....DIALOGUE O. 284 292
HIM YET, AND GIVE US GOOD REASON. NO, HE'S ON ....DIALOGUE O. 284 295
ALL ABSOLUTES THAT ANGELS GIVE   INSOLENT STORM STRIKES AT THE SKULL 326 23
GIVEN (10)
"TEA LEAVES I'VE GIVEN UP, ...RECANTATION 41 1
TO GOVERN MORE SIGHT THAN GIVEN TO A WOMAN ....CRYSTAL GAZER 55 32
NEVER GIVEN; HIDDEN, YET ....THE GREAT CARBUNCLE 72 12
GIVEN HER LIPS THAT LEMON-TASTING DROOP: ....VIRGIN IN A TREE 82 42
GIVEN AN INCH. NOT THAT THEY'RE GROSS (ALTHOUGH .....POEMS, POTATOES 106 6
I HAVE GIVEN MY NAME AND MY DAY-CLOTHES UP TO THE NURSES ....TULIPS 160 6
THERE IS NO HOPE, IT IS GIVEN UP. ....BERCK-PLAGE 201 126
WHY AM I GIVEN ....THE NIGHT DANCES 250 22
A SPACE FOR THE THING I AM GIVEN, ...THALIDOMIDE 252 18
THESE GIFTS ARE GIVEN. AND WHEN WITHHELD, YOU'LL SAY ...DIALOGUE O. 279 126
GIVES (10)
AUGUST GIVES OVER ITS MIDAS TOUCH, ...IN MIDAS' COUNTRY 100 24
PUT UP WITH UNTIL CHAGRIN GIVES PLACE ....THE COMPANIONABLE ILLS 105 3
THE MIRROR GIVES BACK A WOMAN WITHOUT DEFORMITY. ....THREE WOMEN 183 240
THAT GIVES IT A KINGLINESS, A RIGHT. ....PHEASANT 191 10
THE SUN GIVES YOU ULCERS, THE WIND GIVES YOU T.B. ....LESBOS 228 39
THE SUN GIVES YOU ULCERS, THE WIND GIVES YOU T.B. ....LESBOS 228 39
THE YOUNGEST NEPHEW GIVES A FRETFUL WHINE ....FAMILY REUNION 301 23
NO VIOLATION BUT GIVES DIVIDENDS .........METAMORPHOSES OF THE MOON 307 13
RAISED TO TOAST A THOUSAND KINGS, FOR ALL GIVES ....SONNET: TO TIME 311 11
THE MAESTRO GIVES THE SINGING BIRDS THEIR PAY ....DENOUEMENT 326 4
GIVING (6)
GIVING A LEG UP ....WORDS FOR A NURSERY 73 9
COMET COOLLY GIVING MY ....MUSSEL HUNTER AT ROCK HARBOR 96 57
GIVING EVERYBODY A FAIR HEARING. ....CANDLES 149 11
SPACE! SPACE! THE BED LINEN WAS GIVING OUT ENTIRELY. ....WAKING. 151 11
NOW THEY ARE GIVING ME A FASHIONABLE WHITE STRAW ITALIAN HAT ...BEE. 211 21
GIVING A SHRIEK AND POP ....BALLOONS 271 7
GIZZARD (2)
INTO THE ROCKY GIZZARD OF THE EARTH, ...THE GHOST'S LEAVETAKING 90 24
THE SEA IN ITS COLD GIZZARD GROUND THOSE ROUNDS. .....POINT SHIRLEY 110 24
GLAD (2)
HE SAUNTERS IN; HOW BUT MOST GLAD ....ODE FOR TED 29 21
AND WE ARE GLAD IN THIS BRIGHT METAL SEASON. ....GOLD MOUTHS CRY 302 8
GLADIOLAS (1)
WILL THE HIVE SURVIVE, WILL THE GLADIOLAS ....WINTERING 219 46
GLADLY (1)
I WOULD HAVE KILLED MYSELF GLADLY THAT TIME ANY POSSIBLE WAY. ...
... A BIRTHDAY PRESENT 206 15
GLANCE (1)
CASTLES WHEN WE GLANCE ASIDE. THAT'S THAT. ....DIALOGUE O. 286 356
GLARE (6)
AND DARKLY GLARE, ...PROSPECT 28 8
STRAIGHT INTO YELLOW GLARE ....ELLA MASON AND HER ELEVEN CATS 54 27
GOD'S WORK STOOD ANCHORED IN THAT GLARE ....CRYSTAL GAZER 55 38
AND BY THAT GLARE, MY LOVE WILL SEE ....TO A JILTED LOVER 310 25
TRANSFIXED BY GLARE OF BLUE FROM GORGON'S EYE; ..PROLOGUE TO SPRING 322 2
TO SEEK THE STAIRCASE BY THE GLARE OF DAY. ....THE PRINCESS. 334 53

```
                                                   TITLE              PAGE  LINE
GLARED (1)
    THE COUCH GLARED OUT AT THE PROSAIC EYE.  ................YADWIGHA.    85   20
GLASS (46)
    OF BROKEN GLASS,  .....................MISS DRAKE PROCEEDS TO SUPPER   41   20
    WITH SHINGLES BURNISHED AS GLASS,  ..........DREAM WITH CLAM-DIGGERS   43    7
    STILL AS A SHELL: HEAR WHAT AN AGE OF GLASS  ........EPITAPH FOR F.    45   16
    FROM THE MERCURY-BACKED GLASS  ....................ALL THE DEAD DEARS  70   19
    RISES TO THE GLASS FROM HIS BLACK FATHOMS.  ................OUIJA      77    2
    THE GLASS MOUTH SUCKS BLOOD-HEAT FROM MY FOREFINGER.  .........OUIJA   77   10
    DOUBLING THEMSELVES IN A GLASS  .............................LORELEI   94    8
    THE SKY'S GREAT BELL GLASS AND BRIEFLY ENGRAVE  ...IN MIDAS' COUNTRY   99    8
    STILLED, SILVERED AS WATER IN A GLASS  ................WATERCOLOR.    111    2
    SUNSET LOOKED AT THROUGH MILK GLASS.  .....................MEDALLION  124   20
    YOU HANDED ME GIN IN A GLASS BUD VASE.  ...............LEAVING EARLY  146   41
    MY FINGER-LENGTH GREW LUCENT AS GLASS.  ...................LOVE LETTER 147   30
    FLICK THE GLASS WITH YOUR FINGERNAIL:  ......................A LIFE   150    6
    BLUE SHRUB BEHIND THE GLASS  ...............PARLIAMENT HILL FIELDS    153   45
    CLAMBERING ROUND ITS GLASS BOX LIKE AN EIGHT-FINGERED HAND.  ZOO K.   155   31
    TO WANT THE WORLD IN A GLASS HAT.  ..........NEW YEAR ON DARTMOOR     176    9
    SHE IS CRYING THROUGH THE GLASS THAT SEPARATES US.  .....THREE WOMEN  182  205
    THEY HAVE LIVED BEHIND GLASS ALL THEIR LIVES, THEY HAVE BEEN CARED
         FOR TENDERLY.  ......................................THREE WOMEN 184  264
    BEHIND THE GLASS OF THIS CAR  ............................BERCK-PLAGE 200  109
    COLD GLASS, HOW YOU INSERT YOURSELF  ....................THE OTHER    202   26
    OR YOUR LIQUORS SEEP TO ME, IN THIS GLASS CAPSULE,  POPPIES IN JULY   203   13
    A GLASS CASE  ...............................BURNING THE LETTERS      204   16
    WITH HER LION-RED BODY, HER WINGS OF GLASS?  ................STINGS    215   55
    A GLASS EYE, FALSE TEETH OR A CRUTCH,  ...............THE APPLICANT   221    3
    MILLIONS OF NEEDLY GLASS CAKES!  ..........................THE TOUR   238   18
    FLOATED ON A GLASS THAT WAS INVISIBLE.  ....................GULLIVER  251    4
    THE GLASS CRACKS ACROSS,  ...............................THALIDOMIDE  252   24
    GO GET THE GLASS, THEN. BUT I KNOW TONIGHT WILL BE  .....DIALOGUE O.  276    1
    SO THE ARTFUL GLASS WON'T CHANGE ITS CHILL FOR HEART'S  DIALOGUE O.   277   17
    ALWAYS, THE GLASS WILL BLURT WHAT I DON'T WANT  .........DIALOGUE O.  278   68
    THE GLASS YET AS HE GLIDES. P-L-U-  .....DIALOGUE OVER A OUIJA BOARD  278   77
    OUR SEPARATE VEINS AND THIS GLASS MOUTH. OH YOU'RE  ....DIALOGUE O.   280  147
    ONE OF A GIANT'S EAR? I GUESS THIS GLASS*DIALOGUE OVER A OUIJA BOARD  281  201
    MIGHT WORK ON THIS GLASS MEDIUM. BELIEF, YES,  ..........DIALOGUE O.  282  225
    (BREAKING GLASS)  .................DIALOGUE OVER A OUIJA BOARD        284   SD
    I SMASHED A GLASS, AND EVER SINCE THAT DREAM  ...........DIALOGUE O.  285  302
    THOSE GLASS BITS IN THE GRATE STRIKE ME CHILL:  ........DIALOGUE O.   285  306
    AS THE GLASS FLEW TO ITS FRAGMENTS. LET US STAKE  ......DIALOGUE O.   285  328
    MY GLASS OF WATER REFRACTS THE MORNING.  ................FEVER./DR    294   11
    THE WHOLE REVOLVING TALL GLASS PALACE HALL  ..............CINDERELLA  304    5
    IN GLASS PAGODAS HUNG WITH VEILS OF GREEN  ............APRIL AUBADE   312    2
    FRACTURED GLASS FLIES DOWN IN SMITHEREENS;  ...............DOOMSDAY   316   10
    AIR ALTERS INTO GLASS AND THE WHOLE SKY  ........PROLOGUE TO SPRING   322    4
    IN THE SCORCHING GLASS,  ..ON LOOKING INTO THE EYES OF A DEMON LOVER  325   18
    TO TRAVERSE GLASS FLOOR  ................................AERIALIST    331   27
    SUNLIGHT STRIKES A GLASS OF GRAPEFRUIT JUICE,  ..MORNING IN THE HOS.  332    1
GLASSED (2)
    IN A GLASSED TABLEAU OF AFFLUENCE.  ...........................OWL    102    7
    IGNITED WITH A GLASSED FLAME  ...........................MEDALLION    124   10
GLASSES (2)
    THAT SUMMER WE WORE BLACK GLASSES TO HIDE OUR EYES. *THE BABYSITTERS  174    3
    IS IT ANY WONDER HE PUTS ON DARK GLASSES?  .............BERCK-PLAGE   196   12
GLASS-WRAPPED (1)
    OBSTACLE GLASS-WRAPPED AND PECULIAR,  .........NEW YEAR ON DARTMOOR   176    2
GLASSY (3)
    ENCASED IN A GLASSY PELLICLE.  ......................A WINTER SHIP    113   28
    RIPPLED AND PULSED IN THE GLASSY UPDRAUGHT.  ...SUICIDE OFF EGG ROCK  115    5
    THE GLASSY LIGHT WAS A CLEAR WALL,  ..............THE RABBIT CATCHER  194   19
GLAUCOUS (1)
    EXHIBITS ITS GLAUCOUS SILKS,  ...............................WHITSUN  154   15
GLAZE (1)
    THE GLAZE, THE MIRRORY VARIETY OF IT.  ...........A BIRTHDAY PRESENT  207   25
GLAZED (1)
    OF THE GLAZED WATER  .........................DARK WOOD, DARK WATER   127    9
GLAZES (2)
    GLAZES THE WINDOW OF MY HURT; WHAT SOLACE  ........WINTER LANDSCAPE,   22   13
    GLAZES THE ROCK POOLS YET,  ...........................MAN IN BLACK   119   11
GLEAM (5)
    THEY GLEAM LIKE EASTER EGGSHELLS,  ....................BATTLE-SCENE    84   25
    SO THAT EACH MARCH I MAY GLEAM INTO LEAF,  .............I AM VERTICAL 162    4
    GLEAM LIKE SMALL CHANGE.  ........................WUTHERING HEIGHTS   168   45
    LET US SIT DOWN TO IT, ONE ON EITHER SIDE, ADMIRING THE GLEAM,  ...
                                               ... A BIRTHDAY PRESENT    207   24
    I GLEAM LIKE A MIRROR.  ......................................PURDAH  242   18
GLEAMING (1)
    GLEAMING WITH THE MOUTHS OF CORPSES.  ...............CHILDLESS WOMAN  259   18
GLEAMS (1)
    GLEAMS, WIRED TO A TALL ULMUS  ....................A WINTER'S TALE     86    2
GLIDE (1)
    THAT GLIDE AHEAD OF THE VERY THIRSTY.  ...SLEEP IN THE MOJAVE DESERT  144   13
```

GLIDED (1)
    HE GLIDED BY; HIS EYE HAD A BLACK MEANING. ....THREE WOMEN   178   53
GLIDES (4)
    MOST SOFT, MOST SUAVELY GLIDES THAT STEP, ...PURSUIT   22   5
    WHILE THE DAY OUTSIDE GLIDES BY LIKE TICKER TAPE. ....PARALYTIC   266   10
    KINDNESS GLIDES ABOUT MY HOUSE. ....KINDNESS   269   1
    THE GLASS YET AS HE GLIDES. P-L-U- .....DIALOGUE OVER A OUIJA BOARD   278   77
GLIDING (3)
    WITH GREEN ROCK GLIDING, A DELICATE SCHOONER*DREAM WITH CLAM-DIGGERS   44   17
    GLIDING UP IN LOW GEAR BEHIND THE CART. ....BERCK-PLAGE   200 112
    WHERE GUESTS SLIDE GLIDING INTO LIGHT LIKE WINE; ....CINDERELLA   304   6
GLIMPSE (2)
    TO SUCH CROSS-PURPOSES? AT LAST YOU GLIMPSE ....DIALOGUE O.   284 289
    SOME LIGHT. I GLIMPSE NO LIGHT AT ALL AS LONG ....DIALOGUE O.   284 290
GLINTING (1)
    GLINTING AND CLINKING IN A SAINT'S FALSETTO. ONLY YOU   NEW YEAR ON. 176   3
GLINTS (2)
    SUN MANAGES TO STRIKE SUCH TIN GLINTS ....PARLIAMENT HILL FIELDS 152   10
    WATCHING FOR GLINTS, ...BURNING THE LETTERS 204   26
GLISSANDO (1)
    BLOOD RUNS IN A GLISSANDO FROM THE HAND .....EPITAPH IN THREE PARTS 337   18
GLISTER (1)
    CAN BE MADE TO GLISTER ....TINKER JACK AND THE TIDY WIVES   34   13
GLITTER (7)
    THEY GLITTER LIKE EYES, AND I COLLECT THEM ALL. .....PRIVATE GROUND 131   22
    ITS ENDLESS GLITTER. POEM.3.MAENAD. 133   20
    A GLITTER OF WHEAT AND CRUDE EARTH. ....BERCK-PLAGE   200   96
    FOAM TO WHEAT, A GLITTER OF SEAS. ....ARIEL   239   23
    MASTURBATING A GLITTER, ...DEATH & CO.   254   24
    THERE IS NO MERCY IN THE GLITTER OF CLEAVERS, ...TOTEM   264   9
    GLITTER LIKE FONTAINEBLEAU ....GIGOLO   268   28
GLITTERED (2)
    EVERYTHING GLITTERED LIKE BLANK PAPER. ....SUICIDE OFF EGG ROCK 115   20
    TREE AND STONE GLITTERED, WITHOUT SHADOWS. ....LOVE LETTER   147   29
GLITTERING (7)
    ITS GLITTERING SURFACES ARE BLANK AND TRUE. ....TALE OF A TUB   25   32
    ON THE BALCONIES OF THE HOTEL, THINGS ARE GLITTERING. ..BERCK-PLAGE 197   37
    THEY WOULD FLUTTER OFF, BLACK AND GLITTERING, THEY WOULD BE COAL
        ANGELS ....BURNING THE LETTERS   204   33
    WHITE AS BABIES' BEDDING AND GLITTERING WITH DEAD BREATH. O
        IVORY! ....A BIRTHDAY PRESENT   206   18
    GLITTERING ....THE MUNICH MANNEQUINS   263   25
    GLITTERING AND DIGESTING ....THE MUNICH MANNEQUINS   263   26
    GLITTERING AND DRUNK AS FLIES ....MYSTIC   268   3
GLITTERS (3)
    EACH WAVE-TIP GLITTERS LIKE A KNIFE. ....A WINTER SHIP 113   30
    WHILE THE HEATH GRASS GLITTERS AND THE SPINDLING RIVULETS ...
        ... PARLIAMENT HILL FIELDS   153   34
    AND THE BOTTLES OF EMPTY GLITTERS --- ....WINTERING   218   9
GLITTERY (2)
    SOUND, WITH A GLITTERY WISP ....MUSSEL HUNTER AT ROCK HARBOR   96   47
    OR THOSE GLITTERY FICTIONS OF SPILT WATER*SLEEP IN THE MOJAVE DESERT 144   12
GLOAT (1)
    A THIRD TIME. DON'T GLOAT. YOUR WILL MISFIRED TWICE ....DIALOGUE O. 284 281
GLOBE (4)
    THUMB CAN MAKE ANYONE WINCE, BUT THE WHOLE GLOBE ....PERSEUS   83   28
    BUT TRUNDLE ROUND THE GLOBE ....FEVER. 231   16
    LULLED IN THE AMPLE WOMB OF THE FULL-TILT GLOBE. ....THE DEAD 320   4
    LIGHTNING CONJURES GOD'S GLOBE OFF ITS ....INSOLENT STORM. 326   25
GLOBED (1)
    WE HEFT GLOBED FLINT, RACKED IN VEINS' BARBED BINDINGS; ...FIRESONG   30   18
GLOBES (3)
    THESE LITTLE GLOBES OF LIGHT ARE SWEET AS PEARS. ....CANDLES   149   24
    GLOBES OF THIN AIR, RED, GREEN, ...BALLOONS   271   14
    DULL LUNAR GLOBES ....AQUATIC NOCTURNE   306   16
GLOOM (1)
    TO LOOM IN THE LEAF-FILTERED GLOOM ....CHILD'S PARK STONES   100   4
GLOOMY (1)
    NOW IT IS ONLY GLOOMY, A DUMP OF ROCKS -- ....FINISTERRE   169   6
GLORIFIED (1)
    GLORIFIED FOR PRIME FLESH AND GOLDEN CRACKLING ....SOW   60   15
GLORY (5)
    NO GLORY DESCENDS ....RESOLVE   52   12
    BEEN STRUCK TO KEEP ALL GLORY IN THE GRIP ....VIRGIN IN A TREE   82   32
    MORNING GLORY POOL! ....THE TOUR 238   28
    THE GLORY ....BRASILIA   259   23
    THE POWER, THE GLORY. ....BRASILIA   259   24
GLOSS (1)
    NO LAME EXCUSES CAN GLOSS OVER ....GREEN ROCK, WINTHROP BAY   104   1
GLOTTAL (1)
    WORMS IN THE GLOTTAL STOPS. ....THE FEARFUL   256   9
GLOVE (1)
    WHAT GLOVE ....THALIDOMIDE   252   7
GLOVED (2)
    GLOVED MY ARM TO THE ELBOW. ....ZOO KEEPER'S WIFE   155   37

GLOVED (CONT.)
    AND THEY ARE ALL GLOVED AND COVERED, WHY DID NOBODY TELL ME? ..BEE.   211   4
GLOVES (4)
    SHAPELESS AS FLUNG GLOVES, A FEW FEET APART -- ....BLUE MOLES   126   3
    SMALL DROPS SPOT THEIR COATS, THEIR GLOVES: ....ON DECK   143   16
    SHINING GLOVES AND WHITE SUIT. ....THE BEE MEETING   211   29
    THEIR DEATH-PEGS STUD YOUR GLOVES, IT IS NO USE RUNNING. STINGS/DR   293   8
GLOW (4)
    IN THEIR JARS THE SNAIL-NOSED BABIES MOON AND GLOW. .....TWO VIEWS.   114   10
    IN YOUR SISTER'S BIRTHDAY PICTURE START TO GLOW. .....PARLIAMENT H.   153   42
    MY VEINS GLOW LIKE TREES. ....BURNING THE LETTERS   205   48
    GLOW MILKGREEN: ....AQUATIC NOCTURNE   306   18
GLOWED (1)
    THE OVENS GLOWED LIKE HEAVENS, INCANDESCENT. ....MARY'S SONG   257   18
GLOWER (1)
    AS WE TWO GLOWER FROM OUR SEPARATE CAMPS, ...DIALOGUE O.   284 291
GLOWERING (2)
    GLOWERING AT THE COAL-FIRE: "COME FIND ME" -- HER LAST TAUNT. ...
                                  ... THE SNOWMAN ON THE MOOR   58   5
    GLOWERING SULLEN AND POMPOUS FROM AN ASH-HEAP, ...LADY AND T.   69   11
GLOWING (3)
    SO POSSESSED BY THE GLOWING RED OF THE COUCH WHICH YOU, ..YADWIGHA.   86   36
    THE HIGH GREEN MEADOWS ARE GLOWING, AS IF LIT FROM WITHIN.*BLACKBER. 168   14
    GLOWING AND COMING AND GOING, FLUSH ON FLUSH. ....FEVER.   232   42
GLOWS (1)
    PANSY, IT GLOWS. O IT'S ....POLLY'S TREE   128   28
GLOWWORM (1)
    AND SINGING THE GLOWWORM SONG, I COULD ....THE DISQUIETING MUSES   75   27
GLUE (2)
    OOZING THE GLUE DROPS, ...POEM.2.DARK.   132   5
    AND THEY STUCK ME TOGETHER WITH GLUE. ....DADDY   224   62
GLUED (2)
    PIECED, GLUED, AND PROPERLY JOINTED. ....THE COLOSSUS   129   2
    UNDER THE GLUED SHEET FROM WHICH HIS POWDERY BEAK ......BERCK-PLAGE   198   63
GLUEPOTS (1)
    SCALING LITTLE LADDERS WITH GLUEPOTS AND PAILS OF LYSOL*THE COLOSSUS   129   11
GLUING (1)
    ALL DAY, GLUING MY CHURCH OF BURNT MATCHSTICKS, ...THE JAILER   227   26
GLUT (3)
    MEAT MUST GLUT HIS MOUTH'S RAW WOUND. ....PURSUIT   22   16
    GLUT THESE HUNTERS AFTER AN OLD MEAT, ...AFTERMATH   113   7
    UNTIL IN DISENCHANTMENT OUR EYES GLUT ....METAMORPHOSES OF THE MOON   308   34
GLUTTED (1)
    ANNOUNCING AFTER GLUTTED BIRDS HAVE FLOWN: ..EPITAPH IN THREE PARTS   337   21
GLUTTON (1)
    THE GLUTTON ....THE GLUTTON   40   T
GLUTTONIES (1)
    PRODIGIOUS IN GLUTTONIES AS THAT HOG WHOSE WANT ....SOW   61   41
G-MEN (1)
    "O MAY G-MEN ALL DIE OF THE CHOLER, ...DIALOGUE EN ROUTE   308   15
GNAT (1)
    YOUR CRY FADES LIKE THE CRY OF A GNAT. ......PARLIAMENT HILL FIELDS   153   32
GNAW (1)
    RED CLOVER OR GNAW BEETROOT .....WATERCOLOR OF GRANTCHESTER MEADOWS   112   17
GNAWED (1)
    "IN LIFE, LOVE GNAWED MY SKIN ....DIALOGUE BETWEEN GHOST AND PRIEST   39   27
GNAWING (1)
    OF GILDED HARPS OR GNAWING FIRE: SIMPLY TELL ....DIALOGUE B.   39   23
GNAWINGS (1)
    WHILE THE GNAWINGS OF LOVE BEGIN. ....CIRCUS IN THREE RINGS   322   12
GNAWN (1)
    ...WOMAN HAS BEEN SLIGHTLY GNAWN. ....ALL THE DEAD DEARS   70 E/4
GNAWS (1)
    GNAWS ME THROUGH." ....DIALOGUE BETWEEN GHOST AND PRIEST   39   30
GO (66)
    RAT-SHREWD GO HER SQUINT EYES, ...TWO SISTERS OF PERSEPHONE   31   11
    BY A MAD MIRACLE I GO INTACT ....STREET SONG   35   1
    GOODBYES WERE SAID, TRAINS LET GO, ...MONOLOGUE AT 3 A.M.   40   12
    GO TO YOUR GREENHORN YOUTH ....RECANTATION   42   17
    LET FLESH BE KNIT, AND EACH STEP HENCE GO FAMOUS. ....WREATH F.   45   24
    VILLAGE STORIES GO THAT IN OLDEN DAYS*ELLA MASON AND HER ELEVEN CATS   53   13
    MAKING THE WORLD GO THIN AS A WASP'S NEST ....THE THIN PEOPLE   65   46
    AND THE OPULENT AIR GO STUDDED WITH SEED, ...CONJURING.   66   36
    AND TACK OF THE CLOCK, UNTIL WE GO, ...ALL THE DEAD DEARS   71   33
    I SHALL GO DOWN THE SHABBY STAIR AND MEET,*ON THE DECLINE OF ORACLES   78   27
    SO FABLES GO. ....BATTLE-SCENE   85   31
    DIDN'T GO DOWN IN SUCH A HURRY. HOW IT MEMOIRS OF A SPINACH-PICKER   89   2
    GO, GHOST OF OUR MOTHER AND FATHER, GHOST OF US, ...GHOST'S.   91   32
    I'LL GO OUT AND SIT IN WHITE LIKE THEY DO, ...MOONRISE   98   2
    YEARS, GO DOWN TO DRINK THE RIVER: ....CHILD'S PARK STONES   101   29
    A SERVICE AND IGNORE IT, I GO A LIAR ......GREEN ROCK, WINTHROP BAY   105   20
    WHERE THE MOST WATCHFUL COOKS GO JOBLESS ....THE TIMES ARE TIDY   107   3
    THEY GO BEFORE: OPENING THE VEINS, ...BLUE MOLES   126   29
    I NEED HARDLY GO OUT AT ALL. ....PRIVATE GROUND   130   14
    O I AM TOO BIG TO GO BACKWARD: POEM.3.MAENAD.   133   8

GO (CONT.)
    ALREADY YOUR DOLL GRIP LETS GO. ....PARLIAMENT HILL FIELDS 152   25
    I USED TO THINK WE MIGHT MAKE A GO OF IT TOGETHER -- ....IN PLASTER 160   50
    IT LOOKS IN ON, AND MUST GO ON LOOKING IN ON. ....WIDOW 165   40
    HOLLOW DOORSTEPS GO FROM GRASS TO GRASS; ....WUTHERING HEIGHTS   168   31
    OVERHEAD GO THE CHOUGHS IN BLACK, CACOPHONOUS FLOCKS -- ..BLACKBER.   168   10
    THEY GO UP WITHOUT HOPE, LIKE SIGHS. ....FINISTERRE   169   16
    AND THE SEVEN-YEAR-OLD WOULDN'T GO OUT UNLESS HIS JERSEY
        STRIPES ....THE BABYSITTERS   174   8
    THEY WOULD GO MAD WITH IT. ....THREE WOMEN   180 119
    I SHALL NOT LET GO. ....THREE WOMEN   181 174
    I DO NOT EVEN NEED A HOLIDAY; I CAN GO TO WORK TODAY. ..THREE WOMEN   183 249
    THERE IS VERY LITTLE TO GO INTO MY SUITCASE. ....THREE WOMEN   184 266
    I AM A WOUND THAT THEY ARE LETTING GO. ....THREE WOMEN   184 271
    WHO WOULD ADHERE TO ME: I UNDO HER FINGERS LIKE BANDAGES: I GO. ...
                                                     ... THREE WOMEN   184 273
    COLD CLOUDS GO OVER. ....LITTLE FUGUE   187   2
    WHERE DO THE BLACK TREES GO THAT DRINK HERE? ....CROSSING THE WATER   190   2
    I LET HER GO. I LET HER GO ....ELM 192   25
    I LET HER GO. I LET HER GO ....ELM 192   25
    THE WORLD WILL GO UP IN A SHRIEK, AND YOUR HEAD WITH IT, BIRTHDAY.   207   29
    I WILL ONLY TAKE IT AND GO ASIDE QUIETLY. ....A BIRTHDAY PRESENT   207   33
    IS IT IMPOSSIBLE FOR YOU TO LET SOMETHING GO AND HAVE IT GO WHOLE? ...
                                          ... A BIRTHDAY PRESENT   207   45
    IS IT IMPOSSIBLE FOR YOU TO LET SOMETHING GO AND HAVE IT GO WHOLE? ...
                                          ... A BIRTHDAY PRESENT   207   45
    OVER YOUR BODY THE CLOUDS GO ....GULLIVER 251   1
    DISCHARGES ITSELF FROM THE TREE WITH NOWHERE TO GO. *CHILDLESS WOMAN 259   3
    INTO WHICH BROAD TOES WILL GO TOMORROW. ......THE MUNICH MANNEQUINS   263   20
    IT HAPPENS. WILL IT GO ON? --- ....PARALYTIC 266   1
    GO GET THE GLASS, THEN. BUT I KNOW TONIGHT WILL BE .....DIALOGUE O.   276   1
    THEY'LL GO BY, TRUNDLING LIKE MARBLE STATUES WAY OUT ...DIALOGUE O.   276   6
    TO ALTER HER WILL OUR WAY. SHALL WE GO ON ....DIALOGUE O.   277   49
    TO KNOW AT ALL. AND YET I GO AHEAD. ....DIALOGUE OVER A OUIJA BOARD   278   69
    AND GET US CLEAR OF THIS. OH, HE'LL GO CLEVER ....DIALOGUE O.   281 175
    THEM ANY MORE THAN YOU DID. OH, LET IT GO. ....DIALOGUE O.   283 265
    TO OUR MEANING WELL. WHEN LIGHTS GO OUT *DIALOGUE OVER A OUIJA BOARD 286 363
    THE MOON IS LET GO, LIKE A DEAD THING. ....ELM/DR   292   8
    OLD ENOUGH TO GO. ....BITTER STRAWBERRIES   299   11
    IN SOLAR SCHEMES THE TILTED SUNS GO TURNING; ....TO EVA DESCENDING.   303   11
    NOW THERE IS NOWHERE I CAN GO ....TO A JILTED LOVER   310   16
    MY LOVE AND I GO GARLANDED WITH GRASS. ....APRIL AUBADE   312   12
    GO GET THE GOODLY SQUAB ....GO GET THE GOODLY SQUAB   313   T
    GO GET THE GOODLY SQUAB IN GOLD-LOBED CORN   GO GET THE GOODLY SQUAB 313   1
    GO SNARE THE SLEEPING BEAR IN LEAF-LINED DEN*GO GET THE GOODLY SQUAB 313   9
    GO CULL THE PURPLE SNAILS FROM SLOTHFUL SHELLS ....GO GET.   313   17
    FIRST LET THE HEAVENLY FOLIAGE GO, ...SONG FOR A REVOLUTIONARY LOVE   322   2
    BUT, GO! THEY CRY, AND THE SWING ....TOUCH-AND-GO   335   13
    GO! AND THE MERRY-GO-ROUND ....TOUCH-AND-GO   335   15
    GO BAD TO THE CORE. ....TEMPER OF TIME 336   4
    THE THIRD CRIES OUT AS ALL THE SHIPS GO DOWN:*EPITAPH IN THREE PARTS 337   10
GOAL (2)
    A PERIODIC GOAL. ....TRIO OF LOVE SONGS   314   36
    TO KEEP THE YOUNG GIRL FROM HER CROWNING GOAL. ....THE PRINCESS.   333   18
GOAT (2)
    VAMPIRING DRY OF MILK EACH GREAT GOAT UDDER. ....GOATSUCKER 111   4
    YET IT NEVER MILKED ANY GOAT, NOR DEALT COW DEATH ....GOATSUCKER   111   12
GOATHERDS (1)
    OLD GOATHERDS SWEAR HOW ALL NIGHT LONG THEY HEAR ....GOATSUCKER   111   1
GOATHERD'S (1)
    BEHIND A GOATHERD'S HUT: ....SPIDER 48 10
GOAT-HORNS (1)
    GOAT-HORNS. MARKED HOW GOD ROSE ....FAUN 35 14
GOATISH (1)
    THESE GOATISH TRAGEDIANS WHO ....THE BEGGARS   47   2
GOATS (3)
    GOATS SHAMBLE, MOROSE, RANK-HAIRED, ...DEPARTURE   51   19
    BELLS, HOOVES, OF THE HIGH-STEPPING BLACK GOATS WOKE US. OTHER TWO. 68   3
    THE HOUSES ARE WHITE AS SEA-SALT GOATS LICK FROM THE ROCKS. ..NET-. 121   10
GOATSUCKER (3)
    GOATSUCKER ....GOATSUCKER   111   T
    BY CLAW-CUTS OF THE GOATSUCKER, ALIAS DEVIL-BIRD, ...GOATSUCKER   111   7
    SO FABLES SAY THE GOATSUCKER MOVES, MASKED FROM MEN'S SIGHT ...
                                          ... GOATSUCKER   111   9
GOAT-THIGHED (1)
    WHETHER GOAT-THIGHED OR GOD-HALOED. EVER SINCE THAT FIRST DAPHNE ...
                                          ... VIRGIN IN A TREE   81   9
GOBBLEDYGOO (1)
    WITH YOUR LUFTWAFFE, YOUR GOBBLEDYGOO. ....DADDY   223   42
GO-BETWEEN (1)
    TO COLLECT HIS BEATINGS. AND IF HE'S A GO-BETWEEN ......DIALOGUE O.   281 185
GOBLETS (1)
    PITCHERS AND CORONATION GOBLETS ....LEAVING EARLY   145   9
GOBLIN (3)
    THIS MINER'S BOY FROM GOBLIN BODYGUARD.*THE PRINCESS AND THE GOBLINS 333 25

                                                          TITLE   PAGE   LINE
GOBLIN (CONT.)
    ABOUT A GOBLIN RAID ON MINER'S HUT   ....THE PRINCESS AND THE GOBLINS   334   38
    GAILY CURSING THE WHOLE GOBLIN HORDE.   THE PRINCESS AND THE GOBLINS   334   46
GOBLINS (2)
    THE PRINCESS AND THE GOBLINS   ....THE PRINCESS AND THE GOBLINS   333   T
    GRASSHOPPER GOBLINS WITH GREEN POINTED EARS   EPITAPH IN THREE PARTS   337   23
GO-BY (1)
    ORBIT THE GO-BY, MADE KNOWN   ....MUSSEL HUNTER AT ROCK HARBOR   96   58
GOD (41)
    GOAT-HORNS. MARKED HOW GOD ROSE   ....FAUN   35   14
    GOD ORDAINED TO FOLLOW UP YOUR DAYS. IS IT SUCH TROUBLE *DIALOGUE B.   39   25
    GOD KNOWS HOW OUR NEIGHBOR MANAGED TO BREED   ....SOW   60   1
    IT IS A CHILLY GOD, A GOD OF SHADES, ...OUIJA   77   1
    IT IS A CHILLY GOD, A GOD OF SHADES, ...OUIJA   77   1
    THE OLD GOD DRIBBLES, IN RETURN, HIS WORDS.   ....OUIJA   77   11
    THE OLD GOD, TOO, WRITES AUREATE POETRY   ....OUIJA   77   12
    DIMINISHES, AND GOD KNOWS WHAT IS THERE.   ...THE GHOST'S LEAVETAKING   91   26
    OPEN-MOUTHED, THE BABY GOD   ....I WANT, I WANT   106   1
    MOUTHPIECE OF THE DEAD, OR OF SOME GOD OR OTHER.   ....THE COLOSSUS   129   7
    AND HOW A GOD FLIMSY AS A BABY'S FINGER POEM.5.F.   135   19
    BY THE ROOTS OF MY HAIR SOME GOD GOT HOLD OF ME.   ...THE HANGING MAN   141   1
    NOW I RESEMBLE A SORT OF GOD   ....LOVE LETTER   147   34
    THE VOICE OF GOD IS FULL OF DRAFTINESS, ...WIDOW   164   22
    THE GRASSES UNLOAD THEIR GRIEFS ON MY FEET AS IF I WERE GOD,   MOON.   172   3
    THE EYE OF A LITTLE GOD, FOUR-CORNERED.   ....MIRROR   173   5
    O GOD, HOW SHALL I EVER CLEAN THE PHONE TABLE?   .....WORDS HEARD.   202   8
    MY GOD, WHAT A LAUGH!"   ....A BIRTHDAY PRESENT   206   10
    BUT MY GOD, THE CLOUDS ARE LIKE COTTON.   ....A BIRTHDAY PRESENT   207   39
    SMALL, TAKEN ONE BY ONE, BUT MY GOD, TOGETHER!   ....THE ARRIVAL.   213   20
    TOMORROW I WILL BE SWEET GOD, I WILL SET THEM FREE.   ...THE ARRIVAL.   213   35
    IT THINKS THEY ARE THE VOICE OF GOD   ....THE SWARM   216   21
    MY GOD, THERE GOES THE STOPPER!   ....A SECRET   220   37
    MARBLE-HEAVY, A BAG FULL OF GOD, ...DADDY   222   8
    NOT GOD BUT A SWASTIKA   ....DADDY   223   46
    HURTS ME AS THE WORLD HURTS GOD. I AM A LANTERN ---   ....FEVER.   232   36
    THAT THE BIG GOD   ....LYONNESSE   234   20
    LAST SUMMER, MY GOD, LAST SUMMER   ....THE TOUR   238   32
    O MY GOD, WHAT AM I   ....POPPIES IN OCTOBER   240   10
    HERR GOD, HERR LUCIFER   ....LADY LAZARUS   246   79
    O GOD, I AM NOT LIKE YOU   ....YEARS   255   6
    THAT WATCHES, LIKE GOD, OR THE SKY   .....................EAVESDROPPER   261   44
    MY GOD THE IRON LUNG   ....PARALYTIC   266   4
    ONCE ONE HAS SEEN GOD, WHAT IS THE REMEDY?   ....MYSTIC   268   9
    INCANDESCENT AS A GOD;   ....TO A JILTED LOVER   310   15
    HE COUNTED THE GUNS OF GOD A BOTHER, ...LAMENT   315   13
    DESIGNED BY A DRUNKEN GOD   ....CIRCUS IN THREE RINGS   321   2
    GOD HEARS FROM HIS GREAT SUNSTRUCK HELL   ....SONG FOR A REVOLU.   323   19
    THAT ONE MAN'S DEVIL IS ANOTHER'S GOD   ....LOVE IS A PARALLAX   329   8
    AND GOD OR VOID APPALL US TILL WE DROWN   ....LOVE IS A PARALLAX   330   74
    ENORMOUS BOX OF GRAY WHERE GOD HAS GONE   .....EPITAPH IN THREE PARTS   338   30
GODAWFUL (2)
    THE SMALL SKULLS, THE SMASHED BLUE HILLS, THE GODAWFUL HUSH.   ...
                                            ... FOR A FATHERLESS SON   206   13
    GODAWFUL!   ....EAVESDROPPER   260   12
GOD-BALL (1)
    YOU HOUSE YOUR UNNERVING HEAD -- GOD-BALL, ...MEDUSA   224   4
GOD-BIT (1)
    GOD-BIT IN HIM   ....YEARS   255   21
GODDAM (1)
    WITH A GODDAM BABY SCREAMING OFF SOMEWHERE.   ....STOPPED DEAD   230   12
GODDESS (2)
    O CACOPHONY, GODDESS OF JAZZ AND OF QUARRELS, ...ALICANTE LULLABY   43   15
    AND HONOR THE GREAT GODDESS OF THE AIR *THE PRINCESS AND THE GOBLINS   335   62
GODDESSES (1)
    THOSE GREAT GODDESSES OF PEACE.   ....LORELEI   95   35
GOD-FATHERED (1)
    GOD-FATHERED INTO THE WORLD FROM MY MOTHER'S BELLY: ....ELECTRA ON.   116   7
GODFOLK (1)
    THEY MISTAKE THEIR STAR, THESE PAPERY GODFOLK.   ....MAGI   148   15
GOD-HALOED (1)
    WHETHER GOAT-THIGHED OR GOD-HALOED. EVER SINCE THAT FIRST DAPHNE   ...
                                            ... VIRGIN IN A TREE   81   9
GOD-HEAD (1)
    FRUITS OF YOUR WILLFUL TREE: GOD-HEAD, GOD-PIE   ....DIALOGUE O.   283   267
GODHOOD (2)
    YOU DEFY OTHER GODHOOD.   ....FULL FATHOM FIVE   93   40
    EATING YOUR WORDS: YOU'LL REVOKE HIS GODHOOD SOON AS   ...DIALOGUE O.   281   189
GODIVA (1)
    GODIVA, I UNPEEL ---   ....ARIEL   239   20
GODLING (1)
    TILL, SICK OF THEIR RULER'S GODLING AIRS, ...NATURAL HISTORY   71   7
GODLY (2)
    HE, GODLY, DODDERING, SPELLS   ....OUIJA   78   30
    OF SOME GODLY UTTERANCE WAKENED HEADS IGNORE: ....GHOST'S.   90   17

GODMOTHER (2)
   HER LEGENDARY GODMOTHER LEANS DOWN,   ...THE PRINCESS AND THE GOBLINS 333 15
   AT HIS WORDS, THE INDIGNANT GODMOTHER   THE PRINCESS AND THE GOBLINS 335 69
GODMOTHERS (2)
   GODMOTHERS, AND YOU CRIED AND CRIED: ....THE DISQUIETING MUSES   75 31
   THE HORRORS THAT STAND AND IDLE, THE SLIGHTED GODMOTHERS*THREE WOMEN 180 137
GODPIE (2)
   E. GODPIE! THAT'S RICH. THE JACKANAPES   DIALOGUE OVER A OUIJA BOARD 282 210
   OF WATER. WAIT. GODPIE I DON'T BEGRUDGE *DIALOGUE OVER A OUIJA BOARD 282 213
GOD-PIE (2)
   GOD-PIE. WHY, THEN, DID YOU DEIGN TO INTRODUCE ....DIALOGUE O. 283 251
   FRUITS OF YOUR WILLFUL TREE: GOD-HEAD, GOD-PIE ....DIALOGUE O. 283 267
GOD-PLUMED (1)
   YOU'D PRESUME YOUR INNER VOICE GOD-PLUMED ENOUGH ....DIALOGUE O. 280 168
GODS (11)
   AS THE GODS BEGAN ONE WORLD, AND MAN ANOTHER, ...SNAKECHARMER   79   1
   EXPRESSIVE OF GRIEF TURNS GODS, LIKE KINGS, TO ROCKS. ......PERSEUS   83 29
   THE GREAT GODS, STONE-HEAD, CLAW-FOOT,*THE HERMIT AT OUTERMOST HOUSE 118   4
   HARD GODS WERE THERE, NOTHING ELSE. ..THE HERMIT AT OUTERMOST HOUSE 119 13
   NOW THE PILLS ARE WORN-OUT AND SILLY, LIKE CLASSICAL GODS.*INSOMNIAC 163 20
   I IMAGINE THEM WITHOUT FATHERS OR MOTHERS, LIKE THE FIRST GODS. ...
                                                        ... LAST WORDS 172   8
   THEY ARE SO JEALOUS OF ANYTHING THAT IS NOT FLAT! THEY ARE
        JEALOUS GODS ....THREE WOMEN 179 86
   FIXED TO THEIR ARCS LIKE GODS, ...GETTING THERE 248 14
   ALL THE GODS KNOW IS DESTINATIONS. ....GETTING THERE 248 17
   GODS GROW TOO PROUD TO PRACTICE DOORMAN DUTIES ....DIALOGUE O. 280 127
   GODS AND REAR THEM LIKE BEANSTALKS FROM OUT THESE RIBS   DIALOGUE O. 280 170
GOD'S (15)
   REPENT, DEPART, BEFORE GOD'S TRUMP-CRACK SPLITS THE SKY." ...
                        ... DIALOGUE BETWEEN GHOST AND PRIEST   39 46
   GOD'S WORK STOOD ANCHORED IN THAT GLARE ....CRYSTAL GAZER   55 38
   OF GOD'S CITY AND BABYLON'S ....A LESSON IN VENGEANCE   80 10
   ART'S SAKE THAN GOD'S. FAR FROM SEA -- *MUSSEL HUNTER AT ROCK HARBOR   97 82
   DUG IN FIRST AS GOD'S SPURS ....THE COMPANIONABLE ILLS 105   5
   GOD'S LIONESS, ...ARIEL 239   4
   MIGHT DO AS A GOD'S MOUTHPIECE IF A WHIRLWIND ....DIALOGUE O. 281 202
   BECAUSE PAN BLUNTLY SPELT OUT GOD'S HEAD, NOT ....DIALOGUE O. 282 237
   BREATHING THE GOD'S WORD, OR THE DEVIL'S WORD, ...DIALOGUE O. 286 350
   AND AT THE JET-PLANE ANGER OF GOD'S ROAR ....THE TRIAL OF MAN 312   7
   GOD'S MONKEY WRENCH HAS BLASTED ALL MACHINES; ....DOOMSDAY 316 13
   NOR CAN GOD'S STERN, SHOCKED ANGELS CRY THEM UP ....THE DEAD 320 13
   AND TURN GOD'S RADIANT PHOTOGRAPH TO SHADE. ....SONNET TO SATAN 323   8
   LIGHTNING CONJURES GOD'S GLOBE OFF ITS ....INSOLENT STORM. 326 25
   OBSCURE GOD'S EYE WITH CORKSCREW FLECK; ....BLACK PINE TREE. 328   9
GOERS (1)
   THE ANTS -- A FILE OF COMERS, A FILE OF GOERS -- ....SPIDER   49 29
GOES (17)
   NOW HE GOES FROM HIS RIGHTFUL ROAD ....BUCOLICS   24 21
   GOES GRAVEWARD WITH FLESH LAID WASTE, ...TWO SISTERS OF PERSEPHONE   32 27
   "LOOK! THERE SHE GOES, CAT-LADY MASON!" ....ELLA MASON A.   54 31
   THAT NEVER BRIGHTENS OR GOES DOWN. ....THE DISQUIETING MUSES   76 53
   FRINGE OF MUNDANE VISION, THIS GHOST GOES ..THE GHOST'S LEAVETAKING   90 22
   THE ROUND SKY GOES ON MINDING ITS BUSINESS. PARLIAMENT HILL FIELDS 152   3
   I AM IMPORTANT TO HER. SHE COMES AND GOES. ....MIRROR 174 15
   AND THE STUFFED EXPRESSION, BUT GOES ON ....BURNING THE LETTERS 205 53
   IN WHICH A TORTURE GOES ON ONE CAN ONLY WATCH. ....COURAGE. 210 28
   MY GOD, THERE GOES THE STOPPER! ....A SECRET 220 37
   IT REALLY GOES. ....LADY LAZARUS 246 60
   IS ANYBODY THERE? IT GOES. IT GOES .....DIALOGUE OVER A OUIJA BOARD 277 26
   IS ANYBODY THERE? IT GOES. IT GOES .....DIALOGUE OVER A OUIJA BOARD 277 26
   HE GOES . . . I-N-G-O-D-P-I- ....DIALOGUE OVER A OUIJA BOARD 282 209
   SOONER OR LATER SOMETHING GOES AMISS; ....NEVER TRY TO TRICK. 320 16
   GOES THE GRASS-EMBROIDERED BOX. ....DANSE MACABRE 320   3
   OF THAT MERCURIAL STRAND, THE GIRL GOES DOWN ....THE PRINCESS. 334 27
GOING (17)
   JUTTED EARLY TO MARK OUR GOING, WHILE SKY ....CHANNEL CROSSING   27 23
   BY GOING FAR; MY LOOK'S LEASH ....SOLILOQUY OF THE SOLIPSIST   37 13
   IN GOING UP FOR THE COMING DOWN IF THE POST ....ABOVE THE OXBOW   88 18
   A WHITE MIST IS GOING UP. ....THE SLEEPERS 123 16
   GOING UNDER THE CHAINMAIL, ...MEDALLION 124 17
   ANYTHING CAN HAPPEN WHERE THEY ARE GOING. ....ON DECK 143 18
   LOVE SET YOU GOING LIKE A FAT GOLD WATCH. ....MORNING SONG 156   1
   COMING AND GOING, BREATH BY BREATH, WITHOUT ANY FUSS. ....TULIPS 161 51
   A BLACKBERRY ALLEY, GOING DOWN IN HOOKS, AND A SEA ...BLACKBERRYING 168   3
   WHERE ARE YOU GOING ....THE OTHER 202 23
   AND THE NOISE IT FLAYS FROM THE AIR, ONCE IT GETS GOING! ..COURAGE. 210 20
   TATE AND LYLE KEEPS THEM GOING, ...WINTERING 218 27
   GLOWING AND COMING AND GOING, FLUSH ON FLUSH. ....FEVER. 232 42
   I THINK I AN GOING UP, ...FEVER. 232 43
   WE THOUGHT WE'D TRAINED HIM, BEFORE GOING HAYWIRE. TRUTH*DIALOGUE O. 277 41
   GOING TO GET GABRIEL'S THUMB INTO THE PIE ....DIALOGUE O. 280 148
   THE SECRET OF THEIR ECSTASY'S IN GOING; ....LOVE IS A PARALLAX 330 62
GOING'S (1)
   GOING'S BEEN TAME DEVIATION. WHITE, ...WHITENESS I REMEMBER 102   4

	TITLE	PAGE	LINE

GOLD (23)
HEARING TICKS BLOWN GOLD ....TWO SISTERS OF PERSEPHONE 32 14
WITH GOLD; ....SOLILOQUY OF THE SOLIPSIST 37 23
MY JILTING LADY SQUANDER COIN, GOLD LEAF STOCK DITCHES, CONJURING. 66 35
MEADOWS OF GOLD DUST. THE SILVER ....IN MIDAS' COUNTRY 99 1
AND GOLDENROD AS ON GOLD LEAF. ....IN MIDAS' COUNTRY 99 10
PLENTITUDE: APPLES GOLD ON THE BOUGH, ...IN MIDAS' COUNTRY 99 12
WHERE BEES, STRIPED BLACK AND GOLD, SLEEP OUT THE BLIZZARD ...
                    ... ELECTRA ON AZALEA PATH 116 3
GOLD CARP LOOM IN THE POOLS. ....YADDO: THE GRAND MANOR 123 8
LOVE SET YOU GOING LIKE A FAT GOLD WATCH. ....MORNING SONG 156 1
STARS AND SHOWERS OF GOLD -- CONCEPTIONS, CONCEPTIONS! THREE WOMEN 178 48
IN FIFTY, GOLD. ....THE APPLICANT 221 32
OF JAPANESE PAPER, MY GOLD BEATEN SKIN ....FEVER. 232 38
ALL COGS, WEIRD SPARKLE AND EVERY COG SOLID GOLD. ....THE TOUR 237 5
THE PURE GOLD BABY ....LADY LAZARUS 246 69
A GOLD FILLING. ....LADY LAZARUS 246 78
A RING OF GOLD WITH THE SUN IN IT? ....THE COURIERS 247 5
GOLD LEAVES METAL AND BREATHLESS. ....LETTER IN NOVEMBER 253 30
A WINDOW, HOLY GOLD. ....MARY'S SONG 257 4
GOLD JOINTS, MY WAY OF TURNING ....GIGOLO 268 22
GOLD MOUTHS CRY ....GOLD MOUTHS CRY 302 T
GOLD MOUTHS CRY WITH THE GREEN YOUNG ....GOLD MOUTHS CRY 302 1
WE IGNORE THE COMING DOOM OF GOLD ....GOLD MOUTHS CRY 302 7
AND ALL THE GOLD APPLES ....TEMPER OF TIME 336 3
GOLDEN (10)
HONEYCOMBED WITH GOLDEN EGGS, ...RHYME 50 2
GLORIFIED FOR PRIME FLESH AND GOLDEN CRACKLING ....SOW 60 15
GOLDFINCH, GOLDFISH, GOLDEN TIGER CAT STOCK- .....IN MIDAS' COUNTRY 99 13
THE GOLDEN RAIN TREE DRIPS ITS POWDERS DOWN. ....BEEKEEPER'S. 118 9
THE APPLES ARE GOLDEN, ...LETTER IN NOVEMBER 253 24
O GOLDEN CHILD THE WORLD WILL KILL AND EAT. ....MARY'S SONG 257 21
BLAZING IN MY GOLDEN HELL. ....TO A JILTED LOVER 310 27
TOLLING HER GRAVE WITH GOLDEN GONGS, ...LAMENT 315 11
AS THEIR GOLDEN JAILER ....MOONSONG AT MORNING 317 27
THE MAGIC GOLDEN APPLES ALL LOOK GOOD ....ADMONITIONS 319 4
GOLDENROD (2)
AND GOLDENROD AS ON GOLD LEAF. ....IN MIDAS' COUNTRY 99 10
EVEN THE DEAD LAUGH AMONG THE GOLDENROD. ....GOLD MOUTHS CRY 302 9
GOLDFINCH (1)
GOLDFINCH, GOLDFISH, GOLDEN TIGER CAT STOCK- .....IN MIDAS' COUNTRY 99 13
GOLDFISH (2)
GOLDFINCH, GOLDFISH, GOLDEN TIGER CAT STOCK- .....IN MIDAS' COUNTRY 99 13
HAS BEEN DRAINING THE GOLDFISH PONDS. ....PRIVATE GROUND 130 8
GOLD-LOBED (1)
GO GET THE GOODLY SQUAB IN GOLD-LOBED CORN   GO GET THE GOODLY SQUAB 313 1
GOLDPIECES (1)
DRIFT OF GOLDPIECES ....DARK WOOD, DARK WATER 127 20
GOLD-RUDDY (1)
HOLDING THEIR GOLD-RUDDY BALLS ....LETTER IN NOVEMBER 253 27
GOLDS (1)
GOLDS BLEED AND DEEPEN, THE MOUTHS OF THERMOPYLAE. ..LETTER IN NOV. 254 35
GOLGOTHA (1)
OF GOLGOTHA AT THE TIP OF A REED, ...POEM.5.F. 135 18
GONDOLA (1)
GONDOLA OF PAPER ....BATTLE-SCENE 84 12
GONE (32)
IN RITUAL, TO STRIKE -- IS DEFINITELY GONE; ....TALE OF A TUB 25 22
WITH WHITE FROST GONE ....STRUMPET SONG 33 1
GONE BLACK OF POLISH ....TINKER JACK AND THE TIDY WIVES 34 2
NO FORM'S GONE SO AWRY, ...TINKER JACK AND THE TIDY WIVES 34 15
LIKE A LAST STORM-CROSSED LEAF? BEST GET YOU GONE ......DIALOGUE B. 39 44
SACKED LARDER'S GONE BONE-BARE. ....THE GLUTTON 40 14
LONG GONE TO WHEEZE AND SEED, ELLA MASON ....ELLA MASON A. 53 8
LEAN FACE GONE TAWN WITH SEASONS, ...CRYSTAL GAZER 54 2
ALL THE LONG GONE DARLINGS: THEY ....ALL THE DEAD DEARS 71 25
CLAIM AND WEIGHT GONE OUT OF THEM. ....THE GREAT CARBUNCLE 72 8
WORTHLESS SUCH VISION TO EYES GONE DULL ..ON THE DECLINE OF ORACLES 78 30
SORROWS OF MALFI'S GENTLE DUCHESS? GONE ....PERSEUS 83 42
FUNICULAR RAILWAY, WITNESS TO GONE ....ABOVE THE OXBOW 88 38
TIME, AND TO GRACES GONE WITH THE TIME. A STATE VIEW- ......OXBOW. 88 39
HE GAVE ME. I'VE GONE NOWHERE SINCE BUT ....WHITENESS I REMEMBER 102 3
A PLACE, A TIME GONE OUT OF MIND. ....THE EYE-MOTE 109 30
THEY SHOULD HAVE GONE OUT WITH BALLOON FLIGHTS AND THE
        STEREOPTICON. ....CANDLES 149 12
THOUGHTS GONE DIM. ....I AM VERTICAL 162 16
THE SWANS ARE GONE. STILL THE RIVER ....THREE WOMEN 186 344
LISTEN: THESE ARE ITS HOOVES: IT HAS GONE OFF, LIKE A HORSE. ...ELM 192 9
A DEATH TREE, COLOR GONE, AN AUSTRALIAN GUM TREE -- ....FATHERLESS. 205 3
NOW HE IS GONE ....STINGS 215 40
SOMETHING IS GONE ....THE JAILER 226 11
THE TOP QUITE GONE ....CUT 235 3
A-W-W. HE'S GONE OFF: WHAT ENGLISH .....DIALOGUE OVER A OUIJA BOARD 279 93
AND HIS EYES GONE BLIND WITH LEAVES. ....GOLD MOUTHS CRY 302 14
THE TELEGRAM SAYS YOU HAVE GONE AWAY ....DENOUEMENT 326 1

	TITLE	PAGE	LINE

GONE (CONT.)
THE TELEGRAM SAYS YOU HAVE GONE AWAY. ....DENOUEMENT 326 6
THE TELEGRAM SAYS YOU HAVE GONE AWAY. ....DENOUEMENT 327 12
THE TELEGRAM SAYS YOU HAVE GONE AWAY; ....DENOUEMENT 327 18
WHITE WHALES ARE GONE WITH THE WHITE OCEAN. ....TWO LOVERS. 327 12
ENORMOUS BOX OF GRAY WHERE GOD HAS GONE .....EPITAPH IN THREE PARTS 338 30
GONG (1)
OF A SUNKEN GONG. ....AQUATIC NOCTURNE 306 28
GONGING (1)
BLOOD QUICKENS, GONGING IN MY EARS: ....PURSUIT 23 48
GONGS (1)
TOLLING HER GRAVE WITH GOLDEN GONGS, ...LAMENT 315 11
GOOD (37)
HER ANTELOPE WHO MEANT HIM NAUGHT BUT GOOD. ..THE QUEEN'S COMPLAINT 28 10
WHEN IN GOOD HUMOR, ...SOLILOQUY OF THE SOLIPSIST 37 20
AND DO GOOD ....RECANTATION 42 19
FOR NO GOOD REASON ....ELLA MASON AND HER ELEVEN CATS 53 9
IF ROOT'S FIRM-FIXED AND RESOLUTION GOOD. ....MAYFLOWER 60 4
AND LOSE THEIR GOOD BROWNS ....THE THIN PEOPLE 65 44
I LEARN, GOOD CIRCUS ....WORDS FOR A NURSERY 73 11
EXILED TO NO GOOD. ....FULL FATHOM FIVE 93 42
GOOD OF THE CAPE LIGHT THAT SCOURS ....MUSSEL HUNTER AT ROCK HARBOR 95 3
WE GAVE GOOD USE AS SHIP AND HOUSE IS BLACK*GREEN ROCK, WINTHROP BAY 105 11
FLITS NIMBLE-WINGED IN THICKETS, AND OF GOOD COLOR. ....WATERCOLOR. 112 7
IT WAS GOOD FOR TWENTY YEARS, THAT WINTERING -- ....ELECTRA ON. 116 5
I SHALL BE GOOD AS NEW. POEM.7.S. 137 45
FOR WHOM THE GOOD LORD PROVIDES (HE GAVE ....ON DECK 143 20
THE REAL THING, ALL RIGHT: THE GOOD, THE TRUE -- ....MAGI 148 6
THEY RING TRUE, LIKE GOOD CHINA. ....A LIFE 150 18
YOU BRING ME GOOD NEWS FROM THE CLINIC, ...FACE LIFT 155 1
THEIR POPPY-SLEEPY COLORS DO HIM NO GOOD. ....INSOMNIAC 163 21
BLOOM ABOUT ME LIKE NIGHT FLOWERS, WITH A GOOD SMELL. ...LAST WORDS 172 22
I SHALL BE A SKY AND A HILL OF GOOD: O LET ME BE! ......THREE WOMEN 180 140
IT UTTERS SUCH DARK SOUNDS IT CANNOT BE GOOD. ....THREE WOMEN 182 217
IT IS SUCH A GOOD SHAPE, SO VIVID. ....PHEASANT 191 19
AND AT LEAST IT WILL BE A GOOD PLACE NOW, THE ATTIC. ......BURNING. 204 22
IT IS GOOD FOR ME ....FOR A FATHERLESS SON 205 10
YOU SAY YOUR HUSBAND IS JUST NO GOOD TO YOU. ....LESBOS 228 26
I AM PACKING THE HARD POTATOES LIKE GOOD CLOTHES, ...LESBOS 229 68
THAN FINANCIER. WHAT GOOD IS HE, IF NOT *DIALOGUE OVER A OUIJA BOARD 277 44
LIKE A GOOD BOY. BE CAREFUL. I'M NOT SURE THAT HE ......DIALOGUE O. 282 207
HIM YET, AND GIVE US GOOD REASON. NO, HE'S ON ....DIALOGUE O. 284 295
OR AFTER GAY DAYS, OR COLORS THE GROWER FOUND GOOD. ..QUEEN MARY'S. 290 18
WHAT GOOD IS ALL THAT SPACE IF IT CAN'T DRAW YOU OFF? ..DIALOGUE O. 291 13
THE MAGIC GOLDEN APPLES ALL LOOK GOOD ....ADMONITIONS 319 4
AND PAGE BY PRIDE THE GOOD BOOKS BLOW;*SONG FOR A REVOLUTIONARY LOVE 322 3
DEMARCATING GOOD FROM EVIL, ...INSOLENT STORM STRIKES AT THE SKULL 326 20
"THERE IS MORE THAN ONE GOOD WAY TO DROWN." EPITAPH IN THREE PARTS 337 11
"THERE IS MORE THAN ONE GOOD WAY TO DROWN." EPITAPH IN THREE PARTS 337 22
"THERE IS MORE THAN ONE GOOD WAY TO DROWN." EPITAPH IN THREE PARTS 338 33
GOODBYE (7)
HAND ALOFT, GOODBYE, GOODBYE, NOT DOWN .....THE GHOST'S LEAVETAKING 90 23
HAND ALOFT, GOODBYE, GOODBYE, NOT DOWN .....THE GHOST'S LEAVETAKING 90 23
HAIL AND FAREWELL. HELLO, GOODBYE. O KEEPER *THE GHOST'S LEAVETAKING 91 39
AND I AM A WHITE SHIP HOOTING: GOODBYE, GOODBYE. ....THREE WOMEN 184 261
AND I AM A WHITE SHIP HOOTING: GOODBYE, GOODBYE. ....THREE WOMEN 184 261
AND FOLDED HIS HANDS, THAT WERE SHAKING: GOODBYE, GOODBYE. ..BERCK. 198 66
AND FOLDED HIS HANDS, THAT WERE SHAKING: GOODBYE, GOODBYE. ..BERCK. 198 66
GOODBYES (1)
GOODBYES WERE SAID, TRAINS LET GO, ...MONOLOGUE AT 3 A.M. 40 12
GOODLY (3)
GO GET THE GOODLY SQUAB ....GO GET THE GOODLY SQUAB 313 T
GO GET THE GOODLY SQUAB IN GOLD-LOBED CORN GO GET THE GOODLY SQUAB 313 1
ROLLED ROUND WITH GOODLY LOAM AND CRADLED DEEP, ...THE DEAD 320 9
GOODWILL (2)
INDOORS WITH POLITIC GOODWILL, NOT HASTE ...THE SNOWMAN ON THE MOOR 58 11
ON HAWTHORN BOUGHS, WITH GOODWILL TO ENDURE ....MAYFLOWER 60 13
GOODWIVES (1)
JIGGLES HIS TIN CUP AT THE GOODWIVES. ....THE BEGGARS 48 12
GOOSE (3)
AND, MORE DAFT THAN ANY GOOSE, ...STREET SONG 36 29
I'VE GOT A STUBBORN GOOSE WHOSE GUT'S ....RHYME 50 1
IF YOU MUST BUTCHER MOTHER GOOSE TO DO IT. ....DIALOGUE O. 280 149
GOOSE-WIT (1)
SHE, ADDLED IN HER GOOSE-WIT, STRUTS ....RHYME 50 4
GORGED (1)
THOUGH HE BEDDED IN ERMINE, GORGED ON ROAST, ...NATURAL HISTORY 71 3
GORGON-GRIMACE (1)
IN SAFE PERSPECTIVE, COULD OUTFACE THE GORGON-GRIMACE ......PERSEUS 83 14
GORGON-PROSPECTS (1)
AT GORGON-PROSPECTS WITH POWER TO STRIKE TO STONE ....CRYSTAL GAZER 55 41
GORGON'S (1)
TRANSFIXED BY GLARE OF BLUE FROM GORGON'S EYE; ..PROLOGUE TO SPRING 322 2
GORILLA (1)
THE GIGANTIC GORILLA INTERIOR ....GETTING THERE 247 3

GORING (1)
  THE GORING ....GORING 47 T
GORSE (3)
  ABOVE WHORLED, SPINDLING GORSE, ...TWO VIEWS OF WITHENS 71 1
  I TASTED THE MALIGNITY OF THE GORSE, ...THE RABBIT CATCHER 193 6
  I CANNOT RUN, I AM ROOTED, AND THE GORSE HURTS ME ..THE BEE MEETING 211 31
GOSPEL (1)
  COULD GROPE ITS WAY TO GOSPEL THROUGH THAT WELTER ......DIALOGUE O. 286 346
GOSSIP (1)
  I ENJOY PETTICOATS AND VELVETS AND GOSSIP OF COURT, ..QUEEN MARY'S. 290 21
GOSSIPING (1)
  PROFITLESS, THEIR GOSSIPING IMAGES ....ON THE DECLINE OF ORACLES 78 22
GOSSIPS (2)
  AND GOSSIPS IN ITS LOOSE VERNACULAR, ...A WINTER SHIP 113 19
  GOSSIPS LATE AND SOON, ...JILTED 304 6
GOSSIP'S (1)
  THEIR SHRILL, GRAVELLY GOSSIP'S FUNNELED OFF.*PARLIAMENT HILL FIELDS 152 18
GOT (12)
  I'VE GOT A STUBBORN GOOSE WHOSE GUT'S ....RHYME 50 1
  "MISS ELLA'S GOT LOONY FROM KEEPING IN CAHOOTS ....ELLA MASON A. 54 35
  GOT BAKED INTO GINGERBREAD, I WONDER ....THE DISQUIETING MUSES 75 12
  THE LAST CRONE GOT BURNT UP ....THE TIMES ARE TIDY 107 11
  HE WON'T BE GOT RID OF: POEM.4.BEAST. 134 11
  BY THE ROOTS OF MY HAIR SOME GOD GOT HOLD OF ME. ...THE HANGING MAN 141 1
  THE BEES HAVE GOT SO FAR. SEVENTY FEET HIGH! ....THE SWARM 216 26
  THEY HAVE GOT RID OF THE MEN, ...WINTERING 218 40
  I KNEW HE'D GOT IT MIXED BEFORE: VISIONS*DIALOGUE OVER A OUIJA BOARD 282 219
  DEEPER THAN YOUR OWN OCEAN FLOOR, AND GOT ....DIALOGUE O. 283 243
  MARY SAID SLOWLY, "I'VE GOT A FELLA ....BITTER STRAWBERRIES 299 10
  GOT UP TO LET THE SUAVE BLUE POLICEMAN IN. ....THE TRIAL OF MAN 312 8
GOTHIC (2)
  THE YEW TREE POINTS UP. IT HAS A GOTHIC SHAPE. ....MOON. 173 15
  GOTHIC AND BARBAROUS, PURE GERMAN. ....LITTLE FUGUE 188 26
GOURMET (1)
  TURNING THE TABLES OF THIS GRAVE GOURMET, ...TERMINAL 328 9
GOVERN (2)
  TO GOVERN MORE SIGHT THAN GIVEN TO A WOMAN ....CRYSTAL GAZER 55 32
  GOVERN A LIFE ....WORDS 270 20
GOVERNMENTS (1)
  GOVERNMENTS, PARLIAMENTS, SOCIETIES, ...THREE WOMEN 179 83
GOWN (2)
  MY BLACK GOWN IS A LITTLE FUNERAL: ....THREE WOMEN 185 303
  TRAILING HER SCRUPULOUSLY SIMPLE GOWN THE PRINCESS AND THE GOBLINS 333 11
GOWNS (2)
  THEY STAND THEIR VIGIL IN GOWNS OF STONE, ...THE DISQUIETING MUSES 76 50
  IN A SHOWER OF CHANEL, DIOR GOWNS, ...DIALOGUE EN ROUTE 308 9
GRAB (2)
  TOWARD WHAT I CAN GRAB, ...WORDS FOR A NURSERY 73 6
  TO HAVE YOU GRAB MY NOSE, A LADDER RUNG. ......FOR A FATHERLESS SON 205 11
GRACE (5)
  TO JUDGMENT IN A HIGHER COURT OF GRACE. ....DIALOGUE B. 39 45
  FILENE'S SHOW WINDOWS. GRANT US GRACE, ...A WINTER'S TALE 87 19
  FROM WHAT GRACE AM I FALLEN. TONGUES ARE STRANGE, ...INCOMMUNICADO 100 12
  OUR QUESTIONS IN HUMBLE HABIT TO GAIN GRACE ....DIALOGUE O. 281 187
  WAITING FOR HIS GRACE TO CONSECRATE. ....TERMINAL 328 14
GRACES (1)
  TIME, AND TO GRACES GONE WITH THE TIME. A STATE VIEW- ....OXBOW. 88 39
GRACIOUS (1)
  O SHE IS GRACIOUS AND AUSTERE, ...THE BURNT-OUT SPA 138 27
GRACIOUSNESS (1)
  AND THOUGH YOUR GRACIOUSNESS MIGHT STREAM, ...POINT SHIRLEY 111 44
GRACKLES (1)
  FOR PIES. THE FIR TREE'S THICK WITH GRACKLES.*YADDO: THE GRAND MANOR 123 7
GRADE (1)
  LABORING ON THE TILT OF THAT STEEP GRADE ....THE PRINCESS. 334 35
GRADED (1)
  OF MERCURY IN GRADED TUBES, WHERE ILLS ....MORNING IN THE HOS. 332 17
GRAFTERS (1)
  THE GRAFTERS ARE CHEERFUL, ...POEM.7.S. 137 27
GRAIL (2)
  OF THE PROFANE GRAIL, THE DREAMING SKULL. ..THE GHOST'S LEAVETAKING 91 40
  WHAT PRINCE HAS EVER SEIZED THE SHINING GRAIL .......METAMORPHOSES. 307 19
GRAIN (11)
  BRIGHT GRAIN SPRUNG SO RARELY ....ODE FOR TED 29 16
  HOW PERILOUS NEEDLES GRAIN THE FLOORBOARDS ....MISS DRAKE P. 41 16
  SHE FATTENS ON THE FINEST GRAIN. ....RHYME 50 10
  ON THE RENDERING, GRAIN BY GRAIN, *THE LADY AND THE EARTHENWARE HEAD 69 26
  ON THE RENDERING, GRAIN BY GRAIN, *THE LADY AND THE EARTHENWARE HEAD 69 26
  FROM GRAIN OF THE MARROW AND THE RIVER-BED GRAINS. ....LESSON. 80 25
  ABRADING MY LID, THE SMALL GRAIN BURNS*..............THE EYE-MOTE 109 16
  SITTING UNDER A POTLID, TINY AND INERT AS A RICE GRAIN. ..POEM.6.W. 135 15
  GRAIN BY GRAIN, THEY UNROLLED ....BURNING THE LETTERS 204 6
  GRAIN BY GRAIN, THEY UNROLLED ....BURNING THE LETTERS 204 6
  A GRAIN OF SAND IS ALL WE HAVE. ....TWO LOVERS. 327 20

GRAINED (2)
   ANCHORED ITSELF, GRIFFIN-LEGGED AND DARKLY GRAINED. ..THE OTHER TWO   68   9
   OF YOUR GRAINED FACE SHED TIME IN RUNNELS: ....FULL FATHOM FIVE   93   26
GRAINS (4)
   FROM GRAIN OF THE MARROW AND THE RIVER-BED GRAINS. ....LESSON.   80   25
   DOMINOES OF THEIR DOORWAYS. SUN GRAINS THEIR CROW-COLORS, ...NET-. 121   6
   THE SMALL GRAINS MAKE ROOM. ....MUSHROOMS 139   9
   HOT GRAINS, SIMPLY. IT IS DRY, DRY. .....SLEEP IN THE MOJAVE DESERT 143   2
GRAND (6)
   AT THIS WHARF THERE ARE NO GRAND LANDINGS TO SPEAK OF.*A WINTER SHIP 112   1
   YADDO: THE GRAND MANOR ....YADDO: THE GRAND MANOR 123   T
   MUSEUM WITHOUT STATUES, GRAND WITH PILLARS, PORTICOES, ROTUNDAS. ...
    ... BARREN WOMAN 157   2
   SO MUCH FOR THE CHARIOTEERS, THE OUTRIDERS, THE GRAND ARMY! SWARM. 217   39
   SHOULD BE GRAND AND CLASSICAL ....CHILD 265   9
   I'M THROUGH WITH THIS GRAND LOOKING-GLASS HOTEL ......A SORCERER B. 324   1
GRANDAM (1)
   THE GREAT GRANDAM! -- OUR MARVEL BLAZONED A KNIGHT, ...SOW   61   29
GRANDCHILDREN (1)
   GRANDCHILDREN NOBODY KNOWS. ....OLD LADIES' HOME 120   12
GRANDFATHER (1)
   AND MY GRANDFATHER MOPED IN THE TYROL, ...CANDLES 149   20
GRANDILOQUENT (1)
   HOWEVER THE GRANDILOQUENT MIND MAY SCORN ....NOVEMBER GRAVEYARD   56   5
GRANDIOSE (1)
   THAT GRANDIOSE COLOSSUS WHO ....LETTER TO A PURIST   36   1
GRANDMOTHER (3)
   MOTHER, GRANDMOTHER, GREATGRANDMOTHER ....ALL THE DEAD DEARS   70   20
   GRANDMOTHER, STONES ARE NOTHING OF HOME ....POINT SHIRLEY 111   46
   AND I REMEMBER BY MATERNAL GRANDMOTHER FROM VIENNA. ....CANDLES 149   17
GRANDMOTHERLY (1)
   THEY STAND ABOUT IN GRANDMOTHERLY DISGUISE, ...WUTHERING HEIGHTS 167   25
GRANDMOTHER'S (1)
   IN MY GRANDMOTHER'S SAND YARD. SHE IS DEAD, ...POINT SHIRLEY 110   9
GRANDSIRES (1)
   NEVER GRIP, AS THEIR GRANDSIRES DID, THAT DEVIL WHO CHUCKLES*LESSON.   80   24
GRANITE (5)
   GRANITE RUFFS, THEIR SHADOWS ....HARDCASTLE CRAGS   63   36
   WITH A GRANITE GRIN ....ALL THE DEAD DEARS   70   2
   NIGHTLONG, IN THE GRANITE YARD, INVISIBLE CATS ....INSOMNIAC 163   29
   TO THE GRANITE GRIN OF BONE. ....NOTES TO A NEOPHYTE 306   12
   MAJOR FAULTS IN GRANITE ....TRIO OF LOVE SONGS 313   1
GRANT (2)
   MY EYELIDS UP, AND GRANT ....BLACK ROOK IN RAINY WEATHER   57   30
   FILENE'S SHOW WINDOWS. GRANT US GRACE, ...A WINTER'S TALE   87   19
GRANTA (1)
   THE BLAND GRANTA DOUBLE THEIR WHITE AND GREEN ....WATERCOLOR. 112   9
GRANTCHESTER (1)
   WATERCOLOR OF GRANTCHESTER MEADOWS ....WATERCOLOR. 111   T
GRANTS (1)
   GERD WHIRLS THE BALL ABLAZE: "ROUGH STORM," SHE GRANTS, "MAY WREAK ...
    ... CRYSTAL GAZER   55   22
GRANULAR (1)
   OVER AND OVER THE OLD, GRANULAR MOVIE ....INSOMNIAC 163   8
GRAPEBLUE (1)
   GRAPEBLUE MUSSELS ....AQUATIC NOCTURNE 305   13
GRAPEFRUIT (1)
   SUNLIGHT STRIKES A GLASS OF GRAPEFRUIT JUICE, ..MORNING IN THE HOS. 332   1
GRAPELEAVES (1)
   THE DEAD RIPEN IN THE GRAPELEAVES. POEM.3.MAENAD. 133   12
GRAPES (2)
   GREEN, ALSO, THE GRAPES ON THE GREEN VINE ....DEPARTURE   51   2
   MUSSELS CLUSTER BLUE AS GRAPES: ....MAGNOLIA SHOALS 122   17
GRAPHS (1)
   GRAPHS A FEVER CHART, ...TRIO OF LOVE SONGS 313   6
GRASS (27)
   SWEET GRASS SPRANG FOR THEIR GRAZING. ......SONG FOR A SUMMER'S DAY   31   5
   GIVE GRASS ITS GREEN ....SOLILOQUY OF THE SOLIPSIST   37   21
   TO ELEGIAC DRYADS, AND DOUR GRASS ....NOVEMBER GRAVEYARD   56   3
   BUT FROM LEAF, FROM GRASS,*ON THE DIFFICULTY OF CONJURING UP A DRYAD   66   39
   VALLEYS OF GRASS ALTERING ....THE GREAT CARBUNCLE   72   4
   NO FLOOR: A WAVE OF FLICKERING GRASS TONGUES .........SNAKECHARMER   79   9
   ON GRASS THAT ONCE FED BOSTON COWS. ....A WINTER'S TALE   87   23
   EYEING ME. GRASS PUT FORTH CLAWS; .....MUSSEL HUNTER AT ROCK HARBOR   96   25
   GREEN GRASS STREAMING, HOUSES A RIVER ......WHITENESS I REMEMBER 102   19
   TO THIS CREST OF GRASS. INLAND, THEY ARGUE, PARLIAMENT HILL FIELDS 152   7
   WHILE THE HEATH GRASS GLITTERS AND THE SPINDLING RIVULETS ...
    ... PARLIAMENT HILL FIELDS 153   34
   HOLLOW DOORSTEPS GO FROM GRASS TO GRASS; ....WUTHERING HEIGHTS 168   31
   HOLLOW DOORSTEPS GO FROM GRASS TO GRASS; ....WUTHERING HEIGHTS 168   31
   THE GRASS IS BEATING ITS HEAD DISTRACTEDLY. ......WUTHERING HEIGHTS 168   39
   I AM SOLITARY AS GRASS. WHAT IS IT I MISS? ....THREE WOMEN 186 342
   THROUGH THE UNCUT GRASS ON THE ELM'S HILL. ....PHEASANT 191   4
   SIX ROUND BLACK HATS IN THE GRASS AND A LOZENGE OF WOOD,*BERCK-PLAGE 201 123
   SURELY THE GRASS SHOULD BE RIPPLING. ....THE JAILER 226   25

```
                                          TITLE        PAGE  LINE
GRASS (CONT.)
  A SMILE FELL IN THE GRASS.  .....................THE NIGHT DANCES  249    1
  OF YOUR SMALL BREATH, THE DRENCHED GRASS  ..........THE NIGHT DANCES  250    9
  DISPATCHED, INTO TRENCHES OF GRASS.  ......................STINGS/DR  293   13
  IN THE TALL GRASS,  .............................BITTER STRAWBERRIES  299   15
  AND IN A FEW FATAL YARDS OF GRASS  ........................APRIL 18  302   12
  MY LOVE AND I GO GARLANDED WITH GRASS.  ................APRIL AUBADE  312   12
  ACROSS THE FROSTED GRASS SHE MARKS THE SHEEN  .........THE PRINCESS.  334   31
  OF SNAKE IN THE GRASS.  ............................TEMPER OF TIME  336   16
  A WAVE OF GRASS ENGRAVES UPON THE STONE:  ....EPITAPH IN THREE PARTS  338   32
GRASS-COUCHED (1)
  GRASS-COUCHED IN HER LABOR'S PRIDE,  ......TWO SISTERS OF PERSEPHONE   32   23
GRASS-EMBROIDERED (1)
  GOES THE GRASS-EMBROIDERED BOX.  ......................DANSE MACABRE  320    3
GRASSES (10)
  GAVE WAY TO FIELDS AND THE INCESSANT SEETHE OF GRASSES*HARDCASTLE C.   62    9
  SHEEPFOOT-FLATTENED GRASSES,  ..................TWO VIEWS OF WITHENS   71    2
  OF THE DENSE GRASSES I FOUND  .........MUSSEL HUNTER AT ROCK HARBOR   97   68
  ON THIS AMBER BANK WHERE GRASSES BLEACH.  .........IN MIDAS' COUNTRY  100   22
  KEEP HOUSE AMONG THE GRASSES. KNEELING DOWN*THE BEEKEEPER'S DAUGHTER  118   16
  FLATTEN THE DOPED SNAKES TO RIBBON. IN HERE, THE GRASSES *PRIVATE G.  130   17
  THE GRASSES UNLOAD THEIR GRIEFS ON MY FEET AS IF I WERE GOD,  MOON.  172    3
  THE SHADOWS OF THE GRASSES INCHED ROUND LIKE HANDS OF A CLOCK,*BABY.  175   43
  THE CITY WAITS AND ACHES. THE LITTLE GRASSES  ..........THREE WOMEN  187  370
  CIRCLE, WITH ITS TAWN SILK GRASSES -- BABIES' HAIR.  LETTER IN NOV.  253    7
GRASSHEADS (1)
  OF GRASSHEADS AND IS HEARD.  .....WATERCOLOR OF GRANTCHESTER MEADOWS  112    5
GRASSHOPPER (1)
  GRASSHOPPER GOBLINS WITH GREEN POINTED EARS   EPITAPH IN THREE PARTS  337   23
GRASSINESS (1)
  GUARDS THE HARD-HEARTED EMERALD OF ITS GRASSINESS*NOVEMBER GRAVEYARD   56    4
GRASS-ROOT (1)
  CLUMPED LIKE BULBS AT THE GRASS-ROOT  ..MUSSEL HUNTER AT ROCK HARBOR   95   10
GRASSTOPS (1)
  THERE IS NO LIFE HIGHER THAN THE GRASSTOPS  .......WUTHERING HEIGHTS  167   10
GRATE (2)
  HER CRIES ARE HOOKS THAT CATCH AND GRATE LIKE CATS.  ....THREE WOMEN  182  207
  THOSE GLASS BITS IN THE GRATE STRIKE ME CHILL:  .........DIALOGUE O.  285  306
GRATEFUL (2)
  WITHOUT ME, SHE WOULDN'T EXIST, SO OF COURSE SHE WAS GRATEFUL.  ...
                                       ...  IN PLASTER  159   15
  TO MY WATER ROD, DAZZLING AND GRATEFUL,  .....................MEDUSA  225   19
GRATIFIED (2)
  HE IS GRATIFIED BY THE ABSENCE OF ICECAKES.  .................ON DECK  143   27
  GRATIFIED,  ..............................................GIGOLO  268   29
GRAVE (4)
  PAVING THIS GRAVE GROUND. HERE'S HONEST ROT  .....NOVEMBER GRAVEYARD   56    8
  THE GRAVE CAVE ATE WILL BE  ...........................LADY LAZARUS  244   17
  TOLLING HER GRAVE WITH GOLDEN GONGS,  ........................LAMENT  315   11
  TURNING THE TABLES OF THIS GRAVE GOURMET,  .................TERMINAL  328    9
GRAVEL (2)
  OF GRAVEL? THE WAVES'  ...............................POINT SHIRLEY  110   31
  SIX FEET OF YELLOW GRAVEL COVER YOU.  ........ELECTRA ON AZALEA PATH  117   23
GRAVELLY (1)
  THEIR SHRILL, GRAVELLY GOSSIP'S FUNNELED OFF.*PARLIAMENT HILL FIELDS  152   18
GRAVES (1)
  GRAVES ALL CAROL IN REPLY.  .....................LOVE IS A PARALLAX  330   42
GRAVESTONES (1)
  POISON OF STILLED LAWNS, THE LITTLE CLAPBOARD GRAVESTONES,  WAKING.  151    7
GRAVEWARD (1)
  GOES GRAVEWARD WITH FLESH LAID WASTE,  ....TWO SISTERS OF PERSEPHONE   32   27
GRAVEYARD (1)
  NOVEMBER GRAVEYARD  .............................NOVEMBER GRAVEYARD   56    T
GRAVITY (1)
  I WOULD ADMIRE THE DEEP GRAVITY OF IT, ITS TIMELESS EYES. *BIRTHDAY.  208   57
GRAVITY'S (3)
  TABLES AND CHAIRS. GRAVITY'S  ....................THE GREAT CARBUNCLE   73   22
  THAN AGAINST GRAVITY'S GRIP, TABLES RISING; THE DRINK  ..DIALOGUE O.  279  122
  BREAKING THROUGH GRAVITY'S GARRISON,  ............DIALOGUE EN ROUTE  309   31
GRAY (33)
  GRAY AS RATS,  ...........................................PROSPECT   28    4
  ALREADY VEILING THE GRAY SPOOL OF STONE  .......................SPIDER   48   18
  LAPS ITS GRAY PAW  .......................................RESOLVE   52    6
  OF IDENTICAL GRAY BRICK HOUSES,  .......................LANDOWNERS   53    4
  MEAGER OF DIMENSION AS THE GRAY PEOPLE  ............THE THIN PEOPLE   64    2
  A RUDDY SKYLIGHT PAINTS THE GRAY OXBOW  .............ABOVE THE OXBOW   88   42
  TO SAFE GRAY NEVER GRAYED HIS TEMPER.  .........WHITENESS I REMEMBER  102   11
  GULLS CIRCLE GRAY UNDER SHADOW OF A STEELIER FLIGHT.  ...GREEN ROCK.  105   17
  AND SUCK OF THE GRAY SEA  .............................MAN IN BLACK  119    3
  CHEWING AT THE GRAY PAPER,  ............................POEM.2.DARK.  132    4
  THE FUTURE IS A GRAY SEAGULL  ...............................A LIFE  150   31
  INCHING OFF IN THE GRAY CHEVROLET, DRINKING THE GREEN  ......WAKING.  151    6
  THE STAR, THE WISE GRAY MEN.  ...........................HEAVY WOMEN  158   21
  HIS HEAD IS A LITTLE INTERIOR OF GRAY MIRRORS.  .........INSOMNIAC  163   22
  BLINDED TO ALL BUT THE GRAY, SPIRITLESS ROOM  .................WIDOW  165   39
```

	TITLE	PAGE	LINE

GRAY (CONT.)
GRAY AS THE WEATHER. ....WUTHERING HEIGHTS 167 21
GRAY FACES, SHUTTERED BY DRUGS, FOLLOW ME LIKE FLOWERS. ...SURGEON. 171 50
SPRY, WRY, AND GRAY AS THESE MARCH STICKS, ...AMONG THE NARCISSI 190   1
A GRAY WALL NOW, CLAWED AND BLOODY. ...................APPREHENSIONS 195   6
TWO GRAY, PAPERY BAGS -- ..............................APPREHENSIONS 195 13
THE GRAY SKY LOWERS, THE HILLS LIKE A GREEN SEA ....BERCK-PLAGE 199 73
BROOD CELLS GRAY AS THE FOSSILS OF SHELLS ....STINGS 214 12
THE MAN WITH GRAY HANDS STANDS UNDER THE HONEYCOMB ....THE SWARM 216 33
THE MAN WITH GRAY HANDS SMILES -- ....THE SWARM 217 51
GHASTLY STATUE WITH ONE GRAY TOE ....DADDY 222   9
GRAY, INDETERMINATE GILT ....LYONNESSE 234   6
THE SEA SHATTERING ITS GRAY ONE --- ....THE COURIERS 247 12
IN A THICK GRAY DEATH-SOUP, ...LETTER IN NOVEMBER 253 28
GRAY BIRDS OBSESS MY HEART, ...MARY'S SONG 257 13
GRAY TALLOW, FROM BONE AND BONE. .....................EAVESDROPPER 260 23
FROM GRAY CHILD FACES CRYING IN THE STREETS. ....FEMALE AUTHOR 301 14
MY ROOM IS A TWITTERING GRAY BOX WITH A WALL *EPITAPH IN THREE PARTS 337 26
ENORMOUS BOX OF GRAY WHERE GOD HAS GONE .....EPITAPH IN THREE PARTS 338 30
GRAYBEARDS (1)
OF GRAYBEARDS WAKES US UP. ....BATTLE-SCENE   85 40
GRAYED (1)
TO SAFE GRAY NEVER GRAYED HIS TEMPER. ....WHITENESS I REMEMBER 102 11
GRAYER (1)
AND GRAYER; NOT EVEN MOVING THEIR BONES. ....THE THIN PEOPLE   65 47
GRAYNESS (1)
GRAYNESS BLUES, REDDENS, AND THE OUTLINE ....THE THIN PEOPLE   65 34
GRAYS (1)
A MULTITUDE OF SHADED GRAYS; SUSPENSE ....LOVE IS A PARALLAX 329 10
GRAZING (3)
THEN, HONOR-BOUND, MUTE GRAZING CATTLE; ....BUCOLICS   24 11
SWEET GRASS SPRANG FOR THEIR GRAZING. ......SONG FOR A SUMMER'S DAY   31   5
GRAZING AT THE MARGINS OF A BAD MONOCHROME, ...THE EYE-MOTE 109 14
GREASE (2)
MY NIGHT SWEATS GREASE HIS BREAKFAST PLATE. ....THE JAILER 226   1
HE SHRIEKS IN HIS GREASE ....BRASILIA 258   9
GREASED (1)
WITHOUT STOP THOSE GREASED MACHINES, ...NIGHT SHIFT   77 22
GREASES (1)
WARM RAIN GREASES MY HAIR, EXTINGUISHES NOTHING.*BURNING THE LETTERS 205 47
GREASING (1)
GREASING THE BODIES OF ADULTERERS ....FEVER. 231 25
GREASY (1)
A GREASY SMACK ON EVERY CHEEK ....FAMILY REUNION 300 14
GREAT (57)
AND THAT GREAT WOUND ....STREET SONG   36 18
O MY GREAT IDIOT, WHO ....LETTER TO A PURIST   37   9
"WHAT LOVE," ASKED FATHER SHAWN, "BUT TOO GREAT LOVE ...DIALOGUE B.   39 31
AND I, GREAT MAGNANIMOUS FOOL, THUS WRENCHED FROM ..MONOLOGUE AT 3.   40 13
JANGLING THEIR GREAT MONEY BAGS. ....RHYME   50   8
HIS GREAT SOW: ....SOW   60   2
THE GREAT GRANDAM! -- OUR MARVEL BLAZONED A KNIGHT, ...SOW   61 29
LIKE A PLANET, A STONE, SWALLOWED IN A GREAT DARKNESS,*THE OTHER TWO   68 25
THE GREAT CARBUNCLE ....THE GREAT CARBUNCLE   72   T
TOWARD THAT GREAT JEWEL: SHOWN OFTEN, ...THE GREAT CARBUNCLE   72 11
IN THE MIDST OF ALL THAT GREEN AND THOSE GREAT LILIES! ...YADWIGHA.   86 39
DRUNKENNESS OF THE GREAT DEPTHS. ....LORELEI   95 32
THOSE GREAT GODDESSES OF PEACE. ....LORELEI   95 35
THE SKY'S GREAT BELL GLASS AND BRIEFLY ENGRAVE ...IN MIDAS' COUNTRY   99   8
ABOUT SAM: WHITENESS AND THE GREAT RUN ....WHITENESS I REMEMBER 102   2
INIMICAL NOW. THE GREAT GREEN ROCK ....GREEN ROCK, WINTHROP BAY 105 10
THE GREAT BRONZE GATE BEGAN TO CRACK, ...THE BULL OF BENDYLAW 108 13
THE PURPLE EGG-STONES: FROM GREAT HEAD'S KNOB ....POINT SHIRLEY 110 22
VAMPIRING DRY OF MILK EACH GREAT GOAT UDDER. ....GOATSUCKER 111   4
THE GREAT COROLLAS DILATE, PEELING BACK THEIR SILKS. ..BEEKEEPER'S. 118   2
THE GREAT GODS, STONE-HEAD, CLAW-FOOT,*THE HERMIT AT OUTERMOST HOUSE 118   4
OVER A GREAT STONE SPIT ....MAN IN BLACK 119 13
BONES OF THE GREAT TREES. ....DARK WOOD, DARK WATER 127   5
PROCEED FROM YOUR GREAT LIPS. ....THE COLOSSUS 129   4
UNWINDS FROM THE GREAT UMBILICUS OF THE SUN POEM.3.MAENAD. 133 19
I LIE ON A GREAT ANVIL. POEM.7.S. 136   2
AND A DROWNED MAN, COMPLAINING OF THE GREAT COLD, ...A LIFE 150 34
I IMAGINE MYSELF WITH A GREAT PUBLIC, ...BARREN WOMAN 157   6
THEY ARE OPENING LIKE THE MOUTH OF SOME GREAT AFRICAN CAT, ...TULIPS 162 59
WIDOW: THAT GREAT, VACANT ESTATE! ....WIDOW 164 21
THEY ARE SCRUBBED AND SELF-ASSURED AS THE GREAT PLANETS. ....STARS. 165 16
BOTH OF YOU ARE GREAT LIGHT BORROWERS. ....THE RIVAL 166   4
THAT LOOKS OUT ON NOTHING, NOTHING BUT A GREAT SPACE   BLACKBERRYING 169 25
EIGHT GREAT TONGUES AFFIRMING THE RESURRECTION. ....MOON. 173 13
WHEN I WALK OUT, I AM A GREAT EVENT. ....THREE WOMEN 176   8
AND THE GREAT SWAN, WITH ITS TERRIBLE LOOK, ...THREE WOMEN 178 50
DAWN FLOWERS IN THE GREAT ELM OUTSIDE THE HOUSE. ....THREE WOMEN 185 309
THERE IS A GREAT DEAL ELSE TO DO. MY HANDS ....THREE WOMEN 187 359
AND YOU, DURING THE GREAT WAR ....LITTLE FUGUE 188 31

```
                                              TITLE           PAGE  LINE
GREAT (CONT.)
   GREAT SILENCE OF ANOTHER ORDER. ......................LITTLE FUGUE    188   37
   I HEAR HER GREAT HEART PURR. ......................AN APPEARANCE    189    3
   I KNOW THE BOTTOM, SHE SAYS. I KNOW IT WITH MY GREAT TAP ROOT:   ELM   192    1
   THEY HAD AN EFFICIENCY, A GREAT BEAUTY, .........THE RABBIT CATCHER   193    9
   THIS IS THE SEA, THEN, THIS GREAT ABEYANCE. ...........BERCK-PLAGE   196    1
   A GREAT SURGEON, NOW A TATTOOIST, .......THE COURAGE OF SHUTTING-UP   210   10
   IN EIGHT GREAT BOUNDS, A GREAT SCAPEGOAT. ...................STINGS   215   41
   IN EIGHT GREAT BOUNDS, A GREAT SCAPEGOAT. ...................STINGS   215   41
   DO NOT THINK I UNDERESTIMATE YOUR GREAT CONCERN. ......LADY LAZARUS   246   72
   AND YOU, GREAT STASIS --- .....................................YEARS   255   16
   WHAT IS SO GREAT IN THAT! ....................................YEARS   255   17
   IS THERE NO GREAT LOVE, ONLY TENDERNESS? ...................MYSTIC   269   24
   A GREAT FRIEZE, EGYPTIAN, PERHAPS, OR GREEK, ...........DIALOGUE O.   276    9
   THE GREAT ROSES, MANY OF THEM SCENTLESS, ..QUEEN MARY'S ROSE GARDEN   290    4
   TIME IS A GREAT MACHINE OF IRON BARS ..............SONNET: TO TIME   311   13
   GOD HEARS FROM HIS GREAT SUNSTRUCK HELL ........SONG FOR A REVOLU.   323   19
   AS GREAT WEIGHTS DROP ALL ABOUT HER ....................AERIALIST   331   17
   AND HONOR THE GREAT GODDESS OF THE AIR *THE PRINCESS AND THE GOBLINS  335   62
GREAT-GRANDCHILDREN (1)
   A MARVEL TO YOUR GREAT-GRANDCHILDREN. ..........A BIRTHDAY PRESENT   207   31
GREATGRANDMOTHER (1)
   MOTHER, GRANDMOTHER, GREATGRANDMOTHER ..........ALL THE DEAD DEARS    70   20
GREAT-TALONED (1)
   ADRIFT IN THE GUISE OF SOME GREAT-TALONED BIRD .........DIALOGUE O.   285  311
GRECIAN (1)
   COMPOSED IN GRECIAN TUNIC AND PSYCHE-KNOT, ..........CONVERSATION.    21   11
GREED (2)
   HIS GREED HAS SET THE WOODS AFLAME, ........................PURSUIT    22    3
   IN THE FURNACE OF GREED. CLOUDS, CLOUDS. ..................THE SWARM   216   16
GREEK (3)
   OF THE GREEK BEAUTIES YOU BROUGHT ..................PRIVATE GROUND   130    2
   THE ILLUSION OF A GREEK NECESSITY ............................EDGE   272    4
   A GREAT FRIEZE, EGYPTIAN, PERHAPS, OR GREEK, ...........DIALOGUE O.   276    9
GREEN (116)
   GROW GREEN AGAIN? WHO'D WALK IN THIS BLEAK PLACE? *WINTER LANDSCAPE,   22   15
   THEY PITCHED THEIR COATS, COME TO GREEN BED. ..............BUCOLICS    23    8
   WAVER, FAINTLY GREEN, SHUDDERING AWAY ...............TALE OF A TUB    25   26
   IN THE GREEN OF EDEN, PRETEND FUTURE'S SHINING FRUIT   TALE OF A TUB   25   39
   ON ARMS AND LEGS IN A FRINGE OF KELP; GREEN SOAP .....TALE OF A TUB    25   43
   A GREEN CRESCENT OF PALMS ......................SOUTHERN SUNRISE    26   10
   END: GREEN SHORES APPEAR; WE ASSUME OUR NAMES, ...CHANNEL CROSSING    27   40
   GREEN OAT-SPROUTS JUT: ...................................ODE FOR TED   29    2
   BORN GREEN WE WERE .........................................FIRESONG   30    1
   ON THAT GREEN ALTAR .....................TWO SISTERS OF PERSEPHONE    32   20
   AND ALL GREEN DREAMS NOT WORTH MUCH, .................STRUMPET SONG    33    2
   GIVE GRASS ITS GREEN ...................SOLILOQUY OF THE SOLIPSIST    37   21
   A MILLION GREEN COUNTIES FROM HERE, ...........MONOLOGUE AT 3 A.M.    40    7
   SILENT AND SHINING ON A GREEN ROCK BEDDED IN MUD, ....DREAM WITH C.   44   15
   WITH GREEN ROCK GLIDING, A DELICATE SCHOONER .........DREAM WITH C.   44   17
   WHAT THOUGH GREEN LEAVES ONLY WITNESS ..........WREATH FOR A BRIDAL    44    1
   THIS WAVE'S GREEN PEAK ON WIRE .........EPITAPH FOR FIRE AND FLOWER    45    2
   BRIGHT GREEN AND THUMBABLE ...........................FIESTA MELONS    46    5
   OF TURTLE-DARK GREEN. ................................FIESTA MELONS    46    7
   THE FIGS ON THE FIG TREE IN THE YARD ARE GREEN; .........DEPARTURE    51    1
   GREEN, ALSO, THE GRAPES ON THE GREEN VINE ...............DEPARTURE    51    2
   GREEN, ALSO, THE GRAPES ON THE GREEN VINE ...............DEPARTURE    51    2
   ON THE ARCHED GREEN ........................................RESOLVE    52   14
   TWO ENTER TO TAP HER SIGHT, A GREEN PAIR .............CRYSTAL GAZER    55    7
   NOW, AS GREEN SAP ASCENDS THE STEEPLED WOOD, ...........MAYFLOWER    60    5
   BUT NO HOCUS-POCUS OF GREEN ANGELS .....................CONJURING.    66   17
   ON A GREEN BALLOON BRIGHT WITH A MILLION .....THE DISQUIETING MUSES   76   43
   WITH MOON-EYE, MOUTH-PIPE. HE PIPES. PIPES GREEN. PIPES WATER. ....
                                              ... SNAKECHARMER    79    3
   PIPES WATER GREEN UNTIL GREEN WATERS WAVER ...........SNAKECHARMER    79    4
   PIPES WATER GREEN UNTIL GREEN WATERS WAVER ...........SNAKECHARMER    79    4
   AND AS HIS NOTES TWINE GREEN, THE GREEN RIVER ........SNAKECHARMER    79    6
   AND AS HIS NOTES TWINE GREEN, THE GREEN RIVER ........SNAKECHARMER    79    6
   FROM HIS THIN PIPE. OUT OF THIS GREEN NEST ..........SNAKECHARMER    79   18
   TO A MELTING OF GREEN WATERS, TILL NO SNAKE ..........SNAKECHARMER    79   25
   SHOWS ITS HEAD, AND THOSE GREEN WATERS BACK TO .......SNAKECHARMER    79   26
   WATER, TO GREEN, TO NOTHING LIKE A SNAKE. ...........SNAKECHARMER    79   27
   GREEN VIRGINS, CONSECRATING LIMB AND LIP ..........VIRGIN IN A TREE   82   27
   SET IN AN INTRICATE WILDERNESS OF GREEN ................YADWIGHA.    85    5
   TO CHOOSE BETWEEN YOUR WORLD OF JUNGLE GREEN ...........YADWIGHA.    85    9
   STOOD STUBBORN IN ITS JUNGLE: RED AGAINST GREEN, .......YADWIGHA.    85   18
   RED AGAINST FIFTY VARIANTS OF GREEN, ..................YADWIGHA.    85   19
   MARVELINGLY NUMBERED THE MANY SHADES OF GREEN. ........YADWIGHA.    86   34
   IN THE MIDST OF ALL THAT GREEN AND THOSE GREAT LILIES! ...YADWIGHA.   86   39
   GREEN, WHOLLY GREEN, THEY STAND THEIR KNOBBY SPINE   ABOVE THE OXBOW   88   10
   GREEN, WHOLLY GREEN, THEY STAND THEIR KNOBBY SPINE   ABOVE THE OXBOW   88   10
   BLINDERED BY GREEN, UNDER A GREEN-GRAINED SKY ......ABOVE THE OXBOW   88   28
   BY CORRECT GREEN LINES AND NO SEEDY FREE-FOR-ALL ...ABOVE THE OXBOW   89   49
   STRAIGHTFORWARDLY ACROSS THE SPRINGING GREEN. ......ABOVE THE OXBOW   89   52
```

                                                          TITLE   PAGE   LINE
GREEN (CONT.)
    OF THE SPINACH PATCH. BUNCH AFTER BUNCH OF GREEN ...SPINACH-PICKER.   89   7
    SUN AND SKY MIRRORED THE GREEN OF THE SPINACH. .....SPINACH-PICKER.   89   12
    ITS ROUND PERIOD, DISPLACED AND GREEN, ...THE GHOST'S LEAVETAKING   91   29
    HIS WORLD OF MUD -- GREEN COLOR ......MUSSEL HUNTER AT ROCK HARBOR   97   71
    GREEN TO THE POINT OF BLACKNESS, SOME ....CHILD'S PARK STONES   100   2
    UNSETTLING THE STEADY-ROOTED GREEN ....WHITENESS I REMEMBER   102   15
    GREEN GRASS STREAMING, HOUSES A RIVER ....WHITENESS I REMEMBER   102   19
    LET DROP ITS SPITTLE OF SLUGGISH GREEN ..............RHODODENDRON.   103   6
    GREEN ROCK, WINTHROP BAY ....GREEN ROCK, WINTHROP BAY   104   T
    INIMICAL NOW. THE GREAT GREEN ROCK ....GREEN ROCK, WINTHROP BAY   105   10
    TAILS STREAMING AGAINST THE GREEN ....THE EYE-MOTE   109   3
    HORSES WARPED ON THE ALTERING GREEN, ...THE EYE-MOTE   109   12
    COCKCHAFERS AND THE WAN, GREEN LUNA MOTH. ....GOATSUCKER   111   14
    THE BLAND GRANTA DOUBLE THEIR WHITE AND GREEN ....WATERCOLOR.   112   9
    ARCADIAN GREEN ....WATERCOLOR OF GRANTCHESTER MEADOWS   112   20
    MOTHER MEDEA IN A GREEN SMOCK ....AFTERMATH   114   9
    I'VE EATEN A BAG OF GREEN APPLES, ...METAPHORS   116   8
    ROUND, GREEN, DISCONSOLATE AS A TEAR. .....THE BEEKEEPER'S DAUGHTER   118   18
    BUT A CERTAIN MEANING GREEN. ....THE HERMIT AT OUTERMOST HOUSE 119   16
    ROCK-FACE, CRAB-CLAW VERGED ON GREEN. *THE HERMIT AT OUTERMOST HOUSE   119   18
    HEN HUTS AND CATTLE GREEN ....MAN IN BLACK   119   9
    RUST-RED OR GREEN AS LICHENS. ....OLD LADIES' HOME   120   14
    THEIR EYES REVOLVE THE WHOLE TOWN LIKE A BLUE AND GREEN BALL. *NET-.   121   12
    THOUGH THE GREEN SEA GARDENS STALL, ...MAGNOLIA SHOALS   121   6
    THE SMALL GREEN NOSTRILS BREATHE, ...THE SLEEPERS   123   17
    THE RED TOMATO'S IN, THE GREEN BEAN; ....YADDO: THE GRAND MANOR   123   4
    IT FLOWS OFF BELOW THE GREEN AND WHITE ....THE BURNT-OUT SPA 138   22
    NO ANIMAL SPOILS ON HER GREEN DOORSTEP. ....THE BURNT-OUT SPA   138   30
    INCHING OFF IN THE GRAY CHEVROLET, DRINKING THE GREEN ......WAKING.   151   6
    GREEN AS A POOL TABLE, WHERE CABBAGE BUTTERFLIES ....WHITSUN   154   19
    ON THE GREEN HILL, UNDER THE THORN TREES, ...HEAVY WOMEN   158   12
    SCARED AND BARE ON THE GREEN PLASTIC-PILLOWED TROLLEY ......TULIPS   161   25
    THEY STAND LIKE SHADOWS ABOUT THE GREEN LANDSCAPE -- ....WIDOW   164   28
    THE HIGH, GREEN MEADOWS ARE GLOWING, AS IF LIT FROM WITHIN. ...
                                                     ... BLACKBERRYING   168   14
    THESE HILLS ARE TOO GREEN AND SWEET TO HAVE TASTED SALT. BLACKBER.   169   22
    AND RENTED AN OLD GREEN BOAT. I ROWED. YOU READ ....THE BABYSITTERS   175   31
    HOW LONG CAN I BE A WALL AROUND MY GREEN PROPERTY? .....THREE WOMEN   185   295
    CRACK THROUGH STONE, AND THEY ARE GREEN WITH LIFE. .....THREE WOMEN   187   371
    IT RATTLES THEIR STARS ON THE GREEN HILL WHERE PERCY .....NARCISSI.   190   5
    A HUNDRED, ON THAT HILL -- GREEN AND RED, ...PHEASANT   191   17
    INFINITE, GREEN, UTTERLY UNTOUCHABLE. ................APPREHENSIONS   195   2
    THEY ARE HANDLING THE BLACK AND GREEN LOZENGES LIKE THE PARTS
                OF A BODY. ....BERCK-PLAGE   196   16
    WHILE A GREEN POOL OPENS ITS EYE, ...BERCK-PLAGE   197   27
    THE GRAY SKY LOWERS, THE HILLS LIKE A GREEN SEA ....BERCK-PLAGE   199   73
    POLLARDED GREEN BALLS, THE TREES MARCH TO CHURCH. ......BERCK-PLAGE   199   92
    THIS APPARITION IN A GREEN HELMET, ...THE BEE MEETING 211   28
    WHERE IT POURS BEAN GREEN OVER BLUE ....DADDY   222   12
    GREEN AS EUNUCHS, YOUR WISHES ....MEDUSA   226   38
    A GREEN DRINK, ONE A BLUE. ....AMNESIAC   233   22
    THE BLUE, GREEN, ...LYONNESSE   234   5
    THE CLEAR, GREEN, QUITE BREATHABLE ATMOSPHERE, ...LYONNESSE   234   16
    OF WHAT GREEN STARS CAN MAKE IT TO OUR GATE. ....BY CANDLELIGHT   236   5
    SIDE OF GREEN ADAM, I ....PURDAH   242   4
    THERE IS A GREEN IN THE AIR, ...LETTER IN NOVEMBER   253   8
    GLOBES OF THIN AIR, RED, GREEN, ...BALLOONS   271   14
    AND HALE ITS GREEN LATTICEWORK OF LEAVES. YOU NEED .....DIALOGUE O.   280   159
    A SEA OF DREAMS WASHES THE EDGE OF MY GREEN ISLAND ...QUEEN MARY'S.   290   2
    GOLD MOUTHS CRY WITH THE GREEN YOUNG ....GOLD MOUTHS CRY   302   1
    HER GREEN EYES SLANT, HAIR FLARING IN A FAN ....CINDERELLA   303   2
    PUNY, GREEN, AND TART, ...JILTED   304   10
    IN GLASS PAGODAS HUNG WITH VEILS OF GREEN ....APRIL AUBADE   312   2
    GATHER IDLE OYSTERS FROM GREEN SHOALS, ...GO GET THE GOODLY SQUAB   313   19
    GREEN ALLEYS WHERE WE REVELED HAVE BECOME ....DOOM OF EXILES   318   5
    TANGLING IN THE TIDE'S GREEN FALL ....TWO LOVERS.   327   6
    FLARING GREEN THROUGH PHILODENDRON LEAVES ......MORNING IN THE HOS.   332   2
    BEYOND THE INCONSTANT GREEN ....TOUCH-AND-GO   335   6
    DEVOURING GREEN GARDENS INCH BY INCH. ....EPITAPH IN THREE PARTS   337   17
    GRASSHOPPER GOBLINS WITH GREEN POINTED EARS   EPITAPH IN THREE PARTS   337   23
GREENCHEESE (1)
    INFREQUENT AS A MOON OF GREENCHEESE ....APRIL 18   302   8
GREEN-COPSE-CASTLED (1)
    AND THE GREEN-COPSE-CASTLED ....SOW   61   36
GREENERY (1)
    THROUGH THE AFRICAN GIRAFFE IN ITS EDENY GREENERY, ...A SECRET   219   12
GREENEST (1)
    GULLS MULLED IN THE GREENEST LIGHT. ..THE HERMIT AT OUTERMOST HOUSE 119   19
GREEN-EYED (1)
    BLINKING GREEN-EYED AND SOLITARY ....ELLA MASON AND HER ELEVEN CATS   54   38
GREEN-GRAINED (1)
    BLINDERED BY GREEN, UNDER A GREEN-GRAINED SKY ......ABOVE THE OXBOW   88   28
GREEN-HEARTED (1)
    A DRESSING OF MULE EARS, MOTHY PELTS, BUT GREEN-HEARTED,*POEM.1.WHO.   131   17

GREENHORN (4)
    NONE OF THAT GREENHORN LOT MATCHED HER BRIGHT CROWN. ...
                              ... THE QUEEN'S COMPLAINT   29   20
    GO TO YOUR GREENHORN YOUTH ....RECANTATION   42   17
    WHAT GREENHORN VENTS HIS VENOM AGAINST GIANTS ....DIALOGUE O. 281 199
    SHE TELLS THE GREENHORN MINER TO BOW DOWN ....THE PRINCESS. 335   61
GREENING (1)
    THEY CLEAVE THE RIVER'S GREENING PATINAS; ....IN MIDAS' COUNTRY 100   18
GREEN-LEAVED (1)
    THE BABY LACE, THE GREEN-LEAVED CONFECTIONERY,*THE MUNICH MANNEQUINS 263   22
GREEN-LIT (1)
    THROUGH AIR STREAMING AND GREEN-LIT, ...THE GREAT CARBUNCLE   72   2
GREENLY (1)
    AS A GREENLY ESCAPED IDIOT, ...STREET SONG   36   12
GREENNESS (1)
    BUT GREENNESS, DARKNESS SO PURE ....YEARS 255   4
GREEN-POCKED (1)
    FATTEN IN GREEN-POCKED PODS, THE THREE NET-MENDERS SIT OUT, ..NET-. 121   3
GREEN-REEDED (1)
    SOME DUCKS STEP DOWN OFF THEIR GREEN-REEDED SHELF ....QUEEN MARY'S. 290   11
GREENS (4)
    SHEEP GREENS, FINNED FALLS, "I SHALL COMPOSE A CRISIS ...CONJURING.   66   11
    REDS, GREENS, BLUES. ....ON THE PLETHORA OF DRYADS   68   36
    OF BROWNS AND GREENS. EACH WORE ONE ...MUSSEL HUNTER AT ROCK HARBOR   96   32
    EATEN BY WEEDY GREENS. ....WORDS 270   13
GREEN-SHADED (1)
    AND THE MAID SMOKED AND SHOT POOL UNDER A GREEN-SHADED LAMP. BABY. 175   24
GREEN-SINGING (1)
    GREEN-SINGING BIRDS EXPLODE FROM ALL THE ROCKS.   PROLOGUE TO SPRING 322   15
GREEN-STRIPED (1)
    THOSE GREEN-STRIPED OVALS OF SILVER TISSUE? ....LEAVING EARLY 146   15
GREEN-TESSELLATED (1)
    ON A RED VELVET COUCH WITHIN YOUR GREEN-TESSELLATED ......YADWIGHA.   86 26-7
GREEN-TIPPED (1)
    IT WERE A GREEN-TIPPED LEAF ....SONG FOR A SUMMER'S DAY   31   13
GREEN-VAULTED (1)
    THE MIMIC HEAD -- IN A CROTCHED WILLOW, GREEN-VAULTED ..LADY AND T.   69 23-4
GREETING (1)
    THE LAUGHTER AND THE SCREAMS OF GREETING: ....FAMILY REUNION 300   12
GREW (7)
    GREW SO LEAN AND WOULD NOT ROUND ....THE THIN PEOPLE   64   8
    THEY GREW THEIR TOES AND FINGERS WELL ENOUGH, ...STILLBORN 142   2
    MY FINGER-LENGTH GREW LUCENT AS GLASS. ....LOVE LETTER 147   30
    IN TIME OUR RELATIONSHIP GREW MORE INTENSE. ....IN PLASTER 159   28
    THE WAY SHE LAID HIS LETTERS, TILL THEY GREW WARM ....WIDOW 164   18
    AND THEN GREW NORMAL, ...LESBOS 229   57
    US IN: A THIRD UNDID THEM. AND WE GREW ONE ....DIALOGUE O. 285 327
GREY (1)
    GREY WAVES THE STUB-NECKED EIDERS RIDE. ....POINT SHIRLEY 110   33
GRID (2)
    THERE IS ONLY A LITTLE GRID, NO EXIT. ...THE ARRIVAL OF THE BEE BOX 213   10
    I PUT MY EYE TO THE GRID. ....THE ARRIVAL OF THE BEE BOX 213   11
GRIEF (4)
    EXPRESSIVE OF GRIEF TURNS GODS, LIKE KINGS, TO ROCKS. ......PERSEUS   83   29
    GRIEF AND ANGER, EXORCIZED, ...A LIFE 150   29
    LIES. LIES AND A GRIEF. ....THE COURIERS 247   6
    BEHIND MOCK-CEREMONY OF YOUR GRIEF ....DIRGE FOR A JOKER 302   5
GRIEFS (2)
    UNLOAD THEIR GRIEFS ON MY SHOES, ...PRIVATE GROUND 130   18
    THE GRASSES UNLOAD THEIR GRIEFS ON MY FEET AS IF I WERE GOD, MOON. 172   3
GRIEF'S (1)
    GRIEF'S HONEST GRIMACE, DEBASED BY TIME, ...THE BEGGARS   47   7
GRIEVANCES (2)
    OLD GRIEVANCES JOSTLING EACH OTHER, SO MANY LOOSE TEETH. ....ZOO K. 154   13
    TATTOOING OVER AND OVER THE SAME BLUE GRIEVANCES, ...COURAGE. 210   11
GRIEVE (4)
    THINKING NEVER TO HAVE LEFT THE WORLD, YOU GRIEVE ......DIALOGUE B.   39   34
    THEY POISE AND GRIEVE AS IN SOME OLD TRAGEDY. ....THE OTHER TWO   68   21
    SULFUROUS ADULTERIES GRIEVE IN A DREAM. ....THE OTHER 202   25
    FOR NAIVE LARKS WHO STARVE AND GRIEVE. ...METAMORPHOSES OF THE MOON 307   18
GRIEVES (4)
    FOR WHICH THE GHOST OF BOCKLIN GRIEVES. ....OUIJA   78   15
    SURVIVES, GRIEVES ....POINT SHIRLEY 110   29
    HER O-MOUTH GRIEVES AT THE WORLD; YOURS IS UNAFFECTED, ...THE RIVAL 166   5
    AND NEVER GRIEVES, ...GOLD MOUTHS CRY 302   11
GRIEVING (1)
    OPEN IN ITS GAPE OF PERPETUAL GRIEVING. ....THREE WOMEN 182 185
GRIEVOUSLY (1)
    GRIEVOUSLY PURPLED, MOUTH SKEWERED ON A GROAN, ...THE RAVAGED FACE 115   6
GRIFFIN-LEGGED (1)
    ANCHORED ITSELF, GRIFFIN-LEGGED AND DARKLY GRAINED. ..THE OTHER TWO   68   9
GRILLS (1)
    ON THE PUBLIC GRILLS, AND THE OCHREOUS SALT FLATS, ...SUICIDE. 115   2
GRIM (2)
    GRIM AS GARGOYLES FROM YEARS SPENT SQUATTING AT SEA'S BORDER ...

| | | TITLE | PAGE | LINE |

GRIM (CONT.)

                             ... DREAM WITH CLAM-DIGGERS   44   25
    BUT SAT ON, GUARDING HIS GRIM BATTLEMENT. ..THE SNOWMAN ON THE MOOR   58   7
GRIMACE (3)
    TO PATCH WITH BRAND OF LOVE THIS RANK GRIMACE ....STRUMPET SONG   34   16
    GRIEF'S HONEST GRIMACE, DEBASED BY TIME, ...THE BEGGARS   47   7
    GRIMACED AS SKULLS GRIMACE: IT ....MUSSEL HUNTER AT ROCK HARBOR   97   78
GRIMACED (1)
    GRIMACED AS SKULLS GRIMACE: IT ....MUSSEL HUNTER AT ROCK HARBOR   97   78
GRIMACES (1)
    THEIR ROUND EYES, THEIR TEETH, THEIR GRIMACES ....TOTEM 264   17
GRIMLY (2)
    BUT GROWN GRIMLY, AND GRIMLY ....MUSSEL HUNTER AT ROCK HARBOR   96   36
    BUT GROWN GRIMLY, AND GRIMLY ....MUSSEL HUNTER AT ROCK HARBOR   96   36
GRIN (9)
    PUTS ON A PUBLIC GRIN, REPEATS OUR NAME ....TALE OF A TUB   24   7
    AND CRIMP THEIR WRINKLES IN A GRIN, ...RHYME   50   7
    WITH A GRANITE GRIN ....ALL THE DEAD DEARS   70   2
    THE BONNETED LADIES GRIN. ....OLD LADIES' HOME 120   18
    UNHINGED AND HIS GRIN CROOKED, ...MEDALLION 124   6
    WHEN I GRIN, THE STITCHES TAUTEN. I GROW BACKWARD. I'M TWENTY,*FACE. 156   21
    CONDONING THE BEAK, THE CLAW, THE GRIN OF THE DOG ....THE SWARM 216   22
    TO THE GRANITE GRIN OF BONE. ....NOTES TO A NEOPHYTE 306   12
    MAN WHO CAN MANGLE THE GRIN OF KINGS: ....LAMENT 316   17
GRIND (1)
    TO GRIND OUR KNIVES AND SCISSORS: ....THE DEATH OF MYTH-MAKING 104   2
GRINDING (1)
    STARS GRINDING, CRUMB BY CRUMB, ...ALL THE DEAD DEARS   70   11
GRINDS (1)
    GRINDS ROUND, BEARING DOWN WITH THE STRAW, ...HEAVY WOMEN 158   20
GRINNED (1)
    GRINNED LIKE A GETAWAY CAR. ....BURNING THE LETTERS 204   8
GRINNING (3)
    AND, FIXED IN THE CRYSTAL CENTER, GRINNING FIERCE: ...CRYSTAL GAZER   56   47
    GRINNING OVER ITS BONE OF IVORY ....THE SWARM 216   24
    TIGER-TAMER AND GRINNING CLOWN ....AERIALIST 331   29
GRIP (7)
    GRIP THE RAIL, SQUINT AHEAD, AND WONDER HOW MUCH LONGER   CHANNEL C.   26   6
    HOW THEY GRIP US THROUGH THIN AND THICK, ...ALL THE DEAD DEARS   70   13
    NEVER GRIP, AS THEIR GRANDSIRES DID, THAT DEVIL WHO CHUCKLES*LESSON.   80   24
    BEEN STRUCK TO KEEP ALL GLORY IN THE GRIP ....VIRGIN IN A TREE   82   32
    ALREADY YOUR DOLL GRIP LETS GO. ....PARLIAMENT HILL FIELDS 152   25
    NO FINGERS TO GRIP, NO TONGUE, ...PARALYTIC 266   3
    THAN AGAINST GRAVITY'S GRIP, TABLES RISING; THE DRINK ..DIALOGUE O. 279 122
GRIPPING (1)
    IN THE DEEP CONVULSION GRIPPING YOUR FACE, MUSCLES ....PERSEUS   83   43
GRIPS (1)
    THE WATERCOLORIST GRIPS ....MAGNOLIA SHOALS 122   19
GRISLY (1)
    YET, SHRINED ON HER SHELF, THE GRISLY VISAGE ENDURED, ..LADY AND T.   70   29
GRISLY-BRISTLED (1)
    BY A GRISLY-BRISTLED ....SOW   61   32
GRISLY-THEWED (1)
    DOWN FROM PRIDE'S SIZE: INSTEAD, A GRISLY-THEWED, ...SNOWMAN O.   59   29
GRIST (1)
    OUR OWN GRIST DOWN TO ITS BONY FACE. ....ALL THE DEAD DEARS   70   12
GRIT (4)
    HER DOWN TO MERE QUARTZ GRIT IN THAT STONY LIGHT ..HARDCASTLE CRAGS   63   44
    AND SUCH GRIT CORRUPTS MY EYES ....ON THE PLETHORA OF DRYADS   67   31
    YOU HAVE IT IN HAND. GRIT IN THE EYE OR A SORE ....PERSEUS   83   27
    SAND GRIT TO SIDED CRYSTAL ....MUSSEL HUNTER AT ROCK HARBOR   95   4
GRITS (3)
    WHILE I EAT GRITS ....RHYME   50   9
    THE SILK GRITS. ....LESBOS 229   62
    COLD GRITS UNDERFOOT, ...LYONNESSE 234   17
GRITTED (1)
    THE GRITTED WAVE LEAPS ....POINT SHIRLEY 110   5
GROAN (2)
    HE KINGS IT, NAVEL-KNIT TO NO GROAN, ...MAUDLIN   51   6
    GRIEVOUSLY PURPLED, MOUTH SKEWERED ON A GROAN, ...THE RAVAGED FACE 115   6
GROANS (1)
    BUT ALL THE ACCUMULATED LAST GRUNTS, GROANS, ...PERSEUS   83   17
GROCER (1)
    IS IT THE BUTCHER, THE GROCER, THE POSTMAN, SOMEONE I KNOW? ...BEE. 211   30
GROOM (2)
    IN A STILL PLACE, AND THE GROOM IS RED AND FORGETFUL, HE IS
        FEATURELESS ....BERCK-PLAGE 200 108
    OUR WORLD AND THEIRS WE'D BEST PLAY SAFE AND GROOM .....DIALOGUE O. 281 186
GROOVE (2)
    A GROOVE OF OLD FAULTS, DEEP AND BITTER. ....EVENT 195   15
    THE NEEDLE JOURNEYING IN ITS GROOVE, ...THE COURAGE OF SHUTTING-UP 210   8
GROPE (1)
    COULD GROPE ITS WAY TO GOSPEL THROUGH THAT WELTER ......DIALOGUE O. 286 346
GROSS (7)
    HIS NEXT MARTYR TO THE GROSS CAUSE ....SPIDER   49   26

218

TITLE   PAGE LINE

GROSS (CONT.)
FAR DEEPER IN GROSS WOOD ....ON THE PLETHORA OF DRYADS 67 11
TO THE GROSS EATING GAME ....ALL THE DEAD DEARS 70   9
FROM A GROSS COMIC STRIP, AND TOWARD ....OUIJA 78 24
TREE-TWIST WILL APE THIS GROSS ANATOMY ....VIRGIN IN A TREE 82 44
GIVEN AN INCH. NOT THAT THEY'RE GROSS (ALTHOUGH ....POEMS, POTATOES 106   6
AS IF TEMPTING OUR GROSS GULLIBILITY ...DIALOGUE OVER A OUIJA BOARD 281 178
GROSSE (1)
THE YEW HEDGE OF THE GROSSE FUGE. ....LITTLE FUGUE 188 20
GROSSNESS (2)
BLOOD FAULTLESSLY BROACHED REDEEMED THE SULLIED AIR, THE EARTH'S
                         GROSSNESS. ....THE GORING 47 10
"LET US FLATTEN AND LAUNDER THE GROSSNESS FROM THESE SOULS." *THREE. 179 91
GROTESQUE (1)
TO THE FINAL GROTESQUE JOKE OF DEATH ....DIRGE FOR A JOKER 303 10
GROUND (8)
HE STAMPED AND CRACKED STALKS TO THE GROUND ....BUCOLICS 24 19
PAVING THIS GRAVE GROUND. HERE'S HONEST ROT .....NOVEMBER GRAVEYARD 56   8
SHOOK THE GROUND WITH ITS POUNDING. ....NIGHT SHIFT 76 11
WISH FOR EVEN GROUND, AND IT'S THE LAST CLIFF ......ABOVE THE OXBOW 88 22
THE SEA IN ITS COLD GIZZARD GROUND THOSE ROUNDS. ....POINT SHIRLEY 110 24
LIKE HIERATIC STONES, AND THE GROUND IS HARD.*ELECTRA ON AZALEA PATH 116   4
PRIVATE GROUND ....PRIVATE GROUND 130   T
OLD GROUND WITH A FEATHER ....BALLOONS 272 18
GROUNDHOG (1)
THE GROUNDHOG ON THE MOUNTAIN DID NOT RUN ...........INCOMMUNICADO 100   1
GROUNDHOGS (1)
WHERE LOVE-MET GROUNDHOGS LOVE ONE IN RETURN, ...INCOMMUNICADO 100   9
GROUND-WORK (1)
TO MAKE AWAY WITH THE GROUND-WORK ....FULL FATHOM FIVE 93 31-2
GROVE (9)
MIDNIGHT CLOAKS THE SULTRY GROVE; ....PURSUIT 22 26
FROM GROVE OF MOON-GLINT AND FEN-FROST ....FAUN 35   2
WHITE HOUSE AND ALMOND GROVE. THE BEGGARS ....THE BEGGARS 48 18
UNHORSED AND SHREDDED IN THE GROVE OF COMBAT ....SOW 61 31
THEIR MULTIFARIOUS SILKS IN THE HOLY GROVE*ON THE PLETHORA OF DRYADS 68 33
SAWS DOWN A REED AND SWIMS FROM HIS LIMBER GROVE, ...WATERCOLOR. 112 23
THEY ARE LEADING ME TO THE SHORN GROVE, THE CIRCLE OF HIVES. ..BEE. 211 23
SMOKE ROLLS AND SCARVES IN THE GROVE. ....THE BEE MEETING 212 36
WHOSE IS THAT LONG WHITE BOX IN THE GROVE, WHAT HAVE THEY
        ACCOMPLISHED, WHY AM I COLD. ....THE BEE MEETING 212 55
GROVES (1)
HALFWAY DOWN FROM GROVES WHERE THE THIN, BITTER ALMOND PIPS ..NET-. 121   2
GROW (11)
GROW GREEN AGAIN? WHO'D WALK IN THIS BLEAK PLACE? *WINTER LANDSCAPE, 22 15
THOSE ROCKS, CLEFT AND WORN, THEMSELVES THEN GROW ....PERSEUS 83 30
WE ARE FULL OF STARCH, MY SMALL WHITE FELLOWS. WE GROW. ..POEM.6.W. 135 17
WHEN I GRIN, THE STITCHES TAUTEN. I GROW BACKWARD. I'M TWENTY,*FACE. 156 21
WHEN THE SOLES OF MY FEET GROW COLD, ...LAST WORDS 172 19
THE BODY OF A STARFISH CAN GROW BACK ITS ARMS ....THREE WOMEN 184 257
THE SHEETS GROW HEAVY AS A LECHER'S KISS. ....FEVER. 231 30
HOW ONE WE GROW, ...ARIEL 239   5
I SHALL NEVER GROW OLD. NEW OYSTERS ....GIGOLO 268 26
GODS GROW TOO PROUD TO PRACTICE DOORMAN DUTIES ....DIALOGUE O. 280 127
OR THAT THE HEAT WITHIN WOULD GROW ....TO A JILTED LOVER 310 13
GROWER (2)
NOSY GROWER, ...EAVESDROPPER 260   3
OR AFTER GAY DAYS, OR COLORS THE GROWER FOUND GOOD. ..QUEEN MARY'S. 290 18
GROWING (3)
A POWER IS GROWING ON ME, AN OLD TENACITY. ....THREE WOMEN 180 141
GROWING BESIDE YOU, LIKE A TREE, ...FOR A FATHERLESS SON 205   2
MEMORIES GROWING, RING ON RING, ...WINTER TREES 257   4
GROWN (4)
A SOUL GROWN FEVERISH, CLUTCHING ITS DEAD BODY-TREE ....DIALOGUE B. 39 43
GROWN GARGANTUAN BY TRADE, ...MUSSEL HUNTER AT ROCK HARBOR 96 35
BUT GROWN GRIMLY, AND GRIMLY ....MUSSEL HUNTER AT ROCK HARBOR 96 36
GROWN MILKY, ALMOST CLEAR, LIKE THE BODIES OF SAINTS. ......CANDLES 148   4
GROWNUPS (2)
BUT OH, SAGE GROWNUPS KNOW ....BATTLE-SCENE 85 35
GROWNUPS COFFINED IN STOCKINGS AND JACKETS, ...WHITSUN 153   4
GROWNUPS' (1)
WE LIFTED A SUGARED HAM AND A PINEAPPLE FROM THE GROWNUPS' ICEBOX ...
                         ... THE BABYSITTERS 175 30
GROWS (4)
GROWS QUICK WITH SEED. ....TWO SISTERS OF PERSEPHONE 32 22
SUMMER GROWS OLD, COLD-BLOODED MOTHER. ....FROG AUTUMN 99   1
GROWS TALL. YOU CLUTCH YOUR BARS. ....BY CANDLELIGHT 237 22
GROWS BRITTLE AS A TILTED CHINA BOWL; ....PROLOGUE TO SPRING 322   5
GRUBBERS (1)
PALMING THE EARTH ASIDE, GRUBBERS ....BLUE MOLES 126 24
GRUBS (2)
WHERE SMALL ANTS ROLL THEIR EGGS, WHERE GRUBS FATTEN. .....MOONRISE 98 17
THE WHEELS, TWO RUBBER GRUBS, BITE THEIR SWEET TAILS. STOPPED DEAD 230   6
GRUB-WHITE (1)
GRUB-WHITE MULBERRIES REDDEN AMONG LEAVES. ....MOONRISE 98   1

	TITLE	PAGE	LINE

GRUDGES (1)
    OTHER ROCKS HIDE THEIR GRUDGES UNDER THE WATER. ....FINISTERRE 169 9
GRUFF (2)
    WHICH NO GRUFF ANIMAL MISINTERPRETS. .................INCOMMUNICADO 100 11
    HE HEARS THE GRUFF KNOCKING ....TEMPER OF TIME 336 19
GRUFF-TIMBRED (1)
    ONE GRUFF-TIMBRED PURR ROLLING FROM FURRED THROATS: ..ELLA MASON A. 54 23
GRUNT (2)
    SLOWLY, GRUNT ....SOW 61 38
    ON GRUNT, UP IN THE FLICKERING LIGHT TO SHAPE ....SOW 61 39
GRUNTS (1)
    BUT ALL THE ACCUMULATED LAST GRUNTS, GROANS, ...PERSEUS 83 17
GRYPHON (1)
    OF MUSHROOM SIMILE AND GRYPHON GARB. ....A SORCERER B. 324 8
GUARANTEED (1)
    IT IS GUARANTEED ....THE APPLICANT 221 15
GUARD (3)
    "MAY COCKCROW GUARD US SAFE," SAID HE; ....BUCOLICS 23 6
    WIELDS GUARD OF HONOR OVER THESE!" STARRED WITH WORDS ...WREATH F. 45 16
    THESE STONES GUARD A DARK REPOSE ....CHILD'S PARK STONES 101 11
GUARDED (1)
    GUARDED BROODS AND LITTERS ....HARDCASTLE CRAGS 63 31
GUARDIAN (1)
    OF GUARDIAN CATS CROUCHED ROUND THEIR IDOL, ...ELLA MASON A. 54 28
GUARDING (2)
    BUT SAT ON, GUARDING HIS GRIM BATTLEMENT. ..THE SNOWMAN ON THE MOOR 58 7
    AND THE TOAD GUARDING HIS HEART'S DROPLET. ....SLEEP. 144 16
GUARDS (4)
    GUARDS THE HARD-HEARTED EMERALD OF ITS GRASSINESS*NOVEMBER GRAVEYARD 56 4
    THE TUMULUS, EVEN AT NOON, GUARDS ITS BLACK SHADOW: ..PARLIAMENT H. 153 26
    HIS JEW-MAMA GUARDS HIS SWEET SEX LIKE A PEARL. ....LESBOS 228 27
    DOLL HE GUARDS LIKE A HEART -- ....PURDAH 244 54
GUESS (5)
    NOR GUESS THAT IF I CHOOSE TO BLINK .....SOLILOQUY OF THE SOLIPSIST 37 17
    NOT A PATCH ON YOUR PLACE, I GUESS, WITH THE JAVANESE .....THE TOUR 237 9
    I GUESS YOU COULD SAY I'VE A CALL. ....LADY LAZARUS 245 48
    ONE OF A GIANT'S EAR? I GUESS THIS GLASS*DIALOGUE OVER A OUIJA BOARD 281 201
    AND BOLT IT UP BY TAKING OATH NO GUESS   DIALOGUE OVER A OUIJA BOARD 286 345
GUESSING (1)
    GUESSING OF IT. SIBILANT ....MUSSEL HUNTER AT ROCK HARBOR 96 38
GUESSWORK (1)
    CONFOUNDED INEPT GUESSWORK: ....NIGHT SHIFT 76 14
GUEST (3)
    THE LATE GUEST ....YADDO: THE GRAND MANOR 124 18
    YOU HAD A ROSE GARDEN AND A GUEST COTTAGE AND A MODEL APOTHECARY
        SHOP ....THE BABYSITTERS 174 20
    PAN AS OUR EVENING GUEST IF HE'S SO FREE*DIALOGUE OVER A OUIJA BOARD 283 252
GUESTS (4)
    GUESTS IN THE STUDIOS ....YADDO: THE GRAND MANOR 123 11
    THE SHADOWS STOOP OVER LIKE GUESTS AT A CHRISTENING. ....CANDLES 149 35
    THE DEATHLY GUESTS HAD NOT BEEN SATISFIED ....WAKING IN WINTER 151 14
    WHERE GUESTS SLIDE GLIDING INTO LIGHT LIKE WINE; ....CINDERELLA 304 6
GUIDED (1)
    GUIDED ONLY BY THE TUG AND TWITCH .....THE PRINCESS AND THE GOBLINS 334 26
GUIDES (1)
    IT IS HIMSELF HE GUIDES ....PURDAH 242 21
GUILE (1)
    THERE IS NO GUILE OR WARP IN HIM. MAY HE KEEP SO. ......THREE WOMEN 181 175
GUILELESS (1)
    GUILELESS AND CLEAR, ...BALLOONS 271 2
GUILLOTINE (1)
    THE BUTCHER'S GUILLOTINE THAT WHISPERS: "HOW'S THIS, HOW'S THIS?" ...
                                                         ... TOTEM 264 10
GUILLOTINES (1)
    BULLDOZERS, GUILLOTINES, WHITE CHAMBERS OF SHRIEKS PROCEED, THREE. 177 19
GUILT (3)
    I SHUT MY DOORS ON THAT DARK GUILT, ...PURSUIT 23 46
    MOURNFULLY THE DRY TONGUES CLACKED THEIR GUILT: ....SNOWMAN O. 59 39
    I HAD NOTHING TO DO WITH GUILT OR ANYTHING ..ELECTRA ON AZALEA PATH 116 9
GUILT-STRICKEN (1)
    GUILT-STRICKEN HALTS, PALES, CLINGS TO THE PRINCE ....CINDERELLA 304 12
GUILTY (2)
    JUST HOW GUILTY ARE WE WHEN THE CEILING ....TALE OF A TUB 24 9
    I AM GUILTY OF NOTHING. ....LITTLE FUGUE 188 28
GUISE (4)
    AND GALLOPED WOODWARD IN THAT GUISE. ....FAUN 35 15
    THE GUISE OF LEAVES. THE WHOLE LANDSCAPE ....HARDCASTLE CRAGS 63 37
    UNDER THE GUISE OF NONCHALANCE. PAN'S LAUGH ....DIALOGUE O. 282 228
    ADRIFT IN THE GUISE OF SOME GREAT-TALONED BIRD ....DIALOGUE O. 285 311
GULL (5)
    A GULL HOLDS HIS POSE ON A SHANTY RIDGEPOLE, ...A WINTER SHIP 113 6
    HUSTLED A GULL FLOCK TO FLAP OFF THE SANDSPIT. *SUICIDE OFF EGG ROCK 115 13
    UP HERE AMONG THE GULL CRIES ....MAGNOLIA SHOALS 121 1
    BELOW US A WHITE GULL KEEPS ....MAGNOLIA SHOALS 122 13
    ALOFT, A LONE GULL HALTS UPON THE WIND, ...EPITAPH IN THREE PARTS 337 20

                                                    TITLE   PAGE LINE
GULL-COLORED (1)
  GULL-COLORED LACES FLAP IN THE SEA DRAFTS ....FINISTERRE   170   28
GULL-FOULED (1)
  GULL-FOULED, A STONE HUT ....DEPARTURE   51   16
GULLIBILITY (1)
  AS IF TEMPTING OUR GROSS GULLIBILITY ...DIALOGUE OVER A OUIJA BOARD 281 178
GULLIBLE (1)
  A GULLIBLE HEAD UNTOUCHED BY THEIR ANIMOSITY, ...THE BEE MEETING 212   40
GULLIVER (2)
  EACH SKULLED-AND-CROSSBONED GULLIVER ....ALL THE DEAD DEARS   71   34
  GULLIVER ....GULLIVER 251   T
GULLS (15)
  WOULD BE FULL OF SUN, WHITE GULLS, AND WATER DRENCHED ...CHANNEL C.   27   21
  HIGH AGAINST HEAVEN, GULLS WENT WHEELING SOUNDLESS ...DREAM WITH C.   44   13
  SIZE. THE CRIES OF SCAVENGING GULLS SOUND THIN ....GREEN ROCK.   105   14
  GULLS CIRCLE GRAY UNDER SHADOW OF A STEELIER FLIGHT. ...GREEN ROCK.   105   17
  GULLS MULLED IN THE GREENEST LIGHT. ..THE HERMIT AT OUTERMOST HOUSE   119   19
  HUSTLES OTHER GULLS OFF. CRABS ....MAGNOLIA SHOALS   122   15
  HE PAINTS A BLIZZARD OF GULLS, ...MAGNOLIA SHOALS   122   23
  GULLS HAVE THREADED THE RIVER'S MUD BED BACK *PARLIAMENT HILL FIELDS   152   6
  GULLS STIFFEN TO THEIR CHILL VIGIL IN THE DRAFTY HALF-LIGHT; ...
                                  ... PARLIAMENT HILL FIELDS   153   49
  PEEL OFF TO SEA AS GULLS DO, ...WHITSUN   154   20
  THEY PASS THE WAY GULLS PASS INLAND IN THEIR WHITE CAPS, ...TULIPS   160   12
  THE BOLD GULLS DOVE AS IF THEY OWNED IT ALL. ....THE BABYSITTERS   175   37
  GULLS IN A FEATHERED FUGUE OF WINGS. OUTDO ....MIDSUMMER MOBILE   324   4
  UNDER A TENT OF TAUNTING GULLS. ....TWO LOVERS.   327   16
  A CROWD OF SHINING GULLS THAT PLUNGE TO LAUNCH ...EPITAPH IN THREE.   337   13
GULLS' (1)
  MUD STENCH, SHELL GUTS, GULLS' LEAVINGS; ....MUSSEL HUNTER.   95   13
GULP (3)
  BUT WHO'D VOLUNTEER TO GULP THE LAOCOON, ...PERSEUS   82   8
  GULP AT MY BULK ....GIGOLO   267   11
  THE OCEAN IN ONE GULP: YOU SAY A MARK ....LOVE IS A PARALLAX   329   28
GULPS (1)
  GULPS AND RECOVERS ITS SMALL ALTITUDE, ...NICK AND THE CANDLESTICK   241   21
GUM (1)
  A DEATH TREE, COLOR GONE, AN AUSTRALIAN GUM TREE -- ....FATHERLESS.   205   3
GUNS (3)
  NOT GUNS, NOT ABUSES, ...THE THIN PEOPLE   64   16
  THUNDER AND GUNS. ....GETTING THERE   249   50
  HE COUNTED THE GUNS OF GOD A BOTHER, ...LAMENT   315   13
GUT (3)
  LOOK UPON? RATS' TEETH GUT THE CITY ....OWL   102   15
  TO THE FILLED-IN GUT ....POINT SHIRLEY   110   23
  BLUNT AS THE FACELESS GUT ....NOTES TO A NEOPHYTE   306   2
GUT-END (1)
  I HOUSEKEEP IN TIME'S GUT-END POEM.4.BEAST.   134   23
GUTS (4)
  ITS HEART AND GUTS HUNG HOOKED ....STREET SONG   36   8
  INDISSOLUBLE ENOUGH TO RIDDLE THE GUTS ....PERSEUS   82   4
  MUD STENCH, SHELL GUTS, GULLS' LEAVINGS; ....MUSSEL HUNTER.   95   13
  GUTS BAG WOULD CLACK LIKE A CHILD'S RATTLE, ...ZOO KEEPER'S WIFE   154   12
GUT'S (1)
  I'VE GOT A STUBBORN GOOSE WHOSE GUT'S ....RHYME   50   1
GUTTED (3)
  THE GUTTED FOREST FALLS TO ASH; ....PURSUIT   23   42
  OF GUTTED STAR, ...STREET SONG   36   28
  EACH LOVE BLAZING BLIND TO ITS GUTTED END -- ....CRYSTAL GAZER   56   46
GUTTER (1)
  THE LONE WIND RAVING IN THE GUTTER, HIS ....SONNET: TO TIME   311   7
GUTTERS (1)
  NOR DO THESE DRY, DRY GUTTERS DREAM OF RAIN. ....THREE WOMEN   184 279
GUTTURALS (2)
  PALE EYES, PATENT-LEATHER GUTTURALS! ....BURNING THE LETTERS   205   46
  HORNS TWIRLING AND JUNGLE GUTTURALS! ....A SECRET   220   41
GYNDES (1)
  TO REBUKE THE HORSE-SWALLOWING RIVER GYNDES: A LESSON IN VENGEANCE   80   18
HABIT (3)
  HABIT WHICH DEFLECTS ....VIRGIN IN A TREE   81   6
  STAYING PUT ACCORDING TO HABIT. ....LOVE LETTER   147   4
  OUR QUESTIONS IN HUMBLE HABIT TO GAIN GRACE ....DIALOGUE O.   281 187
HABITATIONS (1)
  QUIT THEIR USUAL HABITATIONS. ....THE MANOR GARDEN   125   18
HABITS (1)
  AS IF MY HABITS OFFENDED HER IN SOME WAY. ....IN PLASTER   159   31
HACK (2)
  NOW OUR WHOLE TASK'S TO HACK ....FIRESONG   30   8
  I WORM AND HACK IN A PURPLE WILDERNESS. ......THE SURGEON AT 2 A.M.   171   20
HACKS (1)
  BOLD BEANSTALK; LIE AND LOVE TILL SHARP SCYTHE HACKS *LOVE IS A PAR.   330   71
HAD (54)
HADLEY (1)
  FLATS OF HADLEY FARMS, THEY'RE LOFTY ENOUGH ....ABOVE THE OXBOW   88   8

HADN'T (1)
   I HADN'T A CAT YET. ....FACE LIFT 156 24
HAG (4)
   BEAUTY FROM HAG. ....TINKER JACK AND THE TIDY WIVES 34 18
   MUD-MATTRESSED UNDER THE SIGN OF THE HAG ....MAUDLIN 51   1
   REACH HAG HANDS TO HAUL ME IN, ...ALL THE DEAD DEARS 70 21
   SAD HAG. "EVERY WOMAN'S A WHORE. ....LESBOS 229 83
HAGGARD (1)
   HAGGARD THROUGH THE HOT WHITE NOON. ....PURSUIT 22 10
HAG-HEAD (1)
   AN ANTIQUE HAG-HEAD, TOO TOUGH FOR KNIFE TO FINISH, ...LADY AND T. 70 33
HAGS (2)
   THE BARNYARD LIKE THOSE TALONED HAGS ....RHYME 50   5
   HENNA HAGS: CLOTH OF YOUR CLOTH. ....LEAVING EARLY 146 21
HAIL (1)
   HAIL AND FAREWELL. HELLO, GOODBYE. O KEEPER *THE GHOST'S LEAVETAKING 91 39
HAIR (34)
   HAIR PRICKLING ON HIS HEAD, ...DIALOGUE BETWEEN GHOST AND PRIEST 38   8
   WITH ORANGE DUCK-FEET WINNOWING HIS HAIR -- .....ALL THE DEAD DEARS 71 24
   HE HYMNS THE ROTTEN QUEEN WITH SAFFRON HAIR ....OUIJA 77 22
   CAPPED: WHITE HAIR, WHITE BEARD, FAR-FLUNG, ...FULL FATHOM FIVE 92   4
   OF YOUR SPREAD HAIR, IN WHICH WRINKLING SKEINS ....FULL FATHOM FIVE 92   8
   WITH RICHNESS, HAIR HEAVIER ....LORELEI 94 13
   BLACK HAIR TILL THERE YOU STOOD, ...MAN IN BLACK 120 18
   YOUR FLUTED BONES AND ACANTHINE HAIR ARE LITTERED ....THE COLOSSUS 130 20
   BY THE ROOTS OF MY HAIR SOME GOD GOT HOLD OF ME. ...THE HANGING MAN 141   1
   AND THE CRICKETS COME CREEPING INTO OUR HAIR ....SLEEP. 144 25
   NODDING AND ROCKING AND FINGERING HER THIN HAIR. ....FACE LIFT 156 30
   SHAWLED IN BLOND HAIR AND THE SALT ....HEAVY WOMEN 158   3
   THERE ARE SOME WITH THICK BLACK HAIR, THERE ARE SOME BALD. ..THREE. 183 222
   THE WIND GAGGING MY MOUTH WITH MY OWN BLOWN HAIR,*THE RABBIT CATCHER 193   2
   BRIGHT HAIR, SHOE-BLACK, OLD PLASTIC, ...THE OTHER 201   8
   WARM RAIN GREASES MY HAIR, EXTINGUISHES NOTHING.*BURNING THE LETTERS 205 47
   AND DRIED PLATES WITH MY DENSE HAIR. ....STINGS 214 25
   DRAGGING THEIR JESUS HAIR. ....MEDUSA 225 11
   THE FEVER TRICKLES AND STIFFENS IN MY HAIR. ....THE JAILER 226 21
   I SHOULD SIT ON A ROCK OFF CORNWALL AND COMB MY HAIR. ....LESBOS 228 29
   OUR BONES, OUR HAIR. ....LESBOS 228 37
   AND THAT'S WHY I HAVE NO HAIR, AUNTIE, THAT'S WHY I CHOKE ...THE TOUR 238 24
   THIGHS, HAIR; ....ARIEL 239 17
   OR A PIECE OF MY HAIR OR MY CLOTHES. ....LADY LAZARUS 246 64
   I RISE WITH MY RED HAIR ....LADY LAZARUS 247 83
   ON MY EYES, MY LIPS, MY HAIR ....THE NIGHT DANCES 250 26
   CIRCLE, WITH ITS TAWN SILK GRASSES -- BABIES' HAIR. LETTER IN NOV. 253   7
   HIS HAIR LONG AND PLAUSIVE. ....DEATH & CO. 254 22
   THEY CONTORT YOUR HAIR ....STINGS/DR 293   5
   RED THE UNRAVELED ROSE SINGS IN YOUR HAIR: ......TO EVA DESCENDING. 303   7
   HER GREEN EYES SLANT, HAIR FLARING IN A FAN ....CINDERELLA 303   2
   A ROSE OF JEOPARDY FLAMES IN MY HAIR ....CIRCUS IN THREE RINGS 321   9
   WITH ORANGE SCALLOPS TANGLED IN WET HAIR, ...MIDSUMMER MOBILE 324 11
   THOUGHTS THAT FOUND A MAZE OF MERMAID HAIR ....TWO LOVERS. 327   5
HAIRS (1)
   LIKE ICEBERGS, WHILE MINUTE BROWN HAIRS RISE ....TALE OF A TUB 25 42
HAIRTUSK'S (1)
   HAIRTUSK'S BRIDE. POEM.4.BEAST. 134 26
HAIRY (3)
   I AM INTIMATE WITH A HAIRY SPIRIT. POEM.6.W. 135 11
   SHE MAY BE A SAINT, AND I MAY BE UGLY AND HAIRY, ...IN PLASTER 160 53
   AND A WEED, HAIRY AS PRIVATES. ....BERCK-PLAGE 197 36
HALE (1)
   AND HALE ITS GREEN LATTICEWORK OF LEAVES. YOU NEED .....DIALOGUE O. 280 159
HALF (9)
   THE EARTH TURNS NOW. IN HALF AN HOUR .....ON THE DECLINE OF ORACLES 78 26
   ALREADY HALF UNSTRUNG. A VINEGARY FUME   TWO VIEWS OF A CADAVER ROOM 114   3
   WAVING AND CRUTCHLESS, HALF THEIR OLD SIZE. ....BERCK-PLAGE 196   9
   O HALF MOON -- ....THALIDOMIDE 252   1
   A SIX AND A HALF FOOT WEDDING-CAKE. ....................EAVESDROPPER 260 26
   TAKING UP HALF THE SPACE, ...BALLOONS 271   4
   OF MANDATORY VOICES YOU HALF EXPECT ...DIALOGUE OVER A OUIJA BOARD 279 110
   PUT ORANGE MISTRESS HALF IN SUN, *BLACK PINE TREE IN AN ORANGE LIGHT 328 10
   HALF IN SHADE, UNTIL HER SKIN ...BLACK PINE TREE IN AN ORANGE LIGHT 328 11
HALF-BELIEVE (1)
   TO HALF-BELIEVE: YOUR REAPPEARANCE ....FULL FATHOM FIVE 93 23
HALF-BELIEVED (1)
   AS IF I'D HALF-BELIEVED IN HIM, AND HE, *DIALOGUE OVER A OUIJA BOARD 285 307
HALF-BRAIN (1)
   HALF-BRAIN, LUMINOSITY -- ....THALIDOMIDE 252   2
HALF-CORPSE (1)
   WASTING HER DAYS WAITING ON A HALF-CORPSE! ....IN PLASTER 159 38
HALF-DOLLARS (1)
   KEEPER COLLECTS HALF-DOLLARS FOR THE SLOPES ....ABOVE THE OXBOW 88 40
HALF-HEARTED (1)
   IF EITHER OF US HAD IT: BUT NOT THE HALF-HEARTED ......DIALOGUE O. 282 226-7
HALF-HINTS (2)
   OF HALF-HINTS. YOU PERSIST IN SPELLING HALF-HINTS ......DIALOGUE O. 279 98

HALF-HINTS (CONT.)
    OF HALF-HINTS. YOU PERSIST IN SPELLING HALF-HINTS ......DIALOGUE O.   279   98
HALF-LIGHT (1)
    GULLS STIFFEN TO THEIR CHILL VIGIL IN THE DRAFTY HALF-LIGHT; ...
                              ... PARLIAMENT HILL FIELDS   153   49
HALF-MOONS (1)
    ENOUGH FOR FINGERNAILS TO MAKE HALF-MOONS ....MOONRISE   98   10
HALF-SHELL (1)
    AS VENUS, PEDESTALED ON A HALF-SHELL ....HEAVY WOMEN   158   2
HALFWAY (2)
    HALFWAY UP FROM THE LITTLE HARBOR OF SARDINE BOATS, *THE NET-MENDERS 121   1
    HALFWAY DOWN FROM GROVES WHERE THE THIN, BITTER ALMOND PIPS ..NET-. 121   2
HALL (3)
    DO STEP INTO THE HALL! ....THE TOUR 237   2
    THE WHOLE REVOLVING TALL GLASS PALACE HALL ....CINDERELLA   304   5
    IN A GIGANTIC HALL, ...AERIALIST 331   9
HALLEY'S (1)
    AT THE CLEAR TAIL OF HALLEY'S ....MUSSEL HUNTER AT ROCK HARBOR   96   56
HALLOWING (1)
    THUS HALLOWING AN INTERVAL ....BLACK ROOK IN RAINY WEATHER   57   19
HALLS (3)
    AMUSED COURT HALLS: ....THE SNOWMAN ON THE MOOR   59   42
    STALLS IN HALLS WHERE THE LAMP WICK ....OLD LADIES' HOME 120   20
    THESE HALLS ARE FULL OF WOMEN WHO THINK THEY ARE BIRDS. *POEM.1.WHO. 131   21
HALO (2)
    IN A PARSLEY HALO; ....SOW   61   16
    AS THE HALO ....POLLY'S TREE 128   18
HALOES (2)
    HALOES LUSTROUS AS SIRIUS -- ....A WINTER'S TALE   87   11
    AND THE FINGERS, TAKEN IN BY THEIR OWN HALOES. ....CANDLES   148   3
HALOEY (1)
    THIS HALOEY RADIANCE THAT SEEMS TO BREATHE ....BY CANDLELIGHT   236   11
HALT (12)
    I HURL MY HEART TO HALT HIS PACE, ...PURSUIT   23   37
    OUR LUGGAGE, AS DOCKS HALT OUR BRIEF EPIC; NO DEBT *CHANNEL CROSSING   27   41
    TO HALT FOR A SWIG AT THE PINK TEATS. NO. THIS VAST ....SOW   61   23
    DULLED TO A HALT UNDER BOWLERS. ....POPPIES IN OCTOBER   240   9
    (PROUD YOU HALT UPON THE SPIRAL STAIR.) *TO EVA DESCENDING THE STAIR 303   3
    (PROUD YOU HALT UPON THE SPIRAL STAIR.) *TO EVA DESCENDING THE STAIR 303   9
    (PROUD YOU HALT UPON THE SPIRAL STAIR.) *TO EVA DESCENDING THE STAIR 303   15
    (PROUD YOU HALT UPON THE SPIRAL STAIR.) *TO EVA DESCENDING THE STAIR 303   19
    TO HALT OUR CAR IN HEADLONG COURSE. ....THE DREAM   310   12
    YOU'LL HALT THE CLOCK ....TRIO OF LOVE SONGS   315   51
    WHILE ALL THE ACTORS HALT IN MORTAL SHOCK: ....DOOMSDAY   316   5
    IF YOU'VE A PLOT TO HALT THE LETHAL FLOW ....THE DISPOSSESSED   318   7
HALTS (3)
    GUILT-STRICKEN HALTS, PALES, CLINGS TO THE PRINCE ....CINDERELLA   304   12
    SHE STEPS, HALTS, HUNG ....AERIALIST   331   15
    ALOFT, A LONE GULL HALTS UPON THE WIND, ...EPITAPH IN THREE PARTS   337   20
HAM (3)
    WE LIFTED A SUGARED HAM AND A PINEAPPLE FROM THE GROWNUPS' ICEBOX ...
                              ... THE BABYSITTERS   175   30
    YOU ARE SUNK IN YOUR SEVEN CHINS, STILL AS A HAM. .....STOPPED DEAD   230   16
    LURKED THE BURLESQUE INSTINCT OF THE HAM; ....DIRGE FOR A JOKER   302   6
HAMLET (1)
    SAD HAMLET, WITH A KNIFE? ....STOPPED DEAD   230   19
HAMMER (1)
    AS A SLEDGE HAMMER, AS A MAN'S BUNCHED FIST, ...SPIDER   48   4
HAMMERS (5)
    HAMMERS HOISTED, WHEELS TURNING, ...NIGHT SHIFT   76   17
    AN ANVIL, HOOVES FOUR HAMMERS TO JOLT ....WHITENESS I REMEMBER   102   21
    HAMMERS HER RARE AND ....DARK WOOD, DARK WATER 127   13
    HEATING THE PINCERS, HOISTING THE DELICATE HAMMERS. POEM.7.S.   137   28
    OUR HAMMERS, OUR RAMS, ...MUSHROOMS   139   14
HAMMOCK (1)
    TO ROCK ON ALL FOURS LIKE A PADDED HAMMOCK. ....MAGI   148   11
HAND (39)
    FILCHED BY HIS HAND, ...THE GLUTTON   40   8
    HAND HONES HIS TACKS AND NEEDLES, ...A LESSON IN VENGEANCE   80   12
    YOU HAVE IT IN HAND. GRIT IN THE EYE OR A SORE ....PERSEUS   83   27
    A WHOLE SEA OF SPINACH-HEADS LEANED TO MY HAND. ....SPINACH-PICKER.   90   22
    UPRAISED, AS A HAND, EMBLEMATIC OF FAREWELL.*THE GHOST'S LEAVETAKING   90   11
    HAND ALOFT, GOODBYE, GOODBYE, NOT DOWN .....THE GHOST'S LEAVETAKING   90   23
    YET TODAY, A YELLOW BUD IN MY HAND, ...RHODODENDRON.   103   17
    OF HER HAND, THE HOUSE STILL HUGS IN EACH DRAB ....POINT SHIRLEY   110   20
    FOOLISH, DELICATE, IN THE LOWER RIGHT HAND CORNER. ....TWO VIEWS. 114   22
    OVER MY HAND I HUNG HIM. ....MEDALLION   124   8
    RIBBED LIKE A HAND, ...POLLY'S TREE   129   36
    WAITED ON HIM HAND AND FOOT. POEM.4.BEAST.   134   6
    MOTHER OF BEETLES, ONLY UNCLENCH YOUR HAND: POEM.6.W. 135   19
    ON HIM HAND AND FOOT, QUIET AS A DIAMOND. ....ON DECK   143   33
    CLAMBERING ROUND ITS GLASS BOX LIKE AN EIGHT-FINGERED HAND. ZOO K.   155   31
    EFFACEMENT AT THE WIND'S HAND. ....MORNING SONG   157   9
    THE MOON LAYS A HAND ON MY FOREHEAD, ...BARREN WOMAN   157   9
    HAND FOLDING HAND, AND NOTHING IN BETWEEN. ....WIDOW   164   31

	TITLE	PAGE	LINE

HAND (CONT.)
    HAND FOLDING HAND, AND NOTHING IN BETWEEN. ....WIDOW 164 31
    YOUR DISSATISFACTIONS, ON THE OTHER HAND, ...THE RIVAL 166 13
    GENTLING THE SUN WITH THE SHADE OF MY HAND, ...THREE WOMEN 185 290
    A SNAG IS LIFTING A VALEDICTORY, PALE HAND; ....CROSSING THE WATER 190 9
    MY RED FILAMENTS BURN AND STAND, A HAND OF WIRES. ....ELM 192 18
    BARE-HANDED, I HAND THE COMBS. ....STINGS 214 1
    OPEN YOUR HAND. ....THE APPLICANT 221 9
    EMPTY? EMPTY. HERE IS A HAND ....THE APPLICANT 221 10
    THEM UNWRAP ME HAND AND FOOT --- ....LADY LAZARUS 245 28
    MY LANDSCAPE IS A HAND WITH NO LINES, ...CHILDLESS WOMAN 259 4
    YOU HAND ME TWO CHILDREN, TWO ROSES. ....KINDNESS 270 20
    IF NOTHING COMES OF IT. ON THE OTHER HAND, ...DIALOGUE O. 281 198
    OPPOSE WHAT WE FACED EARLIER. FEEL MY HAND. ....DIALOGUE O. 285 332
    THOUGH HUNDREDS OF LONDONERS KNOW IT LIKE THE PALM OF THEIR HAND. ...
        ... QUEEN MARY'S ROSE GARDEN 290 16
    WARNING ME TO HOLD HER HAND ....THE DREAM 311 20
    SCATTER SMUG ANGELS WITH YOUR HAND. ..SONG FOR A REVOLUTIONARY LOVE 322 4
    THE THRUSTING HAND ....ON LOOKING INTO THE EYES OF A DEMON LOVER 325 14
    WHOSE HOLY BLUE ANOINTS HER INJURED HAND. ....THE PRINCESS. 333 6
    HAND IN HAND, THEY SCALE MERIDIAN, ...THE PRINCESS AND THE GOBLINS 334 54
    HAND IN HAND, THEY SCALE MERIDIAN, ...THE PRINCESS AND THE GOBLINS 334 54
    BLOOD RUNS IN A GLISSANDO FROM THE HAND .....EPITAPH IN THREE PARTS 337 18
HANDBAG (1)
    OPEN YOUR HANDBAG. WHAT IS THAT BAD SMELL? ....THE OTHER 201 13
HANDED (1)
    YOU HANDED ME GIN IN A GLASS BUD VASE. ....LEAVING EARLY 146 41
HANDFUL (1)
    YOUR HANDFUL OF NOTES; ....MORNING SONG 157 17
HANDFULS (1)
    WE KEPT PICKING UP HANDFULS, LOVING IT, ...LESBOS 229 60
HANDICAPS (1)
    UNDER SHUTTER OF THEIR HANDICAPS. ....SONNET TO SATAN 323 4
HANDKERCHIEF (2)
    A BIG HANDKERCHIEF WITH BLUE ....MUSSEL HUNTER AT ROCK HARBOR 97 63
    BENEATH THE FLAT HANDKERCHIEF YOU WEAR INSTEAD OF A HAT. STINGS/DR 293 6
HANDLES (1)
    OLD TOOLS, HANDLES AND RUSTY TUSKS. POEM.1.WHO. 131 5
HANDLING (2)
    WARMED BY MUCH HANDLING. THEY ALMOST PURR. ....LAST WORDS 172 18
    THEY ARE HANDLING THE BLACK AND GREEN LOZENGES LIKE THE PARTS
        OF A BODY. ....BERCK-PLAGE 196 16
HAND-MADE (1)
    FINE AS HAND-MADE ....SOUTHERN SUNRISE 26 5-6
HANDS (58)
    WITH HANDS LIKE DERRICKS, ...THE QUEEN'S COMPLAINT 28 3
    ROUSED BY THORNED HANDS, FEET, HEAD, ...STREET SONG 36 17
    WITH YOUR WHITE HANDS." ....RECANTATION 42 20
    WITH HANDS ....RESOLVE 52 2
    THE BURNISHED BALL HANGS FIRE IN HER HANDS, A LENS ...CRYSTAL GAZER 54 5
    DESPITE HER WRUNG HANDS, HER TEARS, HER PRAYING: VANISH!*LADY AND T. 70 30
    REACH HAG HANDS TO HAUL ME IN, ...ALL THE DEAD DEARS 70 21
    NOR NIGHTFALL, OUR HANDS, FACES ....THE GREAT CARBUNCLE 72 6
    HANDS MOVING MOVE PRIESTLIER ....SCULPTOR 91 5
    THAN PRIEST'S HANDS, INVOKE NO VAIN ....SCULPTOR 91 6
    HANDS LACED, IN A MOONY INDOLENCE OF LOVE -- ....WATERCOLOR. 112 25
    HE HANDS HER THE CUT-OUT HEART LIKE A CRACKED HEIRLOOM. TWO VIEWS. 114 11
    BOTH OF THEM DEAF TO THE FIDDLE IN THE HANDS ....TWO VIEWS. 114 18
    THEIR CORKSCREW NOSES, THEIR WHITE HANDS ....BLUE MOLES 126 15
    OUTSIZE HANDS PREPARE A PATH, ...BLUE MOLES 126 28
    THE BEAN LEAVES ARE DUMB AS HANDS. POEM.3.MAENAD. 133 10
    WITHER LIKE PITHLESS HANDS. THERE IS LITTLE SHELTER. POEM.5.F. 134 4
    TO TRADE THEIR HOOKS FOR HANDS. POEM.7.S. 137 37
    CLOWNLIKE, HAPPIEST ON YOUR HANDS, ...YOU'RE 141 1
    LITTERED WITH CHINESE HANDS. NOW I'M STARED AT ....LEAVING EARLY 146 30
    OR THE HANDS OF AN INVALID. THE WAN ....PARLIAMENT HILL FIELDS 152 9
    AS THE LIGHT LIES ON THESE WHITE WALLS, THIS BED, THESE HANDS. ...
        ... TULIPS 160 4
    DOING THINGS WITH THEIR HANDS, ONE JUST THE SAME AS ANOTHER, *TULIPS 160 13
    TO LIE WITH MY HANDS TURNED UP AND BE UTTERLY EMPTY. ....TULIPS 161 30
    FROM THE SCALPELS AND THE RUBBER HANDS. ......THE SURGEON AT 2 A.M. 170 4
    THE BODY UNDER IT IS IN MY HANDS. ....THE SURGEON AT 2 A.M. 170 6
    THEIR HANDS AND FACES STIFF WITH HOLINESS.*THE MOON AND THE YEW TREE 173 26
    SHE REWARDS ME WITH TEARS AND AN AGITATION OF HANDS. ....MIRROR 174 14
    THE SHADOWS OF THE GRASSES INCHED ROUND LIKE HANDS OF A CLOCK,*BABY. 175 43
    TURN UP THEIR HANDS, THEIR PALLORS. IT IS SO QUIET HERE.*THREE WOMEN 179 94
    THIS RAM OF BLACKNESS. I FOLD MY HANDS ON A MOUNTAIN. ..THREE WOMEN 180 143
    HOW LONG CAN MY HANDS ....THREE WOMEN 185 296
    WHO INJURE MY SLEEP WITH THEIR WHITE EYES, THEIR FINGERLESS
        HANDS. ....THREE WOMEN 185 321
    THERE IS A GREAT DEAL ELSE TO DO. MY HANDS ....THREE WOMEN 187 359
    IT IS ONLY TIME THAT WEIGHS UPON OUR HANDS. ....THREE WOMEN 187 363
    SAFE ON THE MATTRESS, HANDS BRACED, AS FOR A FALL. .....THREE WOMEN 187 367
    I FELT HANDS ROUND A TEA MUG, DULL, BLUNT, ...THE RABBIT CATCHER 194 22
    BY PALE GIRLS, TRAVEL THE AIR IN SCORCHED HANDS. ....BERCK-PLAGE 196 4

HANDS (CONT.)
   AND FOLDED HIS HANDS, THAT WERE SHAKING: GOODBYE, GOODBYE. ..BERCK. 198 66
   THE PALLORS OF HANDS AND NEIGHBORLY FACES, ...BERCK-PLAGE 199 85
   I PUT MY HANDS AMONG THE FLAMES. NOTHING BURNS. ....POPPIES IN JULY 203   4
   HE HAS SEEN TOO MUCH DEATH, HIS HANDS ARE FULL OF IT. .....COURAGE. 210 15
   FEATHER DUSTERS FANNING THEIR HANDS IN A SEA OF BEAN FLOWERS, BEE. 211 17
   THE VILLAGERS ARE UNTYING THEIR DISGUISES, THEY ARE SHAKING HANDS. ...
       ... THE BEE MEETING 212 54
   WITH THE SWARMY FEELING OF AFRICAN HANDS *THE ARRIVAL OF THE BEE BOX 213 13
   THE MAN WITH GRAY HANDS STANDS UNDER THE HONEYCOMB ....THE SWARM 216 33
   THE MAN WITH GRAY HANDS SMILES -- ....THE SWARM 217 51
   THEY ARE NOT HANDS AT ALL ....THE SWARM 217 53
   DEAD HANDS, DEAD STRINGENCIES. ....ARIEL 239 21
   THESE ARE MY HANDS ....LADY LAZARUS 245 31
   HANDS WILL BE OPENING DOORS AND SETTING ......THE MUNICH MANNEQUINS 263 18
   WRINGING OF HANDS, THIS DARK ....CHILD 265 11
   OF COOL MOUTHS AND HANDS OPEN AND NATURAL AS ROSES. ......FEVER./DR 294 10
   WITH QUICK PRACTICED HANDS, ...BITTER STRAWBERRIES 300 36
   AND HANDS LIKE NERVOUS BUTTERFLIES; ....FAMILY REUNION 300 19
   YOUR HANDS WILL CRUSH ....TRIO OF LOVE SONGS 315 47
   HANDS REACH BACK TO RELICS OF ....DANSE MACABRE 321   7
   OUR DRASTIC JARGON, BUT CLOCK HANDS THAT MOVE ...LOVE IS A PARALLAX 329 17
HAND'S (2)
   AT HIS HAND'S STAUNCH HEST, BIRDS BUILD. ....ODE FOR TED   29 18
   WHY, YOUR HAND'S COLD AS ICE! THEN CHAFE THE COLD ......DIALOGUE O. 285 333
HANDSOME (1)
   IN THE TWO HUGE, WHITE, HANDSOME HOUSES IN SWAMPSCOTT. ....BABY. 174   5
HANDYMAN (1)
   ALL MORNING, WITH SMOKING BREATH, THE HANDYMAN .....PRIVATE GROUND 130   7
HANG (6)
   NOW IN THE CRUX OF THEIR VOWS HANG YOUR EAR, ...EPITAPH FOR F.   45 15
   AND HAVE EVERY WEATHERCOCK KISS HANG FIRE ....EPITAPH FOR F.   46 23
   ONE CRY. IT IS THE HOOK I HANG ON. ....THREE WOMEN 183 236
   PAYS TO BE POLITIC. OH, I'M NOT ONE TO HANG ....DIALOGUE O. 281 196
   IF YOU CAN HANG RELIGION ON THE RIM ...DIALOGUE OVER A OUIJA BOARD 283 248
   HANG RIDDLED WITH SHOT, ...TEMPER OF TIME 336 22
HANGING (9)
   A BEDRAGGLED SNAKE, HANGING LIMP AS THE ABSURD MOUTH ....PERSEUS   83 38
   THE HANGING MAN ....THE HANGING MAN 141   T
   HANGING FROM THEIR SCORCHED HOOKS IN THE MOIST ...ZOO KEEPER'S WIFE 155 18
   STUBBORNLY HANGING ON TO MY NAME AND ADDRESS. ....TULIPS 161 23
   HANGING SHYLY UNDER THE STUDDED HORIZON ...STARS OVER THE DORDOGNE 165 19
   HANGING THEIR BLUEGREEN BELLIES AND THEIR WING PANES IN A CHINESE
      SCREEN. ....BLACKBERRYING 168 16
   THIS IS THE TIME OF HANGING ON FOR THE BEES -- THE BEES ..WINTERING 218 22
   HANGING ITS HANGING GARDEN IN THE AIR, ...FEVER. 231 21
   HANGING ITS HANGING GARDEN IN THE AIR, ...FEVER. 231 21
HANGS (5)
   HANGS HIGH. ....SOLILOQUY OF THE SOLIPSIST   37   9
   THE BURNISHED BALL HANGS FIRE IN HER HANDS, A LENS ...CRYSTAL GAZER   54   5
   HANGS IN ITS LUGUBRIOUS POUT. WHERE ARE ....PERSEUS   83 39
   HANGS ITSELF ON ITS OWN ROPE. ...........METAMORPHOSES OF THE MOON 308 42
   THE WINTER LANDSCAPE HANGS IN BALANCE NOW, ...PROLOGUE TO SPRING 322   1
HANKIE (1)
   O I SHOULDN'T DIP MY HANKIE IN, IT HURTS! ....THE TOUR 238 31
HAPHAZARD (1)
   NATURE'S PARTIAL, HAPHAZARD THUMB. ....THE BEGGARS   47   5
HAPPEN (9)
   WARY (FOR IT COULD HAPPEN ....BLACK ROOK IN RAINY WEATHER   57 23
   ANYTHING CAN HAPPEN WHERE THEY ARE GOING. ....ON DECK 143 18
   INSTEAD, THE DEAD INJURE ME WITH ATTENTIONS, AND NOTHING
      CAN HAPPEN. ....BARREN WOMAN 157   8
   IS SHE SORRY FOR WHAT WILL HAPPEN? I DO NOT THINK SO. ..THREE WOMEN 176   6
   WHAT HAPPENS IN ME WILL HAPPEN WITHOUT ATTENTION. ......THREE WOMEN 176 10
   I AM NOT READY FOR ANYTHING TO HAPPEN. ....THREE WOMEN 180 125
   IT IS USUAL, THEY SAY, FOR SUCH A THING TO HAPPEN. .....THREE WOMEN 183 242
   IF ANYTHING SHOULD HAPPEN . . ." ....BITTER STRAWBERRIES 299 12
   "IF ONLY SOMETHING WOULD HAPPEN!" ....DIALOGUE EN ROUTE 308   1
HAPPENED (5)
   O I CANNOT UNDERSTAND WHAT HAPPENED TO THEM! ....STILLBORN 142   6
   THE PILGRIMS AND INDIANS MIGHT NEVER HAVE HAPPENED. ......TWO CAMP. 145 22
   EVERYTHING HAS HAPPENED. ....THE BABYSITTERS 175 45
   I AM FLAT AND VIRGINAL, WHICH MEANS NOTHING HAS HAPPENED, ...THREE. 184 276
   THE FIRST TIME IT HAPPENED I WAS TEN. ....LADY LAZARUS 245 35
HAPPENING (2)
   THE HAPPENING OF THIS HAPPENING ....ON THE DECLINE OF ORACLES   78 25
   THE HAPPENING OF THIS HAPPENING ....ON THE DECLINE OF ORACLES   78 25
HAPPENINGS (1)
   OLD HAPPENINGS ....AMNESIAC 233   9
HAPPENS (6)
   FROM THE DOOR AS EVER. WHAT HAPPENS BETWEEN US ....BLUE MOLES 127 34
   HAPPENS IN DARKNESS, VANISHES ....BLUE MOLES 127 35
   WHAT HAPPENS IN ME WILL HAPPEN WITHOUT ATTENTION. ......THREE WOMEN 176 10
   IT HAPPENS. WILL IT GO ON? --- ....PARALYTIC 266   1
   CRACKS RED. HOTHING HAPPENS. WAIT. ITS TRIP ....DIALOGUE O. 277 20

	TITLE	PAGE	LINE

HAPPENS (CONT.)
THAT HAPPENS TO CONCEAL THE LID OF ONE ......EPITAPH IN THREE PARTS 338 29
HAPPIER (1)
YOU'RE NO HAPPIER THAN I ABOUT IT. ....WHITSUN 154 17
HAPPIEST (1)
CLOWNLIKE, HAPPIEST ON YOUR HANDS, ...YOU'RE 141   1
HAPPY (8)
MUD-SUMP, HAPPY STY-FACE POEM.4.BEAST. 134 17
I CIRCLE THE WRITHEN TREES. I AM TOO HAPPY.   PARLIAMENT HILL FIELDS 153 29
THEY CONCENTRATE MY ATTENTION, THAT WAS HAPPY ....TULIPS 161 55
IT IS A PLACE OF SHRIEKS. IT IS NOT HAPPY. ....THREE WOMEN 180 122
NEITHER A WOMAN, HAPPY TO BE LIKE A MAN, NOR A MAN .....THREE WOMEN 182 192
THE TALKING DUCKS, THE HAPPY LAMBS. ....THREE WOMEN 185 318
"NO, NO, IT IS HAPPY THERE." ....A SECRET 220 34
I AM SO STUPIDLY HAPPY, ...LETTER IN NOVEMBER 253 13
HARA-KIRI (1)
OF COMET HARA-KIRI THROUGH THE DARK ....LOVE IS A PARALLAX 329 29
HARBOR (7)
OF MAKING HARBOR THROUGH THIS RACKETING FLUX ......CHANNEL CROSSING   27 19
ALONGSIDE THE SIBILANT HARBOR THE LOVERS ....ALICANTE LULLABY   43 11
MUSSEL HUNTER AT ROCK HARBOR ....MUSSEL HUNTER AT ROCK HARBOR   95   T
UNLESS YOU DO THIS TAWDRY HARBOR ....GREEN ROCK, WINTHROP BAY 105 19
THE WHOLE FLAT HARBOR ANCHORED IN ....A WINTER SHIP 113   9
HALFWAY UP FROM THE LITTLE HARBOR OF SARDINE BOATS, *THE NET-MENDERS 121   1
UP OVER THE HARBOR LIGHTS. ....LESBOS 229 56
HARBORAGE (1)
PROMISING SURE HARBORAGE; ....LORELEI   94 25
HARD (17)
HE, HUNGER-STUNG, HARD TO SLAKE, ...THE GLUTTON   40   1
TWINED TO HER HARD LIMBS LIKE IVY: THE PURITAN LIP *VIRGIN IN A TREE   81 12
OF PALE FRONTS, STRAW THATCHINGS, THE HARD ROAD*WHITENESS I REMEMBER 102 20
WHO WAKES WITH DARKNESS AND TILL DAWN WORKS HARD ....GOATSUCKER 111   3
LIKE HIERATIC STONES, AND THE GROUND IS HARD.*ELECTRA ON AZALEA PATH 116   4
HARD GODS WERE THERE, NOTHING ELSE. ..THE HERMIT AT OUTERMOST HOUSE 119 13
HOURS OF BLANKNESS. SOME HARD STARS ....THE MANOR GARDEN 125 14
PROMISING SIMPLY THE HARD STARS, THE SPACE ....WIDOW 164 23
I AM OVERLOOKING THEM BY LOOKING TOO HARD.   STARS OVER THE DORDOGNE 165 23
AND HARD, MARBLY BAAS. ....WUTHERING HEIGHTS 167 27
ON THAT DAY-OFF THE TWO OF US CRIED SO HARD TO GET   THE BABYSITTERS 175 29
I HAVE TRIED NOT TO THINK TOO HARD. I HAVE TRIED TO BE NATURAL. ...
... THREE WOMEN 178 74
AND THAT MAD, HARD FACE AT THE END OF IT, THAT O-MOUTH   THREE WOMEN 182 184
A RED, HARD WOOD, EYES SHUT AND MOUTH WIDE OPEN. ....THREE WOMEN 182 212
THEN THERE ARE THE STARS -- INERADICABLE, HARD. ....EVENT 194 10
HARD AND APART AND WHITE. ....LESBOS 229 58
I AM PACKING THE HARD POTATOES LIKE GOOD CLOTHES, ...LESBOS 229 68
HARDCASTLE (1)
HARDCASTLE CRAGS ....HARDCASTLE CRAGS   62   T
HARDEN (1)
SAW HOOF HARDEN FROM FOOT, SAW SPROUT ....FAUN   35 13
HARDER (1)
THESE WERE HARDER, TWO WHITE STONES. ....THE DETECTIVE 209 32
HARDEST (1)
TO THE HARDEST SUBSTANCE KNOWN. ....NOTES TO A NEOPHYTE 307 24
HARD-HEARTED (1)
GUARDS THE HARD-HEARTED EMERALD OF ITS GRASSINESS*NOVEMBER GRAVEYARD   56   4
HARDIHOOD (1)
HOW BEST BEAUTY'S BORN OF HARDIHOOD ....MAYFLOWER   60   8
HARDLY (5)
I NEED HARDLY GO OUT AT ALL. ....PRIVATE GROUND 130 14
I HARDLY KNEW HIM. POEM.4.BEAST. 134 10
I SHALL HARDLY KNOW MYSELF. IT WILL BE DARK, ...LAST WORDS 172 25
SO SLOW I HARDLY KNOW THEM, ...WINTERING 218 23
I COULD HARDLY SPEAK. ....DADDY 223 28
HARDSHIP (2)
"NO HARDSHIP THEN?" HE ASKS. "WE'LL TAKE ....CRYSTAL GAZER   55 19
NURSES THE HARDSHIP OF HIS STITCHES, AND WALKS AND WALKS. *NARCISSI. 190   6
HARE (1)
IN THE BOWL THE HARE IS ABORTED, ...TOTEM 264 11
HARLEQUINS (1)
MULTIPLY PINK HARLEQUINS AND SING ....LOVE IS A PARALLAX 330 46
HARM (4)
UNTIL SWEET WIND CHANGED TUNE, BLEW HARM: ....BUCOLICS   24 15
NO HARM CAN COME TO THEM. ....THE SLEEPERS 123 22
IF I AM A LITTLE ONE, I CAN DO NO HARM. POEM.6.W. 135 13
DO YOU DO NO HARM? ....POPPIES IN JULY 203   2
HARMONY (1)
DERANGING BY HARMONY ....LORELEI   94 21
HARMS (1)
WITH THE PILOT WHO DARES ALL HEAVEN'S HARMS .........METAMORPHOSES. 307   2
HARNESS (1)
SHE DRAWS APPLAUSE; BRIGHT HARNESS ....AERIALIST 331 23
HARPS (1)
OF GILDED HARPS OR GNAWING FIRE: SIMPLY TELL ....DIALOGUE B.   39 23

HARVEST (3)
    WILL BRING CROP'S INCREASE, AND HARVEST FRUIT ....CRYSTAL GAZER   55   17
    BE A HARVEST OF SILVER IN THE NETS, AND THE LAMPS ..THE NET-MENDERS   121   18
    HIS BEAK BRINGS THE HARVEST IN. ....MAGNOLIA SHOALS   122   18
HAS (62)
HASN'T (1)
    A DEVIL. WAIT: HE SHIFTS. HE HASN'T COME*DIALOGUE OVER A OUIJA BOARD   282 216
HASTE (1)
    INDOORS WITH POLITIC GOODWILL, NOT HASTE ...THE SNOWMAN ON THE MOOR   58   11
HAT (11)
    FLEW OFF LIKE THE HAT OF A DOLL POEM.7.S.   136   4
    DEATH IS THE DRESS SHE WEARS, HER HAT AND COLLAR. ....WIDOW   164   13
    TO WANT THE WORLD IN A GLASS HAT. ....NEW YEAR ON DARTMOOR   176   9
    NOW THEY ARE GIVING ME A FASHIONABLE WHITE STRAW ITALIAN HAT ..BEE.   211   21
    HE WORE INSTEAD OF A HAT. ....STINGS   215   44
    THE SWARM IS KNOCKED INTO A COCKED STRAW HAT. ....THE SWARM   217   42
    A FLAP LIKE A HAT, ...CUT   235   6
    TODDLE ON HOME TO TEA NOW IN YOUR FLAT HAT. ....THE TOUR   238   37
    ALL, IF YOU'LL HIDE HOPES OF HEAVEN IN A HAT ....DIALOGUE O.   282 231
    BENEATH THE FLAT HANDKERCHIEF YOU WEAR INSTEAD OF A HAT.   STINGS/DR 293   6
    MAD HATTER'S HAT YIELDS NO NEW METAPHOR, ...A SORCERER B.   324   10
HAT-BRIMS (1)
    BLOATS LIKE A SPINNAKER. HAT-BRIMS ....WHITSUN   154   10
HATCH (2)
    NOW HILLS HATCH MENACE, SPAWNING SHADE; ....PURSUIT   22   25
    WHICH AT TWELVE WILL QUAINTLY HATCH ....BLACK PINE TREE.   328   5
HATCHED (1)
    HATCHED WITH A CLARET HOGSHEAD TO SWIG ....MAUDLIN   51   5
HATCHES (1)
    HATCHES NO FORTUNE, ...ON THE DIFFICULTY OF CONJURING UP A DRYAD   66   38
HATE (5)
    HOLDING IN ITS HATE ....BURNING THE LETTERS 204 12
    WILL THEY HATE ME, ...STINGS   214   28
    NOW I AM SILENT, HATE ....LESBOS   229   64
    IT IS LOVE YOU ARE FULL OF. YOU KNOW WHO YOU HATE. ....LESBOS   229   72
    HOW THEY HATE YOU. ....GULLIVER   251   16
HATED (1)
    AT THE BEGINNING I HATED HER, SHE HAD NO PERSONALITY -- IN PLASTER   158   5
HATES (1)
    SHE HATES ....THE FEARFUL   256   10
HATFUL (1)
    CREEPING UP WITH HER HATFUL OF TRIVIAL REPETITIONS. ......INSOMNIAC   163   32
HATING (2)
    HATING MYSELF, HATING AND FEARING. AND NOW THE WORLD CONCEIVES ...
                                                    ... THREE WOMEN   181 150
    HATING MYSELF, HATING AND FEARING. AND NOW THE WORLD CONCEIVES ...
                                                    ... THREE WOMEN   181 150
HATPIN (1)
    HER A POCKETBOOK, A PEARL HATPIN ....ON DECK   143   21
HATS (3)
    FULL OF DRESSES AND HATS AND CHINA AND MARRIED DAUGHTERS. ...BERCK.   199   77
    SIX ROUND BLACK HATS IN THE GRASS AND A LOZENGE OF WOOD,*BERCK-PLAGE 201 123
    THEY ARE SMILING AND TAKING OUT VEILS TACKED TO ANCIENT HATS. BEE. 211   5
HATTER'S (1)
    MAD HATTER'S HAT YIELDS NO NEW METAPHOR, ...A SORCERER B.   324   10
HAUGHTY (1)
    ELLA FLOUNCED ABOUT, MINX-THIN AND HAUGHTY, ...ELLA MASON A.   53   14
HAUL (4)
    WHICH HUNGERS TO HAUL THE WHITE REFLECTION DOWN. WINTER LANDSCAPE,   21   5
    YOU MIGHT AS WELL HAUL UP ....EPITAPH FOR FIRE AND FLOWER   45   1
    AS TO SEIZE MY SENSES, HAUL ....BLACK ROOK IN RAINY WEATHER   57   29
    REACH HAG HANDS TO HAUL ME IN, ...ALL THE DEAD DEARS   70   21
HAULED (4)
    THE BLACK MARAUDER, HAULED BY LOVE ....PURSUIT   22   27
    HAULED SUDDEN FROM SOLITUDE, ...DIALOGUE BETWEEN GHOST AND PRIEST   38   7
    SO WE ARE HAULED, THOUGH WE WOULD STOP ....IN MIDAS' COUNTRY   100   21
    WOULDN'T SLOW FOR THE HAULED REINS, HIS NAME, WHITENESS I REMEMBER 103   24
HAULS (4)
    HE HAULS TO HIS WILL EARLY; ....ODE FOR TED   29   17
    WHICH HAULS DOWN BUCK, COCK, TROUT, TILL ALL MOST FAIR ....FIRESONG   30   6
    HAULS ME THROUGH AIR --- ....ARIEL   239   16
    HAULS THEM ROUND WITH IT. ....TOUCH-AND-GO   335   16
HAUNCHED (1)
    HAUNCHED LIKE A FAUN, HE HOOED ....FAUN   35   1
HAUNCHES (2)
    ON FLUENT HAUNCHES, KEEPS MY SPEED, ...PURSUIT   23   28
    FAT HAUNCHES AND BLOOD ON THEIR MINDS. ....TOTEM   264   8
HAUNT (3)
    EARTH IS MY HAUNT." ....DIALOGUE BETWEEN GHOST AND PRIEST   38   20
    CAN ONLY HAUNT. STURDY AS POTATOES. ....POEMS, POTATOES   106   4
    THE INFERNAL HAUNT OF DEMON DANGERS; ....DOOM OF EXILES   318   6
HAUNTERS (1)
    OURSELVES THE HAUNTERS, AND THEY, FLESH AND BLOOD; ...THE OTHER TWO   69   33
HAUTEUR (1)
    SKIES ONCE WEARING A BLUE, DIVINE HAUTEUR ....OUIJA   77   19

	TITLE	PAGE	LINE

HAVE (162)

HAVING (3)
BUT A DOZEN WOULD BE WORTH HAVING, ...PHEASANT 191 16
I COULD NOT RUN WITHOUT HAVING TO RUN FOREVER. .....THE BEE MEETING 212 33
HAVING NO REFLECTIONS; ....GULLIVER 251 6

HAVOC (3)
WHAT CEREMONY OF WORDS CAN PATCH THE HAVOC? ..........CONVERSATION. 21 14
FROM GAUNT HEMLOCK, ROOKS CROAK HAVOC: ....PURSUIT 22 7
SOME HAVOC ON TENDER LIMB, AND YET ....CRYSTAL GAZER 55 23

HAVOC-SICK (1)
BELOW, ROCKED HAVOC-SICK, VOYAGERS LIE ....CHANNEL CROSSING 26 9

HAVOC-SPLIT (1)
STREETS CRACK THROUGH IN HAVOC-SPLIT RAVINES ....DOOMSDAY 316 7

HAWK (1)
HAWK MISFORTUNE LIKE FIGS AND CHICKENS ....THE BEGGARS 47 3

HAWS (1)
THROUGHOUT BLACK WINTER THE RED HAWS WITHSTOOD ....MAYFLOWER 60 1

HAWTHORN (5)
ON HAWTHORN BOUGHS, WITH GOODWILL TO ENDURE ....MAYFLOWER 60 13
THE BLOOD-BERRIED HAWTHORN HIDES ITS SPINES WITH WHITE. *WATERCOLOR. 112 21
AND WE PICNIC IN THE DEATH-STENCH OF A HAWTHORN. ....WHITSUN 154 21
IS IT THE HAWTHORN THAT SMELLS SO SICK? ....THE BEE MEETING 211 24
THE BARREN BODY OF HAWTHORN, ETHERIZING ITS CHILDREN. ....BEE. 211 25

HAY (1)
VANISHES IN A LABYRINTH OF HAY ....THE PRINCESS AND THE GOBLINS 335 70

HAYWIRE (1)
WE THOUGHT WE'D TRAINED HIM, BEFORE GOING HAYWIRE. TRUTH*DIALOGUE O. 277 41

HAZARD (2)
HUNG OUT OVER HAZARD, OVER HOOVES ....WHITENESS I REMEMBER 103 30
HISTORY'S BEATEN THE HAZARD. ....THE TIMES ARE TIDY 107 10

HAZARDOUS (3)
CAUGHT IN A HAZARDOUS MEDIUM THAT MIGHT ....VANITY FAIR 32 3
HAZARDOUS AND LONG, ...BATTLE-SCENE 85 34
THROUGH HOOP OF THAT HAZARDOUS DREAM ....AERIALIST 332 40

HAZARD'S (1)
NOW, FREE, BY HAZARD'S QUIRK, FROM THE COMMON ILL CHANNEL CROSSING 27 26

HAZE (1)
EACH THORN; SPIRING FROM WET EARTH, A BLUE HAZE ....DIALOGUE B. 38 5

HE (186)

HEAD (58)
THE GESTURE, BEND AND HOLD THE PRONE MAN'S HEAD. ..CHANNEL CROSSING 27 36
ROUSED BY THORNED HANDS, FEET, HEAD, ...STREET SONG 36 17
DENYING YOU SPRANG OUT OF MY HEAD, ...SOLILOQUY OF THE SOLIPSIST 38 31
HAIR PRICKLING ON HIS HEAD, ...DIALOGUE BETWEEN GHOST AND PRIEST 38 8
AND FURY MAKE HEAD, ...MONOLOGUE AT 3 A.M. 40 2
MY HEAD ON THE PILLOW ....ALICANTE LULLABY 43 19
HIVED LIKE HONEY IN YOUR HEAD. ....EPITAPH FOR FIRE AND FLOWER 45 14
EARTH'S EVER-GREEN DEATH'S HEAD. ....CRYSTAL GAZER 56 48
HER HEAD CUPPED THE BABEL. ....HARDCASTLE CRAGS 63 25
IN THE CONTRACTED COUNTRY OF THE HEAD ....THE THIN PEOPLE 64 25
"WITH MY FANTASY ALONE," BRAGS THE IMPORTUNATE HEAD, ...CONJURING. 66 9
THE LADY AND THE EARTHENWARE HEAD *THE LADY AND THE EARTHENWARE HEAD 69 T
FIRED IN SANGUINE CLAY, THE MODEL HEAD ....LADY AND T. 69 1
HEARTHSTONE AT ONCE OF THE OUTRAGEOUS HEAD; ....LADY AND T. 69 6
MALTREAT THE HOSTAGE HEAD IN SHOCKING WISE, ...LADY AND T. 69 13
THE MIMIC HEAD -- IN A CROTCHED WILLOW, GREEN- ....LADY AND T. 69 23
TO PROVE IT. AS I THINK NOW OF HER HEAD, ...ALL THE DEAD DEARS 70 18
AND NOD AT NOD AT FOOT AND HEAD ....THE DISQUIETING MUSES 75 7
MOUTHLESS, EYELESS, WITH STITCHED BALD HEAD. THE DISQUIETING MUSES 75 16
DAY NOW, NIGHT NOW, AT HEAD, SIDE, FEET, ...THE DISQUIETING MUSES 76 49
SHOWS ITS HEAD, AND THOSE GREEN WATERS BACK TO ......SNAKECHARMER 79 26
HEAD ALONE SHOWS YOU IN THE PRODIGIOUS ACT ....PERSEUS 82 1
NOT NAILS, AND A MIRROR TO KEEP THE SNAKY HEAD ....PERSEUS 83 13
FISTED TO A FOETUS HEAD, RAVINED, SEAMED ....PERSEUS 83 25
TO THE BEHEADED HEAD OF A SULLEN DOLL, ONE BRAID, ...PERSEUS 83 37
WITH FANGED AND DREADFUL HEAD. ....BATTLE-SCENE 84 18
BRING HOME EACH STORIED HEAD. ....BATTLE-SCENE 84 28
IRREPROACHABLE AS ANY LETTUCE HEAD, ...MEMOIRS OF A SPINACH-PICKER 89 10
WHERE THE WAKING HEAD RUBBISHES OUT THE DRAGGLED LOT ......GHOST'S. 90 3
SEEN BY ANY MAN WHO KEPT HIS HEAD, ...FULL FATHOM FIVE 93 38
THE HEAD OF HIS CADAVER HAD CAVED IN, ..TWO VIEWS OF A CADAVER ROOM 114 6
CROWD FOOT TO FOOT, HEAD TO HEAD, NO FLOWER ELECTRA ON AZALEA PATH 117 20
CROWD FOOT TO FOOT, HEAD TO HEAD, NO FLOWER ELECTRA ON AZALEA PATH 117 20
A SCORPION STUNG ITS HEAD, AN ILL-STARRED THING; ....ELECTRA ON. 117 35
HEAD, TOE AND FINGER ....THE MANOR GARDEN 125 7
OF HOLOFERNES' HEAD, DIPPED IN THE SAME ....LEAVING EARLY 146 32
EACH DEAD HEAD HAD A VISOR OF ICE. ....LOVE LETTER 147 18
THEY HAVE PROPPED MY HEAD BETWEEN THE PILLOW AND THE SHEET-CUFF ...
                                                       ... TULIPS 160 8
SINK OUT OF SIGHT, AND THE WATER WENT OVER MY HEAD. ....TULIPS 161 27
HIS HEAD IS A LITTLE INTERIOR OF GRAY MIRRORS. ....INSOMNIAC 163 22
I SEE THOSE CONSTELLATIONS IN MY HEAD, ...STARS OVER THE DORDOGNE 166 35
THE GRASS IS BEATING ITS HEAD DISTRACTEDLY. .....WUTHERING HEIGHTS 168 39
I THINK HER LITTLE HEAD IS CARVED IN WOOD, ...THREE WOMEN 182 211
THE JUT OF THAT ODD, DARK HEAD, PACING ....PHEASANT 191 3

TITLE   PAGE LINE

HEAD (CONT.)
```
TILL YOUR HEAD IS A STONE, YOUR PILLOW A LITTLE TURF, .........ELM            192  11
I HAVE YOUR HEAD ON MY WALL. .............................THE OTHER           202  17
THE WORLD WILL GO UP IN A SHRIEK, AND YOUR HEAD WITH IT,  BIRTHDAY.           207  29
EVERYBODY IS NODDING A SQUARE BLACK HEAD, THEY ARE KNIGHTS IN
     VISORS, ..........................................THE BEE MEETING        211  13
A GULLIBLE HEAD UNTOUCHED BY THEIR ANIMOSITY, ......THE BEE MEETING           212  40
THAT BIG BLUE HEAD -- ...........................................A SECRET     220  26
NOW YOUR HEAD, EXCUSE ME, IS EMPTY. ...................THE APPLICANT          221  26
AND A HEAD IN THE FREAKISH ATLANTIC .........................DADDY            222  11
YOU HOUSE YOUR UNNERVING HEAD -- GOD-BALL, ...................MEDUSA          224   4
MY HEAD A MOON .................................................FEVER.        232  37
ITS BABY HEAD OUT OF THE WAY, EMBALMED IN SPICE, .............TOTEM           264  12
BECAUSE PAN BLUNTLY SPELT OUT GOD'S HEAD, NOT .........DIALOGUE O.            282 237
YOUR HEAD AFTER ALL. IT SEEMS HIS LAUGH *DIALOGUE OVER A OUIJA BOARD          282 238
WE HEARD THE HEAD WOMAN SAY, ...................BITTER STRAWBERRIES           299   5
```
HEADACHE (1)
```
AND A HURRICANE HEADACHE ROCKS   INSOLENT STORM STRIKES AT THE SKULL          326  11
```
HEADACHES (1)
```
TO BRING TEACUPS AND ROLL AWAY HEADACHES .............THE APPLICANT           221  12
```
HEADLAND (1)
```
BARB-WIRED HEADLAND OF ...............................MAN IN BLACK            119   6
```
HEADLINE (1)
```
THE MORNING PAPER CLOCKED THE HEADLINE HOUR .......THE TRIAL OF MAN           312   5
```
HEADLINES (1)
```
IN A WAR MAKING EVIL HEADLINES WHEN WE .............THE THIN PEOPLE            64   6
```
HEADLONG (2)
```
PLUNGES HEADLONG INTO THAT BLACK POND ............WINTER LANDSCAPE,            21   2
TO HALT OUR CAR IN HEADLONG COURSE. ......................THE DREAM           310  12
```
HEADS (16)
```
WITH HEADS LIKE DARNING-EGGS TO NOD .........THE DISQUIETING MUSES             75   6
NODDED THEIR PETALED HEADS AROUND YOUR COUCH. ...........YADWIGHA.             86  30
OF ASPARAGUS HEADS. CARS RUN THEIR SUAVE ...........ABOVE THE OXBOW            89  50
OF SOME GODLY UTTERANCE WAKENED HEADS IGNORE: .............GHOST'S.            90  17
THE ANTHERS NOD THEIR HEADS, POTENT AS KINGS ..........BEEKEEPER'S.           118  11
I AM AT HOME HERE AMONG THE DEAD HEADS. .................POEM.1.WHO.          131   6
MOLDERING HEADS CONSOLE ME, ..............................POEM.1.WHO.         131  13
HERE THEY CAN DOCTOR HEADS, OR ANY LIMB. ................POEM.7.S.            137  35
WHERE THE HEADS AND TAILS OF MY SISTERS DECOMPOSE.*ZOO KEEPER'S WIFE          154   7
SWIVEL THEIR HEADS AND CRY. ............................APPREHENSIONS         195  17
AND THE FOX HEADS, THE OTTER HEADS, THE HEADS OF DEAD RABBITS. ...
                           ... THE COURAGE OF SHUTTING-UP                     210  23
AND THE FOX HEADS, THE OTTER HEADS, THE HEADS OF DEAD RABBITS. ...
                           ... THE COURAGE OF SHUTTING-UP                     210  23
AND THE FOX HEADS, THE OTTER HEADS, THE HEADS OF DEAD RABBITS. ...
                           ... THE COURAGE OF SHUTTING-UP                     210  23
FLOATS OUR HEADS, TWO VENOMOUS OPPOSITES, ...................LESBOS           228  36
THEIR MAGNIFIED HEADS AND PLAN TO KILL ME AS SOON AS
     POSSIBLE. .........................................THE RIVAL/DR          291   3
CAPER WITH CANDLES IN THEIR HEADS; .............LOVE IS A PARALLAX            329  33
```
HEAD'S (1)
```
THE PURPLE EGG-STONES: FROM GREAT HEAD'S KNOB ........POINT SHIRLEY           110  22
```
HEADSTONE (2)
```
ROTS, AND SMELLS OF ROT UNDER ITS HEADSTONE ..............MOONRISE            98  14
AT THE HEADSTONE NEXT TO YOURS, NOR DOES IT ROT, .......ELECTRA ON.          117  26
```
HEAD-STONE (1)
```
THE HEAD-STONE QUIET, JOSTLED BY NOTHING. .................POEM.7.S.          136  10
```
HEADSTONES (2)
```
SEPARATED FROM MY HOUSE BY A ROW OF HEADSTONES. ..............MOON.           173   6
WITH THE SAME TREES AND HEADSTONES. .....................THE JAILER           226   3
```
HEADSTRONG (1)
```
OR HEADSTRONG COLUMBUS CRAB. ..........MUSSEL HUNTER AT ROCK HARBOR            97  76
```
HEADWAITER (1)
```
IMAGINING HIMSELF A HEADWAITER IN AMERICA, ..................CANDLES          149  21
```
HEALING (3)
```
I HAD AN OLD WOUND ONCE, BUT IT IS HEALING. ............THREE WOMEN           185 306
A TENDERNESS THAT DID NOT TIRE, SOMETHING HEALING. .....THREE WOMEN           186 357
I WAIT AND ACHE. I THINK I HAVE BEEN HEALING. ..........THREE WOMEN           187 358
```
HEALS (3)
```
NEITHER NOURISHES NOR HEALS. .....................THE BURNT-OUT SPA           138  34
OLD BLOOD OF CAKED WALLS THE SUN HEALS, ................BERCK-PLAGE           200  98
AND, DROPPING, DIE, TO TRACE A WOUND THAT HEALS   LOVE IS A PARALLAX          330  64
```
HEALTH (3)
```
AND COMES FROM A COUNTRY FAR AWAY AS HEALTH. .............TULIPS              162  63
THEY HUG THEIR FLATNESS LIKE A KIND OF HEALTH. .........THREE WOMEN           180 117
I LEAVE MY HEALTH BEHIND. I LEAVE SOMEONE ............THREE WOMEN             184 272
```
HEAP (1)
```
OFF EUROPE'S RELIC HEAP ...............................PRIVATE GROUND         130   3
```
HEAPED (1)
```
BROOD, ROOTED IN THEIR HEAPED LOSSES. .......PARLIAMENT HILL FIELDS           153  31
```
HEAR (21)
```
ALONE CAN HEAR .......................................STREET SONG             36  25
HEAR LOUDSPEAKERS BOOM ...........................ALICANTE LULLABY            43  12
STILL AS A SHELL: HEAR WHAT AN AGE OF GLASS .........EPITAPH FOR F.           45  16
WE'D WINK AT IF WE DIDN'T HEAR ..................ALL THE DEAD DEARS           70  10
```

HEAR (CONT.)
    TO HEAR THE SEA HE COULD NOT HEAR. ....ON THE DECLINE OF ORACLES   78   6
    TO HEAR THE SEA HE COULD NOT HEAR. ....ON THE DECLINE OF ORACLES   78   6
    OLD GOATHERDS SWEAR HOW ALL NIGHT LONG THEY HEAR ....GOATSUCKER   111   1
    EVEN THROUGH THE GIFT PAPER I COULD HEAR THEM BREATHE ....TULIPS   161   37
    SHE DOES NOT HEAR WHAT THE SAILOR OR THE PEASANT IS SAYING -- ...
                                                       ... FINISTERRE   170   26
    I HEAR THE SOUND OF THE HOURS ....THREE WOMEN   185 311
    WIDEN AND DIE IN THE HEDGEROWS. I HEAR THE MOO OF COWS. *THREE WOMEN   185 312
    HE COULD HEAR BEETHOVEN: ....LITTLE FUGUE   187   13
    I HEAR HER GREAT HEART PURR. ....AN APPEARANCE   189   3
    IS IT THE SEA YOU HEAR IN ME, ...ELM   192   4
    BACK TO BACK. I HEAR AN OWL CRY ....EVENT 194   4
    YOU WILL NOT EVEN HEAR ME OPENING IT, NO PAPER CRACKLE, ..BIRTHDAY.   207   34
    WHERE THEY CRAP AND PUKE AND CRY AND SHE CAN'T HEAR. ....LESBOS   228   14
    OUTSIDE IN THE STREET I HEAR ....FAMILY REUNION   300   1
    OH, HEAR THE CLASH OF PEOPLE MEETING -- ....FAMILY REUNION   300   11
    MOST PLASTIC-WINDOWED CITY, I CAN HEAR ....SONNET: TO TIME   311   6
    WE NEVER THOUGHT TO HEAR THE HOLY COCK:................DOOMSDAY   316   14
HEARD (16)
    STONE-BUILT TOWN, THAT SHE HEARD THE QUICK AIR IGNITE *HARDCASTLE C.   62   4
    HEARD A QUEER CRUSTY SCRABBLE ....MUSSEL HUNTER AT ROCK HARBOR   95   14
    OF GRASSHEADS AND IS HEARD. .....WATERCOLOR OF GRANTCHESTER MEADOWS   112   5
    HE HEARD WHEN HE WALKED INTO THE WATER ....SUICIDE OFF EGG ROCK   115   23
    THE PEOPLE OF THE CITY HEARD IT. POEM.7.S.   136   14
    YOU SNORED, AND I HEARD THE PETALS UNLATCH, ...LEAVING EARLY   146   26
    WORDS HEARD, BY ACCIDENT, OVER THE PHONE ....WORDS HEARD.   202   T
    THE DISKS REVOLVE, THEY ASK TO BE HEARD -- ....COURAGE.   209   5
    OF A COUNTRY NO LONGER HEARD OF, ...THE COURAGE OF SHUTTING-UP   210   33
    WHOEVER HEARD A SUNSET YOWL LIKE THAT? ....STOPPED DEAD   230   15
    IN HER PROPHETIC FIT HEARD WHAT WE HEARD, ...DIALOGUE O.   286 348
    IN HER PROPHETIC FIT HEARD WHAT WE HEARD, ...DIALOGUE O.   286 348
    ALL NIGHT I HAVE HEARD ....FEVER./DR   294   3
    WE HEARD THE HEAD WOMAN SAY, ...BITTER STRAWBERRIES   299   5
    "BEHIND ME THEN I HEARD A VOICE ....THE DREAM   311   19
    SUDDENLY A BRAZEN SONG IS HEARD ....THE PRINCESS AND THE GOBLINS   334   44
HEARING (9)
    HEARING TICKS BLOWN GOLD ....TWO SISTERS OF PERSEPHONE   32   14
    HEARING A WHITE SAINT RAVE ....ON THE PLETHORA OF DRYADS   67   1
    TESSELLATED BOUDOIR. HEARING FLUTES, YOU ....YADWIGHA.   86   27
    I FORGET YOU, HEARING THE CUT FLOWERS ....LEAVING EARLY   145   5
    GIVING EVERYBODY A FAIR HEARING. ....CANDLES   149   11
    FOR THE HEARING OF MY HEART --- ....LADY LAZARUS   246   59
    HEARING THE FIERCE MASK MAGNIFY ....THE FEARFUL   256   15
    DANGERS, BUT DON'T MIND HEARING ABOUT THE ONES ....DIALOGUE O.   278   64
    HEARING A WEIRD CACKLE FROM AFAR, ...THE PRINCESS AND THE GOBLINS   334   41
HEARS (5)
    SHE HEARS THE CAUSTIC TICKING OF THE CLOCK. ....CINDERELLA   304   14
    GOD HEARS FROM HIS GREAT SUNSTRUCK HELL ....SONG FOR A REVOLU.   323   19
    THE PRINCESS HEARS THE THUNDER AND THE POMP ....THE PRINCESS.   333   21
    UNTIL SHE HEARS THE TWITTERING MACHINE *THE PRINCESS AND THE GOBLINS   334   56
    HE HEARS THE GRUFF KNOCKING ....TEMPER OF TIME   336   19
HEARSE (2)
    WHY SHOULD IT, IT IS THE HEARSE OF A DEAD FOOT, ...BERCK-PLAGE   197   20
    DOWN THE DARK IN A BLACK HEARSE ....THE DREAM 310   8
HEART (62)
    I HURL MY HEART TO HALT HIS PACE, ...PURSUIT   23   37
    TOOK MY HEART AS IF ....SONG FOR A SUMMER'S DAY   31   12
    INTO CRACKED HEART ....TINKER JACK AND THE TIDY WIVES   34   24
    ITS HEART AND GUTS HUNG HOOKED ....STREET SONG   36   8
    THAN MAN'S RED HEART." ....DIALOGUE BETWEEN GHOST AND PRIEST   39   50
    LAST BLOOD-DROP OF THAT TRUANT HEART. ....THE SHRIKE   42   23
    TO UNPICK THE HEART, PARE BONE ....NOVEMBER GRAVEYARD   56   9
    OF HER HEART, WAS THE HUMPED INDIFFERENT IRON .....HARDCASTLE CRAGS   63   28
    VISIBLE ONLY TO THE PARAGON HEART, ...ON THE PLETHORA OF DRYADS   67   3
    BY HEART HERE I HOLD ....WORDS FOR A NURSERY   74   38
    IT WAS NOT A HEART, BEATING, ...NIGHT SHIFT   76   1
    TO KNOW THE STILL HEART OF THE STONES: ....CHILD'S PARK STONES 101   22
    HE HANDS HER THE CUT-OUT HEART LIKE A CRACKED HEIRLOOM. TWO VIEWS.   114   11
    WHEN I WORMED BACK UNDER MY MOTHER'S HEART. ELECTRA ON AZALEA PATH   116   10
    MY HEART UNDER YOUR FOOT, SISTER OF A STONE. ....BEEKEEPER'S.   118   7
    MY HEART IS A STOPPED GERANIUM. POEM.1.WHO.   131   9
    AND STILL THE LUNGS WON'T FILL AND THE HEART WON'T START. *STILLBORN   142   10
    LET THEM ASTOUND HIS HEART WITH THEIR MERIT. ....MAGI   148   17
    NO AIRBUBBLES START FROM MY HEART, I AM LUNGLESS ZOO KEEPER'S WIFE   154   5
    THE KNOCK OF THE SMALL, NEW HEART. ....HEAVY WOMEN   158   14
    AND I AM AWARE OF MY HEART: IT OPENS AND CLOSES ....TULIPS   162   60
    THAT WILL PUT HER HEART OUT LIKE AN ONLY EYE. ....WIDOW   164   5
    A PAPER IMAGE TO LAY AGAINST HER HEART ....WIDOW   164   17
    THE HEART IS A RED-BELL-BLOOM, IN DISTRESS. ..THE SURGEON AT 2 A.M.   171   17
    THEY WILL ROLL ME UP IN BANDAGES, THEY WILL STORE MY HEART LAST W.   172   23
    I THINK IT IS A PART OF MY HEART. BUT IT FLICKERS. ....MIRROR   173   8
    WHAT DID MY HEART DO, WITH ITS LOVE? ....THREE WOMEN   181 170
    TO BE SO OPEN: IT IS AS IF MY HEART ....THREE WOMEN   185 300

```
                                                  TITLE          PAGE  LINE
HEART (CONT.)
   OR SITS IN THE DESERT AND HURTS HIS MOTHER'S HEART.  ....THREE WOMEN    186  333
   I HEAR HER GREAT HEART PURR. ......................AN APPEARANCE        189    3
   O HEART, SUCH DISORGANIZATION! ...................AN APPEARANCE         189   16
   IS IT FOR SUCH I AGITATE MY HEART? ..............................ELM    193   36
   INTOLERABLE VOWELS ENTER MY HEART. ............................EVENT    194    6
   AND MY HEART TOO SMALL TO BANDAGE THEIR TERRIBLE FAULTS.  ....BERCK.    198   45
   BUT THE SPAWN PERCOLATE IN MY HEART. THEY ARE FERTILE. *WORDS HEARD.    203   13
   AT THE HEART OF THE HOUSE ..............................WINTERING       218    7
   BRUTE HEART OF A BRUTE LIKE YOU. ............................DADDY      223   50
   BIT MY PRETTY RED HEART IN TWO. .............................DADDY      224   56
   THERE'S A STAKE IN YOUR FAT BLACK HEART ....................DADDY       224   76
   STRAIGHT FROM THE HEART. .......................................CUT     235   13
   PULP OF YOUR HEART .............................................CUT     236   34
   WHOSE RED HEART BLOOMS THROUGH HER COAT SO ASTOUNDINGLY ---*POP.OCT.    240    3
   DOLL HE GUARDS LIKE A HEART -- ..........................PURDAH         244   54
   FOR THE HEARING OF MY HEART --- ........................LADY LAZARUS    246   59
   GRAY BIRDS OBSESS MY HEART, .............................MARY'S SONG    257   13
   IT IS A HEART, .........................................MARY'S SONG     257   19
   FIELDS MELT MY HEART. ...................................SHEEP IN FOG   262   12
   THE HEART HAS NOT STOPPED. ...............................MYSTIC        269   31
   THE HEART SHUTS, .......................................CONTUSION       271   10
   THE HEART LIKE WISHES OR FREE ..........................BALLOONS        272   16
   THEIR LIGHTS WHITEN MY HEART. .......................THE RIVAL/DR       291   26
   SHE PULSES LIKE A HEART ON MY HILL. .....................ELM/DR         292    2
   O IGNORANT HEART! .....................................FEVER.//DR       294    2
   BLOOD SPRINGS ETERNAL IF THE HEART BE BURNING. ..TO EVA DESCENDING.     303    8
   MY LEAN, UNRIPENED HEART. ...................................JILTED     304   12
   MY X-RAYED HEART, DISSECTED BODY: .......................BLUEBEARD      305    6
   EXIT FROM THE HEART. ...........................TRIO OF LOVE SONGS      314    8
   IF YOU PLUCK OUT MY HEART ......................TRIO OF LOVE SONGS      315   49
   A STONE CAN MASQUERADE WHERE NO HEART IS .......NEVER TRY TO TRICK.     319    4
   MY EXTRAVAGANT HEART BLOWS UP AGAIN ..........CIRCUS IN THREE RINGS     321    3
   THE SIMPLE SUM OF HEART PLUS HEART. .............LOVE IS A PARALLAX     331   78
   THE SIMPLE SUM OF HEART PLUS HEART. .............LOVE IS A PARALLAX     331   78
HEARTBEATS' (1)
   IN THEIR HEARTBEATS' BLAZING WAKE UNTIL RED COCK  ....EPITAPH FOR F.     46   27
HEARTEN (1)
   ITS YELLOWS HEARTEN. ....................NICK AND THE CANDLESTICK       241   22
HEARTH (1)
   OF THE HOMELAND HEARTH TO PLOUGH THEIR PILGRIM WAY .......MAYFLOWER      60   10
HEARTHSTONE (1)
   HEARTHSTONE AT ONCE OF THE OUTRAGEOUS HEAD; ...........LADY AND T.       69    6
HEARTHSTONES (1)
   OUT HERE THERE ARE NO HEARTHSTONES, .....SLEEP IN THE MOJAVE DESERT     143    1
HEARTS (12)
   THEIR FOND HEARTS CHARRED AS ANY MATCH. *EPITAPH FOR FIRE AND FLOWER     45    7
   HEARTS OF THOSE WHO PIERCED TIME'S CORE. .............CRYSTAL GAZER      55   42
   BLEEDING HEARTS ON ITS SLEEVE .........................POLLY'S TREE     129   40
   THE STOREROOMS ARE FULL OF HEARTS. .......................POEM.7.S.     137   32
   UPSIDE DOWN HEARTS OF LIGHT TIPPING WAX FINGERS, ..........CANDLES      148    2
   THE WAVES PULSE AND PULSE LIKE HEARTS. ....................WHITSUN      154   22
   OR THE HEARTS OF SHEEP, AND THE WIND ..........WUTHERING HEIGHTS        167   11
   WITH THEIR HEARTS THAT TICK AND TICK, WITH THEIR SATCHELS OF
   INSTRUMENTS. ............................................THREE WOMEN    180  138
   I HAVE PAINTED LITTLE HEARTS ON EVERYTHING. .............THREE WOMEN    186  329
   OLD BLOOD OF LIMB STUMPS, BURNT HEARTS. .................BERCK-PLAGE    200   99
   CREAMY BEAN FLOWERS WITH BLACK EYES AND LEAVES LIKE BORED HEARTS. ...
                                               ...  THE BEE MEETING       211   18
   PUSHING BY LIKE HEARTS, ....................................MEDUSA      225    8
HEART'S (6)
   CAN BE STRUCK FROM ROCK TO MAKE HEART'S WASTE ....WINTER LANDSCAPE,      22   14
   AND WHAT HEART'S OVEN .................................VANITY FAIR       32   15
   TO BELIEVE BEYOND HEART'S FLARE ......................VANITY FAIR        33   26
   AND HEART'S FROSTY DISCIPLINE ...........................SPINSTER        50   17
   AND THE TOAD GUARDING HIS HEART'S DROPLET. ..................SLEEP.     144   16
   SO THE ARTFUL GLASS WON'T CHANGE ITS CHILL FOR HEART'S  DIALOGUE O.     277   17
HEART-SHAPED (1)
   HEART-SHAPED LEAVES, LIKE CATALPA LEAVES, AND LILIES .....YADWIGHA.      85    6
HEAT (13)
   FROM THEIR WHITE HEAT ...............TINKER JACK AND THE TIDY WIVES      35   31
   (WITH HEAT SUCH AS NO MAN COULD HAVE ...................THE GLUTTON      40    3
   BOAR, FABULOUS ENOUGH TO STRADDLE THAT SOW'S HEAT. .............SOW      61   33
   OF HER SMALL HEAT OUT, BUT BEFORE THE WEIGHT ......HARDCASTLE CRAGS      63   42
   WHOSE STONES KEEP A LITTLE HEAT. ....................OLD LADIES' HOME   120    7
   TO FUNNEL MY HEAT AWAY. ............................WUTHERING HEIGHTS   167   15
   DOES NOT MY HEAT ASTOUND YOU. AND MY LIGHT. ..................FEVER.    232   40
   IS ON THE TWO OF US FOR LENDING HEAT ...DIALOGUE OVER A OUIJA BOARD     282  229
   THE DOORBELL RENDS THE NOONDAY HEAT .................FAMILY REUNION     300    5
   HEAT FURNACE OF PARADOX ..........................NOTES TO A NEOPHYTE   306   14
   OR THAT THE HEAT WITHIN WOULD GROW ...............TO A JILTED LOVER     310   13
   HEAT SHADOWS WAVER NOISELESS IN ...MORNING IN THE HOSPITAL SOLARIUM     332    6
   CLAMBERING UP THE CREAKING HEIGHTS OF HEAT ..........THE PRINCESS.      334   55
HEAT-CRACKED (1)
   THE HEAT-CRACKED CRICKETS CONGREGATE ....SLEEP IN THE MOJAVE DESERT     144   22
```

	TITLE	PAGE	LINE
HEATH (1)			
WHILE THE HEATH GRASS GLITTERS AND THE SPINDLING RIVULETS ...			
... PARLIAMENT HILL FIELDS		153	34
HEATHER (3)			
THROUGH BARE WHISTLING HEATHER, OVER STILES OF BLACK STONE, ...			
... THE SNOWMAN ON THE MOOR		58	21
YOU INHERIT WHITE HEATHER, A BEE'S WING, ...THE MANOR GARDEN		125	12
IF I PAY THE ROOTS OF THE HEATHER ....WUTHERING HEIGHTS		167	16
HEATING (1)			
HEATING THE PINCERS, HOISTING THE DELICATE HAMMERS. ......POEM.7.S.		137	28
HEAT-LIGHTNING (1)			
ON THE INCESSANT HEAT-LIGHTNING FLICKER OF SITUATIONS. ...INSOMNIAC		163	28
HEAVED (2)			
GIANT HEAVED INTO THE DISTANCE, STONE-HATCHETED, ...SNOWMAN O.		59	31
BEFORE ONE HEAVED HIMSELF THROUGH HEAVEN'S TENT ....DIALOGUE O.		281	171
HEAVEN (18)			
ATTACH HER TO HEAVEN. ....VANITY FAIR		32	5
THAT NOBLE MIEN, PERHAPS YOU'VE LATE QUITTED HEAVEN?" ..DIALOGUE B.		38	16
HIGH AGAINST HEAVEN, GULLS WENT WHEELING SOUNDLESS ...DREAM WITH C.		44	13
THE HEAVEN THOSE TWO DREAMED OF, IN DESPAIR. ....THE OTHER TWO		69	35
FOR THE RELISH OF HEAVEN, RELENTLESS, DOUSING WITH PRICKLES *LESSON.		80	14
IT MIGHT BE HEAVEN, THIS STATIC ....IN MIDAS' COUNTRY		99	11
OVER AND OVER. AND STILL THE HEAVEN ....BLUE MOLES		127	32
A TREE OF HEAVEN, THOUGH ....POLLY'S TREE		129	31
AND NO BODIES, SINGING LIKE ARROWS UP TO HEAVEN. ....WIDOW		164	25
THE HONEY-FEAST OF THE BERRIES HAS STUNNED THEM; THEY BELIEVE IN			
HEAVEN. ....BLACKBERRYING		169	17
THE WHITE LIGHT IS ARTIFICIAL, AND HYGIENIC AS HEAVEN. ....SURGEON.		170	1
"LET US MAKE A HEAVEN," THEY SAY. ....THREE WOMEN		179	90
THE UPFLIGHT OF THE MURDERESS INTO A HEAVEN THAT LOVES HER. ...BEE.		212	48
EVEN IN YOUR ZEN HEAVEN WE SHAN'T MEET. ....LESBOS		230	92
HEAVEN WOULD BE SOMETHING ELSE, ...LYONNESSE		234	12
THROUGH THE BLACK AMNESIAS OF HEAVEN. ....THE NIGHT DANCES		250	21
TO LET ME THROUGH TO A HEAVEN ....SHEEP IN FOG		262	14
ALL, IF YOU'LL HIDE HOPES OF HEAVEN IN A HAT ....DIALOGUE O.		282	231
HEAVENLY (1)			
FIRST LET THE HEAVENLY FOLIAGE GO, ...SONG FOR A REVOLUTIONARY LOVE		322	2
HEAVENS (3)			
ALREADY YELLOW THE HEAVENS. ....THE MANOR GARDEN		125	15
THE OVENS GLOWED LIKE HEAVENS, INCANDESCENT. ....MARY'S SONG		257	18
AND HEAVENS TILL THE SPIRITS SQUEAK ....LOVE IS A PARALLAX		330	69
HEAVEN'S (3)			
BEFORE ONE HEAVED HIMSELF THROUGH HEAVEN'S TENT ....DIALOGUE O.		281	171
WITH THE PILOT WHO DARES ALL HEAVEN'S HARMS .........METAMORPHOSES.		307	2
WITH HEAVEN'S AUTOCRATIC STATION, ...INSOLENT STORM.		326	30
HEAVENWARD (1)			
NUN-SOULED, THEY BURN HEAVENWARD AND NEVER MARRY. ....CANDLES		149	27
HEAVES (2)			
HEAVES FORTH STALK, LEAF, FRUIT-NUBBED EMERALD; ....ODE FOR TED		29	15
BY DAY, ONLY THE TOPSOIL HEAVES. ....BLUE MOLES		126	26
HEAVIER (1)			
WITH RICHNESS, HAIR HEAVIER ....LORELEI		94	13
HEAVING (2)			
HEAVING THE NEEDLES, ...MUSHROOMS		139	11
SOMEWHERE AT THE END OF IT, HEAVING. BLACKBERRIES ....BLACKBERRYING		168	4
HEAVY (6)			
HEAVY AS STATUARY, SHAPES NOT OURS ....THE OTHER TWO		68	15
FOR HER, THE HEAVY NOTION OF EVIL ....MAGI		148	12
HEAVY WOMEN ....HEAVY WOMEN		158	T
WAITING LIES HEAVY ON MY LIDS. IT LIES LIKE SLEEP, ...THREE WOMEN		179	108
SQUARE AS A CHAIR AND ALMOST TOO HEAVY TO LIFT. ....THE ARRIVAL.		212	2
THE SHEETS GROW HEAVY AS A LECHER'S KISS. ....FEVER.		231	30
HEAVY-FOOTED (1)			
BUT, HEAVY-FOOTED, STOOD ASIDE ....THE DISQUIETING MUSES		75	29
HEBETUDE (1)			
OF HEBETUDE, FROM THE LEDGE ....LORELEI		94	27
HECKLING (1)			
FOR THRIFTY CHILDREN, NOR DOLT PIG RIPE FOR HECKLING, ...SOW		60	13
HECTIC (1)			
AS AMID THE HECTIC MUSIC AND COCKTAIL TALK ....CINDERELLA		304	13
HE'D (5)			
SEASONED HOW HE'D MOST APPROVE; ....THE GLUTTON		40	6
THERE WAS NO TELLING IF HE'D ....MUSSEL HUNTER AT ROCK HARBOR		97	74
HE'D HAD SO MANY WARS! ....LYONNESSE		234	26
AN ORIGINAL NOTE. IF HE'D SAID, HOWEVER, MERELY: ....DIALOGUE O.		278	81
I KNEW HE'D GOT IT MIXED BEFORE: VISIONS*DIALOGUE OVER A OUIJA BOARD		282	219
HEDGE (6)			
TO SPRIGGED HEDGE OF BRAMBLE, ...ODE FOR TED		29	5
OUTSIDE, THE LITTLE HEDGE LEAVES ARE ....RESOLVE		52	8
EACH HEDGE WITH SUCH WHITE BLOOM ASTOUNDS OUR EYES ....MAYFLOWER		60	6
DARK THICKETS HEDGE THE HOUSE. ....THE SLEEPERS		123	11
THE YEW HEDGE OF THE GROSSE FUGE. ....LITTLE FUGUE		188	20
A YEW HEDGE OF ORDERS, ...LITTLE FUGUE		188	25
HEDGED (2)			
ON THE MOVE, HEDGED BY A LITTER OF FEAT-FOOT NINNIES ....SOW		61	21
232

HEDGED (CONT.)
    HEDGED IN AND EVIDENTLY INVIOLATE ....QUEEN MARY'S ROSE GARDEN 290   15
HEDGEHOG (2)
    A FLYING HEDGEHOG, ALL PRICKLES. ....THE SWARM 216   32
    BALLED HEDGEHOG, ...BY CANDLELIGHT 236   20
HEDGEROW (1)
    NOT EVEN NODDING, A PERSONAGE IN A HEDGEROW. ....THE BEE MEETING 212   41
HEDGEROWS (2)
    OF COUNTRY HEDGEROWS AND COW PASTURES ....WHITENESS I REMEMBER 102   16
    WIDEN AND DIE IN THE HEDGEROWS. I HEAR THE MOO OF COWS. *THREE WOMEN 185 312
HEDGES (3)
    DOZENS DROPPED DEAD IN THE HEDGES: O SHE FELT ....SNOWMAN O.   59   35
    EBON IN THE HEDGES, FAT .................................BLACKBERRYING 168   6
    YOUR BROTHER WILL TRIM MY HEDGES! ....................EAVESDROPPER 260   1
HEDGING (1)
    HEDGING MEADOWS OF BENIGN ....WATERCOLOR OF GRANTCHESTER MEADOWS 112   19
HEED (1)
    DEAD MEN RENDER LOVE AND WAR NO HEED, ...THE DEAD 320   3
HEEL (2)
    WHO DRAG OUR ANCIENT FATHER AT THE HEEL, ...MOONRISE   98   28
    HE FLEW INTO THE ROOM, A SHRIEK AT HIS HEEL. ....THREE WOMEN 181 165
HEEL-HUNG (1)
    ON THE INFERNO OF AFRICAN ORANGES, THE HEEL-HUNG PIGS.   THREE WOMEN 184 283
HEEL-PRINTS (1)
    POOLING IN HEEL-PRINTS, FUMBLING PEBBLE AND STEM. ....PARLIAMENT H. 153   36
HEELS (7)
    I SAT AT MY DESK IN MY STOCKINGS, MY HIGH HEELS, ...THREE WOMEN 177   21
    HOLES IN THE HEELS OF SOCKS, THE WHITE MUTE FACES ......THREE WOMEN 182 199
    AT HIS HEELS A PILE OF FIVE BRASS CANNONBALLS, ...BY CANDLELIGHT 237   33
    PIVOT OF HEELS AND KNEES! -- THE FURROW ....ARIEL 239   6
    FLAKES FROM MY HEELS. ....ARIEL 239   18
    AND HIGH HEELS CLICKING UP THE WALK; ....FAMILY REUNION 300   4
    THE PRINCE LEANS TO THE GIRL IN SCARLET HEELS, ...CINDERELLA 303   1
HEFT (1)
    WE HEFT GLOBED FLINT, RACKED IN VEINS' BARBED BINDINGS; ...FIRESONG   30   18
HEFTING (2)
    BLUE FUR, MOLES HAVE; HEFTING CHALK-HULLED FLINT ....ODE FOR TED   29   9
    HEFTING HIS WHITE PILLAR WITH THE LIGHT ....BY CANDLELIGHT 237   28
HEIGHT (1)
    STILL, THEY'RE OUR BEST MUSTERING OF HEIGHT: BY ....ABOVE THE OXBOW   88   5
HEIGHTS (2)
    WUTHERING HEIGHTS ....WUTHERING HEIGHTS 167   T
    CLAMBERING UP THE CREAKING HEIGHTS OF HEAT ....THE PRINCESS. 334   55
HEIR (1)
    HEIR OF THE FIRST FIVE ....WORDS FOR A NURSERY   73   2
HEIRLOOM (3)
    HE HANDS HER THE CUT-OUT HEART LIKE A CRACKED HEIRLOOM. TWO VIEWS. 114   11
    POOR HEIRLOOM, ALL YOU HAVE, ...BY CANDLELIGHT 237   32
    IN THE WINGS SOMEWHERE, OR LIKE HEIRLOOM FURNITURE .....DIALOGUE O. 276   7
HELD (7)
    OLD BOCKLIN MISSED, WHO HELD A SHELL .....ON THE DECLINE OF ORACLES   78   5
    SHUT AGAINST ME. ALL HELD STILL. ......MUSSEL HUNTER AT ROCK HARBOR   95   20
    LIT, BUT UNPEOPLED, HELD ITS WINDOWS ....OWL 101   3
    A SALLOW PIECE OF STRING HELD IT TOGETHER. ....TWO VIEWS. 114   9
    WHEN I HIT HER SHE HELD STILL, LIKE A TRUE PACIFIST. ....IN PLASTER 159   12
    ITS END AND RUNS TOWARD IT, ARMS HELD OUT IN LOVE. .....THREE WOMEN 181 151
    WHAT DID MY FINGERS DO BEFORE THEY HELD HIM? ....THREE WOMEN 181 169
HELEN (1)
    ECLIPSING EVA, CLEO AND HELEN OF TROY: ....VIRGIN IN A TREE   81   19
HELL (12)
    OF HELL, AND NOT THE FIERY PART. YET TO JUDGE BY THAT DAZZLED LOOK, ...
                              ... DIALOGUE BETWEEN GHOST AND PRIEST   38   15
    SHE CAME, AND CALLED HELL TO SUBDUE AN UNRULY MAN ....SNOWMAN O.   59   23
    NOW WORKS HIS HELL OF MONDAYS IN THE MOON'S BALL,*EVERLASTING MONDAY   62   11
    LITTLE POPPIES, LITTLE HELL FLAMES, ...POPPIES IN JULY 203   1
    THE SMOG OF COOKING, THE SMOG OF HELL ....LESBOS 228   35
    THE TONGUES OF HELL ....FEVER. 231   2
    I DO IT SO IT FEELS LIKE HELL. ....LADY LAZARUS 245   46
    IN HELL, SINCE HELL'S A FAIRYTALE. I WOULD ....DIALOGUE O. 278   65
    AND LIKE A CUCKOO IN THE NEST MAKES HELL   METAMORPHOSES OF THE MOON 307   17
    BLAZING IN MY GOLDEN HELL. ....TO A JILTED LOVER 310   27
    AND BURN TO DEATH WITHIN YOUR NEON HELL. ....THE TRIAL OF MAN 312   11
    GOD HEARS FROM HIS GREAT SUNSTRUCK HELL ....SONG FOR A REVOLU. 323   19
HE'LL (9)
    HE'LL NOT SPARE ....THE GLUTTON   40   12
    ILL-SERVED HE'LL BE WHEN ....WORDS FOR A NURSERY   74   41
    CALL HIM ANY NAME, HE'LL COME TO IT. POEM.4.BEAST. 134   16
    HE'LL BE RICH IN A YEAR (AND HE SHOULD KNOW) ....ON DECK 143   28
    IS HE, THEN? HE SPELLS. I-N. HE'LL LIFT *DIALOGUE OVER A OUIJA BOARD 278   76
    AN ANGEL. PLUMAGE. O-F-R. HE'LL ....DIALOGUE OVER A OUIJA BOARD 279   90
    AND GET US CLEAR OF THIS. OH, HE'LL GO CLEVER ....DIALOGUE O. 281 175
    SURFACED IN OURSELVES: HE'LL SPELL A LINE ....DIALOGUE O. 283 255
    ROUND TO EARN HIS PAY: HE'LL HAVE US KEEP ....DIALOGUE O. 284 294
HELLO (3)
    HAIL AND FAREWELL. HELLO, GOODBYE. O KEEPER *THE GHOST'S LEAVETAKING   91   39

```
                                              TITLE              PAGE  LINE
HELLO (CONT.)
    HELLO, AND THEN HELLO AGAIN IN DEAF  ............LOVE IS A PARALLAX  330  40
    HELLO, AND THEN HELLO AGAIN IN DEAF  ............LOVE IS A PARALLAX  330  40
HELLS (1)
    OF WITHERED WORLDS, AND STAMP OUT PUNY HELLS  ....LOVE IS A PARALLAX  330  68
HELL'S (2)
    IN HELL, SINCE HELL'S A FAIRYTALE. I WOULD  ............DIALOGUE O.  278  65
    FOR FEAST THE SWEETEST MEAT OF HELL'S CHEF D'OEUVRES:  .....TERMINAL  328  11
HELMED (1)
    HELMED, IN CUIRASS,  ..............................................SOW   61  30
HELMET (1)
    THIS APPARITION IN A GREEN HELMET,  .................THE BEE MEETING  211  28
HELP (6)
    WILL BREAK BEFORE IT HELP;  ...........................RECANTATION   41   7
    HELP OVER HILL  .............................TWO VIEWS OF WITHENS   72  10
    FROM HER AMAZINGLY WHITE TORSO, AND I COULDN'T HELP BUT NOTICE  ...
                                                        ... IN PLASTER  159  24
    I CANNOT HELP SMILING AT WHAT IT IS I KNOW.  ............THREE WOMEN  177  13
    THERE IS NO HELP IN HIS WEEPING WIFE.  ..................BERCK-PLAGE  198  52
    WORK AT ALL? HOW CAN WE HELP BUT BATTLE *DIALOGUE OVER A OUIJA BOARD  284  286
HELPED (1)
    AND HELPED THE TWO OF US TO CHOIR:  ...........THE DISQUIETING MUSES   75  21
HELPER (1)
    THUMBHEAD, BLUNT HELPER,  .......................WORDS FOR A NURSERY   73  15
HELPLESS (2)
    IS HELPLESS HERE, QUITE EXTRA, YET WE MUST MAKE  ...CHANNEL CROSSING   27  35
    I AM HELPLESS AS THE SEA AT THE END OF HER STRING.  .....THREE WOMEN  182  188
HEMLOCK (1)
    FROM GAUNT HEMLOCK, ROOKS CROAK HAVOC:  .....................PURSUIT   22   7
HEN (2)
    SAGE HEN AND SPRY RABBIT,  ...................TWO VIEWS OF WITHENS   72   8
    HEN HUTS AND CATTLE GREEN  ........................MAN IN BLACK  119   9
HENCE (2)
    LET FLESH BE KNIT, AND EACH STEP HENCE GO FAMOUS.  ........WREATH F.   45  24
    PREDICTING THREE BOYS AN HOUR HENCE WILL PLAY  ..........DIALOGUE O.  279  124
HENNA (1)
    HENNA HAGS: CLOTH OF YOUR CLOTH.  ....................LEAVING EARLY  146  21
HENS (1)
    WHILE THE COCKS AND HENS  ..........................ALICANTE LULLABY   43   5
HER (272)
HERALD (1)
    HERALD DISTRACTION: A FLOCK OF PASTEL PILLS,  ...MORNING IN THE HOS.  332  13
HERALDIC (1)
    NOT OF HERALDIC STALLIONS: OFF-WHITE  ..........WHITENESS I REMEMBER  102   5
HERALDRY (1)
    HERALDRY OF A STARKER AGE,  ...............ON THE DECLINE OF ORACLES   78  19
HERALDS (1)
    A HUNDRED HERALDS SHE SENT OUT  ...............THE QUEEN'S COMPLAINT   29  16
HERB (1)
    WITH THE LOVE-HOT HERB, THE TALKING CAT,  ........THE TIMES ARE TIDY  107  13
HERBAGE (1)
    THESE ROCKS OFFER NO PURCHASE TO HERBAGE OR PEOPLE:  ......TWO CAMP.  145  18
HERCULES (1)
    INTO SALT SEAS. HERCULES HAD A SIMPLE TIME,  .................PERSEUS   82   6
HERDS (1)
    BEHIND SHUT DOORS; THE DAIRY HERDS  .................HARDCASTLE CRAGS   63  32
HERE (63)
    IS HELPLESS HERE, QUITE EXTRA, YET WE MUST MAKE  ...CHANNEL CROSSING   27  35
    A MILLION GREEN COUNTIES FROM HERE,  ...........MONOLOQUE AT 3 A.M.   40   7
    CALL HERE WITH FLYING COLORS ALL WATCHFUL BIRDS *WREATH FOR A BRIDAL   45  13
    BUT HERE -- A BURGEONING  ...............................SPINSTER   50  19
    BY HEART HERE I HOLD  .........................WORDS FOR A NURSERY   74  38
    LIKE A SOAP-BUBBLE AS YOU CALLED: COME HERE!  THE DISQUIETING MUSES   76  47
    NO SUCCINCT GABRIEL FROM THE LETTERS HERE  ....................OUIJA   78  31
    MUST WAIT, WHILE HERE SUSO'S  .................A LESSON IN VENGEANCE   80  11
    HERE IN THIS VALLEY OF DISCREET ACADEMIES  ..........ABOVE THE OXBOW   87   1
    HERE ON A MOUNT OVERLAID WITH LEAVES. THE PAINT-PEELED  ......OXBOW.   88  34
    HERE, IN A WELL-STEERED COUNTRY,  ...........................LORELEI   94  19
    I SMELL THAT WHITENESS HERE, BENEATH THE STONES  ...........MOONRISE   98  16
    WHOSE LAUNDRY SNAPPED AND FROZE HERE, WHO  ............POINT SHIRLEY  110  10
    HERE IS A QUEENSHIP NO MOTHER CAN CONTEST --  .........BEEKEEPER'S.  118  13
    THE OLD WOMEN CREEP OUT HERE  .....................OLD LADIES' HOME  120   4
    UP HERE AMONG THE GULL CRIES  .....................MAGNOLIA SHOALS  121   1
    FLATTEN THE DOPED SNAKES TO RIBBON. IN HERE, THE GRASSES *PRIVATE G.  130  17
    I AM AT HOME HERE AMONG THE DEAD HEADS.  .................POEM.1.WHO.  131   6
    DOWN HERE THE SKY IS ALWAYS FALLING.  ..................POEM.4.BEAST.  134  20
    SICKNESS BEGINS HERE: I AM A DARTBOARD FOR WITCHES.  ......POEM.6.W.  135   4
    HERE THEY CAN DOCTOR HEADS, OR ANY LIMB.  ...............POEM.7.S.  137  35
    OUT HERE THERE ARE NO HEARTHSTONES,  .....SLEEP IN THE MOJAVE DESERT  143   1
    HERE ON THE LAST FRONTIER OF THE BIG, BRASH SPIRIT  .......TWO CAMP.  145  12
    I LEAN TO YOU, NUMB AS A FOSSIL. TELL ME I'M HERE.  .......TWO CAMP.  145  21
    ME, SITTING HERE BORED AS A LEOPARD  .................LEAVING EARLY  145   3
    THE TULIPS ARE TOO EXCITABLE, IT IS WINTER HERE.  ............TULIPS  160   1
    AND WHAT IF THE SKY HERE IS NO DIFFERENT,  ..STARS OVER THE DORDOGNE  166  25
    THERE IS TOO MUCH EASE HERE; THESE STARS TREAT ME TOO WELL.  STARS.  166  37
```

	TITLE	PAGE	LINE

HERE (CONT.)
    I WAKE TO A MAUSOLEUM; YOU ARE HERE, ...THE RIVAL   166   7
    WITH THE O-GAPE OF COMPLETE DESPAIR. I LIVE HERE. ....MOON.   173   11
    TURN UP THEIR HANDS, THEIR PALLORS. IT IS SO QUIET HERE.*THREE WOMEN   179   94
    HERE IS MY SON. ....THREE WOMEN   183 233
    I AM BEAUTIFUL AS A STATISTIC. HERE IS MY LIPSTICK. ....THREE WOMEN   183 245
    WHERE DO THE BLACK TREES GO THAT DRINK HERE? ....CROSSING THE WATER   190   2
    LOVE CANNOT COME HERE. ....EVENT   195   16
    HERE HE COMES NOW, AMONG THE MACKEREL GATHERERS ....BERCK-PLAGE   196   14
    IT IS SO BEAUTIFUL UP HERE: IT IS A STOPPING PLACE. ....BERCK-PLAGE   199   90
    IS HE HERE? ....WORDS HEARD, BY ACCIDENT, OVER THE PHONE   203   10
    AND HERE IS AN END TO THE WRITING, ...BURNING THE LETTERS   204   20
    THIS IS THE SMELL OF YEARS BURNING, HERE IN THE KITCHEN, *DETECTIVE.   208   12
    YES, HERE IS THE SECRETARY OF BEES WITH HER WHITE SHOP SMOCK ..BEE.   211   7
    HERE THEY COME, THE OUTRIDERS, ON THEIR HYSTERICAL ELASTICS. ..BEE.   212   38
    HERE IS MY HONEY-MACHINE, ...STINGS   214   33
    HERE IS HIS SLIPPER, HERE IS ANOTHER, ...STINGS   215   42
    HERE IS HIS SLIPPER, HERE IS ANOTHER, ...STINGS   215   42
    AND HERE THE SQUARE OF WHITE LINEN ....STINGS   215   43
    EMPTY? EMPTY. HERE IS A HAND ....THE APPLICANT   221   10
    COME HERE, SWEETIE, OUT OF THE CLOSET. ....THE APPLICANT   221   28
    HOW DID I GET HERE? ....THE JAILER   227   32
    AND HERE WE ARE, HUNG OUT OVER THE DEAD DROP ....STOPPED DEAD   230   3
    IT'S VIOLENT. WE'RE HERE ON A VISIT, ...STOPPED DEAD   230   11
    O LOVE, HOW DID YOU GET HERE? ....NICK AND THE CANDLESTICK   241   23
    HERE THERE IS SUCH MUD. ....GETTING THERE   248   21
    AND HERE YOU COME, WITH A CUP OF TEA ....KINDNESS   270   16
    ON THE ROUND BASE OF THE INVERTED WINE-GLASS HERE, ...DIALOGUE O.   276   5
    HERE IS A WHITE SKY. HERE IS THE BEAUTY ....FEVER./DR   294   9
    HERE IS A WHITE SKY. HERE IS THE BEAUTY ....FEVER./DR   294   9
    FROM HERE THE MOON SEEMS SMOOTH AS ANGEL-FOOD, ...ADMONITIONS   319   7
    FROM HERE YOU CAN'T SEE SPOTS UPON THE SUN; ....ADMONITIONS   319   8
    PRETENDING THAT THE BIRDS ARE HERE TO STAY; ....NEVER TRY TO TRICK.   319   2
    HERE ARE TWO PUPILS ......ON LOOKING INTO THE EYES OF A DEMON LOVER   325   1
    BEYOND THE INTERVAL OF NOW AND HERE: ....TWO LOVERS.   327   11
    TRAIN TRACKS ALWAYS MEET, NOT HERE, BUT ONLY ...LOVE IS A PARALLAX   329   2
HERE'S (8)
    PAVING THIS GRAVE GROUND. HERE'S HONEST ROT .....NOVEMBER GRAVEYARD   56   8
    THIS LADY HERE'S NO KIN ....ALL THE DEAD DEARS   70   15
    AND MOCKS! HERE'S THE PARODY OF THAT MORAL MOUSETRAP ....VIRGIN.   81   2
    HERE'S A CUDDLY MOTHER. POEM.2.DARK.   133   28
    HERE'S YESTERDAY, LAST YEAR -- ....A LIFE   149   3
    HERE'S A SPOT I THOUGHT YOU'D LOVE -- ....THE TOUR   238   27
    HERE'S YOUR SPECS, DEAR, HERE'S YOUR PURSE. ....THE TOUR   238   36
    HERE'S YOUR SPECS, DEAR, HERE'S YOUR PURSE. ....THE TOUR   238   36
HERESIES (1)
    IN HERESIES OF HOLOCAUST. ......INSOLENT STORM STRIKES AT THE SKULL   326   36
HERETICS (1)
    MELTING THE TALLOW HERETICS, ...MARY'S SONG   257   7
HERMETIC (1)
    IN SQUARE HERMETIC BOTTLES, WHILE THE SUN ....THE TRIAL OF MAN   312   3
HERMIT (2)
    THE HERMIT AT OUTERMOST HOUSE ....THE HERMIT AT OUTERMOST HOUSE   118   T
    HE WITHSTOOD THEM, THAT HERMIT. ......THE HERMIT AT OUTERMOST HOUSE   119   17
HERO (1)
    UNLUCKY THE HERO BORN ....THE TIMES ARE TIDY   107   1
HEROES (3)
    SQUANDERS A SUMMER AND THE BRAWN OF HIS HEROES ....LESSON.   80   17
    GELDED AND WINGLESS. NOT HEROES. NOT HEROES. ....STINGS/DR   293   15
    GELDED AND WINGLESS. NOT HEROES. NOT HEROES. ....STINGS/DR   293   15
HEROIC (4)
    WHILE YOU STAND HEROIC IN COAT AND TIE, I SIT ........CONVERSATION.   21   10
    OF MIXIE BLACKSHORT THE HEROIC BEAR, ...THE DISQUIETING MUSES   75   10
    CRIES AND HEROIC COUPLETS CONCLUDING THE MILLION ....PERSEUS   83   18
    PERSUADED BY HIS BRONZE HEROIC REASON. ....GOLD MOUTHS CRY   302   6
HEROINE (1)
    I SHALL BE A HEROINE OF THE PERIPHERAL. ....THREE WOMEN   182 197
HERON (1)
    HUNG CAUGHT IN DARK-WEBBED BRANCHES LIKE A FABULOUS HERON. ...
                      ... DIALOGUE BETWEEN GHOST AND PRIEST   38   6
HERR (4)
    SO, SO, HERR DOKTOR. ....LADY LAZARUS   246   65
    SO, HERR ENEMY. ....LADY LAZARUS   246   66
    HERR GOD, HERR LUCIFER ....LADY LAZARUS   246   79
    HERR GOD, HERR LUCIFER ....LADY LAZARUS   246   79
HERS (1)
    OF LOVE: CLAWS BRACED, AT BAY, MY CURRENCY NOT HERS. INCOMMUNICADO   100   7
HERSELF (4)
    FOUND HERSELF, OF A SUDDEN, INTOLERABLY STRUCK ....SPINSTER   49   4
    I FELT HER CRITICIZING ME IN SPITE OF HERSELF, ...IN PLASTER   159   30
    THE OLD QUEEN DOES NOT SHOW HERSELF, IS SHE SO UNGRATEFUL? ....BEE.   212   50
    NOW SHE HERSELF IS DARKENING ....ELM/DR   292   9
HE'S (17)
    A STONY HOLE. HE'S TO BLAME. POEM.2.DARK.   132   20
    HE'S A FAT SORT. POEM.2.DARK.   132   21

HE'S (CONT.)
   YOU COULD EAT HIM. HE'S A BOY. ....LESBOS 228 25
   COME ON CALL LIKE THAT BUT PAN? HE'S ...DIALOGUE OVER A OUIJA BOARD 277 28
   BORED HIM. HE'S MORE PHILOSOPHER, IT SEEMS, ...DIALOGUE O. 277 43
   DO YOU KNOW HOW MY FATHER IS? HE'S LEFT *DIALOGUE OVER A OUIJA BOARD 278 74
   YOU'RE MELTING NOW, BECAUSE YOU THINK HE'S HIT ....DIALOGUE O. 278 80
   A-W-W. HE'S GONE OFF: WHAT ENGLISH .....DIALOGUE OVER A OUIJA BOARD 279 93
   LIKE ALL THE OTHERS AND SWEAR THAT HE'S A PUMA ....DIALOGUE O. 281 176
   ON HIM SOMETIMES. HE'S LAZY. LIKE ANY YOUNG ....DIALOGUE O. 281 182
   TO COLLECT HIS BEATINGS. AND IF HE'S A GO-BETWEEN ......DIALOGUE O. 281 185
   WHERE DO YOU LIVE? HE MOVES. HE'S MOVING BRISK ....DIALOGUE O. 281 206
   CHIMERA ON THE HOOK, WHO CLAIMS HE'S LATE ....DIALOGUE O. 283 245
   PAN AS OUR EVENING GUEST IF HE'S SO FREE*DIALOGUE OVER A OUIJA BOARD 283 252
   YOU SAY HE'S TOLD TWO LIES . . . CALL THEM TWO PLUCKED DIALOGUE O. 283 266
   HIM YET, AND GIVE US GOOD REASON. NO, HE'S ON ....DIALOGUE O. 284 295
   A BINGE OF JEERS. LOOK. HE'S RUNNING THROUGH ....DIALOGUE O. 284 296
HEST (1)
   AT HIS HAND'S STAUNCH HEST, BIRDS BUILD. ....ODE FOR TED 29 18
HEX (1)
   THERE'S A HEX ON THE CRADLE ....TEMPER OF TIME 336 23
HEYDAY (1)
   THEIR FABULOUS HEYDAY ENDLESS. ....DREAM WITH CLAM-DIGGERS 44 16
HIATUS (1)
   IN THE WHITE HIATUS OF WINTER -- ....LOVE LETTER 147 11
HIBERNACULUM (1)
   INTO THE LIGHTLESS HIBERNACULUM ....ELECTRA ON AZALEA PATH 116 2
HIBERNATE (1)
   INMATES WHO DON'T HIBERNATE. POEM.1.WHO. 131 15
HID (3)
   WHATEVER HIS SHREWD SECRET, HE KEPT IT HID ....SOW 60 3
   TO DISCOVER THAT METAPHYSICAL TREE WHICH HID ...PLETHORA OF DRYADS. 67 9
   WHEN IT THUNDERED I HID UNDER A FLAT STONE. POEM.3.MAENAD. 133 5
HIDDEN (2)
   NEVER GIVEN; HIDDEN, YET ....THE GREAT CARBUNCLE 72 12
   AND HIDDEN ALL THE BRIGHT ANGELIC MEN. ......EPITAPH IN THREE PARTS 338 31
HIDE (15)
   FOR A BAY-TREE HIDE, RESPECT'S ....VIRGIN IN A TREE 81 11
   OTHER ROCKS HIDE THEIR GRUDGES UNDER THE WATER. ....FINISTERRE 169 9
   THAT SUMMER WE WORE BLACK GLASSES TO HIDE OUR EYES. *THE BABYSITTERS 174 3
   OBSCENE BIKINIS HIDE IN THE DUNES, ...BERCK-PLAGE 197 24
   MY VISIBILITIES HIDE. ....PURDAH 242 17
   SHEER-SIDED, WITH HOLES WHERE TO HIDE. ....GIGOLO 267 3
   ALL, IF YOU'LL HIDE HOPES OF HEAVEN IN A HAT ....DIALOGUE O. 282 231
   I TRY TO THINK OF A PLACE TO HIDE YOU ....THE RIVAL/DR 291 8
   TO HIDE FROM HIM: ....TO A JILTED LOVER 310 17
   HIDE, HIDE, IN THE DEEP NEST ....GO GET THE GOODLY SQUAB 313 7
   HIDE, HIDE, IN THE DEEP NEST ....GO GET THE GOODLY SQUAB 313 7
   HIDE, HIDE, IN THE SAFE CAVE ....GO GET THE GOODLY SQUAB 313 15
   HIDE, HIDE, IN THE SAFE CAVE ....GO GET THE GOODLY SQUAB 313 15
   HIDE, HIDE, IN THE WARM PORT ....GO GET THE GOODLY SQUAB 313 23
   HIDE, HIDE, IN THE WARM PORT ....GO GET THE GOODLY SQUAB 313 23
HIDES (3)
   THE BLOOD-BERRIED HAWTHORN HIDES ITS SPINES WITH WHITE. *WATERCOLOR. 112 21
   "THESE ARE THE PRETTY TRINKETS THE SEA HIDES, ...FINISTERRE 170 31
   AS A DESK DRAWER HIDES A POISON PEN LETTER, ...THE RIVAL/DR 291 9
HIDING (2)
   WHY IS IT SO QUIET, WHAT ARE THEY HIDING? ....BERCK-PLAGE 196 5
   IS SHE HIDING, IS SHE EATING HONEY? SHE IS VERY CLEVER. ....BEE. 212 43
HIERATIC (1)
   LIKE HIERATIC STONES, AND THE GROUND IS HARD.*ELECTRA ON AZALEA PATH 116 4
HIERATICAL (1)
   HIERATICAL IN YOUR FROCK COAT, MAESTRO OF THE BEES, ...BEEKEEPER'S. 118 5
HIEROGLYPHS (2)
   CHAIR AND BUREAU ARE THE HIEROGLYPHS ....THE GHOST'S LEAVETAKING 90 16
   VOICES STAND BACK AND FLATTEN. THEIR VISIBLE HIEROGLYPHS*THREE WOMEN 179 96
HIGH (21)
   HANGS HIGH. ....SOLILOQUY OF THE SOLIPSIST 37 9
   HIGH AGAINST HEAVEN, GULLS WENT WHEELING SOUNDLESS ...DREAM WITH C. 44 13
   TO US, SINCE WE SEE NO LEAF EDGE STIR HIGH ....ABOVE THE OXBOW 88 33
   A HIGH HUSH QUIETENS THE CRICKETS' CRY. ....ABOVE THE OXBOW 89 56
   ALSO OF HIGH WINDOWS. WORSE ....LORELEI 94 28
   HIGH ON THE AIRY THATCHING ....MUSSEL HUNTER AT ROCK HARBOR 97 67
   FIRST HORSE UNDER ME, HIGH AS THE ROOFS, ...WHITENESS I REMEMBER 102 13
   GAVE UP THE GHOST LAST NIGHT. HIGH TIME. ....LEAVING EARLY 146 24
   THE HIGH, GREEN MEADOWS ARE GLOWING, AS IF LIT FROM WITHIN. ...
           ... BLACKBERRYING 168 14
   I SAT AT MY DESK IN MY STOCKINGS, MY HIGH HEELS, ...THREE WOMEN 177 21
   THERE IS THE MOON IN THE HIGH WINDOW. IT IS OVER. ......THREE WOMEN 181 176
   THE HIGH, DEAD, TOELESS FOOT OF THIS PRIEST ....BERCK-PLAGE 197 21
   THE BEES HAVE GOT SO FAR. SEVENTY FEET HIGH! ....THE SWARM 216 26
   HIS HIGH COLD MASKS OF AMNESIA. ....THE JAILER 227 31
   TAKE A LOOK AT THE WHITE, HIGH BERG ON HIS FOREHEAD -- ...LYONNESSE 233 3
   HIGH, HIGH AND ICILY ....GULLIVER 251 2
   HIGH, HIGH AND ICILY ....GULLIVER 251 2
   THEY SETTLE. ON THE HIGH ....MARY'S SONG 257 15

| | | TITLE | PAGE | LINE |

HIGH (CONT.)
THE SKY WAS HIGH AND BLUE. ....BITTER STRAWBERRIES 299 13
AND HIGH HEELS CLICKING UP THE WALK; ....FAMILY REUNION 300   4
SURRENDER: TO BUILD OUR BED AS HIGH AS JACK'S ...LOVE IS A PARALLAX 330 70
HIGHBOYS (1)
WHERE POLISHED HIGHBOYS WHISPER CREAKING CURSES ......FEMALE AUTHOR 301   7
HIGH-CHURCH (1)
FLOATING IN A HIGH-CHURCH HUSH ....CANDLES 149 22
HIGHER (3)
TO JUDGMENT IN A HIGHER COURT OF GRACE. ....DIALOGUE B.   39 45
"THERE SITS NO HIGHER COURT ......DIALOGUE BETWEEN GHOST AND PRIEST   39 49
THERE IS NO LIFE HIGHER THAN THE GRASSTOPS ....WUTHERING HEIGHTS 167 10
HIGHER'S (1)
WHERE NOTHING HIGHER'S TO BE LOOKED TO. DOWNWARD LOOKS ......OXBOW.   88 30
HIGH-RISER (1)
O HIGH-RISER, MY LITTLE LOAF. ....YOU'RE 141   9
HIGH-STEPPING (1)
BELLS, HOOVES, OF THE HIGH-STEPPING BLACK GOATS WOKE US. OTHER TWO.   68   3
HIGHWAY (1)
AND THE BULL ON THE KING'S HIGHWAY. ....THE BULL OF BENDYLAW 108 21
HIKERS (1)
HIKERS GET TO: ....TWO VIEWS OF WITHENS   72   6
HILL (23)
ASLANT: THEIR HILL OF STINGING NETTLE; ....BUCOLICS   24 10
HELP OVER HILL ....TWO VIEWS OF WITHENS   72 10
AND HILL, AND THROUGH PEATY WATER. ....TWO VIEWS OF WITHENS   72 11
O LITTLE CITY ON A HILL! ....A WINTER'S TALE   87 31
FROM WATER-TOWER HILL TO THE BRICK PRISON ....POINT SHIRLEY 110   1
THE DAY I WOKE, I WOKE ON CHURCHYARD HILL. ..ELECTRA ON AZALEA PATH 117 15
I OPEN MY LUNCH ON A HILL OF BLACK CYPRESS. ....THE COLOSSUS 130 19
PARLIAMENT HILL FIELDS ....PARLIAMENT HILL FIELDS 152   T
ON THIS BALD HILL THE NEW YEAR HONES ITS EDGE. ....PARLIAMENT H. 152   1
THE BLUE NIGHT PLANTS, THE LITTLE PALE BLUE HILL .....PARLIAMENT H. 153 41
ON THE GREEN HILL, UNDER THE THORN TREES, ...HEAVY WOMEN 158 12
ON THIS HILL, WITH ITS VIEW OF LIT CASTLES, EACH SWUNG BELL STARS. 166 38
THE PHEASANT STANDS ON THE HILL; ....THREE WOMEN 176 11
I SHALL BE A SKY AND A HILL OF GOOD: O LET ME BE! ......THREE WOMEN 180 140
I AM A WARM HILL. ....THREE WOMEN 183 238
IT IS THE EXCEPTION THAT CLIMBS THE SORROWFUL HILL ....THREE WOMEN 186 332
IT RATTLES THEIR STARS ON THE GREEN HILL WHERE PERCY .....NARCISSI. 190   5
THROUGH THE UNCUT GRASS ON THE ELM'S HILL. ....PHEASANT 191   4
A HUNDRED, ON THAT HILL -- GREEN AND RED, ...PHEASANT 191 17
HE LUMPS IT DOWN THE PLASTIC COBBLED HILL, ...LESBOS 228 48
AND THIS HILL AND THIS ....CHILDLESS WOMAN 259 17
SHE PULSES LIKE A HEART ON MY HILL. ....ELM/DR 292   2
HILL AND VALLEY STIFFEN ROW ON ROW. ....PROLOGUE TO SPRING 322   6
HILLOCKS (2)
WE HAVE NOT MOUNTAINS, BUT MOUNTS, TRUNCATED HILLOCKS ....OXBOW.   87   2
THEMSELVES MERE ROCKY HILLOCKS TO AN EVEREST. ......ABOVE THE OXBOW   87   4
HILLS (14)
NOW HILLS HATCH MENACE, SPAWNING SHADE; ....PURSUIT   22 25
OF STARK WIND-HARROWED HILLS AND WELTERING MIST; ....SNOWMAN O.   58 13
OF ITS HILLS, AND ITS PASTURES BORDERED BY BLACK STONE SET ...
                                     ... HARDCASTLE CRAGS   63 29
OF STONES AND HILLS OF STONES COULD BREAK ....HARDCASTLE CRAGS   63 43
ELEVATIONS TO BE CALLED SOMETHING MORE THAN HILLS. ABOVE THE OXBOW   88   9
AND THE IRON HILLS THAT ENCLOSE THEM. EARTHEN FINGERS ......NET-. 121 16
FROM BETWEEN TWO HILLS A SUDDEN WIND FUNNELS AT ME, ..BLACKBERRYING 169 20
THESE HILLS ARE TOO GREEN AND SWEET TO HAVE TASTED SALT. BLACKBER. 169 22
THE GRAY SKY LOWERS, THE HILLS LIKE A GREEN SEA ....BERCK-PLAGE 199 73
ADDRESSING IT, WHILE THE HILLS ROLL THE NOTES OF THE DEAD BELL; ...
                                     ... BERCK-PLAGE 200 95
THE SMALL SKULLS, THE SMASHED BLUE HILLS, THE GODAWFUL HUSH. ...
                                     ... FOR A FATHERLESS SON 206 13
OVER THE SEVEN HILLS, THE RED FURROW, THE BLUE MOUNTAIN? *DETECTIVE. 208   2
THE MILD HILLS, THE SAME OLD MAGENTA ....THE SWARM 216 28
THE HILLS STEP OFF INTO WHITENESS. ....SHEEP IN FOG 262   1
HILLS' (1)
TO THE HILLS' NORTHERN FACE, AND THE FACE IS ORANGE ROCK BLACKBER. 169 24
HILLTOP (1)
STORMING THE HILLTOP. ....BERCK-PLAGE 200 117
HIM (78)
HIMSELF (7)
HOUSES HIMSELF ELSEWHERE. OUR FOLK THIN ....FROG AUTUMN   99 11
HIMSELF WITHERED THESE LATTER-DAYS ....THE TIMES ARE TIDY 107   8
ONE, BY HIMSELF, SEEMED PITIABLE ENOUGH, ...BLUE MOLES 126   5
SHALL UNHUSK HIMSELF AND STEER INTO THE AIR. POEM.5.F. 135 20
IMAGINING HIMSELF A HEADWAITER IN AMERICA, ...CANDLES 149 21
IT IS HIMSELF HE GUIDES ....PURDAH 242 21
BEFORE ONE HEAVED HIMSELF THROUGH HEAVEN'S TENT ....DIALOGUE O. 281 171
HINGE (1)
EXCEPT FOR A SORT OF A HINGE ....CUT 235   4
HINGES (2)
A SLY WORLD'S HINGES HAD SWUNG ....MUSSEL HUNTER AT ROCK HARBOR   95 19
A SWISS WATCH, JEWELED IN THE HINGES! ....AN APPEARANCE 189 15

| | | TITLE | PAGE | LINE |

HINTERLAND (1)
OF FOG IN THAT HINTERLAND FEW ....TWO VIEWS OF WITHENS 72   5
HIP (1)
WHERE SECOND WIND, HIP BOOT ....TWO VIEWS OF WITHENS 72   9
HIPPOPOTAMUS (1)
THE MOROCCAN HIPPOPOTAMUS? ....A SECRET 219 13
HIPS (1)
BREASTS AND HIPS A CONFECTIONER'S SUGAR ....BERCK-PLAGE 197 25
HIRES (1)
WHEREBY ONE HIRES A DEMON. ....CRYSTAL GAZER 55 36
HIRING (1)
TRIED SOBRIETY HIRING HIM OUT ....WHITENESS I REMEMBER 102   8
HIROSHIMA (1)
LIKE HIROSHIMA ASH AND EATING IN. ....FEVER. 231 26
HIS (274)
HISS (6)
THIS CRACKED WORLD'S INCESSANT GABBLE AND HISS. ....STREET SONG 36 30
CREEPS AWAY, MANY-SNAKED, WITH A LONG HISS OF DISTRESS. *BERCK-PLAGE 196 18
HISS AT MY SINS. ....MEDUSA 226 39
THE POTATOES HISS. ....LESBOS 227   2
IN BLUE DISTANCE THE PISTONS HISS. ....YEARS 256 25
WITH A HISS OF DISASTER ....TEMPER OF TIME 336   7
HISSING (1)
AND EVERY PRIVATE TWINGE A HISSING ASP ....PERSEUS 83 20
HISTORIAN (1)
OLD HISTORIAN, ...WORDS FOR A NURSERY 74 26
HISTORICAL (1)
YOU ARE PITHY AND HISTORICAL AS THE ROMAN FORUM. ......THE COLOSSUS 129 18
HISTORY (8)
NATURAL HISTORY ....NATURAL HISTORY 71   T
COME CLEAR OF THE SHADOW. HISTORY ....THE MANOR GARDEN 125   8
AND MY HISTORY TO THE ANESTHETIST AND MY BODY TO SURGEONS. ..TULIPS 160   7
WHERE SPILT LIVES CONGEAL AND STIFFEN TO HISTORY.*A BIRTHDAY PRESENT 208 51
CLEAR OF VOICES AND HISTORY, THE STATICKY ....LESBOS 228 18
OVER THE ENGLISH CLIFF AND UNDER SO MUCH HISTORY! ....LYONNESSE 234 22
I LOVE THEM LIKE HISTORY. ....LETTER IN NOVEMBER 253 23
WAIST-DEEP IN HISTORY -- ....WINTER TREES 258 10
HISTORY'S (2)
OF THE STABLE HORSE WHOSE HISTORY'S ....WHITENESS I REMEMBER 102   6
HISTORY'S BEATEN THE HAZARD. ....THE TIMES ARE TIDY 107 10
HIT (3)
WHEN I HIT HER SHE HELD STILL, LIKE A TRUE PACIFIST. ....IN PLASTER 159 12
YOU'RE MELTING NOW, BECAUSE YOU THINK HE'S HIT ....DIALOGUE O. 278 80
AN ODD DISEASE HAS HIT OUR HOLY COW, ...THE DISPOSSESSED 318   4
HIVE (4)
THE WHITE HIVE IS SNUG AS A VIRGIN, ...THE BEE MEETING 212 34
THE MIND OF THE HIVE THINKS THIS IS THE END OF EVERYTHING. ....BEE. 212 37
AND THE HIVE ITSELF A TEACUP, ...STINGS 214   8
WILL THE HIVE SURVIVE, WILL THE GLADIOLAS ....WINTERING 219 46
HIVED (2)
HIVED LIKE HONEY IN YOUR HEAD. ....EPITAPH FOR FIRE AND FLOWER 45 14
OF THEIR DREAM, THE HIVED STATION ....THE SWARM 216 34
HIVES (2)
YOU MOVE AMONG THE MANY-BREASTED HIVES, ...THE BEEKEEPER'S DAUGHTER 118   6
THEY ARE LEADING ME TO THE SHORN GROVE, THE CIRCLE OF HIVES. ..BEE. 211 23
HOARD (2)
AND HOARD FAITH SAFE IN A FOSSIL. ......EPITAPH FOR FIRE AND FLOWER 45 21
HOARD LAST YEAR'S LEAVES, WON'T MOURN, WEAR SACKCLOTH, OR TURN ...
                                      ... NOVEMBER GRAVEYARD 56   2
HOCK (1)
OUR LUCKY RELICS HAVE BEEN PUT IN HOCK: ....DOOMSDAY 316 11
HOCUS-POCUS (1)
BUT NO HOCUS-POCUS OF GREEN ANGELS ....CONJURING. 66 17
HOEING (1)
HOEING LETTUCE, WEEDING CELERY. ....BITTER STRAWBERRIES 299 19
HOG (1)
PRODIGIOUS IN GLUTTONIES AS THAT HOG WHOSE WANT ....SOW 61 41
HOGBACK (1)
A RISE IN THE LANDSCAPE, HUMMOCK OR HOGBACK, LOOKS ABOVE THE OXBOW 88 16
HOGHOOD (1)
DREAM-FILMED. WHAT A VISION OF ANCIENT HOGHOOD MUST ....SOW 61 27
HOGSHEAD (1)
HATCHED WITH A CLARET HOGSHEAD TO SWIG ....MAUDLIN 51   5
HOGWALLOW'S (1)
HOGWALLOW'S AT THE WINDOW. POEM.4.BEAST. 134 21
HOISTED (1)
HAMMERS HOISTED, WHEELS TURNING, ...NIGHT SHIFT 76 17
HOISTING (1)
HEATING THE PINCERS, HOISTING THE DELICATE HAMMERS. POEM.7.S. 137 28
HOISTS (1)
SUN HOISTS SOUL UP AFTER LIDS FALL SHUT; ....VANITY FAIR 33 28
HOLD (13)
THE GESTURE, BEND AND HOLD THE PRONE MAN'S HEAD. ..CHANNEL CROSSING 27 36
YET, IN MY WINTRIEST MOODS, I HOLD ......SOLILOQUY OF THE SOLIPSIST 37 24
HOWEVER YOU MAY SWEAT TO HOLD SUCH DARLING WRECKS ...EPITAPH FOR F. 45 13

238

HOLD (CONT.)
  BY HEART HERE I HOLD ....WORDS FOR A NURSERY   74   38
  BUT IT'S THE CLEAR CONVERSION AT THE TOP CAN HOLD ..ABOVE THE OXBOW   88   20
  TAKE HOLD ON THE LOAM, ...MUSHROOMS   139   5
  BY THE ROOTS OF MY HAIR SOME GOD GOT HOLD OF ME. ...THE HANGING MAN   141   1
  I HOLD MY FINGERS UP, TEN WHITE PICKETS. ....THREE WOMEN   182 194
  I HOLD YOU ON MY ARM. ....BY CANDLELIGHT   236   6
  I HOLD MY BREATH UNTIL YOU CREAK TO LIFE, ...BY CANDLELIGHT   236   19
  MY BONES HOLD A STILLNESS, THE FAR ....SHEEP IN FOG   262   11
  BUT THERE IS NO DRAWER TO HOLD YOU. ....THE RIVAL/DR   291   10
  WARNING ME TO HOLD HER HAND ....THE DREAM   311   20
HOLDING (7)
  HOLDING THE HORSES, THE CLOUDS, THE LEAVES ....THE EYE-MOTE   109   6
  BREATHING WAS EASY IN HIS AIRY HOLDING. POEM.4.BEAST.   134   3
  THEN MOTHER SWAM UP, HOLDING A TIN BASIN. ....FACE LIFT   156   7
  HOLDING MY BONES IN PLACE SO THEY WOULD MEND PROPERLY. ..IN PLASTER   159   27
  HOLDING IN ITS HATE ....BURNING THE LETTERS   204   12
  HOLDING UP ONE PALM -- ....A SECRET   219   4
  HOLDING THEIR GOLD-RUDDY BALLS ....LETTER IN NOVEMBER   253   27
HOLDS (6)
  OF ALL DECORUM WHICH HOLDS THE WHIRLWIND BACK. .......CONVERSATION.   21   4
  OLD JOSEPH HOLDS AN ALPENSTOCK. ....A WINTER'S TALE   86   5
  A GULL HOLDS HIS POSE ON A SHANTY RIDGEPOLE, ...A WINTER SHIP   113   6
  IT HOLDS ALOOF, A SHROUDED PARACHUTE .........METAMORPHOSES OF THE MOON 307 8
  REPOSE OF SCUPTURE HOLDS THE COUNTRY STILL. .....PROLOGUE TO SPRING   322   9
  THE WAITRESS HOLDS OUR COATS AND WE PUT ON ......LOVE IS A PARALLAX   329   22
HOLE (5)
  A STONY HOLE. HE'S TO BLAME. POEM.2.DARK.   132   20
  DRAINS LIKE WATER OUT THE HOLE AT THE FAR END. ....INSOMNIAC   163   25
  MADE A HOLE IN THE HOT DAY, A VACANCY. ....THE RABBIT CATCHER   194   18
  FOR A MINUTE THE SKY POURS INTO THE HOLE LIKE PLASMA. ..BERCK-PLAGE   201 125
  YOU HAVE A HOLE, IT'S A POULTICE. ....THE APPLICANT   222   37
HOLE-MOUTH (1)
  I SET MY EYE TO A HOLE-MOUTH AND MEET AN EYE ....BEEKEEPER'S.   118   17
HOLES (9)
  OF A WHALE WITH HOLES AND HOLES, AND BLEED HIM WHITE ....PERSEUS   82   5
  OF A WHALE WITH HOLES AND HOLES, AND BLEED HIM WHITE ....PERSEUS   82   5
  SHOULDER THROUGH HOLES. WE ....MUSHROOMS   139   18
  OR EVEN LIKE BLACK HOLES CUT OUT OF IT. ....WIDOW   164   29
  WITH SEVEN HOLES THUMBED IN. THE SOUL IS ANOTHER LIGHT. ...SURGEON.   170   4
  HOLES IN THE HEELS OF SOCKS, THE WHITE MUTE FACES ......THREE WOMEN   182 199
  WHAT HOLES THIS PAPERY DAY IS ALREADY FULL OF! ....THE JAILER   226   17
  THE CLOAK OF HOLES. ....PURDAH   244   57
  SHEER-SIDED, WITH HOLES WHERE TO HIDE. ....GIGOLO   267   3
HOLIDAY (2)
  I DO NOT EVEN NEED A HOLIDAY; I CAN GO TO WORK TODAY. ..THREE WOMEN   183 249
  FOLLOW HOLIDAY REVEL BEGUN LONG SINCE, ...CINDERELLA   304   10
HOLINESS (1)
  THEIR HANDS AND FACES STIFF WITH HOLINESS.*THE MOON AND THE YEW TREE   173   26
HOLLOW (5)
  IN ITS HOLLOW OF SHADOWS, ITS FRINGE OF REEDS, ...CANDLES   148   8
  HOLLOW DOORSTEPS GO FROM GRASS TO GRASS; ....WUTHERING HEIGHTS   168   31
  THE PATHS NARROWED INTO THE HOLLOW. ....THE RABBIT CATCHER   193   13
  ONE HOLLOW THE WHOLE SEA'S PIVOT. ....CONTUSION   271   6
  ROTS IN THE HOLLOW OF MY SKULL ....APRIL 18   301   2
HOLLOWS (3)
  RUN FOLD UPON FOLD FAR OFF, CONCEALING THEIR HOLLOWS, ..BERCK-PLAGE   199   74
  THE HOLLOWS IN WHICH ROCK THE THOUGHTS OF THE WIFE ---   BERCK-PLAGE   199   75
  THE VOICE OF THE WOMAN HOLLOWS -- ....THE FEARFUL   256   7
HOLLY (2)
  THE BARBAROUS HOLLY WITH ITS VIRIDIAN ....LETTER IN NOVEMBER   253   19
  SPACE OF HOLLY WHERE SPIKES ....YEARS   255   2
HOLLYWOOD (2)
  IT IS ALL HOLLYWOOD, WINDOWLESS, ...LESBOS   227   3
  IN NEW YORK, IN HOLLYWOOD, THE MEN SAID: "THROUGH? ....LESBOS   228   41
HOLMESING (1)
  YOUR SHERLOCK HOLMESING STEERED TO A BLANK WALL ....DIALOGUE O.   280 167
HOLOCAUST (3)
  THIS HOLOCAUST I WALK IN, ...MARY'S SONG   257   20
  BACK INTO THE HOLOCAUST ....SONG FOR A REVOLUTIONARY LOVE   323   22
  IN HERESIES OF HOLOCAUST. ......INSOLENT STORM STRIKES AT THE SKULL   326   36
HOLOFERNES' (1)
  OF HOLOFERNES' HEAD, DIPPED IN THE SAME ....LEAVING EARLY   146   32
HOLY (15)
  MAINTAINS IT HAS NO MORE HOLY CALLING ....TALE OF A TUB   24   11
  OF BELLS CALLS HOLY ONES, HER TONGUE ....VANITY FAIR   32   9
  FROM THIS HOLY DAY ON, ALL POLLEN BLOWN ....WREATH FOR A BRIDAL   45   19
  THEIR MULTIFARIOUS SILKS IN THE HOLY GROVE*ON THE PLETHORA OF DRYADS   68   33
  WHO KEEP COOL AND HOLY MAKE ....VIRGIN IN A TREE   81   25
  IN ITS EASY PEACE, COULD ONLY KEEP HOLY SO. ....THREE WOMEN   178   81
  SUCH FLATNESS CANNOT BUT BE HOLY. ....THREE WOMEN   179   89
  THOSE HOLY JOES. ....NICK AND THE CANDLESTICK   241   13
  A WINDOW, HOLY GOLD. ....MARY'S SONG   257   4
  WE NEVER THOUGHT TO HEAR THE HOLY COCK: ....DOOMSDAY   316   14
  AN ODD DISEASE HAS HIT OUR HOLY COW, ...THE DISPOSSESSED   318   4

```
                                              TITLE          PAGE  LINE
HOLY (CONT.)
   COUCHED IN CAULS OF CLAY AS IN HOLY ROBES,  ................THE DEAD          320    2
   WITH STRUTS AND PROPS OF THE HOLY STAGE.  ........SONG FOR A REVOLU.          323    8
   READ BLACK MAGIC OR HOLY BOOK  ...BLACK PINE TREE IN AN ORANGE LIGHT          328   13
   WHOSE HOLY BLUE ANOINTS HER INJURED HAND.  ............THE PRINCESS.          333    6
HOME (34)
   LURCHING HOME ALONG RIVER BANK.  ............................FAUN             35    7
   A CROCK OF DUST IS MY DEAR HOME." *DIALOGUE BETWEEN GHOST AND PRIEST          39   40
   BACK TO HER EARLY SEA-TOWN HOME  ............DREAM WITH CLAM-DIGGERS          43    3
   AND THE FAIR SHIP SANK, ITS CREW KNELLED HOME FOR DINNER.  ...
       ... DREAM WITH CLAM-DIGGERS                                              44   20
   FIT FOR THOSE OUTLAWS TO RIDE HOME ON,  .........ALL THE DEAD DEARS           71   30
   HOME OF UNCATCHABLE  ..........................TWO VIEWS OF WITHENS           72    7
   BRING HOME EACH STORIED HEAD.  ..........................BATTLE-SCENE         84   28
   IN THE PUBLIC PARK; AT HOME FELT THE WANT  ............RHODODENDRON.         103    2
   GRANDMOTHER, STONES ARE NOTHING OF HOME  .............POINT SHIRLEY         111   46
   OLD LADIES' HOME  ...............................OLD LADIES' HOME          120    T
   I AM AT HOME HERE AMONG THE DEAD HEADS.  ................POEM.1.WHO.         131    6
   SNUG AS A BUD AND AT HOME  ..................................YOU'RE         141   13
   WHERE I AM AT HOME, ONLY THE SPARSEST STARS *STARS OVER THE DORDOGNE        165    9
   AND DRINK THE SMALL NIGHT CHILL LIKE NEWS OF HOME. ..........STARS.         166   40
   TO RATTLE IN A BOTTLE AND TAKE HOME,  .........THE SURGEON AT 2 A.M.         171   35
   THIS IS A DISEASE I CARRY HOME, THIS IS A DEATH.  .......THREE WOMEN         177   36
   IT IS A WORLD OF SNOW NOW. I AM NOT AT HOME.  ..........THREE WOMEN         178   64
   I AM AT HOME IN THE LAMPLIGHT. THE EVENINGS ARE LENGTHENING. *THREE.        186  351
   AND SO WE ARE AT HOME TOGETHER, AFTER HOURS.  ..........THREE WOMEN         187  362
   I AM NEVER, NEVER, NEVER COMING HOME!  ....................AMNESIAC         233   27
   TODDLE ON HOME TO TEA NOW IN YOUR FLAT HAT.  ...............THE TOUR         238   37
   TODDLE ON HOME, BEFORE THE WEATHER'S WORSE.  ..............THE TOUR         238   41
   TODDLE ON HOME, AND DON'T TRIP ON THE NURSE! --  ..........THE TOUR         238   42
   TODDLE ON HOME TO TEA!  ...................................THE TOUR         238   49
   AT HOME ON ME  .........................................LADY LAZARUS         244   18
   TRUNDLING THEIR UDDERS HOME  ..........................EAVESDROPPER         261   42
   YOU TO ASK WHO'S HOME, OR I? I WILL. ...DIALOGUE OVER A OUIJA BOARD         277   25
   OF DAVY'S LOCKER, AND THE LORD'S TO HOME,  .............DIALOGUE O.         283  246
   TO NAME HIS HOME A THIRD TIME. GIVE YOUR WILL THREE  ...DIALOGUE O.         283  269
   BY SNAIL UNDER HUMP OF HOME:  ....................NOTES TO A NEOPHYTE         306    6
   OF OUR COLOSSAL SLEEP, COME HOME TO FIND  ............DOOM OF EXILES         318    2
   RIDING HOME FROM CREDULOUS BLUE DOMES,  ...................TERMINAL         328    1
   AND GET SAFE HOME; BUT, TURNING WITH TRAINED EYES,  .......AERIALIST         331   28
   AND LEADS HIM HOME TO BE HER CHOSEN KNIGHT.  ..........THE PRINCESS.         334   50
HOMECOMING (2)
   AT THE COMMON HOMECOMING  ....................THE GREAT CARBUNCLE          73   28
   MY MOTHER UNROLLED AT YOUR LAST HOMECOMING.  ELECTRA ON AZALEA PATH         117   32
HOMELAND (1)
   OF THE HOMELAND HEARTH TO PLOUGH THEIR PILGRIM WAY  .......MAYFLOWER         60   10
HOMES (2)
   AND SO WE SAIL TOWARD CITIES, STREETS AND HOMES  ...CHANNEL CROSSING         27   37
   IN THESE PALUSTRAL HOMES WE ONLY  .......................FROG AUTUMN         99    3
HOMEWARD (2)
   BOWL ONE HOMEWARD TO TASTE  ..........................FIESTA MELONS         46    9
   THE GIRL BENT HOMEWARD, BRIMFUL OF GENTLE TALK  .........SNOWMAN O.         59   50
HOMICIDES (1)
   COLD HOMICIDES.  ..........................NICK AND THE CANDLESTICK         241    8
HOMUNCULUS (1)
   HOMUNCULUS, I AM ILL.  ....................................CUT            235   23
HONE (1)
   NOW, AS I HONE MY KNIFE, SHE BEGS  .........................RHYME          50   11
HONES (2)
   HAND HONES HIS TACKS AND NEEDLES,  ............A LESSON IN VENGEANCE         80   12
   ON THIS BALD HILL THE NEW YEAR HONES ITS EDGE.  .......PARLIAMENT H.         152    1
HONEST (4)
   FANTASTIC FLESH DOWN TO THE HONEST BONE.  .............TALE OF A TUB         25   24
   GRIEF'S HONEST GRIMACE, DEBASED BY TIME,  ................THE BEGGARS         47    7
   PAVING HIS GRAVE GROUND. HERE'S HONEST ROT  .....NOVEMBER GRAVEYARD         56    8
   TO HOODWINK THE HONEST EARTH WHICH POINTBLANK  ..........CONJURING.         66   28
HONESTLY (2)
   FROM THE MUTE SKY, I CAN'T HONESTLY COMPLAIN:  ........BLACK ROOK I.         57   13
   HONESTLY WANT TO FIND IF YOU'LL HAVE A FLING  .........DIALOGUE O.         278   56
HONEY (10)
   HIVED LIKE HONEY IN YOUR HEAD.  .........EPITAPH FOR FIRE AND FLOWER         45   14
   SEALING OFF HER BROOD CELLS, HER HONEY, AND QUIETLY HUMMING.  ..BEE.        212   35
   IS SHE HIDING, IS SHE EATING HONEY? SHE IS VERY CLEVER.  .......BEE.        212   43
   I AM NO SOURCE OF HONEY  ..................THE ARRIVAL OF THE BEE BOX        213   33
   O EUROPE! O TON OF HONEY!  ...............................THE SWARM         217   60
   I HAVE MY HONEY,  ...........................................WINTERING         217    3
   TO MAKE UP FOR THE HONEY I'VE TAKEN.  ....................WINTERING         218   26
   WHAT HONEY SUMMONS THESE ANIMALCULES?  ...................STINGS/DR         293    1
   FOUR O'CLOCK, AND THE FEVER SOAKS FROM ME LIKE HONEY.  ....FEVER./DR         294    1
   NO MILK OR HONEY FILLS THE EMPTY CAN;  ............THE DISPOSSESSED         318    5
HONEY-AIR (1)
   THROUGH SUNDAY'S HONEY-AIR  ................SONG FOR A SUMMER'S DAY         31   17
HONEYCOMB (1)
   THE MAN WITH GRAY HANDS STANDS UNDER THE HONEYCOMB  .......THE SWARM         216   33
```

```
                                                TITLE         PAGE  LINE
HONEYCOMBED (1)
   HONEYCOMBED WITH GOLDEN EGGS,  ...........................RHYME    50    2
HONEYDEWS (1)
   CREAM-SMOOTH HONEYDEWS,  ..........................FIESTA MELONS   46   11
HONEY-DRUDGERS (1)
   HONEY-DRUDGERS.  .........................................STINGS  214   22
HONEY-FEAST (1)
   THE HONEY-FEAST OF THE BERRIES HAS STUNNED THEM; THEY BELIEVE IN
        HEAVEN.  ...................................BLACKBERRYING   169   17
HONEY-MACHINE (1)
   HERE IS MY HONEY-MACHINE,  ...............................STINGS  214   33
HONOR (5)
   AND, UNDER HONOR, WILL DEPART;  .........................BUCOLICS   24   22
   WIELDS GUARD OF HONOR OVER THESE!" STARRED WITH WORDS  ....WREATH F.  45   16
   BY BESTOWING LARGESSE, HONOR,  .........BLACK ROOK IN RAINY WEATHER  57   21
   IT SEEMS BEES HAVE A NOTION OF HONOR,  ................THE SWARM   217   57
   AND HONOR THE GREAT GODDESS OF THE AIR *THE PRINCESS AND THE GOBLINS  335   62
HONOR-BOUND (1)
   THEN, HONOR-BOUND, MUTE GRAZING CATTLE;  ...............BUCOLICS   24   11
HOOD (3)
   SHALL THE HOOD OF THE COBRA APPALL ME ---  .............TOTEM     264   19
   STARING FROM HER HOOD OF BONE.  ...........................EDGE   273   18
   THE SUAVE DISSEMBLING COBRA WEARS A HOOD  .............ADMONITIONS  319   10
HOODLUM (1)
   BORED HOODLUM IN A RED ROOM  .......................THE DETECTIVE  209   19
HOODS (2)
   DUSK HOODS THEM IN MARY-BLUE  .......................HEAVY WOMEN  158   18
   DUSK HOODS ME IN BLUE NOW, LIKE A MARY.  .............THREE WOMEN  179  102
HOODWINK (1)
   TO HOODWINK THE HONEST EARTH WHICH POINTBLANK  ..........CONJURING.  66   28
HOODWINKED (1)
   NOW EMPTY BOXES OF THE HOODWINKED DEAD*SONG FOR A REVOLUTIONARY LOVE  323   17
HOOED (1)
   HAUNCHED LIKE A FAUN, HE HOOED  ...........................FAUN    35    1
HOOF (1)
   SAW HOOF HARDEN FROM FOOT, SAW SPROUT  .....................FAUN   35   13
HOOF-TAPS (1)
   THE INDEFATIGABLE HOOF-TAPS.  ............................WORDS   270   17
HOOK (6)
   ONE MORE HOOK, AND THE BERRIES AND BUSHES END.  .......BLACKBERRYING  169   18
   I FOLLOW THE SHEEP PATH BETWEEN THEM.  A LAST HOOK BRINGS ME  ...
                                             ... BLACKBERRYING  169   23
   A MAT OF ROOTS. MY ASSISTANTS HOOK THEM BACK. *THE SURGEON AT 2 A.M.  170   13
   ONE CRY. IT IS THE HOOK I HANG ON.  ....................THREE WOMEN  183  236
   A BRACE OR A HOOK,  ................................THE APPLICANT  221    4
   CHIMERA ON THE HOOK, WHO CLAIMS HE'S LATE  .............DIALOGUE O.  283  245
HOOKED (3)
   ITS HEART AND GUTS HUNG HOOKED  ........................STREET SONG  36    8
   EVERY LITTLE WORD HOOKED TO EVERY LITTLE WORD, AND ACT TO ACT.  ...
                                             ... THREE WOMEN  178   55
   HUNG, STARVED, BURNED, HOOKED.  .........................THE JAILER  227   35
HOOKING (1)
   HOOKING ITSELF TO ITSELF,  ...............................THE OTHER  201   15
HOOKS (15)
   TO THESE LIMBER HOOKS.  .........................WORDS FOR A NURSERY  73   10
   TO TRADE THEIR HOOKS FOR HANDS.  .........................POEM.7.S.  137   37
   HANGING FROM THEIR SCORCHED HOOKS IN THE MOIST  ...ZOO KEEPER'S WIFE  155   18
   THEIR SMILES CATCH ONTO MY SKIN, LITLE SMILING HOOKS.  .......TULIPS  160   21
   A BLACKBERRY ALLEY, GOING DOWN IN HOOKS, AND A SEA  ...BLACKBERRYING  168    3
   HER CRIES ARE HOOKS THAT CATCH AND GRATE LIKE CATS.  ....THREE WOMEN  182  207
   IT IS BY THESE HOOKS SHE CLIMBS TO MY NOTICE.  .........THREE WOMEN  182  208
   LOOKING, WITH ITS HOOKS, FOR SOMETHING TO LOVE.  ...............ELM  193   30
   THESE CHILDREN ARE AFTER SOMETHING, WITH HOOKS AND CRIES,  ...BERCK.  198   44
   THE SPRY HOOKS THAT BEND AND CRINGE, AND THE SMILES, THE
        SMILES.  ......................................BURNING THE LETTERS  204  21
   IN THAT VALLEY THE TRAIN SHRIEKS ECHO LIKE SOULS ON HOOKS.  ...
                                             ... THE DETECTIVE  208    5
   HOOKS ---  .............................................ARIEL     239   12
   AND THE BLACK PHONES ON HOOKS  .................THE MUNICH MANNEQUINS  263  24
   BRIGHT FISH HOOKS, THE SMILES OF WOMEN  .......................GIGOLO  267  10
   THE AIR IS A MILL OF HOOKS --  ...........................MYSTIC   268    1
HOOP (1)
   THROUGH HOOP OF THAT HAZARDOUS DREAM  .....................AERIALIST  332  40
HOOPS (1)
   THE HOOPS OF BLACKBERRY STEMS MADE ME CRY.  .............POEM.1.WHO.  132  31
HOOTING (1)
   AND I AM A WHITE SHIP HOOTING: GOODBYE, GOODBYE.  .......THREE WOMEN  184  261
HOOVES (9)
   BELLS, HOOVES, OF THE HIGH-STEPPING BLACK GOATS WOKE US. *OTHER TWO.  68    3
   AN ANVIL, HOOVES FOUR HAMMERS TO JOLT  .........WHITENESS I REMEMBER  102  21
   HUNG OUT OVER HAZARD, OVER HOOVES  .............WHITENESS I REMEMBER  103  30
   STARES THROUGH US; HIS HOOVES CHEW THE BREEZE.  .............WHITSUN  154    8
   I AM DRAGGED BY THE HORSES, THE IRON HOOVES.  .........THREE WOMEN  180  128
   LISTEN: THESE ARE ITS HOOVES: IT HAS GONE OFF, LIKE A HORSE.  ...ELM  192    9
   AND THE HOOVES OF THE HORSES,  .............................YEARS   255   14
```

		TITLE	PAGE	LINE

HOOVES (CONT.)
THE HOOVES WILL NOT HAVE IT, ...YEARS 256 24
HOOVES, DOLOROUS BELLS --- ....SHEEP IN FOG 262 7
HOPE (7)
AS NO MERE INGURGENT MAN COULD HOPE TO BREAK ....SPINSTER 50 28
SKYWARD AGAIN, WITHOUT HOPE, OF COURSE, ...LOVE LETTER 147 7
AND SECRETLY SHE BEGAN TO HOPE I'D DIE. ....IN PLASTER 159 39
THEY GO UP WITHOUT HOPE, LIKE SIGHS. ....FINISTERRE 169 16
THERE IS NO HOPE, IT IS GIVEN UP. ....BERCK-PLAGE 201 126
WELL I HOPE YOU'VE ENJOYED IT, AUNTIE! ....THE TOUR 238 48
R-V-E. IN CORE OF NERVE! I HOPE ....DIALOGUE OVER A OUIJA BOARD 284 278
HOPELESS (1)
I AM ONE IN FIVE, SOMETHING LIKE THAT. I AM NOT HOPELESS. ...THREE. 183 244
HOPES (4)
TO FULL CAPACITY. WE CLIMB IN HOPES ....ABOVE THE OXBOW 88 26
WHOSE HOPES ARE SO LOW THEY ARE COMFORTABLE -- ....MYSTIC 269 21
ALL, IF YOU'LL HIDE HOPES OF HEAVEN IN A HAT ....DIALOGUE O. 282 231
FROM ASKING, BUT INVENTIVE, HOPES; IN VAIN*METAMORPHOSES OF THE MOON 307 11
HOPING (1)
HOPING FOR SOME INCREDIBLE DARK MAN*MORNING IN THE HOSPITAL SOLARIUM 333 23
HORDE (1)
GAILY CURSING THE WHOLE GOBLIN HORDE. THE PRINCESS AND THE GOBLINS 334 46
HORDES (1)
MASS-MOTIVED HORDES, THEY SIDLED ......MUSSEL HUNTER AT ROCK HARBOR 96 39
HORIZON (4)
HANGING SHYLY UNDER THE STUDDED HORIZON ....STARS OVER THE DORDOGNE 165 19
OUR LADY OF THE SHIPWRECKED IS STRIDING TOWARD THE HORIZON, ...
... FINISTERRE 169 19
YOU PREOCCUPY MY HORIZON. ....THE RIVAL/DR 291 12
FABLED HORIZON ....MOONSONG AT MORNING 317 11
HORIZON-HINGED (1)
SKY AND SEA, HORIZON-HINGED ....THE HERMIT AT OUTERMOST HOUSE 118 1
HORIZON-LINE (1)
IN THEIR OLD ANARCHY TO THE HORIZON-LINE. ....THE COLOSSUS 130 21
HORIZONS (6)
FUSING TIME'S THREE HORIZONS. ....CRYSTAL GAZER 54 6
HORIZONS BEYOND VISION, SPILL VISION ....ABOVE THE OXBOW 88 24
AFTER THE HORIZONS, STRETCHING THE NARROWED EYE ....ABOVE THE OXBOW 88 25
THE HORIZONS ARE TOO FAR OFF TO BE CHUMMY AS UNCLES; .....TWO CAMP. 145 13
THE HORIZONS RING ME LIKE FAGGOTS, ...WUTHERING HEIGHTS 167 1
HORIZONS BEAT A RETREAT AS WE EMBARK ....LOVE IS A PARALLAX 329 4
HORIZON'S (1)
THE HORIZON'S BARE OF SHIPS, ...MAGNOLIA SHOALS 122 21
HORIZONTAL (1)
BUT I WOULD RATHER BE HORIZONTAL. ....I AM VERTICAL 162 1
HORIZONTALS (1)
AMONG ALL HORIZONTALS. ....WUTHERING HEIGHTS 168 38
HORN (2)
INSTINCT FOR ART BEGAN WITH THE BULL'S HORN LOFTING IN THE MOB'S ...
... THE GORING 47 8
WEAR MASKS OF HORN TO BED. POEM.5.F. 135 14
HORNS (1)
HORNS TWIRLING AND JUNGLE GUTTURALS! ....A SECRET 220 41
HORNY (3)
OF HORSEHAIR AND LICE HIS HORNY LOINS; ....A LESSON IN VENGEANCE 80 15
A BLUE SEA, FOUR HORNY BULL-FEET, ...THE BULL OF BENDYLAW 108 7
THUMBED NO STONY, HORNY POT, ...THE HERMIT AT OUTERMOST HOUSE 119 15
HORNY-SKINNED (1)
I SEE HIM, HORNY-SKINNED AND TOUGH, CONSTRUE ....OUIJA 77 27
HORRIBLE (1)
THIS IS WHAT IT IS TO BE COMPLETE. IT IS HORRIBLE. .....BERCK-PLAGE 198 61
HORRIFIC (1)
THE HORRIFIC COMPLICATIONS. ....LITTLE FUGUE 187 15
HORROR (1)
DISGUISING THE CONSTANT HORROR IN A COAT ....TALE OF A TUB 25 37
HORRORS (2)
I TASTE IT ON MY TONGUE, AND THE WORKABLE HORRORS, ...THREE WOMEN 180 136
THE HORRORS THAT STAND AND IDLE, THE SLIGHTED GODMOTHERS*THREE WOMEN 180 137
HORSE (8)
ONE WHITE HORSE DROWNED, AND ALL THE UNCONQUERED PINNACLES LESSON. 80 9
OF THE STABLE HORSE WHOSE HISTORY'S ....WHITENESS I REMEMBER 102 6
I SEE HIM ONE-TRACKED, STUBBORN, WHITE HORSE, WHITENESS I REMEMBER 102 12
FIRST HORSE UNDER ME, HIGH AS THE ROOFS, ...WHITENESS I REMEMBER 102 13
OR MOTHER A HORSE. MY BELLY MOVES. POEM.2.DARK. 132 13
THE STOPPED HORSE ON HIS CHROMIUM POLE ....WHITSUN 154 7
LISTEN: THESE ARE ITS HOOVES: IT HAS GONE OFF, LIKE A HORSE. ...ELM 192 9
HORSE THE COLOR OF RUST, ...SHEEP IN FOG 262 6
HORSEFLIES (1)
HORSEFLIES BUZZED, PAUSED AND STUNG. ....BITTER STRAWBERRIES 299 7
HORSEHAIR (2)
OF HORSEHAIR AND LICE HIS HORNY LOINS; ....A LESSON IN VENGEANCE 80 15
A SORT OF BLACK HORSEHAIR, ...BY CANDLELIGHT 236 2
HORSES (10)
AT A FIELD OF HORSES, NECKS BENT, MANES BLOWN, ...THE EYE-MOTE 109 2
HOLDING THE HORSES, THE CLOUDS, THE LEAVES ....THE EYE-MOTE 109 6

242

HORSES (CONT.)
  HORSES WARPED ON THE ALTERING GREEN, ...THE EYE-MOTE   109   12
  HORSES, PLANETS AND SPIRES REVOLVE. ....THE EYE-MOTE   109   18
  HORSES FLUENT IN THE WIND, ...THE EYE-MOTE   109   29
  SHORT-REINED, PAWING LIKE PARADEGROUND HORSES. ....A LIFE   150   14
  I AM DRAGGED BY THE HORSES, THE IRON HOOVES. ....THREE WOMEN   180 128
  THE STOLEN HORSES, THE FORNICATIONS ....THE OTHER   202   21
  AND THE HOOVES OF THE HORSES, ...YEARS   255   14
  OFF FROM THE CENTER LIKE HORSES. ....WORDS   270   5
HORSE-SWALLOWING (1)
  TO REBUKE THE HORSE-SWALLOWING RIVER GYNDES: A LESSON IN VENGEANCE   80   18
HOSPITAL (9)
  ABOUT A BALD, HOSPITAL SAUCER. ....A LIFE   150   22
  AS IF IN HOSPITAL. ....WHITSUN   154   12
  DIRTY AS A BOOTSOLE AND BIG AS A HOSPITAL SINK ...ZOO KEEPER'S WIFE   155   35
  NUDE AS CLEOPATRA IN MY WELL-BOILED HOSPITAL SHIFT, ...FACE LIFT   156   10
  I AM A WOUND WALKING OUT OF HOSPITAL. ....THREE WOMEN   184 270
  LET US EAT OUR LAST SUPPER AT IT, LIKE A HOSPITAL PLATE. BIRTHDAY.   207   26
  A HOSPITAL OF DOLLS. ....GETTING THERE   248   28
  THE BABIES LOOK IN THEIR HOSPITAL ....DEATH & CO.   254   14
  MORNING IN THE HOSPITAL SOLARIUM ..MORNING IN THE HOSPITAL SOLARIUM   332   T
HOSTAGE (1)
  MALTREAT THE HOSTAGE HEAD IN SHOCKING WISE, ...LADY AND T.   69   13
HOSTELRY (1)
  THE HOSTELRY OF WORMS, RAPACIOUS BLADES ....TERMINAL   328   6
HOSTESS (1)
  PLAYS HOSTESS TO TABBY, TOM AND INCREASE, ...ELLA MASON A.   53   10
HOSTILE (1)
  WHERE STRAIGHT TALK IS THE RULE, WHETHER WARM OR HOSTILE, ...
                                             ... INCOMMUNICADO   100   10
HOT (19)
  HAGGARD THROUGH THE HOT WHITE NOON. ....PURSUIT   22   10
  CHOICE WASSAIL MAKES, COOKED HOT, ...THE GLUTTON   40   9
  BLINDS LOWERED ON THAT HOT MORNING. ......DREAM WITH CLAM-DIGGERS   43   8
  VOLCANOED HOT ....THE SNOWMAN ON THE MOOR   59   26
  COLD POLE AND HOT PLATE. ....WORDS FOR A NURSERY   74   25
  STILL HE HYMNS JUICE OF HER, HOT NECTARINE. ....OUIJA   77   26
  LIVED UNDER THE SHADOW OF HOT ROOFTOPS ....ABOVE THE OXBOW   89   54
  A MELDING OF SHAPES IN A HOT RAIN: ....THE EYE-MOTE   109   11
  HOT GRAINS, SIMPLY. IT IS DRY, DRY. ....SLEEP IN THE MOJAVE DESERT   143   2
  SO MAGICAL! A HOT SPRING ....THE SURGEON AT 2 A.M.   171   24
  A HOT BLUE DAY HAD BUDDED INTO SOMETHING. ....THREE WOMEN   178   56
  HOT NOON IN THE MEADOWS. THE BUTTERCUPS ....THREE WOMEN   186 337
  MADE A HOLE IN THE HOT DAY, A VACANCY. ....THE RABBIT CATCHER   194   18
  I AM SICK TO DEATH OF HOT SALT. ....MEDUSA   225   37
  RED AND YELLOW, TWO PASSIONATE HOT METALS ....STOPPED DEAD   230   8
  THE BEADS OF HOT METAL FLY, AND I, LOVE, I ....FEVER.   232   45
  EACH COAL A HOT CROSS-STITCH -- A LOVELY LIGHT! ....THE TOUR   238   21
  SPOTS, AND A SPREAD OF HOT PETALS. ....THE NIGHT DANCES   250   14
  A HOT HYPERBOLICAL JOKE!" ....DIALOGUE EN ROUTE   308   18
HOTDOGS (1)
  BEHIND HIM THE HOTDOGS SPLIT AND DRIZZLED .....SUICIDE OFF EGG ROCK   115   1
HOTEL (3)
  HUNDRED-YEAR-OLD HOTEL SUSTAINS ITS RAMSHACKLE .....ABOVE THE OXBOW   88   35
  ON THE BALCONIES OF THE HOTEL, THINGS ARE GLITTERING. ..BERCK-PLAGE   197   37
  I'M THROUGH WITH THIS GRAND LOOKING-GLASS HOTEL ......A SORCERER B.   324   1
HOTELS (1)
  NOBODY'S ABOUT. IN THE HOTELS ....THE MUNICH MANNEQUINS   263   17
HOTHOUSE (2)
  HOTHOUSE BABY IN ITS CRIB, ...FEVER.   231   19
  AND HOTHOUSE ROSES SHED IMMORAL BLOOMS. ....FEMALE AUTHOR   301   8
HOTS (1)
  DOURLY THE LONG HOTS AND COLDS, ...THE HERMIT AT OUTERMOST HOUSE   119   8
HOUND-BITCH (1)
  YOUR GATE, FATHER -- YOUR HOUND-BITCH, DAUGHTER, FRIEND.*ELECTRA ON.   117   45
HOUNDS (1)
  LET HIM SEND POLICE AND HOUNDS TO BRING HER IN. ....SNOWMAN O.   58   19
HOUR (13)
  TO CONQUER CINDER'S KINGDOM IN THE STROKE OF AN HOUR *EPITAPH FOR F.   45   20
  THE EARTH TURNS NOW. IN HALF AN HOUR .....ON THE DECLINE OF ORACLES   78   26
  IN THE BLUE HOUR BEFORE SUNUP. ....SLEEP IN THE MOJAVE DESERT   144   10
  AND KILLED IT IN AN HOUR. ....FEVER.   231   24
  THE DULL BELLS TONGUE THE HOUR. ....BY CANDLELIGHT   236   8
  THE NEXT HOUR --- ....GETTING THERE   248   32
  PREDICTING THREE BOYS AN HOUR HENCE WILL PLAY ....DIALOGUE O.   279 124
  TO CHIRP THE HOUR IN LUNATIC THIRTEENS. ....SONNET: TO EVA   305   14
  THE MORNING PAPER CLOCKED THE HEADLINE HOUR ....THE TRIAL OF MAN   312   5
  THE HOUR IS CROWDED IN LUNATIC THIRTEENS. ....DOOMSDAY   316   3
  THE HOUR IS CROWDED IN LUNATIC THIRTEENS. ....DOOMSDAY   316   9
  THE HOUR IS CROWDED IN LUNATIC THIRTEENS. ....DOOMSDAY   316   15
  THE HOUR IS CROWDED IN LUNATIC THIRTEENS. ....DOOMSDAY   316   19
HOURGLASS (1)
  HOURGLASS SIFTS A ....DARK WOOD, DARK WATER   127   19
HOUR-GLASS (1)
  DWINDLES IN THE HOUR-GLASS. ....TWO LOVERS.   327   4

```
                                                    TITLE          PAGE  LINE
HOURLY (2)
   HOURLY THE EYE OF THE SKY ENLARGES ITS BLANK  ............POEM.5.F.   134    5
   OBLITERATION HOURLY UNLESS OUR EYE  .....DIALOGUE OVER A OUIJA BOARD   279  116
HOURS (7)
   AND THE HOURS OF PRACTICING, MY EAR  ..........THE DISQUIETING MUSES    75   37
   HOURS OF BLANKNESS. SOME HARD STARS  ...............THE MANOR GARDEN   125   14
   MY HOURS ARE MARRIED TO SHADOW.  .........................THE COLOSSUS  130   28
   I HEAR THE SOUND OF THE HOURS  ..........................THREE WOMEN   185  311
   AND SO WE ARE AT HOME TOGETHER, AFTER HOURS.  ...........THREE WOMEN   187  362
   SEVEN HOURS KNOCKED OUT OF MY RIGHT MIND  ...................THE JAILER  226    7
   IT BOILS FOR FORTY HOURS AT A STRETCH.  .....................THE TOUR   238   30
HOUSE (44)
   THROUGH PORTICO OF MY ELEGANT HOUSE YOU STALK  ........CONVERSATION.    21    1
   TWO GIRLS THERE ARE: WITHIN THE HOUSE  ....TWO SISTERS OF PERSEPHONE    31    1
   BESIDE A NEIGHBOR'S HOUSE  .................DREAM WITH CLAM-DIGGERS     43    6
   WHITE HOUSE AND ALMOND GROVE. THE BEGGARS  .............THE BEGGARS     48   18
   AND ROUND HER HOUSE SHE SET  ..................................SPINSTER  50   25
   AND SEE THAT FIRST HOUSE, AS IF BETWEEN  ................LANDOWNERS     53    6
   IN HER RAMSHACKLE HOUSE OFF SOMERSET TERRACE;  ........ELLA MASON A.    53    2
   STAUNCH SAPLINGS; TO THIS HOUSE, THRIVING DAYS  ......CRYSTAL GAZER     55   16
   BUT FROM THE HOUSE  ..........................THE SNOWMAN ON THE MOOR    58   14
   AND THE HOUSE OF EROS  ........................TWO VIEWS OF WITHENS     72   14
   THE DOMED STATE HOUSE.  ..............................A WINTER'S TALE    86    4
   FROM CHARLES STREET TO THE CUSTOM HOUSE,  ...........A WINTER'S TALE    87   35
   TO HIS HOUSE THE BODILESS  ..............................SCULPTOR       91    1
   WE GAVE GOOD USE AS SHIP AND HOUSE IS BLACK*GREEN ROCK, WINTHROP BAY   105   11
   KEPT HOUSE AGAINST  .....................................POINT SHIRLEY  110   11
   OF HER HAND, THE HOUSE STILL HUGS IN EACH DRAB  .......POINT SHIRLEY   110   20
   THEY LOITER AND STARE AS IF THE HOUSE  ....................AFTERMATH   113    2
   PAST KEEPING TO THE HOUSE, PAST ALL DISCRETION --   THE RAVAGED FACE   115    7
   AN ELEPHANT, A PONDEROUS HOUSE,  ..........................METAPHORS   116    2
   KEEP HOUSE AMONG THE GRASSES. KNEELING DOWN*THE BEEKEEPER'S DAUGHTER   118   16
   THE HERMIT AT OUTERMOST HOUSE  ........THE HERMIT AT OUTERMOST HOUSE   118    T
   DARK THICKETS HEDGE THE HOUSE.  ........................THE SLEEPERS   123   11
   DARK HOUSE  .............................................POEM.2.DARK.  132   ST
   THIS IS A DARK HOUSE, VERY BIG.  .......................POEM.2.DARK.   132    1
   WHERE THE DURABLE ONES KEEP HOUSE.  ................THE BURNT-OUT SPA  138   32
   THE OBSOLETE HOUSE, THE SEA, FLATTENED TO A PICTURE  ........A LIFE    150   27
   I ENTER THE LIT HOUSE.  ......................PARLIAMENT HILL FIELDS   153   50
   FUG OF THE SMALL MAMMAL HOUSE.  ....................ZOO KEEPER'S WIFE  155   19
   AND BLACK AS PURSES, THE HOUSE LIGHTS  ..........WUTHERING HEIGHTS     168   44
   SEPARATED FROM MY HOUSE BY A ROW OF HEADSTONES.  ..............MOON.   173    6
   IN YOUR HOUSE, THE MAIN HOUSE, YOU WERE BETTER OFF. *THE BABYSITTERS   174   19
   IN YOUR HOUSE, THE MAIN HOUSE, YOU WERE BETTER OFF. *THE BABYSITTERS   174   19
   DAWN FLOWERS IN THE GREAT ELM OUTSIDE THE HOUSE.  .......THREE WOMEN   185  309
   IN THE PARLOR OF THE STONE HOUSE  .....................BERCK-PLAGE     199   78
   THERE IS NO BODY IN THE HOUSE AT ALL.  .................THE DETECTIVE  209   16
   THE MAUSOLEUM, THE WAX HOUSE.  .............................STINGS     215   60
   AT THE HEART OF THE HOUSE  ................................WINTERING   218    7
   YOU HOUSE YOUR UNNERVING HEAD -- GOD-BALL,  .................MEDUSA    224    4
   NAME, HOUSE, CAR KEYS,  ...................................AMNESIAC    232    3
   THEY DARKEN YOUR HOUSE,  ...............................EAVESDROPPER   260    2
   KINDNESS GLIDES ABOUT MY HOUSE.  ...........................KINDNESS   269    1
   ARGUMENT TO THE HOUSE NEXT DOOR. OR IF   DIALOGUE OVER A OUIJA BOARD   280  166
   SHUTS DOWN ITS FABLED SUMMER HOUSE;  ....................TWO LOVERS.   327    2
   IN THIS SURREALISTIC HOUSE  ........MORNING IN THE HOSPITAL SOLARIUM   332    3
HOUSED (1)
   HOUSED IN EARTH, THOSE MILLION BRIDES SHRIEK OUT.  ......VANITY FAIR    33   33
HOUSEDRESS (2)
   SO I POKE AT THE CARBON BIRDS IN MY HOUSEDRESS. *BURNING THE LETTERS   204   29
   AND I IN SLIPPERS AND HOUSEDRESS WITH NO LIPSTICK!  ........THE TOUR   237    6
HOUSEKEEP (1)
   I HOUSEKEEP IN TIME'S GUT-END  ........................POEM.4.BEAST.   134   23
HOUSELIGHTS (1)
   WHILE FOOTLIGHTS FLARE AND HOUSELIGHTS DIM.  .....LOVE IS A PARALLAX   330   48
HOUSES (9)
   THESE DREAMING HOUSES ALL SNUFF OUT;  ....SOLILOQUY OF THE SOLIPSIST    37    6
   MAKE HOUSES SHRINK  ..................SOLILOQUY OF THE SOLIPSIST        37   11
   OF IDENTICAL GRAY BRICK HOUSES,  ........................LANDOWNERS     53    4
   HOUSES HIMSELF ELSEWHERE. OUR FOLK THIN  ...............FROG AUTUMN     99   11
   GREEN GRASS STREAMING, HOUSES A RIVER  .........WHITENESS I REMEMBER   102   19
   THE HOUSES ARE WHITE AS SEA-SALT GOATS LICK FROM THE ROCKS.  ..NET-.   121   10
   THE VASE, RECONSTRUCTED, HOUSES  ...........................POEM.7.S.  137   41
   ONE CAN REMEMBER MEN AND HOUSES BY.  .....SLEEP IN THE MOJAVE DESERT   143    7
   IN THE TWO HUGE, WHITE, HANDSOME HOUSES IN SWAMPSCOTT.  .......BABY.   174    5
HOUSEWIFE (1)
   MOVES HUMBLY AS ANY HOUSEWIFE THROUGH  ....................AFTERMATH   114   10
HOUSEWIFE'S (1)
   THE HOUSEWIFE'S, DESULTORY.  ..............THE DEATH OF MYTH-MAKING    104   15
HOUSEWIVES (1)
   ONE, HOUSEWIVES AND SHOPKEEPERS.  ..........THE DEATH OF MYTH-MAKING   104    5
HOVE (2)
   PIG HOVE, LETTING LEGEND LIKE DRIED MUD DROP,  ...................SOW    61   37
   HOVE UP AGAINST BENDYLAW.  ....................THE BULL OF BENDYLAW   108    3
```

HOVER (1)
THE ABSTRACTS HOVER LIKE DULL ANGELS: ....MAGI 148 1
HOW (108)
JUST HOW GUILTY ARE WE WHEN THE CEILING ....TALE OF A TUB 24 9
GRIP THE RAIL, SQUINT AHEAD, AND WONDER HOW MUCH LONGER   CHANNEL C. 26 6
"HOW SAD, ALAS, IT IS ....THE QUEEN'S COMPLAINT 29 24
HE SAUNTERS IN; HOW BUT MOST GLAD ....ODE FOR TED 29 21
SHE SEES HOW THEIR RED SILK FLARE ....TWO SISTERS OF PERSEPHONE 32 17
GOAT-HORNS. MARKED HOW GOD ROSE ....FAUN 35 14
WHO, UNAWARE HOW THEY DWINDLE, ...SOLILOQUY OF THE SOLIPSIST 37 15
"HOW NOW," FATHER SHAWN CRISPLY ADDRESSED THE GHOST ....DIALOGUE B. 38 11
SEASONED HOW HE'D MOST APPROVE; ....THE GLUTTON 40 6
HOW PERILOUS NEEDLES GRAIN THE FLOORBOARDS ..▪........MISS DRAKE P. 41 16
NO MATTER HOW FIERCELY LIT; STAUNCH CONTRACTS BREAK   EPITAPH FOR F. 46 32
HOW SHE LONGED FOR WINTER THEN! -- ....SPINSTER 49 13
ACT, BUT -- HOW THOSE FEATHERS SHINE! ....RHYME 50 16
HOW NATURE, SENSING THIS, COMPOUNDS HER BITTERS. ....DEPARTURE 51 5
HOW WE SHALL DO TOGETHER, ...CRYSTAL GAZER 55 9
HOW BEST BEAUTY'S BORN OF HARDIHOOD. ....MAYFLOWER 60 8
GOD KNOWS HOW OUR NEIGHBOR MANAGED TO BREED ....SOW 60 1
HOW THEY PROP EACH OTHER UP! ....THE THIN PEOPLE 65 40
BATTALIONS. SEE, HOW THE TREE BOLES FLATTEN ....THE THIN PEOPLE 65 43
WE DREAMED HOW WE WERE PERFECT,AND WE WERE. ....THE OTHER TWO 68 7
HOW THEY GRIP US THROUGH THIN AND THICK, ...ALL THE DEAD DEARS 70 13
DOG THAT I AM, HOW ....WORDS FOR A NURSERY 73 12
HOW THIS TART FABLE INSTRUCTS ....VIRGIN IN A TREE 81 1
YADWIGHA, THE LITERALISTS ONCE WONDERED HOW YOU ....YADWIGHA. 85 1
DESCRIBED HOW YOU FELL DREAMING AT FULL OF MOON ....YADWIGHA. 86 25
AND NEVER SAW HOW COOLLY WE MIGHT MOVE. FOR ONCE ...ABOVE THE OXBOW 89 55
DIDN'T GO DOWN IN SUCH A HURRY. HOW IT   MEMOIRS OF A SPINACH-PICKER 89 2
OLD GOATHERDS SWEAR HOW ALL NIGHT LONG THEY HEAR ....GOATSUCKER 111 1
HOW IN SUCH MILD AIR ....WATERCOLOR OF GRANTCHESTER MEADOWS 112 27
HOW SHALL I AGE INTO THAT STATE OF MIND? ....ELECTRA ON AZALEA PATH 117 41
DIFFICULT TO IMAGINE HOW FURY STRUCK -- ....BLUE MOLES 126 17
AND HOW A GOD FLIMSY AS A BABY'S FINGER POEM.5.F. 135 19
HOW LONG HIS CARCASS HAS FOUNDERED UNDER ....THE BURNT-OUT SPA 138 8
HOW DID WE MAKE IT UP TO YOUR ATTIC? ....LEAVING EARLY 146 40
HOW SHALL I TELL ANYTHING AT ALL ....CANDLES 149 32
HOW THE BALCONIES ECHOED! HOW THE SUN LIT UP ......WAKING IN WINTER 151 9
HOW THE BALCONIES ECHOED! HOW THE SUN LIT UP ......WAKING IN WINTER 151 9
HOW OUR COURTSHIP LIT THE TINDERY CAGES -- ....ZOO KEEPER'S WIFE 155 33
I HAD EVEN FORGOTTEN HOW TO WALK OR SIT, ...IN PLASTER 159 45
OR BRAG AHEAD OF TIME HOW I'D AVENGE MYSELF. ....IN PLASTER 160 47
LOOK HOW WHITE EVERYTHING IS, HOW QUIET, HOW SNOWED-IN. .....TULIPS 160 2
LOOK HOW WHITE EVERYTHING IS, HOW QUIET, HOW SNOWED-IN. .....TULIPS 160 2
LOOK HOW WHITE EVERYTHING IS, HOW QUIET, HOW SNOWED-IN. .....TULIPS 160 2
SO IT IS IMPOSSIBLE TO TELL HOW MANY THERE ARE. ....TULIPS 160 14
HOW FREE IT IS, YOU HAVE NO IDEA HOW FREE --- ....TULIPS 161 31
HOW FREE IT IS, YOU HAVE NO IDEA HOW FREE --- ....TULIPS 161 31
HOW THEY LIT THE TEDIUM OF THE PROTRACTED EVENING! ....INSOMNIAC 163 16
HOW I ADMIRE THE ROMANS -- ....THE SURGEON AT 2 A.M. 171 27
HOW I WOULD LIKE TO BELIEVE IN TENDERNESS --- ....MOON. 173 19
BUT I DIDN'T KNOW HOW TO COOK, AND BABIES DEPRESSED ME. .....BABY. 174 13
HOW WHITE THESE SHEETS ARE. THE FACES HAVE NO FEATURES. *THREE WOMEN 178 65
HOW WINTER FILLS MY SOUL! AND THAT CHALK LIGHT ....THREE WOMEN 181 177
HOW SHYLY SHE SUPERIMPOSES HER NEAT SELF ....THREE WOMEN 184 282
HOW LONG CAN I BE A WALL, KEEPING THE WIND OFF? ....THREE WOMEN 185 288
HOW LONG CAN I BE ....THREE WOMEN 185 289
HOW SHALL IT SOFTEN THEM, THIS LITTLE LULLABY? ....THREE WOMEN 185 294
HOW LONG CAN I BE A WALL AROUND MY GREEN PROPERTY? .....THREE WOMEN 185 295
HOW LONG CAN MY HANDS ....THREE WOMEN 185 296
REMEMBERS HOW WHITE THEY WERE. ....THREE WOMEN 186 345
HOW BEAUTIFULLY THE LIGHT INCLUDES THESE THINGS. ....THREE WOMEN 186 353
HOW HER BODY OPENS AND SHUTS -- ....AN APPEARANCE 189 14
HOW YOU LIE AND CRY AFTER IT ....ELM 192 8
HOW YOUR BAD DREAMS POSSESS AND ENDOW ME. ....ELM 192 27
HOW THEY AWAITED HIM, THOSE LITTLE DEATHS! ......THE RABBIT CATCHER 194 24
HOW THE ELEMENTS SOLIDIFY! -- ....EVENT 194 1
HOW THE SUN'S POULTICE DRAWS ON MY INFLAMMATION. ....BERCK-PLAGE 196 2
HOW SUPERIOR HE IS NOW. ....BERCK-PLAGE 198 56
HOW FAR HE IS NOW, HIS ACTIONS ....BERCK-PLAGE 199 82
COLD GLASS, HOW YOU INSERT YOURSELF ....THE OTHER 202 26
O MUD, MUD, HOW FLUID! --   WORDS HEARD, BY ACCIDENT, OVER THE PHONE 202 1
O GOD, HOW SHALL I EVER CLEAN THE PHONE TABLE? ....WORDS HEARD. 202 8
IF YOU ONLY KNEW HOW THE VEILS WERE KILLING MY DAYS. .....BIRTHDAY. 207 37
BUT HOW ABOUT THE EYES, THE EYES, THE EYES? ....COURAGE. 210 26
HOW CAN I LET THEM OUT? ....THE ARRIVAL OF THE BEE BOX 213 16
I WONDER HOW HUNGRY THEY ARE. ....THE ARRIVAL OF THE BEE BOX 213 26
HOW INSTRUCTIVE THIS IS! ....THE SWARM 217 46
HOW SUPERIOR. ....A SECRET 219 2
HOW IT BREATHES IN THE BUREAU DRAWER! ....A SECRET 220 27
HOW CAN WE GIVE YOU A THING? ....THE APPLICANT 221 7
HOW ABOUT THIS SUIT --- ....THE APPLICANT 221 20
HOW DID I GET HERE? ....THE JAILER 227 32
HOW THEY'LL TRAVEL, TRAVEL, TRAVEL, SCENERY ....AMNESIAC 233 17

HOW (CONT.)
  HOW YOU JUMP --- ....CUT   236   37
  HOW ONE WE GROW, ...ARIEL   239   5
  O LOVE, HOW DID YOU GET HERE? ....NICK AND THE CANDLESTICK   241   23
  HOW THE SUN POLISHES THIS SHOULDER! ....PURDAH   242   9
  HOW FAR IS IT? ....GETTING THERE   247   1
  HOW FAR IS IT NOW? ....GETTING THERE   247   2
  HOW FAR IS IT? ....GETTING THERE   248   34
  HOW FAR IS IT? ....GETTING THERE   248   43
  AND HOW WILL YOUR NIGHT DANCES ....THE NIGHT DANCES   249   3
  HOW THEY HATE YOU. ....GULLIVER   251   16
  HE TELLS ME HOW BADLY I PHOTOGRAPH. ....DEATH & CO.   254   12
  HE TELLS ME HOW SWEET ....DEATH & CO.   254   13
  HOW YOU JUMPED WHEN I JUMPED ON YOU! ...................EAVESDROPPER   261   37
  THAT'S HOW YOU ALWAYS TALK BEFORE WE START. ....DIALOGUE O.   277   15
  ENOUGH FOR NICKNAMES. HOW ARE YOU, PAN? F- ....DIALOGUE O.   277   31
  DO YOU KNOW HOW MY FATHER IS? HE'S LEFT *DIALOGUE OVER A OUIJA BOARD   278   74
  FOR YES, DRAGGING OUR FINGERS AFTER. HOW*DIALOGUE OVER A OUIJA BOARD   278   75
  PAN SAID. A PLUMAGE OF RAW WORMS. HOW ..DIALOGUE OVER A OUIJA BOARD   279 100
  TO VIEW HOW VERSATILE WE ARE: YOU'VE PAMPERED ....DIALOGUE O.   280 137
  WORK AT ALL? HOW CAN WE HELP BUT BATTLE *DIALOGUE OVER A OUIJA BOARD   284 286
  BUSINESSLIKE SHE ASKED US, "HOW MANY QUARTS?" ..BITTER STRAWBERRIES   300   31
  AND HOW A HUNDRED THOUSAND LEAVES ....GOLD MOUTHS CRY   302   4
  HOW I AM STILL ....TO A JILTED LOVER   310   26
  HOW FLESH CLEAVES FAST TO FROZEN JOINT, ...INSOLENT STORM.   326   10
  SAY HOW CRAFTY THE PAINTER WAS ..BLACK PINE TREE IN AN ORANGE LIGHT   328   17
  HOW ALL THEIR PLAY IS TOUCH-AND-GO: ....TOUCH-AND-GO   335   12
HOWEVER (5)
  HOWEVER YOU MAY SWEAT TO HOLD SUCH DARLING WRECKS ...EPITAPH FOR F.   45   13
  HOWEVER THE GRANDILOQUENT MIND MAY SCORN ....NOVEMBER GRAVEYARD   56   5
  "HOWEVER I WRENCH OBSTINATE BARK AND TRUNK ....CONJURING.   66   25
  BATTLE HOWEVER I WOULD ....ON THE PLETHORA OF DRYADS   67   19
  AN ORIGINAL NOTE. IF HE'D SAID, HOWEVER, MERELY: ....DIALOGUE O.   278   81
HOWLING (2)
  DAMNED, HOWLING IN THEIR SHROUDS ACROSS THE MOOR *NOVEMBER GRAVEYARD   56   16
  HAVE BEEN HOWLING LIKE WOMEN, OR DAMAGED INSTRUMENTS. ....INSOMNIAC   163   30
HOW'S (2)
  THE BUTCHER'S GUILLOTINE THAT WHISPERS: "HOW'S THIS, HOW'S THIS?" ...
                                                      ... TOTEM   264   10
  THE BUTCHER'S GUILLOTINE THAT WHISPERS: "HOW'S THIS, HOW'S THIS?" ...
                                                      ... TOTEM   264   10
HOYDEN (1)
  THEN, A FREE-GADDING HOYDEN, GERD HAD CRAVED ....CRYSTAL GAZER   55   31
HUFF (1)
  RABBITS IN THE LOT. YOU'RE IN A HUFF ...DIALOGUE OVER A OUIJA BOARD   282 236
HUG (1)
  THEY HUG THEIR FLATNESS LIKE A KIND OF HEALTH. ....THREE WOMEN   180 117
HUGE (5)
  EACH DAY CONCLUDES IN A HUGE SPLURGE OF VERMILIONS ....TWO CAMP.   145   15
  IN THE TWO HUGE, WHITE, HANDSOME HOUSES IN SWAMPSCOTT. ....BABY.   174   5
  YOU ARE BLUE AND HUGE, A TRAFFIC POLICEMAN, ...A SECRET   219   3
  ALL BY MYSELF I AM A HUGE CAMELLIA ....FEVER.   232   41
  THEM HUGE AGAIN, VIOLENT GIANTS ON THE WALL. ....BY CANDLELIGHT   236   14
HUGGING (3)
  HE IS HUGGING HIS BALL AND CHAIN DOWN BY THE GATE ....LESBOS   229   73
  HUGGING HIS PILLOW ....AMNESIAC   233   12
  HUGGING THEIR LIGHTS. ....PARALYTIC   267   36
HUGS (1)
  OF HER HAND, THE HOUSE STILL HUGS IN EACH DRAB ....POINT SHIRLEY   110   20
HULK (1)
  SHRILLING HER HULK ....SOW   61   22
HULKED (1)
  THIS GIANT HULKED, I TELL YOU, ON HER SCENE ..THE QUEEN'S COMPLAINT   28   2
HULKS (1)
  WHITE HULKS ON THEIR DAY'S CRUISING; ....SONG FOR A SUMMER'S DAY   31   4
HULL (1)
  WAVES WALLOP, ASSAULTING THE STUBBORN HULL. ....CHANNEL CROSSING   26   4
HULLS (1)
  AND BUFFS AND SLEEKS THE BLUNT HULLS ..MUSSEL HUNTER AT ROCK HARBOR   95   5
HUMAN (4)
  OF TREE AND HUMAN. AND HE WITHIN THIS SNAKEDOM ........SNAKECHARMER   79   15
  OF HUMAN AGONY: A LOOK TO NUMB ....PERSEUS   83   15
  THE BLUE COLOR PALES. HE IS HUMAN AFTER ALL. ....THREE WOMEN   181 166
  WARM AND HUMAN, THEN THEIR PINK LIGHT ....THE NIGHT DANCES   250   19
HUMANITY (1)
  FLAYED OF FUR AND HUMANITY. ....TOTEM   264   13
HUMBLE (2)
  LITTLE HUMBLE LOVES! POEM.2.DARK.   133   24
  OUR QUESTIONS IN HUMBLE HABIT TO GAIN GRACE ....DIALOGUE O.   281 187
HUMBLED (1)
  HUMBLED THEN, AND CRYING, ...THE SNOWMAN ON THE MOOR   59   49
HUMBLY (2)
  SO HUMBLY DONE, I'D TURN THIS KEEN ....RHYME   50   13
  MOVES HUMBLY AS ANY HOUSEWIFE THROUGH ....AFTERMATH   114   10

```
                                        TITLE                    PAGE  LINE
HUMBUG (1)
   TO BURN AWAY THE HUMBUG RUST  ........SONG FOR A REVOLUTIONARY LOVE  323  23
HUMDRUM (1)
   HUMDRUM, UNEXCEPTIONABLE, HIS  .................WHITENESS I REMEMBER  102   7
HUMILITY (1)
   PRICKLING MY ANKLES AND MURMURING OF THEIR HUMILITY.  .........MOON.  172   4
HUMMING (1)
   SEALING OFF HER BROOD CELLS, HER HONEY, AND QUIETLY HUMMING.  ..BEE.  212  35
HUMMINGBIRDS (1)
   AND BREAKABLE HUMMINGBIRDS,  ..........MISS DRAKE PROCEEDS TO SUPPER   41   8
HUMMOCK (1)
   A RISE IN THE LANDSCAPE, HUMMOCK OR HOGBACK, LOOKS   ABOVE THE OXBOW   88  16
HUMOR (3)
   WHEN IN GOOD HUMOR,  ......................SOLILOQUY OF THE SOLIPSIST   37  20
   OF THE OCEAN. SUCH SAGE HUMOR AND  .................FULL FATHOM FIVE   93  29
   AND TOLERATE THE HUMOR OF THE WORM.  .............DIRGE FOR A JOKER  303  14
HUMORED (1)
   SHE HUMORED MY WEAKNESS LIKE THE BEST OF NURSES,  ........IN PLASTER  159  26
HUMOROUS (1)
   FIZZY WITH SEDATIVES AND UNUSUALLY HUMOROUS,  .............FACE LIFT  156  11
HUMP (2)
   THE HUMP OF ELBA ON YOUR SHORT BACK,  .....................THE SWARM  216   8
   BY SNAIL UNDER HUMP OF HOME:  .................NOTES TO A NEOPHYTE  306   6
HUMPBACK (1)
   THE HUMPBACK IN HIS SMALL, WASHED COTTAGE  ...................MYSTIC  269  22
HUMPED (1)
   OF HER HEART, WAS THE HUMPED INDIFFERENT IRON  .....HARDCASTLE CRAGS   63  28
HUNCH (1)
   TWO BLACK ROOKS HUNCH  .......................................PROSPECT   28   7
HUNCHED (1)
   SPRAWLS, HUNCHED IN BLACK, AMONG BAGGAGE, WINCING   CHANNEL CROSSING   26  11
HUNCHES (2)
   HUNCHES A WET BLACK ROOK  ...............BLACK ROOK IN RAINY WEATHER   56   2
   PALMED OFF OUR OWN HUNCHES AS ORACLES.   DIALOGUE OVER A OUIJA BOARD  279 105
HUNDRED (8)
   A HUNDRED HERALDS SHE SENT OUT  .................THE QUEEN'S COMPLAINT   29  16
   HE SPLIT IT INTO THREE HUNDRED AND SIXTY TRICKLES  ..........LESSON.   80  19
   WITH A HUNDRED BUSHEL BASKETS ON THE EDGE  .........SPINACH-PICKER.   89   6
   PURE LEAFAGE. A HUNDRED BASKETS BY DAY'S END.  ......SPINACH-PICKER.   89  11
   GREEN. NOR DO THEY, ONCE IN A HUNDRED  .........CHILD'S PARK STONES  101  28
   A HUNDRED, ON THAT HILL -- GREEN AND RED,  ................PHEASANT  191  17
   FEVER [ONE HUNDRED THREE DEGREES]  .........................FEVER.  231   T
   AND HOW A HUNDRED THOUSAND LEAVES  .................GOLD MOUTHS CRY  302   4
HUNDREDS (1)
   THOUGH HUNDREDS OF LONDONERS KNOW IT LIKE THE PALM OF THEIR HAND.  ...
                               ... QUEEN MARY'S ROSE GARDEN  290  16
HUNDRED-YEAR-OLD (1)
   HUNDRED-YEAR-OLD HOTEL SUSTAINS ITS RAMSHACKLE  .....ABOVE THE OXBOW   88  35
HUNG (15)
   STARS HUNG WATER-SUNK, SO A RANK  .............................FAUN   35   8
   ITS HEART AND GUTS HUNG HOOKED  ..........................STREET SONG   36   8
   HUNG CAUGHT IN DARK-WEBBED BRANCHES LIKE A FABULOUS HERON.  ...
                               ... DIALOGUE BETWEEN GHOST AND PRIEST   38   6
   UP FROM THE FISSURED VALLEY AND HUNG SHOULDER-HIGH *HARDCASTLE CRAGS   62  14
   THE MUSSELS HUNG DULL BLUE AND  .......MUSSEL HUNTER AT ROCK HARBOR   95  17
   I HUNG ON HIS NECK. RESOLUTENESS  .............WHITENESS I REMEMBER  103  28
   HUNG OUT OVER HAZARD, OVER HOOVES  .............WHITENESS I REMEMBER  103  30
   OVER MY HAND I HUNG HIM.  ...............................MEDALLION  124   8
   AND IN PUNISHMENT WAS HUNG OUT LIKE BROWN FRUIT  ......THE DETECTIVE  209  29
   HUNG UP IN THE LIBRARY WITH THE ENGRAVINGS OF RANGOON  .....COURAGE.  210  22
   HUNG, STARVED, BURNED, HOOKED.  ........................THE JAILER  227  35
   AND HERE WE ARE, HUNG OUT OVER THE DEAD DROP  ...........STOPPED DEAD  230   3
   I HAVE HUNG OUR CAVE WITH ROSES,  ..........NICK AND THE CANDLESTICK  241  32
   IN GLASS PAGODAS HUNG WITH VEILS OF GREEN  ............APRIL AUBADE  312   2
   SHE STEPS, HALTS, HUNG  ...................................AERIALIST  331  15
HUNGER (2)
   IMAGINE THEIR DEEP HUNGER, DEEP AS THE DARK  .................OUIJA   77   8
   AND HUNGER OF THE SURF THAT PLUCKS THE LAND, *EPITAPH IN THREE PARTS  337  16
HUNGER-BATTLE (1)
   IT WAS DURING THE LONG HUNGER-BATTLE  ...............THE THIN PEOPLE   64  12
HUNGERED (2)
   SO HUNGERED, SHE MUST WAIT IN RAGE  ......................THE SHRIKE   42  15
   WHILE SUBJECTS HUNGERED, EMPTY-PURSED,  ............NATURAL HISTORY   71   5
HUNGERS (1)
   WHICH HUNGERS TO HAUL THE WHITE REFLECTION DOWN.   WINTER LANDSCAPE.   21   5
HUNGER-STUNG (1)
   HE, HUNGER-STUNG, HARD TO SLAKE,  ........................THE GLUTTON   40   1
HUNGRY (4)
   AND HUNGRY, HUNGRY, THOSE TAUT THIGHS.  ....................PURSUIT   23  32
   AND HUNGRY, HUNGRY, THOSE TAUT THIGHS.  ....................PURSUIT   23  32
   SHOWS, RANK ON RANK, THE HUNGRY SEAS ADVANCING.  ...CHANNEL CROSSING   26   8
   I WONDER HOW HUNGRY THEY ARE.  .........THE ARRIVAL OF THE BEE BOX  213  26
HUNT (1)
   THE HUNT IS ON, AND SPRUNG THE TRAP.  ......................PURSUIT   22   8
```

247

```
                                       TITLE          PAGE  LINE
HUNTED (1)
   THEY HUNTED THE STONES, TACITURN AND SEPARATE, ...........POEM.7.S.   136   15
HUNTER (1)
   MUSSEL HUNTER AT ROCK HARBOR .........MUSSEL HUNTER AT ROCK HARBOR   95    T
HUNTERS (1)
   GLUT THESE HUNTERS AFTER AN OLD MEAT, ....................AFTERMATH   113    7
HUNTING (1)
   THE VILLAGERS OPEN THE CHAMBERS, THEY ARE HUNTING THE QUEEN. ..BEE.   212   42
HURL (2)
   I HURL MY HEART TO HALT HIS PACE, .........................PURSUIT    23    37
   THEN HURL THE BARE WORLD LIKE A BLUEGREEN BALL ..SONG FOR A REVOLU.   323   21
HURRICANE (3)
   IN THE HURRICANE, WHEN FATHER'S TWELVE .......THE DISQUIETING MUSES   75    17
   IN THE CIRCUS TENT OF A HURRICANE ...........CIRCUS IN THREE RINGS   321    1
   AND A HURRICANE HEADACHE ROCKS   INSOLENT STORM STRIKES AT THE SKULL  326   11
HURRY (3)
   DIDN'T GO DOWN IN SUCH A HURRY. HOW IT   MEMOIRS OF A SPINACH-PICKER   89    2
   THEIR LEAVES DO NOT WISH US TO HURRY: ..........CROSSING THE WATER   190    5
   THEY MOVE IN A HURRY. ...................................APPREHENSIONS 196   20
HURT (6)
   GLAZES THE WINDOW OF MY HURT; WHAT SOLACE ........WINTER LANDSCAPE.   22    13
   TRILLS ITS HURT OUT ....................................STREET SONG   36    22
   THE TULIPS ARE TOO RED IN THE FIRST PLACE, THEY HURT ME. ....TULIPS   161   36
   BE A BANDAGE TO HIS HURT, AND MY WORDS ................THREE WOMEN   185   297
   IF MY MOUTH COULD MARRY A HURT LIKE THAT! ..........POPPIES IN JULY   203   12
   "IT WON'T HURT." .........................................A SECRET   220   24
HURTING (1)
   BOOMERANG LIKE ANCHORED ELASTICS, HURTING THE OWNER. ...BERCK-PLAGE   196   11
HURTLE (1)
   DARK TUNNEL, THROUGH WHICH HURTLE THE VISITATIONS, .....THREE WOMEN   180   130
HURTLED (1)
   SHINY AND STRANGE, AS IF HE HAD HURTLED FROM A STAR? ...THREE WOMEN   181   163
HURTS (7)
   IT HURTS AT FIRST. THE RED TONGUES WILL TEACH THE TRUTH.   POEM.6.W.  135   18
   OR SITS IN THE DESERT AND HURTS HIS MOTHER'S HEART. ....THREE WOMEN   186   333
   I CANNOT RUN, I AM ROOTED, AND THE GORSE HURTS ME ..THE BEE MEETING   211   31
   HURTS ME, HE ...........................................THE JAILER   227   29
   HURTS ME AS THE WORLD HURTS GOD. I AM A LANTERN --- .........FEVER.   232   36
   HURTS ME AS THE WORLD HURTS GOD. I AM A LANTERN --- .........FEVER.   232   36
   O I SHOULDN'T DIP MY HANKIE IN, IT HURTS! .................THE TOUR   238   31
HUSBAND (9)
   MY HUSBAND AND CHILD SMILING OUT OF THE FAMILY PHOTO; .......TULIPS   160   20
   THE MOTH-FACE OF HER HUSBAND, MOONWHITE AND ILL, .............WIDOW   164   14
   WHEN THE SPORTY WIFE AND HER DOCTOR HUSBAND WENT ON ONE OF
      THEIR CRUISES ..................................THE BABYSITTERS   174   16
   I CAN LOVE MY HUSBAND, WHO WILL UNDERSTAND. ...........THREE WOMEN   183   250
   I AM MENDING A SILK SLIP: MY HUSBAND IS READING. ......THREE WOMEN   186   352
   CAN STITCH LACE NEATLY ON TO THIS MATERIAL. MY HUSBAND   THREE WOMEN  187   360
   YOU SAY YOUR HUSBAND IS JUST NO GOOD TO YOU. .................LESBOS   228   26
   THE IMPOTENT HUSBAND SLUMPS OUT FOR A COFFEE. ...............LESBOS   228   44
   A DOG PICKED UP YOUR DOGGY HUSBAND. HE WENT ON. .............LESBOS   229   63
HUSBANDS (2)
   OF OUR HUSBANDS AND SONS MOVE SURE AMONG THE LOW STARS. ......NET-.   121   19
   AT NOON, ANEMIC HUSBANDS VISIT THEM. ..........MORNING IN THE HOS.   333   27
HUSBAND'S (1)
   BROODY AND IN LONG SKIRTS ON MY FIRST HUSBAND'S SOFA, MY FINGERS ...
                                                   ... FACE LIFT   156   22
HUSH (6)
   HUSH A LUMPED MAN-SHAPE. THE WHOLE ACT FORMAL, FLUENT AS A DANCE. ...
                                                   ... THE GORING   47    9
   A HIGH HUSH QUIETENS THE CRICKETS' CRY. ...........ABOVE THE OXBOW   89    56
   FLOATING IN A HIGH-CHURCH HUSH ..............................CANDLES   149   22
   THIS IS RAIN NOW, THIS BIG HUSH. ...............................ELM   192   14
   THE SMALL SKULLS, THE SMASHED BLUE HILLS, THE GODAWFUL HUSH. ...
                                                   ... FOR A FATHERLESS SON  206  13
   ROLLS OUT A CARPET, A HUSH. .................................GIGOLO   268   24
HUSHING (1)
   OR THE SEA, HUSHING THEIR PEELED SENSE LIKE OLD MOTHER MORPHIA. ...
                                                   ... WAKING IN WINTER  151   16
HUSK (1)
   THE HUSK OF A FIDDLER-CRAB, ..........MUSSEL HUNTER AT ROCK HARBOR   97    69
HUSTLE (1)
   TO HUSTLE THEM OFF THE LAWN. ......................OLD LADIES' HOME   120   16
HUSTLED (2)
   HUSTLED A GULL FLOCK TO FLAP OFF THE SANDSPIT. *SUICIDE OFF EGG ROCK  115   13
   ARE HUSTLED OVER THE CRESTS AND TROUGHS, ...................ON DECK   143   13
HUSTLES (2)
   HUSTLES OTHER GULLS OFF. CRABS ....................MAGNOLIA SHOALS   122   15
   THE STREAM THAT HUSTLES US ......................THE BURNT-OUT SPA   138   33
HUT (5)
   BEHIND A GOATHERD'S HUT: .....................................SPIDER   48    10
   GULL-FOULED, A STONE HUT .................................DEPARTURE   51    16
   ANY MORE THAN THE OLD WOMAN IN HER MUD HUT COULD ...THE THIN PEOPLE   64    26
   TIMBERS OF HIS UPRIGHT HUT? ..........THE HERMIT AT OUTERMOST HOUSE   119   12
   ABOUT A GOBLIN RAID ON MINER'S HUT ....THE PRINCESS AND THE GOBLINS   334   38
```

```
                                              TITLE        PAGE  LINE
HUTS (1)
   HEN HUTS AND CATTLE GREEN  ............................MAN IN BLACK  119    9
HYDRANGEA (1)
   THEY RATTLE LIKE HYDRANGEA BUSHES.  ....................POEM.1.WHO.  131   12
HYDRAS (1)
   WHERE THE YEW TREES BLOW LIKE HYDRAS,  ........THE MUNICH MANNEQUINS  262    3
HYGIENIC (1)
   THE WHITE LIGHT IS ARTIFICIAL, AND HYGIENIC AS HEAVEN.  ....SURGEON.  170    1
HYMNS (3)
   HE HYMNS THE ROTTEN QUEEN WITH SAFFRON HAIR  ..................OUIJA   77   22
   STILL HE HYMNS JUICE OF HER, HOT NECTARINE.  .....;............OUIJA   77   26
   WHERE DIAMONDS JANGLE HYMNS WITHIN THE BLOOD  ..........APRIL AUBADE  312    3
HYPERBOLICAL (1)
   A HOT HYPERBOLICAL JOKE!"  ...................DIALOGUE EN ROUTE  308   18
HYPOCRITE (1)
   THE VELVET DODGES OF THE HYPOCRITE:  ..............THE RAVAGED FACE  116   11
HYSTERICAL (1)
   HERE THEY COME, THE OUTRIDERS, ON THEIR HYSTERICAL ELASTICS.  ..BEE.  212   38
I (988)
IAMBICS (1)
   IN APT IAMBICS, IF PRODDED TO RECITE  ...DIALOGUE OVER A OUIJA BOARD  280  143
ICARUS (1)
   BEFORE WE FELL, LIKE ICARUS, UNDONE;  ................DOOM OF EXILES  318   10
ICE (16)
   LAST SUMMER'S REEDS ARE ALL ENGRAVED IN ICE  ......WINTER LANDSCAPE,   22   11
   THAN AGAINST THIS ONSLAUGHT, THESE CASUAL BLASTS OF ICE   CHANNEL C.   27   17
   IN BLACK AND WHITE, OR PUT ON ICE  ......EPITAPH FOR FIRE AND FLOWER   45   10
   ICE AND ROCK, EACH SENTIMENT WITHIN BORDER,  ................SPINSTER   49   16
   LEAVING A SALTY MASH OF ICE TO WHITEN  ................POINT SHIRLEY  110    8
   TO THE RIGHT, AND MARCH ICE  ......................MAN IN BLACK  119   10
   EACH DEAD HEAD HAD A VISOR OF ICE.  ....................LOVE LETTER  147   18
   PURE AS A PANE OF ICE. IT'S A GIFT.  ..................LOVE LETTER  147   36
   AMONG ICE BUCKETS, FROSTY NAPKINS.  ........................CANDLES  149   23
   CHRIST! THEY ARE PANES OF ICE,  ..........NICK AND THE CANDLESTICK  241   15
   WITH THE COLD BURN DRY ICE HAS. YET THE CLOCK  ..........DIALOGUE O.  276   11
   WHY, YOUR HAND'S COLD AS ICE! THEN CHAFE THE COLD  .....DIALOGUE O.  285  333
   IN AN ARTIFICE OF ICE:  ......................NOTES TO A NEOPHYTE  306   15
   FRAMED IN DISCIPLINES OF FIRE AND ICE  ....METAMORPHOSES OF THE MOON  307   26
   ARRANGED IN SHEETS OF ICE, THE FOND  .................DANSE MACABRE  321    4
   YET AS WE WONDER WHAT CAN COME OF ICE  ...........PROLOGUE TO SPRING  322   14
ICEBERGS (1)
   LIKE ICEBERGS, WHILE MINUTE BROWN HAIRS RISE  .........TALE OF A TUB   25   42
ICEBOX (3)
   TONIGHT THE PARTS ARE ENTOMBED IN AN ICEBOX.   THE SURGEON AT 2 A.M.  171   37
   WE LIFTED A SUGARED HAM AND A PINEAPPLE FROM THE GROWNUPS'
      ICEBOX  .........................................THE BABYSITTERS  175   30
   ICEBOX, A SIMPLE  .............................................DEATH & CO.  254   15
ICEBOXES (1)
   THE SMILE OF ICEBOXES ANNIHILATES ME.  . .............AN APPEARANCE  189    1
ICECAKES (2)
   FARTHER OUT, THE WAVES WILL BE MOUTHING ICECAKES -- ..A WINTER SHIP  113   21
   HE IS GRATIFIED BY THE ABSENCE OF ICECAKES.  ................ON DECK  143   27
ICE-HEARTED (1)
   OF YOUR ICE-HEARTED CALLING--  ...............................LORELEI   95   31
ICE-MOUNTAINS (1)
   AS KEELED ICE-MOUNTAINS  ..........................FULL FATHOM FIVE   92   12
ICERIBBED (1)
   AND ARE MET, INSTEAD, BY THIS ICERIBBED SHIP,  ........A WINTER SHIP  113   25
ICES (2)
   WHAT BLUE, MOONY RAY ICES THEIR DREAMS?  ..................THREE WOMEN  181  182
   WHERE APPLE BLOOM ICES THE NIGHT  .............................EVENT  195   13
ICH (4)
   ICH, ICH, ICH, ICH,  ..........................................DADDY  223   27
   ICH, ICH, ICH, ICH,  ..........................................DADDY  223   27
   ICH, ICH, ICH, ICH,  ..........................................DADDY  223   27
   ICH, ICH, ICH, ICH,  ..........................................DADDY  223   27
ICHOR (1)
   AND YET THE ICHOR OF THE SPRING  ..................THE BURNT-OUT SPA  138   19
ICICLES (1)
   ICICLES, OLD ECHOER.  .......................NICK AND THE CANDLESTICK  241   11
ICILY (1)
   HIGH, HIGH AND ICILY  .........................................GULLIVER  251    2
I'D (13)
   FROM YOUR BLUE PALLOR, I'D SAY YOU INHABITED THE FROZEN WASTE  ...
                        ... DIALOGUE BETWEEN GHOST AND PRIEST   38   14
   SO HUMBLY DONE, I'D TURN THIS KEEN  ..........................RHYME   50   13
   I'D ONLY TO SET ONE FOOT IN WILDERNESS--*MEMOIRS OF A SPINACH-PICKER   90   21
   BACKTRACKING TAIL. I'D COME FOR  .......MUSSEL HUNTER AT ROCK HARBOR   95    8
   AND I'D BEEN KEEPING HER IN THE DARK, AND SHE WAS RESENTFUL --  ...
                        ...  IN PLASTER  159   37
   AND SECRETLY SHE BEGAN TO HOPE I'D DIE.  ..................IN PLASTER  159   39
   OR BRAG AHEAD OF TIME HOW I'D AVENGE MYSELF.  ............IN PLASTER  160   47
   I'D CALL IT A SUNSET, BUT  ...........................STOPPED DEAD  230   14
   TO COURT REMORSE. OR SOMEONE ELSE. I'D RATHER  .........DIALOGUE O.  278   59
   M-A-G-E. IN PLUMAGE. I'D NEVER HAVE THOUGHT  ...........DIALOGUE O.  278   78
```

I'D (CONT.)
    AND I'D SOONER BE STAKED FOR A WITCH, KINDLED, AND CURLED ...
                      ... DIALOGUE OVER A OUIJA BOARD 280 132
    TO PEOPLE THE BOUGHS WITH TALKING BIRDS. I'D PLANT .....DIALOGUE O. 280 169
    AS IF I'D HALF-BELIEVED IN HIM, AND HE, *DIALOGUE OVER A OUIJA BOARD 285 307
IDEA (1)
    HOW FREE IT IS, YOU HAVE NO IDEA HOW FREE --- ....TULIPS 161 31
IDEALS (1)
    PERFUME, POLITICS, AND FIXED IDEALS. ....SONNET: TO EVA 305 12
IDEAS (1)
    THAT FLAT, FLAT, FLATNESS FROM WHICH IDEAS, DESTRUCTIONS, ...THREE. 177 18
IDENTICAL (3)
    OF IDENTICAL GRAY BRICK HOUSES, ...LANDOWNERS 53   4
    THEY ARE THE REAL MONKS AND NUNS IN THEIR IDENTICAL GARMENTS.*THREE. 183 227
    NEVERTHELESS, I AM THE SAME, IDENTICAL WOMAN. ....LADY LAZARUS 245 34
IDENTITY (3)
    THE NURSES GIVE BACK MY CLOTHES, AND AN IDENTITY. ......THREE WOMEN 183 241
    THE RED MOUTH I PUT BY WITH MY IDENTITY ....THREE WOMEN 183 247
    I CAST OFF MY IDENTITY ....FAMILY REUNION 301 29
IDIOT (9)
    AS A GREENLY ESCAPED IDIOT, ...STREET SONG 36   12
    O MY GREAT IDIOT, WHO ....LETTER TO A PURIST 37   9
    THIS PARK IS FLESHED WITH IDIOT PETALS. ....MOONRISE 98   4
    BETTER THE FLAT LEER OF THE IDIOT, ...THE RAVAGED FACE 116 9
    THE IDIOT BIRD LEAPS UP AND DRUNKEN LEANS ....SONNET: TO EVA 305 13
    THE IDIOT BIRD LEAPS OUT AND DRUNKEN LEANS ....DOOMSDAY 316 1
    THE IDIOT BIRD LEAPS OUT AND DRUNKEN LEANS. ....DOOMSDAY 316 6
    THE IDIOT BIRD LEAPS OUT AND DRUNKEN LEANS. ....DOOMSDAY 316 12
    THE IDIOT BIRD LEAPS OUT AND DRUNKEN LEANS, ...DOOMSDAY 316 18
IDIOTS (1)
    A TREASON NOT TO BE BORNE. LET IDIOTS ....SPINSTER 50   22
IDLE (4)
    DEFLECT THE WATERY DAZZLE; THE PEOPLE IDLE ....WHITSUN 154 11
    THE HORRORS THAT STAND AND IDLE, THE SLIGHTED GODMOTHERS*THREE WOMEN 180 137
    AND IDLE COILS OF JARGON YET UNSPOKEN. ....SONNET: TO EVA 304 8
    GATHER IDLE OYSTERS FROM GREEN SHOALS, ...GO GET THE GOODLY SQUAB 313 19
IDOL (1)
    OF GUARDIAN CATS CROUCHED ROUND THEIR IDOL, ...ELLA MASON A. 54   28
IDOLS (2)
    WITH THE LANGUOR OF IDOLS BELOW ....IN MIDAS' COUNTRY 99   7
    IT MEANS: NO MORE IDOLS BUT ME, ...THE MUNICH MANNEQUINS 263 8
IDOL'S (1)
    WHICH MAR THE IDOL'S SANCTITY. ..........METAMORPHOSES OF THE MOON 308 36
IDYLL (1)
    MY PROMISE OF AN IDYLL. THE BLUE'S WORN OUT: ....GREEN ROCK. 105 8
IF (116)
    TOOK MY HEART AS IF ....SONG FOR A SUMMER'S DAY 31   12
    THIS WITCH SIDLES, FINGERS CROOKED, AS IF ....VANITY FAIR 32   2
    "AND IF THERE BE ....TINKER JACK AND THE TIDY WIVES 35   26
    NOR GUESS THAT IF I CHOOSE TO BLINK .....SOLILOQUY OF THE SOLIPSIST 37   17
    AS IF TO OUTFLAME A PHOENIX, THE MOMENT'S SPUR ......EPITAPH FOR F. 46   24
    AND SEE THAT FIRST HOUSE, AS IF BETWEEN ....LANDOWNERS 53   6
    AS IF A CELESTIAL BURNING TOOK ....BLACK ROOK IN RAINY WEATHER 57   17
    IF YOU CARE TO CALL THOSE SPASMODIC ....BLACK ROOK IN RAINY WEATHER 57   37
    IF ROOT'S FIRM-FIXED AND RESOLUTION GOOD. ....MAYFLOWER 60   4
    IF THE THIN PEOPLE SIMPLY STAND IN THE FOREST, ...THE THIN PEOPLE 65   45
    AS IF, ABOVE LOVE'S RUINAGE, WE WERE ....THE OTHER TWO 69   34
    WE'D WINK AT IF WE DIDN'T HEAR ....ALL THE DEAD DEARS 70   10
    IN GOING UP FOR THE COMING DOWN IF THE POST ....ABOVE THE OXBOW 88   18
    IF THEY COULD SEE, I WAS ONE ....MUSSEL HUNTER AT ROCK HARBOR 97   65
    THERE WAS NO TELLING IF HE'D ....MUSSEL HUNTER AT ROCK HARBOR 97   74
    THEY LOITER AND STARE AS IF THE HOUSE ....AFTERMATH 113 2
    BURNT-OUT WERE THEIRS, OR AS IF THEY THOUGHT ....AFTERMATH 113 3
    HE SMOLDERED, AS IF STONE-DEAF, BLINDFOLD, ...SUICIDE OFF EGG ROCK 115 14
    AS IF YOU HAD NEVER EXISTED, AS IF I CAME ...ELECTRA ON AZALEA PATH 116 6
    AS IF YOU HAD NEVER EXISTED, AS IF I CAME ...ELECTRA ON AZALEA PATH 116 6
    THOSE OLD DESPOTS, IF HE SAT ....THE HERMIT AT OUTERMOST HOUSE 119 9
    AS IF IT WERE SUMMER STILL. ....MAGNOLIA SHOALS 121 4
    THEY LIE AS IF UNDER WATER ....THE SLEEPERS 122 4
    WHERE HIS INNARDS BULGED AS IF ....MEDALLION 125 23
    IF ONLY THE WIND WOULD LEAVE MY LUNGS ALONE. POEM.1.WHO. 131 10
    IF I AM A LITTLE ONE, I CAN DO NO HARM. POEM.6.W. 135 13
    IF I DON'T MOVE ABOUT, I'LL KNOCK NOTHING OVER. SO I SAID,*POEM.6.W. 135 14
    IF HE WERE I, HE WOULD DO WHAT I DID. ....THE HANGING MAN 142 6
    IF THEY MISSED OUT ON WALKING ABOUT LIKE PEOPLE ....STILLBORN 142 4
    IT WOULD BE BETTER IF THEY WERE ALIVE, AND THAT'S WHAT
                      THEY WERE. ....STILLBORN 142 13
    IF I'M ALIVE NOW, THEN I WAS DEAD, ...LOVE LETTER 147 2
    AS IF IN HOSPITAL. ....WHITSUN 154 12
    I CAN STAY AWAKE ALL NIGHT, IF NEED BE -- ....ZOO KEEPER'S WIFE 154 1
    AS IF MY HABITS OFFENDED HER IN SOME WAY. ....IN PLASTER 159 31
    ARE RIDING TO WORK IN ROWS, AS IF RECENTLY BRAINWASHED. ..INSOMNIAC 163 35
    AND WHAT IF THE SKY HERE IS NO DIFFERENT, ..STARS OVER THE DORDOGNE 166 25
    IF THE MOON SMILED, SHE WOULD RESEMBLE YOU. ....THE RIVAL 166 1
    IF I PAY THE ROOTS OF THE HEATHER ....WUTHERING HEIGHTS 167 16

IF (CONT.)
THE HIGH, GREEN MEADOWS ARE GLOWING, AS IF LIT FROM WITHIN. ...
                            ... BLACKBERRYING   168   14
THEY WILL WONDER IF I WAS IMPORTANT. ....LAST WORDS   172   9
THE GRASSES UNLOAD THEIR GRIEFS ON MY FEET AS IF I WERE GOD, MOON.   172   3
THE BOLD GULLS DOVE AS IF THEY OWNED IT ALL. ....THE BABYSITTERS   175   37
WENT ON SHAPING ITSELF WITH LOVE, AS IF I WAS READY. ...THREE WOMEN   178   63
THE DOCTORS MOVE AMONG US AS IF OUR BIGNESS ....THREE WOMEN   179 114
AND WHAT IF THEY FOUND THEMSELVES SURPRISED, AS I DID? THREE WOMEN   180 118
AND WHAT IF TWO LIVES LEAKED BETWEEN MY THIGHS? ....THREE WOMEN   180 120
SHINY AND STRANGE, AS IF HE HAD HURTLED FROM A STAR? ...THREE WOMEN   181 163
THEY ARE STITCHING ME UP WITH SILK, AS IF I WERE A MATERIAL. *THREE.   181 168
AS IF I HAD LOST AN EYE, A LEG, A TONGUE. ....THREE WOMEN   183 252
TO BE SO OPEN: IT IS AS IF MY HEART ....THREE WOMEN   185 300
WITH PINKNESS, AS IF A TENDERNESS AWOKE, ...THREE WOMEN   186 356
AS IF I THOUGHT IT HAD A SPIRIT. ....PHEASANT   191   8
IF I COULD BLEED, OR SLEEP! ....POPPIES IN JULY   203   11
IF MY MOUTH COULD MARRY A HURT LIKE THAT! ....POPPIES IN JULY   203   12
I WOULD NOT MIND IF IT WAS BONES, OR A PEARL BUTTON. .....BIRTHDAY.   206   12
DO NOT BE ASHAMED -- I DO NOT MIND IF IT IS SMALL. ....BIRTHDAY.   206   22
IF YOU ONLY KNEW HOW THE VEILS WERE KILLING MY DAYS. .....BIRTHDAY.   207   37
IF IT WERE DEATH ....A BIRTHDAY PRESENT   208   56
IF I STAND VERY STILL, THEY WILL THINK I AM COW-PARSLEY, ...BEE.   212   39
I WONDER IF THEY WOULD FORGET ME ....THE ARRIVAL OF THE BEE BOX   213   27
IF I JUST UNDID THE LOCKS AND STOOD BACK AND TURNED INTO A TREE. ...
                            ... THE ARRIVAL OF THE BEE BOX   213   28
IF THERE IS, SHE IS OLD, ...STINGS   214   16
IF I'VE KILLED ONE MAN, I'VE KILLED TWO --- ....DADDY   224   71
SEVEN YEARS, IF YOU WANT TO KNOW. ....DADDY   224   74
SHE'LL CUT HER THROAT AT TEN IF SHE'S MAD AT TWO. ....LESBOS   228   22
OFF AND ON, AS IF I JUST HAD TO RETCH. ....THE TOUR   238   25
AND A LITTLE FLAT, AS IF THEY ....GULLIVER   251   3
TO BLEED, IF IT COMES TO THAT. ......................EAVESDROPPER   260   6
AND BACK TO P, AS IF HE KNEW US WELL ....DIALOGUE OVER A OUIJA BOARD   277   30
I SUPPOSE. IF I DIDN'T TRUST YOU AT THIS*DIALOGUE OVER A OUIJA BOARD   277   36
THAN FINANCIER. WHAT GOOD IS HE, IF NOT *DIALOGUE OVER A OUIJA BOARD   277   44
FROM, IF NOT THE POOLS? OH, FROM A LOT   DIALOGUE OVER A OUIJA BOARD   277   46
HONESTLY WANT TO FIND IF YOU'LL HAVE A FLING ....DIALOGUE O.   278   56
BELIEVE, IF THEY COULD MANAGE TO CONVINCE ....DIALOGUE O.   278   66
AN ORIGINAL NOTE. IF HE'D SAID, HOWEVER, MERELY: ....DIALOGUE O.   278   81
AS IF THE AIR WERE LABORING TO PRODUCE   DIALOGUE OVER A OUIJA BOARD   279   89
OF OUR TWO INTUITIONS. AND IF HE IS? ...DIALOGUE OVER A OUIJA BOARD   279 107
THAT'S SOMETHING TO STUDY EVEN IF IT'S NOT ....DIALOGUE O.   279 108
PAN AS IF HE WERE OUR FIRST-BREACHED BRAT ....DIALOGUE O.   280 138
IN APT IAMBICS, IF PRODDED TO RECITE ...DIALOGUE OVER A OUIJA BOARD   280 143
EVEN IF YOU SEEM PACIFIED, PREFER ......DIALOGUE OVER A OUIJA BOARD   280 145
IF YOU MUST BUTCHER MOTHER GOOSE TO DO IT. ....DIALOGUE O.   280 149
IF THAT ELDERBERRY BUSH BESIDE THE GATE *DIALOGUE OVER A OUIJA BOARD   280 157
IF A BUSH BORROWED TONGUES AND SPOKE TO YOU. YOU'D KNEEL*DIALOGUE O.   280 163
ARGUMENT TO THE HOUSE NEXT DOOR. OR IF   DIALOGUE OVER A OUIJA BOARD   280 166
AS IF TEMPTING OUR GROSS GULLIBILITY ...DIALOGUE OVER A OUIJA BOARD   281 178
TO GIVE ANOTHER INCH. IF YOU PREFER, ...DIALOGUE OVER A OUIJA BOARD   281 179
TO COLLECT HIS BEATINGS. AND IF HE'S A GO-BETWEEN ......DIALOGUE O.   281 185
IF NOTHING COMES OF IT. ON THE OTHER HAND, ...DIALOGUE O.   281 198
MIGHT DO AS A GOD'S MOUTHPIECE IF A WHIRLWIND ....DIALOGUE O.   281 202
IT TAKES PATIENCE. IF VERONICAS AND FOUNTAINS ....DIALOGUE O.   282 221
IF EITHER OF US HAD IT: BUT NOT THE HALF- ....DIALOGUE O.   282 226
ALL, IF YOU'LL HIDE HOPES OF HEAVEN IN A HAT ....DIALOGUE O.   282 231
IF YOU CAN HANG RELIGION ON THE RIM ....DIALOGUE OVER A OUIJA BOARD   283 248
PAN AS OUR EVENING GUEST IF HE'S SO FREE*DIALOGUE OVER A OUIJA BOARD   283 252
AS IF BLOODHOUNDS BORE HIM DOWN. I-N-G-O ... .DIALOGUE O.   283 275
IF OUR NERVES ARE THE SOLE NOURISHERS ..DIALOGUE OVER A OUIJA BOARD   284 287
AS IF I'D HALF-BELIEVED IN HIM, AND HE, *DIALOGUE OVER A OUIJA BOARD   285 307
THE TABLE LOOKS AS IF IT WOULD STAY A TABLE ....DIALOGUE O.   286 353
WHAT GOOD IS ALL THAT SPACE IF IT CAN'T DRAW YOU OFF? THE RIVAL/DR   291   13
IF ANYTHING SHOULD HAPPEN . . ." ....BITTER STRAWBERRIES   299   12
AND IF MY STOMACH WOULD CONTRACT ....APRIL 18   301   3
BLOOD SPRINGS ETERNAL IF THE HEART BE BURNING. ..TO EVA DESCENDING.   303   8
LOVE FLAMES FOREVER IF THE FLESH BE YEARNING. ...TO EVA DESCENDING.   303   14
AND REMEMBER, IF TEDIOUS RISK ....NOTES TO A NEOPHYTE   306   17
"IF ONLY SOMETHING WOULD HAPPEN!" ....DIALOGUE EN ROUTE   308   1
WOULD FRACTURE IF HE FELL. ....TRIO OF LOVE SONGS   314   24
IF YOU DISSECT A BIRD ....TRIO OF LOVE SONGS   315   37
IF YOU FLAY A BEAST ....TRIO OF LOVE SONGS   315   41
IF YOU ASSAULT A FISH ....TRIO OF LOVE SONGS   315   45
IF YOU PLUCK OUT MY HEART ....TRIO OF LOVE SONGS   315   49
TOO LATE TO ASK IF END WAS WORTH THE MEANS, ...DOOMSDAY   316   16
SO IF YOU CAN DREAM UP ANY SAVING PLAN ....THE DISPOSSESSED   318   2
IF YOU'VE A PLOT TO HALT THE LETHAL FLOW ....THE DISPOSSESSED   318   7
IF YOU CAN THINK OF MEANS TO MEND THE VOW ....THE DISPOSSESSED   318   13
"WELL THEN, IF WE AGREE, IT IS NOT ODD ....LOVE IS A PARALLAX   329   7
IGNITE (1)
STONE-BUILT TOWN, THAT SHE HEARD THE QUICK AIR IGNITE *HARDCASTLE C.   62   4
IGNITED (1)
IGNITED WITH A GLASSED FLAME ....MEDALLION   124   10

		TITLE	PAGE	LINE

IGNITING (1)
    IGNITING ITS CARBON MONOXIDES, BY EYES ....POPPIES IN OCTOBER 240   8
IGNORANT (4)
    YET POLITIC; IGNORANT ....BLACK ROOK IN RAINY WEATHER   57 25
    AND UTTERLY IGNORANT OF THE WAY IT TOOK. ....WIDOW 165 35
    ONLY IGNORANT. ....WINTERING 218 21
    O IGNORANT HEART! ....FEVER./DR 294   2
IGNORANTS (1)
    A MILLION IGNORANTS. ....PURDAH 243 47
IGNORE (6)
    OF SOME GODLY UTTERANCE WAKENED HEADS IGNORE: ....GHOST'S.   90 17
    A SERVICE AND IGNORE IT, I GO A LIAR ......GREEN ROCK, WINTHROP BAY 105 20
    IT IS TOUCHING, THE WAY THEY'LL IGNORE ....CANDLES 148   5
    THEY MIGHT IGNORE ME IMMEDIATELY ....THE ARRIVAL OF THE BEE BOX 213 31
    THE LABYRINTH AND IGNORE WHAT MANNER OF BEAST ....DIALOGUE O. 286 343
    WE IGNORE THE COMING DOOM OF GOLD ....GOLD MOUTHS CRY 302   7
IGNORED (1)
    SIGNAL THE BLIND, AND ARE IGNORED. ....LITTLE FUGUE 187   4
ILL (8)
    NOW, FREE, BY HAZARD'S QUIRK, FROM THE COMMON ILL   CHANNEL CROSSING   27 26
    WELL OR ILL." GERD SLANTS A LOOK AT EACH: MOST DEAR,   CRYSTAL GAZER   55 10
    TO A GIDDY JOG. THEN FOR ILL WILL ....WHITENESS I REMEMBER 102 17
    O OEDIPUS. O CHRIST. YOU USE ME ILL. ....THE RAVAGED FACE 116 14
    THE MOTH-FACE OF HER HUSBAND, MOONWHITE AND ILL, ...WIDOW 164 14
    I CALL YOU ORPHAN, ORPHAN. YOU ARE ILL. ....LESBOS 228 38
    HOMUNCULUS, I AM ILL. ....CUT 235 23
    AN ILL WIND IS STALKING ....TEMPER OF TIME 336   1
I'LL (10)
    ONE DAY I'LL HAVE MY DEATH OF HIM; ....PURSUIT   22   2
    I'LL CORRECT EACH MAR ....TINKER JACK AND THE TIDY WIVES   34   5
    I'LL GO OUT AND SIT IN WHITE LIKE THEY DO, ...MOONRISE   98   2
    IF I DON'T MOVE ABOUT, I'LL KNOCK NOTHING OVER. SO I SAID,*POEM.6.W. 135 14
    I'LL FLY THROUGH THE CANDLE'S MOUTH LIKE A SINGELESS MOTH.*POEM.6.W. 135 20
    WHEN YOU KICK ME OUT, THAT'S WHAT I'LL REMEMBER, ...LEAVING EARLY 145   2
    I'LL CARRY IT OFF LIKE A RICH PRETTY GIRL, ...STOPPED DEAD 230 23
    I'LL ASK. DO. WE'VE KEPT HIM WAITING LONG ....DIALOGUE O. 281 180
    IS SMALL THESE DAYS. DON'T BE SO SMART. I'LL ASK, ...DIALOGUE O. 281 204
    S. HE CALLS US APES. I'LL SETTLE HIM! ..DIALOGUE OVER A OUIJA BOARD 284 299
ILL-ASSORTED (1)
    KNOTTING AND STOPPING, ILL-ASSORTED, IN BLUE UNIFORMS,*PARLIAMENT H. 152 14
ILLBRED (1)
    MOTHER, MOTHER, WHAT ILLBRED AUNT ....THE DISQUIETING MUSES   74   1
ILLEGITIMATE (1)
    AN ILLEGITIMATE BABY -- ....A SECRET 220 25
ILL-FAMED (1)
    WELL-NAMED, ILL-FAMED A KNAVISH FLY-BY-NIGHT, ...GOATSUCKER 111 11
ILL-JUDGED (1)
    THE RITUAL DEATH EACH TIME BOTCHED AMONG DROPPED CAPES,
                              ILL-JUDGED STABS, ...THE GORING   47   3
ILLS (2)
    THE COMPANIONABLE ILLS ....THE COMPANIONABLE ILLS 105   T
    OF MERCURY IN GRADED TUBES, WHERE ILLS ....MORNING IN THE HOS. 332 17
ILL-SERVED (1)
    ILL-SERVED HE'LL BE WHEN ....WORDS FOR A NURSERY   74 41
ILL-STARRED (1)
    A SCORPION STUNG ITS HEAD, AN ILL-STARRED THING; ....ELECTRA ON. 117 35
ILLUSION (4)
    BALDING, GELDED BY LIGHTNING -- AN ILLUSION, ..FOR A FATHERLESS SON 205   4
    THE ILLUSION OF A GREEK NECESSITY ....EDGE 272   4
    O MOON OF ILLUSION, ...MOONSONG AT MORNING 316   1
    WHICH DREAMERS CALL REAL, AND REALISTS, ILLUSION: ...LOVE IS A PAR. 330 59
I'M (23)
IMAGE (16)
    AS IS YOUR IMAGE IN MY EYE; DRY FROST   WINTER LANDSCAPE, WITH ROOKS   22 12
    DANS LE FOND DES FORETS VOTRE IMAGE ME SUIT. ....PURSUIT   22   E
    AND AN IMAGE LOOMS UNDER THE FISHPOND SURFACE ...ALL THE DEAD DEARS   71 22
    MY BACKWARD IMAGE. ....WORDS FOR A NURSERY   74 35
    AGAINST THE WEIGHTY IMAGE OF THEIR FALL. ....MOONRISE   98 24
    OUR LIMBS' IMAGE ON A FIELD OF STRAW ....IN MIDAS' COUNTRY   99   9
    I LAY DREAMING YOUR EPIC, IMAGE BY IMAGE. ...ELECTRA ON AZALEA PATH 116 12
    I LAY DREAMING YOUR EPIC, IMAGE BY IMAGE. ...ELECTRA ON AZALEA PATH 116 12
    THE WAX IMAGE OF MYSELF, A DOLL'S BODY. POEM.6.W. 135   3
    A PAPER IMAGE TO LAY AGAINST HER HEART ....WIDOW 164 17
    YOU HAVE AN EYE, IT'S AN IMAGE. ....THE APPLICANT 222 38
    THE IMAGE ....THALIDOMIDE 252 25
    LOYAL TO MY IMAGE, ...CHILDLESS WOMAN 259 12
    THE IMAGE OF YOU, TRANSFIXED BY ROOTS, WAX-PALE, ...DIALOGUE O. 285 325
    TO PRINT YOUR FLAMING IMAGE IN BIRTHSPOT ....SONNET TO SATAN 323 11
    I SOUGHT MY IMAGE ....ON LOOKING INTO THE EYES OF A DEMON LOVER 325 17
IMAGES (8)
    PROFITLESS, THEIR GOSSIPING IMAGES ....ON THE DECLINE OF ORACLES   78 22
    SHAPES ITS IMAGES AROUND HIS SONGS. ..................SNAKECHARMER   79   7
    IMAGES OF LIGHT AND AIR ....SCULPTOR   91   7
    MORGUE OF OLD LOGS AND OLD IMAGES, THE LAKE ....PRIVATE GROUND 131 23
    THE DAY EMPTIES ITS IMAGES ....PARLIAMENT HILL FIELDS 153 37

                                                            TITLE   PAGE LINE
IMAGES (CONT.)
   THESE PURE, SMALL IMAGES. THEY SMELL OF MILK. ....THREE WOMEN 183 230
   LIMBS, IMAGES, SHRIEKS. BEHIND THE CONCRETE BUNKERS ....BERCK-PLAGE 197   29
   POOL IN WHICH IMAGES ....CHILD 265   8
IMAGINATION (1)
   COLD AND FINAL, THE IMAGINATION ....TWO LOVERS. 327   1
IMAGINE (10)
   IMAGINE THEIR DEEP HUNGER, DEEP AS THE DARK ....OUIJA   77   8
   ANACONDA. IMAGINE: THE WORLD ....PERSEUS   83   24
   OF A SINGLE ROSE PRESENT TO IMAGINE ...............RHODODENDRON. 103   3
   DIFFICULT TO IMAGINE HOW FURY STRUCK -- ....BLUE MOLES 126   17
   I IMAGINE MYSELF WITH A GREAT PUBLIC, ...BARREN WOMAN 157   6
   IT IS WHAT THE DEAD CLOSE ON, FINALLY; I IMAGINE THEM ....TULIPS 161   34
   I IMAGINE THEM WITHOUT FATHERS OR MOTHERS, LIKE THE FIRST GODS. ...
                                                     ... LAST WORDS 172   8
   I IMAGINE HIM ....THE JAILER 227   36
   IMAGINE IT --- ....LETTER IN NOVEMBER 253   25
   MOVING, BEING MOVED. AND WE'LL IMAGINE DIALOGUE OVER A OUIJA BOARD 276   8
IMAGINED (2)
   WE SHALL BOARD OUR IMAGINED SHIP AND WILDLY SAIL .....TALE OF A TUB   25   46
   IN ESTABLISHMENTS WHICH IMAGINED LINES ....POEMS, POTATOES 106   3
IMAGINING (2)
   I TIRE, IMAGINING WHITE NIAGARAS ....MOONRISE   98   22
   IMAGINING HIMSELF A HEADWAITER IN AMERICA, ...CANDLES 149   21
IMMACULATE (2)
   FROST ON A LEAF, THE IMMACULATE ....THE COURIERS 247   7
   THESE BONE SHANKS WILL NOT WAKE IMMACULATE ....THE DEAD 320   10
IMMEDIATELY (4)
   EACH GESTURE FLEES IMMEDIATELY DOWN AN ALLEY ....INSOMNIAC 163   23
   THEY ARE EATEN IMMEDIATELY BY THE PINES. ...STARS OVER THE DORDOGNE 165   8
   WHATEVER I SEE I SWALLOW IMMEDIATELY ....MIRROR 173   2
   THEY MIGHT IGNORE ME IMMEDIATELY ....THE ARRIVAL OF THE BEE BOX 213   31
IMMENSE (3)
   SILVER FACTORY, IMMENSE ....NIGHT SHIFT   76   16
   IMMENSE, BALD, THOUGH BABY-HEADED, ...I WANT, I WANT 106   2
   TO MEND THE IMMENSE SKULL-PLATES AND CLEAR ....THE COLOSSUS 129   14
IMMINENT (1)
   IT'S NOT SO IMMINENT. AT LEAST I FEEL ..DIALOGUE OVER A OUIJA BOARD 278   61
IMMORAL (1)
   AND HOTHOUSE ROSES SHED IMMORAL BLOOMS. ....FEMALE AUTHOR 301   8
IMMORTAL (5)
   THEN I SAW WHAT THE TROUBLE WAS: SHE THOUGHT SHE WAS IMMORTAL. ...
                                                     ... IN PLASTER 159   35
   COMPARED WITH ME, A TREE IS IMMORTAL ....I AM VERTICAL 162   8
   OF IMMORTAL BLANKNESS BETWEEN STARS ....WIDOW 164   24
   WHAT IMMORTALITY IS. THAT IT IS IMMORTAL. ......BURNING THE LETTERS 205   56
   LOUD THE IMMORTAL NIGHTINGALES DECLARE: ....TO EVA DESCENDING. 303   13
IMMORTALITY (2)
   THERE IS NO TALK OF IMMORTALITY AMONG THESE! .........APPREHENSIONS 196   18
   WHAT IMMORTALITY IS. THAT IT IS IMMORTAL. ......BURNING THE LETTERS 205   56
IMMUNE (1)
   HE IS IMMUNE TO PILLS: RED, PURPLE, BLUE-- ....INSOMNIAC 163   15
IMP (1)
   BUT YET THE PERVERSE IMP WITHIN WILL PROBE*METAMORPHOSES OF THE MOON 308   31
IMPALED (1)
   IMPALED UPON A STERN ANGELIC STARE ....THE TRIAL OF MAN 312   9
IMPASSE (1)
   COME, SO UNLIKE US, TO A STIFF IMPASSE, ...THE OTHER TWO   69   31
IMPATIENT (1)
   "COME, COME," FATHER SHAWN GAVE AN IMPATIENT SHRUG, ...DIALOGUE B.   39   21
IMPECCABLE (2)
   AGAWP AT THE IMPECCABLE MOON. ....LETTER TO A PURIST   37   16
   OF PINK AND BEIGE, IMPECCABLE BAMBOO, ...MORNING IN THE HOS. 332   4
IMPERFECTIONS (2)
   THE NOSE-END THAT TWITCHES, THE OLD IMPERFECTIONS-- COMPANIONABLE. 105   1
   OF IMPERFECTIONS HIS BOWELS WERE PART OF -- ...SUICIDE OFF EGG ROCK 115   4
IMPERISHABLE (1)
   OF THE IMPERISHABLE ....MAGNOLIA SHOALS 122   8
IMPETUOUSLY (1)
   ALL NIGHT I SHALL GALLOP THUS, IMPETUOUSLY, ...ELM 192   10
IMPLACABLE (1)
   MOON-BLANCHED AND IMPLACABLE, HE AND SHE ....THE OTHER TWO   68   22
IMPLACABLY (1)
   IMPLACABLY FROM TWELVE TO ONE. ....LOVE IS A PARALLAX 329   18
IMPORTANT (5)
   THEY WILL WONDER IF I WAS IMPORTANT. ....LAST WORDS 172   9
   I AM IMPORTANT TO HER. SHE COMES AND GOES. ....MIRROR 174   15
   THE FACELESS FACES OF IMPORTANT MEN. ....THREE WOMEN 179   84
   WAS SHE ARRANGING CUPS? IT IS IMPORTANT. ....THE DETECTIVE 208   3
   THESE ARE THE PEOPLE THAT WERE IMPORTANT --- ....TOTEM 264   16
IMPORTUNATE (2)
   WITH MY FANTASY ALONE," BRAGS THE IMPORTUNATE HEAD, ...CONJURING.   66   9
   IMPORTUNATE CRICKET POEM.7.S. 136   12
IMPOSE (2)
   AND WRESTLES TO IMPOSE ...ON THE DIFFICULTY OF CONJURING UP A DRYAD   66   7

	TITLE	PAGE	LINE

IMPOSE (CONT.)
TO IMPOSE ON THE EVENING. ....NIGHT SHIFT   76   5
IMPOSSIBILITY (1)
THAT, IT SEEMS, IS THE IMPOSSIBILITY. ....THE JAILER 227   40
IMPOSSIBLE (4)
SO IT IS IMPOSSIBLE TO TELL HOW MANY THERE ARE. ....TULIPS 160   14
THEY ARE BALD AND IMPOSSIBLE, LIKE THE FACES OF MY CHILDREN, *THREE. 178   66
IS IT IMPOSSIBLE FOR YOU TO LET SOMETHING GO AND HAVE IT GO
    WHOLE? ....A BIRTHDAY PRESENT 207   45
IN THE IMPOSSIBLE MIND'S EYE; ....LOVE IS A PARALLAX 329   3
IMPOSSIBLES (1)
SHEATH OF IMPOSSIBLES, ...PURDAH 243   33
IMPOTENCE (1)
IN IMPOTENCE, TO SUE FOR PEACE, *INSOLENT STORM STRIKES AT THE SKULL 325   4
IMPOTENT (2)
IMPOTENT AS DISTANT THUNDER, ...THE JAILER 227   37
THE IMPOTENT HUSBAND SLUMPS OUT FOR A COFFEE. ....LESBOS 228   44
IMPOUNDED (1)
HE KEPT THE SOW -- IMPOUNDED FROM PUBLIC STARE. ....SOW   60   5
IMPRESS (1)
BUT EVEN HER TONNAGE DOESN'T IMPRESS A DIAMOND. ....THE RIVAL/DR 291   24
IMPRESSION (1)
YOU LEAVE THE SAME IMPRESSION ....THE RIVAL 166   2
IMPROBABLE (1)
BLUE AND IMPROBABLE PERSON ....THE BURNT-OUT SPA 138   25
IMPROMPTU (2)
SNUBS IMPROMPTU SPIELS OF WIND ....CONJURING.   66   6
AND OLD MAIDS ON IMPROMPTU PETTICOATS FLY ....SONG FOR A REVOLU. 323   15
IMPS (1)
MINOR IMPS PIPE UP, SO LONG AS EACH ....DIALOGUE OVER A OUIJA BOARD 280 152
IMPULSE (1)
YOU SCUTTLE OUT ON IMPULSE ....SPIDER   48   2
IN (1138)
I-N (1)
IS HE, THEN? HE SPELLS. I-N. HE'LL LIFT *DIALOGUE OVER A OUIJA BOARD 278   76
INACCESSIBLE (2)
THE BLIND, WHITE, AWFUL, INACCESSIBLE SLANT. ..NEW YEAR ON DARTMOOR 176   5
THE STARCHED, INACCESSIBLE BREAST. ....PARALYTIC 266   16
INANE (4)
CORRIDOR OF INANE REPLICAS, ...LANDOWNERS   53   8
INANE WORLDS OF WIND AND CLOUD. ....SCULPTOR   91   13
COGS AND DISKS, INANE MECHANIC WHIMS, ...SONNET: TO EVA 304   7
WHEN, FROM THE INANE OVERHEAD ....DIALOGUE EN ROUTE 309   40
INAUSPICIOUS (1)
IN SULLEN LIGHT OF THE INAUSPICIOUS DAY. ....CHANNEL CROSSING   27   25
INCALCULABLE (1)
THE INCALCULABLE MALICE OF THE EVERYDAY. ....THREE WOMEN 184 287
INCANDESCENT (3)
LEAN INCANDESCENT ....BLACK ROOK IN RAINY WEATHER   57   15
THE OVENS GLOWED LIKE HEAVENS, INCANDESCENT. ....MARY'S SONG 257   18
INCANDESCENT AS A GOD; ....TO A JILTED LOVER 310   15
INCAPABLE (2)
I AM INCAPABLE OF MORE KNOWLEDGE. ....ELM 193   37
WHO WHEEZES AT THE GATE. INCAPABLE ....FEVER. 231   5
INCENSE (3)
INCENSE OF DEATH. YOUR DAY APPROACHES. ....THE MANOR GARDEN 125   2
INCENSE. PALE MOSS DRIPS ....DARK WOOD, DARK WATER 127   2
INCENSE IN MY TRACK. ....GETTING THERE 249   63
INCESSANT (3)
THIS CRACKED WORLD'S INCESSANT GABBLE AND HISS. ....STREET SONG   36   30
GAVE WAY TO FIELDS AND THE INCESSANT SEETHE OF GRASSES*HARDCASTLE C.   62   9
ON THE INCESSANT HEAT-LIGHTNING FLICKER OF SITUATIONS. ...INSOMNIAC 163   28
INCESSANTLY (1)
LET HER DIE THERE, OR WITHER INCESSANTLY FOR THE NEXT FIFTY
    YEARS, ...FACE LIFT 156   29
INCH (9)
INCH BY BRIGHT INCH ....SOUTHERN SUNRISE   26   14
INCH BY BRIGHT INCH ....SOUTHERN SUNRISE   26   14
GIVEN AN INCH. NOT THAT THEY'RE GROSS (ALTHOUGH ....POEMS, POTATOES 106   6
THE COW MILKS CREAM AN INCH THICK. ....THE TIMES ARE TIDY 107   15
YOU DIDN'T JUST TOE ME AN INCH, NO -- ....LOVE LETTER 147   5
HE FLOATS AN INCH FROM THE CEILING, ...THE SURGEON AT 2 A.M. 171   45
TO GIVE ANOTHER INCH. IF YOU PREFER, ...DIALOGUE OVER A OUIJA BOARD 281 179
DEVOURING GREEN GARDENS INCH BY INCH. ....EPITAPH IN THREE PARTS 337   17
DEVOURING GREEN GARDENS INCH BY INCH. ....EPITAPH IN THREE PARTS 337   17
INCHED (2)
INCHED FROM THEIR PIGMY BURROWS ....MUSSEL HUNTER AT ROCK HARBOR   96   29
THE SHADOWS OF THE GRASSES INCHED ROUND LIKE HANDS OF A CLOCK,*BABY. 175   43
INCHING (1)
INCHING OFF IN THE GRAY CHEVROLET, DRINKING THE GREEN ......WAKING. 151   6
INCHWORMS (1)
THEY CONVERSE IN THE VALLEY OF YOUR FINGERS, THEY ARE INCHWORMS. ...
    ... GULLIVER 251   17
INCLINATION (1)
BETWEEN STEEL PALMS OF INCLINATION, TAKE IT, ...SONNET: TO EVA 304   3

	TITLE	PAGE	LINE

INCLUDES (1)
HOW BEAUTIFULLY THE LIGHT INCLUDES THESE THINGS. ....THREE WOMEN 186 353
I-N-C-O (1)
AS IF BLOODHOUNDS BORE HIM DOWN. I-N-C-O ...   .DIALOGUE O. 283 275
INCOHERENCES (1)
EARS CUPPING THE SEA'S INCOHERENCES, ...MEDUSA 224 3
INCOHERENT (1)
INCOHERENT SCRAPS OF TALK ....FAMILY REUNION 300 3
INCOMMUNICADO (1)
INCOMMUNICADO ....INCOMMUNICADO 100 T
INCOMPARABLE (1)
SWITCHED HER INCOMPARABLE BACK ....VIRGIN IN A TREE 81 10
INCOMPATIBLE (1)
INCOMPATIBLE MODES OF TIME, THE RAW MATERIAL*THE GHOST'S LEAVETAKING 90 13
INCONGRUOUS (1)
WHICH CONCEAL INCONGRUOUS ................METAMORPHOSES OF THE MOON 307 27
INCONSEQUENT (1)
OTHERWISE INCONSEQUENT ....BLACK ROOK IN RAINY WEATHER 57 20
INCONSPICUOUS (1)
YOUR ABSENCE IS INCONSPICUOUS; ....PARLIAMENT HILL FIELDS 152 4
INCONSTANT (1)
BEYOND THE INCONSTANT GREEN ....TOUCH-AND-GO 335 6
INCREASE (2)
PLAYS HOSTESS TO TABBY, TOM AND INCREASE, ...ELLA MASON A. 53 10
WILL BRING CROP'S INCREASE, AND HARVEST FRUIT ....CRYSTAL GAZER 55 17
INCREASES (1)
THE MASK INCREASES, EATS THE WORM, ...THE FEARFUL 256 5
INCREDIBLE (1)
HOPING FOR SOME INCREDIBLE DARK MAN*MORNING IN THE HOSPITAL SOLARIUM 333 23
INCREDULOUS (1)
THE PRINCESS COAXES THE INCREDULOUS BOY*THE PRINCESS AND THE GOBLINS 334 51
INDEFATIGABLE (4)
INDEFATIGABLE FACT. ....NIGHT SHIFT 77 24
INDEFATIGABLE, PURPLE. MUST IT BE CUT OUT? ....COURAGE. 210 18
INDEFATIGABLE COUSIN ....PURDAH 242 12
THE INDEFATIGABLE HOOF-TAPS. ....WORDS 270 17
INDELIBLE (3)
WAVERY, INDELIBLE, TRUE ....A SECRET 219 11
THE INDELIBLE SMELL ....FEVER. 231 9
THE INDELIBLE BUDS, ...THALIDOMIDE 252 11
INDEPENDENCY (1)
AN OBSTINATE INDEPENDENCY ....THE COURAGE OF SHUTTING-UP 210 34
INDEPENDENT (1)
INDEPENDENT REBEL FIRES ....INSOLENT STORM STRIKES AT THE SKULL 326 34
INDESTRUCTIBLE (2)
AND APPARENTLY INDESTRUCTIBLE. ....A WINTER SHIP 112 4
YOUR FACETS ARE INDESTRUCTIBLE; ....THE RIVAL/DR 291 25
INDETERMINATE (2)
INDETERMINATE CRIMINAL, ...THE JAILER 227 33
GRAY, INDETERMINATE GILT ....LYONNESSE 234 6
INDEX (2)
INDEX THE ARROW, ...WORDS FOR A NURSERY 73 14
TABLE, TRYING OUR LUCK, INDEX FINGERS SET ....DIALOGUE O. 276 4
INDIA (1)
ON INDIA, AFRICA, AMERICA, THESE MIRACULOUS ONES, ...THREE WOMEN 183 229
INDIAN (2)
ACROSS THE INDIAN CARPET, THE COLD FLOOR, ...BY CANDLELIGHT 237 25
APRIL SNOWDROP, INDIAN PIPE, ...CHILD 265 5
INDIANS (1)
THE PILGRIMS AND INDIANS MIGHT NEVER HAVE HAPPENED. ......TWO CAMP. 145 22
INDIAN'S (1)
THE INDIAN'S AXED YOUR SCALP. ....CUT 235 10
INDIFFERENCE (3)
THE STOMACH OF INDIFFERENCE, THE WORDLESS CUPBOARD. POEM.7.S. 136 6
ANGELS SWIM IN IT, AND THE STARS, IN INDIFFERENCE ALSO. ...
                                       ... APPREHENSIONS 195 3
OF INDIFFERENCE! ....THALIDOMIDE 252 22
INDIFFERENT (2)
OF HER HEART, WAS THE HUMPED INDIFFERENT IRON .....HARDCASTLE CRAGS 63 28
NEITHER CRUEL NOR INDIFFERENT, ...WINTERING 218 20
INDIGENOUS (1)
INDIGENOUS PEACE. SUCH SUBSTANCE MAKES ....LANDOWNERS 53 11
INDIGESTIBLE (1)
SOME THINGS OF THIS WORLD ARE INDIGESTIBLE. ......ZOO KEEPER'S WIFE 155 16
INDIGNANT (1)
AT HIS WORDS, THE INDIGNANT GODMOTHER   THE PRINCESS AND THE GOBLINS 335 69
INDIGO (4)
PASSENGERS UNDER AN INDIGO FIZZLE ....ALICANTE LULLABY 43 9
EXHALES AN INDIGO NIMBUS, ...PARLIAMENT HILL FIELDS 153 46
FROM ITS COLD INDIGO. ....EVENT 194 5
DEEP IN LIQUID INDIGO ....AQUATIC NOCTURNE 305 1
INDISSOLUBLE (1)
INDISSOLUBLE ENOUGH TO RIDDLE THE GUTS ....PERSEUS 82 4
INDIVIDUAL (1)
YET INDIVIDUAL PLANET ....TRIO OF LOVE SONGS 313 3

| | | TITLE | PAGE | LINE |

INDOLENCE (2)
HANDS LACED, IN A MOONY INDOLENCE OF LOVE -- ....WATERCOLOR. 112 25
THE LIQUOR OF INDOLENCE, AND ALL THINGS SINK POEM.5.F. 134 8
INDOLENT (1)
TAXIS INDOLENT ON WHISPERED WHEELS;*MORNING IN THE HOSPITAL SOLARIUM 332 11
INDOORS (2)
INDOORS WITH POLITIC GOODWILL, NOT HASTE ...THE SNOWMAN ON THE MOOR 58 11
INDOORS, TIFFANY'S PHOENIX RISES ....YADDO: THE GRAND MANOR 123 13
INDULGE (1)
TO INDULGE MY EXTRAVAGANT WANTS." ....DIALOGUE EN ROUTE 308 12
INDUSTRIOUS (1)
OPENING, IN SPRING, LIKE AN INDUSTRIOUS VIRGIN ....STINGS 215 35
INEFFECTUAL (1)
THE SEA, ALSO, IS INEFFECTUAL. ....THE RIVAL/DR 291 15
INELUCTABLY (1)
LAP AT MY BACK INELUCTABLY. ....THREE WOMEN 185 293
INEPT (1)
CONFOUNDED INEPT GUESSWORK: ....NIGHT SHIFT 76 14
INERADICABLE (1)
THEN THERE ARE THE STARS -- INERADICABLE, HARD. ....EVENT 194 10
INERT (2)
INERT AS A SHOELACE; DEAD ....MEDALLION 124 4
SITTING UNDER A POTLID, TINY AND INERT AS A RICE GRAIN. ..POEM.6.W. 135 15
INESCAPABLE (1)
ITS CARGO OF AGONY TOWARD ME, INESCAPABLE, TIDAL. ......THREE WOMEN 179 110
INEVITABLY (1)
DREAM OF A DUEL THEY WILL WIN INEVITABLY, ...THE BEE MEETING 212 46
INEXORABLE (1)
INEXORABLE. AND THEIR PRIDE! ....GETTING THERE 248 16
INFAMOUS (2)
I AM THE GHOST OF AN INFAMOUS SUICIDE, ...ELECTRA ON AZALEA PATH 117 42
FROM THEIR FOND, FINAL, INFAMOUS DECAY. ....THE DEAD 320 14
INFAMOUSLY (1)
OFF-STAGE AND INFAMOUSLY WRAPPED ....SPIDER 49 33
INFANT (1)
TO THIS INFANT STILL IN A BIRTH-DROWSE? ....CANDLES 149 33
INFANTS (1)
PINK-BUTTOCKED INFANTS ATTEND THEM. ....HEAVY WOMEN 158 15
INFECT (1)
COUNTS. SUCH DUELS INFECT BEST FRIENDSHIPS. PAN ....DIALOGUE O. 283 271
INFER (1)
AGAIN WE ARE DELUDED AND INFER ....APRIL AUBADE 312 13
INFERNAL (1)
THE INFERNAL HAUNT OF DEMON DANGERS; ....DOOM OF EXILES 318 6
INFERNO (1)
ON THE INFERNO OF AFRICAN ORANGES, THE HEEL-HUNG PIGS.   THREE WOMEN 184 283
INFINITE (4)
INFINITE NUMBER SEEMS TO BE THE ISSUE UP THERE. ....STARS OVER. 165 21
INFINITE, GREEN, UTTERLY UNTOUCHABLE. ...............APPREHENSIONS 195 2
IN NETS OF THE INFINITE, ...TOTEM 265 32
WHERE ANCIENT, INFINITE, AND BEAUTIFUL,*THE PRINCESS AND THE GOBLINS 333 14
INFINITELY (2)
INFINITELY DELICATE AND INFINITELY EXPENSIVE. ....FEVER. 232 39
INFINITELY DELICATE AND INFINITELY EXPENSIVE. ....FEVER. 232 39
INFINITESIMAL (1)
TONIGHT, IN THE INFINITESIMAL LIGHT OF THE STARS, ...I AM VERTICAL 162 11
INFINITY (1)
MULTIPLIED TO INFINITY LIKE ANGELS ON A PINHEAD ..ZOO KEEPER'S WIFE 155 22
INFLAME (2)
AND INFLAME TO DANGER ....ON LOOKING INTO THE EYES OF A DEMON LOVER 325 15
SHOULD INFLAME THE SLEEPING TOWN. ....LOVE IS A PARALLAX 329 30
INFLAMMATION (1)
HOW THE SUN'S POULTICE DRAWS ON MY INFLAMMATION. ....BERCK-PLAGE 196 2
INFLUENCE (1)
THOSE SUGARY PLANETS WHOSE INFLUENCE WON FOR HIM ....INSOMNIAC 163 17
INFREQUENT (1)
INFREQUENT AS A MOON OF GREENCHEESE ....APRIL 18 302 8
I-N-G-O-D-H-E-A-D (1)
TO THE END OF IT. HE STARTS AGAIN: I-N-G-O-D-H-E-A-D. *DIALOGUE O. 282 217-18
I-N-G-O-D-P-I-E (1)
HE GOES . . . I-N-G-O-D-P-I-E. ......DIALOGUE OVER A OUIJA BOARD 282 209-10
INHABIT (4)
A THICKET OF SHADOWS IS A POOR COAT. I INHABIT POEM.6.W. 135 2
A COOL WIND SHOULD INHABIT THOSE LEAVES   SLEEP IN THE MOJAVE DESERT 144 8
FUMY, SPIRITOUS MISTS INHABIT THIS PLACE   THE MOON AND THE YEW TREE 172 5
YOU INHABIT. PLAINLY AS YOU CAN, ...DIALOGUE OVER A OUIJA BOARD 283 273
INHABITANTS (1)
THE INHABITANTS ARE LIGHT AS CORK, ...A LIFE 150 9
INHABITED (2)
FROM YOUR BLUE PALLOR, I'D SAY YOU INHABITED THE FROZEN WASTE ...
               ... DIALOGUE BETWEEN GHOST AND PRIEST 38 14
I AM INHABITED BY A CRY. ....ELM 193 28
INHALATION (1)
BURN, FOR YOUR INHALATION, ...EAVESDROPPER 260 17

		TITLE	PAGE	LINE

INHERIT (2)
YOU INHERIT WHITE HEATHER, A BEE'S WING, ...THE MANOR GARDEN 125 12
INHERIT THE EARTH. ....MUSHROOMS 140 32
INIMICAL (1)
INIMICAL NOW. THE GREAT GREEN ROCK ....GREEN ROCK. 105 10
INITIATED (1)
INITIATED BY THE LUNAR LAMP, ...THE PRINCESS AND THE GOBLINS 333 19
INJURE (3)
INSTEAD, THE DEAD INJURE ME WITH ATTENTIONS, AND NOTHING CAN HAPPEN. ...
... BARREN WOMAN 157 8
WHO INJURE MY SLEEP WITH THEIR WHITE EYES, THEIR FINGERLESS
HANDS. ....THREE WOMEN 185 321
TURN BACK TO INJURE ......ON LOOKING INTO THE EYES OF A DEMON LOVER 325 13
INJURED (1)
WHOSE HOLY BLUE ANOINTS HER INJURED HAND. ....THE PRINCESS. 333 6
INJURIES (1)
NO DEATHS, NO PRODIGIOUS INJURIES ....AFTERMATH 113 6
INJURY (1)
SOME STRANGE INJURY ....FULL FATHOM FIVE 92 18
INK (1)
COMMANDING THAT CORKSCREW COMET JET FORTH INK .....SONNET TO SATAN 323 5
INKLINGS (1)
HIS DRIFT ENDORSES YOUR INKLINGS OF A DOOM ....DIALOGUE O. 281 190
INKS (1)
THE WET DAWN INKS ARE DOING THEIR BLUE DISSOLVE. ......WINTER TREES 257 1
INLAND (2)
TO THIS CREST OF GRASS. INLAND, THEY ARGUE, PARLIAMENT HILL FIELDS 152 7
THEY PASS THE WAY GULLS PASS INLAND IN THEIR WHITE CAPS, ...TULIPS 160 12
INMATES (1)
INMATES WHO DON'T HIBERNATE. POEM.1.WHO. 131 15
INNARDS (2)
AND INNARDS BLEACHED AND BLOWN OFF ....MUSSEL HUNTER AT ROCK HARBOR 97 72
WHERE HIS INNARDS BULGED AS IF ....MEDALLION 125 23
INNER (3)
WHAT THE SEASHELL SPOKE TO HIS INNER EAR ON THE DECLINE OF ORACLES 78 7
AS YOU ETCH ON THE INNER WINDOW OF YOUR EYE ....VIRGIN IN A TREE 82 34
YOU'D PRESUME YOUR INNER VOICE GOD-PLUMED ENOUGH ....DIALOGUE O. 280 168
INNOCENCE (4)
PLUCKED BACK THUS SUDDEN TO THAT FAR INNOCENCE, ...DREAM WITH C. 44 21
SMALL AS A DOLL IN MY DRESS OF INNOCENCE ...ELECTRA ON AZALEA PATH 116 11
CAN SUCH INNOCENCE KILL AND KILL? IT MILKS MY LIFE. ....THREE WOMEN 180 134
IS ALWAYS TO BE MADE: INNOCENCE .........METAMORPHOSES OF THE MOON 308 40
INNOCENT (1)
WHAT IS IT THAT FLINGS THESE INNOCENT SOULS AT US? .....THREE WOMEN 183 218
INNUMERABLE (3)
OF INNUMERABLE MELONS, ...FIESTA MELONS 46 3
THE DYING GAUL AND THOSE INNUMERABLE PIETAS ....PERSEUS 82 9
BREED INNUMERABLE BILLS, BONA FIDE: ....DIALOGUE EN ROUTE 308 17
INQUIRING (1)
THAT NO STRAIGHT INQUIRING ....FIRESONG 30 11
INSANE (1)
INSANE FOR THE DESTINATION, ...GETTING THERE 249 57
INSATIABLE (1)
IN THE SECOND YEAR. IT HAD BEEN INSATIABLE ....THE DETECTIVE 209 28
INSATIATE (1)
INSATIATE, HE RANSACKS THE LAND ....PURSUIT 22 13
INSCRUTABLE (1)
SKULLS. INSCRUTABLE, ...FULL FATHOM FIVE 93 36
INSECTS (1)
THE INSECTS ARE SCANT, SKINNY. ....FROG AUTUMN 99 2
INSEPARABLE (1)
I SEE US FLOATING THERE YET, INSEPARABLE -- TWO CORK DOLLS. ..BABY. 175 41
INSERT (1)
COLD GLASS, HOW YOU INSERT YOURSELF ....THE OTHER 202 26
INSIDE (2)
INSIDE THE CHURCH, THE SAINTS WILL BE ALL BLUE, ...MOON. 173 24
WHO PEERS INSIDE ....ON LOOKING INTO THE EYES OF A DEMON LOVER 325 6
INSIGHT (1)
AN INSIGHT LIKE THE FLIGHT OF BIRDS: ....LOVE IS A PARALLAX 330 60
INSINUATE (1)
NOW LITTLE WEEDS INSINUATE ....THE BURNT-OUT SPA 138 10
INSIST (1)
SOFT FISTS INSIST ON ....MUSHROOMS 139 10
INSISTS (1)
WHO INSISTS HIS PLAYMATES RUN. ....LOVE IS A PARALLAX 329 24
INSOLENT (2)
INSOLENT STORM STRIKES AT THE SKULL ....INSOLENT STORM. 325 T
INSOLENT STORM STRIKES AT THE SKULL, ...INSOLENT STORM. 325 1
INSOLVENT (1)
INSOLVENT AMONG THE MOUNTAINS. ....THE COURAGE OF SHUTTING-UP 210 35
INSOMNIAC (1)
INSOMNIAC ....INSOMNIAC 163 T
INSPIRES (1)
SCINTILLANT IRONY INSPIRES .....INSOLENT STORM STRIKES AT THE SKULL 326 33

TITLE   PAGE LINE

INSTANT (1)
  MOUTH'S INSTANT FLARE FOR FUTURE LOOKS; *EPITAPH FOR FIRE AND FLOWER   45 11
INSTEAD (14)
  WITH RADIANCE, PEACOCK-COLORED; INSTEAD, BLEAK ROCKS ....CHANNEL C. 27 22
  DOWN FROM PRIDE'S SIZE: INSTEAD, A GRISLY-THEWED, ...SNOWMAN O. 59 29
  INSTEAD, A WANTON FIT ....ON THE PLETHORA OF DRYADS 67 25
  AND ARE MET, INSTEAD, BY THIS ICERIBBED SHIP, ...A WINTER SHIP 113 25
  INSTEAD, THE DEAD INJURE ME WITH ATTENTIONS, AND NOTHING CAN HAPPEN. ...
                  ... BARREN WOMAN 157   8
  AWAY ON WHEELS, INSTEAD OF LEGS, THEY SERVE AS WELL. ...THREE WOMEN 184 254
  HE WORE INSTEAD OF A HAT. ....STINGS 215 44
  IT IS TATE AND LYLE THEY LIVE ON, INSTEAD OF FLOWERS. ....WINTERING 218 29
  A CLEFT IN YOUR CHIN INSTEAD OF YOUR FOOT ....DADDY 223 53
  MY THUMB INSTEAD OF AN ONION. ....CUT 235   2
  INSTEAD OF DEAD FURNITURE! ....BALLOONS 271 11
  INSTEAD OF BREWING US SUCH A BALDERDASH *DIALOGUE OVER A OUIJA BOARD 279 97
  INSTEAD OF FAT FISH ON THE LINE, YOU'VE PLUMBED ....*DIALOGUE O. 282 242
  BENEATH THE FLAT HANDKERCHIEF YOU WEAR INSTEAD OF A HAT.*DIALOGUE O. 293   6
INSTILLED (1)
  THE MILK YOUR LOVE INSTILLED IN THEM. ....POINT SHIRLEY 111 42
INSTINCT (3)
  INSTINCT FOR ART BEGAN WITH THE BULL'S HORN LOFTING IN THE MOB'S ...
                  ... THE GORING 47   8
  OBEYING ORDERS OF INSTINCT TILL SWEPT ....SPIDER 49 32
  LURKED THE BURLESQUE INSTINCT OF THE HAM; ....DIRGE FOR A JOKER 302   6
INSTRUCTIVE (1)
  HOW INSTRUCTIVE THIS IS! ....THE SWARM 217 46
INSTRUCTS (1)
  HOW THIS TART FABLE INSTRUCTS ....VIRGIN IN A TREE 81   1
INSTRUMENT (2)
  I FEEL IT ENTER ME, COLD, ALIEN, LIKE AN INSTRUMENT. ...THREE WOMEN 182 183
  NOW THE ROOM IS AHISS. THE INSTRUMENT ....WORDS HEARD. 203 11
INSTRUMENTS (4)
  HAVE BEEN HOWLING LIKE WOMEN, OR DAMAGED INSTRUMENTS. ....INSOMNIAC 163 30
  I HAVE SEEN THE WHITE CLEAN CHAMBER WITH ITS INSTRUMENTS. ...THREE. 180 121
  WITH THEIR HEARTS THAT TICK AND TICK, WITH THEIR SATCHELS OF
      INSTRUMENTS. ....THREE WOMEN 180 138
  AMONG THE BLANCHED, BOILED INSTRUMENTS, THE VIRGINAL CURTAINS. ...
                  ... FEVER./DR 294   8
INSUFFERABLE (1)
  THE INSUFFERABLE NIMBUS OF THE LOT-DRAWN ....THE THIN PEOPLE 64 21
INSULTS (2)
  STILL RINGING WITH BRUIT OF INSULTS AND DISHONORS ....SNOWMAN O. 58   3
  HIS BOOK OF INSULTS. NERVE OR NOUMENON, *DIALOGUE OVER A OUIJA BOARD 284 297
INSURGENT (1)
  AS NO MERE INSURGENT MAN COULD HOPE TO BREAK ....SPINSTER 50 28
INTACT (3)
  BY A MAD MIRACLE I GO INTACT ....STREET SONG 35   1
  INTACT, STRANGELY STRAYED ABOVE ....MUSSEL HUNTER AT ROCK HARBOR 97 70
  AND KEEP THEIR SHAPES INTACT WHILE SUN ....CHILD'S PARK STONES 101 12
INTELLECTUAL (1)
  NOW YOU, MY INTELLECTUAL LEPRECHAUN, ...LOVE IS A PARALLAX 329 25
INTELLIGENCE (1)
  IS A FAIRY-TALE; INTELLIGENCE ............METAMORPHOSES OF THE MOON 308 41
INTENSE (1)
  IN TIME OUR RELATIONSHIP GREW MORE INTENSE. ....IN PLASTER 159 28
INTENSELY (1)
  THE SMILE OF A MAN OF BUSINESS, INTENSELY PRACTICAL. .....THE SWARM 217 52
INTENSITY (1)
  AND INTENSITY BY MIDNIGHT ....CHILD'S PARK STONES 101 19
INTENT (2)
  I FELT A STILL BUSYNESS, AN INTENT. ....THE RABBIT CATCHER 194 21
  CAN RECTIFY TRUANT INTENT ......INSOLENT STORM STRIKES AT THE SKULL 326 27
INTENTION (1)
  AND I HAVE NO INTENTION OF DISPARAGING THEM*QUEEN MARY'S ROSE GARDEN 290 19
INTERCEPTING (1)
  INTERCEPTING THE BLUE BOLTS OF A COLD MOON? ....THREE WOMEN 185 291
INTERESTS (1)
  IT IS THE EXCEPTION THAT INTERESTS THE DEVIL. ....THREE WOMEN 186 331
INTERIOR (3)
  COOL AS THE PEARLED INTERIOR OF A CONCH. ....THE OTHER TWO 68   2
  HIS HEAD IS A LITTLE INTERIOR OF GRAY MIRRORS. ....INSOMNIAC 163 22
  THE GIGANTIC GORILLA INTERIOR .... GETTING THERE 247   3
INTERIORS (1)
  A GALLERY OF CREAKING PORCHES AND STILL INTERIORS, THE BABYSITTERS 175 34
INTERTWINED (1)
  COUPLED BY BRANCHES INTERTWINED ....CRYSTAL GAZER 55 14
INTERVAL (2)
  THUS HALLOWING AN INTERVAL ....BLACK ROOK IN RAINY WEATHER 57 19
  BEYOND THE INTERVAL OF NOW AND HERE: ....TWO LOVERS. 327 11
INTIMATE (1)
  I AM INTIMATE WITH A HAIRY SPIRIT. POEM.6.W. 135 11
INTIMATELY (1)
  I KNOW HER. I KNOW HER INTIMATELY -- ....THREE WOMEN 181 157
INTO (109)

```
                                                    TITLE          PAGE  LINE
INTOLERABLE (2)
   INTOLERABLE VOWELS ENTER MY HEART.  .........................EVENT   194   6
   INTOLERABLE, WITHOUT MIND.  . ..............THE MUNICH MANNEQUINS   263  15
INTOLERABLY (1)
   FOUND HERSELF, OF A SUDDEN, INTOLERABLY STRUCK  ...........SPINSTER    49   4
INTOLERANT (1)
   INTOLERANT BEAUTY NEVER WILL BE LEARNING.  .......TO EVA DESCENDING.  303  17
INTRACTABLE (3)
   SHE STALKED INTRACTABLE AS A DRIVEN GHOST  ..THE SNOWMAN ON THE MOOR    58  15
   BEATING AND BEATING AT AN INTRACTABLE METAL.  .........BLACKBERRYING   169  27
   A BLACK INTRACTABLE MIND.  ................................THE SWARM   217  58
INTRANSIGENT (1)
   EVER BLUR THE INTRANSIGENT LINES WHICH DRAW  ..........TALE OF A TUB    25  28
INTRICATE (6)
   MIRRORED THE INTRICATE GESTURES OF TWO OTHERS.  .......THE OTHER TWO    68  14
   SET IN AN INTRICATE WILDERNESS OF GREEN  ..................YADWIGHA.    85   5
   THE INTRICATE, BLUE PIPING UNDER THIS PALE MARBLE.  ........SURGEON.   171  26
   THE MOON SNAGS IN HER INTRICATE NERVOUS SYSTEM.  ..............ELM/DR   292   3
   OF INTRICATE SPUNGLASS ROUTINE,  ...MORNING IN THE HOSPITAL SOLARIUM   332  20
   FLEW FROM THE INTRICATE EMBROIDERY  ....THE PRINCESS AND THE GOBLINS   333   8
INTRIGUING (1)
   IS MY LIFE SO INTRIGUING?  ...............................THE OTHER   201   9
INTRODUCE (1)
   GOD-PIE. WHY, THEN, DID YOU DEIGN TO INTRODUCE  .........DIALOGUE O.   283  251
INTRUDES (1)
   INTRUDES EVEN WHEN THE REVOLTED EYE  ..................TALE OF A TUB    25  30
INTUITIONS (1)
   OF OUR TWO INTUITIONS. AND IF HE IS?  ...DIALOGUE OVER A OUIJA BOARD   279  107
INUNDATING (1)
   INUNDATING EDEN'S QUIET;  .......INSOLENT STORM STRIKES AT THE SKULL   326  22
INVADE (2)
   INVADE THE CLOISTRAL EYE LIKE PAGES  ......ON THE DECLINE OF ORACLES    78  23
   I INVADE MY LION'S DEN;  .....................CIRCUS IN THREE RINGS   321   8
INVADES (1)
   INVADES THE DILATE LENS OF GENESIS  .................SONNET TO SATAN   323  10
INVALID (1)
   OR THE HANDS OF AN INVALID. THE WAN  .........PARLIAMENT HILL FIELDS   152   9
INVALIDS (1)
   KINDLY WITH INVALIDS AND MAWKISH WOMEN,  ...................CANDLES   149  25
INVEIGLED (1)
   INVEIGLED TO FORSAKE THE SOD.  ........................DANSE MACABRE   321  18
INVENTIVE (1)
   FROM ASKING, BUT INVENTIVE, HOPES; IN VAIN*METAMORPHOSES OF THE MOON   307  11
INVERTED (1)
   ON THE ROUND BASE OF THE INVERTED WINE-GLASS HERE,  .....DIALOGUE O.   276   5
INVERTS (1)
   THE WORLD INVERTS:  .......ON LOOKING INTO THE EYES OF A DEMON LOVER   325  10
INVETERATE (2)
   DRY-EYED, THE INVETERATE PATRIARCH  ...................I WANT, I WANT   106   9
   EACH ONE AN INVETERATE GALLANT  ..................DIALOGUE EN ROUTE   309  21
INVIOLATE (2)
   HEDGED IN AND EVIDENTLY INVIOLATE  .........QUEEN MARY'S ROSE GARDEN   290  15
   INVIOLATE IN THE CIRCLE OF THAT SKEIN, *THE PRINCESS AND THE GOBLINS   334  47
INVISIBLE (3)
   NIGHTLONG, IN THE GRANITE YARD, INVISIBLE CATS  ...........INSOMNIAC   163  29
   FLOATED ON A GLASS THAT WAS INVISIBLE.  ....................GULLIVER   251   4
   INVISIBLE AIR DRIFTS,  ....................................BALLOONS   271   6
INVISIBLES (2)
   NOTHING WENT MOLDY. THE LITTLE INVISIBLES  ............POEM.4.BEAST.   134   5
   FILLING MY VEINS WITH INVISIBLES, WITH THE MILLION  .......BIRTHDAY.   207  42
INVITE (1)
   TOO CLOSE ATTENTION, THEY WILL INVITE ME  .........WUTHERING HEIGHTS   167  17
INVOKE (1)
   THAN PRIEST'S HANDS, INVOKE NO VAIN  ......................SCULPTOR    91   6
INVOLVED (3)
   AND THE INVOLVED MALADIES OF AUTUMN,  .................LEAVING EARLY   146  18
   INVOLVED IN ITS WEIRD BLUE DREAMS,  ............BURNING THE LETTERS   205  40
   INVOLVED AS A FOETUS.  ........................BURNING THE LETTERS   205  41
INVOLVES (1)
   FOR YOUR FATE INVOLVES A DARK ASSAILANT."  ...EPITAPH IN THREE PARTS   337   9
IONIAN (1)
   THEN THE FLUTINGS OF THEIR IONIAN  ....................DEATH & CO.   254  17
IRATE (1)
   WHILE THERE IRATE CYRUS  ....................A LESSON IN VENGEANCE    80  16
IRELAND (2)
   ON TRIAL, FROM IRELAND, SHE BURNED BATCH AFTER BATCH OF COOKIES ...
                                   ...  THE BABYSITTERS   175  26
   IT ISN'T ENGLAND, IT ISN'T FRANCE, IT ISN'T IRELAND.  ..STOPPED DEAD   230  10
IRIS (2)
   ALTERS SHADOWS OF ROSE AND IRIS --  ............CHILD'S PARK STONES   101  13
   THE ELATE PALLORS OF FLYING IRIS.  ......................BERCK-PLAGE   199  86
IRON (13)
   FOR THAT BRAG, WE BARNACLE THESE IRON THIGHS."  .........SNOWMAN O.    59  43
   OF HER HEART, WAS THE HUMPED INDIFFERENT IRON  .....HARDCASTLE CRAGS    63  28
   SHIES FROM HIS TOUCH: HIS IS AN IRON MOOD.  ...........THE OTHER TWO    68  19

                            259
```

TITLE PAGE LINE
IRON (CONT)
THE WATER HAD AN IRON TASTE, AND THE AIR, ...SPINACH-PICKER. 89 15
YOUR SPECKLED STONE ASKEW BY AN IRON FENCE. ELECTRA ON AZALEA PATH 117 18
AND THE IRON HILLS THAT ENCLOSE THEM. EARTHEN FINGERS ....NET-. 121 16
IRON ENTRAILS, ENAMEL BOWLS, ...THE BURNT-OUT SPA 138 16
OVER THEIR IRON STILE. AND STILL DON'T SLEEP. ....ZOO KEEPER'S WIFE 155 40
I AM DRAGGED BY THE HORSES, THE IRON HOOVES. ....THREE WOMEN 180 128
SCALLOPS, PURE IRON, ...LETTER IN NOVEMBER 253 20
MY GOD THE IRON LUNG ....PARALYTIC 266 4
TIME IS A GREAT MACHINE OF IRON BARS ....SONNET: TO TIME 311 13
AND CONFRONTS A CAIRN OF IRON ORE. ....THE PRINCESS AND THE GOBLINS 334 43
IRONED (1)
STIPPLE OF SHIFTING WAVE-TIPS IS IRONED OUT, LOST ..ABOVE THE OXBOW 89 46
IRONING (1)
WITH TRIANGULAR SCORCH MARKS FROM IRONING TINY RUCHINGS AND PUFFED
SLEEVES. ... .THE BABYSITTERS 174 15
IRONY (1)
SCINTILLANT IRONY INSPIRES .....INSOLENT STORM STRIKES AT THE SKULL 326 33
IRONY'S (1)
TILL IRONY'S BOUGH BREAK. ....VIRGIN IN A TREE 82 45
IRREFUTABLE (1)
IRREFUTABLE, BEAUTIFULLY SMUG ....HEAVY WOMEN 158 1
IRREGULAR (1)
BY THE BIRDS' IRREGULAR BABEL ....SPINSTER 49 5
IRREPLACEABLE (1)
THE IRREPLACEABLE ....LETTER IN NOVEMBER 254 34
IRREPROACHABLE (1)
IRREPROACHABLE AS ANY LETTUCE HEAD, ...MEMOIRS OF A SPINACH-PICKER 89 10
IRRETRIEVABLE (1)
IRRETRIEVABLE! ....THE NIGHT DANCES 249 2
IRRETRIEVABLES (1)
ARE THOSE THE FACES OF LOVE, THOSE PALE IRRETRIEVABLES? ....ELM 193 35
IRRETRIEVABLY (1)
AS EASILY AND IRRETRIEVABLY ....APRIL 18 302 15
IRRITATING (1)
STRETCHING ITS FINE, IRRITATING SAND IN ALL DIRECTIONS. ..INSOMNIAC 163 7
IS (656)
ISADORA'S (1)
FROM ME LIKE ISADORA'S SCARVES, I'M IN A FRIGHT ....FEVER. 231 12
ISHTAR (1)
AND THE SHINE OF THESE SMALL THINGS SWEETER THAN THE FACE OF ISHTAR. ...
... LAST WORDS 172 26
ISLAND (11)
SO WHEN STAUNCH ISLAND STOCK CHOSE FORFEITURE ....MAYFLOWER 60 9
THE DEER ISLAND PRISON ....MAN IN BLACK 119 7
IT IS TEN YEARS, NOW, SINCE WE ROWED TO CHILDREN'S ISLAND. ...BABY. 174 1
SO WE BOBBED OUT TO THE ISLAND. IT WAS DESERTED -- THE BABYSITTERS 175 33
SHE IS A SMALL ISLAND, ASLEEP AND PEACEFUL, ...THREE WOMEN 184 260
I HAD A DREAM OF AN ISLAND, RED WITH CRIES. ....THREE WOMEN 185 307
A SEA OF DREAMS WASHES THE EDGE OF MY GREEN ISLAND ...QUEEN MARY'S. 290 2
"CRYING, SHE CAME TO THE ISLAND ....THE DREAM 311 13
ALONE TO THAT AUTHENTIC ISLAND WHERE ....A SORCERER B. 324 13
CHIRPS THE FIRST; "LIVE ON A SILENT ISLAND ..EPITAPH IN THREE PARTS 337 5
IN THE AIR ABOVE MY ISLAND FLIES ....EPITAPH IN THREE PARTS 337 12
ISLANDS (1)
AMONG SACRED ISLANDS OF THE MAD TILL DEATH ....TALE OF A TUB 25 47
ISN'T (5)
I AM NOT MYSTICAL: IT ISN'T ....PHEASANT 191 7
IT ISN'T ENGLAND, IT ISN'T FRANCE, IT ISN'T IRELAND. ..STOPPED DEAD 230 10
IT ISN'T ENGLAND, IT ISN'T FRANCE, IT ISN'T IRELAND. ..STOPPED DEAD 230 10
IT ISN'T ENGLAND, IT ISN'T FRANCE, IT ISN'T IRELAND. ..STOPPED DEAD 230 10
ISN'T IN HIM. MAYBE. BUT MAYBE THE POOLS*DIALOGUE OVER A OUIJA BOARD 277 42
ISOLATE (2)
I SHALL NOT BE ACCUSED BY ISOLATE BUTTONS, ...THREE WOMEN 182 198
IT PETRIFIES THE WILL. THESE ARE THE ISOLATE, SLOW FAULTS ......ELM 193 41
ISSUE (3)
INFINITE NUMBER SEEMS TO BE THE ISSUE UP THERE. ....STARS OVER. 165 21
AND FROM THE OPEN MOUTH ISSUE SHARP CRIES ....THREE WOMEN 182 213
YOU'LL ISSUE HIM HIS PASS TO ANGELDOM ..DIALOGUE OVER A OUIJA BOARD 281 192
ISSUING (1)
ISSUING FROM THE STEEL NEEDLE THAT FLIES SO BLINDINGLY? *APPEARANCE. 189 11
IT (600)
ITALIAN (1)
NOW THEY ARE GIVING ME A FASHIONABLE WHITE STRAW ITALIAN HAT ..BEE. 211 21
ITALY (1)
AND THE WHITE CHINA FLYING FISH FROM ITALY. ....LEAVING EARLY 145 6
ITCH (2)
I WEAR THE PRESENT ITCH FOR FLESH, ...THE EYE-MOTE 109 22
MY MENDINGS ITCH. THERE IS NOTHING TO DO. POEM.7.S. 137 44
ITCHED (1)
AND MY SKIN ITCHED AND FLAKED AWAY IN SOFT PIECES ....IN PLASTER 159 33
ITCHES (1)
WHIPPER OF ITCHES, ...WORDS FOR A NURSERY 73 17
ITEM (1)
ITEM: CHUCK OUT ROYAL RIGMAROLE OF PROPS ....A SORCERER B. 324 5

	TITLE	PAGE	LINE

ITEMS (1)
    ARMING MYSELF WITH THE MOST REASONABLE ITEMS ....STREET SONG   36   15
IT'LL (1)
    IT'LL BE LEMON TEA FOR ME, ...THE TOUR 238   38
ITS (201)
IT'S (29)
ITSELF (29)
    SPINS ITSELF FROM UNDER MY FEET; ....SOLILOQUY OF THE SOLIPSIST   37   4
    SHAPING ITSELF FROM THAT MIST. ...DIALOGUE BETWEEN GHOST AND PRIEST   38   10
    CARICATURES ITSELF AND THRIVES ....THE BEGGARS   47   8
    ANCHORED ITSELF, GRIFFIN-LEGGED AND DARKLY GRAINED. ..THE OTHER TWO   68   9
    AS ITSELF -- NO FIDDLER'S ARM ....MUSSEL HUNTER AT ROCK HARBOR   96   34
    THE WOODS CREAK AND ACHE, AND THE DAY FORGETS ITSELF.*PRIVATE GROUND 131   19
    NOW SILENCE AFTER SILENCE OFFERS ITSELF. ....PARLIAMENT HILL FIELDS 152   19
    IN MY COURTYARD A FOUNTAIN LEAPS AND SINKS BACK INTO ITSELF,*BARREN. 157   3
    PLAYING AND RESTING WITHOUT COMMITTING ITSELF. ....TULIPS 161   56
    WIDOW. THE WORD CONSUMES ITSELF -- ....WIDOW 164   1
    WENT ON SHAPING ITSELF WITH LOVE, AS IF I WAS READY. ...THREE WOMEN 178   63
    A BLACK GAP DISCLOSES ITSELF. ....EVENT 195   17
    THERE IS THIS WHITE WALL, ABOVE WHICH THE SKY CREATES ITSELF-- ...
        ... APPREHENSIONS 195   1
    ENGRAVING ITSELF IN SILVER WITH MARVELOUS CALM. ....BERCK-PLAGE 199   72
    HOOKING ITSELF TO ITSELF, ...THE OTHER 201   15
    HOOKING ITSELF TO ITSELF, ...THE OTHER 201   15
    WHERE THE WIRELESS TALKS TO ITSELF LIKE AN ELDERLY RELATIVE. ...
        ... THE DETECTIVE 209   20
    AND THE HIVE ITSELF A TEACUP, ...STINGS 214   8
    IT SPREADS ITSELF OUT, A MILE-LONG BODY OF MEISSEN, ...WINTERING 218   35
    KEEPING ITSELF, IT SEEMS, IN A STATE OF MIRACULOUS REPAIR. ..MEDUSA 225   15
    ALL TO ITSELF ON THE TOP OF EACH ....THE COURIERS 247   9
    THE TRAIN IS DRAGGING ITSELF, IT IS SCREAMING --- ....GETTING THERE 249   55
    AND THE TIGER, EMBELLISHING ITSELF --- ....THE NIGHT DANCES 250   13
    DISCHARGES ITSELF FROM THE TREE WITH NOWHERE TO GO. *CHILDLESS WOMAN 259   3
    SPREADING ITSELF, LIKE BUTTER. .......................EAVESDROPPER 261   51
    THROUGH WHICH THE SKY ETERNALLY THREADS ITSELF? ....TOTEM 264   21
    IS ITSELF AGAIN, AND OURS. THE DREAM ...DIALOGUE OVER A OUIJA BOARD 286 358
    ONE CAMOUFLAGING ITSELF BEHIND ANOTHER. ....THE RIVAL/DR 291   5
    HANGS ITSELF ON ITS OWN ROPE. ...........METAMORPHOSES OF THE MOON 308   42
I'VE (14)
IVORY (7)
    O RED FRUIT, IVORY, FINE TIMBERS! ....METAPHORS 116   4
    WHITE AS BABIES' BEDDING AND GLITTERING WITH DEAD BREATH. O IVORY! ...
        ... A BIRTHDAY PRESENT 206   18
    AS THE MOON, FOR ITS IVORY POWDERS, SCOURS THE SEA. ....STINGS 215   37
    STILL FIGURES OF IVORY. ....THE SWARM 216   12
    GRINNING OVER ITS BONE OF IVORY ....THE SWARM 216   24
    AN IVORY PALACE, A CROTCH PINE. ....THE SWARM 217   50
    THIS IVORY ....CHILDLESS WOMAN 259   9
IVY (2)
    TWINED TO HER HARD LIMBS LIKE IVY: THE PURITAN LIP *VIRGIN IN A TREE   81   12
    DISMEMBERED, TO A TOD OF IVY. ....THE SWARM 217   38
JA (1)
    I REMEMBER YOU PLAYING "JA DA" IN A PINK PIQUE DRESS*THE BABYSITTERS 175   22
JABBERWOCK (1)
    THE JABBERWOCK WILL NOT TRANSLATE HIS SONGS: ....A SORCERER B. 324   11
JABBERWOCKY (1)
    JOG OFF IN JABBERWOCKY NOW AND LOSE US, *DIALOGUE OVER A OUIJA BOARD 279   91
JACK (6)
    TINKER JACK AND THE TIDY WIVES ......TINKER JACK AND THE TIDY WIVES   34   T
    BUT TINKER JACK CAN FORGE ....TINKER JACK AND THE TIDY WIVES   34   17
    JACK WILL TOUCH UP ....TINKER JACK AND THE TIDY WIVES   34   21
    JACK SHALL REPAIR. ....TINKER JACK AND THE TIDY WIVES   34   25
    LET JACK CATCH FIRE." ....TINKER JACK AND THE TIDY WIVES   35   33
    FAGGOT-BEARING JACK IN HIS CRACKLESS EGG: ....MAUDLIN   51   4
JACKANAPES (3)
    E. GODPIE! THAT'S RICH. THE JACKANAPES DIALOGUE OVER A OUIJA BOARD 282 210
    THE BRAZEN JACKANAPES ....TRIO OF LOVE SONGS 314   23
    THAT JAR, WHILE EACH POLEMIC JACKANAPES ....LOVE IS A PARALLAX 330   53
JACKET (2)
    AS WOOD AND FORMAL, IN A JACKET OF ASHES, ...A WINTER SHIP 113   8
    THIS MIZZLE FITS ME LIKE A SAD JACKET. ....LEAVING EARLY 146   39
JACKETS (2)
    GROWNUPS COFFINED IN STOCKINGS AND JACKETS, ...WHITSUN 153   4
    DULLY, UNDER A PACK OF MEN IN RED JACKETS, ...BURNING THE LETTERS 204   13
JACK'S (1)
    SURRENDER: TO BUILD OUR BED AS HIGH AS JACK'S ...LOVE IS A PARALLAX 330   70
JADE (2)
    JADE -- ....PURDAH 242   1
    TODAY WE MOVE IN JADE AND CEASE WITH GARNET ....SONNET: TO TIME 311   1
JADES (1)
    THAT VAIN JADES SULK SINGLE DOWN BRIDAL NIGHTS, ...ELLA MASON A.   54   41
JAG (1)
    FENDING OFF JAG AND TOOTH, ...MISS DRAKE PROCEEDS TO SUPPER   41   22
JAGGED (1)
    AMONG THE JAGGED MAZES OF THE ROCKS. ..THE PRINCESS AND THE GOBLINS 334   34

TITLE   PAGE LINE

JAILER (2)
 THE JAILER ....THE JAILER 226 T
 AS THEIR GOLDEN JAILER ....MOONSONG AT MORNING 317 27
JAM (2)
 THERE, SPRING LAMBS JAM THE SHEEPFOLD. IN AIR ....WATERCOLOR. 111 1
 NEXT TO THE LAST TENANT'S RANCID JAM ....WINTERING 218 8
JAMMY (1)
 OOZING THEIR JAMMY SUBSTANCES, ...THE SURGEON AT 2 A.M. 170 12
JANE (1)
 OF COUSIN JANE, OUR SPINSTER WITH ....FAMILY REUNION 300 17
JANGLE (1)
 WHERE DIAMONDS JANGLE HYMNS WITHIN THE BLOOD ....APRIL AUBADE 312 3
JANGLING (2)
 JANGLING THEIR GREAT MONEY BAGS. ....RHYME 50 8
 AND MOCK THE JANGLING RAIN OF SPLINTERED STARS. ..EPITAPH IN THREE. 337 25
JANUARY (1)
 THE DIAPHANOUS SATINS OF A JANUARY WINDOW ....A BIRTHDAY PRESENT 206 17
JAPANESE (2)
 OF JAPANESE PAPER, MY GOLD BEATEN SKIN ....FEVER. 232 38
 MY JAPANESE SILKS, DESPERATE BUTTERFLIES, ...KINDNESS 269 14
JAR (3)
 SMOKE WHEELS FROM THE BEAK OF THIS EMPTY JAR. POEM.6.W. 135 12
 THEY'VE TRAPPED HER IN SOME LABORATORY JAR. ....FACE LIFT 156 28
 THAT JAR, WHILE EACH POLEMIC JACKANAPES ....LOVE IS A PARALLAX 330 53
JARGON (2)
 AND IDLE COILS OF JARGON YET UNSPOKEN. ....SONNET: TO EVA 304 8
 OUR DRASTIC JARGON, BUT CLOCK HANDS THAT MOVE ...LOVE IS A PARALLAX 329 17
JARGONS (1)
 A SAINTLY SPARROW JARGONS MADRIGALS ....APRIL AUBADE 312 5
JARRING (1)
 RASPS THE JARRING BARITONE OF UNCLE PAUL; ....FAMILY REUNION 300 22
JARS (2)
 IN THEIR JARS THE SNAIL-NOSED BABIES MOON AND GLOW. .....TWO VIEWS. 114 10
 SIX JARS OF IT, ...WINTERING 217 4
JAVANESE (1)
 NOT A PATCH ON YOUR PLACE, I GUESS, WITH THE JAVANESE .....THE TOUR 237 9
JAW (3)
 BUT PLIABLE STILL, HIS JAW ....MEDALLION 124 5
 THEY PROPPED HIS JAW WITH A BOOK UNTIL IT STIFFENED ....BERCK-PLAGE 198 65
 THE TONGUE STUCK IN MY JAW. ....DADDY 223 25
JAWS (2)
 SPOTTED COWS REVOLVE THEIR JAWS AND CROP ....WATERCOLOR. 112 16
 THE SPIDERY JAWS, THE SPINE BONES BARED FOR A MOMENT ....ZOO K. 154 9
JAY'S (1)
 THAN MODELS FROM BONWIT'S OR JAY'S, ...A WINTER'S TALE 86 10
JAZZ (1)
 O CACOPHONY, GODDESS OF JAZZ AND OF QUARRELS, ...ALICANTE LULLABY 43 15
JEALOUS (3)
 ON MY JEALOUS STARE, ...ON THE DIFFICULTY OF CONJURING UP A DRYAD 66 15
 THEY ARE SO JEALOUS OF ANYTHING THAT IS NOT FLAT! THEY ARE
  JEALOUS GODS ....THREE WOMEN 179 86
 THEY ARE SO JEALOUS OF ANYTHING THAT IS NOT FLAT! THEY ARE
  JEALOUS GODS ....THREE WOMEN 179 86
JEALOUSY (1)
 JEALOUSY CAN OPEN THE BLOOD, ...THE SWARM 215 3
JEERS (1)
 A BINGE OF JEERS. LOOK. HE'S RUNNING THROUGH ....DIALOGUE O. 284 296
JELLYFISH (2)
 MILL A LITTER OF BREASTS LIKE JELLYFISH. ....GIGOLO 267 13
 OF BULBOUS JELLYFISH ....AQUATIC NOCTURNE 306 17
JELLY-GLASSFULS (1)
 MARBLE FACADES WITH BLUE VEINS, AND JELLY-GLASSFULS OF DAFFODILS. ...
   ... BERCK-PLAGE 199 89
JEOPARDIZE (1)
 SEEMS TO JEOPARDIZE THIS: ....NOTES TO A NEOPHYTE 306 18
JEOPARDY (1)
 A ROSE OF JEOPARDY FLAMES IN MY HAIR ....CIRCUS IN THREE RINGS 321 9
JERK (1)
 BEGINS. A JERK. AND NOW THE FIRST SLOW RAMBLE ....DIALOGUE O. 277 21
JERSEY (1)
 AND THE SEVEN-YEAR-OLD WOULDN'T GO OUT UNLESS HIS JERSEY STRIPES ...
   ... THE BABYSITTERS 174 8
JESUS (1)
 DRAGGING THEIR JESUS HAIR. ....MEDUSA 225 11
JET (3)
 THE BLOOD JET IS POETRY, ...KINDNESS 270 18
 ON MOBILE JET: ....AQUATIC NOCTURNE 305 6
 COMMANDING THAT CORKSCREW COMET JET FORTH INK ......SONNET TO SATAN 323 5
JET-BACKED (1)
 UP FROM THE JET-BACKED ....DARK WOOD, DARK WATER 127 16
JET-PLANE (1)
 AND AT THE JET-PLANE ANGER OF GOD'S ROAR ....THE TRIAL OF MAN 312 7
JEW (6)
 CHUFFING ME OFF LIKE A JEW. ....DADDY 223 32
 A JEW TO DACHAU, AUSCHWITZ, BELSEN. ....DADDY 223 33

262

	TITLE	PAGE	LINE

JEW (CONT.)
I BEGAN TO TALK LIKE A JEW. . ...DADDY 223 34
I THINK I MAY WELL BE A JEW. ....DADDY 223 35
I MAY BE A BIT OF A JEW. ....DADDY 223 40
JEW LINEN. ....LADY LAZARUS 244 9
JEWEL (3)
TOWARD THAT GREAT JEWEL: SHOWN OFTEN, ...THE GREAT CARBUNCLE 72 11
O JEWEL! O VALUABLE! ....LESBOS 229 52
THE BLUE'S A JEWEL. ....THE TOUR 238 29
JEWELED (3)
A SWISS WATCH, JEWELED IN THE HINGES! ....AN APPEARANCE 189 15
FROM THE SMALL JEWELED ....PURDAH 244 53
AMID THE TICKING JEWELED CLOCKS THAT MARK ....SONNET: TO TIME 311 2
JEWELER (1)
AND THE WHITE-HAIRED JEWELER FROM DENMARK IS CARVING ....ON DECK 143 31
JEWELMASTER (1)
THE JEWELMASTER DRIVES HIS CHISEL TO PRY POEM.7.S. 136 20
JEWELS (2)
THE OLD JEWELS SMOLDERING THERE ....MEDALLION 124 18
THE BLUE AND RED JEWELS OF HER RINGS SMOKE ....KINDNESS 269 3
JEW-MAMA (1)
HIS JEW-MAMA GUARDS HIS SWEET SEX LIKE A PEARL. ....LESBOS 228 27
JEWS (1)
OUSTING THE JEWS. ....MARY'S SONG 257 8
JIGGLES (1)
JIGGLES HIS TIN CUP AT THE GOODWIVES. ....THE BEGGARS 48 12
JILTED (2)
JILTED ....JILTED 304 T
TO A JILTED LOVER ....TO A JILTED LOVER 309 T
JILTING (1)
MY JILTING LADY SQUANDER COIN, GOLD LEAF STOCK DITCHES, CONJURING. 66 35
JOB (1)
AS A BAD JOB. WAIT. HE STIRS. HE ROMPS DIALOGUE OVER A OUIJA BOARD 284 293
JOBLESS (1)
WHERE THE MOST WATCHFUL COOKS GO JOBLESS ....THE TIMES ARE TIDY 107 3
JOCULAR (1)
THEN WITH A JOCULAR FIST THWACKED THE BARREL NAPE, ...SOW 61 35
JOES (1)
THOSE HOLY JOES. ....NICK AND THE CANDLESTICK 241 13
JOG (2)
TO A GIDDY JOG. THEN FOR ILL WILL ....WHITENESS I REMEMBER 102 17
JOG OFF IN JABBERWOCKY NOW AND LOSE US, *DIALOGUE OVER A OUIJA BOARD 279 91
JOIN (1)
AND JOIN HER SIEGE. ....THE SNOWMAN ON THE MOOR 59 24
JOINS (2)
WHOSE STARK ACT ALL COMING DOUBLE LUCK JOINS. ..WREATH FOR A BRIDAL 44 6
JOINS HIS ENEMIES' RECRUITS. ....LOVE IS A PARALLAX 330 54
JOINT (2)
AT THIS JOINT BETWEEN TWO WORLDS AND TWO ENTIRELY ....GHOST'S. 90 12
HOW FLESH CLEAVES FAST TO FROZEN JOINT, ...INSOLENT STORM. 326 10
JOINTED (1)
PIECED, GLUED, AND PROPERLY JOINTED. ....THE COLOSSUS 129 2
JOINTS (1)
GOLD JOINTS, MY WAY OF TURNING ....GIGOLO 268 22
JOKE (2)
TO THE FINAL GROTESQUE JOKE OF DEATH ....DIRGE FOR A JOKER 303 10
A HOT HYPERBOLICAL JOKE!" ....DIALOGUE EN ROUTE 308 18
JOKER (1)
DIRGE FOR A JOKER ....DIRGE FOR A JOKER 302 T
JOKING (1)
IS JOKING AT THE PIE-IN-THE-SKY MIRAGE DIALOGUE OVER A OUIJA BOARD 282 211
JOLT (1)
AN ANVIL, HOOVES FOUR HAMMERS TO JOLT ....WHITENESS I REMEMBER 102 21
JONQUILS (1)
AND JONQUILS SPROUT LIKE SOLOMON'S METAPHORS, ...APRIL AUBADE 312 11
JOSEF (1)
AS A SCHOOLGIRL SHE GAVE ROSES TO FRANZ JOSEF. ....CANDLES 149 18
JOSEPH (1)
OLD JOSEPH HOLDS AN ALPENSTOCK. ....A WINTER'S TALE 86 5
JOSEPH'S (1)
AS SPRANG FROM JOSEPH'S ROD, AND TESTIFIES ....MAYFLOWER 60 7
JOSTLE (1)
MEMORIES JOSTLE EACH OTHER FOR FACE-ROOM LIKE OBSOLETE FILM
STARS. ....INSOMNIAC 163 14
JOSTLED (1)
THE HEAD-STONE QUIET, JOSTLED BY NOTHING. POEM.7.S. 136 10
JOSTLING (1)
OLD GRIEVANCES JOSTLING EACH OTHER, SO MANY LOOSE TEETH. ....ZOO K. 154 13
JOT (1)
BY ONE JOT ITS BASILISK-LOOK OF LOVE. ....LADY AND T. 70 35
JOURNEY (2)
TAUNTS US TO VALOR. BLUE SAILORS SANG THAT OUR JOURNEY ..CHANNEL C. 27 20
I LOSE SIGHT OF YOU ON YOUR BLIND JOURNEY, ..PARLIAMENT HILL FIELDS 153 33
JOURNEYING (1)
THE NEEDLE JOURNEYING IN ITS GROOVE, ...THE COURAGE OF SHUTTING-UP 210 8

	TITLE	PAGE	LINE

JOUST (1)
THEY ARE POLISHED FOR THE JOUST .... • . ...BATTLE-SCENE 84 24
JOVIAN (1)
BOOMED WITH BAD DREAMS AND THE JOVIAN VOICES OF SURGEONS. *FACE LIFT 156 6
JOY (3)
KINDLED LIKE TORCHES FOR HIS JOY, ...PURSUIT 22 22
STILL THAN SWALLOWS JOY. YOU ENTER NOW. ....PERSEUS 83 34
MUFFLES THEIR BIRD-FEET: THEY WHISTLE FOR JOY. ....LEAVING EARLY 146 37
JUDGE (1)
OF HELL, AND NOT THE FIERY PART. YET TO JUDGE BY THAT DAZZLED LOOK. ...
... DIALOGUE BETWEEN GHOST AND PRIEST 38 15
JUDGED (1)
SHE JUDGED PETALS IN DISARRAY ....SPINSTER 49 11
JUDGMENT (1)
TO JUDGMENT IN A HIGHER COURT OF GRACE. ....DIALOGUE B. 39 45
JUDICIOUS (1)
DAYLIGHT WOULD BE MORE JUDICIOUS, ...·.....CANDLES 148 10
JUG (3)
LIKE A SPRAT IN A PICKLE JUG. ....YOU'RE 141 14
THE ROSES IN THE TOBY JUG ....LEAVING EARLY 146 23
BACK, FAT JUG ....BALLOONS 272 27
JUGGLE (1)
TO JUGGLE WITH, MY LOVE, WHEN THE SKY FALLS. ....BY CANDLELIGHT 237 36
JUICE (4)
STILL HE HYMNS JUICE OF HER, HOT NECTARINE. ....OUIJA 77 26
UNTONGUED, ALL BEAUTY'S BRIGHT JUICE SOURS. ....VIRGIN IN A TREE 82 43
DOING NOTHING. JULY'S JUICE ROUNDS THEIR NUBS. ....MOONRISE 98 3
SUNLIGHT STRIKES A GLASS OF GRAPEFRUIT JUICE, ..MORNING IN THE HOS. 332 1
JUICES (2)
LOOK, THEY ARE MELTING LIKE COINS IN THE POWERFUL JUICES -- ZOO K. 154 8
WITH BLUE-RED JUICES. THESE THEY SQUANDER ON MY FINGERS. BLACKBER. 168 7
JULY (2)
OF JULY TO ALL FOOLS' DAY. ....YOU'RE 141 8
POPPIES IN JULY ....·....POPPIES IN JULY 203 T
JULY'S (1)
DOING NOTHING. JULY'S JUICE ROUNDS THEIR NUBS. ....MOONRISE 98 3
JUMBO (1)
AND JUMBO SADLY TRUMPETS INTO STONE; ....DENOUEMENT 327 11
JUMP (2)
AND MOO AS THEY JUMP OVER MOONS AS NEW .....THE GHOST'S LEAVETAKING 91 37
HOW YOU JUMP --- ....CUT 236 37
JUMPED (2)
HOW YOU JUMPED WHEN I JUMPED ON YOU! ..................EAVESDROPPER 261 37
HOW YOU JUMPED WHEN I JUMPED ON YOU! ..................EAVESDROPPER 261 37
JUMPY (1)
JUMPY AS A MEXICAN BEAN. ....YOU'RE 141 16
JUNGLE (5)
TO CHOOSE BETWEEN YOUR WORLD OF JUNGLE GREEN ....YADWIGHA. 85 9
STOOD STUBBORN IN ITS JUNGLE: RED AGAINST GREEN, ...YADWIGHA. 85 18
TO A BERYL JUNGLE, AND DREAMED THAT BRIGHT MOON-LILIES ...YADWIGHA. 86 29
IN YOUR JUNGLE OF WINE-BOTTLE LAMPS, ...LEAVING EARLY 145 4
HORNS TWIRLING AND JUNGLE GUTTURALS! ....A SECRET 220 41
JUNK (1)
STILL, SHE FELT LOATH TO JUNK IT. *THE LADY AND THE EARTHENWARE HEAD 69 7
JUNKED (2)
YOU SHOULD HAVE JUNKED THEM BEFORE THEY DIED. ....LEAVING EARLY 146 28
OSSIFYING LIKE JUNKED STATUES -- ....STINGS/DR 293 14
JUST (19)
JUST HOW GUILTY ARE WE WHEN THE CEILING ....TALE OF A TUB 24 9
AND OCTOPUS -- SCRABBLING JUST BEYOND THE VIEW, ...TALE OF A TUB 25 20
AFTER YOUR LIFE'S END. WHAT JUST EPILOGUE ....DIALOGUE B. 39 24
OF FINAL SURFEIT IS JUST AS FAR ....BLUE MOLES 127 33
YOU DIDN'T JUST TOE ME AN INCH, NO -- ....LOVE LETTER 147 5
AND I WAS SCARED, BECAUSE SHE WAS SHAPED JUST THE WAY I WAS*PLASTER. 158 7
DOING THINGS WITH THEIR HANDS, ONE JUST THE SAME AS ANOTHER, *TULIPS 160 13
JUST AS IT IS, UNMISTED BY LOVE OR DISLIKE. ....MIRROR 173 3
OR JUST TO BE VISITED AT ALL. ....PHEASANT 191 6
A MOUTH JUST BLOODIED. ....POPPIES IN JULY 203 7
AT LEAST I WON'T BE STRUNG JUST UNDER THE SURFACE, ...BURNING. 204 23
I AM SURE IT IS UNIQUE, I AM SURE IT IS JUST WHAT I WANT. *BIRTHDAY. 206 3
IF I JUST UNDID THE LOCKS AND STOOD BACK AND TURNED INTO A
TREE. ....THE ARRIVAL OF THE BEE BOX 213 28
THE VOICES JUST CAN'T WORM THROUGH. ....DADDY 224 70
YOU SAY YOUR HUSBAND IS JUST NO GOOD TO YOU. ....LESBOS 228 26
OFF AND ON, AS IF I JUST HAD TO RETCH. .. ..THE TOUR 238 25
JUST TO MAKE SURE -- ...............................EAVESDROPPER 261 62
SIGNING IN. JUST P THIS TIME. AND OFF, DIALOGUE OVER A OUIJA BOARD 277 29
WILL BE OUR BEAT, JUST AS THE GIFT IS OURS, ...DIALOGUE O. 283 257
JUT (4)
IN THIS PARTICULAR TUB, TWO KNEES JUT UP ....TALE OF A TUB 25 41
GREEN OAT-SPROUTS JUT; ....ODE FOR TED 29 2
ACROSS THE JUT OF OCHREOUS ROCK ....DEPARTURE 51 18
THE JUT OF THAT ODD, DARK HEAD, PACING ....PHEASANT 191 3
JUTTED (1)
JUTTED EARLY TO MARK OUR GOING, WHILE SKY ....CHANNEL CROSSING 27 23

KALEIDOSCOPE (1)
    EXPLODES IN A KALEIDOSCOPE OF SHAPES   ....LOVE IS A PARALLAX 330   52
KALEIDOSCOPIC (1)
    OF KALEIDOSCOPIC SHELLS*TWO LOVERS AND A BEACHCOMBER BY THE REAL SEA 327   14
KAMIKAZE (1)
    KAMIKAZE MAN ---   ....CUT 235   28
KARAKUL (1)
    THEIR CHAR OF KARAKUL STILL. I CAN'T TELL   ....THE BURNT-OUT SPA 138   7
KEEL (1)
    NO LONGER DO I LISTEN FOR THE SCRAPE OF A KEEL   ....THE COLOSSUS 130   29
KEELED (1)
    AS KEELED ICE-MOUNTAINS   ....FULL FATHOM FIVE   92   12
KEEL'S (1)
    PLYING THEIR WILD CELLS IN MY KEEL'S SHADOW, ...MEDUSA 225   7
KEEN (4)
    KEEN THE RENDING TEETH AND SWEET   ....PURSUIT   22   17
    SO HUMBLY DONE, I'D TURN THIS KEEN   ....RHYME   50   13
    AND THEIR EYES LOOKING OUT OF IT: KEEN, *DIALOGUE OVER A OUIJA BOARD 276   10
    BITES KEEN INTO EACH BRAVE LIMB   ....AERIALIST 331   24
KEEP (25)
    TO KEEP SOME UNSAID PACT; PERHAPS CONCERN   ....CHANNEL CROSSING   27   34
    AND YET KEEP KIND)   ....THE GLUTTON   40   4
    IN QUARTZ, AS CRACK YOUR SKULL TO KEEP   EPITAPH FOR FIRE AND FLOWER   45   4
    WARNED HER TO KEEP   ....THE SNOWMAN ON THE MOOR   58   10
    KEEP FROM CUTTING FAT MEAT   ....THE THIN PEOPLE   65   27
    COUSIN DID YOU SO UNWISELY KEEP   ....THE DISQUIETING MUSES   74   3
    WILL BETRAY THE COMPANY I KEEP.   ....THE DISQUIETING MUSES   76   56
    BUT I, I KEEP THE VOICES HE   ....ON THE DECLINE OF ORACLES   78   12
    WHO KEEP COOL AND HOLY MAKE   ....VIRGIN IN A TREE   81   25
    BEEN STRUCK TO KEEP ALL GLORY IN THE GRIP   ....VIRGIN IN A TREE   82   32
    NOT NAILS, AND A MIRROR TO KEEP THE SNAKY HEAD   ....PERSEUS   83   13
    AND KEEP THEIR SHAPES INTACT WHILE SUN   ....CHILD'S PARK STONES 101   12
    KEEP HOUSE AMONG THE GRASSES. KNEELING DOWN*THE BEEKEEPER'S DAUGHTER 118   16
    WHOSE STONES KEEP A LITTLE HEAT.   ....OLD LADIES' HOME 120   7
    THEIR EYELIDS KEEP THE SHADE.   ....THE SLEEPERS 123   21
    MOTHER, KEEP OUT OF MY BARNYARD, ...POEM.3.MAENAD. 133   14
    WHERE THE DURABLE ONES KEEP HOUSE.   ....THE BURNT-OUT SPA 138   32
    SOME FEW PASSENGERS KEEP TRACK   ....ON DECK 142   4
    IN ITS EASY PEACE, COULD ONLY KEEP HOLY SO.   ......THREE WOMEN 178   81
    FLATTEN TO PARCHMENT SCREENS TO KEEP THE WIND OFF.   .....THREE WOMEN 179   97
    THERE IS NO GUILE OR WARP IN HIM. MAY HE KEEP SO.   ......THREE WOMEN 181 175
    AND I CAN'T KEEP AWAY FROM IT.   ....THE ARRIVAL OF THE BEE BOX 213   8
    I TRY TO KEEP HIM IN, ...LESBOS 228   45
    ROUND TO EARN HIS PAY: HE'LL HAVE US KEEP   ....DIALOGUE O. 284 294
    TO KEEP THE YOUNG GIRL FROM HER CROWNING GOAL.   ....THE PRINCESS. 333   18
KEEPER (1)
    HAIL AND FAREWELL. HELLO, GOODBYE. O KEEPER *THE GHOST'S LEAVETAKING   91   39
KEEPER'S (1)
    ZOO KEEPER'S WIFE   ....ZOO KEEPER'S WIFE 154   T
KEEPING (5)
    "MISS ELLA'S GOT LOONY FROM KEEPING IN CAHOOTS   ....ELLA MASON A.   54   35
    PAST KEEPING TO THE HOUSE, PAST ALL DISCRETION --   THE RAVAGED FACE 115   7
    AND I'D BEEN KEEPING HER IN THE DARK, AND SHE WAS RESENTFUL --   ...
                                         ... IN PLASTER 159   37
    HOW LONG CAN I BE A WALL, KEEPING THE WIND OFF?   ....THREE WOMEN 185 288
    KEEPING ITSELF, IT SEEMS, IN A STATE OF MIRACULOUS REPAIR.   ..MEDUSA 225   15
KEEPS (8)
    ON FLUENT HAUNCHES, KEEPS MY SPEED.   ....PURSUIT   23   28
    OLD ELLA MASON KEEPS CATS, ELEVEN AT LAST COUNT, ...ELLA MASON A.   53   1
    BELOW US A WHITE GULL KEEPS   ....MAGNOLIA SHOALS 122   13
    A BLACK-SHARDED LADY KEEPS ME IN A PARROT CAGE. POEM.6.W. 135   9
    TATE AND LYLE KEEPS THEM GOING, ...WINTERING 218   27
    THAT KEEPS THE SKY AT BAY, ...BY CANDLELIGHT 237   29
    IT KEEPS WASHING YOU UP LIKE AN OLD BONE.   ....THE RIVAL/DR 291   16
    THE WHEELS REVOLVE, THE UNIVERSE KEEPS RUNNING.   TO EVA DESCENDING. 303   2
KELP (1)
    ON ARMS AND LEGS IN A FRINGE OF KELP; GREEN SOAP   .....TALE OF A TUB   25   43
KEN (1)
    CHURCH CURSE TO KEN THAT CROOKED OATH   ....CRYSTAL GAZER   55   35
KENTISH (1)
    SOUTHWARD, OVER KENTISH TOWN, AN ASHEN SMUDGE*PARLIAMENT HILL FIELDS 152   21
KEPT (13)
    WHATEVER HIS SHREWD SECRET, HE KEPT IT HID   ....SOW   60   3
    HE KEPT THE SOW -- IMPOUNDED FROM PUBLIC STARE, ...SOW   60   5
    MY FATHER KEPT A VAULTED CONCH   ....ON THE DECLINE OF ORACLES   78   1
    WELL-WATER KEPT COOL AT THE START OF THE ROWS.   .....SPINACH-PICKER.   89   14
    SEEN BY ANY MAN WHO KEPT HIS HEAD, ...FULL FATHOM FIVE   93   38
    KEPT HOUSE AGAINST   ....POINT SHIRLEY 110   11
    YET HIS BELLY KEPT ITS FIRE   ....MEDALLION 124   16
    HE KEPT BLOWING ME KISSES. POEM.4.BEAST. 134   9
    WE KICKED AND TALKED. THE THICK SALT KEPT US UP.   ...THE BABYSITTERS 175   40
    WE KEPT PICKING UP HANDFULS, LOVING IT, ...LESBOS 229   60
    IS WHERE I KEPT THE FURNACE, ...THE TOUR 238   20
    BELCHED INTO BLAZE AND THOUGH RED-HOT, KEPT WHOLE   ......DIALOGUE O. 280 158
    I'LL ASK. DO. WE'VE KEPT HIM WAITING LONG   ....DIALOGUE O. 281 180

| | | TITLE | PAGE | LINE |

KETTLE (1)
AND SHINE THAT KETTLE OF COPPER   .....TINKER JACK AND THE TIDY WIVES   34   7
KEY (6)
I SHUT ON THE KEY ....WORDS FOR A NURSERY   73 19
OFF KEY AND LOUD ....A WINTER'S TALE   87 28
AND A COOK AND A MAID, AND KNEW ABOUT THE KEY TO THE BOURBON. *BABY. 175 21
I AM SENDING BACK THE KEY ....BLUEBEARD 305   1
I AM SENDING BACK THE KEY; ....BLUEBEARD 305   4
I AM SENDING BACK THE KEY ....BLUEBEARD 305   7
KEYHOLE (1)
WHAT KEYHOLE HAVE WE SLIPPED THROUGH, WHAT DOOR HAS SHUT? ....BABY. 175 42
KEYS (5)
THE LETTERS PROCEED FROM THESE BLACK KEYS, AND THESE BLACK KEYS
   PROCEED ....THREE WOMEN 177 27
THE LETTERS PROCEED FROM THESE BLACK KEYS, AND THESE BLACK KEYS
   PROCEED ....THREE WOMEN 177 27
FINGER-TRAPS -- A TUMULT OF KEYS. ....LITTLE FUGUE 187 16
THE RATTLER OF KEYS? ....THE JAILER 226   5
NAME, HOUSE, CAR KEYS, ...AMNESIAC 232   3
KICK (1)
WHEN YOU KICK ME OUT, THAT'S WHAT I'LL REMEMBER, ...LEAVING EARLY 145   2
KICKED (1)
WE KICKED AND TALKED. THE THICK SALT KEPT US UP. ...THE BABYSITTERS 175 40
KICKING (2)
PARALYSING THE KICKING LOVERS. ....MEDUSA 225 26
LITTLE UNSTRUNG PUPPET, KICKING TO DISAPPEAR -- ....LESBOS 227   9
KILL (14)
CIRCLES HER LIKE A PREY SHE'D LOVE TO KILL ....WIDOW 164 15
CAN SUCH INNOCENCE KILL AND KILL? IT MILKS MY LIFE. ....THREE WOMEN 180 134
CAN SUCH INNOCENCE KILL AND KILL? IT MILKS MY LIFE. ....THREE WOMEN 180 134
YOU SAID YOU WOULD KILL IT THIS MORNING. ....PHEASANT 191   1
DO NOT KILL IT. IT STARTLES ME STILL, ...PHEASANT 191   2
THAT KILL, THAT KILL, THAT KILL. ....ELM 193 42
THAT KILL, THAT KILL, THAT KILL. ....ELM 193 42
THAT KILL, THAT KILL, THAT KILL. ....ELM 193 42
MUST YOU KILL WHAT YOU CAN? ....A BIRTHDAY PRESENT 207 47
MIRRORS CAN KILL AND TALK, THEY ARE TERRIBLE ROOMS ....COURAGE. 210 27
DADDY, I HAVE HAD TO KILL YOU. ....DADDY 222   6
I HAVE TAKEN A PILL TO KILL ....CUT 235 24
O GOLDEN CHILD THE WORLD WILL KILL AND EAT. ....MARY'S SONG 257 21
THEIR MAGNIFIED HEADS AND PLAN TO KILL ME AS SOON AS POSSIBLE.
   ... THE RIVAL/DR 291   3
KILLED (6)
I WOULD HAVE KILLED MYSELF GLADLY THAT TIME ANY POSSIBLE WAY.
   ... A BIRTHDAY PRESENT 206 15
OVER THE ENGINE THAT KILLED HER --- ....STINGS 215 59
POM! POM! "THEY WOULD HAVE KILLED ME." ....THE SWARM 217 55
IF I'VE KILLED ONE MAN, I'VE KILLED TWO --- ....DADDY 224 71
IF I'VE KILLED ONE MAN, I'VE KILLED TWO --- ....DADDY 224 71
AND KILLED IT IN AN HOUR. ....FEVER. 231 24
KILLER (1)
AND THE EYES OF THE KILLER MOVING SLUGLIKE AND SIDELONG, *DETECTIVE. 208   8
KILLING (4)
THE CONSTRICTION KILLING ME ALSO. ....THE RABBIT CATCHER 194 30
IF YOU ONLY KNEW HOW THE VEILS WERE KILLING MY DAYS. .....BIRTHDAY. 207 37
THE VILLAGERS ARE MOVING THE VIRGINS, THERE WILL BE NO KILLING.*BEE. 212 49
THE ENGINE IS KILLING THE TRACK, THE TRACK IS SILVER, ...TOTEM 264   1
KILLS (1)
A SANDY DAMPER KILLS THE VIBRATIONS; ....BERCK-PLAGE 196   7
KILROY (1)
WHERE KILROY WOULD PASS ....TEMPER OF TIME 336 14
KIN (2)
THIS LADY HERE'S NO KIN ....ALL THE DEAD DEARS   70 15
OF MINE, YET KIN SHE IS: SHE'LL SUCK ....ALL THE DEAD DEARS   70 16
KIND (10)
AND YET KEEP KIND) ....THE GLUTTON   40   4
FOLLOW ON KIND WIND." ....CRYSTAL GAZER   55 18
ANOTHER KIND OF REDNESS BOTHERS ME: ....ELECTRA ON AZALEA PATH 117 29
OUR KIND MULTIPLIES: ....MUSHROOMS 139 30
I ROLL TO AN ANTEROOM WHERE A KIND MAN ....FACE LIFT 156 12
AFTER ALL, IT WAS A KIND OF MARRIAGE, BEING SO CLOSE. ...IN PLASTER 160 51
THEY HUG THEIR FLATNESS LIKE A KIND OF HEALTH. ....THREE WOMEN 180 117
FATTENS US, IS KIND. HER MOUTH IS RED. ....THREE WOMEN 181 156
THERE IS A KIND OF SMOKE IN THE SPRING AIR, ...THREE WOMEN 186 354
A KIND OF BUSH-STINK. ....................................EAVESDROPPER 260   9
KINDER (1)
BUT NOW TURNED KINDER WITH TIME, WE MARK MISS MASON ..ELLA MASON A.   54 37
KINDLE (1)
THAT WILL KINDLE ANGELS' ENVY, SCORCH AND DROP ......EPITAPH FOR F.   45   6
KINDLED (3)
KINDLED LIKE TORCHES FOR HIS JOY, ...PURSUIT   22 22
KINDLED BY MY LOVE'S PLEASING ....SONG FOR A SUMMER'S DAY   31 14
AND I'D SOONER BE STAKED FOR A WITCH, KINDLED, AND CURLED ...
   ... DIALOGUE OVER A OUIJA BOARD 280 132

```
                                                    TITLE            PAGE  LINE
KINDLES (1)
   AND KINDLES A DAY'S-END BLAZE  ...  ...............CHILD'S PARK STONES  101   15
KINDLING (2)
   NO WORD MAKE THEM CARRY WATER OR FIRE THE KINDLING  .......TWO CAMP.    144    5
   KINDLING HER WITHIN A STEEPLED FLAME,  THE PRINCESS AND THE GOBLINS     333   20
KINDLY (2)
   THE GHOSTS, KINDLY. ............................TWO VIEWS OF WITHENS      72   18
   KINDLY WITH INVALIDS AND MAWKISH WOMEN, ....................CANDLES      149   25
KINDNESS (6)
   KINDNESS ..........................................KINDNESS             269    T
   KINDNESS GLIDES ABOUT MY HOUSE. ...........................KINDNESS     269    1
   DAME KINDNESS, SHE IS SO NICE! ............................KINDNESS     269    2
   SUGAR CAN CURE EVERYTHING, SO KINDNESS SAYS. ..............KINDNESS     269    9
   O KINDNESS, KINDNESS ......................................KINDNESS     269   12
   O KINDNESS, KINDNESS ......................................KINDNESS     269   12
KING (7)
   SHE BEARS A KING. TURNED BITTER ..........TWO SISTERS OF PERSEPHONE      32   24
   SO SHE WILLS ALL TO THE BLACK KING. .....................VANITY FAIR     33   29
   KING EGG-HEAD SAW HIS DOMAIN CRACK. ................NATURAL HISTORY      71   10
   SAINT AND KING UNFISTED OBSTRUCTION'S KNUCKLES*A LESSON IN VENGEANCE     80    4
   THE KING FINGERED HIS BEARD. ...................THE BULL OF BENDYLAW    108    6
   KING OF THE DISH, MY LUCKY ANIMAL. ....................POEM.4.BEAST.    134    2
   AND CASTLED IN IT LIKE A KING. .............................ON DECK     143   15
KINGDOM (6)
   MY ONE KINGDOM. .....................................MONOLOGUE AT 3 A.M.  40  14
   TO CONQUER CINDER'S KINGDOM IN THE STROKE OF AN HOUR *EPITAPH FOR F.     45   20
   AND THIS IS THE KINGDOM YOU BORE ME TO. ......THE DISQUIETING MUSES      76   54
   THIS IS THE KINGDOM OF THE FADING APPARITION, .............GHOST'S.      90    8
   TELL US THE TRUTH THIS TIME: TELL US THE KINGDOM .......DIALOGUE O.     283  272
   THEY WANT NO PROUD PATERNAL KINGDOM COME; .................THE DEAD     320    6
KINGDOM'S (1)
   I WALK DRY ON YOUR KINGDOM'S BORDER ...............FULL FATHOM FIVE      93   41
KINGLINESS (1)
   THAT GIVES IT A KINGLINESS, A RIGHT. ....................PHEASANT       191   10
KINGS (8)
   HE KINGS IT, NAVEL-KNIT TO NO GROAN, .......................MAUDLIN      51    6
   OF KINGS, UNMANNED KINGS' SONS: OUR MASTERIES ..........SNOWMAN O.       59   41
   EXPRESSIVE OF GRIEF TURNS GODS, LIKE KINGS, TO ROCKS. ......PERSEUS      83   29
   THE ANTHERS NOD THEIR HEADS, POTENT AS KINGS .........BEEKEEPER'S.      118   11
   RAISED TO TOAST A THOUSAND KINGS, FOR ALL GIVES ....SONNET: TO TIME     311   11
   MAN WHO CAN MANGLE THE GRIN OF KINGS: .....................LAMENT       316   17
   CABBAGES ARE CABBAGES; KINGS: KINGS. ................A SORCERER B.      324   14
   CABBAGES ARE CABBAGES; KINGS: KINGS. ................A SORCERER B.      324   14
KING'S (2)
   O THE KING'S TIDY ACRE IS UNDER THE SEA, ......THE BULL OF BENDYLAW     108   19
   AND THE BULL ON THE KING'S HIGHWAY. ...........THE BULL OF BENDYLAW     108   21
KINGS' (1)
   OF KINGS, UNMANNED KINGS' SONS: OUR MASTERIES ..........SNOWMAN O.       59   41
KINGSHIP (1)
   THEIR WITHERING KINGSHIP. .........................THE THIN PEOPLE       65   39
KISS (16)
   LAUGH, KISS, GET DRUNK, .................SOLILOQUY OF THE SOLIPSIST      37   16
   AND HAVE EVERY WEATHERCOCK KISS HANG FIRE ...........EPITAPH FOR F.      46   23
   THE FOOD TUBES EMBRACE ME. SPONGES KISS MY LICHENS AWAY.  POEM.7.S.    136   19
   ITS SNAKY ACIDS KISS. .........................................ELM      193   40
   THE SHEETS GROW HEAVY AS A LECHER'S KISS. ...................FEVER.     231   30
   WHOSE KISS STINGS UNBEARABLY ...............................MYSTIC      268    4
   ALWAYS IN THE MIDDLE OF A KISS ...................DIRGE FOR A JOKER     302    1
   AND KISS HER ON THE MOUTH FOR SHE ......................THE DREAM       311   21
   NEVER TRY TO TRICK ME WITH A KISS *NEVER TRY TO TRICK ME WITH A KISS    319    T
   NEVER TRY TO TRICK ME WITH A KISS *NEVER TRY TO TRICK ME WITH A KISS    319    1
   NEVER TRY TO TRICK ME WITH A KISS.*NEVER TRY TO TRICK ME WITH A KISS    319    6
   NEVER TRY TO TRICK ME WITH A KISS.*NEVER TRY TO TRICK ME WITH A KISS    320   12
   SO NEVER TRY TO TRICK ME WITH A KISS: ..........NEVER TRY TO TRICK.     320   18
   WITH KISS OF CINDERS, GHOSTS DESCEND, ................DANSE MACABRE     321   25
   SO KISS: THE DRUNKS UPON THE CURB AND DAMES ....LOVE IS A PARALLAX      329   31
   NOW KISS AGAIN: TILL OUR STRICT FATHER LEANS ....LOVE IS A PARALLAX     330   43
KISSES (5)
   HIS KISSES PARCH, EACH PAW'S A BRIAR, .....................PURSUIT       22   19
   HE KEPT BLOWING ME KISSES. ............................POEM.4.BEAST.    134    9
   THE SNAILS BLEW KISSES LIKE BLACK APPLES. ........ZOO KEEPER'S WIFE     155   38
   EXIT LIKE KISSES. ..................................AN APPEARANCE       189    5
   BY KISSES, BY CHERUBIM, ....................................FEVER.      232   49
KITCHEN (5)
   NAPPING IN HER KITCHEN PAVED WITH SAUCERS. ..........ELLA MASON A.       54   20
   OUT OF KITCHEN TABLE OR CHAIR .........BLACK ROOK IN RAINY WEATHER       57   16
   OF KITCHEN SLOPS AND, STOMACHING NO CONSTRAINT, ...........SOW           61   43
   THIS IS THE SMELL OF YEARS BURNING, HERE IN THE KITCHEN, *DETECTIVE.    208   12
   VICIOUSNESS IN THE KITCHEN! ...............................LESBOS       227    1
KITCHENS (1)
   THROUGH CANDID KITCHENS IN THE RISING SUN ............THE PRINCESS.     334   52
KITTENS (2)
   YOU HAVE STUCK HER KITTENS OUTSIDE YOUR WINDOW ..............LESBOS     227   12
   YOU SAY I SHOULD DROWN THE KITTENS. THEIR SMELL! ...........LESBOS     228   20
```

                                          TITLE   PAGE   LINE
KLAN (1)
    GAUZE KU KLUX KLAN ....CUT   235   30
KLEPTOMANIAC (1)
    SWEETHEART, THAT KLEPTOMANIAC. ....LESBOS   229   88
KLUX (1)
    GAUZE KU KLUX KLAN ....CUT   235   30
KNAVISH (1)
    WELL-NAMED, ILL-FAMED A KNAVISH FLY-BY-NIGHT, ...GOATSUCKER   111   11
KNEEDEEP (1)
    THE BRONZE BOY STANDS KNEEDEEP IN CENTURIES, ...GOLD MOUTHS CRY   302   10
KNEE-DEEP (1)
    KNEE-DEEP IN THE COLD AND SWAMPED BY FLOWERS? ....LEAVING EARLY   146   44
KNEEL (4)
    SO, YOU'LL SCOFF, AND YET YOU'D DROP TO KNEEL ....DIALOGUE O.   280   156
    TO PROVE IT GENUINE. YOU'D KNEEL, TOO, DIALOGUE OVER A OUIJA BOARD   280   162
    IF A BUSH BORROWED TONGUES AND SPOKE TO YOU. YOU'D KNEEL*DIALOGUE O.   280   163
    WHY HE SHOULD KNEEL BEFORE A SILLY SCENE ....THE PRINCESS.   335   65
KNEELING (2)
    KEEP HOUSE AMONG THE GRASSES. KNEELING DOWN*THE BEEKEEPER'S DAUGHTER   118   16
    KNEELING OVER THE ROWS, ...BITTER STRAWBERRIES   300   34
KNEELS (2)
    A MARBLE SAILOR KNEELS AT HER FOOT DISTRACTEDLY, AND AT
        HIS FOOT ....FINISTERRE   170   21
    KNEELS, BACK BENT, AS BEST HE CAN ....BY CANDLELIGHT   237   27
KNEES (8)
    IN THIS PARTICULAR TUB, TWO KNEES JUT UP ....TALE OF A TUB   25   41
    HIM TO HIS KNEES -- ....THE SNOWMAN ON THE MOOR   58   18
    BRACING THEIR KNEES. ON UNSEEN TOWLINES ....IN MIDAS' COUNTRY   99   17
    BUTTONING THE CUFFS AT MY WRISTS AND THE SLIT FROM MY NECK TO MY
        KNEES. ....THE BEE MEETING   211   8
    PIVOT OF HEELS AND KNEES! -- THE FURROW ....ARIEL   239   6
    MY KNEES. ....LADY LAZARUS   245   32
    WINGED RABBITS REVOLVING ABOUT HIS KNEES, ...CIRCUS IN THREE RINGS   322   16
    KNOCKING THE WARDEN TO HIS KNEES*INSOLENT STORM STRIKES AT THE SKULL   325   3
KNELLED (2)
    SO, PERHAPS I, KNELLED DUMB BY YOUR ABSENCE, ...STREET SONG   36   24
    AND THE FAIR SHIP SANK, ITS CREW KNELLED HOME FOR DINNER. ...
                                  ... DREAM WITH CLAM-DIGGERS   44   20
KNELT (1)
    KNELT IN THE MEADOW MUTE AS BOULDERS; ....HARDCASTLE CRAGS   63   33
KNEW (14)
    HE KNEW, BUT NO PEASANTS KNOW. ....ON THE DECLINE OF ORACLES   78   8
    KNEW NOTHING OF. SO THE CRABS ....MUSSEL HUNTER AT ROCK HARBOR   97   60
    I HARDLY KNEW HIM. POEM.4.BEAST.   134   10
    I WASN'T FOOLED. I KNEW YOU AT ONCE. ....LOVE LETTER   147   28
    AND A COOK AND A MAID, AND KNEW ABOUT THE KEY TO THE BOURBON. *BABY.   175   21
    I REMEMBER THE MINUTE WHEN I KNEW FOR SURE. ....THREE WOMEN   177   43
    I WAS SEVEN, I KNEW NOTHING. ....LITTLE FUGUE   188   38
    IF YOU ONLY KNEW HOW THE VEILS WERE KILLING MY DAYS. ....BIRTHDAY.   207   37
    AND THEN I KNEW WHAT TO DO. ....DADDY   224   63
    THEY ALWAYS KNEW IT WAS YOU. ....DADDY   224   79
    AND BACK TO P, AS IF HE KNEW US WELL ...DIALOGUE OVER A OUIJA BOARD   277   30
    I NEVER KNEW SUCH CREDULITY TO PITCH ...DIALOGUE OVER A OUIJA BOARD   280   154
    I KNEW HE'D GOT IT MIXED BEFORE: VISIONS*DIALOGUE OVER A OUIJA BOARD   282   219
    FOR ROT. DON'T THINK YOU HAD ME FOOLED. I KNEW ....DIALOGUE O.   283   263
KNIFE (13)
    OVER HER SKULL'S MIDDEN; NO KNIFE ....VANITY FAIR   32   12
    NOW, AS I HONE MY KNIFE, SHE BEGS ....RHYME   50   11
    UNTIL HER KNIFE HAD PARED ....THE THIN PEOPLE   65   30
    AN ANTIQUE HAG-HEAD, TOO TOUGH FOR KNIFE TO FINISH, ...LADY AND T.   70   33
    BEFORE THE BED, BEFORE THE KNIFE, ...THE EYE-MOTE   109   26
    EACH WAVE-TIP GLITTERS LIKE A KNIFE. ....A WINTER SHIP   113   30
    AND THE KNIFE NOT CARVE, BUT ENTER ....A BIRTHDAY PRESENT   208   60
    DID IT COME LIKE AN ARROW, DID IT COME LIKE A KNIFE? THE DETECTIVE   209   21
    A KNIFE THAT CAN BE TAKEN OUT ....A SECRET   220   21
    THE KNIFE IN YOUR BACK. ....A SECRET   220   46
    DO WITHOUT EYES TO KNIFE, WHAT WOULD HE ....THE JAILER   227   44
    SAD HAMLET, WITH A KNIFE? ....STOPPED DEAD   230   19
    SMALL AND CROSS. THE YELLOW KNIFE ....BY CANDLELIGHT   237   21
KNIFELIKE (1)
    KNIFELIKE, HE WAS CHASTE ENOUGH, ...MEDALLION   125   25
KNIGHT (2)
    THE GREAT GRANDAM! -- OUR MARVEL BLAZONED A KNIGHT, ...SOW   61   29
    AND LEADS HIM HOME TO BE HER CHOSEN KNIGHT. ....THE PRINCESS.   334   50
KNIGHTS (2)
    KNIGHTS MIGHT DOFF THEIR CASQUES. THE CRABS ....MUSSEL HUNTER.   96   28
    EVERYBODY IS NODDING A SQUARE BLACK HEAD, THEY ARE KNIGHTS IN
        VISORS, ...THE BEE MEETING   211   13
KNIT (3)
    LET FLESH BE KNIT, AND EACH STEP HENCE GO FAMOUS. ....WREATH F.   45   24
    NEEDLES KNIT IN A BIRD-BEAKED ....OLD LADIES' HOME   120   8
    KNIT UP A GILDED FABLE FOR THE CHILD ..THE PRINCESS AND THE GOBLINS   335   73
KNITS (1)
    THAT KNITS TO EACH ORIGINAL ITS COARSE COPY. A DARK TARN*LADY AND T.   69   15

KNITTING (2)
   IT IS YOUR KNITTING, BUSILY ....THE OTHER 201 14
   THE WOMAN, STILL AT HER KNITTING, ...WINTERING 219 43
KNIVES (4)
   TO GRIND OUR KNIVES AND SCISSORS: ... .THE DEATH OF MYTH-MAKING 104   2
   PILLAR OF WHITE IN A BLACKOUT OF KNIVES. ....THE BEE MEETING 212 52
   IT IS YOU THE KNIVES ARE OUT FOR ....THE SWARM 216   6
   A VICE OF KNIVES, ...NICK AND THE CANDLESTICK 241 16
KNOB (2)
   THAT FOR ECCENTRIC KNOB AND WART ....ON THE PLETHORA OF DRYADS 67   5
   THE PURPLE EGG-STONES: FROM GREAT HEAD'S KNOB ....POINT SHIRLEY 110 22
KNOBBED (1)
   KNOBBED QUARTZ; FLAYED COLORS RIPEN ....ODE FOR TED 29 11
KNOBBY (2)
   GREEN, WHOLLY GREEN, THEY STAND THEIR KNOBBY SPINE ABOVE THE OXBOW 88 10
   BUNCHES ITS KNOBBY BROWNS ON A VASTLY ....POEMS, POTATOES 106 12
KNOBS (1)
   SMALL MUD KNOBS, NUDGED FROM UNDER, ...MUSSEL HUNTER AT ROCK HARBOR 96 26
KNOCK (7)
   IF I DON'T MOVE ABOUT, I'LL KNOCK NOTHING OVER. SO I SAID,*POEM.6.W. 135 14
   THE KNOCK OF THE SMALL, NEW HEART. ....HEAVY WOMEN 158 14
   OH NEVER TRY TO KNOCK ON ROTTEN WOOD ....ADMONITIONS 319   1
   OH NEVER TRY TO KNOCK ON ROTTEN WOOD. ....ADMONITIONS 319   6
   OH NEVER TRY TO KNOCK ON ROTTEN WOOD, ...ADMONITIONS 319 12
   NEVER TRY TO KNOCK ON ROTTEN WOOD, ...ADMONITIONS 319 18
   TO KNOCK THEM DOWN WITH LOGIC OR WITH LUCK ......LOVE IS A PARALLAX 329 20
KNOCKED (3)
   WHAT SCAR'S BEEN KNOCKED ....TINKER JACK AND THE TIDY WIVES 34 23
   THE SWARM IS KNOCKED INTO A COCKED STRAW HAT. ....THE SWARM 217 42
   SEVEN HOURS KNOCKED OUT OF MY RIGHT MIND ....THE JAILER 226   7
KNOCKING (3)
   KNOCKING OUR BROTHERS DOWN, WE STRIKE A STANCE ....CHANNEL CROSSING 27 27
   KNOCKING THE WARDEN TO HIS KNEES*INSOLENT STORM STRIKES AT THE SKULL 325   3
   HE HEARS THE GRUFF KNOCKING ....TEMPER OF TIME 336 19
KNOCKS (2)
   O PARDON THE ONE WHO KNOCKS FOR PARDON AT ...ELECTRA ON AZALEA PATH 117 44
   THAT KNOCKS ME OUT. ....LADY LAZARUS 246 56
KNOT (4)
   ROSEBUD, KNOT OF WORMS, ...WORDS FOR A NURSERY 73   1
   TO A KNOT OF LAUNDRY, WITH A CLASSIC BUNCH OF SHEETS ......GHOST'S. 90 10
   THE ROADS BUNCHED TO A KNOT, ...CHILDLESS WOMAN 259   5
   THE KNOT MYSELF, ...CHILDLESS WOMAN 259   6
KNOTHOLES (1)
   BURNING LIKE KNOTHOLES FROM A NUN'S SHROUD-CIRCLED .....DIALOGUE O. 280 130
KNOTTED (3)
   OF KNOTTED TABLE AND CROOKED CHAIR, ..MISS DRAKE PROCEEDS TO SUPPER 41   4
   KNOTTED, CAUGHT, SURVIVES ....FULL FATHOM FIVE 92   9
   BREASTPLATES OF CHEESECLOTH KNOTTED UNDER THE ARMPITS. ....BEE. 211 14
KNOTTING (1)
   KNOTTING AND STOPPING, ILL-ASSORTED, IN BLUE UNIFORMS,*PARLIAMENT H. 152 14
KNOTWEED (1)
   MAUNCHING THISTLE AND KNOTWEED ON HER SNOUT-CRUISE -- ....SOW 61 19
KNOUT (1)
   WITH SPUR AND KNOUT ....THE SNOWMAN ON THE MOOR 59 28
KNOW (49)
   I DO NOT KNOW ....THE QUEEN'S COMPLAINT 28   8
   KNOW YOU APPEAR ....SOLILOQUY OF THE SOLIPSIST 38 29
   SUDDENLY AT MY ELBOW. I ONLY KNOW THAT A ROOK ....BLACK ROOK I. 57 27
   HE KNEW, BUT NO PEASANTS KNOW. ....ON THE DECLINE OF ORACLES 78   8
   BUT OH, SAGE GROWNUPS KNOW ....BATTLE-SCENE 85 35
   TO KNOW THE STILL HEART OF THE STONES: ....CHILD'S PARK STONES 101 22
   ELEVEN WEEKS, AND I KNOW YOUR ESTATE SO WELL ....PRIVATE GROUND 130 13
   HE'LL BE RICH IN A YEAR (AND HE SHOULD KNOW) ....ON DECK 143 28
   THE RED GERANIUMS I KNOW. ....LEAVING EARLY 146 16
   I DIDN'T KNOW WHAT TO MAKE OF IT. ....LOVE LETTER 147 24
   YOU KNOW ME LESS CONSTANT, ...PARLIAMENT HILL FIELDS 153 27
   BUT WHAT DO YOU KNOW ABOUT THAT ....ZOO KEEPER'S WIFE 155 14
   I DON'T KNOW A THING. ....FACE LIFT 156 16
   THE SHEEP KNOW WHERE THEY ARE, ...WUTHERING HEIGHTS 167 19
   I SHALL HARDLY KNOW MYSELF. IT WILL BE DARK, ...LAST WORDS 172 25
   BUT I DIDN'T KNOW HOW TO COOK, AND BABIES DEPRESSED ME. ......BABY. 174 13
   DON'T KNOW WHAT TO MAKE OF THE SUDDEN SLIPPINESS, ...NEW YEAR ON. 176   4
   THERE'S NO GETTING UP IT BY THE WORDS YOU KNOW.*NEW YEAR ON DARTMOOR 176   6
   I CANNOT HELP SMILING AT WHAT IT IS I KNOW. ....THREE WOMEN 177 13
   THEY ARE TO BLAME FOR WHAT I AM, AND THEY KNOW IT. .....THREE WOMEN 180 116
   I KNOW HER. I KNOW HER INTIMATELY -- ....THREE WOMEN 181 157
   I KNOW HER. I KNOW HER INTIMATELY -- ....THREE WOMEN 181 157
   THERE ARE THE CLOTHES OF A FAT WOMAN I DO NOT KNOW. ....THREE WOMEN 184 267
   I KNOW THE BOTTOM, SHE SAYS. I KNOW IT WITH MY GREAT TAP ROOT: ELM 192   1
   I KNOW THE BOTTOM, SHE SAYS. I KNOW IT WITH MY GREAT TAP ROOT: ELM 192   1
   WHAT DID THEY KNOW THAT I DIDN'T? ....BURNING THE LETTERS 204   5
   I KNOW WHY YOU WILL NOT GIVE IT TO ME, ...A BIRTHDAY PRESENT 207 27
   I WOULD KNOW YOU WERE SERIOUS. ....A BIRTHDAY PRESENT 208 58
   IS IT THE BUTCHER, THE GROCER, THE POSTMAN, SOMEONE I KNOW? ...BEE. 211 30
   SO SLOW I HARDLY KNOW THEM, ...WINTERING 218 23

KNOW (CONT.)
   SEVEN YEARS, IF YOU WANT TO KNOW. ....DADDY 224 74
   IT IS LOVE YOU ARE FULL OF. YOU KNOW WHO YOU HATE. ....LESBOS 229 72
   YOU KNOW WHAT LIES ARE FOR. ....LESBOS 230 91
   ALL THE GODS KNOW IS DESTINATIONS. ....GETTING THERE 248 17
   GO GET THE GLASS, THEN. BUT I KNOW TONIGHT WILL BE .....DIALOGUE O. 276   1
   EVEN A LITTLE? YOU KNOW I DON'T, AND STILL . . . .DIALOGUE O. 277 34
   AND STILL I'M SKEPTIC. I KNOW. I'M BEING FOOLISH ......DIALOGUE O. 277 35
   REALLY WANT TO KNOW ABOUT? EVERYTHING.   DIALOGUE OVER A OUIJA BOARD 278 54
   TO KNOW AT ALL. AND YET I GO AHEAD. ....DIALOGUE OVER A OUIJA BOARD 278 69
   DO YOU KNOW HOW MY FATHER IS? HE'S LEFT *DIALOGUE OVER A OUIJA BOARD 278 74
   KNOW: WHICH IS WHY I, WHEN THE WONDROUS FIST ....DIALOGUE O. 279 119
   IT WAS HIS TONGUE THAT WANTED MENDING. YOU KNOW, ...DIALOGUE O. 285 305
   THOUGH HUNDREDS OF LONDONERS KNOW IT LIKE THE PALM OF THEIR
      HAND. ....QUEEN MARY'S ROSE GARDEN 290 16
   "I KNOW, I KNOW," I TOLD MY FRIEND. ....THE DREAM 311 24
   "I KNOW, I KNOW," I TOLD MY FRIEND. ....THE DREAM 311 24
   NEVER TRY TO KNOW MORE THAN YOU SHOULD. ....ADMONITIONS 319   3
   NEVER TRY TO KNOW MORE THAN YOU SHOULD. ....ADMONITIONS 319   9
   NEVER TRY TO KNOW MORE THAN YOU SHOULD. ....ADMONITIONS 319 15
   NEVER TRY TO KNOW MORE THAN YOU SHOULD. ....ADMONITIONS 319 19
KNOWABLE (1)
   KNOWABLE ONLY BY LIGHT ....THE GREAT CARBUNCLE   72 15
KNOWING (3)
   NOBODY DIES OR IS BORN WITHOUT THEIR KNOWING IT. ...THE NET-MENDERS 121 13
   KNOWING NEITHER ABORTIONS NOR BITCHERY, ...WINTER TREES 258   6
   ARROWS THAT LACERATE THE SKY, WHILE KNOWING .....LOVE IS A PARALLAX 330 61
KNOWLEDGE (3)
   I PRETENDED I WAS THE TREE OF KNOWLEDGE. ....ZOO KEEPER'S WIFE 155 27
   I AM INCAPABLE OF MORE KNOWLEDGE. ....ELM 193 37
   A FACET OF KNOWLEDGE. ....BERCK-PLAGE 198 49
KNOWN (3)
   ORBIT THE GO-BY, MADE KNOWN ....MUSSEL HUNTER AT ROCK HARBOR   96 58
   I SHOULD HAVE KNOWN BETTER. ....GREEN ROCK, WINTHROP BAY 104   3
   TO THE HARDEST SUBSTANCE KNOWN. ....NOTES TO A NEOPHYTE 307 24
KNOWS (6)
   GOD KNOWS HOW OUR NEIGHBOR MANAGED TO BREED ....SOW   60   1
   DIMINISHES, AND GOD KNOWS WHAT IS THERE. ...THE GHOST'S LEAVETAKING   91 26
   GRANDCHILDREN NOBODY KNOWS. ....OLD LADIES' HOME 120 12
   SHE IS OLD, OLD, OLD, SHE MUST LIVE ANOTHER YEAR, AND SHE
      KNOWS IT. ....THE BEE MEETING 212 44
   OF CAMBRIC OR WATERDROPS, WHO KNOWS WHAT BELIEF ....DIALOGUE O. 282 224
   KNOWS NOT OF DEATH NOR CALCULUS ABOVE ....LOVE IS A PARALLAX 331 77
KNUCKLE (1)
   WHITE AS A KNUCKLE AND TERRIBLY UPSET. ...THE MOON AND THE YEW TREE 173   9
KNUCKLEBONES (1)
   SKIN WORN DOWN TO THE KNUCKLEBONES ....CRYSTAL GAZER   54   3
KNUCKLE-BONES (1)
   BLACK AS THE CHARRED KNUCKLE-BONES ....CHILD'S PARK STONES 100   5
KNUCKLED (1)
   THIS WAS THE LAND'S END: THE LAST FINGERS, KNUCKLED AND
      RHEUMATIC, ...FINISTERRE 169   1
KNUCKLES (3)
   SAINT AND KING UNFISTED OBSTRUCTION'S KNUCKLES*A LESSON IN VENGEANCE   80   4
   TO ROOT DEEP AMONG KNUCKLES, SHINBONES, ...FULL FATHOM FIVE   93 35
   KNUCKLES AT SHOULDER-BLADES, THE ....THALIDOMIDE 252 12
KRUPP (1)
   OF KRUPP, BLACK MUZZLES ....GETTING THERE 248   6
KU (1)
   GAUZE KU KLUX KLAN ....CUT 235 30
KUMQUAT-COLORED (1)
   KUMQUAT-COLORED TROLLEYS DING AS THEY TRUNDLE .....ALICANTE LULLABY   43   8
LA (1)
   THE CARS IN THE PLACE DE LA CONCORDE -- ....A SECRET 220 38
LABELED (1)
   AWAY FROM THE LABELED ELMS, THE TAME TEA-ROSES. ....TWO CAMP. 144   9
LABOR (3)
   REDDEN IN WHITE PALMS NO LABOR REDDENS. ....MOONRISE   98 11
   A LABOR OF LOVE, AND THAT LABOR LOST. ....POINT SHIRLEY 110 34
   A LABOR OF LOVE, AND THAT LABOR LOST. ....POINT SHIRLEY 110 34
LABORATORY (1)
   THEY'VE TRAPPED HER IN SOME LABORATORY JAR. ....FACE LIFT 156 28
LABORED (1)
   THIRTY YEARS NOW I HAVE LABORED ....THE COLOSSUS 129   8
LABORER'S (1)
   THE LABORER'S NAILS PARED LEVEL ....THE DEATH OF MYTH-MAKING 104   7
LABORING (3)
   LUCINA, BONY MOTHER, LABORING ....MOONRISE   98 25
   AS IF THE AIR WERE LABORING TO PRODUCE   DIALOGUE OVER A OUIJA BOARD 279 89
   LABORING ON THE TILT OF THAT STEEP GRADE ....THE PRINCESS. 334 35
LABORS (1)
   THOUGH THE MIND LIKE AN OYSTER LABORS ON AND ON, ...TWO LOVERS. 327 19
LABOR'S (2)
   GRASS-COUCHED IN HER LABOR'S PRIDE, ...TWO SISTERS OF PERSEPHONE   32 23
   WHOSE LABOR'S NOT YET SMOKED ....TINKER JACK AND THE TIDY WIVES   35 29

```
                                           TITLE            PAGE  LINE
LABURNUM (2)
  THERE IS THE LABURNUM, ITS BLOND COLONNADES,  ..........THE ARRIVAL.  213   29
  PODS OF THE LABURNUM AT NINE IN THE MORNING.  ....LETTER IN NOVEMBER  253    4
LABYRINTH (2)
  THE LABYRINTH AND IGNORE WHAT MANNER OF BEAST  ..........DIALOGUE O.  286  343
  VANISHES IN A LABYRINTH OF HAY  ........THE PRINCESS AND THE GOBLINS  335   70
LABYRINTHINE (1)
  ONE LABYRINTHINE TANGLE  ...........................FULL FATHOM FIVE   93   34
LACE (4)
  MADE LACE, OR A LEAF-AND-FLOWER PEN-SKETCH.  .......SOUTHERN SUNRISE   26    6
  CURTAINED WITH YELLOW LACE.  .............................THE SLEEPERS  122    7
  CAN STITCH LACE NEATLY ON TO THIS MATERIAL. MY HUSBAND   THREE WOMEN  187  360
  THE BABY LACE, THE GREEN-LEAVED CONFECTIONERY,*THE MUNICH MANNEQUINS  263   22
LACED (2)
  LACED OVER WITH STRIPES  .............................FIESTA MELONS   46    6
  HANDS LACED, IN A MOONY INDOLENCE OF LOVE --  ..........WATERCOLOR.  112   25
LACERATE (1)
  ARROWS THAT LACERATE THE SKY, WHILE KNOWING  .....LOVE IS A PARALLAX  330   61
LACES (1)
  GULL-COLORED LACES FLAP IN THE SEA DRAFTS  ...............FINISTERRE  170   28
LACK (8)
  BY LACK AND LOSS THESE BEGGARS ENCROACH  .................THE BEGGARS   48   13
  TO LEAF-SIZE FROM LACK OF ACTION:  ...............THE TIMES ARE TIDY  107    9
  IT WASN'T FOR ANY LACK OF MOTHER-LOVE.  ....................STILLBORN  142    5
  NOBODY CAN TELL WHAT I LACK.  ................PARLIAMENT HILL FIELDS  152    5
  BLUNT AND FLAT ENOUGH TO FEEL NO LACK, I FEEL A LACK.  ..THREE WOMEN  182  193
  BLUNT AND FLAT ENOUGH TO FEEL NO LACK, I FEEL A LACK.  ..THREE WOMEN  182  193
  AND A SKY LIKE A PIG'S BACKSIDE, AN UTTER LACK OF ATTENTION.  ...
                               ...  FOR A FATHERLESS SON  205    5
  MARK A MORTAL LACK,  ...........................TRIO OF LOVE SONGS  313    2
LACKEY (1)
  THE LEFT MY LACKEY,  ...........................WORDS FOR A NURSERY   74   34
LACKS (1)
  AS PRODIGAL IN WHAT LACKS ME.  .........................THREE WOMEN  184  259
LADDER (2)
  TO HAVE YOU GRAB MY NOSE, A LADDER RUNG.  ......FOR A FATHERLESS SON  205   11
  A VISIONARY LADDER TOWARD THE MOON  ....THE PRINCESS AND THE GOBLINS  333    5
LADDERS (2)
  SO MANY LADDERS  .............................WORDS FOR A NURSERY   73    8
  SCALING LITTLE LADDERS WITH GLUEPOTS AND PAILS OF LYSOL*THE COLOSSUS  129   11
LADEN (1)
  MY WORLD PYRAMIDED WITH LADEN BASKETS.   MEMOIRS OF A SPINACH-PICKER   90   20
LADIES (8)
  SENT THESE LADIES IN HER STEAD  ...............THE DISQUIETING MUSES   74    5
  WORDS TO RID ME OF THOSE THREE LADIES  ........THE DISQUIETING MUSES   75   14
  BUT THOSE LADIES BROKE THE PANES.  ............THE DISQUIETING MUSES   75   24
  THE LORDS AND LADIES RAN.  ....................THE BULL OF BENDYLAW  108   12
  THE BONNETED LADIES GRIN.  ........................OLD LADIES' HOME  120   18
  THE CHINESE LADIES USE  .................................POLLY'S TREE  128   13
  LITTLE SHELLS MADE UP INTO NECKLACES AND TOY LADIES.  ...FINISTERRE  170   32
  GENTLEMEN, LADIES  ....................................LADY LAZARUS  245   30
LADIES' (2)
  LADIES' SHEAVED SKULLS:  .....................THE SNOWMAN ON THE MOOR   59   38
  OLD LADIES' HOME  ...................................OLD LADIES' HOME  120    T
LADY (22)
  "COME LADY, BRING THAT POT  ..........TINKER JACK AND THE TIDY WIVES   34    1
  "COME LADY, BRING THAT FACE  .........TINKER JACK AND THE TIDY WIVES   34   10
  MY JILTING LADY SQUANDER COIN, GOLD LEAF STOCK DITCHES,   CONJURING.   66   35
  THE LADY AND THE EARTHENWARE HEAD *THE LADY AND THE EARTHENWARE HEAD   69    T
  THIS ANTIQUE MUSEUM-CASED LADY  ...................ALL THE DEAD DEARS   70    3
  THIS LADY HERE'S NO KIN  ..........................ALL THE DEAD DEARS   70   15
  DUNGAREES, PROUD AS A LADY IN A SEA  ..MEMOIRS OF A SPINACH-PICKER   90   18
  TO TIMOROUS CHILDREN, TO THE LADY ON THE STREET.  ..THE RAVAGED FACE  116   13
  SOON EACH WHITE LADY WILL BE BOARDED UP  ...........PRIVATE GROUND  130    5
  LADY, WHO ARE THESE OTHERS IN THE MOON'S VAT --  .....POEM.3.MAENAD.  133   22
  A BLACK-SHARDED LADY KEEPS ME IN A PARROT CAGE.  ..........POEM.6.W.  135    9
  THE UNTIDY LADY REVIVALIST  ...............................ON DECK  143   19
  LADY, YOUR ROOM IS LOUSY WITH FLOWERS.  ................LEAVING EARLY  145    1
  WE SLEPT LIKE STONES. LADY, WHAT AM I DOING  ..........LEAVING EARLY  146   42
  NOW SHE'S DONE FOR, THE DEWLAPPED LADY  ...................FACE LIFT  156   25
  OUR LADY OF THE SHIPWRECKED IS STRIDING TOWARD THE HORIZON,
                               ...  FINISTERRE  169   19
  OUR LADY OF THE SHIPWRECKED IS THREE TIMES LIFE SIZE,  ...FINISTERRE  170   24
  MAIDS AND THE LONG ROYAL LADY.  .............................WINTERING  218   39
  LADY LAZARUS  .......................................LADY LAZARUS  244    T
  AND A TITLED LADY MAY FREQUENTLY BE A BEAUTY.  ........QUEEN MARY'S.  290   22
  EACH LOVELY LADY  .........ON LOOKING INTO THE EYES OF A DEMON LOVER  325    5
  EACH NIGHT, THE ADROIT YOUNG LADY  ......................AERIALIST  331    1
LAID (3)
  GOES GRAVEWARD WITH FLESH LAID WASTE,  ....TWO SISTERS OF PERSEPHONE   32   27
  THEY HAD FOUR MEN LAID OUT, BLACK AS BURNT TURKEY,  ......TWO VIEWS.  114    2
  THE WAY SHE LAID HIS LETTERS, TILL THEY GREW WARM  ...........WIDOW  164   18
LAIN (1)
  LAIN SPLAYED TOO LONG IN THE TORTUOUS BOUGHS: OVERRIPE  .....VIRGIN.   82   37
```

```
                                              TITLE              PAGE  LINE
LAKE (10)
    A BLUE MIST IS DRAGGING THE LAKE.  ..................THE MANOR GARDEN  125    4
    CROSSES THE LAKE. THE WORMS  ......................THE MANOR GARDEN  125   17
    BETWEEN THE ROAD AND THE LAKE WATER,  ...................BLUE MOLES  126   12
    A LAKE THICK WITH FISH.  .....................DARK WOOD, DARK WATER  127    7
    MORGUE OF OLD LOGS AND OLD IMAGES, THE LAKE  .........PRIVATE GROUND  131   23
    (ROCK LAKE, CANADA)  ................TWO CAMPERS IN CLOUD COUNTRY  144   ST
    PLANETS PULSE IN THE LAKE LIKE BRIGHT AMOEBAS;  ...........TWO CAMP.  145   23
    LIKE A DEAD LAKE THE DARK ENVELOPS ME,  ..........ZOO KEEPER'S WIFE  154    3
    NOW I AM A LAKE. A WOMAN BENDS OVER ME,  .....................MIRROR  174   10
    BLACK LAKE, BLACK BOAT, TWO BLACK, CUT-PAPER PEOPLE.*CROSSING THE W.  190    1
LAKES (1)
    LOCKED IN CRYSTAL CASKETS ARE THE LAKES,  .......PROLOGUE TO SPRING  322   13
LAMB (1)
    THE SUNDAY LAMB CRACKS IN ITS FAT.  ....................MARY'S SONG  257    1
LAMBS (2)
    THERE, SPRING LAMBS JAM THE SHEEPFOLD. IN AIR  .........WATERCOLOR.  111    1
    THE TALKING DUCKS, THE HAPPY LAMBS.  ...................THREE WOMEN  185  318
LAMBSWOOL (1)
    BURIED IN THE LAMBSWOOL OF THE DEAD POODLE;  .............FACE LIFT  156   23
LAME (2)
    NO LAME EXCUSES CAN GLOSS OVER  ............GREEN ROCK, WINTHROP BAY  104    1
    I AM LAME IN THE MEMORY.  ...............................LITTLE FUGUE  188   44
LAMENT (1)
    LAMENT  ........................................................LAMENT  315    T
LAMENTABLY (1)
    LAMENTABLY.  ..............................................FROG AUTUMN   99   12
LAMP (4)
    LIT THINGS, THAT LAMP OF THE POSSIBLE! WET YET  .....SPINACH-PICKER.   89    3
    STALLS IN HALLS WHERE THE LAMP WICK  ..............OLD LADIES' HOME  120   20
    AND THE MAID SMOKED AND SHOT POOL UNDER A GREEN-SHADED LAMP.  BABY.  175   24
    INITIATED BY THE LUNAR LAMP,  ..........THE PRINCESS AND THE GOBLINS  333   19
LAMP-HEADED (2)
    THE LAMP-HEADED NYMPHS ARE NODDING TO SLEEP LIKE STATUES. *POEM.5.F.  135   12
    THEY WANT THE CRIB OF SOME LAMP-HEADED PLATO.  ..................MAGI  148   16
LAMPLIGHT (1)
    I AM AT HOME IN THE LAMPLIGHT. THE EVENINGS ARE LENGTHENING. *THREE.  186  351
LAMPS (3)
    BE A HARVEST OF SILVER IN THE NETS, AND THE LAMPS  ..THE NET-MENDERS  121   18
    IN YOUR JUNGLE OF WINE-BOTTLE LAMPS,  .................LEAVING EARLY  145    4
    THESE LAMPS, THESE PLANETS.  .......................THE NIGHT DANCES  250   23
LAMPSHADE (1)
    BRIGHT AS A NAZI LAMPSHADE,  ...........................LADY LAZARUS  244    5
LANCED (1)
    A THRESH-TAILED, LANCED  ..............................POINT SHIRLEY  110   15
LAND (9)
    INSATIATE, HE RANSACKS THE LAND  ...............................PURSUIT   22   13
    THAT EVERY BREATH, THUS TEEMING, SET THE LAND  ..WREATH FOR A BRIDAL   45   21
    ENTER THE CHILLY NO-MAN'S LAND OF ABOUT  ....THE GHOST'S LEAVETAKING   90    1
    TO THE CLOUD-CUCKOO LAND OF COLOR WHEELS  ...THE GHOST'S LEAVETAKING   91   35
    TO BE LET LOOSE AT NEWS OF LAND.  ............................ON DECK  143   36
    LIKE A DIVER ON A LOFTY SPAR OF LAND  .................FAMILY REUNION  301   25
    ECLIPSED BENEATH BLIND LID OF LAND  ....................DANSE MACABRE  320    2
    BRIGHT ANGELS BLACK OUT OVER LOGIC'S LAND  ..........SONNET TO SATAN  323    3
    AND HUNGER OF THE SURF THAT PLUCKS THE LAND, *EPITAPH IN THREE PARTS  337   16
LANDING (1)
    ON THE BLANK STONES OF THE LANDING.  ...................THE COLOSSUS  130   30
LANDINGS (1)
    AT THIS WHARF THERE ARE NO GRAND LANDINGS TO SPEAK OF.*A WINTER SHIP  112    1
LANDOWNERS (2)
    LANDOWNERS  .................................................LANDOWNERS   53    T
    FLIMSILY PEOPLED. BUT LANDOWNERS  ........................LANDOWNERS   53    9
LAND'S (1)
    THIS WAS THE LAND'S END: THE LAST FINGERS, KNUCKLED AND
       RHEUMATIC,  ............................................FINISTERRE  169    1
LANDSCAPE (13)
    WINTER LANDSCAPE, WITH ROOKS  ......................WINTER LANDSCAPE,   21    T
    LONGER ON THIS LANDSCAPE OF CHAGRIN;  .............WINTER LANDSCAPE,   21    8
    AT THE ESSENTIAL LANDSCAPE STARE, STARE  ........NOVEMBER GRAVEYARD   56   13
    EVEN IN THIS DULL, RUINOUS LANDSCAPE); SKEPTICAL,  ....BLACK ROOK I.   57   24
    INTO A LANDSCAPE  .........................THE SNOWMAN ON THE MOOR   58   12
    THE GUISE OF LEAVES. THE WHOLE LANDSCAPE  .........HARDCASTLE CRAGS   63   37
    A RISE IN THE LANDSCAPE, HUMMOCK OR HOGBACK, LOOKS   ABOVE THE OXBOW   88   16
    WIND BARES A FLINTIER LANDSCAPE.  ..................IN MIDAS' COUNTRY  100   25
    GAS TANKS, FACTORY STACKS -- THAT LANDSCAPE  ...SUICIDE OFF EGG ROCK  115    3
    ELSEWHERE THE LANDSCAPE IS MORE FRANK.  ......................A LIFE  150   19
    THEY STAND LIKE SHADOWS ABOUT THE GREEN LANDSCAPE --  .........WIDOW  164   28
    MY LANDSCAPE IS A HAND WITH NO LINES,  .............CHILDLESS WOMAN  259    4
    THE WINTER LANDSCAPE HANGS IN BALANCE NOW,  ......PROLOGUE TO SPRING  322    1
LANDSPIT (1)
    OFF THAT LANDSPIT OF STONY MOUTH-PLUGS,  .....................MEDUSA  224    1
LANDSPITS (1)
    WITH FIVE WHORLED LANDSPITS.  ..................WORDS FOR A NURSERY   74   30
LAND-TRACT (1)
    DEATH AS STRIKING ROOT ON ONE LAND-TRACT;  ..............LANDOWNERS   53   14
```

LANE (2)
  NOBODY IN THE LANE, AND NOTHING, NOTHING BUT BLACKBERRIES,*BLACKBER. 168   1
  IN THE LANE I MEET SHEEP AND WAGONS, ...BRASILIA 258 16
LANGUAGE (2)
  SPEAK IN SIGN LANGUAGE OF A LOST OTHERWORLD,*THE GHOST'S LEAVETAKING 90 19
  AND THE LANGUAGE OBSCENE ....DADDY 223 30
LANGUID (1)
  TO FLOAT LIKE DREAM-FISH IN THE LANGUID LIMBO ..MORNING IN THE HOS. 332   8
LANGUOR (2)
  AND A LANGUOR OF WAX CONGEALS THE VEIN EPITAPH FOR FIRE AND FLOWER 46 31
  WITH THE LANGUOR OF IDOLS BELOW ....IN MIDAS' COUNTRY 99   7
LANTERN (1)
  HURTS ME AS THE WORLD HURTS GOD. I AM A LANTERN --- ....FEVER. 232 36
LANTERN-FRAIL (1)
  A LANTERN-FRAIL ....BATTLE-SCENE 84 11
LANTERN-JAWED (1)
  LANTERN-JAWED REASON, SQUAT COMMON SENSE, THE DEATH OF MYTH-MAKING 104   3
LANTERN-LIT (1)
  THROUGH HIS LANTERN-LIT ....SOW 60   8
LAOCOON (1)
  BUT WHO'D VOLUNTEER TO GULP THE LAOCOON, ...PERSEUS 82   8
LAP (3)
  WHAT LULL, WHAT COOL CAN LAP ME IN ....PURSUIT 23 35
  LAP AT MY BACK INELUCTABLY. ....THREE WOMEN 185 293
  SLACK FOAM IN THE LAP. ....A SECRET 220 43
LAPIS (1)
  ROCKING ACROSS THE LAPIS LAZULI SEA ....EPITAPH IN THREE PARTS 337   1
LAPPED (1)
  I PATRONIZED HER A LITTLE, AND SHE LAPPED IT UP -- ......IN PLASTER 159 20
LAPS (1)
  LAPS ITS GRAY PAW ....RESOLVE 52   6
LAPSE (1)
  LEAVES BEHIND US WARP AND LAPSE. ....MAGNOLIA SHOALS 122 11
LAPSED (1)
  ENOUGH AGES LAPSED TO WIN ....MUSSEL HUNTER AT ROCK HARBOR 95 22
LAPSING (2)
  A FULL MOON, RIVER LAPSING ....LORELEI 94   2
  LAPSING INTO RUSSIAN OR SERBO-CROAT. ...DIALOGUE OVER A OUIJA BOARD 279 92
LAPWING (1)
  HE NAMES A LAPWING, STARTS RABBITS IN A ROUT ....ODE FOR TED 29   3
LARDER'S (1)
  SACKED LARDER'S GONE BONE-BARE. ....THE GLUTTON 40 14
LARD-PALE (1)
  LARD-PALE, SIPPING THE THIN ....WHITSUN 153   5
LARGE (7)
  SUCH STARKNESS: ACCURACY MUST NOT STALK AT LARGE: ....TALE OF A TUB 25 35
  CLAW SWOLLEN TO A SHIELD LARGE ....MUSSEL HUNTER AT ROCK HARBOR 96 33
  OR PETTY THIEVERY BY LARGE. .....FABLE OF THE RHODODENDRON STEALERS 104 28
  LITTLE VICTIM UNEARTHED BY SOME LARGE CREATURE ....BLUE MOLES 126   6
  WHAT LARGE EYES THE DEAD HAVE! POEM.6.W. 135 10
  THEY SEEM LARGE, YET THEY DROP, AND NO GAP IS VISIBLE. ....STARS. 165   5
  AND THERE IS A CHARGE, A VERY LARGE CHARGE ....LADY LAZARUS 246 61
LARGESSE (1)
  BY BESTOWING LARGESSE, HONOR, ...BLACK ROOK IN RAINY WEATHER 57 21
LARKS (1)
  FOR NAIVE LARKS WHO STARVE AND GRIEVE. ...METAMORPHOSES OF THE MOON 307 18
LARKS' (1)
  LARKS' NIP AND TUCK ARISING ....SONG FOR A SUMMER'S DAY 31   9
LARKSPUR (1)
  BLUE LARKSPUR STAR. ....POLLY'S TREE 129 42
LAST (38)
  LAST SUMMER'S REEDS ARE ALL ENGRAVED IN ICE ......WINTER LANDSCAPE, 22 11
  SUCH FORCE CAN LAST; BUT BEYOND, THE NEUTRAL VIEW CHANNEL CROSSING 26   7
  THE OTHER, WRY VIRGIN TO THE LAST, ...TWO SISTERS OF PERSEPHONE 32 26
  LIKE A LAST STORM-CROSSED LEAF? BEST GET YOU GONE ......DIALOGUE B. 39 44
  LAST BLOOD-DROP OF THAT TRUANT HEART. ....THE SHRIKE 42 23
  LAST SUMMER I CAME UPON YOUR SPANISH COUSIN, ...SPIDER 48   8
  OLD ELLA MASON KEEPS CATS, ELEVEN AT LAST COUNT, ...ELLA MASON A. 53   1
  HOARD LAST YEAR'S LEAVES, WON'T MOURN, WEAR SACKCLOTH, OR TURN ...
           ... NOVEMBER GRAVEYARD 56   2
  GLOWERING AT THE COAL-FIRE: "COME FIND ME" -- HER LAST TAUNT. ...
           ... THE SNOWMAN ON THE MOOR 58   5
  BUT ALL THE ACCUMULATED LAST GRUNTS, GROANS, ...PERSEUS 83 17
  WISH FOR EVEN GROUND, AND IT'S THE LAST CLIFF ......ABOVE THE OXBOW 88 22
  THE LAST CRONE GOT BURNT UP ....THE TIMES ARE TIDY 107 11
  THE CROWD SUCKS HER LAST TEAR AND TURNS AWAY. ....AFTERMATH 114 14
  MY MOTHER UNROLLED AT YOUR LAST HOMECOMING. ELECTRA ON AZALEA PATH 117 32
  AND SEVEN WINTER COATS LAST AUGUST? ....ON DECK 143 22
  HERE ON THE LAST FRONTIER OF THE BIG, BRASH SPIRIT ....TWO CAMP. 145 12
  GAVE UP THE GHOST LAST NIGHT. HIGH TIME. ....LEAVING EARLY 146 24
  THEY ARE THE LAST ROMANTICS, THESE CANDLES: ....CANDLES 148   1
  HERE'S YESTERDAY, LAST YEAR -- ....A LIFE 149   3
  I FOLLOW THE SHEEP PATH BETWEEN THEM. A LAST HOOK BRINGS ME ...
           ... BLACKBERRYING 169 23

LAST (CONT.)
   THIS WAS THE LAND'S END: THE LAST FINGERS, KNUCKLED AND
      RHEUMATIC, ...FINISTERRE   169   1
   LAST WORDS ....LAST WORDS   172   T
   I LAST. I LAST IT OUT. I ACCOMPLISH A WORK. ....THREE WOMEN   180 129
   I LAST. I LAST IT OUT. I ACCOMPLISH A WORK. ....THREE WOMEN   180 129
   THE PRINT OF ITS BIG FOOT LAST WINTER, ...PHEASANT   191   11
   LET US EAT OUR LAST SUPPER AT IT, LIKE A HOSPITAL PLATE. BIRTHDAY.   207   26
   THE LAST BADGE OF VICTORY.
   NEXT TO THE LAST TENANT'S RANCID JAM ....THE SWARM   217   41
   MY BOY, IT'S YOUR LAST RESORT. ....WINTERING   218   8
   I'M DOPED AND THICK FROM MY LAST SLEEPING PILL. ....THE APPLICANT   222   39
   LAST SUMMER, MY GOD, LAST SUMMER ....LESBOS   228   34
   LAST SUMMER, MY GOD, LAST SUMMER ....THE TOUR   238   32
   LAST SUMMER, MY GOD, LAST SUMMER ....THE TOUR   238   32
   THE LAST OF VICTORIANA. ....NICK AND THE CANDLESTICK   241   34
   TO LAST IT OUT AND NOT COME BACK AT ALL. ....LADY LAZARUS   245   38
   TO SUCH CROSS-PURPOSES? AT LAST YOU GLIMPSE ....DIALOGUE O.   284 289
   "LAST NIGHT," HE SAID, "I SLEPT WELL ....THE DREAM   310   1
   AND WHEN AT LAST THEY BLUNDER INTO BED ....THE DEAD   320   7
   WITH A LAST ARTFUL DODGE SHE LEAPS ....AERIALIST   332   39
LATCH (1)
   THE DARKENING STAIR, UNDOES THE PALACE LATCH ....THE PRINCESS.   334   28
LATE (15)
   COCKED ON THE LONE, LATE, ...PROSPECT   28   11
   THAT NOBLE MIEN, PERHAPS YOU'VE LATE QUITTED HEAVEN?" ..DIALOGUE B.   38   16
   THE TRUTH IS, ONE LATE OCTOBER, AT MY BIRTH-CRY ....ELECTRA ON.   117   34
   THE LATE MONTH WITHERS, AS WELL. ....MAGNOLIA SHOALS   122   12
   THE LATE GUEST ....YADDO: THE GRAND MANOR 124   18
   DOWN THERE THE LATE YEAR ....DARK WOOD, DARK WATER   127   12
   BUT IT WAS TOO LATE FOR THAT. IT WAS TOO LATE, AND THE FACE THREE.   178   62
   BUT IT WAS TOO LATE FOR THAT. IT WAS TOO LATE, AND THE FACE THREE.   178   62
   YOU COME IN LATE, WIPING YOUR LIPS. ....THE OTHER   201   1
   IT IS VERY LATE. ....BY CANDLELIGHT   236   7
   THAT THESE LATE MOUTHS SHOULD CRY OPEN ....POPPIES IN OCTOBER   240   11
   CHIMERA ON THE HOOK, WHO CLAIMS HE'S LATE ....DIALOGUE O.   283 245
   GOSSIPS LATE AND SOON, ...JILTED   304   6
   TOO LATE TO ASK IF END WAS WORTH THE MEANS, ...DOOMSDAY   316   16
   TOO LATE TO CALCULATE THE TOPPLING STOCK: ....DOOMSDAY   316   17
LATELY (1)
   ALL'S PEACE AND DISCIPLINE DOWN THERE. TILL LATELY WE ....OXBOW.   89   53
LATER (3)
   IN THINNESS, TO COME, LATER, ...THE THIN PEOPLE   64   14
   YEARS LATER I ....WORDS   270   14
   SOONER OR LATER SOMETHING GOES AMISS; ....NEVER TRY TO TRICK.   320   16
LATEST (1)
   WITH HER LATEST SUITOR ....SPINSTER   49   3
LATHER (1)
   LIGHTNING LICKED IN A YELLOW LATHER ....LAMENT   315   4
LATIN (1)
   I LAY MY EAR TO FURIOUS LATIN. ....THE ARRIVAL OF THE BEE BOX   213   21
LATTER (1)
   FREELY BECOME SUN'S BRIDE, THE LATTER ....TWO SISTERS OF PERSEPHONE   32   21
LATTER-DAY (1)
   STILL, LATTER-DAY SAGES, ...A LESSON IN VENGEANCE   80   21
LATTER-DAYS (1)
   HIMSELF WITHERED THESE LATTER-DAYS ....THE TIMES ARE TIDY   107   8
LATTICEWORK (1)
   AND HALE ITS GREEN LATTICEWORK OF LEAVES. YOU NEED .....DIALOGUE O.   280 159
LAUD (2)
   LEAPS TO LAUD SUCH MAN'S BLOOD! ....ODE FOR TED   30   24
   STAND STOCK STILL TO LAUD THESE MATED ONES .....WREATH FOR A BRIDAL   44   5
LAUGH (9)
   LAUGH, KISS, GET DRUNK, ...SOLILOQUY OF THE SOLIPSIST   37   16
   LAUGH DOES AWAY WITH THE UNSTITCHING, PLAGUEY WOUNDS ....PERSEUS   83   45
   FLUNG BRICK PERFECTED HIS LAUGH. ....MEDALLION   125   27
   MY GOD, WHAT A LAUGH!" ....A BIRTHDAY PRESENT   206   10
   UNDER THE GUISE OF NONCHALANCE. PAN'S LAUGH ....DIALOGUE O.   282 228
   YOUR HEAD AFTER ALL. IT SEEMS HIS LAUGH *DIALOGUE OVER A OUIJA BOARD   282 238
   EVEN THE DEAD LAUGH AMONG THE GOLDENROD. ....GOLD MOUTHS CRY   302   9
   LEANED THE DEVIL PROMPTING YOU TO LAUGH. ....DIRGE FOR A JOKER   302   4
   IN THE RARE RIVER WINK AND LAUGH; WE LAVISH .... LOVE IS A PARALLAX   330   38
LAUGHED (3)
   AND THE MAN I WORK FOR LAUGHED: "HAVE YOU SEEN SOMETHING AWFUL? ...
                                                ... THREE WOMEN   177   22
   TWO CHILDREN LAUGHED AT TAG ....BITTER STRAWBERRIES   299   14
   LAUGHED AT THE AMBUSH OF ANGELS' TONGUES, ...LAMENT   315   14
LAUGHING (4)
   LAUGHING, LAUGHING ....BATTLE-SCENE   85   39
   LAUGHING, LAUGHING ....BATTLE-SCENE   85   39
   STOPPED AND AWFUL AS A PHOTOGRAPH OF SOMEBODY LAUGHING, ...BABY.   175   35
   LAUGHING ALOUD, THE DAZZLED BOY DEMANDS*THE PRINCESS AND THE GOBLINS   335   64
LAUGH-SHAKEN (1)
   LAUGH-SHAKEN ON HIS DOORSILL, ...THE HERMIT AT OUTERMOST HOUSE   119   10
LAUGHTER (1)
   THE LAUGHTER AND THE SCREAMS OF GREETING: ....FAMILY REUNION   300   12

LAUNCH (1)
    A CROWD OF SHINING GULLS THAT PLUNGE TO LAUNCH   . .EPITAPH IN THREE. 337 13
LAUNDER (2)
    "LET US FLATTEN AND LAUNDER THE GROSSNESS FROM THESE SOULS." *THREE. 179 91
    LAUNDER AND PRESENT THEMSELVES. ....AN APPEARANCE 189   7
LAUNDRY (4)
    TO A KNOT OF LAUNDRY, WITH A CLASSIC BUNCH OF SHEETS ......GHOST'S.   90 10
    WHOSE LAUNDRY SNAPPED AND FROZE HERE, WHO ....POINT SHIRLEY 110 10
    THEIR WHITENESS BEARS NO RELATION TO LAUNDRY, ...MAGI 148   4
    SLAPPING ITS PHANTOM LAUNDRY IN MY FACE. ............BLACKBERRYING 169 21
LAUREL (1)
    FROM THE LAUREL THICKET. NO ONE APPROACHED. ..........RHODODENDRON. 103 19
LAURELED (1)
    BUT OUT OF THE WATERY ASPIC, LAURELED BY FINS, ...LADY AND T.   69 18
LAVATORY (1)
    THE STRANGER IN THE LAVATORY MIRROR ....TALE OF A TUB   24   6
LAVENDER (1)
    IN PINK AND LAVENDER ....BATTLE-SCENE   84   3
LAVISH (1)
    IN THE RARE RIVER WINK AND LAUGH; WE LAVISH .....LOVE IS A PARALLAX 330 38
LAW (1)
    ORBIT; NEITHER LAW NOR PROPHETS *INSOLENT STORM STRIKES AT THE SKULL 326 26
LAWN (2)
    TO HUSTLE THEM OFF THE LAWN. ....OLD LADIES' HOME 120 16
    AND SLIPS UNSEEN PAST WATCHMEN ON THE LAWN ....THE PRINCESS. 334 29
LAWNS (1)
    POISON OF STILLED LAWNS, THE LITTLE CLAPBOARD GRAVESTONES,   WAKING. 151   7
LAY (13)
    ALL AFTERNOON THESE LOVERS LAY ....BUCOLICS   24 13
    TORPID WARNING, OR LAY STILL ....SPIDER   49 20
    YET WON'T LAY ONE. ....RHYME   50   3
    I NOSE OUT THE LAY ....WORDS FOR A NURSERY   74 23
    LAY OVER THE LEAVES LIKE A CLEAR CELLOPHANE, ...SPINACH-PICKER   89   4
    YOUR VOICES LAY SIEGE. YOU LODGE ....LORELEI   94 23
    I LAY DREAMING YOUR EPIC, IMAGE BY IMAGE. ...ELECTRA ON AZALEA PATH 116 12
    THE BRONZE SNAKE LAY IN THE SUN ....MEDALLION 124   3
    LIMPID AS SPIRITS. MANY STONES LAY ....LOVE LETTER 147 22
    SHE LAY IN BED WITH ME LIKE A DEAD BODY ....IN PLASTER 158   6
    A PAPER IMAGE TO LAY AGAINST HER HEART ....WIDOW 164 17
    I LAY MY EAR TO FURIOUS LATIN. ....THE ARRIVAL OF THE BEE BOX 213 21
    AND VIRGINS RISE WHERE LUSTFUL VENUS LAY: .....NEVER TRY TO TRICK. 319   5
LAYER (4)
    LAYER ON LAYER, AND YOU HAD A BASKET ...MEMOIRS OF A SPINACH-PICKER   89   9
    LAYER ON LAYER, AND YOU HAD A BASKET ...MEMOIRS OF A SPINACH-PICKER   89   9
    NOW COLDNESS COMES SIFTING DOWN, LAYER AFTER LAYER, ...POEM.5.F. 134   1
    NOW COLDNESS COMES SIFTING DOWN, LAYER AFTER LAYER, ...POEM.5.F. 134   1
LAYING (1)
    LAYING ITS SCALES ON THE WINDOWS, THE WINDOWS OF EMPTY OFFICES, ...
                                                    ... THREE WOMEN 181 178
LAYS (3)
    LAYS ALL WALLS WASTE; PRIVATE ESTATES ARE TORN, ...CHANNEL CROSSING   27 31
    AND DAYLIGHT LAYS ITS SAMENESS ON THE WALL. POEM.7.S. 137 26
    THE MOON LAYS A HAND ON MY FOREHEAD, ...BARREN WOMAN 157   9
LAZARUS (1)
    LADY LAZARUS ....LADY LAZARUS 244   T
LAZILY (1)
    HAD LAZILY CLOSED ONE EYE AND LET THEM SLIP ....LYONNESSE 234 21
LAZULI (1)
    ROCKING ACROSS THE LAPIS LAZULI SEA ....EPITAPH IN THREE PARTS 337   1
LAZY (1)
    ON HIM SOMETIMES. HE'S LAZY. LIKE ANY YOUNG ....DIALOGUE O. 281 182
LE (1)
    DANS LE FOND DES FORETS VOTRE IMAGE ME SUIT. ....PURSUIT   22   E
LEAD (4)
    TO PEOPLE THE TWIGGED AISLES; LEAD BABEL TONGUES*WREATH FOR A BRIDAL   45 14
    WHO BORROWED FEATHERS FOR YOUR FEET, NOT LEAD, ...PERSEUS   83 12
    THE MOON LEANS, A STONE MADONNA, OVER THE LEAD SEA   THE NET-MENDERS 121 15
    A DOZEN RED LEAD SINKERS ROUND MY NECK. ....TULIPS 161 42
LEADEN (2)
    THE LEADEN SLAG OF THE WORLD -- ....DEPARTURE   51 11
    I MALIGN THE LEADEN PERSPECTIVE ....LANDOWNERS   53   3
LEADING (1)
    THEY ARE LEADING ME TO THE SHORN GROVE, THE CIRCLE OF HIVES. ..BEE. 211 23
LEADS (2)
    A BLACK SHEEP LEADS THE SHEPHERDS' FLOCK. ....A WINTER'S TALE   86   7
    AND LEADS HIM HOME TO BE HER CHOSEN KNIGHT. ....THE PRINCESS. 334 50
LEAF (18)
    HEAVES FORTH STALK, LEAF, FRUIT-NUBBED EMERALD; ....ODE FOR TED   29 15
    IT WERE A GREEN-TIPPED LEAF ....SONG FOR A SUMMER'S DAY   31 13
    CROW'S-FEET COPY VEINING ON STAINED LEAF; ....VANITY FAIR   32   7
    LIKE A LAST STORM-CROSSED LEAF? BEST GET YOU GONE ......DIALOGUE B.   39 44
    MY JILTING LADY SQUANDER COIN, GOLD LEAF STOCK DITCHES,   CONJURING.   66 35
    BUT FROM LEAF, FROM GRASS,*ON THE DIFFICULTY OF CONJURING UP A DRYAD   66 39
    NOT ONE LEAF WRINKLED IN THE CLEARING AIR. ....THE OTHER TWO   68   5
    LEAF, BECOME EYELID; SNAKE-BODIES, BOUGH, BREAST ......SNAKECHARMER   79 14

LEAF (CONT.)   TITLE   PAGE   LINE

Entry	Title	Page	Line
TO US, SINCE WE SEE NO LEAF EDGE STIR HIGH	ABOVE THE OXBOW	88	33
AND GOLDENROD AS ON GOLD LEAF.	IN MIDAS' COUNTRY	99	10
LEAF UNLIKE ANY	POLLY'S TREE	128	5
GHOST OF A LEAF, GHOST OF A BIRD.	PARLIAMENT HILL FIELDS	153	28
SO THAT EACH MARCH I MAY GLEAM INTO LEAF,	I AM VERTICAL	162	4
IT UNCLAPS, BROWN AS A LEAF, AND LOUD,	PHEASANT	191	21
THE WORD OF A SNAIL ON THE PLATE OF A LEAF?	THE COURIERS	247	1
FROST ON A LEAF, THE IMMACULATE	THE COURIERS	247	7
EACH FALLEN LEAF IS TRAPPED BY SPELL OF STEEL,	PROLOGUE TO SPRING	322	7
OF CHILD, LEAF AND CLOUD,	TOUCH-AND-GO	336	21
LEAFAGE (1)			
PURE LEAFAGE. A HUNDRED BASKETS BY DAY'S END.	SPINACH-PICKER.	89	11
LEAF-AND-FLOWER (1)			
MADE LACE, OR A LEAF-AND-FLOWER PEN-SKETCH.	SOUTHERN SUNRISE	26	6
LEAF-FILTERED (1)			
TO LOOM IN THE LEAF-FILTERED GLOOM	CHILD'S PARK STONES	100	4
LEAFLET (1)			
FINGERING A LEAFLET OF MUSIC, OVER HIM,	*TWO VIEWS OF A CADAVER ROOM	114	17
LEAF-LINED (1)			
GO SNARE THE SLEEPING BEAR IN LEAF-LINED DEN	*GO GET THE GOODLY SQUAB	313	9
LEAF'S (1)			
PURPLES THE FIG IN THE LEAF'S SHADOW, TURNS THE DUST PINK.	NET-.	121	7
LEAF-SHUTTERED (1)			
OF SUCH SEEING UP THE LEAF-SHUTTERED ESCARPMENTS,	ABOVE THE OXBOW	88	27
LEAF-SIZE (1)			
TO LEAF-SIZE FROM LACK OF ACTION:	THE TIMES ARE TIDY	107	9
LEAF-STALK (1)			
CAPER ON LEAFSTALK LEGS ACROSS MY DOORSILL,	EPITAPH IN THREE PARTS	337	24
LEAF-WRAITHED (1)			
ABOVE: LEAF-WRAITHED WHITE AIR, WHITE CLOUD.	BUCOLICS	24	12
LEAFY (3)			
THEIR LEAFY CROWNS, THEIR FAME SOARS,	VIRGIN IN A TREE	81	18
THE LEAFY BEDDING,	MUSHROOMS	139	12
BLACK AND LEAFY, AS IN MY CHILDHOOD,	LITTLE FUGUE	188	24
LEAGUES (1)			
STEP OFF SEVEN LEAGUES, LIKE THOSE DISTANCES	GULLIVER	251	21
LEAKED (1)			
AND WHAT IF TWO LIVES LEAKED BETWEEN MY THIGHS?	THREE WOMEN	180	120
LEAKING (2)			
IS LEAKING FROM THE FINGER-VENTS. AT THE COUNT OF TWO	FACE LIFT	156	14
SEE, THE DARKNESS IS LEAKING FROM THE CRACKS.	THREE WOMEN	182	195
LEAKS (1)			
MEANING LEAKS FROM THE MOLECULES.	MYSTIC	269	27
LEAKY (1)			
MAUDLIN FROM LEAKY EYE TO SWOLLEN NOSE.	THE RAVAGED FACE	115	4
LEAN (11)			
LEAN TO MY WOUND; BURN ON, BURN ON.	FIRESONG	30	21
AFTER A LEAN DAY'S WORK	STRUMPET SONG	33	3
LEAN FACE GONE TAWN WITH SEASONS,	CRYSTAL GAZER	54	2
LEAN INCANDESCENT	BLACK ROOK IN RAINY WEATHER	57	15
MADE LEAN LENT	SOW	61	42
GREW SO LEAN AND WOULD NOT ROUND	THE THIN PEOPLE	64	8
I LEAN TO YOU, NUMB AS A FOSSIL. TELL ME I'M HERE.	TWO CAMP.	145	21
SOLID THE SPACES LEAN ON, ENVIOUS.	NICK AND THE CANDLESTICK	242	41
THESE MANNEQUINS LEAN TONIGHT	THE MUNICH MANNEQUINS	263	11
LEAN AND SEE ME.	GIGOLO	268	32
MY LEAN, UNRIPENED HEART.	JILTED	304	12
LEANED (2)			
A WHOLE SEA OF SPINACH-HEADS LEANED TO MY HAND.	SPINACH-PICKER.	90	22
LEANED THE DEVIL PROMPTING YOU TO LAUGH.	DIRGE FOR A JOKER	302	4
LEANING (2)			
AGAINST MY LEANING DOWN, WOULD NOT EXCHANGE	INCOMMUNICADO	100	5
LEANING OVER, I ENCOUNTER ONE	THE BURNT-OUT SPA	138	24
LEANS (12)			
LEANS TO PECK OPEN THOSE LOCKED LIDS, TO EAT	THE SHRIKE	42	18
THE MOON LEANS, A STONE MADONNA, OVER THE LEAD SEA	THE NET-MENDERS	121	15
THE SKY LEANS ON ME, ME, THE ONE UPRIGHT	WUTHERING HEIGHTS	168	37
THE PRINCE LEANS TO THE GIRL IN SCARLET HEELS,	CINDERELLA	303	1
THE IDIOT BIRD LEAPS UP AND DRUNKEN LEANS	SONNET: TO EVA	305	13
THE IDIOT BIRD LEAPS OUT AND DRUNKEN LEANS.	DOOMSDAY	316	1
THE IDIOT BIRD LEAPS OUT AND DRUNKEN LEANS.	DOOMSDAY	316	6
THE IDIOT BIRD LEAPS OUT AND DRUNKEN LEANS.	DOOMSDAY	316	12
THE IDIOT BIRD LEAPS OUT AND DRUNKEN LEANS,	DOOMSDAY	316	18
THE MOON LEANS DOWN TO LOOK; THE TILTING FISH	LOVE IS A PARALLAX	330	37
NOW KISS AGAIN: TILL OUR STRICT FATHER LEANS	LOVE IS A PARALLAX	330	43
HER LEGENDARY GODMOTHER LEANS DOWN,	THE PRINCESS AND THE GOBLINS	333	15
LEAP (1)			
THE CHILDREN LEAP IN THEIR COTS.	MYSTIC	269	29
LEAPING (1)			
LEAPING AWKWARD AND LONG-LEGGED	BITTER STRAWBERRIES	299	16
LEAPS (10)			
LEAPS TO LAUD SUCH MAN'S BLOOD!	ODE FOR TED	30	24
THE GRITTED WAVE LEAPS	POINT SHIRLEY	110	5
IN MY COURTYARD A FOUNTAIN LEAPS AND SINKS BACK INTO ITSELF,	*BARREN.	157	3

```
                                              TITLE        PAGE  LINE
LEAPS (CONT.)
   SUCH PURE LEAPS AND SPIRALS --- . ..................THE NIGHT DANCES  249   5
   THE IDIOT BIRD LEAPS UP AND DRUNKEN LEANS .. .......SONNET: TO EVA    305  13
   THE IDIOT BIRD LEAPS OUT AND DRUNKEN LEANS ................DOOMSDAY  316   1
   THE IDIOT BIRD LEAPS OUT AND DRUNKEN LEANS. ..............DOOMSDAY.  316   6
   THE IDIOT BIRD LEAPS OUT AND DRUNKEN LEANS. .............DOOMSDAY.  316  12
   THE IDIOT BIRD LEAPS OUT AND DRUNKEN LEANS, ..............DOOMSDAY  316  18
   WITH A LAST ARTFUL DODGE SHE LEAPS .......................AERIALIST  332  39
LEARN (3)
   I LEARN, GOOD CIRCUS ...........................WORDS FOR A NURSERY   73  11
   AND LEARN TO SPEAK WITH FINGERS, NOT A TONGUE. .........THREE WOMEN  184 255
   EACH TIME MUST LEARN THE LETTERS NEW. ARE ..............DIALOGUE O.  277  24
LEARNED (4)
   I LEARNED, I LEARNED, I LEARNED ELSEWHERE, ...THE DISQUIETING MUSES   75  39
   I LEARNED, I LEARNED, I LEARNED ELSEWHERE, ...THE DISQUIETING MUSES   75  39
   I LEARNED, I LEARNED, I LEARNED ELSEWHERE, ...THE DISQUIETING MUSES   75  39
   NOR BY ANY LEARNED MAN. ......................THE BULL OF BENDYLAW  108  18
LEARNING (2)
   I AM LEARNING PEACEFULNESS, LYING BY MYSELF QUIETLY .........TULIPS  160   3
   INTOLERANT BEAUTY NEVER WILL BE LEARNING. .......TO EVA DESCENDING.  303  17
LEASH (3)
   BY GOING FAR; MY LOOK'S LEASH ..........SOLILOQUY OF THE SOLIPSIST   37  13
   RAVE ON THE LEASH OF THE STARVING MIND ..........NOVEMBER GRAVEYARD   56  17
   THE SILVER LEASH OF THE WILL --- ....................GETTING THERE  248  15
LEAST (5)
   FOR HIS LEAST LOOK, SCANT ACRES YIELD: .................ODE FOR TED   29  13
   EMPTY, I ECHO TO THE LEAST FOOTFALL, ...................BARREN WOMAN  157   1
   AND AT LEAST IT WILL BE A GOOD PLACE NOW, THE ATTIC. ......BURNING.  204  22
   AT LEAST I WON'T BE STRUNG JUST UNDER THE SURFACE, ........BURNING.  204  23
   IT'S NOT SO IMMINENT. AT LEAST I FEEL ..DIALOGUE OVER A OUIJA BOARD  278  61
LEATHER (2)
   IN THAT RUBBLE OF SKULL PLATES AND OLD LEATHER. .........TWO VIEWS.  114   8
   MY PATENT LEATHER OVERNIGHT CASE LIKE A BLACK PILLBOX, ......TULIPS  160  19
LEATHERINESS (1)
   WHAT LEATHERINESS .........................................THALIDOMIDE  252   8
LEATHER-KNEED (1)
   I BENT OVER THE PLANTS IN MY LEATHER-KNEED .........SPINACH-PICKER.   89  17
LEATHERY (1)
   LEATHERY, TREELESS, .............................WORDS FOR A NURSERY   74  29
LEAVE (14)
   BY LEAVE OF THE PARK COMMISSION ......................A WINTER'S TALE   87  22
   IF ONLY THE WIND WOULD LEAVE MY LUNGS ALONE. ...........POEM.1.WHO.  131  10
   DEAD MEN LEAVE EYES FOR OTHERS. .........................POEM.7.S.  137  38
   NOR LEAVE ME TO SET MY SMALL BALD EYE ...................LOVE LETTER  147   6
   LEAVE HER ALONE NOW. ......................................A LIFE  150  30
   SHE WANTED TO LEAVE ME, SHE THOUGHT SHE WAS SUPERIOR, ...IN PLASTER  159  36
   YOU LEAVE THE SAME IMPRESSION .............................THE RIVAL  166   2
   I LEAVE MY HEALTH BEHIND. I LEAVE SOMEONE ..............THREE WOMEN  184 272
   I LEAVE MY HEALTH BEHIND. I LEAVE SOMEONE ..............THREE WOMEN  184 272
   WHAT DID I LEAVE UNTOUCHED ON THE DOORSTEP -- ............THE OTHER  201   2
   LEAVE AND ARRIVE, AND THERE IS NO END TO THE COUNTRY. .....THE SWARM  217  36
   PEOPLE LIKE LIGHT RAYS, LEAVE ............................BRASILIA  259  19
   TO LEAVE OUR REASON ........................MOONSONG AT MORNING  317   9
   TO LEAVE HER BED OF FEVER AND ASCEND ..THE PRINCESS AND THE GOBLINS  333   4
LEAVED (1)
   FRESH LEAVED OUT IN VOWS: "COME TELL .................CRYSTAL GAZER   55   8
LEAVES (42)
   "TEA LEAVES I'VE GIVEN UP, ..............................RECANTATION   41   1
   THIS DREAM BUDDED BRIGHT WITH LEAVES AROUND THE EDGES,*DREAM WITH C.   43   1
   WHAT THOUGH GREEN LEAVES ONLY WITNESS ..........WREATH FOR A BRIDAL   44   1
   OUTSIDE, THE LITTLE HEDGE LEAVES ARE .......................RESOLVE   52   8
   HOARD LAST YEAR'S LEAVES, WON'T MOURN, WEAR SACKCLOTH, OR TURN ...
                                         ... NOVEMBER GRAVEYARD   56   2
   BUT LET SPOTTED LEAVES FALL AS THEY FALL, .............BLACK ROOK I.   57   9
   THE GUISE OF LEAVES. THE WHOLE LANDSCAPE ...........HARDCASTLE CRAGS   63  37
   HEART-SHAPED LEAVES, LIKE CATALPA LEAVES, AND LILIES .....YADWIGHA.   85   6
   HEART-SHAPED LEAVES, LIKE CATALPA LEAVES, AND LILIES .....YADWIGHA.   85   6
   LEAVES AND LILIES FLATTENED TO PAPER BEHIND YOU ..........YADWIGHA.   85  16
   HERE ON A MOUNT OVERLAID WITH LEAVES. THE PAINT-PEELED .....OXBOW.   88  34
   LAY OVER THE LEAVES LIKE A CLEAR CELLOPHANE, .......SPINACH-PICKER.   89   4
   GRUB-WHITE MULBERRIES REDDEN AMONG LEAVES. .................MOONRISE   98   1
   HOLDING THE HORSES, THE CLOUDS, THE LEAVES ............THE EYE-MOTE  109   6
   LEAVES BEHIND US WARP AND LAPSE. ....................MAGNOLIA SHOALS  122  11
   THE SNAIL LEAVES A SILVER TRACK; ......................THE SLEEPERS  122  10
   AND LEAVES STEADFAST IN SHAPE .........................THE SLEEPERS  123  14
   LEAVES, UNDOING THEIR YELLOW CAVES .....................BLUE MOLES  126  11
   THE BEAN LEAVES ARE DUMB AS HANDS. ..................POEM.3.MAENAD.  133  10
   IN THE MONTH OF RED LEAVES I CLIMB TO A BED OF FIRE. .....POEM.6.W.  135   6
   A COOL WIND SHOULD INHABIT THOSE LEAVES  SLEEP IN THE MOJAVE DESERT  144   8
   ARE THOSE PETALS OR LEAVES YOU'VE PAIRED THEM WITH -- *LEAVING EARLY  146  14
   WHEN ONE OF THEM FALLS IT LEAVES A SPACE, ..STARS OVER THE DORDOGNE  166  32
   LEAVES AND PETALS ATTEND ME. I AM READY. ..............THREE WOMEN  177  14
   THE YELLOW MINUTE BEFORE THE WIND WALKS, WHEN THE LEAVES*THREE WOMEN  179  93
   THEIR LEAVES DO NOT WISH US TO HURRY: ...........CROSSING THE WATER  190   5
   THE NATURAL FATNESS OF THESE LIME LEAVES! --- .........BERCK-PLAGE  199  91
```

LEAVES (CONT.)
    TELLING THE PARTICLES OF THE CLOUDS, THE LEAVES, THE WATER *BURNING. 205   55
    CREAMY BEAN FLOWERS WITH BLACK EYES AND LEAVES LIKE BORED HEARTS. ...
                                    ... THE BEE MEETING 211   18
    GOLD LEAVES METAL AND BREATHLESS. ....LETTER IN NOVEMBER 253   30
    O MOTHER OF LEAVES AND SWEETNESS ....WINTER TREES 258   13
    THE TRAIN LEAVES A LINE OF BREATH. ....SHEEP IN FOG 262   4
    AND HALE ITS GREEN LATTICEWORK OF LEAVES. YOU NEED .....DIALOGUE O. 280 159
    NOVEMBER'S DONE WITH. THE BLOWN LEAVES MAKE BAT-SHAPES, *DIALOGUE O. 286 337
    WE REACHED AMONG THE LEAVES ....BITTER STRAWBERRIES 300   35
    NOURISHING AS VIOLET LEAVES ....APRIL 18 302   10
    AND HOW A HUNDRED THOUSAND LEAVES ....GOLD MOUTHS CRY 302   4
    AND HIS EYES GONE BLIND WITH LEAVES. ....GOLD MOUTHS CRY 302   14
    TATTOOS BLACK LEAVES ON TANGERINE. ....BLACK PINE TREE. 328   12
    THE LEAVES APPLAUD, AND SANTA CLAUS FLIES IN ....LOVE IS A PARALLAX 329   34
    FLARING GREEN THROUGH PHILODENDRON LEAVES ......MORNING IN THE HOS. 332   2
    SIBYL'S LEAVES BLOW. ....TEMPER OF TIME 336   8
LEAVES'(2)
    AND THE LEAVES' LITTER. ....SPINSTER   49   6
    OF LEAVES' BICKER AND WHISK IN BABEL TONGUES, ..PLETHORA OF DRYADS.   67   21
LEAVETAKING (2)
    UNGIFTED, UNGRIEVED, OUR LEAVETAKING. ....DEPARTURE   51   6
    THE GHOST'S LEAVETAKING ....THE GHOST'S LEAVETAKING   90   T
LEAVING (3)
    LEAVING NO SPARKY TRACK, SETTING UP NO RIPPLE. ....THE OTHER TWO   68   26
    LEAVING A SALTY MASH OF ICE TO WHITEN ....POINT SHIRLEY 110   8
    LEAVING EARLY ....LEAVING EARLY 145   T
LEAVINGS (1)
    MUD STENCH, SHELL GUTS, GULLS' LEAVINGS; ....MUSSEL HUNTER.   95   13
LECHER'S (1)
    THE SHEETS GROW HEAVY AS A LECHER'S KISS. ....FEVER. 231   30
LED (1)
    THEIR SMILES AND THEIR VOICES ARE CHANGING. I AM LED THROUGH A
            BEANFIELD. ....THE BEE MEETING 211   15
LEDAS (1)
    IN THIS, THEY ARE LEDAS. ....WINTER TREES 258   12
LEDGE (3)
    LEDGE WILL DISLODGE OUR CRAMPED CONCEPT OF SPACE, UNWALL ....OXBOW.   88   23
    OF HEBETUDE, FROM THE LEDGE ....LORELEI   94   27
    AND FACED ME, BACK TO A LEDGE OF DIRT, TO RATTLE .....INCOMMUNICADO 100   3
LEDGES (1)
    THE FORGETFUL SURF CREAMING ON THOSE LEDGES. ..SUICIDE OFF EGG ROCK 115   24
LEECHES (1)
    HE LEECHES BY OUR LENIENCE. HE STILL BORES ....DIALOGUE O. 283 259
LEER (1)
    BETTER THE FLAT LEER OF THE IDIOT, ...THE RAVAGED FACE 116   9
LEERED (1)
    THE SIMULACRUM LEERED, ...THE LADY AND THE EARTHENWARE HEAD   69   19
LEERS (1)
    A WHIRLPOOL LEERS AT ME, ...FAMILY REUNION 301   27
LEFT (21)
    THINKING NEVER TO HAVE LEFT THE WORLD, YOU GRIEVE ......DIALOGUE B.   39   34
    AND IN FURY LEFT HIM ....THE SNOWMAN ON THE MOOR   58   4
    NIGHTLY WE LEFT THEM IN THEIR DESERT PLACE. ....THE OTHER TWO   68   27
    THE LEFT MY LACKEY, ...WORDS FOR A NURSERY   74   34
    AND AT THE LEFT SIDE OF MY CRIB? ....THE DISQUIETING MUSES   75   8
    AND LEFT THE COBS TO RATTLE, BITTEN CLEAN. ....OUIJA   77   18
    A PANE OF DRAGONFLY WING, WHEN THEY LEFT ME ....SPINACH-PICKER.   89   5
    AWAY TO THE LEFT LIKE REEDS IN A SEA ....THE EYE-MOTE 109   8
    TO THE LEFT, AND THE WAVE ....MAN IN BLACK 119   4
    OF YOUR LEFT EAR, OUT OF THE WIND, ...THE COLOSSUS 130   25
    I AM LEFT WITH AN ARM OR A LEG, ...THE SURGEON AT 2 A.M. 171   33
    THEY LEFT ME A BORROWED MAID NAMED ELLEN, "FOR PROTECTION", ..BABY. 174   17
    MY LIMBS, ALSO, HAVE LEFT ME. ....EVENT 195   20
    AND THE MEN, WHAT IS LEFT OF THE MEN ....GETTING THERE 248   29
    A FLOWER LEFT OUT. ....SHEEP IN FOG 262   10
    WITHOUT A PART LEFT OVER, ...MYSTIC 268   11
    DO YOU KNOW HOW MY FATHER IS? HE'S LEFT *DIALOGUE OVER A OUIJA BOARD 278   74
    SO CRY FOR THE PAGAN GIRL LEFT PICKING OLIVES ......SONNET: TO TIME 311   9
    LET NOTHING BE LEFT TO SWADDLE US. ...SONG FOR A REVOLUTIONARY LOVE 323   12
    AND LEFT OUR BANKRUPT CIRCUS ON ITS OWN: ....DENOUEMENT 326   2
    BLESSINGS RIGHT AND LEFT AND CRY ....LOVE IS A PARALLAX 330   39
LEFTOVER (1)
    LEFTOVER SOLDIERS FROM OLD, MESSY WARS. ....FINISTERRE 169   7
LEG (7)
    FISH-TAILED GIRLS PURCHASE EACH WHITE LEG. ....MAUDLIN   51   8
    GIVING A LEG UP ....WORDS FOR A NURSERY   73   9
    AN ARM AND A LEG, AN ARM, A LEG. ....LOVE LETTER 147   32
    AN ARM AND A LEG, AN ARM, A LEG. ....LOVE LETTER 147   32
    I AM LEFT WITH AN ARM OR A LEG, ...THE SURGEON AT 2 A.M. 171   33
    AS IF I HAD LOST AN EYE, A LEG, A TONGUE. ....THREE WOMEN 183 252
    YOU HAD ONE LEG, AND A PRUSSIAN MIND. ....LITTLE FUGUE 188   40
LEGAL (1)
    YOU WERE CONDEMNED TO SERVE THE LEGAL LIMIT ....THE TRIAL OF MAN 312   10

LEGEND (1)
  PIG HOVE, LETTING LEGEND LIKE DRIED MUD DROP, ...SOW   61   37
LEGENDARY (3)
  BREAKING ON LEGENDARY BEACHES; IN FAITH ....TALE OF A TUB   25   45
  SORROW; WEEP FOR THE LEGENDARY DRAGON. ....SONNET: TO TIME   311   12
  HER LEGENDARY GODMOTHER LEANS DOWN, ...THE PRINCESS AND THE GOBLINS   333   15
LEGGING (1)
  LEGGING IT MOST NIMBLE ....ODE FOR TED   29   4
LEGGY (1)
  ONE-THIRD ANT-SIZE, A LEGGY SPOT, ...SPIDER   48   12
LEGION (1)
  SPROUTING FRUIT, FLOWERS, CHILDREN MOST FAIR IN LEGION ...WREATH F.   45   22
LEGS (10)
  ON ARMS AND LEGS IN A FRINGE OF KELP; GREEN SOAP .....TALE OF A TUB   25   43
  FROM WHICH COILS, CAUGHT ANTS WAVED LEGS IN ....SPIDER   49   19
  A MONGREL WORKING HIS LEGS TO A GALLOP ....SUICIDE OFF EGG ROCK   115   12
  MY SWADDLED LEGS AND ARMS SMELL SWEET AS RUBBER. POEM.7.S.   137   34
  COT LEGS MELTED IN TERRIBLE ATTITUDES, AND THE NURSES -- ...WAKING.   151   12
  AWAY ON WHEELS, INSTEAD OF LEGS, THEY SERVE AS WELL. ...THREE WOMEN   184 254
  AND NEWTS ARE PRODIGAL IN LEGS. AND MAY I BE ....THREE WOMEN   184 258
  I HAVE TWO LEGS, AND I MOVE SMILINGLY. ....BERCK-PLAGE   196   6
  LEGS, ARMS PILED OUTSIDE ....GETTING THERE   248   26
  CAPER ON LEAFSTALK LEGS ACROSS MY DOORSILL, EPITAPH IN THREE PARTS   337   24
LEG-STUMP (1)
  PROPS A LEG-STUMP UPON A CRUTCH, ...THE BEGGARS   48   11
LEMON (6)
  COLOR OF LEMON, MANGO, PEACH, ...SOUTHERN SUNRISE   26   1
  AND SALLOW AS ANY LEMON, ...TWO SISTERS OF PERSEPHONE   32   25
  LEMON WATER, CHICKEN ....FEVER.   232   32
  IT'LL BE LEMON TEA FOR ME, ...THE TOUR   238   38
  LEMON TEA AND EARWIG BISCUITS -- CREEPY-CREEPY. ....THE TOUR   238   39
  THE SOUR LEMON MOON. ....JILTED   304   8
LEMON-TASTING (1)
  GIVEN HER LIPS THAT LEMON-TASTING DROOP: ....VIRGIN IN A TREE   82   42
LENDING (1)
  IS ON THE TWO OF US FOR LENDING HEAT ...DIALOGUE OVER A OUIJA BOARD   282 229
LENGTH (1)
  CATASTROPHE A WRITHING LENGTH OF COBRA, ...PERSEUS   83   22
LENGTHEN (1)
  THAT LENGTHEN FROM ANCIENT CATHEDRALS ....MYSTIC   268   14
LENGTHENING (1)
  I AM AT HOME IN THE LAMPLIGHT. THE EVENINGS ARE LENGTHENING. *THREE.   186 351
LENGTHS (1)
  WITH REEDY LENGTHS AND NECKS AND UNDULATINGS. .........SNAKECHARMER   79   5
LENIENCE (1)
  HE LEECHES BY OUR LENIENCE. HE STILL BORES ....DIALOGUE O.   283 259
LENS (3)
  THE BURNISHED BALL HANGS FIRE IN HER HANDS, A LENS ...CRYSTAL GAZER   54   5
  LENS OF MERCIES, ...MEDUSA   224   5
  INVADES THE DILATE LENS OF GENESIS ....SONNET TO SATAN   323   10
LENT (1)
  MADE LEAN LENT ....SOW   61   42
LEO (1)
  THE ASTROLOGER AT HER ELBOW (A LEO) ....ON DECK   143   25
LEONARD (1)
  FOR LEONARD BASKIN ....SCULPTOR   91   D
LEOPARD (2)
  ME, SITTING HERE BORED AS A LEOPARD ....LEAVING EARLY   145   3
  DEVILISH LEOPARD! ....FEVER.   231   22
LEPRECHAUN (1)
  NOW YOU, MY INTELLECTUAL LEPRECHAUN, ...LOVE IS A PARALLAX   329   25
LEPROUS (1)
  HIS TEETH ARE CHATTERING AMONG THE LEPROUS ..THE EVERLASTING MONDAY   62   5
LEROY (NOT COUNTED)
  LEROY ....DIALOGUE OVER A OUIJA BOARD   276   DP
LESBOS (1)
  LESBOS ....LESBOS   227   T
LESS (8)
  LESS THAN PRESENT, PAST -- THIS FUTURE. ..ON THE DECLINE OF ORACLES   78   29
  ON A TIGER TOOTH, LESS FOR ....MUSSEL HUNTER AT ROCK HARBOR   97   81
  THE PARK OF LESS RED THAN WITHERING DID. .............RHODODENDRON.   103   12
  ATTENDING HER COT IS LESS THAN A BELLY ACHE, ...MAGI   148   13
  YOU KNOW ME LESS CONSTANT, ...PARLIAMENT HILL FIELDS   153   27
  BUT NO LESS A DEVIL FOR THAT, NO NOT ....DADDY   223   54
  ANY LESS THE BLACK MAN WHO ....DADDY   223   55
  LESS DREAD OF THE WORLD BEYOND THAN OURS. THAT'S BECAUSE*DIALOGUE O.   278   62
LESSON (2)
  DEMURE ONES, LITHE ONES, NEEDING NO LESSON ....ELLA MASON A.   54   40
  A LESSON IN VENGEANCE ....A LESSON IN VENGEANCE   80   T
LESSONED (1)
  LESSONED THUS, THE GIRL ....AERIALIST   331   19
LESSONS (1)
  MOTHER, YOU SENT ME TO PIANO LESSONS ....THE DISQUIETING MUSES   75   33
LEST (4)
  LEST THE LIGHTNING STRIKE YOU TO CINDER. ...GO GET THE GOODLY SQUAB   313   8

                                                      TITLE   PAGE LINE
LEST (CONT.)
    LEST THE BLIZZARD DRIVE YOU BLIND. . . . . . . .GO GET THE GOODLY SQUAB 313   16
    LEST THE WATER DRAG YOU TO DROWN. . . . . .GO GET THE GOODLY SQUAB 313   24
    LEST, OUT OF SPITE, THE WHOLE .AERIALIST 332   46
LET (74)
    CRYING: BLOOD, LET BLOOD BE SPILT; . . . . .PURSUIT   22   15
    LET JACK CATCH FIRE." . . . . .TINKER JACK AND THE TIDY WIVES   35   33
    GOODBYES WERE SAID, TRAINS LET GO, ...MONOLOGUE AT 3 A.M.   40   12
    LET BE YOUR CON BRIOS, YOUR CAPRICCIOSOS, ...ALICANTE LULLABY   43   17
    LOW MOOS OF APPROVE; LET SUN SURPLICED IN BRIGHTNESS . . . . .WREATH F.   44   4
    LET NIGHT BLESS THAT LUCK-ROOTED MEAD OF CLOVER *WREATH FOR A BRIDAL   45   17
    LET FLESH BE KNIT, AND EACH STEP HENCE GO FAMOUS. . . . . .WREATH F.   45   24
    A TREASON NOT TO BE BORNE. LET IDIOTS . . . . .SPINSTER   50   22
    BUT LET SPOTTED LEAVES FALL AS THEY FALL, ...BLACK ROOK I.   57   9
    LET HIM SEND POLICE AND HOUNDS TO BRING HER IN. . . . . .SNOWMAN O.   58   19
    LET BELL-TONGUED BIRDS DESCANT IN BLACKEST FEATHER . . . . .LADY AND T.   69   25
    STALLED, LET FALL THEIR VERTICAL .NIGHT SHIFT   76   18
    OF SNAKY GENERATIONS: LET THERE BE SNAKES! . . . . .SNAKECHARMER   79   20
    LET DROP ITS SPITTLE OF SLUGGISH GREEN . . . . .RHODODENDRON. 103   6
    LET ME SIT IN A FLOWERPOT, ...POEM.1.WHO. 131   7
    TO BE LET LOOSE AT NEWS OF LAND. . . . . .ON DECK 143   36
    LET THEM ASTOUND HIS HEART WITH THEIR MERIT. . . . . .MAGI 148   17
    LET HER DIE THERE, OR WITHER INCESSANTLY FOR THE NEXT FIFTY
         YEARS, ...FACE LIFT 156   29
    SHE LET IN THE DRAFTS AND BECAME MORE AND MORE ABSENT-MINDED,
                                   . . . IN PLASTER 159   32
    I HAVE LET THINGS SLIP, A THIRTY-YEAR-OLD CARGO BOAT . . . . .TULIPS 161   22
    I MUST SEAL OFF AND LET FILL . . . . .THE SURGEON AT 2 A.M. 171   25
    LET ME HAVE MY COPPER COOKING POTS, LET MY ROUGE POTS . . .LAST WORDS 172   21
    LET ME HAVE MY COPPER COOKING POTS, LET MY ROUGE POTS . . .LAST WORDS 172   21
    WITH A POLISHED MAHOGANY STAIR TO LET INTO THE WATER*THE BABYSITTERS 174   11
    "LET US MAKE A HEAVEN," THEY SAY. . . . . .THREE WOMEN 179   90
    "LET US FLATTEN AND LAUNDER THE GROSSNESS FROM THESE SOULS." *THREE. 179   91
    I SHALL BE A SKY AND A HILL OF GOOD: O LET ME BE! . . . . . .THREE WOMEN 180 140
    I SHALL NOT LET GO. . . . . .THREE WOMEN 181 174
    I TRESPASS STUPIDLY. LET BE, LET BE. . . . . .PHEASANT 191   24
    I TRESPASS STUPIDLY. LET BE, LET BE. . . . . .PHEASANT 191   24
    I LET HER GO. I LET HER GO . . . . .ELM 192   25
    I LET HER GO. I LET HER GO . . . . .ELM 192   25
    LET US SIT DOWN TO IT, ONE ON EITHER SIDE, ADMIRING THE GLEAM, . . .
                                   . . . A BIRTHDAY PRESENT 207   24
    LET US EAT OUR LAST SUPPER AT IT, LIKE A HOSPITAL PLATE. BIRTHDAY. 207   26
    IS IT IMPOSSIBLE FOR YOU TO LET SOMETHING GO AND HAVE IT GO
         WHOLE? . . . . .A BIRTHDAY PRESENT 207   45
    LET IT NOT COME BY THE MAIL, FINGER BY FINGER. . .A BIRTHDAY PRESENT 208   52
    LET IT NOT COME BY WORD OF MOUTH, I SHOULD BE SIXTY . . . . . .BIRTHDAY. 208   53
    ONLY LET DOWN THE VEIL, THE VEIL, THE VEIL. . . . .A BIRTHDAY PRESENT 208   55
    HOW CAN I LET THEM OUT? . . . . .THE ARRIVAL OF THE BEE BOX 213   16
    HAD LAZILY CLOSED ONE EYE AND LET THEM SLIP . . . . .LYONNESSE 234   21
    LET THE STARS .NICK AND THE CANDLESTICK 241   35
    LET THE MERCURIC .NICK AND THE CANDLESTICK 242   37
    LET THEIR SOULS WRITHE IN A DEW, ...GETTING THERE 249   62
    LET THIS EYE BE AN EAGLE, ...GULLIVER 251   23
    LET ME ROOST IN YOU! . . . . .EAVESDROPPER 260   19
    LET THEM START THE QUEER ALCHEMY . . . . .EAVESDROPPER 260   21
    TO LET ME THROUGH TO A HEAVEN .SHEEP IN FOG 262   14
    LET US EAT IT LIKE PLATO'S AFTERBIRTH, ...TOTEM 264   14
    LET US EAT IT LIKE CHRIST. . . . . .TOTEM 264   15
    LET ME RELAPSE . . . . .PARALYTIC 266   9
    WOULD TRAFFIC IN. LET HIM FINISH WHAT HE BEGAN. . . .DIALOGUE O. 278   84
    AT THE WHIM OF A WINE-GLASS AND LET US INTO WORLDS . . . . .DIALOGUE O. 280 128
    THEM ANY MORE THAN YOU DID. OH, LET IT GO. . . . . .DIALOGUE O. 283 265
    AS THE GLASS FLEW TO ITS FRAGMENTS. LET US STAKE . . . . . . .DIALOGUE O. 285 328
    AT THE UNREAL FRONTIER. LET OUR BACKS, NOW BOLD, ...DIALOGUE O. 285 331
    AND LET THE DEAD SLEEP AS THEY DESERVE. . . . . .THE RIVAL/DR 291   28
    THE MOON IS LET GO, LIKE A DEAD THING. . . . . .ELM/DR 292   8
    THAT LET ME INTO BLUEBEARD'S STUDY; . . . . .BLUEBEARD 305   2
    THAT LET ME INTO BLUEBEARD'S STUDY. . . . . .BLUEBEARD 305   8
    THE SHUTTERS TO LET WARM WIND FEATHER . . . . .THE DREAM 310   5
    GOT UP TO LET THE SUAVE BLUE POLICEMAN IN. . . . . .THE TRIAL OF MAN 312   8
    BUT LET THE FAST-FEATHERED EAGLE FLY. . . . . . .GO GET THE GOODLY SQUAB 313   4
    LET THE FAST-FEATHERED EAGLE FLY . . . . .GO GET THE GOODLY SQUAB 313   5
    BUT LET THE GALLOPING ANTELOPE RUN. . . . . .GO GET THE GOODLY SQUAB 313   12
    LET THE GALLOPING ANTELOPE RUN . . . . .GO GET THE GOODLY SQUAB 313   13
    BUT LET THE QUICKSILVER MACKEREL SWIM. . . . . . .GO GET THE GOODLY SQUAB 313   20
    LET THE QUICKSILVER MACKEREL SWIM . . . . .GO GET THE GOODLY SQUAB 313   21
    WHICH LET LOVER THINK LOVER . . . . .MOONSONG AT MORNING 317   15
    WHILE STRICKEN PATIENTS LET HIM HAVE HIS SAY; . .NEVER TRY TO TRICK. 320   8
    FIRST LET THE HEAVENLY FOLIAGE GO, . . .SONG FOR A REVOLUTIONARY LOVE 322   2
    LET NOTHING BE LEFT TO SWADDLE US. . . .SONG FOR A REVOLUTIONARY LOVE 323   12
    THE TESSELLATED WAVE. NOW NIMBLY LET . . . . .MIDSUMMER MOBILE 324   7
    THEN LET THE BLUE TENT TOPPLE, STARS RAIN DOWN, LOVE IS A PARALLAX 330   73
    LET MY TRANSIENT EYE BREAK A TEAR . . . . .TOUCH-AND-GO 336   19
LETHAL (1)
    IF YOU'VE A PLOT TO HALT THE LETHAL FLOW . . . . .THE DISPOSSESSED 318   7

	TITLE	PAGE	LINE

LETHE (3)
SLEEPILY AS LETHE. TRYING TO GET IN. ..TWO CAMPERS IN CLOUD COUNTRY 145 26
SWEET LETHE IS MY LIFE. ....AMNESIAC 233 26
STEP TO YOU FROM THE BLACK CAR OF LETHE, ...GETTING THERE 249 67
LETS (2)
ALREADY YOUR DOLL GRIP LETS GO. ....PARLIAMENT HILL FIELDS 152 25
AND LETS OUR SHADOWS WITHER ....BY CANDLELIGHT 236 12
LET'S (4)
WELL WHAT, THEN? THAT'S THE TROUBLE. LET'S SAY HE ....DIALOGUE O. 278 51
THIS BOARD OUR BATTLEFIELD. LET'S GIVE PAN UP ....DIALOGUE O. 284 292
TO NORMAL. LET'S CLOSE THE CURTAINS. IT LOOKS WILD .....DIALOGUE O. 286 335
ALL RIGHT, LET'S SAY YOU COULD TAKE A SKULL AND BREAK IT*SONNET:EVA. 304 1
LETTER (7)
LETTER TO A PURIST ....LETTER TO A PURIST 36 T
LOVE LETTER ....LOVE LETTER 147 T
OF UNANSWERED LETTERS, COFFINED IN A LETTER CASE. ......THREE WOMEN 182 200
I AM A LETTER IN THIS SLOT --- ....GETTING THERE 248 18
LETTER IN NOVEMBER ....LETTER IN NOVEMBER 253 T
LEVERING LETTER FLAPS, ...EAVESDROPPER 261 56
AS A DESK DRAWER HIDES A POISON PEN LETTER, ...THE RIVAL/DR 291 9
LETTERS (11)
NO SUCCINCT GABRIEL FROM THE LETTERS HERE ....OUIJA 78 31
THE WAY SHE LAID HIS LETTERS, TILL THEY GREW WARM ....WIDOW 164 18
OF UNANSWERED LETTERS, COFFINED IN A LETTER CASE. ......THREE WOMEN 182 200
THE LETTERS PROCEED FROM THESE BLACK KEYS, AND THESE BLACK KEYS
PROCEED ....THREE WOMEN 177 27
BURNING THE LETTERS ....BURNING THE LETTERS 204 T
LETTERS AND THEIR DEATH RATTLE ....BURNING THE LETTERS 204 3
DOWN TO A CIRCLE OF LETTERS: TWENTY-SIX *DIALOGUE OVER A OUIJA BOARD 276 13
THE LETTERS LIVE IN THE SAME PLACE. OR ELSE ....DIALOGUE O. 277 23
EACH TIME MUST LEARN THE LETTERS NEW. ARE ....DIALOGUE O. 277 24
THOSE LETTERS SEPARATED INTO SENSE ....DIALOGUE OVER A OUIJA BOARD 279 96
OF POETRY FROM THESE LETTERS, BUT THE BEAT ....DIALOGUE O. 283 256
LETTING (3)
PIG HOVE, LETTING LEGEND LIKE DRIED MUD DROP, ...SOW 61 37
LETTING IN THE LIGHT, PEEPHOLE AFTER PEEPHOLE -- ....INSOMNIAC 163 3
I AM A WOUND THAT THEY ARE LETTING GO. ....THREE WOMEN 184 271
LETTUCE (2)
IRREPROACHABLE AS ANY LETTUCE HEAD, ...MEMOIRS OF A SPINACH-PICKER 89 10
HOEING LETTUCE, WEEDING CELERY. ....BITTER STRAWBERRIES 299 19
LETTUCES (1)
BETWEEN THE YELLOW LETTUCES AND THE GERMAN CABBAGE ....BURNING. 205 39
LETUP (1)
THE LIGHT FALLS WITHOUT LETUP, BLINDINGLY. ....A LIFE 150 20
LEVEL (3)
THEN, TO SQUALL ABOVE THE LEVEL ....OWL 102 10
THE LABORER'S NAILS PARED LEVEL ....THE DEATH OF MYTH-MAKING 104 7
RIVER FLOODS TRANSCEND THE LEVEL*INSOLENT STORM STRIKES AT THE SKULL 326 19
LEVELS (1)
FOUNDERED THROUGH LEVELS OF LIGHT SEAGREEN AND STRANGE. OTHER TWO. 68 5
LEVER (2)
TO LEVER THE DIRT. ....A SECRET 220 23
LEVER OF HIS WET DREAMS. ....THE JAILER 226 10
LEVERING (1)
LEVERING LETTER FLAPS, ...EAVESDROPPER 261 56
LEVITATING (1)
LEVITATING A NUMB MINUTE IN THE UPDRAFT ....WIDOW 164 3
LEWDLY (1)
LEWDLY BECKONING, AND HER COURAGE WAVERED: ....LADY AND T. 69 20
LIAR (2)
A SERVICE AND IGNORE IT, I GO A LIAR ......GREEN ROCK, WINTHROP BAY 105 20
AND I, LOVE, AM A PATHOLOGICAL LIAR, ...LESBOS 227 7
LIARS (1)
THEN SHE TURNS TO THOSE LIARS, THE CANDLES OR THE MOON. .....MIRROR 174 12
LIBERAL (1)
WOULD UMBRELLA LIKE LIBERAL TOADSTOOLS ....DIALOGUE EN ROUTE 308 8
LIBRARY (1)
HUNG UP IN THE LIBRARY WITH THE ENGRAVINGS OF RANGOON .....COURAGE. 210 22
LICE (1)
OF HORSEHAIR AND LICE HIS HORNY LOINS; ....A LESSON IN VENGEANCE 80 15
LICHEN-BITTEN (1)
AS A CHILD I LOVED A LICHEN-BITTEN NAME. ....THREE WOMEN 177 41
LICHEN-LID (1)
THROUGH LICHEN-LID AND PASSING BIRD-FOOT ....TOUCH-AND-GO 335 4
LICHENS (2)
RUST-RED OR GREEN AS LICHENS. ....OLD LADIES' HOME 120 14
THE FOOD TUBES EMBRACE ME. SPONGES KISS MY LICHENS AWAY. POEM.7.S. 136 19
LICK (3)
TO LICK THE SEA-SALT. ....DEPARTURE 51 20
THE HOUSES ARE WHITE AS SEA-SALT GOATS LICK FROM THE ROCKS. ..NET-. 121 10
THIS FIRE MAY LICK AND FAWN, BUT IT IS MERCILESS: ....BURNING. 204 15
LICKED (1)
LIGHTNING LICKED IN A YELLOW LATHER ....LAMENT 315 4
LICKING (1)
OF LICKING CLEAN ....FEVER. 231 6

	TITLE	PAGE	LINE

LICKS (1)
ALL-MOUTH LICKS UP THE BUSHES POEM.2.DARK 132 17
LID (7)
NOBODY BLINKS A LID, GAPES, ...STREET SONG 35 5
PIERCED MY DENSE LID. ....ON THE PLETHORA OF DRYADS 67 24
FIT NOWHERE: BRICKDUST-COMPLECTED, EYE UNDER A DENSE LID, ...
   ... THE LADY AND THE EARTHENWARE HEAD 69 2
ABRADING MY LID, THE SMALL GRAIN BURNS: ....THE EYE-MOTE 109 16
DAYBREAK DISCOVERED THE BUREAU LID ....LEAVING EARLY 146 29
ECLIPSED BENEATH BLIND LID OF LAND ....DANSE MACABRE 320 2
THAT HAPPENS TO CONCEAL THE LID OF ONE ......EPITAPH IN THREE PARTS 338 29
LIDDED (1)
THE ONE WHO NEVER LOOKS UP, WHOSE EYES ARE LIDDED ......DEATH & CO. 254 3
LIDLESS (1)
HE LIVES WITHOUT PRIVACY IN A LIDLESS ROOM, ...INSOMNIAC 163 26
LIDS (7)
SUN HOISTS SOUL UP AFTER LIDS FALL SHUT; ....VANITY FAIR 33 28
LEANS TO PECK OPEN THOSE LOCKED LIDS, TO EAT ....THE SHRIKE 42 18
PUTS UP HIS PIPE, AND LIDS HIS MOONY EYE. ............SNAKECHARMER 79 28
THE LIDS WON'T SHUT. TIME POEM.3.MAENAD. 133 18
LIKE AN EYE BETWEEN TWO WHITE LIDS THAT WILL NOT SHUT. .....TULIPS 160 9
WAITING LIES HEAVY ON MY LIDS. IT LIES LIKE SLEEP, ...THREE WOMEN 179 108
HIS LIDS ARE LIKE THE LILAC-FLOWER ....THREE WOMEN 181 172
LIE (23)
CHARRED AND RAVENED WOMEN LIE, ...PURSUIT 22 23
BELOW, ROCKED HAVOC-SICK, VOYAGERS LIE ....CHANNEL CROSSING 26 9
THEY LIE, CUT-GRASS ASSAULTING EACH SEPARATE SENSE ....WREATH F. 44 8
RIDDLED WITH GHOSTS, TO LIE ....ALL THE DEAD DEARS 71 35
THEY LIE AS IF UNDER WATER ....THE SLEEPERS 122 4
I LIE ON A GREAT ANVIL. POEM.7.S. 136 2
THE SUN PUTS ITS CINDER OUT. WHERE WE LIE*SLEEP IN THE MOJAVE DESERT 144 21
BEACHED UNDER THE SPUMY BLOOMS, WE LIE ....WHITSUN 154 23
FOR FIVE DAYS I LIE IN SECRET, ...FACE LIFT 156 17
TO LIE WITH MY HANDS TURNED UP AND BE UTTERLY EMPTY. ....TULIPS 161 30
AND I SHALL BE USEFUL WHEN I LIE DOWN FINALLY: ....I AM VERTICAL 162 19
AND WHERE I LIE NOW, BACK TO MY OWN DARK STAR, ...STARS. 166 34
HOW YOU LIE AND CRY AFTER IT ....ELM 192 8
IN WHOSE RIFT WE LIE ....EVENT 194 3
DADDY, YOU CAN LIE BACK NOW. ....DADDY 224 75
DEAD EGG, I LIE ....PARALYTIC 266 17
CLOCKS CRY: STILLNESS IS A LIE, MY DEAR;*TO EVA DESCENDING THE STAIR 303 1
CLOCKS CRY: STILLNESS IS A LIE, MY DEAR.*TO EVA DESCENDING THE STAIR 303 6
CLOCKS CRY: STILLNESS IS A LIE, MY DEAR.*TO EVA DESCENDING THE STAIR 303 12
CLOCKS CRY: STILLNESS IS A LIE, MY DEAR.*TO EVA DESCENDING THE STAIR 303 18
COLD ON MY NARROW COT I LIE ....TO A JILTED LOVER 309 1
AND PLUCK THE DROLL-FLECKED QUAIL WHERE THICK THEY LIE; ...GO GET. 313 2
BOLD BEANSTALK; LIE AND LOVE TILL SHARP SCYTHE HACKS *LOVE IS A PAR. 330 71
LIES (17)
BRONZED AS EARTH, THE SECOND LIES, ...TWO SISTERS OF PERSEPHONE 32 13
CANNOT FOLLOW AFTER, BUT LIES ....THE SHRIKE 42 8
LIES, COMPANIONED BY THE GIMCRACK ....ALL THE DEAD DEARS 70 4
AS THE LIGHT LIES ON THESE WHITE WALLS, THIS BED, THESE HANDS. ...
   ... TULIPS 160 4
BEHIND WHICH THE SECRET PASSAGE LIES -- STALE AIR, ...WIDOW 164 8
WAITING LIES HEAVY ON MY LIDS. IT LIES LIKE SLEEP, ...THREE WOMEN 179 108
WAITING LIES HEAVY ON MY LIDS. IT LIES LIKE SLEEP, ...THREE WOMEN 179 108
IN HER GARDEN THE LIES WERE SHAKING OUT THEIR MOIST SILKS*DETECTIVE. 208 7
MOLDING ONTO HIS LIPS LIKE LIES, ...STINGS 215 49
LIES AND SMILES. ....THE JAILER 226 23
YOU KNOW WHAT LIES ARE FOR. ....LESBOS 230 91
LIES. LIES AND A GRIEF. ....THE COURIERS 247 6
LIES. LIES AND A GRIEF. ....THE COURIERS 247 6
YOU SAY HE'S TOLD TWO LIES . . . CALL THEM TWO PLUCKED DIALOGUE O. 283 266
BEYOND THE WINDOW) SHE LIES ON CUSHIONS CURLED ....FEMALE AUTHOR 301 3
PARSLEYED WITH ELEGIES, SHE LIES IN STATE ....TERMINAL 328 13
LIES AMONG SHEETS ....AERIALIST 331 2
LIFE (30)
"IN LIFE, LOVE GNAWED MY SKIN ....DIALOGUE BETWEEN GHOST AND PRIEST 39 27
LIFE, ITS OWN VAPOROUS WAYFARINGS. ....LANDOWNERS 53 15
THEM LIFE LIVELIER THAN OURS, ...SCULPTOR 92 23
A LIFE ....A LIFE 149 T
A LIFE BAPTIZED IN NO-LIFE FOR A WHILE, ...INSOMNIAC 163 18
THERE IS NO LIFE HIGHER THAN THE GRASSTOPS ....WUTHERING HEIGHTS 167 10
FOR A LIFE IN SUCH COMPANY; ....WUTHERING HEIGHTS 168 41
OUR LADY OF THE SHIPWRECKED IS THREE TIMES LIFE SIZE, ...FINISTERRE 170 24
THEY HAVE TOO MANY COLORS, TOO MUCH LIFE. THEY ARE NOT QUIET,*THREE. 178 69
I HAVE STITCHED LIFE INTO ME LIKE A RARE ORGAN, ...THREE WOMEN 178 72
CAN SUCH INNOCENCE KILL AND KILL? IT MILKS MY LIFE. ....THREE WOMEN 180 134
I LOSE LIFE AFTER LIFE. THE DARK EARTH DRINKS THEM. ....THREE WOMEN 181 154
I LOSE LIFE AFTER LIFE. THE DARK EARTH DRINKS THEM. ....THREE WOMEN 181 154
I CANNOT CONTAIN IT. I CANNOT CONTAIN MY LIFE. ....THREE WOMEN 182 196
IT IS USUAL IN MY LIFE, AND THE LIVES OF OTHERS. ....THREE WOMEN 183 243
CRACK THROUGH STONE, AND THEY ARE GREEN WITH LIFE. .....THREE WOMEN 187 371
IS MY LIFE SO INTRIGUING? ....THE OTHER 201 9
PROBABLE MOTES THAT TICK THE YEARS OFF MY LIFE. A BIRTHDAY PRESENT 207 43

LIFE (CONT.)
    WE SHOULD MEET IN ANOTHER LIFE, WE SHOULD MEET IN AIR, ...LESBOS   228 31
    WHERE DO YOU STASH YOUR LIFE? ....STOPPED DEAD   230 20
    SWEET LETHE IS MY LIFE. ....AMNESIAC   233 26
    I HOLD MY BREATH UNTIL YOU CREAK TO LIFE, ...BY CANDLELIGHT   236 19
    SHE CAN BRING THE DEAD TO LIFE ....THE TOUR   238 46
    THE TREE OF LIFE AND THE TREE OF LIFE ....THE MUNICH MANNEQUINS   262   4
    THE TREE OF LIFE AND THE TREE OF LIFE ....THE MUNICH MANNEQUINS   262   4
    ASKS NOTHING OF LIFE. ....PARALYTIC   267 40
    GOVERN A LIFE. ....WORDS   270 20
    A LIFE AFTER THIS LIFE? HE SHOOTS SO SWIFT ....DIALOGUE O.   278 72
    A LIFE AFTER THIS LIFE? HE SHOOTS SO SWIFT ....DIALOGUE O.   278 72
    THAT LIFE WAS A MERE MONUMENTAL SHAM. ....DIRGE FOR A JOKER   302   8
LIFE'S (2)
    AFTER YOUR LIFE'S END, WHAT JUST EPILOGUE .. ..DIALOGUE B.   39 24
    IS OUR LIFE'S WHOLE NEMESIS." ....LOVE IS A PARALLAX   329 12
LIFT (7)
    AS LIFT HIM APART ....THE SHRIKE   42   3
    LOST IN THE LIFT AND DRIFT OF ....THE GREAT CARBUNCLE   73 23
    NOT LIFT A FOOT IN THE TWINKLE-DRESS ....THE DISQUIETING MUSES   75 28
    FACE LIFT ....FACE LIFT   155   T
    THE EYES LIFT AFTER IT AND FIND THE MOON. *THE MOON AND THE YEW TREE   173 16
    SQUARE AS A CHAIR AND ALMOST TOO HEAVY TO LIFT. ....THE ARRIVAL.   212   2
    IS HE, THEN? HE SPELLS. I-N. HE'LL LIFT *DIALOGUE OVER A OUIJA BOARD   278 76
LIFTED (1)
    WE LIFTED A SUGARED HAM AND A PINEAPPLE FROM THE GROWNUPS' ICEBOX ...
                                                 ... THE BABYSITTERS   175 30
LIFTING (1)
    A SNAG IS LIFTING A VALEDICTORY, PALE HAND; .....CROSSING THE WATER   190   9
LIFTS (3)
    SHE LIFTS ONE WEBBED FOOT AFTER THE OTHER ....MISS DRAKE P.   41 24
    HE LIFTS AN ARM TO BRING HER CLOSE, BUT SHE ....THE OTHER TWO   68 18
    THAT LIFTS TO CONSECRATE THE SUNKEN MAN. ....EPITAPH IN THREE PARTS   337 19
LIGHT (78)
    ABOVE THE APPALLING RUIN; IN BLEAK LIGHT ..............CONVERSATION.   21   6
    RECORDS BARE PAINTED WALLS, WHILE AN ELECTRIC LIGHT .TALE OF A TUB   24   2
    IN SULLEN LIGHT OF THE INAUSPICIOUS DAY. ....CHANNEL CROSSING   27 25
    DAYLONG A DUET OF SHADE AND LIGHT ....TWO SISTERS OF PERSEPHONE   31   3
    AND RECOIL IN THE ALTERING LIGHT: THE RADIANT LIMB ..EPITAPH FOR F.   46 33
    A CERTAIN MINOR LIGHT MAY STILL ....BLACK ROOK IN RAINY WEATHER   57 14
    ON GRUNT. UP IN THE FLICKERING LIGHT TO SHAPE ....SOW   61 39
    OF STICKS. THE LIGHT FALLS CHALK AND COLD ...THE EVERLASTING MONDAY   62   3
    HER DOWN TO MERE QUARTZ GRIT IN THAT STONY LIGHT ..HARDCASTLE CRAGS   63 44
    THE MOON TO A RIND OF LITTLE LIGHT. ....THE THIN PEOPLE   65 31
    E.G., BY CANT OF LIGHT ...ON THE DIFFICULTY OF CONJURING UP A DRYAD   66 22
    FOUNDERED THROUGH LEVELS OF LIGHT SEAGREEN AND STRANGE.   OTHER TWO.   68   5
    IN A LIGHT NEITHER OF DAWN ....THE GREAT CARBUNCLE   72   5
    KNOWABLE ONLY BY LIGHT ....THE GREAT CARBUNCLE   72 15
    LIGHT WITHDRAWS. CHAIRS, TABLES DROP ....THE GREAT CARBUNCLE   73 29
    FOR EYES TO LIGHT ME ....WORDS FOR A NURSERY   73   5
    IMAGES OF LIGHT AND AIR .... SCULPTOR   91   7
    THE FLIMSY LIGHT; ARMS FOLDED ....SCULPTOR   91 11
    GOOD OF THE CAPE LIGHT THAT SCOURS ....MUSSEL HUNTER AT ROCK HARBOR   95   3
    FROM A SMOKE-CHOKED CLOSET INTO LIGHT; ....AFTERMATH   113   5
    GULLS MULLED IN THE GREENEST LIGHT. ..THE HERMIT AT OUTERMOST HOUSE   119 19
    IN A BLUE, UNCHANGING LIGHT, ...THE SLEEPERS   122   5
    AS I TURNED HIM IN THE LIGHT; ....MEDALLION   124 11
    NOW THEY LIGHT ME UP LIKE AN ELECTRIC BULB. POEM.1.WHO.   132 32
    I SEE BY MY OWN LIGHT. POEM.2.DARK.   132 11
    IN THIS LIGHT THE BLOOD IS BLACK. POEM.3.MAENAD.   133 24
    I AM LOST, I AM LOST, IN THE ROBES OF ALL THIS LIGHT. POEM.6.W.   136 24
    WHEN I FELL OUT OF THE LIGHT. I ENTERED POEM.7.S.   136   5
    THIS IS THE AFTER-HELL: I SEE THE LIGHT. POEM.7.S.   136 22
    TO THEIR OWNERS' WRISTS, THE LIGHT DREAMS FLOAT ....ON DECK   143 35
    UPSIDE DOWN HEARTS OF LIGHT TIPPING WAX FINGERS, ...CANDLES   148   2
    WHEN I LIGHT THEM, MY NOSTRILS PRICKLE. ....CANDLES   149 14
    THESE LITTLE GLOBES OF LIGHT ARE SWEET AS PEARS. ....CANDLES   149 24
    TONIGHT, LIKE A SHAWL, THE MILD LIGHT ENFOLDS HER, ...CANDLES   149 34
    THE INHABITANTS ARE LIGHT AS CORK, ...A LIFE   150   9
    THE LIGHT FALLS WITHOUT LETUP, BLINDINGLY. ....A LIFE   150 20
    LIGHT UP. EACH RABBIT-EARED ....PARLIAMENT HILL FIELDS   153 44
    AS THE LIGHT LIES ON THESE WHITE WALLS, THIS BED, THESE HANDS. ...
                                                        ... TULIPS   160   4
    WHERE ONCE A DAY THE LIGHT SLOWLY WIDENS AND SLOWLY THINS, ..TULIPS   161 45
    TONIGHT, IN THE INFINITESIMAL LIGHT OF THE STARS, ...I AM VERTICAL   162 11
    LETTING IN THE LIGHT, PEEPHOLE AFTER PEEPHOLE -- ....INSOMNIAC   163   3
    A BONEWHITE LIGHT, LIKE DEATH, BEHIND ALL THINGS. ....INSOMNIAC   163   4
    BOTH OF YOU ARE GREAT LIGHT BORROWERS. ....THE RIVAL   166   4
    THE WHITE LIGHT IS ARTIFICIAL, AND HYGIENIC AS HEAVEN. ...SURGEON.   170   1
    WITH SEVEN HOLES THUMBED IN. THE SOUL IS ANOTHER LIGHT. ...SURGEON.   170   8
    TONIGHT IT HAS RECEDED LIKE A SHIP'S LIGHT. ..THE SURGEON AT 2 A.M.   170 10
    OVER ONE BED IN THE WARD, A SMALL BLUE LIGHT   THE SURGEON AT 2 A.M.   171 41
    THIS IS THE LIGHT OF THE MIND, COLD AND PLANETARY. ....MOON.   172   1
    THE TREES OF THE MIND ARE BLACK. THE LIGHT IS BLUE. ....MOON.   172   2
    HOW WINTER FILLS MY SOUL! AND THAT CHALK LIGHT ......THREE WOMEN   181 177

		TITLE	PAGE	LINE

LIGHT (CONT.)
```
THEIR FEATURES ARE SLEEPING, LIKE LIGHT ON QUIET WATER. *THREE WOMEN    183  226
HOW BEAUTIFULLY THE LIGHT INCLUDES THESE THINGS. .......THREE WOMEN     186  353
A LITTLE LIGHT IS FILTERING FROM THE WATER FLOWERS. *CROSSING THE W.    190    4
THE GLASSY LIGHT WAS A CLEAR WALL, ...............THE RABBIT CATCHER    194   19
OF LITTLE CRYSTALS, TITILLATING THE LIGHT, .............BERCK-PLAGE     197   26
NO LIGHT ...................................................WINTERING   218   14
COBRA LIGHT ..................................................MEDUSA    225   27
WHAT WOULD THE LIGHT ......................................THE JAILER    227   43
THE FLUORESCENT LIGHT WINCING ON AND OFF LIKE A TERRIBLE MIGRAINE, ...
                                                       ... LESBOS       227    4
DOES NOT MY HEAT ASTOUND YOU. AND MY LIGHT. ................FEVER.      232   40
HEFTING HIS WHITE PILLAR WITH THE LIGHT .............BY CANDLELIGHT     237   28
EACH COAL A HOT CROSS-STITCH -- A LOVELY LIGHT! ............THE TOUR    238   21
I AM A MINER. THE LIGHT TURNS BLUE. .......NICK AND THE CANDLESTICK     240    1
WARM AND HUMAN, THEN THEIR PINK LIGHT ............THE NIGHT DANCES      250   19
PEOPLE LIKE LIGHT RAYS, LEAVE ............................BRASILIA      259   19
SOME LIGHT. I GLIMPSE NO LIGHT AT ALL AS LONG .........DIALOGUE O.      284  290
SOME LIGHT. I GLIMPSE NO LIGHT AT ALL AS LONG .........DIALOGUE O.      284  290
THE SKY OF THE CITY IS WHITE; THE LIGHT FROM THE COUNTRY. ...
                             ... QUEEN MARY'S ROSE GARDEN               290   10
WHERE GUESTS SLIDE GLIDING INTO LIGHT LIKE WINE; .......CINDERELLA      304    6
OF DILUTE LIGHT ...............................AQUATIC NOCTURNE         305    3
A LIGHT, AND RIGHT AWAY A RAVING ......................THE DREAM        310   10
THE LIGHT OF LOGIC ...........................MOONSONG AT MORNING       317   17
STEEPLING SNAKE IN THAT CONTRARY LIGHT ...........SONNET TO SATAN       323    9
BEGIN BY DIPPING YOUR BRUSH INTO CLEAR LIGHT. .....MIDSUMMER MOBILE     324    1
BLACK PINE TREE IN AN ORANGE LIGHT ...............BLACK PINE TREE.      328    T
BLACK AGAINST THE ORANGE LIGHT:   BLACK PINE TREE IN AN ORANGE LIGHT    328    3
THE SOURCE OF BLANCHING LIGHT THAT CONJURED HER ......THE PRINCESS.     333    3
GALLOP AND FLICK OF LIGHT ............................TOUCH-AND-GO      335    7
```
LIGHTER (1)
```
BURDENED IN SUCH A WAY WE SEEMED THE LIGHTER -- ......THE OTHER TWO     69   32
```
LIGHTEST (1)
```
THE PINES BLOT OUR VOICES UP IN THEIR LIGHTEST SIGHS. ....TWO CAMP.    145   24
```
LIGHTING (1)
```
LIGHTING PLANT OF THE UNIVERSE. .........................THE DREAM     311   18
```
LIGHTLESS (1)
```
INTO THE LIGHTLESS HIBERNACULUM ............ELECTRA ON AZALEA PATH     116    2
```
LIGHTLY (1)
```
LIGHTLY, THROUGH THEIR WHITE SWADDLINGS, LIKE AN AWFUL BABY. *TULIPS   161   38
```
LIGHTNING (6)
```
SMILINGLY, BLUE LIGHTNING ...............................THE OTHER     201    5
BALDING, GELDED BY LIGHTNING -- AN ILLUSION, ..FOR A FATHERLESS SON    205    4
AN OLD POLE FOR THE LIGHTNING, ............................LESBOS      228   46
LEST THE LIGHTNING STRIKE YOU TO CINDER. ...GO GET THE GOODLY SQUAB    313    8
LIGHTNING LICKED IN A YELLOW LATHER .......................LAMENT      315    4
LIGHTNING CONJURES GOD'S GLOBE OFF ITS ...........INSOLENT STORM.      326   25
```
LIGHTNINGS (1)
```
NO VISIONARY LIGHTNINGS ..................ON THE PLETHORA OF DRYADS    67   23
```
LIGHTNING-STROKE (1)
```
IT WOULD TAKE MORE THAN A LIGHTNING-STROKE ...........THE COLOSSUS    130   22
```
LIGHTS (16)
```
HIS ARDOR SNARES ME, LIGHTS THE TREES, .....................PURSUIT    23   33
LIGHTS OUT, THEY DOGGED US, SLEEPLESS AND ENVIOUS: ...THE OTHER TWO    68   28
AND THE SHADOW STRETCHED, THE LIGHTS WENT OUT.*THE DISQUIETING MUSES   75   32
THE DAY-MOON LIGHTS UP LIKE A SORRY MOTHER, .................SLEEP.   144   24
AND BLACK AS PURSES, THE HOUSE LIGHTS ...........WUTHERING HEIGHTS    168   44
OF WHITE AND PEWTER LIGHTS, AND A DIN LIKE SILVERSMITHS ..BLACKBER.   169   26
THE RED NIGHT LIGHTS ARE FLAT MOONS. THEY ARE DULL WITH BLOOD.
                         ... THE SURGEON AT 2 A.M.                    171   48
THE NIGHT LIGHTS ARE FLAT RED MOONS. THEY ARE DULL WITH BLOOD. ...
                            ... THREE WOMEN                           180  124
IT STRIVES AFTER THEM WITH ITS LIGHTS. ..................THREE WOMEN  186  346
BLINDING ME WITH ITS LIGHTS, THE LIVES OF THE DEAD .....THE RABBIT.   193    4
THE SUN DISSOLVES ON THIS WALL, BLEEDING ITS LIGHTS.  APPREHENSIONS   195    5
UP OVER THE HARBOR LIGHTS. .................................LESBOS    229   56
LIGHTS, ................................................PARALYTIC     266   13
HUGGING THEIR LIGHTS. ..................................PARALYTIC     267   36
TO OUR MEANING WELL. WHEN LIGHTS GO OUT *DIALOGUE OVER A OUIJA BOARD   286  363
THEIR LIGHTS WHITEN MY HEART. .......................THE RIVAL/DR     291   26
```
LIGHT'S (2)
```
QUICK AS THEY. TO FOLLOW THE LIGHT'S TINT ......CHILD'S PARK STONES   101   18
LIGHT'S DEATH TO THEM: THEY SHRIVEL IN IT. ............BLUE MOLES     126   22
```
LIKE (396)
```
LIKE A DAUNTED WITCH, QUITTING CASTLE WHEN REAL DAYS BREAK. ...
                        ... CONVERSATION AMONG THE RUINS              21    8
FEATHERED DARK IN THOUGHT, I STALK LIKE A ROOK, ..WINTER LANDSCAPE,   21    9
KINDLED LIKE TORCHES FOR HIS JOY, .........................PURSUIT    22   22
LIKE ICEBERGS, WHILE MINUTE BROWN HAIRS RISE .........TALE OF A TUB   25   42
THAT WRESTLE WITH US LIKE ANGELS; THE MERE CHANCE  CHANNEL CROSSING   27   18
WITH HANDS LIKE DERRICKS, ...................THE QUEEN'S COMPLAINT    28    3
LIKE POLLEN ON BRIGHT AIR. LULLED ........TWO SISTERS OF PERSEPHONE   32   15
HAUNCHED LIKE A FAUN, HE HOOED ...............................FAUN    35    1
```

LIKE (CONT.)
HUNG CAUGHT IN DARK-WEBBED BRANCHES LIKE A FABULOUS HERON. ...
                      ... DIALOGUE BETWEEN GHOST AND PRIEST   38   6
LIKE A LAST STORM-CROSSED LEAF? BEST GET YOU GONE ......DIALOGUE B.   39   44
WHERE, BEDDED LIKE ANGELS, TWO BURN ONE IN FEVER. ....WREATH F.   45   18
HIVED LIKE HONEY IN YOUR HEAD. ....EPITAPH FOR FIRE AND FLOWER   45   14
TO STREW LIKE CONFETTI ....FIESTA MELONS   47   17
HAWK MISFORTUNE LIKE FIGS AND CHICKENS ....THE BEGGARS 47   3
THE BARNYARD LIKE THOSE TALONED HAGS ....RHYME 50   5
A FLASH LIKE DOOMCRACK RENT NIGHT'S BLACK: ....CRYSTAL GAZER   55   37
PIG HOVE, LETTING LEGEND LIKE DRIED MUD DROP, ...SOW 61   37
IN THE WHORL OF HER EAR, AND LIKE A SCOOPED-OUT PUMPKIN CROWN ...
                      ... HARDCASTLE CRAGS   63   24
LIKE A PLANET, A STONE, SWALLOWED IN A GREAT DARKNESS,*THE OTHER TWO   68   25
DOWN: THE BODY WEIGHS LIKE STONE. ....THE GREAT CARBUNCLE 73   30
WITH HEADS LIKE DARNING-EGGS TO NOD ....THE DISQUIETING MUSES   75   6
LIKE BUBBLES ABOUT TO BREAK, YOU FED ....THE DISQUIETING MUSES   75   19
BLINKING FLASHLIGHTS LIKE FIREFLIES ....THE DISQUIETING MUSES   75   26
LIKE A SOAP-BUBBLE AS YOU CALLED: COME HERE! THE DISQUIETING MUSES   76   47
WHEN WORDS, LIKE LOCUSTS, DRUMMED THE DARKENING AIR ....OUIJA   77   17
INVADE THE CLOISTRAL EYE LIKE PAGES ......ON THE DECLINE OF ORACLES   78   23
WATER, TO GREEN, TO NOTHING LIKE A SNAKE. ..............SNAKECHARMER 79   27
TWINED TO HER HARD LIMBS LIKE IVY: THE PURITAN LIP *VIRGIN IN A TREE   81   12
TO CHASTITY'S SERVICE: LIKE PROPHETS, LIKE PREACHERS, ...VIRGIN.   82   28
TO CHASTITY'S SERVICE: LIKE PROPHETS, LIKE PREACHERS, ...VIRGIN.   82   28
EXPRESSIVE OF GRIEF TURNS GODS, LIKE KINGS, TO ROCKS. ......PERSEUS   83   31
THEY GLEAM LIKE EASTER EGGSHELLS, ...BATTLE-SCENE   84   25
HEART-SHAPED LEAVES, LIKE CATALPA LEAVES, AND LILIES .....YADWIGHA.   85   6
OF MONSTROUS SIZE, LIKE NO WELL-BRED LILIES. ....YADWIGHA.   85   7
LAY OVER THE LEAVES LIKE A CLEAR CELLOPHANE, ...SPINACH-PICKER.   89   6
IN RINGING ORANGE LIKE A STELLAR CARROT. ...THE GHOST'S LEAVETAKING   91   28
AGES BEAT LIKE RAINS ....FULL FATHOM FIVE   93   27
SCRIM AFTER SCRIM LIKE FISHNETS ....LORELEI   94   5
CLUMPED LIKE BULBS AT THE GRASS-ROOT ..MUSSEL HUNTER AT ROCK HARBOR   95   10
I'LL GO OUT AND SIT IN WHITE LIKE THEY DO, ...MOONRISE   98   2
THEY STUNT LIKE CLOWNS IN THE CIRCUS. ....IN MIDAS' COUNTRY 100   20
HER SALLOW RODENT TEETH LIKE CASTANETS ...............INCOMMUNICADO 100   4
AWAY TO THE LEFT LIKE REEDS IN A SEA ....THE EYE-MOTE 109   8
A BLIMP SWIMS UP LIKE A DAY-MOON OR TIN ....A WINTER SHIP 113   11
EACH WAVE-TIP GLITTERS LIKE A KNIFE. ....A WINTER SHIP 113   30
HE HANDS HER THE CUT-OUT HEART LIKE A CRACKED HEIRLOOM. TWO VIEWS.   114   11
SUN STRUCK THE WATER LIKE A DAMNATION. ....SUICIDE OFF EGG ROCK 115   6
EVERYTHING GLITTERED LIKE BLAND PAPER. ......SUICIDE OFF EGG ROCK   115   20
LIKE HIERATIC STONES, AND THE GROUND IS HARD.*ELECTRA ON AZALEA PATH 116   4
THE FLAT SEA PURPLED LIKE THAT EVIL CLOTH ..ELECTRA ON AZALEA PATH   117   31
MY MOTHER SAID; YOU DIED LIKE ANY MAN. ......ELECTRA ON AZALEA PATH 117   40
SHARDED IN BLACK, LIKE BEETLES, ...OLD LADIES' HOME 120   1
FROM BEDS BOXED-IN LIKE COFFINS ....OLD LADIES' HOME 120   17
WINKS LIKE MONEY UNDER THE RINGED TOES OF THE CHICKENS. ......NFT-. 121   10
THEIR EYES REVOLVE THE WHOLE TOWN LIKE A BLUE AND GREEN BALL. *NET-. 121   13
THE GARNET BITS BURNED LIKE THAT. ....MEDALLION   124   13
THE PEARS FATTEN LIKE LITTLE BUDDHAS. ....THE MANOR GARDEN   125   3
RIBBED LIKE A HAND, ...POLLY'S TREE   129   36
I CRAWL LIKE AN ANT IN MOURNING ....THE COLOSSUS   129   12
THEY COLLAPSE LIKE LUNGS, THE ESCAPED WATER ....PRIVATE GROUND 130   9
LITTER THE MUD LIKE ORANGEPEEL. ....PRIVATE GROUND 130   12
THEY GLITTER LIKE EYES, AND I COLLECT THEM ALL. ......PRIVATE GROUND 131   22
THEY RATTLE LIKE HYDRANGEA BUSHES. POEM.1.WHO. 131   12
NOW THEY LIGHT ME UP LIKE AN ELECTRIC BULB. POEM.1.WHO. 132   32
WITHER LIKE PITHLESS HANDS. THERE IS LITTLE SHELTER. POEM.5.F. 134   4
THE LAMP-HEADED NYMPHS ARE NODDING TO SLEEP LIKE STATUES. *POEM.5.F. 135   12
I'LL FLY THROUGH THE CANDLE'S MOUTH LIKE A SINGELESS MOTH.*POEM.6.W. 135   20
FLEW OFF LIKE THE HAT OF A DOLL POEM.7.S.   136   4
I PICK AND PRY LIKE A DOCTOR OR ....THE BURNT-OUT SPA 138   14
GILLED LIKE A FISH. A COMMON-SENSE ....YOU'RE   141   3
WRAPPED UP IN YOURSELF LIKE A SPOOL, ...YOU'RE   141   5
VAGUE AS FOG AND LOOKED FOR LIKE MAIL. ....YOU'RE   141   10
LIKE A SPRAT IN A PICKLE JUG. ....YOU'RE   141   14
RIGHT, LIKE A WELL-DONE SUM. ....YOU'RE   141   17
I SIZZLED IN HIS BLUE VOLTS LIKE A DESERT PROPHET. THE HANGING MAN   141   2
THE NIGHTS SNAPPED OUT OF SIGHT LIKE A LIZARD'S EYELID:*THE HANGING. 141   3
IF THEY MISSED OUT ON WALKING ABOUT LIKE PEOPLE ....STILLBORN 142   4
LIT LIKE A TWO-TIERED WEDDING CAKE ....ON DECK   142   7
AND CASTLED IN IT LIKE A KING. ....ON DECK   143   15
WE SWELTER LIKE FIREDOGS IN THE WIND. ...SLEEP IN THE MOJAVE DESERT 144   20
THE DAY-MOON LIGHTS UP LIKE A SORRY MOTHER, ...SLEEP. 144   24
LIKE LOCAL TROLLS IN THE SPELL OF A SUPERIOR BEING. .....TWO CAMP.   144   6
PLANETS PULSE IN THE LAKE LIKE BRIGHT AMOEBAS; ....TWO CAMP.   145   23
LIKE MONDAY DRUNKARDS. THE MILKY BERRIES ....LEAVING EARLY   145   10
TAPPING AND TICKING LIKE NERVOUS FINGERS. ....LEAVING EARLY   146   27
THIS MIZZLE FITS ME LIKE A SAD JACKET. ....LEAVING EARLY   146   39
WE SLEPT LIKE STONES. LADY, WHAT AM I DOING ....LEAVING EARLY   146   42
THOUGH, LIKE A STONE, UNBOTHERED BY IT, ...LOVE LETTER 147   3
LIKE MY NEIGHBORS, TAKING NO PLEASURE ....LOVE LETTER 147   12

TITLE   PAGE LINE

LIKE (CONT.)
AND I SLEPT ON LIKE A BENT FINGER. ....LOVE LETTER   147   19
TO POUR MYSELF OUT LIKE A FLUID ....LOVE LETTER   147   26
I STARTED TO BUD LIKE A MARCH TWIG: ....LOVE LETTER   147   31
THE ABSTRACTS HOVER LIKE DULL ANGELS: ....MAGI   148   1
TO ROCK ON ALL FOURS LIKE A PADDED HAMMOCK. ....MAGI   148   11
GROWN MILKY, ALMOST CLEAR, LIKE THE BODIES OF SAINTS. ......CANDLES   148   4
TONIGHT, LIKE A SHAWL, THE MILD LIGHT ENFOLDS HER, ...CANDLES   149   34
THE SHADOWS STOOP OVER LIKE GUESTS AT A CHRISTENING. ....CANDLES   149   35
TOUCH IT: IT WON'T SHRINK LIKE AN EYEBALL, ...A LIFE   149   1
IT WILL PING LIKE A CHINESE CHIME IN THE SLIGHTEST AIR STIR A LIFE   150   7
SHORT-REINED, PAWING LIKE PARADEGROUND HORSES. ....A LIFE   150   14
THEY RING TRUE, LIKE GOOD CHINA. ....A LIFE   150   18
WITH NO ATTACHMENTS, LIKE A FOETUS IN A BOTTLE, ...A LIFE   150   26
AGE AND TERROR, LIKE NURSES, ATTEND HER, ...A LIFE   150   33
THE TREES STIFFEN INTO PLACE LIKE BURNT NERVES. ...WAKING IN WINTER   151   3
OR THE SEA, HUSHING THEIR PEELED SENSE LIKE OLD MOTHER MORPHIA. ...
                                              ... WAKING IN WINTER   151   16
SETTLING AND STIRRING LIKE BLOWN PAPER ......PARLIAMENT HILL FIELDS   152   8
AND BRIM; THE CITY MELTS LIKE SUGAR. ....PARLIAMENT HILL FIELDS   152   12
THE WIND STOPS MY BREATH LIKE A BANDAGE. ....PARLIAMENT HILL FIELDS   152   20
YOUR CRY FADES LIKE THE CRY OF A GNAT. ......PARLIAMENT HILL FIELDS   153   32
LIKE A CUP OR A ROOM. THE MOON'S CROOK WHITENS, ...PARLIAMENT H.   153   38
AIR LIKE A MEDICINE. ....WHITSUN   153   6
BLOATS LIKE A SPINNAKER. HAT-BRIMS ....WHITSUN   154   10
BOWING AND TRUCKLING LIKE AN OLD-SCHOOL ORIENTAL. ....WHITSUN   154   16
THE WAVES PULSE AND PULSE LIKE HEARTS. ....WHITSUN   154   22
LIKE A DEAD LAKE THE DARK ENVELOPS ME, ...ZOO KEEPER'S WIFE   154   3
LOOK, THEY ARE MELTING LIKE COINS IN THE POWERFUL JUICES -- ZOO K.   154   8
LIKE THE WHITE LINES ON A BLUEPRINT. ....ZOO KEEPER'S WIFE   154   10
GUTS BAG WOULD CLACK LIKE A CHILD'S RATTLE, ...ZOO KEEPER'S WIFE   154   12
MULTIPLIED TO INFINITY LIKE ANGELS ON A PINHEAD .ZOO KEEPER'S WIFE   155   22
CLAMBERING ROUND ITS GLASS BOX LIKE AN EIGHT-FINGERED HAND. ZOO K.   155   31
THE SNAILS BLEW KISSES LIKE BLACK APPLES. ....ZOO KEEPER'S WIFE   155   38
DARKNESS WIPES ME OUT LIKE CHALK ON A BLACKBOARD... .....FACE LIFT   156   15
TAPPED LIKE A CASK, THE YEARS DRAINING INTO MY PILLOW. ..FACE LIFT   156   18
LOVE SET YOU GOING LIKE A FAT GOLD WATCH. ....MORNING SONG   156   1
THE CLEAR VOWELS RISE LIKE BALLOONS. ....MORNING SONG   157   18
EXHALE THEIR PALLOR LIKE SCENT. ....BARREN WOMAN   157   5
SHE LAY IN BED WITH ME LIKE A DEAD BODY ....IN PLASTER   158   6
WHEN I HIT HER SHE HELD STILL, LIKE A TRUE PACIFIST. ....IN PLASTER   159   12
SHE HUMORED MY WEAKNESS LIKE THE BEST OF NURSES, ...IN PLASTER   159   26
LIVING WITH HER WAS LIKE LIVING WITH MY OWN COFFIN: .....IN PLASTER   160   48
LIKE AN EYE BETWEEN TWO WHITE LIDS THAT WILL NOT SHUT. ....TULIPS   160   9
MY PATENT LEATHER OVERNIGHT CASE LIKE A BLACK PILLBOX, ...TULIPS   160   19
SHUTTING THEIR MOUTHS ON IT, LIKE A COMMUNION TABLET. ....TULIPS   161   35
LIGHTLY, THROUGH THEIR WHITE SWADDLINGS, LIKE AN AWFUL BABY. *TULIPS   161   38
THEN THE TULIPS FILLED IT UP LIKE A LOUD NOISE. ....TULIPS   161   52
THE TULIPS SHOULD BE BEHIND BARS LIKE DANGEROUS ANIMALS; ...TULIPS   162   58
THEY ARE OPENING LIKE THE MOUTH OF SOME GREAT AFRICAN CAT, ..TULIPS   162   59
THE WATER I TASTE IS WARM AND SALT, LIKE THE SEA, ...TULIPS   162   62
A BONEWHITE LIGHT, LIKE DEATH, BEHIND ALL THINGS. ....INSOMNIAC   163   4
MEMORIES JOSTLE EACH OTHER FOR FACE-ROOM LIKE OBSOLETE FILM
    STARS. ....INSOMNIAC   163   14
NOW THE PILLS ARE WORN-OUT AND SILLY, LIKE CLASSICAL GODS.*INSOMNIAC   163   20
DRAINS LIKE WATER OUT THE HOLE AT THE FAR END. ....INSOMNIAC   163   25
HAVE BEEN HOWLING LIKE WOMEN, OR DAMAGED INSTRUMENTS. ....INSOMNIAC   163   30
THAT WILL PUT HER HEART OUT LIKE AN ONLY EYE. ....WIDOW   164   5
CIRCLES HER LIKE A PREY SHE'D LOVE TO KILL ....WIDOW   164   15
AND SEEMED TO GIVE HER WARMTH, LIKE A LIVE SKIN. ....WIDOW   164   19
AND NO BODIES, SINGING LIKE ARROWS UP TO HEAVEN. ....WIDOW   164   25
THEY STAND LIKE SHADOWS ABOUT THE GREEN LANDSCAPE -- ....WIDOW   164   28
OR EVEN LIKE BLACK HOLES CUT OUT OF IT. ....WIDOW   164   29
LIKE BLUE MARY'S ANGEL, DOVELIKE AGAINST A PANE ....WIDOW   165   38
LIKE A CHILD'S TOO-SIMPLE MATHEMATICAL PROBLEM. ....STARS.   165   20
AND DRINK THE SMALL NIGHT CHILL LIKE NEWS OF HOME. ....STARS.   166   40
THE HORIZONS RING ME LIKE FAGGOTS, ...WUTHERING HEIGHTS   167   1
LIKE A SERIES OF PROMISES, AS I STEP FORWARD. ....WUTHERING HEIGHTS   167   9
POURS BY LIKE DESTINY, BENDING ....WUTHERING HEIGHTS   167   12
IT IS LIKE BEING MAILED INTO SPACE, ...WUTHERING HEIGHTS   167   23
GLEAM LIKE SMALL CHANGE. ....WUTHERING HEIGHTS   168   45
OF WHITE AND PEWTER LIGHTS, AND A DIN LIKE SILVERSMITHS ..BLACKBER.   169   26
THEY GO UP WITHOUT HOPE, LIKE SIGHS. ....FINISTERRE   169   16
TONIGHT IT HAS RECEDED LIKE A SHIP'S LIGHT. ..THE SURGEON AT 2 A.M.   170   10
THESE ORCHIDS ARE SPLENDID. THEY SPOT AND COIL LIKE SNAKES.*SURGEON.   170   16
IN VINEGAR LIKE SAINTS' RELICS. ....THE SURGEON AT 2 A.M.   171   39
GRAY FACES, SHUTTERED BY DRUGS, FOLLOW ME LIKE FLOWERS. ...SURGEON.   171   50
I IMAGINE THEM WITHOUT FATHERS OR MOTHERS, LIKE THE FIRST GODS. ...
                                                    ... LAST WORDS   172   8
I SHOULD SUGAR AND PRESERVE MY DAYS LIKE FRUIT! ....LAST WORDS   172   10
I DO NOT TRUST THE SPIRIT. IT ESCAPES LIKE STEAM ....LAST WORDS   172   14
ONE DAY IT WON'T COME BACK. THINGS AREN'T LIKE THAT. ....LAST WORDS   172   16
BLOOM ABOUT ME LIKE NIGHT FLOWERS, WITH A GOOD SMELL. ...LAST WORDS   172   22
IT DRAGS THE SEA AFTER IT LIKE A DARK CRIME; IT IS QUIET .....MOON.   173   10
THE MOON IS MY MOTHER. SHE IS NOT SWEET LIKE MARY. ....MOON.   173   17

```
                                                    TITLE        PAGE  LINE
LIKE (CONT.)
   HOW I WOULD LIKE TO BELIEVE IN TENDERNESS --- ................MOON.   173   19
   RISES TOWARD HER DAY AFTER DAY, LIKE A TERRIBLE FISH. .......MIRROR   174   18
   THE SHADOWS OF THE GRASSES INCHED ROUND LIKE HANDS OF A CLOCK,*BABY.  175   43
   THERE WAS SOMETHING ABOUT THEM LIKE CARDBOARD, AND NOW I HAD
      CAUGHT IT, ................................................THREE WOMEN  177   17
   THE WHITE SKY EMPTIES OF ITS PROMISE, LIKE A CUP. ......THREE WOMEN   177   33
   IT HAD A CONSEQUENTIAL LOOK, LIKE EVERYTHING ELSE, .....THREE WOMEN   177   46
   COMING AT ME, LIKE A CASTLE, FROM THE TOP OF THE RIVER. *THREE WOMEN  178   51
   THEY ARE BALD AND IMPOSSIBLE, LIKE THE FACES OF MY CHILDREN, *THREE.  178   66
   QUIET, LIKE THE LITTLE EMPTINESSES I CARRY. ............THREE WOMEN   178   70
   I HAVE STITCHED LIFE INTO ME LIKE A RARE ORGAN, ........THREE WOMEN   178   72
   AND WALKED CAREFULLY, PRECARIOUSLY, LIKE SOMETHING RARE.*THREE WOMEN  178   73
   I HAVE TRIED TO BE BLIND IN LOVE, LIKE OTHER WOMEN, ...THREE WOMEN    178   75
   THE SHEETS, THE FACES, ARE WHITE AND STOPPED, LIKE CLOCKS. ..THREE.   179   95
   DUSK HOODS ME IN BLUE NOW, LIKE A MARY. ................THREE WOMEN   179  102
   WAITING LIES HEAVY ON MY LIDS. IT LIES LIKE SLEEP, .....THREE WOMEN   179  108
   LIKE A BIG SEA. FAR OFF, FAR OFF, I FEEL THE FIRST WAVE TUG  THREE.   179  109
   FRIGHTENED THE MIND. THEY SMILE LIKE FOOLS. ............THREE WOMEN   179  115
   THEY HUG THEIR FLATNESS LIKE A KIND OF HEALTH. .........THREE WOMEN   180  117
   I AM BREAKING APART LIKE THE WORLD. THERE IS THIS BLACKNESS, *THREE.  180  142
   HIS LIDS ARE LIKE THE LILAC-FLOWER .....................ELM          181  172
   I FEEL IT ENTER ME, COLD, ALIEN, LIKE AN INSTRUMENT. ...THREE WOMEN   182  183
   NEITHER A WOMAN, HAPPY TO BE LIKE A MAN, NOR A MAN .....THREE WOMEN   182  192
   HER CRIES ARE HOOKS THAT CATCH AND GRATE LIKE CATS. ...THREE WOMEN    182  207
   SCRATCHING AT MY SLEEP LIKE ARROWS, ....................THREE WOMEN   182  214
   THEIR FEATURES ARE SLEEPING, LIKE LIGHT ON QUIET WATER. *THREE WOMEN  183  226
   I SEE THEM SHOWERING LIKE STARS ON TO THE WORLD -- ....THREE WOMEN    183  228
   HE IS TURNING TO ME LIKE A LITTLE, BLIND, BRIGHT PLANT. *THREE WOMEN  183  235
   I AM ONE IN FIVE, SOMETHING LIKE THAT. I AM NOT HOPELESS. ...THREE.   183  244
   WHO WOULD ADHERE TO ME: I UNDO HER FINGERS LIKE BANDAGES: I GO. ...
                                                ... THREE WOMEN          184  273
   SO NEAT SHE IS TRANSPARENT, LIKE A SPIRIT. .............THREE WOMEN   184  281
   THE SWIFTS ARE BACK. THEY ARE SHRIEKING LIKE PAPER ROCKETS.  THREE.   185  310
   I LIKE BLACK STATEMENTS. ...............................LITTLE FUGUE  187    5
   RED, MOTTLED, LIKE CUT NECKS. .........................LITTLE FUGUE   188   35
   DEATH OPENED, LIKE A BLACK TREE, BLACKLY. .............LITTLE FUGUE   188   48
   EXIT LIKE KISSES. .....................................AN APPEARANCE  189    5
   THE STARS ARE FLASHING LIKE TERRIBLE NUMERALS. ........AN APPEARANCE  189   17
   THE NARCISSI LOOK UP LIKE CHILDREN, QUICKLY AND WHITELY. NARCISSI.    190   12
   LISTEN: THESE ARE ITS HOOVES: IT HAS GONE OFF, LIKE A HORSE. ...ELM   192    9
   AND THIS IS THE FRUIT OF IT: TIN-WHITE, LIKE ARSENIC. ..........ELM   192   15
   NOW I BREAK UP IN PIECES THAT FLY ABOUT LIKE CLUBS. ............ELM   192   19
   UNREELING IN IT, SPREADING LIKE OIL. ............THE RABBIT CATCHER   193    5
   AND WERE EXTRAVAGANT, LIKE TORTURE. .............THE RABBIT CATCHER   193   10
   SET CLOSE, LIKE BIRTH PANGS. ....................THE RABBIT CATCHER   194   16
   THEY WAITED LIKE SWEETHEARTS. THEY EXCITED HIM.  THE RABBIT CATCHER   194   25
   PEGS TOO DEEP TO UPROOT, AND A MIND LIKE A RING  THE RABBIT CATCHER   194   28
   THE DARK IS MELTING. WE TOUCH LIKE CRIPPLES. ................EVENT    195   22
   BOOMERANG LIKE ANCHORED ELASTICS, HURTING THE OWNER. ...BERCK-PLAGE   196   11
   THEY ARE HANDLING THE BLACK AND GREEN LOZENGES LIKE THE PARTS
      OF A BODY. ..........................................BERCK-PLAGE   196   16
   THE BENT PRINT BULGING BEFORE HIM LIKE SCENERY. ........BERCK-PLAGE   197   23
   DRAWN LIKE A LONG MATERIAL .............................BERCK-PLAGE   197   34
   THE NERVES BURSTING LIKE TREES, AND THIS IS THE SURGEON:*BERCK-PLAGE  198   47
   IT IS LIKE POSSESSING A SAINT. ........................BERCK-PLAGE    198   57
   THEY ARE BROWNING, LIKE TOUCHED GARDENIAS. ............BERCK-PLAGE    198   59
   THE GRAY SKY LOWERS, THE HILLS LIKE A GREEN SEA .......BERCK-PLAGE    199   73
   AROUND HIM LIKE LIVINGROOM FURNITURE, LIKE A DECOR. ...BERCK-PLAGE    199   83
   AROUND HIM LIKE LIVINGROOM FURNITURE, LIKE A DECOR. ...BERCK-PLAGE    199   83
   ENFOLDS HER FACE LIKE FINE LINEN, ....................BERCK-PLAGE     200  102
   FOLLOWING THE COFFIN ON ITS FLOWERY CART LIKE A BEAUTIFUL WOMAN, ...
                                                ... BERCK-PLAGE         200  115
   FOR A MINUTE THE SKY POURS INTO THE HOLE LIKE PLASMA. ..BERCK-PLAGE   201  125
   ASSUMES, LIKE A MEATHOOK, THE BURDEN OF HIS PARTS. ........THE OTHER  201    6
   SHRIEK FROM MY BELLY LIKE ARROWS, AND THESE I RIDE. ......THE OTHER   202   19
   THAT YOU SUCK BREATH LIKE MILEAGE? .......................THE OTHER   202   24
   I SCRATCH LIKE A CAT. ....................................THE OTHER   202   28
   THEY ARE PLOPPING LIKE MUD.*WORDS HEARD, BY ACCIDENT, OVER THE PHONE  202    7
   FLICKERING LIKE THAT, WRINKLY AND CLEAR RED, LIKE THE SKIN OF A
      MOUTH. ............................................POPPIES IN JULY  203    6
   FLICKERING LIKE THAT, WRINKLY AND CLEAR RED, LIKE THE SKIN OF A
      MOUTH. ............................................POPPIES IN JULY  203    6
   IF MY MOUTH COULD MARRY A HURT LIKE THAT! ..........POPPIES IN JULY   203   12
   GRINNED LIKE A GETAWAY CAR. .....................BURNING THE LETTERS   204    8
   I FLAKE UP PAPERS THAT BREATHE LIKE PEOPLE, ...BURNING THE LETTERS    204   37
   MY VEINS GLOW LIKE TREES. ......................BURNING THE LETTERS   205   48
   THE DOGS ARE TEARING A FOX. THIS IS WHAT IT IS LIKE -- ....BURNING.   205   49
   GROWING BESIDE YOU, LIKE A TREE, ...............FOR A FATHERLESS SON  205    2
   AND A SKY LIKE A PIG'S BACKSIDE, AN UTTER LACK OF ATTENTION. ...
                                                ... FOR A FATHERLESS SON  205    5
   NOW THERE ARE THESE VEILS, SHIMMERING LIKE CURTAINS, .....BIRTHDAY.   206   16
   LET US EAT OUR LAST SUPPER AT IT, LIKE A HOSPITAL PLATE.  BIRTHDAY.   207   26
   BUT MY GOD, THE CLOUDS ARE LIKE COTTON. ..........A BIRTHDAY PRESENT  207   39
```

                                                          TITLE   PAGE   LINE
LIKE (CONT.)
    IN THAT VALLEY THE TRAIN SHRIEKS ECHO LIKE SOULS ON HOOKS. ...
                                        ... THE DETECTIVE   208   5
    THESE ARE THE DECEITS, TACKED UP LIKE FAMILY PHOTOGRAPHS,*DETECTIVE. 208   13
    WHERE THE WIRELESS TALKS TO ITSELF LIKE AN ELDERLY RELATIVE. ...
                                        ... THE DETECTIVE   209   20
    DID IT COME LIKE AN ARROW, DID IT COME LIKE A KNIFE?   THE DETECTIVE   209   21
    DID IT COME LIKE AN ARROW, DID IT COME LIKE A KNIFE?   THE DETECTIVE   209   21
    AND IN PUNISHMENT WAS HUNG OUT LIKE BROWN FRUIT ......THE DETECTIVE   209   29
    SO THE DISKS OF THE BRAIN REVOLVE, LIKE THE MUZZLES OF CANNON. ...
                                        ... THE COURAGE OF SHUTTING-UP   210   16
    THEIR DEATH RAYS FOLDED LIKE FLAGS ......THE COURAGE OF SHUTTING-UP   210   32
    STRIPS OF TINFOIL WINKING LIKE PEOPLE, ...THE BEE MEETING   211   16
    CREAMY BEAN FLOWERS WITH BLACK EYES AND LEAVES LIKE BORED HEARTS. ...
                                        ... THE BEE MEETING   211   18
    IT IS LIKE A ROMAN MOB, ...THE ARRIVAL OF THE BEE BOX   213   19
    OPENING, IN SPRING, LIKE AN INDUSTRIOUS VIRGIN ....STINGS   215   35
    MOLDING ONTO HIS LIPS LIKE LIES, ...STINGS   215   49
    LIKE THE PACK, THE PACK, LIKE EVERYBODY. ....THE SWARM   216   25
    LIKE THE PACK, THE PACK, LIKE EVERYBODY. ....THE SWARM   216   25
    THE BLACK BUNCHED IN THERE LIKE A BAT, ...WINTERING   218   13
    FILING LIKE SOLDIERS ....WINTERING   218   24
    IN WHICH I HAVE LIVED LIKE A FOOT ....DADDY   222   3
    CHUFFING ME OFF LIKE A JEW. ....DADDY   223   32
    I BEGAN TO TALK LIKE A JEW. ....DADDY   223   34
    BRUTE HEART OF A BRUTE LIKE YOU ....DADDY   223   50
    PUSHING BY LIKE HEARTS, ...MEDUSA   225   8
    OVEREXPOSED, LIKE AN X-RAY. ....MEDUSA   225   31
    THE FLUORESCENT LIGHT WINCING ON AND OFF LIKE A TERRIBLE MIGRAINE, ...
                                        ... LESBOS   227   4
    YOU WHO HAVE BLOWN YOUR TUBES LIKE A BAD RADIO ....LESBOS   228   17
    HIS JEW-MAMA GUARDS HIS SWEET SEX LIKE A PEARL. ....LESBOS   228   27
    SPLITTING LIKE QUARTZ INTO A MILLION BITS. ....LESBOS   228   51
    WORKING IT LIKE DOUGH, A MULATTO BODY, ...LESBOS   229   61
    I AM PACKING THE HARD POTATOES LIKE GOOD CLOTHES, ...LESBOS   229   68
    EVERY DAY YOU FILL HIM WITH SOUL-STUFF, LIKE A PITCHER. .....LESBOS   229   77
    CLOSE ON YOU LIKE THE FIST OF A BABY ....LESBOS   229   86
    WHOEVER HEARD A SUNSET YOWL LIKE THAT? ....STOPPED DEAD   230   15
    I'LL CARRY IT OFF LIKE A RICH PRETTY GIRL, ...STOPPED DEAD   230   23
    FROM ME LIKE ISADORA'S SCARVES, I'M IN A FRIGHT ....FEVER.   231   12
    LIKE HIROSHIMA ASH AND EATING IN. ....FEVER.   231   26
    LIKE THE RED-HEADED SISTER HE NEVER DARED TO TOUCH, ...AMNESIAC   233   13
    THEY RISE ON EITHER SIDE OF HIM LIKE STARS. ....AMNESIAC   233   23
    TURN, LIKE AN ANIMAL, ...LYONNESSE   234   24
    A FLAP LIKE A HAT, ...CUT   235   6
    I ROCK YOU LIKE A BOAT ....BY CANDLELIGHT   237   24
    THOUGH IT LOOKS LIKE A CAT, WITH ITS FLUFFY STUFF, PURE WHITE.*TOUR.   237   16
    THEY WELD TO ME LIKE PLUMS. ....NICK AND THE CANDLESTICK   241   9
    I GLEAM LIKE A MIRROR. ....PURDAH   242   18
    ONE FEATHER, LIKE THE PEACOCK. ....PURDAH   243   39
    DOLL HE GUARDS LIKE A HEART -- ....PURDAH   244   54
    AND LIKE THE CAT I HAVE NINE TIMES TO DIE. ....LADY LAZARUS   244   21
    AND PICK THE WORMS OFF ME LIKE STICKY PEARLS. ....LADY LAZARUS   245   42
    IS AN ART, LIKE EVERYTHING ELSE. ....LADY LAZARUS   245   44
    I DO IT SO IT FEELS LIKE HELL. ....LADY LAZARUS   245   46
    AND I EAT MEN LIKE AIR. ....LADY LAZARUS   247   84
    PUNCHING OUT ABSENCE! LIKE CANNON. ....GETTING THERE   248   8
    FIXED TO THEIR ARCS LIKE GODS, ...GETTING THERE   248   14
    READY TO ROLL, LIKE A DEVIL'S, ...GETTING THERE   248   40
    I SHALL BURY THE WOUNDED LIKE PUPAS, ...GETTING THERE   249   60
    FALLING LIKE BLESSINGS, LIKE FLAKES ....THE NIGHT DANCES   250   24
    FALLING LIKE BLESSINGS, LIKE FLAKES ....THE NIGHT DANCES   250   24
    STEP OFF SEVEN LEAGUES, LIKE THOSE DISTANCES ....GULLIVER   251   21
    NEGRO, MASKED LIKE A WHITE, ...THALIDOMIDE   252   3
    FLEES AND ABORTS LIKE DROPPED MERCURY. ....THALIDOMIDE   252   26
    I LOVE THEM LIKE HISTORY. ....LETTER IN NOVEMBER   253   23
    AND BALLED, LIKE BLAKE'S, ...DEATH & CO.   254   4
    ARE NOT THE THOUGHTS I TURN ON, LIKE A YOGI, ...YEARS   255   3
    O GOD, I AM NOT LIKE YOU ....YEARS   255   6
    AND CRAWLS BEHIND IT LIKE A WORM. ....THE FEARFUL   256   2
    MORE AND MORE LIKE A DEAD ONE, ...THE FEARFUL   256   8
    DEAD AND PERFECT LIKE NEFERTIT, ...THE FEARFUL   256   14
    THE OVENS GLOWED LIKE HEAVENS, INCANDESCENT. ....MARY'S SONG   257   18
    PEOPLE LIKE LIGHT RAYS, LEAVE ....BRASILIA   259   19
    THAT WATCHES, LIKE GOD, OR THE SKY .................EAVESDROPPER   261   44
    SPREADING ITSELF, LIKE BUTTER. .....................EAVESDROPPER   261   51
    EYES LIKE MICE ....................................EAVESDROPPER   261   54
    WHERE THE YEW TREES BLOW LIKE HYDRAS, ...THE MUNICH MANNEQUINS   262   3
    DAWN GILDS THE FARMERS LIKE PIGS, ...TOTEM   264   5
    LET US EAT IT LIKE PLATO'S AFTERBIRTH, ...TOTEM   264   14
    LET US EAT IT LIKE CHRIST. ....TOTEM   264   15
    OUT OF WHICH THE SAME SELF UNFOLDS LIKE A SUIT ....TOTEM   264   25
    THEY BUZZ LIKE BLUE CHILDREN ....TOTEM   265   31
    WHILE THE DAY OUTSIDE GLIDES BY LIKE TICKER TAPE. ....PARALYTIC   266   10
    FALLING FROM ME LIKE RINGS ....PARALYTIC   267   35

```
                                                        TITLE          PAGE  LINE
LIKE (CONT.)
  MILL A LITTER OF BREASTS LIKE JELLYFISH.  .... ..............GIGOLO     267   13
  GLITTER LIKE FONTAINEBLEAU  ................................. ....GIGOLO  268   28
  OFF FROM THE CENTER LIKE HORSES.  ............................WORDS      270    5
  WELLS LIKE TEARS, LIKE THE  ..................................WORDS      270    7
  WELLS LIKE TEARS. LIKE THE  ..................................WORDS      270    7
  THE HEART LIKE WISHES OR FREE  ............................BALLOONS      272   16
  HIS BALLOON SQUEAK LIKE A CAT. ............................BALLOONS      272   22
  IN EVERY RESPECT LIKE EVERY OTHER NIGHT:*DIALOGUE OVER A OUIJA BOARD     276    2
  THEY'LL GO BY, TRUNDLING LIKE MARBLE STATUES WAY OUT  ...DIALOGUE O.     276    6
  IN THE WINGS SOMEWHERE, OR LIKE HEIRLOOM FURNITURE  .....DIALOGUE O.     276    7
  COME ON CALL LIKE THAT BUT PAN? HE'S ...DIALOGUE OVER A OUIJA BOARD      277   28
  LIKE AN OLIVE-BEAKED DOVE ABOVE THE ENGULFING FACT:  ....DIALOGUE O.     279  112
  BURNING LIKE KNOTHOLES FROM A NUN'S SHROUD-CIRCLED  .....DIALOGUE O.     280  130
  FOR LOUDSPEAKER WIRES RUNNING LIKE A LOGICAL  ...........DIALOGUE O.     280  165
  GODS AND REAR THEM LIKE BEANSTALKS FROM OUT THESE RIBS   DIALOGUE O.     280  170
  LIKE ALL THE OTHERS AND SWEAR THAT HE'S A PUMA  .........DIALOGUE O.     281  176
  ON HIM SOMETIMES. HE'S LAZY. LIKE ANY YOUNG  ...........DIALOGUE O.      281  182
  LIKE A GOOD BOY. BE CAREFUL. I'M NOT SURE THAT HE  ......DIALOGUE O.     282  207
  WHICH PROPS YOU THROUGH THIS DESERT LIKE A DREAM  .......DIALOGUE O.     282  212
  LIKE LIVE WHITE RABBITS, READY TO BEGIN *DIALOGUE OVER A OUIJA BOARD     282  234
  OF ONE WINE-GLASS, YOU'LL PIN IT LIKE A PRIZE  ..........DIALOGUE O.     283  249
  LIKE RIVAL PARENTS OVER A PRECOCIOUS  ...DIALOGUE OVER A OUIJA BOARD     284  283
  LIKE THE UNDERSIDE OF MUSHROOMS. DO YOU FEEL  ..........DIALOGUE O.      285  315
  RULE THEIR BEDS LIKE BEHEADED AND RESURRECTED AND ALL SILENT
      ROYALTY,  ............................ QUEEN MARY'S ROSE GARDEN      290    5
  THOUGH HUNDREDS OF LONDONERS KNOW IT LIKE THE PALM OF THEIR HAND. ...
                                ... QUEEN MARY'S ROSE GARDEN              290   16
  THE WRINKLES CREEP UP LIKE WAVES,  ......................THE RIVAL/DR    291    4
  I SHOULD HAVE A STEEL COMPLEXION LIKE YOURS  ...........THE RIVAL/DR     291    6
  IT KEEPS WASHING YOU UP LIKE AN OLD BONE.  .............THE RIVAL/DR     291   16
  FIND YOU OVER AND OVER, LIPPED LIKE A SKATE AND SMILING,  ...
                                            ... THE RIVAL/DR              291   18
  SHE PULSES LIKE A HEART ON MY HILL.  .........................ELM/DR     292    2
  IT IS LIKE SOMETHING SHE HAS CAUGHT FOR ME.  ................ELM/DR      292    5
  THE MOON IS LET GO, LIKE A DEAD THING.  .....................ELM/DR      292    8
  THEY ARE ASSAILING YOUR BRAIN LIKE NUMERALS,  .............STINGS/DR     293    4
  OSSIFYING LIKE JUNKED STATUES --  .........................STINGS/DR     293   14
  FOUR O'CLOCK, AND THE FEVER SOAKS FROM ME LIKE HONEY. ....FEVER./DR      294    1
  AND HANDS LIKE NERVOUS BUTTERFLIES;  ................FAMILY REUNION      300   19
  LIKE A DIVER ON A LOFTY SPAR OF LAND  ...............FAMILY REUNION      301   25
  WHERE GUESTS SLIDE GLIDING INTO LIGHT LIKE WINE;  ........CINDERELLA     304    6
  MY TEARS LIKE VINEGAR,  .......................................JILTED    304    2
  WHILE LIKE AN EARLY SUMMER PLUM,  .............................JILTED    304    9
  LIKE THE BRONZE TONE  ...............................AQUATIC NOCTURNE    306   27
  AND LIKE A CUCKOO IN THE NEST MAKES HELL   METAMORPHOSES OF THE MOON     307   17
  ELEMENTS LIKE DIRTY SOCKS AND SCRAPS  .....METAMORPHOSES OF THE MOON     307   28
  WOULD UMBRELLA LIKE LIBERAL TOADSTOOLS  ...........DIALOGUE EN ROUTE     308    8
  YOU DRANK YOUR COFFEE LIKE ORIGINAL SIN,  ..........THE TRIAL OF MAN     312    6
  WHILE TULIPS BOW LIKE A COLLEGE OF CARDINALS  .........APRIL AUBADE      312    7
  AND JONQUILS SPROUT LIKE SOLOMON'S METAPHORS,  ........APRIL AUBADE      312   11
  TROUNCING THE SEA LIKE A RAGING BATHER,  .....................LAMENT     315    7
  BEFORE WE FELL, LIKE ICARUS, UNDONE;  .................DOOM OF EXILES    318   10
  AND SWAGGERS LIKE A PROPER GENTLEMAN;  ..................ADMONITIONS     319   11
  NEEDLES NAG LIKE UNICORNS,  ...........................DANSE MACABRE     321   13
  AND THE FRAGMENTS WHIR LIKE A WEATHER VANE  ...CIRCUS IN THREE RINGS     321    5
  CRIMPED LIKE FERN IN THE QUARTZ ATMOSPHERE;  .....PROLOGUE TO SPRING     322    8
  THEN HURL THE BARE WORLD LIKE A BLUEGREEN BALL  ..SONG FOR A REVOLU.     323   21
  IT'S TIME TO VANISH LIKE THE CHESHIRE CAT  ............A SORCERER B.     324   12
  LIKE A RARE CALDER MOBILE IN YOUR MIND.  ...........MIDSUMMER MOBILE     324   14
  NOW FOLD THEIR WINGS LIKE BATS AND DISAPPEAR  .........TWO LOVERS.       327    7
  THOUGH THE MIND LIKE AN OYSTER LABORS ON AND ON,  .......TWO LOVERS.     327   19
  THE PINE TREE LIKE A RORSCHACH-BLOT  .............BLACK PINE TREE.       328    2
  SPRUNG UP LIKE PLAGUE OF TOADSTOOLS OVERNIGHT:  ............TERMINAL     328    4
  WE RAISE OUR ARGUMENTS LIKE SITTING DUCKS  .......LOVE IS A PARALLAX     329   19
  THE RAW WIND LIKE A SCARF; LOVE IS A FAUN  .......LOVE IS A PARALLAX     329   23
  LIKE AN ENORMOUS OYSTER, DOWN  ...................LOVE IS A PARALLAX     329   27
  AN INSIGHT LIKE THE FLIGHT OF BIRDS:  ............LOVE IS A PARALLAX     330   60
  WITH A THUNDER LIKE LIONS; ALL AIMS  .....................AERIALIST      331   32
  TO FLOAT LIKE DREAM-FISH IN THE LANGUID LIMBO  ...MORNING IN THE HOS.    332    8
  LIKE PETULANT PARAKEETS CORKED UP IN CAGES  .....MORNING IN THE HOS.     332   19
  AND LIKE A BURGLAR STEAL THEIR FANCY:  ..........MORNING IN THE HOS.     333   26
  LOOPING LIKE FAITH ABOUT HER BLEEDING FEET,  ..........THE PRINCESS.     334   48
  LIKE COLORED TOPS THROUGH TIME  .....................TOUCH-AND-GO        335   10
  AND I, LIKE THE CHILDREN, CAUGHT  ...................TOUCH-AND-GO        336   17
LIKED (1)
  AND THE VILLAGERS NEVER LIKED YOU. .........................DADDY        224   77
LIKELY (1)
  IT'S LIKELY THAT EACH SECRET SOUGHT  ......METAMORPHOSES OF THE MOON     307   21
LIKING (1)
  FOR BEING TOO WELL-BRED AND SMELLESS AND LIKING THE CITY. ...
                                ... QUEEN MARY'S ROSE GARDEN              290   20
LILAC (1)
  ROSE CANDLES FLICKER ON THE LILAC WALL  .................CINDERELLA      304    7
```

289

```
                                                    TITLE            PAGE  LINE
LILAC-FLOWER (1)
  HIS LIDS ARE LIKE THE LILAC-FLOWER  ...................THREE WOMEN   181  172
LILIES (13)
  YADWIGHA, ON A RED COUCH, AMONG LILIES  ........... .........YADWIGHA.    85   T
  HEART-SHAPED LEAVES, LIKE CATALPA LEAVES, AND LILIES  .....YADWIGHA.     85   6
  OF MONSTROUS SIZE, LIKE NO WELL-BRED LILIES.  . ...........YADWIGHA.     85   7
  AND BODY WHITER THAN ITS FRILL OF LILIES:  ...............YADWIGHA.      85  14
  LEAVES AND LILIES FLATTENED TO PAPER BEHIND YOU  .........YADWIGHA.      85  16
  PERSISTED IN THE PICTURE WITH THE LILIES,  .... ..........YADWIGHA.      86  22
  AND THE SNAKECHARMER'S SONG AND THE GIGANTIC LILIES,  ......YADWIGHA.    86  33
  IN THE MIDST OF ALL THAT GREEN AND THOSE GREAT LILIES!  ...YADWIGHA.     86  39
  NUN-HEARTED AND BLIND TO THE WORLD. MARBLE LILIES  .....BARREN WOMAN    157   4
  STARS OPEN AMONG THE LILIES.  .....................CROSSING THE WATER   190  10
  THE THROATS OF OUR WRISTS BRAVE LILIES.  ....................STINGS     214   4
  SMELL OF YOUR SLEEPS, LILIES, LILIES.  ............THE NIGHT DANCES     250   4
  SMELL OF YOUR SLEEPS, LILIES, LILIES.  ............THE NIGHT DANCES     250  10
LILY (2)
  TO OUR BOWER AT THE LILY ROOT.  ...........................POEM.5.F.    134   2
  PALM-SPEAR AND LILY DISTINCT AS FLORA IN THE VAST  ...........A LIFE    149   4
LIMB (9)
  AND RECOIL IN THE ALTERING LIGHT: THE RADIANT LIMB  ..EPITAPH FOR F.    46  33
  SOME HAVOC ON TENDER LIMB, AND YET  ..................CRYSTAL GAZER     55  23
  STEPS OUT RADIANT IN LIMB, EYE, LIP,  .....................CONJURING.    66  27
  GREEN VIRGINS, CONSECRATING LIMB AND LIP  .........VIRGIN IN A TREE     82  27
  HERE THEY CAN DOCTOR HEADS, OR ANY LIMB.  .................POEM.7.S.   137  35
  TOMORROW THE PATIENT WILL HAVE A CLEAN, PINK PLASTIC LIMB. *SURGEON.   171  40
  OLD BLOOD OF LIMB STUMPS, BURNT HEARTS.  ...............BERCK-PLAGE    200  99
  THE RADIANT LIMB.  .............................MOONSONG AT MORNING    317  36
  BITES KEEN INTO EACH BRAVE LIMB  ..........................AERIALIST   331  24
LIMBER (2)
  TO THESE LIMBER HOOKS.  ........................WORDS FOR A NURSERY     73  10
  SAWS DOWN A REED AND SWIMS FROM HIS LIMBER GROVE,  ......WATERCOLOR.   112  23
LIMBO (2)
  THE SILVER LIMBO OF EACH EYE  .........................THE FEARFUL     256  16
  TO FLOAT LIKE DREAM-FISH IN THE LANGUID LIMBO  ..MORNING IN THE HOS.   332   8
LIMBS (9)
  WE TAKE THE PLUNGE; UNDER WATER OUR LIMBS  ...........TALE OF A TUB      25  25
  OUT THEIR STALKY LIMBS AGAIN THOUGH PEACE  .........THE THIN PEOPLE     64   9
  TWINED TO HER HARD LIMBS LIKE IVY: THE PURITAN LIP *VIRGIN IN A TREE    81  12
  LIMBS: NOT A BASILISK-BLINK, NOR A DOUBLE WHAMMY,  .. .......PERSEUS    83  16
  THE CLASSIC LIMBS OF STUBBORN ANTIGONE?  .....................PERSEUS   83  40
  THEY RISE, THEIR LIMBS PONDEROUS  ...........................LORELEI    94  12
  SLEEPDRUNK, THEIR LIMBS AT ODDS?  ....................POEM.3.MAENAD.   133  23
  MY LIMBS, ALSO, HAVE LEFT ME.  ..............................EVENT     195  20
  LIMBS, IMAGES, SHRIEKS. BEHIND THE CONCRETE BUNKERS  ....BERCK-PLAGE   197  29
LIMBS' (1)
  OUR LIMBS' IMAGE ON A FIELD OF STRAW  ..............IN MIDAS' COUNTRY   99   9
LIME (1)
  THE NATURAL FATNESS OF THESE LIME LEAVES! ---  ..........BERCK-PLAGE   199  91
LIME-GREEN (1)
  WHEN I WAS NINE, A LIME-GREEN ANESTHETIST  ................FACE LIFT   155   4
LIMIT (1)
  YOU WERE CONDEMNED TO SERVE THE LEGAL LIMIT  .......THE TRIAL OF MAN   312  10
LIMP (2)
  A BEDRAGGLED SNAKE, HANGING LIMP AS THE ABSURD MOUTH  .......PERSEUS    83  38
  SHE'D SUPPORTED ME FOR SO LONG I WAS QUITE LIMP --  ......IN PLASTER   159  44
LIMPID (2)
  LIMPID AS SPIRITS. MANY STONES LAY  ......................LOVE LETTER  147  22
  LIMPID AS THE SOLITUDES  .........................WUTHERING HEIGHTS    167  29
LINE (13)
  AND THAT CROOKED LINE  ....................................RECANTATION  41   2
  THE WORD, DEFINING, MUZZLES; THE DRAWN LINE  .......POEMS, POTATOES    106   1
  STONES, WITHOUT CONSCIENCE, WORD AND LINE ENDURE,  ..POEMS, POTATOES   106   5
  ON THE MIND'S EYE, ERECTING A LINE  .....SLEEP IN THE MOJAVE DESERT    143   4
  I WATCHED SETTLE, LINE BY LINE, IN MY MIRROR --  .........FACE LIFT    156  26
  I WATCHED SETTLE, LINE BY LINE, IN MY MIRROR --  .........FACE LIFT    156  26
  THE LINE PINK AND QUIET, A WORM, BASKING.*THE COURAGE OF SHUTTING-UP   209   2
  TREMULOUS BREATH AT THE END OF MY LINE,  .....................MEDUSA   225  17
  THE TRAIN LEAVES A LINE OF BREATH.  ...................SHEEP IN FOG    262   4
  INSTEAD OF FAT FISH ON THE LINE, YOU'VE PLUMBED  ........DIALOGUE O.   282 242
  SURFACED IN OURSELVES: HE'LL SPELL A LINE  .............DIALOGUE O.    283 255
  AND DROOLS AT THE RECEPTION LINE.  ....................FAMILY REUNION  301  24
  THERE BURNS THROUGHOUT THE LINE OF WORDS,  .......LOVE IS A PARALLAX   330  57
LINED (1)
  AND THE OUTRAGE OF A SKY, THE LINED BRAIN OF IT.  .........COURAGE.    209   4
LINEN (7)
  THOUGH THE BODY WALK OUT IN CLEAN LINEN.  ...................MOONRISE   98  15
  SPACE! SPACE! THE BED LINEN WAS GIVING OUT ENTIRELY.  .......WAKING.   151  11
  YOUR SHIRT OF CRISP LINEN  ...................................WHITSUN  154   9
  I WATCHED MY TEASET, MY BUREAUS OF LINEN, MY BOOKS  .........TULIPS    161  26
  ENFOLDS HER FACE LIKE FINE LINEN,  ......................BERCK-PLAGE   200 102
  AND HERE THE SQUARE OF WHITE LINEN  .........................STINGS    215  43
  JEW LINEN.  .............................................LADY LAZARUS  244   9
LINES (9)
  EVER BLUR THE INTRANSIGENT LINES WHICH DRAW  ..........TALE OF A TUB    25  28
```

LINES (CONT.)
    AS OUT OF EDEN'S NAVEL TWIST THE LINES ................SNAKECHARMER   79   19
    BY CORRECT GREEN LINES AND NO SEEDY FREE-FOR-ALL ...ABOVE THE OXBOW   89   49
    FOR THE ARCHAIC TRENCHED LINES ....FULL FATHOM FIVE   93   25
    IN ESTABLISHMENTS WHICH IMAGINED LINES ....POEMS, POTATOES   106   3
    LIKE THE WHITE LINES ON A BLUEPRINT. ....ZOO KEEPER'S WIFE 154   10
    AND THEIR FINE LINES SINGE ....WUTHERING HEIGHTS   167   4
    THE LINES OF THE EYE, SCALDED BY THESE BALD SURFACES, ..BERCK-PLAGE   196   10
    MY LANDSCAPE IS A HAND WITH NO LINES, ...CHILDLESS WOMAN   259   4
LINGERIE (1)
    "IS THAT LINGERIE, PET? ....A SECRET 220   28
LINK (1)
    LINK TO HIS LYRIC ACTION ....TRIO OF LOVE SONGS   314   35
LINKED (1)
    FROM THE LINKED PONDS THAT MY EYES WINCE ....PARLIAMENT HILL FIELDS   152   11
LINOLEUM (1)
    FROM THE POLISHED LOZENGES OF ORANGE LINOLEUM. ....LESBOS   228   24
LINTEL (3)
    BARES ITS LOW LINTEL TO CORRODING WEATHERS: ....DEPARTURE   51   17
    MAZE OF BARNS TO THE LINTEL OF THE SUNK STY DOOR ....SOW   60   9
    LINTEL AND SILL HAVE UNHINGED THEMSELVES. ....WUTHERING HEIGHTS   168   32
LION (1)
    THE LION AND THE TIGERS TURN TO CLAY ....DENOUEMENT   327   10
LIONESS (2)
    GOD'S LIONESS, ...ARIEL   239   4
    THE LIONESS, ...PURDAH   244   55
LION-HEAD (1)
    THE STONE LION-HEAD SET IN THE WALL ................RHODODENDRON.   103   5
LION-RED (1)
    WITH HER LION-RED BODY, HER WINGS OF GLASS? ....STINGS   215   55
LIONS (1)
    WITH A THUNDER LIKE LIONS; ALL AIMS ....AERIALIST   331   32
LION'S (1)
    I INVADE MY LION'S DEN; ....CIRCUS IN THREE RINGS   321   8
LIP (10)
    STEPS OUT RADIANT IN LIMB, EYE, LIP, ...CONJURING.   66   27
    TWINED TO HER HARD LIMBS LIKE IVY: THE PURITAN LIP *VIRGIN IN A TREE   81   12
    GREEN VIRGINS, CONSECRATING LIMB AND LIP ....VIRGIN IN A TREE   82   27
    SAND ABRADED THE MILKLESS LIP. ....I WANT, I WANT   106   5
    WATER MOLLIFIES THE FLINT LIP, ...POEM.7.S.   137   25
    FROM THE BROKEN THROAT, THE MARSHY LIP. ....THE BURNT-OUT SPA   138   21
    ON THE OPPOSITE LIP ....EVENT   195   18
    ATTENDANTS OF THE LIP! ....PURDAH   243   40
    THE SHADOW OF THIS LIP, AN ABYSS. ....GULLIVER   251   24
    BLOOD AND BANK WRIST, ELBOW, SHOULDER, LIP ....DIALOGUE O.   277   18
LIPPED (1)
    FIND YOU OVER AND OVER, LIPPED LIKE A SKATE AND SMILING, ...
                                               ... THE RIVAL/DR   291   18
LIPS (12)
    GIVEN HER LIPS THAT LEMON-TASTING DROOP: ....VIRGIN IN A TREE   82   42
    PROCEED FROM YOUR GREAT LIPS. ....THE COLOSSUS   129   4
    HER LIPS SWEET WITH DIVINITY. ....FINISTERRE 170   25
    FROM HER LIPS AMPERSANDS AND PERCENT SIGNS ....AN APPEARANCE   189   4
    A CREST OF BREASTS, EYELIDS AND LIPS ....BERCK-PLAGE   200 116
    YOU COME IN LATE, WIPING YOUR LIPS. ....THE OTHER   201   1
    THERE WAS NO ABSENCE OF LIPS, THERE WERE TWO CHILDREN,*THE DETECTIVE   209   34
    MOLDING ONTO HIS LIPS LIKE LIES, ...STINGS   215   49
    ON MY EYES, MY LIPS, MY HAIR ....THE NIGHT DANCES   250   26
    WRAP MY LIPS, ...PARALYTIC   266   28
    THE BLACK VEIL MOLDS TO YOUR LIPS: ....STINGS/DR   293   9
    WITH SUNLIGHT OF A THOUSAND YEARS UPON HIS LIPS ....GOLD MOUTHS CRY   302   13
LIPSTICK (2)
    I AM BEAUTIFUL AS A STATISTIC. HERE IS MY LIPSTICK. ....THREE WOMEN   183 245
    AND I IN SLIPPERS AND HOUSEDRESS WITH NO LIPSTICK! ....THE TOUR   237   6
LIQUID (1)
    DEEP IN LIQUID INDIGO ....AQUATIC NOCTURNE   305   1
LIQUIDS (1)
    SIPPING THEIR LIQUIDS FROM ASSORTED POTS, ...LEAVING EARLY   145   8
LIQUOR (1)
    THE LIQUOR OF INDOLENCE, AND ALL THINGS SINK POEM.5.F.   134   8
LIQUORS (1)
    OR YOUR LIQUORS SEEP TO ME, IN THIS GLASS CAPSULE,   POPPIES IN JULY   203   13
LIST (1)
    RED AND ORANGE BARGES LIST AND BLISTER ....A WINTER SHIP   112   2
LISTEN (5)
    NO LONGER DO I LISTEN FOR THE SCRAPE OF A KEEL ....THE COLOSSUS   130   29
    LISTEN: YOUR TENANT MICE ....LEAVING EARLY   146   35
    FLICKERS AMONG THE FLAT PINK ROSES. I WAKE TO LISTEN: MORNING SONG   157   11
    THEY LISTEN FOR THE MILLENNIUM, ...HEAVY WOMEN   158   13
    LISTEN: THESE ARE ITS HOOVES: IT HAS GONE OFF, LIKE A HORSE. ...ELM   192   9
LISTENED (2)
    AND AS I LISTENED ITS COLD TEETH SEETHED   ON THE DECLINE OF ORACLES   78   3
    WE LISTENED. ....BITTER STRAWBERRIES   299   4
LISTENER (1)
    THEY ARE PRESSING OUT OF THE MANY-HOLED EARPIECE, THEY ARE LOOKING

TITLE   PAGE LINE

LISTENER (CONT.)
    FOR A LISTENER. ......WORDS HEARD, BY ACCIDENT, OVER THE PHONE 203   9
LISTENING (2)
    FOR THE WHORLED EAR'S LISTENING ....LORELEI   94 18
    WAS SHE AT THE WINDOW, LISTENING? ....THE DETECTIVE 208   4
LIT (14)
    OF DOUBLE STAR-EYES LIT ....FAUN   35   9
    NO MATTER HOW FIERCELY LIT; STAUNCH CONTRACTS BREAK   EPITAPH FOR F.   46 32
    UNTIL HIS OWN LIT ROOM OUTSHONE ....THE EVERLASTING MONDAY   62   9
    LIT THINGS, THAT LAMP OF THE POSSIBLE! WET YET .....SPINACH-PICKER.   89   3
    LONG, SHORT, LONG -- IN THE LIT GARDEN ....CHILD'S PARK STONES 101 14
    PALELY LIT BY ....POLLY'S TREE 128 24
    LIT LIKE A TWO-TIERED WEDDING CAKE ....ON DECK 142   7
    HOW THE BALCONIES ECHOED! HOW THE SUN LIT UP .....WAKING IN WINTER 151   9
    I ENTER THE LIT HOUSE. ....PARLIAMENT HILL FIELDS 153 50
    HOW OUR COURTSHIP LIT THE TINDERY CAGES -- ....ZOO KEEPER'S WIFE 155 33
    HOW THEY LIT THE TEDIUM OF THE PROTRACTED EVENING! ....INSOMNIAC 163 16
    ON THIS HILL, WITH ITS VIEW OF LIT CASTLES, EACH SWUNG BELL   STARS. 166 38
    THE HIGH, GREEN MEADOWS ARE GLOWING, AS IF LIT FROM WITHIN. ...
                          ... BLACKBERRYING 168 14
    LIT (YOU ARE READING), ...EAVESDROPPER 260 30
LITERALISTS (1)
    YADWIGHA, THE LITERALISTS ONCE WONDERED HOW YOU ....YADWIGHA.   85   1
LITHE (3)
    LURKS THE LITHE ONE; IN DREAMS' AMBUSH ....PURSUIT   23 30
    DEMURE ONES, LITHE ONES, NEEDING NO LESSON ....ELLA MASON A.   54 40
    DILATE LITHE AND ....AQUATIC NOCTURNE 305 14
LITTER (5)
    AND THE LEAVES' LITTER. ....SPINSTER   49   6
    ON THE MOVE, HEDGED BY A LITTER OF FEAT-FOOT NINNIES ....SOW   61 21
    LITTER THE MUD LIKE ORANGEPEEL. ....PRIVATE GROUND 130 12
    ANY DAY I MAY LITTER PUPPIES POEM.2.DARK. 132 12
    MILL A LITTER OF BREASTS LIKE JELLYFISH. ....GIGOLO 267 13
LITTERED (3)
    SHARK LITTERED IN THE GERANIUM BED -- ....POINT SHIRLEY 110 16
    YOUR FLUTED BONES AND ACANTHINE HAIR ARE LITTERED .....THE COLOSSUS 130 20
    LITTERED WITH CHINESE HANDS. NOW I'M STARED AT ....LEAVING EARLY 146 30
LITTERS (1)
    GUARDED BROODS AND LITTERS ....HARDCASTLE CRAGS   63 31
LITTLE (84)
    OUTSIDE, THE LITTLE HEDGE LEAVES ARE ....RESOLVE   52   8
    THE MOON TO A RIND OF LITTLE LIGHT. ....THE THIN PEOPLE   65 31
    BUT THE LITTLE PLANET BOBBED AWAY ....THE DISQUIETING MUSES   76 46
    THIS LITTLE ODYSSEY ....BATTLE-SCENE   84   2
    O LITTLE CITY ON A HILL! ....A WINTER'S TALE   87 31
    THEY ARE UNLOADING THREE BARRELS OF LITTLE CRABS. ....A WINTER SHIP 113 14
    YET DESOLATION, STALLED IN PAINT, SPARES THE LITTLE COUNTRY ...
                ... TWO VIEWS OF A CADAVER ROOM 114 21
    IN THESE LITTLE BOUDOIRS STREAKED WITH ORANGE AND RED BEEKEEPER'S. 118 10
    WHOSE STONES KEEP A LITTLE HEAT. ....OLD LADIES' HOME 120   7
    HALFWAY UP FROM THE LITTLE HARBOR OF SARDINE BOATS, *THE NET-MENDERS 121   1
    HIS LITTLE VERMILION EYE ....MEDALLION 124   9
    THE PEARS FATTEN LIKE LITTLE BUDDHAS. ....THE MANOR GARDEN 125   3
    LITTLE VICTIM UNEARTHED BY SOME LARGE CREATURE ....BLUE MOLES 126   6
    SCALING LITTLE LADDERS WITH GLUEPOTS AND PAILS OF LYSOL*THE COLOSSUS 129 11
    LITTLE HUMBLE LOVES! POEM.2.DARK. 133 24
    THIS MONTH IS FIT FOR LITTLE. POEM.3.MAENAD. 133 11
    NOTHING WENT MOLDY. THE LITTLE INVISIBLES POEM.4.BEAST. 134   5
    WITHER LIKE PITHLESS HANDS. THERE IS LITTLE SHELTER. POEM.5.F. 134   4
    IF I AM A LITTLE ONE, I CAN DO NO HARM. POEM.6.W. 135 13
    ON FRIDAYS THE LITTLE CHILDREN COME POEM.7.S. 137 36
    NOW LITTLE WEEDS INSINUATE ....THE BURNT-OUT SPA 138 10
    LITTLE OR NOTHING. ....MUSHROOMS 139 22
    O HIGH-RISER, MY LITTLE LOAF. ....YOU'RE 141   9
    THEIR LITTLE FOREHEADS BULGED WITH CONCENTRATION. ....STILLBORN 142   3
    IT IS COMFORTABLE, FOR A CHANGE, TO MEAN SO LITTLE. ......TWO CAMP. 145 17
    THESE LITTLE GLOBES OF LIGHT ARE SWEET AS PEARS. ....CANDLES 149 24
    POISON OF STILLED LAWNS, THE LITTLE CLAPBOARD GRAVESTONES, WAKING. 151   7
    THE BLUE NIGHT PLANTS, THE LITTLE PALE BLUE HILL .....PARLIAMENT H. 153 41
    I PATRONIZED HER A LITTLE, AND SHE LAPPED IT UP -- .....IN PLASTER 159 20
    THEIR SMILES CATCH ONTO MY SKIN, LITTLE SMILING HOOKS. ......TULIPS 160 21
    HIS HEAD IS A LITTLE INTERIOR OF GRAY MIRRORS. ....INSOMNIAC 163 22
    LITTLE SHELLS MADE UP INTO NECKLACES AND TOY LADIES. ...FINISTERRE 170 32
    THEY STAY, THEIR LITTLE PARTICULAR LUSTERS ....LAST WORDS 172 17
    THE EYE OF A LITTLE GOD, FOUR-CORNERED. ....MIRROR 173   5
    WE WERE ALWAYS CRYING, IN OUR SPARE ROOMS, LITTLE PUT-UPON
        SISTERS, ...THE BABYSITTERS 174   4
    THIS IS NEWNESS: EVERY LITTLE TAWDRY ....NEW YEAR ON DARTMOOR 176   1
    EVERY LITTLE WORD HOOKED TO EVERY LITTLE WORD, AND ACT TO ACT. ...
                 ... THREE WOMEN 178 55
    EVERY LITTLE WORD HOOKED TO EVERY LITTLE WORD, AND ACT TO ACT. ...
                 ... THREE WOMEN 178 55
    THOSE LITTLE SICK ONES THAT ELUDE MY ARMS. ....THREE WOMEN 178 67
    QUIET, LIKE THE LITTLE EMPTINESSES I CARRY. ....THREE WOMEN 178 70
    I THINK HER LITTLE HEAD IS CARVED IN WOOD, ...THREE WOMEN 182 211

LITTLE (CONT.)
    THE LITTLE SILVER TROPHIES THEY'VE COME SO FAR FOR. ....THREE WOMEN 183 221
    HE IS TURNING TO ME LIKE A LITTLE, BLIND, BRIGHT PLANT. *THREE WOMEN 183 235
    AND SO I STAND, A LITTLE SIGHTLESS. SO I WALK ....THREE WOMEN 184 253
    THERE IS VERY LITTLE TO GO INTO MY SUITCASE. ....THREE WOMEN 184 266
    THESE LITTLE BLACK TWIGS DO NOT THINK TO BUD, ...THREE WOMEN 184 278
    HOW SHALL IT SOFTEN THEM, THIS LITTLE LULLABY? ....THREE WOMEN 185 294
    MY BLACK GOWN IS A LITTLE FUNERAL: . ...THREE WOMEN 185 303
    I SHALL MEDITATE UPON MY LITTLE SON. ....THREE WOMEN 186 324
    I HAVE PAINTED LITTLE HEARTS ON EVERYTHING. ....THREE WOMEN 186 329
    A SMOKE THAT TAKES THE PARKS, THE LITTLE STATUES ....THREE WOMEN 186 355
    THE CITY WAITS AND ACHES. THE LITTLE GRASSES ....THREE WOMEN 187 370
    LITTLE FUGUE ....LITTLE FUGUE 187   T
    IT WILL MAKE LITTLE DRESSES AND COATS, ...AN APPEARANCE 189   12
    A LITTLE LIGHT IS FILTERING FROM THE WATER FLOWERS. *CROSSING THE W. 190   4
    AND THE OCTOGENARIAN LOVES THE LITTLE FLOCKS. ...AMONG THE NARCISSI 190   10
    IT'S A LITTLE CORNUCOPIA. ....PHEASANT 191   20
    TILL YOUR HEAD IS A STONE, YOUR PILLOW A LITTLE TURF, ...ELM 192   11
    HOW THEY AWAITED HIM, THOSE LITTLE DEATHS! ......THE RABBIT CATCHER 194   24
    HIS LITTLE FACE IS CARVED IN PAINED, RED WOOD. ....EVENT 194   9
    OF LITTLE CRYSTALS, TITILLATING THE LIGHT, ...BERCK-PLAGE 197   26
    LITTLE POPPIES, LITTLE HELL FLAMES, ...POPPIES IN JULY 203   1
    LITTLE POPPIES, LITTLE HELL FLAMES, ...POPPIES IN JULY 203   1
    LITTLE BLOODY SKIRTS! ....POPPIES IN JULY 203   8
    THERE IS ONLY A LITTLE GRID, NO EXIT. ...THE ARRIVAL OF THE BEE BOX 213   10
    O LITTLE GIMLETS -- ....THE JAILER 226   16
    LITTLE UNSTRUNG PUPPET, KICKING TO DISAPPEAR -- ....LESBOS 227   9
    THE LITTLE TOY WIFE -- ....AMNESIAC 233   4
    LITTLE PILGRIM, ...CUT 235   9
    HE IS YOURS, THE LITTLE BRASSY ATLAS -- ....BY CANDLELIGHT 237   31
    GECKO, THE LITTLE FLICK! ....THE TOUR 237   4
    LITTLE BUSHY POLYPS, ...PURDAH 242   15
    LITTLE NETS, ...PURDAH 242   16
    AND A LITTLE FLAT, AS IF THEY ....GULLIVER 251   3
    THIS LITTLE BLACK ....LETTER IN NOVEMBER 253   6
    THEN TWO LITTLE FEET. ....DEATH & CO. 254   19
    LITTLE WHORE TONGUE, ...EAVESDROPPER 260   32
    LITTLE ....CHILD 265   6
    ITS CRYSTALS A LITTLE POULTICE. ....KINDNESS 269   11
    SHRED IN HIS LITTLE FIST. ....BALLOONS 272   30
    ONE AT EACH LITTLE ....EDGE 272   10
    EVEN A LITTLE? YOU KNOW I DON'T, AND STILL . . ..DIALOGUE O. 277   34
    "DON'T," PLEADED THE LITTLE GIRL ....BITTER STRAWBERRIES 299   22
    NO LITTLE MAN LIVES IN THE EXACTING MOON ....TWO LOVERS. 327   23
LITTLESOUL (1)
    FIDO LITTLESOUL, THE BOWEL'S FAMILIAR. POEM.4.BEAST. 134   13
LIVE (16)
    TO PEOPLE WHO LIVE IN THE BOTTOM OF VALLEYS ......ABOVE THE OXBOW   88   15
    THESE POEMS DO NOT LIVE: IT'S A SAD DIAGNOSIS. ....STILLBORN 142   1
    AND SEEMED TO GIVE HER WARMTH, LIKE A LIVE SKIN. ....WIDOW 164   19
    WITH THE O-GAPE OF COMPLETE DESPAIR. I LIVE HERE. ....MOON. 173   11
    SHE IS OLD, OLD, OLD, SHE MUST LIVE ANOTHER YEAR, AND SHE KNOWS IT. ...
                                   ... THE BEE MEETING 212   44
    I HAVE TO LIVE WITH IT OVERNIGHT ....THE ARRIVAL OF THE BEE BOX 213   7
    IT IS TATE AND LYLE THEY LIVE ON, INSTEAD OF FLOWERS. ...WINTERING 218   29
    BOTTLE IN WHICH I LIVE, ...MEDUSA 225   35
    AND LIVE IN GIBRALTAR ON AIR, ON AIR. ....STOPPED DEAD 230   25
    ITS FIRST COMMUNION OUT OF MY LIVE TOES. ..NICK AND THE CANDLESTICK 241   19
    SUCH QUEER MOONS WE LIVE WITH ....BALLOONS 271   10
    THE LETTERS LIVE IN THE SAME PLACE. OR ELSE ....DIALOGUE O. 277   23
    WHERE DO YOU LIVE? HE MOVES. HE'S MOVING BRISK ....DIALOGUE O. 281 206
    LIKE LIVE WHITE RABBITS, READY TO BEGIN *DIALOGUE OVER A OUIJA BOARD 282 234
    TELL US THE TRUTH. WHERE DO YOU LIVE? HE STARTS .....DIALOGUE O. 283 274
    CHIRPS THE FIRST; "LIVE ON A SILENT ISLAND ..EPITAPH IN THREE PARTS 337   5
LIVED (6)
    LIVED UNDER THE SHADOW OF HOT ROOFTOPS ....ABOVE THE OXBOW   89   54
    MONKEY LIVED UNDER THE DUNCE CAP. POEM.4.BEAST. 134   8
    THEY HAVE LIVED BEHIND GLASS ALL THEIR LIVES, THEY HAVE BEEN
                CARED FOR TENDERLY. ....THREE WOMEN 184 264
    THE FACE THAT LIVED IN THIS MIRROR IS THE FACE OF A DEAD MAN. ...
                               ... THE COURAGE OF SHUTTING-UP 210   29
    IN WHICH I HAVE LIVED LIKE A FOOT ....DADDY 222   3
    SINCE CHRISTMAS THEY HAVE LIVED WITH US, ...BALLOONS 271   1
LIVELIER (2)
    AND SUFFERED THEIR LIVELIER FELLOWS TO STRUGGLE. ....SPIDER   49   21
    THEM LIFE LIVELIER THAN OURS, ...SCULPTOR   92   23
LIVES (12)
    PLATONIC TABLE WHERE IT LIVES. THE BABY CARP ....PRIVATE GROUND 130   11
    HE LIVES IN AN OLD WELL, ...POEM.2.DARK. 132   19
    SHE LIVES QUIETLY ....A LIFE 150   25
    HE LIVES WITHOUT PRIVACY IN A LIDLESS ROOM, ...INSOMNIAC 163   26
    AND WHAT IF TWO LIVES LEAKED BETWEEN MY THIGHS? ....THREE WOMEN 180 120
    IT IS USUAL IN MY LIFE, AND THE LIVES OF OTHERS. ....THREE WOMEN 183 243
    THEY HAVE LIVED BEHIND GLASS ALL THEIR LIVES, THEY HAVE BEEN
                CARED FOR TENDERLY. ....THREE WOMEN 184 264

LIVES (CONT.)
   BLINDING ME WITH ITS LIGHTS, THE LIVES OF THE DEAD   .....THE RABBIT.   193   4
   WHERE SPILT LIVES CONGEAL AND STIFFEN TO HISTORY.*A BIRTHDAY PRESENT   208   51
   HE LIVES. HIS ANSWER WILL PUT AN END TO GIBES   ....DIALOGUE O.   281 174
   NO LITTLE MAN LIVES IN THE EXACTING MOON   ....TWO LOVERS.   327   23
   HER NINE SO SLIPPERY LIVES.   ....AERIALIST   332   36
LIVING (3)
   LIVING WITH HER WAS LIKE LIVING WITH MY OWN COFFIN: .....IN PLASTER 160   48
   LIVING WITH HER WAS LIKE LIVING WITH MY OWN COFFIN: .....IN PLASTER 160   48
   A LIVING DOLL, EVERYWHERE YOU LOOK.   ....THE APPLICANT 221   33
LIVINGROOM (3)
   AROUND HIM LIKE LIVINGROOM FURNITURE, LIKE A DECOR.   ....BERCK-PLAGE 199   83
   DILATING TO CRATERS IN THIS LIVINGROOM, *DIALOGUE OVER A OUIJA BOARD   285 320
   AS SURE AS THOSE COALS BURN, THE LIVINGROOM   ....DIALOGUE O.   286 357
LIZARD (1)
   OF RIDING AGAINST THE LIZARD, ...THE TIMES ARE TIDY 107   7
LIZARDS (1)
   I THINK OF THE LIZARDS AIRING THEIR TONGUES   ....SLEEP. 144   14
LIZARD'S (1)
   THE NIGHTS SNAPPED OUT OF SIGHT LIKE A LIZARD'S EYELID:*THE HANGING.   141   3
LIZARD-SCALES (1)
   BLUE AS LIZARD-SCALES. FROST SHEENS THE STREET.   ....DIALOGUE O. 286 340
LIZARDY (1)
   THE STREETS ARE LIZARDY CREVICES   ....GIGOLO 267   2
LLAMA (1)
   IN TIBET, OR A LLAMA IN ZANZIBAR   ....DIALOGUE OVER A OUIJA BOARD 281 177
LOADED (1)
   LOADED, AS THEY ARE, WITH ACCOUNTS OF BASTARDIES.   ....COURAGE. 210   6
LOAF (2)
   O HIGH-RISER, MY LITTLE LOAF.   ....YOU'RE 141   9
   COMPARED TO YOU, I AM CORRUPTIBLE AS A LOAF OF BREAD.   THE RIVAL/DR   291   1
LOAF'S (1)
   THIS LOAF'S BIG WITH ITS YEASTY RISING.   ....METAPHORS 116   5
LOAM (2)
   TAKE HOLD ON THE LOAM, ...MUSHROOMS 139   5
   ROLLED ROUND WITH GOODLY LOAM AND CRADLED DEEP, ...THE DEAD 320   9
LOAM-HUMPS (1)
   LOAM-HUMPS, HE SAYS, MOLES SHUNT   ....ODE FOR TED   29   7
LOATH (1)
   STILL, SHE FELT LOATH TO JUNK IT. *THE LADY AND THE EARTHENWARE HEAD   69   7
LOAVES (2)
   A BEGGAR STOPS AMONG EGGS AND LOAVES, ...THE BEGGARS   48   10
   HER WHEAT LOAVES   ....POINT SHIRLEY 110   27
LOBED (1)
   FOUNDING FATHER SET THESE LOBED, WARPED STONES   CHILD'S PARK STONES 100   3
LOBSTER-LIMBED (1)
   A BARNACLE-PATED, MOSS-WIGGED, LOBSTER-LIMBED   ....DIALOGUE O. 283 244
LOBSTERS (1)
   ADROIT LOBSTERS   ....AQUATIC NOCTURNE   306   22
LOCAL (3)
   LIKE LOCAL TROLLS IN THE SPELL OF A SUPERIOR BEING.   ......TWO CAMP. 144   6
   BOW DOWN, A LOCAL CONSTELLATION, ...LEAVING EARLY 145   11
   YOU MAY BE LOCAL, ...EAVESDROPPER 260   10
LOCATIONS (1)
   THE MOUTH-HOLE CRYING THEIR LOCATIONS. POEM.7.S.   136   16
LOCK (2)
   THESE LOVERS PROPHESY TO LOCK EMBRACE   ..EPITAPH FOR FIRE AND FLOWER   45   17
   TO CAST LOCK, STOCK AND BARREL UNDER BAN;   ....THE DISPOSSESSED 318   11
LOCKED (4)
   LEANS TO PECK OPEN THOSE LOCKED LIDS, TO EAT   ....THE SHRIKE   42   18
   AND THE LOCKED DROPS RISING IN A DEW   ....LOVE LETTER 147   21
   THE BOX IS LOCKED, IT IS DANGEROUS.   .....THE ARRIVAL OF THE BEE BOX 213   6
   LOCKED IN CRYSTAL CASKETS ARE THE LAKES, ...PROLOGUE TO SPRING   322   13
LOCKER (1)
   OF DAVY'S LOCKER, AND THE LORD'S TO HOME, ...DIALOGUE O.   283 246
LOCKS (1)
   IF I JUST UNDID THE LOCKS AND STOOD BACK AND TURNED INTO A TREE.   ...
                                ... THE ARRIVAL OF THE BEE BOX 213   28
LOCUST (1)
   OF WEEVIL TRIBE AND LOCUST CARAVAN   ....THE DISPOSSESSED   318   8
LOCUSTS (1)
   WHEN WORDS, LIKE LOCUSTS, DRUMMED THE DARKENING AIR   ....OUIJA   77   17
LODGE (2)
   AND RESOLVED MORE CEREMONIOUSLY TO LODGE   ....LADY AND T.   69   22
   YOUR VOICES LAY SIEGE. YOU LODGE   ....LORELEI   94   23
LOFTING (1)
   INSTINCT FOR ART BEGAN WITH THE BULL'S HORN LOFTING IN THE MOB'S   ...
                                           ... THE GORING   47   8
LOFTY (3)
   THAT LOFTY MONARCH, MONARCH MIND, ...NATURAL HISTORY 71   1
   FLATS OF HADLEY FARMS, THEY'RE LOFTY ENOUGH   ....ABOVE THE OXBOW   88   8
   LIKE A DIVER ON A LOFTY SPAR OF LAND   ....FAMILY REUNION   301   25
LOGAN (1)
   FROM LOGAN AIRPORT OPPOSITE.   ....GREEN ROCK, WINTHROP BAY 105   16

LOGIC (4)
    TO BE MEANT FOR CLIMBING. A PECULIAR LOGIC ....ABOVE THE OXBOW   88   17
    MAKE LOVE AND LOGIC MIX, ...NOTES TO A NEOPHYTE   306   16
    THE LIGHT OF LOGIC ....MOONSONG AT MORNING   317   17
    TO KNOCK THEM DOWN WITH LOGIC OR WITH LUCK ......LOVE IS A PARALLAX   329   20
LOGICAL (1)
    FOR LOUDSPEAKER WIRES RUNNING LIKE A LOGICAL ....DIALOGUE O.   280 165
LOGIC'S (1)
    BRIGHT ANGELS BLACK OUT OVER LOGIC'S LAND ....SONNET TO SATAN   323   3
LOGS (1)
    MORGUE OF OLD LOGS AND OLD IMAGES, THE LAKE ....PRIVATE GROUND   131   23
LOINS (1)
    OF HORSEHAIR AND LICE HIS HORNY LOINS; ....A LESSON IN VENGEANCE   80   15
LOITER (1)
    THEY LOITER AND STARE AS IF THE HOUSE ....AFTERMATH   113   2
LOLL (1)
    THEY LOLL FOREVER IN COLOSSAL SLEEP; ....THE DEAD   320   12
LOLLIES (1)
    ORANGE LOLLIES ON SILVER STICKS, ...THE MUNICH MANNEQUINS   263   14
LOLLS (1)
    A MERMAID ODALISQUE LOLLS AT HER EASE ....MIDSUMMER MOBILE   324   10
LONDONERS (1)
    THOUGH HUNDREDS OF LONDONERS KNOW IT LIKE THE PALM OF THEIR HAND. ...
                               ... QUEEN MARY'S ROSE GARDEN   290   16
LONE (5)
    OUR LONE LUCK NOW, COMPELLED BY BOND, BY BLOOD, ...CHANNEL CROSSING   27   33
    COCKED ON THE LONE, LATE, ...PROSPECT   28   11
    THE LONE WIND RAVING IN THE GUTTER, HIS ....SONNET: TO TIME   311   7
    A LONE BEACHCOMBER SQUATS AMONG THE WRACK ....TWO LOVERS.   327   13
    ALOFT, A LONE GULL HALTS UPON THE WIND, ...EPITAPH IN THREE PARTS   337   20
LONELINESS (3)
    THE TREES OF LONELINESS, THE TREES OF MOURNING. ....WIDOW   164   27
    THE VOICES OF LONELINESS, THE VOICES OF SORROW ....THREE WOMEN   185 292
    THE LONELINESS OF ITS EYE, THE EYE OF THE MOUNTAINS ....TOTEM   264   20
LONG (43)
    SOME BURN SHORT, SOME LONG, ...VANITY FAIR   33   34
    LONG GONE TO WHEEZE AND SEED, ELLA MASON ....ELLA MASON A.   53   8
    THE LONG WAIT FOR THE ANGEL, ...BLACK ROOK IN RAINY WEATHER   57   39
    THE LONG WIND, PARING HER PERSON DOWN ....HARDCASTLE CRAGS   63   22
    IT WAS DURING THE LONG HUNGER-BATTLE ....THE THIN PEOPLE   64   12
    ON THE LONG BOOKSHELF IT STOOD ...THE LADY AND THE EARTHENWARE HEAD   69   3
    ALL THE LONG GONE DARLINGS: THEY ....ALL THE DEAD DEARS   71   25
    THEIR SHADOWS LONG IN THE SETTING SUN ....THE DISQUIETING MUSES   76   52
    LAIN SPLAYED TOO LONG IN THE TORTUOUS BOUGHS: OVERRIPE .....VIRGIN.   82   37
    HAZARDOUS AND LONG, ...BATTLE-SCENE   85   34
    CREST AND TROUGH. MILES LONG ....FULL FATHOM FIVE   92   6
    LONG, SHORT, LONG -- IN THE LIT GARDEN ....CHILD'S PARK STONES   101   14
    LONG, SHORT, LONG -- IN THE LIT GARDEN ....CHILD'S PARK STONES   101   14
    OLD GOATHERDS SWEAR HOW ALL NIGHT LONG THEY HEAR ....GOATSUCKER   111   1
    THESE FLEMISH LOVERS FLOURISH; NOT FOR LONG. ....TWO VIEWS.   114   20
    DOURLY THE LONG HOTS AND COLDS, ...THE HERMIT AT OUTERMOST HOUSE   119   8
    HOW LONG HIS CARCASS HAS FOUNDERED UNDER ....THE BURNT-OUT SPA   138   8
    BROODY AND IN LONG SKIRTS ON MY FIRST HUSBAND'S SOFA, MY
        FINGERS ....FACE LIFT   156   22
    SHE'D SUPPORTED ME FOR SO LONG I WAS QUITE LIMP -- ....IN PLASTER   159   44
    I HAVE FALLEN A LONG WAY. CLOUDS ARE FLOWERING ....MOON.   173   22
    IT IS PINK, WITH SPECKLES. I HAVE LOOKED AT IT SO LONG ......MIRROR   173   7
    I SHALL MOVE NORTH. I SHALL MOVE INTO A LONG BLACKNESS. *THREE WOMEN   182 190
    HOW LONG CAN I BE A WALL, KEEPING THE WIND OFF? ....THREE WOMEN   185 288
    HOW LONG CAN I BE ....THREE WOMEN   185 289
    HOW LONG CAN I BE A WALL AROUND MY GREEN PROPERTY? .....THREE WOMEN   185 295
    HOW LONG CAN MY HANDS ....THREE WOMEN   185 296
    FROM THE LONG FALL, AND FIND MYSELF IN BED, ...THREE WOMEN   187 366
    CREEPS AWAY, MANY-SNAKED, WITH A LONG HISS OF DISTRESS. *BERCK-PLAGE   196   18
    DRAWN LIKE A LONG MATERIAL ....BERCK-PLAGE   197   34
    THE LONG COFFIN OF SOAP-COLORED OAK, ...BERCK-PLAGE   199   70
    WHOSE IS THAT LONG WHITE BOX IN THE GROVE, WHAT HAVE THEY
        ACCOMPLISHED, WHY AM I COLD. ....THE BEE MEETING   212   55
    HER WINGS TORN SHAWLS, HER LONG BODY ....STINGS   214   17
    MAIDS AND THE LONG ROYAL LADY. ....WINTERING   218   39
    HIS HAIR LONG AND PLAUSIVE. ....DEATH & CO.   254   22
    LONG NICOTINE-FINGER ..................................EAVESDROPPER   260   14
    THE STIFFNESS OF SAILS, THE LONG SALT WINDING SHEETS. ....MYSTIC   268   8
    TO BUILD HIS CANTING TOWERS. WHILE YOU, YOU LONG ....DIALOGUE O.   280 136
    MINOR IMPS PIPE UP, SO LONG AS EACH ....DIALOGUE OVER A OUIJA BOARD   280 152
    I'LL ASK. DO. WE'VE KEPT HIM WAITING LONG ....DIALOGUE O.   281 180
    SOME LIGHT. I GLIMPSE NO LIGHT AT ALL AS LONG ....DIALOGUE O.   284 290
    ALL NIGHT LONG, EVEN SHOULD OUR EYES SHUT ....DIALOGUE O.   286 354
    "WE OUGHT TO HAVE BOMBED THEM LONG AGO." ....BITTER STRAWBERRIES   299   21
    FOLLOW HOLIDAY REVEL BEGUN LONG SINCE, ...CINDERELLA   304   10
LONGED (1)
    HOW SHE LONGED FOR WINTER THEN! -- ....SPINSTER   49   13
LONGER (5)
    LONGER ON THIS LANDSCAPE OF CHAGRIN; ....WINTER LANDSCAPE, .   21   8

LONGER (CONT.)
    GRIP THE RAIL, SQUINT AHEAD, AND WONDER HOW MUCH LONGER   CHANNEL C.   26   6
    NO LONGER DO I LISTEN FOR THE SCRAPE OF A KEEL   ....THE COLOSSUS   130   29
    THE NURSES IN THEIR WING-CAPS ARE NO LONGER SO BEAUTIFUL; ...BERCK.   198   58
    OF A COUNTRY NO LONGER HEARD OF, ...THE COURAGE OF SHUTTING-UP   210   33
LONGEVITY (1)
    AND I WANT THE ONE'S LONGEVITY AND THE OTHER'S DARING.*I AM VERTICAL   162   10
LONGING (1)
    TO MORTAL CHILDREN LONGING TO BE GAY: ....NEVER TRY TO TRICK.   320   14
LONG-LEGGED (1)
    LEAPING AWKWARD AND LONG-LEGGED ....BITTER STRAWBERRIES   299   16
LONG-USED (1)
    IT STABLED IN; LONG-USED, BECAME WELL-LOVED   THE COMPANIONABLE ILLS   105   7
LOOK (49)
    ROOTED TO YOUR BLACK LOOK, THE PLAY TURNED TRAGIC: ...CONVERSATION.   21   12
    AN ORANGE CYCLOPS-EYE, SCORNING TO LOOK ....WINTER LANDSCAPE,   21   7
    FOR HIS LEAST LOOK, SCANT ACRES YIELD: ....ODE FOR TED   29   13
    RIVALS HER WHETTED LOOK, DIVINING WHAT CONCEIT ....VANITY FAIR   32   13
    FLAPPED BLACK TO LOOK AND BROOD ....FAUN   35   4
    OF HELL, AND NOT THE FIERY PART. YET TO JUDGE BY THAT DAZZLED LOOK, ...
                      ... DIALOGUE BETWEEN GHOST AND PRIEST   38   15
    OF ANIMALS TO CHOIR: "LOOK WHAT THRESH OF WINGS *WREATH FOR A BRIDAL   45   15
    BLOWS ASH IN EACH LOVER'S EYE; THE ARDENT LOOK ......EPITAPH FOR F.   46   34
    "LOOK! THERE SHE GOES, CAT-LADY MASON!" ....ELLA MASON A.   54   31
    WELL OR ILL." GERD SLANTS A LOOK AT EACH: MOST DEAR,   CRYSTAL GAZER   55   10
    SO BEGGAR GERD MIGHT AIM HER LOOK ....CRYSTAL GAZER   55   40
    FROM MY WORLDLING LOOK ITS BRILLIANT VEIN *ON THE PLETHORA OF DRYADS   67   10
    APE OF HER LOOK. BEST RID ....THE LADY AND THE EARTHENWARE HEAD   69   5
    BED OF A REED. LOOK: ....VIRGIN IN A TREE   81   15
    OF HUMAN AGONY: A LOOK TO NUMB ....PERSEUS   83   15
    AGAINST OUR SKY: THEY ARE WHAT WE LOOK SOUTHWARD TO *ABOVE THE OXBOW   88   11
    CANNOT LOOK MUCH BUT YOUR FORM SUFFERS ....SCULPTOR   92   17
    HAD AN ORIENTAL LOOK, ...MUSSEL HUNTER AT ROCK HARBOR   97   79
    LOOK UPON? RATS' TEETH GUT THE CITY ....OWL   102   15
    AND WOULDN'T PAUSE FOR MY STRAIGHT LOOK. ..........RHODODENDRON.   104   25
    BOW, AND RECOVER THEIR LOOK ....MAGNOLIA SHOALS   122   7
    WE TAKE A BACKWARD LOOK. ....THE SLEEPERS   123   12
    THE MOLES LOOK NEUTRAL AS THE STONES. ....BLUE MOLES   126   14
    NOW THERE IS NOTHING MUCH TO LOOK AT. ....ON DECK   142   9
    LOOK, THEY ARE MELTING LIKE COINS IN THE POWERFUL JUICES --   ZOO K.   154   8
    LOOK HOW WHITE EVERYTHING IS, HOW QUIET, HOW SNOWED-IN. .....TULIPS   160   2
    WE HAVE ONLY COME TO LOOK. YOU ARE TOO NEW ....NEW YEAR ON DARTMOOR   176   8
    IT HAD A CONSEQUENTIAL LOOK, LIKE EVERYTHING ELSE, ...THREE WOMEN   177   46
    AND THE GREAT SWAN, WITH ITS TERRIBLE LOOK, ...THREE WOMEN   178   50
    I DID NOT LOOK. BUT STILL THE FACE WAS THERE, ...THREE WOMEN   178   78
    LOOK, THEY ARE SO EXHAUSTED, THEY ARE ALL FLAT OUT ....THREE WOMEN   183 219
    THE NARCISSI LOOK UP LIKE CHILDREN, QUICKLY AND WHITELY. *NARCISSI.   190   12
    THE EMPTY BENCHES OF MEMORY LOOK OVER STONES, ...BERCK-PLAGE   199   88
    THE BLIND MIRROR OF IT. I LOOK IN ....FOR A FATHERLESS SON   205   8
    AND THIS IS A MAN, LOOK AT HIS SMILE, ...THE DETECTIVE   208   14
    LOOK, LOOK! IT IS WANTING TO CRAWL. ....A SECRET   220   36
    LOOK, LOOK! IT IS WANTING TO CRAWL." ....A SECRET   220   36
    A LIVING DOLL, EVERYWHERE YOU LOOK. ....THE APPLICANT   221   33
    A MAN IN BLACK WITH A MEINKAMPF LOOK ....DADDY   224   65
    AND MY CHILD -- LOOK AT HER, FACE DOWN ON THE FLOOR, ...LESBOS   227   8
    TAKE A LOOK AT THE WHITE, HIGH BERG ON HIS FOREHEAD -- ...LYONNESSE   233   3
    THE BABIES LOOK IN THEIR HOSPITAL ....DEATH & CO.   254   14
    UNTIL IT FINISHED, AND THEN LOOK FURTIVELY ....DIALOGUE O.   280 164
    A BINGE OF JEERS. LOOK. HE'S RUNNING THROUGH ....DIALOGUE O.   284 296
    AND IN SORROW LOOK ....TO A JILTED LOVER   309   2
    THE MAGIC GOLDEN APPLES ALL LOOK GOOD ....ADMONITIONS   319   4
    ALL WHO LOOK: ....ON LOOKING INTO THE EYES OF A DEMON LOVER   325   4
    THE MOON LEANS DOWN TO LOOK; THE TILTING FISH ...LOVE IS A PARALLAX   330   37
    THOSE STONIER EYES LOOK, ...TOUCH-AND-GO   336   23
LOOKED (5)
    WHERE NOTHING HIGHER'S TO BE LOOKED TO. DOWNWARD LOOKS ......OXBOW.   88   30
    SUNSET LOOKED AT THROUGH MILK GLASS. ....MEDALLION   124   20
    VAGUE AS FOG AND LOOKED FOR LIKE MAIL. ....YOU'RE   141   10
    SIMPLY BECAUSE SHE LOOKED AFTER ME SO BADLY. ....IN PLASTER   159   34
    IT IS PINK, WITH SPECKLES. I HAVE LOOKED AT IT SO LONG ......MIRROR   173   7
LOOKER (1)
    YET THERE IS NO WALKER AND LOOKER BUT MYSELF. ....QUEEN MARY'S.   290   9
LOOKING (15)
    THE AIR WAS BRIGHT FOR LOOKING: ....SONG FOR A SUMMER'S DAY   31   6
    BLAMELESS AS DAYLIGHT I STOOD LOOKING ....THE EYE-MOTE   109   1
    MOBS OF EYEBALLS LOOKING UP. ....LEAVING EARLY   146   13
    IT LOOKS IN ON, AND MUST GO ON LOOKING IN ON. ....WIDOW   165   40
    I AM OVERLOOKING THEM BY LOOKING TOO HARD.   STARS OVER THE DORDOGNE   165   23
    TICKING YOUR FINGERS ON THE MARBLE TABLE, LOOKING FOR
            CIGARETTES, ...THE RIVAL   166   8
    I WANT TO BE LOOKING AT THEM WHEN THEY COME ....LAST WORDS   172   4
    NOT LOOKING, THROUGH THE THICK DARK, FOR THE FACE OF ANOTHER.*THREE.   178   77
    HE IS LOOKING SO ANGRILY! ....THREE WOMEN   181 164
    I COULDN'T STOP LOOKING. ....LITTLE FUGUE   187   12
    LOOKING, WITH ITS HOOKS, FOR SOMETHING TO LOVE. ....ELM   193   30

LOOKING (CONT.)
    THEY ARE PRESSING OUT OF THE MANY-HOLED EARPIECE, THEY ARE LOOKING
        FOR A LISTENER. ......WORDS HEARD, BY ACCIDENT, OVER THE PHONE   203   9
    WHEN I AM QUIET AT MY COOKING I FEEL IT LOOKING, I FEEL IT THINKING   ...
                                          ... A BIRTHDAY PRESENT   206   4
    AND THEIR EYES LOOKING OUT OF IT: KEEN, *DIALOGUE OVER A OUIJA BOARD   276   10
    ON LOOKING INTO THE EYES OF A DEMON LOVER *ON LOOKING INTO THE EYES.   325   T
LOOKING-GLASS (1)
    I'M THROUGH WITH THIS GRAND LOOKING-GLASS HOTEL ......A SORCERER B.   324   1
LOOKOUT (1)
    THEY CALLED THE PLACE LOOKOUT FARM. BACK THEN, THE SUN ...
                          ... MEMOIRS OF A SPINACH-PICKER   89   1
LOOKS (13)
    LOOKS FIERCE AND BLACK AS ROOKS; ....THE QUEEN'S COMPLAINT   28   4
    LOOKS UP. ....STRUMPET SONG   34   19
    MOUTH'S INSTANT FLARE FOR FUTURE LOOKS; *EPITAPH FOR FIRE AND FLOWER   45   11
    MARY LOOKS MILD. ....A WINTER'S TALE   86   8
    A RISE IN THE LANDSCAPE, HUMMOCK OR HOGBACK, LOOKS ABOVE THE OXBOW   88   16
    WHERE NOTHING HIGHER'S TO BE LOOKED TO. DOWNWARD LOOKS ......OXBOW.   88   30
    THOUGH NOBODY IN THERE LOOKS UP OR BOTHERS TO ANSWER. ....A LIFE   150   8
    IT LOOKS IN ON, AND MUST GO ON LOOKING IN ON. ....WIDOW   165   40
    THAT LOOKS OUT ON NOTHING, NOTHING BUT A GREAT SPACE   BLACKBERRYING   169   25
    THOUGH IT LOOKS LIKE A CAT, WITH ITS FLUFFY STUFF, PURE WHITE.*TOUR.   237   16
    THE ONE WHO NEVER LOOKS UP, WHOSE EYES ARE LIDDED ......DEATH & CO.   254   3
    TO NORMAL. LET'S CLOSE THE CURTAINS. IT LOOKS WILD ....DIALOGUE O.   286 335
    THE TABLE LOOKS AS IF IT WOULD STAY A TABLE ....DIALOGUE O.   286 353
LOOK'S (1)
    BY GOING FAR; MY LOOK'S LEASH ....SOLILOQUY OF THE SOLIPSIST   37   13
LOOM (2)
    TO LOOM IN THE LEAF-FILTERED GLOOM ....CHILD'S PARK STONES   100   4
    GOLD CARP LOOM IN THE POOLS. ....YADDO: THE GRAND MANOR   123   8
LOOMED (1)
    LOOMED ABSOLUTE AS THE ANTIQUE WORLD WAS ....HARDCASTLE CRAGS   63   38
LOOMS (1)
    AND AN IMAGE LOOMS UNDER THE FISHPOND SURFACE ...ALL THE DEAD DEARS   71   22
LOONY (1)
    "MISS ELLA'S GOT LOONY FROM KEEPING IN CAHOOTS ....ELLA MASON A.   54   35
LOOP (1)
    OF THE AIR EDDIES' LOOP AND ARC THOUGH AIR'S AT REST*ABOVE THE OXBOW   88   32
LOOPHOLE (1)
    OR MUST TAKE LOOPHOLE AND BLAME TIME ......GREEN ROCK, WINTHROP BAY   105   22
LOOPING (2)
    LOOPING WOOL, DOING NOTHING IN PARTICULAR, ...HEAVY WOMEN   158   16
    LOOPING LIKE FAITH ABOUT HER BLEEDING FEET, ...THE PRINCESS.   334   48
LOOPS (1)
    REVOLVING IN OVAL LOOPS OF SOLAR SPEED, ...THE DEAD   320   1
LOOSE (4)
    AND GOSSIPS IN ITS LOOSE VERNACULAR, ...A WINTER SHIP   113   19
    TO BE LET LOOSE AT NEWS OF LAND. ....ON DECK   143   36
    OLD GRIEVANCES JOSTLING EACH OTHER, SO MANY LOOSE TEETH. ....ZOO K.   154   13
    I AM MYSELF AGAIN. THERE ARE NO LOOSE ENDS. ....THREE WOMEN   184 274
LOOSED (1)
    PUPPETS, LOOSED FROM THE STRINGS OF THE PUPPET-MASTER, ...POEM.5.F.   135   13
LOPPED (2)
    THE TREES ARE LOPPED, THE POODLES TRIM, ...THE DEATH OF MYTH-MAKING   104   6
    THE LOPPED ....THALIDOMIDE   252   15
LOPPING (1)
    LOPPING THE SAUSAGES! ....LITTLE FUGUE   188   33
LORD (3)
    FOR MONEY. LORD, THE CROWDS ARE FIERCE! ....A WINTER'S TALE   87   15
    FOR WHOM THE GOOD LORD PROVIDES (HE GAVE ....ON DECK   143   20
    LORD OF THE MIRRORS! ....PURDAH   242   20
LORDLY (1)
    HE PROWLS MORE LORDLY THAN THE SUN. ....PURSUIT   22   4
LORDS (1)
    THE LORDS AND LADIES RAN. ....THE BULL OF BENDYLAW   108   12
LORD'S (1)
    OF DAVY'S LOCKER, AND THE LORD'S TO HOME, ...DIALOGUE O.   283 246
LORELEI (1)
    LORELEI ....LORELEI   94   T
LOSE (8)
    AND LOSE THEIR GOOD BROWNS ....THE THIN PEOPLE   65   44
    A WORLD WE LOSE BY MERELY WAKING UP. ....THE GHOST'S LEAVETAKING   90   20
    STONES THAT TAKE THE WHOLE SUMMER TO LOSE ......CHILD'S PARK STONES   101   23
    I LOSE SIGHT OF YOU ON YOUR BLIND JOURNEY, ..PARLIAMENT HILL FIELDS   153   33
    I AM DYING AS I SIT. I LOSE A DIMENSION. ....THREE WOMEN   177   30
    I LOSE LIFE AFTER LIFE. THE DARK EARTH DRINKS THEM. ....THREE WOMEN   181 154
    LOSE THEMSELVES. IN MATHEMATICS? ....THE NIGHT DANCES   249   4
    JOG OFF IN JABBERWOCKY NOW AND LOSE US, *DIALOGUE OVER A OUIJA BOARD   279   91
LOSING (1)
    AND RETURN, LOSING THEMSELVES ....MUSSEL HUNTER AT ROCK HARBOR   97   88
LOSS (2)
    BY LACK AND LOSS THESE BEGGARS ENCROACH ....THE BEGGARS   48   13
    LOSS CANCELS PROFIT. ....GREEN ROCK, WINTHROP BAY   105   18

| | | TITLE | PAGE | LINE |

LOSSES (1)
BROOD, ROOTED IN THEIR HEAPED LOSSES. ....PARLIAMENT HILL FIELDS 153 31
LOST (15)
WHATEVER LOST GHOSTS FLARE, ...NOVEMBER GRAVEYARD 56 15
LOST LUSTRE UNDER HER FOOTSOLES. ....HARDCASTLE CRAGS 63 21
LOST IN THE LIFT AND DRIFT OF ....THE GREAT CARBUNCLE 73 23
STIPPLE OF SHIFTING WAVE-TIPS IS IRONED OUT, LOST ..ABOVE THE OXBOW 89 46
SPEAK IN SIGN LANGUAGE OF A LOST OTHERWORLD,*THE GHOST'S LEAVETAKING 90 19
A LABOR OF LOVE, AND THAT LABOR LOST. ....POINT SHIRLEY 110 34
WE HAVE LOST TRACK OF IT. ....THE SLEEPERS 122 3
I AM LOST, I AM LOST, IN THE ROBES OF ALL THIS LIGHT. POEM.6.W. 136 24
I AM LOST, I AM LOST, IN THE ROBES OF ALL THIS LIGHT. POEM.6.W. 136 24
NOW I HAVE LOST MYSELF I AM SICK OF BAGGAGE --- ....TULIPS 160 18
THEY ARE ORPHANS. I CANNOT SEE THEM. THEY ARE LOST. ....STARS. 165 14
AS IF I HAD LOST AN EYE, A LEG, A TONGUE. ....THREE WOMEN 183 252
AND LOST IN SUBTLE METAPHOR, RETREATS ....FEMALE AUTHOR 301 13
A FUTURE WAS LOST YESTERDAY ....APRIL 18 302 14
TILL THE ANNOUNCER'S VOICE IS LOST ....INSOLENT STORM. 326 35
LOT (7)
NONE OF THAT GREENHORN LOT MATCHED HER BRIGHT CROWN. ....QUEEN'S C. 29 20
AND THEIR FUTURE LOT, SHE BRAVED ....CRYSTAL GAZER 55 34
WHERE THE WAKING HEAD RUBBISHES OUT THE DRAGGLED LOT ......GHOST'S. 90 3
BARREN, THE LOT ARE BARREN! ....AMNESIAC 233 15
FROM, IF NOT THE POOLS? OH, FROM A LOT DIALOGUE OVER A OUIJA BOARD 277 46
RABBITS IN THE LOT. YOU'RE IN A HUFF ...DIALOGUE OVER A OUIJA BOARD 282 236
BUT I AM CONTENT WITH THIS MORE POMPOUS LOT. ....QUEEN MARY'S. 290 25
LOT-DRAWN (1)
THE INSUFFERABLE NIMBUS OF THE LOT-DRAWN ....THE THIN PEOPLE 64 21
LOTUS (1)
A RED LOTUS OPENS IN ITS BOWL OF BLOOD; ....THREE WOMEN 181 167
LOUD (6)
OFF KEY AND LOUD ....A WINTER'S TALE 87 28
LOUD ON EARTH'S BEDROCK. ALMOST THROWN, NOT ...WHITENESS I REMEMBER 103 31
THEN THE TULIPS FILLED IT UP LIKE A LOUD NOISE. ....TULIPS 161 52
IT UNCLAPS, BROWN AS A LEAF, AND LOUD, ...PHEASANT 191 21
LOUD THE IMMORTAL NIGHTINGALES DECLARE: *TO EVA DESCENDING THE STAIR 303 13
AS THE LOUD ALARMCLOCK STOPS. ....AERIALIST 332 42
LOUDSPEAKER (2)
WOODSMOKE AND A DISTANT LOUDSPEAKER ....YADDO: THE GRAND MANOR 123 1
FOR LOUDSPEAKER WIRES RUNNING LIKE A LOGICAL ....DIALOGUE O. 280 165
LOUDSPEAKERS (1)
HEAR LOUDSPEAKERS BOOM ....ALICANTE LULLABY 43 12
LOUNGED (2)
TABLE-TOP, CUPBOARD SHELF, CATS LOUNGED BRAZEN, ...ELLA MASON A. 54 22
OF A SOW LOUNGED BELLY-BEDDED ON THAT BLACK COMPOST, ...SOW 61 25
LOUNGING (1)
DUPE THE DULL SOW LOUNGING SNOUT IN MUD, ...GO GET THE GOODLY SQUAB 313 11
LOUSY (1)
LADY, YOUR ROOM IS LOUSY WITH FLOWERS. ....LEAVING EARLY 145 1
LOVE (110)
THE BLACK MARAUDER, HAULED BY LOVE ....PURSUIT 22 27
BRAVE LOVE, DREAM ....FIRESONG 30 19
WITH MY OWN COUNTRY LOVE ....SONG FOR A SUMMER'S DAY 30 2
TO PATCH WITH BRAND OF LOVE THIS RANK GRIMACE ....STRUMPET SONG 34 16
O MY LOVE, ...LETTER TO A PURIST 36 8
LOVE FIERY ENOUGH TO PROVE FLESH REAL, ..SOLILOQUY OF THE SOLIPSIST 38 33
"IN LIFE, LOVE GNAWED MY SKIN ....DIALOGUE BETWEEN GHOST AND PRIEST 39 27
WHAT LOVE DID THEN, LOVE DOES NOW: ....DIALOGUE B. 39 29
WHAT LOVE DID THEN, LOVE DOES NOW: ....DIALOGUE B. 39 29
"WHAT LOVE," ASKED FATHER SHAWN, "BUT TOO GREAT LOVE ...DIALOGUE B. 39 31
"WHAT LOVE," ASKED FATHER SHAWN, "BUT TOO GREAT LOVE ...DIALOGUE B. 39 31
TO TRAP THIS WAYWARD GIRL AT HER FIRST MOVE OF LOVE, DREAM WITH C. 44 27
OR LOVE, EITHER. ....SPINSTER 50 30
EACH LOVE BLAZING BLIND TO ITS GUTTED END -- ....CRYSTAL GAZER 56 46
ONE MIGHT SAY LOVE. AT ANY RATE, I NOW WALK ....BLACK ROOK I. 57 22
NO LOVE IN HIS EYE. ....THE SNOWMAN ON THE MOOR 59 36
HAD ALL MY LOVE. ....ON THE PLETHORA OF DRYADS 67 6
BY ONE JOT ITS BASILISK-LOOK OF LOVE. ....LADY AND T. 70 35
PURE PHILOSOPHY HIS LOVE ENGROSSED ....NATURAL HISTORY 71 4
AS PONDERABLE TOKENS OF HER LOVE. ....OUIJA 77 29
OF LOVE: CLAWS BRACED, AT BAY, MY CURRENCY NOT HERS. INCOMMUNICADO 100 7
WHERE LOVE-MET GROUNDHOGS LOVE ONE IN RETURN, ...INCOMMUNICADO 100 9
WHETHER NICETY STOOD CONFOUNDED BY LOVE, ...RHODODENDRON. 104 27
A LABOR OF LOVE, AND THAT LABOR LOST. ....POINT SHIRLEY 110 34
THE MILK YOUR LOVE INSTILLED IN THEM. ....POINT SHIRLEY 111 42
HANDS LACED, IN A MOONY INDOLENCE OF LOVE -- ....WATERCOLOR. 112 25
I BROUGHT MY LOVE TO BEAR, AND THEN YOU DIED.*ELECTRA ON AZALEA PATH 117 38
IT WAS MY LOVE THAT DID US BOTH TO DEATH. ..ELECTRA ON AZALEA PATH 117 46
THE MOTHER OF MOUTHS DIDN'T LOVE ME. POEM.3.MAENAD. 133 6
LOVE IS THE UNIFORM OF MY BALD NURSE. POEM.7.S. 137 39
LOVE IS THE BONE AND SINEW OF MY CURSE. POEM.7.S. 137 40
THE BINGO PLAYERS, THE PLAYERS AT LOVE ....ON DECK 142 11
LOVE LETTER ....LOVE LETTER 147 T
AND LOVE THE MOTHER OF MILK, NO THEORY. ....MAGI 148 14
LOVE SET YOU GOING LIKE A FAT GOLD WATCH. ....MORNING SONG 156 1

298

LOVE (CONT.)
    THEN I REALIZED WHAT SHE WANTED WAS FOR ME TO LOVE HER: IN PLASTER 159   13
    ITS BOWL OF RED BLOOMS OUT OF SHEER LOVE OF ME. ....TULIPS   162   61
    SUCKING UP MINERALS AND MOTHERLY LOVE ....I AM VERTICAL   162   3
    CIRCLES HER LIKE A PREY SHE'D LOVE TO KILL ....WIDOW   164   15
    I HAD NOT ASKED FOR SUCH A BLOOD SISTERHOOD; THEY MUST LOVE ME. ...
                                                 ... BLACKBERRYING   168   8
    SHE IS IN LOVE WITH THE BEAUTIFUL FORMLESSNESS OF THE SEA. ...
                                                 ... FINISTERRE   170   27
    JUST AS IT IS, UNMISTED BY LOVE OR DISLIKE. ....MIRROR   173   3
    IS THIS THE ONE SIN THEN, THIS OLD DEAD LOVE OF DEATH?   THREE WOMEN 177   42
    WENT ON SHAPING ITSELF WITH LOVE, AS IF I WAS READY.   ...THREE WOMEN 178   63
    I HAVE TRIED TO BE BLIND IN LOVE, LIKE OTHER WOMEN,   ...THREE WOMEN 178   75
    ITS END AND RUNS TOWARD IT, ARMS HELD OUT IN LOVE. .....THREE WOMEN 181 151
    IT IS A LOVE OF DEATH THAT SICKENS EVERYTHING. ....THREE WOMEN 181 152
    WHAT DID MY HEART DO, WITH ITS LOVE? ....THREE WOMEN   181 170
    I CAN LOVE MY HUSBAND, WHO WILL UNDERSTAND. ....THREE WOMEN   183 250
    WHO WILL LOVE ME THROUGH THE BLUR OF MY DEFORMITY ......THREE WOMEN   183 251
    TO LOVE ME AS I LOVE HIM, ...THREE WOMEN   186 335
    TO LOVE ME AS I LOVE HIM, ...THREE WOMEN   186 335
    IS THIS LOVE THEN, THIS RED MATERIAL ....AN APPEARANCE 189   10
    LOVE IS A SHADOW. ....ELM   192   7
    LOOKING, WITH ITS HOOKS, FOR SOMETHING TO LOVE. ....ELM 193   30
    ARE THOSE THE FACES OF LOVE, THOSE PALE IRRETRIEVABLES? ....ELM   193   35
    LOVE CANNOT COME HERE. ....EVENT   195   16
    THE POLICE LOVE YOU, YOU CONFESS EVERYTHING. ....THE OTHER   201   7
    LOVE, LOVE, AND WELL, I WAS TIRED ....BURNING THE LETTERS   204   10
    LOVE, LOVE, AND WELL, I WAS TIRED ....BURNING THE LETTERS   204   10
    AND I LOVE YOUR STUPIDITY, ...FOR A FATHERLESS SON   205   7
    I AM NUDE AS A CHICKEN NECK, DOES NOBODY LOVE ME? ..THE BEE MEETING   211   6
    WITH EXCESSIVE LOVE I ENAMELED IT ....STINGS   214   10
    AND A LOVE OF THE RACK AND THE SCREW. ....DADDY   224   66
    AND I, LOVE, AM A PATHOLOGICAL LIAR, ...LESBOS   227   7
    IT IS LOVE YOU ARE FULL OF. YOU KNOW WHO YOU HATE. ....LESBOS   229   72
    LOVE, LOVE, THE LOW SMOKES ROLL ....FEVER.   231   11
    LOVE, LOVE, THE LOW SMOKES ROLL ....FEVER.   231   11
    THE BEADS OF HOT METAL FLY, AND I, LOVE, I ....FEVER.   232   45
    THIS IS WINTER, THIS IS NIGHT, SMALL LOVE -- ....BY CANDLELIGHT   236   1
    TO JUGGLE WITH, MY LOVE, WHEN THE SKY FALLS. ....BY CANDLELIGHT   237   36
    HERE'S A SPOT I THOUGHT YOU'D LOVE -- ....THE TOUR   238   27
    A GIFT, A LOVE GIFT ....POPPIES IN OCTOBER   240   4
    O LOVE, HOW DID YOU GET HERE? ....NICK AND THE CANDLESTICK   241   23
    LOVE, LOVE, ...NICK AND THE CANDLESTICK   241   31
    LOVE, LOVE, ...NICK AND THE CANDLESTICK   241   31
    LOVE, LOVE, MY SEASON. ....THE COURIERS   247   13
    LOVE, LOVE, MY SEASON. ....THE COURIERS   247   13
    A LOVE ....THALIDOMIDE   252   19
    LOVE, THE WORLD ....LETTER IN NOVEMBER   253   1
    I LOVE THEM. ....LETTER IN NOVEMBER   253   22
    I LOVE THEM LIKE HISTORY. ....LETTER IN NOVEMBER   253   23
    O LOVE, O CELIBATE. ....LETTER IN NOVEMBER   254   31
    WHAT I LOVE IS ....YEARS   255   11
    MIRROR TALK YOU LOVE TO CATCH ME AT. ..............EAVESDROPPER   260   36
    THE BLOOD FLOOD IS THE FLOOD OF LOVE, ...THE MUNICH MANNEQUINS 263   6
    IS THERE NO GREAT LOVE, ONLY TENDERNESS? ....MYSTIC   269   24
    OUR WORK. LOVE. THE AFTER-LIFE . . . DO YOU ....DIALOGUE O.   278   55
    AT FAME OR NOT? AS FOR LOVE, I FIGURE WHEN WE'RE ....DIALOGUE O. 278   57
    LOVE FLAMES FOREVER IF THE FLESH BE YEARNING. ...TO EVA DESCENDING. 303   14
    TONIGHT THE CAUSTIC WIND, LOVE, ...JILTED   304   5
    BECAUSE HE WOULD MAKE LOVE TO ME ....BLUEBEARD   305   3
    MAKE LOVE AND LOGIC MIX, ...NOTES TO A NEOPHYTE   306   16
    AND BY THAT GLARE, MY LOVE WILL SEE ....TO A JILTED LOVER   310   25
    MY LOVE AND I GO GARLANDED WITH GRASS. ....APRIL AUBADE   312   12
    TRIO OF LOVE SONGS ....TRIO OF LOVE SONGS   313   T
    MOVES TO OUR MINOR LOVE. ....TRIO OF LOVE SONGS   314   16
    MY LOVE FOR YOU IS MORE ....TRIO OF LOVE SONGS   314   17
    DESCRIBING ARCS OF LOVE. ....TRIO OF LOVE SONGS   314   28
    THAT SYNCOPATES OUR LOVE. ....TRIO OF LOVE SONGS   315   52
    DEAD MEN RENDER LOVE AND WAR NO HEED, ...THE DEAD   320   3
    FROZEN IN DESIGNS OF LOVE. ....DANSE MACABRE 321   9
    WHILE THE GNAWINGS OF LOVE BEGIN. ....CIRCUS IN THREE RINGS 322   12
    SONG FOR A REVOLUTIONARY LOVE ....SONG FOR A REVOLUTIONARY LOVE 322   T
    OR LYRIC OF LOVE IN THE ORANGE AND BLACK ....BLACK PINE TREE.   328   14
    LOVE IS A PARALLAX ....LOVE IS A PARALLAX   329   T
    THE RAW WIND LIKE A SCARF; LOVE IS A FAUN ......LOVE IS A PARALLAX   329   23
    BOLD BEANSTALK; LIE AND LOVE TILL SHARP SCYTHE HACKS *LOVE IS A PAR. 330   71
    TO PAY THE PIPER WITH EACH BREATH, YET LOVE ....LOVE IS A PARALLAX   331   76
    THAT STING NO MORE THAN LOVE: A ROOM WHERE TIME *MORNING IN THE HOS. 332   15
LOVEBED (1)
    MUSKY AS A LOVEBED THE MORNING AFTER. ....LEAVING EARLY 146   19
LOVED (6)
    AS A CHILD I LOVED A LICHEN-BITTEN NAME. ....THREE WOMEN 177   41
    THE FACE OF THE UNBORN ONE THAT LOVED ITS PERFECTIONS,   THREE WOMEN 178   79
    SUCH BLUE CURRENTS IN THE VEINS OF MY LOVED ONE! .....AN APPEARANCE 189   2
    HE WANTS TO BE LOVED. ....DEATH & CO. 254   25

LOVED (CONT.)
    OF ONE I LOVED. I SAW DIVISION BLOOM ...DIALOGUE OVER A OUIJA BOARD 285 322
    LOVED ME AND A BRAVE EMBRACE ....THE DREAM 311   22
LOVE-HOT (1)
    WITH THE LOVE-HOT HERB, THE TALKING CAT, ...THE TIMES ARE TIDY 107   13
LOVELESS (2)
    LOVELESS AS THE MULTIPLICATION TABLE. ....MAGI 148   8
    AND SITS IN THE CENTER OF HER LOVELESS SPOKES. ....WIDOW 164   12
LOVELINESS (1)
    SO, IN THEIR SULFUR LOVELINESS, IN THEIR SMILES ....MUNICH. 263   10
LOVELY (3)
    PURPLE AND RED MOUTHS, UTTERLY LOVELY. POEM.1.WHO. 132   30
    EACH COAL A HOT CROSS-STITCH -- A LOVELY LIGHT! ....THE TOUR 238   21
    EACH LOVELY LADY ....ON LOOKING INTO THE EYES OF A DEMON LOVER 325   5
LOVE-MET (1)
    WHERE LOVE-MET GROUNDHOGS LOVE ONE IN RETURN, ...INCOMMUNICADO 100   9
LOVER (6)
    IS THIS MY LOVER THEN? THIS DEATH, THIS DEATH? ....THREE WOMEN 177   40
    IT IS THE BOWEL-PULSE, LOVER OF DIGESTIBLES. ....WORDS HEARD. 202   4
    TO A JILTED LOVER ....TO A JILTED LOVER 309   T
    WHICH LET LOVER THINK LOVER ....MOONSONG AT MORNING 317   15
    WHICH LET LOVER THINK LOVER ....MOONSONG AT MORNING 317   15
    ON LOOKING INTO THE EYES OF A DEMON LOVER *ON LOOKING INTO THE EYES. 325   T
LOVERS (13)
    ALL AFTERNOON THESE LOVERS LAY ....BUCOLICS   24   13
    ALONGSIDE THE SIBILANT HARBOR THE LOVERS ....ALICANTE LULLABY   43   11
    THESE TWO MOST PERISHABLE LOVERS FROM THE TOUCH ....EPITAPH FOR F.   45   5
    THESE LOVERS PROPHESY TO LOCK EMBRACE ..EPITAPH FOR FIRE AND FLOWER   45   17
    AND LOVERS AFFABLE, DOVELIKE. ....IN MIDAS' COUNTRY   99   15
    A POOR MONTH FOR PARK-SLEEPERS AND LOVERS. ....A WINTER SHIP 113   22
    THESE FLEMISH LOVERS FLOURISH; NOT FOR LONG. ....TWO VIEWS. 114   20
    THEY TALK OF BRIDE-LACE, OF LOVERS SPUNKY AS GAMECOCKS. ......NET-. 121   14
    SWELTER AND MELT, AND THE LOVERS ....THREE WOMEN 186 338
    TWO LOVERS UNSTICK THEMSELVES. ....BERCK-PLAGE 197   30
    PARALYSING THE KICKING LOVERS. ....MEDUSA 225   26
    WERE BEWITCHED TO ASSIDUOUS LOVERS, ...DIALOGUE EN ROUTE 309   20
    TWO LOVERS AND A BEACHCOMBER BY THE REAL SEA ....TWO LOVERS. 327   T
LOVER'S (4)
    BLOWS ASH IN EACH LOVER'S EYE; THE ARDENT LOOK ......EPITAPH FOR F.   46   34
    OBSERVED HER LOVER'S GESTURES UNBALANCE THE AIR, ...SPINSTER   49   8
    BY WITS ALONE: TO FORESEE HER LOVER'S FAITH ....CRYSTAL GAZER   55   33
    WHILE FROM THE MOON, MY LOVER'S EYE ....TO A JILTED LOVER 309   7
LOVES (5)
    LITTLE HUMBLE LOVES! POEM.2.DARK. 133   24
    AND THE OCTOGENARIAN LOVES THE LITTLE FLOCKS. ...AMONG THE NARCISSI 190   10
    THE UPFLIGHT OF THE MURDERESS INTO A HEAVEN THAT LOVES HER. ...BEE. 212   48
    THAT LOVES ME, PUMPS ....PARALYTIC 266   5
    THIS WAS A WOMAN: HER LOVES AND STRATAGEMS ....SONNET: TO EVA 304   5
LOVE'S (8)
    CAME IN FOR MY LOVE'S PRAISING. ....SONG FOR A SUMMER'S DAY   31   10
    KINDLED BY MY LOVE'S PLEASING ....SONG FOR A SUMMER'S DAY   31   14
    FOR WEDLOCK WROUGHT WITHIN LOVE'S PROPER CHAPEL.*WREATH FOR A BRIDAL   44   12
    EVEN AS LOVE'S DEAR FOOLS CRY EVERGREEN,*EPITAPH FOR FIRE AND FLOWER   46   30
    FLAWED BY LOVE'S PRINTS. ....ON THE PLETHORA OF DRYADS   67   18
    AS IF, ABOVE LOVE'S RUINAGE, WE WERE ....THE OTHER TWO   69   34
    AND HIS LOVE'S BODY. ....WORDS FOR A NURSERY   74   40
    LOVE'S PALING SPHERE. ....MOONSONG AT MORNING 317   24
LOVESICK (1)
    LOVESICK AT FIRST FOND SONG, ...VANITY FAIR   33   24
LOVING (3)
    THEY HAVE SWABBED ME CLEAR OF MY LOVING ASSOCIATIONS. ....TULIPS 161   24
    ARRIVE THROUGH THE MAILSLOT WITH LOVING REGULARITY, ...THE RIVAL 166   14
    WE KEPT PICKING UP HANDFULS, LOVING IT, ...LESBOS 229   60
LOVINGLY (1)
    IT CUSHIONS ME LOVINGLY. ....LETTER IN NOVEMBER 253   10
LOW (9)
    LOW MOOS OF APPROVE; LET SUN SURPLICED IN BRIGHTNESS .....WREATH F.   44   4
    BARES ITS LOW LINTEL TO CORRODING WEATHERS: ....DEPARTURE   51   17
    HIS CROWN USURPED BY THE LOW BROW ....NATURAL HISTORY   71   11
    DAWN TIDE STOOD DEAD LOW. I SMELT .....MUSSEL HUNTER AT ROCK HARBOR   95   12
    OF OUR HUSBANDS AND SONS MOVE SURE AMONG THE LOW STARS. ......NET-. 121   19
    GLIDING UP IN LOW GEAR BEHIND THE CART. ....BERCK-PLAGE 200 112
    LOVE, LOVE, THE LOW SMOKES ROLL ....FEVER. 231   11
    BELGE TROLL, THE LOW ...............................EAVESDROPPER 261   49
    WHOSE HOPES ARE SO LOW THEY ARE COMFORTABLE -- ....MYSTIC 269   21
LOWER (1)
    FOOLISH, DELICATE, IN THE LOWER RIGHT HAND CORNER. ......TWO VIEWS. 114   22
LOWERED (1)
    BLINDS LOWERED ON THAT HOT MORNING. ....DREAM WITH CLAM-DIGGERS   43   8
LOWERS (1)
    THE GRAY SKY LOWERS, THE HILLS LIKE A GREEN SEA ....BERCK-PLAGE 199   73
LOW-LINTELLED (1)
    LOW-LINTELLED, NO PALACE; ....TWO VIEWS OF WITHENS   72   15
LOYAL (1)
    LOYAL TO MY IMAGE, ...CHILDLESS WOMAN 259   12

LOZENGE (1)
    SIX ROUND BLACK HATS IN THE GRASS AND A LOZENGE OF WOOD,*BERCK-PLAGE   201 123
LOZENGES (2)
    THEY ARE HANDLING THE BLACK AND GREEN LOZENGES LIKE THE PARTS
        OF A BODY. ....BERCK-PLAGE   196   16
    FROM THE POLISHED LOZENGES OF ORANGE LINOLEUM. ....LESBOS   228   24
LUCENT (3)
    LUCENT AS PORCELAIN, THE EARTH'S ....THE GREAT CARBUNCLE   72   7
    MY FINGER-LENGTH GREW LUCENT AS GLASS. ....LOVE LETTER   147   30
    NAVEL CORDS, BLUE-RED AND LUCENT, ...THE OTHER   202   18
LUCIFER (1)
    HERR GOD, HERR LUCIFER ....LADY LAZARUS   246   79
LUCINA (1)
    LUCINA, BONY MOTHER, LABORING ....MOONRISE   98   25
LUCK (8)
    OUR LONE LUCK NOW, COMPELLED BY BOND, BY BLOOD, ...CHANNEL CROSSING   27   33
    SO FITTED IS FOR MY BLACK LUCK ....THE GLUTTON   40   2
    WHOSE STARK ACT ALL COMING DOUBLE LUCK JOINS. ..WREATH FOR A BRIDAL   44   6
    OF TOTAL NEUTRALITY. WITH LUCK, ...BLACK ROOK IN RAINY WEATHER   57   32
    WITH MY GIPSY ANCESTRESS AND MY WEIRD LUCK ....DADDY   223   38
    TABLE, TRYING OUR LUCK, INDEX FINGERS SET ....DIALOGUE O.   276   4
    TO KNOCK THEM DOWN WITH LOGIC OR WITH LUCK ......LOVE IS A PARALLAX   329   20
    FALL RACKETING FINALE ON HER LUCK. ....AERIALIST   332   48
LUCKIER (1)
    YOU, LUCKIER, ...TWO VIEWS OF WITHENS   72   16
LUCK-ROOTED (1)
    LET NIGHT BLESS THAT LUCK-ROOTED MEAD OF CLOVER WREATH FOR A BRIDAL   45   17
LUCKY (3)
    KING OF THE DISH, MY LUCKY ANIMAL. POEM.4.BEAST.   134   2
    OUR LUCKY RELICS HAVE BEEN PUT IN HOCK: ....DOOMSDAY   316   11
    AND LUCKY STARS ALL EXIT ON THE RUN: ....ADMONITIONS   319   17
LUFTWAFFE (1)
    WITH YOUR LUFTWAFFE, YOUR GOBBLEDYGOO. ....DADDY   223   42
LUGGAGE (1)
    OUR LUGGAGE, AS DOCKS HALT OUR BRIEF EPIC; NO DEBT *CHANNEL CROSSING   27   41
LUGS (1)
    THE COOK LUGS A PUMPKIN ....YADDO: THE GRAND MANOR   123   5
LUGUBRIOUS (2)
    HANGS IN ITS LUGUBRIOUS POUT. WHERE ARE ....PERSEUS   83   39
    MYSELF, MYSELF! -- OBSCENE, LUGUBRIOUS. ....THE RAVAGED FACE   115   8
LULL (1)
    WHAT LULL, WHAT COOL CAN LAP ME IN ....PURSUIT   23   35
LULLABY (3)
    ALICANTE LULLABY ....ALICANTE LULLABY   43   T
    HOW SHALL IT SOFTEN THEM, THIS LITTLE LULLABY? ....THREE WOMEN   185 294
    UNTIL THE STARS TICK OUT A LULLABY ....LOVE IS A PARALLAX   329   14
LULLAYED (1)
    LULLAYED BY SUSURROUS LYRES AND VIOLS. ....ALICANTE LULLABY   43   21
LULLED (2)
    LIKE POLLEN ON BRIGHT AIR. LULLED ....TWO SISTERS OF PERSEPHONE   32   15
    LULLED IN THE AMPLE WOMB OF THE FULL-TILT GLOBE. ....THE DEAD   320   4
LUMBERING (2)
    THE MAMMOTH, LUMBERING STATUARY OF SORROW, ...PERSEUS   82   3
    AND LUMBERING MOVES ....AERIALIST 331   33
LUMINOSITY (1)
    HALF-BRAIN, LUMINOSITY -- ....THALIDOMIDE   252   2
LUMINOUS (4)
    TO MY SWEET WILL, NO LUMINOUS SHAPE ....CONJURING.   66   26
    TO TURN YOU LUMINOUS, WITHOUT THE EYE ....YADWIGHA.   85   12
    SHE PASSES AND REPASSES, LUMINOUS AS A NURSE. ....THREE WOMEN   176   5
    LUMINOUS, THE TOWN OF STONE ....DANSE MACABRE   321   22
LUMP (2)
    FOR THE ROCK'S DWARFED LUMP, FOR THE DRABBLED SCUM, ...GREEN ROCK.   105   23
    AS USUAL THERE IS NO FACE. A LUMP OF CHINESE WHITE ....SURGEON.   170   7
LUMPED (1)
    HUSH A LUMPED MAN-SHAPE. THE WHOLE ACT FORMAL, FLUENT AS A DANCE. ...
        ... THE GORING   47   9
LUMPS (2)
    FIRE SMELTED HIS EYES TO LUMPS ....THE BURNT-OUT SPA   137   3
    HE LUMPS IT DOWN THE PLASTIC COBBLED HILL, ...LESBOS   228   48
LUNA (1)
    COCKCHAFERS AND THE WAN, GREEN LUNA MOTH. ....GOATSUCKER   111   14
LUNAR (4)
    OF SULFUROUS DREAMSCAPES AND OBSCURE LUNAR CONUNDRUMS .....GHOST'S.   90   4
    DULL LUNAR GLOBES ....AQUATIC NORTURNE   306   16
    YET ORDERED LUNAR MOTION ....TRIO OF LOVE SONGS   314   11
    INITIATED BY THE LUNAR LAMP, ...THE PRINCESS AND THE GOBLINS   333   19
LUNATIC (5)
    TO CHIRP THE HOUR IN LUNATIC THIRTEENS. ....SONNET: TO EVA   305   14
    THE HOUR IS CROWED IN LUNATIC THIRTEENS. ....DOOMSDAY   316   3
    THE HOUR IS CROWED IN LUNATIC THIRTEENS. ....DOOMSDAY   316   9
    THE HOUR IS CROWED IN LUNATIC THIRTEENS. ....DOOMSDAY   316   15
    THE HOUR IS CROWED IN LUNATIC THIRTEENS. ....DOOMSDAY   316   19
LUNCH (1)
    I OPEN MY LUNCH ON A HILL OF BLACK CYPRESS. ....THE COLOSSUS   130   19

```
                                                         TITLE          PAGE  LINE
LUNG (3)
   WITH A LUNG FULL OF DUST AND A TONGUE OF WOOD,  .......LEAVING EARLY   146   43
   HE IS RECUPERATING FROM SOMETHING ON THE LUNG.  ..AMONG THE NARCISSI   190    3
   MY GOD THE IRON LUNG  ........................................PARALYTIC  266    4
LUNGE (1)
   PARRIES THE LUNGE AND MENACE  ............................AERIALIST   331   20
LUNGLESS (1)
   NO AIRBUBBLES START FROM MY HEART, I AM LUNGLESS   ZOO KEEPER'S WIFE   154    5
LUNGS (3)
   THEY COLLAPSE LIKE LUNGS, THE ESCAPED WATER  .........PRIVATE GROUND   130    9
   IF ONLY THE WIND WOULD LEAVE MY LUNGS ALONE.  ...........POEM.1.WHO.   131   10
   AND STILL THE LUNGS WON'T FILL AND THE HEART WON'T START. *STILLBORN   142   10
LUNG-TREE (1)
   THIS IS THE LUNG-TREE.  .....................THE SURGEON AT 2 A.M.    170   15
LURCHING (1)
   LURCHING HOME ALONG RIVER BANK.  ................................FAUN    35    7
LURED (2)
   TO ATONE AS SHADE FOR SIN THAT LURED BLIND MAN."  .......DIALOGUE B.    39   36
   LURED BY BRIGANDS IN THE BLOOD,  .....................DANSE MACABRE   321   16
LURID (2)
   PARADES THE MARKETPLACE, LURID AND STRICKEN  .......THE RAVAGED FACE   115    2
   SWABBED AND LURID WITH DISINFECTANTS, SACRIFICIAL.  .....THREE WOMEN   179  107
LURK (1)
   DRYLY DISCLAIMS THAT FIERCE TROLL FACES LURK  .........TALE OF A TUB    24   13
LURKED (1)
   LURKED THE BURLESQUE INSTINCT OF THE HAM;  ........DIRGE FOR A JOKER   302    6
LURKS (2)
   LURKS THE LITHE ONE; IN DREAMS' AMBUSH  .......................PURSUIT    23   30
   LURKS THE SICKLE-SHAPED SHADOW  .....................TEMPER OF TIME   336   15
LUSTER (2)
   FALLEN FROM LUSTER.  .................TINKER JACK AND THE TIDY WIVES    34   11
   ALL'S POLISHED TO A DULL LUSTER  ..................IN MIDAS' COUNTRY    99    5
LUSTERS (1)
   THEY STAY, THEIR LITTLE PARTICULAR LUSTERS  .............LAST WORDS   172   17
LUSTFUL (1)
   AND VIRGINS RISE WHERE LUSTFUL VENUS LAY:  .............ADMONITIONS   319    5
LUSTRE (1)
   LOST LUSTRE UNDER HER FOOTSOLES.  ..................HARDCASTLE CRAGS    63   21
LUSTROUS (1)
   HALOES LUSTROUS AS SIRIUS --  .......................A WINTER'S TALE    87   11
LUTES (1)
   AND THE FABULOUS LUTES AND PEACOCKS, RENDING THE NET   CONVERSATION.    21    3
LUXURY (1)
   SUCH A LUXURY OF STARS WOULD EMBARRASS ME.   STARS OVER THE DORDOGNE  166   27
LYING (3)
   CAME TO BE LYING ON THIS BAROQUE COUCH  ...................YADWIGHA.    85    2
   I AM LEARNING PEACEFULNESS, LYING BY MYSELF QUIETLY  .........TULIPS   160    3
   IT IS MORE NATURAL TO ME, LYING DOWN.  .................I AM VERTICAL   162   17
LYLE (2)
   TATE AND LYLE KEEPS THEM GOING,  .......................WINTERING   218   27
   IT IS TATE AND LYLE THEY LIVE ON, INSTEAD OF FLOWERS.  ....WINTERING   218   29
LYMPH (1)
   ONCE, IN ITS EARLIEST SWAY OF LYMPH AND SAP,  ......HARDCASTLE CRAGS    63   39
LYONIANS (1)
   THE LYONIANS HAD ALWAYS THOUGHT  .........................LYONNESSE   234   11
LYONNESSE (2)
   LYONNESSE  ..............................................LYONNESSE   233    T
   NO USE WHISTLING FOR LYONNESSE!  ...........................LYONNESSE   233    1
LYRES (1)
   LULLAYED BY SUSURROUS LYRES AND VIOLS.  ...........ALICANTE LULLABY    43   21
LYRIC (2)
   LINK TO HIS LYRIC ACTION  .......................TRIO OF LOVE SONGS   314   35
   OR LYRIC OF LOVE IN THE ORANGE AND BLACK  .........BLACK PINE TREE.   328   14
LYSOL (1)
   SCALING LITTLE LADDERS WITH GLUEPOTS AND PAILS OF LYSOL*THE COLOSSUS  129   11
MACABRE (1)
   DANSE MACABRE  ....................................DANSE MACABRE   320    T
MACAWS (1)
   AMONG THESE PARAKEETS, MACAWS!  ...........................PURDAH   243   35
MACHINA (1)
   EX MACHINA. NOR DID THEY SEEM DETERRED BY THIS.  .............SPIDER    49   35
MACHINE (6)
   A MATHEMATICAL MACHINE.  ..................TWO SISTERS OF PERSEPHONE    31    7
   A MACHINE TO BREATHE AND BEAT FOREVER.  .......SUICIDE OFF EGG ROCK   115   16
   YOU ARE SILVER-SUITED FOR THE OCCASION. O ADDING MACHINE --- ...
                                     ...  A BIRTHDAY PRESENT   207   44
   A BIT OF A WILD MACHINE, A BIT OF A MESS!  ..................THE TOUR   237   12
   TIME IS A GREAT MACHINE OF IRON BARS  ...............SONNET: TO TIME   311   13
   UNTIL SHE HEARS THE TWITTERING MACHINE *THE PRINCESS AND THE GOBLINS  334   56
MACHINES (2)
   WITHOUT STOP THOSE GREASED MACHINES,  .................NIGHT SHIFT    77   22
   GOD'S MONKEY WRENCH HAS BLASTED ALL MACHINES;  ..........DOOMSDAY   316   13
MACKEREL (3)
   HERE HE COMES NOW, AMONG THE MACKEREL GATHERERS  ........BERCK-PLAGE   196   14
   BUT LET THE QUICKSILVER MACKEREL SWIM.  .....GO GET THE GOODLY SQUAB   313   20
```

                                                             TITLE   PAGE LINE
MACKEREL (CONT.)
  LET THE QUICKSILVER MACKEREL SWIM ....GO GET THE GOODLY SQUAB 313   21
MAD (10)
  AMONG SACRED ISLANDS OF THE MAD TILL DEATH ....TALE OF A TUB   25   47
  BY A MAD MIRACLE I GO INTACT ....STREET SONG   35   1
  TO STUN SKY BLACK OUT, DRIVE GIBBERING MAD ....CONJURING.   66   12
  OBJECT BESIDE THE MAD, STRAIGHT ROAD ....SLEEP IN THE MOJAVE DESERT 143   6
  THEY WOULD GO MAD WITH IT. ....THREE WOMEN 180 119
  AND THAT MAD, HARD FACE AT THE END OF IT, THAT O-MOUTH   THREE WOMEN 182 184
  SHE'LL CUT HER THROAT AT TEN IF SHE'S MAD AT TWO. ....LESBOS 228   22
  THE ZOO YOWL, THE MAD SOFT ..............................EAVESDROPPER 260   35
  I AM MAD, CALLS THE SPIDER, WAVING ITS MANY ARMS. ....TOTEM 265   28
  MAD HATTER'S HAT YIELDS NO NEW METAPHOR, ...A SORCERER B.   324   10
MADCAP (1)
  IN PREPOSTEROUS PROVINCES OF THE MADCAP ....LETTER TO A PURIST   37   14
MADDENING (1)
  EVEN THAN YOUR MADDENING ....LORELEI   94   29
MADE (27)
  HE MADE HER SHOULDERS BARE ....THE QUEEN'S COMPLAINT   28   14
  MADE TO DO VIOLENCE ON, ...STRUMPET SONG   33   10
  CAN BE MADE TO GLISTER ....TINKER JACK AND THE TIDY WIVES   34   13
  ON THE CALL THIS MAN MADE. ....FAUN   35   5
  SUCH PACT AS IS MADE ONCE ONLY; WHAT MATTER ....WREATH FOR A BRIDAL   44   2
  "OUR WIT MADE FOOLS ....THE SNOWMAN ON THE MOOR   59   40
  MADE LEAN LENT ....SOW   61   42
  MOTHER, WHO MADE TO ORDER STORIES ....THE DISQUIETING MUSES   75   9
  ORBIT THE GO-BY, MADE KNOWN ....MUSSEL HUNTER AT ROCK HARBOR   96   58
  THE HOOPS OF BLACKBERRY STEMS MADE ME CRY. POEM.1.WHO. 132   51
  I MADE IT MYSELF, ...POEM.2.DARK. 132   2
  THE BIRDS MADE MILK. POEM.3.MAENAD. 133   4
  THE COILS AND PIPES THAT MADE HIM RUN. ....THE BURNT-OUT SPA 138   17
  NOT EASY TO STATE THE CHANGE YOU MADE. ....LOVE LETTER 147   1
  WEARS THE FACE OF A PHARAOH, THOUGH IT'S MADE OF MUD AND WATER. ...
                                                      ... IN PLASTER 159   42
  A GARDEN OF BUGGY ROSES THAT MADE HIM CRY. ....INSOMNIAC 163   12
  LITTLE SHELLS MADE UP INTO NECKLACES AND TOY LADIES. ....FINISTERRE 170   32
  I THINK THEY ARE MADE OF WATER; THEY HAVE NO EXPRESSION.*THREE WOMEN 183 225
  MADE A HOLE IN THE HOT DAY, A VACANCY. ....THE RABBIT CATCHER 194   18
  THIS IS WHAT I AM MADE OF, THIS AND A TERROR ........APPREHENSIONS 195   14
  I MADE A FIRE; BEING TIRED ....BURNING THE LETTERS 204   1
  I MADE A MODEL OF YOU, ...DADDY 224   64
  HE MADE OF THE FOOTBALL POOLS -- TEASING US WITH ....DIALOGUE O. 277   39
  BEFORE IT MADE THE BULL'S-EYE. DO WE HAVE TO BATTLE ....DIALOGUE O. 284 282
  IS ALWAYS TO BE MADE: INNOCENCE ..........METAMORPHOSES OF THE MOON 308   40
  THE CHITTERING CRACKPOTS THAT HE MADE.*SONG FOR A REVOLUTIONARY LOVE 323   20
  MADE BY MINERS UP THE MOUNTAINSIDE ....THE PRINCESS AND THE GOBLINS 334   33
MADNESS (2)
  WHICH WEIGHS OUR MADNESS WITH OUR SANITY. ....PERSEUS   84   49
  OR THE VOICE OF NOTHING, THAT WAS YOUR MADNESS? ....ELM 192   6
MADONNA (1)
  THE MOON LEANS, A STONE MADONNA, OVER THE LEAD SEA   THE NET-MENDERS 121   15
MADRIGALS (1)
  A SAINTLY SPARROW JARGONS MADRIGALS ....APRIL AUBADE 312   5
MAENAD (1)
  MAENAD ....POEM.3.MAENAD. 133   ST
MAESTRO (2)
  HIERATICAL IN YOUR FROCK COAT, MAESTRO OF THE BEES, ...BEEKEEPER'S. 118   5
  THE MAESTRO GIVES THE SINGING BIRDS THEIR PAY ....DENOUEMENT 326   4
MAESTRO'S (1)
  WHICH SPEAK HER MAESTRO'S WILL. ....AERIALIST 331   12
MAGAZINES (1)
  OF MAGAZINES IN ELEGANT ENNUI, ...MORNING IN THE HOSPITAL SOLARIUM 332   22
MAGENTA (3)
  WHERE THE THREE MAGENTA ....MAN IN BLACK 119   1
  MAGENTA AS THIS FUBSY SOFA. ....LEAVING EARLY 146   33
  THE MILD HILLS, THE SAME OLD MAGENTA ....THE SWARM 216   28
MAGGOT (1)
  A SMALL WHITE SOUL IS WAVING, A SMALL WHITE MAGGOT. ....EVENT 195   19
MAGGOTS (1)
  AND I SAW WHITE MAGGOTS COIL ....MEDALLION 124   21
MAGI (2)
  AMERICANA. MAGI NEAR ....A WINTER'S TALE   86   3
  MAGI ....MAGI 148   T
MAGIC (6)
  OF YOUR STORMY EYE, MAGIC TAKES FLIGHT ...............CONVERSATION.   21   7
  THE SIZE OF MY DEMAND TO MAGIC: NO MORE *DIALOGUE OVER A OUIJA BOARD 279 121
  ALL MOONSTRUCK MAGIC ....MOONSONG AT MORNING 317   19
  THE MAGIC GOLDEN APPLES ALL LOOK GOOD ....ADMONITIONS 319   4
  THE MAGIC SAWDUST WRITES: ADDRESS UNKNOWN. ....DENOUEMENT 327   17
  READ BLACK MAGIC OR HOLY BOOK ...BLACK PINE TREE IN AN ORANGE LIGHT 328   13
MAGICAL (1)
  SO MAGICAL! A HOT SPRING ....THE SURGEON AT 2 A.M. 171   24
MAGICIAN'S (2)
  I AM THE MAGICIAN'S GIRL WHO DOES NOT FLINCH. ......THE BEE MEETING 212   53
  ECLIPSED BY MAGICIAN'S DISGUISE, ...CIRCUS IN THREE RINGS 322   14

```
                                          TITLE        PAGE  LINE
MAGNANIMOUS (1)
  AND I, GREAT MAGNANIMOUS FOOL, THUS WRENCHED FROM  ..MONOLOGUE AT 3.   40   13
MAGNET (1)
  COMPELLED BY CALAMITY'S MAGNET  ..........................AFTERMATH   113    1
MAGNIFIED (1)
  THEIR MAGNIFIED HEADS AND PLAN TO KILL ME AS SOON AS POSSIBLE.  ...
                                          ...  THE RIVAL/DR   291    3
MAGNIFY (1)
  HEARING THE FIERCE MASK MAGNIFY  ......................THE FEARFUL   256   15
MAGNIFYING (1)
  OUR VOICES ECHO, MAGNIFYING YOUR ARRIVAL. NEW STATUE.   MORNING SONG   157    4
MAGNOLIA (2)
  MAGNOLIA SHOALS  .......................................MAGNOLIA SHOALS   121    T
  OF THE MAGNOLIA,  ....................................PARALYTIC   267   38
MAHOGANY (2)
  WITH A POLISHED MAHOGANY STAIR TO LET INTO THE WATER*THE BABYSITTERS   174   11
  WHAT AM I BUYING, WORMY MAHOGANY?  ....................STINGS   214   14
MAID (4)
  THEY LEFT ME A BORROWED MAID NAMED ELLEN, "FOR PROTECTION",  ..BABY.   174   17
  AND A COOK AND A MAID, AND KNEW ABOUT THE KEY TO THE BOURBON. *BABY.   175   21
  AND THE MAID SMOKED AND SHOT POOL UNDER A GREEN-SHADED LAMP.   BABY.   175   24
  THE OLD MAID IN THE GABLE CRIES ALL DAY:  ......NEVER TRY TO TRICK.   320   11
MAIDEN (1)
  O MAIDEN AUNT, YOU HAVE COME TO CALL.  .....................THE TOUR   237    1
MAIDS (3)
  MAIDS AND THE LONG ROYAL LADY.  .........................WINTERING   218   39
  IT ATE SEVEN MAIDS AND A PLUMBER  .........................THE TOUR   238   33
  AND OLD MAIDS ON IMPROMPTU PETTICOATS FLY  .......SONG FOR A REVOLU.   323   15
MAIL (3)
  CAMOUFLAGED IN MOTTLED MAIL  ..........MUSSEL HUNTER AT ROCK HARBOR    96   31
  VAGUE AS FOG AND LOOKED FOR LIKE MAIL.  ....................YOU'RE   141   10
  LET IT NOT COME BY THE MAIL, FINGER BY FINGER.  ..A BIRTHDAY PRESENT   208   52
MAILED (1)
  IT IS LIKE BEING MAILED INTO SPACE,  ..............WUTHERING HEIGHTS   167   23
MAILSLOT (1)
  ARRIVE THROUGH THE MAILSLOT WITH LOVING REGULARITY,  ......THE RIVAL   166   14
MAIN (4)
  FRAMED IN WINDOWS OF MAIN STREET'S  .....................NIGHT SHIFT    76   15
  UP PLEASANT STREET AT MAIN. POISING THEIR SHAPES  ...ABOVE THE OXBOW    88   12
  CLOCKS BELLED TWELVE. MAIN STREET SHOWED OTHERWISE  ............OWL   101    1
  IN YOUR HOUSE, THE MAIN HOUSE, YOU WERE BETTER OFF. *THE BABYSITTERS   174   19
MAINLY (1)
  BLACKBERRIES ON EITHER SIDE, THOUGH ON THE RIGHT MAINLY,   BLACKBER.   168    2
MAINTAINS (1)
  MAINTAINS IT HAS NO MORE HOLY CALLING  ................TALE OF A TUB    24   11
MAJESTIC (1)
  BY NO MIRACLE OR MAJESTIC MEANS,  .............A LESSON IN VENGEANCE    80    5
MAJOR (1)
  MAJOR FAULTS IN GRANITE  .........................TRIO OF LOVE SONGS   313    1
MAKE (40)
  CAN BE STRUCK FROM ROCK TO MAKE HEART'S WASTE  ....WINTER LANDSCAPE,    22   14
  IS HELPLESS HERE, QUITE EXTRA, YET WE MUST MAKE  ..CHANNEL CROSSING    27   35
  MAKE HOUSES SHRINK  ....................SOLILOQUY OF THE SOLIPSIST    37   11
  AND FURY MAKE HEAD,  ...........................MONOLOGUE AT 3 A.M.    40    2
  PEOPLE MAKE QUERIES  .................ELLA MASON AND HER ELEVEN CATS    53    3
  RULES THE WRITINGS WHICH MAKE MANIFEST  .............SNAKECHARMER     79   16
  WHO KEEP COOL AND HOLY MAKE  ......................VIRGIN IN A TREE    81   25
  THUMB CAN MAKE ANYONE WINCE, BUT THE WHOLE GLOBE  .......PERSEUS      83   28
  EMULOUS SPIRITS MAKE DISCORD,  ........................SCULPTOR       92   20
  TO MAKE AWAY WITH THE GROUND-  .....................FULL FATHOM FIVE    93   31
  ENOUGH FOR FINGERNAILS TO MAKE HALF-MOONS  .................MOONRISE    98   10
  AND SHE COULD SCARCELY MAKE OUT ANYTHING*TWO VIEWS OF A CADAVER ROOM   114    7
  I MUST MAKE MORE MAPS.  ...................................POEM.2.DARK.   132   14
  THE SMALL GRAINS MAKE ROOM.  ..........................MUSHROOMS     139    9
  NO WORD MAKE THEM CARRY WATER OR FIRE THE KINDLING  .......TWO CAMP.   144    5
  HOW DID WE MAKE IT UP TO YOUR ATTIC?  ................LEAVING EARLY   146   40
  I DIDN'T KNOW WHAT TO MAKE OF IT.  ...................LOVE LETTER    147   24
  I USED TO THINK WE MIGHT MAKE A GO OF IT TOGETHER --  ....IN PLASTER   160   50
  DON'T KNOW WHAT TO MAKE OF THE SUDDEN SLIPPINESS,  .....NEW YEAR ON.   176    4
  "LET US MAKE A HEAVEN," THEY SAY.  ...............THREE WOMEN        179   90
  THE SUN IS DOWN. I DIE. I MAKE A DEATH.  ..........THREE WOMEN      181  161
  WHAT AM I TO MAKE OF THESE CONTRADICTIONS?  ..........AN APPEARANCE   189    8
  IT WILL MAKE LITTLE DRESSES AND COATS,  ..............AN APPEARANCE   189   12
  THERE IS ONLY A CROW IN A TREE. MAKE NOTES.  ..........THE DETECTIVE   209   40
  IT CAN MAKE BLACK ROSES.  ...............................THE SWARM    216    4
  TO MAKE UP FOR THE HONEY I'VE TAKEN.  ....................WINTERING   218   26
  MAKE A SACHET OR  ......................................A SECRET     220   31
  WE MAKE NEW STOCK FROM THE SALT.  ....................THE APPLICANT   221   18
  MAKE THEIR OWN ELEMENT. THEY WILL NOT RISE,  ..............FEVER.    231   15
  WATER, WATER MAKE ME RETCH.  .........................FEVER.        232   33
  OF WHAT GREEN STARS CAN MAKE IT TO OUR GATE.  ........BY CANDLELIGHT   236    5
  JUST TO MAKE SURE --  ..............................EAVESDROPPER     261   62
  NOVEMBER'S DONE WITH. THE BLOWN LEAVES MAKE BAT-SHAPES, *DIALOGUE O.   286  337
  AND MAKE THE FATAL PLUNGE.  ....................FAMILY REUNION      301   30
  BECAUSE HE WOULD MAKE LOVE TO ME  .....................BLUEBEARD    305    3
```
                                    304

	TITLE	PAGE	LINE

MAKE (CONT.)
MAKE LOVE AND LOGIC MIX, ...NOTES TO A NEOPHYTE 306 16
A CRAFT WITH PAINT AND POWDER THAT CAN MAKE .........METAMORPHOSES. 307 23
OR WALK INTO THE ORANGE AND MAKE *BLACK PINE TREE IN AN ORANGE LIGHT 328 7
TO MAKE ORANGE AND BLACK AMBIGUOUS. ....BLACK PINE TREE. 328 18
TO ASSAULT THE SCENE AND MAKE SOME *MORNING IN THE HOSPITAL SOLARIUM 333 24
MAKER (1)
O MAKER OF PROUD PLANET'S NEGATIVE, ...SONNET TO SATAN 323 13
MAKES (16)
SHATTERS THE FABULOUS STARS AND MAKES US REAL. ....TALE OF A TUB 25 48
CHOICE WASSAIL MAKES, COOKED HOT, ...THE GLUTTON 40 9
INDIGENOUS PEACE. SUCH SUBSTANCE MAKES ....LANDOWNERS 53 11
MAKES OFF WITH THIS ROSE, ...WORDS FOR A NURSERY 74 48
THE SECOND CARCASS MAKES A DUEL OF THE AFFAIR: ....BLUE MOLES 126 8
FISTS MY FINGERS FOR ME. HE MAKES ME FEEL SOMETHING PRECIOUS FACE. 156 13
ONE MATCH SCRATCH MAKES YOU REAL. ....BY CANDLELIGHT 236 15
MY SINGING MAKES YOU ROAR. ....BY CANDLELIGHT 237 23
YOU SHOULD SEE THE OBJECTS IT MAKES! ....THE TOUR 238 17
THE FROST MAKES A FLOWER, ...DEATH & CO. 255 27
THE DEW MAKES A STAR, ...DEATH & CO. 255 28
THIS MAN MAKES A PSEUDONYM ....THE FEARFUL 256 1
THE FIRE MAKES IT PRECIOUS, ...MARY'S SONG 257 5
AND LIKE A CUCKOO IN THE NEST MAKES HELL METAMORPHOSES OF THE MOON 307 17
TO FIND WHAT MAKES IT MOVE, ...TRIO OF LOVE SONGS 315 50
OF CLOCKWORK THAT MAKES THE ROYAL BLOOD RUN COLD. ....THE PRINCESS. 335 75
MAKESHIFT (1)
MAKESHIFT OF A VIEW TO QUIT ....GREEN ROCK, WINTHROP BAY 105 7
MAKING (8)
OF MAKING HARBOR THROUGH THIS RACKETING FLUX ......CHANNEL CROSSING 27 19
IN A WAR MAKING EVIL HEADLINES WHEN WE ....THE THIN PEOPLE 64 6
MAKING THE WORLD GO THIN AS A WASP'S NEST ....THE THIN PEOPLE 65 46
AND YOUR FIRST GIFT IS MAKING STONE OUT OF EVERYTHING. ...THE RIVAL 166 6
AND A BLACK VEIL THAT MOLDS TO MY FACE, THEY ARE MAKING ME
ONE OF THEM. ....THE BEE MEETING 211 22
BROTHER IS MAKING ....BALLOONS 272 21
AROUND THE RING. I THINK IT MUST BE MAKING SURE ....DIALOGUE O. 277 22
THEY ARE MAKING A CAT'S CRADLE, THEY ARE SUICIDAL. ....STINGS/DR 293 7
MALADIES (1)
AND THE INVOLVED MALADIES OF AUTUMN, ...LEAVING EARLY 146 18
MALADY (1)
YOUR MALADY OF SACRILEGIOUS MIRTH ....DIRGE FOR A JOKER 303 11
MALE (1)
THAT NIGHTLONG STOLE HER MALE, ...THE SHRIKE 42 20
MALFI'S (1)
SORROWS OF MALFI'S GENTLE DUCHESS? GONE ....PERSEUS 83 42
MALICE (3)
WHICH ALLAY THE MALICE ....MISS DRAKE PROCEEDS TO SUPPER 41 3
THE INCALCULABLE MALICE OF THE EVERYDAY. ....THREE WOMEN 184 287
SHE MOUNTS THROUGH MALICE OF THE NEEDLE'S EYE, ...THE PRINCESS. 333 10
MALICIOUS (1)
AND HE WAS NOT EVEN MALICIOUS. .......................EAVESDROPPER 260 27
MALIGN (1)
I MALIGN THE LEADEN PERSPECTIVE ....LANDOWNERS 53 3
MALIGNITY (2)
ALL DAY I FEEL ITS SOFT, FEATHERY TURNINGS, ITS MALIGNITY. .....ELM 193 33
I TASTED THE MALIGNITY OF THE GORSE, ...THE RABBIT CATCHER 193 6
MALLEABLE (1)
MALLEABLE MASK ....NOTES TO A NEOPHYTE 306 11
MALTREAT (1)
MALTREAT THE HOSTAGE HEAD IN SHOCKING WISE, ...LADY AND T. 69 13
MAMMAL (1)
FUG OF THE SMALL MAMMAL HOUSE. ....ZOO KEEPER'S WIFE 155 19
MAMMOTH (2)
MORE MAMMOTH AND BLOWSY WITH EVERY SEASON; ....ELLA MASON A. 54 34
THE MAMMOTH, LUMBERING STATUARY OF SORROW, ...PERSEUS 82 3
MAN (60)
AT THIS RARE RUMPUS WHICH NO MAN CAN CONTROL: .....CHANNEL CROSSING 27 29
UNTIL EVERY MAN, ...STRUMPET SONG 33 6
WALKS THERE NOT SOME SUCH ONE MAN ....STRUMPET SONG 34 14
ON THE CALL THIS MAN MADE. ....FAUN 35 5
TO ATONE AS SHADE FOR SIN THAT LURED BLIND MAN." ....DIALOGUE B. 39 36
(WITH HEAT SUCH AS NO MAN COULD HAVE ....THE GLUTTON 40 3
SUCH ROYAL DREAMS BECKON THIS MAN ....THE SHRIKE 42 2
AS NO MERE INSURGENT MAN COULD HOPE TO BREAK ....SPINSTER 50 28
GIBBETS WITH HER CURSE THE MOON'S MAN, ...MAUDLIN 51 3
SHE CAME, AND CALLED HELL TO SUBDUE AN UNRULY MAN ....SNOWMAN O. 59 23
THE MOON'S MAN STANDS IN HIS SHELL, ...THE EVERLASTING MONDAY 62 1
STAR-LUCKY SLEIGHT-OF-HAND MAN WATCHES ....CONJURING. 66 34
AS THE GODS BEGAN ONE WORLD, AND MAN ANOTHER, ...SNAKECHARMER 79 1
OLD MAN, YOU SURFACE SELDOM. ....FULL FATHOM FIVE 92 1
SEEN BY ANY MAN WHO KEPT HIS HEAD, ...FULL FATHOM FIVE 93 38
NOR BY ANY LEARNED MAN. ....THE BULL OF BENDYLAW 108 18
THE STONE FACE OF THE MAN WHO DOESN'T FEEL, ...THE RAVAGED FACE 116 10
MY MOTHER SAID; YOU DIED LIKE ANY MAN. ......ELECTRA ON AZALEA PATH 117 40
CLAPPED SHUT, FLATTEN THIS MAN OUT. ..THE HERMIT AT OUTERMOST HOUSE 118 3

```
                                              TITLE              PAGE  LINE
MAN (CONT.)
    MAN IN BLACK  ................. . .........................MAN IN BLACK   119    T
    THE OLD MAN SHRANK TO A DOLL.  .......................POEM.3.MAENAD.     133    7
    THE HANGING MAN  .........................................THE HANGING MAN 141   T
    AND A DROWNED MAN, COMPLAINING OF THE GREAT COLD, ...........A LIFE       150    34
    I ROLL TO AN ANTEROOM WHERE A KIND MAN ....................FACE LIFT      156    12
    AND THE MAN I WORK FOR LAUGHED: "HAVE YOU SEEN SOMETHING AWFUL?  ...
                                          ...   THREE WOMEN     177    22
    I SEE MYSELF AS A SHADOW, NEITHER MAN NOR WOMAN,  ......THREE WOMEN       182   191
    NEITHER A WOMAN, HAPPY TO BE LIKE A MAN, NOR A MAN  .....THREE WOMEN      182   192
    NEITHER A WOMAN, HAPPY TO BE LIKE A MAN, NOR A MAN  .....THREE WOMEN      182   192
    THIS WAS A MAN, THEN!  ...................................LITTLE FUGUE    188    47
    THE FLOWERS VIVID AS BANDAGES, AND THE MAN MENDING.  ......NARCISSI.      190     8
    THIS IS THE SIDE OF A MAN: HIS RED RIBS,  ...............BERCK-PLAGE      198    46
    AN OLD MAN IS VANISHING.  .................................BERCK-PLAGE   198    51
    THIS IS THE TONGUE OF THE DEAD MAN: REMEMBER, REMEMBER. *BERCK-PLAGE     199    81
    AND THIS IS A MAN, LOOK AT HIS SMILE, .................THE DETECTIVE      208    14
    THE FACE THAT LIVED IN THIS MIRROR IS THE FACE OF A DEAD MAN.  ...
                                    ...   THE COURAGE OF SHUTTING-UP         210    29
    WHICH IS THE RECTOR NOW, IS IT THAT MAN IN BLACK?  ..THE BEE MEETING     211    11
    THE MAN IN WHITE SMILES, BARE-HANDED, .........................STINGS    214     2
    THE MAN WITH GRAY HANDS STANDS UNDER THE HONEYCOMB  .......THE SWARM      216    33
    THE MAN WITH GRAY HANDS SMILES --  .........................THE SWARM    217    51
    THE SMILE OF A MAN OF BUSINESS, INTENSELY PRACTICAL.  .....THE SWARM      217    52
    ANY LESS THE BLACK MAN WHO  .....................................DADDY    223    55
    A MAN IN BLACK WITH A MEINKAMPF LOOK  ........................DADDY       224    65
    IF I'VE KILLED ONE MAN, I'VE KILLED TWO ---  ................DADDY        224    71
    KAMIKAZE MAN ---  .............................................CUT        235    28
    WHILE THE BRASS MAN  ...............................BY CANDLELIGHT        237    26
    THIS MAN MAKES A PSEUDONYM  ...........................THE FEARFUL        256     1
    SAYS SHE IS A MAN, NOT A WOMAN.  ......................THE FEARFUL        256     4
    THAT EMPTIED ONE MAN INTO SPACE  .....................MARY'S SONG         257    17
    NOW YOU MUST PLAY THE STRAIGHT MAN FOR A TERM  ....DIRGE FOR A JOKER      303    13
    NOT MAN NOR DEMIGOD COULD PUT TOGETHER  ..............SONNET: TO EVA      305     9
    THE FALLING MAN WHO NEVER WILL ABSTAIN  ...METAMORPHOSES OF THE MOON     307    10
    THE TRIAL OF MAN  ...................................THE TRIAL OF MAN     312    T
    MAN WHO CAN MANGLE THE GRIN OF KINGS:  .........................LAMENT    316    17
    THE DYING MAN WILL SCOFF IN SCORN AT THIS.  .....NEVER TRY TO TRICK.     319     3
    THE DYING MAN WILL SCOFF IN SCORN AT THIS.  .....NEVER TRY TO TRICK.     320     9
    THE DYING MAN WILL SCOFF IN SCORN AT THIS.  .....NEVER TRY TO TRICK.     320    15
    THE DYING MAN WILL SCOFF IN SCORN AT THIS.  .....NEVER TRY TO TRICK.     320    19
    NO LITTLE MAN LIVES IN THE EXACTING MOON  ................TWO LOVERS.     327    23
    HOPING FOR SOME INCREDIBLE DARK MAN*MORNING IN THE HOSPITAL SOLARIUM     333    23
    THAT LIFTS TO CONSECRATE THE SUNKEN MAN.  ....EPITAPH IN THREE PARTS     337    19
MANAGE (4)
    I'M COLLECTING MY STRENGTH; ONE DAY I SHALL MANAGE WITHOUT HER,  ...
                                          ...   IN PLASTER     160    55
    EVEN THE SUN-CLOUDS THIS MORNING CANNOT MANAGE SUCH SKIRTS.*POP.OCT.     240     1
    I MANAGE IT ---  .................................................LADY LAZARUS   244     3
    BELIEVE, IF THEY COULD MANAGE TO CONVINCE  .............DIALOGUE O.      278    66
MANAGED (1)
    GOD KNOWS HOW OUR NEIGHBOR MANAGED TO BREED  ....................SOW      60     1
MANAGES (1)
    SUN MANAGES TO STRIKE SUCH TIN GLINTS  .......PARLIAMENT HILL FIELDS     152    10
MANDATORY (1)
    OF MANDATORY VOICES YOU HALF EXPECT  ....DIALOGUE OVER A OUIJA BOARD     279   110
MANE (1)
    TO MARVEL AT THE MANE,  ...........................TRIO OF LOVE SONGS    315    42
MANES (2)
    OF THE MOON, MANES TO THE WIND,  ....................HARDCASTLE CRAGS     62    11
    AT A FIELD OF HORSES, NECKS BENT, MANES BLOWN,  ........THE EYE-MOTE     109     2
MANGLE (1)
    MAN WHO CAN MANGLE THE GRIN OF KINGS:  ........................LAMENT    316    17
MANGLED (2)
    EVEN AS MY EACH MANGLED NERVE-END  .......................STREET SONG     36    21
    IS MANGLED BY STUDY  .............................MOONSONG AT MORNING    317    31
MANGO (1)
    COLOR OF LEMON, MANGO, PEACH,  .....................SOUTHERN SUNRISE      26     1
MANHANDLES (1)
    AGE MANHANDLES ME  .............................WORDS FOR A NURSERY       74    42
MANIACS (1)
    I HAVE SIMPLY ORDERED A BOX OF MANIACS.   THE ARRIVAL OF THE BEE BOX     213    23
MANIFEST (1)
    RULES THE WRITINGS WHICH MAKE MANIFEST  ...............SNAKECHARMER       79    16
MANIFESTATIONS (1)
    THE VISITATIONS, THE MANIFESTATIONS, THE STARTLED FACES.*THREE WOMEN     180   131
MANNEQUINS (4)
    RUDDY ON THE WAX MANNEQUINS  ...........................................OWL    101     6
    AND MUTE AS MANNEQUINS IN A DRESS SHOP,  ....................ON DECK     142     3
    THE MUNICH MANNEQUINS  .........................THE MUNICH MANNEQUINS     262    T
    THESE MANNEQUINS LEAN TONIGHT  .................THE MUNICH MANNEQUINS     263    11
MANNER (2)
    "WHAT MANNER OF BUSINESS ARE YOU ON?  ....................DIALOGUE B.     38    13
    THE LABYRINTH AND IGNORE WHAT MANNER OF BEAST  .........DIALOGUE O.      286   343
```

```
                                                      TITLE          PAGE  LINE
MANNERS (2)
   AND USED HER GENTLE DOVES WITH MANNERS RUDE:   THE QUEEN'S COMPLAINT   28    7
   HIS MANNERS ARE ATROCIOUS. A-P-E-  ......DIALOGUE OVER A OUIJA BOARD  284  298
MANOR (2)
   YADDO: THE GRAND MANOR  .....................YADDO: THE GRAND MANOR   123    T
   THE MANOR GARDEN  ...................  ...............THE MANOR GARDEN   125    T
MAN'S (9)
   THE GESTURE, BEND AND HOLD THE PRONE MAN'S HEAD.  ..CHANNEL CROSSING   27   36
   FROM UNDER CRUNCH OF MY MAN'S BOOT  ...........THE QUEEN'S COMPLAINT   29    1
   LEAPS TO LAUD SUCH MAN'S BLOOD!  ........................ODE FOR TED   30   24
   THAN MAN'S RED HEART."  ...........DIALOGUE BETWEEN GHOST AND PRIEST   39   50
   AS A SLEDGE HAMMER, AS A MAN'S BUNCHED FIST,  ................SPIDER   48    4
   FROST FORMS. NO MAN'S CROWBAR COULD  ...........CHILD'S PARK STONES  101   26
   THE DESERT IS WHITE AS A BLIND MAN'S EYE,*SLEEP IN THE MOJAVE DESERT  144   17
   OF THE MAN'S PANTS  .....................................EAVESDROPPER  261   58
   THAT ONE MAN'S DEVIL IS ANOTHER'S GOD  ...........LOVE IS A PARALLAX  329    8
MAN-SHAMING (1)
   THE PASSAGE, SAY, OF THESE MAN-SHAMING CLOUDS.  ...........TWO CAMP.  144    3
MAN-SHAPE (1)
   HUSH A LUMPED MAN-SHAPE. THE WHOLE ACT FORMAL, FLUENT AS A DANCE.  ...
                                                  ... THE GORING   47    9
MANUSCRIPT (2)
   M-S. MANUSCRIPT. HE STOPS. I WISH  ......DIALOGUE OVER A OUIJA BOARD  279   95
   AND BLOOD REFLECTS ACROSS THE MANUSCRIPT;  ............FEMALE AUTHOR  301   10
MANY (19)
   THAT MANY CATS."  .................ELLA MASON AND HER ELEVEN CATS   53    6
   SO MANY LADDERS  ...............................WORDS FOR A NURSERY   73    8
   MARVELINGLY NUMBERED THE MANY SHADES OF GREEN.  ...........YADWIGHA   86   34
   YOUR DANGERS ARE MANY. I  ...........................FULL FATHOM FIVE   92   16
   IT HAS SO MANY CELLARS,  ...............................POEM.2.DARK.  132    8
   SO MANY OF US!  .............................................MUSHROOMS  139   23
   SO MANY OF US!  .............................................MUSHROOMS  139   24
   LIMPID AS SPIRITS. MANY STONES LAY  .....................LOVE LETTER  147   22
   SHE HAS ONE TOO MANY DIMENSIONS TO ENTER.  ...................A LIFE  150   28
   OLD GRIEVANCES JOSTLING EACH OTHER, SO MANY LOOSE TEETH.  ....ZOO K.  154   13
   SO IT IS IMPOSSIBLE TO TELL HOW MANY THERE ARE.  ...........TULIPS  160   14
   THEY HAVE TOO MANY COLORS, TOO MUCH LIFE. THEY ARE NOT QUIET,*THREE.  178   69
   HE'D HAD SO MANY WARS!  .....................................LYONNESSE  234   26
   SO MANY SILKS.  .............................................GULLIVER  251   15
   I AM MAD, CALLS THE SPIDER, WAVING ITS MANY ARMS.  ...........TOTEM  265   28
   DEATH WITH ITS MANY STICKS.  ...............................TOTEM  265   34
   THE GREAT ROSES, MANY OF THEM SCENTLESS,  ..QUEEN MARY'S ROSE GARDEN  290    4
   BUSINESSLIKE SHE ASKED US, "HOW MANY QUARTS?"  ..BITTER STRAWBERRIES  300   31
   WITH MANY MEN UNTIL I CRASHED  ...........................THE DREAM  310    9
MANY-BREASTED (1)
   YOU MOVE AMONG THE MANY-BREASTED HIVES,  ...THE BEEKEEPER'S DAUGHTER  118    6
MANY-COLORED (1)
   OF MANY-COLORED FICTIONS; WE MASK OUR PAST  ...........TALE OF A TUB   25   38
MANY-HOLED (1)
   THEY ARE PRESSING OUT OF THE MANY-HOLED EARPIECE, THEY ARE LOOKING
      FOR A LISTENER.  ......WORDS HEARD, BY ACCIDENT, OVER THE PHONE  203    9
MANY-SNAKED (1)
   CREEPS AWAY, MANY-SNAKED, WITH A LONG HISS OF DISTRESS. *BERCK-PLAGE  196   18
MAP (3)
   NO MAP TRACES THE STREET  .............................THE SLEEPERS  122    1
   THE CITY IS A MAP OF CHEERFUL TWITTERS NOW,  ...............INSOMNIAC  163   33
   "BOMB THEM OFF THE MAP."  .......................BITTER STRAWBERRIES  299    6
MAPLIKE (1)
   LORDED PERSPECTIVES. MAPLIKE, THE FAR FIELDS ARE RULED  ......OXBOW.   89   48
MAPS (1)
   I MUST MAKE MORE MAPS.  .................................POEM.2.DARK.  132   14
MAR (3)
   BRIGHT THOSE CLAWS THAT MAR THE FLESH  .......................PURSUIT   23   31
   I'LL CORRECT EACH MAR  ...............TINKER JACK AND THE TIDY WIVES   34    5
   WHICH MAR THE IDOL'S SANCTITY.  ...........METAMORPHOSES OF THE MOON  308   36
MARAUDER (1)
   THE BLACK MARAUDER, HAULED BY LOVE  .........................PURSUIT   22   27
MARBLE (11)
   FROM MARBLE SNOW-HEAP OF MOOR TO RIDE THAT WOMAN  ........SNOWMAN O.   59   27
   THAN SCULPTED MARBLE. THEY SING  .............................LORELEI   94   14
   FIRST FROST, AND I WALK AMONG THE ROSE-FRUIT, THE MARBLE TOES  ...
                                                  ... PRIVATE GROUND  130    1
   NUN-HEARTED AND BLIND TO THE WORLD. MARBLE LILIES  .....BARREN WOMAN  157    4
   TICKING YOUR FINGERS ON THE MARBLE TABLE, LOOKING FOR CIGARETTES,  ...
                                                  ... THE RIVAL  166    8
   HER MARBLE SKIRTS BLOWN BACK IN TWO PINK WINGS.  .........FINISTERRE  169   20
   A MARBLE SAILOR KNEELS AT HER FOOT DISTRACTEDLY, AND AT HIS FOOT  ...
                                                  ... FINISTERRE  170   21
   THE INTRICATE, BLUE PIPING UNDER THIS PALE MARBLE.  ........SURGEON.  171   26
   MARBLE FACADES WITH BLUE VEINS, AND JELLY-GLASSFULS OF DAFFODILS. ...
                                                  ... BERCK-PLAGE  199   89
   CIRCLE A WOMB OF MARBLE.  ...............................THE OTHER  202   22
   THEY'LL GO BY, TRUNDLING LIKE MARBLE STATUES WAY OUT  ...DIALOGUE O.  276    6
MARBLEHEAD (1)
   THE SUN FLAMED STRAIGHT DOWN THAT NOON ON THE WATER OFF
                                    307
```

```
                                           TITLE            PAGE  LINE
MARBLEHEAD (CONT.)
      MARBLEHEAD.  .... ..........................THE BABYSITTERS  174    2
MARBLE-HEAVY (1)
   MARBLE-HEAVY, A BAG FULL OF GOD,  ........................DADDY  222    8
MARBLY (1)
   AND HARD, MARBLY BAAS.  ....... ..............WUTHERING HEIGHTS  167   27
MARCH (5)
   TO THE RIGHT, AND MARCH ICE  ......................MAN IN BLACK  119   10
   I STARTED TO BUD LIKE A MARCH TWIG:  ...............LOVE LETTER  147   31
   SO THAT EACH MARCH I MAY GLEAM INTO LEAF,  ..........I AM VERTICAL 162    4
   SPRY, WRY, AND GRAY AS THESE MARCH STICKS,  ......AMONG THE NARCISSI 190    1
   POLLARDED GREEN BALLS, THE TREES MARCH TO CHURCH.  ......BERCK-PLAGE 199   92
MARCHEN (1)
   SUCH MEETINGS NEVER OCCUR IN MARCHEN  .................INCOMMUNICADO 100    8
MARGIN (1)
   MARGIN OF THE TIDAL POOLS.  ............MUSSEL HUNTER AT ROCK HARBOR  95   11
MARGINS (1)
   GRAZING AT THE MARGINS OF A BAD MONOCHROME,  ..........THE EYE-MOTE 109   14
MARK (11)
   JUTTED EARLY TO MARK OUR GOING, WHILE SKY  ........CHANNEL CROSSING  27   23
   DRY TICKS MARK TIME  .....................TWO SISTERS OF PERSEPHONE  31    8
   MARK, I CRY, THAT MOUTH  ..............................STRUMPET SONG  33    9
   BUT NOW TURNED KINDER WITH TIME, WE MARK MISS MASON  ..ELLA MASON A.  54   37
   THE DOOM MARK  .............................................CONTUSION 271    8
   AMID THE TICKING JEWELED CLOCKS THAT MARK  ..........SONNET: TO TIME 311    2
   MARK A MORTAL LACK,  .........................TRIO OF LOVE SONGS 313    2
   BUT MISSED THE MARK WITH SNAKING FANGS:  .....................LAMENT 315    5
   ON SOPHIST SEAS TO OVERTAKE THAT MARK  .........LOVE IS A PARALLAX 329    5
   THE OCEAN IN ONE GULP: YOU SAY A MARK  ..........LOVE IS A PARALLAX 329   28
   AT SOME STEADFAST MARK  ...............................TOUCH-AND-GO 335    5
MARKED (1)
   GOAT-HORNS. MARKED HOW GOD ROSE  ...............................FAUN  35   14
MARKET (2)
   THIS MARKET OF MELON-EATING  ........................FIESTA MELONS  47   19
   TO MARKET FOR HER DEARIES,  ..........ELLA MASON AND HER ELEVEN CATS  54   33
MARKETPLACE (2)
   PARADES THE MARKETPLACE, LURID AND STRICKEN  .......THE RAVAGED FACE 115    2
   IN THE MARKETPLACE THEY ARE PILING THE DRY STICKS.  .......POEM.6.W. 135    1
MARKS (3)
   A POINT OF EXCLAMATION MARKS THAT SKY  ......THE GHOST'S LEAVETAKING  91   27
   WITH TRIANGULAR SCORCH MARKS FROM IRONING TINY RUCHINGS AND PUFFED
   SLEEVES.  ........................................THE BABYSITTERS 174   15
   ACROSS THE FROSTED GRASS SHE MARKS THE SHEEN  .........THE PRINCESS. 334   31
MARRIAGE (3)
   THICKENING WITH MOTES, TO A MARRIAGE WITH THE MIRE.  ..........OUIJA  77   21
   AFTER ALL, IT WAS A KIND OF MARRIAGE, BEING SO CLOSE.  ...IN PLASTER 160   51
   THE CLOUDS ARE A MARRIAGE DRESS, OF THAT PALLOR.  ......LITTLE FUGUE 189   52
MARRIED (3)
   MY HOURS ARE MARRIED TO SHADOW.  ......................THE COLOSSUS 130   28
   I'VE MARRIED A CUPBOARD OF RUBBISH.  .................POEM.4.BEAST. 134   18
   FULL OF DRESSES AND HATS AND CHINA AND MARRIED DAUGHTERS.  ...BERCK. 199   77
MARRIES (1)
   THE QUEEN BEE MARRIES THE WINTER OF YOUR YEAR.  ........BEEKEEPER'S. 118   21
MARROW (3)
   BLOOD AND WHISTLE MY MARROW CLEAN  ...............ALL THE DEAD DEARS  70   17
   STUNNED THE MARROW. MEN IN WHITE  ......................NIGHT SHIFT  77   20
   FROM GRAIN OF THE MARROW AND THE RIVER-BED GRAINS.  .........LESSON.  80   25
MARROWLESS (1)
   HER WINTER-BEHEADED DAISIES, MARROWLESS, GAUNT,  .........SNOWMAN O.  58    9
MARROWY (2)
   THESE MARROWY TUNNELS!  .............................POEM.2.DARK. 132   15
   MY FAT PORK, MY MARROWY SWEETHEART, FACE-TO-THE-WALL?  .......ZOO K. 155   15
MARRY (10)
   AT GIRLS WHO MARRY --  ...............ELLA MASON AND HER ELEVEN CATS  54   39
   IT MARRY QUARTZ-FLAKE,  .................................POLLY'S TREE 129   32
   NUN-SOULED, THEY BURN HEAVENWARD AND NEVER MARRY.  .........CANDLES 149   27
   AND TO MARRY WHAT HE WANTS AND WHERE HE WILL.  ..........THREE WOMEN 186  336
   IF MY MOUTH COULD MARRY A HURT LIKE THAT!  ..........POPPIES IN JULY 203   12
   WILL YOU MARRY IT?  ..................................THE APPLICANT 221   14
   WILL YOU MARRY IT?  ..................................THE APPLICANT 221   22
   WILL YOU MARRY IT, MARRY IT, MARRY IT.  ..............THE APPLICANT 222   40
   WILL YOU MARRY IT, MARRY IT, MARRY IT.  ..............THE APPLICANT 222   40
   WILL YOU MARRY IT, MARRY IT, MARRY IT.  ..............THE APPLICANT 222   40
MARSHALING (1)
   AND THE SNOW, MARSHALING ITS BRILLIANT CUTLERY  ..........THE SWARM 216    9
MARSHALS (1)
   THE WHITE BUSTS OF MARSHALS, ADMIRALS, GENERALS  ........THE SWARM 217   44
MARSHY (1)
   FROM THE BROKEN THROAT, THE MARSHY LIP.  ........THE BURNT-OUT SPA 138   21
MARTYR (1)
   HIS NEXT MARTYR TO THE GROSS CAUSE  ..........................SPIDER  49   26
MARVEL (4)
   AND MARVEL AT THE SMASHING NONCHALANCE  ...........CHANNEL CROSSING  27   15
   THE GREAT GRANDAM! -- OUR MARVEL BLAZONED A KNIGHT,  ...........SOW  61   29
   A MARVEL TO YOUR GREAT-GRANDCHILDREN.  ..........A BIRTHDAY PRESENT 207   31
```

```
                                              TITLE              PAGE  LINE
MARVEL (CONT.)
   TO MARVEL AT THE MANE,    ........... ...............TRIO OF LOVE SONGS  315   42
MARVELINGLY (1)
   MARVELINGLY NUMBERED THE MANY SHADES OF GREEN.  ...........YADWIGHA.  86   34
MARVELOUS (2)
   ENGRAVING ITSELF IN SILVER WITH MARVELOUS CALM.  ........BERCK-PLAGE  199   72
   IT IS A MARVELOUS OBJECT --  .............THE COURAGE OF SHUTTING-UP  210   24
MARY (6)
   MARY LOOKS MILD.  .....................................A WINTER'S TALE  86    8
   THE MOON IS MY MOTHER. SHE IS NOT SWEET LIKE MARY.  ...........MOON.  173   17
   DUSK HOODS ME IN BLUE NOW, LIKE A MARY.  .................THREE WOMEN  179  102
   A COMMUNION WAFER? BLUBBERY MARY?  ...........................MEDUSA  225   33
   IN THE CENTER OF THE GARDEN NAMED AFTER QUEEN MARY.  ..QUEEN MARY'S.  290    3
   MARY SAID SLOWLY, "I'VE GOT A FELLA  ............BITTER STRAWBERRIES  299   10
MARY-BLUE (1)
   DUSK HOODS THEM IN MARY-BLUE  ..........................HEAVY WOMEN  158   18
MARY'S (3)
   LIKE BLUE MARY'S ANGEL, DOVELIKE AGAINST A PANE  .............WIDOW  165   38
   MARY'S SONG  ..............................................MARY'S SONG  257    T
   QUEEN MARY'S ROSE GARDEN  ..................QUEEN MARY'S ROSE GARDEN  290    T
MASH (1)
   LEAVING A SALTY MASH OF ICE TO WHITEN  ................POINT SHIRLEY  110    8
MASK (6)
   OF MANY-COLORED FICTIONS; WE MASK OUR PAST  ...........TALE OF A TUB   25   38
   UNDER THE STRICT MASK OF HIS AGONY.  ................CHANNEL CROSSING   26   12
   A SAMURAI DEATH MASK DONE  .........MUSSEL HUNTER AT ROCK HARBOR   97   80
   THE MASK INCREASES, EATS THE WORM,  .....................THE FEARFUL  256    5
   HEARING THE FIERCE MASK MAGNIFY  .......................THE FEARFUL  256   15
   MALLEABLE MASK  ..................................NOTES TO A NEOPHYTE  306   11
MASKED (3)
   SO FABLES SAY THE GOATSUCKER MOVES, MASKED FROM MEN'S SIGHT  ...
                                                  ... GOATSUCKER  111    9
   MASKED AMONG BLACK ROCKS AS A BLACK ROCK  ..............LOVE LETTER  147   10
   NEGRO, MASKED LIKE A WHITE,  .............................THALIDOMIDE  252    3
MASKS (3)
   WEAR MASKS OF HORN TO BED.  ..............................POEM.5.F.  135   14
   DOZE BEHIND THE OLD MASKS OF FURY.  ......SLEEP IN THE MOJAVE DESERT  144   19
   HIS HIGH COLD MASKS OF AMNESIA.  ..........................THE JAILER  227   31
MASON (6)
   ELLA MASON AND HER ELEVEN CATS  ......ELLA MASON AND HER ELEVEN CATS   53    T
   OLD ELLA MASON KEEPS CATS, ELEVEN AT LAST COUNT,  .....ELLA MASON A.   53    1
   LONG GONE TO WHEEZE AND SEED, ELLA MASON  ............ELLA MASON A.   53    8
   ONCE WE CHILDREN SNEAKED OVER TO SPY MISS MASON  ......ELLA MASON A.   54   19
   "LOOK! THERE SHE GOES, CAT-LADY MASON!"  ............ELLA MASON A.   54   31
   BUT NOW TURNED KINDER WITH TIME, WE MARK MISS MASON  .ELLA MASON A.   54   37
MASQUERADE (1)
   A STONE CAN MASQUERADE WHERE NO HEART IS  .......NEVER TRY TO TRICK.  319    4
MASS (4)
   TWO PINLEGS STAGGER UNDERNEATH THE MASS.  ..........THE RAVAGED FACE  115    5
   MASS AFTER MASS, SAYING SHH!  .............................THE SWARM  216   10
   MASS AFTER MASS, SAYING SHH!  .............................THE SWARM  216   10
   NOW THEY BALL IN A MASS,  ...................................WINTERING  218   31
MASSACRES (1)
   I AM ACCUSED. I DREAM OF MASSACRES.  ....................THREE WOMEN  180  148
MASSES (2)
   SPEWED RELICS CLICKER MASSES IN THE WIND,  ...........POINT SHIRLEY  110   32
   AWAITING MASSES  ...........................................BRASILIA  258    4
MASSIVE (1)
   THE MASSIVE CASTLE TURRETS  ....................................LORELEI   94    7
MASS-MOTIVED (1)
   MASS-MOTIVED HORDES, THEY SIDLED  ......MUSSEL HUNTER AT ROCK HARBOR   96   39
MASTER (2)
   AND WHATEVER PAN THIS MENDING MASTER *TINKER JACK AND THE TIDY WIVES   34    3
   CHANCES TO MASTER MINE. THEY SAY THE THIRD TIME  ........DIALOGUE O.  283  270
MASTERIES (1)
   OF KINGS, UNMANNED KINGS' SONS: OUR MASTERIES  ...........SNOWMAN O.   59   41
MASTERS (1)
   BEDFELLOWS OF THE SPIRIT'S DEBAUCH, FOND MASTERS.  ...COMPANIONABLE.  105    8
MASTER'S (1)
   MY MASTER'S FETCHER,  ...........................WORDS FOR A NURSERY   73   16
MASTURBATING (1)
   MASTURBATING A GLITTER,  ....................................DEATH & CO.  254   24
MAT (1)
   A MAT OF ROOTS. MY ASSISTANTS HOOK THEM BACK. *THE SURGEON AT 2 A.M.  170   13
MATADOR (3)
   TO ADAM THE ARROGANT MATADOR  .....................DIALOGUE EN ROUTE  308    3
   SHAM ADAM THE MATADOR CRIED:  .....................DIALOGUE EN ROUTE  308   14
   AND ADAM THE ARROGANT MATADOR  ....................DIALOGUE EN ROUTE  309   33
MATCH (3)
   THEIR FOND HEARTS CHARRED AS ANY MATCH. *EPITAPH FOR FIRE AND FLOWER   45    7
   TOUCHED BY A MATCH, THEY MIGHT WARM ME,  .........WUTHERING HEIGHTS  167    3
   ONE MATCH SCRATCH MAKES YOU REAL.  ....................BY CANDLELIGHT  236   15
MATCHED (2)
   NONE OF THAT GREENHORN LOT MATCHED HER BRIGHT CROWN.  ....QUEEN'S C.   29   20
   MATCHED THE STRIPES OF HIS SOCKS.  ...................THE BABYSITTERS  174    9
```

MATCHSTICKS (1)
   ALL DAY, GLUING MY CHURCH OF BURNT MATCHSTICKS, ...THE JAILER 227 26
MATE (1)
   THE STUFFED SHAPE OF HER FLOWN MATE ....THE SHRIKE 42 13
MATED (1)
   STAND STOCK STILL TO LAUD THESE MATED ONES .....WREATH FOR A BRIDAL 44 5
MATERIAL (6)
   INCOMPATIBLE MODES OF TIME, THE RAW MATERIAL*THE GHOST'S LEAVETAKING 90 13
   THEY ARE STITCHING ME UP WITH SILK, AS IF I WERE A MATERIAL. *THREE. 181 168
   CAN STITCH LACE NEATLY ON TO THIS MATERIAL. MY HUSBAND   THREE WOMEN 187 360
   IT IS ONLY TIME, AND THAT IS NOT MATERIAL. ....THREE WOMEN 187 364
   IS THIS LOVE THEN, THIS RED MATERIAL ....AN APPEARANCE 189 10
   DRAWN LIKE A LONG MATERIAL ....BERCK-PLAGE 197 34
MATERNAL (1)
   AND I REMEMBER MY MATERNAL GRANDMOTHER FROM VIENNA. ....CANDLES 149 17
MATERNITY (1)
   SETTING: A MATERNITY WARD AND ROUND ABOUT ....THREE WOMEN 176 SD
MATHEMATICAL (2)
   A MATHEMATICAL MACHINE. ....TWO SISTERS OF PERSEPHONE 31 7
   LIKE A CHILD'S TOO-SIMPLE MATHEMATICAL PROBLEM. ....STARS. 165 20
MATHEMATICS (1)
   LOSE THEMSELVES. IN MATHEMATICS? ....THE NIGHT DANCES 249 4
MATISSE (1)
   FRESH FROM THE MELLOW PALETTE OF MATISSE: ....MIDSUMMER MOBILE 324 12
MATS (1)
   STRAW MATS, WHITE WALLS ....BALLOONS 271 12
MATTER (3)
   SUCH PACT AS IS MADE ONCE ONLY; WHAT MATTER ....WREATH FOR A BRIDAL 44 2
   NO MATTER HOW FIERCELY LIT; STAUNCH CONTRACTS BREAK   EPITAPH FOR F. 46 32
   BUT SHE'LL SOON FIND OUT THAT THAT DOESN'T MATTER A BIT. ..PLASTER. 160 54
MATTRESS (2)
   SAFE ON THE MATTRESS, HANDS BRACED, AS FOR A FALL. .....THREE WOMEN 187 367
   ON A STRIPED MATTRESS IN ONE ROOM ....BERCK-PLAGE 198 50
MAUDLIN (2)
   MAUDLIN ....MAUDLIN 51 T
   MAUDLIN FROM LEAKY EYE TO SWOLLEN NOSE. ....THE RAVAGED FACE 115 4
MAUNCHING (1)
   MAUNCHING THISTLE AND KNOTWEED ON HER SNOUT-CRUISE -- ....SOW 61 19
MAUNDERING (1)
   IN TARNISHED MODES, MAUNDERING AMONG THE WASTES, ...OUIJA 77 13
MAUSOLEUM (3)
   I WAKE TO A MAUSOLEUM; YOU ARE HERE, ...THE RIVAL 166 7
   THE MAUSOLEUM, THE WAX HOUSE. ....STINGS 215 60
   INTO A NEW MAUSOLEUM, ...THE SWARM 217 49
MAUVE (1)
   TURQUOISE, ROSE, SIERRA MAUVE; NEEDLES ....MORNING IN THE HOS. 332 14
MAWKISH (1)
   KINDLY WITH INVALIDS AND MAWKISH WOMEN, ...CANDLES 149 25
MAY (43)
   "MAY COCKCROW GUARD US SAFE," SAID HE; ....BUCOLICS 23 6
   HOWEVER YOU MAY SWEAT TO HOLD SUCH DARLING WRECKS ...EPITAPH FOR F. 45 13
   GERD WHIRLS THE BALL ABLAZE: "ROUGH STORM," SHE GRANTS, "MAY WREAK ...
                          ... CRYSTAL GAZER 55 22
   HOWEVER THE GRANDILOQUENT MIND MAY SCORN ....NOVEMBER GRAVEYARD 56 5
   A CERTAIN MINOR LIGHT MAY STILL ....BLACK ROOK IN RAINY WEATHER 57 14
   OF WHATEVER ANGEL MAY CHOOSE TO FLARE ..BLACK ROOK IN RAINY WEATHER 57 26
   THEY NAMED THEIR SHIP AFTER THE FLOWER OF MAY. ....MAYFLOWER 60 14
   PERSEUS, THE PALM, AND MAY YOU POISE ....PERSEUS 84 47
   WAIST DOWN, YOU MAY WIND ....FULL FATHOM FIVE 93 33
   DEATH MAY WHITEN IN SUN OR OUT OF IT. ....MOONRISE 98 18
   AND BLEED. THE WHITE STOMACH MAY RIPEN YET. ....MOONRISE 98 30
   TWIST OLD WORDS INTO THE WEB-THREADS: TONIGHT MAY THE FISH ...NET-. 121 17
   ANY DAY I MAY LITTER PUPPIES POEM.2.DARK. 132 12
   PRAYS UNDER HER BREATH THAT SHE MAY SAVE ....ON DECK 143 23
   SHE MAY BE A SAINT, AND I MAY BE UGLY AND HAIRY, ...IN PLASTER 160 53
   SHE MAY BE A SAINT, AND I MAY BE UGLY AND HAIRY, ...IN PLASTER 160 53
   SO THAT EACH MARCH I MAY GLEAM INTO LEAF, ...I AM VERTICAL 162 4
   THEN THE TREES MAY TOUCH ME FOR ONCE, AND THE FLOWERS HAVE TIME
       FOR ME. ....I AM VERTICAL 162 20
   HIS SOUL MAY BEAT AND BE BEATING AT HER DULL SENSE ....WIDOW 165 37
   THERE IS NO GUILE OR WARP IN HIM. MAY HE KEEP SO. ......THREE WOMEN 181 175
   AND NEWTS ARE PRODIGAL IN LEGS. AND MAY I BE ....THREE WOMEN 184 258
   THE STREETS MAY TURN TO PAPER SUDDENLY, BUT I RECOVER ..THREE WOMEN 187 365
   THIS FIRE MAY LICK AND FAWN, BUT IT IS MERCILESS: ....BURNING. 204 15
   ONE DAY YOU MAY TOUCH WHAT'S WRONG ....FOR A FATHERLESS SON 205 12
   THEY MAY BE WHITE AND SHY THEY ARE NO STOOL PIGEONS, ...COURAGE. 210 31
   I THINK I MAY WELL BE A JEW. ....DADDY 223 35
   I MAY BE A BIT OF A JEW. ....*DADDY 223 40
   I SAY I MAY BE BACK. ....LESBOS 230 90
   I THINK I MAY RISE --- ....FEVER. 232 44
   SHE MAY BE BALD, SHE MAY HAVE NO EYES, ...THE TOUR 238 43
   SHE MAY BE BALD, SHE MAY HAVE NO EYES, ...THE TOUR 238 43
   I MAY BE SKIN AND BONE, ...LADY LAZARUS 245 33
   I THINK I MAY BE ENORMOUS, ...LETTER IN NOVEMBER 253 12
   YOU MAY BE LOCAL, ...EAVESDROPPER 260 10

MAY (CONT.)
    A RABBIT'S CRY MAY BE WILDER ....KINDNESS   269   7
    MAY BE PINNED ANY MINUTE, ANESTHETIZED. ....KINDNESS   269   15
    OR YOUR WHITE-HAIRED BENEFACTRESS, WHO MAY SEE FIT .....DIALOGUE O.   277   48
    MAY TESTIFY TO DRIVE YOUR DOUBTING OUT. *DIALOGUE OVER A OUIJA BOARD   280   153
    A SOLID SHAPE ON AIR. MAY THE DECORUM ..DIALOGUE OVER A OUIJA BOARD   286   360
    OF OUR DAYS SUSTAIN US. MAY EACH THOUGHT*DIALOGUE OVER A OUIJA BOARD   286   361
    MAY TWO REAL PEOPLE BREATHE IN A REAL ROOM. ....DIALOGUE O.   286   364
    AND A TITLED LADY MAY FREQUENTLY BE A BEAUTY. ....QUEEN MARY'S.   290   22
    "O MAY G-MEN ALL DIE OF THE CHOLER, ...DIALOGUE EN ROUTE   308   15
MAYBE (4)
    I MISS ORION AND CASSIOPEIA'S CHAIR. MAYBE THEY ARE ....STARS.   165   18
    WALKING ABOUT IN AFRICA MAYBE, BUT THINKING OF ME. ....THE RIVAL   167   17
    ISN'T IN HIM. MAYBE. BUT MAYBE THE POOLS*DIALOGUE OVER A OUIJA BOARD   277   42
    ISN'T IN HIM. MAYBE. BUT MAYBE THE POOLS*DIALOGUE OVER A OUIJA BOARD   277   42
MAYDAY (1)
    MAYDAY: TWO CAME TO FIELD IN SUCH WISE: ....BUCOLICS   23   1
MAYFLOWER (1)
    MAYFLOWER ....MAYFLOWER   60   T
MAYOR'S (1)
    AND THE MAYOR'S ROTISSERIE TURNS ....THE TIMES ARE TIDY   107   4
MAZE (3)
    MAZE OF BARNS TO THE LINTEL OF THE SUNK STY DOOR ....SOW   60   9
    WE STROLL THROUGH A MAZE OF PALE ....MAGNOLIA SHOALS   121   2
    THOUGHTS THAT FOUND A MAZE OF MERMAID HAIR ....TWO LOVERS.   327   5
MAZES (1)
    AMONG THE JAGGED MAZES OF THE ROCKS. ..THE PRINCESS AND THE GOBLINS   334   34
ME (273)
MEAD (2)
    "A DAISIED MEAD," EACH SAID TO EACH, ...BUCOLICS   23   2
    LET NIGHT BLESS THAT LUCK-ROOTED MEAD OF CLOVER *WREATH FOR A BRIDAL   45   17
MEADOW (3)
    KNELT IN THE MEADOW MUTE AS BOULDERS; ....HARDCASTLE CRAGS   63   33
    A DEVON MEADOW MIGHT OFFER A SIMPLER SORT   QUEEN MARY'S ROSE GARDEN   290   23
    IN THE RAMSHACKLE MEADOW ....TEMPER OF TIME   336   13
MEADOWS (5)
    MEADOWS OF GOLD DUST. THE SILVER ....IN MIDAS' COUNTRY   99   1
    WATERCOLOR OF GRANTCHESTER MEADOWS ....WATERCOLOR.   111   T
    HEDGING MEADOWS OF BENIGN ....WATERCOLOR OF GRANTCHESTER MEADOWS   112   19
    THE HIGH, GREEN MEADOWS ARE GLOWING, AS IF LIT FROM WITHIN. ...
                                             ... BLACKBERRYING   168   14
    HOT NOON IN THE MEADOWS. THE BUTTERCUPS ....THREE WOMEN   186   337
MEAGER (2)
    ROOT-PALE HER MEAGER FRAME. ....TWO SISTERS OF PERSEPHONE   31   12
    MEAGER OF DIMENSION AS THE GRAY PEOPLE ....THE THIN PEOPLE   64   2
MEAL (1)
    THOUGH PRIME PARTS CRAM EACH RICH MEAL, ...THE GLUTTON   40   11
MEAN (8)
    WHICH SEEMED, WHEN DREAMED, TO MEAN SO PROFOUNDLY MUCH, ...GHOST'S.   90   5
    IT IS COMFORTABLE, FOR A CHANGE, TO MEAN SO LITTLE. ......TWO CAMP.   145   17
    I SAW THE WORLD IN IT -- SMALL, MEAN AND BLACK, ...THREE WOMEN   178   54
    IT WAS A DREAM, AND DID NOT MEAN A THING. ....THREE WOMEN   185   308
    DO NOT BE MEAN, I AM READY FOR ENORMITY. ....A BIRTHDAY PRESENT   207   23
    PURE? WHAT DOES IT MEAN? ....FEVER.   231   1
    BY WHATEVER THESE PINK THINGS MEAN. ....FEVER.   232   50
    UNDER YOUR FINGER? I MEAN, YOU DON'T PUSH ....DIALOGUE O.   277   33
MEANDER (1)
    AND MEANDER IN BLAND PLEATINGS UNDER ....IN MIDAS' COUNTRY   99   3
MEANEST (1)
    UNDER THE MEANEST TABLE. ....THE THIN PEOPLE   64   11
MEANING (4)
    BUT A CERTAIN MEANING GREEN. ....THE HERMIT AT OUTERMOST HOUSE   119   16
    HE GLIDED BY; HIS EYE HAD A BLACK MEANING. ....THREE WOMEN   178   53
    MEANING LEAKS FROM THE MOLECULES. ....MYSTIC   269   27
    TO OUR MEANING WELL. WHEN LIGHTS GO OUT *DIALOGUE OVER A OUIJA BOARD   286   363
MEANINGLESS (1)
    THE MEANINGLESS CRY OF BABIES. SUCH A SEA ....DIALOGUE O.   294   4
MEANLY (1)
    MEN HAVE USED HER MEANLY. SHE WILL EAT THEM. ....THREE WOMEN   181   159
MEANS (7)
    BUT NEARING MEANS DISTANCING: ....THE GREAT CARBUNCLE   73   27
    BY NO MIRACLE OR MAJESTIC MEANS, ...A LESSON IN VENGEANCE   80   5
    I'M A MEANS, A STAGE, A COW IN CALF. ....METAPHORS   116   7
    I AM FLAT AND VIRGINAL, WHICH MEANS NOTHING HAS HAPPENED, ...THREE.   184   276
    IT MEANS: NO MORE IDOLS BUT ME, ...THE MUNICH MANNEQUINS   263   8
    TOO LATE TO ASK IF END WAS WORTH THE MEANS, ...DOOMSDAY   316   16
    IF YOU CAN THINK OF MEANS TO MEND THE VOW ....THE DISPOSSESSED   318   13
MEANT (5)
    HER ANTELOPE WHO MEANT HIM NAUGHT BUT GOOD. ..THE QUEEN'S COMPLAINT   28   10
    TWO OF US IN A PLACE MEANT FOR TEN MORE -- ....THE OTHER TWO   68   10
    TO BE MEANT FOR CLIMBING. A PECULIAR LOGIC ....ABOVE THE OXBOW   88   17
    THIS IS NOT WHAT I MEANT: ....WHITSUN   153   1
    THE SECOND TIME I MEANT ....LADY LAZARUS   245   37
MEANWHILE (1)
    MEANWHILE THERE'S A STINK OF FAT AND BABY CRAP. ....LESBOS   228   33

	TITLE	PAGE	LINE

MEASURE (2)
IN THIS COUNTRY THERE IS NEITHER MEASURE NOR BALANCE .....TWO CAMP. 144 1
TO CHART THE MEASURE OF FORTUNE'S WHEEL; ....SONG FOR A REVOLU. 323 11
MEASURING (1)
MEASURING THE FLOUR, CUTTING OFF THE SURPLUS, ...A BIRTHDAY PRESENT 206 7
MEAT (8)
MEAT MUST GLUT HIS MOUTH'S RAW WOUND. ....PURSUIT 22 16
THAT ALL MERIT'S IN BEING MEAT ....THE GLUTTON 40 5
KEEP FROM CUTTING FAT MEAT ....THE THIN PEOPLE 65 27
WITHOUT MEAT OR DRINK I SAT ....ON THE PLETHORA OF DRYADS 67 7
GLUT THESE HUNTERS AFTER AN OLD MEAT, ...AFTERMATH 113 7
AND THE POTS OF MEAT. POEM.2.DARK. 132 18
I AM RED MEAT. HIS BEAK ....DEATH & CO. 254 10
FOR FEAST THE SWEETEST MEAT OF HELL'S CHEF D'OEUVRES: ....TERMINAL 328 11
MEAT-AND-POTATO (1)
OF OUR MEAT-AND-POTATO THOUGHTS ASSUMES THE NIMBUS ....GHOST'S. 90 14
MEATHOOK (1)
ASSUMES, LIKE A MEATHOOK, THE BURDEN OF HIS PARTS. ....THE OTHER 201 6
MECHANIC (1)
COGS AND DISKS, INANE MECHANIC WHIMS, ...SONNET: TO EVA 304 7
MECHANICAL (1)
THESE ARE MY FEET, THESE MECHANICAL ECHOES. ....THREE WOMEN 177 34
MEDALLION (1)
MEDALLION ....MEDALLION 124 T
MEDEA (1)
MOTHER MEDEA IN A GREEN SMOCK ....AFTERMATH 114 9
MEDICINE (1)
AIR LIKE A MEDICINE. ....WHITSUN 153 6
MEDITATE (5)
SMILING TO THEMSELVES, THEY MEDITATE ....HEAVY WOMEN 158 8
MOST OF THE TIME I MEDITATE ON THE OPPOSITE WALL. ....MIRROR 173 6
I SHALL MEDITATE UPON NORMALITY. ....THREE WOMEN 186 323
I SHALL MEDITATE UPON MY LITTLE SON. ....THREE WOMEN 186 324
WHOSE NAMES YOU MEDITATE -- ....CHILD 265 4
MEDIUM (3)
CAUGHT IN A HAZARDOUS MEDIUM THAT MIGHT ....VANITY FAIR 32 3
THEY ARE MY MEDIUM. ...................................APPREHENSIONS 195 4
MIGHT WORK ON THIS GLASS MEDIUM. BELIEF, YES, ...DIALOGUE O. 282 225
MEDUSA (1)
MEDUSA ....MEDUSA 224 T
MEEK (3)
MEEK AND PROUD BOTH FALL; STARK VIOLENCE ....CHANNEL CROSSING 27 30
TABLES, WE ARE MEEK, ...MUSHROOMS 139 26
CHOKING THE AGED AND THE MEEK, ...FEVER. 231 17
MEET (12)
I SHALL GO DOWN THE SHABBY STAIR AND MEET,*ON THE DECLINE OF ORACLES 78 27
MEET THE THIN AND SLUGGISH THREAD .....MUSSEL HUNTER AT ROCK HARBOR 96 42
I SET MY EYE TO A HOLE-MOUTH AND MEET AN EYE ....BEEKEEPER'S. 118 17
WHO ARE THESE PEOPLE AT THE BRIDGE TO MEET ME? THEY ARE THE
VILLAGERS --- ....THE BEE MEETING 211 1
WE SHOULD MEET IN ANOTHER LIFE, WE SHOULD MEET IN AIR, ...LESBOS 228 31
WE SHOULD MEET IN ANOTHER LIFE, WE SHOULD MEET IN AIR, ...LESBOS 228 31
EVEN IN YOUR ZEN HEAVEN WE SHAN'T MEET. ....LESBOS 230 92
THIS IS THE FLUID IN WHICH WE MEET EACH OTHER, ...BY CANDLELIGHT 236 10
IN THE LANE I MEET SHEEP AND WAGONS, ...BRASILIA 258 16
IT IS BEST TO MEET IN A CUL-DE-SAC, ...GIGOLO 267 4
TO A CINDER, THAN MEET A POOR UPSTART OF OUR NETHER ....DIALOGUE O. 280 133
TRAIN TRACKS ALWAYS MEET, NOT HERE, BUT ONLY ....LOVE IS A PARALLAX 329 2
MEETING (2)
THE BEE MEETING ....THE BEE MEETING 211 T
OH, HEAR THE CLASH OF PEOPLE MEETING -- ....FAMILY REUNION 300 11
MEETINGS (1)
SUCH MEETINGS NEVER OCCUR IN MARCHEN ..................INCOMMUNICADO 100 8
MEETS (2)
THIS WOMAN WHO MEETS ME IN WINDOWS -- SHE IS NEAT. .....THREE WOMEN 184 280
MEETS THE CORPSE AT THE GATE, ...BERCK-PLAGE 200 94
MEINKAMPF (1)
A MAN IN BLACK WITH A MEINKAMPF LOOK ....DADDY 224 65
MEISSEN (1)
IT SPREADS ITSELF OUT, A MILE-LONG BODY OF MEISSEN, ...WINTERING 218 35
MELDING (1)
A MELDING OF SHAPES IN A HOT RAIN: ....THE EYE-MOTE 109 11
MELLOW (1)
FRESH FROM THE MELLOW PALETTE OF MATISSE: ....MIDSUMMER MOBILE 324 12
MELON (1)
A MELON STROLLING ON TWO TENDRILS. ....METAPHORS 116 3
MELON-EATING (1)
THIS MARKET OF MELON-EATING ....FIESTA MELONS 47 19
MELONS (3)
FIESTA MELONS ....FIESTA MELONS 46 T
IN BENIDORM THERE ARE MELONS, ...FIESTA MELONS 46 1
OF INNUMERABLE MELONS, ...FIESTA MELONS 46 3
MELT (6)
CHEEKS ALIGHTING EACH MOMENT TO MELT ....LOVE LETTER 147 14
SWELTER AND MELT, AND THE LOVERS ....THREE WOMEN 186 338

312

MELT (CONT.)
   SMELL THE MELT OF SHOE-BLACKING, ...BERCK-PLAGE   201 119
   THEY MELT AND SAG, THEY ARE TOLD   ....BURNING THE LETTERS   204   18
   THE GILT AND PINK DOMES OF RUSSIA MELT AND FLOAT OFF   .....THE SWARM   216   15
   FIELDS MELT MY HEART.   ....SHEEP IN FOG   262   12
MELTED (1)
   COT LEGS MELTED IN TERRIBLE ATTITUDES, AND THE NURSES --   ...WAKING.   151   12
MELTING (7)
   TANGED BY MELTING TAR, ...DREAM WITH CLAM-DIGGERS   44   10
   TO A MELTING OF GREEN WATERS, TILL NO SNAKE   ..........SNAKECHARMER   79   25
   LOOK, THEY ARE MELTING LIKE COINS IN THE POWERFUL JUICES --   ZOO K.   154   8
   THE DARK IS MELTING. WE TOUCH LIKE CRIPPLES.   ....EVENT   195   22
   TOUCHING AND MELTING.   ....THE NIGHT DANCES   250   27
   MELTING THE TALLOW HERETICS, ...MARY'S SONG   257   7
   YOU'RE MELTING NOW, BECAUSE YOU THINK HE'S HIT   ....DIALOGUE O.   278   80
MELTS (4)
   AND BRIM; THE CITY MELTS LIKE SUGAR.   ....PARLIAMENT HILL FIELDS   152   12
   MELTS IN THE WALL.   ....ARIEL   239   25
   THAT MELTS TO A SHRIEK.   ....LADY LAZARUS   246   70
   THAT MELTS THE SKIN   .....................................EAVESDROPPER   260   22
MEMBER (1)
   AND I AM DARK-SUITED AND STILL, A MEMBER OF THE PARTY,   BERCK-PLAGE   200 111
MEMOIRS (1)
   MEMOIRS OF A SPINACH-PICKER   ....MEMOIRS OF A SPINACH-PICKER   89   T
MEMORIES (2)
   MEMORIES JOSTLE EACH OTHER FOR FACE-ROOM LIKE OBSOLETE FILM
      STARS.   ....INSOMNIAC   163   14
   MEMORIES GROWING, RING ON RING, ...WINTER TREES   257   4
MEMORY (4)
   PROFITED MEMORY, BUT DID AWAY WITH THE OLD SCENERY   .....GREEN ROCK.   105   5
   I AM LAME IN THE MEMORY.   ....LITTLE FUGUE   188   44
   THE EMPTY BENCHES OF MEMORY LOOK OVER STONES, ...BERCK-PLAGE   199   88
   THE WALKING BESIDE STILL WATER? MEMORY?   ....MYSTIC   268   17
MEN (29)
   OF OTHER MEN, WHERE STATUES CELEBRATE   ....CHANNEL CROSSING   27   38
   TO SUMMON IN HER SLIGHT ALL DOUGHTY MEN   ......THE QUEEN'S COMPLAINT   29   17
   WHO OGLE MEN   ....RHYME   50   6
   STUNNED THE MARROW. MEN IN WHITE   ....NIGHT SHIFT   77   20
   BUT THREE MEN ENTERING THE YARD, ...ON THE DECLINE OF ORACLES   78   20
   AND THOSE MEN COMING UP THE STAIR.   ......ON THE DECLINE OF ORACLES   78   21
   RAISED HIS MEN OF SKIN AND BONE, ...I WANT, I WANT   106   10
   THEY HAD FOUR MEN LAID OUT, BLACK AS BURNT TURKEY, ...TWO VIEWS.   114   2
   THIS IS THE CITY WHERE MEN ARE MENDED. POEM.7.S.   136   1
   DEAD MEN LEAVE EYES FOR OTHERS. POEM.7.S.   137   38
   ONE CAN REMEMBER MEN AND HOUSES BY.   .....SLEEP IN THE MOJAVE DESERT   143   7
   THE STAR, THE WISE GRAY MEN.   ....HEAVY WOMEN   158   21
   I WATCHED THE MEN WALK ABOUT ME IN THE OFFICE. THEY WERE SO
      FLAT!   ....THREE WOMEN   177   16
   THE FACELESS FACES OF IMPORTANT MEN.   ....THREE WOMEN   179   84
   IT IS THESE MEN I MIND: ....THREE WOMEN   179   85
   MEN HAVE USED HER MEANLY. SHE WILL EAT THEM.   ....THREE WOMEN   181 159
   DEAD MEN CRY FROM IT.   ....LITTLE FUGUE   188   27
   DULLY, UNDER A PACK OF MEN IN RED JACKETS, ...BURNING THE LETTERS   204   13
   THEY HAVE GOT RID OF THE MEN, ...WINTERING   218   40
   IN NEW YORK, IN HOLLYWOOD, THE MEN SAID: "THROUGH?   ....LESBOS   228   41
   AND I EAT MEN LIKE AIR.   ....LADY LAZARUS   247   84
   THE MEN THE BLOOD STILL PUMPS FORWARD, ...GETTING THERE   248   25
   AND THE MEN, WHAT IS LEFT OF THE MEN   ....GETTING THERE   248   29
   AND THE MEN, WHAT IS LEFT OF THE MEN   ....GETTING THERE   248   29
   THE FIELDS WERE FULL OF BRONZED YOUNG MEN   .....BITTER STRAWBERRIES   299   18
   WITH MANY MEN UNTIL I CRASHED   ....THE DREAM   310   9
   ENCHANTING MEN   ....MOONSONG AT MORNING   316   2
   DEAD MEN RENDER LOVE AND WAR NO HEED, ...THE DEAD   320   3
   AND HIDDEN ALL THE BRIGHT ANGELIC MEN.   ......EPITAPH IN THREE PARTS   338   31
MENACE (3)
   NOW HILLS HATCH MENACE, SPAWNING SHADE;   ....PURSUIT   22   25
   INTO OUR BAD DREAMS, THEIR MENACE   ....THE THIN PEOPLE   64   15
   PARRIES THE LUNGE AND MENACE   ....AERIALIST   331   20
MEND (3)
   TO MEND THE IMMENSE SKULL-PLATES AND CLEAR   ....THE COLOSSUS   129   14
   HOLDING MY BONES IN PLACE SO THEY WOULD MEND PROPERLY.   ..IN PLASTER   159   27
   IF YOU CAN THINK OF MEANS TO MEND THE VOW   ....THE DISPOSSESSED   318   13
MENDED (1)
   THIS IS THE CITY WHERE MEN ARE MENDED. POEM.7.S.   136   1
MENDING (5)
   AND WHATEVER PAN THIS MENDING MASTER *TINKER JACK AND THE TIDY WIVES   34   3
   I AM MENDING A SILK SLIP: MY HUSBAND IS READING.   ....THREE WOMEN   186 352
   THE FLOWERS VIVID AS BANDAGES, AND THE MAN MENDING.   .....NARCISSI.   190   8
   IT'S DONE. IT'S DONE, AND THERE'S NO MENDING HIM.   ......DIALOGUE O.   285 304
   IT WAS HIS TONGUE THAT WANTED MENDING. YOU KNOW.   ....DIALOGUE O.   285 305
MENDINGS (1)
   MY MENDINGS ITCH. THERE IS NOTHING TO DO. POEM.7.S.   137   44
MEN'S (2)
   SUCH POVERTY. NO DEAD MEN'S CRIES   ....NOVEMBER GRAVEYARD   56   6

```
                                              TITLE            PAGE  LINE
MEN'S (CONT.)
    SO FABLES SAY THE GOATSUCKER MOVES, MASKED FROM MEN'S SIGHT ...
                                        ... GOATSUCKER  111    9
MENTALITY (1)
    YOU COULD TELL ALMOST AT ONCE SHE HAD A SLAVE MENTALITY. *IN PLASTER 159   21
MEPHISTOPHELES (1)
    MOCKING AS MEPHISTOPHELES, ...................CIRCUS IN THREE RINGS  322   13
MERCIES (1)
    LENS OF MERCIES, ................................................MEDUSA  224    5
MERCILESS (3)
    THE MOON, ALSO, IS MERCILESS: SHE WOULD DRAG ME ................ELM  192   22
    THIS FIRE MAY LICK AND FAWN, BUT IT IS MERCILESS: .........BURNING.  204   15
    THEIR MERCILESS CHURN. .......................................YEARS  255   15
MERCURIAL (1)
    OF THAT MERCURIAL STRAND, THE GIRL GOES DOWN .........THE PRINCESS.  334   27
MERCURIC (1)
    LET THE MERCURIC ..........................NICK AND THE CANDLESTICK  242   37
MERCURY (2)
    FLEES AND ABORTS LIKE DROPPED MERCURY. ..................THALIDOMIDE  252   26
    OF MERCURY IN GRADED TUBES, WHERE ILLS .........MORNING IN THE HOS.  332   17
MERCURY-BACKED (1)
    FROM THE MERCURY-BACKED GLASS ....................ALL THE DEAD DEARS   70   19
MERCY (2)
    THIS BLACK BOOT HAS NO MERCY FOR ANYBODY. .............BERCK-PLAGE   197   19
    THERE IS NO MERCY IN THE GLITTER OF CLEAVERS, .................TOTEM  264    9
MERE (7)
    THAT WRESTLE WITH US LIKE ANGELS, THE MERE CHANCE   CHANNEL CROSSING   27   18
    MERE BRUIT OF HER TAKES OUR STREET ...................STRUMPET SONG   33    5
    AS NO MERE INSURGENT MAN COULD HOPE TO BREAK .............SPINSTER   50   28
    HER DOWN TO MERE QUARTZ GRIT IN THE STONY LIGHT ...HARDCASTLE CRAGS   63   44
    THEMSELVES MERE ROCKY HILLOCKS TO AN EVEREST. ......ABOVE THE OXBOW   87    4
    I WAS PERFECTLY RIGHT: PAN'S A MERE PUPPET ...........DIALOGUE O.   279  106
    THAT LIFE WAS A MERE MONUMENTAL SHAM. ...........DIRGE FOR A JOKER   302    8
MERELY (5)
    NAKED IN THE MERELY ACTUAL ROOM, ......................TALE OF A TUB   24    5
    MERELY BY ITS CONTINUING ..................................VANITY FAIR   32    4
    A WORLD WE LOSE BY MERELY WAKING UP. .......THE GHOST'S LEAVETAKING   90   20
    AN ORIGINAL NOTE. IF HE'D SAID, HOWEVER, MERELY: .......DIALOGUE O.  278   81
    THE MUTE AIR MERELY THINS AND THINS. ....METAMORPHOSES OF THE MOON   307    6
MERIDIAN (1)
    HAND IN HAND, THEY SCALE MERIDIAN, ....THE PRINCESS AND THE GOBLINS  334   54
MERIT (1)
    LET THEM ASTOUND HIS HEART WITH THEIR MERIT. ...................MAGI  148   17
MERIT'S (1)
    THAT ALL MERIT'S IN BEING MEAT ........................THE GLUTTON   40    5
MERMAID (2)
    A MERMAID ODALISQUE LOLLS AT HER EASE ............MIDSUMMER MOBILE   324   10
    THOUGHTS THAT FOUND A MAZE OF MERMAID HAIR .............TWO LOVERS.  327    5
MERMAIDS (1)
    ON MERMAIDS AND TWO-LEGGED DREAMGIRLS. ..THE COURAGE OF SHUTTING-UP  210   13
MERRY-GO-ROUND (1)
    GO! AND THE MERRY-GO-ROUND ...........................TOUCH-AND-GO   335   15
MESH (1)
    WHILE THEIR FINGERS WORK WITH THE COARSE MESH AND THE FINE ...NET-.  121   11
MESS (2)
    A BIT OF A WILD MACHINE, A BIT OF A MESS! .................THE TOUR  237   12
    IN PAN: IT'S BEEN EBBING EVER SINCE THE MESS ...........DIALOGUE O.  277   38
MESSAGE (2)
    A THIN, SILLY MESSAGE. .........................WUTHERING HEIGHTS   167   24
    AND THE MESSAGE OF THE YEW TREE IS BLACKNESS -- BLACKNESS AND
            SILENCE. ..........................THE MOON AND THE YEW TREE  173   28
MESSY (1)
    LEFTOVER SOLDIERS FROM OLD, MESSY WARS. ..................FINISTERRE  169    7
MET (2)
    NO CHANGE MET HER: GARDEN TERRACE, ALL SUMMER ........DREAM WITH C.   44    9
    AND ARE MET, INSTEAD, BY THIS ICERIBBED SHIP, ........A WINTER SHIP  113   25
METAL (9)
    A METAL DETONATING .......................................NIGHT SHIFT   76    7
    TONNAGE OF METAL AND WOOD; ..............................NIGHT SHIFT   77   19
    EVEN, A TANG OF METAL. DAY IN, DAY OUT, ............ABOVE THE OXBOW   89   16
    WINTER DAWN IS THE COLOR OF METAL, ...................WAKING IN WINTER  151    2
    BEATING AND BEATING AT AN INTRACTABLE METAL. ........BLACKBERRYING   169   27
    THE BEADS OF HOT METAL FLY, AND I, LOVE, I ..................FEVER.  232   45
    GOLD LEAVES METAL AND BREATHLESS. .............LETTER IN NOVEMBER   253   30
    AND WE ARE GLAD IN THIS BRIGHT METAL SEASON. .......GOLD MOUTHS CRY  302    8
    OBSERVING THE WRECK OF METAL AND RARE STONE. .......SONNET: TO EVA  304    4
METALS (3)
    VARIOUS METALS. ........................DARK WOOD, DARK WATER   127   14
    RED AND YELLOW, TWO PASSIONATE HOT METALS ............STOPPED DEAD   230    8
    BEATEN IN STARRY METALS. ................................BALLOONS   272   19
METAMORPHOSE (1)
    METAMORPHOSE THE MOLLUSK .....................NOTES TO A NEOPHYTE   306    7
METAMORPHOSES (1)
    METAMORPHOSES OF THE MOON ...............METAMORPHOSES OF THE MOON   307    T
```

	TITLE	PAGE	LINE

METAPHOR (2)
    AND LOST IN SUBTLE METAPHOR, RETREATS ....FEMALE AUTHOR   301   13
    MAD HATTER'S HAT YIELDS NO NEW METAPHOR, ...A SORCERER B.   324   10
METAPHORS (2)
    METAPHORS ....METAPHORS   116   T
    AND JONQUILS SPROUT LIKE SOLOMON'S METAPHORS, ...APRIL AUBADE   312   11
METAPHYSICAL (1)
    TO DISCOVER THAT METAPHYSICAL TREE WHICH HID ...PLETHORA OF DRYADS.   67   9
METHINKS (1)
    METHINKS I SHALL ABSENT ME FOR A WHILE ....A SORCERER B.   324   3
METRONOMES (1)
    METRONOMES THE BLOOD, ...TRIO OF LOVE SONGS   314   10
METROPOLIS (2)
    A TALL METROPOLIS OF CATACOMBS ....DOOM OF EXILES   318   3
    WIND WAKES THE WHOLE METROPOLIS.*INSOLENT STORM STRIKES AT THE SKULL   325   6
MEXICAN (1)
    JUMPY AS A MEXICAN BEAN. ....YOU'RE   141   16
MICA (2)
    ON THE ROAD NAMED FOR TOMAS ORTUNIO, MICA ....THE NET-MENDERS   121   8
    THE CHOICE BETWEEN THE MICA MYSTERY ......METAMORPHOSES OF THE MOON   308   37
MICA-SCALED (1)
    I SHONE, MICA-SCALED, AND UNFOLDED ....LOVE LETTER   147   25
MICA-SILVER (1)
    AND EVERYWHERE PEOPLE, EYES MICA-SILVER AND BLANK, ...INSOMNIAC   163   34
MICE (5)
    PLUMPED THE BELLIES OF THE MICE ....THE THIN PEOPLE   64   10
    LISTEN: YOUR TENANT MICE ....LEAVING EARLY   146   35
    OBSCENE AND BALD AS A PIG, THE WHITE MICE ....ZOO KEEPER'S WIFE   155   21
    EYES LIKE MICE ....EAVESDROPPER   261   54
    NINE BLACK MICE WITH EBON COACH, *BLACK PINE TREE IN AN ORANGE LIGHT   328   6
MICROBES (1)
    THE MICROBES CANNOT SURVIVE IT. ....THE SURGEON AT 2 A.M.   170   2
MICROSCOPE (1)
    OF MICROSCOPE: ....MOONSONG AT MORNING   317   32
MIDAIR (1)
    STALLING IN MIDAIR, ...A LIFE   150   13
MIDAS (1)
    AUGUST GIVES OVER ITS MIDAS TOUCH, ...IN MIDAS' COUNTRY   100   24
MIDAS' (1)
    IN MIDAS' COUNTRY ....IN MIDAS' COUNTRY   99   T
MID-ATLANTIC (1)
    MIDNIGHT IN THE MID-ATLANTIC. ON DECK. ....ON DECK   142   1
MIDDEN (2)
    FROM HIS CRABBED MIDDEN WHERE ALL'S WROUGHT SO AWRY ....FIRESONG   30   10
    OVER HER SKULL'S MIDDEN; NO KNIFE ....VANITY FAIR   32   12
MIDDLE (3)
    OF POPLARS IN THE MIDDLE DISTANCE, THE ONLY ....SLEEP.   143   5
    TURNING AND TURNING IN THE MIDDLE AIR, ...GETTING THERE   249   53
    ALWAYS IN THE MIDDLE OF A KISS ....DIRGE FOR A JOKER   302   1
MIDGET (1)
    I WOULD SAY IT WAS THE COFFIN OF A MIDGET*THE ARRIVAL OF THE BEE BOX   212   3
MIDNIGHT (6)
    MIDNIGHT CLOAKS THE SULTRY GROVE; ....PURSUIT   22   26
    THE MIDNIGHT STREET ....SOLILOQUY OF THE SOLIPSIST   37   3
    AND INTENSITY BY MIDNIGHT ....CHILD'S PARK STONES   101   19
    MIDNIGHT IN THE MID-ATLANTIC. ON DECK. ....ON DECK   142   1
    MIDNIGHT, FOUR O'CLOCK, ...EAVESDROPPER   260   29
    FIGURED IN THE MIDNIGHT SKY, ...TO A JILTED LOVER   309   4
MIDST (1)
    IN THE MIDST OF ALL THAT GREEN AND THOSE GREAT LILIES! ...YADWIGHA.   86   39
MIDSUMMER (1)
    MIDSUMMER MOBILE ....MIDSUMMER MOBILE   324   T
MIDWIFE (4)
    THE MIDWIFE SLAPPED YOUR FOOTSOLES, AND YOUR BALD CRY   MORNING SONG   156   2
    THE RECTOR, THE MIDWIFE, THE SEXTON, THE AGENT FOR BEES. ......BEE.   211   2
    WHICH IS THE MIDWIFE, IS THAT HER BLUE COAT? ....THE BEE MEETING   211   12
    SHE'S PINK, SHE'S A BORN MIDWIFE -- ....THE TOUR   238   45
MIDWIFE'S (1)
    I HAVE WHIRLED THE MIDWIFE'S EXTRACTOR, ...WINTERING   217   2
MIEN (1)
    THAT NOBLE MIEN, PERHAPS YOU'VE LATE QUITTED HEAVEN?" ..DIALOGUE B.   38   16
MIGHT (32)
    WHOSE FORCE MIGHT FIT ....THE QUEEN'S COMPLAINT   29   18
    CAUGHT IN A HAZARDOUS MEDIUM THAT MIGHT ....VANITY FAIR   32   3
    YOU MIGHT AS WELL HAUL UP ....EPITAPH FOR FIRE AND FLOWER   45   1
    SO BEGGAR GERD MIGHT AIM HER LOOK ....CRYSTAL GAZER   55   40
    ONE MIGHT SAY LOVE. AT ANY RATE, I NOW WALK ....BLACK ROOK I.   57   22
    BUT BEFORE I MIGHT BLIND SENSE ....ON THE PLETHORA OF DRYADS   67   13
    WE MIGHT EMBRACE, BUT THOSE TWO NEVER DID, ...THE OTHER TWO   69   30
    MIGHT WELL SEIZE THIS PRIZE, ...THE LADY AND THE EARTHENWARE HEAD   69   12
    HIS SNAKEHOOD AND HIS MIGHT WITH PLIANT TUNES .........SNAKECHARMER   79   17
    DARK FACE. SO MIGHT RIGOR MORTIS COME TO STIFFEN ....PERSEUS   83   32
    AND NEVER SAW HOW COOLLY WE MIGHT MOVE. FOR ONCE ...ABOVE THE OXBOW   89   55
    KNIGHTS MIGHT DOFF THEIR CASQUES. THE CRABS ....MUSSEL HUNTER.   96   28
    ORDER AS I MIGHT PUZZLE ....MUSSEL HUNTER AT ROCK HARBOR   96   55

315

TITLE PAGE LINE

MIGHT (CONT)
IT MIGHT BE HEAVEN, THIS STATIC ....IN MIDAS' COUNTRY 99 11
AND THOUGH YOUR GRACIOUSNESS MIGHT STREAM, ...POINT SHIRLEY 111 44
SOME SCANDAL MIGHT ANY MINUTE OOZE ....AFTERMATH 113 4
ONE BREATH MIGHT SHIVER TO BITS, ...OLD LADIES' HOME 120 3
THE PILGRIMS AND INDIANS MIGHT NEVER HAVE HAPPENED. ......TWO CAMP. 145 22
OF VALENTINE-FACES MIGHT PLEASE A COLLECTOR: ....A LIFE 150 17
I USED TO THINK WE MIGHT MAKE A GO OF IT TOGETHER -- ....IN PLASTER 160 50
TOUCHED BY A MATCH, THEY MIGHT WARM ME, ...WUTHERING HEIGHTS 167 3
SUCH AS FINGERS MIGHT EMBROIDER, CLOSE TO DEATH, ...FINISTERRE 169 11
THEY MIGHT IGNORE ME IMMEDIATELY ....THE ARRIVAL OF THE BEE BOX 213 31
AUNTIE, IT MIGHT BITE! ....THE TOUR 237 14
A FUNNY PINK WORLD HE MIGHT EAT ON THE OTHER SIDE OF IT, ..BALLOONS 272 24
MIGHT DO AS A GOD'S MOUTHPIECE IF A WHIRLWIND ....DIALOGUE O. 281 202
MIGHT WORK ON THIS GLASS MEDIUM. BELIEF, YES, ...DIALOGUE O. 282 225
MIGHT RANGE IN IT. I ONLY SHUT THE DOOR *DIALOGUE OVER A OUIJA BOARD 286 344
A DEVON MEADOW MIGHT OFFER A SIMPLER SORT   QUEEN MARY'S ROSE GARDEN 290 23
I THOUGHT EARTH MIGHT USE YOU. ....THE RIVAL/DR 291 22
AND SUSPENDED ALL THAT MIGHT OCCUR? ....PROLOGUE TO SPRING 322 12
WE ARE NOT WHAT WE MIGHT BE; WHAT WE ARE ....TWO LOVERS. 327 9
MIGNON (1)
FILET MIGNON AND WALLOPING WINES, ...DIALOGUE EN ROUTE 308 10
MIGRAINE (2)
THE FLUORESCENT LIGHT WINCING ON AND OFF LIKE A TERRIBLE MIGRAINE, ...
... LESBOS 227 4
FINE FOR THE MIGRAINE OR THE BELLYACHE. AND THIS ....THE TOUR 238 19
MILD (6)
AND MILD OBEYING. ....THE SNOWMAN ON THE MOOR 59 51
MARY LOOKS MILD. ....A WINTER'S TALE 86 8
HOW IN SUCH MILD AIR ....WATERCOLOR OF GRANTCHESTER MEADOWS 112 27
TONIGHT, LIKE A SHAWL, THE MILD LIGHT ENFOLDS HER, ...CANDLES 149 34
BENDING, ON ME IN PARTICULAR, ITS MILD EYES. ....MOON. 173 21
THE MILD HILLS, THE SAME OLD MAGENTA ....THE SWARM 216 28
MILDNESS (1)
OR MUCH COMPANY, OR THE MILDNESS OF THE SOUTH. ....STARS. 166 30
MILE (1)
INTO THE NEXT MILE, ...GETTING THERE 248 31
MILEAGE (1)
THAT YOU SUCK BREATH LIKE MILEAGE? ....THE OTHER 202 24
MILE-LONG (1)
IT SPREADS ITSELF OUT, A MILE-LONG BODY OF MEISSEN, ...WINTERING 218 35
MILES (2)
CREST AND TROUGH. MILES LONG ....FULL FATHOM FIVE 92 6
IT STRETCHES FOR MILES, THE SHRUNK VOICES ....BERCK-PLAGE 196 8
MILK (14)
FOR THE MILK VAN ....RESOLVE 52 4
BLOAT TUN OF MILK ....SOW 61 20
THE MILK YOUR LOVE INSTILLED IN THEM. ....POINT SHIRLEY 111 42
VAMPIRING DRY OF MILK EACH GREAT GOAT UDDER. ....GOATSUCKER 111 4
SUNSET LOOKED AT THROUGH MILK GLASS. ....MEDALLION 124 20
THE BIRDS MADE MILK. POEM.3.MAENAD. 133 4
AND LOVE THE MOTHER OF MILK, NO THEORY. ....MAGI 148 14
THESE PURE, SMALL IMAGES. THEY SMELL OF MILK. ....THREE WOMEN 183 230
AND I AM A RIVER OF MILK. ....THREE WOMEN 183 237
THE MILK CAME YELLOW, THEN BLUE AND SWEET AS WATER. ..THE DETECTIVE 209 33
PITCHER OF MILK, NOW EMPTY. ....EDGE 272 11
THAT DRAINS ETERNALLY THE MILK OF STARS. ....SONNET: TO TIME 311 14
NO MILK OR HONEY FILLS THE EMPTY CAN; ....THE DISPOSSESSED 318 5
COUPLES COURT BY MILK OF MOON: ....DANSE MACABRE 321 20
MILKBOTTLE (1)
THEY ACCOMMODATE THEMSELVES TO MY MILKBOTTLE, FLATTENING THEIR
SIDES. ....BLACKBERRYING 168 9
MILKED (1)
YET IT NEVER MILKED ANY GOAT, NOR DEALT COW DEATH ....GOATSUCKER 111 12
MILKER (1)
TO THE ELECTRIC MILKER, THE WIFEY, THE BIG BLUE EYE ...EAVESDROPPER 261 43
MILK-FILM (1)
A MILK-FILM BLURS ....RESOLVE 52 10
MILKGREEN (1)
GLOW MILKGREEN: ....AQUATIC NOCTURNE 306 18
MILKING (1)
BUT THAT IT TURNED INTO A MILKING PAIL? ..METAMORPHOSES OF THE MOON 307 20
MILKLESS (1)
SAND ABRADED THE MILKLESS LIP. ....I WANT, I WANT 106 5
MILKMAN (1)
THE ORDINARY MILKMAN BROUGHT THAT DAWN ....THE TRIAL OF MAN 312 1
MILKS (2)
THE COW MILKS CREAM AN INCH THICK. ....THE TIMES ARE TIDY 107 15
CAN SUCH INNOCENCE KILL AND KILL? IT MILKS MY LIFE. ....THREE WOMEN 180 134
MILK-SPOUT (1)
MILK-SPOUT, BIG FINGER ....WORDS FOR A NURSERY 73 7
MILKWEED (2)
HAIRED SEED OF THE MILKWEED ....POLLY'S TREE 128 16
NOW I AM MILKWEED SILK, THE BEES WILL NOT NOTICE. ..THE BEE MEETING 211 9

	TITLE	PAGE	LINE

MILKY (4)
    LIKE MONDAY DRUNKARDS. THE MILKY BERRIES ....LEAVING EARLY 145 10
    GROWN MILKY, ALMOST CLEAR, LIKE THE BODIES OF SAINTS. ......CANDLES 148 4
    TO WAKEN DREAMERS IN THE MILKY DAWN, ...APRIL AUBADE 312 6
    ALONG BRIGHT ASTERISKS BY MILKY WAY. ..THE PRINCESS AND THE GOBLINS 333 12
MILL (3)
    MILL OF SILENCE ....CUT 236 36
    MILL A LITTER OF BREASTS LIKE JELLYFISH. ....GIGOLO 267 13
    THE AIR IS A MILL OF HOOKS -- ....MYSTIC 268 1
MILLE-FLEURS (1)
    OR, AT MOST, TO A MILLE-FLEURS TAPESTRY. BUT THE COUCH ...YADWIGHA. 85 17
MILLENNIUM (1)
    THEY LISTEN FOR THE MILLENNIUM, ...HEAVY WOMEN 158 13
MILLION (12)
    HOUSED IN EARTH, THOSE MILLION BRIDES SHRIEK OUT. ......VANITY FAIR 33 33
    A MILLION GREEN COUNTIES FROM HERE, ...MONOLOGUE AT 3 A.M. 40 7
    ON A GREEN BALLOON BRIGHT WITH A MILLION .....THE DISQUIETING MUSES 76 43
    CRIES AND HEROIC COUPLETS CONCLUDING THE MILLION ....PERSEUS 83 18
    IN THE MILLION PERFECTLY-CHISELED ....LOVE LETTER 147 13
    FILLING MY VEINS WITH INVISIBLES, WITH THE MILLION ....BIRTHDAY. 207 42
    SPLITTING LIKE QUARTZ INTO A MILLION BITS. ....LESBOS 228 51
    A MILLION SOLDIERS RUN, ...CUT 235 19
    A MILLION IGNORANTS. ....PURDAH 243 47
    WHAT A MILLION FILAMENTS. ....LADY LAZARUS 245 25
    THEIR MILLION ....LETTER IN NOVEMBER 253 29
    REFLECTING IN A MILLION FLAGONS' SHINE, ...CINDERELLA 304 8
MILLIONAIRE (2)
    UNCLE, PANTS FACTORY FATSO, MILLIONAIRE. ....STOPPED DEAD 230 4
    "I WISH MILLIONAIRE UNCLES AND AUNTS ....DIALOGUE EN ROUTE 308 7
MILLIONS (1)
    MILLIONS OF NEEDLY GLASS CAKES! ....THE TOUR 238 18
MILLRACE (1)
    WATER IN THE MILLRACE, THROUGH A SLUICE OF STONE, WINTER LANDSCAPE, 21 1
MIMIC (1)
    THE MIMIC HEAD -- IN A CROTCHED WILLOW, GREEN- ....LADY AND T. 69 23
MINCED (1)
    AND MINCED THE MUDDLING DEVIL ....THE DEATH OF MYTH-MAKING 104 10
MIND (38)
    FLOATS CHASTE AS SNOW, TAUNTING THE CLOUDED MIND WINTER LANDSCAPE, 21 4
    WHAT GERD SAW THEN ENGRAVED HER MIND ....CRYSTAL GAZER 56 43
    HOWEVER THE GRANDILOQUENT MIND MAY SCORN ....NOVEMBER GRAVEYARD 56 5
    RAVE ON THE LEASH OF THE STARVING MIND ....NOVEMBER GRAVEYARD 56 17
    THE VAUNTING MIND ....ON THE DIFFICULTY OF CONJURING UP A DRYAD 66 5
    THAT LOFTY MONARCH, MONARCH MIND, ...NATURAL HISTORY 71 1
    OF HIS MIND. AND NOW NOTHING BUT SNAKES ...............SNAKECHARMER 79 12
    WHITE: IT IS A COMPLEXION OF THE MIND. ....MOONRISE 98 21
    A PLACE, A TIME GONE OUT OF MIND. ....THE EYE-MOTE 109 30
    HOW SHALL I AGE INTO THAT STATE OF MIND? ....ELECTRA ON AZALEA PATH 117 41
    UNSPOOL AND SPEND THEMSELVES. MY MIND RUNS WITH THEM, *PARLIAMENT H. 153 35
    I CAN'T GET IT OUT OF MY MIND ....ZOO KEEPER'S WIFE 155 32
    I DIDN'T MIND HER WAITING ON ME, AND SHE ADORED IT. ......IN PLASTER 159 22
    THIS IS THE LIGHT OF THE MIND, COLD AND PLANETARY. ....MOON. 172 1
    THE TREES OF THE MIND ARE BLACK. THE LIGHT IS BLUE. ....MOON. 172 2
    IT IS THESE MEN I MIND: ....THREE WOMEN 179 85
    FRIGHTENED THE MIND. THEY SMILE LIKE FOOLS. ....THREE WOMEN 179 115
    YOU HAD ONE LEG, AND A PRUSSIAN MIND. ....LITTLE FUGUE 188 40
    IT IS MONDAY IN HER MIND: MORALS ....AN APPEARANCE 189 6
    PEGS TOO DEEP TO UPROOT, AND A MIND LIKE A RING THE RABBIT CATCHER 194 28
    IS THERE NO WAY OUT OF THE MIND? .....................APPREHENSIONS 195 7
    I WOULD NOT MIND IF IT WAS BONES, OR A PEARL BUTTON. .....BIRTHDAY. 206 12
    CAN YOU NOT SEE I DO NOT MIND WHAT IT IS. ....A BIRTHDAY PRESENT 206 20
    DO NOT BE ASHAMED -- I DO NOT MIND IF IT IS SMALL. ....BIRTHDAY. 206 22
    THE MIND OF THE HIVE THINKS THIS IS THE END OF EVERYTHING. ....BEE. 212 37
    A BLACK INTRACTABLE MIND. ....THE SWARM 217 58
    MIND AGAINST ALL THAT WHITE. ....WINTERING 218 33
    MY MIND WINDS TO YOU ....MEDUSA 225 13
    SEVEN HOURS KNOCKED OUT OF MY RIGHT MIND ....THE JAILER 226 7
    THE WHITE GAPE OF HIS MIND WAS THE REAL TABULA RASA. .....LYONNESSE 234 27
    INTOLERABLE, WITHOUT MIND. ....THE MUNICH MANNEQUINS 263 15
    MY MIND A ROCK, ...PARALYTIC 266 2
    DANGERS, BUT DON'T MIND HEARING ABOUT THE ONES ....DIALOGUE O. 278 64
    OVER MY MIND, CASTING A SHADOW. SORROW DIALOGUE OVER A OUIJA BOARD 285 312
    ERECTED DOWN THE GANGWAYS OF OUR MIND. ....DOOM OF EXILES 318 4
    IN DARKROOM OF YOUR EYE THE MOONLY MIND ....SONNET TO SATAN 323 1
    LIKE A RARE CALDER MOBILE IN YOUR MIND. ....MIDSUMMER MOBILE 324 14
    THOUGH THE MIND LIKE AN OYSTER LABORS ON AND ON, ...TWO LOVERS. 327 19
MINDING (1)
    THE ROUND SKY GOES ON MINDING ITS BUSINESS. PARLIAMENT HILL FIELDS 152 3
MINDS (1)
    FAT HAUNCHES AND BLOOD ON THEIR MINDS. ....TOTEM 264 8
MIND'S (2)
    ON THE MIND'S EYE, ERECTING A LINE ......SLEEP IN THE MOJAVE DESERT 143 4
    IN THE IMPOSSIBLE MIND'S EYE; ....LOVE IS A PARALLAX 329 3
MINE (8)
    THROUGH A WHIM OF MINE ....SOLILOQUY OF THE SOLIPSIST 37 7

MINE (CONT.)
    OF MINE, YET KIN SHE IS: SHE'LL SUCK ....ALL THE DEAD DEARS   70   16
    MOTHER, MOTHER. BUT NO FROWN OF MINE ....THE DISQUIETING MUSES   76   55
    NO GESTURE OF YOURS OR MINE COULD CATCH THEIR ATTENTION, TWO CAMP.   144   4
    THE FACE IN THE POOL WAS BEAUTIFUL, BUT NOT MINE -- ....THREE WOMEN   177   45
    THEY ARE NOT MINE. THEY DO NOT BELONG TO ME. ....THREE WOMEN   185 322
    IT IS NOT MINE. DO NOT ACCEPT IT. ....THE COURIERS   247   2
    CHANCES TO MASTER MINE. THEY SAY THE THIRD TIME ....DIALOGUE O.   283 270
MINER (3)
    I AM A MINER. THE LIGHT BURNS BLUE. ....NICK AND THE CANDLESTICK   240   1
    THE PRINCESS FREES THE MINER, STONE BY STONE, ...THE PRINCESS.   334   49
    SHE TELLS THE GREENHORN MINER TO BOW DOWN ....THE PRINCESS.   335   61
MINERALS (3)
    SUCKING UP MINERALS AND MOTHERLY LOVE ....I AM VERTICAL 162   3
    PICKING AMONG THE DUMB MINERALS, THE ROOTS. ....LAST WORDS   172   5
    SHE HAS A TERRIBLE WAY WITH MINERALS, ...THE RIVAL/DR   291   23
MINERS (1)
    MADE BY MINERS UP THE MOUNTAINSIDE ....THE PRINCESS AND THE GOBLINS 334   33
MINER'S (2)
    THIS MINER'S BOY FROM GOBLIN BODYGUARD.*THE PRINCESS AND THE GOBLINS 333   25
    ABOUT A GOBLIN RAID ON MINER'S HUT ....THE PRINCESS AND THE GOBLINS 334   38
MINNOWS (1)
    AGILE MINNOWS ....AQUATIC NOCTURNE 305   11
MINOR (3)
    A CERTAIN MINOR LIGHT MAY STILL ....BLACK ROOK IN RAINY WEATHER   57   14
    MINOR IMPS PIPE UP, SO LONG AS EACH ....DIALOGUE OVER A OUIJA BOARD 280 152
    MOVES TO OUR MINOR LOVE. ....TRIO OF LOVE SONGS   314   16
MINUTE (13)
    LIKE ICEBERGS, WHILE MINUTE BROWN HAIRS RISE ....TALE OF A TUB   25   42
    SOME SCANDAL MIGHT ANY MINUTE OOZE ....AFTERMATH 113   4
    EACH STALLED IN HIS PARTICULAR MINUTE ....ON DECK 143   14
    LEVITATING A NUMB MINUTE IN THE UPDRAFT ....WIDOW 164   3
    I REMEMBER THE MINUTE WHEN I KNEW FOR SURE. ....THREE WOMEN   177   43
    THE YELLOW MINUTE BEFORE THE WIND WALKS, WHEN THE LEAVES*THREE WOMEN 179   93
    FOR A MINUTE THE SKY POURS INTO THE HOLE LIKE PLASMA. ..BERCK-PLAGE 201 125
    MINUTE AND SHRUNK FOR EXPORT, ...THE ARRIVAL OF THE BEE BOX 213   14
    NURSES THE SIZE OF WORMS AND A MINUTE DOCTOR ....AMNESIAC 233   7
    THERE IS A MINUTE AT THE END OF IT ....GETTING THERE   248   41
    A MINUTE, A DEWDROP. ....GETTING THERE   248   42
    MAY BE PINNED ANY MINUTE, ANESTHETIZED. ....KINDNESS   269   15
    WE BROKE THE MINUTE THAT THE WORLD BEGAN ....THE DISPOSSESSED   318   14
MINUTES (1)
    IN WHICH THE MINUTES COULD ADMIRE THEIR REFLECTIONS AND
        FORGET ABOUT ME. ....THE RIVAL/DR   291   7
MINX-THIN (1)
    ELLA FLOUNCED ABOUT, MINX-THIN AND HAUGHTY, ...ELLA MASON A.   53   14
MIRACLE (9)
    BY A MAD MIRACLE I GO INTACT ....STREET SONG   35   1
    I DO NOT EXPECT A MIRACLE ....BLACK ROOK IN RAINY WEATHER   56   4
    BY NO MIRACLE OR MAJESTIC MEANS, ...A LESSON IN VENGEANCE   80   5
    THERE IS NO MIRACLE MORE CRUEL THAN THIS. ....THREE WOMEN 180 127
    A SORT OF WALKING MIRACLE, MY SKIN ....LADY LAZARUS 244   4
    "A MIRACLE!" ....LADY LAZARUS 246   55
    NOTHING SHORT OF A MIRACLE TO NAIL .....DIALOGUE OVER A OUIJA BOARD 280 160
    FAITH FAST: A MIRACLE AND THE SMELL OF BLOOD ....DIALOGUE O. 280 161
    GAUDY MIRACLE OCCUR, TO COME ......MORNING IN THE HOSPITAL SOLARIUM 333   25
MIRACLES (3)
    OF SORTS. MIRACLES OCCUR, ...BLACK ROOK IN RAINY WEATHER   57   36
    TRICKS OF RADIANCE MIRACLES. THE WAIT'S BEGUN AGAIN, BLACK ROOK I.   57   38
    I AM SIMPLE AGAIN. I BELIEVE IN MIRACLES. ....THREE WOMEN   185 319
MIRACULOUS (3)
    NOW, SNARED BY THIS MIRACULOUS ART, ...ON THE PLETHORA OF DRYADS   67   28
    ON INDIA, AFRICA, AMERICA, THESE MIRACULOUS ONES, ...THREE WOMEN 183 229
    KEEPING ITSELF, IT SEEMS, IN A STATE OF MIRACULOUS REPAIR. ..MEDUSA 225   15
MIRAGE (1)
    IS JOKING AT THE PIE-IN-THE-SKY MIRAGE   DIALOGUE OVER A OUIJA BOARD 282 211
MIRE (1)
    THICKENING WITH MOTES, TO A MARRIAGE WITH THE MIRE. ....OUIJA   77   21
MIRE-SMIRCHED (1)
    MIRE-SMIRCHED, BLOWZY, ...SOW   61   18
MIRROR (21)
    THE STRANGER IN THE LAVATORY MIRROR ....TALE OF A TUB   24   6
    NOT NAILS, AND A MIRROR TO KEEP THE SNAKY HEAD ....PERSEUS   83   13
    AND A FUN-HOUSE MIRROR THAT TURNS THE TRAGIC MUSE ....PERSEUS   83   36
    AS ROSES BROACH THEIR CARMINE IN A MIRROR. FLUX ....ABOVE THE OXBOW   89   44
    THE MIRROR QUIVERS TO SMITHEREENS. ....IN MIDAS' COUNTRY   100   19
    MIRROR OF WATER ....DARK WOOD, DARK WATER 127   17
    IN THE MIRROR THEIR DOUBLES BACK THEM UP. ....LEAVING EARLY   146   34
    I WATCHED SETTLE, LINE BY LINE, IN MY MIRROR -- ....FACE LIFT   156   26
    THAN THE CLOUD THAT DISTILLS A MIRROR TO REFLECT ITS OWN SLOW ...
                                            ... MORNING SONG   157   8
    MY MIRROR IS CLOUDING OVER -- ....LAST WORDS 172   11
    MIRROR ....MIRROR   173   T
    THE MIRROR GIVES BACK A WOMAN WITHOUT DEFORMITY. ....THREE WOMEN 183 240
    THE BLIND MIRROR OF IT. I LOOK IN ....FOR A FATHERLESS SON 205   8

TITLE   PAGE LINE

MIRROR (CONT.)
  THE FACE THAT LIVED IN THIS MIRROR IS THE FACE OF A DEAD MAN. ...
                          ... THE COURAGE OF SHUTTING-UP   210   29
  THE MIRROR FLOATS US AT ONE CANDLE POWER. ....BY CANDLELIGHT 236   9
  I GLEAM LIKE A MIRROR. ....PURDAH 242   18
  MIRROR SAFE, UNREDEEMED ....BRASILIA 259   21
  MIRROR TALK YOU LOVE TO CATCH ME AT. ...................EAVESDROPPER 260   36
  TO RE-ESTABLISH ITS MIRROR ....WORDS 270   9
  DIVE AT YOUR MIRROR ....MOONSONG AT MORNING 317   39
  "DESTROY YOUR MIRROR AND AVOID MISHAPS," ...EPITAPH IN THREE PARTS 337   4
MIRRORED (2)
  MIRRORED THE INTRICATE GESTURES OF TWO OTHERS. ....THE OTHER TWO   68   14
  SUN AND SKY MIRRORED THE GREEN OF THE SPINACH. .....SPINACH-PICKER.   89   12
MIRRORS (12)
  THIS SORCERESS SETS MIRRORS ENOUGH ....VANITY FAIR   33   22
  MIRRORS, ENGENDERING A SPECTRAL ....LANDOWNERS   53   7
  HIS HEAD IS A LITTLE INTERIOR OF GRAY MIRRORS. ....INSOMNIAC 163   22
  MIRRORS CAN KILL AND TALK, THEY ARE TERRIBLE ROOMS ....COURAGE. 210   27
  LORD OF THE MIRRORS! ....PURDAH 242   20
  A DISTURBANCE IN MIRRORS, ...THE COURIERS 247   11
  SPIDERLIKE, I SPIN MIRRORS, ...CHILDLESS WOMAN 259   11
  NOTIONS AND TICKETS, SHORT CIRCUITS AND FOLDING MIRRORS. .....TOTEM 265   27
  WITH WINDOWS OF MIRRORS. ....GIGOLO 267   6
  IN THE WINDOWS, THE MIRRORS ....KINDNESS 269   4
  THE MIRRORS ARE SHEETED. ....CONTUSION 271   12
  WITHIN THESE MIRRORS .....ON LOOKING INTO THE EYES OF A DEMON LOVER 325   9
MIRROR-SHEEN (1)
  BLACK BENEATH BLAND MIRROR-SHEEN, ...LORELEI   94   3
MIRRORY (2)
  ONE MIRRORY EYE --- ....BERCK-PLAGE 198   48
  THE GLAZE, THE MIRRORY VARIETY OF IT. ....A BIRTHDAY PRESENT 207   25
MIRTH (1)
  YOUR MALADY OF SACRILEGIOUS MIRTH ....DIRGE FOR A JOKER 303   11
MISCARRY (1)
  SCARED MOTHERS TO MISCARRY, ...THE DEATH OF MYTH-MAKING 104   12
MISCHIEF'S (1)
  DISGUISE BEGUILES AND MORTAL MISCHIEF'S DONE: ....ADMONITIONS 319   14
MISFIRED (1)
  A THIRD TIME. DON'T GLOAT. YOUR WILL MISFIRED TWICE ....DIALOGUE O. 284 281
MISFORTUNE (1)
  HAWK MISFORTUNE LIKE FIGS AND CHICKENS ....THE BEGGARS   47   3
MISHAP (1)
  BOTTOM OF YOUR BRAIN. BY SOME MISHAP, ..DIALOGUE OVER A OUIJA BOARD 282 241
MISHAPS (1)
  "DESTROY YOUR MIRROR AND AVOID MISHAPS," ....EPITAPH IN THREE PARTS 337   4
MISINTERPRETS (1)
  WHICH NO GRUFF ANIMAL MISINTERPRETS. .................INCOMMUNICADO 100   11
MISLAID (1)
  AND MISLAID EVERY VITAL TALISMAN; ....THE DISPOSSESSED 319   17
MISS (8)
  MISS DRAKE PROCEEDS TO SUPPER ....MISS DRAKE PROCEEDS TO SUPPER   41   T
  ONCE WE CHILDREN SNEAKED OVER TO SPY MISS MASON ......ELLA MASON A.   54   19
  "MISS ELLA'S GOT LOONY FROM KEEPING IN CAHOOTS ....ELLA MASON A.   54   35
  BUT NOW TURNED KINDER WITH TIME, WE MARK MISS MASON ..ELLA MASON A.   54   37
  AND SHE'LL PERISH WITH EMPTINESS THEN, AND BEGIN TO MISS ME. ...
                                        ... IN PLASTER 160   56
  I MISS ORION AND CASSIOPEIA'S CHAIR. MAYBE THEY ARE ....STARS. 165   18
  I AM SOLITARY AS GRASS. WHAT IS IT I MISS? ....THREE WOMEN 186 342
  I AM YOUNG AS EVER, IT SAYS. WHAT IS IT I MISS? ....THREE WOMEN 186 350
MISSED (3)
  OLD BOCKLIN MISSED, WHO HELD A SHELL .....ON THE DECLINE OF ORACLES   78   5
  IF THEY MISSED OUT ON WALKING ABOUT LIKE PEOPLE ....STILLBORN 142   4
  BUT MISSED THE MARK WITH SNAKING FANGS: ....LAMENT 315   5
MISSING (1)
  STITCHES TO SHOW SOMETHING'S MISSING? NO, NO? THEN ...THE APPLICANT 221   6
MIST (6)
  SHAPING ITSELF FROM THAT MIST. ...DIALOGUE BETWEEN GHOST AND PRIEST   38   10
  FROM THAT PALE MIST ....DIALOGUE BETWEEN GHOST AND PRIEST   39   47
  DAY OF MIST: DAY OF TARNISH ....RESOLVE   52   1
  OF STARK WIND-HARROWED HILLS AND WELTERING MIST; ....SNOWMAN O.   58   13
  A WHITE MIST IS GOING UP. ....THE SLEEPERS 123   16
  A BLUE MIST IS DRAGGING THE LAKE. ....THE MANOR GARDEN 125   4
MISTAKE (1)
  THEY MISTAKE THEIR STAR, THESE PAPERY GODFOLK. ....MAGI 148   15
MISTIER (1)
  OUSTS MISTIER PEERS AND THRIVES, MURDEROUS, ...POEMS, POTATOES 106   2
MISTILY (1)
  RAVEL ABOVE US, MISTILY DESCEND, ...OUIJA   77   20
MISTRESS (2)
  CRACK-THROATED MISTRESS OF BAGPIPES AND CYMBALS, ..ALICANTE LULLABY   43   16
  PUT ORANGE MISTRESS HALF IN SUN, *BLACK PINE TREE IN AN ORANGE LIGHT 328   10
MISTS (5)
  TILL THE NIGHT MISTS CAME RISING. ....SONG FOR A SUMMER'S DAY   31   20
  BLUE MISTS MOVE OVER ....DARK WOOD, DARK WATER 127   6
  ALMOST TOO SMALL FOR THE MISTS TO BOTHER WITH. ....FINISTERRE 169   12

                              319

MISTS (CONT.)
    THE MISTS ARE PART OF THE ANCIENT PARAPHERNALIA -- ......FINISTERRE 169 13
    FUMY, SPIRITOUS MISTS INHABIT THIS PLACE   THE MOON AND THE YEW TREE 172   5
MIST-WRAITH (1)
    MOVES ON ITS ROOT. THOUGH A MIST-WRAITH WOUND .....HARDCASTLE CRAGS   62 13
MIX (1)
    MAKE LOVE AND LOGIC MIX, ...NOTES TO A NEOPHYTE 306 16
MIXED (1)
    I KNEW HE'D GOT IT MIXED BEFORE: VISIONS*DIALOGUE OVER A OUIJA BOARD 282 219
MIXIE (1)
    OF MIXIE BLACKSHORT THE HEROIC BEAR, ...THE DISQUIETING MUSES   75 10
MIZZLE (1)
    THIS MIZZLE FITS ME LIKE A SAD JACKET. ....LEAVING EARLY 146 39
MIZZLING (1)
    EXPOSES EMBARRASSMENTS -- THE MIZZLING DAYS ....INSOMNIAC 163   9
MOANINGLY (1)
    IT REHEARSES THEM MOANINGLY: ....WUTHERING HEIGHTS 168 35
MOANS (1)
    THE CELLOS OF MOANS I EAT EGGS -- ....GIGOLO 267 15
MOB (1)
    IT IS LIKE A ROMAN MOB, ...THE ARRIVAL OF THE BEE BOX 213 19
MOBILE (3)
    ON MOBILE JET: ....AQUATIC NOCTURNE 305   6
    MIDSUMMER MOBILE ....MIDSUMMER MOBILE 324   T
    LIKE A RARE CALDER MOBILE IN YOUR MIND. ....MIDSUMMER MOBILE 324 14
MOBS (1)
    MOBS OF EYEBALLS LOOKING UP. ....LEAVING EARLY 146 13
MOB'S (1)
    INSTINCT FOR ART BEGAN WITH THE BULL'S HORN LOFTING IN THE MOB'S ...
            ... THE GORING   47   8
MOCK (3)
    TO MOCK YOUR FACE ....MOONSONG AT MORNING 316   6
    BRAZEN ACTORS MOCK AT HIM, ...LOVE IS A PARALLAX 330 45
    AND MOCK THE JANGLING RAIN OF SPLINTERED STARS. ..EPITAPH IN THREE. 337 25
MOCK-CEREMONY (1)
    BEHIND MOCK-CEREMONY OF YOUR GRIEF ....DIRGE FOR A JOKER 302   5
MOCK-HEROIC (1)
    MOST MOCK-HEROIC, TO CLOAK OUR WAKING AWE ....CHANNEL CROSSING   27 28
MOCKING (1)
    MOCKING AS MEPHISTOPHELES, ...CIRCUS IN THREE RINGS 322 13
MOCKS (1)
    AND MOCKS! HERE'S THE PARODY OF THAT MORAL MOUSETRAP ....VIRGIN.   81   2
MODE (1)
    THUMBS-DOWN ON THE DODO'S MODE. ....YOU'RE 141   4
MODEL (3)
    FIRED IN SANGUINE CLAY, THE MODEL HEAD ....LADY AND T.   69   1
    YOU HAD A ROSE GARDEN AND A GUEST COTTAGE AND A MODEL APOTHECARY
       SHOP ....THE BABYSITTERS 174 20
    I MADE A MODEL OF YOU, ...DADDY 224 64
MODELS (1)
    THAN MODELS FROM BONWIT'S OR JAY'S, ...A WINTER'S TALE   86 10
MODES (2)
    IN TARNISHED MODES, MAUNDERING AMONG THE WASTES, ...OUIJA   77 13
    INCOMPATIBLE MODES OF TIME, THE RAW MATERIAL*THE GHOST'S LEAVETAKING 90 13
MODISH (1)
    WITH HIS MODISH OPPOSABLE THUMB: ....DIALOGUE EN ROUTE 309 26
MOIST (2)
    HANGING FROM THEIR SCORCHED HOOKS IN THE MOIST ...ZOO KEEPER'S WIFE 155 18
    IN HER GARDEN THE LIES WERE SHAKING OUT THEIR MOIST SILKS*DETECTIVE. 208   7
MOJAVE (1)
    SLEEP IN THE MOJAVE DESERT ....SLEEP IN THE MOJAVE DESERT 143   T
MOLD (1)
    WINDING UP THE RAVELED MOLD. ....DANSE MACABRE 321 12
MOLDERING (1)
    MOLDERING HEADS CONSOLE ME, ...POEM.1.WHO. 131 13
MOLDING (1)
    MOLDING ONTO HIS LIPS LIKE LIES, ...STINGS 215 49
MOLDS (2)
    AND A BLACK VEIL THAT MOLDS TO MY FACE, THEY ARE MAKING ME
       ONE OF THEM. .... THE BEE MEETING 211 22
    THE BLACK VEIL MOLDS TO YOUR LIPS: ....STINGS/DR 293   9
MOLDY (1)
    NOTHING WENT MOLDY. THE LITTLE INVISIBLES POEM.4.BEAST. 134   5
MOLE (2)
    I ENTER THE SOFT PELT OF THE MOLE. ....BLUE MOLES 126 21
    MOLE ON MY SHOULDER, ...EAVESDROPPER 260   4
MOLECULES (1)
    MEANING LEAKS FROM THE MOLECULES. ....MYSTIC 269 27
MOLES (6)
    LOAM-HUMPS, HE SAYS, MOLES SHUNT ....ODE FOR TED   29   7
    BLUE FUR, MOLES HAVE; HEFTING CHALK-HULLED FLINT ....ODE FOR TED   29   9
    TOLERABLE NOW AS MOLES ON THE FACE ....THE COMPANIONABLE ILLS 105   2
    BLUE MOLES ....BLUE MOLES 126   T
    MOLES DEAD IN THE PEBBLED RUT, ...BLUE MOLES 126   2
    THE MOLES LOOK NEUTRAL AS THE STONES. ....BLUE MOLES 126 14

                                                    TITLE   PAGE LINE
MOLESTING (1)
    FREE FROM ALL MOLESTING. ROUGH BOYS, ...LADY AND T.   69   9
MOLEY-HANDED (1)
    MOLEY-HANDED, I EAT MY WAY. POEM.2.DARK.   132   16
MOLLIFIES (1)
    WATER MOLLIFIES THE FLINT LIP, ...POEM.7.S.   137   25
MOLLIFY (1)
    THEY MOLLIFY THE BALD MOON. ....CANDLES   149   26
MOLLUSK (1)
    METAMORPHOSE THE MOLLUSK ....NOTES TO A NEOPHYTE   306   7
MOLLUSKS (1)
    AMONG EMMETS AND MOLLUSKS, ...POEM.4.BEAST.   134   24
MOLTEN (1)
    GAVE MOLTEN EARTH A FRAME, ...NOTES TO A NEOPHYTE   306   20
MOLTS (1)
    THE MOLTS ARE TONGUELESS THAT SANG FROM ABOVE THE WATER ..POEM.5.F.   135   17
MOMENT (2)
    CHEEKS ALIGHTING EACH MOMENT TO MELT ....LOVE LETTER   147   14
    THE SPIDERY JAWS, THE SPINE BONES BARED FOR A MOMENT ....ZOO K.   154   9
MOMENT'S (1)
    AS IF TO OUTFLAME A PHOENIX, THE MOMENT'S SPUR ......EPITAPH FOR F.   46   24
MONADNOCK (1)
    TO THE ADIRONDACKS, TO NORTHERN MONADNOCK, ...ABOVE THE OXBOW   87   3
MONARCH (2)
    THAT LOFTY MONARCH, MONARCH MIND, ...NATURAL HISTORY   71   1
    THAT LOFTY MONARCH, MONARCH MIND, ...NATURAL HISTORY   71   1
MONDAY (5)
    THE EVERLASTING MONDAY ....THE EVERLASTING MONDAY   62   T
    MONDAY AND STAND IN THE MOON. ....THE EVERLASTING MONDAY   62 E/2
    LIKE MONDAY DRUNKARDS. THE MILKY BERRIES ....LEAVING EARLY   145   10
    IT IS MONDAY IN HER MIND: MORALS ....AN APPEARANCE   189   6
    IN DUBIOUS DOORWAYS FORGET THEIR MONDAY NAMES, ..LOVE IS A PARALLAX   329   32
MONDAYS (1)
    NOW WORKS HIS HELL OF MONDAYS IN THE MOON'S BALL,*EVERLASTING MONDAY   62   11
MONDE (1)
    AND THE FASHIONABLE MONDE OF THE RED COUCH ....YADWIGHA.   85   10
MONEY (7)
    JANGLING THEIR GREAT MONEY BAGS. ....RHYME   50   8
    FOR MONEY. LORD, THE CROWDS ARE FIERCE! ....A WINTER'S TALE   87   15
    WINKS LIKE MONEY UNDER THE RINGED TOES OF THE CHICKENS. ......NET-.   121   9
    AND A DEW COLLECT ON THEM, DEARER THAN MONEY, ...SLEEP.   144   9
    TILL THEN YOUR SMILES ARE FOUND MONEY. ....FOR A FATHERLESS SON   206   14
    AND MONEY THE SPERM FLUID OF IT ALL. ....AMNESIAC   233   20
    ASKING ABOUT MONEY? I'M SICK OF THAT. ..DIALOGUE OVER A OUIJA BOARD   277   50
MONEYLESS (1)
    DEAD AND MONEYLESS, ...MEDUSA   225   30
MONEY'S (2)
    THE MONEY'S RUN OUT. ....DEPARTURE   51   4
    MONEY'S NEW-MINTED IN THIS FAT PURSE. ....METAPHORS   116   6
MONGREL (1)
    A MONGREL WORKING HIS LEGS TO A GALLOP ....SUICIDE OFF EGG ROCK   115   12
MONKEY (3)
    MONKEY LIVED UNDER THE DUNCE CAP. POEM.4.BEAST.   134   8
    GEESE AND THE MONKEY TREES. ....THE TOUR   237   10
    GOD'S MONKEY WRENCH HAS BLASTED ALL MACHINES; ....DOOMSDAY   316   13
MONKEYS (1)
    BEHIND TWO EYES IN WHICH NOTHING IS REFLECTED BUT MONKEYS. *A SECRET   219   20
MONKS (1)
    THEY ARE THE REAL MONKS AND NUNS IN THEIR IDENTICAL GARMENTS.*THREE.   183 227
MONOCHROME (1)
    GRAZING AT THE MARGINS OF A BAD MONOCHROME, ...THE EYE-MOTE   109   14
MONOLOGUE (1)
    MONOLOGUE AT 3 A.M. ....MONOLOGUE AT 3 A.M.   40   T
MONOXIDE (2)
    WHITE AND BLANK, EXPANSIVE AS CARBON MONOXIDE. ....THE RIVAL   166   15
    ARMIES OF THEM. THEY ARE CARBON MONOXIDE. ....A BIRTHDAY PRESENT   207   40
MONOXIDES (1)
    IGNITING ITS CARBON MONOXIDES, BY EYES ....POPPIES IN OCTOBER   240   8
MONSTER (1)
    A MONSTER OF WOOD AND RUSTY TEETH. ....THE BURNT-OUT SPA   137   2
MONSTERS (1)
    MONSTERS WHICH UPREAR ....BATTLE-SCENE   84   16
MONSTROUS (1)
    OF MONSTROUS SIZE, LIKE NO WELL-BRED LILIES. ....YADWIGHA.   85   7
MONTH (12)
    A POOR MONTH FOR PARK-SLEEPERS AND LOVERS. ....A WINTER SHIP   113   22
    THE LATE MONTH WITHERS, AS WELL. ....MAGNOLIA SHOALS   122   12
    THE MONTH OF FLOWERING'S FINISHED. THE FRUIT'S IN, ...POEM.1.WHO.   131   1
    OCTOBER'S THE MONTH FOR STORAGE. POEM.1.WHO.   131   3
    THIS MONTH IS FIT FOR LITTLE. POEM.3.MAENAD.   133   11
    THE STAR BUGS WON'T SAVE ME THIS MONTH. POEM.4.BEAST.   134   22
    IN THE MONTH OF RED LEAVES I CLIMB TO A BED OF FIRE. POEM.6.W.   135   6
    IN A MONTH WE'LL WONDER WHAT PLATES AND FORKS ARE FOR. ...TWO CAMP.   145   20
    MONTH AFTER MONTH, WITH ITS VOICES OF FAILURE. ....THREE WOMEN   182 187
    MONTH AFTER MONTH, WITH ITS VOICES OF FAILURE. ....THREE WOMEN   182 187

MONTH (CONT.)
    UNLOOSING THEIR MOONS, MONTH AFTER MONTH, TO NO PURPOSE. ...MUNICH. 263   5
    UNLOOSING THEIR MOONS, MONTH AFTER MONTH, TO NO PURPOSE. ...MUNICH. 263   5
MONTHS (2)
    SIX MONTHS IN THE WORLD, AND SHE IS ABLE ....MAGI 148 10
    NINE MONTHS TOO SOON FOR COMFORT, BUT A BRIGHT ....DIALOGUE O. 280 141
MONUMENT (2)
    A MONUMENT ....SOW   61 40
    IS PRAYING TO THE MONUMENT OF THE SAILOR PRAYING. ....FINISTERRE 170 23
MONUMENTAL (1)
    THAT LIFE WAS A MERE MONUMENTAL SHAM. ....DIRGE FOR A JOKER 302   8
MOO (3)
    AND PRISTINE ALPHABETS AND COWS THAT MOO ...THE GHOST'S LEAVETAKING   91 36
    AND MOO AS THEY JUMP OVER MOONS AS NEW .....THE GHOST'S LEAVETAKING   91 37
    WIDEN AND DIE IN THE HEDGEROWS. I HEAR THE MOO OF COWS. *THREE WOMEN 185 312
MOOD (4)
    SHIRR SONGS TO SUIT WHICH MOOD ....ODE FOR TED   29 20
    THE BLANK MOOD SHE WALKED IN. ONCE PAST ....HARDCASTLE CRAGS   63 18
    SHIES FROM HIS TOUCH: HIS IS AN IRON MOOD. ....THE OTHER TWO   68 19
    WORSHIP THIS WORLD OF WATERCOLOR MOOD ....APRIL AUBADE 312   1
MOODS (1)
    YET, IN MY WINTRIEST MOODS, I HOLD ......SOLILOQUY OF THE SOLIPSIST   37 24
MOON (61)
    AGAWP AT THE IMPECCABLE MOON. ....LETTER TO A PURIST   37 16
    PLAGUE-PITTED AS THE MOON: EACH BUD ....CRYSTAL GAZER   56 44
    MONDAY AND STAND IN THE MOON. ....THE EVERLASTING MONDAY   62 E/2
    OF THE MOON, MANES TO THE WIND, ...HARDCASTLE CRAGS   62 11
    OUT OF THE SIDE OF THE GENEROUS MOON WHEN IT ....THE THIN PEOPLE   65 28
    THE MOON TO A RIND OF LITTLE LIGHT. ....THE THIN PEOPLE   65 31
    OTHER THAN NOON, THAN MOON, STARS -- ....THE GREAT CARBUNCLE   72 16
    OF UNCAGED TIGERS AND A TROPICAL MOON, ...YADWIGHA.   85   4
    WITH ITS PRIM BRIC-A-BRAC, WITHOUT A MOON ....YADWIGHA.   85 11
    THEY'D HAVE HAD YELLOW SILK SCREENING THE MOON, ...YADWIGHA.   85 15
    AND BIRDS OF PARADISE, AND THE ROUND MOON, ...YADWIGHA.   86 24
    DESCRIBED HOW YOU FELL DREAMING AT FULL OF MOON ....YADWIGHA.   86 25
    ACCOMPANIED YOU. SO THEY NODDED AT THE COUCH WITH THE MOON*YADWIGHA.   86 32
    TO FEED HIS EYE WITH RED: SUCH RED! UNDER THE MOON, ...YADWIGHA.   86 38
    A FULL MOON, RIVER LAPSING ....LORELEI   94   2
    MOON FULL, MOON DARK, THE CHARY DAIRY FARMER ....GOATSUCKER 111   5
    MOON FULL, MOON DARK, THE CHARY DAIRY FARMER ....GOATSUCKER 111   5
    IN THEIR JARS THE SNAIL-NOSED BABIES MOON AND GLOW. .....TWO VIEWS. 114 10
    THE MOON LEANS, A STONE MADONNA, OVER THE LEAD SEA   THE NET-MENDERS 121 15
    BY THE GATE WITH STAR AND MOON ....MEDALLION 124   1
    THEY MOLLIFY THE BALD MOON. ....CANDLES 149 26
    IT RESEMBLES THE MOON, OR A SHEET OF BLANK PAPER ....A LIFE 150 23
    THE MOON LAYS A HAND ON MY FOREHEAD, ...BARREN WOMAN 157   9
    FLOATS CALM AS A MOON OR A CLOUD. ....HEAVY WOMEN 158   7
    IF THE MOON SMILED, SHE WOULD RESEMBLE YOU. ....THE RIVAL 166   1
    THE MOON, TOO, ABASES HER SUBJECTS, ...THE RIVAL 166 11
    ROUND AS THE MOON, TO STARE UP. ....LAST WORDS 172   3
    THE MOON AND THE YEW TREE ....THE MOON AND THE YEW TREE 172   T
    THE MOON IS NO DOOR. IT IS A FACE IN ITS OWN RIGHT, ...MOON. 173   8
    THE EYES LIFT AFTER IT AND FIND THE MOON. *THE MOON AND THE YEW TREE 173 16
    THE MOON IS MY MOTHER. SHE IS NOT SWEET LIKE MARY. ....MOON. 173 17
    THE MOON SEES NOTHING OF THIS. SHE IS BALD AND WILD. ....MOON. 173 27
    THEN SHE TURNS TO THOSE LIARS, THE CANDLES OR THE MOON. .....MIRROR 174 12
    THERE IS THE MOON IN THE HIGH WINDOW. IT IS OVER. ......THREE WOMEN 181 176
    INTERCEPTING THE BLUE BOLTS OF A COLD MOON? ....THREE WOMEN 185 291
    THE MOON, ALSO, IS MERCILESS: SHE WOULD DRAG ME ....ELM 192 22
    BUT THEIR BONES SHOWED, AND THE MOON SMILED. ....THE DETECTIVE 209 35
    THERE IS ONLY THE MOON, EMBALMED IN PHOSPHORUS. ....THE DETECTIVE 209 39
    IN MY MOON SUIT AND FUNERAL VEIL. ....THE ARRIVAL OF THE BEE BOX 213 32
    AS THE MOON, FOR ITS IVORY POWDERS, SCOURS THE SEA. ....STINGS 215 37
    THAT NIGHT THE MOON ....LESBOS 229 53
    MY HEAD A MOON ....FEVER. 232 37
    THE MOON, MY ....PURDAH 242 11
    O HALF MOON -- ....THALIDOMIDE 252   1
    RATTLES ITS POD, THE MOON ....CHILDLESS WOMAN 259   2
    THE MOON HAS NOTHING TO BE SAD ABOUT, ...EDGE 273 17
    CAN ONCE IN A BLUE MOON CATCH THE SHADOWS OF ....DIALOGUE O. 282 222
    THE MOON SNAGS IN HER INTRICATE NERVOUS SYSTEM. ....ELM/DR 292   3
    THE MOON IS LET GO, LIKE A DEAD THING. ....ELM/DR 292   8
    INFREQUENT AS A MOON OF GREENCHEESE ....APRIL 18 302   8
    THE SOUR LEMON MOON. ....JILTED 304   8
    METAMORPHOSES OF THE MOON .............METAMORPHOSES OF THE MOON 307   T
    WHILE FROM THE MOON, MY LOVER'S EYE ....TO A JILTED LOVER 309   7
    MOON AND SUN REFLECT HIS FLAME. ....TO A JILTED LOVER 310 18
    O MOON OF ILLUSION, ...MOONSONG AT MORNING 316   1
    FROM HERE THE MOON SEEMS SMOOTH AS ANGEL-FOOD, ...ADMONITIONS 319   7
    COUPLES COURT BY MILK OF MOON: ....DANSE MACABRE 321 20
    NO LITTLE MAN LIVES IN THE EXACTING MOON ....TWO LOVERS. 327 23
    THE MOON LEANS DOWN TO LOOK; THE TILTING FISH ...LOVE IS A PARALLAX 330 37
    A VISIONARY LADDER TOWARD THE MOON ....THE PRINCESS AND THE GOBLINS 333   5
    BEHIND WHICH THE DECLINING MOON HAS SET, ...THE PRINCESS. 334 36

MOON-BLANCHED (1)
   MOON-BLANCHED AND IMPLACABLE, HE AND SHE ....THE OTHER TWO   68   22
MOON-BLUED (1)
   TACKING IN MOON-BLUED CROOKS FROM THE BLACK ....HARDCASTLE CRAGS   62   3
MOON-BOUND (1)
   TIRELESS, TIED, AS A MOON-BOUND SEA ....HARDCASTLE CRAGS   62   12
MOON-EYE (1)
   WITH MOON-EYE, MOUTH-PIPE. HE PIPES. PIPES GREEN. PIPES WATER. ...
                                              ... SNAKECHARMER   79   3
MOON-EYED (1)
   "NO DOUBT NOW IN DREAM-PROPERTIED FALL SOME MOON-EYED, ..CONJURING.   66   33
MOON-GLINT (1)
   FROM GROVE OF MOON-GLINT AND FEN-FROST ....FAUN   35   2
MOON-GLOW (1)
   O MOON-GLOW, O SICK ONE, ...THE OTHER   202   20
MOONLIGHT (3)
   THE MOONLIGHT, THAT CHALK CLIFF ....EVENT   194   2
   WEB-WINGED AND FURIOUS. THE FULL MOONLIGHT ....DIALOGUE O.   286 338
   OF MOONLIGHT OR THE POCKMARKED FACE WE SEE*METAMORPHOSES OF THE MOON 308   38
MOON-LILIES (1)
   TO A BERYL JUNGLE, AND DREAMED THAT BRIGHT MOON-LILIES ...YADWIGHA.   86   29
MOONLY (1)
   IN DARKROOM OF YOUR EYE THE MOONLY MIND ....SONNET TO SATAN 323   1
MOON-PLUMAGED (1)
   ESCAPED AMONG MOON-PLUMAGED STRANGERS; ....THE SHRIKE   42   14
MOON-POCKED (1)
   THIS MOON-POCKED CRYSTAL BALL ....RECANTATION   41   6
MOONRISE (1)
   MOONRISE ....MOONRISE   98   T
MOONS (8)
   AND MOO AS THEY JUMP OVER MOONS AS NEW .....THE GHOST'S LEAVETAKING   91   37
   THE RED NIGHT LIGHTS ARE FLAT MOONS. THEY ARE DULL WITH BLOOD. ...
                                              ... THE SURGEON AT 2 A.M. 171   48
   THE NIGHT LIGHTS ARE FLAT RED MOONS. THEY ARE DULL WITH BLOOD. ...
                                              ... THREE WOMEN   180 124
   UNLOOSING THEIR MOONS, MONTH AFTER MONTH, TO NO PURPOSE. ...MUNICH.   263   5
   SUCH QUEER MOONS WE LIVE WITH ....BALLOONS 271   10
   COLD MOONS WITHDRAW, REFUSING TO COME TO TERMS ......METAMORPHOSES.   307   1
   NIPPLED MOONS, EXTINCT AND COLD, ...DANSE MACABRE   321   8
   WHOSE MOONS OF BLACK .....ON LOOKING INTO THE EYES OF A DEMON LOVER 325   2
MOON'S (11)
   OVER GABLES THE MOON'S CELESTIAL ONION ..SOLILOQUY OF THE SOLIPSIST   37   8
   SUN'S BRASS, THE MOON'S STEELY PATINAS, ...DEPARTURE   51   10
   GIBBETS WITH HER CURSE THE MOON'S MAN, ...MAUDLIN   51   3
   THE MOON'S MAN STANDS IN HIS SHELL, ...THE EVERLASTING MONDAY   62   1
   NOW WORKS HIS HELL OF MONDAYS IN THE MOON'S BALL,*EVERLASTING MONDAY   62   11
   DREAMED YOURSELF AWAY IN THE MOON'S EYE ....YADWIGHA. 86   28
   POINT OF EDEN, NEXT THE NEW MOON'S CURVE. ..THE GHOST'S LEAVETAKING   91   31
   LADY, WHO ARE THESE OTHERS IN THE MOON'S VAT -- POEM.3.MAENAD. 133   22
   LIKE A CUP OR A ROOM. THE MOON'S CROOK WHITENS, ...PARLIAMENT H.   153   38
   UNDER THE EYES OF THE STARS AND THE MOON'S RICTUS ....INSOMNIAC   163   5
   THE MOON'S CONCERN IS MORE PERSONAL: ....THREE WOMEN   176   4
MOON-SKULLED (1)
   FEET TO THE STARS, AND MOON-SKULLED, ...YOU'RE   141   2
MOONSONG (1)
   MOONSONG AT MORNING ....MOONSONG AT MORNING   316   T
MOONSTRUCK (1)
   ALL MOONSTRUCK MAGIC ....MOONSONG AT MORNING   317   19
MOONWHITE (1)
   THE MOTH-FACE OF HER HUSBAND, MOONWHITE AND ILL, ...WIDOW   164   14
MOONY (5)
   FIVE MOONY CRESCENTS ....WORDS FOR A NURSERY   73   4
   PUTS UP HIS PIPE, AND LIDS HIS MOONY EYE. .............SNAKECHARMER   79   28
   HANDS LACED, IN A MOONY INDOLENCE OF LOVE -- ....WATERCOLOR.   112   25
   MOONY BALLOONS TIED BY A STRING ....ON DECK   143   34
   WHAT BLUE, MOONY RAY ICES THEIR DREAMS? ....THREE WOMEN 181 182
MOOR (5)
   DAMNED, HOWLING IN THEIR SHROUDS ACROSS THE MOOR *NOVEMBER GRAVEYARD   56   16
   THE SNOWMAN ON THE MOOR ....THE SNOWMAN ON THE MOOR   58   T
   ACROSS MOOR SNOWS ....THE SNOWMAN ON THE MOOR   58   16
   FROM MARBLE SNOW-HEAP OF MOOR TO RIDE THAT WOMAN ....SNOWMAN O.   59   27
   I FOUND BARE MOOR, ...TWO VIEWS OF WITHENS   72   12
MOORISH (1)
   UNDER WHITE WALL AND MOORISH WINDOW ....THE BEGGARS   47   6
MOOR-TOP (2)
   WE CAME OVER THE MOOR-TOP ....THE GREAT CARBUNCLE   72   1
   ON MOOR-TOP, AT SEA-BOTTOM, ...THE GREAT CARBUNCLE   72   14
MOOS (1)
   LOW MOOS OF APPROVE; LET SUN SURPLICED IN BRIGHTNESS .....WREATH F.   44   4
MOPED (1)
   AND MY GRANDFATHER MOPED IN THE TYROL, ...CANDLES   149   20
MORAL (1)
   AND MOCKS! HERE'S THE PARODY OF THAT MORAL MOUSETRAP ....VIRGIN.   81   2
MORALS (1)
   IT IS MONDAY IN HER MIND: MORALS ....AN APPEARANCE   189   6

	TITLE	PAGE	LINE

MORBID (1)
```
    THE MORBID COBRA'S WITS HAVE RUN ASTRAY:  ...............DENOUEMENT    327   13
MORE (64)
    HE PROWLS MORE LORDLY THAN THE SUN. ........................PURSUIT     22    4
    MAINTAINS IT HAS NO MORE HOLY CALLING  ................TALE OF A TUB    24   11
    AND, MORE DAFT THAN ANY GOOSE,  ..........................STREET SONG    36   29
    IS NO MORE MY CONCERN. ................................RECANTATION    41    4
    OF CONCUPISCENCE. ONCE MORE  ................................SPIDER    49   27
    MORE MAMMOTH AND BLOWSY WITH EVERY SEASON; ..........ELLA MASON A.    54   34
    TO GOVERN MORE SIGHT THAN GIVEN TO A WOMAN ..........CRYSTAL GAZER    55   32
    ANY MORE IN THE DESULTORY WEATHER SOME DESIGN, ......BLACK ROOK I.    57    8
    ANY MORE THAN THE OLD WOMAN IN HER MUD HUT COULD  ...THE THIN PEOPLE    64   26
    EVERY POCK AND STAIN BULKED MORE BEAUTIFUL*ON THE PLETHORA OF DRYADS    67   16
    TWO OF US IN A PLACE MEANT FOR TEN MORE --  ..........THE OTHER TWO    68   10
    AND RESOLVED MORE CEREMONIOUSLY TO LODGE  ...............LADY AND T.    69   22
    ANGELS -- MORE FEMININE AND DOUCE  .................A WINTER'S TALE    86    9
    ELEVATIONS TO BE CALLED SOMETHING MORE THAN HILLS.  ABOVE THE OXBOW    88    9
    OF A WORLD MORE FULL AND CLEAR  ............................LORELEI    94   15
    MORE OR OTHER, THEY STILL DISSATISFY.  .............POEMS, POTATOES   106   10
    MORE THAN EIGHT DECADES BACK  .....................THE TIMES ARE TIDY   107   12
    BETTER, BETTER, AND MORE ACCEPTABLE  ...............THE RAVAGED FACE   116   12
    MORE FINICAL THAN  ......................................POLLY'S TREE   128   11
    IT WOULD TAKE MORE THAN A LIGHTNING-STROKE  ............THE COLOSSUS   130   22
    I MUST MAKE MORE MAPS.  ................................POEM.2.DARK.   132   14
    THE WINGY MYTHS WON'T TUG AT US ANY MORE:  ................POEM.5.F.   135   16
    DAYLIGHT WOULD BE MORE JUDICIOUS,  .........................CANDLES   148   10
    ELSEWHERE THE LANDSCAPE IS MORE FRANK. .....................A LIFE   150   19
    I'M NO MORE YOUR MOTHER  .............................MORNING SONG   157    7
    IN TIME OUR RELATIONSHIP GREW MORE INTENSE. ..............IN PLASTER   159   28
    SHE LET IN THE DRAFTS AND BECAME MORE AND MORE ABSENT-MINDED. ...
                                                      ...  IN PLASTER   159   32
    SHE LET IN THE DRAFTS AND BECAME MORE AND MORE ABSENT-MINDED.
                                                      ...  IN PLASTER   159   32
    AND A FLOWER-HEAD NOT TALL, BUT MORE STARTLING,  .......I AM VERTICAL   162    9
    IT IS MORE NATURAL TO ME, LYING DOWN.  .................I AM VERTICAL   162   17
    THE SMALLER AND MORE TIMID NEVER ARIVE AT ALL  ..............STARS.   165   12
    ONE MORE HOOK, AND THE BERRIES AND BUSHES END.  .......BLACKBERRYING   169   18
    A FEW MORE BREATHS, AND IT WILL REFLECT NOTHING AT ALL.  LAST WORDS   172   12
    THE MOON'S CONCERN IS MORE PERSONAL:  ....................THREE WOMEN   176    4
    IT DOES NOT WISH TO BE MORE, OR DIFFERENT.  ............THREE WOMEN   179  101
    THERE IS NO MIRACLE MORE CRUEL THAN THIS. ..............THREE WOMEN   180  127
    I AM INCAPABLE OF MORE KNOWLEDGE.  .............................ELM   193   37
    THEY ARE MORE BEAUTIFUL THAN MY BODILESS OWL,  ..BURNING THE LETTERS   204   30
    MORE TERRIBLE THAN SHE EVER WAS, RED  .........................STINGS   215   57
    ANY MORE, BLACK SHOE  ..........................................DADDY   222    2
    MORE AND MORE LIKE A DEAD ONE,  .........................THE FEARFUL   256    8
    MORE AND MORE LIKE A DEAD ONE,  .........................THE FEARFUL   256    8
    IT MEANS: NO MORE IDOLS BUT ME, ...........THE MUNICH MANNEQUINS   263    8
    BORED HIM. HE'S MORE PHILOSOPHER, IT SEEMS,  ...........DIALOGUE O.   277   43
    BULKING MORE REAL THAN WE THINK WE ARE: WE FACE  ........DIALOGUE O.   279  115
    THE SIZE OF MY DEMAND TO MAGIC: NO MORE *DIALOGUE OVER A OUIJA BOARD   279  121
    THEM ANY MORE THAN YOU DID. OH, LET IT GO. .............DIALOGUE O.   283  265
    ON DARKNESS, MORE VIVID AND UNNATURAL ..DIALOGUE OVER A OUIJA BOARD   285  323
    OF DREAMERS IS DISPELLED. ONCE MORE WE CUT .............DIALOGUE O.   286  359
    BUT I AM CONTENT WITH THIS MORE POMPOUS LOT.  ..........QUEEN MARY'S.   290   25
    MY LOVE FOR YOU IS MORE  ...........................TRIO OF LOVE SONGS   314   17
    NEVER TRY TO KNOW MORE THAN YOU SHOULD.  ...............ADMONITIONS   319    3
    NEVER TRY TO KNOW MORE THAN YOU SHOULD.  ...............ADMONITIONS   319    9
    NEVER TRY TO KNOW MORE THAN YOU SHOULD.  ...............ADMONITIONS   319   15
    NEVER TRY TO KNOW MORE THAN YOU SHOULD.  ...............ADMONITIONS   319   19
    THERE IS NOTHING MORE FOR ME TO SAY.  ..................DENOUEMENT   326    3
    THERE IS NOTHING MORE FOR ME TO SAY.  ..................DENOUEMENT   326    9
    THERE IS NOTHING MORE FOR ME TO SAY.  ..................DENOUEMENT   327   15
    THERE IS NOTHING MORE FOR ME TO SAY.  ..................DENOUEMENT   327   19
    BUT MORE PRAGMATIC THAN ALL OF THIS, .............BLACK PINE TREE   328   16
    THAT STING NO MORE THAN LOVE: A ROOM WHERE TIME *MORNING IN THE HOS.   332   15
    "THERE IS MORE THAN ONE GOOD WAY TO DROWN."  EPITAPH IN THREE PARTS   337   11
    "THERE IS MORE THAN ONE GOOD WAY TO DROWN."  EPITAPH IN THREE PARTS   337   22
    "THERE IS MORE THAN ONE GOOD WAY TO DROWN."  EPITAPH IN THREE PARTS   338   33
MORES (1)
    BEREFT OF MOSES AND OF MORES;  ..INSOLENT STORM STRIKES AT THE SKULL   326   16
MORGUE (2)
    MORGUE OF OLD LOGS AND OLD IMAGES, THE LAKE  .........PRIVATE GROUND   131   23
    IN MUNICH, MORGUE BETWEEN PARIS AND ROME,  ....THE MUNICH MANNEQUINS   263   12
MORNING (24)
    BLINDS LOWERED ON THAT HOT MORNING.  ........DREAM WITH CLAM-DIGGERS    43    8
    FIVE O'CLOCK IN THE MORNING, THE NO-COLOR VOID  ............GHOST'S.    90    2
    ALL MORNING, WITH SMOKING BREATH, THE HANDYMAN  ......PRIVATE GROUND   130    7
    WE SHALL BY MORNING  ....................................MUSHROOMS   140   31
    MUSKY AS A LOVEBED THE MORNING AFTER.  ................LEAVING EARLY   146   19
    MORNING SONG  .........................................MORNING SONG   156    T
    IN THE MORNING SHE WOKE ME EARLY, REFLECTING THE SUN  ....IN PLASTER   159   23
    EACH MORNING IT IS HER FACE THAT REPLACES THE DARKNESS.  .....MIRROR   174   16
    ARRANGING MY MORNING.  ...............................LITTLE FUGUE   189   50
    YOU SAID YOU WOULD KILL IT THIS MORNING.  ................PHEASANT   191    1
```

```
                                              TITLE          PAGE  LINE
MORNING (CONT.)
    MORNING GLORY POOL!  ..................................THE TOUR    238   28
    EYE, THE CAULDRON OF MORNING. ...........................ARIEL    240   31
    EVEN THE SUN-CLOUDS THIS MORNING CANNOT MANAGE SUCH SKIRTS.*POP.OCT.  240    1
    PODS OF THE LABURNUM AT NINE IN THE MORNING.  ....LETTER IN NOVEMBER  253    4
    ALL MORNING THE  .................................SHEEP IN FOG    262    8
    MORNING HAS BEEN BLACKENING, .....................SHEEP IN FOG    262    9
    IT IS SIX IN THE MORNING AND FINER THAN ANY SUNDAY -- *QUEEN MARY'S.  290    8
    MY GLASS OF WATER REFRACTS THE MORNING. ............FEVER./DR    294   11
    ALL THAT MORNING IN THE STRAWBERRY FIELD  .......BITTER STRAWBERRIES  299    1
    IN THE MORNING ALL SHALL BE  ...................TO A JILTED LOVER  310   19
    THE MORNING PAPER CLOCKED THE HEADLINE HOUR  .......THE TRIAL OF MAN  312    5
    MOONSONG AT MORNING  .........................MOONSONG AT MORNING  316    T
    MORNING IN THE HOSPITAL SOLARIUM  ..MORNING IN THE HOSPITAL SOLARIUM  332    T
    MORNING: ANOTHER DAY, AND TALK  ...MORNING IN THE HOSPITAL SOLARIUM  332   10
MORNINGS (2)
    MORNINGS DISSIPATE IN SOMNOLENCE. .....................FROG AUTUMN   99    5
    WAKENS, MORNINGS, TO A COBALT SKY, ..........YADDO: THE GRAND MANOR  124   19
MOROCCAN (1)
    THE MOROCCAN HIPPOPOTAMUS?  ..............................A SECRET  219   13
MOROSE (1)
    GOATS SHAMBLE, MOROSE, RANK-HAIRED, ....................DEPARTURE   51   19
MORPHIA (2)
    OR THE SEA, HUSHING THEIR PEELED SENSE LIKE OLD MOTHER MORPHIA. ...
                                        ... WAKING IN WINTER  151   16
    THE ANGELS OF MORPHIA HAVE BORNE HIM UP.  .....THE SURGEON AT 2 A.M.  171   44
MORTAL (5)
    MARK A MORTAL LACK, ..........................TRIO OF LOVE SONGS  313    2
    WHILE ALL THE ACTORS HALT IN MORTAL SHOCK: ...............DOOMSDAY  316    5
    DISGUISE BEGUILES AND MORTAL MISCHIEF'S DONE: ..........ADMONITIONS  319   14
    TO MORTAL CHILDREN LONGING TO BE GAY;  ..........NEVER TRY TO TRICK.  320   14
    IN THE MORTAL ACTIVE VERB, .......................TOUCH-AND-GO    336   18
MORTGAGE (4)
    THE ENORMOUS MORTGAGE MUST BE PAID SOMEHOW, .......THE DISPOSSESSED  318    1
    THE ENORMOUS MORTGAGE MUST BE PAID SOMEHOW. .......THE DISPOSSESSED  318    6
    THE ENORMOUS MORTGAGE MUST BE PAID SOMEHOW. .......THE DISPOSSESSED  318   12
    THE ENORMOUS MORTGAGE MUST BE PAID SOMEHOW: .......THE DISPOSSESSED  319   18
MORTIS (1)
    DARK FACE. SO MIGHT RIGOR MORTIS COME TO STIFFEN  ...........PERSEUS   83   32
MOSAIC (1)
    A MOSAIC OF STARS  ...............................TO A JILTED LOVER  309    5
MOSES (1)
    BEREFT OF MOSES AND OF MORES; ..INSOLENT STORM STRIKES AT THE SKULL  326   16
MOSS (1)
    INCENSE. PALE MOSS DRIPS .....................DARK WOOD, DARK WATER  127    2
MOSS-WIGGED (1)
    A BARNACLE-PATED, MOSS-WIGGED, LOBSTER-LIMBED  ..........DIALOGUE O.  283  244
MOST (26)
    MOST SOFT, MOST SUAVELY GLIDES THAT STEP,  ...................PURSUIT   22    5
    MOST SOFT, MOST SUAVELY GLIDES THAT STEP,  ...................PURSUIT   22    5
    RUEFUL, MOST VEXED, THAT TENDER SKIN ......................BUCOLICS   24   17
    MOST MOCK-HEROIC, TO CLOAK OUR WAKING AWE  .......CHANNEL CROSSING   27   28
    SHE SPOKE MOST CHIDING IN HIS EAR  ............THE QUEEN'S COMPLAINT   28   11
    LEGGING IT MOST NIMBLE  ................................ODE FOR TED   29    4
    HE SAUNTERS IN; HOW BUT MOST GLAD  ....................ODE FOR TED   29   21
    WHICH HAULS DOWN BUCK, COCK, TROUT, TILL ALL MOST FAIR  ....FIRESONG   30    6
    MOST FAR IN BLUE, ALOFT,  ...................SONG FOR A SUMMER'S DAY   31    7
    CRAVES MOST TO COOK BATTER  ...........................VANITY FAIR   33   16
    INTO MY MOST CHASTE OWN EYES  .......................STRUMPET SONG   34   18
    ARMING MYSELF WITH THE MOST REASONABLE ITEMS  ...........STREET SONG   36   15
    SEASONED HOW HE'D MOST APPROVE;  .......................THE GLUTTON   40    6
    SPROUTING FRUIT, FLOWERS CHILDREN MOST FAIR IN LEGION  ....WREATH F.   45   22
    THESE TWO MOST PERISHABLE LOVERS FROM THE TOUCH  .....EPITAPH FOR F.   45    5
    WELL OR ILL." GERD SLANTS A LOOK AT EACH: MOST DEAR,  CRYSTAL GAZER   55   10
    POSSESSION OF THE MOST OBTUSE OBJECTS NOW AND THEN -- *BLACK ROOK I.   57   18
    OR, AT MOST, TO A MILLE-FLEURS TAPESTRY. BUT THE COUCH  ...YADWIGHA.   85   17
    WHERE THE MOST WATCHFUL COOKS GO JOBLESS  ........THE TIMES ARE TIDY  107    3
    I MUST MOST PERFECTLY RESEMBLE THEM --  ................I AM VERTICAL  162   15
    MOST OF THE TIME I MEDITATE ON THE OPPOSITE WALL.  ..........MIRROR  173    6
    IT IS THE NOISE THAT APPALLS ME MOST OF ALL,  ..........THE ARRIVAL.  213   17
    OUTSIDE THE CAVE WHOSE CONTOURS MOST REMIND  ...........DIALOGUE O.  281  200
    RUNNING NECK AND NECK WITH THE MOST DEVOUT  ...........DIALOGUE O.  282  235
    FOR MOST EXQUISITE TRUTHS ARE ARTIFICE  ...METAMORPHOSES OF THE MOON  307   25
    MOST PLASTIC-WINDOWED CITY, I CAN HEAR  ...........SONNET: TO TIME  311    6
MOTES (4)
    THICKENING WITH MOTES, TO A MARRIAGE WITH THE MIRE. ..........OUIJA   77   21
    IS IT FOR THIS THE AIR MOTES DEPART? .....................THE OTHER  201   11
    THEY ARE NOT AIR MOTES, THEY ARE CORPUSCLES. .............THE OTHER  201   12
    PROBABLE MOTES THAT TICK THE YEARS OFF MY LIFE.  A BIRTHDAY PRESENT  207   43
MOTH (3)
    COCKCHAFERS AND THE WAN, GREEN LUNA MOTH. ...............GOATSUCKER  111   14
    I'LL FLY THROUGH THE CANDLE'S MOUTH LIKE A SINGELESS MOTH.*POEM.6.V.  135   20
    AND SOFT AS A MOTH, HIS BREATH. ......................THREE WOMEN  181  173
MOTH-BREATH (1)
    ALL NIGHT YOUR MOTH-BREATH .........................MORNING SONG  157   10
```

```
                                                      TITLE            PAGE  LINE
MOTHER (40)
    MOTHER, GRANDMOTHER, GREATGRANDMOTHER  ...........ALL THE DEAD DEARS  70   20
    MOTHER, MOTHER, WHAT ILLBRED AUNT  ...........THE DISQUIETING MUSES   74    1
    MOTHER, MOTHER, WHAT ILLBRED AUNT  ...........THE DISQUIETING MUSES   74    1
    MOTHER, WHO MADE TO ORDER STORIES  ...........THE DISQUIETING MUSES   75    9
    MOTHER, WHOSE WITCHES ALWAYS, ALWAYS  ........THE DISQUIETING MUSES   75   11
    MOTHER, YOU SENT ME TO PIANO LESSONS  ........THE DISQUIETING MUSES   75   33
    FROM MUSES UNHIRED BY YOU, DEAR MOTHER.  .....THE DISQUIETING MUSES   75   40
    I WOKE ONE DAY TO SEE YOU, MOTHER,  ..........THE DISQUIETING MUSES   75   41
    MOTHER, MOTHER. BUT NO FROWN OF MINE  ........THE DISQUIETING MUSES   76   55
    MOTHER, MOTHER. BUT NO FROWN OF MINE  ........THE DISQUIETING MUSES   76   55
    GO, GHOST OF OUR MOTHER AND FATHER, GHOST OF US,  ..........GHOST'S.  91   32
    LUCINA, BONY MOTHER, LABORING  ...........................MOONRISE    98   25
    SUMMER GROWS OLD, COLD-BLOODED MOTHER.  ................FROG AUTUMN   99    1
    MOTHER MEDEA IN A GREEN SMOCK  .........................AFTERMATH    114    9
    MY MOTHER UNROLLED AT YOUR LAST HOMECOMING.  ELECTRA ON AZALEA PATH  117   32
    MY MOTHER DREAMED YOU FACE DOWN IN THE SEA.  ELECTRA ON AZALEA PATH  117   36
    MY MOTHER SAID; YOU DIED LIKE ANY MAN.  .....ELECTRA ON AZALEA PATH  117   40
    HERE IS A QUEENSHIP NO MOTHER CAN CONTEST --  ..........BEEKEEPER'S. 118   13
    MOTHER, YOU ARE THE ONE MOUTH  .......................POEM.1.WHO.    132   25
    I WOULD BE A TONGUE TO. MOTHER OF OTHERNESS  ............POEM.1.WHO. 132   26
    OR MOTHER A HORSE. MY BELLY MOVES.  ...................POEM.2.DARK.  132   13
    HERE'S A CUDDLY MOTHER.  .............................POEM.2.DARK.   133   28
    THE MOTHER OF MOUTHS DIDN'T LOVE ME.  ................POEM.3.MAENAD. 133    6
    MOTHER, KEEP OUT OF MY BARNYARD,  ....................POEM.3.MAENAD. 133   14
    MOTHER OF BEETLES, ONLY UNCLENCH YOUR HAND:  .............POEM.6.W.  135   19
    THE MOTHER OF PESTLES DIMINISHED ME.  ....................POEM.7.S.  136    7
    BUT THEY ARE DEAD, AND THEIR MOTHER NEAR DEAD WITH DISTRACTION,  ...
                                                       ... STILLBORN    142   14
    THE DAY-MOON LIGHTS UP LIKE A SORRY MOTHER,  ...................SLEEP. 144  24
    AND LOVE THE MOTHER OF MILK, NO THEORY.  ......................MAGI  148   14
    OR THE SEA, HUSHING THEIR PEELED SENSE LIKE OLD MOTHER MORPHIA.  ...
                                                  ... WAKING IN WINTER  151   16
    THEN MOTHER SWAM UP, HOLDING A TIN BASIN.  .................FACE LIFT 156   7
    MOTHER TO MYSELF, I WAKE SWADDLED IN GAUZE,  ..............FACE LIFT 156   31
    I'M NO MORE YOUR MOTHER  ............................MORNING SONG    157    7
    MOTHER OF A WHITE NIKE AND SEVERAL BALD-EYED APOLLOS.  BARREN WOMAN  157    7
    THE MOON IS MY MOTHER. SHE IS NOT SWEET LIKE MARY.  ...........MOON. 173   17
    WALKING THE PLANK DRAPED WITH MOTHER FRANCE'S UPHOLSTERY  THE SWARM  217   48
    O SISTER, MOTHER, WIFE,  ...........................AMNESIAC        233   25
    O MOTHER OF LEAVES AND SWEETNESS  .................WINTER TREES      258   13
    IF YOU MUST BUTCHER MOTHER GOOSE TO DO IT.  .............DIALOGUE O. 280  149
    A SCOWL OF SUN STRUCK DOWN MY MOTHER,  ......................LAMENT  315   10
MOTHERING (1)
    WHAT PAINS, WHAT SORROWS MUST I BE MOTHERING?  .........THREE WOMEN  180  133
MOTHER-LOVE (1)
    IT WASN'T FOR ANY LACK OF MOTHER-LOVE.  ....................STILLBORN 142   5
MOTHERLY (3)
    SUCKING UP MINERALS AND MOTHERLY LOVE  .................I AM VERTICAL 162   3
    THE BROWN MOTHERLY FURROWS, THE WHOLE ESTATE.  ........THE DETECTIVE 209   37
    RED EARTH, MOTHERLY BLOOD.  ...............................BRASILIA  258   17
MOTHERS (3)
    SCARED MOTHERS TO MISCARRY,  ............THE DEATH OF MYTH-MAKING    104   12
    SELLING THE WELSH AND ENGLISH MOTHERS  .....................ON DECK  143   29
    I IMAGINE THEM WITHOUT FATHERS OR MOTHERS, LIKE THE FIRST GODS. ...
                                                  ... LAST WORDS        172    8
MOTHER'S (4)
    CRIED OUT FOR THE MOTHER'S DUG.  ....................I WANT, I WANT  106    3
    GOD-FATHERED INTO THE WORLD FROM MY MOTHER'S BELLY:  ....ELECTRA ON. 116    7
    WHEN I WORMED BACK UNDER MY MOTHER'S HEART.  ELECTRA ON AZALEA PATH 116   10
    OR SITS IN THE DESERT AND HURTS HIS MOTHER'S HEART.  ....THREE WOMEN 186  333
MOTH-FACE (1)
    THE MOTH-FACE OF HER HUSBAND, MOONWHITE AND ILL,  .............WIDOW 164   14
MOTHS (1)
    ASSEMBLE WITH THE FRAIL PALENESS OF MOTHS,  ...................OUIJA  77    4
MOTHY (1)
    A DRESSING OF MULE EARS, MOTHY PELTS, BUT GREEN-HEARTED,*POEM.1.WHO. 131   17
MOTION (2)
    THE PISTON IN MOTION ---  .................................YEARS    255   12
    YET ORDERED LUNAR MOTION  ......................TRIO OF LOVE SONGS   314   11
MOTLEY (1)
    INTO VULGAR MOTLEY --  ..................................SPINSTER     50   21
MOTTLE (1)
    STREAK AND MOTTLE OF TAWN BARK,  ..........ON THE PLETHORA OF DRYADS  67   22
MOTTLED (2)
    CAMOUFLAGED IN MOTTLED MAIL  ..........MUSSEL HUNTER AT ROCK HARBOR   96   31
    RED, MOTTLED, LIKE CUT NECKS.  ......................LITTLE FUGUE    188   35
MOUND (1)
    THEY MOUND A SUMMER COOLNESS IN OUR VIEW.  .........ABOVE THE OXBOW   88   14
MOUNDED (1)
    THESE BODIES MOUNDED AROUND ME NOW, THESE POLAR SLEEPERS --  THREE. 181  181
MOUNT (2)
    ON PINCKNEY, MOUNT VERNON, CHESTNUT,  ...............A WINTER'S TALE  87   25
    HERE ON A MOUNT OVERLAID WITH LEAVES. THE PAINT-PEELED  ......OXBOW.  88   34
```

MOUNTAIN (4)
    THE GROUNDHOG ON THE MOUNTAIN DID NOT RUN ............INCOMMUNICADO 100   1
    I AM A MOUNTAIN NOW, AMONG MOUNTAINY WOMEN. ....THREE WOMEN 179 113
    THIS RAM OF BLACKNESS. I FOLD MY HANDS ON A MOUNTAIN. ..THREE WOMEN 180 143
    OVER THE SEVEN HILLS, THE RED FURROW, THE BLUE MOUNTAIN? *DETECTIVE. 208   2
MOUNTAINING (1)
    MOUNTAINING THEM ON SPREAD NEWSPAPER. .................RHODODENDRON. 104   23
MOUNTAINS (4)
    WE HAVE NOT MOUNTAINS, BUT MOUNTS, TRUNCATED HILLOCKS ....OXBOW.   87   2
    INSOLVENT AMONG THE MOUNTAINS. ....THE COURAGE OF SHUTTING-UP 210   35
    THE LONELINESS OF ITS EYE, THE EYE OF THE MOUNTAINS ....TOTEM 264   20
    DIAGRAM OF MOUNTAINS ....TRIO OF LOVE SONGS 313   5
MOUNTAINSIDE (1)
    MADE BY MINERS UP THE MOUNTAINSIDE ....THE PRINCESS AND THE GOBLINS 334   33
MOUNTAINY (1)
    I AM A MOUNTAIN NOW, AMONG MOUNTAINY WOMEN. ....THREE WOMEN 179 113
MOUNTS (2)
    WE HAVE NOT MOUNTAINS, BUT MOUNTS, TRUNCATED HILLOCKS ....OXBOW.   87   2
    SHE MOUNTS THROUGH MALICE OF THE NEEDLE'S EYE, ...THE PRINCESS. 333   10
MOURN (2)
    HOARD LAST YEAR'S LEAVES, WON'T MOURN, WEAR SACKCLOTH, OR TURN ...
                                          ... NOVEMBER GRAVEYARD   56   2
    BESIDE A SUNBLUE SEA, AND MOURN THE FLAGON ....SONNET: TO TIME 311   10
MOURNED (1)
    MOURNED BY RELIGIOUS FIGURES, BY GARLANDED CHILDREN. GETTING THERE 249   48
MOURNFUL (1)
    THE DAY IS BLAZING. IT IS VERY MOURNFUL. ....THREE WOMEN 184 262
MOURNFULLY (1)
    MOURNFULLY THE DRY TONGUES CLACKED THEIR GUILT: ....SNOWMAN O.   59   39
MOURNING (3)
    DRESSED IN BLACK, EVERYBODY IN MOURNING FOR SOMEONE.*THE NET-MENDERS 121   4
    I CRAWL LIKE AN ANT IN MOURNING ....THE COLOSSUS 129   12
    THE TREES OF LONELINESS, THE TREES OF MOURNING. ....WIDOW 164   27
MOUSE (4)
    FOOTING SALLOW AS A MOUSE ....MISS DRAKE PROCEEDS TO SUPPER   41   9
    ...OF A WOMAN, A MOUSE AND A SHREW. THE ANKLE-BONE
        OF THE... ....ALL THE DEAD DEARS   70 E/3
    RELICS OF A MOUSE AND A SHREW ....ALL THE DEAD DEARS   70   5
    HE WERE DIGESTING A MOUSE. ....MEDALLION 125   24
MOUSETRAP (1)
    AND MOCKS! HERE'S THE PARODY OF THAT MORAL MOUSETRAP ....VIRGIN.   81   2
MOUTH (43)
    MARK, I CRY, THAT MOUTH ... .STRUMPET SONG   33   9
    CUPPED QUICK TO MOUTH; ....THE GLUTTON   40   10
    THE STRAIGHT MOUTH. ....RECANTATION   42   16
    THE GLASS MOUTH SUCKS BLOOD-HEAT FROM MY FOREFINGER. ....OUIJA   77   10
    A BEDRAGGLED SNAKE, HANGING LIMP AS THE ABSURD MOUTH ......PERSEUS   83   38
    NOEL! NOEL! NO MOUTH IS SHUT. ....A WINTER'S TALE   87   27
    GRIEVOUSLY PURPLED, MOUTH SKEWERED ON A GROAN, ...THE RAVAGED FACE 115   6
    THEY SLEEP ON, MOUTH TO MOUTH. ....THE SLEEPERS 123   15
    THEY SLEEP ON, MOUTH TO MOUTH. ....THE SLEEPERS 123   15
    EATEN OR ROTTEN. I AM ALL MOUTH. POEM.1.WHO. 131   2
    MOTHER, YOU ARE THE ONE MOUTH POEM.1.WHO. 132   25
    IT IS EASY TO BLAME THE DARK: THE MOUTH OF A DOOR, ...POEM.6.W. 135   7
    I'LL FLY THROUGH THE CANDLE'S MOUTH LIKE A SINGELESS MOTH.*POEM.6.W. 135   20
    YOUR TWO-HORNED RHINOCEROS OPENED A MOUTH ....ZOO KEEPER'S WIFE 155   34
    YOUR MOUTH OPENS CLEAN AS A CAT'S. THE WINDOW SQUARE ..MORNING SONG 157   15
    THEN SHE COULD COVER MY MOUTH AND EYES, COVER ME ENTIRELY, *PLASTER. 159   40
    THEY ARE OPENING LIKE THE MOUTH OF SOME GREAT AFRICAN CAT, ..TULIPS 162   59
    I WALK AMONG THEM, AND THEY STUFF MY MOUTH WITH COTTON. FINISTERRE 169   17
    IT HAS SHUT ITS MOUTH ON THE STONE PILL OF REPOSE. ....SURGEON. 171   30
    FOR THE SPIRIT TO CONCEIVE A FACE, A MOUTH? ....THREE WOMEN 177   26
    FATTENS US, IS KIND. HER MOUTH IS RED. ....THREE WOMEN 181 156
    A RED, HARD WOOD, EYES SHUT AND MOUTH WIDE OPEN. ....THREE WOMEN 182 212
    AND FROM THE OPEN MOUTH ISSUE SHARP CRIES ....THREE WOMEN 182 213
    MY DAUGHTER HAS NO TEETH. HER MOUTH IS WIDE. ....THREE WOMEN 182 216
    I DRAW ON THE OLD MOUTH. ....THREE WOMEN 183 246
    THE RED MOUTH I PUT BY WITH MY IDENTITY ....THREE WOMEN 183 247
    THE WIND GAGGING MY MOUTH WITH MY OWN BLOWN HAIR,*THE RABBIT CATCHER 193   2
    OPENS ITS MOUTH NOW, DEMANDING. ....EVENT 194   8
    AND A NAKED MOUTH, RED AND AWKWARD. ....BERCK-PLAGE 201 124
    FLICKERING LIKE THAT, WRINKLY AND CLEAR RED, LIKE THE SKIN
        OF A MOUTH. ....POPPIES IN JULY 203   6
    A MOUTH JUST BLOODIED. ....POPPIES IN JULY 203   7
    IF MY MOUTH COULD MARRY A HURT LIKE THAT! ....POPPIES IN JULY 203   12
    LET IT NOT COME BY WORD OF MOUTH, I SHOULD BE SIXTY ......BIRTHDAY. 208   53
    THE MOUTH FIRST, ITS ABSENCE REPORTED ....THE DETECTIVE 209   27
    THE COURAGE OF THE SHUT MOUTH, IN SPITE OF ARTILLERY! .....COURAGE. 209   1
    I BREATHE, AND THE MOUTH ....PURDAH 243   24
    STRIPES FOR MOUTH AND EYES AND NOSE, ...THE FEARFUL 256   6
    MOUTH FULL OF PEARLS, ...PARALYTIC 266   24
    MY MOUTH SAGS, ...GIGOLO 267   18
    THE MOUTH OF CHRIST ....GIGOLO 267   19
    OUR SEPARATE VEINS AND THIS GLASS MOUTH. OH YOU'RE .....DIALOGUE O. 280 147

MOUTH (CONT.)
    WITH THE SOUND OF THE SEA IN YOUR MOUTH. ....THE RIVAL/DR 291 19
    AND KISS HER ON THE MOUTH FOR SHE ....THE DREAM 311 21
MOUTH-ASH (1)
    MOUTH-ASH, ASH OF EYE. ....MARY'S SONG 257 14
MOUTHFULS (1)
    BLACK SWEET BLOOD MOUTHFULS, ...ARIEL 239 13
MOUTH-HOLE (3)
    ONLY THE MOUTH-HOLE PIPED OUT, ...POEM.7.S. 136 11
    THE MOUTH-HOLE CRYING THEIR LOCATIONS. POEM.7.S. 136 16
    IN DREAMS, THROUGH MOUTH-HOLE OR EYE-HOLE. I CAN'T STOP IT. *LAST W. 172 15
MOUTHING (1)
    FARTHER OUT, THE WAVES WILL BE MOUTHING ICECAKES -- ..A WINTER SHIP 113 21
MOUTHINGS (1)
    A GARDEN OF MOUTHINGS. PURPLE, SCARLET-SPECKLED, BLACK *BEEKEEPER'S. 118   1
MOUTHLESS (1)
    MOUTHLESS, EYELESS, WITH STITCHED BALD HEAD. THE DISQUIETING MUSES 75 16
MOUTHPIECE (2)
    MOUTHPIECE OF THE DEAD, OR OF SOME GOD OR OTHER. ......THE COLOSSUS 129   7
    MIGHT DO AS A GOD'S MOUTHPIECE IF A WHIRLWIND ....DIALOGUE O. 281 202
MOUTH-PIPE (1)
    WITH MOON-EYE, MOUTH-PIPE. HE PIPES. PIPES GREEN. PIPES WATER. ...
            ... SNAKECHARMER 79   3
MOUTH-PLUGS (1)
    OFF THAT LANDSPIT OF STONY MOUTH-PLUGS, ...MEDUSA 224   1
MOUTHS (10)
    PURPLE AND RED MOUTHS, UTTERLY LOVELY. POEM.1.WHO. 132 30
    THE MOTHER OF MOUTHS DIDN'T LOVE ME. POEM.3.MAENAD. 133   6
    SHUTTING THEIR MOUTHS ON IT, LIKE A COMMUNION TABLET. ....TULIPS 161 35
    POPPING UPWARD FROM THE MOUTHS OF BELLS ....LYONNESSE 234   9
    THAT THESE LATE MOUTHS SHOULD CRY OPEN ....POPPIES IN OCTOBER 240 11
    GOLDS BLEED AND DEEPEN, THE MOUTHS OF THERMOPYLAE. ..LETTER IN NOV. 254 35
    GLEAMING WITH THE MOUTHS OF CORPSES. ....CHILDLESS WOMAN 259 18
    OF COOL MOUTHS AND HANDS OPEN AND NATURAL AS ROSES. ......FEVER./DR 294 10
    GOLD MOUTHS CRY ....GOLD MOUTHS CRY 302   T
    GOLD MOUTHS CRY WITH THE GREEN YOUNG ....GOLD MOUTHS CRY 302   1
MOUTH'S (2)
    MEAT MUST GLUT HIS MOUTH'S RAW WOUND. ....PURSUIT 22 16
    MOUTH'S INSTANT FLARE FOR FUTURE LOOKS; *EPITAPH FOR FIRE AND FLOWER 45 11
MOVE (25)
    I SAW SLOW FLOCKED COWS MOVE ....SONG FOR A SUMMER'S DAY 30   3
    TO TRAP THIS WAYWARD GIRL AT HER FIRST MOVE OF LOVE,   DREAM WITH C. 44 27
    ON THE MOVE, HEDGED BY A LITTER OF FEAT-FOOT NINNIES ....SOW 61 21
    TO MOVE, SERVE, STEER FOOD, ...WORDS FOR A NURSERY 73 13
    AND NEVER SAW HOW COOLLY WE MIGHT MOVE. FOR ONCE ...ABOVE THE OXBOW 89 55
    HANDS MOVING MOVE PRIESTLIER ....SCULPTOR 91   5
    OF YOUR BURIAL MOVE ME ....FULL FATHOM FIVE 93 22
    IN THE SULFUROUS NOON. WE MOVE ....IN MIDAS' COUNTRY 99   6
    YOU MOVE AMONG THE MANY-BREASTED HIVES, ...THE BEEKEEPER'S DAUGHTER 118   6
    OF OUR HUSBANDS AND SONS MOVE SURE AMONG THE LOW STARS. ......NET-. 121 19
    YOU MOVE THROUGH THE ERA OF FISHES, ...THE MANOR GARDEN 125   5
    THEY MOVE THROUGH THEIR MUTE ROOMS WHILE I SLEEP, ...BLUE MOLES 126 23
    BLUE MISTS MOVE OVER ....DARK WOOD, DARK WATER 127   6
    IF I DON'T MOVE ABOUT, I'LL KNOCK NOTHING OVER. SO I SAID,*POEM.6.W. 135 14
    STILL NOBODY WILL MOVE OR SPEAK -- ....ON DECK 142 10
    THE DOCTORS MOVE AMONG US AS IF OUR BIGNESS ....THREE WOMEN 179 114
    I SHALL MOVE NORTH. I SHALL MOVE INTO A LONG BLACKNESS. *THREE WOMEN 182 190
    I SHALL MOVE NORTH. I SHALL MOVE INTO A LONG BLACKNESS. *THREE WOMEN 182 190
    THEY MOVE IN A HURRY. ...................................APPREHENSIONS 196 20
    I HAVE TWO LEGS, AND I MOVE SMILINGLY. ....BERCK-PLAGE 196   6
    OF THE WHEELS MOVE, THEY APPALL ME --- ....GETTING THERE 248   4
    TODAY WE MOVE IN JADE AND CEASE WITH GARNET ....SONNET: TO TIME 311   1
    TO FIND WHAT MAKES IT MOVE, ...TRIO OF LOVE SONGS 315 50
    OBSCURE THE SCALDING SUN TILL NO CLOCKS MOVE. ......SONNET TO SATAN 323 14
    OUR DRASTIC JARGON, BUT CLOCK HANDS THAT MOVE ...LOVE IS A PARALLAX 329 17
MOVED (5)
    ALL SUMMER WE MOVED IN A VILLA BRIMFUL OF ECHOES, ...THE OTHER TWO 68   1
    SOME SUCH TRANSFIGURING MOVED ....THE GREAT CARBUNCLE 72   9
    OR TO AVOID ME. THEY MOVED ....MUSSEL HUNTER AT ROCK HARBOR 96 45
    WHAT MOVED THE PALE, RAPTORIAL OWL ....OWL 102   9
    MOVING, BEING MOVED. AND WE'LL IMAGINE   DIALOGUE OVER A OUIJA BOARD 276   8
MOVES (8)
    MOVES ON ITS ROOT. THOUGH A MIST-WRAITH WOUND .....HARDCASTLE CRAGS 62 13
    SO FABLES SAY THE GOATSUCKER MOVES, MASKED FROM MEN'S SIGHT ...
            ... GOATSUCKER 111   9
    MOVES HUMBLY AS ANY HOUSEWIFE THROUGH ....AFTERMATH 114 10
    OR MOTHER A HORSE. MY BELLY MOVES. POEM.2.DARK. 132 13
    A FAR SEA MOVES IN MY EAR. ....MORNING SONG 157 12
    WHERE DO YOU LIVE? HE MOVES. HE'S MOVING BRISK ....DIALOGUE O. 281 206
    MOVES TO OUR MINOR LOVE. ....TRIO OF LOVE SONGS 314 16
    AND LUMBERING MOVES ....AERIALIST 331 33
MOVIE (2)
    IT WAS ONLY IN A MOVIE, IT WAS ONLY ....THE THIN PEOPLE 64   5
    OVER AND OVER THE OLD, GRANULAR MOVIE ....INSOMNIAC 163   8

                                                               TITLE   PAGE LINE
MOVIE-SCREEN (1)
    ON A MOVIE-SCREEN. THEY ....THE THIN PEOPLE   64   3
MOVING (8)
    AND GRAYER; NOT EVEN MOVING THEIR BONES. ....THE THIN PEOPLE   65   47
    HANDS MOVING MOVE PRIESTLIER ....SCULPTOR   91   5
    AND THE EYES OF THE KILLER MOVING SLUGLIKE AND SIDELONG, *DETECTIVE. 208   8
    THE VILLAGERS ARE MOVING THE VIRGINS, THERE WILL BE NO KILLING.*BEE. 212   49
    MOVING AND RUBBING ON THE SILK ....BALLOONS 271   5
    MOVING, BEING MOVED. AND WE'LL IMAGINE   DIALOGUE OVER A OUIJA BOARD 276   8
    WHERE DO YOU LIVE? HE MOVES. HE'S MOVING BRISK ....DIALOGUE O. 281 206
    SOME DAY, MOVING, ONE WILL DROP, ...LOVE IS A PARALLAX 330   63
M-S (1)
    M-S. MANUSCRIPT? HE STOPS. I WISH ......DIALOGUE OVER A OUIJA BOARD 279   95
MUCH (20)
    GRIP THE RAIL, SQUINT AHEAD, AND WONDER HOW MUCH LONGER   CHANNEL C.   26   6
    AND ALL GREEN DREAMS NOT WORTH MUCH, ...STRUMPET SONG   33   2
    WHICH SEEMED, WHEN DREAMED, TO MEAN SO PROFOUNDLY MUCH, ...GHOST'S.   90   5
    CANNOT LOOK MUCH BUT YOUR FORM SUFFERS ....FULL FATHOM FIVE   92   17
    SOMEWHERE BY MUCH SUN AND WIND; ....MUSSEL HUNTER AT ROCK HARBOR   97   73
    WINDED BY MUCH ROCK-BUMPING ....THE HERMIT AT OUTERMOST HOUSE 118   5
    NOW THERE IS NOTHING MUCH TO LOOK AT. ....ON DECK 142   9
    ONLY MUCH WHITER AND UNBREAKABLE AND WITH NO COMPLAINTS. *IN PLASTER 158   8
    AND THEY ARE WAN, DULLED BY MUCH TRAVELLING.*STARS OVER THE DORDOGNE 165   11
    OR MUCH COMPANY, OR THE MILDNESS OF THE SOUTH. ....STARS. 166   30
    THERE IS TOO MUCH EASE HERE; THESE STARS TREAT ME TOO WELL.   STARS. 166   37
    WARMED BY MUCH HANDLING. THEY ALMOST PURR. ....LAST WORDS 172   18
    THEY HAVE TOO MANY COLORS, TOO MUCH LIFE. THEY ARE NOT QUIET,*THREE. 178   69
    EMPTY SCHOOLROOMS, EMPTY CHURCHES. O SO MUCH EMPTINESS! *THREE WOMEN 181 179
    I DO NOT WANT MUCH OF A PRESENT, ANYWAY, THIS YEAR. ......BIRTHDAY. 206   13
    HE HAS SEEN TOO MUCH DEATH, HIS HANDS ARE FULL OF IT. .....COURAGE. 210   15
    SO MUCH FOR THE CHARIOTEERS, THE OUTRIDERS, THE GRAND ARMY!   SWARM. 217   39
    OVER THE ENGLISH CLIFF AND UNDER SO MUCH HISTORY! ....LYONNESSE 234   22
    SO I SAW YOUR MUCH SICKER ..............................EAVESDROPPER 260   24
    NOW, YOU REALLY DON'T MUCH CARE WHICH, OR WHAT ....DIALOGUE O. 280 151
MUCH-POKED (1)
    BLUEBLACK, WITH THE MUCH-POKED PERIODS OF STARS ....INSOMNIAC 163   2
MUCK (3)
    WITH TARRY MUCK ....GREEN ROCK, WINTHROP BAY 105   12
    MUCK FUNNEL, MUCK FUNNEL --*WORDS HEARD, BY ACCIDENT, OVER THE PHONE 203   14
    MUCK FUNNEL, MUCK FUNNEL --*WORDS HEARD, BY ACCIDENT, OVER THE PHONE 203   14
MUCK-TRAP (1)
    CAUGHT (AS IT WERE) IN THE MUCK-TRAP ....LETTER TO A PURIST   37   11
MUD (21)
    TO UNMADE MUD CLOAKED BY SOUR SKY. ....FIRESONG   30   14
    SILENT AND SHINING ON A GREEN ROCK BEDDED IN MUD, ...DREAM WITH C.   44   15
    PIG HOVE, LETTING LEGEND LIKE DRIED MUD DROP, ...SOW   61   37
    ANY MORE THAN THE OLD WOMAN IN HER MUD HUT COULD ...THE THIN PEOPLE   64   26
    MUD STENCH, SHELL GUTS, GULLS' LEAVINGS; ....MUSSEL HUNTER.   95   13
    SMALL MUD KNOBS, NUDGED FROM UNDER, ...MUSSEL HUNTER AT ROCK HARBOR   96   26
    AND FROM THE TRENCH-DUG MUD, ALL ......MUSSEL HUNTER AT ROCK HARBOR   96   30
    AND TRICKLE. COULD THEY FEEL MUD ......MUSSEL HUNTER AT ROCK HARBOR   96   48
    HIS WORLD OF MUD -- GREEN COLOR ....MUSSEL HUNTER AT ROCK HARBOR   97   71
    TO START THE SPIRIT OUT OF THE MUD ....THE COMPANIONABLE ILLS 105   6
    LITTER THE MUD LIKE ORANGEPEEL. ....PRIVATE GROUND 130   12
    FLEX AS THE MUD FREEZES. ....PRIVATE GROUND 131   21
    GULLS HAVE THREADED THE RIVER'S MUD BED BACK *PARLIAMENT HILL FIELDS 152   6
    WEARS THE FACE OF A PHARAOH, THOUGH IT'S MADE OF MUD AND WATER. ...
                                                     ... IN PLASTER 159   42
    O MUD, MUD, HOW FLUID! --   WORDS HEARD, BY ACCIDENT, OVER THE PHONE 202   1
    O MUD, MUD, HOW FLUID! --   WORDS HEARD, BY ACCIDENT, OVER THE PHONE 202   1
    THEY ARE PLOPPING LIKE MUD.*WORDS HEARD, BY ACCIDENT, OVER THE PHONE 202   7
    THE MUD SQUIRMS WITH THROATS, ...THE SWARM 216   13
    HERE THERE IS SUCH MUD. ....GETTING THERE 248   21
    THERE IS MUD ON MY FEET, ...GETTING THERE 248   35
    DUPE THE DULL SOW LOUNGING SNOUT IN MUD, ...GO GET THE GOODLY SQUAB 313   11
MUDDLING (1)
    AND MINCED THE MUDDLING DEVIL ....THE DEATH OF MYTH-MAKING 104   10
MUDDY (1)
    THE MUDDY RUMORS ....FULL FATHOM FIVE   93   21
MUD-MATTRESSED (1)
    MUD-MATTRESSED UNDER THE SIGN OF THE HAG ....MAUDLIN   51   1
MUD-SUMP (1)
    MUD-SUMP, HAPPY STY-FACE. POEM.4.BEAST. 134   17
MUFFLE (1)
    RUMBAS AND SAMBAS NO EAR-FLAPS CAN MUFFLE. ....ALICANTE LULLABY   43   14
MUFFLES (1)
    MUFFLES THEIR BIRD-FEET: THEY WHISTLE FOR JOY. ....LEAVING EARLY 146   37
MUG (1)
    I FELT HANDS ROUND A TEA MUG, DULL, BLUNT, ...THE RABBIT CATCHER 194   22
MULATTO (1)
    WORKING IT LIKE DOUGH, A MULATTO BODY, ...LESBOS 229   61
MULBERRIES (1)
    GRUB-WHITE MULBERRIES REDDEN AMONG LEAVES. ....MOONRISE   98   1
MULBERRY (1)
    THE QUEEN IN THE MULBERRY ARBOR STARED ....THE BULL OF BENDYLAW 108   4

		TITLE	PAGE	LINE

MULE (1)
   A DRESSING OF MULE EARS, MOTHY PELTS, BUT GREEN-HEARTED,*POEM.1.WHO. 131 17
MULE-BRAY (1)
   MULE-BRAY, PIG-GRUNT AND BAWDY CACKLES ....THE COLOSSUS 129   3
MULISH (1)
   SUCH COLLUSION OF MULISH ELEMENTS ....POINT SHIRLEY 110 17
MULLED (1)
   GULLS MULLED IN THE GREENEST LIGHT. ..THE HERMIT AT OUTERMOST HOUSE 119 19
MULTIFARIOUS (1)
   THEIR MULTIFARIOUS SILKS IN THE HOLY GROVE*ON THE PLETHORA OF DRYADS   68 33
MULTIPLICATION (1)
   LOVELESS AS THE MULTIPLICATION TABLE. ....MAGI 148   8
MULTIPLIED (3)
   OUR FOOTSTEPS MULTIPLIED IN THE SHADOWY CHAMBERS, ...THE OTHER TWO   68 11
   MULTIPLIED TO INFINITY LIKE ANGELS ON A PINHEAD ..ZOO KEEPER'S WIFE 155 22
   MULTIPLIED IN THE EYES OF THE FLIES. ....TOTEM 265 30
MULTIPLIES (2)
   OUR KIND MULTIPLIES: ....MUSHROOMS 139 30
   PARTS, BITS, COGS, THE SHINING MULTIPLES. ....THREE WOMEN 177 29
MULTIPLY (2)
   THE PEASANTS FEAST AND MULTIPLY. ....ON THE DECLINE OF ORACLES   78 16
   MULTIPLY PINK HARLEQUINS AND SING ....-...LOVE IS A PARALLAX 330 46
MULTITUDE (1)
   A MULTITUDE OF SHADED GRAYS; SUSPENSE ....LOVE IS A PARALLAX 329 10
MUM (1)
   BLANK-FACED AND MUM AS A NURSE. ....BARREN WOMAN 157 10
MUMBLE (1)
   TAKE THE GENERAL MUMBLE, ...NOTES TO A NEOPHYTE 306   1
MUMBLEPAWS (1)
   MUMBLEPAWS, TEARY AND SORRY, ...POEM.4.BEAST. 134 12
MUMMY-CASE (1)
   AND WEAR MY PAINTED FACE THE WAY A MUMMY-CASE ....IN PLASTER 159 41
MUMMY-CLOTHS (1)
   MUMMY-CLOTHS, SMILING: I'M ALL RIGHT. ....FACE LIFT 155   3
MUMMY'S (1)
   THIS SHED'S FUSTY AS A MUMMY'S STOMACH: POEM.1.WHO. 131   4
MUMMY-WISE (1)
   ALOOF, SQUATTING MUMMY-WISE, GERD SCANS ....CRYSTAL GAZER   55 28
MUNDANE (2)
   FRINGE OF MUNDANE VISION, THIS GHOST GOES ..THE GHOST'S LEAVETAKING   90 22
   BEYOND THE MUNDANE ORDER, ...LORELEI   94 22
MUNICH (2)
   THE MUNICH MANNEQUINS ....THE MUNICH MANNEQUINS 262   T
   IN MUNICH, MORGUE BETWEEN PARIS AND ROME, ...THE MUNICH MANNEQUINS 263 12
MURDER (1)
   NOW WITH STAKE AND PITCHFORK THEY ADVANCE, FLINT EYES FIXED
      ON MURDER. .... DREAM WITH CLAM-DIGGERS   44 28
MURDERED (1)
   I SHOULD HAVE MURDERED THIS, THAT MURDERS ME. ....THREE WOMEN 180 126
MURDERESS (1)
   THE UPFLIGHT OF THE MURDERESS INTO A HEAVEN THAT LOVES HER. ...BEE. 212 48
MURDEROUS (3)
   FATHER, THIS THICK AIR IS MURDEROUS. ....FULL FATHOM FIVE   93 44
   OUSTS MISTIER PEERS AND THRIVES, MURDEROUS, ...POEMS, POTATOES 106   2
   SO MURDEROUS IN ITS STRANGLE OF BRANCHES? --- ....ELM 193 39
MURDERS (1)
   I SHOULD HAVE MURDERED THIS, THAT MURDERS ME. ....THREE WOMEN 180 126
MURMURING (1)
   PRICKLING MY ANKLES AND MURMURING OF THEIR HUMILITY. ....MOON. 172   4
MUSCLES (1)
   IN THE DEEP CONVULSION GRIPPING YOUR FACE, MUSCLES ....PERSEUS   83 43
MUSE (3)
   AND A FUN-HOUSE MIRROR THAT TURNS THE TRAGIC MUSE ....PERSEUS   83 36
   MUSE, COMPOSE. ....YADDO: THE GRAND MANOR 123 12
   SEND MY MUSE ALICE PACKING WITH GAUDY SCRAPS ....A SORCERER B. 324   7
MUSES (3)
   THE DISQUIETING MUSES ....THE DISQUIETING MUSES   74   T
   FROM MUSES UNHIRED BY YOU, DEAR MOTHER. .....THE DISQUIETING MUSES   75 40
   SHE MUSES ON THE ODOR, SWEET AND SICK, ...FEMALE AUTHOR 301 11
MUSEUM (4)
   SECURE IN MUSEUM DIAMOND FOR THE STARE   EPITAPH FOR FIRE AND FLOWER   45 18
   IN THE ARCHAEOLOGICAL MUSEUM IN CAMBRIDGE IS A STONE...
      ... ALL THE DEAD DEARS   70 E/1
   IN A DRAFTY MUSEUM, YOUR NAKEDNESS ....MORNING SONG 157   5
   MUSEUM WITHOUT STATUES, GRAND WITH PILLARS, PORTICOES, ROTUNDAS. ...
      ... BARREN WOMAN 157   2
MUSEUM-CASED (1)
   THIS ANTIQUE MUSEUM-CASED LADY ....ALL THE DEAD DEARS   70   3
MUSEUMS (1)
   MUSEUMS AND SEPULCHERS? YOU. YOU ....PERSEUS   82 11
MUSHROOM (1)
   OF MUSHROOM SIMILE AND GRYPHON GARB. ....A SORCERER B. 324   8
MUSHROOMS (2)
   MUSHROOMS ....MUSHROOMS 139   T
   LIKE THE UNDERSIDE OF MUSHROOMS. DO YOU FEEL ....DIALOGUE O. 285 315

330

                                                                    TITLE   PAGE   LINE
MUSIC (3)
      CONSUME THIS PIPER AND HE TIRES OF MUSIC ..............SNAKECHARMER   79   22
      FINGERING A LEAFLET OF MUSIC, OVER HIM, *TWO VIEWS OF A CADAVER ROOM   114   17
      AS AMID THE HECTIC MUSIC AND COCKTAIL TALK ....CINDERELLA   304   13
MUSK (2)
      MUSK SATISFIED MY NOSE, RED MY EYE, ...RHODODENDRON.   103   13
      THEIR MUSK ENCROACHES, CIRCLE AFTER CIRCLE,*THE BEEKEEPER'S DAUGHTER   118   3
MUSKRAT (1)
      AND TRAP THE MUSKRAT NAPPING IN SLACK SUN;   GO GET THE GOODLY SQUAB   313   10
MUSKY (1)
      MUSKY AS A LOVEBED THE MORNING AFTER. ....LEAVING EARLY   146   19
MUSSEL (1)
      MUSSEL HUNTER AT ROCK HARBOR ....MUSSEL HUNTER AT ROCK HARBOR   95   T
MUSSEL-PICKER (1)
      TWO-LEGGED MUSSEL-PICKER ....MUSSEL HUNTER AT ROCK HARBOR   97   66
MUSSELS (5)
      FREE FISH-BAIT: THE BLUE MUSSELS ......MUSSEL HUNTER AT ROCK HARBOR   95   9
      THE MUSSELS HUNG DULL BLUE AND ....MUSSEL HUNTER AT ROCK HARBOR   95   17
      MUSSELS. FROM WHAT THE CRABS SAW, ...MUSSEL HUNTER AT ROCK HARBOR   97   64
      MUSSELS CLUSTER BLUE AS GRAPES: ....MAGNOLIA SHOALS   122   17
      GRAPEBLUE MUSSELS ....AQUATIC NOCTURNE   305   13
MUST (42)
      MEAT MUST GLUT HIS MOUTH'S RAW WOUND. ....PURSUIT   22   16
      SUCH STARKNESS; ACCURACY MUST NOT STALK AT LARGE: ....TALE OF A TUB   25   35
      IS HELPLESS HERE, QUITE EXTRA, YET WE MUST MAKE ...CHANNEL CROSSING   27   35
      SO HUNGERED, SHE MUST WAIT IN RAGE ....THE SHRIKE   42   15
      POCKED BY ROOK-CLAW AND RABBIT-TRACK: SHE MUST YET WIN ..SNOWMAN O.   58   17
      DREAM-FILMED. WHAT A VISION OF ANCIENT HOGHOOD MUST ....SOW   61   27
      I MUST WATCH SLUTTISH DRYADS TWITCH ......ON THE PLETHORA OF DRYADS   67   32
      MUST WAIT, WHILE HERE SUSO'S ....A LESSON IN VENGEANCE   80   11
      OR MUST TAKE LOOPHOLE AND BLAME TIME ......GREEN ROCK, WINTHROP BAY   105   22
      I SAID: I MUST REMEMBER THIS, BEING SMALL. POEM.1.WHO.   132   28
      I MUST MAKE MORE MAPS. POEM.2.DARK.   132   14
      I MUST SWALLOW IT ALL. POEM.3.MAENAD.   133   21
      NOW I SEE IT MUST BE ONE OR THE OTHER OF US. ....IN PLASTER   160   52
      TENDS TO THE PEBBLES IT MUST RUN OVER, SMOOTHING THEM GENTLY.*TULIPS   160   16
      UNKNOWING I MUST SOON UNPETAL. ....I AM VERTICAL   162   7
      I MUST MOST PERFECTLY RESEMBLE THEM -- ....I AM VERTICAL   162   15
      IT LOOKS IN ON, AND MUST GO ON LOOKING IN ON. ....WIDOW   165   40
      I HAD NOT ASKED FOR SUCH A BLOOD SISTERHOOD; THEY MUST LOVE ME. ...
                                                         ... BLACKBERRYING   168   8
      I MUST SEAL OFF AND LET FILL ....THE SURGEON AT 2 A.M.   171   25
      WHAT PAINS, WHAT SORROWS MUST I BE MOTHERING? ....THREE WOMEN   180   133
      THEIR SHADOWS MUST COVER CANADA. ....CROSSING THE WATER   190   3
      WILL TOLERATE NO BYSTANDING: I MUST SHRIEK. ....ELM   192   21
      YOU ARE TOO BIG. THEY MUST TAKE YOU BACK! ....WORDS HEARD.   203   15
      IT MUST BE A TUSK THERE, A GHOST-COLUMN. ....A BIRTHDAY PRESENT   206   19
      MUST YOU STAMP EACH PIECE IN PURPLE, ...A BIRTHDAY PRESENT   207   46
      MUST YOU KILL WHAT YOU CAN? ....A BIRTHDAY PRESENT   207   47
      INDEFATIGABLE, PURPLE. MUST IT BE CUT OUT? ....COURAGE.   210   18
      SHE IS OLD, OLD, OLD, SHE MUST LIVE ANOTHER YEAR, AND SHE
                   KNOWS IT. ....THE BEE MEETING 212   44
      IT MUST BE SHOT DOWN. POM! POM! ....THE SWARM   216   19
      AROUND THE RING. I THINK IT MUST BE MAKING SURE ....DIALOGUE O.   277   22
      EACH TIME MUST LEARN THE LETTERS NEW. ARE ....DIALOGUE O.   277   24
      TO YES, HIS SURENESS MUST BE HIS, NOT OURS. ....DIALOGUE O.   278   73
      TO SAY THAT. THAT MUST BE HIS: HIS WORD. YOU SEE, ...DIALOGUE O.   278   79
      IF YOU MUST BUTCHER MOTHER GOOSE TO DO IT. ....DIALOGUE O.   280   149
      MUST HAVE BEEN WHOLLY SOMEONE ELSE. IT'S ABSURD, ...DIALOGUE O.   285   309
      TOAD-STONE! I SEE I MUST WEAR YOU IN THE CENTRE OF MY FOREHEAD ...
                                                         ... THE RIVAL/DR   291   27
      NOW YOU MUST PLAY THE STRAIGHT MAN FOR A TERM ....DIRGE FOR A JOKER   303   13
      THE ENORMOUS MORTGAGE MUST BE PAID SOMEHOW, ...THE DISPOSSESSED   318   1
      THE ENORMOUS MORTGAGE MUST BE PAID SOMEHOW. ....THE DISPOSSESSED   318   6
      THE ENORMOUS MORTGAGE MUST BE PAID SOMEHOW. ....THE DISPOSSESSED   318   12
      THE ENORMOUS MORTGAGE MUST BE PAID SOMEHOW: ....THE DISPOSSESSED   319   18
      BY DAY SHE MUST WALK IN DREAD ....:....AERIALIST   332   44
MUSTACHE (1)
      AND YOUR NEAT MUSTACHE ....DADDY   223   43
MUSTERING (1)
      STILL, THEY'RE OUR BEST MUSTERING OF HEIGHT: BY ....ABOVE THE OXBOW   88   5
MUTE (10)
      THEN, HONOR-BOUND, MUTE GRAZING CATTLE; ....BUCOLICS   24   11
      THAN TO SIT MUTE, TWITCHING SO ....MONOLOGUE AT 3 A.M.   40   8
      FROM THE MUTE SKY, I CAN'T HONESTLY COMPLAIN: ....BLACK ROOK I.   57   13
      KNELT IN THE MEADOW MUTE AS BOULDERS; ....HARDCASTLE CRAGS   63   33
      THEY MOVE THROUGH THEIR MUTE ROOMS WHILE I SLEEP, ...BLUE MOLES   126   23
      MUTE AS A TURNIP FROM THE FOURTH ....YOU'RE   141   7
      AND MUTE AS MANNEQUINS IN A DRESS SHOP, ...ON DECK   142   3
      HOLES IN THE HEELS OF SOCKS, THE WHITE MUTE FACES ......THREE WOMEN   182   199
      BETRAYED IN MUTE GEOMETRY OF BROKEN ....SONNET: TO EVA   304   6
      THE MUTE AIR MERELY THINS AND THINS. .....METAMORPHOSES OF THE MOON   307   6
MUTED (1)
      THAT MUTED BOOM, THAT CLANGOR ....NIGHT SHIFT   76   2

MUTINOUS (1)
    AGAINST MUTINOUS WEATHER ....SPINSTER   50   27
MUZZLES (3)
    THE WORD, DEFINING, MUZZLES; THE DRAWN LINE ....POEMS, POTATOES   106   1
    SO THE DISKS OF THE BRAIN REVOLVE, LIKE THE MUZZLES OF CANNON. ...
                                   ... THE COURAGE OF SHUTTING-UP   210   16
    OF KRUPP, BLACK MUZZLES ....GETTING THERE   248   6
MY (531)
MYSELF (34)
    ARMING MYSELF WITH THE MOST REASONABLE ITEMS ....STREET SONG   36   15
    STEEL ON MYSELF BEFORE PROFIT ....RHYME   50   14
    RED CINDER AROUND WHICH I MYSELF, ...THE EYE-MOTE   109   17
    MYSELF, MYSELF! -- OBSCENE, LUGUBRIOUS. ....THE RAVAGED FACE   115   8
    MYSELF, MYSELF! -- OBSCENE, LUGUBRIOUS. ....THE RAVAGED FACE   115   8
    I MADE IT MYSELF, ...POEM.2.DARK.   132   2
    THE WAX IMAGE OF MYSELF, A DOLL'S BODY. POEM.6.W.   135   3
    TO POUR MYSELF OUT LIKE A FLUID ....LOVE LETTER   147   26
    MOTHER TO MYSELF, I WAKE SWADDLED IN GAUZE, ...FACE LIFT   156   31
    I IMAGINE MYSELF WITH A GREAT PUBLIC, ...BARREN WOMAN   157   6
    OR BRAG AHEAD OF TIME HOW I'D AVENGE MYSELF. ....IN PLASTER   160   47
    I AM LEARNING PEACEFULNESS, LYING BY MYSELF QUIETLY ....TULIPS   160   3
    NOW I HAVE LOST MYSELF I AM SICK OF BAGGAGE --- ....TULIPS   160   18
    AND I SEE MYSELF, FLAT, RIDICULOUS, A CUT-PAPER SHADOW ......TULIPS   161   46
    AND I HAVE NO FACE, I HAVE WANTED TO EFFACE MYSELF. ....TULIPS   161   48
    I SHALL HARDLY KNOW MYSELF. IT WILL BE DARK, ...LAST WORDS   172   25
    I TALK TO MYSELF, MYSELF ONLY, SET APART -- ....THREE WOMEN   179   106
    I TALK TO MYSELF, MYSELF ONLY, SET APART -- ....THREE WOMEN   179   106
    HATING MYSELF, HATING AND FEARING. AND NOW THE WORLD CONCEIVES ...
                                   ... THREE WOMEN   181   150
    I SEE MYSELF AS A SHADOW, NEITHER MAN NOR WOMAN, ...THREE WOMEN   182   191
    I AM MYSELF AGAIN. THERE ARE NO LOOSE ENDS. ....THREE WOMEN   184   274
    FROM THE LONG FALL, AND FIND MYSELF IN BED, ...THREE WOMEN   187   366
    I FIND MYSELF AGAIN. I AM NO SHADOW ....THREE WOMEN   187   368
    BETWEEN MYSELF AND MYSELF. ....THE OTHER   202   27
    BETWEEN MYSELF AND MYSELF. ....THE OTHER   202   27
    I WOULD HAVE KILLED MYSELF GLADLY THAT TIME ANY POSSIBLE WAY. ...
                                   ... A BIRTHDAY PRESENT   206   15
    I AM MYSELF. THAT IS NOT ENOUGH. ....THE JAILER   226   20
    ALL BY MYSELF I AM A HUGE CAMELLIA ....FEVER.   232   41
    I CANNOT UNDO MYSELF, AND THE TRAIN IS STEAMING. .....GETTING THERE   248   38
    THE KNOT MYSELF, ...CHILDLESS WOMAN   259   6
    MYSELF THE ROSE YOU ACHIEVE -- ....CHILDLESS WOMAN   259   7
    I WOULDN'T TRUST MYSELF. THE FAULT'S MY FAITH ....DIALOGUE O.   277   37
    INTO MYSELF AND INTO MY CONVICTION .....DIALOGUE OVER A OUIJA BOARD   285   318
    YET THERE IS NO WALKER AND LOOKER BUT MYSELF. ....QUEEN MARY'S.   290   9
MYSTERY (1)
    THE CHOICE BETWEEN THE MICA MYSTERY ......METAMORPHOSES OF THE MOON   308   37
MYSTIC (1)
    MYSTIC ....MYSTIC   268   T
MYSTICAL (2)
    BLUE AND MYSTICAL OVER THE FACE OF THE STARS. ....MOON.   173   23
    I AM NOT MYSTICAL: IT ISN'T ....PHEASANT   191   7
MYTH (1)
    THE OLD MYTH OF ORIGINS ....FULL FATHOM FIVE   92   10
MYTH-MAKING (1)
    THE DEATH OF MYTH-MAKING ....THE DEATH OF MYTH-MAKING   104   T
MYTHS (1)
    THE WINGY MYTHS WON'T TUG AT US ANY MORE: POEM.5.F.   135   16
NADIR (1)
    OF QUIET. FROM THE NADIR ....LORELEI   94   11
NAG (2)
    TWO VIRTUES RIDE, BY STALLION, BY NAG, ...THE DEATH OF MYTH-MAKING   104   1
    NEEDLES NAG LIKE UNICORNS, ...DANSE MACABRE   321   13
NAIL (2)
    AND MY BABY A NAIL ....BRASILIA   258   7
    NOTHING SHORT OF A MIRACLE TO NAIL .....DIALOGUE OVER A OUIJA BOARD   280   160
NAILED (1)
    NAILED TO THE RAFTERS YESTERDAY: POEM.1.WHO.   131   14
NAILS (3)
    NOT NAILS, AND A MIRROR TO KEEP THE SNAKY HEAD ....PERSEUS   83   13
    THE LABORER'S NAILS PARED LEVEL ....THE DEATH OF MYTH-MAKING   104   7
    TO PARE NAILS, ...A SECRET   220   22
NAIVE (1)
    FOR NAIVE LARKS WHO STARVE AND GRIEVE. ...METAMORPHOSES OF THE MOON   307   18
NAKED (5)
    NAKED IN THE MERELY ACTUAL ROOM, ...TALE OF A TUB   24   5
    AND A NAKED MOUTH, RED AND AWKWARD. ....BERCK-PLAGE   201   124
    I NOTICE YOU ARE STARK NAKED. ....THE APPLICANT   221   19
    NAKED AS PAPER TO START ....THE APPLICANT   221   30
    NAKED AND BALD IN THEIR FURS, ...THE MUNICH MANNEQUINS   263   13
NAKEDNESS (1)
    IN A DRAFTY MUSEUM, YOUR NAKEDNESS ....MORNING SONG   157   5
NAME (17)
    PUTS ON A PUBLIC GRIN, REPEATS OUR NAME ....TALE OF A TUB   24   7
    NOR DID ANY WORD BODY WITH A NAME ....HARDCASTLE CRAGS   63   17

NAME (CONT.)
   BY A FAMILY NAME IT ....MUSSEL HUNTER AT ROCK HARBOR   96   59
   WOULDN'T SLOW FOR THE HAULED REINS, HIS NAME,   WHITENESS I REMEMBER 103   24
   I FOUND YOUR NAME, I FOUND YOUR BONES AND ALL*ELECTRA ON AZALEA PATH 117   16
   TELL ME MY NAME. POEM.3.MAENAD. 133   25
   CALL HIM ANY NAME, HE'LL COME TO IT. POEM.4.BEAST. 134   16
   I HAVE GIVEN MY NAME AND MY DAY-CLOTHES UP TO THE NURSES   ....TULIPS 160   6
   STUBBORNLY HANGING ON TO MY NAME AND ADDRESS. ....TULIPS 161   23
   AND IT ASKS NOTHING, A NAME TAG, A FEW TRINKETS. ....TULIPS 161   33
   AS A CHILD I LOVED A LICHEN-BITTEN NAME. ....THREE WOMEN 177   41
   WHAT IS THE NAME OF THAT COLOR? --- ....BERCK-PLAGE 200   97
   AND A NAME WITH BLACK EDGES ....BURNING THE LETTERS 205   42
   BUT THE NAME OF THE TOWN IS COMMON. ....DADDY 222   19
   NAME, HOUSE, CAR KEYS, ...AMNESIAC 232   3
   I FLY TO A NAME, TWO EYES. ....GETTING THERE 248   19
   TO NAME HIS HOME A THIRD TIME. GIVE YOUR WILL THREE   ...DIALOGUE O. 283 269
NAMED (5)
   THEY NAMED THEIR SHIP AFTER THE FLOWER OF MAY. ....MAYFLOWER   60   14
   ON THE ROAD NAMED FOR TOMAS ORTUNIO, MICA ....THE NET-MENDERS 121   8
   THEY LEFT ME A BORROWED MAID NAMED ELLEN, "FOR PROTECTION", ...
                                          ... THE BABYSITTERS 174   17
   IN THE CENTER OF THE GARDEN NAMED AFTER QUEEN MARY. ..QUEEN MARY'S. 290   3
   THE ROSES ARE NAMED AFTER QUEENS AND PEOPLE OF NOTE ..QUEEN MARY'S. 290   17
NAMES (6)
   END: GREEN SHORES APPEAR; WE ASSUME OUR NAMES, ...CHANNEL CROSSING   27   40
   HE NAMES A LAPWING, STARTS RABBITS IN A ROUT ....ODE FOR TED   29   3
   AT THE END, THEY SOBERLY BONG OUT THEIR NAMES. ....MOON. 173   14
   IN THEIR CANVAS-SIDED COTS, NAMES TIED TO THEIR WRISTS, *THREE WOMEN 183 220
   WHOSE NAMES YOU MEDITATE -- ....CHILD 265   4
   IN DUBIOUS DOORWAYS FORGET THEIR MONDAY NAMES, ..LOVE IS A PARALLAX 329   32
NAP (2)
   (A CRAB TO NAP ON ....WORDS FOR A NURSERY   74   43
   THE PETALS' NAP MY FINGERTIPS: ..FABLE OF THE RHODODENDRON STEALERS 103   14
NAPE (1)
   THEN, WITH A JOCULAR FIST THWACKED THE BARREL NAPE, ...SOW   61   35
NAPKIN (1)
   PEEL OFF THE NAPKIN ....LADY LAZARUS 244   10
NAPKINS (1)
   AMONG ICE BUCKETS, FROSTY NAPKINS. ....CANDLES 149   23
NAPOLEON (3)
   AT WATERLOO, WATERLOO, NAPOLEON, ...THE SWARM 216   7
   A RED TATTER, NAPOLEON! ....THE SWARM 217   40
   NAPOLEON IS PLEASED, HE IS PLEASED WITH EVERYTHING. ......THE SWARM 217   59
NAPPING (2)
   NAPPING IN HER KITCHEN PAVED WITH SAUCERS. ....ELLA MASON A.   54   20
   AND TRAP THE MUSKRAT NAPPING IN SLACK SUN;   GO GET THE GOODLY SQUAB 313   10
NARCISSI (6)
   THE NARCISSI OPEN WHITE FACES IN THE ORCHARD. ....THREE WOMEN 185 315
   AMONG THE NARCISSI ....AMONG THE NARCISSI 190   T
   PERCY BOWS, IN HIS BLUE PEAJACKET, AMONG THE NARCISSI. ...NARCISSI. 190   2
   THE NARCISSI, TOO, ARE BOWING TO SOME BIG THING: *AMONG THE NARCISSI 190   4
   THE NARCISSI LOOK UP LIKE CHILDREN, QUICKLY AND WHITELY. NARCISSI. 190   12
   IT WAS SUNNING IN THE NARCISSI. ....PHEASANT 191   23
NARROW (4)
   IN BURROWS NARROW AS A FINGER, SOLITARY BEES ....BEEKEEPER'S. 118   15
   THROUGH THE NARROW CRACK ....THE SLEEPERS 122   8
   NOW, IN VALLEYS NARROW ....WUTHERING HEIGHTS 168   43
   COLD ON MY NARROW COT I LIE ....TO A JILTED LOVER 309   1
NARROWED (2)
   AFTER THE HORIZONS, STRETCHING THE NARROWED EYE   ....ABOVE THE OXBOW   88   25
   THE PATHS NARROWED INTO THE HOLLOW. ....THE RABBIT CATCHER 193   13
NATIONS (1)
   AND THEN THERE WERE OTHER FACES. THE FACES OF NATIONS,   THREE WOMEN 179   82
NATIVE (2)
   NATIVE, EVIDENTLY, TO ....NIGHT SHIFT   76   8
   MY NATIVE SLEIGHT-OF-HAND IS WEARING OUT: ....A SORCERER B. 324   9
NATIVITIES (1)
   NATIVITIES AT TWO-AND-SIX. ....ON DECK 143   30
NATURAL (6)
   NATURAL HISTORY ....NATURAL HISTORY   71   T
   IT IS MORE NATURAL TO ME, LYING DOWN. ....I AM VERTICAL 162   17
   I HAVE TRIED NOT TO THINK TOO HARD. I HAVE TRIED BE BE NATURAL. ...
                                          ... THREE WOMEN 178   74
   THE NATURAL FATNESS OF THESE LIME LEAVES! --- ....BERCK-PLAGE 199   91
   IT SEEMS PERFECTLY NATURAL NOW --- ....DEATH & CO. 254   2
   OF COOL MOUTHS AND HANDS OPEN AND NATURAL AS ROSES. ......FEVER./DR 294   10
NATURE (3)
   OF NATURE: WHAT BETTER WAY TO TEST TAUT FIBER .....CHANNEL CROSSING   27   16
   HOW NATURE, SENSING THIS, COMPOUNDS HER BITTERS. ....DEPARTURE   51   5
   BLIND TWINS BITTEN BY BAD NATURE. ....BLUE MOLES 126   9
NATURES (1)
   ANGELS WEEPING OVER DULL NATURES, ...LOVE LETTER 147   16
NATURE'S (2)
   NATURE'S PARTIAL, HAPHAZARD THUMB. ....THE BEGGARS   47   5
   NEIGHBORHOOD COCKCROW -- ALL NATURE'S PRODIGAL BACKTALK, CONJURING.   66   4

<pre>
                                                    TITLE   PAGE LINE
NAUGHT (1)
    HER ANTELOPE WHO MEANT HIM NAUGHT BUT GOOD. ..THE QUEEN'S COMPLAINT 28   10
NAUSEOUS (2)
    FED ME BANANA GAS THROUGH A FROG-MASK. THE NAUSEOUS VAULT *FACE LIFT 156   5
    WHERE ARE YOUR OPIATES, YOUR NAUSEOUS CAPSULES? ....POPPIES IN JULY 203   10
NAUSET (1)
    IN THE WATERS OFF BEAUTIFUL NAUSET. ....DADDY 222   13
NAVEL (3)
    CAN SPROUT FROM THE NAVEL OF THIS PRESENT WASTE. .....TALE OF A TUB   25   40
    AS OUT OF EDEN'S NAVEL TWIST THE LINES ...............SNAKECHARMER   79   19
    NAVEL CORDS, BLUE-RED AND LUCENT, ...THE OTHER 202   18
NAVEL-KNIT (1)
    HE KINGS IT, NAVEL-KNIT TO NO GROAN, ...MAUDLIN   51   6
NAVIGATE (1)
    TO NAVIGATE THIS FINAL DARK. ...INSOLENT STORM STRIKES AT THE SKULL 326   18
NAVIGATES (1)
    NAVIGATES THE TIDAL SLOSH OF SEAS ....TALE OF A TUB   25   44
NAZI (1)
    BRIGHT AS A NAZI LAMPSHADE, ...LADY LAZARUS 244   5
NEAR (11)
    NEAR A BED OF POPPIES, ...TWO SISTERS OF PERSEPHONE   32   16
    NEAR HIS SMALL STONEHENGE ABOVE THE ANTS' ROUTE, ...SPIDER   48   11
    AMERICANA. MAGI NEAR ....A WINTER'S TALE   86   3
    UNIMAGINABLE. YOU FLOAT NEAR ....FULL FATHOM FIVE   92   11
    REST ON ORANGE PLUSH NEAR THE NEWEL POST. ...YADDO: THE GRAND MANOR 124   16
    BUT THEY ARE DEAD, AND THEIR MOTHER NEAR DEAD WITH DISTRACTION, ...
                                                      ... STILLBORN 142   14
    A SECOND TIME, TO HAVE HIM NEAR AGAIN -- ....WIDOW 164   16
    NEAR WINS, WEEK BY WEEK, WAITING UNTIL   DIALOGUE OVER A OUIJA BOARD 277   40
    A CAR DOOR SLAM; VOICES COMING NEAR; ....FAMILY REUNION 300   2
    UNTIL NEAR TWELVE THE STRANGE GIRL ALL AT ONCE ....CINDERELLA 304   11
    BECAUSE NEW EXCAVATIONS CAME TOO NEAR   THE PRINCESS AND THE GOBLINS 334   39
NEARED (1)
    CEASE, AND I NEARED THE SILENCED ......MUSSEL HUNTER AT ROCK HARBOR   95   15
NEARER (1)
    DOMINION. THE STARS ARE NO NEARER. POEM.5.F. 134   6
NEAREST (1)
    RIDING THE RIP TIDE TO THE NEAREST POINT OF DEPARTURE, ...MEDUSA 225   10
NEARING (1)
    BUT NEARING MEANS DISTANCING: ....THE GREAT CARBUNCLE   73   27
NEARLY (1)
    AND I, NEARLY EXTINCT, ...BRASILIA 258   11
NEAT (7)
    HIS NEAT TROT PITCHING MY TENSE POISE UP, ...WHITENESS I REMEMBER 102   14
    UNDER MY FEET IN A NEAT PARCEL. ....LAST WORDS 172   24
    THIS WOMAN WHO MEETS ME IN WINDOWS -- SHE IS NEAT. .....THREE WOMEN 184 280
    SO NEAT SHE IS TRANSPARENT, LIKE A SPIRIT. ....THREE WOMEN 184 281
    HOW SHYLY SHE SUPERIMPOSES HER NEAT SELF ....THREE WOMEN 184 282
    OUR CHEESECLOTH GAUNTLETS NEAT AND SWEET, ...STINGS 214   3
    AND YOUR NEAT MUSTACHE ....DADDY 223   43
NEATLY (3)
    SHE WITHDREW NEATLY. ....SPINSTER   50   24
    NEATLY, NICELY, BY DISBELIEF OR BRIDGES, ...A LESSON IN VENGEANCE   80   23
    CAN STITCH LACE NEATLY ON TO THIS MATERIAL. MY HUSBAND   THREE WOMEN 187 360
NECESSARY (2)
    NECESSARY AMONG THE FLOWERS, ...BERCK-PLAGE 200 101
    SUGAR IS A NECESSARY FLUID, ...KINDNESS 269   10
NECESSITY (1)
    THE ILLUSION OF A GREEK NECESSITY ....EDGE 272   4
NECK (10)
    I HUNG ON HIS NECK. RESOLUTENESS ....WHITENESS I REMEMBER 103   28
    TO SWEETEN YOUR NECK OF THE NEW YORK WOODS. ....PRIVATE GROUND 130   4
    A DOZEN RED LEAD SINKERS ROUND MY NECK. ....TULIPS 161   42
    I AM NUDE AS A CHICKEN NECK, DOES NOBODY LOVE ME? ..THE BEE MEETING 211   6
    BUTTONING THE CUFFS AT MY WRISTS AND THE SLIT FROM MY NECK TO MY
        KNEES. ....THE BEE MEETING 211   8
    UP TO MY NECK, ...LESBOS 229   65
    OF THE NECK I CANNOT CATCH, ...ARIEL 239   9
    FRILL AT THE NECK, ...DEATH & CO. 254   16
    RUNNING NECK AND NECK WITH THE MOST DEVOUT ....DIALOGUE O. 282 235
    RUNNING NECK AND NECK WITH THE MOST DEVOUT ....DIALOGUE O. 282 235
NECKLACES (1)
    LITTLE SHELLS MADE UP INTO NECKLACES AND TOY LADIES. ....FINISTERRE 170   32
NECKS (3)
    WITH REEDY LENGTHS AND NECKS AND UNDULATINGS. .........SNAKECHARMER   79   5
    AT A FIELD OF HORSES, NECKS BENT, MANES BLOWN, ...THE EYE-MOTE 109   2
    RED, MOTTLED, LIKE CUT NECKS. ....LITTLE FUGUE 188   35
NECROPOLIS (1)
    ENLISTED IN A CRAMPED NECROPOLIS, ...ELECTRA ON AZALEA PATH 117   17
NECTARINE (1)
    STILL HE HYMNS JUICE OF HER, HOT NECTARINE. ....OUIJA   77   26
NEED (7)
    HE EATS, AND STILL HIS NEED SEEKS FOOD, ...PURSUIT   23   39
    I NEED HARDLY GO OUT AT ALL. ....PRIVATE GROUND 130   14
    I CAN STAY AWAKE ALL NIGHT, IF NEED BE -- ....ZOO KEEPER'S WIFE 154   1
</pre>

334

NEED (CONT.)
    SHE DOESN'T NEED FOOD, SHE IS ONE OF THE REAL SAINTS. ...IN PLASTER   158   4
    I DO NOT EVEN NEED A HOLIDAY; I CAN GO TO WORK TODAY. ..THREE WOMEN   183 249
    THEY CAN DIE. I NEED FEED THEM NOTHING, I AM THE OWNER.*THE ARRIVAL.   213   25
    AND HALE ITS GREEN LATTICEWORK OF LEAVES. YOU NEED .....DIALOGUE O.   280 159
NEEDING (1)
    DEMURE ONES, LITHE ONES, NEEDING NO LESSON ....ELLA MASON A.   54   40
NEEDLE (2)
    ISSUING FROM THE STEEL NEEDLE THAT FLIES SO BLINDINGLY? *APPEARANCE.   189   11
    THE NEEDLE JOURNEYING IN ITS GROOVE, ...THE COURAGE OF SHUTTING-UP   210   8
NEEDLES (7)
    HOW PERILOUS NEEDLES GRAIN THE FLOORBOARDS ....MISS DRAKE P.   41   16
    HAND HONES HIS TACKS AND NEEDLES, ...A LESSON IN VENGEANCE   80   12
    NEEDLES KNIT IN A BIRD-BEAKED ....OLD LADIES' HOME   120   8
    HEAVING THE NEEDLES, ...MUSHROOMS   139   11
    THEY BRING ME NUMBNESS IN THEIR BRIGHT NEEDLES, THEY BRING ME
        SLEEP. ....TULIPS   160   17
    NEEDLES NAG LIKE UNICORNS, ...DANSE MACABRE   321   13
    TURQUOISE, ROSE, SIERRA MAUVE; NEEDLES ....MORNING IN THE HOS.   332   14
NEEDLE'S (1)
    SHE MOUNTS THROUGH MALICE OF THE NEEDLE'S EYE, ...THE PRINCESS.   333   10
NEEDLING (2)
    NEEDLING SPUMILY DOWN FROM THE WIRES: ....ALICANTE LULLABY   43   10
    NEEDLING IT DARK. THEN I WAS SEEING ....THE EYE-MOTE   109   10
NEEDLY (1)
    MILLIONS OF NEEDLY GLASS CAKES! ....THE TOUR   238   18
NEEDN'T (1)
    TO QUICKEN HIS SLUGGARD'S BLOOD. BUT HE NEEDN'T COME ...DIALOGUE O.   281 184
NEEDS (1)
    BOY, HE NEEDS A BEATING NOW AND THEN ...DIALOGUE OVER A OUIJA BOARD   281 183
NEFERTIT (1)
    DEAD AND PERFECT, LIKE NEFERTIT, ...THE FEARFUL   256   14
NEGATIVE (1)
    O MAKER OF PROUD PLANET'S NEGATIVE, ...SONNET TO SATAN   323   13
NEGLECT'S (1)
    THOUGH DOOMSDAY BUD. NEGLECT'S ....VIRGIN IN A TREE   82   41
NEGRESS (1)
    PRETENDING I AM A NEGRESS WITH PINK PAWS. ....THE JAILER   226   19
NEGRO (1)
    NEGRO, MASKED LIKE A WHITE, ...THALIDOMIDE   252   3
NEIGHBOR (2)
    GOD KNOWS HOW OUR NEIGHBOR MANAGED TO BREED ....SOW   60   1
    TOAD-STONE! SISTER-BITCH! SWEET NEIGHBOR! .............EAVESDROPPER   261   63
NEIGHBORHOOD (1)
    NEIGHBORHOOD COCKCROW -- ALL NATURE'S PRODIGAL BACKTALK, CONJURING.   66   4
NEIGHBORLY (1)
    THE PALLORS OF HANDS AND NEIGHBORLY FACES, ...BERCK-PLAGE   199   85
NEIGHBORS (2)
    LIKE MY NEIGHBORS, TAKING NO PLEASURE ....LOVE LETTER   147   12
    IT IS THE SURGEON MY NEIGHBORS ARE WAITING FOR, ...THE BEE MEETING   211   27
NEIGHBOR'S (3)
    BESIDE A NEIGHBOR'S HOUSE ....DREAM WITH CLAM-DIGGERS   43   6
    STEM OF MY NEIGHBOR'S ROSE BUSH ....RESOLVE   52   15
    ON SEEING OUR NEIGHBOR'S CAT-HAUNT, ELLA MASON AND HER ELEVEN CATS   53   4
NEIGHBORS' (1)
    STRIKES THE TILES OF THE NEIGHBORS' GABLE-TOPS ....DIALOGUE O.   286 339
NEITHER (13)
NELDA (1)
    "OH, STOP WORRYING, NELDA," ....BITTER STRAWBERRIES   300   27
NEMATODES (1)
    SAID EVE: "I WISH VENOMOUS NEMATODES ....DIALOGUE EN ROUTE   309   19
NEMESIS (1)
    IS OUR LIFE'S WHOLE NEMESIS." ....LOVE IS A PARALLAX   329   12
NEON (2)
    WE VAUNT OUR DAYS IN NEON AND SCORN THE DARK. ......SONNET: TO TIME   311   4
    AND BURN TO DEATH WITHIN YOUR NEON HELL. ....THE TRIAL OF MAN   312   11
NEON-LIT (1)
    FROM EACH NEON-LIT PALM ....ALICANTE LULLABY   43   13
NEOPHYTE (1)
    NOTES TO A NEOPHYTE ....NOTES TO A NEOPHYTE   306   T
NEPHEW (1)
    THE YOUNGEST NEPHEW GIVES A FRETFUL WHINE ....FAMILY REUNION   301   23
NERVE (3)
    AND WAKEN THE SLY NERVE UP ....THE LADY AND THE EARTHENWARE HEAD   69   14
    R-V-E. IN CORE OF NERVE! I HOPE ....DIALOGUE OVER A OUIJA BOARD   284 278
    HIS BOOK OF INSULTS. NERVE OR NOUMENON, *DIALOGUE OVER A OUIJA BOARD   284 297
NERVE-CURLERS (1)
    WHICH OF THE NERVE-CURLERS, THE CONVULSORS? DID IT ELECTRIFY? ...
                                                    ... THE DETECTIVE   209   23
NERVE-END (1)
    EVEN AS MY EACH MANGLED NERVE-END ....STREET SONG   36   21
NERVES (6)
    FLAYS THE CHROMIUM NERVES OF PLUMBING RAW; ....TALE OF A TUB   24   3
    ROSE UP AND PUT ROYAL NERVES TO THE RACK: ....NATURAL HISTORY   71   9
    THE TREES STIFFEN INTO PLACE LIKE BURNT NERVES. ...WAKING IN WINTER   151   3

NERVES (CONT.)
    THE NERVES BURSTING LIKE TREES, AND THIS IS THE SURGEON:*BERCK-PLAGE 198   47
    IF OUR NERVES ARE THE SOLE NOURISHERS ..DIALOGUE OVER A OUIJA BOARD 284 287
    OF PAN'S PRONOUNCEMENTS, AND OUR NERVES ARE STRUNG .....DIALOGUE O. 284 288
NERVOUS (5)
    TAPPING AND TICKING LIKE NERVOUS FINGERS. ....LEAVING EARLY 146   27
    SPITEFUL AS A WOMAN, BUT NOT SO NERVOUS, ...THE RIVAL 166   9
    THE COOK HAD ONE WALL EYE AND COULDN'T SLEEP, SHE WAS SO
       NERVOUS. ....THE BABYSITTERS 175   25
    THE MOON SNAGS IN HER INTRICATE NERVOUS SYSTEM. ....ELM/DR 292   3
    AND HANDS LIKE NERVOUS BUTTERFLIES; ....FAMILY REUNION 300   19
NEST (5)
    MAKING THE WORLD GO THIN AS A WASP'S NEST ....THE THIN PEOPLE   65   46
    FROM HIS THIN PIPE. OUT OF THIS GREEN NEST ............SNAKECHARMER   79   18
    IN A NEST OF ROOT-HAIRS AND BOREDOM -- ....BURNING THE LETTERS 205   45
    AND LIKE A CUCKOO IN THE NEST MAKES HELL   METAMORPHOSES OF THE MOON 307   17
    HIDE, HIDE, IN THE DEEP NEST ....GO GET THE GOODLY SQUAB 313   7
NET (1)
    AND THE FABULOUS LUTES AND PEACOCKS, RENDING THE NET   CONVERSATION.   21   3
NETHER (1)
    TO A CINDER, THAN MEET A POOR UPSTART OF OUR NETHER ....DIALOGUE O. 280 133
NET-MENDERS (2)
    THE NET-MENDERS ....THE NET-MENDERS 121   T
    FATTEN IN GREEN-POCKED PODS, THE THREE NET-MENDERS SIT OUT, ..NET-. 121   3
NETS (3)
    BE A HARVEST OF SILVER IN THE NETS, AND THE LAMPS ..THE NET-MENDERS 121   18
    LITTLE NETS, ...PURDAH 242   16
    IN NETS OF THE INFINITE, ...TOTEM 265   32
NETTLE (2)
    ASLANT: THEIR HILL OF STINGING NETTLE; ....BUCOLICS   24   10
    COUCHED DAYLONG IN CLOISTERS OF STINGING NETTLE *WREATH FOR A BRIDAL   44   7
NETTLES (2)
    CRUEL NETTLES STUNG HER ANKLES RAW. ....BUCOLICS   24   16
    NIGHTSHADE AND NETTLES ....TEMPER OF TIME 336   11
NETWORK (1)
    ALONG RED NETWORK OF HIS VEINS ....PURSUIT   22   11
NEUTRAL (2)
    SUCH FORCE CAN LAST; BUT BEYOND, THE NEUTRAL VIEW   CHANNEL CROSSING   26   7
    THE MOLES LOOK NEUTRAL AS THE STONES. ....BLUE MOLES 126   14
NEUTRALITY (1)
    OF TOTAL NEUTRALITY. WITH LUCK, ...BLACK ROOK I.   57   32
NEVER (62)
    THINKING NEVER TO HAVE LEFT THE WORLD, YOU GRIEVE ......DIALOGUE B.   39   34
    WE MIGHT EMBRACE, BUT THOSE TWO NEVER DID, ...THE OTHER TWO   69   30
    NEVER GIVEN; HIDDEN, YET ....THE GREAT CARBUNCLE   72   12
    FLOWERS AND BLUEBIRDS THAT NEVER WERE ....THE DISQUIETING MUSES   76   44
    NEVER, NEVER, FOUND ANYWHERE. ....THE DISQUIETING MUSES   76   45
    NEVER, NEVER, FOUND ANYWHERE. ....THE DISQUIETING MUSES   76   45
    THAT NEVER BRIGHTENS OR GOES DOWN. ....THE DISQUIETING MUSES   76   53
    NEVER GRIP, AS THEIR GRANDSIRES DID, THAT DEVIL WHO CHUCKLES*LESSON.   80   24
    AND NEVER SAW HOW COOLLY WE MIGHT MOVE. FOR ONCE   ...ABOVE THE OXBOW   89   55
    SUCH MEETINGS NEVER OCCUR IN MARCHEN .................INCOMMUNICADO 100   8
    TO SAFE GRAY NEVER GRAYED HIS TEMPER. ....WHITENESS I REMEMBER 102   11
    YET IT NEVER MILKED ANY GOAT, NOR DEALT COW DEATH ....GOATSUCKER 111   12
    AS IF YOU HAD NEVER EXISTED, AS IF I CAME ...ELECTRA ON AZALEA PATH 116   6
    I SHALL NEVER GET YOU PUT TOGETHER ENTIRELY, ...THE COLOSSUS 129   1
    AND WE SHALL NEVER ENTER THERE ....THE BURNT-OUT SPA 138   31
    THE PILGRIMS AND INDIANS MIGHT NEVER HAVE HAPPENED. ......TWO CAMP. 145   22
    NUN-SOULED, THEY BURN HEAVENWARD AND NEVER MARRY. ....CANDLES 149   27
    NEVER TRESPASSING IN BAD TEMPER: ....A LIFE 150   12
    I SHALL NEVER GET OUT OF THIS! THERE ARE TWO OF ME NOW: IN PLASTER 158   1
    I AM A NUN NOW, I HAVE NEVER BEEN SO PURE. ....TULIPS 161   28
    IN THIS CLEAR AIR AND NEVER NOTICE IT -- ....WIDOW 164   33
    THE SMALLER AND MORE TIMID NEVER ARRIVE AT ALL ....STARS. 165   12
    WE HAVE NEVER BEEN TO. ....FINISTERRE 170   35
    I HAVE NEVER SEEN A THING SO CLEAR. ....THREE WOMEN 181 171
    THIS IS THE ROOM I HAVE NEVER BEEN IN. ....WINTERING 218   11
    THIS IS THE ROOM I COULD NEVER BREATHE IN. ....WINTERING 218   12
    SO I NEVER COULD TELL WHERE YOU ....DADDY 223   22
    I NEVER COULD TALK TO YOU. ....DADDY 223   24
    AND THE VILLAGERS NEVER LIKED YOU. ....DADDY 224   77
    LIKE THE RED-HEADED SISTER HE NEVER DARED TO TOUCH, ...AMNESIAC 233   13
    I AM NEVER, NEVER, NEVER COMING HOME! ....AMNESIAC 233   27
    I AM NEVER, NEVER, NEVER COMING HOME! ....AMNESIAC 233   27
    I AM NEVER, NEVER, NEVER COMING HOME! ....AMNESIAC 233   27
    IT NEVER OCCURRED THAT THEY HAD BEEN FORGOT, ...LYONNESSE 234   19
    THE ONE WHO NEVER LOOKS UP, WHOSE EYES ARE LIDDED ......DEATH & CO. 254   3
    I NEVER WANTED IT. ....YEARS 255   10
    WHERE THE CHILD CAN NEVER SWIM, ...THE FEARFUL 256   17
    I SHALL NEVER GROW OLD. NEW OYSTERS ....GIGOLO 268   26
    HAS NEVER FAILED TO SEE OUR FABLING SHEARED ....DIALOGUE O. 276   12
    M-A-G-E. IN PLUMAGE. I'D NEVER HAVE THOUGHT ....DIALOGUE O. 278   78
    I NEVER KNEW SUCH CREDULITY TO PITCH ...DIALOGUE OVER A OUIJA BOARD 280 154
    AND NEVER GRIEVES, ...GOLD MOUTHS CRY 302   11
    YOU NEVER ALTERED YOUR AMUSED BELIEF ....DIRGE FOR A JOKER 302   7

                                            TITLE   PAGE LINE
NEVER (CONT.)
    INTOLERANT BEAUTY NEVER WILL BE LEARNING. ....TO EVA DESCENDING. 303   17
    THE FALLING MAN WHO NEVER WILL ABSTAIN ...METAMORPHOSES OF THE MOON   307   10
    I NEVER THOUGHT HIS FLESH WOULD BURN ....TO A JILTED LOVER   310   12
    WE NEVER THOUGHT TO HEAR THE HOLY COCK: ....DOOMSDAY   316   14
    OH NEVER TRY TO KNOCK ON ROTTEN WOOD ....ADMONITIONS   319   1
    NEVER TRY TO KNOW MORE THAN YOU SHOULD. ....ADMONITIONS   319   3
    OH NEVER TRY TO KNOCK ON ROTTEN WOOD. ....ADMONITIONS   319   6
    NEVER TRY TO KNOW MORE THAN YOU SHOULD. ....ADMONITIONS   319   9
    OH NEVER TRY TO KNOCK ON ROTTEN WOOD. ....ADMONITIONS   319   12
    NEVER TRY TO KNOW MORE THAN YOU SHOULD. ....ADMONITIONS   319   15
    NEVER TRY TO KNOCK ON ROTTEN WOOD, ...ADMONITIONS   319   18
    NEVER TRY TO KNOW MORE THAN YOU SHOULD. ....ADMONITIONS   319   19
    NEVER TRY TO TRICK ME WITH A KISS *NEVER TRY TO TRICK ME WITH A KISS   319   T
    NEVER TRY TO TRICK ME WITH A KISS *NEVER TRY TO TRICK ME WITH A KISS   319   1
    NEVER TRY TO TRICK ME WITH A KISS.*NEVER TRY TO TRICK ME WITH A KISS   319   6
    NEVER TRY TO TRICK ME WITH A KISS.*NEVER TRY TO TRICK ME WITH A KISS   320   12
    SO NEVER TRY TO TRICK ME WITH A KISS: ....NEVER TRY TO TRICK.   320   18
    CYCLING PHOENIX NEVER STOPS. ....LOVE IS A PARALLAX   330   66
    O NEVER AGAIN WILL THE EXTRAVAGANT STRAW ....THE PRINCESS.   335   72
NEVERTHELESS (4)
    NEVERTHELESS, NEVERTHELESS ....MEDUSA   225   23
    NEVERTHELESS, NEVERTHELESS ....MEDUSA   225   23
    NEVERTHELESS, I AM THE SAME, IDENTICAL WOMAN. ....LADY LAZARUS   245   34
    IT STRETCHES INTO THE DISTANCE. IT WILL BE EATEN NEVERTHELESS.*TOTEM   264   2
NEW (23)
    THE NEW WOMAN IN THE WARD ....MISS DRAKE P.   41   5
    POINT OF EDEN, NEXT THE NEW MOON'S CURVE. ..THE GHOST'S LEAVETAKING   91   31
    AND MOO AS THEY JUMP OVER MOONS AS NEW .....THE GHOST'S LEAVETAKING   91   37
    TO SWEETEN YOUR NECK OF THE NEW YORK WOODS. ....PRIVATE GROUND   130   4
    I SHALL BE GOOD AS NEW. POEM.7.S.   137   45
    ON THIS BALD HILL THE NEW YEAR HONES ITS EDGE. ......PARLIAMENT H.   152   1
    OUR VOICES ECHO, MAGNIFYING YOUR ARRIVAL. NEW STATUE.   MORNING SONG   157   4
    THE KNOCK OF THE SMALL, NEW HEART. ....HEAVY WOMEN   158   14
    THIS NEW ABSOLUTELY WHITE PERSON AND THE OLD YELLOW ONE, *IN PLASTER   158   2
    ANNOUNCES A NEW SOUL. THE BED IS BLUE. ....THE SURGEON AT 2 A.M.   171   42
    NEW YEAR ON DARTMOOR ....NEW YEAR ON DARTMOOR   176   T
    WE HAVE ONLY COME TO LOOK. YOU ARE TOO NEW ....NEW YEAR ON DARTMOOR   176   8
    WHILE IN THEIR FINGERJOINT CELLS THE NEW VIRGINS ...THE BEE MEETING   212   45
    INTO A NEW MAUSOLEUM, ...THE SWARM   217   49
    WE MAKE NEW STOCK FROM THE SALT. ....THE APPLICANT   221   18
    NOISE OF THE NEW. ....LESBOS   228   19
    IN NEW YORK, IN HOLLYWOOD, THE MEN SAID: "THROUGH? ....LESBOS   228   41
    HE DREAMS OF A NEW ONE -- ....AMNESIAC   233   14
    THE ZOO OF THE NEW ....CHILD   265   3
    I SHALL NEVER GROW OLD. NEW OYSTERS ....GIGOLO   268   26
    EACH TIME MUST LEARN THE LETTERS NEW. ARE ....DIALOGUE O.   277   24
    MAD HATTER'S HAT YIELDS NO NEW METAPHOR, ...A SORCERER B.   324   10
    BECAUSE NEW EXCAVATIONS CAME TOO NEAR   THE PRINCESS AND THE GOBLINS   334   39
NEWEL (1)
    REST ON ORANGE PLUSH NEAR THE NEWEL POST. ...YADDO: THE GRAND MANOR   124   16
NEW-MINTED (1)
    MONEY'S NEW-MINTED IN THIS FAT PURSE. ....METAPHORS   116   6
NEWNESS (1)
    THIS IS NEWNESS: EVERY LITTLE TAWDRY ....NEW YEAR ON DARTMOOR   176   1
NEWS (5)
    TO BE LET LOOSE AT NEWS OF LAND. ....ON DECK   143   36
    YOU BRING ME GOOD NEWS FROM THE CLINIC, ...FACE LIFT   155   1
    AND DRINK THE SMALL NIGHT CHILL LIKE NEWS OF HOME. ....STARS.   166   40
    NO DAY IS SAFE FROM NEWS OF YOU, ...THE RIVAL   167   16
    WHOSE NEWS IS THE OPEN CHERRY, THE OPEN CLOVER? ....STINGS   214   30
NEWSPAPER (1)
    MOUNTAINING THEM ON SPREAD NEWSPAPER. .................RHODODENDRON.   104   23
NEWSPRINT (3)
    BODY, A SHEET OF NEWSPRINT ON THE FIRE ....WIDOW   164   2
    A DEAD SUN STAINS THE NEWSPRINT. IT IS RED. ....THREE WOMEN   181 153
    BROODS IN THE NEWSPRINT! ....FEVER./DR   294   5
NEWTS (2)
    AND NEWTS ARE PRODIGAL IN LEGS. AND MAY I BE ....THREE WOMEN   184 258
    EVEN THE NEWTS ARE WHITE, ...NICK AND THE CANDLESTICK   241   12
NEXT (13)
    HIS NEXT MARTYR TO THE GROSS CAUSE ....SPIDER   49   26
    POINT OF EDEN, NEXT THE NEW MOON'S CURVE. ..THE GHOST'S LEAVETAKING   91   31
    RETROGRESSED TO BLOWZE, I NEXT CHOSE RED; .........RHODODENDRON.   103   10
    AT THE HEADSTONE NEXT TO YOURS, NOR DOES IT ROT, ...ELECTRA ON.   117   26
    LET HER DIE THERE, OR WITHER INCESSANTLY FOR THE NEXT FIFTY
        YEARS, ...FACE LIFT   156   29
    THE BREASTS NEXT. ....THE DETECTIVE   209   31
    NEXT TO THE LAST TENANT'S RANCID JAM ....WINTERING   218   8
    AND AT HIS NEXT STEP ....PURDAH   243   50
    INTO THE NEXT MILE, ...GETTING THERE   248   31
    THE NEXT HOUR --- ....GETTING THERE   248   32
    ARGUMENT TO THE HOUSE NEXT DOOR. OR IF   DIALOGUE OVER A OUIJA BOARD   280 166
    BEFORE HE SPELLS AGAIN, SHOULD HIS NEXT WRIT ....DIALOGUE O.   281 193
    DISRUPT THE CALENDARS NEXT; SEND THE DUTEOUS ....SONG FOR A REVOLU.   323   9

337

```
                                        TITLE              PAGE  LINE
NIAGARAS (1)
    I TIRE, IMAGINING WHITE NIAGARAS  .. ...................MOONRISE    98   22
NIBBLES (1)
    AND NIBBLES AN OCCASIONAL BONBON OF SIN.  ............FEMALE AUTHOR  301    4
NICE (2)
    BUT AUNTIE, SHE'S AWFULLY NICE.  ..........................THE TOUR  238   44
    DAME KINDNESS, SHE IS SO NICE!  ...........................KINDNESS  269    2
NICELY (2)
    NEATLY, NICELY, BY DISBELIEF OR BRIDGES,  .....A LESSON IN VENGEANCE  80   23
    THEY SIT SO NICELY IN THE PICKLING FLUID!  ................STILLBORN 142    8
NICETY (1)
    WHETHER NICETY STOOD CONFOUNDED BY LOVE,  .............RHODODENDRON. 104   27
NICHES (1)
    WORMING THEMSELVES INTO NICHES.  .........................THE SWARM  217   45
NICK (2)
    SHE CAN SEE IN THE NICK OF TIME  ......MISS DRAKE PROCEEDS TO SUPPER  41   15
    NICK AND THE CANDLESTICK  ..................NICK AND THE CANDLESTICK 240    T
NICKNAMES (1)
    ENOUGH FOR NICKNAMES. HOW ARE YOU, PAN? F-  .............DIALOGUE O. 277   31
NICOTINE-FINGER (1)
    LONG NICOTINE-FINGER  ..................................EAVESDROPPER 260   14
NIGGARD (1)
    IT'S A NIGGARD ESTATE,  ...................GREEN ROCK, WINTHROP BAY  105    9
NIGGER-EYE (1)
    NIGGER-EYE  ..................................................ARIEL  239   10
NIGHT (45)
    BROODING AS THE WINTER NIGHT COMES ON.  ...........WINTER LANDSCAPE,  21   10
    WATCHING FOR NIGHT, ................................................PROSPECT  28    9
    TILL THE NIGHT MISTS CAME RISING.  ..........SONG FOR A SUMMER'S DAY  31   20
    WHEN NIGHT COMES BLACK  ...................................THE SHRIKE  42    1
    LET NIGHT BLESS THAT LUCK-ROOTED MEAD OF CLOVER *WREATH FOR A BRIDAL  45   17
    ALL THE NIGHT GAVE HER, IN RETURN  .................HARDCASTLE CRAGS  63   26
    NODDING BY NIGHT AROUND MY BED, .............THE DISQUIETING MUSES    75   15
    DAY NOW, NIGHT NOW, AT HEAD, SIDE, FEET,  .....THE DISQUIETING MUSES  76   49
    NIGHT SHIFT  ...........................................NIGHT SHIFT  76    T
    IT IS NO NIGHT TO DROWN IN:  ................................LORELEI  94    1
    OLD GOATHERDS SWEAR HOW ALL NIGHT LONG THEY HEAR  ......GOATSUCKER   111    1
    TO FIDDLE THE SHORT NIGHT AWAY.  .........SLEEP IN THE MOJAVE DESERT 144   26
    AND NIGHT ARRIVES IN ONE GIGANTIC STEP.*TWO CAMPERS IN CLOUD COUNTRY 145   16
    GAVE UP THE GHOST LAST NIGHT. HIGH TIME.....LEAVING EARLY           146   24
    ALL NIGHT I HAVE DREAMED OF DESTRUCTION, ANNIHILATIONS -- ..WAKING. 151    4
    THE BLUE NIGHT PLANTS, THE LITTLE PALE BLUE HILL ....PARLIAMENT H.  153   41
    I CAN STAY AWAKE ALL NIGHT, IF NEED BE --  ........ZOO KEEPER'S WIFE 154    1
    ALL NIGHT YOUR MOTH-BREATH  .........................MORNING SONG   157   10
    THE NIGHT SKY IS ONLY A SORT OF CARBON PAPER,  ...........INSOMNIAC 163    1
    AND DRINK THE SMALL NIGHT CHILL LIKE NEWS OF HOME.  .........STARS. 166   40
    THE RED NIGHT LIGHTS ARE FLAT MOONS. THEY ARE DULL WITH BLOOD.  ...
                          ...  THE SURGEON AT 2 A.M.                    171   48
    BLOOM ABOUT ME LIKE NIGHT FLOWERS, WITH A GOOD SMELL.  ...LAST WORDS 172   22
    THE NIGHT LIGHTS ARE FLAT RED MOONS. THEY ARE DULL WITH BLOOD.  ...
                          ...  THREE WOMEN                              180  124
    ALL NIGHT I SHALL GALLOP THUS, IMPETUOUSLY,  ...................ELM  192   10
    WHERE APPLE BLOOM ICES THE NIGHT  .............................EVENT 195   13
    MY NIGHT SWEATS GREASE HIS BREAKFAST PLATE.  .............THE JAILER 226    1
    THAT NIGHT THE MOON  .........................................LESBOS 229   53
    DARLING, ALL NIGHT  ..........................................FEVER. 231   28
    THIS IS WINTER, THIS IS NIGHT, SMALL LOVE --  ........BY CANDLELIGHT 236    1
    IT SIMPLY EXPLODED ONE NIGHT,  ............................THE TOUR  238   22
    THE NIGHT DANCES  ....................................THE NIGHT DANCES 249   T
    AND HOW WILL YOUR NIGHT DANCES  ....................THE NIGHT DANCES 249    3
    ALL NIGHT I CARPENTER  ...................................THALIDOMIDE 252   17
    THE NIGHT BRINGS VIOLETS,  .................................PARALYTIC 266   11
    FROM THE SWEET, DEEP THROATS OF THE NIGHT FLOWER.  ...........EDGE  273   16
    IN EVERY RESPECT LIKE EVERY OTHER NIGHT:*DIALOGUE OVER A OUIJA BOARD 276    2
    AND TRICKED US TO TRUST HIS VISION, WHILE NIGHT AFTER NIGHT HE  ...
                          ...  DIALOGUE OVER A OUIJA BOARD              279  104
    AND TRICKED US TO TRUST HIS VISION, WHILE NIGHT AFTER NIGHT HE  ...
                          ...  DIALOGUE OVER A OUIJA BOARD              279  104
    SPRUNG TO BEING ON OUR WEDDING NIGHT  ...DIALOGUE OVER A OUIJA BOARD 280  140
    ALL NIGHT LONG, EVEN SHOULD OUR EYES SHUT  ............DIALOGUE O.  286  354
    THE NIGHT IS A BLUE POOL; SHE IS VERY STILL.  ................ELM/DR 292    6
    ALL NIGHT I HAVE HEARD  ..................................FEVER./DR 294    3
    "LAST NIGHT," HE SAID, "I SLEPT WELL  ...................THE DREAM  310    1
    NIGHT YIELDED UP  ............................MOONSONG AT MORNING   317   30
    EACH NIGHT, THIS ADROIT YOUNG LADY  ......................AERIALIST 331    1
NIGHTFALL (4)
    NIGHTFALL, COLD EYE -- NEITHER DISHEARTENS  ............THE BEGGARS  47    1
    OF FINEST CONSCIENCE. NIGHTFALL OBSCURES  .............THE BEGGARS   48   16
    NOR NIGHTFALL, OUR HANDS, FACES  ...............THE GREAT CARBUNCLE  72    6
    AT NIGHTFALL THERE IS THE BEAUTY OF DROWNED FIELDS,  .......TOTEM   264    4
NIGHTGOWN (1)
    IN MY VICTORIAN NIGHTGOWN. ............................MORNING SONG 157   14
NIGHTINGALES (1)
    LOUD THE IMMORTAL NIGHTINGALES DECLARE: *TO EVA DESCENDING THE STAIR 303   13
```

338

	TITLE	PAGE	LINE

NIGHTLONG (3)
```
    THAT NIGHTLONG STOLE HER MALE, .........................THE SHRIKE    42  20
    FOR A WISH TO TETHER: THEY RIDE NIGHTLONG ...........EPITAPH FOR F.    46  26
    NIGHTLONG, IN THE GRANITE YARD, INVISIBLE CATS ...........INSOMNIAC   163  29
```
NIGHTLY (6)
```
    SET FOOT NIGHTLY IN HER YARD ......................THE THIN PEOPLE    65  29
    NIGHTLY WE LEFT THEM IN THEIR DESERT PLACE. ..........THE OTHER TWO    68  27
    NIGHTLY THE BATTLE-SHOUTS START UP .....................BLUE MOLES   126  19
    NIGHTLY NOW I FLOG APES OWLS BEARS SHEEP .........ZOO KEEPER'S WIFE   155  39
    NIGHTLY IT FLAPS OUT ..............................................ELM   193  29
    NIGHTLY SHE BALANCES ...............................AERIALIST   331   7
```
NIGHTMARE (2)
```
    ON THE PITCHED REEFS OF NIGHTMARE, .........................LORELEI    94  24
    I DO NOT TELL YOU THE NIGHTMARE .........................THE DREAM   311  29
```
NIGHTMARES (1)
```
    TRY ENTRY, ENTER NIGHTMARES .............................SCULPTOR    92  21
```
NIGHTS (5)
```
    THAT VAIN JADES SULK SINGLE DOWN BRIDAL NIGHTS, ......ELLA MASON A.    54  41
    NIGHTS, I SQUAT IN THE CORNUCOPIA .....................THE COLOSSUS   130  24
    THE NIGHTS SNAPPED OUT OF SIGHT LIKE A LIZARD'S EYELID:*THE HANGING.   141   3
    NIGHTS, I WROTE IN MY DIARY SPITEFULLY, MY FINGERS RED .......BABY.   174  14
    THREE DAYS. THREE NIGHTS. ......................................FEVER.   232  31
```
NIGHT'S (1)
```
    A FLASH LIKE DOOMCRACK RENT NIGHT'S BLACK: ..........CRYSTAL GAZER    55  37
```
NIGHTSHADE (1)
```
    NIGHTSHADE AND NETTLES ............................TEMPER OF TIME   336  11
```
NIKE (2)
```
    MOTHER OF A WHITE NIKE AND SEVERAL BALD-EYED APOLLOS.   BARREN WOMAN   157   7
    WHITE NIKE, ..................................................THE OTHER   201   3
```
NIMBLE (5)
```
    LEGGING IT MOST NIMBLE ..............................ODE FOR TED    29   4
    DRIVES NIMBLE BLOOD TOO QUICK ..........EPITAPH FOR FIRE AND FLOWER    46  25
    OF HIS REDOUBT HE RAN HIS NIMBLE FILAMENT, ..................SPIDER    48  15
    NIMBLE AS A NOUN, ...........................TRIO OF LOVE SONGS   314  29
    TO TRAP THIS OUTRAGEOUS NIMBLE QUEEN .....................AERIALIST   332  34
```
NIMBLE-WINGED (1)
```
    FLITS NIMBLE-WINGED IN THICKETS, AND OF GOOD COLOR. ....WATERCOLOR.   112   7
```
NIMBLY (1)
```
    THE TESSELLATED WAVE. NOW NIMBLY LET ..............MIDSUMMER MOBILE   324   7
```
NIMBUS (5)
```
    THE INSUFFERABLE NIMBUS OF THE LOT-DRAWN ...........THE THIN PEOPLE    64  21
    OF OUR MEAT-AND-POTATO THOUGHTS ASSUMES THE NIMBUS ........GHOST'S.    90  14
    BELLIED ON A NIMBUS OF SUN-GLAZED BUTTERCUP. ..........WATERCOLOR.   112  18
    NIMBUS, OR PUFF .......................................POLLY'S TREE   128  21
    EXHALES AN INDIGO NIMBUS, ...................PARLIAMENT HILL FIELDS   153  46
```
NIMBUS-LIT (1)
```
    THAN ITS SUBURB OF WOODS: NIMBUS-LIT, ...........................OWL   101 2-3
```
NINE (9)
```
    I'M A RIDDLE IN NINE SYLLABLES, ........................METAPHORS   116   1
    WHEN I WAS NINE, A LIME-GREEN ANESTHETIST .................FACE LIFT   155   4
    IT HAS NINE TAILS, IT IS DANGEROUS. .....THE COURAGE OF SHUTTING-UP   210  19
    AND LIKE THE CAT I HAVE NINE TIMES TO DIE. ...........LADY LAZARUS   244  21
    OF NINE BLACK ALPS. .................................THE COURIERS   247  10
    PODS OF THE LABURNUM AT NINE IN THE MORNING. ....LETTER IN NOVEMBER   253   4
    NINE MONTHS TOO SOON FOR COMFORT, BUT A BRIGHT .........DIALOGUE O.   280 141
    NINE BLACK MICE WITH EBON COACH, *BLACK PINE TREE IN AN ORANGE LIGHT   328   6
    HER NINE SO SLIPPERY LIVES. ...........................AERIALIST   332  36
```
NINETEEN-TWENTY (1)
```
    MY WIFE, DEAD AND FLAT, IN [NINETEEN-TWENTY] FURS, .......PARALYTIC   266  23
```
NINETY-FOURTH (1)
```
    SHOT PAST THE NINETY-FOURTH FLOOR .................DIALOGUE EN ROUTE   309  34
```
NINNIES (1)
```
    ON THE MOVE, HEDGED BY A LITTER OF FEAT-FOOT NINNIES ...........SOW    61  21
```
NIP (1)
```
    LARKS' NIP AND TUCK ARISING ................SONG FOR A SUMMER'S DAY    31   9
```
NIPPLED (1)
```
    NIPPLED MOONS, EXTINCT AND COLD, .....................DANSE MACABRE   321   8
```
NIPPLE-FLOWERS (1)
```
    UNFACED, UNFORMED, THE NIPPLE-FLOWERS ............VIRGIN IN A TREE    81  23
```
NO (242)
NOAH'S (1)
```
    DROWNS NOAH'S PRAYERS WITH DISTAIN, .................INSOLENT STORM.   326  14
```
NOBILITY (1)
```
    THERE WOULD BE A NOBILITY THEN, THERE WOULD BE A BIRTHDAY.*BIRTHDAY.   208  59
```
NOBLE (2)
```
    THAT NOBLE MIEN, PERHAPS YOU'VE LATE QUITTED HEAVEN?" ..DIALOGUE B.    38  16
    OUR NOBLE DOCTOR CLAIMS THE PAIN IS HIS, .......NEVER TRY TO TRICK.   320   7
```
NOBODY (17)
```
    NOBODY BLINKS A LID, GAPES, ...........................STREET SONG    35   5
    THESE STILLED SUBURBS: NOBODY ...........................NIGHT SHIFT    76   9
    NOBODY WINTERING NOW BEHIND ...........................POINT SHIRLEY   110  25
    NOBODY DIED OR WITHERED ON THAT STAGE. ......ELECTRA ON AZALEA PATH   116  13
    GRANDCHILDREN NOBODY KNOWS. .......................OLD LADIES' HOME   120  12
    NOBODY DIES OR IS BORN WITHOUT THEIR KNOWING IT. ...THE NET-MENDERS   121  13
    NOBODY SEES US, ....................................MUSHROOMS   139   7
```

NOBODY (CONT.)
    STILL NOBODY WILL MOVE OR SPEAK -- ....ON DECK 142   10
    THOUGH NOBODY IN THERE LOOKS UP OR BOTHERS TO ANSWER. ....A LIFE 150   8
    NOBODY CAN TELL WHAT I LACK. ....PARLIAMENT HILL FIELDS 152   5
    I AM NOBODY; I HAVE NOTHING TO DO WITH EXPLOSIONS. ....TULIPS 160   5
    NOBODY WATCHED ME BEFORE, NOW I AM WATCHED. ....TULIPS 161   43
    NOBODY IN THE LANE, AND NOTHING, NOTHING BUT BLACKBERRIES,*BLACKBER. 168   1
    AND THEY ARE ALL GLOVED AND COVERED, WHY DID NOBODY TELL ME? ..BEE. 211   4
    I AM NUDE AS A CHICKEN NECK, DOES NOBODY LOVE ME? ..THE BEE MEETING 211   6
    NOBODY BUT ME ....LETTER IN NOVEMBER 254   32
    IN THIS DAY BEFORE THE DAY NOBODY IS ABOUT.*QUEEN MARY'S ROSE GARDEN 290   1
NOBODY'S (1)
    NOBODY'S ABOUT. IN THE HOTELS ....THE MUNICH MANNEQUINS 263   17
NO-COLOR (1)
    FIVE O'CLOCK IN THE MORNING, THE NO-COLOR VOID ....GHOST'S.   90   2
NOCTURNE (1)
    AQUATIC NOCTURNE ....AQUATIC NOCTURNE 305   T
NOD (6)
    WITH HEADS LIKE DARNING-EGGS TO NOD ....THE DISQUIETING MUSES   75   6
    AND NOD AND NOD AT FOOT AND HEAD ....THE DISQUIETING MUSES   75   7
    AND NOD AND NOD AT FOOT AND HEAD ....THE DISQUIETING MUSES   75   7
    THE ANTHERS NOD THEIR HEADS, POTENT AS KINGS ....BEEKEEPER'S. 118   11
    WHILE I SLEEP, THE BLACK SPORES NOD ....THE RIVAL/DR 291   2
    COLONNADES OF ANGELS NOD HER IN ....THE PRINCESS AND THE GOBLINS 333   13
NODDED (2)
    NODDED THEIR PETALED HEADS AROUND YOUR COUCH. ....YADWIGHA.   86   30
    ACCOMPANIED YOU. SO THEY NODDED AT THE COUCH WITH THE MOON*YADWIGHA.   86   32
NODDING (6)
    NODDING IN A SOMNOLENCE ....SPIDER   49   23
    NODDING BY NIGHT AROUND MY BED, ...THE DISQUIETING MUSES   75   15
    THE LAMP-HEADED NYMPHS ARE NODDING TO SLEEP LIKE STATUES. *POEM.5.F. 135   12
    NODDING AND ROCKING AND FINGERING HER THIN HAIR. ....FACE LIFT 156   30
    EVERYBODY IS NODDING A SQUARE BLACK HEAD, THEY ARE KNIGHTS IN
        VISORS, ...THE BEE MEETING 211   13
    NOT EVEN NODDING, A PERSONAGE IN A HEDGEROW. ....THE BEE MEETING 212   41
NOEL (2)
    NOEL! NOEL! NO MOUTH IS SHUT. ....A WINTER'S TALE   87   27
    NOEL! NOEL! NO MOUTH IS SHUT. ....A WINTER'S TALE   87   27
NOISE (5)
    THE NOISE CAME FROM OUTSIDE: ....NIGHT SHIFT   76   6
    THEN THE TULIPS FILLED IT UP LIKE A LOUD NOISE. ....TULIPS 161   52
    AND THE NOISE IT FLAYS FROM THE AIR, ONCE IT GETS GOING! ..COURAGE. 210   20
    IT IS THE NOISE THAT APPALLS ME MOST OF ALL, ...THE ARRIVAL. 213   17
    NOISE OF THE NEW. ....LESBOS 228   19
NOISELESS (2)
    NOISELESS, ON RUBBER WHEELS, ON THE WAY TO THE SEA RESORT. WAKING. 151   8
    HEAT SHADOWS WAVER NOISELESS IN ...MORNING IN THE HOSPITAL SOLARIUM 332   6
NOISES (1)
    I ENVY THE BIG NOISES, ...LITTLE FUGUE 188   19
NOISY (1)
    I STALLED AT SUDDEN NOISY CRASHES*FABLE OF THE RHODODENDRON STEALERS 103   18
NO-LIFE (1)
    A LIFE BAPTIZED IN NO-LIFE FOR A WHILE, ...INSOMNIAC 163   18
NO-MAN'S (1)
    ENTER THE CHILLY NO-MAN'S LAND OF ABOUT ....THE GHOST'S LEAVETAKING   90   1
NONCHALANCE (2)
    AND MARVEL AT THE SMASHING NONCHALANCE ....CHANNEL CROSSING   27   15
    UNDER THE GUISE OF NONCHALANCE. PAN'S LAUGH ....DIALOGUE O. 282 228
NONE (4)
    NONE OF THAT GREENHORN LOT MATCHED HER BRIGHT CROWN. ....QUEEN'S C.   29   20
    I AM NONE THE WISER. ....THE COLOSSUS 129   10
    NONE OF THEM SEEM TO NOTICE. ....PARLIAMENT HILL FIELDS 152   17
    I WALK AMONG THEM, BUT NONE OF THEM ARE NOTICING. ....I AM VERTICAL 162   13
NOON (11)
    HAGGARD THROUGH THE HOT WHITE NOON. ....PURSUIT   22   10
    SHEEN OF THE NOON SUN STRIKING ....SONG FOR A SUMMER'S DAY   31   11
    IN THE WHITEHOT NOON: ....FIESTA MELONS   46   10
    OTHER THAN NOON, THAN MOON, STARS -- ....THE GREAT CARBUNCLE   72   16
    IN THE SULFUROUS NOON. WE MOVE ....IN MIDAS' COUNTRY   99   6
    BY NOON AND THROUGHOUT THE BRUNT ....CHILD'S PARK STONES 101   20
    THE TUMULUS, EVEN AT NOON, GUARDS ITS BLACK SHADOW: ..PARLIAMENT H. 153   26
    THE SUN FLAMED STRAIGHT DOWN THAT NOON ON THE WATER OFF
        MARBLEHEAD. ....THE BABYSITTERS 174   2
    HOT NOON IN THE MEADOWS. THE BUTTERCUPS ....THREE WOMEN 186 337
    UNTIL THE PEAK OF NOON HAS COME ....TO A JILTED LOVER 310   24
    AT NOON, ANEMIC HUSBANDS VISIT THEM. ....MORNING IN THE HOS. 333   27
NOONDAY (3)
    AND THE AIR DANGEROUS. NOONDAY ACTS QUEERLY ....SLEEP. 143   3
    THE DOORBELL RENDS THE NOONDAY HEAT ....FAMILY REUNION 300   5
    YOU OVERCAST ALL ORDER'S NOONDAY RANK ....SONNET TO SATAN 323   7
NOR (40)
NORMAL (2)
    AND THEN GREW NORMAL, ...LESBOS 229   57
    TO NORMAL. LET'S CLOSE THE CURTAINS. IT LOOKS WILD .....DIALOGUE O. 286 335

```
                                              TITLE         PAGE  LINE
NORMALITY (1)
  I SHALL MEDITATE UPON NORMALITY.  .. .....................THREE WOMEN  186  323
NORTH (6)
  SAW EVIL BREAK OUT OF THE NORTH.  .........ON THE DECLINE OF ORACLES   78   32
  FROM SOUTH STATION TO NORTH.  ......................A WINTER'S TALE     87   36
  OF THE NORTH, TO BE STEERED CLEAR  ..................FULL FATHOM FIVE   92   13
  TRADING THEIR POISONS, THE NORTH AND SOUTH BOUND CARS  ...PRIVATE G.  130   16
  IT TOOK THREE DAYS DRIVING NORTH TO FIND A CLOUD  .........TWO CAMP.  145   10
  I SHALL MOVE NORTH. I SHALL MOVE INTO A LONG BLACKNESS. *THREE WOMEN  182  190
NORTHERN (2)
  TO THE ADIRONDACKS, TO NORTHERN MONADNOCK,  .........ABOVE THE OXBOW   87    3
  TO THE HILLS' NORTHERN FACE, AND THE FACE IS ORANGE ROCK   BLACKBER.  169   24
NOSE (11)
  I NOSE OUT THE LAY  ...............................WORDS FOR A NURSERY  74   23
  MUSK SATISFIED MY NOSE, RED MY EYE,  ..................RHODODENDRON.  103   13
  MAUDLIN FROM LEAKY EYE TO SWOLLEN NOSE.  ...........THE RAVAGED FACE  115    4
  AND YOU DOZE ON, NOSE TO THE WALL.  ...................LEAVING EARLY  146   38
  NOTHING SO VULGAR AS A NOSE OR AN EYE  .......................MAGI   148    2
  AQUEDUCTS, THE BATHS OF CARACALLA, THE EAGLE NOSE!  ........SURGEON.  171   28
  TO HAVE YOU GRAB MY NOSE, A LADDER RUNG.  ......FOR A FATHERLESS SON  205   11
  THE NOSE, THE EYE PITS, THE FULL SET OF TEETH?  ........LADY LAZARUS  244   13
  STRIPES FOR MOUTH AND EYES AND NOSE,  ..................THE FEARFUL  256    6
  EYES, NOSE AND EARS,  ...................................PARALYTIC  266   29
  NO RINGS THROUGH THE NOSE, NO CRIES.  ....................GIGOLO  267    9
NOSE-END (1)
  THE NOSE-END THAT TWITCHES, THE OLD IMPERFECTIONS -- *COMPANIONABLE.  105    1
NOSES (5)
  THEIR CORKSCREW NOSES, THEIR WHITE HANDS  ................BLUE MOLES  126   15
  DOGBODY NOSES THE PETALS. THEY BLOOM UPSIDE DOWN.  ......POEM.1.WHO.  131   11
  FOOTLINGS, BONELESS AS NOSES,  ..........................POEM.2.DARK.  133   25
  OUR TOES, OUR NOSES  ....................................MUSHROOMS  139    4
  HIS FINGERS HAD THE NOSES OF WEASELS.  ................LITTLE FUGUE  187   11
NOSING (1)
  BONES NOSING FOR DISTANCES.  ..............................BRASILIA  258   10
NOSTALGIA (1)
  MY NOSTRILS PRICKLE WITH NOSTALGIA.  ..................LEAVING EARLY  146   20
NOSTALGIAS (1)
  BUT FLORIDLY, HIS AMOROUS NOSTALGIAS.  ....................OUIJA   78   32
NOSTRILS (4)
  THE SMALL GREEN NOSTRILS BREATHE,  ....................THE SLEEPERS  123   17
  SMALL NOSTRILS ARE BREATHING.  ........................POEM.2.DARK.  133   23
  MY NOSTRILS PRICKLE WITH NOSTALGIA.  ..................LEAVING EARLY  146   20
  WHEN I LIGHT THEM, MY NOSTRILS PRICKLE.  ..................CANDLES  149   14
NOSY (1)
  NOSY GROWER,  ...........................................EAVESDROPPER  260    3
NOTABLE (1)
  NOTABLE ROBBER BARON,  ........................................SPIDER   48    9
NOTCHED (1)
  OF NOTCHED TIN PLATITUDES CONCERNING WEATHER,  .......SONNET: TO EVA  305   11
NOTE (3)
  ONE NOTE  .................................................PURDAH  243   42
  AN ORIGINAL NOTE. IF HE'D SAID, HOWEVER, MERELY:  .......DIALOGUE O.  278   81
  THE ROSES ARE NAMED AFTER QUEENS AND PEOPLE OF NOTE  ..QUEEN MARY'S.  290   17
NOTEBOOK (1)
  SHE RECORDED THE TOTAL IN HER NOTEBOOK,  ........BITTER STRAWBERRIES  300   32
NOTES (6)
  AND AS HIS NOTES TWINE GREEN, THE GREEN RIVER  .........SNAKECHARMER   79    6
  FLUTE NOTES FROM A REEDY POND  ...........................POEM.5.F.  134   ST
  YOUR HANDFUL OF NOTES;  .............................MORNING SONG  157   17
  ADDRESSING IT, WHILE THE HILLS ROLL THE NOTES OF THE DEAD BELL;  ...
                                           ... BERCK-PLAGE  200   95
  THERE IS ONLY A CROW IN A TREE. MAKE NOTES.  ..........THE DETECTIVE  209   40
  NOTES TO A NEOPHYTE  ...........................NOTES TO A NEOPHYTE  306    T
NOTHING (71)
  HAS NOTHING ON YOU,  ..............................LETTER TO A PURIST   36    7
  THAN EARTH, AND THERE IS NOTHING  ...............THE GREAT CARBUNCLE   73   25
  OF HIS MIND. AND NOW NOTHING BUT SNAKES  .............SNAKECHARMER   79   12
  WATER, TO GREEN, TO NOTHING LIKE A SNAKE.  ............SNAKECHARMER   79   27
  WHERE NOTHING HIGHER'S TO BE LOOKED TO. DOWNWARD LOOKS  ......OXBOW.   88   30
  SO THESE POSED SHEETS, BEFORE THEY THIN TO NOTHING,  .......GHOST'S.   90   18
  KNEW NOTHING OF. SO THE CRABS  .........MUSSEL HUNTER AT ROCK HARBOR   97   60
  DOING NOTHING. JULY'S JUICE ROUNDS THEIR NUBS.  ...........MOONRISE   98    3
  SIGNS SAY NOTHING. THE FALCON WHO SPOKE CLEAR  .......INCOMMUNICADO  100   13
  GRANDMOTHER, STONES ARE NOTHING OF HOME  .............POINT SHIRLEY  111   46
  NOTHING IS BIG OR FAR.  .........WATERCOLOR OF GRANTCHESTER MEADOWS  111    3
  I HAD NOTHING TO DO WITH GUILT OR ANYTHING  ..ELECTRA ON AZALEA PATH  116    9
  HARD GODS WERE THERE, NOTHING ELSE.  ..THE HERMIT AT OUTERMOST HOUSE  119   13
  FOR WEEKS I CAN REMEMBER NOTHING AT ALL.  ...........POEM.1.WHO.  132   33
  NOTHING WENT MOLDY. THE LITTLE INVISIBLES  .............POEM.4.BEAST.  134    5
  DUCHESS OF NOTHING,  ....................................POEM.4.BEAST.  134   25
  IF I DON'T MOVE ABOUT, I'LL KNOCK NOTHING OVER. SO I SAID,*POEM.6.W.  135   14
  THE HEAD-STONE QUIET, JOSTLED BY NOTHING.  ...............POEM.7.S.  136   10
  MY MENDINGS ITCH. THERE IS NOTHING TO DO.  ...............POEM.7.S.  137   44

                              341
```

	TITLE	PAGE	LINE
NOTHING (CONT.)

LITTLE OR NOTHING. ....MUSHROOMS 139 22
NOW THERE IS NOTHING MUCH TO LOOK AT. ....ON DECK 142 9
NOTHING SO VULGAR AS A NOSE OR AN EYE ....MAGI 148 2
INSTEAD, THE DEAD INJURE ME WITH ATTENTIONS, AND NOTHING CAN
  HAPPEN. ....BARREN WOMAN 157 8
LOOPING WOOL, DOING NOTHING IN PARTICULAR, ...HEAVY WOMEN 158 16
I AM NOBODY; I HAVE NOTHING TO DO WITH EXPLOSIONS. ....TULIPS 160 5
AND IT ASKS NOTHING, A NAME TAG, A FEW TRINKETS. ....TULIPS 161 33
THAT OPENS AT THE TOP ONTO NOTHING AT ALL. . . .   .WIDOW 164 10
HAND FOLDING HAND, AND NOTHING IN BETWEEN. ....WIDOW 164 31
NOBODY IN THE LANE, AND NOTHING, NOTHING BUT BLACKBERRIES,*BLACKBER. 168 1
NOBODY IN THE LANE, AND NOTHING, NOTHING BUT BLACKBERRIES,*BLACKBER. 168 1
THAT LOOKS OUT ON NOTHING, NOTHING BUT A GREAT SPACE   BLACKBERRYING 169 25
THAT LOOKS OUT ON NOTHING, NOTHING BUT A GREAT SPACE   BLACKBERRYING 169 25
CRAMPED ON NOTHING. BLACK ....FINISTERRE 169 2
NOW THEY ARE NOTHING, THEY ARE NOT EVEN BABIES. ....LAST WORDS 172 7
A FEW MORE BREATHS, AND IT WILL REFLECT NOTHING AT ALL.   LAST WORDS 172 12
THE MOON SEES NOTHING OF THIS. SHE IS BALD AND WILD. ....MOON. 173 27
YOU ARE SO WHITE, SUDDENLY." AND I SAID NOTHING. ....THREE WOMEN 177 23
I SEE NOTHING. ....THREE WOMEN 180 147
I AM FLAT AND VIRGINAL, WHICH MEANS NOTHING HAS HAPPENED, ...THREE. 184 276
NOTHING THAT CANNOT BE ERASED, RIPPED UP AND SCRAPPED,
  BEGUN AGAIN. ....THREE WOMEN 184 277
I AM GUILTY OF NOTHING. ....LITTLE FUGUE 188 28
I WAS SEVEN, I KNEW NOTHING. ....LITTLE FUGUE 188 38
DO YOU SAY NOTHING? ....LITTLE FUGUE 188 43
OR THE VOICE OF NOTHING, THAT WAS YOUR MADNESS? ....ELM 192 6
ZEROS, SHUTTING ON NOTHING, ...THE RABBIT CATCHER 194 15
THEY ARE FLYING OFF INTO NOTHING: REMEMBER US. ....BERCK-PLAGE 199 87
I PUT MY HANDS AMONG THE FLAMES. NOTHING BURNS. ...POPPIES IN JULY 203 4
ONLY THEY HAVE NOTHING TO SAY TO ANYBODY. ......BURNING THE LETTERS 204 34
WARM RAIN GREASES MY HAIR, EXTINGUISHES NOTHING.*BURNING THE LETTERS 205 47
THEY CAN DIE, I NEED FEED THEM NOTHING, I AM THE OWNER.*THE ARRIVAL. 213 25
HE HAS NOTHING TO DO WITH THE BEE-SELLER OR WITH ME. ....STINGS 215 39
THIS IS THE EASY TIME, THERE IS NOTHING DOING. ....WINTERING 217 1
BEHIND TWO EYES IN WHICH NOTHING IS REFLECTED BUT MONKEYS. *A SECRET 219 20
IT WORKS, THERE IS NOTHING WRONG WITH IT. ....THE APPLICANT 222 36
THERE IS NOTHING BETWEEN US. ....MEDUSA 226 41
THERE IS NOTHING TO DO WITH SUCH A BEAUTIFUL BLANK BUT SMOOTH IT. ...
  ... AMNESIAC 232 2
TO ALMOST NOTHING, TO A DULL BLUE DUD. ....BY CANDLELIGHT 236 18
FLESH, BONE, THERE IS NOTHING THERE --- ....LADY LAZARUS 246 75
THE SHADOWS OF RINGDOVES CHANTING, BUT EASING NOTHING. *WINTER TREES 258 15
UTTERING NOTHING BUT BLOOD -- ....CHILDLESS WOMAN 259 13
ASKS NOTHING OF LIFE. ....PARALYTIC 267 40
THE MOON HAS NOTHING TO BE SAD ABOUT, ...EDGE 273 17
CRACKS RED. NOTHING HAPPENS. WAIT. ITS TRIP ....DIALOGUE O. 277 20
NOTHING SHORT OF A MIRACLE TO NAIL .....DIALOGUE OVER A OUIJA BOARD 280 160
IF NOTHING COMES OF IT. ON THE OTHER HAND, ...DIALOGUE O. 281 198
LET NOTHING BE LEFT TO SWADDLE US. ...SONG FOR A REVOLUTIONARY LOVE 323 12
THERE IS NOTHING MORE FOR ME TO SAY. ....DENOUEMENT 326 3
THERE IS NOTHING MORE FOR ME TO SAY. ....DENOUEMENT 326 9
THERE IS NOTHING MORE FOR ME TO SAY. ....DENOUEMENT 327 15
THERE IS NOTHING MORE FOR ME TO SAY. ....DENOUEMENT 327 19
NOTHING CHANGES, FOR ALL THE BLAZING OF ....LOVE IS A PARALLAX 329 16
NOTHINGNESS (1)
CAN NOTHINGNESS BE SO PRODIGAL? ....THREE WOMEN 183 232
NOTICE (9)
THE SPIDERS WON'T NOTICE. POEM.1.WHO. 131 8
WHERE TREES AND CLOUDS AND ANIMALS PAY NO NOTICE; ....TWO CAMP. 144 8
NONE OF THEM SEEM TO NOTICE. ....PARLIAMENT HILL FIELDS 152 17
FROM HER AMAZINGLY WHITE TORSO, AND I COULDN'T HELP BUT NOTICE ...
  ... IN PLASTER 159 24
IN THIS CLEAR AIR AND NEVER NOTICE IT -- ....WIDOW 164 33
IT IS BY THESE HOOKS SHE CLIMBS TO MY NOTICE. ....THREE WOMEN 182 208
NOW I AM MILKWEED SILK, THE BEES WILL NOT NOTICE. ..THE BEE MEETING 211 9
I NOTICE YOU ARE STARK NAKED. ....THE APPLICANT 221 19
DO NOT THINK I DON'T NOTICE YOUR CURTAIN -- ..........EAVESDROPPER 260 28
NOTICING (1)
I WALK AMONG THEM, BUT NONE OF THEM ARE NOTICING. .....I AM VERTICAL 162 13
NOTION (2)
FOR HER, THE HEAVY NOTION OF EVIL ....MAGI 148 12
IT SEEMS BEES HAVE A NOTION OF HONOR, ...THE SWARM 217 57
NOTIONS (1)
NOTIONS AND TICKETS, SHORT CIRCUITS AND FOLDING MIRRORS. .....TOTEM 265 27
NOUMENON (1)
HIS BOOK OF INSULTS. NERVE OR NOUMENON, *DIALOGUE OVER A OUIJA BOARD 284 297
NOUN (1)
NIMBLE AS A NOUN, ...TRIO OF LOVE SONGS 314 29
NOUNS (1)
WHERE ADJECTIVES PLAY CROQUET WITH FLAMINGO NOUNS; ...A SORCERER B. 324 2
NOURISH (1)
TO NOURISH ....GIGOLO 267 14

342

NOURISHERS (1)
  IF OUR NERVES ARE THE SOLE NOURISHERS ..DIALOGUE OVER A OUIJA BOARD 284 287
NOURISHES (2)
  NOURISHES THESE BROKEN FLUTINGS, ...THE MANOR GARDEN 125   9
  NEITHER NOURISHES NOR HEALS. ....THE BURNT-OUT SPA 138 34
NOURISHING (1)
  NOURISHING AS VIOLET LEAVES ....APRIL 18 302 10
NOVEMBER (3)
  IN BLACK NOVEMBER. AFTER A SLIDING RAIN ....DIALOGUE B.   38   3
  NOVEMBER GRAVEYARD ....NOVEMBER GRAVEYARD   56   T
  LETTER IN NOVEMBER ....LETTER IN NOVEMBER 253   T
NOVEMBER'S (1)
  NOVEMBER'S DONE WITH. THE BLOWN LEAVES MAKE BAT-SHAPES, *DIALOGUE O. 286 337
NOVICE (1)
  NO NOVICE ....MISS DRAKE PROCEEDS TO SUPPER   41   1
NOVICES (1)
  TO NOVICES AND TO THE TIMID. ....WHITENESS I REMEMBER 102   9
NOW (143)
  NOW, RICH ORDER OF WALLS IS FALLEN; ROOKS CROAK ......CONVERSATION.   21   5
  NOW HILLS HATCH MENACE, SPAWNING SHADE; ....PURSUIT   22 25
  NOW HE GOES FROM HIS RIGHTFUL ROAD ....BUCOLICS   24 21
  BRED AN AMPLE BATCH OF OMENS; BUT NOW ....TALE OF A TUB   25 18
  NOW, FREE, BY HAZARD'S QUIRK, FROM THE COMMON ILL   CHANNEL CROSSING   27 26
  OUR LONE LUCK NOW, COMPELLED BY BOND, BY BLOOD, ...CHANNEL CROSSING   27 33
  NOW OUR WHOLE TASK'S TO HACK ....FIRESONG   30   8
  "HOW NOW," FATHER SHAWN CRISPLY ADDRESSED THE GHOST ....DIALOGUE B.   38 11
  WHAT LOVE DID THEN, LOVE DOES NOW: ....DIALOGUE B.   39 29
  NOW THROUGH HER AMBUSHED AIR, ...MISS DRAKE PROCEEDS TO SUPPER   41 18
  NOW WITH STAKE AND PITCHFORK THEY ADVANCE, FLINT EYES FIXED
    ON MURDER. .... DREAM WITH CLAM-DIGGERS   44 28
  NOW SPEAK SOME SACRAMENT TO PARRY SCRUPLE .....WREATH FOR A BRIDAL   44 11
  NOW IN THE CRUX OF THEIR VOWS HANG YOUR EAR, ...EPITAPH FOR F.   45 15
  NOW THIS PARTICULAR GIRL ....SPINSTER   49   1
  NOW, AS I HONE MY KNIFE, SHE BEGS ....RHYME   50 11
  NOW, RUN TO FAT, SHE'S A SPINSTER WHOSE DOOR SHUTS ...ELLA MASON A.   54 17
  BUT NOW TURNED KINDER WITH TIME, WE MARK MISS MASON ..ELLA MASON A.   54 37
  POSSESSION OF THE MOST OBTUSE OBJECTS NOW AND THEN -- *BLACK ROOK I.   57 18
  ONE MIGHT SAY LOVE. AT ANY RATE, I NOW WALK ....BLACK ROOK I.   57 22
  NOW, AS GREEN SAP ASCENDS THE STEEPLED WOOD, ...MAYFLOWER   60   5
  NOW WORKS HIS HELL OF MONDAYS IN THE MOON'S BALL,*EVERLASTING MONDAY   62 11
  NOW THE THIN PEOPLE DO NOT OBLITERATE ....THE THIN PEOPLE   65 32
  "NO DOUBT NOW IN DREAM-PROPERTIED FALL SOME MOON-EYED, ..CONJURING.   66 33
  NOW, SNARED BY THIS MIRACULOUS ART, ...ON THE PLETHORA OF DRYADS   67 28
  THESE THREE, UNMASKED NOW, BEAR ....ALL THE DEAD DEARS   70   7
  TO PROVE IT. AS I THINK NOW OF HER HEAD, ...ALL THE DEAD DEARS   70 18
  DAY NOW, NIGHT NOW, AT HEAD, SIDE, FEET, ...THE DISQUIETING MUSES   76 49
  DAY NOW, NIGHT NOW, AT HEAD, SIDE, FEET, ...THE DISQUIETING MUSES   76 49
  THE EARTH TURNS NOW. IN HALF AN HOUR .....ON THE DECLINE OF ORACLES   78 26
  OF HIS MIND. AND NOW NOTHING BUT SNAKES ...............SNAKECHARMER   79 12
  NOW, DOUR-FACED, HER FINGERS ....VIRGIN IN A TREE   82 38
  STILL THAN SWALLOWS JOY. YOU ENTER NOW, ...PERSEUS   83 34
  AS THAT CRISP CUSP TOWARDS WHICH YOU VOYAGE NOW. ....GHOST'S.   91 38
  BUT NOW THE WATER-SKIERS RACE, ...IN MIDAS' COUNTRY   99 16
  INIMICAL NOW. THE GREAT GREEN ROCK ....GREEN ROCK, WINTHROP BAY 105 10
  TOLERABLE NOW AS MOLES ON THE FACE ....THE COMPANIONABLE ILLS 105   2
  NOBODY WINTERING NOW BEHIND ....POINT SHIRLEY 110 25
  DISSOLVED NOW, SMOKE OF AN OLD WAR. ....BLUE MOLES 126 18
  THIRTY YEARS NOW I HAVE LABORED ....THE COLOSSUS 129   8
  NOW THEY LIGHT ME UP LIKE AN ELECTRIC BULB. POEM.1.WHO. 132 32
  NOW COLDNESS COMES SIFTING DOWN, LAYER AFTER LAYER, ...POEM.5.F. 134   1
  NOW LITTLE WEEDS INSINUATE ....THE BURNT-OUT SPA 138 10
  NOW THERE IS NOTHING MUCH TO LOOK AT. ....ON DECK 142   9
  LITTERED WITH CHINESE HANDS. NOW I'M STARED AT ....LEAVING EARLY 146 30
  IF I'M ALIVE NOW, THEN I WAS DEAD, ...LOVE LETTER 147   2
  NOW I RESEMBLE A SORT OF GOD ....LOVE LETTER 147 34
  LEAVE HER ALONE NOW. ....A LIFE 150 30
  NOW SILENCE AFTER SILENCE OFFERS ITSELF. ....PARLIAMENT HILL FIELDS 152 19
  NOW, ON THE NURSERY WALL, ...PARLIAMENT HILL FIELDS 153 40
  NIGHTLY NOW I FLOG APES OWLS BEARS SHEEP ....ZOO KEEPER'S WIFE 155 39
  NOW SHE'S DONE FOR, THE DEWLAPPED LADY ....FACE LIFT 156 25
  WHITENS AND SWALLOWS ITS DULL STARS. AND NOW YOU TRY ..MORNING SONG 157 16
  I SHALL NEVER GET OUT OF THIS! THERE ARE TWO OF ME NOW: IN PLASTER 158   1
  NOW I SEE IT MUST BE ONE OR THE OTHER OF US. ....IN PLASTER 160 52
  NOW I HAVE LOST MYSELF I AM SICK OF BAGGAGE --- ....TULIPS 160 18
  I AM A NUN NOW, I HAVE NEVER BEEN SO PURE. ....TULIPS 161 28
  NOBODY WATCHED ME BEFORE, NOW I AM WATCHED. ....TULIPS 161 43
  NOW THE AIR SNAGS AND EDDIES ROUND THEM THE WAY A RIVER .....TULIPS 161 53
  NOW THE PILLS ARE WORN-OUT AND SILLY, LIKE CLASSICAL GODS.*INSOMNIAC 163 20
  THE CITY IS A MAP OF CHEERFUL TWITTERS NOW, ...INSOMNIAC 163 33
  BUT IT IS SHE WHO IS PAPER NOW, WARMED BY NO ONE. ....WIDOW 164 20
  AND WHERE I LIE NOW, BACK TO MY OWN DARK STAR. ....STARS. 166 34
  NOW, IN VALLEYS NARROW ....WUTHERING HEIGHTS 168 43
  THE ONLY THING TO COME NOW IS THE SEA. ...............BLACKBERRYING 169 19
  NOW IT IS ONLY GLOOMY, A DUMP OF ROCKS -- ....FINISTERRE 169   6
  NOW THEY ARE NOTHING, THEY ARE NOT EVEN BABIES. ....LAST WORDS 172   7

NOW (CONT.)
NOW I AM A LAKE. A WOMAN BENDS OVER ME. ....MIRROR 174 10
IT IS TEN YEARS, NOW, SINCE WE ROWED TO CHILDREN'S ISLAND. ...BABY. 174   1
THERE WAS SOMETHING ABOUT THEM LIKE CARDBOARD, AND NOW I HAD
       CAUGHT IT, ...THREE WOMEN 177 17
IT IS A WORLD OF SNOW NOW. I AM NOT AT HOME. ....THREE WOMEN 178 64
DUSK HOODS ME IN BLUE NOW, LIKE A MARY. ....THREE WOMEN 179 102
I AM A MOUNTAIN NOW, AMONG MOUNTAINY WOMEN. ....THREE WOMEN 179 113
HATING MYSELF, HATING AND FEARING. AND NOW THE WORLD CONCEIVES ...
                                                ... THREE WOMEN 181 150
THESE BODIES MOUNDED AROUND ME NOW, THESE POLAR SLEEPERS -- THREE. 181 181
NOW THEY FACE A WINTER OF WHITE SHEETS, WHITE FACES. ...THREE WOMEN 184 265
THE FEATURELESSNESS OF THAT CLOUD, NOW! ....LITTLE FUGUE 187   6
NOW SIMILAR CLOUDS ....LITTLE FUGUE 188 41
THIS IS RAIN NOW, THIS BIG HUSH. ....ELM 192 14
NOW I BREAK UP IN PIECES THAT FLY ABOUT LIKE CLUBS. ....ELM 192 19
OPENS ITS MOUTH NOW, DEMANDING. ....EVENT 194   8
A GRAY WALL NOW, CLAWED AND BLOODY. ...................APPREHENSIONS 195   6
HERE HE COMES NOW, AMONG THE MACKEREL GATHERERS ....BERCK-PLAGE 196 14
HOW SUPERIOR HE IS NOW. ....BERCK-PLAGE 198 56
NOW THE WASHED SHEETS FLY IN THE SUN, ...BERCK-PLAGE 198 67
HOW FAR HE IS NOW, HIS ACTIONS ....BERCK-PLAGE 199 82
NOW THE ROOM IS AHISS. THE INSTRUMENT ....WORDS HEARD. 203 11
AND AT LEAST IT WILL BE A GOOD PLACE NOW, THE ATTIC. .....BURNING. 204 22
BUT RIGHT NOW YOU ARE DUMB. ....FOR A FATHERLESS SON 205   6
NOW THERE ARE THESE VEILS, SHIMMERING LIKE CURTAINS, ...BIRTHDAY. 206 16
A GREAT SURGEON, NOW A TATTOOIST, ...THE COURAGE OF SHUTTING-UP 210 10
NOW I AM MILKWEED SILK, THE BEES WILL NOT NOTICE. ..THE BEE MEETING 211   9
WHICH IS THE RECTOR NOW, IS IT THAT MAN IN BLACK? ..THE BEE MEETING 211 11
NOW THEY ARE GIVING ME A FASHIONABLE WHITE STRAW ITALIAN HAT ..BEE. 211 21
NOW HE IS GONE ....STINGS 215 40
NOW SHE IS FLYING ....STINGS 215 56
NOW THEY BALL IN A MASS, ...WINTERING 218 31
NOW YOUR HEAD, EXCUSE ME, IS EMPTY. ....THE APPLICANT 221 26
DADDY, YOU CAN LIE BACK NOW. ....DADDY 224 75
NOW I AM SILENT, HATE ....LESBOS 229 64
NO USE, NO USE, NOW, BEGGING RECOGNIZE! ....AMNESIAC 232   1
TODDLE ON HOME TO TEA NOW IN YOUR FLAT HAT. ....THE TOUR 238 37
AND NOW I ....ARIEL 239 22
HOW FAR IS IT NOW? ....GETTING THERE 247   2
NOW IS THE TIME FOR BRIBERY. ....GETTING THERE 248 12
AND NOW DETONATIONS --- ....GETTING THERE 249 49
IT SEEMS PERFECTLY NATURAL NOW --- ....DEATH & CO. 254   2
PITCHER OF MILK, NOW EMPTY. ....EDGE 272 11
BEGINS. A JERK. AND NOW THE FIRST SLOW RAMBLE ....DIALOGUE O. 277 21
YOU'RE MELTING NOW, BECAUSE YOU THINK HE'S HIT ....DIALOGUE O. 278 80
JOG OFF IN JABBERWOCKY NOW AND LOSE US, *DIALOGUE OVER A OUIJA BOARD 279 91
NOW, YOU REALLY DON'T MUCH CARE WHICH, OR WHAT ....DIALOGUE O. 280 151
BOY, HE NEEDS A BEATING NOW AND THEN ...DIALOGUE OVER A OUIJA BOARD 281 183
AND WE'LL SEE WHO'S SMARTEST. PAN, TELL US NOW: ....DIALOGUE O. 281 205
IS ON YOU NOW, FOR PLANNING TO DREDGE UP*DIALOGUE OVER A OUIJA BOARD 282 239
TO R NOW. E. IN CORE . . . O-F-N-E- ....DIALOGUE OVER A OUIJA BOARD 284 277
I'VE DREAMED OF DOING IT AGAIN. AND NOW *DIALOGUE OVER A OUIJA BOARD 285 303
BUT NOW THAT ANGER COOLS, I'VE A SENSE OF SORROW ....DIALOGUE O. 285 310
SETTLES IN THE ROOM NOW. ITS WINGS BLACKEN THE TABLE. ..DIALOGUE O. 285 313
AT THE UNREAL FRONTIER. LET OUR BACKS, NOW BOLD, ...DIALOGUE O. 285 331
NOW SHE HERSELF IS DARKENING ....ELM/DR 292   9
THE DOOR NOW OPENS FROM WITHIN. ....FAMILY REUNION 300 10
NOW YOU MUST PLAY THE STRAIGHT MAN FOR A TERM ...DIRGE FOR A JOKER 303 13
OF SILVER AS THE RONDO SLOWS; NOW REELS ....CINDERELLA 303   3
NOW THERE IS NOWHERE I CAN GO ....TO A JILTED LOVER 310 16
NOW, DISCIPLINED IN THE STRICT ANCESTRAL CHAIR, ...THE TRIAL OF MAN 312 12
NOW WE, RETURNING FROM THE VAULTED DOMES ....DOOM OF EXILES 318   1
TELL ME QUICK, DARLING, TELL ME NOW. ....THE DISPOSSESSED 318   3
TELL ME QUICK, DARLING, TELL ME NOW. ....THE DISPOSSESSED 318   9
TELL ME QUICK, DARLING, TELL ME NOW. ....THE DISPOSSESSED 318 15
TELL ME QUICK, DARLING, TELL ME NOW! ....THE DISPOSSESSED 319 19
SHANKS OF BONE NOW RESURRECT, ...DANSE MACABRE 321 17
THE WINTER LANDSCAPE HANGS IN BALANCE NOW, ...PROLOGUE TO SPRING 322   1
NOW EMPTY BOXES OF THE HOODWINKED DEAD*SONG FOR A REVOLUTIONARY LOVE 323 17
THE TESSELLATED WAVE. NOW NIMBLY LET ....MIDSUMMER MOBILE 324   7
NOW EARTH REJECTS COMMUNICATION *INSOLENT STORM STRIKES AT THE SKULL 326 29
NOW FOLD THEIR WINGS LIKE BATS AND DISAPPEAR ....TWO LOVERS 327   7
BEYOND THE INTERVAL OF NOW AND HERE: ....TWO LOVERS. 327 11
NOW YOU, MY INTELLECTUAL LEPRECHAUN, ...LOVE IS A PARALLAX 329 25
NOW KISS AGAIN: TILL OUR STRICT FATHER LEANS ....LOVE IS A PARALLAX 330 43
TELL NOW, WE TAUNT, WHERE BLACK OR WHITE BEGINS LOVE IS A PARALLAX 330 49
NOW AS PENALTY FOR HER SKILL, ...AERIALIST 332 43
NOW BOUND AROUND HER WRIST TILL SHE REDEEM ....THE PRINCESS 333 24
NOW PROWL ON THE BOUGH; ....TEMPER OF TIME 336   6
NOWHERE (5)
FIT NOWHERE: BRICKDUST-COMPLECTED, EYE UNDER A DENSE LID, ...
              ... THE LADY AND THE EARTHENWARE HEAD 69   2
HE GAVE ME. I'VE GONE NOWHERE SINCE BUT ....WHITENESS I REMEMBER 102   3
NOWHERE. ....THE NIGHT DANCES 250 28

	TITLE	PAGE	LINE

NOWHERE (CONT.)
DISCHARGES ITSELF FROM THE TREE WITH NOWHERE TO GO. *CHILDLESS WOMAN 259 3
NOW THERE IS NOWHERE I CAN GO ....TO A JILTED LOVER 310 16
NUB (1)
SHE WORE HER BROOM STRAWS TO THE NUB. ....POINT SHIRLEY 110 18
NUBS (2)
BUMBLINGLY OVER THE NUBS OF THE COBBLES ....ALICANTE LULLABY 43 2
DOING NOTHING. JULY'S JUICE ROUNDS THEIR NUBS. ....MOONRISE 98 3
NUDE (4)
YET ALWAYS THE RIDICULOUS NUDE FLANKS URGE ....TALE OF A TUB 25 33
NUDE AS CLEOPATRA IN MY WELL-BOILED HOSPITAL SHIFT, ...FACE LIFT 156 10
I AM NUDE AS A CHICKEN NECK, DOES NOBODY LOVE ME? ..THE BEE MEETING 211 6
THE NUDE ....DEATH & CO. 254 8
NUDGED (1)
SMALL MUD KNOBS, NUDGED FROM UNDER, ...MUSSEL HUNTER AT ROCK HARBOR 96 26
NUDGERS (1)
NUDGERS AND SHOVERS ....MUSHROOMS 139 28
NUMB (4)
OF HUMAN AGONY: A LOOK TO NUMB ....PERSEUS 83 15
I LEAN TO YOU, NUMB AS A FOSSIL. TELL ME I'M HERE. ......TWO CAMP. 145 21
LEVITATING A NUMB MINUTE IN THE UPDRAFT ....WIDOW 164 3
BY THE TIME THE WHOLE OF IT WAS DELIVERED, AND TOO NUMB
TO USE IT. ....A BIRTHDAY PRESENT 208 54
NUMBER (3)
THEY ARE PROPER IN SHAPE AND NUMBER AND EVERY PART. ......STILLBORN 142 7
INFINITE NUMBER SEEMS TO BE THE ISSUE UP THERE. ....STARS. 165 21
THIS IS NUMBER THREE. ....LADY LAZARUS 245 22
NUMBERED (1)
MARVELINGLY NUMBERED THE MANY SHADES OF GREEN. ....YADWIGHA. 86 34
NUMBNESS (1)
THEY BRING ME NUMBNESS IN THEIR BRIGHT NEEDLES, THEY BRING ME
SLEEP. ....TULIPS 160 17
NUMERALS (2)
THE STARS ARE FLASHING LIKE TERRIBLE NUMERALS. ....AN APPEARANCE 189 17
THEY ARE ASSAILING YOUR BRAIN LIKE NUMERALS, ...STINGS/DR 293 4
NUN (1)
I AM A NUN NOW, I HAVE NEVER BEEN SO PURE. ....TULIPS 161 28
NUN-BLACK (1)
AND PUT ON BARK'S NUN-BLACK ....VIRGIN IN A TREE 81 5
NUN-HEARTED (1)
NUN-HEARTED AND BLIND TO THE WORLD. MARBLE LILIES .....BARREN WOMAN 157 4
NUNNERY (1)
UNDERGOING THE FAUCET WATER, ITS VEILS, VEILS IN A NUNNERY,*GETTING. 248 23
NUNS (1)
THEY ARE THE REAL MONKS AND NUNS IN THEIR IDENTICAL GARMENTS.*THREE. 183 227
NUN'S (1)
BURNING LIKE KNOTHOLES FROM A NUN'S SHROUD-CIRCLED .....DIALOGUE O. 280 130
NUN-SOULED (1)
NUN-SOULED, THEY BURN HEAVENWARD AND NEVER MARRY. ....CANDLES 149 27
NURSE (9)
LOVE IS THE UNIFORM OF MY BALD NURSE. POEM.7.S. 137 39
THE EYES OF THE CHILD I NURSE ARE SCARCELY OPEN. ....CANDLES 149 28
EACH NURSE PATCHED HER SOUL TO A WOUND AND DISAPPEARED. ....WAKING. 151 13
BLANK-FACED AND MUM AS A NURSE. ....BARREN WOMAN 157 10
SHE PASSES AND REPASSES, LUMINOUS AS A NURSE. ....THREE WOMEN 176 5
I AM NOT A NURSE, WHITE AND ATTENDANT, ...BERCK-PLAGE 197 42
ONE NURSE BRINGS IN ....AMNESIAC 233 21
TODDLE ON HOME, AND DON'T TRIP ON THE NURSE! -- ....THE TOUR 238 42
SHE RECALLS QUEER STORIES HER NURSE READ ....THE PRINCESS. 334 37
NURSERY (4)
WORDS FOR A NURSERY ....WORDS FOR A NURSERY 73 T
IT IS A COUNTRY ON A NURSERY PLATE. ....WATERCOLOR. 112 15
NOW, ON THE NURSERY WALL, ...PARLIAMENT HILL FIELDS 153 40
THESE ARE THE CLEAR BRIGHT COLORS OF THE NURSERY, ...THREE WOMEN 185 317
NURSES (12)
AGE AND TERROR, LIKE NURSES, ATTEND HER, ...A LIFE 150 33
COT LEGS MELTED IN TERRIBLE ATTITUDES, AND THE NURSES -- ...WAKING. 151 12
THE DARK STILL NURSES ITS SECRET. ....HEAVY WOMEN 158 11
SHE HUMORED MY WEAKNESS LIKE THE BEST OF NURSES, ...IN PLASTER 159 26
I HAVE GIVEN MY NAME AND MY DAY-CLOTHES UP TO THE NURSES ....TULIPS 160 6
THE NURSES PASS AND PASS, THEY ARE NO TROUBLE, ...TULIPS 160 11
THE NURSES GIVE BACK MY CLOTHES, AND AN IDENTITY. ......THREE WOMEN 183 241
NURSES THE HARDSHIP OF HIS STITCHES, AND WALKS AND WALKS. *NARCISSI. 190 6
THE NURSES IN THEIR WING-CAPS ARE NO LONGER SO BEAUTIFUL; ...BERCK. 198 58
NURSES THE SIZE OF WORMS AND A MINUTE DOCTOR ....AMNESIAC 233 7
IT IS A TRAINSTOP, THE NURSES ....GETTING THERE 248 22
PRIM, PINK-BREASTED, FEMININE, SHE NURSES ....FEMALE AUTHOR 301 5
NURSING (1)
NURSING HER RAGE ....THE SNOWMAN ON THE MOOR 58 20
NUT (1)
STILL, STUBBORNLY WE TRY TO CRACK THE NUT ....DOOM OF EXILES 318 13
NYMPHS (2)
AS NYMPHS; COLD VISION ...ON THE DIFFICULTY OF CONJURING UP A DRYAD 66 30
THE LAMP-HEADED NYMPHS ARE NODDING TO SLEEP LIKE STATUES. *POEM.5.F. 135 12

345

O (69)
O MY LOVE, ...LETTER TO A PURIST   36   8
O MY GREAT IDIOT, WHO ....LETTER TO A PURIST   37   9
O CACOPHONY, GODDESS OF JAZZ AND OF QUARRELS, ...ALICANTE LULLABY   43   15
O BENT BOW OF THORNS ....RESOLVE   52   16
DOZENS DROPPED DEAD IN THE HEDGES: O SHE FELT ....SNOWMAN O.   59   35
O LITTLE CITY ON A HILL! ....A WINTER'S TALE   87   31
HAIL AND FAREWELL. HELLO, GOODBYE. O KEEPER *THE GHOST'S LEAVETAKING   91   39
O RIVER, I SEE DRIFTING ....LORELEI   95   33
O THE KING'S TIDY ACRE IS UNDER THE SEA, ...THE BULL OF BENDYLAW   108   19
O OEDIPUS. O CHRIST. YOU USE ME ILL. ....THE RAVAGED FACE   116   14
O OEDIPUS. O CHRIST. YOU USE ME ILL. ....THE RAVAGED FACE   116   14
O RED FRUIT, IVORY, FINE TIMBERS! ....METAPHORS   116   4
O PARDON THE ONE WHO KNOCKS FOR PARDON AT ...ELECTRA ON AZALEA PATH   117   44
PANSY, IT GLOWS. O IT'S ....POLLY'S TREE   128   28
ARCHES ABOVE US. O FATHER, ALL BY YOURSELF ....THE COLOSSUS   129   17
O THE BEAUTY OF USAGE! POEM.1.WHO.   131   19
O I AM TOO BIG TO GO BACKWARD: POEM.3.MAENAD.   133   8
O SHE IS GRACIOUS AND AUSTERE, ...THE BURNT-OUT SPA   138   27
O HIGH-RISER, MY LITTLE LOAF. ....YOU'RE   141   9
O I CANNOT UNDERSTAND WHAT HAPPENED TO THEM! ....STILLBORN   142   6
O I WAS SICK. ....FACE LIFT   156   8
O IT WAS RICHNESS! -- ELEVEN ROOMS AND A YACHT .....THE BABYSITTERS   174   10
O WHAT HAS COME OVER US, MY SISTER! ....THE BABYSITTERS   175   28
O COLOR OF DISTANCE AND FORGETFULNESS! -- ....THREE WOMEN   179 103
I SHALL BE A SKY AND A HILL OF GOOD: O LET ME BE! ......THREE WOMEN   180 140
EMPTY SCHOOLROOMS, EMPTY CHURCHES. O SO MUCH EMPTINESS! *THREE WOMEN   181 179
O HEART, SUCH DISORGANIZATION! ....AN APPEARANCE   189   16
O WHITE SEA-CROCKERY, ...BERCK-PLAGE   197   31
O MOON-GLOW, O SICK ONE, ...THE OTHER   202   20
O MOON-GLOW, O SICK ONE, ...THE OTHER   202   20
O MUD, MUD, HOW FLUID! --   WORDS HEARD, BY ACCIDENT, OVER THE PHONE   202   1
O GOD, HOW SHALL I EVER CLEAN THE PHONE TABLE? ....WORDS HEARD.   202   8
WHITE AS BABIES' BEDDING AND GLITTERING WITH DEAD BREATH. O IVORY! ...
                  A BIRTHDAY PRESENT   206   18
YOU ARE SILVER-SUITED FOR THE OCCASION. O ADDING MACHINE ---
                  A BIRTHDAY PRESENT   207   44
O EUROPE! O TON OF HONEY! ....THE SWARM   217   60
O EUROPE! O TON OF HONEY! ....THE SWARM   217   60
PANZER-MAN, PANZER-MAN, O YOU --- ....DADDY   223   45
O LITTLE GIMLETS -- ....THE JAILER   226   16
O JEWEL! O VALUABLE! ....LESBOS   229   52
O JEWEL! O VALUABLE! ....LESBOS   229   52
O VASE OF ACID, ...LESBOS   229   71
O SISTER, MOTHER, WIFE, ...AMNESIAC   233   25
O MY ....CUT   235   22
O MAIDEN AUNT, YOU HAVE COME TO CALL. ....THE TOUR   237   1
O I SHOULDN'T PUT MY FINGER IN THAT ....THE TOUR   237   13
O I SHOULDN'T DIP MY HANKIE IN, IT HURTS! ....THE TOUR   238   31
O MY GOD, WHAT AM I ....POPPIES IN OCTOBER   240   10
O LOVE, HOW DID YOU GET HERE? ....NICK AND THE CANDLESTICK   241   23
O EMBRYO ....NICK AND THE CANDLESTICK   241   24
O CHATTERERS ....PURDAH   243   36
O MY ENEMY. ....LADY LAZARUS   244   11
O HALF MOON -- ....THALIDOMIDE   252   1
O LOVE, O CELIBATE. ....LETTER IN NOVEMBER   254   31
O LOVE, O CELIBATE. ....LETTER IN NOVEMBER   254   31
O GOD, I AM NOT LIKE YOU ....YEARS   255   6
O GOLDEN CHILD THE WORLD WILL KILL AND EAT ....MARY'S SONG   257   21
O MOTHER OF LEAVES AND SWEETNESS ....WINTER TREES   258   13
O YOU WHO EAT ....BRASILIA   258   18
O SLOW ....SHEEP IN FOG   262   5
O THE DOMESTICITY OF THESE WINDOWS, ...THE MUNICH MANNEQUINS   263   21
O KINDNESS, KINDNESS ....KINDNESS   269   12
O IGNORANT HEART! ....FEVER./DR   294   2
"O MAY G-MEN ALL DIE OF THE CHOLER, ...DIALOGUE EN ROUTE   308   15
"O FOR UBIQUITOUS FREE APHRODISIACS, ...DIALOGUE EN ROUTE   309   27
O RANSACK THE FOUR WINDS AND FIND ANOTHER ....LAMENT   316   16
O MOON OF ILLUSION, ...MOONSONG AT MORNING   316   1
O THROW IT AWAY, THROW IT ALL AWAY ON THE WND: ..SONG FOR A REVOLU.   322   1
O MAKER OF PROUD PLANET'S NEGATIVE, ...SONNET TO SATAN   323   13
O NEVER AGAIN WILL THE EXTRAVAGANT STRAW ....THE PRINCESS.   335   72
OAF (1)
RICH IN STRAYINGS WITH EVERY AMOROUS OAF, ...VANITY FAIR   33   17
OAK (1)
THE LONG COFFIN OF SOAP-COLORED OAK, ...BERCK-PLAGE   199   70
OAR (1)
COLD WORLDS SHAKE FROM THE OAR. ....CROSSING THE WATER   190   7
OASIS (1)
BEASTS OF OASIS, A BETTER TIME. ....THE EYE-MOTE   109   15
OATH (2)
CHURCH CURSE TO KEN THAT CROOKED OATH ....CRYSTAL GAZER   55   35
AND BOLT IT UP BY TAKING OATH NO GUESS   DIALOGUE OVER A OUIJA BOARD   286 345
OAT-SPROUTS (1)
GREEN OAT-SPROUTS JUT; ....ODE FOR TED   29   2

TITLE   PAGE LINE

OBDURATE (1)
   OBDURATE, IN DENSE-GRAINED WOOD, ...SCULPTOR   91   9
OBESE (1)
   THE STRONGEST WILL SEEMED A WILL TOWARD CEREMONY. OBESE, DARK- ...
                                      ... THE GORING   47   4
OBEYING (2)
   OBEYING ORDERS OF INSTINCT TILL SWEPT ....SPIDER   49 32
   AND MILD OBEYING. ....THE SNOWMAN ON THE MOOR   59 51
OBJECT (2)
   OBJECT BESIDE THE MAD, STRAIGHT ROAD ....SLEEP IN THE MOJAVE DESERT 143   6
   IT IS A MARVELOUS OBJECT -- ....THE COURAGE OF SHUTTING-UP 210 24
OBJECTS (4)
   POSSESSION OF THE MOST OBTUSE OBJECTS NOW AND THEN -- *BLACK ROOK I.   57 18
   A WHOLE FAMILY OF PROMINENT OBJECTS ....CANDLES 148   6
   CHINESE YELLOW ON APPALLING OBJECTS --- ....WINTERING 218 16
   YOU SHOULD SEE THE OBJECTS IT MAKES! ....THE TOUR 238 17
OBLIQUE (1)
   US TO THE OBLIQUE ROAD, IN SPITE OF A FITFUL ....ABOVE THE OXBOW   88 21
OBLIQUELY (1)
   OBLIQUELY WITH A DRY-WET ....MUSSEL HUNTER AT ROCK HARBOR   96 46
OBLITERATE (1)
   NOW THE THIN PEOPLE DO NOT OBLITERATE ....THE THIN PEOPLE   65 32
OBLITERATION (1)
   OBLITERATION HOURLY UNLESS OUR EYE .....DIALOGUE OVER A OUIJA BOARD 279 116
OBLIVION (1)
   WORLD-WRECKED, THEY SEEK ONLY OBLIVION. ....THE DEAD 320   8
OBSCENE (4)
   MYSELF, MYSELF! -- OBSCENE, LUGUBRIOUS. ....THE RAVAGED FACE 115   8
   OBSCENE AND BALD AS A PIG, THE WHITE MICE ....ZOO KEEPER'S WIFE 155 21
   OBSCENE BIKINIS HIDE IN THE DUNES, ...BERCK-PLAGE 197 24
   AND THE LANGUAGE OBSCENE ....DADDY 223 30
OBSCURE (3)
   OF SULFUROUS DREAMSCAPES AND OBSCURE LUNAR CONUNDRUMS .....GHOST'S.   90   4
   OBSCURE THE SCALDING SUN TILL NO CLOCKS MOVE. ......SONNET TO SATAN 323 14
   OBSCURE GOD'S EYE WITH CORKSCREW FLECK; ....BLACK PINE TREE. 328   9
OBSCURED (1)
   SHE THOUGHT OF THEN, THICK-SILTED, WITH WEEDS OBSCURED, *LADY AND T.   69 16
OBSCURES (1)
   OF FINEST CONSCIENCE. NIGHTFALL OBSCURES ....THE BEGGARS   48 16
OBSCURITY (1)
   OF, NOT FATHOMED. ALL OBSCURITY ....FULL FATHOM FIVE   92 14
OBSERVED (1)
   OBSERVED HER LOVER'S GESTURES UNBALANCE THE AIR, ...SPINSTER   49   8
OBSERVING (1)
   OBSERVING THE WRECK OF METAL AND RARE STONE. ....SONNET: TO EVA 304   4
OBSESS (1)
   GRAY BIRDS OBSESS MY HEART, ...MARY'S SONG 257 13
OBSESSIVELY (1)
   THE SEA SUCKS OBSESSIVELY, ...CONTUSION 271   5
OBSOLETE (2)
   THE OBSOLETE HOUSE, THE SEA, FLATTENED TO A PICTURE ....A LIFE 150 27
   MEMORIES JOSTLE EACH OTHER FOR FACE-ROOM LIKE OBSOLETE FILM
       STARS. ....INSOMNIAC 163 14
OBSTACLE (1)
   OBSTACLE GLASS-WRAPPED AND PECULIAR, ...NEW YEAR ON DARTMOOR 176   2
OBSTACLES (1)
   THE PLACE I AM GETTING TO, WHY ARE THERE THESE OBSTACLES --- ...
                                   ... GETTING THERE 249 45
OBSTINATE (3)
   "HOWEVER I WRENCH OBSTINATE BARK AND TRUNK ....CONJURING.   66 25
   SO, OVER THIS BATTERED, OBSTINATE SPIT ....POINT SHIRLEY 110 30
   AN OBSTINATE INDEPENDENCY ....THE COURAGE OF SHUTTING-UP 210 34
OBSTRUCTION'S (1)
   SAINT AND KING UNFISTED OBSTRUCTION'S KNUCKLES*A LESSON IN VENGEANCE   80   4
OBTUSE (1)
   POSSESSION OF THE MOST OBTUSE OBJECTS NOW AND THEN -- *BLACK ROOK I.   57 18
OCCASION (1)
   YOU ARE SILVER-SUITED FOR THE OCCASION. O ADDING MACHINE ---
                              ... A BIRTHDAY PRESENT 207 44
OCCASIONAL (1)
   AND NIBBLES AN OCCASIONAL BONBON OF SIN. ....FEMALE AUTHOR 301   4
OCCASIONALLY (1)
   OCCASIONALLY, SOME BACKTALK ....BLACK ROOK IN RAINY WEATHER   57 12
OCCUR (5)
   OF SORTS. MIRACLES OCCUR, ...BLACK ROOK IN RAINY WEATHER   57 36
   SUCH MEETINGS NEVER OCCUR IN MARCHEN .................INCOMMUNICADO 100   8
   WILL THEY OCCUR, ...BRASILIA 258   1
   AND SUSPENDED ALL THAT MIGHT OCCUR? ....PROLOGUE TO SPRING 322 12
   GAUDY MIRACLE OCCUR, TO COME ......MORNING IN THE HOSPITAL SOLARIUM 333 25
OCCURRED (3)
   THE WORLD OCCURRED. ....LITTLE FUGUE 188 39
   IT NEVER OCCURRED THAT THEY HAD BEEN FORGOT, ...LYONNESSE 234 19
   WHICH OCCURRED TO ME IN CHINA." ....THE DREAM 311 30
OCEAN (5)
   OF THE OCEAN. SUCH SAGE HUMOR AND ....FULL FATHOM FIVE   93 29

TITLE   PAGE LINE

OCEAN (CONT.)
```
  DEEPER THAN YOUR OWN OCEAN FLOOR, AND GOT  ..............DIALOGUE O.  283  243
  TEMPO OF STRICT OCEAN  ....................TRIO OF LOVE SONGS  314    9
  WHITE WHALES ARE GONE WITH THE WHITE OCEAN.  ...........TWO LOVERS.  327   12
  THE OCEAN IN ONE GULP: YOU SAY A MARK  ..........LOVE IS A PARALLAX  329   28
OCEAN-FLOOR (1)
  OFF THE OCEAN-FLOOR  ...................................BATTLE-SCENE   84   17
OCHRE (1)
  DUST DULLED HIS BACK TO OCHRE  ............................MEDALLION  124   14
OCHREOUS (2)
  ACROSS THE JUT OF OCHREOUS ROCK  .........................DEPARTURE   51   18
  ON THE PUBLIC GRILLS, AND THE OCHREOUS SALT FLATS,  ........SUICIDE.  115    2
O'CLOCK (3)
  FIVE O'CLOCK IN THE MORNING, THE NO-COLOR VOID  ...........GHOST'S.   90    2
  MIDNIGHT, FOUR O'CLOCK,  ...............................EAVESDROPPER  260   29
  FOUR O'CLOCK, AND THE FEVER SOAKS FROM ME LIKE HONEY.  ....FEVER./DR  294    1
OCTOBER (2)
  THE TRUTH IS, ONE LATE OCTOBER, AT MY BIRTH-CRY  ........ELECTRA ON.  117   34
  POPPIES IN OCTOBER  ...........................POPPIES IN OCTOBER  240    T
OCTOBER'S (1)
  OCTOBER'S THE MONTH FOR STORAGE.  ......................POEM.1.WHO.  131    3
OCTOGENARIAN (1)
  AND THE OCTOGENARIAN LOVES THE LITTLE FLOCKS.  ...AMONG THE NARCISSI  190   10
OCTOPUS (1)
  AND OCTOPUS -- SCRABBLING JUST BEYOND THE VIEW,  ......TALE OF A TUB   25   20
ODALISQUE (1)
  A MERMAID ODALISQUE LOLLS AT HER EASE  .............MIDSUMMER MOBILE  324   10
ODD (5)
  OF WINDOWS WITH ODD VIOLET PANES.  ..................A WINTER'S TALE   87   30
  REMEMBERS A FEW ODD SYLLABLES.  ..................WUTHERING HEIGHTS  168   34
  THE JUT OF THAT ODD, DARK HEAD, PACING  ...................PHEASANT  191    3
  AN ODD DISEASE HAS HIT OUR HOLY COW,  ..............THE DISPOSSESSED  318    4
  "WELL THEN, IF WE AGREE, IT IS NOT ODD  ..........LOVE IS A PARALLAX  329    7
ODDLY (1)
  ODDLY WOODEN IN SPITE OF SCALES  ..............THE DISQUIETING MUSES   75   36
ODDS (1)
  SLEEPDRUNK, THEIR LIMBS AT ODDS?  .....................POEM.3.MAENAD.  133   23
ODE (1)
  ODE FOR TED  ...........................................ODE FOR TED   29    T
ODOR (1)
  SHE MUSES ON THE ODOR, SWEET AND SICK,  ...............FEMALE AUTHOR  301   11
ODORS (3)
  ODORS OF WET EARTH RISE.  .............................THE SLEEPERS  122    9
  THE TREES AND FLOWERS HAVE BEEN STREWING THEIR COOL ODORS.  ...
                                                ... I AM VERTICAL  162   12
  STIFFENS AND ODORS BLEED  .....................................EDGE  273   15
ODYSSEY (1)
  THIS LITTLE ODYSSEY  ..................................BATTLE-SCENE   84    2
OEDIPUS (2)
  I DREAM THAT I AM OEDIPUS.  ...........................THE EYE-MOTE  109   24
  O OEDIPUS. O CHRIST. YOU USE ME ILL.  .............THE RAVAGED FACE  116   14
OF (1744)
OFF (81)
  TO WARD OFF, AT ALL COST, SUSPICIONS  ....................STREET SONG   36   16
  FENDING OFF JAG AND TOOTH,  ...........MISS DRAKE PROCEEDS TO SUPPER   41   22
  IN HER RAMSHACKLE HOUSE OFF SOMERSET TERRACE;  ........ELLA MASON A.   53    2
  PALMED OFF ON IT.  ......................................CONJURING.   66   32
  MAKES OFF WITH THIS ROSE,  .....................WORDS FOR A NURSERY   74   48
  FAR OFF, NOT BLOOD IN THE EARS  ..........................NIGHT SHIFT   76    3
  OFF THE OCEAN-FLOOR  ..................................BATTLE-SCENE   84   17
  OFF KEY AND LOUD  ....................................A WINTER'S TALE   87   28
  OF STATE SCENERY, SELLS SODA, SHOWS OFF VIEWPOINTS. *ABOVE THE OXBOW   88   41
  AND INNARDS BLEACHED AND BLOWN OFF  ....MUSSEL HUNTER AT ROCK HARBOR   97   72
  ME OFF INTO THEIR SPACE OF BEATING,  ..........WHITENESS I REMEMBER  102   22
  SUICIDE OFF EGG ROCK  ...........................SUICIDE OFF EGG ROCK  115    T
  HUSTLED A GULL FLOCK TO FLAP OFF THE SANDSPIT. *SUICIDE OFF EGG ROCK  115   13
  THE WORDS IN HIS BOOK WORMED OFF THE PAGES.  ...SUICIDE OFF EGG ROCK  115   19
  BOARDED THE TRAIN THERE'S NO GETTING OFF.  ................METAPHORS  116    9
  TO HUSTLE THEM OFF THE LAWN.  ....................OLD LADIES' HOME  120   16
  HUSTLES OTHER GULLS OFF. CRABS  ...................MAGNOLIA SHOALS  122   15
  OFF EUROPE'S RELIC HEAP  ...........................PRIVATE GROUND  130    3
  A SUPERHIGHWAY SEALS ME OFF.  ......................PRIVATE GROUND  130   15
  FLEW OFF LIKE THE HAT OF A DOLL  .........................POEM.7.S.  136    4
  IT FLOWS OFF BELOW THE GREEN AND WHITE  ...........THE BURNT-OUT SPA  138   22
  FARTHER OFF THAN AUSTRALIA.  .................................YOU'RE  141   11
  CARRIES ITS CANDLES SLOWLY OFF.  ..........................ON DECK  142    8
  THE HORIZONS ARE TOO FAR OFF TO BE CHUMMY AS UNCLES;  .....TWO CAMP.  145   13
  INCHING OFF IN THE GRAY CHEVROLET, DRINKING THE GREEN  ......WAKING.  151    6
  THEIR SHRILL, GRAVELLY GOSSIP'S FUNNELED OFF.*PARLIAMENT HILL FIELDS  152   18
  PEEL OFF TO SEA AS GULLS DO,  ...............................WHITSUN  154   20
  WHIPPING OFF YOUR SILK SCARF, EXHIBITING THE TIGHT WHITE   FACE LIFT  155    2
  WHILE FAR OFF, THE AXLE OF WINTER  ....................HEAVY WOMEN  158   19
  I MUST SEAL OFF AND LET FILL  .................THE SURGEON AT 2 A.M.  171   25
  IT IS A STATUE THE ORDERLIES ARE WHEELING OFF.*THE SURGEON AT 2 A.M.  171   31
```

348

OFF (CONT.)
    THE SUN FLAMED STRAIGHT DOWN THAT NOON ON THE WATER OFF
      MARBLEHEAD. ....THE BABYSITTERS   174   2
    IN YOUR HOUSE, THE MAIN HOUSE, YOU WERE BETTER OFF. *THE BABYSITTERS 174   19
    WE PICKED UP STICKS OF DRIFTWOOD AND BEAT THEM OFF, *THE BABYSITTERS 175   38
    FLATTEN TO PARCHMENT SCREENS TO KEEP THE WIND OFF. .....THREE WOMEN 179   97
    LIKE A BIG SEA. FAR OFF, FAR OFF, I FEEL THE FIRST WAVE TUG THREE. 179 109
    LIKE A BIG SEA. FAR OFF, FAR OFF, I FEEL THE FIRST WAVE TUG THREE. 179 109
    HOW LONG CAN I BE A WALL, KEEPING THE WIND OFF? ....THREE WOMEN 185 288
    LISTEN: THESE ARE ITS HOOVES: IT HAS GONE OFF, LIKE A HORSE. ...ELM 192   9
    TEARING OFF MY VOICE, AND THE SEA ....THE RABBIT CATCHER 193   3
    OF BEING WHEELED OFF UNDER CROSSES AND A RAIN OF PIETAS. ...
                                                   ... APPREHENSIONS   195   15
    RUN FOLD UPON FOLD FAR OFF, CONCEALING THEIR HOLLOWS, ..BERCK-PLAGE 199   74
    THEY ARE FLYING OFF INTO NOTHING: REMEMBER US. ....BERCK-PLAGE 199   87
    THEY WOULD FLUTTER OFF, BLACK AND GLITTERING, THEY WOULD BE COAL
      ANGELS ....BURNING THE LETTERS   204   33
    MEASURING THE FLOUR, CUTTING OFF THE SURPLUS, ...A BIRTHDAY PRESENT 206   7
    PROBABLE MOTES THAT TICK THE YEARS OFF MY LIVE. A BIRTHDAY PRESENT 207   43
    SEALING OFF HER BROOD CELLS, HER HONEY, AND QUIETLY HUMMING. ..BEE. 212   35
    THE GILT AND PINK DOMES OF RUSSIA MELT AND FLOAT OFF .....THE SWARM 216   15
    IN THE WATERS OFF BEAUTIFUL NAUSET. ....DADDY 222   13
    CHUFFING ME OFF LIKE A JEW. ....DADDY 223   32
    THE BLACK TELEPHONE'S OFF AT THE ROOT, ...DADDY 224   69
    OFF THAT LANDSPIT OF STONY MOUTH-PLUGS, ...MEDUSA 224   1
    OFF, OFF, EELY TENTACLE! ....MEDUSA 226   40
    OFF, OFF, EELY TENTACLE! ....MEDUSA 226   40
    THE FLUORESCENT LIGHT WINCING ON AND OFF LIKE A TERRIBLE MIGRAINE, ...
                                                         ... LESBOS   227   4
    I SHOULD SIT ON A ROCK OFF CORNWALL AND COMB MY HAIR. ....LESBOS   228   29
    THE ACID BATHS, THE SKYFULS OFF OF YOU. ....LESBOS 228   47
    WITH A GODDAM BABY SCREAMING OFF SOMEWHERE. ....STOPPED DEAD 230   12
    I'LL CARRY IT OFF LIKE A RICH PRETTY GIRL, ...STOPPED DEAD   230   23
    I HAVE BEEN FLICKERING, OFF, ON, OFF, ON. ....FEVER. 231   29
    I HAVE BEEN FLICKERING, OFF, ON, OFF, ON. ....FEVER. 231   29
    SPARKING OFF THEIR BROTHER-SISTER REARS ....AMNESIAC 233   18
    OFF AND ON, AS IF I JUST HAD TO RETCH. ....THE TOUR 238   25
    PEEL OFF THE NAPKIN ....LADY LAZARUS 244   10
    AND PICK THE WORMS OFF ME LIKE STICKY PEARLS. ....LADY LAZARUS   245   42
    SO YOUR GESTURES FLAKE OFF --- ....THE NIGHT DANCES 250   18
    STEP OFF! ....GULLIVER 251   20
    STEP OFF SEVEN LEAGUES, LIKE THOSE DISTANCES ....GULLIVER 251   21
    THE HILLS STEP OFF INTO WHITENESS. ....SHEEP IN FOG 262   1
    OFF FROM THE CENTER LIKE HORSES. ....WORDS   270   5
    SIGNING IN. JUST P THIS TIME. AND OFF, DIALOGUE OVER A OUIJA BOARD 277   29
    JOG OFF IN JABBERWOCKY NOW AND LOSE US, *DIALOGUE OVER A OUIJA BOARD 279   91
    A-W-W. HE'S GONE OFF: WHAT ENGLISH ....DIALOGUE OVER A OUIJA BOARD   279   93
    PALMED OFF OUR OWN HUNCHES AS ORACLES. DIALOGUE OVER A OUIJA BOARD 279 105
    SOME DUCKS STEP DOWN OFF THEIR GREEN-REEDED SHELF ....QUEEN MARY'S. 290   11
    WHAT GOOD IS ALL THAT SPACE IF IT CAN'T DRAW YOU OFF? THE RIVAL/DR 291   13
    "BOMB THEM OFF THE MAP." ....BITTER STRAWBERRIES   299   6
    SNAPPING OFF THE STEM .... BITTER STRAWBERRIES 300   38
    I CAST OFF MY IDENTITY ....FAMILY REUNION 301   29
    AND AUCTION OFF EACH RARE WHITE-RABBIT VERB; ....A SORCERER B. 324   6
    LIGHTNING CONJURES GOD'S GLOBE OFF ITS ....INSOLENT STORM. 326   25
OFFENDED (1)
    AS IF MY HABITS OFFENDED HER IN SOME WAY. ....IN PLASTER 159   31
OFFENSE (1)
    CLAM-DIGGERS ROSE UP OUT OF DARK SLIME AT HER OFFENSE.*DREAM WITH C. 44   24
OFFER (2)
    THESE ROCKS OFFER NO PURCHASE TO HERBAGE OR PEOPLE: ......TWO CAMP. 145   18
    A DEVON MEADOW MIGHT OFFER A SIMPLER SORT   QUEEN MARY'S ROSE GARDEN 290   23
OFFERS (1)
    NOW SILENCE AFTER SILENCE OFFERS ITSELF. ....PARLIAMENT HILL FIELDS 152   19
OFFICE (1)
    I WATCHED THE MEN WALK ABOUT ME IN THE OFFICE. THEY WERE
      SO FLAT! ....THREE WOMEN   177   16
OFFICES (1)
    LAYING ITS SCALES ON THE WINDOWS, THE WINDOWS OF EMPTY OFFICES, ...
                                                   ... THREE WOMEN   181 178
OFFISH (1)
    SHE STOPPED FITTING ME SO CLOSELY AND SEEMED OFFISH. ....IN PLASTER 159   29
OFF-STAGE (1)
    OFF-STAGE AND INFAMOUSLY WRAPPED ....SPIDER   49   33
OFF-WHITE (1)
    NOT OF HERALDIC STALLIONS: OFF-WHITE ....WHITENESS I REMEMBER   102   5
O-F-N-E-R-V-E (1)
    TO R NOW. E. IN CORE . . . O-F-N-E-R-V-E. ....DIALOGUE O. 284 277-78
O-F-R (1)
    AN ANGEL. PLUMAGE. O-F-R. HE'LL ....DIALOGUE OVER A OUIJA BOARD 279   90
OFTEN (3)
    TOWARD THAT GREAT JEWEL: SHOWN OFTEN, ...THE GREAT CARBUNCLE   72   11
    AFTERTHOUGHT OFTEN WOULD HAVE THEM ALTER ....POEMS, POTATOES   106   7
    EASY AND OFTEN AS EACH BREATH. ....BLUE MOLES 127   36

```
                                                 TITLE         PAGE  LINE
O-GAPE (1)
    WITH THE O-GAPE OF COMPLETE DESPAIR. I LIVE HERE.  ...........MOON.  173   11
OGLE (1)
    WHO OGLE MEN  ...............................................RHYME   50    6
OGLED (1)
    IT OGLED THROUGH ROCK-FAULT, WIND-FLAW AND FISTED WAVE--*LADY AND T.  70   32
OH (12)
    OH NO, FOR I STRUT IT CLEVER  ........................STREET SONG    36   11
    BUT OH, SAGE GROWNUPS KNOW  .........................BATTLE-SCENE    85   35
    FROM, IF NOT THE POOLS? OH, FROM A LOT   DIALOGUE OVER A OUIJA BOARD  277  46
    OUR SEPARATE VEINS AND THIS GLASS MOUTH. OH YOU'RE  ....DIALOGUE O.  280  147
    AND GET US CLEAR OF THIS. OH, HE'LL GO CLEVER  .........DIALOGUE O.  281  175
    PAYS TO BE POLITIC. OH, I'M NOT ONE TO HANG  ..........DIALOGUE O.   281  196
    THEM ANY MORE THAN YOU DID. OH, LET IT GO.  ...........DIALOGUE O.   283  265
    "OH, STOP WORRYING, NELDA,"  .....................BITTER STRAWBERRIES 300  27
    OH, HEAR THE CLASH OF PEOPLE MEETING --  ............FAMILY REUNION  300  11
    OH NEVER TRY TO KNOCK ON ROTTEN WOOD  .................ADMONITIONS   319   1
    OH NEVER TRY TO KNOCK ON ROTTEN WOOD.  ................ADMONITIONS   319   6
    OH NEVER TRY TO KNOCK ON ROTTEN WOOD.  ................ADMONITIONS   319   12
OIL (3)
    THE SEA PULSES UNDER A SKIN OF OIL.  ................A WINTER SHIP   112   5
    UNREELING IN IT, SPREADING LIKE OIL.............THE RABBIT CATCHER   193   5
    OF PLACES: THE OIL WELL MY UNCLE OWNS, FOR ONE;  ......DIALOGUE O.   277  47
OLD (90)
    TO SATISFY THE QUESTIONS OF A CURIOUS OLD FOOL?"  .......DIALOGUE B.  39   26
    OLD ELLA MASON KEEPS CATS, ELEVEN AT LAST COUNT,  .....ELLA MASON A.  53   1
    ANY MORE THAN THE OLD WOMAN IN HER MUD HUT COULD  ...THE THIN PEOPLE  64  26
    THEY POISE AND GRIEVE AS IN SOME OLD TRAGEDY.  ........THE OTHER TWO  68  21
    OLD HISTORIAN,  .............................WORDS FOR A NURSERY      74  26
    THE OLD GOD DRIBBLES, IN RETURN, HIS WORDS.  ..................OUIJA  77  11
    THE OLD GOD, TOO, WRITES AUREATE POETRY  .....................OUIJA   77  12
    OLD BOCKLIN MISSED, WHO HELD A SHELL  .....ON THE DECLINE OF ORACLES  78  5
    OLD JOSEPH HOLDS AN ALPENSTOCK.  ................A WINTER'S TALE      86  5
    OLD MAN, YOU SURFACE SELDOM.  .....................FULL FATHOM FIVE   92  1
    THE OLD MYTH OF ORIGINS  ..........................FULL FATHOM FIVE   92  10
    SUMMER GROWS OLD, COLD-BLOODED MOTHER.  ...................FROG AUTUMN 99  1
    PROFITED MEMORY, BUT DID AWAY WITH THE OLD SCENERY  .....GREEN ROCK. 105  5
    THE NOSE-END THAT TWITCHES, THE OLD IMPERFECTIONS -- *COMPANIONABLE. 105  1
    OLD GOATHERDS SWEAR HOW ALL NIGHT LONG THEY HEAR  ......GOATSUCKER   111  1
    THE PROSPECT IS DULL AS AN OLD ETCHING.  .............A WINTER SHIP  113  13
    GLUT THESE HUNTERS AFTER AN OLD MEAT,  ...................AFTERMATH   113  7
    IN THAT RUBBLE OF SKULL PLATES AND OLD LEATHER.  .........TWO VIEWS.  114  8
    AND HIS BLOOD BEATING THE OLD TATTOO  .........SUICIDE OFF EGG ROCK  115  8
    I BORROW THE STILTS OF AN OLD TRAGEDY.  .....ELECTRA ON AZALEA PATH  117  33
    THOSE OLD DESPOTS, IF HE SAT  .........THE HERMIT AT OUTERMOST HOUSE 119  9
    OLD LADIES' HOME  .................................OLD LADIES' HOME  120  T
    THE OLD WOMEN CREEP OUT HERE  ....................OLD LADIES' HOME   120  4
    AT OWL-CALL THE OLD GHOSTS FLOCK  ................OLD LADIES' HOME    120  15
    TWIST OLD WORDS INTO THE WEB-THREADS: TONIGHT MAY THE FISH  ...NET-. 121  17
    THE OLD JEWELS SMOLDERING THERE  .....................MEDALLION      124  18
    DISSOLVED NOW, SMOKE OF AN OLD WAR.  ................BLUE MOLES       126  18
    OLD PEWTER ROOTS TWIST  ....................DARK WOOD, DARK WATER    127  15
    IN THEIR OLD ANARCHY TO THE HORIZON-LINE.  ..............THE COLOSSUS 130  21
    MORGUE OF OLD LOGS AND OLD IMAGES, THE LAKE  .........PRIVATE GROUND 131  23
    MORGUE OF OLD LOGS AND OLD IMAGES, THE LAKE  .........PRIVATE GROUND 131  23
    OLD TOOLS, HANDLES AND RUSTY TUSKS.  .................POEM.1.WHO.    131  5
    HE LIVES IN AN OLD WELL,  ............................POEM.2.DARK.   132  19
    THE OLD MAN SHRANK TO A DOLL.  ...................POEM.3.MAENAD.     133  7
    OVERHEAD THE OLD UMBRELLAS OF SUMMER  ................POEM.5.F.      134  3
    OF THE EAR, OLD WORRIER.  ............................POEM.7.S.      136  24
    AN OLD BEAST ENDED IN THIS PLACE:  ..............THE BURNT-OUT SPA   137  1
    OF THE OLD STAR-MAP ON THE CEILING.  ....................ON DECK     142  5
    DOZE BEHIND THE OLD MASKS OF FURY.  ......SLEEP IN THE MOJAVE DESERT 144  19
    AROUND OUR TENT THE OLD SIMPLICITIES SOUGH  .............TWO CAMP.   145  25
    THEY TOE OLD WATER THICK AS FOG.  ....................LEAVING EARLY  146  22
    OR THE SEA, HUSHING THEIR PEELED SENSE LIKE OLD MOTHER MORPHIA.  ...
                                                 WAKING IN WINTER       151  16
    THE OLD DREGS, THE OLD DIFFICULTIES TAKE ME TO WIFE.  PARLIAMENT H.  153  48
    THE OLD DREGS, THE OLD DIFFICULTIES TAKE ME TO WIFE.  PARLIAMENT H.  153  48
    OLD GRIEVANCES JOSTLING EACH OTHER, SO MANY LOOSE TEETH.  ....ZOO K. 154  13
    OLD SOCK-FACE, SAGGED ON A DARNING EGG.  ................FACE LIFT   156  27
    THIS NEW ABSOLUTELY WHITE PERSON AND THE OLD YELLOW ONE, *IN PLASTER 158  2
    OVER AND OVER THE OLD, GRANULAR MOVIE  ....................INSOMNIAC 163  8
    A SENSE OF ABSENCE IN ITS OLD SHINING PLACE.*STARS OVER THE DORDOGNE 166  33
    LEFTOVER SOLDIERS FROM OLD, MESSY WARS.  .................FINISTERRE 169  7
    IN ME SHE HAS DROWNED A YOUNG GIRL, AND IN ME AN OLD WOMAN ..MIRROR  174  17
    AND RENTED AN OLD GREEN BOAT. I ROWED. YOU READ  ....THE BABYSITTERS 175  31
    IS THIS THE ONE SIN THEN, THIS OLD DEAD LOVE OF DEATH?  THREE WOMEN  177  42
    A POWER IS GROWING ON ME, AN OLD TENACITY.  ..........THREE WOMEN    180  141
    OLD WINTER-FACE, OLD BARREN ONE, OLD TIME BOMB.  ......THREE WOMEN   181  158
    OLD WINTER-FACE, OLD BARREN ONE, OLD TIME BOMB.  ......THREE WOMEN   181  158
    OLD WINTER-FACE, OLD BARREN ONE, OLD TIME BOMB.  ......THREE WOMEN   181  158
    I DRAW ON THE OLD MOUTH.  .............................THREE WOMEN   183  246
    I HAD AN OLD WOUND ONCE, BUT IT IS HEALING.  .........THREE WOMEN    185  306
    A GROOVE OF OLD FAULTS, DEEP AND BITTER.  ..................EVENT    195  15
```

                                                         TITLE   PAGE LINE
OLD (CONT.)
  WAVING AND CRUTCHLESS, HALF THEIR OLD SIZE. ....BERCK-PLAGE 196   9
  AN OLD MAN IS VANISHING. ....BERCK-PLAGE 198   51
  OLD BLOOD OF CAKED WALLS THE SUN HEALS, ...BERCK-PLAGE 200   98
  OLD BLOOD OF LIMB STUMPS, BURNT HEARTS. ....BERCK-PLAGE 200   99
  BRIGHT HAIR, SHOE-BLACK, OLD PLASTIC, ...THE OTHER 201   8
  OF THE WHITE FISTS OF OLD ....BURNING THE LETTERS 204   2
  SHE IS OLD, OLD, OLD, SHE MUST LIVE ANOTHER YEAR, AND SHE KNOWS IT. ...
                                    ... THE BEE MEETING 212   44
  SHE IS OLD, OLD, OLD, SHE MUST LIVE ANOTHER YEAR, AND SHE KNOWS IT. ...
                                    ... THE BEE MEETING 212   44
  SHE IS OLD, OLD, OLD, SHE MUST LIVE ANOTHER YEAR, AND SHE KNOWS IT. ...
                                    ... THE BEE MEETING 212   44
  THE OLD QUEEN DOES NOT SHOW HERSELF, IS SHE SO UNGRATEFUL? ....BEE. 212   50
  TERRIFY ME, THEY SEEM SO OLD. ....STINGS 214   13
  IF THERE IS, SHE IS OLD, ...STINGS 214   16
  THE MILD HILLS, THE SAME OLD MAGENTA ....THE SWARM 216   28
  OLD BARNACLED UMBILICUS, ATLANTIC CABLE, ...MEDUSA 225   14
  AN OLD POLE FOR THE LIGHTNING, ...LESBOS 228   46
  (MY SELVES DISSOLVING, OLD WHORE PETTICOATS) --- ....FEVER. 232   53
  OLD HAPPENINGS ....AMNESIAC 233   9
  OLD CAVE OF CALCIUM ....NICK AND THE CANDLESTICK 241   10
  ICICLES, OLD ECHOER. ....NICK AND THE CANDLESTICK 241   11
  OF OLD BANDAGES, BOREDOMS, OLD FACES ....GETTING THERE 249   66
  OF OLD BANDAGES, BOREDOMS, OLD FACES ....GETTING THERE 249   66
  AND THE WALL OF OLD CORPSES. ....LETTER IN NOVEMBER 253   21
  THE OLD STORY. ....BRASILIA 258   15
  I SHALL NEVER GROW OLD. NEW OYSTERS ....GIGOLO 268   26
  OLD GROUND WITH A FEATHER ....BALLOONS 272   18
  IT KEEPS WASHING YOU UP LIKE AN OLD BONE. ....THE RIVAL/DR 291   16
  OLD ENOUGH TO GO. ....BITTER STRAWBERRIES 299   11
  AND PLANETS PLOT WITH OLD ELLIPTIC CUNNING; .....TO EVA DESCENDING. 303   5
  THE OLD MAID IN THE GABLE CRIES ALL DAY: ....NEVER TRY TO TRICK. 320   11
  AND OLD MAIDS ON IMPROMPTU PETTICOATS FLY ....SONG FOR A REVOLU. 323   15
OLDEN (1)
  VILLAGE STORIES GO THAT IN OLDEN DAYS*ELLA MASON AND HER ELEVEN CATS 53   13
OLD-SCHOOL (1)
  BOWING AND TRUCKLING LIKE AN OLD-SCHOOL ORIENTAL. ....WHITSUN 154   16
OLIVE (1)
  AMBLE DARKLY OLIVE ....AQUATIC NOVTURNE 306   23
OLIVE-BEAKED (1)
  LIKE AN OLIVE-BEAKED DOVE ABOVE THE ENGULFING FACT: ...DIALOGUE O. 279 112
OLIVES (1)
  SO CRY FOR THE PAGAN GIRL LEFT PICKING OLIVES ......SONNET: TO TIME 311   9
OMEN (1)
  BLACK BIRDS OF OMEN ....TEMPER OF TIME 336   5
OMENS (1)
  BRED AN AMPLE BATCH OF OMENS; BUT NOW ....TALE OF A TUB   25   18
O-MOUTH (2)
  HER O-MOUTH GRIEVES AT THE WORLD; YOURS IS UNAFFECTED, ...THE RIVAL 166   5
  AND THAT MAD, HARD FACE AT THE END OF IT, THAT O-MOUTH   THREE WOMEN 182 184
ON (440)
ONCE (33)
  SUCH PACT AS IS MADE ONCE ONLY; WHAT MATTER ....WREATH FOR A BRIDAL   44   2
  OF CONCUPISCENCE. ONCE MORE ....SPIDER   49   27
  ONCE WE CHILDREN SNEAKED OVER TO SPY MISS MASON ....ELLA MASON A.   54   19
  THAT CLAIRVOYANT QUARTZ WHICH ONCE, AT HER OWN WISHING, ...
                                    ... CRYSTAL GAZER   55   29
  THE BLANK MOOD SHE WALKED IN. ONCE PAST ....HARDCASTLE CRAGS   63   18
  ONCE, IN ITS EARLIEST SWAY OF LYMPH AND SAP, ...HARDCASTLE CRAGS   63   39
  HEARTHSTONE AT ONCE OF THE OUTRAGEOUS HEAD; ....LADY AND T.   69   6
  SKIES ONCE WEARING A BLUE, DIVINE HAUTEUR ....OUIJA   77   19
  THAT ONCE DESCRIED TROY'S TOWERS FALL, ...ON THE DECLINE OF ORACLES   78   31
  YADWIGHA, THE LITERALISTS ONCE WONDERED HOW YOU ......YADWIGHA.   85   1
  ON GRASS THAT ONCE FED BOSTON COWS. ....A WINTER'S TALE   87   23
  THE FALLEN TIMBERS OF ITS ONCE REMARKABLE ....ABOVE THE OXBOW   88   37
  AND NEVER SAW HOW COOLLY WE MIGHT MOVE. FOR ONCE ...ABOVE THE OXBOW   89   55
  BELOW SHOULDERS NOT ONCE ....FULL FATHOM FIVE   93   37
  STOOD SHUT OUT, FOR ONCE, FOR ALL, ...MUSSEL HUNTER AT ROCK HARBOR   96   52
  GREEN. NOR DO THEY, ONCE IN A HUNDRED ....CHILD'S PARK STONES 101   28
  SQUALL WAVES ONCE DANCED ....POINT SHIRLEY 110   13
  ONCE I WAS ORDINARY: POEM.3.MAENAD. 133   1
  THE SMALL DELL EATS WHAT ATE IT ONCE. ....THE BURNT-OUT SPA 138   18
  I WASN'T FOOLED. I KNEW YOU AT ONCE. ....LOVE LETTER 147   28
  YOU COULD TELL ALMOST AT ONCE SHE HAD A SLAVE MENTALITY. *IN PLASTER 159   21
  WHERE ONCE A DAY THE LIGHT SLOWLY WIDENS AND SLOWLY THINS, ..TULIPS 161   45
  THEN THE TREES MAY TOUCH ME FOR ONCE, AND THE FLOWERS HAVE TIME
        FOR ME. ....I AM VERTICAL 162   20
  I HAD AN OLD WOUND ONCE, BUT IT IS HEALING. ....THREE WOMEN 185 306
  AND THE NOISE IT FLAYS FROM THE AIR, ONCE IT GETS GOING! ..COURAGE. 210   20
  ONCE YOU WERE BEAUTIFUL. ....LESBOS 228   40
  ONCE ONE HAS SEEN GOD, WHAT IS THE REMEDY? ....MYSTIC 268   9
  ONCE ONE HAS BEEN SEIZED UP ....MYSTIC 268   10
  CAN ONCE IN A BLUE MOON CATCH THE SHADOWS OF ....DIALOGUE O. 282 222
  MY WISH ONE WITH YOUR AIM. ONCE, IN A DREAM, ...DIALOGUE O. 284 301

ONCE (CONT.)
    OF DREAMERS IS DISPELLED. ONCE MORE WE CUT ....DIALOGUE O.   286 359
    UNTIL NEAR TWELVE THE STRANGE GIRL ALL AT ONCE ....CINDERELLA 304   11
    ONCE I WOUNDED HIM WITH SO ....TO A JILTED LOVER   310   10
ONCE-KNOWN (1)
    THE ONCE-KNOWN WAY BECOMING ....THE GREAT CARBUNCLE   72   17
ONCOMING (1)
    STALLING CURBSIDE AT HIS ONCOMING, ...WHITENESS I REMEMBER 103   26
ONE (171)
    ONE DAY I'LL HAVE MY DEATH OF HIM; ....PURSUIT   22   2
    LURKS THE LITHE ONE; IN DREAMS' AMBUSH ....PURSUIT   23   30
    SO WERE THEY ONE; SO SOUGHT THEY COUCH, ...BUCOLICS   23   3
    ONE SITS; THE OTHER, WITHOUT. ....TWO SISTERS OF PERSEPHONE   31   2
    WALKS THERE NOT SOME SUCH ONE MAN ....STRUMPET SONG   34   14
    WITH ONE FOOT ....LETTER TO A PURIST   37   10
    PACED BRISK FATHER SHAWN. A COLD DAY, A SODDEN ONE IT WAS ...
                        ... DIALOGUE BETWEEN GHOST AND PRIEST   38   2
    MY ONE KINGDOM. ....MONOLOGUE AT 3 A.M.   40   14
    SHE LIFTS ONE WEBBED FOOT AFTER THE OTHER ....MISS DRAKE P.   41   24
    WALKING EAGER TOWARD WATER, WHEN THERE, ONE BY ONE, ..DREAM WITH C.   44   23
    WALKING EAGER TOWARD WATER, WHEN THERE, ONE BY ONE, ..DREAM WITH C.   44   23
    WHERE, BEDDED LIKE ANGELS, TWO BURN ONE IN FEVER. ....WREATH F.   45   18
    BOWL ONE HOMEWARD TO TASTE ....FIESTA MELONS   46   9
    YET WON'T LAY ONE. ....RHYME   50   3
    DEATH AS STRIKING ROOT ON ONE LAND-TRACT. ....LANDOWNERS   53   14
    ONE GRUFF-TIMBRED PURR ROLLING FROM FURRED THROATS: ..ELLA MASON A.   54   23
    WHEREBY ONE HIRES A DEMON. ....CRYSTAL GAZER   55   36
    FOCUSING ALL TIME'S DAY-SUNS IN ONE ....CRYSTAL GAZER   55   39
    FREE OF THE FICTIVE VEIN. WHEN ONE STARK SKELETON*NOVEMBER GRAVEYARD   56   10
    ONE MIGHT SAY LOVE. AT ANY RATE, I NOW WALK ....BLACK ROOK I.   57   22
    BUT ONE DUSK OUR QUESTIONS COMMENDED US TO A TOUR ....SOW   60   7
    NOR EVEN ONE OF THE COMMON BARNYARD SOWS, ...SOW   61   17
    NOT ONE LEAF WRINKLED IN THE CLEARING AIR. ....THE OTHER TWO   68   6
    SHE BLENCHED, AS ONE WHO DROWNS,   THE LADY AND THE EARTHENWARE HEAD   69   21
    BY ONE JOT ITS BASILISK-LOOK OF LOVE. ....LADY AND T.   70   35
    IN ONE BODY THOSE EARTHBORN COMMONERS ....NATURAL HISTORY   71   8
    I WOKE ONE DAY TO SEE YOU, MOTHER, ...THE DISQUIETING MUSES   75   41
    AS THE GODS BEGAN ONE WORLD, AND MAN ANOTHER, ...SNAKECHARMER   79   1
    TWISTING OF THUMBSCREWS: ONE SOUL TIED IN SINEWS, ...LESSON.   80   8
    ONE WHITE HORSE DROWNED, AND ALL THE UNCONQUERED PINNACLES LESSON.   80   9
    TO THE BEHEADED HEAD OF A SULLEN DOLL, ONE BRAID, ...PERSEUS   83   37
    ONE THRUST, ONE THRUST, ...BATTLE-SCENE   84   29
    ONE THRUST, ONE THRUST, ...BATTLE-SCENE   84   29
    ONE THRUST: AND THEY ARE SPED. ....BATTLE-SCENE   84   30
    I'D ONLY TO SET ONE FOOT IN WILDERNESS--*MEMOIRS OF A SPINACH-PICKER   90   21
    ONE LABYRINTHINE TANGLE ....FULL FATHOM FIVE   93   34
    OF BROWNS AND GREENS. EACH WORE ONE ...MUSSEL HUNTER AT ROCK HARBOR   96   32
    IF THEY COULD SEE, I WAS ONE ....MUSSEL HUNTER AT ROCK HARBOR   97   65
    STILL IN ONE GIGANTIC TAPESTRY -- ....IN MIDAS' COUNTRY   99   14
    WHERE LOVE-MET GROUNDHOGS LOVE ONE IN RETURN, ...INCOMMUNICADO 100   9
    THROWN: FEAR, WISDOM, AT ONE: ALL COLORS ......WHITENESS I REMEMBER 103   32
    SPINNING TO STILL IN HIS ONE WHITENESS. ......WHITENESS I REMEMBER 103   33
    FROM THE LAUREL THICKET. NO ONE APPROACHED. .........RHODODENDRON. 103   19
    ONE COURTING DOCTORS OF ALL SORTS, ...THE DEATH OF MYTH-MAKING 104   4
    ONE, HOUSEWIVES AND SHOPKEEPERS. ....THE DEATH OF MYTH-MAKING 104   5
    THE TRUTH IS, ONE LATE OCTOBER, AT MY BIRTH-CRY ....ELECTRA ON. 117   34
    O PARDON THE ONE WHO KNOCKS FOR PARDON AT ...ELECTRA ON AZALEA PATH 117   44
    ONE BREATH MIGHT SHIVER TO BITS, ...OLD LADIES' HOME 120   3
    WHEN I SPLIT A ROCK ONE TIME ....MEDALLION 124   12
    ONE, BY HIMSELF, SEEMED PITIABLE ENOUGH, ...BLUE MOLES 126   5
    DOWN THERE ONE IS ALONE. ....BLUE MOLES 126   27
    SLIDING THEIR QUOITS ONE ....DARK WOOD, DARK WATER 127   22
    AND, CROWNING IT, ONE ....POLLY'S TREE 129   41
    MOTHER, YOU ARE THE ONE MOUTH POEM.1.WHO. 132   25
    IF I AM A LITTLE ONE, I CAN DO NO HARM. POEM.6.W. 135   13
    OPEN ONE STONE EYE. POEM.7.S. 136   21
    LEANING OVER, I ENCOUNTER ONE ....THE BURNT-OUT SPA 138   24
    ONE CAN REMEMBER MEN AND HOUSES BY. .....SLEEP IN THE MOJAVE DESERT 143   7
    WELL, ONE WEARIES OF THE PUBLIC GARDENS: ONE WANTS A VACATION ...
                        ... TWO CAMPERS IN CLOUD COUNTRY 144   7
    WELL, ONE WEARIES OF THE PUBLIC GARDENS: ONE WANTS A VACATION ...
                        ... TWO CAMPERS IN CLOUD COUNTRY 144   7
    AND NIGHT ARRIVES IN ONE GIGANTIC STEP.*TWO CAMPERS IN CLOUD COUNTRY 145   16
    EVERY ONE OF THEM PERMANENTLY BUSY. ....A LIFE 150   10
    SHE HAS ONE TOO MANY DIMENSIONS TO ENTER. ....A LIFE 150   28
    ONE CHILD DROPS A BARRETTE OF PINK PLASTIC;   PARLIAMENT HILL FIELDS 152   16
    ONE CRY, AND I STUMBLE FROM BED, COW-HEAVY AND FLORAL   MORNING SONG 157   13
    THIS NEW ABSOLUTELY WHITE PERSON AND THE OLD YELLOW ONE, *IN PLASTER 158   2
    AND THE WHITE PERSON IS CERTAINLY THE SUPERIOR ONE. ......IN PLASTER 158   3
    SHE DOESN'T NEED FOOD, SHE IS ONE OF THE REAL SAINTS. ...IN PLASTER 158   4
    NOW I SEE IT MUST BE ONE OR THE OTHER OF US. ....IN PLASTER 160   52
    I'M COLLECTING MY STRENGTH; ONE DAY I SHALL MANAGE WITHOUT HER, ...
                        ... IN PLASTER 160   55
    DOING THINGS WITH THEIR HANDS, ONE JUST THE SAME AS ANOTHER, *TULIPS 160   13
    BUT IT IS SHE WHO IS PAPER NOW, WARMED BY NO ONE. ....WIDOW 164   20

	TITLE	PAGE	LINE

ONE (CONT.)
ONE SOUL PASS THROUGH THE OTHER, FRAIL AS SMOKE ....WIDOW 165 34
WHEN ONE OF THEM FALLS IT LEAVES A SPACE, ..STARS OVER THE DORDOGNE 166 32
EVERYTHING IN ONE DIRECTION. ....WUTHERING HEIGHTS 167 13
THE SKY LEANS ON ME, ME, THE ONE UPRIGHT ....WUTHERING HEIGHTS 168 37
I COME TO ONE BUSH OF BERRIES SO RIPE IT IS A BUSH OF FLIES, ...
                                             ... BLACKBERRYING 168 15
ONE MORE HOOK, AND THE BERRIES AND BUSHES END. .......BLACKBERRYING 169 18
THE PEASANTS ANCHOR THEM WITH CONCHES. ONE IS TOLD: .....FINISTERRE 170 30
OVER ONE BED IN THE WARD, A SMALL BLUE LIGHT   THE SURGEON AT 2 A.M. 171 41
ONE DAY IT WON'T COME BACK. THINGS AREN'T LIKE THAT. ....LAST WORDS 172 16
WHEN THE SPORTY WIFE AND HER DOCTOR HUSBAND WENT ON ONE OF
      THEIR CRUISES ....THE BABYSITTERS 174 16
THE COOK HAD ONE WALL EYE AND COULDN'T SLEEP, SHE WAS SO NERVOUS. ...
                                             ... THE BABYSITTERS 175 25
IS THIS THE ONE SIN THEN, THIS OLD DEAD LOVE OF DEATH?   THREE WOMEN 177 42
BLIND IN MY BED, WITH MY DEAR BLIND SWEET ONE, ...THREE WOMEN 178 76
THE FACE OF THE UNBORN ONE THAT LOVED ITS PERFECTIONS,   THREE WOMEN 178 79
THE FACE OF THE DEAD ONE THAT COULD ONLY BE PERFECT ....THREE WOMEN 178 80
OLD WINTER-FACE, OLD BARREN ONE, OLD TIME BOMB. ....THREE WOMEN 181 158
ONE CRY. IT IS THE HOOK I HANG ON. ....THREE WOMEN 183 236
I AM ONE IN FIVE, SOMETHING LIKE THAT. I AM NOT HOPELESS. ...THREE. 183 244
YOU HAD ONE LEG, AND A PRUSSIAN MIND. ....LITTLE FUGUE 188 40
SUCH BLUE CURRENTS IN THE VEINS OF MY LOVED ONE! .....AN APPEARANCE 189 2
THERE WAS ONLY ONE PLACE TO GET TO. ....THE RABBIT CATCHER 193 11
ONE TOUCH: IT BURNS AND SICKENS. ....EVENT 194 11
ONE MIRRORY EYE --- ....BERCK-PLAGE 198 48
ON A STRIPED MATTRESS IN ONE ROOM ....BERCK-PLAGE 198 50
ONE CURTAIN IS FLICKERING FROM THE OPEN WINDOW, ...BERCK-PLAGE 199 79
O MOON-GLOW, O SICK ONE, ...THE OTHER 202 20
WITH ONE TIN EYE, ...BURNING THE LETTERS 204 25
ONE DAY YOU MAY TOUCH WHAT'S WRONG ....FOR A FATHERLESS SON 205 12
"IS THIS THE ONE I AM TO APPEAR FOR, ...A BIRTHDAY PRESENT 206 5
IS THIS THE ELECT ONE, THE ONE WITH BLACK EYE-PITS AND A SCAR? ...
                                             ... A BIRTHDAY PRESENT 206 6
IS THIS THE ELECT ONE, THE ONE WITH BLACK EYE-PITS AND A SCAR? ...
                                             ... A BIRTHDAY PRESENT 206 6
IS THIS THE ONE FOR THE ANNUNCIATION? ....A BIRTHDAY PRESENT 206 9
LET US SIT DOWN TO IT, ONE ON EITHER SIDE, ADMIRING THE GLEAM, ...
                                             ... A BIRTHDAY PRESENT 207 24
THERE IS THIS ONE THING I WANT TODAY, AND ONLY YOU CAN GIVE
      IT TO ME. ....A BIRTHDAY PRESENT 207 48
THE DEATH WEAPON? NO ONE IS DEAD. ....THE DETECTIVE 208 15
IN WHICH A TORTURE GOES ON ONE CAN ONLY WATCH. ....COURAGE. 210 28
NO, NO, IT IS SCARLET FLOWERS THAT WILL ONE DAY BE EDIBLE. ....BEE. 211 20
AND A BLACK VEIL THAT MOLDS TO MY FACE, THEY ARE MAKING ME ONE
      OF THEM. ....THE BEE MEETING 211 22
SMALL, TAKEN ONE BY ONE, BUT MY GOD, TOGETHER! ....THE ARRIVAL. 213 20
SMALL, TAKEN ONE BY ONE, BUT MY GOD, TOGETHER! ....THE ARRIVAL. 213 20
HOLDING UP ONE PALM -- ....A SECRET 219 4
I HAVE ONE EYE, YOU HAVE TWO. ....A SECRET 219 6
ONE A FOOL, THE OTHER A FOOL. ....A SECRET 219 16
GHASTLY STATUE WITH ONE GRAY TOE ....DADDY 222 9
IF I'VE KILLED ONE MAN, I'VE KILLED TWO --- ....DADDY 224 71
YOU HAVE ONE BABY, I HAVE TWO. ....LESBOS 228 28
FEVER [ONE HUNDRED THREE DEGREES] ....FEVER. 231 T
ONE SCARF WILL CATCH AND ANCHOR IN THE WHEEL. ....FEVER. 231 13
HE DREAMS OF A NEW ONE -- ....AMNESIAC 233 14
ONE NURSE BRINGS IN ....AMNESIAC 233 21
A GREEN DRINK, ONE A BLUE. ....AMNESIAC 233 22
HAD LAZILY CLOSED ONE EYE AND LET THEM SLIP ....LYONNESSE 234 21
REDCOATS, EVERY ONE. ....CUT 235 20
THE MIRROR FLOATS US AT ONE CANDLE POWER. ....BY CANDLELIGHT 236 9
ONE MATCH SCRATCH MAKES YOU REAL. ....BY CANDLELIGHT 236 15
IT SIMPLY EXPLODED ONE NIGHT, ...THE TOUR 238 22
HOW ONE WE GROW, ...ARIEL 239 5
SUICIDAL, AT ONE WITH THE DRIVE ....ARIEL 240 29
YOU ARE THE ONE ....NICK AND THE CANDLESTICK 242 40
ONE FEATHER, LIKE THE PEACOCK. ....PURDAH 243 39
ONE NOTE ....PURDAH 243 42
ONE YEAR IN EVERY TEN ....LADY LAZARUS 244 2
THE SEA SHATTERING ITS GRAY ONE --- ....THE COURIERS 247 12
THE ONE WHO NEVER LOOKS UP, WHOSE EYES ARE LIDDED ......DEATH & CO. 254 3
MORE AND MORE LIKE A DEAD ONE, ...THE FEARFUL 256 8
THAT EMPTIED ONE MAN INTO SPACE ....MARY'S SONG 257 17
THIS ONE ....BRASILIA 259 20
YOUR BODY ONE ....EAVESDROPPER 260 13
ROPED IN AT THE END BY THE ONE ....TOTEM 265 33
YOUR CLEAR EYE IS THE ONE ABSOLUTELY BEAUTIFUL THING. ....CHILD 265 1
THERE IS SAFE, ...GIGOLO 267 7
ONCE ONE HAS SEEN GOD, WHAT IS THE REMEDY? ....MYSTIC 268 7
ONCE ONE HAS BEEN SEIZED UP ....MYSTIC 268 10
ONE HOLLOW THE WHOLE SEA'S PIVOT. ....CONTUSION 271 6
ONE AT EACH LITTLE ....EDGE 272 10
OF PLACES: THE OIL WELL MY UNCLE OWNS, FOR ONE; ....DIALOGUE O. 277 47

ONE (CONT.)
    BEFORE ONE HEAVED HIMSELF THROUGH HEAVEN'S TENT ....DIALOGUE O.   281 171
    PAYS TO BE POLITIC. OH, I'M NOT ONE TO HANG ....DIALOGUE O.   281 196
    ONE OF A GIANT'S EAR? I GUESS THIS GLASS*DIALOGUE OVER A OUIJA BOARD   281 201
    WITH BLACKBIRDS -- TWENTY-FOUR, AND EVERY ONE ....DIALOGUE O.   282 215
    OF ONE WINE-GLASS, YOU'LL PIN IT LIKE A PRIZE ....DIALOGUE O.   283 249
    WHEN HE RECITES ONE OF MY SIMILES ......DIALOGUE OVER A OUIJA BOARD   283 262
    CHILD TO SEE WHICH ONE OF US CAN CALL ..DIALOGUE OVER A OUIJA BOARD   284 284
    MY WISH ONE WITH YOUR AIM. ONCE, IN A DREAM, ...DIALOGUE O.   284 301
    OF ONE I LOVED. I SAW DIVISION BLOOM ...DIALOGUE OVER A OUIJA BOARD   285 322
    US IN: A THIRD UNDID THEM. AND WE GREW ONE ....DIALOGUE O.   285 327
    ONE CAMOUFLAGING ITSELF BEHIND ANOTHER. ....THE RIVAL/DR 291   5
    YOU ARE THE ONE EYE OUT THERE. ....THE RIVAL/DR 291   14
    EACH ONE AN INVETERATE GALLANT ....DIALOGUE EN ROUTE   309   21
    ALTHOUGH THE WICKED WITCH HAS POISONED ONE. ....ADMONITIONS   319   5
    THEY SHOOT THE DICE FOR ONE REMAINING BONE; ....DENOUEMENT   326   8
    THAT ONE MAN'S DEVIL IS ANOTHER'S GOD ....LOVE IS A PARALLAX   329   8
    IMPLACABLY FROM TWELVE TO ONE. ....LOVE IS A PARALLAX   329   18
    THE OCEAN IN ONE GULP: YOU SAY A MARK ....LOVE IS A PARALLAX   329   28
    SOME DAY, MOVING, ONE WILL DROP, ...LOVE IS A PARALLAX   330   63
    "THERE IS MORE THAN ONE GOOD WAY TO DROWN."   EPITAPH IN THREE PARTS 337   11
    "THERE IS MORE THAN ONE GOOD WAY TO DROWN."   EPITAPH IN THREE PARTS 337   22
    THAT HAPPENS TO CONCEAL THE LID OF ONE .....EPITAPH IN THREE PARTS   338   29
    "THERE IS MORE THAN ONE GOOD WAY TO DROWN."   EPITAPH IN THREE PARTS 338   33
ONE-EARED (1)
    THE ONE-EARED CAT ....RESOLVE 52   5
O'NEILL (1)
    FOR SUSAN O'NEILL ROE ....CUT 235   D
ONES (10)
    OF BELLS CALLS HOLY ONES, HER TONGUE ....VANITY FAIR   32   9
    STAND STOCK STILL TO LAUD THESE MATED ONES .....WREATH FOR A BRIDAL   44   5
    DEMURE ONES, LITHE ONES, NEEDING NO LESSON ....ELLA MASON A.   54   40
    DEMURE ONES, LITHE ONES, NEEDING NO LESSON ....ELLA MASON A.   54   40
    THEIR SMALL PRICE PAID, THESE WEDDED ONES ....CRYSTAL GAZER   55   25
    WHERE THE DURABLE ONES KEEP HOUSE. ....THE BURNT-OUT SPA 138   32
    THOSE LITTLE SICK ONES THAT ELUDE MY ARMS. ....THREE WOMEN 178   67
    ON INDIA, AFRICA, AMERICA, THESE MIRACULOUS ONES, ...THREE WOMEN   183 229
    THE TAME FLOWER-NIBBLERS, THE ONES ....MYSTIC   269   20
    DANGERS, BUT DON'T MIND HEARING ABOUT THE ONES ....DIALOGUE O.   278   64
ONE'S (1)
    AND I WANT THE ONE'S LONGEVITY AND THE OTHER'S DARING. ......TULIPS   162   10
ONE-THIRD (1)
    ONE-THIRD ANT-SIZE, A LEGGY SPOT, ...SPIDER   48   12
ONE-TRACKED (1)
    I SEE HIM ONE-TRACKED, STUBBORN, WHITE HORSE,   WHITENESS I REMEMBER 102   12
ONION (2)
    OVER GABLES THE MOON'S CELESTIAL ONION ..SOLILOQUY OF THE SOLIPSIST   37   8
    MY THUMB INSTEAD OF AN ONION. ....CUT   235   2
ONLOOKER (1)
    AND THE ONLOOKER, TREMBLING, ...BERCK-PLAGE   197   33
ONLY (73)
    WHAT THOUGH GREEN LEAVES ONLY WITNESS ....WREATH FOR A BRIDAL   44   1
    SUCH PACT AS IS MADE ONCE ONLY; WHAT MATTER ....WREATH FOR A BRIDAL   44   2
    SUDDENLY AT MY ELBOW. I ONLY KNOW THAT A ROOK ....BLACK ROOK I.   57   27
    IT WAS ONLY IN A MOVIE, IT WAS ONLY ....THE THIN PEOPLE   64   5
    IT WAS ONLY IN A MOVIE, IT WAS ONLY ....THE THIN PEOPLE   64   5
    VISIBLE ONLY TO THE PARAGON HEART, ...ON THE PLETHORA OF DRYADS   67   3
    KNOWABLE ONLY BY LIGHT ....THE GREAT CARBUNCLE   72   15
    SHROUDED TO SUCKLE DARKNESS? ONLY THEY ....VIRGIN.   81   24
    I'D ONLY TO SET ONE FOOT IN WILDERNESS--*MEMOIRS OF A SPINACH-PICKER   90   21
    TRAILING ITS TELLTALE TATTERS ONLY AT THE OUTERMOST ....GHOST'S.   90   21
    IN THESE PALUSTRAL HOMES WE ONLY ....FROG AUTUMN   99   3
    WARMING AT CORE ONLY AS ....CHILD'S PARK STONES   101   25
    CAN ONLY HAUNT. STURDY AS POTATOES, ...POEMS, POTATOES 106   4
    BONES, BONES ONLY, PAWED AND TOSSED, ...POINT SHIRLEY   111   38
    AND SHADOWS ONLY -- CAVE-MOUTH BRISTLE BESET -- ....GOATSUCKER   111   13
    TWO PEOPLE ONLY ARE BLIND TO THE CARRION ARMY: ....TWO VIEWS.   114   13
    BY DAY, ONLY THE TOPSOIL HEAVES. ....BLUE MOLES   126   26
    IF ONLY THE WIND WOULD LEAVE MY LUNGS ALONE. POEM.1.WHO.   131   10
    ONLY THE DEVIL CAN EAT THE DEVIL OUT. POEM.6.W.   135   5
    MOTHER OF BEETLES, ONLY UNCLENCH YOUR HAND: POEM.6.W.   135   19
    ONLY THE MOUTH-HOLE PIPED OUT, ...POEM.7.S.   136   11
    OF POPLARS IN THE MIDDLE DISTANCE, THE ONLY ....SLEEP.   143   5
    ONLY MUCH WHITER AND UNBREAKABLE AND WITH NO COMPLAINTS. *IN PLASTER 158   8
    I DIDN'T WANT ANY FLOWERS, I ONLY WANTED ....TULIPS   161   29
    THE NIGHT SKY IS ONLY A SORT OF CARBON PAPER, ...INSOMNIAC   163   1
    THAT WILL PUT HER HEART OUT LIKE AN ONLY EYE. ....WIDOW   164   5
    WHERE I AM AT HOME, ONLY THE SPARSEST STARS *STARS OVER THE DORDOGNE 165   9
    THE BIG DIPPER IS MY ONLY FAMILIAR. ....STARS OVER THE DORDOGNE   165   17
    BUT THEY ONLY DISSOLVE AND DISSOLVE ....WUTHERING HEIGHTS   167   8
    OF PEOPLE THE AIR ONLY ....WUTHERING HEIGHTS   168   33
    THEIRS IS THE ONLY VOICE, PROTESTING, PROTESTING. ....BLACKBERRYING 168   12
    THE ONLY THING TO COME NOW IS THE SEA. ..............BLACKBERRYING   169   19
    NOW IT IS ONLY GLOOMY, A DUMP OF ROCKS -- ....FINISTERRE 169   6
    I AM NOT CRUEL, ONLY TRUTHFUL -- ....MIRROR   173   4

ONLY (CONT.)
    GLINTING AND CLINKING IN A SAINT'S FALSETTO. ONLY YOU   NEW YEAR ON. 176   3
    WE HAVE ONLY COME TO LOOK. YOU ARE TOO NEW ....NEW YEAR ON DARTMOOR 176   8
    THE FACE OF THE DEAD ONE THAT COULD ONLY BE PERFECT ....THREE WOMEN 178   80
    IN ITS EASY PEACE, COULD ONLY KEEP HOLY SO. ....THREE WOMEN 178   81
    I TALK TO MYSELF, MYSELF ONLY, SET APART -- ....THREE WOMEN 179 106
    IT IS ONLY TIME THAT WEIGHS UPON OUR HANDS. ....THREE WOMEN 187 363
    IT IS ONLY TIME, AND THAT IS NOT MATERIAL. ....THREE WOMEN 187 364
    THERE WAS ONLY ONE PLACE TO GET TO. ....THE RABBIT CATCHER 193   11
    THERE IS ONLY A SOURNESS. ............................APPREHENSIONS 195   10
    ONLY THEY HAVE NOTHING TO SAY TO ANYBODY. ......BURNING THE LETTERS 204   34
    AFTER ALL I AM ALIVE ONLY BY ACCIDENT. ....A BIRTHDAY PRESENT 206   14
    I WILL ONLY TAKE IT AND GO ASIDE QUIETLY. ....A BIRTHDAY PRESENT 207   33
    IF YOU ONLY KNEW HOW THE VEILS WERE KILLING MY DAYS. ....BIRTHDAY. 207   37
    TO YOU THEY ARE ONLY TRANSPARENCIES, CLEAR AIR.   A BIRTHDAY PRESENT 207   38
    THERE IS THIS ONE THING I WANT TODAY, AND ONLY YOU CAN GIVE
        IT TO ME. ....A BIRTHDAY PRESENT 207   48
    ONLY LET DOWN THE VEIL, THE VEIL, THE VEIL. .....A BIRTHDAY PRESENT 208   55
    THERE IS ONLY THE MOON, EMBALMED IN PHOSPHORUS. ....THE DETECTIVE 209   39
    THERE IS ONLY A CROW IN A TREE. MAKE NOTES. ....THE DETECTIVE 209   40
    IN WHICH A TORTURE GOES ON ONE CAN ONLY WATCH. ....COURAGE. 210   28
    THERE IS ONLY A LITTLE GRID, NO EXIT. ...THE ARRIVAL OF THE BEE BOX 213   10
    THE BOX IS ONLY TEMPORARY. ....THE ARRIVAL OF THE BEE BOX 213   36
    THESE WOMEN WHO ONLY SCURRY, ...STINGS 214   29
    ONLY IGNORANT. ....WINTERING 218   21
    THEY CAN ONLY CARRY THEIR DEAD. ....WINTERING 218   37
    ONLY TO BLOW ....BY CANDLELIGHT 236   13
    I AM ONLY THIRTY. ....LADY LAZARUS 244   20
    WHERE THERE IS ONLY HIM AND HIM. ....THE FEARFUL 256   18
    THERE IS NO TERMINUS, ONLY SUITCASES ....TOTEM 264   24
    IS THERE NO GREAT LOVE, ONLY TENDERNESS? ....MYSTIC 269   24
    BY SCOLDINGS, OR BY SUBTLE PRAISE. ONLY I, ...DIALOGUE O. 280 144
    AREN'T VOUCHSAFED TO ANTIQUE VIRGINS ONLY: ....DIALOGUE O. 282 220
    MIGHT RANGE IN IT. I ONLY SHUT THE DOOR *DIALOGUE OVER A OUIJA BOARD 286 344
    THE ONLY FARE ON MY BARE BREAKFAST PLATE.   QUEEN MARY'S ROSE GARDEN 290   6
    "IF ONLY SOMETHING WOULD HAPPEN!" ....DIALOGUE EN ROUTE 308   1
    WORLD-WRECKED, THEY SEEK ONLY OBLIVION. ....THE DEAD 320   8
    ONLY TO VANISH WITH DEVILISH EASE ....CIRCUS IN THREE RINGS 322   17
    TRAIN TRACKS ALWAYS MEET, NOT HERE, BUT ONLY ....LOVE IS A PARALLAX 329   2
    ONLY TO REOPEN AS FLESH CONGEALS: ....LOVE IS A PARALLAX 330   65
    GUIDED ONLY BY THE TUG AND TWITCH .....THE PRINCESS AND THE GOBLINS 334   26
ONSLAUGHT (1)
    THAN AGAINST THIS ONSLAUGHT, THESE CASUAL BLASTS OF ICE CHANNEL C.   27   17
ONTO (4)
    THE SEAWALL AND DROPS ONTO A BIER ....POINT SHIRLEY 110   6
    THEIR SMILES CATCH ONTO MY SKIN, LITTLE SMILING HOOKS. ......TULIPS 160   21
    THAT OPENS AT THE TOP ONTO NOTHING AT ALL. . . . .WIDOW 164   10
    MOLDING ONTO HIS LIPS LIKE LIES, ...STINGS 215   49
OOZE (1)
    SOME SCANDAL MIGHT ANY MINUTE OOZE ....AFTERMATH 113   4
OOZED (1)
    AS RESIN DROPS OOZED FROM PINE BARK. ....THE BURNT-OUT SPA 137   5
OOZING (2)
    OOZING THE GLUE DROPS, ...POEM.2.DARK. 132   5
    OOZING THEIR JAMMY SUBSTANCES, ...THE SURGEON AT 2 A.M. 170   12
OPACITY (1)
    SACRIFICES ITS OPACITY.... ....MARY'S SONG 257   3
OPAQUE (2)
    IN EACH OPAQUE BELLY-SCALE: ....MEDALLION 124   19
    OF PALE BLUE VITREOUS STUFF, OPAQUE ....THE BURNT-OUT SPA 137   4
OPEN (27)
    HE WITH ROCK SPLITS OPEN ....ODE FOR TED   29   10
    BURNS OPEN TO SUN'S BLADE. ....TWO SISTERS OF PERSEPHONE   32   19
    LEANS TO PECK OPEN THOSE LOCKED LIDS, TO EAT ....THE SHRIKE   42   18
    SHAPERS, I OPEN: ....WORDS FOR A NURSERY   73   3
    THE WREATHED DOORS OPEN TO THE CROWD. ....A WINTER'S TALE   87   26
    TRUMPET-THROATS OPEN TO THE BEAKS OF BIRDS.*THE BEEKEEPER'S DAUGHTER 118   8
    OUT IN THE OPEN ....DARK WOOD, DARK WATER 127   11
    I OPEN MY LUNCH ON A HILL OF BLACK CYPRESS. ....THE COLOSSUS 130   19
    OPEN ONE STONE EYE. POEM.7.S. 136   21
    THE EYES OF THE CHILD I NURSE ARE SCARCELY OPEN. ....CANDLES 149   28
    THEN THE SKY AND I ARE IN OPEN CONVERSATION, ...I AM VERTICAL 162   18
    OPEN IN ITS GAPE OF PERPETUAL GRIEVING. ....THREE WOMEN 182 185
    A RED, HARD WOOD, EYES SHUT AND MOUTH WIDE OPEN. ....THREE WOMEN 182 212
    AND FROM THE OPEN MOUTH ISSUE SHARP CRIES ....THREE WOMEN 182 213
    TO BE SO OPEN: IT IS AS IF MY HEART ....THREE WOMEN 185 300
    THE NARCISSI OPEN WHITE FACES IN THE ORCHARD. ....THREE WOMEN 185 315
    STARS OPEN AMONG THE LILIES. ....CROSSING THE WATER 190   10
    ONE CURTAIN IS FLICKERING FROM THE OPEN WINDOW, ...BERCK-PLAGE 199   79
    OPEN YOUR HANDBAG. WHAT IS THAT BAD SMELL? ....THE OTHER 201   13
    THE VILLAGERS OPEN THE CHAMBERS, THEY ARE HUNTING THE QUEEN. ..BEE. 212   42
    WHOSE NEWS IS THE OPEN CHERRY, THE OPEN CLOVER? ....STINGS 214   30
    WHOSE NEWS IS THE OPEN CHERRY, THE OPEN CLOVER? ....STINGS 214   30
    JEALOUSY CAN OPEN THE BLOOD, ...THE SWARM 215   3
    OPEN YOUR HAND. ....THE APPLICANT 221   9

TITLE   PAGE   LINE

OPEN (CONT.)
    SIMPLY OPEN THE DOOR AND STEP OUT OF THE CAR ....STOPPED DEAD   230   24
    THAT THESE LATE MOUTHS SHOULD CRY OPEN ....POPPIES IN OCTOBER   240   11
    OF COOL MOUTHS AND HANDS OPEN AND NATURAL AS ROSES. ......FEVER./DR   294   10
OPENED (4)
    IT HAD OPENED ITS ORANGE IN MY VASE, ...RHODODENDRON.   103   9
    YOUR TWO-HORNED RHINOCEROS OPENED A MOUTH ....ZOO KEEPER'S WIFE   155   34
    DEATH OPENED, LIKE A BLACK TREE, BLACKLY. ....LITTLE FUGUE   188   48
    WHEN I ROSE AND OPENED ALL ....THE DREAM   310   4
OPENING (10)
    WHICH ARE SLOWLY OPENING THEIR FURRED PETALS ....MISS DRAKE P.   41   11
    VOCATION ENOUGH: OPENING, SHUTTING ....MOONRISE   98   8
    THEY GO BEFORE: OPENING THE VEINS, ...BLUE MOLES   126   29
    THEY ARE OPENING LIKE THE MOUTH OF SOME GREAT AFRICAN CAT, ..TULIPS   162   59
    A RED FIST, OPENING AND CLOSING, ...APPREHENSIONS   195   12
    THEIR EYES OPENING ....BERCK-PLAGE   201   121
    YOU WILL NOT EVEN HEAR ME OPENING IT, NO PAPER CRACKLE, ..BIRTHDAY.   207   34
    OPENING, IN SPRING, LIKE AN INDUSTRIOUS VIRGIN ....STINGS   215   35
    OPENING THE FAT SMILES, THE EYES ...................EAVESDROPPER   261   60
    HANDS WILL BE OPENING DOORS AND SETTING ......THE MUNICH MANNEQUINS   263   18
OPEN-MOUTHED (1)
    OPEN-MOUTHED, THE BABY GOD ....I WANT, I WANT   106   1
OPENS (12)
    A FIELD OF BURDOCK OPENS TO THE SOUTH. ......ELECTRA ON AZALEA PATH   117   22
    OPENS AND SHUTS, ACCEPTING THEM AMONG ITS REFLECTIONS. ..PRIVATE G.   131   24
    OPENS TO SWALLOW ME. I'M A STONE, A STICK, ..PARLIAMENT HILL FIELDS   152   15
    YOUR MOUTH OPENS CLEAN AS A CAT'S. THE WINDOW SQUARE ..MORNING SONG   157   15
    AND I AM AWARE OF MY HEART: IT OPENS AND CLOSES ....TULIPS   162   60
    THAT OPENS AT THE TOP ONTO NOTHING AT ALL. . . . .WIDOW   164   10
    A RED LOTUS OPENS IN ITS BOWL OF BLOOD; ....THREE WOMEN   181   167
    HOW HER BODY OPENS AND SHUTS -- ....AN APPEARANCE   189   14
    OPENS ITS MOUTH NOW, DEMANDING. ....EVENT   194   8
    WHILE A GREEN POOL OPENS ITS EYE, ...BERCK-PLAGE   197   27
    THAT OPENS TO THE SEA ....LESBOS   229   35
    THE DOOR NOW OPENS FROM WITHIN. ....FAMILY REUNION   300   10
OPERATIC (1)
    FROM THE COMIC OPERATIC FANTASY THE SEAFARER ....BATTLE-SCENE   84   ST
OPERATION (1)
    IS IT SOME OPERATION THAT IS TAKING PLACE? ....THE BEE MEETING   211   26
OPIATES (1)
    WHERE ARE YOUR OPIATES, YOUR NAUSEOUS CAPSULES? ....POPPIES IN JULY   203   10
OPPOSABLE (1)
    WITH HIS MODISH OPPOSABLE THUMB: ....DIALOGUE EN ROUTE   309   26
OPPOSE (1)
    OPPOSE WHAT WE FACED EARLIER. FEEL MY HAND. ....DIALOGUE O.   285   332
OPPOSITE (4)
    FROM LOGAN AIRPORT OPPOSITE. ....GREEN ROCK, WINTHROP BAY   105   16
    MOST OF THE TIME I MEDITATE ON THE OPPOSITE WALL. ....MIRROR   173   6
    AND FROM OUR OPPOSITE CONTINENTS WE WAVE AND CALL.   THE BABYSITTERS   175   44
    ON THE OPPOSITE LIP ....EVENT   195   18
OPPOSITES (1)
    FLOATS OUR HEADS, TWO VENOMOUS OPPOSITES, ...LESBOS   228   36
OPULENT (1)
    AND THE OPULENT AIR GO STUDDED WITH SEED, ...CONJURING.   66   36
OPUS (1)
    I AM YOUR OPUS, ...LADY LAZARUS   246   67
OR (188)
O-R (1)
    WORD WEARS TWO W'S? O-R. OR WHAT? ......DIALOGUE OVER A OUIJA BOARD   279   94
ORACLE (1)
    PERHAPS YOU CONSIDER YOURSELF AN ORACLE, ...THE COLOSSUS   129   6
ORACLES (2)
    ON THE DECLINE OF ORACLES ....ON THE DECLINE OF ORACLES   78   T
    PALMED OFF OUR OWN HUNCHES AS ORACLES.   DIALOGUE OVER A OUIJA BOARD   279   105
ORACULAR (1)
    THE ORACULAR GHOST WHO DWINDLES ON PIN-LEGS *THE GHOST'S LEAVETAKING   90   9
ORANGE (29)
    AN ORANGE CYCLOPS-EYE, SCORNING TO LOOK ....WINTER LANDSCAPE,   21   7
    RETCHING IN BRIGHT ORANGE BASINS; A REFUGEE ....CHANNEL CROSSING   26   10
    WITH ORANGE CORES. ....FIESTA MELONS   46   14
    ORANGE ROOF-TILES, ORANGE CHIMNEY POTS, ...LANDOWNERS   53   5
    ORANGE ROOF-TILES, ORANGE CHIMNEY POTS, ...LANDOWNERS   53   5
    WITH ORANGE DUCK-FEET WINNOWING HIS HAIR -- .....ALL THE DEAD DEARS   71   24
    IN RINGING ORANGE LIKE A STELLAR CARROT. ...THE GHOST'S LEAVETAKING   91   28
    BY THE ORANGE AND FUCHSIA BONFIRE ....CHILD'S PARK STONES   101   9
    AN ORANGE BUD, POCKETED IT. WHEN *FABLE OF THE RHODODENDRON STEALERS   103   8
    IT HAD OPENED ITS ORANGE IN MY VASE, ...RHODODENDRON.   103   9
    RED AND ORANGE BARGES LIST AND BLISTER ....A WINTER SHIP   112   2
    IN THESE LITTLE BOUDOIRS STREAKED WITH ORANGE AND RED   BEEKEEPER'S.   118   10
    REST ON ORANGE PLUSH NEAR THE NEWEL POST. ...YADDO: THE GRAND MANOR   124   16
    WORKED INTO THE PEELED ORANGE WOOD ....MEDALLION   124   2
    THE ORANGE PUMPKINS HAVE NO EYES. POEM.1.WHO.   131   20
    THE ORANGE POMPONS, THE EGYPTIAN PAPYRUS ....PARLIAMENT HILL FIELDS   153   43
    THE AIR TO ORANGE ....WUTHERING HEIGHTS   167   5
    TO THE HILLS' NORTHERN FACE, AND THE FACE IS ORANGE ROCK   BLACKBER.   169   24

	TITLE	PAGE	LINE

ORANGE (CONT.)
FROM THE POLISHED LOZENGES OF ORANGE LINOLEUM. ....LESBOS 228 24
ORANGE LOLLIES ON SILVER STICKS, ...THE MUNICH MANNEQUINS 263 14
WITH ORANGE SCALLOPS TANGLED IN WET HAIR, ...MIDSUMMER MOBILE 324 11
BLACK PINE TREE IN AN ORANGE LIGHT ....BLACK PINE TREE. 328 T
BLACK AGAINST THE ORANGE LIGHT: BLACK PINE TREE IN AN ORANGE LIGHT 328 3
PLANT AN ORANGE PUMPKIN PATCH ...BLACK PINE TREE IN AN ORANGE LIGHT 328 4
OR WALK INTO THE ORANGE AND MAKE *BLACK PINE TREE IN AN ORANGE LIGHT 328 7
PUT ORANGE MISTRESS HALF IN SUN, *BLACK PINE TREE IN AN ORANGE LIGHT 328 10
OR LYRIC OF LOVE IN THE ORANGE AND BLACK ....BLACK PINE TREE. 328 14
TILL DARK IS CONQUERED BY ORANGE COCK, ...BLACK PINE TREE. 328 15
TO MAKE ORANGE AND BLACK AMBIGUOUS. ....BLACK PINE TREE. 328 18
ORANGEPEEL (1)
LITTER THE MUD LIKE ORANGEPEEL. ....PRIVATE GROUND 130 12
ORANGES (1)
ON THE INFERNO OF AFRICAN ORANGES, THE HEEL-HUNG PIGS. THREE WOMEN 184 283
ORANGE-TILE (1)
AMONG ORANGE-TILE ROOFTOPS ....PROSPECT 28 1
ORBIT (4)
ORBIT THE GO-BY, MADE KNOWN ....MUSSEL HUNTER AT ROCK HARBOR 96 58
FROM HIS ORBIT UNDER THE ELM ROOT. ....BLUE MOLES 126 7
AS THE WORLD SWIVELED ROUND IN ITS ORBIT ....DIALOGUE EN ROUTE 309 38
ORBIT; NEITHER LAW NOR PROPHETS *INSOLENT STORM STRIKES AT THE SKULL 326 26
ORCHARD (3)
STRENGTHEN THAT ORCHARD THEREBY." ....CRYSTAL GAZER 55 24
UNWARMED BY THE SWEET AIR OF THIS PEACH ORCHARD. ....STARS. 166 36
THE NARCISSI OPEN WHITE FACES IN THE ORCHARD. ....THREE WOMEN 185 315
ORCHID (2)
THE GHASTLY ORCHID ....FEVER. 231 20
THAN ANY ORCHID. YOU BROKE HIM THEN. I BROKE ....DIALOGUE O. 285 324
ORCHIDS (1)
THESE ORCHIDS ARE SPLENDID. THEY SPOT AND COIL LIKE SNAKES.*SURGEON. 170 16
ORCHIS (1)
SINUOUS ORCHIS ....BURNING THE LETTERS 205 44
ORDAINED (1)
GOD ORDAINED TO FOLLOW UP YOUR DAYS. IS IT SUCH TROUBLE *DIALOGUE B. 39 25
ORDER (7)
NOW, RICH ORDER OF WALLS IS FALLEN; ROOKS CROAK ......CONVERSATION. 21 5
SCRUPULOUSLY AUSTERE IN ITS ORDER ....SPINSTER 49 14
ITS OWN ORDER ON WHAT IS. *ON THE DIFFICULTY OF CONJURING UP A DRYAD 66 8
MOTHER, WHO MADE TO ORDER STORIES ....THE DISQUIETING MUSES 75 9
BEYOND THE MUNDANE ORDER, ...LORELEI 94 22
ORDER AS I MIGHT PUZZLE ....MUSSEL HUNTER AT ROCK HARBOR 96 55
GREAT SILENCE OF ANOTHER ORDER. ....LITTLE FUGUE 188 37
ORDERED (3)
I ORDERED THIS, THIS CLEAN WOOD BOX .....THE ARRIVAL OF THE BEE BOX 212 1
I HAVE SIMPLY ORDERED A BOX OF MANIACS. THE ARRIVAL OF THE BEE BOX 213 23
YET ORDERED LUNAR MOTION ....TRIO OF LOVE SONGS 314 11
ORDERING (2)
ORDERING ITS BLACK FEATHERS CAN SO SHINE ....BLACK ROOK I. 57 28
FROM MY ALPHABETICAL FINGERS, ORDERING PARTS, ...THREE WOMEN 177 28
ORDERLIES (1)
IT IS A STATUE THE ORDERLIES ARE WHEELING OFF.*THE SURGEON AT 2 A.M. 171 31
ORDERINGS (1)
IN THE SIMPLIFIED ORDERINGS OF SKY- ....ABOVE THE OXBOW 89 47
ORDERLY (1)
THE SEA, TILL THAT DAY ORDERLY, ...THE BULL OF BENDYLAW 108 2
ORDERS (2)
OBEYING ORDERS OF INSTINCT TILL SWEPT ....SPIDER 49 32
A YEW HEDGE OF ORDERS, ...LITTLE FUGUE 188 25
ORDER'S (1)
YOU OVERCAST ALL ORDER'S NOONDAY RANK ....SONNET TO SATAN 323 7
ORDINARY (3)
ONCE I WAS ORDINARY: POEM.3.MAENAD. 133 1
STIFFEN THE ORDINARY ....NOTES TO A NEOPHYTE 306 10
THE ORDINARY MILKMAN BROUGHT THAT DAWN ....THE TRIAL OF MAN 312 1
ORE (1)
AND CONFRONTS A CAIRN OF IRON ORE. ....THE PRINCESS AND THE GOBLINS 334 43
ORESTEIA (1)
A BLUE SKY OUT OF THE ORESTEIA ....THE COLOSSUS 129 16
ORGAN (1)
I HAVE STITCHED LIFE INTO ME LIKE A RARE ORGAN, ...THREE WOMEN 178 72
ORGANS (1)
IN COMPARISON TO THESE ORGANS! ....THE SURGEON AT 2 A.M. 171 19
ORIENTAL (2)
HAD AN ORIENTAL LOOK, ...MUSSEL HUNTER AT ROCK HARBOR 97 79
BOWING AND TRUCKLING LIKE AN OLD-SCHOOL ORIENTAL. ....WHITSUN 154 16
ORIGIN (2)
WHICH SIGNIFY OUR ORIGIN AND END, ...THE GHOST'S LEAVETAKING 91 34
AT ITS CRYPTIC CELESTIAL ORIGIN. ....DIALOGUE EN ROUTE 309 36
ORIGINAL (3)
THAT KNITS TO EACH ORIGINAL ITS COARSE COPY. A DARK TARN*LADY AND T. 69 15
AN ORIGINAL NOTE. IF HE'D SAID, HOWEVER, MERELY: ....DIALOGUE O. 278 81
YOU DRANK YOUR COFFEE LIKE ORIGINAL SIN, ...THE TRIAL OF MAN 312 6

```
                                     TITLE              PAGE  LINE
ORIGINS (1)
   THE OLD MYTH OF ORIGINS  ........................FULL FATHOM FIVE    92   10
ORION (1)
   I MISS ORION AND CASSIOPEIA'S CHAIR. MAYBE THEY ARE  .........STARS.  165   18
ORPHAN (2)
   I CALL YOU ORPHAN, ORPHAN. YOU ARE ILL.  .....................LESBOS  228   38
   I CALL YOU ORPHAN, ORPHAN. YOU ARE ILL.  .....................LESBOS  228   38
ORPHANS (1)
   THEY ARE ORPHANS. I CANNOT SEE THEM. THEY ARE LOST.  .........STARS.  165   14
ORTHODOX (1)
   THE TEMPLES OF THE ORTHODOX.  ...INSOLENT STORM STRIKES AT THE SKULL  326   12
ORTUNIO (1)
   ON THE ROAD NAMED FOR TOMAS ORTUNIO, MICA  ..........THE NET-MENDERS  121    8
OSSIFYING (1)
   OSSIFYING LIKE JUNKED STATUES --  ........................STINGS/DR  293   14
OTHER (36)
   OF OTHER MEN, WHERE STATUES CELEBRATE  .............CHANNEL CROSSING   27   38
   ONE SITS; THE OTHER, WITHOUT.  ............TWO SISTERS OF PERSEPHONE   31    2
   THE OTHER, WRY VIRGIN TO THE LAST,  .......TWO SISTERS OF PERSEPHONE   32   26
   DITHERS WITH THE OTHER WAY OUT  ...................LETTER TO A PURIST   37   13
   SHE LIFTS ONE WEBBED FOOT AFTER THE OTHER  ...........MISS DRAKE P.    41   24
   EACH TO THE OTHER; FIT FIBER FOR STERN WEATHER.  ......CRYSTAL GAZER   55   11
   HOW THEY PROP EACH OTHER UP!  ......................THE THIN PEOPLE    65   40
   THE OTHER TWO  ................................................THE OTHER TWO   68    T
   OTHER THAN NOON, THAN MOON, STARS --  .........THE GREAT CARBUNCLE    72   16
   WHOLLY OTHER, AND OURSELVES  ....................THE GREAT CARBUNCLE   73   18
   YOU DEFY OTHER GODHOOD.  ........................FULL FATHOM FIVE     93   40
   MORE OR OTHER, THEY STILL DISSATISFY.  ..............POEMS, POTATOES  106   10
   HUSTLES OTHER GULLS OFF. CRABS  ....................MAGNOLIA SHOALS   122   15
   AFTER THE OTHER  ...............................DARK WOOD, DARK WATER  127   23
   OTHER ON IT  .................................................POLLY'S TREE  128    6
   MOUTHPIECE OF THE DEAD, OR OF SOME GOD OR OTHER.  ......THE COLOSSUS  129    7
   OLD GRIEVANCES JOSTLING EACH OTHER, SO MANY LOOSE TEETH. ....ZOO K.  154   13
   NOW I SEE IT MUST BE ONE OR THE OTHER OF US. .........IN PLASTER     160   52
   MEMORIES JOSTLE EACH OTHER FOR FACE-ROOM LIKE OBSOLETE FILM
      STARS. ..................................................INSOMNIAC  163   14
   ONE SOUL PASS THROUGH THE OTHER, FRAIL AS SMOKE  .............WIDOW   165   34
   YOUR DISSATISFACTIONS, ON THE OTHER HAND,  .................THE RIVAL  166   13
   WITH NO BOTTOM, OR ANYTHING ON THE OTHER SIDE OF IT,  ....FINISTERRE  169    4
   OTHER ROCKS HIDE THEIR GRUDGES UNDER THE WATER.  .........FINISTERRE  169    9
   OTHER CHILDREN DO NOT TOUCH ME: THEY ARE TERRIBLE. ....THREE WOMEN   178   68
   I HAVE TRIED TO BE BLIND IN LOVE, LIKE OTHER WOMEN,  ....THREE WOMEN  178   75
   AND THEN THERE WERE OTHER FACES. THE FACES OF NATIONS,  THREE WOMEN  179   82
   THE OTHER  .................................................THE OTHER  201    T
   ONE A FOOL, THE OTHER A FOOL.  ...............................A SECRET  219   16
   THIS IS THE FLUID IN WHICH WE MEET EACH OTHER,  ......BY CANDLELIGHT  236   10
   IT IS RUSSIA I HAVE TO GET ACROSS, IT IS SOME WAR OR OTHER.*GETTING.  248    9
   THE OTHER DOES THAT,  .......................................DEATH & CO.  254   21
   A FUNNY PINK WORLD HE MIGHT EAT ON THE OTHER SIDE OF IT,  ..BALLOONS  272   24
   IN EVERY RESPECT LIKE EVERY OTHER NIGHT:*DIALOGUE OVER A OUIJA BOARD  276    2
   TO PICTURE SOME OTHER PARTY SPEAKING THROUGH  ..........DIALOGUE O.  280  146
   IF NOTHING COMES OF IT. ON THE OTHER HAND,  ............DIALOGUE O.  281  198
   OTHER THAN YOUR OWN. AS HE BORES YOU ...DIALOGUE OVER A OUIJA BOARD  283  261
OTHERNESS (1)
   I WOULD BE A TONGUE TO. MOTHER OF OTHERNESS  ...........POEM.1.WHO.  132   26
OTHERS (5)
   MIRRORED THE INTRICATE GESTURES OF TWO OTHERS.  .......THE OTHER TWO   68   14
   LADY, WHO ARE THESE OTHERS IN THE MOON'S VAT --  .....POEM.3.MAENAD.  133   22
   DEAD MEN LEAVE EYES FOR OTHERS.  .........................POEM.7.S.  137   38
   IT IS USUAL IN MY LIFE, AND THE LIVES OF OTHERS. .........THREE WOMEN  183  243
   LIKE ALL THE OTHERS AND SWEAR THAT HE'S A PUMA  .........DIALOGUE O.  281  176
OTHER'S (2)
   AND I WANT THE ONE'S LONGEVITY AND THE OTHER'S DARING.*I AM VERTICAL  162   10
   PAN'S PROWESS OUR OWN CREATION, AND NOT THE OTHER'S  ...DIALOGUE O.  284  285
OTHERWISE (2)
   OTHERWISE INCONSEQUENT  ..................BLACK ROOK IN RAINY WEATHER   57   20
   CLOCKS BELLED TWELVE. MAIN STREET SHOWED OTHERWISE  ...........OWL   101    1
OTHERWORLD (2)
   SPEAK IN SIGN LANGUAGE OF A LOST OTHERWORLD,*THE GHOST'S LEAVETAKING   90   19
   IN THE WARY OTHERWORLD  ...............MUSSEL HUNTER AT ROCK HARBOR   96   24
OTHERWORLDLINESS (1)
   FULL OF WINGS, OTHERWORLDLINESS.  ......................WINTER TREES  258   11
OTTER (1)
   AND THE FOX HEADS, THE OTTER HEADS, THE HEADS OF DEAD RABBITS.  ...
                            ... THE COURAGE OF SHUTTING-UP  210   23
OUGHT (1)
   "WE OUGHT TO HAVE BOMBED THEM LONG AGO."  .......BITTER STRAWBERRIES  299   21
OUIJA (2)
   OUIJA  ..............................................................OUIJA   77    T
   DIALOGUE OVER A OUIJA BOARD  ............DIALOGUE OVER A OUIJA BOARD  276    T
OUR (158)
OURS (7)
   HEAVY AS STATUARY, SHAPES NOT OURS  ...................THE OTHER TWO   68   15
   THEM LIFE LIVELIER THAN OURS,  ...............................SCULPTOR   92   23
   LESS DREAD OF THE WORLD BEYOND THAN OURS. THAT'S BECAUSE*DIALOGUE O.  278   62
```

	TITLE	PAGE	LINE
OURS (CONT.)			
TO YES, HIS SURENESS MUST BE HIS, NOT OURS.	DIALOGUE O.	278	73
WITH FIBS? THE FIBS ARE OURS, NOT HIS. PAN'S FINE	DIALOGUE O.	283	253
WILL BE OUR BEAT, JUST AS THE GIFT IS OURS,	DIALOGUE O.	283	257
IS ITSELF AGAIN, AND OURS. THE DREAM	DIALOGUE OVER A OUIJA BOARD	286	358
OURSELVES (5)			
OURSELVES THE HAUNTERS, AND THEY, FLESH AND BLOOD;	THE OTHER TWO	69	33
WHOLLY OTHER, AND OURSELVES	THE GREAT CARBUNCLE	73	18
IN SPITE OF OURSELVES.	MUSHROOMS	139	29
SURFACED IN OURSELVES: HE'LL SPELL A LINE	DIALOGUE O.	283	255
AND CONTRADICT OURSELVES FOR FUN;	LOVE IS A PARALLAX	329	21
OUSTED (1)			
OUSTED FROM THAT WARM BED	THE SLEEPERS	123	19
OUSTING (1)			
OUSTING THE JEWS.	MARY'S SONG	257	8
OUSTS (1)			
OUSTS MISTIER PEERS AND THRIVES, MURDEROUS,	POEMS, POTATOES	106	2
OUT (175)			
AND OUT OF THE BLUE DRENCH	SOUTHERN SUNRISE	26	16
BRAVE ACTS PLAYED OUT IN PEACE, IN WAR; ALL DANGERS	*CHANNEL CROSSING	27	39
A HUNDRED HERALDS SHE SENT OUT	THE QUEEN'S COMPLAINT	29	16
OUT OF THE SUN'S BRUISING)	SONG FOR A SUMMER'S DAY	31	19
HOUSED IN EARTH, THOSE MILLION BRIDES SHRIEK OUT.	VANITY FAIR	33	33
WHICH OUT FROM BLACK TARN, DITCH AND CUP	STRUMPET SONG	34	17
PARCELED OUT BY WHITE-JACKETED ASSASSINS.	STREET SONG	36	10
TRILLS ITS HURT OUT	STREET SONG	36	22
DITHERS WITH THE OTHER WAY OUT	LETTER TO A PURIST	37	13
THESE DREAMING HOUSES ALL SNUFF OUT;	SOLILOQUY OF THE SOLIPSIST	37	6
DENYING YOU SPRANG OUT OF MY HEAD,	SOLILOQUY OF THE SOLIPSIST	38	31
RATHER THAN CROAK OUT	RECANTATION	42	8
SPIKE AND SUCK OUT	THE SHRIKE	42	22
CLAM-DIGGERS ROSE UP OUT OF DARK SLIME AT HER OFFENSE.	*DREAM WITH C.	44	24
DAWN SNUFFS OUT STAR'S SPENT WICK,	EPITAPH FOR FIRE AND FLOWER	46	29
RODE OUT AGAINST THE FIFTH BULL TO BRACE HIS PIKE AND SLOWLY BEAR ...	... THE GORING	47	6
YOU SCUTTLE OUT ON IMPULSE	SPIDER	48	2
THE MONEY'S RUN OUT.	DEPARTURE	51	4
FRESH LEAVED OUT IN VOWS: "COME TELL	CRYSTAL GAZER	55	8
OUT OF KITCHEN TABLE OR CHAIR	BLACK ROOK IN RAINY WEATHER	57	16
OF HER SMALL HEAT OUT, BUT BEFORE THE WEIGHT	HARDCASTLE CRAGS	63	42
OUT THEIR STALKY LIMBS AGAIN THOUGH PEACE	THE THIN PEOPLE	64	9
OUT OF THE SIDE OF THE GENEROUS MOON WHEN IT	THE THIN PEOPLE	65	28
TO STUN SKY BLACK OUT, DRIVE GIBBERING MAD	CONJURING.	66	12
STEPS OUT RADIANT IN LIMB, EYE, LIP,	CONJURING.	66	27
DAY IN, DAY OUT,	ON THE PLETHORA OF DRYADS	67	30
LIGHTS OUT, THEY DOGGED US, SLEEPLESS AND ENVIOUS:	THE OTHER TWO	68	28
BUT OUT OF THE WATERY ASPIC, LAURELED BY FINS,	LADY AND T.	69	18
CLAIM AND WEIGHT GONE OUT OF THEM.	THE GREAT CARBUNCLE	72	8
I NOSE OUT THE LAY	WORDS FOR A NURSERY	74	23
AND THE SHADOW STRETCHED, THE LIGHTS WENT OUT.	*THE DISQUIETING MUSES	75	32
SAW EVIL BREAK OUT OF THE NORTH.	ON THE DECLINE OF ORACLES	78	32
FROM HIS THIN PIPE. OUT OF THIS GREEN NEST	SNAKECHARMER	79	18
AS OUT OF EDEN'S NAVEL TWIST THE LINES	SNAKECHARMER	79	19
THE COUCH GLARED OUT AT THE PROSAIC EYE.	YADWIGHA.	85	20
STIPPLE OF SHIFTING WAVE-TIPS IS IRONED OUT, LOST	..ABOVE THE OXBOW	89	46
EVEN, A TANG OF METAL. DAY IN, DAY OUT,	*MEMOIRS OF A SPINACH-PICKER	89	16
WHERE THE WAKING HEAD RUBBISHES OUT THE DRAGGLED LOT	GHOST'S.	90	3
OUT IN A CONVERGING STREAM	MUSSEL HUNTER AT ROCK HARBOR	96	40
STOOD SHUT OUT, FOR ONCE, FOR ALL,	MUSSEL HUNTER AT ROCK HARBOR	96	52
I'LL GO OUT AND SIT IN WHITE LIKE THEY DO,	MOONRISE	98	2
THOUGH THE BODY WALK OUT IN CLEAN LINEN.	MOONRISE	98	15
DEATH MAY WHITEN IN SUN OR OUT OF IT.	MOONRISE	98	18
DEATH WHITENS IN THE EGG AND OUT OF IT.	MOONRISE	98	19
OF THE AZALEAS, YET BURNT OUT	CHILD'S PARK STONES	101	17
TRIED SOBRIETY HIRING HIM OUT	WHITENESS I REMEMBER	102	8
HUNG OUT OVER HAZARD, OVER HOOVES	WHITENESS I REMEMBER	103	30
MY PROMISE OF AN IDYLL. THE BLUE'S WORN OUT:	GREEN ROCK.	105	8
TO START THE SPIRIT OUT OF THE MUD	THE COMPANIONABLE ILLS	105	6
CRIED OUT FOR THE MOTHER'S DUG.	I WANT, I WANT	106	3
A PLACE, A TIME GONE OUT OF MIND.	THE EYE-MOTE	109	30
TWENTY YEARS OUT	POINT SHIRLEY	110	19
THE OWL SHALL STOOP FROM HIS TURRET, THE RAT CRY OUT.	..WATERCOLOR.	112	28
FARTHER OUT, THE WAVES WILL BE MOUTHING ICECAKES --	..A WINTER SHIP	113	21
THEY HAD FOUR MEN LAID OUT, BLACK AS BURNT TURKEY,	TWO VIEWS.	114	2
AND SHE COULD SCARCELY MAKE OUT ANYTHING	*TWO VIEWS OF A CADAVER ROOM	114	7
WHERE BEES, STRIPED BLACK AND GOLD, SLEEP OUT THE BLIZZARD ...	... ELECTRA ON AZALEA PATH	116	3
CLAPPED SHUT, FLATTEN THIS MAN OUT.	..THE HERMIT AT OUTERMOST HOUSE	118	3
STILL HE THUMBED OUT SOMETHING ELSE.	THE HERMIT AT OUTERMOST HOUSE	119	14
STONES, STRODE OUT IN YOUR DEAD	MAN IN BLACK	120	16
THE OLD WOMEN CREEP OUT HERE	OLD LADIES' HOME	120	4
FATTEN IN GREEN-POCKED PODS, THE THREE NET-MENDERS SIT OUT,	..NET-.	121	3
THEY'RE OUT OF THE DARK'S RAGBAG, THESE TWO	BLUE MOLES	126	1
OUT IN THE OPEN	DARK WOOD, DARK WATER	127	11
A BLUE SKY OUT OF THE ORESTEIA	THE COLOSSUS	129	16

```
                                              TITLE           PAGE  LINE
OUT (CONT.)
  OF YOUR LEFT EAR, OUT OF THE WIND,  .....................THE COLOSSUS  130   25
  I NEED HARDLY GO OUT AT ALL.  ..........................PRIVATE GROUND  130   14
  MOTHER, KEEP OUT OF MY BARNYARD,  ....................POEM.3.MAENAD.  133   14
  ONLY THE DEVIL CAN EAT THE DEVIL OUT.  ..................POEM.6.W.  135    5
  THE CELLAR'S BELLY. THEY'VE BLOWN MY SPARKLER OUT.  .......POEM.6.W.  135    8
  WHEN I FELL OUT OF THE LIGHT. I ENTERED  .................POEM.7.S.  136    5
  ONLY THE MOUTH-HOLE PIPED OUT,  .........................POEM.7.S.  136   11
  THE NIGHTS SNAPPED OUT OF SIGHT LIKE A LIZARD'S EYELID:*THE HANGING.  141    3
  IF THEY MISSED OUT ON WALKING ABOUT LIKE PEOPLE  .........STILLBORN  142    4
  OUT HERE THERE ARE NO HEARTHSTONES,  ....SLEEP IN THE MOJAVE DESERT  143    1
  THE SUN PUTS ITS CINDER OUT. WHERE WE LIE*SLEEP IN THE MOJAVE DESERT  144   21
  WHEN YOU KICK ME OUT, THAT'S WHAT I'LL REMEMBER,  ....LEAVING EARLY  145    2
  TO POUR MYSELF OUT LIKE A FLUID  .......................LOVE LETTER  147   26
  THEY SHOULD HAVE GONE OUT WITH BALLOON FLIGHTS AND THE
      STEREOPTICON.  ........................................CANDLES  149   12
  CRAWLS UP OUT OF THE SEA.  ...............................A LIFE  150   35
  SPACE! SPACE! THE BED LINEN WAS GIVING OUT ENTIRELY.  .......WAKING.  151   11
  A POLICEMAN POINTS OUT A VACANT CLIFF  .....................WHITSUN  154   18
  OUT OF SHEER BOREDOM. TANGLED IN THE SWEAT-WET SHEETS  ......ZOO K.  155   23
  I CAN'T GET IT OUT OF MY MIND  .....................ZOO KEEPER'S WIFE  155   32
  DARKNESS WIPES ME OUT LIKE CHALK ON A BLACKBOARD...  .....FACE LIFT  156   15
  I SHALL NEVER GET OUT OF THIS! THERE ARE TWO OF ME NOW:  IN PLASTER  158    1
  I GAVE HER A SOUL, I BLOOMED OUT OF HER AS A ROSE  .......IN PLASTER  159   16
  BLOOMS OUT OF A VASE OF NOT VERY VALUABLE PORCELAIN, ...IN PLASTER  159   17
  BUT SHE'LL SOON FIND OUT THAT THAT DOESN'T MATTER A BIT. *IN PLASTER  160   54
  MY HUSBAND AND CHILD SMILING OUT OF THE FAMILY PHOTO;  .......TULIPS  160   20
  SINK OUT OF SIGHT, AND THE WATER WENT OVER MY HEAD.  ........TULIPS  161   27
  ITS BOWL OF RED BLOOMS OUT OF SHEER LOVE OF ME.  ............TULIPS  162   61
  DRAINS LIKE WATER OUT THE HOLE AT THE FAR END.  .........INSOMNIAC  163   25
  THAT WILL PUT HER HEART OUT LIKE AN ONLY EYE.  .................WIDOW  164    5
  OR EVEN LIKE BLACK HOLES CUT OUT OF IT.  .....................WIDOW  164   29
  BUT STAY, SITTING FAR OUT, IN THEIR OWN DUST.  .............STARS.  165   13
  AND YOUR FIRST GIFT IS MAKING STONE OUT OF EVERYTHING.  ...THE RIVAL  166    6
  THAT LOOKS OUT ON NOTHING, NOTHING BUT A GREAT SPACE  BLACKBERRYING  169   25
  THEY BRUISE THE ROCKS OUT OF EXISTENCE, THEN RESURRECT THEM. ...
                                              ... FINISTERRE  169   15
  AT THE END, THEY SOBERLY BONG OUT THEIR NAMES.  ...............MOON.  173   14
  AND THE SEVEN-YEAR-OLD WOULDN'T GO OUT UNLESS HIS JERSEY STRIPES ...
                                              ... THE BABYSITTERS  174    8
  ON THE GAMEROOM PIANO, WHEN THE "BIG PEOPLE" WERE OUT,  .......BABY.  175   23
  SO WE BOBBED OUT TO THE ISLAND. IT WAS DESERTED --  THE BABYSITTERS  175   33
  WHEN I WALK OUT, I AM A GREAT EVENT.  ...................THREE WOMEN  176    8
  I LAST. I LAST IT OUT. I ACCOMPLISH A WORK.  ...........THREE WOMEN  180  129
  ITS END AND RUNS TOWARD IT, ARMS HELD OUT IN LOVE.  ....THREE WOMEN  181  151
  LOOK, THEY ARE SO EXHAUSTED, THEY ARE ALL FLAT OUT  ....THREE WOMEN  183  219
  I AM A WOUND WALKING OUT OF HOSPITAL.  ................THREE WOMEN  184  270
  NIGHTLY IT FLAPS OUT  ........................................ELM  193   29
  IS THERE NO WAY OUT OF THE MIND?  .....................APPREHENSIONS  195    7
  THEY ARE PRESSING OUT OF THE MANY-HOLED EARPIECE, THEY ARE LOOKING
      FOR A LISTENER.  ......WORDS HEARD, BY ACCIDENT, OVER THE PHONE  203    9
  I FAN THEM OUT  ..............................BURNING THE LETTERS  205   38
  IN HER GARDEN THE LIES WERE SHAKING OUT THEIR MOIST SILKS*DETECTIVE.  208    7
  AND IN PUNISHMENT WAS HUNG OUT LIKE BROWN FRUIT  ......THE DETECTIVE  209   29
  INDEFATIGABLE, PURPLE. MUST IT BE CUT OUT?  .................COURAGE.  210   18
  THEY ARE SMILING AND TAKING OUT VEILS TACKED TO ANCIENT HATS.  BEE.  211    5
  HOW CAN I LET THEM OUT?  .................THE ARRIVAL OF THE BEE BOX  213   16
  THE BEES FOUND HIM OUT,  ...................................STINGS  215   48
  IT IS YOU THE KNIVES ARE OUT FOR  ........................THE SWARM  216    6
  IT SPREADS ITSELF OUT, A MILE-LONG BODY OF MEISSEN,  ......WINTERING  218   35
  WILL IT COME OUT  .........................................A SECRET  219   10
  A KNIFE THAT CAN BE TAKEN OUT  ............................A SECRET  220   21
  "BUT IT WANTS TO GET OUT!  ................................A SECRET  220   35
  WATCH OUT!  ...............................................A SECRET  220   39
  YOU STUMBLE OUT,  .........................................A SECRET  220   44
  THE SECRET IS OUT.  .......................................A SECRET  220   48
  COME HERE, SWEETIE, OUT OF THE CLOSET.  ................THE APPLICANT  221   28
  BUT THEY PULLED ME OUT OF THE SACK,  .........................DADDY  224   61
  SEVEN HOURS KNOCKED OUT OF MY RIGHT MIND  .................THE JAILER  226    7
  THE IMPOTENT HUSBAND SLUMPS OUT FOR A COFFEE.  .............LESBOS  228   44
  AND HERE WE ARE, HUNG OUT OVER THE DEAD DROP  .........STOPPED DEAD  230    3
  AND YOU OUT COLD BESIDE ME IN YOUR CHAIR.  ...........STOPPED DEAD  230    5
  SIMPLY OPEN THE DOOR AND STEP OUT OF THE CAR  ........STOPPED DEAD  230   24
  OUT OF A GAP  ..................................................CUT  235   18
  ITS FIRST COMMUNION OUT OF MY LIVE TOES.  ..NICK AND THE CANDLESTICK  241   19
  TO LAST IT OUT AND NOT COME BACK AT ALL.  .............LADY LAZARUS  245   38
  THAT KNOCKS ME OUT.  .................................LADY LAZARUS  246   56
  OUT OF THE ASH  .....................................LADY LAZARUS  247   82
  PUNCHING OUT ABSENCE! LIKE CANNON.  ...................GETTING THERE  248    8
  YOU CRAWLED OUT,  .....................................EAVESDROPPER  261   47
  A FLOWER LEFT OUT.  ...................................SHEEP IN FOG  262   10
  ITS BABY HEAD OUT OF THE WAY, EMBALMED IN SPICE,  ............TOTEM  264   12
  OUT OF WHICH THE SAME SELF UNFOLDS LIKE A SUIT  .............TOTEM  264   25
  DUST BAGS IN AND OUT,  ..................................PARALYTIC  266    7
  ROLLS OUT A CARPET, A HUSH.  .............................GIGOLO  268   24
```

	TITLE	PAGE	LINE

OUT (CONT.)
```
    THE REST OF THE BODY IS ALL WASHED OUT, ..................CONTUSION     271   2
    THEY'LL GO BY, TRUNDLING LIKE MARBLE STATUES WAY OUT  ...DIALOGUE O.     276   6
    AND THEIR EYES LOOKING OUT OF IT: KEEN, *DIALOGUE OVER A OUIJA BOARD     276  10
    OUT OF IT WILL BE TIME AND PLENTY FOR US*DIALOGUE OVER A OUIJA BOARD     278  58
    OUT OF A WHOLENESS. WORMS, NOT WINGS IS WHAT ..........DIALOGUE O.       279  99
    OUT OF OUR VERY COUNTENANCE BY SIMPLY  ..DIALOGUE OVER A OUIJA BOARD     279 114
    MAY TESTIFY TO DRIVE YOUR DOUBTING OUT. *DIALOGUE OVER A OUIJA BOARD     280 153
    GODS AND REAR THEM LIKE BEANSTALKS FROM OUT THESE RIBS   DIALOGUE O.     280 170
    ANGEL'S EYE IN THE AUDIENCE, THEN WHISK THEM OUT  .......DIALOGUE O.     282 233
    BECAUSE PAN BLUNTLY SPELT OUT GOD'S HEAD, NOT  .........DIALOGUE O.      282 237
    OUT OF IT. THERE. THE ROOM RETURNS  ....DIALOGUE OVER A OUIJA BOARD      285 334
    TO OUR MEANING WELL. WHEN LIGHTS GO OUT *DIALOGUE OVER A OUIJA BOARD     286 363
    YOU ARE THE ONE EYE OUT THERE. .....................THE RIVAL/DR         291  14
    FAT ALWAYS, AND OUT OF BREATH, .....................FAMILY REUNION       300  13
    WALTZING UP TO ME OUT OF HER COCKLE-SHELL." ......DIALOGUE EN ROUTE      309  30
    IF YOU PLUCK OUT MY HEART .........................TRIO OF LOVE SONGS    315  49
    THE IDIOT BIRD LEAPS OUT AND DRUNKEN LEANS  ...............DOOMSDAY      316   1
    THE IDIOT BIRD LEAPS OUT AND DRUNKEN LEANS. ..............DOOMSDAY       316   6
    THE IDIOT BIRD LEAPS OUT AND DRUNKEN LEANS. ..............DOOMSDAY       316  12
    THE IDIOT BIRD LEAPS OUT AND DRUNKEN LEANS, ..............DOOMSDAY       316  18
    CHUCK THE BROKEN ACROPOLIS OUT, ......SONG FOR A REVOLUTIONARY LOVE      323   6
    BRIGHT ANGELS BLACK OUT OVER LOGIC'S LAND ..........SONNET TO SATAN      323   3
    ITEM: CHUCK OUT ROYAL RIGMAROLE OF PROPS .............A SORCERER B.      324   5
    MY NATIVE SLEIGHT-OF-HAND IS WEARING OUT: .............A SORCERER B.     324   9
    HE RENTS HIS POISONS OUT BY TELEPHONE; ..................DENOUEMENT      327  14
    UNTIL THE STARS TICK OUT A LULLABY ..............LOVE IS A PARALLAX      329  14
    OF WITHERED WORLDS, AND STAMP OUT PUNY HELLS  ...LOVE IS A PARALLAX      330  68
    LEST, OUT OF SPITE, THE WHOLE .......................... AERIALIST       332  46
    WHERE THE WATER BLOTS OUT ALL FOOTSTEPS." ...EPITAPH IN THREE PARTS      337   6
    THE THIRD CRIES OUT AS ALL THE SHIPS GO DOWN:*EPITAPH IN THREE PARTS     337  10
```
OUTDO (1)
```
    GULLS IN A FEATHERED FUGUE OF WINGS. OUTDO ........MIDSUMMER MOBILE      324   4
```
OUTER (2)
```
    AGAINST WHICH THE BRUNT OF OUTER SEA .....................DEPARTURE       51  14
    THEY ENTER AS ANIMALS FROM THE OUTER ........................YEARS       255   1
```
OUTERMOST (2)
```
    TRAILING ITS TELLTALE TATTERS ONLY AT THE OUTERMOST .......GHOST'S.       90  21
    THE HERMIT AT OUTERMOST HOUSE ........THE HERMIT AT OUTERMOST HOUSE      118   T
```
OUTFACE (1)
```
    IN SAFE PERSPECTIVE, COULD OUTFACE THE GORGON-GRIMACE ......PERSEUS       83  14
```
OUTFLAME (1)
```
    AS IF TO OUTFLAME A PHOENIX, THE MOMENT'S SPUR .....EPITAPH FOR F.        46  24
```
OUTLANDISH (3)
```
    COULD NOT REMAIN OUTLANDISH VICTIMS .................THE THIN PEOPLE      64  24
    OUTLANDISH AS DOUBLE-HUMPED CAMELS OR UNICORNS, .......THE EYE-MOTE      109  13
    OUTLANDISH AS A CIRCUS, THE RAVAGED FACE ..........THE RAVAGED FACE      115   1
```
OUTLAWS (2)
```
    FIT FOR THOSE OUTLAWS TO RIDE HOME ON, ..........ALL THE DEAD DEARS       71  30
    OUTLAWS ALL EXTRAPOLATION ...............................TWO LOVERS.     327  10
```
OUTLINE (1)
```
    GRAYNESS BLUES, REDDENS, AND THE OUTLINE ..........THE THIN PEOPLE        65  34
```
OUTLOOK (1)
```
    TO THE BARBAROUS OUTLOOK, FROM THERE CHOSE ..................SPIDER       49  25
```
OUT-OF-SEASON (1)
```
    WHERE, ABSURD AND OUT-OF-SEASON, A SINGLE SWAN ...WINTER LANDSCAPE,       21   3
```
OUTLAST (1)
```
    OUTLAST THEIR EVILEST STAR, WRYLY ......................THE BEGGARS       48  19
```
OUTMODED (1)
```
    SHACKLED TO THE DOCK, OUTMODED, GAUDY, ...............A WINTER SHIP      112   3
```
OUTRAGE (2)
```
    THERE ARE BLACK DISKS BEHIND IT, THE DISKS OF OUTRAGE, ....COURAGE.      209   3
    AND THE OUTRAGE OF A SKY, THE LINED BRAIN OF IT. .........COURAGE.       209   4
```
OUTRAGEOUS (2)
```
    HEARTHSTONE AT ONCE OF THE OUTRAGEOUS HEAD; ...........LADY AND T.        69   6
    TO TRAP THIS OUTRAGEOUS NIMBLE QUEEN ....................AERIALIST       332  34
```
OUTRIDERS (2)
```
    HERE THEY COME, THE OUTRIDERS, ON THEIR HYSTERICAL ELASTICS. ..BEE.      212  38
    SO MUCH FOR THE CHARIOTEERS, THE OUTRIDERS, THE GRAND ARMY!  SWARM.      217  39
```
OUTSHONE (1)
```
    UNTIL HIS OWN LIT ROOM OUTSHONE .................EVERLASTING MONDAY       62   9
```
OUTSIDE (9)
```
    OUTSIDE, THE LITTLE HEDGE LEAVES ARE .......................RESOLVE       52   8
    THE NOISE CAME FROM OUTSIDE: ...........................NIGHT SHIFT       76   6
    DAWN FLOWERS IN THE GREAT ELM OUTSIDE THE HOUSE. .......THREE WOMEN      185 309
    YOU HAVE STUCK HER KITTENS OUTSIDE YOUR WINDOW .............LESBOS       227  12
    LEGS, ARMS PILED OUTSIDE ............................GETTING THERE       248  26
    WHILE THE DAY OUTSIDE GLIDES BY LIKE TICKER TAPE. ........PARALYTIC      266  10
    OUTSIDE THE CAVE WHOSE CONTOURS MOST REMIND ...........DIALOGUE O.       281 200
    OUTSIDE IN THE STREET I HEAR .....................FAMILY REUNION         300   1
    BUT OUTSIDE THE DIABOLIC STEEL OF THIS .............SONNET: TO TIME      311   5
```
OUTSIZE (1)
```
    OUTSIZE HANDS PREPARE A PATH, .........................BLUE MOLES       126  28
```
OUTSTRIP (1)
```
    TO CONTRADICT ME. YOUR SHOULDERING WORDS OUTSTRIP ......DIALOGUE O.      281 172
```

	TITLE	PAGE	LINE

OUTWIT (1)
    AND OUTWIT THEIR BRAMBLED PLAN; ......MISS DRAKE PROCEEDS TO SUPPER   41   17
OVAL (3)
    OVAL SOUL-ANIMALS, ...BALLOONS   271   3
    AND ECLIPSE THAT OVAL ....MOONSONG AT MORNING   317   7
    REVOLVING IN OVAL LOOPS OF SOLAR SPEED, ...THE DEAD   320   1
OVALS (2)
    OVALS AND BALLS, ...FIESTA MELONS   46   4
    THOSE GREEN-STRIPED OVALS OF SILVER TISSUE? ....LEAVING EARLY   146   15
OVALTINE (1)
    MY BROTHER AND ME COOKIES AND OVALTINE ....THE DISQUIETING MUSES   75   20
OVEN (1)
    AND WHAT HEART'S OVEN ....VANITY FAIR   32   15
OVENS (1)
    THE OVENS GLOWED LIKE HEAVENS, INCANDESCENT. ....MARY'S SONG   257   18
OVER (95)
    EACH DAY DEMANDS WE CREATE OUR WHOLE WORLD OVER, ...TALE OF A TUB   25   36
    CURDED OVER WITH CLOUDS AND CHALK CLIFFS BLANCHED   CHANNEL CROSSING   27   24
    OVER HER SKULL'S MIDDEN; NO KNIFE ....VANITY FAIR   32   12
    VIES WITH BEST QUEEN OVER ....VANITY FAIR   33   31
    OVER GABLES THE MOON'S CELESTIAL ONION ..SOLILOQUY OF THE SOLIPSIST   37   8
    BUMBLINGLY OVER THE NUBS OF THE COBBLES ....ALICANTE LULLABY   43   2
    OVER TIDAL-FLATS WHERE THREE CHILDREN PLAYED ....DREAM WITH C.   44   14
    WIELDS GUARD OF HONOR OVER THESE!" STARRED WITH WORDS ....WREATH F.   45   16
    LACED OVER WITH STRIPES ....FIESTA MELONS   46   6
    ONCE WE CHILDREN SNEAKED OVER TO SPY MISS MASON ......ELLA MASON A.   54   19
    THROUGH BARE WHISTLING HEATHER, OVER STILES OF BLACK STONE, ...
                                 ... THE SNOWMAN ON THE MOOR   58   21
    HELP OVER HILL ....TWO VIEWS OF WITHENS   72   10
    WE CAME OVER THE MOOR-TOP ....THE GREAT CARBUNCLE   72   1
    THE TRIUMPH OF WIT OVER SUFFERING ....PERSEUS   82   ST
    OVER A SURFACE OF GENTLY- ....BATTLE-SCENE   84   4
    LAY OVER THE LEAVES LIKE A CLEAR CELLOPHANE, ...SPINACH-PICKER.   89   4
    I BENT OVER THE PLANTS IN MY LEATHER-KNEED ....SPINACH-PICKER.   89   17
    AND MOO AS THEY JUMP OVER MOONS AS NEW .....THE GHOST'S LEAVETAKING   91   37
    AUGUST GIVES OVER ITS MIDAS TOUCH, ...IN MIDAS' COUNTRY   100   24
    HUNG OUT OVER HAZARD, OVER HOOVES ....WHITENESS I REMEMBER   103   30
    HUNG OUT OVER HAZARD, OVER HOOVES ....WHITENESS I REMEMBER   103   30
    NO LAME EXCUSES CAN GLOSS OVER ....GREEN ROCK, WINTHROP BAY   104   1
    WHILE CHAPEL PINNACLES OVER THE ROOFS ....THE EYE-MOTE   109   5
    SO, OVER THIS BATTERED, OBSTINATE SPIT ....POINT SHIRLEY   110   30
    CLOUDWRACK AND OWL-HOLLOWED WILLOWS SLANTING OVER ....WATERCOLOR.   112   8
    CIGAR OVER HIS RINK OF FISHES. ....A WINTER SHIP   113   12
    FINGERING A LEAFLET OF MUSIC, OVER HIM, *TWO VIEWS OF A CADAVER ROOM   114   17
    OVER A GREAT STONE SPIT ....MAN IN BLACK   119   13
    THE MOON LEANS, A STONE MADONNA, OVER THE LEAD SEA   THE NET-MENDERS   121   15
    ROVE OVER HIS FIELD OF STONE; ....MAGNOLIA SHOALS   122   16
    OVER WINDFALLS TO SIP CIDER-JUICE. ....YADDO: THE GRAND MANOR   123   10
    OVER MY HAND I HUNG HIM. ....MEDALLION   124   8
    THE FOUNTAINS ARE DRY AND THE ROSES OVER. ....THE MANOR GARDEN   125   1
    OVER AND OVER. AND STILL THE HEAVEN ....BLUE MOLES   127   32
    OVER AND OVER. AND STILL THE HEAVEN ....BLUE MOLES   127   32
    BLUE MISTS MOVE OVER ....DARK WOOD, DARK WATER   127   6
    OVER THE WEEDY ACRES OF YOUR BROW ....THE COLOSSUS   129   13
    I BEND OVER THIS DRAINED BASIN WHERE THE SMALL FISH   PRIVATE GROUND   131   20
    IF I DON'T MOVE ABOUT, I'LL KNOCK NOTHING OVER. SO I SAID,*POEM.6.W.   135   14
    LEANING OVER, I ENCOUNTER ONE ....THE BURNT-OUT SPA   138   24
    ARE HUSTLED OVER THE CRESTS AND TROUGHS, ...ON DECK   143   13
    THE POLITE SKIES OVER BOSTON COULDN'T POSSIBLY ACCOMMODATE. ...
                                 ... TWO CAMPERS IN CLOUD COUNTRY   145   11
    ANGELS WEEPING OVER DULL NATURES, ...LOVE LETTER   147   16
    THE SHADOWS STOOP OVER LIKE GUESTS AT A CHRISTENING. ....CANDLES   149   35
    SOUTHWARD, OVER KENTISH TOWN, AN ASHEN SMUDGE*PARLIAMENT HILL FIELDS   152   21
    OVER THEIR IRON STILE. AND STILL DON'T SLEEP. ....ZOO KEEPER'S WIFE   155   40
    OVER EACH WEIGHTY STOMACH A FACE ....HEAVY WOMEN   158   6
    TENDS TO THE PEBBLES IT MUST RUN OVER, SMOOTHING THEM GENTLY.*TULIPS   160   16
    SINK OUT OF SIGHT, AND THE WATER WENT OVER MY HEAD. ....TULIPS   161   27
    OVER AND OVER THE OLD, GRANULAR MOVIE ....INSOMNIAC   163   8
    OVER AND OVER THE OLD, GRANULAR MOVIE ....INSOMNIAC   163   8
    OVER THE SCALDING, RED TOPOGRAPHY ....WIDOW   164   4
    STARS OVER THE DORDOGNE ....STARS OVER THE DORDOGNE   165   T
    OVER ONE BED IN THE WARD, A SMALL BLUE LIGHT   THE SURGEON AT 2 A.M.   171   34
    MY MIRROR IS CLOUDING OVER -- ....LAST WORDS   172   11
    BLUE AND MYSTICAL OVER THE FACE OF THE STARS. ....MOON.   173   23
    FLOATING ON THEIR DELICATE FEET OVER THE COLD PEWS, ...MOON.   173   25
    FACES AND DARKNESS SEPARATE US OVER AND OVER. ....MIRROR   173   9
    FACES AND DARKNESS SEPARATE US OVER AND OVER. ....MIRROR   173   9
    NOW I AM A LAKE. A WOMAN BENDS OVER ME, ...MIRROR   174   10
    O WHAT HAS COME OVER US, MY SISTER! ....THE BABYSITTERS   175   28
    THERE IS THE MOON IN THE HIGH WINDOW. IT IS OVER. ......THREE WOMEN   181   176
    COLD CLOUDS GO OVER. ....LITTLE FUGUE   187   2
    WHITE AS AN EYE ALL OVER! ....LITTLE FUGUE   187   7
    THE EMPTY BENCHES OF MEMORY LOOK OVER STONES, ...BERCK-PLAGE   199   88
    WORDS HEARD, BY ACCIDENT, OVER THE PHONE ....WORDS HEARD.   202   T
    OVER THE SEVEN HILLS, THE RED FURROW, THE BLUE MOUNTAIN? *DETECTIVE.   208   2

OVER (CONT.)
   TATTOOING OVER AND OVER THE SAME BLUE GRIEVANCES, ...COURAGE. 210 11
   TATTOOING OVER AND OVER THE SAME BLUE GRIEVANCES, ...COURAGE. 210 11
   IT IS ALMOST OVER. ....STINGS 214 31
   OVER THE ENGINE THAT KILLED HER --- ....STINGS 215 59
   GRINNING OVER ITS BONE OF IVORY ....THE SWARM 216 24
   WHERE IT POURS BEAN GREEN OVER BLUE ....DADDY 222 12
   YOU STEAMED TO ME OVER THE SEA, ...MEDUSA 225 24
   UP OVER THE HARBOR LIGHTS. ....LESBOS 229 56
   AND HERE WE ARE, HUNG OUT OVER THE DEAD DROP ....STOPPED DEAD 230   3
   SEA OF HIS EYES WASHING OVER IT ....LYONNESSE 234   7
   OVER THE ENGLISH CLIFF AND UNDER SO MUCH HISTORY! ....LYONNESSE 234 22
   OVER YOUR BODY THE CLOUDS GO ....GULLIVER 251   1
   STARS STUCK ALL OVER, BRIGHT STUPID CONFETTI. ....YEARS 255   8
   OVER THE CICATRIX OF POLAND, BURNT-OUT ....MARY'S SONG 257 10
   FLICKING OVER MY PROPERTY, ...EAVESDROPPER 261 55
   OVER WHOSE POOL I TENDERLY ....GIGOLO 268 31
   WITHOUT A PART LEFT OVER, ...MYSTIC 268 11
   OVER THE ROCK ....WORDS 270 10
   WE HAVE COME SO FAR, IT IS OVER. ....EDGE 272   8
   DIALOGUE OVER A OUIJA BOARD ....DIALOGUE OVER A OUIJA BOARD 276   T
   LIKE RIVAL PARENTS OVER A PRECOCIOUS ...DIALOGUE OVER A OUIJA BOARD 284 283
   OVER MY MIND, CASTING A SHADOW. SORROW   DIALOGUE OVER A OUIJA BOARD 285 312
   STUCK TO HER TRIPOD, OVER THE FUMING CREVICE, ...DIALOGUE O. 286 349
   FIND YOU OVER AND OVER, LIPPED LIKE A SKATE AND SMILING,*DIALOGUE O. 291 18
   FIND YOU OVER AND OVER, LIPPED LIKE A SKATE AND SMILING,*DIALOGUE O. 291 18
   OVER SCOURED POLAND, BURNT-OUT ....MARY'S SONG/DR 294   1
   KNEELING OVER THE ROWS, ...BITTER STRAWBERRIES 300 34
   BRIGHT ANGELS BLACK OUT OVER LOGIC'S LAND ....SONNET TO SATAN 323   3
OVERCAST (1)
   YOU OVERCAST ALL ORDER'S NOONDAY RANK ....SONNET TO SATAN 323   7
OVEREXPOSED (1)
   OVEREXPOSED, LIKE AN X-RAY. ....MEDUSA 225 31
OVERHEAD (5)
   OVERHEAD THE OLD UMBRELLAS OF SUMMER POEM.5.F. 134   3
   OVERHEAD, THE CLOUDS SIT TASSELED AND FANCY ....A LIFE 150 15
   OVERHEAD GO THE CHOUGHS IN BLACK, CACOPHONOUS FLOCKS -- ..BLACKBER. 168 10
   WHEN, FROM THE INANE OVERHEAD ....DIALOGUE EN ROUTE 309 40
   ELABORATE SCAFFOLD OF SKY OVERHEAD ....AERIALIST 332 47
OVERLAID (1)
   HERE ON A MOUNT OVERLAID WITH LEAVES. THE PAINT-PEELED ......OXBOW.   88 34
OVERLOOKING (1)
   I AM OVERLOOKING THEM BY LOOKING TOO HARD.   STARS OVER THE DORDOGNE 165 23
OVERNIGHT (4)
   OVERNIGHT, VERY ....MUSHROOMS 139   1
   MY PATENT LEATHER OVERNIGHT CASE LIKE A BLACK PILLBOX, ...TULIPS 160 19
   I HAVE TO LIVE WITH IT OVERNIGHT ....THE ARRIVAL OF THE BEE BOX 213   7
   SPRUNG UP LIKE PLAGUE OF TOADSTOOLS OVERNIGHT: ....TERMINAL 328   4
OVERRIPE (1)
   LAIN SPLAYED TOO LONG IN THE TORTUOUS BOUGHS: OVERRIPE .....VIRGIN.   82 37
OVERSCRUPULOUS (1)
   AS SMACK OF SPITE AND THE OVERSCRUPULOUS .....A LESSON IN VENGEANCE   80   7
OVERTAKE (1)
   ON SOPHIST SEAS TO OVERTAKE THAT MARK ....LOVE IS A PARALLAX 329   5
OVERWHELM (1)
   FACE THE VOICES THAT OVERWHELM, THE TERRIBLE ELEMENT. ..THREE WOMEN 179 112
OW (1)
   OF THE BASE, BARBAROUS PRINCE OW. ....NATURAL HISTORY   71 12
OWL (9)
   THAT OWL VOICE SOLE "YES", WHILE COWS UTTER ....WREATH FOR A BRIDAL   44   3
   OWL ....OWL 101   T
   WHAT MOVED THE PALE, RAPTORIAL OWL ....OWL 102   9
   SHAKEN BY OWL CRY. ....OWL 102 16
   THE OWL SHALL STOOP FROM HIS TURRET, THE RAT CRY OUT. ..WATERCOLOR. 112 28
   I AM A ROOT, A STONE, AN OWL PELLET, ...POEM.1.WHO. 132 23
   I AM ROUND AS AN OWL, ...POEM.2.DARK. 132 10
   BACK TO BACK. I HEAR AN OWL CRY ....EVENT 194   4
   THEY ARE MORE BEAUTIFUL THAN MY BODILESS OWL, ..BURNING THE LETTERS 204 30
OWL-CALL (1)
   AT OWL-CALL THE OLD GHOSTS FLOCK ....OLD LADIES' HOME 120 15
OWL-EYES (1)
   WHOSE OWL-EYES IN THE SCRAGGLY WOOD ....THE DEATH OF MYTH-MAKING 104 11
OWL-HOLLOWED (1)
   CLOUDWRACK AND OWL-HOLLOWED WILLOWS SLANTING OVER ......WATERCOLOR. 112   8
OWL-HOURS (1)
   TO SQUANDER OWL-HOURS ON BRACKEN BEDDING, ...VANITY FAIR   33 19
OWLS (5)
   UNTIL ALL OWLS IN THE TWIGGED FOREST ....FAUN   35   3
   BOUGHS WHERE THOSE OWLS SAT. ....FAUN   35 10
   TRAWLING YOUR DARK AS OWLS DO. ....YOU'RE 141   6
   NIGHTLY NOW I FLOG APES OWLS BEARS SHEEP ....ZOO KEEPER'S WIFE 155 39
   HER BLUE GARMENTS UNLOOSE SMALL BATS AND OWLS. ....MOON. 173 18
OWN (41)
   WITH MY OWN COUNTRY LOVE ....SONG FOR A SUMMER'S DAY   30   2

	TITLE	PAGE	LINE

OWN (CONT.)
INTO MY MOST CHASTE OWN EYES ....STRUMPET SONG 34 18
TO CALL MY OWN EXCEPT THE AIR-MOTES, ...LANDOWNERS 53 2
OWN THEIR CABBAGE ROOTS, A SPACE OF STARS, ...LANDOWNERS 53 10
LIFE, ITS OWN VAPOROUS WAYFARINGS. ....LANDOWNERS 53 15
THAT CLAIRVOYANT QUARTZ WHICH ONCE, AT HER OWN WISHING, ...
... CRYSTAL GAZER 55 29
UNTIL HIS OWN LIT ROOM OUTSHONE ....THE EVERLASTING MONDAY 62 9
WE OWN NO WILDERNESSES RICH AND DEEP ENOUGH ....THE THIN PEOPLE 65 41
ITS OWN ORDER ON WHAT IS. *ON THE DIFFICULTY OF CONJURING UP A DRYAD 66 8
OUR OWN GRIST DOWN TO ITS BONY FACE. ....ALL THE DEAD DEARS 70 12
SCOURGING TO SORES HIS OWN RED SLUICES ....A LESSON IN VENGEANCE 80 13
ROUND OF ITS OWN ACCORD. ....THE TIMES ARE TIDY 107 5
MY OWN BLUE RAZOR RUSTING IN MY THROAT. .....ELECTRA ON AZALEA PATH 117 43
THE WEED-SLICKED SHELF FOR HIS OWN, ...MAGNOLIA SHOALS 122 14
THE SPIDER ON ITS OWN STRING ....THE MANOR GARDEN 125 16
I SEE BY MY OWN LIGHT. POEM.2.DARK. 132 11
A CLEAN SLATE, WITH YOU OWN FACE ON. ....YOU'RE 141 18
AND THE FINGERS, TAKEN IN BY THEIR OWN HALOES, ...CANDLES 148 3
THAN THE CLOUD THAT DISTILLS A MIRROR TO REFLECT ITS OWN SLOW ...
... MORNING SONG 157 8
LIVING WITH HER WAS LIKE LIVING WITH MY OWN COFFIN: .....IN PLASTER 160 48
BUT STAY, SITTING FAR OUT, IN THEIR OWN DUST. ....STARS. 165 13
AND WHERE I LIE NOW, BACK TO MY OWN DARK STAR, ...STARS. 166 34
THE MOON IS NO DOOR. IT IS A FACE IN ITS OWN RIGHT, ...MOON. 173 8
IT IS SOMETHING TO OWN A PHEASANT, ...PHEASANT 191 5
THE WIND GAGGING MY MOUTH WITH MY OWN BLOWN HAIR,*THE RABBIT CATCHER 193 2
AND FIND NO FACE BUT MY OWN, AND YOU THINK THAT'S FUNNY.*FATHERLESS. 205 9
IT IS THEY WHO OWN ME. ....WINTERING 218 19
MAKE THEIR OWN ELEMENT. THEY WILL NOT RISE, ...FEVER. 231 15
DRUNK ON ITS OWN SCENTS, ...PARALYTIC 267 39
DEAD, YOU'D SWEAR HIM A VICTIM OF OUR OWN VAIN ....DIALOGUE O. 278 82
PALMED OFF OUR OWN HUNCHES AS ORACLES. DIALOGUE OVER A OUIJA BOARD 279 105
PEBBLES WE PRESERVE IN OUR OWN CUPBOARDS*DIALOGUE OVER A OUIJA BOARD 280 135
DEEPER THAN YOUR OWN OCEAN FLOOR, AND GOT ....DIALOGUE O. 283 243
OTHER THAN YOUR OWN. AS HE BORES YOU ...DIALOGUE OVER A OUIJA BOARD 283 261
FEED YOUR OWN WISHFUL THINKING. TRY ASKING HIM ....DIALOGUE O. 283 268
PAN'S PROWESS OUR OWN CREATION, AND NOT THE OTHER'S ...DIALOGUE O. 284 285
OR HER OWN WORD, AMBUSHED IN AN EQUIVOCAL ....DIALOGUE O. 286 351
HANGS ITSELF ON ITS OWN ROPE. ...........METAMORPHOSES OF THE MOON 308 42
AND LEFT OUR BANKRUPT CIRCUS ON ITS OWN; ....DENOUEMENT 326 2
HIS OWN PALE BRIDE UPON A FLAMING TRAY: ....TERMINAL 328 12
IN OUR OWN TEARS: TODAY WE START ....LOVE IS A PARALLAX 330 75
OWNED (1)
THE BOLD GULLS DOVE AS IF THEY OWNED IT ALL. ....THE BABYSITTERS 175 37
OWNER (3)
AND THE OWNER PAST THIRTY, NO BEAUTY AT ALL. ....CANDLES 148 9
BOOMERANG LIKE ANCHORED ELASTICS, HURTING THE OWNER. ...BERCK-PLAGE 196 11
THEY CAN DIE, I NEED FEED THEM NOTHING, I AM THE OWNER.*THE ARRIVAL. 213 25
OWNERS' (1)
TO THEIR OWNERS' WRISTS, THE LIGHT DREAMS FLOAT ....ON DECK 143 35
OWNS (1)
OF PLACES: THE OIL WELL MY UNCLE OWNS, FOR ONE: ....DIALOGUE O. 277 47
OX (1)
ECLIPSING THE SPITTED OX I SEE ....ON THE DECLINE OF ORACLES 78 17
OXBOW (2)
ABOVE THE OXBOW ....ABOVE THE OXBOW 87 T
A RUDDY SKYLIGHT PAINTS THE GRAY OXBOW ....ABOVE THE OXBOW 88 42
OXEN (1)
TWO WAXEN OXEN FLANK THE CHILD. ....A WINTER'S TALE 86 6
OXYGEN (1)
THE VIVID TULIPS EAT MY OXYGEN. ....TULIPS 161 49
OYSTER (2)
THOUGH THE MIND LIKE AN OYSTER LABORS ON AND ON, ...TWO LOVERS. 327 19
LIKE AN ENORMOUS OYSTER, DOWN ....LOVE IS A PARALLAX 329 27
OYSTERS (2)
I SHALL NEVER GROW OLD. NEW OYSTERS ....GIGOLO 268 26
GATHER IDLE OYSTERS FROM GREEN SHOALS, ...GO GET THE GOODLY SQUAB 313 19
P (3)
SIGNING IN. JUST P THIS TIME. AND OFF, DIALOGUE OVER A OUIJA BOARD 277 29
AND BACK TO P, AS IF HE KNEW US WELL ...DIALOGUE OVER A OUIJA BOARD 277 30
PLUMAGE OF WHAT, PAN? P ... HE STARTS AGAIN, ...DIALOGUE O. 279 85
PACE (2)
I HURL MY HEART TO HALT HIS PACE, ...PURSUIT 23 37
I PACE IT, SNIFFING ....LETTER IN NOVEMBER 253 18
PACED (1)
PACED BRISK FATHER SHAWN. A COLD DAY, A SODDEN ONE IT WAS ...
... DIALOGUE BETWEEN GHOST AND PRIEST 38 2
PACIFIED (1)
EVEN IF YOU SEEM PACIFIED, PREFER ......DIALOGUE OVER A OUIJA BOARD 280 145
PACIFIST (1)
WHEN I HIT HER SHE HELD STILL, LIKE A TRUE PACIFIST. ....IN PLASTER 159 12
PACING (1)
THE JUT OF THAT ODD, DARK HEAD, PACING ....PHEASANT 191 3

PACK (8)
    OF CARDBOARD CARTONS THE COLOR OF CEMENT OR A DOG PACK   ....BURNING.   204   11
    DULLY, UNDER A PACK OF MEN IN RED JACKETS, ...BURNING THE LETTERS   204   13
    LIKE THE PACK, THE PACK, LIKE EVERYBODY.   ....THE SWARM   216   25
    LIKE THE PACK, THE PACK, LIKE EVERYBODY.   ....THE SWARM   216   25
    AND MY TAROC PACK AND MY TAROC PACK   ....DADDY   223   39
    AND MY TAROC PACK AND MY TAROC PACK   ....DADDY   223   39
    A PACK OF PHILANTHROPICAL FOOLS   ....DIALOGUE EN ROUTE   308   11
    THE SINGING BIRDS PACK UP AND FLY AWAY;   ....NEVER TRY TO TRICK.   320   17
PACK-DOG (1)
    YELLOW-HAUNCHED, A PACK-DOG, ...THE SWARM   216   23
PACKETS (1)
    ARE RATTLING THE CRACKER PACKETS. FINE FLOUR   ....LEAVING EARLY   146   36
PACKING (5)
    I AM PACKING THE HARD POTATOES LIKE GOOD CLOTHES, ...LESBOS   229   68
    I AM PACKING THE BABIES, ...LESBOS   229   69
    I AM PACKING THE SICK CATS.   ....LESBOS   229   70
    PACKING WITHOUT A COMPASS OR SCALE   ...SONG FOR A REVOLUTIONARY LOVE   323   10
    SEND MY MUSE ALICE PACKING WITH GAUDY SCRAPS   ....A SORCERER B.   324   7
PACT (2)
    TO KEEP SOME UNSAID PACT; PERHAPS CONCERN   ....CHANNEL CROSSING   27   34
    SUCH PACT AS IS MADE ONCE ONLY; WHAT MATTER   ....WREATH FOR A BRIDAL   44   2
PACT'S (1)
    BE CERTAIN SOME SUCH PACT'S   ....VIRGIN IN A TREE   82   31
PADDED (1)
    TO ROCK ON ALL FOURS LIKE A PADDED HAMMOCK.   ....MAGI   148   11
PAGAN (1)
    SO CRY FOR THE PAGAN GIRL LEFT PICKING OLIVES   ......SONNET: TO TIME   311   9
PAGE (3)
    MY PAGE THIS DESERT   ....WORDS FOR A NURSERY   74   27
    SUPERIOR PAGE; THE BLUNT STONE ALSO.   ....POEMS, POTATOES   106   13
    AND PAGE BY PRIDE THE GOOD BOOKS BLOW;*SONG FOR A REVOLUTIONARY LOVE   322   3
PAGES (4)
    INVADE THE CLOISTRAL EYE LIKE PAGES   ......ON THE DECLINE OF ORACLES   78   23
    THE WORDS IN HIS BOOK WORMED OFF THE PAGES.   ...SUICIDE OFF EGG ROCK   115   19
    CAN TURN AND TURN THE PAGES OF A BOOK.   ....THREE WOMEN   187 361
    THE WOMEN WAIT, FLUTTERING, TURNING PAGES   ......MORNING IN THE HOS.   332   21
PAGODAS (1)
    IN GLASS PAGODAS HUNG WITH VEILS OF GREEN   ....APRIL AUBADE   312   2
PAID (5)
    THEIR SMALL PRICE PAID, THESE WEDDED ONES   ....CRYSTAL GAZER   55   25
    THE ENORMOUS MORTGAGE MUST BE PAID SOMEHOW, ...THE DISPOSSESSED   318   1
    THE ENORMOUS MORTGAGE MUST BE PAID SOMEHOW.   ....THE DISPOSSESSED   318   6
    THE ENORMOUS MORTGAGE MUST BE PAID SOMEHOW.   ....THE DISPOSSESSED   318   12
    THE ENORMOUS MORTGAGE MUST BE PAID SOMEHOW: ....THE DISPOSSESSED   319   18
PAIL (2)
    IN THE TIN PAIL SHADED BY YELLOW PAPER   MEMOIRS OF A SPINACH-PICKER   89   13
    BUT THAT IT TURNED INTO A MILKING PAIL?   ..METAMORPHOSES OF THE MOON   307   20
PAILS (1)
    SCALING LITTLE LADDERS WITH GLUEPOTS AND PAILS OF LYSOL*THE COLOSSUS   129   11
PAIN (3)
    WHICH HAD CAUSED HIS DEAR GIRL PAIN.   ....BUCOLICS   24   20
    THE PAIN   ....NICK AND THE CANDLESTICK   241   29
    OUR NOBLE DOCTOR CLAIMS THE PAIN IS HIS, ...NEVER TRY TO TRICK.   320   7
PAINED (1)
    HIS LITTLE FACE IS CARVED IN PAINED, RED WOOD.   ....EVENT   194   9
PAINS (1)
    WHAT PAINS, WHAT SORROWS MUST I BE MOTHERING?   ....THREE WOMEN   180 133
PAINT (4)
    THE GARDEN'S REMAINDER IN FULL PAINT.   ................RHODODENDRON.   103   4
    YET DESOLATION, STALLED IN PAINT, SPARES THE LITTLE COUNTRY   ...
                                   ... TWO VIEWS OF A CADAVER ROOM   114   21
    THEY PAINT SUCH SECRETS IN ARABIC, CHINESE!   ....THREE WOMEN   179   98
    A CRAFT WITH PAINT AND POWDER THAT CAN MAKE   .........METAMORPHOSES.   307   23
PAINTED (5)
    RECORDS BARE PAINTED WALLS, WHILE AN ELECTRIC LIGHT   ..TALE OF A TUB   24   2
    AND WEAR MY PAINTED FACE THE WAY A MUMMY-CASE   ....IN PLASTER   159   41
    ATTRACTING MY SHARE OF AHS AND SPECTACULARLY PAINTED, *I AM VERTICAL   162   6
    I HAVE PAINTED LITTLE HEARTS ON EVERYTHING.   ....THREE WOMEN   186 329
    OUR PAINTED STAGES FALL APART BY SCENES   ....DOOMSDAY   316   4
PAINTER (1)
    SAY HOW CRAFTY THE PAINTER WAS   ..BLACK PINE TREE IN AN ORANGE LIGHT   328   17
PAINT-PEELED (1)
    HERE ON A MOUNT OVERLAID WITH LEAVES. THE PAINT-PEELED   ......OXBOW.   88   34
PAINTS (3)
    A RUDDY SKYLIGHT PAINTS THE GRAY OXBOW   ....ABOVE THE OXBOW   88   42
    AND PAINTS THE RIVER'S PALE CIRCUMFLUENT STILLNESS   ABOVE THE OXBOW   89   43
    HE PAINTS A BLIZZARD OF GULLS, ...MAGNOLIA SHOALS   122   23
PAIR (3)
    THIS PAIR SEEK SINGLE STATE FROM THAT DUAL BATTLE.   ....WREATH F.   44   10
    TWO ENTER TO TAP HER SIGHT, A GREEN PAIR   ....CRYSTAL GAZER   55   7
    (TOO QUICK FOR THE PAIR TO ABSORB IT), ...DIALOGUE EN ROUTE   309   41
PAIRED (1)
    ARE THOSE PETALS OR LEAVES YOU'VE PAIRED THEM WITH -- *LEAVING EARLY   146   14

PAJAMAS (1)
    IS HE WEARING PAJAMAS OR AN EVENING SUIT ....BERCK-PLAGE 198   62
PALACE (6)
    CROWNS, PALACE, ALL ....THE SHRIKE   42   19
    LOW-LINTELLED, NO PALACE; ....TWO VIEWS OF WITHENS   72   15
    AN IVORY PALACE, A CROTCH PINE. ....THE SWARM 217   50
    A PALACE OF VELVET ....GIGOLO 267   5
    THE WHOLE REVOLVING TALL GLASS PALACE HALL ....CINDERELLA 304   5
    THE DARKENING STAIR, UNDOES THE PALACE LATCH ....THE PRINCESS. 334   28
PALATES (1)
    WITH CREAM AND CHICKEN-GUT FEASTING THE PALATES ......ELLA MASON A.   53   11
PALE (24)
    UNTIL THE SUN TURNED PALE FROM WARM, ...BUCOLICS   24   14
    RED, PALE OR DARK, ...STRUMPET SONG   33   7
    FROM THAT PALE MIST ....DIALOGUE BETWEEN GHOST AND PRIEST   39   47
    WON HER THE FROG-COLORED SKIN, PALE PITH AND WATERY*VIRGIN IN A TREE   81   14
    AND PAINTS THE RIVER'S PALE CIRCUMFLUENT STILLNESS   ABOVE THE OXBOW   89   43
    WHAT MOVED THE PALE, RAPTORIAL OWL ....OWL 102   9
    OF PALE FRONTS, STRAW THATCHINGS, THE HARD ROAD*WHITENESS I REMEMBER 102   20
    WE STROLL THROUGH A MAZE OF PALE ....MAGNOLIA SHOALS 121   2
    AMONG PETALS PALE AS DEATH ....THE SLEEPERS 123   13
    INCENSE. PALE MOSS DRIPS ....DARK WOOD, DARK WATER 127   2
    OF PALE BLUE VITREOUS STUFF, OPAQUE ....THE BURNT-OUT SPA 137   4
    THEIR PALE, TENTATIVE YELLOWS ....CANDLES 149   15
    FACELESS AND PALE AS CHINA ....PARLIAMENT HILL FIELDS 152   2
    THE BLUE NIGHT PLANTS, THE LITTLE PALE BLUE HILL .....PARLIAMENT H. 153   41
    WEIGHTING THE PALE SKY WITH A SOLIDER COLOR. .....WUTHERING HEIGHTS 167   7
    THE INTRICATE, BLUE PIPING UNDER THIS PALE MARBLE. ....SURGEON. 171   26
    I SEE THEM ALREADY -- THE PALE, STAR-DISTANCE FACES. ....LAST WORDS 172   6
    A SNAG IS LIFTING A VALEDICTORY, PALE HAND; .....CROSSING THE WATER 190   9
    ARE THOSE THE FACES OF LOVE, THOSE PALE IRRETRIEVABLES? ....ELM 193   35
    BY PALE GIRLS, TRAVEL THE AIR IN SCORCHED HANDS. ......BERCK-PLAGE 196   4
    PALE EYES, PATENT-LEATHER GUTTURALS! ....BURNING THE LETTERS 205   46
    PALE FLOUNDER ....AQUATIC NOCTURNE 305   7
    STARS PALE BEFORE THE ANGRY DAWN; ....TO A JILTED LOVER 310   21
    HIS OWN PALE BRIDE UPON A FLAMING TRAY: ....TERMINAL 328   12
PALELY (2)
    PALELY LIT BY ....POLLY'S TREE 128   24
    PALELY AND FLAMILY ....POPPIES IN OCTOBER 240   7
PALENESS (1)
    ASSEMBLE WITH THE FRAIL PALENESS OF MOTHS, ...OUIJA   77   4
PALES (3)
    FRIEZE OF CABBAGE-ROSES AND CORNFLOWERS PALES ......THE THIN PEOPLE   65   37
    THE BLUE COLOR PALES. HE IS HUMAN AFTER ALL. ....THREE WOMEN 181 166
    GUILT-STRICKEN HALTS, PALES, CLINGS TO THE PRINCE ....CINDERELLA 304   12
PALETTE (1)
    FRESH FROM THE MELLOW PALETTE OF MATISSE: ....MIDSUMMER MOBILE 324   12
PALING (1)
    LOVE'S PALING SPHERE. ....MOONSONG AT MORNING 317   24
PALLID (1)
    BELLIES PALLID AND UPTURNED, ...MUSSEL HUNTER AT ROCK HARBOR   97   85
PALLOR (4)
    FROM YOUR BLUE PALLOR, I'D SAY YOU INHABITED THE FROZEN WASTE ...
                              ... DIALOGUE BETWEEN GHOST AND PRIEST   38   14
    EXHALE THEIR PALLOR LIKE SCENT. ....BARREN WOMAN 157   5
    THE CLOUDS ARE A MARRIAGE DRESS, OF THAT PALLOR. ......LITTLE FUGUE 189   52
    THE WONDER OF IT, IN THAT PALLOR, ...PHEASANT 191   13
PALLORS (6)
    TURN UP THEIR HANDS, THEIR PALLORS. IT IS SO QUIET HERE.*THREE WOMEN 179   94
    AS THE PALLORS GATHER --- ....BERCK-PLAGE 199   84
    THE PALLORS OF HANDS AND NEIGHBORLY FACES, ...BERCK-PLAGE 199   85
    THE ELATE PALLORS OF FLYING IRIS. ....BERCK-PLAGE 199   86
    RISE, WITH HER CANCEROUS PALLORS, ...PURDAH 242   13
    MY DISTRACTIONS, MY PALLORS. .........................EAVESDROPPER 260   20
PALLS (1)
    THEIR THICK PALLS FLOAT ....MARY'S SONG 257   9
PALM (5)
    ON THE QUEEN'S PALM ....RECANTATION   41   3
    FROM EACH NEON-LIT PALM ....ALICANTE LULLABY   43   13
    PERSEUS, THE PALM, AND MAY YOU POISE ....PERSEUS   84   47
    HOLDING UP ONE PALM -- ....A SECRET 219   4
    THOUGH HUNDREDS OF LONDONERS KNOW IT LIKE THE PALM OF THEIR HAND. ...
                              ... QUEEN MARY'S ROSE GARDEN 290   16
PALMED (2)
    PALMED OFF ON IT. ....ON THE DIFFICULTY OF CONJURING UP A DRYAD   66   32
    PALMED OFF OUR OWN HUNCHES AS ORACLES.   DIALOGUE OVER A OUIJA BOARD 279 105
PALMING (1)
    PALMING THE EARTH ASIDE, GRUBBERS ....BLUE MOLES 126   24
PALMS (3)
    A GREEN CRESCENT OF PALMS ....SOUTHERN SUNRISE   26   10
    REDDEN IN WHITE PALMS NO LABOR REDDENS. ....MOONRISE   98   11
    BETWEEN STEEL PALMS OF INCLINATION, TAKE IT, ...SONNET: TO EVA 304   3
PALM-SPEAR (1)
    PALM-SPEAR AND LILY DISTINCT AS FLORA IN THE VAST ....A LIFE 149   4

PALPABLE (1)
PALPABLE AS HIS, AND WEIGHTY. ....SCULPTOR   91   4
PALTRY (2)
FOR THE PALTRY GIFT OF HER BULK AND THE BEAT ......HARDCASTLE CRAGS   63   27
SOME PALTRY SCENE ON THE SOUP-KITCHEN STAIR: ....DIALOGUE O. 279 125
PALUSTRAL (1)
IN THESE PALUSTRAL HOMES WE ONLY ....FROG AUTUMN   99   3
PAMPERED (1)
TO VIEW HOW VERSATILE WE ARE: YOU'VE PAMPERED ....DIALOGUE O. 280 137
PAN (17)
AND WHATEVER PAN THIS MENDING MASTER *TINKER JACK AND THE TIDY WIVES   34   3
DIRECT TO YES. I BET IT'S PAN. WHO'LL ..DIALOGUE OVER A OUIJA BOARD 277   27
COME ON CALL LIKE THAT BUT PAN? HE'S ...DIALOGUE OVER A OUIJA BOARD 277   28
ENOUGH FOR NICKNAMES. HOW ARE YOU PAN? F- ....DIALOGUE O. 277   31
IN PAN: IT'S BEEN EBBING EVER SINCE THE MESS ....DIALOGUE O. 277   38
PAN, ARE YOU STILL THERE? SEE, HIS SPRINT ....DIALOGUE O. 278   70
TO YES SAYS HE IS READY. PAN, IS THERE   DIALOGUE OVER A OUIJA BOARD 278   71
PLUMAGE OF WHAT, PAN? P ... HE STARTS AGAIN, ...DIALOGUE O. 279   85
PAN SAID. A PLUMAGE OF RAW WORMS. HOW ..DIALOGUE OVER A OUIJA BOARD 279 100
PAN AS IF HE WERE OUR FIRST-BREACHED BRAT ....DIALOGUE O. 280 138
THE STINT OF SISYPHUS. ASK PAN, THEN, WHERE ....DIALOGUE O. 281 173
AND WE'LL SEE WHO'S SMARTEST. PAN, TELL US NOW: ....DIALOGUE O. 281 205
BECAUSE PAN BLUNTLY SPELT OUT GOD'S HEAD, NOT ....DIALOGUE O. 282 237
PAN AS OUR EVENING GUEST IF HE'S SO FREE*DIALOGUE OVER A OUIJA BOARD 283 252
COUNTS. SUCH DUELS INFECT BEST FRIENDSHIPS. PAN ....DIALOGUE O. 283 271
CURTSEYED TO YOURS. TOO BAD YOU CALLED PAN UP ....DIALOGUE O. 284 280
THIS BOARD OUR BATTLEFIELD. LET'S GIVE PAN UP ....DIALOGUE O. 284 292
PANE (3)
A PANE OF DRAGONFLY WING, WHEN THEY LEFT ME ....SPINACH-PICKER.   89   5
PURE AS A PANE OF ICE. IT'S A GIFT. ....LOVE LETTER 147   36
LIKE BLUE MARY'S ANGEL, DOVELIKE AGAINST A PANE ....WIDOW 165   38
PANEL (1)
OF AN ECHO, EXPOSES THE PANEL IN THE WALL ....WIDOW 164   7
PANES (4)
BUT THOSE LADIES BROKE THE PANES. ....THE DISQUIETING MUSES   75   24
OF WINDOWS WITH ODD VIOLET PANES. ....A WINTER'S TALE   87   30
HANGING THEIR BLUEGREEN BELLIES AND THEIR WING PANES IN A CHINESE
SCREEN. ....BLACKBERRYING 168   16
CHRIST! THEY ARE PANES OF ICE, ...NICK AND THE CANDLESTICK 241   15
PANGS (1)
SET CLOSE, LIKE BIRTH PANGS. ....THE RABBIT CATCHER 194   16
PANIC (2)
HER FACE RED AND WHITE, A PANIC, ...LESBOS 227   11
IN PANIC AT THE CROP OF CATACOMBS ....TERMINAL 328   3
PANORAMA (1)
IN BRUEGHEL'S PANORAMA OF SMOKE AND SLAUGHTER ....TWO VIEWS. 114   12
PAN'S (6)
PITYS FROM PAN'S ASSAULT! AND THOUGH AGE DROP .....VIRGIN IN A TREE   81   17
I WAS PERFECTLY RIGHT: PAN'S A MERE PUPPET ....DIALOGUE O. 279 106
UNDER THE GUISE OF NONCHALANCE. PAN'S LAUGH ....DIALOGUE O. 282 228
WITH FIBS? THE FIBS ARE OURS, NOT HIS. PAN'S FINE .....DIALOGUE O. 283 253
PAN'S PROWESS OUR OWN CREATION, AND NOT THE OTHER'S ...DIALOGUE O. 284 285
OF PAN'S PRONOUNCEMENTS, AND OUR NERVES ARE STRUNG ....DIALOGUE O. 284 288
PANSY (1)
PANSY, IT GLOWS. O IT'S ....POLLY'S TREE 128   28
PANTHER (1)
THERE IS A PANTHER STALKS ME DOWN: ....PURSUIT   22   1
PANTHER'S (1)
THE PANTHER'S TREAD IS ON THE STAIRS, ...PURSUIT   23   49
PANTS (3)
I SHOULD WEAR TIGER PANTS, I SHOULD HAVE AN AFFAIR. ....LESBOS 228   30
UNCLE, PANTS FACTORY FATSO, MILLIONAIRE. ....STOPPED DEAD 230   4
OF THE MAN'S PANTS ......................................EAVESDROPPER 261   58
PANZER-MAN (2)
PANZER-MAN, PANZER-MAN, O YOU --- ....DADDY 223   45
PANZER-MAN, PANZER-MAN, O YOU --- ....DADDY 223   45
PAPAL (1)
BEFORE THAT PAPAL PARAGON, THE SUN ....APRIL AUBADE 312   8
PAPER (22)
GONDOLA OF PAPER ....BATTLE-SCENE   84   12
LEAVES AND LILIES FLATTENED TO PAPER BEHIND YOU ....YADWIGHA.   85   16
IN THE TIN PAIL SHADED BY YELLOW PAPER   MEMOIRS OF A SPINACH-PICKER   89   13
EVERYTHING GLITTERED LIKE BLANK PAPER. ....SUICIDE OFF EGG ROCK 115   20
FLAT AS PAPER AND ....POLLY'S TREE 128   8
CHEWING AT THE GRAY PAPER, ...POEM.2.DARK. 132   4
IT RESEMBLES THE MOON, OR A SHEET OF BLANK PAPER ....A LIFE 150   23
SETTLING AND STIRRING LIKE BLOWN PAPER ......PARLIAMENT HILL FIELDS 152   8
SKIN DOESN'T HAVE ROOTS, IT PEELS AWAY EASY AS PAPER. ....FACE LIFT 156   20
EVEN THROUGH THE GIFT PAPER I COULD HEAR THEM BREATHE ....TULIPS 161   37
THE NIGHT SKY IS ONLY A SORT OF CARBON PAPER, ...INSOMNIAC 163   1
A PAPER IMAGE TO LAY AGAINST HER HEART ....WIDOW 164   17
BUT IT IS SHE WHO IS PAPER NOW, WARMED BY NO ONE. ....WIDOW 164   20
BITS OF BURNT PAPER WHEELING IN A BLOWN SKY. .........BLACKBERRYING 168   11
THE SWIFTS ARE BACK. THEY ARE SHRIEKING LIKE PAPER ROCKETS.   THREE. 185 310
THE STREETS MAY TURN TO PAPER SUDDENLY, BUT I RECOVER ..THREE WOMEN 187 365

PAPER (CONT.)
    A WEDDING-CAKE FACE IN A PAPER FRILL. ....BERCK-PLAGE   198   55
    YOU WILL NOT EVEN HEAR ME OPENING IT, NO PAPER CRACKLE, ..BIRTHDAY.   207   34
    NAKED AS PAPER TO START ....THE APPLICANT   221   30
    COY PAPER STRIPS FOR DOORS -- ....LESBOS   227   5
    OF JAPANESE PAPER, MY GOLD BEATEN SKIN ....FEVER.   232   38
    THE MORNING PAPER CLOCKED THE HEADLINE HOUR ....THE TRIAL OF MAN   312   5
PAPERED (1)
    I HAVE PAPERED HIS ROOM WITH BIG ROSES, ...THREE WOMEN   186 328
PAPERS (1)
    I FLAKE UP PAPERS THAT BREATHE LIKE PEOPLE, ...BURNING THE LETTERS   204   37
PAPERWEIGHT (1)
    A PAPERWEIGHT, ...LADY LAZARUS   244   7
PAPERY (4)
    THEY MISTAKE THEIR STAR, THESE PAPERY GODFOLK. ....MAGI   148   15
    TWO GRAY, PAPERY BAGS -- ...........................APPREHENSIONS   195   13
    WHAT HOLES THIS PAPERY DAY IS ALREADY FULL OF! ....THE JAILER   226   17
    PAPERY FEELING. ....CUT   235   26
PAPS (1)
    I SUCK AT THE PAPS OF DARKNESS. POEM.7.S.   136   18
PAPYRUS (1)
    THE ORANGE POMPONS, THE EGYPTIAN PAPYRUS ....PARLIAMENT HILL FIELDS   153   43
PARACHUTE (1)
    IT HOLDS ALOOF, A SHROUDED PARACHUTE .....METAMORPHOSES OF THE MOON   307   8
PARADEGROUND (1)
    SHORT-REINED, PAWING LIKE PARADEGROUND HORSES. ....A LIFE   150   14
PARADES (1)
    PARADES THE MARKETPLACE, LURID AND STRICKEN ....THE RAVAGED FACE   115   2
PARADISE (2)
    AND BIRDS OF PARADISE, AND THE ROUND MOON, ...YADWIGHA.   86   24
    TO PARADISE. ....FEVER.   232   54
PARADOX (2)
    HEAT FURNACE OF PARADOX ....NOTES TO A NEOPHYTE   306   14
    THE PARADOX IS THAT "THE PLAY'S THE THING": .....LOVE IS A PARALLAX   330   55
PARAGON (2)
    VISIBLE ONLY TO THE PARAGON HEART, ...ON THE PLETHORA OF DRYADS   67   3
    BEFORE THAT PAPAL PARAGON, THE SUN. ....APRIL AUBADE   312   8
PARAGONS (1)
    WITH SAVOR; COUPLED SO, PURE PARAGONS OF CONSTANCE, ...WREATH F.   44   9
PARAKEETS (2)
    AMONG THESE PARAKEETS, MACAWS! ....PURDAH   243   35
    LIKE PETULANT PARAKEETS CORKED UP IN CAGES .....MORNING IN THE HOS.   332   19
PARALLAX (1)
    LOVE IS A PARALLAX ....LOVE IS A PARALLAX   329   T
PARALYSING (1)
    PARALYSING THE KICKING LOVERS. ....MEDUSA   225   26
PARALYSIS (1)
    EACH VIRILE BACHELOR DREADS PARALYSIS, ...NEVER TRY TO TRICK.   320   10
PARALYTIC (1)
    PARALYTIC ....PARALYTIC   266   T
PARAPHERNALIA (1)
    THE MISTS ARE PART OF THE ANCIENT PARAPHERNALIA -- ......FINISTERRE   169   13
PARCEL (1)
    UNDER MY FEET IN A NEAT PARCEL. ....LAST WORDS   172   24
PARCELED (1)
    PARCELED OUT BY WHITE-JACKETED ASSASSINS. ....STREET SONG   36   10
PARCH (1)
    HIS KISSES PARCH, EACH PAW'S A BRIAR, ...PURSUIT   22   19
PARCHED (1)
    SUN'S PARCHED SCREAM, ...STREET SONG   36   26
PARCHMENT (1)
    FLATTEN TO PARCHMENT SCREENS TO KEEP THE WIND OFF. .....THREE WOMEN   179   97
PARDON (3)
    PARDON, AND THAT'S ....RHYME   50   12
    O PARDON THE ONE WHO KNOCKS FOR PARDON AT ...ELECTRA ON AZALEA PATH   117   44
    O PARDON THE ONE WHO KNOCKS FOR PARDON AT ...ELECTRA ON AZALEA PATH   117   44
PARE (2)
    TO UNPICK THE HEART, PARE BONE ....NOVEMBER GRAVEYARD   56   9
    TO PARE NAILS, ...A SECRET   220   22
PARED (2)
    UNTIL HER KNIFE HAD PARED ....THE THIN PEOPLE   65   30
    THE LABORER'S NAILS PARED LEVEL ....THE DEATH OF MYTH-MAKING   104   7
PARENTAL (1)
    PARENTAL FACES ON TALL STALKS, ALTERNATELY STERN AND TEARFUL, ...
                                                  ... INSOMNIAC   163   11
PARENTHESIS (1)
    FIXED ME IN THIS PARENTHESIS; ....THE EYE-MOTE   109   28
PARENTS (1)
    LIKE RIVAL PARENTS OVER A PRECOCIOUS ...DIALOGUE OVER A OUIJA BOARD   284 283
PARES (1)
    OF CANDOR PARES WHITE FLESH TO THE WHITE BONE, ...MOONRISE   98   27
PARING (1)
    THE LONG WIND, PARING HER PERSON DOWN ....HARDCASTLE CRAGS   63   22
PARINGS (1)
    A FRUIT THAT'S DEATH TO TASTE: DARK FLESH, DARK PARINGS. ...

PARINGS (CONT.)
    ... THE BEEKEEPER'S DAUGHTER 118 14
PARIS (1)
  IN MUNICH, MORGUE BETWEEN PARIS AND ROME, ...THE MUNICH MANNEQUINS 263 12
PARK (6)
  BY LEAVE OF THE PARK COMMISSION ....A WINTER'S TALE 87 22
  THIS PARK IS FLESHED WITH IDIOT PETALS. ....MOONRISE 98 4
  CHILD'S PARK STONES ....CHILD'S PARK STONES 100 T
  IN THE PUBLIC PARK; AT HOME FELT THE WANT ............RHODODENDRON. 103 2
  THE PARK OF LESS RED THAN WITHERING DID. .............RHODODENDRON. 103 12
  IN THIS PRECARIOUS PARK ....TOUCH-AND-GO 335 8
PARKS (1)
  A SMOKE THAT TAKES THE PARKS, THE LITTLE STATUES ....THREE WOMEN 186 355
PARK-SLEEPERS (1)
  A POOR MONTH FOR PARK-SLEEPERS AND LOVERS. ....A WINTER SHIP 113 22
PARLIAMENT (1)
  PARLIAMENT HILL FIELDS ....PARLIAMENT HILL FIELDS 152 T
PARLIAMENTS (1)
  GOVERNMENTS, PARLIAMENTS, SOCIETIES, ...THREE WOMEN 179 83
PARLOR (2)
  IN THE PARLOR OF THE STONE HOUSE ....BERCK-PLAGE 199 78
  WILL PROVE TO BE SOME COMMON PARLOR FAKE: *METAMORPHOSES OF THE MOON 307 22
PARODY (1)
  AND MOCKS! HERE'S THE PARODY OF THAT MORAL MOUSETRAP ....VIRGIN. 81 2
PARRIES (1)
  PARRIES THE LUNGE AND MENACE ....AERIALIST 331 20
PARROT (1)
  A BLACK-SHARDED LADY KEEPS ME IN A PARROT CAGE. POEM.6.W. 135 9
PARRY (1)
  NOW SPEAK SOME SACRAMENT TO PARRY SCRUPLE ......WREATH FOR A BRIDAL 44 11
PARSLEY (1)
  IN A PARSLEY HALO; ....SOW 61 16
PARSLEYED (1)
  PARSLEYED WITH ELEGIES, SHE LIES IN STATE ....TERMINAL 328 13
PART (8)
  BEFORE HE PART ....TINKER JACK AND THE TIDY WIVES 35 32
  OF HELL, AND NOT THE FIERY PART. YET TO JUDGE BY THAT DAZZLED LOOK, ...
    ... DIALOGUE BETWEEN GHOST AND PRIEST 38 15
  CAT-TAILS PART WHERE THE TAME CYGNETS STEER. ....WATERCOLOR. 112 14
  OF IMPERFECTIONS HIS BOWELS WERE PART OF -- ...SUICIDE OFF EGG ROCK 115 4
  THEY ARE PROPER IH SHAPE AND NUMBER AND EVERY PART. ......STILLBORN 142 7
  THE MISTS ARE PART OF THE ANCIENT PARAPHERNALIA -- ......FINISTERRE 169 13
  I THINK IT IS A PART OF MY HEART. BUT IT FLICKERS. ....MIRROR 173 8
  WITHOUT A PART LEFT OVER, ...MYSTIC 268 11
PARTIAL (1)
  NATURE'S PARTIAL, HAPHAZARD THUMB. ....THE BEGGARS 47 5
PARTICLES (2)
  THE PARTICLES OF DESTRUCTION I SUCK UP? AM I A PULSE ...THREE WOMEN 177 38
  TELLING THE PARTICLES OF THE CLOUDS, THE LEAVES, THE WATER *BURNING. 205 55
PARTICULAR (7)
  IN THIS PARTICULAR TUB, TWO KNEES JUT UP ....TALE OF A TUB 25 41
  NOW THIS PARTICULAR GIRL ....SPINSTER 49 1
  EACH PARTICULAR QUIRK SO RAVISHED ME .....ON THE PLETHORA OF DRYADS 67 15
  EACH STALLED IN HIS PARTICULAR MINUTE ....ON DECK 143 14
  LOOPING WOOL, DOING NOTHING IN PARTICULAR, ...HEAVY WOMEN 158 16
  THEY STAY, THEIR LITTLE PARTICULAR LUSTERS ....LAST WORDS 172 17
  BENDING, ON ME IN PARTICULAR, ITS MILD EYES. ....MOON. 173 21
PARTS (8)
  THOUGH PRIME PARTS CRAM EACH RICH MEAL, ...THE GLUTTON 40 11
  THIS IS THE CITY OF SPARE PARTS. POEM.7.S. 137 33
  TONIGHT THE PARTS ARE ENTOMBED IN AN ICEBOX. THE SURGEON AT 2 A.M. 171 37
  FROM MY ALPHABETICAL FINGERS, ORDERING PARTS, ...THREE WOMEN 177 28
  PARTS, BITS, COGS, THE SHINING MULTIPLES. ....THREE WOMEN 177 29
  THEY ARE HANDLING THE BLACK AND GREEN LOZENGES LIKE THE PARTS
    OF A BODY. ....BERCK-PLAGE 196 16
  ASSUMES, LIKE A MEATHOOK, THE BURDEN OF HIS PARTS. ....THE OTHER 201 6
  EPITAPH IN THREE PARTS ....EPITAPH IN THREE PARTS 337 T
PARTY (2)
  AND I AM DARK-SUITED AND STILL, A MEMBER OF THE PARTY, BERCK-PLAGE 200 111
  TO PICTURE SOME OTHER PARTY SPEAKING THROUGH ....DIALOGUE O. 280 146
PASS (15)
  SO SHE IS COME TO THIS RARE PASS ....THE QUEEN'S COMPLAINT 29 21
  OF FLAWED EARTH-FLESH COULD CAUSE THIS SORRY PASS? .....DIALOGUE B. 39 32
  THE NURSES PASS AND PASS, THEY ARE NO TROUBLE, ...TULIPS 160 11
  THE NURSES PASS AND PASS, THEY ARE NO TROUBLE, ...TULIPS 160 11
  THEY PASS THE WAY GULLS PASS INLAND IN THEIR WHITE CAPS, ...TULIPS 160 12
  THEY PASS THE WAY GULLS PASS INLAND IN THEIR WHITE CAPS, ...TULIPS 160 12
  A BODILESS SOUL COULD PASS ANOTHER SOUL ....WIDOW 164 32
  ONE SOUL PASS THROUGH THE OTHER, FRAIL AS SMOKE ....WIDOW 165 34
  PASS BY, PASS BY. ....THREE WOMEN 186 339
  PASS BY, PASS BY. ....THREE WOMEN 186 339
  CLOUDS PASS AND DISPERSE. ....ELM 193 34
  TARTING WITH THE DRAFTS THAT PASS, ...EAVESDROPPER 260 31
  YOU'LL ISSUE HIM HIS PASS TO ANGELDOM ..DIALOGUE OVER A OUIJA BOARD 281 192
  WHERE ON PINK-FLUTED FEET THE PIGEONS PASS ....APRIL AUBADE 312 10

TITLE   PAGE LINE

PASS (CONT.)
    WHERE KILROY WOULD PASS ....TEMPER OF TIME 336 14
PASSAGE (3)
    PUZZLING THE PASSAGE OF THEIR ....MUSSEL HUNTER AT ROCK HARBOR 96 53
    THE PASSAGE, SAY, OF THESE MAN-SHAMING CLOUDS. ....TWO CAMP. 144 3
    BEHIND WHICH THE SECRET PASSAGE LIES -- STALE AIR, ...WIDOW 164 8
PASSED (1)
    "THE DRAFT IS PASSED," THE WOMAN SAID. ....BITTER STRAWBERRIES 299 20
PASSENGERS (2)
    PASSENGERS UNDER AN INDIGO FIZZLE ....ALICANTE LULLABY 43 9
    SOME FEW PASSENGERS KEEP TRACK ....ON DECK 142 4
PASSER-BY (1)
    PASSER-BY. ....PROSPECT 28 12
PASSES (3)
    SHE PASSES AND REPASSES, LUMINOUS AS A NURSE. ....THREE WOMEN 176 5
    PASSES CLOUD AFTER CLOUD. ....BERCK-PLAGE 200 105
    SPLITS AND PASSES, SISTER TO ....ARIEL 239 7
PASSING (3)
    THE PASSING DAZZLE OF EACH FACE ....EPITAPH FOR FIRE AND FLOWER 45 9
    THEIR PASSING ON A PERISHABLE SCREEN ...DIALOGUE OVER A OUIJA BOARD 282 223
    THROUGH LICHEN-LID AND PASSING BIRD-FOOT ....TOUCH-AND-GO 335 4
PASSIONATE (1)
    RED AND YELLOW, TWO PASSIONATE HOT METALS ....STOPPED DEAD 230 8
PAST (10)
    OF MANY-COLORED FICTIONS; WE MASK OUR PAST ....TALE OF A TUB 25 38
    PAST THE YELLOW-PAELLA EATERIES, ...ALICANTE LULLABY 43 3
    THE BLANK MOOD SHE WALKED IN. ONCE PAST ....HARDCASTLE CRAGS 63 18
    LESS THAN PRESENT, PAST -- THIS FUTURE. ..ON THE DECLINE OF ORACLES 78 29
    PAST KEEPING TO THE HOUSE, PAST ALL DISCRETION --   THE RAVAGED FACE 115 7
    PAST KEEPING TO THE HOUSE, PAST ALL DISCRETION --   THE RAVAGED FACE 115 7
    AND THE OWNER PAST THIRTY, NO BEAUTY AT ALL. ....CANDLES 148 9
    AS THEY SHOT PAST THE FORTY-NINTH FLOOR ....DIALOGUE EN ROUTE 308 4
    SHOT PAST THE NINETY-FOURTH FLOOR ....DIALOGUE EN ROUTE 309 34
    AND SLIPS UNSEEN PAST WATCHMEN ON THE LAWN ....THE PRINCESS. 334 29
PASTEBOARD (1)
    FOR PASTEBOARD, AND SIREN-SONG ....BATTLE-SCENE 85 37
PASTEL (2)
    WHO POISES HIS PASTEL SPEAR ....BATTLE-SCENE 84 14
    HERALD DISTRACTION: A FLOCK OF PASTEL PILLS, ...MORNING IN THE HOS. 332 13
PASTRIES (1)
    OF WEDDING PASTRIES, ...OWL 101 4
PASTRY (1)
    YOU: A PRIEST-BAKED PASTRY STUFFED TO THE BRIM ....DIALOGUE O. 282 214
PASTURES (2)
    OF ITS HILLS, AND ITS PASTURES BORDERED BY BLACK STONE SET ...
                                             HARDCASTLE CRAGS 63 29
    OF COUNTRY HEDGEROWS AND COW PASTURES ....WHITENESS I REMEMBER 102 16
PATCH (6)
    WHAT CEREMONY OF WORDS CAN PATCH THE HAVOC? ..........CONVERSATION. 21 14
    TO PATCH WITH BRAND OF LOVE THIS RANK GRIMACE ....STRUMPET SONG 34 16
    PATCH TOGETHER A CONTENT ....BLACK ROOK IN RAINY WEATHER 57 35
    OF THE SPINACH PATCH. BUNCH AFTER BUNCH OF GREEN ...SPINACH-PICKER. 89 7
    NOT A PATCH ON YOUR PLACE, I GUESS, WITH THE JAVANESE .....THE TOUR 237 9
    PLANT AN ORANGE PUMPKIN PATCH ...BLACK PINE TREE IN AN ORANGE LIGHT 328 4
PATCHED (2)
    AND PATCHED THIS SHODDY ....GREEN ROCK, WINTHROP BAY 105 6
    EACH NURSE PATCHED HER SOUL TO A WOUND AND DISAPPEARED. ....WAKING. 151 13
PATCHWORK (1)
    TO BREAK THROUGH THAT PATCHWORK ....ON THE PLETHORA OF DRYADS 67 20
PATE (1)
    SPYING A PATE TO SPARE ....THE LADY AND THE EARTHENWARE HEAD 69 10
PATENT (1)
    MY PATENT LEATHER OVERNIGHT CASE LIKE A BLACK PILLBOX, ...TULIPS 160 19
PATENT-LEATHER (1)
    PALE EYES, PATENT-LEATHER GUTTURALS! ....BURNING THE LETTERS 205 46
PATERNAL (1)
    THEY WANT NO PROUD PATERNAL KINGDOM COME; ....THE DEAD 320 6
PATH (4)
    ELECTRA ON AZALEA PATH ....ELECTRA ON AZALEA PATH 116 T
    BREAKS THE SOIL. THIS IS AZALEA PATH. ....ELECTRA ON AZALEA PATH 117 21
    OUTSIZE HANDS PREPARE A PATH, ...BLUE MOLES 126 28
    I FOLLOW THE SHEEP PATH BETWEEN THEM. A LAST HOOK BRINGS ME ...
                                            BLACKBERRYING 169 23
PATHOLOGICAL (2)
    AND TISSUE IN SLICES -- A PATHOLOGICAL SALAMI.*THE SURGEON AT 2 A.M. 171 36
    AND I, LOVE, AM A PATHOLOGICAL LIAR, ...LESBOS 227 7
PATHS (1)
    THE PATHS NARROWED INTO THE HOLLOW. ....THE RABBIT CATCHER 193 13
PATIENCE (2)
    HER TIDINESS AND HER CALMNESS AND HER PATIENCE: ....IN PLASTER 159 25
    IT TAKES PATIENCE. IF VERONICAS AND FOUNTAINS ....DIALOGUE O. 282 221
PATIENT (2)
    TOMORROW THE PATIENT WILL HAVE A CLEAN, PINK PLASTIC LIMB. *SURGEON. 171 40
    I AM SLOW AS THE WORLD. I AM VERY PATIENT, ...THREE WOMEN 176 1

	TITLE	PAGE	LINE

PATIENTS (1)
   WHILE STRICKEN PATIENTS LET HIM HAVE HIS SAY; ..NEVER TRY TO TRICK. 320 8
PATIENTS' (1)
   OF THE PATIENTS' DINING ROOM. ....MISS DRAKE PROCEEDS TO SUPPER 41 26
PATINAS (2)
   SUN'S BRASS, THE MOON'S STEELY PATINAS, ...DEPARTURE 51 10
   THEY CLEAVE THE RIVER'S GREENING PATINAS; ....IN MIDAS' COUNTRY 100 18
PATRIARCH (1)
   DRY-EYED, THE INVETERATE PATRIARCH ....I WANT, I WANT 106 9
PATRONIZED (2)
   I PATRONIZED HER A LITTLE, AND SHE LAPPED IT UP -- ......IN PLASTER 159 20
   PATRONIZED BY CONVALESCENT WIVES; MORNING IN THE HOSPITAL SOLARIUM 332 5
PAUL (1)
   RASPS THE JARRING BARITONE OF UNCLE PAUL; ....FAMILY REUNION 300 22
PAUSE (4)
   AND WOULDN'T PAUSE FOR MY STRAIGHT LOOK. .............RHODODENDRON. 104 25
   BUT GAVE ME PAUSE, MY ROSE A CHARGE, ...RHODODENDRON. 104 26
   THE STONY ACTORS POISE AND PAUSE FOR BREATH. *ELECTRA ON AZALEA PATH 117 37
   A SECOND'S PAUSE. ....FAMILY REUNION 300 7
PAUSED (1)
   HORSEFLIES BUZZED, PAUSED AND STUNG. ....BITTER STRAWBERRIES 299 7
PAVED (1)
   NAPPING IN HER KITCHEN PAVED WITH SAUCERS. ....ELLA MASON A. 54 20
PAVING (2)
   PAVING THIS GRAVE GROUND. HERE'S HONEST ROT .....NOVEMBER GRAVEYARD 56 8
   EVEN THE PAVING. ....MUSHROOMS 139 13
PAW (2)
   LAPS ITS GRAY PAW ....RESOLVE 52 6
   THE STARCHED WHITE COAT, THE CAT'S PAW WALK, ...MORNING IN THE HOS. 332 12
PAWED (1)
   BONES, BONES ONLY, PAWED AND TOSSED, ...POINT SHIRLEY 111 38
PAWING (1)
   SHORT-REINED, PAWING LIKE PARADEGROUND HORSES. ....A LIFE 150 14
PAWS (1)
   PRETENDING I AM A NEGRESS WITH PINK PAWS. ....THE JAILER 226 19
PAW'S (1)
   HIS KISSES PARCH, EACH PAW'S A BRIAR, ...PURSUIT 22 19
PAY (6)
   WHERE TREES AND CLOUDS AND ANIMALS PAY NO NOTICE; ....TWO CAMP. 144 8
   IF I PAY THE ROOTS OF THE HEATHER ....WUTHERING HEIGHTS 167 16
   ROUND TO EARN HIS PAY: HE'LL HAVE US KEEP ....DIALOGUE O. 284 294
   DEMANDED THAT I PAY A FINE ....THE DREAM 311 15
   THE MAESTRO GIVES THE SINGING BIRDS THEIR PAY ....DENOUEMENT 326 4
   TO PAY THE PIPER WITH EACH BREATH, YET LOVE .....LOVE IS A PARALLAX 331 76
PAYS (1)
   PAYS TO BE POLITIC. OH, I'M NOT ONE TO HANG ....DIALOGUE O. 281 196
PEACE (7)
   BRAVE ACTS PLAYED OUT IN PEACE, IN WAR; ALL DANGERS*CHANNEL CROSSING 27 39
   INDIGENOUS PEACE. SUCH SUBSTANCE MAKES ....LANDOWNERS 53 11
   OUT THEIR STALKY LIMBS AGAIN THOUGH PEACE ....THE THIN PEOPLE 64 9
   ALL'S PEACE AND DISCIPLINE DOWN THERE. TILL LATELY WE ....OXBOW. 89 53
   THOSE GREAT GODDESSES OF PEACE. ....LORELEI 95 35
   IN ITS EASY PEACE, COULD ONLY KEEP HOLY SO. ....THREE WOMEN 178 81
   IN IMPOTENCE, TO SUE FOR PEACE, *INSOLENT STORM STRIKES AT THE SKULL 325 4
PEACEABLE (1)
   THE STONES OF THE BELLY WERE PEACEABLE, ...POEM.7.S. 136 9
PEACEFUL (3)
   THE SCALDED SHEET IS A SNOWFIELD, FROZEN AND PEACEFUL. ....SURGEON. 170 5
   SHE IS A SMALL ISLAND, ASLEEP AND PEACEFUL, ...THREE WOMEN 184 260
   SHE IS NOT EASY, SHE IS NOT PEACEFUL; ....ELM/DR 292 1
PEACEFULNESS (2)
   I AM LEARNING PEACEFULNESS, LYING BY MYSELF QUIETLY ....TULIPS 160 3
   THE PEACEFULNESS IS SO BIG IT DAZES YOU, ...TULIPS 161 32
PEACH (2)
   COLOR OF LEMON, MANGO, PEACH, ...SOUTHERN SUNRISE 26 1
   UNWARMED BY THE SWEET AIR OF THIS PEACH ORCHARD. ....STARS. 166 36
PEACOCK (1)
   ONE FEATHER, LIKE THE PEACOCK. ....PURDAH 243 39
PEACOCK-COLORED (1)
   WITH RADIANCE, PEACOCK-COLORED; INSTEAD, BLEAK ROCKS ....CHANNEL C. 27 22
PEACOCKS (2)
   AND THE FABULOUS LUTES AND PEACOCKS, RENDING THE NET ...
      ... CONVERSATION AMONG THE RUINS 21 3
   PEACOCKS BLESSING ....BALLOONS 272 17
PEAJACKET (1)
   PERCY BOWS, IN HIS BLUE PEAJACKET, AMONG THE NARCISSI. ...NARCISSI. 190 2
PEAK (2)
   THIS WAVE'S GREEN PEAK ON WIRE ....EPITAPH FOR FIRE AND FLOWER 45 2
   UNTIL THE PEAK OF NOON HAS COME ....TO A JILTED LOVER 310 24
PEAKS (1)
   PEAKS AND CRATERS OF THOSE EXTINCT VOLCANOES.*THE EVERLASTING MONDAY 62 6
PEANUT-CRUNCHING (1)
   THE PEANUT-CRUNCHING CROWD ....LADY LAZARUS 245 26
PEARL (5)
   HER A POCKETBOOK, A PEARL HATPIN ....ON DECK 143 21

	TITLE	PAGE	LINE

PEARL (CONT.)
I WOULD NOT MIND IF IT WAS BONES, OR A PEARL BUTTON. .....BIRTHDAY. 206 12
HIS JEW-MAMA GUARDS HIS SWEET SEX LIKE A PEARL. ....LESBOS 228 27
IS IT A PENNY, A PEARL -- ....STOPPED DEAD 230 21
THE COLOR OF PEARL. ....CONTUSION 271 3
PEARLED (1)
COOL AS THE PEARLED INTERIOR OF A CONCH. ....THE OTHER TWO 68 2
PEARLS (3)
I WATCH THEIR SPILT TEARS CLOUD AND DULL TO PEARLS. ....CANDLES 149 31
AND PICK THE WORMS OFF ME LIKE STICKY PEARLS. ....LADY LAZARUS 245 42
MOUTH FULL OF PEARLS, ...PARALYTIC 266 24
PEARS (2)
THE PEARS FATTEN LIKE LITTLE BUDDHAS. ....THE MANOR GARDEN 125 3
THESE LITTLE GLOBES OF LIGHT ARE SWEET AS PEARS. ....CANDLES 149 24
PEASANT (2)
A PEASANT WOMAN IN BLACK ....FINISTERRE 170 22
SHE DOES NOT HEAR WHAT THE SAILOR OR THE PEASANT IS SAYING -- ...
... FINISTERRE 170 26
PEASANTS (3)
HE KNEW, BUT NO PEASANTS KNOW. ....ON THE DECLINE OF ORACLES 78 8
THE PEASANTS FEAST AND MULTIPLY. ....ON THE DECLINE OF ORACLES 78 16
THE PEASANTS ANCHOR THEM WITH CONCHES. ONE IS TOLD: ....FINISTERRE 170 30
PEATY (1)
AND HILL, AND THROUGH PEATY WATER. ....TWO VIEWS OF WITHENS 72 11
PEBBLE (4)
PEBBLE SMELLS, TURNIPY CHAMBERS. POEM.2.DARK. 133 22
I BECAME A STILL PEBBLE. POEM.7.S. 136 8
POOLING IN HEEL-PRINTS, FUMBLING PEBBLE AND STEM. ....PARLIAMENT H. 153 36
MY BODY IS A PEBBLE TO THEM, THEY TEND IT AS WATER ....TULIPS 160 15
PEBBLED (1)
MOLES DEAD IN THE PEBBLED RUT, ...BLUE MOLES 126 2
PEBBLES (3)
WHAT FLINTY PEBBLES THE PLOUGHBLADE UPTURNS ....OUIJA 77 28
TENDS TO THE PEBBLES IT MUST RUN OVER, SMOOTHING THEM GENTLY.*TULIPS 160 16
PEBBLES WE PRESERVE IN OUR OWN CUPBOARDS*DIALOGUE OVER A OUIJA BOARD 280 135
PECK (1)
LEANS TO PECK OPEN THOSE LOCKED LIDS, TO EAT ....THE SHRIKE 42 18
PECULIAR (2)
TO BE MEANT FOR CLIMBING. A PECULIAR LOGIC ....ABOVE THE OXBOW 88 17
OBSTACLE GLASS-WRAPPED AND PECULIAR, ...NEW YEAR ON DARTMOOR 176 2
PEDESTRIAN (1)
ABOVE PITCH OF PEDESTRIAN EAR, ...STREET SONG 36 23
PEDESTALED (1)
AS VENUS, PEDESTALED ON A HALF-SHELL ....HEAVY WOMEN 158 2
PEEL (3)
PEEL OFF TO SEA AS GULLS DO, ...WHITSUN 154 20
PEEL FROM HIS SKIN. ....AMNESIAC 233 10
PEEL OFF THE NAPKIN ....LADY LAZARUS 244 10
PEELED (2)
WORKED INTO THE PEELED ORANGE WOOD ....MEDALLION 124 2
OR THE SEA, HUSHING THEIR PEELED SENSE LIKE OLD MOTHER MORPHIA. ...
... WAKING IN WINTER 151 16
PEELING (2)
THE GREAT COROLLAS DILATE, PEELING BACK THEIR SILKS. ..BEEKEEPER'S. 118 2
BLEEDING AND PEELING ....THE NIGHT DANCES 250 20
PEELS (1)
SKIN DOESN'T HAVE ROOTS, IT PEELS AWAY EASY AS PAPER. ....FACE LIFT 156 20
PEEPHOLE (2)
LETTING IN THE LIGHT, PEEPHOLE AFTER PEEPHOLE -- ....INSOMNIAC 163 3
LETTING IN THE LIGHT, PEEPHOLE AFTER PEEPHOLE -- ....INSOMNIAC 163 3
PEER (1)
YOU PEER FROM THE DOOR, ...LESBOS 229 82
PEERED (1)
WE PEERED AGOG THROUGH THE COBWEBBED DOOR ....ELLA MASON A. 54 26
PEERS (2)
OUSTS MISTIER PEERS AND THRIVES, MURDEROUS, ...POEMS, POTATOES 106 2
WHO PEERS INSIDE ....ON LOOKING INTO THE EYES OF A DEMON LOVER 325 6
PEGS (2)
TAP, TAP, TAP, STEEL PEGS. I AM FOUND WANTING. ....THREE WOMEN 177 35
PEGS TOO DEEP TO UPROOT, AND A MIND LIKE A RING THE RABBIT CATCHER 194 28
PELLET (1)
I AM A ROOT, A STONE, AN OWL PELLET, ...POEM.1.WHO. 132 23
PELLICLE (1)
ENCASED IN A GLASSY PELLICLE. ....A WINTER SHIP 113 28
PELLMELL (1)
PELLMELL, BLUEBLACK. ....THE BULL OF BENDYLAW 108 15
PELT (1)
I ENTER THE SOFT PELT OF THE MOLE. ....BLUE MOLES 126 21
PELTS (1)
A DRESSING OF MULE EARS, MOTHY PELTS, BUT GREEN-HEARTED,*POEM.1.WHO. 131 17
PEN (1)
AS A DESK DRAWER HIDES A POISON PEN LETTER, ...THE RIVAL/DR 291 9
PENALTY (2)
WOULD AVOID ALL PENALTY. ....THE DREAM 311 23
NOW AS PENALTY FOR HER SKILL, ...AERIALIST 332 43

```
                                                          TITLE            PAGE  LINE
PENBEARER (1)
  PENBEARER, SCRUBNURSE,  .......................WORDS FOR A NURSERY    74   36
PENCILS (1)
  OF BLUNT PENCILS, ROSE-SPRIGGED COFFEE CUP,  .............CONJURING.   65    2
PENDULUM (1)
  OF EVERY PENDULUM;  .........................................AERIALIST  331   21
PENNY (3)
  WITH A PENNY SLOT  ...............................................SOW    60   12
  FIELDS SHRUNK TO A PENNY  ................................THE SWARM    216   29
  IS IT A PENNY, A PEARL --  ............................STOPPED DEAD    230   21
PEN-SKETCH (1)
  MADE LACE, OR A LEAF-AND-FLOWER PEN-SKETCH.  .......SOUTHERN SUNTISE    26    6
PENURY (1)
  RETROSPECT SHALL NOT SOFTEN SUCH PENURY --  ...............DEPARTURE    51    9
PEOPLE (33)
  TO SEE MY PEOPLE SHRUNK SO SMALL, SO SMALL."  THE QUEEN'S COMPLAINT    29   25
  TO PEOPLE THE TWIGGED AISLES; LEAD BABEL TONGUES  ........WREATH F.    45   14
  PEOPLE MAKE QUERIES  .................ELLA MASON AND HER ELEVEN CATS    53    3
  THE THIN PEOPLE  ...................................THE THIN PEOPLE    64    T
  THEY ARE ALWAYS WITH US, THE THIN PEOPLE  ..........THE THIN PEOPLE    64    1
  MEAGER OF DIMENSION AS THE GRAY PEOPLE  .............THE THIN PEOPLE    64    2
  NOW THE THIN PEOPLE DO NOT OBLITERATE  ..............THE THIN PEOPLE    65   32
  IF THE THIN PEOPLE SIMPLY STAND IN THE FOREST,  .....THE THIN PEOPLE    65   45
  TO PEOPLE WHO LIVE IN THE BOTTOM OF VALLEYS  ........ABOVE THE OXBOW    88   15
  COLORED BEADS ON THE STRUNG ROADS, AND THE PEOPLE STROLL  ....OXBOW.    89   51
  TWO PEOPLE ONLY ARE BLIND TO THE CARRION ARMY:  .........TWO VIEWS.    114   13
  THE PEOPLE OF THE CITY HEARD IT.  .........................POEM.7.S.    136   14
  IF THEY MISSED OUT ON WALKING ABOUT LIKE PEOPLE  ..........STILLBORN    142    4
  THESE ROCKS OFFER NO PURCHASE TO HERBAGE OR PEOPLE:  ......TWO CAMP.    145   18
  DEFLECT THE WATERY DAZZLE; THE PEOPLE IDLE  ................WHITSUN    154   11
  AND EVERYWHERE PEOPLE, EYES MICA-SILVER AND BLANK,  ......INSOMNIAC    163   34
  OF PEOPLE THE AIR ONLY  ...........................WUTHERING HEIGHTS    168   33
  ON THE GAMEROOM PIANO, WHEN THE "BIG PEOPLE" WERE OUT,  .......BABY.    175   23
  BLACK LAKE, BLACK BOAT, TWO BLACK, CUT-PAPER PEOPLE.*CROSSING THE W.    190    1
  I FLAKE UP PAPERS THAT BREATHE LIKE PEOPLE,  ...BURNING THE LETTERS    204   37
  WHO ARE THESE PEOPLE AT THE BRIDGE TO MEET ME? THEY ARE THE
    VILLAGERS ---  ...................................THE BEE MEETING    211    1
  STRIPS OF TINFOIL WINKING LIKE PEOPLE,  .............THE BEE MEETING    211   16
  SHH! THESE ARE CHESS PEOPLE YOU PLAY WITH,  .............THE SWARM    216   11
  PEOPLE AND COWS.  .......................................LYONNESSE    234   10
  THESE PEOPLE WITH TORSOS OF STEEL  .......................BRASILIA    258    2
  PEOPLE LIKE LIGHT RAYS, LEAVE  ..........................BRASILIA    259   19
  IN A DESERT OF COW PEOPLE  ...........................EAVESDROPPER    261   41
  PEOPLE OR STARS  ........................................SHEEP IN FOG    262    2
  THESE ARE THE PEOPLE THAT WERE IMPORTANT ---  .................TOTEM    264   16
  TO PEOPLE THE BOUGHS WITH TALKING BIRDS. I'D PLANT  ....DIALOGUE O.    280  169
  MAY TWO REAL PEOPLE BREATHE IN A REAL ROOM.  ..........DIALOGUE O.    286  364
  THE ROSES ARE NAMED AFTER QUEENS AND PEOPLE OF NOTE  ..QUEEN MARY'S.    290   17
  OH, HEAR THE CLASH OF PEOPLE MEETING --  ............FAMILY REUNION    300   11
PEOPLED (1)
  FLIMSILY PEOPLED. BUT LANDOWNERS  .......................LANDOWNERS    53    9
PEOPLES (1)
  WHICH PEOPLES THE BARE ROOM, THE BLANK, UNTENANTED AIR. *NOVEMBER G.    56   18
PERCEIVED (1)
  FATHER SHAWN PERCEIVED A GHOST  ...DIALOGUE BETWEEN GHOST AND PRIEST    38    9
PERCENT (1)
  FROM HER LIPS AMPERSANDS AND PERCENT SIGNS  ...........AN APPEARANCE    189    4
PERCOLATE (1)
  BUT THE SPAWN PERCOLATE IN MY HEART. THEY ARE FERTILE. *WORDS HEARD.    203   13
PERCY (2)
  PERCY BOWS, IN HIS BLUE PEAJACKET, AMONG THE NARCISSI.  ...NARCISSI.    190    2
  IT RATTLES THEIR STARS ON THE GREEN HILL WHERE PERCY  .....NARCISSI.    190    5
PERFECT (5)
  WE DREAMED HOW WE WERE PERFECT, AND WE WERE.  .........THE OTHER TWO    68    7
  THEY ARE CONCEIVING A DYNASTY OF PERFECT COLD.  ...........TWO CAMP.    145   19
  THE FACE THE DEAD ONE THAT COULD ONLY BE PERFECT  .......THREE WOMEN    178   80
  BUT HE IS PINK AND PERFECT. HE SMILES SO FREQUENTLY.  ...THREE WOMEN    186  327
  DEAD AND PERFECT, LIKE NEFERTIT,  .......................THE FEARFUL    256   14
PERFECTED (3)
  FLUNG BRICK PERFECTED HIS LAUGH.  .......................MEDALLION    125   27
  I HAVE PERFECTED IT.  .......................THE SURGEON AT 2 A.M.    171   32
  THE WOMAN IS PERFECTED.  ........................................EDGE    272    1
PERFECTION (1)
  PERFECTION IS TERRIBLE, IT CANNOT HAVE CHILDREN.  ..........MUNICH.    262    1
PERFECTIONS (1)
  THE FACE OF THE UNBORN ONE THAT LOVED ITS PERFECTIONS,  THREE WOMEN    178   79
PERFECTLY (5)
  PERFECTLY VOICELESS,  ....................................MUSHROOMS    139   16
  A PERFECTLY FACETED WIFE TO WAIT  ..........................ON DECK    143   32
  I MUST MOST PERFECTLY RESEMBLE THEM --  .................I AM VERTICAL    162   15
  IT SEEMS PERFECTLY NATURAL NOW ---  .....................DEATH & CO.    254    2
  I WAS PERFECTLY RIGHT: PAN'S A MERE PUPPET  ............DIALOGUE O.    279  106
PERFECTLY-CHISELED (1)
  IN THE MILLION PERFECTLY-CHISELED  ....................LOVE LETTER    147   13
```

373

	TITLE	PAGE	LINE

PERFIDIOUS (1)
    AND WITH A PERFIDIOUS VERVE ....THE BEGGARS   48   20
PERFORM (1)
    PERFORM THEIR SHAMBLING WALTZES ....MUSSEL HUNTER AT ROCK HARBOR   97   86
PERFORMED (1)
    PERFORMED A DUMBSHOW IN THE POLISHED WOOD, ...THE OTHER TWO   68   16
PERFUME (1)
    PERFUME, POLITICS, AND FIXED IDEALS. ....SONNET: TO EVA 305   12
PERFUMED (2)
    SIMMERING, PERFUMED, ...THE RABBIT CATCHER 193   12
    OF PERSONAGE -- SINGLE-SKIRTED, PERFUMED, A GEM -- ...QUEEN MARY'S. 290   24
PERHAPS (9)
    TO KEEP SOME UNSAID PACT; PERHAPS CONCERN ....CHANNEL CROSSING   27   34
    SO, PERHAPS I, KNELLED DUMB BY YOUR ABSENCE, ...STREET SONG   36   24
    THAT NOBLE MIEN, PERHAPS YOU'VE LATE QUITTED HEAVEN?" ..DIALOGUE B.   38   16
    TOWARD THE POOL-MOUTH, PERHAPS TO .....MUSSEL HUNTER AT ROCK HARBOR   96   41
    PERHAPS YOU CONSIDER YOURSELF AN ORACLE, ...THE COLOSSUS   129   6
    PERHAPS IT IS THE SEASON THAT IS NOT RIGHT. *STARS OVER THE DORDOGNE 165   24
    HER RADIANCE SCATHES ME. OR PERHAPS I HAVE CAUGHT HER. ....ELM 192   24
    A GREAT FRIEZE, EGYPTIAN, PERHAPS, OR GREEK, ...DIALOGUE O.   276   9
    OF DAY-OLD BREAD AND EGG-STAINED PLATES; PERHAPS ....METAMORPHOSES. 307   29
PERILOUS (5)
    FAR FROM THE SWEET STENCH OF THAT PERILOUS AIR ....CHANNEL CROSSING   27   13
    HOW PERILOUS NEEDLES GRAIN THE FLOORBOARDS ....MISS DRAKE P.   41   16
    WE POISE ON PERILOUS POLES THAT FREEZE US IN ........METAMORPHOSES. 308   46
    DEFENDING MY PERILOUS WOUNDS WITH A CHAIR ....CIRCUS IN THREE RINGS 322   11
    CAT-CLEVER ON PERILOUS WIRE ....AERIALIST 331   8
PERIOD (1)
    ITS ROUND PERIOD, DISPLACED AND GREEN, ...THE GHOST'S LEAVETAKING   91   29
PERIODIC (1)
    A PERIODIC GOAL. ....TRIO OF LOVE SONGS   314   36
PERIODS (1)
    BLUEBLACK, WITH THE MUCH-POKED PERIODS OF STARS ....INSOMNIAC 163   2
PERIPHERAL (1)
    I SHALL BE A HEROINE OF THE PERIPHERAL. ....THREE WOMEN 182 197
PERISH (1)
    AND SHE'LL PERISH WITH EMPTINESS THEN, AND BEGIN TO MISS ME. ...
                                                    ... IN PLASTER   160   56
PERISHABLE (2)
    THESE TWO MOST PERISHABLE LOVERS FROM THE TOUCH .....EPITAPH FOR F.   45   5
    THEIR PASSING ON A PERISHABLE SCREEN ...DIALOGUE OVER A OUIJA BOARD 282 223
PERIWINKLES (1)
    AND PERIWINKLES, SHRUNK TO COMMON ....GREEN ROCK, WINTHROP BAY   105   13
PERMANENTLY (1)
    EVERY ONE OF THEM PERMANENTLY BUSY. ....A LIFE 150   10
PERPETUAL (1)
    OPEN IN ITS GAPE OF PERPETUAL GRIEVING. ....THREE WOMEN 182 185
PERPETUALLY (1)
    TO UNDO HIM, PERPETUALLY), ...LETTER TO A PURIST   36   6
PERPLEXITIES (1)
    AS HE STOLE OUR PERPLEXITIES ABOUT THE POOLS ....DIALOGUE O.   279 103
PERSEPHONE (1)
    TWO SISTERS OF PERSEPHONE ....TWO SISTERS OF PERSEPHONE   31   T
PERSEUS (2)
    PERSEUS ....PERSEUS   82   T
    PERSEUS, THE PALM, AND MAY YOU POISE ....PERSEUS   84   47
PERSEVERE (1)
    THEY FOUND THEIR TALENT TO PERSEVERE ....THE THIN PEOPLE   64   13
PERSEVERED (1)
    PERSEVERED ON A SET COURSE ....SPIDER   49   30
PERSIST (2)
    THEY PERSIST IN THE SUNLIT ROOM: THE WALLPAPER .....THE THIN PEOPLE   65   36
    OF HALF-HINTS. YOU PERSIST IN SPELLING HALF-HINTS ......DIALOGUE O. 279   98
PERSISTED (1)
    PERSISTED IN THE PICTURE WITH THE LILIES, ...YADWIGHA.   86   22
PERSISTENT (1)
    RAVENING THROUGH THE PERSISTENT BRIC-A-BRAC ....CONJURING.   65   1
PERSON (7)
    THE LONG WIND, PARING HER PERSON DOWN ....HARDCASTLE CRAGS   63   22
    BLUE AND IMPROBABLE PERSON ....THE BURNT-OUT SPA   138   25
    THIS NEW ABSOLUTELY WHITE PERSON AND THE OLD YELLOW ONE, *IN PLASTER 158   2
    AND THE WHITE PERSON IS CERTAINLY THE SUPERIOR ONE. .....IN PLASTER 158   3
    TONIGHT, FOR THIS PERSON, BLUE IS A BEAUTIFUL COLOR. ......SURGEON. 171   43
    A THIRD PERSON IS WATCHING. ....STINGS   215   38
    FIRST, ARE YOU OUR SORT OF A PERSON? ....THE APPLICANT 221   1
PERSONAGE (2)
    NOT EVEN NODDING, A PERSONAGE IN A HEDGEROW. ....THE BEE MEETING 212   41
    OF PERSONAGE -- SINGLE-SKIRTED, PERFUMED, A GEM -- ...QUEEN MARY'S. 290   24
PERSONAL (2)
    THE MOON'S CONCERN IS MORE PERSONAL: ....THREE WOMEN   176   4
    THE WORLD IS BLOOD-HOT AND PERSONAL ....TOTEM   264   22
PERSONALITY (1)
    AT THE BEGINNING I HATED HER, SHE HAD NO PERSONALITY --   IN PLASTER 158   5
PERSPECTIVE (3)
    I MALIGN THE LEADEN PERSPECTIVE ....LANDOWNERS   53   3

	TITLE	PAGE	LINE

PERSPECTIVE (CONT.)
   IN SAFE PERSPECTIVE, COULD OUTFACE THE GORGON-GRIMACE ......PERSEUS   83 14
   "PERSPECTIVE BETRAYS WITH ITS DICHOTOMY: ....LOVE IS A PARALLAX 329   1
PERSPECTIVES (2)
   LORDED PERSPECTIVES. MAPLIKE, THE FAR FIELDS ARE RULED ......OXBOW. 89 48
   OF DIMINISHING PERSPECTIVES, AND ITS SIGNIFICANCE ....INSOMNIAC 163 24
PERSUADED (1)
   PERSUADED BY HIS BRONZE HEROIC REASON. ....GOLD MOUTHS CRY 302   6
PERVERSE (1)
   BUT YET THE PERVERSE IMP WITHIN WILL PROBE*METAMORPHOSES OF THE MOON 308 31
PESTLES (1)
   THE MOTHER OF PESTLES DIMINISHED ME. POEM.7.S. 136   7
PET (1)
   "IS THAT LINGERIE, PET? ....A SECRET 220 28
PETALED (2)
   OF PETALED BLOOD ....TWO SISTERS OF PERSEPHONE   32 18
   NODDED THEIR PETALED HEADS AROUND YOUR COUCH. ....YADWIGHA.   86 30
PETALS (14)
   WHICH ARE SLOWLY OPENING THEIR FURRED PETALS ....MISS DRAKE P.   41 11
   STARS SHOOT THEIR PETALS, AND SUNS RUN TO SEED, ...EPITAPH FOR F.   45 12
   SHE JUDGED PETALS IN DISARRAY, ...SPINSTER   49 11
   THIS PARK IS FLESHED WITH IDIOT PETALS. ....MOONRISE   98   4
   WHITE PETALS, WHITE FAN-TAILS, TEN WHITE FINGERS. ....MOONRISE   98   9
   THE ERSATZ PETALS DRIP, AND THEY DRIP RED. ..ELECTRA ON AZALEA PATH 117 28
   AMONG PETALS PALE AS DEATH ....THE SLEEPERS 123 13
   DOGBODY NOSES THE PETALS. THEY BLOOM UPSIDE DOWN. POEM.1.WHO. 131 11
   ARE THOSE PETALS OR LEAVES YOU'VE PAIRED THEM WITH -- *LEAVING EARLY 146 14
   YOU SNORED, AND I HEARD THE PETALS UNLATCH, ...LEAVING EARLY 146 26
   FORMING ITS TWENTY PETALS. ....HEAVY WOMEN 158 10
   LEAVES AND PETALS ATTEND ME. I AM READY. ....THREE WOMEN 177 14
   SPOTS AND A SPREAD OF HOT PETALS. ....THE NIGHT DANCES 250 14
   THEM BACK INTO HER BODY AS PETALS ....EDGE 273 13
PETALS' (1)
   THE PETALS' NAP MY FINGERTIPS: ..FABLE OF THE RHODODENDRON STEALERS 103 14
PETRIFIED (1)
   BALD EYES OR PETRIFIED EGGS, ...WHITSUN 153   3
PETRIFIES (1)
   IT PETRIFIES THE WILL. THESE ARE THE ISOLATE, SLOW FAULTS ......ELM 193 41
PETRIFY (1)
   TO PETRIFY YOUR EYES, AND EVERY VILLAGE ....PERSEUS   83 21
PETTICOATS (4)
   AND THE PETTICOATS OF THE CHERRY. ....THE ARRIVAL OF THE BEE BOX 213 30
   (MY SELVES DISSOLVING, OLD WHORE PETTICOATS)--- ....FEVER. 232 53
   I ENJOY PETTICOATS AND VELVETS AND GOSSIP OF COURT, ..QUEEN MARY'S. 290 21
   AND OLD MAIDS ON IMPROMPTU PETTICOATS FLY ....SONG FOR A REVOLU. 323 15
PETTISHLY (1)
   SHE ADDED PETTISHLY, "I CAN'T SEE WHY ....BITTER STRAWBERRIES 300 25
PETTY (2)
   OR PETTY THIEVERY BY LARGE. ..........................RHODODENDRON. 104 28
   WINDING AND TWINING THEIR PETTY FETTERS, ...GULLIVER 251 13
PETULANT (1)
   LIKE PETULANT PARAKEETS CORKED UP IN CAGES .....MORNING IN THE HOS. 332 19
PEWS (1)
   FLOATING ON THEIR DELICATE FEET OVER THE COLD PEWS, ...MOON. 173 25
PEWTER (2)
   OLD PEWTER ROOTS TWIST ....DARK WOOD, DARK WATER 127 15
   OF WHITE AND PEWTER LIGHTS, AND A DIN LIKE SILVERSMITHS ..BLACKBER. 169 26
PHANTOM (3)
   "FOND PHANTOM," CRIED SHOCKED FATHER SHAWN, ...DIALOGUE B.   39 41
   SLAPPING ITS PHANTOM LAUNDRY IN MY FACE. .............BLACKBERRYING 169 21
   SHEER SILVER BLURS THEIR PHANTOM ACT. ....DANSE MACABRE 321 21
PHARAOH (1)
   WEARS THE FACE OF A PHARAOH, THOUGH IT'S MADE OF MUD AND WATER. ...
   ... IN PLASTER 159 42
PHEASANT (3)
   THE PHEASANT STANDS ON THE HILL; ....THREE WOMEN 176 11
   PHEASANT ....PHEASANT 191   T
   IT IS SOMETHING TO OWN A PHEASANT, ...PHEASANT 191   5
PHEDRE (1)
   THE RED, ROYAL ROBES OF PHEDRE? THE TEAR-DAZZLED ....PERSEUS   83 41
PHENOMENON (1)
   BECAUSE OF SOME EXPLICABLE PHENOMENON ....APRIL 18 301   4
PHILANTHROPICAL (1)
   A PACK OF PHILANTHROPICAL FOOLS ....DIALOGUE EN ROUTE 308 11
PHILODENDRON (1)
   FLARING GREEN THROUGH PHILODENDRON LEAVES ......MORNING IN THE HOS. 332   2
PHILOSOPHER (1)
   BORED HIM. HE'S MORE PHILOSOPHER, IT SEEMS, ...DIALOGUE O. 277 43
PHILOSOPHY (1)
   PURE PHILOSOPHY HIS LOVE ENGROSSED: ....NATURAL HISTORY   71   4
PHOENIX (3)
   AS IF TO OUTFLAME A PHOENIX, THE MOMENT'S SPUR ......EPITAPH FOR F.   46 24
   INDOORS, TIFFANY'S PHOENIX RISES ....YADDO: THE GRAND MANOR 123 13
   CYCLING PHOENIX NEVER STOPS. ....LOVE IS A PARALLAX 330 66

		TITLE	PAGE	LINE

PHONE (2)
WORDS HEARD, BY ACCIDENT, OVER THE PHONE ....WORDS HEARD. 202 T
O GOD, HOW SHALL I EVER CLEAN THE PHONE TABLE? ....WORDS HEARD. 202 8
PHONES (1)
AND THE BLACK PHONES ON HOOKS ....THE MUNICH MANNEQUINS 263 24
PHOSPHORESCENCE (1)
AN ENVIOUS PHOSPHORESCENCE IN THEIR WINGS ....OUIJA 77 5
PHOSPHORUS (1)
THERE IS ONLY THE MOON, EMBALMED IN PHOSPHORUS. ......THE DETECTIVE 209 39
PHOTO (1)
MY HUSBAND AND CHILD SMILING OUT OF THE FAMILY PHOTO; ....TULIPS 160 20
PHOTOGRAPH (3)
STOPPED AND AWFUL AS A PHOTOGRAPH OF SOMEBODY LAUGHING, ...BABY. 175 35
HE TELLS ME HOW BADLY I PHOTOGRAPH. ....DEATH & CO. 254 12
AND TURN GOD'S RADIANT PHOTOGRAPH TO SHADE. ....SONNET TO SATAN 323 8
PHOTOGRAPHIC (1)
THE PHOTOGRAPHIC CHAMBER OF THE EYE ....TALE OF A TUB 24 1
PHOTOGRAPHS (3)
THESE ARE THE DECEITS, TACKED UP LIKE FAMILY PHOTOGRAPHS,*DETECTIVE. 208 13
PHOTOGRAPHS VISIT ME --- ....PARALYTIC 266 22
THERE ARE NO FAMILY PHOTOGRAPHS, ...GIGOLO 267 8
PHOTOS (1)
DISTANT AND COLD AS PHOTOS, ...OLD LADIES' HOME 120 11
PHRASE (1)
PLUNGES FOR A PHRASE ....TRIO OF LOVE SONGS 314 27
PHYSICAL (1)
THAN PHYSICAL ABLUTION, AND THE TOWEL ....TALE OF A TUB 24 12
PIANISSIMO (1)
(PIANO, PIANISSIMO) ....ALICANTE LULLABY 43 20
PIANIST (1)
THE EYE OF THE BLIND PIANIST ....LITTLE FUGUE 187 8
PIANO (3)
(PIANO, PIANISSIMO) ....ALICANTE LULLABY 43 20
MOTHER, YOU SENT ME TO PIANO LESSONS ....THE DISQUIETING MUSES 75 33
ON THE GAMEROOM PIANO, WHEN THE "BIG PEOPLE" WERE OUT, ...BABY. 175 23
PICADOR (1)
FACED IN HIS RICH YELLOWS, TASSELS, POMPONS, BRAID, THE PICADOR ...
... THE GORING 47 5
PICK (3)
WOULD PICK STICKS, WOULD NOT REST ....THE EVERLASTING MONDAY 62 8
I PICK AND PRY LIKE A DOCTOR OR ....THE BURNT-OUT SPA 138 14
AND PICK THE WORMS OFF ME LIKE STICKY PEARLS. ....LADY LAZARUS 245 42
PICKED (4)
THEY BRASSILY PICKED, SLOWED BY NO CHAGRIN, ...RHODODENDRON. 104 24
PICKED HIS TRIP-DATE BY THE STARS. ....ON DECK 143 26
WE PICKED UP STICKS OF DRIFTWOOD AND BEAT THEM OFF, *THE BABYSITTERS 175 38
A DOG PICKED UP YOUR DOGGY HUSBAND. HE WENT ON. ....LESBOS 229 63
PICKET (1)
PICKET OF TREES WHOSE SILHOUETTE IS DARKER   STARS OVER THE DORDOGNE 165 2
PICKETS (1)
I HOLD MY FINGERS UP, TEN WHITE PICKETS. ....THREE WOMEN 182 194
PICKING (6)
PICKING AMONG THE DUMB MINERALS, THE ROOTS. ....LAST WORDS 172 5
WE KEPT PICKING UP HANDFULS, LOVING IT, ...LESBOS 229 60
OR PICKING UP THE BRIGHT PIECES ....MYSTIC 269 18
SWEETLY PICKING UP PIECES! ....KINDNESS 269 13
AND WE ALL TURNED BACK TO PICKING. ....BITTER STRAWBERRIES 300 33
SO CRY FOR THE PAGAN GIRL LEFT PICKING OLIVES ......SONNET: TO TIME 311 9
PICKLE (1)
LIKE A SPRAT IN A PICKLE JUG. ....YOU'RE 141 14
PICKLING (1)
THEY SIT SO NICELY IN THE PICKLING FLUID! ....STILLBORN 142 8
PICNIC (1)
AND WE PICNIC IN THE DEATH-STENCH OF A HAWTHORN. ....WHITSUN 154 21
PICTURE (5)
PERSISTED IN THE PICTURE WITH THE LILIES, ...YADWIGHA. 86 22
THE OBSOLETE HOUSE, THE SEA, FLATTENED TO A PICTURE ....A LIFE 150 27
IN YOUR SISTER'S BIRTHDAY PICTURE START TO GLOW. .....PARLIAMENT H. 153 42
IN THE PICTURE I HAVE OF YOU, ...DADDY 223 52
TO PICTURE SOME OTHER PARTY SPEAKING THROUGH ....DIALOGUE O. 280 146
PIE (1)
GOING TO GET GABRIEL'S THUMB INTO THE PIE ....DIALOGUE O. 280 148
PIECE (3)
A SALLOW PIECE OF STRING HELD IT TOGETHER. ....TWO VIEWS. 114 9
MUST YOU STAMP EACH PIECE IN PURPLE, ...A BIRTHDAY PRESENT 207 46
OR A PIECE OF MY HAIR OR MY CLOTHES. ....LADY LAZARUS 246 64
PIECED (1)
PIECED, GLUED, AND PROPERLY JOINTED. ....THE COLOSSUS 129 2
PIECES (5)
AND MY SKIN ITCHED AND FLAKED AWAY IN SOFT PIECES ....IN PLASTER 159 33
NOW I BREAK UP IN PIECES THAT FLY ABOUT LIKE CLUBS. ....ELM 192 19
THE SNOW DROPS ITS PIECES OF DARKNESS, ...THE MUNICH MANNEQUINS 263 16
OR PICKING UP THE BRIGHT PIECES ....MYSTIC 269 18
SWEETLY PICKING UP PIECES! ....KINDNESS 269 13

```
                                                  TITLE           PAGE  LINE
PIE-IN-THE-SKY (1)
   IS JOKING AT THE PIE-IN-THE-SKY MIRAGE    DIALOGUE OVER A OUIJA BOARD  282  211
PIER (2)
   BARGE-TAR CLOTTED AT THE TIDE-LINE, THE WRECKED PIER  ...GREEN ROCK.  104    2
   THE PIER PILINGS SEEM ABOUT TO COLLAPSE  ..............A WINTER SHIP  113   15
PIERCE (2)
   BY S. S. PIERCE, BY S. S. PIERCE,  ...................A WINTER'S TALE   87   13
   BY S. S. PIERCE, BY S. S. PIERCE,  ...................A WINTER'S TALE   87   13
PIERCED (3)
   HEARTS OF THOSE WHO PIERCED TIME'S CORE.  ..............CRYSTAL GAZER   55   42
   PIERCED MY DENSE LID.  .....................ON THE PLETHORA OF DRYADS   67   24
   THE THINGS IT HAS PIERCED IN ITS TIME.  ..THE COURAGE OF SHUTTING-UP  210   25
PIES (1)
   FOR PIES. THE FIR TREE'S THICK WITH GRACKLES.*YADDO: THE GRAND MANOR  123    7
PIETAS (3)
   THE DYING GAUL AND THOSE INNUMERABLE PIETAS  .................PERSEUS   82    9
   OF BEING WHEELED OFF UNDER CROSSES AND A RAIN OF PIETAS.  ...
                                               ...  APPREHENSIONS  195   15
   WHO ARE THESE PIETAS?  .................................WINTER TREES  258   14
PIG (5)
   PRIZE RIBBON AND PIG SHOW.  .........................................SOW   60    6
   FOR THRIFTY CHILDREN, NOR DOLT PIG RIPE FOR HECKLING,  ..........SOW   60   13
   PIG HOVE, LETTING LEGEND LIKE DRIED MUD DROP,  ..................SOW   61   37
   THE SMUG CENTURIES OF THE PIG --  ..................THE MANOR GARDEN  125    6
   OBSCENE AND BALD AS A PIG, THE WHITE MICE  ........ZOO KEEPER'S WIFE  155   21
PIGEON (2)
   A PIGEON RUDDERS DOWN. ITS FAN-TAIL'S WHITE.  .............MOONRISE   98    7
   REAP THE ROUND BLUE PIGEON FROM ROOF RIDGE, *GO GET THE GOODLY SQUAB  313    3
PIGEONS (4)
   FROST-BITTEN PIGEONS, EDDY FORTH  ...................A WINTER'S TALE   87   34
   THEY MAY BE WHITE AND SHY, THEY ARE NO STOOL PIGEONS,  ....COURAGE.  210   31
   WHERE ON PINK-FLUTED FEET THE PIGEONS PASS  ...........APRIL AUBADE  312   10
   WHERE PIGEONS PROMENADE THE GABLE-ENDS *THE PRINCESS AND THE GOBLINS  335   66
PIGGERIES (1)
   WITH ITS TRIM PIGGERIES,  .............................MAN IN BLACK  119    8
PIG-GRUNT (1)
   MULE-BRAY, PIG-GRUNT AND BAWDY CACKLES  .................THE COLOSSUS  129    3
PIGGY (1)
   THOUGH THEY HAVE A PIGGY AND A FISHY AIR --  .............STILLBORN  142   12
PIGMENT (1)
   COLORED TO DULL THE PIGMENT  ....................CHILD'S PARK STONES  101   16
PIGMY (1)
   INCHED FROM THEIR PIGMY BURROWS  .......MUSSEL HUNTER AT ROCK HARBOR   96   29
PIGS (3)
   THEY ARE NOT PIGS, THEY ARE NOT EVEN FISH,  ..............STILLBORN  142   11
   ON THE INFERNO OF AFRICAN ORANGES, THE HEEL-HUNG PIGS.  THREE WOMEN  184  283
   DAWN GILDS THE FARMERS LIKE PIGS,  ..........................TOTEM  264    5
PIG'S (1)
   AND A SKY LIKE A PIG'S BACKSIDE, AN UTTER LACK OF ATTENTION.  ...
                                               ...  FOR A FATHERLESS SON  205    5
PIKE (1)
   RODE OUT AGAINST THE FIFTH BULL TO BRACE HIS PIKE AND SLOWLY BEAR  ...
                                               ...  THE GORING   47    6
PILE (1)
   AT HIS HEELS A PILE OF FIVE BRASS CANNONBALLS,  ......BY CANDLELIGHT  237   33
PILED (1)
   LEGS, ARMS PILED OUTSIDE  ...........................GETTING THERE  248   26
PILGRIM (2)
   OF THE HOMELAND HEARTH TO PLOUGH THEIR PILGRIM WAY  .......MAYFLOWER   60   10
   LITTLE PILGRIM,  ...................................................CUT  235    9
PILGRIMAGE (1)
   ON MY BLACK PILGRIMAGE  .............................RECANTATION   41    5
PILGRIMAGES (1)
   SCATHED, STAINED AFTER TEDIOUS PILGRIMAGES.  ..........DREAM WITH C.   43    4
PILGRIMS (2)
   THE EIGHT PILGRIMS TOWARDS ITS SOURCE --  .......THE GREAT CARBUNCLE   72   10
   THE PILGRIMS AND INDIANS MIGHT NEVER HAVE HAPPENED.  ......TWO CAMP.  145   22
PILING (1)
   IN THE MARKETPLACE THEY ARE PILING THE DRY STICKS.  .......POEM.6.W.  135    1
PILINGS (1)
   THE PIER PILINGS SEEM ABOUT TO COLLAPSE  ..............A WINTER SHIP  113   15
PILL (4)
   IT HAS SHUT ITS MOUTH ON THE STONE PILL OF REPOSE.  .......SURGEON.  171   30
   I'M DOPED AND THICK FROM MY LAST SLEEPING PILL.  ............LESBOS  228   34
   I HAVE TAKEN A PILL TO KILL  ...................................CUT  235   24
   THE PILL OF THE COMMUNION TABLET,  ........................MYSTIC  268   16
PILLAR (3)
   THE SUN RISES UNDER THE PILLAR OF YOUR TONGUE.  ........THE COLOSSUS  130   27
   PILLAR OF WHITE IN A BLACKOUT OF KNIVES.  ...........THE BEE MEETING  212   52
   HEFTING HIS WHITE PILLAR WITH THE LIGHT  ............BY CANDLELIGHT  237   28
PILLARS (3)
   FRACTURED PILLARS FRAME PROSPECTS OF ROCK;  ..........CONVERSATION.   21    9
   REPORT WHITE PILLARS, A BLUE SKY,  .........TWO VIEWS OF WITHENS   72   17
   MUSEUM WITHOUT STATUES, GRAND WITH PILLARS, PORTICOES,
        ROTUNDAS.  .......................................BARREN WOMAN  157    2
```

377

PILLBOX (1)
MY PATENT LEATHER OVERNIGHT CASE LIKE A BLACK PILLBOX, ...TULIPS   160   19
PILLOW (8)
MY HEAD ON THE PILLOW ....ALICANTE LULLABY   43   19
IT SPRANG FROM HER PILLOW ....POLLY'S TREE   129   34
TAPPED LIKE A CASK, THE YEARS DRAINING INTO MY PILLOW. ...FACE LIFT   156   18
THEY HAVE PROPPED MY HEAD BETWEEN THE PILLOW AND THE SHEET-CUFF ...
     ... TULIPS   160   8
HE SUFFERS HIS DESERT PILLOW, SLEEPLESSNESS ....INSOMNIAC   163   6
TILL YOUR HEAD IS A STONE, YOUR PILLOW A LITTLE TURF, ...ELM   192   11
THE PILLOW CASES ARE SWEETENING. ....BERCK-PLAGE   198   68
HUGGING HIS PILLOW ....AMNESIAC   233   12
PILLOWS (1)
VELVET PILLOWS THE COLOUR OF BLOOD PUDDING ....LEAVING EARLY   145   5
PILLS (3)
HE IS IMMUNE TO PILLS: RED, PURPLE, BLUE -- ....INSOMNIAC   163   15
NOW THE PILLS ARE WORN-OUT AND SILLY, LIKE CLASSICAL GODS.*INSOMNIAC   163   20
HERALD DISTRACTION: A FLOCK OF PASTEL PILLS, ...MORNING IN THE HOS.   332   13
PILOT (1)
WITH THE PILOT WHO DARES ALL HEAVEN'S HARMS .........METAMORPHOSES.   307   2
PIN (3)
BEFORE THE DISTANCES THEY PIN EVAPORATE, ...WUTHERING HEIGHTS   167   6
OF ONE WINE-GLASS, YOU'LL PIN IT LIKE A PRIZE ....DIALOGUE O.   283 249
WITH FINGER BANDAGED WHERE THE WASPISH PIN ....THE PRINCESS.   333   7
PINCERS (1)
HEATING THE PINCERS, HOISTING THE DELICATE HAMMERS. POEM.7.S.   137   28
PINCH (1)
TO A PINCH OF FLAME, BLEW ITS BURDENED WHISTLE ....HARDCASTLE CRAGS   63   23
PINCKNEY (1)
ON PINCKNEY, MOUNT VERNON, CHESTNUT, ...A WINTER'S TALE   87   25
PINE (5)
AS RESIN DROPS OOZED FROM PINE BARK. ....THE BURNT-OUT SPA   137   5
SEVENTY FEET UP, IN A BLACK PINE TREE. ....THE SWARM   216   18
AN IVORY PALACE, A CROTCH PINE. ....THE SWARM   217   50
BLACK PINE TREE IN AN ORANGE LIGHT ....BLACK PINE TREE.   328   T
THE PINE TREE LIKE A RORSCHACH-BLOT ....BLACK PINE TREE.   328   2
PINEAPPLE (1)
WE LIFTED A SUGARED HAM AND A PINEAPPLE FROM THE GROWNUPS' ICEBOX ...
     ... THE BABYSITTERS   175   30
PINEAPPLE-BARKED (1)
PINEAPPLE-BARKED, ...SOUTHERN SUNRISE   26   9
PINE-NEEDLE (1)
PINE-NEEDLE ARMOR PROTECTS ....VIRGIN IN A TREE   81   16
PINES (4)
IN SUNLESS AIR, UNDER PINES ....CHILD'S PARK STONES   100   1
THE PINES BLOT OUR VOICES UP IN THEIR LIGHTEST SIGHS. ....TWO CAMP.   145   24
THEY ARE EATEN IMMEDIATELY BY THE PINES. ...STARS OVER THE DORDOGNE   165   8
IN THE FETID WOMBS OF BLACK AIR UNDER PINES IN SUMMER. ......MYSTIC   268   5
PING (1)
IT WILL PING LIKE A CHINESE CHIME IN THE SLIGHTEST AIR STIR   A LIFE   150   7
PINHEAD (1)
MULTIPLIED TO INFINITY LIKE ANGELS ON A PINHEAD ..ZOO KEEPER'S WIFE   155   22
PINK (28)
TO HALT FOR A SWIG AT THE PINK TEATS. NO. THIS VAST ....SOW   61   23
IN PINK AND LAVENDER ....BATTLE-SCENE   84   3
IN HIS PINK PLUME AND ARMOR. ....BATTLE-SCENE   84   10
OF CERISE AND PINK FROM THE RHODODENDRON, ...RHODODENDRON.   104   22
PURPLES THE FIG IN THE LEAF'S SHADOW, TURNS THE DUST PINK. ...NET-.   121   7
A WORKMAN WALKS BY CARRYING A PINK TORSO. POEM.7.S.   137   31
ONE CHILD DROPS A BARRETTE OF PINK PLASTIC;   PARLIAMENT HILL FIELDS   152   16
SHOULD I STIR, I THINK THIS PINK AND PURPLE PLASTIC ....ZOO K.   154   11
PINK AND SMOOTH AS A BABY. ....FACE LIFT   156   32
FLICKERS AMONG THE FLAT PINK ROSES. I WAKE TO LISTEN: MORNING SONG   157   11
HER MARBLE SKIRTS BLOWN BACK IN TWO PINK WINGS. ....FINISTERRE   169   20
TOMORROW THE PATIENT WILL HAVE A CLEAN, PINK PLASTIC LIMB. *SURGEON.   171   40
IT IS PINK, WITH SPECKLES. I HAVE LOOKED AT IT SO LONG ......MIRROR   173   7
I REMEMBER YOU PLAYING "JA DA" IN A PINK PIQUE DRESS*THE BABYSITTERS   175   22
THEIR SKIN TINTS ARE PINK OR SALLOW, BROWN OR RED; .....THREE WOMEN   183 223
BUT HE IS PINK AND PERFECT. HE SMILES SO FREQUENTLY. ...THREE WOMEN   186 327
THE LINE PINK AND QUIET, A WORM, BASKING.*THE COURAGE OF SHUTTING-UP   209   2
WHITE WITH PINK FLOWERS ON IT, ...STINGS   214   9
THE GILT AND PINK DOMES OF RUSSIA MELT AND FLOAT OFF .....THE SWARM   216   15
PRETENDING I AM A NEGRESS WITH PINK PAWS. ....THE JAILER   226   19
BY WHATEVER THESE PINK THINGS MEAN. ....FEVER.   232   50
OF PINK FIZZ. ....CUT   235   16
SHE'S PINK, SHE'S A BORN MIDWIFE -- ....THE TOUR   238   45
WARM AND HUMAN, THEN THEIR PINK LIGHT ....THE NIGHT DANCES   250   19
A FUNNY PINK WORLD HE MIGHT EAT ON THE OTHER SIDE OF IT, ..BALLOONS   272   24
THERE, THAT'S THE PINK, PLEASED SQUEAK ....FAMILY REUNION   300   16
MULTIPLY PINK HARLEQUINS AND SING ....LOVE IS A PARALLAX   330   46
OF PINK AND BEIGE, IMPECCABLE BAMBOO, ...MORNING IN THE HOS.   332   4
PINK-BREASTED (1)
PRIM, PINK-BREASTED, FEMININE, SHE NURSES ....FEMALE AUTHOR   301   5
PINK-BUTTOCKED (1)
PINK-BUTTOCKED INFANTS ATTEND THEM. ....HEAVY WOMEN   158   15

	TITLE	PAGE	LINE

PINK-FLUTED (1)
  WHERE ON PINK-FLUTED FEET THE PIGEONS PASS ....APRIL AUBADE 312 10
PINKNESS (1)
  WITH PINKNESS, AS IF A TENDERNESS AWOKE, ...THREE WOMEN 186 356
PINK-PULPED (1)
  PINK-PULPED WHOPPERS, ...FIESTA MELONS   46 12
PINKY-PURPLE (1)
  TOWARD THREE PINKY-PURPLE ....BATTLE-SCENE   84 15
PINLEGS (1)
  TWO PINLEGS STAGGER UNDERNEATH THE MASS. ....THE RAVAGED FACE 115   5
PIN-LEGS (1)
  THE ORACULAR GHOST WHO DWINDLES ON PIN-LEGS *THE GHOST'S LEAVETAKING 90   9
PINNACLES (2)
  ONE WHITE HORSE DROWNED, AND ALL THE UNCONQUERED PINNACLES LESSON.   80   9
  WHILE CHAPEL PINNACLES OVER THE ROOFS, ...THE EYE-MOTE 109   5
PINNED (2)
  A VULTUROUS BOREDOM PINNED ME IN THIS TREE. ....THE HANGING MAN 142   5
  MAY BE PINNED ANY MINUTE, ANESTHETIZED. ....KINDNESS 269 15
PINS (2)
  THIN AS PINS IN THE DARK BRUISE ....MEDALLION 125 22
  STINGS BIG AS DRAWING PINS! ....THE SWARM 217 56
PIN-STITCHED (1)
  BUT AT THE PRICE OF A PIN-STITCHED SKIN ....MAUDLIN   51   7
PIPE (5)
  FROM HIS THIN PIPE. OUT OF THIS GREEN NEST ............SNAKECHARMER   79 18
  PUTS UP HIS PIPE, AND LIDS HIS MOONY EYE. .............SNAKECHARMER   79 28
  A BODY INTO A PIPE, AND THE SMOKE RISING. ....THE DETECTIVE 208 11
  APRIL SNOWDROP, INDIAN PIPE, ...CHILD 265   5
  MINOR IMPS PIPE UP, SO LONG AS EACH ....DIALOGUE OVER A OUIJA BOARD 280 152
PIPED (1)
  ONLY THE MOUTH-HOLE PIPED OUT, ...POEM.7.S. 136 11
PIPER (2)
  CONSUME THIS PIPER AND HE TIRES OF MUSIC ..............SNAKECHARMER   79 22
  TO PAY THE PIPER WITH EACH BREATH, YET LOVE ....LOVE IS A PARALLAX 331 76
PIPES (9)
  WITH MOON-EYE, MOUTH-PIPE. HE PIPES. PIPES GREEN. PIPES WATER. ...
                                             ... SNAKECHARMER   79   3
  WITH MOON-EYE, MOUTH-PIPE. HE PIPES. PIPES GREEN. PIPES WATER. ...
                                             ... SNAKECHARMER   79   3
  WITH MOON-EYE, MOUTH-PIPE. HE PIPES. PIPES GREEN. PIPES WATER. ...
                                             ... SNAKECHARMER   79   3
  PIPES WATER GREEN UNTIL GREEN WATERS WAVER ...........SNAKECHARMER   79   4
  HE PIPES A PLACE TO STAND ON, BUT NO ROCKS, ...SNAKECHARMER   79   8
  SUPPORTS HIS FOOT. HE PIPES A WORLD OF SNAKES, ...SNAKECHARMER   79 10
  AND PIPES THE WORLD BACK TO THE SIMPLE FABRIC ........SNAKECHARMER   79 23
  OF SNAKE-WARP, SNAKE-WEFT. PIPES THE CLOTH OF SNAKES ..SNAKECHARMER   79 24
  THE COILS AND PIPES THAT MADE HIM RUN. ....THE BURNT-OUT SPA 138 17
PIPING (1)
  THE INTRICATE, BLUE PIPING UNDER THIS PALE MARBLE. ....SURGEON. 171 26
PIPS (1)
  HALFWAY DOWN FROM GROVES WHERE THE THIN, BITTER ALMOND PIPS ..NET-. 121   2
PIQUE (1)
  I REMEMBER YOU PLAYING "JA DA" IN A PINK PIQUE DRESS*THE BABYSITTERS 175 22
PIRANHA (1)
  A PIRANHA ....NICK AND THE CANDLESTICK 241 17
PISTON (1)
  THE PISTON IN MOTION --- ....YEARS 255 12
PISTONS (2)
  PUMPED AHEAD BY THESE PISTONS, THIS BLOOD ....GETTING THERE 248 30
  IN BLUE DISTANCE THE PISTONS HISS. ....YEARS 256 25
PIT (2)
  NO PIT OF SHADOW TO CRAWL INTO, ...SUICIDE OFF EGG ROCK 115   7
  IN A PIT OF ROCK ....CONTUSION 271   4
PITCH (4)
  ABOVE PITCH OF PEDESTRIAN EAR, ...STREET SONG   36 23
  UNRULY ENOUGH TO PITCH HER FIVE QUEENLY WITS ....SPINSTER   50 20
  I NEVER KNEW SUCH CREDULITY TO PITCH ...DIALOGUE OVER A OUIJA BOARD 280 154
  TO PITCH THE WHITE WORLD DOWN IN SWIVELING FLOOD, ..SONNET TO SATAN 323   6
PITCHED (3)
  THEY PITCHED THEIR COATS, COME TO GREEN BED. ....BUCOLICS   23   8
  ON THE PITCHED REEFS OF NIGHTMARE, ...LORELEI   94 24
  DEEPER WITHIN THE DARK, AND AS I PITCHED FURTHER ....DIALOGUE O. 285 317
PITCHER (2)
  EVERY DAY YOU FILL HIM WITH SOUL-STUFF, LIKE A PITCHER. .....LESBOS 229 77
  PITCHER OF MILK, NOW EMPTY. ....EDGE 272 11
PITCHERS (1)
  PITCHERS AND CORONATION GOBLETS ....LEAVING EARLY 145   9
PITCHFORK (1)
  NOW WITH STAKE AND PITCHFORK THEY ADVANCE, FLINT EYES FIXED
           ON MURDER. .... DREAM WITH CLAM-DIGGERS   44 28
PITCHFORKED (1)
  "NO PITCHFORKED FARMER, PLEASE," SHE SAID; ....BUCOLICS   23   5
PITCHING (1)
  HIS NEAT TROT PITCHING MY TENSE POISE UP, ...WHITENESS I REMEMBER 102 14

```
                                                    TITLE          PAGE  LINE
PITH (1)
   WON HER THE FROG-COLORED SKIN, PALE PITH AND WATERY*VIRGIN IN A TREE    81   14
PITHLESS (2)
   AMONG THE PITHLESS REEDS. FLIES FAIL US. ...........FROG AUTUMN    99    7
   WITHER LIKE PITHLESS HANDS. THERE IS LITTLE SHELTER. .....POEM.5.F.  134    4
PITHY (1)
   YOU ARE PITHY AND HISTORICAL AS THE ROMAN FORUM. ......THE COLOSSUS  129   18
PITIABLE (1)
   ONE, BY HIMSELF, SEEMED PITIABLE ENOUGH, ................BLUE MOLES  126    5
PITIFUL (1)
   FLICKERING AND POURING, A PITIFUL CANDLE. ..............BERCK-PLAGE  199   80
PITS (1)
   THE NOSE, THE EYE PITS, THE FULL SET OF TEETH? ........LADY LAZARUS  244   13
PITY (2)
   TILL HE SOME PITY TOOK UPON HER CRYING;  ......THE QUEEN'S COMPLAINT   28   12
   ON THE COINS OF PITY. AT RANDOM  .......................THE BEGGARS   47    9
PITYING (1)
   BAFFLE THE DARK, THE PITYING EYE.  .....................THE BEGGARS   48   21
PITYS (1)
   PITYS FROM PAN'S ASSAULT! AND THOUGH AGE DROP  .....VIRGIN IN A TREE   81   17
PIVOT (2)
   PIVOT OF HEELS AND KNEES! -- THE FURROW  ....................ARIEL   239    6
   ONE HOLLOW THE WHOLE SEA'S PIVOT.  .......................CONTUSION  271    6
PIZZICATO (1)
   A TINSEL PIZZICATO ON FISH FIN  ..................MIDSUMMER MOBILE  324    8
PLACARD (1)
   THE SAME PLACARD OF BLUE FOG IS WHEELED INTO POSITION  ...THE JAILER  226    2
PLACATE (1)
   SUCH SOPHISTRY CAN PLACATE US.  ..........METAMORPHOSES OF THE MOON  307   30
PLACE (35)
   GROW GREEN AGAIN? WHO'D WALK IN THIS BLEAK PLACE? *WINTER LANDSCAPE,   22   15
   TWO OF US IN A PLACE MEANT FOR TEN MORE --  ...........THE OTHER TWO   68   10
   NIGHTLY WE LEFT THEM IN THEIR DESERT PLACE.  ..........THE OTHER TWO   68   27
   NO PLACE, IT SEEMED, FOR THE EFFIGY TO FARE  ............LADY AND T.   69    8
   HE PIPES A PLACE TO STAND ON, BUT NO ROCKS,  ...........SNAKECHARMER   79    8
   ON WINTER STREET, ON TEMPLE PLACE. ...................A WINTER'S TALE   87   17
   THEY CALLED THE PLACE LOOKOUT FARM. BACK THEN, THE SUN ...
                        ... MEMOIRS OF A SPINACH-PICKER   89    1
   OF PLACE, TIME, AND THEIR BODIES. ........................SCULPTOR   92   19
   PUT UP WITH UNTIL CHAGRIN GIVES PLACE  .......THE COMPANIONABLE ILLS  105    3
   A PLACE, A TIME GONE OUT OF MIND. ....................THE EYE-MOTE  109   30
   EVERYTHING TOOK PLACE IN A DURABLE WHITENESS.*ELECTRA ON AZALEA PATH  117   14
   AN OLD BEAST ENDED IN THIS PLACE: ...............THE BURNT-OUT SPA  137    1
   THE TREES STIFFEN INTO PLACE LIKE BURNT NERVES. ...WAKING IN WINTER  151    3
   TOOK ITS PLACE AMONG THE ELEMENTS. ....................MORNING SONG  156    3
   HOLDING MY BONES IN PLACE SO THEY WOULD MEND PROPERLY. ..IN PLASTER  159   27
   THE TULIPS ARE TOO RED IN THE FIRST PLACE, THEY HURT ME. ....TULIPS  161   36
   A SENSE OF ABSENCE IN ITS OLD SHINING PLACE.*STARS OVER THE DORDOGNE  166   33
   BUT FROM ANOTHER PLACE, TROPICAL AND BLUE, ............FINISTERRE  170   34
   FUMY, SPIRITOUS MISTS INHABIT THIS PLACE  THE MOON AND THE YEW TREE  172    5
   IT IS A PLACE OF SHRIEKS. IT IS NOT HAPPY. .........THREE WOMEN  180  122
   THAT RIVET IN PLACE ABYSS AFTER ABYSS. .................THREE WOMEN  182  203
   IT WAS A PLACE OF FORCE -- ....................THE RABBIT CATCHER  193    1
   THERE WAS ONLY ONE PLACE TO GET TO. .............THE RABBIT CATCHER  193   11
   IT IS SO BEAUTIFUL UP HERE: IT IS A STOPPING PLACE. ....BERCK-PLAGE  199   90
   IN A STILL PLACE, AND THE GROOM IS RED AND FORGETFUL, HE IS
                         FEATURELESS. .......................BERCK-PLAGE  200  108
   AND AT LEAST IT WILL BE A GOOD PLACE NOW, THE ATTIC. ......BURNING.  204   22
   IS IT SOME OPERATION THAT IS TAKING PLACE? .........THE BEE MEETING  211   26
   THE CARS IN THE PLACE DE LA CONCORDE -- ...................A SECRET  220   38
   NOT A PATCH ON YOUR PLACE, I GUESS, WITH THE JAVANESE .....THE TOUR  237    9
   TO THE SAME PLACE, THE SAME FACE, THE SAME BRUTE ......LADY LAZARUS  246   53
   THE PLACE I AM GETTING TO, WHY ARE THERE THESE OBSTACLES ---
                        ... GETTING THERE  249   45
   IS THERE NO STILL PLACE  .............................GETTING THERE  249   52
   THE LETTERS LIVE IN THE SAME PLACE. OR ELSE  ...........DIALOGUE O.  277   23
   I TRY TO THINK OF A PLACE TO HIDE YOU  .................THE RIVAL/DR  291    8
   DEMANDING SATISFACTION; NO DUEL TAKES PLACE:  ........METAMORPHOSES.  307    5
PLACENTA (1)
   FAT AND RED, A PLACENTA  ........................................MEDUSA  225   25
PLACES (3)
   INTO THE BLUE. TOPS DEFINE THEMSELVES AS PLACES  ....ABOVE THE OXBOW   88   29
   THE SAME PLACES... ...................................LYONNESSE  234   14
   OF PLACES: THE OIL WELL MY UNCLE OWNS, FOR ONE;  ........DIALOGUE O.  277   47
PLAGUE (1)
   SPRUNG UP LIKE PLAGUE OF TOADSTOOLS OVERNIGHT:  ............TERMINAL  328    4
PLAGUE-PITTED (1)
   PLAGUE-PITTED AS THE MOON: EACH BUD  ..................CRYSTAL GAZER   56   44
PLAGUEY (1)
   LAUGH DOES AWAY WITH THE UNSTITCHING, PLAGUEY WOUNDS  .......PERSEUS   83   45
PLAIN (2)
   THE FEW I AM USED TO ARE PLAIN AND DURABLE; *STARS OVER THE DORDOGNE  166   28
   I DO NOT WANT A PLAIN BOX, I WANT A SARCOPHAGUS  .........LAST WORDS  172    1
PLAINLY (1)
   YOU INHABIT. PLAINLY AS YOU CAN,  .......DIALOGUE OVER A OUIJA BOARD  283  273
```

PLAINTIFF (1)
   AND, PLAINTIFF AGAINST EACH DAY, DECRY ....THE BEGGARS   47   4
PLAN (4)
   AND OUTWIT THEIR BRAMBLED PLAN; ......MISS DRAKE PROCEEDS TO SUPPER 41   17
   THEIR MAGNIFIED HEADS AND PLAN TO KILL ME AS SOON AS POSSIBLE. ...
                                              ... THE RIVAL/DR   291   3
   SO IF YOU CAN DREAM UP ANY SAVING PLAN ....THE DISPOSSESSED 318   2
   AND STUNG ACCORDING TO THE WITCH'S PLAN, ...THE PRINCESS. 333   9
PLANE (1)
   FLINGS SILVER GAUNLET OF HIS PLANE AT SPACE, ...METAMORPHOSES. 307   4
PLANES (1)
   IN THE TRAFFIC OF PLANES ....GREEN ROCK, WINTHROP BAY   105   15
PLANET (4)
   LIKE A PLANET, A STONE, SWALLOWED IN A GREAT DARKNESS,*THE OTHER TWO 68   25
   BUT THE LITTLE PLANET BOBBED AWAY ....THE DISQUIETING MUSES   76   46
   AGE, ANOTHER PLANET SURELY. FLANKED ....CHILD'S PARK STONES 101   8
   YET INDIVIDUAL PLANET ....TRIO OF LOVE SONGS 313   3
PLANETARY (2)
   THIS IS THE LIGHT OF THE MIND, COLD AND PLANETARY. ....MOON. 172   1
   A PLANETARY SWOON ....TRIO OF LOVE SONGS 314   31
PLANETS (6)
   HORSES, PLANETS AND SPIRES REVOLVE. ....THE EYE-MOTE 109   18
   PLANETS PULSE IN THE LAKE LIKE BRIGHT AMOEBAS; ....TWO CAMP.   145   23
   THOSE SUGARY PLANETS WHOSE INFLUENCE WON FOR HIM ....INSOMNIAC 163   17
   THEY ARE SCRUBBED AND SELF-ASSURED AS THE GREAT PLANETS ....STARS.   165   16
   THESE LAMPS, THESE PLANETS ....THE NIGHT DANCES   250   23
   AND PLANETS PLOT WITH OLD ELLIPTIC CUNNING; .....TO EVA DESCENDING. 303   5
PLANET'S (1)
   O MAKER OF PROUD PLANET'S NEGATIVE, ...SONNET TO SATAN 323   13
PLANET-SHINE (1)
   SUSPENDED ALOFT WITHIN HER PLANET-SHINE. ....THE PRINCESS. 335   63
PLANK (2)
   SURVIVES ARRIVAL; WE WALK THE PLANK WITH STRANGERS.*SOUTHERN SUNRISE 27   42
   WALKING THE PLANK DRAPED WITH MOTHER FRANCE'S UPHOLSTERY THE SWARM 217   48
PLANKED-UP (1)
   THE PLANKED-UP WINDOWS WHERE SHE SET ....POINT SHIRLEY 110   26
PLANNING (1)
   IS ON YOU NOW, FOR PLANNING TO DREDGE UP*DIALOGUE OVER A OUIJA BOARD 282   239
PLANT (4)
   HE IS TURNING TO ME LIKE A LITTLE, BLIND, BRIGHT PLANT. *THREE WOMEN 183   235
   TO PEOPLE THE BOUGHS WITH TALKING BIRDS. I'D PLANT ....DIALOGUE O.   280   169
   LIGHTING PLANT OF THE UNIVERSE. ....THE DREAM   311   18
   PLANT AN ORANGE PUMPKIN PATCH ...BLACK PINE TREE IN AN ORANGE LIGHT 328   4
PLANTS (4)
   I BENT OVER THE PLANTS IN MY LEATHER-KNEED ....SPINACH-PICKER.   89   17
   AMONG BIRD FEET AND THE STEMS OF PLANTS. ....LOVE LETTER 147   27
   WITH THE ROOMS, OR THE SMILES, OR THE BEAUTIFUL RUBBER PLANTS, ...
                                              ... WAKING IN WINTER   151   15
   THE BLUE NIGHT PLANTS, THE LITTLE PALE BLUE HILL ......PARLIAMENT H. 153   41
PLASMA (1)
   FOR A MINUTE THE SKY POURS INTO THE HOLE LIKE PLASMA. ..BERCK-PLAGE 201   125
PLASTER (1)
   IN PLASTER ....IN PLASTER 158 T
PLASTIC (6)
   IN THE BASKET OF PLASTIC EVERGREENS THEY PUT *ELECTRA ON AZALEA PATH 117   25
   ONE CHILD DROPS A BARRETTE OF PINK PLASTIC;   PARLIAMENT HILL FIELDS 152   16
   SHOULD I STIR, I THINK THIS PINK AND PURPLE PLASTIC ....ZOO K. 154   11
   TOMORROW THE PATIENT WILL HAVE A CLEAN, PINK PLASTIC LIMB. *SURGEON. 171   40
   BRIGHT HAIR, SHOE-BLACK, OLD PLASTIC, ...THE OTHER 201   8
   HE LUMPS IT DOWN THE PLASTIC COBBLED HILL, ...LESBOS 228   48
PLASTIC-PILLOWED (1)
   SCARED AND BARE ON THE GREEN PLASTIC-PILLOWED TROLLEY ....TULIPS 161   25
PLASTIC-WINDOWED (1)
   MOST PLASTIC-WINDOWED CITY, I CAN HEAR ....SONNET: TO TIME 311   6
PLATE (6)
   COLD POLE AND HOT PLATE. ....WORDS FOR A NURSERY 74   25
   IT IS A COUNTRY ON A NURSERY PLATE. ....WATERCOLOR.   112   15
   LET US EAT OUR LAST SUPPER AT IT, LIKE A HOSPITAL PLATE. BIRTHDAY. 207   26
   MY NIGHT SWEATS GREASE HIS BREAKFAST PLATE. ....THE JAILER 226   1
   THE WORD OF A SNAIL ON THE PLATE OF A LEAF? ....THE COURIERS   247   1
   THE ONLY FARE ON MY BARE BREAKFAST PLATE.   QUEEN MARY'S ROSE GARDEN 290   6
PLATES (5)
   IN THAT RUBBLE OF SKULL PLATES AND OLD LEATHER. ....TWO VIEWS. 114   8
   IN A MONTH WE'LL WONDER WHAT PLATES AND FORKS ARE FOR. ....TWO CAMP. 145   20
   EMPTY AND SILLY AS PLATES, ...LITTLE FUGUE   188   17
   AND DRIED PLATES WITH MY DENSE HAIR. ....STINGS 214   25
   OF DAY-OLD BREAD AND EGG-STAINED PLATES; PERHAPS ....METAMORPHOSES. 307   29
PLATITUDES (1)
   OF NOTCHED TIN PLATITUDES CONCERNING WEATHER, ...SONNET: TO EVA 305   11
PLATO (1)
   THEY WANT THE CRIB OF SOME LAMP-HEADED PLATO. ....MAGI 148   16
PLATONIC (1)
   PLATONIC TABLE WHERE IT LIVES. THE BABY CARP ....PRIVATE GROUND 130   11
PLATO'S (1)
   LET US EAT IT LIKE PLATO'S AFTERBIRTH, ...TOTEM   264   14

	TITLE	PAGE	LINE

PLAUSIVE (1)
   HIS HAIR LONG AND PLAUSIVE. ....DEATH & CO.   254   22
PLAY (10)
   ROOTED TO YOUR BLACK LOOK, THE PLAY TURNED TRAGIC: ...CONVERSATION.   21   12
   CATS PLAY IN THE STALKS. ....DEPARTURE   51   8
   YOU CHECKED THE DIET CHARTS AND TOOK ME TO PLAY ..ZOO KEEPER'S WIFE   155   25
   SHH! THESE ARE CHESS PEOPLE YOU PLAY WITH, ...THE SWARM   216   11
   PREDICTING THREE BOYS AN HOUR HENCE WILL PLAY ....DIALOGUE O.   279 124
   OUR WORLD AND THEIRS WE'D BEST PLAY SAFE AND GROOM .....DIALOGUE O.   281 186
   NOW YOU MUST PLAY THE STRAIGHT MAN FOR A TERM ....DIRGE FOR A JOKER   303   13
   OR PLAY ANOTHER CARD GAME WHEN YOU'VE WON; ....ADMONITIONS   319   2
   WHERE ADJECTIVES PLAY CROQUET WITH FLAMINGO NOUNS; ...A SORCERER B.   324   2
   HOW ALL THEIR PLAY IS TOUCH-AND-GO: ....TOUCH-AND-GO   335   12
PLAYED (2)
   BRAVE ACTS PLAYED OUT IN PEACE, IN WAR; ALL DANGERS*CHANNEL CROSSING   27   39
   OVER TIDAL-FLATS WHERE THREE CHILDREN PLAYED ....DREAM WITH C.   44   14
PLAYERS (2)
   THE BINGO PLAYERS, THE PLAYERS AT LOVE ....ON DECK   142   11
   THE BINGO PLAYERS, THE PLAYERS AT LOVE ....ON DECK   142   11
PLAYFULNESS (1)
   TO PROPEL HIS PLAYFULNESS, BUT ON YOU, ABOVE ....DIALOGUE O.   282 230
PLAYING (5)
   STIFF AS A QUEEN ON A PLAYING CARD. ....THE BULL OF BENDYLAW   108   5
   PLAYING AND RESTING WITHOUT COMMITTING ITSELF. ....TULIPS   161   56
   I REMEMBER YOU PLAYING "JA DA" IN A PINK PIQUE DRESS*THE BABYSITTERS   175   22
   THERE IS THE SUNLIGHT, PLAYING ITS BLADES, ...THE DETECTIVE   209   18
   PLAYING HIS PRODIGAL CHARADES. ....LOVE IS A PARALLAX   329   36
PLAYMATES (1)
   WHO INSISTS HIS PLAYMATES RUN. ....LOVE IS A PARALLAX   329   24
PLAYS (3)
   PLAYS BETWEEN THESE. ....TWO SISTERS OF PERSEPHONE   31   4
   PLAYS HOSTESS TO TABBY, TOM AND INCREASE, ...ELLA MASON A.   53   10
   ALL DAY SHE PLAYS AT CHESS WITH THE BONES OF THE WORLD: ..FEMALE A.   301   1
PLAY'S (1)
   THE PARADOX IS THAT "THE PLAY'S THE THING": .....LOVE IS A PARALLAX   330   55
PLEADED (1)
   "DON'T," PLEADED THE LITTLE GIRL ....BITTER STRAWBERRIES   299   22
PLEASANT (1)
   UP PLEASANT STREET AT MAIN. POISING THEIR SHAPES ...ABOVE THE OXBOW   88   12
PLEASE (2)
   "NO PITCHFORKED FARMER, PLEASE," SHE SAID; ....BUCOLICS   23   5
   OF VALENTINE-FACES MIGHT PLEASE A COLLECTOR: ....A LIFE   150   17
PLEASED (3)
   NAPOLEON IS PLEASED, HE IS PLEASED WITH EVERYTHING. ......THE SWARM   217   59
   NAPOLEON IS PLEASED, HE IS PLEASED WITH EVERYTHING. ......THE SWARM   217   59
   THERE, THAT'S THE PINK, PLEASED SQUEAK ....FAMILY REUNION   300   16
PLEASING (1)
   KINDLED BY MY LOVE'S PLEASING ....SONG FOR A SUMMER'S DAY   31   14
PLEASURABLE (1)
   PLEASURABLE UNDER CLAWS ....MUSSEL HUNTER AT ROCK HARBOR   96   49
PLEASURE (1)
   LIKE MY NEIGHBORS, TAKING NO PLEASURE ....LOVE LETTER   147   12
PLEATINGS (1)
   AND MEANDER IN BLAND PLEATINGS UNDER ....IN MIDAS' COUNTRY   99   3
PLENITUDE (2)
   THE GENIUS OF PLENITUDE ....FROG AUTUMN   99   10
   PLENITUDE: APPLES GOLD ON THE BOUGH, ...IN MIDAS' COUNTRY   99   12
PLENTY (1)
   OUT OF IT WILL BE TIME AND PLENTY FOR US*DIALOGUE OVER A OUIJA BOARD   278   58
PLETHORA (1)
   ON THE PLETHORA OF DRYADS ....ON THE PLETHORA OF DRYADS   67   T
PLIABLE (1)
   BUT PLIABLE STILL, HIS JAW ....MEDALLION   124   5
PLIANT (2)
   HIS SNAKEHOOD AND HIS MIGHT WITH PLIANT TUNES .........SNAKECHARMER   79   17
   PLIANT VALVES: ....AQUATIC NOCTURNE   305   15
PLOPPING (1)
   THEY ARE PLOPPING LIKE MUD.*WORDS HEARD, BY ACCIDENT, OVER THE PHONE   202   7
PLOT (2)
   AND PLANETS PLOT WITH OLD ELLIPTIC CUNNING; .....TO EVA DESCENDING.   303   5
   IF YOU'VE A PLOT TO HALT THE LETHAL FLOW ....THE DISPOSSESSED   318   7
PLOTS (1)
   PLOTS DOOM FROM ABOVE, ...TRIO OF LOVE SONGS   314   14
PLOUGH (1)
   OF THE HOMELAND HEARTH TO PLOUGH THEIR PILGRIM WAY ....MAYFLOWER   60   10
PLOUGHBLADE (1)
   WHAT FLINTY PEBBLES THE PLOUGHBLADE UPTURNS ....OUIJA   77   28
PLUCK (3)
   THE AUTHENTIC SEA DENIES THEM AND WILL PLUCK ....TALE OF A TUB   25   23
   AND PLUCK THE DROLL-FLECKED QUAIL WHERE THICK THEY LIE; ....GO GET.   313   2
   IF YOU PLUCK OUT MY HEART ....TRIO OF LOVE SONGS   315   49
PLUCKED (3)
   PLUCKED BACK THUS SUDDEN TO THAT FAR INNOCENCE, ...DREAM WITH C.   44   21
   YOU SAY HE'S TOLD TWO LIES . . . CALL THEM TWO PLUCKED   DIALOGUE O.   283 266
   BE PLUCKED FROM CAVES OF DAPPLED AMBER WHERE ......MIDSUMMER MOBILE   324   9

382

	TITLE	PAGE	LINE

PLUCKS (2)
PLUCKS BARE THAT COMET'S FLOWERING. ....EPITAPH FOR FIRE AND FLOWER 46 28
AND HUNGER OF THE SURF THAT PLUCKS THE LAND, *EPITAPH IN THREE PARTS 337 16
PLUM (2)
BLUEBLACK, A SPECTACULAR PLUM FRUIT. ....ZOO KEEPER'S WIFE 154 4
WHILE LIKE AN EARLY SUMMER PLUM, ...JILTED 304 9
PLUMAGE (6)
M-A-G-E. IN PLUMAGE. I'D NEVER HAVE THOUGHT ....DIALOGUE O. 278 78
PLUMAGE OF WHAT, PAN? P ... HE STARTS AGAIN, ...DIALOGUE O. 279 85
TUGGING US THROUGH PLUMAGE. I ALMOST FEEL ....DIALOGUE O. 279 86
AN ANGEL. PLUMAGE. O-F-R. HE'LL ....DIALOGUE OVER A OUIJA BOARD 279 90
PAN SAID. A PLUMAGE OF RAW WORMS. HOW ..DIALOGUE OVER A OUIJA BOARD 279 100
WITH WET PLUMAGE THROUGH MY ROOMS. ....THE DREAM 310 6
P-L-U-M-A-G-E (1)
THE GLASS YET AS HE GLIDES. P-L-U-M-A-G-E. ....DIALOGUE O. 278 77-8
PLUMB (1)
SIMPLY TO PLUMB THE DEEPS OF AN EYE ....CANDLES 148 7
PLUMBED (1)
INSTEAD OF FAT FISH ON THE LINE, YOU'VE PLUMBED ....DIALOGUE O. 282 242
PLUMBER (1)
IT ATE SEVEN MAIDS AND A PLUMBER ....THE TOUR 238 33
PLUMBING (1)
FLAYS THE CHROMIUM NERVES OF PLUMBING RAW; ....TALE OF A TUB 24 3
PLUMBS (1)
WHO PLUMBS THE WELL OF HIS BOOK, ...BERCK-PLAGE 197 22
PLUM-COLOR (1)
COUNTING THE RED STARS AND THOSE OF PLUM-COLOR. ....THE COLOSSUS 130 26
PLUME (1)
IN HIS PINK PLUME AND ARMOR. ....BATTLE-SCENE 84 10
PLUMMET (1)
PLUMMET TO THEIR DARK ADDRESS, ...NICK AND THE CANDLESTICK 241 36
PLUMMETS (1)
AND SERENELY PLUMMETS DOWN ....AERIALIST 331 26
PLUMPED (1)
PLUMPED THE BELLIES OF THE MICE ....THE THIN PEOPLE 64 10
PLUMS (1)
THEY WELD TO ME LIKE PLUMS. ....NICK AND THE CANDLESTICK 241 9
PLUNGE (4)
WE TAKE THE PLUNGE; UNDER WATER OUR LIMBS ....TALE OF A TUB 25 25
SLOPED SEAWARD TO PLUNGE IN BLUE; FED BY WHITE FIRE, DREAM WITH C. 44 11
AND MAKE THE FATAL PLUNGE. ....FAMILY REUNION 301 30
A CROWD OF SHINING GULLS THAT PLUNGE TO LAUNCH ...EPITAPH IN THREE. 337 13
PLUNGES (2)
PLUNGES HEADLONG INTO THAT BLACK POND ....WINTER LANDSCAPE, 21 2
PLUNGES FOR A PHRASE ....TRIO OF LOVE SONGS 314 27
PLUS (3)
IN ALL. PLUS YES. PLUS NO. AND THIS BARE BOARD. ....DIALOGUE O. 276 14
IN ALL. PLUS YES. PLUS NO. AND THIS BARE BOARD. ....DIALOGUE O. 276 14
THE SIMPLE SUM OF HEART PLUS HEART. ....LOVE IS A PARALLAX 331 78
PLUSH (4)
REST ON ORANGE PLUSH NEAR THE NEWEL POST. ...YADDO: THE GRAND MANOR 124 16
THERE IS THE SMELL OF POLISH, THERE ARE PLUSH CARPETS.*THE DETECTIVE 209 18
RUBBED OF ITS PLUSH --- ....STINGS 214 18
THEN THAT RED PLUSH. ....CUT 235 8
PLYING (1)
PLYING THEIR WILD CELLS IN MY KEEL'S SHADOW, ...MEDUSA 225 7
POACHING (1)
SELVES POSING AS PROPHET AND SLYLY POACHING ....DIALOGUE O. 280 134
POCK (1)
EVERY POCK AND STAIN BULKED MORE BEAUTIFUL*ON THE PLETHORA OF DRYADS 67 16
POCKED (1)
POCKED BY ROOK-CLAW AND RABBIT-TRACK: SHE MUST YET WIN SNOWMAN O. 58 17
POCKET (2)
NO POCKET DOZER, ...WORDS FOR A NURSERY 73 18
POCKET WATCH, I TICK WELL. ....GIGOLO 267 1
POCKETBOOK (2)
HER A POCKETBOOK, A PEARL HATPIN ....ON DECK 143 21
THE WIDOW WITH HER BLACK POCKETBOOK AND THREE DAUGHTERS,*BERCK-PLAGE 200 100
POCKETED (1)
AN ORANGE BUD, POCKETED IT. WHEN *FABLE OF THE RHODODENDRON STEALERS 103 8
POCKETS (1)
BALD AND SHINY, WITH POCKETS OF WISHES, ...TOTEM 264 26
POCKMARKED (1)
OF MOONLIGHT OR THE POCKMARKED FACE WE SEE*METAMORPHOSES OF THE MOON 308 38
POD (1)
RATTLES ITS POD, THE MOON ....CHILDLESS WOMAN 259 2
PODS (2)
FATTEN IN GREEN-POCKED PODS, THE THREE NET-MENDERS SIT OUT, ..NET-. 121 3
PODS OF THE LABURNUM AT NINE IN THE MORNING. ....LETTER IN NOVEMBER 253 4
POEM (2)
POEM FOR A BIRTHDAY ....POEM FOR A BIRTHDAY 131 T
A POEM FOR THREE VOICES ....THREE WOMEN 176 ST
POEMS (2)
POEMS, POTATOES ....POEMS, POTATOES 106 T
THESE POEMS DO NOT LIVE: IT'S A SAD DIAGNOSIS. ....STILLBORN 142 1

	TITLE	PAGE	LINE

POETRY (5)
    THE OLD GOD, TOO, WRITES AUREATE POETRY ....OUIJA 77 12
    I CONSIDERED THE POETRY I RESCUED*FABLE OF THE RHODODENDRON STEALERS 103 15
    THE BLOOD JET IS POETRY, ...KINDNESS 270 18
    BOY, PRONE TO COMPOSE QUEER POETRY .....DIALOGUE OVER A OUIJA BOARD 280 142
    OF POETRY FROM THESE LETTERS, BUT THE BEAT ....DIALOGUE O. 283 256
POINT (10)
    A POINT OF EXCLAMATION MARKS THAT SKY ......THE GHOST'S LEAVETAKING 91 27
    SUSPENDS BESIDE IT THE FIRST POINT, THE STARTING ....GHOST'S. 91 30
    POINT OF EDEN, NEXT THE NEW MOON'S CURVE. ..THE GHOST'S LEAVETAKING 91 31
    GREEN TO THE POINT OF BLACKNESS, SOME ....CHILD'S PARK STONES 100 2
    POINT SHIRLEY ....POINT SHIRLEY 110 T
    EATS AT POINT SHIRLEY. SHE DIED BLESSED, ...POINT SHIRLEY 111 36
    THIS IS NO TIME FOR THE PRIVATE POINT OF VIEW. ....CANDLES 149 13
    RIDING THE RIP TIDE TO THE NEAREST POINT OF DEPARTURE, ...MEDUSA 225 10
    POLEMIC GALES PROVE POINT BY POINT ....INSOLENT STORM. 325 9
    POLEMIC GALES PROVE POINT BY POINT ....INSOLENT STORM. 325 9
POINTBLANK (1)
    TO HOODWINK THE HONEST EARTH WHICH POINTBLANK ....CONJURING. 66 28
POINTED (1)
    GRASSHOPPER GOBLINS WITH GREEN POINTED EARS EPITAPH IN THREE PARTS 337 23
POINTING (1)
    POINTING TOWARD THE SPINDLE'S CRYPTIC WHIR, ...THE PRINCESS. 335 60
POINTLESS (1)
    I SUPPOSE IT'S POINTLESS TO THINK OF YOU AT ALL. .....PARLIAMENT H. 152 24
POINTS (2)
    A POLICEMAN POINTS OUT A VACANT CLIFF ....WHITSUN 154 18
    THE YEW TREE POINTS UP. IT HAS A GOTHIC SHAPE. ....MOON. 173 15
POISE (7)
    TWO WATER DROPS POISE ....RESOLVE 52 13
    THEY POISE AND GRIEVE AS IN SOME OLD TRAGEDY. ....THE OTHER TWO 68 21
    PERSEUS, THE PALM, AND MAY YOU POISE ....PERSEUS 84 47
    HIS NEAT TROT PITCHING MY TENSE POISE UP, ...WHITENESS I REMEMBER 102 14
    TO DELICACY, TO POISE) BUT THAT THEY ....POEMS, POTATOES 106 8
    THE STONY ACTORS POISE AND PAUSE FOR BREATH. *ELECTRA ON AZALEA PATH 117 37
    WE POISE ON PERILOUS POLES THAT FREEZE US IN ........METAMORPHOSES. 308 46
POISES (1)
    WHO POISES HIS PASTEL SPEAR ....BATTLE-SCENE 84 14
POISING (1)
    UP PLEASANT STREET AT MAIN. POISING THEIR SHAPES ...ABOVE THE OXBOW 88 12
POISON (2)
    POISON OF STILLED LAWNS, THE LITTLE CLAPBOARD GRAVESTONES, WAKING. 151 7
    AS A DESK DRAWER HIDES A POISON PEN LETTER, ...THE RIVAL/DR 291 9
POISONED (1)
    ALTHOUGH THE WICKED WITCH HAS POISONED ONE. ....ADMONITIONS 319 5
POISONS (4)
    TRADING THEIR POISONS, THE NORTH AND SOUTH BOUND CARS ...PRIVATE G. 130 16
    OR SHALL I BRING YOU THE SOUND OF POISONS? ....ELM 192 13
    WHICH OF THE POISONS IS IT? ....THE DETECTIVE 209 22
    HE RENTS HIS POISONS OUT BY TELEPHONE; ....DENOUEMENT 327 14
POKE (3)
    WITH POKE AND GIGGLE, READY TO SKEDADDLE, ...ELLA MASON A. 54 25
    SO I POKE AT THE CARBON BIRDS IN MY HOUSEDRESS. *BURNING THE LETTERS 204 29
    YOU POKE AND STIR. ....LADY LAZARUS 246 74
POKER-STIFF (1)
    RIGGED POKER-STIFF ON HER BACK ....ALL THE DEAD DEARS 70 1
POLACK (1)
    MY POLACK FRIEND ....DADDY 222 20
POLAND (3)
    RUSSIA, POLAND AND GERMANY! ....THE SWARM 216 27
    OVER THE CICATRIX OF POLAND, BURNT-OUT ....MARY'S SONG 257 10
    OVER SCOURED POLAND, BURNT-OUT ....MARY'S SONG/DR 294 1
POLAR (1)
    THESE BODIES MOUNDED AROUND ME NOW, THESE POLAR SLEEPERS --   THREE. 181 181
POLE (4)
    COLD POLE AND HOT PLATE. ....WORDS FOR A NURSERY 74 25
    THE PUNTER SINKS HIS POLE. ......WATERCOLOR OF GRANTCHESTER MEADOWS 112 12
    THE STOPPED HORSE ON HIS CHROMIUM POLE ....WHITSUN 154 7
    AN OLD POLE FOR THE LIGHTNING, ...LESBOS 228 46
POLEMIC (2)
    POLEMIC GALES PROVE POINT BY POINT ....INSOLENT STORM. 325 9
    THAT JAR, WHILE EACH POLEMIC JACKANAPES ....LOVE IS A PARALLAX 330 53
POLES (1)
    WE POISE ON PERILOUS POLES THAT FREEZE US IN ........METAMORPHOSES. 308 46
POLICE (2)
    LET HIM SEND POLICE AND HOUNDS TO BRING HER IN. ....SNOWMAN O. 58 19
    THE POLICE LOVE YOU, YOU CONFESS EVERYTHING. ....THE OTHER 201 7
POLICEMAN (3)
    A POLICEMAN POINTS OUT A VACANT CLIFF ....WHITSUN 154 18
    YOU ARE BLUE AND HUGE, A TRAFFIC POLICEMAN, ...A SECRET 219 3
    GOT UP TO LET THE SUAVE BLUE POLICEMAN IN. ...THE TRIAL OF MAN 312 8
POLISH (4)
    GONE BLACK OF POLISH ....TINKER JACK AND THE TIDY WIVES 34 2
    THERE IS THE SMELL OF POLISH, THERE ARE PLUSH CARPETS.*THE DETECTIVE 209 17
    IN THE GERMAN TONGUE, IN THE POLISH TOWN ....DADDY 222 16

384

```
                                                      TITLE           PAGE  LINE
POLISH (CONT.)
    DOWN SHOES FOR A POLISH OF CARBON  ...........THE MUNICH MANNEQUINS  263   19
POLISHED (6)
    PERFORMED A DUMBSHOW IN THE POLISHED WOOD,  ...........THE OTHER TWO   68   16
    THEY ARE POLISHED FOR THE JOUST,  .....................BATTLE-SCENE   84   24
    ALL'S POLISHED TO A DULL LUSTER  ...................IN MIDAS' COUNTRY   99    5
    WITH A POLISHED MAHOGANY STAIR TO LET INTO THE WATER*THE BABYSITTERS  174   11
    FROM THE POLISHED LOZENGES OF ORANGE LINOLEUM.  ..............LESBOS  228   24
    WHERE POLISHED HIGHBOYS WHISPER CREAKING CURSES  ......FEMALE AUTHOR  301    7
POLISHES (1)
    HOW THE SUN POLISHES THIS SHOULDER!  .....................PURDAH  242    9
POLITE (2)
    THE POLITE SKIES OVER BOSTON COULDN'T POSSIBLY ACCOMMODATE.  ...
                               ... TWO CAMPERS IN CLOUD COUNTRY  145   11
    ENOUGH. BUT BE POLITE. YOU'RE TOO SEVERE*DIALOGUE OVER A OUIJA BOARD  281  181
POLITIC (3)
    YET POLITIC; IGNORANT  ..................BLACK ROOK IN RAINY WEATHER   57   25
    INDOORS WITH POLITIC GOODWILL, NOT HASTE  ...THE SNOWMAN ON THE MOOR   58   11
    PAYS TO BE POLITIC. OH, I'M NOT ONE TO HANG  ...........DIALOGUE O.  281  196
POLITICS (1)
    PERFUME, POLITICS, AND FIXED IDEALS.  ...............SONNET: TO EVA  305   12
POLLARDED (1)
    POLLARDED GREEN BALLS, THE TREES MARCH TO CHURCH.  ......BERCK-PLAGE  199   92
POLLEN (2)
    LIKE POLLEN ON BRIGHT AIR. LULLED  ........TWO SISTERS OF PERSEPHONE   32   15
    FROM THIS HOLY DAY ON, POLLEN BLOWN  ............WREATH FOR A BRIDAL   45   19
POLLY'S (4)
    POLLY'S TREE  .............................................POLLY'S TREE  128    T
    A DREAM TREE, POLLY'S TREE:  .............................POLLY'S TREE  128    1
    POLLY'S TREE, NOR  .......................................POLLY'S TREE  128   30
    A DREAM TREE. POLLY'S TREE  .............................POLLY'S TREE  129   37
POLYPS (1)
    LITTLE BUSHY POLYPS,  .........................................PURDAH  242   15
POM (8)
    A DULL POM, POM IN THE SUNDAY STREET.  .....................THE SWARM  215    2
    A DULL POM, POM IN THE SUNDAY STREET.  .....................THE SWARM  215    2
    IT MUST BE SHOT DOWN. POM! POM!  ...........................THE SWARM  216   19
    IT MUST BE SHOT DOWN. POM! POM!  ...........................THE SWARM  216   19
    POM! POM! THEY FALL  .......................................THE SWARM  217   37
    POM! POM! THEY FALL  .......................................THE SWARM  217   37
    POM! POM! "THEY WOULD HAVE KILLED ME."  ...................THE SWARM  217   55
    POM! POM! "THEY WOULD HAVE KILLED ME."  ...................THE SWARM  217   55
POMP (1)
    THE PRINCESS HEARS THE THUNDER AND THE POMP  ..........THE PRINCESS.  333   21
POMPONS (2)
    FACED IN HIS RICH YELLOWS, TASSELS, POMPONS, BRAID, THE PICADOR  ...
                               ... THE GORING   47    5
    THE ORANGE POMPONS, THE EGYPTIAN PAPYRUS  ....PARLIAMENT HILL FIELDS  153   43
POMPOUS (2)
    GLOWERING SULLEN AND POMPOUS FROM AN ASH-HEAP,  ........LADY AND T.   69   11
    BUT I AM CONTENT WITH THIS MORE POMPOUS LOT.  ........QUEEN MARY'S.  290   25
POND (3)
    PLUNGES HEADLONG INTO THAT BLACK POND  ...........WINTER LANDSCAPE,   21    2
    FLUTE NOTES FROM A REEDY POND  ...........................POEM.5.F.  134   ST
    AND INTO THE SILVER ELEMENT OF THE POND.  ..QUEEN MARY'S ROSE GARDEN  290   12
PONDERABLE (1)
    AS PONDERABLE TOKENS OF HER LOVE.  ............................OUIJA   77   29
PONDEROUS (3)
    PONDEROUS AND EXTEND DESPAIR ON EARTH'S  ....................PERSEUS   83   31
    THEY RISE, THEIR LIMBS PONDEROUS  ..........................LORELEI   94   12
    AN ELEPHANT, A PONDEROUS HOUSE,  .........................METAPHORS  116    2
PONDS (2)
    HAS BEEN DRAINING THE GOLDFISH PONDS.  ...............PRIVATE GROUND  130    8
    FROM THE LINKED PONDS THAT MY EYES WINCE  ....PARLIAMENT HILL FIELDS  152   11
POODLE (1)
    BURIED IN THE LAMBSWOOL OF THE DEAD POODLE;  ...............FACE LIFT  156   23
POODLES (2)
    POODLES ARE BAKING COOKIES IN  ......................A WINTER'S TALE   87   18
    THE TREES ARE LOPPED, THE POODLES TRIM,  ...THE DEATH OF MYTH-MAKING  104    6
POOL (10)
    IN BYRON'S POOL  .................WATERCOLOR OF GRANTCHESTER MEADOWS  112   13
    GREEN AS A POOL TABLE, WHERE CABBAGE BUTTERFLIES  ...........WHITSUN  154   19
    AND THE MAID SMOKED AND SHOT POOL UNDER A GREEN-SHADED LAMP.  BABY.  175   24
    THE FACE IN THE POOL WAS BEAUTIFUL, BUT NOT MINE --  ...THREE WOMEN  177   45
    WHILE A GREEN POOL OPENS ITS EYE,  .....................BERCK-PLAGE  197   27
    MORNING GLORY POOL!  .......................................THE TOUR  238   28
    POOL IN WHICH IMAGES  .........................................CHILD  265    8
    OVER WHOSE POOL I TENDERLY  .................................GIGOLO  268   31
    FROM THE BOTTOM OF THE POOL, FIXED STARS  ....................WORDS  270   19
    THE NIGHT IS A BLUE POOL; SHE IS VERY STILL.  ...............ELM/DR  292    6
POOL-BED (1)
    EDGE OF A CRATERED POOL-BED  ..........MUSSEL HUNTER AT ROCK HARBOR   95   16
POOLING (1)
    POOLING IN HEEL-PRINTS, FUMBLING PEBBLE AND STEM.  ....PARLIAMENT H.  153   36
```

TITLE   PAGE LINE

POOL-MOUTH (1)
  TOWARD THE POOL-MOUTH, PERHAPS TO .....MUSSEL HUNTER AT ROCK HARBOR   96   41
POOLS (9)
  MARGIN OF THE TIDAL POOLS. ....MUSSEL HUNTER AT ROCK HARBOR   95   11
  GLAZES THE ROCK POOLS YET, ...MAN IN BLACK   119   11
  GOLD CARP LOOM IN THE POOLS. ....YADDO: THE GRAND MANOR 123   8
  HE MADE OF THE FOOTBALL POOLS -- TEASING US WITH ....DIALOGUE O.   277   39
  ISN'T IN HIM. MAYBE. BUT MAYBE THE POOLS*DIALOGUE OVER A OUIJA BOARD   277   42
  FROM, IF NOT THE POOLS? OH, FROM A LOT   DIALOGUE OVER A OUIJA BOARD   277   46
  POOLS ASIDE, WILLS ASIDE, DO WE ....DIALOGUE OVER A OUIJA BOARD   278   53
  AS HE STOLE OUR PERPLEXITIES ABOUT THE POOLS ....DIALOGUE O.   279 103
  POOLS, PROPHECIES AND SUCH FROM THE UNFATHOMED ....DIALOGUE O.   282 240
POOR (6)
  A POOR MONTH FOR PARK-SLEEPERS AND LOVERS. ....A WINTER SHIP   113   22
  A THICKET OF SHADOWS IS A POOR COAT. I INHABIT POEM.6.W.   135   2
  POOR AND BARE AND UNQUEENLY AND EVEN SHAMEFUL. ....STINGS   214   19
  FOR THIRTY YEARS, POOR AND WHITE, ...DADDY   222   4
  POOR HEIRLOOM, ALL YOU HAVE, ...BY CANDLELIGHT   237   32
  TO A CINDER, THAN MEET A POOR UPSTART OF OUR NETHER ....DIALOGUE O.   280 133
POORHOUSE (1)
  IN THIS CHARITY WARD, THIS POORHOUSE, WHERE THE DEAD ...ELECTRA ON.   117   19
POP (1)
  GIVING A SHRIEK AND POP ....BALLOONS   271   7
POPLARS (1)
  OF POPLARS IN THE MIDDLE DISTANCE, THE ONLY ....SLEEP.   143   5
POPPIES (4)
  NEAR A BED OF POPPIES, ...TWO SISTERS OF PERSEPHONE   32   16
  POPPIES IN JULY ....POPPIES IN JULY   203   T
  LITTLE POPPIES, LITTLE HELL FLAMES, ...POPPIES IN JULY   203   1
  POPPIES IN OCTOBER ....POPPIES IN OCTOBER   240   T
POPPING (1)
  POPPING UPWARD FROM THE MOUTHS OF BELLS ....LYONNESSE   234   9
POPPY-SLEEPY (1)
  THEIR POPPY-SLEEPY COLORS DO HIM NO GOOD. ....INSOMNIAC   163   21
POPULACE (1)
  THE POPULACE SINGS TOWARD THE SILL ....A WINTER'S TALE   87   29
PORCELAIN (2)
  LUCENT AS PORCELAIN, THE EARTH'S ....THE GREAT CARBUNCLE   72   7
  BLOOMS OUT OF A VASE OF NOT VERY VALUABLE PORCELAIN, ...IN PLASTER   159   17
PORCH (1)
  SHADING THE BRICKRED PORCH TILES. ....DEPARTURE   51   3
PORCHES (1)
  A GALLERY OF CREAKING PORCHES AND STILL INTERIORS,   THE BABYSITTERS   175   34
PORK (1)
  MY FAT PORK, MY MARROWY SWEETHEART, FACE-TO-THE-WALL? ....ZOO K.   155   15
PORKFAT (1)
  THEIR VEINS WHITE AS PORKFAT. POEM.1.WHO.   131   18
PORTENT (1)
  WITHOUT CEREMONY, OR PORTENT. ....BLACK ROOK IN RAINY WEATHER   57   10
PORT (2)
  HIDE, HIDE, IN THE WARM PORT ....GO GET THE GOODLY SQUAB   313   23
  WHO SEEKS TO DALLY IN THE PORT TILL DAWN, ...EPITAPH IN THREE PARTS   337   8
PORTICO (1)
  THROUGH PORTICO OF MY ELEGANT HOUSE YOU STALK ........CONVERSATION.   21   1
PORTICOES (1)
  MUSEUM WITHOUT STATUES, GRAND WITH PILLARS, PORTICOES, ROTUNDAS. ...
                                           ... BARREN WOMAN   157   2
POSE (3)
  YADWIGHA, POSE ON, THAT HE PUT YOU ON THE COUCH ....YADIWGHA.   86   37
  A GULL HOLDS HIS POSE ON A SHANTY RIDGEPOLE, ...A WINTER SHIP   113   6
  UPLIFTED, STIFFEN IN A FAMILY POSE. ....BLUE MOLES   126   16
POSED (1)
  SO THESE POSED SHEETS, BEFORE THEY THIN TO NOTHING, ...GHOST'S.   90   18
POSING (1)
  SELVES POSING AS PROPHET AND SLYLY POACHING ....DIALOGUE O.   280 134
POSITION (3)
  I WASN'T IN ANY POSITION TO GET RID OF HER. ....IN PLASTER   159   43
  THE SAME PLACARD OF BLUE FOG IS WHEELED INTO POSITION ...THE JAILER   226   2
  YOUR CROSSED POSITION. ....NICK AND THE CANDLESTICK   241   26
POSSESS (1)
  HOW YOUR BAD DREAMS POSSESS AND ENDOW ME. ....ELM   192   27
POSSESSED (1)
  SO POSSESSED BY THE GLOWING RED OF THE COUCH WHICH YOU, ..YADWIGHA.   86   36
POSSESSING (1)
  IT IS LIKE POSSESSING A SAINT. ....BERCK-PLAGE   198   57
POSSESSION (2)
  POSSESSION OF THE MOST OBTUSE OBJECTS NOW AND THEN -- *BLACK ROOK I.   57   18
  POSSESSION. ....WINTERING   218   18
POSSIBLE (3)
  LIT THINGS, THAT LAMP OF THE POSSIBLE! WET YET .....SPINACH-PICKER.   89   3
  I WOULD HAVE KILLED MYSELF GLADLY THAT TIME ANY POSSIBLE WAY. ...
                                           ... A BIRTHDAY PRESENT   206   15
  THEIR MAGNIFIED HEADS AND PLAN TO KILL ME AS SOON AS POSSIBLE. ...
                                           ... THE RIVAL/DR   291   3

386

		TITLE	PAGE	LINE

POSSIBLY (1)
THE POLITE SKIES OVER BOSTON COULDN'T POSSIBLY ACCOMMODATE. ...
        ... TWO CAMPERS IN CLOUD COUNTRY 145 11
POST (3)
IN GOING UP FOR THE COMING DOWN IF THE POST ....ABOVE THE OXBOW 88 18
WE START AT'S THE SAME POST WE FINISH BY, ...ABOVE THE OXBOW 88 19
REST ON ORANGE PLUSH NEAR THE NEWEL POST. ...YADDO: THE GRAND MANOR 124 16
POSTAGE (1)
POSTAGE STAMPS, STACKED BOOKS' CLAMOR AND YAWP, ...CONJURING. 65 3
POSTCARD (1)
BESIDE THE POSTCARD STALLS. ....FINISTERRE 170 29
POSTMAN (1)
IS IT THE BUTCHER, THE GROCER, THE POSTMAN, SOMEONE I KNOW? ...BEE. 211 30
POSTMARKS (1)
AND THE EYES AND TIMES OF THE POSTMARKS. ....BURNING THE LETTERS 204 14
POT (3)
"COME LADY, BRING THAT POT ....TINKER JACK AND THE TIDY WIVES 34 1
THUMBED NO STONY, HORNY POT, ...THE HERMIT AT OUTERMOST HOUSE 119 15
AND DEATH IN THE POT. ....TEMPER OF TIME 336 24
POTATO (1)
UNPOEMED, UNPICTURED, THE POTATO ....POEMS, POTATOES 106 11
POTATOES (4)
POEMS, POTATOES ....POEMS, POTATOES 106 T
CAN ONLY HAUNT. STURDY AS POTATOES, ...POEMS, POTATOES 106 4
THE POTATOES HISS. ....LESBOS 227 2
I AM PACKING THE HARD POTATOES LIKE GOOD CLOTHES, ...LESBOS 229 68
POTENT (1)
THE ANTHERS NOD THEIR HEADS, POTENT AS KINGS ....BEEKEEPER'S. 118 11
POTLID (1)
SITTING UNDER A POTLID, TINY AND INERT AS A RICE GRAIN. ..POEM.6.W. 135 15
POTS (6)
AND CHIMNEY POTS ....PROSPECT 28 2
ORANGE ROOF-TILES, ORANGE CHIMNEY POTS, ...LANDOWNERS 53 5
AND THE POTS OF MEAT. POEM.2.DARK. 132 18
SIPPING THEIR LIQUIDS FROM ASSORTED POTS, ...LEAVING EARLY 145 8
LET ME HAVE MY COPPER COOKING POTS, LET MY ROUGE POTS ...LAST WORDS 172 21
LET ME HAVE MY COPPER COOKING POTS, LET MY ROUGE POTS ...LAST WORDS 172 21
POTTED (1)
DIAMOND RINGS, POTTED ROSES, FOX-SKINS ....OWL 101 5
POULTICE (3)
HOW THE SUN'S POULTICE DRAWS ON MY INFLAMMATION. ....BERCK-PLAGE 196 2
YOU HAVE A HOLE, IT'S A POULTICE. ....THE APPLICANT 222 37
ITS CRYSTALS A LITTLE POULTICE. ....KINDNESS 269 11
POUNDING (1)
SHOOK THE GROUND WITH ITS POUNDING. ....NIGHT SHIFT 76 11
POUR (2)
TO POUR MYSELF OUT LIKE A FLUID ....LOVE LETTER 147 26
POUR OF TOR AND DISTANCES. ....ARIEL 239 3
POURING (2)
FLICKERING AND POURING, A PITIFUL CANDLE. ....BERCK-PLAGE 199 80
UPON THE POURING AIR UNTIL ....SONG FOR A REVOLUTIONARY LOVE 323 18
POURS (3)
POURS BY LIKE DESTINY, BENDING ....WUTHERING HEIGHTS 167 12
FOR A MINUTE THE SKY POURS INTO THE HOLE LIKE PLASMA. ..BERCK-PLAGE 201 125
WHERE IT POURS BEAN GREEN OVER BLUE ....DADDY 222 12
POUT (1)
HANGS IN ITS LUGUBRIOUS POUT. WHERE ARE ....PERSEUS 83 39
POUTS (1)
THOUGH PRIMA DONNA POUTS AND CRITIC STINGS, ...LOVE IS A PARALLAX 330 56
POVERTY (2)
SUCH POVERTY ASSAULTS THE EGO; CAUGHT ....TALE OF A TUB 24 4
SUCH POVERTY. NO DEAD MEN'S CRIES ....NOVEMBER GRAVEYARD 56 6
POWDER (1)
A CRAFT WITH PAINT AND POWDER THAT CAN MAKE .........METAMORPHOSES. 307 23
POWDERS (2)
THE GOLDEN RAIN TREE DRIPS ITS POWDERS DOWN. ....BEEKEEPER'S. 118 9
AS THE MOON, FOR ITS IVORY POWDERS, SCOURS THE SEA. ....STINGS 215 37
POWDERY (1)
UNDER THE GLUED SHEET FROM WHICH HIS POWDERY BEAK ......BERCK-PLAGE 198 63
POWER (5)
ABSOLUTE POWER ....SOLILOQUY OF THE SOLIPSIST 37 25
AT GORGON-PROSPECTS WITH POWER TO STRIKE TO STONE ....CRYSTAL GAZER 55 41
A POWER IS GROWING ON ME, AN OLD TENACITY. ....THREE WOMEN 180 141
THE MIRROR FLOATS US AT ONE CANDLE POWER. ....BY CANDLELIGHT 236 9
THE POWER, THE GLORY. ....BRASILIA 259 24
POWERFUL (1)
LOOK, THEY ARE MELTING LIKE COINS IN THE POWERFUL JUICES -- ZOO K. 154 8
PRACTICAL (2)
BLUNT, PRACTICAL BOATS ....BERCK-PLAGE 199 76
THE SMILE OF A MAN OF BUSINESS, INTENSELY PRACTICAL. .....THE SWARM 217 52
PRACTICE (3)
AND THAT DAMN SCRUPULOUS TREE WON'T PRACTICE WILES ......CONJURING. 66 20
GODS GROW TOO PROUD TO PRACTICE DOORMAN DUTIES ....DIALOGUE O. 280 127
HEARTED GAMBLING-GAME YOU WARILY PRACTICE ....DIALOGUE O. 282 227

```
                                                    TITLE            PAGE  LINE
PRACTICED (1)
    WITH QUICK PRACTICED HANDS,  ....................BITTER STRAWBERRIES  300   36
PRACTICING (1)
    AND THE HOURS OF PRACTICING, MY EAR  ..........THE DISQUIETING MUSES   75   37
PRAGMATIC (2)
    BUT MORE PRAGMATIC THAN ALL OF THIS,  ..............BLACK PINE TREE.  328   16
    FROM THE PRAGMATIC BOY CONFINED WITHIN,*THE PRINCESS AND THE GOBLINS  334   45
PRAISE (2)
    BY SCOLDINGS, OR BY SUBTLE PRAISE. ONLY I,  .............DIALOGUE O.  280  144
    SING PRAISE FOR STATUARY:  .............................TOUCH-AND-GO  335    1
PRAISED (1)
    AND PRAISED MY ARABESQUES AND TRILLS  .........THE DISQUIETING MUSES   75   34
PRAISING (1)
    CAME IN FOR MY LOVE'S PRAISING.  ............SONG FOR A SUMMER'S DAY   31   10
PRAWN (1)
    BENT-BACKED ATLAS, OUR TRAVELED PRAWN.  ......................YOU'RE  141   12
PRAY (1)
    I USED TO PRAY TO RECOVER YOU.  ..............................DADDY  222   14
PRAYER (1)
    AGAINST VIRGIN PRAYER  .....................................VANITY FAIR   33   21
PRAYERS (1)
    DROWNS NOAH'S PRAYERS WITH DISTAIN,  .................INSOLENT STORM.  326   14
PRAYING (3)
    DESPITE HER WRUNG HANDS, HER TEARS, HER PRAYING: VANISH!*LADY AND T.   70   30
    IS PRAYING TO THE MONUMENT OF THE SAILOR PRAYING.  .......FINISTERRE  170   23
    IS PRAYING TO THE MONUMENT OF THE SAILOR PRAYING.  .......FINISTERRE  170   23
PRAYS (1)
    PRAYS UNDER HER BREATH THAT SHE MAY SAVE  ....................ON DECK  143   23
PREACHERS (1)
    TO CHASTITY'S SERVICE: LIKE PROPHETS, LIKE PREACHERS,  ......VIRGIN.   82   28
PREAMBLE (1)
    OF A SLUG OR SMALL PREAMBLE  ....................NOTES TO A NEOPHYTE  306    5
PRECARIOUS (1)
    IN THIS PRECARIOUS PARK  ................................TOUCH-AND-GO  335    8
PRECARIOUSLY (1)
    AND WALKED CAREFULLY, PRECARIOUSLY, LIKE SOMETHING RARE.*THREE WOMEN  178   73
PRECIOUS (2)
    FISTS MY FINGERS FOR ME. HE MAKES ME FEEL SOMETHING PRECIOUS   FACE.  156   13
    THE FIRE MAKES IT PRECIOUS,  ...........................MARY'S SONG  257    5
PRECIPICE (1)
    PRECIPICE  ............................................MARY'S SONG  257   16
PRECOCIOUS (1)
    LIKE RIVAL PARENTS OVER A PRECOCIOUS  ...DIALOGUE OVER A OUIJA BOARD  284  283
PRECONCEPTIONS (1)
    I AM SILVER AND EXACT. I HAVE NO PRECONCEPTIONS.  ............MIRROR  173    1
PREDECESSOR (1)
    PREDECESSOR WRAPPED UP,  ..............................EAVESDROPPER  260   25
PREDICTING (1)
    PREDICTING THREE BOYS AN HOUR HENCE WILL PLAY  ..........DIALOGUE O.  279  124
PREFER (2)
    EVEN IF YOU SEEM PACIFIED, PREFER  ......DIALOGUE OVER A OUIJA BOARD  280  145
    TO GIVE ANOTHER INCH. IF YOU PREFER,  ...DIALOGUE OVER A OUIJA BOARD  281  179
PREGNANCY (1)
    SUCH AS PREGNANCY OR CONSTIPATION  .........................APRIL 18  301    5
PREOCCUPY (1)
    YOU PREOCCUPY MY HORIZON.  .............................THE RIVAL/DR  291   12
PREPARE (1)
    OUTSIZE HANDS PREPARE A PATH,  ...........................BLUE MOLES  126   28
PREPOSTEROUS (1)
    IN PREPOSTEROUS PROVINCES OF THE MADCAP  .........LETTER TO A PURIST   37   14
PRESENT (8)
    CAN SPROUT FROM THE NAVEL OF THIS PRESENT WASTE.  .....TALE OF A TUB   25   40
    LESS THAN PRESENT, PAST -- THIS FUTURE.  ..ON THE DECLINE OF ORACLES   78   29
    OF A SINGLE ROSE PRESENT TO IMAGINE  ..................RHODODENDRON.  103    3
    I WEAR THE PRESENT ITCH FOR FLESH,  ....................THE EYE-MOTE  109   22
    OR ELSE THEY ARE PRESENT, AND THEIR DISGUISE SO BRIGHT  ......STARS.  165   22
    LAUNDER AND PRESENT THEMSELVES.  ......................AN APPEARANCE  189    7
    A BIRTHDAY PRESENT  ............................A BIRTHDAY PRESENT  206    T
    I DO NOT WANT MUCH OF A PRESENT, ANYWAY, THIS YEAR.  ......BIRTHDAY.  206   13
PRESENTLY (1)
    YOU WILL BE AWARE OF AN ABSENCE, PRESENTLY,  ...FOR A FATHERLESS SON  205    1
PRESERVE (2)
    I SHOULD SUGAR AND PRESERVE MY DAYS LIKE FRUIT!  .........LAST WORDS  172   10
    PEBBLES WE PRESERVE IN OUR OWN CUPBOARDS*DIALOGUE OVER A OUIJA BOARD  280  135
PRESSED (1)
    AND RETURNED THEM STEAMED AND PRESSED AND STIFF AS SHIRTS. *THE TOUR  238   34
PRESSING (1)
    THEY ARE PRESSING OUT OF THE MANY-HOLED EARPIECE, THEY ARE LOOKING
        FOR A LISTENER.  ......WORDS HEARD, BY ACCIDENT, OVER THE PHONE  203    9
PRESTISSIMOS (1)
    CRESCENDOS, CADENZAS, PRESTOS AND PRESTISSIMOS,  ...ALICANTE LULLABY   43   18
PRESTOS (1)
    CRESCENDOS, CADENZAS, PRESTOS AND PRESTISSIMOS,  ...ALICANTE LULLABY   43   18
PRESUME (1)
    YOU'D PRESUME YOUR INNER VOICE GOD-PLUMED ENOUGH  .......DIALOGUE O.  280  168
```

	TITLE	PAGE	LINE

PRETEND (1)
    IN THE GREEN OF EDEN, PRETEND FUTURE'S SHINING FRUIT   TALE OF A TUB   25   39
PRETENDED (1)
    I PRETENDED I WAS THE TREE OF KNOWLEDGE. ....ZOO KEEPER'S WIFE   155   27
PRETENDING (2)
    PRETENDING I AM A NEGRESS WITH PINK PAWS. ....THE JAILER   226   19
    PRETENDING THAT THE BIRDS ARE HERE TO STAY; ....NEVER TRY TO TRICK.   319   2
PRETENDS (1)
    WHERE WAVE PRETENDS TO DRENCH REAL SKY." ....LOVE IS A PARALLAX   329   6
PRETTY (3)
    "THESE ARE THE PRETTY TRINKETS THE SEA HIDES, ...FINISTERRE   170   31
    BIT MY PRETTY RED HEART IN TWO. ....DADDY   224   56
    I'LL CARRY IT OFF LIKE A RICH PRETTY GIRL, ...STOPPED DEAD   230   23
PREVENT (1)
    TO PREVENT FALL, OR ANCHOR THE FLUENT AIR ....EPITAPH FOR F.   45   3
PREY (1)
    CIRCLES HER LIKE A PREY SHE'D LOVE TO KILL ....WIDOW   164   15
PRICE (2)
    BUT AT THE PRICE OF A PIN-STITCHED SKIN ....MAUDLIN   51   7
    THEIR SMALL PRICE PAID, THESE WEDDED ONES ....CRYSTAL GAZER   55   25
PRICELESS (1)
    PRICELESS AND QUIET ....PURDAH   243   34
PRICKLE (2)
    MY NOSTRILS PRICKLE WITH NOSTALGIA. ....LEAVING EARLY   146   20
    WHEN I LIGHT THEM, MY NOSTRILS PRICKLE. ....CANDLES   149   14
PRICKLES (2)
    FOR THE RELISH OF HEAVEN, RELENTLESS, DOUSING WITH PRICKLES *LESSON.   80   14
    A FLYING HEDGEHOG, ALL PRICKLES. ....THE SWARM   216   32
PRICKLING (3)
    HAIR PRICKLING ON HIS HEAD, ...DIALOGUE BETWEEN GHOST AND PRIEST   38   8
    UNDER PRICKLING STARS, ...MONOLOGUE AT 3 A.M.   40   9
    PRICKLING MY ANKLES AND MURMURING OF THEIR HUMILITY. ....MOON.   172   4
PRIDE (4)
    GRASS-COUCHED IN HER LABOR'S PRIDE, ...TWO SISTERS OF PERSEPHONE   32   23
    INEXORABLE. AND THEIR PRIDE! ....GETTING THERE   248   16
    HE RODE THE FLOOD IN A PRIDE OF PRONGS ....LAMENT   315   9
    AND PAGE BY PRIDE THE GOOD BOOKS BLOW;*SONG FOR A REVOLUTIONARY LOVE   322   3
PRIDE'S (2)
    STAKED IN PRIDE'S COVEN. ....VANITY FAIR   33   35
    DOWN FROM PRIDE'S SIZE: INSTEAD, A GRISLY-THEWED, ...SNOWMAN O.   59   29
PRIEST (7)
    DIALOGUE BETWEEN GHOST AND PRIEST *DIALOGUE BETWEEN GHOST AND PRIEST   38   T
    GHOST SAID TO PRIEST: ....DIALOGUE BETWEEN GHOST AND PRIEST   38   18
    GHOST SWORE TO PRIEST: ....DIALOGUE BETWEEN GHOST AND PRIEST   39   48
    THE HIGH, DEAD, TOELESS FOOT OF THIS PRIEST ....BERCK-PLAGE   197   21
    THE VOICE OF THE PRIEST, IN THIN AIR, ...BERCK-PLAGE   200   93
    AND THE PRIEST IS A VESSEL, ...BERCK-PLAGE   200   113
    DRIVES PRIEST AND PROSTITUTE IN DOORWAYS, ...INSOLENT STORM.   326   15
PRIEST-BAKED (1)
    YOU: A PRIEST-BAKED PASTY STUFFED TO THE BRIM ....DIALOGUE O.   282   214
PRIESTLIER (1)
    HANDS MOVING MOVE PRIESTLIER ....SCULPTOR   91   5
PRIEST'S (1)
    THAN PRIEST'S HANDS, INVOKE NO VAIN ....SCULPTOR   91   6
PRIM (2)
    WITH ITS PRIM BRIC-A-BRAC, WITHOUT A MOON ....YADWIGHA.   85   11
    PRIM, PINK-BREASTED, FEMININE, SHE NURSES ....FEMALE AUTHOR   301   5
PRIMA (1)
    THOUGH PRIMA DONNA POUTS AND CRITIC STINGS, ...LOVE IS A PARALLAX   330   56
PRIME (2)
    THOUGH PRIME PARTS CRAM EACH RICH MEAL, ...THE GLUTTON   40   11
    GLORIFIED FOR PRIME FLESH AND GOLDEN CRACKLING ....SOW   60   15
PRINCE (4)
    OF THE BASE, BARBAROUS PRINCE OW. ....NATURAL HISTORY   71   12
    THE PRINCE LEANS TO THE GIRL IN SCARLET HEELS, ...CINDERELLA   303   1
    GUILT-STRICKEN HALTS, PALES, CLINGS TO THE PRINCE ....CINDERELLA   304   12
    WHAT PRINCE HAS EVER SEIZED THE SHINING GRAIL .......METAMORPHOSES.   307   19
PRINCESS (5)
    THE PRINCESS AND THE GOBLINS ....THE PRINCESS AND THE GOBLINS   333   T
    UP WHICH THE WAKEFUL PRINCESS CLIMBS TO FIND ....THE PRINCESS.   333   2
    THE PRINCESS HEARS THE THUNDER AND THE POMP ....THE PRINCESS.   333   21
    THE PRINCESS FREES THE MINER, STONE BY STONE, ...THE PRINCESS.   334   49
    THE PRINCESS COAXES THE INCREDULOUS BOY*THE PRINCESS AND THE GOBLINS   334   51
PRINT (3)
    THE PRINT OF ITS BIG FOOT LAST WINTER, ...PHEASANT   191   11
    THE BENT PRINT BULGING BEFORE HIM LIKE SCENERY. ....BERCK-PLAGE   197   23
    TO PRINT YOUR FLAMING IMAGE IN BIRTHSPOT ....SONNET TO SATAN   323   11
PRINTS (1)
    FLAWED BY LOVE'S PRINTS. ....ON THE PLETHORA OF DRYADS   67   18
PRISON (2)
    FROM WATER-TOWER HILL TO THE BRICK PRISON ....POINT SHIRLEY   110   1
    THE DEER ISLAND PRISON ....MAN IN BLACK   119   7
PRISONER (1)
    WITH BLACK ALACRITY BOUND ROUND HIS PRISONER. ....SPIDER   49   28

	TITLE	PAGE	LINE

PRISTINE (1)
AND PRISTINE ALPHABETS AND COWS THAT MOO ...THE GHOST'S LEAVETAKING   91   36
PRIVACY (1)
HE LIVES WITHOUT PRIVACY IN A LIDLESS ROOM, ...INSOMNIAC   163   26
PRIVATE (7)
LAYS ALL WALLS WASTE; PRIVATE ESTATES ARE TORN, ...CHANNEL CROSSING   27   31
AND EVERY PRIVATE TWINGE A HISSING ASP ....PERSEUS   83   20
BUT TO A FRIEND, IN PRIVATE, ROUSSEAU CONFESSED HIS EYE ..YADWIGHA.   86   35
PRIVATE GROUND ....PRIVATE GROUND   130   T
THIS IS NO TIME FOR THE PRIVATE POINT OF VIEW. ....CANDLES   149   13
AND APPEARS TO HAVE SUFFERED A SORT OF PRIVATE BLITZKRIEG. ..A LIFE   150   24
PROCEEDS FROM PRIVATE FLOOD. ....TRIO OF LOVE SONGS   314   12
PRIVATES (1)
AND A WEED, HAIRY AS PRIVATES. ....BERCK-PLAGE   197   36
PRIZE (4)
PRIZE RIBBON AND PIG SHOW. ....SOW   60   6
MIGHT WELL SEIZE THIS PRIZE, ...THE LADY AND THE EARTHENWARE HEAD   69   12
OF PRIZE ROSES, CULLING THE FULLEST FLORETS; ....SPINACH-PICKER.   90   19
OF ONE WINE-GLASS, YOU'LL PIN IT LIKE A PRIZE ....DIALOGUE O.   283 249
PRO (1)
ABOUT EACH COSMIC PRO AND CON; ....LOVE IS A PARALLAX   329   15
PROBABLE (1)
PROBABLE MOTES THAT TICK THE YEARS OFF MY LIFE.   A BIRTHDAY PRESENT   207   43
PROBE (1)
BUT YET THE PERVERSE IMP WITHIN WILL PROBE*METAMORPHOSES OF THE MOON   308   31
PROBING (1)
PROBING FRACTURED VENUS WITH A STICK ....TWO LOVERS.   327   15
PROBLEM (1)
LIKE A CHILD'S TOO-SIMPLE MATHEMATICAL PROBLEM. ....STARS.   165   20
PROBLEMS (1)
THE FIRST WORKS PROBLEMS ON ....TWO SISTERS OF PERSEPHONE   31   6
PROCEED (5)
PROCEED FROM YOUR GREAT LIPS. ....THE COLOSSUS   129   4
BULLDOZERS, GUILLOTINES, WHITE CHAMBERS OF SHRIEKS PROCEED,   THREE.   177   19
ENDLESSLY PROCEED -- AND THE COLD ANGELS, THE ABSTRACTIONS.   THREE.   177   20
THE LETTERS PROCEED FROM THESE BLACK KEYS, AND THESE BLACK KEYS
PROCEED ....THREE WOMEN   177   27
THE LETTERS PROCEED FROM THESE BLACK KEYS, AND THESE BLACK KEYS
PROCEED ....THREE WOMEN   177   27
PROCEEDED (1)
PROCEEDED TO SWILL ....SOW   61   44
PROCEEDS (3)
MISS DRAKE PROCEEDS TO SUPPER ....MISS DRAKE PROCEEDS TO SUPPER   41   T
PROCEEDS CLEAR AS IT EVER DID ....THE BURNT-OUT SPA   138   20
PROCEEDS FROM PRIVATE FLOOD. ....TRIO OF LOVE SONGS   314   12
PRODDED (1)
IN APT IAMBICS, IF PRODDED TO RECITE ...DIALOGUE OVER A OUIJA BOARD   280 143
PRODIGAL (5)
NEIGHBORHOOD COCKCROW -- ALL NATURE'S PRODIGAL BACKTALK, *CONJURING.   66   4
CAN NOTHINGNESS BE SO PRODIGAL? ....THREE WOMEN   183 232
AND NEWTS ARE PRODIGAL IN LEGS. AND MAY I BE ....THREE WOMEN   184 258
AS PRODIGAL IN WHAT LACKS ME. ....THREE WOMEN   184 259
PLAYING HIS PRODIGAL CHARADES. ....LOVE IS A PARALLAX   329   36
PRODIGIOUS (3)
PRODIGIOUS IN GLUTTONIES AS THAT HOG WHOSE WANT ....SOW   61   41
HEAD ALONE SHOWS YOU IN THE PRODIGIOUS ACT ....PERSEUS   82   1
NO DEATHS, NO PRODIGIOUS INJURIES ....AFTERMATH   113   6
PRODUCE (1)
AS IF THE AIR WERE LABORING TO PRODUCE   DIALOGUE OVER A OUIJA BOARD   279   89
PROFANE (3)
OF THE PROFANE GRAIL, THE DREAMING SKULL. ..THE GHOST'S LEAVETAKING   91   40
CAME THE PROFANE STIMULUS TO COUGH; ....DIRGE FOR A JOKER   302   2
AND PROFANE WORDS SCRAWLED BLACK ACROSS THE SUN. ....DOOM OF EXILES   318   12
PROFIT (2)
STEEL ON MYSELF BEFORE PROFIT ....RHYME   50   14
LOSS CANCELS PROFIT. ....GREEN ROCK, WINTHROP BAY   105   18
PROFITED (1)
PROFITED MEMORY, BUT DID AWAY WITH THE OLD SCENERY .....GREEN ROCK.   105   5
PROFITLESS (1)
PROFITLESS, THEIR GOSSIPING IMAGES ....ON THE DECLINE OF ORACLES   78   22
PROFOUNDER (1)
OUR VOICES FATHOMED A PROFOUNDER SOUND: ....THE OTHER TWO   68   12
PROFOUNDLY (1)
WHICH SEEMED, WHEN DREAMED, TO MEAN SO PROFOUNDLY MUCH, ...GHOST'S.   90   5
PROLOGUE (1)
PROLOGUE TO SPRING ....PROLOGUE TO SPRING   322   T
PROMENADE (1)
WHERE PIGEONS PROMENADE THE GABLE-ENDS *THE PRINCESS AND THE GOBLINS   335   66
PROMINENT (1)
A WHOLE FAMILY OF PROMINENT OBJECTS ....CANDLES   148   6
PROMISE (4)
TO SLAY SPAWN OF DRAGON'S TEETH: SPEAKING THIS PROMISE, ..WREATH F.   45   23
MY PROMISE OF AN IDYLL. THE BLUE'S WORN OUT: ....GREEN ROCK.   105   8
THE WHITE SKY EMPTIES OF ITS PROMISE, LIKE A CUP. ......THREE WOMEN   177   33
THE SUAVE ETERNAL SERPENTS PROMISE BLISS ....NEVER TRY TO TRICK.   320   13

		TITLE	PAGE	LINE
PROMISED (1)				
THAT SKEIN OF VOICES. WE PROMISED TO FORGET	...........DIALOGUE O.	286	342
PROMISES (1)				
LIKE A SERIES OF PROMISES, AS I STEP FORWARD.	....WUTHERING HEIGHTS	167	9
PROMISING (2)				
PROMISING SURE HARBORAGE;	......................................LORELEI	94	25
PROMISING SIMPLY THE HARD STARS, THE SPACE	....................WIDOW	164	23
PROMPTING (1)				
LEANED THE DEVIL PROMPTING YOU TO LAUGH.	.........DIRGE FOR A JOKER	302	4
PRONE (2)				
THE GESTURE, BEND AND HOLD THE PRONE MAN'S HEAD.	..CHANNEL CROSSING	27	36
BOY, PRONE TO COMPOSE QUEER POETRY	.....DIALOGUE OVER A OUIJA BOARD	280	142
PRONGS (1)				
HE RODE THE FLOOD IN A PRIDE OF PRONGS	......................LAMENT	315	8
PRONOUNCEMENTS (1)				
OF PAN'S PRONOUNCEMENTS, AND OUR NERVES ARE STRUNG	.....DIALOGUE O.	284	288
PROOF (2)				
NO FIRE IS, NOR IN ANY BOOK PROOF	......................VANITY FAIR	33	27
IT IS WATERPROOF, SHATTERPROOF, PROOF	................THE APPLICANT	221	23
PROP (2)				
HOW THEY PROP EACH OTHER UP!	.......................THE THIN PEOPLE	65	40
TO SUN ON THE ROCKS OR PROP	.......................OLD LADIES' HOME	120	5
PROPEL (1)				
TO PROPEL HIS PLAYFULNESS, BUT ON YOU, ABOVE	...........DIALOGUE O.	282	230
PROPER (3)				
FOR WEDLOCK WROUGHT WITHIN LOVE'S PROPER CHAPEL.	.........WREATH F.	44	12
THEY ARE PROPER IN SHAPE AND NUMBER AND EVERY PART.	......STILLBORN	142	7
AND SWAGGERS LIKE A PROPER GENTLEMAN;	...................ADMONITIONS	319	11
PROPERLY (2)				
PIECED, GLUED, AND PROPERLY JOINTED.	...................THE COLOSSUS	129	2
HOLDING MY BONES IN PLACE SO THEY WOULD MEND PROPERLY.	..IN PLASTER	159	27
PROPERTY (3)				
HOW LONG CAN I BE A WALL AROUND MY GREEN PROPERTY?	.....THREE WOMEN	185	295
THIS IS MY PROPERTY.	...........................LETTER IN NOVEMBER	253	16
FLICKING OVER MY PROPERTY,	...........................EAVESDROPPER	261	55
PROPHECIES (1)				
POOLS, PROPHECIES AND SUCH FROM THE UNFATHOMED	.........DIALOGUE O.	282	240
PROPHESY (1)				
THESE LOVERS PROPHESY TO LOCK EMBRACE	..EPITAPH FOR FIRE AND FLOWER	45	17
PROPHET (2)				
I SIZZLED IN HIS BLUE VOLTS LIKE A DESERT PROPHET.	..........YOU'RE	141	2
SELVES POSING AS PROPHET AND SLYLY POACHING	.............DIALOGUE O.	280	134
PROPHETIC (1)				
IN HER PROPHETIC FIT HEARD WHAT WE HEARD,	.............DIALOGUE O.	286	348
PROPHETS (2)				
TO CHASTITY'S SERVICE: LIKE PROPHETS, LIKE PREACHERS,	......VIRGIN.	82	28
ORBIT; NEITHER LAW NOR PROPHETS *INSOLENT STORM STRIKES AT THE SKULL		326	26
PROPPED (2)				
THEY HAVE PROPPED MY HEAD BETWEEN THE PILLOW AND THE SHEET-CUFF ...			
	... TULIPS	160	8
THEY PROPPED HIS JAW WITH A BOOK UNTIL IT STIFFENED	....BERCK-PLAGE	198	65
PROPPING (1)				
STOLIDLY PROPPING THICK VOLUMES OF PROSE: SPITE-SET	....LADY AND T.	69	4
PROPS (4)				
PROPS A LEG-STUMP UPON A CRUTCH,	......................THE BEGGARS	48	11
WHICH PROPS YOU THROUGH THIS DESERT LIKE A DREAM	........DIALOGUE O.	282	212
WITH STRUTS AND PROPS OF THE HOLY STAGE.	........SONG FOR A REVOLU.	323	8
ITEM: CHUCK OUT ROYAL RIGMAROLE OF PROPS	.............A SORCERER B.	324	5
PROSAIC (1)				
THE COUCH GLARED OUT AT THE PROSAIC EYE.	................YADWIGHA.	85	20
PROSE (2)				
STOLIDLY PROPPING THICK VOLUMES OF PROSE: SPITE-SET	....LADY AND T.	69	4
AGE, AND AGES OF PROSE, HAVE UNCOILED	........................OUIJA	77	15
PROSPECT (2)				
PROSPECT	....PROSPECT	28	T
THE PROSPECT IS DULL AS AN OLD ETCHING.	..............A WINTER SHIP	113	13
PROSPECTS (2)				
FRACTURED PILLARS FRAME PROSPECTS OF ROCK;	..........CONVERSATION.	21	9
WHICH SHROUDS OUR PROSPECTS IN AMBIGUOUS SHADOW?	.....TALE OF A TUB	24	16
PROSTITUTE (1)				
DRIVES PRIEST AND PROSTITUTE IN DOORWAYS,	..........INSOLENT STORM.	326	15
PROTECTED (1)				
HAS PROTECTED	....THALIDOMIDE	252	9
PROTECTING (1)				
I SHALL BE A WALL AND A ROOF, PROTECTING.	..............THREE WOMEN	180	139
PROTECTION (2)				
THEY LEFT ME A BORROWED MAID NAMED ELLEN, "FOR PROTECTION",	..BABY.	174	17
IN MY SLEEVELESS SUMMERY DRESS I HAVE NO PROTECTION,*THE BEE MEETING		211	3
PROTECTIVELY (1)				
CUPPING THE BERRY PROTECTIVELY BEFORE	..........BITTER STRAWBERRIES	300	37
PROTECTS (1)				
PINE-NEEDLE ARMOR PROTECTS	.......................VIRGIN IN A TREE	81	16
PROTESTING (2)				
THEIRS IS THE ONLY VOICE, PROTESTING, PROTESTING.	....BLACKBERRYING	168	12
THEIRS IS THE ONLY VOICE, PROTESTING, PROTESTING.	....BLACKBERRYING	168	12

	TITLE	PAGE	LINE

PROTRACTED (1)
    HOW THEY LIT THE TEDIUM OF THE PROTRACTED EVENING! ....INSOMNIAC 163 16
PROUD (9)
    MEEK AND PROUD BOTH FALL; STARK VIOLENCE ....CHANNEL CROSSING 27 30
    DUNGAREES, PROUD AS A LADY IN A SEA ....MEMOIRS OF A SPINACH-PICKER 90 18
    GODS GROW TOO PROUD TO PRACTICE DOORMAN DUTIES ....DIALOGUE O. 280 127
    (PROUD YOU HALT UPON THE SPIRAL STAIR.) *TO EVA DESCENDING THE STAIR 303 3
    (PROUD YOU HALT UPON THE SPIRAL STAIR.) *TO EVA DESCENDING THE STAIR 303 9
    (PROUD YOU HALT UPON THE SPIRAL STAIR.) *TO EVA DESCENDING THE STAIR 303 15
    (PROUD YOU HALT UPON THE SPIRAL STAIR.) *TO EVA DESCENDING THE STAIR 303 19
    THEY WANT NO PROUD PATERNAL KINGDOM COME; ....THE DEAD 320 6
    O MAKER OF PROUD PLANET'S NEGATIVE, ...SONNET TO SATAN 323 13
PROVE (5)
    LOVE FIERY ENOUGH TO PROVE FLESH REAL, ..SOLILOQUY OF THE SOLIPSIST 38 33
    TO PROVE IT. AS I THINK NOW OF HER HEAD, ...ALL THE DEAD DEARS 70 18
    TO PROVE IT GENUINE. YOU'D KNEEL, TOO, DIALOGUE OVER A OUIJA BOARD 280 162
    WILL PROVE TO BE SOME COMMON PARLOR FAKE: *METAMORPHOSES OF THE MOON 307 22
    POLEMIC GALES PROVE POINT BY POINT ....INSOLENT STORM. 325 9
PROVED (1)
    AND, BRIGHT AS BLOOD-DROPS, PROVED NO BRAVE BRANCH DIES ..MAYFLOWER 60 3
PROVERBS (1)
    SET IN THE PROVERBS STITCHED ON SAMPLERS ....VIRGIN IN A TREE 81 3
PROVES (2)
    PROVES RUMORS SHALLOW, ...FULL FATHOM FIVE 93 24
    A WINDOW WHICH PROVES THE SKY SHEER RIGMAROLE*EPITAPH IN THREE PARTS 337 28
PROVIDES (1)
    FOR WHOM THE GOOD LORD PROVIDES (HE GAVE ....ON DECK 143 20
PROVINCE (1)
    IN THIS PROVINCE OF THE STUCK RECORD ....THE TIMES ARE TIDY 107 2
PROVINCES (1)
    IN PREPOSTEROUS PROVINCES OF THE MADCAP ....LETTER TO A PURIST 37 14
PROWESS (1)
    PAN'S PROWESS OUR OWN CREATION, AND NOT THE OTHER'S ....DIALOGUE O. 284 285
PROWL (1)
    NOW PROWL ON THE BOUGH; ....TEMPER OF TIME 336 6
PROW-LIKE (1)
    PROW-LIKE THROUGH BLURS ....TWO VIEWS OF WITHENS 72 4
PROWLS (1)
    HE PROWLS MORE LORDLY THAN THE SUN. ....PURSUIT 22 4
PRUSSIAN (1)
    YOU HAD ONE LEG, AND A PRUSSIAN MIND. ....LITTLE FUGUE 188 40
PRY (2)
    THE JEWELMASTER DRIVES HIS CHISEL TO PRY POEM.7.S. 136 20
    I PICK AND PRY LIKE A DOCTOR OR ....THE BURNT-OUT SPA 138 14
PSEUDONYM (1)
    THIS MAN MAKES A PSEUDONYM ....THE FEARFUL 256 1
PSYCHE-KNOT (1)
    COMPOSED IN GRECIAN TUNIC AND PSYCHE-KNOT, ...CONVERSATION. 21 11
PSYCHES (1)
    STARS, NOT OUR CHEESEPARING PSYCHES. IT *DIALOGUE OVER A OUIJA BOARD 281 195
PSYCHIC (1)
    FUSING TWO TALENTS, A SORT OF PSYCHIC BASTARD ....DIALOGUE O. 280 139
PUBLIC (7)
    PUTS ON A PUBLIC GRIN, REPEATS OUR NAME ....TALE OF A TUB 24 7
    RANSACKED IN THE PUBLIC EYE. WE FORSAKE ....CHANNEL CROSSING 27 32
    HE KEPT THE SOW -- IMPOUNDED FROM PUBLIC STARE, ...SOW 60 5
    IN THE PUBLIC PARK; AT HOME FELT THE WANT ...........RHODODENDRON. 103 2
    ON THE PUBLIC GRILLS, AND THE OCHREOUS SALT FLATS, ...SUICIDE. 115 2
    WELL, ONE WEARIES OF THE PUBLIC GARDENS: ONE WANTS A VACATION ...
              ... TWO CAMPERS IN CLOUD COUNTRY 144 7
    I IMAGINE MYSELF WITH A GREAT PUBLIC, ...BARREN WOMAN 157 6
PUCKER (1)
    AND I WEAR THE WRY-FACED PUCKER OF ....JILTED 304 7
PUDDING (1)
    VELVET PILLOWS THE COLOUR OF BLOOD PUDDING ....LEAVING EARLY 145 5
PUDDLE (1)
    I BED IN A FISH PUDDLE. POEM.4.BEAST. 134 19
PUFF (1)
    NIMBUS, OR PUFF ....POLLY'S TREE 128 21
PUFFED (1)
    WITH TRIANGULAR SCORCH MARKS FROM IRONING TINY RUCHINGS AND
        PUFFED SLEEVES. ....THE BABYSITTERS 174 15
PUKE (1)
    WHERE THEY CRAP AND PUKE AND CRY AND SHE CAN'T HEAR. ....LESBOS 228 14
PULL (1)
    I-N-E, HE SAYS. YOU FEEL HIM PULL ......DIALOGUE OVER A OUIJA BOARD 277 32
PULLED (1)
    BUT THEY PULLED ME OUT OF THE SACK, ...DADDY 224 61
PULP (1)
    PULP OF YOUR HEART ....CUT 236 34
PULPIT (1)
    ALWAYS FROM THE PULPIT DURING SERVICE ....DIRGE FOR A JOKER 302 3
PULSE (5)
    PLANETS PULSE IN THE LAKE LIKE BRIGHT AMOEBAS; ....TWO CAMP. 145 23
    THE WAVES PULSE AND PULSE LIKE HEARTS. ....WHITSUN 154 22

	TITLE	PAGE	LINE

PULSE (CONT.)
  THE WAVES PULSE AND PULSE LIKE HEARTS. ....WHITSUN 154 22
  THE PARTICLES OF DESTRUCTION I SUCK UP? AM I A PULSE ...THREE WOMEN 177 38
  THICK AS FOREIGN COFFEE, AND WITH A SLUGGY PULSE. .....WORDS HEARD. 202 2
PULSED (1)
  RIPPLED AND PULSED IN THE GLASSY UPDRAUGHT. ...SUICIDE OFF EGG ROCK 115 5
PULSES (3)
  THE SEA PULSES UNDER A SKIN OF OIL. ....A WINTER SHIP 112 5
  SHE PULSES LIKE A HEART ON MY HILL. ....ELM/DR 292 2
  THE DULL DRUMS OF MY PULSES BEAT ....FAMILY REUNION 300 8
PUMA (1)
  LIKE ALL THE OTHERS AND SWEAR THAT HE'S A PUMA ....DIALOGUE O. 281 176
PUMPED (1)
  PUMPED AHEAD BY THESE PISTONS, THIS BLOOD ....GETTING THERE 248 30
PUMPKIN (3)
  IN THE WHORL OF HER EAR, AND LIKE A SCOOPED-OUT PUMPKIN CROWN ...
    ... HARDCASTLE CRAGS 63 24
  THE COOK LUGS A PUMPKIN ....YADDO: THE GRAND MANOR 123 5
  PLANT AN ORANGE PUMPKIN PATCH ...BLACK PINE TREE IN AN ORANGE LIGHT 328 4
PUMPKINS (2)
  THE ORANGE PUMPKINS HAVE NO EYES. POEM.1.WHO. 131 20
  AND FOR PUMPKINS TO PURR INTO CADILLACS ....DIALOGUE EN ROUTE 309 28
PUMPS (2)
  THE MEN THE BLOOD STILL PUMPS FORWARD, ...GETTING THERE 248 25
  THAT LOVES ME, PUMPS ....PARALYTIC 266 5
PUNCHING (1)
  PUNCHING OUT ABSENCE! LIKE CANNON. ....GETTING THERE 248 8
PUNISH (1)
  WILL PUNISH US FOR SAYING WHICH IS WHICH; *METAMORPHOSES OF THE MOON 308 44
PUNISHMENT (1)
  AND IN PUNISHMENT WAS HUNG OUT LIKE BROWN FRUIT ......THE DETECTIVE 209 29
PUNTER (1)
  THE PUNTER SINKS HIS POLE. ......WATERCOLOR OF GRANTCHESTER MEADOWS 112 12
PUNY (2)
  PUNY, GREEN, AND TART, ...JILTED 304 10
  OF WITHERED WORLDS, AND STAMP OUT PUNY HELLS ....LOVE IS A PARALLAX 330 68
PUPAS (1)
  I SHALL BURY THE WOUNDED LIKE PUPAS, ...GETTING THERE 249 60
PUPIL (1)
  STUPID PUPIL, IT HAS TO TAKE EVERYTHING IN. ....TULIPS 160 10
PUPILS (2)
  THE BLACK SLOTS OF THEIR PUPILS TAKE ME IN. ......WUTHERING HEIGHTS 167 22
  HERE ARE TWO PUPILS ......ON LOOKING INTO THE EYES OF A DEMON LOVER 325 1
PUPPET (2)
  LITTLE UNSTRUNG PUPPET, KICKING TO DISAPPEAR -- ....LESBOS 227 9
  I WAS PERFECTLY RIGHT: PAN'S A MERE PUPPET ....DIALOGUE O. 279 106
PUPPET-MASTER (1)
  PUPPETS, LOOSED FROM THE STRINGS OF THE PUPPET-MASTER, ...POEM.5.F. 135 13
PUPPET-PEOPLE (1)
  DANGLES THE PUPPET-PEOPLE ....SOLILOQUY OF THE SOLIPSIST 37 14
PUPPETS (1)
  PUPPETS, LOOSED FROM THE STRINGS OF THE PUPPET-MASTER, ...POEM.5.F. 135 13
PUPPIES (1)
  ANY DAY I MAY LITTER PUPPIES POEM.2.DARK. 132 12
PURCHASE (2)
  FISH-TAILED GIRLS PURCHASE EACH WHITE LEG. ....MAUDLIN 51 8
  THESE ROCKS OFFER NO PURCHASE TO HERBAGE OR PEOPLE: ......TWO CAMP. 145 18
PURDAH (1)
  PURDAH ....PURDAH 242 T
PURE (21)
  WITH SAVOR; COUPLED SO, PURE PARAGONS OF CONSTANCE, ...WREATH F. 44 9
  PURE PHILOSOPHY HIS LOVE ENGROSSED: ....NATURAL HISTORY 71 4
  PURE LEAFAGE. A HUNDRED BASKETS BY DAY'S END. ......SPINACH-PICKER. 89 11
  PURE DEATH'S-METAL. THE YARDMAN'S ....MEDALLION 125 26
  THREADING BACK, FILAMENT BY FILAMENT, TO THE PURE ...PRIVATE GROUND 130 10
  PURE AS A PANE OF ICE. IT'S A GIFT. ....LOVE LETTER 147 36
  SALUTARY AND PURE AS BOILED WATER, ...MAGI 148 7
  I AM A NUN NOW, I HAVE NEVER BEEN SO PURE. ....TULIPS 161 28
  THESE PURE, SMALL IMAGES. THEY SMELL OF MILK. ....THREE WOMEN 183 230
  GOTHIC AND BARBAROUS, PURE GERMAN. ....LITTLE FUGUE 188 26
  PURE AND CLEAN AS THE CRY OF A BABY, ...A BIRTHDAY PRESENT 208 61
  ARE NOT VERY PURE OR TRUE. ....DADDY 223 37
  PURE? WHAT DOES IT MEAN? ....FEVER. 231 1
  I AM TOO PURE FOR YOU OR ANYONE. ....FEVER. 232 34
  AM A PURE ACETYLENE ....FEVER. 232 46
  THOUGH IT LOOKS LIKE A CAT, WITH ITS FLUFFY STUFF, PURE WHITE.*TOUR. 237 16
  THE PURE GOLD BABY ....LADY LAZARUS 246 69
  PURE AS A BABY. ....GETTING THERE 249 68
  SUCH PURE LEAPS AND SPIRALS --- ....THE NIGHT DANCES 249 5
  SCALLOPS, PURE IRON, ...LETTER IN NOVEMBER 253 20
  BUT GREENNESS, DARKNESS SO PURE ....YEARS 255 4
PURGATORY (1)
  OF TENDERNESS DOVE THROUGH THEIR PURGATORY ....THE OTHER TWO 68 24
PURIST (1)
  LETTER TO A PURIST ....LETTER TO A PURIST 36 T

PURITAN (2)
    TWINED TO HER HARD LIMBS LIKE IVY: THE PURITAN LIP *VIRGIN IN A TREE   81   12
    THEY ARE TOO PURITAN AND SOLITARY FOR THAT -- ....STARS.   166   31
PURPLE (13)
    WEARS PURPLE, STEPS CAREFULLY ....MISS DRAKE PROCEEDS TO SUPPER   41   6
    WHITE-BEARDED, WEARY. THE BERRIES PURPLE ....MOONRISE   98   29
    THE PURPLE EGG-STONES: FROM GREAT HEAD'S KNOB ....POINT SHIRLEY   110   22
    A GARDEN OF MOUTHINGS. PURPLE, SCARLET-SPECKLED, BLACK *BEEKEEPER'S.   118   1
    CABBAGEHEADS: WORMY PURPLE, SILVER-GLAZE, ...POEM.1.WHO.   131   16
    PURPLE AND RED MOUTHS, UTTERLY LOVELY. POEM.1.WHO.   132   30
    SHOULD I STIR, I THINK THIS PINK AND PURPLE PLASTIC ....ZOO K.   154   11
    HE IS IMMUNE TO PILLS: RED, PURPLE, BLUE -- ....INSOMNIAC   163   15
    I WORM AND HACK IN A PURPLE WILDERNESS. ......THE SURGEON AT 2 A.M.   171   20
    MUST YOU STAMP EACH PIECE IN PURPLE, ...A BIRTHDAY PRESENT   207   46
    INDEFATIGABLE, PURPLE. MUST IT BE CUT OUT? ....COURAGE.   210   18
    COLOR FLOODS TO THE SPOT, DULL PURPLE. ....CONTUSION   271   1
    GO CULL THE PURPLE SNAILS FROM SLOTHFUL SHELLS ....GO GET.   313   17
PURPLED (2)
    GRIEVOUSLY PURPLED, MOUTH SKEWERED ON A GROAN, ...THE RAVAGED FACE   115   6
    THE FLAT SEA PURPLED LIKE THAT EVIL CLOTH ...ELECTRA ON AZALEA PATH   117   31
PURPLES (1)
    PURPLES THE FIG IN THE LEAF'S SHADOW, TURNS THE DUST PINK. ...NET-.   121   7
PURPOSE (1)
    UNLOOSING THEIR MOONS, MONTH AFTER MONTH, TO NO PURPOSE. ...MUNICH.   263   5
PURR (4)
    ONE GRUFF-TIMBRED PURR ROLLING FROM FURRED THROATS: ..ELLA MASON A.   54   23
    WARMED BY MUCH HANDLING. THEY ALMOST PURR. ....LAST WORDS   172   18
    I HEAR HER GREAT HEART PURR. ....AN APPEARANCE   189   3
    AND FOR PUMPKINS TO PURR INTO CADILLACS ....DIALOGUE EN ROUTE   309   28
PURRS (1)
    THE WORLD PURRS, SHUT-OFF AND GENTLE. ....BERCK-PLAGE   200 110
PURSE (2)
    MONEY'S NEW-MINTED IN THIS FAT PURSE. ....METAPHORS   116   6
    HERE'S YOUR SPECS, DEAR, HERE'S YOUR PURSE. ....THE TOUR   238   36
PURSES (2)
    AND BLACK AS PURSES, THE HOUSE LIGHTS ....WUTHERING HEIGHTS   168   44
    WITH ITS YELLOW PURSES, ITS SPIKY ARMORY. ....THE BEE MEETING   211   32
PURSUERS (1)
    IN A SCABBARD OF WOOD BAFFLES PURSUERS, ...VIRGIN IN A TREE   81   8
PURSUING (1)
    SHE SHIED SIDEWAYS: A WHITE FIZZ! AND THE GIANT, PURSUING, ...
                                    ... THE SNOWMAN ON THE MOOR   59   47
PUSH (1)
    UNDER YOUR FINGER? I MEAN, YOU DON'T PUSH ....DIALOGUE O.   277   33
PUSHING (1)
    PUSHING BY LIKE HEARTS, ...MEDUSA   225   8
PUT (24)
    IN BLACK AND WHITE, OR PUT ON ICE ......EPITAPH FOR FIRE AND FLOWER   45   10
    ROSE UP AND PUT ROYAL NERVES TO THE RACK: ....NATURAL HISTORY   71   9
    AND PUT ON BARK'S NUN-BLACK ....VIRGIN IN A TREE   81   5
    YADWIGHA, POSE ON, THAT HE PUT YOU ON THE COUCH ....YADIWGHA.   86   37
    EYEING ME. GRASS PUT FORTH CLAWS; .....MUSSEL HUNTER AT ROCK HARBOR   96   25
    PUT UP WITH UNTIL CHAGRIN GIVES PLACE ....THE COMPANIONABLE ILLS   105   3
    A BULL-SNOUTED SEA THAT WOULDN'T STAY PUT, ...THE BULL OF BENDYLAW   108   8
    IN THE BASKET OF PLASTIC EVERGREENS THEY PUT *ELECTRA ON AZALEA PATH   117   25
    I SHALL NEVER GET YOU PUT TOGETHER ENTIRELY, ...THE COLOSSUS   129   1
    STAYING PUT ACCORDING TO HABIT. ....LOVE LETTER   147   4
    THAT WILL PUT HER HEART OUT LIKE AN ONLY EYE. ....WIDOW   164   5
    THE RED MOUTH I PUT BY WITH MY IDENTITY ....THREE WOMEN   183 247
    PUT ON A FACE AND WALKED INTO THE WORLD. ....THREE WOMEN   185 301
    I PUT MY HANDS AMONG THE FLAMES. NOTHING BURNS. ....POPPIES IN JULY   203   4
    NO, THE TONGUE, TOO, HAS BEEN PUT BY, ...THE COURAGE OF SHUTTING-UP   210   21
    I PUT MY EYE TO THE GRID. ....THE ARRIVAL OF THE BEE BOX   213   11
    PUT YOUR FOOT, YOUR ROOT, ...DADDY   223   23
    O I SHOULDN'T PUT MY FINGER IN THAT ....THE TOUR   237   13
    IT'S EASY ENOUGH TO DO IT AND STAY PUT. ....LADY LAZARUS   245   50
    HE LIVES. HIS ANSWER WILL PUT AN END TO GIBES ....DIALOGUE O.   281 174
    NOT MAN NOR DEMIGOD COULD PUT TOGETHER ....SONNET: TO EVA   305   9
    OUR LUCKY RELICS HAVE BEEN PUT IN HOCK: ....DOOMSDAY   316   11
    PUT ORANGE MISTRESS HALF IN SUN, *BLACK PINE TREE IN AN ORANGE LIGHT   328   10
    THE WAITRESS HOLDS OUR COATS AND WE PUT ON ......LOVE IS A PARALLAX   329   22
PUT-BY (1)
    WHILE A SKY, WORMY WITH PUT-BY SMILES, ...BERCK-PLAGE   200 104
PUTS (4)
    PUTS ON A PUBLIC GRIN, REPEATS OUR NAME ....TALE OF A TUB   24   7
    PUTS UP HIS PIPE, AND LIDS HIS MOONY EYE. .............SNAKECHARMER   79   28
    THE SUN PUTS ITS CINDER OUT. WHERE WE LIE*SLEEP IN THE MOJAVE DESERT   144   21
    IS IT ANY WONDER HE PUTS ON DARK GLASSES? ....BERCK-PLAGE   196   12
PUT-UPON (1)
    WE WERE ALWAYS CRYING, IN OUR SPARE ROOMS, LITTLE PUT-UPON SISTERS, ...
                                            ... THE BABYSITTERS   174   4
PUZZLE (1)
    ORDER AS I MIGHT PUZZLE ....MUSSEL HUNTER AT ROCK HARBOR   96   55
PUZZLING (1)
    PUZZLING THE PASSAGE OF THEIR ....MUSSEL HUNTER AT ROCK HARBOR   96   53

	TITLE	PAGE	LINE
PYRAMIDED (1)			
MY WORLD PYRAMIDED WITH LADEN BASKETS. MEMOIRS OF A SPINACH-PICKER		90	20
PYRE (1)			
CHEATED OF THE PYRE AND THE RACK, ...AFTERMATH		114	13
PYTHONESS (1)			
OF CONTENDING WORDS. SOME PYTHONESS ....DIALOGUE OVER A OUIJA BOARD		286	347
QUADRILLES (1)			
AND COO QUADRILLES ABOUT THE BLIGHTED CORE ....THE PRINCESS.		335	67
QUAHOG (1)			
OF QUAHOG CHIPS, ...POINT SHIRLEY		110	7
QUAIL (1)			
AND PLUCK THE DROLL-FLECKED QUAIL WHERE THICK THEY LIE; ....GO GET.		313	2
QUAINTLY (2)			
WHICH AT TWELVE WILL QUAINTLY HATCH ....BLACK PINE TREE.		328	5
WHICH QUAINTLY WOVE THE FABRIC OF HER FATE ....THE PRINCESS.		335	57
QUARRELS (1)			
O CACOPHONY, GODDESS OF JAZZ AND OF QUARRELS, ...ALICANTE LULLABY		43	15
QUARRY (1)			
IN A QUARRY OF SILENCES. ....POEM.7.S.		136	13
QUARTERED (1)			
I REMEMBER THE BLOODIED CHICKS AND THE QUARTERED RABBITS. ...ZOO K.		155	24
QUARTS (1)			
BUSINESSLIKE SHE ASKED US, "HOW MANY QUARTS?" ..BITTER STRAWBERRIES		300	31
QUARTZ (6)			
KNOBBED QUARTZ; FLAYED COLORS RIPEN ....ODE FOR TED		29	11
IN QUARTZ, AS CRACK YOUR SKULL TO KEEP EPITAPH FOR FIRE AND FLOWER		45	4
THAT CLAIRVOYANT QUARTZ WHICH ONCE, AT HER OWN WISHING, ...			
... CRYSTAL GAZER		55	29
HER DOWN TO MERE QUARTZ GRIT IN THAT STONY LIGHT ..HARDCASTLE CRAGS		63	44
SPLITTING LIKE QUARTZ INTO A MILLION BITS. ....LESBOS		228	51
CRIMPED LIKE FERN IN THE QUARTZ ATMOSPHERE; .....PROLOGUE TO SPRING		322	8
QUARTZ-CLEAR (1)			
A QUARTZ-CLEAR DAWN ....SOUTHERN SUNRISE		26	13
QUARTZ-FLAKE (1)			
IT MARRY QUARTZ-FLAKE, ...POLLY'S TREE		129	32
QUEEN (14)			
VIES WITH BEST QUEEN OVER ....VANITY FAIR		33	31
HE HYMNS THE ROTTEN QUEEN WITH SAFFRON HAIR ....OUIJA		77	22
THAN VIRGINS' TEARS. THAT BAWDY QUEEN OF DEATH, ...OUIJA		77	24
THE QUEEN IN THE MULBERRY ARBOR STARED ....THE BULL OF BENDYLAW		108	4
STIFF AS A QUEEN ON A PLAYING CARD. ....THE BULL OF BENDYLAW		108	5
THE QUEEN BEE MARRIES THE WINTER OF YOUR YEAR. ....BEEKEEPER'S.		118	21
THE VILLAGERS OPEN THE CHAMBERS, THEY ARE HUNTING THE QUEEN. ..BEE.		212	42
THE OLD QUEEN DOES NOT SHOW HERSELF, IS SHE SO UNGRATEFUL? ....BEE.		212	50
IS THERE ANY QUEEN AT ALL IN IT? ....STINGS		214	15
HAVE A SELF TO RECOVER, A QUEEN. ....STINGS		215	52
QUEEN MARY'S ROSE GARDEN ....QUEEN MARY'S ROSE GARDEN		290	T
IN THE CENTER OF THE GARDEN NAMED AFTER QUEEN MARY. ..QUEEN MARY'S.		290	3
TO TRAP THIS OUTRAGEOUS NIMBLE QUEEN ....AERIALIST		332	34
THE CHAMBERS WHERE THEIR FIENDISH QUEEN WOULD SIT. ...THE PRINCESS.		334	40
QUEENLY (1)			
UNRULY ENOUGH TO PITCH HER FIVE QUEENLY WITS ....SPINSTER		50	20
QUEENS (2)			
THE ROSES ARE NAMED AFTER QUEENS AND PEOPLE OF NOTE ..QUEEN MARY'S.		290	17
FROM RHETORIC OF THESE ROCOCO QUEENS. ....A SORCERER B.		324	4
QUEEN'S (2)			
THE QUEEN'S COMPLAINT ....THE QUEEN'S COMPLAINT		28	T
ON THE QUEEN'S PALM ....RECANTATION		41	3
QUEENSHIP (1)			
HERE IS A QUEENSHIP NO MOTHER CAN CONTEST -- ....BEEKEEPER'S.		118	13
QUEER (6)			
HEARD A QUEER CRUSTY SCRABBLE ....MUSSEL HUNTER AT ROCK HARBOR		95	14
QUEER CANDELABRUM. ....POLLY'S TREE		128	23
LET THEM START THE QUEER ALCHEMY ......................EAVESDROPPER		260	21
SUCH QUEER MOONS WE LIVE WITH ....BALLOONS		271	10
BOY, PRONE TO COMPOSE QUEER POETRY .....DIALOGUE OVER A OUIJA BOARD		280	142
SHE RECALLS QUEER STORIES HER NURSE READ ....THE PRINCESS.		334	37
QUEERLY (1)			
AND THE AIR DANGEROUS. NOONDAY ACTS QUEERLY ....SLEEP.		143	3
QUENCH (1)			
TO QUENCH HIS THIRST I SOUANDER BLOOD; ....PURSUIT		23	38
QUERIES (1)			
PEOPLE MAKE QUERIES ....ELLA MASON AND HER ELEVEN CATS		53	3
QUESTION (1)			
THAT QUESTION ENDED IT -- I ....MUSSEL HUNTER AT ROCK HARBOR		96	51
QUESTIONS (5)			
TO SATISFY THE QUESTIONS OF A CURIOUS OLD FOOL?" ....DIALOGUE B.		39	26
BUT ONE DUSK OUR QUESTIONS COMMENDED US TO A TOUR ....SOW		60	7
YOU DEFY QUESTIONS; ....FULL FATHOM FIVE		93	39
QUESTIONS WITHOUT ANSWER, ...MYSTIC		268	2
OUR QUESTIONS IN HUMBLE HABIT TO GAIN GRACE ....DIALOGUE O.		281	187
QUIBBLE (1)			
IN RUCK AND QUIBBLE OF COURTFOLK ....THE QUEEN'S COMPLAINT		28	1
QUICK (15)			
GROWS QUICK WITH SEED. ....TWO SISTERS OF PERSEPHONE		32	22

395

QUICK (CONT.)
CUPPED QUICK TO MOUTH; ....THE GLUTTON   40   10
DRIVES NIMBLE BLOOD TOO QUICK ....EPITAPH FOR FIRE AND FLOWER 46   25
STONE-BUILT TOWN, THAT SHE HEARD THE QUICK AIR IGNITE *HARDCASTLE C. 62   4
ENOUGH TO SNUFF THE QUICK ....HARDCASTLE CRAGS 63   41
QUICK AS THEY. TO FOLLOW THE LIGHT'S TINT ......CHILD'S PARK STONES 101   18
SLIDING SHUT ON SOME QUICK THING, ...THE RABBIT CATCHER 194   29
WITH QUICK PRACTICED HANDS, ...BITTER STRAWBERRIES 300   36
THE GARNETS ON HER FINGERS TWINKLE QUICK ....FEMALE AUTHOR 301   9
(TOO QUICK FOR THE PAIR TO ABSORB IT), ...DIALOGUE EN ROUTE 309   41
TELL ME QUICK, DARLING, TELL ME NOW. ....THE DISPOSSESSED 318   3
TELL ME QUICK, DARLING, TELL ME NOW. ....THE DISPOSSESSED 318   9
TELL ME QUICK, DARLING, TELL ME NOW. ....THE DISPOSSESSED 318   15
TELL ME QUICK, DARLING, TELL ME NOW! ....THE DISPOSSESSED 319   19
FOR EACH QUICK, FLARING GAME ....TOUCH-AND-GO 336   20
QUICKEN (1)
TO QUICKEN HIS SLUGGARD'S BLOOD. BUT HE NEEDN'T COME ...DIALOGUE O. 281 184
QUICKENED (1)
WALK FORTH INTO SUN-MONEYED AIR, QUICKENED ....CRYSTAL GAZER 55   26
QUICKENS (1)
BLOOD QUICKENS, GONGING IN MY EARS: ....PURSUIT 23   48
QUICKLY (1)
THE NARCISSI LOOK UP LIKE CHILDREN, QUICKLY AND WHITELY. NARCISSI. 190   12
QUICKSANDS (1)
ON THE QUICKSANDS OF AMBIVALENCE ....LOVE IS A PARALLAX 329   11
QUICKSILVER (2)
BUT LET THE QUICKSILVER MACKEREL SWIM. .....GO GET THE GOODLY SQUAB 313   20
LET THE QUICKSILVER MACKERAL SWIM ....GO GET THE GOODLY SQUAB 313   21
QUIET (18)
BULKS REAL, ALL SAINTS' TONGUES FALL QUIET: .....NOVEMBER GRAVEYARD 56   11
OF QUIET. FROM THE NADIR ....LORELEI 94   11
CELL BY CELL FROM A QUIET CORNER, ...POEM.2.DARK. 132   3
THE HEAD-STONE QUIET, JOSTLED BY NOTHING. POEM.7.S. 136   10
ON HIM HAND AND FOOT, QUIET AS A DIAMOND. ....ON DECK 143   33
LOOK HOW WHITE EVERYTHING IS, HOW QUIET, HOW SNOWED-IN. .....TULIPS 160   2
IT DRAGS THE SEA AFTER IT LIKE A DARK CRIME; IT IS QUIET .....MOON. 173   10
THEY HAVE TOO MANY COLORS, TOO MUCH LIFE. THEY ARE NOT QUIET,*THREE. 178   69
QUIET, LIKE THE LITTLE EMPTINESSES I CARRY. ....THREE WOMEN 178   70
TURN UP THEIR HANDS, THEIR PALLORS. IT IS SO QUIET HERE.*THREE WOMEN 179   94
THEIR FEATURES ARE SLEEPING, LIKE LIGHT ON QUIET WATER. *THREE WOMEN 183 226
THE THICKETS QUIET. ....THE RABBIT CATCHER 194   20
WHY IS IT SO QUIET, WHAT ARE THEY HIDING? ....BERCK-PLAGE 196   5
WHEN I AM QUIET AT MY COOKING I FEEL IT LOOKING, I FEEL IT
     THINKING ....A BIRTHDAY PRESENT 206   4
THE LINE PINK AND QUIET, A WORM, BASKING.*THE COURAGE OF SHUTTING-UP 209   2
THE SURGEON IS QUIET, HE DOES NOT SPEAK. *THE COURAGE OF SHUTTING-UP 210   14
PRICELESS AND QUIET ....PURDAH 243   34
INUNDATING EDEN'S QUIET: ....INSOLENT STORM STRIKES AT THE SKULL 326   22
QUIETENS (1)
A HIGH HUSH QUIETENS THE CRICKETS' CRY. ....ABOVE THE OXBOW 89   56
QUIETLY (6)
VERY QUIETLY ....MUSHROOMS 139   3
SHE LIVES QUIETLY ....A LIFE 150   25
I AM LEARNING PEACEFULNESS, LYING BY MYSELF QUIETLY ....TULIPS 160   3
I WILL ONLY TAKE IT AND GO ASIDE QUIETLY. ....A BIRTHDAY PRESENT 207   33
SEALING OFF HER BROOD CELLS, HER HONEY, AND QUIETLY HUMMING. ..BEE. 212   35
QUIETLY THROUGH THE STRAW OF THE BOXCARS. ....GETTING THERE 248   11
QUINTESSENTIAL (1)
ABOUT A QUINTESSENTIAL BEAUTY ....ON THE PLETHORA OF DRYADS 67   2
QUIRK (2)
NOW, FREE, BY HAZARD'S QUIRK, FROM THE COMMON ILL   CHANNEL CROSSING 27   26
EACH PARTICULAR QUIRK SO RAVISHED ME .....ON THE PLETHORA OF DRYADS 67   15
QUIT (3)
AND SOLACED HER, BUT QUIT HER AT COCK'S CROWING. *QUEEN'S COMPLAINT. 28   15
MAKESHIFT OF A VIEW TO QUIT ....GREEN ROCK, WINTHROP BAY 105   7
QUIT THEIR USUAL HABITATIONS. ....THE MANOR GARDEN 125   18
QUITE (9)
IS HELPLESS HERE, QUITE EXTRA, YET WE MUST MAKE ...CHANNEL CROSSING 27   35
THOUGH IT'S QUITE CLEAR ....SOLILOQUY OF THE SOLIPSIST 38   34
BECOME QUITE YELLOW ....RESOLVE 52   9
SHE'D SUPPORTED ME FOR SO LONG I WAS QUITE LIMP -- ......IN PLASTER 159   44
THAN THE DARK OF THE SKY BECAUSE IT IS QUITE STARLESS. ......STARS. 165   3
HE IS QUITE BLUE; THE TERRIBLE WIND TRIES HIS BREATHING. NARCISSI. 190   11
THE CLEAR, GREEN, QUITE BREATHABLE ATMOSPHERE, ...LYONNESSE 234   16
THE TOP QUITE GONE ....CUT 235   3
YOU DON'T QUITE BELIEVE IN IT. YOU'RE DEAF TO REAL .....DIALOGUE O. 278   63
QUITTED (1)
THAT NOBLE MIEN, PERHAPS YOU'VE LATE QUITTED HEAVEN?" ..DIALOGUE B. 38   16
QUITTING (1)
LIKE A DAUNTED WITCH, QUITTING CASTLE WHEN REAL DAYS BREAK. ...
          ... CONVERSATION AMONG THE RUINS 21   8
QUIVER (1)
QUIVER IN THIN STREAKS ....AQUATIC NOCTURNE 305   4
QUIVERING (1)
A TREMOLO OF TURQUOISE QUIVERING IN ....MIDSUMMER MOBILE 324   6

	TITLE	PAGE	LINE

QUIVERS (1)
    THE MIRROR QUIVERS TO SMITHEREENS. ....IN MIDAS' COUNTRY 100   19
QUOITS (1)
    SLIDING THEIR QUOITS ONE ....DARK WOOD, DARK WATER 127   22
R (1)
    TO R NOW. E. IN CORE . . . O-F-N-E- ....DIALOGUE OVER A OUIJA BOARD 284 277
RABBIT (2)
    SAGE HEN AND SPRY RABBIT, ...TWO VIEWS OF WITHENS   72   8
    THE RABBIT CATCHER ....THE RABBIT CATCHER 193   T
RABBIT-EARED (1)
    LIGHT UP. EACH RABBIT-EARED ....PARLIAMENT HILL FIELDS 153   44
RABBITS (6)
    HE NAMES A LAPWING, STARTS RABBITS IN A ROUT ....ODE FOR TED   29   3
    I REMEMBER THE BLOODIED CHICKS AND THE QUARTERED RABBITS. ...ZOO K. 155   24
    AND THE FOX HEADS, THE OTTER HEADS, THE HEADS OF DEAD RABBITS. ...
                            ... THE COURAGE OF SHUTTING-UP 210   23
    LIKE LIVE WHITE RABBITS, READY TO BEGIN *DIALOGUE OVER A OUIJA BOARD 282 234
    RABBITS IN THE LOT. YOU'RE IN A HUFF ...DIALOGUE OVER A OUIJA BOARD 282 236
    WINGED RABBITS REVOLVING ABOUT HIS KNEES, ...CIRCUS IN THREE RINGS 322   16
RABBIT'S (1)
    A RABBIT'S CRY MAY BE WILDER ....KINDNESS 269   7
RABBIT-TRACK (1)
    POCKED BY ROOK-CLAW AND RABBIT-TRACK: SHE MUST YET WIN ..SNOWMAN O.   58   17
RACE (3)
    SO WEEDY A RACE COULD NOT REMAIN IN DREAMS, ...THE THIN PEOPLE   64   23
    BUT NOW THE WATER-SKIERS RACE, ...IN MIDAS' COUNTRY   99   16
    IN WHICH THE RIDDLE OF OUR RACE IS SHUT. ....DOOM OF EXILES 318   14
RACINE (1)
    RACINE ....PURSUIT   22   E
RACK (6)
    ROSE UP AND PUT ROYAL NERVES TO THE RACK: ....NATURAL HISTORY   71   9
    THIS VIRGIN ON HER RACK: ....VIRGIN IN A TREE   82   35
    CHEATED OF THE PYRE AND THE RACK, ...AFTERMATH 114   13
    AND A LOVE OF THE RACK AND THE SCREW. ....DADDY 224   66
    THE RACK OF TIME ....TO A JILTED LOVER 310   23
    TURNS THE RACK; ....MOONSONG AT MORNING 317   28
RACKED (2)
    WE HEFT GLOBED FLINT, RACKED IN VEINS' BARBED BINDINGS; ...FIRESONG   30   18
    A CROSS OF CONTRADICTION, RACKED BETWEEN   METAMORPHOSES OF THE MOON 308   47
RACKET (1)
    SUCH A RACKET OF ECHOES FROM THE STEELY STREET, ...HARDCASTLE CRAGS   62   2
RACKETING (2)
    OF MAKING HARBOR THROUGH THIS RACKETING FLUX ......CHANNEL CROSSING   27   19
    FALL RACKETING FINALE ON HER LUCK. ....AERIALIST 332   48
RADIAL (1)
    EXTEND THE RADIAL SHEAVES ....FULL FATHOM FIVE   92   7
RADIANCE (6)
    FROM SUCH ASSAULT OF RADIANCE. ....PURSUIT   23   44
    WITH RADIANCE, PEACOCK-COLORED; INSTEAD, BLEAK ROCKS ....CHANNEL C.   27   22
    TRICKS OF RADIANCE MIRACLES. THE WAIT'S BEGUN AGAIN,   BLACK ROOK I.   57   38
    HER RADIANCE SCATHES ME. OR PERHAPS I HAVE CAUGHT HER. ....ELM 192   24
    THIS HALOEY RADIANCE THAT SEEMS TO BREATHE ....BY CANDLELIGHT 236   11
    WITH RADIANCE OF HIS FROZEN FAITH. ....TO A JILTED LOVER 309   9
RADIANT (5)
    AND RECOIL IN THE ALTERING LIGHT: THE RADIANT LIMB ..EPITAPH FOR F.   46   33
    STEPS OUT RADIANT IN LIMB, EYE, LIP, ...CONJURING.   66   27
    THE RADIANT LIMB. ....MOONSONG AT MORNING 317   36
    AND TURN GOD'S RADIANT PHOTOGRAPH TO SHADE. ....SONNET TO SATAN 323   8
    BUT FOUND RADIANT VENUS ..ON LOOKING INTO THE EYES OF A DEMON LOVER 325   23
RADIATION (1)
    RADIATION TURNED IT WHITE ....FEVER. 231   23
RADICAL (1)
    DIMINISHED AND FLAT, AS AFTER RADICAL SURGERY. ....ELM 192   26
RADIO (1)
    YOU WHO HAVE BLOWN YOUR TUBES LIKE A BAD RADIO ....LESBOS 228   17
RAFTERS (2)
    NAILED TO THE RAFTERS YESTERDAY: POEM.1.WHO. 131   14
    THE RAFTERS AND STRUTS OF HIS BODY WEAR ....THE BURNT-OUT SPA 138   6
RAGBAG (1)
    THEY'RE OUT OF THE DARK'S RAGBAG, THESE TWO ....BLUE MOLES 126   1
RAGE (2)
    SO HUNGERED, SHE MUST WAIT IN RAGE ....THE SHRIKE   42   15
    NURSING HER RAGE ....THE SNOWMAN ON THE MOOR   58   20
RAGGY (1)
    WRAP ME, RAGGY SHAWLS, ...NICK AND THE CANDLESTICK 241   7
RAGING (1)
    TROUNCING THE SEA LIKE A RAGING BATHER, ...LAMENT 315   7
RAID (2)
    TO RAID THE ZONE WHERE FATE BEGINS, ...METAMORPHOSES OF THE MOON 307   3
    ABOUT A GOBLIN RAID ON MINER'S HUT ....THE PRINCESS AND THE GOBLINS 334   38
RAIL (1)
    GRIP THE RAIL, SQUINT AHEAD, AND WONDER HOW MUCH LONGER   CHANNEL C.   26   6
RAILWAY (1)
    FUNICULAR RAILWAY, WITNESS TO GONE ....ABOVE THE OXBOW   88   38

RAIN (14)
   IN BLACK NOVEMBER. AFTER A SLIDING RAIN ....DIALOGUE B.   38   3
   ARRANGING AND REARRANGING ITS FEATHERS IN THE RAIN. ..BLACK ROOK I. 56   3
   A MELDING OF SHAPES IN A HOT RAIN: ....THE EYE-MOTE 109   11
   THE GOLDEN RAIN TREE DRIPS ITS POWDERS DOWN. ....BEEKEEPER'S. 118   9
   THE TREES WITHER IN THE STREET. THE RAIN IS CORROSIVE.   THREE WOMEN 180 135
   NOR DO THESE DRY, DRY GUTTERS DREAM OF RAIN. ....THREE WOMEN   184 279
   THIS IS RAIN NOW, THIS BIG HUSH. ....ELM   192   14
   OF BEING WHEELED OFF UNDER CROSSES AND A RAIN OF PIETAS. ...
   ... APPREHENSIONS 195   15
   WARM RAIN GREASES MY HAIR, EXTINGUISHES NOTHING.*BURNING THE LETTERS 205   47
   THE SWEAT OF HIS EFFORTS A RAIN ....STINGS 215   46
   IN A RAMPAGE OF CHAMPAGNE-COLORED RAIN ....CIRCUS IN THREE RINGS   321   4
   ABRACADABRA OF THE RAIN ....INSOLENT STORM STRIKES AT THE SKULL   326   13
   THEN LET THE BLUE TENT TOPPLE, STARS RAIN DOWN,   LOVE IS A PARALLAX   330   73
   AND MOCK THE JANGLING RAIN OF SPLINTERED STARS. ..EPITAPH IN THREE.   337   25
RAINBOWS (1)
   A CONCATENATION OF RAINBOWS. ....PURDAH   243   28
RAINS (3)
   AGES BEAT LIKE RAINS ....FULL FATHOM FIVE 93   27
   ALTHOUGH THE RAINS DISSOLVE A BLOODY DYE: ...ELECTRA ON AZALEA PATH   117   27
   FAVORED (WHILE SUDDENLY THE RAINS BEGIN ....FEMALE AUTHOR   301   2
RAINY (1)
   BLACK ROOK IN RAINY WEATHER ....BLACK ROOK IN RAINY WEATHER   56   T
RAISE (2)
   GILT TRUMPETS RAISE. ....A WINTER'S TALE 87 12
   WE RAISE OUR ARGUMENTS LIKE SITTING DUCKS ....LOVE IS A PARALLAX   329   19
RAISED (2)
   RAISED HIS MEN OF SKIN AND BONE, ...I WANT, I WANT 106   10
   RAISED TO TOAST A THOUSAND KINGS, FOR ALL GIVES ....SONNET: TO TIME   311   11
RAKE (1)
   WITH THE BUTT OF A RAKE ....BURNING THE LETTERS 204   36
RAM (2)
   TROUT, COCK, RAM, ...ON THE DIFFICULTY OF CONJURING UP A DRYAD   66   13
   THIS RAM OF BLACKNESS. I FOLD MY HANDS ON A MOUNTAIN. ..THREE WOMEN   180 143
RAMBLE (1)
   BEGINS. A JERK. AND NOW THE FIRST SLOW RAMBLE ....DIALOGUE O.   277   21
RAMPAGE (1)
   IN A RAMPAGE OF CHAMPAGNE-COLORED RAIN ....CIRCUS IN THREE RINGS   321   4
RAMPED (1)
   HER DAINTY ACRES HE RAMPED THROUGH ....THE QUEEN'S COMPLAINT   28   6
RAMS (1)
   OUR HAMMERS, OUR RAMS, ...MUSHROOMS   139   14
RAMSHACKLE (4)
   BELOW THE RAMSHACKLE BACK-ALLEY BALCONIES, ...ALICANTE LULLABY   43   4
   IN HER RAMSHACKLE HOUSE OFF SOMERSET TERRACE: ....ELLA MASON A.   53   2
   HUNDRED-YEAR-OLD HOTEL SUSTAINS ITS RAMSHACKLE .....ABOVE THE OXBOW   88   35
   IN THE RAMSHACKLE MEADOW ....TEMPER OF TIME   336   13
RAM'S-HORN (1)
   WITH COILS OF RAM'S-HORN. ....DARK WOOD, DARK WATER   127   10
RAN (2)
   OF HIS REDOUBT HE RAN HIS NIMBLE FILAMENT, ...SPIDER   48   15
   THE LORDS AND LADIES RAN. ....THE BULL OF BENDYLAW 108   12
RANCID (1)
   NEXT TO THE LAST TENANT'S RANCID JAM ....WINTERING 218   8
RANDOM (2)
   ON THE COINS OF PITY. AT RANDOM ....THE BEGGARS   47   9
   FOR THAT RARE, RANDOM DESCENT. ....BLACK ROOK IN RAINY WEATHER   57   40
RANGE (1)
   MIGHT RANGE IN IT. I ONLY SHUT THE DOOR *DIALOGUE OVER A OUIJA BOARD   286 344
RANGOON (1)
   HUNG UP IN THE LIBRARY WITH THE ENGRAVINGS OF RANGOON .....COURAGE.   210   22
RANK (7)
   SHOWS, RANK ON RANK, THE HUNGRY SEAS ADVANCING. ...CHANNEL CROSSING   26   8
   SHOWS, RANK ON RANK, THE HUNGRY SEAS ADVANCING. ...CHANNEL CROSSING   26   8
   OF WEEDS WE TACKLE TOWARDS WAY'S RANK ENDING; ....FIRESONG   30   16
   TO PATCH WITH BRAND OF LOVE THIS RANK GRIMACE ....STRUMPET SONG   34   16
   STARS HUNG WATER-SUNK, SO A RANK ....FAUN   35   8
   THROUGH A RANK WILDERNESS OF FERN AND FLOWER. ....SPINSTER   49   10
   YOU OVERCAST ALL ORDER'S NOONDAY RANK ....SONNET TO SATAN 323   7
RANK-HAIRED (1)
   GOATS SHAMBLE, MOROSE, RANK-HAIRED, ...DEPARTURE   51   19
RANSACK (1)
   O RANSACK THE FOUR WINDS AND FIND ANOTHER ....LAMENT   316   16
RANSACKED (1)
   RANSACKED IN THE PUBLIC EYE. WE FORSAKE ....CHANNEL CROSSING   27   32
RANSACKS (1)
   INSATIATE, HE RANSACKS THE LAND ....PURSUIT 22   13
RAPACIOUS (1)
   THE HOSTELRY OF WORMS, RAPACIOUS BLADES ....TERMINAL   328   6
RAPED (1)
   I HAVE BEEN DRUGGED AND RAPED. ....THE JAILER   226   6
RAPTORIAL (1)
   WHAT MOVED THE PALE, RAPTORIAL OWL ....OWL   102   9

	TITLE	PAGE	LINE

RARE (13)
    AT THIS RARE RUMPUS WHICH NO MAN CAN CONTROL: .....CHANNEL CROSSING   27 29
    SO SHE IS COME TO THIS RARE PASS ....THE QUEEN'S COMPLAINT   29 21
    SHALL STREW BROADCAST SO RARE A SEED ON WIND ....WREATH F.   45 20
    FOR THAT RARE, RANDOM DESCENT. ....BLACK ROOK IN RAINY WEATHER   57 40
    HAMMERS HER RARE AND ....DARK WOOD, DARK WATER   127 13
    I HAVE STITCHED LIFE INTO ME LIKE A RARE ORGAN, ...THREE WOMEN   178 72
    AND WALKED CAREFULLY, PRECARIOUSLY, LIKE SOMETHING RARE.*THREE WOMEN   178 73
    IS IT ITS RARENESS, THEN? IT IS RARE. ....PHEASANT   191 15
    GEE BABY, YOU ARE RARE." ....LESBOS   228 42
    OBSERVING THE WRECK OF METAL AND RARE STONE. ....SONNET: TO EVA   304   4
    AND AUCTION OFF EACH RARE WHITE-RABBIT VERB; ....A SORCERER B.   324   6
    LIKE A RARE CALDER MOBILE IN YOUR MIND. ....MIDSUMMER MOBILE   324 14
    IN THE RARE RIVER WINK AND LAUGH; WE LAVISH .....LOVE IS A PARALLAX   330 38
RARELY (1)
    BRIGHT GRAIN SPRUNG SO RARELY ....ODE FOR TED   29 16
RARENESS (1)
    IS IT ITS RARENESS, THEN? IT IS RARE. ....PHEASANT   191 15
RASA (1)
    THE WHITE GAPE OF HIS MIND WAS THE REAL TABULA RASA. .....LYONNESSE   234 27
RASPS (1)
    RASPS THE JARRING BARITONE OF UNCLE PAUL; ....FAMILY REUNION   300 22
RAT (2)
    DROLL, VEGETARIAN, THE WATER RAT *WATERCOLOR OF GRANTCHESTER MEADOWS   112 22
    THE OWL SHALL STOOP FROM HIS TURRET, THE RAT CRY OUT. ..WATERCOLOR.   112 28
RATE (1)
    ONE MIGHT SAY LOVE. AT ANY RATE, I NOW WALK ....BLACK ROOK I.   57 22
RATHER (4)
    RATHER THAN CROAK OUT ....RECANTATION   42   8
    BUT I WOULD RATHER BE HORIZONTAL. ....I AM VERTICAL   162   1
    SHE WOULD RATHER BE DEAD THAN FAT, ...THE FEARFUL   256 13
    TO COURT REMORSE. OR SOMEONE ELSE. I'D RATHER ....DIALOGUE O.   278 59
RATION (1)
    IN WHOSE SHADOW I HAVE EATEN MY GHOST RATION. ....THE JAILER   227 38
RATIONED (1)
    AWAY OUR RATIONED DAYS AND WEEKS. ....LOVE IS A PARALLAX   330 72
RATS (1)
    GRAY AS RATS, ...PROSPECT   28   4
RATS' (1)
    LOOK UPON? RATS' TEETH GUT THE CITY ....OWL   102 15
RAT-SHREWD (1)
    RAT-SHREWD GO HER SQUINT EYES, ...TWO SISTERS OF PERSEPHONE   31 11
RAT'S-TAIL (1)
    SPLITS THROUGH THE RAT'S-TAIL ....LETTER IN NOVEMBER   253   3
RATTLE (6)
    AND LEFT THE COBS TO RATTLE, BITTEN CLEAN. ....OUIJA   77 18
    AND FACED ME, BACK TO A LEDGE OF DIRT, TO RATTLE .....INCOMMUNICADO   100   3
    THEY RATTLE LIKE HYDRANGEA BUSHES. POEM.1.WHO.   131 12
    GUTS BAG WOULD CLACK LIKE A CHILD'S RATTLE, ...ZOO KEEPER'S WIFE   154 12
    TO RATTLE IN A BOTTLE AND TAKE HOME, ...THE SURGEON AT 2 A.M.   171 35
    LETTERS AND THEIR DEATH RATTLE ....BURNING THE LETTERS   204   3
RATTLER (1)
    THE RATTLER OF KEYS? ....THE JAILER   226   5
RATTLES (3)
    IT RATTLES THEIR STARS ON THE GREEN HILL WHERE PERCY .....NARCISSI.   190   5
    RATTLES ITS POD, THE MOON ....CHILDLESS WOMAN   259   2
    ON A STICK THAT RATTLES AND CLICKS, A COUNTERFEIT SNAKE. .....TOTEM   264 18
RATTLING (1)
    ARE RATTLING THE CRACKER PACKETS. FINE FLOUR ....LEAVING EARLY   146 36
RAVAGED (2)
    THE RAVAGED FACE ....THE RAVAGED FACE   115   T
    OUTLANDISH AS A CIRCUS, THE RAVAGED FACE ....THE RAVAGED FACE   115   1
RAVE (3)
    RAVE ON THE LEASH OF THE STARVING MIND ....NOVEMBER GRAVEYARD   56 17
    HEARING A WHITE SAINT RAVE ....ON THE PLETHORA OF DRYADS   67   1
    SO WE COULD RAVE ON, DARLING, YOU AND I, ...LOVE IS A PARALLAX   329 13
RAVEL (2)
    RAVEL ABOVE US, MISTILY DESCEND, ...OUIJA   77 20
    RAVEL TO CLEARNESS ON THE DAWN SEA. ....FULL FATHOM FIVE   93 20
RAVELED (3)
    RAVELED WIND-RIPPED FROM THE CREST OF THE WAVE.*SUICIDE OFF EGG ROCK   115 11
    WINDING UP THE RAVELED MOLD. ....DANSE MACABRE   321 12
    IN A BATCH OF RAVELED APPLE RINDS. ....THE PRINCESS AND THE GOBLINS   335 68
RAVEN (1)
    BACKTALKS AT THE RAVEN ....VANITY FAIR   32 10
RAVENED (1)
    CHARRED AND RAVENED WOMEN LIE, ...PURSUIT   22 23
RAVENING (1)
    RAVENING THROUGH THE PERSISTENT BRIC-A-BRAC ....CONJURING.   65   1
RAVENS (1)
    MY DARLING RAVENS ARE FLOWN. ....RECANTATION   42 10
RAVINED (1)
    FISTED TO A FOETUS HEAD, RAVINED, SEAMED ....PERSEUS   83 25
RAVINES (1)
    STREETS CRACK THROUGH IN HAVOC-SPLIT RAVINES ....DOOMSDAY   316   7

RAVING (2)
    A LIGHT, AND RIGHT AWAY A RAVING ....THE DREAM   310   10
    THE LONE WIND RAVING IN THE GUTTER, HIS ....SONNET: TO TIME   311   7
RAVISHED (1)
    EACH PARTICULAR QUIRK SO RAVISHED ME .....ON THE PLETHORA OF DRYADS   67   15
RAW (9)
    MEAT MUST GLUT HIS MOUTH'S RAW WOUND. ....PURSUIT   22   16
    CRUEL NETTLES STUNG HER ANKLES RAW. ....BUCOLICS   24   16
    FLAYS THE CHROMIUM NERVES OF PLUMBING RAW; ....TALE OF A TUB   24   3
    OR CRIES THAT THIS RAW FLESH ....STREET SONG   35   6
    INCOMPATIBLE MODES OF TIME, THE RAW MATERIAL*THE GHOST'S LEAVETAKING   90   13
    THE CURIOUS BEARERS AND THE RAW DATE ....BERCK-PLAGE   199   71
    I AM STILL RAW. ....LESBOS   229   89
    PAN SAID. A PLUMAGE OF RAW WORMS. HOW ..DIALOGUE OVER A OUIJA BOARD   279   100
    THE RAW WIND LIKE A SCARF; LOVE IS A FAUN ....LOVE IS A PARALLAX   329   23
RAY (2)
    RAY BUT EGG ROCK ON THE BLUE WASTAGE. ....SUICIDE OFF EGG ROCK   115   22
    WHAT BLUE, MOONY RAY ICES THEIR DREAMS? ....THREE WOMEN   181   182
RAYED (1)
    RAYED ROUND A CANDLE FLAME, ...POLLY'S TREE   128   19
RAYS (2)
    THEIR DEATH RAYS FOLDED LIKE FLAGS ......THE COURAGE OF SHUTTING-UP   210   32
    PEOPLE LIKE LIGHT RAYS, LEAVE ....BRASILIA   259   19
RAZOR (1)
    MY OWN BLUE RAZOR RUSTING IN MY THROAT. .....ELECTRA ON AZALEA PATH   117   43
REACH (2)
    REACH HAG HANDS TO HAUL ME IN, ...ALL THE DEAD DEARS   70   21
    HANDS REACH BACK TO RELICS OF ....DANSE MACABRE   321   7
REACHED (1)
    WE REACHED AMONG THE LEAVES ....BITTER STRAWBERRIES   300   35
REACHES (2)
    SEARCHING MY REACHES FOR WHAT SHE REALLY IS. ....MIRROR   174   11
    WHEN MY ENGINE REACHES THE END OF IT. ....GIGOLO   267   20
READ (3)
    AND RENTED AN OLD GREEN BOAT. I ROWED. YOU READ ....THE BABYSITTERS   175   31
    READ BLACK MAGIC OR HOLY BOOK ...BLACK PINE TREE IN AN ORANGE LIGHT   328   13
    SHE RECALLS QUEER STORIES HER NURSE READ ....THE PRINCESS.   334   37
READING (2)
    I AM MENDING A SILK SLIP: MY HUSBAND IS READING. ....THREE WOMEN   186   352
    LIT (YOU ARE READING), ...EAVESDROPPER   260   30
READY (15)
    READY, FOR A TRINKET, ...VANITY FAIR   33   18
    WITH POKE AND GIGGLE, READY TO SKEDADDLE, ...ELLA MASON A.   54   25
    GETS READY TO FACE THE READY-MADE CREATION   THE GHOST'S LEAVETAKING   90   6
    GIVE ME BACK MY SHAPE. I AM READY TO CONSTRUE THE DAYS   POEM.6.W.   136   21
    THEIR YELLOW CORSETS WERE READY TO SPLIT. ....LEAVING EARLY   146   25
    LEAVES AND PETALS ATTEND ME. I AM READY. ....THREE WOMEN   177   14
    I WASN'T READY. THE WHITE CLOUDS REARING ....THREE WOMEN   178   57
    I WASN'T READY. ....THREE WOMEN   178   59
    WENT ON SHAPING ITSELF WITH LOVE, AS IF I WAS READY. ...THREE WOMEN   178   63
    "THIS IS WHERE YOU WILL COME WHEN YOU ARE READY." .....THREE WOMEN   180   123
    I AM NOT READY FOR ANYTHING TO HAPPEN. ....THREE WOMEN   180   125
    DO NOT BE MEAN, I AM READY FOR ENORMITY. ....A BIRTHDAY PRESENT   207   23
    READY TO ROLL, LIKE A DEVIL'S. ....GETTING THERE   248   40
    TO YES SAYS HE IS READY. PAN, IS THERE   DIALOGUE OVER A OUIJA BOARD   278   71
    LIKE LIVE WHITE RABBITS, READY TO BEGIN *DIALOGUE OVER A OUIJA BOARD   282   234
READY-MADE (1)
    GETS READY TO FACE THE READY-MADE CREATION   THE GHOST'S LEAVETAKING   90   6
REAL (19)
    LIKE A DAUNTED WITCH, QUITTING CASTLE WHEN REAL DAYS BREAK. ...
                          ... CONVERSATION AMONG THE RUINS   21   8
    SHATTERS THE FABULOUS STARS AND MAKES US REAL. ....TALE OF A TUB   25   48
    LOVE FIERY ENOUGH TO PROVE FLESH REAL, ..SOLILOQUY OF THE SOLIPSIST   38   33
    BULKS REAL, ALL SAINTS' TONGUES FALL QUIET: .....NOVEMBER GRAVEYARD   56   11
    THE REAL THING, ALL RIGHT: THE GOOD, THE TRUE -- ....MAGI   148   6
    I CAN TASTE THE TIN OF THE SKY -- THE REAL TIN THING. ......WAKING.   151   1
    SHE DOESN'T NEED FOOD, SHE IS ONE OF THE REAL SAINTS. ...IN PLASTER   158   4
    THEY ARE THE REAL MONKS AND NUNS IN THEIR IDENTICAL GARMENTS.*THREE.   183   227
    THE WHITE GAPE OF HIS MIND WAS THE REAL TABULA RASA. .....LYONNESSE   234   27
    ONE MATCH SCRATCH MAKES YOU REAL. ....BY CANDLELIGHT   236   15
    I DO IT SO IT FEELS REAL. ....LADY LAZARUS   245   47
    WHAT IS SO REAL AS THE CRY OF A CHILD? ....KINDNESS   269   6
    YOU DON'T QUITE BELIEVE IN IT. YOU'RE DEAF TO REAL .....DIALOGUE O.   278   63
    BULKING MORE REAL THAN WE THINK WE ARE: WE FACE ....DIALOGUE O.   279   115
    MAY TWO REAL PEOPLE BREATHE IN A REAL ROOM. ....DIALOGUE O.   286   364
    MAY TWO REAL PEOPLE BREATHE IN A REAL ROOM. ....DIALOGUE O.   286   364
    TWO LOVERS AND A BEACHCOMBER BY THE REAL SEA ....TWO LOVERS.   327   T
    WHERE WAVE PRETENDS TO DRENCH REAL SKY." ....LOVE IS A PARALLAX   329   6
    WHICH DREAMERS CALL REAL, AND REALISTS, ILLUSION:*LOVE IS A PARALLAX   330   59
REALISTS (1)
    WHICH DREAMERS CALL REAL, AND REALISTS, ILLUSION:*LOVE IS A PARALLAX   330   59
REALITY (1)
    SHE IS DEFERRING TO REALITY. ....THREE WOMEN   184   284
REALIZED (2)
    AND CLAW-THREAT, REALIZED THAT. ......THE HERMIT AT OUTERMOST HOUSE   118   6

		TITLE	PAGE	LINE

REALIZED (CONT.)
THEN I REALIZED WHAT SHE WANTED WAS FOR ME TO LOVE HER: IN PLASTER   159   13
REALLY (5)
SEARCHING MY REACHES FOR WHAT SHE REALLY IS. ....MIRROR   174   11
IT REALLY GOES. ....LADY LAZARUS   246   60
REALLY CAN SEE INTO THE FUTURE. WHAT, ..DIALOGUE OVER A OUIJA BOARD   278   52
REALLY WANT TO KNOW ABOUT? EVERYTHING.   DIALOGUE OVER A OUIJA BOARD   278   54
NOW, YOU REALLY DON'T MUCH CARE WHICH, OR WHAT ....DIALOGUE O.   280 151
REAP (1)
REAP THE ROUND BLUE PIGEON FROM ROOF RIDGE, *GO GET THE GOODLY SQUAB   313   3
REAPPEARANCE (1)
TO HALF-BELIEVE: YOUR REAPPEARANCE ....FULL FATHOM FIVE   93   23
REAR (1)
GODS AND REAR THEM LIKE BEANSTALKS FROM OUT THESE RIBS   DIALOGUE O.   280 170
REARING (1)
I WASN'T READY. THE WHITE CLOUDS REARING ....THREE WOMEN   178   57
REARRANGING (1)
ARRANGING AND REARRANGING ITS FEATHERS IN THE RAIN.   BLACK ROOK I.   56   3
REARS (1)
SPARKING OFF THEIR BROTHER-SISTER REARS ....AMNESIAC   233   18
REASON (7)
FOR NO GOOD REASON ....ELLA MASON AND HER ELEVEN CATS   53   9
LANTERN-JAWED REASON, SQUAT COMMON SENSE,   THE DEATH OF MYTH-MAKING   104   3
HIM YET, AND GIVE US GOOD REASON. NO, HE'S ON ....DIALOGUE O.   284 295
I AM RESOLVED. NO REASON COULD UNTWIST   DIALOGUE OVER A OUIJA BOARD   286 341
PERSUADED BY HIS BRONZE HEROIC REASON. ....GOLD MOUTHS CRY   302   6
YET ALL ANGELIC REASON ....TRIO OF LOVE SONGS   314   15
TO LEAVE OUR REASON ....MOONSONG AT MORNING   317   9
REASONABLE (1)
ARMING MYSELF WITH THE MOST REASONABLE ITEMS ....STREET SONG   36   15
REASSURED (2)
I AM REASSURED. I AM REASSURED. ....THREE WOMEN   185 316
I AM REASSURED. I AM REASSURED. ....THREE WOMEN   185 316
REBEL (1)
INDEPENDENT REBEL FIRES ....INSOLENT STORM STRIKES AT THE SKULL   326   34
REBUKE (1)
TO REBUKE THE HORSE-SWALLOWING RIVER GYNDES: A LESSON IN VENGEANCE   80   18
RECALLS (1)
SHE RECALLS QUEER STORIES HER NURSE READ ....THE PRINCESS.   334   37
RECANTATION (1)
RECANTATION ....RECANTATION   41   T
RECEDE (1)
YET THEY RECEDE, UNTOUCHABLE AS TOMORROW,*SLEEP IN THE MOJAVE DESERT   144   11
RECEDED (1)
TONIGHT IT HAS RECEDED LIKE A SHIP'S LIGHT. ..THE SURGEON AT 2 A.M.   170   10
RECEIVE (1)
THE SECOND SINGS: "RECEIVE NO ROVING GALLANT *EPITAPH IN THREE PARTS   337   7
RECENTLY (1)
ARE RIDING TO WORK IN ROWS, AS IF RECENTLY BRAINWASHED. ..INSOMNIAC   163   35
RECEPTACLES (1)
BUT ASBESTOS RECEPTACLES. ....THE SWARM   217   54
RECEPTION (1)
AND DROOLS AT THE RECEPTION LINE. ....FAMILY REUNION   301   24
RECITE (1)
IN APT IAMBICS, IF PRODDED TO RECITE ...DIALOGUE OVER A OUIJA BOARD   280 143
RECITES (1)
WHEN HE RECITES ONE OF MY SIMILES ......DIALOGUE OVER A OUIJA BOARD   283 262
RECLAIM (2)
FOR THE BLOOD-HEAT THAT WOULD RUDDLE OR RECLAIM. ....OUIJA   77   9
BACKWARD WE TRAVELED TO RECLAIM THE DAY ....DOOM OF EXILES   318   9
RECLUSE (1)
DIED RECLUSE OR SUICIDE ....MUSSEL HUNTER AT ROCK HARBOR   97   75
RECOGNIZE (1)
NO USE, NO USE, NOW, BEGGING RECOGNIZE! ....AMNESIAC   232   1
RECOIL (1)
AND RECOIL IN THE ALTERING LIGHT: THE RADIANT LIMB ..EPITAPH FOR F.   46   33
RECOLLECTION'S (1)
WITH RECOLLECTION'S TICKING THORNS ....DANSE MACABRE   321   11
RECONSTRUCTED (1)
THE VASE, RECONSTRUCTED, HOUSES POEM.7.S.   137   41
RECORD (1)
IN THIS PROVINCE OF THE STUCK RECORD ....THE TIMES ARE TIDY   107   2
RECORDED (1)
SHE RECORDED THE TOTAL IN HER NOTEBOOK, ...BITTER STRAWBERRIES   300   32
RECORDS (1)
RECORDS BARE PAINTED WALLS, WHILE AN ELECTRIC LIGHT ..TALE OF A TUB   24   2
RECOVER (4)
BOW, AND RECOVER THEIR LOOK ....MAGNOLIA SHOALS   122   7
THE STREETS MAY TURN TO PAPER SUDDENLY, BUT I RECOVER ..THREE WOMEN   187 365
HAVE A SELF TO RECOVER, A QUEEN. ....STINGS   215   52
I USED TO PRAY TO RECOVER YOU. ....DADDY   222   14
RECOVERS (1)
GULPS AND RECOVERS ITS SMALL ALTITUDE, ...NICK AND THE CANDLESTICK   241   21
RECREATION (1)
FOR RECREATION DOWN UNDER THE COVERS: ....DIALOGUE EN ROUTE   309   23

```
                                          TITLE              PAGE  LINE
RECROSSING (1)
    CROSSING AND RECROSSING: A FINE THING!  .................PHEASANT     191   18
RECRUITS (1)
    JOINS HIS ENEMIES' RECRUITS.  .................LOVE IS A PARALLAX     330   54
RECTIFY (1)
    CAN RECTIFY TRUANT INTENT  ......INSOLENT STORM STRIKES AT THE SKULL   326   27
RECTOR (2)
    THE RECTOR, THE MIDWIFE, THE SEXTON, THE AGENT FOR BEES.  ......BEE.  211    2
    WHICH IS THE RECTOR NOW, IS IT THAT MAN IN BLACK?  ..THE BEE MEETING  211   11
RECTORY (1)
    IN THE RECTORY GARDEN ON HIS EVENING WALK  .............DIALOGUE B.    38    1
RECUPERATING (1)
    HE IS RECUPERATING FROM SOMETHING ON THE LUNG.  ..AMONG THE NARCISSI  190    3
RED (101)
    ALONG RED NETWORK OF HIS VEINS  .............................PURSUIT   22   11
    RISES THE ROUND RED WATERMELON SUN.  .................SOUTHERN SUNRISE  26   18
    STALKS RED FOX, SHREWD STOAT.  ...........................ODE FOR TED   29    6
    SCORCHED BY RED SUN  .......................................FIRESONG   30   17
    SHE SEES HOW THEIR RED SILK FLARE  ........TWO SISTERS OF PERSEPHONE   32   17
    RED, PALE OR DARK,  ....................................STRUMPET SONG   33    7
    SQUANDERING RED  ...........................................STREET SONG  36   19
    THAN MAN'S RED HEART."  ..........DIALOGUE BETWEEN GHOST AND PRIEST    39   50
    AND WITH RED BEAK  ..........................................THE SHRIKE  42   21
    IN THEIR HEARTBEATS' BLAZING WAKE UNTIL RED COCK  ....EPITAPH FOR F.   46   27
    THROUGHOUT BLACK WINTER THE RED HAWS WITHSTOOD  ...........MAYFLOWER   60    1
    SCOURING TO SORES HIS OWN RED SLUICES  .......A LESSON IN VENGEANCE    80   13
    THE RED, ROYAL ROBES OF PHEDRE? THE TEAR-DAZZLED  ...........PERSEUS   83   41
    YADWIGHA, ON A RED COUCH, AMONG LILIES  ..................YADWIGHA.    85    T
    UPHOLSTERED IN RED VELVET, UNDER THE EYE  ................YADWIGHA.    85    3
    AND THE FASHIONABLE MONDE OF THE RED COUCH  ..............YADWIGHA.    85   10
    STOOD STUBBORN IN ITS JUNGLE: RED AGAINST GREEN,  ........YADWIGHA.    85   18
    RED AGAINST FIFTY VARIANTS OF GREEN,  ....................YADWIGHA.    85   19
    SO ROUSSEAU, TO EXPLAIN WHY THE RED COUCH  ...............YADWIGHA.    86   21
    ON A RED VELVET COUCH WITHIN YOUR GREEN-  ................YADWIGHA.    86   26
    SO POSSESSED BY THE GLOWING RED OF THE COUCH WHICH YOU,  .YADWIGHA.    86   36
    TO FEED HIS EYE WITH RED: SUCH RED! UNDER THE MOON,  .....YADWIGHA.    86   38
    TO FEED HIS EYE WITH RED: SUCH RED! UNDER THE MOON,  .....YADWIGHA.    86   38
    ON BOSTON COMMON A RED STAR  .........................A WINTER'S TALE  86    1
    BETWEEN THE SNUFF AND RED TAR-PAPER APARTMENTS,  ....ABOVE THE OXBOW   88   13
    RETROGRESSED TO BLOWZE, I NEXT CHOSE RED:  ............RHODODENDRON.   103   10
    THE PARK OF LESS RED THAN WITHERING DID.  ............RHODODENDRON.   103   12
    MUSK SATISFIED MY NOSE, RED MY EYE,  .................RHODODENDRON.   103   13
    RED CINDER AROUND WHICH I MYSELF,  .....................THE EYE-MOTE  109   17
    THE SUN SINKS UNDER BOSTON, BLOODY RED.  ..............POINT SHIRLEY  111   40
    RED CLOVER OR GNAW BEETROOT  .....WATERCOLOR OF GRANTCHESTER MEADOWS  112   17
    RED AND ORANGE BARGES LIST AND BLISTER  .................A WINTER SHIP  112    2
    O RED FRUIT, IVORY, FINE TIMBERS,  ........................METAPHORS  116    4
    THE ARTIFICIAL RED SAGE DOES NOT STIR  .......ELECTRA ON AZALEA PATH  117   24
    THE ERSATZ PETALS DRIP, AND THEY DRIP RED.  ..ELECTRA ON AZALEA PATH  117   28
    IN THESE LITTLE BOUDOIRS STREAKED WITH ORANGE AND RED    BEEKEEPER'S.  118   10
    THE RED TOMATO'S IN, THE GREEN BEAN:  ........YADDO: THE GRAND MANOR  123    4
    COUNTING THE RED STARS AND THOSE OF PLUM-COLOR.  .......THE COLOSSUS  130   26
    PURPLE AND RED MOUTHS, UTTERLY LOVELY.  ................POEM.1.WHO.   132   30
    A RED TONGUE IS AMONG US.  ...........................POEM.3.MAENAD.  133   13
    IN THE MONTH OF RED LEAVES I CLIMB TO A BED OF FIRE.  .....POEM.6.W.  135    6
    IT HURTS AT FIRST. THE RED TONGUES WILL TEACH THE TRUTH.   POEM.6.W.  135   18
    THE RED GERANIUMS I KNOW.  ..........................GETTING THERE   146   16
    THE TULIPS ARE TOO RED IN THE FIRST PLACE, THEY HURT ME.  ....TULIPS  161   36
    A DOZEN RED LEAD SINKERS ROUND MY NECK.  ....................TULIPS  161   42
    ITS BOWL OF RED BLOOMS OUT OF SHEER LOVE OF ME.  ............TULIPS  162   61
    HE IS IMMUNE TO PILLS: RED, PURPLE, BLUE --  .............INSOMNIAC  163   15
    OVER THE SCALDING, RED TOPOGRAPHY  ..........................WIDOW   164    4
    I AM UP TO MY ELBOWS IN IT, RED AND SQUEAKING.*THE SURGEON AT 2 A.M.  171   22
    THE RED NIGHT LIGHTS ARE FLAT MOONS. THEY ARE DULL WITH BLOOD.  ...
                              ...  THE SURGEON AT 2 A.M.                  171   48
    NIGHTS, I WROTE IN MY DIARY SPITEFULLY, MY FINGERS RED  .......BABY.  174   14
    WHEN I FIRST SAW IT, THE SMALL RED SEEP, I DID NOT BELIEVE IT.  ...
                              ...  THREE WOMEN                           177   15
    THE NIGHT LIGHTS ARE FLAT RED MOONS. THEY ARE DULL WITH BLOOD.  ...
                              ...  THREE WOMEN                           180  124
    I AM A GARDEN OF BLACK AND RED AGONIES. I DRINK THEM,  ..THREE WOMEN  180  149
    A DEAD SUN STAINS THE NEWSPRINT. IT IS RED.  ...........THREE WOMEN  181  153
    FATTENS US, IS KIND. HER MOUTH IS RED.  ...............THREE WOMEN  181  156
    A RED LOTUS OPENS IN ITS BOWL OF BLOOD;  ..............THREE WOMEN  181  167
    I SEE HER IN MY SLEEP, MY RED, TERRIBLE GIRL.  ........THREE WOMEN  182  204
    A RED, HARD WOOD, EYES SHUT AND MOUTH WIDE OPEN.  ......THREE WOMEN  182  212
    THEIR SKIN TINTS ARE PINK OR SALLOW, BROWN OR RED;  ...THREE WOMEN  183  223
    THE RED MOUTH I PUT BY WITH MY IDENTITY  ..............THREE WOMEN  183  247
    THE FLOWERS IN THIS ROOM ARE RED AND TROPICAL.  .......THREE WOMEN  184  263
    I HAD A DREAM OF AN ISLAND, RED WITH CRIES.  ..........THREE WOMEN  185  307
    RED, MOTTLED, LIKE CUT NECKS.  .......................LITTLE FUGUE  188   35
    IS THIS LOVE THEN, THIS RED MATERIAL  .................AN APPEARANCE  189   10
    A HUNDRED, ON THAT HILL -- GREEN AND RED,  ................PHEASANT  191   17
    MY RED FILAMENTS BURN AND STAND, A HAND OF WIRES.  ...........ELM   192   18
    HIS LITTLE FACE IS CARVED IN PAINED, RED WOOD.  ...........EVENT   194    9
```

	TITLE	PAGE	LINE

RED (CONT.)
THIS RED WALL WINCES CONTINUALLY: .....................APPREHENSIONS 195 11
A RED FIST, OPENING AND CLOSING, ...APPREHENSIONS 195 12
THIS IS THE SIDE OF A MAN: HIS RED RIBS, ...BERCK-PLAGE 198 46
IN A STILL PLACE, AND THE GROOM IS RED AND FORGETFUL, HE IS
FEATURELESS. .... BERCK-PLAGE 200 108
AND A NAKED MOUTH, RED AND AWKWARD. ....BERCK-PLAGE 201 124
FLICKERING LIKE THAT, WRINKLY AND CLEAR RED, LIKE THE SKIN
OF A MOUTH. .... POPPIES IN JULY 203 6
DULLY, UNDER A PACK OF MEN IN RED JACKETS, ...BURNING THE LETTERS 204 13
A RED BURST AND A CRY ....BURNING THE LETTERS 205 50
OVER THE SEVEN HILLS, THE RED FURROW, THE BLUE MOUNTAIN? *DETECTIVE. 208 2
BORED HOODLUM IN A RED ROOM ....THE DETECTIVE 209 19
MORE TERRIBLE THAN SHE EVER WAS, RED ....STINGS 215 57
SCAR IN THE SKY, RED COMET ....STINGS 215 58
A RED TATTER, NAPOLEON! ....THE SWARM 217 40
BIT MY PRETTY RED HEART IN TWO. ....DADDY 224 56
RED STIGMATA AT THE VERY CENTER, ...MEDUSA 225 9
FAT AND RED, A PLACENTA ....MEDUSA 225 25
MY SLEEPING CAPSULE, MY RED AND BLUE ZEPPELIN ....THE JAILER 226 12
HER FACE RED AND WHITE, A PANIC, ...LESBOS 227 11
RED AND YELLOW, TWO PASSIONATE HOT METALS ....STOPPED DEAD 230 8
THEN THAT RED PLUSH. ....CUT 235 8
INTO THE RED ....ARIEL 240 30
WHOSE RED HEART BLOOMS THROUGH HER COAT SO ASTOUNDINGLY ---*POP.OCT. 240 3
I RISE WITH MY RED HAIR ....LADY LAZARUS 247 83
THICK, RED AND SLIPPING. IT IS ADAM'S SIDE, ...GETTING THERE 248 36
SQUELCHING AND SQUELCHING THROUGH THE BEAUTIFUL RED. *LETTER IN NOV. 253 15
I AM RED MEAT. HIS BEAK ....DEATH & CO. 254 10
RED EARTH, MOTHERLY BLOOD. ....BRASILIA 258 17
TASTE IT, DARK RED! ....CHILDLESS WOMAN 259 14
THE BLUE AND RED JEWELS OF HER RINGS SMOKE ....KINDNESS 269 3
GLOBES OF THIN AIR, RED, GREEN, ...BALLOONS 271 14
A RED ....BALLOONS 272 29
CRACKS RED. NOTHING HAPPENS. WAIT. ITS TRIP ....DIALOGUE O. 277 20
RED THE UNRAVELED ROSE SINGS IN YOUR HAIR: ......TO EVA DESCENDING. 303 7
RED-BELL-BLOOM (1)
THE HEART IS A RED-BELL-BLOOM, IN DISTRESS. ..THE SURGEON AT 2 A.M. 171 17
REDCOATS (1)
REDCOATS, EVERY ONE. ....CUT 235 20
REDDEN (3)
GRUB-WHITE MULBERRIES REDDEN AMONG LEAVES. ....MOONRISE 98 1
REDDEN IN WHITE PALMS NO LABOR REDDENS. ....MOONRISE 98 11
BERRIES REDDEN. A BODY OF WHITENESS ....MOONRISE 98 13
REDDENS (2)
GRAYNESS BLUES, REDDENS, AND THE OUTLINE ....THE THIN PEOPLE 65 34
REDDEN IN WHITE PALMS NO LABOR REDDENS. ....MOONRISE 98 11
REDEEM (1)
NOW BOUND AROUND HER WRIST TILL SHE REDEEM ....THE PRINCESS. 333 24
REDEEMED (1)
BLOOD FAULTLESSLY BROACHED REDEEMED THE SULLIED AIR, THE EARTH'S
GROSSNESS. ....THE GORING 47 10
RED-FACED (1)
RUM AND RED-FACED AS A WATER-MELON, HER VOICE ....ELLA MASON A. 53 7
RED-FRECKLED (1)
WHERE RED-FRECKLED CRAB-BACKS, CLAWS ..MUSSEL HUNTER AT ROCK HARBOR 97 83
RED-HEADED (1)
LIKE THE RED-HEADED SISTER HE NEVER DARED TO TOUCH, ...AMNESIAC 233 13
RED-HOT (1)
BELCHED INTO BLAZE AND, THOUGH RED-HOT, KEPT WHOLE .....DIALOGUE O. 280 158
RED-MOTTLED (1)
RED-MOTTLED RELICS, SHELLS, CLAWS ....MAGNOLIA SHOALS 121 3
REDNESS (3)
ARENA DUST RUSTED BY FOUR BULLS' BLOOD TO A DULL REDNESS,*THE GORING 47 1
ANOTHER KIND OF REDNESS BOTHERS ME: ....ELECTRA ON AZALEA PATH 117 29
THEIR REDNESS TALKS TO MY WOUND, IT CORRESPONDS. ....TULIPS 161 39
RED-NOSED (1)
THE RED-NOSED, BLUE-CAPED WOMEN RING ....A WINTER'S TALE 87 14
REDOUBT (1)
OF HIS REDOUBT HE RAN HIS NIMBLE FILAMENT, ...SPIDER 48 15
REDRESS (1)
TO REDRESS THE DOMINANCE OF ROCKS AND WOODS, ...TWO CAMP. 144 2
REDS (1)
REDS, GREENS, BLUES. ....ON THE PLETHORA OF DRYADS 68 36
REED (3)
BED OF A REED. LOOK: ....VIRGIN IN A TREE 81 15
SAWS DOWN A REED AND SWIMS FROM HIS LIMBER GROVE, ...WATERCOLOR. 112 23
OF GOLGOTHA AT THE TIP OF A REED, ...POEM.5.F. 135 18
REEDS (4)
LAST SUMMER'S REEDS ARE ALL ENGRAVED IN ICE ......WINTER LANDSCAPE, 22 11
AMONG THE PITHLESS REEDS. FLIES FAIL US. ....FROG AUTUMN 99 7
AWAY TO THE LEFT LIKE REEDS IN A SEA ....THE EYE-MOTE 109 8
IN ITS HOLLOW OF SHADOWS, ITS FRINGE OF REEDS, ...CANDLES 148 8
REEDY (2)
WITH REEDY LENGTHS AND NECKS AND UNDULATINGS. .........SNAKECHARMER 79 5

	TITLE	PAGE	LINE

REEDY (CONT.)
    FLUTE NOTES FROM A REEDY POND ....POEM.5.F. 134 ST
REEFS (1)
    ON THE PITCHED REEFS OF NIGHTMARE, ...LORELEI   94 24
REEKS (1)
    REEKS OF THE BUTCHER'S CLEAVER, ...STREET SONG   36   7
REEL (1)
    REEL GIDDY IN BEDLAM SPRING: ....SPINSTER   50 23
REELS (1)
    OF SILVER AS THE RONDO SLOWS: NOW REELS ....CINDERELLA 303   3
RE-ESTABLISH (1)
    TO RE-ESTABLISH ITS MIRROR ....WORDS 270   9
REFECTORIES (1)
    REFECTORIES WHERE HE REVELED HAVE BECOME ....TERMINAL 328   5
REFINED (1)
    THE REFINED SNOW. ....WINTERING 218 28
REFLECT (5)
    THAN THE CLOUD THAT DISTILLS A MIRROR TO REFLECT ITS OWN SLOW ...
                                     ... MORNING SONG 157   8
    A FEW MORE BREATHS, AND IT WILL REFLECT NOTHING AT ALL. LAST WORDS 172 12
    I SEE HER BACK, AND REFLECT IT FAITHFULLY. ....MIRROR 174 13
    MOON AND SUN REFLECT HIS FLAME. ....TO A JILTED LOVER 310 18
    REFLECT IN TERROR ....MOONSONG AT MORNING 317 37
REFLECTED (2)
    BEHIND TWO EYES IN WHICH NOTHING IS REFLECTED BUT MONKEYS. *A SECRET 219 20
    REFLECTED THERE. ....ON LOOKING INTO THE EYES OF A DEMON LOVER 325 24
REFLECTING (2)
    IN THE MORNING SHE WOKE ME EARLY, REFLECTING THE SUN ....IN PLASTER 159 23
    REFLECTING IN A MILLION FLAGONS' SHINE, ...CINDERELLA 304   8
REFLECTION (1)
    WHICH HUNGERS TO HAUL THE WHITE REFLECTION DOWN. WINTER LANDSCAPE,   21   5
REFLECTIONS (4)
    MY EYEFUL OF REFLECTIONS A GHOST'S ....LANDOWNERS   53 12
    OPENS AND SHUTS, ACCEPTING THEM AMONG ITS RELFECTIONS. ..PRIVATE G. 131 24
    HAVING NO REFLECTIONS; ....GULLIVER 251   6
    IN WHICH THE MINUTES COULD ADMIRE THEIR REFLECTIONS AND
            FORGET ABOUT ME. ....THE RIVAL/DR 291   7
REFLECTS (3)
    BUT SCRUPULOUSLY REFLECTS THE USUAL TERROR. ....TALE OF A TUB   24   8
    YOU TO TAUNTS THOUGH, WHEN HE REFLECTS A FACE ....DIALOGUE O. 283 260
    AND BLOOD REFLECTS ACROSS THE MANUSCRIPT; ....FEMALE AUTHOR 301 10
REFRACTS (1)
    MY GLASS OF WATER REFRACTS THE MORNING. ....FEVER./DR 294 11
REFUGEE (1)
    RETCHING IN BRIGHT ORANGE BASINS; A REFUGEE ....CHANNEL CROSSING   26 10
REFUSE (1)
    FISH-GREASE, FISH-BONES, REFUSE OF ATROCITIES. ....FEVER./DR 294   6
REFUSING (2)
    REFUSING TO DIMINISH ....THE LADY AND THE EARTHENWARE HEAD   70 34
    COLD MOONS WITHDRAW, REFUSING TO COME TO TERMS ......METAMORPHOSES. 307   1
REGARD (1)
    REGARD ME SADLY, I DISAPPOINT THEM. ....SHEEP IN FOG 262   3
REGARDING (1)
    REGARDING ME WITH ATTENTION. ....THREE WOMEN 176   3
REGION (1)
    BUT TOWARD A REGION WHERE OUR THICK ATMOSPHERE ....GHOST'S.   90 25
REGRETFULLY (1)
    YET I STILL DEPENDED ON HER, THOUGH I DID IT REGRETFULLY.*IN PLASTER 160 49
REGULARITY (1)
    ARRIVE THROUGH THE MAILSLOT WITH LOVING REGULARITY, ...THE RIVAL 166 14
REHEARSE (1)
    I DO NOT HAVE TO THINK, OR EVEN REHEARSE. ....THREE WOMEN 176   9
REHEARSES (1)
    IT REHEARSES THEM MOANINGLY: ....WUTHERING HEIGHTS 168 35
REIGNED (1)
    BLUE-BLOODED IN COARSE COUNTRY REIGNED: ....NATURAL HISTORY   71   2
REINS (2)
    WOULDN'T SLOW FOR THE HAULED REINS, HIS NAME, WHITENESS I REMEMBER 103 24
    THE DREAMER REINS HIS WAKING APPETITE ....TERMINAL 328   2
REJECTS (1)
    NOW EARTH REJECTS COMMUNICATION *INSOLENT STORM STRIKES AT THE SKULL 326 29
RELAPSE (1)
    LET ME RELAPSE ....PARALYTIC 266   9
RELATION (2)
    THEIR WHITENESS BEARS NO RELATION TO LAUNDRY, ...MAGI 148   4
    THEIR FLESH BEARS NO RELATION. ....THE NIGHT DANCES 250 11
RELATIONSHIP (2)
    IN TIME OUR RELATIONSHIP GREW MORE INTENSE. ....IN PLASTER 159 28
    AND WE, TOO, HAD A RELATIONSHIP -- ....THE RABBIT CATCHER 194 26
RELATIVE (2)
    WHERE THE WIRELESS TALKS TO ITSELF LIKE AN ELDERLY RELATIVE. ...
                                     ... THE DETECTIVE 209 20
    FLOUNDER IN THE RELATIVE. ......INSOLENT STORM STRIKES AT THE SKULL 326 24
RELAX (1)
    WHERE I RELAX, FOETUS OR CAT, ...THE JAILER 226   9

```
                                                     TITLE              PAGE  LINE
RELEASED (1)
   WOULD NOT BE EASED, RELEASED. OUR EACH EXAMPLE  .......THE OTHER TWO  68   23
RELENTLESS (1)
   FOR THE RELISH OF HEAVEN, RELENTLESS, DOUSING WITH PRICKLES *LESSON.  80   14
RELIC (4)
   ELEMENT -- THIS RELIC SAVED  ..........MUSSEL HUNTER AT ROCK HARBOR   97   90
   RELIC OF TOUGH WEATHER, EVERY WINCH AND STAY  .........A WINTER SHIP 113   27
   OFF EUROPE'S RELIC HEAP  ..........................PRIVATE GROUND    130    3
   THIS TOE AND THAT TOE, A RELIC.  ..........................GULLIVER  251   19
RELICS (6)
   RELICS OF A MOUSE AND A SHREW  ...................ALL THE DEAD DEARS  70    5
   SPEWED RELICS CLICKER MASSES IN THE WIND,  ...........POINT SHIRLEY  110   32
   RED-MOTTLED RELICS, SHELLS, CLAWS  .................MAGNOLIA SHOALS  121    3
   IN VINEGAR LIKE SAINTS' RELICS.  ............THE SURGEON AT 2 A.M.   171   39
   OUR LUCKY RELICS HAVE BEEN PUT IN HOCK:  .................DOOMSDAY   316   11
   HANDS REACH BACK TO RELICS OF  .....................DANSE MACABRE    321    7
RELIGION (2)
   RELIGION, DRINKING  .....................NICK AND THE CANDLESTICK    241   18
   IF YOU CAN HANG RELIGION ON THE RIM  ....DIALOGUE OVER A OUIJA BOARD 283  248
RELIGIOUS (1)
   MOURNED BY RELIGIOUS FIGURES, BY GARLANDED CHILDREN.  GETTING THERE  249   48
RELISH (1)
   FOR THE RELISH OF HEAVEN, RELENTLESS, DOUSING WITH PRICKLES  LESSON.  80   14
REMAIN (2)
   SO WEEDY A RACE COULD NOT REMAIN IN DREAMS,  ........THE THIN PEOPLE  64   23
   COULD NOT REMAIN OUTLANDISH VICTIMS  ................THE THIN PEOPLE  64   24
REMAINDER (1)
   THE GARDEN'S REMAINDER IN FULL PAINT.  ................RHODODENDRON. 103    4
REMAINING (1)
   THEY SHOOT THE DICE FOR ONE REMAINING BONE;  ............DENOUEMENT  326    8
REMARKABLE (1)
   THE FALLEN TIMBERS OF ITS ONCE REMARKABLE  ..........ABOVE THE OXBOW  88   37
REMEDY (2)
   ONCE ONE HAS SEEN GOD, WHAT IS THE REMEDY?  ...................MYSTIC 268    9
   WHAT IS THE REMEDY?  ...........................................MYSTIC 268   15
REMEMBER (21)
   YOUR SHELLED BED I REMEMBER.  ...................FULL FATHOM FIVE    93   43
   WHITENESS I REMEMBER  ......................WHITENESS I REMEMBER    102    T
   WHITENESS BEING WHAT I REMEMBER  .............WHITENESS I REMEMBER   102    1
   I SAID: I MUST REMEMBER THIS, BEING SMALL.  ............POEM.1.WHO.  132   28
   FOR WEEKS I CAN REMEMBER NOTHING AT ALL.  ..............POEM.1.WHO.  132   33
   ONE CAN REMEMBER MEN AND HOUSES BY.  .....SLEEP IN THE MOJAVE DESERT 143    7
   WHEN YOU KICK ME OUT, THAT'S WHAT I'LL REMEMBER  .....LEAVING EARLY  145    2
   AND I REMEMBER MY MATERNAL GRANDMOTHER FROM VIENNA.  ........CANDLES 149   17
   I REMEMBER THE BLOODIED CHICKS AND THE QUARTERED RABBITS.  ...ZOO K. 155   24
   I REMEMBER YOU PLAYING "JA DA" IN A PINK PIQUE DRESS*THE BABYSITTERS 175   22
   I REMEMBER THE MINUTE WHEN I KNEW FOR SURE.  ...........THREE WOMEN  177   43
   I REMEMBER A WHITE, COLD WING  .........................THREE WOMEN  178   49
   THEY ARE BEGINNING TO REMEMBER THEIR DIFFERENCES.  .....THREE WOMEN  183  224
   I REMEMBER A BLUE EYE,  ...............................LITTLE FUGUE  188   45
   THIS IS THE TONGUE OF THE DEAD MAN: REMEMBER, REMEMBER. *BERCK-PLAGE 199   81
   THIS IS THE TONGUE OF THE DEAD MAN: REMEMBER, REMEMBER. *BERCK-PLAGE 199   81
   THEY ARE FLYING OFF INTO NOTHING: REMEMBER US.  ........BERCK-PLAGE  199   87
   I REMEMBER  ............................................MYSTIC       268    6
   REMEMBER THE WALKER UPON IT?  ...........................MYSTIC      269   26
   I WOULD NOT REMEMBER YOU  ...................................APRIL 18 301    6
   AND REMEMBER, IF TEDIOUS RISK  .................NOTES TO A NEOPHYTE  306   17
REMEMBERING (4)
   REMEMBERING THE WHITE, TRIUMPHANT SPRAY  .................MAYFLOWER   60   12
   REMEMBERING, EVEN IN SLEEP,  .............NICK AND THE CANDLESTICK   241   25
   REMEMBERING A THOUSAND AUTUMNS  ..................GOLD MOUTHS CRY    302    3
   REMEMBERING A THOUSAND AUTUMNS,  .................GOLD MOUTHS CRY    302   12
REMEMBERS (2)
   REMEMBERS A FEW ODD SYLLABLES.  ................WUTHERING HEIGHTS    168   34
   REMEMBERS HOW WHITE THEY WERE.  .....................THREE WOMEN     186  345
REMEMBRANCES (1)
   FUSTY REMEMBRANCES, THE COILED-SPRING STAIR  ..................WIDOW 164    9
REMIND (1)
   OUTSIDE THE CAVE WHOSE CONTOURS MOST REMIND  ...........DIALOGUE O.  281  200
REMORSE (1)
   TO COURT REMORSE. OR SOMEONE ELSE. I'D RATHER  .........DIALOGUE O.  278   59
RENDER (1)
   DEAD MEN RENDER LOVE AND WAR NO HEED,  ....................THE DEAD  320    3
RENDERING (1)
   ON THE RENDERING, GRAIN BY GRAIN,  THE LADY AND THE EARTHENWARE HEAD  69   26
RENDING (2)
   AND THE FABULOUS LUTES AND PEACOCKS, RENDING THE NET  CONVERSATION.  21    3
   KEEN THE RENDING TEETH AND SWEET  .........................PURSUIT   22   17
RENDS (1)
   THE DOORBELL RENDS THE NOONDAY HEAT  ................FAMILY REUNION  300    5
RENT (1)
   A FLASH LIKE DOOMCRACK RENT NIGHT'S BLACK:  ..........CRYSTAL GAZER   55   37
RENTED (2)
   FROM MY RENTED ATTIC WITH NO EARTH  .....................LANDOWNERS   53    1
   AND RENTED AN OLD GREEN BOAT. I ROWED. YOU READ  ....THE BABYSITTERS 175   31
```

RENTS (1)
  HE RENTS HIS POISONS OUT BY TELEPHONE: ....DENOUEMENT 327 14
REOPEN (1)
  ONLY TO REOPEN AS FLESH CONGEALS: ....LOVE IS A PARALLAX 330 65
REPAIR (2)
  JACK SHALL REPAIR. ....TINKER JACK AND THE TIDY WIVES 34 25
  KEEPING ITSELF, IT SEEMS, IN A STATE OF MIRACULOUS REPAIR. ..MEDUSA 225 15
REPASSES (1)
  SHE PASSES AND REPASSES, LUMINOUS AS A NURSE. ....THREE WOMEN 176   5
REPEATS (1)
  PUTS ON A PUBLIC GRIN, REPEATS OUR NAME ....TALE OF A TUB 24   7
REPENT (1)
  REPENT, DEPART, BEFORE GOD'S TRUMP-CRACK SPLITS THE SKY." ...
                     ... DIALOGUE BETWEEN GHOST AND PRIEST 39 46
REPETITIONS (1)
  CREEPING UP WITH HER HATFUL OF TRIVIAL REPETITIONS. ......INSOMNIAC 163 32
REPLACES (1)
  EACH MORNING IT IS HER FACE THAT REPLACES THE DARKNESS. .....MIRROR 174 16
REPLENISH (1)
  THE COLORS REPLENISH THEMSELVES, AND THE WET ....THREE WOMEN 185 313
REPLICAS (1)
  CORRIDOR OF INANE REPLICAS, ...LANDOWNERS 53   8
REPLY (1)
  GRAVES ALL CAROL IN REPLY. ....LOVE IS A PARALLAX 330 42
REPOISE (1)
  AND REPOISE UNTIL TIME STOP, THE CELESTIAL BALANCE ....PERSEUS 84 48
REPORT (1)
  REPORT WHITE PILLARS, A BLUE SKY, ...TWO VIEWS OF WITHENS 72 17
REPORTED (1)
  THE MOUTH FIRST, ITS ABSENCE REPORTED ....THE DETECTIVE 209 27
REPOSE (5)
  SCUTTLE REPOSE WITH CROWNS AND CACKLES. ....ALICANTE LULLABY 43   7
  A SOLIDER REPOSE THAN DEATH'S. ....SCULPTOR 92 24
  THESE STONES GUARD A DARK REPOSE ....CHILD'S PARK STONES 101 11
  IT HAS SHUT ITS MOUTH ON THE STONE PILL OF REPOSE. ....SURGEON. 171 30
  REPOSE OF SCULPTURE HOLDS THE COUNTRY STILL. ....PROLOGUE TO SPRING 322   9
REPRESENT (1)
  THAT REPRESENT A SEA ....BATTLE-SCENE 84   6
RESCUED (1)
  I CONSIDERED THE POETRY I RESCUED*FABLE OF THE RHODODENDRON STEALERS 103 15
RESEMBLE (3)
  NOW I RESEMBLE A SORT OF GOD ....LOVE LETTER 147 34
  I MUST MOST PERFECTLY RESEMBLE THEM -- ....I AM VERTICAL 162 15
  IF THE MOON SMILED, SHE WOULD RESEMBLE YOU ....THE RIVAL 166   1
RESEMBLES (2)
  IT RESEMBLES THE MOON, OR A SHEET OF BLANK PAPER ....A LIFE 150 23
  A WIDOW RESEMBLES THEM, A SHADOW-THING, ...WIDOW 164 30
RESENTFUL (1)
  AND I'D BEEN KEEPING HER IN THE DARK, AND SHE WAS RESENTFUL -- ...
                     ... IN PLASTER 159 37
RESIGN (1)
  AS IS THE USE WITH VAMPIRES, AND RESIGN OUR STAND ......DIALOGUE O. 285 330
RESIN (1)
  AS RESIN DROPS OOZED FROM PINE BARK. ....THE BURNT-OUT SPA 137   5
RESISTIVE (1)
  RESISTIVE, RUDDY-BODIED, ...SCULPTOR 92 15
RESOLUTENESS (1)
  I HUNG ON HIS NECK. RESOLUTENESS ....WHITENESS I REMEMBER 103 28
RESOLUTION (1)
  IF ROOT'S FIRM-FIXED AND RESOLUTION GOOD. ....MAYFLOWER 60   4
RESOLVE (1)
  RESOLVE ....RESOLVE 52   T
RESOLVED (2)
  AND RESOLVED MORE CEREMONIOUSLY TO LODGE ....LADY AND T. 69 22
  I AM RESOLVED. NO REASON COULD UNTWIST   DIALOGUE OVER A OUIJA BOARD 286 341
RESORT (2)
  NOISELESS, ON RUBBER WHEELS, ON THE WAY TO THE SEA RESORT.   WAKING. 151   8
  MY BOY, IT'S YOUR LAST RESORT. ....THE APPLICANT 222 39
RESOURCEFUL (1)
  THE BODY IS RESOURCEFUL. ....THREE WOMEN 184 256
RESPECT (1)
  IN EVERY RESPECT LIKE EVERY OTHER NIGHT:*DIALOGUE OVER A OUIJA BOARD 276   2
RESPECT'S (1)
  FOR A BAY-TREE HIDE, RESPECT'S ....VIRGIN IN A TREE 81 11
RESPITE (1)
  A BRIEF RESPITE FROM FEAR ....BLACK ROOK IN RAINY WEATHER 57 31
REST (6)
  WOULD PICK STICKS, WOULD NOT REST ....THE EVERLASTING MONDAY 62   8
  OF THE AIR EDDIES' LOOP AND ARC THOUGH AIR'S AT REST*ABOVE THE OXBOW 88 32
  REST ON ORANGE PLUSH NEAR THE NEWEL POST. ...YADDO: THE GRAND MANOR 124 16
  THE REST OF THE BODY IS ALL WASHED OUT, ...CONTUSION 271   2
  WHEN ATTACKED, THEN SCOOTING TO REST, BARELY TREMBLING. ...BALLOONS 271   8
  YOU'LL WRECK THE REST ....TRIO OF LOVE SONGS 315 43
RESTING (1)
  PLAYING AND RESTING WITHOUT COMMITTING ITSELF. ....TULIPS 161 56

	TITLE	PAGE	LINE

RESTLESS (2)
    I AM RESTLESS. RESTLESS AND USELESS. I, TOO, CREATE CORPSES. *THREE. 182 189
    I AM RESTLESS. RESTLESS AND USELESS. I, TOO, CREATE CORPSES. *THREE. 182 189
RESURRECT (2)
    THEY BRUISE THE ROCKS OUT OF EXISTENCE, THEN RESURRECT THEM. ...
                                                ... FINISTERRE 169 15
    SHANKS OF BONE NOW RESURRECT, ...DANSE MACABRE 321 17
RESURRECTED (1)
    RULE THEIR BEDS LIKE BEHEADED AND RESURRECTED AND ALL SILENT
        ROYALTY, ... QUEEN MARY'S ROSE GARDEN 290   5
RESURRECTION (1)
    EIGHT GREAT TONGUES AFFIRMING THE RESURRECTION. ....MOON. 173 13
RESURRECTIONS (1)
    FLIES WATCH NO RESURRECTIONS IN THE SUN. ....NOVEMBER GRAVEYARD   56 12
RETCH (2)
    WATER, WATER MAKE ME RETCH. ....FEVER. 232 33
    OFF AND ON, AS IF I JUST HAD TO RETCH. ....THE TOUR 238 25
RETCHING (1)
    RETCHING IN BRIGHT ORANGE BASINS: A REFUGEE ....CHANNEL CROSSING   26 10
RETRACING (1)
    OF SEA RETRACING ITS TIDE- ....MUSSEL HUNTER AT ROCK HARBOR   96 43
RETREAT (1)
    HORIZONS BEAT A RETREAT AS WE EMBARK ....LOVE IS A PARALLAX 329   4
RETREATS (1)
    AND LOST IN SUBTLE METAPHOR, RETREATS ....FEMALE AUTHOR 301 13
RETROGRADE (1)
    IN TWENTY YEARS I SHALL BE RETROGRADE ....CANDLES 149 29
RETROGRESSED (1)
    RETROGRESSED TO BLOWZE, I NEXT CHOSE RED; ...........RHODODENDRON. 103 10
RETROSPECT (1)
    RETROSPECT SHALL NOT SOFTEN SUCH PENURY -- ....DEPARTURE   51   9
RETURN (4)
    ALL THE NIGHT GAVE HER, IN RETURN ....HARDCASTLE CRAGS   63 26
    THE OLD GOD DRIBBLES, IN RETURN, HIS WORDS. ....OUIJA   77 11
    AND RETURN, LOSING THEMSELVES ....MUSSEL HUNTER AT ROCK HARBOR   97 88
    WHERE LOVE-MET GROUNDHOGS LOVE ONE IN RETURN, ...INCOMMUNICADO 100   9
RETURNED (1)
    AND RETURNED THEM STEAMED AND PRESSED AND STIFF AS SHIRTS. *THE TOUR 238 34
RETURNING (2)
    BAREFOOT, SHE STOOD, IN SHOCK OF THAT RETURNING, ...DREAM WITH C.   43   5
    NOW WE, RETURNING FROM THE VAULTED DOMES ....DOOM OF EXILES 318   1
RETURNS (1)
    OUT OF IT. THERE. THE ROOM RETURNS .....DIALOGUE OVER A OUIJA BOARD 285 334
REUNION (1)
    FAMILY REUNION ....FAMILY REUNION 300   T
REVEALS (1)
    REVEALS NO CRACKS THAT CAN BE DECODED? WHEN WASHBOWL   TALE OF A TUB   24 10
REVELATION (1)
    OF AMBROSIAL REVELATION. AND SO DEPARTS. ...THE GHOST'S LEAVETAKING   90 15
REVEL (1)
    FOLLOW HOLIDAY REVEL BEGUN LONG SINCE, ...CINDERELLA 304 10
REVELED (2)
    GREEN ALLEYS WHERE WE REVELED HAVE BECOME ....DOOM OF EXILES 318   5
    REFECTORIES WHERE HE REVELED HAVE BECOME ....TERMINAL 328   5
REVERENCE (1)
    I HAD NO REVERENCE. ....THREE WOMEN 178 60
REVERIE (1)
    THE SCRAPS OF RUSTED REVERIE, THE WHEELS ....SONNET: TO EVA 305 10
REVIVALIST (1)
    THE UNTIDY LADY REVIVALIST ....ON DECK 143 19
REVOKE (1)
    EATING YOUR WORDS: YOU'LL REVOKE HIS GODHOOD SOON AS ...DIALOGUE O. 281 189
REVOLTED (1)
    INTRUDES EVEN WHEN THE REVOLTED EYE ....TALE OF A TUB   25 30
REVOLUTIONARY (1)
    SONG FOR A REVOLUTIONARY LOVE ....SONG FOR A REVOLUTIONARY LOVE 322   T
REVOLVE (9)
    HORSES, PLANETS AND SPIRES REVOLVE. ....THE EYE-MOTE 109 18
    SPOTTED COWS REVOLVE THEIR JAWS AND CROP ....WATERCOLOR. 112 16
    THEIR EYES REVOLVE THE WHOLE TOWN LIKE A BLUE AND GREEN BALL. *NET-. 121 12
    THE DISKS REVOLVE, THEY ASK TO BE HEARD -- ....COURAGE. 209   5
    SO THE DISKS OF THE BRAIN REVOLVE, LIKE THE MUZZLES OF CANNON. ...
                                        ... THE COURAGE OF SHUTTING-UP 210 16
    REVOLVE IN MY ....PURDAH 243 32
    THAT REVOLVE IN CRIVELLI, UNTOUCHABLE. ....GULLIVER 251 22
    THE DARK FRUITS REVOLVE AND FALL. ....THALIDOMIDE 252 23
    THE WHEELS REVOLVE, THE UNIVERSE KEEPS RUNNING.   TO EVA DESCENDING. 303   2
REVOLVED (1)
    WITH TILTED SPARS OF SLOOPS REVOLVED BY WHITE .....MIDSUMMER MOBILE 324   3
REVOLVES (1)
    THE CHILD IN THE WHITE CRIB REVOLVES AND SIGHS, ...EVENT 194   7
REVOLVING (4)
    REVOLVING, THE SOUND ....GETTING THERE 248   7
    THE WHOLE REVOLVING TALL GLASS PALACE HALL ....CINDERELLA 304   5
    REVOLVING IN OVAL LOOPS OF SOLAR SPEED, ...THE DEAD 320   1

```
                                                       TITLE        PAGE  LINE
REVOLVING (CONT.)
   WINGED RABBITS REVOLVING ABOUT HIS KNEES,  ....CIRCUS IN THREE RINGS  322  16
REWARDS (1)
   SHE REWARDS ME WITH TEARS AND AN AGITATION OF HANDS.  ........MIRROR  174  14
RHETORIC (1)
   FROM RHETORIC OF THESE ROCOCO QUEENS.  ................A SORCERER B.  324   4
RHEUMATIC (1)
   THIS WAS THE LAND'S END: THE LAST FINGERS, KNUCKLED AND
      RHEUMATIC,  ....................................FINISTERRE  169   1
RHINOCEROS (1)
   YOUR TWO-HORNED RHINOCEROS OPENED A MOUTH  ........ZOO KEEPER'S WIFE  155  34
RHODODENDRON (3)
   FABLE OF THE RHODODENDRON STEALERS  ...................RHODODENDRON.  103   T
   A SPASM TOOK THE RHODODENDRON BUSHES:  ................RHODODENDRON.  103  20
   OF CERISE AND PINK FROM THE RHODODENDRON,  ...........RHODODENDRON.  104  22
RHYME (1)
   RHYME  .............................................................RHYME   50   T
RIBBED (1)
   RIBBED LIKE A HAND,  .....................................POLLY'S TREE  129  36
RIBBON (2)
   PRIZE RIBBON AND PIG SHOW.  ....................................SOW   60   6
   FLATTEN THE DOPED SNAKES TO RIBBON. IN HERE, THE GRASSES *PRIVATE G.  130  17
RIBBONS (1)
   NO FALLING RIBBONS, NO SCREAM AT THE END.  .......A BIRTHDAY PRESENT  207  35
RIBS (3)
   THIS IS THE SIDE OF A MAN: HIS RED RIBS,  ...............BERCK-PLAGE  198  46
   MY RIBS SHOW. WHAT HAVE I EATEN?  ...................THE JAILER  226  22
   GODS AND REAR THEM LIKE BEANSTALKS FROM OUT THESE RIBS   DIALOGUE O.  280 170
RICE (1)
   SITTING UNDER A POTLID, TINY AND INERT AS A RICE GRAIN.  ..POEM.6.W.  135  15
RICH (12)
   NOW, RICH ORDER OF WALLS IS FALLEN: ROOKS CROAK  ......CONVERSATION.   21   5
   OF RICH ATTIRE  .........................THE QUEEN'S COMPLAINT   28  13
   RICH, BROWN, SUDDEN IN SUNGLINT  .........................ODE FOR TED   29  12
   RICH IN STRAYINGS WITH EVERY AMOROUS OAF,  .............VANITY FAIR   33  17
   THOUGH PRIME PARTS CRAM EACH RICH MEAL,  ................THE GLUTTON   40  11
   FACED IN HIS RICH YELLOWS, TASSELS, POMPONS, BRAID, THE PICADOR ...
                                                       ... THE GORING   47   5
   WE OWN NO WILDERNESSES RICH AND DEEP ENOUGH  .......THE THIN PEOPLE   65  41
   TO FATHER DYNASTIES. THE AIR IS RICH.  .....THE BEEKEEPER'S DAUGHTER  118  12
   HE'LL BE RICH IN A YEAR (AND HE SHOULD KNOW)  ................ON DECK  143  28
   I'LL CARRY IT OFF LIKE A RICH PRETTY GIRL,  ..........STOPPED DEAD  230  23
   E. GODPIE! THAT'S RICH. THE JACKANAPES   DIALOGUE OVER A OUIJA BOARD  282 210
   A CAVIARE DECAY OF RICH BROCADES.  ........................TERMINAL  328   8
RICHNESS (2)
   WITH RICHNESS, HAIR HEAVIER  ...............................LORELEI   94  13
   O IT WAS RICHNESS! -- ELEVEN ROOMS AND A YACHT  .....THE BABYSITTERS  174  10
RICKETY (1)
   AND WITH THEM THAT RICKETY EDIFICE  ...................A WINTER SHIP  113  16
RICTUS (1)
   UNDER THE EYES OF THE STARS AND THE MOON'S RICTUS  ........INSOMNIAC  163   5
RID (5)
   APE OF HER LOOK. BEST RID  ........THE LADY AND THE EARTHENWARE HEAD   69   5
   WORDS TO RID ME OF THOSE THREE LADIES  ........THE DISQUIETING MUSES   75  14
   HE WON'T BE GOT RID OF:  ...............................POEM.4.BEAST.  134  11
   I WASN'T IN ANY POSITION TO GET RID OF HER.  ............IN PLASTER  159  43
   THEY HAVE GOT RID OF THE MEN,  ..........................WINTERING  218  40
RIDDLE (3)
   INDISSOLUBLE ENOUGH TO RIDDLE THE GUTS  ...................PERSEUS   82   4
   I'M A RIDDLE IN NINE SYLLABLES,  .........................METAPHORS  116   1
   IN WHICH THE RIDDLE OF OUR RACE IS SHUT.  .........DOOM OF EXILES  318  14
RIDDLED (2)
   RIDDLED WITH GHOSTS, TO LIE  .......................ALL THE DEAD DEARS   71  35
   HANG RIDDLED WITH SHOT,  .............................TEMPER OF TIME  336  22
RIDE (8)
   FOR A WISH TO TETHER: THEY RIDE NIGHTLONG  ...........EPITAPH FOR F.   46  26
   FROM MARBLE SNOW-HEAP OF MOOR TO RIDE THAT WOMAN  ........SNOWMAN O.   59  27
   I RIDE EARTH'S BURNING CARROUSEL  .........ON THE PLETHORA OF DRYADS   67  29
   FIT FOR THOSE OUTLAWS TO RIDE HOME ON,  ..........ALL THE DEAD DEARS   71  30
   TWO VIRTUES RIDE, BY STALLION, BY NAG,  ....THE DEATH OF MYTH-MAKING  104   1
   GREY WAVES THE STUB-NECKED EIDERS RIDE.  ...............POINT SHIRLEY  110  33
   AND RIDE THAT FLUX AT ANCHOR, UPSIDE DOWN.  ............WATERCOLOR.  112  11
   SHRIEK FROM MY BELLY LIKE ARROWS, AND THESE I RIDE.  ......THE OTHER  202  19
RIDER (1)
   SIMPLIFIED ME: A RIDER, RIDING  .............WHITENESS I REMEMBER  103  29
RIDERLESS (1)
   WORDS DRY AND RIDERLESS,  .......................................WORDS  270  16
RIDGE (1)
   REAP THE ROUND BLUE PIGEON FROM ROOF RIDGE, *GO GET THE GOODLY SQUAB  313   3
RIDGEPOLE (3)
   STONE WALL AND RIDGEPOLE RISE  ..................TWO VIEWS OF WITHENS   71   3
   WORK OF THE EARTH AND THE SKY'S RIDGEPOLE.  ........FULL FATHOM FIVE   93  32
   A GULL HOLDS HIS POSE ON A SHANTY RIDGEPOLE,  .........A WINTER SHIP  113   6
RIDICULOUS (4)
   YET ALWAYS THE RIDICULOUS NUDE FLANKS URGE  ..........TALE OF A TUB   25  33
```

```
                                                          TITLE              PAGE  LINE
RIDICULOUS (CONT.)
  "I DON'T ASK YOU TO SPIN SOME RIDICULOUS FABLE  .........DIALOGUE B.         39   22
  AND I SEE MYSELF, FLAT, RIDICULOUS, A CUT-PAPER SHADOW  ......TULIPS        161   46
  BUT IN THE DAYTIME SHE IS RIDICULOUS.  ....................THE RIVAL        166   12
RIDING (8)
  RIDING IN THE FULL  ..............................HARDCASTLE CRAGS           62   10
  SIMPLIFIED ME: A RIDER, RIDING  ................WHITENESS I REMEMBER        103   29
  OF RIDING AGAINST THE LIZARD,  ...................THE TIMES ARE TIDY        107    7
  RIDING THE TIDE OF THE WIND, STEADY  ..................A WINTER SHIP        113    7
  ARE RIDING TO WORK IN ROWS, AS IF RECENTLY BRAINWASHED.  ..INSOMNIAC        163   35
  RIDING MY ARCTIC  ............................BURNING THE LETTERS           204   27
  RIDING THE RIP TIDE TO THE NEAREST POINT OF DEPARTURE,  ......MEDUSA        225   10
  RIDING HOME FROM CREDULOUS BLUE DOMES,  ....................TERMINAL        328    1
RIFT (2)
  IN WHOSE RIFT WE LIE  ...................................EVENT             194    3
  AND YOU, SHACKLED ASHEN ACROSS THE RIFT, A SPECTER  .....DIALOGUE O.       285  321
RIGGED (1)
  RIGGED POKER-STIFF ON HER BACK  ..................ALL THE DEAD DEARS        70    1
RIGHT (19)
  RIGHT TO BLAZE AS SATAN'S WIFE;  .........................VANITY FAIR       33   32
  FOOLISH, DELICATE, IN THE LOWER RIGHT HAND CORNER.  ......TWO VIEWS.       114   22
  TO THE RIGHT, AND MARCH ICE  ............................MAN IN BLACK      119   10
  RIGHT, LIKE A WELL-DONE SUM.  ...............................YOU'RE        141   17
  THE REAL THING, ALL RIGHT: THE GOOD, THE TRUE --  ..............MAGI       148    6
  I CAN SMELL THE SALT, ALL RIGHT.  ..........................WHITSUN        154   13
  MUMMY-CLOTHS, SMILING: I'M ALL RIGHT.  ...................FACE LIFT        155    3
  PERHAPS IT IS THE SEASON THAT IS NOT RIGHT. *STARS OVER THE DORDOGNE       165   24
  BLACKBERRIES ON EITHER SIDE, THOUGH ON THE RIGHT MAINLY,    BLACKBER.      168    2
  THE MOON IS NO DOOR. IT IS A FACE IN ITS OWN RIGHT,  .........MOON.        173    8
  THAT GIVES IT A KINGLINESS, A RIGHT.  ....................PHEASANT         191   10
  BUT RIGHT NOW YOU ARE DUMB.  ...............FOR A FATHERLESS SON           205    6
  SEVEN HOURS KNOCKED OUT OF MY RIGHT MIND  ...............THE JAILER        226    7
  MY RIGHT FOOT  .........................................LADY LAZARUS       244    6
  TALKERS: "YOU ALL RIGHT?"  ..............................PARALYTIC         266   15
  I WAS PERFECTLY RIGHT: PAN'S A MERE PUPPET  ............DIALOGUE O.        279  106
  ALL RIGHT, LET'S SAY YOU COULD TAKE A SKULL AND BREAK IT*SONNET:EVA.       304    1
  A LIGHT, AND RIGHT AWAY A RAVING  .......................THE DREAM         310   10
  BLESSINGS RIGHT AND LEFT AND CRY  ................LOVE IS A PARALLAX       330   39
RIGHTFUL (1)
  NOW HE GOES FROM HIS RIGHTFUL ROAD  ......................BUCOLICS          24   21
RIGMAROLE (2)
  ITEM: CHUCK OUT ROYAL RIGMAROLE OF PROPS  .............A SORCERER B.       324    5
  A WINDOW WHICH PROVES THE SKY SHEER RIGMAROLE*EPITAPH IN THREE PARTS       337   28
RIGOR (2)
  DARK FACE. SO MIGHT RIGOR MORTIS COME TO STIFFEN  ..........PERSEUS         83   32
  A RIGOR SEIZED ME: I SAW CRACKS APPEAR, *DIALOGUE OVER A OUIJA BOARD       285  319
RIM (1)
  IF YOU CAN HANG RELIGION ON THE RIM  ...DIALOGUE OVER A OUIJA BOARD        283  248
RIND (1)
  THE MOON TO A RIND OF LITTLE LIGHT.  ................THE THIN PEOPLE        65   31
RINDS (1)
  IN A BATCH OF RAVELED APPLE RINDS.  ....THE PRINCESS AND THE GOBLINS       335   68
RING (12)
  THE RED-NOSED, BLUE-CAPED WOMEN RING  ................A WINTER'S TALE       87   14
  THEY ARE TURNING THE BURNERS UP, RING AFTER RING.  ........POEM.6.W.       135   16
  THEY ARE TURNING THE BURNERS UP, RING AFTER RING.  ........POEM.6.W.       135   16
  THEY RING TRUE, LIKE GOOD CHINA.  ...........................A LIFE        150   18
  THE HORIZONS RING ME LIKE FAGGOTS,  ...............WUTHERING HEIGHTS       167    1
  PEGS TOO DEEP TO UPROOT, AND A MIND LIKE A RING   THE RABBIT CATCHER       194   28
  I WALK IN A RING,  .........................................EVENT         195   14
  A WEDDING RING,  .......................................LADY LAZARUS       246   77
  A RING OF GOLD WITH THE SUN IN IT?  ....................THE COURIERS       247    5
  MEMORIES GROWING, RING ON RING,  ........................WINTER TREES      257    4
  MEMORIES GROWING, RING ON RING,  ........................WINTER TREES      257    4
  AROUND THE RING. I THINK IT MUST BE MAKING SURE  ........DIALOGUE O.       277   22
RINGDOVES (2)
  RINGDOVES ROOST WELL WITHIN HIS WOOD,  ..................ODE FOR TED        29   19
  THE SHADOWS OF RINGDOVES CHANTING, BUT EASING NOTHING. *WINTER TREES       258   15
RINGED (1)
  WINKS LIKE MONEY UNDER THE RINGED TOES OF THE CHICKENS.  ......NET-.       121    9
RINGING (3)
  STILL RINGING WITH BRUIT OF INSULTS AND DISHONORS  .......SNOWMAN O.        58    3
  IN RINGING ORANGE LIKE A STELLAR CARROT.  ...THE GHOST'S LEAVETAKING        91   28
  RINGING THE WHITE CHINA.  ........................THE RABBIT CATCHER       194   23
RINGS (6)
  DIAMOND RINGS, POTTED ROSES, FOX-SKINS  .......................OWL        101    5
  FALLING FROM ME LIKE RINGS  .............................PARALYTIC        267   35
  NO RINGS THROUGH THE NOSE, NO CRIES.  ......................GIGOLO        267    9
  THE BLUE AND RED JEWELS OF HER RINGS SMOKE  ...............KINDNESS       269    3
  AFTER WHOSE STROKE THE WOOD RINGS,  ........................WORDS         270    2
  CIRCUS IN THREE RINGS  ......................CIRCUS IN THREE RINGS        321    T
RINK (1)
  CIGAR OVER HIS RINK OF FISHES.  .......................A WINTER SHIP       113   12
RINSING (1)
  RINSING THOSE STABLES: A BABY'S TEARS WOULD DO IT.  .........PERSEUS        82    7
```

TITLE   PAGE LINE

RIOT (1)
  AND CASUIST ARGUMENTS RUN RIOT   INSOLENT STORM STRIKES AT THE SKULL 326 21
RIP (1)
  RIDING THE RIP TIDE TO THE NEAREST POINT OF DEPARTURE, ...MEDUSA 225 10
RIPE (3)
  FOR THRIFTY CHILDREN, NOR DOLT PIG RIPE FOR HECKLING, ...SOW 60 13
  SHE, RIPE AND UNPLUCKED, 'S ....VIRGIN IN A TREE 82 36
  I COME TO ONE BUSH OF BERRIES SO RIPE IT IS A BUSH OF FLIES, ...
                 ... BLACKBERRYING 168 15
RIPEN (3)
  KNOBBED QUARTZ; FLAYED COLORS RIPEN ....ODE FOR TED 29 11
  AND BLEED. THE WHITE STOMACH MAY RIPEN YET. ....MOONRISE 98 30
  THE DEAD RIPEN IN THE GRAPELEAVES. POEM.3.MAENAD. 133 12
RIPPED (2)
  NOTHING THAT CANNOT BE ERASED, RIPPED UP AND SCRAPPED,
      BEGUN AGAIN. ....THREE WOMEN 184 277
  THAT SPLITS FROM ITS RIPPED BAG AND DOES NOT STOP ....BURNING. 205 51
RIPPLE (1)
  LEAVING NO SPARKY TRACK, SETTING UP NO RIPPLE. ....THE OTHER TWO 68 26
RIPPLED (1)
  RIPPLED AND PULSED IN THE GLASSY UPDRAUGHT. ...SUICIDE OFF EGG ROCK 115 5
RIPPLES (2)
  A CREEL OF EELS, ALL RIPPLES. ....YOU'RE 141 15
  BITCHES TO RIPPLES OF SILVER ....GIGOLO 268 23
RIPPLING (1)
  SURELY THE GRASS SHOULD BE RIPPLING. ....THE JAILER 226 25
RISE (15)
  LIKE ICEBERGS, WHILE MINUTE BROWN HAIRS RISE ....TALE OF A TUB 25 42
  STONE WALL AND RIDGEPOLE RISE ....TWO VIEWS OF WITHENS 71 3
  A RISE IN THE LANDSCAPE, HUMMOCK OR HOGBACK, LOOKS ABOVE THE OXBOW 88 16
  THEY RISE, THEIR LIMBS PONDEROUS ....LORELEI 94 12
  SNUFF-COLORED SAND CLIFFS RISE ....MAN IN BLACK 119 12
  ODORS OF WET EARTH RISE. ....THE SLEEPERS 122 9
  THE CLEAR VOWELS RISE LIKE BALLOONS. ....MORNING SONG 157 18
  MAKE THEIR OWN ELEMENT. THEY WILL NOT RISE, ...FEVER. 231 15
  I THINK I MAY RISE --- ....FEVER. 232 44
  THEY RISE ON EITHER SIDE OF HIM LIKE STARS. ....AMNESIAC 233 23
  RISE, WITH HER CANCEROUS PALLORS, ...PURDAH 242 13
  I RISE WITH MY RED HAIR ....LADY LAZARUS 247 83
  THIS EARTH I RISE FROM, AND I IN AGONY. ....GETTING THERE 248 37
  AND VIRGINS RISE WHERE LUSTFUL VENUS LAY: .....NEVER TRY TO TRICK. 319 5
  WILL SCRUPULOUSLY RISE AND SET; ....TWO LOVERS. 327 22
RISES (6)
  RISES THE ROUND RED WATERMELON SUN. ....SOUTHERN SUNRISE 26 18
  RISES TO THE GLASS FROM HIS BLACK FATHOMS. ....OUIJA 77 2
  INDOORS, TIFFANY'S PHOENIX RISES ....YADDO: THE GRAND MANOR 123 13
  THE SUN RISES UNDER THE PILLAR OF YOUR TONGUE. ....THE COLOSSUS 130 27
  RISES TOWARD HER DAY AFTER DAY, LIKE A TERRIBLE FISH. ....MIRROR 174 18
  RISES SO WHITELY UNBUFFETED? ....BERCK-PLAGE 198 64
RISING (8)
  TILL THE NIGHT MISTS CAME RISING. ....SONG FOR A SUMMER'S DAY 31 20
  A DRAGNET, RISING, FALLING, AS WAVES ....FULL FATHOM FIVE 92 5
  THIS LOAF'S BIG WITH ITS YEASTY RISING. ....METAPHORS 116 5
  AND THE LOCKED DROPS RISING IN A DEW ....LOVE LETTER 147 21
  RISING AND FLYING, BUT BLINDED. ....BURNING THE LETTERS 204 32
  A BODY INTO A PIPE, AND THE SMOKE RISING. ....THE DETECTIVE 208 11
  THAN AGAINST GRAVITY'S GRIP, TABLES RISING; THE DRINK ..DIALOGUE O. 279 122
  THROUGH CANDID KITCHENS IN THE RISING SUN ....THE PRINCESS. 334 52
RISK (1)
  AND REMEMBER, IF TEDIOUS RISK ....NOTES TO A NEOPHYTE 306 17
RITUAL (2)
  IN RITUAL, TO STRIKE -- IS DEFINITELY GONE; ....TALE OF A TUB 25 22
  THE RITUAL DEATH EACH TIME BOTCHED AMONG DROPPED CAPES,
                ILL-JUDGED STABS, ...THE GORING 47 3
RITUALS (1)
  IN THOSE ELABORATE RITUALS ....MISS DRAKE PROCEEDS TO SUPPER 41 2
RIVAL (3)
  THE RIVAL ....THE RIVAL 166 T
  LIKE RIVAL PARENTS OVER A PRECOCIOUS ...DIALOGUE OVER A OUIJA BOARD 284 283
  COCKS CROW UP A RIVAL ....MOONSONG AT MORNING 316 5
RIVALS (1)
  RIVALS HER WHETTED LOOK, DIVINING WHAT CONCEIT ....VANITY FAIR 32 13
RIVER (16)
  LURCHING HOME ALONG RIVER BANK. ....FAUN 35 7
  AND AS HIS NOTES TWINE GREEN, THE GREEN RIVER .........SNAKECHARMER 79 6
  TO REBUKE THE HORSE-SWALLOWING RIVER GYNDES: A LESSON IN VENGEANCE 80 18
  A FULL MOON, RIVER LAPSING ....LORELEI 94 2
  O RIVER, I SEE DRIFTING ....LORELEI 95 33
  YEARS, GO DOWN TO DRINK THE RIVER: ....CHILD'S PARK STONES 101 29
  GREEN GRASS STREAMING, HOUSES A RIVER ....WHITENESS I REMEMBER 102 19
  NOW THE AIR SNAGS AND EDDIES ROUND THEM THE WAY A RIVER ....TULIPS 161 53
  BUT TONIGHT THEY HAVE DISCOVERED THIS RIVER WITH NO TROUBLE, *STARS. 165 15
  COMING AT ME, LIKE A CASTLE, FROM THE TOP OF THE RIVER. *THREE WOMEN 178 51
  AND I AM A RIVER OF MILK. ....THREE WOMEN 183 237
  THE SWANS ARE GONE. STILL THE RIVER ....THREE WOMEN 186 344

RIVER (CONT.)
   SPUN INTO A RIVER, THE RIVER CROSSED. ....THE SWARM 216 30
   SPUN INTO A RIVER, THE RIVER CROSSED. ....THE SWARM 216 30
   RIVER FLOODS TRANSCEND THE LEVEL*INSOLENT STORM STRIKES AT THE SKULL 326 19
   IN THE RARE RIVER WINK AND LAUGH; WE LAVISH ....LOVE IS A PARALLAX 330 38
RIVER-BASIN (1)
   WAY UP THE RIVER-BASIN. ....MUSSEL HUNTER AT ROCK HARBOR   96 44
RIVER-BED (1)
   FROM GRAIN OF THE MARROW AND THE RIVER-BED GRAINS. ....LESSON.   80 25
RIVER-LEVEL (1)
   BACK OF THE CONNECTICUT, THE RIVER-LEVEL ....ABOVE THE OXBOW   88   7
RIVER'S (4)
   AND PAINTS THE RIVER'S PALE CIRCUMFLUENT STILLNESS ABOVE THE OXBOW   89 43
   ON THE BANK OF THE RIVER'S ....MUSSEL HUNTER AT ROCK HARBOR   95   7
   THEY CLEAVE THE RIVER'S GREENING PATINAS; ....IN MIDAS' COUNTRY 100 18
   GULLS HAVE THREADED THE RIVER'S MUD BED BACK *PARLIAMENT HILL FIELDS 152   6
RIVER-VERGE (1)
   RIVER-VERGE FARMS WHERE RYE-HEADS WHITEN. ....IN MIDAS' COUNTRY   99   4
RIVET (2)
   BUT THOUGH THEY'D RIVET SINEWS IN ROCK EPITAPH FOR FIRE AND FLOWER   46 22
   THAT RIVET IN PLACE ABYSS AFTER ABYSS. ....THREE WOMEN 182 203
RIVETING (1)
   TIP, RIVETING STONES, AIR, ...MAN IN BLACK 120 20
RIVULETS (1)
   WHILE THE HEATH GRASS GLITTERS AND THE SPINDLING RIVULETS ...
               ... PARLIAMENT HILL FIELDS 153 34
ROAD (9)
   NOW HE GOES FROM HIS RIGHTFUL ROAD ....BUCOLICS   24 21
   US TO THE OBLIQUE ROAD, IN SPITE OF A FITFUL ....ABOVE THE OXBOW   88 21
   OF PALE FRONTS, STRAW THATCHINGS, THE HARD ROAD*WHITENESS I REMEMBER 102 20
   THEY SET THEIR STOUT CHAIRS BACK TO THE ROAD AND FACE THE DARK*NET-. 121   5
   ON THE ROAD NAMED FOR TOMAS ORTUNIO, MICA ....THE NET MENDERS 121   8
   BETWEEN THE ROAD AND THE LAKE WATER, ...BLUE MOLES 126 12
   OBJECT BESIDE THE MAD, STRAIGHT ROAD ....SLEEP IN THE MOJAVE DESERT 143   6
   ENCOUNTER THEM ON THE ROAD --- ....WORDS 270 15
   ACROSS THE RUTTED ROAD. ....BITTER STRAWBERRIES 299 17
ROADS (2)
   COLORED BEADS ON THE STRUNG ROADS, AND THE PEOPLE STROLL ....OXBOW   89 51
   THE ROADS BUNCHED TO A KNOT, ...CHILDLESS WOMAN 259   5
ROAMER (1)
   THE WHOLE SCENE FLARED WELCOME TO THIS ROAMER. ....DREAM WITH C.   44 12
ROAR (5)
   TRAINS ROAR IN MY EARS, DEPARTURES, DEPARTURES! ....THREE WOMEN 177 31
   MY SINGING MAKES YOU ROAR. ....BY CANDLELIGHT 237 23
   IS IT A TIGER THIS YEAR, THIS ROAR AT THE DOOR? ....YEARS 255 18
   AND AT THE JET-PLANE ANGER OF GOD'S ROAR ....THE TRIAL OF MAN 312   7
   TO WHIPCRACK AND ROAR ....AERIALIST 331 11
ROARED (1)
   OF A BLIZZARD, THE GIANT ROARED UP WITH HIS CHITTERING TROPHIES. ...
              ... THE SNOWMAN ON THE MOOR   59 45
ROAST (1)
   THOUGH HE BEDDED IN ERMINE, GORGED ON ROAST, ...NATURAL HISTORY   71   3
ROBBED (1)
   ARGUED MY CONSCIENCE CLEAR WHICH ROBBED ..............RHODODENDRON. 103 11
ROBBER (1)
   NOTABLE ROBBER BARON, ...SPIDER   48   9
ROBE (1)
   BENEATH THE FRINGES OF FORBIDDEN ROBE, ...METAMORPHOSES OF THE MOON 308 32
ROBES (3)
   THE RED, ROYAL ROBES OF PHEDRE? THE TEAR-DAZZLED ....PERSEUS   83 41
   I AM LOST, I AM LOST, IN THE ROBES OF ALL THIS LIGHT. POEM.6.W. 136 24
   COUCHED IN CAULS OF CLAY AS IN HOLY ROBES, ...THE DEAD 320   2
ROBIN'S (1)
   TO STIR ROBIN'S EGG ....POLLY'S TREE 128 14
ROCK (31)
   FRACTURED PILLARS FRAME PROSPECTS OF ROCK; ..........CONVERSATION.   21   9
   CAN BE STRUCK FROM ROCK TO MAKE HEART'S WASTE ....WINTER LANDSCAPE,   22 14
   HE WITH ROCK SPLITS OPEN ....ODE FOR TED   29 10
   SILENT AND SHINING ON A GREEN ROCK BEDDED IN MUD, ...DREAM WITH C.   44 15
   WITH GREEN ROCK GLIDING, A DELICATE SCHOONER*DREAM WITH CLAM-DIGGERS   44 17
   BUT THOUGH THEY'D RIVET SINEWS IN ROCK EPITAPH FOR FIRE AND FLOWER   46 22
   ICE AND ROCK, EACH SENTIMENT WITHIN BORDER, ...SPINSTER   49 16
   THE SCRAGGY ROCK SPIT SHIELDING THE TOWN'S BLUE BAY ......DEPARTURE   51 13
   ACROSS THE JUT OF OCHREOUS ROCK ....DEPARTURE   51 18
   DEADLOCKED WITH THEM, TAKING ROOT AS CRADLES ROCK. ...
              ... ALL THE DEAD DEARS   71 36
   MUSSEL HUNTER AT ROCK HARBOR ....MUSSEL HUNTER AT ROCK HARBOR   95   T
   BUILD UP FROM A ROCK ROOT, AS FOUNTAINS BUILD ....MOONRISE   98 23
   GREEN ROCK, WINTHROP BAY ....GREEN ROCK, WINTHROP BAY 104   T
   INIMICAL NOW. THE GREAT GREEN ROCK ....GREEN ROCK, WINTHROP BAY 105 10
   SUICIDE OFF EGG ROCK ....SUICIDE OFF EGG ROCK 115   T
   RAY BUT EGG ROCK ON THE BLUE WASTAGE. ....SUICIDE OFF EGG ROCK 115 22
   GLAZES THE ROCK POOLS YET, ...MAN IN BLACK 119 11
   WHEN I SPLIT A ROCK ONE TIME ....MEDALLION 124 12
   AFTER THE FAT CHILDREN OF ROOT AND ROCK. ....BLUE MOLES 126 25

TITLE   PAGE   LINE

ROCK (CONT.)
    (ROCK LAKE, CANADA) ....TWO CAMPERS IN CLOUD COUNTRY 144 ST
    MASKED AMONG BLACK ROCKS AS A BLACK ROCK ....LOVE LETTER 147 10
    TO ROCK ON ALL FOURS LIKE A PADDED HAMMOCK. ....MAGI 148 11
    TO THE HILLS' NORTHERN FACE, AND THE FACE IS ORANGE ROCK BLACKBER. 169 24
    THE HOLLOWS IN WHICH ROCK THE THOUGHTS OF THE WIFE --- BERCK-PLAGE 199 75
    I SHOULD SIT ON A ROCK OFF CORNWALL AND COMB MY HAIR. ....LESBOS 228 29
    I ROCK YOU LIKE A BOAT ....BY CANDLELIGHT 237 24
    THE CARRIAGES ROCK, THEY ARE CRADLES. ....GETTING THERE 249 64
    MY MIND A ROCK, ...PARALYTIC 266   2
    OVER THE ROCK ....WORDS 270 10
    IN A PIT OF ROCK ....CONTUSION 271   4
    SAFE-SOCKETED IN ROCK. ....TOUCH-AND-GO 336 24
ROCK-BUMPING (1)
    WINDED BY MUCH ROCK-BUMPING ....THE HERMIT AT OUTERMOST HOUSE 118   5
ROCKED (2)
    BELOW, ROCKED HAVOC-SICK, VOYAGERS LIE ....CHANNEL CROSSING   26   9
    I ROCKED SHUT ....LADY LAZARUS 245 39
ROCKETING (1)
    IN A ROCKETING VERTICAL CLOCKCASE, ...DIALOGUE EN ROUTE 308   5
ROCKETS (1)
    THE SWIFTS ARE BACK. THEY ARE SHRIEKING LIKE PAPER ROCKETS.   THREE. 185 310
ROCK-FACE (1)
    ROCK-FACE, CRAB-CLAW VERGED ON GREEN. *THE HERMIT AT OUTERMOST HOUSE 119 18
ROCK-FAULT (1)
    IT OGLED THROUGH ROCK-FAULT, WIND-FLAW AND FISTED WAVE--*LADY AND T.   70 32
ROCKING (2)
    NODDING AND ROCKING AND FINGERING HER THIN HAIR. ....FACE LIFT 156 30
    ROCKING ACROSS THE LAPIS LAZULI SEA ....EPITAPH IN THREE PARTS 337   1
ROCKS (20)
    FLAYED BY THORNS I TREK THE ROCKS, ...PURSUIT   22   9
    WITH RADIANCE, PEACOCK-COLORED; INSTEAD, BLEAK ROCKS ....CHANNEL C.   27 22
    HE PIPES A PLACE TO STAND ON, BUT NO ROCKS, ...SNAKECHARMER   79   8
    EXPRESSIVE OF GRIEF TURNS GODS, LIKE KINGS, TO ROCKS. ....PERSEUS   83 29
    THOSE ROCKS, CLEFT AND WORN, THEMSELVES THEN GROW ....PERSEUS   83 30
    TO SUN ON THE ROCKS OR PROP ....OLD LADIES' HOME 120   5
    THE HOUSES ARE WHITE AS SEA-SALT GOATS LICK FROM THE ROCKS. ..NET-. 121 10
    THE BEACH AND THE ROCKS ARE BARE. ....MAGNOLIA SHOALS 122 22
    TO REDRESS THE DOMINANCE OF ROCKS AND WOODS, ...TWO CAMP. 144   2
    THESE ROCKS OFFER NO PURCHASE TO HERBAGE OR PEOPLE: ......TWO CAMP. 145 18
    MASKED AMONG BLACK ROCKS AS A BLACK ROCK ....LOVE LETTER 147 10
    STUCCO ARCHES, THE BANKED ROCKS SUNNING IN ROWS, ...WHITSUN 153   2
    HIS FOREHEAD IS BUMPY AS A SACK OF ROCKS. ....INSOMNIAC 163 13
    NOW IT IS ONLY GLOOMY, A DUMP OF ROCKS -- ....FINISTERRE 169   6
    OTHER ROCKS HIDE THEIR GRUDGES UNDER THE WATER. ....FINISTERRE 169   9
    THEY BRUISE THE ROCKS OUT OF EXISTENCE, THEN RESURRECT THEM. ...
                                                        ... FINISTERRE 169 15
    DOWN AMONG STRICT ROOTS AND ROCKS, ...DANSE MACABRE 320   1
    GREEN-SINGING BIRDS EXPLODE FROM ALL THE ROCKS. PROLOGUE TO SPRING 322 15
    AND A HURRICANE HEADACHE ROCKS   INSOLENT STORM STRIKES AT THE SKULL 326 11
    AMONG THE JAGGED MAZES OF THE ROCKS. ..THE PRINCESS AND THE GOBLINS 334 34
ROCK'S (1)
    FOR THE ROCK'S DWARFED LUMP, FOR THE DRABBLED SCUM, ...GREEN ROCK. 105 23
ROCKY (2)
    THEMSELVES MERE ROCKY HILLOCKS TO AN EVEREST. ....ABOVE THE OXBOW   87   4
    INTO THE ROCKY GIZZARD OF THE EARTH, ...THE GHOST'S LEAVETAKING   90 24
ROCOCO (1)
    FROM RHETORIC OF THESE ROCOCO QUEENS. ....A SORCERER B. 324   4
ROD (2)
    AS SPRANG FROM JOSEPH'S ROD, AND TESTIFIES ....MAYFLOWER   60   7
    TO MY WATER ROD, DAZZLING AND GRATEFUL, ...MEDUSA 225 19
RODE (2)
    RODE OUT AGAINST THE FIFTH BULL TO BRACE HIS PIKE AND SLOWLY BEAR ...
                                                        ... THE GORING   47   6
    HE RODE THE FLOOD IN A PRIDE OF PRONGS ....LAMENT 315   8
RODENT (1)
    HER SALLOW RODENT TEETH LIKE CASTANETS ...............INCOMMUNICADO 100   4
RODENTS (1)
    OF CHRIST IN THE FACES OF RODENTS, ...MYSTIC 269 19
ROE (1)
    FOR SUSAN O'NEILL ROE ....CUT 235   D
ROGUE'S (1)
    BY SUCH A ROGUE'S ....RHYME   50 15
ROLL (8)
    WHERE SMALL ANTS ROLL THEIR EGGS, WHERE GRUBS FATTEN. .....MOONRISE   98 17
    I ROLL TO AN ANTEROOM WHERE A KIND MAN ....FACE LIFT 156 12
    THEY WILL ROLL ME UP IN BANDAGES, THEY WILL STORE MY HEART LAST W. 172 23
    ADDRESSING IT, WHILE THE HILLS ROLL THE NOTES OF THE DEAD BELL; ...
                                                        ... BERCK-PLAGE 200 95
    TO BRING TEACUPS AND ROLL AWAY HEADACHES ....THE APPLICANT 221 12
    LOVE, LOVE, THE LOW SMOKES ROLL ....FEVER. 231 11
    READY TO ROLL, LIKE A DEVIL'S. ....GETTING THERE 248 40
    TALL TRUCKS ROLL IN ....AERIALIST 331 31
ROLLED (4)
    SOULS, ROLLED IN THE DOOM-NOISE OF THE SEA. ....FINISTERRE 169 14

412

ROLLED (CONT.)
    THE BED IS ROLLED FROM THE WALL. ....BERCK-PLAGE 198   60
    EYES ROLLED BY WHITE STICKS, ...MEDUSA   224   2
    ROLLED ROUND WITH GOODLY LOAM AND CRADLED DEEP, ...THE DEAD 320   9
ROLLER (1)
    SCRAPED FLAT BY THE ROLLER ....DADDY 222   17
ROLLING (1)
    ONE GRUFF-TIMBRED PURR ROLLING FROM FURRED THROATS: ..ELLA MASON A. 54   23
ROLLS (3)
    SMOKE ROLLS AND SCARVES IN THE GROVE. ....THE BEE MEETING 212   36
    CARPET ROLLS ....CUT   235   12
    ROLLS OUT A CARPET, A HUSH. ....GIGOLO   268   24
ROMAN (3)
    YOU ARE PITHY AND HISTORICAL AS THE ROMAN FORUM. ....THE COLOSSUS 129   18
    THE BODY IS A ROMAN THING. ....THE SURGEON AT 2 A.M. 171   29
    IT IS LIKE A ROMAN MOB, ...THE ARRIVAL OF THE BEE BOX 213   19
ROMANS (1)
    HOW I ADMIRE THE ROMANS -- ....THE SURGEON AT 2 A.M. 171   27
ROMANTICS (1)
    THEY ARE THE LAST ROMANTICS, THESE CANDLES: ....CANDLES 148   1
ROME (1)
    IN MUNICH, MORGUE BETWEEN PARIS AND ROME, ...THE MUNICH MANNEQUINS 263   12
ROMPS (1)
    AS A BAD JOB. WAIT. HE STIRS. HE ROMPS DIALOGUE OVER A OUIJA BOARD 284 293
RONDO (1)
    OF SILVER AS THE RONDO SLOWS: NOW REELS ....CINDERELLA 303   3
ROOF (4)
    SWADDLES ROOF AND TREE. ....PARLIAMENT HILL FIELDS 152   22
    I SHALL BE A WALL AND A ROOF, PROTECTING. ....THREE WOMEN 180 139
    AGAINST FIRE AND BOMBS THROUGH THE ROOF. ....THE APPLICANT 221   24
    REAP THE ROUND BLUE PIGEON FROM ROOF RIDGE, *GO GET THE GOODLY SQUAB 313   3
ROOFGARDENS (1)
    IN THE ROOFGARDENS ....ALICANTE LULLABY   43   6
ROOFS (2)
    FIRST HORSE UNDER ME, HIGH AS THE ROOFS, ...WHITENESS I REMEMBER 102   13
    WHILE CHAPEL PINNACLES OVER THE ROOFS, ...THE EYE-MOTE 109   5
ROOF-TILES (1)
    ORANGE ROOF-TILES, ORANGE CHIMNEY POTS, ...LANDOWNERS   53   5
ROOFTOPS (2)
    AMONG ORANGE-TILE ROOFTOPS ....PROSPECT   28   1
    LIVED UNDER THE SHADOW OF HOT ROOFTOPS ....ABOVE THE OXBOW   89   54
ROOK (4)
    FEATHERED DARK IN THOUGHT, I STALK LIKE A ROOK, ..WINTER LANDSCAPE,   21   9
    BLACK ROOK IN RAINY WEATHER ....BLACK ROOK IN RAINY WEATHER   56   T
    HUNCHES A WET BLACK ROOK ....BLACK ROOK IN RAINY WEATHER   56   2
    SUDDENLY AT MY ELBOW. I ONLY KNOW THAT A ROOK ....BLACK ROOK I.   57   27
ROOK-CLAW (1)
    POCKED BY ROOK-CLAW AND RABBIT-TRACK: SHE MUST YET WIN ..SNOWMAN O.   58   17
ROOKS (5)
    NOW, RICH ORDER OF WALLS IS FALLEN; ROOKS CROAK .....CONVERSATION.   21   5
    WINTER LANDSCAPE, WITH ROOKS ....WINTER LANDSCAPE, WITH ROOKS   21   T
    FROM GAUNT HEMLOCK, ROOKS CROAK HAVOC: *WINTER LANDSCAPE, WITH ROOKS   22   7
    TWO BLACK ROOKS HUNCH ....PROSPECT   28   7
    LOOKS FIERCE AND BLACK AS ROOKS; ....THE QUEEN'S COMPLAINT   28   4
ROOK-TONGUED (1)
    ARROGANT AMONG ROOK-TONGUED SPACES, ...CONJURING.   66   10
ROOM (29)
    NAKED IN THE MERELY ACTUAL ROOM, ...TALE OF A TUB   24   5
    IN HER DARK WAINSCOTED ROOM ....TWO SISTERS OF PERSEPHONE   31   5
    OF THE PATIENTS' DINING ROOM. ....MISS DRAKE PROCEEDS TO SUPPER   41   26
    WHICH PEOPLES THE BARE ROOM, THE BLANK, UNTENANTED AIR. *NOVEMBER G.   56   18
    SHE FLUNG FROM A ROOM ....THE SNOWMAN ON THE MOOR   58   2
    UNTIL HIS OWN LIT ROOM OUTSHONE ....THE EVERLASTING MONDAY   62   9
    THEY PERSIST IN THE SUNLIT ROOM: THE WALLPAPER .....THE THIN PEOPLE   65   36
    TWO VIEWS OF A CADAVER ROOM ....TWO VIEWS OF A CADAVER ROOM 114   T
    THE DAY SHE VISITED THE DISSECTING ROOM *TWO VIEWS OF A CADAVER ROOM 114   1
    THE SMALL GRAINS MAKE ROOM. ....MUSHROOMS 139   9
    LADY, YOUR ROOM IS LOUSY WITH FLOWERS. ....LEAVING EARLY 145   1
    LIKE A CUP OR A ROOM. THE MOON'S CROOK WHITENS, ...PARLIAMENT H. 153   38
    HE LIVES WITHOUT PRIVACY IN A LIDLESS ROOM, ...INSOMNIAC 163   26
    BLINDED TO ALL BUT THE GRAY, SPIRITLESS ROOM ....WIDOW 165   39
    I HAD TO SLEEP IN THE SAME ROOM WITH THE BABY ON A TOO-SHORT
        COT. ....THE BABYSITTERS 174   7
    HE FLEW INTO THE ROOM, A SHRIEK AT HIS HEEL. ....THREE WOMEN 181 165
    THE FLOWERS IN THIS ROOM ARE RED AND TROPICAL. ....THREE WOMEN 184 263
    I HAVE PAPERED HIS ROOM WITH BIG ROSES, ...THREE WOMEN 186 328
    ON A STRIPED MATTRESS IN ONE ROOM ....BERCK-PLAGE 198   50
    NOW THE ROOM IS AHISS. THE INSTRUMENT ....WORDS HEARD. 203   11
    BORED HOODLUM IN A RED ROOM ....THE DETECTIVE 209   19
    THIS IS THE ROOM I HAVE NEVER BEEN IN. ....WINTERING 218   11
    THIS IS THE ROOM I COULD NEVER BREATHE IN. ....WINTERING 218   12
    FEATHERS WINNOWING THE ROOM. A THIN ....DIALOGUE OVER A OUIJA BOARD 279   87
    SETTLES IN THE ROOM NOW. ITS WINGS BLACKEN THE TABLE. ..DIALOGUE O. 285 313
    OUT OF IT. THERE. THE ROOM RETURNS .....DIALOGUE OVER A OUIJA BOARD 285 334
    MAY TWO REAL PEOPLE BREATHE IN A REAL ROOM. ....DIALOGUE O. 286 364

	TITLE	PAGE	LINE

ROOM (CONT.)
THAT STING NO MORE THAN LOVE: A ROOM WHERE TIME *MORNING IN THE HOS. 332 15
MY ROOM IS A TWITTERING GRAY BOX WITH A WALL *EPITAPH IN THREE PARTS 337 26
ROOMS (7)
THEY MOVE THROUGH THEIR MUTE ROOMS WHILE I SLEEP, ...BLUE MOLES 126 23
WITH THE ROOMS, OR THE SMILES, OR THE BEAUTIFUL RUBBER PLANTS, ...
... WAKING IN WINTER 151 15
WE WERE ALWAYS CRYING, IN OUR SPARE ROOMS, LITTLE PUT-UPON
SISTERS, ...THE BABYSITTERS 174 4
O IT WAS RICHNESS! -- ELEVEN ROOMS AND A YACHT .....THE BABYSITTERS 174 10
MIRRORS CAN KILL AND TALK, THEY ARE TERRIBLE ROOMS ....COURAGE. 210 27
CHOCOLATE FANCIES IN ROSE-PAPERED ROOMS ....FEMALE AUTHOR 301 6
WITH WET PLUMAGE THROUGH MY ROOMS. ....THE DREAM 310 6
ROOST (3)
RINGDOVES ROOST WELL WITHIN HIS WOOD, ...ODE FOR TED 29 19
COMES TO ROOST THERE, FRAIL ....POLLY'S TREE 128 17
LET ME ROOST IN YOU! .................................EAVESDROPPER 260 19
ROOSTING (1)
ROOSTING AND COOING "YOU, YOU" ....A SECRET 219 19
ROOT (18)
DEATH AS STRIKING ROOT ON ONE LAND-TRACT; ....LANDOWNERS 53 14
MOVES ON ITS ROOT. THOUGH A MIST-WRAITH WOUND .....HARDCASTLE CRAGS 62 13
DEADLOCKED WITH THEM, TAKING ROOT AS CRADLES ROCK. ...
... ALL THE DEAD DEARS 71 36
IT TOOK ROOT AT MY COMING ....NIGHT SHIFT 76 12
WHITE BODIES IN A WOODEN GIRDLE, ROOT TO TOP ......VIRGIN IN A TREE 81 22
TO ROOT DEEP AMONG KNUCKLES, SHINBONES, ...FULL FATHOM FIVE 93 35
BUILD UP FROM A ROCK ROOT, AS FOUNTAINS BUILD ....MOONRISE 98 23
FROM HIS ORBIT UNDER THE ELM ROOT. ....BLUE MOLES 126 7
AFTER THE FAT CHILDREN OF ROOT AND ROCK. ....BLUE MOLES 126 25
I AM A ROOT, A STONE, AN OWL PELLET, ...POEM.1.WHO. 132 23
IN THE BOWEL OF THE ROOT. POEM.2.DARK. 133 27
TO OUR BOWER AT THE LILY ROOT. POEM.5.F. 134 2
I AM NOT A TREE WITH MY ROOT IN THE SOIL ....I AM VERTICAL 162 2
I KNOW THE BOTTOM, SHE SAYS. I KNOW IT WITH MY GREAT TAP ROOT: ELM 192 1
SCORCHED TO THE ROOT ....ELM 192 17
PUT YOUR FOOT, YOUR ROOT, ...DADDY 223 23
THE BLACK TELEPHONE'S OFF AT THE ROOT, ...DADDY 224 69
FEEDING AT THE ROOT OF THINGS. HE STOLE THAT, TOO, ...DIALOGUE O. 279 102
ROOTED (4)
ROOTED TO YOUR BLACK LOOK, THE PLAY TURNED TRAGIC: ...CONVERSATION. 21 12
STEADILY ROOTED THOUGH THEY WERE ALL FLOWING ....THE EYE-MOTE 109 7
BROOD, ROOTED IN THEIR HEAPED LOSSES. ....PARLIAMENT HILL FIELDS 153 31
I CANNOT RUN, I AM ROOTED, AND THE GORSE HURTS ME ..THE BEE MEETING 211 31
ROOT-HAIRS (1)
IN A NEST OF ROOT-HAIRS AND BOREDOM -- ....BURNING THE LETTERS 205 45
ROOT-PALE (1)
ROOT-PALE HER MEAGER FRAME. ....TWO SISTERS OF PERSEPHONE 31 12
ROOTS (9)
OWN THEIR CABBAGE ROOTS, A SPACE OF STARS, ...LANDOWNERS 53 10
OLD PEWTER ROOTS TWIST ....DARK WOOD, DARK WATER 127 15
BY THE ROOTS OF MY HAIR SOME GOD GOT HOLD OF ME. ...THE HANGING MAN 141 1
SKIN DOESN'T HAVE ROOTS, IT PEELS AWAY EASY AS PAPER. ...FACE LIFT 156 20
IF I PAY THE ROOTS OF THE HEATHER ....WUTHERING HEIGHTS 167 16
A MAT OF ROOTS. MY ASSISTANTS HOOK THEM BACK. *THE SURGEON AT 2 A.M. 170 13
PICKING AMONG THE DUMB MINERALS, THE ROOTS. ....LAST WORDS 172 5
THE IMAGE OF YOU, TRANSFIXED BY ROOTS, WAX-PALE, ...DIALOGUE O. 285 325
DOWN AMONG STRICT ROOTS AND ROCKS, ...DANSE MACABRE 320 1
ROOT'S (1)
IF ROOT'S FIRM-FIXED AND RESOLUTION GOOD. ....MAYFLOWER 60 4
ROPE (2)
HE TRIPPED AN ANT WITH A ROPE ....SPIDER 48 13
HANGS ITSELF ON ITS OWN ROPE. ............METAMORPHOSES OF THE MOON 308 42
ROPED (1)
ROPED IN AT THE END BY THE ONE ....TOTEM 265 33
RORSCHACH-BLOT (1)
THE PINE TREE LIKE A RORSCHACH-BLOT ....BLACK PINE TREE. 328 2
ROSE (22)
GOAT-HORNS. MARKED HOW GOD ROSE ....FAUN 35 14
CLAM-DIGGERS ROSE UP OUT OF DARK SLIME AT HER OFFENSE.*DREAM WITH C. 44 24
STEM OF MY NEIGHBOR'S ROSE BUSH ....RESOLVE 52 15
ROSE UP AND PUT ROYAL NERVES TO THE RACK: ....NATURAL HISTORY 71 9
MAKES OFF WITH THIS ROSE, ...WORDS FOR A NURSERY 74 48
ROSE AND AMETHYST. ....BATTLE-SCENE 84 26
ALTERS SHADOWS OF ROSE AND IRIS -- ....CHILD'S PARK STONES 101 13
OF A SINGLE ROSE PRESENT TO IMAGINE ...................RHODODENDRON. 103 3
BUT GAVE ME PAUSE, MY ROSE A CHARGE, ...RHODODENDRON. 104 26
AND THE ROYAL ROSE IN THE BULL'S BELLY, ...THE BULL OF BENDYLAW 108 20
FEATHER AND ROSE. ....POLLY'S TREE 129 33
THE ELUSIVE ROSE. POEM.7.S. 137 42
I GAVE HER A SOUL, I BLOOMED OUT OF HER AS A ROSE ....IN PLASTER 159 16
YOU HAD A ROSE GARDEN AND A GUEST COTTAGE AND A MODEL APOTHECARY
SHOP ....THE BABYSITTERS 174 20
MYSELF THE ROSE YOU ACHIEVE -- ....CHILDLESS WOMAN 259 7
OF A ROSE CLOSE WHEN THE GARDEN ....EDGE 273 14

	TITLE	PAGE	LINE

ROSE (CONT.)
QUEEN MARY'S ROSE GARDEN ....QUEEN MARY'S ROSE GARDEN 290 T
RED THE UNRAVELED ROSE SINGS IN YOUR HAIR: ......TO EVA DESCENDING. 303 7
ROSE CANDLES FLICKER ON THE LILAC WALL ....CINDERELLA 304 7
WHEN I ROSE AND OPENED ALL ....THE DREAM 310 4
A ROSE OF JEOPARDY FLAMES IN MY HAIR ....CIRCUS IN THREE RINGS 321 9
TURQUOISE, ROSE, SIERRA MAUVE; NEEDLES ....MORNING IN THE HOS. 332 14
ROSE-AND-LARKSPURRED (1)
THIS WAS NO ROSE-AND-LARKSPURRED CHINA SUCKLING ....SOW 60 11
ROSE-BEDS (1)
I WALKED THE UNWALKED GARDEN OF ROSE-BEDS ...........RHODODENDRON. 103 1
ROSEBUD (1)
ROSEBUD, KNOT OF WORMS, ...WORDS FOR A NURSERY 73 1
ROSE-COLORED (1)
TONGUE A ROSE-COLORED ARROW. ....MEDALLION 124 7
ROSE-FRUIT (1)
FIRST FROST, AND I WALK AMONG THE ROSE-FRUIT, THE MARBLE TOES ...
... PRIVATE GROUND 130 1
ROSE-PAPERED (1)
CHOCOLATE FANCIES IN ROSE-PAPERED ROOMS ....FEMALE AUTHOR 301 6
ROSES (19)
AS ROSES BROACH THEIR CARMINE IN A MIRROR. FLUX ....ABOVE THE OXBOW 89 44
OF PRIZE ROSES, CULLING THE FULLEST FLORETS; ....SPINACH-PICKER. 90 19
DIAMOND RINGS, POTTED ROSES, FOX-SKINS ....OWL 101 5
UNDER THE CORONAL OF SUGAR ROSES ....THE BEEKEEPER'S DAUGHTER 118 20
THE FOUNTAINS ARE DRY AND THE ROSES OVER. ....THE MANOR GARDEN 125 1
THE ROSES IN THE TOBY JUG ....LEAVING EARLY 146 23
AS A SCHOOLGIRL SHE GAVE ROSES TO FRANZ JOSEF. ....CANDLES 149 18
FLICKERS AMONG THE FLAT PINK ROSES. I WAKE TO LISTEN: MORNING SONG 157 11
A GARDEN OF BUGGY ROSES THAT MADE HIM CRY. ....INSOMNIAC 163 12
I HAVE PAPERED HIS ROOM WITH BIG ROSES, ...THREE WOMEN 186 328
IT CAN MAKE BLACK ROSES. ....THE SWARM 216 4
WHAT WILL THEY TASTE OF, THE CHRISTMAS ROSES? ....WINTERING 219 49
ATTENDED BY ROSES, ...FEVER. 232 48
I HAVE HUNG OUR CAVE WITH ROSES, ...NICK AND THE CANDLESTICK 241 32
YOU HAND ME TWO CHILDREN, TWO ROSES. ....KINDNESS 270 20
THE GREAT ROSES, MANY OF THEM SCENTLESS, ..QUEEN MARY'S ROSE GARDEN 290 4
THE ROSES ARE NAMED AFTER QUEENS AND PEOPLE OF NOTE ..QUEEN MARY'S. 290 17
OF COOL MOUTHS AND HANDS OPEN AND NATURAL AS ROSES. ......FEVER./DR 294 10
AND HOTHOUSE ROSES SHED IMMORAL BLOOMS. ....FEMALE AUTHOR 301 8
ROSE-SPRIGGED (1)
OF BLUNT PENCILS, ROSE-SPRIGGED COFFEE CUP, ...CONJURING. 65 2
ROSE-STEM (1)
THORNS ON THE BLOODY ROSE-STEM. ....I WANT, I WANT 106 12
ROT (5)
PAVING THIS GRAVE GROUND. HERE'S HONEST ROT .....NOVEMBER GRAVEYARD 56 8
ROTS, AND SMELLS OF ROT UNDER ITS HEADSTONE ....MOONRISE 98 14
AT THE HEADSTONE NEXT TO YOURS, NOR DOES IT ROT, ...ELECTRA ON. 117 26
TEDIOUS. THAT'S WHAT WE'D SAY. ABOUT ROT*DIALOGUE OVER A OUIJA BOARD 279 101
FOR ROT. DON'T THINK YOU HAD ME FOOLED. I KNEW ....DIALOGUE O. 283 263
ROTISSERIE (1)
AND THE MAYOR'S ROTISSERIE TURNS ....THE TIMES ARE TIDY 107 4
ROTS (2)
ROTS, AND SMELLS OF ROT UNDER ITS HEADSTONE ....MOONRISE 98 14
ROTS IN THE HOLLOW OF MY SKULL ....APRIL 18 301 2
ROTTEN (6)
HE HYMNS THE ROTTEN QUEEN WITH SAFFRON HAIR ....OUIJA 77 22
EATEN OR ROTTEN. I AM ALL MOUTH. POEM.1.WHO. 131 2
OH NEVER TRY TO KNOCK ON ROTTEN WOOD. ....ADMONITIONS 319 1
OH NEVER TRY TO KNOCK ON ROTTEN WOOD. ....ADMONITIONS 319 6
OH NEVER TRY TO KNOCK ON ROTTEN WOOD. ....ADMONITIONS 319 12
NEVER TRY TO KNOCK ON ROTTEN WOOD, ...ADMONITIONS 319 18
ROTUNDAS (1)
MUSEUM WITHOUT STATUES, GRAND WITH PILLARS, PORTICOES,
ROTUNDAS. ....BARREN WOMAN 157 2
ROUGE (1)
LET ME HAVE MY COPPER COOKING POTS, LET MY ROUGE POTS ...LAST WORDS 172 21
ROUGH (4)
GERD WHIRLS THE BALL ABLAZE: "ROUGH STORM," SHE GRANTS, "MAY WREAK ...
... CRYSTAL GAZER 55 22
FREE FROM ALL MOLESTING. ROUGH BOYS, ...LADY AND T. 69 9
A ROUGH, DUMB COUNTRY STUFF ....BY CANDLELIGHT 236 3
WHILE ROUGH AS SPLINTERED WOOD ....FAMILY REUNION 300 20
ROUND (39)
RISES THE ROUND RED WATERMELON SUN. ....SOUTHERN SUNRISE 26 18
TIME COMES ROUND FOR THAT FOUL SLUT: ....STRUMPET SONG 33 4
THEY SAILED TILL TIDE FOAMED ROUND THEIR ANKLES ......DREAM WITH C. 44 19
EACH TIME ROUND WINDING THAT ANT ....SPIDER 48 16
WITH BLACK ALACRITY BOUND ROUND HIS PRISONER. ....SPIDER 49 28
AND ROUND HER HOUSE SHE SET ....SPINSTER 50 25
OF GUARDIAN CATS CROUCHED ROUND THEIR IDOL, ...ELLA MASON A. 54 28
GREW SO LEAN AND WOULD NOT ROUND ....THE THIN PEOPLE 64 8
AND BIRDS OF PARADISE, AND THE ROUND MOON, ...YADWIGHA. 86 24
ITS ROUND PERIOD, DISPLACED AND GREEN, ...THE GHOST'S LEAVETAKING 91 29
CAST A ROUND WHITE SHADOW IN THEIR DYING. ....MOONRISE 98 6

ROUND (CONT.)
    ROUND OF ITS OWN ACCORD. ....THE TIMES ARE TIDY 107   5
    THE ROUND OF HIS YELLOW EYE-BUTTON. ....A WINTER SHIP 113   10
    ROUND, GREEN, DISCONSOLATE AS A TEAR. .....THE BEEKEEPER'S DAUGHTER 118   18
    RAYED ROUND A CANDLE FLAME, ...POLLY'S TREE 128   19
    I AM ROUND AS AN OWL, ...POEM.2.DARK. 132   10
    DENSE AND EXPRESSIONLESS ROUND ABOUT. ....LOVE LETTER 147   23
    THE ROUND SKY GOES ON MINDING ITS BUSINESS. PARLIAMENT HILL FIELDS 152   3
    CLAMBERING ROUND ITS GLASS BOX LIKE AN EIGHT-FINGERED HAND.   ZOO K. 155   31
    SHADOWS OUR SAFETY. WE STAND ROUND BLANKLY AS WALLS. ..MORNING SONG 157   6
    GRINDS ROUND, BEARING DOWN WITH THE STRAW, ...HEAVY WOMEN 158   20
    A DOZEN RED LEAD SINKERS ROUND MY NECK. ....TULIPS 161   42
    NOW THE AIR SNAGS AND EDDIES ROUND THEM THE WAY A RIVER .....TULIPS 161   53
    SNAGS AND EDDIES ROUND A SUNKEN RUST-RED ENGINE. ....TULIPS 161   54
    ROUND AS THE MOON, TO STARE UP. ....LAST WORDS 172   3
    THE SHADOWS OF THE GRASSES INCHED ROUND LIKE HANDS OF A CLOCK,*BABY. 175   43
    SETTING: A MATERNITY WARD AND ROUND ABOUT ....THREE WOMEN 176   SD
    THEY ARE ROUND AND FLAT AND FULL OF DARK ADVICE. *CROSSING THE WATER 190   6
    I FELT HANDS ROUND A TEA MUG, DULL, BLUNT, ...THE RABBIT CATCHER 194   22
    SIX ROUND BLACK HATS IN THE GRASS AND A LOZENGE OF WOOD,*BERCK-PLAGE 201 123
    BUT TRUNDLE ROUND THE GLOBE ....FEVER. 231   16
    AND A ROUND BUBBLE ....LYONNESSE 234   8
    THEIR ROUND EYES, THEIR TEETH, THEIR GRIMACES ....TOTEM 264   17
    ON THE ROUND BASE OF THE INVERTED WINE-GLASS HERE, ...DIALOGUE O. 276   5
    ROUND TO EARN HIS PAY: HE'LL HAVE US KEEP ....DIALOGUE O. 284 294
    AS THE WORLD SWIVELED ROUND IN ITS ORBIT ....DIALOGUE EN ROUTE 309   38
    REAP THE ROUND BLUE PIGEON FROM ROOF RIDGE, *GO GET THE GOODLY SQUAB 313   3
    ROLLED ROUND WITH GOODLY LOAM AND CRADLED DEEP, ...THE DEAD 320   9
    HAULS THEM ROUND WITH IT. ....TOUCH-AND-GO 335   16
ROUNDS (2)
    DOING NOTHING. JULY'S JUICE ROUNDS THEIR NUBS. ....MOONRISE   98   3
    THE SEA IN ITS COLD GIZZARD GROUND THOSE ROUNDS. .....POINT SHIRLEY 110   24
ROUSE (1)
    OF BELLRINGERS AND SINGERS ROUSE ....A WINTER'S TALE   87   33
ROUSED (1)
    ROUSED BY THORNED HANDS, FEET, HEAD, ...STREET SONG   36   17
ROUSSEAU (3)
    SO ROUSSEAU, TO EXPLAIN WHY THE RED COUCH ....YADWIGHA.   86   21
    AND THAT, ROUSSEAU TOLD THE CRITICS, WAS WHY THE COUCH ...YADWIGHA.   86   31
    BUT TO A FRIEND, IN PRIVATE, ROUSSEAU CONFESSED HIS EYE ..YADWIGHA.   86   35
ROUT (2)
    HE NAMES A LAPWING, STARTS RABBITS IN A ROUT ....ODE FOR TED   29   3
    AMONG THE COMMON ROUT ....STREET SONG   35   2
ROUTE (2)
    NEAR HIS SMALL STONEHENGE ABOVE THE ANTS' ROUTE, ...SPIDER   48   11
    DIALOGUE EN ROUTE ....DIALOGUE EN ROUTE 308   T
ROUTINE (2)
    DOWN DEEP INTO THE BENT BULL-NECK. CUMBROUS ROUTINE, NOT ARTWORK. ...
                                                        ... THE GORING   47   7
    OF INTRICATE SPUNGLASS ROUTINE, ...MORNING IN THE HOSPITAL SOLARIUM 332   20
ROVE (1)
    ROVE OVER HIS FIELD OF STONE; ....MAGNOLIA SHOALS 122   16
ROVING (1)
    THE SECOND SINGS: "RECEIVE NO ROVING GALLANT *EPITAPH IN THREE PARTS 337   7
ROW (3)
    SEPARATED FROM MY HOUSE BY A ROW OF HEADSTONES. ....MOON. 173   6
    HILL AND VALLEY STIFFEN ROW ON ROW. ....PROLOGUE TO SPRING 322   6
    HILL AND VALLEY STIFFEN ROW ON ROW. ....PROLOGUE TO SPRING 322   6
ROWDY (1)
    TOWARD THE ROWDY BELLOW AND BACK AGAIN ....THE BULL OF BENDYLAW 108   11
ROWED (2)
    IT IS TEN YEARS, NOW, SINCE WE ROWED TO CHILDREN'S ISLAND. ...BABY. 174   1
    AND RENTED AN OLD GREEN BOAT. I ROWED. YOU READ ....THE BABYSITTERS 175   31
ROWS (5)
    WELL-WATER KEPT COOL AT THE START OF THE ROWS. .....SPINACH-PICKER.   89   14
    STUCCO ARCHES, THE BANKED ROCKS SUNNING IN ROWS, ...WHITSUN 153   2
    ARE RIDING TO WORK IN ROWS, AS IF RECENTLY BRAINWASHED. ..INSOMNIAC 163   35
    SQUATTED DOWN BETWEEN THE ROWS ....BITTER STRAWBERRIES 299   3
    KNEELING OVER THE ROWS, ...BITTER STRAWBERRIES 300   34
ROYAL (7)
    SUCH ROYAL DREAMS BECKON THIS MAN ....THE SHRIKE   42   2
    ROSE UP AND PUT ROYAL NERVES TO THE RACK: ....NATURAL HISTORY   71   9
    THE RED, ROYAL ROBES OF PHEDRE? THE TEAR-DAZZLED ....PERSEUS   83   41
    AND THE ROYAL ROSE IN THE BULL'S BELLY, ...THE BULL OF BENDYLAW 108   20
    MAIDS AND THE LONG ROYAL LADY. ....WINTERING 218   39
    ITEM: CHUCK OUT ROYAL RIGMAROLE OF PROPS ....A SORCERER B. 324   5
    OF CLOCKWORK THAT MAKES THE ROYAL BLOOD RUN COLD. ....THE PRINCESS. 335   75
ROYALTY (1)
    RULE THEIR BEDS LIKE BEHEADED AND RESURRECTED AND ALL SILENT ROYALTY, ...
                                        ... QUEEN MARY'S ROSE GARDEN 290   5
RUBBED (1)
    RUBBED OF ITS PLUSH --- ....STINGS 214   18
RUBBER (7)
    MY SWADDLED LEGS AND ARMS SMELL SWEET AS RUBBER. POEM.7.S. 137   34
    NOISELESS, ON RUBBER WHEELS, ON THE WAY TO THE SEA RESORT. WAKING. 151   8

	TITLE	PAGE	LINE
RUBBER (CONT.)			
WITH THE ROOMS, OR THE SMILES, OR THE BEAUTIFUL RUBBER PLANTS, ...			
... WAKING IN WINTER	151	15
FROM THE SCALPELS AND THE RUBBER HANDS. ......THE SURGEON AT 2 A.M.	170	4
RUBBER BREASTS OR A RUBBER CROTCH, ...THE APPLICANT	221	5
RUBBER BREASTS OR A RUBBER CROTCH, ...THE APPLICANT	221	5
THE WHEELS, TWO RUBBER GRUBS, BITE THEIR SWEET TAILS. STOPPED DEAD	230	6
RUBBING (1)			
MOVING AND RUBBING ON THE SILK ....BALLOONS	271	5
RUBBISH (2)			
I'VE MARRIED A CUPBOARD OF RUBBISH. ....POEM.4.BEAST.	134	18
THE RUBBISH OF SUMMERS, THE BLACK-LEAVED FALLS. ..THE BURNT-OUT SPA	138	9
RUBBISHES (1)			
WHERE THE WAKING HEAD RUBBISHES OUT THE DRAGGLED LOT ......GHOST'S.	90	3
RUBBLE (1)			
IN THAT RUBBLE OF SKULL PLATES AND OLD LEATHER. ....TWO VIEWS.	114	8
RUBY (3)			
HER RUBY DREGS. ....RHYME	50	18
ITS EYE, FLASHLIT, A CHIP OF RUBY FIRE. ....GOATSUCKER	111	8
IN YOU, RUBY. ....NICK AND THE CANDLESTICK	241	28
RUCHINGS (1)			
WITH TRIANGULAR SCORCH MARKS FROM IRONING TINY RUCHINGS AND PUFFED			
SLEEVES. ....THE BABYSITTERS	174	15
RUCK (1)			
IN RUCK AND QUIBBLE OF COURTFOLK ....THE QUEEN'S COMPLAINT	28	1
RUDDERS (1)			
A PIGEON RUDDERS DOWN. ITS FAN-TAIL'S WHITE. ....MOONRISE	98	7
RUDDLE (1)			
FOR THE BLOOD-HEAT THAT WOULD RUDDLE OR RECLAIM. ....OUIJA	77	9
RUDDY (2)			
A RUDDY SKYLIGHT PAINTS THE GRAY OXBOW ....ABOVE THE OXBOW	88	42
RUDDY ON THE WAX MANNEQUINS ....OWL	101	6
RUDDY-BODIED (1)			
RESISTIVE, RUDDY-BODIED, ...SCULPTOR	92	15
RUDE (2)			
AND USED HER GENTLE DOVES WITH MANNERS RUDE; THE QUEEN'S COMPLAINT	28	7
FOR BEING SUCH A RUDE ASSAILANT ....THE DREAM	311	16
RUEFUL (1)			
RUEFUL, MOST VEXED, THAT TENDER SKIN ....BUCOLICS	24	17
RUFFS (1)			
GRANITE RUFFS, THEIR SHADOWS ....HARDCASTLE CRAGS	63	36
RUGS (1)			
WITH SOFT RUGS --- ....NICK AND THE CANDLESTICK	241	33
RUIN (2)			
ABOVE THE APPALLING RUIN; IN BLEAK LIGHT .............CONVERSATION.	21	6
TO CREATE SUCH A RUIN. ....THE COLOSSUS	130	23
RUINAGE (1)			
AS IF ABOVE LOVE'S RUINAGE, WE WERE ....THE OTHER TWO	69	34
RUINED (1)			
HER RUINED APARTMENTS, TAKING STOCK ....AFTERMATH	114	11
RUINOUS (1)			
EVEN IN THIS DULL, RUINOUS LANDSCAPE); SKEPTICAL, ...BLACK ROOK I.	57	24
RUINS (2)			
CONVERSATION AMONG THE RUINS ..........CONVERSATION AMONG THE RUINS	21	T
THE WAY SUN RUINS A TROUT. ....MEDALLION	124	15
RULE (3)			
WHERE STRAIGHT TALK IS THE RULE, WHETHER WARM OR HOSTILE, ...			
... INCOMMUNICADO	100	10
RULE THEIR BEDS LIKE BEHEADED AND RESURRECTED AND ALL SILENT ROYALTY, ...			
... QUEEN MARY'S ROSE GARDEN	290	5
WATER WILL RUN BY RULE; THE ACTUAL SUN ....TWO LOVERS.	327	21
RULED (2)			
LORDED PERSPECTIVES. MAPLIKE, THE FAR FIELDS ARE RULED ......OXBOW.	89	48
RULED DECREE OF DOOMSDAY ON THE FLOOR. ....THE TRIAL OF MAN	312	4
RULER (1)			
UNDER A BALANCED RULER. ....LORELEI	94	20
RULER'S (1)			
TILL, SICK OF THEIR RULER'S GODLING AIRS, ...NATURAL HISTORY	71	7
RULES (4)			
RULES THE WRITHINGS WHICH MAKE MANIFEST ...............SNAKECHARMER	79	16
ADHERING TO RULES, TO RULES, TO RULES. ....A BIRTHDAY PRESENT	206	8
ADHERING TO RULES, TO RULES, TO RULES. ....A BIRTHDAY PRESENT	206	8
ADHERING TO RULES, TO RULES, TO RULES. ....A BIRTHDAY PRESENT	206	8
RUM (1)			
RUM AND RED-FACED AS A WATER-MELON, HER VOICE ....ELLA MASON A.	53	7
RUMBAS (1)			
RUMBAS AND SAMBAS NO EAR-FLAPS CAN MUFFLE. ....ALICANTE LULLABY	43	14
RUMORED (1)			
ANGELS ARE RUMORED, CLEARLY ....THE GREAT CARBUNCLE	73	20
RUMORS (2)			
THE MUDDY RUMORS ....FULL FATHOM FIVE	93	21
PROVES RUMORS SHALLOW, ...FULL FATHOM FIVE	93	24
RUMPUS (1)			
AT THIS RARE RUMPUS WHICH NO MAN CAN CONTROL: .....CHANNEL CROSSING	27	29

	TITLE	PAGE	LINE

RUN (24)
WHAT FIRES RUN, WHAT CRAVING WAKES? ....PURSUIT 22 12
AND I RUN FLARING IN MY SKIN; ....PURSUIT 23 34
STARS SHOOT THEIR PETALS, AND SUNS RUN TO SEED, ...EPITAPH FOR F. 45 12
THE MONEY'S RUN OUT. ....DEPARTURE 51 4
NOW, RUN TO FAT, SHE'S A SPINSTER WHOSE DOOR SHUTS ...ELLA MASON A. 54 17
OF ASPARAGUS HEADS. CARS RUN THEIR SUAVE ....ABOVE THE OXBOW 89 50
THE GROUNDHOG ON THE MOUNTAIN DID NOT RUN ...........INCOMMUNICADO 100 1
ABOUT SAM: WHITENESS AND THE GREAT RUN ....WHITENESS I REMEMBER 102 2
THE WORLD SUBDUED TO HIS RUN OF IT. ....WHITENESS I REMEMBER 103 27
THE COILS AND PIPES THAT MADE HIM RUN. ....THE BURNT-OUT SPA 138 17
TENDS TO THE PEBBLES IT MUST RUN OVER, SMOOTHING THEM GENTLY.*TULIPS 160 16
RUN FOLD UPON FOLD FAR OFF, CONCEALING THEIR HOLLOWS, ..BERCK-PLAGE 199 74
I CANNOT RUN, I AM ROOTED, AND THE GORSE HURTS ME ..THE BEE MEETING 211 31
I COULD NOT RUN WITHOUT HAVING TO RUN FOREVER. .....THE BEE MEETING 212 33
I COULD NOT RUN WITHOUT HAVING TO RUN FOREVER. .....THE BEE MEETING 212 33
A MILLION SOLDIERS RUN, ...CUT 235 19
BUT LET THE GALLOPING ANTELOPE RUN. ....GO GET THE GOODLY SQUAB 313 12
LET THE GALLOPING ANTELOPE RUN ....GO GET THE GOODLY SQUAB 313 13
AND LUCKY STARS ALL EXIT ON THE RUN: ....ADMONITIONS 319 17
AND CASUIST ARGUMENTS RUN RIOT INSOLENT STORM STRIKES AT THE SKULL 326 21
THE MORBID COBRA'S WITS HAVE RUN ASTRAY; ....DENOUEMENT 327 13
WATER WILL RUN BY RULE; THE ACTUAL SUN ....TWO LOVERS. 327 21
WHO INSISTS HIS PLAYMATES RUN. ....LOVE IS A PARALLAX 329 24
OF CLOCKWORK THAT MAKES THE ROYAL BLOOD RUN COLD. ....THE PRINCESS. 335 75
RUNG (1)
TO HAVE YOU GRAB MY NOSE, A LADDER RUNG. ......FOR A FATHERLESS SON 205 11
RUNNELS (1)
OF YOUR GRAINED FACE SHED TIME IN RUNNELS: ....FULL FATHOM FIVE 93 26
RUNNING (6)
ITS RUNNING IS USELESS. ....TOTEM 264 3
FOR LOUDSPEAKER WIRES RUNNING LIKE A LOGICAL ....DIALOGUE O. 280 165
RUNNING NECK AND NECK WITH THE MOST DEVOUT ....DIALOGUE O. 282 235
A BINGE OF JEERS. LOOK. HE'S RUNNING THROUGH ....DIALOGUE O. 284 296
THEIR DEATH-PEGS STUD YOUR GLOVES, IT IS NO USE RUNNING. STINGS/DR 293 8
THE WHEELS REVOLVE, THE UNIVERSE KEEPS RUNNING. TO EVA DESCENDING. 303 2
RUNS (5)
AGAINST BOTH BAR AND TOWER THE BLACK SEA RUNS. ....POINT SHIRLEY 111 48
UNSPOOL AND SPEND THEMSELVES. MY MIND RUNS WITH THEM, *PARLIAMENT 153 35
ITS END AND RUNS TOWARD IT, ARMS HELD OUT IN LOVE. .....THREE WOMEN 181 151
THE BLOOD THAT RUNS IS DARK FRUIT -- ....THE OTHER 202 29
BLOOD RUNS IN A GLISSANDO FROM THE HAND .....EPITAPH IN THREE PARTS 337 18
RUSH (1)
APPALLED BY SECRET WANT, I RUSH ....PURSUIT 23 43
RUSHED (1)
WOMAN FOLLOWED US AND RUSHED ....THE DREAM 310 11
RUSSIA (3)
THE GILT AND PINK DOMES OF RUSSIA MELT AND FLOAT OFF .....THE SWARM 216 15
RUSSIA, POLAND AND GERMANY! ....THE SWARM 216 27
IT IS RUSSIA I HAVE TO GET ACROSS, IT IS SOME WAR OR OTHER.*GETTING. 248 9
RUSSIAN (1)
LAPSING INTO RUSSIAN OR SERBO-CROAT. ...DIALOGUE OVER A OUIJA BOARD 279 92
RUSSIANS (1)
THEY TALKED ABOUT THE RUSSIANS. ....BITTER STRAWBERRIES 299 2
RUST (2)
HORSE THE COLOR OF RUST, ...SHEEP IN FOG 262 6
TO BURN AWAY THE HUMBUG RUST ....SONG FOR A REVOLUTIONARY LOVE 323 23
RUSTED (2)
ARENA DUST RUSTED BY FOUR BULLS' BLOOD TO A DULL REDNESS,*THE GORING 47 1
THE SCRAPS OF RUSTED REVERIE, THE WHEELS ....SONNET: TO EVA 305 10
RUSTING (1)
MY OWN BLUE RAZOR RUSTING IN MY THROAT. .....ELECTRA ON AZALEA PATH 117 43
RUSTLING (1)
SCREENS, THESE RUSTLING APPURTENANCES. ....PURDAH 243 23
RUST-RED (2)
RUST-RED OR GREEN AS LICHENS. ....OLD LADIES' HOME 120 14
SNAGS AND EDDIES ROUND A SUNKEN RUST-RED ENGINE. ....TULIPS 161 54
RUSTY (2)
OLD TOOLS, HANDLES AND RUSTY TUSKS. POEM.1.WHO. 131 5
A MONSTER OF WOOD AND RUSTY TEETH. ....THE BURNT-OUT SPA 137 2
RUT (1)
MOLES DEAD IN THE PEBBLED RUT, ...BLUE MOLES 126 2
RUTH (1)
FOR RUTH FAINLIGHT ....ELM 192 D
RUTS (1)
I COME TO WHEEL RUTS, AND WATER ....WUTHERING HEIGHTS 167 28
RUTTED (2)
WHAT THE SLUTTISH, RUTTED SEA COULD DO. ....POINT SHIRLEY 110 12
ACROSS THE RUTTED ROAD. ....BITTER STRAWBERRIES 299 17
RYE-HEADS (1)
RIVER-VERGE FARMS WHERE RYE-HEADS WHITEN. ....IN MIDAS' COUNTRY 99 4
S. (4)
BY S. S. PIERCE, BY S. S. PIERCE, ...A WINTER'S TALE 87 13
BY S. S. PIERCE, BY S. S. PIERCE, ...A WINTER'S TALE 87 13
BY S. S. PIERCE, BY S. S. PIERCE, ...A WINTER'S TALE 87 13

```
                                              TITLE            PAGE   LINE
S. (CONT.)
    BY S. S. PIERCE, BY S. S. PIERCE,  .................A WINTER'S TALE    87   13
SABOTEUR (1)
    SABOTEUR,  .......................................................CUT   235   27
SACHET (1)
    MAKE A SACHET OR  ..........................................A SECRET   220   31
SACK (4)
    HIS FOREHEAD IS BUMPY AS A SACK OF ROCKS.  .................INSOMNIAC   163   13
    BUT THEY PULLED ME OUT OF THE SACK,  ...........................DADDY   224   61
    INTO A BLACK SACK  ........................................THE JAILER   226    8
    THE SACK OF BLACK! IT IS EVERYWHERE, TIGHT, TIGHT!  ..BY CANDLELIGHT   237   30
SACKCLOTH (1)
    HOARD LAST YEAR'S LEAVES, WON'T MOURN, WEAR SACKCLOTH, OR TURN ...
                                              ... NOVEMBER GRAVEYARD   56    2
SACKED (1)
    SACKED LARDER'S GONE BONE-BARE.  ........................THE GLUTTON    40   14
SACRAMENT (1)
    NOW SPEAK SOME SACRAMENT TO PARRY SCRUPLE  ......WREATH FOR A BRIDAL    44   11
SACRED (4)
    AMONG SACRED ISLANDS OF THE MAD TILL DEATH  ...........TALE OF A TUB    25   47
    WITH THE SACRED BABOON IN HIS WIG AND WAX EARS  ...ZOO KEEPER'S WIFE   155   29
    EACH SACRED BODY  ................................MOONSONG AT MORNING   317   29
    OF STRICT AND SACRED SKELETON;   INSOLENT STORM STRIKES AT THE SKULL   325    8
SACRIFICE (2)
    COMPELS A TOTAL SACRIFICE.  ................................PURSUIT    23   40
    THE ABSOLUTE SACRIFICE.  .....................THE MUNICH MANNEQUINS   263    7
SACRIFICES (1)
    SACRIFICES ITS OPACITY....  ............................MARY'S SONG   257    3
SACRIFICIAL (1)
    SWABBED AND LURID WITH DISINFECTANTS, SACRIFICIAL.  .....THREE WOMEN   179  107
SACRILEGIOUS (1)
    YOUR MALADY OF SACRILEGIOUS MIRTH  ...............DIRGE FOR A JOKER   303   11
SACROSANCT (1)
    OF AZALEAS, SACROSANCT  ..........................CHILD'S PARK STONES   101   10
SAD (6)
    "HOW SAD, ALAS, IT IS  .......................THE QUEEN'S COMPLAINT    29   24
    THESE POEMS DO NOT LIVE: IT'S A SAD DIAGNOSIS.  ...........STILLBORN   142    1
    THIS MIZZLE FITS ME LIKE A SAD JACKET.  .................LEAVING EARLY   146   39
    SAD HAG. "EVERY WOMAN'S A WHORE.  .............................LESBOS   229   83
    SAD HAMLET, WITH A KNIFE?  ...........................STOPPED DEAD   230   19
    THE MOON HAS NOTHING TO BE SAD ABOUT,  .........................EDGE   273   17
SADLY (2)
    REGARD ME SADLY, I DISAPPOINT THEM.  ...................SHEEP IN FOG   262    3
    AND JUMBO SADLY TRUMPETS INTO STONE;  ...................DENOUEMENT   327   11
SAFE (11)
    "MAY COCKCROW GUARD US SAFE," SAID HE;  ....................BUCOLICS    23    6
    AND HOARD FAITH SAFE IN A FOSSIL.  ......EPITAPH FOR FIRE AND FLOWER    45   21
    IN SAFE PERSPECTIVE, COULD OUTFACE THE GORGON-GRIMACE  ......PERSEUS    83   14
    TO SAFE GRAY NEVER GRAYED HIS TEMPER.  .........WHITENESS I REMEMBER   102   11
    NO DAY IS SAFE FROM NEWS OF YOU,  .........................THE RIVAL   167   16
    SAFE ON THE MATTRESS, HANDS BRACED, AS FOR A FALL.  .....THREE WOMEN   187  367
    MIRROR SAFE, UNREDEEMED  ......................................BRASILIA   259   21
    THERE ONE IS SAFE,  ...........................................GIGOLO   267    7
    OUR WORLD AND THEIRS WE'D BEST PLAY SAFE AND GROOM  .....DIALOGUE O.   281  186
    HIDE, HIDE, IN THE SAFE CAVE  .............GO GET THE GOODLY SQUAB   313   15
    AND GET SAFE HOME; BUT, TURNING WITH TRAINED EYES,  .......AERIALIST   331   28
SAFE-CONDUCT (1)
    CONFIDENCE OF SAFE-CONDUCT  ..........MUSSEL HUNTER AT ROCK HARBOR    95   23
SAFER (1)
    THIS IS NOT DEATH, IT IS SOMETHING SAFER.  ...............POEM.5.F.   135   15
SAFE-SOCKETED (1)
    SAFE-SOCKETED IN ROCK.  ...............................TOUCH-AND-GO   336   24
SAFETY (1)
    SHADOWS OUR SAFETY. WE STAND ROUND BLANKLY AS WALLS.  ..MORNING SONG   157    6
SAFFRON (1)
    HE HYMNS THE ROTTEN QUEEN WITH SAFFRON HAIR  .................OUIJA    77   22
SAG (1)
    THEY MELT AND SAG, THEY ARE TOLD  ..............BURNING THE LETTERS   204   18
SAG-BACKED (1)
    BALUSTRADE OF A SAG-BACKED BRIDGE.  ...............THE BURNT-OUT SPA   138   23
SAGE (4)
    SAGE HEN AND SPRY RABBIT,  .....................TWO VIEWS OF WITHENS    72    8
    BUT OH, SAGE GROWNUPS KNOW  .............................BATTLE-SCENE    85   35
    OF THE OCEAN. SUCH SAGE HUMOR AND  ...................FULL FATHOM FIVE    93   29
    THE ARTIFICIAL RED SAGE DOES NOT STIR  .......ELECTRA ON AZALEA PATH   117   24
SAGES (1)
    STILL, LATTER-DAY SAGES,  .....................A LESSON IN VENGEANCE    80   21
SAGGED (1)
    OLD SOCK-FACE, SAGGED ON A DARNING EGG.  ...................FACE LIFT   156   27
SAGS (1)
    MY MOUTH SAGS,  ..............................................GIGOLO   267   18
SAID (20)
    "A DAISIED MEAD," EACH SAID TO EACH,  .....................BUCOLICS    23    2
    "NO PITCHFORKED FARMER, PLEASE," SHE SAID;  ...............BUCOLICS    23    5
    "MAY COCKCROW GUARD US SAFE," SAID HE;  ...................BUCOLICS    23    6
```

SAID (CONT.)
    GHOST SAID TO PRIEST: ....DIALOGUE BETWEEN GHOST AND PRIEST   38   18
    GOODBYES WERE SAID, TRAINS LET GO, ...MONOLOGUE AT 3 A.M.   40   12
    WHETHER YOU SAW THEM, WHETHER YOU SAID ....THE DISQUIETING MUSES   75   13
    MY MOTHER SAID; YOU DIED LIKE ANY MAN. ......ELECTRA ON AZALEA PATH   117   40
    I SAID: I MUST REMEMBER THIS, BEING SMALL. POEM.1.WHO.   132   28
    IF I DON'T MOVE ABOUT, I'LL KNOCK NOTHING OVER. SO I SAID,*POEM.6.W. 135   14
    YOU ARE SO WHITE, SUDDENLY." AND I SAID NOTHING. ....THREE WOMEN   177   23
    YOU SAID YOU WOULD KILL IT THIS MORNING. ....PHEASANT 191   1
    AND I SAID I DO, I DO. ....DADDY   224   67
    THE VAMPIRE WHO SAID HE WAS YOU ....DADDY   224   72
    IN NEW YORK, IN HOLLYWOOD, THE MEN SAID: "THROUGH? ....LESBOS   228   41
    AN ORIGINAL NOTE. IF HE'D SAID, HOWEVER, MERELY: ....DIALOGUE O.   278   81
    PAN SAID. A PLUMAGE OF RAW WORMS. HOW ..DIALOGUE OVER A OUIJA BOARD 279 100
    MARY SAID SLOWLY, "I'VE GOT A FELLA ....BITTER STRAWBERRIES   299   10
    "THE DRAFT IS PASSED," THE WOMAN SAID. ....BITTER STRAWBERRIES   299   20
    SAID EVE: "I WISH VENOMOUS NEMATODES ....DIALOGUE EN ROUTE   309   19
    "LAST NIGHT," HE SAID, "I SLEPT WELL ....THE DREAM   310   1
SAIL (4)
    WE SHALL BOARD OUR IMAGINED SHIP AND WILDLY SAIL .....TALE OF A TUB   25   46
    AND SO WE SAIL TOWARD CITIES, STREETS AND HOMES ...CHANNEL CROSSING   27   37
    BY TWO BRONZE BOOKENDS OF SHIPS IN SAIL,   ON THE DECLINE OF ORACLES 78   2
    THE DAY YOUR SLACK SAIL DRANK MY SISTER'S BREATH ......ELECTRA ON.   117   30
SAILED (1)
    THEY SAILED TILL TIDE FOAMED ROUND THEIR ANKLES ......DREAM WITH C.   44   19
SAILOR (4)
    A MARBLE SAILOR KNEELS AT HER FOOT DISTRACTEDLY, AND AT HIS FOOT ...
                                            ... FINISTERRE 170   21
    IS PRAYING TO THE MONUMENT OF THE SAILOR PRAYING. ....FINISTERRE 170   23
    SHE DOES NOT HEAR WHAT THE SAILOR OR THE PEASANT IS SAYING -- ...
                                            ... FINISTERRE 170   26
    OF THE BOLD SAILOR FALLING UNDER DRENCH .....EPITAPH IN THREE PARTS 337   15
SAILORS (1)
    TAUNTS US TO VALOR. BLUE SAILORS SANG THAT OUR JOURNEY ..CHANNEL C.   27   20
SAILS (1)
    THE STIFFNESS OF SAILS, THE LONG SALT WINDING SHEETS. ....MYSTIC 268   8
SAINT (5)
    HEARING A WHITE SAINT RAVE ....ON THE PLETHORA OF DRYADS   67   1
    SAINT AND KING UNFISTED OBSTRUCTION'S KNUCKLES*A LESSON IN VENGEANCE 80   4
    SHE MAY BE A SAINT, AND I MAY BE UGLY AND HAIRY, ...IN PLASTER 160   53
    IT IS LIKE POSSESSING A SAINT. ....BERCK-PLAGE 198   57
    SAVED FOR THE ACORN-STOMACHED SAINT OR EYES ....DIALOGUE O.   280 129
SAINTLY (1)
    A SAINTLY SPARROW JARGONS MADRIGALS ....APRIL AUBADE 312   5
SAINTS (3)
    GROWN MILKY, ALMOST CLEAR, LIKE THE BODIES OF SAINTS. ......CANDLES 148   4
    SHE DOESN'T NEED FOOD, SHE IS ONE OF THE REAL SAINTS. ...IN PLASTER 158   4
    INSIDE THE CHURCH, THE SAINTS WILL BE ALL BLUE, ...MOON.   173   24
SAINT'S (1)
    GLINTING AND CLINKING IN A SAINT'S FALSETTO. ONLY YOU   NEW YEAR ON. 176   3
SAINTS' (3)
    BULKS REAL, ALL SAINTS' TONGUES FALL QUIET: .....NOVEMBER GRAVEYARD   56   11
    IN VINEGAR LIKE SAINTS' RELICS. ....THE SURGEON AT 2 A.M. 171   39
    SMIRK. SAINTS' DOOR APART, BACKDOOR'S A DOOR, ...DIALOGUE O.   280 131
SAKE (2)
    OF VIRGINS FOR VIRGINITY'S SAKE." ....VIRGIN IN A TREE   82   30
    ART'S SAKE THAN GOD'S. FAR FROM SEA -- *MUSSEL HUNTER AT ROCK HARBOR 97   82
SALAMI (1)
    AND TISSUE IN SLICES -- A PATHOLOGICAL SALAMI.*THE SURGEON AT 2 A.M. 171   36
SALLOW (6)
    AND SALLOW AS ANY LEMON, ...TWO SISTERS OF PERSEPHONE   32   25
    FOOTING SALLOW AS A MOUSE ....MISS DRAKE PROCEEDS TO SUPPER   41   9
    HER SALLOW RODENT TEETH LIKE CASTANETS ...............INCOMMUNICADO 100   4
    A SALLOW PIECE OF STRING HELD IT TOGETHER. ....TWO VIEWS. 114   9
    THEIR SKIN TINTS ARE PINK OR SALLOW, BROWN OR RED; .....THREE WOMEN 183 223
    MY THOUGHTS ARE CRABBED AND SALLOW, ...JILTED   304   1
SALT (13)
    INTO SALT SEAS. HERCULES HAD A SIMPLE TIME, ...PERSEUS   82   6
    ON THE PUBLIC GRILLS, AND THE OCHREOUS SALT FLATS, ...SUICIDE. 115   2
    COMFORTLESS AS SALT. SNAKE AND BIRD .....SLEEP IN THE MOJAVE DESERT 144   18
    I CAN SMELL THE SALT, ALL RIGHT. ....WHITSUN   154   13
    SHAWLED IN BLOND HAIR AND THE SALT ....HEAVY WOMEN 158   3
    THE WATER I TASTE IS WARM AND SALT, LIKE THE SEA, ...TULIPS   162   62
    THESE HILLS ARE TOO GREEN AND SWEET TO HAVE TASTED SALT.   BLACKBER. 169   22
    WE KICKED AND TALKED. THE THICK SALT KEPT US UP. ...THE BABYSITTERS 175   40
    WHAT CUPPED SIGHS, WHAT SALT IN THE THROAT.... ......BERCK-PLAGE   197   32
    "IT SMELLS OF SALT COD, YOU HAD BETTER ....A SECRET   220   29
    WE MAKE NEW STOCK FROM THE SALT. ....THE APPLICANT   221   18
    I AM SICK TO DEATH OF HOT SALT. ....MEDUSA   225   37
    THE STIFFNESS OF SAILS, THE LONG SALT WINDING SHEETS. ....MYSTIC 268   8
SALTIER (1)
    WHO HAS SALTIER APHRODISIACS ....OUIJA   77   23
SALTS (1)
    SWEET SALTS WARPED STEM ....FIRESONG   30   15

	TITLE	PAGE	LINE

SALT-SWEETNESS (1)
    SUCH SALT-SWEETNESS. WHY SHOULD I WALK ....BERCK-PLAGE 197 40
SALTY (1)
    LEAVING A SALTY MASH OF ICE TO WHITEN ....POINT SHIRLEY 110 8
SALUTARY (1)
    SALUTARY AND PURE AS BOILED WATER, ...MAGI 148 7
SALVE (1)
    BEFORE THE BROOCH-PIN AND THE SALVE ....THE EYE-MOTE 109 27
SAM (1)
    ABOUT SAM: WHITENESS AND THE GREAT RUN ....WHITENESS I REMEMBER 102 2
SAMBAS (1)
    RUMBAS AND SAMBAS NO EAR-FLAPS CAN MUFFLE. ....ALICANTE LULLABY 43 14
SAME (22)
    IN THE SAME WAY ....SOW 60 4
    WE START AT'S THE SAME POST WE FINISH BY, ...ABOVE THE OXBOW 88 19
    OF HOLOFERNES' HEAD, DIPPED IN THE SAME ....LEAVING EARLY 146 32
    DOING THINGS WITH THEIR HANDS, ONE JUST THE SAME AS ANOTHER, *TULIPS 160 13
    YOU LEAVE THE SAME IMPRESSION ....THE RIVAL 166 2
    I HAD TO SLEEP IN THE SAME ROOM WITH THE BABY ON A TOO-SHORT COT, ...
                ... THE BABYSITTERS 174 7
    TATTOOING OVER AND OVER THE SAME BLUE GRIEVANCES, ...COURAGE. 210 11
    THE MILD HILLS, THE SAME OLD MAGENTA ....THE SWARM 216 28
    THE SAME PLACARD OF BLUE FOG IS WHEELED INTO POSITION ...THE JAILER 226 2
    WITH THE SAME TREES AND HEADSTONES. ....THE JAILER 226 3
    BUT WITH THE SAME FACES, ...LYONNESSE 234 13
    THE SAME PLACES. . . ..LYONNESSE 234 14
    NEVERTHELESS, I AM THE SAME, IDENTICAL WOMAN. ....LADY LAZARUS 245 34
    TO THE SAME PLACE, THE SAME FACE, THE SAME BRUTE ......LADY LAZARUS 246 53
    TO THE SAME PLACE, THE SAME FACE, THE SAME BRUTE ......LADY LAZARUS 246 53
    TO THE SAME PLACE, THE SAME FACE, THE SAME BRUTE ......LADY LAZARUS 246 53
    THE SAME FIRE ....MARY'S SONG 257 6
    OUT OF WHICH THE SAME SELF UNFOLDS LIKE A SUIT ....TOTEM 264 25
    THE LETTERS LIVE IN THE SAME PLACE. OR ELSE ....DIALOGUE O. 277 23
    ALWAYS THE SAME DISTANCE FROM ............METAMORPHOSES OF THE MOON 307 9
    THE SAME AGAIN: ....TO A JILTED LOVER 310 20
    WHILE ON THIS SAME FUGUE, UNMOVED, ...TOUCH-AND-GO 336 22
SAMENESS (1)
    AND DAYLIGHT LAYS ITS SAMENESS ON THE WALL. POEM.7.S. 137 26
SAMPLERS (2)
    SET IN THE PROVERBS STITCHED ON SAMPLERS ....VIRGIN IN A TREE 81 3
    UNRAVEL ANTIQUE SAMPLERS, UNWIND THE CLOCKS, ...SONG FOR A REVOLU. 323 13
SAMURAI (1)
    A SAMURAI DEATH MASK DONE ....MUSSEL HUNTER AT ROCK HARBOR 97 80
SANCTITY (1)
    WHICH MAR THE IDOL'S SANCTITY. ..........METAMORPHOSES OF THE MOON 308 36
SANCTUARY (1)
    AND TO SANCTUARY: USURPING THE ARMCHAIR ....ALL THE DEAD DEARS 71 31
SANCTUM (1)
    A SANCTUM TO ATTRACT ....VIRGIN IN A TREE 82 26
SAND (7)
    SAND GRIT TO SIDED CRYSTAL ....MUSSEL HUNTER AT ROCK HARBOR 95 4
    SAND ABRADED THE MILKLESS LIP. ....I WANT, I WANT 106 5
    IN MY GRANDMOTHER'S SAND YARD. SHE IS DEAD, ...POINT SHIRLEY 110 9
    SNUFF-COLORED SAND CLIFFS RISE ....MAN IN BLACK 119 12
    STRETCHING ITS FINE, IRRITATING SAND IN ALL DIRECTIONS. ..INSOMNIAC 163 1
    THE SCALE-SHEEN ON THE SAND SCARED ME TO DEATH. ....LESBOS 229 59
    A GRAIN OF SAND IS ALL WE HAVE. ....TWO LOVERS. 327 20
SANDBIN (1)
    THE ARMADILLO DOZED IN HIS SANDBIN ....ZOO KEEPER'S WIFE 155 20
SANDMAN'S (1)
    AND THE SANDMAN'S DUST ....HARDCASTLE CRAGS 63 20
SANDS (2)
    SANDS WHERE A DREAM OF CLEAR WATER ....BURNING THE LETTERS 204 7
    AND I, ON THE SKY-MIRRORING, BLAND SANDS*DIALOGUE OVER A OUIJA BOARD 291 17
SANDSPIT (1)
    HUSTLED A GULL FLOCK TO FLAP OFF THE SANDSPIT. *SUICIDE OFF EGG ROCK 115 13
SANDY (1)
    A SANDY DAMPER KILLS THE VIBRATIONS; ....BERCK-PLAGE 196 7
SANE (1)
    THE SKY'S FAR DOME IS SANE AND CLEAR. ....BLUE MOLES 126 10
SANG (2)
    TAUNTS US TO VALOR. BLUE SAILORS SANG THAT OUR JOURNEY ..CHANNEL C. 27 20
    THE MOLTS ARE TONGUELESS THAT SANG FROM ABOVE THE WATER ..POEM.5.F. 135 17
SANGUINE (1)
    FIRED IN SANGUINE CLAY, THE MODEL HEAD ....LADY AND T. 69 1
SANITY (1)
    WHICH WEIGHS OUR MADNESS WITH OUR SANITY. ....PERSEUS 84 49
SANK (1)
    AND THE FAIR SHIP SANK, ITS CREW KNELLED HOME FOR DINNER. ...
              ... DREAM WITH CLAM-DIGGERS 44 20
SANTA (1)
    THE LEAVES APPLAUD, AND SANTA CLAUS FLIES IN ....LOVE IS A PARALLAX 329 34
SANTA'S (1)
    AND ALL YOU SANTA'S DEER WHO BROWSE ....A WINTER'S TALE 87 21

	TITLE	PAGE	LINE

SAP (4)
NOW, AS GREEN SAP ASCENDS THE STEEPLED WOOD, ...MAYFLOWER 60 5
ONCE, IN ITS EARLIEST SWAY OF LYMPH AND SAP, ...HARDCASTLE CRAGS 63 39
THE SAP ....WORDS 270 6
AND SAP ASCENDS THE STEEPLE OF THE VEIN. ....APRIL AUBADE 312 4
SAPLINGS (1)
STAUNCH SAPLINGS; TO THIS HOUSE, THRIVING DAYS ....CRYSTAL GAZER 55 16
SAPPHIRE (1)
AND THE TONGUE, SAPPHIRE OF ASH. ....BERCK-PLAGE 198 54
SARCASM (1)
CAN SPELL SARCASM THROUGH OUR FINGERTIPS. ....DIALOGUE O. 282 208
SARCOPHAGI (1)
I WALK AMONG SLEEPERS IN GAUZE SARCOPHAGI. ...THE SURGEON AT 2 A.M. 171 47
SARCOPHAGUS (1)
I DO NOT WANT A PLAIN BOX, I WANT A SARCOPHAGUS ....LAST WORDS 172 1
SARDINE (1)
HALFWAY UP FROM THE LITTLE HARBOR OF SARDINE BOATS, *THE NET-MENDERS 121 1
SAT (7)
BOUGHS WHERE THOSE OWLS SAT. ....FAUN 35 10
BUT SAT ON, GUARDING HIS GRIM BATTLEMENT. ..THE SNOWMAN ON THE MOOR 58 7
WITHOUT MEAT OR DRINK I SAT ....ON THE PLETHORA OF DRYADS 67 7
THOSE OLD DESPOTS, IF HE SAT ....THE HERMIT AT OUTERMOST HOUSE 119 9
SAT BY MY FATHER'S BEAN TREE POEM.3.MAENAD. 133 2
THE SUN SAT IN HIS ARMPIT. POEM.4.BEAST. 134 4
I SAT AT MY DESK IN MY STOCKINGS, MY HIGH HEELS, ...THREE WOMEN 177 21
SATAN (1)
SONNET TO SATAN ....SONNET TO SATAN 323 T
SATAN'S (1)
RIGHT TO BLAZE AS SATAN'S WIFE: ....VANITY FAIR 33 32
SATCHELS (1)
WITH THEIR HEARTS THAT TICK AND TICK, WITH THEIR SATCHELS OF
     INSTRUMENTS. ....THREE WOMEN 180 138
SATIN (1)
HE, AFLOAT IN THE SEA OF HER BLUE SATIN *TWO VIEWS OF A CADAVER ROOM 114 14
SATINS (1)
THE DIAPHANOUS SATINS OF A JANUARY WINDOW ....A BIRTHDAY PRESENT 206 17
SATISFACTION (1)
DEMANDING SATISFACTION: NO DUEL TAKES PLACE: ........METAMORPHOSES. 307 5
SATISFIED (3)
MUSK SATISFIED MY NOSE, RED MY EYE, ...RHODODENDRON. 103 13
THE DEATHLY GUESTS HAD NOT BEEN SATISFIED ....WAKING IN WINTER 151 14
YOU'RE SATISFIED. MY WILL HAS EVIDENTLY *DIALOGUE OVER A OUIJA BOARD 284 279
SATISFY (1)
TO SATISFY THE QUESTIONS OF A CURIOUS OLD FOOL?" ....DIALOGUE B. 39 26
SAUCER (1)
ABOUT A BALD, HOSPITAL SAUCER. ....A LIFE 150 22
SAUCERS (1)
NAPPING IN HER KITCHEN PAVED WITH SAUCERS. ....ELLA MASON A. 54 20
SAUNTERS (2)
HE SAUNTERS IN: HOW BUT MOST GLAD ....ODE FOR TED 29 21
THE FIENDISH BUTLER SAUNTERS IN AND SERVES ....TERMINAL 328 10
SAUSAGES (1)
LOPPING THE SAUSAGES! ....LITTLE FUGUE 188 33
SAVE (2)
THE STAR BUGS WON'T SAVE ME THIS MONTH. POEM.4.BEAST. 134 22
PRAYS UNDER HER BREATH THAT SHE MAY SAVE ....ON DECK 143 23
SAVED (2)
ELEMENT -- THIS RELIC SAVED ....MUSSEL HUNTER AT ROCK HARBOR 97 90
SAVED FOR THE ACORN-STOMACHED SAINT OR EYES ....DIALOGUE O. 280 129
SAVING (1)
SO IF YOU CAN DREAM UP ANY SAVING PLAN ....THE DISPOSSESSED 318 2
SAVOR (2)
WITH SAVOR: COUPLED SO, PURE PARAGONS OF CONSTANCE, ...WREATH F. 44 9
TO SAVOR THEIR SPAN OF FLOURISHING. ....CRYSTAL GAZER 55 27
SAW (20)
I SAW SLOW FLOCKED COWS MOVE ....SONG FOR A SUMMER'S DAY 30 3
SAW HOOF HARDEN FROM FOOT, SAW SPROUT ....FAUN 35 13
SAW HOOF HARDEN FROM FOOT, SAW SPROUT ....FAUN 35 13
WHAT GERD SAW THEN ENGRAVED HER MIND ....CRYSTAL GAZER 56 43
WORSE -- SAW DANGLING FROM THAT SPIKE-STUDDED BELT ......SNOWMAN O. 59 37
KING EGG-HEAD SAW HIS DOMAIN CRACK, ...NATURAL HISTORY 71 10
WHETHER YOU SAW THEM, WHETHER YOU SAID ....THE DISQUIETING MUSES 75 13
SAW EVIL BREAK OUT OF THE NORTH. ....ON THE DECLINE OF ORACLES. 78 32
AND NEVER SAW HOW COOLLY WE MIGHT MOVE. FOR ONCE ...ABOVE THE OXBOW 89 55
MUSSELS. FROM WHAT THE CRABS SAW, ...MUSSEL HUNTER AT ROCK HARBOR 97 64
AND I SAW WHITE MAGGOTS COIL ....MEDALLION 124 21
THE FIRST THING I SAW WAS SHEER AIR ....LOVE LETTER 147 20
SHE BEGAN TO WARM UP, AND I SAW HER ADVANTAGES. ....IN PLASTER 159 14
THEN I SAW WHAT THE TROUBLE WAS: SHE THOUGHT SHE WAS IMMORTAL. ...
                                          ... IN PLASTER 159 35
WHEN I FIRST SAW IT, THE SMALL RED SEEP, I DID NOT BELIEVE IT. ...
                                       THREE WOMEN 177 15
I SAW DEATH IN THE BARE TREES, A DEPRIVATION. ....THREE WOMEN 177 24
I SAW THE WORLD IN IT -- SMALL, MEAN AND BLACK, ...THREE WOMEN 178 54
SO I SAW YOUR MUCH SICKER ............................EAVESDROPPER 260 24

SAW (CONT.)
    A RIGOR SEIZED ME: I SAW CRACKS APPEAR, *DIALOGUE OVER A OUIJA BOARD 285 319
    OF ONE I LOVED. I SAW DIVISION BLOOM ...DIALOGUE OVER A OUIJA BOARD 285 322
SAWDUST (1)
    THE MAGIC SAWDUST WRITES: ADDRESS UNKNOWN. ....DENOUEMENT 327   17
SAWS (1)
    SAWS DOWN A REED AND SWIMS FROM HIS LIMBER GROVE, ...WATERCOLOR. 112   23
SAY (36)
    FROM YOUR BLUE PALLOR, I'D SAY YOU INHABITED THE FROZEN WASTE ...
              ... DIALOGUE BETWEEN GHOST AND PRIEST   38   14
    WHATEVER TRIAL'S TO COME, SO SAY TRUE." ....CRYSTAL GAZER   55   20
    ONE MIGHT SAY LOVE. AT ANY RATE, I NOW WALK ....BLACK ROOK I.   57   22
    ARE UNREAL, WE SAY: ....THE THIN PEOPLE   64   4
    SIGNS SAY NOTHING. THE FALCON WHO SPOKE CLEAR ........INCOMMUNICADO 100   13
    SO FABLES SAY THE GOATSUCKER MOVES, MASKED FROM MEN'S SIGHT ...
                                  ... GOATSUCKER 111   9
    THE PASSAGE, SAY, OF THESE MAN-SHAMING CLOUDS. ....TWO CAMP. 144   3
    THAT WASN'T IT. I SLEPT, SAY: A SNAKE ....LOVE LETTER 147   9
    AND DYING TO SAY SOMETHING UNANSWERABLE. ....THE RIVAL 166   10
    "LET US MAKE A HEAVEN," THEY SAY. ....THREE WOMEN 179   90
    IT IS USUAL, THEY SAY, FOR SUCH A THING TO HAPPEN. .....THREE WOMEN 183 242
    DO YOU SAY NOTHING? ....LITTLE FUGUE 188   43
    ABC, HER EYELIDS SAY. ....AN APPEARANCE 189   18
    ONLY THEY HAVE NOTHING TO SAY TO ANYBODY. ......BURNING THE LETTERS 204   34
    I WOULD SAY IT WAS THE COFFIN OF A MIDGET*THE ARRIVAL OF THE BEE BOX 212   3
    YOU SAY YOU CAN'T STAND HER, ...LESBOS 228   15
    YOU SAY I SHOULD DROWN THE KITTENS. THEIR SMELL! ....LESBOS 228   20
    YOU SAY I SHOULD DROWN MY GIRL. ....LESBOS 228   21
    YOU SAY YOUR HUSBAND IS JUST NO GOOD TO YOU. ....LESBOS 228   26
    I SAY I MAY BE BACK. ....LESBOS 230   90
    I GUESS YOU COULD SAY I'VE A CALL. ....LADY LAZARUS 245   48
    WELL WHAT, THEN? THAT'S THE TROUBLE. LET'S SAY HE ....DIALOGUE O. 278   51
    TO SAY THAT. THAT MUST BE HIS: HIS WORD. YOU SEE, ...DIALOGUE O. 278   79
    TEDIOUS. THAT'S WHAT WE'D SAY. ABOUT ROT*DIALOGUE OVER A OUIJA BOARD 279 101
    THESE GIFTS ARE GIVEN. AND WHEN WITHHELD, YOU'LL SAY ...DIALOGUE O. 279 126
    YOU SAY HE'S TOLD TWO LIES . . . CALL THEM TWO PLUCKED DIALOGUE O. 283 266
    CHANCES TO MASTER MINE. THEY SAY THE THIRD TIME ....DIALOGUE O. 283 270
    WE HEARD THE HEAD WOMAN SAY, ...BITTER STRAWBERRIES 299   5
    ALL RIGHT, LET'S SAY YOU COULD TAKE A SKULL AND BREAK IT*SONNET:EVA. 304   1
    WHILE STRICKEN PATIENTS LET HIM HAVE HIS SAY: ..NEVER TRY TO TRICK. 320   8
    THERE IS NOTHING MORE FOR ME TO SAY. ....DENOUEMENT 326   3
    THERE IS NOTHING MORE FOR ME TO SAY. ....DENOUEMENT 326   9
    THERE IS NOTHING MORE FOR ME TO SAY. ....DENOUEMENT 327   15
    THERE IS NOTHING MORE FOR ME TO SAY. ....DENOUEMENT 327   19
    SAY HOW CRAFTY THE PAINTER WAS ..BLACK PINE TREE IN AN ORANGE LIGHT 328   17
    THE OCEAN IN ONE GULP: YOU SAY A MARK ....LOVE IS A PARALLAX 329   28
SAYING (5)
    SAYING: "SOMETHING'S ADDLED IN A WOMAN WHO ACCOMMODATES ...
              ... ELLA MASON AND HER ELEVEN CATS   53   5
    SHE DOES NOT HEAR WHAT THE SAILOR OR THE PEASANT IS SAYING -- ...
                                  ... FINISTERRE 170   26
    MASS AFTER MASS, SAYING SHH! ....THE SWARM 216   10
    FEET SEEM TO BE SAYING: ....EDGE 272   7
    WILL PUNISH US FOR SAYING WHICH IS WHICH; *METAMORPHOSES OF THE MOON 308   44
SAYS (13)
    LOAM-HUMPS, HE SAYS, MOLES SHUNT ....ODE FOR TED   29   7
    I AM YOUNG AS EVER, IT SAYS. WHAT IS IT I MISS? ....THREE WOMEN 186 350
    I KNOW THE BOTTOM, SHE SAYS. I KNOW IT WITH MY GREAT TAP ROOT: ELM 192   1
    SAYS THERE ARE A DOZEN OR TWO. ....DADDY 223   21
    SAYS SHE IS A MAN, NOT A WOMAN. ....THE FEARFUL 256   4
    DAWN SAYS, WITH ITS BLOOD-FLUSH. ....TOTEM 264   23
    SUGAR CAN CURE EVERYTHING, SO KINDNESS SAYS. ....KINDNESS 269   9
    I-N-E, HE SAYS. YOU FEEL HIM PULL ......DIALOGUE OVER A OUIJA BOARD 277   32
    TO YES SAYS HE IS READY. PAN, IS THERE DIALOGUE OVER A OUIJA BOARD 278   71
    THE TELEGRAM SAYS YOU HAVE GONE AWAY ....DENOUEMENT 326   1
    THE TELEGRAM SAYS YOU HAVE GONE AWAY. ....DENOUEMENT 326   6
    THE TELEGRAM SAYS YOU HAVE GONE AWAY. ....DENOUEMENT 327   12
    THE TELEGRAM SAYS YOU HAVE GONE AWAY; ....DENOUEMENT 327   18
SCABBARD (1)
    IN A SCABBARD OF WOOD BAFFLES PURSUERS, ...VIRGIN IN A TREE   81   8
SCAFFOLD (1)
    ELABORATE SCAFFOLD OF SKY OVERHEAD ....AERIALIST 332   47
SCALD (1)
    THE SCALD SCAR OF WATER, ...DEATH & CO. 254   7
SCALDED (2)
    THE SCALDED SHEET IS A SNOWFIELD, FROZEN AND PEACEFUL. ....SURGEON. 170   5
    THE LINES OF THE EYE, SCALDED BY THESE BALD SURFACES, ..BERCK-PLAGE 196   10
SCALDING (2)
    OVER THE SCALDING, RED TOPOGRAPHY ....WIDOW 164   4
    OBSCURE THE SCALDING SUN TILL NO CLOCKS MOVE. ......SONNET TO SATAN 323   14
SCALE (2)
    PACKING WITHOUT A COMPASS OR SCALE ...SONG FOR A REVOLUTIONARY LOVE 323   10
    HAND IN HAND, THEY SCALE MERIDIAN, ...THE PRINCESS AND THE GOBLINS 334   54
SCALED (1)
    THEN BRISKLY SCALED HIS ALTAR TIERED WITH TETHERED ANTS, ...SPIDER   49   22

TITLE PAGE LINE

SCALES (3)
 ODDLY WOODEN IN SPITE OF SCALES ....THE DISQUIETING MUSES 75 36
 BUT FINS AND SCALES ....BATTLE-SCENE 84 21
 LAYING ITS SCALES ON THE WINDOWS, THE WINDOWS OF EMPTY OFFICES, ...
   ... THREE WOMEN 181 178
SCALE-SHEEN (1)
 THE SCALE-SHEEN ON THE SAND SCARED ME TO DEATH. ....LESBOS 229 59
SCALING (1)
 SCALING LITTLE LADDERS WITH GLUEPOTS AND PAILS OF LYSOL*THE COLOSSUS 129 11
SCALLOPS (2)
 SCALLOPS, PURE IRON, ...LETTER IN NOVEMBER 253 20
 WITH ORANGE SCALLOPS TANGLED IN WET HAIR, ...MIDSUMMER MOBILE 324 11
SCALP (1)
 THE INDIAN'S AXED YOUR SCALP. ....CUT 235 10
SCALPELS (1)
 FROM THE SCALPELS AND THE RUBBER HANDS. ......THE SURGEON AT 2 A.M. 170 4
SCANDAL (1)
 SOME SCANDAL MIGHT ANY MINUTE OOZE ....AFTERMATH 113 4
SCANS (1)
 ALOOF, SQUATTING MUMMY-WISE, GERD SCANS ....CRYSTAL GAZER 55 28
SCANT (4)
 FOR HIS LEAST LOOK, SCANT ACRES YEILD: ....ODE FOR TED 29 13
 NOR SCANT HIS WANT UNTIL ....THE GLUTTON 40 13
 THOUGH I COUNTED SCANT SECONDS, ...MUSSEL HUNTER AT ROCK HARBOR 95 21
 THE INSECTS ARE SCANT, SKINNY. ....FROG AUTUMN 99 2
SCAPEGOAT (2)
 SCAPEGOAT. BUT SO THIN, ...THE THIN PEOPLE 64 22
 IN EIGHT GREAT BOUNDS, A GREAT SCAPEGOAT. ....STINGS 215 41
SCAR (5)
 ASKEW WITH BLOTCH, DINT, SCAR ....STRUMPET SONG 33 12
 THIN AS THE SKIN SEAMING A SCAR. ....PARLIAMENT HILL FIELDS 153 39
 IS THIS THE ELECT ONE, THE ONE WITH BLACK EYE-PITS AND A SCAR? ...
   ... A BIRTHDAY PRESENT 206 6
 SCAR IN THE SKY, RED COMET ....STINGS 215 58
 THE SCALD SCAR OF WATER, ...DEATH & CO. 254 7
SCARCELY (3)
 SCARCELY VISIBLE. ABOUT AND ABOUT THE SLOPE ....SPIDER 48 14
 AND SHE COULD SCARCELY MAKE OUT ANYTHING*TWO VIEWS OF A CADAVER ROOM 114 7
 THE EYES OF THE CHILD I NURSE ARE SCARCELY OPEN. ....CANDLES 149 28
SCARED (5)
 SCARED MOTHERS TO MISCARRY, ...THE DEATH OF MYTH-MAKING 104 12
 AND I WAS SCARED, BECAUSE SHE WAS SHAPED JUST THE WAY I WAS *PLASTER 158 7
 SCARED AND BARE ON THE GREEN PLASTIC-PILLOWED TROLLEY ....TULIPS 161 25
 I HAVE ALWAYS BEEN SCARED OF YOU, ...DADDY 223 41
 THE SCALE-SHEEN ON THE SAND SCARED ME TO DEATH. ....LESBOS 229 59
SCARF (3)
 WHIPPING OFF YOUR SILK SCARF, EXHIBITING THE TIGHT WHITE FACE LIFT 155 2
 ONE SCARF WILL CATCH AND ANCHOR IN THE WHEEL. ....FEVER. 231 13
 THE RAW WIND LIKE A SCARF: LOVE IS A FAUN ....LOVE IS A PARALLAX 329 23
SCARLET (3)
 NO, NO, IT IS SCARLET FLOWERS THAT WILL ONE DAY BE EDIBLE. ......BEE. 211 20
 THE PRINCE LEANS TO THE GIRL IN SCARLET HEELS, ...CINDERELLA 303 1
 THE SCARLET WOUND. ....ON LOOKING INTO THE EYES OF A DEMON LOVER 325 16
SCARLET-SPECKLED (1)
 A GARDEN OF MOUTHINGS. PURPLE, SCARLET-SPECKLED, BLACK *BEEKEEPER'S. 118 1
SCARS (1)
 FOR THE EYEING OF MY SCARS, THERE IS A CHARGE ....LADY LAZARUS 246 58
SCAR'S (1)
 WHAT SCAR'S BEEN KNOCKED ....TINKER JACK AND THE TIDY WIVES 34 23
SCARVES (2)
 SMOKE ROLLS AND SCARVES IN THE GROVE. ....THE BEE MEETING 212 36
 FROM ME LIKE ISADORA'S SCARVES, I'M IN A FRIGHT ....FEVER. 231 12
SCATH (1)
 "WHATEVER SCATH ....TINKER JACK AND THE TIDY WIVES 34 19
SCATHED (1)
 SCATHED, STAINED AFTER TEDIOUS PILGRIMAGES. DREAM WITH CLAM-DIGGERS 43 4
SCATHES (1)
 HER RADIANCE SCATHES ME. OR PERHAPS I HAVE CAUGHT HER. ....ELM 192 24
SCATTER (1)
 SCATTER SMUG ANGELS WITH YOUR HAND. ..SONG FOR A REVOLUTIONARY LOVE 322 4
SCATTERING (1)
 SCATTERING CANDY FROM A ZEPPELIN, ...LOVE IS A PARALLAX 329 35
SCAVENGING (1)
 SIZE. THE CRIES OF SCAVENGING GULLS SOUND THIN ....GREEN ROCK. 105 14
SCENE (6)
 THIS GIANT HULKED, I TELL YOU, ON HER SCENE ..THE QUEEN'S COMPLAINT 28 2
 THE WHOLE SCENE FLARED WELCOME TO THIS ROAMER. ....DREAM WITH C. 44 12
 THE SCENE STANDS STUBBORN: SKINFLINT TREES ......NOVEMBER GRAVEYARD 56 1
 SOME PALTRY SCENE ON THE SOUP-KITCHEN STAIR: ....DIALOGUE O. 279 125
 TO ASSAULT THE SCENE AND MAKE SOME *MORNING IN THE HOSPITAL SOLARIUM 333 24
 WHY HE SHOULD KNEEL BEFORE A SILLY SCENE ....THE PRINCESS. 335 65
SCENERY (5)
 OF STATE SCENERY, SELLS SODA, SHOWS OFF VIEWPOINTS. *ABOVE THE OXBOW 88 41
 PROFITED MEMORY, BUT DID AWAY WITH THE OLD SCENERY .....GREEN ROCK. 105 5
 THE BENT PRINT BULGING BEFORE HIM LIKE SCENERY. ....BERCK-PLAGE 197 23

SCENERY (CONT.)
    WRITHING AND SIGHING, WHAT SORT OF A SCENERY IS IT? ...STOPPED DEAD   230   9
    HOW THEY'LL TRAVEL, TRAVEL, TRAVEL, SCENERY ....AMNESIAC   233   17
SCENES (2)
    OUR PAINTED STAGES FALL APART BY SCENES ....DOOMSDAY   316   4
    TO CALL FOR CURTAIN ON OUR THOUSAND SCENES; .....LOVE IS A PARALLAX   330   44
SCENT (1)
    EXHALE THEIR PALLOR LIKE SCENT. ....BARREN WOMAN   157   5
SCENTLESS (1)
    THE GREAT ROSES, MANY OF THEM SCENTLESS, ..QUEEN MARY'S ROSE GARDEN   290   4
SCENTS (2)
    A WELL OF SCENTS ALMOST TOO DENSE TO BREATHE IN. ......BEEKEEPER'S.   118   4
    DRUNK ON ITS OWN SCENTS, ...PARALYTIC   267   39
SCHEMES (1)
    IN SOLAR SCHEMES THE TILTED SUNS GO TURNING; ....TO EVA DESCENDING.   303   11
SCHIZOPHRENIC (1)
    WHY SHE IS SCHIZOPHRENIC, ...LESBOS   227   10
SCHOOL (2)
    THIS IS A DULL SCHOOL. POEM.1.WHO.   132   22
    THE BLUE SISTERS SENT ME TO ANOTHER SCHOOL. POEM.4.BEAST.   134   7
SCHOOLGIRL (1)
    AS A SCHOOLGIRL SHE GAVE ROSES TO FRANZ JOSEF. ....CANDLES   149   18
SCHOOLGIRLS (1)
    WHEN ON TIPTOE THE SCHOOLGIRLS DANCED, ...THE DISQUIETING MUSES   75   25
SCHOOLROOMS (1)
    EMPTY SCHOOLROOMS, EMPTY CHURCHES. O SO MUCH EMPTINESS! *THREE WOMEN   181 179
SCHOONER (2)
    WITH GREEN ROCK GLIDING, A DELICATE SCHOONER*DREAM WITH CLAM-DIGGERS   44   17
    SEURAT: FLECK SCHOONER FLANKS WITH SUN AND SET ....MIDSUMMER MOBILE   324   5
SCINTILLANT (1)
    SCINTILLANT IRONY INSPIRES .....INSOLENT STORM STRIKES AT THE SKULL   326   33
SCISSORS (1)
    TO GRIND OUR KNIVES AND SCISSORS: ....THE DEATH OF MYTH-MAKING   104   2
SCOFF (5)
    SO, YOU'LL SCOFF, AND YET YOU'D DROP TO KNEEL ....DIALOGUE O.   280 156
    THE DYING MAN WILL SCOFF IN SCORN AT THIS. .....NEVER TRY TO TRICK.   319   3
    THE DYING MAN WILL SCOFF IN SCORN AT THIS. .....NEVER TRY TO TRICK.   320   9
    THE DYING MAN WILL SCOFF IN SCORN AT THIS. .....NEVER TRY TO TRICK.   320   15
    THE DYING MAN WILL SCOFF IN SCORN AT THIS. .....NEVER TRY TO TRICK.   320   19
SCOLDINGS (1)
    BY SCOLDINGS, OR BY SUBTLE PRAISE. ONLY I, ...DIALOGUE O.   280 144
SCOOPED (1)
    ELECTRIFYINGLY-COLORED SHERBETS, SCOOPED FROM THE FREEZE*BERCK-PLAGE   196   3
SCOOPED-OUT (1)
    IN THE WHORL OF HER EAR, AND LIKE A SCOOPED-OUT PUMPKIN CROWN ...
                                            ... HARDCASTLE CRAGS   63   24
SCOOTING (1)
    WHEN ATTACKED, THEN SCOOTING TO REST, BARELY TREMBLING. ...BALLOONS   271   8
SCORCH (2)
    THAT WILL KINDLE ANGELS' ENVY, SCORCH AND DROP ......EPITAPH FOR F.   45   6
    WITH TRIANGULAR SCORCH MARKS FROM IRONING TINY RUCHINGS AND
        PUFFED SLEEVES. ....THE BABYSITTERS   174   15
SCORCHED (4)
    SCORCHED BY RED SUN ....FIRESONG   30   17
    HANGING FROM THEIR SCORCHED HOOKS IN THE MOIST ...ZOO KEEPER'S WIFE   155   18
    SCORCHED TO THE ROOT ....ELM   192   17
    BY PALE GIRLS, TRAVEL THE AIR IN SCORCHED HANDS. ....BERCK-PLAGE   196   4
SCORCHING (2)
    THE SCORCHING SUN: ....MOONSONG AT MORNING   317   38
    IN THE SCORCHING GLASS, ..ON LOOKING INTO THE EYES OF A DEMON LOVER   325   18
SCORN (7)
    HOWEVER THE GRANDILOQUENT MIND MAY SCORN ....NOVEMBER GRAVEYARD   56   5
    OF FORMAL SCORN, UNTIL THE FIRST SIGN OF AN ....DIALOGUE O.   282 232
    WE VAUNT OUR DAYS IN NEON AND SCORN THE DARK. ......SONNET: TO TIME   311   4
    THE DYING MAN WILL SCOFF IN SCORN AT THIS. .....NEVER TRY TO TRICK.   319   3
    THE DYING MAN WILL SCOFF IN SCORN AT THIS. .....NEVER TRY TO TRICK.   320   9
    THE DYING MAN WILL SCOFF IN SCORN AT THIS. .....NEVER TRY TO TRICK.   320   15
    THE DYING MAN WILL SCOFF IN SCORN AT THIS. .....NEVER TRY TO TRICK.   320   19
SCORNED (4)
    AND SCORNED THE TICK OF THE FALLING WEATHER. ....LAMENT   315   3
    AND SCORNED THE TICK OF THE FALLING WEATHER. ....LAMENT   315   9
    AND SCORNED THE TICK OF THE FALLING WEATHER. ....LAMENT   315   15
    WHO SCORNED THE TICK OF THE FALLING WEATHER. ....LAMENT   316   19
SCORNING (1)
    AN ORANGE CYCLOPS-EYE, SCORNING TO LOOK ....WINTER LANDSCAPE,   21   7
SCORPION (1)
    A SCORPION STUNG ITS HEAD, AN ILL-STARRED THING; ....ELECTRA ON.   117   35
SCOURGING (1)
    SCOURGING TO SORES HIS OWN RED SLUICES ....A LESSON IN VENGEANCE   80   13
SCOUR (1)
    TO SCOUR THE CREAMING CRESTS ....STINGS   215   36
SCOURED (1)
    OVER SCOURED POLAND, BURNT-OUT ....MARY'S SONG/DR   294   1
SCOURS (2)
    GOOD OF THE CAPE LIGHT THAT SCOURS ....MUSSEL HUNTER AT ROCK HARBOR   95   3

	TITLE	PAGE	LINE

SCOURS (CONT.)
AS THE MOON, FOR ITS IVORY POWDERS, SCOURS THE SEA. ....STINGS 215 37
SCOWL (1)
A SCOWL OF SUN STRUCK DOWN MY MOTHER, ...LAMENT 315 10
SCRABBLE (1)
HEARD A QUEER CRUSTY SCRABBLE ....MUSSEL HUNTER AT ROCK HARBOR 95 14
SCRABBLING (1)
AND OCTOPUS -- SCRABBLING JUST BEYOND THE VIEW, ...TALE OF A TUB 25 20
SCRAGGLY (1)
WHOSE OWL-EYES IN THE SCRAGGLY WOOD ....THE DEATH OF MYTH-MAKING 104 11
SCRAGGY (1)
THE SCRAGGY ROCK SPIT SHIELDING THE TOWN'S BLUE BAY ......DEPARTURE 51 13
SCRAPE (1)
NO LONGER DO I LISTEN FOR THE SCRAPE OF A KEEL ....THE COLOSSUS 130 29
SCRAPED (1)
SCRAPED FLAT BY THE ROLLER ....DADDY 222 17
SCRAPPED (1)
NOTHING THAT CANNOT BE ERASED, RIPPED UP AND SCRAPPED,
BEGUN AGAIN. ....THREE WOMEN 184 277
SCRAPS (4)
INCOHERENT SCRAPS OF TALK ....FAMILY REUNION 300 3
THE SCRAPS OF RUSTED REVERIE, THE WHEELS ....SONNET: TO EVA 305 10
ELEMENTS LIKE DIRTY SOCKS AND SCRAPS .....METAMORPHOSES OF THE MOON 307 28
SEND MY MUSE ALICE PACKING WITH GAUDY SCRAPS ....A SORCERER B. 324 7
SCRATCH (2)
I SCRATCH LIKE A CAT. ....THE OTHER 202 28
ONE MATCH SCRATCH MAKES YOU REAL. ....BY CANDLELIGHT 236 15
SCRATCHED (1)
TO BE SCRATCHED ABSENTLY, ...EAVESDROPPER 260 5
SCRATCHING (2)
SCRATCHING AT MY SLEEP LIKE ARROWS, ...THREE WOMEN 182 214
SCRATCHING AT MY SLEEP, AND ENTERING MY SIDE. ....THREE WOMEN 182 215
SCRAWLED (1)
AND PROFANE WORDS SCRAWLED BLACK ACROSS THE SUN. ....DOOM OF EXILES 318 12
SCREAM (2)
SUN'S PARCHED SCREAM, ...STREET SONG 36 26
NO FALLING RIBBONS, NO SCREAM AT THE END. ....A BIRTHDAY PRESENT 207 35
SCREAMING (2)
WITH A GODDAM BABY SCREAMING OFF SOMEWHERE. ....STOPPED DEAD 230 12
THE TRAIN IS DRAGGING ITSELF, IT IS SCREAMING --- ....GETTING THERE 249 55
SCREAMS (1)
THE LAUGHTER AND THE SCREAMS OF GREETING: ....FAMILY REUNION 300 12
SCREECH (1)
OF TWO WET EYES AND A SCREECH. ....THALIDOMIDE 252 20
SCREEN (2)
HANGING THEIR BLUEGREEN BELLIES AND THEIR WING PANES IN A CHINESE
SCREEN. ....BLACKBERRYING 168 16
THEIR PASSING ON A PERISHABLE SCREEN ...DIALOGUE OVER A OUIJA BOARD 282 223
SCREENING (1)
THEY'D HAVE HAD YELLOW SILK SCREENING THE MOON, ...YADWIGHA. 85 15
SCREENS (2)
FLATTEN TO PARCHMENT SCREENS TO KEEP THE WIND OFF. .....THREE WOMEN 179 97
SCREENS, THESE RUSTLING APPURTENANCES. ....PURDAH 243 23
SCREW (1)
AND A LOVE OF THE RACK AND THE SCREW. ....DADDY 224 66
SCRIM (3)
SCRIM AFTER SCRIM LIKE FISHNETS ....LORELEI 94 5
SCRIM AFTER SCRIM LIKE FISHNETS ....LORELEI 94 5
SCRIM OF A SEA BREEZE, THE WOMEN ....HEAVY WOMEN 158 4
SCROLL (1)
SNAILS SCROLL THE BORDER ....DARK WOOD, DARK WATER 127 8
SCROLLED (1)
OF EACH SCROLLED SEA-BEAST ....BATTLE-SCENE 84 22
SCROLLS (1)
FLOWS IN THE SCROLLS OF HER TOGA, ...EDGE 272 5
SCRUBBED (1)
THEY ARE SCRUBBED AND SELF-ASSURED AS THE GREAT PLANETS. ....STARS. 165 16
SCRUBNURSE (1)
PENBEARER, SCRUBNURSE, ...WORDS FOR A NURSERY 74 36
SCRUPLE (2)
NOW SPEAK SOME SACRAMENT TO PARRY SCRUPLE ......WREATH FOR A BRIDAL 44 11
NO SCRUPLE COULD DISRUPT, ...SPIDER 49 31
SCRUPULOUS (2)
AND THAT DAMN SCRUPULOUS TREE WON'T PRACTICE WILES ......CONJURING. 66 20
THROUGH THE SCRUPULOUS TELESCOPE .........METAMORPHOSES OF THE MOON 308 39
SCRUPULOUSLY (4)
BUT SCRUPULOUSLY REFLECTS THE USUAL TERROR. ....TALE OF A TUB 24 8
SCRUPULOUSLY AUSTERE IN ITS ORDER ....SPINSTER 49 14
WILL SCRUPULOUSLY RISE AND SET; ....TWO LOVERS. 327 22
TRAILING HER SCRUPULOUSLY SIMPLE GOWN THE PRINCESS AND THE GOBLINS 333 11
SCRUTINIZING (1)
SCRUTINIZING THE FLY ................................EAVESDROPPER 261 57
SCULPTED (1)
THAN SCULPTED MARBLE. THEY SING ....LORELEI 94 14

426

SCULPTOR (1)
   SCULPTOR ....SCULPTOR   91   T
SCULPTURE (1)
   REPOSE OF SCULPTURE HOLDS THE COUNTRY STILL. ....PROLOGUE TO SPRING 322   9
SCUM (1)
   FOR THE ROCK'S DWARFED LUMP, FOR THE DRABBLED SCUM, ...GREEN ROCK. 105   23
SCURRY (1)
   THESE WOMEN WHO ONLY SCURRY, ...STINGS   214   29
SCUTTLE (2)
   SCUTTLE REPOSE WITH CROWNS AND CACKLES. ....ALICANTE LULLABY   43   7
   YOU SCUTTLE OUT ON IMPULSE ....SPIDER   48   2
SCUTTLED (1)
   BUT FATLY SCUTTLED INTO THE SPLAYED FERN .............INCOMMUNICADO 100   2
SCYTHE (1)
   BOLD BEANSTALK: LIE AND LOVE TILL SHARP SCYTHE HACKS *LOVE IS A PAR. 330   71
SEA (82)
   THE AUTHENTIC SEA DENIES THEM AND WILL PLUCK ....TALE OF A TUB   25   23
   THE ENVIOUS ASSAULTS OF SEA ....LETTER TO A PURIST   36   3
   AGAINST WHICH THE BRUNT OF OUTER SEA ....DEPARTURE   51   14
   TIRELESS, TIED, AS A MOON-BOUND SEA ....HARDCASTLE CRAGS   62   12
   SWIM THE SEA OF DO. ....WORDS FOR A NURSERY   74   33
   WITH VOICES OF THAT AMBIGUOUS SEA ....ON THE DECLINE OF ORACLES   78   4
   TO HEAR THE SEA HE COULD NOT HEAR. ......ON THE DECLINE OF ORACLES   78   6
   THE BOOKS BURNED UP, SEA TOOK THE SHELL,   ON THE DECLINE OF ORACLES   78   11
   THAT REPRESENT A SEA ....BATTLE-SCENE   84   6
   DUNGAREES, PROUD AS A LADY IN A SEA ....MEMOIRS OF A SPINACH-PICKER   90   18
   A WHOLE SEA OF SPINACH-HEADS LEANED TO MY HAND. ....SPINACH-PICKER.   90   22
   RAVEL TO CLEARNESS ON THE DAWN SEA. ....FULL FATHOM FIVE   93   20
   OF SEA RETRACING ITS TIDE- ....MUSSEL HUNTER AT ROCK HARBOR   96   43
   ART'S SAKE THAN GOD'S. FAR FROM SEA -- *MUSSEL HUNTER AT ROCK HARBOR   97   82
   THE BLACK BULL BELLOWED BEFORE THE SEA. ....THE BULL OF BENDYLAW 108   1
   THE SEA, TILL THAT DAY ORDERLY, ...THE BULL OF BENDYLAW   108   2
   A BLUE SEA, FOUR HORNY BULL-FEET, ...THE BULL OF BENDYLAW 108   7
   A BULL-SNOUTED SEA THAT WOULDN'T STAY PUT, ...THE BULL OF BENDYLAW 108   8
   THE SEA BROKE IN AT EVERY CRACK, ...THE BULL OF BENDYLAW   108   14
   O THE KING'S TIDY ACRE IN UNDER THE SEA, ...THE BULL OF BENDYLAW 108   19
   AWAY TO THE LEFT LIKE REEDS IN A SEA ....THE EYE-MOTE   109   8
   WHAT THE SLUTTISH, RUTTED SEA COULD DO. ....POINT SHIRLEY   110   12
   THE SEA IN ITS COLD GIZZARD GROUND THOSE ROUNDS. .....POINT SHIRLEY 110   24
   STEADILY THE SEA ....POINT SHIRLEY   110   35
   A DOG-FACED SEA. ....POINT SHIRLEY   111   39
   AGAINST BOTH BAR AND TOWER THE BLACK SEA RUNS. ....POINT SHIRLEY 111   48
   THE SEA PULSES UNDER A SKIN OF OIL. ....A WINTER SHIP   112   5
   HE, AFLOAT IN THE SEA OF HER BLUE SATIN *TWO VIEWS OF A CADAVER ROOM 114   14
   THE FLAT SEA PURPLED LIKE THAT EVIL CLOTH ...ELECTRA ON AZALEA PATH 117   31
   MY MOTHER DREAMED YOU FACE DOWN IN THE SEA.   ELECTRA ON AZALEA PATH 117   36
   SKY AND SEA, HORIZON-HINGED ....THE HERMIT AT OUTERMOST HOUSE 118   1
   AND SUCK OF THE GRAY SEA ....MAN IN BLACK 119   3
   THE MOON LEANS, A STONE MADONNA, OVER THE LEAD SEA   THE NET-MENDERS 121   15
   THOUGH THE GREEN SEA GARDENS STALL, ...MAGNOLIA SHOALS 121   6
   AT THEIR FEET, THE SEA WAVES BOW IN SINGLE FILE, ...A LIFE 150   11
   THE OBSOLETE HOUSE, THE SEA, FLATTENED TO A PICTURE ....A LIFE 150   27
   CRAWLS UP OUT OF THE SEA. ....A LIFE 150   35
   NOISELESS, ON RUBBER WHEELS, ON THE WAY TO THE SEA RESORT. WAKING.   151   8
   OR THE SEA, HUSHING THEIR PEELED SENSE LIKE OLD MOTHER MORPHIA. ...
                                         ... WAKING IN WINTER 151   16
   AT OUR FEET, THE WEED-MUSTACHIOED SEA ....WHITSUN 154   14
   PEEL OFF TO SEA AS GULLS DO, ...WHITSUN 154   20
   A FAR SEA MOVES IN MY EAR. ....MORNING SONG 157   12
   SCRIM OF A SEA BREEZE, THE WOMEN ....HEAVY WOMEN 158   4
   THE WATER I TASTE IS WARM AND SALT, LIKE THE SEA, ...TULIPS 162   62
   A BLACKBERRY ALLEY, GOING IN HOOKS, AND A SEA ...BLACKBERRYING   168   3
   I DO NOT THINK THE SEA WILL APPEAR AT ALL. ..........BLACKBERRYING   168   13
   THE ONLY THING TO COME NOW IS THE SEA. .............BLACKBERRYING   169   19
   ADMONITORY CLIFFS, AND THE SEA EXPLODING ....FINISTERRE   169   3
   THE SEA CANNONS INTO THEIR EAR, BUT THEY DON'T BUDGE. ..FINISTERRE   169   8
   SOULS, ROLLED IN THE DOOM-NOISE OF THE SEA. ....FINISTERRE   169   14
   SHE IS IN LOVE WITH THE BEAUTIFUL FORMLESSNESS OF THE SEA. ...
                                             ... FINISTERRE 170   27
   GULL-COLORED LACES FLAP IN THE SEA DRAFTS ....FINISTERRE   170   28
   "THESE ARE THE PRETTY TRINKETS THE SEA HIDES, ...FINISTERRE   170   31
   IT DRAGS THE SEA AFTER IT LIKE A DARK CRIME; IT IS QUIET .....MOON. 173   10
   LIKE A BIG SEA. FAR OFF, FAR OFF, I FEEL THE FIRST WAVE TUG   THREE. 179 109
   IT IS SHE THAT DRAGS THE BLOOD-BLACK SEA AROUND ....THREE WOMEN 182 186
   I AM HELPLESS AS THE SEA AT THE END OF HER STRING. .....THREE WOMEN 182 188
   IS IT THE SEA YOU HEAR IN ME, ...ELM   192   4
   TEARING OFF MY VOICE, AND THE SEA ....THE RABBIT CATCHER 193   3
   THIS IS THE SEA, THEN, THIS GREAT ABEYANCE. ....BERCK-PLAGE   196   1
   THE SEA, THAT CRYSTALLIZED THESE, ...BERCK-PLAGE   196   17
   THE GRAY SKY LOWERS, THE HILLS LIKE A GREEN SEA ....BERCK-PLAGE   199   73
   FEATHER DUSTERS FANNING THEIR HANDS IN A SEA OF BEAN FLOWERS, BEE.   211   17
   AS THE MOON, FOR ITS IVORY POWDERS, SCOURS THE SEA. ....STINGS   215   37
   ELBA, ELBA, BLEB ON THE SEA! ....THE SWARM 217   43
   YOU STEAMED TO ME OVER THE SEA, ...MEDUSA   225   24
   THAT OPENS TO THE SEA ....LESBOS 229   74

	TITLE	PAGE	LINE

SEA (CONT.)
OR AN ANEMONE, THAT SEA ....LESBOS 229 87
SEA OF HIS EYES WASHING OVER IT ....LYONNESSE 234 7
THE SEA SHATTERING ITS GRAY ONE --- ....THE COURIERS 247 12
SHRIEK IN THE SEA AND I ....GIGOLO 268 27
DOES THE SEA ....MYSTIC 269 25
THE SEA SUCKS OBSESSIVELY, ...CONTUSION 271 5
THE SEA SLIDES BACK, ...CONTUSION 271 11
A SEA OF DREAMS WASHES THE EDGE OF MY GREEN ISLAND ...QUEEN MARY'S. 290 2
THE SEA, ALSO, IS INEFFECTUAL. ....THE RIVAL/DR 291 15
WITH THE SOUND OF THE SEA IN YOUR MOUTH. ....THE RIVAL/DR 291 19
THE MEANINGLESS CRY OF BABIES. SUCH A SEA ....FEVER./DR 294 4
BESIDE A SUNBLUE SEA, AND MOURN THE FLAGON ......SONNET: TO TIME 311 10
TROUNCING THE SEA LIKE A RAGING BATHER, ...LAMENT 315 7
TWO LOVERS AND A BEACHCOMBER BY THE REAL SEA ....TWO LOVERS. 327 T
ROCKING ACROSS THE LAPIS LAZULI SEA ....EPITAPH IN THREE PARTS 337 1
SEA-BEAST (1)
OF EACH SCROLLED SEA-BEAST ....BATTLE-SCENE 84 22
SEA-BOTTOM (1)
ON MOOR-TOP, AT SEA-BOTTOM, ...THE GREAT CARBUNCLE 72 14
SEA-CHANGE (1)
NO SEA-CHANGE DECKS THE SUNKEN SHANK OF BONE ....TWO LOVERS. 327 17
SEA-COLD (2)
SEA-COLD, SEA-COLD IT CERTAINLY IS. ....LYONNESSE 233 2
SEA-COLD, SEA-COLD IT CERTAINLY IS. ....LYONNESSE 233 2
SEA-CROCKERY (1)
O WHITE SEA-CROCKERY, ...BERCK-PLAGE 197 31
SEA-DRAGON (1)
SEA-DRAGON FOR SOFA, FANG ....BATTLE-SCENE 85 36
SEAFARER (2)
FROM THE COMIC OPERATIC FANTASY THE SEAFARER ....BATTLE-SCENE 84 ST
BEAR UP THE SEAFARER, ...BATTLE-SCENE 84 8
SEAGREEN (1)
FOUNDERED THROUGH LEVELS OF LIGHT SEAGREEN AND STRANGE. OTHER TWO. 68 5
SEAGULL (1)
THE FUTURE IS A GRAY SEAGULL ....A LIFE 150 31
SEAL (2)
I MUST SEAL OFF AND LET FILL ....THE SURGEON AT 2 A.M. 171 25
BIG AS A FRISCO SEAL ....DADDY 222 10
SEALED (2)
ACETIC ACID IN A SEALED TIN? ....THE COURIERS 247 3
SUCH SKEPTIC CRACKS. WITH SENSE SEALED WATERTIGHT ......DIALOGUE O. 280 155
SEALING (1)
SEALING OFF HER BROOD CELLS, HER HONEY, AND QUIETLY HUMMING. ..BEE. 212 35
SEALS (1)
A SUPERHIGHWAY SEALS ME OFF. ....PRIVATE GROUND 130 15
SEAMED (2)
THAT SEAMED FACE ....STRUMPET SONG 33 11
FISTED TO A FOETUS HEAD, RAVINED, SEAMED ....PERSEUS 83 25
SEAMING (1)
THIN AS THE SKIN SEAMING A SCAR. ....PARLIAMENT HILL FIELDS 153 39
SEARCHING (1)
SEARCHING MY REACHES FOR WHAT SHE REALLY IS. ....MIRROR 174 11
SEARS (1)
IN A SMOKE THAT SEARS MY EYES. ....CIRCUS IN THREE RINGS 322 18
SEAS (8)
NAVIGATES THE TIDAL SLOSH OF SEAS ....TALE OF A TUB 25 44
SHOWS, RANK ON RANK, THE HUNGRY SEAS ADVANCING. ...CHANNEL CROSSING 26 8
THE SEVEN TROUGHED SEAS AND EVERY EARTHQUAKING CONTINENT. ......SOW 61 45
FIRELESS, SEVEN CHILL SEAS CHAINED TO HIS ANKLE. EVERLASTING MONDAY 62 12
INTO SALT SEAS. HERCULES HAD A SIMPLE TIME, ...PERSEUS 82 6
WHEN SEAS WASH COLD, FOAM- ....FULL FATHOM FIVE 92 3
FOAM TO WHEAT, A GLITTER OF SEAS. ....ARIEL 239 23
ON SOPHIST SEAS TO OVERTAKE THAT MARK ....LOVE IS A PARALLAX 329 5
SEA'S (5)
GRIM AS GARGOYLES FROM YEARS SPENT SQUATTING AT SEA'S BORDER ...
                        ... DREAM WITH CLAM-DIGGERS 44 25
THE SEA'S COLLAPSE. ....POINT SHIRLEY 110 3
HIS BODY BEACHED WITH THE SEA'S GARBAGE, ...SUICIDE OFF EGG ROCK 115 15
EARS CUPPING THE SEA'S INCOHERENCES, ...MEDUSA 224 3
ONE HOLLOW THE WHOLE SEA'S PIVOT. ....CONTUSION 271 6
SEA-SALT (2)
TO LICK THE SEA-SALT. ....DEPARTURE 51 20
THE HOUSES ARE WHITE AS SEA-SALT GOATS LICK FROM THE ROCKS. ..NET-. 121 10
SEASHELL (2)
WHAT THE SEASHELL SPOKE TO HIS INNER EAR   ON THE DECLINE OF ORACLES 78 7
AS A SEASHELL. ....LADY LAZARUS 245 40
SEASICK (1)
SEASICK AND FEVER-DRY. ....WHITSUN 154 24
SEASON (9)
THE WHOLE SEASON, SLOVEN. ....SPINSTER 49 12
MORE MAMMOTH AND BLOWSY WITH EVERY SEASON; ....ELLA MASON A. 54 34
TREKKING STUBBORN THROUGH THIS SEASON ..BLACK ROOK IN RAINY WEATHER 57 33
THAT SEASON HAS TURNED ITS BACK. ....MAGNOLIA SHOALS 121 5
PERHAPS IT IS THE SEASON THAT IS NOT RIGHT. *STARS OVER THE DORDOGNE 165 24

	TITLE	PAGE	LINE

SEASON (CONT.)
  LOVE, LOVE, MY SEASON. ....THE COURIERS 247 13
  AND WE ARE GLAD IN THIS BRIGHT METAL SEASON. ....GOLD MOUTHS CRY 302 8
  DRAMA OF EACH SEASON ....TRIO OF LOVE SONGS 314 13
  WHICH HAS STOPPED THE SEASON IN ITS TRACKS ......PROLOGUE TO SPRING 322 11
SEASONED (1)
  SEASONED HOW HE'D MOST APPROVE; ....THE GLUTTON 40 6
SEASONS (1)
  LEAN FACE GONE TAWN WITH SEASONS, ...CRYSTAL GAZER 54 2
SEAT (1)
  ALOUD, CROSSLEGGED ON THE STERN SEAT, FROM THE GENERATION
        OF VIPERS. .... THE BABYSITTERS 175 32
SEATED (1)
  SEATED BENEATH THE TONELESS WATER! ....THE BURNT-OUT SPA 138 28
SEA-TOWN (1)
  BACK TO HER EARLY SEA-TOWN HOME ....DREAM WITH CLAM-DIGGERS 43 3
SEAWALL (1)
  THE SEAWALL AND DROPS ONTO A BIER ....POINT SHIRLEY 110 6
SEAWARD (1)
  SLOPED SEAWARD TO PLUNGE IN BLUE; FED BY WHITE FIRE, DREAM WITH C. 44 11
SECEDING (1)
  BY SECEDING FROM THE SOLAR SYSTEM. ....INSOLENT STORM. 326 32
SECOND (9)
  BRONZED AS EARTH, THE SECOND LIES, ...TWO SISTERS OF PERSEPHONE 32 13
  EXACTED HER FIRST SIMPLE SIGHT FOR THIS STRICT SECOND.*CRYSTAL GAZER 55 30
  WHERE SECOND WIND, HIP BOOT ....TWO VIEWS OF WITHENS 72 9
  THE SECOND CARCASS MAKES A DUEL OF THE AFFAIR: ....BLUE MOLES 126 8
  A SECOND TIME, TO HAVE HIM NEAR AGAIN -- ....WIDOW 164 16
  WHEN WILL IT BE, THE SECOND WHEN TIME BREAKS ....THREE WOMEN 179 104
  IN THE SECOND YEAR. IT HAD BEEN INSATIABLE ....THE DETECTIVE 209 28
  THE SECOND TIME I MEANT ....LADY LAZARUS 245 37
  THE SECOND SINGS: "RECEIVE NO ROVING GALLANT *EPITAPH IN THREE PARTS 337 7
SECONDS (1)
  THOUGH I COUNTED SCANT SECONDS, ...MUSSEL HUNTER AT ROCK HARBOR 95 21
SECOND'S (1)
  A SECOND'S PAUSE. ....FAMILY REUNION 300 7
SECRET (14)
  APPALLED BY SECRET WANT, I RUSH ....PURSUIT 23 43
  AMONG HER SECRET COMBINATIONS OF EGGSHELLS ....MISS DRAKE P. 41 7
  WHATEVER HIS SHREWD SECRET, HE KEPT IT HID ....SOW 60 3
  FOR FIVE DAYS I LIE IN SECRET, ...FACE LIFT 156 17
  THE DARK STILL NURSES ITS SECRET. ....HEAVY WOMEN 158 11
  BEHIND WHICH THE SECRET PASSAGE LIES -- STALE AIR, ...WIDOW 164 8
  A SECRET ....A SECRET 219 T
  A SECRET! A SECRET! ....A SECRET 219 1
  A SECRET! A SECRET! ....A SECRET 219 1
  THE SECRET IS STAMPED ON YOU, ...A SECRET 219 7
  A SECRET ... AN EXTRA AMBER ....A SECRET 219 17
  THE SECRET IS OUT. ....A SECRET 220 48
  IT'S LIKELY THAT EACH SECRET SOUGHT ......METAMORPHOSES OF THE MOON 307 21
  THE SECRET OF THEIR ECSTASY'S IN GOING; ....LOVE IS A PARALLAX 330 62
SECRETARY (1)
  YES, HERE IS THE SECRETARY OF BEES WITH HER WHITE SHOP SMOCK, BEE. 211 7
SECRETLY (1)
  AND SECRETLY SHE BEGAN TO HOPE I'D DIE. ....IN PLASTER 159 39
SECRETS (2)
  THEY PAINT SUCH SECRETS IN ARABIC, CHINESE! ....THREE WOMEN 179 98
  FOR DEADLY SECRETS STRIKE WHEN UNDERSTOOD ....ADMONITIONS 319 16
SECURE (1)
  SECURE IN MUSEUM DIAMOND FOR THE STARE   EPITAPH FOR FIRE AND FLOWER 45 18
SEDATIVES (1)
  FIZZY WITH SEDATIVES AND UNUSUALLY HUMOROUS, ...FACE LIFT 156 11
SEDUCED (1)
  SEDUCED BY CURIOSITY, ...METAMORPHOSES OF THE MOON 308 33
SEDUCTIVE (1)
  UNDER FLUX OF THOSE SEDUCTIVE ....ON THE PLETHORA OF DRYADS 68 35
SEE (62)
  TO SEE MY PEOPLE SHRUNK SO SMALL, SO SMALL."   THE QUEEN'S COMPLAINT 29 25
  SHE CAN SEE IN THE NICK OF TIME ....MISS DRAKE PROCEEDS TO SUPPER 41 15
  AND SEE THAT FIRST HOUSE, AS IF BETWEEN ....LANDOWNERS 53 6
  "I SEE TWO STALWART APPLE TREES ....CRYSTAL GAZER 55 13
  BATTALIONS. SEE, HOW THE TREE BOLES FLATTEN ....THE THIN PEOPLE 65 43
  "MY TROUBLE, DOCTOR, IS: I SEE A TREE, ...CONJURING. 66 19
  TO SEE WITH THE SPOTLESS SOUL, ...ON THE PLETHORA OF DRYADS 67 14
  I WOKE ONE DAY TO SEE YOU, MOTHER, ...THE DISQUIETING MUSES 75 41
  I SEE HIM, HORNY-SKINNED AND TOUGH, CONSTRUE ....OUIJA 77 27
  ECLIPSING THE SPITTED OX I SEE ....ON THE DECLINE OF ORACLES 78 17
  TO US, SINCE WE SEE NO LEAF EDGE STIR HIGH ....ABOVE THE OXBOW 88 33
  O RIVER, I SEE DRIFTING ....LORELEI 95 33
  IF THEY COULD SEE, I WAS ONE ....MUSSEL HUNTER AT ROCK HARBOR 97 65
  I CAN SEE NO COLOR FOR THIS WHITENESS. ....MOONRISE 98 20
  I SEE HIM ONE-TRACKED, STUBBORN, WHITE HORSE,   WHITENESS I REMEMBER 102 12
  WE WANTED TO SEE THE SUN COME UP ....A WINTER SHIP 113 24
  I SEE BY MY OWN LIGHT. POEM.2.DARK. 132 11
  THIS IS THE AFTER-HELL: I SEE THE LIGHT. POEM.7.S. 136 22

	TITLE	PAGE	LINE

SEE (CONT.)
NOW I SEE IT MUST BE ONE OR THE OTHER OF US. ....IN PLASTER 160 52
AND I SEE MYSELF, FLAT, RIDICULOUS, A CUT-PAPER SHADOW ......TULIPS 161 46
THEY ARE ORPHANS. I CANNOT SEE THEM. THEY ARE LOST. ....STARS. 165 14
I SEE THOSE CONSTELLATIONS IN MY HEAD. .....STARS OVER THE DORDOGNE 166 35
I SEE THEM ALREADY -- THE PALE, STAR-DISTANCE FACES. ....LAST WORDS 172 6
I SIMPLY CANNOT SEE WHERE THERE IS TO GET TO. ....MOON. 173 7
WHATEVER I SEE I SWALLOW IMMEDIATELY ....MIRROR 173 2
I SEE HER BACK, AND REFLECT IT FAITHFULLY. ....MIRROR 174 13
I SEE US FLOATING THERE YET, INSEPARABLE -- TWO CORK DOLLS. ..BABY. 175 41
AND ALL I COULD SEE WAS DANGERS: DOVES AND WORDS, ...THREE WOMEN 178 47
I SEE THE FATHER CONVERSING WITH THE SON. ....THREE WOMEN 179 88
I SEE NOTHING. ....THREE WOMEN 180 147
I SEE MYSELF AS A SHADOW, NEITHER MAN NOR WOMAN, ...THREE WOMEN 182 191
SEE, THE DARKNESS IS LEAKING FROM THE CRACKS. ....THREE WOMEN 182 195
I SEE HER IN MY SLEEP, MY RED, TERRIBLE GIRL. ....THREE WOMEN 182 204
I SEE THEM SHOWERING LIKE STARS ON TO THE WORLD -- .....THREE WOMEN 183 228
I SEE YOUR VOICE ....LITTLE FUGUE 188 23
I CANNOT SEE YOUR EYES. ....EVENT 194 12
CAN YOU NOT SEE I DO NOT MIND WHAT IT IS. ....A BIRTHDAY PRESENT 206 20
THERE ARE NO WINDOWS, SO I CAN'T SEE WHAT IS IN THERE. *THE ARRIVAL. 213 9
I SEE YOUR CUTE DECOR ....LESBOS 229 85
THEY DID NOT SEE HIM SMILE. ....LYONNESSE 234 23
YOU SHOULD SEE THE OBJECTS IT MAKES! ....THE TOUR 238 17
SHOVES IN TO SEE ....LADY LAZARUS 245 27
LEAN AND SEE ME. ....GIGOLO 268 32
SEEMING TO SEE ....BALLOONS 272 23
HAS NEVER FAILED TO SEE OUR FABLING SHEARED ....DIALOGUE O. 276 12
OR YOUR WHITE-HAIRED BENEFACTRESS, WHO MAY SEE FIT .....DIALOGUE O. 277 48
REALLY CAN SEE INTO THE FUTURE. WHAT, ..DIALOGUE OVER A OUIJA BOARD 278 52
PAN, ARE YOU STILL THERE? SEE, HIS SPRINT ....DIALOGUE O. 278 70
TO SAY THAT. THAT MUST BE HIS: HIS WORD. YOU SEE, ...DIALOGUE O. 278 79
GABRIEL OR BEELZEBUB: I SEE, ...DIALOGUE OVER A OUIJA BOARD 280 150
AND WE'LL SEE WHO'S SMARTEST. PAN, TELL US NOW: ....DIALOGUE O. 281 205
G-O-D-H-E-A-D. THERE, SEE! ....DIALOGUE OVER A OUIJA BOARD 282 218
CHILD TO SEE WHICH ONE OF US CAN CALL .DIALOGUE OVER A OUIJA BOARD 284 284
I SEE THEM START TO CRUISE AND DIP FOR FOOD*QUEEN MARY'S ROSE GARDEN 290 13
TOAD-STONE! I SEE I MUST WEAR YOU IN THE CENTRE OF MY
     FOREHEAD I ....THE RIVAL/DR 291 27
INTO A DARK WORLD I CANNOT SEE AT ALL. ....ELM/DR 292 10
SHE ADDED PETTISHLY, "I CAN'T SEE WHY ....BITTER STRAWBERRIES 300 25
IN HIS EYE'S DARKROOM I CAN SEE ....BLUEBEARD 305 5
OF MOONLIGHT OR THE POCKMARKED FACE WE SEE*METAMORPHOSES OF THE MOON 308 38
AND BY THAT GLARE, MY LOVE WILL SEE ....TO A JILTED LOVER 310 25
FROM HERE YOU CAN'T SEE SPOTS UPON THE SUN; ....ADMONITIONS 319 8
TELL ME WHAT YOU SEE IN IT: .....BLACK PINE TREE IN AN ORANGE LIGHT 328 1

SEED (8)
GROWS QUICK WITH SEED. ....TWO SISTERS OF PERSEPHONE 32 22
SHALL STREW BROADCAST SO RARE A SEED ON WIND ...WREATH FOR A BRIDAL 45 20
STARS SHOOT THEIR PETALS, AND SUNS RUN TO SEED, ...EPITAPH FOR F. 45 12
LONG GONE TO WHEEZE AND SEED, ELLA MASON ....ELLA MASON A. 53 8
AND THE OPULENT AIR GO STUDDED WITH SEED, ...CONJURING. 66 36
HAIRED SEED OF THE MILKWEED ....POLLY'S TREE 128 16
I AM DUMB AND BROWN. I AM A SEED ABOUT TO BREAK. ....THREE WOMEN 179 99
THEY SEED SO EFFORTLESSLY! ....WINTER TALES 258 8

SEEDS (2)
OF BLANCHED SEEDS OR BLACK SEEDS ....FIESTA MELONS 47 16
OF BLANCHED SEEDS OR BLACK SEEDS ....FIESTA MELONS 47 16

SEEDY (1)
BY CORRECT GREEN LINES AND NO SEEDY FREE-FOR-ALL ...ABOVE THE OXBOW 89 49

SEEING (5)
ON SEEING OUR NEIGHBOR'S CAT-HAUNT, ELLA MASON AND HER ELEVEN CATS 53 4
SEEING HER FREEZE, HE TURNS HIS FACE AWAY. ....THE OTHER TWO 68 20
OF SUCH SEEING UP THE LEAF-SHUTTERED ESCARPMENTS, ..ABOVE THE OXBOW 88 27
NEEDLING IT DARK. THEN I WAS SEEING ....THE EYE-MOTE 109 10
I AM EXCITED, SEEING IT THERE. ....ELM/DR 292 4

SEEK (5)
THIS PAIR SEEK SINGLE STATE FROM THAT DUAL BATTLE. ....WREATH F. 44 10
SEEK NO STONY CAMERA-EYE TO FIX ....EPITAPH FOR FIRE AND FLOWER 45 8
IN MY EYE, NOR SEEK ....BLACK ROOK IN RAINY WEATHER 57 7
WORLD-WRECKED, THEY SEEK ONLY OBLIVION. ....THE DEAD 320 8
TO SEEK THE STAIRCASE BY THE GLARE OF DAY. ....THE PRINCESS. 334 53

SEEKS (2)
HE EATS, AND STILL HIS NEED SEEKS FOOD, ...PURSUIT 23 39
WHO SEEKS TO DALLY IN THE PORT TILL DAWN, ...EPITAPH IN THREE PARTS 337 8

SEEM (12)
EX MACHINA. NOR DID THEY SEEM DETERRED BY THIS. ....SPIDER 49 35
THE PIER PILINGS SEEM ABOUT TO COLLAPSE ....A WINTER SHIP 113 15
NONE OF THEM SEEM TO NOTICE. ....PARLIAMENT HILL FIELDS 152 17
THEY ARE SUBTLE: THEY SEEM TO FLOAT, THOUGH THEY WEIGH ME DOWN, ...
     ... TULIPS 161 40
THE WALLS, ALSO, SEEM TO BE WARMING THEMSELVES. ....TULIPS 162 57
THEY SEEM LARGE, YET THEY DROP, AND NO GAP IS VISIBLE. ......STARS. 165 5
TERRIFY ME, THEY SEEM SO OLD. ....STINGS 214 13
SEEM A BOTANICAL DRAWING -- ....WINTER TREES 257 3

SEEM (CONT.)
FEET SEEM TO BE SAYING: ....EDGE   272   7
EVEN IF YOU SEEM PACIFIED, PREFER ......DIALOGUE OVER A OUIJA BOARD   280 145
A SORCERER BIDS FAREWELL TO SEEM ..A SORCERER BIDS FAREWELL TO SEEM   324   T
BRIGHT WINDOW-SQUARES UNTIL THE WOMEN SEEM .....MORNING IN THE HOS.   332   7
SEEMED (8)
THE STRONGEST WILL SEEMED A WILL TOWARD CEREMONY. OBESE, DARK- ...
                                            ... THE GORING   47   4
BURDENED IN SUCH A WAY WE SEEMED THE LIGHTER -- ......THE OTHER TWO   69   32
NO PLACE, IT SEEMED, FOR THE EFFIGY TO FARE ....LADY AND T.   69   8
WHICH SEEMED, WHEN DREAMED, TO MEAN SO PROFOUNDLY MUCH, ...GHOST'S.   90   5
CONSPICUOUS, YET IT SEEMED ....MUSSEL HUNTER AT ROCK HARBOR   95   18
ONE, BY HIMSELF, SEEMED PITIABLE ENOUGH, ...BLUE MOLES 126   5
SHE STOPPED FITTING ME SO CLOSELY AND SEEMED OFFISH. ....IN PLASTER 159   29
AND SEEMED TO GIVE HER WARMTH, LIKE A LIVE SKIN. ....WIDOW 164   19
SEEMING (1)
SEEMING TO SEE ....BALLOONS 272   23
SEEMS (12)
IT SEEMS THE CONSISTENT CRITICS WANTED YOU ....YADWIGHA.   85   8
AND SEEMS TO DIE: SO VAPORS ....FULL FATHOM FIVE   93   19
INFINITE NUMBER SEEMS TO BE THE ISSUE UP THERE. ....STARS.   165   21
IT SEEMS BEES HAVE A NOTION OF HONOR, ...THE SWARM 217   57
KEEPING ITSELF, IT SEEMS, IN A STATE OF MIRACULOUS REPAIR. ..MEDUSA 225   15
THAT, IT SEEMS, IS THE IMPOSSIBILITY. ....THE JAILER 227   40
THIS HALOEY RADIANCE THAT SEEMS TO BREATHE ....BY CANDLELIGHT 236   11
IT SEEMS PERFECTLY NATURAL NOW --- ....DEATH & CO. 254   2
BORED HIM. HE'S MORE PHILOSOPHER, IT SEEMS, ...DIALOGUE O. 277   43
YOUR HEAD AFTER ALL. IT SEEMS HIS LAUGH *DIALOGUE OVER A OUIJA BOARD 282 238
SEEMS TO JEOPARDIZE THIS: ....NOTES TO A NEOPHYTE 306   18
FROM HERE THE MOON SEEMS SMOOTH AS ANGEL-FOOD, ...ADMONITIONS 319   7
SEEN (10)
SIMULTANEOUSLY SEEN ....THE GREAT CARBUNCLE   72   13
SEEN BY ANY MAN WHO KEPT HIS HEAD, ...FULL FATHOM FIVE   93   38
I HAVE NOT SEEN IT; IT DOES NOT FLY UP. ......THE SURGEON AT 2 A.M. 170   9
AND THE MAN I WORK FOR LAUGHED: "HAVE YOU SEEN SOMETHING AWFUL? ...
                                            ... THREE WOMEN 177   22
I HAVE SEEN THE WHITE CLEAN CHAMBER WITH ITS INSTRUMENTS. ..THREE. 180 121
I HAVE NEVER SEEN A THING SO CLEAR. ....THREE WOMEN 181 171
I HAVE SEEN TO THAT. ....BURNING THE LETTERS 204   35
HE HAS SEEN TOO MUCH DEATH, HIS HANDS ARE FULL OF IT. .....COURAGE. 210   15
AND SEEN MY STRANGENESS EVAPORATE, ...STINGS 214   26
ONCE ONE HAS SEEN GOD, WHAT IS THE REMEDY? ....MYSTIC 268   9
SEEP (2)
WHEN I FIRST SAW IT, THE SMALL RED SEEP, I DID NOT BELIEVE IT. ...
                                            ... THREE WOMEN 177   15
OR YOUR LIQUORS SEEP TO ME, IN THIS GLASS CAPSULE, POPPIES IN JULY 203   13
SEEPS (1)
STILL IT SEEPS UP, IT IS NOT EXHAUSTED. ....THE SURGEON AT 2 A.M. 171   23
SEES (3)
SHE SEES HOW THEIR RED SILK FLARE ....TWO SISTERS OF PERSEPHONE   32   17
NOBODY SEES US. ....MUSHROOMS 139   7
THE MOON SEES NOTHING OF THIS. SHE IS BALD AND WILD. ....MOON. 173   27
SEETHE (1)
GAVE WAY TO FIELDS AND THE INCESSANT SEETHE OF GRASSES*HARDCASTLE C.   62   9
SEETHED (1)
AND AS I LISTENED ITS COLD TEETH SEETHED   ON THE DECLINE OF ORACLES   78   3
SEIZE (2)
AS TO SEIZE MY SENSES, HAUL ....BLACK ROOK IN RAINY WEATHER   57   29
MIGHT WELL SEIZE THIS PRIZE, ...THE LADY AND THE EARTHENWARE HEAD   69   12
SEIZED (3)
ONCE ONE HAS BEEN SEIZED UP ....MYSTIC 268   10
A RIGOR SEIZED ME: I SAW CRACKS APPEAR, *DIALOGUE OVER A OUIJA BOARD 285 319
WHAT PRINCE HAS EVER SEIZED THE SHINING GRAIL .......METAMORPHOSES. 307   19
SEIZURE (1)
DRUNK, AND TEA-LEAVES CANDID; THE CLAIRVOYANT SEIZURE ..DIALOGUE O. 279 123
SELDOM (1)
OLD MAN, YOU SURFACE SELDOM. ....FULL FATHOM FIVE   92   1
SELF (4)
THE BROWNNESS IS MY DEAD SELF, AND IT IS SULLEN: ....THREE WOMEN 179 100
HOW SHYLY SHE SUPERIMPOSES HER NEAT SELF ....THREE WOMEN 184 282
HAVE A SELF TO RECOVER, A QUEEN. ....STINGS 215   52
OUT OF WHICH THE SAME SELF UNFOLDS LIKE A SUIT ....TOTEM 264   25
SELF-ASSURED (1)
THEY ARE SCRUBBED AND SELF-ASSURED AS THE GREAT PLANETS. ....STARS. 165   16
SELF-INTEREST (1)
BLUNT IN SELF-INTEREST ....SPIDER   48   3
SELF-SUFFICIENT (1)
SELF-SUFFICIENT AS THEY ARE." ....CONJURING.   66   16
SELLING (1)
SELLING THE WELSH AND ENGLISH MOTHERS ....ON DECK 143   29
SELLS (1)
OF STATE SCENERY, SELLS SODA, SHOWS OFF VIEWPOINTS. *ABOVE THE OXBOW   88   41
SELVES (2)
(MY SELVES DISSOLVING, OLD WHORE PETTICOATS) --- ....FEVER. 232   53
SELVES POSING AS PROPHET AND SLYLY POACHING ....DIALOGUE O. 280 134

SEND (4)
    LET HIM SEND POLICE AND HOUNDS TO BRING HER IN. ....SNOWMAN O.   58   19
    NOR DO THEY SEND UP FIRES WHERE THEY FALL ..STARS OVER THE DORDOGNE   165   6
    DISRUPT THE CALENDARS NEXT: SEND THE DUTEOUS ....SONG FOR A REVOLU.   323   9
    SEND MY MUSE ALICE PACKING WITH GAUDY SCRAPS ....A SORCERER B.   324   7
SENDING (3)
    I AM SENDING BACK THE KEY ....BLUEBEARD   305   1
    I AM SENDING BACK THE KEY; ....BLUEBEARD   305   4
    I AM SENDING BACK THE KEY ....BLUEBEARD   305   7
SENDS (1)
    SENDS UP ITS FORKED ....SOUTHERN SUNRISE   26   11
SENSE (10)
    THEY LIE, CUT-GRASS ASSAULTING EACH SEPARATE SENSE ....WREATH F.   44   8
    BUT BEFORE I MIGHT BLIND SENSE ....ON THE PLETHORA OF DRYADS   67   13
    DRAGGED EACH DAZZLED SENSE APART ....ON THE PLETHORA OF DRYADS   67   26
    LANTERN-JAWED REASON, SQUAT COMMON SENSE,   THE DEATH OF MYTH-MAKING 104   3
    OR THE SEA, HUSHING THEIR PEELED SENSE LIKE OLD MOTHER MORPHIA. ...
                                                     ... WAKING IN WINTER 151   16
    HIS SOUL MAY BEAT AND BE BEATING AT HER DULL SENSE ....WIDOW   165   37
    A SENSE OF ABSENCE IN ITS OLD SHINING PLACE.*STARS OVER THE DORDOGNE 166   33
    THOSE LETTERS SEPARATED INTO SENSE .....DIALOGUE OVER A OUIJA BOARD   279   96
    SUCH SKEPTIC CRACKS. WITH SENSE SEALED WATERTIGHT .....DIALOGUE O.   280 155
    BUT NOW THAT ANGER COOLS, I'VE A SENSE OF SORROW ....DIALOGUE O.   285 310
SENSES (1)
    AS TO SEIZE MY SENSES, HAUL ....BLACK ROOK IN RAINY WEATHER   57   29
SENSING (1)
    HOW NATURE, SENSING THIS, COMPOUNDS HER BITTERS. ....DEPARTURE   51   5
SENT (5)
    A HUNDRED HERALDS SHE SENT OUT ....THE QUEEN'S COMPLAINT   29   16
    SENT THESE LADIES IN HER STEAD ....THE DISQUIETING MUSES   74   5
    MOTHER, YOU SENT ME TO PIANO LESSONS ....THE DISQUIETING MUSES   75   33
    THE BLUE SISTERS SENT ME TO ANOTHER SCHOOL. POEM.4.BEAST.   134   7
    THEY CAN BE SENT BACK. ....THE ARRIVAL OF THE BEE BOX   213   24
SENTIMENT (1)
    ICE AND ROCK, EACH SENTIMENT WITHIN BORDER, ...SPINSTER   49   16
SENTIMENTS (1)
    DRAG UP FALSE, EDWARDIAN SENTIMENTS, ...CANDLES   149   16
SENTRY (1)
    DOZING AROUND THEIR SILVERED SENTRY BOX. ....THE PRINCESS.   334   30
SEPARATE (6)
    THEY LIE, CUT-GRASS ASSAULTING EACH SEPARATE SENSE ....WREATH F.   44   8
    THEY HUNTED THE STONES, TACITURN AND SEPARATE, ...POEM.7.S. 136   15
    FACES AND DARKNESS SEPARATE US OVER AND OVER. ....MIRROR   173   9
    OUR SEPARATE VEINS AND THIS GLASS MOUTH. OH YOU'RE .....DIALOGUE O.   280 147
    AS WE TWO GLOWER FROM OUR SEPARATE CAMPS, ...DIALOGUE O.   284 291
    AND SEPARATE THE FLUTES FROM VIOLINS: ....LOVE IS A PARALLAX   330   50
SEPARATED (2)
    SEPARATED FROM MY HOUSE BY A ROW OF HEADSTONES. ....MOON.   173   6
    THOSE LETTERS SEPARATED INTO SENSE .....DIALOGUE OVER A OUIJA BOARD   279   96
SEPARATES (1)
    SHE IS CRYING THROUGH THE GLASS THAT SEPARATES US. .....THREE WOMEN   182 205
SEPULCHERS (1)
    MUSEUMS AND SEPULCHERS? YOU. YOU ....PERSEUS   82   11
SERAPH (1)
    BOTH SERAPH SONG AND VIOLINS ARE DUMB; ....DOOM OF EXILES   318   7
SERAPHIC (1)
    THEY DESCANT ON THE SERENE AND SERAPHIC BEAUTY ....VIRGIN IN A TREE   82   29
SERBO-CROAT (1)
    LAPSING INTO RUSSIAN OR SERBO-CROAT. ...DIALOGUE OVER A OUIJA BOARD   279   92
SERE (1)
    THEIR FINE SKIN SERE, ...TINKER JACK AND THE TIDY WIVES   35   30
SERENE (1)
    THEY DESCANT ON THE SERENE AND SERAPHIC BEAUTY ....VIRGIN IN A TREE   82   29
SERENELY (1)
    AND SERENELY PLUMMETS DOWN ....AERIALIST   331   26
SERIES (2)
    LIKE A SERIES OF PROMISES, AS I STEP FORWARD. ....WUTHERING HEIGHTS   167   9
    A SERIES OF WEDDINGS. ....WINTER TREES 257   5
SERIOUS (2)
    IT SHOWS I AM SERIOUS. ....THREE WOMEN   185 304
    I WOULD KNOW YOU WERE SERIOUS. ....A BIRTHDAY PRESENT   208   58
SERPENT (1)
    EACH DEAD CHILD COILED, A WHITE SERPENT, ...EDGE   272   9
SERPENTS (1)
    THE SUAVE ETERNAL SERPENTS PROMISE BLISS ....NEVER TRY TO TRICK.   320   13
SERUM (1)
    SLOWLY CONCEDE TO SUN AND SERUM. ..MORNING IN THE HOSPITAL SOLARIUM   332   18
SERVANTS (1)
    SINCE THOSE TWO CIVIL SERVANTS SET ....THE DEATH OF MYTH-MAKING   104   8
SERVE (4)
    TO SERVE HER EXACTING TURN: ....LADY AND T.   69   17
    TO MOVE, SERVE, STEER FOOD, ...WORDS FOR A NURSERY   73   13
    AWAY ON WHEELS, INSTEAD OF LEGS, THEY SERVE AS WELL. ...THREE WOMEN   184 254
    YOU WERE CONDEMNED TO SERVE THE LEGAL LIMIT ....THE TRIAL OF MAN   312   10

	TITLE	PAGE	LINE

SERVES (1)
    THE FIENDISH BUTLER SAUNTERS IN AND SERVES ....TERMINAL 328 10
SERVICE (3)
    TO CHASTITY'S SERVICE: LIKE PROPHETS, LIKE PREACHERS, ...VIRGIN. 82 28
    A SERVICE AND IGNORE IT, I GO A LIAR ......GREEN ROCK, WINTHROP BAY 105 20
    ALWAYS FROM THE PULPIT DURING SERVICE ....DIRGE FOR A JOKER 302 3
SESTINA (1)
    A SESTINA FOR THE DOUANIER ..YADWIGHA, ON A RED COUCH, AMONG LILIES 85 ST
SET (32)
    HIS GREED HAS SET THE WOODS AFLAME, ...PURSUIT 22 3
    THAT EVERY BREATH, THUS TEEMING, SET THE LAND ..WREATH FOR A BRIDAL 45 21
    PERSEVERED ON A SET COURSE ....SPIDER 49 30
    AND ROUND HER HOUSE SHE SET ....SPINSTER 50 25
    TO SET THE SIGHT ON FIRE ....BLACK ROOK IN RAINY WEATHER 57 6
    OF ITS HILLS, AND ITS PASTURES BORDERED BY BLACK STONE SET ...
                                          ... HARDCASTLE CRAGS 63 29
    SET FOOT NIGHTLY IN HER YARD ....THE THIN PEOPLE 65 29
    SET IN MY EAR, AND IN MY EYE ....ON THE DECLINE OF ORACLES 78 13
    SET IN THE PROVERBS STITCHED ON SAMPLERS ....VIRGIN IN A TREE 81 3
    SET IN AN INTRICATE WILDERNESS OF GREEN ....YADWIGHA. 85 5
    I'D ONLY TO SET ONE FOOT IN WILDERNESS--*MEMOIRS OF A SPINACH-PICKER 90 21
    THE CRAB-FACE, ETCHED AND SET THERE, ..MUSSEL HUNTER AT ROCK HARBOR 97 77
    FOUNDING FATHER SET THESE LOBED, WARPED STONES CHILD'S PARK STONES 100 3
    OR TO TRY ME HE SUDDENLY SET ....WHITENESS I REMEMBER 102 18
    THE STONE LION-HEAD SET IN THE WALL ..................RHODODENDRON. 103 5
    SINCE THOSE TWO CIVIL SERVANTS SET ....THE DEATH OF MYTH-MAKING 104 8
    WHO SET WASP, WOLF AND SHARK TO WORK, ...I WANT, I WANT 106 7
    THE PLANKED-UP WINDOWS WHERE SHE SET ....POINT SHIRLEY 110 26
    I SET MY EYE TO A HOLE-MOUTH AND MEET AN EYE ....BEEKEEPER'S. 118 17
    THEY SET THEIR STOUT CHAIRS BACK TO THE ROAD AND FACE THE DARK*NET-- 121 5
    NOR LEAVE ME TO SET MY SMALL BALD EYE ....LOVE LETTER 147 6
    LOVE SET YOU GOING LIKE A FAT GOLD WATCH. ....MORNING SONG 156 1
    A SET OF TEETH, OR STONES ....THE SURGEON AT 2 A.M. 171 34
    I TALK TO MYSELF, MYSELF ONLY, SET APART -- ....THREE WOMEN 179 106
    SET CLOSE, LIKE BIRTH PANGS. ....THE RABBIT CATCHER 194 16
    TOMORROW I WILL BE SWEET GOD, I WILL SET THEM FREE. ...THE ARRIVAL. 213 35
    THE NOSE, THE EYE PITS, THE FULL SET OF TEETH? ....LADY LAZARUS 244 13
    TABLE, TRYING OUR LUCK, INDEX FINGERS SET ....DIALOGUE O. 276 4
    WHAT FEAR? IT HAS SET THEM ZINGING ....STINGS/DR 293 2
    SEURAT: FLECK SCHOONER FLANKS WITH SUN AND SET ....MIDSUMMER MOBILE 324 5
    WILL SCRUPULOUSLY RISE AND SET; ....TWO LOVERS. 327 22
    BEHIND WHICH THE DECLINING MOON HAS SET, ...THE PRINCESS. 334 36
SETS (2)
    THIS SORCERESS SETS MIRRORS ENOUGH ....VANITY FAIR 33 22
    THEY TAKE IT. THE COLD SETS IN. ....WINTERING 218 30
SETTING (4)
    LEAVING NO SPARKY TRACK, SETTING UP NO RIPPLE. ....THE OTHER TWO 68 26
    THEIR SHADOWS LONG IN THE SETTING SUN ....THE DISQUIETING MUSES 76 52
    SETTING: A MATERNITY WARD AND ROUND ABOUT ....THREE WOMEN 176 SD
    HANDS WILL BE OPENING DOORS AND SETTING ......THE MUNICH MANNEQUINS 263 18
SETTLE (4)
    I WATCHED SETTLE, LINE BY LINE, IN MY MIRROR -- ....FACE LIFT 156 26
    SETTLE IN THEIR BELLING DRESSES. ....HEAVY WOMEN 158 5
    THEY SETTLE. ON THE HIGH ....MARY'S SONG 257 15
    S. HE CALLS US APES. I'LL SETTLE HIM! ..DIALOGUE OVER A OUIJA BOARD 284 299
SETTLES (3)
    AND THE CROW SETTLES HER GARMENTS. ....THE MANOR GARDEN 125 11
    SETTLES IN THE ELM, AND IS EASY. ....PHEASANT 191 22
    SETTLES IN THE ROOM NOW. ITS WINGS BLACKEN THE TABLE. ..DIALOGUE O. 285 313
SETTLING (1)
    SETTLING AND STIRRING LIKE BLOWN PAPER ......PARLIAMENT HILL FIELDS 152 8
SEURAT (1)
    SEURAT: FLECK SCHOONER FLANKS WITH SUN AND SET ....MIDSUMMER MOBILE 324 5
SEVEN (12)
    THE SEVEN TROUGHED SEAS AND EVERY EARTHQUAKING CONTINENT. ......SOW 61 45
    FIRELESS, SEVEN CHILL SEAS CHAINED TO HIS ANKLE. *EVERLASTING MONDAY 62 12
    AND SEVEN WINTER COATS LAST AUGUST) ....ON DECK 143 22
    WITH SEVEN HOLES THUMBED IN. THE SOUL IS ANOTHER LIGHT. ...SURGEON. 170 8
    I WAS SEVEN, I KNEW NOTHING. ....LITTLE FUGUE 188 38
    OVER THE SEVEN HILLS, THE RED FURROW, THE BLUE MOUNTAIN? *DETECTIVE. 208 2
    SEVEN YEARS, IF YOU WANT TO KNOW. ....DADDY 224 74
    SEVEN HOURS KNOCKED OUT OF MY RIGHT MIND ....THE JAILER 226 7
    YOU ARE SUNK IN YOUR SEVEN CHINS, STILL AS A HAM. .....STOPPED DEAD 230 16
    IT ATE SEVEN MAIDS AND A PLUMBER ....THE TOUR 238 33
    STEP OFF SEVEN LEAGUES, LIKE THOSE DISTANCES ....GULLIVER 251 21
    FLING THE SEVEN WONDERS AFTER THAT ...SONG FOR A REVOLUTIONARY LOVE 323 7
SEVENTY (3)
    SEVENTY FEET UP, IN A BLACK PINE TREE. ....THE SWARM 216 18
    THE BEES HAVE GOT SO FAR. SEVENTY FEET HIGH! ....THE SWARM 216 26
    MY SEVENTY TREES ....LETTER IN NOVEMBER 253 26
SEVEN-YEAR-OLD (1)
    AND THE SEVEN-YEAR-OLD WOULDN'T GO OUT UNLESS HIS JERSEY STRIPES ...
                                          ... THE BABYSITTERS 174 8
SEVERAL (1)
    MOTHER OF A WHITE NIKE AND SEVERAL BALD-EYED APOLLOS. BARREN WOMAN 157 7

TITLE   PAGE LINE

SEVERE (1)
  ENOUGH. BUT BE POLITE. YOU'RE TOO SEVERE*DIALOGUE OVER A OUIJA BOARD 281 181
SEW (1)
  IT CAN SEW, IT CAN COOK, ...THE APPLICANT 222 34
SEX (1)
  HIS JEW-MAMA GUARDS HIS SWEET SEX LIKE A PEARL. ....LESBOS 228 27
SEXTON (1)
  THE RECTOR, THE MIDWIFE, THE SEXTON, THE AGENT FOR BEES. ......BEE. 211 2
SHABBY (2)
  SHE, IN HER SHABBY TRAVEL GARB, BEGAN ......DREAM WITH CLAM-DIGGERS 44 22
  I SHALL GO DOWN THE SHABBY STAIR AND MEET,*ON THE DECLINE OF ORACLES 78 27
SHACKLED (2)
  SHACKLED TO THE DOCK, OUTMODED, GAUDY, ...A WINTER SHIP 112 3
  AND YOU, SHACKLED ASHEN ACROSS THE RIFT, A SPECTER .....DIALOGUE O. 285 321
SHADE (7)
  NOW HILLS HATCH MENACE, SPAWNING SHADE; ....PURSUIT 22 25
  DAYLONG A DUET OF SHADE AND LIGHT ....TWO SISTERS OF PERSEPHONE 31 3
  TO ATONE AS SHADE FOR SIN THAT LURED BLIND MAN." ....DIALOGUE B. 39 36
  THEIR EYELIDS KEEP THE SHADE. ....THE SLEEPERS 123 21
  GENTLING THE SUN WITH THE SHADE OF MY HAND, ...THREE WOMEN 185 290
  AND TURN GOD'S RADIANT PHOTOGRAPH TO SHADE. ....SONNET TO SATAN 323 8
  HALF IN SHADE, UNTIL HER SKIN ...BLACK PINE TREE IN AN ORANGE LIGHT 328 11
SHADED (2)
  IN THE TIN PAIL SHADED BY YELLOW PAPER MEMOIRS OF A SPINACH-PICKER 89 13
  A MULTITUDE OF SHADED GRAYS; SUSPENSE ....LOVE IS A PARALLAX 329 10
SHADELESS (1)
  A WORLD OF BALD WHITE DAYS IN A SHADELESS SOCKET. ..THE HANGING MAN 141 4
SHADES (2)
  IT IS A CHILLY GOD, A GOD OF SHADES, ...OUIJA 77 1
  MARVELINGLY NUMBERED THE MANY SHADES OF GREEN. ....YADWIGHA. 86 34
SHADING (1)
  SHADING THE BRICKRED PORCH TILES. ....DEPARTURE 51 3
SHADOW (28)
  WHICH SHROUDS OUR PROSPECTS IN AMBIGUOUS SHADOW? .....TALE OF A TUB 24 16
  IN THE SHADOW CAST BY MY DISMAL-HEADED ....THE DISQUIETING MUSES 75 30
  AND THE SHADOW STRETCHED, THE LIGHTS WENT OUT.*THE DISQUIETING MUSES 75 32
  LIVED UNDER THE SHADOW OF HOT ROOFTOPS ....ABOVE THE OXBOW 89 54
  CAST A ROUND WHITE SHADOW IN THEIR DYING. ....MOONRISE 98 6
  GULLS CIRCLE GRAY UNDER SHADOW OF A STEELIER FLIGHT. ...GREEN ROCK 105 17
  NO PIT OF SHADOW TO CRAWL INTO, ...SUICIDE OFF EGG ROCK 115 7
  PURPLES THE FIG IN THE LEAF'S SHADOW, TURNS THE DUST PINK. ...NET-. 121 7
  COME CLEAR OF THE SHADOW. HISTORY ....THE MANOR GARDEN 125 8
  MY HOURS ARE MARRIED TO SHADOW. ....THE COLOSSUS 130 28
  EAT ME. WASTEBASKET GAPER, SHADOW OF DOORWAY. POEM.1.WHO. 132 27
  I COUPLED WITH DUST IN THE SHADOW OF A STONE. POEM.6.W. 136 22
  ON CRUMBS OF SHADOW, ...MUSHROOMS 139 20
  IN THE CREVICE OF AN EXTREMELY SMALL SHADOW ....SLEEP. 144 15
  A WOMAN IS DRAGGING HER SHADOW IN A CIRCLE ....A LIFE 150 21
  THE TUMULUS, EVEN AT NOON, GUARDS ITS BLACK SHADOW: ..PARLIAMENT H. 153 26
  AND I SEE MYSELF, FLAT, RIDICULOUS, A CUT-PAPER SHADOW ......TULIPS 161 46
  WIDOW. THE DEAD SYLLABLE, WITH ITS SHADOW ....WIDOW 164 6
  I SEE MYSELF AS A SHADOW, NEITHER MAN NOR WOMAN, ...THREE WOMEN 182 191
  I FIND MYSELF AGAIN. I AM NO SHADOW ....THREE WOMEN 187 368
  THOUGH THERE IS A SHADOW STARTING FROM MY FEET. I AM A WIFE. *THREE. 187 369
  LOVE IS A SHADOW. ....ELM 192 7
  PLYING THEIR WILD CELLS IN MY KEEL'S SHADOW, ...MEDUSA 225 7
  IN WHOSE SHADOW I HAVE EATEN MY GHOST RATION. ....THE JAILER 227 38
  THE SHADOW OF THIS LIP, AN ABYSS. ....GULLIVER 251 24
  ME FROM THAT SHADOW -- ....THALIDOMIDE 252 10
  OVER MY MIND, CASTING A SHADOW. SORROW DIALOGUE OVER A OUIJA BOARD 285 312
  LURKS THE SICKLE-SHAPED SHADOW ....TEMPER OF TIME 336 15
SHADOWING (1)
  OF THE DEATH'S-HEAD SHADOWING THEIR SONG. ....TWO VIEWS. 114 19
SHADOWS (20)
  GRANITE RUFFS, THEIR SHADOWS ....HARDCASTLE CRAGS 63 36
  THEIR SHADOWS LONG IN THE SETTING SUN ....THE DISQUIETING MUSES 76 52
  ALTERS SHADOWS OF ROSE AND IRIS -- ....CHILD'S PARK STONES 101 13
  AND SHADOWS ONLY -- CAVE-MOUTH BRISTLE BESET -- ....GOATSUCKER 111 13
  EVEN OUR SHADOWS ARE BLUE WITH COLD. ....A WINTER SHIP 113 23
  A THICKET OF SHADOWS IS A POOR COAT. I INHABIT POEM.6.W. 135 2
  TEN FINGERS SHAPE A BOWL FOR SHADOWS. POEM.7.S. 137 43
  TREE AND STONE GLITTERED, WITHOUT SHADOWS. ....LOVE LETTER 147 29
  IN ITS HOLLOW OF SHADOWS, ITS FRINGE OF REEDS, ...CANDLES 148 8
  THE SHADOWS STOOP OVER LIKE GUESTS AT A CHRISTENING. ....CANDLES 149 35
  SHADOWS OUR SAFETY. WE STAND ROUND BLANKLY AS WALLS. ..MORNING SONG 157 6
  THEY STAND LIKE SHADOWS ABOUT THE GREEN LANDSCAPE -- ....WIDOW 164 28
  THE SHADOWS OF THE GRASSES INCHED ROUND LIKE HANDS OF A CLOCK,*BABY. 175 43
  THEY ARE BLACK AND FLAT AS SHADOWS. ....THREE WOMEN 186 340
  THEIR SHADOWS MUST COVER CANADA. ....CROSSING THE WATER 190 3
  AND LETS OUR SHADOWS WITHER ....BY CANDLELIGHT 236 12
  SHADOWS. ....ARIEL 239 14
  THE SHADOWS OF RINGDOVES CHANTING, BUT EASING NOTHING. *WINTER TREES 258 15
  CAN ONCE IN A BLUE MOON CATCH THE SHADOWS OF ....DIALOGUE O. 282 222
  HEAT SHADOWS WAVER NOISELESS IN ...MORNING IN THE HOSPITAL SOLARIUM 332 6

```
                                          TITLE        PAGE  LINE
SHADOW-THING (1)
   A WIDOW RESEMBLES THEM, A SHADOW-THING,  .....................WIDOW  164   30
SHADOWY (1)
   OUR FOOTSTEPS MULTIPLIED IN THE SHADOWY CHAMBERS,  ....THE OTHER TWO  68   11
SHAKE (2)
   ITS TINDER AND SHAKE  .............................HARDCASTLE CRAGS   62    5
   COLD WORLDS SHAKE FROM THE OAR.  .................CROSSING THE WATER  190    7
SHAKEN (1)
   SHAKEN BY OWL CRY.  ................................................OWL  102   16
SHAKING (4)
   SHAKING IN HER SKULL'S CAGE  .........................THE SHRIKE   42   12
   AND FOLDED HIS HANDS, THAT WERE SHAKING: GOODBYE, GOODBYE.  ..BERCK.  198   66
   IN HER GARDEN THE LIES WERE SHAKING OUT THEIR MOIST SILKS*DETECTIVE.  208    7
   THE VILLAGERS ARE UNTYING THEIR DISGUISES, THEY ARE SHAKING HANDS.  ...
                                            ... THE BEE MEETING  212   54
SHALL (54)
   WE SHALL BOARD OUR IMAGINED SHIP AND WILDLY SAIL  .....TALE OF A TUB   25   46
   JACK SHALL REPAIR.  ...................TINKER JACK AND THE TIDY WIVES   34   25
   SHALL STREW BROADCAST SO RARE A SEED ON WIND  ...WREATH FOR A BRIDAL   45   20
   RETROSPECT SHALL NOT SOFTEN SUCH PENURY --  ...............DEPARTURE   51    9
   HOW WE SHALL DO TOGETHER,  ...........................CRYSTAL GAZER   55    9
   OF FATIGUE, I SHALL  ....................BLACK ROOK IN RAINY WEATHER   57   34
   SHEEP GREENS, FINNED FALLS, "I SHALL COMPOSE A CRISIS  ...CONJURING.   66   11
   I SHALL GO DOWN THE SHABBY STAIR AND MEET,*ON THE DECLINE OF ORACLES   78   27
   THE OWL SHALL STOOP FROM HIS TURRET, THE RAT CRY OUT.  ..WATERCOLOR.  112   28
   HOW SHALL I AGE INTO THAT STATE OF MIND?  ....ELECTRA ON AZALEA PATH  117   41
   I SHALL NEVER GET YOU PUT TOGETHER ENTIRELY,  ..........THE COLOSSUS  129    1
   SHALL UNHUSK HIMSELF AND STEER INTO THE AIR.  .............POEM.5.F.  135   20
   I SHALL BE GOOD AS NEW.  ...................................POEM.7.S.  137   45
   AND WE SHALL NEVER ENTER THERE  ...................THE BURNT-OUT SPA  138   31
   WE SHALL BY MORNING  .......................................MUSHROOMS  140   31
   IN TWENTY YEARS I SHALL BE RETROGRADE  .......................CANDLES  149   29
   HOW SHALL I TELL ANYTHING AT ALL  ...........................CANDLES  149   32
   I SHALL NEVER GET OUT OF THIS! THERE ARE TWO OF ME NOW:  IN PLASTER  158    1
   I'M COLLECTING MY STRENGTH; ONE DAY I SHALL MANAGE WITHOUT HER,  ...
                                            ... IN PLASTER  160   55
   AND I SHALL BE USEFUL WHEN I LIE DOWN FINALLY:  ........I AM VERTICAL  162   19
   I SHALL HARDLY KNOW MYSELF. IT WILL BE DARK,  ...........LAST WORDS  172   25
   I SHALL BE A WALL AND A ROOF, PROTECTING.  .............THREE WOMEN  180  139
   I SHALL BE A SKY AND A HILL OF GOOD: O LET ME BE!  ......THREE WOMEN  180  140
   I SHALL NOT LET GO.  ..................................THREE WOMEN  181  174
   I SHALL MOVE NORTH. I SHALL MOVE INTO A LONG BLACKNESS. *THREE WOMEN  182  190
   I SHALL MOVE NORTH. I SHALL MOVE INTO A LONG BLACKNESS. *THREE WOMEN  182  190
   I SHALL BE A HEROINE OF THE PERIPHERAL.  ...............THREE WOMEN  182  197
   I SHALL NOT BE ACCUSED BY ISOLATE BUTTONS,  ............THREE WOMEN  182  198
   I SHALL NOT BE ACCUSED, I SHALL NOT BE ACCUSED.  .......THREE WOMEN  182  201
   I SHALL NOT BE ACCUSED, I SHALL NOT BE ACCUSED.  .......THREE WOMEN  182  201
   THE CLOCK SHALL NOT FIND ME WANTING, NOR THESE STARS  ...THREE WOMEN  182  202
   HOW SHALL IT SOFTEN THEM, THIS LITTLE LULLABY?  ........THREE WOMEN  185  294
   I SHALL MEDITATE UPON NORMALITY.  .....................THREE WOMEN  186  323
   I SHALL MEDITATE UPON MY LITTLE SON.  .................THREE WOMEN  186  324
   SHALL I EVER FIND IT, WHATEVER IT IS?  ................THREE WOMEN  186  343
   ALL NIGHT I SHALL GALLOP THUS, IMPETUOUSLY,  ....................ELM  192   10
   OR SHALL I BRING YOU THE SOUND OF POISONS?  ....................ELM  192   13
   O GOD, HOW SHALL I EVER CLEAN THE PHONE TABLE?  ......WORDS HEARD.  202    8
   I SHALL TAKE NO BITE OF YOUR BODY,  .........................MEDUSA  225   34
   I SHALL UNLOOSE  ............................................PURDAH  243   38
   I SHALL UNLOOSE  ............................................PURDAH  243   41
   I SHALL UNLOOSE  ............................................PURDAH  243   51
   I SHALL UNLOOSE --  .........................................PURDAH  244   52
   I SHALL BURY THE WOUNDED LIKE PUPAS,  ..................GETTING THERE  249   60
   I SHALL COUNT AND BURY THE DEAD.  .....................GETTING THERE  249   61
   THE WORLD FOREVER, I SHALL NOT ENTIRELY  ............THE NIGHT DANCES  250    7
   SHALL THE HOOD OF THE COBRA APPALL ME ---  ...................TOTEM  264   19
   I SHALL NEVER GROW OLD. NEW OYSTERS  ........................GIGOLO  268   26
   TO ALTER HER WILL OUR WAY. SHALL WE GO ON  ............DIALOGUE O.  277   49
   IN THE MORNING ALL SHALL BE  ....................TO A JILTED LOVER  310   19
   ELOQUENTLY SHALL  ...............................TRIO OF LOVE SONGS  314   34
   DAWN SHALL DISSEVER  .........................MOONSONG AT MORNING  317   13
   METHINKS I SHALL ABSENT ME FOR A WHILE  ..............A SORCERER B.  324    3
   SO WE SHALL WALK BAREFOOT ON WALNUT SHELLS  ......LOVE IS A PARALLAX  330   67
SHALLOW (1)
   PROVES RUMORS SHALLOW,  ............................FULL FATHOM FIVE   93   24
SHALLOWS (1)
   IN THE SHALLOWS  .................................AQUATIC NOCTURNE  305   10
SHALT (1)
   THOU SHALT HAVE AN EVERLASTING . . .    .....THE EVERLASTING MONDAY   62  E/1
SHAM (2)
   THAT LIFE WAS A MERE MONUMENTAL SHAM.  ............DIRGE FOR A JOKER  302    8
   SHAM ADAM THE MATADOR CRIED:  .....................DIALOGUE EN ROUTE  308   14
SHAMBLE (1)
   GOATS SHAMBLE, MOROSE, RANK-HAIRED,  ......................DEPARTURE   51   19
SHAMBLED (1)
   WE SNICKERED AS SHE SHAMBLED DOWN SOMERSET TERRACE  ...ELLA MASON A.   54   32
```

                                                         TITLE   PAGE   LINE
SHAMBLING (1)
    PERFORM THEIR SHAMBLING WALTZES ....MUSSEL HUNTER AT ROCK HARBOR   97   86
SHAMEFUL (1)
    POOR AND BARE AND UNQUEENLY AND EVEN SHAMEFUL. ....STINGS   214   19
SHANK (1)
    NO SEA-CHANGE DECKS THE SUNKEN SHANK OF BONE ....TWO LOVERS.   327   17
SHANKS (2)
    THESE BONE SHANKS WILL NOT WAKE IMMACULATE ....THE DEAD   320   10
    SHANKS OF BONE NOW RESURRECT, ...DANSE MACABRE   321   17
SHAN'T (1)
    EVEN IN YOUR ZEN HEAVEN WE SHAN'T MEET. ....LESBOS   230   92
SHANTY (1)
    A GULL HOLDS HIS POSE ON A SHANTY RIDGEPOLE, ...A WINTER SHIP   113   6
SHAPE (16)
    THE SHAPE THAT SHUTS US IN? ABSOLUTE FACT ....TALE OF A TUB   25   29
    SHAPE OF HER SLEEP, HER THOUGHT -- ....THE QUEEN'S COMPLAINT   29   19
    SHOULD TRIM BACK TO SHAPE. ....TINKER JACK AND THE TIDY WIVES   34   4
    WATCHED THE CHANGING SHAPE HE CUT, ...FAUN   35   12
    THE STUFFED SHAPE OF HER FLOWN MATE ....THE SHRIKE   42   13
    ON GRUNT, UP IN THE FLICKERING LIGHT TO SHAPE ....SOW   61   39
    TO MY SWEET WILL, NO LUMINOUS SHAPE ....CONJURING.   66   26
    OF THAT UNCOUTH SHAPE TO SIMPLE SOD AGAIN ....LADY AND T.   70   27
    ALL AMOROUS ARROWS. FOR TO SHEATHE THE VIRGIN SHAPE*VIRGIN IN A TREE 81   7
    AND LEAVES STEADFAST IN SHAPE ....THE SLEEPERS   123   14
    GIVE ME BACK MY SHAPE. I AM READY TO CONSTRUE THE DAYS ...POEM.6.W.   136   21
    TEN FINGERS SHAPE A BOWL FOR SHADOWS. POEM.7.S.   137   43
    THEY ARE PROPER IN SHAPE AND NUMBER AND EVERY PART. ......STILLBORN   142   7
    THE YEW TREE POINTS UP. IT HAS A GOTHIC SHAPE. ....MOON.   173   15
    IT IS SUCH A GOOD SHAPE, SO VIVID. ....PHEASANT   191   19
    A SOLID SHAPE ON AIR. MAY THE DECORUM ..DIALOGUE OVER A OUIJA BOARD   286 360
SHAPED (1)
    AND I WAS SCARED, BECAUSE SHE WAS SHAPED JUST THE WAY I WAS*PLASTER.   158   7
SHAPELESS (1)
    SHAPELESS AS FLUNG GLOVES, A FEW FEET APART -- ....BLUE MOLES   126   3
SHAPERS (1)
    SHAPERS, I OPEN: ....WORDS FOR A NURSERY   73   3
SHAPES (9)
    HEAVY AS STATUARY, SHAPES NOT OURS ....THE OTHER TWO   68   15
    SHAPES ITS IMAGES AROUND HIS SONGS. ................SNAKECHARMER   79   7
    UP PLEASANT STREET AT MAIN. POISING THEIR SHAPES ...ABOVE THE OXBOW   88   12
    A BALD ANGEL BLOCKS AND SHAPES ....SCULPTOR   91   10
    ALL STILLNESS. YET THESE SHAPES FLOAT ....LORELEI   94   9
    AND KEEP THEIR SHAPES INTACT WHILE SUN ....CHILD'S PARK STONES   101   12
    A MELDING OF SHAPES IN A HOT RAIN: ....THE EYE-MOTE   109   11
    IT FINDS THEIR SHAPES IN A CLOUD. ....THREE WOMEN   186 347
    EXPLODES IN A KALEIDOSCOPE OF SHAPES ....LOVE IS A PARALLAX   330   52
SHAPING (2)
    SHAPING ITSELF FROM THAT MIST. ...DIALOGUE BETWEEN GHOST AND PRIEST   38   10
    WENT ON SHAPING ITSELF WITH LOVE, AS IF I WAS READY. ...THREE WOMEN   178   63
SHARDED (1)
    SHARDED IN BLACK, LIKE BEETLES, ...OLD LADIES' HOME   120   1
SHARDS (2)
    ADAZZLE WITH BRIGHT SHARDS ....MISS DRAKE PROCEEDS TO SUPPER   41   19
    OF BEETLES, SWEETBREADS, SHARDS -- TO BE EATEN ....BLUE MOLES   126   31
SHARE (1)
    ATTRACTING MY SHARE OF AHS AND SPECTACULARLY PAINTED, *I AM VERTICAL 162   6
SHARK (3)
    THE WHALE, THE SHARK, THE SQUID. ....BATTLE-SCENE   84   20
    WHO SET WASP, WOLF AND SHARK TO WORK, ...I WANT, I WANT   106   7
    SHARK LITTERED IN THE GERANIUM BED -- ....POINT SHIRLEY   110   16
SHARP (2)
    AND FROM THE OPEN MOUTH ISSUE SHARP CRIES ....THREE WOMEN   182 213
    BOLD BEANSTALK; LIE AND LOVE TILL SHARP SCYTHE HACKS *LOVE IS A PAR. 330   71
SHARPENING (1)
    AND IT IS MY EYES THAT HAVE BEEN SHARPENING THEMSELVES? .....STARS.   166   26
SHARPER (1)
    IN WAIT FOR SHARPER SMART TO FADE. ....BUCOLICS   24   24
SHARPLY (1)
    SNAPPED THE WOMAN SHARPLY. ....BITTER STRAWBERRIES   300   28
SHATTER (1)
    AND SHATTER TO ATOMS ....AERIALIST   332   35
SHATTERING (2)
    SHATTERING ....PURDAH   243   43
    THE SEA SHATTERING ITS GRAY ONE --- ....THE COURIERS   247   12
SHATTERPROOF (1)
    IT IS WATERPROOF, SHATTERPROOF, PROOF ....THE APPLICANT   221   23
SHATTERS (1)
    SHATTERS THE FABULOUS STARS AND MAKES US REAL. ....TALE OF A TUB   25   48
SHAWL (1)
    TONIGHT, LIKE A SHAWL, THE MILD LIGHT ENFOLDS HER, ...CANDLES   149   34
SHAWLED (1)
    SHAWLED IN BLOND HAIR AND THE SALT ....HEAVY WOMEN   158   3
SHAWLS (2)
    HER WINGS TORN SHAWLS, HER LONG BODY ....STINGS   214   17
    WRAP ME, RAGGY SHAWLS, ...NICK AND THE CANDLESTICK   241   7
                                     436

SHAWN (6)
```
  PACED BRISK FATHER SHAWN. A COLD DAY, A SODDEN ONE IT WAS   ...
                         ... DIALOGUE BETWEEN GHOST AND PRIEST   38    2
  FATHER SHAWN PERCEIVED A GHOST  ...DIALOGUE BETWEEN GHOST AND PRIEST   38    9
  "HOW NOW," FATHER SHAWN CRISPLY ADDRESSED THE GHOST  ....DIALOGUE B.   38   11
  "COME, COME," FATHER SHAWN GAVE AN IMPATIENT SHRUG  ....DIALOGUE B.   39   21
  "WHAT LOVE," ASKED FATHER SHAWN, "BUT TOO GREAT LOVE  ...DIALOGUE B.   39   31
  "FOND PHANTOM," CRIED SHOCKED FATHER SHAWN,  ...........DIALOGUE B.   39   41
```
SHE (188)
SHEARED (1)
```
  HAS NEVER FAILED TO SEE OUR FABLING SHEARED  ...........DIALOGUE O.  276   12
```
SHEATH (1)
```
  SHEATH OF IMPOSSIBLES,  ................................PURDAH  243   33
```
SHEATHE (1)
```
  ALL AMOROUS ARROWS. FOR TO SHEATHE THE VIRGIN SHAPE*VIRGIN IN A TREE   81    7
```
SHEAVED (1)
```
  LADIES' SHEAVED SKULLS:  ...................THE SNOWMAN ON THE MOOR   59   38
```
SHEAVES (1)
```
  EXTEND THE RADIAL SHEAVES  ........................FULL FATHOM FIVE   92    7
```
SHED (2)
```
  OF YOUR GRAINED FACE SHED TIME IN RUNNELS:  ........FULL FATHOM FIVE   93   26
  AND HOTHOUSE ROSES SHED IMMORAL BLOOMS.  .............FEMALE AUTHOR  301    8
```
SHE'D (2)
```
  SHE'D SUPPORTED ME FOR SO LONG I WAS QUITE LIMP --  ......IN PLASTER  159   44
  CIRCLES HER LIKE A PREY SHE'D LOVE TO KILL  ...................WIDOW  164   15
```
SHED'S (1)
```
  THIS SHED'S FUSTY AS A MUMMY'S STOMACH:  .................POEM.1.WHO.  131    4
```
SHEEN (3)
```
  SHEEN OF THE NOON SUN STRIKING  .............SONG FOR A SUMMER'S DAY   31   11
  STEELED WITH THE SHEEN  ..............................BY CANDLELIGHT  236    4
  ACROSS THE FROSTED GRASS SHE MARKS THE SHEEN  .........THE PRINCESS.  334   31
```
SHEENS (1)
```
  BLUE AS LIZARD-SCALES. FROST SHEENS THE STREET.  ........DIALOGUE O.  286  340
```
SHEEP (9)
```
  SHEEP DROWSED STONEWARD IN THEIR TUSSOCKS OF WOOL, AND BIRDS,  ...
                            ... HARDCASTLE CRAGS   63   34
  SHEEP GREENS, FINNED FALLS, "I SHALL COMPOSE A CRISIS  ...CONJURING.   66   11
  A BLACK SHEEP LEADS THE SHEPHERDS' FLOCK.  ..........A WINTER'S TALE   86    7
  NIGHTLY NOW I FLOG APES OWLS BEARS SHEEP  ............ZOO KEEPER'S WIFE  155   39
  OR THE HEARTS OF SHEEP, AND THE WIND  .............WUTHERING HEIGHTS  167   11
  THE SHEEP KNOW WHERE THEY ARE,  ...................WUTHERING HEIGHTS  167   19
  I FOLLOW THE SHEEP PATH BETWEEN THEM. A LAST HOOK BRINGS ME  ...
                            ... BLACKBERRYING  169   23
  IN THE LANE I MEET SHEEP AND WAGONS,  ....................BRASILIA  258   16
  SHEEP IN FOG  .........................................SHEEP IN FOG  262    T
```
SHEEPFOLD (1)
```
  THERE, SPRING LAMBS JAM THE SHEEPFOLD. IN AIR  .........WATERCOLOR.  111    1
```
SHEEPFOOT-FLATTENED (1)
```
  SHEEPFOOT-FLATTENED GRASSES,  .................TWO VIEWS OF WITHENS   71    2
```
SHEER (7)
```
  THE BAY'S SHEER, EXTRAVAGANT BLUE,  .....................THE BEGGARS   48   17
  WORLD UNDER THE SHEER WATER  .....WATERCOLOR OF GRANTCHESTER MEADOWS  112   10
  THE FIRST THING I SAW WAS SHEER AIR  ....................LOVE LETTER  147   20
  OUT OF SHEER BOREDOM. TANGLED IN THE SWEAT-WET SHEETS  .......ZOO K.  155   23
  ITS BOWL OF RED BLOOMS OUT OF SHEER LOVE OF ME.  .............TULIPS  162   61
  SHEER SILVER BLURS THEIR PHANTOM ACT.  .............DANSE MACABRE  321   21
  A WINDOW WHICH PROVES THE SKY SHEER RIGMAROLE*EPITAPH IN THREE PARTS  337   28
```
SHEER-SIDED (1)
```
  SHEER-SIDED, WITH HOLES WHERE TO HIDE.  .....................GIGOLO  267    3
```
SHEET (6)
```
  TWISTING CURSES IN THE TANGLED SHEET  ...................THE SHRIKE   42   10
  IT RESEMBLES THE MOON, OR A SHEET OF BLANK PAPER  ...........A LIFE  150   23
  BODY, A SHEET OF NEWSPRINT ON THE FIRE  .....................WIDOW  164    2
  THE SCALDED SHEET IS A SNOWFIELD, FROZEN AND PEACEFUL.  ...SURGEON.  170    5
  THE FLOWERS AND THE FACES WHITEN TO A SHEET.  ..........LAST WORDS  172   13
  UNDER THE GLUED SHEET FROM WHICH HIS POWDERY BEAK  ......BERCK-PLAGE  198   63
```
SHEET-CUFF (1)
```
  THEY HAVE PROPPED MY HEAD BETWEEN THE PILLOW AND THE SHEET-CUFF  ...
                            ... TULIPS  160    8
```
SHEETED (1)
```
  THE MIRRORS ARE SHEETED.  .............................CONTUSION  271   12
```
SHEETS (15)
```
  OF CHAIRS AND BUREAUS AND SLEEP-TWISTED SHEETS.  ...........GHOST'S.   90    7
  TO A KNOT OF LAUNDRY, WITH A CLASSIC BUNCH OF SHEETS  ......GHOST'S.   90   10
  SO THESE POSED SHEETS, BEFORE THEY THIN TO NOTHING,  ......GHOST'S.   90   18
  AND GHOST OF OUR DREAMS' CHILDREN, IN THOSE SHEETS  ........GHOST'S.   91   33
  OUT OF SHEER BOREDOM. TANGLED IN THE SWEAT-WET SHEETS  .......ZOO K.  155   23
  HOW WHITE THESE SHEETS ARE. THE FACES HAVE NO FEATURES. *THREE WOMEN  178   65
  THE SHEETS, THE FACES, ARE WHITE AND STOPPED, LIKE CLOCKS.  ..THREE.  179   95
  NOW THEY FACE A WINTER OF WHITE SHEETS, WHITE FACES.  ...THREE WOMEN  184  265
  ARE SPREADING THEIR VACUOUS SHEETS.  ..................LITTLE FUGUE  188   42
  NOW THE WASHED SHEETS FLY IN THE SUN,  .................BERCK-PLAGE  198   67
  IT BREATHES FROM MY SHEETS, THE COLD DEAD CENTER *A BIRTHDAY PRESENT  207   50
  THE SHEETS GROW HEAVY AS A LECHER'S KISS.  ..................FEVER.  231   30
  THE STIFFNESS OF SAILS, THE LONG SALT WINDING SHEETS.  .......MYSTIC  268    8
```

                                                          TITLE   PAGE   LINE
SHEETS (CONT.)
    ARRANGED IN SHEETS OF ICE, THE FOND ....DANSE MACABRE   321   4
    LIES AMONG SHEETS ....AERIALIST   331   2
SHELF (5)
    TABLE-TOP, CUPBOARD SHELF, CATS LOUNGED BRAZEN, ...ELLA MASON A.   54   22
    YET, SHRINED ON HER SHELF, THE GRISLY VISAGE ENDURED, ..LADY AND T.   70   29
    THE WEED-SLICKED SHELF FOR HIS OWN, ...MAGNOLIA SHOALS   122   14
    THEN STEPPED DOWN THE STEEP BEACH SHELF AND INTO THE WATER. ..BABY.   175   39
    SOME DUCKS STEP DOWN OFF THEIR GREEN-REEDED SHELF ...QUEEN MARY'S.   290   11
SHELL (8)
    STILL AS A SHELL: HEAR WHAT AN AGE OF GLASS ....EPITAPH FOR F.   45   16
    THE MOON'S MAN STANDS IN HIS SHELL, ...THE EVERLASTING MONDAY   62   1
    OLD BOCKLIN MISSED, WHO HELD A SHELL .....ON THE DECLINE OF ORACLES   78   5
    HE WILLED HIS BOOKS AND SHELL AWAY. ......ON THE DECLINE OF ORACLES   78   10
    THE BOOKS BURNED UP, SEA TOOK THE SHELL,   ON THE DECLINE OF ORACLES   78   11
    MUD STENCH, SHELL GUTS, GULLS' LEAVINGS: ....MUSSEL HUNTER.   95   13
    AND I, A SHELL, ECHOING ON THIS WHITE BEACH ....THREE WOMEN   179 111
    UNDERSTANDING BREAKS THROUGH THE SKULL'S SHELL ......METAMORPHOSES.   307   16
SHE'LL (6)
    OF MINE, YET KIN SHE IS: SHE'LL SUCK ....ALL THE DEAD DEARS   70   16
    ASKEW, SHE'LL ACHE AND WAKE ....VIRGIN IN A TREE   82   40
    BUT SHE'LL SOON FIND OUT THAT THAT DOESN'T MATTER A BIT. *IN PLASTER   160   54
    AND SHE'LL PERISH WITH EMPTINESS THEN, AND BEGIN TO MISS ME. ...
                                                      ... IN PLASTER   160   56
    BUT IN TWENTY-FIVE YEARS SHE'LL BE SILVER, ...THE APPLICANT   221   31
    SHE'LL CUT HER THROAT AT TEN IF SHE'S MAD AT TWO. ....LESBOS   228   22
SHELLED (1)
    YOUR SHELLED BED I REMEMBER. ....FULL FATHOM FIVE   93   43
SHELLS (6)
    RED-MOTTLED RELICS, SHELLS, CLAWS ....MAGNOLIA SHOALS   121   3
    LITTLE SHELLS MADE UP INTO NECKLACES AND TOY LADIES. ....FINISTERRE   170   32
    BROOD CELLS GRAY AS THE FOSSILS OF SHELLS ....STINGS   214   12
    GO CULL THE PURPLE SNAILS FROM SLOTHFUL SHELLS ....GO GET.   313   17
    OF KALEIDOSCOPIC SHELLS*TWO LOVERS AND A BEACHCOMBER BY THE REAL SEA   327   14
    SO WE SHALL WALK BAREFOOT ON WALNUT SHELLS ......LOVE IS A PARALLAX   330   67
SHELTER (1)
    WITHER LIKE PITHLESS HANDS. THERE IS LITTLE SHELTER. POEM.5.F.   134   4
SHELVES (1)
    WE ARE SHELVES, WE ARE ....MUSHROOMS   139   25
SHEPHERDS' (1)
    A BLACK SHEEP LEADS THE SHEPHERDS' FLOCK. ....A WINTER'S TALE   86   7
SHERBETS (1)
    ELECTRIFYINGLY-COLORED SHERBETS, SCOOPED FROM THE FREEZE*BERCK-PLAGE   196   3
SHERLOCK (1)
    YOUR SHERLOCK HOLMESING STEERED TO A BLANK WALL ....DIALOGUE O.   280 167
SHE'S (7)
    NOW, RUN TO FAT, SHE'S A SPINSTER WHOSE DOOR SHUTS ...ELLA MASON A.   54   17
    SHE, RIPE AND UNPLUCKED, 'S ....VIRGIN IN A TREE   82   36
    NOW SHE'S DONE FOR, THE DEWLAPPED LADY ....FACE LIFT   156   25
    SHE'LL CUT HER THROAT AT TEN IF SHE'S MAD AT TWO. ....LESBOS   228   22
    BUT AUNTIE, SHE'S AWFULLY NICE. ....THE TOUR   238   44
    SHE'S PINK, SHE'S A BORN MIDWIFE -- ....THE TOUR   238   45
    SHE'S PINK, SHE'S A BORN MIDWIFE -- ....THE TOUR   238   45
SHH (2)
    MASS AFTER MASS, SAYING SHH! ....THE SWARM   216   10
    SHH! THESE ARE CHESS PEOPLE YOU PLAY WITH, ...THE SWARM   216   11
SHIED (1)
    SHE SHIED SIDEWAYS: A WHITE FIZZ! AND THE GIANT, PURSUING, ...
                                          ... THE SNOWMAN ON THE MOOR   59   47
SHIELD (2)
    CLAW SWOLLEN TO A SHIELD LARGE ....MUSSEL HUNTER AT ROCK HARBOR   96   33
    BOSSED, BRAZEN, AN ANTIQUE SHIELD, ...A BIRTHDAY PRESENT   207   30
SHIELDING (1)
    THE SCRAGGY ROCK SPIT SHIELDING THE TOWN'S BLUE BAY ......DEPARTURE   51   13
SHIES (1)
    SHIES FROM HIS TOUCH: HIS IS AN IRON MOOD. ....THE OTHER TWO   68   19
SHIFT (2)
    NIGHT SHIFT ....NIGHT SHIFT   76   T
    NUDE AS CLEOPATRA IN MY WELL-BOILED HOSPITAL SHIFT, ...FACE LIFT   156   10
SHIFTING (2)
    STIPPLE OF SHIFTING WAVE-TIPS IS IRONED OUT, LOST ..ABOVE THE OXBOW   89   46
    SHIFTING MY CLARITIES. ....PURDAH   242   7
SHIFTS (1)
    A DEVIL. WAIT: HE SHIFTS. HE HASN'T COME*DIALOGUE OVER A OUIJA BOARD   282 216
SHIMMERING (2)
    IT IS SHIMMERING, HAS IT BREASTS, HAS IT EDGES?   A BIRTHDAY PRESENT   206   2
    NOW THERE ARE THESE VEILS, SHIMMERING LIKE CURTAINS, ...BIRTHDAY.   206   16
SHIMMERS (1)
    BUT IT SHIMMERS, IT DOES NOT STOP, AND I THINK IT WANTS ME. ...
                                          ... A BIRTHDAY PRESENT   206   11
SHINBONES (1)
    TO ROOT DEEP AMONG KNUCKLES, SHINBONES, ...FULL FATHOM FIVE   93   35
SHINE (6)
    AND SHINE THAT KETTLE OF COPPER .....TINKER JACK AND THE TIDY WIVES   34   7
    ACT, BUT -- HOW THOSE FEATHERS SHINE! ....RHYME   50   16

438

SHINE (CONT.)
   ORDERING ITS BLACK FEATHERS CAN SO SHINE*BLACK ROOK IN RAINY WEATHER   57   28
   AND THE SHINE OF THESE SMALL THINGS SWEETER THAN THE FACE OF
      ISHTAR. ....LAST WORDS   172   26
   THAT AT SUCH A DISTANCE FROM US SHINE AND WHIRL. ....THREE WOMEN   182   210
   REFLECTING IN A MILLION FLAGONS' SHINE, ...CINDERELLA   304   8
SHINES (1)
   THE SUN SHINES ON UNRIPE CORN. ....DEPARTURE   51   7
SHINGLE (1)
   THE SHINGLE BOOMS, BICKERING UNDER ....POINT SHIRLEY   110   2
SHINGLES (1)
   WITH SHINGLES BURNISHED AS GLASS, ...DREAM WITH CLAM-DIGGERS   43   7
SHINING (7)
   IN THE GREEN OF EDEN, PRETEND FUTURE'S SHINING FRUIT   TALE OF A TUB   25   39
   SILENT AND SHINING ON A GREEN ROCK BEDDED IN MUD, ...DREAM WITH C.   44   15
   A SENSE OF ABSENCE IN ITS OLD SHINING PLACE.*STARS OVER THE DORDOGNE   166   33
   PARTS, BITS, COGS, THE SHINING MULTIPLES. ....THREE WOMEN   177   29
   SHINING GLOVES AND WHITE SUIT. ....THE BEE MEETING   211   29
   WHAT PRINCE HAS EVER SEIZED THE SHINING GRAIL .......METAMORPHOSES.   307   19
   A CROWD OF SHINING GULLS THAT PLUNGE TO LAUNCH ...EPITAPH IN THREE.   337   13
SHINS (1)
   A GIRL COULD WADE WITHOUT WETTING HER SHINS.   A LESSON IN VENGEANCE   80   20
SHINY (2)
   SHINY AND STRANGE, AS IF HE HAD HURTLED FROM A STAR? ...THREE WOMEN   181   163
   BALD AND SHINY, WITH POCKETS OF WISHES, ...TOTEM   264   26
SHIP (11)
   WE SHALL BOARD OUR IMAGINED SHIP AND WILDLY SAIL .....TALE OF A TUB   25   46
   WITH EACH TILT, SHOCK AND SHUDDER, OUR BLUNT SHIP   CHANNEL CROSSING   26   2
   AND THE FAIR SHIP SANK, ITS CREW KNELLED HOME FOR DINNER. ...
                                      ... DREAM WITH CLAM-DIGGERS   44   20
   THEY NAMED THEIR SHIP AFTER THE FLOWER OF MAY. ....MAYFLOWER   60   14
   WE GAVE GOOD USE AS SHIP AND HOUSE IS BLACK*GREEN ROCK, WINTHROP BAY   105   11
   SHIP TIMBERS IN THROUGH THE CELLAR WINDOW; ....POINT SHIRLEY   110   14
   A WINTER SHIP ....A WINTER SHIP   112   T
   AND ARE MET, INSTEAD, BY THIS ICERIBBED SHIP, ...A WINTER SHIP   113   25
   TINY AND FAR, A SINGLE SHIP ....ON DECK   142   6
   AND I AM A WHITE SHIP HOOTING: GOODBYE, GOODBYE. ....THREE WOMEN   184   261
   AT MY TABLE ON THE SHIP. ....LITTLE FUGUE   187   9
SHIPS (3)
   BY TWO BRONZE BOOKENDS OF SHIPS IN SAIL,   ON THE DECLINE OF ORACLES   78   2
   THE HORIZON'S BARE OF SHIPS, ...MAGNOLIA SHOALS   122   21
   THE THIRD CRIES OUT AS ALL THE SHIPS GO DOWN:*EPITAPH IN THREE PARTS   337   10
SHIP'S (1)
   TONIGHT IT HAS RECEDED LIKE A SHIP'S LIGHT. ..THE SURGEON AT 2 A.M.   170   10
SHIPWRECKED (2)
   OUR LADY OF THE SHIPWRECKED IS STRIDING TOWARD THE HORIZON, ...
                                      ... FINISTERRE   169   19
   OUR LADY OF THE SHIPWRECKED IS THREE TIMES LIFE SIZE, ...FINISTERRE   170   24
SHIRLEY (2)
   POINT SHIRLEY ....POINT SHIRLEY   110   T
   EATS AT POINT SHIRLEY. SHE DIED BLESSED, ...POINT SHIRLEY   111   36
SHIRR (1)
   SHIRR SONGS TO SUIT WHICH MOOD ....ODE FOR TED   29   20
SHIRT (1)
   YOUR SHIRT OF CRISP LINEN ....WHITSUN   154   9
SHIRTS (1)
   AND RETURNED THEM STEAMED AND PRESSED AND STIFF AS SHIRTS. *THE TOUR   238   34
SHIVER (1)
   ONE BREATH MIGHT SHIVER TO BITS, ...OLD LADIES' HOME   120   3
SHOALS (2)
   MAGNOLIA SHOALS ....MAGNOLIA SHOALS   121   T
   GATHER IDLE OYSTERS FROM GREEN SHOALS, ...GO GET THE GOODLY SQUAB   313   19
SHOCK (4)
   WITH EACH TILT, SHOCK AND SHUDDER, OUR BLUNT SHIP   CHANNEL CROSSING   26   2
   BAREFOOT, SHE STOOD, IN SHOCK OF THAT RETURNING, ...DREAM WITH C.   43   5
   IT WAS NOT A SHOCK -- ....LYONNESSE   234   15
   WHILE ALL THE ACTORS HALT IN MORTAL SHOCK: ....DOOMSDAY   316   5
SHOCKED (2)
   "FOND PHANTOM," CRIED SHOCKED FATHER SHAWN, ...DIALOGUE B.   39   41
   NOR CAN GOD'S STERN, SHOCKED ANGELS CRY THEM UP ....THE DEAD   320   13
SHOCKING (1)
   MALTREAT THE HOSTAGE HEAD IN SHOCKING WISE, ...LADY AND T.   69   13
SHODDY (1)
   AND PATCHED THIS SHODDY ....GREEN ROCK, WINTHROP BAY   105   6
SHOE (2)
   NO GETTING UP BY ELEPHANT OR WHEEL OR SHOE. ...NEW YEAR ON DARTMOOR   176   7
   ANY MORE, BLACK SHOE ....DADDY   222   2
SHOE-BLACK (1)
   BRIGHT HAIR, SHOE-BLACK, OLD PLASTIC, ...THE OTHER   201   8
SHOE-BLACKING (1)
   SMELL THE MELT OF SHOE-BLACKING, ...BERCK-PLAGE   201   119
SHOELACE (1)
   INERT AS A SHOELACE; DEAD ....MEDALLION   124   4
SHOES (4)
   OF CHARRED SHOES, THE SODDEN UPHOLSTERY: ....AFTERMATH   114   12

SHOES (CONT.)
    BLACK COAT, BLACK SHOES, AND YOUR   ....MAN IN BLACK   120   17
    UNLOAD THEIR GRIEFS ON MY SHOES, ...PRIVATE GROUND   130   18
    DOWN SHOES FOR A POLISH OF CARBON   ....THE MUNICH MANNEQUINS   263   19
SHONE (1)
    I SHONE, MICA-SCALED, AND UNFOLDED   ....LOVE LETTER   147   25
SHOOK (1)
    SHOOK THE GROUND WITH ITS POUNDING.   ....NIGHT SHIFT   76   11
SHOOT (2)
    STARS SHOOT THEIR PETALS, AND SUNS RUN TO SEED, ...EPITAPH FOR F.   45   12
    THEY SHOOT THE DICE FOR ONE REMAINING BONE;   ....DENOUEMENT   326   8
SHOOTING (3)
    SOMEBODY IS SHOOTING AT SOMETHING IN OUR TOWN --   ....THE SWARM   215   1
    WHO ARE THEY SHOOTING AT?   ....THE SWARM   216   5
    WARRANT HIM WHELPED IN THE WAKE OF TWO SHOOTING   ....DIALOGUE O.   281 194
SHOOTS (1)
    A LIFE AFTER THIS LIFE? HE SHOOTS SO SWIFT   ....DIALOGUE O.   278   72
SHOP (3)
    AND MUTE AS MANNEQUINS IN A DRESS SHOP, ...ON DECK   142   3
    YOU HAD A ROSE GARDEN AND A GUEST COTTAGE AND A MODEL APOTHECARY
        SHOP   ....THE BABYSITTERS   174   20
    YES, HERE IS THE SECRETARY OF BEES WITH HER WHITE SHOP SMOCK,   BEE.   211   7
SHOPKEEPERS (1)
    ONE, HOUSEWIVES AND SHOPKEEPERS.   ....THE DEATH OF MYTH-MAKING   104   5
SHOPS (1)
    AND BICKERING SHOPS;   ....STREET SONG   35   4
SHORES (1)
    END: GREEN SHORES APPEAR; WE ASSUME OUR NAMES, ...CHANNEL CROSSING   27   40
SHORN (1)
    THEY ARE LEADING ME TO THE SHORN GROVE, THE CIRCLE OF HIVES. ..BEE.   211   23
SHORT (7)
    SOME BURN SHORT, SOME LONG, ...VANITY FAIR   33   34
    LONG, SHORT, LONG -- IN THE LIT GARDEN   ....CHILD'S PARK STONES   101   14
    TO FIDDLE THE SHORT NIGHT AWAY.   ....SLEEP IN THE MOJAVE DESERT   144   26
    THE HUMP OF ELBA ON YOUR SHORT BACK, ...THE SWARM   216   8
    NOTIONS AND TICKETS, SHORT CIRCUITS AND FOLDING MIRRORS.   .....TOTEM   265   27
    NOTHING SHORT OF A MIRACLE TO NAIL   .....DIALOGUE OVER A OUIJA BOARD   280 160
    THEMSELVES ON THE CLAY TOES AND SHORT CLUBFOOT   ......METAMORPHOSES.   308   35
SHORTCHANGE (1)
    SHORTCHANGE ME CONTINUOUSLY: WHETHER   ....POEMS, POTATOES   106   9
SHORTENS (1)
    SHORTENS WITH EACH BREATH DRAWN.   ....OLD LADIES' HOME   120   21
SHORT-REINED (1)
    SHORT-REINED, PAWING LIKE PARADEGROUND HORSES.   ....A LIFE   150   14
SHOT (5)
    AND THE MAID SMOKED AND SHOT POOL UNDER A GREEN-SHADED LAMP. BABY.   175   24
    IT MUST BE SHOT DOWN. POM! POM!   ....THE SWARM   216   19
    AS THEY SHOT PAST THE FORTY-NINTH FLOOR   ....DIALOGUE EN ROUTE   308   4
    SHOT PAST THE NINETY-FOURTH FLOOR   ....DIALOGUE EN ROUTE   309   34
    HANG RIDDLED WITH SHOT, ...TOUCH-AND-GO   336   22
SHOULD (37)
    SHOULD ACCEPT SO FELL A WOUND, ...BUCOLICS   24   18
    SHOULD TRIM BACK TO SHAPE.   ....TINKER JACK AND THE TIDY WIVES   34   4
    I SHOULD HAVE KNOWN BETTER.   ....GREEN ROCK, WINTHROP BAY   104   3
    HE'LL BE RICH IN A YEAR (AND HE SHOULD KNOW)   ....ON DECK   143   28
    A COOL WIND SHOULD INHABIT THOSE LEAVES   SLEEP IN THE MOJAVE DESERT   144   8
    YOU SHOULD HAVE JUNKED THEM BEFORE THEY DIED.   ....LEAVING EARLY   146   28
    THEY SHOULD HAVE GONE OUT WITH BALLOON FLIGHTS AND THE
        STEREOPTICON.   ....CANDLES   149   12
    SHOULD I STIR, I THINK THIS PINK AND PURPLE PLASTIC   ....ZOO K.   154   11
    THE TULIPS SHOULD BE BEHIND BARS LIKE DANGEROUS ANIMALS;   ....TULIPS   162   58
    I SHOULD SUGAR AND PRESERVE MY DAYS LIKE FRUIT!   ....LAST WORDS   172   10
    I SHOULD HAVE MURDERED THIS, THAT MURDERS ME.   ....THREE WOMEN   180 126
    WHY SHOULD IT, IT IS THE HEARSE OF A DEAD FOOT, ...BERCK-PLAGE   197   20
    SUCH SALT-SWEETNESS. WHY SHOULD I WALK   ....BERCK-PLAGE   197   40
    LET IT NOT COME BY WORD OF MOUTH, I SHOULD BE SIXTY   .....BIRTHDAY.   208   53
    SO WHY SHOULD THEY TURN ON ME?   ....THE ARRIVAL OF THE BEE BOX   213   34
    SURELY THE GRASS SHOULD BE RIPPLING.   ....THE JAILER   226   25
    YOU SAY I SHOULD DROWN THE KITTENS. THEIR SMELL!   ....LESBOS   228   20
    YOU SAY I SHOULD DROWN MY GIRL.   ....LESBOS   228   21
    I SHOULD SIT ON A ROCK OFF CORNWALL AND COMB MY HAIR.   ......LESBOS   228   29
    I SHOULD WEAR TIGER PANTS, I SHOULD HAVE AN AFFAIR.   ....LESBOS   228   30
    I SHOULD WEAR TIGER PANTS, I SHOULD HAVE AN AFFAIR.   ....LESBOS   228   30
    WE SHOULD MEET IN ANOTHER LIFE, WE SHOULD MEET IN AIR, ...LESBOS   228   31
    WE SHOULD MEET IN ANOTHER LIFE, WE SHOULD MEET IN AIR, ...LESBOS   228   31
    YOU SHOULD SEE THE OBJECTS IT MAKES!   ....THE TOUR   238   17
    THAT THESE LATE MOUTHS SHOULD CRY OPEN   ....POPPIES IN OCTOBER   240   11
    AND SHOULD   ....PURDAH   242   10
    SHOULD BE GRAND AND CLASSICAL   ....CHILD   265   9
    BEFORE HE SPELLS AGAIN, SHOULD HIS NEXT WRIT   ....DIALOGUE O.   281 193
    ALL NIGHT LONG, EVEN SHOULD OUR EYES SHUT   ....DIALOGUE O.   286 354
    I SHOULD HAVE A STEEL COMPLEXION LIKE YOURS   ....THE RIVAL/DR   291   6
    IF ANYTHING SHOULD HAPPEN . . ."   ....BITTER STRAWBERRIES   299   12
    NEVER TRY TO KNOW MORE THAN YOU SHOULD.   ....ADMONITIONS   319   3
    NEVER TRY TO KNOW MORE THAN YOU SHOULD.   ....ADMONITIONS   319   9

SHOULD (CONT.)
    NEVER TRY TO KNOW MORE THAN YOU SHOULD. ....ADMONITIONS   319   15
    NEVER TRY TO KNOW MORE THAN YOU SHOULD. ....ADMONITIONS   319   19
    SHOULD INFLAME THE SLEEPING TOWN. ....LOVE IS A PARALLAX   329   30
    WHY HE SHOULD KNEEL BEFORE A SILLY SCENE ....THE PRINCESS.   335   65
SHOULDER (5)
    OF HER BARE SHOULDER, WHILE SHE BENDS,   TWO VIEWS OF A CADAVER ROOM   114   16
    SHOULDER THROUGH HOLES. WE ....MUSHROOMS   139   18
    HOW THE SUN POLISHES THIS SHOULDER! ....PURDAH   242   9
    MOLE ON MY SHOULDER, ...EAVESDROPPER   260   4
    BLOOD AND BANK WRIST, ELBOW, SHOULDER, LIP ....DIALOGUE O.   277   18
SHOULDERBLADES (1)
    CAME SLIDING DOWN HIS SHOULDERBLADES ....GOLD MOUTHS CRY   302   5
SHOULDER-BLADES (1)
    KNUCKLES AT SHOULDER-BLADES, THE ....THALIDOMIDE   252   12
SHOULDER-HIGH (1)
    UP FROM THE FISSURED VALLEY AND HUNG SHOULDER-HIGH *HARDCASTLE CRAGS   62   14
SHOULDERING (1)
    TO CONTRADICT ME. YOUR SHOULDERING WORDS OUTSTRIP ......DIALOGUE O.   281 172
SHOULDERS (2)
    HE MADE HER SHOULDERS BARE ....THE QUEEN'S COMPLAINT   28   14
    BELOW SHOULDERS NOT ONCE ....FULL FATHOM FIVE   93   37
SHOULDN'T (2)
    O I SHOULDN'T PUT MY FINGER IN THAT ....THE TOUR   237   13
    O I SHOULDN'T DIP MY HANKIE IN, IT HURTS! ....THE TOUR   238   31
SHOUT (1)
    AMUSED SHOUT: ....LADY LAZARUS   246   54
SHOUTS (1)
    OR SHOUTS OF WALKERS: CROSSROAD TRAFFIC ....WHITENESS I REMEMBER   103   25
SHOVE (2)
    BREAKWATERS TAKE THE SHOVE ....MAN IN BLACK   119   2
    SHOVE INTO BEING, DRAGGING ....THALIDOMIDE   252   14
SHOVERS (1)
    NUDGERS AND SHOVERS ....MUSHROOMS   139   28
SHOVES (1)
    SHOVES IN TO SEE ....LADY LAZARUS   245   27
SHOW (7)
    PRIZE RIBBON AND PIG SHOW. ....SOW   60   6
    FILENE'S SHOW WINDOWS. GRANT US GRACE, ...A WINTER'S TALE   87   19
    THE OLD QUEEN DOES NOT SHOW HERSELF, IS SHE SO UNGRATEFUL? ....BEE.   212   50
    WILL IT SHOW IN THE BLACK DETECTOR? ....A SECRET   219   9
    STITCHES TO SHOW SOMETHING'S MISSING? NO, NO? THEN ...THE APPLICANT   221   6
    MY RIBS SHOW. WHAT HAVE I EATEN? ....THE JAILER   226   22
    WILL SHOW US THAT ....MOONSONG AT MORNING   317   18
SHOWED (2)
    CLOCKS BELLED TWELVE. MAIN STREET SHOWED OTHERWISE ....OWL   101   1
    BUT THEIR BONES SHOWED, AND THE MOON SMILED. ....THE DETECTIVE   209   35
SHOWER (1)
    IN A SHOWER OF CHANEL, DIOR GOWNS, ...DIALOGUE EN ROUTE   308   9
SHOWERING (1)
    I SEE THEM SHOWERING LIKE STARS ON TO THE WORLD -- .....THREE WOMEN   183 228
SHOWERS (1)
    STARS AND SHOWERS OF GOLD -- CONCEPTIONS, CONCEPTIONS!   THREE WOMEN   178   48
SHOWN (2)
    TOWARD THAT GREAT JEWEL: SHOWN OFTEN, ...THE GREAT CARBUNCLE   72   11
    AND YOU WANT TO BE SHOWN ABOUT! ....THE TOUR   237   7
SHOWS (5)
    SHOWS, RANK ON RANK, THE HUNGRY SEAS ADVANCING. ...CHANNEL CROSSING   26   8
    SHOWS ITS HEAD, AND THOSE GREEN WATERS BACK TO ........SNAKECHARMER   79   26
    HEAD ALONE SHOWS YOU IN THE PRODIGIOUS ACT ....PERSEUS   82   1
    OF STATE SCENERY, SELLS SODA, SHOWS OFF VIEWPOINTS. *ABOVE THE OXBOW   88   41
    IT SHOWS I AM SERIOUS. ....THREE WOMEN   185 304
SHRANK (2)
    EVERYTHING SHRANK IN THE SUN'S CORROSIVE ......SUICIDE OFF EGG ROCK   115   21
    THE OLD MAN SHRANK TO A DOLL. POEM.3.MAENAD.   133   7
SHRED (1)
    SHRED IN HIS LITTLE FIST. ....BALLOONS   272   30
SHREDDED (2)
    UNHORSED AND SHREDDED IN THE GROVE OF COMBAT ....SOW   61   31
    SHREDDED FINE AS SNOWFLAKES ....AERIALIST   331   3
SHREW (3)
    ...OF A WOMAN, A MOUSE AND A SHREW. THE ANKLE-BONE
        OF THE... ....ALL THE DEAD DEARS   70 E/3
    RELICS OF A MOUSE AND A SHREW ....ALL THE DEAD DEARS   70   5
    THE SMALL SHREW CHITTERS FROM ITS WILDERNESS ....WATERCOLOR.   112   4
SHREWD (4)
    STALKS RED FOX, SHREWD STOAT. ....ODE FOR TED   29   6
    SHREWD CATCH SILTING OUR EACH BRIGHT ACT BACK ....FIRESONG   30   13
    WHATEVER HIS SHREWD SECRET, HE KEPT IT HID ....SOW   60   3
    ON SHREWD CLAWS: ....AQUATIC NOCTURNE   306   24
SHRIEK (10)
    HOUSED IN EARTH, THOSE MILLION BRIDES SHRIEK OUT. ......VANITY FAIR   33   33
    HE FLEW INTO THE ROOM, A SHRIEK AT HIS HEEL. ....THREE WOMEN   181 165
    WILL TOLERATE NO BYSTANDING: I MUST SHRIEK. ....ELM   192   21
    SHRIEK FROM MY BELLY LIKE ARROWS, AND THESE I RIDE. ......THE OTHER   202   19

		TITLE	PAGE	LINE

SHRIEK (CONT.)
THE WORLD WILL GO UP IN A SHRIEK, AND YOUR HEAD WITH IT,   BIRTHDAY. 207 29
THE SHRIEK IN THE BATH, ...PURDAH 244 56
THAT MELTS TO A SHRIEK. ....LADY LAZARUS 246 70
UNGODLY AS A CHILD'S SHRIEK. ....CHILDLESS WOMAN 259 10
SHRIEK IN THE SEA AND I ....GIGOLO 268 27
GIVING A SHRIEK AND POP ....BALLOONS 271 7
SHRIEKING (1)
THE SWIFTS ARE BACK. THEY ARE SHRIEKING LIKE PAPER ROCKETS.   THREE. 185 310
SHRIEKS (6)
BULLDOZERS, GUILLOTINES, WHITE CHAMBERS OF SHRIEKS PROCEED,   THREE. 177 19
IT IS A PLACE OF SHRIEKS. IT IS NOT HAPPY. ....THREE WOMEN 180 122
THE ABSENCE OF SHRIEKS ....THE RABBIT CATCHER 194 17
LIMBS, IMAGES, SHRIEKS. BEHIND THE CONCRETE BUNKERS ....BERCK-PLAGE 197 29
IN THAT VALLEY THE TRAIN SHRIEKS ECHO LIKE SOULS ON HOOKS. ...
                                                ... THE DETECTIVE 208 5
HE SHRIEKS IN HIS GREASE ....BRASILIA 258 9
SHRIKE (1)
THE SHRIKE ....THE SHRIKE 42 T
SHRIKE-FACE (1)
WHEN HER SHRIKE-FACE ....THE SHRIKE 42 17
SHRILL (1)
THEIR SHRILL, GRAVELLY GOSSIP'S FUNNELED OFF.*PARLIAMENT HILL FIELDS 152 18
SHRILLING (1)
SHRILLING HER HULK ....SOW 61 22
SHRINED (1)
YET, SHRINED ON HER SHELF, THE GRISLY VISAGE ENDURED, ..LADY AND T. 70 29
SHRINK (3)
MAKE HOUSES SHRINK ....SOLILOQUY OF THE SOLIPSIST 37 11
TOUCH IT: IT WON'T SHRINK LIKE AN EYEBALL, ...A LIFE 149 1
FAILS TO APPEAR, TURN, AND, TURNING, SHRINK ....DIALOGUE O. 279 120
SHRIVEL (1)
LIGHT'S DEATH TO THEM: THEY SHRIVEL IN IT. ....BLUE MOLES 126 22
SHRIVELING (2)
AS THOUGH ALIVE, SHRIVELING IN TORMENT THUS ....DIALOGUE B. 39 35
SHRIVELING TO CINDERS AT ITS SOURCE, ...CRYSTAL GAZER 56 45
SHROUD (2)
WHO WALKED IN A SWARMING SHROUD OF WINGS ....LAMENT 315 2
ASSAULT A SLEEPING VIRGIN'S SHROUD ....DANSE MACABRE 321 14
SHROUD-CIRCLED (1)
BURNING LIKE KNOTHOLES FROM A NUN'S SHROUD-CIRCLED .....DIALOGUE O. 280 130
SHROUDED (2)
SHROUDED TO SUCKLE DARKNESS? ONLY THEY ....VIRGIN IN A TREE 81 24
IT HOLDS ALOOF, A SHROUDED PARACHUTE .....METAMORPHOSES OF THE MOON 307 8
SHROUDS (2)
WHICH SHROUDS OUR PROSPECTS IN AMBIGUOUS SHADOW? .....TALE OF A TUB 24 16
DAMNED, HOWLING IN THEIR SHROUDS ACROSS THE MOOR *NOVEMBER GRAVEYARD 56 16
SHRUB (1)
BLUE SHRUB BEHIND THE GLASS ....PARLIAMENT HILL FIELDS 153 45
SHRUG (1)
"COME, COME," FATHER SHAWN GAVE AN IMPATIENT SHRUG .....DIALOGUE B. 39 21
SHRUNK (5)
TO SEE MY PEOPLE SHRUNK SO SMALL, SO SMALL."   THE QUEEN'S COMPLAINT 29 25
AND PERIWINKLES, SHRUNK TO COMMON ....GREEN ROCK, WINTHROP BAY 105 13
IT STRETCHES FOR MILES, THE SHRUNK VOICES ....BERCK-PLAGE 196 8
MINUTE AND SHRUNK FOR EXPORT, ...THE ARRIVAL OF THE BEE BOX 213 14
FIELDS SHRUNK TO A PENNY ....THE SWARM 216 29
SHUDDER (1)
WITH EACH TILT, SHOCK AND SHUDDER, OUR BLUNT SHIP   CHANNEL CROSSING 26 2
SHUDDERING (1)
WAVER, FAINTLY GREEN, SHUDDERING AWAY ....TALE OF A TUB 25 26
SHUNT (1)
LOAM-HUMPS, HE SAYS, MOLES SHUNT ....ODE FOR TED 29 7
SHUT (22)
I SHUT MY DOORS ON THAT DARK GUILT, ...PURSUIT 23 46
SUN HOISTS SOUL UP AFTER LIDS FALL SHUT; ....VANITY FAIR 33 28
WHEN MY EYES SHUT ....SOLILOQUY OF THE SOLIPSIST 37 5
BEHIND SHUT DOORS; THE DAIRY HERDS ....HARDCASTLE CRAGS 63 32
I SHUT ON THE KEY ....WORDS FOR A NURSERY 73 19
NOEL! NOEL! NO MOUTH IS SHUT. ....A WINTER'S TALE 87 27
SHUT AGAINST ME. ALL HELD STILL. ......MUSSEL HUNTER AT ROCK HARBOR 95 20
STOOD SHUT OUT, FOR ONCE, FOR ALL, ...MUSSEL HUNTER AT ROCK HARBOR 96 52
CLAPPED SHUT, FLATTEN THIS MAN OUT. ..THE HERMIT AT OUTERMOST HOUSE 118 3
THE LIDS WON'T SHUT. TIME POEM.3.MAENAD. 133 18
LIKE AN EYE BETWEEN TWO WHITE LIDS THAT WILL NOT SHUT. ......TULIPS 160 9
IS ACCOUNTING FOR ITS COW. I SHUT MY EYES ..STARS OVER THE DORDOGNE 166 39
IT HAS SHUT ITS MOUTH ON THE STONE PILL OF REPOSE. ....SURGEON. 171 30
WHAT KEYHOLE HAVE WE SLIPPED THROUGH, WHAT DOOR HAS SHUT? ....BABY. 175 42
A RED, HARD WOOD, EYES SHUT AND MOUTH WIDE OPEN. ....THREE WOMEN 182 212
SLIDING SHUT ON SOME QUICK THING, ...THE RABBIT CATCHER 194 29
THE COURAGE OF THE SHUT MOUTH, IN SPITE OF ARTILLERY! .....COURAGE. 209 1
TO THUMB SHUT YOUR EYES AT THE END ....THE APPLICANT 221 16
I ROCKED SHUT ....LADY LAZARUS 245 39
MIGHT RANGE IN IT. I ONLY SHUT THE DOOR *DIALOGUE OVER A OUIJA BOARD 286 344
ALL NIGHT LONG, EVEN SHOULD OUR EYES SHUT ....DIALOGUE O. 286 354

442

	TITLE	PAGE	LINE

SHUT (CONT.)
IN WHICH THE RIDDLE OF OUR RACE IS SHUT. ....DOOM OF EXILES 318 14
SHUT-OFF (1)
THE WORLD PURRS, SHUT-OFF AND GENTLE. ....BERCK-PLAGE 200 110
SHUTS (7)
THE SHAPE THAT SHUTS US IN? ABSOLUTE FACT ....TALE OF A TUB 25 29
NOW, RUN TO FAT, SHE'S A SPINSTER WHOSE DOOR SHUTS ...ELLA MASON A. 54 17
OPENS AND SHUTS, ACCEPTING THEM AMONG ITS REFLECTIONS. ..PRIVATE G. 131 24
HOW HER BODY OPENS AND SHUTS -- ....AN APPEARANCE 189 14
THE HEART SHUTS, ...CONTUSION 271 10
THERE! THAT SHUTS HIM UP! SO. BETTER SO,*DIALOGUE OVER A OUIJA BOARD 284 300
SHUTS DOWN ITS FABLED SUMMER HOUSE; ....TWO LOVERS. 327 2
SHUTTER (1)
UNDER SHUTTER OF THEIR HANDICAPS. ....SONNET TO SATAN 323 4
SHUTTERED (1)
GRAY FACES, SHUTTERED BY DRUGS, FOLLOW ME LIKE FLOWERS. ...SURGEON. 171 50
SHUTTERS (2)
SHUTTERS, THEIR BALCONIES ....SOUTHERN SUNRISE 26 4
THE SHUTTERS TO LET WARM WIND FEATHER ....THE DREAM 310 5
SHUTTING (3)
VOCATION ENOUGH: OPENING, SHUTTING ....MOONRISE 98 8
SHUTTING THEIR MOUTHS ON IT, LIKE A COMMUNION TABLET. ....TULIPS 161 35
ZEROS, SHUTTING ON NOTHING, ...THE RABBIT CATCHER 194 15
SHUTTING-UP (1)
THE COURAGE OF SHUTTING-UP ....THE COURAGE OF SHUTTING-UP 209 T
SHY (1)
THEY MAY BE WHITE AND SHY, THEY ARE NO STOOL PIGEONS, ...COURAGE. 210 31
SHYLY (2)
HANGING SHYLY UNDER THE STUDDED HORIZON ....STARS OVER THE DORDOGNE 165 19
HOW SHYLY SHE SUPERIMPOSES HER NEAT SELF ....THREE WOMEN 184 282
SIBILANT (2)
ALONGSIDE THE SIBILANT HARBOR THE LOVERS ....ALICANTE LULLABY 43 11
GUESSING OF IT. SIBILANT ....MUSSEL HUNTER AT ROCK HARBOR 96 38
SIBYL (NOT COUNTED)
SIBYL ....DIALOGUE OVER A OUIJA BOARD 276 DP
SIBYL'S (1)
SIBYL'S LEAVES BLOW. ....TEMPER OF TIME 336 8
SICK (12)
TILL, SICK OF THEIR RULER'S GODLING AIRS, ...NATURAL HISTORY 71 7
O I WAS SICK. ....FACE LIFT 156 8
NOW I HAVE LOST MYSELF I AM SICK OF BAGGAGE --- ....TULIPS 160 18
THOSE LITTLE SICK ONES THAT ELUDE MY ARMS. ....THREE WOMEN 178 67
SICK WITH WHAT IT HAS SWALLOWED --- ....BERCK-PLAGE 197 28
O MOON-GLOW, O SICK ONE, ...THE OTHER 202 20
IS IT THE HAWTHORN THAT SMELLS SO SICK? ....THE BEE MEETING 211 24
I AM SICK TO DEATH OF HOT SALT. ....MEDUSA 225 37
DRAGGED ITS BLOOD BAG, SICK ....LESBOS 229 54
I AM PACKING THE SICK CATS. ....LESBOS 229 70
ASKING ABOUT MONEY? I'M SICK OF THAT. ..DIALOGUE OVER A OUIJA BOARD 277 50
SHE MUSES ON THE ODOR, SWEET AND SICK, ...FEMALE AUTHOR 301 11
SICKENS (3)
THE FEN SICKENS. ....FROG AUTUMN 99 8
IT IS A LOVE OF DEATH THAT SICKENS EVERYTHING. ....THREE WOMEN 181 152
ONE TOUCH: IT BURNS AND SICKENS. ....EVENT 194 11
SICKER (1)
SO I SAW YOUR MUCH SICKER ............................EAVESDROPPER 260 24
SICKLE-SHAPED (1)
LURKS THE SICKLE-SHAPED SHADOW ....TEMPER OF TIME 336 15
SICKNESS (1)
SICKNESS BEGINS HERE: I AM A DARTBOARD FOR WITCHES. POEM.6.W. 135 4
SIDE (19)
FROM THE FLAYED SIDE. ....STREET SONG 36 20
VIVID AT MY SIDE, ...SOLILOQUY OF THE SOLIPSIST 38 30
FROM HIS EARTH-WIFE'S SIDE ....THE SHRIKE 42 4
OUT OF THE SIDE OF THE GENEROUS MOON WHEN IT ....THE THIN PEOPLE 65 28
AND AT THE LEFT SIDE OF MY CRIB? ....THE DISQUIETING MUSES 75 8
DAY NOW, NIGHT NOW, AT HEAD, SIDE, FEET, ...THE DISQUIETING MUSES 76 49
BLACKBERRIES ON EITHER SIDE, THOUGH ON THE RIGHT MAINLY, BLACKBER. 168 2
WITH NO BOTTOM, OR ANYTHING ON THE OTHER SIDE OF IT, ...FINISTERRE 169 4
SCRATCHING AT MY SLEEP, AND ENTERING MY SIDE. ....THREE WOMEN 182 215
THE BOOKS I CARRY WEDGE INTO MY SIDE. ....THREE WOMEN 185 305
THIS IS THE SIDE OF A MAN: HIS RED RIBS, ...BERCK-PLAGE 198 46
LET US SIT DOWN TO IT, ONE ON EITHER SIDE, ADMIRING THE GLEAM, ...
... A BIRTHDAY PRESENT 207 24
AND THE UNIVERSE SLIDE FROM MY SIDE. ....A BIRTHDAY PRESENT 208 62
THEY RISE ON EITHER SIDE OF HIM LIKE STARS. ....AMNESIAC 233 23
WHOSE SIDE ARE THEY ON? ....CUT 235 21
STONE OF THE SIDE, ...PURDAH 242 2
SIDE OF GREEN ADAM, I ....PURDAH 242 4
THICK, RED AND SLIPPING. IT IS ADAM'S SIDE, ...GETTING THERE 248 36
A FUNNY PINK WORLD HE MIGHT EAT ON THE OTHER SIDE OF IT, ..BALLOONS 272 24
SIDED (1)
SAND GRIT TO SIDED CRYSTAL ....MUSSEL HUNTER AT ROCK HARBOR 95 4
SIDELONG (1)
AND THE EYES OF THE KILLER MOVING SLUGLIKE AND SIDELONG, *DETECTIVE. 208 8

443

                                                          TITLE   PAGE   LINE
SIDES (1)
  THEY ACCOMMODATE THEMSELVES TO MY MILKBOTTLE, FLATTENING
     THEIR SIDES. .... BLACKBERRYING   168   9
SIDEWALK (1)
  THRONGING SIDEWALK, STREET, ...STREET SONG   35   3
SIDEWAYS (2)
  UNTIL, TURNING SIDEWAYS, ...MISS DRAKE PROCEEDS TO SUPPER   41   23
  SHE SHIED SIDEWAYS: A WHITE FIZZ! AND THE GIANT, PURSUING, ...
                                    ... THE SNOWMAN ON THE MOOR   59   47
SIDEWISE (1)
  CLAPS SIDEWISE: I AM NOT HIS YET. ....DEATH & CO.   254   11
SIDLED (1)
  MASS-MOTIVED HORDES, THEY SIDLED ......MUSSEL HUNTER AT ROCK HARBOR   96   39
SIDLES (1)
  THIS WITCH SIDLES, FINGERS CROOKED, AS IF ....VANITY FAIR   32   2
SIEGE (2)
  AND JOIN HER SIEGE. ....THE SNOWMAN ON THE MOOR   59   24
  YOUR VOICES LAY SIEGE. YOU LODGE ....LORELEI   94   23
SIERRA (1)
  TURQUOISE, ROSE, SIERRA MAUVE; NEEDLES ....MORNING IN THE HOS. 332   14
SIFT (1)
  SIFT HIM ABOUT THE AFTER-LIFE THAN THIS:*DIALOGUE OVER A OUIJA BOARD 278   60
SIFTING (1)
  NOW COLDNESS COMES SIFTING DOWN, LAYER AFTER LAYER, ...POEM.5.F. 134   1
SIFTS (1)
  HOURGLASS SIFTS A ....DARK WOOD, DARK WATER   127   19
SIGH (2)
  ERASED, SIGH, SIGH. ....AMNESIAC   233   5
  ERASED, SIGH, SIGH. ....AMNESIAC   233   5
SIGHED (1)
  SIGHED EVE, THE ELEVATOR-GIRL ACE, ...DIALOGUE EN ROUTE   308   2
SIGHING (1)
  WRITHING AND SIGHING, WHAT SORT OF A SCENERY IS IT? ...STOPPED DEAD   230   9
SIGHS (4)
  THE PINES BLOT OUR VOICES UP IN THEIR LIGHTEST SIGHS. ....TWO CAMP. 145   24
  THEY GO UP WITHOUT HOPE, LIKE SIGHS. ....FINISTERRE 169   16
  THE CHILD IN THE WHITE CRIB REVOLVES AND SIGHS, ...EVENT 194   7
  WHAT CUPPED SIGHS, WHAT SALT IN THE THROAT.... ....BERCK-PLAGE 197   32
SIGHT (12)
  "FORSWEAR THOSE FREEZING TRICKS OF SIGHT ....RECANTATION   42   11
  TWO ENTER TO TAP HER SIGHT, A GREEN PAIR ....CRYSTAL GAZER   55   7
  EXACTED HER FIRST SIMPLE SIGHT FOR THIS STRICT SECOND.*CRYSTAL GAZER   55   30
  TO GOVERN MORE SIGHT THAN GIVEN TO A WOMAN ....CRYSTAL GAZER   55   32
  TO SET THE SIGHT ON FIRE ....BLACK ROOK IN RAINY WEATHER   57   6
  TO BEGUILE SIGHT: ....ON THE DIFFICULTY OF CONJURING UP A DRYAD   66   21
  I TRIED MY SIGHT ON AN APPLE-TREE ....ON THE PLETHORA OF DRYADS   67   4
  THE SIGHT OF THOSE BLUE, UNSEEN WAVES ....ON THE DECLINE OF ORACLES   78   14
  SO FABLES SAY THE GOATSUCKER MOVES, MASKED FROM MEN'S SIGHT ...
                                         ... GOATSUCKER   111   9
  THE NIGHTS SNAPPED OUT OF SIGHT LIKE A LIZARD'S EYELID:*THE HANGING. 141   3
  I LOSE SIGHT OF YOU ON YOUR BLIND JOURNEY, ..PARLIAMENT HILL FIELDS 153   33
  SINK OUT OF SIGHT, AND THE WATER WENT OVER MY HEAD. ....TULIPS   161   27
SIGHTING (1)
  SIGHTING THE STRATAGEM ....AERIALIST 332   37
SIGHTLESS (1)
  AND SO I STAND, A LITTLE SIGHTLESS. SO I WALK ....THREE WOMEN   184 253
SIGN (3)
  MUD-MATTRESSED UNDER THE SIGN OF THE HAG ....MAUDLIN   51   1
  SPEAK IN SIGN LANGUAGE OF A LOST OTHERWORLD,*THE GHOST'S LEAVETAKING   90   19
  OF FORMAL SCORN, UNTIL THE FIRST SIGN OF AN ....DIALOGUE O. 282 232
SIGNAL (2)
  OR ANY SIGNAL OF DISTRESS OR ANXIOUSNESS. ..STARS OVER THE DORDOGNE 165   7
  SIGNAL THE BLIND, AND ARE IGNORED. ....LITTLE FUGUE 187   4
SIGNIFICANCE (1)
  OF DIMINISHING PERSPECTIVES, AND ITS SIGNIFICANCE ....INSOMNIAC 163   24
SIGNIFY (1)
  WHICH SIGNIFY OUR ORIGIN AND END, ...THE GHOST'S LEAVETAKING   91   34
SIGNING (1)
  SIGNING IN. JUST P THIS TIME. AND OFF, DIALOGUE OVER A OUIJA BOARD   277   29
SIGNS (2)
  SIGNS SAY NOTHING. THE FALCON WHO SPOKE CLEAR ........INCOMMUNICADO 100   13
  FROM HER LIPS AMPERSANDS AND PERCENT SIGNS ....AN APPEARANCE 189   4
SILENCE (10)
  BUT A THIN SILENCE. ....THE THIN PEOPLE   64   17
  SONG, YOUR SILENCE. AT THE SOURCE ....LORELEI   94   30
  NOW SILENCE AFTER SILENCE OFFERS ITSELF. ....PARLIAMENT HILL FIELDS 152   19
  NOW SILENCE AFTER SILENCE OFFERS ITSELF. ....PARLIAMENT HILL FIELDS 152   19
  AND THE MESSAGE OF THE YEW TREE IS BLACKNESS -- BLACKNESS AND
     SILENCE. ....THE MOON AND THE YEW TREE   173   28
  THERE WAS A SILENCE! ....LITTLE FUGUE   188   36
  GREAT SILENCE OF ANOTHER ORDER. ....LITTLE FUGUE   188   37
  THIS IS THE SILENCE OF ASTOUNDED SOULS. ....CROSSING THE WATER 190   12
  MILL OF SILENCE ....CUT   236   36
  AGAINST A SILENCE WEARING THIN. ....FAMILY REUNION   300   9

444

		TITLE	PAGE	LINE

SILENCED (1)
 CEASE, AND I NEARED THE SILENCED ......MUSSEL HUNTER AT ROCK HARBOR   95 15
SILENCES (1)
 IN A QUARRY OF SILENCES. POEM.7.S.   136 13
SILENT (5)
 SILENT AND SHINING ON A GREEN ROCK BEDDED IN MUD, ...DREAM WITH C.   44 15
 NOW I AM SILENT, HATE ....LESBOS 229 64
 RULE THEIR BEDS LIKE BEHEADED AND RESURRECTED AND ALL SILENT
  ROYALTY, ... QUEEN MARY'S ROSE GARDEN 290   5
 CHALLENGES THE SILENT DOME. ..............METAMORPHOSES OF THE MOON 307 12
 CHIRPS THE FIRST: "LIVE ON A SILENT ISLAND ..EPITAPH IN THREE PARTS 337   5
SILENTLY (1)
 THE WOODS ARE A WELL. THE STARS DROP SILENTLY. ....STARS OVER. 165   4
SILHOUETTE (1)
 PICKET OF TREES WHOSE SILHOUETTE IS DARKER   STARS OVER THE DORDOGNE 165   2
SILK (14)
 SHE SEES HOW THEIR RED SILK FLARE ....TWO SISTERS OF PERSEPHONE   32 17
 OF THISTLE AND SILK, ...WORDS FOR A NURSERY   74 24
 THEY'D HAVE HAD YELLOW SILK SCREENING THE MOON, ...YADWIGHA.   85 15
 ANY SILK FAN ....POLLY'S TREE 128 12
 CADDIS WORMS DROWSE IN THEIR SILK CASES, ...POEM.5.F. 135 11
 AND UGLY, MY BELLY A SILK STOCKING ....ZOO KEEPER'S WIFE 154   6
 WHIPPING OFF YOUR SILK SCARF, EXHIBITING THE TIGHT WHITE   FACE LIFT 155   2
 THEY ARE STITCHING ME UP WITH SILK, AS IF I WERE A MATERIAL. *THREE. 181 168
 I AM MENDING A SILK SLIP: MY HUSBAND IS READING. ......THREE WOMEN 186 352
 NOW I AM MILKWEED SILK, THE BEES WILL NOT NOTICE. ..THE BEE MEETING 211   9
 THE SILK GRITS. ....LESBOS 229 62
 IN AMONG THESE SILK ....PURDAH 243 22
 CIRCLE, WITH ITS TAWN SILK GRASSES -- BABIES' HAIR.   LETTER IN NOV. 253   7
 MOVING AND RUBBING ON THE SILK ....BALLOONS 271   5
SILKS (6)
 THEIR MULTIFARIOUS SILKS IN THE HOLY GROVE*ON THE PLETHORA OF DRYADS   68 33
 THE GREAT COROLLAS DILATE, PEELING BACK THEIR SILKS. ..BEEKEEPER'S. 118   2
 EXHIBITS ITS GLAUCOUS SILKS, ...WHITSUN 154 15
 IN HER GARDEN THE LIES WERE SHAKING OUT THEIR MOIST SILKS*DETECTIVE. 208   7
 SO MANY SILKS. ....GULLIVER 251 15
 MY JAPANESE SILKS, DESPERATE BUTTERFLIES, ...KINDNESS 269 14
SILL (2)
 THE POPULACE SINGS TOWARD THE SILL ....A WINTER'S TALE   87 29
 LINTEL AND SILL HAVE UNHINGED THEMSELVES. ....WUTHERING HEIGHTS 168 32
SILLY (4)
 NOW THE PILLS ARE WORN-OUT AND SILLY, LIKE CLASSICAL GODS.*INSOMNIAC 163 20
 A THIN, SILLY MESSAGE. ....WUTHERING HEIGHTS 167 24
 EMPTY AND SILLY AS PLATES, ...LITTLE FUGUE 188 17
 WHY HE SHOULD KNEEL BEFORE A SILLY SCENE ....THE PRINCESS. 335 65
SILT (1)
 TO DREDGE THE SILT FROM YOUR THROAT. ....THE COLOSSUS 129   9
SILTING (1)
 SHREWD CATCH SILTING OUR EACH BRIGHT ACT BACK ....FIRESONG   30 13
SILVER (24)
 ON SILVER DISH, ...TINKER JACK AND THE TIDY WIVES   34   6
 SILVER FACTORY, IMMENSE ....NIGHT SHIFT   76 16
 DEEP IN YOUR FLUX OF SILVER ....LORELEI   95 34
 MEADOWS OF GOLD DUST. THE SILVER ....IN MIDAS' COUNTRY   99   1
 BE A HARVEST OF SILVER IN THE NETS, AND THE LAMPS ..THE NET-MENDERS 121 18
 THE SNAIL LEAVES A SILVER TRACK; ....THE SLEEPERS 122 10
 THOSE GREEN-STRIPED OVALS OF SILVER TISSUE? ....LEAVING EARLY 146 15
 I AM SILVER AND EXACT. I HAVE NO PRECONCEPTIONS.............MIRROR 173   1
 THE SILVER TRACK OF TIME EMPTIES INTO THE DISTANCE, ...THREE WOMEN 177 32
 THE LITTLE SILVER TROPHIES THEY'VE COME SO FAR FOR. ....THREE WOMEN 183 221
 ENGRAVING ITSELF IN SILVER WITH MARVELOUS CALM. ....BERCK-PLAGE 199 72
 SILVER BEAST BETWEEN TWO DARK CANYONS, ..THE COURAGE OF SHUTTING-UP 210   9
 BUT IN TWENTY-FIVE YEARS SHE'LL BE SILVER, ...THE APPLICANT 221 31
 THE SILVER LEASH OF THE WILL --- ....GETTING THERE 248 15
 THE SILVER LIMBO OF EACH EYE ....THE FEARFUL 256 16
 ORANGE LOLLIES ON SILVER STICKS, ...THE MUNICH MANNEQUINS 263 14
 THE ENGINE IS KILLING THE TRACK, THE TRACK IS SILVER, ...TOTEM 264   1
 BITCHES TO RIPPLES OF SILVER ....GIGOLO 268 23
 AND INTO THE SILVER ELEMENT OF THE POND. ..QUEEN MARY'S ROSE GARDEN 290 12
 OF SILVER AS THE RONDO SLOWS; NOW REELS ....CINDERELLA 303   3
 TILTING SILVER: ....AQUATIC NOCTURNE 305   9
 FLINGS SILVER GAUNTLET OF HIS PLANE AT SPACE, ...METAMORPHOSES. 307   4
 YOUR SILVER VEIL ....MOONSONG AT MORNING 317 14
 SHEER SILVER BLURS THEIR PHANTOM ACT. ....DANSE MACABRE 321 21
SILVERED (2)
 STILLED, SILVERED AS WATER IN A GLASS ....WATERCOLOR. 111   2
 DOZING AROUND THEIR SILVERED SENTRY BOX. ....THE PRINCESS. 334 30
SILVER-GLAZE (1)
 CABBAGEHEADS: WORMY PURPLE, SILVER-GLAZE, ...POEM.1.WHO. 131 16
SILVER-GRIZZLED (1)
 COMPARISON WITH THE SUNKEN SILVER-GRIZZLED ....ABOVE THE OXBOW   88   6
SILVER-HAIRED (1)
 AIR. THE SILVER-HAIRED ....POLLY'S TREE 128 15-6
SILVERSMITHS (1)
 OF WHITE AND PEWTER LIGHTS, AND A DIN LIKE SILVERSMITHS ..BLACKBER. 169 26

445

TITLE   PAGE   LINE

SILVER-SUITED (1)
  YOU ARE SILVER-SUITED FOR THE OCCASION. O ADDING MACHINE--- ...
                              ... A BIRTHDAY PRESENT   207   44
SIMIAN (1)
  ADDED ADAM, THAT SIMIAN SWELL, ...DIALOGUE EN ROUTE   309   25
SIMILAR (1)
  NOW SIMILAR CLOUDS ....LITTLE FUGUE   188   41
SIMILE (1)
  OF MUSHROOM SIMILE AND GRYPHON GARB. ....A SORCERER B.   324   8
SIMILES (1)
  WHEN HE RECITES ONE OF MY SIMILES ......DIALOGUE OVER A OUIJA BOARD   283   262
SIMMERING (1)
  SIMMERING, PERFUMED, ...THE RABBIT CATCHER   193   12
SIMPLE (10)
  WAYLAYS SIMPLE GIRLS, CHURCH-GOING, ...VANITY FAIR   32   14
  ABOVE THE SIMPLE VEIN, ...RECANTATION   42   15
  EXACTED HER FIRST SIMPLE SIGHT FOR THIS STRICT SECOND.*CRYSTAL GAZER   55   30
  OF THAT UNCOUTH SHAPE TO SIMPLE SOD AGAIN ....LADY AND T.   70   27
  AND PIPES THE WORLD BACK TO THE SIMPLE FABRIC .........SNAKECHARMER   79   23
  INTO SALT SEAS. HERCULES HAD A SIMPLE TIME, ...PERSEUS   82   6
  I AM SIMPLE AGAIN. I BELIEVE IN MIRACLES. ....THREE WOMEN   185   319
  ICEBOX, A SIMPLE ....DEATH & CO.   254   15
  THE SIMPLE SUM OF HEART PLUS HEART. ....LOVE IS A PARALLAX   331   78
  TRAILING HER SCRUPULOUSLY SIMPLE GOWN   THE PRINCESS AND THE GOBLINS   333   11
SIMPLER (1)
  A DEVON MEADOW MIGHT OFFER A SIMPLER SORT   QUEEN MARY'S ROSE GARDEN   290   23
SIMPLICITIES (1)
  AROUND OUR TENT THE OLD SIMPLICITIES SOUGH ....TWO CAMP.   145   25
SIMPLIFIED (2)
  SIMPLIFIED ME: A RIDER, RIDING ....WHITENESS I REMEMBER   103   29
  IN THE SIMPLIFIED ORDERINGS OF SKY- ....ABOVE THE OXBOW   89   47
SIMPLY (13)
  OF GILDED HARPS OR GNAWING FIRE: SIMPLY TELL ....DIALOGUE B.   39   23
  IF THE THIN PEOPLE SIMPLY STAND IN THE FOREST, ...THE THIN PEOPLE   65   45
  HOT GRAINS, SIMPLY. IT IS DRY, DRY. .....SLEEP IN THE MOJAVE DESERT   143   2
  SIMPLY TO PLUMB THE DEEPS OF AN EYE ....CANDLES   148   7
  SIMPLY BECAUSE SHE LOOKED AFTER ME SO BADLY. ....IN PLASTER   159   34
  PROMISING SIMPLY THE HARD STARS, THE SPACE ....WIDOW   164   23
  I SIMPLY CANNOT SEE WHERE THERE IS TO GET TO. ....MOON.   173   7
  SHE IS SIMPLY ASTONISHED AT FERTILITY. ....THREE WOMEN   176   7
  IT IS SIMPLY IN ITS ELEMENT. ....PHEASANT   191   9
  I HAVE SIMPLY ORDERED A BOX OF MANIACS. ....THE BEE MEETING   213   23
  SIMPLY OPEN THE DOOR AND STEP OUT OF THE CAR ....STOPPED DEAD   230   24
  IT SIMPLY EXPLODED ONE NIGHT, ...THE TOUR   238   22
  OUT OF OUR VERY COUNTENANCE BY SIMPLY ..DIALOGUE OVER A OUIJA BOARD   279   114
SIMULACRUM (1)
  THE SIMULACRUM LEERED, ...THE LADY AND THE EARTHENWARE HEAD   69   19
SIMULTANEOUSLY (1)
  SIMULTANEOUSLY SEEN ....THE GREAT CARBUNCLE   72   13
SIN (9)
  TO ATONE AS SHADE FOR SIN THAT LURED BLIND MAN." ....DIALOGUE B.   39   36
  IS THIS THE ONE SIN THEN, THIS OLD DEAD LOVE OF DEATH?   THREE WOMEN   177   42
  THE AGUEY TENDON, THE SIN, THE SIN. ....FEVER.   231   7
  THE AGUEY TENDON, THE SIN, THE SIN. ....FEVER.   231   7
  THE SIN. THE SIN. ....FEVER.   231   27
  THE SIN. THE SIN. ....FEVER.   231   27
  STILL URINOUS ON YOU, A SIN. .......................EAVESDROPPER   260   8
  AND NIBBLES AN OCCASIONAL BONBON OF SIN. ....FEMALE AUTHOR   301   4
  YOU DRANK YOUR COFFEE LIKE ORIGINAL SIN, ...THE TRIAL OF MAN   312   6
SINCE (10)
  WHETHER GOAT-THIGHED OR GOD-HALOED. EVER SINCE THAT FIRST DAPHNE ...
                              ... VIRGIN IN A TREE   81   9
  TO US, SINCE WE SEE NO LEAF EDGE STIR HIGH ....ABOVE THE OXBOW   88   33
  HE GAVE ME. I'VE GONE NOWHERE SINCE BUT ....WHITENESS I REMEMBER   102   3
  SINCE THOSE TWO CIVIL SERVANTS SET ....THE DEATH OF MYTH-MAKING   104   8
  IT IS TEN YEARS, NOW, SINCE WE ROWED TO CHILDREN'S ISLAND. ...BABY.   174   1
  SINCE CHRISTMAS THEY HAVE LIVED WITH US, ...BALLOONS   271   1
  IN PAN: IT'S BEEN EBBING EVER SINCE THE MESS ....DIALOGUE O.   277   38
  IN HELL, SINCE HELL'S A FAIRYTALE. I WOULD ....DIALOGUE O.   278   65
  I SMASHED A GLASS, AND EVER SINCE THAT DREAM ....DIALOGUE O.   285   302
  FOLLOW HOLIDAY REVEL BEGUN LONG SINCE, ...CINDERELLA   304   10
SINDBAD (1)
  FERRIES THE FISHPOND SINDBAD ....BATTLE-SCENE   84   13
SINEW (1)
  LOVE IS THE BONE AND SINEW OF MY CURSE. POEM.7.S.   137   40
SINEWS (3)
  BUT THOUGH THEY'D RIVET SINEWS IN ROCK   EPITAPH FOR FIRE AND FLOWER   46   22
  TWISTING OF THUMBSCREWS: ONE SOUL TIED IN SINEWS, ...LESSON.   80   8
  AND SINEWS BUNCHED, VICTORIOUS, AS THE COSMIC ....PERSEUS   83   44
SING (4)
  AND SO ALL CHILDREN SING ....BATTLE-SCENE   85   32
  THAN SCULPTED MARBLE. THEY SING ....LORELEI   94   14
  MULTIPLY PINK HARLEQUINS AND SING ....LOVE IS A PARALLAX   330   46
  SING PRAISE FOR STATUARY: ....TOUCH-AND-GO   335   1

                                                               TITLE   PAGE   LINE
SINGE (1)
    AND THEIR FINE LINES SINGE ....WUTHERING HEIGHTS   167   4
SINGEING (1)
    THE SINGEING FURY OF HIS FUR: ....PURSUIT   22   18
SINGELESS (1)
    I'LL FLY THROUGH THE CANDLE'S MOUTH LIKE A SINGELESS MOTH.*POEM.6.W.   135   20
SINGERS (1)
    OF BELLRINGERS AND SINGERS ROUSE ....A WINTER'S TALE   87   33
SINGING (5)
    AND SINGING THE GLOWWORM SONG, I COULD ....THE DISQUIETING MUSES   75   27
    AND NO BODIES, SINGING LIKE ARROWS UP TO HEAVEN. ....WIDOW   164   25
    MY SINGING MAKES YOU ROAR. ....BY CANDLELIGHT   237   23
    THE SINGING BIRDS PACK UP AND FLY AWAY; ....NEVER TRY TO TRICK.   320   17
    THE MAESTRO GIVES THE SINGING BIRDS THEIR PAY ....DENOUEMENT   326   4
SINGLE (7)
    WHERE, ABSURD AND OUT-OF-SEASON, A SINGLE SWAN ...WINTER LANDSCAPE,   21   3
    THIS PAIR SEEK SINGLE STATE FROM THAT DUAL BATTLE. ....WREATH F.   44   10
    THAT VAIN JADES SULK SINGLE DOWN BRIDAL NIGHTS, ...ELLA MASON A.   54   41
    OF A SINGLE ROSE PRESENT TO IMAGINE ...................RHODODENDRON.   103   3
    TINY AND FAR, A SINGLE SHIP ....ON DECK   142   6
    AT THEIR FEET, THE SEA WAVES BOW IN SINGLE FILE, ...A LIFE   150   11
    SPINNING A SINGLE STUBBORN THREAD OF WOOL ....THE PRINCESS.   333   16
SINGLE-SKIRTED (1)
    OF PERSONAGE -- SINGLE-SKIRTED, PERFUMED, A GEM -- ...QUEEN MARY'S.   290   24
SINGS (5)
    AND SINGS YOU THUS: ....THE QUEEN'S COMPLAINT   29   23
    THE POPULACE SINGS TOWARD THE SILL ....A WINTER'S TALE   87   29
    SKIRTS, SINGS IN THE DIRECTION ....TWO VIEWS OF A CADAVER ROOM   114   15
    RED THE UNRAVELED ROSE SINGS IN YOUR HAIR: ......TO EVA DESCENDING.   303   7
    THE SECOND SINGS: RECEIVE NO ROVING GALLANT   EPITAPH IN THREE PARTS   337   7
SINGULAR (1)
    THE SINGULAR AIR, ...THE SHRIKE   42   6
SINGULARLY (1)
    SUSPEND THIS DAY, SO SINGULARLY DESIGNED, ...MIDSUMMER MOBILE   324   13
SINISTER (1)
    BARE NO SINISTER SPACES. ALREADY ....BLUE MOLES   126   13
SINK (4)
    THE LIQUOR OF INDOLENCE, AND ALL THINGS SINK POEM.5.F.   134   8
    DIRTY AS A BOOTSOLE AND BIG AS A HOSPITAL SINK ...ZOO KEEPER'S WIFE   155   35
    SINK OUT OF SIGHT, AND THE WATER WENT OVER MY HEAD. ....TULIPS   161   27
    THEY BOTH WATCHED THE BAROMETER SINK ....DIALOGUE EN ROUTE   309   37
SINKERS (1)
    A DOZEN RED LEAD SINKERS ROUND MY NECK. ....TULIPS   161   42
SINKS (3)
    THE SUN SINKS UNDER BOSTON, BLOODY RED. ....POINT SHIRLEY   111   40
    THE PUNTER SINKS HIS POLE. ......WATERCOLOR OF GRANTCHESTER MEADOWS   112   12
    IN MY COURTYARD A FOUNTAIN LEAPS AND SINKS BACK INTO ITSELF,*BARREN.   157   3
SINS (1)
    HISS AT MY SINS. ....MEDUSA   226   39
SINUOUS (1)
    SINUOUS ORCHIS ....BURNING THE LETTERS   205   44
SIP (1)
    OVER WINDFALLS TO SIP CIDER-JUICE. ....YADDO: THE GRAND MANOR   123   10
SIPPING (2)
    SIPPING THEIR LIQUIDS FROM ASSORTED POTS, ...LEAVING EARLY   145   8
    LARD-PALE, SIPPING THE THIN ....WHITSUN   153   5
SIR (1)
    SIR SO-AND-SO'S GIN. ....WINTERING   218   10
SIRENS (2)
    ON STORM-STRUCK DECK, WIND SIRENS CATERWAUL; ......CHANNEL CROSSING   26   1
    ARE YOU NOT BLINDED BY SUCH EXPRESSIONLESS SIRENS?   CROSSING THE W.   190   11
SIREN-SONG (1)
    FOR PASTEBOARD, AND SIREN-SONG ....BATTLE-SCENE   85   37
SIRIUS (1)
    HALOES LUSTROUS AS SIRIUS -- ....A WINTER'S TALE   87   11
SIRS (1)
    OF UGLY SPINSTERS AND BARREN SIRS ....VIRGIN IN A TREE   82   33
SISTER (5)
    MY HEART UNDER YOUR FOOT, SISTER OF A STONE. ....BEEKEEPER'S.   118   7
    O WHAT HAS COME OVER US, MY SISTER! ....THE BABYSITTERS   175   28
    LIKE THE RED-HEADED SISTER HE NEVER DARED TO TOUCH, ...AMNESIAC   233   13
    O SISTER, MOTHER, WIFE, ...AMNESIAC   233   25
    SPLITS AND PASSES, SISTER TO ....ARIEL   239   7
SISTER-BITCH (1)
    TOAD-STONE! SISTER-BITCH! SWEET NEIGHBOR! ...........EAVESDROPPER   261   63
SISTERHOOD (1)
    I HAD NOT ASKED FOR SUCH A BLOOD SISTERHOOD: THEY MUST LOVE ME. ...
                                             ... BLACKBERRYING   168   8
SISTERS (5)
    TWO SISTERS OF PERSEPHONE ....TWO SISTERS OF PERSEPHONE   31   T
    THAN CAN BE. SISTERS, YOUR SONG ....LORELEI   94   16
    THE BLUE SISTERS SENT ME TO ANOTHER SCHOOL. POEM.4.BEAST.   134   7
    WHERE THE HEADS AND TAILS OF MY SISTERS DECOMPOSE.*ZOO KEEPER'S WIFE   154   7
    WE WERE ALWAYS CRYING, IN OUR SPARE ROOMS, LITTLE PUT-UPON
        SISTERS, ...THE BABYSITTERS   174   4

```
                                                    TITLE            PAGE  LINE
SISTER'S (2)
   THE DAY YOUR SLACK SAIL DRANK MY SISTER'S BREATH  .......ELECTRA ON.  117   30
   IN YOUR SISTER'S BIRTHDAY PICTURE START TO GLOW.  .....PARLIAMENT H.  153   42
SISYPHUS (1)
   THE STINT OF SISYPHUS. ASK PAN, THEN, WHERE  ...........DIALOGUE O.   281  173
SIT (16)
   WHILE YOU STAND HEROIC IN COAT AND TIE, I SIT  ........CONVERSATION.   21   10
   THAN TO SIT MUTE, TWITCHING SO  .................MONOLOGUE AT 3 A.M.   40    8
   I'LL GO OUT AND SIT IN WHITE LIKE THEY DO,  ................MOONRISE   98    2
   WHILE THE STUDENTS STROLL OR SIT,*WATERCOLOR OF GRANTCHESTER MEADOWS  112   24
   FATTEN IN GREEN-POCKED PODS, THE THREE NET-MENDERS SIT OUT,  ..NET-.  121    3
   LET ME SIT IN A FLOWERPOT,  ............................POEM.1.WHO.   131    7
   THEY SIT SO NICELY IN THE PICKLING FLUID!  .................STILLBORN  142    8
   OVERHEAD, THE CLOUDS SIT TASSELED AND FANCY  ................A LIFE   150   15
   I HAD EVEN FORGOTTEN HOW TO WALK OR SIT,  ...............IN PLASTER   159   45
   I AM DYING AS I SIT. I LOSE A DIMENSION.  .............THREE WOMEN   177   30
   LET US SIT DOWN TO IT, ONE ON EITHER SIDE, ADMIRING THE GLEAM, ...
                                            ... A BIRTHDAY PRESENT   207   24
   I SHOULD SIT ON A ROCK OFF CORNWALL AND COMB MY HAIR.  .......LESBOS   228   29
   SIT EMPTIED OF BEAUTIES, THE GIFT  .................THE NIGHT DANCES   250    8
   YOU SIT, SOLEMN-EYED, ABOUT TO VOMIT,  ............THE TRIAL OF MAN   312   13
   TO SIT UP STARK AWAKE  ...................................AERIALIST   332   41
   THE CHAMBERS WHERE THEIR FIENDISH QUEEN WOULD SIT.  ...THE PRINCESS.   334   40
SITS (7)
   ONE SITS; THE OTHER, WITHOUT.  ............TWO SISTERS OF PERSEPHONE   31    2
   "THERE SITS NO HIGHER COURT  ......DIALOGUE BETWEEN GHOST AND PRIEST   39   49
   GERD SITS SPINDLE-SHANKED IN HER DARK TENT,  ..........CRYSTAL GAZER   54    1
   WIDOW. THE BITTER SPIDER SITS  ................................WIDOW  164   11
   AND SITS IN THE CENTER OF HER LOVELESS SPOKES.  ...............WIDOW  164   12
   OR SITS IN THE DESERT AND HURTS HIS MOTHER'S HEART.  ...THREE WOMEN  186  333
   THEN SITS  .................................................BALLOONS  272   26
SITTING (5)
   SITTING UNDER A POTLID, TINY AND INERT AS A RICE GRAIN.  ..POEM.6.W.  135   15
   ME, SITTING HERE BORED AS A LEOPARD  .................LEAVING EARLY   145    3
   BUT STAY, SITTING FAR OUT, IN THEIR OWN DUST.  .........STARS OVER.   165   13
   WHILE WE'RE SITTING, FACE TO FACE ACROSS THE COFFEE-  ...DIALOGUE O.  276    3
   WE RAISE OUR ARGUMENTS LIKE SITTING DUCKS  .......LOVE IS A PARALLAX  329   19
SITUATIONS (1)
   ON THE INCESSANT HEAT-LIGHTNING FLICKER OF SITUATIONS.  ...INSOMNIAC  163   28
SIX (7)
   SIX FEET OF YELLOW GRAVEL COVER YOU.  ........ELECTRA ON AZALEA PATH  117   23
   SIX MONTHS IN THE WORLD, AND SHE IS ABLE  ....................MAGI   148   10
   SIX ROUND BLACK HATS IN THE GRASS AND A LOZENGE OF WOOD,*BERCK-PLAGE  201  123
   SIX JARS OF IT,  .......................................WINTERING   217    4
   SIX CAT'S EYES IN THE WINE CELLAR,  ....................WINTERING   217    5
   A SIX AND A HALF FOOT WEDDING-CAKE.  ...................EAVESDROPPER  260   26
   IT IS SIX IN THE MORNING AND FINER THAN ANY SUNDAY -- *QUEEN MARY'S.  290    8
SIX-COLORED (1)
   AND A CABIN BOY WHO COULD DECORATE CAKES IN SIX-COLORED
                    FROSTING. ........................THE BABYSITTERS  174   12
SIX-SIDED (1)
   SIX-SIDED, WHITE  ...............................THE NIGHT DANCES   250   25
SIXTY (2)
   HE SPLIT IT INTO THREE HUNDRED AND SIXTY TRICKLES  .........LESSON.   80   19
   LET IT NOT COME BY WORD OF MOUTH, I SHOULD BE SIXTY  ......BIRTHDAY.  208   53
SIZE (9)
   DOWN FROM PRIDE'S SIZE: INSTEAD, A GRISLY-THEWED,  .......SNOWMAN O.   59   29
   OF MONSTROUS SIZE, LIKE NO WELL-BRED LILIES. .............YADWIGHA.   85    7
   SIZE. THE CRIES OF SCAVENGING GULLS SOUND THIN  .........GREEN ROCK.  105   14
   BY CHRYSANTHEMUMS THE SIZE  ...................LEAVING EARLY   146   31
   OUR LADY OF THE SHIPWRECKED IS THREE TIMES LIFE SIZE,  ...FINISTERRE  170   24
   WAVING AND CRUTCHLESS, HALF THEIR OLD SIZE.  .........BERCK-PLAGE   196    9
   NURSES THE SIZE OF WORMS AND A MINUTE DOCTOR  .............AMNESIAC   233    7
   THE SIZE OF A FLY,  ......................................CONTUSION   271    7
   THE SIZE OF MY DEMAND TO MAGIC: NO MORE *DIALOGUE OVER A OUIJA BOARD  279  121
SIZZLED (1)
   I SIZZLED IN HIS BLUE VOLTS LIKE A DESERT PROPHET.  THE HANGING MAN  141    2
SKATE (1)
   FIND YOU OVER AND OVER, LIPPED LIKE A SKATE AND SMILING, ...
                                            ... THE RIVAL/DR  291   18
SKATERS (1)
   THE SKATERS FREEZE WITHIN A STONE TABLEAU.  ......PROLOGUE TO SPRING  322    3
SKATE'S (1)
   FLIES FILING IN THROUGH A DEAD SKATE'S EYEHOLE *SUICIDE OFF EGG ROCK  115   17
SKEDADDLE (1)
   WITH POKE AND GIGGLE, READY TO SKEDADDLE,  ...........ELLA MASON A.   54   25
SKEIN (2)
   THAT SKEIN OF VOICES. WE PROMISED TO FORGET  ...........DIALOGUE O.  286  342
   INVIOLATE IN THE CIRCLE OF THAT SKEIN, *THE PRINCESS AND THE GOBLINS  334   47
SKEINS (1)
   OF YOUR SPREAD HAIR, IN WHICH WRINKLING SKEINS  ....FULL FATHOM FIVE   92    8
SKELETON (3)
   FREE OF THE FICTIVE VEIN.  WHEN ONE STARK SKELETON  .....NOVEMBER G.   56   10
   SKELETON STILL CRAVES TO HAVE  .....................DANSE MACABRE   321    5
   OF STRICT AND SACRED SKELETON;  INSOLENT STORM STRIKES AT THE SKULL  325    8
```

SKELETONS (2)
    ...COFFIN OF THE FOURTH CENTURY A.D. CONTAINING THE
        SKELETONS . . .   .ALL THE DEAD DEARS   70 E/2
    TALL SKELETONS WALK;   ....TEMPER OF TIME   336   10
SKELETON'S (1)
    WHO WEAVE WITHIN THE SKELETON'S WHITE WOMB ....TERMINAL   328   7
SKEPTIC (3)
    AND STILL I'M SKEPTIC. I KNOW. I'M BEING FOOLISH ....DIALOGUE O.   277   35
    SUCH SKEPTIC CRACKS. WITH SENSE SEALED WATERTIGHT ......DIALOGUE O.   280 155
    SKEPTIC CYCLONES TRY THE BONE ..INSOLENT STORM STRIKES AT THE SKULL   325   7
SKEPTICAL (1)
    EVEN IN THIS DULL, RUINOUS LANDSCAPE): SKEPTICAL, ...BLACK ROOK I.   57   24
SKEWERED (1)
    GRIEVOUSLY PURPLED, MOUTH SKEWERED ON A GROAN, ...THE RAVAGED FACE   115   6
SKIES (4)
    ASSAULT OF SNOW-FLAWED WINDS FROM THE DOUR SKIES ....MAYFLOWER   60   2
    SKIES ONCE WEARING A BLUE, DIVINE HAUTEUR ....OUIJA   77   19
    THE POLITE SKIES OVER BOSTON COULDN'T POSSIBLY ACCOMMODATE. ...
                          ... TWO CAMPERS IN CLOUD COUNTRY   145   11
    AND THE SKIES CRACK THROUGH WITH THUNDER; ..GO GET THE GOODLY SQUAB   313   6
SKILL (1)
    NOW AS PENALTY FOR HER SKILL, ...AERIALIST   332   43
SKIN (28)
    AND I RUN FLARING IN MY SKIN; ....PURSUIT   23   34
    RUEFUL, MOST VEXED, THAT TENDER SKIN ....BUCOLICS   24   17
    FROM THE GENUINE COLOR OF SKIN; CAN OUR DREAMS ....TALE OF A TUB   25   27
    THEIR FINE SKIN SERE, ...TINKER JACK AND THE TIDY WIVES   35   30
    OF SKIN AND BONE, ...LETTER TO A PURIST 37   12
    "IN LIFE, LOVE GNAWED MY SKIN ....DIALOGUE B.   39   27
    BUT AT THE PRICE OF A PIN-STITCHED SKIN ....MAUDLIN   51   7
    SKIN WORN DOWN TO THE KNUCKLEBONES ....CRYSTAL GAZER   54   3
    WON HER THE FROG-COLORED SKIN, PALE PITH AND WATERY*VIRGIN IN A TREE   81   14
    RAISED HIS MEN OF SKIN AND BONE, ...I WANT, I WANT   106   10
    THE SEA PULSES UNDER A SKIN OF OIL. ....A WINTER SHIP   112   5
    THIN AS THE SKIN SEAMING A SCAR. ....PARLIAMENT HILL FIELDS   153   39
    SKIN DOESN'T HAVE ROOTS, IT PEELS AWAY EASY AS PAPER. ....FACE LIFT   156   20
    AND MY SKIN ITCHED AND FLAKED AWAY IN SOFT PIECES ....IN PLASTER   159   33
    THEIR SMILES CATCH ONTO MY SKIN, LITTLE SMILING HOOKS. ......TULIPS   160   21
    AND SEEMED TO GIVE HER WARMTH, LIKE A LIVE SKIN. ....WIDOW   164   19
    WHEN THE SWEETHEART FROM ENGLAND APPEARED, WITH HER CREAM SKIN AND
        YARDLEY COSMETICS, ...THE BABYSITTERS   174   6
    THEIR SKIN TINTS ARE PINK OR SALLOW, BROWN OR RED; ....THREE WOMEN   183 223
    FLICKERING LIKE THAT, WRINKLY AND CLEAR RED, LIKE THE SKIN
        OF A MOUTH. ....POPPIES IN JULY   203   6
    BLUE DEW FROM DANGEROUS SKIN. ....STINGS   214   27
    OF JAPANESE PAPER, MY GOLD BEATEN SKIN ....FEVER.   232   38
    PEEL FROM HIS SKIN. ....AMNESIAC   233   10
    OF SKIN, ...CUT   235   5
    A SORT OF WALKING MIRACLE, MY SKIN ....LADY LAZARUS   244   4
    I MAY BE SKIN AND BONE, ...LADY LAZARUS   245   33
    AND I, STEPPING FROM THIS SKIN ....GETTING THERE   249   65
    THAT MELTS THE SKIN .................................EAVESDROPPER   260   22
    HALF IN SHADE, UNTIL HER SKIN ...BLACK PINE TREE IN AN ORANGE LIGHT   328   11
SKINFLINT (1)
    THE SCENE STANDS STUBBORN: SKINFLINT TREES ......NOVEMBER GRAVEYARD   56   1
SKINNY (1)
    THE INSECTS ARE SCANT, SKINNY. ....FROG AUTUMN   99   2
SKINS (2)
    WRAPPED IN FLEA-RIDDEN DONKEY SKINS, ...THE THIN PEOPLE   64   18
    WE CAST OUR SKINS AND SLIDE ....THE SLEEPERS   123   23
SKIRTS (6)
    SKIRTS, SINGS IN THE DIRECTION ....TWO VIEWS OF A CADAVER ROOM   114   15
    BROODY AND IN LONG SKIRTS ON MY FIRST HUSBAND'S SOFA, MY
        FINGERS ....FACE LIFT   156   22
    HER MARBLE SKIRTS BLOWN BACK IN TWO PINK WINGS. ....FINISTERRE   169   20
    LITTLE BLOODY SKIRTS! ....POPPIES IN JULY   203   8
    EVEN THE SUN-CLOUDS THIS MORNING CANNOT MANAGE SUCH SKIRTS.*POP.OCT.   240   1
    CHARRED SKIRTS AND DEATHMASK ....GETTING THERE   249   47
SKULKS (1)
    SPITEFULLY SKULKS OUR WARDEN, ...FIRESONG   30   4
SKULL (11)
    IN QUARTZ, AS CRACK YOUR SKULL TO KEEP   EPITAPH FOR FIRE AND FLOWER   45   4
    OF THE PROFANE GRAIL, THE DREAMING SKULL. ..THE GHOST'S LEAVETAKING   91   40
    IN THAT RUBBLE OF SKULL PLATES AND OLD LEATHER. ....TWO VIEWS.   114   8
    A WHITE SKULL, ...WORDS   270   12
    ROTS IN THE HOLLOW OF MY SKULL ....APRIL 18   301   2
    ALL RIGHT, LET'S SAY YOU COULD TAKE A SKULL AND BREAK IT*SONNET:EVA.   304   1
    THE FUTURE AN ELECTRODE IN YOUR SKULL. ....THE TRIAL OF MAN   312   14
    AT TWELVE, EACH SKULL IS AUREOLED ....DANSE MACABRE   321   10
    INSOLENT STORM STRIKES AT THE SKULL ....INSOLENT STORM.   325   T
    INSOLENT STORM STRIKES AT THE SKULL, ...INSOLENT STORM.   325   1
    INTO THE ATTIC OF THE SKULL. ....TWO LOVERS.   327   8
SKULLED-AND-CROSSBONED (1)
    EACH SKULLED-AND-CROSSBONED GULLIVER ....ALL THE DEAD DEARS   71   34

                                            TITLE   PAGE LINE
SKULL-PLATES (1)
     TO MEND THE IMMENSE SKULL-PLATES AND CLEAR ....THE COLOSSUS 129   14
SKULLS (5)
     LADIES' SHEAVED SKULLS: ....THE SNOWMAN ON THE MOOR   59   38
     SKULLS. INSCRUTABLE, ...FULL FATHOM FIVE   93   36
     GRIMACED AS SKULLS GRIMACE: IT ....MUSSEL HUNTER AT ROCK HARBOR   97   78
     THE SKULLS, THE UNBUCKLED BONES FACING THE VIEW! ..WAKING IN WINTER 151   10
     THE SMALL SKULLS, THE SMASHED BLUE HILLS, THE GODAWFUL HUSH. ...
                                          ... FOR A FATHERLESS SON   206   13
SKULL'S (3)
     OVER HER SKULL'S MIDDEN: NO KNIFE ....VANITY FAIR   32   12
     SHAKING IN HER SKULL'S CAGE ....THE SHRIKE 42   12
     UNDERSTANDING BREAKS THROUGH THE SKULL'S SHELL ......METAMORPHOSES. 307   16
SKY (59)
     JUTTED EARLY TO MARK OUR GOING, WHILE SKY ....CHANNEL CROSSING   27   23
     TO UNMADE MUD CLOAKED BY SOUR SKY. ....FIRESONG   30   14
     BLAZON SKY BLUE, AND ENDOW THE SUN .....SOLILOQUY OF THE SOLIPSIST   37   22
     REPENT, DEPART, BEFORE GOD'S TRUMP-CRACK SPLITS THE SKY." ...
                           ... DIALOGUE BETWEEN GHOST AND PRIEST   39   46
     FROM THE MUTE SKY, I CAN'T HONESTLY COMPLAIN: ....BLACK ROOK I.   57   13
     TO STUN SKY BLACK OUT, DRIVE GIBBERING MAD ....CONJURING.   66   12
     REPORT WHITE PILLARS, A BLUE SKY ....TWO VIEWS OF WITHENS   72   17
     AGAINST OUR SKY: THEY ARE WHAT WE LOOK SOUTHWARD TO *ABOVE THE OXBOW   88   11
     BLINDERED BY GREEN, UNDER A GREEN-GRAINED SKY ......ABOVE THE OXBOW   88   28
     SUN AND SKY MIRRORED THE GREEN OF THE SPINACH. ......SPINACH-PICKER. 89   12
     A POINT OF EXCLAMATION MARKS THAT SKY ......THE GHOST'S LEAVETAKING   91   27
     SKY AND SEA, HORIZON-HINGED ....THE HERMIT AT OUTERMOST HOUSE 118   1
     WAKENS, MORNINGS, TO A COBALT SKY, ...YADDO: THE GRAND MANOR 124   19
     A BLUE SKY OUT OF THE ORESTEIA ....THE COLOSSUS 129   16
     DOWN HERE THE SKY IS ALWAYS FALLING. POEM.4.BEAST.   134   20
     HOURLY THE EYE OF THE SKY ENLARGES ITS BLANK POEM.5.F. 134   5
     I CAN TASTE THE TIN OF THE SKY -- THE REAL TIN THING. ......WAKING. 151   1
     THE ROUND SKY GOES ON MINDING ITS BUSINESS. PARLIAMENT HILL FIELDS 152   3
     THEN THE SKY AND I ARE IN OPEN CONVERSATION, ...I AM VERTICAL 162   18
     THE NIGHT SKY IS ONLY A SORT OF CARBON PAPER, ...INSOMNIAC 163   1
     THAN THE DARK OF THE SKY BECAUSE IT IS QUITE STARLESS. ......STARS. 165   3
     AND WHAT IF THE SKY HERE IS NO DIFFERENT, ..STARS OVER THE DORDOGNE 166   25
     WEIGHTING THE PALE SKY WITH A SOLIDER COLOR. .....WUTHERING HEIGHTS 167   7
     THE SKY LEANS ON ME, ME, THE ONE UPRIGHT ....WUTHERING HEIGHTS 168   37
     BITS OF BURNT PAPER WHEELING IN A BLOWN SKY. .........BLACKBERRYING 168   11
     TWICE ON SUNDAY, THE BELLS STARTLE THE SKY --- ....MOON. 173   12
     THE WHITE SKY EMPTIES OF ITS PROMISE, LIKE A CUP. ......THREE WOMEN 177   33
     I SHALL BE A SKY AND A HILL OF GOOD: O LET ME BE! ......THREE WOMEN 180 140
     BRIGHT BIRDS IN THE SKY, CONSOLING, CONSOLING? ....THREE WOMEN 185 298
     THERE IS THIS WHITE WALL, ABOVE WHICH THE SKY CREATES ITSELF -- ...
                                        ... APPREHENSIONS   195   1
     THE GRAY SKY LOWERS, THE HILLS LIKE A GREEN SEA ....BERCK-PLAGE 199   73
     WHILE A SKY, WORMY WITH PUT-BY SMILES, ...BERCK-PLAGE 200 104
     FOR A MINUTE THE SKY POURS INTO THE HOLE LIKE PLASMA. ..BERCK-PLAGE 201 125
     AND A SKY LIKE A PIG'S BACKSIDE, AN UTTER LACK OF ATTENTION. ...
                                        ... FOR A FATHERLESS SON   205   5
     IT STANDS AT MY WINDOW, BIG AS THE SKY. ....A BIRTHDAY PRESENT 207   49
     AND THE OUTRAGE OF A SKY, THE LINED BRAIN OF IT. ....COURAGE. 209   4
     SCAR IN THE SKY, RED COMET ....STINGS 215   58
     SO BLACK NO SKY COULD SQUEAK THROUGH. ....THE DADDY 223   47
     SURELY THE SKY IS NOT THAT COLOR, ...THE JAILER 226   24
     THAT KEEPS THE SKY AT BAY, ...BY CANDLELIGHT   237   29
     TO JUGGLE WITH, MY LOVE, WHEN THE SKY FALLS. ....BY CANDLELIGHT   237   36
     BY A SKY ....POPPIES IN OCTOBER 240   6
     EYES TO THE SKY. ....GULLIVER   251   11
     THAT WATCHES, LIKE GOD, OR THE SKY ...................EAVESDROPPER   261   44
     THROUGH WHICH THE SKY ETERNALLY THREADS ITSELF? ....TOTEM 264   21
     THE SKY OF THE CITY IS WHITE; THE LIGHT FROM THE COUNTRY. ...
                           ... QUEEN MARY'S ROSE GARDEN   290   10
     BLUE SKY OR BLACK ....THE RIVAL/DR 291 11
     HERE IS A WHITE SKY. HERE IS THE BEAUTY ....FEVER./DR   294   9
     THE SKY WAS HIGH AND BLUE. ....BITTER STRAWBERRIES 299   13
     IN A FEW SPACES OF SKY AND TREETOPS ....APRIL 18 302   13
     SKY WON'T BE DRAWN CLOSER: ABSOLUTE, ...METAMOSPHOSES OF THE MOON 307   7
     FIGURED IN THE MIDNIGHT SKY, ...TO A JILTED LOVER 309   4
     AIR ALTERS INTO GLASS AND THE WHOLE SKY ....PROLOGUE TO SPRING 322   4
     TILL UNRULY CHILDREN STREAM DOWN THE SKY ....SONG FOR A REVOLU. 323 14
     THEN SYNCOPATE A SKY OF DUFY-BLUE ....MIDSUMMER MOBILE   324   2
     WHERE WAVE PRETENDS TO DRENCH REAL SKY." ....LOVE IS A PARALLAX   329   6
     ARROWS THAT LACERATE THE SKY, WHILE KNOWING ....LOVE IS A PARALLAX   330   61
     ELABORATE SCAFFOLD OF SKY OVERHEAD ....AERIALIST   332   47
     A WINDOW WHICH PROVES THE SKY SHEER RIGMAROLE*EPITAPH IN THREE PARTS 337   28
SKY-CIRCLE (1)
     THE FLAT BLUE SKY-CIRCLE POEM.7.S. 136   3
SKYFULS (1)
     THE ACID BATHS, THE SKYFULS OFF OF YOU. ....LESBOS   228   47
SKY-HIGH (1)
     SKY-HIGH, AND SNOW ....THE SNOWMAN ON THE MOOR   59   32
SKYLIGHT (1)
     A RUDDY SKYLIGHT PAINTS THE GRAY OXBOW ....ABOVE THE OXBOW   88   42

SKY-LORDED (1)
    IN THE SIMPLIFIED ORDERINGS OF SKY-LORDED ....ABOVE THE OXBOW   89 47-8
SKY-MIRRORING (1)
    AND I, ON THE SKY-MIRRORING, BLAND SANDS ....THE RIVAL/DR 291   17
SKY'S (4)
    COLD SQUINT STEALS SKY'S COLOR; WHILE BRUIT ....VANITY FAIR   32   8
    WORK OF THE EARTH AND THE SKY'S RIDGEPOLE. ....FULL FATHOM FIVE   93   32
    THE SKY'S GREAT BELL GLASS AND BRIEFLY ENGRAVE ...IN MIDAS' COUNTRY   99   8
    THE SKY'S FAR DOME IS SANE AND CLEAR. ....BLUE MOLES 126   10
SKYWARD (1)
    SKYWARD AGAIN, WITHOUT HOPE, OF COURSE, ...LOVE LETTER 147   7
SLABS (1)
    ELOPING FROM THEIR SLABS, ABSTRACT ....DANSE MACABRE 321   19
SLACK (3)
    THE DAY YOUR SLACK SAIL DRANK MY SISTER'S BREATH ....ELECTRA ON. 117   30
    SLACK FOAM IN THE LAP. ....A SECRET 220   43
    AND TRAP THE MUSKRAT NAPPING IN SLACK SUN;   GO GET THE GOODLY SQUAB 313   10
SLAG (1)
    THE LEADEN SLAG OF THE WORLD -- ....DEPARTURE   51   11
SLAKE (1)
    HE, HUNGER-STUNG, HARD TO SLAKE, ...THE GLUTTON   40   1
SLAM (1)
    A CAR DOOR SLAM: VOICES COMING NEAR; ....FAMILY REUNION 300   2
SLANT (2)
    THE BLIND, WHITE, AWFUL, INACCESSIBLE SLANT. ..NEW YEAR ON DARTMOOR 176   5
    HER GREEN EYES SLANT, HAIR FLARING IN A FAN ....CINDERELLA 303   2
SLANTING (1)
    CLOUDWRACK AND OWL-HOLLOWED WILLOWS SLANTING OVER ......WATERCOLOR. 112   8
SLANTS (1)
    WELL OR ILL." GERD SLANTS A LOOK AT EACH: MOST DEAR,   CRYSTAL GAZER   55   10
SLAPPED (1)
    THE MIDWIFE SLAPPED YOUR FOOTSOLES, AND YOUR BALD CRY   MORNING SONG 156   2
SLAPPING (1)
    SLAPPING ITS PHANTOM LAUNDRY IN MY FACE. .............BLACKBERRYING 169   21
SLATE (1)
    A CLEAN SLATE, WITH YOUR OWN FACE ON. ....YOU'RE 141   18
SLAUGHTER (1)
    IN BRUEGHEL'S PANORAMA OF SMOKE AND SLAUGHTER ....TWO VIEWS. 114   12
SLAVE (1)
    YOU COULD TELL ALMOST AT ONCE SHE HAD A SLAVE MENTALITY. *IN PLASTER 159   21
SLAY (2)
    WHAT FURY URGED HIM SLAY ....THE QUEEN'S COMPLAINT   28   9
    TO SLAY SPAWN OF DRAGON'S TEETH: SPEAKING THIS PROMISE, ..WREATH F.   45   23
SLAYING (1)
    SLAYING THE DANDIES WITH HER EMERALD EYES; ....ELLA MASON A.   54   16
SLEDGE (1)
    AS A SLEDGE HAMMER, AS A MAN'S BUNCHED FIST, ...SPIDER   48   4
SLEEK (1)
    WHILE ELLA DROWSED WHISKERED WITH SLEEK FACE, SLY WITS: ...
                        ... ELLA MASON AND HER ELEVEN CATS   54   29
SLEEKS (1)
    AND BUFFS AND SLEEKS THE BLUNT HULLS ..MUSSEL HUNTER AT ROCK HARBOR   95   5
SLEEP (28)
    SHAPE OF HER SLEEP, HER THOUGHT -- ....THE QUEEN'S COMPLAINT   29   19
    FOR FEVER IN A SLEEP. ....BATTLE-SCENE   85   38
    WHERE BEES, STRIPED BLACK AND GOLD, SLEEP OUT THE BLIZZARD ...
                        ... ELECTRA ON AZALEA PATH 116   3
    THEY SLEEP ON, MOUTH TO MOUTH. ....THE SLEEPERS 123   15
    AND THEY TURN IN THEIR SLEEP. ....THE SLEEPERS 123   18
    THEY MOVE THROUGH THEIR MUTE ROOMS WHILE I SLEEP, ...BLUE MOLES 126   23
    THE LAMP-HEADED NYMPHS ARE NODDING TO SLEEP LIKE STATUES. *POEM.5.F. 135   12
    SLEEP IN THE MOJAVE DESERT ....SLEEP IN THE MOJAVE DESERT 143   T
    OVER THEIR IRON STILE. AND STILL DON'T SLEEP. ....ZOO KEEPER'S WIFE 155   40
    I COULDN'T SLEEP FOR A WEEK, SHE WAS SO COLD. ....IN PLASTER 158   9
    THEY BRING ME NUMBNESS IN THEIR BRIGHT NEEDLES, THEY BRING ME
            SLEEP. ....TULIPS 160   17
    I HAD TO SLEEP IN THE SAME ROOM WITH THE BABY ON A TOO-SHORT COT, ...
                        ... THE BABYSITTERS 174   7
    THE COOK HAD ONE WALL EYE AND COULDN'T SLEEP, SHE WAS SO NERVOUS. ...
                        ... THE BABYSITTERS 175   25
    WAITING LIES HEAVY ON MY LIDS. IT LIES LIKE SLEEP, ...THREE WOMEN 179 108
    I SEE HER IN MY SLEEP, MY RED, TERRIBLE GIRL. ....THREE WOMEN 182 204
    SCRATCHING AT MY SLEEP LIKE ARROWS, ...THREE WOMEN 182 214
    SCRATCHING AT MY SLEEP, AND ENTERING MY SIDE. ....THREE WOMEN 182 215
    WHO INJURE MY SLEEP WITH THEIR WHITE EYES, THEIR FINGERLESS
            HANDS. ....THREE WOMEN 185 321
    THEY COLOR MY SLEEP, ...LITTLE FUGUE 188   34
    IF I COULD BLEED, OR SLEEP! --- ....POPPIES IN JULY 203   11
    REMEMBERING, EVEN IN SLEEP, ...NICK AND THE CANDLESTICK 241   25
    THEY WOULD HAVE YOU SLEEP IN THEIR CABINETS, ...GULLIVER 251   18
    IN SLEEP. THE CHAIRS WON'T VANISH OR BECOME ....DIALOGUE O. 286 355
    WHILE I SLEEP, THE BLACK SPORES NOD ....THE RIVAL/DR 291   2
    AND LET THE DEAD SLEEP AS THEY DESERVE. ....THE RIVAL/DR 291   28
    OR THAT BECAUSE OF SLEEP ....APRIL 18 302   7
    OF OUR COLOSSAL SLEEP, COME HOME TO FIND ....DOOM OF EXILES 318   2

	TITLE	PAGE	LINE

SLEEP (CONT.)
THEY LOLL FOREVER IN COLOSSAL SLEEP; ....THE DEAD 320 12
SLEEPDRUNK (1)
SLEEPDRUNK, THEIR LIMBS AT ODDS? POEM.3.MAENAD. 133 23
SLEEPERS (5)
THE SLEEPERS ....THE SLEEPERS 122 T
WHERE THOSE TWO SLEEPERS ARE. ....THE SLEEPERS 122 2
I WALK AMONG SLEEPERS IN GAUZE SARCOPHAGI. ...THE SURGEON AT 2 A.M. 171 47
THESE BODIES MOUNDED AROUND ME NOW, THESE POLAR SLEEPERS -- THREE. 181 181
THE SLEEPERS WAKE ....MOONSONG AT MORNING 317 26
SLEEP-FEATHERED (1)
TO WING, SLEEP-FEATHERED, ...THE SHRIKE 42 5
SLEEPILY (1)
SLEEPILY AS LETHE, TRYING TO GET IN. ..TWO CAMPERS IN CLOUD COUNTRY 145 26
SLEEPING (12)
THOUGH FISHERMEN ARE SLEEPING, ...LORELEI 94 6
SOMETIMES I THINK THAT WHEN I AM SLEEPING ....I AM VERTICAL 162 14
THEIR FEATURES ARE SLEEPING, LIKE LIGHT ON QUIET WATER. *THREE WOMEN 183 226
IS SHE DEAD, IS SHE SLEEPING? ....STINGS 215 53
MY SLEEPING CAPSULE, MY RED AND BLUE ZEPPELIN ....THE JAILER 226 12
I'M DOPED AND THICK FROM MY LAST SLEEPING PILL. ....LESBOS 228 34
DRUM OF MY SLEEPING COUCH ....PARALYTIC 266 21
MY BABY IS SLEEPING. ....FEVER. 294 12
GO SNARE THE SLEEPING BEAR IN LEAF-LINED DEN*GO GET THE GOODLY SQUAB 313 9
ASSAULT A SLEEPING VIRGIN'S SHROUD ....DANSE MACABRE 321 14
ASSAULTS THE SLEEPING CITADEL, INSOLENT STORM STRIKES AT THE SKULL 325 2
SHOULD INFLAME THE SLEEPING TOWN. ....LOVE IS A PARALLAX 329 30
SLEEPLESS (1)
LIGHTS OUT, THEY DOGGED US, SLEEPLESS AND ENVIOUS: ...THE OTHER TWO 68 28
SLEEPLESSNESS (1)
HE SUFFERS HIS DESERT PILLOW, SLEEPLESSNESS ....INSOMNIAC 163 6
SLEEPS (2)
THAT SLEEPS IN ME; ....ELM 193 32
SMELL OF YOUR SLEEPS, LILIES, LILIES. ....THE NIGHT DANCES 250 10
SLEEP-TALKING (1)
IN A CLENCH OF BLOOD, THE SLEEP-TALKING VIRGIN ....MAUDLIN 51 2
SLEEP-TWISTED (1)
OF CHAIRS AND BUREAUS AND SLEEP-TWISTED SHEETS. ....GHOST'S. 90 7
SLEEVE (1)
BLEEDING HEARTS ON ITS SLEEVE ....POLLY'S TREE 129 40
SLEEVELESS (1)
IN MY SLEEVELESS SUMMERY DRESS I HAVE NO PROTECTION,*THE BEE MEETING 211 3
SLEEVES (1)
WITH TRIANGULAR SCORCH MARKS FROM IRONING TINY RUCHINGS AND PUFFED
SLEEVES. ....THE BABYSITTERS 174 15
SLEIGHS (1)
TWO CARVED SLEIGHS ....YADDO: THE GRAND MANOR 123 15
SLEIGHT-OF-HAND (2)
STAR-LUCKY SLEIGHT-OF-HAND MAN WATCHES ....CONJURING. 66 34
MY NATIVE SLEIGHT-OF-HAND IS WEARING OUT: ....A SORCERER B. 324 9
SLEPT (4)
WE SLEPT LIKE STONES. LADY, WHAT AM I DOING ....LEAVING EARLY 146 42
THAT WASN'T IT. I SLEPT, SAY: A SNAKE ....LOVE LETTER 147 9
AND I SLEPT ON LIKE A BENT FINGER. ....LOVE LETTER 147 19
"LAST NIGHT," HE SAID, "I SLEPT WELL ....THE DREAM 310 1
SLICES (1)
AND TISSUE IN SLICES -- A PATHOLOGICAL SALAMI.*THE SURGEON AT 2 A.M. 171 36
SLIDE (3)
WE CAST OUR SKINS AND SLIDE ....THE SLEEPERS 123 23
AND THE UNIVERSE SLIDE FROM MY SIDE. ....A BIRTHDAY PRESENT 208 62
WHERE GUESTS SLIDE GLIDING INTO LIGHT LIKE WINE; ....CINDERELLA 304 6
SLIDES (1)
THE SEA SLIDES BACK, ...CONTUSION 271 11
SLIDING (4)
IN BLACK NOVEMBER. AFTER A SLIDING RAIN ....DIALOGUE B. 38 3
SLIDING THEIR QUOITS ONE ....DARK WOOD, DARK WATER 127 22
SLIDING SHUT ON SOME QUICK THING, ...THE RABBIT CATCHER 194 29
CAME SLIDING DOWN HIS SHOULDERBLADES ....GOLD MOUTHS CRY 302 5
SLIGHT (1)
TO SUMMON IN HER SLIGHT ALL DOUGHTY MEN ......THE QUEEN'S COMPLAINT 29 17
SLIGHTED (1)
THE HORRORS THAT STAND AND IDLE, THE SLIGHTED GODMOTHERS*THREE WOMEN 180 137
SLIGHTEST (1)
IT WILL PING LIKE A CHINESE CHIME IN THE SLIGHTEST AIR STIR A LIFE 150 7
SLIGHTLY (2)
...WOMAN HAS BEEN SLIGHTLY GNAWN. ....ALL THE DEAD DEARS 70 E/4
SWAYING SLIGHTLY IN THEIR THICK SUITS, ...TOTEM 264 6
SLIME (3)
CLAM-DIGGERS ROSE UP OUT OF DARK SLIME AT HER OFFENSE.*DREAM WITH C. 44 24
TROLL NO SLIME, NO WEED. ....BATTLE-SCENE 84 23
THE SLIME OF ALL MY YESTERDAYS ....APRIL 18 301 1
SLIP (3)
I HAVE LET THINGS SLIP, A THIRTY-YEAR-OLD CARGO BOAT ....TULIPS 161 22
I AM MENDING A SILK SLIP: MY HUSBAND IS READING. ....THREE WOMEN 186 352
HAD LAZILY CLOSED ONE EYE AND LET THEM SLIP ....LYONNESSE 234 21

	TITLE	PAGE	LINE

SLIPPED (1)
   WHAT KEYHOLE HAVE WE SLIPPED THROUGH, WHAT DOOR HAS SHUT? ....BABY. 175 42
SLIPPER (1)
   HERE IS HIS SLIPPER, HERE IS ANOTHER, ...STINGS 215 42
SLIPPERS (1)
   AND I IN SLIPPERS AND HOUSEDRESS WITH NO LIPSTICK! ....THE TOUR 237 ˙6
SLIPPERY (1)
   HER NINE SO SLIPPERY LIVES. ....AERIALIST 332 36
SLIPPINESS (1)
   DON'T KNOW WHAT TO MAKE OF THE SUDDEN SLIPPINESS, ...NEW YEAR ON. 176 4
SLIPPING (1)
   THICK, RED AND SLIPPING. IT IS ADAM'S SIDE, ...GETTING THERE 248 36
SLIPS (3)
   THE FEN FOG SLIPS, ...PROSPECT 28 3
   IN THE DISTANCE. ALL AROUND US THE WATER SLIPS ....A WINTER SHIP 113 18
   AND SLIPS UNSEEN PAST WATCHMEN ON THE LAWN ....THE PRINCESS. 334 29
SLIT (2)
   EXIT FROM A SMOKING SLIT ....RHYME 50 17
   BUTTONING THE CUFFS AT MY WRISTS AND THE SLIT FROM MY NECK TO MY
      KNEES. ....THE BEE MEETING 211 8
SLIVERS (1)
   TURQUOISE SLIVERS ....AQUATIC NOCTURNE 305 2
SLOOPS (1)
   WITH TILTED SPARS OF SLOOPS REVOLVED BY WHITE .....MIDSUMMER MOBILE 324 3
SLOPE (1)
   SCARCELY VISIBLE. ABOUT AND ABOUT THE SLOPE ....SPIDER 48 14
SLOPED (1)
   SLOPED SEAWARD TO PLUNGE IN BLUE; FED BY WHITE FIRE, DREAM WITH C. 44 11
SLOPES (1)
   KEEPER COLLECTS HALF-DOLLARS FOR THE SLOPES ....ABOVE THE OXBOW 88 40
SLOPS (1)
   OF KITCHEN SLOPS AND STOMACHING NO CONSTRAINT, ...SOW 61 43
SLOSH (1)
   NAVIGATES THE TIDAL SLOSH OF SEAS ....TALE OF A TUB 25 44
SLOT (2)
   WITH A PENNY SLOT ....OWL 60 12
   I AM A LETTER IN THIS SLOT --- ....GETTING THERE 248 18
SLOTHFUL (1)
   GO CULL THE PURPLE SNAILS FROM SLOTHFUL SHELLS ....GO GET. 313 17
SLOTS (2)
   THE BALD SLOTS OF HIS EYES STIFFENED WIDE-OPEN ....INSOMNIAC 163 27
   THE BLACK SLOTS OF THEIR PUPILS TAKE ME IN. ......WUTHERING HEIGHTS 167 22
SLOUCH (1)
   VEERS TO HER SLOUCH. ....STRUMPET SONG 33 8
SLOVEN (2)
   THE WORST SLOVEN ....VANITY FAIR 33 30
   THE WHOLE SEASON, SLOVEN. ....SPINSTER 49 12
SLOW (10)
   I SAW SLOW FLOCKED COWS MOVE ....SONG FOR A SUMMER'S DAY 30 3
   WOULDN'T SLOW FOR THE HAULED REINS, HIS NAME, WHITENESS I REMEMBER 103 24
   THAN THE CLOUD THAT DISTILLS A MIRROR TO REFLECT ITS OWN SLOW ...
              ... MORNING SONG 157 8
   I AM SLOW AS THE WORLD. I AM VERY PATIENT, ...THREE WOMEN 176 1
   IT PETRIFIES THE WILL. THESE ARE THE ISOLATE, SLOW FAULTS ......ELM 193 41
   THEIR FACES TURNING, WORDLESS AND SLOW, ...BERCK-PLAGE 201 120
   SO SLOW I HARDLY KNOW THEM, ...WINTERING 218 23
   O SLOW ....SHEEP IN FOG 262 5
   BEGINS. A JERK. AND NOW THE FIRST SLOW RAMBLE ....DIALOGUE O. 277 21
   OF SLOW DISASTER: THE BITTEN APPLE ENDS ..METAMORPHOSES OF THE MOON 307 14
SLOWED (1)
   THEY BRASSILY PICKED, SLOWED BY NO CHAGRIN, ...RHODODENDRON. 104 24
SLOWLY (9)
   WHICH ARE SLOWLY OPENING THEIR FURRED PETALS ....MISS DRAKE P. 41 11
   RODE OUT AGAINST THE FIFTH BULL TO BRACE HIS PIKE AND SLOWLY BEAR ...
              ... THE GORING 47 6
   SLOWLY SHE SPINS THE BALL: ....CRYSTAL GAZER 55 12
   SLOWLY, GRUNT ....SOW 61 38
   CARRIES ITS CANDLES SLOWLY OFF. ....ON DECK 142 8
   WHERE ONCE A DAY THE LIGHT SLOWLY WIDENS AND SLOWLY THINS, ..TULIPS 161 45
   WHERE ONCE A DAY THE LIGHT SLOWLY WIDENS AND SLOWLY THINS, ..TULIPS 161 45
   MARY SAID SLOWLY, "I'VE GOT A FELLA ....BITTER STRAWBERRIES 299 10
   SLOWLY CONCEDE TO SUN AND SERUM. ..MORNING IN THE HOSPITAL SOLARIUM 332 18
SLOWS (1)
   OF SILVER AS THE RONDO SLOWS; NOW REELS ....CINDERELLA 303 3
SLUG (1)
   OF A SLUG OR SMALL PREAMBLE ....NOTES TO A NEOPHYTE 306 5
SLUGGARD'S (1)
   TO QUICKEN HIS SLUGGARD'S BLOOD. BUT HE NEEDN'T COME ...DIALOGUE O. 281 184
SLUGGISH (2)
   MEET THE THIN AND SLUGGISH THREAD .....MUSSEL HUNTER AT ROCK HARBOR 96 42
   LET DROP ITS SPITTLE OF SLUGGISH GREEN ..............RHODODENDRON. 103 6
SLUGGY (1)
   THICK AS FOREIGN COFFEE, AND WITH A SLUGGY PULSE. .....WORDS HEARD. 202 2
SLUGLIKE (1)
   AND THE EYES OF THE KILLER MOVING SLUGLIKE AND SIDELONG, *DETECTIVE. 208 8

	TITLE	PAGE	LINE

SLUICE (1)
    WATER IN THE MILLRACE, THROUGH A SLUICE OF STONE, WINTER LANDSCAPE, 21   1
SLUICES (1)
    SCOURGING TO SORES HIS OWN RED SLUICES ....A LESSON IN VENGEANCE   80 13
SLUMBERING (1)
    THE THICK GERMANS SLUMBERING IN THEIR BOTTOMLESS STOLZ. ....MUNICH. 263 23
SLUMPS (1)
    THE IMPOTENT HUSBAND SLUMPS OUT FOR A COFFEE. ....LESBOS 228 44
SLUT (2)
    TIME COMES ROUND FOR THAT FOUL SLUT: ....STRUMPET SONG   33   4
    CLEOPATRA FROM A SLUT. ...................METAMORPHOSES OF THE MOON 307 24
SLUTTISH (2)
    I MUST WATCH SLUTTISH DRYADS TWITCH ......ON THE PLETHORA OF DRYADS   67 32
    WHAT THE SLUTTISH, RUTTED SEA COULD DO. ....POINT SHIRLEY 110 12
SLY (3)
    WHILE ELLA DROWSED WHISKERED WITH SLEEK FACE, SLY WITS: ...
                        ... ELLA MASON AND HER ELEVEN CATS   54 29
    AND WAKEN THE SLY NERVE UP ....THE LADY AND THE EARTHENWARE HEAD   69 14
    A SLY WORLD'S HINGES HAD SWUNG ....MUSSEL HUNTER AT ROCK HARBOR   95 19
SLYLY (1)
    SELVES POSING AS PROPHET AND SLYLY POACHING ....DIALOGUE O. 280 134
SMACK (2)
    AS SMACK OF SPITE AND THE OVERSCRUPULOUS .....A LESSON IN VENGEANCE   80   7
    A GREASY SMACK ON EVERY CHEEK ....FAMILY REUNION 300 14
SMACKS (1)
    OF THE THREE FISHING SMACKS BEACHED ...MUSSEL HUNTER AT ROCK HARBOR   95   6
SMALL (58)
    TO SEE MY PEOPLE SHRUNK SO SMALL, SO SMALL."   THE QUEEN'S COMPLAINT   29 25
    TO SEE MY PEOPLE SHRUNK SO SMALL, SO SMALL."   THE QUEEN'S COMPLAINT   29 25
    FOR SMALL CHARGE. ....TINKER JACK AND THE TIDY WIVES   34 14
    NEAR HIS SMALL STONEHENGE ABOVE THE ANTS' ROUTE, ...SPIDER   48 11
    THEIR SMALL PRICE PAID, THESE WEDDED ONES ....CRYSTAL GAZER   55 25
    OF HER SMALL HEAT OUT, BUT BEFORE THE WEIGHT ......HARDCASTLE CRAGS   63 42
    WERE SMALL THAT THEY FAMISHED AND ....THE THIN PEOPLE   64   7
    SMALL MUD KNOBS, NUDGED FROM UNDER, ...MUSSEL HUNTER AT ROCK HARBOR   96 26
    WHERE SMALL ANTS ROLL THEIR EGGS, WHERE GRUBS FATTEN. .....MOONRISE   98 17
    ABRADING MY LID, THE SMALL GRAIN BURNS: ....THE EYE-MOTE 109 16
    THE SMALL SHREW CHITTERS FROM ITS WILDERNESS ....WATERCOLOR. 112   4
    SMALL AS A DOLL IN MY DRESS OF INNOCENCE ....ELECTRA ON AZALEA PATH 116 11
    THE SMALL GREEN NOSTRILS BREATHE, ...THE SLEEPERS 123 17
    THE SMALL BIRDS CONVERGE, CONVERGE ....THE MANOR GARDEN 125 19
    I BEND OVER THIS DRAINED BASIN WHERE THE SMALL FISH   PRIVATE GROUND 131 20
    I SAID: I MUST REMEMBER THIS, BEING SMALL. POEM.1.WHO. 132 28
    SMALL NOSTRILS ARE BREATHING. POEM.2.DARK. 133 23
    WE ARE FULL OF STARCH, MY SMALL WHITE FELLOWS. WE GROW. ..POEM.6.W. 135 17
    THE SMALL DELL EATS WHAT ATE IT ONCE. ....THE BURNT-OUT SPA 138 18
    THE SMALL GRAINS MAKE ROOM. ....MUSHROOMS 139   9
    SMALL DROPS SPOT THEIR COATS, THEIR GLOVES: ....ON DECK 143 16
    IN THE CREVICE OF AN EXTREMELY SMALL SHADOW ....SLEEP. 144 15
    NOR LEAVE ME TO SET MY SMALL BALD EYE ....LOVE LETTER 147   6
    A CROCODILE OF SMALL GIRLS ....PARLIAMENT HILL FIELDS 152 13
    FUG OF THE SMALL MAMMAL HOUSE. ....ZOO KEEPER'S WIFE 155 19
    THE KNOCK OF THE SMALL, NEW HEART. ....HEAVY WOMEN 158 14
    AND DRINK THE SMALL NIGHT CHILL LIKE NEWS OF HOME. ....STARS. 166 40
    GLEAM LIKE SMALL CHANGE. ....WUTHERING HEIGHTS 168 45
    ALMOST TOO SMALL FOR THE MISTS TO BOTHER WITH. ....FINISTERRE 169 12
    I AM SO SMALL ....THE SURGEON AT 2 A.M. 171 18
    OVER ONE BED IN THE WARD, A SMALL BLUE LIGHT   THE SURGEON AT 2 A.M. 171 41
    AND THE SHINE OF THESE SMALL THINGS SWEETER THAN THE FACE
        OF ISHTAR. .... LAST WORDS 172 26
    HER BLUE GARMENTS UNLOOSE SMALL BATS AND OWLS. ....MOON. 173 18
    AND A SMALL DALMATIAN. ....THE BABYSITTERS 174 18
    WHEN I FIRST SAW IT, THE SMALL RED SEEP, I DID NOT BELIEVE IT. ...
                        ... THREE WOMEN 177 15
    I SAW THE WORLD IN IT -- SMALL, MEAN AND BLACK, ...THREE WOMEN 178 54
    THESE PURE, SMALL IMAGES. THEY SMELL OF MILK. ....THREE WOMEN 183 230
    SHE IS A SMALL ISLAND, ASLEEP AND PEACEFUL, ...THREE WOMEN 184 260
    A SMALL WHITE SOUL IS WAVING, A SMALL WHITE MAGGOT. ....EVENT 195 19
    A SMALL WHITE SOUL IS WAVING, A SMALL WHITE MAGGOT. ....EVENT 195 19
    AND MY HEART TOO SMALL TO BANDAGE THEIR TERRIBLE FAULTS.*BERCK-PLAGE 198 45
    THE SMALL SKULLS, THE SMASHED BLUE HILLS, THE GODAWFUL HUSH. ...
                        ... FOR A FATHERLESS SON 206 13
    DO NOT BE ASHAMED -- I DO NOT MIND IF IT IS SMALL. ....BIRTHDAY. 206 22
    SMALL, TAKEN ONE BY ONE, BUT MY GOD, TOGETHER! ....THE ARRIVAL. 213 20
    CONFRONTS ITS SMALL ....CUT 236 35
    THIS IS WINTER, THIS IS NIGHT, SMALL LOVE -- ....BY CANDLELIGHT 236   1
    SMALL AND CROSS. THE YELLOW KNIFE ....BY CANDLELIGHT 237 21
    WITH HER WIGGLY FINGERS AND FOR A VERY SMALL FEE. ....THE TOUR 238 47
    GULPS AND RECOVERS ITS SMALL ALTITUDE, ...NICK AND THE CANDLESTICK 241 21
    FROM THE SMALL JEWELED ....PURDAH 244 53
    IT IS SO SMALL ....GETTING THERE 249 44
    OF YOUR SMALL BREATH, THE DRENCHED GRASS ....THE NIGHT DANCES 250   9
    THE HUMPBACK IN HIS SMALL, WASHED COTTAGE ....MYSTIC 269 22
    YOUR SMALL ....BALLOONS 272 20
    DID. IT'S SMALL, BUT THE VOLUME OF THE VOICE ....DIALOGUE O. 281 203

SMALL (CONT.)
    IS SMALL THESE DAYS. DON'T BE SO SMART. I'LL ASK. ....DIALOGUE O.   281 204
    OF A SLUG OR SMALL PREAMBLE ....NOTES TO A NEOPHYTE   306   5
    SMALL A THORN ....TO A JILTED LOVER   310 11
SMALLER (1)
    THE SMALLER AND MORE TIMID NEVER ARRIVE AT ALL ....STARS. 165 12
SMART (2)
    IN WAIT FOR SHARPER SMART TO FADE. ....BUCOLICS   24 24
    IS SMALL THESE DAYS. DON'T BE SO SMART. I'LL ASK, ...DIALOGUE O.   281 204
SMARTEST (1)
    AND WE'LL SEE WHO'S SMARTEST. PAN, TELL US NOW: ....DIALOGUE O.   281 205
SMASHED (3)
    THE SMALL SKULLS, THE SMASHED BLUE HILLS, THE GODAWFUL HUSH. ...
                                           ... FOR A FATHERLESS SON   206 13
    CARAPACE SMASHED, ...THE JAILER 226 14
    I SMASHED A GLASS, AND EVER SINCE THAT DREAM ....DIALOGUE O.   285 302
SMASHING (1)
    AND MARVEL AT THE SMASHING NONCHALANCE ....CHANNEL CROSSING   27 15
SMELL (17)
    SURFEITING EYE, EAR, TASTE, TOUCH, SMELL; ON THE PLETHORA OF DRYADS   67 27
    I SMELL THAT WHITENESS HERE, BENEATH THE STONES ....MOONRISE   98 16
    MY SWADDLED LEGS AND ARMS SMELL SWEET AS RUBBER. POEM.7.S. 137 34
    I CAN SMELL THE SALT, ALL RIGHT. ....WHITSUN 154 13
    BLOOM ABOUT ME LIKE NIGHT FLOWERS, WITH A GOOD SMELL. ...LAST WORDS 172 22
    THESE PURE, SMALL IMAGES. THEY SMELL OF MILK. ....THREE WOMEN 183 230
    SMELL THE MELT OF SHOE-BLACKING, ...BERCK-PLAGE 201 119
    OPEN YOUR HANDBAG. WHAT IS THAT BAD SMELL? ....THE OTHER 201 13
    THIS IS THE SMELL OF YEARS BURNING, HERE IN THE KITCHEN, *DETECTIVE. 208 12
    THERE IS THE SMELL OF POLISH, THERE ARE PLUSH CARPETS.*THE DETECTIVE 209 17
    THEY WILL NOT SMELL MY FEAR, MY FEAR, MY FEAR. .....THE BEE MEETING 211 10
    YOU SAY I SHOULD DROWN THE KITTENS. THEIR SMELL! ....LESBOS 228 20
    THE INDELIBLE SMELL ....FEVER. 231   9
    SMELL OF YOUR SLEEPS, LILIES, LILIES. ....THE NIGHT DANCES 250 10
    THE DEAD SMELL OF SUN ON WOOD CABINS, ...MYSTIC 268   7
    FAITH FAST: A MIRACLE AND THE SMELL OF BLOOD ....DIALOGUE O. 280 161
    THE CHAIRS BELONG TO ITS DARKNESS. I SMELL DECAY ....DIALOGUE O. 285 314
SMELLESS (1)
    FOR BEING TOO WELL-BRED AND SMELLESS AND LIKING THE CITY. ...
                                     ... QUEEN MARY'S ROSE GARDEN   290 20
SMELLING (2)
    WAVERING THERE, GAUZE-EDGED, SMELLING OF WOODSMOKE, ...DIALOGUE B.   38 12
    SMELLING THE DAWN DRAFTS. ....THE SURGEON AT 2 A.M. 171 46
SMELLS (5)
    ROTS, AND SMELLS OF ROT UNDER ITS HEADSTONE ....MOONRISE   98 14
    FERRYING THE SMELLS OF DEAD COD AND TAR. ....A WINTER SHIP 113 20
    PEBBLE SMELLS, TURNIPY CHAMBERS. POEM.2.DARK. 133 22
    IS IT THE HAWTHORN THAT SMELLS SO SICK? ....THE BEE MEETING 211 24
    "IT SMELLS OF SALT COD, YOU HAD BETTER ....A SECRET 220 29
SMELT (1)
    DAWN TIDE STOOD DEAD LOW. I SMELT .....MUSSEL HUNTER AT ROCK HARBOR   95 12
SMELTED (1)
    FIRE SMELTED HIS EYES TO LUMPS ....THE BURNT-OUT SPA 137   3
SMILE (19)
    THEY SMILE AND SMILE AND SMILE AND SMILE AT ME. ....STILLBORN 142   9
    THEY SMILE AND SMILE AND SMILE AND SMILE AT ME. ....STILLBORN 142   9
    THEY SMILE AND SMILE AND SMILE AND SMILE AT ME. ....STILLBORN 142   9
    THEY SMILE AND SMILE AND SMILE AND SMILE AT ME. ....STILLBORN 142   9
    FRIGHTENED THE MIND. THEY SMILE LIKE FOOLS. ....THREE WOMEN 179 115
    SO THE BLIND SMILE. ....LITTLE FUGUE 188 18
    THE SMILE OF ICEBOXES ANNIHILATES ME. ....AN APPEARANCE 189   1
    I AM NOT A SMILE. ....BERCK-PLAGE 198 43
    YOU SMILE. ....THE OTHER 202 31
    AND THIS IS A MAN, LOOK AT HIS SMILE, ...THE DETECTIVE 208 14
    THE SMILE OF A MAN OF BUSINESS, INTENSELY PRACTICAL. .....THE SWARM 217 52
    THE SMILE OF THE SNOW IS WHITE. ....WINTERING 218 34
    THEY DID NOT SEE HIM SMILE, ...LYONNESSE 234 23
    SMILE, CROSS-LEGGED, ...PURDAH 242   5
    A SMILE FELL IN THE GRASS. ....THE NIGHT DANCES 249   1
    HE DOES NOT SMILE OR SMOKE. ....DEATH & CO. 254 20
    CHURCH SMILE ....EAVESDROPPER 261 50
    I SMILE, A BUDDHA, ALL ....PARALYTIC 267 33
    BODY WEARS THE SMILE OF ACCOMPLISHMENT, ...EDGE 272   3
SMILED (2)
    IF THE MOON SMILED, SHE WOULD RESEMBLE YOU. ....THE RIVAL 166   1
    BUT THEIR BONES SHOWED, AND THE MOON SMILED. ....THE DETECTIVE 209 35
SMILES (18)
    UNDER THEIR THIN-LIPPED SMILES, ...THE THIN PEOPLE   65 38
    WHILE THE CHILD SMILES INTO THIN AIR. ....MAGI 148   9
    WITH THE ROOMS, OR THE SMILES, OR THE BEAUTIFUL RUBBER PLANTS, ...
                                        ... WAKING IN WINTER 151 15
    THEIR SMILES CATCH ONTO MY SKIN, LITTLE SMILING HOOKS. ......TULIPS 160 21
    BUT HE IS PINK AND PERFECT. HE SMILES SO FREQUENTLY. ...THREE WOMEN 186 327
    WHILE A SKY, WORMY WITH PUT-BY SMILES, ...BERCK-PLAGE 200 104
    THE SPRY HOOKS THAT BEND AND CRINGE, AND THE SMILES, THE SMILES. ...
                                     ... BURNING THE LETTERS 204 21

SMILES (CONT.)
THE SPRY HOOKS THAT BEND AND CRINGE, AND THE SMILES, THE SMILES. ...
    ... BURNING THE LETTERS 204   21
TILL THEN YOUR SMILES ARE FOUND MONEY. ....FOR A FATHERLESS SON 206   14
THEIR SMILES AND THEIR VOICES ARE CHANGING. I AM LED THROUGH A
   BEANFIELD. ....THE BEE MEETING 211   15
THE MAN IN WHITE SMILES, BARE-HANDED, ...STINGS 214   2
THE MAN WITH GRAY HANDS SMILES -- ....THE SWARM 217   51
LIES AND SMILES. ....THE JAILER 226   23
THE BABY SMILES, FAT SNAIL, ...LESBOS 228   23
OPENING THE FAT SMILES, THE EYES ......................EAVESDROPPER 261   60
SO, IN THEIR SULFUR LOVELINESS, IN THEIR SMILES ....MUNICH. 263   10
BRIGHT FISH HOOKS, THE SMILES OF WOMEN ....GIGOLO 267   10
ARE FILLING WITH SMILES. ....KINDNESS 269   5
SMILING (9)
SMILING AT THIS BEHAVIOR, SUBJUGATING THEIR ENEMIES ....LESSON.   80   22
MUMMY-CLOTHS, SMILING: I'M ALL RIGHT. ....FACE LIFT 155   3
SMILING TO THEMSELVES, THEY MEDITATE ....HEAVY WOMEN 158   8
MY HUSBAND AND CHILD SMILING OUT OF THE FAMILY PHOTO; ....TULIPS 160   20
THEIR SMILES CATCH ONTO MY SKIN, LITTLE SMILING HOOKS. ......TULIPS 160   21
I CANNOT HELP SMILING AT WHAT IT IS I KNOW. ....THREE WOMEN 177   13
THEY ARE SMILING AND TAKING OUT VEILS TACKED TO ANCIENT HATS. BEE. 211   5
AND I A SMILING WOMAN. ....LADY LAZARUS 244   19
FIND YOU OVER AND OVER, LIPPED LIKE A SKATE AND SMILING, ...
    ... THE RIVAL/DR 291   18
SMILINGLY (2)
I HAVE TWO LEGS, AND I MOVE SMILINGLY. ....BERCK-PLAGE 196   6
SMILINGLY, BLUE LIGHTNING ....THE OTHER 201   5
SMIRK (1)
SMIRK. SAINTS' DOOR APART, BACKDOOR'S A DOOR, ...DIALOGUE O. 280 131
SMITHEREENS (2)
THE MIRROR QUIVERS TO SMITHEREENS. ....IN MIDAS' COUNTRY 100   19
FRACTURED GLASS FLIES DOWN IN SMITHEREENS; ....DOOMSDAY 316   10
SMITHFIELD (1)
WHITE TOWERS OF SMITHFIELD AHEAD, ...TOTEM 264   7
SMOCK (2)
MOTHER MEDEA IN A GREEN SMOCK ....AFTERMATH 114   9
YES, HERE IS THE SECRETARY OF BEES WITH HER WHITE SHOP SMOCK, BEE. 211   7
SMOG (2)
THE SMOG OF COOKING, THE SMOG OF HELL ....LESBOS 228   35
THE SMOG OF COOKING, THE SMOG OF HELL ....LESBOS 228   35
SMOKE (13)
CRUMBLED TO SMOKE. ....THE SNOWMAN ON THE MOOR   59   48
IN BRUEGHEL'S PANORAMA OF SMOKE AND SLAUGHTER ....TWO VIEWS. 114   12
DISSOLVED NOW, SMOKE OF AN OLD WAR. ....BLUE MOLES 126   18
SMOKE WHEELS FROM THE BEAK OF THIS EMPTY JAR. POEM.6.W. 135   12
ONE SOUL PASS THROUGH THE OTHER, FRAIL AS SMOKE ....WIDOW 165   34
THERE IS A KIND OF SMOKE IN THE SPRING AIR, ...THREE WOMEN 186 354
A SMOKE THAT TAKES THE PARKS, THE LITTLE STATUES ....THREE WOMEN 186 355
A BODY INTO A PIPE, AND THE SMOKE RISING. ....THE DETECTIVE 208   11
SMOKE ROLLS AND SCARVES IN THE GROVE. ....THE BEE MEETING 212   36
IT WENT UP IN SMOKE. ....THE TOUR 238   23
HE DOES NOT SMILE OR SMOKE. ....DEATH & CO. 254   20
THE BLUE AND RED JEWELS OF HER RINGS SMOKE ....KINDNESS 269   3
IN A SMOKE THAT SEARS MY EYES. ....CIRCUS IN THREE RINGS 322   18
SMOKE-CHOKED (1)
FROM A SMOKE-CHOKED CLOSET INTO LIGHT; ....AFTERMATH 113   5
SMOKED (2)
WHOSE LABOR'S NOT YET SMOKED ....TINKER JACK AND THE TIDY WIVES   35   29
AND THE MAID SMOKED AND SHOT POOL UNDER A GREEN-SHADED LAMP. BABY. 175   24
SMOKES (3)
THATCH SMOKES IN THE SUN. ....THREE WOMEN 185 314
LOVE, LOVE, THE LOW SMOKES ROLL ....FEVER. 231   11
SUCH YELLOW SULLEN SMOKES ....FEVER. 231   14
SMOKESTACKS (1)
OF WAREHOUSES, DERRICKS, SMOKESTACKS AND BRIDGES .....A WINTER SHIP 113   17
SMOKING (2)
EXIT FROM A SMOKING SLIT ....RHYME   50   17
ALL MORNING, WITH SMOKING BREATH, THE HANDYMAN ......PRIVATE GROUND 130   7
SMOLDERED (1)
HE SMOLDERED, AS IF STONE-DEAF, BLINDFOLD, ...SUICIDE OFF EGG ROCK 115   14
SMOLDERING (1)
THE OLD JEWELS SMOLDERING THERE ....MEDALLION 124   18
SMOOTH (3)
PINK AND SMOOTH AS A BABY. ....FACE LIFT 156   32
THERE IS NOTHING TO DO WITH SUCH A BEAUTIFUL BLANK BUT SMOOTH IT. ...
    ... AMNESIAC 232   2
FROM HERE THE MOON SEEMS SMOOTH AS ANGEL-FOOD, ...ADMONITIONS 319   7
SMOOTHING (1)
TENDS TO THE PEBBLES IT MUST RUN OVER, SMOOTHING THEM GENTLY.*TULIPS 160   16
SMUDGE (1)
SOUTHWARD, OVER KENTISH TOWN, AN ASHEN SMUDGE*PARLIAMENT HILL FIELDS 152   21
SMUG (3)
THE SMUG CENTURIES OF THE PIG -- ....THE MANOR GARDEN 125   6
IRREFUTABLE, BEAUTIFULLY SMUG ....HEAVY WOMEN 158   1

TITLE   PAGE LINE

SMUG (CONT.)
    SCATTER SMUG ANGELS WITH YOU HAND. ...SONG FOR A REVOLUTIONARY LOVE 322   4
SMUG-SHAPED (1)
    CASTLES UPON THE SMUG-SHAPED CHAIRS. ALL THIS I ....DIALOGUE O. 279 118
SNAG (1)
    A SNAG IS LIFTING A VALEDICTORY, PALE HAND; .....CROSSING THE WATER 190   9
SNAGS (3)
    NOW THE AIR SNAGS AND EDDIES ROUND THEM THE WAY A RIVER .....TULIPS 161 53
    SNAGS AND EDDIES ROUND A SUNKEN RUST-RED ENGINE. ....TULIPS 161 54
    THE MOON SNAGS IN HER INTRICATE NERVOUS SYSTEM. ....ELM/DR 292   3
SNAIL (4)
    THE SNAIL LEAVES A SILVER TRACK; ....THE SLEEPERS 122 10
    THE BABY SMILES, FAT SNAIL, ...LESBOS 228 23
    THE WORD OF A SNAIL ON THE PLATE OF A LEAF? ....THE COURIERS 247   1
    BY SNAIL UNDER HUMP OF HOME: ....NOTES TO A NEOPHYTE 306   6
SNAIL-NOSED (1)
    IN THEIR JARS THE SNAIL-NOSED BABIES MOON AND GLOW. .....TWO VIEWS. 114 10
SNAILS (3)
    SNAILS SCROLL THE BORDER ....DARK WOOD, DARK WATER 127   8
    THE SNAILS BLEW KISSES LIKE BLACK APPLES. ....ZOO KEEPER'S WIFE 155 38
    GO CULL THE PURPLE SNAILS FROM SLOTHFUL SHELLS ....GO GET. 313 17
SNAKE (10)
    TO A MELTING OF GREEN WATERS, TILL NO SNAKE .........SNAKECHARMER   79 25
    WATER, TO GREEN, TO NOTHING LIKE A SNAKE. ..............SNAKECHARMER   79 27
    A BEDRAGGLED SNAKE, HANGING LIMP AS THE ABSURD MOUTH ....PERSEUS   83 38
    THE BRONZE SNAKE LAY IN THE SUN ....MEDALLION 124   3
    COMFORTLESS AS SALT. SNAKE AND BIRD .....SLEEP IN THE MOJAVE DESERT 144 18
    THAT WASN'T IT. I SLEPT, SAY: A SNAKE ....LOVE LETTER 147   9
    THERE IS A SNAKE IN SWANS. ....THREE WOMEN 178 52
    ON A STICK THAT RATTLES AND CLICKS, A COUNTERFEIT SNAKE. .....TOTEM 264 18
    STEEPLING SNAKE IN THAT CONTRARY LIGHT ....SONNET TO SATAN 323   9
    OF SNAKE IN THE GRASS. ....TEMPER OF TIME 336 16
SNAKE-BODIES (1)
    LEAF, BECOME EYELID: SNAKE-BODIES, BOUGH, BREAST ......SNAKECHARMER   79 14
SNAKECHARMER (3)
    SNAKECHARMER ....SNAKECHARMER   79   T
    SO THE SNAKECHARMER BEGINS A SNAKY SPHERE .............SNAKECHARMER   79   2
    TIGERS, SNAKES, AND THE SNAKECHARMER AND YOU, ...YADWIGHA.   86 23
SNAKECHARMER'S (1)
    AND THE SNAKECHARMER'S SONG AND THE GIGANTIC LILIES, ...YADWIGHA.   86 33
SNAKEDOM (1)
    OF TREE AND HUMAN. AND HE WITHIN THIS SNAKEDOM ........SNAKECHARMER   79 15
SNAKE-FIGURED (1)
    AND THE SNAKE-FIGURED ALMANAC ....MONOLOGUE AT 3 A.M.   40   5
SNAKEHOOD (1)
    HIS SNAKEHOOD AND HIS MIGHT WITH PLIANT TUNES .........SNAKECHARMER   79 17
SNAKE-ROOTED (1)
    OF SWAYS AND COILINGS, FROM THE SNAKE-ROOTED BOTTOM ...SNAKECHARMER   79 11
SNAKES (9)
    SUPPORTS HIS FOOT. HE PIPES A WORLD OF SNAKES, ...SNAKECHARMER   79 10
    OF HIS MIND. AND NOW NOTHING BUT SNAKES ..............SNAKECHARMER   79 12
    OF SNAKY GENERATIONS: LET THERE BE SNAKES! ...........SNAKECHARMER   79 20
    AND SNAKES THERE WERE, ARE, WILL BE -- TILL YAWNS .....SNAKECHARMER   79 21
    OF SNAKE-WARP, SNAKE-WEFT. PIPES THE CLOTH OF SNAKES ..SNAKECHARMER   79 24
    TIGERS, SNAKES, AND THE SNAKECHARMER AND YOU, ...YADWIGHA.   86 23
    FLATTEN THE DOPED SNAKES TO RIBBON. IN HERE, THE GRASSES *PRIVATE G. 130 17
    THESE ORCHIDS ARE SPLENDID. THEY SPOT AND COIL LIKE SNAKES.*SURGEON. 170 16
    THE SNAKES, THE BABIES, THE TITS ....THE COURAGE OF SHUTTING-UP 210 12
SNAKE-SCALES (1)
    IS VISIBLE. THE SNAKE-SCALES HAVE BECOME .............SNAKECHARMER   79 13
SNAKE-WARP (1)
    OF SNAKE-WARP, SNAKE-WEFT. PIPES THE CLOTH OF SNAKES ..SNAKECHARMER   79 24
SNAKE-WEFT (1)
    OF SNAKE-WARP, SNAKE-WEFT. PIPES THE CLOTH OF SNAKES ..SNAKECHARMER   79 24
SNAKING (1)
    BUT MISSED THE MARK WITH SNAKING FANGS: ....LAMENT 315   5
SNAKY (4)
    SO THE SNAKECHARMER BEGINS A SNAKY SPHERE .............SNAKECHARMER   79   2
    OF SNAKY GENERATIONS: LET THERE BE SNAKES! ...........SNAKECHARMER   79 20
    NOT NAILS, AND A MIRROR TO KEEP THE SNAKY HEAD ....PERSEUS   83 13
    ITS SNAKY ACIDS KISS. ....ELM 193 40
SNAPPED (3)
    WHOSE LAUNDRY SNAPPED AND FROZE HERE, WHO ....POINT SHIRLEY 110 10
    THE NIGHTS SNAPPED OUT OF SIGHT LIKE A LIZARD'S EYELID:*THE HANGING. 141   3
    SNAPPED THE WOMAN SHARPLY. ....BITTER STRAWBERRIES 300 28
SNAPPING (1)
    SNAPPING OFF THE STEM ....BITTER STRAWBERRIES 300 38
SNARE (4)
    FIXING HIS SNARE ....FIRESONG   30   5
    IT STUCK IN A BARB WIRE SNARE. ....DADDY 223 26
    GO SNARE THE SLEEPING BEAR IN LEAF-LINED DEN*GO GET THE GOODLY SQUAB 313   9
    WHAT COUNTERMAGIC CAN UNDO THE SNARE ....PROLOGUE TO SPRING 322 10
SNARED (1)
    NOW, SNARED BY THIS MIRACULOUS ART, ...ON THE PLETHORA OF DRYADS   67 28

	TITLE	PAGE	LINE

SNARES (2)
HIS ARDOR SNARES ME, LIGHTS THE TREES, ...PURSUIT   23   33
AND THE SNARES ALMOST EFFACED THEMSELVES -- .....THE RABBIT CATCHER   194   14
SNARLED (2)
BEHIND SNARLED THICKETS OF MY EYES ....PURSUIT   23   29
IN WAIT AMID SNARLED WEED AND WRACK OF WAVE *DREAM WITH CLAM-DIGGERS   44   26
SNAZZY (1)
AND I, IN MY SNAZZY BLACKS, ...GIGOLO   267   12
SNEAKED (1)
ONCE WE CHILDREN SNEAKED OVER TO SPY MISS MASON ......ELLA MASON A.   54   19
SNEER (1)
IN THE WIND'S SNEER. ....RESOLVE   52   23
SNICKERED (1)
WE SNICKERED AS SHE SHAMBLED DOWN SOMERSET TERRACE ...ELLA MASON A.   54   32
SNIFFING (1)
I PACE IT, SNIFFING ....LETTER IN NOVEMBER   253   18
SNIPPED (1)
INTO THE STONE BASIN. I SNIPPED   FABLE OF THE RHODODENDRON STEALERS   103   7
SNORED (1)
YOU SNORED, AND I HEARD THE PETALS UNLATCH, ...LEAVING EARLY   146   26
SNOUT (1)
DUPE THE DULL SOW LOUNGING SNOUT IN MUD, ...GO GET THE GOODLY SQUAB   313   11
SNOUT-CRUISE (1)
MAUNCHING THISTLE AND KNOTWEED ON HER SNOUT-CRUISE -- ....SOW   61   19
SNOW (13)
FLOATS CHASTE AS SNOW, TAUNTING THE CLOUDED MIND   WINTER LANDSCAPE.   21   4
SKY-HIGH, AND SNOW ....THE SNOWMAN ON THE MOOR   59   32
ZINC-WHITE SNOW. ....YADDO: THE GRAND MANOR   124   21
SNOW, CHALK OR SUCHLIKE. THEY'RE ....MAGI   148   5
IT IS A WORLD OF SNOW NOW. I AM NOT AT HOME. ....THREE WOMEN   178   64
THE TAIL-TRACK, ON THE SNOW IN OUR COURT -- ....PHEASANT   191   12
AND THE SNOW, MARSHALING ITS BRILLIANT CUTLERY ....THE SWARM   216   9
THE REFINED SNOW. ....WINTERING   218   28
THE SMILE OF THE SNOW IS WHITE. ....WINTERING   218   34
COLD AS SNOW BREATH, IT TAMPS THE WOMB ....THE MUNICH MANNEQUINS   262   2
THE SNOW DROPS ITS PIECES OF DARKNESS, ...THE MUNICH MANNEQUINS   263   16
VOICELESSNESS. THE SNOW HAS NO VOICE. ....THE MUNICH MANNEQUINS   263   27
AND THE SNOW BLOW UP BEHIND; ....GO GET THE GOODLY SQUAB   313   14
SNOWCAKES (1)
SNOWCAKES BREAK AND WELTER. THIS YEAR ....POINT SHIRLEY   110   4
SNOWDROP (2)
APRIL SNOWDROP, INDIAN PIPE, ...CHILD   265   5
CHRISTENED IN A SPINDRIFT OF SNOWDROP STARS, ...APRIL AUBADE   312   9
SNOWED-IN (1)
LOOK HOW WHITE EVERYTHING IS, HOW QUIET, HOW SNOWED-IN. .....TULIPS   160   2
SNOWFIELD (2)
IT COULD BE A SNOWFIELD OR A CLOUDBANK. .....PARLIAMENT HILL FIELDS   152   23
THE SCALDED SHEET IS A SNOWFIELD, FROZEN AND PEACEFUL. ....SURGEON.   170   5
SNOWFLAKE (1)
EXACT AS A SNOWFLAKE. ....SPINSTER   50   18
SNOWFLAKES (1)
SHREDDED FINE AS SNOWFLAKES ....AERIALIST   331   3
SNOW-FLAWED (1)
ASSAULT OF SNOW-FLAWED WINDS FROM THE DOUR SKIES ....MAYFLOWER   60   2
SNOW-HEAP (1)
FROM MARBLE SNOW-HEAP OF MOOR TO RIDE THAT WOMAN ....SNOWMAN O.   59   27
SNOWMAN (1)
THE SNOWMAN ON THE MOOR ....THE SNOWMAN ON THE MOOR   58   T
SNOWS (2)
ACROSS MOOR SNOWS ....THE SNOWMAN ON THE MOOR   58   16
THE SNOWS OF THE TYROL, THE CLEAR BEER OF VIENNA ....DADDY   223   36
SNUBS (1)
SNUBS IMPROMPTU SPIELS OF WIND ....CONJURING.   66   6
SNUFF (3)
THESE DREAMING HOUSES ALL SNUFF OUT: ....SOLILOQUY OF THE SOLIPSIST   37   6
ENOUGH TO SNUFF THE QUICK ....HARDCASTLE CRAGS   63   41
BETWEEN THE SNUFF AND RED TAR-PAPER APARTMENTS, ...ABOVE THE OXBOW   88   13
SNUFF-COLORED (1)
SNUFF-COLORED SAND CLIFFS RISE ....MAN IN BLACK   119   12
SNUFFED (1)
OF A SNUFFED CANDLE! ....FEVER.   231   10
SNUFF-RUFFED (1)
SNUFF-RUFFED DANDELIONS, ...POLLY'S TREE   128   25
SNUFFS (2)
DAWN SNUFFS OUT STAR'S SPENT WICK, ...EPITAPH FOR FIRE AND FLOWER   46   29
IT SNUFFS ITS BUD ....BY CANDLELIGHT   236   17
SNUG (2)
SNUG AS A BUD AND AT HOME ....YOU'RE   141   13
THE WHITE HIVE IS SNUG AS A VIRGIN, ...THE BEE MEETING   212   34
SO (172)
SO WERE THEY ONE; SO SOUGHT THEY COUCH, ...BUCOLICS   23   3
SO WERE THEY ONE; SO SOUGHT THEY COUCH, ...BUCOLICS   23   3
SHOULD ACCEPT SO FELL A WOUND, ...BUCOLICS   24   18
AND SO WE SAIL TOWARD CITIES, STREETS AND HOMES ...CHANNEL CROSSING   27   37
SO SHE IS COME TO THIS RARE PASS ....THE QUEEN'S COMPLAINT   29   21

TITLE PAGE LINE

SO (CONT.)
TO SEE MY PEOPLE SHRUNK SO SMALL, SO SMALL." THE QUEEN'S COMPLAINT 29 25
TO SEE MY PEOPLE SHRUNK SO SMALL, SO SMALL." THE QUEEN'S COMPLAINT 29 25
BRIGHT GRAIN SPRUNG SO RARELY ....ODE FOR TED 29 16
FROM HIS CRABBED MIDDEN WHERE ALL'S WROUGHT SO AWRY ....FIRESONG 30 10
AND SO, TOGETHER, TALKING, ...SONG FOR A SUMMER'S DAY 31 16
SO SHE WILLS ALL TO THE BLACK KING. ....VANITY FAIR 33 29
NO FORM'S GONE SO AWRY, ...TINKER JACK AND THE TIDY WIVES 34 15
STARS HUNG WATER-SUNK, SO A RANK ....FAUN 35 8
SO, PERHAPS I, KNELLED DUMB BY YOUR ABSENCE. ....STREET SONG 36 24
SO FITTED IS FOR MY BLACK LUCK ....THE GLUTTON 40 2
THAN TO SIT MUTE, TWITCHING SO ....MONOLOGUE AT 3 A.M. 40 8
SO HUNGERED, SHE MUST WAIT IN RAGE ....THE SHRIKE 42 15
WITH SAVOR; COUPLED SO, PURE PARAGONS OF CONSTANCE, ...WREATH F. 44 9
SHALL STREW BROADCAST SO RARE A SEED ON WIND ...WREATH FOR A BRIDAL 45 20
SO HUMBLY DONE, I'D TURN THIS KEEN ....RHYME 50 13
WHATEVER TRIAL'S TO COME, SO SAY TRUE." ....CRYSTAL GAZER 55 20
SO BEGGAR GERD MIGHT AIM HER LOOK ....CRYSTAL GAZER 55 40
ORDERING ITS BLACK FEATHERS CAN SO SHINE*BLACK ROOK IN RAINY WEATHER 57 28
SO WHEN STAUNCH ISLAND STOCK CHOSE FORFEITURE ....MAYFLOWER 60 9
GREW SO LEAN AND WOULD NOT ROUND ....THE THIN PEOPLE 64 8
SCAPEGOAT. BUT SO THIN, ...THE THIN PEOPLE 64 22
SO WEEDY A RACE COULD NOT REMAIN IN DREAMS, ...THE THIN PEOPLE 64 23
THAT BULK SO CALM ....ON THE DIFFICULTY OF CONJURING UP A DRYAD 66 14
EACH PARTICULAR QUIRK SO RAVISHED ME .....ON THE PLETHORA OF DRYADS 67 15
COME, SO UNLIKE US, TO A STIFF IMPASSE, ...THE OTHER TWO 69 31
SO FINE WE CANNOT DO IT. ....THE GREAT CARBUNCLE 73 26
SO MANY LADDERS ....WORDS FOR A NURSERY 73 8
COUSIN DID YOU SO UNWISELY KEEP ....THE DISQUIETING MUSES 74 3
SO THE SNAKECHARMER BEGINS A SNAKY SPHERE .............SNAKECHARMER 79 2
DARK FACE. SO MIGHT RIGOR MORTIS COME TO STIFFEN ....PERSEUS 83 32
SO FABLES GO. ....BATTLE-SCENE 85 31
AND SO ALL CHILDREN SING ....BATTLE-SCENE 85 32
SO ROUSSEAU, TO EXPLAIN WHY THE RED COUCH ....YADWIGHA. 86 21
ACCOMPANIED YOU. SO THEY NODDED AT THE COUCH WITH THE MOON*YADWIGHA. 86 32
SO POSSESSED BY THE GLOWING RED OF THE COUCH WHICH YOU, ..YADWIGHA. 86 36
WHICH SEEMED, WHEN DREAMED, TO MEAN SO PROFOUNDLY MUCH, ...GHOST'S. 90 5
OF AMBROSIAL REVELATION. AND SO DEPARTS. ...THE GHOST'S LEAVETAKING 90 15
SO THESE POSED SHEETS, BEFORE THEY THIN TO NOTHING, ...GHOST'S. 90 18
AND SEEMS TO DIE: SO VAPORS ....FULL FATHOM FIVE 93 19
KNEW NOTHING OF. SO THE CRABS ....MUSSEL HUNTER AT ROCK HARBOR 97 60
SO WE ARE HAULED, THOUGH WE WOULD STOP ....IN MIDAS' COUNTRY 100 21
SO, OVER THIS BATTERED, OBSTINATE SPIT ....POINT SHIRLEY 110 30
SO FABLES SAY THE GOATSUCKER MOVES, MASKED FROM MEN'S SIGHT ...
... GOATSUCKER 111 9
ELEVEN WEEKS, AND I KNOW YOUR ESTATE SO WELL ....PRIVATE GROUND 130 13
IT HAS SO MANY CELLARS, ...POEM.2.DARK. 132 8
IF I DON'T MOVE ABOUT, I'LL KNOCK NOTHING OVER. SO I SAID,*POEM.6.W. 135 14
SO MANY OF US! ....MUSHROOMS 139 23
SO MANY OF US! ....MUSHROOMS 139 24
THEY SIT SO NICELY IN THE PICKLING FLUID! ....STILLBORN 142 8
IT IS COMFORTABLE, FOR A CHANGE, TO MEAN SO LITTLE. ......TWO CAMP. 145 17
FROM STONE TO CLOUD, SO I ASCENDED. ....LOVE LETTER 147 33
NOTHING SO VULGAR AS A NOSE OR AN EYE ....MAGI 148 2
OLD GRIEVANCES JOSTLING EACH OTHER, SO MANY LOOSE TEETH. ....ZOO K. 154 13
I COULDN'T SLEEP FOR A WEEK, SHE WAS SO COLD. ....IN PLASTER 158 9
WITHOUT ME, SHE WOULDN'T EXIST, SO OF COURSE SHE WAS GRATEFUL. ...
... IN PLASTER 159 15
HOLDING MY BONES IN PLACE SO THEY WOULD MEND PROPERLY. ..IN PLASTER 159 27
SHE STOPPED FITTING ME SO CLOSELY AND SEEMED OFFISH. ....IN PLASTER 159 29
SIMPLY BECAUSE SHE LOOKED AFTER ME SO BADLY. ....IN PLASTER 159 34
SHE'D SUPPORTED ME FOR SO LONG I WAS QUITE LIMP -- ......IN PLASTER 159 44
SO I WAS CAREFUL NOT TO UPSET HER IN ANY WAY ....IN PLASTER 160 46
AFTER ALL, IT WAS A KIND OF MARRIAGE, BEING SO CLOSE. ...IN PLASTER 160 51
SO IT IS IMPOSSIBLE TO TELL HOW MANY THERE ARE. ....TULIPS 160 14
I AM A NUN NOW, I HAVE NEVER BEEN SO PURE. ....TULIPS 161 28
THE PEACEFULNESS IS SO BIG IT DAZES YOU, ...TULIPS 161 32
SO THAT EACH MARCH I MAY GLEAM INTO LEAF, ...I AM VERTICAL 162 4
OR ELSE THEY ARE PRESENT, AND THEIR DISGUISE SO BRIGHT ......STARS. 165 22
SPITEFUL AS A WOMAN, BUT NOT SO NERVOUS, ...THE RIVAL 166 9
I COME TO ONE BUSH OF BERRIES SO RIPE IT IS A BUSH OF FLIES, ...
... BLACKBERRYING 168 15
I AM SO SMALL ....THE SURGEON AT 2 A.M. 171 18
SO MAGICAL! A HOT SPRING ....THE SURGEON AT 2 A.M. 171 24
IT IS PINK, WITH SPECKLES, I HAVE LOOKED AT IT SO LONG ......MIRROR 173 7
THE COOK HAD ONE WALL EYE AND COULDN'T SLEEP, SHE WAS SO NERVOUS. ...
... THE BABYSITTERS 175 25
ON THAT DAY-OFF THE TWO OF US CRIED SO HARD TO GET THE BABYSITTERS 175 29
SO WE BOBBED OUT TO THE ISLAND. IT WAS DESERTED -- THE BABYSITTERS 175 33
IS SHE SORRY FOR WHAT WILL HAPPEN? I DO NOT THINK SO. ..THREE WOMEN 176 6
I WATCHED THE MEN WALK ABOUT ME IN THE OFFICE. THEY WERE SO
FLAT! ....THREE WOMEN 177 16
YOU ARE SO WHITE, SUDDENLY." AND I SAID NOTHING. ....THREE WOMEN 177 23
I COULD NOT BELIEVE IT. IS IT SO DIFFICULT ....THREE WOMEN 177 25
IN ITS EASY PEACE, COULD ONLY KEEP HOLY SO. ....THREE WOMEN 178 81

SO (CONT.)

THEY ARE SO JEALOUS OF ANYTHING THAT IS NOT FLAT! THEY ARE
    JEALOUS GODS ....THREE WOMEN 179   86
TURN UP THEIR HANDS, THEIR PALLORS. IT IS SO QUIET HERE.*THREE WOMEN 179   94
SHE IS THE VAMPIRE OF US ALL. SO SHE SUPPORTS US, ...THREE WOMEN 181 155
HE IS LOOKING SO ANGRILY! ....THREE WOMEN 181 164
I HAVE NEVER SEEN A THING SO CLEAR. ....THREE WOMEN 181 171
THERE IS NO GUILE OR WARP IN HIM. MAY HE KEEP SO. .....THREE WOMEN 181 175
EMPTY SCHOOLROOMS, EMPTY CHURCHES. O SO MUCH EMPTINESS! *THREE WOMEN 181 179
LOOK, THEY ARE SO EXHAUSTED, THEY ARE ALL FLAT OUT ....THREE WOMEN 183 219
THE LITTLE SILVER TROPHIES THEY'VE COME SO FAR FOR. ...THREE WOMEN 183 221
CAN NOTHINGNESS BE SO PRODIGAL? ....THREE WOMEN 183 232
AND SO I STAND, A LITTLE SIGHTLESS. SO I WALK ....THREE WOMEN 184 253
AND SO I STAND, A LITTLE SIGHTLESS. SO I WALK ....THREE WOMEN 184 253
I AM SO VULNERABLE SUDDENLY. ....THREE WOMEN 184 269
SO NEAT SHE IS TRANSPARENT, LIKE A SPIRIT. ....THREE WOMEN 184 281
TO BE SO OPEN: IT IS AS IF MY HEART ....THREE WOMEN 185 300
BUT HE IS PINK AND PERFECT. HE SMILES SO FREQUENTLY. ...THREE WOMEN 186 327
IT IS SO BEAUTIFUL TO HAVE NO ATTACHMENTS! ....THREE WOMEN 186 341
AND SO WE ARE AT HOME TOGETHER, AFTER HOURS. ....THREE WOMEN 187 362
SO THE DEAF AND DUMB ....LITTLE FUGUE 187   3
SO THE BLIND SMILE. ....LITTLE FUGUE 188   18
ISSUING FROM THE STEEL NEEDLE THAT FLIES SO BLINDINGLY? *APPEARANCE. 189   11
IT IS SUCH A GOOD SHAPE, SO VIVID. ....PHEASANT 191   19
SO MURDEROUS IN ITS STRANGLE OF BRANCHES? --- ....ELM 193   39
WHY IS IT SO QUIET, WHAT ARE THEY HIDING? ....BERCK-PLAGE 196   5
THE NURSES IN THEIR WING-CAPS ARE NO LONGER SO BEAUTIFUL; ...BERCK. 198   58
RISES SO WHITELY UNBUFFETED? ....BERCK-PLAGE 198   64
IT IS SO BEAUTIFUL UP HERE: IT IS A STOPPING PLACE. ....BERCK-PLAGE 199   90
IS MY LIFE SO INTRIGUING? ....THE OTHER 201   9
SO I POKE AT THE CARBON BIRDS IN MY HOUSEDRESS. *BURNING THE LETTERS 204   29
DO NOT BE AFRAID, IT IS NOT SO. ....A BIRTHDAY PRESENT 207   32
SO THE DISKS OF THE BRAIN REVOLVE, LIKE THE MUZZLES OF CANNON. ...
                ... THE COURAGE OF SHUTTING-UP 210   16
IS IT THE HAWTHORN THAT SMELLS SO SICK? ....THE BEE MEETING 211   24
THE OLD QUEEN DOES NOT SHOW HERSELF, IS SHE SO SICK? ....BEE. 212   50
THERE ARE NO WINDOWS, SO I CAN'T SEE WHAT IS IN THERE. *THE ARRIVAL. 213   9
SO WHY SHOULD THEY TURN ON ME? ....THE ARRIVAL OF THE BEE BOX 213   34
TERRIFY ME, THEY SEEM SO OLD. ....STINGS 214   13
SO THE SWARM BALLS AND DESERTS ....THE SWARM 216   17
SO DUMB IT THINKS BULLETS ARE THUNDER. ....THE SWARM 216   20
THE BEES HAVE GOT SO FAR. SEVENTY FEET HIGH! ....THE SWARM 216   26
SO MUCH FOR THE CHARIOTEERS, THE OUTRIDERS, THE GRAND ARMY! SWARM. 217   39
SO SLOW I HARDLY KNOW THEM, ...WINTERING 218   23
SO I NEVER COULD TELL WHERE YOU ....DADDY 223   22
SO BLACK NO SKY COULD SQUEAK THROUGH. ....DADDY 223   47
SO DADDY, I'M FINALLY THROUGH. ....DADDY 224   68
YOU ARE SO EXHAUSTED. ....LESBOS 229   78
OVER THE ENGLISH CLIFF AND UNDER SO MUCH HISTORY! ....LYONNESSE 234   22
HE'D HAD SO MANY WARS! ....LYONNESSE 234   26
WHOSE RED HEART BLOOMS THROUGH HER COAT SO ASTOUNDINGLY ---*POP.OCT. 240   3
SO VALUABLE! ....PURDAH 242   8
I DO IT SO IT FEELS LIKE HELL. ....LADY LAZARUS 245   46
I DO IT SO IT FEELS REAL. ....LADY LAZARUS 245   47
SO, SO, HERR DOKTOR. ....LADY LAZARUS 246   65
SO, SO, HERR DOKTOR. ....LADY LAZARUS 246   65
SO, HERR ENEMY. ....LADY LAZARUS 246   66
IT IS SO SMALL ....GETTING THERE 249   44
SO YOUR GESTURES FLAKE OFF --- ....THE NIGHT DANCES 250   18
SO MANY SILKS. ....GULLIVER 251   15
I AM SO STUPIDLY HAPPY, ...LETTER IN NOVEMBER 253   13
BUT GREENNESS, DARKNESS SO PURE ....YEARS 255   4
WHAT IS SO GREAT IN THAT! ....YEARS 255   17
THEY SEED SO EFFORTLESSLY! ....WINTER TREES 258   8
SO I SAW YOUR MUCH SICKER ..............................EAVESDROPPER 260   24
SO, IN THEIR SULFUR LOVELINESS, IN THEIR SMILES ....MUNICH. 263   10
WHOSE HOPES ARE SO LOW THEY ARE COMFORTABLE -- ....MYSTIC 269   21
DAME KINDNESS, SHE IS SO NICE! ....KINDNESS 269   2
WHAT IS SO REAL AS THE CRY OF A CHILD? ....KINDNESS 269   6
SUGAR CAN CURE EVERYTHING, SO KINDNESS SAYS. ....KINDNESS 269   9
WE HAVE COME SO FAR, IT IS OVER. ....EDGE 272   8
SO THE ARTFUL GLASS WON'T CHANGE ITS CHILL FOR HEART'S DIALOGUE O. 277   17
IT'S NOT SO IMMINENT. AT LEAST I FEEL ..DIALOGUE OVER A OUIJA BOARD 278   61
A LIFE AFTER THIS LIFE? HE SHOOTS SO SWIFT ....DIALOGUE O. 278   72
MINOR IMPS PIPE UP, SO LONG AS EACH ....DIALOGUE OVER A OUIJA BOARD 280 152
SO, YOU'LL SCOFF, AND YET YOU'D DROP TO KNEEL ....DIALOGUE O. 280 156
IS SMALL THESE DAYS. DON'T BE SO SMART. I'LL ASK ....DIALOGUE O. 281 204
PAN AS OUR EVENING GUEST IF HE'S SO FREE*DIALOGUE OVER A OUIJA BOARD 283 252
THERE! THAT SHUTS HIM UP! SO. BETTER SO,*DIALOGUE OVER A OUIJA BOARD 284 300
THERE! THAT SHUTS HIM UP! SO. BETTER SO,*DIALOGUE OVER A OUIJA BOARD 284 300
SURELY IT IS NOT I YOU WANT SO BADLY ....THE RIVAL/DR 291   21
ONCE I WOUNDED HIM WITH SO ....TO A JILTED LOVER 310   10
SO CRY FOR THE PAGAN GIRL LEFT PICKING OLIVES ......SONNET: TO TIME 311   9
SO IF YOU CAN DREAM UP ANY SAVING PLAN ....THE DISPOSSESSED 318   2
SO NEVER TRY TO TRICK ME WITH A KISS: ....NEVER TRY TO TRICK. 320   18

	TITLE	PAGE	LINE

SO (CONT.)
    SUSPEND THIS DAY, SO SINGULARLY DESIGNED, ...MIDSUMMER MOBILE 324 13
    SO I STARED IN THAT FURNACE ....ON LOOKING INTO THE EYES. 325 21
    SO WE COULD RAVE ON, DARLING, YOU AND I, ...LOVE IS A PARALLAX 329 13
    SO KISS: THE DRUNKS UPON THE CURB AND DAMES .....LOVE IS A PARALLAX 329 31
    SO WE SHALL WALK BAREFOOT ON WALNUT SHELLS .....LOVE IS A PARALLAX 330 67
    HER NINE SO SLIPPERY LIVES. ....AERIALIST 332 36
SOAKS (1)
    FOUR O'CLOCK, AND THE FEVER SOAKS FROM ME LIKE HONEY. ....FEVER./DR 294 1
SO-AND-SO'S (1)
    SIR SO-AND-SO'S GIN. ....WINTERING 218 10
SOAP (2)
    ON ARMS AND LEGS IN A FRINGE OF KELP; GREEN SOAP .....TALE OF A TUB 25 43
    A CAKE OF SOAP, ...LADY LAZARUS 246 76
SOAP-BUBBLE (1)
    LIKE A SOAP-BUBBLE AS YOU CALLED: COME HERE! THE DISQUIETING MUSES 76 47
SOAP-COLORED (1)
    THE LONG COFFIN OF SOAP-COLORED OAK, ...BERCK-PLAGE 199 70
SOARS (1)
    THEIR LEAFY CROWNS, THEIR FAME SOARS, ...VIRGIN IN A TREE 81 18
SOBERLY (1)
    AT THE END, THEY SOBERLY BONG OUT THEIR NAMES. ....MOON. 173 14
SOBRIETY (1)
    TRIED SOBRIETY HIRING HIM OUT ....WHITENESS I REMEMBER 102 8
SOCIETIES (1)
    GOVERNMENTS, PARLIAMENTS, SOCIETIES, ...THREE WOMEN 179 83
SOCKET (2)
    STUCCO SOCKET ....POINT SHIRLEY 110 21
    A WORLD OF BALD WHITE DAYS IN A SHADELESS SOCKET. ..THE HANGING MAN 141 4
SOCKETED (1)
    AMONG THE SOCKETED WHITE STARS, YOUR FACE ....MOONRISE 98 26
SOCK-FACE (1)
    OLD SOCK-FACE, SAGGED ON A DARNING EGG. ....FACE LIFT 156 27
SOCKS (3)
    MATCHED THE STRIPES OF HIS SOCKS. ....THE BABYSITTERS 174 9
    HOLES IN THE HEELS OF SOCKS, THE WHITE MUTE FACES ......THREE WOMEN 182 199
    ELEMENTS LIKE DIRTY SOCKS AND SCRAPS .....METAMORPHOSES OF THE MOON 307 28
SOD (2)
    OF THAT UNCOUTH SHAPE TO SIMPLE SOD AGAIN ....LADY AND T. 70 27
    INVEIGLED TO FORSAKE THE SOD. ....DANSE MACABRE 321 18
SODA (1)
    OF STATE SCENERY, SELLS SODA, SHOWS OFF VIEWPOINTS. *ABOVE THE OXBOW 88 41
SODDEN (2)
    PACED BRISK FATHER SHAWN. A COLD DAY, A SODDEN ONE IT WAS ...
                ... DIALOGUE BETWEEN GHOST AND PRIEST 38 2
    OF CHARRED SHOES, THE SODDEN UPHOLSTERY: ....AFTERMATH 114 12
SOFA (3)
    SEA-DRAGON FOR SOFA, FANG ....BATTLE-SCENE 85 36
    MAGENTA AS THIS FUBSY SOFA. ....LEAVING EARLY 146 33
    BROODY AND IN LONG SKIRTS ON MY FIRST HUSHAND'S SOFA, MY
        FINGERS ....FACE LIFT 156 22
SOFT (13)
    MOST SOFT, MOST SUAVELY GLIDES THAT STEP. ....PURSUIT 22 5
    DENSE-FEATHERED, FEARFULLY SOFT TO ....OWL 102 14
    I ENTER THE SOFT PELT OF THE MOLE. ....BLUE MOLES 126 21
    INTO A SOFT CAUL OF FORGETFULNESS. POEM.5.F. 135 9
    SOFT SUEDE TONGUES BETWEEN HIS BONES. ....THE BURNT-OUT SPA 138 11
    SOFT FISTS INSIST ON ....MUSHROOMS 139 10
    AND MY SKIN ITCHED AND FLAKED AWAY IN SOFT PIECES ....IN PLASTER 159 33
    AND SOFT AS A MOTH, HIS BREATH. ....THREE WOMEN 181 173
    ALL DAY I FEEL ITS SOFT, FEATHERY TURNINGS, ITS MALIGNITY. .....ELM 193 33
    WITH SOFT RUGS --- ....NICK AND THE CANDLESTICK 241 33
    SOFT, DELECTABLE. ....LETTER IN NOVEMBER 253 9
    THE ZOO YOWL, THE MAD SOFT .............................EAVESDROPPER 260 35
    THE SOFT ANONYMOUS ....PARALYTIC 266 14
SOFTEN (2)
    RETROSPECT SHALL NOT SOFTEN SUCH PENURY -- ....DEPARTURE 51 9
    HOW SHALL IT SOFTEN THEM, THIS LITTLE LULLABY? ....THREE WOMEN 185 294
SOGGY (1)
    AND WHOLE CRABS, DEAD, THEIR SOGGY ....MUSSEL HUNTER AT ROCK HARBOR 97 84
SOIL (2)
    BREAKS THE SOIL. THIS IS AZALEA PATH. ....ELECTRA ON AZALEA PATH 117 21
    I AM NOT A TREE WITH MY ROOT IN THE SOIL ....I AM VERTICAL 162 2
SOLACE (1)
    GLAZES THE WINDOW OF MY HURT: WHAT SOLACE ....WINTER LANDSCAPE. 22 13
SOLACED (1)
    AND SOLACED HER, BUT QUIT HER AT COCK'S CROWING. ....QUEEN'S C. 28 15
SOLAR (5)
    IN SOLAR SCHEMES THE TILTED SUNS GO TURNING; ....TO EVA DESCENDING. 303 11
    IT WAS A SOLAR TURBINE ....NOTES TO A NEOPHYTE 306 19
    REVOLVING IN OVAL LOOPS OF SOLAR SPEED, ...THE DEAD 320 1
    BY SECEDING FROM THE SOLAR SYSTEM. ....INSOLENT STORM. 326 32
    OR THAT THE SOLAR SPECTRUM IS ....LOVE IS A PARALLAX 329 9
SOLARIUM (1)
    MORNING IN THE HOSPITAL SOLARIUM ..MORNING IN THE HOSPITAL SOLARIUM 332 T

<pre>
                                            TITLE   PAGE LINE
SOLDIERS (3)
    LEFTOVER SOLDIERS FROM OLD, MESSY WARS. ....FINISTERRE   169   7
    FILING LIKE SOLDIERS ....WINTERING   218   24
    A MILLION SOLDIERS RUN, ...CUT   235   19
SOLE (2)
    THAT OWL VOICE SOLE "YES", WHILE COWS UTTER ....WREATH FOR A BRIDAL   44   3
    IF OUR NERVES ARE THE SOLE NOURISHERS ..DIALOGUE OVER A OUIJA BOARD   284 287
SOLEMN-EYED (1)
    YOU SIT, SOLEMN-EYED, ABOUT TO VOMIT, ...THE TRIAL OF MAN   312   13
SOLES (1)
    WHEN THE SOLES OF MY FEET GROW COLD, ...LAST WORDS   172   19
SOLID (3)
    ALL COGS, WEIRD SPARKLE AND EVERY COG SOLID GOLD. ....THE TOUR   237   5
    SOLID THE SPACES LEAN ON, ENVIOUS. ....NICK AND THE CANDLESTICK   242   41
    A SOLID SHAPE ON AIR. MAY THE DECORUM ..DIALOGUE OVER A OUIJA BOARD   286 360
SOLIDER (2)
    A SOLIDER REPOSE THAN DEATH'S. ....SCULPTOR   92   24
    WEIGHTING THE PALE SKY WITH A SOLIDER COLOR. .....WUTHERING HEIGHTS   167   7
SOLIDIFY (1)
    HOW THE ELEMENTS SOLIDIFY! -- ....EVENT   194   1
SOLILOQUY (1)
    SOLILOQUY OF THE SOLIPSIST ....SOLILOQUY OF THE SOLIPSIST   37   T
SOLIPSIST (1)
    SOLILOQUY OF THE SOLIPSIST ....SOLILOQUY OF THE SOLIPSIST   37   T
SOLITARY (4)
    BLINKING GREEN-EYED AND SOLITARY ....ELLA MASON AND HER ELEVEN CATS   54   38
    IN BURROWS NARROW AS A FINGER, SOLITARY BEES ....BEEKEEPER'S.   118   15
    THEY ARE TOO PURITAN AND SOLITARY FOR THAT -- ....STARS.   166   31
    I AM SOLITARY AS GRASS. WHAT IS IT I MISS? ....THREE WOMEN   186 342
SOLITUDE (1)
    HAULED SUDDEN FROM SOLITUDE, ...DIALOGUE BETWEEN GHOST AND PRIEST   38   7
SOLITUDES (1)
    LIMPID AS THE SOLITUDES ....WUTHERING HEIGHTS   167   29
SOLOMON'S (1)
    AND JONQUILS SPROUT LIKE SOLOMON'S METAPHORS, ...APRIL AUBADE   312   11
SOME (53)
    WAITING FOR SOME ACCIDENTAL BREAK ....TALE OF A TUB   25   21
    THE FABRICATION OF SOME CLOTH TO COVER ....TALE OF A TUB   25   34
    TO KEEP SOME UNSAID PACT; PERHAPS CONCERN ....CHANNEL CROSSING   27   34
    TILL HE SOME PITY TOOK UPON HER CRYING; ......THE QUEEN'S COMPLAINT   28   12
    SOME ANGEL-SHAPE WORTH WEARING ....FIRESONG   30   9
    SOME BURN SHORT, SOME LONG, ...VANITY FAIR   33   34
    SOME BURN SHORT, SOME LONG, ...VANITY FAIR   33   34
    WALKS THERE NOT SOME SUCH ONE MAN ....STRUMPET SONG   34   14
    "I DON'T ASK YOU TO SPIN SOME RIDICULOUS FABLE ....DIALOGUE B.   39   22
    SOME DAMNED CONDITION YOU ARE IN: DIALOGUE BETWEEN GHOST AND PRIEST   39   33
    NOW SPEAK SOME SACRAMENT TO PARRY SCRUPLE ......WREATH FOR A BRIDAL   44   11
    SOME HAVOC ON TENDER LIMB, AND YET ....CRYSTAL GAZER   55   23
    ANY MORE IN THE DESULTORY WEATHER SOME DESIGN, ...BLACK ROOK I.   57   8
    OCCASIONALLY, SOME BACKTALK ....BLACK ROOK IN RAINY WEATHER   57   12
    "NO DOUBT NOW IN DREAM-PROPERTIED FALL SOME MOON-EYED, ..CONJURING.   66   33
    THEY POISE AND GRIEVE AS IN SOME OLD TRAGEDY. ....THE OTHER TWO   68   21
    SOME SUCH TRANSFIGURING MOVED ....THE GREAT CARBUNCLE   72   9
    BE CERTAIN SOME SUCH PACT'S ....VIRGIN IN A TREE   82   31
    OF SOME GODLY UTTERANCE WAKENED HEADS IGNORE: ....GHOST'S.   90   17
    SOME STRANGE INJURY ....FULL FATHOM FIVE   92   18
    GREEN TO THE POINT OF BLACKNESS, SOME ....CHILD'S PARK STONES 100   2
    SOME SCANDAL MIGHT ANY MINUTE OOZE ....AFTERMATH   113   4
    BY SOME UNUTTERABLE CHAGRIN, ...THE RAVAGED FACE   115   3
    HOURS OF BLANKNESS. SOME HARD STARS ....THE MANOR GARDEN 125   14
    LITTLE VICTIM UNEARTHED BY SOME LARGE CREATURE ....BLUE MOLES   126   6
    MOUTHPIECE OF THE DEAD, OR OF SOME GOD OR OTHER. ....THE COLOSSUS   129   7
    BY THE ROOTS OF MY HAIR SOME GOD GOT HOLD OF ME. ...THE HANGING MAN 141   1
    SOME FEW PASSENGERS KEEP TRACK ....ON DECK   142   4
    THEY WANT THE CRIB OF SOME LAMP-HEADED PLATO. ....MAGI   148   16
    SOME THINGS OF THIS WORLD ARE INDIGESTIBLE. ......ZOO KEEPER'S WIFE   155   16
    THEY'VE TRAPPED HER IN SOME LABORATORY JAR. ....FACE LIFT   156   28
    AS IF MY HABITS OFFENDED HER IN SOME WAY. ....IN PLASTER   159   31
    THEY ARE OPENING LIKE THE MOUTH OF SOME GREAT AFRICAN CAT, ..TULIPS 162   59
    ARRIVE AT TWILIGHT, AND THEN AFTER SOME EFFORT. ....STARS.   165   10
    THERE ARE SOME WITH THICK BLACK HAIR, THERE ARE SOME BALD. ..THREE. 183 222
    THERE ARE SOME WITH THICK BLACK HAIR, THERE ARE SOME BALD. ..THREE. 183 222
    THE NARCISSI, TOO, ARE BOWING TO SOME BIG THING: *AMONG THE NARCISSI 190   4
    SLIDING SHUT ON SOME QUICK THING, ...THE RABBIT CATCHER 194   29
    IS IT SOME OPERATION THAT IS TAKING PLACE? ....THE BEE MEETING 211   26
    IT IS RUSSIA I HAVE TO GET ACROSS, IT IS SOME WAR OR OTHER.*GETTING. 248   9
    SOME PALTRY SCENE ON THE SOUP-KITCHEN STAIR: ....DIALOGUE O. 279 125
    TO PICTURE SOME OTHER PARTY SPEAKING THROUGH ....DIALOGUE O. 280 146
    BOTTOM OF YOUR BRAIN. BY SOME MISHAP, ..DIALOGUE OVER A OUIJA BOARD 282 241
    SOME LIGHT. I GLIMPSE NO LIGHT AT ALL AS LONG ....DIALOGUE O. 284 290
    ADRIFT IN THE GUISE OF SOME GREAT-TALONED BIRD ....DIALOGUE O. 285 311
    OF CONTENDING WORDS. SOME PYTHONESS ....DIALOGUE OVER A OUIJA BOARD 286 347
    SOME DUCKS STEP DOWN OFF THEIR GREEN-REEDED SHELF ....QUEEN MARY'S. 290   11
    BECAUSE OF SOME EXPLICABLE PHENOMENON ....APRIL 18   301   4
    WILL PROVE TO BE SOME COMMON PARLOR FAKE: *METAMORPHOSES OF THE MOON 307   22
</pre>

SOME (CONT.)
    SOME DAY, MOVING, ONE WILL DROP, ...LOVE IS A PARALLAX   330   63
    HOPING FOR SOME INCREDIBLE DARK MAN*MORNING IN THE HOSPITAL SOLARIUM   333   23
    TO ASSAULT THE SCENE AND MAKE SOME *MORNING IN THE HOSPITAL SOLARIUM   333   24
    AT SOME STEADFAST MARK ....TOUCH-AND-GO   335   5
SOMEBODY (2)
    STOPPED AND AWFUL AS A PHOTOGRAPH OF SOMEBODY LAUGHING, ...BABY.   175   35
    SOMEBODY IS SHOOTING AT SOMETHING IN OUR TOWN -- ....THE SWARM   215   1
SOMEBODY'S (1)
    SOMEBODY'S DONE FOR. ....DEATH & CO.   255   31
SOMEHOW (5)
    THAT SOMEHOW WE ARE YOUNGER THAN WE WERE. ....APRIL AUBADE   312   14
    THE ENORMOUS MORTGAGE MUST BE PAID SOMEHOW, ...THE DISPOSSESSED   318   1
    THE ENORMOUS MORTGAGE MUST BE PAID SOMEHOW. ....THE DISPOSSESSED   318   6
    THE ENORMOUS MORTGAGE MUST BE PAID SOMEHOW. ....THE DISPOSSESSED   318   12
    THE ENORMOUS MORTGAGE MUST BE PAID SOMEHOW: ....THE DISPOSSESSED   319   18
SOMEONE (6)
    DRESSED IN BLACK, EVERYBODY IN MOURNING FOR SOMEONE.*THE NET-MENDERS   121   4
    I LEAVE MY HEALTH BEHIND. I LEAVE SOMEONE ....THREE WOMEN   184 272
    IS IT THE BUTCHER, THE GROCER, THE POSTMAN, SOMEONE I KNOW? ...BEE.   211   30
    I DREAM OF SOMEONE ELSE ENTIRELY. ....THE JAILER   227   27
    TO COURT REMORSE. OR SOMEONE ELSE. I'D RATHER ....DIALOGUE O.   278   59
    MUST HAVE BEEN WHOLLY SOMEONE ELSE. IT'S ABSURD, ...DIALOGUE O.   285 309
SOMERSAULTS (1)
    SOMERSAULTS TO COUNTERFEIT ECLIPSE: ....SONNET TO SATAN   323   2
SOMERSET (2)
    IN HER RAMSHACKLE HOUSE OFF SOMERSET TERRACE; ....ELLA MASON A.   53   2
    WE SNICKERED AS SHE SHAMBLED DOWN SOMERSET TERRACE ...ELLA MASON A.   54   32
SOMETHING (28)
    ELEVATIONS TO BE CALLED SOMETHING MORE THAN HILLS.   ABOVE THE OXBOW   88   9
    STILL HE THUMBED OUT SOMETHING ELSE.   THE HERMIT AT OUTERMOST HOUSE 119   14
    THINKING OF SOMETHING ELSE. POEM.2.DARK. 132   7
    THIS IS NOT DEATH, IT IS SOMETHING SAFER. POEM.5.F.   135   15
    FISTS MY FINGERS FOR ME. HE MAKES ME FEEL SOMETHING PRECIOUS   FACE. 156   13
    OF SOMETHING BEAUTIFUL, BUT ANNIHILATING. ....THE RIVAL 166   3
    AND DYING TO SAY SOMETHING UNANSWERABLE. ....THE RIVAL 166   10
    THERE WAS SOMETHING ABOUT THEM LIKE CARDBOARD, AND NOW I HAD
        CAUGHT IT, ...THREE WOMEN   177   17
    AND THE MAN I WORK FOR LAUGHED: "HAVE YOU SEEN SOMETHING AWFUL? ...
                                    ... THREE WOMEN   177   22
    A HOT BLUE DAY HAD BUDDED INTO SOMETHING. ....THREE WOMEN 178   56
    AND WALKED CAREFULLY, PRECARIOUSLY, LIKE SOMETHING RARE.*THREE WOMEN 178   73
    I AM CALM. I AM CALM. IT IS THE CALM BEFORE SOMETHING AWFUL: *THREE. 179   92
    I AM ONE IN FIVE, SOMETHING LIKE THAT. I AM NOT HOPELESS. ...THREE.   183 244
    A TENDERNESS THAT DID NOT TIRE, SOMETHING HEALING. .....THREE WOMEN   186 357
    DEAFNESS IS SOMETHING ELSE. ....LITTLE FUGUE   188   21
    HE IS RECUPERATING FROM SOMETHING ON THE LUNG. ..AMONG THE NARCISSI   190   3
    IT IS SOMETHING TO OWN A PHEASANT, ...PHEASANT   191   5
    LOOKING, WITH ITS HOOKS, FOR SOMETHING TO LOVE. ....ELM   193   30
    THESE CHILDREN ARE AFTER SOMETHING, WITH HOOKS AND CRIES, ...BERCK.   198   44
    IS IT IMPOSSIBLE FOR YOU TO LET SOMETHING GO AND HAVE IT GO WHOLE? ...
                                    ... A BIRTHDAY PRESENT   207   45
    SOMEBODY IS SHOOTING AT SOMETHING IN OUR TOWN -- ....THE SWARM   215   1
    SOMETHING IS GONE. ....THE JAILER 226   11
    HEAVEN WOULD BE SOMETHING ELSE, ...LYONNESSE   234   12
    SOMETHING ELSE ....ARIEL 239   15
    THAT'S SOMETHING TO STUDY EVEN IF IT'S NOT ....DIALOGUE O.   279 108
    IT IS LIKE SOMETHING SHE HAS CAUGHT FOR ME. ....ELM/DR   292   5
    "IF ONLY SOMETHING WOULD HAPPEN!" ....DIALOGUE EN ROUTE   308   1
    SOONER OR LATER SOMETHING GOES AMISS; ....NEVER TRY TO TRICK.   320   16
SOMETHING'S (2)
    SAYING: "SOMETHING'S ADDLED IN A WOMAN WHO ACCOMMODATES ...
                        ... ELLA MASON AND HER ELEVEN CATS   53   5
    STITCHES TO SHOW SOMETHING'S MISSING? NO, NO? THEN ...THE APPLICANT 221   6
SOMETIMES (2)
    SOMETIMES I THINK THAT WHEN I AM SLEEPING ....I AM VERTICAL 162   14
    ON HIM SOMETIMES. HE'S LAZY. LIKE ANY YOUNG ....DIALOGUE O.   281 182
SOMEWHERE (4)
    SOMEWHERE BY MUCH SUN AND WIND; ....MUSSEL HUNTER AT ROCK HARBOR   97   73
    SOMEWHERE AT THE END OF IT, HEAVING. BLACKBERRIES ....BLACKBERRYING   168   4
    WITH A GODDAM BABY SCREAMING OFF SOMEWHERE. ....STOPPED DEAD   230   12
    IN THE WINGS SOMEWHERE, OR LIKE HEIRLOOM FURNITURE .....DIALOGUE O.   276   7
SOMNOLENCE (2)
    NODDING IN A SOMNOLENCE ....SPIDER   49   23
    MORNINGS DISSIPATE IN SOMNOLENCE. ....FROG AUTUMN   99   5
SON (4)
    I SEE THE FATHER CONVERSING WITH THE SON. ....THREE WOMEN   179   88
    HERE IS MY SON. ....THREE WOMEN   183 233
    I SHALL MEDITATE UPON MY LITTLE SON. ....THREE WOMEN   186 324
    FOR A FATHERLESS SON ....FOR A FATHERLESS SON   205   T
SONG (15)
    SONG FOR A SUMMER'S DAY ....SONG FOR A SUMMER'S DAY   30   T
    LOVESICK AT FIRST FOND SONG, ...VANITY FAIR   33   24
    STRUMPET SONG ....STRUMPET SONG   33   T
    STREET SONG ....STREET SONG   35   T

SONG (CONT.)
AND SINGING THE GLOWWORM SONG, I COULD ....THE DISQUIETING MUSES   75   27
AND THE SNAKECHARMER'S SONG AND THE GIGANTIC LILIES, ...YADWIGHA.   86   33
THAN CAN BE. SISTERS, YOUR SONG ....LORELEI   94   16
SONG, YOUR SILENCE. AT THE SOURCE ....LORELEI   94   30
OF THE DEATH'S-HEAD SHADOWING THEIR SONG. ....TWO VIEWS. 114   19
MORNING SONG ....MORNING SONG 156   T
MARY'S SONG ....MARY'S SONG 257   T
ARTICULATING SONG. ....TRIO OF LOVE SONGS 315   40
BOTH SERAPH SONG AND VIOLINS ARE DUMB; ....DOOM OF EXILES 318   7
SONG FOR A REVOLUTIONARY LOVE ....SONG FOR A REVOLUTIONARY LOVE   322   T
SUDDENLY A BRAZEN SONG IS HEARD ....THE PRINCESS AND THE GOBLINS   334   44
SONGS (4)
SHIRR SONGS TO SUIT WHICH MOOD ....ODE FOR TED   29   20
SHAPES ITS IMAGES AROUND HIS SONGS. ...................SNAKECHARMER   79   7
TRIO OF LOVE SONGS ....TRIO OF LOVE SONGS 313   T
THE JABBERWOCK WILL NOT TRANSLATE HIS SONGS: ....A SORCERER B.   324   11
SONNET (3)
SONNET: TO EVA ....SONNET: TO EVA 304   T
SONNET: TO TIME ....SONNET: TO TIME 311   T
SONNET TO SATAN ....SONNET TO SATAN 323   T
SONS (4)
OF KINGS, UNMANNED KINGS' SONS: OUR MASTERIES ....SNOWMAN O.   59   41
SONS, DAUGHTERS, DAUGHTERS AND SONS, ...OLD LADIES' HOME   120   10
SONS, DAUGHTERS, DAUGHTERS AND SONS, ...OLD LADIES' HOME   120   10
OF OUR HUSBANDS AND SONS MOVE SURE AMONG THE LOW STARS. ......NET-.   121   19
SOON (12)
GET BACK, THOUGH, SOON, ...ALL THE DEAD DEARS   71   26
SOON: BE IT BY WAKES, WEDDINGS, ...ALL THE DEAD DEARS   71   27
THE SUN WILL DIMINISH IT SOON ENOUGH: ....A WINTER SHIP 113   29
SOON EACH WHITE LADY WILL BE BOARDED UP ....PRIVATE GROUND   130   5
BUT SHE'LL SOON FIND OUT THAT THAT DOESN'T MATTER A BIT. *IN PLASTER 160   54
UNKNOWING I MUST SOON UNPETAL. ....I AM VERTICAL   162   7
SOON, SOON THE FLESH ....LADY LARARUS   244   16
SOON, SOON THE FLESH ....LADY LARARUS   244   16
NINE MONTHS TOO SOON FOR COMFORT, BUT A BRIGHT ....DIALOGUE O.   280 141
EATING YOUR WORDS: YOU'LL REVOKE HIS GODHOOD SOON AS ...DIALOGUE O.   281 189
THEIR MAGNIFIED HEADS AND PLAN TO KILL ME AS SOON
    AS POSSIBLE. ....THE RIVAL/DR 291   3
GOSSIPS LATE AND SOON, ...JILTED 304   6
SOONER (2)
AND I'D SOONER BE STAKED FOR A WITCH, KINDLED, AND CURLED ...
                    ... DIALOGUE OVER A OUIJA BOARD 280 132
SOONER OR LATER SOMETHING GOES AMISS; ....NEVER TRY TO TRICK.   320   16
SOOT (1)
TIME'S SOOT IN BLEARED EYE ....TINKER JACK AND THE TIDY WIVES   34   12
SOPHIST (1)
ON SOPHIST SEAS TO OVERTAKE THAT MARK ....LOVE IS A PARALLAX   329   5
SOPHISTRY (1)
SUCH SOPHISTRY CAN PLACATE US. ............METAMORPHOSES OF THE MOON 307   30
SORCERER (1)
A SORCERER BIDS FAREWELL TO SEEM ..A SORCERER BIDS FAREWELL TO SEEM   324   T
SORCERESS (1)
THIS SORCERESS SETS MIRRORS ENOUGH ....VANITY FAIR   33   22
SORE (1)
YOU HAVE IT IN HAND. GRIT IN THE EYE OR A SORE ....PERSEUS   83   27
SORES (1)
SCOURGING TO SORES HIS OWN RED SLUICES ....A LESSON IN VENGEANCE   80   13
SORROW (8)
THE MAMMOTH, LUMBERING STATUARY OF SORROW, ...PERSEUS   82   3
THE VOICES OF LONELINESS, THE VOICES OF SORROW ....THREE WOMEN 185 292
WITH SUCH SORROW IN ITS VOICE? ....THREE WOMEN 186 349
AND DISSOLVE OF SORROW. ....THE APPLICANT 221   17
BUT NOW THAT ANGER COOLS, I'VE A SENSE OF SORROW ....DIALOGUE O.   285 310
OVER MY MIND, CASTING A SHADOW. SORROW   DIALOGUE OVER A OUIJA BOARD 285 312
AND IN SORROW LOOK ....TO A JILTED LOVER   309   2
SORROW; WEEP FOR THE LEGENDARY DRAGON. ....SONNET: TO TIME   311   12
SORROWFUL (1)
IT IS THE EXCEPTION THAT CLIMBS THE SORROWFUL HILL .....THREE WOMEN 186 332
SORROWS (2)
SORROWS OF MALFI'S GENTLE DUCHESS? GONE ....PERSEUS   83   42
WHAT PAINS, WHAT SORROWS MUST I BE MOTHERING? ....THREE WOMEN 180 133
SORRY (5)
OF FLAWED EARTH-FLESH COULD CAUSE THIS SORRY PASS? .....DIALOGUE B.   39   32
MUMBLEPAWS, TEARY AND SORRY, ...POEM.4.BEAST.   134   12
THE DAY-MOON LIGHTS UP LIKE A SORRY MOTHER, ...SLEEP.   144   24
IS SHE SORRY FOR WHAT WILL HAPPEN? I DO NOT THINK SO. ..THREE WOMEN 176   6
A TARRED FABRIC, SORRY AND DULL, ...BERCK-PLAGE   200 114
SORT (16)
WITHOUT DREAMS OF ANY SORT. POEM.1.WHO.   132   24
HE'S A FAT SORT. POEM.2.DARK.   132   21
THE COLORS ASSERT THEMSELVES WITH A SORT OF VENGEANCE. ...TWO CAMP.   145   14
NOW I RESEMBLE A SORT OF GOD ....LOVE LETTER   147   34
AND APPEARS TO HAVE SUFFERED A SORT OF PRIVATE BLITZKRIEG. ..A LIFE   150   24
A SORT OF CELLOPHANE BALLOON. ....PARLIAMENT HILL FIELDS   153   47

SORT (CONT.)
    THE NIGHT SKY IS ONLY A SORT OF CARBON PAPER, ...INSOMNIAC   163   1
    FIRST, ARE YOU OUR SORT OF A PERSON? ....THE APPLICANT   221   1
    IN A SORT OF CEMENT WELL ....LESBOS   227   13
    WRITHING AND SIGHING, WHAT SORT OF A SCENERY IS IT? ...STOPPED DEAD   230   9
    EXCEPT FOR A SORT OF A HINGE ....CUT   235   4
    A SORT OF BLACK HORSEHAIR, ...BY CANDLELIGHT   236   2
    A SORT OF WALKING MIRACLE, MY SKIN ....LADY LAZARUS   244   4
    SHE IS USED TO THIS SORT OF THING. ....EDGE   273   19
    FUSING TWO TALENTS, A SORT OF PSYCHIC BASTARD ....DIALOGUE O.   280 139
    A DEVON MEADOW MIGHT OFFER A SIMPLER SORT   QUEEN MARY'S ROSE GARDEN   290   23
SORTS (2)
    OF SORTS. MIRACLES OCCUR, ...BLACK ROOK IN RAINY WEATHER   57   36
    ONE COURTING DOCTORS OF ALL SORTS, ...THE DEATH OF MYTH-MAKING   104   4
SOUGH (1)
    AROUND OUR TENT THE OLD SIMPLICITIES SOUGH ....TWO CAMP.   145   25
SOUGHT (3)
    SO WERE THEY ONE; SO SOUGHT THEY COUCH, ...BUCOLICS   23   3
    IT'S LIKELY THAT EACH SECRET SOUGHT ......METAMORPHOSES OF THE MOON   307   21
    I SOUGHT MY IMAGE ....ON LOOKING INTO THE EYES OF A DEMON LOVER   325   17
SOUL (19)
    SUN HOISTS SOUL UP AFTER LIDS FALL SHUT; ....VANITY FAIR   33   28
    A SOUL GROWN FEVERISH, CLUTCHING ITS DEAD BODY-TREE ....DIALOGUE B.   39   43
    TO SEE WITH THE SPOTLESS SOUL, ...ON THE PLETHORA OF DRYADS   67   14
    TWISTING OF THUMBSCREWS: ONE SOUL TIED IN SINEWS, ...LESSON.   80   8
    EACH NURSE PATCHED HER SOUL TO A WOUND AND DISAPPEARED. ....WAKING.   151   13
    I GAVE HER A SOUL, I BLOOMED OUT OF HER AS A ROSE ....IN PLASTER   159   16
    A BODILESS SOUL COULD PASS ANOTHER SOUL ....WIDOW   164   32
    A BODILESS SOUL COULD PASS ANOTHER SOUL ....WIDOW   164   32
    ONE SOUL PASS THROUGH THE OTHER, FRAIL AS SMOKE ....WIDOW   165   34
    HIS SOUL MAY BEAT AND BE BEATING AT HER DULL SENSE ....WIDOW   165   37
    WITH SEVEN HOLES THUMBED IN. THE SOUL IS ANOTHER LIGHT. ...SURGEON.   170   8
    ANNOUNCES A NEW SOUL. THE BED IS BLUE. ....THE SURGEON AT 2 A.M.   171   42
    HOW WINTER FILLS MY SOUL! AND THAT CHALK LIGHT ....THREE WOMEN   181 177
    A SMALL WHITE SOUL IS WAVING, A SMALL WHITE MAGGOT. ....EVENT   195   19
    AND THE SOUL IS A BRIDE ....BERCK-PLAGE   200 107
    YOUR SOUL, YOUR SOUL? ....STOPPED DEAD   230   22
    YOUR SOUL, YOUR SOUL? ....STOPPED DEAD   230   22
    MY SOUL DIES BEFORE IT. ....YEARS   255   13
    BUT IT HAS NO SOUL. ....KINDNESS   269   8
SOUL-ANIMALS (1)
    OVAL SOUL-ANIMALS, ...BALLOONS   271   3
SOULS (6)
    SOULS, ROLLED IN THE DOOM-NOISE OF THE SEA. ....FINISTERRE   169   14
    "LET US FLATTEN AND LAUNDER THE GROSSNESS FROM THESE SOULS." *THREE.   179   91
    WHAT IS IT THAT FLINGS THESE INNOCENT SOULS AT US? .....THREE WOMEN   183 218
    THIS IS THE SILENCE OF ASTOUNDED SOULS. ....CROSSING THE WATER   190   12
    IN THAT VALLEY THE TRAIN SHRIEKS ECHO LIKE SOULS ON HOOKS. ...
                                                  ... THE DETECTIVE   208   5
    LET THEIR SOULS WRITHE IN A DEW, ...GETTING THERE   249   62
SOUL-SHIFT (1)
    FLOATING THROUGH THE AIR IN MY SOUL-SHIFT ....LOVE LETTER   147   35
SOUL-STUFF (1)
    EVERY DAY YOU FILL HIM WITH SOUL-STUFF, LIKE A PITCHER. .....LESBOS   229   77
SOUND (12)
    NO SOUND BUT A DRUNKEN COOT ....FAUN   35   6
    OUR VOICES FATHOMED A PROFOUNDER SOUND: ....THE OTHER TWO   68   12
    STARTLED AT IT, THOUGH THE SOUND ....NIGHT SHIFT   76   10
    SOUND, WITH A GLITTERY WISP ....MUSSEL HUNTER AT ROCK HARBOR   96   47
    FOR THAT WARY CLATTER SOUND OR GESTURE ..............INCOMMUNICADO   100   6
    SIZE. THE CRIES OF SCAVENGING GULLS SOUND THIN ....GREEN ROCK.   105   14
    I HEAR THE SOUND OF THE HOURS ....THREE WOMEN   185 311
    OR SHALL I BRING YOU THE SOUND OF POISONS? ....ELM   192   13
    REVOLVING, THE SOUND ....GETTING THERE   248   7
    WITH THE SOUND OF THE SEA IN YOUR MOUTH. ....THE RIVAL/DR   291   19
    DOWN WHERE SOUND ....AQUATIC NOCTURNE   306   25
    ANTICIPATES THE WARNING SOUND ....DANSE MACABRE   321   23
SOUNDING (1)
    FOR SOUNDING SYLLABLES WE HAVEN'T YET ..DIALOGUE OVER A OUIJA BOARD   283 254
SOUNDLESS (1)
    HIGH AGAINST HEAVEN, GULLS WENT WHEELING SOUNDLESS ...DREAM WITH C.   44   13
SOUNDS (1)
    IT UTTERS SUCH DARK SOUNDS IT CANNOT BE GOOD. ....THREE WOMEN   182 217
SOUP-KITCHEN (1)
    SOME PALTRY SCENE ON THE SOUP-KITCHEN STAIR: ....DIALOGUE O.   279 125
SOUR (4)
    TO UNMADE MUD CLOAKED BY SOUR SKY. ....FIRESONG   30   14
    THE SOUR BREATH ....LADY LAZARUS   244   14
    TURNED THICK AND SOUR. ....BITTER STRAWBERRIES   299   9
    THE SOUR LEMON MOON. ....JILTED   304   8
SOURCE (6)
    SHRIVELING TO CINDERS AT ITS SOURCE, ...CRYSTAL GAZER   56   45
    THE EIGHT PILGRIMS TOWARDS ITS SOURCE -- ....THE GREAT CARBUNCLE   72   10
    TILL THE THUDDING SOURCE, EXPOSED, ...NIGHT SHIFT   76   13
    SONG, YOUR SILENCE. AT THE SOURCE ....LORELEI   94   30

```
                                                              TITLE          PAGE  LINE
SOURCE (CONT.)
     I AM NO SOURCE OF HONEY ..................THE ARRIVAL OF THE BEE BOX  213   33
     THE SOURCE OF BLANCHING LIGHT THAT CONJURED HER  ......THE PRINCESS.  333    3
SOURNESS (1)
     THERE IS ONLY A SOURNESS. .............................APPREHENSIONS  195   10
SOURS (1)
     UNTONGUED, ALL BEAUTY'S BRIGHT JUICE SOURS.  .......VIRGIN IN A TREE   82   43
SOUTH (4)
     FROM SOUTH STATION TO NORTH. ......................A WINTER'S TALE     87   36
     A FIELD OF BURDOCK OPENS TO THE SOUTH.  ......ELECTRA ON AZALEA PATH  117   22
     TRADING THEIR POISONS, THE NORTH AND SOUTH BOUND CARS*PRIVATE GROUND  130   16
     OR MUCH COMPANY, OR THE MILDNESS OF THE SOUTH. ...............STARS.  166   30
SOUTHERN (1)
     SOUTHERN SUNRISE ...............................SOUTHERN SUNRISE       26    T
SOUTHWARD (2)
     AGAINST OUR SKY: THEY ARE WHAT WE LOOK SOUTHWARD TO *ABOVE THE OXBOW   88   11
     SOUTHWARD, OVER KENTISH TOWN, AN ASHEN SMUDGE*PARLIAMENT HILL FIELDS  152   21
SOW (5)
     SOW ...............................................................SOW   60    T
     HIS GREAT SOW: ....................................................SOW   60    2
     HE KEPT THE SOW --  IMPOUNDED FROM PUBLIC STARE, .................SOW   60    5
     OF A SOW LOUNGED BELLY-BEDDED ON THAT BLACK COMPOST, ...........SOW    61   25
     DUPE THE DULL SOW LOUNGING SNOUT IN MUD, ...GO GET THE GOODLY SQUAB  313   11
SOWS (1)
     NOR EVEN ONE OF THE COMMON BARNYARD SOWS, ......................SOW    61   17
SOW'S (1)
     BOAR, FABULOUS ENOUGH TO STRADDLE THAT SOW'S HEAT. .............SOW    61   33
SPA (1)
     THE BURNT-OUT SPA ..................................THE BURNT-OUT SPA  137    T
SPACE (18)
     OWN THEIR CABBAGE ROOTS, A SPACE OF STARS, ...............LANDOWNERS   53   10
     LEDGE WILL DISLODGE OUR CRAMPED CONCEPT OF SPACE, UNWALL ....OXBOW.    88   23
     ME OFF INTO THEIR SPACE OF BEATING, ..........WHITENESS I REMEMBER    102   22
     SPACE! SPACE! THE BED LINEN WAS GIVING OUT ENTIRELY. .......WAKING.   151   11
     SPACE! SPACE! THE BED LINEN WAS GIVING OUT ENTIRELY. .......WAKING.   151   11
     PROMISING SIMPLY THE HARD STARS, THE SPACE ...................WIDOW   164   23
     WHEN ONE OF THEM FALLS IT LEAVES A SPACE, ..STARS OVER THE DORDOGNE   166   32
     IT IS LIKE BEING MAILED INTO SPACE, ..............WUTHERING HEIGHTS   167   23
     THAT LOOKS OUT ON NOTHING, NOTHING BUT A GREAT SPACE   BLACKBERRYING  169   25
     HAVE SUCH A SPACE TO CROSS, .......................THE NIGHT DANCES   250   16
     A SPACE FOR THE THING I AM GIVEN, .....................THALIDOMIDE    252   18
     SPACE OF HOLLY WHERE SPIKES ...............................YEARS      255    2
     THAT EMPTIED ONE MAN INTO SPACE .......................MARY'S SONG    257   17
     TAKING UP HALF THE SPACE, .................................BALLOONS   271    4
     WHAT GOOD IS ALL THAT SPACE IF IT CAN'T DRAW YOU OFF?   THE RIVAL/DR  291   13
     FLINGS SILVER GAUNTLET OF HIS PLANE AT SPACE, .......METAMORPHOSES.   307    4
     TO CORRAL THE CONUNDRUM OF SPACE ..............DIALOGUE EN ROUTE      309   35
     ACROBAT OF SPACE, ............................TRIO OF LOVE SONGS      314   25
SPACES (4)
     ARROGANT AMONG ROOK-TONGUED SPACES, .....................CONJURING.   66   10
     BARE NO SINISTER SPACES. ALREADY .......................BLUE MOLES   126   13
     SOLID THE SPACES LEAN ON, ENVIOUS. ........NICK AND THE CANDLESTICK  242   41
     IN A FEW SPACES OF SKY AND TREETOPS ....................APRIL 18     302   13
SPAIN (1)
     IS THAT SPAIN DOWN THERE? .............................STOPPED DEAD   230    7
SPAN (2)
     TO SAVOR THEIR SPAN OF FLOURISHING. .................CRYSTAL GAZER    55   27
     BEGIN ON TILTED VIOLINS TO SPAN .........................CINDERELLA  303    4
SPANISH (2)
     LAST SUMMER I CAME UPON YOUR SPANISH COUSIN, ..............SPIDER     48    8
     AT THE CRADLE OF SPANISH WALNUT, .........................WINTERING  219   44
SPAR (1)
     LIKE A DIVER ON A LOFTY SPAR OF LAND .................FAMILY REUNION  301   25
SPARE (5)
     AS CAN SPARE BREATH .................................STRUMPET SONG    34   15
     HE'LL NOT SPARE .......................................THE GLUTTON    40   12
     SPYING A PATE TO SPARE ........THE LADY AND THE EARTHENWARE HEAD      69   10
     THIS IS THE CITY OF SPARE PARTS. ......................POEM.7.S.     137   33
     WE WERE ALWAYS CRYING, IN OUR SPARE ROOMS, LITTLE PUT-UPON
          SISTERS, ....................................THE BABYSITTERS   174    4
SPARES (1)
     YET DESOLATION, STALLED IN PAINT, SPARES THE LITTLE COUNTRY ...
          ... TWO VIEWS OF A CADAVER ROOM                               114   21
SPARKING (1)
     SPARKING OFF THEIR BROTHER-SISTER REARS ...................AMNESIAC  233   18
SPARKLE (1)
     ALL COGS, WEIRD SPARKLE AND EVERY COG SOLID GOLD. .........THE TOUR  237    5
SPARKLER (1)
     THE CELLAR'S BELLY. THEY'VE BLOWN MY SPARKLER OUT. .......POEM.6.W.  135    8
SPARKS (2)
     FLOGGED TROLLEY. THE SPARKS ARE BLUE. .......................LESBOS  228   49
     THE BLUE SPARKS SPILL, ......................................LESBOS  228   50
SPARKY (1)
     LEAVING NO SPARKY TRACK, SETTING UP NO RIPPLE. .......THE OTHER TWO   68   26
```

		TITLE	PAGE	LINE

SPARROW (2)
THROUGH CROSSHATCH OF SPARROW AND STARLING. ....PHEASANT   191   14
A SAINTLY SPARROW JARGONS MADRIGALS ....APRIL AUBADE   312   5
SPARS (1)
WITH TILTED SPARS OF SLOOPS REVOLVED BY WHITE .....MIDSUMMER MOBILE   324   3
SPARSEST (1)
WHERE I AM AT HOME, ONLY THE SPARSEST STARS *STARS OVER THE DORDOGNE   165   9
SPASM (1)
A SPASM TOOK THE RHODODENDRON BUSHES: ................RHODODENDRON.   103   20
SPASMODIC (1)
IF YOU CARE TO CALL THOSE SPASMODIC ....BLACK ROOK IN RAINY WEATHER   57   37
SPAWN (3)
WATER FAUCETS SPAWN NO DANGER; EACH CRAB ....TALE OF A TUB   25   19
TO SLAY SPAWN OF DRAGON'S TEETH: SPEAKING THIS PROMISE, ..WREATH F.   45   23
BUT THE SPAWN PERCOLATE IN MY HEART. THEY ARE FERTILE. *WORDS HEARD.   203   13
SPAWNING (1)
NOW HILLS HATCH MENACE, SPAWNING SHADE; ....PURSUIT   22   25
SPEAK (14)
NOW SPEAK SOME SACRAMENT TO PARRY SCRUPLE ......WREATH FOR A BRIDAL   44   11
FOR WHICH OF THOSE WOULD SPEAK ....VIRGIN IN A TREE   81   20
SPEAK IN SIGN LANGUAGE OF A LOST OTHERWORLD,*THE GHOST'S LEAVETAKING   90   19
AT THIS WHARF THERE ARE NO GRAND LANDINGS TO SPEAK OF.*A WINTER SHIP   112   1
AND THEY STUPIDLY STARE, AND DO NOT SPEAK OF HER. ....STILLBORN   142   15
STILL NOBODY WILL MOVE OR SPEAK -- ....ON DECK   142   10
AND LEARN TO SPEAK WITH FINGERS, NOT A TONGUE. ....THREE WOMEN   184 255
HE DOES NOT WALK. HE DOES NOT SPEAK A WORD. ....THREE WOMEN   186 325
SPEAK, SPEAK! WHO IS IT? ..WORDS HEARD, BY ACCIDENT, OVER THE PHONE   202   3
SPEAK, SPEAK! WHO IS IT? ..WORDS HEARD, BY ACCIDENT, OVER THE PHONE   202   3
THE SURGEON IS QUIET, HE DOES NOT SPEAK. *THE COURAGE OF SHUTTING-UP   210   14
I COULD HARDLY SPEAK. ....DADDY   223   28
I DO NOT SPEAK. ....LESBOS   229   67
WHICH SPEAK HER MAESTRO'S WILL. ....AERIALIST   331   12
SPEAKING (2)
TO SLAY SPAWN OF DRAGON'S TEETH: SPEAKING THIS PROMISE, ..WREATH F.   45   23
TO PICTURE SOME OTHER PARTY SPEAKING THROUGH ....DIALOGUE O.   280 146
SPEAR (1)
WHO POISES HIS PASTEL SPEAR ....BATTLE-SCENE   84   14
SPECK (1)
OF EYEBATHS CAN UNSEAT THE SPECK: ....THE EYE-MOTE   109   20
SPECKLED (3)
BUT IN SPECKLED THICKETS, WARTED AS A TOAD, ...FIRESONG   30   3
YOUR SPECKLED STONE ASKEW BY AN IRON FENCE. ....ELECTRA ON.   117   18
EACH SPECKLED TWIG ....POLLY'S TREE   128   3
SPECKLES (1)
IT IS PINK, WITH SPECKLES. I HAVE LOOKED AT IT SO LONG ......MIRROR   173   7
SPECS (1)
HERE'S YOUR SPECS, DEAR, HERE'S YOUR PURSE. ....THE TOUR   238   36
SPECTACULAR (1)
BLUEBLACK, A SPECTACULAR PLUM FRUIT. ....ZOO KEEPER'S WIFE   154   4
SPECTACULARLY (1)
ATTRACTING MY SHARE OF AHS AND SPECTACULARLY PAINTED, *I AM VERTICAL   162   6
SPECTER (1)
AND YOU, SHACKLED ASHEN ACROSS THE RIFT, A SPECTER .....DIALOGUE O.   285 321
SPECTRAL (1)
MIRRORS, ENGENDERING A SPECTRAL ....LANDOWNERS   53   7
SPECTRUM (1)
OR THAT THE SOLAR SPECTRUM IS ....LOVE IS A PARALLAX   329   9
SPED (1)
ONE THRUST: AND THEY ARE SPED. ....BATTLE-SCENE   84   30
SPEED (2)
ON FLUENT HAUNCHES, KEEPS MY SPEED. ....PURSUIT   23   28
REVOLVING IN OVAL LOOPS OF SOLAR SPEED, ...THE DEAD   320   1
SPELL (4)
LIKE LOCAL TROLLS IN THE SPELL OF A SUPERIOR BEING. ......TWO CAMP.   144   6
CAN SPELL SARCASM THROUGH OUR FINGERTIPS. ....DIALOGUE O.   282 208
SURFACED IN OURSELVES: HE'LL SPELL A LINE ....DIALOGUE O.   283 255
EACH FALLEN LEAF IS TRAPPED BY SPELL OF STEEL, ..PROLOGUE TO SPRING   322   7
SPELLING (1)
OF HALF-HINTS. YOU PERSIST IN SPELLING HALF-HINTS ......DIALOGUE O.   279   98
SPELLS (4)
HIS VOICE WAYLAYS ME, SPELLS A TRANCE, ...PURSUIT   23   41
HE, GODLY, DODDERING, SPELLS ....OUIJA   78   30
IS HE, THEN? HE SPELLS. I-N. HE'LL LIFT *DIALOGUE OVER A OUIJA BOARD   278   76
BEFORE HE SPELLS AGAIN, SHOULD HIS NEXT WRIT ....DIALOGUE O.   281 193
SPELT (1)
BECAUSE PAN BLUNTLY SPELT OUT GOD'S HEAD, NOT ....DIALOGUE O.   282 237
SPEND (1)
UNSPOOL AND SPEND THEMSELVES. MY MIND RUNS WITH THEM, *PARLIAMENT H.   153   35
SPENT (2)
GRIM AS GARGOYLES FROM YEARS SPENT SQUATTING AT SEA'S BORDER ...
                            ... DREAM WITH CLAM-DIGGERS   44   25
DAWN SNUFFS OUT STAR'S SPENT WICK, ...EPITAPH FOR FIRE AND FLOWER   46   29
SPERM (1)
AND MONEY THE SPERM FLUID OF IT ALL. ....AMNESIAC   233   20

		TITLE	PAGE	LINE

SPEWED (1)
  SPEWED RELICS CLICKER MASSES IN THE WIND, ...POINT SHIRLEY 110 32
SPEWS (1)
  THEN SPEWS IT BACK. ....LESBOS 229 76
SPHERE (2)
  SO THE SNAKECHARMER BEGINS A SNAKY SPHERE .............SNAKECHARMER 79 2
  LOVE'S PALING SPHERE. ....MOONSONG AT MORNING 317 24
SPHINX-QUEEN (1)
  SPHINX-QUEEN OF CATS. ....ELLA MASON AND HER ELEVEN CATS 54 30
SPICE (1)
  ITS BABY HEAD OUT OF THE WAY, EMBALMED IN SPICE, ...TOTEM 264 12
SPIDER (6)
  SPIDER ....SPIDER 48 T
  FROST DROPS EVEN THE SPIDER. CLEARLY ....FROG AUTUMN 99 9
  THE SPIDER ON ITS OWN STRING ....THE MANOR GARDEN 125 16
  AND THE BEAR-FURRED, BIRD-EATING SPIDER ....ZOO KEEPER'S WIFE 155 30
  WIDOW. THE BITTER SPIDER SITS ....WIDOW 164 11
  I AM MAD, CALLS THE SPIDER, WAVING ITS MANY ARMS. ....TOTEM 265 28
SPIDERLIKE (1)
  SPIDERLIKE, I SPIN MIRRORS, ...CHILDLESS WOMAN 259 11
SPIDER-MEN (1)
  THE SPIDER-MEN HAVE CAUGHT YOU, ...GULLIVER 251 12
SPIDERS (1)
  THE SPIDERS WON'T NOTICE. POEM.1.WHO. 131 8
SPIDERY (3)
  THE SPIDERY JAWS, THE SPINE BONES BARED FOR A MOMENT ....ZOO K. 154 9
  AND THE SPIDERY WATER-DAZZLE ON FIELD AND STREET. ....LYONNESSE 234 18
  SPIDERY, UNSAFE. ....THALIDOMIDE 252 6
SPIELS (1)
  SNUBS IMPROMPTU SPIELS OF WIND ....CONJURING. 66 6
SPIKE (1)
  SPIKE AND SUCK OUT ....THE SHRIKE 42 22
SPIKES (2)
  ITS BLACK SPIKES, ...THE RABBIT CATCHER 193 7
  SPACE OF HOLLY WHERE SPIKES ....YEARS 255 2
SPIKE-STUDDED (1)
  WORSE -- SAW DANGLING FROM THAT SPIKE-STUDDED BELT ......SNOWMAN O. 59 37
SPIKY (1)
  WITH ITS YELLOW PURSES, ITS SPIKY ARMORY. ....THE BEE MEETING 211 32
SPILL (2)
  HORIZONS BEYOND VISION, SPILL VISION ....ABOVE THE OXBOW 88 24
  THE BLUE SPARKS SPILL, ...LESBOS 228 50
SPILT (5)
  CRYING: BLOOD, LET BLOOD BE SPILT; ....PURSUIT 22 15
  IS TRICKED TO FALTER IN SPILT BLOOD. ....FIRESONG 30 7
  OR THOSE GLITTERY FICTIONS OF SPILT WATER*SLEEP IN THE MOJAVE DESERT 144 12
  I WATCH THEIR SPILT TEARS CLOUD AND DULL TO PEARLS. ....CANDLES 149 31
  WHERE SPILT LIVES CONGEAL AND STIFFEN TO HISTORY.*A BIRTHDAY PRESENT 208 51
SPIN (2)
  "I DON'T ASK YOU TO SPIN SOME RIDICULOUS FABLE ....DIALOGUE B. 39 22
  SPIDERLIKE, I SPIN MIRRORS, ...CHILDLESS WOMAN 259 11
SPINACH (2)
  OF THE SPINACH PATCH. BUNCH AFTER BUNCH OF GREEN ...SPINCAH-PICKER. 89 7
  SUN AND SKY MIRRORED THE GREEN OF THE SPINACH. .....SPINACH-PICKER. 89 12
SPINACH-HEADS (1)
  A WHOLE SEA OF SPINACH-HEADS LEANED TO MY HAND. ....SPINACH-PICKER. 90 22
SPINACH-PICKER (1)
  MEMOIRS OF A SPINACH-PICKER ....MEMOIRS OF A SPINACH-PICKER 89 T
SPINACH-TIPS (1)
  UPSTANDING SPINACH-TIPS WEDGED IN A CIRCLE -- ......SPINACH-PICKER. 89 8
SPINDLE'S (1)
  POINTING TOWARD THE SPINDLE'S CRYPTIC WHIR, ...THE PRINCESS. 335 60
SPINDLE-SHANKED (1)
  GERD SITS SPINDLE-SHANKED IN HER DARK TENT, ...CRYSTAL GAZER 54 1
SPINDLING (2)
  ABOVE WHORLED, SPINDLING GORSE, ...TWO VIEWS OF WITHENS 71 1
  WHILE THE HEATH GRASS GLITTERS AND THE SPINDLING RIVULETS ...
                    ... PARLIAMENT HILL FIELDS 153 34
SPINDRIFT (2)
  WERE SQUEALING WHERE COMBERS BROKE AND THE SPINDRIFT ......SUICIDE. 115 10
  CHRISTENED IN A SPINDRIFT OF SNOWDROP STARS, ...APRIL AUBADE 312 9
SPINE (2)
  GREEN, WHOLLY GREEN, THEY STAND THEIR KNOBBY SPINE ABOVE THE OXBOW 88 10
  THE SPIDERY JAWS, THE SPINE BONES BARED FOR A MOMENT ....ZOO K. 154 9
SPINES (1)
  THE BLOOD-BERRIED HAWTHORN HIDES ITS SPINES WITH WHITE. *WATERCOLOR. 112 21
SPINNAKER (1)
  BLOATS LIKE A SPINNAKER. HAT-BRIMS ....WHITSUN 154 10
SPINNING (2)
  SPINNING TO STILL IN HIS ONE WHITENESS. ....WHITENESS I REMEMBER 103 33
  SPINNING A SINGLE STUBBORN THREAD OF WOOL ....THE PRINCESS. 333 16
SPINS (2)
  SPINS ITSELF FROM UNDER MY FEET: ....SOLILOQUY OF THE SOLIPSIST 37 4
  SLOWLY SHE SPINS THE BALL: ....CRYSTAL GAZER 55 12

                                              TITLE   PAGE LINE
SPINSTER (3)
    SPINSTER ....SPINSTER   49   T
    NOW, RUN TO FAT, SHE'S A SPINSTER WHOSE DOOR SHUTS ...ELLA MASON A.   54 17
    OF COUSIN JANE, OUR SPINSTER WITH ....FAMILY REUNION 300 17
SPINSTERS (1)
    OF UGLY SPINSTERS AND BARREN SIRS ....VIRGIN IN A TREE   82 33
SPIRAL (6)
    STEPS AT MY BACK SPIRAL INTO A WELL. ................APPREHENSIONS   195   8
    (PROUD YOU HALT UPON THE SPIRAL STAIR.) *TO EVA DESCENDING THE STAIR 303   3
    (PROUD YOU HALT UPON THE SPIRAL STAIR.) *TO EVA DESCENDING THE STAIR 303   9
    (PROUD YOU HALT UPON THE SPIRAL STAIR.) *TO EVA DESCENDING THE STAIR 303 15
    (PROUD YOU HALT UPON THE SPIRAL STAIR.) *TO EVA DESCENDING THE STAIR 303 19
    FROM FABRICATION SPRINGS THE SPIRAL STAIR ....THE PRINCESS.   333   1
SPIRALS (2)
    SUCH PURE LEAPS AND SPIRALS --- ....THE NIGHT DANCES 249   5
    IN WILY SPIRALS ....AQUATIC NOCTURNE 306 20
SPIRES (1)
    HORSES, PLANETS AND SPIRES REVOLVE. ....THE EYE-MOTE 109 18
SPIRING (1)
    EACH THORN; SPIRING FROM WET EARTH, A BLUE HAZE ....DIALOGUE B.   38   5
SPIRIT (8)
    TO START THE SPIRIT OUT OF THE MUD ....THE COMPANIONABLE ILLS 105   6
    I AM INTIMATE WITH A HAIRY SPIRIT. POEM.6.W. 135 11
    HERE ON THE LAST FRONTIER OF THE BIG, BRASH SPIRIT ....TWO CAMP.   145 12
    I DO NOT TRUST THE SPIRIT. IT ESCAPES LIKE STEAM ....LAST WORDS 172 14
    FOR THE SPIRIT TO CONCEIVE A FACE, A MOUTH? ....THREE WOMEN 177 26
    SO NEAT SHE IS TRANSPARENT, LIKE A SPIRIT. ....THREE WOMEN 184 281
    THE SPIRIT OF BLACKNESS IS IN US, IT IS IN THE FISHES. ...
                                          ... CROSSING THE WATER 190   8
    AS IF I THOUGHT IT HAD A SPIRIT. ....PHEASANT 191   8
SPIRITLESS (1)
    BLINDED TO ALL BUT THE GRAY, SPIRITLESS ROOM ....WIDOW 165 39
SPIRITOUS (1)
    FUMY, SPIRITOUS MISTS INHABIT THIS PLACE   THE MOON AND THE YEW TREE 172   5
SPIRITS (4)
    ON SPIRITS TENDERER THAN THEIRS, ...THE BEGGARS   48 14
    EMULOUS SPIRITS MAKE DISCORD, ...SCULPTOR   92 20
    LIMPID AS SPIRITS. MANY STONES LAY ....LOVE LETTER 147 22
    AND HEAVENS TILL THE SPIRITS SQUEAK ....LOVE IS A PARALLAX 330 69
SPIRIT'S (1)
    BEDFELLOWS OF THE SPIRIT'S DEBAUCH, FOND MASTERS. ...COMPANIONABLE. 105   8
SPIRITUAL (1)
    NO SPIRITUAL CAESARS ARE THESE DEAD: ....THE DEAD 320   5
SPIT (5)
    THE SCRAGGY ROCK SPIT SHIELDING THE TOWN'S BLUE BAY ......DEPARTURE   51 13
    THE DRY VOLCANOES CRACKED AND SPIT, ...I WANT, I WANT 106   4
    SO, OVER THIS BATTERED, OBSTINATE SPIT ....POINT SHIRLEY 110 30
    OVER A GREAT STONE SPIT ....MAN IN BLACK 119 13
    WHITE SPIT ....THALIDOMIDE 252 21
SPITE (7)
    ODDLY WOODEN IN SPITE OF SCALES ....THE DISQUIETING MUSES   75 36
    AS SMACK OF SPITE AND THE OVERSCRUPULOUS .....A LESSON IN VENGEANCE   80   7
    US TO THE OBLIQUE ROAD, IN SPITE OF A FITFUL ....ABOVE THE OXBOW   88 21
    IN SPITE OF OURSELVES. ....MUSHROOMS 139 29
    I FELT HER CRITICIZING ME IN SPITE OF HERSELF, ...IN PLASTER 159 30
    THE COURAGE OF THE SHUT MOUTH, IN SPITE OF ARTILLERY! .....COURAGE. 209   1
    LEST, OUT OF SPITE, THE WHOLE ....AERIALIST 332 46
SPITEFUL (1)
    SPITEFUL AS A WOMAN, BUT NOT SO NERVOUS, ...THE RIVAL 166   9
SPITEFULLY (2)
    SPITEFULLY SKULKS OUR WARDEN, ...FIRESONG   30   4
    NIGHTS, I WROTE IN MY DIARY SPITEFULLY, MY FINGERS RED ....BABY. 174 14
SPITE-SET (1)
    STOLIDLY PROPPING THICK VOLUMES OF PROSE: SPITE-SET ....LADY AND T.   69   4
SPITTED (1)
    ECLIPSING THE SPITTED OX I SEE ....ON THE DECLINE OF ORACLES   78 17
SPITTLE (1)
    LET DROP ITS SPITTLE OF SLUGGISH GREEN ..............RHODODENDRON.   103   6
SPLAYED (2)
    LAIN SPLAYED TOO LONG IN THE TORTUOUS BOUGHS: OVERRIPE .....VIRGIN.   82 37
    BUT FATLY SCUTTLED INTO THE SPLAYED FERN ............INCOMMUNICADO 100   2
SPLENDID (1)
    THESE ORCHIDS ARE SPLENDID. THEY SPOT AND COIL LIKE SNAKES.*SURGEON. 170 16
SPLINTER (1)
    WHEN THE SPLINTER FLEW IN AND STUCK MY EYE, ...THE EYE-MOTE 109   9
SPLINTERED (2)
    WHILE ROUGH AS SPLINTERED WOOD ....FAMILY REUNION 300 20
    AND MOCK THE JANGLING RAIN OF SPLINTERED STARS. ..EPITAPH IN THREE. 337 25
SPLIT (5)
    AND BLOODIED AS A COW'S SPLIT FRAME ....STREET SONG   36   9
    HE SPLIT IT INTO THREE HUNDRED AND SIXTY TRICKLES ....LESSON.   80 19
    BEHIND HIM THE HOTDOGS SPLIT AND DRIZZLED .....SUICIDE OFF EGG ROCK 115   1
    WHEN I SPLIT A ROCK ONE TIME ....MEDALLION 124 12
    THEIR YELLOW CORSETS WERE READY TO SPLIT. ....LEAVING EARLY 146 25

	TITLE	PAGE	LINE

SPLITS (5)
HE WITH ROCK SPLITS OPEN ....ODE FOR TED   29   10
REPENT, DEPART, BEFORE GOD'S TRUMP-CRACK SPLITS THE SKY." ...
    ... DIALOGUE BETWEEN GHOST AND PRIEST   39   46
THAT SPLITS FROM ITS RIPPED BAG AND DOES NOT STOP ....BURNING. 205   51
SPLITS AND PASSES, SISTER TO ....ARIEL 239   7
SPLITS THROUGH THE RAT'S-TAIL ....LETTER IN NOVEMBER 253   3
SPLITTING (1)
SPLITTING LIKE QUARTZ INTO A MILLION BITS. ....LESBOS 228   51
SPLURGE (1)
EACH DAY CONCLUDES IN A HUGE SPLURGE OF VERMILIONS ....TWO CAMP. 145   15
SPOILS (1)
NO ANIMAL SPOILS ON HER GREEN DOORSTEP. ....THE BURNT-OUT SPA 138   30
SPOKE (4)
SHE SPOKE MOST CHIDING IN HIS EAR ....THE QUEEN'S COMPLAINT   28   11
WHAT THE SEASHELL SPOKE TO HIS INNER EAR   ON THE DECLINE OF ORACLES   78   7
SIGNS SAY NOTHING. THE FALCON WHO SPOKE CLEAR ........INCOMMUNICADO 100   13
IF A BUSH BORROWED TONGUES AND SPOKE TO YOU. YOU'D KNEEL*DIALOGUE O. 280 163
SPOKES (2)
AND SITS IN THE CENTER OF HER LOVELESS SPOKES. ....WIDOW 164   12
UNDER THE SPOKES OF THE CLEMATIS. ....MYSTIC 269   23
SPONGE (1)
ABSORBENT AS A SPONGE; ....FAMILY REUNION 301   28
SPONGES (1)
THE FOOD TUBES EMBRACE ME. SPONGES KISS MY LICHENS AWAY.   POEM.7.S. 136   19
SPOOL (2)
ALREADY VEILING THE GRAY SPOOL OF STONE ....SPIDER   48   18
WRAPPED UP IN YOURSELF LIKE A SPOOL, ...YOU'RE 141   5
SPORES (1)
WHILE I SLEEP, THE BLACK SPORES NOD ....THE RIVAL/DR 291   2
SPORTY (1)
WHEN THE SPORTY WIFE AND HER DOCTOR HUSBAND WENT ON ONE OF
THEIR CRUISES ....THE BABYSITTERS 174   16
SPOT (5)
ONE-THIRD ANT-SIZE, A LEGGY SPOT, ...SPIDER   48   12
SMALL DROPS SPOT THEIR COATS, THEIR GLOVES: ....ON DECK 143   16
THESE ORCHIDS ARE SPLENDID. THEY SPOT AND COIL LIKE SNAKES.*SURGEON. 170   16
HERE'S A SPOT I THOUGHT YOU'D LOVE -- ....THE TOUR 238   27
COLOR FLOODS TO THE SPOT, DULL PURPLE. ....CONTUSION 271   1
SPOTLESS (1)
TO SEE WITH THE SPOTLESS SOUL, ...ON THE PLETHORA OF DRYADS   67   14
SPOTS (2)
SPOTS, AND A SPREAD OF HOT PETALS. ....THE NIGHT DANCES 250   14
FROM HERE YOU CAN'T SEE SPOTS UPON THE SUN; ....ADMONITIONS 319   8
SPOTTED (3)
WHILE ON SPOTTED BRANCH ....PROSPECT   28   5
BUT LET SPOTTED LEAVES FALL AS THEY FALL, ...BLACK ROOK I.   57   9
SPOTTED COWS REVOLVE THEIR JAWS AND CROP ....WATERCOLOR. 112   16
SPOTTY (1)
BEYOND THE BREAKWATER, SPOTTY WITH BARNACLES? ....BERCK-PLAGE 197   41
SPRANG (4)
SWEET GRASS SPRANG FOR THEIR GRAZING. ......SONG FOR A SUMMER'S DAY   31   5
DENYING YOU SPRANG OUT OF MY HEAD, ...SOLILOQUY OF THE SOLIPSIST   38   31
AS SPRANG FROM JOSEPH'S ROD, AND TESTIFIES ....MAYFLOWER   60   7
IT SPRANG FROM HER PILLOW ....POLLY'S TREE 129   34
SPRAT (1)
LIKE A SPRAT IN A PICKLE JUG. ....YOU'RE 141   14
SPRAWLS (1)
SPRAWLS, HUNCHED IN BLACK, AMONG BAGGAGE, WINCING   CHANNEL CROSSING   26   11
SPRAY (3)
BY BLACKTHORN THICKET, FLOWER SPRAY ....BUCOLICS   23   7
FLAYED BY SPRAY, WE TAKE THE CHALLENGE UP, ...CHANNEL CROSSING   26   5
REMEMBERING THE WHITE, TRIUMPHANT SPRAY ....MAYFLOWER   60   12
SPREAD (6)
OF YOUR SPREAD HAIR, IN WHICH WRINKLING SKEINS ....FULL FATHOM FIVE   92   8
MOUNTAINING THEM ON SPREAD NEWSPAPER. .................RHODODENDRON. 104   23
NOT TO BE SPREAD AGAIN. ....BERCK-PLAGE 200 103
I SPREAD TO THE BEAKS OF BIRDS. ....THE JAILER 226   15
SPOTS, AND A SPREAD OF HOT PETALS. ....THE NIGHT DANCES 250   14
SPREAD GAY CONTAGION WITH EACH CLEVER BREATH. ....DIRGE FOR A JOKER 303   12
SPREADING (3)
ARE SPREADING THEIR VACUOUS SHEETS. ....LITTLE FUGUE 188   42
UNREELING IN IT, SPREADING LIKE OIL. ....THE RABBIT CATCHER 193   5
SPREADING ITSELF, LIKE BUTTER. .......................EAVESDROPPER 261   51
SPREADS (1)
IT SPREADS ITSELF OUT, A MILE-LONG BODY OF MEISSEN, ...WINTERING 218   35
SPRIGGED (1)
TO SPRIGGED HEDGE OF BRAMBLE, ...ODE FOR TED   29   5
SPRING (9)
REEL GIDDY IN BEDLAM SPRING: ....SPINSTER   50   23
THERE, SPRING LAMBS JAM THE SHEEPFOLD. IN AIR ....WATERCOLOR. 111   1
AND YET THE ICHOR OF THE SPRING ....THE BURNT-OUT SPA 138   19
SO MAGICAL! A HOT SPRING ....THE SURGEON AT 2 A.M. 171   24
TODAY THE COLLEGES ARE DRUNK WITH SPRING. ....THREE WOMEN 185 302
THERE IS A KIND OF SMOKE IN THE SPRING AIR, ...THREE WOMEN 186 354

	TITLE	PAGE	LINE
SPRING (CONT.)			
OPENING, IN SPRING, LIKE AN INDUSTRIOUS VIRGIN ....STINGS	215	35
THE BEES ARE FLYING. THEY TASTE THE SPRING. ....WINTERING	219	50
PROLOGUE TO SPRING ....PROLOGUE TO SPRING	322	T
SPRINGING (2)			
AND, SPRINGING ALL ABOUT, ...CRYSTAL GAZER	55	15
STRAIGHTFORWARDLY ACROSS THE SPRINGING GREEN. ......ABOVE THE OXBOW	89	52
SPRINGS (2)			
BLOOD SPRINGS ETERNAL IF THE HEART BE BURNING. ..TO EVA DESCENDING.	303	8
FROM FABRICATION SPRINGS THE SPIRAL STAIR ....THE PRINCESS.	333	1
SPRINT (1)			
PAN, ARE YOU STILL THERE? SEE, HIS SPRINT ....DIALOGUE O.	278	70
SPROUT (3)			
CAN SPROUT FROM THE NAVEL OF THIS PRESENT WASTE. .....TALE OF A TUB	25	40
SAW HOOF HARDEN FROM FOOT, SAW SPROUT ....FAUN	35	13
AND JONQUILS SPROUT LIKE SOLOMON'S METAPHORS, ...APRIL AUBADE	312	11
SPROUTING (1)			
SPROUTING FRUIT, FLOWERS, CHILDREN MOST FAIR IN LEGION ...WREATH F.	45	22
SPRUNG (4)			
THE HUNT IS ON, AND SPRUNG THE TRAP. ....PURSUIT	22	8
BRIGHT GRAIN SPRUNG SO RARELY ....ODE FOR TED	29	16
SPRUNG TO BEING ON OUR WEDDING NIGHT ...DIALOGUE OVER A OUIJA BOARD	280	140
SPRUNG UP LIKE PLAGUE OF TOADSTOOLS OVERNIGHT: ....TERMINAL	328	4
SPRY (4)			
UP BY A SPRY BLACK DEUS ....SPIDER	49	34
SAGE HEN AND SPRY RABBIT, ...TWO VIEWS OF WITHENS	72	8
SPRY, WRY, AND GRAY AS THESE MARCH STICKS, ...AMONG THE NARCISSI	190	1
THE SPRY HOOKS THAT BEND AND CRINGE, AND THE SMILES, THE SMILES. ...		
... BURNING THE LETTERS	204	21
SPUMIEST (1)			
TO THAT SPUMIEST DOVE. ....POINT SHIRLEY	111	47
SPUMILY (1)			
NEEDLING SPUMILY DOWN FROM THE WIRES: ....ALICANTE LULLABY	43	10
SPUMY (1)			
BEACHED UNDER THE SPUMY BLOOMS, WE LIE ....WHITSUN	154	23
SPUN (2)			
YOU SPUN THE COSMIC WEB: YOU SQUINT FROM CENTER FIELD. ......SPIDER	48	7
SPUN INTO A RIVER, THE RIVER CROSSED. ....THE SWARM	216	30
SPUNGLASS (1)			
OF INTRICATE SPUNGLASS ROUTINE, ...MORNING IN THE HOSPITAL SOLARIUM	332	20
SPUNKY (1)			
THEY TALK OF BRIDE-LACE, OF LOVERS SPUNKY AS GAMECOCKS. ......NET-.	121	14
SPUR (2)			
AS IF TO OUTFLAME A PHOENIX, THE MOMENT'S SPUR ......EPITAPH FOR F.	46	24
WITH SPUR AND KNOUT ....THE SNOWMAN ON THE MOOR	59	28
SPURNS (1)			
SPURNS SUCH FICTION ......ON THE DIFFICULTY OF CONJURING UP A DRYAD	66	29
SPURS (1)			
DUG IN FIRST AS GOD'S SPURS ....THE COMPANIONABLE ILLS	105	5
SPY (1)			
ONCE WE CHILDREN SNEAKED OVER TO SPY MISS MASON ......ELLA MASON A.	54	19
SPYING (1)			
SPYING A PATE TO SPARE ....THE LADY AND THE EARTHENWARE HEAD	69	10
SQUAB (2)			
GO GET THE GOODLY SQUAB ....GO GET THE GOODLY SQUAB	313	T
GO GET THE GOODLY SQUAB IN GOLD-LOBED CORN GO GET THE GOODLY SQUAB	313	1
SQUADRONS (1)			
OF SQUADRONS UNDERGROUND ABDUCTING HIM *THE PRINCESS AND THE GOBLINS	333	22
SQUALL (3)			
WHEREBY SHE TREKS IN BLOOD THROUGH SUN AND SQUALL ....QUEEN'S C.	29	22
THEN, TO SQUALL ABOVE THE LEVEL ....OWL	102	10
SQUALL WAVES ONCE DANCED ....POINT SHIRLEY	110	13
SQUALOR (1)			
IN GARDENS OF SQUALOR ....MOONSONG AT MORNING	317	25
SQUANDER (4)			
TO QUENCH HIS THIRST I SQUANDER BLOOD; ....PURSUIT	23	38
TO SQUANDER OWL-HOURS ON BRACKEN BEDDING, ...VANITY FAIR	33	19
MY JILTING LADY SQUANDER COIN, GOLD LEAF STOCK DITCHES, CONJURING.	66	35
WITH BLUE-RED JUICES. THESE THEY SQUANDER ON MY FINGERS. BLACKBER.	168	7
SQUANDERED (1)			
WE'VE SQUANDERED ALL THE BANKER WILL ALLOW ....THE DISPOSSESSED	319	16
SQUANDERING (1)			
SQUANDERING RED ....STREET SONG	36	19
SQUANDERS (1)			
SQUANDERS A SUMMER AND THE BRAWN OF HIS HEROES*A LESSON IN VENGEANCE	80	17
SQUARE (8)			
ON A SQUARE NO BIGGER THAN A CARPET ....ON DECK	142	12
YOUR MOUTH OPENS CLEAN AS A CAT'S. THE WINDOW SQUARE ..MORNING SONG	157	15
EVERYBODY IS NODDING A SQUARE BLACK HEAD, THEY ARE KNIGHTS IN		
VISORS, ...THE BEE MEETING	211	13
SQUARE AS A CHAIR AND ALMOST TOO HEAVY TO LIFT. ....THE ARRIVAL.	212	2
OR A SQUARE BABY ....THE ARRIVAL OF THE BEE BOX	212	4
AND HERE THE SQUARE OF WHITE LINEN ....STINGS	215	43
THEY STARE FROM A SQUARE, STIFF FRILL. ....A SECRET	219	14
IN SQUARE HERMETIC BOTTLES, WHILE THE SUN ....THE TRIAL OF MAN	312	3

	TITLE	PAGE	LINE

SQUAT (3)
LANTERN-JAWED REASON, SQUAT COMMON SENSE,   THE DEATH OF MYTH-MAKING 104   3
NIGHTS, I SQUAT IN THE CORNUCOPIA ....THE COLOSSUS 130 24
SQUAT, BOWLING BLACK BALLS AT HER. ....AERIALIST 331 30
SQUATS (1)
A LONE BEACHCOMBER SQUATS AMONG THE WRACK ....TWO LOVERS. 327 13
SQUATTED (1)
SQUATTED DOWN BETWEEN THE ROWS ....BITTER STRAWBERRIES 299   3
SQUATTING (2)
GRIM AS GARGOYLES FROM YEARS SPENT SQUATTING AT SEA'S BORDER ...
        ... DREAM WITH CLAM-DIGGERS   44 25
ALOOF, SQUATTING MUMMY-WISE, GERD SCANS ....CRYSTAL GAZER   55 28
SQUEAK (4)
SO BLACK NO SKY COULD SQUEAK THROUGH. ....DADDY 223 47
HIS BALLOON SQUEAK LIKE A CAT. ....BALLOONS 272 22
THERE, THAT'S THE PINK, PLEASED SQUEAK ....FAMILY REUNION 300 16
AND HEAVENS TILL THE SPIRITS SQUEAK ....LOVE IS A PARALLAX 330 69
SQUEAKING (1)
I AM UP TO MY ELBOWS IN IT, RED AND SQUEAKING.*THE SURGEON AT 2 A.M. 171 22
SQUEAL (1)
A SQUEAL OF BRAKES. ....STOPPED DEAD 230   1
SQUEALING (1)
WERE SQUEALING WHERE COMBERS BROKE AND THE SPINDRIFT ......SUICIDE. 115 10
SQUEEZED (1)
MY EYES ARE SQUEEZED BY THIS BLACKNESS. ....THREE WOMEN 180 146
SQUEEZING (1)
SQUEEZING THE BREATH FROM THE BLOOD BELLS ....MEDUSA 225 28
SQUELCHING (2)
SQUELCHING AND SQUELCHING THROUGH THE BEAUTIFUL RED. *LETTER IN NOV. 253 15
SQUELCHING AND SQUELCHING THROUGH THE BEAUTIFUL RED. *LETTER IN NOV. 253 15
SQUID (2)
THE WHALE, THE SHARK, THE SQUID. ....BATTLE-SCENE   84 20
THE APHRODISIAC SQUID. ....GIGOLO 267 17
SQUINT (4)
GRIP THE RAIL, SQUINT AHEAD, AND WONDER HOW MUCH LONGER CHANNEL C.   26   6
RAT-SHREWD GO HER SQUINT EYES, ...TWO SISTERS OF PERSEPHONE   31 11
COLD SQUINT STEALS SKY'S COLOR; WHILE BRUIT ....VANITY FAIR   32   8
YOU SPUN THE COSMIC WEB: YOU SQUINT FROM CENTER FIELD. ......SPIDER   48   7
SQUIRMS (1)
THE MUD SQUIRMS WITH THROATS, ...THE SWARM 216 13
STAB (1)
STAB A FEW CLOVES IN AN APPLE, ...A SECRET 220 30
STABLE (1)
OF THE STABLE HORSE WHOSE HISTORY'S ....WHITENESS I REMEMBER 102   6
STABLED (1)
IT STABLED IN: LONG-USED, BECAME WELL-LOVED THE COMPANIONABLE ILLS 105   7
STABLES (1)
RINSING THOSE STABLES: A BABY'S TEARS WOULD DO IT. ....PERSEUS   82   7
STABS (1)
THE RITUAL DEATH EACH TIME BOTCHED AMONG DROPPED CAPES,
    ILL-JUDGED STABS, ...THE GORING   47   3
STACKED (1)
POSTAGE STAMPS, STACKED BOOKS' CLAMOR AND YAWP, ...CONJURING.   65   3
STACKS (1)
GAS TANKS, FACTORY STACKS -- THAT LANDSCAPE ...SUICIDE OFF EGG ROCK 115   3
STAGE (4)
I'M A MEANS, A STAGE, A COW IN CALF. ....METAPHORS 116   7
NOBODY DIED OR WITHERED ON THAT STAGE. ......ELECTRA ON AZALEA PATH 116 13
STAGE CURTAINS, A WIDOW'S FRIZZ. ....LESBOS 227   6
WITH STRUTS AND PROPS OF THE HOLY STAGE. ....SONG FOR A REVOLU. 323   8
STAGES (1)
OUR PAINTED STAGES FALL APART BY SCENES ....DOOMSDAY 316   4
STAGGER (2)
TWO PINLEGS STAGGER UNDERNEATH THE MASS. ....THE RAVAGED FACE 115   5
AFTER, THEY STAGGER AND WEAVE, UNDER NO BANNER. ....STINGS/DR 293 11
STAIN (4)
EVERY POCK AND STAIN BULKED MORE BEAUTIFUL*ON THE PLETHORA OF DRYADS   67 16
HER WIDE BED WORE THE STAIN OF DIVINITY. ....ELECTRA ON AZALEA PATH 116   8
THE STAIN ON YOUR ....CUT 235 29
THE STAIN OF THE TROPICS .............................EAVESDROPPER 260   7
STAINED (2)
CROW'S-FEET COPY VEINING ON STAINED LEAF; ....VANITY FAIR   32   7
SCATHED, STAINED AFTER TEDIOUS PILGRIMAGES. DREAM WITH CLAM-DIGGERS   43   4
STAINS (2)
A DEAD SUN STAINS THE NEWSPRINT. IT IS RED. ....THREE WOMEN 181 153
USED UTTERLY, IN THE SUN'S CONFLAGRATIONS, THE STAINS .....MYSTIC 268 13
STAIR (12)
AND THOSE MEN COMING UP THE STAIR. ....ON THE DECLINE OF ORACLES   78 21
I SHALL GO DOWN THE SHABBY STAIR AND MEET,*ON THE DECLINE OF ORACLES   78 27
FUSTY REMEMBRANCES, THE COILED-SPRING STAIR ....WIDOW 164   9
WITH A POLISHED MAHOGANY STAIR TO LET INTO THE WATER*THE BABYSITTERS 174 11
SOME PALTRY SCENE ON THE SOUP-KITCHEN STAIR: ....DIALOGUE O. 279 125
TO EVA DESCENDING THE STAIR ....TO EVA DESCENDING THE STAIR 303   T
(PROUD YOU HALT UPON THE SPIRAL STAIR.) *TO EVA DESCENDING THE STAIR 303   3
(PROUD YOU HALT UPON THE SPIRAL STAIR.) *TO EVA DESCENDING THE STAIR 303   9

```
                                          TITLE            PAGE  LINE
STAIR (CONT.)
    (PROUD YOU HALT UPON THE SPIRAL STAIR.) *TO EVA DESCENDING THE STAIR   303   15
    (PROUD YOU HALT UPON THE SPIRAL STAIR.) *TO EVA DESCENDING THE STAIR   303   19
    FROM FABRICATION SPRINGS THE SPIRAL STAIR ............THE PRINCESS.    333    1
    THE DARKENING STAIR, UNDOES THE PALACE LATCH .........THE PRINCESS.    334   28
STAIRCASE (1)
    TO SEEK THE STAIRCASE BY THE GLARE OF DAY. ...........THE PRINCESS.    334   53
STAIRS (3)
    THE PANTHER'S TREAD IS ON THE STAIRS, ......................PURSUIT     23   49
    COMING UP AND UP THE STAIRS. ...............................PURSUIT     23   50
    ATOP THE FLIGHT OF STAIRS I STAND. ..................FAMILY REUNION    301   26
STAKE (3)
    NOW WITH STAKE AND PITCHFORK THEY ADVANCE, FLINT EYES FIXED
        ON MURDER. .......................... DREAM WITH CLAM-DIGGERS      44   28
    THERE'S A STAKE IN YOUR FAT BLACK HEART ......................DADDY    224   76
    AS THE GLASS FLEW TO ITS FRAGMENTS. LET US STAKE .......DIALOGUE O.    285  328
STAKED (2)
    STAKED IN PRIDE'S COVEN. ................................VANITY FAIR    33   35
    AND I'D SOONER BE STAKED FOR A WITCH, KINDLED, AND CURLED ...
                           ... DIALOGUE OVER A OUIJA BOARD    280  132
STALACTITES (1)
    WAXY STALACTITES ...........................NICK AND THE CANDLESTICK   240    2
STALE (1)
    BEHIND WHICH THE SECRET PASSAGE LIES -- STALE AIR, ..........WIDOW     164    8
STALEMATED (1)
    STALEMATED THEIR ARMIES STOOD, WITH TOTTERING BANNERS: ..SNOWMAN O.    58    1
STALK (6)
    THROUGH PORTICO OF MY ELEGANT HOUSE YOU STALK ........CONVERSATION.    21    1
    FEATHERED DARK IN THOUGHT, I STALK LIKE A ROOK, ..WINTER LANDSCAPE,    21    9
    SUCH STARKNESS; ACCURACY MUST NOT STALK AT LARGE: ....TALE OF A TUB    25   35
    HEAVES FORTH STALK, LEAF, FRUIT-NUBBED EMERALD: ........ODE FOR TED    29   15
    DEW STOOD IN CHILL SWEAT ON EACH STALK, .................DIALOGUE B.   38    4
    STALK WITHOUT WRINKLE, ..........................................CHILD 265    7
STALKED (2)
    WHY, ALL THE WINDOWS BROKE WHEN HE STALKED IN.*THE QUEEN'S COMPLAINT   28    5
    SHE STALKED INTRACTABLE AS A DRIVEN GHOST ..THE SNOWMAN ON THE MOOR    58   15
STALKING (1)
    AN ILL WIND IS STALKING ...........................TEMPER OF TIME     336    1
STALKS (5)
    THERE IS A PANTHER STALKS ME DOWN: ..........................PURSUIT    22    1
    HE STAMPED AND CRACKED STALKS TO THE GROUND ...............BUCOLICS    24   19
    STALKS RED FOX, SHREWD STOAT. ...........................ODE FOR TED   29    6
    CATS PLAY IN THE STALKS. .................................DEPARTURE    51    8
    PARENTAL FACES ON TALL STALKS, ALTERNATELY STERN AND TEARFUL, ...
                           ... INSOMNIAC    163   11
STALKY (1)
    OUT THEIR STALKY LIMBS AGAIN THOUGH PEACE ..........THE THIN PEOPLE    64    9
STALL (1)
    THOUGH THE GREEN SEA GARDENS STALL, ................MAGNOLIA SHOALS   121    6
STALLED (4)
    STALLED, LET FALL THEIR VERTICAL ......................NIGHT SHIFT     76   18
    I STALLED AT SUDDEN NOISY CRASHES*FABLE OF THE RHODODENDRON STEALERS  103   18
    YET DESOLATION, STALLED IN PAINT, SPARES THE LITTLE COUNTRY ...
                           ... TWO VIEWS OF A CADAVER ROOM    114   21
    EACH STALLED IN HIS PARTICULAR MINUTE .....................ON DECK    143   14
STALLING (2)
    STALLING CURBSIDE AT HIS ONCOMING, ...........WHITENESS I REMEMBER    103   26
    STALLING IN MIDAIR, .................................................A LIFE 150 13
STALLION (1)
    TWO VIRTUES RIDE, BY STALLION, BY NAG, ....THE DEATH OF MYTH-MAKING   104    1
STALLIONS (1)
    NOT OF HERALDIC STALLIONS: OFF-WHITE ..........WHITENESS I REMEMBER   102    5
STALLS (2)
    STALLS IN HALLS WHERE THE LAMP WICK ..............OLD LADIES' HOME    120   20
    BESIDE THE POSTCARD STALLS. ..............................FINISTERRE   170   29
STALWART (1)
    "I SEE TWO STALWART APPLE TREES ......................CRYSTAL GAZER    55   13
STAMP (2)
    MUST YOU STAMP EACH PIECE IN PURPLE, ............A BIRTHDAY PRESENT   207   46
    OF WITHERED WORLDS, AND STAMP OUT PUNY HELLS ....LOVE IS A PARALLAX   330   68
STAMPED (2)
    HE STAMPED AND CRACKED STALKS TO THE GROUND ...............BUCOLICS    24   19
    THE SECRET IS STAMPED ON YOU, ............................A SECRET    219    7
STAMPEDE (2)
    A STAMPEDE, A STAMPEDE! ..................................A SECRET    220   40
    A STAMPEDE, A STAMPEDE! ..................................A SECRET    220   40
STAMPING (1)
    THEY ARE DANCING AND STAMPING ON YOU. ......................DADDY    224   78
STAMPS (1)
    POSTAGE STAMPS, STACKED BOOKS' CLAMOR AND YAWP, .........CONJURING.    65    3
STANCE (1)
    KNOCKING OUR BROTHERS DOWN, WE STRIKE A STANCE ....CHANNEL CROSSING    27   27
STAND (21)
    WHILE YOU STAND HEROIC IN COAT AND TIE, I SIT ........CONVERSATION.    21   10
    STAND STOCK STILL TO LAUD THESE MATED ONES .....WREATH FOR A BRIDAL    44    5
```

	TITLE	PAGE	LINE

STAND (CONT.)
MONDAY AND STAND IN THE MOON. ....THE EVERLASTING MONDAY 62 E/2
IF THE THIN PEOPLE SIMPLY STAND IN THE FOREST, ...THE THIN PEOPLE 65 45
THEY STAND THEIR VIGIL IN GOWNS OF STONE, ...THE DISQUIETING MUSES 76 50
HE PIPES A PLACE TO STAND ON, BUT NO ROCKS, ...SNAKECHARMER 79 8
GREEN, WHOLLY GREEN, THEY STAND THEIR KNOBBY SPINE ABOVE THE OXBOW 88 10
SHADOWS OUR SAFETY. WE STAND ROUND BLANKLY AS WALLS. ..MORNING SONG 157 6
THEY STAND LIKE SHADOWS ABOUT THE GREEN LANDSCAPE -- ....WIDOW 164 28
THEY STAND ABOUT IN GRANDMOTHERLY DISGUISE, ...WUTHERING HEIGHTS 167 25
VOICES STAND BACK AND FLATTEN. THEIR VISIBLE HIEROGLYPHS*THREE WOMEN 179 96
THE HORRORS THAT STAND AND IDLE, THE SLIGHTED GODMOTHERS*THREE WOMEN 180 137
AND SO I STAND, A LITTLE SIGHTLESS. SO I WALK ....THREE WOMEN 184 253
THEY BOW AND STAND: THEY SUFFER SUCH ATTACKS! ...AMONG THE NARCISSI 190 9
MY RED FILAMENTS BURN AND STAND, A HAND OF WIRES. ....ELM 192 18
IF I STAND VERY STILL, THEY WILL THINK I AM COW-PARSLEY, ...BEE. 212 39
I STAND IN A COLUMN ....STINGS 214 20
YOU STAND AT THE BLACKBOARD, DADDY, ...DADDY 223 51
YOU SAY YOU CAN'T STAND HER, ...LESBOS 228 15
AS IS THE USE WITH VAMPIRES, AND RESIGN OUR STAND ......DIALOGUE O. 285 330
ATOP THE FLIGHT OF STAIRS I STAND. ....FAMILY REUNION 301 26
STANDS (8)
WHILE SHE STANDS BURNING, VENOM-GIRT, ...BUCOLICS 24 23
NOT WEALTH NOR WISDOM STANDS ....RECANTATION 42 14
THE SCENE STANDS STUBBORN: SKINFLINT TREES ......NOVEMBER GRAVEYARD 56 1
THE MOON'S MAN STANDS IN HIS SHELL, ...THE EVERLASTING MONDAY 62 1
THE PHEASANT STANDS ON THE HILL; ....THREE WOMEN 176 11
IT STANDS AT MY WINDOW, BIG AS THE SKY. ....A BIRTHDAY PRESENT 207 49
THE MAN WITH GRAY HANDS STANDS UNDER THE HONEYCOMB ....THE SWARM 216 33
THE BRONZE BOY STANDS KNEEDEEP IN CENTURIES, ...GOLD MOUTHS CRY 302 10
STAR (16)
OF GUTTED STAR, ...STREET SONG 36 28
OUTLAST THEIR EVILEST STAR, WRYLY ....THE BEGGARS 48 19
NEITHER BRAZEN SWAN NOR BURNING STAR, ...ON THE DECLINE OF ORACLES 78 18
ON BOSTON COMMON A RED STAR ....A WINTER'S TALE 86 1
BY THE GATE WITH STAR AND MOON ....MEDALLION 124 1
BLUE LARKSPUR STAR. ....POLLY'S TREE 129 42
THE STAR BUGS WON'T SAVE ME THIS MONTH. POEM.4.BEAST. 134 22
THEY MISTAKE THEIR STAR, THESE PAPERY GODFOLK. ....MAGI 148 15
THE STAR, THE WISE GRAY MEN. ....HEAVY WOMEN 158 21
AND WHERE I LIE NOW, BACK TO MY OWN DARK STAR, ...STARS OVER. 166 34
SHINY AND STRANGE, AS IF HE HAD HURTLED FROM A STAR? ...THREE WOMEN 181 163
THE DEW MAKES A STAR, ...DEATH & CO. 255 28
AND THE STAR, ...BRASILIA 258 14
CEILING WITHOUT A STAR. ....CHILD 265 12
OF AN ACETIC STAR. ....JILTED 304 4
AGILE AS A STAR ....TRIO OF LOVE SONGS 314 19
STARCH (1)
WE ARE FULL OF STARCH, MY SMALL WHITE FELLOWS. WE GROW. ..POEM.6.W. 135 17
STARCHED (2)
THE STARCHED, INACCESSIBLE BREAST. ....PARALYTIC 266 16
THE STARCHED WHITE COAT, THE CAT'S PAW WALK, ...MORNING IN THE HOS. 332 12
STAR-DISTANCE (1)
I SEE THEM ALREADY -- THE PALE, STAR-DISTANCE FACES. ....LAST WORDS 172 6
STARE (13)
WITH STARE, WITH CURSE ....MONOLOGUE AT 3 A.M. 40 10
SECURE IN MUSEUM DIAMOND FOR THE STARE EPITAPH FOR FIRE AND FLOWER 45 18
AT THE ESSENTIAL LANDSCAPE STARE, STARE ....NOVEMBER GRAVEYARD 56 13
AT THE ESSENTIAL LANDSCAPE STARE, STARE ....NOVEMBER GRAVEYARD 56 13
HE KEPT THE SOW -- IMPOUNDED FROM PUBLIC STARE, ...SOW 60 5
ON MY JEALOUS STARE, ...ON THE DIFFICULTY OF CONJURING UP A DRYAD 66 15
THEY LOITER AND STARE AS IF THE HOUSE ....AFTERMATH 113 2
AND THEY STUPIDLY STARE, AND DO NOT SPEAK OF HER. ....STILLBORN 142 15
ROUND AS THE MOON, TO STARE UP. ....LAST WORDS 172 3
THEY STARE FROM A SQUARE, STIFF FRILL. ....A SECRET 219 14
IMPALED UPON A STERN ANGELIC STARE ....THE TRIAL OF MAN 312 9
WITHSTAND THAT STARE ....MOONSONG AT MORNING 317 22
AND STAUNCH STONE EYES THAT STARE ....TOUCH-AND-GO 335 3
STARED (3)
THE QUEEN IN THE MULBERRY ARBOR STARED ....THE BULL OF BENDYLAW 108 4
LITTERED WITH CHINESE HANDS. NOW I'M STARED AT ....LEAVING EARLY 146 30
SO I STARED IN THAT FURNACE ....ON LOOKING INTO THE EYES. 325 21
STARES (1)
STARES THROUGH US; HIS HOOVES CHEW THE BREEZE. ....WHITSUN 154 8
STAR-EYES (1)
OF DOUBLE STAR-EYES LIT ....FAUN 35 9
STARFISH (1)
THE BODY OF A STARFISH CAN GROW BACK ITS ARMS ....THREE WOMEN 184 257
STARING (1)
STARING FROM HER HOOD OF BONE. ....EDGE 273 18
STARK (6)
MEEK AND PROUD BOTH FALL: STARK VIOLENCE ....CHANNEL CROSSING 27 30
WHOSE STARK ACT ALL COMING DOUBLE LUCK JOINS. ..WREATH FOR A BRIDAL 44 6
FREE OF THE FICTIVE VEIN. WHEN ONE STARK SKELETON*NOVEMBER GRAVEYARD 56 10
OF STARK WIND-HARROWED HILLS AND WELTERING MIST; ....SNOWMAN O. 58 13
I NOTICE YOU ARE STARK NAKED. ....THE APPLICANT 221 19

474

STARK (CONT.)
   TO SIT UP STARK AWAKE ....AERIALIST 332 41
STARKER (1)
   HERALDRY OF A STARKER AGE, ...ON THE DECLINE OF ORACLES   78 19
STARKNESS (1)
   SUCH STARKNESS; ACCURACY MUST NOT STALK AT LARGE: ....TALE OF A TUB   25 35
STARLESS (2)
   THAN THE DARK OF THE SKY BECAUSE IT IS QUITE STARLESS. ......STARS. 165   3
   STARLESS AND FATHERLESS, A DARK WATER. ....SHEEP IN FOG 262 15
STARLING (1)
   THROUGH CROSSHATCH OF SPARROW AND STARLING. ....PHEASANT 191 14
STARLIT (1)
   CHURCHYARD EARS UNTIL THE STARLIT STIFF ....LOVE IS A PARALLAX 330 41
STAR-LUCKY (1)
   STAR-LUCKY SLEIGHT-OF-HAND MAN WATCHES ....CONJURING.   66 34
STAR-MAP (1)
   OF THE OLD STAR-MAP ON THE CEILING. ....ON DECK 142   5
STARRED (1)
   WIELDS GUARD OF HONOR OVER THESE!" STARRED WITH WORDS ....WREATH F.   45 16
STARRY (1)
   BEATEN IN STARRY METALS. ....BALLOONS 272 19
STARS (59)
   SHATTERS THE FABULOUS STARS AND MAKES US REAL. ......TALE OF A TUB   25 48
   STARS HUNG WATER-SUNK, SO A RANK ....FAUN   35   8
   UNDER PRICKLING STARS, ...MONOLOGUE AT 3 A.M.   40   9
   STARS SHOOT THEIR PETALS, AND SUNS RUN TO SEED, ...EPITAPH FOR F.   45 12
   OWN THEIR CABBAGE ROOTS, A SPACE OF STARS, ...LANDOWNERS   53 10
   STARS GRINDING, CRUMB BY CRUMB, ...ALL THE DEAD DEARS   70 11
   WITH STARS, WITH ANGELS, HE CONVERSED ....NATURAL HISTORY   71   6
   OTHER THAN NOON, THAN MOON, STARS -- ....THE GREAT CARBUNCLE   72 16
   AMONG THE SOCKETED WHITE STARS, YOUR FACE ....MOONRISE   98 26
   OF OUR HUSBANDS AND SONS MOVE SURE AMONG THE LOW STARS. ......NET-. 121 19
   HOURS OF BLANKNESS. SOME HARD STARS ....THE MANOR GARDEN 125 14
   COUNTING THE RED STARS AND THOSE OF PLUM-COLOR. ....THE COLOSSUS 130 26
   DOMINION. THE STARS ARE NO NEARER. POEM.5.F. 134   6
   FEET TO THE STARS, AND MOON-SKULLED, ...YOU'RE 141   2
   PICKED HIS TRIP-DATE BY THE STARS. ....ON DECK 143 26
   OF APPREHENDING BLUENESS, OR STARS. ....LOVE LETTER 147   8
   WHITENS AND SWALLOWS ITS DULL STARS. AND NOW YOU TRY ..MORNING SONG 157 16
   TONIGHT, IN THE INFINITESIMAL LIGHT OF THE STARS, ...I AM VERTICAL 162 11
   BLUEBLACK, WITH THE MUCH-POKED PERIODS OF STARS ....INSOMNIAC 163   2
   UNDER THE EYES OF THE STARS AND THE MOON'S RICTUS ....INSOMNIAC 163   5
   MEMORIES JOSTLE EACH OTHER FOR FACE-ROOM LIKE OBSOLETE FILM
       STARS. ....INSOMNIAC 163 14
   PROMISING SIMPLY THE HARD STARS, THE SPACE ....WIDOW 164 23
   OF IMMORTAL BLANKNESS BETWEED STARS ....WIDOW 164 24
   STARS OVER THE DORDOGNE ....STARS OVER THE DORDOGNE 165   T
   STARS ARE DROPPING THICK AS STONES INTO THE TWIGGY .....STARS OVER. 165   1
   THE WOODS ARE A WELL. THE STARS DROP SILENTLY. ....STARS OVER. 165   4
   WHERE I AM AT HOME, ONLY THE SPARSEST STARS *STARS OVER THE DORDOGNE 165   9
   SUCH A LUXURY OF STARS WOULD EMBARRASS ME. STARS OVER THE DORDOGNE 166 27
   THERE IS TOO MUCH EASE HERE; THESE STARS TREAT ME TOO WELL. STARS. 166 37
   THE CLIFFS ARE EDGED WITH TREFOILS, STARS AND BELLS .....FINISTERRE 169 10
   BLUE AND MYSTICAL OVER THE FACE OF THE STARS. ....MOON. 173 23
   TURNING THROUGH MY TIME, THE SUNS AND STARS ....THREE WOMEN 176   2
   STARS AND SHOWERS OF GOLD -- CONCEPTIONS, CONCEPTIONS! THREE WOMEN 178 48
   THE CLOCK SHALL NOT FIND ME WANTING, NOR THESE STARS ...THREE WOMEN 182 202
   SHE IS CRYING AT THE DARK, OR AT THE STARS ....THREE WOMEN 182 209
   I SEE THEM SHOWERING LIKE STARS ON TO THE WORLD -- .....THREE WOMEN 183 228
   THE STARS ARE FLASHING LIKE TERRIBLE NUMERALS. ....AN APPEARANCE 189 17
   STARS OPEN AMONG THE LILIES. ....CROSSING THE WATER 190 10
   IT RATTLES THEIR STARS ON THE GREEN HILL WHERE PERCY .....NARCISSI. 190   5
   THEN THERE ARE THE STARS -- INERADICABLE, HARD. ....EVENT 194 10
   ANGELS SWIM IN IT, AND THE STARS, IN INDIFFERENCE ALSO. ...
                                    APPREHENSIONS 195   3
   THEY RISE ON EITHER SIDE OF HIM LIKE STARS. ....AMNESIAC 233 23
   IN HIS CAGE OF ETHER, HIS CAGE OF STARS. ....LYONNESSE 234 25
   OF WHAT GREEN STARS CAN MAKE IT TO OUR GATE. ....BY CANDLELIGHT 236   5
   LET THE STARS ....NICK AND THE CANDLESTICK 241 35
   STARS STUCK ALL OVER, BRIGHT STUPID CONFETTI. ....YEARS 255   8
   PEOPLE OR STARS ....SHEEP IN FOG 262   2
   FROM THE BOTTOM OF THE POOL, FIXED STARS ....WORDS 270 19
   STARS, NOT OUR CHEESEPARING PSYCHES. IT *DIALOGUE OVER A OUIJA BOARD 281 195
   CRYPTIC STARS WIND UP THE ATMOSPHERE, ..TO EVA DESCENDING THE STAIR 303 10
   A MOSAIC OF STARS ....TO A JILTED LOVER 309   5
   STARS PALE BEFORE THE ANGRY DAWN; ....TO A JILTED LOVER 310 21
   THAT DRAINS ETERNALLY THE MILK OF STARS. ....SONNET: TO TIME 311 14
   CHRISTENED IN A SPINDRIFT OF SNOWDROP STARS, ...APRIL AUBADE 312   9
   AND LUCKY STARS ALL EXIT ON THE RUN: ....ADMONITIONS 319 17
   UNTIL THE STARS TICK OUT A LULLABY ....LOVE IS A PARALLAX 329 14
   THEN LET THE BLUE TENT TOPPLE, STARS RAIN DOWN, LOVE IS A PARALLAX 330 73
   WHILE EVIL STARS WHIR ....TEMPER OF TIME 336   2
   AND MOCK THE JANGLING RAIN OF SPLINTERED STARS. ..EPITAPH IN THREE. 337 25
STAR'S (1)
   DAWN SNUFFS OUT STAR'S SPENT WICK, ...EPITAPH FOR FIRE AND FLOWER   46 29

	TITLE	PAGE	LINE

START (12)
WE START AT'S THE SAME POST WE FINISH BY, ...ABOVE THE OXBOW 88 19
WELL-WATER KEPT COOL AT THE START OF THE ROWS. .....SPINACH-PICKER. 89 14
TO START THE SPIRIT OUT OF THE MUD ....THE COMPANIONABLE ILLS 105 6
NIGHTLY THE BATTLE-SHOUTS START UP ....BLUE MOLES 126 19
AND STILL THE LUNGS WON'T FILL AND THE HEART WON'T START. *STILLBORN 142 10
IN YOUR SISTER'S BIRTHDAY PICTURE START TO GLOW. .....PARLIAMENT H. 153 42
NO AIRBUBBLES START FROM MY HEART, I AM LUNGLESS ZOO KEEPER'S WIFE 154 5
NAKED AS PAPER TO START ....THE APPLICANT 221 30
LET THEM START THE QUEER ALCHEMY ......................EAVESDROPPER 260 21
THAT'S HOW YOU ALWAYS TALK BEFORE WE START. ....DIALOGUE O. 277 15
I SEE THEM START TO CRUISE AND DIP FOR FOOD*QUEEN MARY'S ROSE GARDEN 290 13
IN OUR OWN TEARS: TODAY WE START ....LOVE IS A PARALLAX 330 75
STARTED (2)
THE WHITE-SMOCKED BOYS STARTED WORKING. *TWO VIEWS OF A CADAVER ROOM 114 5
I STARTED TO BUD LIKE A MARCH TWIG; ....LOVE LETTER 147 31
STARTING (2)
SUSPENDS BESIDE IT THE FIRST POINT, THE STARTING ....GHOST'S. 91 30
THOUGH THERE IS A SHADOW STARTING FROM MY FEET. I AM A WIFE. *THREE. 187 369
STARTLE (1)
TWICE ON SUNDAY, THE BELLS STARTLE THE SKY --- ....MOON. 173 12
STARTLED (2)
STARTLED AT IT, THOUGH THE SOUND ....NIGHT SHIFT 76 10
THE VISITATIONS, THE MANIFESTATIONS, THE STARTLED FACES.*THREE WOMEN 180 131
STARTLES (1)
DO NOT KILL IT. IT STARTLES ME STILL, ...PHEASANT 191 2
STARTLING (1)
AND A FLOWER-HEAD NOT TALL, BUT MORE STARTLING, ...I AM VERTICAL 162 9
STARTS (5)
HE NAMES A LAPWING, STARTS RABBITS IN A ROUT ....ODE FOR TED 29 3
STARTS WITH A DANGER: ....FULL FATHOM FIVE 92 15
PLUMAGE OF WHAT, PAN? P . . . HE STARTS AGAIN, ...DIALOGUE O. 279 85
TO THE END OF IT. HE STARTS AGAIN: I-N- *DIALOGUE OVER A OUIJA BOARD 282 217
TELL US THE TRUTH. WHERE DO YOU LIVE? HE STARTS ....DIALOGUE O. 283 274
STARVE (1)
FOR NAIVE LARKS WHO STARVE AND GRIEVE. ...METAMORPHOSES OF THE MOON 307 18
STARVED (2)
WITH HER BLANK BROWN EYES STARVED WIDE, ...THE SHRIKE 42 9
HUNG, STARVED, BURNED, HOOKED. ....THE JAILER 227 35
STARVING (3)
BECOME HIS STARVING BODY'S BAIT. ....PURSUIT 22 24
RAVE ON THE LEASH OF THE STARVING MIND ....NOVEMBER GRAVEYARD 56 17
STARVING MY FANTASY DOWN ....ON THE PLETHORA OF DRYADS 67 8
STASH (1)
WHERE DO YOU STASH YOUR LIFE? ....STOPPED DEAD 230 20
STASIS (2)
STASIS IN DARKNESS. ....ARIEL 239 1
AND YOU, GREAT STASIS --- ....YEARS 255 16
STATE (8)
THIS PAIR SEEK SINGLE STATE FROM THAT DUAL BATTLE. ....WREATH F. 44 10
THE DOMED STATE HOUSE. ....A WINTER'S TALE 86 4
TIME, AND TO GRACES GONE WITH THE TIME. A STATE VIEW- ....OXBOW. 88 39
OF STATE SCENERY, SELLS SODA, SHOWS OFF VIEWPOINTS. *ABOVE THE OXBOW 88 41
HOW SHALL I AGE INTO THAT STATE OF MIND? ...ELECTRA ON AZALEA PATH 117 41
NOT EASY TO STATE THE CHANGE YOU MADE. ....LOVE LETTER 147 1
KEEPING ITSELF, IT SEEMS, IN A STATE OF MIRACULOUS REPAIR. ..MEDUSA 225 15
PARSLEYED WITH ELEGIES, SHE LIES IN STATE ....TERMINAL 328 13
STATEMENTS (1)
I LIKE BLACK STATEMENTS. ....LITTLE FUGUE 187 5
STATIC (1)
IT MIGHT BE HEAVEN, THIS STATIC ....IN MIDAS' COUNTRY 99 11
STATICKY (1)
CLEAR OF VOICES AND HISTORY, THE STATICKY ....LESBOS 228 18
STATION (3)
FROM SOUTH STATION TO NORTH. ....A WINTER'S TALE 87 36
OF THEIR DREAM, THE HIVED STATION ....THE SWARM 216 34
WITH HEAVEN'S AUTOCRATIC STATION, ...INSOLENT STORM. 326 30
STATIONS (1)
BUT SURE STATIONS IN BRONZE, WOOD, STONE. ....SCULPTOR 91 8
STATISTIC (1)
I AM BEAUTIFUL AS A STATISTIC. HERE IS MY LIPSTICK. ....THREE WOMEN 183 245
STATUARY (3)
HEAVY AS STATUARY, SHAPES NOT OURS ....THE OTHER TWO 68 15
THE MAMMOTH, LUMBERING STATUARY OF SORROW, ...PERSEUS 82 3
SING PRAISE FOR STATUARY: ....TOUCH-AND-GO 335 1
STATUE (3)
OUR VOICES ECHO, MAGNIFYING YOUR ARRIVAL. NEW STATUE. MORNING SONG 157 4
IT IS A STATUE THE ORDERLIES ARE WHEELING OFF.*THE SURGEON AT 2 A.M. 171 31
GHASTLY STATUE WITH ONE GRAY TOE ....DADDY 222 9
STATUES (6)
OF OTHER MEN, WHERE STATUES CELEBRATE ....CHANNEL CROSSING 27 38
THE LAMP-HEADED NYMPHS ARE NODDING TO SLEEP LIKE STATUES. *POEM.5.F. 135 12
MUSEUM WITHOUT STATUES, GRAND WITH PILLARS, PORTICOES, ROTUNDAS. ...
... BARREN WOMAN 157 2
A SMOKE THAT TAKES THE PARKS, THE LITTLE STATUES ......THREE WOMEN 186 355

476

STATUES (CONT.)
    THEY'LL GO BY, TRUNDLING LIKE MARBLE STATUES WAY OUT ...DIALOGUE O. 276   6
    OSSIFYING LIKE JUNKED STATUES -- ....STINGS/DR 293 14
STAUNCH (5)
    AT HIS HAND'S STAUNCH HEST, BIRDS BUILD. ....ODE FOR TED   29 18
    NO MATTER HOW FIERCELY LIT; STAUNCH CONTRACTS BREAK EPITAPH FOR F.   46 32
    STAUNCH SAPLINGS; TO THIS HOUSE, THRIVING DAYS ....CRYSTAL GAZER   55 16
    SO WHEN STAUNCH ISLAND STOCK CHOSE FORFEITURE ....MAYFLOWER   60   9
    AND STAUNCH STONE EYES THAT STARE ....TOUCH-AND-GO 335   3
STAUNCHING (1)
    NOT OF STAUNCHING SUCH STRICT FLAME, BUT COME, ...FIRESONG   30 20
STAY (8)
    A BULL-SNOUTED SEA THAT WOULDN'T STAY PUT, ...THE BULL OF BENDYLAW 108   8
    RELIC OF TOUGH WEATHER, EVERY WINCH AND STAY ....A WINTER SHIP 113 27
    I CAN STAY AWAKE ALL NIGHT, IF NEED BE -- ....ZOO KEEPER'S WIFE 154   1
    BUT STAY, SITTING FAR OUT, IN THEIR OWN DUST. ....STARS. 165 13
    THEY STAY, THEIR LITTLE PARTICULAR LUSTERS ....LAST WORDS 172 17
    IT'S EASY ENOUGH TO DO IT AND STAY PUT. ....LADY LAZARUS 245 50
    THE TABLE LOOKS AS IF IT WOULD STAY A TABLE ....DIALOGUE O. 286 353
    PRETENDING THAT THE BIRDS ARE HERE TO STAY; ....NEVER TRY TO TRICK. 319   2
STAYED (1)
    NOT TO BE STAYED BY A DAISY CHAIN ....THE BULL OF BENDYLAW 108 17
STAYING (1)
    STAYING PUT ACCORDING TO HABIT. ....LOVE LETTER 147   4
STAYS (1)
    MY TREE STAYS TREE. ......ON THE DIFFICULTY OF CONJURING UP A DRYAD   66 24
STEAD (1)
    SENT THESE LADIES IN HER STEAD ....THE DISQUIETING MUSES   74   5
STEADFAST (3)
    STEADFAST AND EVIL-STARRED, ...THE LADY AND THE EARTHENWARE HEAD   70 31
    AND LEAVES STEADFAST IN SHAPE ....THE SLEEPERS 123 14
    AT SOME STEADFAST MARK ....TOUCH-AND-GO 335   5
STEADILY (2)
    STEADILY ROOTED THOUGH THEY WERE ALL FLOWING ....THE EYE-MOTE 109   7
    STEADILY THE SEA ....POINT SHIRLEY 110 35
STEADY (1)
    RIDING THE TIDE OF THE WIND, STEADY ....A WINTER SHIP 113   7
STEADY-ROOTED (1)
    UNSETTLING THE STEADY-ROOTED GREEN ....WHITENESS I REMEMBER 102 15
STEAL (1)
    AND LIKE A BURGLAR STEAL THEIR FANCY: ....MORNING IN THE HOS. 333 26
STEALER (2)
    STEALER OF CELLS, STEALER OF BEAUTY -- ....THE FEARFUL 256 12
    STEALER OF CELLS, STEALER OF BEAUTY -- ....THE FEARFUL 256 12
STEALERS (1)
    FABLE OF THE RHODODENDRON STEALERS ....................RHODODENDRON. 103   T
STEALS (1)
    COLD SQUINT STEALS SKY'S COLOR; WHILE BRUIT ....VANITY FAIR   32   8
STEAM (3)
    BLIND WITH STEAM, WILL NOT ADMIT THE DARK ....TALE OF A TUB   24 15
    I DO NOT TRUST THE SPIRIT. IT ESCAPES LIKE STEAM ....LAST WORDS 172 14
    WREATHED IN STEAM. ....KINDNESS 270 17
STEAMED (2)
    YOU STEAMED TO ME OVER THE SEA, ...MEDUSA 225 24
    AND RETURNED THEM STEAMED AND PRESSED AND STIFF AS SHIRTS. *THE TOUR 238 34
STEAMING (2)
    I CANNOT UNDO MYSELF, AND THE TRAIN IS STEAMING. .....GETTING THERE 248 38
    STEAMING AND BREATHING, ITS TEETH ....GETTING THERE 248 39
STEEL (12)
    STEEL ON MYSELF BEFORE PROFIT ....RHYME   50 14
    TAP, TAP, TAP, STEEL PEGS. I AM FOUND WANTING. ....THREE WOMEN 177 35
    ISSUING FROM THE STEEL NEEDLE THAT FLIES SO BLINDINGLY? *APPEARANCE. 189 11
    TUBULAR STEEL WHEELCHAIRS, ALUMINUM CRUTCHES. ....BERCK-PLAGE 197 39
    WHERE TRAINS, FAITHFUL TO THEIR STEEL ARCS, ...THE SWARM 216 35
    THESE PEOPLE WITH TORSOS OF STEEL ....BRASILIA 258   2
    I SHOULD HAVE A STEEL COMPLEXION LIKE YOURS ....THE RIVAL/DR 291   6
    BETWEEN STEEL PALMS OF INCLINATION, TAKE IT, ...SONNET: TO EVA 304   3
    OUR YEARS. DEATH COMES IN A CASUAL STEEL CAR, YET ..SONNET: TO TIME 311   3
    BUT OUTSIDE THE DIABOLIC STEEL OF THIS ....SONNET: TO TIME 311   5
    EACH FALLEN LEAF IS TRAPPED BY SPELL OF STEEL, ..PROLOGUE TO SPRING 322   7
    STEEL GAUNTLETS OF TRAFFIC, TERROR-STRUCK ....AERIALIST 332 45
STEELED (1)
    STEELED WITH THE SHEEN ....BY CANDLELIGHT 236   4
STEELIER (1)
    GULLS CIRCLE GRAY UNDER SHADOW OF A STEELIER FLIGHT. ...GREEN ROCK. 105 17
STEELY (2)
    SUN'S BRASS, THE MOON'S STEELY PATINAS, ...DEPARTURE   51 10
    SUCH A RACKET OF ECHOES FROM THE STEELY STREET, ...HARDCASTLE CRAGS   62   2
STEEP (2)
    THEN STEPPED DOWN THE STEEP BEACH SHELF AND INTO THE WATER. ..BABY. 175 39
    LABORING ON THE TILT OF THAT STEEP GRADE ....THE PRINCESS. 334 35
STEEPLE (1)
    AND SAP ASCENDS THE STEEPLE OF THE VEIN. ....APRIL AUBADE 312   4
STEEPLED (2)
    NOW, AS GREEN SAP ASCENDS THE STEEPLED WOOD, ...MAYFLOWER   60   5

	TITLE	PAGE	LINE

STEEPLED (CONT.)
    KINDLING HER WITHIN A STEEPLED FLAME,   THE PRINCESS AND THE GOBLINS 333 20
STEEPLING (1)
    STEEPLING SNAKE IN THAT CONTRARY LIGHT ....SONNET TO SATAN 323   9
STEER (3)
    TO MOVE, SERVE, STEER FOOD, ...WORDS FOR A NURSERY   73 13
    CAT-TAILS PART WHERE THE TAME CYGNETS STEER. ....WATERCOLOR. 112 14
    SHALL UNHUSK HIMSELF AND STEER INTO THE AIR. POEM.5.F. 135 20
STEERED (3)
    CLOUDS STEERED A BURNISHED DRIFT; ....SONG FOR A SUMMER'S DAY   31   8
    OF THE NORTH, TO BE STEERED CLEAR ....FULL FATHOM FIVE   92 13
    YOUR SHERLOCK HOLMESING STEERED TO A BLANK WALL ....DIALOGUE O. 280 167
STELLAR (1)
    IN RINGING ORANGE LIKE A STELLAR CARROT. ...THE GHOST'S LEAVETAKING   91 28
STEM (5)
    SWEET SALTS WARPED STEM ....FIRESONG   30 15
    STEM OF MY NEIGHBOR'S ROSE BUSH ....RESOLVE   52 15
    POOLING IN HEEL-PRINTS, FUMBLING PEBBLE AND STEM. ...PARLIAMENT H. 153 36
    SNAPPING OFF THE STEM ....BITTER STRAWBERRIES 300 38
    DROOPS UPON ITS WIZENED STEM ....JILTED 304 11
STEMS (3)
    ON ARROWY STEMS, ...SOUTHERN SUNRISE   26   8
    THE HOOPS OF BLACKBERRY STEMS MADE ME CRY. POEM.1.WHO. 132 31
    AMONG BIRD FEET AND THE STEMS OF PLANTS. ....LOVE LETTER 147 27
STENCH (2)
    FAR FROM THE SWEET STENCH OF THAT PERILOUS AIR ....CHANNEL CROSSING   27 13
    MUD STENCH, SHELL GUTS, GULLS' LEAVINGS; ....MUSSEL HUNTER.   95 13
STENCHES (1)
    STENCHES AND COLORS ASSAIL ME. ....THE SURGEON AT 2 A.M. 170 14
STENTORIAN (1)
    SUCH STENTORIAN CATS! ....ELLA MASON AND HER ELEVEN CATS   54 24
STEP (14)
    MOST SOFT, MOST SUAVELY GLIDES THAT STEP, ...PURSUIT   22   5
    LET FLESH BE KNIT, AND EACH STEP HENCE GO FAMOUS. ....WREATH F.   45 24
    AND NIGHT ARRIVES IN ONE GIGANTIC STEP.*TWO CAMPERS IN CLOUD COUNTRY 145 16
    THEY STEP AMONG THE ARCHETYPES. ....HEAVY WOMEN 158 17
    LIKE A SERIES OF PROMISES, AS I STEP FORWARD. ....WUTHERING HEIGHTS 167   9
    SIMPLY OPEN THE DOOR AND STEP OUT OF THE CAR ....STOPPED DEAD 230 24
    I STEP ON IT, ...CUT 235 14
    DO STEP INTO THE HALL! ....THE TOUR 237   2
    AND AT HIS NEXT STEP ....PURDAH 243 50
    STEP TO YOU FROM THE BLACK CAR OF LETHE, ...GETTING THERE 249 67
    STEP OFF! ....GULLIVER 251 20
    STEP OFF SEVEN LEAGUES, LIKE THOSE DISTANCES ....GULLIVER 251 21
    THE HILLS STEP OFF INTO WHITENESS. ....SHEEP IN FOG 262   1
    SOME DUCKS STEP DOWN OFF THEIR GREEN-REEDED SHELF ....QUEEN MARY'S. 290 11
STEPPED (1)
    THEN STEPPED DOWN THE STEEP BEACH SHELF AND INTO THE WATER. ..BABY. 175 39
STEPPING (2)
    STEPPING STONES FOR FRENCH BOOTSOLES. ....THE SWARM 216 14
    AND I, STEPPING FROM THIS SKIN ....GETTING THERE 249 65
STEPS (4)
    WEARS PURPLE, STEPS CAREFULLY ....MISS DRAKE PROCEEDS TO SUPPER   41   6
    STEPS OUT RADIANT IN LIMB, EYE, LIP, ...CONJURING.   66 27
    STEPS AT MY BACK SPIRAL INTO A WELL. ..................APPREHENSIONS 195   8
    SHE STEPS, HALTS, HUNG ....AERIALIST 331 15
STEREOPTICON (1)
    THEY SHOULD HAVE GONE OUT WITH BALLOON FLIGHTS AND THE
        STEREOPTICON. ....CANDLES 149 12
STERN (6)
    EACH TO THE OTHER; FIT FIBER FOR STERN WEATHER. ......CRYSTAL GAZER   55 11
    PARENTAL FACES ON TALL STALKS, ALTERNATELY STERN AND TEARFUL, ...
                                              ... INSOMNIAC 163 11
    ALOUD, CROSSLEGGED ON THE STERN SEAT, FROM THE GENERATION OF
        VIPERS. ....THE BABYSITTERS 175 32
    IMPALED UPON A STERN ANGELIC STARE ....THE TRIAL OF MAN 312   9
    AND STERN TRUTH TWISTED ....MOONSONG AT MORNING 317 35
    NOR CAN GOD'S STERN, SHOCKED ANGELS CRY THEM UP ....THE DEAD 320 13
STICK (3)
    OPENS TO SWALLOW ME. I'M A STONE, A STICK, ...PARLIAMENT HILL FIELDS 152 15
    ON A STICK THAT RATTLES AND CLICKS, A COUNTERFEIT SNAKE. .....TOTEM 264 18
    PROBING FRACTURED VENUS WITH A STICK ....TWO LOVERS. 327 15
STICKS (10)
    OF STICKS. THE LIGHT FALLS CHALK AND COLD ...THE EVERLASTING MONDAY   62   3
    WOULD PICK STICKS, WOULD NOT REST ....THE EVERLASTING MONDAY   62   8
    IT STICKS, AND IT HAS STUCK A WEEK. ....THE EYE-MOTE 109 21
    A THICKET OF STICKS, ...POLLY'S TREE 128   2
    IN THE MARKETPLACE THEY ARE PILING THE DRY STICKS. POEM.6.W. 135   1
    WE PICKED UP STICKS OF DRIFTWOOD AND BEAT THEM OFF, *THE BABYSITTERS 175 38
    SPRY, WRY, AND GRAY AS THESE MARCH STICKS, ...AMONG THE NARCISSI 190   1
    EYES ROLLED BY WHITE STICKS, ...MEDUSA 224   2
    ORANGE LOLLIES ON SILVER STICKS, ...THE MUNICH MANNEQUINS 263 14
    DEATH WITH ITS MANY STICKS. ....TOTEM 265 34
STICKY (3)
    OF CHILDHOOD AND ADOLESCENCE, STICKY WITH DREAMS, ...INSOMNIAC 163 10

                                                      TITLE   PAGE LINE
STICKY (CONT.)
    IT IS YOUR STICKY CANDIES. ....THE OTHER   201   16
    AND PICK THE WORMS OFF ME LIKE STICKY PEARLS. ....LADY LAZARUS   245   42
STIFF (10)
    ON THE STIFF TWIG UP THERE ....BLACK ROOK IN RAINY WEATHER   56   1
    FOR STRONGHOLD AGAINST THEIR STIFF ....THE THIN PEOPLE   65   42
    COME, SO UNLIKE US, TO A STIFF IMPASSE, ...THE OTHER TWO   69   31
    STIFF AS TWIGS, HER BODY WOODENLY ....VIRGIN IN A TREE   82   39
    STIFF AS A QUEEN ON A PLAYING CARD. ....THE BULL OF BENDYLAW   108   5
    THEIR HANDS AND FACES STIFF WITH HOLINESS.*THE MOON AND THE YEW TREE   173   26
    THEY STARE FROM A SQUARE, STIFF FRILL. ....A SECRET   219   14
    BLACK AND STIFF, BUT NOT A BAD FIT. ....THE APPLICANT   221   21
    AND RETURNED THEM STEAMED AND PRESSED AND STIFF AS SHIRTS. *THE TOUR   238   34
    CHURCHYARD EARS UNTIL THE STARLIT STIFF ....LOVE IS A PARALLAX   330   41
STIFFEN (7)
    DARK FACE. SO MIGHT RIGOR MORTIS COME TO STIFFEN ....PERSEUS   83   32
    UPLIFTED, STIFFEN IN A FAMILY POSE. ....BLUE MOLES   126   16
    THE TREES STIFFEN INTO PLACE LIKE BURNT NERVES. ...WAKING IN WINTER   151   3
    GULLS STIFFEN TO THEIR CHILL VIGIL IN THE DRAFTY HALF-LIGHT, ...
                              ... PARLIAMENT HILL FIELDS   153   49
    WHERE SPILT LIVES CONGEAL AND STIFFEN TO HISTORY.*A BIRTHDAY PRESENT   208   51
    STIFFEN THE ORDINARY ....NOTES TO A NEOPHYTE   306   10
    HILL AND VALLEY STIFFEN ROW ON ROW. ....PROLOGUE TO SPRING   322   6
STIFFENED (2)
    THE BALD SLOTS OF HIS EYES STIFFENED WIDE-OPEN ....INSOMNIAC   163   27
    THEY PROPPED HIS JAW WITH A BOOK UNTIL IT STIFFENED ....BERCK-PLAGE   198   65
STIFFENS (2)
    THE FEVER TRICKLES AND STIFFENS IN MY HAIR. ....THE JAILER   226   21
    STIFFENS AND ODORS BLEED ....EDGE   273   15
STIFFNESS (1)
    THE STIFFNESS OF SAILS, THE LONG SALT WINDING SHEETS. ....MYSTIC   268   8
STIGMATA (1)
    RED STIGMATA AT THE VERY CENTER, ...MEDUSA   225   9
STILE (2)
    ACROSS BARBED STILE, THROUGH FLOCKED BROWN COWS. ....BUCOLICS   23   4
    OVER THEIR IRON STILE. AND STILL DON'T SLEEP. ....ZOO KEEPER'S WIFE   155   40
STILES (1)
    THROUGH BARE WHISTLING HEATHER, OVER STILES OF BLACK STONE, ...
                              ... THE SNOWMAN ON THE MOOR   58   21
STILL (66)
    HE EATS, AND STILL HIS NEED SEEKS FOOD, ...PURSUIT   23   39
    STILL DREAM BEHIND ....SOUTHERN SUNRISE   26   3
    WE WALKED (AND STILL WALK THERE -- ....SONG FOR A SUMMER'S DAY   31   18
    YOUNG WIVES STILL BLITHE, ...TINKER JACK AND THE TIDY WIVES   35   27
    STILL FAIR, ...TINKER JACK AND THE TIDY WIVES   35   28
    INTO THE STILL, SULTRY WEATHER ....MISS DRAKE PROCEEDS TO SUPPER   41   25
    STAND STOCK STILL TO LAUD THESE MATED ONES .....WREATH FOR A BRIDAL   44   5
    STILL AS A SHELL: HEAR WHAT AN AGE OF GLASS ....EPITAPH FOR F.   45   16
    TORPID WARNING, OR LAY STILL ....SPIDER   49   20
    A CERTAIN MINOR LIGHT MAY STILL ....BLACK ROOK IN RAINY WEATHER   57   14
    STILL RINGING WITH BRUIT OF INSULTS AND DISHONORS ....SNOWMAN O.   58   3
    STILL, SHE FELT LOATH TO JUNK IT. *THE LADY AND THE EARTHENWARE HEAD   69   7
    STILL HE HYMNS JUICE OF HER, HOT NECTARINE. ....OUIJA   77   26
    STILL, LATTER-DAY SAGES, ...A LESSON IN VENGEANCE   80   21
    STILL THAN SWALLOWS JOY. YOU ENTER NOW, ...PERSEUS   83   34
    STILL, THEY'RE OUR BEST MUSTERING OF HEIGHT: BY ....ABOVE THE OXBOW   88   5
    SHUT AGAINST ME. ALL HELD STILL. ......MUSSEL HUNTER AT ROCK HARBOR   95   20
    TO KNOW THE STILL HEART OF THE STONES: ....CHILD'S PARK STONES   101   22
    SPINNING TO STILL IN HIS ONE WHITENESS. ....WHITENESS I REMEMBER   103   33
    MORE OR OTHER, THEY STILL DISSATISFY. ....POEMS, POTATOES   106   10
    OF HER HAND, THE HOUSE STILL HUGS IN EACH DRAB ....POINT SHIRLEY   110   20
    STILL HE THUMBED OUT SOMETHING ELSE. THE HERMIT AT OUTERMOST HOUSE   119   14
    AS IF IT WERE SUMMER STILL. ....MAGNOLIA SHOALS   121   4
    BUT PLIABLE STILL, HIS JAW ....MEDALLION   124   5
    OVER AND OVER. AND STILL THE HEAVEN ....BLUE MOLES   127   32
    I BECAME A STILL PEBBLE. POEM.7.S.   136   8
    THEIR CHAR OF KARAKUL STILL. I CAN'T TELL ....THE BURNT-OUT SPA   138   7
    AND STILL THE LUNGS WON'T FILL AND THE HEART WON'T START. *STILLBORN   142   10
    STILL NOBODY WILL MOVE OR SPEAK -- ....ON DECK   142   10
    TO THIS INFANT STILL IN A BIRTH-DROWSE? ....CANDLES   149   33
    OVER THEIR IRON STILE. AND STILL DON'T SLEEP. ....ZOO KEEPER'S WIFE   155   40
    THE DARK STILL NURSES ITS SECRET. ....HEAVY WOMEN   158   11
    WHEN I HIT HER SHE HELD STILL, LIKE A TRUE PACIFIST. ....IN PLASTER   159   12
    YET I STILL DEPENDED ON HER, THOUGH I DID IT REGRETFULLY.*IN PLASTER   160   49
    STILL IT SEEPS UP, IT IS NOT EXHAUSTED. ......THE SURGEON AT 2 A.M.   171   23
    A GALLERY OF CREAKING PORCHES AND STILL INTERIORS, THE BABYSITTERS   175   34
    I DID NOT LOOK. BUT STILL THE FACE WAS THERE, ...THREE WOMEN   178   78
    HE IS STILL SWADDLED IN WHITE BANDS. ....THREE WOMEN   186 326
    THE SWANS ARE GONE. STILL THE RIVER ....THREE WOMEN   186 344
    DO NOT KILL IT. IT STARTLES ME STILL, ...PHEASANT   191   2
    I FELT A STILL BUSYNESS, AN INTENT. ....THE RABBIT CATCHER   194   21
    THROUGH A STILL VIRULENCE, ...BERCK-PLAGE   197   35
    IN A STILL PLACE, AND THE GROOM IS RED AND FORGETFUL, HE IS
          FEATURELESS. .... BERCK-PLAGE   200 108
    AND I AM DARK-SUITED AND STILL, A MEMBER OF THE PARTY, BERCK-PLAGE   200 111

		TITLE	PAGE	LINE

STILL (CONT.)
IF I STAND VERY STILL, THEY WILL THINK I AM COW-PARSLEY, ...BEE. 212 39
STILL FIGURES OF IVORY. ....THE SWARM 216 12
THE WOMAN, STILL AT HER KNITTING, ...WINTERING 219 43
I AM STILL RAW. ....LESBOS 229 89
YOU ARE SUNK IN YOUR SEVEN CHINS, STILL AS A HAM. .....STOPPED DEAD 230 16
THE MEN THE BLOOD STILL PUMPS FORWARD, ...GETTING THERE 248 25
IS THERE NO STILL PLACE ....GETTING THERE 249 52
THE BLOOD BERRIES ARE THEMSELVES, THEY ARE VERY STILL. ....YEARS 255 23
STILL URINOUS ON YOU, A SIN. ..........................EAVESDROPPER 260 8
THE STILL WATERS ....PARALYTIC 266 27
THE WALKING BESIDE STILL WATER? MEMORY? ....MYSTIC 268 17
EVEN A LITTLE? YOU KNOW I DON'T, AND STILL . . ..DIALOGUE O. 277 34
AND STILL I'M SKEPTIC. I KNOW. I'M BEING FOOLISH ....DIALOGUE O. 277 35
PAN, ARE YOU STILL THERE? SEE, HIS SPRINT ....DIALOGUE O. 278 70
HE LEECHES BY OUR LENIENCE. HE STILL BORES ....DIALOGUE O. 283 259
THE NIGHT IS A BLUE POOL; SHE IS VERY STILL. ....ELM/DR 292 6
AT THE CENTER SHE IS STILL, VERY STILL WITH WISDOM. ....ELM/DR 292 7
AT THE CENTER SHE IS STILL, VERY STILL WITH WISDOM. ....ELM/DR 292 7
HOW I AM STILL ....TO A JILTED LOVER 310 26
STILL, STUBBORNLY WE TRY TO CRACK THE NUT ....DOOM OF EXILES 318 13
SKELETON STILL CRAVES TO HAVE ....DANSE MACABRE 321 5
REPOSE OF SCULPTURE HOLDS THE COUNTRY STILL. ....PROLOGUE TO SPRING 322 9
STILLBORN (1)
STILLBORN ....STILLBORN 142 T
STILLED (4)
THESE STILLED SUBURBS: NOBODY ....NIGHT SHIFT 76 9
OF TIGERS TO BE STILLED BY YOUR DARK EYE ....YADWIGHA. 85 13
STILLED, SILVERED AS WATER IN A GLASS ....WATERCOLOR. 111 2
POISON OF STILLED LAWNS, THE LITTLE CLAPBOARD GRAVESTONES, WAKING. 151 7
STILLING (1)
DULLING AND STILLING. ....POPPIES IN JULY 203 14
STILLNESS (7)
AND PAINTS THE RIVER'S PALE CIRCUMFLUENT STILLNESS ABOVE THE OXBOW 89 43
ALL STILLNESS. YET THESE SHAPES FLOAT ....LORELEI 94 9
MY BONES HOLD A STILLNESS, THE FAR ....SHEEP IN FOG 262 11
CLOCKS CRY: STILLNESS IS A LIE, MY DEAR.*TO EVA DESCENDING THE STAIR 303 1
CLOCKS CRY: STILLNESS IS A LIE, MY DEAR.*TO EVA DESCENDING THE STAIR 303 6
CLOCKS CRY: STILLNESS IS A LIE, MY DEAR.*TO EVA DESCENDING THE STAIR 303 12
CLOCKS CRY: STILLNESS IS A LIE, MY DEAR.*TO EVA DESCENDING THE STAIR 303 18
STILTS (1)
I BORROW THE STILTS OF AN OLD TRAGEDY. ......ELECTRA ON AZALEA PATH 117 33
STIMULUS (1)
CAME THE PROFANE STIMULUS TO COUGH; ....DIRGE FOR A JOKER 302 2
STING (5)
THE STING OF BEES TOOK AWAY MY FATHER. ....LAMENT 315 1
THE STING OF BEES TOOK AWAY MY FATHER. ....LAMENT 315 6
BUT THE STING OF BEES TOOK AWAY MY FATHER. ....LAMENT 315 12
THE STING OF BEES TOOK AWAY MY FATHER. ....LAMENT 316 18
THAT STING NO MORE THAN LOVE: A ROOM WHERE TIME *MORNING IN THE HOS. 332 15
STINGING (2)
ASLANT: THEIR HILL OF STINGING NETTLE; ....BUCOLICS 24 10
COUCHED DAYLONG IN CLOISTERS OF STINGING NETTLE *WREATH FOR A BRIDAL 44 7
STINGS (4)
STINGS ....STINGS 214 T
STINGS BIG AS DRAWING PINS! ....THE SWARM 217 56
WHOSE KISS STINGS UNBEARABLY ....MYSTIC 268 4
THOUGH PRIMA DONNA POUTS AND CRITIC STINGS, ...LOVE IS A PARALLAX 330 56
STINK (2)
FRIENDS, FRIENDS. THEY STINK OF ARMPITS ....LEAVING EARLY 146 17
MEANWHILE THERE'S A STINK OF FAT AND BABY CRAP. ....LESBOS 228 33
STINT (2)
THE STINT OF SISYPHUS. ASK PAN, THEN, WHERE ....DIALOGUE O. 281 173
THEN, THIS TOUGH STINT DONE, SHE CURTSIES ....AERIALIST 331 25
STIPPLE (1)
STIPPLE OF SHIFTING WAVE-TIPS IS IRONED OUT, LOST ..ABOVE THE OXBOW 89 46
STIR (7)
TO US, SINCE WE SEE NO LEAF EDGE STIR HIGH ....ABOVE THE OXBOW 88 33
THE ARTIFICIAL RED SAGE DOES NOT STIR ....ELECTRA ON AZALEA PATH 117 24
TO STIR ROBIN'S EGG ....POLLY'S TREE 128 14
IT WILL PING LIKE A CHINESE CHIME IN THE SLIGHTEST AIR STIR A LIFE 150 7
SHOULD I STIR, I THINK THIS PINK AND PURPLE PLASTIC ....ZOO K. 154 11
YOU POKE AND STIR. ....LADY LAZARUS 246 74
I DO NOT STIR. ....DEATH & CO. 255 26
STIRRING (1)
SETTLING AND STIRRING LIKE BLOWN PAPER ......PARLIAMENT HILL FIELDS 152 8
STIRRUPS (1)
STIRRUPS UNDONE, AND DECORUM. AND ....WHITENESS I REMEMBER 103 23
STIRS (2)
VEIL STIRS ITS CURTAIN ....PURDAH 243 25
AS A BAD JOB. WAIT. HE STIRS. HE ROMPS DIALOGUE OVER A OUIJA BOARD 284 293
STITCH (1)
CAN STITCH LACE NEATLY ON TO THIS MATERIAL. MY HUSBAND THREE WOMEN 187 360
STITCHED (3)
MOUTHLESS, EYELESS, WITH STITCHED BALD HEAD. THE DISQUIETING MUSES 75 16

STITCHED (CONT.)
    SET IN THE PROVERBS STITCHED ON SAMPLERS ....VIRGIN IN A TREE   81   3
    I HAVE STITCHED LIFE INTO ME LIKE A RARE ORGAN, ...THREE WOMEN   178   72
STITCHES (4)
    WHEN I GRIN, THE STITCHES TAUTEN. I GROW BACKWARD. I'M TWENTY,*FACE.   156   21
    NURSES THE HARDSHIP OF HIS STITCHES, AND WALKS AND WALKS. *NARCISSI.   190   6
    VOLT UPON VOLT. CATGUT STITCHES MY FISSURES. POEM.7.S.   137   30
    STITCHES TO SHOW SOMETHING'S MISSING? NO, NO? THEN   ...THE APPLICANT 221   6
STITCHING (1)
    THEY ARE STITCHING ME UP WITH SILK, AS IF I WERE A MATERIAL. *THREE.   181 168
STOAT (1)
    STALKS RED FOX, SHREWD STOAT. ....ODE FOR TED   29   6
STOCK (7)
    STAND STOCK STILL TO LAUD THESE MATED ONES .....WREATH FOR A BRIDAL   44   5
    SO WHEN STAUNCH ISLAND STOCK CHOSE FORFEITURE ....MAYFLOWER   60   9
    MY JILTING LADY SQUANDER COIN, GOLD LEAF STOCK DITCHES, CONJURING.   66   35
    HER RUINED APARTMENTS, TAKING STOCK ....AFTERMATH   114   11
    WE MAKE NEW STOCK FROM THE SALT. ....THE APPLICANT   221   18
    TOO LATE TO CALCULATE THE TOPPLING STOCK: ....DOOMSDAY   316   17
    TO CAST LOCK, STOCK AND BARREL UNDER BAN; ....THE DISPOSSESSED   318   11
STOCKING (1)
    AND UGLY, MY BELLY A SILK STOCKING ....ZOO KEEPER'S WIFE   154   6
STOCKINGS (2)
    GROWNUPS COFFINED IN STOCKINGS AND JACKETS, ...WHITSUN   153   4
    I SAT AT MY DESK IN MY STOCKINGS, MY HIGH HEELS, ...THREE WOMEN   177   21
STOCK-STILL (1)
    GOLDFINCH, GOLDFISH, GOLDEN TIGER CAT STOCK-STILL *IN MIDAS' COUNTRY   99 13-4
STOLE (3)
    THAT NIGHTLONG STOLE HER MALE, ...THE SHRIKE   42   20
    FEEDING AT THE ROOT OF THINGS. HE STOLE THAT, TOO, ...DIALOGUE O.   279 102
    AS HE STOLE OUR PERPLEXITIES ABOUT THE POOLS ....DIALOGUE O.   279 103
STOLEN (1)
    THE STOLEN HORSES, THE FORNICATIONS ....THE OTHER   202   21
STOLIDLY (1)
    STOLIDLY PROPPING THICK VOLUMES OF PROSE: SPITE-SET ....LADY AND T.   69   4
STOLZ (1)
    THE THICK GERMANS SLUMBERING IN THEIR BOTTOMLESS STOLZ. ....MUNICH.   263   23
STOMACH (5)
    AND BLEED. THE WHITE STOMACH MAY RIPEN YET. ....MOONRISE   98   30
    THIS SHED'S FUSTY AS A MUMMY'S STOMACH: POEM.1.WHO. 131   4
    THE STOMACH OF INDIFFERENCE, THE WORDLESS CUPBOARD. POEM.7.S.   136   6
    OVER EACH WEIGHTY STOMACH A FACE ....HEAVY WOMEN   158   6
    AND IF MY STOMACH WOULD CONTRACT ....APRIL 18   301   3
STOMACHING (1)
    OF KITCHEN SLOPS AND STOMACHING NO CONSTRAINT, ...SOW   61   43
STONE (52)
    WATER IN THE MILLRACE, THROUGH A SLUICE OF STONE, WINTER LANDSCAPE,   21   1
    ALREADY VEILING THE GRAY SPOOL OF STONE ....SPIDER   48   18
    GULL-FOULED, A STONE HUT ....DEPARTURE   51   16
    AT GORGON-PROSPECTS WITH POWER TO STRIKE TO STONE ....CRYSTAL GAZER   55   41
    THROUGH BARE WHISTLING HEATHER, OVER STILES OF BLACK STONE, ...
                                     ... THE SNOWMAN ON THE MOOR   58   21
    OF ITS HILLS, AND ITS PASTURES BORDERED BY BLACK STONE SET ...
                                     ... HARDCASTLE CRAGS   63   29
    ON BLACK STONE. BARNS ....HARDCASTLE CRAGS   63   30
    LIKE A PLANET, A STONE, SWALLOWED IN A GREAT DARKNESS,*THE OTHER TWO   68   25
    IN THE ARCHAEOLOGICAL MUSEUM IN CAMBRIDGE IS A STONE . . . ...
                                     ... ALL THE DEAD DEARS   70 E/1
    STONE WALL AND RIDGEPOLE RISE ....TWO VIEWS OF WITHENS   71   3
    STONE FARMS FOUNDERING IN IT, ...THE GREAT CARBUNCLE   72   3
    DOWN: THE BODY WEIGHS LIKE STONE. ....THE GREAT CARBUNCLE   73   30
    THEY STAND THEIR VIGIL IN GOWNS OF STONE, ...THE DISQUIETING MUSES   76   50
    BUT SURE STATIONS IN BRONZE, WOOD, STONE. ....SCULPTOR   91   8
    STONE, STONE, FERRY ME DOWN THERE. ....LORELEI   95   36
    STONE, STONE, FERRY ME DOWN THERE. ....LORELEI   95   36
    THE STONE LION-HEAD SET IN THE WALL ..................RHODODENDRON.   103   5
    INTO THE STONE BASIN. I SNIPPED FABLE OF THE RHODODENDRON STEALERS   103   7
    SUPERIOR PAGE; THE BLUNT STONE ALSO. ....POEMS, POTATOES   106   13
    THE STONE FACE OF THE MAN WHO DOESN'T FEEL, ...THE RAVAGED FACE   116   10
    YOUR SPECKLED STONE ASKEW BY AN IRON FENCE. ELECTRA ON AZALEA PATH   117   18
    MY HEART UNDER YOUR FOOT, SISTER OF A STONE. ....BEEKEEPER'S. 118   7
    OVER A GREAT STONE SPIT ....MAN IN BLACK   119   13
    THE MOON LEANS, A STONE MADONNA, OVER THE LEAD SEA   THE NET-MENDERS   121   15
    ROVE OVER HIS FIELD OF STONE; ....MAGNOLIA SHOALS   122   16
    I AM A ROOT, A STONE, AN OWL PELLET, ...POEM.1.WHO.   132   23
    WHEN IT THUNDERED I HID UNDER A FLAT STONE. POEM.3.MAENAD.   133   5
    I COUPLED WITH DUST IN THE SHADOW OF A STONE. POEM.6.W.   136   22
    OPEN ONE STONE EYE. POEM.7.S.   136   21
    THOUGH, LIKE A STONE, UNBOTHERED BY IT, ...LOVE LETTER   147   3
    TREE AND STONE GLITTERED, WITHOUT SHADOWS. ....LOVE LETTER   147   29
    FROM STONE TO CLOUD, SO I ASCENDED. ....LOVE LETTER   147   33
    OPENS TO SWALLOW ME.. I'M A STONE, A STICK, ..PARLIAMENT HILL FIELDS   152   15
    AND YOUR FIRST GIFT IS MAKING STONE OUT OF EVERYTHING. ...THE RIVAL   166   6
    BLACK STONE, BLACK STONE. ....WUTHERING HEIGHTS   168   36
    BLACK STONE, BLACK STONE. ....WUTHERING HEIGHTS   168   36

STONE (CONT.)
    IT HAS SHUT ITS MOUTH ON THE STONE PILL OF REPOSE. ....SURGEON. 171 30
    CRACK THROUGH STONE, AND THEY ARE GREEN WITH LIFE. .....THREE WOMEN 187 371
    TILL YOUR HEAD IS A STONE, YOUR PILLOW A LITTLE TURF, ...ELM 192 11
    IN THE PARLOR OF THE STONE HOUSE ....BERCK-PLAGE 199 78
    STONE OF THE SIDE, ...PURDAH 242 2
    UNDER A STONE. THOSE TWO DREAMED DEATHS TOOK ....DIALOGUE O. 285 326
    OBSERVING THE WRECK OF METAL AND RARE STONE. ....SONNET: TO EVA 304 4
    AND IT TOOK THE DIAMOND STONE ....NOTES TO A NEOPHYTE 307 21
    A STONE CAN MASQUERADE WHERE NO HEART IS ....NEVER TRY TO TRICK. 319 4
    LUMINOUS, THE TOWN OF STONE ....DANSE MACABRE 321 22
    THE SKATERS FREEZE WITHIN A STONE TABLEAU. ......PROLOGUE TO SPRING 322 3
    AND JUMBO SADLY TRUMPETS INTO STONE; ....DENOUEMENT 327 11
    THE PRINCESS FREES THE MINER, STONE BY STONE, ...THE PRINCESS. 334 49
    THE PRINCESS FREES THE MINER, STONE BY STONE, ...THE PRINCESS. 334 49
    AND STAUNCH STONE EYES THAT STARE ....TOUCH-AND-GO 335 3
    A WAVE OF GRASS ENGRAVES UPON THE STONE: ....EPITAPH IN THREE PARTS 338 32
STONE-BUILT (1)
    STONE-BUILT TOWN, THAT SHE HEARD THE QUICK AIR IGNITE *HARDCASTLE C. 62 4
STONE-DEAF (1)
    HE SMOLDERED, AS IF STONE-DEAF, BLINDFOLD, ...SUICIDE OFF EGG ROCK 115 14
STONE-HATCHETED (1)
    GIANT HEAVED INTO THE DISTANCE, STONE-HATCHETED, ...SNOWMAN O. 59 31
STONE-HEAD (1)
    THE GREAT GODS, STONE-HEAD, CLAW-FOOT,*THE HERMIT AT OUTERMOST HOUSE 118 4
STONEHENGE (1)
    NEAR HIS SMALL STONEHENGE ABOVE THE ANTS' ROUTE, ...SPIDER 48 11
STONES (30)
    FLOWER FORGET-ME-NOTS BETWEEN THE STONES ....NOVEMBER GRAVEYARD 56 7
    OF STONES AND HILLS OF STONES COULD BREAK ....HARDCASTLE CRAGS 63 43
    OF STONES AND HILLS OF STONES COULD BREAK ....HARDCASTLE CRAGS 63 43
    I SMELL THAT WHITENESS HERE, BENEATH THE STONES ....MOONRISE 98 16
    CHILD'S PARK STONES ....CHILD'S PARK STONES 100 T
    FOUNDING FATHER SET THESE LOBED, WARPED STONES CHILD'S PARK STONES 100 3
    THESE STONES GUARD A DARK REPOSE ....CHILD'S PARK STONES 101 11
    TO KNOW THE STILL HEART OF THE STONES: ....CHILD'S PARK STONES 101 22
    STONES THAT TAKE THE WHOLE SUMMER TO LOSE .....CHILD'S PARK STONES 101 23
    THEIR DREAM OF THE WINTER'S COLD; STONES ......CHILD'S PARK STONES 101 24
    STONES, WITHOUT CONSCIENCE, WORD AND LINE ENDURE, ..POEMS, POTATOES 106 5
    I WOULD GET FROM THESE DRY-PAPPED STONES ....POINT SHIRLEY 111 41
    GRANDMOTHER, STONES ARE NOTHING OF HOME ....POINT SHIRLEY 111 46
    LIKE HIERATIC STONES, AND THE GROUND IS HARD.*ELECTRA ON AZALEA PATH 116 4
    STONES, STRODE OUT IN YOUR DEAD ....MAN IN BLACK 120 16
    TIP, RIVETING STONES, AIR, ...MAN IN BLACK 120 20
    WHOSE STONES KEEP A LITTLE HEAT. ....OLD LADIES' HOME 120 7
    THE MOLES LOOK NEUTRAL AS THE STONES. ....BLUE MOLES 126 14
    ON THE BLANK STONES OF THE LANDING. ....THE COLOSSUS 130 30
    THE STONES ....POEM.7.S. 136 ST
    THE STONES OF THE BELLY WERE PEACEABLE, ...POEM.7.S. 136 9
    THEY HUNTED THE STONES, TACITURN AND SEPARATE, ...POEM.7.S. 136 15
    HIS ARMORPLATE, HIS TOPPLED STONES ....THE BURNT-OUT SPA 138 12
    WE SLEPT LIKE STONES. LADY, WHAT AM I DOING ....LEAVING EARLY 146 42
    LIMPID AS SPIRITS. MANY STONES LAY ....LOVE LETTER 147 22
    STARS ARE DROPPING THICK AS STONES INTO THE TWIGGY ....STARS. 165 1
    A SET OF TEETH, OR STONES ....THE SURGEON AT 2 A.M. 171 34
    THE EMPTY BENCHES OF MEMORY LOOK OVER STONES, ...BERCK-PLAGE 199 88
    THESE WERE HARDER, TWO WHITE STONES. ....THE DETECTIVE 209 32
    STEPPING STONES FOR FRENCH BOOTSOLES. ....THE SWARM 216 14
STONE'S (1)
    NO THIRST DISTURBS A STONE'S BED. ....CHILD'S PARK STONES 101 30
STONEWARD (1)
    SHEEP DROWSED STONEWARD IN THEIR TUSSOCKS OF WOOL, AND BIRDS, ...
                                        ... HARDCASTLE CRAGS 63 34
STONIER (1)
    THOSE STONIER EYES LOOK, ...TOUCH-AND-GO 336 23
STONY (6)
    SEEK NO STONY CAMERA-EYE TO FIX ....EPITAPH FOR FIRE AND FLOWER 45 8
    HER DOWN TO MERE QUARTZ GRIT IN THAT STONY LIGHT ..HARDCASTLE CRAGS 63 44
    THE STONY ACTORS POISE AND PAUSE FOR BREATH. *ELECTRA ON AZALEA PATH 117 37
    THUMBED NO STONY, HORNY POT, ...THE HERMIT AT OUTERMOST HOUSE 119 15
    A STONY HOLE. HE'S TO BLAME. POEM.2.DARK. 132 20
    OFF THAT LANDSPIT OF STONY MOUTH-PLUGS, ...MEDUSA 224 1
STOOD (17)
    BELOW: A FEN WHERE WATER STOOD; ....BUCOLICS 24 9
    STOOD ASTRIDE ....LETTER TO A PURIST 36 2
    DEW STOOD IN CHILL SWEAT ON EACH STALK, ...DIALOGUE B. 38 4
    BAREFOOT, SHE STOOD IN SHOCK OF THAT RETURNING, ...DREAM WITH C. 43 5
    GOD'S WORK STOOD ANCHORED IN THAT GLARE ....CRYSTAL GAZER 55 38
    STALEMATED THEIR ARMIES STOOD, WITH TOTTERING BANNERS: ..SNOWMAN O. 58 1
    ON THE LONG BOOKSHELF IT STOOD ...THE LADY AND THE EARTHENWARE HEAD 69 3
    BUT, HEAVY-FOOTED, STOOD ASIDE ....THE DISQUIETING MUSES 75 29
    STOOD STUBBORN IN ITS JUNGLE: RED AGAINST GREEN, ...YADWIGHA. 85 18
    DAWN TIDE STOOD DEAD LOW. I SMELT .....MUSSEL HUNTER AT ROCK HARBOR 95 12
    STOOD SHUT OUT, FOR ONCE, FOR ALL, ...MUSSEL HUNTER AT ROCK HARBOR 96 52
    WHETHER NICETY STOOD CONFOUNDED BY LOVE, ...RHODODENDRON. 104 27

	TITLE	PAGE	LINE

STOOD (CONT.)
    BLAMELESS AS DAYLIGHT I STOOD LOOKING ....THE EYE-MOTE 109   1
    BLACK HAIR TILL THERE YOU STOOD, ...MAN IN BLACK 120 18
    IF I JUST UNDID THE LOCKS AND STOOD BACK AND TURNED INTO A TREE. ...
                                    ... THE ARRIVAL OF THE BEE BOX 213 28
    SHE STOOD UP, A THIN COMMANDING FIGURE ....BITTER STRAWBERRIES 300 29
    UNTIL HE STOOD ....TO A JILTED LOVER 310 14
STOOGES (1)
    YOUR STOOGES ....MEDUSA 225   6
STOOL (1)
    THEY MAY BE WHITE AND SHY, THEY ARE NO STOOL PIGEONS, ...COURAGE. 210 31
STOOP (2)
    THE OWL SHALL STOOP FROM HIS TURRET, THE RAT CRY OUT. ..WATERCOLOR. 112 28
    THE SHADOWS STOOP OVER LIKE GUESTS AT A CHRISTENING. ....CANDLES 149 35
STOP (11)
    WITHOUT STOP THOSE GREASED MACHINES, ...NIGHT SHIFT   77 22
    TENDING, WITHOUT STOP, THE BLUNT ....NIGHT SHIFT   77 23
    AND REPOISE UNTIL TIME STOP, THE CELESTIAL BALANCE ....PERSEUS   84 48
    SO WE ARE HAULED, THOUGH WE WOULD STOP ....IN MIDAS' COUNTRY 100 21
    IN DREAMS, THROUGH MOUTH-HOLE OR EYE-HOLE. I CAN'T STOP IT. *LAST W. 172 15
    I COULDN'T STOP LOOKING. ....LITTLE FUGUE 187 12
    THAT SPLITS FROM ITS RIPPED BAG AND DOES NOT STOP ....BURNING. 205 51
    BUT IT SHIMMERS, IT DOES NOT STOP, AND I THINK IT WANTS ME. ...
                                    ... A BIRTHDAY PRESENT 206 11
    STOP CRYING. ....THE APPLICANT 221   8
    "OH, STOP WORRYING, NELDA," ....BITTER STRAWBERRIES 300 27
    NOR STOP TO UNDERSTAND ....TOUCH-AND-GO 335 11
STOPPED (9)
    MY HEART IS A STOPPED GERANIUM. POEM.1.WHO. 131   9
    THE STOPPED HORSE ON HIS CHROMIUM POLE ....WHITSUN 154   7
    SHE STOPPED FITTING ME SO CLOSELY AND SEEMED OFFISH. ....IN PLASTER 159 29
    STOPPED AND AWFUL AS A PHOTOGRAPH OF SOMEBODY LAUGHING, ...BABY. 175 35
    THE SHEETS, THE FACES, ARE WHITE AND STOPPED, LIKE CLOCKS. ..THREE. 179 95
    STOPPED DEAD ....STOPPED DEAD 230   T
    THE HEART HAS NOT STOPPED. ....MYSTIC 269 31
    WHERE WE STOPPED, AND WITH A CURSE ....THE DREAM 311 14
    WHICH HAS STOPPED THE SEASON IN ITS TRACKS ......PROLOGUE TO SPRING 322 11
STOPPER (1)
    MY GOD, THERE GOES THE STOPPER! ....A SECRET 220 37
STOPPING (3)
    KNOTTING AND STOPPING, ILL-ASSORTED, IN BLUE UNIFORMS,*PARLIAMENT H. 152 14
    IT IS SO BEAUTIFUL UP HERE: IT IS A STOPPING PLACE. ....BERCK-PLAGE 199 90
    THERE IS NO STOPPING IT. ....KINDNESS 270 19
STOPS (7)
    A BEGGAR STOPS AMONG EGGS AND LOAVES, ...THE BEGGARS   48 10
    STOPS US, BETRAYS US; ....MUSHROOMS 139   8
    THE WIND STOPS MY BREATH LIKE A BANDAGE. ...PARLIAMENT HILL FIELDS 152 20
    WORMS IN THE GLOTTAL STOPS. ....THE FEARFUL 256   9
    M-S. MANUSCRIPT? HE STOPS. I WISH ......DIALOGUE OVER A OUIJA BOARD 279 95
    CYCLING PHOENIX NEVER STOPS. ....LOVE IS A PARALLAX 330 66
    AS THE LOUD ALARMCLOCK STOPS. ....AERIALIST 332 42
STORAGE (1)
    OCTOBER'S THE MONTH FOR STORAGE. POEM.1.WHO. 131   3
STORE (1)
    THEY WILL ROLL ME UP IN BANDAGES, THEY WILL STORE MY HEART   LAST W. 172 23
STOREROOMS (1)
    THE STOREROOMS ARE FULL OF HEARTS. POEM.7.S. 137 32
STORIED (1)
    BRING HOME EACH STORIED HEAD. ....BATTLE-SCENE   84 28
STORIES (3)
    VILLAGE STORIES GO THAT IN OLDEN DAYS*ELLA MASON AND HER ELEVEN CATS   53 13
    MOTHER, WHO MADE TO ORDER STORIES ....THE DISQUIETING MUSES   75   9
    SHE RECALLS QUEER STORIES HER NURSE READ ....THE PRINCESS. 334 37
STORM (3)
    GERD WHIRLS THE BALL ABLAZE: "ROUGH STORM," SHE GRANTS, "MAY WREAK ...
                                    ... CRYSTAL GAZER   55 22
    INSOLENT STORM STRIKES AT THE SKULL ....INSOLENT STORM. 325   T
    INSOLENT STORM STRIKES AT THE SKULL, ...INSOLENT STORM. 325   1
STORM-CROSSED (1)
    LIKE A LAST STORM-CROSSED LEAF? BEST GET YOU GONE ......DIALOGUE B.   39 44
STORMING (1)
    STORMING THE HILLTOP. ....BERCK-PLAGE 200 117
STORM-STRUCK (1)
    ON STORM-STRUCK DECK, WIND SIRENS CATERWAUL: ......CHANNEL CROSSING   26   1
STORMY (1)
    OF YOUR STORMY EYE, MAGIC TAKES FLIGHT .................CONVERSATION.   21   7
STORY (1)
    THE OLD STORY. ....BRASILIA 258 15
STORYBOOK (1)
    THESE STORYBOOK VILLAS ....SOUTHERN SUNRISE   26   2
STOUT (2)
    THEY SET THEIR STOUT CHAIRS BACK TO THE ROAD AND FACE THE DARK*NET-. 121   5
    AN EXPLODED BOTTLE OF STOUT, ...A SECRET 220 42
STOVES (1)
    WOOD STOVES BURN WARM AS TOAST. ....YADDO: THE GRAND MANOR 124 17

	TITLE	PAGE	LINE

STRADDLE (1)
    BOAR, FABULOUS ENOUGH TO STRADDLE THAT SOW'S HEAT. ....SOW   61   33
STRAIGHT (9)
    THAT NO STRAIGHT INQUIRING ....FIRESONG   30   11
    THE STRAIGHT MOUTH. ....RECANTATION   42   16
    STRAIGHT INTO YELLOW GLARE ....ELLA MASON AND HER ELEVEN CATS   54   27
    WHERE STRAIGHT TALK IS THE RULE, WHETHER WARM OR HOSTILE, ...
        ... INCOMMUNICADO   100   10
    AND WOULDN'T PAUSE FOR MY STRAIGHT LOOK. ..............RHODODENDRON.   104   25
    OBJECT BESIDE THE MAD, STRAIGHT ROAD ....SLEEP IN THE MOJAVE DESERT   143   6
    THE SUN FLAMED STRAIGHT DOWN THAT NOON ON THE WATER OFF
        MARBLEHEAD. ....THE BABYSITTERS   174   2
    STRAIGHT FROM THE HEART. ....CUT   235   13
    NOW YOU MUST PLAY THE STRAIGHT MAN FOR A TERM ....DIRGE FOR A JOKER   303   13
STRAIGHTFORWARDLY (1)
    STRAIGHTFORWARDLY ACROSS THE SPRINGING GREEN. ......ABOVE THE OXBOW   89   52
STRAINS (1)
    THE CORDIAL STRAINS ....A WINTER'S TALE   87   32
STRAND (1)
    OF THAT MERCURIAL STRAND, THE GIRL GOES DOWN ....THE PRINCESS.   334   27
STRANGE (5)
    FOUNDERED THROUGH LEVELS OF LIGHT SEAGREEN AND STRANGE. OTHER TWO.   68   5
    SOME STRANGE INJURY ....FULL FATHOM FIVE   92   18
    FROM WHAT GRACE AM I FALLEN. TONGUES ARE STRANGE, ...INCOMMUNICADO   100   12
    SHINY AND STRANGE, AS IF HE HAD HURTLED FROM A STAR? ...THREE WOMEN   181   163
    UNTIL NEAR TWELVE THE STRANGE GIRL ALL AT ONCE ....CINDERELLA   304   11
STRANGELY (1)
    INTACT, STRANGELY STRAYED ABOVE ....MUSSEL HUNTER AT ROCK HARBOR   97   70
STRANGENESS (1)
    AND SEEN MY STRANGENESS EVAPORATE, ...STINGS   214   26
STRANGER (1)
    THE STRANGER IN THE LAVATORY MIRROR ....TALE OF A TUB   24   6
STRANGERS (3)
    SURVIVES ARRIVAL; WE WALK THE PLANK WITH STRANGERS.*CHANNEL CROSSING   27   42
    ESCAPED AMONG MOON-PLUMAGED STRANGERS; ....THE SHRIKE   42   14
    EACH CLOCK TICK CONSECRATES THE DEATH OF STRANGERS. DOOM OF EXILES   318   8
STRANGLE (1)
    SO MURDEROUS IN ITS STRANGLE OF BRANCHES? --- ....ELM   193   39
STRATAGEM (1)
    SIGHTING THE STRATAGEM ....AERIALIST   332   37
STRATAGEMS (1)
    THIS WAS A WOMAN: HER LOVES AND STRATAGEMS ....SONNET: TO EVA   304   5
STRAW (8)
    OUR LIMBS' IMAGE ON A FIELD OF STRAW ....IN MIDAS' COUNTRY   99   9
    OF PALE FRONTS, STRAW THATCHINGS, THE HARD ROAD*WHITENESS I REMEMBER   102   20
    GRINDS ROUND, BEARING DOWN WITH THE STRAW, ...HEAVY WOMEN   158   20
    NOW THEY ARE GIVING ME A FASHIONABLE WHITE STRAW ITALIAN HAT ..BEE.   211   21
    THE SWARM IS KNOCKED INTO A COCKED STRAW HAT. ....THE SWARM   217   42
    QUIETLY THROUGH THE STRAW OF THE BOXCARS. ....GETTING THERE   248   11
    STRAW MATS, WHITE WALLS ....BALLOONS   271   12
    O NEVER AGAIN WILL THE EXTRAVAGANT STRAW ....THE PRINCESS.   335   72
STRAWBERRIES (2)
    BITTER STRAWBERRIES ....BITTER STRAWBERRIES   299   T
    AND THE TASTE OF STRAWBERRIES ....BITTER STRAWBERRIES   299   8
STRAWBERRY (1)
    ALL THAT MORNING IN THE STRAWBERRY FIELD ....BITTER STRAWBERRIES   299   1
STRAWS (1)
    SHE WORE HER BROOM STRAWS TO THE NUB. ....POINT SHIRLEY   110   18
STRAY (1)
    HIS GAIT STRAY UNEVEN ....SPINSTER   49   9
STRAYED (1)
    INTACT, STRANGELY STRAYED ABOVE ....MUSSEL HUNTER AT ROCK HARBOR   97   70
STRAYINGS (1)
    RICH IN STRAYINGS WITH EVERY AMOROUS OAF, ...VANITY FAIR   33   17
STREAK (1)
    STREAK AND MOTTLE OF TAWN BARK, ...ON THE PLETHORA OF DRYADS   67   22
STREAKED (1)
    IN THESE LITTLE BOUDOIRS STREAKED WITH ORANGE AND RED BEEKEEPER'S.   118   10
STREAKS (1)
    QUIVER IN THIN STREAKS ....AQUATIC NOCTURNE   305   4
STREAM (4)
    OUT IN A CONVERGING STREAM ....MUSSEL HUNTER AT ROCK HARBOR   96   40
    AND THOUGH YOUR GRACIOUSNESS MIGHT STREAM, ...POINT SHIRLEY   111   44
    THE STREAM THAT HUSTLES US ....THE BURNT-OUT SPA   138   33
    TILL UNRULY CHILDREN STREAM DOWN THE SKY ....SONG FOR A REVOLU.   323   14
STREAMING (4)
    THROUGH AIR STREAMING AND GREEN-LIT, ...THE GREAT CARBUNCLE   72   2
    GREEN GRASS STREAMING, HOUSES A RIVER ....WHITENESS I REMEMBER   102   19
    TAILS STREAMING AGAINST THE GREEN ....THE EYE-MOTE   109   3
    STREAMING BETWEEN MY WALLS? ....THE OTHER   201   4
STREET (16)
    MERE BRUIT OF HER TAKES OUR STREET ....STRUMPET SONG   33   5
    STREET SONG ....STREET SONG   35   T
    THRONGING SIDEWALK, STREET, ...STREET SONG   35   3
    THE MIDNIGHT STREET ....SOLILOQUY OF THE SOLIPSIST   37   3

	TITLE	PAGE	LINE

STREET (CONT.)
SUCH A RACKET OF ECHOES FROM THE STEELY STREET, ...HARDCASTLE CRAGS 62 2
ON WINTER STREET, ON TEMPLE PLACE. ....A WINTER'S TALE 87 17
FROM CHARLES STREET TO THE CUSTOM HOUSE, ...A WINTER'S TALE 87 35
UP PLEASANT STREET AT MAIN. POISING THEIR SHAPES ...ABOVE THE OXBOW 88 12
CLOCKS BELLED TWELVE. MAIN STREET SHOWED OTHERWISE ....OWL 101 1
TO TIMOROUS CHILDREN, TO THE LADY ON THE STREET. ..THE RAVAGED FACE 116 13
NO MAP TRACES THE STREET ....THE SLEEPERS 122 1
THE TREES WITHER IN THE STREET. THE RAIN IS CORROSIVE. THREE WOMEN 180 135
A DULL POM, POM IN THE SUNDAY STREET. ....THE SWARM 215 2
AND THE SPIDERY WATER-DAZZLE ON FIELD AND STREET. ....LYONNESSE 234 18
BLUE AS LIZARD-SCALES. FROST SHEENS THE STREET. ....DIALOGUE O. 286 340
OUTSIDE IN THE STREET I HEAR ....FAMILY REUNION 300 1
STREETLIGHT (1)
SUDDENLY TURNS, TURNS COLOR. THE STREETLIGHT ....LETTER IN NOVEMBER 253 2
STREETLIGHTS (1)
OF STREETLIGHTS AND WIRES, ITS WALL TO WALL ....OWL 102 11
STREETS (5)
AND SO WE SAIL TOWARD CITIES, STREETS AND HOMES ..CHANNEL CROSSING 27 37
THE STREETS MAY TURN TO PAPER SUDDENLY, BUT I RECOVER ..THREE WOMEN 187 365
THE STREETS ARE LIZARDY CREVICES ....GIGOLO 267 2
FROM GRAY CHILD FACES CRYING IN THE STREETS. ....FEMALE AUTHOR 301 14
STREETS CRACK THROUGH IN HAVOC-SPLIT RAVINES ....DOOMSDAY 316 7
STREET'S (1)
FRAMED IN WINDOWS OF MAIN STREET'S ....NIGHT SHIFT 76 15
STRENGTH (1)
I'M COLLECTING MY STRENGTH: ONE DAY I SHALL MANAGE WITHOUT HER, ...
... IN PLASTER 160 55
STRENGTHEN (1)
STRENGTHEN THAT ORCHARD THEREBY." ....CRYSTAL GAZER 55 24
STRETCH (1)
IT BOILS FOR FORTY HOURS AT A STRETCH. ....THE TOUR 238 30
STRETCHED (1)
AND THE SHADOW STRETCHED, THE LIGHTS WENT OUT.*THE DISQUIETING MUSES 75 32
STRETCHES (2)
IT STRETCHES FOR MILES, THE SHRUNK VOICES ....BERCK-PLAGE 196 8
IT STRETCHES INTO THE DISTANCE. IT WILL BE EATEN NEVERTHELESS. ...
... TOTEM 264 2
STRETCHING (2)
AFTER THE HORIZONS, STRETCHING THE NARROWED EYE ....ABOVE THE OXBOW 88 25
STRETCHING ITS FINE, IRRITATING SAND IN ALL DIRECTIONS. ..INSOMNIAC 163 7
STREW (2)
SHALL STREW BROADCAST SO RARE A SEED ON WIND ...WREATH FOR A BRIDAL 45 20
TO STREW LIKE CONFETTI ....FIESTA MELONS 47 17
STREWING (1)
THE TREES AND FLOWERS HAVE BEEN STREWING THEIR COOL ODORS.*VERTICAL. 162 12
STRICKEN (2)
PARADES THE MARKETPLACE, LURID AND STRICKEN ....THE RAVAGED FACE 115 2
WHILE STRICKEN PATIENTS LET HIM HAVE HIS SAY; ..NEVER TRY TO TRICK. 320 8
STRICT (9)
UNDER THE STRICT MASK OF HIS AGONY. ....CHANNEL CROSSING 26 12
NOT OF STAUNCHING SUCH STRICT FLAME, BUT COME, ...FIRESONG 30 20
EXACTED HER FIRST SIMPLE SIGHT FOR THIS STRICT SECOND.*CRYSTAL GAZER 55 30
NOW, DISCIPLINED IN THE STRICT ANCESTRAL CHAIR, ...THE TRIAL OF MAN 312 12
TEMPO OF STRICT OCEAN ....TRIO OF LOVE SONGS 314 9
DOWN AMONG STRICT ROOTS AND ROCKS, ...DANSE MACABRE 320 1
OF STRICT AND SACRED SKELETON; INSOLENT STORM STRIKES AT THE SKULL 325 8
NOW KISS AGAIN: TILL OUR STRICT FATHER LEANS ....LOVE IS A PARALLAX 330 43
FROM BED TO STRICT TRYOUTS ....AERIALIST 331 5
STRICKEN (1)
WE DREAMED THEIR ARGUMENTS, THEIR STRICKEN VOICES. ...THE OTHER TWO 69 29
STRIDING (1)
OUR LADY OF THE SHIPWRECKED IS STRIDING TOWARD THE HORIZON, ...
... FINISTERRE 169 19
STRIKE (7)
IN RITUAL, TO STRIKE -- IS DEFINITELY GONE; ....TALE OF A TUB 25 22
KNOCKING OUR BROTHERS DOWN, WE STRIKE A STANCE ....CHANNEL CROSSING 27 27
AT GORGON-PROSPECTS WITH POWER TO STRIKE TO STONE ....CRYSTAL GAZER 55 41
SUN MANAGES TO STRIKE SUCH TIN GLINTS ....PARLIAMENT HILL FIELDS 152 10
THOSE GLASS BITS IN THE GRATE STRIKE ME CHILL: ....DIALOGUE O. 285 306
LEST THE LIGHTNING STRIKE YOU TO CINDER. ...GO GET THE GOODLY SQUAB 313 8
FOR DEADLY SECRETS STRIKE WHEN UNDERSTOOD ....ADMONITIONS 319 16
STRIKES (4)
STRIKES THE TILES OF THE NEIGHBORS' GABLE-TOPS ....DIALOGUE O. 286 339
INSOLENT STORM STRIKES AT THE SKULL ....INSOLENT STORM. 325 T
INSOLENT STORM STRIKES AT THE SKULL, ...INSOLENT STORM. 325 1
SUNLIGHT STRIKES A GLASS OF GRAPEFRUIT JUICE, ..MORNING IN THE HOS. 332 1
STRIKING (3)
SHEEN OF THE NOON SUN STRIKING ....SONG FOR A SUMMER'S DAY 31 11
DEATH AS STRIKING ROOT ON ONE LAND-TRACT; ....LANDOWNERS 53 14
BACKDROP OF SYCAMORES. SUN WAS STRIKING ....THE EYE-MOTE 109 4
STRING (5)
A SALLOW PIECE OF STRING HELD IT TOGETHER. ....TWO VIEWS. 114 9
THE SPIDER ON ITS OWN STRING ....THE MANOR GARDEN 125 16
MOONY BALLOONS TIED BY A STRING ....ON DECK 143 34

	TITLE	PAGE	LINE

STRING (CONT.)
I AM HELPLESS AS THE SEA AT THE END OF HER STRING. .....THREE WOMEN 182 188
IS IT BLOOD CLOTS THE TENDRILS ARE DRAGGING UP THAT STRING? ...BEE. 211 19
STRINGENCIES (1)
DEAD HANDS, DEAD STRINGENCIES. ....ARIEL 239 21
STRINGENT (1)
HIS BRUSH IN THE STRINGENT AIR. ....MAGNOLIA SHOALS 122 20
STRINGS (3)
PUPPETS, LOOSED FROM THE STRINGS OF THE PUPPET-MASTER, ...POEM.5.F. 135 13
WITH NO STRINGS ATTACHED. ....GULLIVER 251 8
ON ENVIOUS STRINGS, AND YOU ARE THE CENTER. ....STINGS/DR 293 3
STRIP (2)
FROM A GROSS COMIC STRIP, AND TOWARD .....ON THE DECLINE OF ORACLES 78 24
THE BIG STRIP TEASE. ....LADY LAZARUS 245 29
STRIPED (2)
WHERE BEES, STRIPED BLACK AND GOLD, SLEEP OUT THE BLIZZARD ...
... ELECTRA ON AZALEA PATH 116 3
ON A STRIPED MATTRESS IN ONE ROOM ....BERCK-PLAGE 198 50
STRIPES (5)
LACED OVER WITH STRIPES ....FIESTA MELONS 46 6
WITH TIGERY STRIPES, AND A FACE ON IT ....LAST WORDS 172 2
AND THE SEVEN-YEAR-OLD WOULDN'T GO OUT UNLESS HIS JERSEY
STRIPES ....THE BABYSITTERS 174 8
MATCHED THE STRIPES OF HIS SOCKS. ....THE BABYSITTERS 174 9
STRIPES FOR MOUTH AND EYES AND NOSE, ...THE FEARFUL 256 6
STRIPS (2)
STRIPS OF TINFOIL WINKING LIKE PEOPLE, ...THE BEE MEETING 211 16
COY PAPER STRIPS FOR DOORS -- ....LESBOS 227 5
STRIVES (1)
IT STRIVES AFTER THEM WITH ITS LIGHTS. ....THREE WOMEN 186 346
STRIVING (1)
WATER STRIVING ....WORDS 270 8
STRODE (1)
STONES, STRODE OUT IN YOUR DEAD ....MAN IN BLACK 120 16
STROKE (2)
TO CONQUER CINDER'S KINGDOM IN THE STROKE OF AN HOUR *EPITAPH FOR F. 45 20
AFTER WHOSE STROKE THE WOOD RINGS, ...WORDS 270 2
STROLL (3)
COLORED BEADS ON THE STRUNG ROADS, AND THE PEOPLE STROLL ....OXBOW. 89 51
WHILE THE STUDENTS STROLL OR SIT,*WATERCOLOR OF GRANTCHESTER MEADOWS 112 24
WE STROLL THROUGH A MAZE OF PALE ....MAGNOLIA SHOALS 121 2
STROLLING (1)
A MELON STROLLING ON TWO TENDRILS. ....METAPHORS 116 3
STRONGEST (1)
THE STRONGEST WILL SEEMED A WILL TOWARD CEREMONY. OBESE, DARK- ...
... THE GORING 47 4
STRONGHOLD (1)
FOR STRONGHOLD AGAINST THEIR STIFF ....THE THIN PEOPLE 65 42
STRUCK (8)
CAN BE STRUCK FROM ROCK TO MAKE HEART'S WASTE ....WINTER LANDSCAPE, 22 14
STRUCK BY EACH DOUR YEAR. ....STRUMPET SONG 34 13
FOUND HERSELF, OF A SUDDEN, INTOLERABLY STRUCK ....SPINSTER 49 4
FLINTLIKE, HER FEET STRUCK ....HARDCASTLE CRAGS 62 1
BEEN STRUCK TO KEEP ALL GLORY IN THE GRIP ....VIRGIN IN A TREE 82 32
SUN STRUCK THE WATER LIKE A DAMNATION. ....SUICIDE OFF EGG ROCK 115 6
DIFFICULT TO IMAGINE HOW FURY STRUCK -- ....BLUE MOLES 126 17
A SCOWL OF SUN STRUCK DOWN MY MOTHER, ...LAMENT 315 10
STRUCTURAL (1)
WITH STRUCTURAL DISCIPLINE: ....NOTES TO A NEOPHYTE 306 9
STRUGGLE (1)
AND SUFFERED THEIR LIVELIER FELLOWS TO STRUGGLE. ....SPIDER 49 21
STRUMPET (1)
STRUMPET SONG ....STRUMPET SONG 33 T
STRUNG (3)
COLORED BEADS ON THE STRUNG ROADS, AND THE PEOPLE STROLL ....OXBOW. 89 51
AT LEAST I WON'T BE STRUNG JUST UNDER THE SURFACE, ...BURNING. 204 23
OF PAN'S PRONOUNCEMENTS, AND OUR NERVES ARE STRUNG .....DIALOGUE O. 284 288
STRUT (2)
OH NO, FOR I STRUT IT CLEVER ....STREET SONG 36 11
VERNACULAR AS THE STRUT ....NOTES TO A NEOPHYTE 306 4
STRUTS (3)
SHE, ADDLED IN HER GOOSE-WIT, STRUTS ....RHYME 50 4
THE RAFTERS AND STRUTS OF HIS BODY WEAR ....THE BURNT-OUT SPA 138 6
WITH STRUTS AND PROPS OF THE HOLY STAGE. ....SONG FOR A REVOLU. 323 8
STUBBORN (9)
WAVES WALLOP, ASSAULTING THE STUBBORN HULL. ....CHANNEL CROSSING 26 4
I'VE GOT A STUBBORN GOOSE WHOSE GUT'S ....RHYME 50 1
THE SCENE STANDS STUBBORN: SKINFLINT TREES ......NOVEMBER GRAVEYARD 56 1
TREKKING STUBBORN THROUGH THIS SEASON ..BLACK ROOK IN RAINY WEATHER 57 33
THE CLASSIC LIMBS OF STUBBORN ANTIGONE? ....PERSEUS 83 40
STOOD STUBBORN IN ITS JUNGLE: RED AGAINST GREEN, ...YADWIGHA. 85 18
I SEE HIM ONE-TRACKED, STUBBORN, WHITE HORSE, WHITENESS I REMEMBER 102 12
TILL HER STUBBORN BODY BURNS. ....DANSE MACABRE 321 15
SPINNING A SINGLE STUBBORN THREAD OF WOOL ....THE PRINCESS. 333 16

486

	TITLE	PAGE	LINE

STUBBORNLY (2)
STUBBORNLY HANGING ON TO MY NAME AND ADDRESS. ....TULIPS 161 23
STILL, STUBBORNLY WE TRY TO CRACK THE NUT ....DOOM OF EXILES 318 13
STUBBORNNESS (1)
"CAN THERE BE SUCH STUBBORNNESS --*DIALOGUE BETWEEN GHOST AND PRIEST 39 42
STUB-NECKED (1)
GREY WAVES THE STUB-NECKED EIDERS RIDE. ....POINT SHIRLEY 110 33
STUCCO (2)
STUCCO SOCKET ....POINT SHIRLEY 110 21
STUCCO ARCHES, THE BANKED ROCKS SUNNING IN ROWS, ...WHITSUN 153 2
STUCK (9)
IN THIS PROVINCE OF THE STUCK RECORD ....THE TIMES ARE TIDY 107 2
WHEN THE SPLINTER FLEW IN AND STUCK MY EYE, ...THE EYE-MOTE 109 9
IT STICKS, AND IT HAS STUCK A WEEK. ....THE EYE-MOTE 109 21
THE TONGUE STUCK IN MY JAW. ....DADDY 223 25
IT STUCK IN A BARB WIRE SNARE. ....DADDY 223 26
AND THEY STUCK ME TOGETHER WITH GLUE. ....DADDY 224 62
YOU HAVE STUCK HER KITTENS OUTSIDE YOUR WINDOW ....LESBOS 227 12
STARS STUCK ALL OVER, BRIGHT STUPID CONFETTI. ....YEARS 255 8
STUCK TO HER TRIPOD, OVER THE FUMING CREVICE, ...DIALOGUE O. 286 349
STUD (1)
THEIR DEATH-PEGS STUD YOUR GLOVES, IT IS NO USE RUNNING. STINGS/DR 293 8
STUDDED (2)
AND THE OPULENT AIR GO STUDDED WITH SEED, ...CONJURING. 66 36
HANGING SHYLY UNDER THE STUDDED HORIZON ....STARS OVER THE DORDOGNE 165 19
STUDDING (1)
EACH WEDGE WEARS A STUDDING ....FIESTA MELONS 47 15
STUDENTS (2)
WHILE THE STUDENTS STROLL OR SIT,*WATERCOLOR OF GRANTCHESTER MEADOWS 112 24
THE ART STUDENTS IN WEST BERLIN. ....ON DECK 143 24
STUDIOS (1)
GUESTS IN THE STUDIOS ....YADDO: THE GRAND MANOR 123 11
STUDY (5)
STUDY WINDOWS BELLIED IN ....THE DISQUIETING MUSES 75 18
THAT'S SOMETHING TO STUDY EVEN IF IT'S NOT ....DIALOGUE O. 279 108
THAT LET ME INTO BLUEBEARD'S STUDY; ....BLUEBEARD 305 2
THAT LET ME INTO BLUEBEARD'S STUDY. ....BLUEBEARD 305 8
IS MANGLED BY STUDY ....MOONSONG AT MORNING 317 31
STUFF (5)
OF PALE BLUE VITREOUS STUFF, OPAQUE ....THE BURNT-OUT SPA 137 4
I WALK AMONG THEM, AND THEY STUFF MY MOUTH WITH COTTON. FINISTERRE 169 11
A ROUGH, DUMB COUNTRY STUFF ....BY CANDLELIGHT 236 3
THOUGH IT LOOKS LIKE A CAT, WITH ITS FLUFFY STUFF, PURE WHITE.*TOUR. 237 16
COAL GAS IS GHASTLY STUFF. ....THE TOUR 238 26
STUFFED (3)
THE STUFFED SHAPE OF HER FLOWN MATE ....THE SHRIKE 42 13
AND THE STUFFED EXPRESSION, BUT GOES ON ....BURNING THE LETTERS 205 53
YOU: A PRIEST-BAKED PASTY STUFFED TO THE BRIM ....DIALOGUE O. 282 214
STUMBLE (2)
ONE CRY, AND I STUMBLE FROM BED, COW-HEAVY AND FLORAL MORNING SONG 157 13
YOU STUMBLE OUT, ...A SECRET 220 44
STUMBLERS (1)
THE BLUNT, CLUMSY STUMBLERS, THE BOORS. ....WINTERING 219 41
STUMP (1)
THUMB STUMP. ....CUT 236 40
STUMPS (1)
OLD BLOOD OF LIMB STUMPS, BURNT HEARTS. ....BERCK-PLAGE 200 99
STUN (1)
TO STUN SKY BLACK OUT, DRIVE GIBBERING MAD ....CONJURING. 66 12
STUNG (4)
CRUEL NETTLES STUNG HER ANKLES RAW. ....BUCOLICS 24 16
A SCORPION STUNG ITS HEAD, AN ILL-STARRED THING; ....ELECTRA ON. 117 35
HORSEFLIES BUZZED, PAUSED AND STUNG........BITTER STRAWBERRIES 299 7
AND STUNG ACCORDING TO THE WITCH'S PLAN, ...THE PRINCESS. 333 9
STUNNED (2)
STUNNED THE MARROW. MEN IN WHITE ....NIGHT SHIFT 77 20
THE HONEY-FEAST OF THE BERRIES HAS STUNNED THEM; THEY BELIEVE
IN HEAVEN. ....BLACKBERRYING 169 17
STUNT (1)
THEY STUNT LIKE CLOWNS IN THE CIRCUS. ....IN MIDAS' COUNTRY 100 20
STUPID (3)
I COULDN'T UNDERSTAND HER STUPID BEHAVIOR! ....IN PLASTER 159 11
STUPID PUPIL, IT HAS TO TAKE EVERYTHING IN. ....TULIPS 160 10
STARS STUCK ALL OVER, BRIGHT STUPID CONFETTI. ....YEARS 255 8
STUPIDITY (1)
AND I LOVE YOUR STUPIDITY, ...FOR A FATHERLESS SON 205 7
STUPIDLY (3)
AND THEY STUPIDLY STARE, AND DO NOT SPEAK OF HER. ....STILLBORN 142 15
I TRESPASS STUPIDLY. LET BE, LET BE. ....PHEASANT 191 24
I AM SO STUPIDLY HAPPY, ...LETTER IN NOVEMBER 253 13
STURDY (1)
CAN ONLY HAUNT. STURDY AS POTATOES, ...POEMS, POTATOES 106 4
STY (1)
MAZE OF BARNS TO THE LINTEL OF THE SUNK STY DOOR ....SOW 60 9

<pre>
                                           TITLE   PAGE LINE
STY-FACE (1)
   MUD-SUMP, HAPPY STY-FACE. POEM.4.BEAST. 134 17
SUAVE (4)
   OF ASPARAGUS HEADS. CARS RUN THEIR SUAVE ....AVOVE THE OXBOW   89 50
   GOT UP TO LET THE SUAVE BLUE POLICEMAN IN. ....THE TRIAL OF MAN 312   8
   THE SUAVE DISSEMBLING COBRA WEARS A HOOD ....ADMONITIONS 319 10
   THE SUAVE ETERNAL SERPENTS PROMISE BLISS ....NEVER TRY TO TRICK. 320 13
SUAVELY (1)
   MOST SOFT, MOST SUAVELY GLIDES THAT STEP, ...PURSUIT   22   5
SUBDUE (1)
   SHE CAME, AND CALLED HELL TO SUBDUE AN UNRULY MAN ....SNOWMAN O.   59 23
SUBDUED (1)
   THE WORLD SUBDUED TO HIS RUN OF IT. ....WHITENESS I REMEMBER 103 27
SUBJECTS (2)
   WHILE SUBJECTS HUNGERED, EMPTY-PURSED, ...NATURAL HISTORY   71   5
   THE MOON, TOO, ABASES HER SUBJECTS, ...THE RIVAL 166 11
SUBJUGATING (1)
   SMILING AT THIS BEHAVIOR, SUBJUGATING THEIR ENEMIES ....LESSON.   80 22
SUBPOENA (1)
   AND TOOK THE WOMAN'S BRIGHT SUBPOENA ....THE DREAM 311 26
SUBSTANCE (2)
   INDIGENOUS PEACE. SUCH SUBSTANCE MAKES ....LANDOWNERS   53 11
   TO THE HARDEST SUBSTANCE KNOWN. ....NOTES TO A NEOPHYTE 307 24
SUBSTANCELESS (1)
   THEN THE SUBSTANCELESS BLUE ....ARIEL 239   2
SUBSTANCES (1)
   OOZING THEIR JAMMY SUBSTANCES, ...THE SURGEON AT 2 A.M. 170 12
SUBTLE (4)
   THEY ARE SUBTLE: THEY SEEM TO FLOAT, THOUGH THEY WEIGH ME DOWN, ...
                                                   ... TULIPS 161 40
   I AM NOT SUBTLE ....BURNING THE LETTERS 204   9
   BY SCOLDINGS, OR BY SUBTLE PRAISE. ONLY I, ...DIALOGUE O. 280 144
   AND LOST IN SUBTLE METAPHOR, RETREATS ....FEMALE AUTHOR 301 13
SUBURB (1)
   THAN ITS SUBURB OF WOODS: NIMBUS- ....OWL 101   2
SUBURBS (1)
   THESE STILLED SUBURBS: NOBODY ....NIGHT SHIFT   76   9
SUBVERSION (1)
   AND HE, FOR THIS SUBVERSION, ...THE JAILER 227 28
SUCCEED (1)
   SUCCEED IN BANKING THEIR FIRES ....WINTERING 219 47
SUCCINCT (1)
   NO SUCCINCT GABRIEL FROM THE LETTERS HERE ....OUIJA   78 31
SUCH (83)
   WITH SUCH BLIGHT WROUGHT ON OUR BANKRUPT ESTATE, ...CONVERSATION.   21 13
   FROM SUCH ASSAULT OF RADIANCE. ....PURSUIT   23 44
   MAYDAY: TWO CAME TO FIELD IN SUCH WISE: ....BUCOLICS   23   1
   SUCH POVERTY ASSAULTS THE EGO; CAUGHT ....TALE OF A TUB   24   4
   SUCH STARKNESS; ACCURACY MUST NOT STALK AT LARGE: ....TALE OF A TUB   25 35
   SUCH FORCE CAN LAST; BUT BEYOND, THE NEUTRAL VIEW   CHANNEL CROSSING   26   7
   LEAPS TO LAUD SUCH MAN'S BLOOD! ....ODE FOR TED   30 24
   NOT OF STAUNCHING SUCH STRICT FLAME, BUT COME, ...FIRESONG   30 20
   WALKS THERE NOT SOME SUCH ONE MAN ....STRUMPET SONG   34 14
   GOD ORDAINED TO FOLLOW UP YOUR DAYS. IS IT SUCH TROUBLE *DIALOGUE B.   39 25
   "CAN THERE BE SUCH STUBBORNNESS --*DIALOGUE BETWEEN GHOST AND PRIEST   39 42
   (WITH HEAT SUCH AS NO MAN COULD HAVE ....THE GLUTTON   40   3
   SUCH ROYAL DREAMS BECKON THIS MAN ....THE SHRIKE   42   2
   SUCH PACT AS IS MADE ONCE ONLY; WHAT MATTER ....WREATH FOR A BRIDAL   44   2
   HOWEVER YOU MAY SWEAT TO HOLD SUCH DARLING WRECKS ...EPITAPH FOR F.   45 13
   SUCH A BARRICADE OF BARB AND CHECK ....SPINSTER   50 26
   BY SUCH A ROGUE'S ....RHYME   50 15
   RETROSPECT SHALL NOT SOFTEN SUCH PENURY -- ....DEPARTURE   51   9
   INDIGENOUS PEACE. SUCH SUBSTANCE MAKES ....LANDOWNERS   53 11
   SUCH STENTORIAN CATS! ....ELLA MASON AND HER ELEVEN CATS   54 24
   SUCH POVERTY. NO DEAD MEN'S CRIES ....NOVEMBER GRAVEYARD   56   6
   EACH HEDGE WITH SUCH WHITE BLOOM ASTOUNDS OUR EYES ....MAYFLOWER   60   6
   SUCH A RACKET OF ECHOES FROM THE STEELY STREET, ...HARDCASTLE CRAGS   62   2
   SPURNS SUCH FICTION ......ON THE DIFFICULTY OF CONJURING UP A DRYAD   66 29
   AND SUCH GRIT CORRUPTS MY EYES ....ON THE PLETHORA OF DRYADS   67 31
   BURDENED IN SUCH A WAY WE SEEMED THE LIGHTER -- ......THE OTHER TWO   69 32
   SOME SUCH TRANSFIGURING MOVED ....THE GREAT CARBUNCLE   72   9
   WORTHLESS SUCH VISION TO EYES GONE DULL ..ON THE DECLINE OF ORACLES   78 30
   BUT BY SUCH ABUSES ....A LESSON IN VENGEANCE   80   6
   BE CERTAIN SOME SUCH PACT'S ....VIRGIN IN A TREE   82 31
   TO FEED HIS EYE WITH RED: SUCH RED! UNDER THE MOON, ...YADWIGHA.   86 38
   OF SUCH SEEING UP THE LEAF-SHUTTERED ESCARPMENTS, ..ABOVE THE OXBOW   88 27
   DIDN'T GO DOWN IN SUCH A HURRY. HOW IT MEMOIRS OF A SPINACH-PICKER   89   2
   OF THE OCEAN. SUCH SAGE HUMOR AND ....FULL FATHOM FIVE   93 29
   SUCH MEETINGS NEVER OCCUR IN MARCHEN ................INCOMMUNICADO 100   8
   SUCH COLLUSION OF MULISH ELEMENTS ....POINT SHIRLEY 110 17
   HOW IN SUCH MILD AIR ....WATERCOLOR OF GRANTCHESTER MEADOWS 112 27
   TO CREATE SUCH A RUIN. ....THE COLOSSUS 130 23
   THERE WERE SUCH ENORMOUS FLOWERS, ...POEM.1.WHO. 132 29
   SUCH EELISH DELVINGS! POEM.2.DARK. 132   9
   WHAT GIRL EVER FLOURISHED IN SUCH COMPANY? ....MAGI 148 18
</pre>

	TITLE	PAGE	LINE

SUCH (CONT.)
SUN MANAGES TO STRIKE SUCH TIN GLINTS ....PARLIAMENT HILL FIELDS   152   10
SUCH A LUXURY OF STARS WOULD EMBARRASS ME.   STARS OVER THE DORDOGNE 166   27
FOR A LIFE IN SUCH COMPANY; ....WUTHERING HEIGHTS   168   41
I HAD NOT ASKED FOR SUCH A BLOOD SISTERHOOD; THEY MUST LOVE ME.   ...
                                               ... BLACKBERRYING   168   8
SUCH AS FINGERS MIGHT EMBROIDER, CLOSE TO DEATH, ...FINISTERRE   169   11
SUCH FLATNESS CANNOT BE HOLY. ....THREE WOMEN   179   89
THEY PAINT SUCH SECRETS IN ARABIC, CHINESE! ....THREE WOMEN   179   98
CAN SUCH INNOCENCE KILL AND KILL? IT MILKS MY LIFE. ....THREE WOMEN   180 134
THAT AT SUCH A DISTANCE FROM US SHINE AND WHIRL. ....THREE WOMEN   182 210
IT UTTERS SUCH DARK SOUNDS IT CANNOT BE GOOD. ....THREE WOMEN   182 217
IT IS USUAL, THEY SAY, FOR SUCH A THING TO HAPPEN. .....THREE WOMEN   183 242
WITH SUCH SORROW IN ITS VOICE? ....THREE WOMEN   186 349
SUCH A DARK FUNNEL, MY FATHER! ....LITTLE FUGUE   188   22
SUCH BLUE CURRENTS IN THE VEINS OF MY LOVED ONE! .....AN APPEARANCE   189   2
O HEART, SUCH DISORGANIZATION! ....AN APPEARANCE   189   16
ARE YOU NOT BLINDED BY SUCH EXPRESSIONLESS SIRENS?   CROSSING THE W.   190   11
THEY BOW AND STAND: THEY SUFFER SUCH ATTACKS! ...AMONG THE NARCISSI   190   9
IT IS SUCH A GOOD SHAPE, SO VIVID. ....PHEASANT   191   19
A WIND OF SUCH VIOLENCE ....ELM   192   20
IS IT FOR SUCH I AGITATE MY HEART? ....ELM   193   36
SUCH SALT-SWEETNESS. WHY SHOULD I WALK ....BERCK-PLAGE   197   40
WERE THERE NOT SUCH A DIN IN IT. ....THE ARRIVAL OF THE BEE BOX   212   5
SUCH YELLOW SULLEN SMOKES ....FEVER.   231   14
THERE IS NOTHING TO DO WITH SUCH A BEAUTIFUL BLANK BUT
   SMOOTH IT. ....AMNESIAC   232   2
EVEN THE SUN-CLOUDS THIS MORNING CANNOT MANAGE SUCH SKIRTS.*POP.OCT.   240   1
HERE THERE IS SUCH MUD. ....GETTING THERE   248   21
SUCH PURE LEAPS AND SPIRALS --- ....THE NIGHT DANCES   249   5
HAVE SUCH A SPACE TO CROSS, ...THE NIGHT DANCES   250   16
SUCH COLDNESS, FORGETFULNESS. ....THE NIGHT DANCES   250   17
SUCH QUEER MOONS WE LIVE WITH ....BALLOONS   271   10
INSTEAD OF BREWING US SUCH A BALDERDASH *DIALOGUE OVER A OUIJA BOARD   279   97
I NEVER KNEW SUCH CREDULITY TO PITCH ...DIALOGUE OVER A OUIJA BOARD   280 154
SUCH SKEPTIC CRACKS. WITH SENSE SEALED WATERTIGHT .....DIALOGUE O.   280 155
POOLS, PROPHECIES AND SUCH FROM THE UNFATHOMED ....DIALOGUE O.   282 240
COUNTS. SUCH DUELS INFECT BEST FRIENDSHIPS. PAN ....DIALOGUE O.   283 271
TO SUCH CROSS-PURPOSES? AT LAST YOU GLIMPSE ....DIALOGUE O.   284 289
SUCH A WASTE OF BRIGHTNESS I CAN'T UNDERSTAND. ....QUEEN MARY'S.   290   7
THE MEANINGLESS CRY OF BABIES. SUCH A SEA ....FEVER./DR   294   4
SUCH AS PREGNANCY OR CONSTIPATION ....APRIL 18   301   5
FOR SUCH A TEMPERING TASK, ...NOTES TO A NEOPHYTE   306   13
SUCH SOPHISTRY CAN PLACATE US. ..........METAMORPHOSES OF THE MOON   307   30
FOR BEING SUCH A RUDE ASSAILANT ....THE DREAM   311   16
SUCHLIKE (1)
SNOW, CHALK OR SUCHLIKE. THEY'RE ....MAGI   148   5
SUCK (6)
SPIKE AND SUCK OUT ....THE SHRIKE   42   22
OF MINE, YET KIN SHE IS: SHE'LL SUCK ....ALL THE DEAD DEARS   70   16
AND SUCK OF THE GRAY SEA ....MAN IN BLACK   119   3
I SUCK AT THE PAPS OF DARKNESS. POEM.7.S.   136   18
THE PARTICLES OF DESTRUCTION I SUCK UP? AM I A PULSE ...THREE WOMEN   177   38
THAT YOU SUCK BREATH LIKE MILEAGE? ....THE OTHER   202   24
SUCKING (3)
SUCKING UP MINERALS AND MOTHERLY LOVE ....I AM VERTICAL   162   3
TOUCHING AND SUCKING. ....MEDUSA   225   20
FLAPPING AND SUCKING, BLOOD-LOVING BAT. ....LESBOS   229   80
SUCKLE (1)
SHROUDED TO SUCKLE DARKNESS? ONLY THEY ....VIRGIN IN A TREE   81   24
SUCKLING (1)
THIS WAS NO ROSE-AND-LARKSPURRED CHINA SUCKLING ....SOW   60   11
SUCKS (3)
THE GLASS MOUTH SUCKS BLOOD-HEAT FROM MY FOREFINGER. ....OUIJA   77   10
THE CROWD SUCKS HER LAST TEAR AND TURNS AWAY. ....AFTERMATH   114   14
THE SEA SUCKS OBSESSIVELY. ....CONTUSION   271   5
SUDDEN (8)
RICH, BROWN, SUDDEN IN SUNGLINT. ....ODE FOR TED   29   12
HAULED SUDDEN FROM SOLITUDE, ...DIALOGUE BETWEEN GHOST AND PRIEST   38   7
PLUCKED BACK THUS SUDDEN TO THAT FAR INNOCENCE, ...DREAM WITH C.   44   21
FOUND HERSELF, OF A SUDDEN, INTOLERABLY STRUCK ....SPINSTER   49   4
I STALLED AT SUDDEN NOISY CRASHES*FABLE OF THE RHODODENDRON STEALERS   103   18
UPSETTING ME WITH THEIR SUDDEN TONGUES AND THEIR COLOR, ...TULIPS   161   41
FROM BETWEEN TWO HILLS A SUDDEN WIND FUNNELS AT ME, ..BLACKBERRYING   169   20
DON'T KNOW WHAT TO MAKE OF THE SUDDEN SLIPPINESS, ...NEW YEAR ON.   176   4
SUDDENLY (8)
SUDDENLY AT MY ELBOW. I ONLY KNOW THAT A ROOK ....BLACK ROOK I.   57   27
OR TO TRY ME HE SUDDENLY SET ....WHITENESS I REMEMBER   102   18
YOU ARE SO WHITE, SUDDENLY." AND I SAID NOTHING. ....THREE WOMEN   177   23
I AM SO VULNERABLE SUDDENLY. ....THREE WOMEN   184 269
THE STREETS MAY TURN TO PAPER SUDDENLY, BUT I RECOVER ..THREE WOMEN   187 365
SUDDENLY TURNS, TURNS COLOR. THE STREETLIGHT ....LETTER IN NOVEMBER   253   2
FAVORED (WHILE SUDDENLY THE RAINS BEGIN ....FEMALE AUTHOR   301   2
SUDDENLY A BRAZEN SONG IS HEARD ....THE PRINCESS AND THE GOBLINS   334   44

	TITLE	PAGE	LINE

SUE (1)
     IN IMPOTENCE, TO SUE FOR PEACE, *INSOLENT STORM STRIKES AT THE SKULL   325   4
SUEDE (2)
     BLUE SUEDE A DOG OR FOX HAS CHEWED. ....BLUE MOLES   126   4
     SOFT SUEDE TONGUES BETWEEN HIS BONES. ....THE BURNT-OUT SPA   138   11
SUFFER (1)
     THEY BOW AND STAND: THEY SUFFER SUCH ATTACKS! ...AMONG THE NARCISSI   190   9
SUFFERED (3)
     AND SUFFERED THEIR LIVELIER FELLOWS TO STRUGGLE. ....SPIDER   49   21
     AND APPEARS TO HAVE SUFFERED A SORT OF PRIVATE BLITZKRIEG. ..A LIFE   150   24
     I HAVE SUFFERED THE ATROCITY OF SUNSETS. ....ELM   192   16
SUFFERER (1)
     OF AN ETERNAL SUFFERER. TO YOU ....PERSEUS   83   46
SUFFERING (2)
     THE TRIUMPH OF WIT OVER SUFFERING ....PERSEUS   82   ST
     WITH SUFFERING FROM CONCEPTION UPWARDS, AND THERE ....PERSEUS   83   26
SUFFERING-TOUGHENED (1)
     SUFFERING-TOUGHENED BEYOND THE FETCH ....THE BEGGARS   48   15
SUFFERS (3)
     UNTIL NO CHASTE TREE BUT SUFFERS BLOTCH ..ON THE PLETHORA OF DRYADS   68   34
     CANNOT LOOK MUCH BUT YOUR FORM SUFFERS ....FULL FATHOM FIVE   92   17
     HE SUFFERS HIS DESERT PILLOW, SLEEPLESSNESS ....INSOMNIAC   163   6
SUGAR (7)
     UNDER THE CORONAL OF SUGAR ROSES ....THE BEEKEEPER'S DAUGHTER   118   20
     AND BRIM; THE CITY MELTS LIKE SUGAR. ....PARLIAMENT HILL FIELDS   152   12
     FOR MY CUBE OF SUGAR: ITS BOG BREATH ....ZOO KEEPER'S WIFE   155   36
     I SHOULD SUGAR AND PRESERVE MY DAYS LIKE FRUIT! ....LAST WORDS   172   10
     BREASTS AND HIPS A CONFECTIONER'S SUGAR ....BERCK-PLAGE   197   25
     SUGAR CAN CURE EVERYTHING, SO KINDNESS SAYS. ....KINDNESS   269   9
     SUGAR IS A NECESSARY FLUID, ...KINDNESS   269   10
SUGARED (1)
     WE LIFTED A SUGARED HAM AND A PINEAPPLE FROM THE GROWNUPS' ICEBOX ...
                                               ... THE BABYSITTERS   175   30
SUGARY (1)
     THOSE SUGARY PLANETS WHOSE INFLUENCE WON FOR HIM ....INSOMNIAC   163   17
SUICIDAL (2)
     SUICIDAL, AT ONE WITH THE DRIVE ....ARIEL   240   29
     THEY ARE MAKING A CAT'S CRADLE, THEY ARE SUICIDAL. ....STINGS/DR   293   7
SUICIDE (3)
     DIED RECLUSE OR SUICIDE ....MUSSEL HUNTER AT ROCK HARBOR   97   75
     SUICIDE OFF EGG ROCK ....SUICIDE OFF EGG ROCK   115   T
     I AM THE GHOST OF AN INFAMOUS SUICIDE, ...ELECTRA ON AZALEA PATH   117   42
SUICIDES (1)
     TWO SUICIDES, THE FAMILY WOLVES, ...THE MANOR GARDEN   125   13
SUIT (7)
     DANS LE FOND DES FORETS VOTRE IMAGE ME SUIT. ....PURSUIT   22   E
     SHIRR SONGS TO SUIT WHICH MOOD ....ODE FOR TED   29   20
     IS HE WEARING PAJAMAS OR AN EVENING SUIT ....BERCK-PLAGE   198   62
     SHINING GLOVES AND WHITE SUIT. ....THE BEE MEETING   211   29
     IN MY MOON SUIT AND FUNERAL VEIL. ....THE ARRIVAL OF THE BEE BOX   213   32
     HOW ABOUT THIS SUIT --- ....THE APPLICANT   221   20
     OUT OF WHICH THE SAME SELF UNFOLDS LIKE A SUIT ....TOTEM   264   25
SUITCASE (1)
     THERE IS VERY LITTLE TO GO INTO MY SUITCASE. ....THREE WOMEN   184 266
SUITCASES (1)
     THERE IS NO TERMINUS, ONLY SUITCASES ....TOTEM   264   24
SUITOR (1)
     WITH HER LATEST SUITOR ....SPINSTER   49   3
SUITS (1)
     SWAYING SLIGHTLY IN THEIR THICK SUITS, ...TOTEM   264   6
SULFUR (1)
     SO, IN THEIR SULFUR LOVELINESS, IN THEIR SMILES ....MUNICH.   263   10
SULFUROUS (3)
     OF SULFUROUS DREAMSCAPES AND OBSCURE LUNAR CONUNDRUMS .....GHOST'S.   90   4
     IN THE SULFUROUS NOON. WE MOVE ....IN MIDAS' COUNTRY   99   6
     SULFUROUS ADULTERIES GRIEVE IN A DREAM. ....THE OTHER   202   25
SULK (1)
     THAT VAIN JADES SULK SINGLE DOWN BRIDAL NIGHTS, ...ELLA MASON A.   54   41
SULLEN (5)
     IN SULLEN LIGHT OF THE INAUSPICIOUS DAY. ....CHANNEL CROSSING   27   25
     GLOWERING SULLEN AND POMPOUS FROM AN ASH-HEAP, ...LADY AND T.   69   11
     TO THE BEHEADED HEAD OF A SULLEN DOLL, ONE BRAID, ...PERSEUS   83   37
     THE BROWNNESS IS MY DEAD SELF, AND IT IS SULLEN: ....THREE WOMEN   179 100
     SUCH YELLOW SULLEN SMOKES ....FEVER.   231   14
SULLIED (1)
     BLOOD FAULTLESSLY BROACHED REDEEMED THE SULLIED AIR, THE EARTH'S
                                    GROSSNESS. ....THE GORING   47   10
SULTRY (3)
     MIDNIGHT CLOAKS THE SULTRY GROVE: ....PURSUIT   22   26
     INTO THE STILL, SULTRY WEATHER ....MISS DRAKE PROCEEDS TO SUPPER   41   25
     ACROSS THAT SULTRY AIR, ...AERIALIST   331   14
SUM (3)
     AS SHE CALCULATES EACH SUM. ....TWO SISTERS OF PERSEPHONE   31   9
     RIGHT, LIKE A WELL-DONE SUM. ....YOU'RE   141   17
     THE SIMPLE SUM OF HEART PLUS HEART. ....LOVE IS A PARALLAX   331   78

```
                                                      TITLE            PAGE  LINE
SUMMER (15)
   NO CHANGE MET HER: GARDEN TERRACE, ALL SUMMER  ........DREAM WITH C.   44    9
   LAST SUMMER I CAME UPON YOUR SPANISH COUSIN, ................SPIDER    48    8
   ALL SUMMER WE MOVED IN A VILLA BRIMFUL OF ECHOES. ....THE OTHER TWO    68    1
   SQUANDERS A SUMMER AND THE BRAWN OF HIS HEROES*A LESSON IN VENGEANCE   80   17
   THEY MOUND A SUMMER COOLNESS IN OUR VIEW. ..........ABOVE THE OXBOW    88   14
   SUMMER GROWS OLD, COLD-BLOODED MOTHER. .................FROG AUTUMN    99    1
   STONES THAT TAKE THE WHOLE SUMMER TO LOSE ......CHILD'S PARK STONES   101   23
   AS IF IT WERE SUMMER STILL. .......................MAGNOLIA SHOALS    121    4
   OVERHEAD THE OLD UMBRELLAS OF SUMMER ....................POEM.5.F.    134    3
   THAT SUMMER WE WORE BLACK GLASSES TO HIDE OUR EYES. *THE BABYSITTERS  174    3
   LAST SUMMER, MY GOD, LAST SUMMER ........................THE TOUR    238   32
   LAST SUMMER, MY GOD, LAST SUMMER ........................THE TOUR    238   32
   IN THE FETID WOMBS OF BLACK AIR UNDER PINES IN SUMMER. ......MYSTIC   268    5
   WHILE LIKE AN EARLY SUMMER PLUM, ...........................JILTED   304    9
   SHUTS DOWN ITS FABLED SUMMER HOUSE; ...................TWO LOVERS.   327    2
SUMMERS (1)
   THE RUBBISH OF SUMMERS, THE BLACK-LEAVED FALLS. ..THE BURNT-OUT SPA  138    9
SUMMER'S (2)
   LAST SUMMER'S REEDS ARE ALL ENGRAVED IN ICE ......WINTER LANDSCAPE,   22   11
   SONG FOR A SUMMER'S DAY ...................SONG FOR A SUMMER'S DAY    30    T
SUMMERY (1)
   IN MY SLEEVELESS SUMMERY DRESS I HAVE NO PROTECTION,*THE BEE MEETING  211    3
SUMMON (2)
   TO SUMMON IN HER SLIGHT ALL DOUGHTY MEN ......THE QUEEN'S COMPLAINT    29   17
   WHEN ALL EARTH HIS WORDS DO SUMMON .....................ODE FOR TED    30   23
SUMMONS (1)
   WHAT HONEY SUMMONS THESE ANIMALCULES? ....................STINGS/DR   293    1
SUN (71)
   THE AUSTERE SUN DESCENDS ABOVE THE FEN, ...........WINTER LANDSCAPE,   21    6
   HE PROWLS MORE LORDLY THAN THE SUN. ........................PURSUIT    22    4
   UNTIL THE SUN TURNED PALE FROM WARM, ......................BUCOLICS    24   14
   RISES THE ROUND RED WATERMELON SUN. ...............SOUTHERN SUNRISE    26   18
   WOULD BE FULL OF SUN, WHITE GULLS, AND WATER DRENCHED ...CHANNEL C.    27   21
   WHEREBY SHE TREKS IN BLOOD THROUGH SUN AND SQUALL ......QUEEN'S C.    29   22
   SCORCHED BY RED SUN .......................................FIRESONG    30   17
   SHEEN OF THE NOON SUN STRIKING .............SONG FOR A SUMMER'S DAY    31   11
   SUN HOISTS SOUL UP AFTER LIDS FALL SHUT; ...............VANITY FAIR    33   28
   BLAZON SKY BLUE, AND ENDOW THE SUN .....SOLILOQUY OF THE SOLIPSIST    37   22
   LOW MOOS OF APPROVE; LET SUN SURPLICED IN BRIGHTNESS .....WREATH F.    44    4
   THE SUN SHINES ON UNRIPE CORN. ..........................DEPARTURE    51    7
   FLIES WATCH NO RESURRECTIONS IN THE SUN. ........NOVEMBER GRAVEYARD    56   12
   SUNDAY'S GHOST OF SUN; ...................THE EVERLASTING MONDAY    62   10
   THEIR SHADOWS LONG IN THE SETTING SUN ........THE DISQUIETING MUSES    76   52
   VERMILIONS, BRONZES, COLORS OF THE SUN ........................OUIJA   77    6
   THEY CALLED THE PLACE LOOKOUT FARM. BACK THEN, THE SUN ...
                             ...  MEMOIRS OF A SPINACH-PICKER    89    1
   SUN AND SKY MIRRORED THE GREEN OF THE SPINACH. .....SPINACH-PICKER.   89   12
   SOMEWHERE BY MUCH SUN AND WIND; .......MUSSEL HUNTER AT ROCK HARBOR    97   73
   FACE, TO FACE THE BALD-FACED SUN. .....MUSSEL HUNTER AT ROCK HARBOR    97   91
   DEATH MAY WHITEN IN SUN OR OUT OF IT. .....................MOONRISE    98   18
   THE SUN BRIGHTENS TARDILY .............................FROG AUTUMN    99    6
   AND KEEP THEIR SHAPES INTACT WHILE SUN .........CHILD'S PARK STONES   101   12
   ALONG BOX-LINED WALKS IN THE FLORID SUN .......THE BULL OF BENDYLAW   108   10
   BACKDROP OF SYCAMORES. SUN WAS STRIKING ...............THE EYE-MOTE   109    4
   THE SUN SINKS UNDER BOSTON, BLOODY RED. ...............POINT SHIRLEY  111   40
   WE WANTED TO SEE THE SUN COME UP ....................A WINTER SHIP   113   24
   THE SUN WILL DIMINISH IT SOON ENOUGH: ...............A WINTER SHIP   113   29
   SUN STRUCK THE WATER LIKE A DAMNATION. .......SUICIDE OFF EGG ROCK    115    6
   TO SUN ON THE ROCKS OR PROP ....................OLD LADIES' HOME    120    5
   DOMINOES OF THEIR DOORWAYS. SUN GRAINS THEIR CROW-COLORS, ....NET-.   121    6
   THE BRONZE SNAKE LAY IN THE SUN ..........................MEDALLION   124    3
   THE WAY SUN RUINS A TROUT. ..............................MEDALLION   124   15
   THE SUN RISES UNDER THE PILLAR OF YOUR TONGUE. ........THE COLOSSUS   130   27
   UNWINDS FROM THE GREAT UMBILICUS OF THE SUN .........POEM.3.MAENAD.   133   19
   THE SUN SAT IN HIS ARMPIT. ...........................POEM.4.BEAST.   134    4
   THE SUN PUTS ITS CINDER OUT. WHERE WE LIE*SLEEP IN THE MOJAVE DESERT  144   21
   HOW THE BALCONIES ECHOED! HOW THE SUN LIT UP ......WAKING IN WINTER   151    9
   SUN MANAGES TO STRIKE SUCH TIN GLINTS .......PARLIAMENT HILL FIELDS   152   10
   IN THE MORNING SHE WOKE ME EARLY, REFLECTING THE SUN ....IN PLASTER   159   23
   BETWEEN THE EYE OF THE SUN AND THE EYES OF THE TULIPS, ......TULIPS   161   47
   I AM THE SUN, IN MY WHITE COAT, .............THE SURGEON AT 2 A.M.    171   49
   THE SUN FLAMED STRAIGHT DOWN THAT NOON ON THE WATER OFF MARBLEHEAD. ...
                             ...  THE BABYSITTERS    174    2
   A DEAD SUN STAINS THE NEWSPRINT. IT IS RED .............THREE WOMEN   181  153
   THE SUN IS DOWN. I DIE. I MAKE A DEATH. .................THREE WOMEN  181  161
   GENTLING THE SUN WITH THE SHADE OF MY HAND, ...........THREE WOMEN   185  290
   THATCH SMOKES IN THE SUN. ............................THREE WOMEN   185  314
   THE SUN DISSOLVES ON THIS WALL, BLEEDING ITS LIGHTS. APPREHENSIONS   195    5
   NOW THE WASHED SHEETS FLY IN THE SUN, ...................BERCK-PLAGE  198   67
   OLD BLOOD OF CAKED WALLS THE SUN HEALS, .................BERCK-PLAGE  200   98
   THE SUN GIVES YOU ULCERS, THE WIND GIVES YOU T.B. ...........LESBOS   228   39
   HOW THE SUN POLISHES THIS SHOULDER! .......................PURDAH    242    9
   A RING OF GOLD WITH THE SUN IN IT? ....................THE COURIERS   247    5
   THE DEAD SMELL OF SUN ON WOOD CABINS, .....................MYSTIC   268    7
```

	TITLE	PAGE	LINE

SUN (CONT.)
THE SUN BLOOMS, IT IS A GERANIUM. ....MYSTIC 269 30
MOON AND SUN REFLECT HIS FLAME. ....TO A JILTED LOVER 310 18
IN SQUARE HERMETIC BOTTLES, WHILE THE SUN ....THE TRIAL OF MAN 312 3
BEFORE THAT PAPAL PARAGON, THE SUN. ....APRIL AUBADE 312 8
AND TRAP THE MUSKRAT NAPPING IN SLACK SUN; GO GET THE GOODLY SQUAB 313 10
THE TENTS OF SUN ABSORB. ....TRIO OF LOVE SONGS 314 20
A SCOWL OF SUN STRUCK DOWN MY MOTHER, ...LAMENT 315 10
THE SCORCHING SUN: ....MOONSONG AT MORNING 317 38
AND PROFANE WORDS SCRAWLED BLACK ACROSS THE SUN. ....DOOM OF EXILES 318 12
FROM HERE YOU CAN'T SEE SPOTS UPON THE SUN; ....ADMONITIONS 319 8
OBSCURE THE SCALDING SUN TILL NO CLOCKS MOVE. ......SONNET TO SATAN 323 14
SEURAT: FLECK SCHOONER FLANKS WITH SUN AND SET ....MIDSUMMER MOBILE 324 5
WATER WILL RUN BY RULE: THE ACTUAL SUN ....TWO LOVERS. 327 21
PUT ORANGE MISTRESS HALF IN SUN, *BLACK PINE TREE IN AN ORANGE LIGHT 328 10
WOULD HAVE ME SWALLOW THE ENTIRE SUN ....LOVE IS A PARALLAX 329 26
SLOWLY CONCEDE TO SUN AND SERUM. ..MORNING IN THE HOSPITAL SOLARIUM 332 18
THROUGH CANDID KITCHENS IN THE RISING SUN ....THE PRINCESS. 334 52
SUNBLUE (1)
BESIDE A SUNBLUE SEA, AND MOURN THE FLAGON ....SONNET: TO TIME 311 10
SUN-CLOUDS (1)
EVEN THE SUN-CLOUDS THIS MORNING CANNOT MANAGE SUCH SKIRTS.*POP.OCT. 240 1
SUNDAY (4)
TWICE ON SUNDAY, THE BELLS STARTLE THE SKY --- ....MOON. 173 12
A DULL POM, POM IN THE SUNDAY STREET. ....THE SWARM 215 2
THE SUNDAY LAMB CRACKS IN ITS FAT. ....MARY'S SONG 257 1
IT IS SIX IN THE MORNING AND FINER THAN ANY SUNDAY -- QUEEN MARY'S. 290 8
SUNDAY'S (2)
THROUGH SUNDAY'S HONEY-AIR ....SONG FOR A SUMMER'S DAY 31 17
SUNDAY'S GHOST OF SUN; ....THE EVERLASTING MONDAY 62 10
SUN-GLAZED (1)
BELLIED ON A NIMBUS OF SUN-GLAZED BUTTERCUP. ....WATERCOLOR. 112 18
SUNGLINT (1)
RICH, BROWN, SUDDEN IN SUNGLINT. ....ODE FOR TED 29 12
SUNK (3)
MAZE OF BARNS TO THE LINTEL OF THE SUNK STY DOOR ....SOW 60 9
YOU ARE SUNK IN YOUR SEVEN CHINS, STILL AS A HAM. .....STOPPED DEAD 230 16
THERE'S WHERE IT SUNK. ....LYONNESSE 234 4
SUNKEN (5)
COMPARISON WITH THE SUNKEN SILVER-GRIZZLED ....ABOVE THE OXBOW 88 6
SNAGS AND EDDIES ROUND A SUNKEN RUST-RED ENGINE. ....TULIPS 161 54
OF A SUNKEN GONG. ....AQUATIC NORTURNE 306 28
NO SEA-CHANGE DECKS THE SUNKEN SHANK OF BONE ....TWO LOVERS. 327 17
THAT LIFTS TO CONSECRATE THE SUNKEN MAN. ....EPITAPH IN THREE PARTS 337 19
SUNLESS (1)
IN SUNLESS AIR, UNDER PINES ....CHILD'S PARK STONES 100 1
SUNLIGHT (4)
THERE IS THE SUNLIGHT, PLAYING ITS BLADES, ...THE DETECTIVE 209 18
WITH SUNLIGHT OF A THOUSAND YEARS UPON HIS LIPS ....GOLD MOUTHS CRY 302 13
SUNLIGHT STRIKES A GLASS OF GRAPEFRUIT JUICE, ..MORNING IN THE HOS. 332 1
WHILE SUNLIGHT WINDS ITS YARN UPON THE FLOOR. ....THE PRINCESS. 335 71
SUNLIT (1)
THEY PERSIST IN THE SUNLIT ROOM: THE WALLPAPER .....THE THIN PEOPLE 65 36
SUN-MONEYED (1)
WALK FORTH INTO SUN-MONEYED AIR, QUICKENED ....CRYSTAL GAZER 55 26
SUNNING (2)
STUCCO ARCHES, THE BANKED ROCKS SUNNING IN ROWS, ...WHITSUN 153 2
IT WAS SUNNING IN THE NARCISSI. ....PHEASANT 191 23
SUNRISE (1)
SOUTHERN SUNRISE ....SOUTHERN SUNRISE 26 T
SUNS (3)
STARS SHOOT THEIR PETALS, AND SUNS RUN TO SEED, ...EPITAPH FOR F. 45 12
TURNING THROUGH MY TIME, THE SUNS AND STARS ....THREE WOMEN 176 2
IN SOLAR SCHEMES THE TILTED SUNS GO TURNING; ....TO EVA DESCENDING. 303 11
SUN'S (8)
OUT OF THE SUN'S BRUISING) ....SONG FOR A SUMMER'S DAY 31 19
BURNS OPEN TO SUN'S BLADE. ....TWO SISTERS OF PERSEPHONE 32 19
FREELY BECOME SUN'S BRIDE, THE LATTER ....TWO SISTERS OF PERSEPHONE 32 21
SUN'S PARCHED SCREAM, ...STREET SONG 36 26
SUN'S BRASS, THE MOON'S STEELY PATINAS, ...DEPARTURE 51 10
EVERYTHING SHRANK IN THE SUN'S CORROSIVE ......SUICIDE OFF EGG ROCK 115 21
HOW THE SUN'S POULTICE DRAWS ON MY INFLAMMATION. ....BERCK-PLAGE 196 2
USED UTTERLY, IN THE SUN'S CONFLAGRATIONS, THE STAINS ....MYSTIC 268 13
SUNSET (4)
SUNSET LOOKED AT THROUGH MILK GLASS. ....MEDALLION 124 20
THE BLOOD IS A SUNSET. I ADMIRE IT. ....THE SURGEON AT 2 A.M. 171 21
I'D CALL IT A SUNSET, BUT ....STOPPED DEAD 230 14
WHOEVER HEARD A SUNSET YOWL LIKE THAT? ....STOPPED DEAD 230 15
SUNSETS (1)
I HAVE SUFFERED THE ATROCITY OF SUNSETS. ....ELM 192 16
SUNSTRUCK (1)
GOD HEARS FROM HIS GREAT SUNSTRUCK HELL ....SONG FOR A REVOLU. 323 19
SUNUP (1)
IN THE BLUE HOUR BEFORE SUNUP. ....SLEEP IN THE MOJAVE DESERT 144 10

	TITLE	PAGE	LINE

SUPERHIGHWAY (1)
   A SUPERHIGHWAY SEALS ME OFF. ....PRIVATE GROUND 130 15
SUPERIMPOSES (1)
   HOW SHYLY SHE SUPERIMPOSES HER NEAT SELF ....THREE WOMEN 184 282
SUPERIOR (6)
   SUPERIOR PAGE; THE BLUNT STONE ALSO. ....POEMS, POTATOES 106 13
   LIKE LOCAL TROLLS IN THE SPELL OF A SUPERIOR BEING. ......TWO CAMP. 144   6
   AND THE WHITE PERSON IS CERTAINLY THE SUPERIOR ONE. .....IN PLASTER 158   3
   SHE WANTED TO LEAVE ME, SHE THOUGHT SHE WAS SUPERIOR, ...IN PLASTER 159 36
   HOW SUPERIOR HE IS NOW. ....BERCK-PLAGE 198 56
   HOW SUPERIOR. ....A SECRET 219   2
SUPER-PEOPLE (1)
   THESE SUPER-PEOPLE! -- ....BRASILIA 258   6
SUPPER (2)
   MISS DRAKE PROCEEDS TO SUPPER ....MISS DRAKE PROCEEDS TO SUPPER   41   T
   LET US EAT OUR LAST SUPPER AT IT, LIKE A HOSPITAL PLATE. BIRTHDAY. 207 26
SUPPORTED (1)
   SHE'D SUPPORTED ME FOR SO LONG I WAS QUITE LIMP -- ......IN PLASTER 159 44
SUPPORTS (2)
   SUPPORTS HIS FOOT. HE PIPES A WORLD OF SNAKES, ...SNAKECHARMER   79 10
   SHE IS THE VAMPIRE OF US ALL. SO SHE SUPPORTS US, ...THREE WOMEN 181 155
SUPPOSE (2)
   I SUPPOSE IT'S POINTLESS TO THINK OF YOU AT ALL. .....PARLIAMENT H. 152 24
   I SUPPOSE. IF I DIDN'T TRUST YOU AT THIS*DIALOGUE OVER A OUIJA BOARD 277 36
SUPPOSED (2)
   NOT HER WHITENESS AND BEAUTY, AS I HAD AT FIRST SUPPOSED.*IN PLASTER 159 19
   AND NOT EXTINCT, AS EVERYONE SUPPOSED. DIALOGUE OVER A OUIJA BOARD 283 247
SURE (10)
   BUT SURE STATIONS IN BRONZE, WOOD, STONE. ....SCULPTOR   91   8
   PROMISING SURE HARBORAGE; ....LORELEI   94 25
   OF OUR HUSBANDS AND SONS MOVE SURE AMONG THE LOW STARS. ......NET-. 121 19
   I REMEMBER THE MINUTE WHEN I KNEW FOR SURE. ....THREE WOMEN 177 43
   I AM SURE IT IS UNIQUE, I AM SURE IT IS JUST WHAT I WANT. *BIRTHDAY. 206   3
   I AM SURE IT IS UNIQUE, I AM SURE IT IS JUST WHAT I WANT. *BIRTHDAY. 206   3
   JUST TO MAKE SURE -- .....................................EAVESDROPPER 261 62
   AROUND THE RING. I THINK IT MUST BE MAKING SURE ....DIALOGUE O. 277 22
   LIKE A GOOD BOY. BE CAREFUL. I'M NOT SURE THAT HE ......DIALOGUE O. 282 207
   AS SURE AS THOSE COALS BURN, THE LIVINGROOM ....DIALOGUE O. 286 357
SURELY (5)
   AGE, ANOTHER PLANET SURELY. FLANKED ....CHILD'S PARK STONES 101   8
   SURELY THE SKY IS NOT THAT COLOR, ...THE JAILER 226 24
   SURELY THE GRASS SHOULD BE RIPPLING. ....THE JAILER 226 25
   SURELY THEY TRAVEL ....THE NIGHT DANCES 249   6
   SURELY IT IS NOT I YOU WANT SO BADLY. ....THE RIVAL/DR 291 21
SURENESS (1)
   TO YES, HIS SURENESS MUST BE HIS, NOT OURS. ....DIALOGUE O. 278 73
SURF (2)
   THE FORGETFUL SURF CREAMING ON THOSE LEDGES. ..SUICIDE OFF EGG ROCK 115 24
   AND HUNGER OF THE SURF THAT PLUCKS THE LAND, *EPITAPH IN THREE PARTS 337 16
SURFACE (5)
   AND AN IMAGE LOOMS UNDER THE FISHPOND SURFACE ...ALL THE DEAD DEARS   71 22
   OVER A SURFACE OF GENTLY- ....BATTLE-SCENE   84   4
   OLD MAN, YOU SURFACE SELDOM. ....FULL FATHOM FIVE   92   1
   AT LEAST I WON'T BE STRUNG JUST UNDER THE SURFACE, ...BURNING. 204 23
   BLEACHED AND FINISHED, I SURFACE ....FEVER./DR 294   7
SURFACED (1)
   SURFACED IN OURSELVES: HE'LL SPELL A LINE ....DIALOGUE O. 283 255
SURFACES (2)
   ITS GLITTERING SURFACES ARE BLANK AND TRUE. ....TALE OF A TUB   25 32
   THE LINES OF THE EYE, SCALDED BY THESE BALD SURFACES, ..BERCK-PLAGE 196 10
SURFEIT (1)
   OF FINAL SURFEIT IS JUST AS FAR ....BLUE MOLES 127 33
SURFEITING (1)
   SURFEITING EYE, EAR, TASTE, TOUCH, SMELL; ON THE PLETHORA OF DRYADS   67 27
SURGED (2)
   THE BULL SURGED UP, THE BULL SURGED DOWN, ...THE BULL OF BENDYLAW 108 16
   THE BULL SURGED UP, THE BULL SURGED DOWN, ...THE BULL OF BENDYLAW 108 16
SURGEON (5)
   THE SURGEON AT 2 A.M. ....THE SURGEON AT 2 A.M. 170   T
   THE NERVES BURSTING LIKE TREES, AND THIS IS THE SURGEON:*BERCK-PLAGE 198 47
   A GREAT SURGEON, NOW A TATTOOIST, ...THE COURAGE OF SHUTTING-UP 210 10
   THE SURGEON IS QUIET, HE DOES NOT SPEAK. *THE COURAGE OF SHUTTING-UP 210 14
   IT IS THE SURGEON MY NEIGHBORS ARE WAITING FOR, ...THE BEE MEETING 211 27
SURGEONS (2)
   BOOMED WITH BAD DREAMS AND THE JOVIAN VOICES OF SURGEONS. *FACE LIFT 156   6
   AND MY HISTORY TO THE ANESTHETIST AND MY BODY TO SURGEONS. ..TULIPS 160   7
SURGERY (1)
   DIMINISHED AND FLAT, AS AFTER RADICAL SURGERY. ....ELM 192 26
SURPLICED (1)
   LOW MOOS OF APPROVE; LET SUN SURPLICED IN BRIGHTNESS .....WREATH F.   44   4
SURPLUS (1)
   MEASURING THE FLOUR, CUTTING OFF THE SURPLUS, ...A BIRTHDAY PRESENT 206   7
SURPRISED (1)
   AND WHAT IF THEY FOUND THEMSELVES SURPRISED, AS I DID? THREE WOMEN 180 118

SURREALISTIC (1)
    IN THIS SURREALISTIC HOUSE ....MORNING IN THE HOSPITAL SOLARIUM 332   3
SURRENDER (1)
    SURRENDER: TO BUILD OUR BED AS HIGH AS JACK'S ...LOVE IS A PARALLAX 330   70
SURVIVE (3)
    THE MICROBES CANNOT SURVIVE IT. ....THE SURGEON AT 2 A.M. 170   2
    I SURVIVE THE WHILE, ...LITTLE FUGUE 189   49
    WILL THE HIVE SURVIVE, WILL THE GLADIOLAS ....WINTERING 219   46
SURVIVES (3)
    SURVIVES ARRIVAL; WE WALK THE PLANK WITH STRANGERS.*CHANNEL CROSSING   27   42
    KNOTTED, CAUGHT, SURVIVES ....FULL FATHOM FIVE   92   9
    SURVIVES, GRIEVES ....POINT SHIRLEY 110   29
SUSAN (1)
    FOR SUSAN O'NEILL ROE ....CUT 235   D
SUSO'S (1)
    MUST WAIT, WHILE HERE SUSO'S ....A LESSON IN VENGEANCE   80   11
SUSPEND (1)
    SUSPEND THIS DAY, SO SINGULARLY DESIGNED, ...MIDSUMMER MOBILE 324   13
SUSPENDED (3)
    ESTRANGED, CHANGED, SUSPENDED WHERE ....THE GREAT CARBUNCLE   73   19
    AND SUSPENDED ALL THAT MIGHT OCCUR? ....PROLOGUE TO SPRING 322   12
    SUSPENDED ALOFT WITHIN HER PLANET-SHINE. ....THE PRINCESS. 335   63
SUSPENDS (1)
    SUSPENDS BESIDE IT THE FIRST POINT, THE STARTING ....GHOST'S.   91   30
SUSPENSE (1)
    A MULTITUDE OF SHADED GRAYS; SUSPENSE ....LOVE IS A PARALLAX 329   10
SUSPICIONS (1)
    TO WARD OFF, AT ALL COST, SUSPICIONS ....STREET SONG   36   16
SUSTAIN (1)
    OF OUR DAYS SUSTAIN US. MAY EACH THOUGHT*DIALOGUE OVER A OUIJA BOARD 286 361
SUSTAINS (1)
    HUNDRED-YEAR-OLD HOTEL SUSTAINS ITS RAMSHACKLE .....ABOVE THE OXBOW   88   35
SUSURROUS (1)
    LULLAYED BY SUSURROUS LYRES AND VIOLS. ....ALICANTE LULLABY   43   21
SWABBED (2)
    THEY HAVE SWABBED ME CLEAR OF MY LOVING ASSOCIATIONS. ....TULIPS 161   24
    SWABBED AND LURID WITH DISINFECTANTS, SACRIFICIAL. .....THREE WOMEN 179 107
SWADDLE (1)
    LET NOTHING BE LEFT TO SWADDLE US. ...SONG FOR A REVOLUTIONARY LOVE 323   12
SWADDLED (3)
    MY SWADDLED LEGS AND ARMS SMELL SWEET AS RUBBER. POEM.7.S. 137   34
    MOTHER TO MYSELF, I WAKE SWADDLED IN GAUZE, ...FACE LIFT 156   31
    HE IS STILL SWADDLED IN WHITE BANDS. ....THREE WOMEN 186 326
SWADDLES (1)
    SWADDLES ROOF AND TREE. ....PARLIAMENT HILL FIELDS 152   22
SWADDLINGS (1)
    LIGHTLY, THROUGH THEIR WHITE SWADDLINGS, LIKE AN AWFUL BABY. *TULIPS 161   38
SWAGGERS (1)
    AND SWAGGERS LIKE A PROPER GENTLEMAN; ....ADMONITIONS 319   11
SWALLOW (4)
    I MUST SWALLOW IT ALL. POEM.3.MAENAD. 133   21
    OPENS TO SWALLOW ME. I'M A STONE, A STICK, ..PARLIAMENT HILL FIELDS 152   15
    WHATEVER I SEE I SWALLOW IMMEDIATELY ....MIRROR 173   2
    WOULD HAVE ME SWALLOW THE ENTIRE SUN ....LOVE IS A PARALLAX 329   26
SWALLOWED (2)
    LIKE A PLANET, A STONE, SWALLOWED IN A GREAT DARKNESS,*THE OTHER TWO   68   25
    SICK WITH WHAT IT HAS SWALLOWED --- ....BERCK-PLAGE 197   28
SWALLOWS (2)
    STILL THAN SWALLOWS JOY. YOU ENTER NOW, ...PERSEUS   83   34
    WHITENS AND SWALLOWS ITS DULL STARS. AND NOW YOU TRY ..MORNING SONG 157   16
SWAM (2)
    THEN MOTHER SWAM UP, HOLDING A TIN BASIN. ....FACE LIFT 156   7
    HER BLUE EYES SWAM WITH VAGUE TERROR. ....BITTER STRAWBERRIES 300   24
SWAMPED (1)
    KNEE-DEEP IN THE COLD AND SWAMPED BY FLOWERS? ....LEAVING EARLY 146   44
SWAMPSCOTT (1)
    IN THE TWO HUGE, WHITE, HANDSOME HOUSES IN SWAMPSCOTT. ....BABY. 174   5
SWAN (3)
    WHERE, ABSURD AND OUT-OF-SEASON, A SINGLE SWAN ...WINTER LANDSCAPE.   21   3
    NEITHER BRAZEN SWAN NOR BURNING STAR, ...ON THE DECLINE OF ORACLES   78   18
    AND THE GREAT SWAN, WITH ITS TERRIBLE LOOK, ...THREE WOMEN 178   50
SWANS (3)
    THERE IS A SNAKE IN SWANS. ....THREE WOMEN 178   52
    THE SWANS ARE GONE. STILL THE RIVER ....THREE WOMEN 186 344
    UNLIKE SWANS, ...GULLIVER 251   5
SWARM (3)
    THE SWARM ....THE SWARM 215   T
    SO THE SWARM BALLS AND DESERTS ....THE SWARM 216   17
    THE SWARM IS KNOCKED INTO A COCKED STRAW HAT. ....THE SWARM 217   42
SWARMING (1)
    WHO WALKED IN A SWARMING SHROUD OF WINGS ....LAMENT 315   2
SWARMY (1)
    WITH THE SWARMY FEELING OF AFRICAN HANDS *THE ARRIVAL OF THE BEE BOX 213   13
SWASTIKA (1)
    NOT GOD BUT A SWASTIKA ....DADDY 223   46

	TITLE	PAGE	LINE

SWAY (1)
ONCE, IN ITS EARLIEST SWAY OF LYMPH AND SAP, ...HARDCASTLE CRAGS   63   39
SWAYING (1)
SWAYING SLIGHTLY IN THEIR THICK SUITS, ...TOTEM   264   6
SWAYS (1)
OF SWAYS AND COILINGS, FROM THE SNAKE-ROOTED BOTTOM   ...SNAKECHARMER   79   11
SWEAR (4)
OLD GOATHERDS SWEAR HOW ALL NIGHT LONG THEY HEAR   ....GOATSUCKER   111   1
DEAD, YOU'D SWEAR HIM A VICTIM OF OUR OWN VAIN   ....DIALOGUE O.   278   82
LIKE ALL THE OTHERS AND SWEAR THAT HE'S A PUMA   ....DIALOGUE O.   281   176
WHERE THOSE WORMS CAME FROM. I SWEAR I DIDN'T EXPECT   ...DIALOGUE O.   283   264
SWEAT (3)
DEW STOOD IN CHILL SWEAT ON EACH STALK, ...DIALOGUE B.   38   4
HOWEVER YOU MAY SWEAT TO HOLD SUCH DARLING WRECKS   ...EPITAPH FOR F.   45   13
THE SWEAT OF HIS EFFORTS A RAIN   ....STINGS   215   46
SWEATED (1)
THE BURGHERS SWEATED AND WEPT. THE CHILDREN WORE WHITE.   ....CANDLES   149   19
SWEATS (2)
MY NIGHT SWEATS GREASE HIS BREAKFAST PLATE.   ....THE JAILER   226   1
THE CHIMNEYS OF THE CITY BREATHE, THE WINDOW SWEATS, ...MYSTIC   269   28
SWEAT-WET (1)
OUT OF SHEER BOREDOM. TANGLED IN THE SWEAT-WET SHEETS   ....ZOO K.   155   23
SWEET (28)
KEEN THE RENDING TEETH AND SWEET   ....PURSUIT   22   17
UNTIL SWEET WIND CHANGED TUNE, BLEW HARM: ....BUCOLICS   24   15
FAR FROM THE SWEET STENCH OF THAT PERILOUS AIR   ....CHANNEL CROSSING   27   13
SWEET SALTS WARPED STEM   ....FIRESONG   30   15
SWEET GRASS SPRANG FOR THEIR GRAZING.   ......SONG FOR A SUMMER'S DAY   31   5
TO MY SWEET WILL, NO LUMINOUS SHAPE   ....CONJURING   66   26
MY SWADDLED LEGS AND ARMS SMELL SWEET AS RUBBER. POEM.7.S.   137   34
THESE LITTLE GLOBES OF LIGHT ARE SWEET AS PEARS.   ....CANDLES   149   24
AND THE SWEET, DRUGGED WAKING OF A FORGETFUL BABY.   ....INSOMNIAC   163   19
UNWARMED BY THE SWEET AIR OF THIS PEACH ORCHARD.   ....STARS.   166   36
THESE HILLS ARE TOO GREEN AND SWEET TO HAVE TASTED SALT.   BLACKBER.   169   22
HER LIPS SWEET WITH DIVINITY.   ....FINISTERRE   170   25
THE MOON IS MY MOTHER. SHE IS NOT SWEET LIKE MARY.   ....MOON.   173   17
BLIND IN MY BED, WITH MY DEAR BLIND SWEET ONE, ...THREE WOMEN   178   76
THE MILK CAME YELLOW, THEN BLUE AND SWEET AS WATER.   ..THE DETECTIVE   209   33
TOMORROW I WILL BE SWEET GOD, I WILL SET THEM FREE.   ...THE ARRIVAL.   213   35
OUR CHEESECLOTH GAUNTLETS NEAT AND SWEET, ...STINGS   214   3
HE WAS SWEET, ...STINGS   215   45
HIS JEW-MAMA GUARDS HIS SWEET SEX LIKE A PEARL.   ....LESBOS   228   27
THE WHEELS, TWO RUBBER GRUBS, BITE THEIR SWEET TAILS.   STOPPED DEAD   230   6
SWEET LETHE IS MY LIFE.   ....AMNESIAC   233   26
BLACK SWEET BLOOD MOUTHFULS, ...ARIEL   239   13
HE TELLS ME HOW SWEET   ....DEATH & CO.   254   13
TOAD-STONE! SISTER-BITCH! SWEET NEIGHBOR!   ............EAVESDROPPER   261   63
FROM THE SWEET, DEEP THROATS OF THE NIGHT FLOWER.   ....EDGE   273   16
SHE MUSES ON THE ODOR, SWEET AND SICK, ...FEMALE AUTHOR   301   11
NO SWEET DISGUISES   ....MOONSONG AT MORNING   317   21
BLUE VIEWS ARE BOARDED UP; OUR SWEET VACATION   ....TWO LOVERS.   327   3
SWEETBREADS (1)
OF BEETLES, SWEETBREADS, SHARDS -- TO BE EATEN   ....BLUE MOLES   126   31
SWEETEN (1)
TO SWEETEN YOUR NECK OF THE NEW YORK WOODS.   ....PRIVATE GROUND   130   4
SWEETENING (1)
THE PILLOW CASES ARE SWEETENING.   ....BERCK-PLAGE   198   68
SWEETER (1)
AND THE SHINE OF THESE SMALL THINGS SWEETER THAN THE FACE OF
ISHTAR.   ....   LAST WORDS   172   26
SWEETEST (1)
FOR FEAST THE SWEETEST MEAT OF HELL'S CHEF D'OEUVRES: .....TERMINAL   328   11
SWEETHEART (3)
MY FAT PORK, MY MARROWY SWEETHEART, FACE-TO-THE-WALL?   ....ZOO K.   155   15
WHEN THE SWEETHEART FROM ENGLAND APPEARED, WITH HER CREAM SKIN AND
YARDLEY COSMETICS.   ....THE BABYSITTERS   174   6
SWEETHEART, THAT KLEPTOMANIAC.   ....LESBOS   229   88
SWEETHEARTS (1)
THEY WAITED LIKE SWEETHEARTS. THEY EXCITED HIM.   THE RABBIT CATCHER   194   25
SWEETIE (1)
COME HERE, SWEETIE, OUT OF THE CLOSET.   ....THE APPLICANT   221   28
SWEETLY (3)
SWEETLY, SWEETLY I BREATHE IN, ...A BIRTHDAY PRESENT   207   41
SWEETLY, SWEETLY I BREATHE IN, ...A BIRTHDAY PRESENT   207   41
SWEETLY PICKING UP PIECES!   ....KINDNESS   269   13
SWEETNESS (3)
THINKING "SWEETNESS, SWEETNESS".   ....STINGS   214   11
THINKING "SWEETNESS, SWEETNESS".   ....STINGS   214   11
O MOTHER OF LEAVES AND SWEETNESS   ....WINTER TREES   258   13
SWELL (1)
ADDED ADAM, THAT SIMIAN SWELL, ...DIALOGUE EN ROUTE   309   25
SWELTER (2)
WE SWELTER LIKE FIREDOGS IN THE WIND.   ...SLEEP IN THE MOJAVE DESERT   144   20
SWELTER AND MELT, AND THE LOVERS   ....THREE WOMEN   186   338

	TITLE	PAGE	LINE

SWEPT (1)
    OBEYING ORDERS OF INSTINCT TILL SWEPT ....SPIDER   49   32
SWIFT (1)
    A LIFE AFTER THIS LIFE? HE SHOOTS SO SWIFT ....DIALOGUE O. 278   72
SWIFTS (2)
    FOLLOW THE BLACK ARROW-BACKS OF SWIFTS ON THEIR TRACK ....OXBOW.   88   31
    THE SWIFTS ARE BACK. THEY ARE SHRIEKING LIKE PAPER ROCKETS.   THREE. 185 310
SWIG (2)
    HATCHED WITH A CLARET HOGSHEAD TO SWIG ....MAUDLIN   51   5
    TO HALT FOR A SWIG AT THE PINK TEATS. NO. THIS VAST ....SOW   61   23
SWILL (1)
    PROCEEDED TO SWILL ....SOW   61   44
SWIM (6)
    SWIM THE SEA OF DO, ...WORDS FOR A NURSERY   74   33
    TOMORROW THEY WILL SWIM ....THE SURGEON AT 2 A.M. 171   38
    ANGELS SWIM IN IT, AND THE STARS, IN INDIFFERENCE ALSO.
                                              ... APPREHENSIONS 195   3
    WHERE THE CHILD CAN NEVER SWIM, ...THE FEARFUL 256   17
    BUT LET THE QUICKSILVER MACKEREL SWIM. .....GO GET THE GOODLY SQUAB 313   20
    LET THE QUICKSILVER MACKEREL SWIM ....GO GET THE GOODLY SQUAB 313   21
SWIMS (2)
    SAWS DOWN A REED AND SWIMS FROM HIS LIMBER GROVE, ...WATERCOLOR. 112   23
    A BLIMP SWIMS UP LIKE A DAY-MOON OR TIN ....A WINTER SHIP 113   11
SWING (2)
    AND COMMENCE TO SWING. ....AERIALIST 331   18
    BUT, GO! THEY CRY, AND THE SWING ....TOUCH-AND-GO 335   13
SWISS (1)
    A SWISS WATCH, JEWELED IN THE HINGES! ....AN APPEARANCE 189   15
SWITCHED (1)
    SWITCHED HER INCOMPARABLE BACK ....VIRGIN IN A TREE   81   10
SWIVEL (1)
    SWIVEL THEIR HEADS AND CRY. .........................APPREHENSIONS 195   17
SWIVELED (1)
    AS THE WORLD SWIVELED ROUND IN ITS ORBIT ....DIALOGUE EN ROUTE 309   38
SWIVELING (1)
    TO PITCH THE WHITE WORLD DOWN IN SWIVELING FLOOD, ..SONNET TO SATAN 323   6
SWOLLEN (2)
    CLAW SWOLLEN TO A SHIELD LARGE ....MUSSEL HUNTER AT ROCK HARBOR   96   33
    MAUDLIN FROM LEAKY EYE TO SWOLLEN NOSE. ....THE RAVAGED FACE 115   4
SWOON (1)
    A PLANETARY SWOON ....TRIO OF LOVE SONGS 314   31
SWORE (1)
    GHOST SWORE TO PRIEST: ....DIALOGUE BETWEEN GHOST AND PRIEST   39   48
SWUNG (2)
    A SLY WORLD'S HINGES HAD SWUNG ....MUSSEL HUNTER AT ROCK HARBOR   95   19
    ON THIS HILL, WITH ITS VIEW OF LIT CASTLES, EACH SWUNG BELL   STARS. 166   38
SYCAMORE (1)
    OF THE SYCAMORE ....PROSPECT   28   6
SYCAMORES (1)
    BACKDROP OF SYCAMORES. SUN WAS STRIKING ....THE EYE-MOTE 109   4
SYLLABLE (2)
    WIDOW. THE DEAD SYLLABLE, WITH ITS SHADOW ....WIDOW 164   6
    OF EACH SYLLABLE, ...TRIO OF LOVE SONGS 314   22
SYLLABLES (5)
    I'M A RIDDLE IN NINE SYLLABLES, ...METAPHORS 116   1
    REMEMBERS A FEW ODD SYLLABLES. ....WUTHERING HEIGHTS 168   34
    IT IS HE WHO HAS ACHIEVED THESE SYLLABLES. ....WORDS HEARD. 202   5
    THE UNINTELLIGIBLE SYLLABLES. ....THE ARRIVAL OF THE BEE BOX 213   18
    FOR SOUNDING SYLLABLES WE HAVEN'T YET ..DIALOGUE OVER A OUIJA BOARD 283 254
SYNCOPATE (1)
    THEN SYNCOPATE A SKY OF DUFY-BLUE ....MIDSUMMER MOBILE 324   2
SYNCOPATES (1)
    THAT SYNCOPATES OUR LOVE. ....TRIO OF LOVE SONGS 315   52
SYRINX (1)
    CRIES: "CELEBRATE SYRINX WHOSE DEMURS ....VIRGIN IN A TREE   81   13
SYRUP (1)
    TO THE SYRUP TIN ....WINTERING 218   25
SYSTEM (2)
    THE MOON SNAGS IN HER INTRICATE NERVOUS SYSTEM. ....ELM/DR 292   3
    BY SECEDING FROM THE SOLAR SYSTEM. ....INSOLENT STORM. 326   32
TABBY (1)
    PLAYS HOSTESS TO TABBY, TOM AND INCREASE, ...ELLA MASON A.   53   10
TABLE (13)
    OF KNOTTED TABLE AND CROOKED CHAIR, ..MISS DRAKE PROCEEDS TO SUPPER   41   4
    OUT OF KITCHEN TABLE OR CHAIR ....BLACK ROOK IN RAINY WEATHER   57   16
    UNDER THE MEANEST TABLE. ....THE THIN PEOPLE   64   11
    THE WALNUT BANQUET TABLE, THE TWELVE CHAIRS ....THE OTHER TWO   68   13
    PLATONIC TABLE WHERE IT LIVES. THE BABY CARP ....PRIVATE GROUND 130   11
    LOVELESS AS THE MULTIPLICATION TABLE. ....MAGI 148   8
    GREEN AS A POOL TABLE, WHERE CABBAGE BUTTERFLIES ....WHITSUN 154   19
    TICKING YOUR FINGERS ON THE MARBLE TABLE, LOOKING FOR
                    CIGARETTES, ...THE RIVAL 166   8
    AT MY TABLE ON THE SHIP. ....LITTLE FUGUE 187   9
    O GOD, HOW SHALL I EVER CLEAN THE PHONE TABLE? ....WORDS HEARD. 202   8
    SETTLES IN THE ROOM NOW. ITS WINGS BLACKEN THE TABLE. ..DIALOGUE O. 285 313

		TITLE	PAGE	LINE

TABLE (CONT.)
THE TABLE LOOKS AS IF IT WOULD STAY A TABLE ....DIALOGUE O. 286 353
THE TABLE LOOKS AS IF IT WOULD STAY A TABLE ....DIALOGUE O. 286 353
TABLEAU (3)
IN A GLASSED TABLEAU OF AFFLUENCE. ....OWL 102 7
THE SKATERS FREEZE WITHIN A STONE TABLEAU. ......PROLOGUE TO SPRING 322 3
WHO WEEPS BEFORE THE DESOLATE TABLEAU   THE PRINCESS AND THE GOBLINS 335 74
TABLES (8)
TABLES AND CHAIRS. GRAVITY'S ....THE GREAT CARBUNCLE 73 22
LIGHT WITHDRAWS. CHAIRS, TABLES DROP ....THE GREAT CARBUNCLE 73 29
CHAIRARMS AND TABLES, ...WORDS FOR A NURSERY 74 44
TABLES, WE ARE MEEK, ...MUSHROOMS 139 26
TABLES AND CHAIRS CAN ELBOW US WITH EASE*DIALOGUE OVER A OUIJA BOARD 279 113
CAN WHIPCRACK THE TABLES INTO TIGERS AND FOIST ....DIALOGUE O. 279 117
THAN AGAINST GRAVITY'S GRIP, TABLES RISING; THE DRINK ..DIALOGUE O. 279 122
TURNING THE TABLES OF THIS GRAVE GOURMET, ...TERMINAL 328 9
TABLET (2)
SHUTTING THEIR MOUTHS ON IT, LIKE A COMMUNION TABLET. ....TULIPS 161 35
THE PILL OF THE COMMUNION TABLET, ...MYSTIC 268 16
TABLETOP (1)
TOWARD THEIR ADMIRERS IN THE TABLETOP: ....LEAVING EARLY 146 12
TABLE-TOP (1)
TABLE-TOP, CUPBOARD SHELF, CATS LOUNGED BRAZEN, ...ELLA MASON A. 54 22
TABLETS (1)
TABLETS OF BLANK BLUE, COULDN'T, ...THE HERMIT AT OUTERMOST HOUSE 118 2
TABULA (1)
THE WHITE GAPE OF HIS MIND WAS THE REAL TABULA RASA. .....LYONNESSE 234 27
TACITURN (1)
THEY HUNTED THE STONES, TACITURN AND SEPARATE, ...POEM.7.S. 136 15
TACK (1)
AND TACK OF THE CLOCK, UNTIL WE GO, ...ALL THE DEAD DEARS 71 33
TACKED (2)
THESE ARE THE DECEITS, TACKED UP LIKE FAMILY PHOTOGRAPHS,*DETECTIVE. 208 13
THEY ARE SMILING AND TAKING OUT VEILS TACKED TO ANCIENT HATS. BEE. 211 5
TACKING (1)
TACKING IN MOON-BLUED CROOKS FROM THE BLACK ....HARDCASTLE CRAGS 62 3
TACKLE (1)
OF WEEDS WE TACKLE TOWARDS WAY'S RANK ENDING; ....FIRESONG 30 16
TACKS (1)
HAND HONES HIS TACKS AND NEEDLES, ...A LESSON IN VENGEANCE 80 12
TAG (2)
AND IT ASKS NOTHING, A NAME TAG, A FEW TRINKETS. ....TULIPS 161 33
TWO CHILDREN LAUGHED AT TAG ....BITTER STRAWBERRIES 299 14
TAIL (4)
BACKTRACKING TAIL. I'D COME FOR ....MUSSEL HUNTER AT ROCK HARBOR 95 8
AT THE CLEAR TAIL OF HALLEY'S ....MUSSEL HUNTER AT ROCK HARBOR 96 56
A COMET TAIL! ....AMNESIAC 233 19
TAIL ON EACH TOY DONKEY THAT WILL BRAY   DIALOGUE OVER A OUIJA BOARD 283 250
TAILS (5)
TAILS STREAMING AGAINST THE GREEN ....THE EYE-MOTE 109 3
WHERE THE HEADS AND TAILS OF MY SISTERS DECOMPOSE.*ZOO KEEPER'S WIFE 154 7
IT HAS NINE TAILS, IT IS DANGEROUS. .....THE COURAGE OF SHUTTING-UP 210 19
THE WHEELS, TWO RUBBER GRUBS, BITE THEIR SWEET TAILS. STOPPED DEAD 230 6
ON ELUSIVE TAILS: ....AQUATIC NOCTURNE 306 21
TAIL-TRACK (1)
THE TAIL-TRACK, ON THE SNOW IN OUR COURT -- ....PHEASANT 191 12
TAINT (1)
AT HER TOUGH TRADE; WITHOUT TIME'S TAINT ....CRYSTAL GAZER 54 4
TAKE (21)
WE TAKE THE PLUNGE; UNDER WATER OUR LIMBS ....TALE OF A TUB 25 25
FLAYED BY SPRAY, WE TAKE THE CHALLENGE UP, ...CHANNEL CROSSING 26 5
"NO HARDSHIP THEN?" HE ASKS. "WE'LL TAKE ....CRYSTAL GAZER 55 19
STONES THAT TAKE THE WHOLE SUMMER TO LOSE ......CHILD'S PARK STONES 101 23
OR MUST TAKE LOOPHOLE AND BLAME TIME ......GREEN ROCK, WINTHROP BAY 105 22
BREAKWATERS TAKE THE SHOVE ....MAN IN BLACK 119 2
WE TAKE A BACKWARD LOOK. ....THE SLEEPERS 123 12
IT WOULD TAKE MORE THAN A LIGHTNING-STROKE ....THE COLOSSUS 130 22
TAKE HOLD ON THE LOAM, ...MUSHROOMS 139 5
THE OLD DREGS, THE OLD DIFFICULTIES TAKE ME TO WIFE. PARLIAMENT H. 153 48
STUPID PUPIL, IT HAS TO TAKE EVERYTHING IN. ....TULIPS 160 10
THE BLACK SLOTS OF THEIR PUPILS TAKE ME IN. ......WUTHERING HEIGHTS 167 22
TO RATTLE IN A BOTTLE AND TAKE HOME, ...THE SURGEON AT 2 A.M. 171 35
YOU ARE TOO BIG. THEY MUST TAKE YOU BACK! ....WORDS HEARD. 203 15
I WILL ONLY TAKE IT AND GO ASIDE QUIETLY. ....A BIRTHDAY PRESENT 207 33
THEY TAKE IT. THE COLD SETS IN. ....WINTERING 218 30
I SHALL TAKE NO BITE OF YOUR BODY, ...MEDUSA 225 34
TAKE A LOOK AT THE WHITE, HIGH BERG ON HIS FOREHEAD -- ...LYONNESSE 233 3
ALL RIGHT, LET'S SAY YOU COULD TAKE A SKULL AND BREAK IT*SONNET:EVA. 304 1
BETWEEN STEEL PALMS OF INCLINATION, TAKE IT, ...SONNET: TO EVA 304 3
TAKE THE GENERAL MUMBLE, ...NOTES TO A NEOPHYTE 306 1
TAKEN (5)
AND THE FINGERS, TAKEN IN BY THEIR OWN HALOES, ...CANDLES 148 3
SMALL, TAKEN ONE BY ONE, BUT MY GOD, TOGETHER! ....THE ARRIVAL. 213 20
TO MAKE UP FOR THE HONEY I'VE TAKEN. ....WINTERING 218 26
A KNIFE THAT CAN BE TAKEN OUT ....A SECRET 220 21

TAKEN (CONT.)
  I HAVE TAKEN A PILL TO KILL ....CUT 235 24
TAKES (7)
  OF YOUR STORMY EYE, MAGIC TAKES FLIGHT ................CONVERSATION. 21   7
  MERE BRUIT OF HER TAKES OUR STREET ....STRUMPET SONG 33   5
  A SMOKE THAT TAKES THE PARKS, THE LITTLE STATUES ....THREE WOMEN 186 355
  IT TAKES PATIENCE. IF VERONICAS AND FOUNTAINS ....DIALOGUE O. 282 221
  DEMANDING SATISFACTION: NO DUEL TAKES PLACE: ........METAMORPHOSES. 307   5
  TAKES ON THE BODY ....ON LOOKING INTO THE EYES OF A DEMON LOVER 325   7
  UNTIL DREAM TAKES HER BODY ....AERIALIST 331   4
TAKING (7)
  DEADLOCKED WITH THEM, TAKING ROOT AS CRADLES ROCK. ...
                                          ... ALL THE DEAD DEARS 71 36
  HER RUINED APARTMENTS, TAKING STOCK ....AFTERMATH 114 11
  LIKE MY NEIGHBORS, TAKING NO PLEASURE ....LOVE LETTER 147 12
  THEY ARE SMILING AND TAKING OUT VEILS TACKED TO ANCIENT HATS. BEE. 211 11
  IS IT SOME OPERATION THAT IS TAKING PLACE? ....THE BEE MEETING 211 26
  TAKING UP HALF THE SPACE, ...BALLOONS 271   4
  AND BOLT IT UP BY TAKING OATH NO GUESS DIALOGUE OVER A OUIJA BOARD 286 345
TALE (2)
  TALE OF A TUB ....TALE OF A TUB 24   T
  A WINTER'S TALE ....A WINTER'S TALE 86   T
TALENT (2)
  THEY FOUND THEIR TALENT TO PERSEVERE ....THE THIN PEOPLE 64 13
  WITH VALENTINO'S CRACK TECHNICAL TALENT ....DIALOGUE EN ROUTE 309 22
TALENTS (1)
  FUSING TWO TALENTS, A SORT OF PSYCHIC BASTARD ....DIALOGUE O. 280 139
TALISMAN (1)
  AND MISLAID EVERY VITAL TALISMAN; ....THE DISPOSSESSED 319 17
TALISMANIC (1)
  SHE CLUTCHES AT THE TALISMANIC CORD ...THE PRINCESS AND THE GOBLINS 334 42
TALK (16)
  THE GIRL BENT HOMEWARD, BRIMFUL OF GENTLE TALK ....SNOWMAN O. 59 50
  WHERE STRAIGHT TALK IS THE RULE, WHETHER WARM OR HOSTILE, ...
                                          ... INCOMMUNICADO 100 10
  THEY TALK OF BRIDE-LACE, OF LOVERS SPUNKY AS GAMECOCKS. ......NET-. 121 14
  I TALK TO MYSELF, MYSELF ONLY, SET APART -- ....THREE WOMEN 179 106
  THERE IS NO TALK OF IMMORTALITY AMONG THESE! .........APPREHENSIONS 196 18
  MIRRORS CAN KILL AND TALK, THEY ARE TERRIBLE ROOMS ....COURAGE. 210 27
  IT CAN TALK, TALK, TALK. ....THE APPLICANT 222 35
  IT CAN TALK, TALK, TALK. ....THE APPLICANT 222 35
  IT CAN TALK, TALK, TALK. ....THE APPLICANT 222 35
  I NEVER COULD TALK TO YOU. ....DADDY 223 24
  I BEGAN TO TALK LIKE A JEW. ....DADDY 223 34
  MIRROR TALK YOU LOVE TO CATCH ME AT. ...............EAVESDROPPER 260 36
  THAT'S HOW YOU ALWAYS TALK BEFORE WE START. ....DIALOGUE O. 277 15
  INCOHERENT SCRAPS OF TALK ....FAMILY REUNION 300   3
  AS AMID THE HECTIC MUSIC AND COCKTAIL TALK ....CINDERELLA 304 13
  MORNING: ANOTHER DAY, AND TALK ....MORNING IN THE HOSPITAL SOLARIUM 332 10
TALKED (2)
  WE KICKED AND TALKED. THE THICK SALT KEPT US UP. ...THE BABYSITTERS 175 40
  THEY TALKED ABOUT THE RUSSIANS. ....BITTER STRAWBERRIES 299   2
TALKERS (1)
  TALKERS: "YOU ALL RIGHT?" ....PARALYTIC 266 15
TALKING (7)
  AND SO, TOGETHER, TALKING, ...SONG FOR A SUMMER'S DAY 31 16
  HIS TALKING WHIRLWIND, ABATED HIS EXCESSIVE TEMPER ....OUIJA 77 16
  WITH THE LOVE-HOT HERB, THE TALKING CAT, ...THE TIMES ARE TIDY 107 13
  THE TALKING DUCKS, THE HAPPY LAMBS. ....THREE WOMEN 185 318
  CAULDRON, TALKING AND CRACKLING ....THE COURIERS 247   8
  TO PEOPLE THE BOUGHS WITH TALKING BIRDS. I'D PLANT .....DIALOGUE O. 280 169
  YOU'RE ALWAYS TALKING THIS WAY . . ." ....BITTER STRAWBERRIES 300 26
TALKS (2)
  THEIR REDNESS TALKS TO MY WOUND, IT CORRESPONDS. ....TULIPS 161 39
  WHERE THE WIRELESS TALKS TO ITSELF LIKE AN ELDERLY RELATIVE. ...
                                          ... THE DETECTIVE 209 20
TALL (10)
  GLEAMS, WIRED TO A TALL ULMUS ....A WINTER'S TALE 86   2
  AND A FLOWER-HEAD NOT TALL, BUT MORE STARTLING, ...I AM VERTICAL 162   9
  PARENTAL FACES ON TALL STALKS, ALTERNATELY STERN AND TEARFUL, ...
                                          ... INSOMNIAC 163 11
  GROWS TALL. YOU CLUTCH YOUR BARS. ....BY CANDLELIGHT 237 22
  IN THE TALL GRASS, ...BITTER STRAWBERRIES 299 15
  THE WHOLE REVOLVING TALL GLASS PALACE HALL ....CINDERELLA 304   5
  A TALL METROPOLIS OF CATACOMBS ....DOOM OF EXILES 318   3
  TALL TRUCKS ROLL IN ....AERIALIST 331 31
  ARCS UP TO THE TALL TREE TIP; ....TOUCH-AND-GO 335 14
  TALL SKELETONS WALK; ....TEMPER OF TIME 336 10
TALLOW (2)
  MELTING THE TALLOW HERETICS, ...MARY'S SONG 257   7
  GRAY TALLOW, FROM BONE AND BONE. .....................EAVESDROPPER 260 23
TALONED (2)
  WITH TALONED FINGERS, ...THE SHRIKE 42 11
  THE BARNYARD LIKE THOSE TALONED HAGS ....RHYME 50   5

TAME (4)
   GOING'S BEEN TAME DEVIATION. WHITE, ...WHITENESS I REMEMBER 102   4
   CAT-TAILS PART WHERE THE TAME CYGNETS STEER. ....WATERCOLOR. 112 14
   AWAY FROM THE LABELED ELMS, THE TAME TEA-ROSES. ....TWO CAMP. 144   9
   THE TAME FLOWER-NIBBLERS, THE ONES ....MYSTIC 269 20
TAMPING (1)
   THE FINGERS WERE TAMPING A WOMAN INTO A WALL, ...THE DETECTIVE 208 10
TAMPS (1)
   COLD AS SNOW BREATH, IT TAMPS THE WOMB ....THE MUNICH MANNEQUINS 262   2
TANG (1)
   EVEN, A TANG OF METAL. DAY IN, DAY OUT, *MEMOIRS OF A SPINACH-PICKER 89 16
TANGED (1)
   TANGED BY MELTING TAR, ...DREAM WITH CLAM-DIGGERS   44 10
TANGERINE (1)
   TATTOOS BLACK LEAVES ON TANGERINE. ....BLACK PINE TREE. 328 12
TANGERINES (1)
   A BRIEFCASE OF TANGERINES. ....LITTLE FUGUE 188 46
TANGLE (2)
   ONE LABYRINTHINE TANGLE ....FULL FATHOM FIVE   93 34
   TANGLE THE TRACK. ....TEMPER OF TIME 336 12
TANGLED (3)
   TWISTING CURSES IN THE TANGLED SHEET ....THE SHRIKE   42 10
   OUT OF SHEER BOREDOM. TANGLED IN THE SWEAT-WET SHEETS ....ZOO K. 155 23
   WITH ORANGE SCALLOPS TANGLED IN WET HAIR, ...MIDSUMMER MOBILE 324 11
TANGLING (1)
   TANGLING IN THE TIDE'S GREEN FALL ....TWO LOVERS. 327   6
TANG'S (1)
   ANY TOUCH, TASTE, TANG'S ....ALL THE DEAD DEARS   71 29
TANKS (1)
   GAS TANKS, FACTORY STACKS -- THAT LANDSCAPE ...SUICIDE OFF EGG ROCK 115   3
TAP (5)
   TWO ENTER TO TAP HER SIGHT, A GREEN PAIR ....CRYSTAL GAZER   55   7
   TAP, TAP, TAP, STEEL PEGS. I AM FOUND WANTING. ....THREE WOMEN 177 35
   TAP, TAP, TAP, STEEL PEGS. I AM FOUND WANTING. ....THREE WOMEN 177 35
   TAP, TAP, TAP, STEEL PEGS. I AM FOUND WANTING. ....THREE WOMEN 177 35
   I KNOW THE BOTTOM, SHE SAYS. I KNOW IT WITH MY GREAT TAP ROOT: ELM 192   1
TAPE (1)
   WHILE THE DAY OUTSIDE GLIDES BY LIKE TICKER TAPE. ....PARALYTIC 266 10
TAPESTRIES (2)
   OR TAPESTRIES ON A WALL, ...MAGNOLIA SHOALS 122 10
   TAPESTRIES OF EYES, ...PARALYTIC 266 12
TAPESTRY (3)
   OR, AT MOST, TO A MILLE-FLEURS TAPESTRY. BUT THE COUCH ...YADWIGHA.   85 17
   STILL IN ONE GIGANTIC TAPESTRY -- ....IN MIDAS' COUNTRY   99 14
   WINDLESS THREADWORK OF A TAPESTRY. ....A LIFE 149   5
TAPPED (1)
   TAPPED LIKE A CASK, THE YEARS DRAINING INTO MY PILLOW. ...FACE LIFT 156 18
TAPPING (1)
   TAPPING AND TICKING LIKE NERVOUS FINGERS. ....LEAVING EARLY 146 27
TAR (2)
   TANGED BY MELTING TAR, ...DREAM WITH CLAM-DIGGERS   44 10
   FERRYING THE SMELLS OF DEAD COD AND TAR. ....A WINTER SHIP 113 20
TARDILY (1)
   THE SUN BRIGHTENS TARDILY ....FROG AUTUMN   99   6
TARN (2)
   WHICH OUT FROM BLACK TARN, DITCH AND CUP ....STRUMPET SONG   34 17
   THAT KNITS TO EACH ORIGINAL ITS COARSE COPY. A DARK TARN*LADY AND T.   69 15
TARNISH (1)
   DAY OF MIST: DAY OF TARNISH ....RESOLVE   52   1
TARNISHED (1)
   IN TARNISHED MODES, MAUNDERING AMONG THE WASTES, ...OUIJA   77 13
TARNISHES (1)
   DARKENS AND TARNISHES AND WHEN ....CUT 236 32
TAROC (2)
   AND MY TAROC PACK AND MY TAROC PACK ....DADDY 223 39
   AND MY TAROC PACK AND MY TAROC PACK ....DADDY 223 39
TAR-PAPER (1)
   BETWEEN THE SNUFF AND RED TAR-PAPER APARTMENTS, ...ABOVE THE OXBOW   88 13
TARRED (1)
   A TARRED FABRIC, SORRY AND DULL, ...BERCK-PLAGE 200 114
TARRY (1)
   WITH TARRY MUCK ....GREEN ROCK, WINTHROP BAY 105 12
TART (2)
   HOW THIS TART FABLE INSTRUCTS ....VIRGIN IN A TREE   81   1
   PUNY, GREEN, AND TART, ...JILTED 304 10
TARTING (1)
   TARTING WITH THE DRAFTS THAT PASS, ...EAVESDROPPER 260 31
TASK (1)
   FOR SUCH A TEMPERING TASK, ...NOTES TO A NEOPHYTE 306 13
TASK'S (1)
   NOW OUR WHOLE TASK'S TO HACK ....FIRESONG   30   8
TASSELED (1)
   OVERHEAD, THE CLOUDS SIT TASSELED AND FANCY ....A LIFE 150 15
TASSELS (1)
   FACED IN HIS RICH YELLOWS, TASSELS, POMPONS, BRAID, THE PICADOR ...
                                                    ... THE GORING   47   5

```
                                              TITLE              PAGE  LINE
TASTE (12)
   BOWL ONE HOMEWARD TO TASTE  ..........................FIESTA MELONS    46    9
   SURFEITING EYE, EAR, TASTE, TOUCH, SMELL: *ON THE PLETHORA OF DRYADS   67   27
   ANY TOUCH, TASTE, TANG'S  .........................ALL THE DEAD DEARS  71   29
   THE WATER HAD AN IRON TASTE, AND THE AIR,  ..........SPINACH-PICKER.   89   15
   A FRUIT THAT'S DEATH TO TASTE: DARK FLESH, DARK PARINGS. ...
                              ...  THE BEEKEEPER'S DAUGHTER  118   14
   I CAN TASTE THE TIN OF THE SKY -- THE REAL TIN THING.  ......WAKING.  151    1
   THE WATER I TASTE IS WARM AND SALT, LIKE THE SEA,  ..........TULIPS  162   62
   I TASTE IT ON MY TONGUE, AND THE WORKABLE HORRORS,  .....THREE WOMEN  180  136
   WHAT WILL THEY TASTE OF, THE CHRISTMAS ROSES?  ............WINTERING  219   49
   THE BEES ARE FLYING. THEY TASTE THE SPRING.  .............WINTERING  219   50
   TASTE IT, DARK RED!  ...........................CHILDLESS WOMAN  259   14
   AND THE TASTE OF STRAWBERRIES  ..................BITTER STRAWBERRIES  299    8
TASTED (2)
   THESE HILLS ARE TOO GREEN AND SWEET TO HAVE TASTED SALT.   BLACKBER.  169   22
   I TASTED THE MALIGNITY OF THE GORSE,  ...........THE RABBIT CATCHER  193    6
TASTING (2)
   TASTING THE BITTERNESS BETWEEN MY TEETH.  ...............THREE WOMEN  184  286
   TASTING THE WINDS, THAT ARE FOOTLESS,  .................WINTER TREES  258    9
TATE (2)
   TATE AND LYLE KEEPS THEM GOING,  .......................WINTERING  218   27
   IT IS TATE AND LYLE THEY LIVE ON, INSTEAD OF FLOWERS.  ....WINTERING  218   29
TATTER (1)
   A RED TATTER, NAPOLEON!  ..................................THE SWARM  217   40
TATTERS (1)
   TRAILING ITS TELLTALE TATTERS ONLY AT THE OUTERMOST  .......GHOST'S.   90   21
TATTLE (1)
   THE TATTLE OF MY  .............................................GIGOLO  268   21
TATTLING (1)
   TATTLING IN ITS CAT-VOICE OF DEPARTURE, DEPARTURE.  ..........A LIFE  150   32
TATTOO (1)
   AND HIS BLOOD BEATING THE OLD TATTOO  .........SUICIDE OFF EGG ROCK  115    8
TATTOOING (1)
   TATTOOING OVER AND OVER THE SAME BLUE GRIEVANCES,  ........COURAGE.  210   11
TATTOOIST (1)
   A GREAT SURGEON, NOW A TATTOOIST,  .......THE COURAGE OF SHUTTING-UP  210   10
TATTOOS (1)
   TATTOOS BLACK LEAVES ON TANGERINE.  ................BLACK PINE TREE.  328   12
TAUGHT (1)
   AND ALL ELSE I'VE TAUGHT  .................................RECANTATION   42   12
TAUNT (2)
   GLOWERING AT THE COAL-FIRE: "COME FIND ME" -- HER LAST TAUNT.  ...
                              ...  THE SNOWMAN ON THE MOOR   58    5
   TELL NOW, WE TAUNT, WHERE BLACK OR WHITE BEGINS   LOVE IS A PARALLAX  330   49
TAUNTING (2)
   FLOATS CHASTE AS SNOW, TAUNTING THE CLOUDED MIND   WINTER LANDSCAPE,   21    4
   UNDER A TENT OF TAUNTING GULLS.  .......................TWO LOVERS.  327   16
TAUNTS (2)
   TAUNTS US TO VALOR. BLUE SAILORS SANG THAT OUR JOURNEY  ..CHANNEL C.   27   20
   YOU TO TAUNTS THOUGH, WHEN HE REFLECTS A FACE  .........DIALOGUE O.  283  260
TAUT (2)
   AND HUNGRY, HUNGRY, THOSE TAUT THIGHS.  .....................PURSUIT   23   32
   OF NATURE: WHAT BETTER WAY TO TEST TAUT FIBER  .....CHANNEL CROSSING   27   16
TAUTEN (1)
   WHEN I GRIN, THE STITCHES TAUTEN. I GROW BACKWARD. I'M TWENTY,*FACE.  156   21
TAWDRY (2)
   UNLESS YOU DO THIS TAWDRY HARBOR  ..........GREEN ROCK, WINTHROP BAY  105   19
   THIS IS NEWNESS: EVERY LITTLE TAWDRY  ..........NEW YEAR ON DARTMOOR  176    1
TAWN (3)
   LEAN FACE GONE TAWN WITH SEASONS,  .....................CRYSTAL GAZER   54    2
   STREAK AND MOTTLE OF TAWN BARK,  ..........ON THE PLETHORA OF DRYADS   67   22
   CIRCLE, WITH ITS TAWN SILK GRASSES -- BABIES' HAIR.   LETTER IN NOV.  253    7
TAXIS (1)
   TAXIS INDOLENT ON WHISPERED WHEELS;*MORNING IN THE HOSPITAL SOLARIUM  332   11
T.B. (1)
   THE SUN GIVES YOU ULCERS, THE WIND GIVES YOU T.B.  ..........LESBOS  228   39
TEA (7)
   "TEA LEAVES I'VE GIVEN UP,  ............................RECANTATION   41    1
   I FELT HANDS ROUND A  TEA MUG, DULL, BLUNT,  .....THE RABBIT CATCHER  194   22
   TODDLE ON HOME TO TEA NOW IN YOUR FLAT HAT.  .............THE TOUR  238   37
   IT'LL BE LEMON TEA FOR ME,  ..............................THE TOUR  238   38
   LEMON TEA AND EARWIG BISCUITS -- CREEPY-CREEPY.  ...........THE TOUR  238   39
   TODDLE ON HOME TO TEA!  .....................................THE TOUR  238   49
   AND HERE YOU COME, WITH A CUP OF TEA  .....................KINDNESS  270   16
TEACH (1)
   IT HURTS AT FIRST. THE RED TONGUES WILL TEACH THE TRUTH.   POEM.6.W.  135   18
TEACHER (1)
   ALTHOUGH EACH TEACHER FOUND MY TOUCH  .........THE DISQUIETING MUSES   75   35
TEACUP (1)
   AND THE HIVE ITSELF A TEACUP,  .............................STINGS  214    8
TEACUPS (1)
   TO BRING TEACUPS AND ROLL AWAY HEADACHES  ............THE APPLICANT  221   12
TEA-LEAVES (1)
   DRUNK, AND TEA-LEAVES CANDID; THE CLAIRVOYANT SEIZURE  ..DIALOGUE O.  279  123
```

```
                                              TITLE             PAGE  LINE
TEAR (4)
    THE CROWD SUCKS HER LAST TEAR AND TURNS AWAY. ...........AFTERMATH  114  14
    ROUND, GREEN, DISCONSOLATE AS A TEAR. .....THE BEEKEEPER'S DAUGHTER  118  18
    THIS EGG-SHAPED BAILIWICK, CLEAR AS A TEAR. ...............A LIFE  149   2
    LET MY TRANSIENT EYE BREAK A TEAR .....................TOUCH-AND-GO  336  19
TEAR-DAZZLED (1)
    THE RED, ROYAL ROBES OF PHEDRE? THE TEAR-DAZZLED ...........PERSEUS  83  41
TEARFUL (1)
    PARENTAL FACES ON TALL STALKS, ALTERNATELY STERN AND TEARFUL, ...
                                                  ... INSOMNIAC  163  11
TEARING (2)
    TEARING OFF MY VOICE, AND THE SEA ...............THE RABBIT CATCHER  193   3
    THE DOGS ARE TEARING A FOX. THIS IS WHAT IT IS LIKE -- ....BURNING.  205  49
TEA-ROSES (1)
    AWAY FROM THE LABELED ELMS, THE TAME TEA-ROSES. ..........TWO CAMP.  144   9
TEAR-PEARLED (1)
    ARC OF TEAR-PEARLED ....................................POLLY'S TREE  129  39
TEARS (14)
    DESPITE HER WRUNG HANDS, HER TEARS, HER PRAYING: VANISH!*LADY AND T.  70  30
    THAN VIRGINS' TEARS. THAT BAWDY QUEEN OF DEATH, ..............OUIJA  77  24
    RINSING THOSE STABLES: A BABY'S TEARS WOULD DO IT. .........PERSEUS  82   7
    NEITHER TEARS NOR THE EASING FLUSH .....................THE EYE-MOTE  109  19
    MY CHEEK OF BASALT. THEY TURNED TO TEARS, ..............LOVE LETTER  147  15
    BUT DIDN'T CONVINCE ME. THOSE TEARS FROZE. ............LOVE LETTER  147  17
    I WATCH THEIR SPILT TEARS CLOUD AND DULL TO PEARLS. ........CANDLES  149  31
    WHEN THEY FREE ME, I AM BEADED WITH TEARS. ............FINISTERRE  169  18
    SHE REWARDS ME WITH TEARS AND AN AGITATION OF HANDS. ........MIRROR  174  14
    DRIP AND THICKEN, TEARS .....................NICK AND THE CANDLESTICK  240   3
    WELLS LIKE TEARS, LIKE THE .......................................WORDS  270   7
    MY TEARS LIKE VINEGAR, ...........................................JILTED  304   2
    (WHILE SHE WASHED THE WAY WITH TEARS), ...................THE DREAM  311  27
    IN OUR OWN TEARS: TODAY WE START .................LOVE IS A PARALLAX  330  75
TEARY (1)
    MUMBLEPAWS, TEARY AND SORRY, ........................POEM.4.BEAST.  134  12
TEASE (1)
    THE BIG STRIP TEASE. ....................................LADY LAZARUS  245  29
TEASET (1)
    I WATCHED MY TEASET, MY BUREAUS OF LINEN, MY BOOKS ..........TULIPS  161  26
TEASING (1)
    HE MADE OF THE FOOTBALL POOLS -- TEASING US WITH .......DIALOGUE O.  277  39
TEATS (1)
    TO HALT FOR A SWIG AT THE PINK TEATS. NO. THIS VAST ............SOW  61  23
TECHNICAL (1)
    WITH VALENTINO'S CRACK TECHNICAL TALENT ..........DIALOGUE EN ROUTE  309  22
TED (1)
    ODE FOR TED ............................................ODE FOR TED  29   T
TEDIOUS (3)
    SCATHED, STAINED AFTER TEDIOUS PILGRIMAGES. *DREAM WITH CLAM-DIGGERS  43   4
    TEDIOUS. THAT'S WHAT WE'D SAY. ABOUT ROT*DIALOGUE OVER A OUIJA BOARD  279 101
    AND REMEMBER, IF TEDIOUS RISK .... ...........NOTES TO A NEOPHYTE  306  17
TEDIUM (1)
    HOW THEY LIT THE TEDIUM OF THE PROTRACTED EVENING! .......INSOMNIAC  163  16
TEEMING (1)
    THAT EVERY BREATH, THUS TEEMING, SET THE LAND ..WREATH FOR A BRIDAL  45  21
TEETH (17)
    KEEN THE RENDING TEETH AND SWEET ............................PURSUIT  22  17
    TO SLAY SPAWN OF DRAGON'S TEETH: SPEAKING THIS PROMISE, ..WREATH F.  45  23
    HIS TEETH ARE CHATTERING AMONG THE LEPROUS ..THE EVERLASTING MONDAY  62   5
    AND AS I LISTENED ITS COLD TEETH SEETHED   ON THE DECLINE OF ORACLES  78   3
    HER SALLOW RODENT TEETH LIKE CASTANETS ...............INCOMMUNICADO  100   4
    LOOK UPON? RATS' TEETH GUT THE CITY ............................OWL  102  15
    A MONSTER OF WOOD AND RUSTY TEETH. ..............THE BURNT-OUT SPA  137   2
    OLD GRIEVANCES JOSTLING EACH OTHER, SO MANY LOOSE TEETH. ....ZOO K.  154  13
    ALL WIG CURLS AND YELLOW TEETH ..................WUTHERING HEIGHTS  167  26
    A SET OF TEETH, OR STONES ..................THE SURGEON AT 2 A.M.  171  34
    MY DAUGHTER HAS NO TEETH. HER MOUTH IS WIDE. ...........THREE WOMEN  182 216
    TASTING THE BITTERNESS BETWEEN MY TEETH. ..............THREE WOMEN  184 286
    A GLASS EYE, FALSE TEETH OR A CRUTCH, .................THE APPLICANT  221   3
    THE NOSE, THE EYE PITS, THE FULL SET OF TEETH? .......LADY LAZARUS  244  13
    STEAMING AND BREATHING, ITS TEETH ....................GETTING THERE  248  39
    HIS THREE TEETH CUTTING ....................................BRASILIA  258  12
    THEIR ROUND EYES, THEIR TEETH, THEIR GRIMACES ...............TOTEM  264  17
TELEGRAM (5)
    THE TELEGRAM SAYS YOU HAVE GONE AWAY .................DENOUEMENT  326   1
    THE TELEGRAM SAYS YOU HAVE GONE AWAY. ................DENOUEMENT  326   6
    THE TELEGRAM SAYS YOU HAVE GONE AWAY. ................DENOUEMENT  327  12
    THE TELEGRAM SAYS YOU HAVE GONE AWAY; ...............DENOUEMENT  327  18
    EACH WITH A TELEGRAM ADDRESSED TO ME. .......EPITAPH IN THREE PARTS  337   3
TELEPHONE (2)
    THIS WOMAN ON THE TELEPHONE ..........................THE FEARFUL  256   3
    HE RENTS HIS POISONS OUT BY TELEPHONE; ..................DENOUEMENT  327  14
TELEPHONE'S (1)
    THE BLACK TELEPHONE'S OFF AT THE ROOT, .. ....................DADDY  224  69
TELESCOPE (1)
    THROUGH THE SCRUPULOUS TELESCOPE ........METAMORPHOSES OF THE MOON  308  39
```

501

TELL (28)
    THIS GIANT HULKED, I TELL YOU, ON HER SCENE ..THE QUEEN'S COMPLAINT   28   2
    OF GILDED HARPS OR GNAWING FIRE: SIMPLY TELL ....DIALOGUE B.   39   23
    FRESH LEAVED OUT IN VOWS: "COME TELL ....CRYSTAL GAZER   55   8
    TELL ME MY NAME. POEM.3.MAENAD.   133   25
    THEIR CHAR OF KARAKUL STILL. I CAN'T TELL ....THE BURNT-OUT SPA   138   7
    I LEAN TO YOU, NUMB AS A FOSSIL. TELL ME I'M HERE. ....TWO CAMP.   145   21
    HOW SHALL I TELL ANYTHING AT ALL ....CANDLES 149   32
    NOBODY CAN TELL WHAT I LACK. ....PARLIAMENT HILL FIELDS   152   5
    YOU COULD TELL ALMOST AT ONCE SHE HAD A SLAVE MENTALITY. *IN PLASTER 159   21
    SO IT IS IMPOSSIBLE TO TELL HOW MANY THERE ARE. ....TULIPS 160   14
    AND THEY ARE ALL GLOVED AND COVERED, WHY DID NOBODY TELL ME? ..BEE. 211   4
    AND DO WHATEVER YOU TELL IT. ....THE APPLICANT   221   13
    SO I NEVER COULD TELL WHERE YOU ....DADDY 223   22
    AND WE'LL SEE WHO'S SMARTEST. PAN, TELL US NOW: ....DIALOGUE O.   281 205
    TELL US THE TRUTH THIS TIME: TELL US THE KINGDOM ......DIALOGUE O.   283 272
    TELL US THE TRUTH THIS TIME: TELL US THE KINGDOM ......DIALOGUE O.   283 272
    TELL US THE TURTH. WHERE DO YOU LIVE? HE STARTS ....DIALOGUE O.   283 274
    I DO NOT TELL YOU THE NIGHTMARE ....THE DREAM 311   29
    TELL ME QUICK, DARLING, TELL ME NOW. ....THE DISPOSSESSED   318   3
    TELL ME QUICK, DARLING, TELL ME NOW. ....THE DISPOSSESSED   318   3
    TELL ME QUICK, DARLING, TELL ME NOW. ....THE DISPOSSESSED   318   9
    TELL ME QUICK, DARLING, TELL ME NOW. ....THE DISPOSSESSED   318   9
    TELL ME QUICK, DARLING, TELL ME NOW. ....THE DISPOSSESSED   318   15
    TELL ME QUICK, DARLING, TELL ME NOW. ....THE DISPOSSESSED   318   15
    TELL ME QUICK, DARLING, TELL ME NOW! ....THE DISPOSSESSED   319   19
    TELL ME QUICK, DARLING, TELL ME NOW! ....THE DISPOSSESSED   319   19
    TELL ME WHAT YOU SEE IN IT: ....BLACK PINE TREE IN AN ORANGE LIGHT   328   1
    TELL NOW, WE TAUNT, WHERE BLACK OR WHITE BEGINS   LOVE IS A PARALLAX 330   49
TELLING (2)
    THERE WAS NO TELLING IF HE'D ....MUSSEL HUNTER AT ROCK HARBOR   97   74
    TELLING THE PARTICLES OF THE CLOUDS, THE LEAVES, THE WATER *BURNING. 205   55
TELLS (3)
    HE TELLS ME HOW BADLY I PHOTOGRAPH. ....DEATH & CO. 254   12
    HE TELLS ME HOW SWEET ....DEATH & CO.   254   13
    SHE TELLS THE GREENHORN MINER TO BOW DOWN ....THE PRINCESS.   335   61
TELLTALE (1)
    TRAILING ITS TELLTALE TATTERS ONLY AT THE OUTERMOST ....GHOST'S.   90   21
TEMPER (5)
    HIS TALKING WHIRLWIND, ABATED HIS EXCESSIVE TEMPER ....OUIJA   77   16
    TO SAFE GRAY NEVER GRAYED HIS TEMPER. ....WHITENESS I REMEMBER 102   11
    AND TURNED THE FARMBOY'S TEMPER WOLFISH, ..THE DEATH OF MYTH-MAKING 104   14
    NEVER TRESPASSING IN BAD TEMPER: ....A LIFE 150   12
    TEMPER OF TIME ....TEMPER OF TIME   336   T
TEMPERING (1)
    FOR SUCH A TEMPERING TASK, ...NOTES TO A NEOPHYTE   306   13
TEMPLE (1)
    ON WINTER STREET, ON TEMPLE PLACE. ....A WINTER'S TALE   87   17
TEMPLES (1)
    THE TEMPLES OF THE ORTHODOX. ...INSOLENT STORM STRIKES AT THE SKULL 326   12
TEMPO (2)
    TEMPO OF STRICT OCEAN ....TRIO OF LOVE SONGS 314   9
    TICKS TEMPO TO THE CASUAL CLIMB ...MORNING IN THE HOSPITAL SOLARIUM 332   16
TEMPORARY (1)
    THE BOX IS ONLY TEMPORARY. ....THE ARRIVAL OF THE BEE BOX   213   36
TEMPTING (1)
    AS IF TEMPTING OUR GROSS GULLIBILITY ...DIALOGUE OVER A OUIJA BOARD 281 178
TEN (10)
    TWO OF US IN A PLACE MEANT FOR TEN MORE -- ....THE OTHER TWO   68   10
    WHITE PETALS, WHITE FAN-TAILS, TEN WHITE FINGERS. ....MOONRISE   98   9
    TEN FINGERS SHAPE A BOWL FOR SHADOWS. POEM.7.S.   137   43
    IT IS TEN YEARS, NOW, SINCE WE ROWED TO CHILDREN'S ISLAND. ...BABY. 174   1
    BUT TEN YEARS DEAD. ....THE BABYSITTERS   175   36
    I HOLD MY FINGERS UP, TEN WHITE PICKETS. ....THREE WOMEN 182 194
    I WAS TEN WHEN THEY BURIED YOU. ....DADDY   224   57
    SHE'LL CUT HER THROAT AT TEN IF SHE'S MAD AT TWO. ....LESBOS   228   22
    ONE YEAR IN EVERY TEN ....LADY LAZARUS   244   2
    THE FIRST TIME IT HAPPENED I WAS TEN. ....LADY LAZARUS 245   35
TENACITY (1)
    A POWER IS GROWING ON ME, AN OLD TENACITY. ....THREE WOMEN   180 141
TENANT (1)
    LISTEN: YOUR TENANT MICE ....LEAVING EARLY 146   35
TENANT'S (1)
    NEXT TO THE LAST TENANT'S RANCID JAM ....WINTERING   218   8
TEND (1)
    MY BODY IS A PEBBLE TO THEM, THEY TEND IT AS WATER ....TULIPS   160   15
TENDER (2)
    RUEFUL, MOST VEXED, THAT TENDER SKIN ....BUCOLICS   24   17
    SOME HAVOC ON TENDER LIMB, AND YET ....CRYSTAL GAZER   55   23
TENDERER (1)
    ON SPIRITS TENDERER THAN THEIRS, ...THE BEGGARS   48   14
TENDERLY (2)
    THEY HAVE LIVED BEHIND GLASS ALL THEIR LIVES, THEY HAVE BEEN CARED
        FOR TENDERLY. ....THREE WOMEN 184 264
    OVER WHOSE POOL I TENDERLY ....GIGOLO   268   31

TENDERNESS (5)
    OF TENDERNESS DOVE THROUGH THEIR PURGATORY ....THE OTHER TWO   68   24
    HOW I WOULD LIKE TO BELIEVE IN TENDERNESS --- ....MOON. 173   19
    WITH PINKNESS, AS IF A TENDERNESS AWOKE, ...THREE WOMEN 186 356
    A TENDERNESS THAT DID NOT TIRE, SOMETHING HEALING. .....THREE WOMEN 186 357
    IS THERE NO GREAT LOVE, ONLY TENDERNESS? ....MYSTIC 269   24
TENDING (2)
    UNDERSHIRTS CIRCLED, TENDING ....NIGHT SHIFT   77   21
    TENDING, WITHOUT STOP, THE BLUNT ....NIGHT SHIFT   77   23
TENDON (1)
    THE AGUEY TENDON, THE SIN, THE SIN. ....FEVER. 231   7
TENDRILS (2)
    A MELON STROLLING ON TWO TENDRILS. ....METAPHORS 116   3
    IS IT BLOOD CLOTS THE TENDRILS ARE DRAGGING UP THAT STRING? ...BEE. 211   19
TENDS (1)
    TENDS TO THE PEBBLES IT MUST RUN OVER, SMOOTHING THEM GENTLY.*TULIPS 160   16
TENNIS (1)
    AS A TENNIS BALL AT TWILIGHT ....APRIL 18 302   16
TENSE (1)
    HIS NEAT TROT PITCHING MY TENSE POISE UP, ...WHITENESS I REMEMBER 102   14
TENT (7)
    GERD SITS SPINDLE-SHANKED IN HER DARK TENT, ...CRYSTAL GAZER   54   1
    AROUND OUR TENT THE OLD SIMPLICITIES SOUGH ....TWO CAMP. 145   25
    THE TENT OF UNENDING CRIES --- ....GETTING THERE 248   27
    BEFORE ONE HEAVED HIMSELF THROUGH HEAVEN'S TENT ....DIALOGUE O. 281 171
    IN THE CIRCUS TENT OF A HURRICANE ....CIRCUS IN THREE RINGS 321   1
    UNDER A TENT OF TAUNTING GULLS. ....TWO LOVERS. 327   16
    THEN LET THE BLUE TENT TOPPLE, STARS RAIN DOWN,   LOVE IS A PARALLAX 330   73
TENTACLE (2)
    WITHDRAWS ITS TENTACLE.   ...WORDS HEARD, BY ACCIDENT, OVER THE PHONE 203   12
    OFF, OFF, EELY TENTACLE! ....MEDUSA 226   40
TENTATIVE (1)
    THEIR PALE, TENTATIVE YELLOWS ....CANDLES 149   15
TENTS (2)
    THE TENTS OF SUN ABSORB. ....TRIO OF LOVE SONGS 314   20
    THE COLORED TENTS ALL TOPPLE IN THE BAY: ....DENOUEMENT 327   16
TERM (1)
    NOW YOU MUST PLAY THE STRAIGHT MAN FOR A TERM ....DIRGE FOR A JOKER 303   13
TERMINAL (1)
    TERMINAL ....TERMINAL 328   T
TERMINUS (1)
    THERE IS NO TERMINUS, ONLY SUITCASES ....TOTEM 264   24
TERMS (1)
    COLD MOONS WITHDRAW, REFUSING TO COME TO TERMS ......METAMORPHOSES. 307   1
TERRACE (3)
    NO CHANGE MET HER: GARDEN TERRACE, ALL SUMMER ....DREAM WITH C.   44   9
    IN HER RAMSHACKLE HOUSE OFF SOMERSET TERRACE; ....ELLA MASON A.   53   2
    WE SNICKERED AS SHE SHAMBLED DOWN SOMERSET TERRACE ...ELLA MASON A.   54   32
TERRIBLE (21)
    COT LEGS MELTED IN TERRIBLE ATTITUDES, AND THE NURSES -- ...WAKING. 151   12
    RISES TOWARD HER DAY AFTER DAY, LIKE A TERRIBLE FISH. ....MIRROR 174   18
    AND THE GREAT SWAN, WITH ITS TERRIBLE LOOK, ...THREE WOMEN 178   50
    OTHER CHILDREN DO NOT TOUCH ME: THEY ARE TERRIBLE. .....THREE WOMEN 178   68
    FACE THE VOICES THAT OVERWHELM, THE TERRIBLE ELEMENT. ..THREE WOMEN 179 112
    THERE IS THIS CESSATION. THIS TERRIBLE CESSATION OF EVERYTHING. ...
                                                    ... THREE WOMEN 181 180
    I SEE HER IN MY SLEEP, MY RED, TERRIBLE GIRL. ....THREE WOMEN 182 204
    IT IS A TERRIBLE THING ....THREE WOMEN 185 299
    I DO NOT BELIEVE IN THOSE TERRIBLE CHILDREN ....THREE WOMEN 185 320
    THE STARS ARE FLASHING LIKE TERRIBLE NUMERALS. ....AN APPEARANCE 189   17
    HE IS QUITE BLUE; THE TERRIBLE WIND TRIES HIS BREATHING. NARCISSI. 190   11
    AND MY HEART TOO SMALL TO BANDAGE THEIR TERRIBLE FAULTS.*BERCK-PLAGE 198   45
    MIRRORS CAN KILL AND TALK, THEY ARE TERRIBLE ROOMS ....COURAGE. 210   27
    MORE TERRIBLE THAN SHE EVER WAS, RED ....STINGS 215   57
    DROPS ME FROM A TERRIBLE ALTITUDE. ....THE JAILER 226   13
    THE FLUORESCENT LIGHT WINCING ON AND OFF LIKE A TERRIBLE MIGRAINE, ...
                                                    ... LESBOS 227   4
    INTO THE TERRIBLE WELL, ...NICK AND THE CANDLESTICK 242   39
    THE TERRIBLE BRAINS ....GETTING THERE 248   5
    PERFECTION IS TERRIBLE, IT CANNOT HAVE CHILDREN. ....MUNICH. 262   1
    AND IN TRUTH IT IS TERRIBLE, ...TOTEM 265   29
    SHE HAS A TERRIBLE WAY WITH MINERALS, ...THE RIVAL/DR 291   23
TERRIBLY (1)
    WHITE AS A KNUCKLE AND TERRIBLY UPSET.   ...THE MOON AND THE YEW TREE 173   9
TERRIFIED (2)
    I AM TERRIFIED BY THIS DARK THING ....ELM 193   31
    YOU ARE TERRIFIED ....A BIRTHDAY PRESENT 207   28
TERRIFIES (1)
    DARKNESS TERRIFIES IT. ....WUTHERING HEIGHTS 168   42
TERRIFY (2)
    TERRIFY ME, THEY SEEM SO OLD. ....STINGS 214   13
    DO I TERRIFY? --- ....LADY LAZARUS 244   12
TERROR (5)
    BUT SCRUPULOUSLY REFLECTS THE USUAL TERROR. ....TALE OF A TUB   24   8
    AGE AND TERROR, LIKE NURSES, ATTEND HER, ...A LIFE 150   33

                                                     TITLE   PAGE LINE
TERROR (CONT.)
    THIS IS WHAT I AM MADE OF, THIS AND A TERROR .........APPREHENSIONS 195   14
    HER BLUE EYES SWAM WITH VAGUE TERROR. ....BITTER STRAWBERRIES 300   24
    REFLECT IN TERROR ....MOONSONG AT MORNING   317   37
TERROR-STRUCK (1)
    STEEL GAUNTLETS OF TRAFFIC, TERROR-STRUCK ....AERIALIST 332   45
TESSELLATED (1)
    THE TESSELLATED WAVE. NOW NIMBLY LET ....MIDSUMMER MOBILE 324   7
TEST (1)
    OF NATURE: WHAT BETTER WAY TO TEST TAUT FIBER .....CHANNEL CROSSING   27   16
TESTIFIES (1)
    AS SPRANG FROM JOSEPH'S ROD, AND TESTIFIES ....MAYFLOWER   60   7
TESTIFY (1)
    MAY TESTIFY TO DRIVE YOUR DOUBTING OUT. *DIALOGUE OVER A OUIJA BOARD 280 153
TETHER (1)
    FOR A WISH TO TETHER: THEY RIDE NIGHTLONG ....EPITAPH FOR F.   46   26
TETHERED (1)
    THEN BRISKLY SCALED HIS ALTAR TIERED WITH TETHERED ANTS, ...SPIDER   49   22
THALIDOMIDE (1)
    THALIDOMIDE ....THALIDOMIDE 252   T
THAN (70)
    HE PROWLS MORE LORDLY THAN THE SUN. ....PURSUIT   22   4
    THAN PHYSICAL ABLUTION, AND THE TOWEL ....TALE OF A TUB   24   12
    THAN AGAINST THIS ONSLAUGHT, THESE CASUAL BLASTS OF ICE   CHANNEL C.   27   17
    AND, MORE DAFT THAN ANY GOOSE, ...STREET SONG   36   29
    THAN MAN'S RED HEART." ....DIALOGUE B.   39   50
    THAN TO SIT MUTE, TWITCHING SO ....MONOLOGUE AT 3 A.M.   40   8
    RATHER THAN CROAK OUT ....RECANTATION   42   8
    ON SPIRITS TENDERER THAN THEIRS, ...THE BEGGARS   48   14
    TO GOVERN MORE SIGHT THAN GIVEN TO A WOMAN ....CRYSTAL GAZER   55   32
    ANY MORE THAN THE OLD WOMAN IN HER MUD HUT COULD ...THE THIN PEOPLE   64   26
    THAN AXE COULD CUT. ....ON THE PLETHORA OF DRYADS   67   12
    THAN FLESH OF ANY BODY ....ON THE PLETHORA OF DRYADS   67   17
    OTHER THAN NOON, THAN MOON, STARS -- ....THE GREAT CARBUNCLE   72   16
    OTHER THAN NOON, THAN MOON, STARS -- ....THE GREAT CARBUNCLE   72   16
    THAN EARTH, AND THERE IS NOTHING ....THE GREAT CARBUNCLE   73   25
    THAN VIRGINS' TEARS. THAT BAWDY QUEEN OF DEATH, ...OUIJA   77   24
    LESS THAN PRESENT, PAST -- THIS FUTURE. ..ON THE DECLINE OF ORACLES   78   29
    STILL THAN SWALLOWS JOY. YOU ENTER NOW, ...PERSEUS   83   34
    AND BODY WHITER THAN ITS FRILL OF LILIES: ....YADWIGHA.   85   14
    THAN MODELS FROM BONWIT'S OR JAY'S, ...A WINTER'S TALE   86   10
    ELEVATIONS TO BE CALLED SOMETHING MORE THAN HILLS. ABOVE THE OXBOW   88   9
    THAN PRIEST'S HANDS, INVOKE NO VAIN ....SCULPTOR   91   6
    THEM LIFE LIVELIER THAN OURS, ...SCULPTOR   92   23
    A SOLIDER REPOSE THAN DEATH'S. ....SCULPTOR   92   24
    THAN SCULPTED MARBLE. THEY SING ....LORELEI   94   14
    THAN CAN BE. SISTERS, YOUR SONG ....LORELEI   94   16
    EVEN THAN YOUR MADDENING ....LORELEI   94   29
    ART'S SAKE THAN GOD'S. FAR FROM SEA -- *MUSSEL HUNTER AT ROCK HARBOR   97   82
    THAN ITS SUBURB OF WOODS: NIMBUS- ....OWL   101   2
    THE PARK OF LESS RED THAN WITHERING DID. ...........RHODODENDRON.   103   12
    MORE THAN EIGHT DECADES BACK ....THE TIMES ARE TIDY   107   12
    MORE FINICAL THAN ....POLLY'S TREE   128   11
    IT'S WORSE THAN A BARNYARD. ....THE COLOSSUS   129   5
    IT WOULD TAKE MORE THAN A LIGHTNING-STROKE ....THE COLOSSUS   130   22
    FARTHER OFF THAN AUSTRALIA. ....YOU'RE   141   11
    ON A SQUARE NO BIGGER THAN A CARPET ....ON DECK   142   12
    AND A DEW COLLECT ON THEM, DEARER THAN MONEY, ...SLEEP.   144   9
    ATTENDING HER COT IS LESS THAN A BELLY ACHE, ...MAGI   148   13
    YOU'RE NO HAPPIER THAN I ABOUT IT. ....WHITSUN   154   17
    THAN THE CLOUD THAT DISTILLS A MIRROR TO REFLECT ITS OWN SLOW ...
                                              ... MORNING SONG   157   8
    THAN THE DARK OF THE SKY BECAUSE IT IS QUITE STARLESS. ......STARS.   165   3
    THERE IS NO LIFE HIGHER THAN THE GRASSTOPS ....WUTHERING HEIGHTS   167   10
    AND THE SHINE OF THESE SMALL THINGS SWEETER THAN THE FACE OF
      ISHTAR. ....LAST WORDS   172   26
    THERE IS NO MIRACLE MORE CRUEL THAN THIS. ....THREE WOMEN   180 127
    THEY ARE MORE BEAUTIFUL THAN MY BODILESS OWL, ..BURNING THE LETTERS   204   30
    MORE TERRIBLE THAN SHE EVER WAS, RED ....STINGS   215   57
    SHE WOULD RATHER BE DEAD THAN FAT, ...THE FEARFUL   256   13
    TRUER THAN WOMEN, ...WINTER TREES   258   7
    THAN FINANCIER. WHAT GOOD IS HE, IF NOT *DIALOGUE OVER A OUIJA BOARD   277   44
    SIFT HIM ABOUT THE AFTER-LIFE THAN THIS:*DIALOGUE OVER A OUIJA BOARD   278   60
    LESS DREAD OF THE WORLD BEYOND THAN OURS. THAT'S BECAUSE*DIALOGUE O.   278   62
    BULKING MORE REAL THAN WE THINK WE ARE: WE FACE .....DIALOGUE O.   279 115
    THAN AGAINST GRAVITY'S GRIP, TABLES RISING; THE DRINK ..DIALOGUE O.   279 122
    TO A CINDER, THAN MEET A POOR UPSTART OF OUR NETHER ....DIALOGUE O.   280 133
    DEEPER THAN YOUR OWN OCEAN FLOOR, AND GOT ....DIALOGUE O.   283 243
    OTHER THAN YOUR OWN. AS HE BORES YOU ...DIALOGUE OVER A OUIJA BOARD   283 261
    THEM ANY MORE THAN YOU DID. OH, LET IT GO. ....DIALOGUE O.   283 265
    THAN ANY ORCHID. YOU BROKE HIM THEN. I BROKE ....DIALOGUE O.   285 324
    IT IS SIX IN THE MORNING AND FINER THAN ANY SUNDAY -- *QUEEN MARY'S.   290   8
    THAT SOMEHOW WE ARE YOUNGER THAN WE WERE. ....APRIL AUBADE   312   14
    ATHLETIC THAN A VERB, ...TRIO OF LOVE SONGS   314   18

THAN (CONT.)
    NEVER TRY TO KNOW MORE THAN YOU SHOULD.   ....ADMONITIONS   319   3
    NEVER TRY TO KNOW MORE THAN YOU SHOULD.   ....ADMONITIONS   319   9
    NEVER TRY TO KNOW MORE THAN YOU SHOULD.   ....ADMONITIONS   319   15
    NEVER TRY TO KNOW MORE THAN YOU SHOULD.   ....ADMONITIONS   319   19
    BUT MORE PRAGMATIC THAN ALL OF THIS, ...BLACK PINE TREE.   328   16
    THAT STING NO MORE THAN LOVE: A ROOM WHERE TIME *MORNING IN THE HOS.   332   15
    "THERE IS MORE THAN ONE GOOD WAY TO DROWN."   EPITAPH IN THREE PARTS   337   11
    "THERE IS MORE THAN ONE GOOD WAY TO DROWN."   EPITAPH IN THREE PARTS   337   22
    "THERE IS MORE THAN ONE GOOD WAY TO DROWN."   EPITAPH IN THREE PARTS   338   33
THAT (391)
THATCH (1)
    THATCH SMOKES IN THE SUN.   ....THREE WOMEN   185 314
THATCHING (1)
    HIGH ON THE AIRY THATCHING   ....MUSSEL HUNTER AT ROCK HARBOR   97   67
THATCHINGS (1)
    OF PALE FRONTS, STRAW THATCHINGS, THE HARD ROAD*WHITENESS I REMEMBER   102   20
THAT'S (16)
    PARDON, AND THAT'S   ....RHYME   50   12
    A FRUIT THAT'S DEATH TO TASTE: DARK FLESH, DARK PARINGS.   ...
                                   ... THE BEEKEEPER'S DAUGHTER   118   14
    IT WOULD BE BETTER IF THEY WERE ALIVE, AND THAT'S WHAT THEY
        WERE.   ....STILLBORN   142   13
    WHEN YOU KICK ME OUT, THAT'S WHAT I'LL REMEMBER, ...LEAVING EARLY   145   2
    AND FIND NO FACE BUT MY OWN, AND YOU THINK THAT'S FUNNY.*FATHERLESS.   205   9
    THAT'S MY FROST BOX, NO CAT, ...THE TOUR   237   15
    AND THAT'S WHY I HAVE NO HAIR, AUNTIE, THAT'S WHY I CHOKE   THE TOUR   238   24
    AND THAT'S WHY I HAVE NO HAIR, AUNTIE, THAT'S WHY I CHOKE   THE TOUR   238   24
    THAT'S HOW YOU ALWAYS TALK BEFORE WE START.   ....DIALOGUE O.   277   15
    WELL WHAT, THEN? THAT'S THE TROUBLE. LET'S SAY HE   ......DIALOGUE O.   278   51
    LESS DREAD OF THE WORLD BEYOND THAN OURS. THAT'S BECAUSE*DIALOGUE O.   278   62
    TEDIOUS. THAT'S WHAT WE'D SAY. ABOUT ROT*DIALOGUE OVER A OUIJA BOARD   279 101
    THAT'S SOMETHING TO STUDY EVEN IF IT'S NOT   ....DIALOGUE O.   279 108
    E. GODPIE! THAT'S RICH. THE JACKANAPES   DIALOGUE OVER A OUIJA BOARD   282 210
    CASTLES WHEN WE GLANCE ASIDE. THAT'S THAT.   ....DIALOGUE O.   286 356
    THERE, THAT'S THE PINK, PLEASED SQUEAK   ....FAMILY REUNION   300   16
THE (3847)
THEATRICAL (1)
    IT'S THE THEATRICAL   ....LADY LAZARUS   245   51
THEIR (284)
THEIRS (4)
    ON SPIRITS TENDERER THAN THEIRS, ...THE BEGGARS   48   14
    BURNT-OUT WERE THEIRS, OR AS IF THEY THOUGHT   ....AFTERMATH   113   3
    THEIRS IS THE ONLY VOICE, PROTESTING, PROTESTING.   ....BLACKBERRYING   168   12
    OUR WORLD AND THEIRS WE'D BEST PLAY SAFE AND GROOM   .....DIALOGUE O.   281 186
THEM (107)
THEMSELVES (25)
    THEMSELVES AS THE DAWN   ....THE THIN PEOPLE   65   33
    THOSE ROCKS, CLEFT AND WORN, THEMSELVES THEN GROW   ....PERSEUS   83   30
    THEMSELVES MERE ROCKY HILLOCKS TO AN EVEREST.   ......ABOVE THE OXBOW   87   4
    INTO THE BLUE. TOPS DEFINE THEMSELVES AS PLACES   ....ABOVE THE OXBOW   88   29
    DOUBLING THEMSELVES IN A GLASS   ....LORELEI   94   8
    AND RETURN, LOSING THEMSELVES   ....MUSSEL HUNTER AT ROCK HARBOR   97   88
    THEMSELVES UP AGAINST THE WALL   ....OLD LADIES' HOME   120   6
    WRAPPED UP IN THEMSELVES AS IN THICK VEILING   ....ON DECK   142   2
    THE COLORS ASSERT THEMSELVES WITH A SORT OF VENGEANCE.   ...TWO CAMP.   145   14
    UNSPOOL AND SPEND THEMSELVES. MY MIND RUNS WITH THEM, *PARLIAMENT H.   153   35
    SMILING TO THEMSELVES, THEY MEDITATE   ....HEAVY WOMEN   158   8
    THE WALLS, ALSO, SEEM TO BE WARMING THEMSELVES.   ....TULIPS   162   57
    AND IT IS MY EYES THAT HAVE BEEN SHARPENING THEMSELVES?   .....STARS.   166   26
    LINTEL AND SILL HAVE UNHINGED THEMSELVES.   ....WUTHERING HEIGHTS   168   32
    THEY ACCOMMODATE THEMSELVES TO MY MILKBOTTLE, FLATTENING THEIR
        SIDES.   ....BLACKBERRYING   168   9
    AND WHAT IF THEY FOUND THEMSELVES SURPRISED, AS I DID?   THREE WOMEN   180 118
    THE COLORS REPLENISH THEMSELVES, AND THE WET   ....THREE WOMEN   185 313
    LAUNDER AND PRESENT THEMSELVES.   ....AN APPEARANCE   189   7
    AND THE SNARES ALMOST EFFACED THEMSELVES --   .....THE RABBIT CATCHER   194   14
    TWO LOVERS UNSTICK THEMSELVES.   ....BERCK-PLAGE   197   30
    WORMING THEMSELVES INTO NICHES.   ....THE SWARM   217   45
    LOSE THEMSELVES. IN MATHEMATICS?   ....THE NIGHT DANCES   249   4
    THE BLOOD BERRIES ARE THEMSELVES, THEY ARE VERY STILL.   ....YEARS   255   23
    THEMSELVES ON MY THUMB --   ....WINTER TREES   258   13
    THEMSELVES ON THE CLAY TOES AND SHORT CLUBFOOT   ......METAMORPHOSES.   308   35
THEN (78)
    THEN, HONOR-BOUND, MUTE GRAZING CATTLE;   ....BUCOLICS   24   11
    WHAT LOVE DID THEN, LOVE DOES NOW:*DIALOGUE BETWEEN GHOST AND PRIEST   39   29
    THEN BRISKLY SCALED HIS ALTAR TIERED WITH TETHERED ANTS, ...SPIDER   49   22
    HOW SHE LONGED FOR WINTER THEN!--   ....SPINSTER   49   13
    "NO HARDSHIP THEN?" HE ASKS. "WE'LL TAKE   ....CRYSTAL GAZER   55   19
    THEN, A FREE-GADDING HOYDEN, GERD HAD CRAVED   ....CRYSTAL GAZER   55   31
    WHAT GERD SAW THEN ENGRAVED HER MIND   ....CRYSTAL GAZER   56   43
    POSSESSION OF THE MOST OBTUSE OBJECTS NOW AND THEN -- *BLACK ROOK I.   57   18
    HUMBLED THEN, AND CRYING, ...THE SNOWMAN ON THE MOOR   59   49
    THEN, WITH A JOCULAR FIST THWACKED THE BARREL NAPE, ...SOW   61   35

THEN (CONT.)
    SHE THOUGHT OF THEN, THICK-SILTED, WITH WEEDS OBSCURED, *LADY AND T.   69   16
    THOSE ROCKS, CLEFT AND WORN, THEMSELVES THEN GROW ....PERSEUS   83   30
    THEY CALLED THE PLACE LOOKOUT FARM. BACK THEN, THE SUN ...
                         ... MEMOIRS OF A SPINACH-PICKER   89   1
    THEN YOU COME IN WITH THE TIDE'S COMING ....FULL FATHOM FIVE   92   2
    THEN, TO SQUALL ABOVE THE LEVEL ....OWL   102   10
    TO A GIDDY JOG. THEN FOR ILL WILL ....WHITENESS I REMEMBER   102   17
    CRIED THEN FOR THE FATHER'S BLOOD ....I WANT, I WANT   106   6
    NEEDLING IT DARK. THEN I WAS SEEING ....THE EYE-MOTE   109   10
    I BROUGHT MY LOVE TO BEAR, AND THEN YOU DIED.*ELECTRA ON AZALEA PATH   117   38
    FOR WHAT, THEN, HAD THEY ENDURED .....THE HERMIT AT OUTERMOST HOUSE   119   7
    IF I'M ALIVE NOW, THEN I WAS DEAD, ...LOVE LETTER   147   2
    THEN MOTHER SWAM UP, HOLDING A TIN BASIN. ....FACE LIFT   156   7
    THEN I REALIZED WHAT SHE WANTED WAS FOR ME TO LOVE HER: IN PLASTER   159   13
    THEN I SAW WHAT THE TROUBLE WAS: SHE THOUGHT SHE WAS IMMORTAL. ...
                         ... IN PLASTER   159   35
    THEN SHE COULD COVER MY MOUTH AND EYES, COVER ME ENTIRELY, *PLASTER.   159   40
    AND SHE'LL PERISH WITH EMPTINESS THEN, AND BEGIN TO MISS ME. ...
                         ... IN PLASTER   160   56
    THEN THE TULIPS FILLED IT UP LIKE A LOUD NOISE. ....TULIPS   161   52
    THEN THE SKY AND I ARE IN OPEN CONVERSATION, ...I AM VERTICAL   162   18
    THEN THE TREES MAY TOUCH ME FOR ONCE, AND THE FLOWERS HAVE
           TIME FOR ME. ....I AM VERTICAL   162   20
    ARRIVE AT TWILIGHT, AND THEN AFTER SOME EFFORT. ....STARS.   165   10
    THEY BRUISE THE ROCKS OUT OF EXISTENCE, THEN RESURRECT THEM. ...
                         ... FINISTERRE   169   15
    THEN SHE TURNS TO THOSE LIARS, THE CANDLES OR THE MOON. .....MIRROR   174   12
    THEN STEPPED DOWN THE STEEP BEACH SHELF AND INTO THE WATER. ..BABY.   175   39
    IS THIS MY LOVER THEN? THIS DEATH, THIS DEATH? ....THREE WOMEN   177   40
    IS THIS THE ONE SIN THEN, THIS OLD DEAD LOVE OF DEATH? THREE WOMEN   177   42
    AND THEN THERE WERE OTHER FACES. THE FACES OF NATIONS, THREE WOMEN   179   82
    THE YEW MY CHRIST, THEN. ....LITTLE FUGUE   188   29
    THIS WAS A MAN, THEN! ....LITTLE FUGUE   188   47
    IS THIS LOVE THEN, THIS RED MATERIAL ....AN APPEARANCE   189   10
    IS IT ITS RARENESS, THEN? IT IS RARE. ....PHEASANT   191   15
    THEN THERE ARE THE STARS -- INERADICABLE, HARD. ....EVENT   194   10
    THIS IS THE SEA, THEN, THIS GREAT ABEYANCE. ....BERCK-PLAGE   196   1
    THEN, FROM THE BARRED YARD, THE CHILDREN ....BERCK-PLAGE   200 118
    TILL THEN YOUR SMILES ARE FOUND MONEY. ....FOR A FATHERLESS SON   206   14
    THERE WOULD BE A NOBILITY THEN, THERE WOULD BE A BIRTHDAY.*BIRTHDAY.   208   59
    THE MILK CAME YELLOW, THEN BLUE AND SWEET AS WATER. ..THE DETECTIVE   209   33
    THEN THE DRY WOOD, THE GATES, ...THE DETECTIVE   209   36
    THEN THERE IS THAT ANTIQUE BILLHOOK, THE TONGUE, ...COURAGE.   210   17
    STITCHES TO SHOW SOMETHING'S MISSING? NO, NO? THEN ...THE APPLICANT   221   6
    AND THEN I KNEW WHAT TO DO. ....DADDY   224   63
    AND THEN GREW NORMAL, ...LESBOS   229   57
    THEN SPEWS IT BACK. ....LESBOS   229   76
    THEN THAT RED PLUSH. ....CUT   235   8
    THEN THE SUBSTANCELESS BLUE ....ARIEL   239   2
    WARM AND HUMAN, THEN THEIR PINK LIGHT ....THE NIGHT DANCES   250   19
    THEN THE FLUTINGS OF THEIR IONIAN ....DEATH & CO.   254   17
    THEN TWO LITTLE FEET. ....DEATH & CO.   254   19
    WHEN ATTACKED, THEN SCOOTING TO REST, BARELY TREMBLING. ...BALLOONS   271   8
    THEN SITS ....BALLOONS   272   26
    GO GET THE GLASS, THEN. BUT I KNOW TONIGHT WILL BE ......DIALOGUE O.   276   1
    WELL WHAT, THEN? THAT'S THE TROUBLE. LET'S SAY HE .....DIALOGUE O.   278   51
    IS HE, THEN? HE SPELLS. I-N. HE'LL LIFT *DIALOGUE OVER A OUIJA BOARD   278   76
    UNTIL IT FINISHED, AND THEN LOOK FURTIVELY ....DIALOGUE O.   280 164
    THE STINT OF SISYPHUS. ASK PAN, THEN, WHERE ....DIALOGUE O.   281 173
    BOY, HE NEEDS A BEATING NOW AND THEN ...DIALOGUE OVER A OUIJA BOARD   281 183
    ANGEL'S EYE IN THE AUDIENCE, THEN WHISK THEM OUT ......DIALOGUE O.   282 233
    GOD-PIE. WHY, THEN, DID YOU DEIGN TO INTRODUCE ....DIALOGUE O.   283 251
    THAN ANY ORCHID. YOU BROKE HIM THEN. I BROKE ....DIALOGUE O.   285 324
    WHY, YOUR HAND'S COLD AS ICE! THEN CHAFE THE COLD .....DIALOGUE O.   285 333
    "BEHIND ME THEN I HEARD A VOICE ....THE DREAM   311   19
    THEN DROVE TO YOU FROM THE WIND. . . . .THE DREAM   311   28
    THEN HURL THE BARE WORLD LIKE A BLUEGREEN BALL ..SONG FOR A REVOLU.   323   21
    THEN SYNCOPATE A SKY OF DUFY-BLUE ....MIDSUMMER MOBILE   324   2
    "WELL THEN, IF WE AGREE, IT IS NOT ODD ....LOVE IS A PARALLAX   329   7
    HELLO, AND THEN HELLO AGAIN IN DEAF ....LOVE IS A PARALLAX   330   40
    THEN LET THE BLUE TENT TOPPLE, STARS RAIN DOWN, LOVE IS A PARALLAX   330   73
    THEN, THIS TOUGH STINT DONE, SHE CURTSIES ....AERIALIST   331   25
    THERE AND THERE AND THERE AGAIN, AND THEN ...EPITAPH IN THREE PARTS   337   27
THEORY (1)
    AND LOVE THE MOTHER OF MILK, NO THEORY. ....MAGI   148   14
THERE (165)
    THERE IS A PANTHER STALKS ME DOWN: ....PURSUIT   22   1
    WE WALKED (AND STILL WALK THERE -- ....SONG FOR A SUMMER'S DAY   31   18
    TWO GIRLS THERE ARE: WITHIN THE HOUSE ....TWO SISTERS OF PERSEPHONE   31   1
    WALKS THERE NOT SOME SUCH ONE MAN ....STRUMPET SONG   34   14
    "AND IF THERE BE ....TINKER JACK AND THE TIDY WIVES   35   26
    WAVERING THERE, GAUZE-EDGED, SMELLING OF WOODSMOKE, ...DIALOGUE B.   38   12
    "CAN THERE BE SUCH STUBBORNNESS --*DIALOGUE BETWEEN GHOST AND PRIEST   39   42
    "THERE SITS NO HIGHER COURT ......DIALOGUE BETWEEN GHOST AND PRIEST   39   49

THERE (CONT.)
  WALKING EAGER TOWARD WATER, WHEN THERE, ONE BY ONE, ..DREAM WITH C.   44   23
  IN BENIDORM THERE ARE MELONS, ...FIESTA MELONS 46   1
  TO THE BARBAROUS OUTLOOK, FROM THERE CHOSE ....SPIDER   49   25
  "LOOK! THERE SHE GOES, CAT-LADY MASON!" ....ELLA MASON A. 54   31
  ON THE STIFF TWIG UP THERE ....BLACK ROOK IN RAINY WEATHER   56   1
  THAN EARTH, AND THERE IS NOTHING ....THE GREAT CARBUNCLE   73   25
  OF SNAKY GENERATIONS: LET THERE BE SNAKES! ...........SNAKECHARMER   79   20
  AND SNAKES THERE WERE, ARE, WILL BE -- TILL YAWNS ....SNAKECHARMER   79   21
  WHILE THERE IRATE CYRUS ....A LESSON IN VENGEANCE   80   16
  WITH SUFFERING FROM CONCEPTION UPWARDS, AND THERE ....PERSEUS   83   26
  ALL'S PEACE AND DISCIPLINE DOWN THERE. TILL LATELY WE ....OXBOW.   89   53
  DIMINISHES, AND GOD KNOWS WHAT IS THERE. ...THE GHOST'S LEAVETAKING   91   26
  STONE, STONE, FERRY ME DOWN THERE. ....LORELEI 95   36
  THERE WAS NO TELLING IF HE'D ....MUSSEL HUNTER AT ROCK HARBOR   97   74
  THE CRAB-FACE, ETCHED AND SET THERE, ..MUSSEL HUNTER AT ROCK HARBOR   97   77
  THERE, SPRING LAMBS JAM THE SHEEPFOLD. IN AIR ....WATERCOLOR.   111   1
  AT THIS WHARF THERE ARE NO GRAND LANDINGS TO SPEAK OF.*A WINTER SHIP   112   1
  HARD GODS WERE THERE, NOTHING ELSE. ..THE HERMIT AT OUTERMOST HOUSE   119   13
  BLACK HAIR TILL THERE YOU STOOD, ...MAN IN BLACK 120   18
  THE OLD JEWELS SMOLDERING THERE ....MEDALLION   124   18
  DOWN THERE ONE IS ALONE. ....BLUE MOLES   126   27
  DOWN THERE THE LATE YEAR ....DARK WOOD, DARK WATER   127   12
  COMES TO ROOST THERE, FRAIL ....POLLY'S TREE   128   17
  THERE WERE SUCH ENORMOUS FLOWERS, ...POEM.1.WHO.   132   29
  WITHER LIKE PITHLESS HANDS. THERE IS LITTLE SHELTER. POEM.5.F.   134   4
  MY MENDINGS ITCH. THERE IS NOTHING TO DO. POEM.7.S.   137   44
  AND WE SHALL NEVER ENTER THERE ....THE BURNT-OUT SPA 138   31
  NOW THERE IS NOTHING MUCH TO LOOK AT. ....ON DECK   142   9
  OUT HERE THERE ARE NO HEARTHSTONES, ...SLEEP IN THE MOJAVE DESERT   143   1
  IN THIS COUNTRY THERE IS NEITHER MEASURE NOR BALANCE .....TWO CAMP.   144   1
  THOUGH NOBODY IN THERE LOOKS UP OR BOTHERS TO ANSWER. ....A LIFE   150   8
  LET HER DIE THERE, OR WITHER INCESSANTLY FOR THE NEXT FIFTY
      YEARS, ...FACE LIFT   156   29
  I SHALL NEVER GET OUT OF THIS! THERE ARE TWO OF ME NOW: IN PLASTER   158   1
  SO IT IS IMPOSSIBLE TO TELL HOW MANY THERE ARE. ....TULIPS   160   14
  INFINITE NUMBER SEEMS TO BE THE ISSUE UP THERE. ....STARS.   165   21
  THERE IS TOO MUCH EASE HERE: THESE STARS TREAT ME TOO WELL.   STARS.   166   37
  THERE IS NO LIFE HIGHER THAN THE GRASSTOPS ......WUTHERING HEIGHTS   167   10
  THEY DO NOT COME FROM THE BAY OF THE DEAD DOWN THERE, ...FINISTERRE   170   33
  AS USUAL THERE IS NO FACE. A LUMP OF CHINESE WHITE ....SURGEON.   170   7
  I SIMPLY CANNOT SEE WHERE THERE IS TO GET TO. ....MOON.   173   7
  I SEE US FLOATING THERE YET, INSEPARABLE -- TWO CORK DOLLS. ..BABY.   175   41
  THERE WAS SOMETHING ABOUT THEM LIKE CARDBOARD, AND NOW I HAD
      CAUGHT IT, ...THREE WOMEN   177   17
  THERE IS A SNAKE IN SWANS. ....THREE WOMEN   178   52
  I DID NOT LOOK. BUT STILL THE FACE WAS THERE, ...THREE WOMEN 178   78
  AND THEN THERE WERE OTHER FACES. THE FACES OF NATIONS, THREE WOMEN   179   82
  THERE IS NO MIRACLE MORE CRUEL THAN THIS. ....THREE WOMEN   180 127
  I AM BREAKING APART LIKE THE WORLD. THERE IS THIS BLACKNESS, *THREE.   180 142
  THERE IS NO GUILE OR WARP IN HIM. MAY HE KEEP SO. ......THREE WOMEN   181 175
  THERE IS THE MOON IN THE HIGH WINDOW. IT IS OVER. ......THREE WOMEN   181 176
  THERE IS THIS CESSATION. THIS TERRIBLE CESSATION OF EVERYTHING. ...
                                           ...   THREE WOMEN   181 180
  THERE ARE SOME WITH THICK BLACK HAIR, THERE ARE SOME BALD. ..THREE.   183 222
  THERE ARE SOME WITH THICK BLACK HAIR, THERE ARE SOME BALD. ..THREE.   183 222
  THERE IS VERY LITTLE TO GO INTO MY SUITCASE. ....THREE WOMEN   184 266
  THERE ARE THE CLOTHES OF A FAT WOMAN I DO NOT KNOW. ....THREE WOMEN   184 267
  THERE IS MY COMB AND BRUSH. THERE IS AN EMPTINESS. .....THREE WOMEN   184 268
  THERE IS MY COMB AND BRUSH. THERE IS AN EMPTINESS. .....THREE WOMEN   184 268
  I AM MYSELF AGAIN. THERE ARE NO LOOSE ENDS. ....THREE WOMEN   184 274
  THERE IS A KIND OF SMOKE IN THE SPRING AIR, ...THREE WOMEN   186 354
  THERE IS A GREAT DEAL ELSE TO DO. MY HANDS ....THREE WOMEN   187 359
  THOUGH THERE IS A SHADOW STARTING FROM MY FEET. I AM A WIFE. *THREE.   187 369
  THERE WAS A SILENCE! ....LITTLE FUGUE 188   36
  THERE IS A DIGNITY TO THIS; THERE IS A FORMALITY -- ......NARCISSI.   190   7
  THERE IS A DIGNITY TO THIS; THERE IS A FORMALITY -- ......NARCISSI.   190   7
  I DO NOT FEAR IT: I HAVE BEEN THERE. ....ELM   192   3
  THERE WAS ONLY ONE PLACE TO GET TO. ....THE RABBIT CATCHER   193   11
  THEN THERE ARE THE STARS -- INERADICABLE, HARD. ....EVENT   194   10
  THERE IS THIS WHITE WALL, ABOVE WHICH THE SKY CREATES ITSELF -- ...
                                           ...   APPREHENSIONS   195   1
  IS THERE NO WAY OUT OF THE MIND? ....................APPREHENSIONS   195   7
  THERE ARE NO TREES OR BIRDS IN THIS WORLD, ...APPREHENSIONS   195   9
  THERE IS ONLY A SOURNESS. ...........................APPREHENSIONS   195   10
  THERE IS NO TALK OF IMMORTALITY AMONG THESE! ........APPREHENSIONS   196   18
  THERE IS NO HELP IN HIS WEEPING WIFE. ....BERCK-PLAGE   198   52
  THERE IS NO HOPE, IT IS GIVEN UP. ....BERCK-PLAGE   201 126
  THERE ARE FUMES THAT I CANNOT TOUCH. ....POPPIES IN JULY   203   9
  NOW THERE ARE THESE VEILS, SHIMMERING LIKE CURTAINS, ...BIRTHDAY.   206   16
  IT MUST BE A TUSK THERE, A GHOST-COLUMN. .....A BIRTHDAY PRESENT   206   19
  THERE IS THIS ONE THING I WANT TODAY, AND ONLY YOU CAN GIVE
      IT TO ME. ....A BIRTHDAY PRESENT   207   48
  THERE WOULD BE A NOBILITY THEN, THERE WOULD BE A BIRTHDAY.*BIRTHDAY.   208   59
  THERE WOULD BE A NOBILITY THEN, THERE WOULD BE A BIRTHDAY.*BIRTHDAY.   208   59

	TITLE	PAGE	LINE

THERE (CONT.)
THERE IS NO BODY IN THE HOUSE AT ALL. ....THE DETECTIVE 209 16
THERE IS THE SMELL OF POLISH, THERE ARE PLUSH CARPETS.*THE DETECTIVE 209 17
THERE IS THE SMELL OF POLISH, THERE ARE PLUSH CARPETS.*THE DETECTIVE 209 17
THERE IS THE SUNLIGHT, PLAYING ITS BLADES, ...THE DETECTIVE 209 18
THERE WAS NO ABSENCE OF LIPS, THERE WERE TWO CHILDREN,*THE DETECTIVE 209 34
THERE WAS NO ABSENCE OF LIPS, THERE WERE TWO CHILDREN,*THE DETECTIVE 209 34
THERE IS ONLY THE MOON, EMBALMED IN PHOSPHORUS. ......THE DETECTIVE 209 39
THERE IS ONLY A CROW IN A TREE. MAKE NOTES. ....THE DETECTIVE 209 40
THERE ARE BLACK DISKS BEHIND IT, THE DISKS OF OUTRAGE, ...COURAGE. 209 3
THEN THERE IS THAT ANTIQUE BILLHOOK, THE TONGUE, ...COURAGE. 210 17
THE VILLAGERS ARE MOVING THE VIRGINS, THERE WILL BE NO KILLING.*BEE. 212 49
WERE THERE NOT SUCH A DIN IN IT. ....THE ARRIVAL OF THE BEE BOX 212 5
THERE ARE NO WINDOWS, SO I CAN'T SEE WHAT IS IS THERE. *THE ARRIVAL. 213 9
THERE ARE NO WINDOWS, SO I CAN'T SEE WHAT IS IS THERE. *THE ARRIVAL. 213 9
THERE IS ONLY A LITTLE GRID, NO EXIT. ...THE ARRIVAL OF THE BEE BOX 213 10
THERE IS THE LABURNUM, ITS BLOND COLONNADES, ...THE ARRIVAL. 213 29
IS THERE ANY QUEEN AT ALL IN IT? ....STINGS 214 15
IF THERE IS, SHE IS OLD, ...STINGS 214 16
LEAVE AND ARRIVE, AND THERE IS NO END TO THE COUNTRY. ....THE SWARM 217 36
THIS IS THE EASY TIME, THERE IS NOTHING DOING. ....WINTERING 217 1
THE BLACK BUNCHED IN THERE LIKE A BAT, ...WINTERING 218 13
"NO, NO, IT IS HAPPY THERE." ....A SECRET 220 34
MY GOD, THERE GOES THE STOPPER! ....A SECRET 220 37
IT WORKS, THERE IS NOTHING WRONG WITH IT. ....THE APPLICANT 222 36
SAYS THERE ARE A DOZEN OR TWO. ....DADDY 223 21
IN ANY CASE, YOU ARE ALWAYS THERE, ...MEDUSA 225 16
THERE IS NOTHING BETWEEN US. ....MEDUSA 226 41
IS THAT SPAIN DOWN THERE? ....STOPPED DEAD 230 7
THERE IS NOTHING TO DO WITH SUCH A BEAUTIFUL BLANK BUT SMOOTH IT. ...
                                              ... AMNESIAC 232 2
THERE IS A CHARGE ....LADY LAZARUS 246 57
FOR THE EYEING OF MY SCARS, THERE IS A CHARGE ....LADY LAZARUS 246 58
AND THERE IS A CHARGE, A VERY LARGE CHARGE ....LADY LAZARUS 246 61
FLESH, BONE, THERE IS NOTHING THERE --- ....LADY LAZARUS 246 75
FLESH, BONE, THERE IS NOTHING THERE --- ....LADY LAZARUS 246 75
GETTING THERE ....GETTING THERE 247 T
WILL THERE BE FIRE, WILL THERE BE BREAD? ....GETTING THERE 248 20
WILL THERE BE FIRE, WILL THERE BE BREAD? ....GETTING THERE 248 20
HERE THERE IS SUCH MUD. ....GETTING THERE 248 21
THERE IS MUD ON MY FEET, ...GETTING THERE 248 35
THERE IS A MINUTE AT THE END OF IT ....GETTING THERE 248 41
THE PLACE I AM GETTING TO, WHY ARE THERE THESE OBSTACLES --- ...
                                        ... GETTING THERE 249 45
IS THERE NO STILL PLACE ....GETTING THERE 249 52
YOU, THERE ON YOUR BACK, ...GULLIVER 251 10
THERE IS A GREEN IN THE AIR, ...LETTER IN NOVEMBER 253 8
TWO, OF COURSE THERE ARE TWO. ....DEATH & CO. 254 1
WHERE THERE IS ONLY HIM AND HIM. ....THE FEARFUL 256 18
AT NIGHTFALL THERE IS THE BEAUTY OF DROWNED FIELDS, ...TOTEM 264 4
THERE IS NO MERCY IN THE GLITTER OF CLEAVERS, ...TOTEM 264 9
THERE IS NO TERMINUS, ONLY SUITCASES ....TOTEM 264 24
THERE ONE IS SAFE, ...GIGOLO 267 7
THERE ARE NO FAMILY PHOTOGRAPHS, ...GIGOLO 267 8
AND THERE IS NO END, NO END OF IT. ....GIGOLO 268 25
IS THERE NO GREAT LOVE, ONLY TENDERNESS? ....MYSTIC 269 24
THERE IS NO STOPPING IT. ....KINDNESS 270 19
IS ANYBODY THERE? IT GOES. IT GOES .....DIALOGUE OVER A OUIJA BOARD 277 26
PAN, ARE YOU STILL THERE? SEE, HIS SPRINT ....DIALOGUE O. 278 70
TO YES SAYS HE IS READY. PAN, IS THERE   DIALOGUE OVER A OUIJA BOARD 278 71
G-O-D-H-E-A-D. THERE, SEE! ....DIALOGUE OVER A OUIJA BOARD 282 218
THERE! THAT SHUTS HIM UP! SO. BETTER SO,*DIALOGUE OVER A OUIJA BOARD 284 300
OUT OF IT. THERE. THE ROOM RETURNS ....DIALOGUE OVER A OUIJA BOARD 285 334
YET THERE IS NO WALKER AND LOOKER BUT MYSELF. ....QUEEN MARY'S. 290 9
BUT THERE IS NO DRAWER TO HOLD YOU. ....THE RIVAL/DR 291 10
YOU ARE THE ONE EYE OUT THERE. ....THE RIVAL/DR 291 14
I AM EXCITED, SEEING IT THERE. ....ELM/DR 292 4
THERE, THAT'S THE PINK, PLEASED SQUEAK ....FAMILY REUNION 300 16
NOW THERE IS NOWHERE I CAN GO ....TO A JILTED LOVER 310 16
REFLECTED THERE. ....ON LOOKING INTO THE EYES OF A DEMON LOVER 325 24
THERE IS NOTHING MORE FOR ME TO SAY. ....DENOUEMENT 326 3
THERE IS NOTHING MORE FOR ME TO SAY. ....DENOUEMENT 326 9
THERE IS NOTHING MORE FOR ME TO SAY. ....DENOUEMENT 327 15
THERE IS NOTHING MORE FOR ME TO SAY. ....DENOUEMENT 327 19
THERE BURNS THROUGHOUT THE LINE OF WORDS, ...LOVE IS A PARALLAX 330 57
"THERE IS MORE THAN ONE GOOD WAY TO DROWN." EPITAPH IN THREE PARTS 337 11
"THERE IS MORE THAN ONE GOOD WAY TO DROWN." EPITAPH IN THREE PARTS 337 22
THERE AND THERE AND THERE AGAIN, AND THEN ...EPITAPH IN THREE PARTS 337 27
THERE AND THERE AND THERE AGAIN, AND THEN ...EPITAPH IN THREE PARTS 337 27
THERE AND THERE AND THERE AGAIN, AND THEN ...EPITAPH IN THREE PARTS 337 27
"THERE IS MORE THAN ONE GOOD WAY TO DROWN." EPITAPH IN THREE PARTS 338 33
THEREBY (1)
STRENGTHEN THAT ORCHARD THEREBY." ....CRYSTAL GAZER 55 24
THERE'S (10)
THERE'S CAROLING ....A WINTER'S TALE 87 16

THERE'S (CONT.)
  THERE'S NO CAREER IN THE VENTURE ....THE TIMES ARE TIDY   107   6
  BOARDED THE TRAIN THERE'S NO GETTING OFF. ....METAPHORS   116   9
  THERE'S NO GETTING UP IT BY THE WORDS YOU KNOW.*NEW YEAR ON DARTMOOR   176   6
  THERE'S A STAKE IN YOUR FAT BLACK HEART ....DADDY   224   76
  MEANWHILE THERE'S A STINK OF FAT AND BABY CRAP. ....LESBOS   228   33
  THERE'S ALWAYS A BLOODY BABY IN THE AIR. ....STOPPED DEAD   230   13
  THERE'S WHERE IT SUNK. ....LYONNESSE   234   4
  IT'S DONE. IT'S DONE, AND THERE'S NO MENDING HIM. ......DIALOGUE O.   285 304
  THERE'S A HEX ON THE CRADLE ....TEMPER OF TIME   336   23
THERMOPYLAE (1)
  GOLDS BLEED AND DEEPEN, THE MOUTHS OF THERMOPYLAE. ..LETTER IN NOV.   254   35
THESE (120)
THEY (354)
THEY'D (2)
  BUT THOUGH THEY'D RIVET SINEWS IN ROCK   EPITAPH FOR FIRE AND FLOWER   46   22
  THEY'D HAVE HAD YELLOW SILK SCREENING THE MOON, ...YADWIGHA.   85   15
THEY'LL (4)
  IT IS TOUCHING, THE WAY THEY'LL IGNORE ....CANDLES   148   5
  BELIEVE ME, THEY'LL BURY YOU IN IT. ....THE APPLICANT   221   25
  HOW THEY'LL TRAVEL, TRAVEL, TRAVEL, SCENERY ....AMNESIAC   233   17
  THEY'LL GO BY, TRUNDLING LIKE MARBLE STATUES WAY OUT ...DIALOGUE O.   276   6
THEY'RE (5)
  STILL, THEY'RE OUR BEST MUSTERING OF HEIGHT: BY ....ABOVE THE OXBOW   88   5
  FLATS OF HADLEY FARMS, THEY'RE LOFTY ENOUGH ....ABOVE THE OXBOW   88   8
  GIVEN AN INCH. NOT THAT THEY'RE GROSS (ALTHOUGH ....POEMS, POTATOES   106   6
  THEY'RE OUT OF THE DARK'S RAGBAG, THESE TWO ....BLUE MOLES   126   1
  SNOW, CHALK OR SUCHLIKE. THEY'RE ....MAGI   148   5
THEY'VE (4)
  THE CELLAR'S BELLY. THEY'VE BLOWN MY SPARKLER OUT. POEM.6.W.   135   8
  THEY'VE CHANGED ALL THAT. TRAVELING ....FACE LIFT   156   9
  THEY'VE TRAPPED HER IN SOME LABORATORY JAR. ....FACE LIFT   156   28
  THE LITTLE SILVER TROPHIES THEY'VE COME SO FAR FOR. ...THREE WOMEN   183 221
THICK (28)
  THRONED IN THE THICK ....THE SNOWMAN ON THE MOOR   59   44
  STOLIDLY PROPPING THICK VOLUMES OF PROSE: SPITE-SET ....LADY AND T.   69   4
  HOW THEY GRIP US THROUGH THIN AND THICK, ...ALL THE DEAD DEARS   70   13
  AND THE DECLINE OF EMPIRES THE THICK COIL OF A VAST ....PERSEUS   83   23
  BUT TOWARD A REGION WHERE OUR THICK ATMOSPHERE ....GHOST'S.   90   25
  FATHER, THIS THICK AIR IS MURDEROUS. ....FULL FATHOM FIVE   93   44
  THE COW MILKS CREAM AN INCH THICK. ....THREE WOMEN   107   15
  FOR PIES. THE FIR TREE'S THICK WITH GRACKLES.*YADDO: THE GRAND MANOR   123   7
  A LAKE THICK WITH FISH. ....DARK WOOD, DARK WATER   127   7
  WRAPPED UP IN THEMSELVES AS IN THICK VEILING ....ON DECK   142   2
  THEY TOE OLD WATER THICK AS FOG. ....LEAVING EARLY   146   22
  STARS ARE DROPPING THICK AS STONES INTO THE TWIGGY ....STARS.   165   1
  WE KICKED AND TALKED. THE THICK SALT KEPT US UP. ...THE BABYSITTERS   175   40
  NOT LOOKING, THROUGH THE THICK DARK, FOR THE FACE OF ANOTHER.*THREE.   178   77
  THE AIR IS THICK. IT IS THICK WITH THIS WORKING. ....THREE WOMEN   180 144
  THE AIR IS THICK. IT IS THICK WITH THIS WORKING. ....THREE WOMEN   180 144
  THERE ARE SOME WITH THICK BLACK HAIR, THERE ARE SOME BALD. ..THREE.   183 222
  THICK AS FOREIGN COFFEE, AND WITH A SLUGGY PULSE. ....WORDS HEARD.   202   2
  I'M DOPED AND THICK FROM MY LAST SLEEPING PILL. ....LESBOS   228   34
  THICK, THICK. ....LESBOS   229   66
  THICK, THICK. ....LESBOS   229   66
  THICK, RED AND SLIPPING. IT IS ADAM'S SIDE, ...GETTING THERE   248   36
  IN A THICK GRAY DEATH-SOUP, ...LETTER IN NOVEMBER   253   28
  THEIR THICK PALLS FLOAT ....MARY'S SONG   257   9
  THE THICK GERMANS SLUMBERING IN THEIR BOTTOMLESS STOLZ. ...MUNICH.   263   23
  SWAYING SLIGHTLY IN THEIR THICK SUITS, ...TOTEM   264   6
  TURNED THICK AND SOUR. ....BITTER STRAWBERRIES   299   9
  AND PLUCK THE DROLL-FLECKED QUAIL WHERE THICK THEY LIE; ...GO GET.   313   2
THICKEN (1)
  DRIP AND THICKEN, TEARS ....NICK AND THE CANDLESTICK   240   3
THICKENING (1)
  THICKENING WITH MOTES, TO A MARRIAGE WITH THE MIRE. ....OUIJA   77   21
THICKET (5)
  BY BLACKTHORN THICKET, FLOWER SPRAY ....BUCOLICS   23   7
  FROM THE LAUREL THICKET. NO ONE APPROACHED. ..........RHODODENDRON.   103   19
  A THICKET OF STICKS, ...POLLY'S TREE   128   2
  A THICKET OF SHADOWS IS A POOR COAT. I INHABIT POEM.6.W.   135   2
  THICKET OF WORDS. THE CURTAIN'S DRAWN ON THAT. ....DIALOGUE O.   286 352
THICKETS (5)
  BEHIND SNARLED THICKETS OF MY EYES ....PURSUIT   23   29
  BUT IN SPECKLED THICKETS, WARTED AS A TOAD, ...FIRESONG   30   3
  FLITS NIMBLE-WINGED IN THICKETS, AND OF GOOD COLOR. ...WATERCOLOR.   112   7
  DARK THICKETS HEDGE THE HOUSE. ....THE SLEEPERS   123   11
  THE THICKETS QUIET. ....THE RABBIT CATCHER   194   20
THICK-SILTED (1)
  SHE THOUGHT OF THEN, THICK-SILTED, WITH WEEDS OBSCURED, *LADY AND T.   69   16
THIEVERY (1)
  OR PETTY THIEVERY BY LARGE. .....FABLE OF THE RHODODENDRON STEALERS   104   28
THIEVES (1)
  THIEVES WHAT IT HAS." ....ON THE DIFFICULTY OF CONJURING UP A DRYAD   66   40

	TITLE	PAGE	LINE
THIGHS (5)			
AND HUNGRY, HUNGRY, THOSE TAUT THIGHS.	PURSUIT	23	32
FOR THAT BRAG, WE BARNACLE THESE IRON THIGHS."	SNOWMAN O.	59	43
MY ANKLES BRIGHTEN. BRIGHTNESS ASCENDS MY THIGHS.	POEM.6.W.	136	23
AND WHAT IF TWO LIVES LEAKED BETWEEN MY THIGHS?	THREE WOMEN	180	120
THIGHS, HAIR;	ARIEL	239	17
THIN (28)			
THE THIN PEOPLE	THE THIN PEOPLE	64	T
THEY ARE ALWAYS WITH US, THE THIN PEOPLE	THE THIN PEOPLE	64	1
BUT A THIN SILENCE.	THE THIN PEOPLE	64	17
SCAPEGOAT. BUT SO THIN, ...	THE THIN PEOPLE	64	22
NOW THE THIN PEOPLE DO NOT OBLITERATE	THE THIN PEOPLE	65	32
IF THE THIN PEOPLE SIMPLY STAND IN THE FOREST.	THE THIN PEOPLE	65	45
MAKING THE WORLD GO THIN AS A WASP'S NEST	THE THIN PEOPLE	65	46
HOW THEY GRIP US THROUGH THIN AND THICK, ...	ALL THE DEAD DEARS	70	13
TO FEED THE THIN CROWS.	WORDS FOR A NURSERY	74	50
FROM HIS THIN PIPE. OUT OF THIS GREEN NEST	SNAKECHARMER	79	18
SO THESE POSED SHEETS, BEFORE THEY THIN TO NOTHING, ...	GHOST'S.	90	18
MEET THE THIN AND SLUGGISH THREAD .....MUSSEL HUNTER AT ROCK HARBOR		96	42
HOUSES HIMSELF ELSEWHERE. OUR FOLK THIN	FROG AUTUMN	99	11
SIZE. THE CRIES OF SCAVENGING GULLS SOUND THIN	GREEN ROCK.	105	14
HALFWAY DOWN FROM GROVES WHERE THE THIN, BITTER ALMOND PIPS .	NET-.	121	2
THIN AS PINS IN THE DARK BRUISE	MEDALLION	125	22
WHILE THE CHILD SMILES INTO THIN AIR.	MAGI	148	9
THIN AS THE SKIN SEAMING A SCAR. ....PARLIAMENT HILL FIELDS		153	39
LARD-PALE, SIPPING THE THIN	WHITSUN	153	5
NODDING AND ROCKING AND FINGERING HER THIN HAIR.	FACE LIFT	156	30
A THIN, SILLY MESSAGE.	WUTHERING HEIGHTS	167	24
THE VOICE OF THE PRIEST, IN THIN AIR, ...	BERCK-PLAGE	200	93
THE THIN	CUT	235	25
GLOBES OF THIN AIR, RED, GREEN, ...	BALLOONS	271	14
FEATHERS WINNOWING THE ROOM. A THIN ....DIALOGUE OVER A OUIJA BOARD		279	87
SHE STOOD UP, A THIN COMMANDING FIGURE ....BITTER STRAWBERRIES		300	29
AGAINST A SILENCE WEARING THIN.	FAMILY REUNION	300	9
QUIVER IN THIN STREAKS	AQUATIC NOCTURNE	305	4
THING (23)			
A SCORPION STUNG ITS HEAD, AN ILL-STARRED THING;	ELECTRA ON.	117	35
THE FIRST THING I SAW WAS SHEER AIR	LOVE LETTER	147	20
THE REAL THING, ALL RIGHT: THE GOOD, THE TRUE --	MAGI	148	6
I CAN TASTE THE TIN OF THE SKY -- THE REAL TIN THING.	WAKING.	151	1
I DON'T KNOW A THING.	FACE LIFT	156	16
THE ONLY THING TO COME NOW IS THE SEA.	BLACKBERRYING	169	19
THE BODY IS A ROMAN THING.	THE SURGEON AT 2 A.M.	171	29
I HAVE NEVER SEEN A THING SO CLEAR.	THREE WOMEN	181	171
IT IS USUAL, THEY SAY, FOR SUCH A THING TO HAPPEN.	THREE WOMEN	183	242
IT IS A TERRIBLE THING	THREE WOMEN	185	299
IT WAS A DREAM, AND DID NOT MEAN A THING.	THREE WOMEN	185	308
THE NARCISSI, TOO, ARE BOWING TO SOME BIG THING: *AMONG THE NARCISSI		190	4
CROSSING AND RECROSSING: A FINE THING!	PHEASANT	191	18
I AM TERRIFIED BY THIS DARK THING	ELM	193	31
SLIDING SHUT ON SOME QUICK THING, ...THE RABBIT CATCHER		194	29
ON A WONDERFUL THING ---	BERCK-PLAGE	201	122
THERE IS THIS ONE THING I WANT TODAY, AND ONLY YOU CAN GIVE			
IT TO ME.	A BIRTHDAY PRESENT	207	48
HOW CAN WE GIVE YOU A THING?	THE APPLICANT	221	7
A SPACE FOR THE THING I AM GIVEN, ...	THALIDOMIDE	252	18
YOUR CLEAR EYE IS THE ONE ABSOLUTELY BEAUTIFUL THING.	CHILD	265	1
SHE IS USED TO THIS SORT OF THING.	EDGE	273	19
THE MOON IS LET GO, LIKE A DEAD THING.	ELM/DR	292	8
THE PARADOX IS THAT "THE PLAY'S THE THING": .....LOVE IS A PARALLAX		330	55
THINGS (15)			
LIT THINGS, THAT LAMP OF THE POSSIBLE! WET YET .....SPINACH-PICKER.		89	3
THE LIQUOR OF INDOLENCE, AND ALL THINGS SINK	POEM.5.F.	134	8
SOME THINGS OF THIS WORLD ARE INDIGESTIBLE. ......ZOO KEEPER'S WIFE		155	16
DOING THINGS WITH THEIR HANDS, ONE JUST THE SAME AS ANOTHER, *TULIPS		160	13
I HAVE LET THINGS SLIP, A THIRTY-YEAR-OLD CARGO BOAT	TULIPS	161	22
A BONEWHITE LIGHT, LIKE DEATH, BEHIND ALL THINGS.	INSOMNIAC	163	4
ONE DAY IT WON'T COME BACK. THINGS AREN'T LIKE THAT.	LAST WORDS	172	16
AND THE SHINE OF THESE SMALL THINGS SWEETER THAN THE FACE OF			
ISHTAR.	LAST WORDS	172	26
HOW BEAUTIFULLY THE LIGHT INCLUDES THESE THINGS.	THREE WOMEN	186	353
ON THE BALCONIES OF THE HOTEL, THINGS ARE GLITTERING. ..	BERCK-PLAGE	197	37
THINGS, THINGS ---	BERCK-PLAGE	197	38
THINGS, THINGS ---	BERCK-PLAGE	197	38
THE THINGS IT HAS PIERCED IN ITS TIME. ..THE COURAGE OF SHUTTING-UP		210	25
BY WHATEVER THESE PINK THINGS MEAN.	FEVER.	232	50
FEEDING AT THE ROOT OF THINGS. HE STOLE THAT, TOO, ...DIALOGUE O.		279	102
THINK (38)			
TO PROVE IT. AS I THINK NOW OF HER HEAD, ...ALL THE DEAD DEARS		70	18
THESE HALLS ARE FULL OF WOMEN WHO THINK THEY ARE BIRDS. *POEM.1.WHO.		131	21
I THINK OF THE LIZARDS AIRING THEIR TONGUES	SLEEP.	144	14
I SUPPOSE IT'S POINTLESS TO THINK OF YOU AT ALL. ....PARLIAMENT H.		152	24
SHOULD I STIR, I THINK THIS PINK AND PURPLE PLASTIC	ZOO K.	154	11
I USED TO THINK WE MIGHT MAKE A GO OF IT TOGETHER -- ....IN PLASTER		160	50
SOMETIMES I THINK THAT WHEN I AM SLEEPING	I AM VERTICAL	162	14

	TITLE	PAGE	LINE

THINK (CONT.)
I THINK THEY WOULD NOT WISH FOR THIS DRESSY BACKCLOTH ....STARS. 166 29
I DO NOT THINK THE SEA WILL APPEAR AT ALL. ...........BLACKBERRYING 168 13
I THINK IT IS A PART OF MY HEART. BUT IT FLICKERS. ....MIRROR 173 8
IS SHE SORRY FOR WHAT WILL HAPPEN? I DO NOT THINK SO. ..THREE WOMEN 176 6
I DO NOT HAVE TO THINK, OR EVEN REHEARSE. ....THREE WOMEN 176 9
I HAVE TRIED NOT TO THINK TOO HARD. I HAVE TRIED TO BE NATURAL. ...
... THREE WOMEN 178 74
I THINK HER LITTLE HEAD IS CARVED IN WOOD, ...THREE WOMEN 182 211
I THINK THEY ARE MADE OF WATER; THEY HAVE NO EXPRESSION.*THREE WOMEN 183 225
THESE LITTLE BLACK TWIGS DO NOT THINK TO BUD, ...THREE WOMEN 184 278
I WAIT AND ACHE. I THINK I HAVE BEEN HEALING. ....THREE WOMEN 187 358
AND FIND NO FACE BUT MY OWN, AND YOU THINK THAT'S FUNNY.*FATHERLESS. 205 9
BUT IT SHIMMERS, IT DOES NOT STOP, AND I THINK IT WANTS ME. ...
... A BIRTHDAY PRESENT 206 11
I DO NOT THINK YOU CREDIT ME WITH THIS DISCRETION. ....BIRTHDAY. 207 36
IF I STAND VERY STILL, THEY WILL THINK I AM COW-PARSLEY, ...BEE. 212 39
HER BODY A BULB IN THE COLD AND TOO DUMB TO THINK. ....WINTERING 219 45
WELL, WHAT DO YOU THINK OF THAT? ....THE APPLICANT 221 29
I THINK I MAY WELL BE A JEW. ....DADDY 223 35
WHO DO YOU THINK YOU ARE? ....MEDUSA 225 32
WHO DO YOU THINK I AM, ...STOPPED DEAD 230 17
I THINK I AM GOING UP, ...FEVER. 232 43
I THINK I MAY RISE --- ....FEVER. 232 44
DO NOT THINK I UNDERESTIMATE YOUR GREAT CONCERN. ......LADY LAZARUS 246 72
I THINK I MAY BE ENORMOUS, ...LETTER IN NOVEMBER 253 12
DO NOT THINK I DON'T NOTICE YOUR CURTAIN -- ..........EAVESDROPPER 260 28
AROUND THE RING. I THINK IT MUST BE MAKING SURE ....DIALOGUE O. 277 22
YOU'RE MELTING NOW, BECAUSE YOU THINK HE'S HIT ....DIALOGUE O. 278 80
BULKING MORE REAL THAN WE THINK WE ARE: WE FACE ....DIALOGUE O. 279 115
FOR ROT. DON'T THINK YOU HAD ME FOOLED. I KNEW ....DIALOGUE O. 283 263
I TRY TO THINK OF A PLACE TO HIDE YOU ....THE RIVAL/DR 291 8
WHICH LET LOVER THINK LOVER ....MOONSONG AT MORNING 317 15
IF YOU CAN THINK OF MEANS TO MEND THE VOW ....THE DISPOSSESSED 318 13
THINKING (7)
THINKING NEVER TO HAVE LEFT THE WORLD, YOU GRIEVE ......DIALOGUE B. 39 34
THINKING OF SOMETHING ELSE. POEM.2.DARK. 132 7
WALKING ABOUT IN AFRICA MAYBE, BUT THINKING OF ME. ....THE RIVAL 167 17
WHEN I AM QUIET AT MY COOKING I FEEL IT LOOKING, I FEEL IT
THINKING ....A BIRTHDAY PRESENT 206 4
THINKING "SWEETNESS, SWEETNESS". ....STINGS 214 11
IT WILL WORK WITHOUT THINKING, ...STINGS 215 34
FEED YOUR OWN WISHFUL THINKING. TRY ASKING HIM ....DIALOGUE O. 283 268
THINKS (4)
EVEN MY BEST FRIEND THINKS I'M IN THE COUNTRY. ....FACE LIFT 156 19
THE MIND OF THE HIVE THINKS THIS IS THE END OF EVERYTHING. ....BEE. 212 37
SO DUMB IT THINKS BULLETS ARE THUNDER. ....THE SWARM 216 20
IT THINKS THEY ARE THE VOICE OF GOD ....THE SWARM 216 21
THIN-LIPPED (1)
UNDER THEIR THIN-LIPPED SMILES, ...THE THIN PEOPLE 65 38
THINNESS (1)
IN THINNESS, TO COME, LATER, ...THE THIN PEOPLE 64 14
THIN-PANED (1)
ENDING IN A THIN-PANED ....POLLY'S TREE 128 4
THINS (3)
WHERE ONCE A DAY THE LIGHT SLOWLY WIDENS AND SLOWLY THINS, ..TULIPS 161 45
THE MUTE AIR MERELY THINS AND THINS. .....METAMORPHOSES OF THE MOON 307 6
THE MUTE AIR MERELY THINS AND THINS. .....METAMORPHOSES OF THE MOON 307 6
THIRD (6)
A THIRD PERSON IS WATCHING. ....STINGS 215 38
TO NAME HIS HOME A THIRD TIME. GIVE YOUR WILL THREE ....DIALOGUE O. 283 269
CHANCES TO MASTER MINE. THEY SAY THE THIRD TIME ....DIALOGUE O. 283 270
A THIRD TIME. DON'T GLOAT. YOUR WILL MISFIRED TWICE ....DIALOGUE O. 284 281
US IN: A THIRD UNDID THEM. AND WE GREW ONE ....DIALOGUE O. 285 327
THE THIRD CRIES OUT AS ALL THE SHIPS GO DOWN:*EPITAPH IN THREE PARTS 337 10
THIRST (2)
TO QUENCH HIS THIRST I SQUANDER BLOOD; ....PURSUIT 23 38
NO THIRST DISTURBS A STONE'S BED. ....CHILD'S PARK STONES 101 30
THIRSTY (1)
THAT GLIDE AHEAD OF THE VERY THIRSTY. ...SLEEP IN THE MOJAVE DESERT 144 13
THIRTEENS (5)
TO CHIRP THE HOUR IN LUNATIC THIRTEENS. ....SONNET: TO EVA 305 14
THE HOUR IS CROWED IN LUNATIC THIRTEENS. ....DOOMSDAY 316 3
THE HOUR IS CROWED IN LUNATIC THIRTEENS. ....DOOMSDAY 316 9
THE HOUR IS CROWED IN LUNATIC THIRTEENS. ....DOOMSDAY 316 15
THE HOUR IS CROWED IN LUNATIC THIRTEENS. ....DOOMSDAY 316 19
THIRTY (4)
THIRTY YEARS NOW I HAVE LABORED ....THE COLOSSUS 129 8
AND THE OWNER PAST THIRTY, NO BEAUTY AT ALL. ....CANDLES 148 9
FOR THIRTY YEARS, POOR AND WHITE, ...DADDY 222 4
I AM ONLY THIRTY. ....LADY LAZARUS 244 20
THIRTY-YEAR-OLD (1)
I HAVE LET THINGS SLIP, A THIRTY-YEAR-OLD CARGO BOAT ....TULIPS 161 22
THIS (294)

	TITLE	PAGE	LINE

THISTLE (2)
MAUNCHING THISTLE AND KNOTWEED ON HER SNOUT-CRUISE -- ....SOW   61 19
OF THISTLE AND SILK, ...WORDS FOR A NURSERY   74 24
THOR (2)
"THOR IS ANGRY: BOOM BOOM BOOM! ....THE DISQUIETING MUSES   75 22
THOR IS ANGRY: WE DON'T CARE!" ....THE DISQUIETING MUSES   75 23
THORN (3)
EACH THORN; SPIRING FROM WET EARTH, A BLUE HAZE ....DIALOGUE B.   38   5
ON THE GREEN HILL, UNDER THE THORN TREES, ...HEAVY WOMEN 158 12
SMALL A THORN ....TO A JILTED LOVER 310 11
THORNED (1)
ROUSED BY THORNED HANDS, FEET, HEAD, ...STREET SONG   36 17
THORNS (4)
FLAYED BY THORNS I TREK THE ROCKS, ...PURSUIT   22   9
O BENT BOW OF THORNS ....RESOLVE   52 16
THORNS ON THE BLOODY ROSE-STEM. ....I WANT, I WANT 106 12
WITH RECOLLECTION'S TICKING THORNS ....DANSE MACABRE 321 11
THOSE (65)
THOU (1)
THOU SHALT HAVE AN EVERLASTING... ....THE EVERLASTING MONDAY   62 E/1
THOUGH (38)
THOUGH IT'S QUITE CLEAR ....SOLILOQUY OF THE SOLIPSIST   38 34
AS THOUGH ALIVE, SHRIVELING IN TORMENT THUS ....DIALOGUE B.   39 35
THOUGH PRIME PARTS CRAM EACH RICH MEAL, ...THE GLUTTON   40 11
WHAT THOUGH GREEN LEAVES ONLY WITNESS ....WREATH FOR A BRIDAL   44   1
BUT THOUGH THEY'D RIVET SINEWS IN ROCK   EPITAPH FOR FIRE AND FLOWER   46 22
MOVES ON ITS ROOT. THOUGH A MIST-WRAITH WOUND .....HARDCASTLE CRAGS   62 13
OUT THEIR STALKY LIMBS AGAIN THOUGH PEACE ....THE THIN PEOPLE   64   9
GET BACK, THOUGH, SOON, ...ALL THE DEAD DEARS   71 26
THOUGH HE BEDDED IN ERMINE, GORGED ON ROAST, ...NATURAL HISTORY   71   3
STARTLED AT IT, THOUGH THE SOUND ....NIGHT SHIFT   76 10
PITYS FROM PAN'S ASSAULT! AND THOUGH AGE DROP .....VIRGIN IN A TREE   81 17
THOUGH DOOMSDAY BUD. NEGLECT'S ....VIRGIN IN A TREE   82 41
OF THE AIR EDDIES' LOOP AND ARC THOUGH AIR'S AT REST*ABOVE THE OXBOW   88 32
THOUGH FISHERMEN ARE SLEEPING, ...LORELEI   94   6
THOUGH I COUNTED SCANT SECONDS, ...MUSSEL HUNTER AT ROCK HARBOR   95 21
THOUGH THE BODY WALK OUT IN CLEAN LINEN. ....MOONRISE   98 15
SO WE ARE HAULED, THOUGH WE WOULD STOP ....IN MIDAS' COUNTRY 100 21
IMMENSE, BALD, THOUGH BABY-HEADED, ...I WANT, I WANT 106   2
STEADILY ROOTED THOUGH THEY WERE ALL FLOWING ....THE EYE-MOTE 109   7
AND THOUGH YOUR GRACIOUSNESS MIGHT STREAM, ...POINT SHIRLEY 111 44
THOUGH THE GREEN SEA GARDENS STALL, ...MAGNOLIA SHOALS 121   6
A TREE OF HEAVEN, THOUGH ....POLLY'S TREE 129 31
THOUGH THEY HAVE A PIGGY AND A FISHY AIR -- ....STILLBORN 142 12
THOUGH, LIKE A STONE, UNBOTHERED BY IT, ...LOVE LETTER 147   3
THOUGH NOBODY IN THERE LOOKS UP OR BOTHERS TO ANSWER. ....A LIFE 150   8
WEARS THE FACE OF A PHARAOH, THOUGH IT'S MADE OF MUD AND WATER. ...
                 ... IN PLASTER 159 42
YET I STILL DEPENDED ON HER, THOUGH I DID IT REGRETFULLY.*IN PLASTER 160 49
THEY ARE SUBTLE: THEY SEEM TO FLOAT, THOUGH THEY WEIGH ME DOWN, ...
                  ... TULIPS 161 40
BLACKBERRIES ON EITHER SIDE, THOUGH ON THE RIGHT MAINLY, BLACKBER. 168   2
THOUGH THERE IS A SHADOW STARTING FROM MY FEET. I AM A WIFE. *THREE. 187 369
THAT IS THE VALLEY OF DEATH, THOUGH THE COWS THRIVE.   THE DETECTIVE 208   6
THOUGH FOR YEARS I HAVE EATEN DUST ....STINGS 214 24
THOUGH IT LOOKS LIKE A CAT, WITH ITS FLUFFY STUFF, PURE WHITE.*TOUR. 237 16
BELCHED INTO BLAZE AND, THOUGH RED-HOT, KEPT WHOLE .....DIALOGUE O. 280 158
YOU TO TAUNTS THOUGH, WHEN HE REFLECTS A FACE ....DIALOGUE O. 283 260
THOUGH HUNDREDS OF LONDONERS KNOW IT LIKE THE PALM OF THEIR HAND. ...
             ... QUEEN MARY'S ROSE GARDEN 290 16
THOUGH THE MIND LIKE AN OYSTER LABORS ON AND ON, ...TWO LOVERS. 327 19
THOUGH PRIMA DONNA POUTS AND CRITIC STINGS, ...LOVE IS A PARALLAX 330 56
THOUGHT (22)
FEATHERED DARK IN THOUGHT, I STALK LIKE A ROOK, ..WINTER LANDSCAPE,   21   9
SHAPE OF HER SLEEP, HER THOUGHT -- ....THE QUEEN'S COMPLAINT   29 19
TO DISTRACT BEAUTY'S THOUGHT; ....VANITY FAIR   33 23
SHE THOUGHT OF THEN, THICK-SILTED, WITH WEEDS OBSCURED, *LADY AND T.   69 16
BURNT-OUT WERE THEIRS, OR AS IF THEY THOUGHT ....AFTERMATH 113   3
THEN I SAW WHAT THE TROUBLE WAS: SHE THOUGHT SHE WAS IMMORTAL. ...
                 ... IN PLASTER 159 35
SHE WANTED TO LEAVE ME, SHE THOUGHT THAT SHE WAS SUPERIOR, ...IN PLASTER 159 36
I THOUGHT I COULD DENY THE CONSEQUENCE -- ....THREE WOMEN 178 61
AS IF I THOUGHT IT HAD A SPIRIT. ....PHEASANT 191   8
THEY THOUGHT DEATH WAS WORTH IT, BUT I ....STINGS 215 51
I THOUGHT EVERY GERMAN WAS YOU. ....DADDY 223 29
I THOUGHT EVEN THE BONES WOULD DO. ....DADDY 224 60
THE LYONIANS HAD ALWAYS THOUGHT ....LYONNESSE 234 11
HERE'S A SPOT I THOUGHT YOU'D LOVE -- ....THE TOUR 238 27
THE THOUGHT OF A BABY -- ....THE FEARFUL 256 11
WE THOUGHT WE'D TRAINED HIM, BEFORE GOING HAYWIRE. TRUTH*DIALOGUE O. 277 41
M-A-G-E. IN PLUMAGE. I'D NEVER HAVE THOUGHT ....DIALOGUE O. 278 78
AND TONGUE, AND THOUGHT, AS WELL AS THE BLOOD-HEAT .....DIALOGUE O. 283 258
OF OUR DAYS SUSTAIN US. MAY EACH THOUGHT*DIALOGUE OVER A OUIJA BOARD 286 361
I THOUGHT EARTH MIGHT USE YOU. ....THE RIVAL/DR 291 22
I NEVER THOUGHT HIS FLESH WOULD BURN ....TO A JILTED LOVER 310 12

THOUGHT (CONT.)
  WE NEVER THOUGHT TO HEAR THE HOLY COCK: ....DOOMSDAY 316 14
THOUGHTS (6)
  OF OUR MEAT-AND-POTATO THOUGHTS ASSUMES THE NIMBUS ....GHOST'S. 90 14
  THOUGHTS GONE DIM. ....I AM VERTICAL 162 16
  THE HOLLOWS IN WHICH ROCK THE THOUGHTS OF THE WIFE ---   BERCK-PLAGE 199 75
  ARE NOT THE THOUGHTS I TURN ON, LIKE A YOGI, ...YEARS 255 3
  MY THOUGHTS ARE CRABBED AND SALLOW, ...JILTED 304 1
  THOUGHTS THAT FOUND A MAZE OF MERMAID HAIR ....TWO LOVERS. 327 5
THOUSAND (7)
  HAVE A THOUSAND CLEAN CELLS BETWEEN US, ...STINGS 214 6
  REMEMBERING A THOUSAND AUTUMNS ....GOLD MOUTHS CRY 302 3
  AND HOW A HUNDRED THOUSAND LEAVES ....GOLD MOUTHS CRY 302 4
  REMEMBERING A THOUSAND AUTUMNS, ...GOLD MOUTHS CRY 302 12
  WITH SUNLIGHT OF A THOUSAND YEARS UPON HIS LIPS ....GOLD MOUTHS CRY 302 13
  RAISED TO TOAST A THOUSAND KINGS, FOR ALL GIVES ....SONNET: TO TIME 311 11
  TO CALL FOR CURTAIN ON OUR THOUSAND SCENES; .....LOVE IS A PARALLAX 330 44
THOUSANDS (1)
  AND THOUSANDS WERE BORN AND DROPPED DEAD, ...DIALOGUE EN ROUTE 309 39
THREAD (3)
  MEET THE THIN AND SLUGGISH THREAD .....MUSSEL HUNTER AT ROCK HARBOR 96 42
  SPINNING A SINGLE STUBBORN THREAD OF WOOL ....THE PRINCESS. 333 16
  OF THREAD CONDUCTING HER TO THE WORN TRACKS ....THE PRINCESS. 334 32
THREADBARE (1)
  DAMASKS WITH DAZZLE THE THREADBARE EYE; ....CONJURING. 66 18
THREADED (1)
  GULLS HAVE THREADED THE RIVER'S MUD BED BACK *PARLIAMENT HILL FIELDS 152 6
THREADING (1)
  THREADING BACK, FILAMENT BY FILAMENT, TO THE PURE ...PRIVATE GROUND 130 10
THREADS (1)
  THROUGH WHICH THE SKY ETERNALLY THREADS ITSELF? ....TOTEM 264 21
THREADWORK (1)
  WINDLESS THREADWORK OF A TAPESTRY. ....A LIFE 149 5
THREAT (1)
  WITH CURSE, FIST, THREAT ....SPINSTER 50 29
THREATEN (1)
  THEY THREATEN ....SHEEP IN FOG 262 13
THREE (30)
  MONOLOGUE AT [THREE] A.M. ....MONOLOGUE AT 3 A.M. 40 T
  OVER TIDAL-FLATS WHERE THREE CHILDREN PLAYED*DREAM WITH CLAM-DIGGERS 44 14
  FUSING TIME'S THREE HORIZONS. ....CRYSTAL GAZER 54 6
  THESE THREE, UNMASKED NOW, BEAR ....ALL THE DEAD DEARS 70 7
  CROSSED BY THREE CAUSEWAYS, ...WORDS FOR A NURSERY 74 28
  WORDS TO RID ME OF THOSE THREE LADIES ....THE DISQUIETING MUSES 75 14
  BUT THREE MEN ENTERING THE YARD, ...ON THE DECLINE OF ORACLES 78 20
  COMING UP, THOSE THREE. WORTH ....ON THE DECLINE OF ORACLES 78 28
  HE SPLIT IT INTO THREE HUNDRED AND SIXTY TRICKLES ....LESSON. 80 19
  TOWARD THREE PINKY-PURPLE ....BATTLE-SCENE 84 15
  OF THE THREE FISHING SMACKS BEACHED ...MUSSEL HUNTER AT ROCK HARBOR 95 6
  THREE GIRLS, ENGROSSED, WERE WRENCHING FULL CLUSTERS   RHODODENDRON. 104 21
  THEY ARE UNLOADING THREE BARRELS OF LITTLE CRABS. ....A WINTER SHIP 113 14
  WHERE THE THREE MAGENTA ....MAN IN BLACK 119 1
  FATTEN IN GREEN-POCKED PODS, THE THREE NET-MENDERS SIT OUT, ..NET-. 121 3
  IT TOOK THREE DAYS DRIVING NORTH TO FIND A CLOUD ....TWO CAMP. 145 10
  OUR LADY OF THE SHIPWRECKED IS THREE TIMES LIFE SIZE, ...FINISTERRE 170 24
  THREE WOMEN ....THREE WOMEN 176 T
  A POEM FOR THREE VOICES ....THREE WOMEN 176 ST
  A DAY AGO, TWO DAYS, THREE DAYS AGO. IT WAS A FRIDAY. ..THREE WOMEN 183 248
  THE WIDOW WITH HER BLACK POCKETBOOK AND THREE DAUGHTERS,*BERCK-PLAGE 200 100
  FEVER [ONE HUNDRED THREE DEGREES] ....FEVER. 231 T
  THREE DAYS. THREE NIGHTS. ....FEVER. 232 31
  THREE DAYS. THREE NIGHTS. ....FEVER. 232 31
  THIS IS NUMBER THREE. ....LADY LAZARUS 245 22
  HIS THREE TEETH CUTTING ....BRASILIA 258 12
  PREDICTING THREE BOYS AN HOUR HENCE WILL PLAY ....DIALOGUE O. 279 124
  TO NAME HIS HOME A THIRD TIME. GIVE YOUR WILL THREE ....DIALOGUE O. 283 269
  CIRCUS IN THREE RINGS ....CIRCUS IN THREE RINGS 321 T
  EPITAPH IN THREE PARTS ....EPITAPH IN THREE PARTS 337 T
THRESH (1)
  OF ANIMALS TO CHOIR: "LOOK WHAT THRESH OF WINGS *WREATH FOR A BRIDAL 45 15
THRESH-TAILED (1)
  A THRESH-TAILED, LANCED ....POINT SHIRLEY 110 15
THRIFTY (1)
  FOR THRIFTY CHILDREN, NOR DOLT PIG RIPE FOR HECKLING, ...SOW 60 13
THRILL (2)
  YOU ACTED, ACTED, ACTED FOR THE THRILL. ....LESBOS 228 43
  WHAT A THRILL --- ....CUT 235 1
THRIVE (1)
  THAT IS THE VALLEY OF DEATH, THOUGH THE COWS THRIVE.   THE DETECTIVE 208 6
THRIVES (2)
  CARICATURES ITSELF AND THRIVES ....THE BEGGARS 47 8
  OUSTS MISTIER PEERS AND THRIVES, MURDEROUS, ...POEMS, POTATOES 106 2
THRIVING (1)
  STAUNCH SAPLINGS; TO THIS HOUSE, THRIVING DAYS ....CRYSTAL GAZER 55 16

	TITLE	PAGE	LINE

THROAT (5)
MY OWN BLUE RAZOR RUSTING IN MY THROAT. .....ELECTRA ON AZALEA PATH 117 43
TO DREDGE THE SILT FROM YOUR THROAT. ....THE COLOSSUS 129 9
FROM THE BROKEN THROAT, THE MARSHY LIP. ....THE BURNT-OUT SPA 138 21
WHAT CUPPED SIGHS, WHAT SALT IN THE THROAT.... ....BERCK-PLAGE 197 32
SHE'LL CUT HER THROAT AT TEN IF SHE'S MAD AT TWO. ....LESBOS 228 22
THROATS (5)
ONE GRUFF-TIMBERED PURR ROLLING FROM FURRED THROATS: ELLA MASON A. 54 23
AN ASSEMBLY-LINE OF CUT THROATS, AND YOU AND I ....WAKING IN WINTER 151 5
THE THROATS OF OUR WRISTS BRAVE LILIES. ....STINGS 214 4
THE MUD SQUIRMS WITH THROATS, ...THE SWARM 216 13
FROM THE SWEET, DEEP THROATS OF THE NIGHT FLOWER. ....EDGE 273 16
THRONED (1)
THRONED IN THE THICK ....THE SNOWMAN ON THE MOOR 59 44
THRONGING (1)
THRONGING SIDEWALK, STREET, ...STREET SONG 35 3
THROUGH (97)
THROUGHOUT (3)
THROUGHOUT BLACK WINTER THE RED HAWS WITHSTOOD ....MAYFLOWER 60 1
BY NOON AND THROUGHOUT THE BRUNT ....CHILD'S PARK STONES 101 20
THERE BURNS THROUGHOUT THE LINE OF WORDS, ...LOVE IS A PARALLAX 330 57
THROW (2)
O THROW IT AWAY, THROW IT ALL AWAY ON THE WIND: SONG FOR A REVOLU. 322 1
O THROW IT AWAY, THROW IT ALL AWAY ON THE WIND: SONG FOR A REVOLU. 322 1
THROWN (2)
LOUD ON EARTH'S BEDROCK. ALMOST THROWN, NOT ...WHITENESS I REMEMBER 103 31
THROWN: FEAR, WISDOM, AT ONE: ALL COLORS .....WHITENESS I REMEMBER 103 32
THRUST (3)
ONE THRUST, ONE THRUST, ...BATTLE-SCENE 84 29
ONE THRUST, ONE THRUST, ...BATTLE-SCENE 84 29
ONE THRUST: AND THEY ARE SPED. ....BATTLE-SCENE 84 30
THRUSTING (1)
THE THRUSTING HAND ....ON LOOKING INTO THE EYES OF A DEMON LOVER 325 14
THUDDING (1)
TILL THE THUDDING SOURCE, EXPOSED, ...NIGHT SHIFT 76 13
THUMB (10)
NATURE'S PARTIAL, HAPHAZARD THUMB. ....THE BEGGARS 47 5
THUMB CAN MAKE ANYONE WINCE, BUT THE WHOLE GLOBE ....PERSEUS 83 28
BIG AS THE BALL OF MY THUMB, AND DUMB AS EYES ........BLACKBERRYING 168 5
TO THUMB SHUT YOUR EYES AT THE END ....THE APPLICANT 221 16
MY THUMB INSTEAD OF AN ONION. ....CUT 235 2
THUMB STUMP. ....CUT 236 40
THEMSELVES ON MY THUMB -- ....BRASILIA 258 13
GOING TO GET GABRIEL'S THUMB INTO THE PIE ....DIALOGUE O. 280 148
BETWEEN THUMB AND FOREFINGER. ....BITTER STRAWBERRIES 300 39
WITH HIS MODISH OPPOSABLE THUMB: ....DIALOGUE EN ROUTE 309 26
THUMBED (3)
STILL HE THUMBED OUT SOMETHING ELSE.   THE HERMIT AT OUTERMOST HOUSE 119 14
THUMBED NO STONY, HORNY POT, ...THE HERMIT AT OUTERMOST HOUSE 119 15
WITH SEVEN HOLES THUMBED IN. THE SOUL IS ANOTHER LIGHT. ...SURGEON. 170 8
THUMBHEAD (1)
THUMBHEAD, BLUNT HELPER, ...WORDS FOR A NURSERY 73 15
THUMBSCREWS (1)
TWISTING OF THUMBSCREWS: ONE SOUL TIED IN SINEWS, ...LESSON. 80 8
THUMBS-DOWN (1)
THUMBS-DOWN ON THE DODO'S MODE. ....YOU'RE 141 4
THUMB-SIZE (1)
EACH THUMB-SIZE BIRD ....WATERCOLOR OF GRANTCHESTER MEADOWS 112 6
THUMPABLE (1)
BRIGHT GREEN AND THUMPABLE ....FIESTA MELONS 46 5
THUNDER (6)
SO DUMB IT THINKS BULLETS ARE THUNDER. ....THE SWARM 216 20
IMPOTENT AS DISTANT THUNDER, ...THE JAILER 227 37
THUNDER AND GUNS. ....GETTING THERE 249 50
AND THE SKIES CRACK THROUGH WITH THUNDER; ..GO GET THE GOODLY SQUAB 313 6
WITH A THUNDER LIKE LIONS; ALL AIMS ....AERIALIST 331 32
THE PRINCESS HEARS THE THUNDER AND THE POMP ....THE PRINCESS. 333 21
THUNDERED (1)
WHEN IT THUNDERED I HID UNDER A FLAT STONE. POEM.3.MAENAD. 133 5
THUS (9)
AND SINGS YOU THUS: ....THE QUEEN'S COMPLAINT 29 23
AS THOUGH ALIVE, SHRIVELING IN TORMENT THUS ....DIALOGUE B. 39 35
AND I, GREAT MAGNANIMOUS FOOL, THUS WRENCHED FROM ...
... MONOLOGUE AT 3 A.M. 40 13
PLUCKED BACK THUS SUDDEN TO THAT FAR INNOCENCE, ..DREAM WITH C. 44 21
THAT EVERY BREATH, THUS TEEMING, SET THE LAND ..WREATH FOR A BRIDAL 45 21
THUS HALLOWING AN INTERVAL ....BLACK ROOK IN RAINY WEATHER 57 19
THUS WHOLLY ENGROSS ....SOW 61 28
ALL NIGHT I SHALL GALLOP THUS, IMPETUOUSLY, ...ELM 192 10
LESSONED THUS, THE GIRL ....AERIALIST 331 19
THWACKED (1)
THEN, WITH A JOCULAR FIST THWACKED THE BARREL NAPE, ...SOW 61 35
TIBET (1)
IN TIBET, OR A LLAMA IN ZANZIBAR ....DIALOGUE OVER A OUIJA BOARD 281 177

TICK (11)
    BETWEEN TICK ....ALL THE DEAD DEARS   71   32
    WITH THEIR HEARTS THAT TICK AND TICK, WITH THEIR SATCHELS OF
        INSTRUMENTS. ....THREE WOMEN 180 138
    WITH THEIR HEARTS THAT TICK AND TICK, WITH THEIR SATCHELS OF
        INSTRUMENTS. ....THREE WOMEN 180 138
    PROBABLE MOTES THAT TICK THE YEARS OFF MY LIFE. A BIRTHDAY PRESENT 207 43
    POCKET WATCH, I TICK WELL. ....GIGOLO 267   1
    AND SCORNED THE TICK OF THE FALLING WEATHER. ....LAMENT 315   3
    AND SCORNED THE TICK OF THE FALLING WEATHER. ....LAMENT 315   9
    AND SCORNED THE TICK OF THE FALLING WEATHER. ....LAMENT 315 15
    WHO SCORNED THE TICK OF THE FALLING WEATHER. ....LAMENT 316 19
    EACH CLOCK TICK CONSECRATES THE DEATH OF STRANGERS. DOOM OF EXILES 318   8
    UNTIL THE STARS TICK OUT A LULLABY ....LOVE IS A PARALLAX 329 14
TICKER (1)
    WHILE THE DAY OUTSIDE GLIDES BY LIKE TICKER TAPE. ......PARALYTIC 266 10
TICKET (1)
    I HAVE THE TICKET FOR THAT. ....THE APPLICANT 221 27
TICKETS (2)
    NOTIONS AND TICKETS, SHORT CIRCUITS AND FOLDING MIRRORS. .....TOTEM 265 27
    AND THEY BUY TICKETS FOR THE TROPIC ZONE; ....DENOUEMENT 326   5
TICKING (5)
    TAPPING AND TICKING LIKE NERVOUS FINGERS. ....LEAVING EARLY 146 27
    TICKING YOUR FINGERS ON THE MARBLE TABLE, LOOKING FOR
        CIGARETTES, ...TULIPS 166   8
    SHE HEARS THE CAUSTIC TICKING OF THE CLOCK. ....CINDERELLA 304 14
    AMID THE TICKING JEWELED CLOCKS THAT MARK ....SONNET: TO TIME 311   2
    WITH RECOLLECTION'S TICKING THORNS ....DANSE MACABRE 321 11
TICKLE (1)
    ARMED WITH FEATHERS TO TICKLE AS WELL AS FLY, ...PERSEUS   83 35
TICKS (3)
    DRY TICKS MARK TIME ....TWO SISTERS OF PERSEPHONE   31   8
    HEARING TICKS BLOWN GOLD ....TWO SISTERS OF PERSEPHONE   32 14
    TICKS TEMPO TO THE CASUAL CLIMB ...MORNING IN THE HOSPITAL SOLARIUM 332 16
TIDAL (3)
    NAVIGATES THE TIDAL SLOSH OF SEAS ....TALE OF A TUB   25 44
    MARGIN OF THE TIDAL POOLS. ....MUSSEL HUNTER AT ROCK HARBOR   95 11
    ITS CARGO OF AGONY TOWARD ME, INESCAPABLE, TIDAL. ......THREE WOMEN 179 110
TIDAL-FLATS (1)
    OVER TIDAL-FLATS WHERE THREE CHILDREN PLAYED*DREAM WITH CLAM-DIGGERS   44 14
TIDE (7)
    TIDE BY TIDE, ...LETTER TO A PURIST   36   5
    TIDE BY TIDE, ...LETTER TO A PURIST   36   5
    THEY SAILED TILL TIDE FOAMED ROUND THEIR ANKLES .....DREAM WITH C.   44 19
    DAWN TIDE STOOD DEAD LOW. I SMELT .....MUSSEL HUNTER AT ROCK HARBOR   95 12
    RIDING THE TIDE OF THE WIND, STEADY ....A WINTER SHIP 113   7
    BARED BY EACH FALLING TIDE, ...MAN IN BLACK 119 14
    RIDING THE RIP TIDE TO THE NEAREST POINT OF DEPARTURE, ...MEDUSA 225 10
TIDE-LINE (1)
    BARGE-TAR CLOTTED AT THE TIDE-LINE, THE WRECKED PIER ...GREEN ROCK. 104   2
TIDE'S (2)
    THEN YOU COME IN WITH THE TIDE'S COMING ....FULL FATHOM FIVE   92   2
    TANGLING IN THE TIDE'S GREEN FALL ....TWO LOVERS. 327   6
TIDE-WAY (1)
    OF SEA RETRACING ITS TIDE-WAY ....MUSSEL HUNTER AT ROCK HARBOR 96 43-4
TIDINESS (1)
    HER TIDINESS AND HER CALMNESS AND HER PATIENCE: ....IN PLASTER 159 25
TIDY (3)
    TINKER JACK AND THE TIDY WIVES ......TINKER JACK AND THE TIDY WIVES   34   T
    THE TIMES ARE TIDY ....THE TIMES ARE TIDY 107   T
    O THE KING'S TIDY ACRE IS UNDER THE SEA, ...THE BULL OF BENDYLAW 108 19
TIE (1)
    WHILE YOU STAND HEROIC IN COAT AND TIE, I SIT ........CONVERSATION.   21 10
TIED (4)
    TIRELESS, TIED, AS A MOON-BOUND SEA ....HARDCASTLE CRAGS   62 12
    TWISTING OF THUMBSCREWS: ONE SOUL TIED IN SINEWS, ...LESSON.   80   8
    MOONY BALLOONS TIED BY A STRING ....ON DECK 143 34
    IN THEIR CANVAS-SIDED COTS, NAMES TIED TO THEIR WRISTS, *THREE WOMEN 183 220
TIERED (1)
    THEN BRISKLY SCALED HIS ALTAR TIERED WITH TETHERED ANTS, ...SPIDER   49 22
TIFFANY'S (1)
    INDOORS, TIFFANY'S PHOENIX RISES ....YADDO: THE GRAND MANOR 123 13
TIGER (5)
    ON A TIGER TOOTH, LESS FOR ....MUSSEL HUNTER AT ROCK HARBOR   97 81
    GOLDFINCH, GOLDFISH, GOLDEN TIGER CAT STOCK- .....IN MIDAS' COUNTRY   99 13
    I SHOULD WEAR TIGER PANTS, I SHOULD HAVE AN AFFAIR. ....LESBOS 228 30
    AND THE TIGER, EMBELLISHING ITSELF --- ....THE NIGHT DANCES 250 13
    IS IT A TIGER THIS YEAR, THIS ROAR AT THE DOOR? ....YEARS 255 18
TIGER-FACED (1)
    A TIGER-FACED ....POLLY'S TREE 128 27
TIGERS (5)
    OF UNCAGED TIGERS AND A TROPICAL MOON, ...YADWIGHA.   85   4
    OF TIGERS TO BE STILLED BY YOUR DARK EYE ....YADWIGHA.   85 13
    TIGERS, SNAKES, AND THE SNAKECHARMER AND YOU, ...YADWIGHA.   86 23
    CAN WHIPCRACK THE TABLES INTO TIGERS AND FOIST ....DIALOGUE O. 279 117

		TITLE	PAGE	LINE
TIGERS (CONT.)				
THE LION AND THE TIGERS TURN TO CLAY ....DENOUEMENT			327	10
TIGER-TAMER (1)				
TIGER-TAMER AND GRINNING CLOWN ....AERIALIST			331	29
TIGERY (1)				
WITH TIGERY STRIPES, AND A FACE ON IT ....LAST WORDS			172	2
TIGHT (5)				
WHIPPING OFF YOUR SILK SCARF, EXHIBITING THE TIGHT WHITE FACE LIFT			155	2
TIGHT WIRES BETWEEN US, ...THE RABBIT CATCHER			194	27
THE SACK OF BLACK! IT IS EVERYWHERE, TIGHT, TIGHT! ..BY CANDLELIGHT			237	30
THE SACK OF BLACK! IT IS EVERYWHERE, TIGHT, TIGHT! ..BY CANDLELIGHT			237	30
AT THE WHITE, TIGHT ....PARALYTIC			266	20
TIGHTER (1)				
TIGHTER TO THE COCOON ....SPIDER			48	17
TIGHTROPE (1)				
IN TIGHTROPE ACROBATICS. ....AERIALIST			331	6
TIGHTROPES (1)				
TREADING CIRCUS TIGHTROPES ....TRIO OF LOVE SONGS			314	21
TILES (3)				
SHADING THE BRICKRED PORCH TILES. ....DEPARTURE			51	3
GRADED TURQUOISE TILES ....BATTLE-SCENE			84	5
STRIKES THE TILES OF THE NEIGHBORS' GABLE-TOPS ....DIALOGUE O.			286	339
TILL (31)				
AMONG SACRED ISLANDS OF THE MAD TILL DEATH ....TALE OF A TUB			25	47
TILL HE SOME PITY TOOK UPON HER CRYING; ......THE QUEEN'S COMPLAINT			28	12
WHICH HAULS DOWN BUCK, COCK, TROUT, TILL ALL MOST FAIR ....FIRESONG			30	6
TILL THE NIGHT MISTS CAME RISING. ....SONG FOR A SUMMER'S DAY			31	20
THEY SAILED TILL TIDE FOAMED ROUND THEIR ANKLES ......DREAM WITH C.			44	19
OBEYING ORDERS OF INSTINCT TILL SWEPT ....SPIDER			49	32
TILL YOUR EYES FOIST A VISION DAZZLING ON THE WIND: ...NOVEMBER G.			56	14
TILL, SICK OF THEIR RULER'S GODLING AIRS, ...NATURAL HISTORY			71	7
TILL THE THUDDING SOURCE, EXPOSED, ...NIGHT SHIFT			76	13
AND SNAKES THERE WERE, ARE, WILL BE -- TILL YAWNS .....SNAKECHARMER			79	21
TO A MELTING OF GREEN WATERS, TILL NO SNAKE ...........SNAKECHARMER			79	25
TILL IRONY'S BOUGH BREAK. ....VIRGIN IN A TREE			82	45
ALL'S PEACE AND DISCIPLINE DOWN THERE. TILL LATELY WE ....OXBOW.			89	53
THE SEA, TILL THAT DAY ORDERLY, ...THE BULL OF BENDYLAW			108	2
WHO WAKES WITH DARKNESS AND TILL DAWN WORKS HARD ....GOATSUCKER			111	3
BLACK HAIR TILL THERE YOU STOOD, ...MAN IN BLACK			120	18
THE WAY SHE LAID HIS LETTERS, TILL THEY GREW WARM ....WIDOW			164	18
TILL SHE WAS FIRED. ....THE BABYSITTERS			175	27
TILL YOUR HEAD IS A STONE, YOUR PILLOW A LITTLE TURF, ...ELM			192	11
TILL THEN YOUR SMILES ARE FOUND MONEY. ....FOR A FATHERLESS SON			206	14
TILL HER STUBBORN BODY BURNS. ....DANSE MACABRE			321	15
TILL UNRULY CHILDREN STREAM DOWN THE SKY ....SONG FOR A REVOLU.			323	14
OBSCURE THE SCALDING SUN TILL NO CLOCKS MOVE. ......SONNET TO SATAN			323	14
TILL THE ANNOUNCER'S VOICE IS LOST ....INSOLENT STORM.			326	35
TILL DARK IS CONQUERED BY ORANGE COCK, ...BLACK PINE TREE.			328	15
NOW KISS AGAIN: TILL OUR STRICT FATHER LEANS ....LOVE IS A PARALLAX			330	43
AND HEAVENS TILL THE SPIRITS SQUEAK ....LOVE IS A PARALLAX			330	69
BOLD BEANSTALK; LIE AND LOVE TILL SHARP SCYTHE HACKS *LOVE IS A PAR.			330	71
AND GOD OR VOID APPALL US TILL WE DROWN ....LOVE IS A PARALLAX			330	74
NOW BOUND AROUND HER WRIST TILL SHE REDEEM ....THE PRINCESS.			333	24
WHO SEEKS TO DALLY IN THE PORT TILL DAWN, ...EPITAPH IN THREE PARTS			337	8
TILT (2)				
WITH EACH TILT, SHOCK AND SHUDDER, OUR BLUNT SHIP CHANNEL CROSSING			26	2
LABORING ON THE TILT OF THAT STEEP GRADE ....THE PRINCESS.			334	35
TILTED (5)				
TILTED AND DISPARATE, AND ALWAYS UNSTABLE. ....WUTHERING HEIGHTS			167	2
IN SOLAR SCHEMES THE TILTED SUNS GO TURNING: ....TO EVA DESCENDING.			303	11
BEGIN ON TILTED VIOLINS TO SPAN ....CINDERELLA			303	4
GROWS BRITTLE AS A TILTED CHINA BOWL; ....PROLOGUE TO SPRING			322	5
WITH TILTED SPARS OF SLOOPS REVOLVED BY WHITE .....MIDSUMMER MOBILE			324	3
TILTING (3)				
TILTING WITH THE WINDS, ...SOUTHERN SUNRISE			26	7
TILTING SILVER: ....AQUATIC NOCTURNE			305	9
THE MOON LEANS DOWN TO LOOK; THE TILTING FISH ...LOVE IS A PARALLAX			330	37
TILTS (1)				
MY DEMON OF DOOM TILTS ON A TRAPEZE, ...CIRCUS IN THREE RINGS			322	15
TIMBERS (4)				
THE FALLEN TIMBERS OF ITS ONCE REMARKABLE ....ABOVE THE OXBOW			88	37
SHIP TIMBERS IN THROUGH THE CELLAR WINDOW; ....POINT SHIRLEY			110	14
O RED FRUIT, IVORY, FINE TIMBERS! ....METAPHORS			116	4
TIMBERS OF HIS UPRIGHT HUT? ....THE HERMIT AT OUTERMOST HOUSE			119	12
TIME (62)				
DRY TICKS MARK TIME ....TWO SISTERS OF PERSEPHONE			31	8
TIME GOMES ROUND FOR THAT FOUL SLUT: ....STRUMPET SONG			33	'4
UNTIL THAT TIME ....DIALOGUE BETWEEN GHOST AND PRIEST			39	39
BLACKENING THE TIME ....MONOLOGUE AT 3 A.M.			40	11
SHE CAN SEE IN THE NICK OF TIME ......MISS DRAKE PROCEEDS TO SUPPER			41	15
BEFORE TIME ENDS ....RECANTATION			42	18
THE RITUAL DEATH EACH TIME BOTCHED AMONG DROPPED CAPES,				
ILL-JUDGED STABS, ...THE GORING			47	3
GRIEF'S HONEST GRIMACE, DEBASED BY TIME, ...THE BEGGARS			47	7
EACH TIME ROUND WINDING THAT ANT ....SPIDER			48	16

TIME (CONT.)
    BUT NOW TURNED KINDER WITH TIME, WE MARK MISS MASON ..ELLA MASON A.   54   37
    INTO SALT SEAS. HERCULES HAD A SIMPLE TIME, ...PERSEUS   82   6
    AND REPOISE UNTIL TIME STOP, THE CELESTIAL BALANCE ....PERSEUS   84   48
    TIME, AND TO GRACES GONE WITH THE TIME. A STATE VIEW- ....OXBOW.   88   39
    TIME, AND TO GRACES GONE WITH THE TIME. A STATE VIEW- ....OXBOW.   88   39
    INCOMPATIBLE MODES OF TIME, THE RAW MATERIAL*THE GHOST'S LEAVETAKING   90   13
    OF PLACE, TIME, AND THEIR BODIES. ....SCULPTOR   92   19
    OF YOUR GRAINED FACE SHED TIME IN RUNNELS: ....FULL FATHOM FIVE   93   26
    OR MUST TAKE LOOPHOLE AND BLAME TIME ......GREEN ROCK, WINTHROP BAY   105   22
    BEASTS OF OASIS, A BETTER TIME. ....THE EYE-MOTE   109   15
    A PLACE, A TIME GONE OUT OF MIND. ....THE EYE-MOTE   109   30
    INTO ANOTHER TIME. ....THE SLEEPERS   123   24
    WHEN I SPLIT A ROCK ONE TIME ....MEDALLION   124   12
    THE LIDS WON'T SHUT. TIME POEM.3.MAENAD.   133   18
    GAVE UP THE GHOST LAST NIGHT. HIGH TIME. ....LEAVING EARLY   146   24
    THIS IS NO TIME FOR THE PRIVATE POINT OF VIEW. ....CANDLES   149   13
    IN TIME OUR RELATIONSHIP GREW MORE INTENSE. ....IN PLASTER   159   28
    OR BRAG AHEAD OF TIME HOW I'D AVENGE MYSELF. ....IN PLASTER   160   47
    THEN THE TREES MAY TOUCH ME FOR ONCE, AND THE FLOWERS HAVE TIME
        FOR ME. ....I AM VERTICAL   162   20
    A SECOND TIME, TO HAVE HIM NEAR AGAIN -- ....WIDOW   164   16
    MOST OF THE TIME I MEDITATE ON THE OPPOSITE WALL. ....MIRROR   173   6
    TURNING THROUGH MY TIME, THE SUNS AND STARS ....THREE WOMEN   176   2
    THE SILVER TRACK OF TIME EMPTIES INTO THE DISTANCE, ...THREE WOMEN   177   32
    WHEN WILL IT BE, THE SECOND WHEN TIME BREAKS ....THREE WOMEN   179 104
    OLD WINTER-FACE, OLD BARREN ONE, OLD TIME BOMB. ....THREE WOMEN   181 158
    IT IS ONLY TIME THAT WEIGHS UPON OUR HANDS. ....THREE WOMEN   187 363
    IT IS ONLY TIME, AND THAT IS NOT MATERIAL. ....THREE WOMEN   187 364
    I WOULD HAVE KILLED MYSELF GLADLY THAT TIME ANY POSSIBLE WAY. ...
        ... A BIRTHDAY PRESENT   206   15
    BY THE TIME THE WHOLE OF IT WAS DELIVERED, AND TOO NUMB TO
        USE IT. ....A BIRTHDAY PRESENT   208   54
    THE THINGS IT HAS PIERCED IN ITS TIME. ..THE COURAGE OF SHUTTING-UP   210   25
    THIS IS THE EASY TIME, THERE IS NOTHING DOING. ....WINTERING   217   1
    THIS IS THE TIME OF HANGING ON FOR THE BEES -- THE BEES ..WINTERING   218   22
    YOU DIED BEFORE I HAD TIME --- ....DADDY   222   7
    THE FIRST TIME IT HAPPENED I WAS TEN. ....LADY LAZARUS   245   35
    THE SECOND TIME I MEANT ....LADY LAZARUS   245   37
    NOW IS THE TIME FOR BRIBERY. ....GETTING THERE   248   12
    EACH TIME MUST LEARN THE LETTERS NEW. ARE ....DIALOGUE O.   277   24
    SIGNING IN. JUST P THIS TIME. AND OFF, DIALOGUE OVER A OUIJA BOARD   277   29
    OUT OF IT WILL BE TIME AND PLENTY FOR US*DIALOGUE OVER A OUIJA BOARD   278   58
    AND CHANCE OF A TRUE ANSWER. YOU WASTE NO TIME ....DIALOGUE O.   281 188
    TO NAME HIS HOME A THIRD TIME. GIVE YOUR WILL THREE ....DIALOGUE O.   283 269
    CHANCES TO MASTER MINE. THEY SAY THE THIRD TIME ....DIALOGUE O.   283 270
    TELL US THE TRUTH THIS TIME: TELL US THE KINGDOM ....DIALOGUE O.   283 272
    A THIRD TIME. DON'T GLOAT. YOUR WILL MISFIRED TWICE ....DIALOGUE O.   284 281
    AND ACT BEAR WITNESS, IN THE CRUX OF TIME, ...DIALOGUE O.   286 362
    A WEIGHT OF WORLD AND TIME ....NOTES TO A NEOPHYTE   307   22
    THE RACK OF TIME ....TO A JILTED LOVER   310   23
    SONNET: TO TIME ....SONNET: TO TIME   311   T
    TIME IS A GREAT MACHINE OF IRON BARS ....SONNET: TO TIME   311   13
    IT'S TIME TO VANISH LIKE THE CHESHIRE CAT ....A SORCERER B.   324   12
    THAT STING NO MORE THAN LOVE: A ROOM WHERE TIME *MORNING IN THE HOS.   332   15
    LIKE COLORED TOPS THROUGH TIME ....TOUCH-AND-GO   335   10
    TEMPER OF TIME ....TEMPER OF TIME   336   T
TIMELESS (1)
    I WOULD ADMIRE THE DEEP GRAVITY OF IT, ITS TIMELESS EYES. *BIRTHDAY.   208   57
TIMES (5)
    THE TIMES ARE TIDY ....THE TIMES ARE TIDY   107   T
    OUR LADY OF THE SHIPWRECKED IS THREE TIMES LIFE SIZE, ...FINISTERRE   170   24
    AND THE EYES AND TIMES OF THE POSTMARKS. ....BURNING THE LETTERS   204   14
    AND LIKE THE CAT I HAVE NINE TIMES TO DIE. ....LADY LAZARUS   244   21
    TWO TIMES A DAY ....LETTER IN NOVEMBER   253   17
TIME'S (6)
    TIME'S SOOT IN BLEARED EYE ....TINKER JACK AND THE TIDY WIVES   34   12
    AT HER TOUGH TRADE: WITHOUT TIME'S TAINT ....CRYSTAL GAZER   54   4
    FUSING TIME'S THREE HORIZONS. ....CRYSTAL GAZER   54   6
    FOCUSING ALL TIME'S DAY-SUNS IN ONE ....CRYSTAL GAZER   55   39
    HEARTS OF THOSE WHO PIERCED TIME'S CORE. ....CRYSTAL GAZER   55   42
    I HOUSEKEEP IN TIME'S GUT-END POEM.4.BEAST.   134   23
TIMID (2)
    TO NOVICES AND TO THE TIMID. ....WHITENESS I REMEMBER   102   9
    THE SMALLER AND MORE TIMID NEVER ARRIVE AT ALL ....STARS.   165   12
TIMOROUS (1)
    TO TIMOROUS CHILDREN, TO THE LADY ON THE STREET. ..THE RAVAGED FACE   116   13
TIN (12)
    JIGGLES HIS TIN CUP AT THE GOODWIVES. ....THE BEGGARS   48   12
    DRINKING VINEGAR FROM TIN CUPS: THEY WORE ....THE THIN PEOPLE   64   20
    IN THE TIN PAIL SHADED BY YELLOW PAPER   MEMOIRS OF A SPINACH-PICKER   89   13
    A BLIMP SWIMS UP LIKE A DAY-MOON OR TIN ....A WINTER SHIP   113   11
    I CAN TASTE THE TIN OF THE SKY -- THE REAL TIN THING. ......WAKING.   151   1
    I CAN TASTE THE TIN OF THE SKY -- THE REAL TIN THING. ......WAKING.   151   1
    SUN MANAGES TO STRIKE SUCH TIN GLINTS ....PARLIAMENT HILL FIELDS   152   10

	TITLE	PAGE	LINE

TIN (CONT.)
    THEN MOTHER SWAM UP, HOLDING A TIN BASIN. ....FACE LIFT   156   7
    WITH ONE TIN EYE, ...BURNING THE LETTERS   204   25
    TO THE SYRUP TIN ....WINTERING   218   25
    ACETIC ACID IN A SEALED TIN? ....THE COURIERS   247   3
    OF NOTCHED TIN PLATITUDES CONCERNING WEATHER, ...SONNET: TO EVA   305   11
TINDER (2)
    ITS TINDER AND SHAKE ....HARDCASTLE CRAGS   62   5
    THE TINDER CRIES. ....FEVER.   231   8
TINDERY (1)
    HOW OUR COURTSHIP LIT THE TINDERY CAGES -- ....ZOO KEEPER'S WIFE   155   33
TINFOIL (2)
    STRIPS OF TINFOIL WINKING LIKE PEOPLE, ...THE BEE MEETING   211   16
    OF BRIGHT TINFOIL ....AQUATIC NOCTURNE   305   5
TINKER (2)
    TINKER JACK AND THE TIDY WIVES ......TINKER JACK AND THE TIDY WIVES   34   T
    BUT TINKER JACK CAN FORGE ....TINKER JACK AND THE TIDY WIVES   34   17
TINSEL (2)
    WITH TINSEL VISION ....MOONSONG AT MORNING   316   3
    A TINSEL PIZZICATO ON FISH FIN ....MIDSUMMER MOBILE   324   8
TINT (1)
    QUICK AS THEY. TO FOLLOW THE LIGHT'S TINT ......CHILD'S PARK STONES   101   18
TINTS (1)
    THEIR SKIN TINTS ARE PINK OR SALLOW, BROWN OR RED; .....THREE WOMEN   183   223
TIN-WHITE (1)
    AND THIS IS THE FRUIT OF IT: TIN-WHITE, LIKE ARSENIC. ....ELM   192   15
TINY (4)
    DISPLACED THEIR DOMES AS TINY ....MUSSEL HUNTER AT ROCK HARBOR   96   27
    SITTING UNDER A POTLID, TINY AND INERT AS A RICE GRAIN. ..POEM.6.W.   135   15
    TINY AND FAR, A SINGLE SHIP ....ON DECK   142   6
    WITH TRIANGULAR SCORCH MARKS FROM IRONING TINY RUCHINGS AND
        PUFFED SLEEVES. ....THE BABYSITTERS   174   15
TIP (3)
    TIP, RIVETING STONES, AIR, ...MAN IN BLACK   120   20
    OF GOLGOTHA AT THE TIP OF A REED, ...POEM.5.F.   135   18
    ARCS UP TO THE TALL TREE TIP; ....TOUCH-AND-GO   335   14
TIPPING (2)
    OF CLOUD-STUFF, TIPPING HER ....POLLY'S TREE   128   22
    UPSIDE DOWN HEARTS OF LIGHT TIPPING WAX FINGERS, ...CANDLES   148   2
TIPTOE (1)
    WHEN ON TIPTOE THE SCHOOLGIRLS DANCED, ...THE DISQUIETING MUSES   75   25
TIRE (2)
    I TIRE, IMAGINING WHITE NIAGARAS ....MOONRISE   98   22
    A TENDERNESS THAT DID NOT TIRE, SOMETHING HEALING. .....THREE WOMEN   186   357
TIRED (2)
    I MADE A FIRE; BEING TIRED ....BURNING THE LETTERS   204   1
    LOVE, LOVE, AND WELL, I WAS TIRED ....BURNING THE LETTERS   204   10
TIRELESS (1)
    TIRELESS, TIED, AS A MOON-BOUND SEA ....HARDCASTLE CRAGS   62   12
TIRES (1)
    CONSUME THIS PIPER AND HE TIRES OF MUSIC ..............SNAKECHARMER   79   22
TISSUE (2)
    THOSE GREEN-STRIPED OVALS OF SILVER TISSUE? ....LEAVING EARLY   146   15
    AND TISSUE IN SLICES -- A PATHOLOGICAL SALAMI.*THE SURGEON AT 2 A.M.   171   36
TITILLATING (1)
    OF LITTLE CRYSTALS, TITILLATING THE LIGHT, ...BERCK-PLAGE   197   26
TITLED (1)
    AND A TITLED LADY MAY FREQUENTLY BE A BEAUTY. ....QUEEN MARY'S.   290   22
TITS (1)
    THE SNAKES, THE BABIES, THE TITS ....THE COURAGE OF SHUTTING-UP   210   12
TO (1003)
TOAD (3)
    BUT IN SPECKLED THICKETS, WARTED AS A TOAD, ...FIRESONG   30   3
    AND THE TOAD GUARDING HIS HEART'S DROPLET. ....SLEEP.   144   16
    OF A TOAD. ....ON LOOKING INTO THE EYES OF A DEMON LOVER   325   8
TOAD-STONE (2)
    TOAD-STONE! SISTER-BITCH! SWEET NEIGHBOR! ............EAVESDROPPER   261   63
    TOAD-STONE! I SEE I MUST WEAR YOU IN THE CENTRE OF MY
        FOREHEAD ....THE RIVAL/DR   291   27
TOADSTOOLS (2)
    WOULD UMBRELLA LIKE LIBERAL TOADSTOOLS ....DIALOGUE EN ROUTE   308   8
    SPRUNG UP LIKE PLAGUE OF TOADSTOOLS OVERNIGHT: ....TERMINAL   328   4
TOAD-YELLOW (1)
    TOAD-YELLOW UNDER THE DROP ..........................EAVESDROPPER   261   39
TOAST (2)
    WOOD STOVES BURN WARM AS TOAST. ....YADDO: THE GRAND MANOR   124   17
    RAISED TO TOAST A THOUSAND KINGS, FOR ALL GIVES ....SONNET: TO TIME   311   11
TOBY (1)
    THE ROSES IN THE TOBY JUG ....LEAVING EARLY   146   23
TOD (1)
    DISMEMBERED, TO A TOD OF IVY. ....THE SWARM   217   38
TODAY (8)
    TODAY ....RESOLVE   52   19
    TODAY I WILL NOT ....RESOLVE   52   20
    YET TODAY, A YELLOW BUD IN MY HAND, ...RHODODENDRON.   103   17

TODAY (CONT.)
    I DO NOT EVEN NEED A HOLIDAY: I CAN GO TO WORK TODAY. ..THREE WOMEN   183 249
    TODAY THE COLLEGES ARE DRUNK WITH SPRING. ....THREE WOMEN   185 302
    THERE IS THIS ONE THING I WANT TODAY, AND ONLY YOU CAN GIVE
        IT TO ME. ....A BIRTHDAY PRESENT   207   48
    TODAY WE MOVE IN JADE AND CEASE WITH GARNET ....SONNET: TO TIME   311   1
    IN OUR OWN TEARS: TODAY WE START ....LOVE IS A PARALLAX   330   75
TODDLE (4)
    TODDLE ON HOME TO TEA NOW IN YOUR FLAT HAT. ....THE TOUR   238   37
    TODDLE ON HOME, BEFORE THE WEATHER'S WORSE. ....THE TOUR   238   41
    TODDLE ON HOME, AND DON'T TRIP ON THE NURSE! ....THE TOUR   238   42
    TODDLE ON HOME TO TEA! ....THE TOUR   238   49
TOE (7)
    HEAD, TOE AND FINGER ....THE MANOR GARDEN   125   7
    THEY TOE OLD WATER THICK AS FOG. ....LEAVING EARLY   146   22
    YOU DIDN'T JUST TOE ME AN INCH, NO -- ....LOVE LETTER   147   5
    GHASTLY STATUE WITH ONE GRAY TOE ....DADDY   222   9
    THIS TOE AND THAT TOE, A RELIC. ....GULLIVER   251   19
    THIS TOE AND THAT TOE, A RELIC. ....GULLIVER   251   19
    NOT A TOE, NOT A FINGER, AND USED, ...MYSTIC   268   12
TOELESS (1)
    THE HIGH, DEAD, TOELESS FOOT OF THIS PRIEST ....BERCK-PLAGE   197   21
TOES (8)
    AS I COULD BETWEEN BARE TOES? ....MUSSEL HUNTER AT ROCK HARBOR   96   50
    WINKS LIKE MONEY UNDER THE RINGED TOES OF THE CHICKENS. ......NET-.   121   9
    FIRST FROST, AND I WALK AMONG THE ROSE-FRUIT, THE MARBLE TOES ...
                                                    ... PRIVATE GROUND   130   1
    OUR TOES, OUR NOSES ....MUSHROOMS   139   4
    THEY GREW THEIR TOES AND FINGERS WELL ENOUGH, ...STILLBORN   142   2
    ITS FIRST COMMUNION OUT OF MY LIVE TOES. ..NICK AND THE CANDLESTICK   241   19
    INTO WHICH BROAD TOES WILL GO TOMORROW. ....THE MUNICH MANNEQUINS   263   20
    THEMSELVES ON THE CLAY TOES AND SHORT CLUBFOOT ......METAMORPHOSES.   308   35
TOGA (1)
    FLOWS IN THE SCROLLS OF HER TOGA, ...EDGE   272   5
TOGETHER (12)
    AND SO, TOGETHER, TALKING, ...SONG FOR A SUMMER'S DAY   31   16
    HOW WE SHALL DO TOGETHER, ...CRYSTAL GAZER   55   9
    PATCH TOGETHER A CONTENT ....BLACK ROOK IN RAINY WEATHER   57   35
    A SALLOW PIECE OF STRING HELD IT TOGETHER. ....TWO VIEWS.   114   9
    ALL OF IT, TOGETHER. ....MAN IN BLACK   120   21
    I SHALL NEVER GET YOU PUT TOGETHER ENTIRELY, ...THE COLOSSUS   129   1
    I USED TO THINK WE MIGHT MAKE A GO OF IT TOGETHER -- ....IN PLASTER   160   50
    AND SO WE ARE AT HOME TOGETHER, AFTER HOURS. ....THREE WOMEN   187 362
    SMALL, TAKEN ONE BY ONE, BUT MY GOD, TOGETHER! ....THE ARRIVAL.   213   20
    AND THEY STUCK ME TOGETHER WITH GLUE. ....DADDY   224   62
    NOT MAN NOR DEMIGOD COULD PUT TOGETHER ....SONNET: TO EVA   305   9
    AND AGAIN TOGETHER BEGIN IT ALL. .....SONG FOR A REVOLUTIONARY LOVE   323   24
TOKENS (1)
    AS PONDERABLE TOKENS OF HER LOVE. ....OUIJA   77   29
TOLD (6)
    TO GET YOUR CAROUSALS TOLD: ....SPIDER   48   6
    AND THAT, ROUSSEAU TOLD THE CRITICS, WAS WHY THE COUCH ...YADWIGHA.   86   31
    THE PEASANTS ANCHOR THEM WITH CONCHES. ONE IS TOLD: .....FINISTERRE   170   30
    THEY MELT AND SAG, THEY ARE TOLD ....BURNING THE LETTERS   204   18
    YOU SAY HE'S TOLD TWO LIES . . . CALL THEM TWO PLUCKED DIALOGUE O.   283 266
    "I KNOW, I KNOW," I TOLD MY FRIEND. ....THE DREAM   311   24
TOLERABLE (2)
    TOLERABLE NOW AS MOLES ON THE FACE ....THE COMPANIONABLE ILLS   105   2
    IT IS WARM AND TOLERABLE POEM.2.DARK.   133   26
TOLERATE (2)
    WILL TOLERATE NO BYSTANDING: I MUST SHRIEK. ....ELM   192   21
    AND TOLERATE THE HUMOR OF THE WORM. ....DIRGE FOR A JOKER   303   14
TOLLING (1)
    TOLLING HER GRAVE WITH GOLDEN GONGS, ...LAMENT   315   11
TOM (1)
    PLAYS HOSTESS TO TABBY, TOM AND INCREASE, ...ELLA MASON A.   53   10
TOMAS (1)
    ON THE ROAD NAMED FOR TOMAS ORTUNIO, MICA ....THE NET-MENDERS   121   8
TOMATO'S (1)
    THE RED TOMATO'S IN, THE GREEN BEAN: ....YADDO: THE GRAND MANOR   123   4
TOMORROW (5)
    YET THEY RECEDE, UNTOUCHABLE AS TOMORROW,*SLEEP IN THE MOJAVE DESERT   144   11
    TOMORROW THEY WILL SWIM ....THE SURGEON AT 2 A.M.   171   38
    TOMORROW THE PATIENT WILL HAVE A CLEAN, PINK PLASTIC LIMB. *SURGEON.   171   40
    TOMORROW I WILL BE SWEET GOD, I WILL SET THEM FREE. ...THE ARRIVAL.   213   35
    INTO WHICH BROAD TOES WILL GO TOMORROW. ......THE MUNICH MANNEQUINS   263   20
TON (1)
    O EUROPE! O TON OF HONEY! ....THE SWARM   217   60
TONE (1)
    LIKE THE BRONZE TONE ....AQUATIC NOCTURNE   306   27
TONE-DEAF (1)
    TONE-DEAF AND YES, UNTEACHABLE. ....THE DISQUIETING MUSES   75   38
TONELESS (1)
    SEATED BENEATH THE TONELESS WATER! ....THE BURNT-OUT SPA   138   28

TONGUE (21)
    OF BELLS CALLS HOLY ONES, HER TONGUE ....VANITY FAIR   32   9
    TONGUE A ROSE-COLORED ARROW. ....MEDALLION   124   7
    THE SUN RISES UNDER THE PILLAR OF YOUR TONGUE. ....THE COLOSSUS   130   27
    I WOULD BE A TONGUE TO. MOTHER OF OTHERNESS POEM.1.WHO.   132   26
    A RED TONGUE IS AMONG US. POEM.3.MAENAD.   133   13
    WITH A LUNG FULL OF DUST AND A TONGUE OF WOOD, ...LEAVING EARLY   146   43
    I TASTE IT ON MY TONGUE, AND THE WORKABLE HORRORS, ...THREE WOMEN   180 136
    AS IF I HAD LOST AN EYE, A LEG, A TONGUE. ....THREE WOMEN   183 252
    AND LEARN TO SPEAK WITH FINGERS, NOT A TONGUE. ....THREE WOMEN   184 255
    AND THE TONGUE, SAPPHIRE OF ASH. ....BERCK-PLAGE   198   54
    THIS IS THE TONGUE OF THE DEAD MAN: REMEMBER, REMEMBER. *BERCK-PLAGE 199   81
    THEN THERE IS THAT ANTIQUE BILLHOOK, THE TONGUE, ...COURAGE.   210   17
    NO, THE TONGUE, TOO, HAS BEEN PUT BY, ...THE COURAGE OF SHUTTING-UP   210   21
    IN THE GERMAN TONGUE, IN THE POLISH TOWN ....DADDY   222   16
    THE TONGUE STUCK IN MY JAW. ....DADDY   223   25
    THE DULL BELLS TONGUE THE HOUR. ....BY CANDLELIGHT   236   8
    LITTLE WHORE TONGUE, ...EAVESDROPPER   260   32
    NO FINGERS TO GRIP, NO TONGUE, ...PARALYTIC   266   3
    AND TONGUE, AND THOUGHT, AS WELL AS THE BLOOD-HEAT .....DIALOGUE O.   283 258
    IT WAS HIS TONGUE THAT WANTED MENDING. YOU KNOW, ...DIALOGUE O.   285 305
    TO DIAGRAM THE TONGUE, ...TRIO OF LOVE SONGS   315   38
TONGUELESS (1)
    THE MOLTS ARE TONGUELESS THAT SANG FROM ABOVE THE WATER ..POEM.5.F. 135   17
TONGUES (15)
    TO PEOPLE THE TWIGGED AISLES: LEAD BABEL TONGUES*WREATH FOR A BRIDAL   45   14
    BULKS REAL, ALL SAINTS' TONGUES FALL QUIET: ....NOVEMBER GRAVEYARD   56   11
    MOURNFULLY THE DRY TONGUES CLACKED THEIR GUILT: ....SNOWMAN O. 59   39
    OF LEAVES' BICKER AND WHISK IN BABEL TONGUES, ..PLETHORA OF DRYADS.   67   21
    NO FLOOR: A WAVE OF FLICKERING GRASS TONGUES ..........SNAKECHARMER   79   9
    FROM WHAT GRACE AM I FALLEN. TONGUES ARE STRANGE, ...INCOMMUNICADO   100   12
    IT HURTS AT FIRST. THE RED TONGUES WILL TEACH THE TRUTH. POEM.6.W. 135   18
    SOFT SUEDE TONGUES BETWEEN HIS BONES. ....THE BURNT-OUT SPA   138   11
    I THINK OF THE LIZARDS AIRING THEIR TONGUES ....SLEEP. 144   14
    UPSETTING ME WITH THEIR SUDDEN TONGUES AND THEIR COLOR, ...TULIPS 161   41
    EIGHT GREAT TONGUES AFFIRMING THE RESURRECTION. ....MOON. 173   13
    THE TONGUES OF HELL ....FEVER.   231   2
    TONGUES OF DULL, FAT CERBERUS ....FEVER.   231   4
    IF A BUSH BORROWED TONGUES AND SPOKE TO YOU. YOU'D KNEEL*DIALOGUE O. 280 163
    LAUGHED AT THE AMBUSH OF ANGELS' TONGUES, ...LAMENT   315   14
TONIGHT (11)
    TWIST OLD WORDS INTO THE WEB-THREADS: TONIGHT MAY THE FISH ...NET-. 121   17
    TONIGHT, LIKE A SHAWL, THE MILD LIGHT ENFOLDS HER, ...CANDLES   149   34
    TONIGHT, IN THE INFINITESIMAL LIGHT OF THE STARS, ...I AM VERTICAL 162   11
    BUT TONIGHT THEY HAVE DISCOVERED THIS RIVER WITH NO TROUBLE, *STARS. 165   15
    TONIGHT IT HAS RECEDED LIKE A SHIP'S LIGHT. ..THE SURGEON AT 2 A.M. 170   10
    TONIGHT THE PARTS ARE ENTOMBED IN AN ICEBOX.   THE SURGEON AT 2 A.M. 171   37
    TONIGHT, FOR THIS PERSON, BLUE IS A BEAUTIFUL COLOR. ......SURGEON. 171   43
    THESE MANNEQUINS LEAN TONIGHT ....THE MUNICH MANNEQUINS 263   11
    GO GET THE GLASS, THEN. BUT I KNOW TONIGHT WILL BE .....DIALOGUE O. 276   1
    BEYOND THE WINDOW-FRAME TONIGHT. WIND WARNS ....DIALOGUE O.   286 336
    TONIGHT THE CAUSTIC WIND, LOVE, ...JILTED   304   5
TONIGHT'S (1)
    WISER FOR TONIGHT'S WISE WORDS? I FELT DRAWN ....DIALOGUE O.   285 316
TONING (1)
    YET THE DAPPLE TONING HIS WHITE DOWN ....WHITENESS I REMEMBER 102   10
TONNAGE (2)
    TONNAGE OF METAL AND WOOD; ....NIGHT SHIFT 77   19
    BUT EVEN HER TONNAGE DOESN'T IMPRESS A DIAMOND. ....THE RIVAL/DR 291   24
TOO (53)
    "WHAT LOVE," ASKED FATHER SHAWN, "BUT TOO GREAT LOVE ...DIALOGUE B.   39   31
    DRIVES NIMBLE BLOOD TOO QUICK ....EPITAPH FOR FIRE AND FLOWER   46   25
    AN ANTIQUE HAG-HEAD, TOO TOUGH FOR KNIFE TO FINISH, ...LADY AND T. 70   33
    THE OLD GOD, TOO, WRITES AUREATE POETRY ....OUIJA 77   12
    LAIN SPLAYED TOO LONG IN THE TORTUOUS BOUGHS: OVERRIPE .....VIRGIN. 82   37
    BEARS A BURDEN TOO WEIGHTY ....LORELEI 94   17
    A WELL OF SCENTS ALMOST TOO DENSE TO BREATHE IN. ......BEEKEEPER'S. 118   4
    O I AM TOO BIG TO GO BACKWARD: POEM.3.MAENAD. 133   8
    THEY FLY TOO FAST TO FEEL THE WET. ....ON DECK   143   17
    THE HORIZONS ARE TOO FAR OFF TO BE CHUMMY AS UNCLES; .....TWO CAMP. 145   13
    SHE HAS ONE TOO MANY DIMENSIONS TO ENTER. ....A LIFE   150   28
    I CIRCLE THE WRITHEN TREES. I AM TOO HAPPY. PARLIAMENT HILL FIELDS 153   29
    THE TULIPS ARE TOO EXCITABLE, IT IS WINTER HERE. ....TULIPS   160   1
    THE TULIPS ARE TOO RED IN THE FIRST PLACE, THEY HURT ME. ...TULIPS   161   36
    I AM OVERLOOKING THEM BY LOOKING TOO HARD.   STARS OVER THE DORDOGNE 165   23
    THEY ARE TOO PURITAN AND SOLITARY FOR THAT -- ....STARS.   166   31
    THERE IS TOO MUCH EASE HERE; THESE STARS TREAT ME TOO WELL. STARS. 166   37
    THERE IS TOO MUCH EASE HERE; THESE STARS TREAT ME TOO WELL. STARS. 166   37
    THE MOON, TOO, ABASES HER SUBJECTS, ...THE RIVAL   166   11
    TOO CLOSE ATTENTION, THEY WILL INVITE ME ....WUTHERING HEIGHTS 167   17
    IT IS TOO DELICATE ....WUTHERING HEIGHTS 168   40
    THESE HILLS ARE TOO GREEN AND SWEET TO HAVE TASTED SALT. BLACKBER. 169   22
    ALMOST TOO SMALL FOR THE MISTS TO BOTHER WITH. ....FINISTERRE 169   12
    WE HAVE ONLY COME TO LOOK. YOU ARE TOO NEW ....NEW YEAR ON DARTMOOR 176   8
    BUT IT WAS TOO LATE FOR THAT. IT WAS TOO LATE, AND THE FACE THREE. 178   62

TOO (CONT.)
    BUT IT WAS TOO LATE FOR THAT. IT WAS TOO LATE, AND THE FACE   THREE.   178 62
    THEY HAVE TOO MANY COLORS, TOO MUCH LIFE. THEY ARE NOT QUIET,*THREE.   178 69
    THEY HAVE TOO MANY COLORS, TOO MUCH LIFE. THEY ARE NOT QUIET,*THREE.   178 69
    I HAVE TRIED NOT TO THINK TOO HARD. I HAVE TRIED TO BE NATURAL. ...
                                                     ... THREE WOMEN   178 74
    I AM RESTLESS. RESTLESS AND USELESS. I, TOO, CREATE CORPSES. *THREE.   182 189
    THE NARCISSI, TOO, ARE BOWING TO SOME BIG THING: *AMONG THE NARCISSI   190   4
    AND WE, TOO, HAD A RELATIONSHIP -- ....THE RABBIT CATCHER   194 26
    PEGS TOO DEEP TO UPROOT, AND A MIND LIKE A RING THE RABBIT CATCHER   194 28
    AND MY HEART TOO SMALL TO BANDAGE THEIR TERRIBLE FAULTS.*BERCK-PLAGE   198 45
    YOU ARE TOO BIG. THEY MUST TAKE YOU BACK! ....WORDS HEARD.   203 15
    WHEN I CAME TOO CLOSE TO THE WASTEBASKET. ......BURNING THE LETTERS   204   4
    BY THE TIME THE WHOLE OF IT WAS DELIVERED, AND TOO NUMB TO USE IT. ...
                                         ... A BIRTHDAY PRESENT   208 54
    HE HAS SEEN TOO MUCH DEATH, HIS HANDS ARE FULL OF IT. .....COURAGE.   210 15
    NO, THE TONGUE, TOO, HAS BEEN PUT BY, ...THE COURAGE OF SHUTTING-UP   210 21
    SQUARE AS A CHAIR AND ALMOST TOO HEAVY TO LIFT. ....THE ARRIVAL.   212   2
    HER BODY A BULB IN THE COLD AND TOO DUMB TO THINK. ....WINTERING   219 45
    I AM TOO PURE FOR YOU OR ANYONE. ....FEVER.   232 34
    FEEDING AT THE ROOT OF THINGS. HE STOLE THAT, TOO, ...DIALOGUE O.   279 102
    GODS GROW TOO PROUD TO PRACTICE DOORMAN DUTIES ....DIALOGUE O.   280 127
    NINE MONTHS TOO SOON FOR COMFORT, BUT A BRIGHT ....DIALOGUE O.   280 141
    TO PROVE IT GENUINE. YOU'D KNEEL, TOO, DIALOGUE OVER A OUIJA BOARD   280 162
    ENOUGH. BUT BE POLITE. YOU'RE TOO SEVERE*DIALOGUE OVER A OUIJA BOARD   281 181
    CURTSEYED TO YOURS. TOO BAD YOU CALLED PAN UP ....DIALOGUE O.   284 280
    FOR BEING TOO WELL-BRED AND SMELLESS AND LIKING THE CITY. ...
                                     ... QUEEN MARY'S ROSE GARDEN   290 20
    (TOO QUICK FOR THE PAIR TO ABSORB IT), ...DIALOGUE EN ROUTE   309 41
    TOO LATE TO ASK IF END WAS WORTH THE MEANS, ...DOOMSDAY   316 16
    TOO LATE TO CALCULATE THE TOPPLING STOCK: ....DOOMSDAY   316 17
    BECAUSE NEW EXCAVATIONS CAME TOO NEAR   THE PRINCESS AND THE GOBLINS   334 39
TOOK (18)
    TILL HE SOME PITY TOOK UPON HER CRYING: ......THE QUEEN'S COMPLAINT   28 12
    TOOK MY HEART AS IF ....SONG FOR A SUMMER'S DAY   31 12
    AS IF A CELESTIAL BURNING TOOK ....BLACK ROOK IN RAINY WEATHER   57 17
    IT TOOK ROOT AT MY COMING ....NIGHT SHIFT   76 12
    THE BOOKS BURNED UP, SEA TOOK THE SHELL, ON THE DECLINE OF ORACLES   78 11
    A SPASM TOOK THE RHODODENDRON BUSHES: ...............RHODODENDRON.   103 20
    EVERYTHING TOOK PLACE IN A DURABLE WHITENESS.*ELECTRA ON AZALEA PATH   117 14
    IT TOOK THREE DAYS DRIVING NORTH TO FIND A CLOUD ....TWO CAMP.   145 10
    YOU CHECKED THE DIET CHARTS AND TOOK ME TO PLAY ..ZOO KEEPER'S WIFE   155 25
    TOOK ITS PLACE AMONG THE ELEMENTS. ....MORNING SONG   156   3
    AND UTTERLY IGNORANT OF THE WAY IT TOOK. ....WIDOW   165 35
    UNDER A STONE. THOSE TWO DREAMED DEATHS TOOK ....DIALOGUE O.   285 326
    AND IT TOOK THE DIAMOND STONE ....NOTES TO A NEOPHYTE   307 21
    AND TOOK THE WOMAN'S BRIGHT SUBPOENA ....THE DREAM   311 26
    THE STING OF BEES TOOK AWAY MY FATHER ....LAMENT   315   1
    THE STING OF BEES TOOK AWAY MY FATHER. ....LAMENT   315   6
    BUT THE STING OF BEES TOOK AWAY MY FATHER ....LAMENT   315 12
    THE STING OF BEES TOOK AWAY MY FATHER ....LAMENT   316 18
TOOLS (1)
    OLD TOOLS, HANDLES AND RUSTY TUSKS. POEM.1.WHO.   131   5
TOO-SHORT (1)
    I HAD TO SLEEP IN THE SAME ROOM WITH THE BABY ON A TOO-SHORT
        COT, ...THE BABYSITTERS   174   7
TOO-SIMPLE (1)
    LIKE A CHILD'S TOO-SIMPLE MATHEMATICAL PROBLEM. ....STARS.   165 20
TOOTH (2)
    FENDING OFF JAG AND TOOTH, ...MISS DRAKE PROCEEDS TO SUPPER   41 22
    ON A TIGER TOOTH, LESS FOR ....MUSSEL HUNTER AT ROCK HARBOR   97 81
TOP (6)
    WHITE BODIES IN A WOODEN GIRDLE, ROOT TO TOP ......VIRGIN IN A TREE   81 22
    BUT IT'S THE CLEAR CONVERSION AT THE TOP CAN HOLD ..ABOVE THE OXBOW   88 20
    THAT OPENS AT THE TOP ONTO NOTHING AT ALL. . . ..WIDOW   164 10
    COMING AT ME, LIKE A CASTLE, FROM THE TOP OF THE RIVER. *THREE WOMEN   178 51
    THE TOP QUITE GONE ....CUT   235   3
    ALL TO ITSELF ON THE TOP OF EACH ....THE COURIERS   247   9
TOPOGRAPHY (1)
    OVER THE SCALDING, RED TOPOGRAPHY ....WIDOW   164   4
TOPPLE (3)
    WHITE CATALPA FLOWERS TOWER, TOPPLE, ...MOONRISE   98   5
    THE COLORED TENTS ALL TOPPLE IN THE BAY: ....DENOUEMENT   327 16
    THEN LET THE BLUE TENT TOPPLE, STARS RAIN DOWN, LOVE IS A PARALLAX   330 73
TOPPLED (1)
    HIS ARMORPLATE, HIS TOPPLED STONES ....THE BURNT-OUT SPA   138 12
TOPPLES (1)
    WHERE THE BLACK WAVE TOPPLES DOWN; ....GO GET THE GOODLY SQUAB   313 22
TOPPLING (1)
    TOO LATE TO CALCULATE THE TOPPLING STOCK: ....DOOMSDAY   316 17
TOPS (2)
    INTO THE BLUE. TOPS DEFINE THEMSELVES AS PLACES ....ABOVE THE OXBOW   88 29
    LIKE COLORED TOPS THROUGH TIME ....TOUCH-AND-GO   335 10
TOPSOIL (1)
    BY DAY, ONLY THE TOPSOIL HEAVES. ....BLUE MOLES   126 26

                                                      TITLE   PAGE LINE
TOR (1)
    POUR OF TOR AND DISTANCES. ....ARIEL   239   3
TORCH (1)
    BUT THE TORCH AND ITS FAINT ....WINTERING   218   15
TORCHES (1)
    KINDLED LIKE TORCHES FOR HIS JOY, ...PURSUIT   22   22
TORMENT (1)
    AS THOUGH ALIVE, SHRIVELING IN TORMENT THUS ....DIALOGUE B.   39   35
TORN (2)
    LAYS ALL WALLS WASTE: PRIVATE ESTATES ARE TORN, ...CHANNEL CROSSING   27   31
    HER WINGS TORN SHAWLS, HER LONG BODY ....STINGS   214   17
TORPID (1)
    TORPID WARNING, OR LAY STILL ....SPIDER   49   20
TORSO (2)
    A WORKMAN WALKS BY CARRYING A PINK TORSO. POEM.7.S.   137   31
    FROM HER AMAZINGLY WHITE TORSO, AND I COULDN'T HELP BUT NOTICE ...
                                                        ... IN PLASTER   159   24
TORSOS (1)
    THESE PEOPLE WITH TORSOS OF STEEL ....BRASILIA   258   2
TORTUOUS (1)
    LAIN SPLAYED TOO LONG IN THE TORTUOUS BOUGHS: OVERRIPE .....VIRGIN.   82   37
TORTURE (2)
    AND WERE EXTRAVAGANT, LIKE TORTURE. ....THE RABBIT CATCHER   193   10
    IN WHICH A TORTURE GOES ON ONE CAN ONLY WATCH. ....COURAGE.   210   28
TORTURED (1)
    IS IT NOT AS TORTURED? ....LITTLE FUGUE   188   30
TOSSED (1)
    BONES, BONES ONLY, PAWED AND TOSSED, ...POINT SHIRLEY   111   38
TOTAL (3)
    COMPELS A TOTAL SACRIFICE. ....PURSUIT   23   40
    OF TOTAL NEUTRALITY. WITH LUCK, ...BLACK ROOK IN RAINY WEATHER   57   32
    SHE RECORDED THE TOTAL IN HER NOTEBOOK, ...BITTER STRAWBERRIES   300   32
TOTEM (1)
    TOTEM ....TOTEM   264   T
TOTTERING (1)
    STALEMATED THEIR ARMIES STOOD, WITH TOTTERING BANNERS: ..SNOWMAN O.   58   1
TOUCH (19)
    JACK WILL TOUCH UP ....TINKER JACK AND THE TIDY WIVES   34   21
    THESE TWO MOST PERISHABLE LOVERS FROM THE TOUCH .....EPITAPH FOR F.   45   5
    SURFEITING EYE, EAR, TASTE, TOUCH, SMELL; *ON THE PLETHORA OF DRYADS   67   27
    SHIES FROM HIS TOUCH: HIS IS AN IRON MOOD. ....THE OTHER TWO   68   19
    ANY TOUCH, TASTE, TANG'S ....ALL THE DEAD DEARS   71   29
    ALTHOUGH EACH TEACHER FOUND MY TOUCH ....THE DISQUIETING MUSES   75   35
    AUGUST GIVES OVER ITS MIDAS TOUCH, ...IN MIDAS' COUNTRY   100   24
    TOUCH IT: IT WON'T SHRINK LIKE AN EYEBALL, ...A LIFE   149   1
    THEN THE TREES MAY TOUCH ME FOR ONCE, AND THE FLOWERS HAVE TIME
        FOR ME. ....I AM VERTICAL   162   20
    OTHER CHILDREN DO NOT TOUCH ME: THEY ARE TERRIBLE. .....THREE WOMEN   178   68
    ONE TOUCH: IT BURNS AND SICKENS. ....EVENT   194   11
    THE DARK IS MELTING. WE TOUCH LIKE CRIPPLES. ....EVENT   195   22
    YOU FLICKER. I CANNOT TOUCH YOU. ....POPPIES IN JULY   203   3
    THERE ARE FUMES THAT I CANNOT TOUCH. ....POPPIES IN JULY   203   9
    DO NOT TOUCH. ....BURNING THE LETTERS   204   19
    ONE DAY YOU MAY TOUCH WHAT'S WRONG ....FOR A FATHERLESS SON   205   12
    LIKE THE RED-HEADED SISTER HE NEVER DARED TO TOUCH, ...AMNESIAC   233   13
    FOR A WORD OR A TOUCH ....LADY LAZARUS   246   62
    ON A WHOLE WORLD I CANNOT TOUCH, ...PARALYTIC   266   19
TOUCH-AND-GO (2)
    TOUCH-AND-GO ....TOUCH-AND-GO   335   T
    HOW ALL THEIR PLAY IS TOUCH-AND-GO: ....TOUCH-AND-GO   335   12
TOUCHED (2)
    TOUCHED BY A MATCH, THEY MIGHT WARM ME, ...WUTHERING HEIGHTS   167   3
    THEY ARE BROWNING, LIKE TOUCHED GARDENIAS. ....BERCK-PLAGE   198   59
TOUCHING (4)
    IT IS TOUCHING, THE WAY THEY'LL IGNORE ....CANDLES   148   5
    TOUCHING AND SUCKING. ....MEDUSA   225   20
    TOUCHING THEIR WOUNDED, ...GETTING THERE   248   24
    TOUCHING AND MELTING. ....THE NIGHT DANCES   250   27
TOUCHY (1)
    TOUCHY ANTENNA, ...WORDS FOR A NURSERY   74   22
TOUGH (5)
    AT HER TOUGH TRADE; WITHOUT TIME'S TAINT ....CRYSTAL GAZER   54   4
    AN ANTIQUE HAG-HEAD, TOO TOUGH FOR KNIFE TO FINISH, ...LADY AND T.   70   33
    I SEE HIM, HORNY-SKINNED AND TOUGH, CONSTRUE ....OUIJA   77   27
    RELIC OF TOUGH WEATHER, EVERY WINCH AND STAY ....A WINTER SHIP   113   27
    THEN, THIS TOUGH STINT DONE, SHE CURTSIES ....AERIALIST   331   25
TOUR (2)
    BUT ONE DUSK OUR QUESTIONS COMMEMDED US TO A TOUR ....SOW   60   7
    THE TOUR ....THE TOUR   237   T
TOWARD (21)
    AND SO WE SAIL TOWARD CITIES, STREETS AND HOMES ...CHANNEL CROSSING   27   37
    WALKING EAGER TOWARD WATER, WHEN THERE, ONE BY ONE, ..DREAM WITH C.   44   23
    THE STRONGEST WILL SEEMED A WILL TOWARD CEREMONY. OBESE, DARK- ...
                                                      ... THE GORING   47   4
    TOWARD THAT GREAT JEWEL: SHOWN OFTEN, ...THE GREAT CARBUNCLE   72   11

TOWARD (CONT.)
    TOWARD WHAT I CAN GRAB, ...WORDS FOR A NURSERY   73   6
    FROM A GROSS COMIC STRIP, AND TOWARD .....ON THE DECLINE OF ORACLES   78   24
    TOWARD THREE PINKY-PURPLE ....BATTLE-SCENE   84   15
    THE POPULACE SINGS TOWARD THE SILL ....A WINTER'S TALE   87   29
    BUT TOWARD A REGION WHERE OUR THICK ATMOSPHERE ....GHOST'S.   90   25
    TOWARD EXTINCTION IN THOSE EYES ....SCULPTOR   92   17
    UP TOWARD ME, TROUBLING THE FACE ....LORELEI   94   10
    TOWARD THE POOL-MOUTH, PERHAPS TO .....MUSSEL HUNTER AT ROCK HARBOR   96   41
    WHITE BRUISES TOWARD COLOR, ELSE COLLAPSES. ....MOONRISE   98   12
    TOWARD THE ROWDY BELLOW AND BACK AGAIN ....THE BULL OF BENDYLAW   108   11
    TOWARD THEIR ADMIRERS IN THE TABLETOP: ....LEAVING EARLY   146   12
    OUR LADY OF THE SHIPWRECKED IS STRIDING TOWARD THE HORIZON, ...
                                          ... FINISTERRE   169   19
    RISES TOWARD HER DAY AFTER DAY, LIKE A TERRIBLE FISH. ....MIRROR   174   18
    ITS CARGO OF AGONY TOWARD ME, INESCAPABLE, TIDAL. ......THREE WOMEN   179 110
    ITS END AND RUNS TOWARD IT, ARMS HELD OUT IN LOVE. .....THREE WOMEN   181 151
    A VISIONARY LADDER TOWARD THE MOON ....THE PRINCESS AND THE GOBLINS   333   5
    POINTING TOWARD THE SPINDLE'S CRYPTIC WHIR, ...THE PRINCESS.   335   60
TOWARDS (3)
    OF WEEDS WE TACKLE TOWARDS WAY'S RANK ENDING; ....FIRESONG   30   16
    THE EIGHT PILGRIMS TOWARDS ITS SOURCE -- ......THE GREAT CARBUNCLE   72   10
    AS THAT CRISP CUSP TOWARDS WHICH YOU VOYAGE NOW. ....GHOST'S.   91   38
TOWEL (1)
    THAN PHYSICAL ABLUTION, AND THE TOWEL ....TALE OF A TUB   24   12
TOWER (3)
    ENTERING THE TOWER OF MY FEARS, ...PURSUIT   23   45
    WHITE CATALPA FLOWERS TOWER, TOPPLE, ...MOONRISE   98   5
    AGAINST BOTH BAR AND TOWER THE BLACK SEA RUNS. ....POINT SHIRLEY   111   48
TOWERS (3)
    THAT ONCE DESCRIED TROY'S TOWERS FALL, ...ON THE DECLINE OF ORACLES   78   31
    WHITE TOWERS OF SMITHFIELD AHEAD, ...TOTEM   264   7
    TO BUILD HIS CANTING TOWERS. WHILE YOU, YOU LONG ....DIALOGUE O.   280 136
TOWLINES (1)
    BRACING THEIR KNEES. ON UNSEEN TOWLINES ....IN MIDAS' COUNTRY   99   17
TOWN (8)
    STONE-BUILT TOWN, THAT SHE HEARD THE QUICK AIR IGNITE *HARDCASTLE C.   62   4
    THEIR EYES REVOLVE THE WHOLE TOWN LIKE A BLUE AND GREEN BALL. *NET-.   121   12
    SOUTHWARD, OVER KENTISH TOWN, AN ASHEN SMUDGE*PARLIAMENT HILL FIELDS   152   21
    SOMEBODY IS SHOOTING AT SOMETHING IN OUR TOWN -- ....THE SWARM   215   1
    IN THE GERMAN TONGUE, IN THE POLISH TOWN ....DADDY   222   16
    BUT THE NAME OF THE TOWN IS COMMON. ....DADDY   222   19
    LUMINOUS, THE TOWN OF STONE ....DANSE MACABRE   321   22
    SHOULD INFLAME THE SLEEPING TOWN. ....LOVE IS A PARALLAX   329   30
TOWN'S (1)
    THE SCRAGGY ROCK SPIT SHIELDING THE TOWN'S BLUE BAY ......DEPARTURE   51   13
TOY (4)
    OF THIS BLUE-GREEN TOY. ....WORDS FOR A NURSERY   73   20
    LITTLE SHELLS MADE UP INTO NECKLACES AND TOY LADIES. ....FINISTERRE   170   32
    THE LITTLE TOY WIFE -- ....AMNESIAC   233   4
    TAIL ON EACH TOY DONKEY THAT WILL BRAY   DIALOGUE OVER A OUIJA BOARD   283 250
TRACE (1)
    AND, DROPPING, DIE, TO TRACE A WOUND THAT HEALS   LOVE IS A PARALLAX   330   64
TRACES (1)
    NO MAP TRACES THE STREET ....THE SLEEPERS   122   1
TRACK (10)
    LEAVING NO SPARKY TRACK, SETTING UP NO RIPPLE. ....THE OTHER TWO   68   26
    FOLLOW THE BLACK ARROW-BACKS OF SWIFTS ON THEIR TRACK ....OXBOW.   88   31
    WE HAVE LOST TRACK OF IT. ....THE SLEEPERS   122   3
    THE SNAIL LEAVES A SILVER TRACK; ....THE SLEEPERS   122   10
    SOME FEW PASSENGERS KEEP TRACK ....ON DECK   142   4
    THE SILVER TRACK OF TIME EMPTIES INTO THE DISTANCE, ...THREE WOMEN   177   32
    INCENSE IN MY TRACK. ....GETTING THERE   249   63
    THE ENGINE IS KILLING THE TRACK, THE TRACK IS SILVER, ...TOTEM   264   1
    THE ENGINE IS KILLING THE TRACK, THE TRACK IS SILVER, ...TOTEM   264   1
    TANGLE THE TRACK. ....TEMPER OF TIME   336   12
TRACKS (3)
    WHICH HAS STOPPED THE SEASON IN ITS TRACKS ......PROLOGUE TO SPRING   322   11
    TRAIN TRACKS ALWAYS MEET, NOT HERE, BUT ONLY ....LOVE IS A PARALLAX   329   2
    OF THREAD CONDUCTING HER TO THE WORN TRACKS ....THE PRINCESS.   334   32
TRADE (3)
    AT HER TOUGH TRADE: WITHOUT TIME'S TAINT ....CRYSTAL GAZER   54   4
    GROWN GARGANTUAN BY TRADE, ...MUSSEL HUNTER AT ROCK HARBOR   96   35
    TO TRADE THEIR HOOKS FOR HANDS. POEM.7.S.   137   37
TRADEMARK (1)
    THE BIRTHMARKS THAT ARE HIS TRADEMARK --- ....DEATH & CO.   254   6
TRADING (1)
    TRADING THEIR POISONS, THE NORTH AND SOUTH BOUND CARS*PRIVATE GROUND   130   16
TRAFFIC (5)
    OR SHOUTS OF WALKERS: CROSSROAD TRAFFIC ....WHITENESS I REMEMBER   103   25
    IN THE TRAFFIC OF PLANES ....GREEN ROCK, WINTHROP BAY   105   15
    YOU ARE BLUE AND HUGE, A TRAFFIC POLICEMAN, ...A SECRET   219   3
    WOULD TRAFFIC IN. LET HIM FINISH WHAT HE BEGAN. ....DIALOGUE O.   278   84
    STEEL GAUNTLETS OF TRAFFIC, TERROR-STRUCK ....AERIALIST   332   45

	TITLE	PAGE	LINE

TRAGEDIANS (1)
    THESE GOATISH TRAGEDIANS WHO ....THE BEGGARS   47   2
TRAGEDIES (2)
    ENACTED TRAGEDIES ON THESE BLOOD-SOAKED BOARDS, ...PERSEUS   83   19
    BLOOD-SPOOR OF THE AUSTERE TRAGEDIES. ....AFTERMATH 113   8
TRAGEDY (2)
    THEY POISE AND GRIEVE AS IN SOME OLD TRAGEDY. ....THE OTHER TWO   68   21
    I BORROW THE STILTS OF AN OLD TRAGEDY. ......ELECTRA ON AZALEA PATH 117   33
TRAGIC (2)
    ROOTED TO YOUR BLACK LOOK, THE PLAY TURNED TRAGIC: ....CONVERSATION. 21   12
    AND A FUN-HOUSE MIRROR THAT TURNS THE TRAGIC MUSE ....PERSEUS   83   36
TRAILING (2)
    TRAILING ITS TELLTALE TATTERS ONLY AT THE OUTERMOST ....GHOST'S. 90   21
    TRAILING HER SCRUPULOUSLY SIMPLE GOWN   THE PRINCESS AND THE GOBLINS 333 11
TRAIN (6)
    BOARDED THE TRAIN THERE'S NO GETTING OFF. ....METAPHORS 116   9
    IN THAT VALLEY THE TRAIN SHRIEKS ECHO LIKE SOULS ON HOOKS. ...
                                                 ... THE DETECTIVE   208   5
    I CANNOT UNDO MYSELF, AND THE TRAIN IS STEAMING. .....GETTING THERE 248 38
    THE TRAIN IS DRAGGING ITSELF, IT IS SCREAMING --- ....GETTING THERE 249 55
    THE TRAIN LEAVES A LINE OF BREATH. ....SHEEP IN FOG 262   4
    TRAIN TRACKS ALWAYS MEET, NOT HERE, BUT ONLY ....LOVE IS A PARALLAX 329   2
TRAINED (2)
    WE THOUGHT WE'D TRAINED HIM, BEFORE GOING HAYWIRE. TRUTH*DIALOGUE O. 277 41
    AND GET SAFE HOME; BUT, TURNING WITH TRAINED EYES, ...AERIALIST 331 28
TRAINS (3)
    GOODBYES WERE SAID, TRAINS LET GO, ...MONOLOGUE AT 3 A.M.   40 12
    TRAINS ROAR IN MY EARS, DEPARTURES, DEPARTURES! ....THREE WOMEN 177 31
    WHERE TRAINS, FAITHFUL TO THEIR STEEL ARCS, ...THE SWARM   216 35
TRAINSTOP (1)
    IT IS A TRAINSTOP, THE NURSES ....GETTING THERE   248 22
TRAITOR (1)
    THE ASTEROIDS TURN TRAITOR IN THE AIR,   TO EVA DESCENDING THE STAIR 303   4
TRANCE (2)
    HIS VOICE WAYLAYS ME, SPELLS A TRANCE, ...PURSUIT   23 41
    AND GILDED COUPLES ALL IN WHIRLING TRANCE ....CINDERELLA 304   9
TRANSCEND (1)
    RIVER FLOODS TRANSCEND THE LEVEL*INSOLENT STORM STRIKES AT THE SKULL 326 19
TRANSFIGURING (1)
    SOME SUCH TRANSFIGURING MOVED ....THE GREAT CARBUNCLE 72   9
TRANSFIXED (2)
    THE IMAGE OF YOU, TRANSFIXED BY ROOTS, WAX-PALE, ...DIALOGUE O. 285 325
    TRANSFIXED BY GLARE OF BLUE FROM GORGON'S EYE: ..PROLOGUE TO SPRING 322   2
TRANSFORM (1)
    TRANSFORM TO CRIPPLES ....ON LOOKING INTO THE EYES OF A DEMON LOVER 325   3
TRANSIENT (1)
    LET MY TRANSIENT EYE BREAK A TEAR ....TOUCH-AND-GO 336 19
TRANSLATE (1)
    THE JABBERWOCK WILL NOT TRANSLATE HIS SONGS: ....A SORCERER B. 324 11
TRANSPARENCIES (1)
    TO YOU THEY ARE ONLY TRANSPARENCIES, CLEAR AIR.   A BIRTHDAY PRESENT 207 38
TRANSPARENT (2)
    THEY ARE DEPARTING IN THEIR TRANSPARENT GARMENTS, TURNED ASIDE ...
                                       ... THE SURGEON AT 2 A.M.   170   3
    SO NEAT SHE IS TRANSPARENT, LIKE A SPIRIT. ....THREE WOMEN 184 281
TRAP (4)
    THE HUNT IS ON, AND SPRUNG THE TRAP. ....PURSUIT   22   8
    TO TRAP THIS WAYWARD GIRL AT HER FIRST MOVE OF LOVE,   DREAM WITH C. 44 27
    AND TRAP THE MUSKRAT NAPPING IN SLACK SUN; GO GET THE GOODLY SQUAB 313 10
    TO TRAP THIS OUTRAGEOUS NIMBLE QUEEN ....AERIALIST 332 34
TRAPEZE (1)
    MY DEMON OF DOOM TILTS ON A TRAPEZE, ...CIRCUS IN THREE RINGS 322 15
TRAPPED (2)
    THEY'VE TRAPPED HER IN SOME LABORATORY JAR. ....FACE LIFT 156 28
    EACH FALLEN LEAF IS TRAPPED BY SPELL OF STEEL, ..PROLOGUE TO SPRING 322   7
TRASH (1)
    WHAT A TRASH ....LADY LAZARUS 245 23
TRAVEL (6)
    SHE, IN HER SHABBY TRAVEL GARB, BEGAN ......DREAM WITH CLAM-DIGGERS   44 22
    BY PALE GIRLS, TRAVEL THE AIR IN SCORCHED HANDS. ....BERCK-PLAGE 196   4
    HOW THEY'LL TRAVEL, TRAVEL, TRAVEL, SCENERY ....AMNESIAC 233 17
    HOW THEY'LL TRAVEL, TRAVEL, TRAVEL, SCENERY ....AMNESIAC 233 17
    HOW THEY'LL TRAVEL, TRAVEL, TRAVEL, SCENERY ....AMNESIAC 233 17
    SURELY THEY TRAVEL ....THE NIGHT DANCES 249   6
TRAVELED (2)
    BENT-BACKED ATLAS, OUR TRAVELED PRAWN. ....YOU'RE 141 12
    BACKWARD WE TRAVELED TO RECLAIM THE DAY ....DOOM OF EXILES 318   9
TRAVELING (4)
    AND I FACED MY TRAVELING COMPANIONS. ....THE DISQUIETING MUSES   76 48
    THEY'VE CHANGED ALL THAT. TRAVELING ....FACE LIFT 156   9
    ECHOES TRAVELING...WORDS   270   4
    AND THESE TRAVELING ....BALLOONS 271 13
TRAVELLING (1)
    AND THEY ARE WAN, DULLED BY MUCH TRAVELLING.*STARS OVER THE DORDOGNE 165 11

```
                                              TITLE            PAGE  LINE
TRAVERSE (1)
  TO TRAVERSE GLASS FLOOR  ...............................AERIALIST  331   27
TRAWLING (1)
  TRAWLING YOUR DARK AS OWLS DO.  ...........................YOU'RE  141    6
TRAY (1)
  HIS OWN PALE BRIDE UPON A FLAMING TRAY:  ................TERMINAL  328   12
TREAD (2)
  THE PANTHER'S TREAD IS ON THE STAIRS,  ...................PURSUIT   23   49
  FLOURED HIS WHIRLING BEARD, AND AT HIS TREAD*THE SNOWMAN ON THE MOOR  59   33
TREADING (1)
  TREADING CIRCUS TIGHTROPES  ....................TRIO OF LOVE SONGS  314   21
TREASON (1)
  A TREASON NOT TO BE BORNE. LET IDIOTS  ...................SPINSTER   50   22
TREAT (1)
  THERE IS TOO MUCH EASE HERE; THESE STARS TREAT ME TOO WELL.   STARS.  166   37
TREE (44)
  THE FIGS ON THE FIG TREE IN THE YARD ARE GREEN:  .........DEPARTURE   51    1
  BATTALIONS. SEE, HOW THE TREE BOLES FLATTEN  ........THE THIN PEOPLE   65   43
  "MY TROUBLE, DOCTOR, IS: I SEE A TREE,  .............CONJURING UP A.   66   19
  AND THAT DAMN SCRUPULOUS TREE WON'T PRACTICE WILES   CONJURING UP A.   66   20
  MY TREE STAYS TREE.  ......ON THE DIFFICULTY OF CONJURING UP A DRYAD   66   24
  MY TREE STAYS TREE.  ......ON THE DIFFICULTY OF CONJURING UP A DRYAD   66   24
  TO DISCOVER THAT METAPHYSICAL TREE WHICH HID  ...PLETHORA OF DRYADS.   67    9
  UNTIL NO CHASTE TREE BUT SUFFERS BLOTCH  ..ON THE PLETHORA OF DRYADS   68   34
  OF TREE AND HUMAN. AND HE WITHIN THIS SNAKEDOM  .......SNAKECHARMER   79   15
  VIRGIN IN A TREE  .................................VIRGIN IN A TREE   81    T
  APPROVING CHASED GIRLS WHO GET THEM TO A TREE  .....VIRGIN IN A TREE   81    4
  THE GOLDEN RAIN TREE DRIPS ITS POWDERS DOWN.  ..........BEEKEEPER'S.  118    9
  POLLY'S TREE  ........................................POLLY'S TREE  128    T
  A DREAM TREE, POLLY'S TREE:  .........................POLLY'S TREE  128    1
  A DREAM TREE, POLLY'S TREE:  .........................POLLY'S TREE  128    1
  NO FAMILY TREE,  .....................................POLLY'S TREE  128   29
  POLLY'S TREE, NOR  ...................................POLLY'S TREE  128   30
  A TREE OF HEAVEN, THOUGH  ............................POLLY'S TREE  129   31
  A DREAM TREE. POLLY'S TREE  ..........................POLLY'S TREE  129   37
  A DREAM TREE. POLLY'S TREE  ..........................POLLY'S TREE  129   37
  SAT BY MY FATHER'S BEAN TREE  ......................POEM.3.MAENAD.  133    2
  A VULTUROUS BOREDOM PINNED ME IN THIS TREE.  .......THE HANGING MAN  142    5
  TREE AND STONE GLITTERED, WITHOUT SHADOWS.  ...........LOVE LETTER  147   29
  SWADDLES ROOF AND TREE.  ....................PARLIAMENT HILL FIELDS  152   22
  I PRETENDED I WAS THE TREE OF KNOWLEDGE.  .........ZOO KEEPER'S WIFE  155   27
  I AM NOT A TREE WITH MY ROOT IN THE SOIL  .............I AM VERTICAL  162    2
  COMPARED WITH ME, A TREE IS IMMORTAL  .................I AM VERTICAL  162    8
  THE MOON AND THE YEW TREE  ................THE MOON AND THE YEW TREE  172    T
  THE YEW TREE POINTS UP. IT HAS A GOTHIC SHAPE.  ...............MOON.  173   15
  AND THE MESSAGE OF THE YEW TREE IS BLACKNESS -- BLACKNESS AND
       SILENCE.  ...........................THE MOON AND THE YEW TREE  173   28
  DEATH OPENED, LIKE A BLACK TREE, BLACKLY.  ...........LITTLE FUGUE  188   48
  GROWING BESIDE YOU, LIKE A TREE,  ..............FOR A FATHERLESS SON  205    2
  A DEATH TREE, COLOR GONE, AN AUSTRALIAN GUM TREE --  ....FATHERLESS.  205    3
  A DEATH TREE, COLOR GONE, AN AUSTRALIAN GUM TREE --  ....FATHERLESS.  205    3
  THERE IS ONLY A CROW IN A TREE. MAKE NOTES.  ........THE DETECTIVE  209   40
  IF I JUST UNDID THE LOCKS AND STOOD BACK AND TURNED INTO A TREE.  ...
       ...  THE ARRIVAL OF THE BEE BOX  213   28
  SEVENTY FEET UP, IN A BLACK PINE TREE.  ...................THE SWARM  216   18
  DISCHARGES ITSELF FROM THE TREE WITH NOWHERE TO GO. *CHILDLESS WOMAN  259    3
  THE TREE OF LIFE AND THE TREE OF LIFE  ........THE MUNICH MANNEQUINS  262    4
  THE TREE OF LIFE AND THE TREE OF LIFE  ........THE MUNICH MANNEQUINS  262    4
  FRUITS OF YOUR WILLFUL TREE: GOD-HEAD, GOD-PIE  .........DIALOGUE O.  283  267
  BLACK PINE TREE IN AN ORANGE LIGHT  ................BLACK PINE TREE.  328    T
  THE PINE TREE LIKE A RORSCHACH-BLOT  ...............BLACK PINE TREE.  328    2
  ARCS UP TO THE TALL TREE TIP;  ........................TOUCH-AND-GO  335   14
TREELESS (1)
  LEATHERY, TREELESS,  ..........................WORDS FOR A NURSERY   74   29
TREES (31)
  HIS ARDOR SNARES ME, LIGHTS THE TREES,  ...................PURSUIT   23   33
  AND TREES DIMINISH  ....................SOLILOQUY OF THE SOLIPSIST   37   12
  "I SEE TWO STALWART APPLE TREES  ....................CRYSTAL GAZER   55   13
  THE SCENE STANDS STUBBORN: SKINFLINT TREES  ......NOVEMBER GRAVEYARD   56    1
  THE TREES ARE LOPPED, THE POODLES TRIM,  ...THE DEATH OF MYTH-MAKING  104    6
  BONES OF THE GREAT TREES.  ...................DARK WOOD, DARK WATER  127    5
  WHERE TREES AND CLOUDS AND ANIMALS PAY NO NOTICE;  .......TWO CAMP.  144    8
  THE TREES STIFFEN INTO PLACE LIKE BURNT NERVES.  ...WAKING IN WINTER  151    3
  I CIRCLE THE WRITHEN TREES. I AM TOO HAPPY.  PARLIAMENT HILL FIELDS  153   29
  ON THE GREEN HILL, UNDER THE THORN TREES,  ...........HEAVY WOMEN  158   12
  THE TREES AND FLOWERS HAVE BEEN STREWING THEIR COOL ODORS.*VERTICAL.  162   12
  THEN THE TREES MAY TOUCH ME FOR ONCE, AND THE FLOWERS HAVE TIME
       FOR ME.  .............................................I AM VERTICAL  162   20
  WIDOW, THE COMPASSIONATE TREES BEND IN,  ....................WIDOW  164   26
  THE TREES OF LONELINESS, THE TREES OF MOURNING.  .............WIDOW  164   27
  THE TREES OF LONELINESS, THE TREES OF MOURNING.  .............WIDOW  164   27
  PICKET OF TREES WHOSE SILHOUETTE IS DARKER   STARS OVER THE DORDOGNE  165    2
  THE TREES OF THE MIND ARE BLACK. THE LIGHT IS BLUE.  .........MOON.  172    2
  I SAW DEATH IN THE BARE TREES, A DEPRIVATION.  .........THREE WOMEN  177   24
  THE TREES WITHER IN THE STREET. THE RAIN IS CORROSIVE.   THREE WOMEN  180  135
```

TITLE   PAGE   LINE

TREES (CONT.)
    WHERE DO THE BLACK TREES GO THAT DRINK HERE? ....CROSSING THE WATER   190   2
    THERE ARE NO TREES OR BIRDS IN THIS WORLD, ...APPREHENSIONS   195   9
    THE NERVES BURSTING LIKE TREES, AND THIS IS THE SURGEON:*BERCK-PLAGE   198   47
    POLLARDED GREEN BALLS, THE TREES MARCH TO CHURCH. ......BERCK-PLAGE   199   92
    MY VEINS GLOW LIKE TREES. ....BURNING THE LETTERS   205   48
    WITH THE SAME TREES AND HEADSTONES. ....THE JAILER   226   3
    GEESE AND THE MONKEY TREES. ....THE TOUR   237   10
    DRAGGING TREES -- ....PURDAH   242   14
    MY SEVENTY TREES ....LETTER IN NOVEMBER   253   26
    WINTER TREES ....WINTER TREES   257   T
    ON THEIR BLOTTER OF FOG THE TREES ....WINTER TREES   257   2
    WHERE THE YEW TREES BLOW LIKE HYDRAS, ...THE MUNICH MANNEQUINS   262   3
TREE'S (1)
    FOR PIES. THE FIR TREE'S THICK WITH GRACKLES.*YADDO: THE GRAND MANOR   123   7
TREETOPS (1)
    IN A FEW SPACES OF SKY AND TREETOPS ....APRIL 18   302   13
TREE-TWIST (1)
    TREE-TWIST WILL APE THIS GROSS ANATOMY ....VIRGIN IN A TREE   82   44
TREFOILS (1)
    THE CLIFFS ARE EDGED WITH TREFOILS, STARS AND BELLS .....FINISTERRE   169   10
TREK (1)
    FLAYED BY THORNS I TREK THE ROCKS, ...PURSUIT   22   9
TREKKING (1)
    TREKKING STUBBORN THROUGH THIS SEASON ..BLACK ROOK IN RAINY WEATHER   57   33
TREKS (1)
    WHEREBY SHE TREKS IN BLOOD THROUGH SUN AND SQUALL *QUEEN'S COMPLAINT   29   22
TREMBLING (2)
    AND THE ONLOOKER, TREMBLING, ...BERCK-PLAGE   197   33
    WHEN ATTACKED, THEN SCOOTING TO REST, BARELY TREMBLING. ...BALLOONS   271   8
TREMOLO (1)
    A TREMOLO OF TURQUOISE QUIVERING IN ....MIDSUMMER MOBILE   324   6
TREMULOUS (1)
    TREMULOUS BREATH AT THE END OF MY LINE, ...MEDUSA   225   17
TRENCH-DUG (1)
    AND FROM THE TRENCH-DUG MUD, ALL ......MUSSEL HUNTER AT ROCK HARBOR   96   30
TRENCHED (1)
    FOR THE ARCHAIC TRENCHED LINES ....FULL FATHOM FIVE   93   25
TRENCHES (1)
    DISPATCHED, INTO TRENCHES OF GRASS. ....STINGS/DR   293   13
TREPANNED (1)
    TREPANNED VETERAN, ...CUT   236   38
TRESPASS (1)
    I TRESPASS STUPIDLY. LET BE, LET BE. ....PHEASANT   191   24
TRESPASSING (1)
    NEVER TRESPASSING IN BAD TEMPER: ....A LIFE   150   12
TRIAL (2)
    ON TRIAL, FROM IRELAND, SHE BURNED BATCH AFTER BATCH OF COOKIES ...
                                             ... THE BABYSITTERS   175   26
    THE TRIAL OF MAN ....THE TRIAL OF MAN   312   T
TRIAL'S (1)
    WHATEVER TRIAL'S TO COME, SO SAY TRUE." ....CRYSTAL GAZER   55   20
TRIANGULAR (1)
    WITH TRIANGULAR SCORCH MARKS FROM IRONING TINY RUCHINGS AND PUFFED
        SLEEVES. ....THE BABYSITTERS   174   15
TRIBE (1)
    OF WEEVIL TRIBE AND LOCUST CARAVAN ....THE DISPOSSESSED   318   8
TRICK (5)
    NEVER TRY TO TRICK ME WITH A KISS *NEVER TRY TO TRICK ME WITH A KISS   319   T
    NEVER TRY TO TRICK ME WITH A KISS *NEVER TRY TO TRICK ME WITH A KISS   319   1
    NEVER TRY TO TRICK ME WITH A KISS.*NEVER TRY TO TRICK ME WITH A KISS   319   6
    NEVER TRY TO TRICK ME WITH A KISS.*NEVER TRY TO TRICK ME WITH A KISS   320   12
    SO NEVER TRY TO TRICK ME WITH A KISS: ....NEVER TRY TO TRICK.   320   18
TRICKED (2)
    IS TRICKED TO FALTER IN SPILT BLOOD. ....FIRESONG   30   7
    AND TRICKED US TO TRUST HIS VISION, WHILE NIGHT AFTER NIGHT HE ...
                                      ... DIALOGUE OVER A OUIJA BOARD   279   104
TRICKLE (1)
    AND TRICKLE. COULD THEY FEEL MUD ......MUSSEL HUNTER AT ROCK HARBOR   96   48
TRICKLES (2)
    HE SPLIT IT INTO THREE HUNDRED AND SIXTY TRICKLES ....LESSON.   80   19
    THE FEVER TRICKLES AND STIFFENS IN MY HAIR. ....THE JAILER   226   21
TRICKS (2)
    "FORSWEAR THOSE FREEZING TRICKS OF SIGHT ....RECANTATION   42   11
    TRICKS OF RADIANCE MIRACLES. THE WAIT'S BEGUN AGAIN,   BLACK ROOK I.   57   38
TRIED (8)
    I TRIED MY SIGHT ON AN APPLE-TREE ....ON THE PLETHORA OF DRYADS   67   4
    TRIED SOBRIETY HIRING HIM OUT ....WHITENESS I REMEMBER 102   8
    I HAVE HAD MY CHANCES. I HAVE TRIED AND TRIED. ....THREE WOMEN   178   71
    I HAVE HAD MY CHANCES. I HAVE TRIED AND TRIED. ....THREE WOMEN   178   71
    I HAVE TRIED NOT TO THINK TOO HARD. I HAVE TRIED TO BE NATURAL. ...
                                             ... THREE WOMEN   178   74
    I HAVE TRIED NOT TO THINK TOO HARD. I HAVE TRIED TO BE NATURAL. ...
                                             ... THREE WOMEN   178   74
    I HAVE TRIED TO BE BLIND IN LOVE, LIKE OTHER WOMEN, ...THREE WOMEN   178   75

```
                                        TITLE              PAGE  LINE
TRIED (CONT.)
   AT TWENTY I TRIED TO DIE  ........................DADDY  224   58
TRIES (1)
   HE IS QUITE BLUE: THE TERRIBLE WIND TRIES HIS BREATHING.  NARCISSI.  190  11
TRIGGER (1)
   COIN, BUTTON, TRIGGER  .........................WORDS FOR A NURSERY  74  39
TRILLS (2)
   TRILLS ITS HURT OUT  ....................................STREET SONG  36  22
   AND PRAISED MY ARABESQUES AND TRILLS  .........THE DISQUIETING MUSES  75  34
TRIM (4)
   SHOULD TRIM BACK TO SHAPE.  .........TINKER JACK AND THE TIDY WIVES   34   4
   THE TREES ARE LOPPED, THE POODLES TRIM,  ...THE DEATH OF MYTH-MAKING  104   6
   WITH ITS TRIM PIGGERIES,  .............................MAN IN BLACK  119   8
   YOUR BROTHER WILL TRIM MY HEDGES!  ....................EAVESDROPPER  260   1
TRINKET (1)
   READY, FOR A TRINKET,  ..............................VANITY FAIR   33  18
TRINKETS (2)
   AND IT ASKS NOTHING, A NAME TAG, A FEW TRINKETS.  ............TULIPS  161  33
   "THESE ARE THE PRETTY TRINKETS THE SEA HIDES,  ..........FINISTERRE  170  31
TRIO (1)
   TRIO OF LOVE SONGS  .............................TRIO OF LOVE SONGS  313   T
TRIP (2)
   TODDLE ON HOME, AND DON'T TRIP ON THE NURSE! --  ...........THE TOUR  238  42
   CRACKS RED. NOTHING HAPPENS. WAIT. ITS TRIP  ..........DIALOGUE O.  277  20
TRIP-DATE (1)
   PICKED HIS TRIP-DATE BY THE STARS.  .........................ON DECK  143  26
TRIPLE (1)
   ARE DULL, DULL AS THE TRIPLE  ..................................FEVER.  231   3
TRIPOD (1)
   STUCK TO HER TRIPOD, OVER THE FUMING CREVICE,  ..........DIALOGUE O.  286 349
TRIPPED (1)
   HE TRIPPED AN ANT WITH A ROPE  .................................SPIDER  48  13
TRIUMPH (1)
   THE TRIUMPH OF WIT OVER SUFFERING  ..........................PERSEUS  82  ST
TRIUMPHANT (1)
   REMEMBERING THE WHITE, TRIUMPHANT SPRAY  ...................MAYFLOWER  60  12
TRIVIAL (1)
   CREEPING UP WITH HER HATFUL OF TRIVIAL REPETITIONS.  ......INSOMNIAC  163  32
TROLL (3)
   DRYLY DISCLAIMS THAT FIERCE TROLL FACES LURK  .........TALE OF A TUB  24  13
   TROLL NO SLIME, NO WEED.  ............................BATTLE-SCENE  84  23
   BELGE TROLL, THE LOW  ...............................EAVESDROPPER  261  49
TROLLEY (2)
   SCARED AND BARE ON THE GREEN PLASTIC-PILLOWED TROLLEY  .......TULIPS  161  25
   FLOGGED TROLLEY. THE SPARKS ARE BLUE.  .......................LESBOS  228  49
TROLLEYS (1)
   KUMQUAT-COLORED TROLLEYS DING AS THEY TRUNDLE  .....ALICANTE LULLABY  43   8
TROLLS (1)
   LIKE LOCAL TROLLS IN THE SPELL OF A SUPERIOR BEING.  ......TWO CAMP.  144   6
TROPHIES (2)
   OF A BLIZZARD, THE GIANT ROARED UP WITH HIS CHITTERING TROPHIES.  ...
                                       ... THE SNOWMAN ON THE MOOR   59  45
   THE LITTLE SILVER TROPHIES THEY'VE COME SO FAR FOR.  ....THREE WOMEN  183 221
TROPIC (1)
   AND THEY BUY TICKETS FOR THE TROPIC ZONE;  ..............DENOUEMENT  326   5
TROPICAL (3)
   OF UNCAGED TIGERS AND A TROPICAL MOON,  ....................YADWIGHA.  85   4
   BUT FROM ANOTHER PLACE, TROPICAL AND BLUE,  ..............FINISTERRE  170  34
   THE FLOWERS IN THIS ROOM ARE RED AND TROPICAL.  .........THREE WOMEN  184 263
TROPICS (1)
   THE STAIN OF THE TROPICS  .............................EAVESDROPPER  260   7
TROT (1)
   HIS NEAT TROT PITCHING MY TENSE POISE UP,  .....WHITENESS I REMEMBER  102  14
TROUBLE (6)
   GOD ORDAINED TO FOLLOW UP YOUR DAYS. IS IT SUCH TROUBLE *DIALOGUE B.  39  25
   "MY TROUBLE, DOCTOR, IS: I SEE A TREE,  .............CONJURING UP A.  66  19
   THEN I SAW WHAT THE TROUBLE WAS: SHE THOUGHT SHE WAS IMMORTAL.  ...
                                       ... IN PLASTER  159  35
   THE NURSES PASS AND PASS, THEY ARE NO TROUBLE,  ..............TULIPS  160  11
   BUT TONIGHT THEY HAVE DISCOVERED THIS RIVER WITH NO TROUBLE, *STARS.  165  15
   WELL WHAT, THEN? THAT'S THE TROUBLE. LET'S SAY HE  ......DIALOGUE O.  278  51
TROUBLING (1)
   UP TOWARD ME, TROUBLING THE FACE  .........................LORELEI   94  10
TROUBLOUS (1)
   NOT THIS TROUBLOUS  ...........................................CHILD  265  10
TROUGH (1)
   CREST AND TROUGH. MILES LONG  .......................FULL FATHOM FIVE  92   6
TROUGHED (1)
   THE SEVEN TROUGHED SEAS AND EVERY EARTHQUAKING CONTINENT.  ......SOW  61  45
TROUGHS (1)
   ARE HUSTLED OVER THE CRESTS AND TROUGHS,  ...................ON DECK  143  13
TROUNCING (1)
   TROUNCING THE SEA LIKE A RAGING BATHER,  ...................LAMENT  315   7
TROUT (4)
   WHICH HAULS DOWN BUCK, COCK, TROUT, TILL ALL MOST FAIR  ....FIRESONG  30   6
```

TROUT (CONT.)
   TROUT, COCK, RAM, ...ON THE DIFFICULTY OF CONJURING UP A DRYAD 66 13
   THE WAY SUN RUINS A TROUT. ....MEDALLION 124 15
   AND BAIT THE DROWSING TROUT BY THE BROOK'S BRIM; ....GO GET. 313 18
TROY (1)
   ECLIPSING EVA, CLEO AND HELEN OF TROY: ....VIRGIN IN A TREE 81 19
TROY'S (1)
   THAT ONCE DESCRIED TROY'S TOWERS FALL, ...ON THE DECLINE OF ORACLES 78 31
TRUANT (2)
   LAST BLOOD-DROP OF THAT TRUANT HEART. ....THE SHRIKE 42 23
   CAN RECTIFY TRUANT INTENT ......INSOLENT STORM STRIKES AT THE SKULL 326 27
TRUCK (1)
   OF BLACK WEIGHT, BLACK BALL, BLACK TRUCK, ...AERIALIST 332 38
TRUCKLING (1)
   BOWING AND TRUCKLING LIKE AN OLD-SCHOOL ORIENTAL. ....WHITSUN 154 16
TRUCKS (1)
   TALL TRUCKS ROLL IN ....AERIALIST 331 31
TRUCULENCE (1)
   THE AFTERNOON AT A BAD END UNDER THE CROWD'S TRUCULENCE, *THE GORING 47 2
TRUE (8)
   ITS GLITTERING SURFACES ARE BLANK AND TRUE. ....TALE OF A TUB 25 32
   WHATEVER TRIAL'S TO COME, SO SAY TRUE." ....CRYSTAL GAZER 55 20
   THE REAL THING, ALL RIGHT: THE GOOD, THE TRUE -- ....MAGI 148 6
   THEY RING TRUE, LIKE GOOD CHINA. ....A LIFE 150 18
   WHEN I HIT HER SHE HELD STILL, LIKE A TRUE PACIFIST. ....IN PLASTER 159 12
   WAVERY, INDELIBLE, TRUE ....A SECRET 219 11
   ARE NOT VERY PURE OR TRUE. ....DADDY 223 37
   AND CHANCE OF A TRUE ANSWER. YOU WASTE NO TIME ....DIALOGUE O. 281 188
TRUER (1)
   TRUER THAN WOMEN, ...WINTER TREES 258 7
TRUMP-CRACK (1)
   REPENT, DEPART, BEFORE GOD'S TRUMP-CRACK SPLITS THE SKY." ...
           ... DIALOGUE BETWEEN GHOST AND PRIEST 39 46
TRUMPETS (2)
   GILT TRUMPETS RAISE. ....A WINTER'S TALE 87 12
   AND JUMBO SADLY TRUMPETS INTO STONE; ....DENOUEMENT 327 11
TRUMPET-THROATS (1)
   TRUMPET-THROATS OPEN TO THE BEAKS OF BIRDS.*THE BEEKEEPER'S DAUGHTER 118 8
TRUMPET-TOPPLING (1)
   TO TRUMPET-TOPPLING DAWN OF DOOMSTRUCK DAY: ....THE DEAD 320 11
TRUNCATED (1)
   WE HAVE NOT MOUNTAINS, BUT MOUNTS, TRUNCATED HILLOCKS ....OXBOW. 87 2
TRUNDLE (2)
   KUMQUAT-COLORED TROLLEYS DING AS THEY TRUNDLE .....ALICANTE LULLABY 43 8
   BUT TRUNDLE ROUND THE GLOBE ....FEVER. 231 16
TRUNDLING (2)
   TRUNDLING THEIR UDDERS HOME ......................EAVESDROPPER 261 42
   THEY'LL GO BY, TRUNDLING LIKE MARBLE STATUES WAY OUT ...DIALOGUE O. 276 6
TRUNK (1)
   "HOWEVER I WRENCH OBSTINATE BARK AND TRUNK ....CONJURING 66 25
TRUST (4)
   I DO NOT TRUST THE SPIRIT. IT ESCAPES LIKE STEAM ....LAST WORDS 172 14
   I SUPPOSE. IF I DIDN'T TRUST YOU AT THIS*DIALOGUE OVER A OUIJA BOARD 277 36
   I WOULDN'T TRUST MYSELF. THE FAULT'S MY FAITH ....DIALOGUE O. 277 37
   AND TRICKED US TO TRUST HIS VISION, WHILE NIGHT AFTER NIGHT HE ...
           ... DIALOGUE OVER A OUIJA BOARD 279 104
TRUTH (7)
   THE TRUTH IS, ONE LATE OCTOBER, AT MY BIRTH-CRY ....ELECTRA ON. 117 34
   IT HURTS AT FIRST. THE RED TONGUES WILL TEACH THE TRUTH. POEM.6.W. 135 18
   AND IN TRUTH IT IS TERRIBLE, ...TOTEM 265 29
   WE THOUGHT WE'D TRAINED HIM, BEFORE GOING HAYWIRE. TRUTH*DIALOGUE O. 277 41
   TELL US THE TRUTH THIS TIME: TELL US THE KINGDOM ....DIALOGUE O. 283 272
   TELL US THE TRUTH. WHERE DO YOU LIVE? HE STARTS ....DIALOGUE O. 283 274
   AND STERN TRUTH TWISTED ....MOONSONG AT MORNING 317 35
TRUTHFUL (1)
   I AM NOT CRUEL, ONLY TRUTHFUL -- ....MIRROR 173 4
TRUTHS (1)
   FOR MOST EXQUISITE TRUTHS ARE ARTIFICE ...METAMORPHOSES OF THE MOON 307 25
TRY (21)
   TRY ENTRY, ENTER NIGHTMARES ....SCULPTOR 92 21
   OR TO TRY ME HE SUDDENLY SET ....WHITENESS I REMEMBER 102 18
   WHITENS AND SWALLOWS ITS DULL STARS. AND NOW YOU TRY ..MORNING SONG 157 16
   I TRY TO KEEP HIM IN, ...LESBOS 228 45
   FEED YOUR OWN WISHFUL THINKING. TRY ASKING HIM ....DIALOGUE O. 283 268
   I TRY TO THINK OF A PLACE TO HIDE YOU ....THE RIVAL/DR 291 8
   STILL, STUBBORNLY WE TRY TO CRACK THE NUT ....DOOM OF EXILES 318 13
   OH NEVER TRY TO KNOCK ON ROTTEN WOOD ....ADMONITIONS 319 1
   NEVER TRY TO KNOW MORE THAN YOU SHOULD. ....ADMONITIONS 319 3
   OH NEVER TRY TO KNOCK ON ROTTEN WOOD. ....ADMONITIONS 319 6
   NEVER TRY TO KNOW MORE THAN YOU SHOULD. ....ADMONITIONS 319 9
   OH NEVER TRY TO KNOCK ON ROTTEN WOOD. ....ADMONITIONS 319 12
   NEVER TRY TO KNOW MORE THAN YOU SHOULD. ....ADMONITIONS 319 15
   NEVER TRY TO KNOCK ON ROTTEN WOOD, ...ADMONITIONS 319 18
   NEVER TRY TO KNOW MORE THAN YOU SHOULD. ....ADMONITIONS 319 19
   NEVER TRY TO TRICK ME WITH A KISS *NEVER TRY TO TRICK ME WITH A KISS 319 T

TRY (CONT.)
    NEVER TRY TO TRICK ME WITH A KISS *NEVER TRY TO TRICK ME WITH A KISS   319   1
    NEVER TRY TO TRICK ME WITH A KISS.*NEVER TRY TO TRICK ME WITH A KISS   319   6
    NEVER TRY TO TRICK ME WITH A KISS.*NEVER TRY TO TRICK ME WITH A KISS   320   12
    SO NEVER TRY TO TRICK ME WITH A KISS: ....NEVER TRY TO TRICK.   320   18
    SKEPTIC CYCLONES TRY THE BONE ..INSOLENT STORM STRIKES AT THE SKULL   325   7
TRYING (3)
    SLEEPILY AS LETHE, TRYING TO GET IN. ..TWO CAMPERS IN CLOUD COUNTRY   145   26
    I CAN FEEL IT TRYING ....WUTHERING HEIGHTS   167   14
    TABLE, TRYING OUR LUCK, INDEX FINGERS SET ....DIALOGUE O.   276   4
TRYOUTS (1)
    FROM BED TO STRICT TRYOUTS ....AERIALIST   331   5
TUB (4)
    TALE OF A TUB ....TALE OF A TUB   24   T
    TWENTY YEARS AGO, THE FAMILIAR TUB ....TALE OF A TUB   25   17
    IS CLOSED; THE TUB EXISTS BEHIND OUR BACK: ....TALE OF A TUB   25   31
    IN THIS PARTICULAR TUB, TWO KNEES JUT UP ....TALE OF A TUB   25   41
TUBERS (1)
    IT IS A GARDEN I HAVE TO DO WITH -- TUBERS AND FRUITS .....SURGEON.   170   11
TUBES (3)
    THE FOOD TUBES EMBRACE ME. SPONGES KISS MY LICHENS AWAY.   POEM.7.S.   136   19
    YOU WHO HAVE BLOWN YOUR TUBES LIKE A BAD RADIO ....LESBOS   228   17
    OF MERCURY IN GRADED TUBES, WHERE ILLS ....MORNING IN THE HOS.   332   17
TUBULAR (1)
    TUBULAR STEEL WHEELCHAIRS, ALUMINUM CRUTCHES. ....BERCK-PLAGE   197   39
TUCK (2)
    LARKS' NIP AND TUCK ARISING ....SONG FOR A SUMMER'S DAY   31   9
    TUCK HIM IN. ....AMNESIAC   233   8
TUG (3)
    THE WINGY MYTHS WON'T TUG AT US ANY MORE: POEM.5.F.   135   16
    LIKE A BIG SEA. FAR OFF, FAR OFF, I FEEL THE FIRST WAVE TUG   THREE.   179   109
    GUIDED ONLY BY THE TUG AND TWITCH .....THE PRINCESS AND THE GOBLINS   334   26
TUGGING (2)
    TUGGING THE WORLD TO FRUIT. ....STINGS   215   47
    TUGGING US THROUGH PLUMAGE. I ALMOST FEEL ....DIALOGUE O.   279   86
TULIPS (9)
    TULIPS ....TULIPS   160   T
    THE TULIPS ARE TOO EXCITABLE, IT IS WINTER HERE. ....TULIPS   160   1
    THE TULIPS ARE TOO RED IN THE FIRST PLACE, THEY HURT ME. ...TULIPS   161   36
    THE TULIPS TURN TO ME, AND THE WINDOW BEHIND ME ....TULIPS   161   44
    BETWEEN THE EYE OF THE SUN AND THE EYES OF THE TULIPS, ...TULIPS   161   47
    THE VIVID TULIPS EAT MY OXYGEN. ....TULIPS   161   49
    THEN THE TULIPS FILLED IT UP LIKE A LOUD NOISE. ....TULIPS   161   52
    THE TULIPS SHOULD BE BEHIND BARS LIKE DANGEROUS ANIMALS; ....TULIPS   162   58
    WHILE TULIPS BOW LIKE A COLLEGE OF CARDINALS ....APRIL AUBADE   312   7
TUMULI (1)
    THE BALD, WHITE TUMULI OF YOUR EYES. ....THE COLOSSUS   129   15
TUMULT (2)
    BY THIS TUMULT AFFLICTED, SHE ....SPINSTER   49   7
    FINGER-TRAPS -- A TUMULT OF KEYS. ....LITTLE FUGUE   187   16
TUMULUS (1)
    THE TUMULUS, EVEN AT NOON, GUARDS ITS BLACK SHADOW: ..PARLIAMENT H.   153   26
TUN (1)
    BLOAT TUN OF MILK ....SOW   61   20
TUNE (1)
    UNTIL SWEET WIND CHANGED TUNE, BLEW HARM: ....BUCOLICS   24   15
TUNES (1)
    HIS SNAKEHOOD AND HIS MIGHT WITH PLIANT TUNES .........SNAKECHARMER   79   17
TUNIC (1)
    COMPOSED IN GRECIAN TUNIC AND PSYCHE-KNOT, ...CONVERSATION.   21   11
TUNNEL (1)
    DARK TUNNEL, THROUGH WHICH HURTLE THE VISITATIONS, ...THREE WOMEN   180   130
TUNNELS (1)
    THESE MARROWY TUNNELS! POEM.2.DARK.   132   15
TURBINE (1)
    IT WAS A SOLAR TURBINE ....NOTES TO A NEOPHYTE   306   19
TURF (1)
    TILL YOUR HEAD IS A STONE, YOUR PILLOW A LITTLE TURF, ...ELM   192   11
TURKEY (2)
    THEY HAD FOUR MEN LAID OUT, BLACK AS BURNT TURKEY, ...TWO VIEWS.   114   2
    YOUR TURKEY WATTLE ....CUT   235   11
TURN (21)
    SO HUMBLY DONE, I'D TURN THIS KEEN ....RHYME   50   13
    HOARD LAST YEAR'S LEAVES, WON'T MOURN, WEAR SACKCLOTH, OR TURN ...
        ... NOVEMBER GRAVEYARD   56   2
    TO SERVE HER EXACTING TURN: ......THE LADY AND THE EARTHENWARE HEAD   69   17
    TO TURN YOU LUMINOUS, WITHOUT THE EYE ....YADWIGHA.   85   12
    ON THE WAVES' DISSOLVING TURN ....MUSSEL HUNTER AT ROCK HARBOR   97   87
    AND THEY TURN IN THEIR SLEEP. ....THE SLEEPERS   123   18
    THE TULIPS TURN TO ME, AND THE WINDOW BEHIND ME ....TULIPS   161   44
    TURN UP THEIR HANDS, THEIR PALLORS. IT IS SO QUIET HERE.*THREE WOMEN   179   94
    CAN TURN AND TURN THE PAGES OF A BOOK. ....THREE WOMEN   187   361
    CAN TURN AND TURN THE PAGES OF A BOOK. ....THREE WOMEN   187   361
    THE STREETS MAY TURN TO PAPER SUDDENLY, BUT I RECOVER ..THREE WOMEN   187   365
    SO WHY SHOULD THEY TURN ON ME? ....THE ARRIVAL OF THE BEE BOX   213   34

```
                                           TITLE            PAGE  LINE
TURN (CONT.)
    TURN, LIKE AN ANIMAL, ........................................LYONNESSE  234   24
    I TURN AND BURN. ..........................................LADY LAZARUS  246   71
    ARE NOT THE THOUGHTS I TURN ON, LIKE A YOGI, ...................YEARS    255    3
    FAILS TO APPEAR, TURN, AND, TURNING, SHRINK ............DIALOGUE O.      279  120
    THE ASTEROIDS TURN TRAITOR IN THE AIR,   TO EVA DESCENDING THE STAIR    303    4
    THE GILDED COCK WILL TURN FOR ME .................TO A JILTED LOVER      310   22
    AND TURN GOD'S RADIANT PHOTOGRAPH TO SHADE. ........SONNET TO SATAN      323    8
    TURN BACK TO INJURE ......ON LOOKING INTO THE EYES OF A DEMON LOVER      325   13
    THE LION AND THE TIGERS TURN TO CLAY ....................DENOUEMENT      327   10
TURNED (16)
    ROOTED TO YOUR BLACK LOOK, THE PLAY TURNED TRAGIC: ...CONVERSATION.       21   12
    UNTIL THE SUN TURNED PALE FROM WARM, .......................BUCOLICS      24   14
    SHE BEARS A KING. TURNED BITTER ..........TWO SISTERS OF PERSEPHONE       32   24
    BUT NOW TURNED KINDER WITH TIME, WE MARK MISS MASON ..ELLA MASON A.       54   37
    SHE TURNED BACK. ....................................HARDCASTLE CRAGS     63   45
    AND TURNED THE FARMBOY'S TEMPER WOLFISH, ..THE DEATH OF MYTH-MAKING      104   14
    THAT SEASON HAS TURNED ITS BACK. ..................MAGNOLIA SHOALS       121    5
    AS I TURNED HIM IN THE LIGHT; ...........................MEDALLION       124   11
    MY CHEEK OF BASALT. THEY TURNED TO TEARS, ..............LOVE LETTER      147   15
    TO LIE WITH MY HANDS TURNED UP AND BE UTTERLY EMPTY. ........TULIPS      161   30
    THEY ARE DEPARTING IN THEIR TRANSPARENT GARMENTS, TURNED ASIDE ...
                                            ... THE SURGEON AT 2 A.M.       170    3
    IF I JUST UNDID THE LOCKS AND STOOD BACK AND TURNED INTO A TREE. ...
                                            ... THE ARRIVAL OF THE BEE BOX  213   28
    RADIATION TURNED IT WHITE .....................................FEVER.   231   23
    TURNED THICK AND SOUR. .........................BITTER STRAWBERRIES     299    9
    AND WE ALL TURNED BACK TO PICKING. ............BITTER STRAWBERRIES      300   33
    BUT THAT IT TURNED INTO A MILKING PAIL? ..METAMORPHOSES OF THE MOON     307   20
TURNING (14)
    UNTIL, TURNING SIDEWAYS, ..............MISS DRAKE PROCEEDS TO SUPPER      41   23
    HAMMERS HOISTED, WHEELS TURNING, ........................NIGHT SHIFT     76   17
    THEY ARE TURNING THE BURNERS UP, RING AFTER RING. .......POEM.6.W.      135   16
    TURNING THROUGH MY TIME, THE SUNS AND STARS ...........THREE WOMEN      176    2
    HE IS TURNING TO ME LIKE A LITTLE, BLIND, BRIGHT PLANT. *THREE WOMEN    183  235
    THEIR FACES TURNING, WORDLESS AND SLOW, ...............BERCK-PLAGE      201  120
    TURNING AND TURNING IN THE MIDDLE AIR, ...............GETTING THERE     249   53
    TURNING AND TURNING IN THE MIDDLE AIR, ...............GETTING THERE     249   53
    GOLD JOINTS, MY WAY OF TURNING ..............................GIGOLO     268   22
    FAILS TO APPEAR, TURN, AND, TURNING, SHRINK ...........DIALOGUE O.      279  120
    IN SOLAR SCHEMES THE TILTED SUNS GO TURNING; ....TO EVA DESCENDING.     303   11
    TURNING THE TABLES OF THIS GRAVE GOURMET, ..................TERMINAL    328    9
    AND GET SAFE HOME; BUT, TURNING WITH TRAINED EYES, .......AERIALIST     331   28
    THE WOMEN WAIT, FLUTTERING, TURNING PAGES ......MORNING IN THE HOS.     332   21
TURNINGS (1)
    ALL DAY I FEEL ITS SOFT, FEATHERY TURNINGS, ITS MALIGNITY. .....ELM     193   33
TURNIP (1)
    MUTE AS A TURNIP FROM THE FOURTH ............................YOU'RE     141    7
TURNIPY (1)
    PEBBLE SMELLS, TURNIPY CHAMBERS. ....................POEM.2.DARK.       133   22
TURNS (13)
    THE WORLD TURNS ...........................................RESOLVE      52   18
    SEEING HER FREEZE, HE TURNS HIS FACE AWAY. ..........THE OTHER TWO       68   20
    THE EARTH TURNS NOW. IN HALF AN HOUR .....ON THE DECLINE OF ORACLES      78   26
    EXPRESSIVE OF GRIEF TURNS GODS, LIKE KINGS, TO ROCKS. ......PERSEUS      83   29
    AND A FUN-HOUSE MIRROR THAT TURNS THE TRAGIC MUSE .........PERSEUS       83   36
    AND THE MAYOR'S ROTISSERIE TURNS ................THE TIMES ARE TIDY     107    4
    THE CROWD SUCKS HER LAST TEAR AND TURNS AWAY. ...........AFTERMATH      114   14
    PURPLES THE FIG IN THE LEAF'S SHADOW, TURNS THE DUST PINK. ...NET-.     121    7
    THEN SHE TURNS TO THOSE LIARS, THE CANDLES OR THE MOON. .....MIRROR     174   12
    SUDDENLY TURNS, TURNS COLOR. THE STREETLIGHT ....LETTER IN NOVEMBER     253    2
    SUDDENLY TURNS, TURNS COLOR. THE STREETLIGHT ....LETTER IN NOVEMBER     253    2
    THAT DROPS AND TURNS, .......................................WORDS      270   11
    TURNS THE RACK; ..............................MOONSONG AT MORNING       317   28
TURQUOISE (5)
    GRADED TURQUOISE TILES ................................BATTLE-SCENE      84    5
    THE BLUE EYE OF MY TURQUOISE WILL COMFORT ME. ..........LAST WORDS      172   20
    TURQUOISE SLIVERS ................................AQUATIC NOCTURNE      305    2
    A TREMOLO OF TURQUOISE QUIVERING IN ..............MIDSUMMER MOBILE      324    6
    TURQUOISE, ROSE, SIERRA MAUVE; NEEDLES .........MORNING IN THE HOS.     332   14
TURRET (1)
    THE OWL SHALL STOOP FROM HIS TURRET, THE RAT CRY OUT. ..WATERCOLOR.     112   28
TURRETS (1)
    THE MASSIVE CASTLE TURRETS ................................LORELEI       94    7
TURTLE-DARK (1)
    OF TURTLE-DARK GREEN. ..............................FIESTA MELONS       46    7
TUSKS (2)
    OLD TOOLS, HANDLES AND RUSTY TUSKS. ....................POEM.1.WHO.     131    5
    IT MUST BE A TUSK THERE, A GHOST-COLUMN. ........A BIRTHDAY PRESENT     206   19
TUSSOCKS (1)
    SHEEP DROWSED STONEWARD IN THEIR TUSSOCKS OF WOOL, AND BIRDS, ...
                                            ... HARDCASTLE CRAGS            63   34
TWELVE (8)
    DISENCHANT MY TWELVE BLACK-GOWNED EXAMINERS ..............RESOLVE        52   21
    THE WALNUT BANQUET TABLE, THE TWELVE CHAIRS ..........THE OTHER TWO      68   13
```

TWELVE (CONT.)
  IN THE HURRICANE, WHEN FATHER'S TWELVE ....THE DISQUIETING MUSES   75 17
  CLOCKS BELLED TWELVE. MAIN STREET SHOWED OTHERWISE ....OWL   101   1
  UNTIL NEAR TWELVE THE STRANGE GIRL ALL AT ONCE ....CINDERELLA   304 11
  AT TWELVE, EACH SKULL IS AUREOLED ....DANSE MACABRE   321 10
  WHICH AT TWELVE WILL QUAINTLY HATCH ....BLACK PINE TREE.   328   5
  IMPLACABLY FROM TWELVE TO ONE. ....LOVE IS A PARALLAX   329 18
TWENTY (7)
  TWENTY YEARS AGO, THE FAMILIAR TUB ....TALE OF A TUB   25 17
  TWENTY YEARS OUT ....POINT SHIRLEY 110 19
  IT WAS GOOD FOR TWENTY YEARS, THAT WINTERING -- ....ELECTRA ON. 116   5
  IN TWENTY YEARS I SHALL BE RETROGRADE ....CANDLES 149 29
  WHEN I GRIN, THE STITCHES TAUTEN. I GROW BACKWARD. I'M TWENTY,*FACE. 156 21
  FORMING ITS TWENTY PETALS. ....HEAVY WOMEN 158 10
  AT TWENTY I TRIED TO DIE ....DADDY 224 58
TWENTY-FIVE (1)
  BUT IN TWENTY-FIVE YEARS SHE'LL BE SILVER, ...THE APPLICANT 221 31
TWENTY-FOUR (1)
  WITH BLACKBIRDS -- TWENTY-FOUR, AND EVERY ONE ....DIALOGUE O. 282 215
TWENTY-SIX (1)
  DOWN TO A CIRCLE OF LETTERS: TWENTY-SIX *DIALOGUE OVER A OUIJA BOARD 276 13
TWICE (2)
  TWICE ON SUNDAY, THE BELLS STARTLE THE SKY --- ....MOON. 173 12
  A THIRD TIME. DON'T GLOAT. YOUR WILL MISFIRED TWICE ....DIALOGUE O. 284 281
TWIG (3)
  ON THE STIFF TWIG UP THERE ....BLACK ROOK IN RAINY WEATHER   56   1
  EACH SPECKLED TWIG ....POLLY'S TREE 128   3
  I STARTED TO BUD LIKE A MARCH TWIG: ....LOVE LETTER 147 31
TWIGGED (2)
  UNTIL ALL OWLS IN THE TWIGGED FOREST ....FAUN   35   3
  TO PEOPLE THE TWIGGED AISLES; LEAD BABEL TONGUES*WREATH FOR A BRIDAL   45 14
TWIGGY (1)
  STARS ARE DROPPING THICK AS STONES INTO THE TWIGGY ....STARS. 165   1
TWIGS (2)
  STIFF AS TWIGS, HER BODY WOODENLY ....VIRGIN IN A TREE   82 39
  THESE LITTLE BLACK TWIGS DO NOT THINK TO BUD, ...THREE WOMEN 184 278
TWIG-SLEEPING (1)
  TWIG-SLEEPING, WORE ....HARDCASTLE CRAGS   63 35
TWILIGHT (2)
  ARRIVE AT TWILIGHT, AND THEN AFTER SOME EFFORT. ....STARS. 165 10
  AS A TENNIS BALL AT TWILIGHT ....APRIL 18 302 16
TWINE (1)
  AND AS HIS NOTES TWINE GREEN, THE GREEN RIVER .........SNAKECHARMER   79   6
TWINED (1)
  TWINED TO HER HARD LIMBS LIKE IVY: THE PURITAN LIP VIRGIN IN A TREE   81 12
TWINGE (1)
  AND EVERY PRIVATE TWINGE A HISSING ASP ....PERSEUS   83 20
TWINING (1)
  WINDING AND TWINING THEIR PETTY FETTERS, ...GULLIVER 251 13
TWINKLE (1)
  THE GARNETS ON HER FINGERS TWINKLE QUICK ....FEMALE AUTHOR 301   9
TWINKLE-DRESS (1)
  NOT LIFT A FOOT IN THE TWINKLE-DRESS ....THE DISQUIETING MUSES   75 28
TWINS (1)
  BLIND TWINS BITTEN BY BAD NATURE. ....BLUE MOLES 126   9
TWIRL (3)
  EELS TWIRL ....AQUATIC NOCTURNE 306 19
  BY DEFT DUCK AND TWIRL ....AERIALIST 331 22
  WHERE VIVID CHILDREN TWIRL ....TOUCH-AND-GO 335   9
TWIRLING (1)
  HORNS TWIRLING AND JUNGLE GUTTURALS! ....A SECRET 220 41
TWIST (3)
  AS OUT OF EDEN'S NAVEL TWIST THE LINES .................SNAKECHARMER   79 19
  TWIST OLD WORDS INTO THE WEB-THREADS: TONIGHT MAY THE FISH ...NET-. 121 17
  OLD PEWTER ROOTS TWIST ....DARK WOOD, DARK WATER 127 15
TWISTED (1)
  AND STERN TRUTH TWISTED ....MOONSONG AT MORNING 317 35
TWISTING (2)
  TWISTING CURSES IN THE TANGLED SHEET ....THE SHRIKE   42 10
  TWISTING OF THUMBSCREWS: ONE SOUL TIED IN SINEWS, ...LESSON.   80   8
TWITCH (2)
  I MUST WATCH SLUTTISH DRYADS TWITCH ......ON THE PLETHORA OF DRYADS   67 32
  GUIDED ONLY BY THE TUG AND TWITCH .....THE PRINCESS AND THE GOBLINS 334 26
TWITCHES (1)
  THE NOSE-END THAT TWITCHES, THE OLD IMPERFECTIONS -- COMPANIONABLE. 105   1
TWITCHING (1)
  THAN TO SIT MUTE, TWITCHING SO ....MONOLOGUE AT 3 A.M.   40   8
TWITTERING (2)
  UNTIL SHE HEARS THE TWITTERING MACHINE *THE PRINCESS AND THE GOBLINS 334 56
  MY ROOM IS A TWITTERING GRAY BOX WITH A WALL *EPITAPH IN THREE PARTS 337 26
TWITTERS (1)
  THE CITY IS A MAP OF CHEERFUL TWITTERS NOW, ...INSOMNIAC 163 33
TWO (87)
  MAYDAY: TWO CAME TO FIELD IN SUCH WISE: ....BUCOLICS   23   1
  IN THIS PARTICULAR TUB, TWO KNEES JUT UP ....TALE OF A TUB   25 41

TITLE		PAGE	LINE
TWO (CONT.)			
TWO BLACK ROOKS HUNCH ....PROSPECT		28	7
TWO SISTERS OF PERSEPHONE ....TWO SISTERS OF PERSEPHONE		31	T
TWO GIRLS THERE ARE: WITHIN THE HOUSE ....TWO SISTERS OF PERSEPHONE		31	1
WHERE, BEDDED LIKE ANGELS, TWO BURN ONE IN FEVER. ....WREATH F.		45	18
THESE TWO MOST PERISHABLE LOVERS FROM THE TOUCH .....EPITAPH FOR F.		45	5
TWO WATER DROPS POISE ....RESOLVE		52	13
TWO ENTER TO TAP HER SIGHT, A GREEN PAIR ....CRYSTAL GAZER		55	7
"I SEE TWO STALWART APPLE TREES ....CRYSTAL GAZER		55	13
THE OTHER TWO ....THE OTHER TWO		68	T
TWO OF US IN A PLACE MEANT FOR TEN MORE -- ....THE OTHER TWO		68	10
MIRRORED THE INTRICATE GESTURES OF TWO OTHERS. ....THE OTHER TWO		68	14
WE MIGHT EMBRACE, BUT THOSE TWO NEVER DID. ....THE OTHER TWO		69	30
THE HEAVEN THOSE TWO DREAMED OF, IN DESPAIR. ....THE OTHER TWO		69	35
TWO VIEWS OF WITHENS ....TWO VIEWS OF WITHENS		71	T
AND HELPED THE TWO OF US TO CHOIR: ....THE DISQUIETING MUSES		75	21
BY TWO BRONZE BOOKENDS OF SHIPS IN SAIL, ON THE DECLINE OF ORACLES		78	2
TWO WAXEN OXEN FLANK THE CHILD. ....A WINTER'S TALE		86	6
AT THIS JOINT BETWEEN TWO WORLDS AND TWO ENTIRELY ....GHOST'S.		90	12
AT THIS JOINT BETWEEN TWO WORLDS AND TWO ENTIRELY ....GHOST'S.		90	12
TWO VIRTUES RIDE, BY STALLION, BY NAG, ...THE DEATH OF MYTH-MAKING		104	1
SINCE THOSE TWO CIVIL SERVANTS SET ....THE DEATH OF MYTH-MAKING		104	8
TWO VIEWS OF A CADAVER ROOM ....TWO VIEWS OF A CADAVER ROOM		114	T
TWO PEOPLE ONLY ARE BLIND TO THE CARRION ARMY: ....TWO VIEWS.		114	13
TWO PINLEGS STAGGER UNDERNEATH THE MASS. ....THE RAVAGED FACE		115	5
A MELON STROLLING ON TWO TENDRILS. ....METAPHORS		116	3
WHERE THOSE TWO SLEEPERS ARE. ....THE SLEEPERS		122	2
TWO CARVED SLEIGHS ....YADDO: THE GRAND MANOR		123	15
TWO SUICIDES, THE FAMILY WOLVES, ...THE MANOR GARDEN		125	13
THEY'RE OUT OF THE DARK'S RAGBAG, THESE TWO ....BLUE MOLES		126	1
TWO CAMPERS IN CLOUD COUNTRY ....TWO CAMPERS IN CLOUD COUNTRY		144	T
IS LEAKING FROM THE FINGER-VENTS. AT THE COUNT OF TWO ....FACE LIFT		156	14
I SHALL NEVER GET OUT OF THIS! THERE ARE TWO OF ME NOW: IN PLASTER		158	1
LIKE AN EYE BETWEEN TWO WHITE LIDS THAT WILL NOT SHUT. .....TULIPS		160	9
FROM BETWEEN TWO HILLS A SUDDEN WIND FUNNELS AT ME, ..BLACKBERRYING		169	20
HER MARBLE SKIRTS BLOWN BACK IN TWO PINK WINGS. ....FINISTERRE		169	20
THE SURGEON AT [TWO] A.M. ....THE SURGEON AT 2 A.M.		170	T
IN THE TWO HUGE, WHITE, HANDSOME HOUSES IN SWAMPSCOTT. ....BABY.		174	5
ON THAT DAY-OFF THE TWO OF US CRIED SO HARD TO GET THE BABYSITTERS		175	29
I SEE US FLOATING THERE YET, INSEPARABLE -- TWO CORK DOLLS. ..BABY.		175	41
AND WHAT IF TWO LIVES LEAKED BETWEEN MY THIGHS? ....THREE WOMEN		180	120
A DAY AGO, TWO DAYS, THREE DAYS AGO. IT WAS A FRIDAY. ..THREE WOMEN		183	248
BLACK LAKE, BLACK BOAT, TWO BLACK, CUT-PAPER PEOPLE.*CROSSING THE W.		190	1
TWO GRAY, PAPERY BAGS -- .............................APPREHENSIONS		195	13
I HAVE TWO LEGS, AND I MOVE SMILINGLY. ....BERCK-PLAGE		196	6
TWO LOVERS UNSTICK THEMSELVES. ....BERCK-PLAGE		197	30
THESE WERE HARDER, TWO WHITE STONES. ....THE DETECTIVE		209	32
THERE WAS NO ABSENCE OF LIPS, THERE WERE TWO CHILDREN,*THE DETECTIVE		209	34
SILVER BEAST BETWEEN TWO DARK CANYONS, ..THE COURAGE OF SHUTTING-UP		210	9
I HAVE ONE EYE, YOU HAVE TWO. ....A SECRET		219	6
BEHIND TWO EYES IN WHICH NOTHING IS REFLECTED BUT MONKEYS. *A SECRET		219	20
SAYS THERE ARE A DOZEN OR TWO. ....DADDY		223	21
BIT MY PRETTY RED HEART IN TWO. ....DADDY		224	56
IF I'VE KILLED ONE MAN, I'VE KILLED TWO --- ....DADDY		224	71
SHE'LL CUT HER THROAT AT TEN IF SHE'S MAD AT TWO. ....LESBOS		228	22
YOU HAVE ONE BABY, I HAVE TWO. ....LESBOS		228	28
FLOATS OUR HEADS, TWO VENOMOUS OPPOSITES, ...LESBOS		228	36
THE WHEELS, TWO RUBBER GRUBS, BITE THEIR SWEET TAILS. STOPPED DEAD		230	6
RED AND YELLOW, TWO PASSIONATE HOT METALS ....STOPPED DEAD		230	8
THE TWO DRINKS FLAME AND FOAM. ....AMNESIAC		233	24
I FLY TO A NAME, TWO EYES. ....GETTING THERE		248	19
OF TWO WET EYES AND A SCREECH. ....THALIDOMIDE		252	20
TWO TIMES A DAY ....LETTER IN NOVEMBER		253	17
TWO, OF COURSE THERE ARE TWO. ....DEATH & CO.		254	1
TWO, OF COURSE THERE ARE TWO. ....DEATH & CO.		254	1
THEN TWO LITTLE FEET. ....DEATH & CO.		254	19
OF TWO BABIES ......................................EAVESDROPPER		261	61
MY TWO ....PARALYTIC		266	6
TWO GIRLS ....PARALYTIC		266	25
YOU HAND ME TWO CHILDREN, TWO ROSES. ....KINDNESS		270	20
YOU HAND ME TWO CHILDREN, TWO ROSES. ....KINDNESS		270	20
WORD WEARS TWO W'S? O-R. OR WHAT? ......DIALOGUE OVER A OUIJA BOARD		279	94
OF OUR TWO INTUITIONS. AND IF HE IS? ...DIALOGUE OVER A OUIJA BOARD		279	107
FUSING TWO TALENTS, A SORT OF PSYCHIC BASTARD ....DIALOGUE O.		280	139
WARRANT HIM WHELPED IN THE WAKE OF TWO SHOOTING ....DIALOGUE O.		281	194
IS ON THE TWO OF US FOR LENDING HEAT ....DIALOGUE OVER A OUIJA BOARD		282	229
YOU SAY HE'S TOLD TWO LIES . . . CALL THEM TWO PLUCKED DIALOGUE O.		283	266
YOU SAY HE'S TOLD TWO LIES . . . CALL THEM TWO PLUCKED DIALOGUE O.		283	266
AS WE TWO GLOWER FROM OUR SEPARATE CAMPS, ...DIALOGUE O.		284	291
UNDER A STONE. THOSE TWO DREAMED DEATHS TOOK ....DIALOGUE O.		285	326
DEATH'S TWO DREAMS DOWN WITH THE BODY THAT BLED THE VEIN, ...			
... DIALOGUE OVER A OUIJA BOARD		285	329
MAY TWO REAL PEOPLE BREATHE IN A REAL ROOM. ....DIALOGUE O.		286	364
TWO CHILDREN LAUGHED AT TAG ....BITTER STRAWBERRIES		299	14
EXCEPT FOR TWO UNCANNY DREAMS ....THE DREAM		310	2

532

	TITLE	PAGE	LINE

TWO (CONT.)
    HERE ARE TWO PUPILS ......ON LOOKING INTO THE EYES OF A DEMON LOVER 325 1
    TWO LOVERS AND A BEACHCOMBER BY THE REAL SEA ....TWO LOVERS. 327 T
TWO-AND-SIX (1)
    NATIVITIES AT TWO-AND-SIX. ....ON DECK 143 30
TWO-HORNED (1)
    YOUR TWO-HORNED RHINOCEROS OPENED A MOUTH ....ZOO KEEPER'S WIFE 155 34
TWO-LEGGED (2)
    TWO-LEGGED MUSSEL-PICKER. ....MUSSEL HUNTER AT ROCK HARBOR 97 66
    ON MERMAIDS AND TWO-LEGGED DREAMGIRLS. ..THE COURAGE OF SHUTTING-UP 210 13
TWO-TIERED (1)
    LIT LIKE A TWO-TIERED WEDDING CAKE ....ON DECK 142 7
TYROL (2)
    AND MY GRANDFATHER MOPED IN THE TYROL, ...CANDLES 149 20
    THE SNOWS OF THE TYROL, THE CLEAR BEER OF VIENNA ....DADDY 223 36
UBIQUITOUS (1)
    "O FOR UBIQUITOUS FREE APHRODISIACS, ...DIALOGUE EN ROUTE 309 27
UDDER (1)
    VAMPIRING DRY OF MILK EACH GREAT GOAT UDDER. ....GOATSUCKER 111 4
UDDERS (1)
    TRUNDLING THEIR UDDERS HOME ...........................EAVESDROPPER 261 42
UGLY (5)
    OF UGLY SPINSTERS AND BARREN SIRS ....VIRGIN IN A TREE 82 33
    AND UGLY, MY BELLY A SILK STOCKING ....ZOO KEEPER'S WIFE 154 6
    SHE MAY BE A SAINT, AND I MAY BE UGLY AND HAIRY, ...IN PLASTER 160 53
    I AM NOT UGLY. I AM EVEN BEAUTIFUL. ....THREE WOMEN 183 239
    WHAT IS THIS, BEHIND THIS VEIL, IS IT UGLY, IS IT BEAUTIFUL? ...
    ... A BIRTHDAY PRESENT 206 1
ULCERS (1)
    THE SUN GIVES YOU ULCERS, THE WIND GIVES YOU T.B. ....LESBOS 228 39
ULMUS (1)
    GLEAMS, WIRED TO A TALL ULMUS ....A WINTER'S TALE 86 2
UMBILICUS (2)
    UNWINDS FROM THE GREAT UMBILICUS OF THE SUN POEM.3.MAENAD. 133 19
    OLD BARNACLED UMBILICUS, ATLANTIC CABLE, ...MEDUSA 225 14
UMBRELLA (1)
    WOULD UMBRELLA LIKE LIBERAL TOADSTOOLS ....DIALOGUE EN ROUTE 308 8
UMBRELLAS (1)
    OVERHEAD THE OLD UMBRELLAS OF SUMMER POEM.5.F. 134 3
UNABLE (1)
    UNABLE TO FACE THE FINGERS, THOSE EGOTISTS. ....THE DETECTIVE 208 9
UNAFFECTED (1)
    HER O-MOUTH GRIEVES AT THE WORLD; YOURS IS UNAFFECTED, ...THE RIVAL 166 5
UNALTERED (1)
    UNALTERED BY EYES, ...HARDCASTLE CRAGS 63 40
UNANSWERABLE (1)
    AND DYING TO SAY SOMETHING UNANSWERABLE. ....THE RIVAL 166 10
UNANSWERED (1)
    OF UNANSWERED LETTERS, COFFINED IN A LETTER CASE. ......THREE WOMEN 182 200
UNASKED (2)
    UNASKED TO MY CHRISTENING, THAT SHE ....THE DISQUIETING MUSES 74 4
    UTTERLY UNASKED FOR ....POPPIES IN OCTOBER 240 5
UNAWARE (2)
    WHO, UNAWARE HOW THEY DWINDLE, ...SOLILOQUY OF THE SOLIPSIST 37 15
    BLACK-GOWNED, BUT UNAWARE ......WATERCOLOR OF GRANTCHESTER MEADOWS 112 26
UNBALANCE (1)
    OBSERVED HER LOVER'S GESTURES UNBALANCE THE AIR, ...SPINSTER 49 8
UNBEARABLY (1)
    WHOSE KISS STINGS UNBEARABLY ....MYSTIC 268 4
UNBEATEN (1)
    ON THE UNBEATEN CHANNELS ....FULL FATHOM FIVE 93 28
UNBENDABLE (1)
    BACKBONE UNBENDABLE AS ....THE HERMIT AT OUTERMOST HOUSE 119 11
UNBORN (2)
    AT THE WINDOW, THOSE UNBORN, THOSE UNDONE ....OUIJA 77 3
    THE FACE OF THE UNBORN ONE THAT LOVED ITS PERFECTIONS, THREE WOMEN 178 79
UNBOTHERED (1)
    THOUGH, LIKE A STONE, UNBOTHERED BY IT, ...LOVE LETTER 147 3
UNBREAKABLE (1)
    ONLY MUCH WHITER AND UNBREAKABLE AND WITH NO COMPLAINTS. *IN PLASTER 158 8
UNBUCKLED (1)
    THE SKULLS, THE UNBUCKLED BONES FACING THE VIEW! ..WAKING IN WINTER 151 10
UNBUFFETED (1)
    RISES SO WHITELY UNBUFFETED? ....BERCK-PLAGE 198 64
UNCAGED (1)
    OF UNCAGED TIGERS AND A TROPICAL MOON, ...YADWIGHA. 85 4
UNCANNY (1)
    EXCEPT FOR TWO UNCANNY DREAMS ....THE DREAM 310 2
UNCATCHABLE (1)
    HOME OF UNCATCHABLE ....TWO VIEWS OF WITHENS 72 7
UNCHANGING (1)
    IN A BLUE, UNCHANGING LIGHT, ...THE SLEEPERS 122 5
UNCLAPS (1)
    IT UNCLAPS, BROWN AS A LEAF, AND LOUD, ...PHEASANT 191 21

	TITLE	PAGE	LINE

UNCLE (5)
UNCLE, PANTS FACTORY FATSO, MILLIONAIRE. ....STOPPED DEAD   230   4
UNCLE, UNCLE? ....STOPPED DEAD   230   18
UNCLE, UNCLE? ....STOPPED DEAD   230   18
OF PLACES: THE OIL WELL MY UNCLE OWNS, FOR ONE; ....DIALOGUE O.   277   47
RASPS THE JARRING BARITONE OF UNCLE PAUL; ....FAMILY REUNION   300   22
UNCLENCH (1)
MOTHER OF BEETLES, ONLY UNCLENCH YOUR HAND: POEM.6.W.   135   19
UNCLES (2)
THE HORIZONS ARE TOO FAR OFF TO BE CHUMMY AS UNCLES; .....TWO CAMP.   145   13
"I WISH MILLIONAIRE UNCLES AND AUNTS ....DIALOGUE EN ROUTE   308   7
UNCOILED (1)
AGE, AND AGES OF PROSE, HAVE UNCOILED ....OUIJA   77   15
UNCONQUERED (1)
ONE WHITE HORSE DROWNED, AND ALL THE UNCONQUERED PINNACLES   LESSON.   80   9
UNCOUTH (1)
OF THAT UNCOUTH SHAPE TO SIMPLE SOD AGAIN ....LADY AND T.   70   27
UNCTION (1)
THE EXTREME UNCTION OF ITS YELLOW CANDLE-FLOWERS.*THE RABBIT CATCHER   193   8
UNCUT (1)
THROUGH THE UNCUT GRASS ON THE ELM'S HILL. ....PHEASANT   191   4
UNDER (79)
AND, UNDER HONOR, WILL DEPART; ....BUCOLICS   24   22
WE TAKE THE PLUNGE; UNDER WATER OUR LIMBS ....TALE OF A TUB   25   25
UNDER THE STRICT MASK OF HIS AGONY. ....CHANNEL CROSSING   26   12
FROM UNDER CRUNCH OF MY MAN'S BOOT ....ODE FOR TED   29   1
SPINS ITSELF FROM UNDER MY FEET; ....SOLILOQUY OF THE SOLIPSIST   37   4
UNDER PRICKLING STARS, ...MONOLOGUE AT 3 A.M.   40   9
PASSENGERS UNDER AN INDIGO FIZZLE ....ALICANTE LULLABY   43   9
UNDER THE FEET OF ....FIESTA MELONS   47   18
THE AFTERNOON AT A BAD END UNDER THE CROWD'S TRUCULENCE, THE GORING   47   2
UNDER WHITE WALL AND MOORISH WINDOW ....THE BEGGARS   47   6
MUD-MATTRESSED UNDER THE SIGN OF THE HAG ....MAUDLIN   51   1
BENT UNDER A BUNDLE ....THE EVERLASTING MONDAY   62   2
LOST LUSTRE UNDER HER FOOTSOLES. ....HARDCASTLE CRAGS   63   21
UNDER THE MEANEST TABLE. ....THE THIN PEOPLE   64   11
UNDER THEIR THIN-LIPPED SMILES, ...THE THIN PEOPLE   65   38
UNDER FLUX OF THOSE SEDUCTIVE ....ON THE PLETHORA OF DRYADS   68   35
FIT NOWHERE: BRICKDUST-COMPLECTED, EYE UNDER A DENSE LID, ...
            ... THE LADY AND THE EARTHENWARE HEAD   69   2
AND AN IMAGE LOOMS UNDER THE FISHPOND SURFACE ...ALL THE DEAD DEARS   71   22
UPHOLSTERED IN RED VELVET, UNDER THE EYE ....YADWIGHA.   85   3
TO FEED HIS EYE WITH RED: SUCH RED! UNDER THE MOON, ...YADWIGHA.   86   38
BLINDERED BY GREEN, UNDER A GREEN-GRAINED SKY ......ABOVE THE OXBOW   88   28
LIVED UNDER THE SHADOW OF HOT ROOFTOPS ....ABOVE THE OXBOW   89   54
UNDER A BALANCED RULER. ....LORELEI   94   20
SMALL MUD KNOBS, NUDGED FROM UNDER, ...MUSSEL HUNTER AT ROCK HARBOR   96   26
PLEASURABLE UNDER CLAWS ....MUSSEL HUNTER AT ROCK HARBOR   96   49
ROTS, AND SMELLS OF ROT UNDER ITS HEADSTONE ....MOONRISE   98   14
AND MEANDER IN BLAND PLEATINGS UNDER ....IN MIDAS' COUNTRY   99   3
IN SUNLESS AIR, UNDER PINES ....CHILD'S PARK STONES   100   1
FIRST HORSE UNDER ME, HIGH AS THE ROOFS, ...WHITENESS I REMEMBER   102   13
GULLS CIRCLE GRAY UNDER SHADOW OF A STEELIER FLIGHT. ...GREEN ROCK.   105   17
O THE KING'S TIDY ACRE IN UNDER THE SEA, ...THE BULL OF BENDYLAW   108   19
THE SHINGLE BOOMS, BICKERING UNDER ....POINT SHIRLEY   110   2
THE SUN SINKS UNDER BOSTON, BLOODY RED. ....POINT SHIRLEY   111   40
WORLD UNDER THE SHEER WATER .....WATERCOLOR OF GRANTCHESTER MEADOWS   112   10
THE SEA PULSES UNDER A SKIN OF OIL. ....A WINTER SHIP   112   5
WHEN I WORMED BACK UNDER MY MOTHER'S HEART. ELECTRA ON AZALEA PATH   116   10
MY HEART UNDER YOUR FOOT, SISTER OF A STONE. ....BEEKEEPER'S.   118   7
UNDER THE CORONAL OF SUGAR ROSES ....THE BEEKEEPER'S DAUGHTER   118   20
WINKS LIKE MONEY UNDER THE RINGED TOES OF THE CHICKENS. ......NET-.   121   9
THEY LIE AS IF UNDER WATER ....THE SLEEPERS   122   4
GOING UNDER THE CHAINMAIL, ...MEDALLION   124   17
FROM HIS ORBIT UNDER THE ELM ROOT. ....BLUE MOLES   126   7
THE SUN RISES UNDER THE PILLAR OF YOUR TONGUE. ....THE COLOSSUS   130   27
WHEN IT THUNDERED I HID UNDER A FLAT STONE. POEM.3.MAENAD.   133   5
MONKEY LIVED UNDER THE DUNCE CAP. POEM.4.BEAST.   134   8
SITTING UNDER A POTLID, TINY AND INERT AS A RICE GRAIN. ..POEM.6.W.   135   15
HOW LONG HIS CARCASS HAS FOUNDERED UNDER ....THE BURNT-OUT SPA   138   8
PRAYS UNDER HER BREATH THAT SHE MAY SAVE ....ON DECK   143   23
BEACHED UNDER THE SPUMY BLOOMS, WE LIE ....WHITSUN   154   23
ON THE GREEN HILL, UNDER THE THORN TREES, ...HEAVY WOMEN   158   12
UNDER THE EYES OF THE STARS AND THE MOON'S RICTUS ....INSOMNIAC   163   5
HANGING SHYLY UNDER THE STUDDED HORIZON ....STARS OVER THE DORDOGNE   165   19
OTHER ROCKS HIDE THEIR GRUDGES UNDER THE WATER. ....FINISTERRE   169   9
THE BODY UNDER IT IS IN MY HANDS. ....THE SURGEON AT 2 A.M.   170   6
THE INTRICATE, BLUE PIPING UNDER THIS PALE MARBLE. ....SURGEON.   171   26
UNDER MY FEET IN A NEAT PARCEL. ....LAST WORDS   172   24
AND THE MAID SMOKED AND SHOT POOL UNDER A GREEN-SHADED LAMP. BABY.   175   24
OF BEING WHEELED OFF UNDER CROSSES AND A RAIN OF PIETAS. ...
            ... APPREHENSIONS   195   15
UNDER THE GLUED SHEET FROM WHICH HIS POWDERY BEAK ......BERCK-PLAGE   198   63
DULLY, UNDER A PACK OF MEN IN RED JACKETS, ...BURNING THE LETTERS   204   13
AT LEAST I WON'T BE STRUNG JUST UNDER THE SURFACE, ...BURNING.   204   23

```
                                                      TITLE        PAGE  LINE
UNDER (CONT.)
   BREASTPLATES OF CHEESECLOTH KNOTTED UNDER THE ARMPITS. ........BEE.  211   14
   THE MAN WITH GRAY HANDS STANDS UNDER THE HONEYCOMB  .......THE SWARM  216   33
   OVER THE ENGLISH CLIFF AND UNDER SO MUCH HISTORY!  ........LYONNESSE  234   22
   DULLED TO A HALT UNDER BOWLERS.  ..................POPPIES IN OCTOBER 240    9
   TOAD-YELLOW UNDER THE DROP  ..........................EAVESDROPPER  261   39
   IN THE FETID WOMBS OF BLACK AIR UNDER PINES IN SUMMER.  ......MYSTIC  268    5
   UNDER THE SPOKES OF THE CLEMATIS.  ..........................MYSTIC  269   23
   UNDER YOUR FINGER? I MEAN, YOU DON'T PUSH ..............DIALOGUE O.  277   33
   UNDER THE GUISE OF NONCHALANCE. PAN'S LAUGH  ...........DIALOGUE O.  282  228
   UNDER A STONE. THOSE TWO DREAMED DEATHS TOOK  ..........DIALOGUE O.  285  326
   UNDER THE BELL-JAR OF A WONDERLAND.  .......QUEEN MARY'S ROSE GARDEN  290   14
   AFTER, THEY STAGGER AND WEAVE, UNDER NO BANNER.  .........STINGS/DR  293   11
   BY SNAIL UNDER HUMP OF HOME:  ....................NOTES TO A NEOPHYTE 306    6
   FOR RECREATION DOWN UNDER THE COVERS:  ...........DIALOGUE EN ROUTE  309   23
   TO CAST LOCK, STOCK AND BARREL UNDER BAN;  ........THE DISPOSSESSED  318   11
   UNDER SHUTTER OF THEIR HANDICAPS.  ...............SONNET TO SATAN    323    4
   UNDER A TENT OF TAUNTING GULLS.  .......................TWO LOVERS.  327   16
   OF THE BOLD SAILOR FALLING UNDER DRENCH  .....EPITAPH IN THREE PARTS  337   15
UNDERESTIMATE (1)
   DO NOT THINK I UNDERESTIMATE YOUR GREAT CONCERN.  ......LADY LAZARUS  246   72
UNDERFOOT (1)
   COLD GRITS UNDERFOOT,  .......................................LYONNESSE  234   17
UNDERGOING (1)
   UNDERGOING THE FAUCET WATER, ITS VEILS, VEILS IN A NUNNERY,*GETTING.  248   23
UNDERGROUND (2)
   COMPELLED TO DEADLOCK UNDERGROUND.  ...................DANSE MACABRE  321   26
   OF SQUADRONS UNDERGROUND ABDUCTING HIM *THE PRINCESS AND THE GOBLINS  333   22
UNDERNEATH (1)
   TWO PINLEGS STAGGER UNDERNEATH THE MASS.  ..........THE RAVAGED FACE  115    5
UNDERSHIRTS (1)
   UNDERSHIRTS CIRCLED, TENDING  ..........................NIGHT SHIFT   77   21
UNDERSIDE (1)
   LIKE THE UNDERSIDE OF MUSHROOMS. DO YOU FEEL  ...........DIALOGUE O.  285  315
UNDERSTAND (5)
   O I CANNOT UNDERSTAND WHAT HAPPENED TO THEM!  .............STILLBORN  142    6
   I COULDN'T UNDERSTAND HER STUPID BEHAVIOR!  .............IN PLASTER  159   11
   I CAN LOVE MY HUSBAND, WHO WILL UNDERSTAND.  .............THREE WOMEN  183  250
   SUCH A WASTE OF BRIGHTNESS I CAN'T UNDERSTAND  ........QUEEN MARY'S.  290    7
   NOR STOP TO UNDERSTAND  ............................TOUCH-AND-GO     335   11
UNDERSTANDING (1)
   UNDERSTANDING BREAKS THROUGH THE SKULL'S SHELL  ......METAMORPHOSES.  307   16
UNDERSTOOD (1)
   FOR DEADLY SECRETS STRIKE WHEN UNDERSTOOD  ..............ADMONITIONS  319   16
UNDID (2)
   IF I JUST UNDID THE LOCKS AND STOOD BACK AND TURNED INTO A TREE.  ...
                                           ... THE ARRIVAL OF THE BEE BOX  213   28
   US IN: A THIRD UNDID THEM. AND WE GREW ONE  ............DIALOGUE O.  285  327
UNDO (5)
   TO UNDO HIM, PERPETUALLY),  .......................LETTER TO A PURIST   36    6
   WHO WOULD ADHERE TO ME: I UNDO HER FINGERS LIKE BANDAGES: I GO.  ...
                                           ... THREE WOMEN  184  273
   I CANNOT UNDO MYSELF, AND THE TRAIN IS STEAMING.  .....GETTING THERE  248   38
   WHAT COUNTERMAGIC CAN UNDO THE SNARE  ..........PROLOGUE TO SPRING   322   10
   UNDO THE DOINGS OF THE FATHERING AGE: *SONG FOR A REVOLUTIONARY LOVE  323    5
UNDOES (1)
   THE DARKENING STAIR, UNDOES THE PALACE LATCH  .........THE PRINCESS.  334   28
UNDOING (1)
   LEAVES, UNDOING THEIR YELLOW CAVES  .....................BLUE MOLES  126   11
UNDONE (3)
   AT THE WINDOW, THOSE UNBORN, THOSE UNDONE  ...................OUIJA   77    3
   STIRRUPS UNDONE, AND DECORUM. AND  ............WHITENESS I REMEMBER  103   23
   BEFORE WE FELL, LIKE ICARUS, UNDONE:  .................DOOM OF EXILES  318   10
UNDULANT (2)
   FAINT, UNDULANT WATERMARK.  ............................A SECRET     219    8
   OF AN UNDULANT AQUARIUM.  ..........MORNING IN THE HOSPITAL SOLARIUM  332    9
UNDULATINGS (1)
   WITH REEDY LENGTHS AND NECKS AND UNDULATINGS.  .........SNAKECHARMER   79    5
UNEARTHED (1)
   LITTLE VICTIM UNEARTHED BY SOME LARGE CREATURE  ..........BLUE MOLES  126    6
UNENDING (1)
   THE TENT OF UNENDING CRIES ---  .......................GETTING THERE  248   27
UNEVEN (1)
   HIS GAIT STRAY UNEVEN  .......................................SPINSTER   49    9
UNEXCEPTIONABLE (1)
   HUMDRUM, UNEXCEPTIONABLE, HIS  .................WHITENESS I REMEMBER  102    7
UNFACED (1)
   UNFACED, UNFORMED, THE NIPPLE-FLOWERS  ............VIRGIN IN A TREE   81   23
UNFATHOMED (1)
   POOLS, PROPHECIES AND SUCH FROM THE UNFATHOMED  .........DIALOGUE O.  282  240
UNFISTED (1)
   SAINT AND KING UNFISTED OBSTRUCTION'S KNUCKLES*A LESSON IN VENGEANCE   80    4
UNFISTS (1)
   UNFISTS AGAINST THE DUN  ...............................MAN IN BLACK  119    5
```

535

                                                          TITLE   PAGE   LINE

UNFOLDED (1)
    I SHONE, MICA-SCALED, AND UNFOLDED ....LOVE LETTER 147   25
UNFOLDS (1)
    OUT OF WHICH THE SAME SELF UNFOLDS LIKE A SUIT ....TOTEM 264   25
UNFORMED (1)
    UNFACED, UNFORMED, THE NIPPLE-FLOWERS ....VIRGIN IN A TREE   81   23
UNGIFTED (1)
    UNGIFTED, UNGRIEVED, OUR LEAVETAKING. ....DEPARTURE   51   6
UNGODLY (1)
    UNGODLY AS A CHILD'S SHRIEK. ....CHILDLESS WOMAN 259   10
UNGRATEFUL (1)
    THE OLD QUEEN DOES NOT SHOW HERSELF, IS SHE SO UNGRATEFUL? ....BEE. 212   50
UNGRIEVED (1)
    UNGIFTED, UNGRIEVED, OUR LEAVETAKING. ....DEPARTURE   51   6
UNHINGED (2)
    UNHINGED AND HIS GRIN CROOKED, ...MEDALLION 124   6
    LINTEL AND SILL HAVE UNHINGED THEMSELVES. ....WUTHERING HEIGHTS 168   32
UNHIRED (1)
    FROM MUSES UNHIRED BY YOU, DEAR MOTHER. ......THE DISQUIETING MUSES   75   40
UNHORSED (1)
    UNHORSED AND SHREDDED IN THE GROVE OF COMBAT ....SOW   61   31
UNHUSK (1)
    SHALL UNHUSK HIMSELF AND STEER INTO THE AIR. POEM.5.F. 135   20
UNICORNS (2)
    OUTLANDISH AS DOUBLE-HUMPED CAMELS OR UNICORNS, ...THE EYE-MOTE 109   13
    NEEDLES NAG LIKE UNICORNS, ...DANSE MACABRE 321   13
UNIDENTIFIABLE (1)
    ON A BLACK WALL, UNIDENTIFIABLE BIRDS ...............APPREHENSIONS 195   16
UNIFORM (1)
    LOVE IS THE UNIFORM OF MY BALD NURSE. POEM.7.S. 137   39
UNIFORMS (1)
    KNOTTING AND STOPPING, ILL-ASSORTED, IN BLUE UNIFORMS,*PARLIAMENT H. 152   14
UNIMAGINABLE (1)
    UNIMAGINABLE. YOU FLOAT NEAR ....FULL FATHOM FIVE   92   11
UNINTELLIGIBLE (1)
    THE UNINTELLIGIBLE SYLLABLES. ....THE ARRIVAL OF THE BEE BOX 213   18
UNIQUE (2)
    OF THE DESULTORY CURRENTS -- ALL THAT UNIQUE ....ABOVE THE OXBOW   89   45
    I AM SURE IT IS UNIQUE, I AM SURE IT IS JUST WHAT I WANT. *BIRTHDAY. 206   3
UNISON (1)
    IN UNISON ....A WINTER'S TALE   87   24
UNIVERSAL (1)
    ATOP THE BROKEN UNIVERSAL CLOCK: ....DOOMSDAY 316   2
UNIVERSE (3)
    AND THE UNIVERSE SLIDE FROM MY SIDE. ....A BIRTHDAY PRESENT 208   62
    THE WHEELS REVOLVE, THE UNIVERSE KEEPS RUNNING.   TO EVA DESCENDING. 303   2
    LIGHTING PLANT OF THE UNIVERSE. ....THE DREAM 311   18
UNKNOWING (1)
    UNKNOWING I MUST SOON UNPETAL. ....I AM VERTICAL 162   7
UNKNOWN (1)
    THE MAGIC SAWDUST WRITES: ADDRESS UNKNOWN. ....DENOUEMENT 327   17
UNLATCH (1)
    YOU SNORED, AND I HEARD THE PETALS UNLATCH, ...LEAVING EARLY 146   26
UNLESS (3)
    UNLESS YOU DO THIS TAWDRY HARBOR ....GREEN ROCK, WINTHROP BAY 105   19
    AND THE SEVEN-YEAR-OLD WOULDN'T GO OUT UNLESS HIS JERSEY
        STRIPES ....THE BABYSITTERS 174   8
    OBLITERATION HOURLY UNLESS OUR EYE .....DIALOGUE OVER A OUIJA BOARD 279 116
UNLIKE (5)
    COME, SO UNLIKE US, TO A STIFF IMPASSE, ...THE OTHER TWO   69   31
    LEAF UNLIKE ANY ....POLLY'S TREE 128   5
    UNLIKE SWANS, ...GULLIVER 251   5
    UNLIKE YOU, ...GULLIVER 251   7
    ALL COOL, ALL BLUE. UNLIKE YOU --- ....GULLIVER 251   9
UNLOAD (2)
    UNLOAD THEIR GRIEFS ON MY SHOES, ...PRIVATE GROUND 130   18
    THE GRASSES UNLOAD THEIR GRIEFS ON MY FEET AS IF I WERE GOD,   MOON. 172   3
UNLOADING (1)
    THEY ARE UNLOADING THREE BARRELS OF LITTLE CRABS. ....A WINTER SHIP 113   14
UNLOCK (1)
    COULD UNLOCK ....FIRESONG   30   12
UNLOOSE (5)
    HER BLUE GARMENTS UNLOOSE SMALL BATS AND OWLS. ....MOON. 173   18
    I SHALL UNLOOSE ....PURDAH 243   38
    I SHALL UNLOOSE ....PURDAH 243   41
    I SHALL UNLOOSE ....PURDAH 243   51
    I SHALL UNLOOSE -- ....PURDAH 244   52
UNLOOSING (1)
    UNLOOSING THEIR MOONS, MONTH AFTER MONTH, TO NO PURPOSE. ...MUNICH. 263   5
UNLUCKY (1)
    UNLUCKY THE HERO BORN ....THE TIMES ARE TIDY 107   1
UNMADE (1)
    TO UNMADE MUD CLOAKED BY SOUR SKY. ....FIRESONG   30   14
UNMANNED (1)
    OF KINGS, UNMANNED KINGS' SONS: OUR MASTERIES ....SNOWMAN O.   59   41

UNMASKED (1)
   THESE THREE, UNMASKED NOW, BEAR ....ALL THE DEAD DEARS   70   7
UNMIRACULOUS (1)
   OF WINGED, UNMIRACULOUS WOMEN, ...STINGS   214   21
UNMISTED (1)
   JUST AS IT IS, UNMISTED BY LOVE OR DISLIKE. ....MIRROR   173   3
UNMOVED (1)
   WHILE ON THIS SAME FUGUE, UNMOVED, ...TOUCH-AND-GO   336   22
UNNATURAL (1)
   ON DARKNESS, MORE VIVID AND UNNATURAL ..DIALOGUE OVER A OUIJA BOARD   285 323
UNNERVING (1)
   YOU HOUSE YOUR UNNERVING HEAD -- GOD-BALL, ...MEDUSA   224   4
UNPEEL (1)
   GODIVA, I UNPEEL --- ....ARIEL   239   20
UNPEOPLED (1)
   LIT, BUT UNPEOPLED, HELD ITS WINDOWS ....OWL   101   3
UNPETAL (1)
   UNKNOWING I MUST SOON UNPETAL. ....I AM VERTICAL   162   7
UNPICK (1)
   TO UNPICK THE HEART, PARE BONE ....NOVEMBER GRAVEYARD   56   9
UNPICTURED (1)
   UNPOEMED, UNPICTURED, THE POTATO ....POEMS, POTATOES   106   11
UNPLUCKED (1)
   SHE, RIPE AND UNPLUCKED, 'S ....VIRGIN IN A TREE   82   36
UNPOEMED (1)
   UNPOEMED, UNPICTURED, THE POTATO ....POEMS, POTATOES   106   11
UNQUEENLY (1)
   POOR AND BARE AND UNQUEENLY AND EVEN SHAMEFUL. ....STINGS   214   19
UNRAVEL (1)
   UNRAVEL ANTIQUE SAMPLERS, UNWIND THE CLOCKS, ...SONG FOR A REVOLU.   323   13
UNRAVELED (1)
   RED THE UNRAVELED ROSE SINGS IN YOUR HAIR: ......TO EVA DESCENDING.   303   7
UNREAL (2)
   ARE UNREAL, WE SAY: ....THE THIN PEOPLE   64   4
   AT THE UNREAL FRONTIER. LET OUR BACKS, NOW BOLD, ...DIALOGUE O.   285 331
UNREDEEMED (1)
   MIRROR SAFE, UNREDEEMED ....BRASILIA   259   21
UNREELING (1)
   UNREELING IN IT, SPREADING LIKE OIL. ....THE RABBIT CATCHER   193   5
UNRIPE (1)
   THE SUN SHINES ON UNRIPE CORN. ....DEPARTURE   51   7
UNRIPENED (1)
   MY LEAN, UNRIPENED HEART. ....JILTED   304   12
UNROLLED (2)
   MY MOTHER UNROLLED AT YOUR LAST HOMECOMING.   ELECTRA ON AZALEA PATH   117   32
   GRAIN BY GRAIN, THEY UNROLLED ....BURNING THE LETTERS   204   6
UNRULY (3)
   UNRULY ENOUGH TO PITCH HER FIVE QUEENLY WITS ....SPINSTER   50   20
   SHE CAME, AND CALLED HELL TO SUBDUE AN UNRULY MAN ....SNOWMAN O.   59   23
   TILL UNRULY CHILDREN STREAM DOWN THE SKY ....SONG FOR A REVOLU.   323   14
UNSAFE (1)
   SPIDERY, UNSAFE. ....THALIDOMIDE   252   6
UNSAID (1)
   TO KEEP SOME UNSAID PACT; PERHAPS CONCERN ....CHANNEL CROSSING   27   34
UNSEAT (1)
   OF EYEBATHS CAN UNSEAT THE SPECK: ....THE EYE-MOTE   109   20
UNSEEN (4)
   THE SIGHT OF THOSE BLUE, UNSEEN WAVES ....ON THE DECLINE OF ORACLES   78   14
   BRACING THEIR KNEES. ON UNSEEN TOWLINES ....IN MIDAS' COUNTRY   99   17
   AND DAMAGING THE WHOLE UNSEEN ....THE DREAM   311   17
   AND SLIPS UNSEEN PAST WATCHMEN ON THE LAWN ....THE PRINCESS.   334   29
UNSERVICEABLE (1)
   UNSERVICEABLE, I WAIT ....RESOLVE   52   3
UNSETTLING (1)
   UNSETTLING THE STEADY-ROOTED GREEN ....WHITENESS I REMEMBER   102   15
UNSHEATHES (1)
   THE CAT UNSHEATHES ITS CLAWS ....RESOLVE   52   17
UNSHRIVEN (1)
   FLESH UNSHRIVEN. ....VANITY FAIR   33   20
UNSIGHTLY (1)
   OR WHAT DISFIGURED AND UNSIGHTLY ....THE DISQUIETING MUSES   74   2
UNSPOKEN (1)
   AND IDLE COILS OF JARGON YET UNSPOKEN. ....SONNET: TO EVA   304   8
UNSPOOL (1)
   UNSPOOL AND SPEND THEMSELVES. MY MIND RUNS WITH THEM, *PARLIAMENT H.   153   35
UNSTABLE (1)
   TILTED AND DISPARATE, AND ALWAYS UNSTABLE. ....WUTHERING HEIGHTS   167   2
UNSTICK (1)
   TWO LOVERS UNSTICK THEMSELVES. ....BERCK-PLAGE   197   30
UNSTITCHING (1)
   LAUGH DOES AWAY WITH THE UNSTITCHING, PLAGUEY WOUNDS ....PERSEUS   83   45
UNSTOPPERS (1)
   A WIND UNSTOPPERS THE CHAMBER POEM.7.S.   136   23
UNSTRUNG (2)
   ALREADY HALF UNSTRUNG. A VINEGARY FUME   TWO VIEWS OF A CADAVER ROOM   114   3

UNSTRUNG (CONT.)
   LITTLE UNSTRUNG PUPPET, KICKING TO DISAPPEAR -- ....LESBOS 227   9
UNSURE (1)
   ACROSS ATLANTIC FURROWS, DARK, UNSURE -- ....MAYFLOWER   60   11
UNTEACHABLE (1)
   TONE-DEAF AND YES, UNTEACHABLE. ....THE DISQUIETING MUSES   75   38
UNTENANTED (1)
   WHICH PEOPLES THE BARE ROOM, THE BLANK, UNTENANTED AIR. *NOVEMBER G.   56   18
UNTIDY (1)
   THE UNTIDY LADY REVIVALIST ....ON DECK 143   19
UNTIL (34)
   UNTIL THE SUN TURNED PALE FROM WARM, ...BUCOLICS   24   14
   UNTIL SWEET WIND CHANGED TUNE, BLEW HARM: ....BUCOLICS   24   15
   UNTIL EVERY MAN, ...STRUMPET SONG   33   6
   UNTIL ALL OWLS IN THE TWIGGED FOREST ....FAUN   35   3
   UNTIL THAT TIME ....DIALOGUE BETWEEN GHOST AND PRIEST   39   39
   NOR SCANT HIS WANT UNTIL ....THE GLUTTON   40   13
   UNTIL, TURNING SIDEWAYS, ...MISS DRAKE PROCEEDS TO SUPPER   41   23
   UNTIL BIRD-RACKETING DAWN ....THE SHRIKE   42   16
   IN THEIR HEARTBEATS' BLAZING WAKE UNTIL RED COCK ....EPITAPH FOR F.   46   27
   UNTIL HIS OWN LIT ROOM OUTSHONE ....THE EVERLASTING MONDAY   62   9
   UNTIL HER KNIFE HAD PARED ....THE THIN PEOPLE   65   30
   UNTIL NO CHASTE TREE BUT SUFFERS BLOTCH ..ON THE PLETHORA OF DRYADS   68   34
   AND TACK OF THE CLOCK, UNTIL WE GO, ...ALL THE DEAD DEARS   71   33
   PIPES WATER GREEN UNTIL GREEN WATERS WAVER ...........SNAKECHARMER   79   4
   AND REPOISE UNTIL TIME STOP, THE CELESTIAL BALANCE ....PERSEUS   84   48
   UNTIL HIS CHISEL BEQUEATHS ....SCULPTOR   92   22
   PUT UP WITH UNTIL CHAGRIN GIVES PLACE ....THE COMPANIONABLE ILLS 105   3
   THEY PROPPED HIS JAW WITH A BOOK UNTIL IT STIFFENED ....BERCK-PLAGE 198   65
   I HOLD MY BREATH UNTIL YOU CREAK TO LIFE, ...CUT 236   19
   NEAR WINS, WEEK BY WEEK, WAITING UNTIL   DIALOGUE OVER A OUIJA BOARD 277   40
   UNTIL IT FINISHED, AND THEN LOOK FURTIVELY ....DIALOGUE O. 280 164
   OF FORMAL SCORN, UNTIL THE FIRST SIGN OF AN ....DIALOGUE O. 282 232
   UNTIL NEAR TWELVE THE STRANGE GIRL ALL AT ONCE ....CINDERELLA 304   11
   UNTIL IN DISENCHANTMENT OUR EYES GLUT ....METAMORPHOSES OF THE MOON 308   34
   UNTIL HE STOOD ....TO A JILTED LOVER 310   14
   UNTIL THE PEAK OF NOON HAS COME ....TO A JILTED LOVER 310   24
   WITH MANY MEN UNTIL I CRASHED ....THE DREAM 310   9
   UPON THE POURING AIR UNTIL ....SONG FOR A REVOLUTIONARY LOVE 323   18
   HALF IN SHADE, UNTIL HER SKIN ...BLACK PINE TREE IN AN ORANGE LIGHT 328   11
   UNTIL THE STARS TICK OUT A LULLABY ....LOVE IS A PARALLAX 329   14
   CHURCHYARD EARS UNTIL THE STARLIT STIFF ....LOVE IS A PARALLAX 330   41
   UNTIL DREAM TAKES HER BODY ....AERIALIST 331   4
   BRIGHT WINDOW-SQUARES UNTIL THE WOMEN SEEM .....MORNING IN THE HOS. 332   7
   UNTIL SHE HEARS THE TWITTERING MACHINE *THE PRINCESS AND THE GOBLINS 334   56
UNTONGUED (1)
   UNTONGUED, ALL BEAUTY'S BRIGHT JUICE SOURS. ....VIRGIN IN A TREE   82   43
UNTOUCHABLE (4)
   YET THEY RECEDE, UNTOUCHABLE AS TOMORROW,*SLEEP IN THE MOJAVE DESERT 144   11
   INFINITE, GREEN, UTTERLY UNTOUCHABLE. ................APPREHENSIONS 195   2
   UNTOUCHED AND UNTOUCHABLE. ....GETTING THERE 249   54
   THAT REVOLVE IN CRIVELLI, UNTOUCHABLE. ....GULLIVER 251   22
UNTOUCHED (4)
   THEIR FOOTSOLES ARE UNTOUCHED. THEY ARE WALKERS OF AIR. *THREE WOMEN 183 231
   WHAT DID I LEAVE UNTOUCHED ON THE DOORSTEP -- ....THE OTHER 201   2
   A GULLIBLE HEAD UNTOUCHED BY THEIR ANIMOSITY, ...THE BEE MEETING 212   40
   UNTOUCHED AND UNTOUCHABLE. ....GETTING THERE 249   54
UNTWIST (1)
   I AM RESOLVED. NO REASON COULD UNTWIST   DIALOGUE OVER A OUIJA BOARD 286 341
UNTYING (1)
   THE VILLAGERS ARE UNTYING THEIR DISGUISES, THEY ARE SHAKING HANDS. ...
                                          ... THE BEE MEETING 212   54
UNUSUALLY (1)
   FIZZY WITH SEDATIVES AND UNUSUALLY HUMOROUS, ...FACE LIFT 156   11
UNUTTERABLE (1)
   BY SOME UNUTTERABLE CHAGRIN, ...THE RAVAGED FACE 115   3
UNWALKED (1)
   I WALKED THE UNWALKED GARDEN OF ROSE-BEDS ...........RHODODENDRON. 103   1
UNWALL (1)
   LEDGE WILL DISLODGE OUR CRAMPED CONCEPT OF SPACE, UNWALL ....OXBOW.   88   23
UNWARMED (1)
   UNWARMED BY THE SWEET AIR OF THIS PEACH ORCHARD. ....STARS. 166   36
UNWIND (1)
   UNRAVEL ANTIQUE SAMPLERS, UNWIND THE CLOCKS, ...SONG FOR A REVOLU. 323   13
UNWINDS (1)
   UNWINDS FROM THE GREAT UMBILICUS OF THE SUN POEM.3.MAENAD. 133   19
UNWISELY (1)
   COUSIN DID YOU SO UNWISELY KEEP ....THE DISQUIETING MUSES   74   3
UNWRAP (1)
   THEM UNWRAP ME HAND AND FOOT --- ....LADY LAZARUS 245   28
UP (158)
   COMING UP AND UP THE STAIRS. ....PURSUIT   23   50
   COMING UP AND UP THE STAIRS. ....PURSUIT   23   50
   IN THIS PARTICULAR TUB, TWO KNEES JUT UP ....TALE OF A TUB   25   41
   SENDS UP ITS FORKED ....SOUTHERN SUNRISE   26   11

UP (CONT.)
FLAYED BY SPRAY, WE TAKE THE CHALLENGE UP, ...CHANNEL CROSSING   26   5
UP FROM DELVED WORM-HAUNT; ....ODE FOR TED   29   8
SUN HOISTS SOUL UP AFTER LIDS FALL SHUT; ....VANITY FAIR   33   28
LOOKS UP. ....STRUMPET SONG   34   19
JACK WILL TOUCH UP ....TINKER JACK AND THE TIDY WIVES   34   21
GOD ORDAINED TO FOLLOW UP YOUR DAYS. IS IT SUCH TROUBLE *DIALOGUE B.   39   25
"TEA LEAVES I'VE GIVEN UP, ...RECANTATION   41   1
CLAM-DIGGERS ROSE UP OUT OF DARK SLIME AT HER OFFENSE.*DREAM WITH C.   44   24
YOU MIGHT AS WELL HAUL UP ....EPITAPH FOR FIRE AND FLOWER   45   1
UP BY A SPRY BLACK DEUS ....SPIDER   49   34
ON THE STIFF TWIG UP THERE ....BLACK ROOK IN RAINY WEATHER   56   1
MY EYELIDS UP, AND GRANT ....BLACK ROOK IN RAINY WEATHER   57   30
OF A BLIZZARD, THE GIANT ROARED UP WITH HIS CHITTERING TROPHIES. ...
                                  ... THE SNOWMAN ON THE MOOR   59   45
ON GRUNT, UP IN THE FLICKERING LIGHT TO SHAPE ....SOW   61   39
UP FROM THE FISSURED VALLEY AND HUNG SHOULDER-HIGH *HARDCASTLE CRAGS   62   14
HOW THEY PROP EACH OTHER UP! ....THE THIN PEOPLE   65   40
ON THE DIFFICULTY OF CONJURING UP A DRYAD ....CONJURING.   65   T
LEAVING NO SPARKY TRACK, SETTING UP NO RIPPLE. ....THE OTHER TWO   68   26
AND WAKEN THE SLY NERVE UP ....THE LADY AND THE EARTHENWARE HEAD   69   14
ROSE UP AND PUT ROYAL NERVES TO THE RACK: ....NATURAL HISTORY   71   9
GIVING A LEG UP ....WORDS FOR A NURSERY   73   9
DRUMMING UP ANY FEVER ....NIGHT SHIFT   76   4
THE BOOKS BURNED UP, SEA TOOK THE SHELL, ON THE DECLINE OF ORACLES   78   11
AND THOSE MEN COMING UP THE STAIR. ....ON THE DECLINE OF ORACLES   78   21
COMING UP, THOSE THREE. WORTH ....ON THE DECLINE OF ORACLES   78   28
PUTS UP HIS PIPE, AND LIDS HIS MOONY EYE. .............SNAKECHARMER   79   28
BEAR UP THE SEAFARER, ...BATTLE-SCENE   84   8
OF GRAYBEARDS WAKES US UP. ....BATTLE-SCENE   85   40
UP PLEASANT STREET AT MAIN. POISING THEIR SHAPES ...ABOVE THE OXBOW   88   12
IN GOING UP FOR THE COMING DOWN IF THE POST ....ABOVE THE OXBOW   88   18
OF SUCH SEEING UP THE LEAF-SHUTTERED ESCARPMENTS, ..ABOVE THE OXBOW   88   27
A WORLD WE LOSE BY MERELY WAKING UP. ....THE GHOST'S LEAVETAKING   90   20
UP TOWARD ME, TROUBLING THE FACE ....LORELEI   94   10
WAY UP THE RIVER-BASIN. ....MUSSEL HUNTER AT ROCK HARBOR   96   44
BUILD UP FROM A ROCK ROOT, AS FOUNTAINS BUILD ....MOONRISE   98   23
HIS NEAT TROT PITCHING MY TENSE POISE UP, ...WHITENESS I REMEMBER   102   14
PUT UP WITH UNTIL CHAGRIN GIVES PLACE ....THE COMPANIONABLE ILLS   105   3
THE LAST CRONE GOT BURNT UP ....THE TIMES ARE TIDY   107   11
HOVE UP AGAINST BENDYLAW. ....THE BULL OF BENDYLAW   108   3
THE BULL SURGED UP, THE BULL SURGED DOWN, ...THE BULL OF BENDYLAW   108   16
A BLIMP SWIMS UP LIKE A DAY-MOON OR TIN ....A WINTER SHIP   113   11
WE WANTED TO SEE THE SUN COME UP ....A WINTER SHIP   113   24
THEMSELVES UP AGAINST THE WALL ....OLD LADIES' HOME   120   6
HALFWAY UP FROM THE LITTLE HARBOR OF SARDINE BOATS, *THE NET-MENDERS   121   1
UP HERE AMONG THE GULL CRIES ....MAGNOLIA SHOALS   121   1
A WHITE MIST IS GOING UP. ....THE SLEEPERS   123   16
NIGHTLY THE BATTLE-SHOUTS START UP ....BLUE MOLES   126   19
UP FROM THE JET-BACKED ....DARK WOOD, DARK WATER   127   16
SOON EACH WHITE LADY WILL BE BOARDED UP ....PRIVATE GROUND   130   5
NOW THEY LIGHT ME UP LIKE AN ELECTRIC BULB. POEM.1.WHO.   132   32
ALL-MOUTH LICKS UP THE BUSHES POEM.2.DARK.   132   17
THEY ARE TURNING THE BURNERS UP, RING AFTER RING. POEM.6.W.   135   16
WRAPPED UP IN YOURSELF LIKE A SPOOL, ...YOU'RE   141   5
WRAPPED UP IN THEMSELVES AS IN THICK VEILING ....ON DECK   142   2
THE DAY-MOON LIGHTS UP LIKE A SORRY MOTHER, ...SLEEP.   144   24
THE PINES BLOT OUR VOICES UP IN THEIR LIGHTEST SIGHS. ....TWO CAMP.   145   24
MOBS OF EYEBALLS LOOKING UP. ....LEAVING EARLY   146   13
GAVE UP THE GHOST LAST NIGHT. HIGH TIME. ....LEAVING EARLY   146   24
IN THE MIRROR THEIR DOUBLES BACK THEM UP. ....LEAVING EARLY   146   34
HOW DID WE MAKE IT UP TO YOUR ATTIC? ....LEAVING EARLY   146   40
DRAG UP FALSE, EDWARDIAN SENTIMENTS, ...CANDLES   149   16
THOUGH NOBODY IN THERE LOOKS UP OR BOTHERS TO ANSWER. ....A LIFE   150   8
CRAWLS UP OUT OF THE SEA. ....A LIFE   150   35
HOW THE BALCONIES ECHOED! HOW THE SUN LIT UP .....WAKING IN WINTER   151   9
LIGHT UP. EACH RABBIT-EARED ....PARLIAMENT HILL FIELDS   153   44
THEN MOTHER SWAM UP, HOLDING A TIN BASIN. ....FACE LIFT   156   7
SHE BEGAN TO WARM UP, AND I SAW HER ADVANTAGES. ....IN PLASTER   159   14
I PATRONIZED HER A LITTLE, AND SHE LAPPED IT UP -- ......IN PLASTER   159   20
I HAVE GIVEN MY NAME AND MY DAY-CLOTHES UP TO THE NURSES ....TULIPS   160   6
TO LIE UP WITH MY HANDS TURNED UP AND BE UTTERLY EMPTY. ....TULIPS   161   6
THEN THE TULIPS FILLED IT UP LIKE A LOUD NOISE. ....TULIPS   161   52
SUCKING UP MINERALS AND MOTHERLY LOVE ....I AM VERTICAL   162   3
CREEPING UP WITH HER HATFUL OF TRIVIAL REPETITIONS. .....INSOMNIAC   163   32
AND NO BODIES, SINGING LIKE ARROWS UP TO HEAVEN. ....WIDOW   164   25
NOR DO THEY SEND UP FIRES WHERE THEY FALL ..STARS OVER THE DORDOGNE   165   6
INFINITE NUMBER SEEMS TO BE THE ISSUE UP THERE. ....STARS.   165   21
THEY GO UP WITHOUT HOPE, LIKE SIGHS. ....FINISTERRE   169   16
LITTLE SHELLS MADE UP INTO NECKLACES AND TOY LADIES. ....FINISTERRE   170   32
I HAVE NOT SEEN IT; IT DOES NOT FLY UP. ......THE SURGEON AT 2 A.M.   170   9
I AM UP TO MY ELBOWS IN IT, RED AND SQUEAKING.*THE SURGEON AT 2 A.M.   171   22
STILL IT SEEPS UP, IT IS NOT EXHAUSTED. ......THE SURGEON AT 2 A.M.   171   23
THE ANGELS OF MORPHIA HAVE BORNE HIM UP. .....THE SURGEON AT 2 A.M.   171   44
ROUND AS THE MOON, TO STARE UP. ....LAST WORDS   172   3

UP (CONT.)   TITLE   PAGE LINE
    THEY WILL ROLL ME UP IN BANDAGES, THEY WILL STORE MY HEART   LAST W.   172   23
    THE YEW TREE POINTS UP. IT HAS A GOTHIC SHAPE. ....MOON.   173   15
    WE PICKED UP STICKS OF DRIFTWOOD AND BEAT THEM OFF, *THE BABYSITTERS   175   38
    WE KICKED AND TALKED. THE THICK SALT KEPT US UP. ...THE BABYSITTERS   175   40
    THERE'S NO GETTING UP IT BY THE WORDS YOU KNOW.*NEW YEAR ON DARTMOOR   176   6
    NO GETTING UP BY ELEPHANT OR WHEEL OR SHOE. ...NEW YEAR ON DARTMOOR   176   7
    THE PARTICLES OF DESTRUCTION I SUCK UP? AM I A PULSE ...THREE WOMEN   177   38
    TURN UP THEIR HANDS, THEIR PALLORS. IT IS SO QUIET HERE.*THREE WOMEN   179   94
    THEY ARE STITCHING ME UP WITH SILK, AS IF I WERE A MATERIAL. *THREE.   181 168
    I HOLD MY FINGERS UP, TEN WHITE PICKETS. ....THREE WOMEN   182 194
    NOTHING THAT CANNOT BE ERASED, RIPPED UP AND SCRAPPED,
          BEGUN AGAIN. ....THREE WOMEN   184 277
    THE NARCISSI LOOK UP LIKE CHILDREN, QUICKLY AND WHITELY.   NARCISSI.   190   12
    NOW I BREAK UP IN PIECES THAT FLY ABOUT LIKE CLUBS. ....ELM   192   19
    WHO WALL UP THEIR BACKS AGAINST HIM. ....BERCK-PLAGE   196   15
    IT IS SO BEAUTIFUL UP HERE: IT IS A STOPPING PLACE. ...BERCK-PLAGE   199   90
    GLIDING UP IN LOW GEAR BEHIND THE CART. ....BERCK-PLAGE   200 112
    THERE IS NO HOPE, IT IS GIVEN UP. ....BERCK-PLAGE   201 126
    I FLAKE UP PAPERS THAT BREATHE LIKE PEOPLE, ...BURNING THE LETTERS   204   37
    THE WORLD WILL GO UP IN A SHRIEK, AND YOUR HEAD WITH IT, BIRTHDAY.   207   29
    THESE ARE THE DECEITS, TACKED UP LIKE FAMILY PHOTOGRAPHS,*DETECTIVE.   208   13
    HUNG UP IN THE LIBRARY WITH THE ENGRAVINGS OF RANGOON .....COURAGE.   210   22
    IS IT BLOOD CLOTS THE TENDRILS ARE DRAGGING UP THAT STRING? ...BEE.   211   19
    SEVENTY FEET UP, IN A BLACK PINE TREE. ....THE SWARM   216   18
    TO MAKE UP FOR THE HONEY I'VE TAKEN. ....WINTERING   218   26
    HOLDING UP ONE PALM -- ....A SECRET   219   4
    IS THAT ALL HE CAN COME UP WITH, ...THE JAILER   226   4
    UP OVER THE HARBOR LIGHTS. ....LESBOS   229   56
    WE KEPT PICKING UP HANDFULS, LOVING IT, ...LESBOS   229   60
    A DOG PICKED UP YOUR DOGGY HUSBAND. HE WENT ON. ....LESBOS   229   63
    UP TO MY NECK, ...LESBOS   229   65
    I THINK I AM GOING UP, ...FEVER.   232   43
    IT WENT UP IN SMOKE. ....THE TOUR   238   23
    THE ONE WHO NEVER LOOKS UP, WHOSE EYES ARE LIDDED ......DEATH & CO.   254   3
    PREDECESSOR WRAPPED UP, ...EAVESDROPPER   260   25
    ONCE ONE HAS BEEN SEIZED UP ....MYSTIC   268   10
    OR PICKING UP THE BRIGHT PIECES ....MYSTIC   269   18
    SWEETLY PICKING UP PIECES! ....KINDNESS   269   13
    TAKING UP HALF THE SPACE, ...BALLOONS   271   4
    BUT I'VE BROUGHT BRANDY AND BUILT THE FIRE UP ....DIALOGUE O.   277   16
    MINOR IMPS PIPE UP, SO LONG AS EACH ....DIALOGUE OVER A OUIJA BOARD   280 152
    IS ON YOU NOW, FOR PLANNING TO DREDGE UP*DIALOGUE OVER A OUIJA BOARD 282 239
    CURTSEYED TO YOURS. TOO BAD YOU CALLED PAN UP ....DIALOGUE O.   284 280
    THIS BOARD OUR BATTLEFIELD. LET'S GIVE PAN UP ....DIALOGUE O.   284 292
    THERE! THAT SHUTS HIM UP! SO. BETTER SO,*DIALOGUE OVER A OUIJA BOARD 284 300
    AND BOLT IT UP BY TAKING OATH NO GUESS   DIALOGUE OVER A OUIJA BOARD 286 345
    THE WRINKLES CREEP UP LIKE WAVES, ...THE RIVAL/DR 291   4
    IT KEEPS WASHING YOU UP LIKE AN OLD BONE. ....THE RIVAL/DR   291   16
    SHE STOOD UP, A THIN COMMANDING FIGURE ....BITTER STRAWBERRIES   300   29
    AND HIGH HEELS CLICKING UP THE WALK; ....FAMILY REUNION   300   4
    CRYPTIC STARS WIND UP THE ATMOSPHERE, ...TO EVA DESCENDING THE STAIR 303   10
    THE IDIOT BIRD LEAPS UP AND DRUNKEN LEANS ....SONNET: TO EVA   305   13
    WALTZING UP TO ME OUT OF HER COCKLE-SHELL." ......DIALOGUE EN ROUTE   309   30
    GOT UP TO LET THE SUAVE BLUE POLICEMAN IN. ....THE TRIAL OF MAN   312   8
    AND THE SNOW BLOW UP BEHIND; ....GO GET THE GOODLY SQUAB   313   14
    COCKS CROW UP A RIVAL ....MOONSONG AT MORNING   316   5
    NIGHT YIELDED UP ....MOONSONG AT MORNING   317   30
    SO IF YOU CAN DREAM UP ANY SAVING PLAN ....THE DISPOSSESSED   318   2
    THE SINGING BIRDS PACK UP AND FLY AWAY; ....NEVER TRY TO TRICK.   320   17
    NOR CAN GOD'S STERN, SHOCKED ANGELS CRY THEM UP ....THE DEAD   320   13
    WINDING UP THE RAVELED MOLD. ....DANSE MACABRE   321   12
    OF COCKCROW CRYING UP THE DAWN. ....DANSE MACABRE   321   24
    MY EXTRAVAGANT HEART BLOWS UP AGAIN ....CIRCUS IN THREE PARTS   321   3
    BLUE VIEWS ARE BOARDED UP; OUR SWEET VACATION ....TWO LOVERS.   327   3
    SPRUNG UP LIKE PLAGUE OF TOADSTOOLS OVERNIGHT: ....TERMINAL   328   4
    TO SIT UP STARK AWAKE ....AERIALIST   332   41
    LIKE PETULANT PARAKEETS CORKED UP IN CAGES .....MORNING IN THE HOS.   332   19
    UP WHICH THE WAKEFUL PRINCESS CLIMBS TO FIND ....THE PRINCESS.   333   2
    MADE BY MINERS UP THE MOUNTAINSIDE ....THE PRINCESS AND THE GOBLINS   334   33
    CLAMBERING UP THE CREAKING HEIGHTS OF HEAT ....THE PRINCESS.   334   55
    KNIT UP A GILDED FABLE FOR THE CHILD ..THE PRINCESS AND THE GOBLINS   335   73
    ARCS UP TO THE TALL TREE TIP; ....TOUCH-AND-GO   335   14
UPDRAFT (1)
    LEVITATING A NUMB MINUTE IN THE UPDRAFT ....WIDOW   164   3
UPDRAUGHT (1)
    RIPPLED AND PULSED IN THE GLASSY UPDRAUGHT. ...SUICIDE OFF EGG ROCK   115   5
UPFLIGHT (1)
    THE UPFLIGHT OF THE MURDERESS INTO A HEAVEN THAT LOVES HER. ...BEE.   212   48
UPHOLSTERED (1)
    UPHOLSTERED IN RED VELVET, UNDER THE EYE ....YADWIGHA.   85   3
UPHOLSTERY (2)
    OF CHARRED SHOES, THE SODDEN UPHOLSTERY: ....AFTERMATH   114   12
    WALKING THE PLANK DRAPED WITH MOTHER FRANCE'S UPHOLSTERY   THE SWARM 217   48

	TITLE	PAGE	LINE

UPLEAPING (1)
   CURVE OF WATER UPLEAPING ....MEDUSA 225 18
UPLIFTED (1)
   UPLIFTED, STIFFEN IN A FAMILY POSE. ....BLUE MOLES 126 16
UPON (28)
   TILL HE SOME PITY TOOK UPON HER CRYING; ......THE QUEEN'S COMPLAINT 28 12
   PROPS A LEG-STUMP UPON A CRUTCH, ...THE BEGGARS 48 11
   LAST SUMMER I CAME UPON YOUR SPANISH COUSIN, ...SPIDER 48 8
   UPON OUR BEDSPREAD. ....THE EVERLASTING MONDAY 62 4
   LOOK UPON? RATS' TEETH GUT THE CITY ....OWL 102 15
   VOLT UPON VOLT. CATGUT STITCHES MY FISSURES. POEM.7.S. 137 30
   I SHALL MEDITATE UPON NORMALITY. ....THREE WOMEN 186 323
   I SHALL MEDITATE UPON MY LITTLE SON. ....THREE WOMEN 186 324
   IT IS ONLY TIME THAT WEIGHS UPON OUR HANDS. ....THREE WOMEN 187 363
   RUN FOLD UPON FOLD FAR OFF, CONCEALING THEIR HOLLOWS, ..BERCK-PLAGE 199 74
   REMEMBER THE WALKER UPON IT? ....MYSTIC 269 26
   CASTLES UPON THE SMUG-SHAPED CHAIRS. ALL THIS I ....DIALOGUE O. 279 118
   WITH SUNLIGHT OF A THOUSAND YEARS UPON HIS LIPS ....GOLD MOUTHS CRY 302 13
   (PROUD YOU HALT UPON THE SPIRAL STAIR.) *TO EVA DESCENDING THE STAIR 303 3
   (PROUD YOU HALT UPON THE SPIRAL STAIR.) *TO EVA DESCENDING THE STAIR 303 9
   (PROUD YOU HALT UPON THE SPIRAL STAIR.) *TO EVA DESCENDING THE STAIR 303 15
   (PROUD YOU HALT UPON THE SPIRAL STAIR.) *TO EVA DESCENDING THE STAIR 303 19
   DROOPS UPON ITS WIZENED STEM ....JILTED 304 11
   THEN DROVE TO YOU UPON THE WIND. . . ..THE DREAM 311 28
   IMPALED UPON A STERN ANGELIC STARE ....THE TRIAL OF MAN 312 9
   FROM HERE YOU CAN'T SEE SPOTS UPON THE SUN; ....ADMONITIONS 319 8
   UPON THE POURING AIR UNTIL ....SONG FOR A REVOLUTIONARY LOVE 323 18
   HIS OWN PALE BRIDE UPON A FLAMING TRAY: ....TERMINAL 328 12
   SO KISS: THE DRUNKS UPON THE CURB AND DAMES .....LOVE IS A PARALLAX 329 31
   WHILE SUNLIGHT WINDS ITS YARN UPON THE FLOOR. ....THE PRINCESS. 335 71
   AN ACCURATE ASSAULT UPON THE EYES ....EPITAPH IN THREE PARTS 337 14
   ALOFT, A LONE GULL HALTS UPON THE WIND, ...EPITAPH IN THREE PARTS 337 20
   A WAVE OF GRASS ENGRAVES UPON THE STONE: ....EPITAPH IN THREE PARTS 338 32
UPRAISED (1)
   UPRAISED, AS A HAND, EMBLEMATIC OF FAREWELL.*THE GHOST'S LEAVETAKING 90 11
UPREAR (1)
   MONSTERS WHICH UPREAR ....BATTLE-SCENE 84 16
UPRIGHT (2)
   TIMBERS OF HIS UPRIGHT HUT? ....THE HERMIT AT OUTERMOST HOUSE 119 12
   THE SKY LEANS ON ME, ME, THE ONE UPRIGHT ....WUTHERING HEIGHTS 168 37
UPROOT (2)
   UPROOT THEM: THEIR BEARDS ARE EVER- ....CHILD'S PARK STONES 101 27
   PEGS TOO DEEP TO UPROOT, AND A MIND LIKE A RING THE RABBIT CATCHER 194 28
UPSET (2)
   SO I WAS CAREFUL NOT TO UPSET HER IN ANY WAY ....IN PLASTER 160 46
   WHITE AS A KNUCKLE AND TERRIBLY UPSET. ...THE MOON AND THE YEW TREE 173 9
UPSETTING (1)
   UPSETTING ME WITH THEIR SUDDEN TONGUES AND THEIR COLOR, ...TULIPS 161 41
UPSIDE (3)
   AND RIDE THAT FLUX AT ANCHOR, UPSIDE DOWN. ....WATERCOLOR. 112 11
   DOGBODY NOSES THE PETALS. THEY BLOOM UPSIDE DOWN. POEM.1.WHO. 131 11
   UPSIDE DOWN HEARTS OF LIGHT TIPPING WAX FINGERS, ...CANDLES 148 2
UPSTANDING (1)
   UPSTANDING SPINACH-TIPS WEDGED IN A CIRCLE -- ......SPINACH-PICKER. 89 8
UPSTART (1)
   TO A CINDER, THAN MEET A POOR UPSTART OF OUR NETHER ....DIALOGUE O. 280 133
UPTURNED (1)
   BELLIES PALLID AND UPTURNED, ...MUSSEL HUNTER AT ROCK HARBOR 97 85
UPTURNS (1)
   WHAT FLINTY PEBBLES THE PLOUGHBLADE UPTURNS ....OUIJA 77 28
UPWARD (1)
   POPPING UPWARD FROM THE MOUTHS OF BELLS ....LYONNESSE 234 9
UPWARDS (1)
   WITH SUFFERING FROM CONCEPTION UPWARDS, AND THERE ....PERSEUS 83 26
URGE (1)
   YET ALWAYS THE RIDICULOUS NUDE FLANKS URGE ....TALE OF A TUB 25 33
URGED (1)
   WHAT FURY URGED HIM SLAY ....THE QUEEN'S COMPLAINT 28 9
URINOUS (1)
   STILL URINOUS ON YOU, A SIN. .........................EAVESDROPPER 260 8
US (100)
USAGE (1)
   O THE BEAUTY OF USAGE! POEM.1.WHO. 131 19
USAGES (1)
   BASTARDIES, USAGES, DESERTIONS AND DOUBLENESS, ...COURAGE. 210 7
USE (13)
   AND FIT FOR USE. ....TINKER JACK AND THE TIDY WIVES 34 22
   BORNE, FOR A USE BEYOND MY ....MUSSEL HUNTER AT ROCK HARBOR 96 37
   WE GAVE GOOD USE AS SHIP AND HOUSE IS BLACK*GREEN ROCK, WINTHROP BAY 105 11
   O OEDIPUS. O CHRIST. YOU USE ME ILL. ....THE RAVAGED FACE 116 14
   THE CHINESE LADIES USE ....POLLY'S TREE 128 13
   I AM USED. I AM DRUMMED INTO USE. ....THREE WOMEN 180 145
   BY THE TIME THE WHOLE OF IT WAS DELIVERED, AND TOO NUMB TO
      USE IT. ....A BIRTHDAY PRESENT 208 54
   NO USE, NO USE, NOW, BEGGING RECOGNIZE! ....AMNESIAC 232 1

USE (CONT.)
    NO USE, NO USE, NOW, BEGGING RECOGNIZE! ....AMNESIAC   232   1
    NO USE WHISTLING FOR LYONNESSE! ....LYONNESSE   233   1
    AS IS THE USE WITH VAMPIRES, AND RESIGN OUR STAND ......DIALOGUE O.   285 330
    I THOUGHT EARTH MIGHT USE YOU. ....THE RIVAL/DR   291   22
    THEIR DEATH-PEGS STUD YOUR GLOVES, IT IS NO USE RUNNING.   STINGS/DR   293   8
USED (9)
    AND USED HER GENTLE DOVES WITH MANNERS RUDE: THE QUEEN'S COMPLAINT   28   7
    I USED TO THINK WE MIGHT MAKE A GO OF IT TOGETHER -- ....IN PLASTER   160   50
    THE FEW I AM USED TO ARE PLAIN AND DURABLE; *STARS OVER THE DORDOGNE 166   28
    I AM USED. I AM DRUMMED INTO USE. ....THREE WOMEN 180 145
    MEN HAVE USED HER MEANLY. SHE WILL EAT THEM. ....THREE WOMEN 181 159
    I USED TO PRAY TO RECOVER YOU. ....DADDY   222   14
    NOT A TOE, NOT A FINGER, AND USED, ...MYSTIC 268   12
    USED UTTERLY, IN THE SUN'S CONFLAGRATIONS, THE STAINS ....MYSTIC 268   13
    SHE IS USED TO THIS SORT OF THING. ....EDGE 273   19
USEFUL (1)
    AND I SHALL BE USEFUL WHEN I LIE DOWN FINALLY: ....I AM VERTICAL 162   19
USELESS (2)
    I AM RESTLESS. RESTLESS AND USELESS. I, TOO, CREATE CORPSES. *THREE. 182 189
    ITS RUNNING IS USELESS. ....TOTEM 264   3
USUAL (5)
    BUT SCRUPULOUSLY REFLECTS THE USUAL TERROR. ....TALE OF A TUB   24   8
    QUIT THEIR USUAL HABITATIONS. ....THE MANOR GARDEN   125   18
    AS USUAL THERE IS NO FACE. A LUMP OF CHINESE WHITE ......SURGEON.   170   7
    IT IS USUAL, THEY SAY, FOR SUCH A THING TO HAPPEN. .....THREE WOMEN 183 242
    IT IS USUAL IN MY LIFE, AND THE LIVES OF OTHERS. ....THREE WOMEN 183 243
USURPED (1)
    HIS CROWN USURPED BY THE LOW BROW ....NATURAL HISTORY   71   11
USURPING (1)
    AND TO SANCTUARY: USURPING THE ARMCHAIR ....ALL THE DEAD DEARS 71   31
UTTER (2)
    THAT OWL VOICE SOLE "YES", WHILE COWS UTTER ....WREATH FOR A BRIDAL   44   3
    AND A SKY LIKE A PIG'S BACKSIDE, AN UTTER LACK OF ATTENTION. ...
                                        ... FOR A FATHERLESS SON 205   5
UTTERANCE (1)
    OF SOME GODLY UTTERANCE WAKENED HEADS IGNORE: ....GHOST'S.   90   17
UTTERING (1)
    UTTERING NOTHING BUT BLOOD -- ....CHILDLESS WOMAN 259   13
UTTERLY (7)
    PURPLE AND RED MOUTHS, UTTERLY LOVELY. POEM.1.WHO.   132   30
    TO LIE WITH MY HANDS TURNED UP AND BE UTTERLY EMPTY. ....TULIPS 161   30
    AND UTTERLY IGNORANT OF THE WAY IT TOOK. ....WIDOW 165   35
    AND ETERNITY ENGULFS IT, AND I DROWN UTTERLY? ....THREE WOMEN 179 105
    INFINITE, GREEN, UTTERLY UNTOUCHABLE. ................APPREHENSIONS 195   2
    UTTERLY UNASKED FOR ....POPPIES IN OCTOBER 240   5
    USED UTTERLY, IN THE SUN'S CONFLAGRATIONS, THE STAINS ....MYSTIC 268   13
UTTERS (1)
    IT UTTERS SUCH DARK SOUNDS IT CANNOT BE GOOD. ....THREE WOMEN 182 217
VACANCY (1)
    MADE A HOLE IN THE HOT DAY, A VACANCY. ....THE RABBIT CATCHER 194   18
VACANT (2)
    A POLICEMAN POINTS OUT A VACANT CLIFF ....WHITSUN 154   18
    WIDOW: THAT GREAT, VACANT ESTATE! ....WIDOW 164   21
VACATION (2)
    WELL, ONE WEARIES OF THE PUBLIC GARDENS: ONE WANTS A VACATION ...
                           ... TWO CAMPERS IN CLOUD COUNTRY 144   7
    BLUE VIEWS ARE BOARDED UP; OUR SWEET VACATION ....TWO LOVERS. 327   3
VACUOUS (2)
    ARE SPREADING THEIR VACUOUS SHEETS. ....LITTLE FUGUE 188   42
    IN YOUR VACUOUS BLACK, ...YEARS 255   7
VAGUE (3)
    VAGUE AS FOG AND LOOKED FOR LIKE MAIL. ....YOU'RE 141   10
    HER BLUE EYES SWAM WITH VAGUE TERROR. ....BITTER STRAWBERRIES 300   24
    OF VAGUE VOCABULARY ....NOTES TO A NEOPHYTE 306   8
VAIN (5)
    EACH VAIN GIRL'S DRIVEN ....VANITY FAIR 33   25
    THAT VAIN JADES SULK SINGLE DOWN BRIDAL NIGHTS, ...ELLA MASON A. 54   41
    THAN PRIEST'S HANDS, INVOKE NO VAIN ....SCULPTOR   91   6
    DEAD, YOU'D SWEAR HIM A VICTIM OF OUR OWN VAIN ....DIALOGUE O. 278   82
    FROM ASKING, BUT INVENTIVE, HOPES: IN VAIN ..........METAMORPHOSES. 307   11
VALEDICTORY (1)
    A SNAG IS LIFTING A VALEDICTORY, PALE HAND; .....CROSSING THE WATER 190   9
VALENTINE (1)
    WEARS A VALENTINE ....POLLY'S TREE 129   38
VALENTINE-FACES (1)
    OF VALENTINE-FACES MIGHT PLEASE A COLLECTOR: ....A LIFE 150   17
VALENTINO'S (1)
    WITH VALENTINO'S CRACK TECHNICAL TALENT ....DIALOGUE EN ROUTE 309   22
VALLEY (6)
    UP FROM THE FISSURED VALLEY AND HUNG SHOULDER-HIGH *HARDCASTLE CRAGS   62   14
    HERE IN THIS VALLEY OF DISCREET ACADEMIES ....ABOVE THE OXBOW   87   1
    IN THAT VALLEY THE TRAIN SHRIEKS ECHO LIKE SOULS ON HOOKS. ...
                                     ... THE DETECTIVE 208   5
    THAT IS THE VALLEY OF DEATH, THOUGH THE COWS THRIVE. THE DETECTIVE 208   6

VALLEY (CONT.)
    THEY CONVERSE IN THE VALLEY OF YOUR FINGERS, THEY ARE INCHWORMS. ...
                                                 ... GULLIVER   251   17
    HILL AND VALLEY STIFFEN ROW ON ROW. ....PROLOGUE TO SPRING   322   6
VALLEYS (3)
    VALLEYS OF GRASS ALTERING ....THE GREAT CARBUNCLE   72   4
    TO PEOPLE WHO LIVE IN THE BOTTOM OF VALLEYS ....ABOVE THE OXBOW   88   15
    NOW, IN VALLEYS NARROW ....WUTHERING HEIGHTS   168   43
VALOR (1)
    TAUNTS US TO VALOR. BLUE SAILORS SANG THAT OUR JOURNEY ..CHANNEL C.   27   20
VALUABLE (5)
    BLOOMS OUT OF A VASE OF NOT VERY VALUABLE PORCELAIN, ...IN PLASTER   159   17
    WHERE ARE THE EYE-STONES, YELLOW AND VALUABLE, ...BERCK-PLAGE   198   53
    O JEWEL! O VALUABLE! ....LESBOS   229   52
    SO VALUABLE! ....PURDAH   242   8
    I AM YOUR VALUABLE, ...LADY LAZARUS   246   68
VALVES (1)
    PLIANT VALVES: ....AQUATIC NOCTURNE   305   15
VAMPIRE (2)
    SHE IS THE VAMPIRE OF US ALL. SO SHE SUPPORTS US, ...THREE WOMEN   181 155
    THE VAMPIRE WHO SAID HE WAS YOU ....DADDY   224   72
VAMPIRES (1)
    AS IS THE USE WITH VAMPIRES, AND RESIGN OUR STAND ......DIALOGUE O.   285 330
VAMPIRING (1)
    VAMPIRING DRY OF MILK EACH GREAT GOAT UDDER. ....GOATSUCKER   111   4
VAN (1)
    FOR THE MILK VAN ....RESOLVE   52   4
VANE (1)
    AND THE FRAGMENTS WHIR LIKE A WEATHER VANE ...CIRCUS IN THREE RINGS   321   5
VANISH (5)
    DESPITE HER WRUNG HANDS, HER TEARS, HER PRAYING: VANISH!*LADY AND T.   70   30
    WILL VANISH IN A DAY. ....LADY LAZARUS   244   15
    IN SLEEP. THE CHAIRS WON'T VANISH OR BECOME ....DIALOGUE O.   286 355
    ONLY TO VANISH WITH DEVILISH EASE ....CIRCUS IN THREE RINGS   322   17
    IT'S TIME TO VANISH LIKE THE CHESHIRE CAT ....A SORCERER B.   324   12
VANISHES (2)
    HAPPENS IN DARKNESS, VANISHES ....BLUE MOLES   127   35
    VANISHES IN A LABYRINTH OF HAY ....THE PRINCESS AND THE GOBLINS   335   70
VANISHING (1)
    AN OLD MAN IS VANISHING. ....BERCK-PLAGE   198   51
VANITY (1)
    VANITY FAIR ....VANITY FAIR   32   T
VAPORISH (1)
    VAPORISH AS FROST-BREATH, ...POLLY'S TREE   128   10
VAPORIZATION (1)
    IT IS A CASE OF VAPORIZATION. ....THE DETECTIVE   209   26
VAPOROUS (1)
    LIFE, ITS OWN VAPOROUS WAYFARINGS. ....LANDOWNERS   53   15
VAPORS (1)
    AND SEEMS TO DIE: SO VAPORS ....FULL FATHOM FIVE   93   19
VARIANTS (1)
    RED AGAINST FIFTY VARIANTS OF GREEN, ...YADWIGHA.   85   19
VARIETY (2)
    THE GLAZE, THE MIRRORY VARIETY OF IT. ....A BIRTHDAY PRESENT   207   25
    I DIE WITH VARIETY -- ....THE JAILER   227   34
VARIOUS (2)
    OF VARIOUS WEATHERS IS ....CHILD'S PARK STONES   101   21
    VARIOUS METALS. ....DARK WOOD, DARK WATER   127   14
VASE (5)
    IT HAD OPENED ITS ORANGE IN MY VASE, ...RHODODENDRON.   103   9
    THE VASE, RECONSTRUCTED, HOUSES POEM.7.S.   137   41
    YOU HANDED ME GIN IN A GLASS BUD VASE. ....LEAVING EARLY   146   41
    BLOOMS OUT OF A VASE OF NOT VERY VALUABLE PORCELAIN, ...IN PLASTER   159   17
    O VASE OF ACID, ...LESBOS   229   71
VAST (3)
    TO HALT FOR A SWIG AT THE PINK TEATS. NO. THIS VAST ....SOW   61   23
    AND THE DECLINE OF EMPIRES THE THICK COIL OF A VAST ....PERSEUS   83   23
    PALM-SPEAR AND LILY DISTINCT AS FLORA IN THE VAST ....A LIFE   149   4
VASTLY (1)
    BUNCHES ITS KNOBBY BROWNS ON A VASTLY ....POEMS, POTATOES   106   12
VAT (1)
    LADY, WHO ARE THESE OTHERS IN THE MOON'S VAT -- POEM.3.MAENAD.   133   22
VATICAN (1)
    GHASTLY VATICAN. ....MEDUSA   225   36
VATS (1)
    OF THE DEATH VATS CLUNG TO THEM; ....TWO VIEWS OF A CADAVER ROOM   114   4
VAULT (1)
    FED ME BANANA GAS THROUGH A FROG-MASK. THE NAUSEOUS VAULT *FACE LIFT   156   5
VAULTED (3)
    MY FATHER KEPT A VAULTED CONCH ....ON THE DECLINE OF ORACLES   78   1
    BUZZED AND ASSAILED THE VAULTED BRAINCHAMBER. SUICIDE OFF EGG ROCK   115   18
    NOW WE, RETURNING FROM THE VAULTED DOMES ....DOOM OF EXILES   318   1
VAUNT (1)
    WE VAUNT OUR DAYS IN NEON AND SCORN THE DARK. ......SONNET: TO TIME   311   4

TITLE   PAGE LINE

VAUNTING (1)
   THE VAUNTING MIND ....ON THE DIFFICULTY OF CONJURING UP A DRYAD 66   5
VEERS (1)
   VEERS TO HER SLOUCH. ....STRUMPET SONG 33   8
VEGETARIAN (1)
   DROLL, VEGETARIAN, THE WATER RAT *WATERCOLOR OF GRANTCHESTER MEADOWS 112 22
VEIL (10)
   WHAT IS THIS, BEHIND THIS VEIL, IS IT UGLY, IS IT BEAUTIFUL? ...
                         ... A BIRTHDAY PRESENT 206   1
   ONLY LET DOWN THE VEIL, THE VEIL, THE VEIL. .....A BIRTHDAY PRESENT 208 55
   ONLY LET DOWN THE VEIL, THE VEIL, THE VEIL. .....A BIRTHDAY PRESENT 208 55
   ONLY LET DOWN THE VEIL, THE VEIL, THE VEIL. .....A BIRTHDAY PRESENT 208 55
   AND A BLACK VEIL THAT MOLDS TO MY FACE, THEY ARE MAKING ME ONE
       OF THEM. ....THE BEE MEETING 211 22
   IN MY MOON SUIT AND FUNERAL VEIL. ....THE ARRIVAL OF THE BEE BOX 213 32
   VEIL STIRS ITS CURTAIN ....PURDAH 243 25
   VEIL IS ....PURDAH 243 27
   THE BLACK VEIL MOLDS TO YOUR LIPS: ....STINGS/DR 293   9
   YOUR SILVER VEIL ....MOONSONG AT MORNING 317 14
VEILING (2)
   ALREADY VEILING THE GRAY SPOOL OF STONE ....SPIDER 48 18
   WRAPPED UP IN THEMSELVES AS IN THICK VEILING ....ON DECK 142   2
VEILS (6)
   NOW THERE ARE THESE VEILS, SHIMMERING LIKE CURTAINS, ...BIRTHDAY. 206 16
   IF YOU ONLY KNEW HOW THE VEILS WERE KILLING MY DAYS. .....BIRTHDAY. 207 37
   THEY ARE SMILING AND TAKING OUT VEILS TACKED TO ANCIENT HATS. BEE. 211   5
   UNDERGOING THE FAUCET WATER, ITS VEILS, VEILS IN A NUNNERY,*GETTING. 248 23
   UNDERGOING THE FAUCET WATER, ITS VEILS, VEILS IN A NUNNERY,*GETTING. 248 23
   IN GLASS PAGODAS HUNG WITH VEILS OF GREEN ....APRIL AUBADE 312   2
VEIN (7)
   ABOVE THE SIMPLE VEIN, ...RECANTATION 42 15
   AND A LANGUOR OF WAX CONGEALS THE VEIN   EPITAPH FOR FIRE AND FLOWER 46 31
   FREE OF THE FICTIVE VEIN. WHEN ONE STARK SKELETON*NOVEMBER GRAVEYARD 56 10
   FROM MY WORLDLING LOOK ITS BRILLIANT VEIN *ON THE PLETHORA OF DRYADS 67 10
   DEATH'S TWO DREAMS DOWN WITH THE BODY THAT BLED THE VEIN, ...
                  ... DIALOGUE OVER A OUIJA BOARD 285 329
   AND SAP ASCENDS THE STEEPLE OF THE VEIN. ....APRIL AUBADE 312   4
   ALONG THE VEIN, ...MOONSONG AT MORNING 316   4
VEINING (1)
   CROW'S-FEET COPY VEINING ON STAINED LEAF; ....VANITY FAIR 32   7
VEINS (8)
   ALONG RED NETWORK OF HIS VEINS ....PURSUIT 22 11
   THEY GO BEFORE: OPENING THE VEINS, ...BLUE MOLES 126 29
   THEIR VEINS WHITE AS PORKFAT. POEM.1.WHO. 131 18
   SUCH BLUE CURRENTS IN THE VIENS OF MY LOVED ONE! .....AN APPEARANCE 189   2
   MARBLE FACADES WITH BLUE VEINS, AND JELLY-GLASSFULS OF DAFFODILS. ...
                           ... BERCK-PLAGE 199 89
   MY VEINS GLOW LIKE TREES. ....BURNING THE LETTERS 205 48
   FILLING MY VEINS WITH INVISIBLES, WITH THE MILLION ....BIRTHDAY. 207 42
   OUR SEPARATE VEINS AND THIS GLASS MOUTH. OH YOU'RE .....DIALOGUE O. 280 147
VEINS' (1)
   WE HEFT GLOBED FLINT, RACKED IN VEINS' BARBED BINDINGS; ...FIRESONG 30 18
VELVET (5)
   UPHOLSTERED IN RED VELVET, UNDER THE EYE ....YADWIGHA. 85   3
   ON A RED VELVET COUCH WITHIN YOUR GREEN- ....YADWIGHA. 86 26
   THE VELVET DODGES OF THE HYPOCRITE: ....THE RAVAGED FACE 116 11
   VELVET PILLOWS THE COLOUR OF BLOOD PUDDING ....LEAVING EARLY 145   5
   A PALACE OF VELVET ....GIGOLO 267   5
VELVETS (1)
   I ENJOY PETTICOATS AND VELVETS AND GOSSIP OF COURT, ..QUEEN MARY'S. 290 21
VENGEANCE (2)
   A LESSON IN VENGEANCE ....A LESSON IN VENGEANCE 80   T
   THE COLORS ASSERT THEMSELVES WITH A SORT OF VENGEANCE. ...TWO CAMP. 145 14
VENOM (1)
   WHAT GREENHORN VENTS HIS VENOM AGAINST GIANTS ....DIALOGUE O. 281 199
VENOM-GIRT (1)
   WHILE SHE STANDS BURNING, VENOM-GIRT, ...BUCOLICS 24 23
VENOMOUS (2)
   FLOATS OUR HEADS, TWO VENOMOUS OPPOSITES, ...LESBOS 228 36
   SAID EVE: "I WISH VENOMOUS NEMATODES ....DIALOGUE EN ROUTE 309 19
VENTRILOQUY (2)
   VENTRILOQUY. BUT WINGS NEITHER YOU NOR I ....DIALOGUE O. 278 83
   IN GAY VENTRILOQUY FROM WING TO WING ....LOVE IS A PARALLAX 330 47
VENTS (1)
   WHAT GREENHORN VENTS HIS VENOM AGAINST GIANTS ....DIALOGUE O. 281 199
VENTURE (1)
   THERE'S NO CAREER IN THE VENTURE ....THE TIMES ARE TIDY 107   6
VENUS (5)
   AS VENUS, PEDESTALED ON A HALF-SHELL ....HEAVY WOMEN 158   2
   AND VOLUPTUOUS VENUS TO COME ....DIALOGUE EN ROUTE 309 29
   AND VIRGINS RISE WHERE LUSTFUL VENUS LAY: ....NEVER TRY TO TRICK. 319   5
   BUT FOUND RADIANT VENUS ..ON LOOKING INTO THE EYES OF A DEMON LOVER 325 23
   PROBING FRACTURED VENUS WITH A STICK ....TWO LOVERS. 327 15
VERANDA (1)
   FOUR-WAY VERANDA, VIEW-KEEPING ABOVE ....ABOVE THE OXBOW 88 36

                                                          TITLE   PAGE LINE
VERB (3)
   ATHLETIC THAN A VERB, ...TRIO OF LOVE SONGS   314   18
   AND AUCTION OFF EACH RARE WHITE-RABBIT VERB; ....A SORCERER B.   324   6
   IN THE MORTAL ACTIVE VERB, ...TOUCH-AND-GO   336   18
VERDIGRIS (1)
   VERDIGRIS OF THE CONDOR. ....DEATH & CO.   254   9
VERGED (1)
   ROCK-FACE, CRAB-CLAW VERGED ON GREEN. *THE HERMIT AT OUTERMOST HOUSE   119   18
VERMILION (1)
   HIS LITTLE VERMILION EYE ....MEDALLION   124   9
VERMILIONS (2)
   VERMILIONS, BRONZES, COLORS OF THE SUN ....OUIJA   77   6
   EACH DAY CONCLUDES IN A HUGE SPLURGE OF VERMILIONS ....TWO CAMP.   145   15
VERNACULAR (2)
   AND GOSSIPS IN ITS LOOSE VERNACULAR, ...A WINTER SHIP   113   19
   VERNACULAR AS THE STRUT ....NOTES TO A NEOPHYTE   306   4
VERNON (1)
   ON PINCKNEY, MOUNT VERNON, CHESTNUT, ...A WINTER'S TALE   87   25
VERONICAS (1)
   IT TAKES PATIENCE. IF VERONICAS AND FOUNTAINS ....DIALOGUE O.   282 221
VERSATILE (1)
   TO VIEW HOW VERSATILE WE ARE: YOU'VE PAMPERED ....DIALOGUE O.   280 137
VERSE (1)
   A VERSE DIALOGUE ....DIALOGUE OVER A OUIJA BOARD   276   ST
VERTICAL (3)
   STALLED, LET FALL THEIR VERTICAL ....NIGHT SHIFT   76   18
   I AM VERTICAL ....I AM VERTICAL   162   T
   IN A ROCKETING VERTICAL CLOCKCASE, ...DIALOGUE EN ROUTE   308   5
VERVE (1)
   AND WITH A PERFIDIOUS VERVE ....THE BEGGARS   48   20
VERY (19)
   THIS IS A DARK HOUSE, VERY BIG. POEM.2.DARK.   132   1
   OVERNIGHT, VERY ....MUSHROOMS 139   1
   VERY QUIETLY ....MUSHROOMS   139   3
   THAT GLIDE AHEAD OF THE VERY THIRSTY. ...SLEEP IN THE MOJAVE DESERT   144   13
   BLOOMS OUT OF A VASE OF NOT VERY VALUABLE PORCELAIN, ...IN PLASTER   159   17
   I AM SLOW AS THE WORLD. I AM VERY PATIENT, ...THREE WOMEN   176   1
   THE DAY IS BLAZING. IT IS VERY MOURNFUL. ....THREE WOMEN   184 262
   THERE IS VERY LITTLE TO GO INTO MY SUITCASE. ....THREE WOMEN   184 266
   IF I STAND VERY STILL, THEY WILL THINK I AM COW-PARSLEY, ...BEE.   212   39
   IS SHE HIDING, IS SHE EATING HONEY? SHE IS VERY CLEVER. ....BEE.   212   43
   ARE NOT VERY PURE OR TRUE. ....DADDY   223   37
   RED STIGMATA AT THE VERY CENTER, ...MEDUSA   225   9
   IT IS VERY LATE. ....BY CANDLELIGHT   236   7
   WITH HER WIGGLY FINGERS AND FOR A VERY SMALL FEE. ....THE TOUR   238   47
   AND THERE IS A CHARGE, A VERY LARGE CHARGE ....LADY LAZARUS   246   61
   THE BLOOD BERRIES ARE THEMSELVES, THEY ARE VERY STILL. ....YEARS   255   23
   OUT OF OUR VERY COUNTENANCE BY SIMPLY ..DIALOGUE OVER A OUIJA BOARD   279 114
   THE NIGHT IS A BLUE POOL; SHE IS VERY STILL. ....ELM/DR   292   6
   AT THE CENTER SHE IS STILL, VERY STILL WITH WISDOM. ....ELM/DR   292   7
VESSEL (1)
   AND THE PRIEST IS A VESSEL, ...BERCK-PLAGE   200 113
VETERAN (2)
   IN THE EAR OF THE VETERAN, AND AGAIN ....BLUE MOLES   126   20
   TREPANNED VETERAN, ...CUT   236   38
VEXED (1)
   RUEFUL, MOST VEXED, THAT TENDER SKIN ....BUCOLICS   24   17
VIBRATIONS (1)
   A SANDY DAMPER KILLS THE VIBRATIONS; ....BERCK-PLAGE   196   7
VICE (1)
   A VICE OF KNIVES, ...NICK AND THE CANDLESTICK   241   16
VICIOUSNESS (1)
   VICIOUSNESS IN THE KITCHEN! ....LESBOS   227   1
VICTIM (2)
   LITTLE VICTIM UNEARTHED BY SOME LARGE CREATURE ....BLUE MOLES   126   6
   DEAD, YOU'D SWEAR HIM A VICTIM OF OUR OWN VAIN ....DIALOGUE O.   278   82
VICTIMS (1)
   COULD NOT REMAIN OUTLANDISH VICTIMS ....THE THIN PEOPLE   64   24
VICTORIAN (2)
   AS VICTORIAN CUSHIONS. THIS FAMILY ....A LIFE   150   16
   IN MY VICTORIAN NIGHTGOWN. ....MORNING SONG   157   14
VICTORIANA (1)
   THE LAST OF VICTORIANA. ....NICK AND THE CANDLESTICK   241   34
VICTORIOUS (1)
   AND SINEWS BUNCHED, VICTORIOUS, AS THE COSMIC ....PERSEUS   83   44
VICTORY (1)
   THE LAST BADGE OF VICTORY. ....THE SWARM   217   41
VIENNA (2)
   AND I REMEMBER MY MATERNAL GRANDMOTHER FROM VIENNA. ....CANDLES   149   17
   THE SNOWS OF THE TYROL, THE CLEAR BEER OF VIENNA ....DADDY   223   36
VIES (1)
   VIES WITH BEST QUEEN OVER ....VANITY FAIR   33   31
VIEW (8)
   AND OCTOPUS -- SCRABBLING JUST BEYOND THE VIEW, ...TALE OF A TUB   25   20
   SUCH FORCE CAN LAST; BUT BEYOND, THE NEUTRAL VIEW   CHANNEL CROSSING   26   7
                                     545

```
                                           TITLE             PAGE  LINE
VIEW (CONT.)
    THEY MOUND A SUMMER COOLNESS IN OUR VIEW. ..........ABOVE THE OXBOW   88   14
    MAKESHIFT OF A VIEW TO QUIT ...............GREEN ROCK, WINTHROP BAY  105    7
    THIS IS NO TIME FOR THE PRIVATE POINT OF VIEW. ............CANDLES  149   13
    THE SKULLS, THE UNBUCKLED BONES FACING THE VIEW! ..WAKING IN WINTER  151   10
    ON THIS HILL, WITH ITS VIEW OF LIT CASTLES, EACH SWUNG BELL   STARS. 166   38
    TO VIEW HOW VERSATILE WE ARE: YOU'VE PAMPERED .........DIALOGUE O.  280  137
VIEW-KEEPER (1)
    TIME, AND TO GRACES GONE WITH THE TIME. A STATE VIEW-KEEPER   OXBOW. 88 39-40
VIEW-KEEPING (1)
    FOUR-WAY VERANDA, VIEW-KEEPING ABOVE ...............ABOVE THE OXBOW   88   36
VIEWPOINTS (1)
    OF STATE SCENERY, SELLS SODA, SHOWS OFF VIEWPOINTS. *ABOVE THE OXBOW  88   41
VIEWS (3)
    TWO VIEWS OF WITHENS .........................TWO VIEWS OF WITHENS   71    T
    TWO VIEWS OF A CADAVER ROOM ...........TWO VIEWS OF A CADAVER ROOM  114    T
    BLUE VIEWS ARE BOARDED UP; OUR SWEET VACATION ..........TWO LOVERS.  327    3
VIGIL (2)
    THEY STAND THEIR VIGIL IN GOWNS OF STONE, ....THE DISQUIETING MUSES   76   50
    GULLS STIFFEN TO THEIR CHILL VIGIL IN THE DRAFTY HALF-LIGHT; ...
                                  ... PARLIAMENT HILL FIELDS  153   49
VILLA (1)
    ALL SUMMER WE MOVED IN A VILLA BRIMFUL OF ECHOES, ....THE OTHER TWO   68    1
VILLAGE (3)
    VILLAGE STORIES GO THAT IN OLDEN DAYS*ELLA MASON AND HER ELEVEN CATS  53   13
    THE DREAM-PEOPLED VILLAGE, HER EYES ENTERTAINED NO DREAM, ...
                                  ... HARDCASTLE CRAGS   63   19
    TO PETRIFY YOUR EYES, AND EVERY VILLAGE ....................PERSEUS   83   21
VILLAGERS (5)
    WHO ARE THESE PEOPLE AT THE BRIDGE TO MEET ME? THEY ARE THE
             VILLAGERS --- ...............................THE BEE MEETING 211    1
    THE VILLAGERS OPEN THE CHAMBERS, THEY ARE HUNTING THE QUEEN. ..BEE.  212   42
    THE VILLAGERS ARE MOVING THE VIRGINS, THERE WILL BE NO KILLING.*BEE.  212   49
    THE VILLAGERS ARE UNTYING THEIR DISGUISES, THEY ARE SHAKING HANDS. ...
                                  ... THE BEE MEETING  212   54
    AND THE VILLAGERS NEVER LIKED YOU. ...........................DADDY  224   77
VILLANELLE (2)
    A VILLANELLE ...........................TO EVA DESCENDING THE STAIR  303   ST
    A VILLANELLE ...........................................LAMENT  315   ST
VILLAS (1)
    THESE STORYBOOK VILLAS ........................SOUTHERN SUNRISE   26    2
VINE (2)
    GREEN, ALSO, THE GRAPES ON THE GREEN VINE ................DEPARTURE   51    2
    FROM THE VINE ...........................YADDO: THE GRAND MANOR  123    6
VINEGAR (3)
    DRINKING VINEGAR FROM TIN CUPS: THEY WORE ..........THE THIN PEOPLE   64   20
    IN VINEGAR LIKE SAINTS' RELICS. ..............THE SURGEON AT 2 A.M.  171   39
    MY TEARS LIKE VINEGAR, ........................................JILTED  304    2
VINEGARY (1)
    ALREADY HALF UNSTRUNG. A VINEGARY FUME   TWO VIEWS OF A CADAVER ROOM  114    3
VIOLATES (1)
    AND VIOLATES CELESTIAL CUSTOM ..INSOLENT STORM STRIKES AT THE SKULL  326   31
VIOLATION (1)
    NO VIOLATION BUT GIVES DIVIDENDS .........METAMORPHOSES OF THE MOON  307   13
VIOLENCE (3)
    MEEK AND PROUD BOTH FALL; STARK VIOLENCE ..........CHANNEL CROSSING   27   30
    MADE TO DO VIOLENCE ON, ...............................STRUMPET SONG   33   10
    A WIND OF SUCH VIOLENCE ....................................ELM  192   20
VIOLENT (2)
    IT'S VIOLENT. WE'RE HERE ON A VISIT, ...................STOPPED DEAD  230   11
    THEM HUGE AGAIN, VIOLENT GIANTS ON THE WALL. ........BY CANDLELIGHT  236   14
VIOLET (2)
    OF WINDOWS WITH ODD VIOLET PANES. ...................A WINTER'S TALE   87   30
    NOURISHING AS VIOLET LEAVES .... ....................APRIL 18  302   10
VIOLETS (1)
    THE NIGHT BRINGS VIOLETS, ...............................PARALYTIC  266   11
VIOLINS (3)
    BEGIN ON TILTED VIOLINS TO SPAN ......................CINDERELLA  303    4
    BOTH SERAPH SONG AND VIOLINS ARE DUMB; .............DOOM OF EXILES  318    7
    AND SEPARATE THE FLUTES FROM VIOLINS: ..........LOVE IS A PARALLAX  330   50
VIOLS (1)
    LULLAYED BY SUSURROUS LYRES AND VIOLS. ............ALICANTE LULLABY   43   21
VIPERS (1)
    ALOUD, CROSSLEGGED ON THE STERN SEAT, FROM THE GENERATION
             OF VIPERS. .............................THE BABYSITTERS  175   32
VIRGIN (9)
    THE OTHER, WRY VIRGIN TO THE LAST, .......TWO SISTERS OF PERSEPHONE   32   26
    AGAINST VIRGIN PRAYER ........................................VANITY FAIR   33   21
    IN A CLENCH OF BLOOD, THE SLEEP-TALKING VIRGIN ............MAUDLIN   51    2
    VIRGIN IN A TREE ....................................VIRGIN IN A TREE   81    T
    ALL AMOROUS ARROWS. FOR TO SHEATHE THE VIRGIN SHAPE*VIRGIN IN A TREE   81    7
    THIS VIRGIN ON HER RACK: ..........................VIRGIN IN A TREE   82   35
    THE WHITE HIVE IS SNUG AS A VIRGIN, ................THE BEE MEETING  212   34
    OPENING, IN SPRING, LIKE AN INDUSTRIOUS VIRGIN ..............STINGS  215   35
    VIRGIN .....................................................FEVER.  232   47
```

```
                                              TITLE            PAGE LINE
VIRGINAL (2)
    I AM FLAT AND VIRGINAL, WHICH MEANS NOTHING HAS HAPPENED,  ...THREE.  184 276
    AMONG THE BLANCHED, BOILED INSTRUMENTS, THE VIRGINAL CURTAINS. ...
                                                  ... FEVER./DR  294    8
VIRGINITY'S (1)
    OF VIRGINS FOR VIRGINITY'S SAKE." ...............VIRGIN IN A TREE   82   30
VIRGINS (6)
    GREEN VIRGINS, CONSECRATING LIMB AND LIP ........VIRGIN IN A TREE   82   27
    OF VIRGINS FOR VIRGINITY'S SAKE." ...............VIRGIN IN A TREE   82   30
    WHILE IN THEIR FINGERJOINT CELLS THE NEW VIRGINS ...THE BEE MEETING 212   45
    THE VILLAGERS ARE MOVING THE VIRGINS, THERE WILL BE NO KILLING.*BEE. 212  49
    AREN'T VOUCHSAFED TO ANTIQUE VIRGINS ONLY: .............DIALOGUE O. 282  220
    AND VIRGINS RISE WHERE LUSTFUL VENUS LAY: ......NEVER TRY TO TRICK. 319    5
VIRGIN'S (1)
    ASSAULT A SLEEPING VIRGIN'S SHROUD ..................DANSE MACABRE 321   14
VIRGINS' (1)
    THAN VIRGINS' TEARS. THAT BAWDY QUEEN OF DEATH, ..............OUIJA  77   24
VIRIDIAN (1)
    THE BARBAROUS HOLLY WITH ITS VIRIDIAN ..........LETTER IN NOVEMBER 253   19
VIRILE (1)
    EACH VIRILE BACHELOR DREADS PARALYSIS, .........NEVER TRY TO TRICK. 320  10
VIRTUES (1)
    TWO VIRTUES RIDE, BY STALLION, BY NAG, ....THE DEATH OF MYTH-MAKING 104    1
VIRULENCE (1)
    THROUGH A STILL VIRULENCE, ............................BERCK-PLAGE 197   35
VISAGE (1)
    YET, SHRINED ON HER SHELF, THE GRISLY VISAGE ENDURED, ..LADY AND T.  70   29
VISIBILITIES (1)
    MY VISIBILITIES HIDE. .......................................PURDAH 242  17
VISIBLE (5)
    SCARCELY VISIBLE. ABOUT AND ABOUT THE SLOPE .................SPIDER  48   14
    VISIBLE ONLY TO THE PARAGON HEART, .......ON THE PLETHORA OF DRYADS  67    3
    IS VISIBLE. THE SNAKE-SCALES HAVE BECOME .............SNAKECHARMER   79   13
    THEY SEEM LARGE, YET THEY DROP, AND NO GAP IS VISIBLE. ......STARS. 165    5
    VOICES STAND BACK AND FLATTEN. THEIR VISIBLE HIEROGLYPHS*THREE WOMEN 179  96
VISION (10)
    TILL YOUR EYES FOIST A VISION DAZZLING ON THE WIND: ....NOVEMBER G.  56   14
    DREAM-FILMED. WHAT A VISION OF ANCIENT HOGHOOD MUST ...........SOW   61   27
    AS NYMPHS; COLD VISION ...ON THE DIFFICULTY OF CONJURING UP A DRYAD  66   30
    WORTHLESS SUCH VISION TO EYES GONE DULL ..ON THE DECLINE OF ORACLES  78   30
    HORIZONS BEYOND VISION, SPILL VISION ...............ABOVE THE OXBOW  88   24
    HORIZONS BEYOND VISION, SPILL VISION ...............ABOVE THE OXBOW  88   24
    FRINGE OF MUNDANE VISION, THIS GHOST GOES ..THE GHOST'S LEAVETAKING  90   22
    VISION, WISDOM, FOR BODIES ................................SCULPTOR  91    3
    AND TRICKED US TO TRUST HIS VISION, WHILE NIGHT AFTER NIGHT HE ...
                                  ... DIALOGUE OVER A OUIJA BOARD 279  104
    WITH TINSEL VISION ..........................MOONSONG AT MORNING   316    3
VISIONARY (2)
    NO VISIONARY LIGHTNINGS ..................ON THE PLETHORA OF DRYADS  67   23
    A VISIONARY LADDER TOWARD THE MOON ....THE PRINCESS AND THE GOBLINS 333    5
VISIONS (1)
    I KNEW HE'D GOT IT MIXED BEFORE: VISIONS*DIALOGUE OVER A OUIJA BOARD 282 219
VISIT (3)
    IT'S VIOLENT. WE'RE HERE ON A VISIT, ..................STOPPED DEAD 230   11
    PHOTOGRAPHS VISIT ME --- ..................................PARALYTIC 266   22
    AT NOON, ANEMIC HUSBANDS VISIT THEM. ..........MORNING IN THE HOS. 333   27
VISITATIONS (2)
    DARK TUNNEL, THROUGH WHICH HURTLE THE VISITATIONS, .....THREE WOMEN 180  130
    THE VISITATIONS, THE MANIFESTATIONS, THE STARTLED FACES.*THREE WOMEN 180 131
VISITED (2)
    THE DAY SHE VISITED THE DISSECTING ROOM *TWO VIEWS OF A CADAVER ROOM 114    1
    OR JUST TO BE VISITED AT ALL. ............................PHEASANT 191    6
VISOR (1)
    EACH DEAD HEAD HAD A VISOR OF ICE. .....................LOVE LETTER 147   18
VISORS (1)
    EVERYBODY IS NODDING A SQUARE BLACK HEAD, THEY ARE KNIGHTS IN
        VISORS, ...........................................THE BEE MEETING 211   13
VITAL (1)
    AND MISLAID EVERY VITAL TALISMAN; ..................THE DISPOSSESSED 319   17
VITREOUS (1)
    OF PALE BLUE VITREOUS STUFF, OPAQUE ..............THE BURNT-OUT SPA 137    4
VIVID (7)
    VIVID AT MY SIDE, .........................SOLILOQUY OF THE SOLIPSIST  38   30
    BLOOD DRENCHING VIVID ......................MONOLOGUE AT 3 A.M.  40    3
    THE VIVID TULIPS EAT MY OXYGEN. ..............................TULIPS 161   49
    THE FLOWERS VIVID AS BANDAGES, AND THE MAN MENDING. ......NARCISSI. 190    8
    IT IS SUCH A GOOD SHAPE, SO VIVID. ........................PHEASANT 191   19
    ON DARKNESS, MORE VIVID AND UNNATURAL ..DIALOGUE OVER A OUIJA BOARD 285 323
    WHERE VIVID CHILDREN TWIRL ...........................TOUCH-AND-GO 335    9
VOCABULARY (1)
    OF VAGUE VOCABULARY ..........................NOTES TO A NEOPHYTE 306    8
VOCATION (1)
    VOCATION ENOUGH: OPENING, SHUTTING ......................MOONRISE  98    8
VOICE (20)
    HIS VOICE WAYLAYS ME, SPELLS A TRANCE, .....................PURSUIT  23   41
                              547
```

	TITLE	PAGE	LINE

VOICE (CONT.)
IN VOICE FURRED WITH FROST, ...DIALOGUE BETWEEN GHOST AND PRIEST 38 17
THAT OWL VOICE SOLE "YES", WHILE COWS UTTER ....WREATH FOR A BRIDAL 44 3
RUM AND RED-FACED AS A WATER-MELON, HER VOICE ....ELLA MASON A. 53 7
THE VOICE OF GOD IS FULL OF DRAFTINESS, ...WIDOW 164 22
THEIRS IS THE ONLY VOICE, PROTESTING, PROTESTING. ....BLACKBERRYING 168 12
WITH SUCH SORROW IN ITS VOICE? ....THREE WOMEN 186 349
I SEE YOUR VOICE ....LITTLE FUGUE 188 23
OR THE VOICE OF NOTHING, THAT WAS YOUR MADNESS? ....ELM 192 6
TEARING OFF MY VOICE, AND THE SEA ....THE RABBIT CATCHER 193 3
THE VOICE OF THE PRIEST, IN THIN AIR, ...BERCK-PLAGE 200 93
IT THINKS THEY ARE THE VOICE OF GOD ....THE SWARM 216 21
YOUR VOICE MY EAR-RING, ...LESBOS 229 79
THE VOICE OF THE WOMAN HOLLOWS -- ....THE FEARFUL 256 7
VOICELESSNESS. THE SNOW HAS NO VOICE. ....THE MUNICH MANNEQUINS 263 27
YOU'D PRESUME YOUR INNER VOICE GOD-PLUMED ENOUGH ....DIALOGUE O. 280 168
DID. IT'S SMALL, BUT THE VOLUME OF THE VOICE ....DIALOGUE O. 281 203
"BEHIND ME THEN I HEARD A VOICE ....THE DREAM 311 19
VOICE CRYING EXCLUSION IN MY EAR. ....SONNET: TO TIME 311 8
TILL THE ANNOUNCER'S VOICE IS LOST ....INSOLENT STORM. 326 35
VOICELESS (1)
PERFECTLY VOICELESS, ...MUSHROOMS 139 16
VOICELESSNESS (1)
VOICELESSNESS. THE SNOW HAS NO VOICE. ....THE MUNICH MANNEQUINS 263 27
VOICES (22)
OUR VOICES FATHOMED A PROFOUNDER SOUND: ....THE OTHER TWO 68 12
WE DREAMED THEIR ARGUMENTS, THEIR STRICKEN VOICES. ...THE OTHER TWO 69 29
WITH VOICES OF THAT AMBIGUOUS SEA ....ON THE DECLINE OF ORACLES 78 4
BUT I, I KEEP THE VOICES HE ....ON THE DECLINE OF ORACLES 78 12
YOUR VOICES LAY SIEGE. YOU LODGE ....LORELEI 94 23
COUNTERPOINT TO THEIR VOICES: ....OLD LADIES' HOME 120 9
THE PINES BLOT OUR VOICES UP IN THEIR LIGHTEST SIGHS. ....TWO CAMP. 145 24
BOOMED WITH BAD DREAMS AND THE JOVIAN VOICES OF SURGEONS. *FACE LIFT 156 6
OUR VOICES ECHO, MAGNIFYING YOUR ARRIVAL. NEW STATUE. MORNING SONG 157 4
A POEM FOR THREE VOICES ....THREE WOMEN 176 ST
VOICES STAND BACK AND FLATTEN. THEIR VISIBLE HIEROGLYPHS*THREE WOMEN 179 96
FACE THE VOICES THAT OVERWHELM, THE TERRIBLE ELEMENT. ..THREE WOMEN 179 112
MONTH AFTER MONTH, WITH ITS VOICES OF FAILURE. ....THREE WOMEN 182 187
THE VOICES OF LONELINESS, THE VOICES OF SORROW ....THREE WOMEN 185 292
THE VOICES OF LONELINESS, THE VOICES OF SORROW ....THREE WOMEN 185 292
IT STRETCHES FOR MILES, THE SHRUNK VOICES ....BERCK-PLAGE 196 8
THEIR SMILES AND THEIR VOICES ARE CHANGING. I AM LED THROUGH
    A BEANFIELD. ....THE BEE MEETING 211 15
THE VOICES JUST CAN'T WORM THROUGH. ....DADDY 224 70
CLEAR OF VOICES AND HISTORY, THE STATICKY ....LESBOS 228 18
OF MANDATORY VOICES YOU HALF EXPECT ..DIALOGUE OVER A OUIJA BOARD 279 110
THAT SKEIN OF VOICES. WE PROMISED TO FORGET ....DIALOGUE O. 286 342
A CAR DOOR SLAM; VOICES COMING NEAR; ....FAMILY REUNION 300 2
VOID (2)
FIVE O'CLOCK IN THE MORNING, THE NO-COLOR VOID ....GHOST'S. 90 2
AND GOD OR VOID APPALL US TILL WE DROWN ....LOVE IS A PARALLAX 330 74
VOLCANOED (1)
VOLCANOED HOT ....THE SNOWMAN ON THE MOOR 59 26
VOLCANOES (2)
PEAKS AND CRATERS OF THOSE EXTINCT VOLCANOES.*THE EVERLASTING MONDAY 62 6
THE DRY VOLCANOES CRACKED AND SPIT, ...I WANT, I WANT 106 4
VOLT (2)
VOLT UPON VOLT. CATGUT STITCHES MY FISSURES. POEM.7.S. 137 30
VOLT UPON VOLT. CATGUT STITCHES MY FISSURES. POEM.7.S. 137 30
VOLTS (1)
I SIZZLED IN HIS BLUE VOLTS LIKE A DESERT PROPHET. THE HANGING MAN 141 2
VOLUME (1)
DID. IT'S SMALL, BUT THE VOLUME OF THE VOICE ....DIALOGUE O. 281 203
VOLUMES (1)
STOLIDLY PROPPING THICK VOLUMES OF PROSE: SPITE-SET ....LADY AND T. 69 4
VOLUNTEER (1)
BUT WHO'D VOLUNTEER TO GULP THE LAOCOON, ...PERSEUS 82 8
VOLUPTUOUS (1)
AND VOLUPTUOUS VENUS TO COME ....DIALOGUE EN ROUTE 309 29
VOMIT (1)
YOU SIT, SOLEMN-EYED, ABOUT TO VOMIT, ...THE TRIAL OF MAN 312 13
VORTEX (1)
FIXED VORTEX ON THE FAR ....MAN IN BLACK 120 19
VOTRE (1)
DANS LE FOND DES FORETS VOTRE IMAGE ME SUIT. ....PURSUIT 22 E
VOUCHING (1)
VOUCHING YOU ARE ....MONOLOGUE AT 3 A.M. 40 6
VOUCHSAFED (1)
AREN'T VOUCHSAFED TO ANTIQUE VIRGINS ONLY: ....DIALOGUE O. 282 220
VOW (1)
IF YOU CAN THINK OF MEANS TO MEND THE VOW ....THE DISPOSSESSED 318 13
VOWELS (2)
THE CLEAR VOWELS RISE LIKE BALLOONS. ....MORNING SONG 157 18
INTOLERABLE VOWELS ENTER MY HEART. ....EVENT 194 6

	TITLE	PAGE	LINE

VOWS (2)
NOW IN THE CRUX OF THEIR VOWS HANG YOUR EAR, ...EPITAPH FOR F.   45   15
FRESH LEAVED OUT IN VOWS: "COME TELL ....CRYSTAL GAZER   55   8
VOYAGE (1)
AS THAT CRISP CUSP TOWARDS WHICH YOU VOYAGE NOW. ....GHOST'S.   91   38
VOYAGERS (1)
BELOW, ROCKED HAVOC-SICK, VOYAGERS LIE ....CHANNEL CROSSING   26   9
VULGAR (2)
INTO VULGAR MOTLEY -- ....SPINSTER   50   21
NOTHING SO VULGAR AS A NOSE OR AN EYE ....MAGI   148   2
VULNERABLE (1)
I AM SO VULNERABLE SUDDENLY. ....THREE WOMEN   184   269
VULTUROUS (1)
A VULTUROUS BOREDOM PINNED ME IN THIS TREE. ....THE HANGING MAN   142   5
WADE (1)
A GIRL COULD WADE WITHOUT WETTING HER SHINS.   A LESSON IN VENGEANCE   80   20
WAFER (1)
A COMMUNION WAFER? BLUBBERY MARY? ....MEDUSA   225   33
WAG (2)
TO WAG AT THE DARK) ....WORDS FOR A NURSERY   74   46
THE YEW'S BLACK FINGERS WAG; ....LITTLE FUGUE   187   1
WAGONS (1)
IN THE LANE I MEET SHEEP AND WAGONS, ...BRASILIA   258   16
WAINSCOTED (1)
IN HER DARK WAINSCOTED ROOM ....TWO SISTERS OF PERSEPHONE   31   5
WAIST (1)
WAIST DOWN, YOU MAY WIND ....FULL FATHOM FIVE   93   33
WAIST-DEEP (1)
WAIST-DEEP IN HISTORY -- ....WINTER TREES   258   10
WAIST-HIGH (1)
WALKS THE WAIST-HIGH WET. ....LETTER IN NOVEMBER   254   33
WAIT (13)
IN WAIT FOR SHARPER SMART TO FADE. ....BUCOLICS   24   24
SO HUNGERED, SHE MUST WAIT IN RAGE ....THE SHRIKE   42   15
IN WAIT AMID SNARLED WEED AND WRACK OF WAVE *DREAM WITH CLAM-DIGGERS   44   26
UNSERVICEABLE, I WAIT ....RESOLVE   52   3
THE LONG WAIT FOR THE ANGEL, ...BLACK ROOK IN RAINY WEATHER   57   39
MUST WAIT, WHILE HERE SUSO'S ....A LESSON IN VENGEANCE   80   11
A PERFECTLY FACETED WIFE TO WAIT ....ON DECK   143   32
I WAIT AND ACHE. I THINK I HAVE BEEN HEALING. ....THREE WOMEN   187   358
CRACKS RED. NOTHING HAPPENS. WAIT. ITS TRIP ....DIALOGUE O.   277   20
OF WATER. WAIT. GODPIE I DON'T BEGRUDGE *DIALOGUE OVER A OUIJA BOARD   282   213
A DEVIL. WAIT: HE SHIFTS. HE HASN'T COME*DIALOGUE OVER A OUIJA BOARD   282   216
AS A BAD JOB. WAIT. HE STIRS. HE ROMPS   DIALOGUE OVER A OUIJA BOARD   284   293
THE WOMEN WAIT, FLUTTERING, TURNING PAGES ......MORNING IN THE HOS.   332   21
WAITED (3)
WAITED ON HIM HAND AND FOOT. POEM.4.BEAST.   134   6
THEY WAITED LIKE SWEETHEARTS. THEY EXCITED HIM.   THE RABBIT CATCHER   194   25
"BUT YET I WAITED TO BE FINED ....THE DREAM   311   25
WAITING (8)
WAITING FOR SOME ACCIDENTAL BREAK ....TALE OF A TUB   25   21
I DIDN'T MIND HER WAITING ON ME, AND SHE ADORED IT. .....IN PLASTER   159   22
WASTING HER DAYS WAITING ON A HALF-CORPSE! ....IN PLASTER   159   38
WAITING LIES HEAVY ON MY LIDS. IT LIES LIKE SLEEP, ...THREE WOMEN   179   108
IT IS THE SURGEON MY NEIGHBORS ARE WAITING FOR, ...THE BEE MEETING   211   27
NEAR WINS, WEEK BY WEEK, WAITING UNTIL   DIALOGUE OVER A OUIJA BOARD   277   40
I'LL ASK. DO. WE'VE KEPT HIM WAITING LONG ....DIALOGUE O.   281   180
WAITING FOR HIS GRACE TO CONSECRATE. ....TERMINAL   328   14
WAITRESS (1)
THE WAITRESS HOLDS OUR COATS AND WE PUT ON ......LOVE IS A PARALLAX   329   22
WAITS (1)
THE CITY WAITS AND ACHES. THE LITTLE GRASSES ....THREE WOMEN   187   370
WAIT'S (1)
TRICKS OF RADIANCE MIRACLES. THE WAIT'S BEGUN AGAIN,   BLACK ROOK I.   57   38
WAKE (11)
IN THE WAKE OF THIS FIERCE CAT, ...PURSUIT   22   21
IN THEIR HEARTBEATS' BLAZING WAKE UNTIL RED COCK ....EPITAPH FOR F.   46   27
ASKEW, SHE'LL ACHE AND WAKE ....VIRGIN IN A TREE   82   40
WE'LL WAKE BLANK-BRAINED AS WATER IN THE DAWN. ....TWO CAMP.   145   27
MOTHER TO MYSELF, I WAKE SWADDLED IN GAUZE, ...FACE LIFT   156   31
FLICKERS AMONG THE FLAT PINK ROSES. I WAKE TO LISTEN: MORNING SONG   157   11
I WAKE TO A MAUSOLEUM; YOU ARE HERE, ...THE RIVAL   166   7
YOU WAKE TO IS NOT YOURS. ....NICK AND THE CANDLESTICK   241   30
WARRANT HIM WHELPED IN THE WAKE OF TWO SHOOTING ....DIALOGUE O.   281   194
THE SLEEPERS WAKE ....MOONSONG AT MORNING   317   26
THESE BONE SHANKS WILL NOT WAKE IMMACULATE ....THE DEAD   320   10
WAKEFUL (2)
WHILE ANGELS WEAR A WAKEFUL ATTITUDE ....ADMONITIONS   319   13
UP WHICH THE WAKEFUL PRINCESS CLIMBS TO FIND ....THE PRINCESS.   333   2
WAKEN (2)
AND WAKEN THE SLY NERVE UP ....THE LADY AND THE EARTHENWARE HEAD   69   14
TO WAKEN DREAMERS IN THE MILKY DAWN, ...APRIL AUBADE   312   6
WAKENED (1)
OF SOME GODLY UTTERANCE WAKENED HEADS IGNORE: ....GHOST'S.   90   17

	TITLE	PAGE	LINE

WAKENS (1)
    WAKENS, MORNINGS, TO A COBALT SKY, ...YADDO: THE GRAND MANOR 124 19
WAKES (5)
    WHAT FIRES RUN, WHAT CRAVING WAKES? ....PURSUIT   22 12
    SOON: BE IT BY WAKES, WEDDINGS, ...ALL THE DEAD DEARS   71 27
    OF GRAYBEARDS WAKES US UP. ....BATTLE-SCENE   85 40
    WHO WAKES WITH DARKNESS AND TILL DAWN WORKS HARD ....GOATSUCKER   111   3
    WIND WAKES THE WHOLE METROPOLIS.*INSOLENT STORM STRIKES AT THE SKULL 325   6
WAKING (6)
    MOST MOCK-HEROIC, TO CLOAK OUR WAKING AWE ....CHANNEL CROSSING   27 28
    WHERE THE WAKING HEAD RUBBISHES OUT THE DRAGGLED LOT ......GHOST'S.   90   3
    A WORLD WE LOSE BY MERELY WAKING UP. ....THE GHOST'S LEAVETAKING   90 20
    WAKING IN WINTER ....WAKING IN WINTER 151   T
    AND THE SWEET, DRUGGED WAKING OF A FORGETFUL BABY. ....INSOMNIAC   163 19
    THE DREAMER REINS HIS WAKING APPETITE ....TERMINAL   328   2
WALK (29)
    GROW GREEN AGAIN? WHO'D WALK IN THIS BLEAK PLACE? *WINTER LANDSCAPE,   22 15
    SURVIVES ARRIVAL: WE WALK THE PLANK WITH STRANGERS.*CHANNEL CROSSING   27 42
    WE WALKED (AND STILL WALK THERE -- ....SONG FOR A SUMMER'S DAY   31 18
    I WALK ALONE; ....SOLILOQUY OF THE SOLIPSIST   37   2
    IN THE RECTORY GARDEN ON HIS EVENING WALK ....DIALOGUE B.   38   1
    DURING A CEREMONIOUS APRIL WALK ....SPINSTER   49   2
    WALK FORTH INTO SUN-MONEYED AIR, QUICKENED ....CRYSTAL GAZER   55 26
    ONE MIGHT SAY LOVE. AT ANY RATE, I NOW WALK ....BLACK ROOK I.   57 22
    I WALK DRY ON YOUR KINGDOM'S BORDER ....FULL FATHOM FIVE   93 41
    THOUGH THE BODY WALK OUT IN CLEAN LINEN. ....MOONRISE   98 15
    FIRST FROST, AND I WALK AMONG THE ROSE-FRUIT, THE MARBLE TOES ...
                                          ... PRIVATE GROUND 130   1
    I HAD EVEN FORGOTTEN HOW TO WALK OR SIT, ...IN PLASTER 159 45
    I WALK AMONG THEM, BUT NONE OF THEM ARE NOTICING. ....I AM VERTICAL   162 13
    I WALK AMONG THEM, AND THEY STUFF MY MOUTH WITH COTTON. FINISTERRE 169 17
    I WALK AMONG SLEEPERS IN GAUZE SARCOPHAGI. ...THE SURGEON AT 2 A.M. 171 47
    WHEN I WALK OUT, I AM A GREAT EVENT. ....THREE WOMEN 176   8
    I WATCHED THE MEN WALK ABOUT ME IN THE OFFICE. THEY WERE SO
                                FLAT! ....THREE WOMEN 177 16
    AND SO I STAND, A LITTLE SIGHTLESS. SO I WALK ....THREE WOMEN 184 253
    HE DOES NOT WALK. HE DOES NOT SPEAK A WORD. ....THREE WOMEN 186 325
    I WALK IN A RING, ...EVENT   195 14
    SUCH SALT-SWEETNESS. WHY SHOULD I WALK ....BERCK-PLAGE   197 40
    WE WALK ON AIR, WATSON. ....THE DETECTIVE 209 38
    THIS HOLOCAUST I WALK IN, ...MARY'S SONG 257 20
    AND HIGH HEELS CLICKING UP THE WALK; ....FAMILY REUNION   300   4
    OR WALK INTO THE ORANGE AND MAKE *BLACK PINE TREE IN AN ORANGE LIGHT 328   7
    SO WE SHALL WALK BAREFOOT ON WALNUT SHELLS ......LOVE IS A PARALLAX 330 67
    BY DAY SHE MUST WALK IN DREAD ....AERIALIST   332 44
    THE STARCHED WHITE COAT, THE CAT'S PAW WALK, ...MORNING IN THE HOS. 332 12
    TALL SKELETONS WALK; ....TEMPER OF TIME 336 10
WALKED (7)
    WE WALKED (AND STILL WALK THERE -- ....SONG FOR A SUMMER'S DAY   31 18
    THE BLANK MOOD SHE WALKED IN. ONCE PAST ....HARDCASTLE CRAGS   63 18
    I WALKED THE UNWALKED GARDEN OF ROSE-BEDS ...........RHODODENDRON.   103   1
    HE HEARD WHEN HE WALKED INTO THE WATER ....SUICIDE OFF EGG ROCK   115 23
    AND WALKED CAREFULLY, PRECARIOUSLY, LIKE SOMETHING RARE.*THREE WOMEN 178 73
    PUT ON A FACE AND WALKED INTO THE WORLD. ....THREE WOMEN 185 301
    WHO WALKED IN A SWARMING SHROUD OF WINGS ....LAMENT   315   2
WALKER (2)
    REMEMBER THE WALKER UPON IT? ....MYSTIC   269 26
    YET THERE IS NO WALKER AND LOOKER BUT MYSELF. ....QUEEN MARY'S.   290   9
WALKERS (2)
    OR SHOUTS OF WALKERS: CROSSROAD TRAFFIC ......WHITENESS I REMEMBER   103 25
    THEIR FOOTSOLES ARE UNTOUCHED. THEY ARE WALKERS OF AIR. *THREE WOMEN 183 231
WALKING (8)
    THROUGH FEN AND FARMLAND WALKING ....SONG FOR A SUMMER'S DAY   30   1
    WALKING EAGER TOWARD WATER, WHEN THERE, ONE BY ONE, ..DREAM WITH C.   44 23
    IF THEY MISSED OUT ON WALKING ABOUT LIKE PEOPLE ....STILLBORN 142   4
    WALKING ABOUT IN AFRICA MAYBE, BUT THINKING OF ME. ....THE RIVAL 167 17
    I AM A WOUND WALKING OUT OF HOSPITAL. ....THREE WOMEN 184 270
    WALKING THE PLANK DRAPED WITH MOTHER FRANCE'S UPHOLSTERY   THE SWARM 217 48
    A SORT OF WALKING MIRACLE, MY SKIN ....LADY LAZARUS   244   4
    THE WALKING BESIDE STILL WATER? MEMORY? ....MYSTIC   268 17
WALKS (7)
    WALKS THERE NOT SOME SUCH ONE MAN ....STRUMPET SONG   34 14
    ALONG BOX-LINED WALKS IN THE FLORID SUN ....THE BULL OF BENDYLAW 108 10
    A WORKMAN WALKS BY CARRYING A PINK TORSO...........POEM.7.S.   137 31
    THE YELLOW MINUTE BEFORE THE WIND WALKS, WHEN THE LEAVES*THREE WOMEN 179 93
    NURSES THE HARDSHIP OF HIS STITCHES, AND WALKS AND WALKS. *NARCISSI. 190   6
    NURSES THE HARDSHIP OF HIS STITCHES, AND WALKS AND WALKS. *NARCISSI. 190   6
    WALKS THE WAIST-HIGH WET. ....LETTER IN NOVEMBER   254 33
WALL (36)
    UNDER WHITE WALL AND MOORISH WINDOW ....THE BEGGARS   47   6
    A FIREWORK OF ECHOES FROM WALL ....HARDCASTLE CRAGS   62   6
    TO WALL OF THE DARK, DWARFED COTTAGES. ....HARDCASTLE CRAGS   62   7
    STONE WALL AND RIDGEPOLE RISE ....TWO VIEWS OF WITHENS   71   3
    OF STREETLIGHTS AND WIRES, ITS WALL TO WALL ....OWL 102 11
    OF STREETLIGHTS AND WIRES, ITS WALL TO WALL ....OWL 102 11

WALL (CONT.)
   THE STONE LION-HEAD SET IN THE WALL ..................RHODODENDRON. 103   5
   THEMSELVES UP AGAINST THE WALL ....OLD LADIES' HOME 120   6
   OR TAPESTRIES ON A WALL, ...MAGNOLIA SHOALS 122 10
   AND DAYLIGHT LAYS ITS SAMENESS ON THE WALL. POEM.7.S. 137 26
   AND YOU DOZE ON, NOSE TO THE WALL. ....LEAVING EARLY 146 38
   NOW, ON THE NURSERY WALL, ...PARLIAMENT HILL FIELDS 153 40
   OF AN ECHO, EXPOSES THE PANEL IN THE WALL ....WIDOW 164   7
   MOST OF THE TIME I MEDITATE ON THE OPPOSITE WALL. ....MIRROR 173   6
   THE COOK HAD ONE WALL EYE AND COULDN'T SLEEP, SHE WAS SO
       NERVOUS. ....THE BABYSITTERS 175 25
   I SHALL BE A WALL AND A ROOF, PROTECTING. ....THREE WOMEN 180 139
   HOW LONG CAN I BE A WALL, KEEPING THE WIND OFF? ......THREE WOMEN 185 288
   HOW LONG CAN I BE A WALL AROUND MY GREEN PROPERTY? .....THREE WOMEN 185 295
   THE GLASSY LIGHT WAS A CLEAR WALL, ...THE RABBIT CATCHER 194 19
   THERE IS THIS WHITE WALL, ABOVE WHICH THE SKY CREATES ITSELF -- ...
                                                  ... APPREHENSIONS 195   1
   THE SUN DISSOLVES ON THIS WALL, BLEEDING ITS LIGHTS. APPREHENSIONS 195   5
   A GRAY WALL NOW, CLAWED AND BLOODY. .................APPREHENSIONS 195   6
   THIS RED WALL WINCES CONTINUALLY: .....................APPREHENSIONS 195 11
   ON A BLACK WALL, UNIDENTIFIABLE BIRDS ................APPREHENSIONS 195 16
   WHO WALL UP THEIR BACKS AGAINST HIM. ....BERCK-PLAGE 196 15
   THE BED IS ROLLED FROM THE WALL. ....BERCK-PLAGE 198 60
   I HAVE YOUR HEAD ON MY WALL. ....THE OTHER 202 17
   THE FINGERS WERE TAMPING A WOMAN INTO A WALL, ...THE DETECTIVE 208 10
   THEM HUGE AGAIN, VIOLENT GIANTS ON THE WALL. ....BY CANDLELIGHT 236 14
   MELTS IN THE WALL. ....ARIEL 239 25
   AND THE WALL OF OLD CORPSES. ....LETTER IN NOVEMBER 253 21
   CRAWLS DOWN THE WALL. ....CONTUSION 271   9
   COLUMN OF DAZZLE DRAWS MY EYES TO THE WALL ....DIALOGUE O. 279 88
   YOUR SHERLOCK HOLMESING STEERED TO A BLANK WALL ....DIALOGUE O. 280 167
   ROSE CANDLES FLICKER ON THE LILAC WALL ....CINDERELLA 304   7
   MY ROOM IS A TWITTERING GRAY BOX WITH A WALL *EPITAPH IN THREE PARTS 337 26
WALLOP (1)
   WAVES WALLOP, ASSAULTING THE STUBBORN HULL. ....CHANNEL CROSSING 26   4
WALLOPING (1)
   FILET MIGNON AND WALLOPING WINES, ...DIALOGUE EN ROUTE 308 10
WALLPAPER (1)
   THEY PERSIST IN THE SUNLIT ROOM: THE WALLPAPER .....THE THIN PEOPLE 65 36
WALLS (13)
   NOW, RICH ORDER OF WALLS IS FALLEN; ROOKS CROAK ......CONVERSATION. 21   5
   RECORDS BARE PAINTED WALLS, WHILE AN ELECTRIC LIGHT ..TALE OF A TUB 24   2
   LAYS ALL WALLS WASTE; PRIVATE ESTATES ARE TORN, ...CHANNEL CROSSING 27 31
   BUT THE ECHOES DIED AT HER BACK AS THE WALLS .....HARDCASTLE CRAGS 62   8
   AGAINST BARE, WHITEWASHED WALLS, THE FURNITURE ....THE OTHER TWO 68   8
   FESTERING ON THE DIM WALLS OF EUROPE'S CHAPELS, ...PERSEUS 82 10
   SHADOWS OUR SAFETY, WE STAND ROUND BLANKLY AS WALLS. ..MORNING SONG 157   6
   AS THE LIGHT LIES ON THESE WHITE WALLS, THIS BED, THESE HANDS. ...
                                                  ... TULIPS 160   4
   THE WALLS, ALSO, SEEM TO BE WARMING THEMSELVES. ....TULIPS 162 57
   OLD BLOOD OF CAKED WALLS THE SUN HEALS, ...BERCK-PLAGE 200 98
   STREAMING BETWEEN MY WALLS? ....THE OTHER 201   4
   STRAW MATS, WHITE WALLS ....BALLOONS 271 12
   TO FRACTURE THESE FOUR WALLS. YOUR FAITH FLIES ....DIALOGUE O. 279 111
WALNUT (3)
   THE WALNUT BANQUET TABLE, THE TWELVE CHAIRS ....THE OTHER TWO 68 13
   AT THE CRADLE OF SPANISH WALNUT, ...WINTERING 219 44
   SO WE SHALL WALK BAREFOOT ON WALNUT SHELLS ......LOVE IS A PARALLAX 330 67
WALTZES (1)
   PERFORM THEIR SHAMBLING WALTZES ....MUSSEL HUNTER AT ROCK HARBOR 97 86
WALTZING (1)
   WALTZING UP TO ME OUT OF HER COCKLE-SHELL." ......DIALOGUE EN ROUTE 309 30
WAN (4)
   COCKCHAFERS AND THE WAN, GREEN LUNA MOTH. ....GOATSUCKER 111 14
   OR THE HANDS OF AN INVALID. THE WAN ....PARLIAMENT HILL FIELDS 152   9
   AND THEY ARE WAN, DULLED BY MUCH TRAVELLING.*STARS OVER THE DORDOGNE 165 11
   COMES BLUNT AND WAN ....AQUATIC NOCTURNE 306 26
WANES (2)
   THAT WANES AND WANES, FACING THE COLD ANGEL? ....THREE WOMEN 177 39
   THAT WANES AND WANES, FACING THE COLD ANGEL? ....THREE WOMEN 177 39
WANT (26)
   APPALLED BY SECRET WANT, I RUSH ....PURSUIT 23 43
   NOR SCANT HIS WANT UNTIL ....THE GLUTTON 40 13
   PRODIGIOUS IN GLUTTONIES AS THAT HOG WHOSE WANT ....SOW 61 41
   IN THE PUBLIC PARK; AT HOME FELT THE WANT ............RHODODENDRON. 103   2
   I WANT, I WANT ....I WANT, I WANT 106   T
   I WANT, I WANT ....I WANT, I WANT 106   T
   WHAT I WANT BACK IS WHAT I WAS ....THE EYE-MOTE 109 25
   THEY WANT THE CRIB OF SOME LAMP-HEADED PLATO. ....MAGI 148 16
   I DIDN'T WANT ANY FLOWERS, I ONLY WANTED ....TULIPS 161 29
   AND I WANT THE ONE'S LONGEVITY AND THE OTHER'S DARING.*I AM VERTICAL 162 10
   I DO NOT WANT A PLAIN BOX. I WANT A SARCOPHAGUS ....LAST WORDS 172   1
   I DO NOT WANT A PLAIN BOX. I WANT A SARCOPHAGUS ....LAST WORDS 172   1
   I WANT TO BE LOOKING AT THEM WHEN THEY COME ....LAST WORDS 172   4
   TO WANT THE WORLD IN A GLASS HAT. ....NEW YEAR ON DARTMOOR 176   9

```
                                            TITLE              PAGE  LINE
WANT (CONT.)
  I AM SURE IT IS UNIQUE, I AM SURE IT IS JUST WHAT I WANT. *BIRTHDAY.  206   3
  I DO NOT WANT MUCH OF A PRESENT, ANYWAY, THIS YEAR.  ......BIRTHDAY.  206  13
  THERE IS THIS ONE THING I WANT TODAY, AND ONLY YOU CAN GIVE
    IT TO ME. ...................................A BIRTHDAY PRESENT   207  48
  SEVEN YEARS, IF YOU WANT TO KNOW. .........................DADDY    224  74
  AND YOU WANT TO BE SHOWN ABOUT! .......................THE TOUR     237   7
  YOU'D NOT WANT THAT. ..................................THE TOUR     238  40
  I WANT TO FILL IT WITH COLOR AND DUCKS, ..................CHILD     265   2
  REALLY WANT TO KNOW ABOUT? EVERYTHING.  DIALOGUE OVER A OUIJA BOARD  278  54
  HONESTLY WANT TO FIND IF YOU'LL HAVE A FLING .........DIALOGUE O.   278  56
  ALWAYS, THE GLASS WILL BLURT WHAT I DON'T WANT ........DIALOGUE O.  278  68
  SURELY IT IS NOT I YOU WANT SO BADLY. ..............THE RIVAL/DR    291  21
  THEY WANT NO PROUD PATERNAL KINGDOM COME; ...............THE DEAD   320   6
WANTED (8)
  IT SEEMS THE CONSISTENT CRITICS WANTED YOU ............YADWIGHA.     85   8
  WE WANTED TO SEE THE SUN COME UP .................A WINTER SHIP     113  24
  THEN I REALIZED WHAT SHE WANTED WAS FOR ME TO LOVE HER:  IN PLASTER 159  13
  SHE WANTED TO LEAVE ME, SHE THOUGHT SHE WAS SUPERIOR, ...IN PLASTER 159  36
  I DIDN'T WANT ANY FLOWERS, I ONLY WANTED ..............TULIPS       161  29
  AND I HAVE NO FACE, I HAVE WANTED TO EFFACE MYSELF. .........TULIPS 161  48
  I NEVER WANTED IT. ....................................YEARS       255  10
  IT WAS HIS TONGUE THAT WANTED MENDING. YOU KNOW, ......DIALOGUE O.  285 305
WANTING (3)
  TAP, TAP, TAP, STEEL PEGS. I AM FOUND WANTING. .........THREE WOMEN 177  35
  THE CLOCK SHALL NOT FIND ME WANTING, NOR THESE STARS ...THREE WOMEN 182 202
  LOOK, LOOK! IT IS WANTING TO CRAWL." ....................A SECRET   220  36
WANTON (1)
  INSTEAD, A WANTON FIT ...................ON THE PLETHORA OF DRYADS   67  25
WANTONLY (1)
  WHILE WANTONLY AMUSED BY THIS,  INSOLENT STORM STRIKES AT THE SKULL 325   5
WANTS (7)
  WELL, ONE WEARIES OF THE PUBLIC GARDENS: ONE WANTS A VACATION ...
               ... TWO CAMPERS IN CLOUD COUNTRY 144   7
  AND TO MARRY WHAT HE WANTS AND WHERE HE WILL. .........THREE WOMEN  186 336
  BUT IT SHIMMERS, IT DOES NOT STOP, AND I THINK IT WANTS ME. ...
               ... A BIRTHDAY PRESENT 206  11
  "BUT IT WANTS TO GET OUT! ............................A SECRET      220  35
  HE WANTS TO BE LOVED. ..............................DEATH & CO.     254  25
  WANTS, DESIRE .......................................PARALYTIC      267  34
  TO INDULGE MY EXTRAVAGANT WANTS." ...........DIALOGUE EN ROUTE      308  12
WAR (6)
  BRAVE ACTS PLAYED OUT IN PEACE, IN WAR; ALL DANGERS*CHANNEL CROSSING  27  39
  IN A WAR MAKING EVIL HEADLINES WHEN WE ...........THE THIN PEOPLE    64   6
  DISSOLVED NOW, SMOKE OF AN OLD WAR. ..................BLUE MOLES    126  18
  AND YOU, DURING THE GREAT WAR ......................LITTLE FUGUE    188  31
  IT IS RUSSIA I HAVE TO GET ACROSS, IT IS SOME WAR OR OTHER.*GETTING. 248  9
  DEAD MEN RENDER LOVE AND WAR NO HEED, ...................THE DEAD   320   3
WARD (5)
  TO WARD OFF, AT ALL COST, SUSPICIONS ...............STREET SONG      36  16
  THE NEW WOMAN IN THE WARD ..........MISS DRAKE PROCEEDS TO SUPPER    41   5
  IN THIS CHARITY WARD, THIS POORHOUSE, WHERE THE DEAD ...ELECTRA ON. 117  19
  OVER ONE BED IN THE WARD, A SMALL BLUE LIGHT  THE SURGEON AT 2 A.M. 171  41
  SETTING: A MATERNITY WARD AND ROUND ABOUT ..........THREE WOMEN     176  SD
WARDEN (2)
  SPITEFULLY SKULKS OUR WARDEN, ...........................FIRESONG    30   4
  KNOCKING THE WARDEN TO HIS KNEES*INSOLENT STORM STRIKES AT THE SKULL 325  3
WAREHOUSES (1)
  OF WAREHOUSES, DERRICKS, SMOKESTACKS AND BRIDGES .....A WINTER SHIP 113  17
WARILY (1)
  HEARTED GAMBLING-GAME YOU WARILY PRACTICE .............DIALOGUE O.  282 227
WARM (16)
  UNTIL THE SUN TURNED PALE FROM WARM, ....................BUCOLICS    24  14
  WHERE STRAIGHT TALK IS THE RULE, WHETHER WARM OR HOSTILE, ...
               ... INCOMMUNICADO 100  10
  OUSTED FROM THAT WARM BED ..........................THE SLEEPERS   123  19
  WOOD STOVES BURN WARM AS TOAST. ............YADDO: THE GRAND MANOR  124  17
  IT IS WARM AND TOLERABLE .........................POEM.2.DARK.      133  26
  SHE BEGAN TO WARM UP, AND I SAW HER ADVANTAGES. .........IN PLASTER 159  14
  THE WATER I TASTE IS WARM AND SALT, LIKE THE SEA, .........TULIPS   162  62
  THE WAY SHE LAID HIS LETTERS, TILL THEY GREW WARM ..........WIDOW   164  18
  TOUCHED BY A MATCH, THEY MIGHT WARM ME, .......WUTHERING HEIGHTS    167   3
  I AM A WARM HILL. ...............................THREE WOMEN        183 238
  WARM RAIN GREASES MY HAIR, EXTINGUISHES NOTHING.*BURNING THE LETTERS 205 47
  INTO WHICH, ON WARM DAYS, .............................WINTERING    218  36
  WARM AND HUMAN, THEN THEIR PINK LIGHT .............THE NIGHT DANCES 250  19
  I AM FLUSHED AND WARM. .........................LETTER IN NOVEMBER  253  11
  THE SHUTTERS TO LET WARM WIND FEATHER ....................THE DREAM 310   5
  HIDE, HIDE, IN THE WARM PORT .............GO GET THE GOODLY SQUAB   313  23
WARMED (2)
  BUT IT IS SHE WHO IS PAPER NOW, WARMED BY NO ONE. ..........WIDOW   164  20
  WARMED BY MUCH HANDLING. THEY ALMOST PURR. .............LAST WORDS  172  18
WARMING (2)
  WARMING AT CORE ONLY AS .....................CHILD'S PARK STONES    101  25
  THE WALLS, ALSO, SEEM TO BE WARMING THEMSELVES. ............TULIPS  162  57
                            552
```

	TITLE	PAGE	LINE

WARMTH (1)
AND SEEMED TO GIVE HER WARMTH, LIKE A LIVE SKIN. ....WIDOW 164 19
WARNED (1)
WARNED HER TO KEEP ....THE SNOWMAN ON THE MOOR 58 10
WARNING (4)
TORPID WARNING, OR LAY STILL ....SPIDER 49 20
THE WARNING WHIRR AND BURRING OF THE BIRD ....GOATSUCKER 111 2
WARNING ME TO HOLD HER HAND ....THE DREAM 311 20
ANTICIPATES THE WARNING SOUND ....DANSE MACABRE 321 23
WARNS (1)
BEYOND THE WINDOW-FRAME TONIGHT. WIND WARNS ....DIALOGUE O. 286 336
WARP (2)
LEAVES BEHIND US WARP AND LAPSE. ....MAGNOLIA SHOALS 122 11
THERE IS NO GUILE OR WARP IN HIM. MAY HE KEEP SO. ......THREE WOMEN 181 175
WARPED (3)
SWEET SALTS WARPED STEM ....FIRESONG 30 15
FOUNDING FATHER SET THESE LOBED, WARPED STONES CHILD'S PARK STONES 100 3
HORSES WARPED ON THE ALTERING GREEN, ...THE EYE-MOTE 109 12
WARRANT (1)
WARRANT HIM WHELPED IN THE WAKE OF TWO SHOOTING ....DIALOGUE O. 281 194
WARS (5)
LEFTOVER SOLDIERS FROM OLD, MESSY WARS. ....FINISTERRE 169 7
OF WARS, WARS, WARS. ....DADDY 222 18
OF WARS, WARS, WARS. ....DADDY 222 18
OF WARS, WARS, WARS. ....DADDY 222 18
HE'D HAD SO MANY WARS! ....LYONNESSE 234 26
WART (1)
THAT FOR ECCENTRIC KNOB AND WART ....ON THE PLETHORA OF DRYADS 67 5
WARTED (1)
BUT IN SPECKLED THICKETS, WARTED AS A TOAD, ...FIRESONG 30 3
WARY (4)
SHE EDGES WITH WARY BREATH, ...MISS DRAKE PROCEEDS TO SUPPER 41 21
WARY (FOR IT COULD HAPPEN ....BLACK ROOK IN RAINY WEATHER 57 23
IN THE WARY OTHERWORLD ....MUSSEL HUNTER AT ROCK HARBOR 96 24
FOR THAT WARY CLATTER SOUND OR GESTURE ...............INCOMMUNICADO 100 6
WAS (104)
WASH (1)
WHEN SEAS WASH COLD, FOAM- ....FULL FATHOM FIVE 92 3
WASHBOWL (1)
REVEALS NO CRACKS THAT CAN BE DECODED? WHEN WASHBOWL TALE OF A TUB 24 10
WASHED (4)
NOW THE WASHED SHEETS FLY IN THE SUN, ...BERCK-PLAGE 198 67
THE HUMPBACK IN HIS SMALL, WASHED COTTAGE ....MYSTIC 269 22
THE REST OF THE BODY IS ALL WASHED OUT, ...CONTUSION 271 2
(WHILE SHE WASHED THE WAY WITH TEARS), ...THE DREAM 311 27
WASHES (1)
A SEA OF DREAMS WASHES THE EDGE OF MY GREEN ISLAND ...QUEEN MARY'S. 290 2
WASHING (2)
SEA OF HIS EYES WASHING OVER IT ....LYONNESSE 234 7
IT KEEPS WASHING YOU UP LIKE AN OLD BONE. ....THE RIVAL/DR 291 16
WASN'T (7)
WASN'T FIDDLING, AND I FILLED ....MUSSEL HUNTER AT ROCK HARBOR 97 62
IT WASN'T FOR ANY LACK OF MOTHER-LOVE. ....STILLBORN 142 5
THAT WASN'T IT. I SLEPT, SAY: A SNAKE ....LOVE LETTER 147 9
I WASN'T FOOLED. I KNEW YOU AT ONCE. ....LOVE LETTER 147 28
I WASN'T IN ANY POSITION TO GET RID OF HER. ....IN PLASTER 159 43
I WASN'T READY. THE WHITE CLOUDS REARING ....THREE WOMEN 178 57
I WASN'T READY. ....THREE WOMEN 178 59
WASP (2)
WHO SET WASP, WOLF AND SHARK TO WORK, ...I WANT, I WANT 106 10
A WASP CRAWLS ....YADDO: THE GRAND MANOR 123 9
WASPISH (1)
WITH FINGER BANDAGED WHERE THE WASPISH PIN ....THE PRINCESS. 333 7
WASP'S (1)
MAKING THE WORLD GO THIN AS A WASP'S NEST ....THE THIN PEOPLE 65 46
WASSAIL (1)
CHOICE WASSAIL MAKES, COOKED HOT, ...THE GLUTTON 40 9
WASTAGE (1)
RAY BUT EGG ROCK ON THE BLUE WASTAGE. ....SUICIDE OFF EGG ROCK 115 22
WASTE (7)
CAN BE STRUCK FROM ROCK TO MAKE HEART'S WASTE ....WINTER LANDSCAPE, 22 14
CAN SPROUT FROM THE NAVEL OF THIS PRESENT WASTE. ......TALE OF A TUB 25 40
LAYS ALL WALLS WASTE: PRIVATE ESTATES ARE TORN, ...CHANNEL CROSSING 27 31
GOES GRAVEWARD WITH FLESH LAID WASTE, ...TWO SISTERS OF PERSEPHONE 32 27
FROM YOUR BLUE PALLOR, I'D SAY YOU INHABITED THE FROZEN WASTE ...
... DIALOGUE BETWEEN GHOST AND PRIEST 38 14
AND CHANCE OF A TRUE ANSWER. YOU WASTE NO TIME ....DIALOGUE O. 281 188
SUCH A WASTE OF BRIGHTNESS I CAN'T UNDERSTAND. ....QUEEN MARY'S. 290 7
WASTEBASKET (2)
EAT ME. WASTEBASKET GAPER, SHADOW OF DOORWAY. POEM.1.WHO. 132 27
WHEN I CAME TOO CLOSE TO THE WASTEBASKET. ......BURNING THE LETTERS 204 4
WASTES (1)
IN TARNISHED MODES, MAUNDERING AMONG THE WASTES, ...OUIJA 77 13
WASTING (1)
WASTING HER DAYS WAITING ON A HALF-CORPSE! ....IN PLASTER 159 38

		TITLE	PAGE	LINE

WATCH (10)
```
        FLIES WATCH NO RESURRECTIONS IN THE SUN. ........NOVEMBER GRAVEYARD     56   12
        I MUST WATCH SLUTTISH DRYADS TWITCH ......ON THE PLETHORA OF DRYADS     67   32
        I WATCH THEIR SPILT TEARS CLOUD AND DULL TO PEARLS. ........CANDLES    149   31
        LOVE SET YOU GOING LIKE A FAT GOLD WATCH. .............MORNING SONG    156    1
        A SWISS WATCH, JEWELED IN THE HINGES!  ................AN APPEARANCE   189   15
        AND IT EXHAUSTS ME TO WATCH YOU ...................POPPIES IN JULY    203    5
        IN WHICH A TORTURE GOES ON ONE CAN ONLY WATCH. ............COURAGE.   210   28
        WATCH OUT! ...........................................A SECRET        220   39
        THE CIPHERS THAT WATCH IT. ...........................EAVESDROPPER    261   45
        POCKET WATCH, I TICK WELL. ..................................GIGOLO   267    1
WATCHED (7)
        WATCHED THE CHANGING SHAPE HE CUT, .............................FAUN   35   12
        I WATCHED SETTLE, LINE BY LINE, IN MY MIRROR -- .........FACE LIFT   156   26
        I WATCHED MY TEASET, MY BUREAUS OF LINEN, MY BOOKS ..........TULIPS  161   26
        NOBODY WATCHED ME BEFORE, NOW I AM WATCHED. ................TULIPS    161   43
        NOBODY WATCHED ME BEFORE, NOW I AM WATCHED. ................TULIPS    161   43
        I WATCHED THE MEN WALK ABOUT ME IN THE OFFICE. THEY WERE SO
                FLAT! ...........................................THREE WOMEN  177   16
        THEY BOTH WATCHED THE BAROMETER SINK .............DIALOGUE EN ROUTE  309   37
WATCHES (3)
        STAR-LUCKY SLEIGHT-OF-HAND MAN WATCHES ...................CONJURING.  66   34
        WATCHES HIS CUMBROUS WORLD ECLIPSE ......................SCULPTOR     91   12
        THAT WATCHES, LIKE GOD, OR THE SKY .................EAVESDROPPER      261   44
WATCHFUL (2)
        CALL HERE WITH FLYING COLORS ALL WATCHFUL BIRDS *WREATH FOR A BRIDAL  45   13
        WHERE THE MOST WATCHFUL COOKS GO JOBLESS ........THE TIMES ARE TIDY   107    3
WATCHING (3)
        WATCHING FOR NIGHT, .........................................PROSPECT  28   9
        WATCHING FOR GLINTS, ........................BURNING THE LETTERS     204   26
        A THIRD PERSON IS WATCHING. ..................................STINGS  215   38
WATCHMEN (1)
        AND SLIPS UNSEEN PAST WATCHMEN ON THE LAWN ..........THE PRINCESS.    334   29
WATER (68)
        WATER IN THE MILLRACE, THROUGH A SLUICE OF STONE, *WINTER LANDSCAPE,   21    1
        BELOW: A FEN WHERE WATER STOOD; .........................BUCOLICS     24    9
        WATER FAUCETS SPAWN NO DANGER; EACH CRAB .............TALE OF A TUB   25   19
        WE TAKE THE PLUNGE; UNDER WATER OUR LIMBS .............TALE OF A TUB   25   25
        WOULD BE FULL OF SUN, WHITE GULLS, AND WATER DRENCHED ...CHANNEL C.   27   21
        WALKING EAGER TOWARD WATER, WHEN THERE, ONE BY ONE, ..DREAM WITH C.   44   23
        TWO WATER DROPS POISE ......................................RESOLVE   52   13
        AND HILL, AND THROUGH PEATY WATER. ...........TWO VIEWS OF WITHENS    72   11
        WITH MOON-EYE, MOUTH-PIPE. HE PIPES. PIPES GREEN. PIPES WATER. ...
                ... SNAKECHARMER     79    3
        PIPES WATER GREEN UNTIL GREEN WATERS WAVER .............SNAKECHARMER   79    4
        WATER, TO GREEN, TO NOTHING LIKE A SNAKE. ...........SNAKECHARMER     79   27
        THE WATER HAD AN IRON TASTE, AND THE AIR, ..........SPINACH-PICKER.   89   15
        I WOULD BREATHE WATER. ...........................FULL FATHOM FIVE    93   45
        STILLED, SILVERED AS WATER IN A GLASS ...................WATERCOLOR.  111    2
        WORLD UNDER THE SHEER WATER ....WATERCOLOR OF GRANTCHESTER MEADOWS   112   10
        DROLL, VEGETARIAN, THE WATER RAT *WATERCOLOR OF GRANTCHESTER MEADOWS 112   22
        IN THE DISTANCE. ALL AROUND US THE WATER SLIPS .......A WINTER SHIP  113   18
        SUN STRUCK THE WATER LIKE A DAMNATION. .........SUICIDE OFF EGG ROCK 115    6
        HE HEARD WHEN HE WALKED INTO THE WATER .........SUICIDE OFF EGG ROCK 115   23
        THEY LIE AS IF UNDER WATER ..........................THE SLEEPERS    122    4
        BETWEEN THE ROAD AND THE LAKE WATER, .....................BLUE MOLES 126   12
        DARK WOOD, DARK WATER ..................DARK WOOD, DARK WATER        127    T
        OF THE GLAZED WATER ...................DARK WOOD, DARK WATER         127    9
        MIRROR OF WATER .......................DARK WOOD, DARK WATER         127   17
        THEY COLLAPSE LIKE LUNGS, THE ESCAPED WATER ........PRIVATE GROUND   130    9
        THE MOLTS ARE TONGUELESS THAT SANG FROM ABOVE THE WATER ..POEM.5.F.  135   17
        WATER MOLLIFIES THE FLINT LIP, ..........................POEM.7.S.   137   25
        SEATED BENEATH THE TONELESS WATER! ...............THE BURNT-OUT SPA  138   28
        DIET ON WATER, ...........................................MUSHROOMS  139   19
        OR THOSE GLITTERY FICTIONS OF SPILT WATER*SLEEP IN THE MOJAVE DESERT 144   12
        NO WORD MAKE THEM CARRY WATER OR FIRE THE KINDLING .......TWO CAMP.  144    5
        WE'LL WAKE BLANK-BRAINED AS WATER IN THE DAWN. ..........TWO CAMP.   145   27
        THEY TOE OLD WATER THICK AS FOG. ....................LEAVING EARLY   146   22
        SALUTARY AND PURE AS BOILED WATER, ...........................MAGI   148    7
        WEARS THE FACE OF A PHARAOH, THOUGH IT'S MADE OF MUD AND WATER. ...
                ... IN PLASTER     159   42
        MY BODY IS A PEBBLE TO THEM, THEY TEND IT AS WATER ..........TULIPS  160   15
        SINK OUT OF SIGHT, AND THE WATER WENT OVER MY HEAD. ........TULIPS   161   27
        THE WATER I TASTE IS WARM AND SALT, LIKE THE SEA, ..........TULIPS   162   62
        DRAINS LIKE WATER OUT THE HOLE AT THE FAR END. .........INSOMNIAC    163   25
        I COME TO WHEEL RUTS, AND WATER ...................WUTHERING HEIGHTS 167   28
        OTHER ROCKS HIDE THEIR GRUDGES UNDER THE WATER. .........FINISTERRE  169    9
        THE SUN FLAMED STRAIGHT DOWN THAT NOON ON THE WATER OFF
                MARBLEHEAD. ...................................THE BABYSITTERS 174    2
        WITH A POLISHED MAHOGANY STAIR TO LET INTO THE WATER*THE BABYSITTERS  174   11
        THEN STEPPED DOWN THE STEEP BEACH SHELF AND INTO THE WATER. ..BABY.  175   39
        I THINK THEY ARE MADE OF WATER; THEY HAVE NO EXPRESSION.*THREE WOMEN 183  225
        THEIR FEATURES ARE SLEEPING, LIKE LIGHT ON QUIET WATER. *THREE WOMEN 183  226
        CROSSING THE WATER ...........................CROSSING THE WATER     190    T
        A LITTLE LIGHT IS FILTERING FROM THE WATER FLOWERS. *CROSSING THE W. 190    4
```

554

WATER (CONT.)
   SANDS WHERE A DREAM OF CLEAR WATER ....BURNING THE LETTERS 204   7
   TELLING THE PARTICLES OF THE CLOUDS, THE LEAVES, THE WATER *BURNING. 205   55
   THE MILK CAME YELLOW, THEN BLUE AND SWEET AS WATER. ..THE DETECTIVE 209   33
   CURVE OF WATER UPLEAPING ....MEDUSA 225   18
   TO MY WATER ROD, DAZZLING AND GRATEFUL, ...MEDUSA 225   19
   LEMON WATER, CHICKEN ....FEVER. 232   32
   WATER, WATER MAKE ME RETCH. ....FEVER. 232   33
   WATER, WATER MAKE ME RETCH. ....FEVER. 232   33
   UNDERGOING THE FAUCET WATER, ITS VEILS, VEILS IN A NUNNERY,*GETTING. 248   23
   THE SCALD SCAR OF WATER, ...DEATH & CO. 254   7
   STARLESS AND FATHERLESS, A DARK WATER. ....SHEEP IN FOG 262   15
   ALL THE FALL OF WATER AN EYE ....GIGOLO 268   30
   THE WALKING BESIDE STILL WATER? MEMORY? ....MYSTIC 268   17
   WATER STRIVING ....WORDS 270   8
   CONTEMPLATING A WORLD CLEAR AS WATER. ....BALLOONS 272   28
   OF WATER. WAIT. GODPIE I DON'T BEGRUDGE *DIALOGUE OVER A OUIJA BOARD 282 213
   MY GLASS OF WATER REFRACTS THE MORNING. ....FEVER./DR 294   11
   LEST THE WATER DRAG YOU TO DROWN. ....GO GET THE GOODLY SQUAB 313   24
   WATER WILL RUN BY RULE; THE ACTUAL SUN ....TWO LOVERS. 327   21
   WHERE THE WATER BLOTS OUT ALL FOOTSTEPS." ...EPITAPH IN THREE PARTS 337   6
WATERCOLOR (2)
   WATERCOLOR OF GRANTCHESTER MEADOWS ....WATERCOLOR. 111   T
   WORSHIP THIS WORLD OF WATERCOLOR MOOD ....APRIL AUBADE 312   1
WATERCOLORIST (1)
   THE WATERCOLORIST GRIPS ....MAGNOLIA SHOALS 122   19
WATER-COLORISTS (1)
   I CAME BEFORE THE WATER-COLORISTS .....MUSSEL HUNTER AT ROCK HARBOR 95 1-2
WATER-DAZZLE (1)
   AND THE SPIDERY WATER-DAZZLE ON FIELD AND STREET. ....LYONNESSE 234   18
WATERDROPS (1)
   OF CAMBRIC OR WATERDROPS, WHO KNOWS WHAT BELIEF ....DIALOGUE O. 282 224
WATERLIGHTS (1)
   BRIGHT WATERLIGHTS ARE ....DARK WOOD, DARK WATER 127   21
WATERLOO (2)
   AT WATERLOO, WATERLOO, NAPOLEON, ...THE SWARM 216   7
   AT WATERLOO, WATERLOO, NAPOLEON, ...THE SWARM 216   7
WATERMARK (1)
   FAINT, UNDULANT WATERMARK. ....A SECRET 219   8
WATERMELON (1)
   RISES THE ROUND RED WATERMELON SUN. ....SOUTHERN SUNRISE   26   18
WATER-MELON (1)
   RUM AND RED-FACED AS A WATER-MELON, HER VOICE ....ELLA MASON A.   53   7
WATER-MISTS (1)
   THE BLUE WATER-MISTS DROPPING ....LORELEI   94   4
WATERPROOF (1)
   IT IS WATERPROOF, SHATTERPROOF, PROOF ....THE APPLICANT 221   23
WATERS (5)
   PIPES WATER GREEN UNTIL GREEN WATERS WAVER ...........SNAKECHARMER   79   4
   TO A MELTING OF GREEN WATERS, TILL NO SNAKE ...........SNAKECHARMER   79   25
   SHOWS ITS HEAD, AND THOSE GREEN WATERS BACK TO .......SNAKECHARMER   79   26
   IN THE WATERS OFF BEAUTIFUL NAUSET. ....DADDY 222   13
   THE STILL WATERS ....PARALYTIC 266   27
WATER-SKIERS (1)
   BUT NOW THE WATER-SKIERS RACE, ...IN MIDAS' COUNTRY   99   16
WATER-SUNK (1)
   STARS HUNG WATER-SUNK, SO A RANK ....FAUN   35   8
WATERTIGHT (1)
   SUCH SKEPTIC CRACKS. WITH SENSE SEALED WATERTIGHT ......DIALOGUE O. 280 155
WATER-TOWER (1)
   FROM WATER-TOWER HILL TO THE BRICK PRISON ....POINT SHIRLEY 110   1
WATERY (3)
   BUT OUT OF THE WATERY ASPIC, LAURELED BY FINS, ...LADY AND T.   69   18
   WON HER THE FROG-COLORED SKIN, PALE PITH AND WATERY*VIRGIN IN A TREE   81   14
   DEFLECT THE WATERY DAZZLE; THE PEOPLE IDLE ....WHITSUN 154   11
WATSON (1)
   WE WALK ON AIR, WATSON. ....THE DETECTIVE 209   38
WATTLE (1)
   YOUR TURKEY WATTLE ....CUT 235   11
WAVE (15)
   (ESSAYING, WAVE BY WAVE, ...LETTER TO A PURIST   36   4
   (ESSAYING, WAVE BY WAVE, ...LETTER TO A PURIST   36   4
   IN WAIT AMID SNARLED WEED AND WRACK OF WAVE *DREAM WITH CLAM-DIGGERS   44   26
   IT OGLED THROUGH ROCK-FAULT, WIND-FLAW AND FISTED WAVE--*LADY AND T.   70   32
   NO FLOOR: A WAVE OF FLICKERING GRASS TONGUES .........SNAKECHARMER   79   9
   THE GRITTED WAVE LEAPS ....POINT SHIRLEY 110   5
   RAVELED WIND-RIPPED FROM THE CREST OF THE WAVE.*SUICIDE OFF EGG ROCK 115   11
   TO THE LEFT, AND THE WAVE ....MAN IN BLACK 119   34
   AND FROM OUR OPPOSITE CONTINENTS WE WAVE AND CALL. THE BABYSITTERS 175   44
   LIKE A BIG SEA. FAR OFF, FAR OFF, I FEEL THE FIRST WAVE TUG   THREE. 179 109
   WHERE THE BLACK WAVE TOPPLES DOWN; ....GO GET THE GOODLY SQUAB 313   14
   THE TESSELLATED WAVE. NOW NIMBLY LET ....MIDSUMMER MOBILE 324   7
   THAT CHUCKLES IN BACKTRACK OF THE WAVE;" ....TWO LOVERS. 327   18
   WHERE WAVE PRETENDS TO DRENCH REAL SKY." ....LOVE IS A PARALLAX 329   6
   A WAVE OF GRASS ENGRAVES UPON THE STONE: ....EPITAPH IN THREE PARTS 338   32

```
                                               TITLE              PAGE  LINE
WAVED (1)
    FROM WHICH COILS, CAUGHT ANTS WAVED LEGS IN  ................SPIDER    49   19
WAVER (4)
    WAVER, FAINTLY GREEN, SHUDDERING AWAY  ................TALE OF A TUB   25   26
    PIPES WATER GREEN UNTIL GREEN WATERS WAVER  ...........SNAKECHARMER    79    4
    WAVER BY  ...........................................AQUATIC NOCTURNE  305    8
    HEAT SHADOWS WAVER NOISELESS IN  ...MORNING IN THE HOSPITAL SOLARIUM  332    6
WAVERED (1)
    LEWDLY BECKONING, AND HER COURAGE WAVERED:  .............LADY AND T.   69   20
WAVERING (1)
    WAVERING THERE, GAUZE-EDGED, SMELLING OF WOODSMOKE,  ....DIALOGUE B.   38   12
WAVERY (1)
    WAVERY, INDELIBLE, TRUE  ....................................A SECRET  219   11
WAVES (10)
    WAVES WALLOP, ASSAULTING THE STUBBORN HULL.  .......CHANNEL CROSSING   26    4
    THE SIGHT OF THOSE BLUE, UNSEEN WAVES  ....ON THE DECLINE OF ORACLES   78   14
    WITH CHEQUERED WAVES AND GAILY  .........................BATTLE-SCENE  84    7
    A DRAGNET, RISING, FALLING, AS WAVES  ..............FULL FATHOM FIVE   92    5
    SQUALL WAVES ONCE DANCED  ............................POINT SHIRLEY   110   13
    GREY WAVES THE STUB-NECKED EIDERS RIDE.  .............POINT SHIRLEY   110   33
    FARTHER OUT, THE WAVES WILL BE MOUTHING ICECAKES --  ..A WINTER SHIP  113   21
    AT THEIR FEET, THE SEA WAVES BOW IN SINGLE FILE,  ...........A LIFE   150   11
    THE WAVES PULSE AND PULSE LIKE HEARTS.  ....................WHITSUN   154   22
    THE WRINKLES CREEP UP LIKE WAVES,  ....................THE RIVAL/DR   291    4
WAVE'S (1)
    THIS WAVE'S GREEN PEAK ON WIRE  .........EPITAPH FOR FIRE AND FLOWER   45    2
WAVES' (2)
    ON THE WAVES' DISSOLVING TURN  .........MUSSEL HUNTER AT ROCK HARBOR   97   87
    OF GRAVEL? THE WAVES'  ...............................POINT SHIRLEY   110   31
WAVE-TIP (1)
    EACH WAVE-TIP GLITTERS LIKE A KNIFE.  .................A WINTER SHIP   113   30
WAVE-TIPS (1)
    STIPPLE OF SHIFTING WAVE-TIPS IS IRONED OUT, LOST  ..ABOVE THE OXBOW   89   46
WAVING (3)
    A SMALL WHITE SOUL IS WAVING, A SMALL WHITE MAGGOT.  .........EVENT   195   19
    WAVING AND CRUTCHLESS, HALF THEIR OLD SIZE.  ...........BERCK-PLAGE   196    9
    I AM MAD, CALLS THE SPIDER, WAVING ITS MANY ARMS.  ...........TOTEM   265   28
WAX (8)
    AND A LANGUOR OF WAX CONGEALS THE VEIN   EPITAPH FOR FIRE AND FLOWER   46   31
    RUDDY ON THE WAX MANNEQUINS  .......................................OWL  101    6
    THE WAX IMAGE OF MYSELF, A DOLL'S BODY.  ...................POEM.6.W.  135    3
    UPSIDE DOWN HEARTS OF LIGHT TIPPING WAX FINGERS,  ..........CANDLES   148    2
    WITH THE SACRED BABOON IN HIS WIG AND WAX EARS  ...ZOO KEEPER'S WIFE  155   29
    I AM BLED WHITE AS WAX, I HAVE NO ATTACHMENTS.  ......THREE WOMEN   184  275
    A CURTAIN OF WAX DIVIDING THEM FROM THE BRIDE FLIGHT,  .........BEE.  212   47
    THE MAUSOLEUM, THE WAX HOUSE.  ...........................STINGS   215   60
WAXEN (1)
    TWO WAXEN OXEN FLANK THE CHILD.  ...................A WINTER'S TALE    86    6
WAX-PALE (1)
    THE IMAGE OF YOU, TRANSFIXED BY ROOTS, WAX-PALE,  .......DIALOGUE O.  285  325
WAXY (1)
    WAXY STALACTITES  .........................NICK AND THE CANDLESTICK   240    2
WAY (36)
    OF NATURE: WHAT BETTER WAY TO TEST TAUT FIBER  .....CHANNEL CROSSING   27   16
    DITHERS WITH THE OTHER WAY OUT  .................LETTER TO A PURIST    37   13
    OF THE HOMELAND HEARTH TO PLOUGH THEIR PILGRIM WAY  .......MAYFLOWER   60   10
    IN THE SAME WAY  ..................................................SOW   60    4
    GAVE WAY TO FIELDS AND THE INCESSANT SEETHE OF GRASSES*HARDCASTLE C.   62    9
    BURDENED IN SUCH A WAY WE SEEMED THE LIGHTER --  ......THE OTHER TWO   69   32
    THE ONCE-KNOWN WAY BECOMING  ....................THE GREAT CARBUNCLE   72   17
    THE WAY SUN RUINS A TROUT.  ..............................MEDALLION   124   15
    MOLEY-HANDED, I EAT MY WAY.  ........................POEM.2.DARK.    132   16
    IT IS TOUCHING, THE WAY THEY'LL IGNORE  .....................CANDLES  148    5
    NOISELESS, ON RUBBER WHEELS, ON THE WAY TO THE SEA RESORT.  WAKING.   151    8
    AND I WAS SCARED, BECAUSE SHE WAS SHAPED JUST THE WAY I WAS*PLASTER.  158    7
    AS IF MY HABITS OFFENDED HER IN SOME WAY.  .................IN PLASTER  159   31
    AND WEAR MY PAINTED FACE THE WAY A MUMMY-CASE  ............IN PLASTER  159   41
    SO I WAS CAREFUL NOT TO UPSET HER IN ANY WAY  ...........IN PLASTER   160   46
    THEY PASS THE WAY GULLS PASS INLAND IN THEIR WHITE CAPS,  ....TULIPS  160   12
    NOW THE AIR SNAGS AND EDDIES ROUND THEM THE WAY A RIVER  .....TULIPS  161   53
    THE WAY SHE LAID HIS LETTERS, TILL THEY GREW WARM  ..........WIDOW   164   18
    AND UTTERLY IGNORANT OF THE WAY IT TOOK.  ....................WIDOW   165   35
    I HAVE FALLEN A LONG WAY. CLOUDS ARE FLOWERING  ..............MOON.   173   22
    IS THERE NO WAY OUT OF THE MIND?  ....................APPREHENSIONS   195    7
    I WOULD HAVE KILLED MYSELF GLADLY THAT TIME ANY POSSIBLE WAY.  ...
                                            ...  A BIRTHDAY PRESENT   206   15
    ITS BABY HEAD OUT OF THE WAY, EMBALMED IN SPICE,  ............TOTEM   264   12
    GOLD JOINTS, MY WAY OF TURNING  ...........................GIGOLO    268   22
    THEY'LL GO BY, TRUNDLING LIKE MARBLE STATUES WAY OUT  ...DIALOGUE O.  276    6
    TO ALTER HER WILL OUR WAY. SHALL WE GO ON  ...........DIALOGUE O.    277   49
    COULD GROPE ITS WAY TO GOSPEL THROUGH THAT WELTER  .....DIALOGUE O.  286  346
    SHE HAS A TERRIBLE WAY WITH MINERALS,  .................THE RIVAL/DR  291   23
    YOU'RE ALWAYS TALKING THIS WAY . . ."  ..........BITTER STRAWBERRIES  300   26
    THE WAY YOU'D CRACK A CLOCK; YOU'D CRUSH THE BONE  ...SONNET: TO EVA  304    2
    EITHER WAY WE CHOOSE, THE ANGRY WITCH  ....METAMORPHOSES OF THE MOON  308   43
```

WAY (CONT.)
   (WHILE SHE WASHED THE WAY WITH TEARS), ...THE DREAM 311   27
   ALONG BRIGHT ASTERISKS BY MILKY WAY. ..THE PRINCESS AND THE GOBLINS 333   12
   "THERE IS MORE THAN ONE GOOD WAY TO DROWN." EPITAPH IN THREE PARTS 337   11
   "THERE IS MORE THAN ONE GOOD WAY TO DROWN." EPITAPH IN THREE PARTS 337   22
   "THERE IS MORE THAN ONE GOOD WAY TO DROWN." EPITAPH IN THREE PARTS 338   33
WAYFARINGS (1)
   LIFE, ITS OWN VAPOROUS WAYFARINGS. ....LANDOWNERS   53   15
WAYLAYS (2)
   HIS VOICE WAYLAYS ME, SPELLS A TRANCE, ...PURSUIT   23   41
   WAYLAYS SIMPLE GIRLS, CHURCH-GOING, ...VANITY FAIR   32   14
WAY'S (1)
   OF WEEDS WE TACKLE TOWARDS WAY'S RANK ENDING; ....FIRESONG   30   16
WAYWARD (1)
   TO TRAP THIS WAYWARD GIRL AT HER FIRST MOVE OF LOVE,   DREAM WITH C.   44   27
WE (162)
WEAK (2)
   "I FEEL WEAK." ....A SECRET 220   47
   THE WEAK ....FEVER. 231   18
WEAKNESS (1)
   SHE HUMORED MY WEAKNESS LIKE THE BEST OF NURSES, ...IN PLASTER 159   26
WEALTH (1)
   NOT WEALTH NOR WISDOM STANDS ....RECANTATION   42   14
WEAPON (1)
   THE DEATH WEAPON? NO ONE IS DEAD. ....THE DETECTIVE 208   15
WEAR (12)
   HOARD LAST YEAR'S LEAVES, WON'T MOURN, WEAR SACKCLOTH, OR TURN ...
                                          ... NOVEMBER GRAVEYARD   56   2
   I WEAR THE PRESENT ITCH FOR FLESH, ...THE EYE-MOTE 109   22
   WEAR MASKS OF HORN TO BED. POEM.5.F. 135   14
   THE RAFTERS AND STRUTS OF HIS BODY WEAR ....THE BURNT-OUT SPA 138   6
   AND WEAR MY PAINTED FACE THE WAY A MUMMY-CASE ....IN PLASTER 159   41
   I WEAR WHITE CUFFS, I BOW. ....AN APPEARANCE 189   9
   DO YOU WEAR ....THE APPLICANT 221   2
   I SHOULD WEAR TIGER PANTS, I SHOULD HAVE AN AFFAIR. ....LESBOS 228   30
   TOAD-STONE! I SEE I MUST WEAR YOU IN THE CENTRE OF MY FOREHEAD ...
                                          ... THE RIVAL/DR 291   27
   BENEATH THE FLAT HANDKERCHIEF YOU WEAR INSTEAD OF A HAT. STINGS/DR 293   6
   AND I WEAR THE WRY-FACED PUCKER OF ....JILTED 304   7
   WHILE ANGELS WEAR A WAKEFUL ATTITUDE ....ADMONITIONS 319   13
WEARIES (1)
   WELL, ONE WEARIES OF THE PUBLIC GARDENS: ONE WANTS A VACATION ...
                                          ... TWO CAMPERS IN CLOUD COUNTRY 144   7
WEARING (5)
   SOME ANGEL-SHAPE WORTH WEARING ....FIRESONG   30   9
   SKIES ONCE WEARING A BLUE, DIVINE HAUTEUR ....OUIJA   77   19
   IS HE WEARING PAJAMAS OR AN EVENING SUIT ....BERCK-PLAGE 198   62
   AGAINST A SILENCE WEARING THIN. ....FAMILY REUNION 300   9
   MY NATIVE SLEIGHT-OF-HAND IS WEARING OUT: ....A SORCERER B. 324   9
WEARS (9)
   WEARS PURPLE, STEPS CAREFULLY ....MISS DRAKE PROCEEDS TO SUPPER   41   6
   EACH WEDGE WEARS A STUDDING ....FIESTA MELONS   47   15
   AGE WEARS THE BEST BLACK FABRIC ....OLD LADIES' HOME 120   13
   WEARS A VALENTINE ....POLLY'S TREE 129   38
   WEARS THE FACE OF A PHARAOH, THOUGH IT'S MADE OF MUD AND WATER. ...
                                          ... IN PLASTER 159   42
   DEATH IS THE DRESS SHE WEARS, HER HAT AND COLLAR. ....WIDOW 164   13
   BODY WEARS THE SMILE OF ACCOMPLISHMENT, ...EDGE 272   3
   WORD WEARS TWO W'S? O-R. OR WHAT? ......DIALOGUE OVER A OUIJA BOARD 279   94
   THE SUAVE DISSEMBLING COBRA WEARS A HOOD ....ADMONITIONS 319   10
WEARY (1)
   WHITE-BEARDED, WEARY. THE BERRIES PURPLE ....MOONRISE   98   29
WEASELS (1)
   HIS FINGERS HAD THE NOSES OF WEASELS. ....LITTLE FUGUE 187   11
WEATHER (18)
   THROUGH FROST-THICK WEATHER ....VANITY FAIR   32   1
   INTO THE STILL, SULTRY WEATHER ....MISS DRAKE PROCEEDS TO SUPPER   41   25
   AGAINST MUTINOUS WEATHER ....SPINSTER   50   27
   EACH TO THE OTHER; FIT FIBER FOR STERN WEATHER. ......CRYSTAL GAZER   55   11
   BLACK ROOK IN RAINY WEATHER ....BLACK ROOK IN RAINY WEATHER   56   T
   ANY MORE IN THE DESULTORY WEATHER SOME DESIGN, ...BLACK ROOK I.   57   8
   THROUGH DREAR AND DULCET WEATHER. *THE LADY AND THE EARTHENWARE HEAD   70   28
   A COLORLESS WEATHER, ...TWO VIEWS OF WITHENS   72   13
   RELIC OF TOUGH WEATHER, EVERY WINCH AND STAY ....A WINTER SHIP 113   27
   GRAY AS THE WEATHER. ....WUTHERING HEIGHTS 167   21
   A WEATHER FIGURE, BOGGLING, ...EAVESDROPPER 261   48
   OF NOTCHED TIN PLATITUDES CONCERNING WEATHER, ...SONNET: TO EVA 305   11
   THAT CAME BEFORE THE CHANGE OF WEATHER ....THE DREAM 310   3
   AND SCORNED THE TICK OF THE FALLING WEATHER. ....LAMENT 315   3
   AND SCORNED THE TICK OF THE FALLING WEATHER. ....LAMENT 315   9
   AND SCORNED THE TICK OF THE FALLING WEATHER. ....LAMENT 315   15
   WHO SCORNED THE TICK OF THE FALLING WEATHER. ....LAMENT 316   19
   AND THE FRAGMENTS WHIR LIKE A WEATHER VANE ...CIRCUS IN THREE RINGS 321   5
WEATHERCOCK (1)
   AND HAVE EVERY WEATHERCOCK KISS HANG FIRE ....EPITAPH FOR F.   46   23

                                   557

	TITLE	PAGE	LINE

WEATHERS (2)
        BARES ITS LOW LINTEL TO CORRODING WEATHERS: ....DEPARTURE   51   17
        OF VARIOUS WEATHERS IS ....CHILD'S PARK STONES 101   21
WEATHER'S (1)
        TODDLE ON HOME, BEFORE THE WEATHER'S WORSE. ....THE TOUR 238   41
WEAVE (2)
        AFTER, THEY STAGGER AND WEAVE, UNDER NO BANNER. ....STINGS/DR 293   11
        WHO WEAVE WITHIN THE SKELETON'S WHITE WOMB ....TERMINAL 328   7
WEB (1)
        YOU SPUN THE COSMIC WEB: YOU SQUINT FROM CENTER FIELD. ......SPIDER   48   7
WEBBED (1)
        SHE LIFTS ONE WEBBED FOOT AFTER THE OTHER ....MISS DRAKE P.   41   24
WEB-THREADS (1)
        TWIST OLD WORDS INTO THE WEB-THREADS: TONIGHT MAY THE FISH ...NET-. 121   17
WEB-WINGED (1)
        WEB-WINGED AND FURIOUS. THE FULL MOONLIGHT ....DIALOGUE O. 286 338
WE'D (4)
        WE'D WINK AT IF WE DIDN'T HEAR ....ALL THE DEAD DEARS   70   10
        WE THOUGHT WE'D TRAINED HIM, BEFORE GOING HAYWIRE. TRUTH*DIALOGUE O. 277   41
        TEDIOUS. THAT'S WHAT WE'D SAY. ABOUT ROT*DIALOGUE OVER A OUIJA BOARD 279 101
        OUR WORLD AND THEIRS WE'D BEST PLAY SAFE AND GROOM .....DIALOGUE O. 281 186
WEDDED (1)
        THEIR SMALL PRICE PAID, THESE WEDDED ONES ....CRYSTAL GAZER   55   25
WEDDING (4)
        OF WEDDING PASTRIES, ...OWL 101   4
        LIT LIKE A TWO-TIERED WEDDING CAKE ....ON DECK 142   7
        A WEDDING RING, ...LADY LAZARUS 246   77
        SPRUNG TO BEING ON OUR WEDDING NIGHT ...DIALOGUE OVER A OUIJA BOARD 280 140
WEDDING-CAKE (2)
        A WEDDING-CAKE FACE IN A PAPER FRILL. ....BERCK-PLAGE 198   55
        A SIX AND A HALF FOOT WEDDING-CAKE. ...................EAVESDROPPER 260   26
WEDDINGS (2)
        SOON: BE IT BY WAKES, WEDDINGS, ...ALL THE DEAD DEARS   71   27
        A SERIES OF WEDDINGS. ....WINTER TREES 257   5
WEDGE (2)
        EACH WEDGE WEARS A STUDDING ....FIESTA MELONS   47   15
        THE BOOKS I CARRY WEDGE INTO MY SIDE. ....THREE WOMEN 185 305
WEDGED (1)
        UPSTANDING SPINACH-TIPS WEDGED IN A CIRCLE -- ......SPINACH-PICKER.   89   8
WEDLOCK (1)
        FOR WEDLOCK WROUGHT WITHIN LOVE'S PROPER CHAPEL.*WREATH FOR A BRIDAL   44   12
WEED (3)
        IN WAIT AMID SNARLED WEED AND WRACK OF WAVE *DREAM WITH CLAM-DIGGERS   44   26
        TROLL NO SLIME, NO WEED. ....BATTLE-SCENE   84   23
        AND A WEED, HAIRY AS PRIVATES. ....BERCK-PLAGE 197   36
WEEDING (1)
        HOEING LETTUCE, WEEDING CELERY. ....BITTER STRAWBERRIES 299   19
WEED-MUSTACHIOED (1)
        AT OUR FEET, THE WEED-MUSTACHIOED SEA ....WHITSUN 154   14
WEEDS (3)
        OF WEEDS WE TACKLE TOWARDS WAY'S RANK ENDING; ....FIRESONG   30   16
        SHE THOUGHT OF THEN, THICK-SILTED, WITH WEEDS OBSCURED, *LADY AND T.   69   16
        NOW LITTLE WEEDS INSINUATE ....THE BURNT-OUT SPA 138   10
WEED-SLICKED (1)
        THE WEED-SLICKED SHELF FOR HIS OWN, ...MAGNOLIA SHOALS 122   14
WEEDY (3)
        SO WEEDY A RACE COULD NOT REMAIN IN DREAMS, ...THE THIN PEOPLE   64   23
        OVER THE WEEDY ACRES OF YOUR BROW ....THE COLOSSUS 129   13
        EATEN BY WEEDY GREENS. ....WORDS 270   13
WEEK (4)
        IT STICKS, AND IT HAS STUCK A WEEK. ....THE EYE-MOTE 109   21
        I COULDN'T SLEEP FOR A WEEK, SHE WAS SO COLD. ....IN PLASTER 158   9
        NEAR WINS, WEEK BY WEEK, WAITING UNTIL   DIALOGUE OVER A OUIJA BOARD 277   40
        NEAR WINS, WEEK BY WEEK, WAITING UNTIL   DIALOGUE OVER A OUIJA BOARD 277   40
WEEKS (3)
        ELEVEN WEEKS, AND I KNOW YOUR ESTATE SO WELL ....PRIVATE GROUND 130   13
        FOR WEEKS I CAN REMEMBER NOTHING AT ALL. POEM.1.WHO. 132   33
        AWAY OUR RATIONED DAYS AND WEEKS. ....LOVE IS A PARALLAX 330   72
WEEP (1)
        SORROW; WEEP FOR THE LEGENDARY DRAGON. ....SONNET: TO TIME 311   12
WEEPING (2)
        ANGELS WEEPING OVER DULL NATURES, ...LOVE LETTER 147   16
        THERE IS NO HELP IN HIS WEEPING WIFE. ....BERCK-PLAGE 198   52
WEEPS (1)
        WHO WEEPS BEFORE THE DESOLATE TABLEAU   THE PRINCESS AND THE GOBLINS 335   74
WEEVIL (1)
        OF WEEVIL TRIBE AND LOCUST CARAVAN ....THE DISPOSSESSED 318   8
WEIGH (1)
        THEY ARE SUBTLE: THEY SEEM TO FLOAT, THOUGH THEY WEIGH ME DOWN, ...
                                                               ... TULIPS 161   40
WEIGHS (3)
        DOWN: THE BODY WEIGHS LIKE STONE. ....THE GREAT CARBUNCLE   73   30
        WHICH WEIGHS OUR MADNESS WITH OUR SANITY. ....PERSEUS   84   49
        IT IS ONLY TIME THAT WEIGHS UPON OUR HANDS. ....THREE WOMEN 187 363

558

WEIGHT (4)
    OF HER SMALL HEAT OUT, BUT BEFORE THE WEIGHT ......HARDCASTLE CRAGS   63   42
    CLAIM AND WEIGHT GONE OUT OF THEM. ....THE GREAT CARBUNCLE   72   8
    A WEIGHT OF WORLD AND TIME ....NOTES TO A NEOPHYTE 307   22
    OF BLACK WEIGHT, BLACK BALL, BLACK TRUCK, ...AERIALIST 332   38
WEIGHTING (1)
    WEIGHTING THE PALE SKY WITH A SOLIDER COLOR. .....WUTHERING HEIGHTS 167   7
WEIGHTS (1)
    AS GREAT WEIGHTS DROP ALL ABOUT HER ....AERIALIST 331   17
WEIGHTY (4)
    PALPABLE AS HIS, AND WEIGHTY. ....SCULPTOR   91   4
    BEARS A BURDEN TOO WEIGHTY ....LORELEI   94   17
    AGAINST THE WEIGHTY IMAGE OF THEIR FALL. ....MOONRISE   98   24
    OVER EACH WEIGHTY STOMACH A FACE ....HEAVY WOMEN 158   6
WEIRD (4)
    INVOLVED IN ITS WEIRD BLUE DREAMS, ...BURNING THE LETTERS 205   40
    WITH MY GIPSY ANCESTRESS AND MY WEIRD LUCK ....DADDY 223   38
    ALL COGS, WEIRD SPARKLE AND EVERY COG SOLID GOLD. ....THE TOUR 237   5
    HEARING A WEIRD CACKLE FROM AFAR, ...THE PRINCESS AND THE GOBLINS 334   41
WELCOME (2)
    THE WHOLE SCENE FLARED WELCOME TO THIS ROAMER. ......DREAM WITH C.   44   12
    FOR A CHURLISH WELCOME. ....GREEN ROCK, WINTHROP BAY 105   24
WELD (1)
    THEY WELD TO ME LIKE PLUMS. ....NICK AND THE CANDLESTICK 241   9
WELL (31)
    RINGDOVES ROOST WELL WITHIN HIS WOOD, ...ODE FOR TED   29   19
    YOU MIGHT AS WELL HAUL UP ....EPITAPH FOR FIRE AND FLOWER   45   1
    WELL OR ILL." GERD SLANTS A LOOK AT EACH: MOST DEAR, CRYSTAL GAZER   55   10
    MIGHT WELL SEIZE THIS PRIZE, ...THE LADY AND THE EARTHENWARE HEAD   69   12
    ARMED WITH FEATHERS TO TICKLE AS WELL AS FLY, ...PERSEUS   83   35
    A WELL OF SCENTS ALMOST TOO DENSE TO BREATHE IN. ......BEEKEEPER'S. 118   4
    THE LATE MONTH WITHERS, AS WELL. ....MAGNOLIA SHOALS 122   12
    ELEVEN WEEKS, AND I KNOW YOUR ESTATE SO WELL ....PRIVATE GROUND 130   13
    HE LIVES IN AN OLD WELL, ...POEM.2.DARK. 132   19
    THEY GREW THEIR TOES AND FINGERS WELL ENOUGH, ...STILLBORN 142   2
    WELL, ONE WEARIES OF THE PUBLIC GARDENS: ONE WANTS A VACATION ...
                                      ... TWO CAMPERS IN CLOUD COUNTRY 144   7
    THE WOODS ARE A WELL. THE STARS DROP SILENTLY. ....STARS. 165   4
    THERE IS TOO MUCH EASE HERE; THESE STARS TREAT ME TOO WELL. STARS. 166   37
    AWAY ON WHEELS, INSTEAD OF LEGS, THEY SERVE AS WELL. ...THREE WOMEN 184 254
    STEPS AT MY BACK SPIRAL INTO A WELL. .................APPREHENSIONS 195   8
    WHO PLUMBS THE WELL OF HIS BOOK, ... BERCK-PLAGE 197   22
    LOVE, LOVE, AND WELL, I WAS TIRED ....BURNING THE LETTERS 204   10
    WELL, WHAT DO YOU THINK OF THAT? ....THE APPLICANT 221   29
    I THINK I MAY WELL BE A JEW. ....DADDY 223   35
    IN A SORT OF CEMENT WELL ....LESBOS 227   13
    WELL I HOPE YOU'VE ENJOYED IT, AUNTIE! ....THE TOUR 238   48
    INTO THE TERRIBLE WELL, ...NICK AND THE CANDLESTICK 242   39
    I DO IT EXCEPTIONALLY WELL. ....LADY LAZARUS 245   45
    POCKET WATCH, I TICK WELL. ....GIGOLO 267   1
    AND BACK TO P, AS IF HE KNEW US WELL ...DIALOGUE OVER A OUIJA BOARD 277   30
    OF PLACES: THE OIL WELL MY UNCLE OWNS, FOR ONE; ....DIALOGUE O. 277   47
    WELL WHAT, THEN? THAT'S THE TROUBLE. LET'S SAY HE ......DIALOGUE O. 278   51
    AND TONGUE, AND THOUGHT, AS WELL AS THE BLOOD-HEAT ....DIALOGUE O. 283 258
    TO OUR MEANING WELL. WHEN LIGHTS GO OUT *DIALOGUE OVER A OUIJA BOARD 286 363
    "LAST NIGHT," HE SAID, "I SLEPT WELL ....THE DREAM 310   1
    "WELL THEN, IF WE AGREE, IT IS NOT ODD ....LOVE IS A PARALLAX 329   7
WE'LL (5)
    "NO HARDSHIP THEN?" HE ASKS. "WE'LL TAKE ....CRYSTAL GAZER   55   19
    IN A MONTH WE'LL WONDER WHAT PLATES AND FORKS ARE FOR. ...TWO CAMP. 145   20
    WE'LL WAKE BLANK-BRAINED AS WATER IN THE DAWN. ....TWO CAMP. 145   27
    MOVING, BEING MOVED. AND WE'LL IMAGINE DIALOGUE OVER A OUIJA BOARD 276   8
    AND WE'LL SEE WHO'S SMARTEST. PAN, TELL US NOW: ....DIALOGUE O. 281 205
WELL-BOILED (1)
    NUDE AS CLEOPATRA IN MY WELL-BOILED HOSPITAL SHIFT, ...FACE LIFT 156   10
WELL-BRED (2)
    OF MONSTROUS SIZE, LIKE NO WELL-BRED LILIES. ....YADWIGHA.   85   7
    FOR BEING TOO WELL-BRED AND SMELLESS AND LIKING THE CITY. ...
                                      ... QUEEN MARY'S ROSE GARDEN 290   20
WELL-DONE (1)
    RIGHT, LIKE A WELL-DONE SUM. ....YOU'RE 141   17
WELLINGTONS (1)
    MY WELLINGTONS ....LETTER IN NOVEMBER 253   14
WELL-LOVED (1)
    IT STABLED IN: LONG-USED, BECAME WELL-LOVED THE COMPANIONABLE ILLS 105   7
WELL-NAMED (1)
    WELL-NAMED, ILL-FAMED A KNAVISH FLY-BY-NIGHT, ...GOATSUCKER 111   11
WELLS (1)
    WELLS LIKE TEARS, LIKE THE ....WORDS 270   7
WELL-STEERED (1)
    HERE, IN A WELL-STEERED COUNTRY, ...LORELEI   94   19
WELL-WATER (1)
    WELL-WATER KEPT COOL AT THE START OF THE ROWS. .....SPINACH-PICKER.   89   14
WELSH (1)
    SELLING THE WELSH AND ENGLISH MOTHERS ....ON DECK 143   29
                                      559

```
                                                     TITLE             PAGE  LINE
WELTER (2)
     SNOWCAKES BREAK AND WELTER. THIS YEAR  ................POINT SHIRLEY   110    4
     COULD GROPE ITS WAY TO GOSPEL THROUGH THAT WELTER  ......DIALOGUE O.   286  346
WELTERING (1)
     OF STARK WIND-HARROWED HILLS AND WELTERING MIST:  ........SNOWMAN O.    58   13
WENT (11)
     HIGH AGAINST HEAVEN, GULLS WENT WHEELING SOUNDLESS  ...DREAM WITH C.    44   13
     WHERE THE DAFT FATHER WENT DOWN  .................ALL THE DEAD DEARS    71   23
     AND THE SHADOW STRETCHED, THE LIGHTS WENT OUT.*THE DISQUIETING MUSES    75   32
     WENT ABOUT THEIR BUSINESS, WHICH  ......MUSSEL HUNTER AT ROCK HARBOR    97   61
     THE DAY YOU DIED I WENT INTO THE DIRT,  ......ELECTRA ON AZALEA PATH   116    1
     NOTHING WENT MOLDY. THE LITTLE INVISIBLES  ............POEM.4.BEAST.   134    5
     SINK OUT OF SIGHT, AND THE WATER WENT OVER MY HEAD. .........TULIPS    161   27
     WHEN THE SPORTY WIFE AND HER DOCTOR HUSBAND WENT ON ONE OF
          THEIR CRUISES  .....................................THE BABYSITTERS   174   16
     WENT ON SHAPING ITSELF WITH LOVE, AS IF I WAS READY.  ...THREE WOMEN   178   63
     A DOG PICKED UP YOUR DOGGY HUSBAND. HE WENT ON. ............LESBOS    229   63
     IT WENT UP IN SMOKE. .........................................THE TOUR   238   23
WEPT (1)
     THE BURGHERS SWEATED AND WEPT. THE CHILDREN WORE WHITE.  ....CANDLES   149   19
WERE (56)
WE'RE (4)
     IT'S VIOLENT. WE'RE HERE ON A VISIT,  .................STOPPED DEAD    230   11
     AS FLAT AS SHE, WHO WHISPER "WE'RE YOUR DAUGHTERS."  ......PARALYTIC   266   26
     WHILE WE'RE SITTING, FACE TO FACE ACROSS THE COFFEE-  ...DIALOGUE O.   276    3
     AT FAME OR NOT? AS FOR LOVE, I FIGURE WHEN WE'RE  .......DIALOGUE O.   278   57
WEST (1)
     THE ART STUDENTS IN WEST BERLIN. ...........................ON DECK   143   24
WET (12)
     EACH THORN; SPIRING FROM WET EARTH, A BLUE HAZE  ........DIALOGUE B.    38    5
     HUNCHES A WET BLACK ROOK  ..............BLACK ROOK IN RAINY WEATHER    56    2
     LIT THINGS, THAT LAMP OF THE POSSIBLE! WET YET  .....SPINACH-PICKER.    89    3
     ODORS OF WET EARTH RISE. .............................THE SLEEPERS    122    9
     THEY FLY TOO FAST TO FEEL THE WET. ........................ON DECK    143   17
     THE COLORS REPLENISH THEMSELVES, AND THE WET  ..........THREE WOMEN    185  313
     LEVER OF HIS WET DREAMS. ................................THE JAILER    226   10
     OF TWO WET EYES AND A SCREECH. .........................THALIDOMIDE    252   20
     WALKS THE WAIST-HIGH WET. .........................LETTER IN NOVEMBER   254   33
     THE WET DAWN INKS ARE DOING THEIR BLUE DISSOLVE. ......WINTER TREES    257    1
     WITH WET PLUMAGE THROUGH MY ROOMS. .......................THE DREAM    310    6
     WITH ORANGE SCALLOPS TANGLED IN WET HAIR, ........MIDSUMMER MOBILE    324   11
WETTING (1)
     A GIRL COULD WADE WITHOUT WETTING HER SHINS.   A LESSON IN VENGEANCE    80   20
WE'VE (2)
     I'LL ASK. DO. WE'VE KEPT HIM WAITING LONG  ............DIALOGUE O.    281  180
     WE'VE SQUANDERED ALL THE BANKER WILL ALLOW  ........THE DISPOSSESSED   319   16
WHALE (2)
     OF A WHALE WITH HOLES AND HOLES, AND BLEED HIM WHITE  .......PERSEUS    82    5
     THE WHALE, THE SHARK, THE SQUID.  .....................BATTLE-SCENE    84   20
WHALES (1)
     WHITE WHALES ARE GONE WITH THE WHITE OCEAN.  ............TWO LOVERS.   327   12
WHAMMY (1)
     LIMBS: NOT A BASILISK-BLINK, NOR A DOUBLE WHAMMY,  .........PERSEUS    83   16
WHARF (1)
     AT THIS WHARF THERE ARE NO GRAND LANDINGS TO SPEAK OF.*A WINTER SHIP   112    1
WHAT (161)
     WHAT CEREMONY OF WORDS CAN PATCH THE HAVOC?  .........CONVERSATION.    21   14
     GLAZES THE WINDOW OF MY HURT; WHAT SOLACE  .......WINTER LANDSCAPE,    22   13
     WHAT FIRES RUN, WHAT CRAVING WAKES? ..........................PURSUIT   22   12
     WHAT FIRES RUN, WHAT CRAVING WAKES? ..........................PURSUIT   22   12
     WHAT LULL, WHAT COOL CAN LAP ME IN  ........................PURSUIT    23   35
     WHAT LULL, WHAT COOL CAN LAP ME IN  ........................PURSUIT    23   35
     OF NATURE: WHAT BETTER WAY TO TEST TAUT FIBER  .....CHANNEL CROSSING    27   16
     WHAT FURY URGED HIM SLAY  ....................THE QUEEN'S COMPLAINT    28    9
     RIVALS HER WHETTED LOOK, DIVINING WHAT CONCEIT  .......VANITY FAIR     32   13
     AND WHAT HEART'S OVEN  ...................................VANITY FAIR    32   15
     WHAT SCAR'S BEEN KNOCKED  ...........TINKER JACK AND THE TIDY WIVES    34   23
     "WHAT MANNER OF BUSINESS ARE YOU ON?  ...................DIALOGUE B.    38   13
     AFTER YOUR LIFE'S END, WHAT JUST EPILOGUE  .............DIALOGUE B.    39   24
     WHAT LOVE DID THEN, LOVE DOES NOW:*DIALOGUE BETWEEN GHOST AND PRIEST    39   29
     "WHAT LOVE," ASKED FATHER SHAWN, "BUT TOO GREAT LOVE ...DIALOGUE B.    39   31
     WHAT THOUGH GREEN LEAVES ONLY WITNESS  .........WREATH FOR A BRIDAL    44    1
     SUCH PACT AS IS MADE ONCE ONLY; WHAT MATTER  ....WREATH FOR A BRIDAL    44    2
     OF ANIMALS TO CHOIR: "LOOK WHAT THRESH OF WINGS *WREATH FOR A BRIDAL    45   15
     STILL AS A SHELL: HEAR WHAT AN AGE OF GLASS  ........EPITAPH FOR F.    45   16
     WHAT GERD SAW THEN ENGRAVED HER MIND  ................CRYSTAL GAZER    56   43
     DREAM-FILMED. WHAT A VISION OF ANCIENT HOGHOOD MUST  ...........SOW    61   27
     ITS OWN ORDER ON WHAT IS   ON THE DIFFICULTY OF CONJURING UP A DRYAD    66    8
     THIEVES WHAT IT HAS."  ....ON THE DIFFICULTY OF CONJURING UP A DRYAD    66   40
     TOWARD WHAT I CAN GRAB,  ........................WORDS FOR A NURSERY    73    6
     MOTHER, MOTHER, WHAT ILLBRED AUNT  ..............THE DISQUIETING MUSES    74    1
     OR WHAT DISFIGURED AND UNSIGHTLY  ............THE DISQUIETING MUSES    74    2
     WHAT FLINTY PEBBLES THE PLOUGHBLADE UPTURNS  ................OUIJA    77   28
     WHAT THE SEASHELL SPOKE TO HIS INNER EAR   ON THE DECLINE OF ORACLES    78    7
     OF DIGESTING WHAT CENTURIES ALONE DIGEST:  ................PERSEUS    82    2
```

	TITLE	PAGE	LINE

WHAT (CONT.)
```
AGAINST OUR SKY: THEY ARE WHAT WE LOOK SOUTHWARD TO *ABOVE THE OXBOW    88   11
DIMINISHES, AND GOD KNOWS WHAT IS THERE.  ...THE GHOST'S LEAVETAKING    91   26
MUSSELS. FROM WHAT THE CRABS SAW,  .....MUSSEL HUNTER AT ROCK HARBOR    97   64
FROM WHAT GRACE AM I FALLEN. TONGUES ARE STRANGE,  ....INCOMMUNICADO   100   12
WHAT MOVED THE PALE, RAPTORIAL OWL  .............................OWL   102    9
WHITENESS BEING WHAT I REMEMBER  ...............WHITENESS I REMEMBER   102    1
BLIND TO WHAT WILL BE AND WHAT WAS.  .....................THE EYE-MOTE  109   23
BLIND TO WHAT WILL BE AND WHAT WAS.  .....................THE EYE-MOTE  109   23
WHAT I WANT BACK IS WHAT I WAS  .........................THE EYE-MOTE  109   25
WHAT I WANT BACK IS WHAT I WAS  .........................THE EYE-MOTE  109   25
WHAT THE SLUTTISH, RUTTED SEA COULD DO.  ..............POINT SHIRLEY   110   12
AND APPLE CAKES TO COOL. WHAT IS IT  ..................POINT SHIRLEY   110   28
FOR WHAT, THEN, HAD THEY ENDURED  .....THE HERMIT AT OUTERMOST HOUSE   119    7
FROM THE DOOR AS EVER. WHAT HAPPENS BETWEEN US  ..........BLUE MOLES   127   34
WHAT LARGE EYES THE DEAD HAVE!  ...........................POEM.6.W.   135   10
THE SMALL DELL EATS WHAT ATE IT ONCE.  .............THE BURNT-OUT SPA   138   18
IF HE WERE I, HE WOULD DO WHAT I DID.  ...........THE HANGING MAN      142    6
O I CANNOT UNDERSTAND WHAT HAPPENED TO THEM!  .............STILLBORN   142    6
IT WOULD BE BETTER IF THEY WERE ALIVE, AND THAT'S WHAT THEY
   WERE.  ...............................................STILLBORN    142   13
IN A MONTH WE'LL WONDER WHAT PLATES AND FORKS ARE FOR.  ...TWO CAMP.   145   20
WHEN YOU KICK ME OUT, THAT'S WHAT I'LL REMEMBER,  .....LEAVING EARLY   145    2
WE SLEPT LIKE STONES. LADY, WHAT AM I DOING  .........LEAVING EARLY   146   42
I DIDN'T KNOW WHAT TO MAKE OF IT.  ......................LOVE LETTER   147   24
WHAT GIRL EVER FLOURISHED IN SUCH COMPANY?  ...................MAGI   148   18
NOBODY CAN TELL WHAT I LACK.  .................PARLIAMENT HILL FIELDS  152    5
THIS IS NOT WHAT I MEANT:  ...................................WHITSUN  153    1
BUT WHAT DO YOU KNOW ABOUT THAT  .................ZOO KEEPER'S WIFE   155   14
THEN I REALIZED WHAT SHE WANTED WAS FOR ME TO LOVE HER:  IN PLASTER   159   13
THEN I SAW WHAT THE TROUBLE WAS: SHE THOUGHT SHE WAS IMMORTAL.  ...
   ...  IN PLASTER    159   35
IT IS WHAT THE DEAD CLOSE ON, FINALLY; I IMAGINE THEM  .......TULIPS   161   34
AND WHAT IF THE SKY HERE IS NO DIFFERENT,  ..STARS OVER THE DORDOGNE   166   25
SHE DOES NOT HEAR WHAT THE SAILOR OR THE PEASANT IS SAYING --  ...
   ...  FINISTERRE    170   26
SEARCHING MY REACHES FOR WHAT SHE REALLY IS.  ...............MIRROR   174   11
O WHAT HAS COME OVER US, MY SISTER!  .................THE BABYSITTERS  175   28
WHAT KEYHOLE HAVE WE SLIPPED THROUGH, WHAT DOOR HAS SHUT?  ....BABY.   175   42
WHAT KEYHOLE HAVE WE SLIPPED THROUGH, WHAT DOOR HAS SHUT?  ....BABY.   175   42
DON'T KNOW WHAT TO MAKE OF THE SUDDEN SLIPPINESS,  .....NEW YEAR ON.   176    4
IS SHE SORRY FOR WHAT WILL HAPPEN? I DO NOT THINK SO.  ..THREE WOMEN   176    6
WHAT HAPPENS IN ME WILL HAPPEN WITHOUT ATTENTION.  ......THREE WOMEN   176   10
I CANNOT HELP SMILING AT WHAT IT IS I KNOW.  ...........THREE WOMEN   177   13
THEY ARE TO BLAME FOR WHAT I AM, AND THEY KNOW IT.  .....THREE WOMEN   180  116
AND WHAT IF THEY FOUND THEMSELVES SURPRISED, AS I DID?  THREE WOMEN   180  118
AND WHAT IF TWO LIVES LEAKED BETWEEN MY THIGHS?  ........THREE WOMEN   180  120
WHAT PAINS, WHAT SORROWS MUST I BE MOTHERING?  .........THREE WOMEN   180  133
WHAT PAINS, WHAT SORROWS MUST I BE MOTHERING?  ..........THREE WOMEN   180  133
WHAT DID MY FINGERS DO BEFORE THEY HELD HIM?  ..........THREE WOMEN   181  169
WHAT DID MY HEART DO, WITH ITS LOVE?  ..................THREE WOMEN   181  170
WHAT BLUE, MOONY RAY ICES THEIR DREAMS?  ...............THREE WOMEN   181  182
WHAT IS IT THAT FLINGS THESE INNOCENT SOULS AT US?  .....THREE WOMEN   183  218
AS PRODIGAL IN WHAT LACKS ME.  ........................THREE WOMEN   184  259
AND TO MARRY WHAT HE WANTS AND WHERE HE WILL.  .........THREE WOMEN   186  336
I AM SOLITARY AS GRASS. WHAT IS IT I MISS?  ............THREE WOMEN   186  342
WHAT IS THAT BIRD THAT CRIES  .........................THREE WOMEN   186  348
I AM YOUNG AS EVER, IT SAYS. WHAT IS IT I MISS?  .......THREE WOMEN   186  350
WHAT AM I TO MAKE OF THESE CONTRADICTIONS?  .........AN APPEARANCE   189    8
IT IS WHAT YOU FEAR.  ......................................ELM   192    2
WHAT IS THIS, THIS FACE  ...................................ELM   193   38
THIS IS WHAT I AM MADE OF, THIS AND A TERROR  .......APPREHENSIONS   195   14
WHY IS IT SO QUIET, WHAT ARE THEY HIDING?  .............BERCK-PLAGE   196    5
SICK WITH WHAT IT HAS SWALLOWED ---  ..................BERCK-PLAGE   197   28
WHAT CUPPED SIGHS, WHAT SALT IN THE THROAT....  .......BERCK-PLAGE   197   32
WHAT CUPPED SIGHS, WHAT SALT IN THE THROAT....  .......BERCK-PLAGE   197   32
THIS IS WHAT IT IS TO BE COMPLETE. IT IS HORRIBLE.  .....BERCK-PLAGE   198   61
WHAT IS THE NAME OF THAT COLOR? ---  ..................BERCK-PLAGE   200   97
WHAT DID I LEAVE UNTOUCHED ON THE DOORSTEP --  ...........THE OTHER   201    2
OPEN YOUR HANDBAG. WHAT IS THAT BAD SMELL?  .............THE OTHER   201   13
WHAT ARE THESE WORDS, THESE WORDS?  ...................WORDS HEARD.   202    6
WHAT DID THEY KNOW THAT I DIDN'T?  .............BURNING THE LETTERS   204    5
THE DOGS ARE TEARING A FOX. THIS IS WHAT IT IS LIKE --  ...BURNING.   205   49
WHAT IMMORTALITY IS. THAT IT IS IMMORTAL.  ....BURNING THE LETTERS   205   56
WHAT IS THIS, BEHIND THIS VEIL, IS IT UGLY, IS IT BEAUTIFUL?  ...
   ...  A BIRTHDAY PRESENT    206    1
I AM SURE IT IS UNIQUE, I AM SURE IT IS JUST WHAT I WANT. *BIRTHDAY.  206    3
MY GOD, WHAT A LAUGH!"  ...................A BIRTHDAY PRESENT   206   10
CAN YOU NOT SEE I DO NOT MIND WHAT IT IS.  .......A BIRTHDAY PRESENT   206   20
MUST YOU KILL WHAT YOU CAN?  .....................A BIRTHDAY PRESENT   207   47
WHAT WAS SHE DOING WHEN IT BLEW IN  .................THE DETECTIVE   208    1
WHOSE IS THAT LONG WHITE BOX IN THE GROVE, WHAT HAVE THEY
   ACCOMPLISHED, WHY AM I COLD.  ................THE BEE MEETING   212   55
THERE ARE NO WINDOWS, SO I CAN'T SEE WHAT IS IN THERE. *THE ARRIVAL.  213    9
WHAT AM I BUYING, WORMY MAHOGANY?  ..........................STINGS   214   14
```

561

```
                                              TITLE           PAGE  LINE
WHAT (CONT.)
   WHAT WILL THEY TASTE OF, THE CHRISTMAS ROSES? ..........WINTERING   219   49
   WELL, WHAT DO YOU THINK OF THAT? .....................THE APPLICANT 221   29
   AND THEN I KNEW WHAT TO DO. .................................DADDY  224   63
   WHAT HOLES THIS PAPERY DAY IS ALREADY FULL OF! .........THE JAILER  226   17
   MY RIBS SHOW. WHAT HAVE I EATEN? ......................THE JAILER   226   22
   THAT BEING FREE. WHAT WOULD THE DARK ..................THE JAILER   227   41
   WHAT WOULD THE LIGHT .................................THE JAILER    227   43
   DO WITHOUT EYES TO KNIFE, WHAT WOULD HE ...............THE JAILER    227   44
   YOU KNOW WHAT LIES ARE FOR. ................................LESBOS  230   91
   WRITHING AND SIGHING, WHAT SORT OF A SCENERY IS IT? ...STOPPED DEAD 230    9
   PURE? WHAT DOES IT MEAN? ...................................FEVER.  231    1
   WHAT A THRILL --- ...........................................CUT    235    1
   OF WHAT GREEN STARS CAN MAKE IT TO OUR GATE. ........BY CANDLELIGHT 236    5
   O MY GOD, WHAT AM I .............................POPPIES IN OCTOBER 240   10
   WHAT A TRASH ........................................LADY LAZARUS   245   23
   WHAT A MILLION FILAMENTS. ...........................LADY LAZARUS   245   25
   WHAT DO WHEELS EAT, THESE WHEELS ....................GETTING THERE  248   13
   AND THE MEN, WHAT IS LEFT OF THE MEN ................GETTING THERE  248   29
   WHAT GLOVE ..........................................THALIDOMIDE    252    7
   WHAT LEATHERINESS ...................................THALIDOMIDE    252    8
   WHAT I LOVE IS .............................................YEARS   255   11
   WHAT IS SO GREAT IN THAT! ..................................YEARS   255   17
   THIS IS WHAT I AM IN FOR -- .........................EAVESDROPPER   261   52
   ONCE ONE HAS SEEN GOD, WHAT IS THE REMEDY? ................MYSTIC   268    9
   WHAT IS THE REMEDY? .......................................MYSTIC   268   15
   WHAT IS SO REAL AS THE CRY OF A CHILD? ..................KINDNESS   269    6
   THAN FINANCIER. WHAT GOOD IS HE, IF NOT *DIALOGUE OVER A OUIJA BOARD 277  44
   WELL WHAT, THEN? THAT'S THE TROUBLE. LET'S SAY HE ......DIALOGUE O. 278   51
   REALLY CAN SEE INTO THE FUTURE. WHAT, ..DIALOGUE OVER A OUIJA BOARD 278   52
   ALWAYS, THE GLASS WILL BLURT WHAT I DON'T WANT ........DIALOGUE O.  278   68
   WOULD TRAFFIC IN. LET HIM FINISH WHAT HE BEGAN. .......DIALOGUE O.  278   84
   PLUMAGE OF WHAT, PAN? P . . HE STARTS AGAIN, .........DIALOGUE O.   279   85
   A-W-W. HE'S GONE OFF: WHAT ENGLISH .....DIALOGUE OVER A OUIJA BOARD 279   93
   WORD WEARS TWO W'S? O-R. OR WHAT? ......DIALOGUE OVER A OUIJA BOARD 279   94
   OUT OF A WHOLENESS. WORMS, NOT WINGS IS WHAT ..........DIALOGUE O.  279   99
   TEDIOUS. THAT'S WHAT WE'D SAY. ABOUT ROT*DIALOGUE OVER A OUIJA BOARD 279 101
   NOW, YOU REALLY DON'T MUCH CARE WHICH, OR WHAT ........DIALOGUE O.  280  151
   WHAT GREENHORN VENTS HIS VENOM AGAINST GIANTS .........DIALOGUE O.  281  199
   OF CAMBRIC OR WATERDROPS, WHO KNOWS WHAT BELIEF .......DIALOGUE O.  282  224
   OPPOSE WHAT WE FACED EARLIER. FEEL MY HAND. ..........DIALOGUE O.   285  332
   THE LABYRINTH AND IGNORE WHAT MANNER OF BEAST ........DIALOGUE O.   286  343
   IN HER PROPHETIC FIT HEARD WHAT WE HEARD, ............DIALOGUE O.   286  348
   WHAT GOOD IS ALL THAT SPACE IF IT CAN'T DRAW YOU OFF? THE RIVAL/DR  291   13
   WHAT HONEY SUMMONS THESE ANIMALCULES? ...................STINGS/DR  293    1
   WHAT FEAR? IT HAS SET THEM ZINGING ......................STINGS/DR  293    2
   WHAT PRINCE HAS EVER SEIZED THE SHINING GRAIL .......METAMORPHOSES. 307   19
   TO FIND WHAT MAKES IT MOVE, .......................TRIO OF LOVE SONGS 315 50
   WHAT COUNTERMAGIC CAN UNDO THE SNARE ...........PROLOGUE TO SPRING  322   10
   YET AS WE WONDER WHAT CAN COME OF ICE ..........PROLOGUE TO SPRING  322   14
   FOR WHAT FIRE COULD DAMAGE*ON LOOKING INTO THE EYES OF A DEMON LOVER 325 19
   WE ARE NOT WHAT WE MIGHT BE; WHAT WE ARE ...............TWO LOVERS. 327    9
   WE ARE NOT WHAT WE MIGHT BE; WHAT WE ARE ...............TWO LOVERS. 327    9
   TELL ME WHAT YOU SEE IN IT: .....BLACK PINE TREE IN AN ORANGE LIGHT 328    1
WHATEVER (10)
   AND WHATEVER PAN THIS MENDING MASTER *TINKER JACK AND THE TIDY WIVES 34   3
   "WHATEVER SCATH ....................TINKER JACK AND THE TIDY WIVES   34   19
   WHATEVER TRIAL'S TO COME, SO SAY TRUE." .............CRYSTAL GAZER   55   20
   WHATEVER LOST GHOSTS FLARE, ....................NOVEMBER GRAVEYARD   56   15
   OF WHATEVER ANGEL MAY CHOOSE TO FLARE ..BLACK ROOK IN RAINY WEATHER 57   26
   WHATEVER HIS SHREWD SECRET, HE KEPT IT HID .......................SOW 60   3
   WHATEVER I SEE I SWALLOW IMMEDIATELY .........................MIRROR 173   2
   SHALL I EVER FIND IT, WHATEVER IT IS? ...............THREE WOMEN    186  343
   AND DO WHATEVER YOU TELL IT. .......................THE APPLICANT   221   13
   BY WHATEVER THESE PINK THINGS MEAN. .......................FEVER.   232   50
WHAT'S (3)
   WHAT'S TO COME, .......................................RECANTATION   42    9
   GILDING WHAT'S EYESORE, ....................GREEN ROCK, WINTHROP BAY 105   21
   ONE DAY YOU MAY TOUCH WHAT'S WRONG ..........FOR A FATHERLESS SON   205   12
WHEAT (3)
   HER WHEAT LOAVES ...................................POINT SHIRLEY   110   27
   A GLITTER OF WHEAT AND CRUDE EARTH. .....................BERCK-PLAGE 200   96
   FOAM TO WHEAT, A GLITTER OF SEAS. .............................ARIEL 239   23
WHEEL (4)
   I COME TO WHEEL RUTS, AND WATER ..................WUTHERING HEIGHTS 167   28
   NO GETTING UP BY ELEPHANT OR WHEEL OR SHOE. ...NEW YEAR ON DARTMOOR 176    7
   ONE SCARF WILL CATCH AND ANCHOR IN THE WHEEL. ...............FEVER. 231   13
   TO CHART THE MEASURE OF FORTUNE'S WHEEL; ........SONG FOR A REVOLU. 323   11
WHEELCHAIRS (1)
   TUBULAR STEEL WHEELCHAIRS, ALUMINUM CRUTCHES. ..........BERCK-PLAGE 197   39
WHEELED (2)
   OF BEING WHEELED OFF UNDER CROSSES AND A RAIN OF PIETAS.
                                          ...      APPREHENSIONS      195   15
   THE SAME PLACARD OF BLUE FOG IS WHEELED INTO POSITION ...THE JAILER 226    2

                                  562
```

WHEELING (3)
   HIGH AGAINST HEAVEN, GULLS WENT WHEELING SOUNDLESS ...DREAM WITH C.   44 13
   BITS OF BURNT PAPER WHEELING IN A BLOWN SKY. .........BLACKBERRYING 168 11
   IT IS A STATUE THE ORDERLIES ARE WHEELING OFF.*THE SURGEON AT 2 A.M. 171 31
WHEELS (13)
   HAMMERS HOISTED, WHEELS TURNING, ...NIGHT SHIFT   76 17
   TO THE CLOUD-CUCKOO LAND OF COLOR WHEELS ...THE GHOST'S LEAVETAKING   91 35
   WHITE DAISY WHEELS AND ....POLLY'S TREE 128 26
   SMOKE WHEELS FROM THE BEAK OF THIS EMPTY JAR. POEM.6.W. 135 12
   NOISELESS, ON RUBBER WHEELS, ON THE WAY TO THE SEA RESORT. WAKING. 151   8
   AWAY ON WHEELS, INSTEAD OF LEGS, THEY SERVE AS WELL. ...THREE WOMEN 184 254
   THE WHEELS, TWO RUBBER GRUBS, BITE THEIR SWEET TAILS. STOPPED DEAD 230   6
   OF THE WHEELS MOVE, THEY APPALL ME --- ....GETTING THERE 248   4
   WHAT DO WHEELS EAT, THESE WHEELS ....GETTING THERE 248 13
   WHAT DO WHEELS EAT, THESE WHEELS ....GETTING THERE 248 13
   THE WHEELS REVOLVE, THE UNIVERSE KEEPS RUNNING. TO EVA DESCENDING. 303   2
   THE SCRAPS OF RUSTED REVERIE, THE WHEELS ....SONNET: TO EVA 305 10
   TAXIS INDOLENT ON WHISPERED WHEELS;*MORNING IN THE HOSPITAL SOLARIUM 332 11
WHEEZE (1)
   LONG GONE TO WHEEZE AND SEED, ELLA MASON ....ELLA MASON A.   53   8
WHEEZES (1)
   WHO WHEEZES AT THE GATE. INCAPABLE ....FEVER. 231   5
WHELPED (1)
   WARRANT HIM WHELPED IN THE WAKE OF TWO SHOOTING ....DIALOGUE O. 281 194
WHEN (76)
   LIKE A DAUNTED WITCH, QUITTING CASTLE WHEN REAL DAYS BREAK. ...
             ... CONVERSATION AMONG THE RUINS   21   8
   WHEN BURNS AND BRANDS THAT YELLOW GAZE? ....PURSUIT   23 36
   JUST HOW GUILTY ARE WE WHEN THE CEILING ....TALE OF A TUB   24   9
   REVEALS NO CRACKS THAT CAN BE DECODED? WHEN WASHBOWL TALE OF A TUB   24 10
   IN ITS EXPLICIT FOLDS? OR WHEN THE WINDOW, ...TALE OF A TUB   24 14
   INTRUDES EVEN WHEN THE REVOLTED EYE ....TALE OF A TUB   25 30
   WHY, ALL THE WINDOWS BROKE WHEN HE STALKED IN.*THE QUEEN'S COMPLAINT   28   5
   WHEN ALL EARTH HIS WORDS DO SUMMON ....ODE FOR TED   30 23
   WHEN MY EYES SHUT ....SOLILOQUY OF THE SOLIPSIST   37   5
   WHEN IN GOOD HUMOR, ...SOLILOQUY OF THE SOLIPSIST   37 20
   WHEN NIGHT COMES BLACK ....THE SHRIKE   42   1
   WHEN HER SHRIKE-FACE ....THE SHRIKE   42 17
   WALKING EAGER TOWARD WATER, WHEN THERE, ONE BY ONE, ..DREAM WITH C.   44 23
   FREE OF THE FICTIVE VEIN. WHEN ONE STARK SKELETON*NOVEMBER GRAVEYARD   56 10
   SO WHEN STAUNCH ISLAND STOCK CHOSE FORFEITURE ....MAYFLOWER   60   9
   IN A WAR MAKING EVIL HEADLINES WHEN WE ....THE THIN PEOPLE   64   6
   OUT OF THE SIDE OF THE GENEROUS MOON WHEN IT ....THE THIN PEOPLE   65 28
   ILL-SERVED HE'LL BE WHEN ....WORDS FOR A NURSERY   74 41
   AND WORSE-SERVED WHEN DEATH ....WORDS FOR A NURSERY   74 47
   IN THE HURRICANE, WHEN FATHER'S TWELVE ....THE DISQUIETING MUSES   75 17
   WHEN ON TIPTOE THE SCHOOLGIRLS DANCED, ...THE DISQUIETING MUSES   75 25
   WHEN WORDS, LIKE LOCUSTS, DRUMMED THE DARKENING AIR ....OUIJA   77 17
   MY FATHER DIED, AND WHEN HE DIED ....ON THE DECLINE OF ORACLES   78   9
   A PANE OF DRAGONFLY WING, WHEN THEY LEFT ME ....SPINACH-PICKER.   89   5
   WHICH SEEMED, WHEN DREAMED, TO MEAN SO PROFOUNDLY MUCH, ...GHOST'S.   90   5
   WHEN SEAS WASH COLD, FOAM- ....FULL FATHOM FIVE   92   3
   AN ORANGE BUD, POCKETED IT. WHEN *FABLE OF THE RHODODENDRON STEALERS 103   8
   WHEN THE SPLINTER FLEW IN AND STUCK MY EYE, ...THE EYE-MOTE 109   9
   HE HEARD WHEN HE WALKED INTO THE WATER ....SUICIDE OFF EGG ROCK 115 23
   WHEN I WORMED BACK UNDER MY MOTHER'S HEART. ELECTRA ON AZALEA PATH 116 10
   WHEN I SPLIT A ROCK ONE TIME ....MEDALLION 124 12
   WHEN IT THUNDERED, I GRIT A FLAT STONE. POEM.3.MAENAD. 133   5
   WHEN I FELL OUT OF THE LIGHT. I ENTERED POEM.7.S. 136   5
   WHEN YOU KICK ME OUT, THAT'S WHAT I'LL REMEMBER, ...LEAVING EARLY 145   2
   WHEN I LIGHT THEM, MY NOSTRILS PRICKLE. ....CANDLES 149 14
   WHEN I WAS NINE, A LIME-GREEN ANESTHETIST ....FACE LIFT 155   4
   WHEN I GRIN, THE STITCHES TAUTEN. I GROW BACKWARD. I'M TWENTY,*FACE. 156 21
   WHEN I HIT HER SHE HELD STILL, LIKE A TRUE PACIFIST. ...IN PLASTER 159 12
   SOMETIMES I THINK THAT WHEN I AM SLEEPING ....I AM VERTICAL 162 14
   AND I SHALL BE USEFUL WHEN I LIE DOWN FINALLY: ....I AM VERTICAL 162 19
   WHEN ONE OF THEM FALLS IT LEAVES A SPACE, ..STARS OVER THE DORDOGNE 166 32
   WHEN THEY FREE ME, I AM BEADED WITH TEARS. ....FINISTERRE 169 18
   I WANT TO BE LOOKING AT THEM WHEN THEY COME ....LAST WORDS 172   4
   WHEN THE SOLES OF MY FEET GROW COLD, ...LAST WORDS 172 19
   WHEN THE SWEETHEART FROM ENGLAND APPEARED, WITH HER CREAM SKIN AND
      YARDLEY COSMETICS, ...THE BABYSITTERS 174   6
   WHEN THE SPORTY WIFE AND HER DOCTOR HUSBAND WENT ON ONE OF THEIR
      CRUISES ....THE BABYSITTERS 174 16
   ON THE GAMEROOM PIANO, WHEN THE "BIG PEOPLE" WERE OUR, ...BABY. 175 23
   WHEN I WALK OUT, I AM A GREAT EVENT. ....THREE WOMEN 176   8
   WHEN I FIRST SAW IT, THE SMALL RED SEEP, I DID NOT BELIEVE IT. ...
             ... THREE WOMEN 177 15
   I REMEMBER THE MINUTE WHEN I KNEW FOR SURE. ....THREE WOMEN 177 43
   THE YELLOW MINUTE BEFORE THE WIND WALKS, WHEN THE LEAVES*THREE WOMEN 179 93
   WHEN WILL IT BE, THE SECOND WHEN TIME BREAKS ....THREE WOMEN 179 104
   WHEN WILL IT BE, THE SECOND WHEN TIME BREAKS ....THREE WOMEN 179 104
   THIS IS WHERE YOU WILL COME WHEN YOU ARE READY." ....THREE WOMEN 180 123
   WHEN I CAME TOO CLOSE TO THE WASTEBASKET. ......BURNING THE LETTERS 204   4

WHEN (CONT.)   TITLE   PAGE LINE
WHEN I AM QUIET AT MY COOKING I FEEL IT LOOKING, I FEEL IT THINKING ...
                                          ... A BIRTHDAY PRESENT   206   4
WHAT WAS SHE DOING WHEN IT BLEW IN ....THE DETECTIVE   208   1
I WAS TEN WHEN THEY BURIED YOU. ....DADDY   224   57
DARKENS AND TARNISHES AND WHEN ....CUT   236   32
TO JUGGLE WITH, MY LOVE, WHEN THE SKY FALLS. ....BY CANDLELIGHT   237   36
HOW YOU JUMPED WHEN I JUMPED ON YOU! ...................EAVESDROPPER   261   37
WHEN MY ENGINE REACHES THE END OF IT. ....GIGOLO   267   20
WHEN ATTACKED, THEN SCOOTING TO REST, BARELY TREMBLING. ...BALLOONS   271   4
OF A ROSE CLOSE WHEN THE GARDEN ....EDGE   273   14
AT FAME OR NOT? AS FOR LOVE, I FIGURE WHEN WE'RE ....DIALOGUE O. 278   57
KNOW: WHICH IS WHY I, WHEN THE WONDROUS FIST ....DIALOGUE O. 279 119
THESE GIFTS ARE GIVEN. AND WHEN WITHHELD, YOU'LL SAY ...DIALOGUE O. 279 126
YOU TO TAUNTS THOUGH, WHEN HE REFLECTS A FACE ....DIALOGUE O. 283 260
WHEN HE RECITES ONE OF MY SIMILES .....DIALOGUE OVER A OUIJA BOARD   283 262
CASTLES WHEN WE GLANCE ASIDE. THAT'S THAT. ....DIALOGUE O.   286 356
TO OUR MEANING WELL. WHEN LIGHTS GO OUT *DIALOGUE OVER A OUIJA BOARD 286 363
WHEN, FROM THE INANE OVERHEAD ....DIALOGUE EN ROUTE 309   40
WHEN I ROSE AND OPENED ALL ....THE DREAM   310   1
OR PLAY ANOTHER CARD GAME WHEN YOU'VE WON; ....ADMONITIONS 319   2
FOR DEADLY SECRETS STRIKE WHEN UNDERSTOOD ....ADMONITIONS   319   16
AND WHEN AT LAST THEY BLUNDER INTO BED ....THE DEAD   320   7
WHERE (108)
WHERE, ABSURD AND OUT-OF-SEASON, A SINGLE SWAN ...WINTER LANDSCAPE,   21   3
BELOW: A FEN WHERE WATER STOOD; ....BUCOLICS   24   9
OF OTHER MEN, WHERE STATUES CELEBRATE ....CHANNEL CROSSING   27   38
FROM HIS CRABBED MIDDEN WHERE ALL'S WROUGHT SO AWRY ....FIRESONG   30   10
BOUGHS WHERE THOSE OWLS SAT. ....FAUN   35   10
OVER TIDAL-FLATS WHERE THREE CHILDREN PLAYED*DREAM WITH CLAM-DIGGERS   44   14
WHERE, BEDDED LIKE ANGELS, TWO BURN ONE IN FEVER. ....WREATH F.   45   18
WHERE THE DAFT FATHER WENT DOWN ....ALL THE DEAD DEARS   71   23
WHERE SECOND WIND, HIP BOOT ....TWO VIEWS OF WITHENS   72   9
ESTRANGED, CHANGED, SUSPENDED WHERE ....THE GREAT CARBUNCLE   73   19
HANGS IN ITS LUGUBRIOUS POUT. WHERE ARE ....PERSEUS   83   39
WHERE NOTHING HIGHER'S TO BE LOOKED TO. DOWNWARD LOOKS .....OXBOW.   88   30
WHERE THE WAKING HEAD RUBBISHES OUT THE DRAGGLED LOT .....GHOST'S.   90   3
BUT TOWARD A REGION WHERE OUR THICK ATMOSPHERE ....GHOST'S.   90   25
WHERE RED-FRECKLED CRAB-BACKS, CLAWS ..MUSSEL HUNTER AT ROCK HARBOR   97   83
WHERE SMALL ANTS ROLL THEIR EGGS, WHERE GRUBS FATTEN. .....MOONRISE   98   17
WHERE SMALL ANTS ROLL THEIR EGGS, WHERE GRUBS FATTEN. .....MOONRISE   98   17
RIVER-VERGE FARMS WHERE RYE-HEADS WHITEN. ....IN MIDAS' COUNTRY   99   4
ON THIS AMBER BANK WHERE GRASSES BLEACH. ....IN MIDAS' COUNTRY 100   22
WHERE LOVE-MET GROUNDHOGS LOVE ONE IN RETURN, ...INCOMMUNICADO   100   9
WHERE STRAIGHT TALK IS THE RULE, WHETHER WARM OR HOSTILE, ...
                                          ... INCOMMUNICADO   100   10
WHERE THE MOST WATCHFUL COOKS GO JOBLESS ....THE TIMES ARE TIDY 107   3
THE PLANKED-UP WINDOWS WHERE SHE SET ....POINT SHIRLEY   110   26
CAT-TAILS PART WHERE THE TAME CYGNETS STEER. ....WATERCOLOR.   112   14
WERE SQUEALING WHERE COMBERS BROKE AND THE SPINDRIFT ......SUICIDE. 115   10
WHERE BEES, STRIPED BLACK AND GOLD, SLEEP OUT THE BLIZZARD ...
                                          ... ELECTRA ON AZALEA PATH 116   3
IN THIS CHARITY WARD, THIS POORHOUSE, WHERE THE DEAD ...ELECTRA ON. 117   19
WHERE THE THREE MAGENTA ....MAN IN BLACK 119   1
STALLS IN HALLS WHERE THE LAMP WICK ....OLD LADIES' HOME 120   20
HALFWAY DOWN FROM GROVES WHERE THE THIN, BITTER ALMOND PIPS ..NET-. 121   2
WHERE THOSE TWO SLEEPERS ARE. ....THE SLEEPERS 122   2
WHERE HIS INNARDS BULGED AS IF ....MEDALLION   125   23
PLATONIC TABLE WHERE IT LIVES. THE BABY CARP ....PRIVATE GROUND 130   11
I BEND OVER THIS DRAINED BASIN WHERE THE SMALL FISH PRIVATE GROUND 131   20
THIS IS THE CITY WHERE MEN ARE MENDED. POEM.7.S. 136   1
WHERE THE DURABLE ONES KEEP HOUSE. ....THE BURNT-OUT SPA 138   32
ANYTHING CAN HAPPEN WHERE THEY ARE GOING. ....ON DECK   143   18
THE SUN PUTS ITS CINDER OUT. WHERE WE LIE*SLEEP IN THE MOJAVE DESERT 144   21
WHERE TREES AND CLOUDS AND ANIMALS PAY NO NOTICE; ....TWO CAMP. 144   8
GREEN AS A POOL TABLE, WHERE CABBAGE BUTTERFLIES ....WHITSUN   154   19
WHERE THE HEADS AND TAILS OF MY SISTERS DECOMPOSE. ....ZOO K.   154   7
I ROLL TO AN ANTEROOM WHERE A KIND MAN ....FACE LIFT 156   12
WHERE ONCE A DAY THE LIGHT SLOWLY WIDENS AND SLOWLY THINS, ..TULIPS 161   45
NOR DO THEY SEND UP FIRES WHERE THEY FALL .STARS OVER THE DORDOGNE 165   6
WHERE I AM AT HOME, ONLY THE SPARSEST STARS *STARS OVER THE DORDOGNE 165   9
AND WHERE I LIE NOW, BACK TO MY OWN DARK STAR, ...STARS.   166   34
THE SHEEP KNOW WHERE THEY ARE, ...WUTHERING HEIGHTS   167   19
I SIMPLY CANNOT SEE WHERE THERE IS TO GET TO. ....MOON. 173   7
THIS IS WHERE YOU WILL COME WHEN YOU ARE READY." ....THREE WOMEN 180 123
AND TO MARRY WHAT HE WANTS AND WHERE HE WILL. ....THREE WOMEN   186 336
WHERE DO THE BLACK TREES GO THAT DRINK HERE? ....CROSSING THE WATER 190   2
IT RATTLES THEIR STARS ON THE GREEN HILL WHERE PERCY .....NARCISSI. 190   5
WHERE APPLE BLOOM ICES THE NIGHT ....EVENT   195   13
WHERE ARE THE EYE-STONES, YELLOW AND VALUABLE, ...BERCK-PLAGE 198   53
WHERE ARE YOU GOING ....THE OTHER   202   23
WHERE ARE YOUR OPIATES, YOUR NAUSEOUS CAPSULES? ...POPPIES IN JULY   203   10
SANDS WHERE A DREAM OF CLEAR WATER ....BURNING THE LETTERS   204   3
WHERE SPILT LIVES CONGEAL AND STIFFEN TO HISTORY.*A BIRTHDAY PRESENT 208   51

WHERE (CONT.)
  WHERE THE WIRELESS TALKS TO ITSELF LIKE AN ELDERLY RELATIVE. ...
                                        ... THE DETECTIVE 209   20
  WHERE HAS SHE BEEN, ...STINGS 215   54
  WHERE TRAINS, FAITHFUL TO THEIR STEEL ARCS, ...THE SWARM 216   35
  WHERE IT POURS BEAN GREEN OVER BLUE ....DADDY 222   12
  SO I NEVER COULD TELL WHERE YOU ....DADDY 223   22
  WHERE I RELAX, FOETUS OR CAT, ...THE JAILER 226   9
  WHERE THEY CRAP AND PUKE AND CRY AND SHE CAN'T HEAR. ....LESBOS 228   14
  WHERE IT DRIVES IN, WHITE AND BLACK, ...LESBOS 229   75
  WHERE DO YOU STASH YOUR LIFE? ....STOPPED DEAD 230   20
  THERE'S WHERE IT SUNK. ....LYONNESSE 234   4
  IS WHERE I KEPT THE FURNACE, ...THE TOUR 238   20
  SPACE OF HOLLY WHERE SPIKES ....YEARS 255   2
  WHERE THE CHILD CAN NEVER SWIM, ...THE FEARFUL 256   17
  WHERE THERE IS ONLY HIM AND HIM. ....THE FEARFUL 256   18
  WHERE THE YEW TREES BLOW LIKE HYDRAS, ...THE MUNICH MANNEQUINS 262   3
  SHEER-SIDED, WITH HOLES WHERE TO HIDE. ....GIGOLO 267   3
  FOR FORTUNE-TELLING? AND WHERE IS IT FORTUNE COMES ....DIALOGUE O. 277   45
  THE STINT OF SISYPHUS. ASK PAN, THEN, WHERE ....DIALOGUE O. 281 173
  WHERE DO YOU LIVE? HE MOVES. HE'S MOVING BRISK ....DIALOGUE O. 281 206
  WHERE THOSE WORMS CAME FROM. I SWEAR I DIDN'T EXPECT ..DIALOGUE O. 283 264
  TELL US THE TRUTH. WHERE DO YOU LIVE? HE STARTS ....DIALOGUE O. 283 274
  WHERE POLISHED HIGHBOYS WHISPER CREAKING CURSES .....FEMALE AUTHOR 301   7
  WHERE GUESTS SLIDE GLIDING INTO LIGHT LIKE WINE; ....CINDERELLA 304   6
  DOWN WHERE SOUND ....AQUATIC NOCTURNE 306   25
  TO RAID THE ZONE WHERE FATE BEGINS, ...METAMORPHOSES OF THE MOON 307   3
  WHERE WE STOPPED, AND WITH A CURSE ....THE DREAM 311   14
  WHERE DIAMONDS JANGLE HYMNS WITHIN THE BLOOD ....APRIL AUBADE 312   3
  WHERE ON PINK-FLUTED FEET THE PIGEONS PASS ....APRIL AUBADE 312   10
  AND PLUCK THE DROLL-FLECKED QUAIL WHERE THICK THEY LIE; ...GO GET. 313   2
  WHERE THE BLACK WAVE TOPPLES DOWN; ....GO GET THE GOODLY SQUAB 313   22
  GREEN ALLEYS WHERE WE REVELED HAVE BECOME ....DOOM OF EXILES 318   5
  A STONE CAN MASQUERADE WHERE NO HEART IS ....NEVER TRY TO TRICK. 319   4
  AND VIRGINS RISE WHERE LUSTFUL VENUS LAY: ......NEVER TRY TO TRICK. 319   5
  WHERE ADJECTIVES PLAY CROQUET WITH FLAMINGO NOUNS; ...A SORCERER B. 324   2
  ALONE TO THAT AUTHENTIC ISLAND WHERE ....A SORCERER B. 324   13
  BE PLUCKED FROM CAVES OF DAPPLED AMBER WHERE ......MIDSUMMER MOBILE 324   9
  WHERE BEAUTIES CHAR ......ON LOOKING INTO THE EYES OF A DEMON LOVER 325   22
  REFECTORIES WHERE HE REVELED HAVE BECOME ....TERMINAL 328   5
  WHERE WAVE PRETENDS TO DRENCH REAL SKY." ....LOVE IS A PARALLAX 329   6
  TELL NOW, WE TAUNT, WHERE BLACK OR WHITE BEGINS LOVE IS A PARALLAX 330   49
  THAT STING NO MORE THAN LOVE: A ROOM WHERE TIME *MORNING IN THE HOS. 332   15
  OF MERCURY IN GRADED TUBES, WHERE ILLS ....MORNING IN THE HOS. 332   17
  WITH FINGER BANDAGED WHERE THE WASPISH PIN ....THE PRINCESS. 333   7
  WHERE ANCIENT, INFINITE, AND BEAUTIFUL,*THE PRINCESS AND THE GOBLINS 333   14
  THE CHAMBERS WHERE THEIR FIENDISH QUEEN WOULD SIT. ...THE PRINCESS. 334   40
  WHERE PIGEONS PROMENADE THE GABLE-ENDS *THE PRINCESS AND THE GOBLINS 335   66
  WHERE VIVID CHILDREN TWIRL ....TOUCH-AND-GO 335   9
  WHERE KILROY WOULD PASS ....TEMPER OF TIME 336   14
  WHERE THE WATER BLOTS OUT ALL FOOTSTEPS." ...EPITAPH IN THREE PARTS 337   6
  ENORMOUS BOX OF GRAY WHERE GOD HAS GONE .....EPITAPH IN THREE PARTS 338   30
WHEREBY (2)
  WHEREBY SHE TREKS IN BLOOD THROUGH SUN AND SQUALL *QUEEN'S COMPLAINT 29   22
  WHEREBY ONE HIRES A DEMON. ....CRYSTAL GAZER 55   36
WHETHER (6)
  WHETHER YOU SAW THEM, WHETHER YOU SAID ....THE DISQUIETING MUSES 75   13
  WHETHER YOU SAW THEM, WHETHER YOU SAID ....THE DISQUIETING MUSES 75   13
  WHETHER GOAT-THIGHED OR GOD-HALOED. EVER SINCE THAT FIRST DAPHNE ...
                                        ... VIRGIN IN A TREE 81   9
  WHERE STRAIGHT TALK IS THE RULE, WHETHER WARM OR HOSTILE, ...
                                        ... INCOMMUNICADO 100   10
  WHETHER NICETY STOOD CONFOUNDED BY LOVE, ...RHODODENDRON. 104   27
  SHORTCHANGE ME CONTINUOUSLY: WHETHER ....POEMS, POTATOES 106   9
WHETSTONE (1)
  THEIR WHETSTONE TO THE BLUNTED EDGE ....THE DEATH OF MYTH-MAKING 104   9
WHETTED (1)
  RIVALS HER WHETTED LOOK, DIVINING WHAT CONCEIT ....VANITY FAIR 32   13
WHICH (81)
  OF ALL DECORUM WHICH HOLDS THE WHIRLWIND BACK. .......CONVERSATION. 21   4
  WHICH HUNGERS TO HAUL THE WHITE REFLECTION DOWN. WINTER LANDSCAPE, 21   5
  WHICH HAD CAUSED HIS DEAR GIRL PAIN. ....BUCOLICS 24   20
  WHICH SHROUDS OUR PROSPECTS IN AMBIGUOUS SHADOW? .....TALE OF A TUB 24   16
  EVER BLUR THE INTRANSIGENT LINES WHICH DRAW ....TALE OF A TUB 25   28
  IN WHICH OUR COMRADES ARE BETRAYED, WE FREEZE .....CHANNEL CROSSING 27   14
  AT THIS RARE RUMPUS WHICH NO MAN CAN CONTROL: ....CHANNEL CROSSING 27   29
  SHIRR SONGS TO SUIT WHICH MOOD ....ODE FOR TED 29   20
  WHICH HAULS DOWN BUCK, COCK, TROUT, TILL ALL MOST FAIR ....FIRESONG 30   6
  WHICH OUT FROM BLACK TARN, DITCH AND CUP ....STRUMPET SONG 34   17
  WHICH ALLAY THE MALICE ....MISS DRAKE PROCEEDS TO SUPPER 41   3
  WHICH ARE SLOWLY OPENING THEIR FURRED PETALS ....MISS DRAKE P. 41   11
  FROM WHICH COILS, CAUGHT ANTS WAVED LEGS IN ....SPIDER 49   19
  AGAINST WHICH THE BRUNT OF OUTER SEA ....DEPARTURE 51   14
  EYEFUL, WHICH, ENVIOUS, WOULD DEFINE ....LANDOWNERS 53   13

WHICH (CONT.)
    THAT CLAIRVOYANT QUARTZ WHICH ONCE, AT HER OWN WISHING, ...
                               ... CRYSTAL GAZER   55   29
    WHICH PEOPLES THE BARE ROOM, THE BLANK, UNTENANTED AIR. NOVEMBER G. 56   18
    TO HOODWINK THE HONEST EARTH WHICH POINTBLANK ....CONJURING. 66   28
    TO DISCOVER THAT METAPHYSICAL TREE WHICH HID ...PLETHORA OF DRYADS. 67   9
    FOR WHICH THE GHOST OF BOCKLIN GRIEVES. ..ON THE DECLINE OF ORACLES 78   15
    RULES THE WRITHINGS WHICH MAKE MANIFEST ................SNAKECHARMER 79   16
    HABIT WHICH DEFLECTS ....VIRGIN IN A TREE 81   6
    FOR WHICH OF THOSE WOULD SPEAK ....VIRGIN IN A TREE 81   20
    WHICH WEIGHS OUR MADNESS WITH OUR SANITY. ....PERSEUS 84   49
    MONSTERS WHICH UPREAR ....BATTLE-SCENE 84   16
    SO POSSESSED BY THE GLOWING RED OF THE COUCH WHICH YOU, ..YADWIGHA. 86   36
    WHICH SEEMED, WHEN DREAMED, TO MEAN SO PROFOUNDLY MUCH, ...GHOST'S. 90   5
    WHICH SIGNIFY OUR ORIGIN AND END, ...THE GHOST'S LEAVETAKING 91   34
    AS THAT CRISP CUSP TOWARDS WHICH YOU VOYAGE NOW. ....GHOST'S. 91   38
    WHICH, WITHOUT HIM, WERE BEGGARED ....SCULPTOR 92   18
    OF YOUR SPREAD HAIR, IN WHICH WRINKLING SKEINS ...FULL FATHOM FIVE 92   8
    WENT ABOUT THEIR BUSINESS, WHICH ......MUSSEL HUNTER AT ROCK HARBOR 97   61
    WHICH NO GRUFF ANIMAL MISINTERPRETS. ...................INCOMMUNICADO 100   11
    ARGUED MY CONSCIENCE CLEAR WHICH ROBBED ............RHODODENDRON. 103   11
    IN ESTABLISHMENTS WHICH IMAGINED LINES ....POEMS, POTATOES 106   3
    RED CINDER AROUND WHICH I MYSELF, ...THE EYE-MOTE 109   17
    BEHIND WHICH THE SECRET PASSAGE LIES -- STALE AIR, ...WIDOW 164   8
    THAT FLAT, FLAT, FLATNESS FROM WHICH IDEAS, DESTRUCTIONS, ...THREE. 177   18
    DARK TUNNEL, THROUGH WHICH HURTLE THE VISITATIONS, ...THREE WOMEN 180   130
    I AM FLAT AND VIRGINAL, WHICH MEANS NOTHING HAS HAPPENED, ...THREE. 184   276
    THERE IS THIS WHITE WALL, ABOVE WHICH THE SKY CREATES ITSELF --
                               ... APPREHENSIONS 195   1
    UNDER THE GLUED SHEET FROM WHICH HIS POWDERY BEAK ......BERCK-PLAGE 198   63
    THE HOLLOWS IN WHICH ROCK THE THOUGHTS OF THE WIFE --- BERCK-PLAGE 199   75
    WHICH OF THE POISONS IS IT? ....THE DETECTIVE 209   22
    WHICH OF THE NERVE-CURLERS, THE CONVULSORS? DID IT ELECTRIFY? ...
                               ... THE DETECTIVE 209   23
    IN WHICH A TORTURE GOES ON ONE CAN ONLY WATCH. ....COURAGE. 210   28
    WHICH IS THE RECTOR NOW, IS IT THAT MAN IN BLACK? ..THE BEE MEETING 211   11
    WHICH IS THE MIDWIFE, IS THAT HER BLUE COAT? ....THE BEE MEETING 211   12
    INTO WHICH, ON WARM DAYS, ...WINTERING 218   36
    BEHIND TWO EYES IN WHICH NOTHING IS REFLECTED BUT MONKEYS. *A SECRET 219   20
    IN WHICH I HAVE LIVED LIKE A FOOT ....DADDY 222   3
    BOTTLE IN WHICH I LIVE, ...MEDUSA 225   35
    THIS IS THE FLUID IN WHICH WE MEET EACH OTHER, ...BY CANDLELIGHT 236   10
    ON WHICH I, ...EAVESDROPPER 260   15
    INTO WHICH BROAD TOES WILL GO TOMORROW. ......THE MUNICH MANNEQUINS 263   20
    THROUGH WHICH THE SKY ETERNALLY THREADS ITSELF? ....TOTEM 264   21
    OUT OF WHICH THE SAME SELF UNFOLDS LIKE A SUIT ....TOTEM 264   25
    POOL IN WHICH IMAGES ....CHILD 265   8
    KNOW: WHICH IS WHY I, WHEN THE WONDROUS FIST ....DIALOGUE O. 279   119
    NOW, YOU REALLY DON'T MUCH CARE WHICH, OR WHAT ....DIALOGUE O. 280   151
    WHICH PROPS YOU THROUGH THIS DESERT LIKE A DREAM ....DIALOGUE O. 282   212
    CHILD TO SEE WHICH ONE OF US CAN CALL ..DIALOGUE OVER A OUIJA BOARD 284   284
    IN WHICH THE MINUTES COULD ADMIRE THEIR REFLECTIONS AND
       FORGET ABOUT ME. ....THE RIVAL/DR 291   7
    WHICH CONCEAL INCONGRUOUS ............METAMORPHOSES OF THE MOON 307   27
    WHICH MAR THE IDOL'S SANCTITY. ..........METAMORPHOSES OF THE MOON 308   36
    WILL PUNISH US FOR SAYING WHICH IS WHICH; *METAMORPHOSES OF THE MOON 308   44
    WILL PUNISH US FOR SAYING WHICH IS WHICH; *METAMORPHOSES OF THE MOON 308   44
    WHICH OCCURRED TO ME IN CHINA." ....THE DREAM 311   30
    FROM WHICH THE FUR BEGAN. ....TRIO OF LOVE SONGS 315   44
    WHICH CONJURED US ....MOONSONG AT MORNING 317   8
    WHICH LET LOVER THINK LOVER ....MOONSONG AT MORNING 317   15
    IN WHICH THE RIDDLE OF OUR RACE IS SHUT. ....DOOM OF EXILES 318   14
    WHICH HAS STOPPED THE SEASON IN ITS TRACKS ......PROLOGUE TO SPRING 322   11
    WHICH AT TWELVE WILL QUAINTLY HATCH ....BLACK PINE TREE. 328   5
    WHICH DREAMERS CALL REAL, AND REALISTS, ILLUSION:*LOVE IS A PARALLAX 330   59
    WHICH SPEAK HER MAESTRO'S WILL. ....AERIALIST 331   12
    UP WHICH THE WAKEFUL PRINCESS CLIMBS TO FIND ....THE PRINCESS. 333   2
    WHICH ALL THE ARTFUL WIZARDS CANNOT CRIMP ....THE PRINCESS. 333   17
    BEHIND WHICH THE DECLINING MOON HAS SET, ...THE PRINCESS. 334   36
    WHICH QUAINTLY WOVE THE FABRIC OF HER FATE ....THE PRINCESS. 335   57
    A WINDOW WHICH PROVES THE SKY SHEER RIGMAROLE*EPITAPH IN THREE PARTS 337   28
WHILE (59)
    WHILE YOU STAND HEROIC IN COAT AND TIE, I SIT ........CONVERSATION. 21   10
    WHILE SHE STANDS BURNING, VENOM-GIRT, ...BUCOLICS 24   23
    RECORDS BARE PAINTED WALLS, WHILE AN ELECTRIC LIGHT ..TALE OF A TUB 24   2
    LIKE ICEBERGS, WHILE MINUTE BROWN HAIRS RISE ....TALE OF A TUB 25   42
    JUTTED EARLY TO MARK OUR GOING, WHILE SKY ....CHANNEL CROSSING 27   23
    WHILE ON SPOTTED BRANCH ....PROSPECT 28   5
    COLD SQUINT STEALS SKY'S COLOR; WHILE BRUIT ....VANITY FAIR 32   8
    WHILE SHE, ENVIOUS BRIDE, ...THE SHRIKE 42   7
    WHILE THE COCKS AND HENS ....ALICANTE LULLABY 43   5
    THAT OWL VOICE SOLE "YES", WHILE COWS UTTER ....WREATH FOR A BRIDAL 44   3
    WHILE I EAT GRITS ....RHYME 50   9
    WHILE ELLA DROWSED WHISKERED WITH SLEEK FACE, SLY WITS: ...
                               ... ELLA MASON AND HER ELEVEN CATS 54   29

WHILE (CONT.)
  WHILE THIS BEGGARED BRAIN *ON THE DIFFICULTY OF CONJURING UP A DRYAD 66 37
  WHILE SUBJECTS HUNGERED, EMPTY-PURSED, ...NATURAL HISTORY 71   5
  MUST WAIT, WHILE HERE SUSO'S ....A LESSON IN VENGEANCE 80 11
  WHILE THERE IRATE CYRUS ....A LESSON IN VENGEANCE 80 16
  AND KEEP THEIR SHAPES INTACT WHILE SUN ....CHILD'S PARK STONES 101 12
  WHILE CHAPEL PINNACLES OVER THE ROOFS, ...THE EYE-MOTE 109   5
  WHILE THE STUDENTS STROLL OR SIT,*WATERCOLOR OF GRANTCHESTER MEADOWS 112 24
  OF HER BARE SHOULDER, WHILE SHE BENDS, TWO VIEWS OF A CADAVER ROOM 114 16
  WHILE THEIR FINGERS WORK WITH THE COARSE MESH AND THE FINE ...NET-. 121 11
  THEY MOVE THROUGH THEIR MUTE ROOMS WHILE I SLEEP, ...BLUE MOLES 126 23
  AND WHILE THE AIR'S CLEAR ....DARK WOOD, DARK WATER 127 18
  WHILE THE CHILD SMILES INTO THIN AIR. ....MAGI 148   9
  WHILE THE HEATH GRASS GLITTERS AND THE SPINDLING RIVULETS ...
                  ... PARLIAMENT HILL FIELDS 153 34
  WHILE FAR OFF, THE AXLE OF WINTER ....HEAVY WOMEN 158 19
  A LIFE BAPTIZED IN NO-LIFE FOR A WHILE, ...INSOMNIAC 163 18
  I SURVIVE THE WHILE, ...LITTLE FUGUE 189 49
  WHILE A GREEN POOL OPENS ITS EYE, ...BERCK-PLAGE 197 27
  ADDRESSING IT, WHILE THE HILLS ROLL THE NOTES OF THE DEAD BELL: ...
                      ... BERCK-PLAGE 200 95
  WHILE A SKY, WORMY WITH PUT-BY SMILES, ...BERCK-PLAGE 200 104
  WHILE IN THEIR FINGERJOINT CELLS THE NEW VIRGINS ...THE BEE MEETING 212 45
  WHILE THE BRASS MAN ....BY CANDLELIGHT 237 26
  WHILE THE DAY OUTSIDE GLIDES BY LIKE TICKER TAPE. ....PARALYTIC 266 10
  WHILE ....WORDS 270 18
  WHILE WE'RE SITTING, FACE TO FACE ACROSS THE COFFEE- ...DIALOGUE O. 276   3
  AND TRICKED US TO TRUST HIS VISION, WHILE NIGHT AFTER NIGHT HE ...
              ... DIALOGUE OVER A OUIJA BOARD 279 104
  TO BUILD HIS CANTING TOWERS. WHILE YOU, YOU LONG ....DIALOGUE O. 280 136
  WHILE I SLEEP, THE BLACK SPORES NOD ....THE RIVAL/DR 291   2
  WHILE ROUGH AS SPLINTERED WOOD ....FAMILY REUNION 300 20
  FAVORED (WHILE SUDDENLY THE RAINS BEGIN ....FEMALE AUTHOR 301   2
  WHILE LIKE AN EARLY SUMMER PLUM, ...JILTED 304   9
  WHILE FROM THE MOON, MY LOVER'S EYE ....TO A JILTED LOVER 309   7
  (WHILE SHE WASHED THE WAY WITH TEARS), ...THE DREAM 311 27
  IN SQUARE HERMETIC BOTTLES, WHILE THE SUN ....THE TRIAL OF MAN 312   3
  WHILE TULIPS BOW LIKE A COLLEGE OF CARDINALS ....APRIL AUBADE 312   7
  WHILE ALL THE ACTORS HALT IN MORTAL SHOCK: ....DOOMSDAY 316   5
  WHILE ANGELS WEAR A WAKEFUL ATTITUDE ....THE DISPOSSESSED 319 13
  WHILE STRICKEN PATIENTS LET HIM HAVE HIS SAY: ..NEVER TRY TO TRICK. 320   8
  WHILE THE ANGELS ALL APPLAUD. ....CIRCUS IN THREE RINGS 321   6
  WHILE THE GNAWINGS OF LOVE BEGIN. ....CIRCUS IN THREE RINGS 322 12
  METHINKS I SHALL ABSENT ME FOR A WHILE ....A SORCERER B. 324   3
  WHILE WANTONLY AMUSED BY THIS, INSOLENT STORM STRIKES AT THE SKULL 325   5
  WHILE FOOTLIGHTS FLARE AND HOUSELIGHTS DIM. .....LOVE IS A PARALLAX 330 48
  THAT JAR, WHILE EACH POLEMIC JACKANAPES ....LOVE IS A PARALLAX 330 53
  ARROWS THAT LACERATE THE SKY, WHILE KNOWING .....LOVE IS A PARALLAX 330 61
  WHILE SUNLIGHT WINDS ITS YARN UPON THE FLOOR. ....THE PRINCESS. 335 71
  WHILE ON THIS SAME FUGUE, UNMOVED, ...TOUCH-AND-GO 336 22
  WHILE EVIL STARS WHIR ....TEMPER OF TIME 336   2
WHIM (2)
  THROUGH A WHIM OF MINE ....SOLILOQUY OF THE SOLIPSIST 37   7
  AT THE WHIM OF A WINE-GLASS AND LET US INTO WORLDS .....DIALOGUE O. 280 128
WHIMS (1)
  COGS AND DISKS, INANE MECHANIC WHIMS, ...SONNET: TO EVA 304   7
WHINE (2)
  DROVE THE DOGS TO CRINGE AND WHINE, ...THE DEATH OF MYTH-MAKING 104 13
  THE YOUNGEST NEPHEW GIVES A FRETFUL WHINE ....FAMILY REUNION 301 23
WHIP (1)
  YET I FLOURISH MY WHIP WITH A FATAL FLAIR ...CIRCUS IN THREE RINGS 322 10
WHIPCRACK (2)
  CAN WHIPCRACK THE TABLES INTO TIGERS AND FOIST ....DIALOGUE O. 279 117
  TO WHIPCRACK AND ROAR ....AERIALIST 331 11
WHIPPER (1)
  WHIPPER OF ITCHES, ...WORDS FOR A NURSERY 73 17
WHIPPING (1)
  WHIPPING OFF YOUR SILK SCARF, EXHIBITING THE TIGHT WHITE FACE LIFT 155   2
WHIR (3)
  AND THE FRAGMENTS WHIR LIKE A WEATHER VANE ...CIRCUS IN THREE RINGS 321   5
  POINTING TOWARD THE SPINDLE'S CRYPTIC WHIR, ...THE PRINCESS. 335 60
  WHILE EVIL STARS WHIR ....TEMPER OF TIME 336   2
WHIRL (1)
  THAT AT SUCH A DISTANCE FROM US SHINE AND WHIRL. ....THREE WOMEN 182 210
WHIRLED (1)
  I HAVE WHIRLED THE MIDWIFE'S EXTRACTOR, ...WINTERING 217   2
WHIRLING (2)
  FLOURED HIS WHIRLING BEARD, AND AT HIS TREAD*THE SNOWMAN ON THE MOOR 59 33
  AND GILDED COUPLES ALL IN WHIRLING TRANCE ....CINDERELLA 304   9
WHIRLPOOL (1)
  A WHIRLPOOL LEERS AT ME, ...FAMILY REUNION 301 27
WHIRLPOOLS (1)
  DURANCE ARE WHIRLPOOLS .. ..FULL FATHOM FIVE 93 30
WHIRLS (1)
  GERD WHIRLS THE BALL ABLAZE: "ROUGH STORM," SHE GRANTS, "MAY WREAK ...
                  ... CRYSTAL GAZER 55 22

                                                                    TITLE   PAGE LINE
WHIRLWIND (3)
   OF ALL DECORUM WHICH HOLDS THE WHIRLWIND BACK. .......CONVERSATION.   21   4
   HIS TALKING WHIRLWIND, ABATED HIS EXCESSIVE TEMPER ....OUIJA   77   16
   MIGHT DO AS A GOD'S MOUTHPIECE IF A WHIRLWIND ....DIALOGUE O.   281 202
WHIRR (1)
   THE WARNING WHIRR AND BURRING OF THE BIRD ....GOATSUCKER   111   2
WHISK (2)
   OF LEAVES' BICKER AND WHISK IN BABEL TONGUES, ..PLETHORA OF DRYADS.   67   21
   ANGEL'S EYE IN THE AUDIENCE, THEN WHISK THEM OUT ....DIALOGUE O.   282 233
WHISKERED (1)
   WHILE ELLA DROWSED WHISKERED WITH SLEEK FACE, SLY WITS: ...
                       ... ELLA MASON AND HER ELEVEN CATS   54   29
WHISPER (2)
   AS FLAT AS SHE, WHO WHISPER "WE'RE YOUR DAUGHTERS." ......PARALYTIC   266   26
   WHERE POLISHED HIGHBOYS WHISPER CREAKING CURSES ......FEMALE AUTHOR   301   7
WHISPERED (1)
   TAXIS INDOLENT ON WHISPERED WHEELS;*MORNING IN THE HOSPITAL SOLARIUM   332   11
WHISPERS (1)
   THE BUTCHER'S GUILLOTINE THAT WHISPERS: "HOW'S THIS, HOW'S THIS?" ...
                                       ... TOTEM   264   10
WHISTLE (3)
   TO A PINCH OF FLAME, BLEW ITS BURDENED WHISTLE ....HARDCASTLE CRAGS   63   23
   BLOOD AND WHISTLE MY MARROW CLEAN ....ALL THE DEAD DEARS   70   17
   MUFFLES THEIR BIRD-FEET: THEY WHISTLE FOR JOY. ....LEAVING EARLY   146   37
WHISTLED (1)
   BUT OUR FARMER WHISTLED, ...SOW   61   34
WHISTLING (3)
   THROUGH BARE WHISTLING HEATHER, OVER STILES OF BLACK STONE, ...
                       ... THE SNOWMAN ON THE MOOR   58   21
   WHISTLING, WIGGLING MY EARS, ...POEM.2.DARK.   132   6
   NO USE WHISTLING FOR LYONNESSE! ....LYONNESSE   233   1
WHITE (166)
   WHICH HUNGERS TO HAUL THE WHITE REFLECTION DOWN. WINTER LANDSCAPE,   21   5
   HAGGARD THROUGH THE HOT WHITE NOON. ....PURSUIT   22   10
   ABOVE: LEAF-WRAITHED WHITE AIR, WHITE CLOUD. ....BUCOLICS   24   12
   ABOVE: LEAF-WRAITHED WHITE AIR, WHITE CLOUD. ....BUCOLICS   24   12
   WOULD BE FULL OF SUN, WHITE GULLS, AND WATER DRENCHED ...CHANNEL C.   27   21
   WHITE HULKS ON THEIR DAY'S CRUISING; ....SONG FOR A SUMMER'S DAY   31   4
   WITH WHITE FROST GONE ....STRUMPET SONG   33   1
   FROM THEIR WHITE HEAT ....TINKER JACK AND THE TIDY WIVES   35   31
   TO THIS WHITE BONE; ....DIALOGUE BETWEEN GHOST AND PRIEST   39   28
   WITH YOUR WHITE HANDS." ....RECANTATION   42   20
   SLOPED SEAWARD TO PLUNGE IN BLUE; FED BY WHITE FIRE, DREAM WITH C.   44   11
   IN BLACK AND WHITE, OR PUT ON ICE ......EPITAPH FOR FIRE AND FLOWER   45   10
   UNDER WHITE WALL AND MOORISH WINDOW ....THE BEGGARS   47   6
   WHITE HOUSE AND ALMOND GROVE. THE BEGGARS ....THE BEGGARS   48   18
   OF WHITE AND BLACK ....SPINSTER   49   15
   FISH-TAILED GIRLS PURCHASE EACH WHITE LEG. ....MAUDLIN   51   8
   TO THE WORLD'S WHITE EDGE ....THE SNOWMAN ON THE MOOR   59   22
   SHE SHIED SIDEWAYS: A WHITE FIZZ! AND THE GIANT, PURSUING, ...
                       ... THE SNOWMAN ON THE MOOR   59   47
   EACH HEDGE WITH SUCH WHITE BLOOM ASTOUNDS OUR EYES ....MAYFLOWER   60   6
   REMEMBERING THE WHITE, TRIUMPHANT SPRAY ....MAYFLOWER   60   12
   HEARING A WHITE SAINT RAVE ....ON THE PLETHORA OF DRYADS   67   1
   REPORT WHITE PILLARS, A BLUE SKY, ...TWO VIEWS OF WITHENS   72   17
   STUNNED THE MARROW. MEN IN WHITE ....NIGHT SHIFT   77   20
   ONE WHITE HORSE DROWNED, AND ALL THE UNCONQUERED PINNACLES LESSON.   80   9
   WHITE BODIES IN A WOODEN GIRDLE, ROOT TO TOP ......VIRGIN IN A TREE   81   22
   OF A WHALE WITH HOLES AND HOLES, AND BLEED HIM WHITE ....PERSEUS   82   5
   CAPPED: WHITE HAIR, WHITE BEARD, FAR-FLUNG, ...FULL FATHOM FIVE   92   4
   CAPPED: WHITE HAIR, WHITE BEARD, FAR-FLUNG, ...FULL FATHOM FIVE   92   4
   I'LL GO OUT AND SIT IN WHITE LIKE THEY DO, ...MOONRISE   98   2
   WHITE CATALPA FLOWERS TOWER, TOPPLE, ...MOONRISE   98   5
   CAST A ROUND WHITE SHADOW IN THEIR DYING. ....MOONRISE   98   6
   A PIGEON RUDDERS DOWN. ITS FAN-TAIL'S WHITE. ....MOONRISE   98   7
   WHITE PETALS, WHITE FAN-TAILS, TEN WHITE FINGERS. ....MOONRISE   98   9
   WHITE PETALS, WHITE FAN-TAILS, TEN WHITE FINGERS. ....MOONRISE   98   9
   WHITE PETALS, WHITE FAN-TAILS, TEN WHITE FINGERS. ....MOONRISE   98   9
   REDDEN IN WHITE PALMS NO LABOR REDDENS. ....MOONRISE   98   11
   WHITE BRUISES TOWARD COLOR, ELSE COLLAPSES. ....MOONRISE   98   12
   WHITE: IT IS A COMPLEXION OF THE MIND. ....MOONRISE   98   21
   I TIRE, IMAGINING WHITE NIAGARAS ....MOONRISE   98   22
   AMONG THE SOCKETED WHITE STARS, YOUR FACE ....MOONRISE   98   26
   OF CANDOR PARES WHITE FLESH TO THE WHITE BONE, ...MOONRISE   98   27
   OF CANDOR PARES WHITE FLESH TO THE WHITE BONE, ...MOONRISE   98   27
   AND BLEED. THE WHITE STOMACH MAY RIPEN YET. ....MOONRISE   98   30
   GOING'S BEEN TAME DEVIATION. WHITE, ...WHITENESS I REMEMBER   102   4
   YET THE DAPPLE TONING HIS WHITE DOWN ....WHITENESS I REMEMBER   102   10
   I SEE HIM ONE-TRACKED, STUBBORN, WHITE HORSE, WHITENESS I REMEMBER   102   12
   THE BLAND GRANTA DOUBLE THEIR WHITE AND GREEN ....WATERCOLOR.   112   9
   THE BLOOD-BERRIED HAWTHORN HIDES ITS SPINES WITH WHITE. *WATERCOLOR.   112   21
   AND YOU, ACROSS THOSE WHITE ....MAN IN BLACK   119   15
   THE HOUSES ARE WHITE AS SEA-SALT GOATS LICK FROM THE ROCKS. ..NET--.   121   10
   BELOW US A WHITE GULL KEEPS ....MAGNOLIA SHOALS   122   13
   A WHITE MIST IS GOING UP. ....THE SLEEPERS   123   16

```
                                                       TITLE       PAGE  LINE
WHITE (CONT.)
   AND I SAW WHITE MAGGOTS COIL  .............................MEDALLION  124   21
   YOU INHERIT WHITE HEATHER, A BEE'S WING,  ..........THE MANOR GARDEN  125   12
   THEIR CORKSCREW NOSES, THEIR WHITE HANDS  ................BLUE MOLES  126   15
   WHITE DAISY WHEELS AND  ................................POLLY'S TREE  128   26
   THE BALD, WHITE TUMULI OF YOUR EYES.  ...................THE COLOSSUS  129   15
   SOON EACH WHITE LADY WILL BE BOARDED UP  ............PRIVATE GROUND  130    5
   THEIR VEINS WHITE AS PORKFAT.  ...........................POEM.1.WHO.  131   18
   WE ARE FULL OF STARCH, MY SMALL WHITE FELLOWS. WE GROW.  ..POEM.6.W.  135   17
   IT FLOWS OFF BELOW THE GREEN AND WHITE  ..........THE BURNT-OUT SPA  138   22
   A WORLD OF BALD WHITE DAYS IN A SHADELESS SOCKET.  ..THE HANGING MAN  141    4
   THE DESERT IS WHITE AS A BLIND MAN'S EYE,*SLEEP IN THE MOJAVE DESERT  144   17
   AND THE WHITE CHINA FLYING FISH FROM ITALY.  ..........LEAVING EARLY  145    6
   IN THE WHITE HIATUS OF WINTER --  ......................LOVE LETTER  147   11
   THE BURGHERS SWEATED AND WEPT. THE CHILDREN WORE WHITE.  ....CANDLES  149   19
   LIKE THE WHITE LINES ON A BLUEPRINT.  .............ZOO KEEPER'S WIFE  154   10
   OBSCENE AND BALD AS A PIG, THE WHITE MICE  ........ZOO KEEPER'S WIFE  155   21
   WHIPPING OFF YOUR SILK SCARF, EXHIBITING THE TIGHT WHITE  FACE LIFT  155    2
   MOTHER OF A WHITE NIKE AND SEVERAL BALD-EYED APOLLOS.  BARREN WOMAN  157    7
   THIS NEW ABSOLUTELY WHITE PERSON AND THE OLD YELLOW ONE, *IN PLASTER  158    2
   AND THE WHITE PERSON IS CERTAINLY THE SUPERIOR ONE.  .....IN PLASTER  158    3
   FROM HER AMAZINGLY WHITE TORSO, AND I COULDN'T HELP BUT NOTICE  ...
                                                     ... IN PLASTER  159   24
   LOOK HOW WHITE EVERYTHING IS, HOW QUIET, HOW SNOWED-IN.  .....TULIPS  160    2
   AS THE LIGHT LIES ON THESE WHITE WALLS, THIS BED, THESE HANDS.  ...
                                                     ... TULIPS  160    4
   LIKE AN EYE BETWEEN TWO WHITE LIDS THAT WILL NOT SHUT.  ....TULIPS  160    9
   THEY PASS THE WAY GULLS PASS INLAND IN THEIR WHITE CAPS,  ...TULIPS  160   12
   LIGHTLY, THROUGH THEIR WHITE SWADDLINGS, LIKE AN AWFUL BABY. *TULIPS  161   38
   ALREADY HE CAN FEEL DAYLIGHT, HIS WHITE DISEASE,  .........INSOMNIAC  163   31
   WHITE AND BLANK, EXPANSIVE AS CARBON MONOXIDE.  ..........THE RIVAL  166   15
   OF WHITE AND PEWTER LIGHTS, AND A DIN LIKE SILVERSMITHS  ..BLACKBER.  169   26
   THE WHITE LIGHT IS ARTIFICIAL, AND HYGIENIC AS HEAVEN.  ....SURGEON.  170    1
   AS USUAL THERE IS NO FACE. A LUMP OF CHINESE WHITE  .......SURGEON.  170    7
   I AM THE SUN, IN MY WHITE COAT,  .............THE SURGEON AT 2 A.M.  171   49
   WHITE AS A KNUCKLE AND TERRIBLY UPSET.  ...THE MOON AND THE YEW TREE  173    9
   IN THE TWO HUGE, WHITE, HANDSOME HOUSES IN SWAMPSCOTT.  ....BABY.  174    5
   THE BLIND, WHITE, AWFUL, INACCESSIBLE SLANT.  ..NEW YEAR ON DARTMOOR  176    5
   BULLDOZERS, GUILLOTINES, WHITE CHAMBERS OF SHRIEKS PROCEED,   THREE.  177   19
   YOU ARE SO WHITE, SUDDENLY." AND I SAID NOTHING.  ......THREE WOMEN  177   23
   THE WHITE SKY EMPTIES OF ITS PROMISE, LIKE A CUP.  ......THREE WOMEN  177   33
   I REMEMBER A WHITE, COLD WING  ........................THREE WOMEN  178   49
   I WASN'T READY. THE WHITE CLOUDS REARING  ..............THREE WOMEN  178   57
   HOW WHITE THESE SHEETS ARE. THE FACES HAVE NO FEATURES. *THREE WOMEN  178   65
   THE SHEETS, THE FACES, ARE WHITE AND STOPPED, LIKE CLOCKS.  ..THREE.  179   95
   AND I, A SHELL, ECHOING ON THIS WHITE BEACH  .........THREE WOMEN  179  111
   I HAVE SEEN THE WHITE CLEAN CHAMBER WITH ITS INSTRUMENTS.  ...THREE.  180  121
   I HOLD MY FINGERS UP, TEN WHITE PICKETS.  .............THREE WOMEN  182  194
   HOLES IN THE HEELS OF SOCKS, THE WHITE MUTE FACES  ......THREE WOMEN  182  199
   AND I AM A WHITE SHIP HOOTING: GOODBYE, GOODBYE.  ......THREE WOMEN  184  261
   NOW THEY FACE A WINTER OF WHITE SHEETS, WHITE FACES.  ...THREE WOMEN  184  265
   NOW THEY FACE A WINTER OF WHITE SHEETS, WHITE FACES.  ...THREE WOMEN  184  265
   I AM BLED WHITE AS WAX, I HAVE NO ATTACHMENTS.  .........THREE WOMEN  184  275
   THE NARCISSI OPEN WHITE FACES IN THE ORCHARD.  ........THREE WOMEN  185  315
   WHO INJURE MY SLEEP WITH THEIR WHITE EYES, THEIR FINGERLESS
      HANDS.  ..........................................THREE WOMEN  185  321
   HE IS STILL SWADDLED IN WHITE BANDS.  .................THREE WOMEN  186  326
   REMEMBERS HOW WHITE THEY WERE.  ......................THREE WOMEN  186  345
   WHITE AS AN EYE ALL OVER!  ..............................LITTLE FUGUE  187    7
   BLACK YEW, WHITE CLOUD,  ................................LITTLE FUGUE  187   14
   I WEAR WHITE CUFFS, I BOW.  ..........................AN APPEARANCE  189    9
   RINGING THE WHITE CHINA.  ......................THE RABBIT CATCHER  194   23
   THE CHILD IN THE WHITE CRIB REVOLVES AND SIGHS,  .............EVENT  194    7
   A SMALL WHITE SOUL IS WAVING, A SMALL WHITE MAGGOT.  .........EVENT  195   19
   A SMALL WHITE SOUL IS WAVING, A SMALL WHITE MAGGOT.  .........EVENT  195   19
   THERE IS THIS WHITE WALL, ABOVE WHICH THE SKY CREATES ITSELF --  ...
                                                   ... APPREHENSIONS  195    1
   O WHITE SEA-CROCKERY,  .................................BERCK-PLAGE  197   31
   I AM NOT A NURSE, WHITE AND ATTENDANT,  ................BERCK-PLAGE  197   42
   WHITE NIKE,  ............................................THE OTHER  201    3
   OF THE WHITE FISTS OF OLD  ....................BURNING THE LETTERS  204    2
   WHITE AS BABIES' BEDDING AND GLITTERING WITH DEAD BREATH. O IVORY!  ...
                                                   ... A BIRTHDAY PRESENT  206   18
   THESE WERE HARDER, TWO WHITE STONES.  ..................THE DETECTIVE  209   32
   THEY MAY BE WHITE AND SHY, THEY ARE NO STOOL PIGEONS,  ....COURAGE.  210   31
   YES, HERE IS THE SECRETARY OF BEES WITH HER WHITE SHOP SMOCK,  BEE.  211    7
   NOW THEY ARE GIVING ME A FASHIONABLE WHITE STRAW ITALIAN HAT  ..BEE.  211   21
   SHINING GLOVES AND WHITE SUIT.  ....................THE BEE MEETING  211   29
   THE WHITE HIVE IS SNUG AS A VIRGIN,  ...............THE BEE MEETING  212   34
   PILLAR OF WHITE IN A BLACKOUT OF KNIVES.  ..........THE BEE MEETING  212   52
   WHOSE IS THAT LONG WHITE BOX IN THE GROVE, WHAT HAVE THEY ACCOMPLISHED,
      WHY AM I COLD.  ..............................THE BEE MEETING  212   55
   THE MAN IN WHITE SMILES, BARE-HANDED,  ......................STINGS  214    2
   WHITE WITH PINK FLOWERS ON IT,  .............................STINGS  214    9
   AND HERE THE SQUARE OF WHITE LINEN  .........................STINGS  215   43
```

	TITLE	PAGE	LINE

WHITE (CONT.)
```
THE WHITE BUSTS OF MARSHALS, ADMIRALS, GENERALS .........THE SWARM    217   44
MIND AGAINST ALL THAT WHITE. .............................WINTERING    218   33
THE SMILE OF THE SNOW IS WHITE. ..........................WINTERING    218   34
FOR THIRTY YEARS, POOR AND WHITE, ...........................DADDY     222    4
EYES ROLLED BY WHITE STICKS, ...............................MEDUSA     224    2
HER FACE RED AND WHITE, A PANIC, ...........................LESBOS     227   11
HARD AND APART AND WHITE. ..................................LESBOS     229   58
WHERE IT DRIVES IN, WHITE AND BLACK, .......................LESBOS     229   75
RADIATION TURNED IT WHITE ..................................FEVER.     231   23
TAKE A LOOK AT THE WHITE, HIGH BERG ON HIS FOREHEAD -- ...LYONNESSE    233    3
THE WHITE GAPE OF HIS MIND WAS THE REAL TABULA RASA. .....LYONNESSE    234   27
DEAD WHITE. ...................................................CUT     235    7
HEFTING HIS WHITE PILLAR WITH THE LIGHT ...............BY CANDLELIGHT   237   28
THOUGH IT LOOKS LIKE A CAT, WITH ITS FLUFFY STUFF, PURE WHITE.*TOUR.   237   16
WHITE .......................................................ARIEL     239   19
EVEN THE NEWTS ARE WHITE, ..................NICK AND THE CANDLESTICK   241   12
SIX-SIDED, WHITE ...................................THE NIGHT DANCES   250   25
NEGRO, MASKED LIKE A WHITE, ............................THALIDOMIDE    252    3
WHITE SPIT .............................................THALIDOMIDE    252   21
WHITE CIGARETTE, .......................................EAVESDROPPER   260   16
WHITE TOWERS OF SMITHFIELD AHEAD, ...........................TOTEM     264    7
AT THE WHITE, TIGHT .....................................PARALYTIC     266   20
A WHITE SKULL, .............................................WORDS      270   12
STRAW MATS, WHITE WALLS .................................BALLOONS      271   12
EACH DEAD CHILD COILED, A WHITE SERPENT, ......................EDGE    272    9
BLED WHITE WITH BRIARS BY A BUSY CONSCIENCE ............DIALOGUE O.    281  197
LIKE LIVE WHITE RABBITS, READY TO BEGIN *DIALOGUE OVER A OUIJA BOARD   282  234
THE SKY OF THE CITY IS WHITE; THE LIGHT FROM THE COUNTRY. ...
                          ... QUEEN MARY'S ROSE GARDEN     290   10
HERE IS A WHITE SKY. HERE IS THE BEAUTY .................FEVER./DR     294    9
TO PITCH THE WHITE WORLD DOWN IN SWIVELING FLOOD, ..SONNET TO SATAN    323    6
WITH TILTED SPARS OF SLOOPS REVOLVED BY WHITE .....MIDSUMMER MOBILE    324    3
WHITE WHALES ARE GONE WITH THE WHITE OCEAN. ............TWO LOVERS.    327   12
WHITE WHALES ARE GONE WITH THE WHITE OCEAN. ............TWO LOVERS.    327   12
WHO WEAVE WITHIN THE SKELETON'S WHITE WOMB ...............TERMINAL     328    7
TELL NOW, WE TAUNT, WHERE BLACK OR WHITE BEGINS   LOVE IS A PARALLAX   330   49
THE STARCHED WHITE COAT, THE CAT'S PAW WALK, ...MORNING IN THE HOS.    332   12
```
WHITE-BEARDED (1)
```
WHITE-BEARDED, WEARY. THE BERRIES PURPLE ..................MOONRISE     98   29
```
WHITE-BELLIED (1)
```
BROWN-BACKED, WHITE-BELLIED ....................WORDS FOR A NURSERY     74   31
```
WHITE-HAIRED (2)
```
AND THE WHITE-HAIRED JEWELER FROM DENMARK IS CARVING .......ON DECK   143   31
OR YOUR WHITE-HAIRED BENEFACTRESS, WHO MAY SEE FIT .....DIALOGUE O.    277   48
```
WHITEHOT (1)
```
IN THE WHITEHOT NOON: .............................FIESTA MELONS       46   10
```
WHITE-JACKETED (1)
```
PARCELED OUT BY WHITE-JACKETED ASSASSINS. .............STREET SONG      36   10
```
WHITELY (3)
```
WHITELY, DISCREETLY, .....................................MUSHROOMS    139    2
THE NARCISSI LOOK UP LIKE CHILDREN, QUICKLY AND WHITELY. .NARCISSI.    190   12
RISES SO WHITELY UNBUFFETED? ...........................BERCK-PLAGE    198   64
```
WHITEN (6)
```
DEATH MAY WHITEN IN SUN OR OUT OF IT. ....................MOONRISE      98   18
RIVER-VERGE FARMS WHERE RYE-HEADS WHITEN. .........IN MIDAS' COUNTRY    99    4
LEAVING A SALTY MASH OF ICE TO WHITEN .............POINT SHIRLEY       110    8
TO WHITEN MY BONES AMONG THEM. ..................WUTHERING HEIGHTS     167   18
THE FLOWERS AND THE FACES WHITEN TO A SHEET. ............LAST WORDS    172   13
THEIR LIGHTS WHITEN MY HEART. ..........................THE RIVAL/DR   291   26
```
WHITENED (1)
```
WHITENED BY THE FACES OF THE DROWNED. ..................FINISTERRE     169    5
```
WHITENESS (11)
```
BERRIES REDDEN. A BODY OF WHITENESS ......................MOONRISE      98   13
I SMELL THAT WHITENESS HERE, BENEATH THE STONES ..........MOONRISE      98   16
I CAN SEE NO COLOR FOR THIS WHITENESS. ...................MOONRISE      98   20
WHITENESS I REMEMBER .........................WHITENESS I REMEMBER    102    T
WHITENESS BEING WHAT I REMEMBER .............WHITENESS I REMEMBER     102    1
ABOUT SAM: WHITENESS AND THE GREAT RUN ......WHITENESS I REMEMBER     102    2
SPINNING TO STILL IN HIS ONE WHITENESS. ......WHITENESS I REMEMBER    103   33
EVERYTHING TOOK PLACE IN A DURABLE WHITENESS.*ELECTRA ON AZALEA PATH   117   14
THEIR WHITENESS BEARS NO RELATION TO LAUNDRY, ...............MAGI     148    4
NOT HER WHITENESS AND BEAUTY, AS I HAD AT FIRST SUPPOSED.*IN PLASTER   159   19
THE HILLS STEP OFF INTO WHITENESS. ....................SHEEP IN FOG    262    1
```
WHITENS (3)
```
DEATH WHITENS IN THE EGG AND OUT OF IT. ..................MOONRISE      98   19
LIKE A CUP OR A ROOM. THE MOON'S CROOK WHITENS, ......PARLIAMENT H.    153   38
WHITENS AND SWALLOWS ITS DULL STARS. AND NOW YOU TRY ..MORNING SONG    157   16
```
WHITER (2)
```
AND BODY WHITER THAN ITS FRILL OF LILIES: ..............YADWIGHA.      85   14
ONLY MUCH WHITER AND UNBREAKABLE AND WITH NO COMPLAINTS. *IN PLASTER   158    8
```
WHITE-RABBIT (1)
```
AND AUCTION OFF EACH RARE WHITE-RABBIT VERB; .........A SORCERER B.    324    6
```
WHITE-SMOCKED (1)
```
THE WHITE-SMOCKED BOYS STARTED WORKING. *TWO VIEWS OF A CADAVER ROOM   114    5
```

WHITEWASHED (1)
   AGAINST BARE, WHITEWASHED WALLS, THE FURNITURE ....THE OTHER TWO   68   8
WHITSUN (1)
   WHITSUN ....WHITSUN   153   T
WHO (80)
   HER ANTELOPE WHO MEANT HIM NAUGHT BUT GOOD. ..THE QUEEN'S COMPLAINT   28   10
   THAT GRANDIOSE COLOSSUS WHO ....LETTER TO A PURIST   36   1
   O MY GREAT IDIOT, WHO .. ..LETTER TO A PURIST   37   9
   WHO, UNAWARE HOW THEY DWINDLE, ...SOLILOQUY OF THE SOLIPSIST   37   15
   THESE GOATISH TRAGEDIANS WHO ....THE BEGGARS   47   2
   WHO OGLE MEN ....RHYME   50   6
   SAYING: "SOMETHING'S ADDLED IN A WOMAN WHO ACCOMMODATES ...
                        ... ELLA MASON AND HER ELEVEN CATS   53   5
   AT GIRLS WHO MARRY -- ....ELLA MASON AND HER ELEVEN CATS   54   39
   HEARTS OF THOSE WHO PIERCED TIME'S CORE. ....CRYSTAL GAZER   55   42
   SHE BLENCHED, AS ONE WHO DROWNS, THE LADY AND THE EARTHENWARE HEAD   69   21
   MOTHER, WHO MADE TO ORDER STORIES ....THE DISQUIETING MUSES   75   9
   WHO HAS SALTIER APHRODISIACS ....OUIJA   77   23
   OLD BOCKLIN MISSED, WHO HELD A SHELL .....ON THE DECLINE OF ORACLES   78   5
   NEVER GRIP, AS THEIR GRANDSIRES DID, THAT DEVIL WHO CHUCKLES*LESSON.   80   24
   APPROVING CHASED GIRLS WHO GET THEM TO A TREE .....VIRGIN IN A TREE   81   4
   WHO KEEP COOL AND HOLY MAKE ....VIRGIN IN A TREE   81   25
   WHO BORROWED FEATHERS FOR YOUR FEET, NOT LEAD, ...PERSEUS   83   12
   WHO POISES HIS PASTEL SPEAR ....BATTLE-SCENE   84   14
   AND ALL YOU SANTA'S DEER WHO BROWSE ....A WINTER'S TALE   87   21
   TO PEOPLE WHO LIVE IN THE BOTTOM OF VALLEYS ......ABOVE THE OXBOW   88   15
   THE ORACULAR GHOST WHO DWINDLES ON PIN-LEGS *THE GHOST'S LEAVETAKING   90   9
   SEEN BY ANY MAN WHO KEPT HIS HEAD, ...FULL FATHOM FIVE   93   38
   WHO DRAG OUR ANCIENT FATHER AT THE HEEL, ...MOONRISE   98   28
   SIGNS SAY NOTHING. THE FALCON WHO SPOKE CLEAR ........INCOMMUNICADO   100   13
   WHO SET WASP, WOLF AND SHARK TO WORK, ...I WANT, I WANT   106   7
   WHOSE LAUNDRY SNAPPED AND FROZE HERE, WHO ....POINT SHIRLEY   110   10
   WHO WAKES WITH DARKNESS AND TILL DAWN WORKS HARD ....GOATSUCKER   111   3
   THE STONE FACE OF THE MAN WHO DOESN'T FEEL, ...THE RAVAGED FACE   116   10
   O PARDON THE ONE WHO KNOCKS FOR PARDON AT ...ELECTRA ON AZALEA PATH   117   44
   WHO ....POEM.1.WHO.   131   ST
   INMATES WHO DON'T HIBERNATE. POEM.1.WHO.   131   15
   THESE HALLS ARE FULL OF WOMEN WHO THINK THEY ARE BIRDS. *POEM.1.WHO.   131   21
   LADY, WHO ARE THESE OTHERS IN THE MOON'S VAT -- POEM.3.MAENAD.   133   22
   AND IT WAS I WHO ATTRACTED EVERYBODY'S ATTENTION, ...IN PLASTER   159   18
   BUT IT IS SHE WHO IS PAPER NOW, WARMED BY NO ONE. ....WIDOW   164   20
   AND A CABIN BOY WHO COULD DECORATE CAKES IN SIX-COLORED
                    FROSTING. ....THE BABYSITTERS   174   12
   WHO IS HE, THIS BLUE, FURIOUS BOY, ...THREE WOMEN   181   162
   I CAN LOVE MY HUSBAND, WHO WILL UNDERSTAND. ....THREE WOMEN   183   250
   WHO WILL LOVE ME THROUGH THE BLUR OF MY DEFORMITY ......THREE WOMEN   183   251
   WHO WOULD ADHERE TO ME; I UNDO HER FINGERS LIKE BANDAGES: I GO. ...
                    ... THREE WOMEN   184   273
   THIS WOMAN WHO MEETS ME IN WINDOWS -- SHE IS NEAT. ....THREE WOMEN   184   280
   WHO INJURE MY SLEEP WITH THEIR WHITE EYES, THEIR FINGERLESS
                    HANDS. ....THREE WOMEN   185   321
   WHO HAS DISMEMBERED US? ....THE RABBIT CATCHER   195   21
   WHO WALL UP THEIR BACKS AGAINST HIM. ....BERCK-PLAGE   196   15
   WHO PLUMBS THE WELL OF HIS BOOK, ...BERCK-PLAGE   197   22
   SPEAK, SPEAK! WHO IS IT? ..WORDS HEARD, BY ACCIDENT, OVER THE PHONE   202   3
   IT IS HE WHO HAS ACHIEVED THESE SYLLABLES. ....WORDS HEARD.   202   5
   WHO ARE THESE PEOPLE AT THE BRIDGE TO MEET ME? THEY ARE THE
                    VILLAGERS --- ....THE BEE MEETING   211   1
   I AM THE MAGICIAN'S GIRL WHO DOES NOT FLINCH. ....THE BEE MEETING   212   53
   THESE WOMEN WHO ONLY SCURRY, ...STINGS   214   29
   WHO ARE THEY SHOOTING AT? ....THE SWARM   216   5
   IT IS THEY WHO OWN ME. ....WINTERING   218   19
   ANY LESS THE BLACK MAN WHO ....DADDY   223   55
   THE VAMPIRE WHO SAID HE WAS YOU ....DADDY   224   72
   WHO DO YOU THINK YOU ARE? ....MEDUSA   225   32
   YOU WHO HAVE BLOWN YOUR TUBES LIKE A BAD RADIO ....LESBOS   228   17
   IT IS LOVE YOU ARE FULL OF. YOU KNOW WHO YOU HATE. ....LESBOS   229   72
   WHO DO YOU THINK I AM, ...STOPPED DEAD   230   17
   WHO WHEEZES AT THE GATE. INCAPABLE ....FEVER.   231   5
   THE ONE WHO NEVER LOOKS UP, WHOSE EYES ARE LIDDED ......DEATH & CO.   254   3
   WHO EXHIBITS ....DEATH & CO.   254   5
   WHO ARE THESE PIETAS? ....WINTER TREES   258   14
   O YOU WHO EAT ....BRASILIA   258   18
   AS FLAT AS SHE, WHO WHISPER "WE'RE YOUR DAUGHTERS." ......PARALYTIC   266   26
   OR YOUR WHITE-HAIRED BENEFACTRESS, WHO MAY SEE FIT .....DIALOGUE O.   277   48
   OF CAMBRIC OR WATERDROPS, WHO KNOWS WHAT BELIEF ....DIALOGUE O.   282   224
   CHIMERA ON THE HOOK, WHO CLAIMS HE'S LATE ....DIALOGUE O.   283   245
   WITH THE PILOT WHO DARES ALL HEAVEN'S HARMS .........METAMORPHOSES.   307   2
   THE FALLING MAN WHO NEVER WILL ABSTAIN ...METAMORPHOSES OF THE MOON   307   10
   FOR NAIVE LARKS WHO STARVE AND GRIEVE. ...METAMORPHOSES OF THE MOON   307   18
   WHO WALKED IN A SWARMING SHROUD OF WINGS ....LAMENT   315   2
   MAN WHO CAN MANGLE THE GRIN OF KINGS: .. ..LAMENT   316   17
   WHO SCORNED THE TICK OF THE FALLING WEATHER. ....LAMENT   316   19
   ALL WHO LOOK: ....ON LOOKING INTO THE EYES OF A DEMON LOVER   325   4
   WHO PEERS INSIDE ....ON LOOKING INTO THE EYES OF A DEMON LOVER   325   6

WHO (CONT.)
    WHO WEAVE WITHIN THE SKELETON'S WHITE WOMB ....TERMINAL   328   7
    WHO INSISTS HIS PLAYMATES RUN. ....LOVE IS A PARALLAX   329   24
    WHO IS THE DESTINATION OF THE CORD ....THE PRINCESS AND THE GOBLINS   333   23
    WHO WEEPS BEFORE THE DESOLATE TABLEAU   THE PRINCESS AND THE GOBLINS   335   74
    WHO SEEKS TO DALLY IN THE PORT TILL DAWN, ...EPITAPH IN THREE PARTS   337   8
WHO'D (2)
    GROW GREEN AGAIN? WHO'D WALK IN THIS BLEAK PLACE? *WINTER LANDSCAPE,   22   15
    BUT WHO'D VOLUNTEER TO GULP THE LAOCOON, ...PERSEUS   82   8
WHOEVER (1)
    WHOEVER HEARD A SUNSET YOWL LIKE THAT? ....STOPPED DEAD   230   15
WHOLE (30)
    EACH DAY DEMANDS WE CREATE OUR WHOLE WORLD OVER, ...TALE OF A TUB   25   36
    NOW OUR WHOLE TASK'S TO HACK ....FIRESONG   30   8
    THE WHOLE SCENE FLARED WELCOME TO THIS ROAMER. ....DREAM WITH C.   44   12
    WHOLE DONKEY-CARTS FULL ....FIESTA MELONS   46   2
    HUSH A LUMPED MAN-SHAPE. THE WHOLE ACT FORMAL, FLUENT AS A DANCE. ...
                                                    ... THE GORING   47   9
    THE WHOLE SEASON, SLOVEN. ....SPINSTER   49   12
    THE GUISE OF LEAVES. THE WHOLE LANDSCAPE ....HARDCASTLE CRAGS   63   37
    THUMB CAN MAKE ANYONE WINCE, BUT THE WHOLE GLOBE ....PERSEUS   83   28
    A WHOLE SEA OF SPINACH-HEADS LEANED TO MY HAND. ....SPINACH-PICKER.   90   22
    AND WHOLE CRABS, DEAD, THEIR SOGGY ....MUSSEL HUNTER AT ROCK HARBOR   97   84
    STONES THAT TAKE THE WHOLE SUMMER TO LOSE ......CHILD'S PARK STONES   101   23
    THE WHOLE FLAT HARBOR ANCHORED IN ....A WINTER SHIP   113   9
    THEIR EYES REVOLVE THE WHOLE TOWN LIKE A BLUE AND GREEN BALL. *NET-.   121   12
    WHOLE AS A COBWEB, ...POLLY'S TREE   129   35
    A WHOLE FAMILY OF PROMINENT OBJECTS ....CANDLES   148   6
    THAT WOULD HAVE THE WHOLE WORLD FLAT BECAUSE THEY ARE. THREE WOMEN   179   87
    IS IT IMPOSSIBLE FOR YOU TO LET SOMETHING GO AND HAVE IT GO
        WHOLE? ....A BIRTHDAY PRESENT   207   45
    BY THE TIME THE WHOLE OF IT WAS DELIVERED, AND TOO NUMB TO USE IT. ...
                                                    ... A BIRTHDAY PRESENT 208   54
    THE BROWN MOTHERLY FURROWS, THE WHOLE ESTATE. ....THE DETECTIVE   209   37
    WHOLE ....PARALYTIC 266   18
    ON A WHOLE WORLD I CANNOT TOUCH, ...PARALYTIC   266   19
    ONE HOLLOW THE WHOLE SEA'S PIVOT. ....CONTUSION   271   6
    BELCHED INTO BLAZE AND, THOUGH RED-HOT, KEPT WHOLE .....DIALOGUE O.   280 158
    THE WHOLE REVOLVING TALL GLASS PALACE HALL ....CINDERELLA   304   5
    AND DAMAGING THE WHOLE UNSEEN ....THE DREAM   311   17
    AIR ALTERS INTO GLASS AND THE WHOLE SKY ....PROLOGUE TO SPRING   322   4
    WIND WAKES THE WHOLE METROPOLIS.*INSOLENT STORM STRIKES AT THE SKULL   325   6
    IS OUR LIFE'S WHOLE NEMESIS." ....LOVE IS A PARALLAX   329   12
    LEST, OUT OF SPITE, THE WHOLE ....AERIALIST 332   46
    GAILY CURSING THE WHOLE GOBLIN HORDE. THE PRINCESS AND THE GOBLINS   334   46
WHOLENESS (1)
    OUT OF A WHOLENESS. WORMS, NOT WINGS IS WHAT ....DIALOGUE O.   279   99
WHO'LL (1)
    DIRECT TO YES. I BET IT'S PAN. WHO'LL ..DIALOGUE OVER A OUIJA BOARD   277   27
WHOLLY (5)
    THUS WHOLLY ENGROSS ....SOW   61   28
    WHOLLY OTHER, AND OURSELVES ....THE GREAT CARBUNCLE   73   18
    IN THE COAL FIRE WILL NOT WHOLLY CONSOLE THEM. ....OUIJA   77   7
    GREEN, WHOLLY GREEN, THEY STAND THEIR KNOBBY SPINE ABOVE THE OXBOW   88   10
    MUST HAVE BEEN WHOLLY SOMEONE ELSE. IT'S ABSURD, ...DIALOGUE O.   285 309
WHOM (1)
    FOR WHOM THE GOOD LORD PROVIDES (HE GAVE ....ON DECK   143   20
WHOPPERS (1)
    PINK-PULPED WHOPPERS, ...FIESTA MELONS   46   12
WHORE (3)
    SAD HAG. "EVERY WOMAN'S A WHORE. ....LESBOS   229   83
    (MY SELVES DISSOLVING, OLD WHORE PETTICOATS) --- ....FEVER.   232   53
    LITTLE WHORE TONGUE, ...EAVESDROPPER   260   32
WHORL (1)
    IN THE WHORL OF HER EAR, AND LIKE A SCOOPED-OUT PUMPKIN CROWN ...
                                                    ... HARDCASTLE CRAGS   63   24
WHORLED (3)
    ABOVE WHORLED, SPINDLING GORSE, ...TWO VIEWS OF WITHENS 71   1
    WITH FIVE WHORLED LANDSPITS. ....WORDS FOR A NURSERY 74   30
    FOR THE WHORLED EAR'S LISTENING ....LORELEI   94   18
WHO'S (2)
    YOU TO ASK WHO'S HOME, OR I? I WILL. ...DIALOGUE OVER A OUIJA BOARD   277   25
    AND WE'LL SEE WHO'S SMARTEST. PAN, TELL US NOW: ....DIALOGUE O.   281 205
WHOSE (30)
    WHOSE FORCE MIGHT FIT ....THE QUEEN'S COMPLAINT   29   18
    WHOSE LABOR'S NOT YET SMOKED ....TINKER JACK AND THE TIDY WIVES   35   29
    WHOSE STARK ACT ALL COMING DOUBLE LUCK JOINS. ..WREATH FOR A BRIDAL   44   6
    I'VE GOT A STUBBORN GOOSE WHOSE GUT'S ....RHYME   50   1
    NOW, RUN TO FAT, SHE'S A SPINSTER WHOSE DOOR SHUTS ...ELLA MASON A.   54   17
    PRODIGIOUS IN GLUTTONIES AS THAT HOG WHOSE WANT ....SOW   61   41
    MOTHER, WHOSE WITCHES ALWAYS, ALWAYS ....THE DISQUIETING MUSES   75   11
    CRIES: "CELEBRATE SYRINX WHOSE DEMURS ....VIRGIN IN A TREE   81   13
    OF THE STABLE HORSE WHOSE HISTORY'S ....WHITENESS I REMEMBER   102   6
    WHOSE OWL-EYES IN THE SCRAGGLY WOOD ....THE DEATH OF MYTH-MAKING   104   11
    WHOSE LAUNDRY SNAPPED AND FROZE HERE, WHO ....POINT SHIRLEY   110   10

WHOSE (CONT.)
     WHOSE STONES KEEP A LITTLE HEAT. ....OLD LADIES' HOME   120   7
     THOSE SUGARY PLANETS WHOSE INFLUENCE WON FOR HIM ....INSOMNIAC   163   17
     PICKET OF TREES WHOSE SILHOUETTE IS DARKER   STARS OVER THE DORDOGNE 165   2
     IN WHOSE RIFT WE LIE ....EVENT 194   3
     WHOSE IS THAT LONG WHITE BOX IN THE GROVE, WHAT HAVE THEY ACCOMPLISHED,
          WHY AM I COLD. ....THE BEE MEETING   212   55
     WHOSE NEWS IS THE OPEN CHERRY, THE OPEN CLOVER? ....STINGS   214   30
     IN WHOSE SHADOW I HAVE EATEN MY GHOST RATION. ....THE JAILER   227   38
     WHOSE SIDE ARE THEY ON? ....CUT 235   21
     WHOSE RED HEART BLOOMS THROUGH HER COAT SO ASTOUNDINGLY ---*POP.OCT.   240   3
     THE ONE WHO NEVER LOOKS UP, WHOSE EYES ARE LIDDED ......DEATH & CO.   254   3
     WHOSE NAMES YOU MEDITATE -- ....CHILD 265   4
     OVER WHOSE POOL I TENDERLY ....GIGOLO   268   31
     WHOSE KISS STINGS UNBEARABLY ....MYSTIC   268   4
     WHOSE HOPES ARE SO LOW THEY ARE COMFORTABLE -- ....MYSTIC   269   21
     AFTER WHOSE STROKE THE WOOD RINGS, ...WORDS   270   2
     OUTSIDE THE CAVE WHOSE CONTOURS MOST REMIND ....DIALOGUE O.   281 200
     WHOSE CANDOR EXPOSES ....MOONSONG AT MORNING   317   23
     WHOSE MOONS OF BLACK .....ON LOOKING INTO THE EYES OF A DEMON LOVER   325   2
     WHOSE HOLY BLUE ANOINTS HER INJURED HAND. ....THE PRINCESS.   333   6
WHY (20)
     WHY, ALL THE WINDOWS BROKE WHEN HE STALKED IN.*THE QUEEN'S COMPLAINT   28   5
     SO ROUSSEAU, TO EXPLAIN WHY THE RED COUCH ....YADWIGHA.   86   21
     AND THAT, ROUSSEAU TOLD THE CRITICS, WAS WHY THE COUCH ...YADWIGHA.   86   31
     WHY IS IT SO QUIET, WHAT ARE THEY HIDING? ....BERCK-PLAGE   196   5
     WHY SHOULD IT, IT IS THE HEARSE OF A DEAD FOOT, ...BERCK-PLAGE   197   20
     SUCH SALT-SWEETNESS. WHY SHOULD I WALK ....BERCK-PLAGE   197   40
     I KNOW WHY YOU WILL NOT GIVE IT TO ME, ...A BIRTHDAY PRESENT   207   27
     AND THEY ARE ALL GLOVED AND COVERED, WHY DID NOBODY TELL ME? ..BEE.   211   4
     WHOSE IS THAT LONG WHITE BOX IN THE GROVE, WHAT HAVE THEY ACCOMPLISHED,
          WHY AM I COLD. ....THE BEE MEETING   212   55
     SO WHY SHOULD THEY TURN ON ME? ....THE ARRIVAL OF THE BEE BOX   213   34
     WHY SHE IS SCHIZOPHRENIC, ...LESBOS   227   10
     AND THAT'S WHY I HAVE NO HAIR, AUNTIE, THAT'S WHY I CHOKE   THE TOUR 238   24
     AND THAT'S WHY I HAVE NO HAIR, AUNTIE, THAT'S WHY I CHOKE   THE TOUR 238   24
     THE PLACE I AM GETTING TO, WHY ARE THERE THESE OBSTACLES --- ...
                                             ... GETTING THERE   249   45
     WHY AM I GIVEN ....THE NIGHT DANCES 250   22
     KNOW: WHICH IS WHY I, WHEN THE WONDROUS FIST ....DIALOGUE O.   279 119
     GOD-PIE. WHY, THEN, DID YOU DEIGN TO INTRODUCE ....DIALOGUE O.   283 251
     WHY, YOUR HAND'S COLD AS ICE! THEN CHAFE THE COLD .....DIALOGUE O.   285 333
     SHE ADDED PETTISHLY, "I CAN'T SEE WHY ....BITTER STRAWBERRIES   300   25
     WHY HE SHOULD KNEEL BEFORE A SILLY SCENE ....THE PRINCESS.   335   65
WICK (2)
     DAWN SNUFFS OUT STAR'S SPENT WICK, ...EPITAPH FOR FIRE AND FLOWER   46   29
     STALLS IN HALLS WHERE THE LAMP WICK ....OLD LADIES' HOME   120   20
WICKED (1)
     ALTHOUGH THE WICKED WITCH HAS POISONED ONE. ....ADMONITIONS   319   5
WICKLESS (1)
     FIVE WICKLESS CANDLES ....WORDS FOR A NURSERY   74   45
WIDE (5)
     WITH HER BLANK BROWN EYES STARVED WIDE, ...THE SHRIKE   42   9
     HER WIDE BED WORE THE STAIN OF DIVINITY. ....ELECTRA ON AZALEA PATH   116   8
     A RED, HARD WOOD, EYES SHUT AND MOUTH WIDE OPEN. ....THREE WOMEN   182 212
     MY DAUGHTER HAS NO TEETH. HER MOUTH IS WIDE. ....THREE WOMEN   182 216
     HIS WIDE EYE IS THAT GENERAL, FLAT BLUE. ....THREE WOMEN   183 234
WIDEN (3)
     WIDEN THE CRANNIES, ...MUSHROOMS   139   17
     WIDEN AND DIE IN THE HEDGEROWS. I HEAR THE MOO OF COWS. *THREE WOMEN   185 312
     IS IT FOR THIS YOU WIDEN YOUR EYE-RINGS? ....THE OTHER   201   10
WIDENS (1)
     WHERE ONCE A DAY THE LIGHT SLOWLY WIDENS AND SLOWLY THINS. ..TULIPS   161   45
WIDE-OPEN (1)
     THE BALD SLOTS OF HIS EYES STIFFENED WIDE-OPEN ....INSOMNIAC   163   27
WIDOW (8)
     WIDOW ....WIDOW   164   T
     WIDOW. THE WORD CONSUMES ITSELF -- ....WIDOW   164   1
     WIDOW. THE DEAD SYLLABLE, WITH ITS SHADOW ....WIDOW   164   6
     WIDOW. THE BITTER SPIDER SITS ....WIDOW   164   11
     WIDOW: THAT GREAT, VACANT ESTATE! ....WIDOW   164   21
     WIDOW, THE COMPASSIONATE TREES BEND IN, ...WIDOW   164   26
     A WIDOW RESEMBLES THEM, A SHADOW-THING, ...WIDOW   164   30
     THE WIDOW WITH HER BLACK POCKETBOOK AND THREE DAUGHTERS,*BERCK-PLAGE   200 100
WIDOW'S (1)
     STAGE CURTAINS, A WIDOW'S FRIZZ. ....LESBOS   227   6
WIELDS (1)
     WIELDS GUARD OF HONOR OVER THESE!" STARRED WITH WORDS ....WREATH F.   45   16
WIFE (13)
     RIGHT TO BLAZE AS SATAN'S WIFE: ....VANITY FAIR   33   32
     A PERFECTLY FACETED WIFE TO WAIT ....ON DECK   143   32
     THE OLD DREGS, THE OLD DIFFICULTIES TAKE ME TO WIFE. PARLIAMENT H.   153   48
     ZOO KEEPER'S WIFE ....ZOO KEEPER'S WIFE   154   T
     WHEN THE SPORTY WIFE AND HER DOCTOR HUSBAND WENT ON ONE OF
          THEIR CRUISES ....THE BABYSITTERS 174   16

TITLE   PAGE LINE

WIFE (CONT.)

THOUGH THERE IS A SHADOW STARTING FROM MY FEET. I AM A WIFE. *THREE. 187 369
THERE IS NO HELP IN HIS WEEPING WIFE. ....BERCK-PLAGE 198 52
THE HOLLOWS IN WHICH ROCK THE THOUGHTS OF THE WIFE ---   BERCK-PLAGE 199 75
THE LITTLE TOY WIFE -- ....AMNESIAC 233   4
O SISTER, MOTHER, WIFE, ...AMNESIAC 233 25
NO CHILD, NO WIFE. ....BY CANDLELIGHT 237 34
MY WIFE, DEAD AND FLAT, IN 1920 FURS, ...PARALYTIC 266 23
HIS WIFE AND HIS CHILDREN ....TEMPER OF TIME 336 21

WIFEY (1)

TO THE ELECTRIC MILKER, THE WIFEY, THE BIG BLUE EYE ...EAVESDROPPER 261 43

WIG (2)

WITH THE SACRED BABOON IN HIS WIG AND WAX EARS ...ZOO KEEPER'S WIFE 155 29
ALL WIG CURLS AND YELLOW TEETH ....WUTHERING HEIGHTS 167 26

WIGGLING (1)

WHISTLING, WIGGLING MY EARS, ...POEM.2.DARK. 132   6

WIGGLY (1)

WITH HER WIGGLY FINGERS AND FOR A VERY SMALL FEE. ....THE TOUR 238 47

WILD (6)

WITH YOUR WILD FURIES, DISTURBING GARLANDS OF FRUIT ..CONVERSATION.   21   2
THE MOON SEES NOTHING OF THIS. SHE IS BALD AND WILD. ....MOON. 173 27
PLYING THEIR WILD CELLS IN MY KEEL'S SHADOW, ...MEDUSA 225   7
A BIT OF A WILD MACHINE, A BIT OF A MESS! ....THE TOUR 237 12
DRIVING THE DULL CELLS WILD. ........................EAVESDROPPER 260 18
TO NORMAL. LET'S CLOSE THE CURTAINS. IT LOOKS WILD ....DIALOGUE O. 286 335

WILD-CATS (1)

ACCURST AS WILD-CATS. ....ELLA MASON AND HER ELEVEN CATS   54 42

WILDER (1)

A RABBIT'S CRY MAY BE WILDER ....KINDNESS 269   7

WILDERNESS (5)

THROUGH A RANK WILDERNESS OF FERN AND FLOWER. ....SPINSTER   49 10
SET IN AN INTRICATE WILDERNESS OF GREEN ....YADWIGHA   85   5
I'D ONLY TO SET ONE FOOT IN WILDERNESS--*MEMOIRS OF A SPINACH-PICKER   90 21
THE SMALL SHREW CHITTERS FROM ITS WILDERNESS ....WATERCOLOR. 112   4
I WORM AND HACK IN A PURPLE WILDERNESS. ......THE SURGEON AT 2 A.M. 171 20

WILDERNESSES (1)

WE OWN NO WILDERNESSES RICH AND DEEP ENOUGH ....THE THIN PEOPLE   65 41

WILDLY (1)

WE SHALL BOARD OUR IMAGINED SHIP AND WILDLY SAIL .....TALE OF A TUB   25 46

WILES (1)

AND THAT DAMN SCRUPULOUS TREE WON'T PRACTICE WILES ......CONJURING.   66 20

WILL (129)

AND, UNDER HONOR, WILL DEPART; ....BUCOLICS   24 22
BLIND WITH STEAM, WILL NOT ADMIT THE DARK ....TALE OF A TUB   24 15
THE AUTHENTIC SEA DENIES THEM AND WILL PLUCK ....TALE OF A TUB   25 23
HE HAULS TO HIS WILL EARLY; ....ODE FOR TED   29 17
JACK WILL TOUCH UP ....TINKER JACK AND THE TIDY WIVES   34 21
WILL BREAK BEFORE IT HELP; ....RECANTATION   41   7
THAT WILL KINDLE ANGELS' ENVY, SCORCH AND DROP ......EPITAPH FOR F.   45   6
THE STRONGEST WILL SEEMED A WILL TOWARD CEREMONY. OBESE, DARK-
                        ... THE GORING   47   4
THE STRONGEST WILL SEEMED A WILL TOWARD CEREMONY. OBESE, DARK-
                        ... THE GORING   47   4
TODAY I WILL NOT ....RESOLVE   52 20
WILL BRING CROP'S INCREASE, AND HARVEST FRUIT ....CRYSTAL GAZER   55 17
TO MY SWEET WILL, NO LUMINOUS SHAPE ....CONJURING.   66 26
WILL HAVE NO COUNTERFEIT   ON THE DIFFICULTY OF CONJURING UP A DRYAD   66 31
WILL BETRAY THE COMPANY I KEEP. ....THE DISQUIETING MUSES   76 56
IN THE COAL FIRE WILL NOT WHOLLY CONSOLE THEM. ....OUIJA   77   7
AND SNAKES THERE WERE, ARE, WILL BE -- TILL YAWNS ....SNAKECHARMER   79 21
TREE-TWIST WILL APE THIS GROSS ANATOMY ....VIRGIN IN A TREE   82 44
LEDGE WILL DISLODGE OUR CRAMPED CONCEPT OF SPACE, UNWALL ....OXBOW.   88 23
TO A GIDDY JOG. THEN FOR ILL WILL ....WHITENESS I REMEMBER 102 17
BLIND TO WHAT WILL BE AND WHAT WAS. ....THE EYE-MOTE 109 23
FARTHER OUT, THE WAVES WILL BE MOUTHING ICECAKES -- ..A WINTER SHIP 113 21
THE SUN WILL DIMINISH IT SOON ENOUGH: ....A WINTER SHIP 113 29
SOON EACH WHITE LADY WILL BE BOARDED UP ....PRIVATE GROUND 130   5
IT HURTS AT FIRST. THE RED TONGUES WILL TEACH THE TRUTH. POEM.6.W. 135 18
STILL NOBODY WILL MOVE OR SPEAK -- ....ON DECK 142 10
IT WILL PING LIKE A CHINESE CHIME IN THE SLIGHTEST AIR STIR A LIFE 150   7
LIKE AN EYE BETWEEN TWO WHITE LIDS THAT WILL NOT SHUT. ......TULIPS 160   9
THAT WILL PUT HER HEART OUT LIKE AN ONLY EYE. ....WIDOW 164   5
TOO CLOSE ATTENTION, THEY WILL INVITE ME ....WUTHERING HEIGHTS 167 17
I DO NOT THINK THE SEA WILL APPEAR AT ALL. ..........BLACKBERRYING 168 13
TOMORROW THEY WILL SWIM ....THE SURGEON AT 2 A.M. 171 38
TOMORROW THE PATIENT WILL HAVE A CLEAN, PINK PLASTIC LIMB. *SURGEON. 171 40
THEY WILL WONDER IF I WAS IMPORTANT. ....LAST WORDS 172   9
A FEW MORE BREATHS, AND IT WILL REFLECT NOTHING AT ALL. LAST WORDS 172 12
THE BLUE EYE OF MY TURQUOISE WILL COMFORT ME. ....LAST WORDS 172 20
THEY WILL ROLL ME UP IN BANDAGES, THEY WILL STORE MY HEART LAST W. 172 23
THEY WILL ROLL ME UP IN BANDAGES, THEY WILL STORE MY HEART LAST W. 172 23
I SHALL HARDLY KNOW MYSELF. IT WILL BE DARK, ...LAST WORDS 172 25
INSIDE THE CHURCH, THE SAINTS WILL BE ALL BLUE, ...MOON. 173 24
IS SHE SORRY FOR WHAT WILL HAPPEN? I DO NOT THINK SO. ..THREE WOMEN 176   6
WHAT HAPPENS IN ME WILL HAPPEN WITHOUT ATTENTION. ......THREE WOMEN 176 10

WILL (CONT.) TITLE PAGE LINE

WHEN WILL IT BE, THE SECOND WHEN TIME BREAKS ....THREE WOMEN 179 104
"THIS IS WHERE YOU WILL COME WHEN YOU ARE READY." ......THREE WOMEN 180 123
MEN HAVE USED HER MEANLY. SHE WILL EAT THEM. ....THREE WOMEN 181 159
I CAN LOVE MY HUSBAND, WHO WILL UNDERSTAND. ....THREE WOMEN 183 250
WHO WILL LOVE ME THROUGH THE BLUR OF MY DEFORMITY .....THREE WOMEN 183 251
I DO NOT WILL HIM TO BE EXCEPTIONAL. ....THREE WOMEN 186 330
I WILL HIM TO BE COMMON, ...THREE WOMEN 186 334
AND TO MARRY WHAT HE WANTS AND WHERE HE WILL. ....THREE WOMEN 186 336
IT WILL MAKE LITTLE DRESSES AND COATS, ...AN APPEARANCE 189 12
IT WILL COVER A DYNASTY. ....AN APPEARANCE 189 13
WILL TOLERATE NO BYSTANDING: I MUST SHRIEK. ....ELM 192 21
IT PETRIFIES THE WILL. THESE ARE THE ISOLATE, SLOW FAULTS ......ELM 193 41
AND AT LEAST IT WILL BE A GOOD PLACE NOW, THE ATTIC. ......BURNING. 204 22
YOU WILL BE AWARE OF AN ABSENCE, PRESENTLY, ...FOR A FATHERLESS SON 205 1
I KNOW WHY YOU WILL NOT GIVE IT TO ME, ...A BIRTHDAY PRESENT 207 27
THE WORLD WILL GO UP IN A SHRIEK, AND YOUR HEAD WITH IT, BIRTHDAY. 207 29
I WILL ONLY TAKE IT AND GO ASIDE QUIETLY. ....A BIRTHDAY PRESENT 207 33
YOU WILL NOT EVEN HEAR ME OPENING IT, NO PAPER CRACKLE, ..BIRTHDAY. 207 34
NOW I AM MILKWEED SILK, THE BEES WILL NOT NOTICE. ..THE BEE MEETING 211 9
THEY WILL NOT SMELL MY FEAR, MY FEAR, MY FEAR. .....THE BEE MEETING 211 10
NO, NO, IT IS SCARLET FLOWERS THAT WILL ONE DAY BE EDIBLE. ....BEE. 211 20
IF I STAND VERY STILL, THEY WILL THINK I AM COW-PARSLEY, ...BEE. 212 39
DREAM OF A DUEL THEY WILL WIN INEVITABLY, ...THE BEE MEETING 212 46
THE VILLAGERS ARE MOVING THE VIRGINS, THERE WILL BE NO KILLING.*BEE. 212 49
TOMORROW I WILL BE SWEET GOD, I WILL SET THEM FREE. ...THE ARRIVAL. 213 35
TOMORROW I WILL BE SWEET GOD, I WILL SET THEM FREE. ...THE ARRIVAL. 213 35
WILL THEY HATE ME, ...STINGS 214 28
IT WILL WORK WITHOUT THINKING, ...STINGS 215 34
WILL THE HIVE SURVIVE, WILL THE GLADIOLAS ....WINTERING 219 46
WILL THE HIVE SURVIVE, WILL THE GLADIOLAS ....WINTERING 219 46
WHAT WILL THEY TASTE OF, THE CHRISTMAS ROSES? ....WINTERING 219 49
WILL IT SHOW IN THE BLACK DETECTOR? ....A SECRET 219 9
WILL IT COME OUT ....A SECRET 219 10
WILL YOU MARRY IT? ....THE APPLICANT 221 14
WILL YOU MARRY IT? ....THE APPLICANT 221 22
WILL YOU MARRY IT, MARRY IT, MARRY IT. ....THE APPLICANT 222 40
ONE SCARF WILL CATCH AND ANCHOR IN THE WHEEL. ....FEVER. 231 13
MAKE THEIR OWN ELEMENT. THEY WILL NOT RISE, ...FEVER. 231 15
AT FIRST THE CANDLE WILL NOT BLOOM AT ALL -- ....BY CANDLELIGHT 236 16
WILL VANISH IN A DAY. ....LADY LAZARUS 244 15
THE GRAVE CAVE ATE WILL BE ....LADY LAZARUS 244 17
THE SILVER LEASH OF THE WILL --- ....GETTING THERE 248 15
WILL THERE BE FIRE, WILL THERE BE BREAD? ....GETTING THERE 248 20
WILL THERE BE FIRE, WILL THERE BE BREAD? ....GETTING THERE 248 20
AND HOW WILL YOUR NIGHT DANCES ....THE NIGHT DANCES 249 3
THE HOOVES WILL NOT HAVE IT, ...YEARS 256 24
O GOLDEN CHILD THE WORLD WILL KILL AND EAT. ....MARY'S SONG 257 21
WILL THEY OCCUR, ...BRASILIA 258 1
YOUR BROTHER WILL TRIM MY HEDGES! .....................EAVESDROPPER 260 1
HANDS WILL BE OPENING DOORS AND SETTING ....THE MUNICH MANNEQUINS 263 18
INTO WHICH BROAD TOES WILL GO TOMORROW. ....THE MUNICH MANNEQUINS 263 20
IT STRETCHES INTO THE DISTANCE. IT WILL BE EATEN NEVERTHELESS.*TOTEM 264 2
IT HAPPENS. WILL IT GO ON? --- ....PARALYTIC 266 1
WILL NOT ....PARALYTIC 266 8
GO GET THE GLASS, THEN. BUT I KNOW TONIGHT WILL BE .....DIALOGUE O. 276 1
YOU TO ASK WHO'S HOME, OR I? I WILL. ...DIALOGUE OVER A OUIJA BOARD 277 25
TO ALTER HER WILL OUR WAY. SHALL WE GO ON ....DIALOGUE O. 277 49
OUT OF IT WILL BE TIME AND PLENTY FOR US*DIALOGUE OVER A OUIJA BOARD 278 58
ALWAYS, THE GLASS WILL BLURT WHAT I DON'T WANT ....DIALOGUE O. 278 63
PREDICTING THREE BOYS AN HOUR HENCE WILL PLAY ....DIALOGUE O. 279 124
HE LIVES. HIS ANSWER WILL PUT AN END TO GIBES ....DIALOGUE O. 281 174
TAIL ON EACH TOY DONKEY THAT WILL BRAY   DIALOGUE OVER A OUIJA BOARD 283 250
WILL BE OUR BEAT, JUST AS THE GIFT IS OURS, ...DIALOGUE O. 283 257
TO NAME HIS HOME A THIRD TIME. GIVE YOUR WILL THREE ...DIALOGUE O. 283 269
YOU'RE SATISFIED. MY WILL HAS EVIDENTLY *DIALOGUE OVER A OUIJA BOARD 284 279
A THIRD TIME. DON'T GLOAT. YOUR WILL MISFIRED TWICE ...DIALOGUE O. 284 281
INTOLERANT BEAUTY NEVER WILL BE LEARNING. ....TO EVA DESCENDING. 303 17
THE FALLING MAN WHO NEVER WILL ABSTAIN ....METAMORPHOSES OF THE MOON 307 10
WILL PROVE TO BE SOME COMMON PARLOR FAKE: *METAMORPHOSES OF THE MOON 307 22
BUT YET THE PERVERSE IMP WITHIN WILL PROBE*METAMORPHOSES OF THE MOON 308 31
WILL PUNISH US FOR SAYING WHICH IS WHICH; *METAMORPHOSES OF THE MOON 308 44
THE GILDED COCK WILL TURN FOR ME ....TO A JILTED LOVER 310 22
AND BY THAT GLARE, MY LOVE WILL SEE ....TO A JILTED LOVER 310 25
YOUR HANDS WILL CRUSH ....TRIO OF LOVE SONGS 315 47
WILL SHOW US THAT ....MOONSONG AT MORNING 317 18
WE'VE SQUANDERED ALL THE BANKER WILL ALLOW ....THE DISPOSSESSED 319 16
THE DYING MAN WILL SCOFF IN SCORN AT THIS. .....NEVER TRY TO TRICK. 319 3
THE DYING MAN WILL SCOFF IN SCORN AT THIS. .....NEVER TRY TO TRICK. 320 9
THE DYING MAN WILL SCOFF IN SCORN AT THIS. .....NEVER TRY TO TRICK. 320 15
THE DYING MAN WILL SCOFF IN SCORN AT THIS. .....NEVER TRY TO TRICK. 320 19
THESE BONE SHANKS WILL NOT WAKE IMMACULATE ....THE DEAD 320 10
THE JABBERWOCK WILL NOT TRANSLATE HIS SONGS: ....A SORCERER B. 324 11
WATER WILL RUN BY RULE; THE ACTUAL SUN ....TWO LOVERS. 327 21
WILL SCRUPULOUSLY RISE AND SET; ....TWO LOVERS. 327 22

	TITLE	PAGE	LINE

WILL (CONT.)
WHICH AT TWELVE WILL QUAINTLY HATCH ....BLACK PINE TREE. 328 5
SOME DAY, MOVING, ONE WILL DROP, ...:LOVE IS A PARALLAX 330 63
WHICH SPEAK HER MAESTRO'S WILL. ....AERIALIST 331 12
O NEVER AGAIN WILL THE EXTRAVAGANT STRAW ....THE PRINCESS. 335 72
WILLED (1)
HE WILLED HIS BOOKS AND SHELL AWAY. ......ON THE DECLINE OF ORACLES 78 10
WILLFUL (1)
FRUITS OF YOUR WILLFUL TREE: GOD-HEAD, GOD-PIE ....DIALOGUE O. 283 267
WILLING (1)
TO FILL IT AND WILLING ....THE APPLICANT 221 11
WILL-O'-THE-WISP (1)
A WILL-O'-THE-WISP ....POLLY'S TREE 128 20
WILLOW (1)
THE MIMIC HEAD -- IN A CROTCHED WILLOW, GREEN- ....LADY AND T. 69 23
WILLOWS (2)
CLOUDWRACK AND OWL-HOLLOWED WILLOWS SLANTING OVER ......WATERCOLOR. 112 8
THE WILLOWS WERE CHILLING, ...THREE WOMEN 177 44
WILLS (2)
SO SHE WILLS ALL TO THE BLACK KING. ....VANITY FAIR 33 29
POOLS ASIDE, WILLS ASIDE, DO WE ....DIALOGUE OVER A OUIJA BOARD 278 53
WILTS (1)
WILTS AT MY FOOT, ...BURNING THE LETTERS 205 43
WILY (1)
IN WILY SPIRALS ....AQUATIC NOCTURNE 306 20
WIN (3)
POCKED BY ROOK-CLAW AND RABBIT-TRACK: SHE MUST YET WIN ..SNOWMAN O. 58 17
ENOUGH AGES LAPSED TO WIN ....MUSSEL HUNTER AT ROCK HARBOR 95 22
DREAM OF A DUEL THEY WILL WIN INEVITABLY, ...THE BEE MEETING 212 46
WINCE (2)
THUMB CAN MAKE ANYONE WINCE, BUT THE WHOLE GLOBE ....PERSEUS 83 28
FROM THE LINKED PONDS THAT MY EYES WINCE ....PARLIAMENT HILL FIELDS 152 11
WINCES (1)
THIS RED WALL WINCES CONTINUALLY: ...................APPREHENSIONS 195 11
WINCH (1)
RELIC OF TOUGH WEATHER, EVERY WINCH AND STAY ....A WINTER SHIP 113 27
WINCING (2)
SPRAWLS, HUNCHED IN BLACK, AMONG BAGGAGE, WINCING   CHANNEL CROSSING 26 11
THE FLUORESCENT LIGHT WINCING ON AND OFF LIKE A TERRIBLE MIGRAINE, ...
... LESBOS 227 4
WIND (42)
UNTIL SWEET WIND CHANGED TUNE, BLEW HARM: ....BUCOLICS 24 15
ON STORM-STRUCK DECK, WIND SIRENS CATERWAUL; ......CHANNEL CROSSING 26 1
SHALL STREW BROADCAST SO RARE A SEED ON WIND ...WREATH FOR A BRIDAL 45 20
FOLLOW ON KIND WIND." ....CRYSTAL GAZER 55 18
TILL YOUR EYES FOIST A VISION DAZZLING ON THE WIND: ...NOVEMBER G. 56 14
OF THE MOON, MANES TO THE WIND, ...HARDCASTLE CRAGS 62 11
THE LONG WIND, PARING HER PERSON DOWN ....HARDCASTLE CRAGS 63 22
SNUBS IMPROMPTU SPIELS OF WIND ....CONJURING. 66 6
WHERE SECOND WIND, HIP BOOT ....TWO VIEWS OF WITHENS 72 9
INANE WORLDS OF WIND AND CLOUD. ....SCULPTOR 91 11
WAIST DOWN, YOU MAY WIND ....FULL FATHOM FIVE 93 33
SOMEWHERE BY MUCH SUN AND WIND; ....MUSSEL HUNTER AT ROCK HARBOR 97 73
WIND BARES A FLINTIER LANDSCAPE. ....IN MIDAS' COUNTRY 100 25
HORSES FLUENT IN THE WIND, ...THE EYE-MOTE 109 29
SPEWED RELICS CLICKER MASSES IN THE WIND, ...POINT SHIRLEY 110 32
RIDING THE TIDE OF THE WIND, STEADY ....A WINTER SHIP 113 7
OF YOUR LEFT EAR, OUT OF THE WIND, ...THE COLOSSUS 130 25
IF ONLY THE WIND WOULD LEAVE MY LUNGS ALONE. POEM.1.WHO. 131 10
A WIND UNSTOPPERS THE CHAMBER POEM.7.S. 136 23
A COOL WIND SHOULD INHABIT THOSE LEAVES   SLEEP IN THE MOJAVE DESERT 144 8
WE SWELTER LIKE FIREDOGS IN THE WIND. ...SLEEP IN THE MOJAVE DESERT 144 20
THE WIND STOPS MY BREATH LIKE A BANDAGE. ....PARLIAMENT HILL FIELDS 152 20
OR THE HEARTS OF SHEEP, AND THE WIND ....WUTHERING HEIGHTS 167 11
FROM BETWEEN TWO HILLS A SUDDEN WIND FUNNELS AT ME, ..BLACKBERRYING 169 20
THE YELLOW MINUTE BEFORE THE WIND WALKS, WHEN THE LEAVES*THREE WOMEN 179 93
FLATTEN TO PARCHMENT SCREENS TO KEEP THE WIND OFF. .....THREE WOMEN 179 97
HOW LONG CAN I BE A WALL, KEEPING THE WIND OFF? ....THREE WOMEN 185 288
HE IS QUITE BLUE; THE TERRIBLE WIND TRIES HIS BREATHING.   NARCISSI. 190 11
A WIND OF SUCH VIOLENCE ....ELM 192 20
THE WIND GAGGING MY MOUTH WITH MY OWN BLOWN HAIR,*THE RABBIT CATCHER 193 2
THE SUN GIVES YOU ULCERS, THE WIND GIVES YOU T.B. ....LESBOS 228 39
BEYOND THE WINDOW-FRAME TONIGHT. WIND WARNS ....DIALOGUE O. 286 336
CRYPTIC STARS WIND UP THE ATMOSPHERE, ..TO EVA DESCENDING THE STAIR 303 10
TONIGHT THE CAUSTIC WIND, LOVE, ...JILTED 304 5
THE SHUTTERS TO LET WARM WIND FEATHER ....THE DREAM 310 5
THEN DROVE TO YOU UPON THE WIND. . . ..THE DREAM 311 28
THE LONE WIND RAVING IN THE GUTTER, HIS ....SONNET: TO TIME 311 7
O THROW IT AWAY, THROW IT ALL AWAY ON THE WIND: SONG FOR A REVOLU. 322 1
WIND WAKES THE WHOLE METROPOLIS.*INSOLENT STORM STRIKES AT THE SKULL 325 6
THE RAW WIND LIKE A SCARF; LOVE IS A FAUN ....LOVE IS A PARALLAX 329 23
AN ILL WIND IS STALKING ....TEMPER OF TIME 336 1
ALOFT, A LONE GULL HALTS UPON THE WIND, ...EPITAPH IN THREE PARTS 337 20
WINDED (1)
WINDED BY MUCH ROCK-BUMPING ....THE HERMIT AT OUTERMOST HOUSE 118 5

576

WINDFALLS (1)
OVER WINDFALLS TO SIP CIDER-JUICE. ....YADDO: THE GRAND MANOR 123 10
WIND-FLAW (1)
IT OGLED THROUGH ROCK-FAULT, WIND-FLAW AND FISTED WAVE--*LADY AND T. 70 32
WIND-HARROWED (1)
OF STARK WIND-HARROWED HILLS AND WELTERING MIST; ....SNOWMAN O. 58 13
WINDING (4)
EACH TIME ROUND WINDING THAT ANT ....SPIDER 48 16
WINDING AND TWINING THEIR PETTY FETTERS, ...GULLIVER 251 13
THE STIFFNESS OF SAILS, THE LONG SALT WINDING SHEETS. ....MYSTIC 268 8
WINDING UP THE RAVELED MOLD. ....DANSE MACABRE 321 12
WINDLESS (1)
WINDLESS THREADWORK OF A TAPESTRY. ....A LIFE 149 5
WINDOW (22)
GLAZES THE WINDOW OF MY HURT; WHAT SOLACE ....WINTER LANDSCAPE, 22 13
IN ITS EXPLICIT FOLDS? OR WHEN THE WINDOW, ...TALE OF A TUB 24 14
UNDER WHITE WALL AND MOORISH WINDOW ....THE BEGGARS 47 6
AT THE WINDOW, THOSE UNBORN, THOSE UNDONE ....OUIJA 77 3
AS YOU ETCH ON THE INNER WINDOW OF YOUR EYE ....VIRGIN IN A TREE 82 34
SHIP TIMBERS IN THROUGH THE CELLAR WINDOW; ....POINT SHIRLEY 110 14
THE FRENCH WINDOW AJAR ....THE SLEEPERS 122 6
A DIAMOND-PANED WINDOW, ...YADDO: THE GRAND MANOR 124 20
HOGWALLOW'S AT THE WINDOW. POEM.4.BEAST. 134 21
YOUR MOUTH OPENS CLEAN AS A CAT'S. THE WINDOW SQUARE ..MORNING SONG 157 15
THE TULIPS TURN TO ME, AND THE WINDOW BEHIND ME ....TULIPS 161 44
THERE IS THE MOON IN THE HIGH WINDOW. IT IS OVER. ......THREE WOMEN 181 176
ONE CURTAIN IS FLICKERING FROM THE OPEN WINDOW, ...BERCK-PLAGE 199 79
THE DIAPHANOUS SATINS OF A JANUARY WINDOW ....A BIRTHDAY PRESENT 206 17
IT STANDS AT MY WINDOW, BIG AS THE SKY. ....A BIRTHDAY PRESENT 207 49
WAS SHE AT THE WINDOW, LISTENING? ....THE DETECTIVE 208 4
WINTERING IN A DARK WITHOUT WINDOW ....WINTERING 218 6
YOU HAVE STUCK HER KITTENS OUTSIDE YOUR WINDOW ....LESBOS 227 12
A WINDOW, HOLY GOLD. ....MARY'S SONG 257 4
THE CHIMNEYS OF THE CITY BREATHE, THE WINDOW SWEATS, ...MYSTIC 269 28
BEYOND THE WINDOW) SHE LIES ON CUSHIONS CURLED ....FEMALE AUTHOR 301 3
A WINDOW WHICH PROVES THE SKY SHEER RIGMAROLE*EPITAPH IN THREE PARTS 337 28
WINDOW-FRAME (1)
BEYOND THE WINDOW-FRAME TONIGHT. WIND WARNS ....DIALOGUE O. 286 336
WINDOWLESS (1)
IT IS ALL HOLLYWOOD, WINDOWLESS, ...LESBOS 227 3
WINDOWS (16)
WHY, ALL THE WINDOWS BROKE WHEN HE STALKED IN.*THE QUEEN'S COMPLAINT 28 5
THAT CABINET WITHOUT WINDOWS OR DOORS: ....THE OTHER TWO 68 17
STUDY WINDOWS BELLIED IN ....THE DISQUIETING MUSES 75 18
FRAMED IN WINDOWS OF MAIN STREET'S ....NIGHT SHIFT 76 15
FILENE'S SHOW WINDOWS. GRANT US GRACE, ...A WINTER'S TALE 87 19
OF WINDOWS WITH ODD VIOLET PANES. ....A WINTER'S TALE 87 30
ALSO OF HIGH WINDOWS. WORSE ....LORELEI 94 28
LIT, BUT UNPEOPLED, HELD ITS WINDOWS ....OWL 101 3
THE PLANKED-UP WINDOWS WHERE SHE SET ....POINT SHIRLEY 110 26
LAYING ITS SCALES ON THE WINDOWS, THE WINDOWS OF EMPTY OFFICES,
                                            ... THREE WOMEN 181 178
LAYING ITS SCALES ON THE WINDOWS, THE WINDOWS OF EMPTY OFFICES, ...
                                            ... THREE WOMEN 181 178
THIS WOMAN WHO MEETS ME IN WINDOWS -- SHE IS NEAT. .....THREE WOMEN 184 280
THERE ARE NO WINDOWS, SO I CAN'T SEE WHAT IS IN THERE. *THE ARRIVAL. 213 9
O THE DOMESTICITY OF THESE WINDOWS, ...THE MUNICH MANNEQUINS 263 21
WITH WINDOWS OF MIRRORS. ....GIGOLO 267 6
IN THE WINDOWS, THE MIRRORS ....KINDNESS 269 4
WINDOWSILL (1)
THE EMPTY BOTTLES ON THE WINDOWSILL ....RESOLVE 52 11
WINDOW-SQUARE (1)
THROUGH MY WINDOW-SQUARE OF BLACK: ....TO A JILTED LOVER 309 3
WINDOW-SQUARES (1)
BRIGHT WINDOW-SQUARES UNTIL THE WOMEN SEEM .....MORNING IN THE HOS. 332 7
WIND-RIPPED (1)
RAVELED WIND-RIPPED FROM THE CREST OF THE WAVE.*SUICIDE OFF EGG ROCK 115 11
WINDS (6)
TILTING WITH THE WINDS, ...SOUTHERN SUNRISE 26 7
ASSAULT OF SNOW-FLAWED WINDS FROM THE DOUR SKIES ....MAYFLOWER 60 2
MY MIND WINDS TO YOU ....MEDUSA 225 13
TASTING THE WINDS, THAT ARE FOOTLESS, ...WINTER TREES 258 9
O RANSACK THE FOUR WINDS AND FIND ANOTHER ....LAMENT 316 16
WHILE SUNLIGHT WINDS ITS YARN UPON THE FLOOR. ....THE PRINCESS. 335 71
WIND'S (2)
IN THE WIND'S SNEER. ....RESOLVE 52 23
EFFACEMENT AT THE WIND'S HAND. ....MORNING SONG 157 9
WINE (3)
BUYING WINE, BREAD, ...STREET SONG 36 13
SIX CAT'S EYES IN THE WINE CELLAR, ...WINTERING 217 5
WHERE GUESTS SLIDE GLIDING INTO LIGHT LIKE WINE: ....CINDERELLA 304 6
WINE-BOTTLE (1)
IN YOUR JUNGLE OF WINE-BOTTLE LAMPS, ...LEAVING EARLY 145 4
WINE-GLASS (3)
ON THE ROUND BASE OF THE INVERTED WINE-GLASS HERE, ...DIALOGUE O. 276 5

WINE-GLASS (CONT.)
   AT THE WHIM OF A WINE-GLASS AND LET US INTO WORLDS   .....DIALOGUE O.   280 128
   OF ONE WINE-GLASS, YOU'LL PIN IT LIKE A PRIZE   ....DIALOGUE O.   283 249
WINES (1)
   FILET MIGNON AND WALLOPING WINES, ...DIALOGUE EN ROUTE   308   10
WING (7)
   TO WING, SLEEP-FEATHERED, ...THE SHRIKE   42   5
   A PANE OF DRAGONFLY WING, WHEN THEY LEFT ME   ....SPINACH-PICKER.   89   5
   YOU INHERIT WHITE HEATHER, A BEE'S WING, ...THE MANOR GARDEN   125   12
   HANGING THEIR BLUEGREEN BELLIES AND THEIR WING PANES IN A CHINESE
      SCREEN.   ....BLACKBERRYING   168   16
   I REMEMBER A WHITE, COLD WING   ....THREE WOMEN   178   49
   IN GAY VENTRILOQUY FROM WING TO WING   ....LOVE IS A PARALLAX   330   47
   IN GAY VENTRILOQUY FROM WING TO WING   ....LOVE IS A PARALLAX   330   47
WING-CAPS (1)
   THE NURSES IN THEIR WING-CAPS ARE NO LONGER SO BEAUTIFUL;   ...BERCK.   198   58
WINGED (3)
   OF WINGED, UNMIRACULOUS WOMEN, ...STINGS   214   21
   WINGED ELBOWS AND EYEHOLES   ....BRASILIA   258   3
   WINGED RABBITS REVOLVING ABOUT HIS KNEES, ...CIRCUS IN THREE RINGS   322   16
WINGLESS (1)
   GELDED AND WINGLESS. NOT HEROES. NOT HEROES.   ....STINGS/DR   293   15
WINGS (15)
   OF ANIMALS TO CHOIR: "LOOK WHAT THRESH OF WINGS *WREATH FOR A BRIDAL   45   15
   AN ENVIOUS PHOSPHORESCENCE IN THEIR WINGS.   ....OUIJA   77   5
   IN AN EBONY AIR, ON WINGS OF WITCH CLOTH, ...GOATSUCKER   111   10
   WINGS DRUMMING IN THE WINTER.   ....MAGNOLIA SHOALS 122   24
   HER MARBLE SKIRTS BLOWN BACK IN TWO PINK WINGS.   ....FINISTERRE   169   20
   HER WINGS TORN SHAWLS, HER LONG BODY   ....STINGS   214   17
   WITH HER LION-RED BODY, HER WINGS OF GLASS?   ....STINGS   215   55
   FULL OF WINGS, OTHERWORLDLINESS.   ....WINTER TREES   258   11
   IN THE WINGS SOMEWHERE, OR LIKE HEIRLOOM FURNITURE   .....DIALOGUE O.   276   7
   VENTRILOQUY. BUT WINGS NEITHER YOU NOR I*DIALOGUE OVER A OUIJA BOARD   278   83
   OUT OF A WHOLENESS. WORMS, NOT WINGS IS WHAT   ....DIALOGUE O.   279   99
   SETTLES IN THE ROOM NOW. ITS WINGS BLACKEN THE TABLE.   ..DIALOGUE O.   285 313
   WHO WALKED IN A SWARMING SHROUD OF WINGS   ....LAMENT   315   2
   GULLS IN A FEATHERED FUGUE OF WINGS. OUTDO   ....MIDSUMMER MOBILE   324   4
   NOW FOLD THEIR WINGS LIKE BATS AND DISAPPEAR   ....TWO LOVERS.   327   7
WINGSPREAD (1)
   WINGSPREAD IN CONTROL   ....OWL   102   12
WINGY (1)
   THE WINGY MYTHS WON'T TUG AT US ANY MORE: POEM.5.F.   135   16
WINK (3)
   WE'D WINK AT IF WE DIDN'T HEAR   ....ALL THE DEAD DEARS   70   10
   CAME A GARGANTUAN GALACTIC WINK.   ....DIALOGUE EN ROUTE   309   42
   IN THE RARE RIVER WINK AND LAUGH; WE LAVISH   .....LOVE IS A PARALLAX   330   38
WINKING (1)
   STRIPS OF TINFOIL WINKING LIKE PEOPLE, ...THE BEE MEETING   211   16
WINKS (1)
   WINKS LIKE MONEY UNDER THE RINGED TOES OF THE CHICKENS.   ......NET-.   121   9
WINNOWED (1)
   ITS CLEAR AIR WINNOWED BY ANGELS; SHE WAS COME   ....DREAM WITH C.   43   2
WINNOWING (2)
   WITH ORANGE DUCK-FEET WINNOWING HIS HAIR --   .....ALL THE DEAD DEARS   71   24
   FEATHERS WINNOWING THE ROOM. A THIN   ....DIALOGUE OVER A OUIJA BOARD   279   87
WINS (1)
   NEAR WINS, WEEK BY WEEK, WAITING UNTIL   DIALOGUE OVER A OUIJA BOARD   277   40
WINTER (22)
   WINTER LANDSCAPE, WITH ROOKS   ....WINTER LANDSCAPE, WITH ROOKS   21   T
   BROODING AS THE WINTER NIGHT COMES ON. *WINTER LANDSCAPE, WITH ROOKS   21   10
   HOW SHE LONGED FOR WINTER THEN! --   ....SPINSTER   49   13
   THROUGHOUT BLACK WINTER THE RED HAWS WITHSTOOD   ....MAYFLOWER   60   1
   ON WINTER STREET, ON TEMPLE PLACE.   ....A WINTER'S TALE   87   17
   A WINTER SHIP   ....A WINTER SHIP   112   T
   THE QUEEN BEE MARRIES THE WINTER OF YOUR YEAR.   ....BEEKEEPER'S.   118   21
   WINGS DRUMMING IN THE WINTER.   ....MAGNOLIA SHOALS   122   24
   AND SEVEN WINTER COATS LAST AUGUST)   ....ON DECK   143   22
   IN THE WHITE HIATUS OF WINTER --   ....LOVE LETTER   147   11
   WAKING IN WINTER   ....WAKING IN WINTER   151   T
   WINTER DAWN IS THE COLOR OF METAL, ...WAKING IN WINTER   151   2
   WHILE FAR OFF, THE AXLE OF WINTER   ....HEAVY WOMEN   158   19
   THE TULIPS ARE TOO EXCITABLE, IT IS WINTER HERE.   ....TULIPS   160   1
   HOW WINTER FILLS MY SOUL! AND THAT CHALK LIGHT   ....THREE WOMEN   181 177
   NOW THEY FACE A WINTER OF WHITE SHEETS, WHITE FACES.   ...THREE WOMEN   184 265
   THE PRINT OF ITS BIG FOOT LAST WINTER, ...PHEASANT   191   11
   WINTER IS FOR WOMEN ---   ....WINTERING   219   42
   THIS IS WINTER, THIS IS NIGHT, SMALL LOVE --   ....BY CANDLELIGHT   236   1
   WINTER TREES   ....WINTER TREES   257   T
   WITH WINTER AS YOU CLAIM IT DOES. THE COAL   ....DIALOGUE O.   277   19
   THE WINTER LANDSCAPE HANGS IN BALANCE NOW, ...PROLOGUE TO SPRING   322   1
WINTER-BEHEADED (1)
   HER WINTER-BEHEADED DAISIES, MARROWLESS, GAUNT, ...SNOWMAN O.   58   9
WINTER-FACE (1)
   OLD WINTER-FACE, OLD BARREN ONE, OLD TIME BOMB.   ....THREE WOMEN   181 158

	TITLE	PAGE	LINE

WINTERING (4)
NOBODY WINTERING NOW BEHIND ....POINT SHIRLEY 110 25
IT WAS GOOD FOR TWENTY YEARS, THAT WINTERING -- ....ELECTRA ON. 116 5
WINTERING ... .WINTERING 217 T
WINTERING IN A DARK WITHOUT WINDOW ....WINTERING 218 6
WINTER'S (2)
A WINTER'S TALE ....A WINTER'S TALE 86 T
THEIR DREAM OF THE WINTER'S COLD; STONES ....CHILD'S PARK STONES 101 24
WINTHROP (1)
GREEN ROCK, WINTHROP BAY ....GREEN ROCK, WINTHROP BAY 104 T
WINTRIEST (1)
YET, IN MY WINTRIEST MOODS, I HOLD ......SOLILOQUY OF THE SOLIPSIST 37 24
WIPES (1)
DARKNESS WIPES ME OUT LIKE CHALK ON A BLACKBOARD... ......FACE LIFT 156 15
WIPING (1)
YOU COME IN LATE, WIPING YOUR LIPS. ....THE OTHER 201 1
WIRE (4)
THIS WAVE'S GREEN PEAK ON WIRE ....EPITAPH FOR FIRE AND FLOWER 45 2
BARBS ON THE CROWN OF GILDED WIRE, ...I WANT, I WANT 106 11
IT STUCK IN A BARB WIRE SNARE. ....DADDY 223 26
CAT-CLEVER ON PERILOUS WIRE ....AERIALIST 331 8
WIRED (1)
GLEAMS, WIRED TO A TALL ULMUS ....A WINTER'S TALE 86 2
WIRELESS (1)
WHERE THE WIRELESS TALKS TO ITSELF LIKE AN ELDERLY RELATIVE. ...
                                           ... THE DETECTIVE 209 20
WIRES (6)
NEEDLING SPUMILY DOWN FROM THE WIRES: ....ALICANTE LULLABY 43 10
OF STREETLIGHTS AND WIRES, ITS WALL TO WALL ....OWL 102 11
A CURRENT AGITATES THE WIRES POEM.7.S. 137 29
MY RED FILAMENTS BURN AND STAND, A HAND OF WIRES. ....ELM 192 18
TIGHT WIRES BETWEEN US, ...THE RABBIT CATCHER 194 27
FOR LOUDSPEAKER WIRES RUNNING LIKE A LOGICAL ....DIALOGUE O. 280 165
WISDOM (5)
NOT WEALTH NOR WISDOM STANDS ....RECANTATION 42 14
VISION, WISDOM, FOR BODIES ....SCULPTOR 91 3
THROWN: FEAR, WISDOM, AT ONE: ALL COLORS ......WHITENESS I REMEMBER 103 32
EATING THE FINGERS OF WISDOM. POEM.3.MAENAD. 133 3
AT THE CENTER SHE IS STILL, VERY STILL WITH WISDOM. ....ELM/DR 292 7
WISE (4)
MAYDAY: TWO CAME TO FIELD IN SUCH WISE: ....BUCOLICS 23 1
MALTREAT THE HOSTAGE HEAD IN SHOCKING WISE, ...LADY AND T. 69 13
THE STAR, THE WISE GRAY MEN. ....HEAVY WOMEN 158 21
WISER FOR TONIGHT'S WISE WORDS? I FELT DRAWN ....DIALOGUE O. 285 316
WISER (2)
I AM NONE THE WISER. ....THE COLOSSUS 129 10
WISER FOR TONIGHT'S WISE WORDS? I FELT DRAWN ....DIALOGUE O. 285 316
WISH (12)
FOR A WISH TO TETHER: THEY RIDE NIGHTLONG ....EPITAPH FOR F. 46 26
WISH FOR EVEN GROUND, AND IT'S THE LAST CLIFF ......ABOVE THE OXBOW 88 22
I THINK THEY WOULD NOT WISH FOR THIS DRESSY BACKCLOTH ....STARS. 166 29
IT DOES NOT WISH TO BE MORE, OR DIFFERENT. ....THREE WOMEN 179 101
THEIR LEAVES DO NOT WISH US TO HURRY: ....CROSSING THE WATER 190 5
BETWEEN THIS WISH AND THAT WISH. ....BURNING THE LETTERS 204 28
BETWEEN THIS WISH AND THAT WISH. ....BURNING THE LETTERS 204 28
I WISH HIM DEAD OR AWAY. ....THE JAILER 227 39
M-S. MANUSCRIPT? HE STOPS. I WISH ......DIALOGUE OVER A OUIJA BOARD 279 95
MY WISH ONE WITH YOUR AIM. ONCE, IN A DREAM, ...DIALOGUE EN ROUTE 284 301
"I WISH MILLIONAIRE UNCLES AND AUNTS ....DIALOGUE EN ROUTE 308 7
SAID EVE: "I WISH VENOMOUS NEMATODES ....DIALOGUE EN ROUTE 309 19
WISHES (3)
GREEN AS EUNUCHS, YOUR WISHES ....MEDUSA 226 38
BALD AND SHINY, WITH POCKETS OF WISHES, ...TOTEM 264 26
THE HEART LIKE WISHES OR FREE ....BALLOONS 272 16
WISHFUL (1)
FEED YOUR OWN WISHFUL THINKING. TRY ASKING HIM ....DIALOGUE O. 283 268
WISHING (1)
THAT CLAIRVOYANT QUARTZ WHICH ONCE, AT HER OWN WISHING, ...
                                           ... CRYSTAL GAZER 55 29
WISP (1)
SOUND, WITH A GLITTERY WISP ....MUSSEL HUNTER AT ROCK HARBOR 96 47
WIT (3)
ALL YOUR BEAUTY, ALL YOUR WIT, IS A GIFT, MY DEAR, ...
                           ... SOLILOQUY OF THE SOLIPSIST 38 35
"OUR WIT MADE FOOLS ....THE SNOWMAN ON THE MOOR 59 40
THE TRIUMPH OF WIT OVER SUFFERING ....PERSEUS 82 ST
WITCH (7)
LIKE A DAUNTED WITCH, QUITTING CASTLE WHEN REAL DAYS BREAK. ...
                           ... CONVERSATION AMONG THE RUINS 21 8
THIS WITCH SIDLES, FINGERS CROOKED, AS IF ....VANITY FAIR 32 2
IN AN EBONY AIR, ON WINGS OF WITCH CLOTH, ...GOATSUCKER 111 10
WITCH BURNING ....POEM.6.W. 135 ST
AND I'D SOONER BE STAKED FOR A WITCH, KINDLED, AND CURLED ...
                           ... DIALOGUE OVER A OUIJA BOARD 280 132
EITHER WAY WE CHOOSE, THE ANGRY WITCH ....METAMORPHOSES OF THE MOON 308 43

WITCH (CONT.)
   ALTHOUGH THE WICKED WITCH HAS POISONED ONE. ....ADMONITIONS   319   5
WITCHES (2)
   MOTHER, WHOSE WITCHES ALWAYS, ALWAYS ....THE DISQUIETING MUSES   75   11
   SICKNESS BEGINS HERE: I AM A DARTBOARD FOR WITCHES. POEM.6.W. 135   4
WITCH'S (2)
   A WITCH'S FACE? ....ON LOOKING INTO THE EYES OF A DEMON LOVER 325   20
   AND STUNG ACCORDING TO THE WITCH'S PLAN, ...THE PRINCESS. 333   9
WITH (445)
WITHDRAW (1)
   COLD MOONS WITHDRAW, REFUSING TO COME TO TERMS ......METAMORPHOSES. 307   1
WITHDRAWS (2)
   LIGHT WITHDRAWS. CHAIRS, TABLES DROP ....THE GREAT CARBUNCLE   73   29
   WITHDRAWS ITS TENTACLE. ...WORDS HEARD, BY ACCIDENT, OVER THE PHONE 203   12
WITHDREW (1)
   SHE WITHDREW NEATLY. ....SPINSTER   50   24
WITHENS (1)
   TWO VIEWS OF WITHENS ....TWO VIEWS OF WITHENS   71   T
WITHER (5)
   CROAK AND WITHER. ....FROG AUTUMN   99   4
   WITHER LIKE PITHLESS HANDS. THERE IS LITTLE SHELTER. POEM.5.F. 134   4
   LET HER DIE THERE, OR WITHER INCESSANTLY FOR THE NEXT FIFTY
          YEARS, ...FACE LIFT 156   29
   THE TREES WITHER IN THE STREET. THE RAIN IS CORROSIVE.   THREE WOMEN 180 135
   AND LETS OUR SHADOWS WITHER ....BY CANDLELIGHT 236   12
WITHERED (3)
   HIMSELF WITHERED THESE LATTER-DAYS ....THE TIMES ARE TIDY 107   8
   NOBODY DIED OR WITHERED ON THAT STAGE. ......ELECTRA ON AZALEA PATH 116   13
   OF WITHERED WORLDS, AND STAMP OUT PUNY HELLS ....LOVE IS A PARALLAX 330   68
WITHERING (2)
   THEIR WITHERING KINGSHIP ....THE THIN PEOPLE   65   39
   THE PARK OF LESS RED THAN WITHERING DID. .............RHODODENDRON. 103   12
WITHERS (1)
   THE LATE MONTH WITHERS, AS WELL. ....MAGNOLIA SHOALS 122   12
WITHHELD (1)
   THESE GIFTS ARE GIVEN. AND WHEN WITHHELD, YOU'LL SAY ...DIALOGUE O. 279 126
WITHIN (20)
   RINGDOVES ROOST WELL WITHIN HIS WOOD, ...ODE FOR TED   29   19
   TWO GIRLS THERE ARE: WITHIN THE HOUSE ....TWO SISTERS OF PERSEPHONE   31   1
   FOR WEDLOCK WROUGHT WITHIN LOVE'S PROPER CHAPEL.*WREATH FOR A BRIDAL   44   12
   ICE AND ROCK, EACH SENTIMENT WITHIN BORDER, ...SPINSTER   49   16
   OF TREE AND HUMAN. AND HE WITHIN THIS SNAKEDOM ........SNAKECHARMER   79   15
   ON A RED VELVET COUCH WITHIN YOUR GREEN- ....YADWIGHA.   86   26
   THE HIGH, GREEN MEADOWS ARE GLOWING, AS IF LIT FROM WITHIN. ...
                                                   ... BLACKBERRYING 168   14
   DEEPER WITHIN THE DARK, AND AS I PITCHED FURTHER ....DIALOGUE O. 285 317
   THE DOOR NOW OPENS FROM WITHIN. ....FAMILY REUNION 300   10
   BUT YET THE PERVERSE IMP WITHIN WILL PROBE*METAMORPHOSES OF THE MOON 308   31
   OR THAT THE HEAT WITHIN WOULD GROW ....TO A JILTED LOVER 310   13
   AND BURN TO DEATH WITHIN YOUR NEON HELL. ....THE TRIAL OF MAN 312   11
   WHERE DIAMONDS JANGLE HYMNS WITHIN THE BLOOD ....APRIL AUBADE 312   3
   AND DROWN WITHIN. ....MOONSONG AT MORNING 317   40
   THE SKATERS FREEZE WITHIN A STONE TABLEAU. ......PROLOGUE TO SPRING 322   3
   WITHIN THESE MIRRORS .....ON LOOKING INTO THE EYES OF A DEMON LOVER 325   9
   WHO WEAVE WITHIN THE SKELETON'S WHITE WOMB ....TERMINAL 328   7
   KINDLING HER WITHIN A STEEPLED FLAME,   THE PRINCESS AND THE GOBLINS 333   20
   FROM THE PRAGMATIC BOY CONFINED WITHIN,*THE PRINCESS AND THE GOBLINS 334   45
   SUSPENDED ALOFT WITHIN HER PLANET-SHINE. ....THE PRINCESS. 335   63
WITHOUT (42)
   ONE SITS; THE OTHER, WITHOUT. ....TWO SISTERS OF PERSEPHONE   31   2
   AT HER TOUGH TRADE; WITHOUT TIME'S TAINT ....CRYSTAL GAZER   54   4
   WITHOUT CEREMONY, OR PORTENT. ....BLACK ROOK IN RAINY WEATHER   57   10
   WITHOUT MEAT OR DRINK I SAT ....ON THE PLETHORA OF DRYADS   67   7
   THAT CABINET WITHOUT WINDOWS OR DOORS: ....THE OTHER TWO   68   17
   WITHOUT STOP THOSE GREASED MACHINES, ...NIGHT SHIFT   77   22
   TENDING, WITHOUT STOP, THE BLUNT ....NIGHT SHIFT   77   23
   OF DRAGONS BREATHING WITHOUT THE FRAME OF FABLES, ...LESSON.   80   3
   A GIRL COULD WADE WITHOUT WETTING HER SHINS.   A LESSON IN VENGEANCE   80   20
   WITH ITS PRIM BRIC-A-BRAC, WITHOUT A MOON ....YADWIGHA.   85   11
   TO TURN YOU LUMINOUS, WITHOUT THE EYE ....YADWIGHA.   85   12
   WHICH, WITHOUT HIM, WERE BEGGARED ....SCULPTOR   92   18
   STONES, WITHOUT CONSCIENCE, WORD AND LINE ENDURE, ...POEMS, POTATOES 106   5
   NOBODY DIES OR IS BORN WITHOUT THEIR KNOWING IT. ...THE NET-MENDERS 121   13
   WITHOUT DREAMS OF ANY SORT. POEM.1.WHO. 132   24
   SKYWARD AGAIN, WITHOUT HOPE, OF COURSE, ...LOVE LETTER 147   7
   TREE AND STONE GLITTERED, WITHOUT SHADOWS. ....LOVE LETTER 147   29
   THE LIGHT FALLS WITHOUT LETUP, BLINDINGLY. ....A LIFE 150   20
   COLD AS AN EEL, WITHOUT EYELIDS. ....ZOO KEEPER'S WIFE 154   2
   MUSEUM WITHOUT STATUES, GRAND WITH PILLARS, PORTICOES,
          ROTUNDAS. ....BARREN WOMAN 157   2
   WITHOUT ME, SHE WOULDN'T EXIST, SO OF COURSE SHE WAS GRATEFUL. ...
                                                   ... IN PLASTER 159   15
   I'M COLLECTING MY STRENGTH; ONE DAY I SHALL MANAGE WITHOUT HER, ...
                                                   ... IN PLASTER 160   55
   COMING AND GOING, BREATH BY BREATH, WITHOUT ANY FUSS. ....TULIPS 161   51

WITHOUT (CONT.)
    PLAYING AND RESTING WITHOUT COMMITTING ITSELF. ....TULIPS   161   56
    HE LIVES WITHOUT PRIVACY IN A LIDLESS ROOM, ...INSOMNIAC   163   26
    THEY GO UP WITHOUT HOPE, LIKE SIGHS. ....FINISTERRE   169   16
    I IMAGINE THEM WITHOUT FATHERS OR MOTHERS, LIKE THE FIRST GODS. ...
                                                      ... LAST WORDS   172   8
    WHAT HAPPENS IN ME WILL HAPPEN WITHOUT ATTENTION. ......THREE WOMEN   176   10
    THE MIRROR GIVES BACK A WOMAN WITHOUT DEFORMITY. ......THREE WOMEN   183 240
    THIS IS A CASE WITHOUT A BODY. ....THE DETECTIVE   209   24
    I COULD NOT RUN WITHOUT HAVING TO RUN FOREVER. .....THE BEE MEETING   212   33
    IT WILL WORK WITHOUT THINKING, ...STINGS   215   34
    WINTERING IN A DARK WITHOUT WINDOW ....WINTERING   218   6
    DO WITHOUT FEVERS TO EAT? ....THE JAILER   227   42
    DO WITHOUT EYES TO KNIFE, WHAT WOULD HE ....THE JAILER   227   44
    DO, DO, DO WITHOUT ME? ....THE JAILER   227   45
    INTOLERABLE, WITHOUT MIND. ....THE MUNICH MANNEQUINS   263   15
    STALK WITHOUT WRINKLE, ...CHILD   265   7
    CEILING WITHOUT A STAR. ....CHILD   265   12
    QUESTIONS WITHOUT ANSWER, ...MYSTIC   268   2
    WITHOUT A PART LEFT OVER, ...MYSTIC   268   11
    PACKING WITHOUT A COMPASS OR SCALE ...SONG FOR A REVOLUTIONARY LOVE   323   10
WITHSTAND (1)
    WITHSTAND THAT STARE ....MOONSONG AT MORNING   317   22
WITHSTOOD (2)
    THROUGHOUT BLACK WINTER THE RED HAWS WITHSTOOD ....MAYFLOWER   60   1
    HE WITHSTOOD THEM, THAT HERMIT. ......THE HERMIT AT OUTERMOST HOUSE   119   17
WITNESS (5)
    WHAT THOUGH GREEN LEAVES ONLY WITNESS ....WREATH FOR A BRIDAL   44   1
    APPALLING TO WITNESS, ...SPIDER   49   24
    DRY WITNESS ....ALL THE DEAD DEARS   70   8
    FUNICULAR RAILWAY, WITNESS TO GONE ....ABOVE THE OXBOW   88   38
    AND ACT BEAR WITNESS, IN THE CRUX OF TIME, ...DIALOGUE O.   286 362
WITS (4)
    UNRULY ENOUGH TO PITCH HER FIVE QUEENLY WITS ....SPINSTER   50   20
    WHILE ELLA DROWSED WHISKERED WITH SLEEK FACE, SLY WITS: ...
                                      ... ELLA MASON AND HER ELEVEN CATS   54   29
    BY WITS ALONE: TO FORSEE HER LOVER'S FAITH ....CRYSTAL GAZER   55   33
    THE MORBID COBRA'S WITS HAVE RUN ASTRAY; ....DENOUEMENT   327   13
WIVES (3)
    TINKER JACK AND THE TIDY WIVES ......TINKER JACK AND THE TIDY WIVES   34   T
    YOUNG WIVES STILL BLITHE, ...TINKER JACK AND THE TIDY WIVES   35   27
    PATRONIZED BY CONVALESCENT WIVES;   MORNING IN THE HOSPITAL SOLARIUM   332   5
WIZARDS (1)
    WHICH ALL THE ARTFUL WIZARDS CANNOT CRIMP ....THE PRINCESS.   333   17
WIZENED (1)
    DROOPS UPON ITS WIZENED STEM ....JILTED   304   11
WOKE (5)
    BELLS, HOOVES, OF THE HIGH-STEPPING BLACK GOATS WOKE US. OTHER TWO.   68   3
    I WOKE ONE DAY TO SEE YOU, MOTHER, ...THE DISQUIETING MUSES   75   41
    THE DAY I WOKE, I WOKE ON CHURCHYARD HILL. ..ELECTRA ON AZALEA PATH   117   15
    THE DAY I WOKE, I WOKE ON CHURCHYARD HILL. ..ELECTRA ON AZALEA PATH   117   15
    IN THE MORNING SHE WOKE ME EARLY, REFLECTING THE SUN ....IN PLASTER   159   23
WOLF (2)
    WHO SET WASP, WOLF AND SHARK TO WORK, ...I WANT, I WANT   106   7
    OF THE WOLF AT THE DOOR. ....TEMPER OF TIME   336   20
WOLF-HEADED (1)
    YOU WOOED ME WITH THE WOLF-HEADED FRUIT BATS .....ZOO KEEPER'S WIFE   155   17
WOLFISH (1)
    AND TURNED THE FARMBOY'S TEMPER WOLFISH, ..THE DEATH OF MYTH-MAKING   104   14
WOLVES (1)
    TWO SUICIDES, THE FAMILY WOLVES, ...THE MANOR GARDEN   125   13
WOMAN (38)
    COULD BE THIS ADAM'S WOMAN ....ODE FOR TED   30   22
    WORM-HUSBANDED, YET NO WOMAN. ....TWO SISTERS OF PERSEPHONE   32   28
    THE NEW WOMAN IN THE WARD ....MISS DRAKE PROCEEDS TO SUPPER   41   5
    SAYING: "SOMETHING'S ADDLED IN A WOMAN WHO ACCOMMODATES ...
                                      ... ELLA MASON AND HER ELEVEN CATS   53   5
    TO GOVERN MORE SIGHT THAN GIVEN TO A WOMAN ....CRYSTAL GAZER   55   32
    FROM MARBLE SNOW-HEAP OF MOOR TO RIDE THAT WOMAN ....SNOWMAN O.   59   27
    ANY MORE THAN THE OLD WOMAN IN HER MUD HUT COULD ...THE THIN PEOPLE   64   26
    ... OF A WOMAN, A MOUSE AND A SHREW. THE ANKLE-BONE OF THE ...
                                      ... ALL THE DEAD DEARS   70 E/3
    ...WOMAN HAS BEEN SLIGHTLY GNAWN. ....ALL THE DEAD DEARS   70 E/4
    A WOMAN IS DRAGGING HER SHADOW IN A CIRCLE ....A LIFE   150   21
    BARREN WOMAN ....BARREN WOMAN   157   T
    SPITEFUL AS A WOMAN, BUT NOT SO NERVOUS, ...THE RIVAL   166   9
    A PEASANT WOMAN IN BLACK ....FINISTERRE   170   22
    NOW I AM A LAKE. A WOMAN BENDS OVER ME, ...MIRROR   174   10
    IN ME SHE HAS DROWNED A YOUNG GIRL, AND IN ME AN OLD WOMAN ...MIRROR   174   17
    I SEE MYSELF AS A SHADOW, NEITHER MAN NOR WOMAN, ...THREE WOMEN   182 191
    NEITHER A WOMAN, HAPPY TO BE LIKE A MAN, NOR A MAN .....THREE WOMEN   182 192
    THE MIRROR GIVES BACK A WOMAN WITHOUT DEFORMITY. ....THREE WOMEN   183 240
    THERE ARE THE CLOTHES OF A FAT WOMAN I DO NOT KNOW. ....THREE WOMEN   184 267
    THIS WOMAN WHO MEETS ME IN WINDOWS -- SHE IS NEAT. .....THREE WOMEN   184 280

WOMAN (CONT.)
```
FOLLOWING THE COFFIN ON ITS FLOWERY CART LIKE A BEAUTIFUL WOMAN, ...
                                              ... BERCK-PLAGE   200  115
THE FINGERS WERE TAMPING A WOMAN INTO A WALL, ........THE DETECTIVE  208   10
THE WOMAN, STILL AT HER KNITTING, ....................WINTERING  219   43
EVERY WOMAN ADORES A FASCIST, ............................DADDY  223   48
NOR THE WOMAN IN THE AMBULANCE ...................POPPIES IN OCTOBER  240    2
AND I A SMILING WOMAN. .................................LADY LAZARUS  244   19
NEVERTHELESS, I AM THE SAME, IDENTICAL WOMAN. ........LADY LAZARUS  245   34
THE BODY OF THIS WOMAN, ............................GETTING THERE  249   46
THIS WOMAN ON THE TELEPHONE ..........................THE FEARFUL  256    3
SAYS SHE IS A MAN, NOT A WOMAN. ......................THE FEARFUL  256    4
THE VOICE OF THE WOMAN HOLLOWS -- ....................THE FEARFUL  256    7
CHILDLESS WOMAN ................................CHILDLESS WOMAN  259    T
THE WOMAN IS PERFECTED. .....................................EDGE  272    1
WE HEARD THE HEAD WOMAN SAY, ...............BITTER STRAWBERRIES  299    5
"THE DRAFT IS PASSED," THE WOMAN SAID. .......BITTER STRAWBERRIES  299   20
SNAPPED THE WOMAN SHARPLY. ..................BITTER STRAWBERRIES  300   28
THIS WAS A WOMAN: HER LOVES AND STRATAGEMS .........SONNET: TO EVA  304    5
WOMAN FOLLOWED US AND RUSHED .........................THE DREAM  310   11
```
WOMAN'S (2)
```
SAD HAG. "EVERY WOMAN'S A WHORE. ............................LESBOS  229   83
AND TOOK THE WOMAN'S BRIGHT SUBPOENA ...................THE DREAM  311   26
```
WOMB (6)
```
CIRCLE A WOMB OF MARBLE. ...............................THE OTHER  202   22
THE EARTHEN WOMB .........................NICK AND THE CANDLESTICK  240    4
THE WOMB ......................................CHILDLESS WOMAN  259    1
COLD AS SNOW BREATH, IT TAMPS THE WOMB ......THE MUNICH MANNEQUINS  262    2
LULLED IN THE AMPLE WOMB OF THE FULL-TILT GLOBE. ..........THE DEAD  320    4
WHO WEAVE WITHIN THE SKELETON'S WHITE WOMB ...............TERMINAL  328    7
```
WOMBS (1)
```
IN THE FETID WOMBS OF BLACK AIR UNDER PINES IN SUMMER. ......MYSTIC  268    5
```
WOMEN (19)
```
CHARRED AND RAVENED WOMEN LIE, ...........................PURSUIT   22   23
THE RED-NOSED, BLUE-CAPED WOMEN RING ...............A WINTER'S TALE   87   14
THE OLD WOMEN CREEP OUT HERE .....................OLD LADIES' HOME  120    4
THESE HALLS ARE FULL OF WOMEN WHO THINK THEY ARE BIRDS. *POEM.1.WHO.  131   21
KINDLY WITH INVALIDS AND MAWKISH WOMEN, ...................CANDLES  149   25
HEAVY WOMEN .........................................HEAVY WOMEN  158    T
SCRIM OF A SEA BREEZE, THE WOMEN .....................HEAVY WOMEN  158    4
HAVE BEEN HOWLING LIKE WOMEN, OR DAMAGED INSTRUMENTS. ....INSOMNIAC  163   30
THREE WOMEN .......................................THREE WOMEN  176    T
I HAVE TRIED TO BE BLIND IN LOVE, LIKE OTHER WOMEN, ....THREE WOMEN  178   75
I AM A MOUNTAIN NOW, AMONG MOUNTAINY WOMEN. .............THREE WOMEN  179  113
OF WINGED, UNMIRACULOUS WOMEN, ............................STINGS  214   21
THESE WOMEN WHO ONLY SCURRY, .............................STINGS  214   29
THE BEES ARE ALL WOMEN, .................................WINTERING  218   38
WINTER IS FOR WOMEN --- .................................WINTERING  219   42
TRUER THAN WOMEN, ...................................WINTER TREES  258    7
BRIGHT FISH HOOKS, THE SMILES OF WOMEN ......................GIGOLO  267   10
BRIGHT WINDOW-SQUARES UNTIL THE WOMEN SEEM .....MORNING IN THE HOS.  332    7
THE WOMEN WAIT, FLUTTERING, TURNING PAGES .....MORNING IN THE HOS.  332   21
```
WON (3)
```
WON HER THE FROG-COLORED SKIN, PALE PITH AND WATERY*VIRGIN IN A TREE   81   14
THOSE SUGARY PLANETS WHOSE INFLUENCE WON FOR HIM .........INSOMNIAC  163   17
OR PLAY ANOTHER CARD GAME WHEN YOU'VE WON; ............ADMONITIONS  319    2
```
WONDER (11)
```
GRIP THE RAIL, SQUINT AHEAD, AND WONDER HOW MUCH LONGER   CHANNEL C.   26    6
GOT BAKED INTO GINGERBREAD, I WONDER .........THE DISQUIETING MUSES   75   12
IN A MONTH WE'LL WONDER WHAT PLATES AND FORKS ARE FOR. ...TWO CAMP.  145   20
THEY WILL WONDER IF I WAS IMPORTANT. ....................LAST WORDS  172    9
THE WONDER OF IT, IN THAT PALLOR, ........................PHEASANT  191   13
IS IT ANY WONDER HE PUTS ON DARK GLASSES? ..............BERCK-PLAGE  196   12
IS IT ANY WONDER HE AFFECTS A BLACK CASSOCK? ..........BERCK-PLAGE  196   13
I WONDER HOW HUNGRY THEY ARE. ...........THE ARRIVAL OF THE BEE BOX  213   26
I WONDER IF THEY WOULD FORGET ME. .......THE ARRIVAL OF THE BEE BOX  213   27
DID I ESCAPE, I WONDER? ...................................MEDUSA  225   12
YET AS WE WONDER WHAT CAN COME OF ICE ..........PROLOGUE TO SPRING  322   14
```
WONDERED (1)
```
YADWIGHA, THE LITERALISTS ONCE WONDERED HOW YOU .........YADWIGHA.   85    1
```
WONDERFUL (1)
```
ON A WONDERFUL THING --- ...............................BERCK-PLAGE  201  122
```
WONDERLAND (1)
```
UNDER THE BELL-JAR OF A WONDERLAND. .......QUEEN MARY'S ROSE GARDEN  290   14
```
WONDERS (1)
```
FLING THE SEVEN WONDERS AFTER THAT ...SONG FOR A REVOLUTIONARY LOVE  323    7
```
WONDROUS (1)
```
KNOW WHICH IS WHY I, WHEN THE WONDROUS FIST ............DIALOGUE O.  279  119
```
WON'T (17)
```
YET WON'T LAY ONE. .........................................RHYME   50    3
HOARD LAST YEAR'S LEAVES, WON'T MOURN, WEAR SACKCLOTH, OR TURN ...
                                      ... NOVEMBER GRAVEYARD   56    2
AND THAT DAMN SCRUPULOUS TREE WON'T PRACTICE WILES ......CONJURING.   66   20
THE SPIDERS WON'T NOTICE. .............................POEM.1.WHO.  131    8
THE LIDS WON'T SHUT. TIME .............................POEM.3.MAENAD.  133   18
```

WON'T (CONT.)
  HE WON'T BE GOT RID OF: POEM.4.BEAST.   134   11
  THE STAR BUGS WON'T SAVE ME THIS MONTH. POEM.4.BEAST.   134   22
  THE WINGY MYTHS WON'T TUG AT US ANY MORE: POEM.5.F.   135   16
  AND STILL THE LUNGS WON'T FILL AND THE HEART WON'T START. *STILLBORN 142   10
  AND STILL THE LUNGS WON'T FILL AND THE HEART WON'T START. *STILLBORN 142   10
  TOUCH IT: IT WON'T SHRINK LIKE AN EYEBALL, ...A LIFE   149   1
  ONE DAY IT WON'T COME BACK. THINGS AREN'T LIKE THAT. ....LAST WORDS   172   16
  AT LEAST I WON'T BE STRUNG JUST UNDER THE SURFACE, ...BURNING.   204   23
  "IT WON'T HURT." ....A SECRET   220   24
  SO THE ARTFUL GLASS WON'T CHANGE ITS CHILL FOR HEART'S DIALOGUE O.   277   17
  IN SLEEP. THE CHAIRS WON'T VANISH OR BECOME ....DIALOGUE O.   286 355
  SKY WON'T BE DRAWN CLOSER: ABSOLUTE, ...METAMORPHOSES OF THE MOON 307   7
WOOD (29)
  RINGDOVES ROOST WELL WITHIN HIS WOOD, ...ODE FOR TED 29   19
  NOW, AS GREEN SAP ASCENDS THE STEEPLED WOOD, ...MAYFLOWER   60   5
  FAR DEEPER IN GROSS WOOD ....ON THE PLETHORA OF DRYADS   67   11
  PERFORMED A DUMBSHOW IN THE POLISHED WOOD, ...THE OTHER TWO   68   16
  TONNAGE OF METAL AND WOOD; ....NIGHT SHIFT   77   19
  IN A SCABBARD OF WOOD BAFFLES PURSUERS, ...VIRGIN IN A TREE   81   8
  BUT SURE STATIONS IN BRONZE, WOOD, STONE. ....SCULPTOR   91   8
  OBDURATE, IN DENSE-GRAINED WOOD, ...SCULPTOR   91   9
  WHOSE OWL-EYES IN THE SCRAGGLY WOOD ....THE DEATH OF MYTH-MAKING 104   11
  AS WOOD AND FORMAL, IN A JACKET OF ASHES, ...A WINTER SHIP 113   8
  WOOD STOVES BURN WARM AS TOAST. ....YADDO: THE GRAND MANOR 124   17
  WORKED INTO THE PEELED ORANGE WOOD ....MEDALLION 124   2
  DARK WOOD, DARK WATER ....DARK WOOD, DARK WATER   127   T
  THIS WOOD BURNS A DARK ....DARK WOOD, DARK WATER   127   1
  A MONSTER OF WOOD AND RUSTY TEETH. ....THE BURNT-OUT SPA 137   2
  WITH A LUNG FULL OF DUST AND A TONGUE OF WOOD, ...LEAVING EARLY 146   43
  I THINK HER LITTLE HEAD IS CARVED IN WOOD, ...THREE WOMEN   182 211
  A RED, HARD WOOD, EYES SHUT AND MOUTH WIDE OPEN. ....THREE WOMEN 182 212
  HIS LITTLE FACE IS CARVED IN PAINED, RED WOOD. ....EVENT   194   9
  SIX ROUND BLACK HATS IN THE GRASS AND A LOZENGE OF WOOD,*BERCK-PLAGE 201 123
  THEN THE DRY WOOD, THE GATES, ...THE DETECTIVE   209   36
  I ORDERED THIS, THIS CLEAN WOOD BOX .....THE ARRIVAL OF THE BEE BOX 212   1
  THE DEAD SMELL OF SUN ON WOOD CABINS, ...MYSTIC 268   7
  AFTER WHOSE STROKE THE WOOD RINGS, ...WORDS   270   2
  WHILE ROUGH AS SPLINTERED WOOD ....FAMILY REUNION 300   20
  OH NEVER TRY TO KNOCK ON ROTTEN WOOD ....ADMONITIONS 319   1
  OH NEVER TRY TO KNOCK ON ROTTEN WOOD. ....ADMONITIONS 319   6
  OH NEVER TRY TO KNOCK ON ROTTEN WOOD. ....ADMONITIONS 319   12
  NEVER TRY TO KNOCK ON ROTTEN WOOD, ...ADMONITIONS   319   18
WOODEN (2)
  ODDLY WOODEN IN SPITE OF SCALES ....THE DISQUIETING MUSES   75   36
  WHITE BODIES IN A WOODEN GIRDLE, ROOT TO TOP ......VIRGIN IN A TREE   81   22
WOODENLY (1)
  STIFF AS TWIGS, HER BODY WOODENLY ....VIRGIN IN A TREE   82   39
WOODS (6)
  HIS GREED HAS SET THE WOODS AFLAME, ...PURSUIT   22   3
  THAN ITS SUBURB OF WOODS: NIMBUS- ....OWL 101   2
  TO SWEETEN YOUR NECK OF THE NEW YORK WOODS. ....PRIVATE GROUND 130   4
  THE WOODS CREAK AND ACHE, AND THE DAY FORGETS ITSELF.*PRIVATE GROUND 131   19
  TO REDRESS THE DOMINANCE OF ROCKS AND WOODS, ...TWO CAMP.   144   2
  THE WOODS ARE A WELL. THE STARS DROP SILENTLY. ....STARS. 165   4
WOODSMOKE (2)
  WAVERING THERE, GAUZE-EDGED, SMELLING OF WOODSMOKE, ...DIALOGUE B.   38   12
  WOODSMOKE AND A DISTANT LOUDSPEAKER ....YADDO: THE GRAND MANOR 123   1
WOODWARD (1)
  AND GALLOPED WOODWARD IN THAT GUISE. ....FAUN   35   15
WOOED (1)
  YOU WOOED ME WITH THE WOLF-HEADED FRUIT BATS .....ZOO KEEPER'S WIFE 155   17
WOOL (3)
  SHEEP DROWSED STONEWARD IN THEIR TUSSOCKS OF WOOL, AND BIRDS, ...
                                    ... HARDCASTLE CRAGS   63   34
  LOOPING WOOL, DOING NOTHING IN PARTICULAR, ...HEAVY WOMEN 158   16
  SPINNING A SINGLE STUBBORN THREAD OF WOOL ....THE PRINCESS. 333   16
WOOL-CLOUDS (1)
  BROWSING IN THEIR DIRTY WOOL-CLOUDS, ...WUTHERING HEIGHTS 167   20
WOOLLY (1)
  THE CLEVER WOOLLY DOGS HAVE HAD THEIR DAY ....DENOUEMENT   326   7
WORD (17)
  HIS BRIDE ECHOES HIS WORD. AT THAT, ...CRYSTAL GAZER   55   21
  NOR DID ANY WORD BODY WITH A NAME ....HARDCASTLE CRAGS   63   17
  THE WORD, DEFINING, MUZZLES; THE DRAWN LINE ....POEMS, POTATOES 106   1
  STONES, WITHOUT CONSCIENCE, WORD AND LINE ENDURE, ..POEMS, POTATOES 106   5
  NO WORD MAKE THEM CARRY WATER OR FIRE THE KINDLING ....TWO CAMP. 144   5
  WIDOW. THE WORD CONSUMES ITSELF -- ....WIDOW   164   1
  EVERY LITTLE WORD HOOKED TO EVERY LITTLE WORD, AND ACT TO ACT. ...
                                    ... THREE WOMEN   178   55
  EVERY LITTLE WORD HOOKED TO EVERY LITTLE WORD, AND ACT TO ACT. ...
                                    ... THREE WOMEN   178   55
  HE DOES NOT WALK. HE DOES NOT SPEAK A WORD. ....THREE WOMEN   186 325
  LET IT NOT COME BY WORD OF MOUTH, I SHOULD BE SIXTY ......BIRTHDAY. 208   53
  FOR A WORD OR A TOUCH ....LADY LAZARUS   246   62

```
                                                    TITLE              PAGE  LINE
WORD (CONT.)
    THE WORD OF A SNAIL ON THE PLATE OF A LEAF?  ...........THE COURIERS   247    1
    TO SAY THAT. THAT MUST BE HIS: HIS WORD. YOU SEE,  ......DIALOGUE O.   278   79
    WORD WEARS TWO W'S? O-R. OR WHAT?  ......DIALOGUE OVER A OUIJA BOARD   279   94
    BREATHING THE GOD'S WORD, OR THE DEVIL'S WORD,  .........DIALOGUE O.   286  350
    BREATHING THE GOD'S WORD, OR THE DEVIL'S WORD,  .........DIALOGUE O.   286  350
    OR HER OWN WORD, AMBUSHED IN AN EQUIVOCAL  .............DIALOGUE O.    286  351
WORDLESS (2)
    THE STOMACH OF INDIFFERENCE, THE WORDLESS CUPBOARD.  ......POEM.7.S.   136    6
    THEIR FACES TURNING, WORDLESS AND SLOW,  ...............BERCK-PLAGE    201  120
WORDS (27)
    WHAT CEREMONY OF WORDS CAN PATCH THE HAVOC?  ...........CONVERSATION.   21   14
    WHEN ALL EARTH HIS WORDS DO SUMMON  ....................ODE FOR TED    30   23
    WIELDS GUARD OF HONOR OVER THESE!" STARRED WITH WORDS  ....WREATH F.   45   16
    WORDS FOR A NURSERY  .............................WORDS FOR A NURSERY   73    T
    WORDS TO RID ME OF THOSE THREE LADIES  ........THE DISQUIETING MUSES   75   14
    THE OLD GOD DRIBBLES, IN RETURN, HIS WORDS.  ...................OUIJA   77   11
    WHEN WORDS, LIKE LOCUSTS, DRUMMED THE DARKENING AIR  ..........OUIJA   77   17
    THE WORDS IN HIS BOOK WORMED OFF THE PAGES.  ...SUICIDE OFF EGG ROCK  115   19
    TWIST OLD WORDS INTO THE WEB-THREADS: TONIGHT MAY THE FISH  ..NET-.   121   17
    LAST WORDS  .............................................LAST WORDS   172    T
    THERE'S NO GETTING UP IT BY THE WORDS YOU KNOW.*NEW YEAR ON DARTMOOR  176    6
    AND ALL I COULD SEE WAS DANGERS: DOVES AND WORDS  ....THREE WOMEN     178   47
    BE A BANDAGE TO HIS HURT, AND MY WORDS  ...............THREE WOMEN    185  297
    WORDS HEARD BY ACCIDENT, OVER THE PHONE  ...............WORDS HEARD.   202    T
    WHAT ARE THESE WORDS, THESE WORDS?  ....................WORDS HEARD.   202    6
    WHAT ARE THESE WORDS, THESE WORDS?  ....................WORDS HEARD.   202    6
    BECKONING MY WORDS IN --  ..............................EAVESDROPPER   260   34
    WORDS  ........................................................WORDS   270    T
    WORDS DRY AND RIDERLESS,  .....................................WORDS   270   16
    TO CONTRADICT ME. YOUR SHOULDERING WORDS OUTSTRIP  ......DIALOGUE O.   281  172
    EATING YOUR WORDS: YOU'LL REVOKE HIS GODHOOD SOON AS  ...DIALOGUE O.   281  189
    WISER FOR TONIGHT'S WISE WORDS? I FELT DRAWN  ..........DIALOGUE O.   285  316
    OF CONTENDING WORDS. SOME PYTHONESS  ....DIALOGUE OVER A OUIJA BOARD   286  347
    THICKET OF WORDS. THE CURTAIN'S DRAWN ON THAT.  ........DIALOGUE O.   286  352
    AND PROFANE WORDS SCRAWLED BLACK ACROSS THE SUN.  ....DOOM OF EXILES   318   12
    THERE BURNS THROUGHOUT THE LINE OF WORDS,  .......LOVE IS A PARALLAX   330   57
    AT HIS WORDS, THE INDIGNANT GODMOTHER   THE PRINCESS AND THE GOBLINS   335   69
WORE (8)
    TWIG-SLEEPING, WORE  .............................HARDCASTLE CRAGS     63   35
    DRINKING VINEGAR FROM TIN CUPS: THEY WORE  ..........THE THIN PEOPLE    64   20
    OF BROWNS AND GREENS. EACH WORE ONE  ...MUSSEL HUNTER AT ROCK HARBOR    96   32
    SHE WORE HER BROOM STRAWS TO THE NUB.  .................POINT SHIRLEY  110   18
    HER WIDE BED WORE THE STAIN OF DIVINITY.  ....ELECTRA ON AZALEA PATH  116    8
    THE BURGHERS SWEATED AND WEPT. THE CHILDREN WORE WHITE.  ....CANDLES  149   19
    THAT SUMMER WE WORE BLACK GLASSES TO HIDE OUR EYES. *THE BABYSITTERS  174    1
    HE WORE INSTEAD OF A HAT.  ...................................STINGS  215   44
WORK (12)
    AFTER A LEAN DAY'S WORK  ...............................STRUMPET SONG   33    3
    GOD'S WORK STOOD ANCHORED IN THAT GLARE  ...............CRYSTAL GAZER   55   38
    WHO SET WASP, WOLF AND SHARK TO WORK,  ...........I WANT, I WANT      106    7
    WHILE THEIR FINGERS WORK WITH THE COARSE MESH AND THE FINE  ...NET-.  121   11
    ARE RIDING TO WORK IN ROWS, AS IF RECENTLY BRAINWASHED.  ...INSOMNIAC  163   35
    AND THE MAN I WORK FOR LAUGHED: "HAVE YOU SEEN SOMETHNG AWFUL?  ...
                                                   ... THREE WOMEN       177   22
    I LAST. I LAST IT OUT. I ACCOMPLISH A WORK.  .........THREE WOMEN     180  129
    I DO NOT EVEN NEED A HOLIDAY; I CAN GO TO WORK TODAY.  ..THREE WOMEN  183  249
    IT WILL WORK WITHOUT THINKING,  ...........................STINGS    215   34
    OUR WORK. LOVE. THE AFTER-LIFE . . . DO YOU  ...........DIALOGUE O.   278   55
    MIGHT WORK ON THIS GLASS MEDIUM. BELIEF, YES,  .........DIALOGUE O.   282  225
    WORK AT ALL? HOW CAN WE HELP BUT BATTLE *DIALOGUE OVER A OUIJA BOARD  284  286
WORKABLE (1)
    I TASTE IT ON MY TONGUE, AND THE WORKABLE HORRORS,  .....THREE WOMEN  180  136
WORKED (1)
    WORKED INTO THE PEELED ORANGE WOOD  ......................MEDALLION   124    2
WORKING (4)
    THE WHITE-SMOCKED BOYS STARTED WORKING. *TWO VIEWS OF A CADAVER ROOM  114    5
    A MONGREL WORKING HIS LEGS TO A GALLOP  .........SUICIDE OFF EGG ROCK  115   12
    THE AIR IS THICK. IT IS THICK WITH THIS WORKING.  .......THREE WOMEN  180  144
    WORKING IT LIKE DOUGH, A MULATTO BODY,  .....................LESBOS   229   61
WORKMAN (1)
    A WORKMAN WALKS BY CARRYING A PINK TORSO.  ...............POEM.7.S.   137   31
WORKS (4)
    THE FIRST WORKS PROBLEMS ON  ...........TWO SISTERS OF PERSEPHONE     31    6
    NOW WORKS HIS HELL OF MONDAYS IN THE MOON'S BALL,*EVERLASTING MONDAY   62   11
    WHO WAKES WITH DARKNESS AND TILL DAWN WORKS HARD  .......GOATSUCKER   111    3
    IT WORKS, THERE IS NOTHING WRONG WITH IT.  ...........THE APPLICANT   222   36
WORLD (59)
    EACH DAY DEMANDS WE CREATE OUR WHOLE WORLD OVER,  .....TALE OF A TUB   25   36
    THINKING NEVER TO HAVE LEFT THE WORLD, YOU GRIEVE  ......DIALOGUE B.   39   34
    THE LEADEN SLAG OF THE WORLD --  .........................DEPARTURE   51   11
    THE WORLD TURNS  .........................................RESOLVE     52   18
    LOOMED ABSOLUTE AS THE ANTIQUE WORLD WAS  .........HARDCASTLE CRAGS    63   38
    OF THE WORLD COMES CLEAR AND FILLS WITH COLOR.  .....THE THIN PEOPLE   65   35
    MAKING THE WORLD GO THIN AS A WASP'S NEST  .........THE THIN PEOPLE    65   46
```

WORLD (CONT.)
  AS THE GODS BEGAN ONE WORLD, AND MAN ANOTHER, ...SNAKECHARMER 79   1
  SUPPORTS HIS FOOT. HE PIPES A WORLD OF SNAKES, ...SNAKECHARMER 79 10
  AND PIPES THE WORLD BACK TO THE SIMPLE FABRIC ........SNAKECHARMER 79 23
  ANACONDA. IMAGINE: THE WORLD ....PERSEUS 83 24
  TO CHOOSE BETWEEN YOUR WORLD OF JUNGLE GREEN ....YADWIGHA. 85   9
  MY WORLD PYRAMIDED WITH LADEN BASKETS. MEMOIRS OF A SPINACH-PICKER 90 20
  A WORLD WE LOSE BY MERELY WAKING UP. ....THE GHOST'S LEAVETAKING 90 20
  WATCHES HIS CUMBROUS WORLD ECLIPSE ....SCULPTOR 91 12
  OF A WORLD MORE FULL AND CLEAR ....LORELEI 94 15
  HIS WORLD OF MUD -- GREEN COLOR ....MUSSEL HUNTER AT ROCK HARBOR 97 71
  THE WORLD SUBDUED TO HIS RUN OF IT. ....WHITENESS I REMEMBER 103 27
  WORLD UNDER THE SHEER WATER .....WATERCOLOR OF GRANTCHESTER MEADOWS 112 10
  GOD-FATHERED INTO THE WORLD FROM MY MOTHER'S BELLY: ....ELECTRA ON. 116   7
  A WORLD OF BALD WHITE DAYS IN A SHADELESS SOCKET. ..THE HANGING MAN 141   4
  SIX MONTHS IN THE WORLD, AND SHE IS ABLE ....MAGI 148 10
  SOME THINGS OF THIS WORLD ARE INDIGESTIBLE. ......ZOO KEEPER'S WIFE 155 16
  NUN-HEARTED AND BLIND TO THE WORLD. MARBLE LILIES .....BARREN WOMAN 157   4
  HER O-MOUTH GRIEVES AT THE WORLD; YOURS IS UNAFFECTED, ...THE RIVAL 166   5
  TO WANT THE WORLD IN A GLASS HAT. ....NEW YEAR ON DARTMOOR 176   9
  I AM SLOW AS THE WORLD. I AM VERY PATIENT, ...THREE WOMEN 176   1
  I SAW THE WORLD IN IT -- SMALL, MEAN AND BLACK, ...THREE WOMEN 178 54
  IT IS A WORLD OF SNOW NOW. I AM NOT AT HOME. ....THREE WOMEN 178 64
  THAT WOULD HAVE THE WHOLE WORLD FLAT BECAUSE THEY ARE. THREE WOMEN 179 87
  I AM BREAKING APART LIKE THE WORLD. THERE IS THIS BLACKNESS, *THREE. 180 142
  HATING MYSELF, HATING AND FEARING. AND NOW THE WORLD CONCEIVES ...
                                     ... THREE WOMEN 181 150
  I SEE THEM SHOWERING LIKE STARS ON TO THE WORLD -- .....THREE WOMEN 183 228
  PUT ON A FACE AND WALKED INTO THE WORLD. ....THREE WOMEN 185 301
  THE WORLD OCCURRED. ....LITTLE FUGUE 188 39
  THERE ARE NO TREES OR BIRDS IN THIS WORLD, ...APPREHENSIONS 195   9
  THE WORLD PURRS, SHUT-OFF AND GENTLE. ....BERCK-PLAGE 200 110
  THE WORLD WILL GO UP IN A SHRIEK, AND YOUR HEAD WITH IT, BIRTHDAY. 207 29
  TUGGING THE WORLD TO FRUIT. ....STINGS 215 47
  HURTS ME AS THE WORLD HURTS GOD. I AM A LANTERN --- ....FEVER. 232 36
  THE WORLD FOREVER, I SHALL NOT ENTIRELY ....THE NIGHT DANCES 250   7
  LOVE, THE WORLD ....LETTER IN NOVEMBER 253   1
  O GOLDEN CHILD THE WORLD WILL KILL AND EAT. ....MARY'S SONG 257 21
  THE WORLD IS BLOOD-HOT AND PERSONAL ....TOTEM 264 22
  ON A WHOLE WORLD I CANNOT TOUCH, ...PARALYTIC 266 19
  A FUNNY PINK WORLD HE MIGHT EAT ON THE OTHER SIDE OF IT, ..BALLOONS 272 24
  CONTEMPLATING A WORLD CLEAR AS WATER. ....BALLOONS 272 28
  LESS DREAD OF THE WORLD BEYOND THAN OURS. THAT'S BECAUSE*DIALOGUE O. 278 62
  OUR WORLD AND THEIRS WE'D BEST PLAY SAFE AND GROOM .....DIALOGUE O. 281 186
  INTO A DARK WORLD I CANNOT SEE AT ALL. ....ELM/DR 292 10
  ALL DAY SHE PLAYS AT CHESS WITH THE BONES OF THE WORLD: ..FEMALE A. 301   1
  A WEIGHT OF WORLD AND TIME ....NOTES TO A NEOPHYTE 307 22
  AS THE WORLD SWIVELED ROUND IN ITS ORBIT ....DIALOGUE EN ROUTE 309 38
  WORSHIP THIS WORLD OF WATERCOLOR MOOD ....APRIL AUBADE 312   1
  WE BROKE THE MINUTE THAT THE WORLD BEGAN ....THE DISPOSSESSED 318 14
  FEVER FROM THE WORLD BEHIND. ....DANSE MACABRE 321   6
  THEN HURL THE BARE WORLD LIKE A BLUEGREEN BALL ..SONG FOR A REVOLU. 323 21
  TO PITCH THE WHITE WORLD DOWN IN SWIVELING FLOOD, ..SONNET TO SATAN 323   6
  THE WORLD INVERTS: ....ON LOOKING INTO THE EYES OF A DEMON LOVER 325 10
WORLDLING (1)
  FROM MY WORLDLING LOOK ITS BRILLIANT VEIN *ON THE PLETHORA OF DRYADS 67 10
WORLDS (5)
  AT THIS JOINT BETWEEN TWO WORLDS AND TWO ENTIRELY ....GHOST'S. 90 12
  INANE WORLDS OF WIND AND CLOUD. ....SCULPTOR 91 13
  COLD WORLDS SHAKE FROM THE OAR. ....CROSSING THE WATER 190   7
  AT THE WHIM OF A WINE-GLASS AND LET US INTO WORLDS .....DIALOGUE O. 280 128
  OF WITHERED WORLDS, AND STAMP OUT PUNY HELLS ...LOVE IS A PARALLAX 330 68
WORLD'S (3)
  THIS CRACKED WORLD'S INCESSANT GABBLE AND HISS. ....STREET SONG 36 30
  TO THE WORLD'S WHITE EDGE ....THE SNOWMAN ON THE MOOR 59 22
  A SLY WORLD'S HINGES HAD SWUNG ....MUSSEL HUNTER AT ROCK HARBOR 95 19
WORLD-SHAPE (1)
  CHOOSE AN EGG-SHAPE, A WORLD-SHAPE, ...FIESTA MELONS 46   8
WORLD-WRECKED (1)
  WORLD-WRECKED, THEY SEEK ONLY OBLIVION. ....THE DEAD 320   8
WORM (6)
  I WORM AND HACK IN A PURPLE WILDERNESS. ....THE SURGEON AT 2 A.M. 171 20
  THE LINE PINK AND QUIET, A WORM, BASKING.*THE COURAGE OF SHUTTING-UP 209   2
  THE VOICES JUST CAN'T WORM THROUGH. ....DADDY 224 70
  AND CRAWLS BEHIND IT LIKE A WORM. ....THE FEARFUL 256   2
  THE MASK INCREASES, EATS THE WORM, ...THE FEARFUL 256   5
  AND TOLERATE THE HUMOR OF THE WORM. ....DIRGE FOR A JOKER 303 14
WORMED (2)
  THE WORDS IN HIS BOOK WORMED OFF THE PAGES. ...SUICIDE OFF EGG ROCK 115 19
  WHEN I WORMED BACK UNDER MY MOTHER'S HEART. ELECTRA ON AZALEA PATH 116 10
WORM-HAUNT (1)
  UP FROM DELVED WORM-HAUNT; ....ODE FOR TED 29   8
WORM-HUSBANDED (1)
  WORM-HUSBANDED, YET NO WOMAN. ....TWO SISTERS OF PERSEPHONE 32 28

	TITLE	PAGE	LINE

WORMING (1)
  WORMING THEMSELVES INTO NICHES. ....THE SWARM 217 45
WORMS (11)
  ROSEBUD, KNOT OF WORMS, ...WORDS FOR A NURSERY 73 1
  FIVE WORMS IN A BOX ....WORDS FOR A NURSERY 74 49
  CROSSES THE LAKE. THE WORMS ....THE MANOR GARDEN 125 17
  CADDIS WORMS DROWSE IN THEIR SILK CASES, ...POEM.5.F. 135 11
  NURSES THE SIZE OF WORMS AND A MINUTE DOCTOR ....AMNESIAC 233 7
  AND PICK THE WORMS OFF ME LIKE STICKY PEARLS. ....LADY LAZARUS 245 42
  WORMS IN THE GLOTTAL STOPS. ....THE FEARFUL 256 9
  OUT OF A WHOLENESS. WORMS, NOT WINGS IS WHAT ....DIALOGUE O. 279 99
  PAN SAID. A PLUMAGE OF RAW WORMS. HOW ..DIALOGUE OVER A OUIJA BOARD 279 100
  WHERE THOSE WORMS CAME FROM. I SWEAR I DIDN'T EXPECT ...DIALOGUE O. 283 264
  THE HOSTELRY OF WORMS, RAPACIOUS BLADES ....TERMINAL 328 6
WORMY (4)
  HER WORMY COURIERS ARE AT HIS BONES. ....OUIJA 77 25
  CABBAGEHEADS: WORMY PURPLE, SILVER-GLAZE, ...POEM.1.WHO. 131 16
  WHILE A SKY, WORMY WITH PUT-BY SMILES, ...BERCK-PLAGE 200 104
  WHAT AM I BUYING, WORMY MAHOGANY? ....STINGS 214 14
WORN (4)
  SKIN WORN DOWN TO THE KNUCKLEBONES ....CRYSTAL GAZER 54 3
  THOSE ROCKS, CLEFT AND WORN, THEMSELVES THEN GROW ....PERSEUS 83 30
  MY PROMISE OF AN IDYLL. THE BLUE'S WORN OUT: ....GREEN ROCK. 105 8
  OF THREAD CONDUCTING HER TO THE WORN TRACKS ....THE PRINCESS. 334 32
WORN-OUT (1)
  NOW THE PILLS ARE WORN-OUT AND SILLY, LIKE CLASSICAL GODS.*INSOMNIAC 163 20
WORRIER (1)
  OF THE EAR, OLD WORRIER. POEM.7.S. 136 24
WORRY (1)
  DO NOT WORRY ABOUT THE EYES -- ....THE COURAGE OF SHUTTING-UP 210 30
WORRYING (1)
  "OH, STOP WORRYING, NELDA," ....BITTER STRAWBERRIES 300 27
WORSE (4)
  WORSE -- SAW DANGLING FROM THAT SPIKE-STUDDED BELT ......SNOWMAN O. 59 37
  ALSO OF HIGH WINDOWS. WORSE ....LORELEI 94 28
  IT'S WORSE THAN A BARNYARD. ....THE COLOSSUS 129 5
  TODDLE ON HOME, BEFORE THE WEATHER'S WORSE. ....THE TOUR 238 41
WORSE-SERVED (1)
  AND WORSE-SERVED WHEN DEATH ....WORDS FOR A NURSERY 74 47
WORSHIP (1)
  WORSHIP THIS WORLD OF WATERCOLOR MOOD ....APRIL AUBADE 312 1
WORST (1)
  THE WORST SLOVEN ....VANITY FAIR 33 30
WORTH (6)
  SOME ANGEL-SHAPE WORTH WEARING ....FIRESONG 30 9
  AND ALL GREEN DREAMS NOT WORTH MUCH, ...STRUMPET SONG 33 2
  COMING UP, THOSE THREE. WORTH ....ON THE DECLINE OF ORACLES 78 28
  BUT A DOZEN WOULD BE WORTH HAVING, ...PHEASANT 191 16
  THEY THOUGHT DEATH WAS WORTH IT, BUT I ....STINGS 215 51
  TOO LATE TO ASK IF END WAS WORTH THE MEANS, ...DOOMSDAY 316 16
WORTHLESS (1)
  WORTHLESS SUCH VISION TO EYES GONE DULL ..ON THE DECLINE OF ORACLES 78 30
WOULD (70)
  WOULD BE FULL OF SUN, WHITE GULLS, AND WATER DRENCHED ...CHANNEL C. 27 21
  EYEFUL, WHICH, ENVIOUS, WOULD DEFINE ....LANDOWNERS 53 13
  WOULD PICK STICKS, WOULD NOT REST ....THE EVERLASTING MONDAY 62 8
  WOULD PICK STICKS, WOULD NOT REST ....THE EVERLASTING MONDAY 62 8
  GREW SO LEAN AND WOULD NOT ROUND ....THE THIN PEOPLE 64 8
  BATTLE HOWEVER I WOULD ....ON THE PLETHORA OF DRYADS 67 19
  WOULD NOT BE EASED, RELEASED. OUR EACH EXAMPLE ....THE OTHER TWO 68 23
  FOR THE BLOOD-HEAT THAT WOULD RUDDLE OR RECLAIM. ....OUIJA 77 9
  FOR WHICH OF THOSE WOULD SPEAK ....VIRGIN IN A TREE 81 20
  RINSING THOSE STABLES: A BABY'S TEARS WOULD DO IT. ....PERSEUS 82 7
  I WOULD BREATHE WATER. ....FULL FATHOM FIVE 93 45
  SO WE ARE HAULED, THOUGH WE WOULD STOP ....IN MIDAS' COUNTRY 100 21
  AGAINST MY LEANING DOWN, WOULD NOT EXCHANGE .........INCOMMUNICADO 100 5
  AFTERTHOUGHT OFTEN WOULD HAVE THEM ALTER ....POEMS, POTATOES 106 7
  I WOULD GET FROM THESE DRY-PAPPED STONES ....POINT SHIRLEY 111 41
  IT WOULD TAKE MORE THAN A LIGHTNING-STROKE ....THE COLOSSUS 130 22
  IF ONLY THE WIND WOULD LEAVE MY LUNGS ALONE. POEM.1.WHO. 131 10
  I WOULD BE A TONGUE TO. MOTHER OF OTHERNESS POEM.1.WHO. 132 26
  IF HE WERE I, HE WOULD DO WHAT I DID. ....THE HANGING MAN 142 6
  IT WOULD BE BETTER IF THEY WERE ALIVE, AND THAT'S WHAT THEY
    WERE. ....STILLBORN 142 13
  DAYLIGHT WOULD BE MORE JUDICIOUS, ...CANDLES 148 10
  GUTS BAG WOULD CLACK LIKE A CHILD'S RATTLE, ...ZOO KEEPER'S WIFE 154 12
  HOLDING MY BONES IN PLACE SO THEY WOULD MEND PROPERLY. ..IN PLASTER 159 27
  BUT I WOULD RATHER BE HORIZONTAL. ....I AM VERTICAL 162 1
  SUCH A LUXURY OF STARS WOULD EMBARRASS ME. STARS OVER THE DORDOGNE 166 27
  I THINK THEY WOULD NOT WISH FOR THIS DRESSY BACKCLOTH ......STARS. 166 29
  IF THE MOON SMILED, SHE WOULD RESEMBLE YOU. ....THE RIVAL 166 1
  HOW I WOULD LIKE TO BELIEVE IN TENDERNESS --- ....MOON. 173 19
  THAT WOULD HAVE THE WHOLE WORLD FLAT BECAUSE THEY ARE. THREE WOMEN 179 87
  THEY WOULD GO MAD WITH IT. ....THREE WOMEN 180 119

WOULD (CONT.)
  WHO WOULD ADHERE TO ME: I UNDO HER FINGERS LIKE BANDAGES: I GO. ...
                                ... THREE WOMEN 184 273
  YOU SAID YOU WOULD KILL IT THIS MORNING. ....PHEASANT 191   1
  BUT A DOZEN WOULD BE WORTH HAVING, ...PHEASANT 191   16
  THE MOON, ALSO, IS MERCILESS: SHE WOULD DRAG ME ....ELM 192   22
  MY FINGERS WOULD ENTER ALTHOUGH ....BURNING THE LETTERS 204   17
  THEY WOULD FLUTTER OFF, BLACK AND GLITTERING, THEY WOULD BE COAL
      ANGELS ....BURNING THE LETTERS 204   33
  THEY WOULD FLUTTER OFF, BLACK AND GLITTERING, THEY WOULD BE COAL
      ANGELS ....BURNING THE LETTERS 204   33
  I WOULD NOT MIND IF IT WAS BONES, OR A PEARL BUTTON. .....BIRTHDAY. 206   12
  I WOULD HAVE KILLED MYSELF GLADLY THAT TIME ANY POSSIBLE WAY. ...
                        ... A BIRTHDAY PRESENT 206   15
  I WOULD ADMIRE THE DEEP GRAVITY OF IT, ITS TIMELESS EYES. *BIRTHDAY. 208   57
  I WOULD KNOW YOU WERE SERIOUS. ....A BIRTHDAY PRESENT 208   58
  THERE WOULD BE A NOBILITY THEN, THERE WOULD BE A BIRTHDAY.*BIRTHDAY. 208   59
  THERE WOULD BE A NOBILITY THEN, THERE WOULD BE A BIRTHDAY.*BIRTHDAY. 208   59
  I WOULD SAY IT WAS THE COFFIN OF A MIDGET*THE ARRIVAL OF THE BEE BOX 212   3
  I WONDER IF THEY WOULD FORGET ME. ....THE ARRIVAL OF THE BEE BOX 213   27
  POM! POM! "THEY WOULD HAVE KILLED ME." ....THE SWARM 217   55
  I THOUGHT EVEN THE BONES WOULD DO. ....DADDY 224   60
  THAT BEING FREE. WHAT WOULD THE DARK ....THE JAILER 227   41
  WHAT WOULD THE LIGHT ....THE JAILER 227   43
  DO WITHOUT EYES TO KNIFE, WHAT WOULD HE ....THE JAILER 227   44
  HEAVEN WOULD BE SOMETHING ELSE, ...LYONNESSE 234   12
  THEY WOULD HAVE YOU SLEEP IN THEIR CABINETS, ...GULLIVER 251   18
  SHE WOULD RATHER BE DEAD THAN FAT, ...THE FEARFUL 256   13
  THAT WOULD NOT, WOULD NOT DROP .........................EAVESDROPPER 261   40
  THAT WOULD NOT, WOULD NOT DROP .........................EAVESDROPPER 261   40
  IN HELL, SINCE HELL'S A FAIRYTALE. I WOULD ....DIALOGUE O. 278   65
  WOULD TRAFFIC IN. LET HIM FINISH WHAT HE BEGAN. ....DIALOGUE O. 278   84
  THE TABLE LOOKS AS IF IT WOULD STAY A TABLE ....DIALOGUE O. 286 353
  AND IF MY STOMACH WOULD CONTRACT ....APRIL 18 301   3
  I WOULD NOT REMEMBER YOU ....APRIL 18 301   6
  BECAUSE HE WOULD MAKE LOVE TO ME ....BLUEBEARD 305   3
  "IF ONLY SOMETHING WOULD HAPPEN!" ....DIALOGUE EN ROUTE 308   1
  WOULD UMBRELLA LIKE LIBERAL TOADSTOOLS ....DIALOGUE EN ROUTE 308   8
  I NEVER THOUGHT HIS FLESH WOULD BURN ....TO A JILTED LOVER 310   12
  OR THAT THE HEAT WITHIN WOULD GROW ....TO A JILTED LOVER 310   13
  WOULD AVOID ALL PENALTY. ....THE DREAM 311   23
  WOULD FRACTURE IF HE FELL. ....TRIO OF LOVE SONGS 314   24
  WOULD HAVE ME SWALLOW THE ENTIRE SUN ....LOVE IS A PARALLAX 329   26
  THE CHAMBERS WHERE THEIR FIENDISH QUEEN WOULD SIT. ...THE PRINCESS. 334   40
  WHERE KILROY WOULD PASS ....TOUCH-AND-GO 336   14
WOULDN'T (6)
  WOULDN'T SLOW FOR THE HAULED REINS, HIS NAME, WHITENESS I REMEMBER 103   24
  AND WOULDN'T PAUSE FOR MY STRAIGHT LOOK. .............RHODODENDRON. 104   25
  A BULL-SNOUTED SEA THAT WOULDN'T STAY PUT, ...THE BULL OF BENDYLAW 108   8
  WITHOUT ME, SHE WOULDN'T EXIST, SO OF COURSE SHE WAS GRATEFUL. ....
                        ... IN PLASTER 159   15
  AND THE SEVEN-YEAR-OLD WOULDN'T GO OUT UNLESS HIS JERSEY
      STRIPES ....THE BABYSITTERS 174   8
  I WOULDN'T TRUST MYSELF. THE FAULT'S MY FAITH ....DIALOGUE O. 277   37
WOUND (12)
  MEAT MUST GLUT HIS MOUTH'S RAW WOUND. ....PURSUIT 22   16
  SHOULD ACCEPT SO FELL A WOUND, ...BUCOLICS 24   18
  LEAN TO MY WOUND; BURN ON, BURN ON. ....FIRESONG 30   21
  AND THAT GREAT WOUND ....STREET SONG 36   18
  MOVES ON ITS ROOT. THOUGH A MIST-WRAITH WOUND .....HARDCASTLE CRAGS 62   13
  EACH NURSE PATCHED HER SOUL TO A WOUND AND DISAPPEARED. ....WAKING. 151   13
  THEIR REDNESS TALKS TO MY WOUND, IT CORRESPONDS. ....TULIPS 161   39
  I AM A WOUND WALKING OUT OF HOSPITAL. ....THREE WOMEN 184 270
  I AM A WOUND THAT THEY ARE LETTING GO. ....THREE WOMEN 184 271
  I HAD AN OLD WOUND ONCE, BUT IT IS HEALING. ....THREE WOMEN 185 306
  THE SCARLET WOUND. ....ON LOOKING INTO THE EYES OF A DEMON LOVER 325   16
  AND, DROPPING, DIE, TO TRACE A WOUND THAT HEALS LOVE IS A PARALLAX 330   64
WOUNDED (3)
  TOUCHING THEIR WOUNDED, ...GETTING THERE 248   24
  I SHALL BURY THE WOUNDED LIKE PUPAS, ...GETTING THERE 249   60
  ONCE I WOUNDED HIM WITH SO ....TO A JILTED LOVER 310   10
WOUNDS (2)
  LAUGH DOES AWAY WITH THE UNSTITCHING, PLAGUEY WOUNDS ....PERSEUS 83   45
  DEFENDING MY PERILOUS WOUNDS WITH A CHAIR ....CIRCUS IN THREE RINGS 322   11
WOVE (1)
  WHICH QUAINTLY WOVE THE FABRIC OF HER FATE .... THE PRINCESS. 335   57
WRACK (2)
  IN WAIT AMID SNARLED WEED AND WRACK OF WAVE DREAM WITH CLAM-DIGGERS 44   26
  A LONE BEACHCOMBER SQUATS AMONG THE WRACK ....TWO LOVERS. 327   13
WRAP (2)
  WRAP ME, RAGGY SHAWLS, ...NICK AND THE CANDLESTICK 241   7
  WRAP MY LIPS, ...PARALYTIC 266   28
WRAPPED (5)
  OFF-STAGE AND INFAMOUSLY WRAPPED ....SPIDER 49   33
  WRAPPED IN FLEA-RIDDEN DONKEY SKINS, ...THE THIN PEOPLE 64   18

                                                    TITLE   PAGE LINE

WRAPPED (CONT.)
    WRAPPED UP IN YOURSELF LIKE A SPOOL, ...YOU'RE 141   5
    WRAPPED UP IN THEMSELVES AS IN THICK VEILING ....ON DECK 142   2
    PREDECESSOR WRAPPED UP, ...EAVESDROPPER 260   25
WREAK (1)
    GERD WHIRLS THE BALL ABLAZE: "ROUGH STORM," SHE GRANTS, "MAY WREAK ...
                                              ... CRYSTAL GAZER   55   22
WREATH (1)
    WREATH FOR A BRIDAL ....WREATH FOR A BRIDAL 44   T
WREATHED (2)
    THE WREATHED DOORS OPEN TO THE CROWD. ....A WINTER'S TALE 87   26
    WREATHED IN STEAM. ....KINDNESS 270   17
WRECK (2)
    OBSERVING THE WRECK OF METAL AND RARE STONE. ....SONNET: TO EVA 304   4
    YOU'LL WRECK THE REST ....TRIO OF LOVE SONGS   315   43
WRECKED (1)
    BARGE-TAR CLOTTED AT THE TIDE-LINE, THE WRECKED PIER ...GREEN ROCK. 104   2
WRECKS (1)
    HOWEVER YOU MAY SWEAT TO HOLD SUCH DARLING WRECKS ...EPITAPH FOR F. 45   13
WRENCH (2)
    "HOWEVER I WRENCH OBSTINATE BARK AND TRUNK ....CONJURING.   66   25
    GOD'S MONKEY WRENCH HAS BLASTED ALL MACHINES; ....DOOMSDAY 316   13
WRENCHED (1)
    AND I, GREAT MAGNANIMOUS FOOL, THUS WRENCHED FROM ...
                                       ... MONOLOGUE AT 3 A.M.   40   13
WRENCHING (1)
    THREE GIRLS, ENGROSSED, WERE WRENCHING FULL CLUSTERS   RHODODENDRON. 104   21
WRESTLE (2)
    THAT WRESTLE WITH US LIKE ANGELS; THE MERE CHANCE   CHANNEL CROSSING 27   18
    OF ASTOUNDED GENERATIONS; THEY WRESTLE   EPITAPH FOR FIRE AND FLOWER 45   19
WRESTLES (1)
    AND WRESTLES TO IMPOSE ...ON THE DIFFICULTY OF CONJURING UP A DRYAD 66   7
WRINGING (1)
    WRINGING OF HANDS, THIS DARK ....CHILD 265   11
WRINKLE (2)
    TO WRINKLE AND DRY. ....THE DETECTIVE 209   30
    STALK WITHOUT WRINKLE, ...CHILD 265   7
WRINKLED (1)
    NOT ONE LEAF WRINKLED IN THE CLEARING AIR. ....THE OTHER TWO   68   6
WRINKLES (2)
    AND CRIMP THEIR WRINKLES IN A GRIN, ...RHYME   50   7
    THE WRINKLES CREEP UP LIKE WAVES, ...THE RIVAL/DR   291   4
WRINKLING (1)
    OF YOUR SPREAD HAIR, IN WHICH WRINKLING SKEINS ....FULL FATHOM FIVE   92   8
WRINKLY (1)
    FLICKERING LIKE THAT, WRINKLY AND CLEAR RED, LIKE THE SKIN OF A MOUTH. ...
                                        ... POPPIES IN JULY 203   6
WRIST (2)
    BLOOD AND BANK WRIST, ELBOW, SHOULDER, LIP ....DIALOGUE O. 277   18
    NOW BOUND AROUND HER WRIST TILL SHE REDEEM ....THE PRINCESS. 333   24
WRISTS (4)
    TO THEIR OWNERS' WRISTS, THE LIGHT DREAMS FLOAT ....ON DECK 143   35
    IN THEIR CANVAS-SIDED COTS, NAMES TIED TO THEIR WRISTS, *THREE WOMEN 183 220
    BUTTONING THE CUFFS AT MY WRISTS AND THE SLIT FROM MY NECK
        TO MY KNEES. ....THE BEE MEETING 211   8
    THE THROATS OF OUR WRISTS BRAVE LILIES. ....STINGS   214   4
WRIT (1)
    BEFORE HE SPELLS AGAIN, SHOULD HIS NEXT WRIT ....DIALOGUE O.   281 193
WRITE (1)
    DOES HE WRITE C FOR G? NO. HE DARTS ....DIALOGUE OVER A OUIJA BOARD 284 276
WRITES (2)
    THE OLD GOD, TOO, WRITES AUREATE POETRY ....OUIJA   77   12
    THE MAGIC SAWDUST WRITES: ADDRESS UNKNOWN. ....DENOUEMENT   327   17
WRITHE (1)
    LET THEIR SOULS WRITHE IN A DEW, ...GETTING THERE   249   62
WRITHEN (1)
    I CIRCLE THE WRITHEN TREES. I AM TOO HAPPY.   PARLIAMENT HILL FIELDS 153   29
WRITHING (2)
    CATASTROPHE A WRITHING LENGTH OF COBRA, ...PERSEUS   83   22
    WRITHING AND SIGHING, WHAT SORT OF A SCENERY IS IT? ...STOPPED DEAD 230   9
WRITHINGS (1)
    RULES THE WRITHINGS WHICH MAKE MANIFEST ...............SNAKECHARMER   79   16
WRITING (1)
    AND HERE IS AN END TO THE WRITING, ...BURNING THE LETTERS   204   20
WRONG (2)
    ONE DAY YOU MAY TOUCH WHAT'S WRONG ....FOR A FATHERLESS SON 205   12
    IT WORKS, THERE IS NOTHING WRONG WITH IT. ....THE APPLICANT 222   36
WROTE (1)
    NIGHTS, I WROTE IN MY DIARY SPITEFULLY, MY FINGERS RED ....BABY. 174   14
WROUGHT (4)
    WITH SUCH BLIGHT WROUGHT ON OUR BANKRUPT ESTATE, ...CONVERSATION.   21   13
    FROM HIS CRABBED MIDDEN WHERE ALL'S WROUGHT SO AWRY ....FIRESONG   30   10
    FIERCE FIRE'S WROUGHT ....TINKER JACK AND THE TIDY WIVES   34   20
    FOR WEDLOCK WROUGHT WITHIN LOVE'S PROPER CHAPEL.*WREATH FOR A BRIDAL   44   12

WRUNG (1)
DESPITE HER WRUNG HANDS, HER TEARS, HER PRAYING: VANISH!*LADY AND T.   70   30
WRY (3)
THE OTHER, WRY VIRGIN TO THE LAST, ...TWO SISTERS OF PERSEPHONE   32   26
TO A WRY COMPLAISANCE -- ....THE COMPANIONABLE ILLS   105   4
SPRY, WRY, AND GRAY AS THESE MARCH STICKS, ...AMONG THE NARCISSI   190   1
WRY-FACED (1)
AND I WEAR THE WRY-FACED PUCKER OF ....JILTED   304   7
WRYLY (1)
OUTLAST THEIR EVILEST STAR, WRYLY ....THE BEGGARS   48   19
W'S (1)
WORD WEARS TWO W'S? O-R. OR WHAT? ......DIALOGUE OVER A OUIJA BOARD   279   94
WUTHERING (1)
WUTHERING HEIGHTS ....WUTHERING HEIGHTS   167   T
X-RAY (1)
OVEREXPOSED, LIKE AN X-RAY. ....MEDUSA   225   31
X-RAYED (1)
MY X-RAYED HEART, DISSECTED BODY: ....BLUEBEARD   305   6
YACHT (1)
O IT WAS RICHNESS! -- ELEVEN ROOMS AND A YACHT .....THE BABYSITTERS   174   10
YADDO (1)
YADDO: THE GRAND MANOR ....YADDO: THE GRAND MANOR   123   T
YADWIGHA (3)
YADWIGHA, ON A RED COUCH, AMONG LILIES ....YADWIGHA.   85   T
YADWIGHA, THE LITERALISTS ONCE WONDERED HOW YOU ....YADWIGHA.   85   1
YADWIGHA, POSE ON, THAT HE PUT YOU ON THE COUCH ....YADWIGHA.   86   37
YARD (6)
THE FIGS ON THE FIG TREE IN THE YARD ARE GREEN: ....DEPARTURE   51   1
SET FOOT NIGHTLY IN HER YARD ....THE THIN PEOPLE   65   29
BUT THREE MEN ENTERING THE YARD, ...ON THE DECLINE OF ORACLES   78   20
IN MY GRANDMOTHER'S SAND YARD. SHE IS DEAD, ...POINT SHIRLEY   110   9
NIGHTLONG, IN THE GRANITE YARD, INVISIBLE CATS ....INSOMNIAC   163   29
THEN, FROM THE BARRED YARD, THE CHILDREN ....BERCK-PLAGE   200   118
YARDLEY (1)
WHEN THE SWEETHEART FROM ENGLAND APPEARED, WITH HER CREAM SKIN
    AND YARDLEY COSMETICS, ...THE BABYSITTERS   174   6
YARDMAN'S (1)
PURE DEATH'S-METAL. THE YARDMAN'S ....MEDALLION   125   26
YARDS (1)
AND IN A FEW FATAL YARDS OF GRASS ....APRIL 18   302   12
YARN (1)
WHILE SUNLIGHT WINDS ITS YARN UPON THE FLOOR. ....THE PRINCESS.   335   71
YAWNS (1)
AND SNAKES THERE WERE, ARE, WILL BE -- TILL YAWNS .....SNAKECHARMER   79   21
YAWP (1)
POSTAGE STAMPS, STACKED BOOKS' CLAMOR AND YAWP, ...CONJURING.   65   3
YEAR (16)
STRUCK BY EACH DOUR YEAR. ....STRUMPET SONG   34   13
SNOWCAKES BREAK AND WELTER. THIS YEAR ....POINT SHIRLEY   110   4
THE QUEEN BEE MARRIES THE WINTER OF YOUR YEAR. ....BEEKEEPER'S.   118   21
DOWN THERE THE LATE YEAR ....DARK WOOD, DARK WATER   127   12
HE'LL BE RICH IN A YEAR (AND HE SHOULD KNOW) ....ON DECK   143   28
HERE'S YESTERDAY, LAST YEAR -- ....A LIFE   149   3
ON THIS BALD HILL THE NEW YEAR HONES ITS EDGE. ....PARLIAMENT H.   152   1
NEW YEAR ON DARTMOOR ....NEW YEAR ON DARTMOOR   176   T
I DO NOT WANT MUCH OF A PRESENT, ANYWAY, THIS YEAR. ......BIRTHDAY.   206   13
IN THE SECOND YEAR. IT HAD BEEN INSATIABLE ....THE DETECTIVE   209   28
SHE IS OLD, OLD, OLD, SHE MUST LIVE ANOTHER YEAR, AND SHE
    KNOWS IT. ....THE BEE MEETING   212   44
TO ENTER ANOTHER YEAR? ....WINTERING   219   48
AND DRANK MY BLOOD FOR A YEAR, ...DADDY   224   73
ONE YEAR IN EVERY TEN ....LADY LAZARUS   244   2
IS IT A TIGER THIS YEAR, THIS ROAR AT THE DOOR? ....YEARS   255   18
CIRCLING ZODIAC COMPELS THE YEAR. ......TO EVA DESCENDING THE STAIR   303   16
YEARNING (1)
LOVE FLAMES FOREVER IF THE FLESH BE YEARNING. ...TO EVA DESCENDING.   303   14
YEARS (23)
TWENTY YEARS AGO, THE FAMILIAR TUB ....TALE OF A TUB   25   17
GRIM AS GARGOYLES FROM YEARS SPENT SQUATTING AT SEA'S BORDER ...
    ... DREAM WITH CLAM-DIGGERS   44   25
YEARS, GO DOWN TO DRINK THE RIVER: ....CHILD'S PARK STONES   101   29
FIFTEEN YEARS BETWEEN ME AND THE BAY ......GREEN ROCK, WINTHROP BAY   105   4
TWENTY YEARS OUT ....POINT SHIRLEY   110   19
IT WAS GOOD FOR TWENTY YEARS, THAT WINTERING -- ....ELECTRA ON.   116   5
THIRTY YEARS NOW I HAVE LABORED ....THE COLOSSUS   129   8
IN TWENTY YEARS I SHALL BE RETROGRADE ....CANDLES   149   29
TAPPED LIKE A CASK, THE YEARS DRAINING INTO MY PILLOW. ...FACE LIFT   156   18
LET HER DIE THERE, OR WITHER INCESSANTLY FOR THE NEXT FIFTY
    YEARS, ...FACE LIFT   156   29
IT IS TEN YEARS, NOW, SINCE WE ROWED TO CHILDREN'S ISLAND. ...BABY.   174   1
BUT TEN YEARS DEAD. ....THE BABYSITTERS   175   36
PROBABLE MOTES THAT TICK THE YEARS OFF MY LIFE. A BIRTHDAY PRESENT   207   43
THIS IS THE SMELL OF YEARS BURNING, HERE IN THE KITCHEN, *DETECTIVE.   208   12
THOUGH FOR YEARS I HAVE EATEN DUST ....STINGS   214   24
BUT IN TWENTY-FIVE YEARS SHE'LL BE SILVER, ...THE APPLICANT   221   31

```
                                                 TITLE      PAGE  LINE
YEARS (CONT.)
   FOR THIRTY YEARS, POOR AND WHITE, ...........................DADDY  222   4
   SEVEN YEARS, IF YOU WANT TO KNOW. ...........................DADDY  224  74
   YEARS ......................................................YEARS  255   T
   YEARS LATER I ..............................................WORDS  270  14
   WITH SUNLIGHT OF A THOUSAND YEARS UPON HIS LIPS  ....GOLD MOUTHS CRY 302  13
   DIAGRAMS THE FALLING YEARS, ......................TO A JILTED LOVER 309   6
   OUR YEARS. DEATH COMES IN A CASUAL STEEL CAR, YET  ..SONNET: TO TIME 311   3
YEAR'S (1)
   HOARD LAST YEAR'S LEAVES, WON'T MOURN, WEAR SACKCLOTH, OR TURN  ...
                                          ... NOVEMBER GRAVEYARD   56   2
YEASTY (1)
   THIS LOAF'S BIG WITH ITS YEASTY RISING. ..................METAPHORS 116   5
YELLOW (30)
   WHEN BURNS AND BRANDS THAT YELLOW GAZE? .....................PURSUIT  23  36
   AN ARENA OF YELLOW EYES .......................................FAUN   35  11
   BECOME QUITE YELLOW ........................................RESOLVE   52   9
   STRAIGHT INTO YELLOW GLARE .........ELLA MASON AND HER ELEVEN CATS   54  27
   THEY'D HAVE HAD YELLOW SILK SCREENING THE MOON, .........YADWIGHA.    85  15
   IN THE TIN PAIL SHADED BY YELLOW PAPER   MEMOIRS OF A SPINACH-PICKER  89  13
   YET TODAY, A YELLOW BUD IN MY HAND, ...................RHODODENDRON.  103  17
   THE ROUND OF HIS YELLOW EYE-BUTTON. ..................A WINTER SHIP  113  10
   SIX FEET OF YELLOW GRAVEL COVER YOU. ........ELECTRA ON AZALEA PATH  117  23
   CURTAINED WITH YELLOW LACE. .........................THE SLEEPERS   122   7
   ALREADY YELLOW THE HEAVENS. ......................THE MANOR GARDEN   125  15
   LEAVES, UNDOING THEIR YELLOW CAVES ....................BLUE MOLES    126  11
   THEIR YELLOW CORSETS WERE READY TO SPLIT. ............LEAVING EARLY  146  25
   THIS NEW ABSOLUTELY WHITE PERSON AND THE OLD YELLOW ONE, *IN PLASTER 158   2
   ALL WIG CURLS AND YELLOW TEETH ...................WUTHERING HEIGHTS  167  26
   THE YELLOW MINUTE BEFORE THE WIND WALKS, WHEN THE LEAVES*THREE WOMEN 179  93
   THE EXTREME UNCTION OF ITS YELLOW CANDLE-FLOWERS.*THE RABBIT CATCHER 193   8
   WHERE ARE THE EYE-STONES, YELLOW AND VALUABLE, .........BERCK-PLAGE  198  53
   BETWEEN THE YELLOW LETTUCES AND THE GERMAN CABBAGE ........BURNING.  205  39
   THE MILK CAME YELLOW, THEN BLUE AND SWEET AS WATER. ..THE DETECTIVE  209  33
   WITH ITS YELLOW PURSES, ITS SPIKY ARMORY. ..........THE BEE MEETING  211  32
   EIGHT COMBS OF YELLOW CUPS, .................................STINGS  214   7
   CHINESE YELLOW ON APPALLING OBJECTS --- ..................WINTERING  218  16
   RED AND YELLOW, TWO PASSIONATE HOT METALS .............STOPPED DEAD  230   8
   SUCH YELLOW SULLEN SMOKES ...................................FEVER.  231  14
   SMALL AND CROSS. THE YELLOW KNIFE ....................BY CANDLELIGHT  237  21
   BUT THAT YELLOW! ......................................EAVESDROPPER  260  11
   YELLOW CATHEAD, BLUE FISH --- .............................BALLOONS  271   9
   OR THE BITTER BLINKING YELLOW ...............................JILTED  304   3
   LIGHTNING LICKED IN A YELLOW LATHER .........................LAMENT  315   4
YELLOW-CASQUED (1)
   YELLOW-CASQUED CHRYSANTHEMUMS -- .......................STREET SONG   36  14
YELLOW-HAUNCHED (1)
   YELLOW-HAUNCHED, A PACK-DOG, ............................THE SWARM  216  23
YELLOW-PAELLA (1)
   PAST THE YELLOW-PAELLA EATERIES, ..................ALICANTE LULLABY   43   3
YELLOWS (3)
   FACED IN HIS RICH YELLOWS, TASSELS, POMPONS, BRAID, THE PICADOR  ...
                                          ... THE GORING   47   5
   THEIR PALE, TENTATIVE YELLOWS ............................CANDLES  149  15
   ITS YELLOWS HEARTEN. ......................NICK AND THE CANDLESTICK  241  22
YES (11)
   THAT OWL VOICE SOLE "YES", WHILE COWS UTTER ....WREATH FOR A BRIDAL   44   3
   TONE-DEAF AND YES, UNTEACHABLE. ..............THE DISQUIETING MUSES   75  38
   YES, HERE IS THE SECRETARY OF BEES WITH HER WHITE SHOP SMOCK, .BEE.  211   7
   YES, YES, THIS IS MY ADDRESS. ...........................THE TOUR   237   8
   YES, YES, THIS IS MY ADDRESS. ...........................THE TOUR   237   8
   IN ALL. PLUS YES. PLUS NO. AND THIS BARE BOARD. ........DIALOGUE O.  276  14
   DIRECT TO YES. I BET IT'S PAN. WHO'LL  ..DIALOGUE OVER A OUIJA BOARD  277  27
   TO YES SAYS HE IS READY. PAN, IS THERE   DIALOGUE OVER A OUIJA BOARD  278  71
   TO YES, HIS SURENESS MUST BE HIS, NOT OURS. ...........DIALOGUE O.  278  73
   FOR YES, DRAGGING OUR FINGERS AFTER. HOW*DIALOGUE OVER A OUIJA BOARD 278  75
   MIGHT WORK ON THIS GLASS MEDIUM. BELIEF, YES, .........DIALOGUE O.  282 225
YESTERDAY (3)
   NAILED TO THE RAFTERS YESTERDAY: ......................POEM.1.WHO.  131  14
   HERE'S YESTERDAY, LAST YEAR -- ............................A LIFE  149   3
   A FUTURE WAS LOST YESTERDAY ..............................APRIL 18  302  14
YESTERDAYS (1)
   THE SLIME OF ALL MY YESTERDAYS ...........................APRIL 18  301   1
YET (53)
   YET ALWAYS THE RIDICULOUS NUDE FLANKS URGE ...........TALE OF A TUB   25  33
   IS HELPLESS HERE, QUITE EXTRA, YET WE MUST MAKE  ...CHANNEL CROSSING  27  35
   WORM-HUSBANDED, YET NO WOMAN. ...........TWO SISTERS OF PERSEPHONE   32  28
   WHOSE LABOR'S NOT YET SMOKED .......TINKER JACK AND THE TIDY WIVES   35  29
   YET, IN MY WINTRIEST MOODS, I HOLD ......SOLILOQUY OF THE SOLIPSIST   37  24
   OF HELL, AND NOT THE FIERY PART. YET TO JUDGE BY THAT DAZZLED LOOK,  ...
                          ... DIALOGUE BETWEEN GHOST AND PRIEST   38  15
   IS NOT YET COME. ..................DIALOGUE BETWEEN GHOST AND PRIEST  39  38
   AND YET KEEP KIND) ......................................THE GLUTTON  40   4
   YET OF DEVILS THE CLEVEREST ................................SPIDER   48   5
   YET WON'T LAY ONE. ..........................................RHYME   50   3
```

YET (CONT.)
  SOME HAVOC ON TENDER LIMB, AND YET ....CRYSTAL GAZER   55   23
  YET POLITIC; IGNORANT ....BLACK ROOK IN RAINY WEATHER   57   25
  POCKED BY ROOK-CLAW AND RABBIT-TRACK: SHE MUST YET WIN ..SNOWMAN O.   58   17
  YET, SHRINED ON HER SHELF, THE GRISLY VISAGE ENDURED, ..LADY AND T.   70   29
  O MINE, YET KIN SHE IS: SHE'LL SUCK ....ALL THE DEAD DEARS   70   16
  NEVER GIVEN; HIDDEN, YET ....THE GREAT CARBUNCLE   72   12
  LIT THINGS, THAT LAMP OF THE POSSIBLE! WET YET .....SPINACH-PICKER.   89   3
  ALL STILLNESS. YET THESE SHAPES FLOAT ....LORELEI   94   9
  CONSPICUOUS, YET IT SEEMED ....MUSSEL HUNTER AT ROCK HARBOR   95   18
  AND BLEED. THE WHITE STOMACH MAY RIPEN YET. ....MOONRISE   98   30
  OF THE AZALEAS, YET BURNT OUT ....CHILD'S PARK STONES   101   17
  YET THE DAPPLE TONING HIS WHITE DOWN ....WHITENESS I REMEMBER   102   10
  YET TODAY, A YELLOW BUD IN MY HAND, ...RHODODENDRON.   103   17
  YET IT NEVER MILKED ANY GOAT, NOR DEALT COW DEATH ....GOATSUCKER.   111   12
  YET DESOLATION, STALLED IN PAINT, SPARES THE LITTLE COUNTRY ...
                                ... TWO VIEWS OF A CADAVER ROOM   114   21
  GLAZES THE ROCK POOLS YET, ...MAN IN BLACK   119   11
  YET HIS BELLY KEPT ITS FIRE ....MEDALLION   124   16
  AND YET THE ICHOR OF THE SPRING ....THE BURNT-OUT SPA   138   19
  YET THEY RECEDE, UNTOUCHABLE AS TOMORROW,*SLEEP IN THE MOJAVE DESERT   144   11
  I HADN'T A CAT YET. ....FACE LIFT   156   24
  YET I STILL DEPENDED ON HER, THOUGH I DID IT REGRETFULLY.*IN PLASTER   160   49
  THEY SEEM LARGE, YET THEY DROP, AND NO GAP IS VISIBLE. ......STARS.   165   5
  I SEE US FLOATING THERE YET, INSEPARABLE -- TWO CORK DOLLS. ..BABY.   175   41
  CLAPS SIDEWISE: I AM NOT HIS YET. ....DEATH & CO.   254   11
  WITH THE COLD BURN DRY ICE HAS. YET THE CLOCK ....DIALOGUE O.   276   11
  TO KNOW AT ALL. AND YET I GO AHEAD. ....DIALOGUE OVER A OUIJA BOARD   278   69
  THE GLASS YET AS HE GLIDES. P-L-U- ....DIALOGUE OVER A OUIJA BOARD   278   77
  SO, YOU'LL SCOFF, AND YET YOU'D DROP TO KNEEL ....DIALOGUE O.   280 156
  DESCENDED ON YOUR FAVORITES, AND YET ..DIALOGUE OVER A OUIJA BOARD   281 191
  FOR SOUNDING SYLLABLES WE HAVEN'T YET ..DIALOGUE OVER A OUIJA BOARD   283 254
  HIM YET, AND GIVE US GOOD REASON. NO, HE'S ON ....DIALOGUE O.   284 295
  YET THERE IS NO WALKER AND LOOKER BUT MYSELF. ....QUEEN MARY'S.   290   9
  AND IDLE COILS OF JARGON YET UNSPOKEN. ....SONNET: TO EVA   304   3
  BUT YET THE PERVERSE IMP WITHIN WILL PROBE*METAMORPHOSES OF THE MOON   308   31
  "BUT YET I WAITED TO BE FINED ....THE DREAM   311   25
  OUR YEARS. DEATH COMES IN A CASUAL STEEL CAR, YET ..SONNET: TO TIME   311   3
  YET INDIVIDUAL PLANET ....TRIO OF LOVE SONGS 313   3
  YET ASTRONOMIC FOUNTAINS ....TRIO OF LOVE SONGS 314   7
  YET ORDERED LUNAR MOTION ....TRIO OF LOVE SONGS 314   11
  YET ALL ANGELIC REASON ....TRIO OF LOVE SONGS 314   15
  YET I FLOURISH MY WHIP WITH A FATAL FLAIR ....CIRCUS IN THREE RINGS   322   10
  YET AS WE WONDER WHAT CAN COME OF ICE ....PROLOGUE TO SPRING   322   14
  TO PAY THE PIPER WITH EACH BREATH, YET LOVE .....LOVE IS A PARALLAX   331   76
YEW (8)
  THE MOON AND THE YEW TREE ....THE MOON AND THE YEW TREE   172   T
  THE YEW TREE POINTS UP. IT HAS A GOTHIC SHAPE. ....MOON.   173   15
  AND THE MESSAGE OF THE YEW TREE IS BLACKNESS -- BLACKNESS AND
         SILENCE. ....THE MOON AND THE YEW TREE   173   28
  BLACK YEW, WHITE CLOUD, ...LITTLE FUGUE   187   14
  THE YEW HEDGE OF THE GROSSE FUGE. ....LITTLE FUGUE   188   20
  A YEW HEDGE OF ORDERS, ...LITTLE FUGUE   188   25
  THE YEW MY CHRIST, THEN. ....LITTLE FUGUE   188   29
  WHERE THE YEW TREES BLOW LIKE HYDRAS, ...THE MUNICH MANNEQUINS   262   3
YEW'S (1)
  THE YEW'S BLACK FINGERS WAG; ....LITTLE FUGUE   187   1
YIELD (1)
  FOR HIS LEAST LOOK, SCANT ACRES YIELD: ....ODE FOR TED   29   13
YIELDED (1)
  NIGHT YIELDED UP ....MOONSONG AT MORNING   317   30
YIELDS (1)
  MAD HATTER'S HAT YIELDS NO NEW METAPHOR, ...A SORCERER B.   324   10
YOGI (1)
  ARE NOT THE THOUGHTS I TURN ON, LIKE A YOGI, ...YEARS   255   3
YORK (2)
  TO SWEETEN YOUR NECK OF THE NEW YORK WOODS. ....PRIVATE GROUND   130   4
  IN NEW YORK, IN HOLLYWOOD, THE MEN SAID: "THROUGH? ....LESBOS   228   41
YOU (393)
YOU'D (9)
  HERE'S A SPOT I THOUGHT YOU'D LOVE -- ....THE TOUR   238   27
  YOU'D NOT WANT THAT. ....THE TOUR   238   40
  DEAD, YOU'D SWEAR HIM A VICTIM OF OUR OWN VAIN ....DIALOGUE O.   278   82
  SO, YOU'LL SCOFF, AND YET YOU'D DROP TO KNEEL ....DIALOGUE O.   280 156
  TO PROVE IT GENUINE. YOU'D KNEEL, TOO, DIALOGUE OVER A OUIJA BOARD   280 162
  IF A BUSH BORROWED TONGUES AND SPOKE TO YOU. YOU'D KNEEL*DIALOGUE O.   280 163
  YOU'D PRESUME YOUR INNER VOICE GOD-PLUMED ENOUGH ....DIALOGUE O.   280 168
  THE WAY YOU'D CRACK A CLOCK; YOU'D CRUSH THE BONE ...SONNET: TO EVA   304   2
  THE WAY YOU'D CRACK A CLOCK; YOU'D CRUSH THE BONE ...SONNET: TO EVA   304   2
YOU'LL (10)
  HONESTLY WANT TO FIND IF YOU'LL HAVE A FLING ....DIALOGUE O.   278   56
  THESE GIFTS ARE GIVEN. AND WHEN WITHHELD, YOU'LL SAY ...DIALOGUE O.   279 126
  SO, YOU'LL SCOFF, AND YET YOU'D DROP TO KNEEL ....DIALOGUE O.   280 156
  EATING YOUR WORDS: YOU'LL REVOKE HIS GODHOOD SOON AS ...DIALOGUE O.   281 189
  YOU'LL ISSUE HIM HIS PASS TO ANGELDOM ..DIALOGUE OVER A OUIJA BOARD   281 192

	TITLE	PAGE	LINE

YOU'LL (CONT.)
```
    ALL, IF YOU'LL HIDE HOPES OF HEAVEN IN A HAT  ..........DIALOGUE O.  282  231
    OF ONE WINE-GLASS, YOU'LL PIN IT LIKE A PRIZE  .........DIALOGUE O.  283  249
    YOU'LL CUT THE CHORD  ...........................TRIO OF LOVE SONGS  315   39
    YOU'LL WRECK THE REST  ..........................TRIO OF LOVE SONGS  315   43
    YOU'LL HALT THE CLOCK  ..........................TRIO OF LOVE SONGS  315   51
YOUNG (8)
    YOUNG WIVES STILL BLITHE,  ...........TINKER JACK AND THE TIDY WIVES   35   27
    IN ME SHE HAS DROWNED A YOUNG GIRL, AND IN ME AN OLD WOMAN  ..MIRROR  174   17
    I AM YOUNG AS EVER, IT SAYS. WHAT IS IT I MISS?  ........THREE WOMEN  186  350
    ON HIM SOMETIMES. HE'S LAZY. LIKE ANY YOUNG  ............DIALOGUE O.  281  182
    THE FIELDS WERE FULL OF BRONZED YOUNG MEN  .....BITTER STRAWBERRIES  299   18
    GOLD MOUTHS CRY WITH THE GREEN YOUNG  ...............GOLD MOUTHS CRY  302    1
    EACH NIGHT, THIS ADROIT YOUNG LADY  .......................AERIALIST  331    1
    TO KEEP THE YOUNG GIRL FROM HER CROWNING GOAL.  .......THE PRINCESS.  333   18
YOUNGER (1)
    THAT SOMEHOW WE ARE YOUNGER THAN WE WERE.  .............APRIL AUBADE  312   14
YOUNGEST (1)
    THE YOUNGEST NEPHEW GIVES A FRETFUL WHINE  ..........FAMILY REUNION  301   23
YOUR (229)
YOU'RE (9)
    YOU'RE  ...................................................YOU'RE  141    T
    YOU'RE NO HAPPIER THAN I ABOUT IT.  ...........................WHITSUN  154   17
    YOU DON'T QUITE BELIEVE IN IT. YOU'RE DEAF TO REAL  .....DIALOGUE O.  278   63
    YOU'RE MELTING NOW, BECAUSE YOU THINK HE'S HIT  .........DIALOGUE O.  278   80
    OUR SEPARATE VEINS AND THIS GLASS MOUTH. OH YOU'RE  .....DIALOGUE O.  280  147
    ENOUGH. BUT BE POLITE. YOU'RE TOO SEVERE*DIALOGUE OVER A OUIJA BOARD  281  181
    RABBITS IN THE LOT. YOU'RE IN A HUFF  ...DIALOGUE OVER A OUIJA BOARD  282  236
    YOU'RE SATISFIED. MY WILL HAS EVIDENTLY *DIALOGUE OVER A OUIJA BOARD  284  279
    YOU'RE ALWAYS TALKING THIS WAY . . ."  ..........BITTER STRAWBERRIES  300   26
YOURS (7)
    AT THE HEADSTONE NEXT TO YOURS, NOR DOES IT ROT,  .......ELECTRA ON.  117   26
    NO GESTURE OF YOURS OR MINE COULD CATCH THEIR ATTENTION  ..TWO CAMP.  144    4
    HER O-MOUTH GRIEVES AT THE WORLD; YOURS IS UNAFFECTED,  ...THE RIVAL  166    5
    HE IS YOURS, THE LITTLE BRASSY ATLAS --  .............BY CANDLELIGHT  237   31
    YOU WAKE TO IS NOT YOURS.  .................NICK AND THE CANDLESTICK  241   30
    CURTSEYED TO YOURS. TOO BAD YOU CALLED PAN UP  .........DIALOGUE O.  284  280
    I SHOULD HAVE A STEEL COMPLEXION LIKE YOURS  ..........THE RIVAL/DR  291    6
YOURSELF (5)
    DREAMED YOURSELF AWAY IN THE MOON'S EYE  ..................YADWIGHA.   86   28
    PERHAPS YOU CONSIDER YOURSELF AN ORACLE,  ..............THE COLOSSUS  129    6
    ARCHES ABOVE US. O FATHER, ALL BY YOURSELF  ...........THE COLOSSUS  129   17
    WRAPPED UP IN YOURSELF LIKE A SPOOL,  .......................YOU'RE  141    5
    COLD GLASS, HOW YOU INSERT YOURSELF  .....................THE OTHER  202   26
YOUTH (1)
    GO TO YOUR GREENHORN YOUTH  ............................RECANTATION   42   17
YOU'VE (7)
    THAT NOBLE MEIN, PERHAPS YOU'VE LATE QUITTED HEAVEN?"  ..DIALOGUE O.   38   16
    ARE THOSE PETALS OR LEAVES YOU'VE PAIRED THEM WITH -- *LEAVING EARLY  146   14
    WELL I HOPE YOU'VE ENJOYED IT, AUNTIE!  ....................THE TOUR  238   48
    TO VIEW HOW VERSATILE WE ARE: YOU'VE PAMPERED  .........DIALOGUE O.  280  137
    INSTEAD OF FAT FISH ON THE LINE, YOU'VE PLUMBED  .......DIALOGUE O.  282  242
    IF YOU'VE A PLOT TO HALT THE LETHAL FLOW  .........THE DISPOSSESSED  318    7
    OR PLAY ANOTHER CARD GAME WHEN YOU'VE WON;  ............ADMONITIONS  319    2
YOWL (2)
    WHOEVER HEARD A SUNSET YOWL LIKE THAT?  .................STOPPED DEAD  230   15
    THE ZOO YOWL, THE MAD SOFT  ...........................EAVESDROPPER  260   35
ZANZIBAR (1)
    IN TIBET, OR A LLAMA IN ZANZIBAR  .......DIALOGUE OVER A OUIJA BOARD  281  177
ZEN (1)
    EVEN IN YOUR ZEN HEAVEN WE SHAN'T MEET.  ....................LESBOS  230   92
ZEPPELIN (2)
    MY SLEEPING CAPSULE, MY RED AND BLUE ZEPPELIN  ...........THE JAILER  226   12
    SCATTERING CANDY FROM A ZEPPELIN,  ...............LOVE IS A PARALLAX  329   35
ZEROS (1)
    ZEROS, SHUTTING ON NOTHING,  .....................THE RABBIT CATCHER  194   15
ZINC-WHITE (1)
    ZINC-WHITE SNOW.  ...........................YADDO: THE GRAND MANOR  124   21
ZINGING (1)
    WHAT FEAR? IT HAS SET THEM ZINGING  .......................STINGS/DR  293    2
ZODIAC (3)
    CIRCLING ZODIAC COMPELS THE YEAR.  .......TO EVA DESCENDING THE STAIR  303   16
    DIRECTS ALL ZODIAC.  ............................TRIO OF LOVE SONGS  313    4
    BEHIND THE ZODIAC ON ATTIC DOOR  .......THE PRINCESS AND THE GOBLINS  335   58
ZONE (2)
    TO RAID THE ZONE WHERE FATE BEGINS,  ......METAMORPHOSES OF THE MOON  307    3
    AND THEY BUY TICKETS FOR THE TROPIC ZONE;  ..............DENOUEMENT  326    5
ZOO (3)
    ZOO KEEPER'S WIFE  ..................................ZOO KEEPER'S WIFE  154    T
    THE ZOO YOWL, THE MAD SOFT  ...........................EAVESDROPPER  260   35
    THE ZOO OF THE NEW  ..........................................CHILD  265    3
```

INDEX WORDS IN ORDER OF FREQUENCY

-3847- THE	-233- NOT	-107- THEM	-70- FACE THAN WOULD	-49- BODY KNOW LOOK
-1744- OF	-229- YOUR	-104- WAS	-69- O	-46- GLASS
-1710- AND	-201- ITS	-101- RED	-68- WATER	-45- ANY NIGHT
-1675- A	-195- ALL	-100- US	-66- GO STILL	-44- HOUSE TREE
-1138- IN	-188- OR SHE	-98- CAN	-65- COME THOSE	-43- LONG MAY MOUTH
-1003- TO	-186- HE	-97- EACH THROUGH	-64- DAY MORE	-42- LEAVES MUST WIND WITHOUT
-988- I	-180- BUT	-95- OVER	-63- HERE	-41- BEFORE GOD OWN
-656- IS	-175- OUT	-91- DOWN	-62- HAS HEART NEVER SEE TIME	-40- MAKE MOTHER NOR
-600- IT	-172- AM SO	-90- OLD	-61- MOON	-39- BETWEEN BRIGHT HAND ROUND
-531- MY	-171- ONE	-88- EYE EYES	-60- AMONG MAN	-38- AWAY EVEN LAST MIND THINK THOUGH WOMAN
-445- WITH	-166- WHITE	-87- TWO	-59- SKY STARS WHILE WORLD	-37- CRY FINGERS GOOD SHOULD
-440- ON	-165- BE THERE	-85- AIR	-58- HANDS HEAD SMALL	-36- CLEAR OTHER SAY WALL WAY
-400- AS	-162- HAVE WE	-84- LITTLE	-57- BLOOD GREAT	-35- DID PLACE
-396- LIKE	-161- WHAT	-83- SUCH	-56- WERE	-34- AGAINST HAIR HOME MYSELF UNTIL
-393- YOU	-158- BLACK OUR UP	-82- DEAD SEA	-55- COULD	-33- EVERY GRAY ONCE PEOPLE
-391- THAT	-155- AN	-81- OFF WHICH	-54- HAD SHALL	
-354- THEY	-143- NOW	-80- WHO	-53- AFTER SOME TOO YET	
-337- ARE	-129- WILL	-79- UNDER	-52- STONE	
-294- THIS	-120- THESE	-78- HIM LIGHT THEN	-51- DEATH	
-284- FOR THEIR	-116- GREEN IF	-76- WHEN	-50- ABOUT COLD	
-279- FROM	-111- DO	-74- LET		
-274- HIS	-110- LOVE	-73- ONLY		
-273- ME	-109- INTO	-72- DARK		
-272- HER	-108- BLUE HOW WHERE	-71- BACK NOTHING SUN		
-262- AT				
-242- NO				
-237- BY				

-32-
GONE
MIGHT
SET

-31-
BEHIND
CHILDREN
FAR
ROCK
TILL
TREES
WELL

-30-
DREAM
END
FIRST
LIFE
STONES
THREE
WHOLE
WHOSE
YELLOW

-29-
AGAIN
BED
BEEN
IT'S
ITSELF
MEN
ORANGE
ROOM
WALK
WOOD

-28-
BREATH
COLOR
DULL
FACES
FLAT
PINK
SHADOW
SKIN
SLEEP
SOMETHING
SWEET
TELL
THICK
THIN
UPON

-27-
BABY
FULL
GET
GRASS
MADE
OPEN
WORDS

-26-
BIG
MOST
WANT

-25-
BONE
CANNOT
ENOUGH
FATHER
FEET
FIRE
FOOT
KEEP
MOVE
THEMSELVES

-24-
BIRDS
FLOWERS
MORNING
PALE
PUT
RUN
SILVER

-23-
ABOVE
ALWAYS
ANOTHER
BLIND
DAWN
DOES
GOLD
HILL
I'M
LIE
NEW
THING
YEARS

-22-
DOOR
EAT
FAT
LADY
PAPER
ROSE
SAME
SHUT
THOUGHT
VOICES
WINDOW
WINTER

-21-
ANGELS
BALD
BEAUTIFUL
CAME
DAYS
DON'T
EARTH
FLESH
HEAR
HIGH
LEFT
MIRROR
MUD
PURE
REMEMBER
STAND
TAKE
TERRIBLE
TONGUE
TOWARD
TRY
TURN

-20-
ACROSS
BARE
FEEL
GHOST
GIRL
MUCH
ROCKS
SAID
SAW
SHADOWS
VOICE
WHY
WITHIN

-19-
BONES
CALL
DREAMS
EVERYTHING
FALL
GARDEN
HOT
JUST
MANY
REAL
RIGHT
ROSES
SIDE
SMILE
SOUL
TOUCH
VERY
WOMEN

-18-
BEES
BEING
CHILD
FISH
HEAVEN
LEAF
QUIET
ROOT
SMILES
SPACE
TOOK
WEATHER

-17-
CLOUDS
COUNTRY
CRIES
DRY
EAR
EMPTY
GOES
GOING
HARD
HE'S
LIES
NAME
NOBODY
PAN
SMELL
STOOD
TEETH
WON'T
WORD

-16-
CLOUD
ELSE
FIND
HEADS
HEARD
ICE
IMAGE
KISS
LIGHTS
LIVE
MAKES
RIVER
SHAPE
SIT
SORT
STAR
STREET
TALK
THAT'S
TURNED
WARM
WINDOWS
YEAR

-15-
AROUND
BEAUTY
BREAK
COMES
COUCH
DARKNESS
DEEP
DIDN'T
FINE
FLY
FOUND
GOD'S
GULLS
HIDE
HOLY
HOOKS
HUNG
LATE
LOOKING
LOST
PASS
QUICK
READY
RISE
SHEETS
SONG
SUMMER
THINGS
TONGUES
WAVE
WINGS

-14-
BLANK
BOX
BURN
CAN'T
CAT
CATS
CITY
COMING
DIE
ENTER
GIVE
HILLS
INSTEAD
I'VE
KILL
KNEW
LEAVE
LIT
MILK
PETALS
QUEEN
RAIN
SECRET
SILK
SPEAK
STEP
TEARS
TURNING

-13-
BAD
BALL
BECAUSE
BEYOND
BIRD
BLUNT
BOY
BREATHE
CLEAN
CRACK
CRYING
DROP
DUMB
FALLING
FIVE
FLIES
FROST
FRUIT
HEAT
HOLD
HOUR
I'D
IRON
KEPT
KNIFE
LANDSCAPE
LAY
LILIES
LINE
LOOKS
LOVERS
MINUTE
NEITHER
NEXT
PURPLE
RARE
SALT
SAYS
SIMPLY
SMOKE
SNOW
SOFT
STARE
TABLE
TURNS
USE
WAIT
WALLS
WHEELS
WIFE

-12-
BEST
BETTER
BLOWN
BRING
COLORS
DEAR
EVER
FINGER
FLOWER
FREE
GOT
HALT
HEARTS
HELL
LEANS
LIPS
LIVES
MEET
MILLION
MIRRORS
MONTH
NURSES
OH
OPENS
RICH
RING
SEEM
SEEMS
SEVEN
SICK
SIGHT
SLEEPING
SOON
SOUND
STAIR
START
STEEL
TASTE
TIN
TOGETHER
WEAR
WET
WISH
WORK
WOUND

-11-
ACT
ALMOST
BELLY
BROWN

598

PERFECT	TAILS	ARROW	CURTAINS	GUARDS
PERFECTLY	TAKEN	ART	DARING	GUESTS
PERILOUS	TAP	ASKEW	DAYLIGHT	GUISE
PICTURE	TELEGRAM	ASKING	DAZZLE	GUTS
PIECES	TEMPER	ATE	DEAF	HAG
PIG	TENDERNESS	ATMOSPHERE	DEPARTURE	HARM
PINE	TERROR	ATTENDANTS	DIALOGUE	HAUL
PIPE	THEY'RE	AUNTIE	DIRTY	HAULED
PLATES	THICKET	BABEL	DISGUISE	HAULS
PLAYING	THICKETS	BALCONIES	DISTANCES	HEROIC
POETRY	THIGHS	BALLOON	DOMES	HERR
POWER	THIRTEENS	BANDAGES	DOUBLE	HERSELF
PRINCESS	THROAT	BANK	DOUR	HIVE
PROCEED	THROATS	BARBAROUS	DOVE	HONEST
PRODIGAL	TICKING	BARNYARD	DRAFTS	HOPES
PROVE	TIGER	BASTARD	DRAW	HORIZON
PULSE	TIGERS	BATCH	DREAMING	HUMAN
QUESTIONS	TIGHT	BATTLE	DRIFT	HUNGRY
RADIANT	TILTED	BEND	DRIP	ICH
REALLY	TIMES	BEWARE	DRIVE	IDLE
REFLECT	TOMORROW	BIRTHDAY	DRIVEN	IGNORANT
REPOSE	TOUGH	BLAME	DRIVES	ILLUSION
RID	TRAFFIC	BLAND	DROPPED	IMMEDIATELY
ROAR	TRICK	BLEEDING	DURING	IMPOSSIBLE
ROOKS	TURQUOISE	BLEW	EAGLE	INANE
ROT	UGLY	BLIZZARD	EASE	INDEFATIGABLE
ROWS	UNCLE	BOARD	EATS	INDIGO
RUNS	UNDERSTAND	BOARDED	ECHO	INFINITE
SAINT	UNDO	BOAT	ECLIPSE	INHABIT
SAYING	UNLIKE	BOOT	EDGES	INNOCENCE
SCAR	UNLOOSE	BORDER	ELEMENTS	INSTRUMENTS
SCARED	USUAL	BORED	ELM	JUICE
SCENERY	VAIN	BOREDOM	EMBRACE	JUT
SCOFF	VALUABLE	BOSTON	EVE	KEEN
SEA'S	VANISH	BOUGH	EVERYBODY	KILLING
SEEING	VASE	BOUGHS	FABLE	KNEEL
SEEK	VELVET	BRASS	FABRIC	KNIVES
SENT	VENUS	BREAD	FACT	KNOT
SHELF	VILLAGERS	BREAKING	FAN	LACE
SHOT	VISIBLE	BRINGS	FAST	LAMP
SHOULDER	WAKES	BROOD	FAULTS	LAUGHING
SHOWS	WARD	BROUGHT	FED	LAUNDRY
SHRUNK	WARS	BRUTE	FIRES	LAYER
SILENT	WATERS	BULK	FLAMES	LEAD
SINGING	WEARING	BUNCH	FLARING	LEARNED
SINGS	WE'LL	BUNCHED	FLINT	LEST
SISTER	WHOLLY	BURNED	FLUENT	LET'S
SISTERS	WIDE	BUSHES	FOLD	LOCKED
SITTING	WILDERNESS	BUSINESS	FOOL	LOGIC
SKULLS	WISDOM	CAGE	FOREHEAD	LOOSE
SLEEPERS	WITHER	CASTLES	FOUNTAINS	LOVER'S
SMELLS	WITNESS	CAT'S	FOX	LUMINOUS
SOLAR	WOKE	CEILING	FRAIL	LUNAR
SOMEHOW	WORLDS	CHAGRIN	FRILL	MAID
SORRY	WRAPPED	CHASTE	FUNNEL	MAIN
SOW	YOURSELF	CINDER	FUR	MANAGE
SPARE		CLAY	FURIOUS	MANNEQUINS
SPILT		CLIFF	FURNACE	MARVEL
SPIT	-4-	CLIFFS	FURNED	MASS
SPLIT	ACCUSED	CLOTHES	GAILY	MAYBE
SPLITS	ACHE	COBRA	GARMENTS	MEANING
SPOT	ADDRESS	COCKCROW	GAY	MELTS
STALKS	ADMIRE	COCKED	GENTLE	MEMORY
STARTS	AFRICAN	COFFEE	GERMAN	MIDWIFE
STAUNCH	AGES	COILS	GESTURE	MILKY
STEM	AGO	COLORED	GHASTLY	MOOD
STING	AGONY	COMMUNION	GILT	MORTGAGE
STOMACH	ALIVE	COMPANY	GLIDES	MOTES
STRANGE	ALOFT	CONCERN	GLOBE	MOTHER'S
STREETS	AMUSED	CONSCIENCE	GLOVES	MOUNTAIN
STRING	ANCHOR	COT	GLOW	MOUNTAINS
STRIPES	ANGER	COUSIN	GRAINS	MOUSE
STUDY	ANGRY	CRAWLS	GRAVE	MUSEUM
STUFF	ANIMALS	CREST	GREENHORN	NARROW
SULLEN	ANKLES	CRIB	GREENS	NEVERTHELESS
SUNKEN	ANTS	CROAK	GRIEF	NIGHTFALL
SURELY	APPALL	CROWED	GRIEVE	NONE
SURFACE	APRIL	CROWN	GRIEVES	NOSTRILS
SURGEON	ARCS	CROWNS	GRIT	NUDE
SYLLABLES	ARRANGING	CRUEL	GROWN	NUMB
	ARRIVE	CURRENTS	GROWS	NURSERY

OBJECTS
OBSCENE
ONTO
OPENED
OPPOSITE
ORBIT
OVERNIGHT
PAGES
PAINT
PALLOR
PANES
PAPERY
PATH
PAUSE
PEBBLE
PETTICOATS
PICKED
PIGEONS
PILL
PINES
PITCH
PLAN
PLANET
PLANT
PLANTS
PLUNGE
PLUSH
POISONS
POLE
POLISH
POLLY'S
POPPIES
POTATOES
PRIDE
PRINCE
PRIZE
PROMISE
PROPS
PURR
PUTS
RAMSHACKLE
RATHER
RECOVER
REEDS
REFLECTIONS
RELIC
REMEMBERING
RETURN
REVOLVING
RIDICULOUS
RIVER'S
ROLLED
ROOF
ROOK
ROOTED
ROUGH
RULES
S.
SACK
SACRED
SAGE
SAIL
SAILOR
SAP
SCANT
SCORCHED
SCORNED
SCRAPS
SCRUPULOUSLY
SELF
SEND
SERVE
SETTING
SETTLE
SHAKING
SHOCK
SHOES
SHREWD
SIGHS
SILLY

SING
SINK
SKIES
SKY'S
SLEPT
SLIDING
SNAIL
SNAKY
SNARE
SOLITARY
SOMEWHERE
SON
SONGS
SONS
SOUR
SOUTH
SPACES
SPELL
SPELLS
SPIRITS
SPOKE
SPRANG
SPRUNG
SPRY
SQUANDER
SQUEAK
SQUINT
STAGE
STAIN
STALLED
STEPS
STILLED
STINGS
STITCHES
STREAM
STREAMING
STRIKES
STUNG
SUAVE
SUBTLE
SUNDAY
SUNLIGHT
SUNSET
SWALLOW
SWEAR
TAIL
TAME
TEAR
THEIRS
THEY'LL
THEY'VE
THINKS
THIRTY
THORNS
TIED
TIMBERS
TINY
TODDLE
TOUCHING
TOY
TRAP
TRAVELING
TRIM
TROUT
TRUST
TUB
UNSEEN
UNTOUCHABLE
UNTOUCHED
WAN
WARNING
WARY
WASHED
WAVER
WE'D
WEDDING
WEEK
WEIGHT
WEIGHTY
WEIRD
WE'RE

WHEEL
WINDING
WINTERING
WIRE
WISE
WITS
WORKING
WORKS
WORMY
WORN
WORSE
WRISTS
WROUGHT

-3-
ABSOLUTELY
ABSURD
ABYSS
ACCEPT
ACID
ACRES
ACTED
ACTORS
ADMIT
ADROIT
ALL'S
ALTERING
AMBER
AMBIGUOUS
AMBUSHED
AMID
AMOROUS
ANGELIC
ANGELS'
ANT
ANTELOPE
ANYBODY
APPALLING
ARC
ARGUMENTS
ARMOR
ARRIVAL
ARROGANT
ARTFUL
ASCENDS
ASKED
ASKS
ASSAULTS
ATLANTIC
ATTACHMENTS
ATTEND
AUNT
AVOID
BADLY
BAGS
BALANCE
BALLED
BALLOONS
BANDAGE
BARK
BARS
BASIN
BASKETS
BAT
BATS
BEACH
BEACHED
BEARD
BEATEN
BEAUTIES
BEAUTY'S
BECAME
BEDDED
BEDDING
BEE
BEETLES
BEGGARS
BEGUN
BELIEF
BELLIES

BIRTH
BITE
BITTEN
BLACKBERRIES
BLANCHED
BLAZE
BLEAK
BLED
BLESSING
BLINDED
BLINKING
BLOND
BLOOD-HEAT
BLOODIED
BLUEBLACK
BLUR
BLURS
BODILESS
BOLT
BORES
BORNE
BORROWED
BOTTLES
BOUND
BOYS
BRANCHES
BREAKS
BRICK
BRIEF
BRIGHTNESS
BRIM
BROTHER
BROWNS
BRUIT
BRUNT
BRUSH
BULB
BULLS'
BUREAU
BURNISHED
BURY
BUTTERFLIES
CABBAGE
CAKES
CALLS
CARE
CARS
CARVED
CASTLE
CASUAL
CATTLE
CELL
CELLOPHANE
CENTURIES
CEREMONY
CERTAIN
CHAMBER
CHANGED
CHOSE
CLAMBERING
CLAW
CLIMB
CLIMBS
CLOAK
CLOVER
COARSE
COGS
COIL
COLDNESS
COLLAPSE
COLLECT
COLORLESS
COMIC
COMPELLED
COMPLETE
COMPOSE
CONSOLE
CONTROL
COOKIES
COOKING
COPPER

CORKSCREW
CORNER
CORPSES
CORRECT
COSMIC
COTTAGE
COUNT
COUNTERFEIT
COUPLED
COURAGE
CRAB
CRADLE
CRAMPED
CREAKING
CREAM
CREATE
CREATION
CRICKETS
CROP
CROSS
CROSSED
CROSSING
CROW
CRYPTIC
CRYSTALS
CUPBOARD
CUPPED
CUPS
CUSHIONS
CUTTING
DANCES
DANGER
DARKENING
DARKLY
DAUGHTER
DAY'S
DAZZLED
DEATHS
DEATH'S
DECK
DECORUM
DEEPER
DEPART
DESCANT
DESPAIR
DESULTORY
DEVIL'S
DIES
DIFFICULT
DIGESTING
DILATE
DIM
DIMINISH
DIRT
DISCIPLINE
DISEASE
DISTANT
DISTRESS
DOGS
DOOMSDAY
DOORSTEP
DOORWAYS
DOZEN
DRAFTY
DRAGGED
DRANK
DRAWER
DRAWS
DREAMERS
DRENCH
DRESSES
DRINKING
DRIVING
DROPPING
DRYADS
DUEL
DULLED
DURABLE
DUSK
DYNASTY
ECHOING

-3- (CONT.)

EDEN	GERMANY	INTRACTABLE	MELONS	PHANTOM
ELBA	GESTURES	INVISIBLE	MENACE	PHEASANT
ELECTRIC	GLASSY	INVOLVED	MEND	PHOENIX
ELEGANT	GLIDING	ISSUE	MERCILESS	PHOTOGRAPH
ELSEWHERE	GLITTERS	JACKANAPES	METALS	PHOTOGRAPHS
EMERALD	GLOBES	JAR	MIDDLE	PIANO
EMPTIES	GLOWING	JAW	MILL	PICK
EMPTINESS	GLUT	JEALOUS	MINER	PIECE
ENDLESSLY	GOATS	JET	MINERALS	PIERCED
ENDS	GOATSUCKER	JEWELL	MINOR	PIETAS
ENGLISH	GOBLIN	JEWELLED	MIRACLES	PIGS
ENTERING	GOODLY	JOY	MIRACULOUS	PILLAR
ESCAPED	GOOSE	JUG	MISSED	PILLARS
ETERNAL	GORSE	KINDLED	MOBILE	PILLS
EVA	GRANDMOTHER	KNIT	MOCK	PIN
EVERYWHERE	GRAVITY'S	KNOCKED	MODEL	PITCHED
EVIDENTLY	GRAZING	KNOCKING	MONKEY	PLACES
EXCEPT	GREEK	KNOTTED	MOO	PLAYS
EXPECT	GRIMACE	KNOWING	MOONLIGHT	PLEASED
EXPOSES	GRINNING	KNOWLEDGE	MOTH	PLUCK
EXPRESSION	GRITS	KNOWN	MOTHERLY	PLUCKED
FABLES	GROWING	KNUCKLES	MOTHERS	PLUS
FACED	GUARD	LABOR	MOURNING	POKE
FACELESS	GUEST	LABORING	MOUTH-HOLE	POLAND
FACTORY	GUILT	LAID	MUCK	POLICEMAN
FAMILIAR	GULP	LAMPS	MULTIPLIED	POLITIC
FANTASY	GUNS	LAP	MURDEROUS	POND
FAREWELL	GUT	LATER	MUSE	PONDEROUS
FARMER	GUTTED	LAUGHED	MUSES	POSE
FARMS	HABIT	LAYS	MUSIC	POSITION
FASHIONABLE	HAIRY	LEAFY	MUZZLES	POSSIBLE
FATE	HALL	LEARN	NAILS	POST
FATHER'S	HALLS	LEASH	NAPOLEON	POT
FATTEN	HALTS	LEAVING	NATURE	POULTICE
FAUN	HAM	LEDGE	NAVEL	POURS
FEATURES	HARVEST	LEGENDARY	NEATLY	PRACTICE
FERN	HATS	LENS	NECKS	PRAYING
FIBER	HAUNT	LETHE	NEIGHBOR'S	PRETTY
FIFTY	HAVING	LETTING	NERVE	PRICKLING
FIGURE	HAVOC	LEVEL	NETS	PRINT
FILAMENT	HAZARDOUS	LICK	NEWSPRINT	PROCEEDS
FILE	HEALING	LIFTS	NIGHTLONG	PRODIGIOUS
FILLING	HEALS	LINTEL	NOONDAY	PROFANE
FILLS	HEALTH	LITHE	NOTE	PROPER
FINALLY	HEATHER	LITTERED	NOVEMBER	PROPERTY
FINISH	HEAVENS	LIVING	NUMBER	PULSES
FINISHED	HEAVEN'S	LIVINGROOM	OBSCURE	PUMPKIN
FISHES	HEDGES	LOCAL	OBSTINATE	QUIT
FISTED	HEIRLOOM	LOFTY	OCCURED	RACE
FISTS	HELLO	LONELINESS	O'CLOCK	RAINS
FLAP	HEROES	LORD	ODORS	RATTLES
FLATNESS	HID	LOVELY	OFTEN	RAVE
FLAWED	HIDES	LOVING	OIL	RAVELED
FLICK	HIGHER	LUCENT	ORCHARD	READ
FLOWN	HIT	LUCKY	ORDERED	REDDEN
FLUNG	HOLLOWS	LULLABY	ORDINARY	REDNESS
FLUSH	HOLOCAUST	LUNG	ORIGINAL	REED
FOAM	HOOD	LUNGS	OUTLANDISH	REFLECTS
FOOTSOLES	HOOKED	LYING	OVAL	RESEMBLE
FORCE	HORNY	MACKEREL	OWNER	RHODODENDRON
FORGETFUL	HOTEL	MAGENTA	P	RIBS
FORGETFULNESS	HUGGING	MAIDS	PAGE	RIDDLE
FORMAL	HUMOR	MAIL	PAIN	RIDGEPOLE
FORWARD	HURRICANE	MALICE	PAINTS	RINGING
FRACTURED	HURRY	MAP	PAIR	RIPE
FRAMED	HYMNS	MAR	PALES	RIPEN
FRINGE	ICEBOX	MARKS	PALMS	RIVAL
FRUITS	IDENTICAL	MARRIAGE	PANE	ROBES
FUGUE	IDENTITY	MARRIED	PANTS	ROLLS
FUNERAL	IMMENSE	MARROW	PARDON	ROMAN
FUTURE'S	INCANDESCENT	MARY'S	PASSAGE	ROOST
GALLOP	INCENSE	MASKED	PASSES	ROUSSEAU
GAME	INCESSANT	MASKS	PASSING	ROW
GAP	INDELIBLE	MATADOR	PEACEFUL	RUBY
GAPE	INDIFFERENCE	MATCH	PEARLS	RULE
GAS	INJURE	MATTER	PEASANTS	RUSSIA
GAUDY	INNER	MAUSOLEUM	PEBBLES	SAINTS
GAUZE	INNUMERABLE	MAZE	PEEL	SAINTS'
GENUINE	INSTINCT	MEADOW	PENNY	SATISFIED
GERANIUM	INTACT	MEDIUM	PERFECTED	SCALES
	INTERIOR	MEEK	PERSPECTIVE	SCARCELY

601

-2- (CONT.)
BURDENED
BUREAUS
BURIED
BURROWS
BUSY
BUTCHER
BUTCHER'S
BUTTON
BUYING
BUZZED
CABBAGE-ROSES
CABBAGES
CACKLES
CADAVER
CAGES
CAKE
CALLING
CANADA
CANDID
CANDOR
CANNON
CAPER
CAPSULE
CARCASS
CARD
CARDBOARD
CAREER
CAREFUL
CAREFULLY
CARGO
CARP
CART
CASES
CATACOMBS
CATALPA
CAT-TAILS
CAULDRON
CAUSE
CAUSTIC
CAVES
CEASE
CELEBRATE
CELLAR
CEMENT
CERTAINLY
CESSATION
CHAIN
CHANCE
CHANCES
CHANGING
CHAPEL
CHAR
CHART
CHEEK
CHEERFUL
CHEESECLOTH
CHERRY
CHESS
CHICKEN
CHICKENS
CHILDHOOD
CHILLY
CHIMNEY
CHISEL
CHITTERING
CHOICE
CHOIR
CHRISTENING
CHRISTMAS
CHROMIUM
CHRYSANTHEMUMS
CHUCK
CHUCKLES
CHURCHYARD
CIGARETTES
CINDERS
CLAIM
CLAIMS
CLAIRVOYANT
CLAM-DIGGERS

CLASSIC
CLASSICAL
CLEARLY
CLEAVES
CLEFT
CLEOPATRA
CLOSED
CLOSET
CLOUD-CUCKOO
CLUTCHING
COCKS
COD
COFFINED
COIN
COINS
COLONNADES
COLOSSAL
COLOSSUS
COLUMN
COMB
COMBS
COMFORT
COMFORTABLE
COMMANDING
COMPARED
COMPARISON
COMPELS
COMPLAINT
COMPLEXION
CON
CONCEAL
CONCEPTIONS
CONCH
CONDEMNED
CONFETTI
CONFOUNDED
CONFRONTS
CONGEALS
CONJURED
CONNECTICUT
CONSECRATE
CONSOLING
CONSTANT
CONSTRUE
CONTAIN
CONTENT
CONTRADICT
CONVERGE
CONVERSATION
CONVINCE
COOLLY
COPY
CORD
CORK
CORN
CORNFLOWERS
CORNUCOPIA
CORROSIVE
COTS
COTTON
COUCHED
COUNTED
COUPLES
COURIERS
CRABBED
CRACKLE
CRACKLING
CRADLES
CRAP
CRATERS
CRAVES
CREAK
CREAMING
CREEP
CREEPING
CRESTS
CREVICE
CRIMP
CRINGE
CRIPPLES
CRISP

CRITICS
CROSSES
CROTCH
CROWNING
CRUMB
CRUSH
CRUTCH
CRUX
CRYSTALLIZED
CUFFS
CUMBROUS
CUPPING
CURIOUS
CURLED
CURSES
CURVE
CUSTOM
CUT-PAPER
DAFT
DAIRY
DAISY
DAMNED
DANCED
DAPHNE
DARKROOM
DARK'S
DARTS
DAYLONG
DAY-MOON
DAZZLING
DECLINE
DECOR
DEER
DEFINE
DEFORMITY
DEFY
DELIVERED
DEMANDING
DEMANDS
DEN
DEPARTURES
DERRICKS
DESCEND
DESCENDS
DESIGN
DESIGNED
DESIRE
DESK
DESTINATION
DESTINY
DESTRUCTION
DEVILISH
DIAGRAM
DIET
DIFFERENT
DIMENSION
DIMINISHED
DIN
DIP
DIRECTION
DIRECTIONS
DISAPPEAR
DISASTER
DISCOVERED
DISCRETION
DISGUISES
DISH
DISMEMBERED
DISPLACED
DISRUPT
DISSATISFACTION
DISSOLVING
DISTRACTEDLY
DISTRACTION
DIVE
DIVINITY
DOCTORS
DOLLS
DOME
DONKEY
DOOMSTRUCK

DOORSILL
DOPED
DOUBT
DOVELIKE
DOVES
DOZE
DRAGS
DRAINING
DRAINS
DRAWING
DREAD
DREAMS'
DREDGE
DREGS
DRENCHED
DRIED
DRINKS
DRIPS
DROVE
DROWNS
DROWSED
DRUGGED
DRUMMED
DRUMMING
DUCHESS
DUG
DUNGAREES
DWARFED
DWINDLE
DWINDLES
EARLIER
EARTHEN
EARTHENWARE
EASING
EASTER
EBON
ECLIPSED
ECLIPSING
EDDIES
EDEN'S
EDIBLE
EELS
EFFIGY
EGGSHELLS
EGO
EGYPTIAN
ELABORATE
ELASTICS
ELEVATOR-GIRL
ELBOWS
ELEPHANT
ELUSIVE
EMBALMED
EMPTIED
ENCOUNTER
ENDED
ENDING
ENDLESS
ENDOW
ENDURE
ENDURED
ENEMY
ENFOLDS
ENGLAND
ENGRAVED
ENGROSSED
ENTERED
ENVY
EPIC
EPITAPH
ERASED
ETERNALLY
ETERNITY
EUROPE'S
EVAPORATE
EVENT
EVER-GREEN
EVERLASTING
EXACT
EXACTING
EXCEPTION

EXCESSIVE
EXCITED
EXHIBITS
EXPLODED
EXPORT
EXPRESSIONLESS
EXTEND
EXTRA
EYEFUL
EYEHOLE
EYEING
EYELESS
EYELID
EYE'S
FABLED
FABRICATION
FACET
FACING
FADED
FAINT
FAITHFUL
FALCON
FALSE
FAME
FANCY
FARE
FARTHER
FAST-FEATHERED
FATHERLESS
FATHOMED
FATTENS
FEAST
FEATHERED
FEATURELESS
FEELING
FEELS
FELLOWS
FEMININE
FERRYING
FESTERING
FIBS
FICTIONS
FIDDLE
FIENDISH
FIERY
FIG
FIGS
FIGURES
FILAMENTS
FILING
FILLED
FIN
FINEST
FINGERING
FINGERTIPS
FINICAL
FINS
FIR
FIRED
FIRE'S
FIREWORK
FISHPOND
FIZZ
FLAKE
FLAKES
FLAMING
FLANKS
FLAPS
FLATS
FLATTENED
FLAYS
FLECK
FLEES
FLICKERS
FLIMSY
FLING
FLINGS
FLOCKED
FLOCKS
FLOODS
FLOUNDER

FLOUR
FLOURISH
FLOWERING
FLOWS
FLUTES
FLUTINGS
FOIST
FOLDING
FOLDS
FOLIAGE
FOOLED
FOOLISH
FOOTING
FOOTSTEPS
FOREFINGER
FORSAKE
FORTUNE
FOSSIL
FOUL
FOUNDERED
FOURTH
FRACTURE
FRAGMENTS
FRENCH
FREQUENTLY
FRESH
FRIENDS
FRIEZE
FRONTIER
FROSTY
FROZE
FUCHSIA
FUNNY
FURROW
FURROWS
FURS
FUSING
FUSTY
GABRIEL
GALLANT
GALLOPING
GARB
GARDENIAS
GARGANTUAN
GARLANDED
GARNET
GATHER
GAUNT
GAUNTLETS
GELDED
GENERAL
GENERATIONS
GETS
GHOST'S
GIANTS
GIDDY
GIFTS
GILDS
GIN
GIZZARD
GLAD
GLASSED
GLASSES
GLAZES
GLIMPSE
GLINTS
GLITTERED
GLITTERY
GLOVED
GLOWERING
GLUE
GLUED
GOAL
GOAT
GOBLINS
GODAWFUL
GODDESS
GODHOOD
GODLY
GODMOTHER

GODMOTHERS
GODPIE
GOD-PIE
GOLDENROD
GOLDFISH
GOODWILL
GOSSIPS
GOTHIC
GOVERN
GOWN
GOWNS
GRAB
GRAIL
GRAINED
GRANT
GRAPES
GRATE
GRATEFUL
GRATIFIED
GRAVEL
GREASE
GREED
GRID
GRIEFS
GRIEVANCES
GRIM
GRIMLY
GROAN
GROOM
GROOVE
GROSSNESS
GROWER
GROWNUPS
GRUBS
GRUFF
GRUNT
GUARDING
GUILTY
GULLIVER
GUTTURALS
HACK
HAGS
HALF-HINTS
HALFWAY
HALO
HALOES
HANDKERCHIEF
HANDLING
HAND'S
HAPPENING
HARDSHIP
HATCH
HATING
HAUNCHES
HAZARD
HEADLONG
HEADSTONE
HEADSTONES
HEARSE
HEAVED
HEAVES
HEAVING
HEDGED
HEDGEHOG
HEDGEROWS
HEEL
HEFTING
HEIGHTS
HELL'S
HELPLESS
HEN
HENCE
HERMIT
HIDDEN
HIDING
HIEROGLYPHS
HILLOCKS
HINGES
HISTORY'S
HIVED
HIVES

HOARD
HOLIDAY
HOLLY
HOLLYWOOD
HOMECOMING
HOMES
HOMEWARD
HONES
HONESTLY
HOODS
HORN
HORRORS
HORSEHAIR
HOTHOUSE
HOURLY
HOUSEDRESS
HOVE
HOWLING
HOW'S
HUMBLE
HUMBLY
HUMP
HUNCHES
HUNGER
HUNGERED
HURL
HUSBANDS
HUSTLED
HUSTLES
ICECAKES
ICES
IDOLS
ILLS
IMAGINED
IMAGINING
IMMACULATE
IMMORTALITY
IMPECCABLE
IMPERFECTIONS
IMPORTUNATE
IMPOSE
IMPOTENT
IMPROMPTU
INACCESSIBLE
INCAPABLE
INCHED
INCREASE
INDESTRUCTIBLE
INDETERMINATE
INDEX
INDIAN
INDIFFERENT
INDOLENCE
INDOORS
INERT
INFAMOUS
INFINITELY
INFLAME
INHABITED
INHERIT
INLAND
INNARDS
INSIDE
INSOLENT
INSTRUMENT
INSULTS
INTENT
INTERVAL
INTOLERABLE
INVADE
INVETERATE
INVIOLATE
INVISIBLES
IRELAND
IRIS
ISOLATE
ITCH
IVY
JACKET
JACKETS
JADE

JAILER
JAM
JANGLING
JAPANESE
JARGON
JARS
JAWS
JELLYFISH
JEWELS
JILTED
JOG
JOINS
JOINT
JOKE
JOURNEY
JUICES
JULY
JUMP
JUMPED
JUNKED
KICKING
KIN
KINDLING
KINDLY
KING'S
KITTENS
KNEELING
KNEELS
KNELLED
KNIGHT
KNIGHTS
KNITTING
KNOB
KNOBBY
KNOCKS
LABOR'S
LABURNUM
LABYRINTH
LACED
LADDER
LADDERS
LADIES'
LAMBS
LAME
LAMP-HEADED
LANDOWNERS
LANE
LANGUAGE
LANGUOR
LAPSING
LAUD
LAUNDER
LAWN
LEADEN
LEADS
LEAKING
LEANED
LEANING
LEARNING
LEATHER
LEAVES'
LEAVETAKING
LEOPARD
LESSON
LETS
LETTUCE
LEVER
LIAR
LICHENS
LIFE'S
LIGHT'S
LILY
LIMBER
LIMBO
LIMP
LIMPID
LIONESS
LIPSTICK
LISTENED
LISTENING
LIVELIER

LOAF
LOAM
LOAVES
LOCK
LODGE
LOOM
LOOPING
LOPPED
LOSS
LOUDSPEAKER
LOUNGED
LOVELESS
LOZENGES
LUGUBRIOUS
LULLED
LUMBERING
LUMP
LUMPS
LURED
LURID
LURKS
LUSTER
LYLE
LYONNESSE
LYRIC
MACHINES
MADNESS
MAESTRO
MAGI
MAGICIAN'S
MAGNOLIA
MAHOGANY
MALIGNITY
MAMMOTH
MANES
MANGLED
MANNER
MANNERS
MANOR
MANUSCRIPT
MARKET
MARKETPLACE
MARROWY
MARVELOUS
MASSES
MASTER
MATCHED
MATHEMATICAL
MATTRESS
MAUDLIN
MEAD
MEAGER
MEASURE
MEETING
MEETS
MEMORIES
MEN'S
MERCURY
MERCY
MERMAID
MESS
MESSAGE
MET
METAPHOR
METAPHORS
METROPOLIS
MICA
MIDDEN
MIGRAINE
MILES
MILKS
MILKWEED
MILLIONAIRE
MIND'S
MINER'S
MIRRORED
MIRRORY
MISTRESS
MODES
MOIST
MOLDS

MOLE
MOMENT
MONARCH
MONEY'S
MONOXIDE
MONTHS
MONUMENT
MOOR-TOP
MORGUE
MORNINGS
MORPHIA
MOTION
MOTTLED
MOUNT
MOUNTS
MOURN
MOUTHPIECE
MOUTH'S
MOVIE
MULTIPLIES
MULTIPLY
MUNDANE
MUNICH
MUSHROOMS
MUSK
MYSTICAL
NAG
NAIL
NAP
NAPPING
NARROWED
NATIVE
NATURE'S
NAUSEOUS
NECESSARY
NEEDLE
NEEDLING
NEIGHBOR
NEIGHBORS
NEON
NET-MENDERS
NETTLE
NETTLES
NEUTRAL
NEWTS
NICE
NICELY
NICK
NIGHTMARE
NIKE
NOBLE
NODDED
NOEL
NOISELESS
NONCHALANCE
NORMAL
NORTHERN
NOTION
NOURISHES
NUBS
NUMERALS
NYMPHS
OATH
OBEYING
OBJECT
OBSOLETE
OCHREOUS
OCTOBER
OEDIPUS
OFFER
O-MOUTH
ONION
OOZING
OPAQUE
ORACLES
ORCHID
ORDERING
ORDERS
ORIENTAL
ORIGIN

ORPHAN
OTHER'S
OTHERWISE
OTHERWORLD
OUIJA
OUTER
OUTERMOST
OUTLAWS
OUTRAGE
OUTRAGEOUS
OUTRIDERS
OVALS
OXBOW
OYSTER
OYSTERS
PACE
PACT
PAIL
PALELY
PALMED
PALTRY
PANIC
PANZER-MAN
PARADISE
PARADOX
PARAGON
PARAKEETS
PARE
PARED
PARLOR
PARTICLES
PARTY
PASSENGERS
PASTEL
PASTURES
PATCHED
PATHOLOGICAL
PATIENCE
PATIENT
PATINAS
PATRONIZED
PAVING
PAW
PEACEFULNESS
PEACH
PEACOCKS
PEAK
PEARS
PEASANT
PECULIAR
PEELED
PEELING
PEEPHOLE
PEERS
PEGS
PENALTY
PERCY
PERFUMED
PERISHABLE
PERSEUS
PERSIST
PERSONAGE
PERSONAL
PERSPECTIVES
PETALED
PETTY
PEWTER
PHONE
PIER
PIERCE
PIGEON
PILGRIM
PILGRIMS
PINNACLES
PINNED
PINS
PIPER
PISTONS
PIT
PITCHER
PITHLESS

PITY
PIVOT
PLAIN
PLANETARY
PLANK
PLAYED
PLAYERS
PLEASE
PLENITUDE
PLIANT
PLOT
PLUCKS
PLUM
PLUNGES
POCKET
POCKETBOOK
PODS
POEM
POEMS
POINTS
POISON
POLEMIC
POLICE
POLITE
POLLEN
POMPONS
POMPOUS
PONDS
POODLES
PORCELAIN
PORT
POSSESSION
POUR
POURING
POVERTY
POWDERS
PRACTICAL
PRAGMATIC
PRAISE
PRECIOUS
PREFER
PRESERVE
PRETENDING
PRICE
PRICKLE
PRICKLES
PRIDE'S
PRIM
PRIME
PRISON
PROFIT
PROMISING
PRONE
PROOF
PROP
PROPERLY
PROPHET
PROPHETS
PROPPED
PROSE
PROSPECT
PROSPECTS
PROTECTION
PROTESTING
PROVES
PRY
PUMPKINS
PUMPS
PUNY
PUPILS
PUPPET
PURCHASE
PURITAN
PURPLED
PURSE
PURSES
QUAINTLY
QUEENS
QUEEN'S
QUICKSILVER
QUIRK

RABBIT
RACKED
RACKETING
RAFTERS
RAGE
RAID
RAISE
RAISED
RAM
RAN
RANDOM
RAT
RAVAGED
RAVEL
RAVING
RAY
RAYS
REACH
REACHES
READING
REALIZED
REASSURED
RECLAIM
RECTOR
REDDENS
REEDY
REFLECTED
REFLECTING
REFUSING
REINS
RELATION
RELATIONSHIP
RELATIVE
RELIGION
REMAIN
REMEDY
REMEMBERS
RENDING
RENTED
REPAIR
RESEMBLES
RESOLVED
RESORT
RESTLESS
RESURRECT
RETCH
RETURNING
REVELED
RIBBON
RICHNESS
RIDDLED
RIFT
RIGMAROLE
RIGOR
RINGDOVES
RIPPED
RIPPLES
RITUAL
RIVET
ROADS
ROCKED
ROCKING
ROCKY
ROD
RODE
ROOFS
ROOFTOPS
ROPE
ROTS
ROUNDS
ROUT
ROUTE
ROUTINE
ROWED
RUBBISH
RUDDY
RUDE
RUIN
RUINS
RULED
RUMORS

RUST
RUSTED
RUST-RED
RUSTY
RUTTED
SACRIFICE
SADLY
SAKE
SAMPLERS
SANDS
SANG
SAUNTERS
SAVE
SAVED
SAVOR
SCALDED
SCALDING
SCALE
SCALLOPS
SCAPEGOAT
SCARVES
SCENES
SCENTS
SCHOOL
SCHOONER
SCORCH
SCORCHING
SCOURS
SCRATCH
SCRATCHING
SCREAM
SCREAMING
SCREEN
SCREENS
SCRUPLE
SCRUPULOUS
SCUTTLE
SEA-COLD
SEAFARER
SEAL
SEALED
SEAMED
SEA-SALT
SEASHELL
SECRETS
SEEDS
SEEKS
SEEP
SEIZE
SELVES
SEPARATED
SERIES
SERIOUS
SETS
SHABBY
SHACKLED
SHADED
SHADES
SHAKE
SHAM
SHANKS
SHAPING
SHARDS
SHARP
SHATTERING
SHAWLS
SHED
SHE'D
SHH
SHIELD
SHIFT
SHIFTING
SHIMMERING
SHINY
SHIPWRECKED
SHIRLEY
SHOALS
SHOCKED
SHOE
SHOOT
SHOULDERS

SHOULDN'T
SHOVE
SHOWED
SHOWN
SHRANK
SHREDDED
SHRIVELING
SHROUD
SHROUDED
SHROUDS
SHUTTERS
SHYLY
SIBILANT
SIDEWAYS
SIEGE
SIGH
SIGNAL
SIGNS
SILL
SILVERED
SIMPLIFIED
SIPPING
SIRENS
SISTER'S
SIXTY
SKEIN
SKELETONS
SKINS
SLANT
SLAY
SLEEPS
SLEIGHT-OF-HAND
SLIGHTLY
SLIT
SLOT
SLOTS
SLOVEN
SLUGGISH
SLUT
SLUTTISH
SMACK
SMART
SMELLING
SMILED
SMILINGLY
SMITHEREENS
SMOCK
SMOG
SMOKED
SMOKING
SNARES
SNARLED
SNOWDROP
SNOWFIELD
SNOWS
SNUFFS
SNUG
SOAP
SOCKET
SOD
SODDEN
SOFTEN
SOIL
SOLE
SOLIDER
SOMEBODY
SOMERSET
SOMETHING'S
SOMETIMES
SOMNOLENCE
SOONER
SORROWS
SORTS
SOUTHWARD
SPAN
SPANISH
SPARKS
SPARROW
SPEAKING
SPEED

SPENT
SPHERE
SPIKES
SPILL
SPIN
SPINACH
SPINDLING
SPINDRIFT
SPINE
SPINNING
SPINS
SPIRALS
SPITEFULLY
SPLAYED
SPLINTERED
SPOKES
SPOOL
SPOTS
SPRINGING
SPRINGS
SPUN
SPUR
SQUAB
SQUATTING
SQUELCHING
SQUID
STAGGER
STAINED
STAINS
STAKED
STALKED
STALLING
STALLS
STAMP
STAMPED
STAMPEDE
STARCHED
STARLESS
STARTED
STARTING
STARTLED
STARVED
STASIS
STEADILY
STEALER
STEAMED
STEAMING
STEELY
STEEP
STEEPLED
STENCH
STEPPING
STIFFENED
STIFFENS
STILE
STINGING
STINK
STINT
STIRS
STOCKINGS
STOOP
STOUT
STRAWBERRIES
STRETCHES
STRETCHING
STREW
STRICKEN
STRIP
STRIPED
STRIPS
STROKE
STRUT
STUBBORNLY
STUCCO
STUDDED
STUDENTS
STUMBLE
STUNNED
SUBJECTS
SUBSTANCE
SUEDE

SUFFERING
SUICIDAL
SUMMER'S
SUMMON
SUNDAY'S
SUNNING
SUPPER
SUPPORTS
SUPPOSE
SUPPOSED
SURF
SURFACES
SURGED
SURGEONS
SWABBED
SWALLOWED
SWALLOWS
SWAM
SWEATS
SWELTER
SWIFTS
SWIG
SWIMS
SWING
SWOLLEN
SWUNG
SYLLABLE
SYSTEM
TABLET
TACKED
TAG
TALE
TALENT
TALKED
TALKS
TALLOW
TALONED
TANGLE
TAPESTRIES
TAR
TARN
TAROC
TART
TASTED
TASTING
TATE
TAUNT
TAUNTING
TAUNTS
TAUT
TAWDRY
TEARING
TELEPHONE
TELLING
TEMPO
TENDER
TENDERLY
TENDING
TENDRILS
TENTACLE
TENTS
TERRIFIED
TERRIFY
THEY'D
THIRST
THISTLE
THOR
THRILL
THRIVES
THROW
THROWN
TICKETS
TIDE'S
TILT
TIMID
TINDER
TINFOIL
TINKER
TINSEL
TIPPING
TIRE

TIRED
TISSUE
TOAD-STONE
TOADSTOOLS
TOAST
TOLERABLE
TOLERATE
TONNAGE
TOOTH
TOPS
TORN
TORSO
TORTURE
TOUCH-AND-GO
TOUCHED
TOUR
TRAGEDIES
TRAGEDY
TRAGIC
TRAILING
TRAINED
TRANCE
TRANSFIXED
TRANSPARENT
TRAPPED
TRAVELED
TREAD
TREMBLING
TRIAL
TRICKED
TRICKLES
TRICKS
TRILLS
TRINKETS
TRIP
TROLLEY
TROPHIES
TRUANT
TRUMPETS
TRUNDLE
TRUNDLING
TUCK
TUGGING
TUMULT
TURKEY
TUSKS
TWICE
TWIGGED
TWIGS
TWILIGHT
TWISTING
TWITCH
TWITTERING
TWO-LEGGED
TYROL
UMBILICUS
UNASKED
UNAWARE
UNBORN
UNCLES
UNDERGROUND
UNDID
UNDULANT
UNHINGED
UNICORNS
UNIQUE
UNLOAD
UNREAL
UNROLLED
UNSTRUNG
UPHOLSTERY
UPRIGHT
UPROOT
UPSET
USELESS
UTTER
VACANT
VACATION
VACUOUS
VAMPIRE
VANISHES

VARIETY
VARIOUS
VEILING
VENGEANCE
VENOMOUS
VENTRILOQUY
VERMILIONS
VERNACULAR
VETERAN
VICTIM
VICTORIAN
VIENNA
VIGIL
VILLANELLE
VINE
VIOLENT
VIOLET
VIRGINAL
VISIONARY
VISITATIONS
VISITED
VOID
VOLCANOES
VOLT
VOWELS
VOWS
VULGAR
WAG
WAKEFUL
WAKEN
WALKER
WALKERS
WANES
WARDEN
WARMED
WARMING
WARP
WASHING
WASP
WASTEBASKET
WATCHFUL
WATERCOLOR
WATERLOO
WAVES'
WAYLAYS
WEAK
WEATHERS
WEAVE
WEDDING-CAKE
WEDDINGS
WEDGE
WEEPING
WELCOME
WELL-BRED
WELTER
WE'VE
WHALE
WHEELED
WHEREBY
WHIM
WHINE
WHIPCRACK
WHIRLING
WHISK
WHISPER
WHITE-HAIRED
WHITER
WHO'D
WHO'S
WICK
WIG
WILLOWS
WILLS
WINCE
WINCING
WIND'S
WINNOWING
WINTER'S
WISER
WITCHES
WITCH'S

-2- (CONT.)	ACROBATICS	ALPHABETS	APT	ATTRACTED
WITHDRAWS	ACROPOLIS	ALPS	AQUARIUM	ATTRACTING
WITHERING	ACTIONS	ALTARS	AQUATIC	AUBADE
WITHSTOOD	ACTIVE	ALTERED	AQUEDUCTS	AUCTION
WOLF	A D	ALTERNATELY	ARABESQUES	AUDIENCE
WOMAN'S	ADAZZLE	ALTOGETHER	ARABIC	AUNTS
WOODEN	ADDING	ALUMINUM	ARBOR	AUREATE
WOODSMOKE	ADDRESSING	AMAZINGLY	ARCADIAN	AUREOLED
WORDLESS	ADHERE	AMBIVALENCE	ARCHAEOLOGICAL	AUSCHWITZ
WORMED	ADHERING	AMBLE	ARCHAEOLOGIST	AUSTRALIA
WOUNDS	ADIRONDACKS	AMBROSIAL	ARCHED	AUSTRALIAN
WRACK	ADJECTIVE	AMBULANCE	ARCHETYPES	AUTHOR
WRAP	ADJECTIVES	AMERICANA	ARDOR	AUTOCRATIC
WREATHED	ADMIRALS	AMETHYST	ARGUED	AVENGE
WRECK	ADMIRERS	AMISS	ARGUMENT	AVENUE
WRENCH	ADMIRER'S	AMNESIA	ARIEL	AVERSE
WRESTLE	ADMIRING	AMNESIAC	ARISING	AWAITED
WRINKLE	ADMONITIONS	AMNESIAS	ARMADILLO	AWAITING
WRINKLES	ADMONITORY	AMOEBAS	ARMCHAIR	AWE
WRIST	ADOLESCENCE	AMPERSANDS	ARMED	AWFULLY
WRITES	ADORED	AMPUTATIONS	ARMING	AWOKE
WRITHING	ADORES	ANACONDA	ARMORY	A-W-W
WRONG	ADRIFT	ANALYSE	ARMPIT	AXE
YORK	ADULTERERS	ANANSI	ARRANGED	AXE-CRACK
YOWL	ADULTERIES	ANARCHY	ARROW-BACKS	AXED
ZEPPELIN	ADVANCE	ANATOMY	ARROWY	AXES
ZONE	ADVANCES	ANCESTRESS	ARSENIC	AXLE
	ADVANTAGES	ANEMIC	ARTICULATING	BAAS
-1-	ADVICE	ANEMONE	ARTILLERY	BABOON
ABASES	AERIALIST	ANESTHETIZED	ART'S	BABUSHKA
ABATED	AFAR	ANGELDOM	ARTWORK	BABY-HEADED
ABC	AFFABLE	ANGEL-FOOD	ARYAN	BABYLON'S
ABDUCTING	AFFECTS	ANGEL-SHAPE	ASBESTOS	BABYSITTERS
ABEYANCE	AFFIRMING	ANIMALCULES	ASCEND	BACHELOR
ABLAZE	AFFLICTED	ANIMOSITY	ASCENDED	BACK-ALLEY
ABLE	AFFLUENCE	ANKLE	ASHAMED	BACKBONE
ABLUTION	AFLAME	ANNIHILATE	ASHES	BACKCLOTH
ABORTED	AFLOAT	ANNIHILATES	ASH-HEAP	BACKDOOR'S
ABORTIONS	AFTERBIRTH	ANNIHILATING	ASININITY	BACKDROP
ABORTS	AFTER-HELL	ANNIHILATION	ASLANT	BACKSIDE
ABRADED	AFTERMATH	ANNIHILATIONS	ASLEEP	BACKTALKS
ABRADING	AFTERTHOUGHT	ANNOUNCER'S	ASP	BACKTRACK
ABSENCES	AGAWP	ANNOUNCES	ASPARAGUS	BACKTRACKING
ABSENT	AGED	ANNOUNCING	ASPIC	BADGE
ABSENTLY	AGENT	ANNUNCIATION	ASSAIL	BAFFLE
ABSENT-MINDED	AGITATE	ANOINTS	ASSAILED	BAFFLES
ABSINTHE	AGITATES	ANOTHER'S	ASSAILING	BAGPIPES
ABSORBANT	AGITATION	ANTENNA	ASSASSINS	BAILIWICK
ABSTAIN	AGOG	ANTEROOM	ASSEMBLE	BAKED
ABSTRACT	AGONIES	ANTHERS	ASSEMBLY-LINE	BAKING
ABSTRACTIONS	AGONIZED	ANTICIPATES	ASSERT	BALANCED
ABSTRACTS	AGREE	ANTIGONE	ASSIDUOUS	BALANCES
ACADEMIES	AGUEY	ANTIMACASSARS	ASSISTANTS	BALDERDASH
ACANTHINE	AHAB	ANTS'	ASSOCIATIONS	BALD-EYED
ACANTHUS	AHISS	ANT-SIZE	ASSORTED	BALD-FACED
ACCEPTABLE	AHS	ANXIOUSNESS	ASSUME	BALD-HEAD
ACCEPTING	AIMS	ANYHOW	ASTERISKS	BALDING
ACCIDENTAL	AIRBUBBLES	ANYWAY	ASTEROIDS	BALUSTRADE
ACCOMMODATES	AIRING	ANYWHERE	ASTONISHED	BAMBOO
ACCOMPANIED	AIR-MOTES	A-P-E-S	ASTOUNDINGLY	BAN
ACCOMPLISH	AIRPORT	APHRODISIAC	ASTOUNDS	BANANA
ACCOMPLISHED	AISLES	APOLLOS	ASTRAY	BANDAGED
ACCOMPLISHMENT	AJAR	APOTHECARY	ASTRIDE	BANDED
ACCORD	ALACRITY	APPALLED	ASTROLOGER	BANDS
ACCOUNTING	ALARMCLOCK	APPALLS	ASTRONOMIC	BANDY-LEG
ACCOUNTS	ALAS	APPARENTLY	ATHLETIC	BANKED
ACCUMULATED	ALBATROSS	APPEARANCE	ATONE	BANKER
ACCURACY	ALCHEMY	APPEARED	ATROCIOUS	BANKING
ACCURATE	ALGEBRA	APPEARS	ATROCITIES	BANNER
ACCURST	ALIAS	APPENDAGES	AT'S	BANNERS
ACETYLENE	ALICE	APPLAUSE	ATTACH	BANQUET
ACH	ALIGHTING	APPLE-TREE	ATTACHED	BAPTIZED
ACHES	ALLAY	APPLICANT	ATTACKED	BAR
ACHIEVE	ALLEYS	APPREHENDING	ATTACKS	BARBECUE
ACHIEVED	ALL-MOUTH	APPREHENSIONS	ATTENDANT	BARBS
ACHOO	ALLOW	APPROACH	ATTENDED	BARB-WIRED
ACIDS	ALMANAC	APPROACHED	ATTENDING	BARGES
ACORN-STOMACHED	ALONGSIDE	APPROACHES	ATTENTIONS	BARGE-TAR
ACQUIRE	ALPENSTOCK	APPROACHING	ATTIRE	BARITONE
ACRE	ALPHABET	APPROVING	ATTITUDE	BARK'S
ACROBAT	ALPHABETICAL	APPURTENANCES	ATTRACT	BARN

-1- (CONT.)
BARNACLED
BARNACLE-PATED
BARNACLES
BAROMETER
BARON
BARONIAL
BAROQUE
BARRED
BARRETTE
BARRICADE
BARTER
BASALT
BASEMENTS
BASILISK-BLINK
BASILISK-LOOK
BASINS
BASKETWORK
BASKIN
BASKING
BASTARD'S
BATH
BATHER
BATHTUB
BATMAN
BAT-SHAPES
BATTALIONS
BATTENED
BATTER
BATTERED
BATTLEFIELD
BATTLEMENT
BATTLES
BATTLE-SCENE
BATTLESHIPS
BATTLE-SHOUTS
BAY'S
BAY-TREE
BEACHES
BEADED
BEANFIELD
BEANSTALK
BEANSTALKS
BEARDED
BEARERS
BEAR-FURRED
BEARING
BEASTS
BEATINGS
BEATS
BECKON
BECKONER
BEDFELLOWS
BEDLAM
BEDRAGGLED
BEDROCK
BEDSPREAD
BEEKEEPER'S
BEELZEBUB
BEER
BEE'S
BEE-SELLER
BEETHOVEN
BEETROOT
BEGGING
BEGONIA
BEGRUDGE
BEGS
BEGUILE
BEIGE
BELCHED
BELGE
BELLED
BELLING
BELL-JAR
BELLOW
BELLOWED
BELLRINGERS
BELL-TONGUED
BELLYACHE
BELLY-BEDDED

BELLY-SCALE
BELSEN
BELT
BENCHES
BENEFACTRESS
BENIDORM
BENIGN
BENT-BACKED
BEQUEATHS
BERCK-PLAGE
BEREFT
BERG
BERLIN
BERRY
BERYL
BESET
BESTOWING
BET
BETRAY
BEWITCHED
BIBLE
BICKER
BIDS
BIER
BIGNESS
BIKINIS
BILLHOOK
BILLS
BINDINGS
BINGE
BINGO
BIRD-BEAKED
BIRD-EATING
BIRD-FEET
BIRD-FOOT
BIRDMILK
BIRD-QUICK
BIRD-RACKETING
BIRDS'
BIRTH-CRY
BIRTH-DROWSE
BIRTHMARKS
BIRTHSPOT
BISCUITS
BITCHERY
BITCHES
BITTERNESS
BITTERS
BLACKBERRYING
BLACKBIRDS
BLACKEN
BLACKENS
BLACKEST
BLACK-LEAVED
BLACKLY
BLACKOUT
BLACK-SHARDED
BLACKSHORT
BLACKTHORN
BLADE
BLAKE'S
BLAMED
BLAMELESS
BLANCHING
BLAND-MANNERED
BLANK-BRAINED
BLANK-FACED
BLANKLY
BLASTS
BLAZON
BLAZONED
BLEACH
BLEARED
BLEB
BLENCHED
BLESS
BLESSED
BLIGHT
BLIGHTED
BLIMP
BLINDERED

BLINDFOLD
BLINDING
BLINDS
BLINK
BLINKS
BLISS
BLISTER
BLITHE
BLITZEN
BLITZKRIEG
BLOAT
BLOATS
BLOOD-BERRIED
BLOOD-BLACK
BLOOD-CAUL
BLOOD-DROP
BLOOD-DROPS
BLOOD-FLUSH
BLOOD-HOT
BLOODHOUNDS
BLOOD-LOVING
BLOOD'S
BLOOD-SOAKED
BLOOD-SPOOR
BLOODSPOT
BLOOMED
BLOT
BLOTS
BLOTTER
BLOWING
BLOWSY
BLOWZE
BLOWZY
BLUBBERY
BLUEBEARD
BLUEBIRDS
BLUE-BLOODED
BLUE-CAPED
BLUE-GREEN
BLUENESS
BLUEST
BLUNDER
BLUNTED
BLUNTLY
BLURT
BOA
BOAR
BOARDS
BOAST
BODYGUARD
BODY'S
BODY-TREE
BOG
BOGGLING
BOILS
BOLTS
BOMBED
BOMBS
BONA
BONBON
BOND
BONE-BARE
BONELESS
BONEWHITE
BONFIRE
BONG
BONNETED
BONWIT'S
BOOKENDS
BOOKS'
BOOKSHELF
BOOMED
BOOMERANG
BOOMS
BOORS
BOOTSOLE
BOOTSOLES
BORDERED
BORDERS
BOREDOMS
BORNING

BORROW
BORROWERS
BOSSED
BOSSING
BOTANICAL
BOTCHED
BOTTOMLESS
BOUDOIR
BOUDOIRS
BOULDERS
BOUNDS
BOURBON
BOWEL
BOWEL-PULSE
BOWELS
BOWEL'S
BOWER
BOWLERS
BOWLING
BOWLS
BOWS
BOXCARS
BOXED-IN
BOXES
BOX-LINED
BOYCOTT
BRACKEN
BRACING
BRAGS
BRAIDS
BRAINCHAMBER
BRAINS
BRAINWASHED
BRAKES
BRAMBLE
BRAMBLED
BRANCHING
BRAND
BRANDS
BRASH
BRASILIA
BRASSILY
BRASSY
BRAT
BRAVED
BRAWN
BRAY
BREAKABLE
BREAKWATER
BREAKWATERS
BREASTPLATES
BREATHABLE
BREATHLESS
BREATHS
BRED
BREWING
BRIAR
BRIARS
BRIBERY
BRIBES
BRICKDUST-
    COMPLECTED
BRICKRED
BRIDE-LACE
BRIDES
BRIEFCASE
BRIEFLY
BRIGANDS
BRIGHTEN
BRIOS
BRISKLY
BRISTLE
BRITTLE
BROACH
BROACHED
BROADCAST
BROBDINGNAG
BROCADES
BRONZES
BROOCH-PIN
BROODING

BROODY
BROOK'S
BROOM
BROTH
BROTHERS
BROTHER-SISTER
BROWN-BACKED
BROWNING
BROWNNESS
BROWSE
BROWSING
BRUEGHEL'S
BRUISES
BRUISING
BRUTAL
BUBBLE
BUBBLES
BUCK
BUCKED
BUCKETS
BUCOLIC
BUCOLICS
BUDDHA
BUDDHAS
BUDGE
BUDS
BUFFS
BUGGY
BUGS
BUILDING
BUILDS
BUILT
BULBOUS
BULBS
BULGING
BULKED
BULKING
BULKS
BULLDOZERS
BULLETS
BULL-FEET
BULLMAN
BULL-NECK
BULL'S-EYE
BULL-SNOUTED
BUMBLINGLY
BUMP-RINDED
BUMPY
BUNCHES
BUNDLE
BUNKERS
BURDOCK
BURGEONING
BURGERS
BURGLAR
BURIAL
BURLESQUE
BURNERS
BURRING
BURST
BURSTING
BUSHEL
BUSH-STINK
BUSHY
BUSILY
BUSINESSLIKE
BUSTS
BUSYBODY
BUSYNESS
BUTLER
BUTT
BUTTER
BUTTERCUP
BUTTERCUPS
BUTTONING
BUTTONS
BUY
BUZZ
BUZZARD
BYRON'S
BYSTANDING

608

C
CABBAGEHEADS
CABIN
CABINET
CABINETS
CABINS
CABLE
CACKLE
CACOPHONOUS
CACOPHONY
CADENZAS
CADDIS
CADILLACS
CAESAR
CAESARS
CAHOOTS
CAIRN
CAKED
CALAMITY'S
CALCIUM
CALCULATE
CALCULATES
CALCULUS
CALDER
CALENDARS
CALF
CALIFORNIA
CALLA
CALMNESS
CAMBRIC
CAMBRIDGE
CAMELLIA
CAMELS
CAMERA-EYE
CAMOUFLAGED
CAMOUFLAGING
CAMPERS
CAMPS
CANACEE
CANCELS
CANCEROUS
CANDELABRUM
CANDIES
CANDLE-FLOWERS
CANDLELIGHT
CANDLE'S
CANDLESTICK
CANDY
CANNONBALLS
CANNONS
CANT
CANTALOUPES
CANTING
CANVAS-SIDED
CANYONS
CAP
CAPACITY
CAPE
CAPES
CAPRICCIOSOS
CAPRICE
CAPS
CAPSULES
CAPTAIN'S
CARACALLA
CARAPACE
CARAVAN
CARBUNCLE
CARDINALS
CARED
CARICATURES
CARMINE
CAROL
CAROLING
CAROUSALS
CARPENTER
CARPETS
CARPET'S
CARRIAGES
CARRIES

CARRION
CARROT
CARROUSEL
CARRYING
CARTONS
CARVE
CARVING
CASK
CASKETS
CASQUES
CASSIOPEIA'S
CASSOCK
CASTANETS
CASTING
CASTLED
CASUIST
CATAPULTS
CATARACT
CATASTROPHE
CATCHER
CAT-CLEVER
CATERWAUL
CATGUT
CAT-HAUNT
CATHEAD
CATHEDRALS
CAT-LADY
CAT-VOICE
CAUL
CAULS
CAUSED
CAUSEWAYS
CAVED
CAVE-MOUTH
CAVIARE
CELEBRATION
CELERY
CELIBATE
CELLARS
CELLAR'S
CELLOS
CENTRE
CENTURY
CERBERUS
CEREMONIOUS
CEREMONIOUSLY
CERISE
CERTAINTY
CHAFE
CHAINED
CHAINMAIL
CHAIRARMS
CHALK-HULLED
CHALLENGE
CHALLENGES
CHAMPAGNE-
  COLORED
CHANDELIER
CHANEL
CHANGES
CHANNEL
CHANNELS
CHANTING
CHAPELS
CHARACTERS
CHARADES
CHARIOTEERS
CHARITY
CHARLES
CHARTS
CHARY
CHASED
CHASTITY'S
CHATTERERS
CHATTERING
CHEATED
CHECK
CHECKED
CHEEKS
CHEESEPARING
CHEF

CHENILLE
CHEQUERED
CHERUBIM
CHESHIRE
CHESTNUT
CHEVROLET
CHEW
CHEWED
CHEWING
CHICKEN-GUT
CHICKS
CHIDING
CHILDBIRTHS
CHILDLESS
CHILDREN'S
CHILLING
CHILLS
CHIME
CHIMERA
CHIMERICAL
CHIMNEYS
CHIN
CHINS
CHIP
CHIPS
CHIRP
CHIRPS
CHITTERS
CHOCOLATE
CHOKE
CHOKING
CHOLER
CHORD
CHORUS
CHOSEN
CHOUGHS
CHRISTENED
CHRISTUS
CHRONICLER
CHUFFING
CHUMMY
CHURCHES
CHURCH-GOING
CHURLISH
CHURN
CICATRIX
CIDER-JUICE
CIGAR
CIGARETTE
CINDERELLA
CINDER'S
CIPHERS
CIRCLED
CIRCLES
CIRCLING
CIRCUITS
CIRCUMFLUENT
CITADEL
CITIES
CIVIL
CLACK
CLACKED
CLAIMING
CLAM
CLAMOR
CLANGOR
CLAPBOARD
CLAPPED
CLAPS
CLARET
CLARITIES
CLASH
CLATTER
CLAUS
CLAW-CUTS
CLAWED
CLAW-FOOT
CLAW-THREAT
CLEARING
CLEARNESS
CLEAVE

CLEAVER
CLEAVERS
CLEAVING
CLEMATIS
CLENCH
CLEO
CLEVEREST
CLICKER
CLICKING
CLICKS
CLIMATE
CLIMAX
CLIMBING
CLINGS
CLINIC
CLINKING
CLOAKED
CLOAKS
CLOCKCASE
CLOCKED
CLOCKWORK
CLOISTERS
CLOISTRAL
CLOSELY
CLOSER
CLOSES
CLOSETS
CLOSING
CLOTS
CLOTTED
CLOUDBANK
CLOUDED
CLOUDING
CLOUD-STUFF
CLOUDWRACK
CLOVES
CLOWN
CLOWNLIKE
CLOWNS
CLUBFOOT
CLUBS
CLUMPED
CLUMSY
CLUNG
CLUSTER
CLUSTERS
CLUTCH
CLUTCHES
CO.
COACH
COAL-FIRE
COALS
COARSENED
COAXES
COBALT
COBBLED
COBBLES
COBRA'S
COBS
COBWEB
COBWEBBED
COCKCHAFERS
COCKLE-SHELL
COCKLE-SHELLS
COCK'S
COCKTAIL
COCOON
COFFEE-TABLE
COFFINS
COG
COILED
COILED-SPRING
COILINGS
COLD-BLOODIED
COLDS
COLLAPSES
COLLAR
COLLECTING
COLLECTOR
COLLECTS
COLLEGE

COLLEGES
COLLUSION
COLOUR
COLUMBUS
COMBAT
COMBERS
COMBINATIONS
COMEBACK
COMERS
COMETS
COMET'S
COMFORTLESS
COMMENCE   .
COMMENDED
COMMISSION
COMMITTING
COMMONERS
COMMON-SENSE
COMMUNICATE
COMMUNICATION
COMPANIONABLE
COMPANIONED
COMPANIONS
COMPASS
COMPASSIONATE
COMPLAIN
COMPLAINING
COMPLAINTS
COMPLAISANCE
COMPLICATING
COMPLICATIONS
COMPOSED
COMPOST
COMPOUNDS
COMRADES
CONCATENATION
CONCEALING
CONCEDE
CONCEIT
CONCEIVE
CONCEIVES
CONCEIVING
CONCENTRATE
CONCENTRATION
CONCEPT
CONCEPTION
CONCERNING
CONCHES
CONCLUDES
CONCLUDING
CONCOCT
CONCORDE
CONCRETE
CONCUPISCENCE
CONDITION
CONDONING
CONDOR
CONDUCTING
CONFECTIONER'S
CONFECTIONERY
CONFESS
CONFESSED
CONFIDENCE
CONFINED
CONFLAGRATIONS
CONGEAL
CONGREGATE
CONJUNCTION
CONJURES
CONJURING
CONQUER
CONQUERED
CONSECRATES
CONSECRATING
CONSEQUENCE
CONSEQUENTIAL
CONSIDER
CONSIDERED
CONSISTENT
CONSPICUOUS
CONSTANCE

-1- (CONT.)
CONSTELLATION
CONSTELLATIONS
CONSTIPATION
CONSTRAINT
CONTRARY
CONSTRICTION
CONSTRICTOR
CONSTRICTS
CONSUME
CONSUMES
CONSUMMATES
CONTAGION
CONTAINING
CONTEMPLATING
CONTENDING
CONTEST
CONTINENT
CONTINENTS
CONTINUALLY
CONTINUING
CONTINUOUSLY
CONTORT
CONTOURS
CONTRACT
CONTRACTED
CONTRACTS
CONTRADICTION
CONTRADICTIONS
CONTRIVE
CONTUSION
CONUNDRUM
CONUNDRUMS
CONVALESCENT
CONVERGING
CONVERSE
CONVERSED
CONVERSING
CONVERSION
CONVICTION
CONVULSION
CONVULSORS
COO
COOING
COOKED
COOKER
COOKS
COOLNESS
COOLS
COOT
COPSES
CORDIAL
CORDS
CORES
CORKED
CORNWALL
COROLLAS
CORONAL
CORONATION
CORPSE
CORPSE-WHITE
CORPUSCLES
CORRAL
CORRESPONDS
CORRIDOR
CORRODING
CORRUPTIBLE
CORRUPTS
CORSETS
COSMETIC
COSMETICS
COST
COTTAGES
COUGH
COUNTENANCE
COUNTERMAGIC
COUNTERPOINT
COUNTIES
COUNTING
COUNTRIES
COUNTS

COUPLETS
COURTFOLK
COURTING
COURTSHIP
COURTYARD
COVEN
COVERED
COVERS
COW-HEAVY
COW-PARSLEY
COW'S
COY
CRAB-BACKS
CRAB-CLAW
CRAB-FACE
CRACKER
CRACKING
CRACKLESS
CRACKPOTS
CRACK-THROATED
CRADLED
CRAFT
CRAFTY
CRAGS
CRAM
CRANNIES
CRASH
CRASHED
CRASHES
CRATERED
CRAVED
CRAVING
CRAWLED
CREAM-SMOOTH
CREAMY
CREATES
CREATURE
CREDIT
CREDITOR
CREDULITY
CREDULOUS
CREEL
CREEPS
CREEPY-CREEPY
CREPES
CRESCENDOS
CRESCENT
CRESCENTS
CREVICES
CREW
CRICKET
CRICKETS'
CRIME
CRIMINAL
CRIMPED
CRIPPLE
CRISIS
CRISPLY
CRITIC
CRITICIZING
CRIVELLI
CROCK
CROCODILE
CRONE
CROOK
CROOK-BACK
CROOKS
CROP'S
CROQUET
CROSSHATCH
CROSSLEGGED
CROSS-LEGGED
CROSS-PURPOSES
CROSSROAD
CROSS-STITCH
CROTCHED
CROUCHED
CROWBAR
CROW-COLORS
CROWDS
CROWD'S

CROWING
CROWS
CROW'S-FEET
CRUDE
CRUELLY
CRUISE
CRUISES
CRUISING
CRUMBLED
CRUMBLES
CRUMBS
CRUNCH
CRUSTY
CRUTCHES
CRUTCHLESS
CRYPT
CUBE
CUCKOO
CUDDLY
CUIRASS
CUL-DE-SAC
CULL
CULLING
CULTIVATED
CUNNING
CUPBOARDS
CURB
CURBSIDE
CURDED
CURE
CURIOSITY
CURLS
CURRENCY
CURRENT
CURSING
CURTAINED
CURTAIN'S
CURTSEYED
CURTSIES
CUSP
CUTE
CUT-GRASS
CUTLERY
CUT-OUT
CYCLING
CYCLONES
CYCLOPS-EYE
CYGNETS
CYMBALS
CYPRESS
CYPRESSES
CYRUS
DA
DACHAU
DAFFODILS
DAINTY
DAISIED
DAISIES
DALLY
DALMATIAN
DAMAGE
DAMAGED
DAMAGING
DAMASKS
DAME
DAMES
DAMN
DAMNATION
DAMPER
DANCE
DANCING
DANDELIONS
DANDIES
DANGLES
DANGLING
DANS
DANSE
DAPPLE
DAPPLED
DARED
DARES

DARK-BOUGHED
DARKEN
DARKENS
DARKER
DARK-FACED
DARK-SUITED
DARK-WEBBED
DARLINGS
DARNING
DARNING-EGGS
DARTBOARD
DARTMOOR
DATE
DAUNTED
DAVY'S
DAYBREAK
DAY-CLOTHES
DAY-OFF
DAY-OLD
DAY'S-END
DAY-SUNS
DAYTIME
DAZES
DE
DEADLOCK
DEADLOCKED
DEADLY
DEAFNESS
DEAL
DEALT
DEARER
DEARIES
DEARS
DEATH-GOWNS
DEATHLY
DEATHMASK
DEATH-PEGS
DEATH'S-HEAD
DEATH'S-METAL
DEATH-SOUP
DEATH-STENCH
DEBASED
DEBAUCH
DEBONAIR
DEBT
DECADE
DECADES
DECEITS
DECKED
DECKS
DECLARE
DECLENSION
DECLINING
DECODED
DECOMPOSE
DECORATE
DECREE
DECRY
DEEPEN
DEEPS
DEEP-SUNK
DEFACE
DEFENDING
DEFERRING
DEFINING
DEFINITELY
DEFLECT
DEFLECTS
DEFT
DEGREES
DEIGN
DELECTABLE
DELICACY
DELICATESSEN
DELIGHTING
DELL
DELUDED
DELVED
DELVING
DELVINGS
DEMAND

DEMANDED
DEMARCATING
DEMIGOD
DEMURE
DEMURS
DENIES
DENMARK
DENOUEMENT
DENSE-FEATHERED
DENSE-GRAINED
DENY
DENYING
DEPARTING
DEPARTS
DEPENDED
DEPRESSED
DEPRIVATION
DEPTHS
DERANGING
DES
DESCENDED
DESCENDING
DESCENT
DESCRIBED
DESCRIBING
DESCRIED
DESERTED
DESERTIONS
DESERTS
DESERVE
DESIGNS
DESOLATE
DESOLATION
DESPERATE
DESPITE
DESPOTS
DESTINATIONS
DESTROY
DESTRUCTIONS
DETECTIVE
DETECTOR
DETERRED
DETONATING
DETONATIONS
DETOUR
DEUS
DEVIATION
DEVIL-BIRD
DEVILS
DEVON
DEVOUR
DEVOURER
DEVOURING
DEVOURS
DEVOUT
DEVOUTLY
DEWDROP
DEWLAPPED
DIABOLIC
DIAGNOSIS
DIAGRAMS
DIAMOND-PANED
DIAMONDS
DIAPHANOUS
DIARY
DICE
DICHOTOMY
DIFFERENCE
DIFFERENCES
DIFFICULTIES
DIFFICULTY
DIGEST
DIGESTIBLES
DIGNITY
DILATING
DILUTE
DIMENSIONS
DIMINISHES
DIMINISHING
DING
DINING

-1- (CONT.)
DINNER
DINT
DIOR
DIPPED
DIPPER
DIPPING
DIRECT
DIRECTS
DIRGE
DISAPPEARED
DISAPPOINT
DISARRAY
DISBELIEF
DISCHARGES
DISCIPLINED
DISCIPLINES
DISCLAIMS
DISCLOSES
DISCONSOLATE
DISCORD
DISCOVER
DISCREET
DISCREETLY
DISENCHANT
DISENCHANTMENT
DISFIGURED
DISGUISING
DISHEARTENS
DISHONORS
DISINFECTANTS
DISLIKE
DISLODGE
DISMAL-HEADED
DISORGANIZATION
DISPARAGING
DISPARATE
DISPATCHED
DISPELLED
DISPERSE
DISPOSSESSED
DISQUIETING
DISSATISFY
DISSECT
DISSECTED
DISSECTING
DISSEMBLING
DISSEVER
DISSIPATE
DISSOLUTE
DISSOLVED
DISSOLVES
DISTAIN
DISTANCING
DISTILLS
DISTINCT
DISTRACT
DISTRACTIONS
DISTURBANCE
DISTURBING
DISTURBS
DITCH
DITCHES
DITHERS
DIVER
DIVIDENDS
DIVIDING
DIVINE
DIVINING
DIVISION
DOCK
DOCKS
DODDERING
DODGE
DODGES
DODO'S
D'OEUVRES
DOFF
DOGBODY
DOG-FACED
DOGGED

DOGGY
DOG-HEAD
DOINGS
DOKTOR
DOLLAR
DOLL'S
DOLOROUS
DOLT
DOMAIN
DOMED
DOMESTICITY
DOMINANCE
DOMINATE
DOMINION
DOMINOES
DONKEY-CARTS
DONNA
DONNER
DOOMCRACK
DOOM-NOISE
DOORBELL
DOORMAN
DOORSTEPS
DOORWAY
DORDOGNE
DOUANIER
DOUBLECROSS
DOUBLE-HUMPED
DOUBLENESS
DOUBLES
DOUBLING
DOUBTING
DOUCE
DOUGH
DOUGHTY
DOUR-FACED
DOURLY
DOUSING
DOVE'S
DOWNFALL
DOWNWARD
DOZED
DOZENS
DOZER
DOZING
DRAB
DRABBLED
DRAFT
DRAFTIER
DRAFTINESS
DRAGGLED
DRAGNET
DRAGON
DRAGONFLY
DRAGONS
DRAGON'S
DRAIN
DRAINED
DRAKE
DRAMA
DRAPED
DRASTIC
DRAUGHTY
DREADFUL
DREADS
DREAMER
DREAM-FILMED
DREAM-FISH
DREAMGIRLS
DREAM-PEOPLED
DREAM-
    PROPERTIED
DREAMSCAPES
DREAR
DRENCHING
DRESSED
DRESSING
DRESSY
DRIBBLES
DRIFTING
DRIFTS

DRIFTWOOD
• DRIZZLED
DROLL
DROLL-FLECKED
DROOLS
DROOP
DROOPS
DROPLET
DROWSE
DROWSING
DRUDGE
DRUGS
DRUM
DRUMS
DRUNKARDS
DRUNKENNESS
DRUNKS
DRYAD
DRY-EYED
DRYLY
DRY-PAPPED
DRY-WET
DU
DUAL
DUBIOUS
DUCK
DUCK-FEET
DUD
DUELS
DUET
DUFY-BLUE
DULCET
DULLING
DULLY
DUMBSHOW
DUMP
DUN
DUNCE
DUNES
DUPE
DURANCE
DUSTBINS
DUSTERS
DUTCH
DUTEOUS
DUTIES
DWARF
DWARFING
DYE
DYEING
DYNASTIES
E
EAGER
EAR-FLAPS
EARLESS
EARLIEST
EARN
EARPIECE
EAR-RING
EAR'S
EARTHBORN
EARTH-FLESH
EARTHQUAKING
EARTH-WIFE'S
EARWIG
EASED
EASIER
EASILY
EATERIES
EAVESDROPPER
EBBING
EBONY
ECCENTRIC
ECHOED
ECHOER
ECSTASY'S
EDDIES'
EDDY
EDENY
EDGED
EDIFICE

EDWARDIAN
EEL
EELISH
EELY
EFFACE
EFFACED
EFFACEMENT
EFFECT
EFFICIENCY
EFFORT
EFFORTLESSLY
EFFORTS
E G.
EGG-HEAD
EGG-SHAPE
EGG-SHAPED
EGG-STAINED
EGGSTONES
EGOTISTS
EIDERS
EIGHTEENTH
EIGHT-FINGERED
ELATE
ELBOW-SCARVES
ELDERBERRY
ELDERLY
ELECT
ELECTRA
ELECTRIFY
ELECTRIFYINGLY-
    COLORED
ELECTRODE
ELEGIAC
ELEGIES
ELEVATIONS
ELIZABETH
ELLA'S
ELLEN
ELLIPTIC
ELMS
ELM'S
ELOPING
ELOQUENTLY
ELUDE
EMBARK
EMBARRASS
EMBARRASSMENTS
EMBELLISHING
EMBLEMATIC
EMBROIDER
EMBROIDERY
EMBRYO
EMMETS
EMPIRES
EMPTINESSES
EMPTY-PURSED
EMULOUS
EN
ENACTED
ENAMEL
ENAMELED
ENCASED
ENCHANTING
ENCLOSE
ENCROACH
ENCROACHES
ENDORSES
ENEMIES
ENEMIES'
ENGENDERING
ENGINEERED
ENGRAVE
ENGRAVES
ENGRAVING
ENGRAVINGS
ENGROSS
ENGULFING
ENGULFS
ENIGMATICAL
ENJOY
ENJOYED

ENLARGES
ENLISTED
ENNUI
ENORMITY
ENTERPRISE
ENTERTAINED
ENTIRE
ENTOMBED
ENTRAILS
ENTRY
ENVELOPS
EPHEMERIDS
EPILOGUE
EPISODES
EQUILIBRIUM
EQUIVOCAL
ERA
ERECT
ERECTED
ERECTING
ERMINE
EROS
EROTIC
ERSATZ
ESCAPE
ESCAPES
ESCARPMENTS
ESPLANADE
ESSAYING
ESSENTIAL
ESSENTIALS
ESTABLISHMENTS
ESTATES
ESTRANGED
ETCH
ETCHED
ETCHING
ETHER
ETHEREAL
ETHERIZING
EUNUCHS
EUROPE
EVENINGS
EVEREST
EVERGREEN
EVERGREENS
EVERYBODY'S
EVERYDAY
EVERYONE
EVILEST
EVIL-STARRED
EX
EXACTED
EXAMINERS
EXAMPLE
EXCAVATIONS
EXCEPTIONAL
EXCEPTIONALLY
EXCHANGE
EXCITABLE
EXCLAMATION
EXCLUSION
EXCUSE
EXCUSES
EXHALE
EXHALES
EXHAUSTS
EXHIBITING
EXILED
EXILES
EXIST
EXISTANCE
EXISTED
EXISTS
EXORCIZED
EXPANSIVE
EXPEND
EXPENSIVE
EXPLAIN
EXPLICABLE
EXPLICIT

EXPLODE
EXPLODES
EXPLODING
EXPLOSIONS
EXPOSE
EXPOSED
EXPRESSIVE
EXQUISITE
EXTINCTION
EXTINGUISHES
EXTRACTOR
EXTRAPOLATION
EXTREME
EXTREMELY
EXUDES
EYEBALL
EYEBALLS
EYEBATHS
EYE-BUTTON
EYEHOLES
EYELASH
EYE-MOTE
EYE-PITS
EYE-RINGS
EYESORE
EYE-STONES
FABLING
FACADES
FACE-OVALS
FACE-ROOM
FACETED
FACETS
FACE-TO-THE-
   WALL
FACTS
FADE
FADES
FADING
FAGGOT-BEARING
FAGGOTS
FAIL
FAILED
FAILS
FAILURE
FAINLIGHT
FAINTLY
FAIRYTALE
FAIRY-TALE
FAITHFULLY
FAITH-MAKER
FAKE
FAKERY
FALLIBLE
FALSETTO
FALTER
FAMILY-FEATURED
FAMISHED
FAMOUS
FANCIES
FANG
FANGED
FANGS
FANNING
FAN-TAILS
FAN-TAIL'S
FANTASTIC
FAR-FLUNG
FARM
FARMBOY'S
FARMERS
FARMER'S
FARMLAND
FASCIST
FASHION
FATHERING
FATHERS
FATHOM
FATHOMS
FATIGUE
FATLY

FATNESS
FAT-RUTTED
FATSO
FATTENED
FATTEST
FAUCET
FAUCETS
FAULT
FAULTLESSLY
FAULT'S
FAVORED
FAVORITES
FAWN
FEARFUL
FEARFULLY
FEARING
FEARS
FEASTING
FEAT-FOOT
FEATHERY
FEATURELESSNESS
FEE
FEEDING
FELLA
FELLOWS'
FEMALE
FENCE
FENDING
FEN-FROST
FERRIES
FERRY
FERTILE
FERTILITY
FETCH
FETCHER
FETID
FETTERS
FEVER-DRY
FEVERED
FEVERISH
FEVERS
FICTION
FICTIVE
FIDDLER-CRAB
FIDDLER'S
FIDDLING
FIDE
FIDO
FIERCELY
FIESTA
FIESTA-GOERS
FIFTEEN
FIFTH
FIGURED
FILCHED
FILENE'S
FILET
FILLED-IN
FILM
FILTER
FILTERING
FINALE
FINANCIER
FINDS
F-I-N-E
FINED
FINER
FINGERED
FINGER-FURROWED
FINGERJOINT
FINGER-LENGTH
FINGERLESS
FINGERNAIL
FINGERNAILS
FINGER-TRAPS
FINGER-VENTS
FINISTERRE
FINNED
FIRE-BLURTING
FIREDOGS
FIREFLIES

FIRELESS
FIREPLACE
FIRESIDE
FIRESONG
FIRMAMENT
FIRM-FIXED
FIRST-BREACHED
FISH-BAIT
FISH-BONES
FISHERMEN
FISH-GREASE
FISHING
FISH-MOUTH
FISHNETS
FISH-TAILED
FISHY
FISSURED
FISSURES
FITFUL
FITS
FITTED
FITTING
FIVE-ANTLERED
FIX
FIXING
FIZZLE
FIZZY
FLAGON
FLAGONS'
FLAGS
FLAIR
FLAKED
FLAMED
FLAMILY
FLAMINGO
FLANK
FLANKED
FLAPPED
FLAPPING
FLARED
FLASH
FLASHING
FLASHLIGHTS
FLASHLIT
FLATFISH
FLATTENING
FLAY
FLEA
FLEA-RIDDEN
FLEE
FLEMISH
FLESHED
FLEX
FLICKING
FLIGHTS
FLIMSILY
FLINCH
FLINTIER
FLINTLIKE
FLINTY
FLITS
FLOATED
FLOG
FLOGGED
FLOORBOARDS
FLORA
FLORAL
FLORETS
FLORID
FLORIDLY
FLOUNCED
FLOURED
FLOURISHED
FLOURISHING
FLOW
FLOWER-HEAD
FLOWERING'S
FLOWER-NIBBLERS
FLOWERPOT
FLOWERY
FLOWING

FLUFFY
FLUORESCENT
FLUSHED
FLUTE
FLUTED
FLUTTER
FLUTTERING
FLY-BY-NIGHT
FOAM-CAPPED
FOAMED
FOCUSING
FOLDEROL
FOLK
FOLKTALES
FOLLOWED
FOLLOWING
FONTAINEBLEAU
FOOLS'
FOOTBALL
FOOTFALL
FOOTLESS
FOOTLIGHTS
FOOTLINGS
FOOT'S
FORBID
FORBIDDEN
FOREHEADS
FOREIGN
FORESEE
FORETS
FORFEITURE
FORGE
FORGET-ME-NOTS
FORGETS
FORGOT
FORGOTTEN
FORKED
FORKS
FORK-TAILED
FORM
FORMALITY
FORMING
FORMLESSNESS
FORMS
FORM'S
FORNICATIONS
FORSWEAR
FORTUNE'S
FORTUNE-TELLING
FORTY
FORTY-NINTH
FORUM
FOSSILS
FOUNDERING
FOUNDING
FOUNTAIN
FOUR-CORNERED
FOURS
FOUR-WAY
FOX-SKINS
FRANCE
FRANCE'S
FRANK
FRANZ
FREAKISH
FREE-FOR-ALL
FREE-GADDING
FREELY
FREES
FREEZES
FREEZING
FREQUENT
FRESHNESS
FRETFUL
FRIDAY
FRIDAYS
FRIENDLY
FRIENDSHIPS
FRIGHT
FRIGHTENED
FRINGES

FRISCO
FRIZZ
FROCK
FROG
FROG-COLORED
FROG-MASK
FROG-MOUTH
FRONDS
FRONTS
FROST-BITTEN
FROST-BREATH
FROSTED
FROSTING
FROST-THICK
FROWN
FRUIT-NUBBED
FRUIT'S
FUBSY
FUG
FUGE
FUGITIVE
FULFILL
FULLEST
FULL-TILT
FUMBLING
FUME
FUMES
FUMING
FUMY
FUN
FUN-HOUSE
FUNICULAR
FUNNELED
FUNNELS
FURIES
FURTHER
FURTIVELY
FUSION
FUSS
G
GABBLE
GABLE
GABLE-ENDS
GABLES
GABLE-TOPS
GABRIEL'S
GAGGING
GAIN
GAIT
GALACTIC
GALES
GALLERY
GALLOPED
GAMBLING-GAME
GAMECOCKS
GAMEROOM
GANGRENE
GANGWAYS
GANNET'S
GAPER
GAPES
GARBAGE
GARDEN'S
GARGOYLES
GARLANDS
GARNETS
GARRISON
GATES
GATHERERS
GAUL
GAUNTLET
GAUZE-EDGED
GAZE
GAZER
GEAR
GECKO
GEE
GEESE
GEM
GENERALS
GENERATING

612

GENERATION
GENEROUS
GENESIS
GENIUS
GENTLED
GENTLEMAN
GENTLEMEN
GENTLING
GENTLY
GENTLY-GRADED
GEOMETRY
GERANIUMS
GERMANS
GETAWAY
GHOST-COLUMN
GIANT'S
GIBBERING
GIBBERISH
GIBBETS
GIBES
GIBRALTER
GIGGLE
GIGOLO
GILDING
GILLED
GIMCRACK
GIMLETS
GINGERBREAD
GIPSY
GIRAFFE
GIRDLE
GIRL'S
GLADIOLAS
GLADLY
GLANCE
GLARED
GLASS-WRAPPED
GLAUCOUS
GLAZE
GLAZED
GLEAMING
GLEAMS
GLIDE
GLIDED
GLINTING
GLISSANDO
GLISTER
GLOAT
GLOBED
GLOOM
GLOOMY
GLORIFIED
GLOSS
GLOTTAL
GLOVE
GLOWED
GLOWER
GLOWS
GLOWWORM
GLUEPOTS
GLUING
GLUTTED
GLUTTON
GLUTTONIES
G-MEN
GNAT
GNAW
GNAWED
GNAWING
GNAWINGS
GNAWN
GNAWS
GOATHERDS
GOATHERD'S
GOAT-HORNS
GOATISH
GOAT-THIGHED
GOBBLEDYGOO
GO-BETWEEN
GOBLETS

GO-BY
GOD-BALL
GOD-BIT
GODDAM
GODDESSES
GOD-FATHERED
GODFOLK
GOD-HALOED
GOD-HEAD
GODIVA
GODLING
GOD-PLUMED
GOERS
GOING'S
GOLDFINCH
GOLD-LOBED
GOLDPIECES
GOLD-RUDDY
GOLDS
GOLGOTHA
GONDOLA
GONG
GONGING
GONGS
GOODBYES
GOODWIVES
GOOSE-WIT
GORGED
GORGON-GRIMACE
GORGON-
    PROSPECTS
GORGON'S
GORILLA
GORING
GOSPEL
GOSSIP
GOSSIPING
GOSSIP'S
GOURMET
GOVERNMENTS
GRACES
GRACIOUS
GRACIOUSNESS
GRACKLES
GRADE
GRADED
GRAFTERS
GRANDAM
GRANDCHILDREN
GRANDFATHER
GRANDILOQUENT
GRANDIOSE
GRANDMOTHERLY
GRANDMOTHER'S
GRANDSIRES
GRANTA
GRANTCHESTER
GRANTS
GRANULAR
GRAPEBLUE
GRAPEFRUIT
GRAPELEAVES
GRAPHS
GRASS-COUCHED
GRASS-
    EMBROIDERED
GRASSHEADS
GRASSHOPPER
GRASSINESS
GRASS-ROOT
GRASSTOPS
GRAVELLY
GRAVES
GRAVESTONES
GRAVEWARD
GRAVEYARD
GRAVITY
GRAYBEARDS
GRAYED
GRAYER
GRAYNESS

GRAYS
GREASED
GREASES
GREASING
GREASY
GREAT-
    GRANDCHILDREN
GREATGRANDMOTHER
GREAT-TALONED
GRECIAN
GREENCHEESE
GREEN-COPSE-
    CASTLED
GREENERY
GREENEST
GREEN-EYED
GREEN-GRAINED
GREEN-HEARTED
GREENING
GREEN-LEAVED
GREEN-LIT
GREENLY
GREENNESS
GREEN-POCKED
GREEN-REEDED
GREEN-SHADED
GREEN-SINGING
GREEN-STRIPED
GREEN-
    TESSELLATED
GREEN-TIPPED
GREEN-VAULTED
GREETING
GREY
GRIEF'S
GRIEVING
GRIEVOUSLY
GRIFFIN-LEGGED
GRILLS
GRIMACED
GRIMACES
GRIND
GRINDING
GRINDS
GRINNED
GRIPPING
GRIPS
GRISLY
GRISLY-BRISTLED
GRISLY-THEWED
GRIST
GRITTED
GROANS
GROCER
GROPE
GROSSE
GROTESQUE
GROUNDHOG
GROUNDHOGS
GROUND-WORK
GROVES
GROWNUPS'
GRUBBERS
GRUB-WHITE
GRUDGES
GRUFF-TIMBRED
GRUNTS
GRYPHON
GUARANTEED
GUARDED
GUARDIAN
GUESSING
GUESSWORK
GUIDED
GUIDES
GUILE
GUILELESS
GUILLOTINE
GUILLOTINES
GUILT-STRICKEN
GULL-COLORED

GULL-FOULED
GULLIBILITY
GULLIBLE
GULLS'
GULPS
GUM
GUT-END
GUT'S
GUTTER
GUTTERS
GYNDES
HABITATIONS
HABITS
HACKS
HADLEY
HADN'T
HAGGARD
HAG-HEAD
HAIL
HAIRS
HAIRTUSK'S
HALE
HALF-BELIEVE
HALF-BELIEVED
HALF-BRAIN
HALF-CORPSE
HALF-DOLLARS
HALF-HEARTED
HALF-LIGHT
HALF-MOONS
HALF-SHELL
HALLEY'S
HALLOWING
HALOEY
HAMLET
HAMMER
HAMMOCK
HANDBAG
HANDED
HANDFUL
HANDFULS
HANDICAPS
HANDLES
HAND-MADE
HANDSOME
HANDYMAN
HANKIE
HAPHAZARD
HAPPENINGS
HAPPIER
HAPPIEST
HARA-KIRI
HARBORAGE
HARDCASTLE
HARDEN
HARDER
HARDEST
HARD-HEARTED
HARDIHOOD
HARE
HARLEQUINS
HARMONY
HARMS
HARNESS
HARPS
HASN'T
HASTE
HAT-BRIMS
HATCHED
HATCHES
HATED
HATES
HATFUL
HATPIN
HATTER'S
HAUGHTY
HAUNCHED
HAUNTERS
HAUTEUR
HAVOC-SICK
HAVOC-SPLIT

HAWK
HAWS
HAY
HAYWIRE
HAZARD'S
HAZE
HEADACHE
HEADACHES
HEADLAND
HEADLINE
HEADLINES
HEAD'S
HEAD-STONE
HEADSTRONG
HEADWAITER
HEAP
HEAPED
HEARTBEATS'
HEARTEN
HEARTH
HEARTHSTONE
HEARTHSTONES
HEART-SHAPED
HEAT-CRACKED
HEATH
HEATING
HEAT-LIGHTNING
HEAVENLY
HEAVENWARD
HEAVIER
HEAVY-FOOTED
HEBETUDE
HECKLING
HECTIC
HEDGEROW
HEDGING
HEED
HEEL-HUNG
HEEL-PRINTS
HEFT
HEIGHT
HEIR
HELEN
HELLS
HELMED
HELMET
HELPED
HELPER
HEMLOCK
HENNA
HENS
HERALD
HERALDIC
HERALDRY
HERALDS
HERB
HERBAGE
HERCULES
HERDS
HERESIES
HERETICS
HERMETIC
HERO
HEROINE
HERON
HERS
HEST
HEX
HEYDAY
HIATUS
HIBERNACULUM
HIBERNATE
HIERATIC
HIERATICAL
HIGHBOYS
HIGH-CHURCH
HIGHER'S
HIGH-RISER
HIGH-STEPPING
HIGHWAY
HIKERS

HILLS'	HOUSELIGHTS	ILL-STARRED	INJURED	ITEM
HILLTOP	HOUSEWIFE	IMAGINATION	INJURIES	ITEMS
HINGE	HOUSEWIFE'S	IMMINENT	INJURY	IT'LL
HINTERLAND	HOUSEWIVES	IMMORAL	INK	JA
HIP	HOVER	IMMUNE	INKLINGS	JABBERWOCK
HIPPOPOTAMUS	HOYDEN	IMP	INKS	JABBERWOCKY
HIPS	HUFF	IMPALED	INMATES	JACK'S
HIRES	HUG	IMPASSE	INNOCENT	JADES
HIRING	HUGS	IMPATIENT	INQUIRING	JAG
HIROSHIMA	HULK	IMPERISHABLE	INSANE	JAGGED
HISSING	HULKED	IMPETUOUSLY	INSATIABLE	JAMMY
HISTORIAN	HULKS	IMPLACABLE	INSATIATE	JANE
HISTORICAL	HULL	IMPLACABLY	INSCRUTABLE	JANGLE
HOCK	HULLS	IMPOSSIBILITY	INSECTS	JANUARY
HOCUS-POCUS	HUMANITY	IMPOSSIBLES	INSEPARABLE	JARGONS
HOEING	HUMBLED	IMPOTENCE	INSERT	JARRING
HOG	HUMBUG	IMPOUNDED	INSIGHT	JAVANESE
HOGBACK	HUMDRUM	IMPRESS	INSINUATE	JAY'S
HOGHOOD	HUMILITY	IMPRESSION	INSIST	JAZZ
HOGSHEAD	HUMMING	IMPROBABLE	INSISTS	JEALOUSY
HOGWALLOW'S	HUMMINGBIRDS	IMPS	INSOLVENT	JEERS
HOISTED	HUMMOCK	IMPULSE	INSOMNIAC	JELLY-
HOISTING	HUMORED	I-N	INSPIRES	GLASSFULS
HOISTS	HUMOROUS	INAUSPICIOUS	INSTANT	JEOPARDIZE
HOLE-MOUTH	HUMPBACK	INCALCULABLE	INSTILLED	JEOPARDY
HOLINESS	HUMPED	INCESSANTLY	INSTRUCTIVE	JERK
HOLMESING	HUNCH	INCHING	INSTRUCTS	JERSEY
HOLOFERNNES'	HUNCHED	INCHWORMS	INSUFFERABLE	JESUS
HOMELAND	HUNDREDS	INCLINATION	INSURGENT	JET-BACKED
HOMICIDES	HUNDRED-	INCLUDES	INTELLECTUAL	JET-PLANE
HOMUNCULUS	YEAR-OLD	I-N-C-O	INTELLIGENCE	JEWELER
HONE	HUNGER-BATTLE	INCOHERENCES	INTENSE	JEWELMASTER
HONEY-AIR	HUNGERS	INCOHERENT	INTENSELY	JEW-MAMA
HONEYCOMB	HUNGER-STUNG	INCOMMUNICADO	INTENSITY	JEWS
HONEYCOMBED	HUNT	INCOMPARABLE	INTENTION	JIGGLES
HONEYDEWS	HUNTED	INCOMPATIBLE	INTERCEPTING	JILTING
HONEY-DRUDGERS	HUNTER	INCONGRUOUS	INTERESTS	JOB
HONEY-FEAST	HUNTERS	INCONSEQUENT	INTERIORS	JOBLESS
HONEY-MACHINE	HUNTING	INCONSPICUOUS	INTERTWINED	JOCULAR
HONOR-BOUND	HURTING	INCONSTANT	INTIMATE	JOES
HOODLUM	HURTLE	INCREASES	INTIMATELY	JOIN
HOODWINK	HURTLED	INCREDIBLE	INTOLERABLY	JOINTED
HOODWINKED	HUSBAND'S	INCREDULOUS	INTOLERANT	JOINTS
HOOED	HUSHING	INDEPENDENCY	INTRANSIGENT	JOKER
HOOF	HUSK	INDEPENDENT	INTRIGUING	JOKING
HOOF-TAPS	HUSTLE	INDIA	INTRODUCE	JOLT
HOOKING	HUTS	INDIANS	INTRUDES	JONQUILS
HOOP	HYDRANGEA	INDIAN'S	INTUITIONS	JOSEF
HOOPS	HYDRAS	INDIGENOUS	INUNDATING	JOSEPH
HOOTING	HYGIENIC	INDIGESTIBLE	INVADES	JOSEPH'S
HOPELESS	HYPERBOLICAL	INDIGNANT	INVALID	JOSTLE
HOPING	HYPOCRITE	INDISSOLUBLE	INVALIDS	JOSTLED
HORDE	HYSTERICAL	INDIVIDUAL	INVEIGLED	JOSTLING
HORDES	IAMBICS	INDOLENT	INVENTIVE	JOT
HORIZON-HINGED	ICARUS	INDULGE	INVERTED	JOURNEYING
HORIZON-LINE	ICEBERGS	INDUSTRIOUS	INVERTS	JOUST
HORIZON'S	ICEBOXES	INEFFECTUAL	INVITE	JOVIAN
HORIZONTAL	ICE-HEARTED	INELUCTABLY	INVOKE	JUDGE
HORIZONTALS	ICE-MOUNTAINS	INEPT	INVOLVES	JUDGED
HORNS	ICERIBBED	INERADICABLE	IONIAN	JUDGMENT
HORNY-SKINNED	ICHOR	INESCAPABLE	IRATE	JUDICIOUS
HORRIBLE	ICICLES	INEVITABLY	IRONED	JUGGLE
HORRIFIC	ICILY	INEXORABLE	IRONING	JULY'S
HORROR	IDEA	INFAMOUSLY	IRONY	JUMBO
HORSEFLIES	IDEALS	INFANT	IRONY'S	JUMPY
HORSE-	IDEAS	INFANTS	IRREFUTABLE	JUNK
SWALLOWING	IDIOTS	INFECT	IRREGULAR	JUTTED
HOSTAGE	IDOL	INFER	IRREPLACEABLE	KALEIDOSCOPE
HOSTELRY	IDOL'S	INFERNAL	IRREPROACHABLE	KALEIDOSCOPIC
HOSTESS	IDYLL	INFERNO	IRRETRIEVABLE	KAMIKAZE
HOSTILE	IGNITE	INFINITESIMAL	IRRETRIEVABLES	KARAKUL
HOTDOGS	IGNITED	INFINITY	IRRETRIEVABLY	KEEL
HOTELS	IGNITING	INFLAMMATION	IRRITATING	KEELED
HOTS	IGNORANTS	INFLUENCE	ISADORA'S	KEEL'S
HOUND-BITCH	IGNORED	INFREQUENT	ISHTAR	KEEPER
HOUNDS	ILL-ASSORTED	I-N-G-O-D-H-E-A-D	ISLANDS	KEEPER'S
HOURGLASS	ILLBRED	I-N-G-O-D-P-I-E	ISSUING	KELP
HOUR-GLASS	ILLEGITIMATE	INHABITANTS	ITALIAN	KEN
HOUSED	ILL-FAMED	INHALATION	ITALY	KENTISH
HOUSEKEEP	ILL-JUDGED	INIMICAL	ITCHED	KETTLE
	ILL-SERVED	INITIATED	ITCHES	KEYHOLE

KICK	LARKSPUR	LEVELS	LONDONERS	MAGGOTS
KICKED	LATCH	LEVERING	LONGED	MAGICAL
KILLER	LATELY	LEVITATING	LONGEVITY	MAGNANIMOUS
KILLS	LATEST	LEWDLY	LONGING	MAGNET
KILROY	LATHER	LIARS	LONG-LEGGED	MAGNIFIED
KINDER	LATIN	LIBERAL	LONG-USED	MAGNIFY
KINDLE	LATTER	LIBRARY	LOOKER	MAGNIFYING
KINDLES	LATTER-DAY	LICE	LOOKING-GLASS	MAIDEN
KINGDOM'S	LATTER-DAYS	LICHEN-BITTEN	LOOKOUT	MAILED
KINGLINESS	LATTICEWORK	LICHEN-LID	LOOK'S	MAILSLOT
KINGS'	LAUGH-SHAKEN	LICKED	LOOMED	MAINLY
KINGSHIP	LAUGHTER	LICKING	LOOMS	MAINTAINS
KITCHENS	LAUNCH	LICKS	LOONY	MAJESTIC
KLAN	LAUREL	LIDDED	LOOP	MAJOR
KLEPTOMANIAC	LAURELED	LIDLESS	LOOPHOLE	MAKER
KLUX	LAVATORY	LIFTED	LOOPS	MAKESHIFT
KNAVISH	LAVENDER	LIFTING	LOOSED	MALADIES
KNEEDEEP	LAVISH	LIGHTER	LOPPING	MALADY
KNEE-DEEP	LAW	LIGHTEST	LORDLY	MALE
KNELT	LAWNS	LIGHTING	LORDS	MALFI'S
KNIFELIKE	LAYING	LIGHTLESS	LORD'S	MALICIOUS
KNITS	LAZARUS	LIGHTLY	LORELEI	MALIGN
KNOBBED	LAZILY	LIGHTNINGS	LOSING	MALLEABLE
KNOBS	LAZULI	LIGHTNING-STROKE	LOSSES	MALTREAT
KNOTHOLES	LAZY	LIKED	LOT-DRAWN	MAMMAL
KNOTTING	LE	LIKELY	LOTUS	MANAGED
KNOTWEED	LEADING	LIKING	LOUDSPEAKERS	MANAGES
KNOUT	LEAFAGE	LILAC	LOUNGING	MANDATORY
KNOWABLE	LEAF-AND-FLOWER	LILAC-FLOWER	LOUSY	MANE
KNUCKLE	LEAF-FILTERED	LIMBS'	LOVEBED	MANGLE
KNUCKLEBONES	LEAFLET	LIME	LOVE-HOT	MANGO
KNUCKLE-BONES	LEAF-LINED	LIME-GREEN	LOVELINESS	MANHANDLES
KNUCKLED	LEAF'S	LIMIT	LOVE-MET	MANIACS
KRUPP	LEAF-SHUTTERED	LINED	LOVESICK	MANIFEST
KU	LEAF-SIZE	LINGERIE	LOVINGLY	MANIFESTATIONS
KUMQUAT-COLORED	LEAF-STALK	LINK	LOWER	MAN-SHAMING
LA	LEAF-WRAITHED	LINKED	LOWERED	MAN-SHAPE
LABELED	LEAGUES	LINOLEUM	LOWERS	MANY-BREASTED
LABORATORY	LEAKED	LION	LOW-LINTELLED	MANY-COLORED
LABORED	LEAKS	LION-HEAD	LOYAL	MANY-HOLED
LABORER'S	LEAKY	LION-RED	LOZENGE	MANY-SNAKED
LABORS	LEAP	LIONS	LUCIFER	MAPLIKE
LABYRINTHINE	LEAPING	LION'S	LUCINA	MAPS
LACERATE	LEATHERINESS	LIPPED	LUCKIER	MARAUDER
LACES	LEATHER-KNEED	LIQUID	LUCK-ROOTED	MARBLEHEAD
LACKEY	LEATHERY	LIQUIDS	LUFTWAFFE	MARBLE-HEAVY
LACKS	LEAVED	LIQUOR	LUGGAGE	MARBLY
LADEN	LEAVINGS	LIQUORS	LUGS	MARCHEN
LAIN	LECHER'S	LIST	LULL	MARGIN
LAKES	LED	LISTENER	LULLAYED	MARGINS
LAMB	LEDAS	LITERALISTS	LUMINOSITY	MARKED
LAMBSWOOL	LEDGES	LITTERS	LUMPED	MARRIES
LAMENT	LEECHES	LITTLESOUL	LUNA	MARROWLESS
LAMENTABLY	LEER	LIZARD	LUNCH	MARSHALING
LAMPLIGHT	LEERED	LIZARDS	LUNGE	MARSHALS
LAMPSHADE	LEERS	LIZARD'S	LUNGLESS	MARSHY
LANCED	LEFTOVER	LIZARD-SCALES	LUNG-TREE	MARTYR
LANDING	LEGAL	LIZARDY	LURCHING	MARVELINGLY
LANDINGS	LEGEND	LLAMA	LURK	MARY-BLUE
LAND'S	LEGGING	LOADED	LURKED	MASH
LANDSPIT	LEGGY	LOAF'S	LUSTERS	MASQUERADE
LANDSPITS	LEGION	LOAM-HUMPS	LUSTFUL	MASSACRES
LAND-TRACT	LEG-STUMP	LOATH	LUSTRE	MASSIVE
LANGUID	LEMON-TASTING	LOBED	LUSTROUS	MASS-MOTIVED
LANTERN	LENDING	LOBSTER-LIMBED	LUTES	MASTERIES
LANTERN-FRAIL	LENGTH	LOBSTERS	LUXURY	MASTERS
LANTERN-JAWED	LENGTHEN	LOCATIONS	LYMPH	MASTER'S
LANTERN-LIT	LENGTHENING	LOCKER	LYONIANS	MASTURBATING
LAOCOON	LENGTHS	LOCKS	LYRES	MAT
LAPIS	LENIENCE	LOCUST	LYSOL	MATCHSTICKS
LAPPED	LENT	LOCUSTS	MACABRE	MATE
LAPS	LEO	LOFTING	MACAWS	MATED
LAPSE	LEONARD	LOGAN	MACHINA	MATERNAL
LAPSED	LEPRECHAUN	LOGICAL	MADCAP	MATERNITY
LAPWING	LEPROUS	LOGIC'S	MADDENING	MATHEMATICS
LARDER'S	LESBOS	LOGS	MADONNA	MATISSE
LARD-PALE	LESSONED	LOINS	MADRIGALS	MATS
LARGESSE	LESSONS	LOITER	MAENAD	MAUNCHING
LARKS	LETHAL	LOLL	MAESTRO'S	MAUNDERING
LARKS'	LETTUCES	LOLLIES	MAGAZINES	MAUVE
	LETUP	LOLLS	MAGGOT	MAWKISH

-1- (CONT.)

MAYDAY	MILLRACE	MOON-LILIES	MUSEUM-CASED	NIGHT'S
MAYFLOWER	MIMIC	MOONLY	MUSEUMS	NIGHTSHADE
MAYOR'S	MINCED	MOON-PLUMAGED	MUSHROOM	NIMBLE-WINGED
MAZES	MINDING	MOON-POCKED	MUSKRAT	NIMBLY
MEAL	MINDS	MOONRISE	MUSKY	NIMBUS-LIT
MEANDER	MINERS	MOON-SKULLED	MUSSEL	NINETEEN-TWENTY
MEANEST	MINNOWS	MOONSONG	MUSSEL-PICKER	NINETY-FOURTH
MEANINGLESS	MINUTES	MOONSTRUCK	MUSTACHE	NINNIES
MEANLY	MINX-THIN	MOONWHITE	MUSTERING	NIP
MEANWHILE	MIRAGE	MOORISH	MUTED	NIPPLED
MEASURING	MIRE	MOOS	MUTINOUS	NIPPLE-FLOWERS
MEAT-AND-POTATO	MIRE-SMIRCHED	MOPED	MYSTERY	NOAH'S
MEATHOOK	MIRROR-SHEEN	MORAL	MYSTIC	NOBILITY
MECHANIC	MIRTH	MORALS	MYTH	NOBODY'S
MECHANICAL	MISCARRY	MORBID	MYTH-MAKING	NO-COLOR
MEDALLION	MISCHIEF'S	MORES	MYTHS	NOCTURNE
MEDEA	MISFIRED	MOROCCAN	NADIR	NOISES
MEDICINE	MISFORTUNE	MOROSE	NAILED	NOISY
MEDUSA	MISHAP	MORTIS	NAIVE	NO-LIFE
MEETINGS	MISHAPS	MOSAIC	NAKEDNESS	NO-MAN'S
MEINKAMPF	MISINTERPRETS	MOSES	NAPE	NORMALITY
MEISSEN	MISLAID	MOSS	NAPKIN	NOSE-END
MELDING	MISSING	MOSS-WIGGED	NAPKINS	NOSING
MELLOW	MISTAKE	MOTH-BREATH	NATIONS	NOSTALGIA
MELON	MISTIER	MOTHERING	NATIVITIES	NOSTALGIAS
MELON-EATING	MISTILY	MOTHER-LOVE	NATURES	NOSY
MELTED	MIST-WRAITH	MOTH-FACE	NAUGHT	NOTABLE
MEMBER	MIX	MOTHS	NAUSET	NOTCHED
MEMOIRS	MIXED	MOTHY	NAVEL-KNIT	NOTEBOOK
MENDED	MIXIE	MOTLEY	NAVIGATE	NOTHINGNESS
MENDINGS	MIZZLE	MOTTLE	NAVIGATES	NOTICING
MENTALITY	MIZZLING	MOUND	NAZI	NOTIONS
MEPHISTOPHELES	MOANINGLY	MOUNDED	NEARED	NOUMENON
MERCIES	MOANS	MOUNTAINING	NEARER	NOUN
MERCURIAL	MOB	MOUNTAINSIDE	NEAREST	NOUNS
MERCURIC	MOBS	MOUNTAINY	NEARING	NOURISH
MERCURY-BACKED	MOB'S	MOURNED	NEARLY	NOURISHERS
MERIDIAN	MOCK-CEREMONY	MOURNFUL	NECESSITY	NOURISHING
MERIT	MOCK-HEROIC	MOURNFULLY	NECKLACES	NOVEMBER'S
MERIT'S	MOCKING	MOUSETRAP	NECROPOLIS	NOVICE
MERMAIDS	MOCKS	MOUTH-ASH	NECTARINE	NOVICES
MERRY-GO-ROUND	MODE	MOUTHFULS	NEEDING	NUB
MESH	MODELS	MOUTHING	NEEDLE'S	NUDGED
MESSY	MODISH	MOUTHINGS	NEEDLY	NUDGERS
METAMORPHOSE	MOJAVE	MOUTHLESS	NEEDN'T	NUMBERED
METAMORPHOSES	MOLD	MOUTH-PIPE	NEEDS	NUMBNESS
METAPHYSICAL	MOLDERING	MOUTH-PLUGS	NEFERTIT	NUN
METHINKS	MOLDING	MOVIE-SCREEN	NEGATIVE	NUN-BLACK
METRONOMES	MOLDY	M-S	NEGLECT'S	NUN-HEARTED
MEXICAN	MOLECULES	MUCH-POKED	NEGRESS	NUNNERY
MICA-SCALED	MOLESTING	MUCK-TRAP	NEGRO	NUNS
MICA-SILVER	MOLEY-HANDED	MUDDLING	NEIGHBORHOOD	NUN'S
MICROBES	MOLLIFIES	MUDDY	NEIGHBORLY	NUN-SOULED
MICROSCOPE	MOLLIFY	MUD-MATTRESSED	NEIGHBORS'	NURSING
MIDAIR	MOLLUSK	MUD-SUMP	NELDA	NUT
MIDAS	MOLLUSKS	MUFFLE	NEMATODES	OAF
MIDAS'	MOLTEN	MUFFLES	NEMESIS	OAK
MID-ATLANTIC	MOLTS	MUG	NEON-LIT	OAR
MIDGET	MOMENT'S	MULATTO	NEOPHYTE	OASIS
MIDST	MONADNOCK	MULBERRIES	NEPHEW	OAT-SPROUTS
MIDSUMMER	MONDAYS	MULBERRY	NERVE-CURLERS	OBDURATE
MIDWIFE'S	MONDE	MULE	NERVE-END	OBESE
MIEN	MONEYLESS	MULE-BRAY	NET	OBLIQUE
MIGON	MONGREL	MULISH	NETHER	OBLIQUELY
MILDNESS	MONKEYS	MULLED	NETWORK	OBLITERATE
MILE	MONKS	MULTIFARIOUS	NEUTRALITY	OBLITERATION
MILEAGE	MONOCHROME	MULTIPLICATION	NEWEL	OBLIVION
MILE-LONG	MONOLOGUE	MULTITUDE	NEW-MINTED	OBSCURED
MILKBOTTLE	MONOXIDES	MUM	NEWNESS	OBSCURES
MILKED	MONSTER	MUMBLE	NEWSPAPER	OBSCURITY
MILKER	MONSTERS	MUMBLEPAWS	NIAGARAS	OBSERVED
MILK-FILM	MONSTROUS	MUMMY-CASE	NIBBLES	OBSERVING
MILKGREEN	MONUMENTAL	MUMMY-CLOTHS	NICETY	OBSESS
MILKING	MOODS	MUMMY'S	NICHES	OBSESSIVELY
MILKLESS	MOON-BLANCHED	MUMMY-WISE	NICKNAMES	OBSTACLE
MILKMAN	MOON-BLUED	MURDER	NICOTINE-FINGER	OBSTACLES
MILK-SPOUT	MOON-BOUND	MURDERED	NIGGARD	OBSTRUCTION'S
MILLE-FLEURS	MOON-EYE	MURDERESS	NIGGER-EYE	OBTUSE
MILLENNIUM	MOON-EYED	MURDERS	NIGHTGOWN	OCCASION
MILLIONS	MOON-GLINT	MURMURING	NIGHTINGALES	OCCASIONAL
	MOON-GLOW	MUSCLES	NIGHTMARES	OCCASIONALLY

OCEAN-FLOOR
OCHRE
OCTOBER'S
OCTOGENARIAN
OCTOPUS
ODALISQUE
ODDLY
ODDS
ODE
ODOR
ODYSSEY
OFFENDED
OFFENSE
OFFERS
OFFICE
OFFICES
OFFISH
OFF-STAGE
OFF-WHITE
O-F-N-E-R-V-E
O-F-R
O-GAPE
OGLE
OGLED
OLDEN
OLD-SCHOOL
OLIVE
OLIVE-BEAKED
OLIVES
OMEN
OMENS
ONCE-KNOWN
ONCOMING
ONE-EARED
O'NEILL
ONE'S
ONE-THIRD
ONE-TRACKED
ONLOOKER
ONSLAUGHT
OOZE
OOZED
OPACITY
OPEN-MOUTHED
OPERATIC
OPERATION
OPIATES
OPPOSABLE
OPPOSE
OPPOSITES
OPULENT
OPUS
O-R
ORACLE
ORACULAR
ORANGEPEEL
ORANGES
ORANGE-TILE
ORCHIDS
ORCHIS
ORDAINED
ORDERLIES
ORDERINGS
ORDERLY
ORDER'S
ORE
ORESTEIA
ORGAN
ORGANS
ORIGINS
ORION
ORPHANS
ORTHODOX
ORTUNIO
OSSIFYING
OTHERNESS
OTHERWORLDLINESS
OTTER
OUGHT
OUSTED

OUSTING
OUSTS
OUTDO
OUTFACE
OUTFLAME
OUTLINE
OUTLOOK
OUT-OF-SEASON
OUTLAST
OUTMODED
OUTSHONE
OUTSIZE
OUTSTRIP
OUTWIT
OVALTINE
OVEN
OVENS
OVERCAST
OVEREXPOSED
OVERLAID
OVERLOOKING
OVERRIPE
OVERSCRUPULOUS
OVERTAKE
OVERWHELM
OW
OWL-CALL
OWL-EYES
OWL-HOLLOWED
OWL-HOURS
OWNED
OWNERS'
OWNS
OX
OXEN
OXYGEN
PACED
PACIFIED
PACIFIST
PACING
PACK-DOG
PACKETS
PACT'S
PADDED
PAGAN
PAGODAS
PAILS
PAINED
PAINS
PAINTER
PAINT-PEELED
PAIRED
PAJAMAS
PALATES
PALENESS
PALETTE
PALING
PALLID
PALLS
PALMING
PALM-SPEAR
PALPABLE
PALUSTRAL
PAMPERED
PANEL
PANGS
PANORAMA
PANSY
PANTHER
PANTHER'S
PAPAL
PAPERED
PAPERS
PAPERWEIGHT
PAPS
PAPYRUS
PARACHUTE
PARADEGROUND
PARADES
PARAGONS
PARALLAX

PARALYSING
PARALYSIS
PARALYTIC
PARAPHERNALIA
PARCEL
PARCELED
PARCH
PARCHED
PARCHMENT
PARENTAL
PARENTHESIS
PARENTS
PARES
PARING
PARINGS
PARIS
PARKS
PARK-SLEEPERS
PARLIAMENT
PARLIAMENTS
PARODY
PARRIES
PARRY
PARSLEY
PARSLEYED
PARTIAL
PASSED
PASSER-BY
PASSIONATE
PASTEBOARD
PASTRIES
PASTRY
PATCHWORK
PATE
PATENT
PATENT-LEATHER
PATERNAL
PATHS
PATIENTS
PATIENTS'
PATRIARCH
PAUL
PAUSED
PAVED
PAWED
PAWING
PAWS
PAW'S
PAYS
PEACEABLE
PEACOCK
PEACOCK-COLORED
PEAJACKET
PEAKS
PEANUT-
   CRUNCHING
PEARLED
PEATY
PEBBLED
PECK
PEDESTRIAN
PEDESTALED
PEELS
PEER
PEERED
PELLET
PELLICLE
PELLMELL
PELT
PELTS
PEN
PENBEARER
PENCILS
PENDULUM
PEN-SKETCH
PENURY
PEOPLED
PEOPLES
PERCEIVED
PERCENT

PERCOLATE
PERFECTION
PERFECTIONS
PERFECTLY-
   CHISELED
PERFIDIOUS
PERFORM
PERFORMED
PERFUME
PERIOD
PERIODIC
PERIODS
PERIPHERAL
PERISH
PERIWINKLES
PERMANENTLY
PERPETUAL
PERPETUALLY
PERPLEXITIES
PERSEPHONE
PERSEVERE
PERSEVERED
PERSISTED
PERSISTENT
PERSONALITY
PERSUADED
PERVERSE
PESTLES
PET
PETALS'
PETRIFIED
PETRIFIES
PETRIFY
PETTISHLY
PETULANT
PEWS
PHARAOH
PHEDRE
PHENOMENON
PHILANTHROPICAL
PHILODENDRON
PHILOSOPHER
PHILOSOPHY
PHONES
PHOSPHORESCENCE
PHOSPHORUS
PHOTO
PHOTOGRAPHIC
PHOTOS
PHRASE
PHYSICAL
PIANISSIMO
PIANIST
PICADOR
PICKET
PICKETS
PICKLE
PICKLING
PICNIC
PIE
PIECED
PIE-IN-THE-SKY
PIES
PIGGERIES
PIG-GRUNT
PIGGY
PIGMENT
PIGMY
PIG'S
PIKE
PILE
PILED
PILGRIMAGE
PILGRIMAGES
PILING
PILINGS
PILLBOX
PILLOWS
PILOT
PINCERS
PINCH

PINCKNEY
PINEAPPLE
PINEAPPLE-
   BARKED
PINE-NEEDLE
PING
PINHEAD
PINK-BREASTED
PINK-BUTTOCKED
PINK-FLUTED
PINKNESS
PINK-PULPED
PINKY-PURPLE
PINLEGS
PIN-LEGS
PIN-STITCHED
PIPED
PIPING
PIPS
PIQUE
PIRANHA
PISTON
PITCHERS
PITCHFORK
PITCHFORKED
PITCHING
PITH
PITHY
PITIABLE
PITIFUL
PITS
PITYING
PITYS
PIZZICATO
PLACARD
PLACATE
PLACENTA
PLAGUE
PLAGUE-PITTED
PLAGUEY
PLAINLY
PLAINTIFF
PLANE
PLANES
PLANET'S
PLANET-SHINE
PLANKED-UP
PLANNING
PLASMA
PLASTER
PLASTIC-
   PILLOWED
PLASTIC-
   WINDOWED
PLATITUDES
PLATO
PLATONIC
PLATO'S
PLAUSIVE
PLAYFULNESS
PLAYMATES
PLAY'S
PLEADED
PLEASANT
PLEASING
PLEASURABLE
PLEASURE
PLEATINGS
PLENTY
PLETHORA
PLIABLE
PLOPPING
PLOTS
PLOUGH
PLOUGHBLADE
P-L-U-M-A-G-E
PLUMB
PLUMBED
PLUMBER
PLUMBING
PLUMBS

PLUM-COLOR
PLUME
PLUMMET
PLUMMETS
PLUMPED
PLUMS
PLYING
POACHING
POCK
POCKED
POCKETED
POCKETS
POCKMARKED
POD
POINTBLANK
POINTED
POINTING
POINTLESS
POISES
POISING
POISONED
POKER-STIFF
POLACK
POLAR
POLES
POLISHES
POLITICS
POLLARDED
POLYPS
POMP
PONDERABLE
POODLE
POOL-BED
POOLING
POOL-MOUTH
POORHOUSE
POP
POPLARS
POPPING
POPPY-SLEEPY
POPULACE
PORCH
PORCHES
PORK
PORKFAT
PORTENT
PORTICO
PORTICOES
POSED
POSING
POSSESS
POSSESSED
POSSESSING
POSSIBLY
POSTAGE
POSTCARD
POSTMAN
POSTMARKS
POTATO
POTENT
POTLID
POTTED
POUNDING
POUT
POUTS
POWDER
POWDERY
POWERFUL
PRACTICED
PRACTICING
PRAISED
PRAISING
PRAWN
PRAY
PRAYER
PRAYERS
PRAYS
PREACHERS
PREAMBLE
PRECARIOUS

PRECARIOUSLY
PRECIPICE
PRECOCIOUS
PRECONCEPTIONS
PREDECESSOR
PREDICTING
PREGNANCY
PREOCCUPY
PREPARE
PREPOSTEROUS
PRESENTLY
PRESSED
PRESSING
PRESTISSIMOS
PRESTOS
PRESUME
PRETEND
PRETENDED
PRETENDS
PREVENT
PREY
PRICELESS
PRIEST-BAKED
PRIESTLIER
PRIEST'S
PRIMA
PRINTS
PRISONER
PRISTINE
PRIVACY
PRIVATES
PRO
PROBABLE
PROBE
PROBING
PROBLEM
PROBLEMS
PROCEEDED
PRODDED
PRODUCE
PROFITED
PROFITLESS
PROFOUNDER
PROFOUNDLY
PROLOGUE
PROMENADE
PROMINENT
PROMISED
PROMISES
PROMPTING
PRONGS
PRONOUNCEMENTS
PROPEL
PROPHECIES
PROPHESY
PROPHETIC
PROPPING
PROSAIC
PROSTITUTE
PROTECTED
PROTECTING
PROTECTIVELY
PROTECTS
PROTRACTED
PROVED
PROVERBS
PROVIDES
PROVINCE
PROVINCES
PROWESS
PROWL
PROW-LIKE
PROWLS
PRUSSIAN
PSEUDONYM
PSYCHE-KNOT
PSYCHES
PSYCHIC
PUCKER
PUDDING
PUDDLE

PUFF
PUFFED
PUKE
PULL
PULLED
PULP
PULPIT
PULSED
PUMA
PUMPED
PUNCHING
PUNISH
PUNISHMENT
PUNTER
PUPAS
PUPIL
PUPPET-MASTER
PUPPET-PEOPLE
PUPPETS
PUPPIES
PURDAH
PURGATORY
PURIST
PURPLES
PURPOSE
PURRS
PURSUERS
PURSUING
PUSH
PUSHING
PUT-BY
PUT-UPON
PUZZLE
PUZZLING
PYRAMIDED
PYRE
PYTHONESS
QUADRILLES
QUAHOG
QUAIL
QUARRELS
QUARRY
QUARTERED
QUARTS
QUARTZ-CLEAR
QUARTZ-FLAKE
QUEENLY
QUEENSHIP
QUEERLY
QUENCH
QUERIES
QUESTION
QUIBBLE
QUICKEN
QUICKENED
QUICKENS
QUICKLY
QUICKSANDS
QUIETENS
QUINTESSENTIAL
QUITTED
QUITTING
QUIVER
QUIVERING
QUIVERS
QUOITS
R
RABBIT-EARED
RABBIT'S
RABBIT-TRACK
RACINE
RACKET
RADIAL
RADIATION
RADICAL
RADIO
RAGBAG
RAGGY
RAGING
RAIL
RAILWAY

RAINBOWS
RAINY
RAKE
RAMBLE
RAMPAGE
RAMPED
RAMS
RAM'S-HORN
RANCID
RANGE
RANGOON
RANK-HAIRED
RANSACK
RANSACKED
RANSACKS
RAPACIOUS
RAPED
RAPTORIAL
RARELY
RARENESS
RASA
RASPS
RATE
RATION
RATIONED
RATS
RATS'
RAT-SHREWD
RAT'S-TAIL
RATTLER
RATTLING
RAVEN
RAVENED
RAVENING
RAVENS
RAVINED
RAVINES
RAVISHED
RAYED
RAZOR
REACHED
READY-MADE
REALISTS
REALITY
REAP
REAPPEARANCE
REAR
REARING
REARRANGING
REARS
REASONABLE
REBEL
REBUKE
RECALLS
RECANTATION
RECEDE
RECEDED
RECEIVE
RECENTLY
RECEPTACLES
RECEPTION
RECITE
RECITES
RECLUSE
RECOGNIZE
RECOIL
RECOLLECTION'S
RECONSTRUCTED
RECORD
RECORDED
RECORDS
RECOVERS
RECREATION
RECROSSING
RECRUITS
RECTIFY
RECTORY
RECUPERATING
RED-BELL-BLOOM
REDCOATS
REDEEM

REDEEMED
RED-FACED
RED-FRECKLED
RED-HEADED
RED-HOT
RED-MOTTLED
RED-NOSED
REDOUBT
REDRESS
REDS
REEFS
REEKS
REEL
REELS
RE-ESTABLISH
REFECTORIES
REFINED
REFLECTION
REFRACTS
REFUGEE
REFUSE
REGARD
REGARDING
REGION
REGRETFULLY
REGULARITY
REHEARSE
REHEARSES
REIGNED
REJECTS
RELAPSE
RELAX
RELEASED
RELENTLESS
RELIGIOUS
RELISH
REMAINDER
REMAINING
REMARKABLE
REMEMBRANCES
REMIND
REMORSE
RENDER
RENDERING
RENDS
RENT
RENTS
REOPEN
REPASSES
REPEATS
REPENT
REPETITIONS
REPLACES
REPLENISH
REPLICAS
REPLY
REPOISE
REPORT
REPORTED
REPRESENT
RESCUED
RESENTFUL
RESIGN
RESIN
RESISTIVE
RESOLUTENESS
RESOLUTION
RESOLVE
RESOURCEFUL
RESPECT
RESPECT'S
RESPITE
RESTING
RESURRECTED
RESURRECTION
RESURRECTIONS
RETCHING
RETRACING
RETREAT
RETREATS
RETROGRADE

-1- (CONT.)
RETROGRESSED
RETROSPECT
RETURNED
RETURNS
REUNION
REVEALS
REVELATION
REVEL
REVERENCE
REVERIE
REVIVALIST
REVOKE
REVOLTED
REVOLUTIONARY
REVOLVED
REVOLVES
REWARDS
RHETORIC
RHEUMATIC
RHINOCEROS
RHYME
RIBBED
RIBBONS
RICE
RICKETY
RICTUS
RIDER
RIDERLESS
RIDGE
RIGGED
RIGHTFUL
RIM
RIND
RINDS
RINGED
RINK
RINSING
RIOT
RIP
RIPPLE
RIPPLED
RIPPLING
RISK
RITUALS
RIVALS
RIVER-BASIN
RIVER-BED
RIVER-LEVEL
RIVER-VERGE
RIVETING
RIVULETS
ROAMER
ROARED
ROAST
ROBBED
ROBBER
ROBE
ROBIN'S
ROCK-BUMPING
ROCKETING
ROCKETS
ROCK-FACE
ROCK-FAULT
ROCK'S
ROCOCO
RODENT
RODENTS
ROE
ROGUE'S
ROLLER
ROLLING
ROMANS
ROMANTICS
ROME
ROMPS
RONDO
ROOFGARDENS
ROOF-TILES
ROOK-CLAW
ROOK-TONGUED

ROOSTING
ROOT-HAIRS
ROOT-PALE
ROOT'S
ROPED
RORSCHACH-BLOT
ROSE-AND-
  LARKSPURRED
ROSE-BEDS
ROSEBUD
ROSE-COLORED
ROSE-FRUIT
ROSE-PAPERED
ROSE-SPRIGGED
ROSE-STEM
ROTISSERIE
ROTUNDAS
ROUGE
ROUSE
ROUSED
ROVE
ROVING
ROWDY
ROYALTY
RUBBED
RUBBING
RUBBISHES
RUBBLE
RUCHINGS
RUCK
RUDDERS
RUDDLE
RUDDY-BODIED
RUEFUL
RUFFS
RUGS
RUINAGE
RUINED
RUINOUS
RULER
RULER'S
RUM
RUMBAS
RUMORED
RUMPUS
RUNG
RUNNELS
RUSH
RUSHED
RUSSIAN
RUSSIANS
RUSTING
RUSTLING
RUT
RUTH
RUTS
RYE-HEADS
SABOTEUR
SACHET
SACKCLOTH
SACKED
SACRAMENT
SACRIFICES
SACRIFICIAL
SACRILEGIOUS
SACROSANCT
SAFE-CONDUCT
SAFER
SAFE-SOCKETED
SAFETY
SAFFRON
SAG
SAG-BACKED
SAGES
SAGGED
SAGS
SAILED
SAILORS
SAILS
SAINTLY
SAINT'S

SALAMI
SALTIER
SALTS
SALT-SWEETNESS
SALTY
SALUTARY
SALVE
SAM
SAMBAS
SAMENESS
SAMURAI
SANCTITY
SANCTUARY
SANCTUM
SANDBIN
SANDMAN'S
SANDSPIT
SANDY
SANE
SANGUINE
SANITY
SANK
SANTA
SANTA'S
SAPLINGS
SAPPHIRE
SARCASM
SARCOPHAGI
SARCOPHAGUS
SARDINE
SATAN
SATAN'S
SATCHELS
SATIN
SATINS
SATISFACTION
SATISFY
SAUCER
SAUCERS
SAUSAGES
SAVING
SAWDUST
SAWS
SCABBARD
SCAFFOLD
SCALD
SCALED
SCALE-SHEEN
SCALING
SCALP
SCALPELS
SCANDAL
SCANS
SCARLET-
  SPECKLED
SCARS
SCAR'S
SCATH
SCATHED
SCATHES
SCATTER
SCATTERING
SCAVENGING
SCENT
SCENTLESS
SCHEMES
SCHIZOPHRENIC
SCHOOLGIRL
SCHOOLGIRLS
SCHOOLROOMS
SCINTILLANT
SCISSORS
SCOLDINGS
SCOOPED
SCOOPED-OUT
SCOOTING
SCORNING
SCORPION
SCOUR
SCOURED
SCOURGING

SCOWL
SCRABBLE
SCRABBLING
SCRAGGLY
SCRAGGY
SCRAPE
SCRAPED
SCRAPPED
SCRATCHED
SCRAWLED
SCREAMS
SCREECH
SCREENING
SCREW
SCROLL
SCROLLED
SCROLLS
SCRUBBED
SCRUBNURSE
SCRUTINIZING
SCULPTED
SCULPTOR
SCULPTURE
SCUM
SCURRY
SCUTTLED
SCYTHE
SEA-BEAST
SEA-BOTTOM
SEA-CHANGE
SEA-CROCKERY
SEA-DRAGON
SEAGREEN
SEAGULL
SEALING
SEALS
SEAMING
SEARCHING
SEARS
SEASICK
SEASONED
SEASONS
SEAT
SEATED
SEA-TOWN
SEAWALL
SEAWARD
SECEDING
SECONDS
SECOND'S
SECRETARY
SECRETLY
SECURE
SEDATIVES
SEDUCED
SEDUCTIVE
SEEDY
SEEMING
SEEPS
SEETHE
SEETHED
SEIZURE
SELDOM
SELF-ASSURED
SELF-INTEREST
SELF-SUFFICIENT
SELLING
SELLS
SENDS
SENSES
SENSING
SENTIMENT
SENTIMENTS
SENTRY
SEPARATES
SEPULCHERS
SERAPH
SERAPHIC
SERBO-CROAT
SERE
SERENE

SERENELY
SERPENT
SERPENTS
SERUM
SERVANTS
SERVES
SESTINA
SETTLING
SEURAT
SEVEN-YEAR-OLD
SEVERAL
SEVERE
SEW
SEX
SEXTON
SHADELESS
SHADING
SHADOWING
SHADOW-THING
SHADOWY
SHAKEN
SHALLOW
SHALLOWS
SHALT
SHAMBLE
SHAMBLED
SHAMBLING
SHAMEFUL
SHANK
SHAN'T
SHANTY
SHAPED
SHAPELESS
SHAPERS
SHARDED
SHARE
SHARPENING
SHARPER
SHARPLY
SHATTER
SHATTERPROOF
SHATTERS
SHAWL
SHAWLED
SHEARED
SHEATH
SHEATHE
SHEAVED
SHEAVES
SHED'S
SHEENS
SHEEPFOLD
SHEEPFOOT-
  FLATTENED
SHEER-SIDED
SHEET-CUFF
SHEETED
SHELLED
SHELTER
SHELVES
SHEPHERDS'
SHERBETS
SHERLOCK
SHIED
SHIELDING
SHIES
SHIFTS
SHIMMERS
SHINBONES
SHINES
SHINGLE
SHINGLES
SHINS
SHIP'S
SHIRR
SHIRT
SHIRTS
SHIVER
SHOCKING
SHODDY
SHOE-BLACK

619

SHOE-BLACKING	SIMMERING	SLIGHT	SO-AND-SO'S	SPIKE
SHOELACE	SIMPLER	SLIGHTED	SOAP-BUBBLE	SPIKE-STUDDED
SHONE	SIMPLICITIES	SLIGHTEST	SOAP-COLORED	SPIKY
SHOOK	SIMULACRUM	SLIPPED	SOARS	SPINACH-HEADS
SHOOTS	SIMULTANEOUSLY	SLIPPER	SOBERLY	SPINACH-PICKER
SHOPKEEPERS	SINDBAD	SLIPPERS	SOBRIETY	SPINACH-TIPS
SHOPS	SINEW	SLIPPERY	SOCIETIES	SPINDLE'S
SHORES	SINGE	SLIPPINESS	SOCKETED	SPINDLE-SHANKED
SHORN	SINGEING	SLIPPING	SOCK-FACE	SPINES
SHORTCHANGE	SINGELESS	SLIVERS	SODA	SPINNAKER
SHORTENS	SINGERS	SLOOPS	SOGGY	SPINSTERS
SHORT-REINED	SINGLE-SKIRTED	SLOPE	SOLACE	SPIRES
SHOULDERBLADES	SINGULAR	SLOPED	SOLACED	SPIRING
SHOULDER-BLADES	SINGULARLY	SLOPES	SOLARIUM	SPIRITLESS
SHOULDER-HIGH	SINISTER	SLOPS	SOLEMN-EYED	SPIRITOUS
SHOULDERING	SINKERS	SLOSH	SOLES	SPIRIT'S
SHOUT	SINS	SLOTHFUL	SOLIDIFY	SPIRITUAL
SHOUTS	SINUOUS	SLOUCH	SOLILOQUY	SPITEFUL
SHOVERS	SIP	SLOWED	SOLIPSIST	SPITE-SET
SHOVES	SIR	SLOWS	SOLITUDE	SPITTED
SHOWER	SIREN-SONG	SLUG	SOLITUDES	SPITTLE
SHOWERING	SIRIUS	SLUGGARD'S	SOLOMON'S	SPLENDID
SHOWERS	SIRS	SLUGGY	SOMEBODY'S	SPLINTER
SHRED	SISTER-BITCH	SLUGLIKE	SOMERSAULTS	SPLITTING
SHRIEKING	SISTERHOOD	SLUICE	SOOT	SPLURGE
SHRIKE	SISYPHUS	SLUICES	SOPHIST	SPOILS
SHRIKE-FACE	SITUATIONS	SLUMBERING	SOPHISTRY	SPONGE
SHRILL	SIX-COLORED	SLUMPS	SORCERER	SPONGES
SHRILLING	SIX-SIDED	SLYLY	SORCERESS	SPORES
SHRINED	SIZZLED	SMACKS	SORE	SPORTY
SHRIVEL	SKATE	SMALLER	SORES	SPOTLESS
SHROUD-CIRCLED	SKATE'S	SMARTEST	SORROWFUL	SPOTTY
SHRUB	SKEDADDLE	SMASHING	SOUGH	SPRAT
SHRUG	SKEINS	SMELLESS	SOUL-ANIMALS	SPRAWLS
SHUDDER	SKELETON'S	SMELT	SOUL-SHIFT	SPREADS
SHUDDERING	SKEPTICAL	SMELTED	SOUL-STUFF	SPRIGGED
SHUNT	SKEWERED	SMIRK	SOUNDING	SPRINT
SHUT-OFF	SKILL	SMITHFIELD	SOUNDLESS	SPROUTING
SHUTTER	SKINFLINT	SMOKE-CHOKED	SOUNDS	SPUMIEST
SHUTTERED	SKINNY	SMOKESTACKS	SOUP-KITCHEN	SPUMILY
SHUTTING-UP	SKULKS	SMOLDERED	SOURNESS	SPUMY
SHY	SKULLED-AND-	SMOLDERING	SOURS	SPUNGLASS
SIBYL'S	CROSSBONED	SMOOTHING	SOUTHERN	SPUNKY
SICKER	SKULL-PLATES	SMUDGE	SOWS	SPURNS
SICKLE-SHAPED	SKY-CIRCLE	SMUG-SHAPED	SOW'S	SPURS
SICKNESS	SKYFULS	SNAG	SPA	SPY
SIDED	SKY-HIGH	SNAIL-NOSED	SPAIN	SPYING
SIDELONG	SKYLIGHT	SNAKE-BODIES	SPAR	SQUADRONS
SIDES	SKY-LORDED	SNAKECHARMER'S	SPARES	SQUALOR
SIDEWALK	SKY-MIRRORING	SNAKEDOM	SPARKING	SQUANDERED
SIDEWISE	SKYWARD	SNAKE-FIGURED	SPARKLE	SQUANDERING
SIDLED	SLABS	SNAKEHOOD	SPARKLER	SQUANDERS
SIDLES	SLAG	SNAKE-ROOTED	SPARKY	SQUATS
SIERRA	SLAKE	SNAKE-SCALES	SPARS	SQUATTED
SIFT	SLAM	SNAKE-WARP	SPARSEST	SQUEAKING
SIFTING	SLANTING	SNAKE-WEFT	SPASM	SQUEAL
SIFTS	SLANTS	SNAKING	SPASMODIC	SQUEALING
SIGHED	SLAPPED	SNAPPING	SPAWNING	SQUEEZED
SIGHING	SLAPPING	SNARED	SPEAR	SQUEEZING
SIGHTING	SLATE	SNAZZY	SPECK	SQUIRMS
SIGHTLESS	SLAUGHTER	SNEAKED	SPECKLES	STAB
SIGNIFICANCE	SLAVE	SNEER	SPECS	STABLE
SIGNIFY	SLAYING	SNICKERED	SPECTACULAR	STABLED
SIGNING	SLEDGE	SNIFFING	SPECTACULARLY	STABLES
SILENCED	SLEEK	SNIPPED	SPECTER	STABS
SILENCES	SLEEKS	SNORED	SPECTRAL	STACKED
SILENTLY	SLEEPDRUNK	SNOUT	SPECTRUM	STACKS
SILHOUETTE	SLEEP-FEATHERED	SNOUT-CRUISE	SPED	STAGES
SILT	SLEEPILY	SNOWCAKES	SPELLING	STAIRCASE
SILTING	SLEEPLESS	SNOWED-IN	SPELT	STALACTITES
SILVER-GLAZE	SLEEPLESSNESS	SNOWFLAKE	SPEND	STALE
SILVER-GRIZZLED	SLEEP-TALKING	SNOWFLAKES	SPERM	STALEMATED
SILVER-HAIRED	SLEEP-TWISTED	SNOW-FLAWED	SPEWED	STALKING
SILVERSMITHS	SLEEVE	SNOW-HEAP	SPEWS	STALKY
SILVER-SUITED	SLEEVELESS	SNOWMAN	SPHINX-QUEEN	STALL
SIMIAN	SLEEVES	SNUBS	SPICE	STALLION
SIMILAR	SLEIGHS	SNUFF-COLORED	SPIDERLIKE	STALLIONS
SIMILE	SLICES	SNUFFED	SPIDER-MEN	STALWART
SIMILES	SLIDES	SNUFF-RUFFED	SPIDERS	STAMPING
		SOAKS	SPIELS	STAMPS

STANCE
STARCH
STAR-DISTANCE
STARES
STAR-EYES
STARFISH
STARING
STARKER
STARKNESS
STARLING
STARLIT
STAR-LUCKY
STAR-MAP
STARRED
STARRY
STAR'S
STARTLE
STARTLES
STARTLING
STARVE
STASH
STATEMENTS
STATIC
STATICKY
STATIONS
STATISTIC
STAUNCHING
STAYED
STAYING
STAYS
STEAD
STEADY
STEADY-ROOTED
STEAL
STEALERS
STEALS
STEELED
STEELIER
STEEPLE
STEEPLING
STELLAR
STENCHES
STENTORIAN
STEPPED
STEREOPTICON
STIFFNESS
STIGMATA
STILES
STILLBORN
STILLING
STILTS
STIMULUS
STIPPLE
STIRRING
STIRRUPS
STITCH
STITCHING
STOAT
STOCKING
STOCK-STILL
STOLEN
STOLIDLY
STOLZ
STOMACHING
STONE-BUILT
STONE-DEAF
STONE-HATCHETED
STONE-HEAD
STONEHENGE
STONE'S
STONEWARD
STONIER
STOOGES
STOOL
STOPPER
STORAGE
STORE
STOREROOMS
STORIED
STORM-CROSSED

STORMING
STORM-STRUCK
STORMY
STORY
STORYBOOK
STOVES
STRADDLE
STRAIGHTFORWARDLY
STRAINS
STRAND
STRANGELY
STRANGENESS
STRANGER
STRANGLE
STRATAGEM
STRATAGEMS
STRAWBERRY
STRAWS
STRAY
STRAYED
STRAYINGS
STREAK
STREAKED
STREAKS
STREETLIGHT
STREETLIGHTS
STREET'S
STRENGTH
STRENGTHEN
STRETCH
STRETCHED
STREWING
STRICKEN
STRIDING
STRINGENCIES
STRINGENT
STRIVES
STRIVING
STRODE
STROLLING
STRONGEST
STRONGHOLD
STRUCTURAL
STRUGGLE
STRUMPET
STUBBORNNESS
STUB-NECKED
STUD
STUDDING
STUDIOS
STUMBLERS
STUMP
STUMPS
STUN
STUNT
STUPIDITY
STURDY
STY
STY-FACE
SUAVELY
SUBDUE
SUBDUED
SUBJUGATING
SUBPOENA
SUBSTANCELESS
SUBSTANCES
SUBURB
SUBURBS
SUBVERSION
SUCCEED
SUCCINCT
SUCHLIKE
SUCKLE
SUCKLING
SUE
SUFFER
SUFFERER
SUFFERING-
    TOUGHENED
SUGARED
SUGARY

SUICIDES
SUITCASE
SUITCASES
SUITOR
SUITS
SULFUR
SULK
SULLIED
SUMMERS
SUMMERY
SUMMONS
SUNBLUE
SUN-CLOUDS
SUN-GLAZED
SUNGLINT
SUNLESS
SUNLIT
SUN-MONEYED
SUNRISE
SUNSETS
SUNSTRUCK
SUNUP
SUPERHIGHWAY
SUPERIMPOSES
SUPER-PEOPLE
SUPPORTED
SURENESS
SURFACED
SURFEIT
SURFEITING
SURGERY
SURPLICED
SURPLUS
SURPRISED
SURREALISTIC
SURRENDER
SUSAN
SUSO'S
SUSPEND
SUSPENDS
SUSPENSE
SUSPICIONS
SUSTAIN
SUSTAINS
SUSURROUS
SWADDLE
SWADDLES
SWADDLINGS
SWAGGERS
SWAMPED
SWAMPSCOTT
SWARMING
SWARMY
SWASTIKA
SWAY
SWAYING
SWAYS
SWEATED
SWEAT-WET
SWEETBREADS
SWEETEN
SWEETENING
SWEETER
SWEETEST
SWEETHEARTS
SWEETIE
SWELL
SWEPT
SWIFT
SWILL
SWISS
SWITCHED
SWIVEL
SWIVELED
SWIVELING
SWOON
SWORE
SYCAMORE
SYCAMORES
SYNCOPATE
SYNCOPATES

SYRINX
SYRUP
TABBY
TABLETOP
TABLE-TOP
TABLETS
TABULA
TACITURN
TACK
TACKING
TACKLE
TACKS
TAIL-TRACK
TAINT
TALENTS
TALISMAN
TALISMANIC
TALKERS
TAMPING
TAMPS
TANG
TANGED
TANGERINE
TANGERINES
TANGLING
TANG'S
TANKS
TAPE
TAPPED
TAPPING
TARDILY
TARNISH
TARNISHED
TARNISHES
TAR-PAPER
TARRED
TARRY
TARTING
TASK
TASK'S
TASSELED
TASSELS
TATTER
TATTERS
TATTLE
TATTLING
TATTOO
TATTOOING
TATTOOIST
TATTOOS
TAUGHT
TAUTEN
TAXIS
T.B.
TEACH
TEACHER
TEACUP
TEACUPS
TEA-LEAVES
TEAR-DAZZLED
TEARFUL
TEA-ROSES
TEAR-PEARLED
TEARY
TEASE
TEASET
TEASING
TEATS
TECHNICAL
TED
TEDIUM
TEEMING
TELEPHONE'S
TELESCOPE
TELLTALE
TEMPERING
TEMPLE
TEMPLES
TEMPORARY
TEMPTING
TENACITY

TENANT
TENANT'S
TEND
TENDERER
TENDON
TENDS
TENNIS
TENSE
TENTATIVE
TERM
TERMINAL
TERMINUS
TERMS
TERRIBLY
TERRIFIES
TERROR-STRUCK
TESSELLATED
TEST
TESTIFIES
TESTIFY
TETHER
TETHERED
THALIDOMIDE
THATCH
THATCHING
THATCHINGS
THEATRICAL
THEORY
THEREBY
THERMOPYLAE
THICKEN
THICKENING
THICK-SILTED
THIEVERY
THIEVES
THIN-LIPPED
THINNESS
THIN-PANED
THIRSTY
THIRTY-YEAR-OLD
THORNED
THOU
THOUSANDS
THREADBARE
THREADED
THREADING
THREADS
THREADWORK
THREAT
THREATEN
THRESH
THRESH-TAILED
THRIFTY
THRIVE
THRIVING
THRONED
THRONGING
THRUSTING
THUDDING
THUMBHEAD
THUMBSCREWS
THUMBS-DOWN
THUMB-SIZE
THUMPABLE
THUNDERED
THWACKED
TIBET
TICKER
TICKET
TICKLE
TIDAL-FLATS
TIDE-LINE
TIDE-WAY
TIDINESS
TIE
TIERED
TIFFANY'S
TIGER-FACED
TIGER-TAMER
TIGERY
TIGHTER

-1- (CONT.)

TIGHTROPE
TIGHTROPES
TILTS
TIMELESS
TIMOROUS
TINDERY
TINT
TINTS
TIN-WHITE
TIPTOE
TIRELESS
TIRES
TITILLATING
TITLED
TITS
TOAD-YELLOW
TOBY
TOD
TOELESS
TOGA
TOKENS
TOLLING
TOM
TOMAS
TOMATO'S
TON
TONE
TONE-DEAF
TONELESS
TONGUELESS
TONIGHT'S
TONING
TOOLS
TOO-SHORT
TOO-SIMPLE
TOPOGRAPHY
TOPPLED
TOPPLES
TOPPLING
TOPSOIL
TOR
TORCH
TORCHES
TORMENT
TORPID
TORSOS
TORTUOUS
TORTURED
TOSSED
TOTEM
TOTTERING
TOUCHY
TOWEL
TOWLINES
TOWN'S
TRACE
TRACES
TRADEMARK
TRADING
TRAGEDIANS
TRAINSTOP
TRAITOR
TRANSCEND
TRANSFIGURING
TRANSFORM
TRANSIENT
TRANSLATE
TRANSPARENCIES
TRAPEZE
TRASH
TRAVELLING
TRAVERSE
TRAWLING
TRAY
TREADING
TREASON
TREAT
TREELESS
TREE'S
TREETOPS

TREE-TWIST
TREFOILS
TREK
TREKKING
TREKS
TREMOLO
TREMULOUS
TRENCH-DUG
TRENCHED
TRENCHES
TREPANNED
TRESPASS
TRESPASSING
TRIAL'S
TRIANGULAR
TRIBE
TRICKLE
TRIES
TRIGGER
TRINKET
TRIO
TRIP-DATE
TRIPLE
TRIPOD
TRIPPED
TRIUMPH
TRIUMPHANT
TRIVIAL
TROLLEYS
TROLLS
TROPIC
TROPICS
TROT
TROUBLING
TROUBLOUS
TROUGH
TROUGHED
TROUGHS
TROUNCING
TROY
TROY'S
TRUCK
TRUCKLING
TRUCKS
TRUCULENCE
TRUER
TRUMP-CRACK
TRUMPET-THROATS
TRUMPET-TOPPLING
TRUNCATED
TRUNK
TRUTHFUL
TRUTHS
TRYOUTS
TUBERS
TUBULAR
TUMULI
TUMULUS
TUN
TUNE
TUNES
TUNIC
TUNNEL
TUNNELS
TURBINE
TURF
TURNINGS
TURNIP
TURNIPY
TURRET
TURRETS
TURTLE-DARK
TUSSOCKS
TWENTY-FIVE
TWENTY-FOUR
TWENTY-SIX
TWIGGY
TWIG-SLEEPING
TWINE
TWINED
TWINGE

TWINING
TWINKLE
TWINKLE-DRESS
TWINS
TWIRLING
TWISTED
TWITCHES
TWITCHING
TWITTERS
TWO-AND-SIX
TWO-HORNED
TWO-TIERED
UBIQUITOUS
UDDER
UDDERS
ULCERS
ULMUS
UMBRELLA
UMBRELLAS
UNABLE
UNAFFECTED
UNALTERED
UNANSWERABLE
UNANSWERED
UNBALANCE
UNBEARABLY
UNBEATEN
UNBENDABLE
UNBOTHERED
UNBREAKABLE
UNBUCKLED
UNBUFFETED
UNCAGED
UNCANNY
UNCATCHABLE
UNCHANGING
UNCLAPS
UNCLENCH
UNCOILED
UNCONQUERED
UNCOUTH
UNCTION
UNCUT
UNDERESTIMATE
UNDERFOOT
UNDERGOING
UNDERNEATH
UNDERSHIRTS
UNDERSIDE
UNDERSTANDING
UNDERSTOOD
UNDOES
UNDOING
UNDULATINGS
UNEARTHED
UNENDING
UNEVEN
UNEXCEPTIONABLE
UNFACED
UNFATHOMED
UNFISTED
UNFISTS
UNFOLDED
UNFOLDS
UNFORMED
UNGIFTED
UNGODLY
UNGRATEFUL
UNGRIEVED
UNHIRED
UNHORSED
UNHUSK
UNIDENTIFIABLE
UNIFORM
UNIFORMS
UNIMAGINABLE
UNINTELLIGIBLE
UNISON
UNIVERSAL
UNKNOWING
UNKNOWN

UNLATCH
UNLOADING
UNLOCK
UNLOOSING
UNLUCKY
UNMADE
UNMANNED
UNMASKED
UNMIRACULOUS
UNMISTED
UNMOVED
UNNATURAL
UNNERVING
UNPEEL
UNPEOPLED
UNPETAL
UNPICK
UNPICTURED
UNPLUCKED
UNPOEMED
UNQUEENLY
UNRAVEL
UNRAVELED
UNREDEEMED
UNREELING
UNRIPE
UNRIPENED
UNSAFE
UNSAID
UNSEAT
UNSERVICEABLE
UNSETTLING
UNSHEATHES
UNSHRIVEN
UNSIGHTLY
UNSPOKEN
UNSPOOL
UNSTABLE
UNSTICK
UNSTITCHING
UNSTOPPERS
UNSURE
UNTEACHABLE
UNTENANTED
UNTIDY
UNTONGUED
UNTWIST
UNTYING
UNUSUALLY
UNUTTERABLE
UNWALKED
UNWALL
UNWARMED
UNWIND
UNWINDS
UNWISELY
UNWRAP
UPDRAFT
UPDRAUGHT
UPFLIGHT
UPHOLSTERED
UPLEAPING
UPLIFTED
UPRAISED
UPREAR
UPSETTING
UPSTANDING
UPSTART
UPTURNED
UPTURNS
UPWARD
UPWARDS
URGE
URGED
URINOUS
USAGE
USAGES
USEFUL
USURPED
USURPING
UTTERANCE

UTTERING
UTTERS
VACANCY
VALEDICTORY
VALENTINE
VALENTINE-FACES
VALENTINO'S
VALOR
VALVES
VAMPIRES
VAMPIRING
VAN
VANE
VANISHING
VANITY
VAPORISH
VAPORIZATION
VAPOROUS
VAPORS
VARIANTS
VASTLY
VAT
VATICAN
VATS
VAULT
VAUNT
VAUNTING
VEERS
VEGETARIAN
VEINING
VEINS'
VELVETS
VENOM
VENOM-GIRT
VENTS
VENTURE
VERANDA
VERDIGRIS
VERGED
VERMILION
VERNON
VERONICAS
VERSATILE
VERSE
VERVE
VESSEL
VEXED
VIBRATIONS
VICE
VICIOUSNESS
VICTIMS
VICTORIANA
VICTORIOUS
VICTORY
VIES
VIEW-KEEPER
VIEW-KEEPING
VIEWPOINTS
VILLA
VILLAS
VINEGARY
VIOLATES
VIOLATION
VIOLETS
VIOLS
VIPERS
VIRGINITY'S
VIRGIN'S
VIRGINS'
VIRIDIAN
VIRILE
VIRTUES
VIRULENCE
VISAGE
VISIBILITIES
VISIONS
VISOR
VISORS
VITAL
VITREOUS
VOCABULARY

VOCATION
VOICELESS
VOICELESSNESS
VOLCANOED
VOLTS
VOLUME
VOLUMES
VOLUNTEER
VOLUPTUOUS
VOMIT
VORTEX
VOTRE
VOUCHING
VOUCHSAFED
VOW
VOYAGE
VOYAGERS
VULNERABLE
VULTUROUS
WADE
WAFER
WAGONS
WAINSCOTED
WAIST
WAIST-DEEP
WAIST-HIGH
WAITRESS
WAITS
WAIT'S
WAKENED
WAKENS
WALLOP
WALLOPING
WALLPAPER
WALTZES
WALTZING
WANTON
WANTONLY
WAREHOUSES
WARILY
WARMTH
WARNED
WARNS
WARRANT
WART
WARTED
WASH
WASHBOWL
WASHES
WASPISH
WASP'S
WASSAIL
WASTAGE
WASTES
WASTING
WATCHMEN
WATERCOLORIST
WATER-COLORISTS
WATER-DAZZLE
WATERDROPS
WATERLIGHTS
WATERMARK
WATERMELON
WATER-MELON
WATER-MISTS
WATERPROOF
WATER-SKIERS
WATER-SUNK
WATERTIGHT
WATER-TOWER
WATSON
WATTLE
WAVED
WAVERED
WAVERING
WAVERY
WAVE'S
WAVE-TIP
WAVE-TIPS
WAXEN

WAX-PALE
WAXY
WAYFARINGS
WAY'S
WAYWARD
WEAKNESS
WEALTH
WEAPON
WEARIES
WEARY
WEASELS
WEATHERCOCK
WEATHER'S
WEB
WEBBED
WEB-THREADS
WEB-WINGED
WEDDED
WEDGED
WEDLOCK
WEEDING
WEED-MUSTACHIOED
WEED-SLICKED
WEEP
WEEPS
WEEVIL
WEIGH
WEIGHTING
WEIGHTS
WELD
WELL-BOILED
WELL-DONE
WELLINGTONS
WELL-LOVED
WELL-NAMED
WELLS
WELL-STEERED
WELL-WATER
WELSH
WELTERING
WEPT
WEST
WETTING
WHALES
WHAMMY
WHARF
WHEELCHAIRS
WHEEZE
WHEEZES
WHELPED
WHETSTONE
WHETTED
WHIMS
WHIP
WHIPPER
WHIPPING
WHIRL
WHIRLED
WHIRLPOOL
WHIRLPOOLS
WHIRLS
WHIRR
WHISKERED
WHISPERED
WHISPERS
WHISTLED
WHITE-BEARDED
WHITE-BELLIED
WHITEHOT
WHITE-JACKETED
WHITENED
WHITE-RABBIT
WHITE-SMOCKED
WHITEWASHED
WHITSUN
WHOEVER
WHOLENESS
WHO'LL
WHOM
WHOPPERS
WHORL

WICKED
WICKLESS
WIDENS
WIDE-OPEN
WIDOW'S
WIELDS
WIFEY
WIGGLING
WIGGLY
WILD-CATS
WILDER
WILDERNESSES
WILDLY
WILES
WILLED
WILLFUL
WILLING
WILL-O'-THE-WISP
WILLOW
WILTS
WILY
WINCES
WINCH
WINDED
WINDFALLS
WIND-FLAW
WIND-HARROWED
WINDLESS
WINDOW-FRAME
WINDOWLESS
WINDOWSILL
WINDOW-SQUARE
WINDOW-SQUARES
WIND-RIPPED
WINE-BOTTLE
WINES
WING-CAPS
WINGLESS
WINGSPREAD
WINGY
WINKING
WINKS
WINNOWED
WINS
WINTER-BEHEADED
WINTER-FACE
WINTHROP
WINTRIEST
WIPES
WIPING
WIRED
WIRELESS
WISHFUL
WISHING
WISP
WITHDRAW
WITHDREW
WITHENS
WITHERS
WITHHELD
WITHSTAND
WIZARDS
WIZENED
WOLF-HEADED
WOLFISH
WOLVES
WOMBS
WONDERED
WONDERFUL
WONDERLAND
WONDERS
WONDROUS
WOODENLY
WOODWARD
WOOED
WOOL-CLOUDS
WOOLLY
WORKABLE
WORKED
WORKMAN
WORLDLING

WORLD-SHAPE
WORLD-WRECKED
WORM-HAUNT
WORM-HUSBANDED
WORMING
WORN-OUT
WORRIER
WORRY
WORRYING
WORSE-SERVED
WORSHIP
WORST
WORTHLESS
WOVE
WREAK
WREATH
WRECKED
WRECKS
WRENCHED
WRENCHING
WRESTLES
WRINGING
WRINKLED
WRINKLING
WRINKLY
WRIT
WRITE
WRITHE
WRITHEN
WRITHINGS
WRITING
WROTE
WRUNG
WRY-FACED
WRYLY
W'S
WUTHERING
X-RAY
X-RAYED
YACHT
YADDO
YARDLEY
YARDMAN'S
YARDS
YARN
YAWNS
YAWP
YEARNING
YEAR'S
YEASTY
YELLOW-CASQUED
YELLOW-HAUNCHED
YELLOW-PAELLA
YESTERDAYS
YEW'S
YIELD
YIELDED
YIELDS
YOGI
YOUNGER
YOUNGEST
YOUTH
ZANZIBAR
ZEN
ZEROS
ZINC-WHITE
ZINGING

THE

OF

AND

&

IS

TO

I

IT

IT

MY

WITH

ON

AS

LIKE

YOU

THAT

THEY

ARE

THIS

FOR
THEIR

FROM

HIS

HER

AT

NO

BY

EYE

ALL

OR
SUS

ONE

WHITE

HAVE
IF

WHAT

PLEASE
FOR

AN

NOW

WILL

RED

OLD

EYE
EYES

TWO

OLD

EYE
EYES

TWO

ACE
THROUGH

UNDER

L
TO